The
Merriam-Webster
Dictionary

The Merriam-Webster Dictionary

Merriam-Webster, Incorporated
Springfield, Massachusetts

A GENUINE MERRIAM-WEBSTER

The name *Webster* alone is no guarantee of excellence. It is used by a number of publishers and may serve mainly to mislead an unwary buyer.

Merriam-Webster™ is the name you should look for when you consider the purchase of dictionaries or other fine reference books. It carries the reputation of a company that has been publishing since 1831 and is your assurance of quality and authority.

Library of Congress Cataloging-in-Publication Data

Names: Merriam-Webster, Inc., issuing body.
Title: The Merriam-Webster dictionary.
Description: Springfield, Massachusetts : Merriam-Webster, Incorporated, [2019]
Identifiers: LCCN 2018060941 | ISBN 9780877796688 (paperback : alk. paper)
Subjects: LCSH: English language—Dictionaries.
Classification: LCC PE1628 .M353 2019 | DDC 423—dc23
LC record available at https://lccn.loc.gov/2018060941

Printed in the United States of America

8th printing   Data Reproductions Corp.   Auburn Hills, MI   December 2023

Contents

Contents

PREFACE

This edition of *The Merriam-Webster Dictionary* is the newest in a line of Merriam=Webster paperback dictionaries which began in 1947. It is based on and preserves the best aspects of preceding editions, but it now includes the most important recent vocabulary that was added to *Merriam-Webster's Collegiate Dictionary, Eleventh Edition* over the past decade. Throughout the dictionary, over 8,000 usage examples illustrate meanings and help to clarify definitions. All the new material has been based on examples of actual use found in the Merriam-Webster citation files and in edited texts online.

The nearly 65,000 entries and more than 75,000 definitions in this dictionary give coverage to the most frequently used words in the language. The heart of the dictionary is the A-Z vocabulary section, where readers will find information about meaning, spelling, pronunciation, etymology, and synonyms. This section is followed by others that users have long found useful: Foreign Words and Phrases, which covers words and phrases from other languages that often occur in English texts but have not become part of the English vocabulary; Biographical Names, which identifies historical and contemporary individuals of note, as well as biblical, legendary, and mythological characters; and Geographical Names, which identifies places of importance, along with population figures. The following sections are also provided for convenient reference: A Brief History of English, English Word Roots, Confused and Misused Words, A Guide to Common Verb Collocations, Irregular English Verbs, Basic English Grammar, A Handbook of Style, Documentation of Sources, Signs and Symbols, and An Overview of the Internet.

The Merriam-Webster Dictionary has been created by a company that has been publishing dictionaries for more than 150 years and continues to maintain an in-house staff of experienced lexicographers. For this edition, the primary editing was done by Karen L. Wilkinson, building on earlier work by former staff member James G. Lowe. Specialist editors included Adrienne M. Scholz for cross-reference, Joshua S. Guenter for pronunciation, James L. Rader for etymology, and Joan I. Narmontas for life science. Data entry and data-file processing were handled by Daniel B. Brandon and Anne E. McDonald. Emily A. Vezina acted as production editor guiding the book through its typesetting stages, assisted by Paul S. Wood. Proofreaders included Susan L. Brady, Serenity H. Carr, Sarah S. Carragher, Allison M. DeJordy, Joanne M. Despres, Neil S. Serven, and Linda Picard Wood, as well as some of the other editors mentioned above. All the editors join in the hope that users will find The *Merriam-Webster Dictionary* to be a concise, handy, and reliable guide to the English language of today.

EXPLANATORY NOTES

The dictionary contains so much information, that it is necessary to condense much of it to accommodate the limitations of the printed page. This section provides information on the conventions used throughout the dictionary, from the styling of entries and pronunciation to how we present information on usage and meaning. An understanding of the information contained in these notes will make the dictionary both easier and more rewarding to use.

ENTRIES

A boldface letter or a combination of such letters, including punctuation marks and diacritics where needed, that is set flush with the left-hand margin of each column of type is a main entry. The main entry may consist of letters set solid, of letters joined by a hyphen or a diagonal, or of letters separated by one or more spaces:

> **alone** . . . *adj*
> **avant–garde** . . . *n*
> **and/or** . . . *conj*
> **assembly language** *n*
> **av·a·lanche** . . . *n*

The material in lightface type that follows each main entry on the same line and on succeeding indented lines presents information about the main entry.

The main entries follow one another in alphabetical order letter by letter: *bill of attainder* follows *billion; Day of Atonement* follows *daylight saving time.* Those containing an Arabic numeral are alphabetized as if the numeral were spelled out: *4-H* comes between *fourfold* and *Four Hundred; 3-D* comes between *three* and *three-dimensional.* Those that often begin with the abbreviation *St.* in common usage have the abbreviation spelled out: *Saint Valentine's Day.* Main entries that begin with *Mc* are alphabetized just as they are spelled.

A pair of guide words is printed at the top of each page. These indicate that the entries falling alphabetically between the words at the top of the outer column of each page are found on that page.

The guide words are the first and last main entries printed on the page:

> **avocation • baby boom**

When one main entry has exactly the same written form as another, the two are distinguished by superscript numerals preceding each word:

> [1]**melt** . . . *vb*
> [2]**melt** *n*
> [1]**pine** . . . *n*
> [2]**pine** *vb*

Full words come before parts of words made up of the same letters; solid compounds come before hyphenated compounds; hyphenated compounds come before open compounds; and lowercase entries come before those with an initial capital:

> [2]**super** *n*
> **super-** . . . *prefix*
> **run·down** . . . *n*
> **run–down** . . . *adj*
> **run down** *vb*
> **dutch** . . . *adv*
> **Dutch** . . . *n*

The centered dots within entry words indicate division points at which a hyphen may be put at the end of a line of print or writing. Thus the noun *cap·puc·ci·no* may be ended on one line and continued on the next in this manner:

> cap-
>
> puccino
>
> cappuc-
>
> cino
>
> cappucci-
>
> no

Centered dots are not shown after a single initial letter or before a single terminal letter because typesetters seldom cut off a single letter:

abyss . . . *n*
flighty . . . *adj*
idea . . . *n*

Nor are they usually shown at the second and succeeding homographs unless they differ among themselves:

¹sig·nal . . . *n*
²signal *vb*
³signal *adj*
  but
¹min·ute . . . *n*
²mi·nute . . . *adj*

There are acceptable alternative end-of-line divisions just as there are acceptable variant spellings and pronunciations, but no more than one division is shown for any entry in this dictionary.

A double hyphen at the end of a line in this dictionary (as in the definition at ¹**pug 1**) stands for a hyphen that is retained when the word is written as a unit on one line. This kind of fixed hyphen is always represented in boldface words in this dictionary with an en dash, longer than an ordinary hyphen.

When a main entry is followed by the word *or* and another spelling, the two spellings are equal variants. Both are standard, and either one may be used according to personal inclination:

ocher *or* ochre

If two variants joined by *or* are out of alphabetical order, they remain equal variants. The one printed first is, however, slightly more common than the second:

¹plow *or* plough

When another spelling is joined to the main entry by the word *also*, the spelling after *also* is a secondary variant and occurs less frequently than the first:

ab·sinthe *also* ab·sinth

Secondary variants belong to standard usage and may be used according to personal inclination. Once the word *also* is used to signal a secondary variant, all following secondary variants are joined by *or*:

²wool·ly *also* wool·ie *or* wooly

Variants whose spelling puts them alphabetically more than a column away from the main entry are entered at their own alphabetical places as well as at the applicable main entry:

²gage *var of* GAUGE
¹gauge *also* gage
²gauge *also* gage

Variants having a usage label appear only at their own alphabetical places:

me·tre . . . *chiefly Brit var of* METER

To show all the stylings that are found for English compounds would require space that can be better used for other information. So this dictionary limits itself to a single styling for a compound:

peace·mak·er
pell–mell
high five

When a compound is widely used and one styling predominates, that styling is shown. When a compound is uncommon or when the evidence indicates that two or three stylings are approximately equal in frequency, the styling shown is based on the comparison of other similar compounds.

A main entry may be followed by one or more derivatives or by a homograph with a different functional label. These are run-on entries. Each is introduced by a long dash and each has a functional label. They are not defined, however, since their meanings are readily understood from the meaning of the root word:

fear·less . . . *adj* . . . — fear·less·ly *adv* —
  fear·less·ness *n*
hic·cup . . . *n* . . . — hiccup *vb*

A main entry may be followed by one or more phrases containing the entry word or an inflected form of it. These are also run-on entries. Each is introduced by a long dash but there is no functional label. They are, however, defined since their meanings are more than the sum of the meanings of their elements:

¹set . . . *vb* . . . — set sail : . . .
¹hand . . . *n* . . . — at hand : . . .

Defined phrases of this sort are run on at the entry defining the first major word in the phrase. When there are variants, however, the run-on appears at the entry defining the first major invariable word in the phrase:

¹seed . . . *n* . . . — go to seed *or* run to seed
  1 : . . .

Boldface words that appear within parentheses (as **coca** at **cocaine** and **jet engine** and **jet propulsion** at **jet–propelled**) are run-in entries. Attention is called to the definition of *vocabulary entry* on page 561. The term *dictionary entry* includes all vocabulary entries as well as all boldface entries in the back sections headed "Foreign Words & Phrases," "Biographical Names," and "Geographical Names."

PRONUNCIATION

The matter between a pair of reversed slashes \ \ following the entry word indicates the pronunciation. The symbols used are explained in the chart at the end of this section.

A hyphen is used in the pronunciation to show syllabic division. These hyphens sometimes coincide with the centered dots in the entry word that indicate end-of-line division:

ab·sen·tee \ˌab-sən-ˈtē\

Sometimes they do not:

met·ric \ˈme-trik\

A high-set mark ˈ indicates major (primary) stress or accent; a low-set mark ˌ indicates minor (secondary) stress or accent:

heart·beat \ˈhärt-ˌbēt\

The stress mark stands at the beginning of the syllable that receives the stress.

A syllable with neither a high-set mark nor a low-set mark is unstressed:

¹**struc·ture** \ˈstrək-chər\

The presence of variant pronunciations indicates that not all educated speakers pronounce words the same way. A second-place variant is not to be regarded as less acceptable than the pronunciation that is given first. It may, in fact, be used by as many educated speakers as the first variant, but the requirements of the printed page are such that one must precede the other:

apri·cot \ˈa-prə-ˌkät, ˈā-\
fore·head \ˈfȯr-əd, ˈfȯr-ˌhed\

Symbols enclosed by parentheses represent elements that are present in the pronunciation of some speakers but are absent from the pronunciation of other speakers, or elements that are present in some but absent from other utterances of the same speaker:

¹**om·ni·bus** \ˈäm-ni-(ˌ)bəs\
ad·di·tion·al \ə-ˈdi-sh(ə-)nəl\

Thus, the above parentheses indicate that some people say \ˈäm-ni-ˌbəs\ and others say \ˈäm-ni-bəs\; some \ə-ˈdi-shə-nəl\, others \ə-ˈdi-shnəl\.

When a main entry has less than a full pronunciation, the missing part is to be supplied from a pronunciation in a preceding entry or within the same pair of reversed slashes:

cham·pi·on·ship \-ˌship\
pa·la·ver \pə-ˈla-vər, -ˈlä-\

The pronunciation of the first three syllables of *championship* is found at the main entry *champion*. The hyphens before and after \ˈlä\ in the pronunciation of *palaver* indicate that both the first and the last parts of the pronunciation are to be taken from the immediately preceding pronunciation.

In general, no pronunciation is indicated for open compounds consisting of two or more English words that have own-place entry:

dental floss *n*

Only the first entry in a sequence of numbered homographs is given a pronunciation if their pronunciations are the same:

¹**re·ward** \ri-ˈwȯrd\ *vb*
²**reward** *n*

The absent but implied pronunciation of derivatives and compounds run on after a main entry is a combination of the pronunciation at the main entry and the pronunciation of the other element as given at its alphabetical place in the vocabulary:

— **quick·ness** *n*
— **hold with**

Thus, the pronunciation of *quickness* is the sum of the pronunciations given at *quick* and *-ness;* that of *hold with*, the sum of the pronunciations of the two elements that make up the phrase.

FUNCTIONAL LABELS

An italic label indicating a part of speech or another functional classification follows the pronunciation or, if no pronunciation is given, the main entry. The eight traditional parts of speech are indicated as follows:

bold . . . *adj*
forth·with . . . *adv*
¹**but** . . . *conj*

ge·sund·heit . . . *interj*
bo·le·ro . . . *n*
²**un·der** . . . *prep*
¹**it** . . . *pron*
slap . . . *vb*

Other italicized labels used to indicate functional classifications that are not traditional parts of speech include:

AT *abbr*
self- *comb form*
un- ... *prefix*
-ial *adj suffix*
²-ly *adv suffix*
²-er ... *n suffix*

-ize *vb suffix*
Fe *symbol*
may ... *verbal auxiliary*

Functional labels are sometimes combined:

afloat ... *adj or adv*

INFLECTED FORMS

NOUNS

The plurals of nouns are shown in this dictionary when suffixation brings about a change of final *-y* to *-i-*, when the noun ends in a consonant plus *-o* or in *-ey*, when the noun ends in *-oo*, when the noun has an irregular plural or an uninflected plural or a foreign plural, when the noun is a compound that pluralizes any element but the last, when a final consonant is doubled, when the noun has variant plurals, and when it is believed that the dictionary user might have reasonable doubts about the spelling of the plural or when the plural is spelled in a way contrary to what is expected:

²spy *n, pl* **spies**
si·lo ... *n, pl* **silos**
val·ley ... *n, pl* **valleys**
²shampoo *n, pl* **shampoos**
mouse ... *n, pl* **mice**
moose ... *n, pl* **moose**
cri·te·ri·on ... *n, pl* **-ria**
son–in–law ... *n, pl* **sons–in–law**
¹quiz ... *n, pl* **quiz·zes**
¹fish ... *n, pl* **fish** *or* **fish·es**

pi ... *n, pl* **pis**
³dry *n, pl* **drys**

Cutback inflected forms are used when the noun has three or more syllables:

ame·ni·ty ... *n, pl* **-ties**

The plurals of nouns are usually not shown when the base word is unchanged by suffixation, when the noun is a compound whose second element is readily recognizable as a regular free form entered at its own place, or when the noun is unlikely to occur in the plural:

night ... *n*
fore·foot ... *n*
mo·nog·a·my ... *n*

Nouns that are plural in form and that are regularly construed as plural are labeled *n pl*:

munch·ies ... *n pl*

Nouns that are plural in form but that are not always construed as plurals are appropriately labeled:

lo·gis·tics ... *n sing or pl*

VERBS

The principal parts of verbs are shown in this dictionary when suffixation brings about a doubling of a final consonant or an elision of a final *-e* or a change of final *-y* to *-i-*, when final *-c* changes to *-ck* in suffixation, when the verb ends in *-ey*, when the inflection is irregular, when there are variant inflected forms, and when it is believed that the dictionary user might have reasonable doubts about the spelling of an inflected form or when the inflected form is spelled in a way contrary to what is expected:

²snag *vb* **snagged; snag·ging**
¹move ... *vb* **moved; mov·ing**
¹cry ... *vb* **cried; cry·ing**
¹frol·ic ... *vb* **frol·icked; frol·ick·ing**
¹sur·vey ... *vb* **sur·veyed; sur·vey·ing**
¹drive ... *vb* **drove** ... **driv·en** ... **driv·ing**
²bus *vb* **bused** *or* **bussed; bus·ing** *or* **bus·sing**

²visa *vb* **vi·saed** ... **vi·sa·ing**
²chagrin *vb* **cha·grined** ... **cha·grin·ing**

The principal parts of a regularly inflected verb are shown when it is desirable to indicate the pronunciation of one of the inflected forms:

learn ... *vb* **learned** \'lərnd, 'lərnt\; **learn·ing**
¹al·ter \'òl-tər\ *vb* **al·tered; al·ter·ing** \-t(ə-)riŋ\

Cutback inflected forms are usually used when the verb has three or more syllables, when it is a two-syllable word that ends in *-l* and has variant spellings, and when it is a compound whose second element is readily recognized as an irregular verb:

elim·i·nate ... *vb* **-nat·ed; -nat·ing**
²quarrel *vb* **-reled** *or* **-relled; -rel·ing** *or* **-rel·ling**
¹re·take ... *vb* **-took** ... **-tak·en** ... **-tak·ing**

The principal parts of verbs are usually not shown when the base word is unchanged by suffixation or when the verb is a compound whose second element is readily recognizable as a regular free form entered at its own place:

¹jump . . . *vb*
pre·judge . . . *vb*

Another inflected form of English verbs is the third person singular of the present tense, which is regularly formed by the addition of *-s* or *-es* to the base form of the verb. This inflected form is not shown except at a handful of entries (as *have* and *do*) for which it is in some way unusual.

ADJECTIVES & ADVERBS

The comparative and superlative forms of adjectives and adverbs are shown in this dictionary when suffixation brings about a doubling of a final consonant or an elision of a final *-e* or a change of final *-y* to *-i-*, when the word ends in *-ey*, when the inflection is irregular, and when there are variant inflected forms:

¹red . . . *adj* red·der; red·dest
¹tame . . . *adj* tam·er; tam·est
¹kind·ly . . . *adj* kind·li·er; -est
hors·ey *also* horsy . . . *adj* hors·i·er; -est
¹good . . . *adj* bet·ter . . . best
¹far . . . *adv* far·ther . . . *or* fur·ther . . . far·thest *or* fur·thest . . .

The superlative forms of adjectives and adverbs of two or more syllables are usually cut back:

³fancy *adj* fan·ci·er; -est
¹ear·ly . . . *adv* ear·li·er; -est

The comparative and superlative forms of regularly inflected adjectives and adverbs are shown when it is desirable to indicate the pronunciation of the inflected forms:

¹young \'yəŋ\ *adj* youn·ger \'yəŋ-gər\; youn·gest \'yəŋ-gəst\

The inclusion of inflected forms in *-er* and *-est* at adjective and adverb entries means nothing more about the use of *more* and *most* with these adjectives and adverbs than that their comparative and superlative degrees may be expressed in either way: *lazier* or *more lazy; laziest* or *most lazy.*

At a few adjective entries only the superlative form is shown:

²mere *adj, superlative* mer·est

The absence of the comparative form indicates that there is no evidence of its use.

The comparative and superlative forms of adjectives and adverbs are usually not shown when the base word is unchanged by suffixation, when the inflected forms of the word are identical with those of a preceding homograph, or when the word is a compound whose second element is readily recognizable as a regular free form entered at its own place:

¹near . . . *adv*
³good *adv*
un·wor·thy . . . *adj*

Inflected forms are not shown at undefined run-ons.

CAPITALIZATION

Most entries in this dictionary begin with a lowercase letter. A few of these have an italicized label *often cap*, which indicates that the word is as likely to be capitalized as not and that it is as acceptable with an uppercase initial as it is with one in lowercase. Some entries begin with an uppercase letter, which indicates that the word is usually capitalized. The absence of an initial capital or of an *often cap* label indicates that the word is not ordinarily capitalized:

salm·on . . . *n*
gar·gan·tuan . . . *adj, often cap*
Mo·hawk . . . *n*

The capitalization of entries that are open or hyphenated compounds is similarly indicated

by the form of the entry or by an italicized label:

dry goods . . . *n pl*
french fry *n, often cap 1st F*
un–Amer·i·can . . . *adj*
Par·kin·son's disease . . . *n*
lazy Su·san . . . *n*
Jack Frost *n*

A word that is capitalized in some senses and lowercase in others shows variations from the form of the main entry by the use of italicized labels at the appropriate senses:

Trin·i·ty . . . *n* . . . 2 *not cap*
To·ry . . . *n* . . . 3 *often not cap*
ti·tan . . . *n* 1 *cap*
re·nais·sance . . . *n* . . . 1 *cap* . . . 2 *often cap*

ETYMOLOGY

This dictionary gives the etymologies for a number of the vocabulary entries. These etymologies are inside square brackets preceding the definition. Meanings given in roman type within these brackets are not definitions of the entry, but are meanings of the Middle English, Old English, or non-English words within the brackets.

The etymology gives the language from which words borrowed into English have come. It also gives the form of the word in that language or a representation of the word in our alphabet if the form in that language differs from that in English:

phi·lo·den·dron . . . [NL, fr. Gk, neut. of *philo-dendros* loving trees . . .]

¹sav·age . . . [ME, fr. AF *salvage, savage,* fr. LL *salvaticus,* alter. of L *silvaticus* of the woods, wild, fr. *silva* forest]

An etymology beginning with the name of a language (including ME or OE) and not giving the foreign (or Middle English or Old English) form indicates that this form is the same as the form of the entry word:

le·gume . . . [F]
¹jour·ney . . . [ME, fr. OF . . .]

An etymology beginning with the name of a language (including ME or OE) and not giving the foreign (or Middle English or Old English) meaning indicates that this meaning is the same as the meaning expressed in the first definition in the entry:

ug·ly . . . *adj* . . . [ME, fr. ON *uggligr* . . .] **1**
: FRIGHTFUL, DIRE

USAGE

Three types of status labels are used in this dictionary—temporal, regional, and stylistic—to signal that a word or a sense of a word is not part of the standard vocabulary of English.

The temporal label *obs* for "obsolete" means that there is no evidence of use since 1755:

³post *n* **1** *obs*

The label *obs* is a comment on the word being defined. When a thing, as distinguished from the word used to designate it, is obsolete, appropriate orientation is usually given in the definition:

cat·a·pult . . . *n* **1** : an ancient military machine for hurling missiles

The temporal label *archaic* means that a word or sense once in common use is found today only sporadically or in special contexts:

¹mete . . . *vb* . . . **1** *archaic*
¹thou . . . *pron, archaic*

A word or sense limited in use to a specific region of the U.S. has an appropriate label. The adverb *chiefly* precedes a label when the word has some currency outside the specified region, and a double label is used to indicate considerable currency in each of two specific regions:

²wash *n* . . . **8** *West*
do·gie . . . *n, chiefly West*
crul·ler . . . *n* . . . **2** *Northern & Midland*

Words current in all regions of the U.S. have no label.

A word or sense limited in use to one of the other countries of the English-speaking world has an appropriate regional label:

chem·ist . . . *n* . . . **2** *Brit*
loch . . . *n, Scot*
²wireless *n* . . . **2** *chiefly Brit*

The label *dial* for "dialect" indicates that the pattern of use of a word or sense is too complex for summary labeling: it usually includes several regional varieties of American English or of American and British English:

²mind *vb* **1** *chiefly dial*

The stylistic label *slang* is used with words or senses that are especially appropriate in contexts of extreme informality:

³can . . . *vb* . . . **2** *slang*
²grand *n* . . . *slang*

There is no satisfactory objective test for slang, especially with reference to a word out of context. No word, in fact, is invariably slang, and many standard words can be given slang applications.

The stylistic labels *offensive* and *disparaging* are used for those words or senses that in common use are intended to hurt or that are likely to give offense even when they are used without such an intent:

dumb . . . *adj* **1** *often offensive*
brat . . . *n, disparaging*

Definitions are sometimes followed by verbal illustrations that show a typical use of the word in context. These illustrations are enclosed in angle brackets, and the word being illustrated is usually replaced by a lightface swung dash. The swung dash stands for the boldface entry word, and it may be followed by an italicized suffix:

> ¹**jump** . . . *vb* . . . **5** . . . ⟨~ town⟩
> **all–around** . . . *adj* **1** . . . ⟨best ~ performance⟩
> ¹**can·on** . . . *n* . . . **3** . . . ⟨the ~s of good taste⟩
> **en·joy** . . . *vb* . . . **2** . . . ⟨~ed the concert⟩

The swung dash is not used when the form of the boldface entry word is changed in suffixation, and it is not used for compounds:

> ²**deal** *vb* . . . **2** . . . ⟨*dealt* him a blow⟩
> **drum up** *vb* **1** . . . ⟨*drum up* business⟩

Definitions are sometimes followed by usage notes that give supplementary information about such matters as idiom, syntax, and semantic relationship. A usage note is introduced by a lightface dash:

> ²**cry** *n* . . . **5** . . . — usu. used in the phrase *a far cry*
> ²**drum** *vb* . . . **4** . . . — usu. used with *out*
> ¹**jaw** . . . *n* . . . **2** . . . — usu. used in pl.
> ¹**ada·gio** . . . *adv or adj* . . . — used as a direction in music
> **hajji** . . . *n* . . . — often used as a title

Sometimes a usage note is used in place of a definition. Some function words (as conjunctions and prepositions) have chiefly grammatical meaning and little or no lexical meaning; most interjections express feelings but are otherwise untranslatable into lexical meaning; and some other words (as honorific titles) are more amenable to comment than to definition:

> **or** . . . *conj* — used as a function word to indicate an alternative
> ¹**at** . . . *prep* **1** — used to indicate a point in time or space
> **auf Wie·der·seh·en** . . . *interj* . . . — used to express farewell
> ¹**grace** . . . *n* . . . **4** — used as a title for a duke, a duchess, or an archbishop

SENSE DIVISION

A boldface colon is used in this dictionary to introduce a definition:

> **equine** . . . *adj* . . . : of or relating to the horse

It is also used to separate two or more definitions of a single sense:

> **no·ti·fy** . . . *vb* . . . **1** : to give notice of : report the occurrence of

Boldface Arabic numerals separate the senses of a word that has more than one sense:

> **add** . . . *vb* **1** : to join to something else so as to increase in number or amount **2** : to say further . . . **3** : to combine (numbers) into one sum

A particular semantic relationship between senses is sometimes suggested by the use of one of the two italic sense dividers *esp* or *also*.
The sense divider *esp* (for *especially*) is used to introduce the most common meaning included in the more general preceding definition:

> **crys·tal** . . . *n* . . . **2** : something resembling crystal (as in transparency); *esp* : a clear colorless glass of superior quality

The sense divider *also* is used to introduce a meaning related to the preceding sense by an easily understood extension of that sense:

> **chi·na** . . . *n* : porcelain ware; *also* : domestic pottery in general

The order of senses is historical: the sense known to have been first used in English is entered first. This is not to be taken to mean, however, that each sense of a multisense word developed from the immediately preceding sense. It is altogether possible that sense 1 of a word has given rise to sense 2 and sense 2 to sense 3, but frequently sense 2 and sense 3 may have developed independently of one another from sense 1.
When an italicized label follows a boldface numeral, the label applies only to that specific numbered sense. It does not apply to any other boldface numbered senses:

> **craft** . . . *n* . . . **3** *pl usu* **craft**
> ¹**fa·ther** . . . *n* . . . **2** *cap* . . . **5** *often cap*
> **dul·ci·mer** . . . *n* . . . **2** *or* **dul·ci·more**
> \ˌmȯr\
> ²**lift** *n* . . . **5** *chiefly Brit*

At *craft* the *pl* label applies to sense 3 but to none of the other numbered senses. At *father* the *cap* label applies only to sense 2 and the *often cap* label only to sense 5. At *dulcimer* the variant spelling and pronunciation apply only to sense 2, and the *chiefly Brit* label at *lift* applies only to sense 5.

CROSS-REFERENCE

Four different kinds of cross-references are used in this dictionary: directional, synonymous, cognate, and inflectional. In each instance the cross-reference is readily recognized by the lightface small capitals in which it is printed.

A cross-reference following a lightface dash and beginning with *see* is a directional cross-reference. It directs the dictionary user to look elsewhere for further information:

eu·ro . . . *n* . . . — see MONEY table

A cross-reference following a boldface colon is a synonymous cross-reference. It may stand alone as the only definition for an entry or for a sense of an entry; it may follow an analytical definition; it may be one of two or more synonymous cross-references separated by commas:

pa·pa . . . *n* : FATHER
¹**par·tic·u·lar** . . . *adj* . . . 4 : attentive to details
    : PRECISE
²**main** *adj* 1 : CHIEF, PRINCIPAL
¹**fig·ure** . . . *n* . . . 6 : SHAPE, FORM, OUTLINE

A synonymous cross-reference indicates that an entry, a definition at the entry, or a specific sense at the entry cross-referred to can be substituted as a definition for the entry or the sense in which the cross-reference appears.

A cross-reference following an italic *var of* ("variant of") is a cognate cross-reference:

pick·a·back . . . *var of* PIGGYBACK

Occasionally a cognate cross-reference has a limiting label preceding *var of* as an indication that the variant is not standard American English:

aero·plane . . . *chiefly Brit var of* AIRPLANE

A cross-reference following an italic label that identifies an entry as an inflected form (as of a noun or verb) is an inflectional cross-reference:

calves *pl of* CALF
woven *past part of* WEAVE

Inflectional cross-references appear only when the inflected form falls at least a column away from the entry cross-referred to.

SYNONYMS

A bold italic **Synonmys** preceded by a small black diamond figure near the end of an entry introduces words that are synonymous with the word being defined:

alone . . . *adj* . . . ✦ **Synonmys** LONELY, LONESOME, LONE, SOLITARY

Synonyms are not definitions although they may often be substituted for each other in context.

COMBINING FORMS, PREFIXES, & SUFFIXES

An entry that begins or ends with a hyphen is a word element that forms part of an English compound:

-wise . . . *adv comb form* . . . ⟨slant*wise*⟩
ex- . . . *prefix* . . . 2 . . . ⟨*ex*-president⟩
-let *n suffix* 1 . . . ⟨book*let*⟩

Combining forms, prefixes, and suffixes are entered in this dictionary for two reasons: to make understandable the meaning of many undefined run-ons and to make recognizable the meaningful elements of words that are not entered in the dictionary.

LISTS OF UNDEFINED WORDS

Many words that begin with the prefixes or combining forms *anti-, in-, non-, over-, re-, self-, semi-, sub-, super-,* and *un-* are self-explanatory combinations of the prefix or combining form and a word entered elsewhere in the dictionary, and they are listed undefined below the entry for the prefix or combining form.

ABBREVIATIONS & SYMBOLS

Abbreviations and symbols for chemical elements are included as main entries in the vocabulary:

RSVP *abbr* . . . please reply
Ca *symbol* calcium

Abbreviations have been normalized to one form. In practice, however, there is considerable variation in the use of periods and in capitalization (as *vhf, v.h.f.,* and *V.H.F.* for the entry **VHF**), and stylings other than those given in this dictionary are often acceptable.

ABBREVIATIONS IN THIS WORK

ab	about	*ft*	feet	*OF*	Old French
abbr	abbreviation	*G, Ger*	German	*OIt*	Old Italian
abl	ablative	*Gk*	Greek	*ON*	Old Norse
acc	accusative	*Gmc*	Germanic	*OPers*	Old Persian
A.D.	anno Domini	*Heb*	Hebrew	*orig*	originally
adj	adjective	*Hung*	Hungarian	*part*	participle
adv	adverb	*Icel*	Icelandic	*Pers*	Persian
AF	Anglo-French	*imit*	imitative	*perh*	perhaps
alter	alteration	*imper*	imperative	*Pg*	Portuguese
Am, Amer	American	*interj*	interjection	*pl*	plural
AmerF	American French	*Ir*	Irish	*Pol*	Polish
AmerInd	American Indian	*irreg*	irregular	*pp*	past participle
AmerSp	American Spanish	*It, Ital*	Italian	*prep*	preposition
Ar	Arabic	*Jp*	Japanese	*pres*	present, president
Aram	Aramaic	*K*	Kelvin	*prob*	probably
B.C.	before Christ	*km*	kilometers	*pron*	pronoun,
Brit	British	*L*	Latin		pronunciation
C	Celsius	*LaF*	Louisiana French	*prp*	present participle
ca	circa	*LG*	Low German	*pseud*	pseudonym
Calif	California	*LGk*	Late Greek	*r*	reigned
Canad	Canadian	*LHeb*	Late Hebrew	*Russ*	Russian
CanF	Canadian French	*lit*	literally	*Sc*	Scotch, Scots
cap	capital, capitalized	*LL*	Late Latin	*Scand*	Scandinavian
Celt	Celtic	*m*	meters	*ScGael*	Scottish Gaelic
cen	central	*masc*	masculine	*Scot*	Scottish
cent	century	*MD*	Middle Dutch	*sing*	singular
Chin	Chinese	*ME*	Middle English	*Skt*	Sanskrit
comb	combining	*MexSp*	Mexican Spanish	*Slav*	Slavic
compar	comparative	*MF*	Middle French	*So*	South
conj	conjunction	*MGk*	Middle Greek	*Sp, Span*	Spanish
constr	construction	*mi*	miles	*St*	Saint
D	Dutch	*ML*	Medieval Latin	*superl*	superlative
Dan	Danish	*modif*	modification	*Sw*	Swedish
dat	dative	*MS*	manuscript	*syn*	synonym, synonymy
deriv	derivative	*Mt*	Mount	*trans*	translation
dial	dialect	*n*	noun	*Turk*	Turkish
dim	diminutive	*neut*	neuter	*US*	United States
E	English	*NewEng*	New England	*USSR*	Union of Soviet
Egypt	Egyptian	*NGk*	New Greek		Socialist Republics
Eng	English	*NHeb*	New Hebrew	*usu*	usually
esp	especially	*NL*	New Latin	*var*	variant
est	estimated	*No*	North	*vb*	verb
F	Fahrenheit, French	*Norw*	Norwegian	*vi*	verb intransitive
fem	feminine	*n pl*	noun plural	*VL*	Vulgar Latin
fl	flourished	*obs*	obsolete	*vt*	verb transitive
fr	from	*OE*	Old English	*W*	Welsh

PRONUNCIATION SYMBOLS

ə	abut, collect, suppose	ȯi	toy
'ə, ˌə	humdrum	p	pepper, lip
ᵊ	(in ᵊl, ᵊn) battle, cotton; (in lᵊ, mᵊ, rᵊ) French table, prisme, titre	r	rarity
		s	source, less
ər	operation, further	sh	shy, mission
a	map, patch	t	tie, attack
ā	day, fate	th	thin, ether
ä	bother, cot, father	th	then, either
är	car, heart	ü	boot, few \'fyü\
au̇	now, out	u̇	put, pure \'pyu̇r\
b	baby, rib	u̇r	boor, tour
ch	chin, catch	œ	French rue, German füllen, fühlen
d	did, adder	v	vivid, give
e	set, red	w	we, away
er	bare, fair	y	yard, cue \'kyü\
ē	beat, easy	ʸ	indicates that a preceding \l\, \n\, or \w\ is modified by having the tongue approximate the position for \y\, as in French digne \dēnʸ\
f	fifty, cuff		
g	go, big		
h	hat, ahead		
hw	whale	z	zone, raise
i	tip, banish	zh	vision, pleasure
ir	near, deer	\	slant line used in pairs to mark the beginning and end of a transcription: \'pen\
ī	site, buy		
j	job, edge		
k	kin, cook	'	mark at the beginning of a syllable that has primary (strongest) stress: \'shə-fəl-ˌbȯrd\
k̲	German Bach, Scots loch		
l	lily, cool		
m	murmur, dim	ˌ	mark at the beginning of a syllable that has secondary (next-strongest) stress: \'shə-fəl-ˌbȯrd\
n	nine, own		
ⁿ	indicates that a preceding vowel is pronounced through both nose and mouth, as in French bon \bōⁿ\	-	mark of a syllable division in pronunciations (the mark of end-of-line division in boldface entries is a centered dot ·)
ŋ	sing, singer, finger, ink	( )	indicate that what is symbolized between sometimes occurs and sometimes does not occur in the pronunciation of the word: bakery \'bā-k(ə-)rē\ = \'bā-kə-rē, 'bā-krē\
ō	bone, hollow		
ȯ	saw		
ȯr	boar, port		
œ	French bœuf, feu, German Hölle, Höhle		

¹a \'ā\ *n, pl* **a's** *or* **as** \'āz\ *often cap* **1** : the 1st letter of the English alphabet **2** : a grade rating a student's work as superior

²a \ə, (')ā\ *indefinite article* : ONE, SOME — used to indicate an unspecified or unidentified individual ⟨there's ~ man outside⟩

³a *abbr, often cap* **1** absent **2** acre **3** alto **4** answer **5** are **6** area

AA *abbr* **1** Alcoholics Anonymous **2** antiaircraft **3** associate in arts

AAA *abbr* American Automobile Association

A and M *abbr* agricultural and mechanical

A and R *abbr* artists and repertory

aard·vark \'ärd-ˌvärk\ *n* [obs. Afrikaans, fr. Afrikaans *aard* earth + *vark* pig] : a large burrowing African mammal that feeds on ants and termites with its long sticky tongue

aardvark

¹ab \'ab\ *n* : an abdominal muscle

²ab *abbr* about

AB *abbr* **1** able-bodied seaman **2** airman basic **3** [NL *artium baccalaureus*] bachelor of arts

ABA *abbr* American Bar Association

aback \ə-'bak\ *adv* : by surprise ⟨taken ~⟩

aba·cus \'a-bə-kəs\ *n, pl* **aba·ci** \-ˌsī, -ˌkē\ *or* **aba·cus·es** : an instrument for making calculations by sliding counters along rods or grooves

¹abaft \ə-'baft\ *prep* : to the rear of

²abaft *adv* : toward or at the stern : AFT

ab·a·lo·ne \ˌa-bə-'lō-nē, 'a-bə-ˌ\ *n* : any of a genus of large edible sea mollusks with a flattened slightly spiral shell with holes along the edge

¹aban·don \ə-'ban-dən\ *vb* [ME *abandounen,* fr. AF *abanduner,* fr. *(mettre) a bandun* to hand over, put in someone's control] : to give up completely : FORSAKE, DESERT — **aban·don·ment** *n*

²abandon *n* : a thorough yielding to natural impulses; *esp* : EXUBERANCE

aban·doned \ə-'ban-dənd\ *adj* : morally unrestrained

✦ **Synonyms** PROFLIGATE, DISSOLUTE, REPROBATE

abase \ə-'bās\ *vb* **abased; abas·ing** : HUMBLE, DEGRADE — **abase·ment** *n*

abash \ə-'bash\ *vb* : to destroy the composure of : EMBARRASS — **abash·ment** *n*

abate \ə-'bāt\ *vb* **abat·ed; abat·ing 1** : to put an end to ⟨~ a nuisance⟩ **2** : to decrease in amount, number, or degree

abate·ment \ə-'bāt-mənt\ *n* **1** : DECREASE **2** : an amount abated; *esp* : a deduction from a tax

ab·at·toir \'a-bə-ˌtwär\ *n* [F] : SLAUGHTERHOUSE

ab·ba·cy \'a-bə-sē\ *n, pl* **-cies** : the office or term of office of an abbot or abbess

ab·bé \a-'bā, 'a-ˌ\ *n* : a member of the French secular clergy — used as a title

ab·bess \'a-bəs\ *n* : the superior of a convent for nuns

ab·bey \'a-bē\ *n, pl* **abbeys 1** : MONASTERY **2** : CONVENT **3** : an abbey church

ab·bot \'a-bət\ *n* [ME *abbod,* fr. OE, fr. LL *abbat-, abbas,* fr. LGk *abbas,* fr. Aramaic *abbā* father] : the superior of a monastery for men

abbr *abbr* abbreviation

ab·bre·vi·ate \ə-'brē-vē-ˌāt\ *vb* **-at·ed; -at·ing** : SHORTEN, CURTAIL; *esp* : to reduce to an abbreviation

ab·bre·vi·a·tion \ə-ˌbrē-vē-'ā-shən\ *n* **1** : the act or result of abbreviating **2** : a shortened form of a word or phrase used for brevity esp. in writing

¹ABC \ˌā-(ˌ)bē-'sē\ *n, pl* **ABC's** *or* **ABCs** \-'sēz\ **1** : ALPHABET — usu. used in pl. **2** : RUDIMENTS — usu. used in pl.

²ABC *abbr* American Broadcasting Company

Ab·di·as \ab-'dī-əs\ *n* : OBADIAH

ab·di·cate \'ab-di-ˌkāt\ *vb* **-cat·ed; -cat·ing** : to give up (as a throne) formally — **ab·di·ca·tion** \ˌab-di-'kā-shən\ *n*

ab·do·men \'ab-də-mən, ab-'dō-\ *n* **1** : the cavity in or area of the body between the chest and the pelvis **2** : the part of the body posterior to the thorax in an arthropod — **ab·dom·i·nal** \ab-'dä-mə-nᵊl\ *adj* — **ab·dom·i·nal·ly** *adv*

ab·duct \ab-'dəkt\ *vb* : to take away (a person) by force : KIDNAP — **ab·duc·tion** \-'dək-shən\ *n* — **ab·duc·tor** \-tər\ *n*

abeam \ə-'bēm\ *adv or adj* : on a line at right angles to a ship's keel

abed \ə-'bed\ *adv or adj* : in bed

Abe·na·ki \ˌa-bə-'nä-kē\ *also* **Ab·na·ki** \ab-'nä-kē\ *n, pl* **Abenaki** *or* **Abenakis** *also* **Abnaki** *or* **Abnakis** : a member of a group of American Indian peoples of northern New England and southern Quebec

ab·er·ra·tion \ˌa-bə-'rā-shən\ *n* **1** : deviation esp. from a moral standard or normal state **2** : failure of a mirror or lens to produce exact point-to-point correspondence between an object and its image **3** : unsoundness of mind : DERANGEMENT — **ab·er·rant** \a-'ber-ənt\ *adj*

abet \ə-'bet\ *vb* **abet·ted; abet·ting** [ME *abetten,* fr. AF *abeter,* fr. *beter* to bait] : INCITE, ENCOURAGE **2** : to assist or support in the achievement of a purpose ⟨~ a fugitive⟩ — **abet·tor** *or* **abet·ter** \-'be-tər\ *n*

abey·ance \ə-'bā-əns\ *n* : a condition of suspended activity — **abey·ant** \-ənt\ *adj*

ab·hor \əb-'hȯr, ab-\ *vb* **ab·horred; ab·hor·ring** [ME *abhorren,* fr. L *abhorrēre,* fr. *ab-* + *horrēre* to shudder] : LOATHE, DETEST — **ab·hor·rence** \-əns\ *n*

ab·hor·rent \-ənt\ *adj* : LOATHSOME, DETESTABLE ⟨~ crimes⟩

abide \ə-'bīd\ *vb* **abode** \-'bōd\ *or* **abid·ed; abid·ing 1** : BEAR, ENDURE **2** : DWELL, REMAIN, LAST — **abide by** : to conform or acquiesce to ⟨*abide by* the law⟩

abil·i·ty \ə-'bi-lə-tē\ *n, pl* **-ties** : the quality of being able : POWER, SKILL

-ability *also* **-ibility** *n suffix* : capacity, fitness, or tendency to act or be acted on in a (specified) way ⟨flamm*ability*⟩

ab·ject \'ab-ˌjekt, ab-'jekt\ *adj* : low in spirit, hope, or state ⟨~ poverty⟩ — **ab·jec·tion** \ab-'jek-shən\ *n* — **ab·ject·ly** *adv* — **ab·ject·ness** *n*

ab·jure \ab-'jùr\ *vb* **ab·jured; ab·jur·ing 1** : to renounce solemnly : RECANT **2** : to abstain from — **ab·ju·ra·tion** \ˌab-jə-'rā-shən\ *n*

abl *abbr* ablative

ab·late \a-'blāt\ *vb* **ab·lat·ed; ab·lat·ing** : to remove or become removed esp. by cutting, abrading, or vaporizing

ab·la·tion \a-'blā-shən\ *n* **1** : surgical cutting and removal **2** : loss of a part (as the outside of a nose cone) by melting or vaporization

ab·la·tive \'ab-lə-tiv\ *adj* : of, relating to, or constituting a grammatical case (as in Latin) expressing typically the relation of separation and source — **ablative** *n*

ablaze \ə-'blāz\ *adj or adv* : being on fire : BLAZING

able \'ā-bəl\ *adj* **abler** \-b(ə-)lər\; **ablest** \-b(ə-)ləst\ [ME, fr. AF, fr. L *habilis* apt, fr. *habēre* to hold, possess] **1** : having sufficient power, skill, or resources to accomplish an object **2** : marked by skill or efficiency — **ably** \-blē\ *adv*

-able *also* **-ible** *adj suffix* **1** : capable of, fit for, or worthy of (being so acted upon or toward) ⟨break*able*⟩ ⟨collect*ible*⟩ **2** : tending, given, or liable to ⟨knowledge*able*⟩ ⟨perish*able*⟩

able–bod·ied \ā-bəl-'bä-dēd\ *adj* : having a sound strong body

abloom \ə-'blüm\ *adj* : BLOOMING

ab·lu·tion \ə-'blü-shən, a-\ *n* : the washing of one's body or part of it

ABM \ā-(ˌ)bē-'em\ *n, pl* **ABM's** *or* **ABMs** : ANTIBALLISTIC MISSILE

Abnaki *var of* ABENAKI

ab·ne·gate \'ab-ni-ˌgāt\ *vb* **-gat·ed; -gat·ing** **1** : DENY, RENOUNCE **2** : SURRENDER, RELINQUISH ⟨~ her powers⟩ — **ab·ne·ga·tion** \ˌab-ni-'gā-shən\ *n*

ab·nor·mal \ab-'nor-məl\ *adj* : deviating from the normal or average — **ab·nor·mal·i·ty** \ˌab-nor-'ma-lə-tē\ *n* — **ab·nor·mal·ly** *adv*

¹aboard \ə-'bord\ *adv* **1** : ALONGSIDE **2** : on, onto, or within a car, ship, or aircraft **3** : in or into a group or association ⟨welcome new workers ~⟩

²aboard *prep* : ON, ONTO, WITHIN

abode \ə-'bōd\ *n* **1** : STAY, SOJOURN **2** : HOME, RESIDENCE

abol·ish \ə-'bä-lish\ *vb* : to do away with : ANNUL ⟨~ slavery⟩ — **ab·o·li·tion** \ˌa-bə-'li-shən\ *n*

ab·o·li·tion·ism \ˌa-bə-'li-shə-ˌni-zəm\ *n* : advocacy of the abolition of slavery — **ab·o·li·tion·ist** \-'li-sh(ə-)nist\ *n or adj*

A–bomb \'ā-ˌbäm\ *n* : ATOMIC BOMB — **A–bomb** *vb*

abom·i·na·ble \ə-'bä-mə-nə-bəl\ *adj* : causing disgust or hatred : DETESTABLE

abominable snow·man \-'snō-mən, -ˌman\ *n, often cap A&S* : a mysterious creature with human or apelike characteristics reported to exist in the high Himalayas

abom·i·nate \ə-'bä-mə-ˌnāt\ *vb* **-nat·ed; -nat·ing** [L *abominari*, lit., to deprecate as an ill omen, fr. *ab-* away + *omen* omen] : to hate or loathe intensely

abom·i·na·tion \ə-ˌbä-mə-'nā-shən\ *n* **1** : something abominable **2** : extreme disgust or hatred : LOATHING

ab·orig·i·nal \ˌa-bə-'ri-jə-nəl\ *adj* : ORIGINAL, INDIGENOUS, PRIMITIVE

ab·orig·i·ne \ˌa-bə-'ri-jə-nē\ *n* : a member of the original race of inhabitants of a region : NATIVE

aborn·ing \ə-'bor-niŋ\ *adv* : while being born or produced

¹abort \ə-'bort\ *vb* **1** : to cause or undergo abortion **2** : to terminate prematurely ⟨~ a spaceflight⟩ — **abor·tive** \-'bor-tiv\ *adj*

²abort *n* : the premature termination of a mission of or a procedure relating to an aircraft or spacecraft

abor·tion \ə-'bor-shən\ *n* : the spontaneous or induced termination of a pregnancy after, accompanied by, resulting in, or closely followed by the death of the embryo or fetus

abor·tion·ist \-sh(ə-)nist\ *n* : one who induces abortions

abound \ə-'baund\ *vb* **1** : to be plentiful : TEEM **2** : to be fully supplied

¹about \ə-'baut\ *adv* **1** : reasonably close to; *also* : on the verge of ⟨~ to join the army⟩ **2** : on all sides **3** : NEARBY

²about *prep* **1** : on every side of **2** : near to **3** : CONCERNING

about–face \-'fās\ *n* : a reversal of direction or attitude — **about–face** *vb*

¹above \ə-'bəv\ *adv* **1** : in the sky; *also* : in or to heaven **2** : in or to a higher place; *also* : higher on the same page or on a preceding page

²above *prep* **1** : in or to a higher place than : OVER ⟨storm clouds ~ the bay⟩ **2** : superior to ⟨he thought her far ~ him⟩ **3** : more than : EXCEEDING **4** : as distinct from ⟨~ the noise⟩

above–board \-ˌbord\ *adv or adj* : without concealment or deception : OPENLY

abp *abbr* archbishop

abr *abbr* abridged; abridgment

ab·ra·ca·dab·ra \ˌa-brə-kə-'da-brə\ *n* **1** : a magical charm or incantation against calamity **2** : GIBBERISH

abrade \ə-'brād\ *vb* **abrad·ed; abrad·ing** **1** : to wear away by friction **2** : to wear down in spirit : IRRITATE — **abra·sion** \-'brā-zhən\ *n*

¹abra·sive \ə-'brā-siv\ *n* : a substance (as pumice) for abrading, smoothing, or polishing

²abrasive *adj* : tending to abrade : causing irritation ⟨~ relationships⟩ — **abra·sive·ly** *adv* — **abra·sive·ness** *n*

abreast \ə-'brest\ *adv or adj* **1** : side by side **2** : up to a standard or level esp. of knowledge ⟨kept ~ of the news⟩

abridge \ə-'brij\ *vb* **abridged; abridg·ing** [ME *abregen*, fr. AF *abreger*, fr. LL *abbreviare*, fr. L *ad* to + *brevis* short] : to lessen in length or extent : SHORTEN — **abridg·ment** *or* **abridge·ment** *n*

abroad \ə-'brod\ *adv or adj* **1** : over a wide area **2** : away from one's home **3** : outside one's country

ab·ro·gate \'a-brə-ˌgāt\ *vb* **-gat·ed; -gat·ing** : ANNUL, REVOKE — **ab·ro·ga·tion** \ˌa-brə-'gā-shən\ *n*

abrupt \ə-'brəpt\ *adj* **1** : broken or as if broken off **2** : SUDDEN, HASTY ⟨an ~ turn⟩ **3** : so quick as to seem rude ⟨an ~ reply⟩ **4** : DISCONNECTED **5** : STEEP — **abrupt·ly** *adv*

abs *abbr* absolute

ab·scess \'ab-ˌses\ *n, pl* **ab·scess·es** [L *abscessus*, lit., act of going away, fr. *abscedere* to go away, fr. *abs-, ab-* away + *cedere* to go] : a localized collection of pus surrounded by inflamed tissue — **ab·scessed** \-ˌsest\ *adj*

ab·scis·sa \ab-'si-sə\ *n, pl* **abscissas** *also* **ab·scis·sae** \-'si-(ˌ)sē\ : the horizontal coordinate of a point in a plane coordinate system obtained by measuring parallel to the x-axis

ab·scis·sion \ab-'si-zhən\ *n* **1** : the act or process of cutting off **2** : the natural separation of flowers, fruits, or leaves from plants — **ab·scise** \ab-'sīz\ *vb*

ab·scond \ab-'skänd\ *vb* : to depart secretly and hide oneself

ab·sence \'ab-səns\ *n* **1** : the state or time of being absent **2** : WANT, LACK **3** : INATTENTION ⟨~ of mind⟩

¹ab·sent \'ab-sənt\ *adj* **1** : not present **2** : LACKING **3** : INATTENTIVE

²ab·sent \ab-'sent\ *vb* : to keep (oneself) away

³ab·sent \'ab-sənt\ *prep* : in the absence of : WITHOUT

ab·sen·tee \ˌab-sən-'tē\ *n* : one that is absent or keeps away

absentee ballot *n* : a ballot submitted (as by mail) in advance of an election by a voter who is unable to be present at the polls

ab·sen·tee·ism \ˌab-sən-'tē-ˌi-zəm\ *n* : chronic absence (as from work or school)

ab·sent–mind·ed \ˌab-sənt-'mīn-dəd\ *adj* : unaware of one's surroundings or actions : INATTENTIVE — **ab·sent·mind·ed·ly** *adv* — **ab·sent·mind·ed·ness** *n*

ab·sinthe *also* **ab·sinth** \'ab-ˌsinth\ *n* [F] : a liqueur flavored esp. with wormwood and anise

ab·so·lute \'ab-sə-ˌlüt, ˌab-sə-'lüt\ *adj* **1** : free from imperfection or mixture **2** : free from control, restriction, or qualification ⟨~ power⟩ **3** : lacking grammatical connection with any other word in a sentence ⟨~ construction⟩ **4** : POSITIVE ⟨~ proof⟩ **5** : relating to the fundamental units of length, mass, and time **6** : FUNDAMENTAL, ULTIMATE ⟨~ knowledge⟩ — **ab·so·lute·ly** *adv*

absolute pitch *n* **1** : the position of a tone in a standard scale independently determined by its rate of vibration **2** : the ability to sing a note asked for or to name a note heard

absolute value *n* : a nonnegative number equal to a given real number with any negative sign removed

absolute zero *n* : a theoretical temperature marked by a complete absence of heat and motion and equivalent to exactly -273.15°C or -459.67°F

ab·so·lu·tion \ˌab-sə-'lü-shən\ *n* : the act of absolving; *esp* : a remission of sins pronounced by a priest in the sacrament of reconciliation

ab·so·lut·ism \'ab-sə-ˌlü-ˌti-zəm\ *n* **1** : the theory that a ruler or government should have unlimited power **2** : government by an absolute ruler or authority

ab·solve \əb-'zälv, -'sälv\ *vb* **ab·solved; ab·solv·ing** : to set free from an obligation or the consequences of guilt

ab·sorb \əb-'sorb, -'zorb\ *vb* **1** : to take in and make part of an existent whole **2** : to suck up or take in the manner of a sponge **3** : to engage (one's attention) : ENGROSS **4** : to receive without recoil or shock ⟨a ceiling that ~s sound⟩ **5** : ASSUME, BEAR ⟨~ all costs⟩ **6** : to transform (radiant energy) into a different form esp. with a resulting rise in temperature — **ab·sorb·ing** *adj* — **ab·sorb·ing·ly** *adv*

ab·sor·bent *also* **ab·sor·bant** \əb-'sȯr-bənt, '-zȯr-\ *adj* : able to absorb ⟨∼ cotton⟩ — **ab·sor·ben·cy** \-bən-sē\ *n* — **absorbent** *also* **absorbant** *n*

ab·sorp·tion \əb-'sȯrp-shən, -'zȯrp-\ *n* **1** : a process of absorbing or being absorbed **2** : concentration of attention ⟨∼ in his work⟩ — **ab·sorp·tive** \-tiv\ *adj*

ab·stain \əb-'stān\ *vb* : to refrain from an action or practice — **ab·stain·er** *n* — **ab·sten·tion** \-'sten-chən\ *n*

ab·ste·mi·ous \ab-'stē-mē-əs\ *adj* : sparing in use of food or drink : TEMPERATE — **ab·ste·mi·ous·ly** *adv* — **ab·ste·mi·ous·ness** *n*

ab·sti·nence \'ab-stə-nəns\ *n* : voluntary refraining esp. from eating certain foods, drinking liquor, or engaging in sexual intercourse — **ab·sti·nent** \-nənt\ *adj*

abstr *abbr* abstract

¹ab·stract \ab-'strakt, 'ab-ˌstrakt\ *adj* **1** : considered apart from a particular instance **2** : expressing a quality apart from an object ⟨*whiteness* is an ∼ word⟩ **3** : having only intrinsic form with little or no pictorial representation ⟨∼ painting⟩ — **ab·stract·ly** *adv* — **ab·stract·ness** *n*

²ab·stract \'ab-ˌstrakt; *2 also* ab-'strakt\ *n* **1** : a written summary **2** : an abstract thing or state

³ab·stract \ab-'strakt, 'ab-ˌstrakt; *2 usu* 'ab-ˌstrakt\ *vb* **1** : REMOVE, SEPARATE **2** : to make an abstract of : SUMMARIZE **3** : to draw away the attention of **4** : STEAL — **ab·stract·ed·ly** \ab-'strak-təd-lē, 'ab-ˌstrak-\ *adv*

abstract expressionism *n* : art that expresses the artist's attitudes and emotions through abstract forms — **abstract expressionist** *n*

ab·strac·tion \ab-'strak-shən\ *n* **1** : the act of abstracting : the state of being abstracted **2** : an abstract idea **3** : an abstract work of art

ab·struse \ab-'strüs\ *adj* : hard to understand : RECONDITE — **ab·struse·ly** *adv* — **ab·struse·ness** *n*

ab·surd \əb-'sərd, -'zərd\ *adj* [MF *absurde*, fr. L *absurdus*, fr. *ab-* from + *surdus* deaf, stupid] : RIDICULOUS, UNREASONABLE — **ab·sur·di·ty** \-'sər-də-tē, -'zər-\ *n* — **ab·surd·ly** *adv*

abun·dant \ə-'bən-dənt\ *adj* [ME, fr. AF, fr. L *abundant-, abundans,* prp. of *abundare* to abound, fr. *ab-* from + *unda* wave] : more than enough : amply sufficient ✦ **Synonyms** COPIOUS, PLENTIFUL, AMPLE, BOUNTIFUL — **abun·dance** \-dəns\ *n* — **abun·dant·ly** *adv*

¹abuse \ə-'byüs\ *n* **1** : a corrupt practice **2** : MISUSE ⟨drug ∼⟩ **3** : coarse and insulting speech ⟨verbal ∼⟩ **4** : MISTREATMENT ⟨child ∼⟩

²abuse \ə-'byüz\ *vb* **abused; abus·ing 1** : to put to a wrong use : MISUSE **2** : to use excessively ⟨∼ alcohol⟩ **3** : MISTREAT **4** : to attack in words : REVILE — **abus·er** *n* — **abu·sive** \-'byü-siv\ *adj* — **abu·sive·ly** *adv* — **abu·sive·ness** *n*

abut \ə-'bət\ *vb* **abut·ted; abut·ting** : to touch along a border : border on

abut·ment \ə-'bət-mənt\ *n* : the part of a structure (as a bridge) that supports weight or withstands lateral pressure

abut·ter \ə-'bə-tər\ *n* : one that abuts; *esp* : the owner of a contiguous property

abuzz \ə-'bəz\ *adj* : filled or resounding with activity or excitement ⟨an office ∼ with rumors⟩

abys·mal \ə-'biz-məl\ *adj* **1** : immeasurably deep : BOTTOMLESS **2** : absolutely wretched ⟨∼ living conditions of the poor⟩ — **abys·mal·ly** *adv*

abyss \ə-'bis\ *n* **1** : the bottomless pit in old accounts of the universe **2** : an immeasurable depth

abys·sal \ə-'bi-səl\ *adj* : of or relating to the bottom waters of the ocean depths

ac *abbr* account

-ac *n suffix* : one affected with ⟨hypochondri*ac*⟩

Ac *symbol* actinium

AC *abbr* **1** air-conditioning **2** alternating current **3** [L *ante Christum*] before Christ **4** [L *ante cibum*] before meals **5** area code

aca·cia \ə-'kā-shə\ *n* : any of a genus of leguminous trees or shrubs with round white or yellow flower clusters and often feathery leaves

acad *abbr* academic; academy

ac·a·deme \'a-kə-ˌdēm, ˌa-kə-'\ *n* : SCHOOL; *also* : academic environment

¹ac·a·dem·ic \ˌa-kə-'de-mik\ *n* : a person who is academic in background, outlook, or methods

²academic *adj* **1** : of, relating to, or associated with schools or colleges **2** : literary or general rather than technical **3** : theoretical rather than practical — **ac·a·dem·i·cal·ly** \-mi-k(ə-)lē\ *adv*

ac·a·de·mi·cian \ˌa-kə-də-'mi-shən, ə-ˌka-də-\ *n* **1** : a member of a society of scholars or artists **2** : ACADEMIC

ac·a·dem·i·cism \ˌa-kə-'de-mə-ˌsi-zəm\ *also* **acad·e·mism** \ə-'ka-də-ˌmi-zəm\ *n* **1** : a formal academic quality **2** : purely speculative thinking

acad·e·my \ə-'ka-də-mē\ *n, pl* **-mies** [Gk *Akadēmeia*, school of philosophy founded by Plato, fr. *Akadēmeia*, gymnasium where Plato taught, fr. *Akadēmos* Greek mythological hero] **1** : a school above the elementary level; *esp* : a private high school **2** : a society of scholars or artists

acan·thus \ə-'kan-thəs\ *n, pl* **acanthus 1** : any of a genus of prickly herbs of the Mediterranean region **2** : an ornamentation (as on a column) representing the leaves of the acanthus

a cap·pel·la *also* **a ca·pel·la** \ˌä-kə-'pe-lə\ *adv or adj* [It *a cappella* in chapel style] : without instrumental accompaniment

acc *abbr* accusative

ac·cede \ak-'sēd\ *vb* **ac·ced·ed; ac·ced·ing 1** : to become a party to an agreement **2** : to express approval **3** : to enter upon an office ✦ **Synonyms** AGREE, ACQUIESCE, ASSENT, CONSENT, SUBSCRIBE

ac·cel·er·ate \ik-'se-lə-ˌrāt, ak-\ *vb* **-at·ed; -at·ing 1** : to bring about earlier **2** : to speed up : QUICKEN — **ac·cel·er·a·tion** \-ˌse-lə-'rā-shən\ *n*

ac·cel·er·a·tor \ik-'se-lə-ˌrā-tər, ak-\ *n* **1** : one that accelerates **2** : a pedal for controlling the speed of a motor-vehicle engine **3** : an apparatus for imparting high velocities to charged particles

ac·cel·er·om·e·ter \ik-ˌse-lə-'rä-mə-tər, ak-\ *n* : an instrument for measuring acceleration or vibrations

¹ac·cent \'ak-ˌsent, ak-'sent\ *vb* : to give stress to : EMPHASIZE

²ac·cent \'ak-ˌsent\ *n* **1** : prominence given to one syllable of a word esp. by stress **2** : a distinctive manner of pronunciation ⟨a foreign ∼⟩ **3** : a mark (as ´, `, ˆ) over a vowel used usu. to indicate a difference in pronunciation from a vowel not so marked — **ac·cen·tu·al** \ak-'sen-chə-wəl\ *adj*

ac·cen·tu·ate \ak-'sen-chə-ˌwāt\ *vb* **-at·ed; -at·ing** : STRESS, EMPHASIZE — **ac·cen·tu·a·tion** \-ˌsen-chə-'wā-shən\ *n*

ac·cept \ik-'sept, ak-\ *vb* **1** : to receive willingly **2** : to agree to **3** : to assume an obligation to pay

ac·cept·able \ik-'sep-tə-bəl, ak-\ *adj* : capable or worthy of being accepted — **ac·cept·abil·i·ty** \ik-ˌsep-tə-'bi-lə-tē, ak-\ *n*

ac·cep·tance \ik-'sep-təns, ak-\ *n* **1** : the act of accepting **2** : the state of being accepted or acceptable **3** : an accepted bill of exchange

ac·cep·ta·tion \ˌak-ˌsep-'tā-shən\ *n* : the generally understood meaning of a word

¹ac·cess \'ak-ˌses\ *n* **1** : capacity to enter or approach **2** : a way of approach : ENTRANCE

²access *vb* : to get at : gain access to

ac·ces·si·ble \ik-'se-sə-bəl, ak-, ek-\ *adj* **1** : capable of being reached ⟨∼ by train⟩ **2** : capable of being used or seen ⟨∼ archives⟩ **3** : capable of being understood ⟨an ∼ film⟩ — **ac·ces·si·bil·i·ty** \-ˌse-sə-'bi-lə-tē\ *n*

ac·ces·sion \ik-'se-shən, ak-\ *n* **1** : increase by something added **2** : something added **3** : the act of coming to a high office or position

ac·ces·so·ry *also* **ac·ces·sa·ry** \ik-'se-sə-rē, ak-\ *n, pl* **-ries 1** : a person who though not present abets or assists in the commission of an offense **2** : something helpful but not essential ✦ **Synonyms** APPURTENANCE, ADJUNCT, APPENDAGE, APPENDIX — **accessory** *adj*

ac·ci·dent \'ak-sə-dənt\ *n* **1** : an event occurring by chance or unintentionally **2** : CHANCE ⟨met by ∼⟩ **3** : a nonessential property

¹ac·ci·den·tal \ˌak-sə-'den-tᵊl\ *adj* **1** : happening unexpectedly or by chance **2** : happening without intent or through carelessness ✦ **Synonyms** CASUAL, FORTUITOUS,

INCIDENTAL, CHANCE — **ac·ci·den·tal·ly** \-'den-tᵊl-ē\ *also* **ac·ci·dent·ly** \-'dent-lē\ *adv*
²**accidental** *n* : a musical note foreign to a key indicated by a signature
ac·claim \ə-'klām\ *vb* **1** : to give strong approval or praise to **2** : to declare by acclamation ✦ *Synonyms* EXTOL, LAUD, COMMEND, HAIL — **acclaim** *n*
ac·cla·ma·tion \ˌa-klə-'mā-shən\ *n* **1** : loud eager applause **2** : an overwhelming affirmative vote by shouting or applause rather than by ballot
ac·cli·mate \'a-klə-ˌmāt, ə-'klī-mət\ *vb* **-mat·ed; -mat·ing** : to accustom or become accustomed to a new climate or situation — **ac·cli·ma·tion** \ˌa-klə-'mā-shən, -ˌklī-\ *n*
ac·cli·ma·tise *Brit var of* ACCLIMATIZE
ac·cli·ma·tize \ə-'klī-mə-ˌtīz\ *vb* **-tized; -tiz·ing** : ACCLIMATE — **ac·cli·ma·ti·za·tion** \-ˌklī-mə-tə-'zā-shən\ *n*
ac·cliv·i·ty \ə-'kli-və-tē\ *n, pl* **-ties** : an ascending slope
ac·co·lade \'a-kə-ˌlād\ *n* [F, fr. *accoler* to embrace, ult. fr. L *ad-* to + *collum* neck] : an expression of praise : AWARD
ac·com·mo·date \ə-'kä-mə-ˌdāt\ *vb* **-dat·ed; -dat·ing 1** : to make fit or suitable : ADAPT, ADJUST **2** : HARMONIZE, RECONCILE **3** : to provide with something needed **4** : to hold without crowding **5** : to undergo visual accommodation
ac·com·mo·dat·ing *adj* : OBLIGING
ac·com·mo·da·tion \ə-ˌkä-mə-'dā-shən\ *n* **1** : something supplied to satisfy a need; *esp* : LODGINGS — usu. used in pl. **2** : the act of accommodating : ADJUSTMENT **3** : the automatic adjustment of the eye for seeing at different distances
ac·com·pa·ni·ment \ə-'kəm-pə-nē-mənt, -'kəmp-nē-\ *n* : something that accompanies another; *esp* : subordinate music to support a principal voice or instrument
ac·com·pa·ny \-nē\ *vb* **-nied; -ny·ing 1** : to go or occur with : ATTEND **2** : to play an accompaniment for — **ac·com·pa·nist** \-nist\ *n*
ac·com·plice \ə-'käm-pləs, -'kəm-\ *n* : an associate in wrongdoing
ac·com·plish \ə-'käm-plish, -'kəm-\ *vb* : to bring to completion ✦ *Synonyms* ACHIEVE, EFFECT, EXECUTE, PERFORM — **ac·com·plish·er** *n*
ac·com·plished \-plisht\ *adj* **1** : EXPERT, SKILLED ⟨an ∼ pianist⟩ **2** : established beyond doubt ⟨an ∼ fact⟩
ac·com·plish·ment \ə-'käm-plish-mənt, -'kəm-\ *n* **1** : COMPLETION **2** : something completed or effected **3** : an acquired excellence or skill
¹**ac·cord** \ə-'kȯrd\ *vb* [ME, fr. AF *acorder*, fr. VL *accordare*, fr. L *ad-* to + *cord-, cor* heart] **1** : GRANT, CONCEDE **2** : AGREE, HARMONIZE ⟨his interpretation does not ∼ with the facts⟩ — **ac·cor·dant** \-'kȯr-dᵊnt\ *adj*
²**accord** *n* **1** : AGREEMENT, HARMONY **2** : willingness to act ⟨gave of their own ∼⟩
ac·cor·dance \ə-'kȯr-dᵊns\ *n* **1** : ACCORD **2** : the act of granting
ac·cord·ing·ly \ə-'kȯr-diŋ-lē\ *adv* **1** : in accordance **2** : CONSEQUENTLY, SO
according *prep* **1** : in conformity with ⟨paid *according* to ability⟩ **2** : as stated or attested by ⟨*according to you*⟩
¹**ac·cor·di·on** \ə-'kȯr-dē-ən\ *n* [G *Akkordion*, fr. *Akkord* chord] : a portable keyboard instrument with a bellows and reeds — **ac·cor·di·on·ist** \-ə-nist\ *n*
²**accordion** *adj* : folding like the bellows of an accordion ⟨∼ pleats⟩
ac·cost \ə-'kȯst\ *vb* [MF *accoster*, ultim. fr. L *ad-* to + *costa* rib, side] : to approach and speak to esp. aggressively
¹**ac·count** \ə-'kaȯnt\ *n* **1** : a statement of business transactions **2** : a formal business arrangement for regular dealings or services ⟨an advertising ∼⟩ ⟨an email ∼⟩ **3** : a statement of reasons, causes, or motives **4** : VALUE, IMPORTANCE ⟨his opinion is of little ∼⟩ **5** : a sum of money deposited in a bank and subject to withdrawal by the depositor — **on account of** : BECAUSE OF — **on no account** : under no circumstances — **on one's own account** : on one's own behalf
²**account** *vb* **1** : CONSIDER ⟨I ∼ him lucky⟩ **2** : to give an explanation ⟨∼ for the money you spent⟩ — used with *for*
ac·count·able \ə-'kaȯn-tə-bəl\ *adj* **1** : ANSWERABLE,

RESPONSIBLE **2** : EXPLICABLE — **ac·count·abil·i·ty** \-ˌkaȯn-tə-'bi-lə-tē\ *n*
ac·coun·tant \ə-'kaȯn-tᵊnt\ *n* : a person skilled in accounting — **ac·coun·tan·cy** \-tᵊn-sē\ *n*
account executive *n* : a business executive in charge of a client's account
ac·count·ing \ə-'kaȯn-tiŋ\ *n* : the art or system of keeping and analyzing financial records
ac·cou·tre *or* **ac·cou·ter** \ə-'kü-tər\ *vb* **-cou·tred** *or* **-coutered; -cou·tring** *or* **-cou·ter·ing** \-'kü-t(ə-)riŋ\ : EQUIP, OUTFIT ⟨the knights were *accoutred* for battle⟩
ac·cou·tre·ment *or* **ac·cou·ter·ment** \ə-'kü-trə-mənt, -'kü-tər-\ *n* [F] **1** : an accessory item — usu. used in pl. **2** : an identifying characteristic
ac·cred·it \ə-'kre-dət\ *vb* **1** : to endorse or approve officially **2** : to attribute — **ac·cred·i·ta·tion** \-ˌkre-də-'tā-shən\ *n*
ac·cre·tion \ə-'krē-shən\ *n* **1** : growth or enlargement esp. by addition from without **2** : a product of accretion
accretion disk *n* : a disk of usu. gaseous matter surrounding and gradually accumulating onto a massive celestial object
ac·crue \ə-'krü\ *vb* **ac·crued; ac·cru·ing 1** : to come by way of increase **2** : to be added by periodic growth — **ac·cru·al** \-əl\ *n*
acct *abbr* account; accountant
ac·cul·tur·a·tion \ə-ˌkəl-chə-'rā-shən\ *n* : cultural modification of an individual or group by borrowing and adapting traits from another culture
ac·cu·mu·late \ə-'kyü-myə-ˌlāt\ *vb* **-lat·ed; -lat·ing** [L *accumulare*, fr. *ad-* to + *cumulare* to heap up] : to heap or pile up ✦ *Synonyms* AMASS, GATHER, COLLECT, STOCKPILE — **ac·cu·mu·la·tion** \-ˌkyü-myə-'lā-shən\ *n* — **ac·cu·mu·la·tive** \-'kyü-myə-lə-tiv\ *adj* — **ac·cu·mu·la·tor** \-'kyü-myə-ˌlā-tər\ *n*
ac·cu·rate \'a-kyə-rət\ *adj* : free from error : EXACT, PRECISE — **ac·cu·ra·cy** \-rə-sē\ *n* — **ac·cu·rate·ly** *adv* — **ac·cu·rate·ness** *n*
ac·cursed \ə-'kərst, -'kər-səd\ *or* **ac·curst** \ə-'kərst\ *adj* **1** : being under a curse **2** : DAMNABLE, EXECRABLE
ac·cus·al \ə-'kyü-zəl\ *n* : ACCUSATION
ac·cu·sa·tive \ə-'kyü-zə-tiv\ *adj* : of, relating to, or being a grammatical case marking the direct object of a verb or the object of a preposition — **accusative** *n*
ac·cu·sa·to·ry \ə-'kyü-zə-ˌtȯr-ē\ *adj* : expressing accusation ⟨an ∼ tone⟩
ac·cuse \ə-'kyüz\ *vb* **ac·cused; ac·cus·ing** : to charge with an offense : BLAME — **ac·cu·sa·tion** \ˌa-kyə-'zā-shən\ *n* — **ac·cus·er** *n*
ac·cused \ə-'kyüzd\ *n, pl* **accused** : the defendant in a criminal case
ac·cus·tom \ə-'kəs-təm\ *vb* : to make familiar through use or experience
ac·cus·tomed \ə-'kəs-təmd\ *adj* : USUAL, CUSTOMARY; *also* : being in the habit ⟨∼ed to winning⟩
¹**ace** \'ās\ *n* [ME *as* a die face marked with one spot, fr. AF, fr. L, unit, a copper coin] **1** : a playing card bearing a single large pip in its center **2** : a point (as in tennis) won on a serve that goes untouched **3** : a golf score of one stroke on a hole **4** : a combat pilot who has downed five or more enemy planes **5** : one that excels **6** : the best pitcher on a baseball team
²**ace** *vb* **aced; ac·ing 1** : to score an ace against (an opponent) or on (a golf hole) **2** : to defeat decisively **3** : to perform extremely well in or on ⟨*aced* the quiz⟩
³**ace** *adj* : of first rank or quality
ACE in·hib·i·tor \ˌā-ˌsē-'ē-in-'hi-bə-tər, 'ās-\ *n* : any of a group of drugs that lower blood pressure by relaxing the arteries
acer·bic \ə-'sər-bik, a-\ *adj* : acid in temper, mood, or tone ⟨∼ wit⟩
acer·bi·ty \ə-'sər-bə-tē\ *n, pl* **-ties** : SOURNESS, BITTERNESS
acet·amin·o·phen \ə-ˌsē-tə-'mi-nə-fən\ *n* : a crystalline compound used in chemical synthesis and in medicine to relieve pain and fever
ac·e·tate \'a-sə-ˌtāt\ *n* **1** : a salt or ester of acetic acid **2** : a textile fiber made from cellulose and acetic acid; *also* : a fabric or plastic made of this fiber
ace·tic acid \ə-'sē-tik-\ *n* : a colorless pungent liquid acid that is the chief acid of vinegar and is used esp. in making chemical compounds

ac·e·tone \'a-sə-ˌtōn\ *n* : a volatile flammable fragrant liquid compound used in making other chemical compounds and as a solvent

ace·tyl·cho·line \ə-ˌsē-tᵊl-'kō-ˌlēn\ *n* : a compound that is released at nerve endings of the autonomic nervous system and is active in the transmission of nerve impulses

acet·y·lene \ə-'se-tᵊl-ən, -tᵊl-ˌēn\ *n* : a colorless flammable gas used as a fuel (as in welding and soldering)

ace·tyl·sal·i·cyl·ic acid \ə-ˌsē-tᵊl-ˌsa-lə-ˌsi-lik-\ *n* : ASPIRIN 1

ache \'āk\ *vb* **ached; ach·ing 1** : to suffer a usu. dull persistent pain ⟨an *aching* back⟩ **2** : LONG, YEARN ⟨*aching* to go home⟩ — **ache** *n* — **ach·ing·ly** \'ā-kiŋ-lē\ *adv*

achieve \ə-'chēv\ *vb* **achieved; achiev·ing** [ME *acheven*, fr. AF *achever* to finish, fr. a- to (fr. L *ad-*) + *chef* end, head, fr. L *caput*] : to gain by work or effort ✦ *Synonyms* ACCOMPLISH, ATTAIN, REALIZE — **achiev·able** \-'chē-və-bəl\ *adj* — **achieve·ment** *n* — **achiev·er** *n*

Achil·les' heel \ə-ˌki-lēz-\ *n* [fr. the story that the Greek warrior Achilles was vulnerable only in the heel] : a vulnerable point

Achil·les tendon \ə-ˌki-lēz-\ *n* : the tendon joining the muscles in the calf of the leg to the bone of the heel

ach·ro·mat·ic \ˌa-krə-'ma-tik\ *adj* : giving an image almost free from extraneous colors ⟨∼ lens⟩

achy \'ā-kē\ *adj* **ach·i·er; ach·i·est** : afflicted with aches — **ach·i·ness** *n*

¹**ac·id** \'a-səd\ *adj* **1** : sour or biting to the taste; *also* : sharp or sour in manner **2** : of or relating to an acid — **acid·i·ty** \ə-'si-də-tē\ *n* — **acid·ly** *adv*

²**acid** *n* **1** : a sour substance **2** : a usu. water-soluble chemical compound that has a sour taste, reacts with a base to form a salt, and reddens litmus **3** : LSD — **acid·ic** \ə-'si-dik\ *adj*

acid·i·fy \ə-'si-də-ˌfī\ *vb* **-fied; -fy·ing 1** : to make or become acid **2** : to change into an acid — **acid·i·fi·ca·tion** \-ˌsi-də-fə-'kā-shən\ *n*

ac·i·do·sis \ˌa-sə-'dō-səs\ *n, pl* **-do·ses** \-ˌsēz\ : an abnormal state of reduced alkalinity of the blood and body tissues

acid precipitation *n* : precipitation with above normal acidity that is caused esp. by atmospheric pollutants

acid rain *n* : acid precipitation in the form of rain

acid test *n* : a severe or crucial test

acid·u·lous \ə-'si-jə-ləs\ *adj* : somewhat acid or harsh in taste or manner

ack acknowledge; acknowledgment

ac·knowl·edge \ik-'nä-lij, ak-\ *vb* **-edged; -edg·ing 1** : to recognize the rights or authority of **2** : to admit as true **3** : to express thanks for; *also* : to report receipt of ⟨∼ a letter⟩ **4** : to recognize as valid — **ac·knowl·edg·ment** *or* **ac·knowl·edge·ment** *n*

ACL \ˌā-ˌsē-'el\ *n* : ANTERIOR CRUCIATE LIGAMENT

ACLU *abbr* American Civil Liberties Union

ac·me \'ak-mē\ *n* [Gk *akmē*] : the highest point

ac·ne \'ak-nē\ *n* [Gk *aknē*, MS var. of *akmē*, lit., point] : a skin disorder marked by inflammation of skin glands and hair follicles and by pimple formation esp. on the face

ac·o·lyte \'a-kə-ˌlīt\ *n* **1** : one who assists a member of the clergy in a liturgical service **2** : FOLLOWER

ac·o·nite \'a-kə-ˌnīt\ *n* **1** : MONKSHOOD **2** : the dried root of a common Eurasian monkshood used formerly as a drug

acorn \'ā-ˌkȯrn, -kərn\ *n* : the nut of the oak

acorn: three different kinds of oak tree

acorn squash *n* : an acorn-shaped dark green winter squash with a ridged surface and yellow to orange flesh

acous·tic \ə-'kü-stik\ *or* **acous·ti·cal** \-sti-kəl\ *adj* **1** : of or relating to the sense or organs of hearing, to sound, or to the science of sounds **2** : deadening sound ⟨∼ tile⟩ **3** : operated by or utilizing sound waves **4** : having a sound that is not electronically modified ⟨∼ guitar⟩ — **acous·ti·cal·ly** \-k(ə-)lē\ *adv*

acous·tics \ə-'kü-stiks\ *n sing or pl* **1** : the science of sound **2** : the qualities in a room that make it easy or hard for a person in it to hear distinctly

ac·quaint \ə-'kwānt\ *vb* [ME, ultim. fr. L *ad-* + *cognoscere* to know] **1** : to cause to know personally **2** : INFORM

ac·quain·tance \ə-'kwān-tᵊns\ *n* **1** : personal knowledge **2** : a person with whom one is acquainted — **ac·quain·tance·ship** *n*

acquaintance rape *n* : rape committed by someone known to the victim

ac·qui·esce \ˌa-kwē-'es\ *vb* **-esced; -esc·ing** : to accept, comply, or submit without open opposition ✦ *Synonyms* CONSENT, AGREE, ASSENT, ACCEDE — **ac·qui·es·cence** \-'e-sᵊns\ *n* — **ac·qui·es·cent** \-sᵊnt\ *adj* — **ac·qui·es·cent·ly** *adv*

ac·quire \ə-'kwī(-ə)r\ *vb* **ac·quired; ac·quir·ing** : to gain possession of : GET — **ac·quir·able** \-'kwī-rə-bəl\ *adj*

acquired *adj* **1** : gained by or as a result of effort or experience **2** : caused by environmental forces and not passed from parent to offspring in the genes ⟨∼ characteristics⟩

acquired immune deficiency syndrome *n* : AIDS

acquired immunodeficiency syndrome *n* : AIDS

ac·quire·ment \-'kwī(-ə)r-mənt\ *n* **1** : ATTAINMENT, ACCOMPLISHMENT **2** : the act of acquiring

ac·qui·si·tion \ˌa-kwə-'zi-shən\ *n* **1** : ACQUIREMENT **2** : something acquired

ac·quis·i·tive \ə-'kwi-zə-tiv\ *adj* : eager to acquire : GREEDY — **ac·quis·i·tive·ly** *adv* — **ac·quis·i·tive·ness** *n*

ac·quit \ə-'kwit\ *vb* **ac·quit·ted; ac·quit·ting 1** : to pronounce not guilty **2** : to conduct (oneself) usu. satisfactorily — **ac·quit·tal** \ə-'kwi-tᵊl\ *n*

acre \'ā-kər\ *n* **1** *pl* : LANDS, ESTATE **2** — see WEIGHT table

acre·age \'ā-k(ə-)rij\ *n* : area in acres

ac·rid \'a-krəd\ *adj* **1** : sharp and biting in taste or odor **2** : deeply bitter : CAUSTIC — **ac·rid·i·ty** \a-'kri-də-tē\ *n* — **ac·rid·ly** *adv* — **ac·rid·ness** *n*

ac·ri·mo·ny \'a-krə-ˌmō-nē\ *n, pl* **-nies** : harsh or biting sharpness of language or feeling — **ac·ri·mo·ni·ous** \ˌa-krə-'mō-nē-əs\ *adj* — **ac·ri·mo·ni·ous·ly** *adv* — **ac·ri·mo·ni·ous·ness** *n*

ac·ro·bat \'a-krə-ˌbat\ *n* [F *acrobate*, fr. Gk *akrobatēs*, fr. *akros* topmost + *bainein* to go] : a performer of gymnastic feats — **ac·ro·bat·ic** \ˌa-krə-'ba-tik\ *adj* — **ac·ro·bat·i·cal·ly** \-ti-k(ə-)lē\ *adv*

ac·ro·bat·ics \ˌa-krə-'ba-tiks\ *n sing or pl* : the performance of an acrobat

ac·ro·nym \'a-krə-ˌnim\ *n* : a word (as *radar*) or abbreviation (as *FBI*) formed from the initial letter or letters of each of the successive parts or major parts of a compound term

ac·ro·pho·bia \ˌa-krə-'fō-bē-ə\ *n* : abnormal dread of being in a high place : fear of heights

acrop·o·lis \ə-'krä-pə-ləs\ *n* [Gk *akropolis*, fr. *akros* topmost + *polis* city] : the upper fortified part of an ancient Greek city

¹**across** \ə-'krȯs\ *adv* **1** : to or on the opposite side **2** : so as to be understandable ⟨get the point ∼⟩

²**across** *prep* **1** : to or on the opposite side of ⟨ran ∼ the street⟩ **2** : on so as to cross or pass at an angle ⟨a log ∼ the road⟩

across–the–board *adj* **1** : placed to win if a competitor wins, places, or shows ⟨an ∼ bet⟩ **2** : including all classes or categories ⟨an ∼ wage increase⟩

acros·tic \ə-'krȯs-tik\ *n* : a composition usu. in verse in which the initial or final letters of the lines taken in order form a word or phrase — **acrostic** *adj*

acryl·ic \ə-'kri-lik\ *n* **1** : ACRYLIC RESIN **2** : a paint in which the vehicle is acrylic resin **3** : a quick-drying synthetic textile fiber

acrylic resin *n* : a glassy thermoplastic used for cast and molded parts or as coatings and adhesives

¹act \'akt\ *n* **1** : a thing done : DEED **2** : STATUTE, DECREE **3** : a main division of a play; *also* : an item on a variety program **4** : an instance of insincere behavior : PRETENSE

²act *vb* **1** : to perform by action esp. on the stage; *also* : FEIGN, SIMULATE, PRETEND **2** : to take action **3** : to conduct oneself : BEHAVE **4** : to perform a specified function **5** : to produce an effect

³act *abbr* **1** active **2** actual

ACT *abbr* Australian Capital Territory

actg *abbr* acting

ACTH \ˌā-(ˌ)sē-(ˌ)tē-'āch\ *n* : a protein hormone of the pituitary gland that stimulates the adrenal cortex

act·ing \'ak-tiŋ\ *adj* : doing duty temporarily or for another ⟨~ president⟩

ac·tin·i·um \ak-'ti-nē-əm\ *n* : a radioactive metallic chemical element

ac·tion \'ak-shən\ *n* **1** : a legal proceeding **2** : the manner or method of performing **3** : ACTIVITY **4** : ACT, DEED **5** : the accomplishment of a thing usu. over a period of time, in stages, or with the possibility of repetition **6** *pl* : CONDUCT **7** : COMBAT, BATTLE ⟨units that saw ~⟩ ⟨soldiers missing in ~⟩ **8** : the events of a literary plot **9** : an operating mechanism ⟨the ~ of a gun⟩; *also* : the way it operates ⟨stiff ~⟩

ac·tion·able \'ak-sh(ə-)nə-bəl\ *adj* : affording ground for an action or suit at law — **ac·tion·ably** \-blē\ *adv*

ac·ti·vate \'ak-tə-ˌvāt\ *vb* **-vat·ed; -vat·ing 1** : to spur into action; *also* : to make active, reactive, or radioactive **2** : to treat (as carbon) so as to improve adsorptive properties **3** : to set up (a military unit) formally; *also* : to call to active duty — **ac·ti·va·tion** \ˌak-tə-'vā-shən\ *n* — **ac·ti·va·tor** \'ak-tə-ˌvā-tər\ *n*

ac·tive \'ak-tiv\ *adj* **1** : causing or involving action or change **2** : asserting that the grammatical subject performs the action represented by the verb ⟨~ voice⟩ **3** : BRISK, LIVELY **4** : erupting or likely to erupt ⟨~ volcano⟩ **5** : presently in operation or use **6** : tending to progress or to cause degeneration ⟨~ tuberculosis⟩ — **active** *n* — **ac·tive·ly** *adv* — **ac·tive·ness** *n*

ac·tive–ma·trix \'ak-tiv-ˌmā-triks\ *adj* : of, relating to, or being an LCD in which each pixel is individually controlled

ac·tive·wear \'ak-tiv-ˌwer\ *n* : clothing designed for recreation or informal wear

ac·tiv·ism \'ak-ti-ˌvi-zəm\ *n* : a doctrine or practice that emphasizes vigorous action for political ends — **ac·tiv·ist** \-vist\ *n or adj*

ac·tiv·i·ty \ak-'ti-və-tē\ *n, pl* **-ties 1** : the quality or state of being active **2** : forceful or energetic action **3** : an occupation in which one is engaged

ac·tor \'ak-tər\ *n* : a person who acts in a play, motion picture, television show, etc.

ac·tress \'ak-trəs\ *n* : a woman or girl who is an actor

Acts \'akts\ *or* **Acts of the Apostles** *n* — see BIBLE table

ac·tu·al \'ak-chə-wəl, -shə-\ *adj* : really existing : REAL — **ac·tu·al·i·ty** \ˌak-chə-'wa-lə-tē, -shə-\ *n* — **ac·tu·al·i·za·tion** \ˌak-chə-wə-lə-'zā-shən, -shə-\ *n* — **ac·tu·al·ize** \'ak-chə-wə-ˌliz, -shə-\ *vb*

ac·tu·al·ly \'ak-chə-wə-lē, -shə-\ *adv* : in fact or in truth : REALLY

ac·tu·ary \'ak-chə-ˌwer-ē, -shə-\ *n, pl* **-ar·ies** : a person who calculates insurance risks and premiums — **ac·tu·ar·i·al** \ˌak-chə-'wer-ē-əl, -shə-\ *adj*

ac·tu·ate \'ak-chə-ˌwāt\ *vb* **-at·ed; -at·ing 1** : to put into action **2** : to move to action — **ac·tu·a·tion** \ˌak-chə-'wā-shən, -shə-\ *n* — **ac·tu·a·tor** \'ak-chə-ˌwā-tər, -shə-\ *n*

act up *vb* **1** : MISBEHAVE **2** : to function improperly ⟨the car is *acting up* again⟩

acu·ity \ə-'kyü-ə-tē\ *n, pl* **-ities** : keenness of perception

acu·men \ə-'kyü-mən\ *n* : mental keenness and penetration ◆ **Synonyms** DISCERNMENT, INSIGHT, PERCIPIENCE, PERSPICACITY

acu·pres·sure \'a-kyu̇-ˌpre-shər\ *n* : a finger massage of those points on the body stimulated in acupuncture

acu·punc·ture \-ˌpəŋk-chər\ *n* : an orig. Chinese practice of inserting thin needles through the skin at specific points esp. to cure disease or relieve pain — **acu·punc·tur·ist** \ˌa-kyu̇-'pəŋk-chə-rist\ *n*

acute \ə-'kyüt\ *adj* **acut·er; acut·est** [ME, fr. L *acutus*, pp. of *acuere* to sharpen, fr. *acus* needle] **1** : SHARP,

POINTED **2** : containing less than 90 degrees ⟨an ~ angle⟩ **3** : sharply perceptive; *esp* : mentally keen **4** : SEVERE ⟨~ distress⟩; *also* : having a sudden onset, sharp rise, and short duration ⟨~ inflammation⟩ **5** : of, marked by, or being an accent mark having the form ´ — **acute·ly** *adv* — **acute·ness** *n*

acy·clo·vir \(ˌ)ā-'sī-klō-ˌvir\ *n* : a drug used esp. to treat the genital form of herpes simplex

ad \'ad\ *n* : ADVERTISEMENT

AD *abbr* **1** after date **2** [L *anno Domini*] in the year of our Lord — often printed in small capitals and often punctuated **3** assistant director **4** athletic director

ad·age \'a-dij\ *n* : an old familiar saying

¹ada·gio \ə-'dä-j(ē-ˌ)ō, -zh(ē-ˌ)ō\ *adv or adj* [It] : at a slow tempo — used as a direction in music

²adagio *n, pl* **-gios 1** : an adagio movement **2** : a ballet duet or trio displaying feats of lifting and balancing

¹ad·a·mant \'a-də-mənt, -ˌmant\ *n* [ME, fr. AF, fr. L *adamant-, adamas* hardest metal, diamond, fr. Gk] : a stone believed to be impenetrably hard — **ad·a·man·tine** \ˌa-də-'man-ˌtēn, -ˌtīn\ *adj*

²adamant *adj* : very determined : INFLEXIBLE, UNYIELDING — **ad·a·man·cy** \'a-də-mən-sē\ *n* — **ad·a·mant·ly** *adv*

Ad·am's apple \'a-dəmz-\ *n* : the projection in front of the neck formed by the largest cartilage of the larynx

adapt \ə-'dapt\ *vb* **1** : to make suitable or fit (as for a new use or for a different situation) **2** : to adjust to environmental conditions ◆ **Synonyms** ADJUST, ACCOMMODATE, CONFORM — **adapt·abil·i·ty** \ə-ˌdap-tə-'bi-lə-tē\ *n* — **adapt·able** *adj* — **ad·ap·ta·tion** \ˌa-ˌdap-'tā-shən\ *n* — **ad·ap·ta·tion·al** \-sh(ə-)nəl\ *adj* — **adap·tive** \ə-'dap-tiv\ *adj* — **ad·ap·tiv·i·ty** \ˌa-ˌdap-'ti-və-tē\ *n*

adapt·er *also* **adap·tor** \ə-'dap-tər\ *n* **1** : one that adapts **2** : a device for connecting two dissimilar parts of an apparatus **3** : an attachment for adapting apparatus for uses not orig. intended

adaptive optics *n sing or pl* : a telescopic system that improves image resolution by compensating for distortions from atmospheric turbulence

ADC *abbr* **1** aide-de-camp **2** Aid to Dependent Children

add \'ad\ *vb* **1** : to join to something else so as to increase in number or amount **2** : to say further ⟨let me ~ this⟩ **3** : to combine (numbers) into one sum

ADD *abbr* attention deficit disorder

ad·dend \'a-ˌdend\ *n* : a number to be added to another

ad·den·dum \ə-'den-dəm\ *n, pl* **-da** \-də\ [L] : something added; *esp* : a supplement to a book

¹ad·der \'a-dər\ *n* [ME, alter. (by false division of *a naddre*) of *naddre*, fr. OE *nædre*] **1** : a poisonous European viper or a related snake **2** : any of various harmless No. American snakes (as the hognose snake)

²add·er \'a-dər\ *n* : one that adds; *esp* : a device that performs addition

¹ad·dict \ə-'dikt\ *vb* **1** : to devote or surrender (oneself) to something habitually or excessively **2** : to cause addiction to a substance in (as a person) — **ad·dic·tive** \-'dik-tiv\ *adj*

²ad·dict \'a-(ˌ)dikt\ *n* : one who is addicted esp. to a substance

ad·dic·tion \ə-'dik-shən\ *n* **1** : the quality or state of being addicted **2** : compulsive need for and use of a habit-forming substance (as heroin, nicotine, or alcohol) characterized by well-defined physiological symptoms upon withdrawal; *also* : persistent compulsive use of a substance known by the user to be harmful

ad·di·tion \ə-'di-shən\ *n* **1** : the act or process of adding; *also* : something added **2** : the operation of combining numbers to obtain their sum ◆ **Synonyms** ACCRETION, INCREMENT, ACCESSION, AUGMENTATION

ad·di·tion·al \ə-'di-sh(ə-)nəl\ *adj* : coming by way of addition : ADDED, EXTRA

ad·di·tion·al·ly \ə-'di-sh(ə-)nə-lē\ *adv* : in or by way of addition : FURTHERMORE

¹ad·di·tive \'a-də-tiv\ *adj* **1** : of, relating to, or characterized by addition **2** : produced by addition — **ad·di·tiv·i·ty** \ˌa-də-'ti-və-tē\ *n*

²additive *n* : a substance added to another in small quantities to effect a desired change in properties ⟨food ~s⟩

ad·dle \'a-dᵊl\ *vb* **ad·dled; ad·dling 1** : to throw into confusion : MUDDLE **2** : to become rotten ⟨*addled* eggs⟩

addn *abbr* addition

addnl *abbr* additional

add—on \'ad-,ȯn, -,än\ *n* : something (as a feature or accessory) added esp. as an enhancement

¹**ad·dress** \ə-'dres\ *vb* **1** : to direct the attention of (oneself) **2** : to direct one's remarks to : deliver an address to **3** : to mark directions for delivery on **4** : to identify (as a memory location) by an address

²**ad·dress** \ə-'dres, 'a-,dres\ *n* **1** : skillful management **2** : a formal speech : LECTURE **3** : the place where a person or organization may be communicated with **4** : the directions for delivery placed on mail; *also* : the designation of a computer account from which one can send or receive e-mail **5** : a location (as in a computer's memory) where particular data is stored; *also* : URL

ad·dress·ee \,a-,dre-'sē, ə-,dre-'sē\ *n* : one to whom something is addressed

ad·duce \ə-'düs, -'dyüs\ *vb* **ad·duced; ad·duc·ing** : to offer as argument, reason, or proof ✦ *Synonyms* ADVANCE, ALLEGE, CITE, SUBMIT — **ad·duc·er** *n*

-ade *suffix* **1** : act : action ⟨block*ade*⟩ **2** : product; *esp* : sweet drink ⟨lime*ade*⟩

ad·e·nine \'a-də-,nēn\ *n* : a purine base that codes genetic information in the molecular chain of DNA and RNA

ad·e·noid \'a-də-,nȯid, 'ad-,nȯid\ *n* : an enlarged mass of tissue near the opening of the nose into the throat — usu. used in pl. — **adenoid** *or* **ad·e·noi·dal** \,a-də-'nȯi-dᵊl\ *adj*

aden·o·sine tri·phos·phate \ə-'de-nə-,sēn-trī-'fäs-,fāt\ *n* : ATP

ad·e·no·vi·rus \,a-dᵊn-ō-'vī-rəs\ *n* : any of a family of viruses causing infections of the respiratory tract, conjunctiva, and gastrointestinal tract

¹**ad·ept** \'a-,dept\ *n* : EXPERT

²**adept** \ə-'dept\ *adj* : highly skilled : EXPERT — **adept·ly** *adv* — **adept·ness** *n*

ad·e·quate \'a-di-kwət\ *adj* : equal to or sufficient for a specific requirement — **ad·e·qua·cy** \-kwə-sē\ *n* — **ad·e·quate·ly** *adv* — **ad·e·quate·ness** *n*

ad·here \ad-'hir\ *vb* — **ad·hered; ad·her·ing 1** : to give support : maintain loyalty **2** : to stick fast : CLING — **ad·her·ence** \-'hir-əns\ *n* — **ad·her·ent** \-ənt\ *adj or n*

ad·he·sion \ad-'hē-zhən\ *n* **1** : the act or state of adhering **2** : the union of bodily tissues abnormally grown together after inflammation; *also* : the newly formed uniting tissue **3** : the molecular attraction between the surfaces of bodies in contact

¹**ad·he·sive** \-'hē-siv, -ziv\ *adj* **1** : tending to adhere : STICKY **2** : prepared for adhering

²**adhesive** *n* : an adhesive substance

adhesive tape *n* : tape coated on one side with an adhesive mixture; *esp* : one used for covering wounds

¹**ad hoc** \'ad-'häk, -'hōk\ *adv* [L, for this] : for the case at hand apart from other applications

²**ad hoc** *adj* : concerned with or formed for a particular purpose ⟨an *ad hoc* committee⟩ ⟨*ad hoc* solutions⟩

adi·a·bat·ic \,a-dē-ə-'ba-tik\ *adj* : occurring without loss or gain of heat — **adi·a·bat·i·cal·ly** \-ti-k(ə-)lē\ *adv*

adieu \ə-'dü, -'dyü\ *n, pl* **adieus** *or* **adieux** \ə-'düz, -'dyüz\ : FAREWELL — often used interjectionally

ad in·fi·ni·tum \,ad-,in-fə-'nī-təm\ *adv or adj* : without end or limit

ad in·ter·im \ad-'in-tə-rəm, -,rim\ *adv* : for the intervening time — **ad interim** *adj*

adi·os \,a-dē-'ōs, ,ä-\ *interj* [Sp adiós, lit., to God] — used to express farewell

ad·i·pose \'a-də-,pōs\ *adj* : of or relating to animal fat : FATTY

adj *abbr* **1** adjective **2** adjutant

ad·ja·cent \ə-'jā-sᵊnt\ *adj* : situated near or next ✦ *Synonyms* ADJOINING, CONTIGUOUS, ABUTTING, JUXTAPOSED, CONTERMINOUS — **ad·ja·cent·ly** *adv*

ad·jec·tive \'a-jik-tiv\ *n* : a word that typically serves as a modifier of a noun — **ad·jec·ti·val** \,a-jik-'tī-vəl\ *adj* — **ad·jec·ti·val·ly** *adv*

ad·join \ə-'jȯin\ *vb* : to be situated next to

ad·join·ing *adj* : touching or bounding at a point or line ⟨~ rooms⟩

ad·journ \ə-'jərn\ *vb* **1** : to suspend indefinitely or until a stated time **2** : to transfer to another place — **ad·journ·ment** *n*

ad·judge \ə-'jəj\ *vb* **ad·judged; ad·judg·ing 1** : JUDGE, ADJUDICATE **2** : to hold or pronounce to be : DEEM **3** : to award by judicial decision

ad·ju·di·cate \ə-'jü-di-,kāt\ *vb* **-cat·ed; -cat·ing** : to settle judicially — **ad·ju·di·ca·tion** \ə-,jü-di-'kā-shən\ *n*

ad·junct \'a-,jəŋkt\ *n* : something joined or added to another but not essentially a part of it ✦ *Synonyms* APPENDAGE, APPURTENANCE, ACCESSORY, APPENDIX — **adjunct** *adj*

ad·jure \ə-'jùr\ *vb* **ad·jured; ad·jur·ing** : to command solemnly : urge earnestly ✦ *Synonyms* BEG, BESEECH, IMPLORE — **ad·ju·ra·tion** \,a-jə-'rā-shən\ *n*

ad·just \ə-'jəst\ *vb* **1** : to bring to agreement : SETTLE **2** : to cause to conform : ADAPT, FIT **3** : REGULATE ⟨~ a watch⟩ — **ad·just·able** *adj* — **ad·just·er** *also* **ad·jus·tor** \ə-'jəs-tər\ *n* — **ad·just·ment** \ə-'jəst-mənt\ *n*

ad·ju·tant \'a-jə-tənt\ *n* : one who assists; *esp* : an officer who assists a commanding officer by handling correspondence and keeping records

ad·ju·vant \'a-jə-vənt\ *n* : one that helps or facilitates; *esp* : something that enhances the effectiveness of medical treatment — **adjuvant** *adj*

¹**ad—lib** \'ad-'lib\ *vb* **ad—libbed; ad—lib·bing** : IMPROVISE — **ad—lib** *n*

²**ad—lib** *adj* : spoken, composed, or performed without preparation

ad lib \'ad-'lib\ *adv* [NL *ad libitum*] **1** : at one's pleasure **2** : without limit

adm *abbr* administration; administrative

ADM *abbr* admiral

ad·man \'ad-,man\ *n* : one who writes, solicits, or places advertisements

admin *abbr* administration; administrative

ad·min·is·ter \əd-'mi-nə-stər\ *vb* **1** : MANAGE, SUPERINTEND **2** : to mete out : DISPENSE ⟨~ punishment⟩ **3** : to give ritually or remedially ⟨~ quinine for malaria⟩ **4** : to perform the office of administrator — **ad·min·is·tra·ble** \-strə-bəl\ *adj* — **ad·min·is·trant** \-strənt\ *n*

ad·min·is·tra·tion \əd-,mi-nə-'strā-shən\ *n* **1** : the act or process of administering **2** : MANAGEMENT **3** : the officials directing the government of a country **4** : the term of office of an administrative officer or body — **ad·min·is·tra·tive** \əd-'mi-nə-,strā-tiv\ *adj* — **ad·min·is·tra·tive·ly** *adv*

ad·min·is·tra·tor \əd-'mi-nə-,strā-tər\ *n* : one that administers; *esp* : one who settles an intestate estate

ad·mi·ra·ble \'ad-m(ə-)rə-bəl\ *adj* : worthy of admiration : EXCELLENT — **ad·mi·ra·bil·i·ty** \,ad-m(ə-)rə-'bi-lə-tē\ *n* — **ad·mi·ra·ble·ness** *n* **ad·mi·ra·bly** \-blē\ *adv*

ad·mi·ral \'ad-m(ə-)rəl\ *n* [ME, ultim. fr. Ar *amīr-al-* commander of the (as in *amīr-al-baḥr* commander of the sea)] : a commissioned officer in the navy ranking next below a fleet admiral

ad·mi·ral·ty \'ad-m(ə-)rəl-tē\ *n* **1** *cap* : a British government department formerly having authority over naval affairs **2** : the court having jurisdiction over questions of maritime law

ad·mire \əd-'mī(-ə)r\ *vb* **ad·mired; ad·mir·ing** [MF *admirer*, fr. L *admirari*, fr. *ad-* to + *mirari* to wonder] : to regard with high esteem — **ad·mi·ra·tion** \,ad-mə-'rā-shən\ *n* — **ad·mir·er** *n* — **ad·mir·ing·ly** \-'mī-riŋ-lē\ *adv*

ad·mis·si·ble \əd-'mi-sə-bəl\ *adj* : that can be or is worthy to be admitted or allowed ⟨ALLOWABLE ⟨~ evidence⟩ — **ad·mis·si·bil·i·ty** \-,mi-sə-'bi-lə-tē\ *n*

ad·mis·sion \əd-'mi-shən\ *n* **1** : the act of admitting **2** : the privilege of being admitted **3** : a fee paid for admission **4** : the granting of an argument **5** : the acknowledgment of a fact

ad·mit \əd-'mit\ *vb* **ad·mit·ted; ad·mit·ting 1** : PERMIT, ALLOW **2** : to recognize as genuine or valid **3** : to allow to enter ⟨*admitted* to the club⟩ **4** : to accept into a hospital as an inpatient

ad·mit·tance \əd-'mi-tᵊns\ *n* : the act or process of admitting : permission to enter

ad·mit·ted·ly \əd-'mi-təd-lē\ *adv* **1** : as has been or must be admitted **2** : it must be admitted

ad·mix \ad-'miks\ *vb* : to mix in

ad·mix·ture \ad-'miks-chər\ *n* **1** : something added in mixing **2** : MIXTURE

ad·mon·ish \ad-'mä-nish\ *vb* : to warn gently : reprove with a warning ✦ *Synonyms* CHIDE, REPROACH, REBUKE, REPRIMAND, REPROVE — **ad·mon·ish·er** *n* — **ad·mon·ish·ing·ly** *adv* — **ad·mon·ish·ment** *n* —

ad·mo·ni·tion \ˌad-mə-ˈni-shən\ n — **ad·mon·i·to·ry** \ad-ˈmä-nə-ˌtȯr-ē\ adj

ad nau·se·am \ad-ˈnȯ-zē-əm\ adv [L] : to a sickening or excessive degree

ado \ə-ˈdü\ n 1 : heightened fuss or concern 2 : TROUBLE

ado·be \ə-ˈdō-bē\ n 1 : sun-dried brick; also : clay for making such bricks 2 : a structure made of adobe bricks

ad·o·les·cence \ˌa-də-ˈles-ᵊns\ n : the process or period of growth between childhood and maturity — **ad·o·les·cent** \-sᵊnt\ adj or n

adopt \ə-ˈdäpt\ vb 1 : to take (a child of other parents) as one's own child 2 : to take up and practice as one's own 3 : to accept formally and put into effect — **adopt·able** \-ˈdäp-tə-bəl\ adj — **adopt·er** n — **adop·tion** \-ˈdäp-shən\ n

adop·tive \ə-ˈdäp-tiv\ adj : made or acquired by adoption ⟨the ∼ father⟩ — **adop·tive·ly** adv

ador·able \ə-ˈdȯr-ə-bəl\ adj 1 : worthy of adoration 2 : extremely charming ⟨an ∼ child⟩ — **ador·able·ness** n — **ador·ably** \-blē\ adv

adore \ə-ˈdȯr\ vb **adored; ador·ing** [ME adouren, fr. AF aurer, adourer, fr. L adorare, fr. ad- to + orare to speak, pray] 1 : to regard with loving admiration ⟨∼s his wife⟩ 3 : to be extremely fond of ⟨∼s pecan pie⟩ — **ad·o·ra·tion** \ˌa-də-ˈrā-shən\ n

adorn \ə-ˈdȯrn\ vb : to enhance the appearance of esp. with ornaments ⟨blouses ∼ed with sequins⟩ — **adorn·ment** n

ad·re·nal \ə-ˈdrē-nᵊl\ adj : of, relating to, or being a pair of endocrine organs (**adrenal glands**) that are located near the kidneys and produce several hormones and esp. epinephrine

adren·a·line \ə-ˈdre-nə-lən\ n : EPINEPHRINE

adrift \ə-ˈdrift\ adv or adj 1 : afloat without motive power or moorings 2 : without guidance or purpose

adroit \ə-ˈdrȯit\ adj [F, fr. OF, fr. a- to + droit right] 1 : dexterous with one's hands 2 : SHREWD, RESOURCEFUL ♦ **Synonyms** CANNY, CLEVER, CUNNING, INGENIOUS — **adroit·ly** adv — **adroit·ness** n

ad·sorb \ad-ˈsȯrb, -ˈzȯrb\ vb : to take up (as molecules of gases) and hold on the surface of a solid or liquid — **ad·sorp·tion** \-ˈsȯrp-shən, -ˈzȯrp-\ n

ad·u·la·tion \ˌa-jə-ˈlā-shən\ n : excessive admiration or flattery — **ad·u·late** \ˈa-jə-ˌlāt\ vb — **ad·u·la·tor** \-ˌlā-tər\ n — **ad·u·la·to·ry** \-lə-ˌtȯr-ē\ adj

¹adult \ə-ˈdəlt, ˈa-ˌ\ adj [L adultus, pp. of adolescere to grow up, fr. ad- to + alescere to grow] : fully developed and mature — **adult·hood** n

²adult n : one that is adult; esp : a human being after an age (as 18) specified by law

adul·ter·ant \ə-ˈdəl-tə-rənt\ n : something used to adulterate another

adul·ter·ate \ə-ˈdəl-tə-ˌrāt\ vb **-at·ed; -at·ing** [L adulterare, fr. ad- to + alter other] : to make impure by mixing in a foreign or inferior substance — **adul·ter·a·tion** \-ˌdəl-tə-ˈrā-shən\ n

adul·tery \ə-ˈdəl-t(ə-)rē\ n, pl **-ter·ies** : sexual unfaithfulness of a married person — **adul·ter·er** \-tər-ər\ n — **adul·ter·ess** \-t(ə-)rəs\ also **adul·tress** \-trəs\ n — **adul·ter·ous** \-t(ə-)rəs\ adj

ad·um·brate \ˈa-dəm-ˌbrāt\ vb **-brat·ed; -brat·ing** 1 : to foreshadow vaguely : INTIMATE 2 : to suggest or disclose partially 3 : SHADE, OBSCURE — **ad·um·bra·tion** \ˌa-dəm-ˈbrā-shən\ n

adv abbr 1 adverb 2 advertisement

ad va·lor·em \ˌad-və-ˈlȯr-əm\ adj [L, according to the value] : imposed at a percentage of the value ⟨an ad valorem tax⟩

¹ad·vance \əd-ˈvans\ vb **ad·vanced; ad·vanc·ing** 1 : to assist the progress of ⟨∼ a cause⟩ 2 : to bring or move forward ⟨∼ a pawn⟩ 3 : to promote in rank 4 : to make earlier in time 5 : PROPOSE 6 : LEND 7 : to raise in rate : INCREASE — **ad·vance·ment** n

²advance n 1 : a forward movement 2 : IMPROVEMENT 3 : a rise esp. in price or value 4 : OFFER — **in advance** : BEFOREHAND

³advance adj : made, sent, or furnished ahead of time ⟨∼ payment⟩

ad·van·tage \əd-ˈvan-tij\ n 1 : superiority of position 2 : BENEFIT, GAIN 3 : the 1st point won in tennis af-

ter deuce — **ad·van·ta·geous** \ˌad-van-ˈtā-jəs\ adj — **ad·van·ta·geous·ly** adv

ad·vent \ˈad-ˌvent\ n 1 cap : a penitential period beginning four Sundays before Christmas 2 cap : the coming of Christ 3 : a coming into being or use

ad·ven·ti·tious \ˌad-vən-ˈti-shəs\ adj 1 : ACCIDENTAL, INCIDENTAL 2 : arising or occurring sporadically or in other than the usual location ⟨∼ buds⟩ — **ad·ven·ti·tious·ly** adv

¹ad·ven·ture \əd-ˈven-chər\ n 1 : a risky undertaking 2 : a remarkable and exciting experience — **ad·ven·tur·ous** \-ch(ə-)rəs\ adj

²adventure vb **-ven·tured; -ven·tur·ing** \-ˈven-ch(ə-)riŋ\ 1 : RISK, HAZARD ⟨∼ their capital in foreign trade⟩ 2 : to engage in adventure

ad·ven·tur·er \əd-ˈven-ch(ə-)rər\ n 1 : a person who engages in new and risky undertakings 2 : a person who follows a military career for adventure or profit 3 : a person who tries to gain wealth by questionable means

ad·ven·ture·some \əd-ˈven-chər-səm\ adj : inclined to take risks

ad·ven·tur·ess \əd-ˈven-ch(ə-)rəs\ n : a female adventurer

ad·verb \ˈad-ˌvərb\ n : a word that typically serves as a modifier of a verb, an adjective, or another adverb — **ad·ver·bi·al** \ad-ˈvər-bē-əl\ adj — **ad·ver·bi·al·ly** adv

¹ad·ver·sary \ˈad-vər-ˌser-ē\ n, pl **-sar·ies** : FOE

²adversary adj : involving antagonistic parties or interests

ad·verse \ad-ˈvərs, ˈad-ˌvərs\ adj 1 : acting against or in a contrary direction ⟨∼ winds⟩ 2 : UNFAVORABLE ⟨∼ criticism⟩ — **ad·verse·ly** adv

ad·ver·si·ty \ad-ˈvər-sə-tē\ n, pl **-ties** : serious difficulty : MISFORTUNE

ad·vert \ad-ˈvərt\ vb : REFER ⟨∼ to a previous remark⟩

ad·ver·tise \ˈad-vər-ˌtīz\ vb **-tised; -tis·ing** 1 : INFORM, NOTIFY 2 : to call public attention to esp. in order to sell — **ad·ver·tis·er** n

ad·ver·tise·ment \ˌad-vər-ˈtīz-mənt; əd-ˈvər-təs-mənt\ n 1 : the act of advertising 2 : a public notice intended to advertise something

ad·ver·tis·ing \ˈad-vər-ˌtī-ziŋ\ n : the business of preparing advertisements

ad·vice \əd-ˈvīs\ n 1 : recommendation with regard to a course of action : COUNSEL 2 : INFORMATION, REPORT

ad·vis·able \əd-ˈvī-zə-bəl\ adj : proper to be done : EXPEDIENT ⟨∼ to stay fit⟩ — **ad·vis·abil·i·ty** \-ˌvī-zə-ˈbi-lə-tē\ n

ad·vise \əd-ˈvīz\ vb **ad·vised; ad·vis·ing** 1 : to give advice to : COUNSEL 2 : INFORM, NOTIFY 3 : CONSULT, CONFER ⟨∼ with your friends⟩ — **ad·vis·er** also **ad·vi·sor** \-ˈvī-zər\ n

ad·vised \əd-ˈvīzd\ adj : thought out : CONSIDERED ⟨well-advised⟩ — **ad·vis·ed·ly** \-ˈvī-zəd-lē\ adv

ad·vise·ment \əd-ˈvīz-mənt\ n 1 : careful consideration ⟨take the matter under ∼⟩ 2 : the act of advising

ad·vi·so·ry \əd-ˈvī-zə-rē\ adj 1 : having or exercising power to advise 2 : containing or giving advice

¹ad·vo·cate \ˈad-və-kət, -ˌkāt\ n [ultim. fr. L advocare to summon, fr. ad- to + vocare to call] 1 : one who pleads another's cause 2 : one who argues or pleads for a cause or proposal — **ad·vo·ca·cy** \-və-kə-sē\ n

²ad·vo·cate \-ˌkāt\ vb **-cat·ed; -cat·ing** : to plead in favor of — **ad·vo·ca·tion** \ˌad-və-ˈkā-shən\ n

advt abbr advertisement

adze also **adz** \ˈadz\ n : a tool with a curved blade set at right angles to the handle that is used in shaping wood

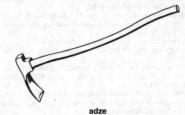

adze

AEC *abbr* Atomic Energy Commission
ae·gis \'ē-jəs\ *n* **1** : SHIELD, PROTECTION ⟨under the ∼ of the constitution⟩ **2** : PATRONAGE, SPONSORSHIP ⟨under the ∼ of the museum⟩
ae·o·li·an harp \ē-'ō-lē-ən-\ *n* : a box with strings that produce musical sounds when the wind blows on them
ae·on *or* **eon** \'ē-ən, -ˌän\ *n* : an indefinitely long time : AGE
aer·ate \'aer-ˌāt\ *vb* **aer·at·ed**; **aer·at·ing** **1** : to supply, impregnate, or combine with a gas and esp. air **2** : to supply (blood) with oxygen by respiration — **aer·a·tion** \ˌer-'ā-shən\ *n* — **aer·a·tor** \'er-ˌā-tər\ *n*
¹ae·ri·al \'er-ē-əl\ *adj* **1** : inhabiting, occurring in, or done in the air **2** : AIRY **3** : of or relating to aircraft
²aer·i·al \'er-ē-əl\ *n* : ANTENNA 2
ae·ri·al·ist \'er-ē-ə-list\ *n* : a performer of feats above the ground esp. on a trapeze
ae·rie \'er-ē, 'ir-ē\ *n* : a highly placed nest (as of an eagle)
aer·o·bat·ics \ˌer-ə-'ba-tiks\ *n sing or pl* : spectacular flying feats and maneuvers
aer·o·bic \er-'rō-bik\ *adj* **1** : living or active only in the presence of oxygen ⟨∼ bacteria⟩ **2** : involving or increasing oxygen consumption; *also* : of or relating to aerobics — **aer·o·bi·cal·ly** \-bi-k(ə-)lē\ *adv*
aer·o·bics \-biks\ *n sing or pl* : strenuous exercises that produce a marked temporary increase in respiration and heart rate; *also* : a system of physical conditioning involving these
aero·drome \'er-ə-ˌdrōm\ *n chiefly Brit* : AIRPORT
aero·dy·nam·ics \ˌer-ō-dī-'na-miks\ *n* : the science dealing with the forces acting on bodies in motion in a gas (as air) — **aero·dy·nam·ic** \-mik\ *also* **aero·dy·nam·i·cal** \-mi-kəl\ *adj* — **aero·dy·nam·i·cal·ly** \-mi-k(ə-)lē\ *adv*
aero·naut \'er-ə-ˌnȯt\ *n* [F *aéronaute*, ultim. fr. Gk *aēr* air + *nautēs* sailor] : one who operates or travels in an airship or balloon
aero·nau·tics \ˌer-ə-'nȯ-tiks\ *n* : the science of aircraft operation — **aero·nau·ti·cal** \-ti-kəl\ *also* **aero·nau·tic** \-tik\ *adj*
aero·pho·bia \ˌer-ō-'fō-bē-ə\ *n* : fear or strong dislike of flying
aero·plane \'er-ə-ˌplān\ *chiefly Brit var of* AIRPLANE
aero·sol \'er-ə-ˌsäl, -ˌsȯl\ *n* **1** : a suspension of fine solid or liquid particles in a gas; *also, pl* : the particles themselves **2** : a substance (as an insecticide) dispensed from a pressurized container as an aerosol
aero·space \'er-ō-ˌspās\ *n* : the earth's atmosphere and the space beyond — **aerospace** *adj*
aery \'er-ē\ *adj* **aer·i·er**; **-est** : having an aerial quality : ETHEREAL ⟨∼ visions⟩
aes·thete *also* **es·thete** \'es-ˌthēt\ *n* : a person having or affecting sensitivity to beauty esp. in art
aes·thet·ic *also* **es·thet·ic** \es-'the-tik\ *adj* **1** : of or relating to aesthetics : ARTISTIC **2** : appreciative of the beautiful — **aes·thet·i·cal·ly** *also* **es·thet·i·cal·ly** \-ti-k(ə-)lē\ *adv*
aes·thet·ics *also* **es·thet·ics** \-tiks\ *n* : a branch of philosophy dealing with the nature, creation, and appreciation of beauty
ae·ti·ol·o·gy *chiefly Brit var of* ETIOLOGY
AF *abbr* **1** air force **2** audio frequency
¹afar \ə-'fär\ *adv* : from, at, or to a great distance
²afar *n* : a great distance
AFB *abbr* air force base
AFC *abbr* **1** American Football Conference **2** automatic frequency control
AFDC *abbr* Aid to Families with Dependent Children
af·fa·ble \'a-fə-bəl\ *adj* : courteous and agreeable in conversation — **af·fa·bil·i·ty** \ˌa-fə-'bi-lə-tē\ *n* — **af·fa·bly** \'a-fə-blē\ *adv*
af·fair \ə-'fer\ *n* [ME *afere*, fr. AF fr. *afaire*, fr. *a faire* to do] **1** : something that relates to or involves one : CONCERN **2** : a romantic or sexual attachment of limited duration
¹af·fect \ə-'fekt, a-\ *vb* **1** : to be fond of using or wearing **2** : to pretend than an attitude or behavior is genuine
²affect *vb* : to produce an effect on : INFLUENCE
³af·fect \'a-ˌfekt\ *n* : EMOTION; *also* : an observable display of emotion ⟨an expressionless ∼⟩
af·fec·ta·tion \ˌa-ˌfek-'tā-shən\ *n* : an attitude or behavior that is assumed by a person but not genuinely felt
af·fect·ed \a-'fek-təd\ *adj* **1** : given to or marked by af-

fectation **2** : artificially assumed to impress others — **af·fect·ed·ly** *adv*
af·fect·ing \a-'fek-tiŋ\ *adj* : arousing pity, sympathy, or sorrow ⟨an ∼ story⟩ — **af·fect·ing·ly** *adv*
af·fec·tion \ə-'fek-shən\ *n* : tender attachment — **af·fec·tion·ate** \-sh(ə-)nət\ *adj* — **af·fec·tion·ate·ly** *adv*
af·fec·tive \a-'fek-tiv\ *adj* : relating to, influencing, or expressing an emotion or feeling : EMOTIONAL ⟨an ∼ disorder⟩
af·fer·ent \'a-fə-rənt, -ˌfer-ənt\ *adj* : bearing or conducting inward toward a more central part and esp. a nerve center (as the central nervous system)
af·fi·ance \ə-'fī-əns\ *vb* **-anced**; **-anc·ing** : to promise oneself or another in marriage
af·fi·da·vit \ˌa-fə-'dā-vət\ *n* [ML, he has made an oath] : a sworn statement in writing
¹af·fil·i·ate \ə-'fi-lē-ˌāt\ *vb* **-at·ed**; **-at·ing** : to associate as a member or branch — **af·fil·i·a·tion** \-ˌfi-lē-'ā-shən\ *n*
²af·fil·i·ate \ə-'fi-lē-ət\ *n* : an affiliated person or organization
af·fin·i·ty \ə-'fi-nə-tē\ *n, pl* **-ties** **1** : KINSHIP, RELATIONSHIP **2** : attractive force : ATTRACTION, SYMPATHY
affinity card *n* : a credit card issued in affiliation with an organization (as a charity or an airline) the use of which benefits the organization or possessor of the card
af·firm \ə-'fərm\ *vb* **1** : CONFIRM **2** : to assert positively **3** : to make a solemn and formal declaration or assertion in place of an oath ♦ **Synonyms** AVER, AVOW, AVOUCH, DECLARE, ASSERT — **af·fir·ma·tion** \ˌa-fər-'mā-shən\ *n*
¹af·fir·ma·tive \ə-'fər-mə-tiv\ *adj* : asserting that the fact is so : POSITIVE
²affirmative *n* **1** : an expression of affirmation or assent **2** : the side that upholds the proposition stated in a debate
affirmative action *n* : an active effort to improve the employment or educational opportunities of members of minority groups and women
¹af·fix \ə-'fiks\ *vb* : ATTACH, ADD
²af·fix \'a-ˌfiks\ *n* : one or more sounds or letters attached to the beginning or end of a word that produce a derivative word or an inflectional form
af·fla·tus \ə-'flā-təs\ *n* : divine inspiration
af·flict \ə-'flikt\ *vb* : to cause pain and distress to ♦ **Synonyms** RACK, TRY, TORMENT, TORTURE — **af·flic·tion** \-'flik-shən\ *n*
af·flic·tive \-'flik-tiv\ *adj* : causing affliction : DISTRESSING ⟨∼ emotions⟩ — **af·flic·tive·ly** *adv*
af·flu·ence \'a-ˌflü-ən(t)s, a-'flü-\ *n* : abundant supply; *also* : WEALTH, RICHES — **af·flu·ent** \-ənt\ *adj*
af·ford \ə-'fȯrd\ *vb* **1** : to manage to bear or bear the cost of without serious harm or loss **2** : PROVIDE, FURNISH ⟨the roof ∼ed a fine view⟩
af·for·es·ta·tion \a-ˌfȯr-ə-'stā-shən\ *n* : the act or process of establishing a forest — **af·for·est** \a-'fȯr-əst, -'fär-\ *vb*
af·fray \ə-'frā\ *n* : FIGHT, FRAY
af·fright \ə-'frīt\ *vb archaic* : FRIGHTEN, ALARM — **affright** *n*
af·front \ə-'frənt\ *vb* **1** : INSULT **2** : CONFRONT ⟨∼ death⟩ — **affront** *n*
af·ghan \'af-ˌgan\ *n* **1** *cap* : a native or inhabitant of Afghanistan **2** : a blanket or shawl of colored wool knitted or crocheted in sections — **Afghan** *or* **Af·ghani** \af-'ga-nē, -'gä-\ *adj*
Afghan hound *n* : any of a breed of tall slim swift hunting dogs with a coat of silky thick hair and a long silky top-knot
af·ghani \af-'ga-nē\ *n* — see MONEY table
afi·cio·na·do \ə-ˌfi-sh(ē-)ə-'nä-dō, -sē-ə-\ *n, pl* **-dos** [Sp, fr. pp. of *aficionar* to inspire affection] : DEVOTEE, FAN
afield \ə-'fēld\ *adv or adj* **1** : to, in, or on the field **2** : away from home **3** : out of the way : ASTRAY
afire \ə-'fī(-ə)r\ *adj or adv* : being on fire : BURNING
AFL *abbr* American Football League
aflame \ə-'flām\ *adj or adv* : FLAMING
AFL–CIO *abbr* American Federation of Labor and Congress of Industrial Organizations
afloat \ə-'flōt\ *adj or adv* **1** : borne on or as if on the water **2** : CIRCULATING ⟨rumors were ∼⟩ **3** : ADRIFT
aflut·ter \ə-'flə-tər\ *adj* **1** : FLUTTERING **2** : nervously excited ⟨∼ at the news⟩
afoot \ə-'fùt\ *adv or adj* **1** : on foot **2** : in action : in progress
afore·men·tioned \ə-'fȯr-'men-chənd\ *adj* : mentioned previously

afore·said \-ˌsed\ *adj* : said or named before
afore·thought \-ˌthȯt\ *adj* : planned beforehand : PRE-MEDITATED ⟨with malice ∼⟩
a for·ti·o·ri \ˌä-ˌfȯr-tē-ˈȯr-ē\ *adv* [NL, lit., from the stronger (argument)] : with even greater reason
afoul of \ə-ˈfaúl-əv\ *prep* **1** : in or into conflict with **2** : in or into collision or entanglement with
Afr *abbr* Africa; African
afraid \ə-ˈfrād\ *adj* **1** : FRIGHTENED, FEARFUL **2** : filled with concern or regret ⟨∼ I won't be able to go⟩
A–frame \ˈā-ˌfrām\ *n* : a building having triangular front and rear walls with the roof reaching to the ground
afresh \ə-ˈfresh\ *adv* : ANEW, AGAIN
Af·ri·can \ˈa-fri-kən\ *n* **1** : a native or inhabitant of Africa **2** : a person of African ancestry — **African** *adj*
African American *n* : an American of African and esp. of black African descent — **African American** *or* **Af·ri·can–Amer·i·can** \-ə-ˈmer-ə-kən\ *adj*
Af·ri·can·ized bee \ˈa-frə-kə-ˌnīzd-\ *n* : a highly aggressive hybrid honeybee accidentally produced from Brazilian and African stocks that has spread from So. America into Mexico and the southern U.S.
Africanized honeybee *n* : AFRICANIZED BEE
African violet *n* : a tropical African plant widely grown indoors for its velvety fleshy leaves and showy purple, pink, or white flowers
Af·ri·kaans \ˌa-fri-ˈkäns\ *n* : a language developed from 17th century Dutch that is one of the official languages of the Republic of So. Africa
Af·ro \ˈa-(ˌ)frō\ *n, pl* **Afros** : a hairstyle of tight curls in a full evenly rounded shape
Af·ro–Amer·i·can \ˌa-frō-ə-ˈmer-ə-kən\ *n* : AFRICAN AMERICAN — **Afro–American** *adj*
aft \ˈaft\ *adv* : near, toward, or in the stern of a ship or the tail of an aircraft
AFT *abbr* American Federation of Teachers
¹af·ter \ˈaf-tər\ *adv* : AFTERWARD, SUBSEQUENTLY
²after *prep* **1** : behind in place **2** : later than ⟨∼ dinner⟩ **3** : in pursuit or search of ⟨he's ∼ your job⟩
³after *conj* : following the time when ⟨we will come ∼ we make plans⟩
⁴after *adj* **1** : LATER ⟨in ∼ years⟩ **2** : located toward the rear
af·ter·birth \ˈaf-tər-ˌbərth\ *n* : the placenta and membranes of the fetus that are expelled after childbirth
af·ter·burn·er \-ˌbər-nər\ *n* : a device incorporated in the tail pipe of a turbojet engine for injecting fuel into the hot exhaust gases and burning it to provide extra thrust
af·ter·care \-ˌker\ *n* : the care, nursing, or treatment of a convalescent patient
af·ter·deck \-ˌdek\ *n* : the rear half of the deck of a ship
af·ter·ef·fect \-ə-ˌfekt\ *n* : an effect that follows its cause after an interval
af·ter·glow \-ˌglō\ *n* : a glow remaining where a light has disappeared
af·ter·im·age \-ˌim-ij\ *n* : a usu. visual sensation continuing after the stimulus causing it has ended
af·ter·life \-ˌlif\ *n* : an existence after death
af·ter·math \-ˌmath\ *n* **1** : a second-growth crop esp. of hay **2** : CONSEQUENCES, EFFECTS ✦ **Synonyms** AFTEREFFECT, UPSHOT, RESULT, OUTCOME
af·ter·noon \ˌaf-tər-ˈnün\ *n* : the time between noon and evening
af·ter·shave \ˈaf-tər-ˌshāv\ *n* : a usu. scented lotion for the face after shaving
af·ter·taste \-ˌtāst\ *n* : a sensation (as of flavor) continuing after the stimulus causing it has ended
af·ter–tax \ˈaf-tər-ˈtaks\ *adj* : remaining after payment of taxes and esp. of income tax ⟨an ∼ profit⟩
af·ter·thought \-ˌthȯt\ *n* : an idea occurring later
af·ter·ward \-wərd\ *or* **af·ter·wards** \-wərdz\ *adv* : at a later time
Ag *symbol* [L *argentum*] silver
AG *abbr* **1** adjutant general **2** attorney general
again \ə-ˈgen, -ˈgin\ *adv* **1** : once more : ANEW ⟨come see us ∼⟩ **2** : on the other hand ⟨we may, and ∼ we may not⟩ **3** : in addition : BESIDES
against \ə-ˈgenst\ *prep* **1** : in opposition to **2** : directly opposite to : FACING **3** : as defense from **4** : so as to touch or strike ⟨threw him ∼ the wall⟩; *also* : TOUCHING

¹aga·pe \ä-ˈgä-pā, ˈä-gə-ˌpā\ *n* [LL, fr. Gk *agapē*, lit., love] : unselfish unconditional love for another
²agape \ə-ˈgāp\ *adj or adv* : having the mouth open in wonder or surprise : GAPING
agar \ˈä-ˌgär\ *n* **1** : a jellylike substance extracted from a red alga and used esp. as a gelling and stabilizing agent in foods **2** : a culture medium containing agar
agar–agar \ˌä-ˌgär-ˈä-ˌgär\ *n* : AGAR
ag·ate \ˈa-gət\ *n* **1** : a striped or clouded quartz **2** : a playing marble of agate or of glass
aga·ve \ə-ˈgä-vē\ *n* : any of a genus of spiny-leaved plants (as a century plant) related to the amaryllis
agcy *abbr* agency
¹age \ˈāj\ *n* **1** : the length of time during which a being or thing has lived or existed **2** : the time of life at which some particular qualification is achieved; *esp* : MAJORITY **3** : the latter part of life **4** : a long time **5** : a period in history
²age *vb* **aged; ag·ing** *or* **age·ing** **1** : to grow old or cause to grow old **2** : to become or cause to become mature or mellow
-age *n suffix* **1** : aggregate : collection ⟨track*age*⟩ **2** : action : process ⟨haul*age*⟩ **3** : cumulative result of ⟨break*age*⟩ **4** : rate of ⟨dos*age*⟩ **5** : house or place of ⟨orphan*age*⟩ **6** : state : rank ⟨vassal*age*⟩ **7** : fee : charge ⟨post*age*⟩
aged \ˈā-jəd *for 1;* ˈäjd *for 2*\ *adj* **1** : of advanced age **2** : having attained a specified age ⟨a man ∼ 40 years⟩
age·ism \ˈā-ˌji-zəm\ *n* : discrimination against persons of a particular age and esp. the elderly — **age·ist** \-jist\ *n*
age·less \ˈāj-ləs\ *adj* **1** : not growing old or showing the effects of age **2** : TIMELESS, ETERNAL ⟨∼ truths⟩
agen·cy \ˈā-jən-sē\ *n, pl* **-cies** **1** : one through which something is accomplished : INSTRUMENTALITY **2** : the office or function of an agent **3** : an establishment doing business for another **4** : an administrative division (as of a government) ✦ **Synonyms** MEANS, MEDIUM, VEHICLE
agen·da \ə-ˈjen-də\ *n* : a list of things to be done
agen·der \(ˌ)ā-ˈjen-dər\ *adj* : of, relating to, or being a person whose gender identity is genderless or neutral
agent \ˈā-jənt\ *n* **1** : one that acts **2** : MEANS, INSTRUMENT **3** : a person acting or doing business for another **4** : a computer program designed to automate certain tasks (as gathering information online) ✦ **Synonyms** ATTORNEY, DEPUTY, PROXY, DELEGATE
Agent Orange *n* : an herbicide widely used in the Vietnam War that is composed of 2,4-D and 2,4,5-T and contains a toxic contaminant
agent pro·vo·ca·teur \ˈä-ˌzhäⁿ-prō-ˌvä-kə-ˈtər, ˈä-jənt-\ *n, pl* **agents provocateurs** \ˈä-ˌzhäⁿ-prō-ˌväk-ə-ˈtər, ˈä-jənts-prō-\ [F] : a person hired to infiltrate a group and incite its members to illegal action
age of consent : the age at which one is legally competent to give consent esp. to marriage or to sexual intercourse
age–old \ˈāj-ˈōld\ *adj* : having existed for ages : ANCIENT
ag·er·a·tum \ˌa-jə-ˈrā-təm\ *n, pl* **-tum** *also* **-tums** : any of a genus of tropical American plants that are related to the daisies and have small showy heads of usu. blue or white flowers
age spots *n pl* : benign flat spots of dark pigmentation on the skin occurring esp. among older people
Ag·ge·us \a-ˈgē-əs\ *n* : HAGGAI
¹ag·glom·er·ate \ə-ˈglä-mə-ˌrāt\ *vb* **-at·ed; -at·ing** [L *agglomerare* to heap up, join, fr. *ad-* to + *glomer-, glomus* ball] : to gather into a mass : CLUSTER — **ag·glom·er·a·tion** \-ˌglä-mə-ˈrā-shən\ *n*
²ag·glom·er·ate \-rət\ *n* : rock composed of volcanic fragments
ag·glu·ti·nate \ə-ˈglü-tᵊn-ˌāt\ *vb* **-nat·ed; -nat·ing** **1** : to cause to adhere : gather into a group or mass **2** : to cause (as red blood cells or bacteria) to collect into clumps — **ag·glu·ti·na·tion** \-ˌglü-tᵊn-ˈā-shən\ *n*
ag·gran·dise *Brit var of* AGGRANDIZE
ag·gran·dize \ə-ˈgran-ˌdīz, ˈa-grən-\ *vb* **-dized; -diz·ing** : to make great or greater ⟨∼ an estate⟩ — **ag·gran·dize·ment** \ə-ˈgran-dəz-mənt, -ˌdīz-; ˌa-grən-ˈdīz-\ *n*
ag·gra·vate \ˈa-grə-ˌvāt\ *vb* **-vat·ed; -vat·ing** **1** : to make more severe : INTENSIFY **2** : IRRITATE — **ag·gra·va·tion** \ˌa-grə-ˈvā-shən\ *n*

¹**ag·gre·gate** \'a-gri-gət\ *adj* : formed by the gathering of units into one mass

²**ag·gre·gate** \-ˌgāt\ *vb* **-gat·ed; -gat·ing** : to collect into one mass

³**ag·gre·gate** \-gət\ *n* : a mass or body of units or parts somewhat loosely associated with one another; *also* : the whole amount

ag·gre·ga·tion \ˌa-gri-'gā-shən\ *n* **1** : a group, body, or mass composed of many distinct parts **2** : the collecting of units or parts into a mass or whole

ag·gres·sion \ə-'gre-shən\ *n* **1** : an unprovoked attack **2** : the practice of making attacks **3** : hostile, injurious, or destructive behavior or outlook esp. when caused by frustration — **ag·gres·sor** \-'gre-sər\ *n*

ag·gres·sive \ə-'gre-siv\ *adj* **1** : tending toward or exhibiting aggression; *esp* : marked by combative readiness **2** : marked by driving energy or initiative : ENTERPRISING **3** : more intensive or comprehensive esp. in dosage or extent — **ag·gres·sive·ly** *adv* — **ag·gres·sive·ness** *n*

ag·grieve \ə-'grēv\ *vb* **ag·grieved; ag·griev·ing** **1** : to cause grief to **2** : to inflict injury on : WRONG

ag·gro \'a-ˌgrō\ *adj* : aggressive or aggressively daring in style or manner ⟨~ music⟩ ⟨~ surfing⟩

aghast \ə-'gast\ *adj* : struck with amazement or horror

ag·ile \'a-jəl\ *adj* : able to move quickly and easily — **ag·ile·ly** *adv* — **agil·i·ty** \ə-'ji-lə-tē\ *n*

ag·i·ta \'a-jə-tə\ *n* [southern It dial. pron. of It *acido*, lit., heartburn, acid] : a feeling of agitation or anxiety

ag·i·tate \'a-jə-ˌtāt\ *vb* **-tat·ed; -tat·ing** **1** : to move with an irregular rapid motion **2** : to stir up : EXCITE **3** : to discuss earnestly **4** : to attempt to arouse public feeling — **ag·i·ta·tion** \ˌa-jə-'tā-shən\ *n* — **ag·i·ta·tor** \'a-jə-ˌtā-tər\ *n*

ag·it·prop \'a-jət-ˌpräp\ *n* [Russ] : political propaganda promulgated esp. through the arts

agleam \ə-'glēm\ *adj* : GLEAMING ⟨eyes ~ with tears⟩

aglit·ter \ə-'gli-tər\ *adj* : GLITTERING

aglow \ə-'glō\ *adj* : GLOWING

ag·nos·tic \ag-'näs-tik\ *adj* [Gk *agnōstos* unknown, unknowable, fr. *a-* un- + *gnōstos* known] : of or relating to the belief that the existence of any ultimate reality (as God) is unknown and prob. unknowable — **agnostic** *n* — **ag·nos·ti·cism** \-'näs-tə-ˌsi-zəm\ *n*

ago \ə-'gō\ *adj or adv* : earlier than the present time ⟨10 years ~⟩

agog \ə-'gäg\ *adj* [MF *en gogues* in mirth] : full of excitement : EAGER

a-go-go \ä-'gō-ˌgō\ *adj* [*Whisky à Gogo*, café and disco in Paris, France, fr. F *à gogo* galore] : GO-GO

ag·o·nise *Brit var of* AGONIZE

ag·o·nize \'a-gə-ˌnīz\ *vb* **-nized; -niz·ing** : to suffer or cause to suffer agony — **ag·o·niz·ing·ly** *adv*

ag·o·ny \'a-gə-nē\ *n, pl* **-nies** [ME *agonie*, fr. L *agonia*, fr. Gk *agōnia* struggle, anguish, fr. *agōn* gathering, contest for a prize] : extreme pain of mind or body ♦ *Synonyms* SUFFERING, DISTRESS, MISERY

ago·ra \ˌä-gə-'rä\ *n, pl* **ago·rot** \-'rōt\ — see *shekel* at MONEY table

ag·o·ra·pho·bia \ˌa-gə-rə-'fō-bē-ə\ *n* : abnormal fear of being in a helpless, embarrassing, or inescapable situation characterized esp. by avoidance of open or public places — **ag·o·ra·pho·bic** \-'fō-bik, -'fä-\ *adj or n*

agr *abbr* agricultural; agriculture

agrar·i·an \ə-'grer-ē-ən\ *adj* **1** : of or relating to land or its ownership ⟨~ reforms⟩ **2** : of or relating to farmers or farming interests — **agrarian** *n* — **agrar·i·an·ism** *n*

agree \ə-'grē\ *vb* **agreed; agree·ing** **1** : ADMIT, CONCEDE ⟨~s that he was wrong⟩ **2** : to be similar : CORRESPOND ⟨both copies ~⟩ **3** : to express agreement or approval **4** : to be in harmony **5** : to settle by common consent **6** : to be fitting or healthful : SUIT ⟨this climate ~s with her⟩

agree·able \ə-'grē-ə-bəl\ *adj* **1** : PLEASING, PLEASANT ⟨an ~ fragrance⟩ **2** : ready to consent ⟨I'm ~ to their proposal⟩ **3** : being in harmony : CONSONANT — **agree·able·ness** *n* — **agree·ably** \-blē\ *adv*

agree·ment \ə-'grē-mənt\ *n* **1** : harmony of opinion or action **2** : mutual understanding or arrangement; *also* : a document containing such an arrangement

ag·ri·busi·ness \'a-grə-ˌbiz-nəs, -nəz\ *n* : an industry en-

gaged in the manufacture and sale of farm equipment and supplies and in the production, processing, storage, and sale of farm commodities

agric *abbr* agricultural; agriculture

ag·ri·cul·ture \'a-gri-ˌkəl-chər\ *n* : FARMING, HUSBANDRY — **ag·ri·cul·tur·al** \ˌa-gri-'kəl-ch(ə-)rəl\ *adj* — **ag·ri·cul·tur·ist** \-ch(ə-)rist\ *or* **ag·ri·cul·tur·al·ist** \-ch(ə-)rə-list\ *n*

agron·o·my \ə-'grä-nə-mē\ *n* : a branch of agriculture that deals with the raising of crops and the care of the soil — **ag·ro·nom·ic** \ˌa-grə-'nä-mik\ *adj* — **agron·o·mist** \ə-'grä-nə-mist\ *n*

aground \ə-'graünd\ *adv or adj* : on or onto the bottom or shore ⟨ran ~⟩

agt *abbr* agent

ague \'ā-gyü\ *n* : a fever (as malaria) with recurrent chills and sweating

ahead \ə-'hed\ *adv or adj* **1** : in or toward the front **2** : into or for the future ⟨plan ~⟩ **3** : in or toward a more advantageous position

ahead of *prep* **1** : in front or advance of **2** : in excess of : ABOVE

ahoy \ə-'hói\ *interj* — used in hailing ⟨ship ~⟩

AI *abbr* artificial intelligence

¹**aid** \'ād\ *vb* : to provide with what is useful in achieving an end : ASSIST

²**aid** *n* **1** : ASSISTANCE **2** : ASSISTANT

AID *abbr* Agency for International Development

aide \'ād\ *n* : a person who acts as an assistant; *esp* : a military officer assisting a superior

aide–de–camp \ˌād-di-'kamp, -'kän̄\ *n, pl* **aides–de–camp** \ˌādz-di-\ [F] : AIDE

AIDS \'ādz\ *n* [*a*cquired *i*mmuno*d*eficiency *s*yndrome] : a serious disease of the human immune system that is characterized by severe reduction in the numbers of helper T cells and increased vulnerability to life-threatening illnesses and that is caused by infection with HIV commonly transmitted in infected blood esp. during illicit intravenous drug use and in bodily secretions (as semen) during sexual intercourse

AIDS–related complex *n* : a group of symptoms (as fever, weight loss, and lymphadenopathy) that is associated with the presence of antibodies to HIV and is followed by the development of AIDS in a certain proportion of cases

AIDS virus *n* : HIV

ai·grette \ā-'gret, 'ā-ˌ\ *n* [F, plume, egret] : a plume or decorative tuft for the head

ail \'āl\ *vb* **1** : to be the matter with : TROUBLE **2** : to be unwell

ai·lan·thus \ā-'lan-thəs\ *n* : any of a genus of Asian trees or shrubs with pinnate leaves and ill-scented greenish flowers; *esp* : TREE OF HEAVEN

ai·le·ron \'ā-lə-ˌrän\ *n* : a movable part of an airplane wing used in banking

ail·ment \'āl-mənt\ *n* : a bodily disorder

¹**aim** \'ām\ *vb* [ME, fr. AF *aesmer* & *esmer*; AF *aesmer*, fr. *a-* to (fr. L *ad-*) + *esmer* to estimate, fr. L *aestimare*] **1** : to point a weapon at an object **2** : to direct one's efforts : ASPIRE **3** : to direct to or toward a specified object or goal

²**aim** *n* **1** : the pointing of a weapon at an object **2** : the ability to hit a target **3** : OBJECT, PURPOSE ⟨my ~ is to win⟩ — **aim·less** \-ləs\ *adj* — **aim·less·ly** *adv* — **aim·less·ness** *n*

AIM *abbr* American Indian Movement

ain't \'ānt\ **1** : are not **2** : is not **3** : am not — though disapproved by many and more common in less educated speech, used in both speech and writing to catch attention and to gain emphasis

Ai·nu \'ī-nü\ *n, pl* **Ainu** *or* **Ainus** **1** : a member of an indigenous people of northern Japan **2** : the language of the Ainu people

¹**air** \'er\ *n* **1** : the gaseous mixture surrounding the earth **2** : a light breeze **3** : MELODY, TUNE **4** : the outward appearance of a person or thing : MANNER **5** : an artificial manner **6** : COMPRESSED AIR ⟨~ sprayer⟩ **7** : AIRCRAFT ⟨traveled by ~⟩ **8** : AVIATION ⟨~ safety⟩ **9** : the medium of transmission of radio waves; *also* : RADIO, TELEVISION

²**air** *vb* **1** : to expose to the air ⟨~ clothes⟩ **2** : to expose to public view **3** : to broadcast on radio or television

air·bag \'er-ˌbag\ *n* : a bag designed to inflate automatically to protect automobile occupants in case of collision

air·boat \'er-ˌbōt\ *n* : a shallow-draft boat driven by an airplane propeller

air·borne \-ˌbȯrn\ *adj* : done or being in the air

air brake *n* 1 : a brake operated by a piston driven by compressed air 2 : a surface projected into the airflow to lower an airplane's speed

air·brush \'er-ˌbrəsh\ *n* : a device for applying a fine spray (as of paint) by compressed air — airbrush *vb*

air con·di·tion·er \ˌer-kən-'di-sh(ə-)nər\ *n* : an apparatus for filtering air and controlling its humidity and temperature — air–con·di·tion \-'di-shən\ *vb*

air·craft \'er-ˌkraft\ *n, pl* aircraft : a vehicle for traveling through the air

aircraft carrier *n* : a warship with a deck on which airplanes can be launched and landed

air·drop \'er-ˌdräp\ *n* : delivery of cargo or personnel by parachute from an airplane in flight — air–drop *vb*

Aire·dale terrier \'er-ˌdāl-\ *n* : any of a breed of large terriers with a hard wiry coat

air·fare \'er-ˌfer\ *n* : fare for travel by airplane

air·field \-ˌfēld\ *n* : AIRPORT

air·flow \-ˌflō\ *n* : the motion of air relative to a body in it

air·foil \-ˌfȯi(-ə)l\ *n* : an airplane surface designed to produce reaction forces from the air through which it moves

air force *n* : the military organization of a nation for air warfare

air·frame \'er-ˌfrām\ *n* : the structure of an aircraft, rocket, or missile without the power plant; *also* : AIRCRAFT

air·freight \-'frāt\ *n* : freight transport by aircraft in volume; *also* : the charge for this service

air gun *n* 1 : a gun operated by compressed air 2 : a hand tool that works by compressed air; *esp* : AIRBRUSH

air·head \'er-ˌhed\ *n* : a mindless or stupid person

air lane *n* : AIRWAY 1

air·lift \'er-ˌlift\ *n* : transportation (as of supplies or passengers) by aircraft — airlift *vb*

air·line \-ˌlīn\ *n* : a transportation system using airplanes

air·lin·er \-ˌlī-nər\ *n* : a large passenger airplane operated by an airline

air lock *n* : an airtight chamber separating areas of different pressure

air·mail \'er-ˌmāl\ *n* : the system of transporting mail by aircraft; *also* : mail so transported — airmail *vb*

air·man \-mən\ *n* 1 : AVIATOR, PILOT 2 : an enlisted person in the air force ranking next below an airman first class

airman basic *n* : an enlisted person of the lowest rank in the air force

airman first class *n* : an enlisted person in the air force ranking next below a senior airman

air mass *n* : a large horizontally homogeneous body of air

air·mo·bile \'er-ˌmō-bəl, -ˌbēl\ *adj* : of, relating to, or being a military unit whose members are transported to combat areas usu. by helicopter

air·plane \'er-ˌplān\ *n* : a powered heavier-than-air aircraft that has fixed wings from which it derives lift

air·play \-ˌplā\ *n* : the playing of a musical recording on the air by a radio station

air pocket *n* : a condition of the atmosphere (as a local downdraft) that causes an airplane to drop suddenly

air police *n* : the military police of an air force

air·port \'er-ˌpȯrt\ *n* : a place from which aircraft operate that usu. has paved runways and a terminal

air rage *n* : an airline passenger's uncontrolled anger that is usu. expressed in aggressive or violent behavior

air raid *n* : an attack by armed airplanes on a surface target

air·ship \'er-ˌship\ *n* : a lighter-than-air aircraft having propulsion and steering systems

air·sick \-ˌsik\ *adj* : affected with motion sickness associated with flying — air·sick·ness *n*

air·space \-ˌspās\ *n* : the space above a nation and under its jurisdiction

air·speed \-ˌspēd\ *n* : the speed of an object (as an airplane) with relation to the surrounding air

air·strip \-ˌstrip\ *n* : a runway without normal airport facilities

air·tight \'er-ˌtīt\ *adj* 1 : so tightly sealed that no air can enter or escape 2 : leaving no opening for attack

air–to–air *adj* : launched from one airplane in flight at another; *also* : involving aircraft in flight

air·waves \'er-ˌwāvz\ *n pl* : AIR 9

air·way \-ˌwā\ *n* 1 : a regular route for airplanes 2 : AIRLINE

air·wor·thy \-ˌwər-thē\ *adj* : fit for operation in the air ⟨an ~ plane⟩ — air·wor·thi·ness *n*

airy \'er-ē\ *adj* air·i·er; -est 1 : LOFTY ⟨~ perches⟩ 2 : lacking in reality : EMPTY 3 : DELICATE 4 : BREEZY

aisle \'ī(-ə)l\ *n* [ME *ile*, fr. AF *ele*, lit., wing, fr. L *ala*] 1 : the side of a church nave separated by piers from the nave proper 2 : a passage between sections of seats

ajar \ə-'jär\ *adj or adv* : partly open

AK *abbr* Alaska

aka *abbr* also known as

AKC *abbr* American Kennel Club

akim·bo \ə-'kim-bō\ *adj or adv* : having the hand on the hip and the elbow turned outward

akin \ə-'kin\ *adj* 1 : related by blood 2 : similar in kind

Al *symbol* aluminum

AL *abbr* 1 Alabama 2 American League 3 American Legion

¹-al *adj suffix* : of, relating to, or characterized by ⟨directional⟩

²-al *n suffix* : action : process ⟨rehearsal⟩

Ala *abbr* Alabama

al·a·bas·ter \'a-lə-ˌbas-tər\ *n* 1 : a compact fine-textured usu. white and translucent gypsum often carved into objects (as vases) 2 : a hard translucent calcite

à la carte \ˌä-lə-'kärt, ˌa-\ *adv or adj* [F] : with a separate price for each item on the menu

alac·ri·ty \ə-'la-krə-tē\ *n* : cheerful readiness : BRISKNESS

à la mode \ˌa-lə-'mōd, ˌä-\ *adj* [F, according to the fashion] 1 : FASHIONABLE, STYLISH 2 : topped with ice cream

¹alarm \ə-'lärm\ *also* ala·rum \ə-'lär-əm, -'ler-\ *n* [ME *alarme*, fr. MF, fr. OIt *all'arme*, lit., to arms] 1 : a warning signal or device 2 : the terror caused by sudden danger

²alarm *also* alarum *vb* 1 : to warn of danger 2 : FRIGHTEN

alarm·ist \ə-'lär-mist\ *n* : a person who alarms others esp. needlessly

alas \ə-'las\ *interj* — used to express unhappiness, pity, or concern

al·ba·core \'al-bə-ˌkȯr\ *n, pl* -core *or* -cores : a large tuna that is a source of canned tuna

Al·ba·nian \al-'bā-nē-ən\ *n* : a native or inhabitant of Albania

al·ba·tross \'al-bə-ˌtrȯs, -ˌträs\ *n, pl* -tross *or* -tross·es : any of a family of large web-footed seabirds

al·be·do \al-'bē-(ˌ)dō\ *n, pl* -dos : the fraction of incident radiation that is reflected by a body or surface

al·be·it \ȯl-'bē-ət, al-\ *conj* : even though : ALTHOUGH

al·bi·no \al-'bī-nō\ *n, pl* -nos : a person or animal lacking coloring matter in the skin, hair, and eyes — al·bi·nism \'al-bə-ˌni-zəm\ *n*

al·bum \'al-bəm\ *n* 1 : a book with blank pages used for making a collection (as of stamps or photographs) 2 : one or more recordings (as on tape or disk) produced as a single unit

al·bu·men \al-'byü-mən\ *n* 1 : the white of an egg 2 : ALBUMIN

al·bu·min \al-'byü-mən\ *n* : any of numerous water-soluble proteins of blood, milk, egg white, and plant and animal tissues

al·bu·min·ous \al-'byü-mə-nəs\ *adj* : containing or resembling albumen or albumin

al·bu·ter·ol \al-'byü-tə-ˌrȯl, -ˌrōl\ *n* : a drug used as an aerosol or in tablet form to treat asthma

alc *abbr* alcohol

al·cal·de \al-'käl-dē\ *n* : the chief administrative and judicial officer of a Spanish or Spanish-American town

al·ca·zar \al-'kä-zər, -'ka-\ *n* [Sp *alcázar*, fr. Ar *al-qaṣr* the castle] : a Spanish fortress or palace

al·che·my \'al-kə-mē\ *n* : medieval chemistry chiefly concerned with efforts to turn base metals into gold — al·che·mist \'al-kə-mist\ *n*

al·co·hol \'al-kə-ˌhȯl\ *n* [NL, fr. ML, powdered antimony, fr. Sp, fr. Ar *al-kuḥul* the powdered antimony] 1 : a colorless flammable liquid that is the intoxicating agent in fermented and distilled liquors **2** : any of various carbon compounds similar to alcohol **3** : beverages containing alcohol

¹al·co·hol·ic \ˌal-kə-ˈhȯ-lik, -ˈhä-\ *adj* **1** : of, relating to, caused by, or containing alcohol **2** : affected with alcoholism — **al·co·hol·i·cal·ly** \-li-k(ə-)lē\ *adv*

²alcoholic *n* : a person affected with alcoholism

al·co·hol·ism \ˈal-kə-ˌhȯ-ˌli-zəm\ *n* : continued excessive and usu. uncontrollable use of alcoholic drinks; *also* : a complex chronic psychological and nutritional disorder associated with such use

al·cove \ˈal-ˌkōv\ *n* **1** : a nook or small recess opening off a larger room **2** : a niche or arched opening (as in a wall)

ald *abbr* alderman

al·der \ˈȯl-dər\ *n* : any of a genus of trees or shrubs related to the birches and growing in wet areas

al·der·man \ˈȯl-dər-mən\ *n* : a member of a city legislative body

ale \ˈāl\ *n* : an alcoholic beverage brewed from malt and hops that is usu. more bitter than beer

ale·a·tor·ic \ˌā-lē-ə-ˈtȯr-ik\ *adj* : characterized by chance or random elements ⟨~ music⟩

ale·a·to·ry \ˈā-lē-ə-ˌtȯr-ē\ *adj* : ALEATORIC

alee \ə-ˈlē\ *adv* : on or toward the lee

ale·house \ˈāl-ˌhau̇s\ *n* : a place where ale is sold to be drunk on the premises

¹alert \ə-ˈlȯrt\ *adj* [It *all'erta*, lit., on the ascent] **1** : watchful against danger **2** : quick to perceive and act — **alert·ly** *adv* — **alert·ness** *n*

²alert *n* **1** : ALARM **2** : the period during which an alert is in effect

³alert *vb* **1** : WARN **2** : to make aware of

Aleut \ə-lē-ˈüt, ə-ˈlüt\ *n* **1** : a member of a people of the Aleutian and Shumagin islands and the western part of Alaska Peninsula **2** : the language of the Aleuts

ale·wife \ˈāl-ˌwīf\ *n, pl* **ale·wives** \-ˌwīvz\ : a food fish related to the herring that is abundant esp. along the Atlantic coast

alewife

Al·ex·an·dri·an \ˌa-lig-ˈzan-drē-ən\ *adj* **1** : HELLENISTIC **2** : of or relating to Alexander the Great

al·ex·an·drine \-ˈzan-drən\ *n, often cap* : a line of six iambic feet

al·fal·fa \al-ˈfal-fə\ *n* : a leguminous plant widely grown for hay and forage

al·fres·co \al-ˈfres-kō\ *adj or adv* [It] : taking place in the open air

alg *abbr* algebra

al·ga \ˈal-gə\ *n, pl* **al·gae** \ˈal-(ˌ)jē\ : any of a group of lower plants having chlorophyll but no vascular system and including seaweeds and related freshwater plants — **al·gal** \-gəl\ *adj*

al·ge·bra \ˈal-jə-brə\ *n* [ML, fr. Ar *al-jabr*] : a generalization of arithmetic in which letters representing numbers are combined according to the rules of arithmetic — **al·ge·bra·ic** \ˌal-jə-ˈbrā-ik\ *adj* — **al·ge·bra·i·cal·ly** \-ˈbrā-ə-k(ə-)lē\ *adv*

Al·gon·qui·an \al-ˈgän-kwē-ən, -ˈgäŋ-\ *or* **Al·gon·quin** \-kwən\ *n* **1** *usu* Algonquin : a member of an American Indian people of the Ottawa River valley **2** *usu* Algonquian : a family of American Indian languages of eastern and central No. America

al·go·rithm \ˈal-gə-ˌri-thəm\ *n* : a procedure for solving a problem esp. in mathematics or computing — **al·go·rith·mic** \ˌal-gə-ˈrith-mik\ *adj* — **al·go·rith·mi·cal·ly** \-mi-k(ə-)lē\ *adv*

¹ali·as \ˈā-lē-əs, ˈāl-yəs\ *adv* [L, otherwise, fr. *alius* other] : otherwise called

²alias *n* : an assumed name

¹al·i·bi \ˈa-lə-ˌbī\ *n* [L, elsewhere, fr. *alius* other] **1** : a plea offered by an accused person of not having been at the scene of an offense **2** : an excuse (as for failure)

²alibi *vb* **-bied; -bi·ing** **1** : to furnish an excuse for **2** : to offer an excuse

¹alien \ˈā-lē-ən, ˈāl-yən\ *adj* **1** : belonging to another : FOREIGN **2** : EXOTIC 1

²alien *n* **1** : a foreign-born resident who has not been naturalized **2** : EXTRATERRESTRIAL

alien·able \ˈā-lyə-nə-bəl, ˈā-lē-ə-nə-\ *adj* : transferable to the ownership of another ⟨~ property⟩

alien·ate \ˈā-lē-ə-ˌnāt, ˈāl-yə-\ *vb* **-at·ed; -at·ing** **1** : to make hostile : ESTRANGE **2** : to transfer (property) to another — **alien·ation** \ˌā-lē-ə-ˈnā-shən, ˌāl-yə-\ *n*

alien·ist \ˈā-lē-ə-nist, ˈāl-yə-\ *n* : PSYCHIATRIST

¹alight \ə-ˈlīt\ *vb* **alight·ed** *also* **alit** \ə-ˈlit;\ **alight·ing** **1** : to get down (as from a vehicle) **2** : to come to rest from the air ♦ *Synonyms* SETTLE, LAND, PERCH

²alight *adj* : lighted up

align *also* **aline** \ə-ˈlīn\ *vb* **1** : to bring into line **2** : to array on the side of or against a cause — **align·er** *n* — **align·ment** *also* **aline·ment** *n*

¹alike \ə-ˈlīk\ *adv* : EQUALLY ⟨denounced by teachers and students ~⟩

²alike *adj* : LIKE ⟨~ in their beliefs⟩ ♦ *Synonyms* AKIN, ANALOGOUS, SIMILAR, COMPARABLE

al·i·ment \ˈa-lə-mənt\ *n* : NOURISHMENT 1 — **aliment** *vb*

al·i·men·ta·ry \ˌa-lə-ˈmen-t(ə-)rē\ *adj* : of, relating to, or functioning in nourishment or nutrition

alimentary canal *n* : the tube that extends from the mouth to the anus and functions in the digestion and absorption of food and the elimination of residues

al·i·mo·ny \ˈa-lə-ˌmō-nē\ *n, pl* **-nies** [L *alimonia* sustenance, fr. *alere* to nourish] : an allowance made to one spouse by the other for support pending or after legal separation or divorce

A—line \ˈā-ˌlīn\ *adj* : having a flared bottom and a close-fitting top ⟨an ~ skirt⟩

alive \ə-ˈlīv\ *adj* **1** : having life **2** : being in force or operation **3** : SENSITIVE ⟨~ to the danger⟩ **4** : ALERT, BRISK **5** : ANIMATED ⟨streets ~ with traffic⟩ — **alive·ness** *n*

alk *abbr* alkaline

al·ka·li \ˈal-kə-ˌlī\ *n, pl* **-lies** *or* **-lis** **1** : a substance (as a hydroxide) that has a bitter taste and neutralizes acids **2** : a mixture of salts in the soil of some dry regions in such amount as to make ordinary farming impossible — **al·ka·line** \-kə-lən, -ˌlīn\ *adj* — **al·ka·lin·i·ty** \ˌal-kə-ˈli-nə-tē\ *n*

al·ka·loid \ˈal-kə-ˌlȯid\ *n* : any of various usu. basic and bitter organic compounds found esp. in seed plants

al·kane \ˈal-ˌkān\ *n* : a hydrocarbon in which each carbon atom is bonded to 4 other atoms

al·kyd \ˈal-kəd\ *n* : any of numerous synthetic resins used esp. for protective coatings and in paint

¹all \ˈȯl\ *adj* **1** : the whole of ⟨sat up ~ night⟩ **2** : every member of **3** : EVERY ⟨~ manner of problems⟩ **4** : any whatever ⟨beyond ~ doubt⟩ **5** : nothing but ⟨~ ears⟩ **6** : being more than one person or thing ⟨who ~ is coming⟩

²all *adv* **1** : WHOLLY ⟨sat ~ alone⟩ **2** : selected as the best — used in combination ⟨*all*-state champs⟩ **3** : so much ⟨~ the better for it⟩ **4** : for each side ⟨the score is two ~⟩

³all *pron sing or pl* **1** : the whole number, quantity, or amount ⟨~ of it is gone⟩ **2** : EVERYBODY, EVERYTHING ⟨~ are members⟩ ⟨that is ~⟩

⁴all *n* : the whole of one's resources ⟨gave his ~⟩

Al·lah \ˈä-lə, ˈa-; ˈā-ˌlä, ä-ˈlä\ *n* [Ar *allāh*] : GOD 1 — used in Islam

all along *adv* : all the time ⟨knew it *all along*⟩

all—Amer·i·can \ˌȯl-ə-ˈmer-ə-kən\ *adj* **1** : selected as the best in the U.S. **2** : composed wholly of American elements **3** : typical of the U.S. — **all—American** *n*

all—around \ˌȯl-ə-ˈrau̇nd\ *adj* **1** : considered in all aspects ⟨best ~ performance⟩ **2** : competent in many fields : VERSATILE ⟨an ~ athlete⟩

al·lay \ə-ˈlā\ *vb* **1** : ALLEVIATE **2** : CALM ♦ *Synonyms* LIGHTEN, RELIEVE, EASE, ASSUAGE

all clear *n* : a signal that a danger has passed

al·lege \ə-'lej\ vb al·leged; al·leg·ing 1 : to assert without proof 2 : to offer as a reason — al·le·ga·tion \,a-li-'gā-shən\ n — al·leged \ə-'lejd, -'le-jəd\ adj — al·leg·ed·ly \ə-'le-jəd-lē\ adv

al·le·giance \ə-'lē-jəns\ n 1 : loyalty owed by a citizen to a government 2 : loyalty to a person or cause

al·le·go·ry \'a-lə-,gȯr-ē\ n, pl -ries : the expression through symbolism of truths or generalizations about human experience — al·le·gor·i·cal \,a-lə-'gȯr-i-kəl\ adj — al·le·gor·i·cal·ly \-k(ə-)lē\ adv

¹al·le·gro \ə-'le-grō, -'lā-\ n, pl -gros : an allegro movement

²allegro adv or adj [It, merry] : at a brisk lively tempo — used as a direction in music

al·lele \ə-'lēl\ n : any of the alternative forms of a gene that may occur at a given site on a chromosome — al·le·lic \-'lē-lik, -'le-\ adj

al·le·lu·ia \,a-lə-'lü-yə\ interj : HALLELUJAH

Al·len wrench \'a-lən-\ n [Allen Manufacturing Company, Hartford, Conn.] : an L-shaped hexagonal metal bar of which either end fits the socket of a screw or bolt

al·ler·gen \'a-lər-jən\ n : something that causes allergy — al·ler·gen·ic \,a-lər-'je-nik\ adj

al·ler·gist \'a-lər-jist\ n : a specialist in allergies

al·ler·gy \'a-lər-jē\ n, pl -gies [G Allergie, fr. Gk allos other + ergon work] : exaggerated or abnormal reaction (as by sneezing) to substances or situations harmless to most people — al·ler·gic \ə-'lər-jik\ adj

al·le·vi·ate \ə-'lē-vē-,āt\ vb -at·ed; -at·ing : RELIEVE, LESSEN ⟨~ pain⟩ ✦ Synonyms LIGHTEN, MITIGATE, ALLAY — al·le·vi·a·tion \ə-,lē-vē-'ā-shən\ n

al·ley \'a-lē\ n, pl alleys 1 : a garden or park walk 2 : a place for bowling 3 : a narrow passageway esp. between buildings

al·ley–oop \,a-lē-'yüp\ n : a basketball play in which a player catches a pass above the basket and immediately dunks the ball

al·ley·way \'a-lē-,wā\ n : ALLEY 3

all–fired \'ȯl-,fī(-ə)rd\ adv : EXTREMELY, EXCESSIVELY ⟨~ stubborn⟩

All·hal·lows \ȯl-'ha-lōz\ n, pl Allhallows : ALL SAINTS' DAY

all hours n pl : a very late time ⟨stayed up until all hours⟩

al·li·ance \ə-'lī-əns\ n : a union to promote common interests ✦ Synonyms LEAGUE, COALITION, CONFEDERACY, FEDERATION

al·li·ga·tor \'a-lə-,gā-tər\ n [Sp el lagarto the lizard] : either of two large short-legged reptiles resembling crocodiles but having a shorter and broader snout

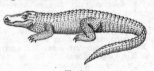

alligator

alligator pear n : AVOCADO

al·lit·er·ate \ə-'li-tə-,rāt\ vb -at·ed; -at·ing 1 : to form an alliteration 2 : to arrange so as to make alliteration

al·lit·er·a·tion \ə-,li-tə-'rā-shən\ n : the repetition of initial sounds in adjacent words or syllables — al·lit·er·a·tive \-'li-tə-,rā-tiv\ adj

al·lo·cate \'a-lə-,kāt\ vb -cat·ed; -cat·ing : ALLOT, ASSIGN — al·lo·ca·tion \,a-lə-'kā-shən\ n

al·lot \ə-'lät\ vb al·lot·ted; al·lot·ting : to distribute as a share ✦ Synonyms ASSIGN, APPORTION, ALLOCATE — al·lot·ment n

all–out \'ȯl-'aút\ adj : made with maximum effort

¹all over adv : EVERYWHERE

²all over prep 1 : in eagerly affectionate, attentive, or aggressive pursuit 2 : in or into a state marked by excessive criticism

al·low \ə-'laú\ vb 1 : to assign as a share ⟨~ time for rest⟩ 2 : to count as a deduction 3 : to make allowance ⟨~ for expansion⟩ 4 : ADMIT, CONCEDE ⟨~ed that the situation was serious⟩ 5 : PERMIT ⟨~s the dog to roam⟩ — al·low·able adj

al·low·ance \-əns\ n 1 : an allotted share 2 : money given regularly for expenses 3 : a taking into account of extenuating circumstances

al·loy \'a-,lȯi, ə-'lȯi\ n 1 : a substance composed of metals melted together 2 : an admixture that lessens value — al·loy \ə-'lȯi, 'a-,lȯi\ vb

all right adv 1 — used interjectionally esp. to express agreement or resignation or to indicate the resumption of a discussion ⟨all right, let's go⟩ 2 : beyond doubt 3 : SATISFACTORILY ⟨does all right in school⟩ — all right adj

All Saints' Day n : a Christian feast on November 1 in honor of all the saints

All Souls' Day n : a day of prayer observed by some Christian churches on November 2 for the souls of the faithful departed

all·spice \'ȯl-,spīs\ n : the berry of a West Indian tree related to the European myrtle; also : the mildly pungent and aromatic spice made from it

all–star \'ȯl-,stär\ n : a member of a team of star performers — all–star adj

all–ter·rain vehicle n : a small motor vehicle with three or four wheels for use on a wide range of terrain

all told adv : with everything or everyone counted ⟨expecting eight guests all told⟩

al·lude \ə-'lüd\ vb al·lud·ed; al·lud·ing [L alludere, lit., to play with] : to refer indirectly — al·lu·sion \-'lü-zhən\ n — al·lu·sive \-'lü-siv\ adj — al·lu·sive·ly adv — al·lu·sive·ness n

al·lure \ə-'lúr\ vb al·lured; al·lur·ing : to attract by something desirable — allure n — al·lur·ing·ly adv

al·lu·vi·um \ə-'lü-vē-əm\ n, pl -vi·ums or -via \-vē-ə\ : soil material (as clay) deposited by running water — al·lu·vi·al \-vē-əl\ adj or n

all–wheel \'ȯl-'wēl\ adj : acting independently on or by means of all four wheels of a vehicle

al·ly \ə-'lī, 'a-,lī\ vb al·lied; al·ly·ing : to enter into an alliance — al·ly \'a-,lī, ə-'lī\ n

-ally adv suffix : ²-LY ⟨specifically⟩

al·ma ma·ter \,al-mə-'mä-tər\ n [L, fostering mother] 1 : an educational institute that one has attended 2 : the song or hymn of an alma mater

al·ma·nac \'ȯl-mə-,nak, 'al-\ n 1 : a publication esp. of astronomical and meteorological data 2 : a usu. annual publication of miscellaneous information

al·man·dite \'al-mən-,dīt\ n : a deep red garnet

al·mighty \ȯl-'mī-tē\ adj 1 often cap : having absolute power over all ⟨Almighty God⟩ 2 : relatively unlimited in power — al·might·i·ness n

Almighty n : GOD 1

al·mond \'ä-mənd, 'a-; 'al-\ n : a small tree related to the peach; also : the edible nutlike kernel of its fruit

al·mo·ner \'al-mə-nər, 'ä-mə-\ n : a person who distributes alms

al·most \'ȯl-,mōst, ȯl-'mōst\ adv : very nearly but not exactly

alms \'ämz, 'almz\ n, pl alms [ME almesse, almes, fr. OE ælmesse, ælms, fr. L eleemosyna alms, fr. Gk eleēmosynē pity, alms, fr. eleēmōn merciful, fr. eleos pity] : something given freely to relieve the poor

alms·house \-,haús\ n : POORHOUSE

al·oe \'a-lō\ n 1 : any of a large genus of succulent chiefly southern African plants related to the lilies 2 pl : the dried juice of the leaves of an aloe used esp. formerly as a laxative

aloe vera \-'ver-ə, -'vir-\ n : an aloe with leaves that yield a jellylike emollient extract used esp. in cosmetics; also : this extract

aloft \ə-'lȯft\ adv 1 : high in the air 2 : in flight

alo·ha \ə-'lō-ə, ä-'lō-hä\ interj [Hawaiian] — used to greet or bid farewell

alone \ə-'lōn\ adj 1 : separated from others 2 : not including anyone or anything else : ONLY ⟨she ~ knows why⟩ ✦ Synonyms LONELY, LONESOME, LONE, SOLITARY — alone adv

¹along \ə-'lȯŋ\ prep 1 : in a line matching the direction of ⟨sail ~ the coast⟩ 2 : at a point on or during ⟨stopped ~ the way⟩

²along adv 1 : FORWARD, ON ⟨move ~⟩ 2 : as a companion ⟨bring her ~⟩ 3 : at an advanced point ⟨plans are far ~⟩

along–shore \ə-'lȯŋ-'shȯr\ adv or adj : along the shore or coast ⟨walked ~⟩

¹along·side \-,sīd\ adv : along or by the side

²**alongside** *prep* **1** : along or by the side of **2** : in association with

alongside of *prep* : ALONGSIDE

aloof \ə-'lüf\ *adj* : removed or distant physically or emotionally — **aloof·ly** *adv* — **aloof·ness** *n*

al·o·pe·cia \ˌa-lə-'pē-sh(ē-)ə\ *n* : BALDNESS

aloud \ə-'laüd\ *adv* : with the speaking voice 〈read ~〉

alp \'alp\ *n* : a high rugged mountain

al·paca \al-'pa-kə\ *n* : a domesticated mammal esp. of Peru that is prob. descended from the vicuña; *also* : its woolly hair or a thin cloth made from this hair

al·pha \'al-fə\ *n* **1** : the 1st letter of the Greek alphabet — A or α **2** : something first : BEGINNING

al·pha·bet \'al-fə-ˌbet\ *n* : the set of letters or characters used in writing a language

al·pha·bet·i·cal \ˌal-fə-'be-ti-kəl\ *or* **al·pha·bet·ic** \-'be-tik\ *adj* **1** : arranged in the order of the letters of the alphabet **2** : of or employing an alphabet — **al·pha·bet·i·cal·ly** \-ti-k(ə-)lē\ *adv*

al·pha·bet·ize \'al-fə-bə-ˌtīz\ *vb* **-ized; -iz·ing** : to arrange in alphabetical order — **al·pha·bet·iz·er** *n*

al·pha·nu·mer·ic \ˌal-fə-nü-'mer-ik, -nyü-\ *adj* : consisting of letters and numbers and often other symbols 〈an ~ code〉; *also* : being a character in an alphanumeric system

alpha particle *n* : a positively charged particle identical with the nucleus of a helium atom that is ejected at high speed in certain radioactive transformations

alpha rhythm *n* : ALPHA WAVE

alpha wave *n* : an electrical rhythm of the brain often associated with a state of wakeful relaxation

Al·pine \'al-ˌpīn\ *adj* **1** : relating to, located in, or resembling the Alps *often not cap* **2** : of, relating to, or growing on upland slopes above timberline **3** : of or relating to competitive ski events consisting of slalom and downhill racing

al·ready \ol-'re-dē\ *adv* : by this time : PREVIOUSLY

al·right \ol-'rīt\ *adv* : ALL RIGHT

al·so \'ol-sō\ *adv* : in addition : TOO

al·so–ran \-ˌran\ *n* **1** : a horse or dog that finishes out of the money in a race **2** : a contestant that does not win

alt *abbr* **1** alternate **2** altitude

Alta *abbr* Alberta

al·tar \'ol-tər\ *n* **1** : a structure on which sacrifices are offered or incense is burned **2** : a table used as a center of ritual or worship

altar server *n* : a boy or girl who assists the celebrant at a church service

¹**al·ter** \'ol-tər\ *vb* **al·tered; al·ter·ing** \-t(ə-)riŋ\ **1** : to make or become different **2** : CASTRATE, SPAY — **al·ter·able** \'ol-tə-rə-bəl\ *adj* — **al·ter·a·tion** \ˌol-tə-'rā-shən\ *n*

²**alter** *abbr* alteration

al·ter·ca·tion \ˌol-tər-'kā-shən\ *n* : a noisy or angry dispute

alter ego \ˌol-tər-'ē-gō\ *n* [L, lit., second I] : a second self; *esp* : a trusted friend

al·ter·i·ty \ol-'ter-ə-tē\ *n* : the quality or state of being radically alien to the conscious self or a particular cultural orientation

¹**al·ter·nate** \'ol-tər-nət, 'al-\ *adj* **1** : arranged or succeeding by turns **2** : every other **3** : being an alternative 〈an ~ route〉 — **al·ter·nate·ly** *adv*

²**al·ter·nate** \-ˌnāt\ *vb* **-nat·ed; -nat·ing** : to occur or cause to occur by turns — **al·ter·na·tion** \ˌol-tər-'nā-shən, ˌal-\ *n*

³**alternate** *n* : SUBSTITUTE

alternating current *n* : an electric current that reverses its direction at regular intervals

al·ter·na·tive \ol-'tər-nə-tiv, al-\ *adj* **1** : offering a choice 〈several ~ plans〉 **2** : different from the usual or conventional — **alternative** *n*

alternative medicine *n* : any of various systems of healing (as homeopathy) not typically practiced in conventional Western medicine

al·ter·na·tor \'ol-tər-ˌnā-tər, 'al-\ *n* : an electric generator for producing alternating current

al·though *also* **al·tho** \ol-'thō\ *conj* : in spite of the fact that : even though

al·tim·e·ter \al-'ti-mə-tər, 'al-tə-ˌmē-tər\ *n* : an instrument for measuring altitude

al·ti·tude \'al-tə-ˌtüd, -ˌtyüd\ *n* **1** : angular distance above the horizon **2** : vertical distance : HEIGHT **3** : the perpendicular distance in a geometric figure from the vertex

to the base, from the vertex of an angle to the side opposite, or from the base to a parallel side or face

al·to \'al-tō\ *n, pl* **altos** [It, lit., high, fr. L *altus*] : the lower female voice part in a 4-part chorus; *also* : a singer having this voice or part

¹**al·to·geth·er** \ˌol-tə-'ge-thər\ *adv* **1** : WHOLLY 〈stopped raining ~〉 **2** : in all 〈spent $100 ~〉 **3** : on the whole 〈~ their efforts were successful〉

²**altogether** *n* : NUDE 〈posed in the ~〉

al·tru·ism \'al-trü-ˌi-zəm\ *n* [F *altruisme*, fr. *autrui* other people, fr. OF, oblique case form of *autre* other, fr. L *alter*] : unselfish interest in the welfare of others — **al·tru·ist** \-ist\ *n* — **al·tru·is·tic** \ˌal-trü-'is-tik\ *adj* — **al·tru·is·ti·cal·ly** \-ti-k(ə-)lē\ *adv*

al·um \'a-ləm\ *n* : either of two colorless crystalline aluminum-containing compounds used esp. as an emetic or as an astringent and styptic

alu·mi·na \ə-'lü-mə-nə\ *n* : the oxide of aluminum occurring in nature as corundum and in bauxite

al·u·min·i·um \ˌal-yə-'mi-nē-əm\ *n chiefly Brit* : ALUMINUM

alu·mi·nize \ə-'lü-mə-ˌnīz\ *vb* **-nized; -niz·ing** : to treat with aluminum

alu·mi·num \ə-'lü-mə-nəm\ *n* : a silver-white malleable ductile light metallic element that is the most abundant metal in the earth's crust

aluminum oxide *n* : ALUMINA

alum·na \ə-'ləm-nə\ *n, pl* **-nae** \-(ˌ)nē\ : a woman or girl who is a graduate or former student of a college or school

alum·nus \ə-'ləm-nəs\ *n, pl* **-ni** \-ˌnī\ [L, foster son, pupil, fr. *alere* to nourish] : a graduate or former student of a college or school

al·ways \'ol-wēz, -wəz, -(ˌ)wāz\ *adv* **1** : at all times : INVARIABLY **2** : FOREVER

Alz·hei·mer's disease \'älts-ˌhī-mərz-, 'alts-\ *n* : a degenerative brain disease of unknown cause that is characterized esp. by progressive mental deterioration and memory loss

am *pres 1st sing of* BE

¹**Am** *abbr* America; American

²**Am** *symbol* americium

¹**AM** \'ā-ˌem\ *n* : a broadcasting system using amplitude modulation; *also* : a radio receiver for broadcasts made by such a system

²**AM** *abbr* **1** ante meridiem — often not cap. and often punctuated **2** [NL *artium magister*] master of arts

AMA *abbr* American Medical Association

amah \'ä-(ˌ)mä\ *n* : a female servant in eastern Asia; *esp* : a Chinese nurse

amain \ə-'mān\ *adv archaic* : with full force or speed

amal·gam \ə-'mal-gəm\ *n* **1** : an alloy of mercury with another metal used in making dental cements **2** : a mixture of different elements

amal·gam·ate \ə-'mal-gə-ˌmāt\ *vb* **-at·ed; -at·ing** : to unite or merge into one body — **amal·ga·ma·tion** \-ˌmal-gə-'mā-shən\ *n*

aman·u·en·sis \ə-ˌman-yə-'wen-səs\ *n, pl* **-en·ses** \-ˌsēz\ : one employed to write from dictation or to copy what another has written : SECRETARY

am·a·ranth \'a-mə-ˌranth\ *n* **1** : any of a large genus of coarse herbs sometimes grown for their showy flowers **2** : a flower that never fades

am·a·ran·thine \ˌa-mə-'ran-thən, -ˌthīn\ *adj* **1** : relating to or resembling an amaranth **2** : UNDYING

am·a·ryl·lis \ˌa-mə-'ri-ləs\ *n* : any of various plants related to the lilies; *esp* : an autumn-flowering South African bulbous herb widely grown for its large showy red to whitish flowers

amass \ə-'mas\ *vb* : ACCUMULATE

am·a·teur \'a-mə-(ˌ)tər, -ˌtur, -ˌtyur, -ˌchur, -chər\ *n* [F, fr. L *amator* lover, fr. *amare* to love] **1** : a person who engages in a pursuit for pleasure and not as a profession **2** : a person who is not expert — **am·a·teur·ish** \ˌa-mə-'tər-ish, -'tur-, -'tyur-, -'chur-, -'chər-\ *adj* — **am·a·teur·ism** \'a-mə-(ˌ)tər-i-zəm, -ˌtur-, -ˌtyur-, -ˌchur-, -ˌchər-\ *n*

am·a·tive \'a-mə-tiv\ *adj* : indicative of love : AMOROUS — **am·a·tive·ly** *adv* — **am·a·tive·ness** *n*

am·a·to·ry \'a-mə-ˌtōr-ē\ *adj* : of or expressing sexual love

amaze \ə-'māz\ *vb* **amazed; amaz·ing** : to fill with wonder : ASTOUND ♦ **Synonyms** ASTONISH, SURPRISE, DUMBFOUND — **amaze·ment** *n* — **amaz·ing·ly** *adv*

am·a·zon \'a-mə-ˌzän, -zən\ *n* **1** *cap* : a member of a race of female warriors of Greek mythology **2** : a tall strong often masculine woman — **am·a·zo·ni·an** \ˌa-mə-ˈzō-nē-ən\ *adj, often cap*

amb *abbr* ambassador

am·bas·sa·dor \am-ˈba-sə-dər\ *n* : a representative esp. of a government — **am·bas·sa·do·ri·al** \-ˌba-sə-ˈdȯr-ē-əl\ *adj* — **am·bas·sa·dor·ship** *n*

am·ber \'am-bər\ *n* : a yellowish or brownish fossil resin used esp. for ornamental objects; *also* : the color of this resin

Amber Alert *n* : a widely publicized bulletin that alerts the public to a recently abducted or missing child

am·ber·gris \'am-bər-ˌgris, -ˌgrēs\ *n* : a waxy substance from the sperm whale used in making perfumes

am·bi·dex·trous \ˌam-bi-ˈdek-strəs\ *adj* : using both hands with equal ease — **am·bi·dex·trous·ly** *adv*

am·bi·ence *or* **am·bi·ance** \'am-bē-əns, äⁿ-ˈbyäⁿs\ *n* : a pervading atmosphere

¹**am·bi·ent** \'am-bē-ənt\ *adj* : existing on all sides

²**ambient** *n* : music intended to serve as an unobtrusive accompaniment to other activities

am·big·u·ous \am-ˈbi-gyə-wəs\ *adj* : capable of being understood in more than one way — **am·bi·gu·i·ty** \ˌam-bə-ˈgyü-ə-tē\ *n* — **am·big·u·ous·ly** *adv*

am·bi·tion \am-ˈbi-shən\ *n* [ME, fr. MF or L; MF, fr. L *ambition-, ambitio*, lit., act of soliciting for votes, fr. *ambire* to go around] : eager desire for success or power

am·bi·tious \-shəs\ *adj* : characterized by ambition — **am·bi·tious·ly** *adv* — **am·bi·tious·ness** *n*

am·biv·a·lence \am-ˈbi-və-ləns\ *n* : simultaneous attraction toward and repulsion from a person, object, or action — **am·biv·a·lent** \-lənt\ *adj*

¹**am·ble** \'am-bəl\ *vb* **am·bled; am·bling** \-b(ə-)liŋ\ : to go at an amble

²**amble** *n* : an easy gait esp. of a horse

am·bro·sia \am-ˈbrō-zh(ē-)ə\ *n* : the food of the Greek and Roman gods — **am·bro·sial** \-zh(ē-)əl\ *adj*

am·bu·lance \'am-byə-ləns\ *n* : a vehicle equipped for carrying the injured or sick

am·bu·lant \'am-byə-lənt\ *adj* : AMBULATORY

¹**am·bu·la·to·ry** \'am-byə-lə-ˌtȯr-ē\ *adj* **1** : of, relating to, or adapted to walking **2** : able to walk or move about

²**ambulatory** *n, pl* **-ries** : a sheltered place (as in a cloister) for walking

am·bus·cade \'am-bə-ˌskād\ *n* : AMBUSH

am·bush \'am-ˌbush\ *n* : a trap in which concealed persons wait to attack by surprise — **ambush** *vb*

amdt *abbr* amendment

ameba, ameboid *var of* AMOEBA, AMOEBOID

ame·lio·rate \ə-ˈmēl-yə-ˌrāt\ *vb* **-rat·ed; -rat·ing** : to make or grow better : IMPROVE — **ame·lio·ra·tion** \-ˌmēl-yə-ˈrā-shən\ *n*

amen \(ˌ)ä-ˈmen, (ˌ)ā-\ *interj* — used esp. at the end of prayers to affirm or express approval

ame·na·ble \ə-ˈmē-nə-bəl, -ˈme-\ *adj* **1** : ANSWERABLE ⟨∼ to the law⟩ **2** : agreeable to something asked for

amend \ə-ˈmend\ *vb* **1** : to change for the better : IMPROVE **2** : to alter formally in phraseology — **amend·able** \-ˈmen-də-bəl\ *adj*

amend·ment \ə-ˈmend-mənt\ *n* **1** : correction of faults **2** : the process of amending a parliamentary motion or a constitution; *also* : the alteration so proposed or made

amends \ə-ˈmendz\ *n sing or pl* : compensation for injury or loss

ame·ni·ty \ə-ˈme-nə-tē, -ˈmē-\ *n, pl* **-ties** **1** : AGREEABLENESS **2** : a gesture observed in social relationships **3** : something that serves as a comfort or convenience

Amer *abbr* America; American

amerce \ə-ˈmərs\ *vb* **amerced; amerc·ing** **1** : to penalize by a fine determined by the court **2** : PUNISH — **amerce·ment** *n*

Amer·i·ca·na \ə-ˌmer-ə-ˈka-nə, -ˈkä-\ *n pl* : materials concerning or characteristic of America, its civilization, or its culture

American Indian *n* : a member of any of the indigenous peoples of No. and So. America except often those distinguished as Eskimos or Inuits

Amer·i·can·ism \ə-ˈmer-ə-kə-ˌni-zəm\ *n* **1** : a characteristic feature of English as used in the U.S. **2** : attachment or loyalty to the traditions, interests, or ideals of

the U.S. **3** : a custom or trait peculiar to the U.S. or to Americans

Amer·i·can·ize \ə-ˈmer-ə-kə-ˌnīz\ *vb* : to make or become American — **Amer·i·can·i·za·tion** \ə-ˌmer-ə-kə-nə-ˈzā-shən\ *n*

Amer·i·can·ness \ə-ˈmer-ə-kən-nəs\ *n* : the quality or state of being American

American plan *n* : a hotel plan whereby the daily rates cover the cost of room and three meals

American Sign Language *n* : a sign language for the deaf in which meaning is conveyed by a system of hand gestures and placement

am·er·i·ci·um \ˌam-ə-ˈrish-ē-əm, -ˈris-\ *n* : a radioactive metallic chemical element produced artificially from plutonium

AmerInd *abbr* American Indian

Am·er·in·di·an \ˌa-mə-ˈrin-dē-ən\ *n* : AMERICAN INDIAN — **Amerindian** *adj*

am·e·thyst \'a-mə-thəst\ *n* [ME *amatiste*, fr. AF & L; AF, fr. L *amethystus*, fr. Gk *amethystos*, lit., remedy against drunkenness, fr. *a-* not + *methyein* to be drunk, fr. *methy* wine] : a gemstone consisting of clear purple or bluish-violet quartz

ami·a·ble \'ā-mē-ə-bəl\ *adj* **1** : AGREEABLE ⟨an ∼ comedy⟩ **2** : having a friendly and sociable disposition — **ami·a·bil·i·ty** \ˌā-mē-ə-ˈbi-lə-tē\ *n* — **ami·a·ble·ness** *n* — **ami·a·bly** \'ā-mē-ə-blē\ *adv*

am·i·ca·ble \'a-mi-kə-bəl\ *adj* : FRIENDLY, PEACEABLE ⟨an ∼ settlement of differences⟩ — **am·i·ca·bil·i·ty** \ˌa-mi-kə-ˈbi-lə-tē\ *n* — **am·i·ca·bly** \'a-mi-kə-blē\ *adv*

amid \ə-ˈmid\ *or* **amidst** \-ˈmidst\ *prep* : in or into the middle of : AMONG

amid·ships \ə-ˈmid-ˌships\ *adv* : in or near the middle of a ship

ami·no acid \ə-ˈmē-nō-\ *n* : any of numerous nitrogen-containing acids that include some which are used by cells to build proteins

amir *var of* EMIR

¹**amiss** \ə-ˈmis\ *adv* **1** : WRONGLY **2** : ASTRAY ⟨something had gone ∼⟩ **3** : IMPERFECTLY

²**amiss** *adj* **1** : WRONG **2** : out of place

am·i·ty \'a-mə-tē\ *n, pl* **-ties** : FRIENDSHIP; *esp* : friendly relations between nations

am·me·ter \'a-ˌmē-tər\ *n* : an instrument for measuring electric current esp. in amperes

am·mo \'a-mō\ *n* : AMMUNITION

am·mo·nia \ə-ˈmō-nyə\ *n* [NL, fr. L *sal ammoniacus* sal ammoniac (ammonium chloride), lit., salt of Ammon, fr. Gk *ammōniakos* of Ammon, fr. *Ammōn* Ammon, an Egyptian god near one of whose temples it was extracted] **1** : a colorless gaseous compound of nitrogen and hydrogen used in refrigeration and in the making of fertilizers and explosives **2** : a solution (**ammonia water**) of ammonia in water

am·mo·ni·um \ə-ˈmō-nē-əm\ *n* : an ion or chemical group derived from ammonia by combination with hydrogen

ammonium chloride *n* : a white crystalline volatile salt used in batteries and as an expectorant

am·mu·ni·tion \ˌam-yə-ˈni-shən\ *n* **1** : projectiles fired from guns **2** : explosive items used in war **3** : material for use in attack or defense

Amn *abbr* airman

am·ne·sia \am-ˈnē-zhə\ *n* **1** : abnormal loss of memory **2** : the selective overlooking of events or acts not favorable to one's purpose — **am·ne·si·ac** \-zhē-ˌak, -zē-\ *or* — **am·ne·sic** \-zik, -sik\ *adj or n*

am·nes·ty \'am-nə-stē\ *n, pl* **-ties** : an act granting a pardon to a group of individuals — **amnesty** *vb*

am·nio·cen·te·sis \ˌam-nē-ō-ˌsen-ˈtē-səs\ *n, pl* **-te·ses** \-ˌsēz\ : the surgical insertion of a hollow needle through the abdominal wall and uterus of a pregnant female esp. to obtain fluid used to check the fetus for chromosomal abnormality and to determine sex

am·ni·ot·ic fluid \ˌam-nē-ˈä-tik-\ *n* : the watery fluid in which the embryo or fetus is immersed

amoe·ba *also* **ame·ba** \ə-ˈmē-bə\ *n, pl* **-bas** *or* **-bae** \-(ˌ)bē\ : any of various tiny one-celled protozoans that lack permanent cell organs and occur esp. in water and soil — **amoe·bic** \-bik\ *adj*

amoe·boid *also* **ame·boid** \-ˌbȯid\ *adj* : resembling an amoeba esp. in moving or readily changing shape

amok \ə-'mək, -'mäk\ *or* **amuck** \-'mək\ *adv* : in a violent, frenzied, or uncontrolled manner ⟨run ~⟩

among \ə-'məŋ\ *also* **amongst** \-'məŋst\ *prep* **1** : in or through the midst of **2** : in the number, class, or company of **3** : in shares to each of **4** : by common action of

amon·til·la·do \ə-ˌmän-tə-'lä-dō\ *n, pl* **-dos** [Sp] : a medium dry sherry

amor·al \ā-'mȯr-əl\ *adj* **1** : neither moral nor immoral; *esp* : being outside the sphere to which moral judgments apply **2** : lacking moral sensibility — **amor·al·ly** *adv*

am·o·rous \'a-mə-rəs\ *adj* **1** : inclined to love **2** : being in love **3** : of or indicative of love — **am·o·rous·ly** *adv* — **am·o·rous·ness** *n*

amor·phous \ə-'mȯr-fəs\ *adj* **1** : SHAPELESS, FORMLESS **2** : not crystallized

am·or·tize \'a-mər-ˌtīz, ə-'mȯr-\ *vb* **-tized; -tiz·ing** : to extinguish (as a mortgage) usu. by payment on the principal at the time of each periodic interest payment — **amor·ti·za·tion** \ˌa-mər-tə-'zā-shən, ə-ˌmȯr-\ *n*

Amos \'ā-məs\ — see BIBLE table

¹amount \ə-'mȧunt\ *vb* **1** : to be equivalent **2** : to reach a total : add up

²amount *n* **1** : the total number or quantity **2** : a principal sum plus the interest on it

amour \ə-'mùr, ä-, a-\ *n* **1** : a love affair esp. when illicit **2** : LOVER

amour pro·pre \ˌa-ˌmùr-'prōpr°, ä-, -'prȯpr°\ *n* [F] : SELF=ESTEEM

¹amp \'amp\ *n* **1** : AMPERE **2** : AMPLIFIER; *also* : a unit consisting of an electronic amplifier and a loudspeaker

²amp *vb* : EXCITE, ENERGIZE ⟨tried to ~ up the crowd⟩

am·per·age \'am-p(ə-)rij\ *n* : the strength of a current of electricity expressed in amperes

am·pere \'am-ˌpir\ *n* : a unit of electric current equivalent to a steady current produced by one volt applied across a resistance of one ohm

am·per·sand \'am-pər-ˌsand\ *n* [alter. of *and per se and,* spoken form of the phrase *& per se and,* lit., (the character) *&* by itself (stands for the word) *and*] : a character *&* used for the word *and*

am·phet·amine \am-'fe-tə-ˌmēn, -mən\ *n* : a compound or one of its derivatives that stimulates the central nervous system and is used esp. to treat hyperactive children and to suppress appetite

am·phib·i·an \am-'fi-bē-ən\ *n* **1** : an amphibious organism; *esp* : any of a class of vertebrate animals (as frogs and salamanders) intermediate between fishes and reptiles **2** : an airplane that can land on and take off from either land or water

am·phib·i·ous \am-'fi-bē-əs\ *adj* [Gk *amphibios,* lit., living a double life, fr. *amphi-* + *bios* mode of life] **1** : able to live both on land and in water **2** : adapted for both land and water **3** : made by joint action of land, sea, and air forces invading from the sea; *also* : trained for such action

am·phi·bole \'am-fə-ˌbōl\ *n* : any of a group of rock-forming minerals of similar crystal structure

am·phi·the·ater \'am-fə-ˌthē-ə-tər\ *n* **1** : an oval or circular structure with rising tiers of seats around an arena **2** : a very large auditorium

am·pho·ra \'am-fə-rə\ *n, pl* **-rae** \-ˌrē\ *or* **-ras** : an ancient Greek jar or vase with two handles that rise almost to the level of the mouth

am·ple \'am-pəl\ *adj* **am·pler** \-plər\; **am·plest** \-pləst\ **1** : LARGE, CAPACIOUS **2** : enough to satisfy : ABUNDANT — **am·ply** \-plē\ *adv*

am·pli·fy \'am-plə-ˌfī\ *vb* **-fied; -fy·ing 1** : to expand by extended treatment **2** : to increase in magnitude or strength; *esp* : to make louder — **am·pli·fi·ca·tion** \ˌam-plə-fə-'kā-shən\ *n* — **am·pli·fi·er** \'am-plə-ˌfī(-ə)r\ *n*

am·pli·tude \-ˌtüd, -ˌtyüd\ *n* **1** : ample extent : FULLNESS **2** : the extent of a vibratory movement (as of a pendulum) **3** : the height or depth of an oscillation (as of an alternating current or a radio wave) compared to its average value

amplitude modulation *n* : modulation of the amplitude of a radio carrier wave in accordance with the strength of the signal; *also* : a broadcasting system using such modulation

am·poule *or* **am·pule** *also* **am·pul** \'am-ˌpyül, -pül\ *n* : a

small sealed bulbous glass vessel used to hold a solution for hypodermic injection

am·pu·tate \'am-pyə-ˌtāt\ *vb* **-tat·ed; -tat·ing** : to cut off ⟨~ a leg⟩ — **am·pu·ta·tion** \ˌam-pyə-'tā-shən\ *n*

am·pu·tee \ˌam-pyə-'tē\ *n* : one who has had a limb amputated

AMSLAN *abbr* American Sign Language

amt *abbr* amount

amuck *var of* AMOK

am·u·let \'am-yə-lət\ *n* : an ornament worn as a charm against evil

amuse \ə-'myüz\ *vb* **amused; amus·ing** : to entertain in a light or playful manner : DIVERT — **amuse·ment** *n* — **amusing** *adj* — **amus·ing·ly** *adv*

amusement park *n* : a commercially operated park having various devices (as a roller coaster) for entertainment and booths for selling refreshments

AM·VETS \'am-ˌvets\ *abbr* American Veterans (of World War II)

am·y·lase \'a-mə-ˌlās, -ˌlāz\ *n* : any of several enzymes that accelerate the breakdown of starch and glycogen

an \ən, (')an\ *indefinite article* : A — used before words beginning with a vowel sound

¹-an *or* **-ian** *also* **-ean** *n suffix* **1** : one that belongs to ⟨American⟩ ⟨crustacean⟩ **2** : one skilled in or specializing in ⟨phonetician⟩

²-an *or* **-ian** *also* **-ean** *adj suffix* **1** : of or belonging to ⟨American⟩ **2** : characteristic of : resembling ⟨Shakespearean⟩

AN *abbr* airman (Navy)

an·a·bol·ic steroid \ˌa-nə-'bä-lik-\ *n* : any of a group of synthetic steroid hormones sometimes abused by athletes in training to increase the size and strength of their muscles

anach·ro·nism \ə-'na-krə-ˌni-zəm\ *n* **1** : the error of placing a person or thing in the wrong period **2** : one that is chronologically out of place — **anach·ro·nis·tic** \ə-ˌna-krə-'nis-tik\ *adj* — **anach·ro·nous** \-'na-krə-nəs\ *adj*

an·a·con·da \ˌa-nə-'kän-də\ *n* : a large So. American snake that suffocates and kills its prey by constriction

anad·ro·mous \ə-'na-drə-məs\ *adj* : ascending rivers from the sea for breeding ⟨shad are ~⟩

anae·mia, anae·mic *chiefly Brit var of* ANEMIA, ANEMIC

an·aer·obe \'a-nə-ˌrōb\ *n* : an anaerobic organism

an·aer·o·bic \ˌa-nə-'rō-bik\ *adj* : living, active, occurring, or existing in the absence of free oxygen

an·aes·the·sia, an·aes·thet·ic *chiefly Brit var of* ANESTHESIA, ANESTHETIC

ana·gram \'a-nə-ˌgram\ *n* : a word or phrase made by transposing the letters of another word or phrase

¹anal \'ā-n°l\ *adj* **1** : of, relating to, situated near, or involving the anus **2** : of, relating to, or characterized by the stage of psychosexual development in psychoanalytic theory during which one is concerned esp. with feces **3** : of, relating to, or characterized by personality traits (as frugality and neatness) considered typical of fixation at the anal stage of development — **anal·ly** *adv*

²anal *abbr* **1** analogy **2** analysis; analytic

an·al·ge·sia \ˌa-n°l-'jē-zhə\ *n* : insensibility to pain — **an·al·ge·sic** \-'jē-zik, -sik\ *adj*

an·al·ge·sic \-'jē-zik, -sik\ *n* : an agent for producing analgesia

analog computer *n* : a computer that operates with numbers represented by directly measurable quantities (as voltages)

anal·o·gous \ə-'na-lə-gəs\ *adj* : similar in one or more respects — **anal·o·gous·ly** *adv*

an·a·logue *or* **an·a·log** \'a-nə-ˌlȯg, -ˌläg\ *n* **1** : something that is analogous to something else **2** : an organ similar in function to one of another animal or plant but different in structure or origin

anal·o·gy \ə-'na-lə-jē\ *n, pl* **-gies 1** : inference that if two or more things agree in some respects they will probably agree in others **2** : a likeness in one or more ways between things otherwise unlike — **an·a·log·i·cal** \ˌa-nə-'lä-ji-kəl\ *adj* — **an·a·log·i·cal·ly** \-k(ə-)lē\ *adv*

anal–re·ten·tive \'ā-n°l-ri-'ten-tiv\ *adj* : ANAL 3

an·a·lyse *chiefly Brit var of* ANALYZE

anal·y·sis \ə-'na-lə-səs\ *n, pl* **-y·ses** \-ˌsēz\ [NL, fr. Gk, fr. *analyein* to break up, fr. *ana-* up + *lyein* to loosen] **1**

: separation of a thing into the parts or elements of which it is composed **2** : an examination of a thing to determine its parts or elements; *also* : a statement showing the results of such an examination **3** : PSYCHOANALYSIS — **an·a·lyst** \'a-nə-list\ *n* — **an·a·lyt·ic** \ˌa-nə-'li-tik\ *or* **an·a·lyt·i·cal** \-ti-kəl\ *adj* — **an·a·lyt·i·cal·ly** *adv*

an·a·lyte \'a-nə-ˌlīt\ *n* : a chemical substance that is the subject of chemical analysis

an·a·lyze \'a-nə-ˌlīz\ *vb* **-lyzed; -lyz·ing** : to make an analysis of

an·a·pest \'a-nə-ˌpest\ *n* : a metrical foot of two unaccented syllables followed by one accented syllable — **an·a·pes·tic** \ˌa-nə-'pes-tik\ *adj or n*

an·ar·chism \'a-nər-ˌki-zəm\ *n* : the theory that all government is undesirable — **an·ar·chist** \-kist\ *n or adj* — **an·ar·chis·tic** \ˌa-nər-'kis-tik\ *adj*

an·ar·chy \'a-nər-kē\ *n* **1** : a social structure without government or law and order **2** : utter confusion — **an·ar·chic** \a-'när-kik\ *adj* — **an·ar·chi·cal·ly** \-ki-k(ə-)lē\ *adv*

anas·to·mo·sis \ə-ˌnas-tə-'mō-səs\ *n, pl* **-mo·ses** \-ˌsēz\ : the union of parts or branches (as of blood vessels) **2** : NETWORK

anat *abbr* anatomical; anatomy

anath·e·ma \ə-'na-thə-mə\ *n* **1** : a solemn curse **2** : a person or thing accursed; *also* : one intensely disliked

anath·e·ma·tize \-ˌtīz\ *vb* **-tized; -tiz·ing** : to pronounce an anathema against : CURSE

anat·o·mise *Brit var of* ANATOMIZE

anat·o·mize \ə-'na-tə-ˌmīz\ *vb* **-mized; -miz·ing** : to dissect so as to examine the structure and parts; *also* : ANALYZE

anat·o·my \ə-'na-tə-mē\ *n, pl* **-mies** [LL *anatomia* dissection, fr. Gk *anatomē*, fr. *anatemnein* to dissect, fr. *ana-* up + *temnein* to cut] **1** : a branch of science dealing with the structure of organisms **2** : structural makeup esp. of an organism or any of its parts **3** : a separating into parts for detailed study : ANALYSIS — **an·a·tom·i·cal** \ˌa-nə-'tä-mi-kəl\ *or* **an·a·tom·ic** \-mik\ *adj* — **an·a·tom·i·cal·ly** \-mi-k(ə-)lē\ *adv* — **anat·o·mist** \ə-'na-tə-mist\ *n*

anc *abbr* ancient

-ance *n suffix* **1** : action or process ⟨further*ance*⟩ : instance of an action or process ⟨perform*ance*⟩ **2** : quality or state : instance of a quality or state ⟨protuber*ance*⟩ **3** : amount or degree ⟨conduct*ance*⟩

an·ces·tor \'an-ˌses-tər\ *n* [ME *ancestre*, fr. AF, fr. L *antecessor* predecessor, fr. *antecedere* to go before, fr. *ante-* before + *cedere* to go] : one from whom an individual is descended

an·ces·tress \'an-ˌses-trəs\ *n* : a female ancestor

an·ces·try \'an-ˌses-trē\ *n* **1** : line of descent : LINEAGE **2** : ANCESTORS — **an·ces·tral** \an-'ses-trəl\ *adj*

an·cho \'än-chō\ *n, pl* **anchos** : a poblano chili pepper esp. when mature and dried to a reddish black

¹an·chor \'aŋ-kər\ *n* **1** : a heavy metal device attached to a ship that catches hold of the bottom and holds the ship in place **2** : something that serves to hold an object firmly **3** : ANCHORPERSON **4** : a large store that attracts customers and other businesses to a shopping mall

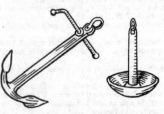

anchor 1: different styles

²anchor *vb* : to hold or become held in place by or as if by an anchor

an·chor·age \'aŋ-k(ə-)rij\ *n* : a place suitable for ships to anchor

an·cho·rite \'aŋ-kə-ˌrīt\ *n* : HERMIT

an·chor·man \'aŋ-kər-ˌman\ *n* **1** : the member of a team who competes last **2** : an anchorperson who is a man

an·chor·per·son \-ˌpər-sən\ *n* : a broadcaster who reads the news and introduces the reports of other broadcasters

an·chor·wom·an \-ˌwù-mən\ *n* : an anchorperson who is a woman

an·cho·vy \'an-ˌchō-vē, an-'chō-\ *n, pl* **-vies** *or* **-vy** : any of a family of small herringlike fishes often used as food

an·cien ré·gime \äⁿs-yaⁿ-rā-'zhēm\ *n* **1** : the political and social system of France before the Revolution of 1789 **2** : a system no longer prevailing

¹an·cient \'ān-shənt\ *adj* **1** : having existed for many years ⟨~ customs⟩ **2** : belonging to times long past; *esp* : belonging to the period before the Middle Ages

²ancient *n* **1** : an aged person **2** *pl* : the peoples of ancient Greece and Rome; *esp* : the classical authors of Greece and Rome

an·cil·lary \'an-sə-ˌler-ē\ *adj* **1** : SUBORDINATE, SUBSIDIARY ⟨a factory's ~ plants⟩ **2** : AUXILIARY, SUPPLEMENTARY ⟨~ evidence⟩ — **ancillary** *n*

-ancy *n suffix* : quality or state ⟨flamboy*ancy*⟩

and \ənd, (')and\ *conj* — used to indicate connection or addition esp. of items within the same class or type or to join words or phrases of the same grammatical rank or function **2** — used to join one finite verb to another so that together they are equivalent to an infinitive of purpose ⟨come ~ see me⟩

¹an·dan·te \än-'dän-ˌtä, -tē\ *adv or adj* [It, lit., going, prp. of *andare* to go] : moderately slow — used as a direction in music

²andante *n* : an andante movement

and·iron \'an-ˌdī(-ə)rn\ *n* : one of a pair of metal supports for firewood in a fireplace

and/or \'and-'ór\ *conj* — used to indicate that either *and* or *or* may apply ⟨apples ~ oranges means that the possibilities include apples, oranges, or both⟩

an·dro·gen \'an-drə-jən\ *n* : a male sex hormone (as testosterone)

an·drog·y·nous \an-'drä-jə-nəs\ *adj* **1** : having the characteristics of both male and female **2** : suitable for either sex ⟨~ clothing⟩ — **an·drog·y·ny** \-nē\ *n*

an·droid \'an-ˌdróid\ *n* : a mobile robot usu. with a human form

an·ec·dot·al \ˌa-nik-'dō-tᵊl\ *adj* **1** : relating to or consisting of anecdotes **2** : based on reports of an unscientific nature — **an·ec·dot·al·ly** *adv*

an·ec·dote \'an-ik-ˌdōt\ *n, pl* **-dotes** *also* **-dota** \ˌa-nik-'dō-tə\ [F, fr. Gk *anekdota* unpublished items, fr. *a-* not + *ekdidonai* to publish] : a brief story of an interesting, amusing, or biographical incident

ane·mia \ə-'nē-mē-ə\ *n* **1** : a condition in which blood is deficient in quantity, in red blood cells, or in hemoglobin and which is marked by pallor, weakness, and irregular heart action **2** : lack of vitality — **ane·mic** \ə-'nē-mik\ *adj*

an·e·mom·e·ter \ˌa-nə-'mä-mə-tər\ *n* : an instrument for measuring the force or speed of the wind

anem·o·ne \ə-'ne-mə-nē\ *n* : any of a large genus of herbs related to the buttercups that have showy flowers without petals but with conspicuous often colored sepals

anent \ə-'nent\ *prep* : CONCERNING

an·es·the·sia \ˌa-nəs-'thē-zhə\ *n* : loss of bodily sensation

an·es·the·si·ol·o·gy \-ˌthē-zē-'ä-lə-jē\ *n* : a branch of medical science dealing with anesthesia and anesthetics — **an·es·the·si·ol·o·gist** \-jist\ *n*

¹an·es·thet·ic \ˌa-nəs-'the-tik\ *adj* : of, relating to, or capable of producing anesthesia

²anesthetic *n* : an agent that produces anesthesia

anes·the·tist \ə-'nes-thə-tist\ *n* : one who administers anesthetics

anes·the·tize \ə-'nes-thə-ˌtīz\ *vb* **-tized; -tiz·ing** : to subject to anesthesia

an·eu·rysm *also* **an·eu·rism** \'an-yə-ˌri-zəm\ *n* : an abnormal blood-filled bulge of a blood vessel

anew \ə-'nü, -'nyü\ *adv* **1** : over again ⟨begin ~⟩ **2** : in a new form ⟨this film tells the story ~⟩

an·gel \'än-jəl\ *n* [ME, fr. OE *engel* & AF *angele*, both fr. L *angelus*, fr. Gk *angelos*, lit., messenger] **1** : a spiritual being superior to humans **2** : an attendant spirit **3** : a winged figure of human form in art **4** : MESSENGER, HARBINGER ⟨~ of death⟩ **5** : a person held to resemble an angel **6** : a financial backer — **an·gel·ic** \an-'je-lik\ *or* **an·gel·i·cal** \-li-kəl\ *adj* — **an·gel·i·cal·ly** \-k(ə-)lē\ *adv*

an·gel·fish \'ăn-jəl-ˌfish\ *n* : any of several brightly colored tropical fishes that are flattened from side to side

an·gel·i·ca \an-'je-li-kə\ *n* : a biennial herb related to the carrot whose roots and fruit furnish a flavoring oil

¹**an·ger** \'aŋ-gər\ *vb* : to make angry

²**anger** *n* [ME, affliction, anger, fr. ON *angr* grief] : a strong feeling of displeasure ◆ *Synonyms* WRATH, IRE, RAGE, FURY, INDIGNATION

an·gi·na \an-'jī-nə\ *n* : a disorder (as of the heart) marked by attacks of intense pain; *esp* : ANGINA PECTORIS — **an·gi·nal** \an-'jī-nᵊl\ *adj*

angina pec·to·ris \-'pek-t(ə-)rəs\ *n* : a heart disease marked by brief attacks of sharp chest pain caused by deficient oxygenation of heart muscles

an·gio·gen·e·sis \ˌan-jē-ō-'je-nə-səs\ *n* : the formation of blood vessels — **an·gio·gen·ic** \-'je-nik\ *adj*

an·gio·gram \'an-jē-ə-ˌgram\ *n* : a radiograph made by angiography

an·gi·og·ra·phy \ˌan-jē-'ä-grə-fē\ *n* : the use of radiography to make blood vessels visible after injection of a substance opaque to radiation

an·gio·plas·ty \'an-jē-ə-ˌplas-tē\ *n* : surgical repair of a blood vessel esp. by using an inflatable catheter to unblock arteries clogged by atherosclerotic deposits

an·gio·sperm \-ˌspərm\ *n* : FLOWERING PLANT

¹**an·gle** \'aŋ-gəl\ *n* 1 : a sharp projecting corner 2 : the figure formed by the meeting of two lines in a point 3 : a point of view 4 : a special technique or plan : GIMMICK — **an·gled** *adj*

²**angle** *vb* **an·gled; an·gling** \-g(ə-)liŋ\ : to turn, move, or direct at an angle

³**angle** *vb* **an·gled; an·gling** \-g(ə-)liŋ\ : to fish with a hook and line — **an·gler** \-glər\ *n* — **an·gling** \-gliŋ\ *n*

an·gle·worm \'aŋ-gəl-ˌwərm\ *n* : EARTHWORM

An·gli·can \'aŋ-gli-kən\ *adj* 1 : of or relating to the established episcopal Church of England 2 : of or relating to England or the English nation — **Anglican** *n* — **An·gli·can·ism** \-kə-ˌni-zəm\ *n*

an·gli·cize \'aŋ-glə-ˌsīz\ *vb* **-cized; -ciz·ing** *often cap* 1 : to make English (as in habits, speech, character, or outlook) 2 : to borrow (a foreign word or phrase) into English without changing form or spelling and sometimes without changing pronunciation — **an·gli·ci·za·tion** \ˌaŋ-glə-sə-'zā-shən\ *n, often cap*

An·glo \'aŋ-glō\ *n, pl* **Anglos** : a non-Hispanic white inhabitant of the U.S.; *esp* : one of English origin and descent

An·glo·cen·tric \ˌaŋ-glō-'sen-trik\ *adj* : centered on or favoring England or things English

An·glo–French \ˌaŋ-glō-'french\ *n* : the French language used in medieval England

An·glo·phile \'aŋ-glə-ˌfī(-ə)l\ *also* **An·glo·phil** \-ˌfil\ *n* : one who greatly admires England and things English

An·glo·phobe \'aŋ-glə-ˌfōb\ *n* : one who is averse to England and things English

An·glo–Sax·on \ˌaŋ-glō-'sak-sən\ *n* 1 : a member of any of the Germanic peoples who invaded England in the 5th century A.D. 2 : a member of the English people 3 : Old English — **Anglo–Saxon** *adj*

an·go·ra \aŋ-'gòr-ə, an-\ *n* 1 : yarn or cloth made from the hair of an Angora goat or rabbit 2 *cap* : any of a breed of cats, goats, or rabbits with a long silky coat

an·gry \'aŋ-grē\ *adj* **an·gri·er; -est** : feeling or showing anger ◆ *Synonyms* ENRAGED, WRATHFUL, IRATE, INDIGNANT, MAD — **an·gri·ly** \-grə-lē\ *adv*

angst \'äŋst\ *n* [G] : a feeling of anxiety

ang·strom \'aŋ-strəm\ *n* : a unit of length equal to one ten-billionth of a meter

an·guish \'aŋ-gwish\ *n* : extreme pain or distress esp. of mind — **an·guished** \-gwisht\ *adj*

an·gu·lar \'aŋ-gyə-lər\ *adj* 1 : sharp-cornered 2 : having one or more angles 3 : being thin and bony — **an·gu·lar·i·ty** \ˌaŋ-gyə-'ler-ə-tē\ *n*

An·gus \'aŋ-gəs\ *n* : any of a breed of usu. black hornless beef cattle originating in Scotland

an·hy·drous \an-'hī-drəs\ *adj* : free from water

an·i·line \'a-nᵊl-ən\ *n* : an oily poisonous liquid used in making dyes, medicines, and explosives

an·i·mad·vert \ˌa-nə-ˌmad-'vərt\ *vb* : to remark critically : express censure — **an·i·mad·ver·sion** \-'vər-zhən\ *n*

¹**an·i·mal** \'a-nə-məl\ *n* 1 : any of a kingdom of living things typically differing from plants in capacity for active movement, in rapid response to stimulation, and in lack of cellulose cell walls 2 : a lower animal as distinguished from human beings; *also* : MAMMAL

²**animal** *adj* 1 : of, relating to, or derived from animals 2 : of or relating to the physical as distinguished from the mental or spiritual ◆ *Synonyms* CARNAL, FLESHLY, SENSUAL

an·i·mal·cule \ˌa-nə-'mal-kyül\ *n* : a tiny animal usu. invisible to the naked eye

¹**an·i·mate** \'a-nə-mət\ *adj* : having life

²**an·i·mate** \-ˌmāt\ *vb* **-mat·ed; -mat·ing** 1 : to impart life to 2 : to give spirit and vigor to 3 : to make appear to move ⟨∼ a cartoon for motion pictures⟩ — **an·i·mat·ed** *adj* — **an·i·mat·ed·ly** *adv*

an·i·ma·tion \ˌa-nə-'mā-shən\ *n* 1 : VIVACITY, LIVELINESS 2 : a motion picture made from a series of drawings, computer graphics, or stop-motion images simulating motions by means of slight progressive changes

an·i·ma·tron·ic \ˌa-nə-mə-'trä-nik\ *adj* : of, relating to, or being an electrically animated mechanical figure (as a puppet)

an·i·mism \'a-nə-ˌmi-zəm\ *n* : attribution of conscious life to objects in and phenomena of nature or to inanimate objects — **an·i·mist** \-mist\ *n* — **an·i·mis·tic** \ˌa-nə-'mis-tik\ *adj*

an·i·mos·i·ty \ˌa-nə-'mä-sə-tē\ *n, pl* **-ties** : ILL WILL, RESENTMENT

an·i·mus \'a-nə-məs\ *n* : deep-seated resentment and hostility

an·ion \'a-ˌnī-ən, -ˌnī-ˌän\ *n* : a negatively charged ion

an·ise \'a-nəs\ *n* : an herb related to the carrot with aromatic seeds (aniseed \-sēd\) used in flavoring

an·is·ette \ˌa-nə-'set, -'zet\ *n* [F] : a usu. colorless sweet liqueur flavored with aniseed

ankh \'äŋk\ *n* : a cross having a loop for its upper vertical arm and serving esp. in ancient Egypt as an emblem of life

an·kle \'aŋ-kəl\ *n* : the joint or region between the foot and the leg

an·kle·bone \'aŋ-kəl-ˌbōn\ *n* : the bone that in human beings bears the weight of the body and with the tibia and fibula forms the ankle joint

an·klet \'aŋ-klət\ *n* 1 : something (as an ornament) worn around the ankle 2 : a short sock reaching slightly above the ankle

ann *abbr* 1 annals 2 annual

an·nals \'a-nᵊlz\ *n pl* 1 : a record of events in chronological order 2 : historical records — **an·nal·ist** \-nᵊl-ist\ *n*

an·neal \ə-'nēl\ *vb* 1 : to make (as glass or steel) less brittle by heating and then cooling 2 : STRENGTHEN, TOUGHEN

¹**an·nex** \ə-'neks, 'a-ˌneks\ *vb* 1 : to attach as an addition 2 : to incorporate (as a territory) within a political domain — **an·nex·a·tion** \ˌa-ˌnek-'sā-shən\ *n*

²**an·nex** \'a-ˌneks, -niks\ *n* : a subsidiary or supplementary structure

an·nexe *chiefly Brit var of* ANNEX

an·ni·hi·late \ə-'nī-ə-ˌlāt\ *vb* **-lat·ed; -lat·ing** : to destroy completely — **an·ni·hi·la·tion** \-ˌnī-ə-'lā-shən\ *n*

an·ni·ver·sa·ry \ˌa-nə-'vər-sə-rē\ *n, pl* **-ries** : the annual return of the date of a notable event and esp. a wedding

an·no Do·mi·ni \ˌa-nō-'dä-mə-nē, -'dō-, -ˌnī\ *adv, often cap A* [ML, in the year of the Lord] — used to indicate that a time division falls within the Christian era

an·no·tate \'a-nə-ˌtāt\ *vb* **-tat·ed; -tat·ing** : to furnish with notes — **an·no·ta·tion** \ˌa-nə-'tā-shən\ *n* — **an·no·ta·tor** \'a-nə-ˌtā-tər\ *n*

an·nounce \ə-'naůns\ *vb* **an·nounced; an·nounc·ing** 1 : to make known publicly 2 : to give notice of the arrival or presence of — **an·nounce·ment** *n*

an·nounc·er \ə-'naůn-sər\ *n* : a person who introduces radio or television programs, makes commercial announcements, or gives station identification

an·noy \ə-'nòi\ *vb* : to disturb or irritate esp. by repeated acts : VEX ◆ *Synonyms* IRK, BOTHER, PESTER, TEASE, HARASS — **an·noy·ing·ly** *adv*

an·noy·ance \ə-'nòi-əns\ *n* 1 : the act of annoying 2 : the state of being annoyed 3 : NUISANCE ⟨the delay was a minor ∼⟩

¹an·nu·al \'an-yə-wəl\ adj 1 : covering the period of a year ⟨~ rainfall⟩ 2 : occurring once a year : YEARLY 3 : completing the life cycle in one growing season ⟨~ plants⟩ — an·nu·al·ly adv

²annual n 1 : a publication appearing once a year 2 : an annual plant

annual ring n : the layer of wood produced by a single year's growth of a woody plant

an·nu·i·tant \ə-'nü-ə-tənt, -'nyü-\ n : a beneficiary of an annuity

an·nu·i·ty \ə-'nü-ə-tē, -'nyü-\ n, pl -i·ties : an amount payable annually; also : the right to receive such a payment

an·nul \ə-'nəl\ vb an·nulled; an·nul·ling : to make legally void — an·nul·ment n

an·nu·lar \'an-yə-lər\ adj : ring-shaped

an·nun·ci·ate \ə-'nən-sē-ˌāt\ vb -at·ed; -at·ing : ANNOUNCE

an·nun·ci·a·tion \ə-ˌnən-sē-'ā-shən\ n 1 cap : March 25 observed as a church festival commemorating the announcement of the Incarnation 2 : ANNOUNCEMENT

an·nun·ci·a·tor \ə-'nən-sē-ˌā-tər\ n : one that annunciates; specif : a usu. electrically controlled signal board or indicator

an·ode \'a-ˌnōd\ n 1 : the positive electrode of an electrolytic cell 2 : the negative terminal of a battery 3 : the electron-collecting electrode of an electron tube — an·od·ic \a-'nä-dik\ also an·od·al \-'nō-d°l\ adj

an·od·ize \'a-nə-ˌdīz\ vb -ized; -iz·ing : to subject (a metal) to electrolytic action as the anode of a cell in order to coat with a protective or decorative film

an·o·dyne \'a-nə-ˌdīn\ n : something that relieves pain : a soothing agent

anoint \ə-'nóint\ vb 1 : to apply oil to esp. as a sacred rite 2 : CONSECRATE — anoint·ment n

anom·a·lous \ə-'nä-mə-ləs\ adj : deviating from a general rule : ABNORMAL

anom·a·ly \ə-'nä-mə-lē\ n, pl -lies : something anomalous : IRREGULARITY

¹anon \ə-'nän\ adv : SOON

²anon abbr anonymous; anonymously

anon·y·mous \ə-'nä-nə-məs\ adj : of unknown or undeclared origin or authorship — an·o·nym·i·ty \ˌa-nə-'ni-mə-tē\ n — anon·y·mous·ly adv

anoph·e·les \ə-'nä-fə-ˌlēz\ n [NL, genus name, fr. Gk anōphelēs useless, fr. a- not + ophelos advantage, help] : any of a genus of mosquitoes that includes all mosquitoes which transmit malaria to human beings

an·o·rec·tic \ˌa-nə-'rek-tik\ adj : ANOREXIC — anorectic n

an·orex·ia \ˌa-nə-'rek-sē-ə\ n 1 : loss of appetite esp. when prolonged 2 : ANOREXIA NERVOSA

anorexia ner·vo·sa \-nər-'vō-sə\ n : a serious disorder in eating behavior marked esp. by a pathological fear of weight gain leading to faulty eating patterns, malnutrition, and usu. excessive weight loss

an·orex·ic \ˌa-nə-'rek-sik\ adj 1 : lacking or causing loss of appetite 2 : affected with or as if with anorexia nervosa — anorexic n

¹an·oth·er \ə-'nə-thər\ adj 1 : some other ⟨do it ~ time⟩ 2 : being one in addition : one more ⟨~ piece of pie⟩

²another pron 1 : an additional one : one more 2 : one that is different from the first or present one

ans abbr answer

¹an·swer \'an-sər\ n 1 : something spoken or written in reply to a question 2 : a solution of a problem

²answer vb 1 : to speak or write in reply to 2 : to be responsible 3 : to be adequate — an·swer·er n

an·swer·able \'an-sə-rə-bəl\ adj 1 : subject to taking blame or responsibility 2 : capable of being refuted

answering machine n : a machine that receives telephone calls by playing a recorded message and usu. by recording messages from callers

answering service n : a commercial service that answers telephone calls for its clients

¹ant \'ant\ n : any of a family of small social insects related to the bees and living in communities usu. in earth or wood

²ant abbr antonym

Ant abbr Antarctica

ant- — see ANTI-

¹-ant n suffix 1 : one that performs or promotes (a specified action) ⟨coolant⟩ 2 : thing that is acted upon (in a specified manner) ⟨inhalant⟩

²-ant adj suffix 1 : performing (a specified action) or be-

ing (in a specified condition) ⟨propellant⟩ 2 : promoting (a specified action or process) ⟨expectorant⟩

ant·ac·id \ˌant-'a-səd\ n : an agent that counteracts acidity — antacid adj

an·tag·o·nism \an-'ta-gə-ˌni-zəm\ n 1 : active opposition or hostility 2 : opposition in physiological action — an·tag·o·nis·tic \-ˌta-gə-'nis-tik\ adj

an·tag·o·nist \-nist\ n : ADVERSARY, OPPONENT

an·tag·o·nize \an-'ta-gə-ˌnīz\ vb -nized; -niz·ing : to provoke the hostility of

ant·arc·tic \ant-'ärk-tik, -'är-tik\ adj, often cap : of or relating to the south pole or the region near it

antarctic circle n, often cap A&C : the parallel of latitude that is approximately 66½ degrees south of the equator

¹an·te \'an-tē\ n : a poker stake put up before the deal to build the pot; also : an amount paid : PRICE

²ante vb an·ted; an·te·ing 1 : to put up (an ante) 2 : PAY

ant·eat·er \'ant-ˌē-tər\ n : any of several mammals (as an aardvark) that feed mostly on ants or termites

an·te·bel·lum \ˌan-ti-'be-ləm\ adj : existing before a war; esp : existing before the U.S. Civil War of 1861-65

an·te·ced·ent \ˌan-tə-'sē-d°nt\ n 1 : a noun, pronoun, phrase, or clause referred to by a personal or relative pronoun 2 : a preceding event or cause 3 pl : the significant conditions of one's earlier life 4 pl : ANCESTORS — antecedent adj

an·te·cham·ber \'an-ti-ˌchām-bər\ n : ANTEROOM

an·te·date \'an-ti-ˌdāt\ vb 1 : to date (a paper) as of an earlier day than that on which the actual writing or signing is done 2 : to precede in time

an·te·di·lu·vi·an \ˌan-ti-də-'lü-vē-ən, -dī-\ adj 1 : of the period before the biblical flood 2 : ANTIQUATED, OUT= OF-DATE

an·te·lope \'an-tə-ˌlōp\ n, pl -lope or -lopes [ME, fabulous heraldic beast, prob. fr. MF antelop savage animal with sawlike horns, fr. ML anthalopus, fr. LGk antholops] : any of various deerlike ruminant mammals that chiefly inhabit Africa and have a slender build and horns extending upward and backward 2 : PRONGHORN

an·te me·ri·di·em \'an-ti-mə-'ri-dē-əm\ adj [L] : being before noon

an·ten·na \an-'te-nə\ n, pl -nae \-(ˌ)nē\ or -nas [ML, fr. L, sail yard] 1 : one of the long slender paired segmented sensory organs on the head of an arthropod (as an insect or crab) 2 pl usu -nas : a metallic device (as a rod or wire) for sending out or receiving radio waves

an·te·pe·nult \ˌan-ti-'pē-ˌnəlt\ also an·te·pen·ul·ti·ma \-pi-'nəl-tə-mə\ n : the 3d syllable of a word counting from the end — an·te·pen·ul·ti·mate \-pi-'nəl-tə-mət\ adj or n

an·te·ri·or \an-'tir-ē-ər\ adj 1 : situated before or toward the front 2 : situated near or nearer to the head 3 : coming before in time ♦ Synonyms PRECEDING, PREVIOUS, PRIOR, ANTECEDENT

anterior cruciate ligament n : a cross-shaped ligament of the knee that connects the tibia and femur

an·te·room \'an-ti-ˌrüm, -ˌrùm\ n : a room forming the entrance to another and often used as a waiting room

an·them \'an-thəm\ n 1 : a sacred vocal composition 2 : a song or hymn of praise or gladness

an·ther \'an-thər\ n : the part of a stamen of a seed plant that produces and contains pollen

ant·hill \'ant-ˌhil\ n : a mound thrown up by ants or termites in digging their nest

an·thol·o·gy \an-'thä-lə-jē\ n, pl -gies [NL anthologia collection of epigrams, fr. MGk, fr. Gk, flower gathering, fr. anthos flower + logia collecting, fr. legein to gather] : a collection of literary selections — an·thol·o·gist \-jist\ n — an·thol·o·gize \-ˌjīz\ vb

an·thra·cite \'an-thrə-ˌsīt\ n : a hard glossy coal that burns without much smoke

an·thrax \'an-ˌthraks\ n : an infectious and usu. fatal bacterial disease of warm-blooded animals (as cattle and sheep) that is transmissible to humans; also : a bacterium causing anthrax

an·thro·po·cen·tric \ˌan-thrə-pə-'sen-trik\ adj : interpreting or regarding the world in terms of human values and experiences

an·thro·poid \'an-thrə-ˌpóid\ n 1 : any of several large tailless apes (as a gorilla) 2 : a person resembling an ape — anthropoid adj

an·thro·pol·o·gy \,an-thrə-'pä-lə-jē\ *n* : the science of human beings and esp. of their physical characteristics, their origin and ancestry, their environment and social relations, and their culture — **an·thro·po·log·i·cal** \-pə-'lä-ji-kəl\ *adj* — **an·thro·pol·o·gist** \-'pä-lə-jist\ *n*

an·thro·po·mor·phism \,an-thrə-pə-'mȯr-,fi-zəm\ *n* : an interpretation of what is not human or personal in terms of human or personal characteristics : HUMANIZATION — **an·thro·po·mor·phic** \-fik\ *adj*

an·ti \'an-,tī, -tē\ *n, pl* **antis** : one who is opposed

anti- \an-ti, -tē, -,tī\ *or* **ant-** *or* **anth-** *prefix* **1** : opposite in kind, position, or action **2** : opposing : hostile toward **3** : counteractive **4** : preventive of : curative of

antiaging	antigovernment
anti-AIDS	anti-HIV
antiaircraft	anti-imperialism
antialcohol	anti-imperialist
anti-American	antiknock
antianxiety	antilabor
antiapartheid	antimalarial
antibacterial	antimicrobial
anticapitalist	antinausea
anti-Catholic	antipoverty
anticholesterol	antislavery
anticlerical	antispasmodic
anticolonial	antistatic
anticommunism	antisubmarine
anticommunist	antitank
antidemocratic	antitumor
antidiscrimination	antiviral
antiestablishment	antiwar
antifascist	

an·ti·abor·tion \,an-tē-ə-'bȯr-shən, ,an-,tī-\ *adj* : opposed to abortion — **an·ti·abor·tion·ist** \-shə-nist\ *n*

an·ti·bal·lis·tic missile \,an-ti-bə-'lis-tik-, ,an-,tī-\ *n* : a missile for intercepting and destroying ballistic missiles

an·ti·bi·ot·ic \-bī-'ä-tik, -bē-\ *n* : a substance produced by or derived by chemical alteration of a substance produced by a microorganism (as a fungus or bacterium) that in dilute solution inhibits or kills another microorganism — **antibiotic** *adj*

an·ti·body \'an-ti-,bä-dē\ *n* : any of a large number of proteins of high molecular weight produced normally by specialized B cells after stimulation by an antigen and acting specifically against the antigen in an immune response

¹an·tic \'an-tik\ *n* [It *antico* ancient thing or person, fr. *antico* ancient, fr. L *antiquus*] : an often wildly playful or funny act or action

²antic *adj* **1** *archaic* : GROTESQUE **2** : PLAYFUL

an·ti·can·cer \,an-ti-'kan-sər, ,an-,tī-\ *adj* : used against or tending to arrest or prevent cancer ⟨~ drugs⟩

An·ti·christ \'an-ti-,krīst\ *n* **1** : one who denies or opposes Christ **2** : a false Christ

an·tic·i·pate \an-'ti-sə-,pāt\ *vb* **-pat·ed; -pat·ing 1** : to foresee and provide for beforehand ⟨~s problems⟩ **2** : to look forward to — **an·tic·i·pa·tion** \-,ti-sə-'pā-shən\ *n* — **an·tic·i·pa·to·ry** \-'ti-sə-pə-,tȯr-ē\ *adj*

an·ti·cli·max \,an-ti-'klī-,maks\ *n* : something (as the ending of a story) that is strikingly less important or dramatic than expected — **an·ti·cli·mac·tic** \-klī-'mak-tik\ *adj*

an·ti·cline \'an-ti-,klīn\ *n* : an arch of layers of rock in the earth's crust

an·ti·co·ag·u·lant \,an-ti-kō-'a-gyə-lənt\ *n* : a substance that hinders the clotting of blood — **anticoagulant** *adj*

an·ti·cy·clone \,an-ti-'sī-,klōn\ *n* : a system of winds that rotates about a center of high atmospheric pressure — **an·ti·cy·clon·ic** \-sī-'klä-nik\ *adj*

an·ti·de·pres·sant \,an-ti-di-'pres-ºnt, ,an-,tī-\ *n* : a drug used to relieve psychic depression — **antidepressant** *adj*

an·ti·dote \'an-ti-,dōt\ *n* : a remedy to counteract the effects of poison

an·ti·drug \'an-,tī-,drəg\ *adj* : acting against or opposing illicit drugs

an·ti·fer·til·i·ty \,an-ti-fər-'ti-lə-tē\ *adj* : tending to reduce or destroy fertility : CONTRACEPTIVE ⟨~ agents⟩

an·ti·freeze \'an-ti-,frēz\ *n* : a substance added to a liquid to lower its freezing temperature

an·ti·fun·gal \,an-tē-'fəŋ-gəl, ,an-,tī-\ *n* : FUNGICIDE — **antifungal** *adj*

an·ti·gen \'an-ti-jən\ *n* : any substance (as a toxin) foreign to the body that induces an immune response — **an·ti·gen·ic** \,an-ti-'je-nik\ *adj* — **an·ti·ge·nic·i·ty** \-jə-'ni-sə-tē\ *n*

an·ti·grav·i·ty \,an-ti-'gra-və-tē, ,an-,tī-\ *adj* : reducing or canceling the effect of gravity

an·ti·he·ro \'an-ti-,hē-rō, 'an-,tī-\ *n* : a protagonist who is notably lacking in heroic qualities (as courage)

an·ti·his·ta·mine \,an-ti-'his-tə-,mēn, ,an-,tī-, -mən\ *n* : any of various drugs used in treating allergies and colds — **antihistamine** *adj*

an·ti·hy·per·ten·sive \-,hī-pər-'ten-siv\ *n* : a substance that is effective against high blood pressure — **antihypertensive** *adj*

an·ti–in·flam·ma·to·ry \-in-'fla-mə-,tȯr-ē\ *adj* : counteracting inflammation — **anti-inflammatory** *n*

an·ti–in·tel·lec·tu·al \-,in-tə-'lek-chə-wəl\ *adj* : opposing or hostile to intellectuals or to an intellectual view or approach

an·ti·lock \'an-ti-,läk, 'an-,tī-\ *adj* : being a braking system designed to prevent the wheels from locking

an·ti·log·a·rithm \,an-ti-'lȯ-gə-,ri-thəm, an-,tī-, -'lä-\ *n* : the number corresponding to a given logarithm ⟨if the logarithm in base *x* of *a* equals *b* then the antilogarithm in base *x* of *b* equals *a*⟩

an·ti·ma·cas·sar \,an-ti-mə-'ka-sər\ *n* : a cover to protect the back or arms of furniture

an·ti·mat·ter \'an-ti-,ma-tər, 'an-,tī-\ *n* : matter composed of antiparticles

an·ti·mo·ny \'an-tə-,mō-nē\ *n* : a brittle silvery white metallic chemical element used esp. in alloys

an·ti·neu·tron \,an-ti-'nü-,trän, ,an-,tī-, -'nyü-\ *n* : the antiparticle of the neutron

an·ti·no·mi·an \,an-ti-'nō-mē-ən\ *n* : one who denies the validity of moral laws

an·tin·o·my \an-'ti-nə-mē\ *n, pl* **-mies** : a contradiction between two seemingly true statements

an·ti·nov·el \'an-ti-,nä-vəl, 'an-,tī-\ *n* : a work of fiction that lacks all or most of the traditional features of the novel

an·ti·nu·cle·ar \,an-ti-'nü-klē-ər, -'nyü-\ *adj* : opposing the use or production of nuclear power

an·ti·ox·i·dant \,an-tē-'äk-sə-dənt, ,an-,tī-\ *n* : a substance that inhibits oxidation — **antioxidant** *adj*

an·ti·par·ti·cle \'an-ti-,pär-ti-kəl, 'an-,tī-\ *n* : a subatomic particle identical to another subatomic particle in mass but opposite to it in electric and magnetic properties

an·ti·pas·to \,an-ti-'pas-tō, ,än-ti-'päs-\ *n, pl* **-ti** \-(,)tē\ : any of various typically Italian hors d'oeuvres

an·tip·a·thy \an-'ti-pə-thē\ *n, pl* **-thies 1** : settled aversion or dislike **2** : an object of aversion — **an·ti·pa·thet·ic** \,an-ti-pə-'the-tik\ *adj*

an·ti·per·son·nel \,an-ti-,pər-sə-'nel, ,an-,tī-\ *adj* : designed for use against military personnel ⟨~ mine⟩

an·ti·per·spi·rant \-'pər-spə-rənt\ *n* : a preparation used to reduce perspiration

an·tiph·o·nal \an-'ti-fə-nºl\ *adj* : performed by two alternating groups — **an·tiph·o·nal·ly** *adv*

an·ti·pode \'an-tə-,pōd\ *n, pl* **an·tip·o·des** \an-'ti-pə-,dēz\ [ME *antipodes*, pl., persons dwelling at opposite points on the globe, fr. L, fr. Gk, fr. pl. of *antipod-, antipous* with feet opposite, fr. *anti-* against + *pod-, pous* foot] : the parts of the earth diametrically opposite — usu. used in pl. — **an·tip·o·dal** \an-'ti-pə-dºl\ *adj* — **an·tip·o·de·an** \(,)an-,ti-pə-'dē-ən\ *adj*

an·ti·pol·lu·tion \,an-ti-pə-'lü-shən\ *adj* : designed to prevent, reduce, or eliminate pollution ⟨~ laws⟩

an·ti·pope \'an-ti-,pōp\ *n* : one elected or claiming to be pope in opposition to the pope canonically chosen

an·ti·pro·ton \,an-ti-'prō-,tän\ *n* : the antiparticle of the proton

an·ti·psy·chot·ic \,an-tē-sī-'kä-tik\ *n* : any of the powerful tranquilizers used to treat psychosis — **antipsychotic** *adj*

an·ti·quar·i·an \,an-tə-'kwer-ē-ən\ *adj* **1** : of or relating to antiquities **2** : dealing in old books — **antiquarian** *n* — **an·ti·quar·i·an·ism** *n*

an·ti·quary \'an-tə-,kwer-ē\ *n, pl* **-quar·ies** : a person who collects or studies antiquities

an·ti·quat·ed \'an-tə-,kwä-təd\ *adj* : OUT-OF-DATE, OLD-FASHIONED

¹an·tique \an-'tēk\ *n* : an object made in a bygone period

²**antique** adj **1** : belonging to antiquity **2** : OLD-FASH-
IONED **3** : of a bygone style or period
³**antique** vb **-tiqued; -tiqu·ing 1** : to finish or refinish in
antique style : give an appearance of age to **2** : to shop
around for antiques — **an·tiqu·er** n
an·tiq·ui·ty \an-ˈti-kwə-tē\ n, pl **-ties 1** : ancient times **2**
: great age **3** pl : relics of ancient times **4** pl : matters
relating to ancient culture
an·ti·re·tro·vi·ral \ˌan-tē-ˈre-trō-ˌvī-rəl, ˌan-ˌtī-\ adj : effective against retroviruses ⟨~ drugs⟩ — **antiretroviral** n
antis pl of ANTI
an·ti–Sem·i·tism \ˌan-ti-ˈse-mə-ˌti-zəm, ˌan-ˌtī-\ n : hostility
toward Jews as a religious or social minority — **an·ti–
Sem·ite** \-ˈse-ˌmīt\ n — **an·ti–Se·mit·ic** \-sə-ˈmi-tik\ adj
an·ti·sep·tic \ˌan-tə-ˈsep-tik\ adj **1** : killing or checking
the growth of germs that cause decay or infection **2**
: scrupulously clean : ASEPTIC **3** : coldly impersonal ⟨an
~ greeting⟩ — **antiseptic** n — **an·ti·sep·ti·cal·ly** adv
an·ti·se·rum \ˈan-ti-ˌsir-əm, ˈan-ˌtī-\ n : a serum containing antibodies
an·ti·so·cial \ˌan-ti-ˈsō-shəl\ adj **1** : disliking the society
of others **2** : contrary or hostile to the well-being of society ⟨crime is ~⟩; esp : deviating sharply from the social norm — **an·ti·so·cial·ly** adv
an·tith·e·sis \an-ˈti-thə-səs\ n, pl **-e·ses** \-ˌsēz\ **1** : the opposition or contrast of ideas **2** : the direct opposite
an·ti·thet·i·cal \ˌan-tə-ˈthe-ti-kəl\ also **an·ti·thet·ic** \-tik\ adj
: constituting or marked by antithesis — **an·ti·thet·i·cal·ly**
\-ti-k(ə-)lē\ adv
an·ti·tox·in \ˌan-ti-ˈtäk-sən\ n : an antibody that is able
to neutralize a particular toxin or disease-causing agent;
also : an antiserum containing an antitoxin
an·ti·trust \ˌan-ti-ˈtrəst\ adj : of or relating to legislation
against trusts; also : consisting of laws to protect trade
and commerce from unlawful restraints and monopolies
or unfair business practices
an·ti·ven·in \-ˈve-nən\ n : an antitoxin to a venom; also : a
serum containing such antitoxin
ant·ler \ˈant-lər\ n [ME aunteler, fr. AF antler, fr. VL
*anteocularis located before the eye, fr. L ante- before +
oculus eye] : one of the paired deciduous solid bone processes on the head of a deer; also : a branch of this —
ant·lered \-lərd\ adj
ant lion n : any of various insects having a long-jawed
larva that digs a conical pit in which it lies in wait for
insects (as ants) on which it feeds
an·to·nym \ˈan-tə-ˌnim\ n : a word of opposite meaning
ant·sy \ˈant-sē\ adj **1** : RESTLESS, IMPATIENT ⟨~ chil-
dren⟩ **2** : APPREHENSIVE ⟨~ investors⟩
anus \ˈā-nəs\ n [L] : the lower or posterior opening of the
alimentary canal
an·vil \ˈan-vəl\ n **1** : a heavy iron block on which metal
is shaped **2** : INCUS
anx·i·ety \aŋ-ˈzī-ə-tē\ n, pl **-et·ies 1** : painful uneasiness
of mind usu. over an anticipated ill **2** : abnormal apprehension and fear often accompanied by physiological
signs (as sweating and increased pulse), by doubt about
the nature and reality of the threat itself, and by self=
doubt
anx·ious \ˈaŋk-shəs\ adj **1** : uneasy in mind : WORRIED
⟨~ parents⟩ **2** : earnestly wishing : EAGER ⟨~ to
leave⟩ — **anx·ious·ly** adv
¹**any** \ˈe-nē\ adj **1** : one chosen at random **2** : of whatever number or quantity
²**any** pron **1** : any one or ones ⟨take ~ of the books you
like⟩ **2** : any amount ⟨~ of the money not used is to
be returned⟩
³**any** adv : to any extent or degree : AT ALL ⟨could not
walk ~ farther⟩
any·body \-ˌbä-dē, -bə-\ pron : ANYONE
any·how \-ˌhaů\ adv **1** : in any way **2** : NEVERTHELESS;
also : in any case
any·more \ˌe-nē-ˈmȯr\ adv **1** : any longer ⟨won't bother
you ~⟩ **2** : at the present time
any·one \ˈe-nē-(ˌ)wən\ pron : any person
any·place \-ˌplās\ adv : ANYWHERE 1
any·thing \-ˌthiŋ\ pron : any thing whatever
any·time \ˈe-nē-ˌtīm\ adv : at any time whatever
any·way \-ˌwā\ adv : ANYHOW
any·where \-ˌhwer\ adv **1** : in or to any place **2** : to any
extent ⟨not ~ near done⟩

any·wise \-ˌwīz\ adv : in any way whatever
A–OK \ˌā-ō-ˈkā\ adv or adj : very definitely OK
A1 \ˈā-ˈwən\ adj : of the finest quality
aor·ta \ā-ˈȯr-tə\ n, pl **-tas** or **-tae** \-tē\ : the main artery
that carries blood from the heart — **aor·tic** \-tik\ adj
ap abbr **1** apostle **2** apothecaries'
AP abbr **1** American plan **2** Associated Press
apace \ə-ˈpās\ adv : SWIFTLY
Apache \ə-ˈpa-chē\ n, pl **Apache** or **Apach·es** \-ˈpa-chēz,
-ˈpa-shəz\ : a member of an American Indian people of
the southwestern U.S.; also : any of the languages of the
Apache people — **Apach·e·an** \ə-ˈpa-chē-ən\ adj or n
apanage var of APPANAGE
apart \ə-ˈpärt\ adv **1** : separately in place or time **2**
: ASIDE **3** : in two or more parts : to pieces
apart·heid \ə-ˈpär-ˌtāt, -ˌtīt\ n [Afrikaans] : a policy of racial segregation formerly practiced in the Republic of So.
Africa
apart·ment \ə-ˈpärt-mənt\ n : a room or set of rooms occupied as a dwelling; also : a building divided into individual dwelling units
ap·a·thy \ˈa-pə-thē\ n **1** : lack of emotion **2** : lack of interest : INDIFFERENCE — **ap·a·thet·ic** \ˌa-pə-ˈthe-tik\ adj
— **ap·a·thet·i·cal·ly** \-ti-k(ə-)lē\ adv
ap·a·tite \ˈa-pə-ˌtīt\ n : any of a group of minerals that are
phosphates of calcium and occur esp. in phosphate rock
and in bones and teeth
apato·sau·rus \ə-ˌpa-tə-ˈsȯr-əs\ n : any of a genus of
large 4-footed dinosaurs of the Jurassic : BRONTOSAU-
RUS
APB abbr all points bulletin
¹**ape** \ˈāp\ n **1** : any of the larger tailless primates (as a baboon or gorilla); also : MONKEY **2** : MIMIC, IMITATOR;
also : a large uncouth person
²**ape** vb aped; ap·ing : IMITATE, MIMIC
ape–man \ˈāp-ˌman\ n : a primate intermediate in character between Homo sapiens and the higher apes
aper·i·tif \ˌä-ˌper-ə-ˈtēf\ n : an alcoholic drink taken as an
appetizer
ap·er·ture \ˈa-pər-ˌchůr, -chər\ n : OPENING, HOLE
apex \ˈā-ˌpeks\ n, pl **apex·es** or **api·ces** \ˈā-pə-ˌsēz, ˈa-\ : the
highest point : PEAK
apha·sia \ə-ˈfā-zh(ē-)ə\ n : loss or impairment of the
power to use or comprehend words — **apha·sic** \-zik\
adj or n
aph·elion \a-ˈfēl-yən\ n, pl **-elia** \-yə\ [NL, fr. apo- away
from + Gk hēlios sun] : the point in an object's orbit
most distant from the sun
aphid \ˈā-fəd\ n : any of numerous small insects that suck
the juices of plants

aphid

aphis \ˈā-fəs, ˈa-\ n, pl **aphi·des** \-fə-ˌdēz\ : APHID
aph·o·rism \ˈa-fə-ˌri-zəm\ n : a short saying stating a general truth : MAXIM — **aph·o·ris·tic** \ˌa-fə-ˈris-tik\ adj
aph·ro·di·si·ac \ˌa-frə-ˈdi-zē-ˌak, -ˈdē-zē-\ n : an agent
that excites sexual desire — **aphrodisiac** adj
api·ary \ˈā-pē-ˌer-ē\ n, pl **-ar·ies** : a place where bees are
kept — **api·a·rist** \-pē-ə-rist\ n
api·cal \ˈā-pi-kəl, ˈa-\ adj : of, relating to, or situated at an
apex — **api·cal·ly** \-k(ə-)lē\ adv
apiece \ə-ˈpēs\ adv : for each one
aplen·ty \ə-ˈplen-tē\ adj : being in plenty or abundance
aplomb \ə-ˈpläm, -ˈpləm\ n [F, lit., perpendicularity, fr.
MF, fr. a plomb, lit., according to the plummet] : complete composure or self-assurance
APO abbr army post office
Apoc abbr **1** Apocalypse **2** Apocrypha
apoc·a·lypse \ə-ˈpä-kə-ˌlips\ n **1** : a writing prophesying

a cataclysm in which evil forces are destroyed **2** *cap* — see BIBLE table — **apoc·a·lyp·tic** \-ˌpä-kə-ˈlip-tik\ *also* **apoc·a·lyp·ti·cal** \-ti-kəl\ *adj*

Apoc·ry·pha \ə-ˈpä-krə-fə\ *n* **1** *not cap* : writings of dubious authenticity **2** : books included in the Septuagint and Vulgate but excluded from the Jewish and Protestant canons of the Old Testament — see BIBLE table **3** : early Christian writings not included in the New Testament

apoc·ry·phal \-fəl\ *adj* **1** : not canonical : SPURIOUS **2** *often cap* : of or resembling the Apocrypha — **apoc·ry·phal·ly** *adv* — **apoc·ry·phal·ness** *n*

apo·gee \ˈa-pə-ˌ(ˌ)jē\ *n* [F *apogée*, fr. NL *apogaeum*, fr. Gk *apogaion*, fr. *apo* away from + *gē, gaia* earth] : the point at which an orbiting object is farthest from the body being orbited

apo·lit·i·cal \ˌā-pə-ˈli-ti-kəl\ *adj* **1** : having an aversion for or no interest in political affairs **2** : having no political significance — **apo·lit·i·cal·ly** \-k(ə-)lē\ *adv*

apol·o·get·ic \ə-ˌpä-lə-ˈje-tik\ *adj* : expressing apology — **apol·o·get·i·cal·ly** \-ti-k(ə-)lē\ *adv*

ap·o·lo·gia \ˌa-pə-ˈlō-j(ē-)ə\ *n* : APOLOGY; *esp* : an argument in support or justification

apol·o·gise *Brit var of* APOLOGIZE

apol·o·gize \ə-ˈpä-lə-ˌjīz\ *vb* **-gized; -giz·ing** : to make an apology : express regret — **apol·o·gist** \-jist\ *n*

apol·o·gy \ə-ˈpä-lə-jē\ *n, pl* **-gies** **1** : a formal justification : DEFENSE **2** : an expression of regret for a wrong

ap·o·plexy \ˈa-pə-ˌplek-sē\ *n* : STROKE **3** — **ap·o·plec·tic** \ˌa-pə-ˈplek-tik\ *adj*

ap·o·pto·sis \ˌa-pəp-ˈtō-səs, -pə-ˈtō-\ *n, pl* **-pto·ses** \-ˌsēz\ : a genetically directed process of cell self-destruction

aport \ə-ˈpȯrt\ *adv* : on or toward the left side of a ship

apos·ta·sy \ə-ˈpäs-tə-sē\ *n, pl* **-sies** : a renunciation or abandonment of a former loyalty (as to a religion) — **apos·tate** \ə-ˈpäs-ˌtāt, -tət\ *adj or n*

a pos·te·ri·o·ri \ˌä-pō-ˌstir-ē-ˈȯr-ē\ *adj* [L, lit., from the latter] : relating to or derived by reasoning from observed facts — **a posteriori** *adv*

apos·tle \ə-ˈpä-səl\ *n* **1** : one of the group composed of Jesus' 12 original disciples and Paul **2** : the first prominent missionary to a region or group **3** : a person who initiates or first advocates a great reform — **apos·tle·ship** *n*

ap·os·tol·ic \ˌa-pə-ˈstä-lik\ *adj* **1** : of or relating to an apostle or to the New Testament apostles **2** : of or relating to a succession of spiritual authority from the apostles **3** : PAPAL ⟨∼ authority⟩

¹apos·tro·phe \ə-ˈpäs-trə-(ˌ)fē\ *n* : the rhetorical addressing of a usu. absent person or a usu. personified thing (as in "O grave, where is thy victory?")

²apostrophe *n* : a punctuation mark ' used esp. to indicate the possessive case or the omission of a letter or figure

apos·tro·phise *Brit var of* APOSTROPHIZE

apos·tro·phize \ə-ˈpäs-trə-ˌfīz\ *vb* **-phized; -phiz·ing** : to address as if present or capable of understanding

apothecaries' weight *n* : a system of weights based on the troy pound and ounce and used chiefly by pharmacists — see WEIGHT table

apoth·e·cary \ə-ˈpä-thə-ˌker-ē\ *n, pl* **-car·ies** [ME *apothecarie*, fr. ML *apothecarius*, fr. LL, shopkeeper, fr. L *apotheca* storehouse, fr. Gk *apothēkē*, fr. *apotithenai* to put away] : DRUGGIST

ap·o·thegm \ˈa-pə-ˌthem\ *n* : APHORISM

apo·the·o·sis \ə-ˌpä-thē-ˈō-səs, ˌa-pə-ˈthē-ə-səs\ *n, pl* **-o·ses** \-ˌsēz\ **1** : DEIFICATION **2** : the perfect example

¹app \ˈap\ *n* : APPLICATION 6

²app *abbr* **1** apparatus **2** appendix

ap·pall *also* **ap·pal** \ə-ˈpȯl\ *vb* **ap·palled; ap·pall·ing** : to overcome with horror : DISMAY

Ap·pa·loo·sa \ˌa-pə-ˈlü-sə\ *n* : any of a breed of saddle horses developed in western No. America and usu. having a white or solid-colored coat with small spots

ap·pa·nage *also* **a·pa·nage** \ˈa-pə-nij\ *n* **1** : provision (as a grant of land) made by a sovereign or legislative body for dependent members of the royal family **2** : a rightful adjunct

ap·pa·ra·tus \ˌa-pə-ˈra-təs, -ˈrä-\ *n, pl* **-tus·es** *or* **-tus** [L] **1** : a set of materials or equipment for a particular use **2** : a complex machine or device : MECHANISM **3** : the organization of a political party or underground movement

¹ap·par·el \ə-ˈper-əl\ *vb* **-eled** *or* **-elled; -el·ing** *or* **-el·ling** **1** : CLOTHE **2** : ADORN

²apparel *n* : CLOTHING, DRESS

ap·par·ent \ə-ˈper-ənt\ *adj* **1** : open to view : VISIBLE **2** : EVIDENT, OBVIOUS **3** : appearing as real or true : SEEMING

ap·par·ent·ly \-lē\ *adv* : it seems apparent

ap·pa·ri·tion \ˌa-pə-ˈri-shən\ *n* : a supernatural appearance : GHOST

ap·peal \ə-ˈpēl\ *vb* **1** : to take steps to have (a case) reheard in a higher court **2** : to plead for help, corroboration, or decision **3** : to arouse a sympathetic response — **appeal** *n*

ap·pear \ə-ˈpir\ *vb* **1** : to become visible **2** : to come formally before an authority **3** : SEEM **4** : to become evident **5** : to come before the public

ap·pear·ance \ə-ˈpir-əns\ *n* **1** : outward aspect : LOOK **2** : the act of appearing **3** : PHENOMENON

ap·pease \ə-ˈpēz\ *vb* **ap·peased; ap·peas·ing** **1** : to cause to subside : ALLAY **2** : PACIFY, CONCILIATE; *esp* : to buy off by concessions — **ap·pease·ment** *n* — **ap·peas·able** \-ˈpē-zə-bəl\ *adj*

ap·pel·lant \ə-ˈpe-lənt\ *n* : one who appeals esp. from a judicial decision

ap·pel·late \ə-ˈpe-lət\ *adj* : having power to review decisions of a lower court

ap·pel·la·tion \ˌa-pə-ˈlā-shən\ *n* : NAME, DESIGNATION

ap·pel·lee \ˌa-pə-ˈlē\ *n* : one against whom an appeal is taken

ap·pend \ə-ˈpend\ *vb* : to attach esp. as something additional : AFFIX

ap·pend·age \ə-ˈpen-dij\ *n* **1** : something appended to a principal or greater thing **2** : a projecting part (as an antenna) of an animal or plant body; *esp* : an arm, leg, or similar part ✦ **Synonyms** ACCESSORY, ADJUNCT, APPENDIX, APPURTENANCE

ap·pen·dec·to·my \ˌa-pən-ˈdek-tə-mē\ *n, pl* **-mies** : surgical removal of the intestinal appendix

ap·pen·di·ci·tis \ə-ˌpen-də-ˈsī-təs\ *n* : inflammation of the intestinal appendix

ap·pen·dix \ə-ˈpen-diks\ *n, pl* **-dix·es** *or* **-di·ces** \-də-ˌsēz\ [L] **1** : supplementary matter added at the end of a book **2** : a narrow blind tube usu. about three or four inches long that extends from the cecum in the lower right-hand part of the abdomen

ap·per·tain \ˌa-pər-ˈtān\ *vb* : to belong as a rightful part or privilege

ap·pe·tis·er, ap·pe·tis·ing *Brit var of* APPETIZER, APPETIZING

ap·pe·tite \ˈa-pə-ˌtīt\ *n* [ME *apetit*, fr. AF, fr. L *appetitus*, fr. *appetere* to strive after, fr. *ad-* to + *petere* to go to] **1** : natural desire for satisfying some want or need esp. for food **2** : TASTE, PREFERENCE ⟨an ∼ for adventure⟩

ap·pe·tiz·er \ˈa-pə-ˌtī-zər\ *n* : a food or drink taken just before a meal to stimulate the appetite

ap·pe·tiz·ing \-ziŋ\ *adj* : tempting to the appetite — **ap·pe·tiz·ing·ly** *adv*

appl *abbr* applied

ap·plaud \ə-ˈplȯd\ *vb* : to show approval esp. by clapping

ap·plause \ə-ˈplȯz\ *n* : approval publicly expressed (as by clapping)

ap·ple \ˈa-pəl\ *n* : a rounded fruit with firm white flesh and a seedy core; *also* : a tree that bears this fruit

ap·ple·jack \-ˌjak\ *n* : a liquor distilled from fermented cider

ap·plet \ˈa-plət\ *n* : a short computer program esp. for performing a simple specific task

ap·pli·ance \ə-ˈplī-əns\ *n* **1** : INSTRUMENT, DEVICE **2** : a piece of household equipment (as a stove or toaster) operated by gas or electricity

ap·pli·ca·ble \ˈa-pli-kə-bəl, ə-ˈpli-kə-\ *adj* : capable of being applied : RELEVANT — **ap·pli·ca·bil·i·ty** \ˌa-pli-kə-ˈbi-lə-tē, ə-ˌpli-kə-\ *n*

ap·pli·cant \ˈa-pli-kənt\ *n* : one who applies ⟨a job ∼⟩

ap·pli·ca·tion \ˌa-pli-ˈkā-shən\ *n* **1** : the act of applying **2** : assiduous attention **3** : REQUEST; *also* : a form used in making a request **4** : something placed or spread on a surface **5** : capacity for use **6** : a program (as a word processor) that performs one of a computer's major tasks

ap·pli·ca·tor \ˈa-pli-ˌkā-tər\ *n* : a device for applying a substance (as medicine or polish)

ap·plied \ə-'plīd\ adj : put to practical use ⟨~ art⟩
ap·pli·qué \ˌa-plə-'kā\ n [F] : a fabric decoration cut out and fastened to a larger piece of material — appliqué vb
ap·ply \ə-'plī\ vb ap·plied; ap·ply·ing 1 : to put to practical use 2 : to place in contact : put or spread on a surface 3 : to employ with close attention 4 : to have reference or connection 5 : to submit a request
ap·point \ə-'pòint\ vb 1 : to fix or set officially ⟨~ a day for trial⟩ 2 : to name officially 3 : to fit out : EQUIP
ap·poin·tee \ə-ˌpòin-'tē, ˌa-\ n : a person appointed
ap·point·ive \ə-'pòin-tiv\ adj : subject to appointment
ap·point·ment \ə-'pòint-mənt\ n 1 : the act of appointing 2 : an arrangement for a meeting 3 pl : FURNISHINGS, EQUIPMENT 4 : a nonelective office or position
ap·por·tion \ə-'pòr-shən\ vb : to distribute proportionately : ALLOT — ap·por·tion·ment n
ap·po·site \'a-pə-zət\ adj : APPROPRIATE, RELEVANT ⟨an ~ quotation⟩ — ap·po·site·ly adv — ap·po·site·ness n
ap·po·si·tion \ˌa-pə-'zi-shən\ n : a grammatical construction in which a noun or pronoun is followed by another that has the same referent (as the poet and Burns in "a biography of the poet Burns")
ap·pos·i·tive \ə-'pä-zə-tiv, a-\ adj : of, relating to, or standing in grammatical apposition — appositive n
ap·praise \ə-'prāz\ vb ap·praised; ap·prais·ing : to set a value on — ap·prais·al \-'prā-zəl\ n — ap·prais·er n
ap·pre·cia·ble \ə-'prē-shə-bəl\ adj : large enough to be recognized and measured — ap·pre·cia·bly adv
ap·pre·ci·ate \ə-'prē-shē-ˌāt\ vb -at·ed; -at·ing 1 : to value justly 2 : to be aware of 3 : to be grateful for 4 : to increase in value — ap·pre·ci·a·tion \-ˌprē-shē-'ā-shən\ n
ap·pre·cia·tive \ə-'prē-shə-tiv, -shē-ˌāt-\ adj : having or showing appreciation — ap·pre·cia·tive·ly adv
ap·pre·hend \ˌa-pri-'hend\ vb 1 : ARREST 2 : to become aware of 3 : to look forward to with dread 4 : UNDERSTAND — ap·pre·hen·sion \-'hen-chən\ n
ap·pre·hen·sive \-'hen-siv\ adj : viewing the future with anxiety — ap·pre·hen·sive·ly adv — ap·pre·hen·sive·ness n
¹ap·pren·tice \ə-'pren-təs\ n 1 : a person learning a craft under a skilled worker 2 : BEGINNER — ap·pren·tice·ship n
²apprentice vb -ticed; -tic·ing : to bind or set at work as an apprentice
ap·prise \ə-'prīz\ vb ap·prised; ap·pris·ing : INFORM ⟨apprised him of his rights⟩
ap·proach \ə-'prōch\ vb 1 : to move nearer to ⟨~ the bench⟩ 2 : to be almost the same as 3 : to make advances to esp. for the purpose of creating a desired result 4 : to take preliminary steps toward ⟨~ the subject carefully⟩ — approach n — ap·proach·able adj
ap·pro·ba·tion \ˌa-prə-'bā-shən\ n : APPROVAL
¹ap·pro·pri·ate \ə-'prō-prē-ˌāt\ vb -at·ed; -at·ing 1 : to take possession of 2 : to set apart for a particular use
²ap·pro·pri·ate \ə-'prō-prē-ət\ adj : fitted to a purpose or use : SUITABLE ♦ Synonyms PROPER, FIT, APT, BEFITTING — ap·pro·pri·ate·ly adv — ap·pro·pri·ate·ness n
ap·pro·pri·a·tion \ə-ˌprō-prē-'ā-shən\ n : something (as money) set aside by formal action for a specific use
ap·prov·al \ə-'prü-vəl\ n : an act of approving — on approval : subject to a prospective buyer's acceptance or refusal
ap·prove \ə-'prüv\ vb ap·proved; ap·prov·ing 1 : to have or express a favorable opinion of 2 : to accept as satisfactory : RATIFY ⟨~ the treaty⟩
approx abbr approximate; approximately
¹ap·prox·i·mate \ə-'präk-sə-mət\ adj : nearly correct or exact ⟨an ~ count⟩ — ap·prox·i·mate·ly adv
²ap·prox·i·mate \-ˌmāt\ vb -mat·ed; -mat·ing : to come or bring near or close — ap·prox·i·ma·tion \ə-ˌpräk-sə-'mā-shən\ n
appt abbr appoint; appointed; appointment
ap·pur·te·nance \ə-'pərt-nəns, -'pər-tə-nəns\ n : something that belongs to or goes with another thing ♦ Synonyms ACCESSORY, ADJUNCT, APPENDAGE, APPENDIX — ap·pur·te·nant \ə-'pərt-nənt, -'pər-tə-nənt\ adj
Apr abbr April
APR abbr annual percentage rate
apri·cot \'a-prə-ˌkät, 'ā-\ n [alter. of earlier abrecock, ultim. fr. Ar al-birqūq, ultim. fr. L (persicum) praecox, lit., early-ripening (peach)] : an oval orange-colored fruit re-

sembling the related peach and plum in flavor; also : a tree bearing apricots
April \'ā-prəl\ n [ME, fr. AF & L; AF avrill, fr. L Aprilis] : the 4th month of the year
a pri·o·ri \ˌä-prē-'òr-ē\ adj [L, from the former] 1 : characterized by or derived by reasoning from self-evident propositions 2 : independent of experience — a priori adv
apron \'ā-prən\ n [ME, alter. (fr. misdivision of a napron) of napron, fr. MF naperon, dim. of nape cloth, modif. of L mappa napkin] 1 : a garment tied over the front of the body to protect the clothes 2 : a paved area for parking or handling airplanes — aproned adj
¹ap·ro·pos \ˌa-prə-'pō, 'a-prə-ˌpō\ adv [F à propos, lit., to the purpose] 1 : OPPORTUNELY 2 : in passing : INCIDENTALLY
²apropos adj : being to the point
apropos of prep : with regard to
apse \'aps\ n : a projecting usu. semicircular and vaulted part of a building (as a church)
¹apt \'apt\ adj 1 : well adapted : SUITABLE 2 : having an habitual tendency : LIKELY 3 : quick to learn — apt·ly adv — apt·ness \'apt-nəs\ n
²apt abbr 1 apartment 2 aptitude
ap·ti·tude \'ap-tə-ˌtüd, -ˌtyüd\ n 1 : natural ability : TALENT 2 : APPROPRIATENESS
aqua \'a-kwə, 'ä-\ n : a light greenish blue color
aqua·cul·ture \'a-kwə-ˌkəl-chər, 'ä-\ n : the cultivation of aquatic organisms (as fish or shellfish) for human use esp. as food — aqua·cul·tur·ist \-chə-rist\ n
aqua·ma·rine \ˌa-kwə-mə-'rēn, ˌä-\ n 1 : a bluish green gem 2 : a pale blue to light greenish blue
aqua·naut \'a-kwə-ˌnòt, 'ä-\ n : a person who lives in an underwater shelter for an extended period
aqua·plane \-ˌplān\ n : a board towed behind a motorboat and ridden by a person standing on it — aquaplane vb
aqua re·gia \ə-kwə-'rē-j(ē-)ə\ n [NL, lit., royal water] : a mixture of nitric and hydrochloric acids that dissolves gold or platinum
aquar·i·um \ə-'kwer-ē-əm\ n, pl -i·ums or -ia \-ē-ə\ 1 : a container (as a glass tank) in which living aquatic animals or plants are kept 2 : a place where aquatic animals and plants are kept and shown
Aquar·i·us \ə-'kwer-ē-əs\ n [L, lit., water carrier] 1 : a zodiacal constellation between Capricorn and Pisces usu. pictured as a man pouring water 2 : the 11th sign of the zodiac in astrology; also : one born under this sign
¹aquat·ic \ə-'kwä-tik, -'kwa-\ adj 1 : growing or living in or frequenting water 2 : performed in or on water
²aquatic n : an aquatic animal or plant
aqua·vit \'ä-kwə-ˌvēt\ n : a clear liquor flavored with caraway seeds
aqua vi·tae \ˌa-kwə-'vī-tē, ˌä-\ n [ME, fr. ML, lit., water of life] : a strong alcoholic liquor (as brandy)
aq·ue·duct \'a-kwə-ˌdəkt\ n 1 : a conduit for carrying running water 2 : a structure carrying a canal over a river or hollow 3 : a passage in a bodily part

aqueduct 2

aque·ous \'ā-kwē-əs, 'a-\ adj 1 : WATERY 2 : made of, by, or with water
aqueous humor n : a clear fluid occupying the space between the lens and the cornea of the eye
aqui·fer \'a-kwə-fər, 'ä-\ n : a water-bearing stratum of permeable rock, sand, or gravel
aq·ui·line \'a-kwə-ˌlīn, -lən\ adj 1 : of or resembling an eagle 2 : hooked like an eagle's beak ⟨an ~ nose⟩
ar abbr arrival; arrive
Ar symbol argon
AR abbr Arkansas
-ar adj suffix : of or relating to ⟨molecular⟩ : being ⟨spectacular⟩ : resembling ⟨oracular⟩

25 Arab • ardor

Ar·ab \'a-rəb\ *n* 1 : a member of a Semitic people of the Arabian peninsula in southwestern Asia 2 : a member of an Arabic-speaking people — **Arab** *adj* — **Ara·bi·an** \ə-'rā-bē-ən\ *adj or n*

ar·a·besque \,a-rə-'besk\ *n* : a design of interlacing lines forming figures of flowers, foliage, and sometimes animals — **arabesque** *adj*

¹Ar·a·bic \'a-rə-bik\ *n* : a Semitic language of southwestern Asia and northern Africa

²Arabic *adj* 1 : of or relating to the Arabs, Arabic, or the Arabian peninsula in southwestern Asia 2 : expressed in or making use of Arabic numerals

Arabic numeral *n* : any of the number symbols 0, 1, 2, 3, 4, 5, 6, 7, 8, 9

ar·a·ble \'a-rə-bəl\ *adj* : fit for or used for the growing of crops ⟨~ land⟩

arach·nid \ə-'rak-nəd\ *n* : any of a class of usu. 8-legged arthropods comprising the spiders, scorpions, mites, and ticks — **arachnid** *adj*

Ar·a·ma·ic \,a-rə-'mā-ik\ *n* : an ancient Semitic language

ar·a·mid \'a-rə-məd, -,mid\ *n* : any of several light but very strong heat-resistant synthetic materials used esp. in textiles and plastics

Arap·a·ho *or* **Arap·a·hoe** \ə-'ra-pə-,hō\ *n, pl* **-ho** *or* **-hos** *or* **-hoe** *or* **-hoes** : a member of an American Indian people of the western U.S.

ar·bi·ter \'är-bə-tər\ *n* : one having power to decide : JUDGE

ar·bi·trage \'är-bə-,träzh\ *n* [F, fr. MF, arbitration] : the purchase and sale of the same or equivalent securities in different markets in order to profit from price discrepancies

ar·bi·tra·geur \,är-bə-bə-(,)trä-'zhər\ *or* **ar·bi·trag·er** \'är-bə-,trä-zhər\ *n* : one who practices arbitrage

ar·bi·tra·ment \är-'bi-trə-mənt\ *n* 1 : the act of deciding a dispute 2 : the judgment given by an arbitrator

ar·bi·trary \'är-bə-,trer-ē\ *adj* 1 : AUTOCRATIC, DESPOTIC 2 : determined by will or caprice : selected at random — **ar·bi·trari·ly** \,är-bə-'trer-ə-lē\ *adv* — **ar·bi·trari·ness** \'är-bə-,trer-ē-nəs\ *n*

ar·bi·trate \'är-bə-,trāt\ *vb* **-trat·ed; -trat·ing** 1 : to act as arbitrator 2 : to act on as arbitrator 3 : to submit for decision to an arbitrator — **ar·bi·tra·tion** \,är-bə-'trā-shən\ *n*

ar·bi·tra·tor \'är-bə-,trā-tər\ *n* : one chosen to settle differences between two parties in a controversy

ar·bor \'är-bər\ *n* [ME *erber, herber* garden, fr. AF, fr. *herbe* herb, grass] : a shelter formed of or covered with vines or branches

ar·bo·re·al \är-'bòr-ē-əl\ *adj* 1 : of, relating to, or resembling a tree 2 : living in trees ⟨~ monkeys⟩

ar·bo·re·tum \,är-bə-'rē-təm\ *n, pl* **-retums** *or* **-re·ta** \-tə\ [L, plantation of trees, fr. *arbor* tree] : a place where trees and plants are grown for scientific and educational purposes

ar·bor·vi·tae \,är-bər-'vī-tē\ *n* : any of various evergreen trees and shrubs with scalelike leaves that are related to the cypresses

ar·bour *chiefly Brit var of* ARBOR

ar·bu·tus \är-'byü-təs\ *n* : TRAILING ARBUTUS

¹arc \'ärk\ *n* 1 : a sustained luminous discharge of electricity (as between two electrodes) 2 : a continuous portion of a curved line (as part of the circumference of a circle)

²arc *vb* **arced** \'ärkt\; **arc·ing** \'är-kiŋ\ : to form an electric arc

ARC *abbr* 1 AIDS-related complex 2 American Red Cross

ar·cade \är-'kād\ *n* 1 : an arched or covered passageway; *esp* : one lined with shops 2 : a row of arches with their supporting columns 3 : an amusement center having coin-operated games

ar·cane \är-'kān\ *adj* : SECRET, MYSTERIOUS

¹arch \'ärch\ *n* 1 : a curved structure spanning an opening (as a door) 2 : something resembling an arch 3 : ARCHWAY

²arch *vb* 1 : to cover with an arch 2 : to form or bend into an arch

³arch *adj* 1 : CHIEF, EMINENT ⟨my ~ enemy⟩ 2 : ROGUISH, MISCHIEVOUS; *also* : deliberately playful or impudent ⟨~ comments⟩ — **arch·ly** *adv* — **arch·ness** *n*

⁴arch *abbr* architect; architectural; architecture

ar·chae·ol·o·gy *or* **ar·che·ol·o·gy** \,är-kē-'ä-lə-jē\ *n* : the study of past human life as revealed by relics left by ancient peoples — **ar·chae·o·log·i·cal** \-ə-'lä-ji-kəl\ *adj* — **ar·chae·ol·o·gist** \-'ä-lə-jist\ *n*

ar·cha·ic \är-'kā-ik\ *adj* 1 : having the characteristics of the language of the past and surviving chiefly in specialized uses ⟨~ words⟩ 2 : belonging to an earlier time : ANTIQUATED — **ar·cha·i·cal·ly** \-i-k(ə-)lē\ *adv*

arch·an·gel \'är-,kān-jəl\ *n* : a chief angel

arch·bish·op \ärch-'bi-shəp\ *n* : a bishop of high rank

arch·bish·op·ric \-shə-(,)prik\ *n* : the jurisdiction or office of an archbishop

arch·con·ser·va·tive \(,)ärch-kən-'sər-və-tiv\ *n* : an extreme conservative — **archconservative** *adj*

arch·dea·con \-'dē-kən\ *n* : a church official who assists a diocesan bishop in ceremonial or administrative functions

arch·di·o·cese \-'dī-ə-səs, -,sēz\ *n* : the diocese of an archbishop

arch·duke \-'dük, -'dyük\ *n* 1 : a sovereign prince 2 : a prince of the imperial family of Austria

Ar·che·an \är-'kē-ən\ *adj* : of, relating to, or being the earliest eon of geologic history — **Archean** *n*

arch·en·e·my \,ärch-'e-nə-mē\ *n, pl* **-mies** : a principal enemy

Ar·cheo·zo·ic \,är-kē-ə-'zō-ik\ *adj* : ARCHEAN — **Archeozoic** *n*

ar·chery \'är-chə-rē\ *n* : the art or practice of shooting with bow and arrows — **ar·cher** \'är-chər\ *n*

ar·che·type \'är-ki-,tīp\ *n* : the original pattern or model of all things of the same type — **ar·che·typ·al** \,är-kə-'tī-pəl\ *adj*

arch·fiend \,ärch-'fēnd\ *n* : a chief fiend; *esp* : SATAN

ar·chi·epis·co·pal \,är-kē-ə-'pis-kə-pəl\ *adj* : of or relating to an archbishop

ar·chi·man·drite \,är-kə-'man-,drīt\ *n* : a dignitary in an Eastern church ranking below a bishop

ar·chi·pel·a·go \,är-kə-'pe-lə-,gō, ,är-chə-\ *n, pl* **-goes** *or* **-gos** : a group of islands

ar·chi·tect \'är-kə-,tekt\ *n* 1 : a person who plans buildings and oversees their construction 2 : a person who designs and guides a plan or undertaking

ar·chi·tec·ture \'är-kə-,tek-chər\ *n* 1 : the art or science of planning and building structures 2 : a method or style of building 3 : the manner in which the elements (as of a design) or components (of a computer) are arranged or organized — **ar·chi·tec·tur·al** \,är-kə-'tek-chə-rəl, -'tek-shrəl\ *adj* — **ar·chi·tec·tur·al·ly** *adv*

ar·chi·trave \'är-kə-,trāv\ *n* : the supporting horizontal member just above the columns in a building in the classical style of architecture

ar·chive \'är-,kīv\ *n* 1 : a place for keeping public records; *also* : public records — often used in pl. 2 : a repository esp. of information

ar·chi·vist \'är-kə-vist, -,kī-\ *n* : a person in charge of archives

ar·chon \'är-,kän, -kən\ *n* : a chief magistrate of ancient Athens

arch·ri·val \'ärch-'rī-vəl\ *n* : a principal rival

arch·way \'ärch-,wā\ *n* : a passageway under an arch; *also* : an arch over a passage

arc lamp *n* : a gas-filled electric lamp that produces light when a current arcs between incandescent electrodes

¹arc·tic \'ärk-tik, 'är-tik\ *adj* [ME *artik*, fr. L *arcticus*, fr. Gk *arktikos*, fr. *arktos* bear, Ursa Major, north] 1 *often cap* : of or relating to the north pole or the region near it 2 : FRIGID

²arc·tic \'är-tik, 'ärk-tik\ *n* : a rubber overshoe that reaches to the ankle or above

arctic circle *n, often cap A&C* : the parallel of latitude that is approximately 66½ degrees north of the equator

-ard *also* **-art** *n suffix* : one that is characterized by performing some action, possessing some quality, or being associated with some thing esp. conspicuously or excessively ⟨brag*art*⟩ ⟨dull*ard*⟩

ar·dent \'är-dᵊnt\ *adj* 1 : characterized by warmth of feeling : PASSIONATE 2 : FIERY, HOT ⟨an ~ sun⟩ 3 : GLOWING ⟨~ eyes⟩ — **ar·dent·ly** *adv*

ar·dor \'är-dər\ *n* 1 : warmth of feeling : ZEAL 2 : sexual excitement

ardour • arrange

ar·dour *chiefly Brit var of* ARDOR
ar·du·ous \'är-jə-wəs, -dyü-wəs\ *adj* : DIFFICULT, LABORIOUS — **ar·du·ous·ly** *adv* — **ar·du·ous·ness** *n*
¹**are** *pres 2d sing or pres pl of* BE
²**are** \'er\ *n* — see METRIC SYSTEM table
ar·ea \'er-ē-ə\ *n* 1 : a flat surface or space 2 : the amount of surface included (as within the lines of a geometric figure) 3 : range or extent of some thing or concept : FIELD 4 : REGION
area code *n* : a usu. 3-digit number that identifies each telephone service area in a country (as the U.S. or Canada)
are·na \ə-'rē-nə\ *n* [L *harena, arena* sand, sandy place] 1 : an enclosed area used for public entertainment 2 : a sphere of activity or competition
ar·gen·tite \'är-jən-ˌtīt\ *n* : a dark gray or black mineral of metallic luster that is an important ore of silver
ar·gon \'är-ˌgän\ *n* [Gk, neut. of *argos* idle, lazy, fr. *a-* not + *ergon* work; fr. its relative inertness] : a colorless odorless gaseous chemical element found in the air and used for filling electric lamps
ar·go·sy \'är-gə-sē\ *n, pl* **-sies** 1 : a large merchant ship 2 : FLEET
ar·got \'är-gət, -ˌgō\ *n* : the language of a particular group or class
argu·able \'är-gyü-ə-bəl\ *adj* : open to argument, dispute, or question
ar·gu·ably \'är-gyü-(ə-)blē\ *adv* : as may be argued or shown by argument
ar·gue \'är-gyü\ *vb* **ar·gued; ar·gu·ing** 1 : to give reasons for or against something 2 : to contend in words : DISPUTE ⟨*argued* about money⟩ 3 : DEBATE 4 : to persuade by giving reasons
ar·gu·ment \'är-gyə-mənt\ *n* 1 : a reason offered in proof 2 : discourse intended to persuade 3 : QUARREL
ar·gu·men·ta·tion \ˌär-gyə-mən-'tā-shən\ *n* : the art of formal discussion
ar·gu·men·ta·tive \ˌär-gyə-'men-tə-tiv\ *adj* : inclined to argue
ar·gyle *also* **ar·gyll** \'är-ˌgīl(-ə)l\ *n, often cap* : a geometric knitting pattern of varicolored diamonds on a single background color; *also* : a sock knit in this pattern
aria \'är-ē-ə\ *n* : an accompanied elaborate vocal solo forming part of a larger work
ari·a·ry \ˌä-rē-'ä-rē\ *n, pl ariary* — see MONEY table
ar·id \'a-rəd\ *adj* : very dry; *esp* : having insufficient rainfall to support agriculture — **arid·i·ty** \ə-'ri-də-tē\ *n*
Ar·i·es \'er-ˌēz, -ē-ˌez\ *n* [L, lit., ram] 1 : a zodiacal constellation between Pisces and Taurus pictured as a ram 2 : the 1st sign of the zodiac in astrology; *also* : one born under this sign
aright \ə-'rīt\ *adv* : RIGHT, CORRECTLY
arise \ə-'rīz\ *vb* **arose** \-'rōz\; **aris·en** \-'ri-zᵊn\; **aris·ing** \-'rī-ziŋ\ 1 : to get up 2 : ORIGINATE 3 : ASCEND
 ✦ **Synonyms** RISE, DERIVE, SPRING, ISSUE
ar·is·toc·ra·cy \ˌa-rə-'stä-krə-sē\ *n, pl* **-cies** 1 : government by a noble or privileged class; *also* : a state so governed 2 : the governing class of an aristocracy 3 : UPPER CLASS — **aris·to·crat** \ə-'ris-tə-ˌkrat\ *n* — **aris·to·crat·ic** \ə-ˌris-tə-'kra-tik\ *adj*
arith *abbr* arithmetic; arithmetical
arith·me·tic \ə-'rith-mə-ˌtik\ *n* 1 : a branch of mathematics that deals with computations usu. with nonnegative real numbers 2 : COMPUTATION, CALCULATION — **ar·ith·met·ic** \ˌer-ith-'me-tik\ *or* **ar·ith·met·i·cal** \-ti-kəl\ *adj* — **ar·ith·met·i·cal·ly** \-ti-k(ə-)lē\ *adv* — **arith·me·ti·cian** \ə-ˌrith-mə-'ti-shən\ *n*
arithmetic mean *n* : the sum of a set of numbers divided by the number of numbers in the set
Ariz *abbr* Arizona
ark \'ärk\ *n* 1 : a boat held to resemble that of Noah's at the time of the Flood 2 : the sacred chest in a synagogue representing to Hebrews the presence of God; *also* : the repository for the scrolls of the Torah
Ark *abbr* Arkansas
¹**arm** \'ärm\ *n* [ME, fr. OE *earm*] 1 : a human upper limb and esp. the part between the shoulder and wrist; *also* : a corresponding limb of a 2-footed vertebrate 2 : something resembling an arm in shape or position ⟨an ~ of a chair⟩ ⟨the eight ~s of an octopus⟩ 3 : POWER, MIGHT ⟨the ~ of the law⟩ — **armed** \'ärmd\ *adj* — **arm·less** *adj*

²**arm** *vb* [ME, fr. AF *armer*, fr. L *armare*, fr. *arma* weapons, tools] : to furnish with weapons
³**arm** *n* 1 : WEAPON 2 : a branch of the military forces 3 *pl* : the hereditary heraldic devices of a family
ar·ma·da \är-'mä-də, -'mā-\ *n* : a fleet of warships
ar·ma·dil·lo \ˌär-mə-'di-lō\ *n, pl* **-los** [Sp, fr. dim. of *armado* armed one] : any of several small burrowing mammals with the head and body protected by an armor of bony plates
Ar·ma·ged·don \ˌär-mə-'ge-dᵊn\ *n* : a final conclusive battle between the forces of good and evil; *also* : the site or time of this
ar·ma·ment \'är-mə-mənt\ *n* 1 : military strength 2 : arms and equipment (as of a tank or combat unit) 3 : the process of preparing for war
ar·ma·ture \'är-mə-ˌchùr, -chər\ *n* 1 : a protective covering or structure (as the spines of a cactus) 2 : the rotating part of an electric generator or motor; *also* : the movable part in an electromagnetic device (as a loudspeaker)
arm·chair \'ärm-ˌcher\ *n* : a chair with armrests
armed forces *n pl* : the combined military, naval, and air forces of a nation
Ar·me·nian \är-'mē-nē-ən\ *n* 1 : a native or inhabitant of Armenia 2 : the Indo-European language of the Armenians
arm·ful \'ärm-ˌfùl\ *n, pl* **armfuls** *or* **arms·ful** \'ärmz-ˌfùl\ : as much as the arm or arms can hold
arm·hole \'ärm-ˌhōl\ *n* : an opening for the arm in a garment
ar·mi·stice \'är-mə-stəs\ *n* : temporary suspension of hostilities by mutual agreement : TRUCE
arm·let \'ärm-lət\ *n* : a band worn around the upper arm
ar·mor \'är-mər\ *n* 1 : protective covering 2 : armored forces and vehicles — **ar·mored** \-mərd\ *adj*
ar·mor·er \'är-mər-ər\ *n* 1 : a person who makes arms and armor 2 : a person who services firearms
ar·mo·ri·al \är-'mȯr-ē-əl\ *adj* : of or bearing heraldic arms
ar·mory \'är-mə-rē\ *n, pl* **ar·mor·ies** 1 : a place where arms are stored 2 : a factory where arms are made
ar·mour, ar·moury *chiefly Brit var of* ARMOR, ARMORY
arm·pit \'ärm-ˌpit\ *n* : the hollow under the junction of the arm and shoulder
arm·rest \-ˌrest\ *n* : a support for the arm
ar·my \'är-mē\ *n, pl* **armies** 1 : a body of persons trained and organized for war 2 *often cap* : the complete military organization of a country for land warfare 3 : a great number 4 : a body of persons organized to advance a cause
army ant *n* : any of various nomadic social ants
ar·my·worm \'är-mē-ˌwərm\ *n* : any of numerous moths whose larvae move about destroying crops
aro·ma \ə-'rō-mə\ *n* : a usu. pleasing odor : FRAGRANCE — **ar·o·mat·ic** \ˌar-ə-'ma-tik\ *adj*
aro·ma·ther·a·py \ə-ˌrō-mə-'ther-ə-pē\ *n* : massage with a preparation of fragrant oils extracted from herbs, flowers, and fruits
arose *past of* ARISE
¹**around** \ə-'raund\ *adv* 1 : in a circle or in circumference ⟨a tree five feet ~⟩ 2 : in or along a circuit ⟨the road goes ~ by the lake⟩ 3 : on all sides ⟨nothing for miles ~⟩ 4 : NEARBY ⟨wait ~ awhile⟩ 5 : from one place to another ⟨travels ~ on business⟩ 6 : in an opposite direction ⟨turn ~⟩ 7 — used with some verbs to indicate continued action ⟨joking ~⟩ 8 : APPROXIMATELY ⟨cost ~ $5⟩
²**around** *prep* 1 : SURROUNDING ⟨trees ~ the house⟩ 2 : to or on another side of ⟨~ the corner⟩ 3 : NEAR ⟨stayed right ~ home⟩ 4 : along the circuit of ⟨go ~ the world⟩
arouse \ə-'raùz\ *vb* **aroused; arous·ing** 1 : to awaken from sleep 2 : to stir up : EXCITE — **arous·al** \-'raù-zəl\ *n*
ar·peg·gio \är-'pe-jē-ˌō, -'pe-jō\ *n, pl* **-gios** [It fr. *arpeggiare* to play on the harp, fr. *arpa* harp] : a chord whose notes are performed in succession and not simultaneously
arr *abbr* 1 arranged 2 arrival; arrive
ar·raign \ə-'rān\ *vb* 1 : to call before a court to answer to an indictment 2 : to accuse of wrong or imperfection — **ar·raign·ment** *n*
ar·range \ə-'rānj\ *vb* **ar·ranged; ar·rang·ing** 1 : to put

in order **2** : PLAN ⟨~ an interview⟩ **3** : to adapt (a musical composition) to voices or instruments other than those for which it was orig. written **4** : to come to an agreement about : SETTLE ⟨~ a business deal⟩ — **ar·range·ment** *n* — **ar·rang·er** *n*

ar·rant \'a-rənt\ *adj* : being notoriously without moderation : EXTREME

ar·ras \'a-rəs\ *n, pl* **arras** **1** : TAPESTRY **2** : a wall hanging or screen of tapestry

¹ar·ray \ə-'rā\ *vb* **1** : to dress esp. splendidly **2** : to arrange in order (as in an array)

²array *n* **1** : a regular arrangement **2** : rich apparel **3** : a large or varied group

ar·rears \ə-'rirz\ *n pl* **1** : a state of being behind in the discharge of obligations ⟨in ~ with the rent⟩ **2** : overdue debts

¹ar·rest \ə-'rest\ *vb* **1** : STOP, CHECK **2** : to take into legal custody

²arrest *n* **1** : the act of stopping; *also* : the state of being stopped **2** : the taking into custody by legal authority

ar·rhyth·mia \ā-'rith-mē-ə\ *n* : an alteration of the heartbeat's rhythm

ar·riv·al \ə-'rī-vəl\ *n* **1** : the act of arriving **2** : one that arrives

ar·rive \ə-'rīv\ *vb* **ar·rived; ar·riv·ing** **1** : to reach a destination **2** : to make an appearance ⟨the guests have *arrived*⟩ **3** : to attain success

ar·ro·gant \'er-ə-gənt\ *adj* : offensively exaggerating one's own importance — **ar·ro·gance** \-gəns\ *n* — **ar·ro·gant·ly** *adv*

ar·ro·gate \-,gāt\ *vb* **-gat·ed; -gat·ing** : to claim or seize without justification as one's right — **ar·ro·ga·tion** \,ar-ə-'gā-shən\ *n*

ar·row \'er-ō\ *n* **1** : a missile shot from a bow and usu. having a slender shaft, a pointed head, and feathers at the butt **2** : a pointed mark used to indicate direction

ar·row·head \'er-ō-,hed\ *n* : the pointed end of an arrow

arrowhead

ar·row·root \-,rüt, -,rút\ *n* : an edible starch from the roots of any of several tropical American plants; *also* : a plant yielding arrowroot

ar·royo \ə-'rói-ə, -ō\ *n, pl* **-royos** [Sp] **1** : a watercourse in a dry region **2** : a water-carved gully or channel

ar·se·nal \'ärs-nəl, 'är-sə-nəl\ *n* [ultim. fr. Ar *dār ṣinā'a* house of manufacture] **1** : a place for making and storing arms and military equipment **2** : STORE, REPERTOIRE ⟨an ~ of tools⟩

ar·se·nic \'ärs-nik, 'är-sə-nik\ *n* **1** : a solid brittle poisonous chemical element of grayish metallic luster **2** : a very poisonous oxygen compound of arsenic used in making insecticides

ar·son \'är-s°n\ *n* : the willful or malicious burning of property — **ar·son·ist** \-ist\ *n*

¹art \'ärt\ *n* **1** : skill acquired by experience or study **2** : a branch of learning; *esp* : one of the humanities **3** : an occupation requiring knowledge or skill **4** : the use of skill and imagination in the production of things of beauty; *also* : works so produced **5** : ARTFULNESS

²art *adj* : produced as an artistic effort ⟨an ~ film⟩

³art *abbr* **1** article **2** artificial **3** artillery

-art — see -ARD

ar·te·fact *chiefly Brit var of* ARTIFACT

ar·te·ri·al \är-'tir-ē-əl\ *adj* **1** : of or relating to an artery; *also* : relating to or being the oxygenated blood found in most arteries **2** : of, relating to, or being a route for through traffic

ar·te·ri·ole \är-'tir-ē-,ōl\ *n* : any of the small terminal branches of an artery that ends in capillaries — **ar·te·ri·o·lar** \-,tir-ē-'ō-lər\ *adj*

ar·te·rio·scle·ro·sis \är-,tir-ē-ō-sklə-'rō-səs\ *n* : a chronic disease in which arterial walls are abnormally thickened and hardened — **ar·te·rio·scle·rot·ic** \-'rä-tik\ *adj or n*

ar·tery \'är-tə-rē\ *n, pl* **-ter·ies** **1** : one of the tubular vessels that carry blood from the heart **2** : a main channel of transportation or communication

ar·te·sian well \är-'tē-zhən-\ *n* : a well from which the water flows to the surface by natural pressure; *also* : a deep well

art·ful \'ärt-fəl\ *adj* **1** : performed with, showing, or using art or skill **2** : CRAFTY — **art·ful·ly** *adv* — **art·ful·ness** *n*

ar·thri·tis \är-'thrī-təs\ *n, pl* **-thri·ti·des** \-'thri-tə-,dēz\ : inflammation of the joints — **ar·thrit·ic** \-'thri-tik\ *adj or n*

ar·thro·pod \'är-thrə-,päd\ *n* : any of a phylum of invertebrate animals comprising those (as insects, spiders, or crabs) with segmented bodies and jointed limbs — **arthropod** *adj*

ar·thros·co·py \är-'thräs-kə-pē\ *n, pl* **-pies** : visual examination of the interior of a joint (as the knee) with a special surgical instrument; *also* : surgery on a joint using arthroscopy — **ar·thro·scope** \'är-thrə-,skōp\ *n* — **ar·thro·scop·ic** \,är-thrə-'skä-pik\ *adj*

ar·ti·choke \'är-tə-,chōk\ *n* [It dial. *articiocco*, ultim. fr. Ar *al-khurshūf*] : a tall thistlelike herb related to the daisies; *also* : its edible flower head

ar·ti·cle \'är-ti-kəl\ *n* [ME, fr. AF, fr. L *articulus* joint, division, dim. of *artus* joint, limb] **1** : a distinct part of a written document **2** : a nonfictional prose composition forming an independent part of a publication **3** : a word (as *an, the*) used with a noun to limit or give definiteness to its application **4** : a member of a class of things; *esp* : COMMODITY

ar·tic·u·lar \är-'ti-kyə-lər\ *adj* : of or relating to a joint ⟨~ cartilage⟩

¹ar·tic·u·late \är-'ti-kyə-lət\ *adj* **1** : divided into meaningful parts : INTELLIGIBLE **2** : able to speak; *also* : expressing oneself readily and effectively ⟨an ~ orator⟩ **3** : JOINTED — **ar·tic·u·late·ly** *adv* — **ar·tic·u·late·ness** *n*

²ar·tic·u·late \-,lāt\ *vb* **-lat·ed; -lat·ing** **1** : to utter distinctly **2** : to unite by or as if by joints — **ar·tic·u·la·tion** \-,ti-kyə-'lā-shən\ *n*

ar·ti·fact \'är-tə-,fakt\ *n* : something made or modified by humans usu. for a purpose; *esp* : an object remaining from another time or culture ⟨prehistoric ~s⟩

ar·ti·fice \'är-tə-fəs\ *n* **1** : TRICK; *also* : TRICKERY **2** : an ingenious device; *also* : INGENUITY

ar·ti·fi·cer \är-'ti-fə-sər, 'är-tə-fə-sər\ *n* : a skilled worker

ar·ti·fi·cial \,är-tə-'fi-shəl\ *adj* **1** : produced by art rather than nature; *also* : made by humans to imitate nature **2** : not genuine : FEIGNED — **ar·ti·fi·ci·al·i·ty** \-,fi-shē-'a-lə-tē\ *n* — **ar·ti·fi·cial·ly** *adv* — **ar·ti·fi·cial·ness** *n*

artificial insemination *n* : introduction of semen into the uterus or oviduct by other than natural means

artificial intelligence *n* : the capability of a machine and esp. a computer to imitate intelligent human behavior

artificial respiration *n* : the rhythmic forcing of air into and out of the lungs of a person whose breathing has stopped

ar·til·lery \är-'ti-lə-rē\ *n, pl* **-ler·ies** **1** : crew-served mounted firearms (as guns) **2** : a branch of the army armed with artillery — **ar·til·ler·ist** \-rist\ *n*

ar·ti·san \'är-tə-zən, -sən\ *n* : a worker who practices a trade or handicraft

art·ist \'är-tist\ *n* **1** : one who practices an art; *esp* : one who creates objects of beauty **2** : ARTISTE

ar·tiste \är-'tēst\ *n* : a skilled public performer

ar·tis·tic \är-'tis-tik\ *adj* : showing taste and skill — **ar·tis·ti·cal·ly** \-ti-k(ə-)lē\ *adv*

art·ist·ry \'är-tə-strē\ *n* : artistic quality or ability

art·less \'ärt-ləs\ *adj* **1** : lacking art or skill **2** : free from artificiality : NATURAL **3** : free from guile : SINCERE — **art·less·ly** *adv* — **art·less·ness** *n*

art nou·veau \,ärt-nü-'vō, ,ärt-\ *n, often cap A&N* [F, lit., new art] : a late 19th century design style characterized by sinuous lines and leaf-shaped forms

art·work \'ärt-,wərk\ *n* : an artistic production or work

arty \'är-tē\ *adj* **art·i·er; -est** : showily or pretentiously artistic — **art·i·ly** \'är-tə-lē\ *adv* — **art·i·ness** *n*

aru·gu·la \ə-'rü-gə-lə\ *n* : a yellowish-flowered herb related to the mustards with edible leaves used esp. in salads

ar·um \\'a-rəm\\ n : any of a family of plants (as the jack=in-the-pulpit or a skunk cabbage) with flowers in a fleshy enclosed spike

ARV abbr American Revised Version

¹-ary n suffix : thing or person belonging to or connected with ⟨function*ary*⟩

²-ary adj suffix : of, relating to, or connected with ⟨budget*ary*⟩

Ary·an \\'a-rē-ən, 'er-e-; 'är-yən\\ adj 1 : INDO-EUROPEAN 2 : NORDIC — **Aryan** n

¹as \\əz, (ˌ)az\\ adv 1 : to the same degree or amount : EQUALLY ⟨~ green as grass⟩ 2 : for instance ⟨various trees, ~ oak or pine⟩ 3 : when considered in a specified relation ⟨my opinion ~ distinguished from his⟩

²as conj 1 : in the same amount or degree in which ⟨green ~ grass⟩ 2 : in the same way that ⟨farmed ~ his father before him had farmed⟩ 3 : WHILE, WHEN ⟨spoke to me ~ I was leaving⟩ 4 : THOUGH ⟨improbable ~ it seems⟩ 5 : SINCE, BECAUSE ⟨~ I'm not wanted, I'll go⟩ 6 : that the result is ⟨so guilty ~ to leave no doubt⟩

³as pron 1 : THAT — used after same or such ⟨it's the same price ~ before⟩ 2 : a fact that ⟨he's rich, ~ you know⟩

⁴as prep : in the capacity or character of ⟨this will serve ~ a substitute⟩

As symbol arsenic

AS abbr 1 American Samoa 2 Anglo-Saxon 3 associate in science

asa·fet·i·da or **asa·foe·ti·da** \\ˌa-sə-'fe-tə-dē, -'fē-\\ n : an ill-smelling plant gum formerly used in medicine

ASAP abbr as soon as possible

as·bes·tos \\as-'bes-təs, az-\\ n : a noncombustible grayish mineral that occurs in fibrous form and has been used as a fireproof material

as·cend \\ə-'send\\ vb 1 : to move upward : MOUNT, CLIMB 2 : to succeed to : OCCUPY ⟨he ~ed the throne⟩

as·cen·dan·cy also **as·cen·den·cy** \\ə-'sen-dən-sē\\ n : controlling influence : DOMINATION

¹as·cen·dant also **as·cen·dent** \\ə-'sen-dənt\\ n : a dominant position

²ascendant also **ascendent** adj 1 : moving upward 2 : DOMINANT

as·cen·sion \\ə-'sen-chən\\ n : the act or process of ascending

Ascension Day n : the Thursday 40 days after Easter observed in commemoration of Christ's ascension into heaven

as·cent \\ə-'sent\\ n 1 : the act of mounting upward : CLIMB 2 : degree of upward slope

as·cer·tain \\ˌa-sər-'tān\\ vb : to learn with certainty — **as·cer·tain·able** adj

as·cet·ic \\ə-'se-tik\\ adj : practicing self-denial esp. for spiritual reasons : AUSTERE — **ascetic** n — **as·cet·i·cism** \\-'se-tə-ˌsi-zəm\\ n

ASCII \\'as-kē\\ n [American Standard Code for Information Interchange] : a computer code for representing alphanumeric information

ascor·bic acid \\ə-'skòr-bik-\\ n : VITAMIN C

as·cot \\'as-kət, -ˌkät\\ n [Ascot Heath, racetrack near Ascot, England] : a broad neck scarf that is looped under the chin

as·cribe \\ə-'skrīb\\ vb **as·cribed; as·crib·ing** : to refer to a supposed cause, source, or author : ATTRIBUTE — **as·crib·able** adj — **as·crip·tion** \\-'skrip-shən\\ n

asep·tic \\ā-'sep-tik\\ adj : free or freed from disease=causing germs

asex·u·al \\ā-'sek-shə-wəl\\ adj 1 : lacking sex or functional sex organs 2 : occurring or formed without the production and union of two kinds of gametes ⟨~ reproduction⟩ 3 : devoid of sexuality 4 : neither male nor female — **asex·u·al·ly** adv

as for prep : with regard to : CONCERNING ⟨as for the others, they were late⟩

¹ash \\'ash\\ n 1 : any of a genus of trees related to the olive and having winged seeds and bark with grooves and ridges 2 : the tough elastic wood of an ash

²ash n 1 : the solid matter left when material is burned 2 : fine mineral particles from a volcano 3 pl : the remains of the dead human body after cremation or disintegration

ashamed \\ə-'shāmd\\ adj 1 : feeling shame 2 : restrained by anticipation of shame ⟨~ to say anything⟩ — **asham·ed·ly** \\-'shā-məd-lē\\ adv

ash·en \\'a-shən\\ adj : resembling ashes (as in color); esp : deadly pale

ash·lar \\'ash-lər\\ n : hewn or squared stone; also : masonry of such stone

ashore \\ə-'shòr\\ adv : on or to the shore

as how conj : THAT ⟨allowed as how she was glad to be here⟩

ash·ram \\'äsh-rəm\\ n : a religious retreat esp. of a Hindu sage

ash·tray \\'ash-ˌtrā\\ n : a receptacle for tobacco ashes

Ash Wednesday n : the 1st day of Lent

ashy \\'a-shē\\ adj **ash·i·er; -est** : ASHEN

Asian \\'ā-zhən\\ adj : of, relating to, or characteristic of the continent of Asia or its people — **Asian** n

¹aside \\ə-'sīd\\ adv 1 : to or toward the side 2 : out of the way ⟨putting ~ savings⟩

²aside n : an actor's words heard by the audience but supposedly not by other characters on stage

aside from prep 1 : BESIDES ⟨aside from being pretty, she's intelligent⟩ 2 : with the exception of ⟨aside from one D his grades are excellent⟩

as if conj 1 : as it would be if ⟨it's as if nothing had changed⟩ 2 : as one would if ⟨he acts as if he'd never been away⟩ 3 : THAT ⟨it seems as if nothing ever happens around here⟩

as·i·nine \\'a-sə-ˌnīn\\ adj [L asininus, fr. asinus ass] : STUPID, FOOLISH — **as·i·nin·i·ty** \\ˌa-sə-'ni-nə-tē\\ n

ask \\'ask\\ vb **asked** \\'askt;\\ **ask·ing** 1 : to call on for an answer ⟨she ~ed him about his trip⟩ 2 : UTTER ⟨~ a question⟩ 3 : to make a request of ⟨~ him for help⟩ 4 : to make a request for ⟨~ help of her⟩ 5 : to set as a price ⟨~ed $800 for the car⟩ 6 : INVITE

askance \\ə-'skans\\ adv 1 : with a side glance 2 : with distrust

askew \\ə-'skyü\\ adv or adj : out of line : AWRY

ASL abbr American Sign Language

¹aslant \\ə-'slant\\ adv or adj : in a slanting direction

²aslant prep : over or across in a slanting direction

asleep \\ə-'slēp\\ adv or adj 1 : in or into a state of sleep 2 : DEAD 3 : NUMB 4 : INACTIVE

as long as conj 1 : provided that ⟨do as you like as long as you get home on time⟩ 2 : INASMUCH AS, SINCE ⟨as long as you're up, turn on the light⟩

aso·cial \\(ˌ)ā-'sō-shəl\\ adj : ANTISOCIAL

as of prep : AT, DURING, FROM, ON ⟨takes effect as of July 1⟩

asp \\'asp\\ n : a small poisonous African snake

as·par·a·gus \\ə-'sper-ə-gəs\\ n : a tall branching perennial herb related to the lilies; also : its edible young stalks

as·par·tame \\'as-pər-ˌtām, ə-'spär-\\ n : a crystalline low=calorie sweetener

ASPCA abbr American Society for the Prevention of Cruelty to Animals

as·pect \\'as-ˌpekt\\ n 1 : a position facing a particular direction 2 : APPEARANCE, LOOK 3 : PHASE

as·pen \\'as-pən\\ n : any of several poplars with leaves that flutter in the slightest breeze

as per \\'az-ˌpər\\ prep : in accordance with ⟨as per instructions⟩

as·per·i·ty \\a-'sper-ə-tē\\ n, pl **-ties** 1 : ROUGHNESS 2 : harshness of temper

as·per·sion \\ə-'spər-zhən\\ n : a slanderous or defamatory remark

as·phalt \\'as-ˌfòlt\\ also **as·phal·tum** \\as-'fòl-təm\\ n : a dark substance found in natural beds or obtained as a residue in petroleum refining and used esp. in paving streets

asphalt jungle n : a big city or a specified part of a big city

as·pho·del \\'as-fə-ˌdel\\ n : any of several Old World herbs related to the lilies and bearing flowers in long erect spikes

as·phyx·ia \\as-'fik-sē-ə\\ n : a lack of oxygen or excess of carbon dioxide in the body that results in unconsciousness and often death and is usu. caused by interruption of breathing

as·phyx·i·ate \\-sē-ˌāt\\ vb **-at·ed; -at·ing** : SUFFOCATE — **as·phyx·i·a·tion** \\-ˌfik-sē-'ā-shən\\ n

as·pic \\'as-pik\\ n [F, lit., asp] : a savory meat jelly

as·pi·rant \'as-pə-rənt, ə-'spī-rənt\ *n* : one who aspires ⟨a presidential ∼⟩ ✦ *Synonyms* CANDIDATE, SEEKER

¹**as·pi·rate** \'as-pə-rət\ *n* 1 : an independent sound \h\ or a character (as the letter *h*) representing it 2 : a consonant having aspiration as its final component

²**as·pi·rate** \'as-pə-ˌrāt\ *vb* -rat·ed; -rat·ing : to draw, remove, or take up or into by suction

as·pi·ra·tion \ˌas-pə-'rā-shən\ *n* 1 : the pronunciation or addition of an aspirate; *also* : the aspirate or its symbol 2 : a drawing of something in, out, up, or through by or as if by suction 3 : a strong desire to achieve something noble; *also* : an object of this desire

as·pire \ə-'spī(-ə)r\ *vb* **as·pired; as·pir·ing** 1 : to seek to attain or accomplish a particular goal 2 : to rise aloft

as·pi·rin \'as-pə-rən\ *n, pl* **aspirin** *or* **aspirins** 1 : a white crystalline drug used to relieve pain and fever 2 : a tablet of aspirin

as regards *also* **as respects** *prep* : in regard to : with respect to

ass \'as\ *n* 1 : any of several long-eared mammals smaller than the related horses; *esp* : one of Africa ancestral to the donkey 2 *impolite* : a stupid person

as·sail \ə-'sāl\ *vb* : to attack violently — **as·sail·able** *adj* — **as·sail·ant** *n*

as·sas·sin \ə-'sa-sᵊn\ *n* [ML *assassinus,* fr. Ar *ḥash-shāshīn,* pl. of *ḥashshāsh* worthless person, lit., hashish= user, fr. *hashīsh* hashish] : a murderer esp. for hire or fanatical reasons

as·sas·si·nate \ə-'sa-sə-ˌnāt\ *vb* -nat·ed; -nat·ing : to murder by sudden or secret attack — **as·sas·si·na·tion** \-ˌsa-sə-'nā-shən\ *n*

as·sault \ə-'sȯlt\ *n* 1 : a violent attack 2 : an unlawful attempt or threat to do harm to another — **assault** *vb* — **as·sault·ive** \-'sȯl-tiv\ *adj*

assault rifle *n* : a military automatic rifle with a large= capacity magazine

¹**as·say** \'a-ˌsā, a-'sā\ *n* : analysis to determine the quantity of one or more components present in a sample (as of an ore or drug)

²**as·say** \a-'sā, 'a-ˌsā\ *vb* 1 : TRY, ATTEMPT 2 : to subject (as an ore or drug) to an assay 3 : JUDGE 3

as·sem·blage \ə-'sem-blij, 3 & 4 *also* ˌäm-'bläzh\ *n* 1 : a collection of persons or things : GATHERING 2 : the act of assembling 3 : an artistic composition made from scraps, junk, and odds and ends 4 : the art of making assemblages

as·sem·ble \ə-'sem-bəl\ *vb* -bled; -bling 1 : to collect into one place : CONGREGATE 2 : to fit together the parts of 3 : to meet together : CONVENE

as·sem·bly \ə-'sem-blē\ *n, pl* -blies 1 : a gathering of persons : MEETING 2 *cap* : a legislative body; *esp* : the lower house of a legislature 3 : a signal for troops to assemble 4 : the fitting together of parts (as of a machine)

assembly language *n* : a computer language consisting of mnemonic codes corresponding to machine-language instructions

as·sem·bly–line \ə-'sem-blē-ˌlīn\ *adj* : made by or as if by an assembly line; *esp* : lacking originality or creativity

assembly line *n* : an arrangement of machines, equipment, and workers in which work passes from operation to operation in a direct line

as·sem·bly·man \ə-'sem-blē-mən\ *n* : a member of an assembly

as·sem·bly·wom·an \-ˌwu̇-mən\ *n* : a woman who is a member of an assembly

as·sent \ə-'sent\ *vb* : AGREE, CONCUR — **assent** *n*

as·sert \ə-'sərt\ *vb* 1 : to state positively 2 : to demonstrate the existence of ✦ *Synonyms* DECLARE, AFFIRM, PROTEST, AVOW, CLAIM — **as·ser·tive** \-'sər-tiv\ *adj* — **as·ser·tive·ly** *adv* — **as·ser·tive·ness** *n*

as·ser·tion \ə-'sər-shən\ *n* : a positive statement

as·sess \ə-'ses\ *vb* 1 : to fix the rate or amount of 2 : to impose (as a tax) at a specified rate 3 : to evaluate for taxation — **as·sess·ment** *n* — **as·ses·sor** \-'se-sər\ *n*

as·set \'a-ˌset\ *n* 1 *pl* : the entire property of a person or company that may be used to pay debts 2 : ADVAN-TAGE, RESOURCE ⟨my wit is my chief ∼⟩

as·sev·er·ate \ə-'se-və-ˌrāt\ *vb* -at·ed; -at·ing : to assert earnestly — **as·sev·er·a·tion** \-ˌse-və-'rā-shən\ *n*

as·sid·u·ous \ə-'si-jə-wəs\ *adj* : steadily attentive : DILI-GENT — **as·si·du·i·ty** \ˌa-sə-'dü-ə-tē, -'dyü-\ *n* — **as·sid-u·ous·ly** *adv* — **as·sid·u·ous·ness** *n*

as·sign \ə-'sīn\ *vb* 1 : to transfer (property) to another 2 : to appoint to or as a duty ⟨∼ a lesson⟩ 3 : FIX, SPECIFY ⟨∼ a limit⟩ 4 : ASCRIBE ⟨∼ a reason⟩ — **as·sign·able** *adj*

as·sig·na·tion \ˌa-sig-'nā-shən\ *n* : an appointment for a meeting; *esp* : TRYST

assigned risk *n* : a poor risk (as an accident-prone motorist) that an insurance company is forced to insure by state law

as·sign·ment \ə-'sīn-mənt\ *n* 1 : the act of assigning 2 : something assigned

as·sim·i·late \ə-'si-mə-ˌlāt\ *vb* -lat·ed; -lat·ing 1 : to take up and absorb as nourishment; *also* : to absorb into a cultural tradition 2 : COMPREHEND 3 : to make or become similar — **as·sim·i·la·tion** \-ˌsi-mə-'lā-shən\ *n*

¹**as·sist** \ə-'sist\ *vb* : HELP, AID — ⟨∼ed the injured⟩ — **as·sis·tance** \-'sis-təns\ *n*

²**assist** *n* 1 : an act of assistance 2 : the action of a player who enables a teammate to make a putout (as in baseball) or score a goal (as in hockey or basketball)

as·sis·tant \ə-'sis-tənt\ *n* : a person who assists : HELPER

as·sis·ted living \ə-'sis-təd-\ *n* : a system of housing and limited care for senior citizens who need assistance with daily activities but do not require care in a nursing home

as·sis·tive \ə-'sis-tiv\ *adj* : providing aid or assistance ⟨∼ technology⟩

as·size \ə-'sīz\ *n* [ME *assise,* fr. AF, session, legal action, fr. *asseer, asseoir* to seat, fr. VL *assedēre,* fr. L *assidēre* to sit beside] 1 : a judicial inquest 2 *pl* : the former regular sessions of superior courts in English counties

assn *abbr* association

assoc *abbr* associate; associated; association

¹**as·so·ci·ate** \ə-'sō-shē-ˌāt, -sē-\ *vb* -at·ed; -at·ing 1 : to join in companionship or partnership 2 : to connect in thought

²**as·so·ciate** \-shē-ət, -sē-; -shət\ *n* 1 : a fellow worker : PARTNER 2 : COMPANION 3 *often cap* : a degree conferred esp. by a junior college ⟨∼ in arts⟩ — **associate** *adj*

as·so·ci·a·tion \ə-ˌsō-shē-'ā-shən, -sē-\ *n* 1 : the act of associating 2 : an organization of persons : SOCIETY

as·so·cia·tive \ə-'sō-shē-ˌā-tiv, -sē-; -shə-tiv\ *adj* 1 : of, relating to, or involved in association esp. of ideas or images 2 : of, having, or being the property of producing the same mathematical value regardless of how an expression's elements are grouped as long as their order is the same

as·so·nance \'a-sə-nəns\ *n* : repetition of vowels esp. as an alternative to rhyme in verse — **as·so·nant** \-nənt\ *adj or n*

as soon as *conj* : immediately at or shortly after the time that ⟨we'll start *as soon as* they arrive⟩

as·sort \ə-'sȯrt\ *vb* 1 : to distribute into like groups : CLASSIFY 2 : HARMONIZE

as·sort·ed \-'sȯr-təd\ *adj* : consisting of various kinds

as·sort·ment \-'sȯrt-mənt\ *n* : a collection of assorted things or persons

asst *abbr* assistant

as·suage \ə-'swāj\ *vb* **as·suaged; as·suag·ing** 1 : to make (as pain or grief) less : EASE 2 : SATISFY ✦ *Synonyms* ALLEVIATE, RELIEVE, LIGHTEN, MITIGATE

as·sume \ə-'süm\ *vb* **as·sumed; as·sum·ing** 1 : to take upon oneself 2 : to pretend to have or be 3 : to take as granted or true though not proved

as·sump·tion \ə-'səmp-shən\ *n* 1 : the taking up of a person into heaven 2 *cap* : August 15 observed in commemoration of the Assumption of the Virgin Mary 3 : a taking upon oneself 4 : PRETENSION 5 : SUPPOSITION

as·sur·ance \ə-'shu̇r-əns\ *n* 1 : PLEDGE 2 *chiefly Brit* : INSURANCE 3 : SECURITY 4 : SELF-CONFIDENCE; *also* : AUDACITY

as·sure \ə-'shu̇r\ *vb* **as·sured; as·sur·ing** 1 : INSURE 2 : to give confidence to 3 : to state confidently to 4 : to make certain the coming or attainment of

as·sured \ə-'shu̇rd\ *n, pl* assured *or* assureds : INSURED

as·ta·tine \'as-tə-ˌtēn\ *n* : an unstable radioactive chemical element

as·ter \'as-tər\ n : any of various mostly fall-blooming leafy-stemmed composite herbs with daisylike purple, white, pink, or yellow flower heads

as·ter·isk \'as-tə-ˌrisk\ n [L asteriscus, fr. Gk asteriskos, lit., little star, dim. of astēr star] : a character * used as a reference mark or as an indication of the omission of letters or words

astern \ə-'stərn\ adv or adj 1 : in, at, or toward the stern 2 : BACKWARD

as·ter·oid \'as-tə-ˌroid\ n : any of the numerous small celestial bodies found esp. between Mars and Jupiter

asth·ma \'az-mə\ n : a chronic lung disorder marked by recurrent episodes of labored breathing, a feeling of tightness in the chest, and coughing — **asth·mat·ic** \az-'ma-tik\ adj or n

as though conj : AS IF

astig·ma·tism \ə-'stig-mə-ˌti-zəm\ n : a defect in a lens or an eye causing improper focusing and blurred vision — **as·tig·mat·ic** \ˌas-tig-'ma-tik\ adj

astir \ə-'stər\ adj 1 : being in action : MOVING 2 : being out of bed

as to prep 1 : ABOUT, CONCERNING ⟨uncertain as to what went on⟩ 2 : ACCORDING TO ⟨graded as to size⟩

as·ton·ish \ə-'stä-nish\ vb : to strike with sudden and usu. great wonder : AMAZE — **as·ton·ish·ing·ly** adv — **as·ton·ish·ment** n

as·tound \ə-'staund\ vb : to fill with bewilderment or wonder — **as·tound·ing·ly** adv

¹**astrad·dle** \ə-'stra-dᵊl\ adv : on or above and extending onto both sides

²**astraddle** prep : ASTRIDE

as·tra·khan \'as-trə-kən, -ˌkan\ n, often cap 1 : karakul of Russian origin 2 : a cloth with a usu. wool, curled, and looped pile resembling karakul

as·tral \'as-trəl\ adj : of, relating to, or coming from the stars

astray \ə-'strā\ adv or adj 1 : off the right path or route 2 : into error

¹**astride** \ə-'strīd\ adv 1 : with one leg on each side 2 : with legs apart

²**astride** prep : with one leg on each side of

¹**as·trin·gent** \ə-'strin-jənt\ adj : able or tending to shrink body tissues — **as·trin·gen·cy** \-jən-sē\ n

²**astringent** n : an astringent agent or substance

astrol abbr astrologer; astrology

as·tro·labe \'as-trə-ˌlāb\ n : an instrument formerly used for observing the positions of celestial bodies

as·trol·o·gy \ə-'strä-lə-jē\ n : divination based on the supposed influence of the stars upon human events — **as·trol·o·ger** \-jər\ n — **as·tro·log·i·cal** \ˌas-trə-'lä-ji-kəl\ adj — **as·tro·log·i·cal·ly** \-kə-lē\ adv

astron abbr astronomer; astronomy

as·tro·naut \'as-trə-ˌnot\ n : a traveler in a spacecraft

as·tro·nau·tics \as-trə-'no-tiks\ n : the science of the construction and operation of spacecraft — **as·tro·nau·tic** \-tik\ or **as·tro·nau·ti·cal** \-ti-kəl\ adj

as·tro·nom·i·cal \ˌas-trə-'nä-mi-kəl\ also **as·tro·nom·ic** \-mik\ adj 1 : of or relating to astronomy 2 : extremely large ⟨an ~ amount of money⟩

astronomical unit n : a unit of length used in astronomy equal to the mean distance of the earth from the sun or about 93 million miles (150 million kilometers)

as·tron·o·my \ə-'strä-nə-mē\ n, pl **-mies** : the science of objects and matter beyond the earth's atmosphere — **as·tron·o·mer** \-mər\ n

as·tro·phys·ics \ˌas-trə-'fi-ziks\ n : astronomy dealing esp. with the physical properties and dynamic processes of celestial objects — **as·tro·phys·i·cal** \-zi-kəl\ adj — **as·tro·phys·i·cist** \-'fi-zə-sist\ n

as·tute \ə-'stüt, -'styüt, a-\ adj [L astutus, fr. astus craft] : shrewdly discerning; also : WILY — ⟨an ~ lawyer⟩ — **as·tute·ly** adv — **as·tute·ness** n

asun·der \ə-'sən-dər\ adv or adj 1 : into separate pieces ⟨torn ~⟩ 2 : separated in position from each other

ASV abbr American Standard Version

¹**as well as** conj : and in addition : and moreover ⟨brave as well as loyal⟩

²**as well as** prep : in addition to : BESIDES ⟨the coach, as well as the team, is ready⟩

asy·lum \ə-'sī-ləm\ n [ME, fr. L, fr. Gk asylon, neut. of asylos inviolable, fr. a- not + sylon right of seizure] 1 : a place of refuge 2 : protection given to esp. political fugitives 3 : an institution for the care of the needy or sick and esp. of the insane

asym·met·ri·cal \ˌā-sə-'me-tri-kəl\ or **asym·met·ric** \-trik\ adj : not symmetrical — **asym·met·ri·cal·ly** \-tri-kə-lē\ adv — **asym·me·try** \(ˌ)ā-'si-mə-trē\ n

asymp·tom·at·ic \ˌā-ˌsimp-tə-'ma-tik\ adj : presenting no symptoms of disease ⟨an ~ infection⟩

as·ymp·tote \'a-səmp-ˌtōt\ n : a straight line that is approached ever more closely by a curve that never coincides with it — **as·ymp·tot·ic** \ˌa-səmp-'tä-tik\ adj — **as·ymp·tot·i·cal·ly** \-ti-k(ə-)lē\ adv

¹**at** \ət, (ˈ)at\ prep 1 — used to indicate a point in time or space ⟨be here ~ 3 o'clock⟩ 2 — used to indicate a goal ⟨swung ~ the ball⟩ 3 — used to indicate position or condition ⟨~ rest⟩ 4 — used to indicate means, cause, or manner ⟨sold ~ auction⟩

²**at** also **att** \'ät\ n, pl **at** also **att** — see kip at MONEY table

At symbol astatine

AT abbr automatic transmission

at all adv : in any way : in any circumstances ⟨not at all likely⟩

at·a·vism \'a-tə-ˌvi-zəm\ n : appearance in an individual of a character typical of an ancestral form; also : such an individual or character — **at·a·vis·tic** \ˌa-tə-'vis-tik\ adj

atax·ia \ə-'tak-sē-ə\ n : an inability to coordinate muscular movements

ate past of EAT

¹**-ate** n suffix 1 : one acted upon (in a specified way) ⟨distillate⟩ 2 : chemical compound or complex derived from a (specified) compound or element ⟨acetate⟩

²**-ate** n suffix 1 : office : function : rank : group of persons holding a (specified) office or rank ⟨episcopate⟩ 2 : state : dominion : jurisdiction ⟨emirate⟩

³**-ate** adj suffix 1 : acted on (in a specified way) : being in a (specified) state ⟨temperate⟩ ⟨degenerate⟩ 2 : marked by having ⟨vertebrate⟩

⁴**-ate** vb suffix : cause to be modified or affected by ⟨pollinate⟩ : cause to become ⟨activate⟩ : furnish with ⟨aerate⟩

ate·lier \ˌa-tᵊl-'yā\ n 1 : an artist's or designer's studio 2 : WORKSHOP

athe·ist \'ā-thē-ist\ n : one who denies the existence of God — **athe·ism** \-ˌi-zəm\ n — **athe·is·tic** \ˌā-thē-'is-tik\ adj

ath·e·nae·um or **ath·e·ne·um** \ˌa-thə-'nē-əm\ n : LIBRARY 1

ath·ero·scle·ro·sis \ˌa-thə-rō-sklə-'rō-səs\ n : arteriosclerosis characterized by the deposition of fatty substances in and the hardening of the inner layer of the arteries — **ath·ero·scle·rot·ic** \-'rä-tik\ adj

athirst \ə-'thərst\ adj 1 archaic : THIRSTY 2 : EAGER, LONGING

ath·lete \'ath-ˌlēt\ n [ME, fr. L athleta, fr. Gk athlētēs, fr. athlein to contend for a prize, fr. athlon prize, contest] : a person who is trained to compete in athletics

athlete's foot n : ringworm of the feet

ath·let·ic \ath-'le-tik\ adj 1 : of or relating to athletes or athletics 2 : VIGOROUS, ACTIVE 3 : STURDY, MUSCULAR — **ath·let·i·cal·ly** \-ti-kə-lē\ adv — **ath·let·i·cism** \-tə-ˌsi-zəm\ n

ath·let·ics \ath-'le-tiks\ n sing or pl : exercises and games requiring physical skill, strength, and endurance

athletic supporter n : an elastic pouch used to support the male genitals and worn esp. during athletic activity

¹**athwart** \ə-'thwort\ prep 1 : ACROSS 2 : in opposition to

²**athwart** adv : obliquely across

atilt \ə-'tilt\ adv or adj 1 : in a tilted position 2 : with lance in hand

-ation n suffix : action or process ⟨flirtation⟩ : something connected with an action or process ⟨discoloration⟩

Atl abbr Atlantic

at-large \'at-'lärj\ adj : of or being a political representative who is elected to serve an entire area rather than one of its subdivisions

at·las \'at-ləs\ n : a book of maps

atm abbr atmosphere; atmospheric

ATM n : a computerized electronic machine that performs basic banking functions

at·mo·sphere \'at-mə-ˌsfir\ n 1 : the gaseous envelope of a celestial body; esp : the mass of air surrounding the earth 2 : a surrounding influence 3 : a unit of pressure equal to the pressure of air at sea level or about 14.7 pounds per square inch (10 newtons per square centimeter) **4** : an intriguing or singular tone, effect, or appeal — **at·mo·spher·ic** \ˌat-mə-'sfir-ik, -'sfer-\ *adj* — **at·mo·spher·i·cal·ly** \-i-k(ə-)lē\ *adv*

at·mo·sphe·rics \at-mə-'sfir-iks, -'sfer-\ *n pl* : radio noise from atmospheric electrical phenomena

atoll \'a-ˌtól, -ˌtäl, 'ä-\ *n* : a coral island consisting of a reef surrounding a lagoon

at·om \'a-təm\ *n* [ME, fr. L *atomus*, fr. Gk *atomos*, fr. *atomos* indivisible, fr. *a-* not + *temnein* to cut] **1** : a tiny particle : BIT **2** : the smallest particle of a chemical element that can exist alone or in combination

atom·ic \ə-'tä-mik\ *adj* **1** : of or relating to atoms; *also* : NUCLEAR 2 ⟨∼ energy⟩ **2** : extremely small

atomic bomb *n* : a very destructive bomb utilizing the energy released by splitting the atom

atomic clock *n* : a very precise clock regulated by the natural vibration of atoms or molecules (as of cesium)

atomic number *n* : the number of protons in the nucleus of an element

atomic weight *n* : the mass of one atom of an element

at·om·ise, at·om·is·er *Brit var of* ATOMIZE, ATOMIZER

at·om·ize \'a-tə-ˌmīz\ *vb* **-ized; -iz·ing** : to reduce to minute particles

at·om·iz·er \'a-tə-ˌmī-zər\ *n* : a device for dispensing a liquid (as perfume) as a mist

atom smasher *n* : ACCELERATOR 3

aton·al \ä-'tō-n°l\ *adj* : marked by avoidance of traditional musical tonality — **ato·nal·i·ty** \ˌä-tō-'na-lə-tē\ *n* — **aton·al·ly** \ä-'tō-nə-lē\ *adv*

atone \ə-'tōn\ *vb* **atoned; aton·ing 1** : to make amends **2** : EXPIATE ⟨∼ for sins⟩

atone·ment \ə-'tōn-mənt\ *n* **1** : the reconciliation of God and mankind through the death of Jesus Christ **2** : reparation for an offense : SATISFACTION

¹atop \ə-'täp\ *adv or adj* : on, to, or at the top

²atop *prep* : on top of

ATP \ˌā-ˌtē-'pē\ *n* [adenosine *tri*phosphate] : a compound that occurs widely in living tissue and supplies energy for many cellular processes by undergoing enzymatic hydrolysis

atri·um \'ā-trē-əm\ *n, pl* **atria** \-trē-ə\ *also* **atri·ums** : the central room of a Roman house; *also* : an open patio or court in the center of a building (as a hotel) **2** : an anatomical cavity or passage; *esp* : one of the chambers of the heart that receives blood from the veins — **atri·al** \-əl\ *adj*

atro·cious \ə-'trō-shəs\ *adj* **1** : savagely brutal, cruel, or wicked **2** : very bad : ABOMINABLE — **atro·cious·ly** *adv* — **atro·cious·ness** *n*

atroc·i·ty \ə-'trä-sə-tē\ *n, pl* **-ties 1** : ATROCIOUSNESS **2** : an atrocious act or object ⟨the *atrocities* of war⟩

at·ro·phy \'a-trə-fē\ *n, pl* **-phies** : decrease in size or wasting away of a bodily part or tissue — **atrophy** *vb*

at·ro·pine \'a-trə-ˌpēn\ *n* : a drug from belladonna and related plants used esp. to relieve spasms and to dilate the pupil of the eye

¹att *var of* AT

²att *abbr* **1** attached **2** attention **3** attorney

at·tach \ə-'tach\ *vb* **1** : to seize legally in order to force payment of a debt **2** : to bind by personal ties **3** : FASTEN, CONNECT **4** : to be fastened or connected

at·ta·ché \ˌa-tə-'shā, ˌa-ˌta-, ə-ˌta-\ *n* [F] : a technical expert on the diplomatic staff of an ambassador

at·ta·ché case \ə-'ta-shā-, ˌa-tə-'shā-\ *n* : a small thin suitcase used esp. for carrying papers; *also* : BRIEFCASE

at·tach·ment \ə-'tach-mənt\ *n* **1** : legal seizure of property **2** : connection by ties of affection and regard **3** : a device attached to a machine or implement **4** : a connection by which one thing is attached to another **5** : a document or image included with an electronic message

¹at·tack \ə-'tak\ *vb* **1** : to set upon with force or words : ASSAIL, ASSAULT **2** : to set to work on

²attack *n* **1** : an offensive action **2** : a fit of sickness **3** : a scoring action in a game

³attack *adj* : designed, planned, or used for a military attack

at·tain \ə-'tān\ *vb* **1** : ACHIEVE, ACCOMPLISH **2** : to arrive at : REACH — **at·tain·abil·i·ty** \-'tā-nə-'bi-lə-tē\ *n* — **at·tain·able** *adj*

at·tain·der \ə-'tān-dər\ *n* : extinction of the civil rights of a person upon sentence of death or outlawry

at·tain·ment \ə-'tān-mənt\ *n* **1** : the act of attaining **2** : ACCOMPLISHMENT

at·tar \'a-tər\ *n* [Pers *'aṭir* perfumed, fr. Ar, fr. *'iṭr* perfume] : a fragrant floral oil

at·tempt \ə-'tempt\ *vb* : to make an effort toward : TRY — **attempt** *n*

at·tend \ə-'tend\ *vb* **1** : to look after : TEND **2** : to be present with **3** : to be present at **4** : to apply oneself **5** : to pay attention **6** : to direct one's attention

at·ten·dance \ə-'ten-dəns\ *n* **1** : the act or fact of attending **2** : the number of persons present; *also* : the number of times a person attends

¹at·ten·dant \ə-'ten-dənt\ *n* : one that attends another to render a service

²attendant *adj* : ACCOMPANYING ⟨∼ circumstances⟩

at·ten·tion \ə-'ten-chən\ *n* **1** : the act or state of applying the mind to an object **2** : CONSIDERATION **3** : an act of courtesy **4** : a position of readiness assumed on command by a soldier — **at·ten·tive** \-'ten-tiv\ *adj* — **at·ten·tive·ly** *adv* — **at·ten·tive·ness** *n*

attention deficit disorder *n* : a behavioral syndrome esp. of children that is marked by hyperactivity, impulsive behavior, and inattention

attention–deficit/hyperactivity disorder *n* : ATTENTION DEFICIT DISORDER

attention span *n* : the length of time during which one is able to concentrate or remain interested

at·ten·u·ate \ə-'ten-yə-ˌwāt\ *vb* **-at·ed; -at·ing 1** : to make or become thin **2** : WEAKEN ⟨sorrows ∼ with time⟩ — **at·tenuate** \-wət\ *adj* — **at·ten·u·a·tion** \-ˌten-yə-'wā-shən\ *n*

at·test \ə-'test\ *vb* **1** : to certify as genuine by signing as a witness **2** : MANIFEST ⟨her record ∼s her integrity⟩ **3** : TESTIFY ⟨∼ to a belief⟩ — **at·tes·ta·tion** \ˌa-ˌtes-'tä-shən\ *n*

at·tic \'a-tik\ *n* : the space or room in a building immediately below the roof

¹at·tire \ə-'tī(-ə)r\ *vb* **at·tired; at·tir·ing** : to put garments on : DRESS, ARRAY

²attire *n* : DRESS, CLOTHES

at·ti·tude \'a-tə-ˌtüd, -ˌtyüd\ *n* **1** : POSTURE **2** : a mental position or feeling with regard to a fact or state **3** : the position of something in relation to something else **4** : a negative or hostile state of mind **5** : a cocky or arrogant manner

at·ti·tu·di·nise *Brit var of* ATTITUDINIZE

at·ti·tu·di·nize \ˌa-tə-'tüd-də-ˌniz, -'tyü-\ *vb* **-nized; -niz·ing** : to assume an affected mental attitude : POSE

attn *abbr* attention

at·tor·ney \ə-'tər-nē\ *n, pl* **-neys** : a legal agent qualified to act for persons in legal proceedings

attorney general *n, pl* **attorneys general** *or* **attorney generals** : the chief legal representative and adviser of a nation or state

at·tract \ə-'trakt\ *vb* **1** : to draw to or toward oneself : cause to approach **2** : to draw by emotional or aesthetic appeal ♦ *Synonyms* CHARM, FASCINATE, ALLURE, CAPTIVATE, ENCHANT — **at·trac·tive** \-'trak-tiv\ *adj* — **at·trac·tive·ly** *adv* — **at·trac·tive·ness** *n*

at·trac·tant \ə-'trak-tənt\ *n* : a substance (as a pheromone) that attracts specific animals (as insects)

at·trac·tion \ə-'trak-shən\ *n* **1** : the act or power of attracting; *esp* : personal charm **2** : an attractive quality, object, or feature **3** : a force tending to draw particles together

attrib *abbr* attributive

¹at·tri·bute \'a-trə-ˌbyüt\ *n* **1** : an inherent characteristic **2** : a word ascribing a quality; *esp* : ADJECTIVE

²at·trib·ute \ə-'tri-ˌbyüt, -byət\ *vb* **-ut·ed; -ut·ing 1** : to explain as to cause or origin ⟨∼ the illness to fatigue⟩ **2** : to regard as a characteristic ♦ *Synonyms* ASCRIBE, CREDIT, CHARGE, IMPUTE — **at·trib·ut·able** *adj* — **at·tri·bu·tion** \ˌa-trə-'byü-shən\ *n*

at·trib·u·tive \ə-'tri-byə-tiv\ *adj* : joined directly to a modified noun without a linking verb ⟨*red* in red *hair* is an ∼ adjective⟩ — **attributive** *n* — **at·trib·u·tive·ly** *adv*

at·tri·tion \ə-'tri-shən\ *n* **1** : the act of wearing away by or as if by rubbing **2** : a reduction in numbers as a result of resignation, retirement, or death

at·tune \ə-'tün, -'tyün\ *vb* : to bring into harmony : TUNE — **at·tune·ment** *n*

atty *abbr* attorney
ATV \ˌā-ˌtē-ˈvē\ *n* : ALL-TERRAIN VEHICLE
atyp·i·cal \ā-ˈti-pi-kəl\ *adj* : not typical : IRREGULAR —
atyp·i·cal·ly \-k(ə-)lē\ *adv*
Au *symbol* [L *aurum*] gold
au·burn \ˈȯ-bərn\ *adj* : reddish brown — **auburn** *n*
au cou·rant \ˌō-kù-ˈränⁿ\ *adj* [F, lit., in the current] : UP-TO-DATE, STYLISH
¹**auc·tion** \ˈȯk-shən\ *n* [L *auction-, auctio,* fr. *augēre* to increase] : public sale of property to the highest bidder
²**auction** *vb* **auc·tioned; auc·tion·ing** \-shə-niŋ\ : to sell at auction
auc·tion·eer \ˌȯk-shə-ˈnir\ *n* : an agent who conducts an auction
aud *abbr* audit; auditor
au·da·cious \ȯ-ˈdā-shəs\ *adj* **1** : DARING, BOLD **2** : INSOLENT — **au·da·cious·ly** *adv* — **au·da·cious·ness** *n* — **au·dac·i·ty** \-ˈda-sə-tē\ *n*
¹**au·di·ble** \ˈȯ-də-bəl\ *adj* : capable of being heard — **au·di·bil·i·ty** \ˌȯ-də-ˈbi-lə-tē\ *n* — **au·di·bly** \ˈȯ-də-blē\ *adv*
²**audible** *n* : a play called at the line of scrimmage — **audible** *vb*
au·di·ence \ˈȯ-dē-əns\ *n* **1** : a formal interview **2** : an opportunity of being heard **3** : an assembly of listeners or spectators
¹**au·dio** \ˈȯ-dē-ˌō\ *adj* **1** : of or relating to frequencies (as of radio waves) corresponding to those of audible sound waves **2** : of or relating to sound or its reproduction and esp. high-fidelity reproduction **3** : relating to or used in the transmission or reception of sound
²**audio** *n* **1** : the transmission, reception, or reproduction of sound **2** : the section of television or motion-picture equipment that deals with sound
au·dio·book \ˈȯ-dē-ō-ˌbùk\ *n* : a recording of a book or magazine being read aloud
au·di·ol·o·gy \ˌȯ-dē-ˈä-lə-jē\ *n* : a branch of science dealing with hearing and esp. with the treatment of individuals having trouble with hearing — **au·di·o·log·i·cal** \-ə-ˈlä-ji-kəl\ *adj* — **au·di·ol·o·gist** \-ˈä-lə-jist\ *n*
au·dio·phile \ˈȯ-dē-ō-ˌfī(-ə)l\ *n* : one who is enthusiastic about high-fidelity sound reproduction
au·dio·tape \ˈȯ-dē-ō-ˌtāp\ *n* : a tape recording of sound
au·dio·vi·su·al \ˌȯ-dē-ō-ˈvi-zhə-wəl\ *adj* : of, relating to, or making use of both hearing and sight
au·dio·vi·su·als \-wəlz\ *n pl* : audiovisual teaching materials (as videotapes)
¹**au·dit** \ˈȯ-dət\ *n* : a formal examination and verification of financial accounts
²**audit** *vb* **1** : to perform an audit on or for **2** : to attend (a course) without expecting formal credit
¹**au·di·tion** \ȯ-ˈdi-shən\ *n* **1** : HEARING **2** : a trial performance to appraise an entertainer's merits
²**audition** *vb* **-tioned; -tion·ing** \-ˈdi-shə-niŋ\ : to give an audition to; *also* : to give a trial performance
au·di·tor \ˈȯ-də-tər\ *n* **1** : LISTENER **2** : a person who audits
au·di·to·ri·um \ˌȯ-də-ˈtȯr-ē-əm\ *n, pl* **-ri·ums** *or* **-ria** \-rē-ə\ **1** : the part of a public building where an audience sits **2** : a hall or building used for public gatherings
au·di·to·ry \ˈȯ-də-ˌtȯr-ē\ *adj* : of or relating to hearing or to the sense or organs of hearing ⟨~ stimuli⟩
auditory tube *n* : EUSTACHIAN TUBE
auf Wie·der·seh·en \aùf-ˈvē-dər-ˌzān\ *interj* [G] — used to express farewell
Aug *abbr* August
au·ger \ˈȯ-gər\ *n* : a tool for boring

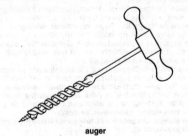

auger

aught \ˈȯt, ˈät\ *n* : ZERO, CIPHER
aug·ment \ȯg-ˈment\ *vb* : ENLARGE, INCREASE — **aug·men·ta·tion** \ˌȯg-mən-ˈtā-shən\ *n*
au gra·tin \ō-ˈgra-tⁿn, ȯ-, -ˈgrä-\ *adj* [F, lit., with the burnt scrapings from the pan] : covered with bread crumbs or grated cheese and browned
¹**au·gur** \ˈȯ-gər\ *n* : DIVINER, SOOTHSAYER
²**augur** *vb* **1** : to foretell esp. from omens **2** : to give promise of ⟨the decision doesn't ~ well⟩
au·gu·ry \ˈȯ-gyə-rē, -gə-\ *n, pl* **-ries 1** : divination from omens **2** : OMEN, PORTENT
au·gust \ȯ-ˈgəst\ *adj* : marked by majestic dignity or grandeur — **au·gust·ly** *adv* — **au·gust·ness** *n*
Au·gust \ˈȯ-gəst\ *n* [ME, fr. OE, fr. L *Augustus,* fr. *Augustus* Caesar] : the 8th month of the year
au jus \ō-ˈzhü, -ˈzhüs, -ˈjüs; ō-zhœ\ *adj* [F] : served in the juice obtained from roasting
auk \ˈȯk\ *n* : any of several stocky black-and-white diving seabirds that breed in colder parts of the northern hemisphere
auld \ˈȯl, ˈȯld, ˈäl, ˈäld\ *adj chiefly Scot* : OLD
aunt \ˈant, ˈänt\ *n* **1** : the sister of one's father or mother **2** : the wife of one's uncle or aunt
aunt·ie \ˈan-tē, ˈän-\ *n* : AUNT
au pair \ō-ˈper\ *n* [F, on even terms] : a usu. young foreign person who does domestic work for a family in return for room and board and to learn the family's language
au·ra \ˈȯr-ə\ *n* **1** : a distinctive atmosphere surrounding a given source **2** : a luminous radiation
au·ral \ˈȯr-əl\ *adj* : of or relating to the ear or to the sense of hearing
aurar *pl of* EYRIR
au·re·ole \ˈȯr-ē-ˌōl\ *or* **au·re·o·la** \ȯ-ˈrē-ə-lə\ *n* : HALO, NIMBUS
au re·voir \ˌō-rə-ˈvwär\ *n* [F, lit., till seeing again] : GOOD-BYE
au·ri·cle \ˈȯr-i-kəl\ *n* : an atrium of the heart
au·ric·u·lar \ȯ-ˈri-kyə-lər\ *adj* **1** : told privately ⟨~ confession⟩ **2** : known or recognized by the sense of hearing
au·ro·ra \ə-ˈrȯr-ə\ *n, pl* **auroras** *or* **au·ro·rae** \-(ˌ)ē\ : a luminous phenomenon of streamers or arches of light appearing in the upper atmosphere esp. of a planet's polar regions — **au·ro·ral** \-əl\ *adj*
aurora aus·tra·lis \-ȯ-ˈstrā-ləs\ *n* : an aurora that occurs in earth's southern hemisphere
aurora bo·re·al·is \-ˌbȯr-ē-ˈa-ləs\ *n* : an aurora that occurs in earth's northern hemisphere
AUS *abbr* Army of the United States
aus·pice \ˈȯ-spəs\ *n, pl* **aus·pic·es** \-spə-səz, -ˌsēz\ [L *auspicium,* fr. *auspic-, auspex* diviner by birds, fr. *avis* bird + *specere* to look, look at] **1** : observation of birds by an augur **2** *pl* : kindly patronage and protection **3** : a prophetic sign or omen
aus·pi·cious \ȯ-ˈspi-shəs\ *adj* **1** : promising success : PROPITIOUS **2** : FORTUNATE, PROSPEROUS ⟨an ~ year⟩ — **aus·pi·cious·ly** *adv* — **aus·pi·cious·ness** *n*
aus·tere \ȯ-ˈstir\ *adj* **1** : STERN, SEVERE, STRICT ⟨~ Puritans⟩ **2** : markedly simple ⟨an ~ lifestyle⟩ **3** : UNADORNED ⟨~ furnishings⟩ — **aus·tere·ly** *adv* — **aus·ter·i·ty** \-ˈster-ə-tē\ *n*
aus·tral \ˈȯs-trəl\ *adj* : SOUTHERN
Aus·tro·ne·sian \ˌȯs-trə-ˈnē-zhən\ *adj* : of, relating to, or constituting a family of languages spoken in the area extending from Madagascar eastward through the Malay Peninsula to Hawaii and Easter Island
auth *abbr* **1** authentic **2** author **3** authorized
au·then·tic \ə-ˈthen-tik, ȯ-\ *adj* : GENUINE, REAL — **au·then·ti·cal·ly** \-ti-k(ə-)lē\ *adv* — **au·then·tic·i·ty** \ˌȯ-ˌthen-ˈti-sə-tē\ *n*
au·then·ti·cate \ə-ˈthen-ti-ˌkāt, ȯ-\ *vb* **-cat·ed; -cat·ing** : to prove genuine — **au·then·ti·ca·tion** \-ˌthen-ti-ˈkā-shən\ *n*
au·thor \ˈȯ-thər\ *n* [ME *auctour,* fr. AF *auctor, autor,* fr. L *auctor* originator, author, fr. *augēre* to increase] **1** : one that originates or creates **2** : one that writes or composes a literary work
au·thor·ess \ˈȯ-thə-rəs\ *n* : a woman or girl who is an author
au·tho·ri·sa·tion, au·tho·rise *Brit var of* AUTHORIZATION, AUTHORIZE

au·thor·i·tar·i·an \ȯ-ˌthär-ə-'ter-ē-ən, ə-, -ˌthȯr-\ *adj* 1
: characterized by or favoring the principle of blind
obedience to authority 2 : characterized by or favoring
concentration of political power in an authority not responsible to the people — **authoritarian** *n*
au·thor·i·ta·tive \ə-'thär-ə-ˌtā-tiv, ȯ-, -'thȯr-\ *adj* : supported by, proceeding from, or being an authority —
au·thor·i·ta·tive·ly *adv* — **au·thor·i·ta·tive·ness** *n*
au·thor·i·ty \ə-'thär-ə-tē, ȯ-, -'thȯr-\ *n, pl* **-ties** 1 : a citation used in support of a statement or in defense of an
action; *also* : the source of such a citation 2 : one ap-
pealed to as an expert 3 : power to influence thought
or behavior 4 : freedom granted : RIGHT 5 : persons
in command; *esp* : GOVERNMENT 6 : convincing force
au·tho·rize \'ȯ-thə-ˌrīz\ *vb* **-rized; -riz·ing** 1 : SANCTION
⟨custom *authorized* by time⟩ 2 : to give legal power to
— **au·tho·ri·za·tion** \ˌȯ-thə-rə-'zā-shən\ *n*
au·thor·ship \'ȯ-thər-ˌship\ *n* 1 : the state of being an
author 2 : the source of a piece of writing, music, or art
au·tism \'ȯ-ˌti-zəm\ *n* : a disorder that appears by age
three and is characterized esp. by impaired ability to
communicate with others and form normal social relationships and by repetitive patterns of behavior —
au·tis·tic \ȯ-'tis-tik\ *adj or n*
¹au·to \'ȯ-tō\ *n, pl* **autos** : AUTOMOBILE
²auto *abbr* automatic
au·to·bahn \'ȯ-tō-ˌbän, 'aü-\ *n* : a German, Swiss, or Austrian expressway
au·to·bi·og·ra·phy \ˌȯ-tə-bī-'ä-grə-fē\ *n* : the biography of
a person narrated by that person — **au·to·bi·og·ra·pher**
\-fər\ *n* — **au·to·bi·o·graph·i·cal** \-ˌbī-ə-'gra-fi-kəl\ *adj*
— **au·to·bi·o·graph·i·cal·ly** \-k(ə-)lē\ *adv*
au·toch·tho·nous \ȯ-'täk-thə-nəs\ *adj* : INDIGENOUS, NA-
TIVE ⟨an ~ people⟩
au·to·clave \'ȯ-tō-ˌklāv\ *n* : an apparatus (as for steriliz-
ing) using superheated high-pressure steam
au·toc·ra·cy \ȯ-'tä-krə-sē\ *n, pl* **-cies** : government by one
person having unlimited power — **au·to·crat** \'ȯ-tə-ˌkrat\
n — **au·to·crat·ic** \ˌȯ-tə-'kra-tik\ *adj* — **au·to·crat·i·cal·ly**
\-ti-k(ə-)lē\ *adv*
au·to·ex·po·sure \ˌȯ-tō-ik-'spō-zhər\ *n* : a camera system
that automatically adjusts the exposure according to ambient light
¹au·to·graph \'ȯ-tə-ˌgraf\ *n* 1 : an original manuscript 2
: a person's signature written by hand
²autograph *vb* : to write one's signature on
au·to·im·mune \ˌȯ-tō-i-'myün\ *adj* : of, relating to, or
caused by antibodies or lymphocytes that attack molecules, cells, or tissues of the organism producing them
⟨~ diseases⟩ — **au·to·im·mu·ni·ty** \-i-'myü-nə-tē\ *n*
au·to·mate \'ȯ-tə-ˌmāt\ *vb* **-mat·ed; -mat·ing** 1 : to operate automatically using mechanical or electronic devices
2 : to convert to automatic operation — **au·to·ma·tion**
\ȯ-tə-'mā-shən\ *n*
automated teller machine *n* : ATM
¹au·to·mat·ic \ˌȯ-tə-'ma-tik\ *adj* 1 : INVOLUNTARY 2
: made so that certain parts act in a desired manner at
the proper time : SELF-ACTING ⟨an ~ transmission⟩ —
au·to·mat·i·cal·ly \-ti-k(ə-)lē\ *adv*
²automatic *n* 1 : an automatic firearm 2 : an automobile
with an automatic transmission
automatic teller *n* : ATM
automatic teller machine *n* : ATM
au·tom·a·ton \ȯ-'tä-mə-tən, -ˌtän\ *n, pl* **-atons** *or* **-a·ta**
\-ə-tə, -ə-ˌtä\ 1 : an automatic machine; *esp* : ROBOT 2
: an individual who acts mechanically
au·to·mo·bile \'ȯ-tə-mō-ˌbēl, ˌȯ-tə-mə-'bēl\ *n* : a usu.
4-wheeled automotive vehicle for conveying passengers
au·to·mo·tive \ˌȯ-tə-'mō-tiv\ *adj* 1 : of or relating to automobiles, trucks, or buses 2 : SELF-PROPELLED
au·to·nom·ic nervous system \ˌȯ-tə-'nä-mik-\ *n* : a part
of the vertebrate nervous system that governs involuntary actions and that consists of the sympathetic nervous
system and the parasympathetic nervous system
au·ton·o·mous \ȯ-'tä-nə-məs\ *adj* : having the right or
power of self-government — **au·ton·o·mous·ly** *adv* —
au·ton·o·my \-mē\ *n*
au·top·sy \'ȯ-ˌtäp-sē, 'ȯ-təp-\ *n, pl* **-sies** [Gk *autopsia* act
of seeing with one's own eyes, fr. *autos* self + *opsis* sight]
: examination of a dead body usu. with dissection suffi-

cient to determine the cause of death or extent of change
produced by disease — **autopsy** *vb*
au·tumn \'ȯ-təm\ *n* : the season between summer and
winter — **au·tum·nal** \ȯ-'təm-nəl\ *adj*
aux *abbr* auxiliary
¹aux·il·ia·ry \ȯg-'zil-yə-rē, -'zi-lə-rē\ *adj* 1 : providing help
2 : functioning in a subsidiary capacity 3 : accompanying
a verb form to express person, number, mood, or tense
⟨~ verbs⟩
²auxiliary *n, pl* **-ries** 1 : an auxiliary person, group, or device 2 : an auxiliary verb
aux·in \'ȯk-sən\ *n* : a plant hormone that stimulates
growth in length
av *abbr* 1 avenue 2 average 3 avoirdupois
AV *abbr* 1 ad valorem 2 audiovisual 3 Authorized Version
¹avail \ə-'vāl\ *vb* : to be of use or advantage : HELP, BENEFIT
²avail *n* : USE ⟨effort was of no ~⟩
avail·able \ə-'vā-lə-bəl\ *adj* 1 : USABLE ⟨~ resources⟩
2 : ACCESSIBLE ⟨~ in any drugstore⟩ — **avail·abil·i·ty**
\-ˌvā-lə-'bi-lə-tē\ *n*
av·a·lanche \'a-və-ˌlanch\ *n* : a mass of snow, ice, earth,
or rock sliding down a mountainside
avant–garde \ä-ˌvänt-'gärd, -ˌvänt-\ *n* [F, vanguard] : those
esp. in the arts who create or apply new or experimental
ideas and techniques — **avant–garde** *adj*
av·a·rice \'a-və-rəs\ *n* : excessive desire for wealth : GREED
— **av·a·ri·cious** \ˌa-və-'ri-shəs\ *adj*
avast \ə-'vast\ *vb imper* — a nautical command to stop
or cease
av·a·tar \'a-və-ˌtär\ *n* [Skt *avatāra* descent] : INCARNATION
avaunt \ə-'vȯnt\ *adv* : AWAY, HENCE
avdp *abbr* avoirdupois
ave *abbr* avenue
Ave Ma·ria \ˌä-ˌvä-mə-'rē-ə\ *n* : HAIL MARY 1
avenge \ə-'venj\ *vb* **avenged; aveng·ing** : to take vengeance for — **aveng·er** *n*
av·e·nue \'a-və-ˌnü, -ˌnyü\ *n* 1 : a way or route to a place
or goal : PATH 2 : a broad street
aver \ə-'vər\ *vb* **averred; aver·ring** : ALLEGE, ASSERT;
also : DECLARE
¹av·er·age \'a-və-rij, 'a-vrij\ *n* [earlier, proportionally distributed charge for damage at sea, modif. of MF *avarie*
damage to ship or cargo, fr. It *avaria*, fr. Ar *'awārīyah*
damaged merchandise] 1 : ARITHMETIC MEAN 2 : a ratio of successful tries to total tries esp. in athletics ⟨bat-
ting ~ of .303⟩
²average *adj* 1 : equaling or approximating an arithmetic mean 2 : being about midway between extremes 3
: not out of the ordinary : COMMON
³average *vb* **av·er·aged; av·er·ag·ing** 1 : to be at or
come to an average 2 : to be, do, or get usually 3 : to
find the average of
averse \ə-'vərs\ *adj* : having an active feeling of dislike or
reluctance ⟨~ to exercise⟩
aver·sion \ə-'vər-zhən\ *n* 1 : a feeling of repugnance for
something with a desire to avoid it 2 : something decidedly disliked
avert \ə-'vərt\ *vb* 1 : to turn aside or away ⟨~ the eyes⟩
2 : to ward off
avg *abbr* average
avi·an \'ā-vē-ən\ *adj* [L *avis* bird] : of, relating to, or derived from birds
avi·ary \'ā-vē-ˌer-ē\ *n, pl* **-ar·ies** : a place for keeping
birds confined
avi·a·tion \ˌā-vē-'ā-shən, ˌa-\ *n* 1 : the operation of heavier=
than-air aircraft 2 : aircraft manufacture, development,
and design
avi·a·tor \'ā-vē-ˌā-tər, 'a-\ *n* : an airplane pilot
avi·a·trix \ˌā-vē-'ā-triks, ˌa-\ *n, pl* **-trix·es** \-trik-səz\ *or*
-tri·ces \-trə-ˌsēz\ : a woman who is an aviator
av·id \'a-vəd\ *adj* 1 : craving eagerly : GREEDY 2
: enthusiastic in pursuit of an interest — **avid·i·ty** \ə-'vi-
də-tē, a-\ *n* — **av·id·ly** *adv* — **av·id·ness** *n*
avi·on·ics \ˌā-vē-'ä-niks, ˌa-\ *n pl* : electronics designed
for use in aerospace vehicles — **avi·on·ic** \-nik\ *adj*
avo \'ä-(ˌ)vō\ *n, pl* **avos** — see MONEY table
av·o·ca·do \ˌa-və-'kä-dō, ˌä-\ *n, pl* **-dos** *also* **-does** [modif.
of Sp *aguacate*, fr. Nahuatl *āhuacatl*, avocado, testicle]
: a pulpy green- to purple-skinned nutty-flavored fruit of
a tropical American tree; *also* : this tree

av·o·ca·tion \ˌa-və-ˈkā-shən\ *n* : HOBBY
av·o·cet \ˈa-və-ˌset\ *n* : any of several long-legged shore-birds with webbed feet and slender upward-curving bills
avoid \ə-ˈvȯid\ *vb* **1** : to keep away from : SHUN **2** : to prevent the occurrence of **3** : to refrain from — **avoid·able** *adj* — **avoid·ably** *adv* — **avoid·ance** \ə-ˈvȯi-dəns\ *n*
av·oir·du·pois \ˌa-vər-də-ˈpȯiz\ *n* [ME *avoir de pois* goods sold by weight, fr. AF, lit., goods of weight] **1** : AVOIRDUPOIS WEIGHT **2** : WEIGHT, HEAVINESS; *esp* : personal weight
avoirdupois weight *n* : a system of weights based on a pound of 16 ounces and an ounce of 16 drams (28 grams) — see WEIGHT table
avouch \ə-ˈvau̇ch\ *vb* **1** : to declare positively : AVER **2** : to vouch for
avow \ə-ˈvau̇\ *vb* : to declare openly — **avow·al** \-ˈvau̇-(ə)l\ *n*
avun·cu·lar \ə-ˈvəŋ-kyə-lər\ *adj* : of, relating to, or resembling an uncle
await \ə-ˈwāt\ *vb* : to wait for : EXPECT
¹awake \ə-ˈwāk\ *vb* **awoke** \-ˈwōk\ *also* **awaked** \-ˈwākt\; **awo·ken** \-ˈwō-kən\ *or* **awaked** *also* **awoke**; **awak·ing** : to bring back to consciousness : wake up
²awake *adj* : not asleep; *also* : ALERT
awak·en \ə-ˈwā-kən\ *vb* **awak·ened**; **awak·en·ing** \-ˈwā-kə-niŋ\ : AWAKE
¹award \ə-ˈwȯrd\ *vb* **1** : to give by judicial decision ⟨∼ damages⟩ **2** : to give in recognition of merit or achievement
²award *n* **1** : a final decision : JUDGMENT **2** : something awarded : PRIZE
aware \ə-ˈwer\ *adj* : having perception or knowledge : CONSCIOUS, INFORMED — **aware·ness** *n*
awash \ə-ˈwȯsh, -ˈwäsh\ *adj* **1** : washed by waves or tide **2** : AFLOAT **3** : FLOODED ⟨the street was ∼ after the storm⟩
¹away \ə-ˈwā\ *adv* **1** : from this or that place ⟨go ∼⟩ **2** : out of the way **3** : in another direction ⟨turn ∼⟩ **4** : out of existence ⟨fade ∼⟩ **5** : from one's possession ⟨give ∼⟩ **6** : without interruption ⟨chatter ∼⟩ **7** : at a distance in space or time ⟨far ∼⟩ ⟨∼ back in 1910⟩
²away *adj* **1** : ABSENT **2** : distant in space or time ⟨a lake 10 miles ∼⟩
¹awe \ˈȯ\ *n* **1** : profound and reverent dread of the supernatural **2** : respectful fear inspired by authority
²awe *vb* **awed**; **aw·ing** : to inspire with awe
aweigh \ə-ˈwā\ *adj* : just clear of the bottom ⟨anchors ∼⟩
awe·some \ˈȯ-səm\ *adj* **1** : expressive of awe ⟨∼ tribute⟩ **2** : inspiring awe
awe·struck \-ˌstrək\ *also* **awe·strick·en** \-ˌstri-kən\ *adj* : filled with awe
aw·ful \ˈȯ-fəl\ *adj* **1** : inspiring awe **2** : extremely dis-

agreeable **3** : very great ⟨an ∼ lot of money⟩
aw·ful·ly *adv*
awhile \ə-ˈhwī(-ə)l\ *adv* : for a while
awhirl \ə-ˈhwərl\ *adj* : being in a whirl
awk·ward \ˈȯ-kwərd\ *adj* **1** : CLUMSY ⟨∼ with needle and thread⟩ **2** : UNGRACEFUL ⟨∼ writing⟩ **3** : difficult to explain : EMBARRASSING **4** : difficult to deal with — **awk·ward·ly** *adv* — **awk·ward·ness** *n*
awl \ˈȯl\ *n* : a pointed instrument for making small holes
aw·ning \ˈȯ-niŋ\ *n* : a rooflike cover (as of canvas) extended over or in front of a place as a shelter
AWOL \ˈā-ˌwȯl, ˌā-ˌdə-bəl-yü-ˌō-ˈel\ *n* : a person who is absent without leave — **AWOL** *adj or adv*
awry \ə-ˈrī\ *adv or adj* **1** : ASKEW ⟨with hair ∼⟩ **2** : AMISS ⟨their plans went ∼⟩
ax *or* **axe** \ˈaks\ *n* : a chopping or cutting tool with an edged head fitted parallel to a handle
ax·i·al \ˈak-sē-əl\ *adj* **1** : of, relating to, or functioning as an axis **2** : situated around, in the direction of, on, or along an axis — **ax·i·al·ly** *adv*
ax·i·om \ˈak-sē-əm\ *n* [L *axioma*, fr. Gk *axiōma*, lit., something worthy, fr. *axioun* to think worthy, fr. *axios* worth, worthy] **1** : a statement generally accepted as true : MAXIM **2** : a proposition regarded as a self= evident truth — **ax·i·om·at·ic** \ˌak-sē-ə-ˈma-tik\ *adj* — **ax·i·om·at·i·cal·ly** \-ti-k(ə-)lē\ *adv*
ax·is \ˈak-səs\ *n, pl* **ax·es** \-ˌsēz\ **1** : a straight line around which a body rotates **2** : a straight line or structure with respect to which a body or figure is symmetrical **3** : one of the reference lines of a system of coordinates **4** : an alliance between major powers
ax·le \ˈak-səl\ *n* : a shaft on which a wheel revolves
ax·on \ˈak-ˌsän\ *n* : the long thin usu. unbranched part of a nerve cell that usu. conducts impulses away from the cell body
ayah \ˈī-ə\ *n* [Hindi & Urdu *āyā*, fr. Pg *aia*, fr. L *avia* grandmother] : a nurse or maid native to India
aya·tol·lah \ˌī-ə-ˈtō-lə\ *n* [Pers *āyatollāh*, lit., sign of God, fr. Ar *aya* sign, miracle + *allāh* God] : an Islamic religious leader — used as a title of respect
¹aye *also* **ay** \ˈā\ *adv* : ALWAYS, EVER
²aye *also* **ay** \ˈī\ *adv* : YES
³aye *also* **ay** \ˈī\ *n, pl* **ayes** : an affirmative vote
AZ *abbr* Arizona
aza·lea \ə-ˈzāl-yə\ *n* : any of numerous rhododendrons with funnel-shaped blossoms and usu. deciduous leaves
az·i·do·thy·mi·dine \ə-ˌzī-dō-ˈthī-mə-ˌdēn\ *n* : AZT
az·i·muth \ˈa-zə-məth\ *n* : horizontal direction expressed as an angular distance from a fixed point
AZT \ˌā-(ˌ)zē-ˈtē\ *n* : an antiviral drug used to treat AIDS
Az·tec \ˈaz-ˌtek\ *n* : a member of a Nahuatl-speaking people that founded the Mexican empire and were conquered by Hernan Cortes in 1519 — **Az·tec·an** *adj*
azure \ˈa-zhər\ *n* : the blue of the clear sky — **azure** *adj*

¹b \ˈbē\ *n, pl* **b's** *or* **bs** \ˈbēz\ *often cap* **1** : the 2d letter of the English alphabet **2** : a grade rating a student's work as good
²b *abbr, often cap* **1** bachelor **2** bass **3** bishop **4** book **5** born
B *symbol* boron
Ba *symbol* barium
BA *abbr* **1** bachelor of arts **2** batting average
bab·ble \ˈba-bəl\ *vb* **bab·bled**; **bab·bling** **1** : to talk enthusiastically or excessively **2** : to utter meaningless sounds — **babble** *n* — **bab·bler** \-b(ə-)lər\ *n*
babe \ˈbāb\ *n* **1** : BABY **2** *slang* : GIRL, WOMAN **3** *slang* : a person who is physically attractive
ba·bel \ˈbā-bəl, ˈba-\ *n, often cap* [fr. the Tower of *Babel*, Gen 11:4–9] : a place or scene of noise and confusion;

also : a confused sound ♦ **Synonyms** HUBBUB, RACKET, DIN, UPROAR, CLAMOR
ba·boon \ba-ˈbün\ *n* [ME *babewin*, fr. MF *babouin*, fr. *baboue* grimace] : any of several large apes of Asia and Africa with doglike muzzles
ba·bush·ka \bə-ˈbüsh-kə, -ˈbüsh-\ *n* [Russ, grandmother, dim. of *baba* old woman] : a kerchief for the head
¹ba·by \ˈbā-bē\ *n, pl* **babies** **1** : a very young child : INFANT **2** : the youngest or smallest of a group **3** : a childish person — **baby** *adj* — **ba·by·hood** *n* — **ba·by·ish** *adj*
²baby *vb* **ba·bied**; **ba·by·ing** : to tend or treat often with excessive care
baby boom *n* : a marked rise in birthrate — **baby boom·er** \-ˈbü-mər\ *n*

baby's breath *n* : any of a genus of herbs that are related to the pinks and have small delicate flowers

ba·by·sit \'bā-bē-ˌsit\ *vb* **-sat** \-ˌsat\; **-sit·ting** : to care for children usu. during a short absence of the parents — **ba·by·sit·ter** *n*

bac·ca·lau·re·ate \ˌba-kə-'lȯr-ē-ət\ *n* **1** : the degree of bachelor conferred by colleges and universities **2** : a sermon delivered to a graduating class

bac·ca·rat \ˌbä-kə-'rä, ˌba-\ *n* : a card game in which three hands are dealt and players may bet either or both hands against the dealer's

bac·cha·nal \'ba-kə-nᵊl, ˌba-kə-'nal, ˌbä-kə-'näl\ *n* **1** : ORGY **2** : REVELER

bac·cha·na·lia \ˌba-kə-'näl-yə\ *n, pl* **bacchanalia** : a drunken orgy — **bac·cha·na·lian** \-'näl-yən\ *adj or n*

bach·e·lor \'bach-lər, 'ba-chə-lər\ *n* **1** : a person who has received the usu. lowest degree conferred by a 4-year college **2** : an unmarried man — **bach·e·lor·hood** *n*

bach·e·lor·ette \ˌbach-lə-'ret, ˌba-chə-\ *n* : a young unmarried woman

bachelor's button *n* : a European plant related to the daisies and having usu. blue, pink, or white flower heads

ba·cil·lus \bə-'si-ləs\ *n, pl* **-li** \-ˌlī\ [NL, fr. ML, small staff, dim. of L *baculus* staff] : any of a genus of rod-shaped bacteria; *also* : a disease-producing bacterium — **bac·il·lary** \'ba-sə-ˌler-ē\ *adj*

¹back \'bak\ *n* **1** : the rear or dorsal part of the human body; *also* : the corresponding part of a lower animal **2** : the part or surface opposite the front **3** : a player in the backfield in football — **back·less** \-ləs\ *adj*

²back *adv* **1** : to, toward, or at the rear **2** : AGO **3** : so as to be restrained or delayed **4** : to, toward, or in a former place or state **5** : in return or reply

³back *adj* **1** : located at or in the back; *also* : REMOTE **2** : OVERDUE ⟨~ rent⟩ **3** : moving or operating backward **4** : not current ⟨~ issues of a magazine⟩

⁴back *vb* **1** : SUPPORT, UPHOLD **2** : to go or cause to go backward or in reverse **3** : to furnish with a back : form the back of — **back·er** *n*

back·ache \-ˌāk\ *n* : a pain in the lower back

back–bench·er \-'ben-chər\ *n* : a rank-and-file member of a British legislature

back·bite \-ˌbīt\ *vb* **-bit** \-ˌbit\; **-bit·ten** \-ˌbi-tᵊn\; **-bit·ing** \-ˌbī-tiŋ\ : to say mean or spiteful things about someone who is absent — **back·bit·er** *n*

back·board \-ˌbȯrd\ *n* : a board placed at or serving as the back of something

back·bone \-ˌbōn\ *n* **1** : the bony column in the back of a vertebrate that is the chief support of the trunk and consists of a jointed series of vertebrae enclosing and protecting the spinal cord **2** : firm resolute character **3** : the primary high-speed hardware and transmission lines of a telecommunication network

back·drop \'bak-ˌdräp\ *n* : a painted cloth hung across the rear of a stage

back·field \-ˌfēld\ *n* : the football players whose positions are behind the line

¹back·fire \-ˌfī(-ə)r\ *n* : a loud noise caused by the improperly timed explosion of fuel in the cylinder of an internal combustion engine

²backfire *vb* **1** : to make or undergo a backfire **2** : to have a result opposite to what was intended

back·flip \-ˌflip\ *n* : a backward somersault esp. in the air

back·gam·mon \'bak-ˌga-mən\ *n* : a game played with pieces on a double board in which the moves are determined by throwing dice

back·ground \'bak-ˌgraúnd\ *n* **1** : the scenery behind something **2** : the setting within which something takes place; *also* : the sum of a person's experience, training, and understanding

back·hand \'bak-ˌhand\ *n* : a stroke (as in tennis) made with the back of the hand turned in the direction of movement; *also* : the side on which such a stroke is made — **back·hand** *vb*

back·hand·ed \'bak-'han-dəd\ *adj* **1** : INDIRECT, DEVIOUS; *esp* : SARCASTIC ⟨a ~ compliment⟩ **2** : using or made with a backhand ⟨a ~ catch⟩

back·hoe \'bak-ˌhō\ *n* : an excavating machine having a bucket that is drawn toward the machine

back·ing \'ba-kiŋ\ *n* **1** : something forming a back **2**

: SUPPORT, AID; ⟨needed financial ~⟩ *also* : a body of supporters

back·lash \'bak-ˌlash\ *n* **1** : a sudden violent backward movement or reaction **2** : a strong adverse reaction

¹back·log \-ˌlȯg, -ˌläg\ *n* **1** : a large log at the back of a hearth fire **2** : an accumulation of tasks unperformed or materials not processed

²backlog *vb* : to accumulate in reserve

back of *prep* : BEHIND

back order *n* : a business order yet to be fulfilled because stock is unavailable — **back–order** *vb*

back out *vb* : to withdraw esp. from a commitment or contest

¹back·pack \'bak-ˌpak\ *n* : a camping pack supported by an aluminum frame and carried on the back

²backpack *vb* : to hike with a backpack — **back·pack·er** *n*

back·ped·al \'bak-ˌpe-dᵊl\ *vb* : RETREAT

back·rest \-ˌrest\ *n* : a rest for the back

back·side \-ˌsīd\ *n* : BUTTOCKS

back·slap \-ˌslap\ *vb* : to display excessive cordiality — **back·slap·per** *n*

back·slide \-ˌslīd\ *vb* **-slid** \-ˌslid\; **-slid** *or* **-slid·den** \-ˌsli-dᵊn\; **-slid·ing** \-ˌslī-diŋ\ : to lapse morally or in religious practice — **back·slid·er** *n*

back·space \-ˌspās\ *vb* : to move back a space in a text with the press of a key — **backspace** *n*

back·spin \-ˌspin\ *n* : a backward rotary motion of a ball

¹back·stage \'bak-'stāj\ *adj* **1** : relating to or occurring in the area behind a stage **2** : of or relating to the private lives of theater people **3** : of or relating to the inner working or operation

²back·stage \'bak-'stāj\ *adv* **1** : in or to a backstage area **2** : SECRETLY ⟨worked ~ to gain support⟩

back·stairs \-ˌsterz\ *adj* : SECRET, FURTIVE; *also* : SORDID, SCANDALOUS

¹back·stop \-ˌstäp\ *n* : something serving as a stop behind something else; *esp* : a screen or fence to keep a ball from leaving the field of play

²backstop *vb* **1** : SUPPORT **2** : to serve as a backstop to

back·sto·ry \-ˌstȯr-ē\ *n* : a story that tells what led up to the main story or plot (as of a film)

back·stretch \'bak-'strech\ *n* : the side opposite the homestretch on a racecourse

back·stroke \-ˌstrōk\ *n* : a swimming stroke executed on the back — **back·strok·er** \-ˌstrō-kər\ *n*

back talk *n* : impudent, insolent, or argumentative replies

back·track \'bak-ˌtrak\ *vb* **1** : to retrace one's course **2** : to reverse a position or stand

back·up \-ˌəp\ *n* **1** : one that serves as a substitute or alternative **2** : a copy of computer data — **back up** *vb*

¹back·ward \'bak-wərd\ *or* **back·wards** \-wərdz\ *adv* **1** : toward the back **2** : with the back foremost ⟨ride ~⟩ **3** : in a reverse or contrary direction or way ⟨count ~⟩ **4** : toward the past; *also* : toward a worse state

²backward *adj* **1** : directed, turned, or done backward **2** : DIFFIDENT, SHY **3** : slow in development or learning — **back·ward·ly** *adv* — **back·ward·ness** *n*

back·wash \'bak-ˌwȯsh, -ˌwäsh\ *n* : a backward flow or movement (as of water or air) produced by a propelling force (as the motion of oars)

back·wa·ter \-ˌwȯ-tər, -ˌwä-\ *n* **1** : water held or turned back in its course **2** : an isolated or backward place or condition

back·woods \-'wùdz\ *n pl* **1** : wooded or partly cleared areas far from cities **2** : a remote or isolated place

ba·con \'bā-kən\ *n* : salted and smoked meat from the sides or back of a pig

bacteria *pl of* BACTERIUM

bac·te·ri·cid·al \bak-ˌtir-ə-'sī-dᵊl\ *adj* : destroying bacteria — **bac·te·ri·cide** \-'tir-ə-ˌsīd\ *n*

bac·te·ri·ol·o·gy \bak-ˌtir-ē-'ä-lə-jē\ *n* : a science dealing with bacteria **2** : bacterial life and phenomena — **bac·te·ri·o·log·ic** \-ə-'lä-jik\ *or* **bac·te·ri·o·log·i·cal** \-ə-'lä-ji-kəl\ *adj* — **bac·te·ri·ol·o·gist** \-'ä-lə-jist\ *n*

bac·te·rio·phage \bak-'tir-ē-ə-ˌfāj\ *n* : any of various viruses that attack specific bacteria

bac·te·ri·um \bak-'tir-ē-əm\ *n, pl* **-ria** \-ē-ə\ [NL, fr. Gk *baktērion* staff] : any of a group of single-celled microorganisms including some that cause disease and others that are valued esp. for their chemical effects (as fermentation) — **bac·te·ri·al** \-ē-əl\ *adj*

bad \\'bad\\ *adj* **worse** \\'wərs\\; **worst** \\'wərst\\ **1** : below standard : POOR; *also* : UNFAVORABLE ⟨a ∼ report⟩ **2** : SPOILED, DECAYED **3** : WICKED; *also* : not well-behaved **4** : DISAGREEABLE ⟨a ∼ taste⟩; *also* : HARMFUL **5** : DEFECTIVE, FAULTY ⟨∼ wiring⟩; *also* : not valid ⟨a ∼ check⟩ **6** : UNWELL, ILL **7** : SORRY, REGRETFUL ⟨feels ∼ about forgetting to call⟩ ✦ *Synonyms* EVIL, WRONG, IMMORAL, INIQUITOUS — **bad·ly** *adv* — **bad·ness** *n*

bade *past and past part of* BID

badge \\'baj\\ *n* : a device or token usu. worn as a sign of status

¹bad·ger \\'ba-jər\\ *n* : any of several sturdy burrowing mammals with long claws on their forefeet

²badger *vb* : to harass or annoy persistently

ba·di·nage \\,ba-də-'näzh\\ *n* [F] : playful talk back and forth : BANTER

bad·land \\'bad-,land\\ *n* : a region marked by intricate erosional sculpturing and scanty vegetation — usu. used in pl.

bad·min·ton \\'bad-,mi-t³n, -,min-t³n\\ *n* : a court game played with light rackets and a shuttlecock volleyed over a net

bad–mouth \\'bad-,mȧu̇th\\ *vb* : to criticize severely

Bae·de·ker \\'bā-di-kər, 'be-\\ *n* : GUIDEBOOK

¹baf·fle \\'ba-fəl\\ *vb* **baf·fled; baf·fling** \\-f(ə-)liŋ\\ : FRUSTRATE, THWART, FOIL; *also* : PERPLEX — **baf·fle·ment** *n*

²baffle *n* : a device (as a wall or screen) to deflect, check, or regulate flow (as of liquid or sound) — **baf·fled** \\'ba-fəld\\ *adj*

¹bag \\'bag\\ *n* **1** : a flexible usu. closable container (as for storing or carrying) **2** : something that bulges and sags like a bag ⟨∼s under the eyes⟩

²bag *vb* **bagged; bag·ging 1** : DISTEND, BULGE **2** : to put in a bag **3** : to get possession of; *esp* : to take in hunting ✦ *Synonyms* TRAP, SNARE, CATCH, CAPTURE, COLLAR

ba·gasse \\bə-'gas\\ *n* [F] : plant residue (as of sugarcane) left after a product (as juice) has been extracted

bag·a·telle \\,ba-gə-'tel\\ *n* [F] : TRIFLE 1

ba·gel \\'bā-gəl\\ *n* [Yiddish *beygl*] : a firm doughnut-shaped roll usu. made by boiling and then baking

bag·gage \\'ba-gij\\ *n* **1** : the traveling bags and personal belongings of a traveler : LUGGAGE **2** : intangible things that get in the way ⟨emotional ∼⟩

bag·gie \\'ba-gē\\ *n* : a usu. small clear plastic bag

bag·gies \\'ba-gēz\\ *n pl* : baggy pants or shorts

bag·gy \\'ba-gē\\ *adj* **bag·gi·er; -est** : puffed out or hanging like a bag ⟨a ∼ sweater⟩ — **bag·gi·ly** \\-gə-lē\\ *adv* — **bag·gi·ness** \\-gē-nəs\\ *n*

bag·man \\'bag-mən\\ *n* : a person who collects or distributes illicitly gained money on behalf of another

ba·gnio \\'ban-yō\\ *n, pl* **bagnios** [It *bagno*, lit., public bath] : BROTHEL

bag of waters : a double-walled fluid-filled sac that encloses and protects the fetus in the womb and that breaks releasing its fluid during the process of birth

bag·pipe \\'bag-,pīp\\ *n* : a musical wind instrument consisting of a bag, a tube with valves, and sounding pipes — often used in pl. — **bag·pip·er** \\-,pī-pər\\ *n*

ba·guette \\ba-'get\\ *n* [F, lit., rod] **1** : a gem having the shape of a narrow rectangle; *also* : the shape itself **2** : a long thin loaf of French bread

baht \\'bät\\ *n, pl* **baht** *also* **bahts** — see MONEY table

¹bail \\'bāl\\ *n* : a container for ladling water out of a boat

²bail *vb* : to dip and throw water from a boat — **bail·er** *n*

³bail *n* : security given to guarantee a prisoner's appearance when legally required; *also* : one giving such security or the release secured

⁴bail *vb* : to release under bail; *also* : to procure the release of by giving bail — **bail·able** \\'bā-lə-bəl\\ *adj*

⁵bail *n* : the arched handle (as of a pail or kettle)

bai·liff \\'bā-ləf\\ *n* **1** : an aide of a British sheriff who serves writs and makes arrests; *also* : a minor officer of a U.S. court **2** : an estate or farm manager esp. in Britain : STEWARD

bai·li·wick \\'bā-li-,wik\\ *n* : one's special province or domain ✦ *Synonyms* TERRITORY, FIELD, SPHERE

bail·out \\'bāl-,ȧu̇t\\ *n* : a rescue from financial distress

bairn \\'bern\\ *n, chiefly Scot* : CHILD

¹bait \\'bāt\\ *vb* **1** : to persecute by continued attacks **2** : to harass with dogs usu. for sport ⟨∼ a bear⟩ **3** : to furnish (as a hook) with bait **4** : ALLURE, ENTICE **5** : to give food and drink to (as an animal) ✦ *Synonyms* BADGER, HECKLE, HOUND

²bait *n* **1** : a lure for catching animals (as fish) **2** : LURE, TEMPTATION ✦ *Synonyms* SNARE, TRAP, DECOY, COME-ON, ENTICEMENT

bait·fish \\'bāt-,fish\\ *n* : a small fish that attracts and is a food source for a larger fish; *also* : a fish used for bait

bai·za \\'bī-(,)zä\\ *n, pl* **baiza** *or* **baizas** — see *rial* at MONEY table

baize \\'bāz\\ *n* : a coarse feltlike fabric

¹bake \\'bāk\\ *vb* **baked; bak·ing 1** : to cook or become cooked in dry heat esp. in an oven **2** : to dry and harden by heat ⟨∼ bricks⟩ — **bak·er** *n*

²bake *n* : a social gathering featuring baked food

baker's dozen *n* : THIRTEEN

bak·ery \\'bā-k(ə-)rē\\ *n, pl* **-er·ies** : a place for baking or selling baked goods

bake sale *n* : a fund-raising event at which usu. home-made foods are sold

bake·shop \\'bāk-,shäp\\ *n* : BAKERY

bake·ware \\-,wer\\ *n* : dishes used for baking and serving food

baking powder *n* : a powder that consists of a carbonate, an acid, and a starch and that makes the dough rise in baking cakes and biscuits

baking soda *n* : SODIUM BICARBONATE

bak·sheesh \\'bak-,shēsh\\ *n* : payment (as a tip or bribe) to expedite service

bal *abbr* balance

bal·a·lai·ka \\,ba-lə-'lī-kə\\ *n* [Russ] : a triangular 3-stringed instrument of Russian origin played by plucking or strumming

¹bal·ance \\'ba-ləns\\ *n* [ME, fr. AF, fr. VL *bilancia*, fr. LL *bilanc-, bilanx* having two scalepans, fr. L *bi* two + *lanc-, lanx* plate] **1** : a weighing device : SCALE **2** : a weight, force, or influence counteracting the effect of another **3** : an oscillating wheel used to regulate a timepiece **4** : a state of equilibrium **5** : REMAINDER, REST; *esp* : an amount in excess esp. on the credit side of an account — **bal·anced** \\-lənst\\ *adj*

²balance *vb* **bal·anced; bal·anc·ing 1** : to compute the balance of an account **2** : to arrange so that one set of elements equals another; *also* : to equal or equalize in weight, number, or proportions **3** : WEIGH **4** : to bring or come to a state or position of balance; *also* : to bring into harmony or proportion

bal·boa \\bal-'bō-ə\\ *n* — see MONEY table

bal·co·ny \\'bal-kə-nē\\ *n, pl* **-nies** **1** : a platform projecting from the side of a building and enclosed by a railing **2** : a gallery inside a building

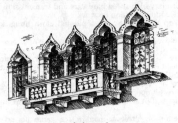

balcony 1

bald \\'bȯld\\ *adj* **1** : lacking a natural or usual covering (as of hair) **2** : UNADORNED, PLAIN ⟨the ∼ truth⟩ **3** : having little or no tread ⟨∼ tires⟩ **4** : not disguised ⟨∼ hate⟩ ✦ *Synonyms* BARE, BARREN, NAKED, NUDE — **bald·ly** *adv* — **bald·ness** *n*

bal·da·chin \\'bȯl-də-kən, 'bal-\\ *or* **bal·da·chi·no** \\,bal-də-'kē-nō\\ *n, pl* **-chins** *or* **-chinos** : a canopylike structure over an altar

bald cypress *n* : either of two coniferous trees of southern U.S. swamps; *also* : their hard red wood

bald eagle *n* : a large brown eagle of No. America that when mature has white head and neck feathers and a white tail

bal·der·dash \\'bȯl-dər-,dash\\ *n* : NONSENSE

bald·ing \'bȯl-diŋ\ *adj* : becoming bald

bal·dric \'bȯl-drik\ *n* : a belt worn over the shoulder to carry a sword or bugle

¹**bale** \'bāl\ *n* : a large or closely packed bundle

²**bale** *vb* **baled; bal·ing** : to pack in a bale — **bal·er** *n*

ba·leen \bə-'lēn\ *n* : a horny substance attached in plates to the upper jaw of some large whales (**baleen whales**)

bale·ful \'bāl-fəl\ *adj* : DEADLY, HARMFUL; *also* : OMINOUS ◆ **Synonyms** SINISTER, MALEFIC, MALEFICENT, MALIGN

¹**balk** \'bȯk\ *n* **1** : HINDRANCE, CHECK, SETBACK **2** : an illegal motion of the pitcher in baseball while in position

²**balk** *vb* **1** : BLOCK, THWART **2** : to stop short and refuse to go on **3** : to commit a balk in sports ◆ **Synonyms** FRUSTRATE, BAFFLE, FOIL, THWART — **balky** \'bȯ-kē\ *adj*

¹**ball** \'bȯl\ *n* **1** : a rounded body or mass (as an object used in a game or as a missile); *also* : a roundish protuberant part of the body ⟨the ~ of the foot⟩ **2** : a game played with a ball **3** : a pitched baseball that misses the strike zone and is not swung at by the batter **4** : a hit or thrown ball in various games ⟨foul ~⟩ — **on the ball** : COMPETENT, KNOWLEDGEABLE, ALERT

²**ball** *vb* : to form into a ball

³**ball** *n* : a large formal dance

bal·lad \'ba-ləd\ *n* **1** : a narrative poem of strongly marked rhythm suitable for singing **2** : a simple song : AIR **3** : a slow romantic song

bal·lad·eer \ba-lə-'dir\ *n* : a singer of ballads

¹**bal·last** \'ba-ləst\ *n* **1** : heavy material used to stabilize a ship or control a balloon's ascent **2** : crushed stone laid in a railroad bed or used in making concrete

²**ballast** *vb* : to provide with ballast ◆ **Synonyms** BALANCE, STABILIZE, STEADY

ball bearing *n* : a bearing in which the revolving part turns upon steel balls that roll easily in a groove; *also* : one of the balls in such a bearing

ball·car·ri·er \'bȯl-ker-ē-ər\ *n* : the football player carrying the ball in an offensive play

ball·er \'bȯ-lər\ *n* : an implement for shaping food into a ball ⟨melon ~⟩

bal·le·ri·na \ba-lə-'rē-nə\ *n* : a female ballet dancer

bal·let \'ba-lā, ba-'lā\ *n* **1** : dancing in which fixed poses and steps are combined with light flowing movements often to convey a story; *also* : a theatrical art form using ballet dancing **2** : a company of ballet dancers

bal·let·o·mane \ba-'le-tə-mān\ *n* : a devotee of ballet

bal·lis·tic missile \bə-'lis-tik-\ *n* : a missile that is guided during ascent and that falls freely during descent

bal·lis·tics \-tiks\ *n sing or pl* **1** : the science of the motion of projectiles (as bullets) in flight **2** : the flight characteristics of a projectile — **ballistic** *adj*

ball of fire : an unusually energetic person

¹**bal·loon** \bə-'lün\ *n* **1** : a bag filled with gas or heated air so as to rise and float in the atmosphere usu. carrying a suspended load **2** : an inflatable bag used as a toy or decoration — **bal·loon·ist** *n*

²**balloon** *vb* **1** : to swell or puff out **2** : to travel in a balloon **3** : to increase rapidly

¹**bal·lot** \'ba-lət\ *n* [It *ballotta* small ball used in secret voting, fr. It dial., dim. of *balla* ball] **1** : a piece of paper used to cast a vote **2** : the action or a system of voting; *also* : the right to vote

²**ballot** *vb* : to decide by ballot : VOTE

¹**ball·park** \'bȯl-park\ *n* : a park in which ball games are played

²**ballpark** *adj* : approximately correct ⟨~ estimate⟩

ball·point \'bȯl-pȯint\ *n* : a pen whose writing point is a small rotating metal ball that inks itself from an inner container

ball·room \'bȯl-rüm, -rum\ *n* : a large room for dances

ballroom dance *n* : any of various dances (as the tango, two-step, and waltz) in which couples perform set moves

bal·ly·hoo \'ba-lē-hü\ *n, pl* **-hoos** : extravagant statements and claims made for publicity — **ballyhoo** *vb*

balm \'bäm, 'bälm\ *n* **1** : a fragrant healing or soothing lotion or ointment **2** : any of several spicy fragrant herbs of the mint family **3** : something that comforts or soothes

balmy \'bä-mē, 'bäl-\ *adj* **balm·i·er; -est** **1** : gently soothing : MILD **2** : FOOLISH, ABSURD ◆ **Synonyms** SOFT, BLAND, MILD, GENTLE — **balm·i·ness** *n*

ba·lo·ney \bə-'lō-nē\ *n* : NONSENSE

bal·sa \'bȯl-sə\ *n* : the extremely light strong wood of a tropical American tree; *also* : the tree

bal·sam \'bȯl-səm\ *n* **1** : a fragrant aromatic and usu. resinous substance oozing from various plants; *also* : a preparation containing or smelling like balsam **2** : a balsam-yielding tree (as balsam fir) **3** : an ornamental garden plant — **bal·sam·ic** \bȯl-'sa-mik\ *adj*

balsam fir *n* : a resinous No. American evergreen tree that is widely used for pulpwood and as a Christmas tree

balsamic vinegar *n* : an aged Italian vinegar made from white grapes

Balt \'bȯlt\ *n* : a native or inhabitant of Lithuania, Latvia, or Estonia

Bal·ti·more oriole \'bȯl-tə-mȯr-\ *n* : a common American oriole in which the male is brightly colored with orange, black, and white

bal·us·ter \'ba-lə-stər\ *n* [F *balustre*, fr. It *balaustro*, fr. *balaustra* wild pomegranate flower, fr. L *balaustium;* fr. its shape] : an upright support for a rail (as of a staircase)

bal·us·trade \'ba-lə-strād\ *n* : a row of balusters topped by a rail

bam·boo \bam-'bü\ *n, pl* **bamboos** : any of various woody mostly tall tropical grasses including some with strong hollow stems used for building, furniture, or utensils

bamboo curtain *n, often cap B&C* : a political, military, and ideological barrier in eastern Asia

bam·boo·zle \bam-'bü-zəl\ *vb* **-boo·zled; -boo·zling** : TRICK, HOODWINK

¹**ban** \'ban\ *vb* **banned; ban·ning** : PROHIBIT, FORBID

²**ban** *n* **1** : CURSE **2** : a legal or formal prohibition ⟨a ~ on beef imports⟩

³**ban** \'bän\ *n, pl* **ban** \-'nē\ — see *leu* at MONEY table

ba·nal \bə-'näl, -'nal; 'bā-nᵊl\ *adj* [F] : COMMONPLACE, TRITE ⟨~ remarks⟩ — **ba·nal·i·ty** \bā-'na-lə-tē\ *n*

ba·nana \bə-'na-nə\ *n* : a treelike tropical plant bearing thick clusters of yellow or reddish finger-shaped fruit; *also* : this fruit

¹**band** \'band\ *n* **1** : something that binds, ties, or goes around **2** : a strip or stripe that can be distinguished (as by color or texture) from nearby matter **3** : a range of wavelengths (as in radio)

²**band** *vb* **1** : to tie up, finish, or enclose with a band **2** : to gather together or unite esp. for some common end — **band·er** *n*

³**band** *n* : a group of persons, animals, or things; *esp* : a group of musicians organized for playing together

¹**ban·dage** \'ban-dij\ *n* : a strip of material used esp. in dressing wounds

²**bandage** *vb* **ban·daged; ban·dag·ing** : to dress or cover with a bandage

Band-Aid \'ban-'dād\ *adj* : offering, making use of, or serving as a temporary or expedient remedy or solution

ban·dan·na *or* **ban·dana** \ban-'da-nə\ *n* : a large colored figured handkerchief

B and B *abbr* bed-and-breakfast

band·box \'band-bäks\ *n* : a usu. cylindrical box for carrying clothing

band·ed \'ban-dəd\ *adj* : having or marked with bands

ban·de·role *or* **ban·de·rol** \'ban-də-rōl\ *n* : a long narrow forked flag or streamer

ban·dit \'ban-dət\ *n* [It *bandito*, fr. *bandire* to banish] **1** *pl also* **ban·dit·ti** \ban-'di-tē\ : an outlaw who lives by plunder; *esp* : a member of a band of marauders **2** : ROBBER — **ban·dit·ry** \ban-də-trē\ *n*

band·lead·er \'band-lē-dər\ *n* : the conductor of a band

ban·do·lier *or* **ban·do·leer** \ban-də-'lir\ *n* : a belt slung over the shoulder esp. to carry ammunition

band saw *n* : a saw in the form of an endless steel belt running over pulleys

band·stand \'band-stand\ *n* : a usu. roofed platform on which a band or orchestra performs outdoors

b and w *abbr* black and white

band·wag·on \'band-wa-gən\ *n* **1** : a wagon carrying musicians in a parade **2** : a movement that attracts growing support ⟨a political ~⟩

band·width \-'width\ *n* : the capacity for data transfer of an electronic communication system

¹**ban·dy** \'ban-dē\ *vb* **ban·died; ban·dy·ing** **1** : to exchange (as blows or quips) esp. in rapid succession **2** : to use in a glib or offhand way

²**bandy** *adj* : curved outward ⟨~ legs⟩

bane \'bān\ *n* **1** : POISON **2** : WOE, HARM; *also* : a source of this — **bane·ful** *adj*
¹bang \'baŋ\ *vb* **1** : BUMP ⟨fell and ~*ed* his knee⟩ **2** : to strike, thrust, or move usu. with a loud noise
²bang *n* **1** : a resounding blow **2** : a sudden loud noise
³bang *adv* : DIRECTLY, RIGHT ⟨ran ~ up against more trouble⟩
⁴bang *n* : a fringe of hair cut short (as across the forehead) — usu. used in pl.
⁵bang *vb* : to cut (as hair) to produce bangs
ban·gle \'baŋ-gəl\ *n* **1** : BRACELET **2** : a loose-hanging ornament
bang–up \'baŋ-ˌəp\ *adj* : FIRST-RATE, EXCELLENT ⟨a ~ job⟩
bani *pl of* ³BAN
ban·ish \'ba-nish\ *vb* **1** : to require by authority to leave a country **2** : to drive out : EXPEL ♦ **Synonyms** EXILE, OSTRACIZE, DEPORT, RELEGATE — **ban·ish·ment** *n*
ban·is·ter \'ba-nə-stər\ *n* **1** : a handrail with its supporting posts **2** : HANDRAIL **3** : BALUSTER
ban·jo \'ban-ˌjō\ *n, pl* **banjos** *also* **banjoes** : a musical instrument with a long neck, a drumlike body, and usu. five strings — **ban·jo·ist** \-ist\ *n*
¹bank \'baŋk\ *n* **1** : a piled-up mass (as of cloud or earth) **2** : an undersea elevation **3** : rising ground bordering a lake, river, or sea **4** : the sideways slope of a surface along a curve or of a vehicle as it rounds a curve
²bank *vb* **1** : to form a bank about **2** : to cover (as a fire) with fuel to keep inactive **3** : to build (a curve) with the roadbed or track inclined laterally upward from the inside edge **4** : to pile or heap in a bank; *also* : to arrange in a tier **5** : to incline (an airplane) laterally
³bank *n* [ME, fr. MF or It; MF *banque*, fr. It *banca*, lit., bench, of Gmc origin] **1** : an establishment concerned esp. with the custody, loan, exchange, or issue of money, the extension of credit, and the transmission of funds **2** : a stock of or a place for holding something in reserve ⟨a blood ~⟩
⁴bank *vb* **1** : to conduct the business of a bank **2** : to deposit money or have an account in a bank — **bank·er** *n* — **bank·ing** *n*
⁵bank *n* : a group of objects arranged close together (as in a row or tier) ⟨a ~ of file drawers⟩
bank·book \'baŋk-ˌbuk\ *n* : the depositor's book in which a bank records deposits and withdrawals
bank·card \-ˌkärd\ *n* : a card (as a credit card or an ATM card) issued by a bank
bank·note \-ˌnōt\ *n* : a promissory note issued by a bank and circulating as money
bank·roll \-ˌrōl\ *n* : supply of money : FUNDS
¹bank·rupt \'baŋk-(ˌ)rəpt\ *n* [modif. of MF *banquerote* bankruptcy, fr. It *bancarotta*, fr. *banca* bank + *rotta* broken] : an insolvent person; *esp* : one whose property is turned over by court action to a trustee to be handled for the benefit of his creditors — **bankrupt** *vb*
²bankrupt *adj* **1** : reduced to financial ruin; *esp* : legally declared a bankrupt **2** : wholly lacking in or deprived of some essential ⟨morally ~⟩ — **bank·rupt·cy** \'baŋk-(ˌ)rəpt-sē\ *n*
¹ban·ner \'ba-nər\ *n* **1** : a piece of cloth attached to a staff and used by a leader as his standard **2** : FLAG **3** : an advertisement that runs usu. across the top of a Web page
²banner *adj* : distinguished from all others esp. in excellence ⟨a ~ year⟩
ban·nock \'ba-nək\ *n* : a flat oatmeal or barley cake usu. cooked on a griddle
banns \'banz\ *n pl* : public announcement esp. in church of a proposed marriage
ban·quet \'baŋ-kwət\ *n* [MF, fr. It *banchetto*, fr. dim. of *banca* bench] : a ceremonial dinner — **banquet** *vb*
ban·quette \baŋ-'ket\ *n* : a long upholstered bench esp. along a wall
ban·shee \'ban-shē\ *n* [Ir *bean sídhe* & ScGael *bean sìth*, lit., woman of fairyland] : a female spirit in Gaelic folklore whose wailing warns a family that one of them will soon die
ban·tam \'ban-təm\ *n* **1** : any of numerous small domestic fowls that are often miniatures of standard breeds **2** : a small but pugnacious person
¹ban·ter \'ban-tər\ *vb* **1** : to speak to in a witty and teasing manner

²banter *n* : good-natured witty joking
Ban·tu \'ban-(ˌ)tü\ *n, pl* **Bantu** *or* **Bantus** **1** : a group of languages spoken in central and southern Africa **2** : a member of a group of African peoples who speak Bantu
ban·yan \'ban-yən\ *n* : a large tropical Asian tree whose aerial roots grow downward to the ground and form new trunks
ban·zai \bän-'zī\ *n* : a Japanese cheer or cry of triumph
bao·bab \'bau̇-ˌbab, 'bā-ə-\ *n* : a tropical African tree with short swollen trunk and sour edible fruits resembling gourds
bap·tism \'bap-ˌti-zəm\ *n* **1** : a Christian sacrament signifying spiritual rebirth and symbolized by the ritual use of water **2** : an act of baptizing — **bap·tis·mal** \bap-'tiz-məl\ *adj*
baptismal name *n* : GIVEN NAME
Bap·tist \'bap-tist\ *n* : a member of any of several Protestant denominations emphasizing baptism by immersion of believers only
bap·tis·tery *or* bap·tis·try \'bap-tə-strē\ *n, pl* **-ter·ies** *or* **-tries** : a place esp. in a church used for baptism
bap·tize \bap-'tīz, 'bap-ˌtīz\ *vb* **bap·tized; bap·tiz·ing** [ME, fr. AF *baptiser*, fr. L *baptizare*, fr. Gk *baptizein* to dip, baptize, fr. *baptein* to dip] **1** : to administer baptism to; *also* : CHRISTEN **2** : to purify esp. by an ordeal
¹bar \'bär\ *n* **1** : a long narrow piece of material (as wood or metal) used esp. for a lever, fastening, or support **2** : BARRIER, OBSTACLE **3** : the railing in a law court at which prisoners are stationed; *also* : the legal profession or the whole body of lawyers **4** : a stripe, band, or line much longer than wide **5** : a counter at which food or esp. drink is served; *also* : BARROOM **6** : a vertical line across the musical staff
²bar *vb* **barred; bar·ring** **1** : to fasten, confine, or obstruct with or as if with a bar or bars **2** : to mark with bars : STRIPE **3** : to shut or keep out : EXCLUDE **4** : FORBID, PREVENT
³bar *prep* : EXCEPT ⟨the most popular actor, ~ none⟩
⁴bar *abbr* barometer; barometric
Bar *abbr* Baruch
barb \'bärb\ *n* **1** : a sharp projection extending backward (as from the point of an arrow) **2** : a biting critical remark — **barbed** \'bärbd\ *adj* — **barb·less** \'bärb-ləs\ *adj*
bar·bar·ian \bär-'ber-ē-ən\ *adj* **1** : of, relating to, or being a land, culture, or people alien to and usu. believed to be inferior to another's **2** : lacking refinement, learning, or artistic or literary culture — **barbarian** *n* — **bar·bar·i·an·ism** \-ē-ə-ˌni-zəm\ *n*
bar·bar·ic \bär-'ber-ik\ *adj* **1** : BARBARIAN ⟨~ tribes⟩ **2** : marked by a lack of restraint : WILD ⟨~ attacks⟩ **3** : PRIMITIVE, UNSOPHISTICATED
bar·ba·rism \'bär-bə-ˌri-zəm\ *n* **1** : the social condition of barbarians; *also* : the use or display of barbarian or barbarous acts, attitudes, or ideas **2** : a word or expression that offends standards of correctness or purity
bar·ba·rous \'bär-bə-rəs\ *adj* **1** : lacking culture or refinement **2** : using linguistic barbarisms **3** : mercilessly harsh or cruel — **bar·bar·i·ty** \bär-'ber-ə-tē\ *n* — **bar·ba·rous·ly** *adv* — **bar·ba·rous·ness** *n*
¹bar·be·cue \'bär-bi-ˌkyü\ *vb* **-cued; -cu·ing** **1** : to cook on a rack or revolving spit over or before a source of heat **2** : to cook in a highly seasoned vinegar sauce
²barbecue *n* : a social gathering at which barbecued food is served
bar·bell \'bär-ˌbel\ *n* : a bar with adjustable weights attached to each end used for exercise and in weight lifting
bar·ber \'bär-bər\ *n* [ME, fr. AF *barbour*, fr. *barbe* beard, fr. L *barba*] : one whose business is cutting and dressing hair and shaving and trimming beards
bar·ber·ry \'bär-ˌber-ē\ *n* : any of a genus of spiny shrubs bearing yellow flowers and oblong red berries
bar·bi·tu·rate \bär-'bi-chə-rət\ *n* : any of various compounds (as a salt or ester) formed from an organic acid (bar·bi·tu·ric acid \ˌbär-bə-'tu̇r-ik-, -'tyu̇r-\); *esp* : one used as a sedative or hypnotic
bar·ca·role *or* bar·ca·rolle \'bär-kə-ˌrōl\ *n* : a Venetian boat song characterized by a beat suggesting a rowing rhythm; *also* : a piece of music imitating this
bar chart *n* : BAR GRAPH
bar·code \'bär-ˌkōd\ *n* : a set of printed and variously spaced bars and sometimes numerals that is designed to be

scanned to provide information about the object it labels —
bar–cod·ed \'bär-ˌkō-dəd\ *adj* — **bar coding** *n*
bard \'bärd\ *n* : POET
¹bare \'ber\ *adj* **bar·er**; **bar·est** **1** : NAKED **2** : UNCON-
CEALED, EXPOSED **3** : EMPTY ⟨the cupboard was ⁓⟩ **4**
: leaving nothing to spare : MERE **5** : PLAIN, UNADORNED
⟨the ⁓ facts⟩ ✦ *Synonyms* NUDE, BALD — **bare·ness** *n*
²bare *vb* **bared**; **bar·ing** : to make or lay bare : UNCOVER
bare·back \-ˌbak\ *or* **bare·backed** \-'bakt\ *adv or adj*
: without a saddle
bare·faced \-'fāst\ *adj* **1** : having the face uncovered;
esp : BEARDLESS **2** : not concealed : OPEN ⟨a ⁓ lie⟩ —
bare·faced·ly \-'fā-səd-lē, -'fāst-lē\ *adv*
bare·foot \-ˌfu̇t\ *or* **bare·foot·ed** \-'fu̇-təd\ *adv or adj*
: with bare feet
bare–hand·ed \-'han-dəd\ *adv or adj* **1** : without gloves
2 : without tools or weapons ⟨⁓ fighting⟩
bare·head·ed \-'he-dəd\ *adv or adj* : without a hat
bare·ly \'ber-lē\ *adv* **1** : PLAINLY, MEAGERLY ⟨a ⁓ furnished room⟩ **2** : by a narrow margin : only just ⟨⁓
enough money⟩
bar·fly \'bär-ˌflī\ *n* : a drinker who frequents bars
¹bar·gain \'bär-gən\ *n* **1** : AGREEMENT **2** : an advantageous purchase **3** : a transaction, situation, or event
regarded in the light of its results
²bargain *vb* **1** : to negotiate over the terms of an agreement; *also* : to come to terms **2** : BARTER
bar·gain–base·ment \'bär-gən-'bās-mənt\ *adj* : markedly
inexpensive
¹barge \'bärj\ *n* **1** : a broad flat-bottomed boat usu. moved
by towing **2** : a motorboat supplied to a flagship (as for
an admiral) **3** : a ceremonial boat elegantly furnished —
barge·man \-mən\ *n*
²barge *vb* **barged**; **barg·ing** **1** : to carry by barge **2** : to
move or thrust oneself clumsily or rudely
bar graph *n* : a graphic technique for comparing amounts
by rectangles whose lengths are proportional to the
amounts they represent
ba·ris·ta \bə-'rēs-tə\ *n* : a person who makes and serves
coffee to the public
bari·tone \'ber-ə-ˌtōn\ *n* [F *baryton* or It *baritono*, fr. Gk
barytonos deep sounding, fr. *barys* heavy + *tonos* tone] : a
male singing voice between bass and tenor; *also* : a person having this voice
bar·i·um \'ber-ē-əm\ *n* : a silver-white metallic chemical
element that occurs only in combination
¹bark \'bärk\ *vb* **1** : to make the short loud cry of a dog
2 : to speak or utter in a curt loud tone : SNAP
²bark *n* : the sound made by a barking dog
³bark *n* : the tough corky outer covering of a woody stem
or root
⁴bark *vb* **1** : to strip the bark from **2** : to rub the skin
from : ABRADE
⁵bark *n* : a ship of three or more masts with the aft mast
fore-and-aft rigged and the others square-rigged
bar·keep \'bär-ˌkēp\ *also* **bar·keep·er** \-ˌkē-pər\ *n* : BAR-
TENDER
bark·er \'bär-kər\ *n* : a person who stands at the entrance
esp. to a show and tries to attract customers to it
bar·ley \'bär-lē\ *n* : a cereal grass with seeds used as food
and in making malt liquors; *also* : its seed
bar mitz·vah \bär-'mits-və\ *n, often cap B&M* [Heb *bar
miṣwāh*, lit., son of the (divine) law] **1** : a Jewish boy
who reaches his 13th birthday and assumes religious responsibilities **2** : the ceremony recognizing a boy as a
bar mitzvah
barn \'bärn\ *n* [ME *bern*, fr. OE *bereærn*, fr. *bere* barley
+ *ærn* house, store] : a building used esp. for storing hay
and grain and for housing livestock or farm equipment
bar·na·cle \'bär-ni-kəl\ *n* : any of numerous small marine
crustaceans free-swimming when young but permanently
fixed (as to rocks, whales, or ships) when adult
barn·storm \'bärn-ˌstȯrm\ *vb* : to travel through the
country making brief stops to entertain (as with shows
or flying stunts) or to campaign for political office
barn·yard \-ˌyärd\ *n* : a usu. fenced area adjoining a barn
baro·graph \'ber-ə-ˌgraf\ *n* : a recording barometer
ba·rom·e·ter \bə-'räm-ə-tər\ *n* : an instrument for measuring atmospheric pressure — **baro·met·ric** \ˌbar-ə-'me-
trik\ *adj*
bar·on \'ber-ən\ *n* : a member of the lowest grade of

the British peerage — **ba·ro·ni·al** \bə-'rō-nē-əl\ *adj* —
bar·ony \'ber-ə-nē\ *n*
bar·on·age \'ber-ə-nij\ *n* : PEERAGE
bar·on·ess \'ber-ə-nəs\ *n* **1** : the wife or widow of a baron
2 : a woman holding a baronial title in her own right
bar·on·et \'ber-ə-nət\ *n* : the holder of a rank of honor
below a baron but above a knight — **bar·on·et·cy** \-sē\ *n*
ba·roque \bə-'rōk, -'räk\ *adj* : marked by the use of complex forms, bold ornamentation, and the juxtapositioning
of contrasting elements
ba·rouche \bə-'rüsh\ *n* [G *Barutsche*, fr. It *biroccio*, ultim.
fr. LL *birotus* two-wheeled, fr. L *bi-* two + *rota* wheel] : a
4-wheeled carriage with a high driver's seat in front and
a folding top
bar·racks \'ber-əks\ *n sing or pl* : a building or group of
buildings for lodging soldiers
bar·ra·cu·da \ˌber-ə-'kü-də\ *n, pl* **-da** *or* **-das** : any of several large slender predaceous sea fishes including some
used for food
bar·rage \bə-'räzh, -'räj\ *n* : a heavy concentration of fire
(as of artillery)
barred \'bärd\ *adj* : STRIPED
¹bar·rel \'ber-əl\ *n* **1** : a round bulging cask with flat ends
of equal diameter **2** : the amount contained in a barrel
3 : a cylindrical or tubular part ⟨gun ⁓⟩ — **bar·reled**
\-əld\ *adj*
²barrel *vb* **-reled** *or* **-relled**; **-rel·ing** *or* **-rel·ling** **1** : to pack
in a barrel **2** : to travel at high speed
bar·rel·head \-ˌhed\ *n* : the flat end of a barrel — **on the
barrelhead** : asking for or granting no credit ⟨paid cash
on the barrelhead⟩
barrel roll *n* : an airplane maneuver in which a complete
revolution about the longitudinal axis is made
¹bar·ren \'ber-ən\ *adj* **1** : STERILE, UNFRUITFUL **2** : unproductive of results ⟨a ⁓ scheme⟩ **3** : lacking interest
or charm **4** : lacking inspiration or ideas — **bar·ren·ness**
\-nəs\ *n*
²barren *n* : a tract of barren land
bar·rette \bä-'ret, bə-\ *n* : a clasp or bar for holding the
hair in place
¹bar·ri·cade \'ber-ə-ˌkād, ˌber-ə-'kād\ *vb* **-cad·ed**; **-cad·ing**
: to block, obstruct, or fortify with a barricade
²barricade *n* [F, fr. MF, fr. *barriquer* to barricade, fr. *bar-
rique* barrel] **1** : a hastily thrown-up obstruction or fortification **2** : BARRIER, OBSTACLE
bar·ri·er \'ber-ē-ər\ *n* : something that separates, demar-
cates, or serves as a barricade ⟨racial ⁓s⟩
barrier island *n* : a long broad sandy island lying parallel
to a shore
barrier reef *n* : a coral reef roughly parallel to a shore
and separated from it usu. by a lagoon
bar·ring \'bär-iŋ\ *prep* : excluding by exception : EX-
CEPTING
bar·rio \'bär-ē-ˌō, 'ber-\ *n, pl* **-ri·os** **1** : a district of a city
or town in a Spanish-speaking country **2** : a Spanish-
speaking quarter in a U.S. city
bar·ris·ter \'ber-ə-stər\ *n* : a British counselor admitted to
plead in the higher courts
bar·room \'bär-ˌrüm, -ˌru̇m\ *n* : a room or establishment
whose main feature is a bar for the sale of liquor
¹bar·row \'ber-ō\ *n* : a large burial mound of earth and stones
²barrow *n* **1** : WHEELBARROW **2** : a cart with a boxlike
body and two shafts for pushing it
Bart *abbr* baronet
bar·tend·er \'bär-ˌten-dər\ *n* : a person who serves liquor
at a bar
bar·ter \'bär-tər\ *vb* : to trade by exchange of goods —
barter *n* — **bar·ter·er** *n*
Ba·ruch \'bär-ˌük, bə-'rük\ *n* — see BIBLE table
bas·al \'bā-səl\ *adj* **1** : situated at or forming the base **2**
: BASIC
basal metabolism *n* : the turnover of energy in a fasting and resting organism using energy solely to maintain
vital cellular activity, respiration, and circulation as measured by the rate at which heat is given off
ba·salt \bə-'sȯlt, 'bā-ˌsȯlt\ *n* : a dark fine-grained igneous
rock — **ba·sal·tic** \bā-'sȯl-tik\ *adj*
¹base \'bās\ *n, pl* **bas·es** \'bā-səz\ **1** : BOTTOM, FOUNDA-
TION **2** : a side or face on which a geometrical figure
stands; *also* : the length of a base **3** : a main ingredient
or fundamental part **4** : the point of beginning an act or

operation **5** : a place on which a force depends for supplies **6** : a number (as 5 in 5⁷) that is raised to a power; *esp* : a number that when raised to a power equal to the logarithm of a number yields the number itself ⟨the logarithm of 100 to ∼ 10 is 2 since 10² = 100⟩ **7** : the number of units in a given digit's place of a number system that is required to give the numeral 1 in the next higher place ⟨the decimal system uses a ∼ of 10⟩; *also* : such a system using an indicated base ⟨convert from ∼ 10 to ∼ 2⟩ **8** : any of the four stations at the corners of a baseball diamond **9** : a chemical compound (as lime or ammonia) that reacts with an acid to form a salt, has a bitter taste, and turns litmus blue ✦ *Synonyms* BASIS, GROUND, GROUNDWORK, FOOTING, FOUNDATION — **base·less** *adj*

²base *vb* **based; bas·ing** **1** : to form or serve as a base for **2** : ESTABLISH

³base *adj* **1** : of low value and inferior quality : DEBASED, ALLOYED **2** : CONTEMPTIBLE, IGNOBLE ⟨∼ motives⟩ **3** : MENIAL, DEGRADING ✦ *Synonyms* LOW, VILE, DESPICABLE, WRETCHED — **base·ly** *adv* — **base·ness** *n*

base·ball \'bās-ˌbȯl\ *n* : a game played with a bat and ball by two teams on a field with four bases arranged in a diamond; *also* : the ball used in this game

baseball cap *n* : a cap of the kind worn by baseball players that has a rounded crown and a long visor

base·board \-ˌbȯrd\ *n* : a line of boards or molding covering the joint of a wall and the adjoining floor

base·born \-'bȯrn\ *adj* **1** : MEAN, IGNOBLE **2** : of humble birth **3** : of illegitimate birth

base exchange *n* : a post exchange at a naval or air force base

base hit *n* : a hit in baseball that enables the batter to reach base safely with no error made and no base runner forced out

BASE jumping \'bās-\ *n* [*b*uilding, *a*ntenna, *s*pan, *e*arth] : the activity of parachuting from a high structure or cliff

base·line \'bās-ˌlīn\ *n* **1** : a line serving as a basis esp. to calculate or locate something **2** : the area within which a baseball player must keep when running between bases

base·ment \-mənt\ *n* **1** : the part of a building that is wholly or partly below ground level **2** : the lowest or fundamental part of something

base on balls : an advance to first base given to a baseball player who receives four balls

base runner *n* : a baseball player who is on base or is attempting to reach a base

¹bash \'bash\ *vb* **1** : to strike violently : HIT **2** : to smash by a blow **3** : to attack physically or verbally

²bash *n* **1** : a heavy blow **2** : a festive social gathering : PARTY

bash·ful \'bash-fəl\ *adj* : inclined to shrink from public attention — **bash·ful·ly** \-fə-lē\ *adv* — **bash·ful·ness** *n*

ba·sic \'bā-sik\ *adj* **1** : of, relating to, or forming the base or essence : FUNDAMENTAL **2** : concerned with fundamental scientific principles : not applied **3** : of, relating to, or having the character of a chemical base ✦ *Synonyms* UNDERLYING, BASAL, PRIMARY — **ba·sic·i·ty** \bā-'si-sə-tē\ *n*

BA·SIC \'bā-sik\ *n* [*B*eginner's *A*ll-purpose *S*ymbolic *I*nstruction *C*ode] : a simplified language for programming a computer

ba·si·cal·ly \'bā-si-k(ə-)lē\ *adv* **1** : at a basic level **2** : for the most part **3** : in a basic manner

ba·sil \'bā-zəl, 'ba-, -səl\ *n* : any of several mints with fragrant leaves used in cooking; *also* : the leaves

ba·sil·i·ca \bə-'si-li-kə, -'zi-\ *n* [L, fr. Gk *basilikē*, fr. fem. of *basilikos* royal, fr. *basileus* king] **1** : an early Christian church building consisting of nave and aisles with clerestory and apse **2** : a Roman Catholic church given ceremonial privileges

bas·i·lisk \'ba-sə-ˌlisk, 'ba-zə-\ *n* [ME, fr. L *basiliscus*, fr. Gk *basiliskos*, fr. dim. of *basileus* king] : a legendary reptile with fatal breath and glance

ba·sin \'bā-sᵊn\ *n* **1** : an open usu. circular vessel with sloping sides for holding liquid (as water) **2** : a hollow or enclosed place containing water; *also* : the region drained by a river

ba·sis \'bā-səs\ *n, pl* **ba·ses** \-ˌsēz\ **1** : FOUNDATION, BASE **2** : a fundamental principle

bask \'bask\ *vb* **1** : to expose oneself to comfortable heat

2 : to enjoy something warmly comforting ⟨∼*ing* in his friends' admiration⟩

bas·ket \'bas-kət\ *n* : a container made of woven material (as twigs or grasses); *also* : any of various lightweight usu. wood containers — **bas·ket·ful** *n*

bas·ket·ball \-ˌbȯl\ *n* : a game played on a court by two teams who try to throw an inflated ball through a raised goal; *also* : the ball used in this game — **bas·ket·ball·er** \-ˌbȯ-lər\ *n*

basket case *n* **1** : a person who has all four limbs amputated **2** : a person who is mentally incapacitated or worn out (as from nervous tension)

basket weave *n* : a textile weave resembling the checkered pattern of a plaited basket

bas·ma·ti rice \ˌbäz-'mä-tē-\ *n* : an aromatic long-grain rice originating in southern Asia

bas mitzvah *var of* BAT MITZVAH

Basque \'bask\ *n* **1** : a member of a people inhabiting a region bordering on the Bay of Biscay in northern Spain and southwestern France **2** : the language of the Basque people — **Basque** *adj*

bas–re·lief \ˌbä-ri-'lēf\ *n* [F] : a sculpture in relief with the design raised very slightly from the background

bas-relief

¹bass \'bas\ *n, pl* **bass** *or* **bass·es** : any of numerous sport and food bony fishes (as a striped bass)

²bass \'bās\ *adj* : of low pitch

³bass \'bās\ *n* **1** : a deep sound or tone **2** : the lower half of the musical pitch range **3** : the lowest part in a 4-part chorus; *also* : a singer having this voice or part

bas·set hound \'ba-sət-\ *n* : any of an old breed of short-legged hunting dogs of French origin having long ears and a short smooth coat

bas·si·net \ˌba-sə-'net\ *n* : a baby's bed that resembles a basket and often has a hood over one end

bas·so \'ba-sō, 'bä-\ *n, pl* **bassos** *or* **bas·si** \'bä-ˌsē\ [It] : a bass singer

bas·soon \bə-'sün\ *n* : a musical wind instrument lower in pitch than the oboe

bass·wood \'bas-ˌwu̇d\ *n* : any of several New World lindens or their wood

bast \'bast\ *n* : BAST FIBER

¹bas·tard \'bas-tərd\ *n* **1** : an illegitimate child **2** : an offensive or disagreeable person

²bastard *adj* **1** : ILLEGITIMATE **2** : of an inferior or nontypical kind, size, or form; *also* : SPURIOUS — **bas·tardy** *n*

bas·tard·ise *Brit var of* BASTARDIZE

bas·tard·ize \'bas-tər-ˌdīz\ *vb* **-ized; -iz·ing** : to reduce from a higher to a lower state : DEBASE

¹baste \'bāst\ *vb* **bast·ed; bast·ing** : to sew with long stitches so as to keep temporarily in place

²baste *vb* **bast·ed; bast·ing** : to moisten (as meat) at intervals with liquid while cooking

bast fiber *n* : a strong woody plant fiber obtained chiefly from phloem and used esp. in making ropes

bas·ti·na·do \ˌbas-tə-'nä-dō, -'nä-\ *or* **bas·ti·nade** \ˌbas-tə-'näd, -'näd\ *n, pl* **-na·does** *or* **-nades** **1** : a blow or beating esp. with a stick **2** : a punishment consisting of beating the soles of the feet

bas·tion \'bas-chən\ *n* : a projecting part of a fortification; *also* : a fortified position

¹bat \'bat\ *n* **1** : a stout stick : CLUB **2** : a sharp blow **3** : an implement (as of wood) used to hit a ball (as in baseball) **4** : a turn at batting — usu. used in the phrase *at bat*

²**bat** vb **bat·ted; bat·ting** : to hit with or as if with a bat

³**bat** n : any of an order of night-flying mammals with forelimbs modified to form wings

⁴**bat** vb **bat·ted; bat·ting** : WINK, BLINK

batch \'bach\ n 1 : a quantity (as of bread) baked at one time 2 : a quantity of material for use at one time or produced at one operation

bate \'bāt\ vb **bat·ed; bat·ing** : MODERATE, REDUCE ⟨he bated his breath⟩

bath \'bath, 'bath\ n, pl **baths** \'bathz, 'baths, 'bāthz, 'bāths\ 1 : a washing of the body 2 : water for washing the body 3 : a liquid in which objects are immersed so that it can act on them 4 : BATHROOM 5 : a financial loss ⟨took a ~ in the market⟩

bathe \'bāth\ vb **bathed; bath·ing** 1 : to wash in liquid and esp. water; also : to apply water or a medicated liquid to ⟨bathed her eyes⟩ 2 : to take a bath; also : to take a swim 3 : to wash along, over, or against so as to wet 4 : to suffuse with or as if with light — **bath·er** n

bath·house \'bath-ˌhaus, 'bāth-\ n 1 : a building equipped for bathing 2 : a building containing dressing rooms for bathers

bathing suit n : SWIMSUIT

ba·thos \'bā-ˌthäs\ n [Gk, lit., depth] 1 : the sudden appearance of the commonplace in otherwise elevated matter or style 2 : insincere or overdone pathos — **ba·thet·ic** \ba-'the-tik\ adj

bath·robe \'bath-ˌrōb, 'bāth-\ n : a loose often absorbent robe worn before and after bathing or as a dressing gown

bath·room \-ˌrüm, -ˌrum\ n : a room containing a bathtub or shower and usu. a sink and toilet

bathroom tissue n : TOILET PAPER

bath·tub \-ˌtəb\ n : a usu. fixed tub for bathing

ba·tik \bə-'tēk, 'ba-tik\ n [Javanese baṭik] 1 : an Indonesian method of hand-printing textiles by coating with wax the parts not to be dyed; also : a design so executed 2 : a fabric printed by batik

ba·tiste \bə-'tēst\ n : a fine sheer fabric of plain weave

bat·man \'bat-mən\ n : an orderly of a British military officer

bat mitz·vah \bät-'mits-və\ also **bas mitzvah** \bäs-\ n, often cap B&M [Heb bath miṣwāh, lit., daughter of the (divine) law] 1 : a Jewish girl who at 12 or more years of age assumes religious responsibilities 2 : the ceremony recognizing a girl as a bat mitzvah

ba·ton \bə-'tän\ n : STAFF, ROD; esp : a stick with which the leader directs an orchestra or band

bats·man \'bats-mən\ n : a batter esp. in cricket

bat·tal·ion \bə-'tal-yən\ n 1 : a large body of troops organized to act together : ARMY 2 : a military unit composed of a headquarters and two or more units (as companies)

¹**bat·ten** \'ba-tᵊn\ vb 1 : to grow or make fat 2 : THRIVE

²**batten** n : a strip of wood used esp. to seal or strengthen a joint

³**batten** vb : to fasten with or as if with battens

¹**bat·ter** \'ba-tər\ vb : to beat or damage with repeated blows

²**batter** n : a soft mixture (as for cake) basically of flour and liquid

³**batter** n : one that bats; esp : the player whose turn it is to bat

battering ram n 1 : an ancient military machine for battering down walls 2 : a heavy metal bar with handles used to batter down doors

bat·tery \'ba-tə-rē\ n, pl **-ter·ies** 1 : BEATING; esp : unlawful beating or use of force on a person 2 : a grouping of artillery pieces for tactical purposes; also : the guns of a warship 3 : a group of electric cells for furnishing electric current; also : a single electric cell ⟨a flashlight ~⟩ 4 : a number of similar items grouped or used as a unit ⟨a ~ of tests⟩ 5 : the pitcher and catcher of a baseball team

bat·ting \'ba-tiŋ\ n : layers or sheets of cotton or wool (as for lining quilts)

batting cage n : a screen around the back and sides of the home plate area to stop baseballs during practice

¹**bat·tle** \'ba-tᵊl\ n [ME batel, fr. AF bataille battle, battalion, fr. LL battalia combat, alter. of battualia fencing exercises, fr. L battuere to beat] : a general military engagement; also : an extended contest or controversy

²**battle** vb **bat·tled; bat·tling** : to engage in battle : CONTEND, FIGHT

bat·tle–ax or **battle–axe** \'ba-tᵊl-ˌaks\ n 1 : a long-handled ax formerly used as a weapon 2 : a quarrelsome domineering woman

battle fatigue n : COMBAT FATIGUE

bat·tle·field \'ba-tᵊl-ˌfēld\ n : a place where a battle is fought

bat·tle·ment \-mənt\ n : a decorative or defensive parapet on top of a wall

bat·tle·ship \-ˌship\ n : a warship of the most heavily armed and armored class

bat·tle·wag·on \-ˌwa-gən\ n : BATTLESHIP

bat·ty \'ba-tē\ adj **bat·ti·er; -est** : CRAZY, FOOLISH

bau·ble \'bo-bəl\ n : TRINKET

baud \'bod, Brit 'bōd\ n, pl **baud** also **bauds** : a unit of data transmission speed

baulk chiefly Brit var of BALK

baux·ite \'bok-ˌsīt\ n : a clayey mixture that is the chief ore of aluminum

bawd \'bod\ n 1 : MADAM 2 2 : PROSTITUTE

bawdy \'bo-dē\ adj **bawd·i·er; -est** : OBSCENE, LEWD — **bawd·i·ly** \'bo-də-lē\ adv — **bawd·i·ness** \-dē-nəs\ n

¹**bawl** \'bol\ vb : to cry or cry out loudly; also : to scold harshly

²**bawl** n : a long loud cry : BELLOW

¹**bay** \'bā\ adj : reddish brown

²**bay** n 1 : a bay-colored animal 2 : a reddish brown color

³**bay** n 1 : a section or compartment of a building or vehicle 2 : a compartment projecting outward from the wall of a building and containing a window (**bay window**)

⁴**bay** vb : to bark with deep long tones

⁵**bay** n 1 : the position of one unable to escape and forced to face danger 2 : a baying of dogs

⁶**bay** n : an inlet of a body of water (as the sea) usu. smaller than a gulf

⁷**bay** n : LAUREL; also : a shrub or tree resembling the laurel

bay·ber·ry \'bā-ˌber-ē\ n : a hardy deciduous shrub of coastal eastern No. America bearing small hard berries coated with a white wax used for candles; also : its fruit

bay leaf n : the dried leaf of the European laurel used in cooking

¹**bay·o·net** \'bā-ə-nət, ˌbā-ə-'net\ n : a daggerlike weapon made to fit on the muzzle end of a rifle

²**bayonet** vb **-net·ed** also **-net·ted; -net·ing** also **-net·ting** : to use or stab with a bayonet

bay·ou \'bī-yü, -ō\ n [Louisiana French, fr. Choctaw bayuk] : a marshy or sluggish body of water

bay rum n : a fragrant liquid used esp. as a cologne or after-shave lotion

ba·zaar \bə-'zär\ n 1 : a group of shops : MARKETPLACE 2 : a fair for the sale of articles usu. for charity

ba·zoo·ka \bə-'zü-kə\ n [bazooka (a crude musical instrument made of pipes and a funnel)] : a weapon consisting of a tube that launches a rocket able to pierce armor

¹**BB** \'bē-(ˌ)bē\ n : a small round shot pellet

²**BB** abbr base on balls

BBB abbr Better Business Bureau

BBC abbr British Broadcasting Corporation

bbl abbr barrel; barrels

BC abbr 1 before Christ — often printed in small capitals and often punctuated 2 British Columbia

¹**bcc** \ˌbē-ˌsē-'sē\ vt 1 : to send a blind carbon copy to 2 : to send as a blind carbon copy

²**bcc** abbr blind carbon copy

B cell n [bone-marrow-derived cell] : any of the lymphocytes that secrete antibodies when mature

B complex n : VITAMIN B COMPLEX

bd abbr 1 board 2 bound

bdl or **bdle** abbr bundle

bdrm abbr bedroom

be \'bē\ vb, past 1st & 3d sing **was** \'wəz, 'wäz\; 2d sing **were** \'wər\; pl **were**; past subjunctive **were**; past part **been** \'bin, 'ben\; pres part **be·ing** \'bē-iŋ\; pres 1st sing **am** \əm, 'am\; 2d sing **are** \ər, 'är\; 3d sing **is** \'iz, əz\; pl **are**; pres subjunctive **be** 1 : to equal in meaning or symbolically ⟨God is love⟩; also : to have a specified qualification or relationship ⟨leaves are green⟩ ⟨this fish is a trout⟩ 2 : to have objective existence ⟨I think, therefore I am⟩; also : to have or occupy a particular place ⟨here is your pen⟩ 3 : to take place : OCCUR ⟨the meeting is

tonight⟩ **4** — used with the past participle of transitive verbs as a passive voice auxiliary ⟨the door *was* opened⟩ **5** — used as the auxiliary of the present participle in expressing continuous action ⟨he *is* sleeping⟩ **6** — used as an auxiliary with the past participle of some intransitive verbs to form archaic perfect tenses **7** — used as an auxiliary with *to* and the infinitive to express futurity, prearrangement, or obligation ⟨you *are* to wait here⟩
Be *symbol* beryllium
¹beach \'bēch\ *n* : a sandy or gravelly part of the shore of an ocean or lake
²beach *vb* : to run or drive ashore
beach buggy *n* : DUNE BUGGY
beach·comb·er \'bēch-ˌkō-mər\ *n* : a person who searches along a shore for something of use or value
beach·head \'bēch-ˌhed\ *n* : a small area on an enemy-held shore occupied in the initial stages of an invasion
bea·con \'bē-kən\ *n* **1** : a signal fire **2** : a guiding or warning signal (as a lighthouse) **3** : a radio transmitter emitting signals for guidance of aircraft
¹bead \'bēd\ *n* [ME *bede* prayer, prayer bead, fr. OE *bed*, *gebed* prayer] **1** *pl* : a series of prayers and meditations made with a rosary **2** : a small piece of material pierced for threading on a line (as in a rosary) **3** : a small globular body **4** : a narrow projecting rim or band — **bead·ing** *n* — **beady** *adj*
²bead *vb* : to form into a bead
bea·dle \'bē-dᵊl\ *n* : a usu. English parish officer whose duties include keeping order in church
bea·gle \'bē-gəl\ *n* : a small short-legged smooth-coated hound
beak \'bēk\ *n* : the bill of a bird and esp. of a bird of prey; *also* : a pointed projecting part — **beaked** \'bēkt\ *adj*
bea·ker \'bē-kər\ *n* **1** : a large widemouthed drinking cup **2** : a widemouthed thin-walled laboratory vessel
¹beam \'bēm\ *n* **1** : a large long piece of timber or metal **2** : the bar of a balance from which the scales hang **3** : the breadth of a ship at its widest part **4** : a ray or shaft of light **5** : a collection of nearly parallel rays (as X-rays) or particles (as electrons) **6** : a constant radio signal transmitted for the guidance of pilots; *also* : the course indicated by this signal
²beam *vb* **1** : to send out light **2** : BROADCAST **3** : to transmit (data) electronically **4** : to smile with joy
¹bean \'bēn\ *n* : the edible seed borne in pods by some leguminous plants; *also* : a plant or a pod bearing beans
²bean *vb* : to strike on the head with an object
bean·bag \'bēn-ˌbag\ *n* : a cloth bag partially filled typically with dried beans and used as a toy
bean·ball \'bēn-ˌbȯl\ *n* : a pitch thrown at a batter's head
bean curd *n* : TOFU
bean·ie \'bē-nē\ *n* : a small round tight-fitting skullcap
beano \'bē-nō\ *n, pl* **beanos** : BINGO
¹bear \'ber\ *n, pl* **bears 1** *or pl* **bear** : any of a family of large heavy mammals with shaggy hair and small tails **2** : a gruff or sullen person **3** : one who sells (as securities) in expectation of a price decline — **bear·ish** *adj*
²bear *vb* **bore** \'bȯr\; **borne** \'bȯrn\ *also* **born** \'bȯrn\; **bear·ing 1** : CARRY **2** : to be equipped with **3** : to give as testimony ⟨~ witness to the facts of the case⟩ **4** : to give birth to; *also* : PRODUCE, YIELD ⟨a tree that ~s regularly⟩ **5** : ENDURE, SUSTAIN ⟨~ pain⟩ ⟨*bore* the weight on piles⟩; *also* : to exert pressure or influence **6** : to go in an indicated direction ⟨~ to the right⟩ — **bear·able** *adj* — **bear·er** *n*
¹beard \'bird\ *n* **1** : the hair that grows on the face of a man **2** : a growth of bristly hairs (as on a goat's chin) — **beard·ed** \'bir-dəd\ *adj* — **beard·less** *adj*
²beard *vb* : to confront boldly
bearing *n* **1** : manner of carrying oneself : COMPORTMENT **2** : a supporting object, purpose, or point **3** : a machine part in which another part (as an axle or pin) turns **4** : an emblem in a coat of arms **5** : the position or direction of one point with respect to another or to the compass; *also* : a determination of position **6** *pl* : comprehension of one's situation **7** : connection with or influence on something; *also* : SIGNIFICANCE
bear market *n* : a market in which securities or commodities are persistently declining in value

bear·skin \'ber-ˌskin\ *n* : an article (as a hat) made of the skin of a bear
beast \'bēst\ *n* **1** : ANIMAL 1; *esp* : a 4-footed mammal **2** : a contemptible person
¹beast·ly \'bēst-lē\ *adj* **beast·li·er; -est 1** : BESTIAL **2** : ABOMINABLE, DISAGREEABLE — **beast·li·ness** \-nəs\ *n*
²beastly *adv* : VERY ⟨a ~ cold day⟩
¹beat \'bēt\ *vb* **beat; beat·en** \'bē-tᵊn\ *or* **beat; beat·ing 1** : to strike repeatedly **2** : TREAD **3** : to affect or alter by beating ⟨~ metal into sheets⟩ **4** : to sound (as an alarm) on a drum **5** : OVERCOME ⟨~ his opponent⟩; *also* : SURPASS ⟨a meal hard to ~⟩ **6** : to act or arrive before ⟨~ his brother home⟩ **7** : THROB — **beat·er** *n*
²beat *n* **1** : a single stroke or blow esp. of a series; *also* : PULSATION **2** : a rhythmic stress in poetry or music or the rhythmic effect of these **3** : a regularly traversed course
³beat *adj* **1** : EXHAUSTED **2** : of or relating to beatniks
be·atif·ic \ˌbē-ə-'ti-fik\ *adj* : giving or indicative of great joy or bliss
be·at·i·fy \bē-'a-tə-ˌfī\ *vb* **-fied; -fy·ing 1** : to make supremely happy **2** : to declare to have attained the blessedness of heaven and authorize the title "Blessed" for — **be·at·i·fi·ca·tion** \-ˌa-tə-fə-'kā-shən\ *n*
be·at·i·tude \bē-'a-tə-ˌtüd, -ˌtyüd\ *n* **1** : a state of utmost bliss **2** : any of the declarations made in the Sermon on the Mount (Mt 5:3–12) beginning "Blessed are"
beat·nik \'bēt-nik\ *n* : a usu. young and artistic person who rejects the mores of established society
beau \'bō\ *n, pl* **beaux** \'bōz\ *or* **beaus** [F, fr. *beau* beautiful, fr. L *bellus* pretty] **1** : a man of fashion : DANDY **2** : BOYFRIEND 2
beau geste \bō-'zhest\ *n, pl* **beaux gestes** *or* **beau gestes** \bō-'zhest\ [F] : a graceful or magnanimous gesture
beau ide·al \ˌbō-ī-'dē(-ə)l\ *n, pl* **beau ideals** [F] : the perfect type or model
Beau·jo·lais \ˌbō-zhō-'lā\ *n* : a light fruity red wine
beau monde \bō-'mänd, -'mōⁿd\ *n, pl* **beau mondes** \-'mänz, -'mändz\ *or* **beaux mondes** \bō-'mōⁿd\ [F] : the world of high society and fashion
beau·te·ous \'byü-tē-əs\ *adj* : BEAUTIFUL — **beau·te·ous·ly** *adv*
beau·ti·cian \byü-'ti-shən\ *n* : COSMETOLOGIST
beau·ti·ful \'byü-ti-fəl\ *adj* : characterized by beauty : LOVELY ♦ *Synonyms* PRETTY, FAIR, COMELY — **beau·ti·ful·ly** \-f(ə-)lē\ *adv*
beautiful people *n pl, often cap B&P* : wealthy or famous people whose lifestyle is usu. expensive and well-publicized
beau·ti·fy \'byü-tə-ˌfī\ *vb* **-fied; -fy·ing** : to make more beautiful — **beau·ti·fi·ca·tion** \ˌbyü-tə-fə-'kā-shən\ *n* — **beau·ti·fi·er** *n*
beau·ty \'byü-tē\ *n, pl* **beauties** : qualities that give pleasure to the senses or exalt the mind : LOVELINESS; *also* : something having such qualities
beauty shop *n* : an establishment where hairdressing, facials, and manicures are done
beaux arts \bō-'zär\ *n pl* [F] : FINE ARTS
bea·ver \'bē-vər\ *n, pl* **beavers** : a large fur-bearing herbivorous rodent that builds dams and underwater houses of mud and sticks; *also* : its fur

beaver

be·calm \bi-'käm, -'kälm\ *vb* : to keep (as a ship) motionless by lack of wind
be·cause \bi-'kȯz, -'kəz\ *conj* : for the reason that ⟨ran away ~ they were afraid⟩
because of *prep* : by reason of
beck \'bek\ *n* : a beckoning gesture; *also* : SUMMONS

beck·on \\'be-kən\\ vb : to summon or signal esp. by a nod or gesture; also : ATTRACT
be·cloud \\bi-'klaud\\ vb : OBSCURE
be·come \\bi-'kəm\\ vb -came \\-'kām\\; -come; -com·ing 1 : to come to be ⟨~ tired⟩ 2 : to suit or be suitable to ⟨her dress ~s her⟩
becoming adj : SUITABLE, FIT; also : ATTRACTIVE — **be·com·ing·ly** adv
¹**bed** \\'bed\\ n 1 : an article of furniture to sleep on 2 : a plot of ground prepared for plants 3 : FOUNDATION, BOTTOM ⟨the ocean ~⟩ 4 : LAYER, STRATUM ⟨a ~ of rice⟩
²**bed** vb **bed·ded; bed·ding** 1 : to put or go to bed 2 : to fix in a foundation : EMBED 3 : to plant in beds 4 : to lay or lie flat or in layers
bed–and–breakfast n : an establishment offering lodging and breakfast
be·daub \\bi-'dȯb\\ vb : SMEAR
be·daz·zle \\bi-'da-zəl\\ vb : to confuse by or as if by a strong light; also : FASCINATE — **be·daz·zle·ment** n
bed·bug \\'bed-ˌbəg\\ n : a wingless bloodsucking bug infesting houses and esp. beds
bed·clothes \\'bed-ˌklōthz\\ n pl : materials for making up a bed
bed·ding \\'be-diŋ\\ n 1 : BEDCLOTHES 2 : FOUNDATION ⟨straw ~⟩
be·deck \\bi-'dek\\ vb : ADORN
be·dev·il \\bi-'de-vəl\\ vb 1 : HARASS, TORMENT 2 : CONFUSE, MUDDLE
be·dew \\bi-'dü, -'dyü\\ vb : to wet with or as if with dew
bed·fast \\'bed-ˌfast\\ adj : BEDRIDDEN
bed·fel·low \\-ˌfe-lō\\ n 1 : one sharing the bed of another 2 : a close associate : ALLY ⟨politics makes strange ~s⟩
be·di·zen \\bi-'dī-z²n, -'di-\\ vb : to dress or adorn with showy or vulgar finery
bed·lam \\'bed-ləm\\ n [Bedlam, popular name for the Hospital of St. Mary of Bethlehem, London, an insane asylum, fr. ME Bedlem Bethlehem] 1 often cap : an insane asylum 2 : a scene of uproar and confusion ⟨~ in the court⟩
bed·ou·in also **bed·u·in** \\'be-də-wən\\ n, pl **bedouin** or **bedouins** also **beduin** or **beduins** often cap [ME Bedoyne, fr. MF bedoïn, fr. Ar badawī desert dweller] : a nomadic Arab of the Arabian, Syrian, or northern African deserts
bed·pan \\'bed-ˌpan\\ n : a shallow vessel used by a bedridden person for urination or defecation
bed·post \\-ˌpōst\\ n : the post of a bed
be·drag·gled \\bi-'dra-gəld\\ adj : soiled and disordered as if by being drenched
bed·rid·den \\'bed-ˌri-d²n\\ adj : kept in bed by illness or weakness
¹**bed·rock** \\-'räk\\ n : the solid rock underlying surface materials (as soil)
²**bedrock** adj : solidly fundamental, basic, or reliable ⟨traditional ~ values⟩
bed·roll \\'bed-ˌrōl\\ n : bedding rolled up for carrying
bed·room \\-ˌrüm, -ˌrum\\ n : a room containing a bed and used esp. for sleeping
bed·side \\-ˌsīd\\ n : the place beside a bed esp. of a sick or dying person
bed·sore \\-ˌsȯr\\ n : an ulceration of tissue deprived of adequate blood supply by prolonged pressure
bed·spread \\-ˌspred\\ n : a usu. ornamental cloth cover for a bed
bed·stead \\-ˌsted\\ n : the framework of a bed
bed·time \\-ˌtīm\\ n : time for going to bed
bed–wet·ting \\-ˌwe-tiŋ\\ n : involuntary discharge of urine esp. in bed during sleep — **bed–wet·ter** n
¹**bee** \\'bē\\ n : any of numerous 4-winged insects (as honeybees or bumblebees) that feed on nectar and pollen and that sometimes produce honey or have a painful sting
²**bee** n : a gathering of people for a specific purpose ⟨a quilting ~⟩
beech \\'bēch\\ n, pl **beech·es** or **beech** : any of a genus of hardwood trees with smooth gray bark and small sweet triangular nuts; also : its wood — **beech·en** \\'bē-chən\\ adj
beech·nut \\'bēch-ˌnət\\ n : the nut of a beech
¹**beef** \\'bēf\\ n, pl **beefs** \\'bēfs\\ or **beeves** \\'bēvz\\ 1 : the flesh of a steer, cow, or bull; also : the dressed carcass of a beef animal 2 : a steer, cow, or bull esp. when fattened for food 3 : MUSCLE, BRAWN 4 pl beefs : COMPLAINT

²**beef** vb 1 : STRENGTHEN — usu. used with up ⟨~ed up security⟩ 2 : COMPLAIN
beef·eat·er \\'bēf-ˌfē-tər\\ n : a yeoman of the guard of an English monarch
beef·steak \\-ˌstāk\\ n : a slice of beef suitable for broiling or frying
beefy \\'bē-fē\\ adj **beef·i·er; -est** : THICKSET, BRAWNY ⟨a ~ wrestler⟩
bee·hive \\'bē-ˌhīv\\ n : HIVE 1, HIVE 3
bee·keep·er \\-ˌkē-pər\\ n : a person who raises bees — **bee·keep·ing** n
bee·line \\-ˌlīn\\ n : a straight direct course
been past part of BE
beep·er \\'bē-pər\\ n : PAGER; esp : one that beeps
beer \\'bir\\ n : an alcoholic beverage brewed from malt and hops — **beery** adj
beer belly n : POTBELLY
bees·wax \\'bēz-ˌwaks\\ n : WAX 1
beet \\'bēt\\ n : a garden plant with edible leaves and a thick sweet root used as a vegetable, as a source of sugar, or as forage; also : its root
¹**bee·tle** \\'bē-t²l\\ n : any of an order of insects having four wings of which the stiff outer pair covers the membranous inner pair when not in flight
²**beetle** vb **bee·tled; bee·tling** : to jut out : PROJECT
be·fall \\bi-'fȯl\\ vb -fell \\-'fel\\; -fall·en \\-'fȯ-lən\\ : to happen to : OCCUR
be·fit \\bi-'fit\\ vb : to be suitable to
be·fog \\bi-'fȯg, -'fäg\\ vb : OBSCURE; also : CONFUSE ⟨drink befogged his senses⟩
¹**be·fore** \\bi-'fȯr\\ adv or adj 1 : in front 2 : EARLIER
²**before** prep 1 : in front of ⟨stood ~ him⟩ 2 : earlier than ⟨got there ~ me⟩ 3 : in a more important category than ⟨put quality ~ quantity⟩
³**before** conj 1 : earlier than the time that ⟨she started ~ I did⟩ 2 : more willingly than ⟨he'd starve ~ he'd steal⟩
be·fore·hand \\bi-'fȯr-ˌhand\\ adv or adj : in advance
be·foul \\bi-'fau̇(-ə)l\\ vb : SOIL
be·friend \\bi-'frend\\ vb : to act as friend to
be·fud·dle \\bi-'fə-d²l\\ vb : MUDDLE, CONFUSE
beg \\'beg\\ vb **begged; beg·ging** 1 : to ask as a charity; also : ENTREAT 2 : EVADE; also : assume as established, settled, or proved ⟨~ the question⟩
be·get \\bi-'get\\ vb -got \\-'gät\\; -got·ten \\-'gä-t²n\\ or -got; -get·ting : to become the father of : SIRE
¹**beg·gar** \\'be-gər\\ n : one that begs; esp : a person who begs as a way of life
²**beggar** vb : IMPOVERISH
beg·gar·ly \\'be-gər-lē\\ adj 1 : contemptibly mean or inadequate 2 : marked by unrelieved poverty ⟨a ~ life⟩
beg·gary \\'be-gə-rē\\ n : extreme poverty
be·gin \\bi-'gin\\ vb **be·gan** \\-'gan\\; **be·gun** \\-'gən\\; **be·gin·ning** 1 : to do the first part of an action : COMMENCE 2 : to come into being : ARISE; also : FOUND ⟨he began the movement⟩ 3 : ORIGINATE, INVENT — **be·gin·ner** n
beg off vb : to ask to be excused from something
be·gone \\bi-'gȯn\\ vb : to go away : DEPART — used esp. in the imperative
be·go·nia \\bi-'gō-nyə\\ n : any of a genus of tropical herbs widely grown for their showy leaves and waxy flowers
be·grime \\bi-'grīm\\ vb **be·grimed; be·grim·ing** : to make dirty
be·grudge \\bi-'grəj\\ vb 1 : to give or concede reluctantly 2 : to be reluctant to grant or allow — **be·grudg·ing·ly** \\-'grə-jiŋ-lē\\ adv
be·guile \\bi-'gī(-ə)l\\ vb **be·guiled; be·guil·ing** 1 : DECEIVE 2 : to while away ⟨beguiled sorrow with music⟩ 3 : to engage the interest of by guile
be·guine \\bi-'gēn\\ n [AmerF béguine, fr. F béguin flirtation] : a vigorous popular dance of the islands of Saint Lucia and Martinique
be·gum \\'bā-gəm, 'bē-\\ n : a Muslim woman of high rank
be·half \\bi-'haf, -'häf\\ n : BENEFIT, SUPPORT, DEFENSE ⟨argued in their ~⟩
be·have \\bi-'hāv\\ vb **be·haved; be·hav·ing** 1 : to bear, comport, or conduct oneself in a particular and esp. a proper way 2 : to act, function, or react in a particular way
be·hav·ior \\bi-'hā-vyər\\ n : way of behaving; esp : personal conduct — **be·hav·ior·al** \\-vyə-rəl\\ adj — **be·hav·ior·al·ly** \\-rə-lē\\ adv

behaviorism • bench

be·hav·ior·ism \bi-'hā-vyə-ˌri-zəm\ *n* : a school of psychology concerned with the objective evidence of behavior without reference to conscious experience

be·hav·ior·ist \-vyə-rist\ *n* 1 : a person who supports behaviorism 2 : a person who studies behavior

be·hav·iour, be·hav·iour·ism *chiefly Brit var of* BEHAVIOR, BEHAVIORISM

be·head \bi-'hed\ *vb* : to cut off the head of

be·he·moth \bi-'hē-məth, 'bē-ə-ˌmäth\ *n* : a huge powerful animal described in Job 40:15–24; *also* : something of monstrous size or power

be·hest \bi-'hest\ *n* 1 : COMMAND 2 : an urgent prompting

¹be·hind \bi-'hīnd\ *adv or adj* 1 : BACK, BACKWARD ⟨look ~⟩ 2 : LATE, SLOW

²behind *prep* 1 : in or to a place or situation in back of or to the rear of ⟨look ~ you⟩ ⟨the staff stayed ~ the troops⟩ 2 : inferior to (as in rank) : BELOW ⟨three games ~ the first-place team⟩ 3 : in support of : SUPPORTING ⟨we're ~ you all the way⟩

be·hind·hand \bi-'hīnd-ˌhand\ *adj* : being in arrears ♦ *Synonyms* TARDY, LATE, OVERDUE, BELATED

be·hold \bi-'hōld\ *vb* -held \-'held\; -hold·ing 1 : to have in sight : SEE 2 — used imperatively to direct the attention ♦ *Synonyms* VIEW, OBSERVE, NOTICE, ESPY —
be·hold·er *n*

be·hold·en \bi-'hōl-dən\ *adj* : OBLIGATED, INDEBTED

be·hoove \bi-'hüv\ *vb* be·hooved; be·hoov·ing : to be necessary, proper, or advantageous for

be·hove *chiefly Brit var of* BEHOOVE

beige \'bāzh\ *n* : a pale dull yellowish brown — beige *adj*

be·ing \'bē-iŋ\ *n* 1 : EXISTENCE; *also* : LIFE 2 : the qualities or constitution of an existent thing 3 : a living thing; *esp* : PERSON

be·la·bor \bi-'lā-bər\ *vb* : to assail (as with words) tiresomely or at length

be·la·bour *chiefly Brit var of* BELABOR

be·lat·ed \bi-'lā-təd\ *adj* : DELAYED, LATE ⟨~ birthday wishes⟩

be·lay \bi-'lā\ *vb* 1 : to wind (a rope) around a pin or cleat in order to hold secure 2 : QUIT, STOP — used in the imperative

belch \'belch\ *vb* 1 : to expel (gas) from the stomach through the mouth 2 : to gush forth ⟨a volcano ~ing lava⟩ — belch *n*

bel·dam *or* bel·dame \'bel-dəm\ *n* [ME *beldam* grandmother, fr. AF *bel* beautiful + ME *dam* lady, mother] : an old woman

be·lea·guer \bi-'lē-gər\ *vb* 1 : BESIEGE 2 : HARASS ⟨~ed parents⟩

bel·fry \'bel-frē\ *n, pl* belfries : a tower for a bell (as on a church); *also* : the part of the tower in which the bell hangs

Belg *abbr* Belgian; Belgium

Bel·gian endive \'bel-jən\ *n* : the blanched shoot of chicory

Belgian waffle *n* : a waffle having large depressions and usu. topped with fruit and whipped cream

be·lie \bi-'lī\ *vb* -lied; -ly·ing 1 : MISREPRESENT 2 : to show (something) to be false 3 : to run counter to

be·lief \bə-'lēf\ *n* 1 : CONFIDENCE, TRUST 2 : something (as a tenet or creed) believed ♦ *Synonyms* CONVICTION, OPINION, PERSUASION, SENTIMENT

be·lieve \bə-'lēv\ *vb* be·lieved; be·liev·ing 1 : to have religious convictions 2 : to have a firm conviction about something : accept as true 3 : to hold as an opinion : SUPPOSE — be·liev·able \-'lē-və-bəl\ *adj* — be·liev·ably \-blē\ *adv* — be·liev·er *n*

be·like \bi-'līk\ *adv, archaic* : PROBABLY

be·lit·tle \bi-'li-t²l\ *vb* -lit·tled; -lit·tling : to make seem little or less; *also* : DISPARAGE ⟨belittled his opponent⟩

¹bell \'bel\ *n* 1 : a hollow metallic device that makes a ringing sound when struck 2 : the sounding or stroke of a bell (as on shipboard to tell the time); *also* : time so indicated 3 : something with the flared form of a bell

²bell *vb* : to provide with a bell

bel·la·don·na \ˌbe-lə-'dä-nə\ *n* [It, lit., beautiful lady] : a medicinal extract (as atropine) from a poisonous European herb related to the potato; *also* : this herb

bell·bot·toms \'bel-ˌbä-təmz\ *n pl* : pants with wide flaring bottoms — bell–bottom *adj*

bell·boy \'bel-ˌbȯi\ *n* : BELLHOP

belle \'bel\ *n* : an attractive and popular girl or woman

belles let·tres \bel-'letrᵉ\ *n pl* [F] : literature that is an end in itself and not practical or purely informative — bel·le·tris·tic \ˌbe-lə-'tris-tik\ *adj*

bell·hop \'bel-ˌhäp\ *n* : a hotel or club employee who takes guests to rooms, carries luggage, and runs errands

bel·li·cose \'be-li-ˌkōs\ *adj* : WARLIKE, PUGNACIOUS ♦ *Synonyms* BELLIGERENT, QUARRELSOME, COMBATIVE, CONTENTIOUS — bel·li·cos·i·ty \ˌbe-li-'kä-sə-tē\ *n*

bel·lig·er·en·cy \bə-'li-jə-rən-sē\ *n* 1 : the status of a nation engaged in war 2 : BELLIGERENCE, TRUCULENCE

bel·lig·er·ent \-rənt\ *adj* 1 : waging war 2 : aggressively self-assertive ♦ *Synonyms* BELLICOSE, PUGNACIOUS, COMBATIVE, CONTENTIOUS, WARLIKE — bel·lig·er·ence \-rəns\ *n* — belligerent *n* — bel·lig·er·ent·ly *adv*

bel·low \'be-lō\ *vb* 1 : to make the deep hollow sound characteristic of a bull 2 : to shout in a deep voice — bellow *n*

bel·lows \-lōz, -ləz\ *n sing or pl* : a closed device with sides that can be spread apart and then pressed together to draw in air and expel it through a tube

bell·weth·er \'bel-'we-thər, -ˌwe-\ *n* : one that takes the lead or initiative; *also* : an indicator of trends

¹bel·ly \'be-lē\ *n, pl* bellies [ME *bely* bellows, belly, fr. OE *belg* bag, skin] 1 : ABDOMEN 1; *also* : POTBELLY 2 : the underpart of an animal's body

²belly *vb* bel·lied; bel·ly·ing : BULGE

¹bel·ly·ache \'be-lē-ˌāk\ *n* : pain in the abdomen : STOMACHACHE

²bellyache *vb* : COMPLAIN

belly button *n* : the human navel

belly dance *n* : a usu. solo dance emphasizing movement of the belly — belly dance *vb* — belly dancer *n*

belly laugh *n* : a deep hearty laugh

be·long \bi-'lȯŋ\ *vb* 1 : to be suitable or appropriate; *also* : to be properly situated ⟨shoes ~ in the closet⟩ 2 : to be the property ⟨this ~s to me⟩; *also* : to be attached (as through birth or membership) ⟨~ to a club⟩ 3 : to form an attribute or part ⟨this wheel ~s to the cart⟩ 4 : to be classified ⟨whales ~ among the mammals⟩

be·long·ings \-'lȯŋ-iŋz\ *n pl* : GOODS, EFFECTS, POSSESSIONS

be·loved \bi-'ləvd, -'lə-vəd\ *adj* : dearly loved — beloved *n*

¹be·low \bi-'lō\ *adv* 1 : in or to a lower place or rank 2 : on earth 3 : in hell

²below *prep* 1 : lower than ⟨~ sea level⟩ 2 : inferior to (as in rank)

be·low·decks \bi-ˌlō-'deks, -'lō-ˌdeks\ *adv* : inside the superstructure of a boat or down to a lower deck

¹belt \'belt\ *n* 1 : a strip (as of leather) worn about the waist 2 : a flexible continuous band to communicate motion or convey material 3 : a region marked by some distinctive feature; *esp* : one suited to a particular crop

²belt *vb* 1 : to encircle or secure with a belt 2 : to beat with or as if with a belt 3 : to mark with an encircling band 4 : to sing loudly

³belt *n* 1 : a jarring blow : WHACK 2 : DRINK ⟨a ~ of whiskey⟩

belt·er \'bel-tər\ *n* : a singer with a powerful voice

belt–tightening *n* : a reduction in spending

belt·way \'belt-ˌwā\ *n* : a highway around a city

be·lu·ga \bə-'lü-gə\ *n* [Russ] 1 : a large white sturgeon of the Black Sea, Caspian Sea, and their tributaries that is a source of caviar; *also* : caviar from beluga roe 2 : a whale of arctic and subarctic waters that is white when mature

bel·ve·dere \'bel-və-ˌdir\ *n* [It, lit., beautiful view] : a structure (as a summerhouse) designed to command a view

be·mire \bi-'mī(-ə)r\ *vb* : to cover or soil with or sink in mire

be·moan \bi-'mōn\ *vb* : LAMENT, DEPLORE ♦ *Synonyms* BEWAIL, GRIEVE, MOAN, WEEP

be·muse \bi-'myüz\ *vb* : BEWILDER, CONFUSE

¹bench \'bench\ *n* 1 : a long seat for two or more persons 2 : the seat of a judge in court; *also* : the office or dignity of a judge 3 : COURT; *also* : JUDGES 4 : a table for holding work and tools ⟨a carpenter's ~⟩

²bench *vb* 1 : to furnish with benches 2 : to seat on a bench 3 : to remove from or keep out of a game

¹**bench·mark** \'bench-ˌmärk\ *n* **1** *usu* **bench mark** : a mark on a permanent object serving as an elevation reference in topographical surveys **2** : a point of reference for measurement; *also* : STANDARD

²**benchmark** *vb* : to study (as a competitor's business practices) in order to improve one's own performance

bench press *n* : an exercise in which a weight is raised by a person lying on a bench — **bench–press** *vb*

bench warrant *n* : a warrant issued by a presiding judge or by a court against a person guilty of contempt or indicted for a crime

¹**bend** \'bend\ *vb* **bent** \'bent\; **bend·ing** **1** : to draw (as a bow) taut **2** : to curve or cause a change of shape in ⟨∼ a bar⟩ **3** : to make fast : SECURE **4** : DEFLECT **5** : to turn in a certain direction ⟨*bent* his steps toward town⟩ **6** : APPLY ⟨*bent* themselves to the task⟩ **7** : SUBDUE **8** : to curve downward **9** : YIELD, SUBMIT

²**bend** *n* **1** : an act or process of bending **2** : something bent; *esp* : CURVE **3** *pl* : a painful and sometimes fatal disorder caused by release of gas bubbles in the tissues upon too rapid decrease in air pressure after a stay in a compressed atmosphere

³**bend** *n* : a knot by which a rope is fastened (as to another rope)

bend·er \'ben-dər\ *n* : SPREE ⟨hungover after a weekend ∼⟩

¹**be·neath** \bi-'nēth\ *adv* : BELOW ⟨the mountains and the town ∼⟩ ♦ *Synonyms* UNDER, UNDERNEATH

²**beneath** *prep* **1** : BELOW, UNDER ⟨stood ∼ a tree⟩ **2** : unworthy of ⟨considered such behavior ∼ her⟩ **3** : concealed by ⟨a warm heart ∼ a gruff manner⟩

bene·dic·tion \ˌbe-nə-'dik-shən\ *n* : the invocation of a blessing esp. at the close of a public worship service

ben·e·fac·tion \-'fak-shən\ *n* : a charitable donation ♦ *Synonyms* CONTRIBUTION, ALMS, BENEFICENCE, OFFERING

ben·e·fac·tor \'ben-ə-ˌfak-tər\ *n* : one that confers a benefit and esp. a benefaction

ben·e·fac·tress \-ˌfak-trəs\ *n* : a woman who is a benefactor

ben·e·fice \'be-nə-fəs\ *n* : an ecclesiastical office to which the revenue from an endowment is attached

be·nef·i·cence \bə-'ne-fə-səns\ *n* **1** : beneficent quality **2** : BENEFACTION

be·nef·i·cent \-sənt\ *adj* : doing or producing good (as by acts of kindness or charity); *also* : BENEFICIAL

ben·e·fi·cial \ˌbe-nə-'fi-shəl\ *adj* : being of benefit or help : HELPFUL ♦ *Synonyms* ADVANTAGEOUS, PROFITABLE, FAVORABLE, PROPITIOUS — **ben·e·fi·cial·ly** *adv*

ben·e·fi·cia·ry \ˌbe-nə-'fi-shē-ˌer-ē, -'fi-shə-rē\ *n, pl* **-ries** : one that receives a benefit (as the income of a trust or the proceeds of an insurance)

¹**ben·e·fit** \'be-nə-ˌfit\ *n* **1** : ADVANTAGE ⟨the ∼s of exercise⟩ **2** : useful aid : HELP; *also* : material aid or service provided or due (as in sickness or unemployment) as a right in addition to regular pay **3** : a performance or event to raise funds

²**benefit** *vb* **-fit·ed** \-ˌfi-təd\ *also* **-fit·ted; -fit·ing** *also* **-fit·ting** **1** : to be useful or profitable to **2** : to receive benefit

be·nev·o·lence \bə-'ne-və-ləns\ *n* **1** : charitable nature **2** : an act of kindness : CHARITY — **be·nev·o·lent** \-lənt\ *adj* — **be·nev·o·lent·ly** *adv*

be·night·ed \bi-'nī-təd\ *adj* **1** : overtaken by darkness or night **2** : living in ignorance

be·nign \bi-'nīn\ *adj* [ME *benigne*, fr. AF, fr. L *benignus*] **1** : of a gentle disposition; *also* : showing kindness **2** : of a mild kind; *esp* : not malignant ⟨∼ tumors⟩ ♦ *Synonyms* BENIGNANT, KIND, KINDLY, GOOD-HEARTED — **be·nig·ni·ty** \-'nig-nə-tē\ *n* — **be·nign·ly** *adv*

be·nig·nant \-'nig-nənt\ *adj* : BENIGN 1 ♦ *Synonyms* KIND, KINDLY, GOOD-HEARTED

ben·i·son \'be-nə-sən, -zən\ *n* : BLESSING, BENEDICTION

¹**bent** \'bent\ *n* **1** : strong inclination or interest; *also* : TALENT **2** : power of endurance ♦ *Synonyms* TALENT, APTITUDE, GIFT, FLAIR, KNACK, GENIUS

²**bent** *adj* **1** : changed by bending : CROOKED ⟨∼ branches⟩ **2** : strongly inclined : DETERMINED ⟨∼ on going⟩

bent grass *n* : any of a genus of stiff velvety grasses used esp. for lawns and pastures

ben·thic \'ben-thik\ *adj* : of, relating to, or occurring at the bottom of a body of water

ben·ton·ite \'ben-tə-ˌnīt\ *n* : an absorptive clay used esp. as a filler (as in paper)

bent·wood \'bent-ˌwu̇d\ *adj* : made of wood bent into shape ⟨a ∼ rocker⟩

be·numb \bi-'nəm\ *vb* **1** : DULL, DEADEN **2** : to make numb esp. by cold

ben·zene \'ben-ˌzēn\ *n* : a colorless volatile flammable liquid hydrocarbon used in organic synthesis and as a solvent — **ben·ze·noid** \-zə-ˌnȯid\ *adj or n*

ben·zine \'ben-ˌzēn\ *n* : any of various flammable petroleum distillates used as solvents or as motor fuels

ben·zo·ate \'ben-zə-ˌwāt\ *n* : a salt or ester of benzoic acid

ben·zo·ic acid \ben-'zō-ik-\ *n* : a white crystalline acid used as a preservative and antiseptic and in synthesizing chemicals

ben·zo·in \'ben-zə-wən, -ˌzȯin\ *n* : a balsamic resin from trees of southern Asia used esp. in medicine and perfumes

be·queath \bi-'kwēth, -'kwēth\ *vb* [ME *bequethen*, fr. OE *becwethan*, fr. *be-* + *cwethan* to say] **1** : to leave by will **2** : to hand down

be·quest \bi-'kwest\ *n* **1** : the action of bequeathing **2** : something bequeathed : LEGACY

be·rate \-'rāt\ *vb* : to scold harshly

Ber·ber \'bər-bər\ *n* : a member of any of various peoples living in northern Africa west of Tripoli

ber·ceuse \ber-'sœz, -'süz\ *n, pl* **ber·ceuses** *same or* -'sü-zəz\ [F, fr. *bercer* to rock] **1** : LULLABY **2** : a musical composition that resembles a lullaby

¹**be·reaved** \bi-'rēvd\ *adj* : suffering the death of a loved one ⟨her ∼ parents⟩ — **be·reave·ment** *n*

²**bereaved** *n, pl* **bereaved** : one who is bereaved

be·reft \-'reft\ *adj* **1** : deprived of or lacking something — usu. used with *of* **2** : BEREAVED ⟨a ∼ mother⟩

be·ret \bə-'rā\ *n* : a round soft cap with no visor

berg \'bərg\ *n* : ICEBERG

beri·beri \ˌber-ē-'ber-ē\ *n* : a deficiency disease marked by weakness, wasting, and nerve damage and caused by lack of thiamine

berke·li·um \'bər-klē-əm\ *n* : an artificially produced radioactive chemical element

berm \'bərm\ *n* : a narrow shelf or path at the top or bottom of a slope; *also* : a mound or bank of earth

Bermuda grass *n* : a creeping grass often used for lawns and pastures

Ber·mu·das \bər-'myü-dəz\ *n pl* : BERMUDA SHORTS

Bermuda shorts *n pl* : knee-length walking shorts

ber·ry \'ber-ē\ *n, pl* **berries** **1** : a small pulpy fruit (as a strawberry) **2** : a simple fruit (as a grape, tomato, or cucumber) with the wall of the ripened ovary thick and pulpy **3** : the dry seed of some plants (as coffee)

ber·serk \bər-'sərk, -'zərk\ *adj* [ON *berserkr* warrior frenzied in battle, prob. fr. *ber-* bear + *serkr* shirt] : FRENZIED, CRAZED ⟨∼ behavior⟩ — **berserk** *adv*

¹**berth** \'bərth\ *n* **1** : adequate distance esp. for a ship to maneuver **2** : the place where a ship is anchored or a vehicle rests **3** : ACCOMMODATIONS **4** : JOB, POSITION ♦ *Synonyms* POST, SITUATION, OFFICE, APPOINTMENT

²**berth** *vb* **1** : to bring or come into a berth **2** : to allot a berth to

ber·yl \'ber-əl\ *n* : a hard silicate mineral occurring as colorless hexagonal crystals when pure

be·ryl·li·um \bə-'ri-lē-əm\ *n* : a light strong metallic chemical element used as a hardener in alloys

be·seech \bi-'sēch\ *vb* **-sought** \-'sȯt\ *or* **-seeched; -seech·ing** : to beg urgently : ENTREAT ♦ *Synonyms* IMPLORE, PLEAD, SUPPLICATE, IMPORTUNE

be·seem \bi-'sēm\ *vb, archaic* : BEFIT

be·set \-'set\ *vb* **-set; -set·ting** **1** : TROUBLE, HARASS ⟨the ills that ∼ humanity⟩ **2** : ASSAIL ⟨∼ by wild dogs⟩; *also* : SURROUND

be·set·ting *adj* : persistently present

¹**be·side** \bi-'sīd\ *prep* **1** : by the side of ⟨sit ∼ me⟩ **2** : BESIDES **3** : not relevant to ⟨∼ the point⟩

²**beside** *adv, archaic* : BESIDES

¹**be·sides** \bi-'sīdz\ *prep* **1** : other than ⟨no one ∼ us⟩ **2** : together with

²**besides** *adv* **1** : as well : ALSO **2** : MOREOVER

be·siege \bi-'sēj\ *vb* : to lay siege to; *also* : to press with requests — **be·sieg·er** *n*

be·smear \-'smir\ vb : SMEAR
be·smirch \-'smərch\ vb : SMIRCH, SOIL
be·som \'bē-zəm\ n : BROOM
be·sot \bi-'sät\ vb be·sot·ted; be·sot·ting 1 : INFATUATE ⟨besotted lovers⟩ 2 : to make dull esp. by drinking
be·spat·ter \-'spa-tər\ vb : SPATTER
be·speak \bi-'spēk\ vb -spoke \-'spōk\; -spo·ken \-'spō-kən\; -speak·ing 1 : PREARRANGE 2 : ADDRESS 3 : REQUEST 4 : INDICATE, SIGNIFY ⟨her new album ~s her talent⟩ 5 : FORETELL
be·sprin·kle \-'sprin-kəl\ vb : SPRINKLE
¹best \'best\ adj, superlative of GOOD 1 : excelling all others 2 : most productive (as of good or satisfaction) ⟨the ~ thing to do⟩ 3 : LARGEST, MOST
²best adv, superlative of WELL 1 : in the best way 2 : MOST
³best n : something that is best
⁴best vb : to get the better of : OUTDO
best friend n : one's closest and dearest friend
bes·tial \'bes-chəl\ adj 1 : of or relating to beasts 2 : resembling a beast esp. in brutality or lack of intelligence
bes·ti·al·i·ty \,bes-chē-'a-lə-tē, ,bēs-\ n, pl -ties 1 : the condition or status of a lower animal 2 : display or gratification of bestial traits or impulses 3 : sexual relations between a human being and a lower animal
bes·ti·ary \'bes-chē-,er-ē\ n, pl -ar·ies : a medieval allegorical or moralizing work on the appearance and habits of animals
best·ie \'be-stē\ n : BEST FRIEND
be·stir \bi-'stər\ vb : to rouse to action
best man n : the principal groomsman at a wedding
be·stow \bi-'stō\ vb 1 : PUT, PLACE, STOW 2 : to present as a gift — be·stow·al n — be·stow·er n
be·stride \bi-'strīd\ vb -strode \-'strōd\; -strid·den \-'strid-ⁿn\; -strid·ing : to ride, sit, or stand astride
¹bet \'bet\ n 1 : something that is wagered, risked, or pledged usu. between two parties on the outcome of a contest; also : the making of such a bet 2 : OPTION ⟨the back road is your best ~⟩
²bet vb bet also bet·ted; bet·ting 1 : to stake on the outcome of an issue or a contest ⟨~ $2 on the race⟩ 2 : to make a bet with 3 : to lay a bet
³bet abbr between
be·ta \'bā-tə\ n 1 : the 2d letter of the Greek alphabet — B or β 2 : a nearly complete form of a new product (as software)
beta–block·er \-,blä-kər\ n : any of a group of drugs that decrease the rate and force of heart contractions and lower high blood pressure
be·ta–car·o·tene \-'ker-ə-,tēn\ n : an isomer of carotene found in dark green and dark yellow vegetables and fruits
be·take \bi-'tāk\ vb -took \-'tůk\; -tak·en \-'tā-kən\; -tak·ing : to cause (oneself) to go
beta particle n : a high-speed electron; esp : one emitted by a radioactive nucleus
beta ray n 1 : BETA PARTICLE 2 : a stream of beta particles
beta test n : a field test of the beta version of a product esp. by outside testers and prior to commercial release — beta test vb
be·tel \'bē-tⁿl\ n : a climbing pepper of southern Asia whose leaves are chewed together with lime and betel nut as a stimulant
betel nut n : the astringent seed of an Asian palm that is chewed with betel leaves
bête noire \,bet-'nwär, ,bāt-\ n, pl bêtes noires \same or -'nwärz\ [F, lit., black beast] : a person or thing strongly disliked or avoided
beth·el \'be-thəl\ n [Heb bēth'ēl house of God] : a place of worship esp. for seamen
be·tide \bi-'tīd\ vb : to happen to
be·times \bi-'tīmz\ adv : in good time : EARLY ✦ Synonyms SOON, SEASONABLY, TIMELY
be·to·ken \bi-'tō-kən\ vb 1 : PRESAGE 2 : to give evidence of ✦ Synonyms INDICATE, ATTEST, BESPEAK, TESTIFY
be·tray \bi-'trā\ vb 1 : to lead astray; esp : SEDUCE 2 : to deliver to an enemy 3 : ABANDON 4 : to prove unfaithful to 5 : to reveal unintentionally; also : SHOW, INDICATE ✦ Synonyms MISLEAD, DELUDE, DECEIVE, BEGUILE — be·tray·al n — be·tray·er n
be·troth \bi-'trōth, -'trȯth\ vb : to promise to marry — be·troth·al n

be·trothed n : the person to whom one is betrothed
¹bet·ter \'be-tər\ adj, comparative of GOOD 1 : greater than half 2 : improved in health 3 : more attractive, favorable, or commendable 4 : more advantageous or effective ⟨a ~ solution⟩ 5 : improved in accuracy or performance
²better vb 1 : to make or become better 2 : SURPASS, EXCEL
³better adv, comparative of WELL 1 : in a superior manner 2 : to a higher or greater degree; also : MORE
⁴better n 1 : something better; also : a superior esp. in merit or rank 2 : ADVANTAGE ⟨got the ~ of his opponent⟩
⁵better verbal auxiliary : had better ⟨you ~ hurry⟩
better half n : SPOUSE
bet·ter·ment \'be-tər-mənt\ n : IMPROVEMENT
bet·tor or bet·ter \'be-tər\ n : one that bets
be·tween \bi-'twēn\ prep 1 : by the common action of ⟨earned $10,000 ~ the two of them⟩ 2 : in the interval separating ⟨an alley ~ two buildings⟩; also : in intermediate relation to 3 : in point of comparison of ⟨choose ~ two cars⟩
²between adv : in an intervening space or interval
be·twixt \bi-'twikst\ adv or prep : BETWEEN
¹bev·el \'be-vəl\ n 1 : a device for adjusting the slant of the surfaces of a piece of work 2 : the angle or slant that one surface or line makes with another when not at right angles
²bevel vb -eled or -elled; -el·ing or -el·ling 1 : to cut or shape to a bevel 2 : INCLINE, SLANT
bev·er·age \'bev-rij\ n : a drinkable liquid
bevy \'be-vē\ n, pl bev·ies 1 : a large group or collection 2 : a group of animals and esp. quail
be·wail \bi-'wāl\ vb : LAMENT ✦ Synonyms DEPLORE, BEMOAN, GRIEVE, MOAN, WEEP
be·ware \-'wer\ vb : to be on one's guard : be wary of
be·wil·der \bi-'wil-dər\ vb : PERPLEX, CONFUSE ✦ Synonyms MYSTIFY, DISTRACT, PUZZLE — be·wil·der·ment n
be·witch \-'wich\ vb 1 : to affect by witchcraft 2 : CHARM, FASCINATE ✦ Synonyms ENCHANT, ATTRACT, CAPTIVATE — be·witch·ment n
bey \'bā\ n 1 : a former Turkish provincial governor 2 : the former native ruler of Tunis or Tunisia
¹be·yond \bē-'änd\ adv 1 : FARTHER ⟨extends to the river and ~⟩ 2 : BESIDES
²beyond prep 1 : on or to the farther side of 2 : out of the reach or sphere of 3 : BESIDES
be·zel \'bē-zəl, 'be-\ n 1 : a rim that holds a transparent covering (as on a watch) 2 : the faceted part of a cut gem that rises above the setting
bf abbr boldface
BFF abbr best friends forever
BG or B Gen abbr brigadier general
Bh symbol bohrium
bhang \'baŋ\ n [Hindi bhāṅg] : HEMP; also : a mildly intoxicating preparation made from hemp leaves
Bi symbol bismuth
BIA abbr Bureau of Indian Affairs
bi·an·nu·al \(,)bī-'an-yə-wəl\ adj : occurring twice a year — bi·an·nu·al·ly adv
¹bi·as \'bī-əs\ n 1 : a line diagonal to the grain of a fabric 2 : PREJUDICE, BENT
²bias adv : on the bias : DIAGONALLY
³bias vb bi·ased or bi·assed; bi·as·ing or bi·as·sing : PREJUDICE
bi·ath·lon \bī-'ath-lən, -,län\ n : a composite athletic contest consisting of cross-country skiing and target shooting with a rifle
¹bib \'bib\ n : a cloth or plastic shield tied under the chin to protect the clothes while eating
²bib abbr Bible; biblical
bi·be·lot \'bē-bə-,lō\ n, pl bibelots \same or -,lōz\ : a small household ornament or decorative object
bi·ble \'bī-bəl\ n [ME, fr. OF, fr. ML biblia, fr. Gk, pl. of biblion book, dim. of byblos papyrus, book, fr. Byblos, ancient Phoenician city from which papyrus was exported] 1 cap : the sacred scriptures of Christians comprising the Old and New Testaments 2 cap : the sacred scriptures of Judaism; also : those of some other religion 3 : a publication that is considered authoritative for its subject — bib·li·cal \'bi-bli-kəl\ adj

BOOKS OF THE BIBLE

JEWISH SCRIPTURE

LAW	PROPHETS		WRITINGS
Genesis	Joshua	Obadiah	Psalms
Exodus	Judges	Jonah	Proverbs
Leviticus	1 & 2 Samuel	Micah	Job
Numbers	1 & 2 Kings	Nahum	Song of Songs
Deuteronomy	Isaiah	Habakkuk	Ruth
	Jeremiah	Zephaniah	Lamentations
	Ezekiel	Haggai	Ecclesiastes
	Hosea	Zechariah	Esther
	Joel	Malachi	Daniel
	Amos		Ezra
			Nehemiah
			1 & 2 Chronicles

CHRISTIAN CANON—OLD TESTAMENT

ROMAN CATHOLIC	PROTESTANT	ROMAN CATHOLIC	PROTESTANT
Genesis	Genesis	Wisdom	
Exodus	Exodus	Sirach	
Leviticus	Leviticus	Isaiah	Isaiah
Numbers	Numbers	Jeremiah	Jeremiah
Deuteronomy	Deuteronomy	Lamentations	Lamentations
Joshua	Joshua	Baruch	
Judges	Judges	Ezekiel	Ezekiel
Ruth	Ruth	Daniel	Daniel
1 & 2 Samuel	1 & 2 Samuel	Hosea	Hosea
1 & 2 Kings	1 & 2 Kings	Joel	Joel
1 & 2 Chronicles	1 & 2 Chronicles	Amos	Amos
Ezra	Ezra	Obadiah	Obadiah
Nehemiah	Nehemiah	Jonah	Jonah
Tobit		Micah	Micah
Judith		Nahum	Nahum
Esther	Esther	Habakkuk	Habakkuk
Job	Job	Zephaniah	Zephaniah
Psalms	Psalms	Haggai	Haggai
Proverbs	Proverbs	Zechariah	Zechariah
Ecclesiastes	Ecclesiastes	Malachi	Malachi
Song of Songs	Song of Solomon	1 & 2 Maccabees	

PROTESTANT APOCRYPHA

1 & 2 Esdras	Baruch
Tobit	Prayer of Azariah and the Song
Judith	of the Three Holy Children
Additions to Esther	Susanna
Wisdom of Solomon	Bel and the Dragon
Ecclesiasticus or the Wisdom of Jesus	The Prayer of Manasses
Son of Sirach	1 & 2 Maccabees

CHRISTIAN CANON—NEW TESTAMENT

Matthew	Ephesians	James
Mark	Philippians	1 & 2 Peter
Luke	Colossians	1, 2, 3 John
John	1 & 2 Thessalonians	Jude
Acts of the Apostles	1 & 2 Timothy	Revelation or
Romans	Titus	Apocalypse
1 & 2 Corinthians	Philemon	
Galatians	Hebrews	

bib·li·og·ra·phy \ˌbi-blē-'ä-grə-fē\ *n, pl* **-phies** **1** : the history or description of writings or publications **2** : a list of writings (as on a subject or of an author) — **bib·li·og·ra·pher** \-fər\ *n* — **bib·li·o·graph·ic** \-ə-'gra-fik\ *also* **bib·li·o·graph·i·cal** \-fi-kəl\ *adj*
bib·lio·phile \'bi-blē-ə-ˌfī(-ə)l\ *n* : a lover of books
bib·u·lous \'bi-byə-ləs\ *adj* **1** : highly absorbent **2** : fond of alcoholic beverages
bi·cam·er·al \'bī-'ka-mə-rəl\ *adj* : having or consisting of two legislative branches
bicarb \(ˌ)bī-'kärb, 'bī-ˌ\ *n* : SODIUM BICARBONATE
bi·car·bon·ate \(ˌ)bī-'kär-bə-ˌnāt, -nət\ *n* : an acid carbonate
bicarbonate of soda : SODIUM BICARBONATE
bi·cen·te·na·ry \ˌbī-sen-'te-nə-rē, bī-'sen-tᵊn-ˌer-ē\ *n* : BI-CENTENNIAL — **bicentenary** *adj*
bi·cen·ten·ni·al \ˌbī-sen-'te-nē-əl\ *n* : a 200th anniversary or its celebration — **bicentennial** *adj*
bi·ceps \'bī-ˌseps\ *n, pl* **biceps** *also* **bi·ceps·es** [NL, fr. L, two-headed, fr. *bi-* two + *caput* head] : a muscle (as in the front of the upper arm) having two points of origin
¹bick·er \'bi-kər\ *n* : ALTERCATION
²bicker *vb* : to engage in a petty quarrel
bi·coast·al \bī-'kōs-tᵊl\ *adj* : living or working on both the east and west coasts of the U.S.
bi·con·cave \ˌbī-(ˌ)kän-'kāv, (ˌ)bī-'kän-ˌkāv\ *adj* : concave on both sides
bi·con·vex \ˌbī-(ˌ)kän-'veks, (ˌ)bī-'kän-ˌveks\ *adj* : convex on both sides
bi·cus·pid \bī-'kəs-pəd\ *n* : PREMOLAR
¹bi·cy·cle \'bī-ˌsi-kəl\ *n* : a light 2-wheeled vehicle with a saddle, pedals, and handlebars for steering
²bicycle *vb* **-cy·cled; -cy·cling** \-ˌsi-k(ə-)liŋ, -ˌsī-\ : to ride a bicycle — **bi·cy·cler** \-k(ə-)lər\ *n* — **bi·cy·clist** \-k(ə-)list\ *n*
¹bid \'bid\ *vb* **bade** \'bad, 'bād\ *or* **bid; bid·den** \'bi-dᵊn\ *or* **bid** *also* **bade; bid·ding** **1** : COMMAND, ORDER **2** : IN-VITE **3** : to give expression to ⟨*bade* a tearful farewell⟩ **4** : to make a bid : OFFER — **bid·der** *n*
²bid *n* **1** : the act of one who bids; *also* : an offer for something **2** : INVITATION **3** : an announcement in a card game of what a player proposes to accomplish **4** : an attempt to win or gain ⟨a ~ for mayor⟩
bid·da·ble \'bi-də-bəl\ *adj* **1** : OBEDIENT, DOCILE **2** : capable of being bid
bid·dy \'bi-dē\ *n, pl* **biddies** : HEN; *also* : a young chicken
bide \'bīd\ *vb* **bode** \'bōd\ *or* **bid·ed; bided; bid·ing** **1** : to wait for **2** : WAIT, TARRY **3** : DWELL
bi·det \bi-'dā\ *n* : a bathroom fixture used esp. for bathing the external genitals and the anal region
bi·di·rec·tion·al \ˌbī-də-'rek-sh(ə-)nəl\ *adj* : involving, moving, or taking place in two usu. opposite directions — **bi·di·rec·tion·al·ly** *adv*
bi·en·ni·al \bī-'e-nē-əl\ *adj* **1** : taking place once in two years **2** : lasting two years **3** : producing leaves the first year and fruiting and dying the second year — **biennial** *n* — **bi·en·ni·al·ly** *adv*
bi·en·ni·um \bī-'e-nē-əm\ *n, pl* **-niums** *or* **-nia** \-ə\ [L, fr. *bi-* two + *annus* year] : a period of two years
bier \'bir\ *n* : a stand bearing a coffin or corpse
bi·fo·cal \'bī-ˌfō-kəl\ *adj* : having two focal lengths
bifocals \-kəlz\ *n pl* : eyeglasses with lenses that have one part that corrects for near vision and one for distant vision
bi·fold \'bī-ˌfōld\ *adj* : designed to fold twice ⟨~ doors⟩
bi·fur·cate \'bī-fər-ˌkāt, bī-'fər-\ *vb* **-cat·ed; -cat·ing** : to divide into two branches or parts — **bi·fur·ca·tion** \ˌbī-fər-'kā-shən\ *n*
big \'big\ *adj* **big·ger; big·gest** **1** : large in size, amount, or scope **2** : PREGNANT; *also* : SWELLING **3** : IMPOR-TANT, IMPOSING **4** : NOBLE, GENEROUS **5** : POPULAR — **big·ness** *n* — **big on** : strongly favoring or liking
big·a·my \'bi-gə-mē\ *n* : the act of marrying one person while still legally married to another — **big·a·mist** \-mist\ *n* — **big·a·mous** \-məs\ *adj*
big bang theory *n* : a theory in astronomy: the universe originated in an explosion (**big bang**) from a single point of nearly infinite energy density
big brother *n* **1** : an older brother **2** : a man who serves as a companion, father figure, and role model for a boy **3** *cap both Bs* : the leader of an authoritarian state or movement **4** : a powerful government or organization that watches and controls people's actions

big cheese *n* : ³BOSS
big crunch *n* : a hypothetical event in which all matter in the universe collapses to a single point of nearly infinite energy density
Big Dipper *n* : the seven principal stars of Ursa Major in a form resembling a dipper
big·foot \'big-ˌfút\ *n* : SASQUATCH
big·horn sheep \'big-ˌhȯrn\ *n* : a wild sheep of mountainous western No. America

bighorn sheep

bight \'bīt\ *n* **1** : a curve in a coast; *also* : the bay formed by such a curve **2** : a slack part in a rope
big–name \'big-'nām\ *adj* : widely popular ⟨a ~ performer⟩ — **big name** *n*
big·ot \'bi-gət\ *n* : one who regards or treats members of a group with hatred and intolerance ♦ **Synonyms** FA-NATIC, ENTHUSIAST, ZEALOT — **big·ot·ed** \-gə-təd\ *adj* — **big·ot·ry** \-trē\ *n*
big screen *n* : the motion picture medium as contrasted to television
big shot \'big-ˌshät\ *n* : an important person
big sister *n* **1** : an older sister **2** : a woman who serves as a companion, mother figure, and role model for a girl
big time \-ˌtīm\ *n* **1** : a high-paying vaudeville circuit requiring only two performances a day **2** : the top rank of an activity or enterprise — **big–tim·er** *n*
big top *n* **1** : the main tent of a circus **2** : CIRCUS
big·wig \'big-ˌwig\ *n* : BIG SHOT
bike \'bīk\ *n* **1** : BICYCLE **2** : MOTORCYCLE
bik·er *n* : MOTORCYCLIST; *esp* : one who is a member of an organized gang
bike·way \'bīk-ˌwā\ *n* : a thoroughfare for bicycles
bi·ki·ni \bə-'kē-nē\ *n* [F, fr. *Bikini*, atoll in the Marshall Islands] : a woman's brief 2-piece bathing suit
bi·lat·er·al \bī-'la-tə-rəl\ *adj* **1** : having or involving two sides **2** : affecting reciprocally two sides or parties — **bi·lat·er·al·ism** \-tə-rə-ˌli-zəm\ *n* — **bi·lat·er·al·ly** *adv*
bile \'bī(-ə)l\ *n* **1** : a bitter greenish fluid secreted by the liver that aids in the digestion of fats **2** : an ill-humored mood
bilge \'bilj\ *n* **1** : the part of a ship that lies between the bottom and the point where the sides go straight up **2** : stale or worthless remarks or ideas
bi·lin·gual \bī-'liŋ-gwəl\ *adj* : expressed in, knowing, or using two languages
bil·ious \'bil-yəs\ *adj* **1** : marked by or suffering from disordered liver function **2** : IRRITABLE, ILL-TEMPERED ⟨a ~ disposition⟩ — **bil·ious·ness** *n*
bilk \'bilk\ *vb* : CHEAT, SWINDLE
¹bill \'bil\ *n* : the jaws of a bird together with their horny covering; *also* : a mouthpart (as of a turtle) resembling these — **billed** \'bild\ *adj*
²bill *vb* : to caress fondly
³bill *n* **1** : an itemized statement of particulars; *also* : IN-VOICE **2** : a written document or note **3** : a printed advertisement (as a poster) announcing an event **4** : a draft of a law presented to a legislature for enactment **5** : a written statement of a legal wrong suffered or of some breach of law **6** : a piece of paper money
⁴bill *vb* **1** : to enter in or prepare a bill; *also* : to submit a bill or account to **2** : to advertise by bills or posters

bill·board \-ˌbȯrd\ *n* : a flat surface on which advertising bills are posted

¹bil·let \ˈbil-lət\ *n* **1** : an order requiring a person to provide lodging for a soldier; *also* : quarters assigned by or as if by such an order **2** : POSITION, APPOINTMENT

²billet *vb* : to assign lodging to by billet

bil·let–doux \ˌbi-lā-ˈdü\ *n, pl* **billets–doux** *same or* -ˈdüz\ [F *billet doux*, lit., sweet letter] : a love letter

bill·fold \ˈbil-ˌfōld\ *n* : WALLET

bil·liards \ˈbil-yərdz\ *n* : any of several games played on an oblong table by driving balls against each other or into pockets with a cue

bil·lings·gate \ˈbi-liŋz-ˌgāt, *Brit usu* -git\ *n* [*Billingsgate*, old gate and fish market, London, England] : coarsely abusive language

bil·lion \ˈbil-yən\ *n* **1** : a thousand millions **2** *Brit* : a million millions — **billion** *adj* — **bil·lionth** \-yənth\ *adj or n*

bill of attainder : a legislative act that imposes punishment without a trial

bill of health : a usu. favorable report following an examination

bill of sale : a legal document transferring ownership of goods

¹bil·low \ˈbi-lō\ *n* **1** : WAVE; *esp* : a great wave **2** : a rolling mass (as of fog or flame) like a great wave — **bil·lowy** \ˈbi-lə-wē\ *adj*

²billow *vb* : to rise and roll in waves; *also* : to swell out ⟨∼*ing* sails⟩

bil·ly \ˈbi-lē\ *n, pl* **billies** : BILLY CLUB

billy club *n* : a heavy usu. wooden club; *esp* : a police officer's club

bil·ly goat \ˈbi-lē-\ *n* : a male goat

bi·met·al \ˈbī-ˌme-tᵊl\ *adj* : BIMETALLIC — **bimetal** *n*

bi·me·tal·lic \ˌbī-mə-ˈta-lik\ *adj* : made of two different metals — often used of devices having a bonded expansive part — **bimetallic** *n*

bi·met·al·lism \bī-ˈme-tᵊl-ˌi-zəm\ *n* : the use of two metals at fixed ratios to form a standard of value for a monetary system

¹bi·month·ly \bī-ˈmənth-lē\ *adj* **1** : occurring every two months **2** : occurring twice a month : SEMIMONTHLY — **bimonthly** *adv*

²bimonthly *n* : a bimonthly publication

bin \ˈbin\ *n* : a box, crib, or enclosure used for storage

bi·na·ry \ˈbī-nə-rē, -ˌner-ē\ *adj* **1** : consisting of two things or parts **2** : relating to, being, or belonging to a system of numbers having 2 as its base ⟨the ∼ digits 0 and 1⟩ **3** : involving a choice between or condition of two alternatives only (as on-off, yes-no) — **binary** *n*

binary star *n* : a system of two stars revolving around each other

binary system *n* : BINARY STAR

bin·au·ral \bī-ˈnȯr-əl\ *adj* : of or relating to sound reproduction involving the use of two separated microphones and two transmission channels to achieve a stereophonic effect

bind \ˈbīnd\ *vb* **bound** \ˈbaȯnd\; **bind·ing 1** : TIE; *also* : to restrain as if by tying **2** : to put under an obligation; *also* : to constrain with legal authority **3** : BANDAGE **4** : to unite into a mass **5** : to compel as if by a pledge ⟨a handshake ∼*s* the deal⟩ **6** : to strengthen or decorate with a band **7** : to fasten together and enclose in a cover ⟨∼ books⟩ **8** : to exert a tying, restraining, or compelling effect — **bind·er** *n*

bind·ing \ˈbīn-diŋ\ *n* : something (as a ski fastening, a cover, or an edging fabric) used to bind

bin·dle \ˈbin-dᵊl\ *n* : a bundle of clothes or bedding

¹binge \ˈbinj\ *n* **1** : SPREE **2** : an act of excessive consumption (as of food)

²binge *vb* **binged; binge·ing** *or* **bing·ing** : to go on a binge — **bing·er** *n*

bin·go \ˈbiŋ-gō\ *n, pl* **bingos** : a game of chance played with cards having numbered squares corresponding to numbered balls drawn at random and won by covering five squares in a row

bin·na·cle \ˈbi-ni-kəl\ *n* [alter. of ME *bitakle*, fr. Pg or Sp; Pg *bitácola* & Sp *bitácula*, fr. L *habitaculum* dwelling place, fr. *habitare* to inhabit] : a container holding a ship's compass

¹bin·oc·u·lar \bī-ˈnä-kyə-lər, bə-\ *adj* : of, relating to, or adapted to the use of both eyes — **bin·oc·u·lar·ly** *adv*

²bin·oc·u·lar \bə-ˈnä-kyə-lər, bī-\ *n* **1** : a binocular optical instrument (as a microscope) **2** : a hand-held optical

instrument composed of two telescopes and a focusing device — usu. used in pl.

bi·no·mi·al \bī-ˈnō-mē-əl\ *n* **1** : a mathematical expression consisting of two terms connected by the sign plus (+) or minus (–) **2** : a biological species name consisting of two terms — **binomial** *adj*

bio·chem·is·try \ˌbī-ō-ˈke-mə-strē\ *n* : chemistry that deals with the chemical compounds and processes occurring in living things — **bio·chem·i·cal** \-mi-kəl\ *adj or n* — **bio·chem·ic·al·ly** \-k(ə-)lē\ *adv* — **bio·chem·ist** \-mist\ *n*

bio·de·grad·able \-di-ˈgrā-də-bəl\ *adj* : capable of being broken down esp. into innocuous products by the actions of living things (as microorganisms) ⟨a ∼ detergent⟩ — **bio·de·grad·abil·i·ty** \-ˌgrā-də-ˈbi-lə-tē\ *n* — **bio·deg·ra·da·tion** \-ˌde-grə-ˈdā-shən\ *n* — **bio·de·grade** \-di-ˈgrād\ *vb*

bio·di·ver·si·ty \-də-ˈvər-sə-tē, -dī-\ *n* : biological diversity in an environment as indicated by numbers of different species of plants and animals

bio·en·gi·neer·ing \-ˌen-jə-ˈnir-iŋ\ *n* **1** : the application of engineering principles to medicine and biology **2** : GENETIC ENGINEERING

bio·eth·ics \-ˈe-thiks\ *n* : the ethics of biological research and its applications esp. in medicine — **bio·eth·i·cal** \-ˈe-thi-kəl\ *adj* — **bio·eth·i·cist** \-ˈe-thə-sist\ *n*

bio·feed·back \-ˈfēd-ˌbak\ *n* : the technique of making unconscious or involuntary bodily processes (as heartbeats or brain waves) perceptible to the senses (as by use of an oscilloscope) in order to manipulate them by conscious mental control

biog *abbr* biographer; biographical; biography

bio·ge·og·ra·phy \ˌbī-ō-jē-ˈä-grə-fē\ *n* : a science that deals with the geographical distribution of plants and animals — **bio·ge·og·ra·pher** *n*

bi·og·ra·phy \bī-ˈä-grə-fē, bē-\ *n, pl* **-phies** : a written history of a person's life; *also* : such writings in general — **bi·og·ra·pher** *n* — **bio·graph·i·cal** \ˌbī-ə-ˈgra-fi-kəl\ *also* **bi·o·graph·ic** \-fik\ *adj*

bio·in·for·mat·ics \ˌbī-ō-in-fər-ˈma-tiks\ *n* : the storage, classification, and analysis of biological information using computers

biol *abbr* biologic; biological; biologist; biology

bi·o·log·i·cal \ˌbī-ə-ˈlä-ji-kəl\ *also* **bi·o·log·ic** \-jik\ *adj* **1** : of, relating to, or produced by biology or life and living processes **2** : connected by direct genetic relationship rather than by adoption or marriage ⟨her ∼ father⟩ — **bi·o·log·i·cal·ly** \-ji-k(ə-)lē\ *adv*

biological clock *n* : an inherent timing mechanism in a living system that is inferred to exist in order to explain the timing of various physiological and behavioral states and processes

biological warfare *n* : warfare in which harmful living organisms (**biological weapons**) are used against an enemy esp. to cause large-scale death or disease

bi·ol·o·gy \bī-ˈä-lə-jē\ *n* [G *Biologie*, fr. Gk *bios* mode of life + *logos* word, discourse] **1** : a science that deals with living beings and life processes **2** : the life processes of an organism or group — **bi·ol·o·gist** \bī-ˈä-lə-jist\ *n*

bio·mass \ˈbī-ō-ˌmas\ *n* **1** : the amount of living matter (as in a unit area) **2** : plant materials and animal waste used esp. as fuel

bio·med·i·cal \ˌbī-ō-ˈme-di-kəl\ *adj* : of, relating to, or involving biological, medical, and physical science

bi·on·ic \bī-ˈä-nik\ *adj* : having normal biological capability or performance enhanced by or as if by electronic or mechanical devices

bio·phys·ics \ˌbī-ō-ˈfi-ziks\ *n* : a branch of science concerned with the application of physical principles and methods to biological problems — **bio·phys·i·cal** \-zi-kəl\ *adj* — **bio·phys·i·cist** \-ˈfi-zə-sist\ *n*

bio·pic \ˈbī-ō-ˌpik\ *n* : a biographical movie

bi·op·sy \ˈbī-ˌäp-sē\ *n, pl* **-sies** : the removal of tissue, cells, or fluids from the living body for examination

bio·rhythm \ˈbī-ō-ˌri-thəm\ *n* : an innately determined rhythmic biological process (as sleep); *also* : the internal mechanism controlling such a process

bio·sci·ence \ˈbī-ˌsī-əns\ *n* : BIOLOGY 1; *also* : LIFE SCIENCE

bio·sphere \ˈbī-ə-ˌsfir\ *n* **1** : the part of the world in which life can exist **2** : living organisms together with their environment

bio·tech \'bī-ō-ˌtek\ n : BIOTECHNOLOGY
bio·tech·nol·ogy \ˌbī-ō-tek-'nä-lə-jē\ n : the manipulation (as through genetic engineering) of living organisms to produce useful products; *also* : biological science so applied
bio·ter·ror·ism \-'ter-ər-ˌi-zəm\ n : terrorism involving the use of biological weapons — **bio·ter·ror·ist** \-ist\ adj or n
bi·ot·ic \bī-'ä-tik\ adj : of, relating to, or caused by living organisms
bi·o·tin \'bī-ə-tən\ n : a vitamin of the vitamin B complex found esp. in yeast, liver, and egg yolk and active in growth promotion
bi·o·tite \'bī-ə-ˌtīt\ n : a dark mica containing iron, magnesium, potassium, and aluminum
bi·par·ti·san \bī-'pär-tə-zən\ adj : marked by or involving cooperation, agreement, and compromise between two major political parties — **bi·par·ti·san·ship** \-ˌship\ n
bi·par·tite \-'pär-ˌtīt\ adj 1 : being in two parts 2 : shared by two ⟨~ treaty⟩
bi·ped \'bī-ˌped\ n : a 2-footed animal — **bi·ped·al** \(ˌ)bī-'pe-dᵊl\ adj
bi·plane \'bī-ˌplān\ n : an aircraft with two wings placed one above the other
bi·po·lar \bī-'pō-lər\ adj : having or involving the use of two poles — **bi·po·lar·i·ty** \ˌbī-pō-'ler-ə-tē\ n
bipolar disorder n : any of several psychological disorders of mood characterized usu. by alternating episodes of depression and mania
bi·ra·cial \bī-'rā-shəl\ adj : of, relating to, or involving members of two races
¹birch \'bərch\ n 1 : any of a genus of mostly short-lived deciduous shrubs and trees with membranous outer bark and pale close-grained wood; *also* : this wood 2 : a birch rod or bundle of twigs for flogging — **birch** or **birch·en** \'bər-chən\ adj
²birch vb : WHIP, FLOG
¹bird \'bərd\ n : any of a class of warm-blooded egg-laying vertebrates having the body feathered and the forelimbs modified to form wings
²bird vb : to observe or identify wild birds in their native habitat — **bird·er** n
bird·bath \'bərd-ˌbath, -ˌbäth\ n : a usu. ornamental basin set up for birds to bathe in
bird·house \-ˌhaůs\ n : an artificial nesting place for birds; *also* : AVIARY
bird·ie \'bər-dē\ n : a score of one under par on a hole in golf
bird·lime \-ˌlīm\ n : a sticky substance smeared on twigs to snare small birds
bird of paradise : any of numerous brilliantly colored plumed birds of the New Guinea area
bird of prey : a carnivorous bird that feeds wholly or chiefly on carrion or on meat taken by hunting
bird·seed \'bərd-ˌsēd\ n : a mixture of small seeds (as of hemp or millet) used for feeding birds
bird's-eye \'bərdz-ˌī\ adj 1 : marked with spots resembling birds' eyes ⟨~ maple⟩ 2 : seen from above as if by a flying bird ⟨~ view⟩; *also* : CURSORY
bi·ret·ta \bə-'re-tə\ n : a square cap with three ridges on top worn esp. by Roman Catholic clergymen
birr \'bir, 'bər\ n, pl **birr** — see MONEY table
¹birth \'bərth\ n 1 : the act or fact of being born or of bringing forth young 2 : LINEAGE, DESCENT 3 : ORIGIN, BEGINNING — **birth** vb
²birth adj : BIOLOGICAL 2 ⟨~ parents⟩
birth canal n : the channel formed by the cervix, vagina, and vulva through which the fetus passes during birth
birth control n : control of the number of children born esp. by preventing or lessening the frequency of conception
birth·day \'bərth-ˌdā\ n : the day or anniversary of one's birth
birth defect n : a physical or biochemical defect present at birth and inherited or environmentally induced
birth·mark \'bərth-ˌmärk\ n : an unusual mark or blemish on the skin at birth
birth·place \-ˌplās\ n : place of birth or origin
birth·rate \-ˌrāt\ n : the number of births per number of individuals in a given area or group during a given time
birth·right \-ˌrīt\ n : a right, privilege, or possession to which one is entitled by birth ♦ **Synonyms** LEGACY, PATRIMONY, HERITAGE, INHERITANCE

birth·stone \-ˌstōn\ n : a gemstone associated symbolically with the month of one's birth
bis·cuit \'bis-kət\ n [ME bisquite, fr. AF besquit, fr. (pain) besquit twice-cooked bread] 1 : a crisp flat cake; *esp*, *Brit* : CRACKER 2 2 : a small quick bread made from dough that has been rolled and cut or dropped from a spoon
bi·sect \'bī-ˌsekt\ vb : to divide into two equal parts; *also* : CROSS, INTERSECT — **bi·sec·tion** \'bī-ˌsek-shən\ n — **bi·sec·tor** \-tər\ n
bi·sex·u·al \bī-'sek-shə-wəl\ adj 1 : possessing characters of both sexes 2 : having sexual or romantic attraction to both sexes 3 : of, relating to, or involving both sexes — **bisexual** n — **bi·sex·u·al·i·ty** \ˌbī-ˌsek-shə-'wal-ə-tē\ n
bish·op \'bi-shəp\ n [ME bisshop, fr. OE bisceop, fr. LL episcopus, fr. Gk episkopos, lit., overseer, fr. epi- on, over + skeptesthai to look] 1 : a member of the clergy ranking above a priest and typically governing a diocese 2 : any of various Protestant church officials who superintend other clergy 3 : a chess piece that can move diagonally across any number of adjoining unoccupied squares
bish·op·ric \'bi-shə-prik\ n 1 : DIOCESE 2 : the office of bishop
bis·muth \'biz-məth\ n : a heavy brittle grayish white metallic chemical element used in alloys and medicine
bi·son \'bī-sᵊn, -zᵊn\ n, pl **bison** : BUFFALO 2
bisque \'bisk\ n : a thick cream soup
bis·tro \'bēs-trō, 'bis-\ n, pl **bistros** [F] 1 : a small or unpretentious restaurant 2 : BAR; *also* : NIGHTCLUB
¹bit \'bit\ n 1 : the biting or cutting edge or part of a tool 2 : the part of a bridle that is placed in a horse's mouth
²bit n 1 : a morsel of food; *also* : a small piece or quantity of something 2 : a small coin; *also* : a unit of value equal to 12½ cents 3 : something small or trivial 4 : an indefinite usu. small degree or extent ⟨a ~ tired⟩
³bit n [binary digit] : a unit of computer information equivalent to the result of a choice between two alternatives; *also* : its physical representation
¹bitch \'bich\ n 1 : a female canine; *esp* : a female dog 2 often offensive : a malicious, spiteful, or overbearing woman 3 : something difficult or impossible
²bitch vb : COMPLAIN
¹bite \'bīt\ vb **bit** \'bit\; **bit·ten** \'bi-tᵊn\ also **bit**; **bit·ing** \'bī-tiŋ\ 1 : to grip with teeth or jaws; *also* : to wound or sting with or as if with fangs 2 : to cut or pierce with or as if with an edged instrument 3 : to cause to smart or sting 4 : CORRODE 5 : to take bait
²bite n 1 : the act or manner of biting 2 : FOOD 3 : a wound made by biting; *also* : a penetrating effect
bite-size \'bīt-ˌsīz\ adj 1 : of a size that can be eaten in one bite 2 : being or made small or brief esp. so as to be easily manageable
biting adj : SHARP, CUTTING
bit·map \'bit-ˌmap\ n : an array of binary data representing a bitmapped image or display
bit·mapped \'bit-ˌmapt\ adj : of, relating to, or being a digital image or display for which an array of binary data specifies the value of each pixel
bit·ter \'bi-tər\ adj 1 : being or inducing the one of the basic taste sensations that is acrid, astringent, or disagreeable and is suggestive of hops 2 : marked by intensity or severity (as of distress or hatred) 3 : extremely harsh or cruel — **bit·ter·ly** adv — **bit·ter·ness** n
bit·tern \'bi-tərn\ n : any of various small or medium-sized herons
bit·ters \'bi-tərz\ n sing or pl : a usu. alcoholic solution of bitter and often aromatic plant products used in mixing drinks and as a mild tonic
¹bit·ter·sweet \'bi-tər-ˌswēt\ n 1 : a poisonous nightshade with purple flowers and reddish berries 2 : a woody vine with yellow capsules that open when ripe to show scarlet seed covers
²bittersweet adj : being at once both bitter and sweet
bi·tu·mi·nous coal \bə-'tü-mə-nəs-, bī-, -'tyü-\ n : a coal that when heated yields considerable volatile waste matter
bi·valve \'bī-ˌvalv\ n : any of a class of mollusks (as clams or scallops) of two separate parts that open and shut — **bivalve** adj
¹biv·ouac \'bi-və-ˌwak\ n [F, fr. LG biwacht, fr. bi at + wacht guard] : a temporary encampment or shelter

²**bivouac** *vb* **-ouacked; -ouack·ing** : to form a bivouac : CAMP
¹**bi·week·ly** \ˌbī-ˈwē-klē\ *adj* **1** : occurring twice a week **2** : occurring every two weeks : FORTNIGHTLY — **biweekly** *adv*
²**biweekly** *n* : a biweekly publication
bi·year·ly \-ˈyir-lē\ *adj* **1** : BIANNUAL **2** : BIENNIAL
bi·zarre \bə-ˈzär\ *adj* : ODD, ECCENTRIC, FANTASTIC ⟨~ costumes⟩ — **bi·zarre·ly** *adv*
bi·zar·ro \bə-ˈzär-ō\ *adj* : characterized by a bizarre, fantastic, or unconventional approach ⟨~ horror movies⟩
bk *abbr* **1** bank **2** book
Bk *symbol* berkelium
bkg *abbr* banking
bkgd *abbr* background
bks *abbr* barracks
bkt *abbr* **1** basket **2** bracket
bl *abbr* **1** bale **2** barrel **3** blue
blab \ˈblab\ *vb* **blabbed; blab·bing** : TATTLE, GOSSIP
¹**black** \ˈblak\ *adj* **1** : of the color black; *also* : very dark **2** : SWARTHY **3** : of or relating to any of various population groups having dark pigmentation of the skin **4** : of or relating to African American people or their culture **5** : SOILED, DIRTY **6** : lacking light ⟨a ~ night⟩ **7** : WICKED, EVIL ⟨~ magic⟩ **8** : DISMAL, GLOOMY ⟨a ~ outlook⟩ **9** : SULLEN ⟨a ~ mood⟩ — **black·ish** *adj* — **black·ly** *adv* — **black·ness** *n*
²**black** *n* **1** : a black pigment or dye; *also* : something (as clothing) that is black **2** : the characteristic color of soot or coal **3** : a person belonging to any of various population groups having dark pigmentation of the skin **4** : AFRICAN AMERICAN
³**black** *vb* : BLACKEN
black–and–blue \ˌbla-kən-ˈblü\ *adj* : darkly discolored from blood effused by bruising
black–and–white \ˌbla-kən-ˈhwīt\ *n* : SQUAD CAR
black·ball \ˈblak-ˌbȯl\ *vb* **1** : to vote against; *esp* : to exclude from membership by casting a negative vote **2** : OSTRACIZE — **black·ball** *n*
black bass *n* : any of several freshwater sunfishes native to eastern and central No. America
black bear *n* : a usu. black-furred bear of No. American forests
¹**black belt** \ˈblak-ˌbelt\ *n, often cap both Bs* : an area densely populated by blacks
²**black belt** \-ˈbelt\ *n* : one who holds the rating of expert (as in judo or karate); *also* : the rating itself
black·ber·ry \-ˌber-ē\ *n* : the usu. black or purple juicy but seedy edible fruit of various brambles; *also* : a plant bearing this fruit
black·bird \-ˌbərd\ *n* : any of various birds (as the red-winged blackbird) of which the male is largely or wholly black
black·board \-ˌbȯrd\ *n* : a smooth usu. dark surface used for writing or drawing on with chalk
black·body \-ˈbä-dē\ *n* : a body or surface that completely absorbs incident radiation with no reflection
black box *n* **1** : a usu. complicated electronic device whose components and workings are unknown or mysterious to the user **2** : a device used in aircraft to record cockpit conversations and flight data
black death *n* : an epidemic of bacterial plague and esp. bubonic plague that spread rapidly in Europe and Asia in the 14th century
black·en \ˈbla-kən\ *vb* **black·ened; black·en·ing** **1** : to make or become black **2** : DEFAME, SULLY ⟨~ed her reputation⟩
black·ened *adj* : coated with spices and quickly seared in a very hot skillet ⟨~ swordfish⟩
black eye *n* : a discoloration of the skin around the eye from bruising
black–eyed Su·san \ˌblak-ˌīd-ˈsü-zᵊn\ *n* : a coarse No. American plant that is related to the daisies and has deep yellow to orange flower heads with dark conical centers
Black·foot \ˈblak-ˌfu̇t\ *n, pl* **Black·feet** *or* **Blackfoot** : a member of an American Indian people of Montana, Alberta, and Saskatchewan
black·guard \ˈbla-gərd, -ˌgärd\ *n* : SCOUNDREL, RASCAL
black·head \ˈblak-ˌhed\ *n* : a small usu. dark oily mass plugging the outlet of a skin gland

black hole *n* : a celestial object with a gravitational field so strong that light cannot escape from it
black ice *n* : a thin layer of ice on a paved road that is very difficult to see
black·ing \ˈbla-kiŋ\ *n* : a substance applied to something to make it black
¹**black·jack** \ˈblak-jak\ *n* **1** : a leather-covered club with a flexible handle **2** : a card game in which the object is to be dealt cards having a higher count than the dealer but not exceeding 21
²**blackjack** *vb* : to hit with or as if with a blackjack
black light *n* : invisible ultraviolet light
black·list \ˈblak-ˌlist\ *n* : a list of persons who are disapproved of and are to be punished or boycotted — **black·list** *vb*
black·mail \ˈblak-ˌmāl\ *n* : extortion by threats esp. of public exposure; *also* : something so extorted — **black·mail** *vb* — **black·mail·er** *n*
black market *n* : illicit trade in goods; *also* : a place where such trade is carried on
Black Mass *n* : a travesty of the Christian Mass ascribed to worshipers of Satan
Black Muslim *n* : a member of a chiefly black group that professes Islamic religious belief
black nationalist *n, often cap B&N* : a member of a group of militant blacks who advocate separatism from whites and the formation of self-governing black communities — **black nationalism** *n, often cap B&N*
black–on–black *adj* : involving a black person against another black person ⟨~ crime⟩
black·out \ˈblak-ˌau̇t\ *n* **1** : a period of darkness due to electrical power failure **2** : a transitory loss or dulling of vision or consciousness **3** : the prohibition or restriction of the telecasting of a sports event — **black out** *vb*
black pepper *n* : a spice that consists of the dried berry of a pepper plant ground with the black husk still on
black power *n* : the mobilization of the political and economic power of black Americans esp. to compel respect for their rights and improve their condition
black sheep *n* : a member of a group who is disreputable or not regarded favorably
black·smith \ˈblak-ˌsmith\ *n* : a smith who forges iron — **black·smith·ing** *n*
black·strap molasses \ˈblak-ˌstrap-\ *n* : a thick dark molasses obtained from successive processing of raw sugar
black·thorn \-ˌthȯrn\ *n* : a European thorny plum
black–tie \ˈblak-ˌtī\ *adj* : characterized by or requiring semiformal evening clothes consisting of a usu. black tie and tuxedo for men and a formal dress for women
black·top \ˈblak-ˌtäp\ *n* : a dark tarry material (as asphalt) used esp. for surfacing roads — **blacktop** *vb*
black widow *n* : a venomous New World spider having the female black with an hourglass-shaped red mark on the underside of the abdomen

black widow

blad·der \ˈbla-dər\ *n* : a sac in which liquid or gas is stored; *esp* : one in a vertebrate into which urine passes from the kidneys
¹**blade** \ˈblād\ *n* **1** : a leaf of a plant and esp. of a grass; *also* : the flat part of a leaf as distinguished from its stalk **2** : something (as the flat part of an oar or an arm of a propeller) resembling the blade of a leaf **3** : the cutting part of an instrument or tool **4** : SWORD; *also* : SWORDSMAN

5 : a dashing fellow ⟨a gay ∼⟩ **6** : the runner of an ice skate — **blad·ed** \'blā-dəd\ *adj*
²**blade** *vb* **blad·ed; blad·ing** : to skate on in-line skates — **blad·er** \'blā-dər\ *n*
blain \'blān\ *n* : an inflammatory swelling or sore
¹**blame** \'blām\ *vb* **blamed; blam·ing** [ME, fr. AF *blamer, blasmer,* fr. L *blasphemare* to blaspheme, fr. Gk *blasphēmein*] **1** : to find fault with **2** : to hold responsible or responsible for ♦ *Synonyms* CENSURE, DENOUNCE, CONDEMN, CRITICIZE — **blam·able** *adj*
²**blame** *n* **1** : CENSURE, REPROOF **2** : responsibility for fault or error ♦ *Synonyms* GUILT, FAULT, CULPABILITY, ONUS — **blame·less** *adj* — **blame·less·ly** *adv* — **blame·less·ness** *n*
blame·wor·thy \-ˌwər-t͟hē\ *adj* : deserving blame — **blame·wor·thi·ness** *n*
blanch \'blanch\ *vb* : to make or become white or pale ⟨fear ∼ed her cheeks⟩
blanc·mange \blə-'mänj, -'mänzh\ *n* : a dessert made from gelatin or a starchy substance and milk usu. sweetened and flavored
bland \'bland\ *adj* **1** : smooth in manner : SUAVE ⟨a ∼ smile⟩ **2** : gently soothing ⟨a ∼ diet⟩; *also* : INSIPID ♦ *Synonyms* GENTLE, MILD, SOFT, BALMY — **bland·ly** *adv* — **bland·ness** *n*
blan·dish·ment \'blan-dish-mənt\ *n* : flattering or coaxing speech or action : CAJOLERY
¹**blank** \'blaŋk\ *adj* **1** : showing or causing an appearance of dazed dismay; *also* : EXPRESSIONLESS **2** : free from writing or marks; *also* : having spaces to be filled in **3** : DULL, EMPTY ⟨∼ moments⟩ **4** : ABSOLUTE, DOWNRIGHT ⟨a ∼ refusal⟩ **5** : not shaped in final form — **blank·ly** *adv* — **blank·ness** *n*
²**blank** *n* **1** : an empty space **2** : a form with spaces for the entry of data **3** : an unfinished form (as of a key) **4** : a cartridge with propellant and a seal but no projectile
³**blank** *vb* **1** : to cover or close up : OBSCURE **2** : to keep from scoring
blank check *n* **1** : a signed check with the amount unspecified **2** : complete freedom of action
¹**blan·ket** \'blan-kət\ *n* **1** : a heavy woven often woolen covering **2** : a covering layer ⟨a ∼ of snow⟩
²**blanket** *vb* : to cover with a blanket
³**blanket** *adj* : covering a group or class ⟨∼ insurance⟩; *also* : applicable in all instances ⟨∼ rules⟩
blank verse *n* : unrhymed iambic pentameter
blare \'bler\ *vb* **blared; blar·ing** : to sound loud and harsh; *also* : to proclaim loudly — **blare** *n*
blar·ney \'blär-nē\ *n* [*Blarney stone,* a stone in Blarney Castle, near Cork, Ireland, held to bestow skill in flattery on those who kiss it] : skillful flattery : BLANDISHMENT
bla·sé \blä-'zā\ *adj* [F] : apathetic to pleasure or excitement as a result of excessive indulgence; *also* : SOPHISTICATED
blas·pheme \blas-'fēm, 'blas-ˌ\ *vb* **blas·phemed; blas·phem·ing** **1** : to speak of or address with irreverence **2** : to utter blasphemy — **blas·phem·er** *n*
blas·phe·my \'blas-fə-mē\ *n, pl* **-mies** **1** : the act of expressing lack of reverence for God **2** : irreverence toward something considered sacred — **blas·phe·mous** \-məs\ *adj*
¹**blast** \'blast\ *n* **1** : a violent gust of wind; *also* : its effect **2** : sound made by a wind instrument **3** : a current of air forced at high pressure through a hole in a furnace (blast furnace) **4** : a sudden withering esp. of plants : BLIGHT **5** : EXPLOSION; *also* : the shock wave of an explosion
²**blast** *vb* : to shatter by or as if by an explosive
blast off *vb* : TAKE OFF **4** — used esp. of rocket-propelled vehicles — **blast-off** \'blast-ˌȯf\ *n*
bla·tant \'blā-t³nt\ *adj* : offensively obtrusive : vulgarly showy ♦ *Synonyms* VOCIFEROUS, BOISTEROUS, CLAMOROUS, OBSTREPEROUS — **bla·tan·cy** \-t³n-sē\ *n* — **bla·tant·ly** *adv*
blath·er \'bla-t͟hər\ *vb* : to talk foolishly at length — **blather** *n*
blath·er·skite \'bla-t͟hər-ˌskīt\ *n* : a person who blathers
¹**blaze** \'blāz\ *n* **1** : FIRE **2** : intense direct light accompanied by heat **3** : something (as a dazzling display or sudden outburst) suggesting fire ⟨a ∼ of autumn leaves⟩ ♦ *Synonyms* GLARE, GLOW, FLAME
²**blaze** *vb* **blazed; blaz·ing** **1** : to burn brightly; *also* : to flare up **2** : to be conspicuously bright : GLITTER

³**blaze** *vb* **blazed; blaz·ing** : to make public or conspicuous
⁴**blaze** *n* **1** : a usu. white stripe on the face of an animal **2** : a trail marker; *esp* : one made on a tree
⁵**blaze** *vb* **blazed; blaz·ing** : to mark (as a tree or trail) with blazes
blaze orange *n* : a very bright orange used in clothing for visibility
blaz·er \'blā-zər\ *n* : a sports jacket often with notched collar and pockets that are stitched on
¹**bla·zon** \'blā-z³n\ *n* **1** : COAT OF ARMS **2** : ostentatious display
²**blazon** *vb* **1** : to publish widely : PROCLAIM **2** : DECK, ADORN
bldg *abbr* building
bldr *abbr* builder
¹**bleach** \'blēch\ *vb* : WHITEN, BLANCH
²**bleach** *n* : a preparation used in bleaching
bleach·ers \'blē-chərz\ *n sing or pl* : a usu. uncovered stand of tiered seats for spectators
bleak \'blēk\ *adj* **1** : desolately barren and often windswept **2** : lacking warm or cheering qualities ⟨the future looks ∼⟩ — **bleak·ly** *adv* — **bleak·ness** *n*
blear \'blir\ *adj* : dim with water or tears ⟨∼ eyes⟩
bleary \'blir-ē\ *adj* **1** : dull or dimmed esp. from fatigue or sleep **2** : poorly outlined or defined ⟨a ∼ view⟩
bleat \'blēt\ *n* : the cry of a sheep or goat or a sound like it — **bleat** *vb*
bleed \'blēd\ *vb* **bled** \'bled\; **bleed·ing** **1** : to lose or shed blood **2** : to be wounded; *also* : to feel pain or distress **3** : to flow or ooze from a wounded surface; *also* : to draw fluid from ⟨∼ a tire⟩ **4** : to extort money from
bleed·er \'blē-dər\ *n* : one that bleeds; *esp* : HEMOPHILIAC
bleeding heart *n* **1** : a garden plant related to the poppies that has usu. deep pink or white drooping heartshaped flowers **2** *disparaging* : a person who shows extravagant sympathy esp. for an object of alleged persecution
¹**blem·ish** \'ble-mish\ *vb* : to spoil by a flaw : MAR
²**blemish** *n* : a noticeable flaw
¹**blench** \'blench\ *vb* [ME, to deceive, blench, fr. OE *blencan* to deceive] : FLINCH, QUAIL ♦ *Synonyms* SHRINK, RECOIL, WINCE, START
²**blench** *vb* : to grow or make pale
¹**blend** \'blend\ *vb* **blend·ed; blend·ing** **1** : to mix thoroughly **2** : to prepare (as coffee) by mixing different varieties **3** : to combine into an integrated whole **4** : HARMONIZE ♦ *Synonyms* FUSE, MERGE, MINGLE, COALESCE — **blend·er** *n*
²**blend** *n* : a product of blending ♦ *Synonyms* COMPOUND, COMPOSITE, ALLOY, MIXTURE
blended family *n* : a family that includes children of a previous marriage of one spouse or both
bless \'bles\ *vb* **blessed** \'blest\ *also* **blest** \'blest\; **bless·ing** [ME, fr. OE *blētsian,* fr. *blōd* blood; fr. the use of blood in consecration] **1** : to consecrate by religious rite or word **2** : to sanctify with the sign of the cross **3** : to invoke divine care for **4** : PRAISE, GLORIFY **5** : to confer happiness upon
bless·ed \'ble-səd\ *also* **blest** \'blest\ *adj* **1** : HOLY **2** : BEATIFIED **3** : DELIGHTFUL ⟨∼ relief from the heat⟩ — **bless·ed·ly** *adv* — **bless·ed·ness** *n*
bless·ing \'ble-siŋ\ *n* **1** : the act or words of one who blesses; *also* : APPROVAL **2** : a thing conducive to happiness ⟨count your ∼s⟩ **3** : grace said at a meal
blew *past of* BLOW
¹**blight** \'blīt\ *n* **1** : a plant disease or injury marked esp. by withering and death of parts; *also* : an organism causing blight **2** : an impairing or frustrating influence; *also* : a deteriorated condition ⟨urban ∼⟩
²**blight** *vb* : to affect with or suffer from blight
blimp \'blimp\ *n* : an airship that maintains its form by pressure of contained gas
¹**blind** \'blīnd\ *adj* **1** : lacking or grossly deficient in ability to see; *also* : intended for blind persons **2** : not based on reason, evidence, or knowledge ⟨∼ faith⟩ **3** : not intelligently controlled or directed ⟨∼ chance⟩ **4** : performed solely by using aircraft instruments ⟨a ∼ landing⟩ **5** : hard to discern or make out : HIDDEN ⟨a ∼

seam⟩ 6 : lacking an opening or outlet ⟨a ∼ alley⟩ — **blind·ly** adv — **blind·ness** \'blīnd-nəs\ n
²**blind** vb 1 : to make blind 2 : DAZZLE 3 : DARKEN; also : HIDE
³**blind** n 1 : something (as a shutter) to hinder vision or keep out light 2 : a place of concealment 3 : SUBTERFUGE
blind carbon copy n : a copy of a message (such as an e-mail) that is sent without the knowledge of the other recipients
blind date n : a date between persons who have not previously met; also : either of these persons
blind·er \'blīn-dər\ n : either of two flaps on a horse's bridle to prevent it from seeing to the side
blind·fold \'blīnd-ˌfōld\ vb : to cover the eyes of with or as if with a bandage — **blindfold** n
¹**blink** \'bliŋk\ vb 1 : WINK 2 : TWINKLE 3 : EVADE, IGNORE 4 : YIELD, GIVE IN
²**blink** n 1 : GLIMMER, SPARKLE 2 : a usu. involuntary shutting and opening of the eye
blink·er \'bliŋ-kər\ n : a blinking light used as a signal
blin·tze \'blint-sə\ or **blintz** \'blints\ n [Yiddish blintse] : a thin rolled pancake with a filling usu. of cream cheese
blip \'blip\ n 1 : a spot on a radar screen 2 : ABERRATION 1
bliss \'blis\ n : complete happiness : JOY ✦ **Synonyms** BEATITUDE, BLESSEDNESS — **bliss·ful** \-fəl\ adj — **bliss·ful·ly** adv
¹**blis·ter** \'blis-tər\ n 1 : a raised area of skin containing watery fluid; also : an agent that causes blisters 2 : something (as a raised spot in paint) suggesting a blister 3 : a disease of plants marked by large raised patches on the leaves
²**blister** vb : to develop a blister; also : to cause blisters
blithe \'blīth, 'blīth\ adj **blith·er**; **blith·est** : happily lighthearted ✦ **Synonyms** MERRY, JOVIAL, JOLLY, JOCUND — **blithe·ly** adv — **blithe·some** \-səm\ adj
blitz \'blits\ n 1 : an intensive series of air raids 2 : a fast intensive campaign 3 : a rush of the passer by the defensive linebackers in football — **blitz** vb
blitz·krieg \-ˌkrēg\ n [G, fr. Blitz lightning + Krieg war] : a sudden violent enemy attack
bliz·zard \'bli-zərd\ n : a long severe snowstorm
blk abbr 1 black 2 block
bloat \'blōt\ vb : to swell by or as if by filling with water or air
blob \'bläb\ n : a small lump or drop of a thick consistency
bloc \'bläk\ n [F, lit., block] : a combination of individuals or groups (as nations) working for a common purpose
¹**block** \'bläk\ n 1 : a solid piece of substantial material (as wood or stone) 2 : HINDRANCE, OBSTRUCTION; also : interruption of normal function of body or mind ⟨heart ∼⟩ 3 : a frame enclosing one or more pulleys and having a hook or strap by which it may be attached 4 : a piece of material with a hand-cut design on its surface from which copies are to be made 5 : a large building divided into separate units (as apartments or offices) 6 : a row of houses or shops 7 : a city square; also : the distance along one of the sides of such a square 8 : a quantity of things considered as a unit ⟨a ∼ of seats⟩
²**block** vb 1 : OBSTRUCT, CHECK 2 : to outline roughly ⟨∼ out a design⟩ 3 : to provide or support with a block ✦ **Synonyms** BAR, IMPEDE, HINDER, OBSTRUCT — **block·er** n
block·ade \blä-'kād\ n : the isolation of a place usu. by troops or ships — **blockade** vb — **block·ad·er** n
block·age \'blä-kij\ n : an act or instance of obstructing : the state of being blocked
block·bust·er \'bläk-ˌbəs-tər\ n : one that is very large, successful, expensive, or extravagant ⟨a ∼ movie⟩
block·head \'bläk-ˌhed\ n : DOLT, DUNCE
block·house \-ˌhaůs\ n : a small strong building used as a shelter (as from enemy fire) or observation post
blog \'blóg, 'bläg\ n [short for Weblog] : a website containing one's reflections, opinions, and comments; also : the contents of such a site — **blog** vb — **blog·ger** n — **blog·ging** \'blö-giŋ, 'blä-\ n
¹**blond** or **blonde** \'bländ\ adj 1 : fair in complexion; also : of a light or bleached color ⟨∼ mahogany⟩ — **blond·ish** \'blän-dish\ adj

²**blond** or **blonde** n : a person having blond hair
blood \'bləd\ n 1 : a usu. red liquid that circulates in the heart, arteries, and veins of animals 2 : LIFEBLOOD; also : LIFE 3 : LINEAGE, STOCK 4 : KINSHIP; also : KINDRED 5 : the taking of life 6 : TEMPER, PASSION 7 : DANDY 1 — **blood·less** adj — **bloody** adj
blood·bath \'bləd-ˌbath, -ˌbäth\ n : MASSACRE
blood count n : the determination of the number of blood cells in a specific volume of blood; also : the number of cells so determined
blood·cur·dling \'bləd-kərd-liŋ, -ˌkər-dᵊl-iŋ\ adj : arousing fright or horror
blood·ed \'blə-dəd\ adj 1 : having blood of a specified kind ⟨warm-blooded animals⟩ 2 : entirely or largely purebred ⟨∼ horses⟩
blood group n : one of the classes into which human beings can be separated by the presence or absence in their blood of specific antigens
blood·hound \'bləd-ˌhaůnd\ n : any of a breed of large powerful hounds with long drooping ears, a wrinkled face, and keen sense of smell
blood·let·ting \-ˌle-tiŋ\ n 1 : PHLEBOTOMY 2 : BLOODSHED
blood·line \-ˌlīn\ n : a sequence of direct ancestors esp. in a pedigree
blood·lust \-ˌləst\ n : desire for bloodshed
blood·mo·bile \-mō-ˌbēl\ n : a motor vehicle equipped for collecting blood from donors
blood poisoning n : invasion of the bloodstream by virulent microorganisms from a focus of infection accompanied esp. by chills, fever, and prostration
blood pressure n : pressure of the blood on the walls of blood vessels and esp. arteries
blood·root \'bləd-ˌrüt, -ˌrůt\ n : a plant related to the poppy that has a red root and sap, a solitary leaf, and a white flower in early spring
blood·shed \-ˌshed\ n : wounding or taking of life : CARNAGE, SLAUGHTER
blood·shot \-ˌshät\ adj : inflamed to redness ⟨∼ eyes⟩
blood·stain \-ˌstān\ n : a discoloration caused by blood — **blood·stained** \-ˌstānd\ adj
blood·stone \-ˌstōn\ n : a green quartz sprinkled with red spots
blood·stream \-ˌstrēm\ n : the flowing blood in a circulatory system
blood·suck·er \-ˌsə-kər\ n : an animal that sucks blood; esp : LEECH — **blood·suck·ing** adj
blood test n : a test of the blood (as to detect disease-causing agents)
blood thinner n : a drug used to prevent the clotting of blood
blood·thirsty \'bləd-ˌthər-stē\ adj : eager to shed blood — **blood·thirst·i·ly** \-ˌthər-stə-lē\ adv — **blood·thirst·i·ness** \-stē-nəs\ n
blood type n : BLOOD GROUP — **blood–typ·ing** n
blood vessel n : a vessel (as a vein or artery) in which blood circulates in the body
Bloody Mary \-'mer-ē\ n, pl **Bloody Marys** : a drink made essentially of vodka and tomato juice
¹**bloom** \'blüm\ n 1 : FLOWER 1; also : flowers or amount of flowers (as of a plant) 2 : the period or state of flowering 3 : a state or time of beauty and vigor 4 : a powdery coating esp. on fruits and leaves 5 : rosy color; also : an appearance of freshness or health — **bloomy** adj
²**bloom** vb 1 : to produce or yield flowers 2 : MATURE 3 : to glow esp. with healthy color ✦ **Synonyms** FLOWER, BLOSSOM
bloo·mers \'blü-mərz\ n pl [Amelia Bloomer †1894 Am. reformer] : a woman's garment of short loose pants gathered at the knee
bloop·er \'blü-pər\ n 1 : a fly ball hit barely beyond a baseball infield 2 : an embarrassing public blunder
¹**blos·som** \'blä-səm\ n 1 : the flower of a plant 2 : the period or state of flowering
²**blossom** vb : FLOWER, BLOOM
¹**blot** \'blät\ n 1 : SPOT, STAIN ⟨ink ∼s⟩ 2 : BLEMISH ✦ **Synonyms** STIGMA, BRAND, SLUR
²**blot** vb blot·ted; blot·ting 1 : SPOT, STAIN 2 : OBSCURE, ECLIPSE ⟨∼ out the sun⟩ 3 obs : MAR; esp : DISGRACE 4 : to dry or remove with or as if with an absorbing material 5 : to make a blot

blotch \'bläch\ *n* : a usu. large and irregular spot or mark (as of ink or color) — **blotch** *vb* — **blotchy** *adj*

blot·ter \'blä-tər\ *n* **1** : a piece of blotting paper **2** : a book for preliminary records (as of sales or arrests)

blot·ting paper *n* : a spongy paper used to absorb ink

blouse \'blaús, 'blaúz\ *n* **1** : a loose outer garment like a smock **2** : a usu. loose garment reaching from the neck to about the waist

¹**blow** \'blō\ *vb* **blew** \'blü\; **blown** \'blōn\; **blow·ing 1** : to be in motion; *esp* : to move forcibly ⟨the wind *blew*⟩ **2** : to send forth a current of gas (as air) **3** : to act on with a current of gas or vapor; *esp* : to drive with such a current **4** : to clear with a current of air **5** : to sound or cause to sound ⟨~ a horn⟩ **6** : PANT, GASP; *also* : to expel moist air in breathing ⟨the whale *blew*⟩ **7** : BOAST; *also* : BLUSTER **8** : ERUPT, EXPLODE **9** : MELT — used of an electrical fuse **10** : to shape or form by blown or injected air ⟨~ glass⟩ **11** : to shatter or destroy by or as if by explosion **12** : to make breathless by exertion **13** : to spend recklessly **14** : BOTCH ⟨*blew* her lines⟩ — **blow·er** *n*

²**blow** *n* **1** : a usu. strong blowing of air : GALE **2** : BOASTING, BRAG **3** : an act or instance of blowing

³**blow** *vb* **blew** \'blü\; **blown** \'blōn\; **blow·ing** : FLOWER, BLOOM

⁴**blow** *n* **1** : a forcible stroke ⟨a ~ to the head⟩ **2** : COMBAT ⟨come to ~*s*⟩ **3** : a severe and usu. unexpected calamity

blow-by-blow *adj* : minutely detailed ⟨~ account⟩

blow-dry \-ˌdrī\ *vb* : to dry and usu. style hair with a blow-dryer

blow-dryer \-ˌdrī(-ə)r\ *n* : a hand-held hair dryer

blow-fly \'blō-ˌflī\ *n* : any of a family of dipteran flies (as a bluebottle) that deposit their eggs or maggots on meat or in wounds

blow-gun \-ˌgən\ *n* : a tube from which an arrow or a dart may be shot by the force of the breath

blow-out \'blō-ˌaút\ *n* **1** : a bursting of something (as a tire) because of pressure of the contents (as air) **2** : a depression created by the wind in sand or soil

blow-sy *also* **blow-zy** \'blaú-zē\ *adj* : DISHEVELED, SLOVENLY

blow-torch \'blō-ˌtòrch\ *n* : a small portable burner whose flame is made hotter by a blast of air or oxygen

blow-up \'blō-ˌəp\ *n* **1** : EXPLOSION **2** : an outburst of temper **3** : a photographic enlargement

blowy \'blō-ē\ *adj* : WINDY

BLT \ˌbē-ˌel-'tē\ *n* : a bacon, lettuce, and tomato sandwich

¹**blub·ber** \'blə-bər\ *vb* : to cry noisily

²**blubber** *n* **1** : the fat of large sea mammals (as whales) **2** : a noisy crying

¹**blud·geon** \'blə-jən\ *n* : a short often loaded club

²**bludgeon** *vb* : to strike with or as if with a bludgeon

¹**blue** \'blü\ *adj* **blu·er; blu·est** [ME, fr. AF *blef, blew,* of Gmc origin] **1** : of the color blue; *also* : BLUISH **2** : MELANCHOLY; *also* : DEPRESSING **3** : PURITANICAL **4** : INDECENT **5** : tending to support Democratic candidates ⟨~ states⟩ — **blue·ness** *n*

²**blue** *n* **1** : a color between green and violet in the spectrum : the color of the clear daytime sky **2** : something (as clothing or the sky) that is blue

blue baby *n* : a baby with bluish skin due to faulty circulation caused by a heart defect

blue·bell \-ˌbel\ *n* : any of various plants with blue bell= shaped flowers

blue·ber·ry \'blü-ˌber-ē, -bə-rē\ *n* : the edible blue or blackish berry of various shrubs of the heath family; *also* : one of these shrubs

blue·bird \-ˌbərd\ *n* : any of three small No. American thrushes that are blue above and reddish-brown or pale blue below

blue·bon·net \'blü-ˌbä-nət\ *n* : either of two low-growing annual lupines of Texas with silky foliage and blue flowers

blue·bot·tle \'blü-ˌbä-t³l\ *n* : any of several blowflies with iridescent blue bodies or abdomens

blue cheese *n* : cheese having veins of greenish-blue mold

blue–col·lar \'blü-'kä-lər\ *adj* : of, relating to, or being the class of workers whose duties call for work clothes

blue·fish \-ˌfish\ *n* : a marine sport and food fish that is bluish above and silvery below

blue·grass \-ˌgras\ *n* **1** : KENTUCKY BLUEGRASS **2** : country music played on stringed instruments having free improvisation and close harmonies

blue jay \-ˌjā\ *n* : a crested bright blue No. American jay

blue jeans *n pl* : pants usu. made of blue denim

blue·nose \-ˌnōz\ *n* : a person who advocates a rigorous moral code

blue·point \-ˌpòint\ *n* : a small oyster typically from the south shore of Long Island, New York

blue·print \-ˌprint\ *n* **1** : a photographic print in white on a blue ground used esp. for copying mechanical drawings and architects' plans **2** : a detailed plan of action — **blueprint** *vb*

blues \'blüz\ *n pl* **1** : MELANCHOLY **2** : music in a style marked by recurrent minor intervals and melancholy lyrics

blue screen *n* : a technique in which a subject is filmed in front of a blue background so as to allow the creation of a composite with other footage

blue·stock·ing \'blü-ˌstä-kiŋ\ *n* : a woman having intellectual interests

blu·et \'blü-ət\ *n* : a low No. American herb with dainty bluish flowers

blue whale *n* : a very large baleen whale that may reach a weight of 150 tons (135 metric tons) and a length of 100 feet (30 meters)

¹**bluff** \'bləf\ *adj* **1** : having a broad flattened front **2** : rising steeply with a broad flat front **3** : OUTSPOKEN, FRANK ✦ *Synonyms* ABRUPT, BLUNT, BRUSQUE, CURT, GRUFF

²**bluff** *n* : a high steep bank : CLIFF

³**bluff** *vb* : to frighten or deceive by pretense or a mere show of strength

⁴**bluff** *n* : an act or instance of bluffing; *also* : one who bluffs

blu·ing *or* **blue·ing** \'blü-iŋ\ *n* : a preparation used in laundering to counteract yellowing of white fabrics

blu·ish \'blü-ish\ *adj* : somewhat blue

¹**blun·der** \'blən-dər\ *vb* **1** : to move clumsily or unsteadily **2** : to make a stupid or needless mistake

²**blunder** *n* : an avoidable and usu. serious mistake

blun·der·buss \'blən-dər-ˌbəs\ *n* [obs. D *donderbus,* fr. D *donder* thunder + obs. D *bus* gun] : an obsolete short= barreled firearm with a flaring muzzle

¹**blunt** \'blənt\ *adj* **1** : not sharp : DULL **2** : lacking in tact : BLUFF ⟨~ criticism⟩ ✦ *Synonyms* BRUSQUE, CURT, GRUFF, ABRUPT, CRUSTY — **blunt·ly** *adv* — **blunt·ness** *n*

²**blunt** *vb* : to make or become dull

¹**blur** \'blər\ *n* **1** : a smear or stain that obscures **2** : something vaguely perceived; *esp* : something moving too quickly to be clearly perceived — **blur·ry** \-ē\ *adj*

²**blur** *vb* **blurred; blur·ring** : DIM, CLOUD, OBSCURE ⟨*blurred* vision⟩

blurb \'blərb\ *n* : a short publicity notice (as on a book jacket)

blurt \'blərt\ *vb* : to utter suddenly and impulsively

blush \'bləsh\ *n* **1** : a reddening of the face (as from modesty or confusion) : FLUSH **2** : a cosmetic used to tint the face — **blush** *vb* — **blush·ful** *adj*

blus·ter \'bləs-tər\ *vb* **1** : to blow in stormy noisy gusts **2** : to talk or act with noisy swaggering threats — **bluster** *n* — **blus·tery** \-tə-rē\ *adj*

blvd *abbr* boulevard

B lymphocyte *n* : B CELL

BM *abbr* bowel movement

B movie *n* : a cheaply produced motion picture

BO *abbr* **1** best offer **2** body odor **3** box office **4** branch office

boa \'bō-ə\ *n* **1** : a large snake (as the **boa con·stric·tor** \-kən-'strik-tər\ or the related anaconda) that suffocates and kills its prey by constriction **2** : a fluffy scarf usu. of fur or feathers

boar \'bòr\ *n* : a male swine; *also* : WILD BOAR

¹**board** \'bòrd\ *n* **1** : the side of a ship **2** : a thin flat length of sawed lumber; *also* : material (as cardboard) or a piece of material formed as a thin flat firm sheet **3** *pl* : STAGE **1 4** : a table spread with a meal; *also* : daily meals esp. when furnished for pay **5** : a table at which a council or magistrates sit **6** : a group or association

of persons organized for a special responsibility (as the management of a business or institution); *also* : an organized commercial exchange **7** : a sheet of insulating material carrying circuit elements and inserted in an electronic device **8** : BULLETIN BOARD
²**board** *vb* **1** : to go or put aboard ⟨∼ a boat⟩ **2** : to cover with boards **3** : to provide or be provided with meals and often lodging — **board·er** *n*
board game *n* : a game of strategy (as checkers or chess) played by moving pieces on a board
board·ing·house \'bȯr-diŋ-ˌhaůs\ *n* : a house at which persons are boarded
board·walk \'bȯrd-ˌwȯk\ *n* : a promenade (as of planking) along a beach
boast \'bōst\ *vb* **1** : to praise oneself **2** : to mention or assert with excessive pride **3** : to prize as a possession; *also* : HAVE ⟨the house ∼s a fireplace⟩ — **boast** *n* — **boast·ful** \-fəl\ *adj* — **boast·ful·ly** *adv*
boat \'bōt\ *n* : a small vessel for travel on water; *also* : SHIP — **boat** *vb*
boat·er \'bō-tər\ *n* **1** : one that travels in a boat **2** : a stiff straw hat
boat·man \'bōt-mən\ *n* : a man who operates, works on, or deals in boats
boat people *n pl* : refugees fleeing by boat
boat·swain *or* **bo·sun** \'bō-sᵊn\ *n* : a subordinate officer of a ship in charge of the hull and related equipment
¹**bob** \'bäb\ *vb* **bobbed; bob·bing 1** : to move up and down jerkily or repeatedly **2** : to emerge, arise, or appear suddenly or unexpectedly
²**bob** *n* : a bobbing movement
³**bob** *n* **1** : a knob, knot, twist, or curl esp. of ribbons, yarn, or hair **2** : a short haircut of a woman or child **3** : FLOAT 2 **4** : a weight hanging from a line
⁴**bob** *vb* **bobbed; bob·bing** : to cut hair in a bob
⁵**bob** *n, pl* **bob** *slang Brit* : SHILLING
bob·bin \'bä-bən\ *n* : a cylinder or spindle for holding or dispensing thread (as in a sewing machine)
bob·ble \'bä-bəl\ *vb* **bob·bled; bob·bling 1** : to move up and down quickly or repeatedly **2** : FUMBLE ⟨the catcher *bobbled* the ball⟩ — **bobble** *n*
bob·by \'bä-bē\ *n, pl* **bobbies** [*Bobby*, nickname for Sir *Robert* Peel, who organized the London police force] *Brit* : a police officer
bobby pin *n* : a flat wire hairpin with prongs that press close together
bob·cat \'bäb-ˌkat\ *n* : a small usu. rusty-colored No. American lynx
bob·o·link \'bä-bə-ˌliŋk\ *n* : an American migratory songbird related to the meadowlarks
bob·sled \'bäb-ˌsled\ *n* **1** : a short sled usu. used as one of a joined pair **2** : a racing sled with two pairs of runners, a steering wheel, and a hand brake — **bobsled** *vb*
bob·white \(ˌ)bäb-'hwīt\ *n* : any of a genus of quail; *esp* : a popular game bird of eastern and central No. America
boc·cie *or* **boc·ci** *or* **boc·ce** \'bä-chē\ *n* : Italian lawn bowling played on a long narrow court
bock \'bäk\ *n* : a strong dark beer usu. sold in early spring
bod \'bäd\ *n* : BODY
¹**bode** \'bōd\ *vb* **bod·ed; bod·ing** : to indicate by signs : PRESAGE
²**bode** *past of* BIDE
bo·de·ga \bō-'dä-gə\ *n* [Sp, fr. L *apotheca* storehouse] : a usu. small store specializing in Hispanic groceries
bod·ice \'bä-dəs\ *n* [alter. of *bodies*, pl. of *body*] : the usu. close-fitting part of a dress above the waist
bodi·less \'bä-di-ləs\ *adj* : lacking a body or material form
¹**bodi·ly** \'bä-dᵊl-ē\ *adj* : of or relating to the body ⟨∼ contact⟩ ⟨∼ organs⟩
²**bodily** *adv* **1** : in the flesh **2** : as a whole ⟨lifted the crate up ∼⟩
bod·kin \'bäd-kən\ *n* **1** : DAGGER **2** : a pointed implement for punching holes in cloth **3** : a blunt needle for drawing tape or ribbon through a loop or hem
body \'bä-dē\ *n, pl* **bod·ies 1** : the physical whole of a living or dead organism; *also* : the trunk or main mass of an organism as distinguished from its appendages **2** : a human being : PERSON **3** : the main part of something **4** : a mass of matter distinct from other masses **5** : GROUP

⟨the student ∼⟩ **6** : VISCOSITY, FIRMNESS **7** : richness of flavor — used esp. of wines — **bod·ied** \'bä-dēd\ *adj*
body·build·ing \'bä-dē-ˌbil-diŋ\ *n* : the developing of the body through exercise and diet — **body·build·er** \-dər\ *n*
body English *n* : bodily motions made in a usu. unconscious effort to influence the movement of a propelled object (as a ball)
body·guard \'bä-dē-ˌgärd\ *n* : a personal guard; *also* : RETINUE
body language *n* : movements (as with the hands) or posture used as a means of communication
body stocking *n* : a sheer close-fitting one-piece garment for the torso that often has sleeves and legs
body·work \'bä-dē-ˌwərk\ *n* : the making or repairing of vehicle bodies
Boer \'bȯr, 'bůr\ *n* [D, lit., farmer] : a South African of Dutch or Huguenot descent
¹**bog** \'bäg, 'bȯg\ *n* : wet, spongy, poorly drained, and usu. acid ground — **bog·gy** *adj*
²**bog** *vb* **bogged; bog·ging** : to sink into or as if into a bog
bo·gey *also* **bo·gie** *or* **bo·gy** \'bů-gē, 'bō- *for 1*; 'bō- *for 2*\ *n, pl* **bogeys** *also* **bogies 1** : SPECTER, HOBGOBLIN; *also* : a source of fear or annoyance **2** : a score of one over par on a hole in golf
bo·gey·man \'bů-gē-ˌman, 'bō-, 'bů- \ *n* : an imaginary monster used in threatening children
bog·gle \'bä-gəl\ *vb* **bog·gled; bog·gling** : to overwhelm or be overwhelmed with fright or amazement
bo·gus \'bō-gəs\ *adj* : SPURIOUS, SHAM
Bo·he·mi·an \bō-'hē-mē-ən\ *n* **1** : a native or inhabitant of Bohemia **2** *often not cap* : VAGABOND, WANDERER **3** *often not cap* : a person (as a writer or artist) living an unconventional life — **bohemian** *adj, often cap*
bohr·i·um \'bȯr-ē-əm\ *n* : an artificially produced radioactive chemical element
¹**boil** \'bȯi(-ə)l\ *n* : an inflamed swelling on the skin containing pus
²**boil** *vb* **1** : to heat or become heated to a temperature (**boil·ing point**) at which vapor is formed and rises in bubbles ⟨water ∼s and changes to steam⟩; *also* : to act on or be acted on by a boiling liquid ⟨∼ eggs⟩ **2** : to be in a state of seething agitation
³**boil** *n* **1** : the act or state of boiling **2** : a boiled dish (as of seafood) **3** : a gathering where boiled food is served
boil·er \'bȯi-lər\ *n* **1** : a container in which something is boiled **2** : a strong vessel used in making steam **3** : a tank holding hot water
boil·er·mak·er \'bȯi-lər-ˌmā-kər\ *n* : whiskey with a beer chaser
bois·ter·ous \'bȯi-st(ə-)rəs\ *adj* : noisily turbulent or exuberant — **bois·ter·ous·ly** *adv*
bok choy \'bäk-'chȯi\ *n* : a Chinese vegetable related to the mustards that forms a loose head of green leaves with long thick white stalks
bo·la \'bō-lə\ *or* **bo·las** \-ləs\, *n, pl* **bolas** \-ləz\ *also* **bo·las·es** [AmerSp *bolas*, fr. Sp *bola* ball] : a cord with weights attached to the ends for hurling at and entangling an animal
bold \'bōld\ *adj* **1** : COURAGEOUS, INTREPID **2** : IMPUDENT **3** : STEEP ⟨∼ cliffs⟩ **4** : ADVENTUROUS, FREE ⟨a ∼ thinker⟩ ◆ **Synonyms** DAUNTLESS, BRAVE, VALIANT — **bold·ly** *adv* — **bold·ness** \'bōld-nəs\ *n*
bold·face \'bōld-ˌfās\ *n* : a heavy-faced type; *also* : printing in boldface — **bold–faced** \-'fāst\ *adj*
bole \'bōl\ *n* : the trunk of a tree
bo·le·ro \bə-'ler-ō\ *n, pl* **-ros 1** : a Spanish dance or its music **2** : a short loose jacket open at the front
bo·li·var \bə-'lē-ˌvär, 'bä-lə-vər\ *n, pl* **-va·res** \ˌbä-lə-'vär-ˌās, ˌbō-\ *or* **-vars** — see MONEY table
Bo·liv·i·an \bə-'li-vē-ən\ *n* : a native or inhabitant of Bolivia — **Bolivian** *adj*
bo·li·vi·a·no \bə-ˌli-vē-'ä-(ˌ)nō\ *n, pl* **-nos** — see MONEY table
boll \'bōl\ *n* : a seed pod (as of cotton)
boll weevil *n* : a small usu. grayish or brown weevil that infests the cotton plant both as a larva and as an adult
boll·worm \'bōl-ˌwərm\ *n* : any of several moths and esp. the corn earworm whose larvae feed on cotton bolls
bo·lo·gna \bə-'lō-nē\ *n* [short for *Bologna sausage*, fr. *Bologna*, Italy] : a large smoked sausage of beef, veal, and pork

Bol·she·vik \'bōl-shə-,vik\ *n, pl* **Bolsheviks** *also* **Bol-she·vi·ki** \,bōl-shə-'vi-kē\ [Russ *bol'shevik*, fr. *bol'shiĭ* larger] **1** : a member of the party that seized power in Russia in the revolution of November 1917 **2** : COMMU-NIST — **Bolshevik** *adj*

bol·she·vism \'bōl-shə-,vi-zəm\ *n, often cap* : the doctrine or program of the Bolsheviks advocating violent over-throw of capitalism

¹bol·ster \'bōl-stər\ *n* : a long pillow or cushion

²bolster *vb* : to support with or as if with a bolster; *also* : REINFORCE

¹bolt \'bōlt\ *n* **1** : a missile (as an arrow) for a crossbow or catapult **2** : a flash of lightning : THUNDERBOLT **3** : a sliding bar used to fasten a door **4** : a roll of cloth or wallpaper of specified length **5** : a rod with a head at one end and a screw thread at the other used with a nut to fas-ten objects together **6** : a metal cylinder that drives the cartridge into the chamber of a firearm

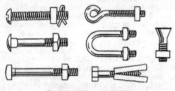

¹bolt 5: different styles

²bolt *vb* **1** : to move suddenly (as in fright or hurry) : START, DASH **2** : to break away (as from association) ⟨~ from a political platform⟩ **3** : to produce seed prematurely **4** : to secure or fasten with a bolt **5** : to swallow hastily or without chewing

³bolt *n* : an act of bolting

bo·lus \'bō-ləs\ *n, pl* **bo·lus·es** **1** : a large pill **2** : a soft mass of chewed food

¹bomb \'bäm\ *n* **1** : a fused explosive device designed to detonate under specified conditions (as impact) **2** : an aerosol or foam dispenser (as of insecticide) : SPRAY CAN **3** : FAILURE, FLOP **4** : a long pass, shot, or hit

²bomb *vb* **1** : to attack with bombs **2** : FAIL ⟨~ed at the audition⟩

bom·bard \bäm-'bärd\ *vb* **1** : to attack esp. with artillery or bombers **2** : to assail persistently **3** : to subject to the impact of rapidly moving particles (as electrons) — **bom·bard·ment** *n*

bom·bar·dier \,bäm-bər-'dir\ *n* : a bomber-crew member who releases the bombs

bom·bast \'bäm-,bast\ *n* [ME, cotton padding, fr. MF *bombace*, fr. ML *bombax* cotton, alter. of L *bombyx* silkworm, silk, fr. Gk] : pretentious wordy speech or writing — **bom·bas·tic** \bäm-'bas-tik\ *adj* — **bom·bas·ti·cal·ly** \-ti-k(ə-)lē\ *adv*

bom·ba·zine \,bäm-bə-'zēn\ *n* **1** : a twilled fabric with silk warp and worsted filling **2** : a silk fabric in twill weave dyed black

bomb·er \'bä-mər\ *n* : one that bombs; *esp* : an airplane for dropping bombs

bomb·proof \'bäm-,prüf\ *adj* : safe against the explosive force of bombs

bomb·shell \'bäm-,shel\ *n* **1** : BOMB 1 **2** : one that stuns, amazes, or completely upsets

bona fide \'bō-nə-,fīd, 'bä-; ,bō-nə-'fī-dē, -də\ *adj* [L, in good faith] **1** : made in good faith ⟨a *bona fide* agree-ment⟩ **2** : GENUINE, REAL ⟨a *bona fide* bargain⟩

bo·nan·za \bə-'nan-zə\ *n* [Sp, lit., calm sea, fr. ML *bo-nacia*, alter. of L *malacia*, fr. Gk *malakia*, lit., softness, fr. *malakos* soft] **1** : something yielding a rich return **2** : a spectacular event

bon·bon \'bän-,bän\ *n* : a candy with a creamy center and a soft covering (as of chocolate)

¹bond \'bänd\ *n* **1** : FETTER **2** : a binding or uniting force or tie ⟨~s of friendship⟩ **3** : an agreement or obligation often made binding by a pledge of money or goods **4** : a person who acts as surety for another **5** : an interest=bearing certificate of public or private indebtedness **6** : the state of goods subject to supervision pending pay-ment of taxes or duties due

²bond *vb* **1** : to assure payment of duties or taxes on (goods) by giving a bond **2** : to insure against losses caused by the acts of ⟨~ a bank teller⟩ **3** : to make or become firmly united as if by bonds ⟨~ iron to copper⟩ **4** : to form a close relationship ⟨~ed with her stepmother⟩

bond·age \'bän-dij\ *n* : SLAVERY, SERVITUDE

bond·hold·er \'bänd-,hōl-dər\ *n* : one that owns a govern-ment or corporation bond

bond·ing \'bän-diŋ\ *n* **1** : the formation of a close per-sonal relationship esp. through frequent or constant as-sociation **2** : the attaching of a material (as porcelain) to a tooth surface esp. for cosmetic purposes

bond·man \'bänd-mən\ *n* : SLAVE, SERF

¹bonds·man \'bändz-mən\ *n* : SURETY

²bondsman *var of* BONDMAN

bond·wom·an \'bänd-,wů-mən\ *n* : a female slave or serf

¹bone \'bōn\ *n* **1** : a hard largely calcareous tissue forming most of the skeleton of a vertebrate animal; *also* : one of the pieces of bone making up a vertebrate skeleton **2** : a hard animal substance (as ivory or baleen) similar to true bone **3** : something made of bone — **bone·less** *adj* — **bony** *also* **bon·ey** \'bō-nē\ *adj*

²bone *vb* **boned; bon·ing** : to free from bones ⟨~ a chicken⟩

bone black *n* : the black carbon residue from calcined bones used esp. as a pigment

bone marrow *n* : MARROW

bone·meal \'bōn-,mēl\ *n* : crushed or ground bone used esp. as fertilizer or feed

bon·er \'bō-nər\ *n* : a stupid and ridiculous blunder

bone up *vb* **1** : CRAM 3 **2** : to refresh one's memory ⟨*boned up* on the speech before giving it⟩

bon·fire \'bän-,fī(-ə)r\ *n* [ME *bonefire* a fire of bones, fr. *bon* bone + *fire*] : a large fire built in the open air

bon·go \'bäŋ-gō\ *n, pl* **bongos** *also* **bongoes** [AmerSp *bongó*] : one of a pair of small tuned drums played with the hands

bon·ho·mie \,bä-nə-'mē\ *n* [F *bonhomie*, fr. *bonhomme* good-natured man, fr. *bon* good + *homme* man] : good=natured easy friendliness

bo·ni·to \bə-'nē-tō\ *n, pl* **-tos** *or* **-to** : any of several medium=sized tunas

bon mot \bōⁿ-'mō\ *n, pl* **bons mots** *same*\ *or* **bon mots** *same*\ [F, lit., good word] : a clever remark

bon·net \'bä-nət\ *n* : a covering (as a cap) for the head; *esp* : a hat for a woman or infant tied under the chin

bon·ny \'bä-nē\ *adj* **bon·ni·er; -est** *chiefly Brit* : ATTRAC-TIVE, FAIR; *also* : FINE, EXCELLENT

bon·sai \bōn-'sī, 'bän-,\ *n, pl* **bonsai** [Jp] : a potted plant (as a tree) dwarfed and trained to an artistic shape; *also* : the art of growing such a plant

bo·nus \'bō-nəs\ *n* : something in addition to what is ex-pected

bon vi·vant \,bän-vē-'vänt, ,bōⁿ-vē-'väⁿ\ *n, pl* **bons vivants** \,bän-vē-'vänts, ,bōⁿ-vē-'väⁿ\ *or* **bon vivants** *same*\ [F, lit., good liver] : a person having cultivated, refined, and sociable tastes esp. in food and drink

bon voy·age \,bōⁿ-,vòi-'äzh, ,bän-; ,bōⁿ-,vwä-'yäzh\ *n* : FAREWELL — often used as an interjection

bony fish *n* : any of a class of fishes (as eels or sturgeons) with a bone rather than a cartilaginous skeleton

bonze \'bänz\ *n* : a Buddhist monk

boo \'bü\ *n, pl* **boos** : a shout of disapproval or contempt — **boo** *vb*

boo·by \'bü-bē\ *n, pl* **boobies** : an awkward foolish person : DOPE

booby hatch *n* : a psychiatric hospital

booby prize *n* : an award for the poorest performance in a contest

booby trap *n* : a trap for the unwary; *esp* : a concealed explosive device set to go off when some harmless=looking object is touched — **booby–trap** *vb*

boo·dle \'bü-d²l\ *n* **1** : bribe money **2** : a large amount of money

¹book \'bůk\ *n* **1** : a set of sheets bound into a volume **2** : a long written or printed narrative or record **3** : a major division of a long literary work **4** *cap* : BIBLE — **in one's book** : in one's own opinion

²book *vb* **1** : to engage, reserve, or schedule by or as if by writing in a book ⟨~ seats on a plane⟩ **2** : to enter charges against in a police register

book·case \-ˌkās\ *n* : a piece of furniture consisting of shelves to hold books

book·end \-ˌend\ *n* : a support to hold up a row of books

book·ie \'bu̇-kē\ *n* : BOOKMAKER

book·ish \'bu̇-kish\ *adj* 1 : fond of books and reading 2 : inclined to rely unduly on book knowledge

book·keep·er \'bu̇k-ˌkē-pər\ *n* : a person who records the accounts or transactions of a business — **book·keep·ing** *n*

book·let \'bu̇k-lət\ *n* : PAMPHLET

book·mak·er \'bu̇k-ˌmā-kər\ *n* : a person who determines odds and receives and pays off bets — **book·mak·ing** *n*

book·mark \-ˌmärk\ *or* **book·mark·er** \-ˌmär-kər\ *n* 1 : a marker for finding a place in a book 2 : a shortcut to a previously viewed location (as a website) on a computer — **bookmark** *vb*

book·mo·bile \'bu̇k-mō-ˌbēl\ *n* : a truck that serves as a traveling library

book·plate \'bu̇k-ˌplāt\ *n* : a label pasted in a book to show who owns it

book·sell·er \'bu̇k-ˌse-lər\ *n* : one that sells books; *esp* : the proprietor of a bookstore

book·shelf \-ˌshelf\ *n* : a shelf for books

book·worm \'bu̇k-ˌwərm\ *n* : a person unusually devoted to reading and study

¹boom \'bu̇m\ *vb* 1 : to make a deep hollow sound : RESOUND 2 : to grow or cause to grow rapidly esp. in number, value, esteem, or importance

²boom *n* 1 : a booming sound or cry 2 : a rapid expansion or increase esp. of economic activity

³boom *n* [D, tree, beam] 1 : a long spar used to extend the bottom of a sail 2 : a line of floating timbers used to obstruct passage or catch floating objects 3 : a beam projecting from the upright pole of a derrick to support or guide the object lifted 4 : a long usu. horizontal supporting arm (as for a microphone)

boom box *n* : a large portable radio and often tape or CD player

boo·mer·ang \'bu̇-mə-ˌraŋ\ *n* [Dharuk (an Australian aboriginal language) *bumarin'*] : a bent or angular club that can be so thrown as to return near the starting point

boom·ing \'bu̇-miŋ\ *adj* 1 : making a loud deep sound ⟨a ~ voice⟩ 2 : powerfully executed ⟨hit a ~ serve⟩

¹boon \'bu̇n\ *n* [ME *bone* prayer, request, the favor requested, fr. ON *bōn* request] : BENEFIT, BLESSING ♦ *Synonyms* FAVOR, GIFT, LARGESS, PRESENT

²boon *adj* [ME *bon*, fr. AF, good] : CONVIVIAL ⟨a ~ companion⟩

boon·docks \'bu̇n-ˌdäks\ *n pl* [Tagalog (language of the Philippines) *bundok* mountain] 1 : rough country filled with dense brush 2 : a rural area

boon·dog·gle \'bu̇n-ˌdä-gəl, -ˌdȯ-\ *n* : a useless or wasteful project or activity

boor \'bu̇r\ *n* 1 : YOKEL 2 : a rude or insensitive person ♦ *Synonyms* CHURL, LOUT, CLOWN, CLODHOPPER — **boor·ish** *adj*

boost \'bu̇st\ *vb* 1 : to push up from below 2 : INCREASE, RAISE ⟨~ prices⟩ 3 : AID, PROMOTE ⟨voted a bonus to ~ morale⟩ — **boost** *n* — **boost·er** *n*

¹boot \'bu̇t\ *n, chiefly dial* : something to equalize a trade — **to boot** : BESIDES

²boot *vb, archaic* : AVAIL, PROFIT

³boot *n* 1 : a covering for the foot and leg 2 : a protective sheath (as of a flower) 3 *Brit* : an automobile trunk 4 : KICK; *also* : a discharge from employment 5 : a navy or marine corps trainee

⁴boot *vb* 1 : KICK 2 : to eject or discharge summarily 3 : to load or become loaded into a computer from a disk 4 : to start or become ready for use esp. by booting a program ⟨~ up the computer⟩

boot·black \'bu̇t-ˌblak\ *n* : a person who shines shoes

boot camp *n* 1 : a navy or marine corps training camp 2 : a facility with a rigorous disciplinary program for young offenders

boo·tee *or* **boo·tie** \'bu̇-tē\ *n* : an infant's knitted or crocheted sock

booth \'bu̇th\ *n, pl* **booths** \'bu̇thz, 'bu̇ths\ 1 : a small enclosed stall (as at a fair) 2 : a small enclosure giving privacy for a person ⟨voting ~⟩ ⟨telephone ~⟩ 3 : a

restaurant accommodation having a table between backed benches

boot·leg \'bu̇t-ˌleg\ *vb* : to make, transport, or sell (as liquor) illegally — **boot·leg** *adj or n* — **boot·leg·ger** *n*

boot·less \'bu̇t-ləs\ *adj* : USELESS ⟨their efforts were ~⟩ ♦ *Synonyms* FUTILE, VAIN, ABORTIVE, FRUITLESS — **boot·less·ly** *adv* — **boot·less·ness** *n*

¹boo·ty \'bu̇-tē\ *n, pl* **booties** : PLUNDER, SPOIL

²booty *also* **boo·tie** \'bü-tē\ *n, pl* **booties** *slang* : BUTTOCKS

¹booze \'bu̇z\ *vb* boozed; booz·ing : to drink liquor to excess — **booz·er** *n*

²booze *n* : intoxicating liquor — **boozy** *adj*

bop \'bäp\ *vb* bopped; bop·ping : HIT, SOCK — **bop** *n*

BOQ *abbr* bachelor officers' quarters

bor *abbr* borough

bo·rate \'bȯr-ˌāt\ *n* : a salt or ester of boric acid

bo·rax \'bȯr-ˌaks\ *n* : a crystalline borate of sodium that occurs as a mineral and is used as a flux and cleanser

bor·del·lo \bȯr-'de-lō\ *n, pl* **-los** [It] : BROTHEL

¹bor·der \'bȯr-dər\ *n* 1 : EDGE, MARGIN 2 : BOUNDARY, FRONTIER ♦ *Synonyms* RIM, BRIM, BRINK, FRINGE, PERIMETER

²border *vb* bor·dered; bor·der·ing 1 : to put a border on 2 : ADJOIN 3 : VERGE

border collie *n, often cap B* : any of a British breed of medium-sized long-haired sheepdogs

bor·der·land \'bȯr-dər-ˌland\ *n* 1 : territory at or near a border 2 : an outlying or intermediate region often not clearly defined

bor·der·line \-ˌlīn\ *adj* : being in an intermediate position or state; *esp* : not quite up to what is standard or expected ⟨~ intelligence⟩

¹bore \'bȯr\ *vb* bored; bor·ing 1 : to make a hole in with or as if with a drill 2 : to make (as a well) by boring or digging away material ♦ *Synonyms* PERFORATE, DRILL, PRICK, PUNCTURE — **bor·er** *n*

²bore *n* 1 : a hole made by or as if by boring 2 : a cylindrical cavity 3 : the diameter of a hole or tube; *esp* : the interior diameter of a gun barrel or engine cylinder

³bore *past of* BEAR

⁴bore *n* : a tidal flood with a high abrupt front

⁵bore *n* : one that causes boredom

⁶bore *vb* bored; bor·ing : to weary with tedious dullness

bo·re·al \'bȯr-ē-əl\ *adj* : of, relating to, or located in northern regions

bore·dom \'bȯr-dəm\ *n* : the condition of being bored

bo·ric acid \'bȯr-ik-\ *n* : a white crystalline weak acid that contains boron and is used esp. as an antiseptic

born \'bȯrn\ *adj* 1 : brought into life by birth 2 : NATIVE ⟨American-*born*⟩ 3 : having special natural abilities or character from birth ⟨a ~ leader⟩

born–again *adj* : having experienced a revival of a personal faith or conviction ⟨a ~ believer⟩ ⟨a ~ liberal⟩

borne *past part of* BEAR

bo·ron \'bȯr-ˌän\ *n* : a chemical element that occurs in nature only in combination (as in borax)

bor·ough \'bər-ō\ *n* [ME *burgh*, fr. OE *burg* fortified town] 1 : a British town that sends one or more members to Parliament; *also* : an incorporated British urban area 2 : an incorporated town or village in some U.S. states; *also* : any of the five political divisions of New York City 3 : a civil division of the state of Alaska corresponding to a county in most other states

bor·row \'bär-ō\ *vb* 1 : to take or receive (something) temporarily and with intent to return ⟨~*ed* my car⟩ 2 : to take into possession or use from another source : DERIVE, APPROPRIATE ⟨~ a metaphor⟩

borscht \'bȯrsht\ *or* **borsch** \'bȯrsh\ *n* [Yiddish *borsht* & Ukrainian & Russ *borshch*] : a soup made mainly from beets

bosh \'bäsh\ *n* [Turk *boş* empty] : foolish talk or action : NONSENSE

bosky \'bäs-kē\ *adj* : covered with trees or shrubs

¹bos·om \'bu̇-zəm, 'bü-\ *n* 1 : the front of the human chest; *esp* : the female breasts 2 : the seat of secret thoughts and feelings 3 : the part of a garment covering the breast — **bos·omed** \-zəmd\ *adj*

²bosom *adj* : CLOSE, INTIMATE

¹boss \'bäs, 'bȯs\ *n* : a knoblike ornament : STUD

²boss *vb* : to ornament with bosses

³**boss** \'bȯs\ *n* **1** : one (as a foreman or manager) exercising control or supervision **2** : a politician who controls votes or dictates policies — **bossy** *adj*

⁴**boss** \'bȯs\ *vb* : to act as or in the manner of a boss

bosun *var of* BOATSWAIN

¹**bot** \'bät\ *n* **1** : ROBOT **2** : a computer program that performs automatic, repetitive, and sometimes harmful tasks **3** : a computer program or character that mimics human actions

²**bot** *abbr* botanical; botanist; botany

bot·a·ny \'bä-tə-nē, 'bät-nē\ *n, pl* **-nies** **1** : a branch of biology dealing with plants and plant life **2** : plant life (as of a given region); *also* : the biology of a plant or plant group — **bo·tan·i·cal** \bə-'ta-ni-kəl\ *adj or n* — **bo·tan·i·cal·ly** \-kə-lē\ *adv* — **bot·a·nist** *n* — **bot·a·nize** \'bät-ə-ˌnīz\ *vb*

botch \'bäch\ *vb* : to foul up hopelessly : BUNGLE — **botch** *n*

¹**both** \'bōth\ *pron* : both ones : the one as well as the other

²**both** *conj* — used as a function word to indicate and stress the inclusion of each of two or more things specified by coordinated words, phrases, or clauses ⟨~ New York and London⟩

³**both** *adj* : being the two : including the one and the other ⟨went to ~ museums⟩

both·er \'bä-thər\ *vb* **1** : PESTER, TROUBLE ⟨was ~ed by bees⟩ **2** : to concern oneself : make an effort ⟨didn't ~ asking⟩ ◆ **Synonyms** VEX, ANNOY, IRK, PROVOKE — **bother** *n* — **both·er·some** \-səm\ *adj*

¹**bot·tle** \'bä-tᵊl\ *n* **1** : a container (as of glass) with a narrow neck and usu. no handles **2** : the quantity held by a bottle **3** : intoxicating liquor

²**bottle** *vb* **bot·tled; bot·tling** **1** : to confine as if in a bottle : RESTRAIN ⟨bottled up his anger⟩ **2** : to put into a bottle

bot·tle·neck \'bä-tᵊl-ˌnek\ *n* **1** : a narrow passage or point of congestion **2** : something that obstructs or impedes

¹**bot·tom** \'bä-təm\ *n* **1** : an under or supporting surface; *also* : BUTTOCKS **2** : the surface on which a body of water lies **3** : the lowest part or place; *also* : an inferior position ⟨start at the ~⟩ **4** : BOTTOMLAND **5** : BASIS, SOURCE ⟨get to the ~ of this mystery⟩ **6** : a quark with a charge of -⅓ and a measured energy of approximately 5 billion electron volts — **bottom** *adj* — **bot·tom·less** *adj*

²**bottom** *vb* **1** : to furnish with a bottom **2** : to reach the bottom **3** : to reach a point where a decline is halted or reversed — usu. used with *out*

bot·tom·land \'bä-təm-ˌland\ *n* : low land along a river

bottom line *n* **1** : the essential point : CRUX **2** : the final result : OUTCOME

bot·u·lism \'bä-chə-ˌli-zəm\ *n* : an acute paralytic disease caused by a bacterial toxin (**bot·u·li·num toxin** \ˌbä-chə-'lī-nəm-\) esp. in tainted food

bou·doir \'bü-ˌdwär, 'bü-, ˌbü-', ˌbü-'\ *n* [F, fr. *bouder* to pout] : a woman's dressing room or bedroom

bouf·fant \bü-'fänt, 'bü-ˌfänt\ *adj* [F] : puffed out ⟨~ hairdos⟩

bough \'baù\ *n* : a usu. large or main branch of a tree

bought *past and past part of* BUY

bouil·la·baisse \ˌbü-yə-'bäs\ *n* [F] : a highly seasoned fish stew made with at least two kinds of fish

bouil·lon \'bü-ˌyän; 'bùl-ˌyän, -yən\ *n* : a clear soup made usu. from beef

boul·der *also* **bowl·der** \'bōl-dər\ *n* : a large detached rounded or worn mass of rock — **boul·dered** \-dərd\ *adj*

bou·le·vard \'bù-lə-ˌvärd, 'bü-\ *n* [F, modif. of MD *bolwerc* bulwark] : a broad often landscaped thoroughfare

bounce \'baùns\ *vb* **bounced; bounc·ing** **1** : to cause to rebound ⟨~ a ball⟩ **2** : to rebound after striking **3** : to issue (a check) from an account with insufficient funds — **bounce** *n* — **bouncy** \'baùn-sē\ *adj*

bounc·er \'baùn-sər\ *n* : a person employed in a public place to remove disorderly persons

¹**bound** \'baùnd\ *adj* : intending to go ⟨homeward ~⟩

²**bound** *n* : LIMIT, BOUNDARY — **bound·less** *adj* — **bound·less·ness** *n*

³**bound** *vb* **1** : to set limits to **2** : to form the boundary of **3** : to name the boundaries of

⁴**bound** *past and past part of* BIND

⁵**bound** *adj* **1** : constrained by or as if by bonds : CONFINED, OBLIGED ⟨was duty ~ to help⟩ **2** : enclosed in a binding or cover **3** : RESOLVED, DETERMINED; *also* : SURE

⁶**bound** *n* **1** : LEAP, JUMP **2** : REBOUND, BOUNCE

⁷**bound** *vb* : SPRING, BOUNCE

bound·ary \'baùn-drē\ *n, pl* **-aries** : something that marks or fixes a limit or extent (as of territory) ◆ **Synonyms** BORDER, FRONTIER, MARCH

bound·en \'baùn-dən\ *adj* : BINDING ⟨our ~ duty⟩

boun·te·ous \'baùn-tē-əs\ *adj* **1** : GENEROUS **2** : ABUNDANT — **boun·te·ous·ly** *adv* — **boun·te·ous·ness** *n*

boun·ti·ful \'baùn-ti-fəl\ *adj* **1** : giving freely **2** : PLENTIFUL — **boun·ti·ful·ly** *adv* — **boun·ti·ful·ness** *n*

boun·ty \'baùn-tē\ *n, pl* **bounties** [ME *bounte* goodness, fr. AF *bunté*, fr. L *bonitas*, fr. *bonus* good] **1** : GENEROSITY **2** : something given liberally **3** : a reward, premium, or subsidy given usu. for doing something

bou·quet \bō-'kā, bü-\ *n* [F, fr. MF, thicket, bunch of flowers, fr. OF (dial. of Normandy and Picardy) *bosquet* thicket, fr. *bosc* forest] **1** : flowers picked and fastened together in a bunch **2** : a distinctive aroma (as of wine) ◆ **Synonyms** SCENT, FRAGRANCE, PERFUME, REDOLENCE

bour·bon \'bər-bən\ *n* : a whiskey distilled from a corn mash

bour·geois \'bùrzh-ˌwä, bùrzh-'wä\ *n, pl* **bourgeois** \same or -ˌwäz, -'wäz\ [MF, fr. OF *burgeis* townsman, fr. *burc, borg* town, fr. L *burgus* fortified place, of Gmc origin] : a middle-class person — **bourgeois** *adj*

bour·geoi·sie \ˌbùrzh-ˌwä-'zē\ *n* : a social order dominated by bourgeois

bourne *also* **bourn** \'bȯrn, 'bùrn\ *n* : BOUNDARY; *also* : DESTINATION

bourse \'bùrs\ *n* : a European stock exchange

bout \'baùt\ *n* **1** : CONTEST, MATCH **2** : OUTBREAK, ATTACK ⟨a ~ of measles⟩

bou·tique \bü-'tēk\ *n* : a small fashionable specialty shop

bou·ton·niere \ˌbü-tᵊn-'iər\ *n* : a flower or bouquet worn in a buttonhole

¹**bo·vine** \'bō-ˌvīn, -ˌvēn\ *adj* **1** : of or relating to bovines **2** : having qualities (as placidity or dullness) characteristic of oxen or cows

²**bovine** *n* : any of a group of mammals including oxen, buffalo, and other like those relatives

bovine spon·gi·form encephalopathy \-'spən-ji-ˌfȯrm-\ *n* : MAD COW DISEASE

¹**bow** \'baù\ *vb* **1** : SUBMIT, YIELD **2** : to bend the head or body (as in submission, courtesy, or assent) **3** : DEBUT ⟨the play ~s next month⟩

²**bow** *n* : an act or posture of bowing

³**bow** \'bō\ *n* **1** : BEND, ARCH; *esp* : RAINBOW **2** : a weapon for shooting arrows; *also* : ARCHER **3** : a knot formed by doubling a line into two or more loops **4** : a wooden rod strung with horsehairs for playing an instrument of the violin family

⁴**bow** \'bō\ *vb* **1** : BEND, CURVE **2** : to play (an instrument) with a bow

⁵**bow** \'baù\ *n* : the forward part of a ship — **bow** *adj*

bowd·ler·ise *Brit var of* BOWDLERIZE

bowd·ler·ize \'bōd-lə-ˌrīz, 'baù-\ *vb* **-ized; -iz·ing** : to expurgate by omitting parts considered vulgar

bow·el \'baù(-ə)l\ *n* **1** : INTESTINE; *also* : one of the divisions of the intestine — usu. used in pl. **2** *pl* : the inmost parts ⟨the ~s of the earth⟩

bowel movement *n* : an act of passing usu. solid waste through the rectum and anus; *also* : STOOL 4

bow·er \'baù(-ə)r\ *n* : a shelter of boughs or vines : ARBOR

¹**bowl** \'bōl\ *n* **1** : a concave vessel used to hold liquids **2** : a drinking vessel **3** : a bowl-shaped part or structure — **bowl·ful** \-ˌfùl\ *n*

²**bowl** *n* **1** : a ball for rolling on a level surface in bowling **2** : a cast of the ball in bowling

³**bowl** *vb* **1** : to play a game of bowling; *also* : to roll a ball in bowling **2** : to travel (as in a vehicle) rapidly and smoothly **3** : to strike or knock down with a moving object

bowlder *var of* BOULDER

bow·legged \'bō-ˌle-gəd\ *adj* : having legs that bow outward at or below the knee — **bow·leg** \'bō-ˌleg\ *n*

¹**bowl·er** \'bō-lər\ *n* : a person who bowls
²**bow·ler** \'bō-lər\ *n* : DERBY 3
bow·line \'bō-lən, -ˌlīn\ *n* : a knot used to form a loop that neither slips nor jams
bowl·ing \'bō-liŋ\ *n* : any of various games in which balls are rolled on a green or alley at an object or a group of objects
bow·man \'bō-mən\ *n* : ARCHER
bow·sprit \'baú-ˌsprit\ *n* : a spar projecting forward from the prow of a ship
bow·string \'bō-ˌstriŋ\ *n* : the cord connecting the two ends of a shooting bow
¹**box** \'bäks\ *n, pl* **box** *or* **box·es** : an evergreen shrub or small tree used esp. for hedges
²**box** *n* 1 : a rigid typically rectangular receptacle often with a cover; *also* : the quantity held by a box 2 : a small compartment (as for a group of theater patrons); *also* : a boxlike receptacle or division 3 : a usu. rectangular space demarcated for a particular purpose ⟨the batter's ~⟩ 4 : a difficult situation : PREDICAMENT — **boxy** \'bäk-sē\ *adj*
³**box** *vb* : to enclose in or as if in a box
⁴**box** *n* : a punch or slap esp. on the ear
⁵**box** *vb* 1 : to strike with the hand 2 : to engage in boxing with
box·car \'bäks-ˌkär\ *n* : a roofed freight car usu. with sliding doors in the sides
box cutter *n* : a small cutting tool with a retractable razor blade
¹**box·er** \'bäk-sər\ *n* 1 : a person who engages in boxing 2 *pl* : BOXER SHORTS
²**boxer** *n* : any of a German breed of compact medium-sized dogs with a short usu. fawn or brindled coat
boxer shorts *n pl* : men's loose-fitting shorts worn as underwear
box·ing \'bäk-siŋ\ *n* : the sport of fighting with the fists
box office *n* : an office (as in a theater) where admission tickets are sold
box turtle *n* : any of several No. American land turtles able to withdraw completely into their shell
box·wood \'bäks-ˌwúd\ *n* : the tough hard wood of the box; *also* : a box tree or shrub
boy \'bói\ *n* 1 : a male child : YOUTH 2 : SON — **boy·hood** \-ˌhúd\ *n* — **boy·ish** *adj* — **boy·ish·ly** *adv* — **boy·ish·ness** *n*
boy·cott \'bói-ˌkät\ *vb* [Charles C. *Boycott* †1897 Eng. land agent in Ireland who was ostracized for refusing to reduce rents] : to refrain from having any dealings with — **boycott** *n*
boy·friend \'bói-ˌfrend\ *n* 1 : a male friend 2 : a frequent or regular male companion in a romantic relationship
Boy Scout *n* : a member of any of various national scouting programs (as the Boy Scouts of America)
boy·sen·ber·ry \'bói-z²n-ˌber-ē, 'bóis-\ *n* : a large reddish-black fruit with a raspberry flavor; *also* : the hybrid bramble bearing it developed by crossing blackberries and raspberries
bo·zo \'bō-ˌzō\ *n, pl* **bozos** : a foolish or incompetent person
bp *abbr* 1 bishop 2 birthplace
BP *abbr* 1 batting practice 2 blood pressure 3 boiling point
bpl *abbr* birthplace
BPOE *abbr* Benevolent and Protective Order of Elks
br *abbr* 1 branch 2 brass 3 brown
¹**Br** *abbr* Britain; British
²**Br** *symbol* bromine
BR *abbr* bedroom
bra \'brä\ *n* : BRASSIERE
¹**brace** \'brās\ *vb* **braced; brac·ing** 1 *archaic* : to make fast : BIND 2 : to tighten preparatory to use; *also* : to get ready for : prepare oneself 3 : INVIGORATE 4 : to furnish or support with a brace; *also* : STRENGTHEN 5 : to set firmly 6 : to gain courage or confidence
²**brace** *n, pl* **brac·es** 1 *or pl* **brace** : two of a kind ⟨a ~ of dogs⟩ 2 : a crank-shaped device for turning a bit 3 : something (as a tie, prop, or clamp) that distributes, directs, or resists pressure or weight 4 *pl* : SUSPENDERS 5 : an appliance for supporting a body part (as the shoulders) 6 *pl* : a dental appliance used to exert pressure to straighten misaligned teeth 7 : one of two

marks { } used to connect words or items to be considered together
brace·let \'brā-slət\ *n* [ME, fr. MF, dim. of *bras* arm, fr. L *bracchium*, fr. Gk *brachiōn*] : an ornamental band or chain worn around the wrist
bra·ce·ro \brä-'ser-ō\ *n, pl* **-ros** : a Mexican laborer admitted to the U.S. esp. for seasonal farm work
brack·en \'bra-kən\ *n* : a large coarse fern; *also* : a growth of such ferns
¹**brack·et** \'bra-kət\ *n* 1 : a projecting framework or arm designed to support weight; *also* : a shelf on such framework 2 : one of a pair of punctuation marks [ ] used esp. to enclose interpolated matter 3 : a continuous section of a series; *esp* : one of a graded series of income groups
²**bracket** *vb* 1 : to furnish or fasten with brackets 2 : to place within brackets; *also* : to separate or group with or as if with brackets
brack·ish \'bra-kish\ *adj* : somewhat salty — **brack·ish·ness** *n*
bract \'brakt\ *n* : an often modified leaf on or at the base of a flower stalk
brad \'brad\ *n* : a slender nail with a small head
brae \'brā\ *n, chiefly Scot* : a hillside esp. along a river
brag \'brag\ *vb* **bragged; brag·ging** : to talk or assert boastfully — **brag** *n* — **brag·ger** *n*
brag·ga·do·cio \ˌbra-gə-'dō-shē-ˌō, -sē-, -chē-\ *n, pl* **-cios** 1 : BRAGGART, BOASTER 2 : empty boasting 3 : arrogant pretension : COCKINESS
brag·gart \'bra-gərt\ *n* : one who brags
Brah·man *or* **Brah·min** \'brä-mən for 1; 'brä-, 'brä-, 'brā-for 2\ *n* 1 : a Hindu of the highest caste traditionally assigned to the priesthood 2 : any of a breed of large vigorous humped cattle developed in the southern U.S. from Indian stock 3 *usu* **Brahmin** : a person of high social standing and cultivated intellect and taste
Brah·man·ism \'brä-mə-ˌni-zəm\ *n* : orthodox Hinduism
¹**braid** \'brād\ *vb* 1 : to form (strands) into a braid : PLAIT; *also* : to make from braids 2 : to ornament with braid
²**braid** *n* 1 : a length of braided hair 2 : a cord or ribbon of three or more interwoven strands; *esp* : a narrow ornamental one
braille \'brāl\ *n, often cap* : a system of writing for the blind that uses characters made up of raised dots

a	b	c	d	e	f	g	h	i	j
1	2	3	4	5	6	7	8	9	0

k	l	m	n	o	p	q	r	s	t

u	v	w	x	y	z		Capital Sign	Numeral Sign	

braille alphabet

¹**brain** \'brān\ *n* 1 : the part of the vertebrate central nervous system enclosed in the skull and continuous with the spinal cord that is composed of neurons and supporting structures and is the center of thought and nervous system control; *also* : a centralized mass of nerve tissue in an invertebrate 2 : INTELLECT, INTELLIGENCE — often used in pl. — **brained** \'brānd\ *adj* — **brain·less** *adj* — **brainy** *adj*
²**brain** *vb* 1 : to kill by smashing the skull 2 : to hit on the head
brain·child \'brān-ˌchī(-ə)ld\ *n* : a product of one's creative imagination
brain death *n* : final cessation of activity in the central nervous system esp. as indicated by a flat electroencephalogram — **brain–dead** \-ˌded\ *adj*
brain drain *n* : the departure of educated or professional people from one country, sector, or field to another usu. for better pay or living conditions
brain·storm \-ˌstòrm\ *n* : a sudden inspiration or idea — **brainstorm** *vb*
brain·teas·er \-ˌtē-zər\ *n* : a challenging puzzle

brain·wash·ing \'brān-ˌwȯ-shiŋ, -ˌwä-\ n 1 : a forcible indoctrination to induce someone to give up basic political, social, or religious beliefs and attitudes and to accept contrasting regimented ideas 2 : persuasion by propaganda or salesmanship — brain·wash vb

brain wave n 1 : BRAINSTORM 2 : rhythmic fluctuations of voltage between parts of the brain; also : a current produced by brain waves

braise \'brāz\ vb braised; brais·ing : to cook slowly in fat and little moisture in a closed pot

¹brake \'brāk\ n : a common bracken fern

²brake n : rough or wet land heavily overgrown (as with thickets or reeds)

³brake n : a device for slowing or stopping motion esp. by friction — brake·less adj

⁴brake vb braked; brak·ing 1 : to slow or stop by or as if by a brake 2 : to apply a brake

brake·man \'brāk-mən\ n : a train crew member who inspects the train and assists the conductor

bram·ble \'bram-bəl\ n : any of a large genus of prickly shrubs (as a blackberry) related to the roses; also : any rough prickly shrub or vine — bram·bly \-b(ə-)lē\ adj

bran \'bran\ n : the edible broken husks of cereal grain sifted from flour or meal

¹branch \'branch\ n [ME, fr. AF branche, fr. LL branca paw] 1 : a natural subdivision (as a bough or twig) of a plant stem 2 : a division (as of an antler or a river) related to a whole like a plant branch to its stem 3 : a discrete element of a complex system ⟨the executive ~⟩; esp : a division of a family descended from one ancestor — branched \'brancht\ adj

²branch vb 1 : to develop branches 2 : DIVERGE 3 : to extend activities ⟨the business is ~ing out⟩

¹brand \'brand\ n 1 : a piece of charred or burning wood 2 : a mark made (as by burning) usu. to identify; also : a mark of disgrace : STIGMA 3 : a class of goods identified as the product of a particular firm or producer 4 : a distinctive kind ⟨my own ~ of humor⟩

²brand vb 1 : to mark with a brand 2 : STIGMATIZE ⟨was ~ed a traitor⟩

bran·dish \'bran-dish\ vb : to shake or wave menacingly ⟨~ a knife⟩ ✦ Synonyms FLOURISH, FLASH, FLAUNT

brand–new \'bran-'nü, -'nyü\ adj : conspicuously new and unused

bran·dy \'bran-dē\ n, pl brandies [short for brandywine, fr. D brandewijn, fr. MD brantwijn, fr. brant distilled + wijn wine] : a liquor distilled from wine or fermented fruit juice — brandy vb

brash \'brash\ adj 1 : IMPETUOUS, AUDACIOUS 2 : aggressively self-assertive — brash·ly adv — brash·ness n

brass \'bras\ n 1 : an alloy of copper and zinc; also : an object of brass 2 : brazen self-assurance 3 : persons of high rank (as in the military) — brassy adj

bras·siere \brə-'zir\ n : a woman's close-fitting undergarment designed to support the breasts

brat \'brat\ n, disparaging : an ill-behaved child — brat·ti·ness n — brat·ty adj

bra·va·do \brə-'vä-dō\ n, pl -does or -dos 1 : blustering swaggering conduct 2 : a show of bravery

¹bra·vo \'brä-vō\ adj brav·er; brav·est [MF, fr. It & Sp bravo courageous, wild, prob. fr. L barbarus barbarous] 1 : showing courage 2 : EXCELLENT, SPLENDID ✦ Synonyms BOLD, INTREPID, COURAGEOUS, VALIANT — brave·ly adv

²brave vb braved; brav·ing : to face or endure bravely

³brave n : an American Indian warrior

brav·ery \'brā-və-rē\ n, pl -er·ies : COURAGE

bra·vo \'brä-vō\ n, pl bravos : a shout of approval — often used as an interjection in applauding

bra·vu·ra \brə-'vyùr-ə, -'vùr-\ n 1 : a florid brilliant musical style 2 : self-assured brilliant performance — bravura adj

brawl \'brȯl\ n : a noisy quarrel ✦ Synonyms FRACAS, ROW, RUMPUS, SCRAP, FRAY, MELEE — brawl vb — brawl·er n

brawn \'brȯn\ n : strong muscles; also : muscular strength — brawn·i·ness n — brawny adj

bray \'brā\ n : the characteristic harsh cry of a donkey — bray vb

braze \'brāz\ vb brazed; braz·ing : to solder with an alloy (as brass) that melts at a lower temperature than the metals being joined — braz·er n

¹bra·zen \'brā-zᵊn\ adj 1 : made of brass 2 : sounding harsh and loud 3 : of the color of brass 4 : marked by contemptuous boldness ⟨a ~ rebuff⟩ — bra·zen·ly adv — bra·zen·ness n

²brazen vb : to face boldly or defiantly

¹bra·zier \'brā-zhər\ n : a worker in brass

²brazier n 1 : a vessel holding burning coals (as for heating) 2 : a device on which food is grilled

Bra·zil nut \brə-'zil-\ n : a triangular oily edible nut borne in large capsules by a tall So. American tree; also : the tree

¹breach \'brēch\ n 1 : a breaking of a law, obligation, tie (as of friendship), or standard (as of conduct) 2 : an interruption or opening made by or as if by breaking through ✦ Synonyms VIOLATION, TRANSGRESSION, INFRINGEMENT, TRESPASS

²breach vb 1 : to make a breach in ⟨the army ~ed the castle wall⟩ 2 : to leap out of water ⟨whales ~ing⟩

¹bread \'bred\ n 1 : baked food made basically of flour or meal 2 : FOOD

²bread vb : to cover with bread crumbs

bread·bas·ket \'bred-ˌbas-kət\ n : a major cereal-producing region

bread·fruit \-ˌfrüt\ n : a round usu. seedless fruit resembling bread in color and texture when baked; also : a tall tropical tree related to the mulberry and bearing breadfruit

bread·stuff \-ˌstəf\ n : GRAIN, FLOUR

breadth \'bredth, 'bretth\ n 1 : WIDTH 2 : comprehensive quality : SCOPE ⟨her ~ of knowledge⟩

bread·win·ner \'bred-ˌwi-nər\ n : a member of a family whose wages supply its livelihood

¹break \'brāk\ vb broke \'brōk\; bro·ken \'brō-kən\; break·ing 1 : to separate into parts usu. suddenly or violently; also : to render inoperable ⟨broke his watch⟩ 2 : TRANSGRESS ⟨~ a law⟩ 3 : to force a way into, out of, or through 4 : to disrupt the order or unity of ⟨~ ranks⟩ ⟨~ up a gang⟩; also : to bring to submission or helplessness 5 : EXCEED, SURPASS ⟨~ a record⟩ 6 : RUIN 7 : to make known ⟨~ the bad news⟩ 8 : HALT, INTERRUPT; also : to act or change abruptly (as a course or activity) 9 : to come esp. suddenly into being or notice ⟨as day ~s⟩ 10 : to fail under stress 11 : HAPPEN, DEVELOP ⟨report news as it ~s⟩ — break·able adj or n — break into 1 : to begin with a sudden throwing off of restraint ⟨broke into tears⟩ 2 : to make entry or entrance into ⟨break into show business⟩

²break n 1 : an act of breaking 2 : a result of breaking; esp : an interruption of continuity ⟨coffee ~⟩ ⟨a ~ for the commercial⟩ 3 : a stroke of luck

break·age \'brā-kij\ n 1 : loss due to things broken 2 : the action of breaking 3 : articles or amount broken

break·down \'brāk-ˌdaùn\ n 1 : functional failure; esp : a physical, mental, or nervous collapse 2 : DISINTEGRATION 3 : DECOMPOSITION 4 : ANALYSIS, CLASSIFICATION — break down vb

break·er \'brā-kər\ n 1 : one that breaks 2 : a wave that breaks into foam (as against the shore)

break·fast \'brek-fəst\ n : the first meal of the day — breakfast vb

break in vb 1 : to enter a building by force 2 : INTERRUPT; also : INTRUDE 3 : TRAIN ⟨break in new employees⟩ — break–in \'brāk-ˌin\ n

break·neck \'brāk-'nek\ adj : very fast or dangerous ⟨~ speed⟩

break out vb 1 : to develop or erupt suddenly or with force 2 : to develop a skin rash

break·through \'brāk-ˌthrü\ n 1 : an act or instance of breaking through an obstruction or defensive line 2 : a sudden advance in knowledge or technique ⟨a scientific ~⟩

break·up \-ˌəp\ n 1 : DISSOLUTION 2 : a division into smaller units — break up vb

break·wa·ter \'brāk-ˌwȯ-tər, -ˌwä-\ n : a structure protecting a harbor or beach from the force of waves

bream \'brim, 'brēm\ n, pl bream or breams : any of various small freshwater sunfishes

breast \'brest\ n 1 : either of the pair of mammary glands extending from the front of the chest esp. in pu-

bescent and adult human females 2 : the front part of
the body between the neck and the abdomen 3 : the
seat of emotion and thought
breast·bone \'brest-ˌbōn\ *n* : STERNUM
breast–feed \-ˌfēd\ *vb* : to feed (a baby) from a mother's
breast
breast·plate \-ˌplāt\ *n* : a metal plate of armor for the
breast
breast·stroke \-ˌstrōk\ *n* : a swimming stroke executed
by extending both arms forward and then sweeping them
back with palms out while kicking backward and outward with both legs
breast·work \-ˌwərk\ *n* : a temporary fortification
breath \'breth\ *n* 1 : the act or power of breathing 2
: a slight breeze 3 : air inhaled or exhaled in breathing 4 : spoken sound 5 : SPIRIT — **breath·less** *adj* —
breath·less·ly *adv* — **breath·less·ness** *n* — **breathy**
\'bre-thē\ *adj*
breathe \'brēth\ *vb* **breathed; breath·ing** 1 : to inhale
and exhale 2 : LIVE 3 : to halt for rest 4 : to utter
softly or secretly — **breath·able** *adj*
breath·er \'brē-thər\ *n* 1 : one that breathes 2 : a short
rest
breath·tak·ing \'breth-ˌtā-kiŋ\ *adj* 1 : making one out
of breath 2 : EXCITING, THRILLING ⟨~ beauty⟩ —
breath·tak·ing·ly *adv*
brec·cia \'bre-chē-ə, -chə\ *n* : a rock composed of sharp
fragments held in fine-grained material
breech \'brēch\ *n* 1 *pl* \usu 'bri-chəz\ : pants ending
near the knee 2 : BUTTOCKS, RUMP 3 : the part of a
firearm at the rear of the barrel
¹breed \'brēd\ *vb* **bred** \'bred\; **breed·ing** 1 : BEGET; *also*
: ORIGINATE 2 : to propagate sexually; *also* : MATE 3
: BRING UP, NURTURE 4 : to produce (fissionable material) from material that is not fissionable ♦ **Synonyms**
GENERATE, REPRODUCE, PROCREATE, PROPAGATE —
breed·er *n*
²breed *n* 1 : a strain of similar and presumably related
plants or animals usu. developed in domestication 2
: KIND, SORT, CLASS
breeding *n* 1 : ANCESTRY 2 : training in polite social
interaction 3 : sexual propagation of plants or animals
¹breeze \'brēz\ *n* 1 : a light wind 2 : CINCH, SNAP —
breeze-less *adj*
²breeze *vb* **breezed; breez·ing** : to progress quickly and
easily
breeze·way \'brēz-ˌwā\ *n* : a roofed open passage connecting two buildings (as a house and garage)
breezy \'brē-zē\ *adj* 1 : swept by breezes 2 : briskly
informal ⟨~ prose⟩ — **breez·i·ly** \'brē-zə-lē\ *adv* —
breez·i·ness \-zē-nəs\ *n*
breth·ren \'breth-rən, 'bre-thə-; 'bre-thərn\ *pl of* BROTHER
— used esp. in formal or solemn address
Brethren *n pl* : members of one of several Protestant denominations originating chiefly in a German religious
movement and stressing personal religious experience
bre·via·ry \'brē-vyə-rē, -vē-ˌer-ē\ *n, pl* **-ries** *often cap* : a
book of prayers, hymns, psalms, and readings used by
Roman Catholic priests
brev·i·ty \'bre-və-tē\ *n, pl* **-ties** 1 : shortness or concise-
ness of expression 2 : shortness of duration
brew \'brü\ *vb* 1 : to prepare (as beer) by steeping, boiling, and fermenting 2 : to prepare (as tea) by steeping in
hot water — **brew** *n* — **brew·er** *n* — **brew·ery** \'brü-ə-rē,
'brù(-ə)r-ē\ *n*
¹bri·ar *also* **bri·er** \'brī-ər\ *n* : a plant (as a bramble or
rose) with a thorny or prickly usu. woody stem; *also* : a
mass or twig of these — **bri·ary** \'brī-ər-ē\ *adj*
²briar *n* : a tobacco pipe made from the root or stem of a
European heath
¹bribe \'brīb\ *n* [ME, morsel given to a beggar, bribe, fr.
AF, morsel] : something (as money or a favor) given or
promised to a person to influence conduct
²bribe *vb* **bribed; brib·ing** : to influence by offering a bribe
— **brib·able** *adj* — **brib·er** *n* — **brib·ery** \'brī-bə-rē\ *n*
bric-a-brac \'bri-kə-ˌbrak\ *n pl* [F] : small ornamental
articles
¹brick \'brik\ *n* : a block molded from moist clay and
hardened by heat used esp. for building
²brick *vb* : to close, cover, or pave with bricks
brick·bat \'brik-ˌbat\ *n* 1 : a piece of a hard material (as

a brick) esp. when thrown as a missile 2 : an uncomplimentary remark
brick·lay·er \'brik-ˌlā-ər\ *n* : a person who builds or paves
with bricks — **brick·lay·ing** *n*
¹brid·al \'brī-dᵊl\ *n* [ME *bridale*, fr. OE *brȳdealu*, fr. *brȳd*
bride + *ealu* ale] : MARRIAGE, WEDDING
²bridal *adj* : of or relating to a bride or a wedding
bride \'brīd\ *n* : a woman just married or about to be
married
bride·groom \'brīd-ˌgrüm, -ˌgrùm\ *n* : a man just married
or about to be married
brides·maid \'brīdz-ˌmād\ *n* : a woman who attends a
bride at her wedding
¹bridge \'brij\ *n* 1 : a structure built over a depression or
obstacle for use as a passageway 2 : something (as the
upper part of the nose) resembling a bridge in form or
function 3 : a curved piece raising the strings of a musical instrument 4 : the forward part of a ship's superstructure from which it is navigated 5 : an artificial
replacement for missing teeth
²bridge *vb* **bridged; bridg·ing** : to build a bridge over —
bridge·able *adj*
³bridge *n* : a card game for four players developed from
whist
bridge·head \-ˌhed\ *n* : an advanced position seized in enemy territory
bridge·work \-ˌwərk\ *n* : dental bridges
¹bri·dle \'brī-dᵊl\ *n* 1 : headgear with which a horse is
controlled 2 : CURB, RESTRAINT
²bridle *vb* **bri·dled; bri·dling** 1 : to put a bridle on; *also*
: to restrain with or as if with a bridle 2 : to show hostility or scorn usu. by tossing the head
Brie \'brē\ *n* : a soft cheese with a whitish rind and a pale
yellow interior
¹brief \'brēf\ *adj* 1 : short in duration or extent 2 : CON-
CISE; *also* : CURT — **brief·ly** *adv* — **brief·ness** *n*
²brief *n* 1 : a concise statement or document; *esp* : one
summarizing a law client's case or a legal argument 2 *pl*
: short snug underpants
³brief *vb* : to give instructions or information to
brief·case \'brēf-ˌkās\ *n* : a flat flexible case for carrying
papers
brier *var of* BRIAR
¹brig \'brig\ *n* : a 2-masted square-rigged sailing ship
²brig *n* : the place of confinement for offenders on a naval
ship
³brig *abbr* brigade
bri·gade \bri-ˈgād\ *n* 1 : a military unit composed of a
headquarters, one or more units of infantry or armored
forces, and supporting units 2 : a group organized for a
particular purpose (as fire fighting)
brig·a·dier general \'bri-gə-ˌdir-\ *n* : a commissioned officer (as in the army) ranking next below a major general
brig·and \'bri-gənd\ *n* : BANDIT — **brig·and·age** \-gən-
dij\ *n*
brig·an·tine \'bri-gən-ˌtēn\ *n* : a 2-masted square-rigged
ship with a fore-and-aft mainsail
Brig Gen *abbr* brigadier general
bright \'brīt\ *adj* 1 : SHINING, RADIANT 2 : ILLUS-
TRIOUS, GLORIOUS 3 : INTELLIGENT, CLEVER; *also*
: LIVELY, CHEERFUL ⟨a ~ smile⟩ ♦ **Synonyms** BRIL-
LIANT, LUSTROUS, BEAMING — **bright** *adv* — **bright·ly**
adv — **bright·ness** *n*
bright·en \'brī-tᵊn\ *vb* : to make or become bright or
brighter ⟨the good news ~ed her mood⟩ — **bright·en·er**
n
¹bril·liant \'bril-yənt\ *adj* [F *brillant*, prp. of *briller* to shine,
fr. It *brillare*] 1 : very bright 2 : STRIKING, DISTINC-
TIVE 3 : very intelligent ⟨a ~ idea⟩ ♦ **Synonyms** RA-
DIANT, LUSTROUS, BEAMING, LUCID, BRIGHT, LAMBENT
— **bril·liance** \-yəns\ *n* — **bril·lian·cy** \-yən-sē\ *n* —
bril·liant·ly *adv*
²brilliant *n* : a gem cut in a particular form with many facets
¹brim \'brim\ *n* : EDGE, RIM ♦ **Synonyms** BRINK, BOR-
DER, VERGE, FRINGE — **brim·less** *adj*
²brim *vb* **brimmed; brim·ming** : to be or become full often
to overflowing
brim·ful \-ˈfùl\ *adj* : full to the brim
brim·stone \'brim-ˌstōn\ *n* : SULFUR

brindled • brontosaurus

brin·dled \'brin-d³ld\ *adj* : having dark streaks or flecks on a gray or tawny ground ⟨a ~ Great Dane⟩

brine \'brīn\ *n* 1 : water saturated with salt 2 : OCEAN — **brin·i·ness** *n* — **briny** \'brī-nē\ *adj*

bring \'briŋ\ *vb* **brought** \'brȯt\; **bring·ing** \'briŋ-iŋ\ 1 : to cause to come with one 2 : INDUCE, PERSUADE, LEAD 3 : PRODUCE, EFFECT 4 : to sell for ⟨~ a good price⟩ — **bring·er** *n*

bring about *vb* : to cause to take place

bring up *vb* 1 : to give a parent's fostering care to 2 : to come or bring to a sudden halt 3 : to call to notice

brink \'briŋk\ *n* 1 : an edge at the top of a steep place 2 : the point of onset

brio \'brē-ō\ *n* : VIVACITY, SPIRIT

bri·quette *or* **bri·quet** \bri-'ket\ *n* : a compacted often brick-shaped mass of fine material ⟨a charcoal ~⟩

bris *also* **briss** \'bris\ *n* : the Jewish rite of circumcision

brisk \'brisk\ *adj* 1 : ALERT, LIVELY 2 : INVIGORATING ⟨~ weather⟩ 3 : highly active ⟨a ~ business⟩ ✦ **Synonyms** AGILE, SPRY, NIMBLE — **brisk·ly** *adv* — **brisk·ness** *n*

bris·ket \'bris-kət\ *n* : the breast or lower chest of a quadruped; *also* : a cut of beef from the brisket

bris·ling \'briz-liŋ, 'bris-\ *n* : SPRAT 1

¹**bris·tle** \'bri-səl\ *n* : a short stiff coarse hair — **bris·tle·like** \'bri-səl-,līk\ *adj* — **bris·tly** *adj*

²**bristle** *vb* **bris·tled; bris·tling** 1 : to stand stiffly erect 2 : to show angry defiance ⟨bristled at the charges⟩ 3 : to appear as if covered with bristles

Brit *abbr* Britain; British

Bri·tan·nic \bri-'ta-nik\ *adj* : BRITISH

britch·es \'bri-chəz\ *n pl* : BREECHES, TROUSERS

Brit·ish \'bri-tish\ *n pl* : the people of Great Britain or the Commonwealth — **British** *adj* — **Brit·ish·ness** *n*

British thermal unit *n* : the quantity of heat needed to raise the temperature of one pound of water one degree Fahrenheit

Brit·on \'bri-t³n\ *n* 1 : a member of a people inhabiting Britain before the Anglo-Saxon invasion 2 : a native or inhabitant of Great Britain

brit·tle \'bri-t³l\ *adj* **brit·tler; brit·tlest** : easily broken : FRAGILE ✦ **Synonyms** CRISP, CRUMBLY, FRIABLE — **brit·tle·ness** *n*

bro \'brō\ *n, pl* **bros** 1 : BROTHER 1 2 : SOUL BROTHER

¹**broach** \'brōch\ *n* : a pointed tool

²**broach** *vb* 1 : to pierce (as a cask) in order to draw the contents 2 : to open up (a subject) for discussion

broad \'brȯd\ *adj* 1 : WIDE 2 : SPACIOUS ⟨the ~ plains⟩ 3 : CLEAR, OPEN ⟨~ daylight⟩ 4 : OBVIOUS ⟨a ~ hint⟩ 5 : COARSE, CRUDE ⟨~ stories⟩ 6 : tolerant in outlook 7 : GENERAL ⟨a ~ rule⟩ 8 : dealing with essential points — **broad·ly** *adv* — **broad·ness** *n*

broad·band \'brȯd-,band\ *n* : a system of high-speed telecommunication in which a frequency range is divided into multiple independent channels for simultaneous transmission of signals

¹**broad·cast** \'brȯd-,kast\ *vb* **broadcast** *also* **broad·cast·ed; broad·cast·ing** 1 : to scatter or sow broadcast 2 : to make widely known 3 : to transmit a broadcast — **broad·cast·er** *n*

²**broadcast** *adv* : to or over a wide area

³**broadcast** *n* 1 : the transmission of sound or images by radio or television 2 : a single radio or television program

broad·cloth \-,klȯth\ *n* 1 : a smooth dense woolen cloth 2 : a fine soft cloth of cotton, silk, or synthetic fiber

broad·en \'brȯ-d³n\ *vb* : WIDEN

broad·loom \-,lüm\ *adj* : woven on a wide loom esp. in a solid color

broad–mind·ed \-'mīn-dəd\ *adj* : tolerant of varied opinions — **broad–mind·ed·ly** *adv* — **broad–mind·ed·ness** *n*

¹**broad·side** \-,sīd\ *n* 1 : a sheet of paper printed usu. on one side (as an advertisement) 2 : all of the guns on one side of a ship; *also* : their simultaneous firing 3 : a volley of abuse or denunciation

²**broadside** *adv* 1 : with one side forward : SIDEWAYS 2 : from the side ⟨the car was hit ~⟩

broad–spectrum *adj* : effective against a wide range of organisms ⟨~ antibiotics⟩

broad·sword \'brȯd-,sȯrd\ *n* : a broad-bladed sword

broad·tail \-,tāl\ *n* : a karakul esp. with flat and wavy fur

bro·cade \brō-'kād\ *n* : a usu. silk fabric with a raised design

broc·co·li \'brä-kə-lē\ *n* [It, pl. of *broccolo* flowering top of a cabbage, dim. of *brocco* small nail, sprout, fr. L *broccus* projecting] : the stems and immature usu. green or purple flower heads of either of two garden vegetable plants closely related to the cabbage; *also* : either of the plants

bro·chette \brō-'shet\ *n* : SKEWER

bro·chure \brō-'shùr\ *n* [F, fr. *brocher* to sew, fr. MF, to prick, fr. OF *brochier*, fr. *broche* pointed tool] : PAMPHLET, BOOKLET

bro·gan \'brō-gən, brō-'gan\ *n* : a heavy shoe

brogue \'brōg\ *n* : a dialect or regional pronunciation; *esp* : an Irish accent

broil \'brȯi(-ə)l\ *vb* : to cook by exposure to radiant heat : GRILL — **broil** *n*

broil·er \'brȯi-lər\ *n* 1 : a utensil for broiling 2 : a young chicken fit for broiling

broil·ing \'brȯi(-ə)-liŋ\ *adj* : extremely hot ⟨a ~ sun⟩

¹**broke** \'brōk\ *past of* BREAK

²**broke** *adj* : PENNILESS

¹**bro·ken** \'brō-kən\ *past part of* BREAK

²**broken** *adj* 1 : SHATTERED ⟨~ glass⟩ 2 : having gaps or breaks : INTERRUPTED, DISRUPTED 3 : SUBDUED, CRUSHED ⟨a ~ spirit⟩ 4 : BANKRUPT 5 : imperfectly spoken ⟨~ English⟩ — **bro·ken·ly** *adv*

bro·ken·heart·ed \,brō-kən-'här-təd\ *adj* : overcome by grief or despair

bro·ker \'brō-kər\ *n* : an agent who negotiates contracts of purchase and sale — **broker** *vb*

bro·ker·age \'brō-kə-rij\ *n* 1 : the business of a broker 2 : the fee or commission charged by a broker

bro·mance \'brō-,man(t)s\ *n* [blend of *bro* and *romance*] : a close nonsexual friendship between men — **bro·man·tic** \brō-'man-tik\ *adj*

bro·me·li·ad \brō-'mē-lē-,ad\ *n* : any of several tropical American ornamental plants related to the pineapple that usu. grow on trees

bro·mide \'brō-,mīd\ *n* : a compound of bromine and another element or chemical group including some (as potassium bromide) used as sedatives

bro·mid·ic \brō-'mi-dik\ *adj* : TRITE, UNORIGINAL

bro·mine \'brō-,mēn\ *n* [F *brome* bromine, fr. Gk *brōmos* stink] : a deep red liquid corrosive chemical element that gives off an irritating vapor

bronc \'bräŋk\ *n* : an unbroken or partly broken range horse of western No. America; *also* : MUSTANG

bron·chi·al \'bräŋ-kē-əl\ *adj* : of, relating to, or affecting the bronchi or their branches

bron·chi·tis \brän-'kī-təs, bräŋ-\ *n* : inflammation of the bronchi and their branches — **bron·chit·ic** \-'ki-tik\ *adj*

bron·chus \'bräŋ-kəs\ *n, pl* **bron·chi** \'bräŋ-,kī, -,kē\ : either of the main divisions of the trachea each leading to a lung

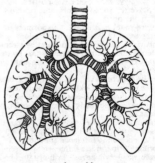

bronchi

bron·co \'bräŋ-kō\ *n, pl* **broncos** [MexSp, fr. Sp, rough, wild] : BRONC

bron·to·sau·rus \,brän-tə-'sȯr-əs\ *also* **bron·to·saur** \'brän-tə-,sȯr\ *n* [NL, fr. Gk *brontē* thunder + *sauros* liz-

ard] : any of a genus of large 4-footed sauropod dinosaurs of the Jurassic : APATOSAURUS
Bronx cheer \'bräŋks-\ *n* : RASPBERRY 2
¹**bronze** \'bränz\ *vb* **bronzed; bronz·ing** : to give the appearance of bronze to
²**bronze** *n* 1 : an alloy of copper and tin and sometimes other elements; *also* : something made of bronze 2 : a yellowish brown color — **bronzy** \'brän-zē\ *adj*
brooch \'brōch, 'brüch\ *n* : an ornamental clasp or pin
¹**brood** \'brüd\ *n* : a family of young animals or children and esp. of birds
²**brood** *adj* : kept for breeding ⟨a ~ mare⟩
³**brood** *vb* 1 : to sit on eggs to hatch them; *also* : to shelter (hatched young) with the wings 2 : to think anxiously or gloomily about something — **brood·ing·ly** *adv*
brood·er \'brü-dər\ *n* 1 : one that broods 2 : a heated structure for raising young birds
¹**brook** \'brúk\ *n* : a small natural stream
²**brook** *vb* : TOLERATE, BEAR ⟨would ~ no nonsense⟩
brook·let \'brú-klət\ *n* : a small brook
brook trout *n* : a common speckled cold-water char of No. America
broom \'brüm, 'brùm\ *n* 1 : any of several shrubs of the legume family with long slender branches and usu. yellow flowers 2 : an implement with a long handle (**broom·stick** \-ˌstik\) used for sweeping
broth \'brōth\ *n, pl* **broths** \'brōths, 'brōthz\ 1 : liquid in which meat or sometimes vegetable food has been cooked 2 : a fluid culture medium
broth·el \'brä-thəl, 'brō-\ *n* : a house of prostitution
broth·er \'brə-thər\ *n, pl* **brothers** *also* **breth·ren** \'breth-rən, 'bre-thə-; 'bre·thərn\ 1 : a male having one or both parents in common with another individual 2 : a man who is a religious but not a priest 3 : KINSMAN; *also* : SOUL BROTHER — **broth·er·li·ness** \-lē-nəs\ *n* — **broth·er·ly** *adj*
broth·er·hood \'brə-thər-ˌhùd\ *n* 1 : the state of being brothers or a brother 2 : ASSOCIATION, FRATERNITY : the whole body of persons in a business or profession ⟨the medical ~⟩
broth·er-in-law \'brə-thə-rən-ˌlò, 'brə-thərn-ˌlò\ *n, pl* **brothers-in-law** \'brə-thər-zən-\ : the brother of one's spouse; *also* : the husband of one's sibling or of one's spouse's sibling
brougham \'brü(-ə)m, 'brō(-ə)m\ *n* : a light closed horse-drawn carriage with the driver outside in front
brought *past and past part of* BRING
brou·ha·ha \'brü-ˌhä-ˌhä\ *n* : HUBBUB, UPROAR
brow \'braú\ *n* 1 : the eyebrow or the ridge on which it grows; *also* : FOREHEAD 2 : the projecting upper part of a steep place
brow·beat \'braú-ˌbēt\ *vb* **-beat; -beat·en** \-ˌbē-tᵊn\ *or* **-beat; -beat·ing** : to intimidate by sternness or arrogance
¹**brown** \'braún\ *adj* : of the color brown; *also* : of dark or tanned complexion
²**brown** *n* : a color like that of coffee or chocolate that is a blend of red and yellow darkened by black — **brown·ish** *adj*
³**brown** *vb* : to make or become brown
brown bag·ging \-'ba-giŋ\ *n* : the practice of carrying one's lunch usu. in a brown bag — **brown bag·ger** *n*
brown bear *n* : any of various large typically brown-furred bears including the grizzly bear
brown·ie \'braú-nē\ *n* 1 : a legendary cheerful elf who performs good deeds at night 2 *cap* : a member of a program of the Girl Scouts for girls in the first through third grades 3 : a small square or rectangle of rich chocolate cake
brown·nose \'braún-ˌnōz\ *vb, disparaging* : to ingratiate oneself with — **brownnose** *n*
brown·out \'braú-ˌnaút\ *n* : a period of reduced voltage of electricity caused esp. by high demand and resulting in reduced illumination
brown rice *n* : hulled but unpolished rice that retains most of the bran layers
brown·stone \'braún-ˌstōn\ *n* : a dwelling faced with reddish-brown sandstone
¹**browse** \'braúz\ *vb* **browsed; brows·ing** 1 : to feed on browse; *also* : GRAZE 2 : to read or look over something in a casual way 3 : to access (a network) with a browser
²**browse** *n* : tender shoots, twigs, and leaves fit for food for cattle

brows·er \'braú-zər\ *n* : a computer program for accessing sites or information on a network (as the World Wide Web)
bru·in \'brü-ən\ *n* : BEAR
¹**bruise** \'brüz\ *vb* **bruised; bruis·ing** 1 : to inflict a bruise on; *also* : to become bruised 2 : to break down (as leaves or berries) by pounding
²**bruise** *n* : a surface injury to flesh : CONTUSION
bruis·er \'brü-zər\ *n* : a big husky man
bruit \'brüt\ *vb* : to make widely known by common report ⟨word of his dismissal was ~ed about⟩
brunch \'brənch\ *n* : a meal that combines a late breakfast and an early lunch
bru·net *or* **bru·nette** \brü-'net\ *adj* [F *brunet*, masc., *brunette*, fem., brownish, fr. OF, fr. *brun* brown, of Gmc origin] : having brown or black hair and usu. a relatively dark complexion — **brunet** *or* **brunette** *n*
brunt \'brənt\ *n* : the main shock, force, or stress esp. of an attack; *also* : the greater burden
bru·schet·ta \brü-'she-tə, -'ske-\ *n* : an appetizer of grilled bread with toppings
¹**brush** \'brəsh\ *n* 1 : BRUSHWOOD 2 : scrub vegetation or land covered with it
²**brush** *n* 1 : a device composed of bristles set in a handle and used esp. for cleaning or painting 2 : a bushy tail (as of a fox) 3 : an electrical conductor that makes contact between a stationary and a moving part (as of a motor) 4 : a quick light touch in passing
³**brush** *vb* 1 : to treat (as in cleaning or painting) with a brush 2 : to remove with or as if with a brush; *also* : to dismiss in an offhand manner 3 : to touch gently in passing
⁴**brush** *n* : SKIRMISH ⟨a ~ with the law⟩ ◆ **Synonyms** ENCOUNTER, RUN-IN
brush fire *n* 1 : a fire involving low-growing plants 2 : a minor conflict or crisis
brush–off \'brəsh-ˌòf\ *n* : a curt offhand dismissal
brush up *vb* : to renew one's skill
brush·wood \'brəsh-ˌwùd\ *n* 1 : small branches of wood esp. when cut 2 : a thicket of shrubs and small trees
brusque \'brəsk\ *adj* [F *brusque*, fr. It *brusco*, fr. ML *bruscus* a plant with stiff twigs used for brooms] : CURT, BLUNT, ABRUPT ⟨a ~ answer⟩ ◆ **Synonyms** GRUFF, BLUFF, CRUSTY, SHORT — **brusque·ly** *adv*
brus·sels sprout \'brəs-əlz-\ *n, often cap B* : one of the edible green heads borne on the stalk of a plant closely related to the cabbage; *also, pl* : this plant
bru·tal \'brü-tᵊl\ *adj* 1 : befitting a brute : UNFEELING, CRUEL 2 : HARSH, SEVERE ⟨~ weather⟩ 3 : unpleasantly accurate ⟨a ~ depiction of war⟩ — **bru·tal·i·ty** \brü-'ta-lə-tē\ *n* — **bru·tal·ly** *adv*
bru·tal·ise *Brit var of* BRUTALIZE
bru·tal·ize \'brü-tᵊl-ˌīz\ *vb* **-ized; -iz·ing** 1 : to make brutal 2 : to treat brutally
¹**brute** \'brüt\ *adj* [ME, fr. MF *brut* rough, fr. L *brutus* brutish, lit., heavy] 1 : of or relating to beasts 2 : BRUTAL 3 : UNREASONING; *also* : purely physical ⟨~ strength⟩
²**brute** *n* 1 : BEAST 1 2 : a brutal person
brut·ish \'brü-tish\ *adj* 1 : BRUTE 1 2 : strongly sensual; *also* : showing little intelligence
BS *abbr* bachelor of science
BSA *abbr* Boy Scouts of America
bskt *abbr* basket
Bt *abbr* baronet
btry *abbr* battery
Btu *abbr* British thermal unit
bu *abbr* bushel
¹**bub·ble** \'bə-bəl\ *n* 1 : a globule of gas in a liquid 2 : a thin film of liquid filled with gas 3 : something lacking firmness or solidity — **bub·bly** *adj*
²**bubble** *vb* **bub·bled; bub·bling** : to form, rise in, or give off bubbles
bub·kes \'bəp-kəs, 'bùp-\ *n pl* [Yiddish] : the least amount ⟨didn't win ~⟩
bu·bo \'bü-bō, 'byü-\ *n, pl* **buboes** : an inflammatory swelling of a lymph gland
bu·bon·ic plague \bü-'bä-nik-, byü-\ *n* : plague caused by a bacterium transmitted to human beings by flea bites and marked esp. by chills and fever and by buboes usu. in the groin
buc·ca·neer \ˌbə-kə-'nir\ *n* : PIRATE
¹**buck** \'bək\ *n, pl* **bucks** 1 *or pl* **buck** : a male animal (as a deer or antelope) 2 : DANDY 3 : DOLLAR

²**buck** *vb* **1** : to spring with an arching leap ⟨a ~*ing* horse⟩ **2** : to charge against something; *also* : to strive for advancement sometimes without regard to ethical behavior

buck·board \-ˌbórd\ *n* : a 4-wheeled horse-drawn wagon with a floor of long springy boards

buck·et \ˈbə-kət\ *n* **1** : PAIL **2** : an object resembling a bucket in collecting, scooping, or carrying something ⟨a tractor's ~⟩ — **buck·et·ful** *n*

bucket list *n* [from *kick the bucket* (to die)] : a list of things one has not done before but wants to do before dying

bucket seat *n* : a low separate seat for one person (as in an automobile)

buck·eye \ˈbə-ˌkī\ *n* : any of various trees or shrubs related to the horse chestnut; *also* : the large nutlike seed of such a shrub or tree

buck fever *n* : nervous excitement of an inexperienced hunter at the sight of game

¹**buck·le** \ˈbə-kəl\ *n* : a clasp (as on a belt) for two loose ends

²**buckle** *vb* **buck·led; buck·ling 1** : to fasten with a buckle **2** : to apply oneself with vigor **3** : to crumple up : BEND, COLLAPSE

³**buckle** *n* : BEND, FOLD, KINK

buck·ler \ˈbə-klər\ *n* : SHIELD

buck·ram \ˈbə-krəm\ *n* : a coarse stiff cloth used esp. for binding books

buck·saw \ˈbək-ˌsò\ *n* : a saw set in a usu. H-shaped frame for sawing wood

buck·shot \ˈbək-ˌshät\ *n* : lead shot that is from .24 to .33 inch (about 6.1 to 8.4 millimeters) in diameter

buck·skin \-ˌskin\ *n* **1** : the skin of a buck **2** : a soft usu. suede-finished leather — **buckskin** *adj*

buck·tooth \-ˈtüth\ *n* : a large protruding front tooth — **buck–toothed** \-ˈtütht\ *adj*

buck·wheat \-ˌhwēt\ *n* : either of two plants grown for their triangular seeds which are used as a cereal grain; *also* : these seeds

bu·col·ic \byü-ˈkä-lik\ *adj* [L *bucolicus*, fr. Gk *boukolikos*, fr. *boukolos* cowherd] : PASTORAL, RURAL ⟨a ~ countryside⟩

¹**bud** \ˈbəd\ *n* **1** : an undeveloped plant shoot (as of a leaf or a flower); *also* : a partly opened flower **2** : an asexual reproductive structure that detaches from the parent and forms a new individual **3** : something not yet fully developed ⟨nipped in the ~⟩

²**bud** *vb* **bud·ded; bud·ding 1** : to form or put forth buds; *also* : to reproduce by asexual buds **2** : to be or develop like a bud **3** : to reproduce a desired variety (as of peach) by inserting a bud in a plant of a different variety

Bud·dhism \ˈbü-ˌdi-zəm, ˈbú-\ *n* : a religion of eastern and central Asia growing out of the teachings of Gautama Buddha — **Bud·dhist** \ˈbü-dist, ˈbú-\ *n or adj*

bud·dy \ˈbə-dē\ *n, pl* **buddies 1** : COMPANION; *also* : FRIEND **2** : FELLOW

budge \ˈbəj\ *vb* **budged; budg·ing** : MOVE, SHIFT; *also* : YIELD

bud·ger·i·gar \ˈbə-jə-rē-ˌgar\ *n* : a small brightly colored Australian parrot often kept as a pet

¹**bud·get** \ˈbə-jət\ *n* [ME *bowgette*, fr. MF *bougette*, dim. of *bouge* leather bag, fr. L *bulga*] **1** : STOCK, SUPPLY **2** : a financial report containing estimates of income and expenses; *also* : a plan for coordinating income and expenses **3** : the amount of money available for a particular use — **bud·get·ary** \ˈbə-jə-ˌter-ē\ *adj*

²**budget** *vb* **1** : to allow for in a budget **2** : to draw up a budget

³**budget** *adj* : INEXPENSIVE

bud·gie \ˈbə-jē\ *n* : BUDGERIGAR

¹**buff** \ˈbəf\ *n* **1** : a yellow to orange yellow color **2** : FAN, ENTHUSIAST

²**buff** *adj* : of the color buff

³**buff** *vb* : POLISH, SHINE

buf·fa·lo \ˈbə-fə-ˌlō\ *n, pl* **-lo** *or* **-loes** *also* **-los 1** : WATER BUFFALO **2** : a large shaggy-maned No. American wild bovine mammal that has short horns and heavy forequarters with a large muscular hump

buffalo soldier *n* : an African American soldier serving in the western U.S. after the Civil War

¹**buf·fer** \ˈbə-fər\ *n* : something or someone that protects or shields (as from physical damage or a financial blow)

²**buffer** *n* : one that buffs

¹**buf·fet** \ˈbə-fət\ *n* : BLOW, SLAP

²**buffet** *vb* **1** : to strike with the hand; *also* : to pound repeatedly **2** : to struggle against or on ♦ **Synonyms** BEAT, BATTER, DRUB, PUMMEL, THRASH

³**buf·fet** \(ˌ)bə-ˈfā, bü-\ *n* **1** : SIDEBOARD **2** : a counter for refreshments; *also* : a meal at which people serve themselves informally

buff leather *n* : a strong supple oil-tanned leather

buf·foon \(ˌ)bə-ˈfün\ *n* [MF *bouffon*, fr. It *buffone*] : CLOWN **2** — **buf·foon·ery** \-ˈfü-nə-rē\ *n* — **buf·foon·ish** \-ˈfü-nish\ *adj*

¹**bug** \ˈbəg\ *n* **1** : an insect or other creeping or crawling invertebrate animal; *esp* : an insect pest (as the cockroach or bedbug) **2** : any of an order of insects with sucking mouthparts and incomplete metamorphosis that includes many plant pests **3** : an unexpected flaw or imperfection ⟨a ~ in a computer program⟩ **4** : a disease-producing germ; *also* : a disease caused by it **5** : a concealed listening device — **bug·gy** \ˈbə-gē\ *adj*

²**bug** *vb* **bugged; bug·ging 1** : BOTHER, ANNOY **2** : to plant a concealed microphone in

³**bug** *vb* **bugged; bug·ging** *of the eyes* : PROTRUDE, BULGE

bug·a·boo \ˈbə-gə-ˌbü\ *n, pl* **-boos** : BOGEY 1

bug·bear \ˈbəg-ˌber\ *n* : BOGEY 1; *also* : a source of dread

bug·gy \ˈbə-gē\ *n, pl* **buggies** : a light horse-drawn carriage; *also* : a carriage for a baby

bu·gle \ˈbyü-gəl\ *n* [ME, buffalo, instrument made of buffalo horn, bugle, fr. AF, fr. L *buculus*, dim. of *bos* head of cattle] : a valveless brass instrument resembling a trumpet and used esp. for military calls — **bu·gler** *n*

bug out *vb* **1** : to flee in panic **2** : to depart in a hurry

¹**build** \ˈbild\ *vb* **built** \ˈbilt\; **build·ing 1** : to form or have formed by ordering and uniting materials ⟨~ a house⟩; *also* : to bring into being or develop **2** : to produce or create gradually ⟨~ an argument on facts⟩ **3** : INCREASE, ENLARGE; *also* : ENHANCE **4** : to engage in building — **build·er** *n*

²**build** *n* : form or mode of structure; *esp* : PHYSIQUE

build·ing \ˈbil-diŋ\ *n* **1** : a usu. roofed and walled structure (as a house) for permanent use **2** : the art or business of constructing buildings

build-up \ˈbild-ˌəp\ *n* : the act or process of building up; *also* : something produced by this

built–in \ˈbilt-ˈin\ *adj* **1** : forming an integral part of a structure **2** : INHERENT

bulb \ˈbəlb\ *n* **1** : an underground resting stage of a plant (as a lily or an onion) consisting of a short stem base bearing one or more buds enclosed in overlapping leaves; *also* : a fleshy plant structure (as a tuber) resembling a bulb **2** : a plant having or growing from a bulb **3** : a rounded more or less bulb-shaped object or part (as for an electric lamp) — **bul·bous** \ˈbəl-bəs\ *adj*

¹**bulge** \ˈbəlj\ *vb* **bulged; bulg·ing** : to become or cause to become protuberant

²**bulge** *n* : a swelling projecting part

bu·li·mia \bü-ˈlē-mē-ə, byü-, -ˈli-\ *n* **1** : an abnormal and constant craving for food **2** : a serious eating disorder chiefly of females that is characterized by compulsive overeating usu. followed by self-induced vomiting or laxative or diuretic abuse — **bu·lim·ic** \-ˈlē-mik, -ˈli-\ *adj or n*

¹**bulk** \ˈbəlk\ *n* **1** : MAGNITUDE, VOLUME **2** : material that forms a mass in the intestine; *esp* : FIBER **2** **3** : a large mass **4** : the major portion

²**bulk** *vb* **1** : to cause to swell or bulge **2** : to appear as a factor : LOOM

buffalo 2

bulk·head \'bəlk-ˌhed\ *n* **1** : a partition separating compartments **2** : a structure built to cover a shaft or a cellar stairway

bulky \'bəl-kē\ *adj* **bulk·i·er; -est** : having bulk; *esp* : being large and unwieldy

¹bull \'bul\ *n* **1** : a male bovine animal; *also* : a usu. adult male of various large animals (as the moose, elephant, or whale) **2** : one who buys securities or commodities in expectation of a price increase — **bull·ish** *adj*

²bull *adj* **1** : of, relating to, or suggestive of a bull : MALE **2** : large of its kind ⟨a ~ lathe⟩

³bull *n* [ME *bulle*, fr. ML *bulla*, fr. L, bubble, amulet] **1** : a papal letter **2** : DECREE

⁴bull *n, slang* : NONSENSE

⁵bull *abbr* bulletin

¹bull·dog \'bul-ˌdog\ *n* : any of a breed of compact muscular short-haired dogs of English origin

²bulldog *vb* : to throw (a steer) by seizing the horns and twisting the neck

bull·doze \-ˌdōz\ *vb* **1** : to move, clear, or level with a tractor-driven machine (**bull·doz·er**) having a broad blade for pushing **2** : to force as if by using a bulldozer

bul·let \'bu-lət\ *n* [MF *boulette* small ball & *boulet* missile, dims. of *boule* ball, fr. L *bulla* bubble] : a missile to be shot from a firearm

bul·le·tin \'bu-lə-tᵊn\ *n* **1** : a brief public report intended for immediate release on a matter of public interest **2** : a periodical publication (as of a college)

bulletin board *n* **1** : a board for posting notices **2** : a public forum on a computer network in which users write or read messages or download files

bul·let·proof \'bu-lət-ˌprüf\ *adj* **1** : impenetrable to bullets **2** : not subject to correction, alteration, or modification **3** : INVINCIBLE

bull·fight \'bul-ˌfīt\ *n* : a spectacle in which people ceremonially fight with and usu. kill bulls in an arena — **bull·fight·er** *n*

bull·frog \-ˌfrog, -ˌfräg\ *n* : a large deep-voiced frog

bull·head \-ˌhed\ *n* : any of several common large-headed freshwater catfishes of the U.S.

bull·head·ed \-'he-dəd\ *adj* : stupidly stubborn : HEADSTRONG

bul·lion \'bul-yən\ *n* : gold or silver esp. in bars or ingots

bull market *n* : a market in which securities or commodities are persistently rising in value

bull·ock \'bu-lək\ *n* : a young bull; *also* : STEER

bull pen *n* : a place on a baseball field where pitchers warm up; *also* : the relief pitchers of a baseball team

bull session *n* : an informal discussion

bull's-eye \'bulz-ˌī\ *n, pl* **bull's-eyes** : the center of a target; *also* : a shot that hits the bull's-eye

¹bul·ly \'bu-lē\ *n, pl* **bul·lies** : a person habitually cruel to others who are weaker

²bully *adj* : EXCELLENT, FIRST-RATE — often used interjectionally ⟨~ for you⟩

³bully *vb* **bul·lied; bul·ly·ing** : to behave as a bully toward : DOMINEER ♦ **Synonyms** BROWBEAT, INTIMIDATE, HECTOR — **bul·ly·ing** *n*

bul·rush \'bul-ˌrəsh\ *n* : any of several large rushes or sedges of wetlands

bul·wark \'bul-(ˌ)wərk, -ˌwork; 'bəl-(ˌ)wərk\ *n* **1** : a wall-like defensive structure **2** : a strong support or protection

¹bum \'bəm\ *adj* **1** : of poor quality ⟨~ advice⟩ **2** : disabled by damage or injury ⟨a ~ knee⟩

²bum *vb* **bummed; bum·ming 1** : to spend time unemployed and wandering; *also* : LOAF **2** : to obtain by begging

³bum *n* **1** : LOAFER **2** : one whose time is devoted to a recreational activity ⟨a ski ~⟩ **3** : TRAMP 1

bum·ble \'bəm-bəl\ *vb* **bum·bled; bum·bling 1** : to speak in a stuttering and faltering manner **2** : to proceed unsteadily **3** : BUNGLE

bum·ble·bee \'bəm-bəl-ˌbē\ *n* : any of numerous large hairy social bees

bum·mer \'bə-mər\ *n* **1** : an unpleasant experience **2** : FAILURE

¹bump \'bəmp\ *n* **1** : a local bulge; *esp* : a swelling of tissue **2** : a sudden forceful blow or impact — **bumpy** *adj*

²bump *vb* **1** : to strike or knock forcibly; *also* : to move by or as if by bumping **2** : to collide with

¹bum·per \'bəm-pər\ *n* **1** : a cup or glass filled to the brim **2** : something unusually large — **bumper** *adj*

²bump·er \'bəm-pər\ *n* : a device for absorbing shock or preventing damage; *esp* : a usu. metal bar at either end of an automobile

bump·kin \'bəmp-kən\ *n* : an awkward and unsophisticated country person

bump·tious \'bəmp-shəs\ *adj* : obtusely and often noisily self-assertive

bun \'bən\ *n* : a sweet or plain round roll

¹bunch \'bənch\ *n* **1** : SWELLING **2** : CLUSTER, GROUP — **bunchy** *adj*

²bunch *vb* : to form into a group or bunch

bun·co *or* **bun·ko** \'bəŋ-kō\ *n, pl* **buncos** *or* **bunkos** : a swindling scheme — **bunco** *vb*

¹bun·dle \'bən-dᵊl\ *n* **1** : several items bunched and fastened together; *also* : something wrapped for carrying **2** : a considerable amount : LOT **3** : a small band of mostly parallel nerve or muscle fibers **4** : a package offering related products or services at a single price

²bundle *vb* **bun·dled; bun·dling** : to gather or tie in a bundle

bundling *n* : a former custom of a courting couple's occupying the same bed without undressing

bung \'bəŋ\ *n* : the stopper in the bunghole of a cask

bun·ga·low \'bəŋ-gə-ˌlō\ *n* [Hindi & Urdu *banglā*, lit., (house) in the Bengal style] : a one-storied house with a low-pitched roof

bun·gee cord \'bən-jē-\ *n* : a long elastic cord used esp. as a fastening or shock-absorbing device

bungee jump *vb* : to jump from a height while attached to a bungee cord — **bungee jumper** *n*

bung·hole \'bəŋ-ˌhōl\ *n* : a hole for emptying or filling a cask

bun·gle \'bəŋ-gəl\ *vb* **bun·gled; bun·gling** : to do badly : BOTCH — **bungle** *n* — **bun·gler** *n*

bun·ion \'bən-yən\ *n* : an inflamed swelling of the first joint of the big toe

¹bunk \'bəŋk\ *n* : BED; *esp* : a built-in bed that is often one of a tier

²bunk *n* : BUNKUM, NONSENSE

bunk bed *n* : one of two single beds usu. placed one above the other

bun·ker \'bəŋ-kər\ *n* **1** : a bin or compartment for storage (as for coal on a ship) **2** : a protective embankment or dugout **3** : a sand trap or embankment constituting a hazard on a golf course

bun·kum *or* **bun·combe** \'bəŋ-kəm\ *n* [*Buncombe* County, N.C.; fr. a remark made by its congressman, who defended an irrelevant speech by claiming that he was speaking to Buncombe] : insincere or foolish talk

bun·ny \'bə-nē\ *n, pl* **-nies** : RABBIT

bunny slope *n* : a gentle incline used by novice skiers

Bun·sen burner \'bən-sən-\ *n* : a gas burner usu. consisting of a straight tube with air holes at the bottom

¹bunt \'bənt\ *vb* **1** : ¹BUTT **2** : to push or tap a baseball lightly without swinging the bat

²bunt *n* : an act or instance of bunting; *also* : a bunted ball

¹bun·ting \'bən-tiŋ\ *n* : any of numerous small stout-billed finches

²bunting *n* : a thin fabric used esp. for flags; *also* : FLAGS

¹buoy \'bü-ē, 'boi\ *n* **1** : a floating object anchored in water to mark something (as a channel) **2** : a float consisting of a ring of buoyant material to support a person who has fallen into the water

²buoy *vb* **1** : to mark by a buoy **2** : to keep afloat **3** : to raise the spirits of

buoy·an·cy \'boi-ən-sē, 'bü-yən-\ *n* **1** : the tendency of a body to float or rise when submerged in a fluid **2** : the power of a fluid to exert an upward force on a body placed in it **3** : resilience of spirit — **buoy·ant** \-ənt, -yənt\ *adj*

¹bur *var of* BURR

²bur *abbr* bureau

burbs \'bərbz\ *n pl* : SUBURBS

¹bur·den \'bər-dᵊn\ *n* **1** : LOAD; *also* : CARE, RESPONSIBILITY **2** : something oppressive : ENCUMBRANCE ⟨the tax ~⟩ **3** : CARGO; *also* : capacity for cargo

²burden *vb* : LOAD, OPPRESS ⟨~ed with guilt⟩ — **bur·den·some** \-səm\ *adj*

³**burden** *n* **1** : REFRAIN, CHORUS **2** : a main theme or idea : GIST

bur·dock \'bər-ˌdäk\ *n* : any of a genus of coarse composite herbs with globe-shaped flower heads surrounded by prickly bracts

bu·reau \'byùr-ō\ *n, pl* **bureaus** *also* **bu·reaux** \-ōz\ [F, desk, cloth covering for desks, fr. OF *burel* woolen cloth, ultim. fr. L *burra* shaggy cloth] **1** : a chest of drawers **2** : an administrative unit (as of a government department) **3** : a branch of a publication or wire service in an important news center

bu·reau·cra·cy \byù-'rä-krə-sē\ *n, pl* **-cies** **1** : a body of appointive government officials **2** : government marked by specialization of functions under fixed rules and a hierarchy of authority; *also* : an unwieldy administrative system burdened with excessive complexity and lack of flexibility — **bu·reau·crat** \'byùr-ə-ˌkrat\ *n* — **bu·reau·crat·ic** \ˌbyùr-ə-'kra-tik\ *adj*

bur·geon \'bər-jən\ *vb* : to put forth fresh growth (as from buds) : grow vigorously : FLOURISH

burgh \'bər-ō\ *n* : a Scottish town

bur·gher \'bər-gər\ *n* **1** : TOWNSMAN **2** : a prosperous solid citizen

bur·glary \'bər-glə-rē\ *n, pl* **-glar·ies** : forcible entry into a building esp. at night with the intent to commit a crime (as theft) — **bur·glar** \-glər\ *n* — **bur·glar·ize** \'bər-glə-ˌrīz\ *vb*

bur·gle \'bər-gəl\ *vb* **bur·gled; bur·gling** : to commit burglary on

bur·go·mas·ter \'bər-gə-ˌmas-tər\ *n* : the chief magistrate of a town in some European countries

bur·gun·dy \'bər-gən-dē\ *n, pl* **-dies** *often cap* **1** : a red or white table wine from the Burgundy region of France **2** : a blended red wine

buri·al \'ber-ē-əl\ *n* : the act or process of burying

bur·ka *or* **bur·qa** \'bùr-kə\ *n* : a loose garment that covers the face and body and is worn in public by certain Muslim women

burl \'bərl\ *n* : a hard woody often flattened hemispherical outgrowth on a tree

bur·lap \'bər-ˌlap\ *n* : a coarse fabric usu. of jute or hemp used esp. for bags

¹**bur·lesque** \(ˌ)bər-'lesk\ *n* [*burlesque*, adj., comic, droll, fr. F, fr. It *burlesco*, fr. *burla* joke, fr. Sp] **1** : a witty or derisive literary or dramatic imitative work **2** : broadly humorous theatrical entertainment consisting of several items (as songs, skits, or dances)

²**burlesque** *vb* **bur·lesqued; bur·lesqu·ing** : to make ludicrous by burlesque ♦ *Synonyms* CARICATURE, PARODY, TRAVESTY

bur·ly \'bər-lē\ *adj* **bur·li·er; -est** : strongly and heavily built. : HUSKY ♦ *Synonyms* MUSCULAR, BRAWNY, BEEFY, HEFTY

¹**burn** \'bərn\ *vb* **burned** \'bərnd, 'bərnt\ *or* **burnt** \'bərnt\; **burn·ing** **1** : to be on fire **2** : to feel or look as if on fire **3** : to alter or become altered by or as if by the action of fire or heat **4** : to use as fuel (~ coal); *also* : to destroy by fire (~ trash) **5** : to cause or make by fire (~ a hole); *also* : to affect as if by heat **6** : to record digital data or music on (an optical disk) using a laser (~ a CD)

²**burn** *n* : an injury or effect produced by or as if by burning

burn·er \'bər-nər\ *n* : the part of a fuel-burning or heat-producing device where the flame or heat is produced

bur·nish \'bər-nish\ *vb* : to make shiny esp. by rubbing : POLISH — **bur·nish·er** *n* — **bur·nish·ing** *adj or n*

bur·noose *or* **bur·nous** \(ˌ)bər-'nüs\ *n* : a hooded cloak worn esp. by Arabs

burn·out \'bərn-ˌaùt\ *n* **1** : the cessation of operation of a jet or rocket engine **2** : exhaustion of one's physical or emotional strength; *also* : a person suffering from burnout

burp \'bərp\ *n* : an act of belching — **burp** *vb*

burp gun *n* : a small submachine gun

burr \'bər\ *n* **1** *usu* **bur** : a rough or prickly envelope of a fruit; *also* : a plant that bears burs **2** : roughness left in cutting or shaping metal **3** : a trilled \r\ as used by some speakers in northern England and Scotland **4** : WHIR — **bur·ry** *adj*

bur·ri·to \bə-'rē-tō\ *n* [AmerSp, fr. Sp, little donkey, dim. of *burro*] : a flour tortilla rolled around a filling and baked

bur·ro \'bər-ō, 'bùr-\ *n, pl* **burros** [Sp] : a usu. small donkey

¹**bur·row** \'bər-ō\ *n* : a hole in the ground made by an animal (as a rabbit)

²**burrow** *vb* **1** : to form by tunneling; *also* : to make a burrow **2** : to progress by or as if by digging — **bur·row·er** *n*

bur·sar \'bər-sər\ *n* : a treasurer esp. of a college

bur·si·tis \(ˌ)bər-'sī-təs\ *n* : inflammation of the serous sac (**bur·sa** \'bər-sə\) of a joint (as the elbow or shoulder)

¹**burst** \'bərst\ *vb* **burst** *or* **burst·ed; burst·ing** **1** : to fly apart or into pieces **2** : to show one's feelings suddenly; *also* : PLUNGE (~ into song) **3** : to enter or emerge suddenly : SPRING **4** : to be filled to the breaking point

²**burst** *n* **1** : a sudden outbreak : SPURT **2** : EXPLOSION **3** : result of bursting

bury \'ber-ē\ *vb* **bur·ied; bury·ing** **1** : to deposit in the earth; *also* : to inter with funeral ceremonies **2** : CONCEAL, HIDE **3** : SUBMERGE, ENGROSS — usu. used with *in* (*buried* himself in work)

¹**bus** \'bəs\ *n, pl* **bus·es** *also* **bus·ses** [short for *omnibus*, fr. F, fr. L, for all, dat. pl. of *omnis* all] : a large motor vehicle for carrying passengers

²**bus** *vb* **bused** *or* **bussed; bus·ing** *or* **bus·sing** **1** : to travel or transport by bus **2** : to work as a busboy

³**bus** *abbr* business

bus·boy \'bəs-ˌbòi\ *n* : a waiter's helper

bus·by \'bəz-bē\ *n, pl* **busbies** : a military full-dress fur hat

bush \'bùsh\ *n* **1** : SHRUB **2** : rough uncleared country **3** : a thick tuft (a ~ of hair) — **bushy** *adj*

bushed \'bùsht\ *adj* : TIRED, EXHAUSTED

bush·el \'bù-shəl\ *n* — see WEIGHT table

bush·ing \'bù-shiŋ\ *n* : a usu. removable cylindrical lining for an opening of a mechanical part to limit the size of the opening, resist wear, or serve as a guide

bush·mas·ter \'bùsh-ˌmas-tər\ *n* : a large venomous pit viper of Central and So. America

bush·whack \-ˌhwak\ *vb* **1** : AMBUSH **2** : to clear a path through esp. by chopping down bushes and branches — **bush·whack·er** *n*

busi·ness \'biz-nəs, -nəz\ *n* **1** : OCCUPATION; *also* : TASK, MISSION **2** : a commercial or industrial enterprise; *also* : TRADE (~ is good) **3** : AFFAIR, MATTER **4** : personal concern

busi·ness·man \-ˌman\ *n* : a man engaged in business esp. as an executive

busi·ness·per·son \-ˌpər-sᵊn\ *n* : a businessman or businesswoman

busi·ness·wom·an \-ˌwù-mən\ *n* : a woman engaged in business esp. as an executive

bus·kin \'bəs-kən\ *n* **1** : a laced boot reaching halfway to the knee **2** : tragic drama

buss \'bəs\ *n* : KISS — **buss** *vb*

¹**bust** \'bəst\ *n* [F *buste*, fr. It *busto*, fr. L *bustum* tomb] **1** : sculpture representing the upper part of the human figure **2** : the part of the human torso between the neck and the waist; *esp* : the breasts of a woman

²**bust** *vb* **bust·ed** *also* **bust; bust·ing** **1** : BREAK, SMASH; *also* : BURST **2** : to ruin financially **3** : TAME **4** : DEMOTE **5** *slang* : ARREST; *also* : RAID

³**bust** *n* **1** : a drinking session **2** : a complete failure : FLOP **3** : a business depression **4** : PUNCH, SOCK **5** *slang* : a police raid; *also* : ARREST

¹**bus·tle** \'bə-səl\ *vb* **bus·tled; bus·tling** : to move or work in a brisk busy manner

²**bustle** *n* : briskly energetic activity

³**bustle** *n* : a pad or frame worn to support the fullness at the back of a woman's skirt

¹**busy** \'bi-zē\ *adj* **busi·er; -est** **1** : engaged in action : not idle **2** : being in use (~ telephones) **3** : full of activity (~ streets) **4** : full of distracting detail (a ~ design) — **busi·ly** \'bi-zə-lē\ *adv*

²**busy** *vb* **bus·ied; busy·ing** : to make or keep busy : OCCUPY

busy·body \'bi-zē-ˌbä-dē\ *n* : MEDDLER

busy·work \-ˌwərk\ *n* : work that appears productive but only keeps one occupied

¹**but** \'bət\ *conj* **1** : except for the fact (would have protested ~ that he was afraid) **2** : THAT (there's no doubt ~ he won) **3** : without the certainty that (never rains

~ it pours⟩ **4** : on the contrary ⟨not one, ~ two job offers⟩ **5** : YET ⟨poor ~ proud⟩ **6** : with the exception of ⟨none ~ the strongest attempt it⟩

²**but** *prep* : other than : EXCEPT ⟨this letter is nothing ~ an insult⟩; *also* : with the exception of ⟨no one here ~ me⟩

bu·tane \'byü-ˌtān\ *n* : either of two gaseous hydrocarbons used as a fuel

butch \'bu̇ch\ *adj* : notably masculine in appearance or manner

¹**butch·er** \'bu̇-chər\ *n* [ME *bocher*, fr. AF, fr. *buc* he=goat] **1** : one who slaughters animals or dresses their flesh; *also* : a dealer in meat **2** : one that kills brutally or needlessly **3** : one that botches — **butch·ery** \-chə-rē\ *n*

²**butcher** *vb* **1** : to slaughter and dress for meat ⟨~ hogs⟩ **2** : to kill barbarously **3** : BOTCH ⟨the band ~ed my favorite song⟩

but·ler \'bət-lər\ *n* [ME *buteler*, fr. AF *butiller*, † fr. OF *botele* bottle] : the chief male servant of a household

¹**butt** \'bət\ *vb* : to strike with the head or horns

²**butt** *n* : a blow or thrust with the head or horns

³**butt** *n* : a large cask

⁴**butt** *n* **1** : TARGET **2** : an object of abuse or ridicule ⟨the ~ of everyone's jokes⟩

⁵**butt** *n* **1** : BUTTOCKS **2** : a large, thicker, or bottom end of something

⁶**butt** *vb* **1** : ABUT — used with *on* or *against* **2** : to place or join edge to edge without overlapping

butte \'byüt\ *n* : an isolated steep hill

¹**but·ter** \'bə-tər\ *n* [ME, fr. OE *butere*, fr. L *butyrum* butter, fr. Gk *boutyron*, fr. *bous* cow + *tyros* cheese] **1** : a solid edible emulsion of fat obtained from cream by churning **2** : a substance resembling butter — **but·tery** *adj*

²**butter** *vb* : to spread with or as if with butter ⟨~ed toast⟩

but·ter–and–eggs \ˌbə-tər-°n-'egz\ *n sing or pl* : a common perennial herb related to the snapdragon that has showy yellow and orange flowers

butter bean *n* **1** : LIMA BEAN **2** : WAX BEAN **3** : a green shell bean

but·ter·cream \'bə-tər-ˌkrēm\ *n* : a sweet butter-based mixture used esp. as a filling or frosting

but·ter·cup \'bə-tər-ˌkəp\ *n* : any of a genus of herbs having usu. yellow flowers with five petals and sepals

but·ter·fat \-ˌfat\ *n* : the natural fat of milk and chief constituent of butter

but·ter·fin·gered \-ˌfiŋ-gərd\ *adj* : likely to let things fall or slip through the fingers — **but·ter·fin·gers** \-gərz\ *n sing or pl*

but·ter·fly \-ˌflī\ *n* : any of a group of slender day-flying insects with broad often brightly-colored wings

but·ter·milk \-ˌmilk\ *n* : the liquid remaining after butter is churned

but·ter·nut \-ˌnət\ *n* : the sweet egg-shaped nut of an American tree related to the walnut; *also* : this tree

butternut squash *n* : a smooth buff-colored cylindrical winter squash

but·ter·scotch \-ˌskäch\ *n* : a candy made from brown sugar, corn syrup, and water; *also* : the flavor of such candy

but·tock \'bə-tək\ *n* **1** : the back of a hip that forms one of the fleshy parts on which a person sits **2** *pl* : the seat of the body : RUMP

¹**but·ton** \'bə-tᵊn\ *n* **1** : a small knob secured to an article (as of clothing) and used as a fastener by passing it through a buttonhole or loop **2** : something that resembles a button **3** : PUSH BUTTON **4** : a hidden sensitivity that can be manipulated to produce a desired response **5** : a usu. box-shaped computer icon that initiates a software function

²**button** *vb* : to close or fasten with or as if with buttons

¹**but·ton·hole** \'bə-tᵊn-ˌhōl\ *n* : a slit or loop for a button to pass through

²**buttonhole** *vb* : to detain in conversation by or as if by holding on to the outer garments of

¹**but·tress** \'bə-trəs\ *n* [ME *butres*, fr. AF (*arche*) *boteraz* thrusting (arch), ultim. fr. *buter* to thrust] **1** : a projecting structure to support a wall **2** : PROP, SUPPORT

²**buttress** *vb* : PROP, SUPPORT

bu·tut \bü-'tüt\ *n, pl* **bututs** *or* **butut** — see *dalasi* at MONEY table

bux·om \'bək-səm\ *adj* : healthily plump; *esp* : full=bosomed

¹**buy** \'bī\ *vb* **bought** \'bȯt\; **buy·ing** **1** : to obtain for a price : PURCHASE; *also* : BRIBE **2** : to accept as true — **buy·er** *n*

²**buy** *n* **1** : PURCHASE 1, 2 **2** : an exceptional value : BARGAIN

¹**buzz** \'bəz\ *vb* **1** : to make a buzz **2** : to fly fast and close to

²**buzz** *n* **1** : a low humming sound **2** : RUMOR, GOSSIP

buz·zard \'bə-zərd\ *n* : any of various usu. large birds of prey and esp. the turkey vulture

buzz·er \'bə-zər\ *n* : a device that signals with a buzzing sound

buzz saw *n* : CIRCULAR SAW

buzz·word \'bəz-ˌwərd\ *n* : a voguish word or phrase often from technical jargon

BVM *abbr* Blessed Virgin Mary

BWI *abbr* British West Indies

bx *abbr* box

BX *abbr* base exchange

¹**by** \'bī, bə\ *prep* **1** : NEAR ⟨stood ~ the window⟩ **2** : through or through the medium of : VIA ⟨left ~ the door⟩ **3** : PAST ⟨drove ~ the house⟩ **4** : DURING, AT ⟨studied ~ night⟩ **5** : no later than ⟨get here ~ 3 p.m.⟩ **6** : through the means or direct agency of ⟨~ force⟩ **7** : in conformity with; *also* : ACCORDING TO ⟨did it ~ the book⟩ **8** : with respect to ⟨a doctor ~ profession⟩ **9** : to the amount or extent of ⟨won ~ a nose⟩ **10** — used to express relationship in multiplication, in division, and in measurements ⟨divide *a* ~ *b*⟩ ⟨multiply ~ 6⟩ ⟨15 feet ~ 20 feet⟩

²**by** \'bī\ *adv* **1** : near at hand; *also* : IN ⟨stop ~⟩ **2** : PAST ⟨saw him go ~⟩ **3** : ASIDE, APART ⟨put some money ~⟩

bye \'bī\ *n* : a position of a participant in a tournament who advances to the next round without playing

by–elec·tion *also* **bye–election** \'bī-ə-ˌlek-shən\ *n* : a special election held between regular elections in order to fill a vacancy

by·gone \'bī-ˌgȯn\ *adj* : gone by : PAST — **bygone** *n*

by·law *also* **bye·law** \'bī-ˌlȯ\ *n* : a rule adopted by an organization for managing its internal affairs

by–line \'bī-ˌlīn\ *n* : a line at the beginning of a news story or magazine article giving the writer's name

BYO *abbr* bring your own

BYOB *abbr* bring your own beer; bring your own booze; bring your own bottle

¹**by·pass** \'bī-ˌpas\ *n* : a passage to one side or around a blocked or congested area; *also* : a surgical procedure establishing this ⟨a coronary ~⟩

²**bypass** *vb* : to avoid by means of a bypass

by·path \-ˌpath, -ˌpäth\ *n* : BYWAY

by·play \'bī-ˌplā\ *n* : action engaged in on the side (as of a stage) while the main action proceeds

by–prod·uct \-ˌprä-(ˌ)dəkt\ *n* : a sometimes unexpected product or result produced in addition to the main product or result

by·stand·er \-ˌstan-dər\ *n* : one present but not participating ✦ *Synonyms* ONLOOKER, WITNESS, SPECTATOR, EYEWITNESS

byte \'bīt\ *n* : a unit of computer information consisting of a group of 8 bits

by·way \'bī-ˌwā\ *n* **1** : a little-traveled side road **2** : a secondary aspect

by·word \-ˌwərd\ *n* **1** : PROVERB **2** : one that is noteworthy or notorious

Byz·an·tine \'biz-ᵊn-ˌtēn, 'bī-, -ˌtīn; bə-'zan-, bī-\ *adj* **1** : of, relating to, or characteristic of the ancient city of Byzantium or the Byzantine Empire **2** *often not cap* : intricately involved and often devious

¹c \'sē\ n, pl c's or cs \'sēz\ often cap 1 : the 3d letter of the English alphabet 2 slang : a sum of $100 3 : a grade rating a student's work as fair
²c abbr, often cap 1 calorie 2 carat 3 Celsius 4 cent 5 centigrade 6 centimeter 7 century 8 chapter 9 circa 10 cocaine 11 copyright
C symbol carbon
ca abbr circa
Ca symbol calcium
CA abbr 1 California 2 chartered accountant 3 chief accountant 4 chronological age
cab \'kab\ n 1 : a light closed horse-drawn carriage 2 : TAXICAB 3 : the covered compartment for the engineer and controls of a locomotive; also : a similar compartment (as on a truck) — cab vb
CAB abbr Civil Aeronautics Board
ca·bal \kə-'bäl, -'bal\ n [F cabale, fr. ML cabbala cabala, fr. Heb qabbālāh, lit., received (lore)] 1 : a secret group of plotters or political conspirators 2 : CLUB, GROUP ⟨a ~ of artists⟩
cabala var of KABBALAH
ca·bana \kə-'ban-yə, -'ba-nə\ n : a shelter at a beach or swimming pool
cab·a·ret \ˌka-bə-'rā\ n : NIGHTCLUB
cab·bage \'ka-bij\ n [ME caboche, fr. MF dial., lit., head, noggin] : a vegetable related to the mustard with a dense head of leaves
cab·bie or cab·by \'ka-bē\ n, pl cabbies : a driver of a cab
cab·er·net sau·vi·gnon \ˌka-bər-'nā-sō-vē-'nyōⁿ\ n : a dry red wine made from a single variety of black grape
cab·in \'ka-bən\ n 1 : a private room on a ship; also : a compartment below deck on a boat for passengers or crew 2 : an aircraft or spacecraft compartment for passengers, crew, or cargo 3 : a small simple one-story house
cabin boy n : a boy working as a servant on a ship
cabin class n : a class of accommodations on a passenger ship superior to tourist class and inferior to first class
cabin cruiser n : CRUISER 3
cab·i·net \'kab-nit\ n 1 : a case or cupboard for holding or displaying articles 2 : the advisory council of a head of state (as a president or sovereign)
cab·i·net·mak·er \-ˌmā-kər\ n : a woodworker who makes fine furniture — cab·i·net·mak·ing n
cab·i·net·work \-ˌwərk\ n : the finished work of a cabinetmaker
¹ca·ble \'kā-bəl\ n 1 : a very strong rope, wire, or chain 2 : a bundle of insulated wires usu. twisted around a central core 3 : CABLEGRAM 4 : CABLE TELEVISION
²cable vb ca·bled; ca·bling : to telegraph by cable
cable car n : a vehicle moved by an endless cable
ca·ble·cast \'kā-bəl-ˌkast\ n : a cable television transmission — cablecast vb
ca·ble·gram \'kā-bəl-ˌgram\ n : a message sent by a submarine telegraph cable
cable modem n : a modem for connecting a computer to a network over a cable television line
cable television n : a system of television reception in which signals from distant stations are sent by cable to the receivers of paying subscribers
cab·o·chon \'ka-bə-ˌshän\ n : a gem or bead cut in convex form and highly polished but not given facets; also : this style of cutting — cabochon adv
ca·boose \kə-'büs\ n : a car usu. at the rear of a freight train for the use of the train crew and railroad workers
cab·ri·o·let \ˌka-brē-ə-'lā\ n [F] 1 : a light 2-wheeled one-horse carriage 2 : a convertible coupe
cab·stand \'kab-ˌstand\ n : a place where cabs wait for passengers
ca·cao \kə-'kaů, -'kā-ō\ n, pl cacaos [Sp, fr. Nahuatl cacahuatl] : a So. American tree whose seeds (cacao beans) are the source of cocoa and chocolate; also : its dried fatty seeds

cac·cia·to·re \ˌkä-chə-'tōr-ē\ adj [It] : cooked with tomatoes and herbs ⟨chicken ~⟩
cache \'kash\ n [F] : a hiding place esp. for preserving provisions; also : something hidden or stored in a cache — cache vb
ca·chet \ka-'shā\ n [F] 1 : a seal used esp. as a mark of official approval 2 : a feature or quality conferring prestige; also : PRESTIGE 3 : a design, inscription, or advertisement printed or stamped on mail
cack·le \'ka-kəl\ vb cack·led; cack·ling 1 : to make the sharp broken cry characteristic of a hen 2 : to laugh or chatter noisily — cackle n — cack·ler n
ca·coph·o·ny \ka-'kä-fə-nē\ n, pl -nies : harsh or discordant sound — ca·coph·o·nous \-nəs\ adj
cac·tus \'kak-təs\ n, pl cac·ti \-ˌtī\ or cac·tus·es also cactus : any of a large family of drought-resistant flowering plants with succulent stems and with leaves replaced by scales or prickles
cad \'kad\ n : a man who deliberately disregards another's feelings — cad·dish \'ka-dish\ adj — cad·dish·ly adv — cad·dish·ness n
ca·dav·er \kə-'da-vər\ n : a dead body
ca·dav·er·ous \kə-'da-və-rəs\ adj : suggesting a corpse esp. in gauntness or pallor ✦ Synonyms WASTED, EMACIATED, GAUNT — ca·dav·er·ous·ly adv
cad·die or cad·dy \'ka-dē\ n, pl caddies [Sc, errand boy, modif. of F cadet military cadet] : a person who assists a golfer esp. by carrying the clubs — caddie or caddy vb
cad·dy \'ka-dē\ n, pl caddies [Malay kati a unit of weight] : a small box, can, or chest; esp : one to keep tea in
ca·dence \'kād-ⁿns\ n : the measure or beat of a rhythmical flow : RHYTHM — ca·denced \-ⁿnst\ adj
ca·den·za \kə-'den-zə\ n [It] : a brilliant sometimes improvised passage usu. toward the close of a musical composition
ca·det \kə-'det\ n [F, fr. Occitan (Gascony) capdet chief, fr. L capitellum, fr. L caput head] 1 : a younger son or brother 2 : a student in a service academy
Ca·dette \kə-'det\ n : a member of a Girl Scout program for girls in sixth through ninth grades
cadge \'kaj\ vb cadged; cadg·ing : SPONGE, BEG ⟨~ a free meal⟩ — cadg·er n
cad·mi·um \'kad-mē-əm\ n : a bluish-white metallic chemical element used esp. in protective platings
cad·re \'ka-ˌdrā, 'kä-, -ˌdrē\ n [F] 1 : FRAMEWORK 2 : a central unit esp. of trained personnel able to assume control and train others 3 : a group of indoctrinated leaders active in promoting the interests of a revolutionary party
ca·du·ceus \kə-'dü-sē-əs, -'dyü-, -shəs\ n, pl -cei \-sē-ˌī\ [L] 1 : the staff of a herald; esp : a representation of a staff with two entwined snakes and two wings at the top 2 : an insignia bearing a caduceus and symbolizing a physician
cae·cum var of CECUM
Cae·sar \'sē-zər\ n 1 : any of the Roman emperors succeeding Augustus Caesar — used as a title 2 often not cap : a powerful ruler : AUTOCRAT, DICTATOR; also : the civil or temporal power
caesarean also caesarian var of CESAREAN
cae·si·um chiefly Brit var of CESIUM
cae·su·ra \si-'zhúr-ə\ n, pl -suras or -su·rae \-'zhúr-(ˌ)ē\ : a break in the flow of sound usu. in the middle of a line of verse
ca·fé \ka-'fā\ n [F, lit., coffee] 1 : RESTAURANT 2 : BARROOM 3 : NIGHTCLUB
ca·fé au lait \(ˌ)ka-ˌfā-ō-'lā\ n : coffee with hot milk in about equal parts
caf·e·te·ria \ˌka-fə-'tir-ē-ə\ n [AmerSp cafetería coffeehouse] : a restaurant in which the customers serve themselves or are served at a counter

caf·fein·at·ed \'ka-fə-ˌnā-təd\ *adj* **1** : stimulated by or as if by caffeine **2** : containing caffeine
caf·feine \ka-'fēn, 'ka-ˌfēn\ *n* : a stimulating alkaloid found esp. in coffee and tea
caf·fe lat·te \'kä-fä-'lä-tä\ *n* [It] : espresso mixed with hot or steamed milk
caf·tan \kaf-'tan, 'kaf-ˌtan\ *n* [Russ *kaftan*, fr. Turk, fr. Pers *qaftān*] : an ankle-length garment with long sleeves worn in countries of the eastern Mediterranean
¹cage \'kāj\ *n* **1** : an openwork enclosure for confining an animal **2** : something resembling a cage
²cage *vb* **caged; cag·ing** : to put or keep in or as if in a cage
ca·gey *also* **ca·gy** \'kā-jē\ *adj* **ca·gi·er; -est** : wary of being trapped or deceived : SHREWD ⟨a ~ dealer⟩ — **ca·gi·ly** \-jə-lē\ *adv* — **ca·gi·ness** \-jē-nəs\ *n*
CAGS *abbr* Certificate of Advanced Graduate Study
ca·hoot \kə-'hüt\ *n* : PARTNERSHIP, LEAGUE — usu. used in pl. ⟨officials in ~s with the underworld⟩
cai·man *also* **cayman** \'kā-mən; kā-'man, kī-\ *n* : any of several Central and So. American reptiles closely related to alligators and crocodiles
cairn \'karn\ *n* : a heap of stones serving as a memorial or a landmark
cais·son \'kā-ˌsän, 'kās-ᵊn\ *n* **1** : a usu. 2-wheeled vehicle for artillery ammunition **2** : a watertight chamber used in underwater construction work or as a foundation
caisson disease *n* : ²BEND 3
cai·tiff \'kā-təf\ *adj* [ME *caitif*, fr. AF *caitif, chaitif* wretched, despicable, fr. L *captivus* captive] : being base, cowardly, or despicable — **caitiff** *n*
ca·jole \kə-'jōl\ *vb* **ca·joled; ca·jol·ing** [F *cajoler*] : to persuade or coax esp. with flattery or false promises — **ca·jole·ment** *n* — **ca·jol·ery** \-'jō-lə-rē\ *n*
Ca·jun \'kā-jən\ *n* : a Louisianian descended from French-speaking immigrants from Acadia (Nova Scotia) — **Cajun** *adj*
¹cake \'kāk\ *n* **1** : a baked or fried breadlike food usu. in a small flat shape **2** : a sweet baked food made from batter or dough usu. containing flour, sugar, shortening, and a leaven (as baking powder) **3** : a hardened or compacted substance ⟨a ~ of soap⟩ **4** : something easily done ⟨the quiz was ~⟩
²cake *vb* **caked; cak·ing** **1** : ENCRUST **2** : to form or harden into a cake
cake·walk \'kāk-ˌwȯk\ *n* **1** : a stage dance typically involving a high prance with backward tilt **2** : a one-sided contest or an easy task
cal *abbr* **1** calendar **2** caliber
Cal *abbr* **1** California **2** calorie
cal·a·bash \'ka-lə-ˌbash\ *n* : the fruit of a gourd; *also* : a utensil made from its hard shell
cal·a·boose \'ka-lə-ˌbüs\ *n* [Sp *calabozo* dungeon] : JAIL
ca·la·di·um \kə-'lā-dē-əm\ *n* : any of a genus of tropical American ornamental plants related to the arums
cal·a·mari \ˌkä-lə-'mär-ē\ *n* [It] : squid used as food
cal·a·mine \'ka-lə-ˌmīn\ *n* : a lotion of oxides of zinc and iron
ca·lam·i·ty \kə-'la-mə-tē\ *n, pl* **-ties** **1** : great distress or misfortune **2** : an event causing great harm or loss and affliction : DISASTER ⟨an economic ~⟩ — **ca·lam·i·tous** \-təs\ *adj* — **ca·lam·i·tous·ly** *adv* — **ca·lam·i·tous·ness** *n*
calc *abbr* calculate; calculated
cal·car·e·ous \kal-'kar-ē-əs\ *adj* : resembling calcium carbonate in hardness; *also* : containing calcium or calcium carbonate
cal·cif·er·ous \kal-'si-fə-rəs\ *adj* : producing or containing calcium carbonate
cal·ci·fy \'kal-sə-ˌfī\ *vb* **-fied; -fy·ing** : to make or become calcareous — **cal·ci·fi·ca·tion** \ˌkal-sə-fə-'kā-shən\ *n*
cal·ci·mine \'kal-sə-ˌmīn\ *n* : a thin water paint used esp. on plastered surfaces — **calcimine** *vb*
cal·cine \kal-'sīn\ *vb* **cal·cined; cal·cin·ing** : to heat to a high temperature but without fusing to drive off volatile matter and often to reduce to powder — **cal·ci·na·tion** \ˌkal-sə-'nā-shən\ *n*
cal·cite \'kal-ˌsīt\ *n* : a crystalline mineral consisting of calcium carbonate — **cal·cit·ic** \kal-'si-tik\ *adj*
cal·ci·um \'kal-sē-əm\ *n* : a silver-white soft metallic chemical element occurring only in combination
calcium carbonate *n* : a substance found in nature as

limestone and marble and in plant ashes, bones, and shells
cal·cu·late \'kal-kyə-ˌlāt\ *vb* **-lat·ed; -lat·ing** [L *calculare*, fr. *calculus* pebble (used in reckoning)] **1** : to determine by mathematical processes : COMPUTE **2** : to reckon by exercise of practical judgment : ESTIMATE **3** : to design or adapt for a purpose **4** : COUNT, RELY — **cal·cu·la·ble** \-lə-bəl\ *adj* — **cal·cu·la·tor** \-ˌlā-tər\ *n*
cal·cu·lat·ed \-ˌlā-təd\ *adj* **1** : undertaken after estimating the chance of success or failure ⟨a ~ risk⟩ **2** : planned purposefully : DELIBERATE ⟨a ~ strategy⟩
cal·cu·lat·ing \-ˌlā-tiŋ\ *adj* : marked by shrewd consideration esp. of self-interest — **cal·cu·lat·ing·ly** *adv*
cal·cu·la·tion \ˌkal-kyə-'lā-shən\ *n* **1** : the process or an act of calculating **2** : the result of an act of calculating **3** : studied care; *also* : cold heartless planning to promote self-interest
cal·cu·lus \'kal-kyə-ləs\ *n, pl* **-li** \-ˌlī\ *also* **-lus·es** [L, pebble (used in reckoning)] **1** : a method of computation or calculation in a special notation (as of logic) **2** : a branch of mathematics concerned with the rate of change of functions and with methods of finding lengths, areas, and volumes **3** : a concretion usu. of mineral salts esp. in hollow organs or ducts
cal·de·ra \kal-'der-ə, kȯl-, -'dir-\ *n* [Sp, lit., cauldron] : a large crater usu. formed by the collapse of a volcanic cone
cal·dron *var of* CAULDRON
¹cal·en·dar \'ka-lən-dər\ *n* **1** : an arrangement of time into days, weeks, months, and years; *also* : a sheet or folder containing such an arrangement for a period **2** : an orderly list
²calendar *vb* : to enter in a calendar
¹cal·en·der \'ka-lən-dər\ *vb* : to press (as cloth or paper) between rollers or plates so as to make smooth or glossy or to thin into sheets
²calender *n* : a machine for calendering
ca·lends \'ka-ləndz, 'kā-\ *n sing or pl* : the first day of the ancient Roman month
ca·len·du·la \kə-'len-jə-lə\ *n* : any of a genus of yellow=flowered herbs related to the daisies
¹calf \'kaf, 'käf\ *n, pl* **calves** \'kavz, 'kävz\ **1** : the young of the domestic cow; *also* : the young of various large mammals (as the elephant or whale) **2** : CALFSKIN
²calf *n, pl* **calves** \'kavz, 'kävz\ : the fleshy back of the leg below the knee
calf·skin \'kaf-ˌskin, 'käf-\ *n* : leather made of the skin of a calf
cal·i·ber *or* **cal·i·bre** \'ka-lə-bər\ *n* [MF *calibre*, fr. It *calibro*, fr. Ar *qālib* shoemaker's last] **1** : degree of mental capacity, excellence, or importance **2** : the diameter of a projectile **3** : the diameter of the bore of a gun
cal·i·brate \'ka-lə-ˌbrāt\ *vb* **-brat·ed; -brat·ing** : to adjust precisely
cal·i·bra·tion \ˌka-lə-'brā-shən\ *n* : a set of graduated marks indicating values or positions — usu. used in pl.
cal·i·co \'ka-li-ˌkō\ *n, pl* **-coes** *or* **-cos** **1** : printed cotton fabric **2** : a mottled or spotted animal — **calico** *adj*
Calif *abbr* California
Cal·i·for·nia poppy \ˌka-lə-'fȯr-nyə-\ *n* : a widely cultivated herb with usu. yellow or orange flowers that is related to the poppies
cal·i·for·ni·um \ˌka-lə-'fȯr-nē-əm\ *n* : an artificially prepared radioactive chemical element
cal·i·per \'ka-lə-pər\ *n* **·1** : any of various instruments having two arms, legs, or jaws used esp. to measure diameter or thickness — usu. used in pl. **2** : a device for pressing a frictional material against the sides of a rotating wheel or disk
ca·liph \'kā-ləf, 'ka-\ *n* : a successor of Muhammad as head of Islam — used as a title — **ca·liph·ate** \-lə-ˌfāt, -fət\ *n*
cal·is·then·ics \ˌka-ləs-'the-niks\ *n sing or pl* [Gk *kalos* beautiful + *sthenos* strength] : bodily exercises usu. done without apparatus — **cal·is·then·ic** *adj*
calk \'kȯk\ *var of* CAULK
¹call \'kȯl\ *vb* **1** : SHOUT, CRY; *also* : to utter a characteristic note or cry **2** : to utter in a loud clear voice ⟨~ed out my name⟩ **3** : to announce authoritatively **4** : SUMMON ⟨was ~ed to testify⟩ **5** : to make a request or demand ⟨~ for an investigation⟩ **6** : to halt (as a baseball game)

because of unsuitable conditions **7** : to demand payment of (a loan); *also* : to demand surrender of (as a bond) for redemption **8** : to get or try to get in communication by telephone **9** : to make a brief visit **10** : to speak of or address by name : give a name to **11** : to estimate or consider for practical purposes ⟨∼ it ten miles⟩ **12** : to temporarily transfer control of computer processing to (as a subroutine or procedure) — **call·er** *n*

²**call** *n* **1** : SHOUT **2** : the cry of an animal (as a bird) **3** : a request or a command to come or assemble : INVITATION, SUMMONS **4** : DEMAND, CLAIM; *also* : REQUEST **5** : a brief usu. formal visit **6** : an act of calling on the telephone **7** : DECISION ⟨a tough ∼⟩ **8** : a temporary transfer of control of computer processing to a particular set of instructions

cal·la lily \'ka-lə-\ *n* : a plant related to the arums and grown for its large white lilylike bract that surrounds a fleshy spike of small yellow flowers

call·back \'kȯl-ˌbak\ *n* : a calling back; *esp* : RECALL 5

call–board \-ˌbȯrd\ *n* : a board for posting notices (as of rehearsal calls)

call down *vb* : REPRIMAND

call girl *n* : a prostitute with whom appointments are made by phone

cal·lig·ra·phy \kə-'li-grə-fē\ *n* : artistic or elegant handwriting; *also* : the art of producing such writing — **cal·lig·ra·pher** \-fər\ *n* — **cal·li·graph·ic** \ˌka-lə-'graf-ik\ *adj*

call–in \'kȯl-ˌin\ *adj* : allowing listeners to engage in broadcast telephone conversations ⟨a ∼ show⟩

call in *vb* **1** : to order to return or be returned **2** : to summon to one's aid **3** : to report by telephone

call·ing \'kȯ-liŋ\ *n* **1** : a strong inner impulse toward a particular course of action **2** : the activity in which one customarily engages as an occupation

cal·li·ope \kə-'lī-ə-(ˌ)pē, 'ka-lē-ˌōp\ *n* [fr. *Calliope*, chief of the Muses, fr. L, fr. Gk *Kalliopē*] : a keyboard musical instrument similar to an organ and made up of a series of whistles

cal·li·per *chiefly Brit var of* CALIPER

call number *n* : a combination of characters assigned to a library book to indicate its place on a shelf

call off *vb* : CANCEL ⟨*called off* the trip⟩

cal·los·i·ty \ka-'lä-sə-tē\ *n, pl* **-ties 1** : the quality or state of being callous ⟨CALLUS 1

¹**cal·lous** \'ka-ləs\ *adj* **1** : being thickened and hardened ⟨∼ skin⟩ **2** : feeling no emotion or sympathy — **cal·lous·ly** *adv* — **cal·lous·ness** *n*

²**callous** *vb* : to make callous

cal·low \'ka-lō\ *adj* [ME *calu* bald, fr. OE] : lacking adult sophistication ⟨a ∼ youth⟩ — **cal·low·ness** *n*

call–up \'kȯ-ˌləp\ *n* : an order to report for active military service

call up *vb* : to summon for active military duty

cal·lus \'ka-ləs\ *n* **1** : a callous area on skin or bark **2** : tissue that is converted into bone in the healing of a bone fracture — **callus** *vb*

call–waiting *n* : a telephone service by which during a call in progress an incoming call is signaled (as by a click)

¹**calm** \'käm, 'kälm\ *n* **1** : a period or a condition free from storms, high winds, or rough water **2** : complete or almost complete absence of wind **3** : a state of tranquillity

²**calm** *vb* : to make or become calm

³**calm** *adj* : marked by calm : STILL, UNRUFFLED — **calm·ly** *adv* — **calm·ness** *n*

cal·o·mel \'ka-lə-məl, -ˌmel\ *n* : a chloride of mercury used esp. as a fungicide

ca·lor·ic \kə-'lȯr-ik\ *adj* **1** : of or relating to heat **2** : of, relating to, or containing calories — **ca·lo·ric·al·ly** \-i-k(ə-)lē\ *adv*

cal·o·rie *also* **cal·o·ry** \'ka-lə-rē\ *n, pl* **-ries** : a unit for measuring heat; *esp* : one for measuring the value of foods for producing heat and energy in the human body equivalent to the amount of heat required to raise the temperature of one kilogram of water one degree Celsius

cal·o·rim·e·ter \ˌka-lə-'ri-mə-tər\ *n* : an apparatus for measuring quantities of heat — **cal·o·rim·e·try** \-trē\ *n*

cal·u·met \'kal-yə-ˌmet, -mət\ *n* : an American Indian ceremonial pipe

ca·lum·ni·ate \kə-'ləm-nē-ˌāt\ *vb* **-at·ed; -at·ing** : to make false and malicious statements about ✦ *Syno-*

nyms DEFAME, MALIGN, LIBEL, SLANDER, TRADUCE — **ca·lum·ni·a·tion** \-ˌləm-nē-'ā-shən\ *n* — **ca·lum·ni·a·tor** \-'ləm-nē-ˌā-tər\ *n*

cal·um·ny \'ka-ləm-nē\ *n, pl* **-nies** : false and malicious accusation — **ca·lum·ni·ous** \kə-'ləm-nē-əs\ *adj*

calve \'kav, 'käv\ *vb* **calved; calv·ing** : to give birth to a calf

calves *pl of* CALF

Cal·vin·ism \'kal-və-ˌni-zəm\ *n* : the theological system of John Calvin and his followers — **Cal·vin·ist** \-nist\ *n or adj* — **Cal·vin·is·tic** \ˌkal-və-'nis-tik\ *adj*

ca·lyp·so \kə-'lip-sō\ *n, pl* **-sos** : a style of music originating in the British West Indies and having lyrics that usu. satirize local personalities and events

ca·lyx \'kā-liks, 'ka-\ *n, pl* **ca·lyx·es** or **ca·ly·ces** \'kā-lə-ˌsēz, 'ka-\ : the usu. green or leaflike outer part of a flower consisting of sepals

cal·zo·ne \kal-'zōn, -'zō-nē\ *n* : a baked or fried turnover of pizza dough stuffed with cheese and various fillings

¹**cam** \'kam\ *n* : a rotating or sliding piece in a mechanical linkage by which rotary motion is transformed into linear motion or vice versa

²**cam** *n* : CAMERA

ca·ma·ra·de·rie \ˌkäm-'rä-də-rē, ˌkam-, -'ra-\ *n* [F] : friendly feeling and goodwill among comrades

cam·bi·um \'kam-bē-əm\ *n, pl* **-bi·ums** or **-bia** \-bē-ə\ : a thin cellular layer between xylem and phloem of most higher plants from which new tissues develop — **cam·bi·al** \-əl\ *adj*

Cam·bri·an \'kam-brē-ən, 'käm-\ *adj* : of, relating to, or being the earliest part of the Paleozoic era — **Cambrian** *n*

cam·bric \'kām-brik\ *n* : a fine thin white linen or cotton fabric

cam·cord·er \'kam-ˌkȯr-dər\ *n* : a small portable combined camera and VCR

came *past of* COME

cam·el \'ka-məl\ *n* : either of two large hoofed cud-chewing mammals used esp. in desert regions of Asia and Africa for carrying and riding

camel hair *also* **camel's hair** *n* **1** : the hair of a camel or a substitute for it **2** : cloth made of camel hair or of camel hair and wool

ca·mel·lia \kə-'mēl-yə\ *n* : any of a genus of shrubs and trees related to the tea plant and grown in warm regions and greenhouses for their showy roselike flowers

Cam·em·bert \'ka-məm-ˌber\ *n* : a soft cheese with a grayish rind and yellow interior

cam·eo \'ka-mē-ˌō\ *n, pl* **-eos 1** : a gem carved in relief; *also* : a small medallion with a profiled head in relief **2** : a brief appearance esp. by a well-known actor in a play or movie

cam·era \'kam-rə, 'ka-mər-ə\ *n* : a device with a lightproof chamber fitted with a lens through which the image of an object is projected onto a surface for recording (as on film) or for conversion into electrical signals (as for television broadcast) — **cam·era·man** \-ˌman, -mən\ *n* — **cam·era·wom·an** *n*

cam·i·sole \'ka-mə-ˌsōl\ *n* : a short sleeveless garment for women

camomile *var of* CHAMOMILE

cam·ou·flage \'ka-mə-ˌfläzh, -ˌfläj\ *n* [F] **1** : the disguising of military equipment with paint, nets, or foliage; *also* : the disguise itself **2** : deceptive behavior — **camouflage** *vb*

¹**camp** \'kamp\ *n* **1** : a place where tents or buildings are erected for usu. temporary shelter **2** : a collection of tents or other shelters **3** : a program offering recreational activities (as boating and hiking) for a limited time ⟨summer ∼⟩ **4** : a body of persons encamped **5** : a training session for athletes outside of the regular season — **camp·ground** \-ˌgraṻnd\ *n* — **camp·site** \-ˌsīt\ *n*

calumet

²camp vb **1** : to make or occupy a camp **2** : to live in a camp or outdoors
³camp n **1** : exaggerated effeminate mannerisms **2** : something so outrageous, inappropriate, or theatrical as to be considered amusing — **camp** adj — **camp·i·ly** \'kam-pə-lē\ adv — **camp·i·ness** \-pē-nəs\ n — **campy** \-pē\ adj
⁴camp vb : to engage in camp : exhibit the qualities of camp
cam·paign \kam-'pān\ n **1** : a series of military operations forming one distinct stage in a war **2** : a series of activities designed to bring about a particular result ⟨advertising ∼⟩ — **campaign** vb — **cam·paign·er** n
cam·pa·ni·le \ₐkam-pə-'nē-lē\ n, pl **-ni·les** or **-ni·li** \-'nē-lē\ : a usu. freestanding bell tower
cam·pa·nol·o·gy \ₐkam-pə-'nä-lə-jē\ n : the art of bell ringing — **cam·pa·nol·o·gist** \-jist\ n
camp·er \'kam-pər\ n **1** : one who camps **2** : a portable dwelling (as a specially equipped vehicle) for use during casual travel and camping
Camp Fire Girl n : a member of a national organization of girls from ages 5 to 18
camp follower n **1** : a civilian (as a prostitute) who follows a military unit to attend or exploit its personnel **2** : a follower of a group who is not an adherent; esp : a politician who joins a movement solely for personal gain
cam·phor \'kam-fər\ n : a gummy volatile aromatic compound obtained from an evergreen Asian tree (**camphor tree**) and used esp. in medicine
camp meeting n : a series of evangelistic meetings usu. held outdoors
camp·o·ree \ₐkam-pə-'rē\ n : a gathering of Boy Scouts or Girl Scouts from a given geographic area
cam·pus \'kam-pəs\ n [L, plain] : the grounds and buildings of a college or school; also : grounds resembling a campus ⟨hospital ∼⟩
cam·shaft \'kam-ₐshaft\ n : a shaft to which a cam is fastened
¹can \kən, 'kan\ vb, past **could** \kəd, 'kùd\; pres sing & pl **can 1** : be able to **2** : may perhaps ⟨∼ he still be alive⟩ **3** : be permitted by conscience or feeling to ⟨you ∼ hardly blame her⟩ **4** : have permission to ⟨you ∼ go now⟩
²can \'kan\ n **1** : a usu. cylindrical container or receptacle ⟨garbage ∼⟩ ⟨coffee ∼⟩ **2** : JAIL **3** : TOILET
³can \'kan\ vb **canned; can·ning 1** : to put in a can : preserve by sealing in airtight cans or jars **2** slang : to discharge from employment **3** slang : to put a stop or an end to — **can·ner** n
Can or **Canad** abbr Canada; Canadian
Can·a·da goose \'ka-nə-də-\ n : a common wild goose of No. America
ca·naille \kə-'nī, -'nāl\ n [F, fr. It canaglia, fr. cane dog] : RABBLE, RIFFRAFF
ca·nal \kə-'nal\ n **1** : a tubular passage in the body : DUCT **2** : an artificial waterway (as for boats or irrigation)
can·a·lize \'kan-ᵊl-ₐīz\ vb **-lized; -liz·ing 1** : to provide with a canal or make into or like a channel **2** : to provide with an outlet; esp : to direct into preferred channels — **ca·nal·i·za·tion** \ₐkan-ᵊl-ə-'zā-shən\ n
can·a·pé \'ka-nə-pē, -ₐpā\ n [F, lit., sofa, fr. ML canopeum, canapeum mosquito net] : a piece of bread or toast or a cracker topped with a savory food
ca·nard \kə-'närd\ n : a false or unfounded report, story or belief
ca·nary \kə-'ner-ē\ n, pl **ca·nar·ies** [fr. the Canary islands] **1** : a usu. sweet wine similar to Madeira **2** : a usu. yellow or greenish finch often kept in a cage as a pet
ca·nas·ta \kə-'nas-tə\ n [Sp, lit., basket] : rummy played with two full decks of cards plus four jokers
canc abbr canceled
can·can \'kan-ₐkan\ n : a woman's dance of French origin characterized by high kicking
¹can·cel \'kan-səl\ vb **-celed** or **-celled; -cel·ing** or **-cel·ling** [ME cancellen, fr. AF canceller, chanceller, fr. LL cancellare, fr. L, to make like a lattice, fr. cancelli lattice] **1** : to destroy the force or validity of : ANNUL **2** : to match in force or effect : OFFSET **3** : to cross out : DELETE **4** : to remove (a common divisor) from a numerator and denominator; also : to remove (equivalents) on opposite sides of an equation or account **5** : to mark (a postage

stamp or check) so that it cannot be reused **6** : to neutralize each other's strength or effect — **can·cel·la·tion** \ₐkan-sə-'lā-shən\ n — **can·cel·er** or **can·cel·ler** n
²cancel n **1** : CANCELLATION **2** : a deleted part
can·cer \'kan-sər\ n [L, lit., crab] **1** cap : a zodiacal constellation between Gemini and Leo usu. pictured as a crab **2** cap : the 4th sign of the zodiac in astrology; also : one born under this sign **3** : a malignant tumor that tends to spread in the body; also : an abnormal state marked by such tumors **4** : a malignant evil that spreads destructively — **can·cer·ous** \-sə-rəs\ adj — **can·cer·ous·ly** adv
can·de·la·bra \ₐkan-də-'lä-brə, -'la-\ n : an ornamental branched candlestick or lamp with several lights
can·de·la·brum \-brəm\ n, pl **-bra** also **-brums** : CANDELABRA
can·did \'kan-dəd\ adj **1** : FRANK, STRAIGHTFORWARD ⟨a ∼ critique⟩ **2** : relating to photography of subjects acting naturally or spontaneously without being posed — **can·did·ly** adv — **can·did·ness** n
can·di·da·cy \'kan-də-də-sē\ n, pl **-cies** : the state of being a candidate
can·di·date \'kan-də-ₐdāt, 'ka-nə-, -dət\ n [L candidatus, fr. candidatus clothed in white, fr. candidus white; fr. the white toga worn by office seekers in ancient Rome] : one who seeks or is proposed for an office, honor, or membership ⟨a ∼ for governor⟩
can·di·da·ture \'kan-də-də-ₐchùr, 'ka-nə-\ n, chiefly Brit : CANDIDACY
can·died \'kan-dēd\ adj : preserved in or encrusted with sugar
¹can·dle \'kan-dᵊl\ n : a usu. slender mass of tallow or wax molded around a wick that is burned to give light
²candle vb **can·dled; can·dling** : to examine (as eggs) by holding between the eye and a light — **can·dler** n
can·dle·light \'kan-dᵊl-līt\ n **1** : the light of a candle; also : any soft artificial light **2** : the time when candles are lit : TWILIGHT
can·dle·lit \-ₐlit\ adj : illuminated by candlelight ⟨a ∼ dinner⟩
Can·dle·mas \'kan-dᵊl-məs\ n : February 2 observed as a church festival in commemoration of the presentation of Christ in the temple
can·dle·stick \-ₐstik\ n : a holder with a socket for a candle
can·dle·wick \-ₐwik\ n : a soft cotton yarn; also : embroidery made with this yarn usu. in tufts
can·dor \'kan-dər\ n : FRANKNESS, OUTSPOKENNESS
can·dour chiefly Brit var of CANDOR
C and W abbr country and western
¹can·dy \'kan-dē\ n, pl **candies** [ME sugre candy, fr. MF sucre candi, fr. OF sucre sugar + Ar qandī candied, fr. qand crystallized sugar] **1** : a confection made from sugar often with flavoring and filling **2** : something that appeals in a light or frivolous way
²candy vb **can·died; can·dy·ing 1** : to encrust in sugar often by cooking in a syrup
candy strip·er \-'strī-pər\ n : a teenage volunteer worker at a hospital
¹cane \'kān\ n **1** : a slender hollow or pithy stem (as of a reed or bramble) **2** : a tall woody grass or reed (as sugarcane or sorghum) **3** : a walking stick; also : a rod for flogging
²cane vb **caned; can·ing 1** : to beat with a cane **2** : to weave or make with cane — **can·er** n
cane·brake \'kān-ₐbrāk\ n : a thicket of cane
¹ca·nine \'kā-ₐnīn\ n **1** : a pointed tooth between the outer incisor and the first premolar **2** : a canine mammal (as a domestic dog)
²canine adj [L caninus, fr. canis dog] : of or relating to dogs or to the family to which they belong
can·is·ter \'ka-nə-stər\ n : an often cylindrical container
can·ker \'kaŋ-kər\ n : a spreading sore that eats into tissue — **can·ker·ous** \-kə-rəs\ adj
can·ker·worm \-ₐwərm\ n : either of two moths and esp. their larvae that are pests of fruit and shade trees
can·na \'ka-nə\ n : any of a genus of tropical herbs with large leaves and racemes of bright-colored flowers
can·na·bis \'ka-nə-bəs\ n : any of the psychoactive preparations (as marijuana) or chemicals (as THC) derived from hemp; also : HEMP

canned \'kand\ *adj* : prepared in standardized form for general use or wide distribution ⟨∼ music⟩

can·nery \'ka-nə-rē\ *n, pl* **-ner·ies** : a factory for the canning of foods

can·ni·bal \'ka-nə-bəl\ *n* [NL *Canibalis* a member of a Caribbean Indian people, fr. Sp *Canibal*] : one that eats the flesh of its own kind — **can·ni·bal·ism** \-bə-ˌli-zəm\ *n* — **can·ni·bal·is·tic** \-bə-'lis-tik\ *adj*

can·ni·bal·ise *Brit var of* CANNIBALIZE

can·ni·bal·ize \'ka-nə-bə-ˌlīz\ *vb* **-ized; -iz·ing** 1 : to take usable parts from (as an inoperative machine) to construct or repair another machine 2 : to practice cannibalism

can·non \'ka-nən\ *n, pl* **cannons** *or* **cannon** [ME *canon*, fr. AF, fr. It *cannone*, lit., large tube, fr. *canna* reed, tube, fr. L, cane, reed] : a large heavy gun; *esp* : one mounted on a carriage

can·non·ade \ˌka-nə-'nād\ *n* : a heavy fire of artillery — **cannonade** *vb*

can·non·ball \'ka-nən-ˌból\ *n* : a usu. round solid missile for a cannon

can·non·eer \ˌka-nə-'nir\ *n* : an artillery gunner

can·not \'ka-ˌnät; kə-'nät\ : can not — **cannot but** : to be unable to do otherwise than ⟨we *cannot but* wonder why⟩

can·nu·la \'kan-yə-lə\ *n, pl* **-las** *or* **-lae** \-ˌlē\ : a small tube for insertion into a body cavity or into a duct or vessel

can·ny \'ka-nē\ *adj* **can·ni·er; -est** : PRUDENT, SHREWD — **can·ni·ly** \'kan-ᵊl-ē\ *adv* — **can·ni·ness** \'ka-nē-nəs\ *n*

ca·noe \kə-'nü\ *n* : a light narrow boat with sharp ends and curved sides that is usu. propelled by paddles — **canoe** *vb* — **ca·noe·ist** *n*

ca·no·la \kə-'nō-lə\ *n* : a rape plant producing seeds that are low in a toxic acid and yield an edible oil (**canola oil**) high in monounsaturated fatty acids; *also* : this oil

¹can·on \'ka-nən\ *n* 1 : a regulation decreed by a church council; *also* : a provision of canon law 2 : an official or authoritative list (as of works of literature) 3 : an accepted principle ⟨the ∼s of good taste⟩

²canon *n* : a member of the clergy on the staff of a cathedral

ca·non·i·cal \kə-'nä-ni-kəl\ *adj* 1 : of, relating to, or forming a canon 2 : conforming to a general rule or acceptable procedure : ORTHODOX 3 : of or relating to a canon of a cathedral — **ca·non·i·cal·ly** \-k(ə-)lē\ *adv*

can·on·ize \'ka-nə-ˌnīz\ *vb* **can·on·ized** \-ˌnīzd\; **can·on·iz·ing** 1 : to declare (a deceased person) an officially recognized saint 2 : GLORIFY, EXALT — **can·on·i·za·tion** \ˌka-nə-nə-'zā-shən\ *n*

canon law *n* : the law governing a church

can·o·py \'ka-nə-pē\ *n, pl* **-pies** [ME *canope*, fr. ML *canopeum* mosquito net, fr. L *conopeum*, fr. Gk *kōnōpion*, fr. *kōnōps* mosquito] 1 : an overhanging cover, shelter, or shade 2 : the uppermost spreading layer of a forest 3 : a transparent cover for an airplane cockpit 4 : the fabric part of a parachute — **canopy** *vb*

¹cant \'kant\ *vb* : to give a slant to

²cant *n* 1 : an oblique or slanting surface 2 : TILT, SLANT

³cant *vb* 1 : to beg in a whining manner 2 : to talk hypocritically

⁴cant *n* 1 : the special idiom of a profession or trade : JARGON 2 : insincere speech; *esp* : insincerely pious words or statements

Cant *abbr* Canticle of Canticles

can·ta·bi·le \kän-'tä-bə-ˌlā\ *adv or adj* [It] : in a singing manner — used as a direction in music

can·ta·loupe *also* **can·ta·loup** \'kant-ᵊl-ˌōp\ *n* : MUSKMELON; *esp* : one with orange flesh and rough skin

can·tan·ker·ous \kan-'taŋ-kə-rəs\ *adj* : difficult to deal with : ILL-NATURED ⟨a ∼ mule⟩ — **can·tan·ker·ous·ly** *adv* — **can·tan·ker·ous·ness** *n*

can·ta·ta \kən-'tä-tə\ *n* [It] : a choral composition usu. sung to instrumental accompaniment

can·teen \kan-'tēn\ *n* [F *cantine* bottle case, canteen (store), fr. It *cantina* wine cellar] 1 : a flask for carrying liquids 2 : a place of recreation and entertainment for military personnel 3 : a small cafeteria or counter at which snacks are served

can·ter \'kan-tər\ *n* : a horse's 3-beat gait resembling but smoother and slower than a gallop — **canter** *vb*

Can·ter·bury bell \'kant-ər-ˌber-ē-\ *n* : any of several plants related to the bluebell that are cultivated for their showy flowers

can·ti·cle \'kan-ti-kəl\ *n* : SONG; *esp* : any of several liturgical songs taken from the Bible

Canticle of Canticles *n* : SONG OF SONGS

¹can·ti·le·ver \'kant-ᵊl-ˌē-vər\ *n* : a projecting beam or structure supported only at one end; *also* : either of a pair of such structures projecting toward each other so that when joined they form a bridge

²cantilever *vb* 1 : to support by a cantilever ⟨a ∼ed shelf⟩ 2 : to build as a cantilever 3 : to project as a cantilever

can·tle \'kant-ᵊl\ *n* : the upwardly projecting rear part of a saddle

can·to \'kan-ˌtō\ *n, pl* **cantos** [It, fr. L *cantus* song] : one of the major divisions of a long poem

can·ton \'kant-ᵊn, 'kan-ˌtän\ *n* : a small territorial division of a country; *esp* : one of the political divisions of Switzerland — **can·ton·al** \'kant-ᵊn-əl, kan-'tän-ᵊl\ *adj*

can·ton·ment \kan-'tōn-mənt, -'tän-\ *n* : usu. temporary quarters for troops

can·tor \'kan-tər\ *n* 1 : a choir leader 2 : a synagogue official who sings liturgical music and leads the congregation in prayer

can·vas *also* **can·vass** \'kan-vəs\ *n* 1 : a strong cloth formerly much used for making tents and sails 2 : a set of sails 3 : a group of tents 4 : a piece of cloth prepared as a surface for a painting; *also* : a painting on this surface 5 : the canvas-covered floor of a boxing or wrestling ring

can·vas·back \'kan-vəs-ˌbak\ *n* : a No. American wild duck with red head and gray back

¹can·vass *also* **can·vas** \'kan-vəs\ *vb* **can·vassed; can·vas·sing** : to go through (a district) or to (persons) to solicit votes or orders for goods or to determine public opinion or sentiment — **can·vass·er** *n*

²canvass *n* : an act or instance of canvassing

can·yon \'kan-yən\ *n* : a deep narrow valley with high steep sides

¹cap \'kap\ *n* 1 : a covering for the head esp. with a visor and no brim; *also* : something resembling such a covering esp. on a tip, knob or end ⟨a bottle ∼⟩ 2 : a container holding an explosive charge (as for a toy gun) 3 : an upper limit (as on expenditures)

²cap *vb* **capped; cap·ping** 1 : to provide or protect with a cap 2 : to form a cap over : CROWN ⟨snow-*capped* mountains⟩ 3 : OUTDO, SURPASS 4 : to bring to a conclusion ⟨∼ off dinner with coffee⟩

³cap *abbr* 1 capacity 2 capital 3 capitalize; capitalized

CAP *abbr* Civil Air Patrol

ca·pa·ble \'kā-pə-bəl\ *adj* : having ability, capacity, or power to do something : ABLE, COMPETENT — **ca·pa·bil·i·ty** \ˌkā-pə-'bi-lə-tē\ *n* — **ca·pa·bly** *adv*

ca·pa·cious \kə-'pā-shəs\ *adj* : able to contain much — **ca·pa·cious·ly** *adv* — **ca·pa·cious·ness** *n*

ca·pac·i·tance \kə-'pa-sə-təns\ *n* : the property of an electric nonconductor that permits the storage of energy

ca·pac·i·tor \kə-'pa-sə-tər\ *n* : an electronic circuit device for temporary storage of electrical energy

¹ca·pac·i·ty \kə-'pa-sə-tē\ *n, pl* **-ties** 1 : legal qualification or fitness ⟨∼ to stand trial⟩ 2 : the ability to contain, receive, or accommodate ⟨seating ∼⟩ 3 : the maximum amount or number that can be contained — see METRIC SYSTEM table, WEIGHT table 4 : ABILITY 5 : position or character assigned or assumed

²capacity *adj* : equaling maximum capacity ⟨a ∼ crowd⟩

cap–a–pie *or* **cap–à–pie** \ˌka-pə-'pē\ *adv* [MF] : from head to foot : at all points

ca·par·i·son \kə-'par-ə-sən\ *n* 1 : an ornamental covering for a horse 2 : TRAPPINGS, ADORNMENT — **caparison** *vb*

¹cape \'kāp\ *n* 1 : a point of land jutting out into water 2 *often cap* : CAPE COD COTTAGE

²cape *n* : a sleeveless garment hanging from the neck over the shoulders — **caped** *adj*

Cape Cod cottage \'kāp-'käd-\ *n* : a compact rectangular dwelling of one or one-and-a-half stories usu. with a steep gable roof

¹ca·per \'kā-pər\ *n* : the greenish flower bud or young berry of a Mediterranean shrub pickled for use as a relish; *also* : this shrub

²**caper** *vb* ca·pered; ca·per·ing : to leap about in a playful manner

³**caper** *n* 1 : a frolicsome leap 2 : a capricious escapade 3 : an illegal or questionable act

cape·skin \'kāp-ˌskin\ *n* : a light flexible leather made from sheepskins

cap·ful \'kap-ˌfúl\ *n, pl* **cap·fuls** *also* **caps·ful** \'kaps-\ : as much as a cap will hold

cap·il·lar·i·ty \ˌka-pə-ˈlar-ə-tē\ *n, pl* **-ties** : the action by which the surface of a liquid where it is in contact with a solid (as in a slender tube) is raised or lowered depending on the relative attraction of the molecules of the liquid for each other and for those of the solid

¹**cap·il·lary** \'ka-pə-ˌler-ē\ *adj* 1 : resembling a hair 2 : having a very small bore ⟨∼ tube⟩ 3 : of or relating to capillaries or to capillarity

²**capillary** *n, pl* **-lar·ies** : any of the tiny thin-walled blood vessels that carry blood between the smallest arteries and their corresponding veins

¹**cap·i·tal** \'ka-pət-ᵊl\ *n* : the top part or piece of an architectural column

¹**capital: different styles**

²**capital** *adj* 1 : conforming to the series A, B, C rather than a, b, c ⟨∼ letters⟩ ⟨∼ G⟩ 2 : punishable by death ⟨a ∼ crime⟩ 3 : most serious ⟨a ∼ error⟩ 4 : first in importance or position : CHIEF; *also* : being the seat of government ⟨the ∼ city⟩ 5 : of or relating to capital ⟨∼ expenditures⟩; *esp* : relating to or being assets that add to the long-term net worth of a corporation 6 : FIRST-RATE, EXCELLENT

³**capital** *n* 1 : accumulated wealth esp. as used to produce more wealth 2 : the total face value of shares of stock issued by a company 3 : persons holding capital 4 : ADVANTAGE, GAIN 5 : a letter larger than the ordinary small letter and often different in form 6 : the capital city of a state, province or country; *also* : a city preeminent in some activity ⟨the fashion ∼⟩

capital gain *n* : the increase in value of an asset (as stock or real estate) between the time it is bought and the time it is sold

capital goods *n pl* : machinery, tools, factories, and commodities used in the production of goods

cap·i·tal·ise *Brit var of* CAPITALIZE

cap·i·tal·ism \'ka-pət-ᵊl-ˌi-zəm\ *n* : an economic system characterized by private or corporate ownership of capital goods and by prices, production, and distribution of goods that are determined mainly by competition in a free market

¹**cap·i·tal·ist** \-ist\ *n* 1 : a person who has capital esp. invested in business 2 : a person of great wealth : PLUTOCRAT 3 : a believer in capitalism

²**capitalist** *or* **cap·i·tal·is·tic** \ˌka-pət-ᵊl-ˈis-tik\ *adj* 1 : owning capital 2 : practicing or advocating capitalism 3 : marked by capitalism — **cap·i·tal·is·ti·cal·ly** \-ti-k(ə-)lē\ *adv*

cap·i·tal·iza·tion \ˌka-pət-ᵊl-ə-ˈzā-shən\ *n* 1 : the act or process of capitalizing 2 : the total amount of money used as capital in a business

cap·i·tal·ize \'ka-pət-ᵊl-ˌīz\ *vb* **-ized; -iz·ing** 1 : to write or print with an initial capital or in capitals 2 : to convert into or use as capital 3 : to supply capital for 4 : to gain by turning something to advantage : PROFIT

cap·i·tal·ly \'ka-pət-ᵊl-ē\ *adv* : ADMIRABLY, EXCELLENTLY

cap·i·ta·tion \ˌka-pə-ˈtā-shən\ *n* : a direct uniform tax levied on each person

cap·i·tol \'ka-pət-ᵊl\ *n* : the building in which a legislature holds its sessions

ca·pit·u·late \kə-ˈpi-chə-ˌlāt\ *vb* **-lat·ed; -lat·ing** 1 : to surrender esp. on conditions agreed upon 2 : to cease resisting : ACQUIESCE ♦ **Synonyms** SUBMIT, YIELD, SUCCUMB, CAVE, DEFER — **ca·pit·u·la·tion** \-ˌpi-chə-ˈlā-shən\ *n*

cap·let \'ka-plət\ *n* : a capsule-shaped medicinal tablet

ca·pon \'kā-ˌpän, -pən\ *n* : a castrated male chicken

cap·puc·ci·no \ˌka-pə-ˈchē-nō, ˌkä-\ *n* [It, lit., Capuchin; fr. the likeness of its color to that of a Capuchin's habit] : espresso mixed with foamy hot milk or cream and often flavored with cinnamon

ca·pric·cio \kə-ˈprē-chē-ˌō, -chō\ *n, pl* **-cios** [It, lit., whim, prank] : an instrumental piece in free form usu. lively in tempo and brilliant in style

ca·price \kə-ˈprēs\ *n* [F, fr. It *capriccio*] 1 : a sudden whim or fancy 2 : an inclination to do things impulsively 3 : CAPRICCIO — **ca·pri·cious** \-ˈpri-shəs\ *adj* — **ca·pri·cious·ly** *adv* — **ca·pri·cious·ness** *n*

Cap·ri·corn \'ka-pri-ˌkòrn\ *n* 1 : a zodiacal constellation between Sagittarius and Aquarius usu. pictured as a goat 2 : the 10th sign of the zodiac in astrology; *also* : one born under this sign

cap·ri·ole \'ka-prē-ˌōl\ *n* : ³CAPER 1; *also* : an upward leap of a horse with a backward kick at the height of the leap — **capriole** *vb*

caps *abbr* 1 capitals 2 capsule

cap·sa·i·cin \kap-ˈsā-ə-sən\ *n* : a colorless compound found in various capsicums that gives hot peppers their hotness

cap·si·cum \'kap-si-kəm\ *n* : PEPPER 2

cap·size \'kap-ˌsīz, kap-ˈsīz\ *vb* **cap·sized; cap·siz·ing** : UPSET, OVERTURN

cap·stan \'kap-stən, -ˌstan\ *n* 1 : a machine for moving or raising heavy weights that consists of a vertical drum which can be rotated and around which cable is turned 2 : a rotating shaft that drives recorder tape

cap·su·lar \'kap-sə-lər\ *adj* : of, relating to, or resembling a capsule

cap·su·lat·ed \-ˌlā-təd\ *adj* : enclosed in a capsule

¹**cap·sule** \'kap-səl, -sül\ *n* 1 : a membrane or sac enclosing a body part (as of a joint) 2 : a case bearing spores or seeds 3 : a shell usu. of gelatin that is used for packaging something (as a drug); *also* : such a shell together with its contents 4 : a small pressurized compartment or vehicle (as for space flight)

²**capsule** *adj* 1 : very brief ⟨a ∼ biography⟩ 2 : very compact ⟨a ∼ camera⟩

Capt *abbr* captain

¹**cap·tain** \'kap-tən\ *n* 1 : a commander of a body of troops 2 : a commissioned officer in the army, air force, or marine corps ranking below a major 3 : an officer in charge of a ship 4 : a commissioned officer in the navy ranking next below a rear admiral or a commodore 5 : a leader of a side or team 6 : a dominant figure — **cap·tain·cy** *n*

²**captain** *vb* : to be captain of : LEAD

cap·tion \'kap-shən\ *n* 1 : a heading esp. of an article or document : TITLE 2 : the explanatory matter accompanying an illustration 3 : a motion-picture subtitle — **cap·tion** *vb*

cap·tious \'kap-shəs\ *adj* : marked by an inclination to find fault — **cap·tious·ly** *adv* — **cap·tious·ness** *n*

cap·ti·vate \'kap-tə-ˌvāt\ *vb* **-vat·ed; -vat·ing** : to attract and hold irresistibly by some special charm or art — **cap·ti·va·tion** \ˌkap-tə-ˈvā-shən\ *n* — **cap·ti·va·tor** \'kap-tə-ˌvā-tər\ *n*

cap·tive \'kap-tiv\ *adj* 1 : made prisoner esp. in war 2 : kept within bounds : CONFINED 3 : held under control — **captive** *n* — **cap·tiv·i·ty** \kap-ˈti-və-tē\ *n*

cap·tor \'kap-tər\ *n* : one that captures

¹**cap·ture** \'kap-chər\ *n* 1 : the act of capturing 2 : one that has been captured

²**capture** *vb* **cap·tured; cap·tur·ing** 1 : to take captive : WIN, GAIN ⟨∼ the enemy⟩ 2 : to preserve in a relatively permanent form ⟨∼ the moment on film⟩

Ca·pu·chin \'ka-pyə-shən\ *n* : a member of an austere branch of the order of St. Francis of Assisi engaged in missionary work and preaching

car \'kär\ *n* 1 : a vehicle moving on wheels 2 : the compartment of an elevator 3 : the part of a balloon or airship that carries passengers or equipment

car·a·cole \'kar-ə-ˌkōl\ *n* : a half turn to right or left executed by a mounted horse — **caracole** *vb*

car·a·cul \'kar-ə-ˌkəl\ *n* : the pelt of a karakul lamb after the curl begins to loosen

ca·rafe \kə-ˈraf, -ˈräf\ *n* 1 : a bottle with a flaring lip used esp. to hold wine   2 : a usu. glass pitcher for pouring coffee

car·am·bo·la \ˌkar-əm-'bō-lə\ *n*   1 : a 5-angled green to yellow edible tropical fruit of star-shaped cross section   2 : a tropical Asian tree widely cultivated for carambolas

car·a·mel \'kar-ə-məl, 'kär-məl\ *n*   1 : an amorphous substance obtained by heating sugar and used for flavoring and coloring   2 : a firm chewy candy

car·a·pace \'kar-ə-ˌpās\ *n* : a protective case or shell on the back of some animals (as turtles or crabs)

¹carat *var of* KARAT

²car·at \'kar-ət\ *n* : a unit of weight for precious stones equal to 200 milligrams

car·a·van \'kar-ə-ˌvan\ *n*   1 : a group of travelers journeying together through desert or hostile regions   2 : a group of vehicles traveling in a file

car·a·van·sa·ry \ˌkar-ə-'van-sə-rē\ *or* **car·a·van·se·rai** \-sə-ˌrī\ *n, pl* **-ries** *or* **-rais** *or* **-rai** [Pers *kārvānsarāī*, fr. *kārvān* caravan + *sarāī* palace, inn]   1 : an inn in eastern countries where caravans rest at night   2 : HOTEL, INN

car·a·vel \'kar-ə-ˌvel\ *n* : a small 15th and 16th century ship with a broad bow, high narrow poop, and usu. three masts

car·a·way \'kar-ə-ˌwā\ *n* : an aromatic herb related to the carrot with fruits (**caraway seed**) used in seasoning and medicine; *also* : its fruit

car·bide \'kär-ˌbīd\ *n* : a compound of carbon with another element

car·bine \'kär-ˌbēn, -ˌbīn\ *n* : a short-barreled lightweight rifle

car·bo·hy·drate \ˌkär-bō-'hī-ˌdrāt, -drət\ *n* : any of various compounds composed of carbon, hydrogen, and oxygen (as sugars and starches)

car·bol·ic acid \ˌkär-'bä-lik-\ *n* : PHENOL

car·bon \'kär-bən\ *n*   1 : a nonmetallic chemical element occurring in nature esp. as diamond and graphite and as a constituent of coal, petroleum, and limestone   2 : a sheet of carbon paper; *also* : CARBON COPY 1 — **car·bon·less** \-ləs\ *adj*

car·bo·na·ceous \ˌkär-bə-'nā-shəs\ *adj* : relating to, containing, or composed of carbon

¹car·bon·ate \'kär-bə-ˌnāt, -nət\ *n* : a salt or ester of carbonic acid

²car·bon·ate \-ˌnāt\ *vb* **-at·ed; -at·ing** : to combine or infuse with carbon dioxide ⟨*carbonated* beverages⟩ — **car·bon·ation** \ˌkär-bə-'nā-shən\ *n*

carbon black *n* : any of various black substances consisting chiefly of carbon and used esp. as pigments

carbon copy *n*   1 : a copy made by carbon paper   2 : DUPLICATE

carbon dating *n* : the determination of the age of old material (as an archaeological specimen) by its content of carbon 14

carbon dioxide *n* : a heavy colorless gas that does not support combustion and is formed in animal respiration and in the combustion and decomposition of organic substances

carbon footprint *n* : the amount of carbon dioxide emitted by something in a given period

carbon 14 *n* : a heavy radioactive form of carbon used esp. in dating old materials (as archaeological specimens)

car·bon·ic acid \kär-'bä-nik-\ *n* : a weak acid that decomposes readily into water and carbon dioxide

car·bon·if·er·ous \ˌkär-bə-'ni-fə-rəs\ *adj*   1 : producing or containing carbon or coal   2 *cap* : of, relating to, or being the period of the Paleozoic era between the Devonian and the Permian — **Carboniferous** *n*

carbon monoxide *n* : a colorless odorless very poisonous gas formed by the incomplete burning of carbon

carbon paper *n* : a thin paper coated with a pigment and used for making copies

carbon tet·ra·chlo·ride \-ˌte-trə-'klōr-ˌīd\ *n* : a colorless nonflammable toxic liquid used esp. as a solvent

carbon 12 *n* : the most abundant isotope of carbon having a nucleus of 6 protons and 6 neutrons and used as a standard for measurements of atomic weight

car·boy \'kär-ˌbȯi\ *n* [Pers *qarāba*, fr. Ar *qarrāba* demijohn] : a large container for liquids

car·bun·cle \'kär-ˌbən-kəl\ *n* : a painful inflammation of the skin and underlying tissue that discharges pus from several openings

car·bu·re·tor \'kär-bə-ˌrā-tər, -byə-\ *n* : an apparatus for premixing vaporized fuel and air and supplying the mixture to an internal combustion engine

car·bu·ret·tor *also* **car·bu·ret·ter** \ˌkär-byə-'re-tər, 'kär-byə-ˌ\ *chiefly Brit var of* CARBURETOR

car·case *Brit var of* CARCASS

car·cass \'kär-kəs\ *n* : a dead body; *esp* : one of an animal dressed for food

car·cin·o·gen \kär-'si-nə-jən\ *n* : a substance or agent causing cancer — **car·ci·no·gen·ic** \ˌkärs-ᵊn-ō-'je-nik\ *adj* — **car·ci·no·ge·nic·i·ty** \-jə-'ni-sə-tē\ *n*

car·ci·no·ma \ˌkärs-ᵊn-'ō-mə\ *n, pl* **-mas** *also* **-ma·ta** \-tə\ : a malignant tumor of epithelial origin — **car·ci·no·ma·tous** \-təs\ *adj*

¹card \'kärd\ *vb* : to comb with a card : cleanse and untangle before spinning ⟨~ed cotton⟩ — **card·er** *n*

²card *n* : an instrument for combing fibers (as wool or cotton)

³card *n*   1 : PLAYING CARD   2 *pl* : a game played with playing cards; *also* : card playing   3 : an emotional issue used to one's advantage (as in a political campaign)   4 : a usu. clownishly amusing person • WAG   5 : a flat stiff usu. small piece of paper, cardboard, or plastic often bearing pictures or information   6 : PROGRAM; *esp* : a sports program — **in the cards** : INEVITABLE

⁴card *vb*   1 : to list or schedule on a card   2 : SCORE   3 : to ask for identification (as at a bar)

⁵card *abbr* cardinal

car·da·mom \'kär-də-məm\ *n* : the aromatic capsular fruit of an Indian herb related to the ginger whose seeds are used as a spice or condiment and in medicine; *also* : this plant

card·board \'kärd-ˌbȯrd\ *n* : a material thicker than paper and made from cellulose fiber

card–car·ry·ing \'kärd-ˌkar-ē-iŋ\ *adj* : being a regularly enrolled member of an organization (as a political party)

card catalog *n* : a catalog (as of books) in which the entries are arranged systematically on cards

car·di·ac \'kär-dē-ˌak\ *adj* [L *cardiacus*, fr. Gk *kardiakos*, fr. *kardia* heart]   1 : of, relating to, or located near the heart   2 : of, relating to, or affected with heart disease ⟨~ patients⟩

car·di·gan \'kär-di-gən\ *n* : a sweater or jacket usu. without a collar and with a full-length opening in the front

¹car·di·nal \'kärd-nəl, 'kär-dᵊn-əl\ *n*   1 : an ecclesiastical official of the Roman Catholic Church ranking next below the pope   2 : a crested No. American finch that is nearly completely red in the male

²cardinal *adj* [ME, fr. LL *cardinalis*, fr. L serving as a hinge, fr. *cardo* hinge]   1 : of basic importance : CHIEF, MAIN, PRIMARY ⟨a ~ principle⟩   2 : very serious ⟨a ~ sin⟩ — **car·di·nal·ly** *adv*

car·di·nal·ate \'kärd-nə-lət, -'kär-dᵊn-ə-let, -ˌlāt\ *n* : the office, rank, or dignity of a cardinal

cardinal flower *n* : a No. American plant that bears a spike of brilliant red flowers

cardinal number *n* : a number (as 1, 5, 82, 357) that is used in simple counting and answers the question "how many?" — compare ORDINAL NUMBER

cardinal point *n* : one of the four principal compass points north, south, east, and west

car·dio \'kär-dē-ō\ *adj* : CARDIOVASCULAR 2

car·di·ol·o·gy \ˌkär-dē-'ä-lə-jē\ *n* : the study of the heart and its action and diseases — **car·di·ol·o·gist** \-jist\ *n*

car·dio·pul·mo·nary resuscitation \ˌkär-dē-ō-'pu̇l-mə-ˌner-ē-\ *n* : a procedure to restore normal breathing after cardiac arrest that includes the clearance of air passages to the lungs, mouth-to-mouth method of artificial respiration, and heart massage by the exertion of pressure on the chest

car·dio·vas·cu·lar \-'vas-kyə-lər\ *adj*   1 : of or relating to the heart and blood vessels   2 : causing a temporary increase in heart rate ⟨a ~ workout⟩

card·sharp \-ˌshärp\ *or* **card·sharp·er** \'kärd-ˌshär-pər\ *n* : a cheater at cards

¹care \'ker\ *n*   1 : a disquieted state of uncertainty and responsibility : ANXIETY   2 : watchful attention : HEED   3 : CHARGE, SUPERVISION ⟨under a doctor's ~⟩   4 : a person or thing that is an object of anxiety or solicitude

²care *vb* **cared; car·ing**   1 : to feel anxiety   2 : to feel interest   3 : to give care   4 : to have a liking, fondness, taste, or inclination **5** : to be concerned about ⟨∼ what happens⟩

CARE *abbr* Cooperative for American Relief to Everywhere

ca·reen \kə-'rēn\ *vb* **1** : to put (a ship or boat) on a beach esp. in order to clean or repair its hull **2** : to sway from side to side **3** : CAREER

¹**ca·reer** \kə-'rir\ *n* [MF *carrière*, fr. Old Occitan *carriera* street, fr. ML *carraria* road for vehicles, fr. L *carrus* car] **1** : COURSE, PASSAGE; *also* : speed in a course ⟨ran at full ∼⟩ **2** : an occupation or profession followed as a life's work

²**career** *vb* : to go at top speed esp. in a headless manner

care-free \'ker-ˌfrē\ *adj* : free from care or worry

care·ful \-fəl\ *adj* **care·ful·ler; care·ful·lest** **1** : using or taking care : VIGILANT **2** : marked by solicitude, caution, or prudence — **care·ful·ly** *adv* — **care·ful·ness** *n*

care·giv·er \-ˌgi-vər\ *n* : a person who provides direct care (as for children, elderly people, or the chronically ill)

care·less \-ləs\ *adj* **1** : free from care : UNTROUBLED **2** : UNCONCERNED, INDIFFERENT ⟨∼ of the consequences⟩ **3** : not taking care **4** : not showing or receiving care — **care·less·ly** *adv* — **care·less·ness** *n*

care package *n* : a package of useful or pleasurable items given as a gift to another

¹**ca·ress** \kə-'res\ *vb* : to touch or stroke tenderly or lovingly — **ca·ress·er** *n*

²**caress** *n* : a tender or loving touch or embrace

car·et \'ker-ət\ *n* [L, there is lacking, fr. *carēre* to lack, be without] : a mark ^ used to indicate the place where something is to be inserted

care·tak·er \'ker-ˌtā-kər\ *n* **1** : one in charge usu. as occupant in place of an absent owner **2** : one temporarily fulfilling the functions of an office

care·worn \-ˌwórn\ *adj* : showing the effects of grief or anxiety

car·fare \'kär-ˌfer\ *n* : passenger fare (as on a streetcar or bus)

car·go \'kär-gō\ *n, pl* **cargoes** *or* **cargos** : the goods carried in a ship, airplane, or vehicle : FREIGHT

Ca·rib·be·an \ˌkar-ə-'bē-ən, kə-'ri-bē-ən\ *adj* : of or relating to the eastern and southern West Indies or the Caribbean Sea

car·i·bou \'ker-ə-ˌbü\ *n, pl* **caribou** *or* **caribous** : a large circumpolar gregarious deer of northern taiga and tundra that usu. has large branched antlers usu. in both sexes — used esp. for one of the New World

car·i·ca·ture \'ker-i-kə-ˌchùr\ *n* **1** : distorted representation to produce a ridiculous effect **2** : a representation esp. in literature or art having the qualities of caricature — **caricature** *vb* — **car·i·ca·tur·ist** \-ist\ *n*

car·ies \'ker-ēz\ *n, pl* **caries** : tooth decay

car·il·lon \'ker-ə-ˌlän\ *n* : a set of tuned bells sounded by hammers controlled from a keyboard

car·i·ous \'ker-ē-əs\ *adj* : affected with caries

car·jack·ing \'kär-ˌja-kiŋ\ *n* : the theft of an automobile by force or intimidation — **car·jack·er** *n*

car·load \'kär-ˌlōd\ *n* : a load that fills a car

car·mi·na·tive \kär-'mi-nə-tiv\ *adj* : expelling gas from the stomach or intestines — **carminative** *n*

car·mine \'kär-mən, -ˌmīn\ *n* : a vivid red

car·nage \'kär-nij\ *n* : great destruction of life : SLAUGHTER

car·nal \'kär-nəl\ *adj* [ME, fr. LL *carnalis*, fr. L *carn-, caro* flesh] **1** : of or relating to the body **2** : relating to or given to sensual pleasures and appetites — **car·nal·i·ty** \kär-'na-lə-tē\ *n* — **car·nal·ly** *adv*

car·na·tion \kär-'nā-shən\ *n* : a cultivated pink of any of numerous usu. double-flowered varieties derived from an Old World species

car·nau·ba wax \kär-'nó-bə-, -'naú-; ˌkär-nə-'ü-bə-\ *n* : a brittle yellowish wax from a Brazilian palm that is used esp. in polishes

car·ne·lian \kär-'nēl-yən\ *n* : a hard red chalcedony used as a gem

car·ni·val \'kär-nə-vəl\ *n* [It *carnevale*, alter. of *carnelevare*, lit., removal of meat] **1** : a festival of merrymaking just before Lent **2** : a boisterous merrymaking **3** : a traveling enterprise offering amusements **4** : an organized program of entertainment

car·ni·val·esque \ˌkär-nə-və-'lesk\ *adj* : suggestive of a carnival

car·niv·o·ra \kär-'ni-və-rə\ *n pl* : carnivorous mammals

car·ni·vore \'kär-nə-ˌvór\ *n* : a flesh-eating animal; *esp* : any of an order of mammals (as dogs, cats, bears, minks, and seals) feeding mostly on animal flesh

car·niv·o·rous \kär-'ni-və-rəs\ *adj* **1** : feeding on animal tissues **2** : of or relating to the carnivores — **car·niv·o·rous·ly** *adv* — **car·niv·o·rous·ness** *n*

car·ny *or* **car·ney** *or* **car·nie** \'kär-nē\ *n, pl* **carnies** *or* **carneys** **1** : CARNIVAL **3 2** : one who works with a carnival

car·ol \'ker-əl\ *n* : a song of joy or devotion — **carol** *vb* — **car·ol·er** *or* **car·ol·ler** *n*

car·om \'ker-əm\ *n* **1** : a shot in billiards in which the cue ball strikes two other balls **2** : a rebounding esp. at an angle — **carom** *vb*

car·o·tene \'ker-ə-ˌtēn\ *n* : any of several orange to red pigments (as beta-carotene) formed esp. in plants and used as a source of vitamin A

ca·rot·en·oid \kə-'rä-tə-ˌnóid\ *n* : any of various usu. yellow to red pigments (as carotenes) found widely in plants and animals

ca·rot·id \kə-'rä-təd\ *adj* : of, relating to, or being the chief artery or pair of arteries that pass up the neck and supply the head — **carotid** *n*

ca·rous·al \kə-'raú-zəl\ *n* : CAROUSE

ca·rouse \kə-'raúz\ *n* [MF *carrousse*, fr. *carous*, adv., all out (in *boire carous* to empty the cup), fr. G *garaus*] : a drunken revel — **carouse** *vb* — **ca·rous·er** *n*

car·ou·sel *also* **car·rou·sel** \ˌker-ə-'sel, 'kar-ə-ˌsel\ *n* **1** : MERRY-GO-ROUND **2** : a circular conveyor ⟨a baggage ∼⟩

¹**carp** \'kärp\ *vb* : to find fault : CAVIL, COMPLAIN — **carp** *n* — **carp·er** *n*

²**carp** *n, pl* **carp** *or* **carps** : a large variable Asian freshwater fish of sluggish waters often raised for food

¹**car·pal** \'kär-pəl\ *adj* : of or relating to the wrist or the bones of the wrist

²**carpal** *n* : a carpal element or bone

carpal tunnel syndrome *n* : a condition characterized esp. by weakness, pain, and disturbances of sensation (as numbness) in the hand and fingers and caused by compression of a nerve in the wrist

car·pe di·em \ˌkär-pe-'dē-ˌem, -'dī-\ *n* [L, lit., pluck the day] : enjoyment of the present without concern for the future

car·pel \'kär-pəl\ *n* : one of the highly modified leaves that together form the ovary of a flower of a seed plant

car·pen·ter \'kär-pən-tər\ *n* : one who builds or repairs wooden structures — **carpenter** *vb* — **car·pen·try** \-trē\ *n*

car·pet \'kär-pət\ *n* : a heavy fabric used as a floor covering — **carpet** *vb*

car·pet·bag \-ˌbag\ *n* : a traveling bag common in the 19th century

car·pet·bag·ger \-ˌba-gər\ *n* : a Northerner in the South after the American Civil War usu. seeking private gain under the reconstruction governments

car·pet·ing \'kär-pə-tiŋ\ *n* : material for carpets; *also* : CARPETS

car pool *n* : an arrangement in which a group of people commute together by car; *also* : a group having this arrangement — **car·pool** \-ˌpül\ *vb*

car·port \'kär-ˌpórt\ *n* : an open-sided automobile shelter

car·pus \'kär-pəs\ *n* : the wrist or its bones

car·ra·geen·an *or* **car·ra·geen·in** \ˌker-ə-'gē-nən\ *n* : a colloid extracted esp. from a dark purple branching seaweed and used in foods esp. to stabilize and thicken them

car·rel \'ker-əl\ *n* : a table often partitioned or enclosed for individual study in a library

car·riage \'ker-ij\ *n* **1** : the act of carrying **2** : manner of holding the body **3** : a wheeled vehicle **4** *Brit* : a railway passenger coach **5** : a movable part of a machine for supporting some other moving part ⟨a typewriter ∼⟩

carriage trade *n* : trade from well-to-do or upper-class people

car·ri·er \'ker-ē-ər\ *n* **1** : one that carries **2** : a person or organization in the transportation business **3** : AIRCRAFT CARRIER **4** : one whose system carries the causative agents of a disease but who is immune to the disease **5** : an individual having a gene for a trait or condition that

is not expressed outwardly **6** : an electromagnetic wave whose amplitude or frequency is varied in order to convey a radio or television signal
carrier pigeon *n* : a pigeon used esp. to carry messages
car·ri·on \\'ker-ē-ən\ *n* : dead and decaying flesh
car·rot \\'ker-ət\ *n* : the elongated usu. orange root of a common garden plant that is eaten as a vegetable; *also* : this plant
carrousel *var of* CAROUSEL
¹**car·ry** \\'ka-rē, 'ker-ē\ *vb* **car·ried; car·ry·ing** [ME *carien*, fr. AF *carier*, fr. *carre* vehicle, fr. L *carrus*] **1** : to move while supporting : TRANSPORT, CONVEY, TAKE **2** : to influence by mental or emotional appeal **3** : to get possession or control of : CAPTURE, WIN **4** : to transfer from one place (as a column) to another ⟨∼ a number in adding⟩ **5** : to have or wear on one's person; *also* : to bear within one **6** : INVOLVE, IMPLY **7** : to hold or bear (oneself) in a specified way **8** : to keep in stock for sale **9** : to sustain the weight or burden of : SUPPORT **10** : to prolong in space, time, or degree **11** : to keep on one's books as a debtor **12** : to succeed in (an election) **13** : to win adoption (as in a legislature) **14** : PUBLISH, PRINT **15** : to reach or penetrate to a distance ⟨voices ∼ well over water⟩
²**carry** *n* **1** : the range of a gun or projectile or of a struck or thrown ball **2** : PORTAGE **3** : an act or method of carrying ⟨fireman's ∼⟩
car·ry·all \-ȯl\ *n* : a capacious bag or case
carry away *vb* : to arouse to a high and often excessive degree of emotion
carrying charge *n* : a charge added to the price of merchandise sold on the installment plan
car·ry·on \-ȯn, -än\ *n* : a piece of luggage suitable for being carried aboard an airplane by a passenger — **carry-on** *adj*
carry on *vb* **1** : CONDUCT, MANAGE **2** : to behave in a foolish, excited, or improper manner **3** : to continue in spite of hindrance or discouragement
carry out *vb* **1** : to bring to a successful conclusion **2** : to put into execution
car·sick \\'kär-ˌsik\ *adj* : affected with motion sickness esp. in an automobile — **car sickness** *n*
¹**cart** \\'kärt\ *n* **1** : a heavy 2-wheeled wagon **2** : a small wheeled vehicle
²**cart** *vb* : to convey in or as if in a cart — **cart·er** *n*
cart·age \\'kär-tij\ *n* : the act of or rate charged for carting
carte blanche \\'kärt-'blä⁵sh\ *n, pl* **cartes blanches** *same or* -'blä⁵-shəz\ [F, lit., blank document] : full discretionary power
car·tel \kär-'tel\ *n* : a combination of independent business enterprises designed to limit competition ♦ **Synonyms** POOL, SYNDICATE, MONOPOLY, TRUST
car·ti·lage \\'kär-tə-lij\ *n* : a usu. translucent somewhat elastic tissue that composes most of the skeleton of young vertebrate embryos and later is mostly converted to bone in higher vertebrates — **car·ti·lag·i·nous** \ˌkär-tə-'la-jə-nəs\ *adj*
cartilaginous fish *n* : any of a class of fishes (as a shark or ray) having the skeleton wholly or largely composed of cartilage
car·tog·ra·phy \kär-'tä-grə-fē\ *n* : the making of maps — **car·tog·ra·pher** *n* — **car·to·graph·ic** \ˌkär-tə-'gra-fik\ *adj*
car·ton \\'kär-tⁿn\ *n* : a cardboard box or container
car·toon \kär-'tün\ *n* **1** : a preparatory sketch (as for a painting) **2** : a drawing intended as humor, caricature, or satire **3** : COMIC STRIP — **cartoon** *vb* — **car·toon·ist** *n*
car·tridge \\'kär-trij\ *n* **1** : a tube containing a complete charge for a firearm **2** : a container of material for insertion into an apparatus **3** : a small case containing a phonograph needle and transducer that is attached to a tonearm **4** : a case containing a magnetic tape or disk **5** : a case for holding integrated circuits containing a computer program
cart·wheel \\'kärt-ˌhwēl\ *n* **1** : a large coin (as a silver dollar) **2** : a lateral handspring with arms and legs extended
carve \\'kärv\ *vb* **carved; carv·ing** **1** : to cut with care or precision : shape by cutting **2** : to cut into pieces or slices **3** : to slice and serve meat at table — **carv·er** *n*
cary·at·id \ˌker-ē-'a-təd\ *n, pl* **-ids** *or* **-i·des** \-'a-tə-ˌdēz\ : a sculptured draped female figure used as an architectural column
CAS *abbr* certificate of advanced study

ca·sa·ba \kə-'sä-bə\ *n* : any of several muskmelons with a yellow rind and sweet flesh
¹**cas·cade** \ˌkas-'kād\ *n* **1** : a steep usu. small waterfall **2** : something arranged in a series or succession of stages so that each stage derives from or acts upon the product of the preceding
²**cas·cade** *vb* **cas·cad·ed; cas·cad·ing** : to fall, pass, or connect in or as if in a cascade ⟨water *cascaded* over the rocks⟩
cas·cara \kas-'ska-rə\ *n* : the dried bark of a small Pacific coastal tree of the U.S. and southern Canada used as a laxative; *also* : this tree
¹**case** \\'kās\ *n* [ME *cas*, fr. AF, fr. L *casus* fall, chance, fr. *cadere* to fall] **1** : a particular instance or situation **2** : an inflectional form of a noun, pronoun, or adjective indicating its grammatical relation to other words; *also* : such a relation whether indicated by inflection or not **3** : what actually exists or happens : FACT **4** : a suit or action in law : CAUSE **5** : a convincing argument **6** : an instance of disease or injury; *also* : PATIENT **7** : INSTANCE, EXAMPLE — **in case** : as a precaution — **in case of** : in the event of
²**case** *n* [ME *cas*, fr. AF *case, chase*, fr. L *capsa*] **1** : a box or container for holding something; *also* : a box with its contents **2** : an outer covering **3** : a divided tray for holding printing type **4** : CASING 2
³**case** *vb* **cased; cas·ing** **1** : to enclose in or cover with a case **2** : to inspect esp. with intent to rob
ca·sein \\'kā-ˌsēn, kā-'\ *n* : any of several phosphorus-containing proteins occurring in or produced from milk
case·ment \\'kās-mənt\ *n* : a window that opens like a door
case·work \-ˌwərk\ *n* : social work that involves the individual person or family — **case·work·er** *n*
¹**cash** \\'kash\ *n* [MF or It; MF *casse* money box, fr. It *cassa*, fr. L *capsa* chest, case] **1** : ready money **2** : money or its equivalent paid at the time of purchase or delivery
²**cash** *vb* : to pay or obtain cash for
ca·shew \\'ka-shü, kə-'shü\ *n* : an edible kidney-shaped nut of a tropical American tree related to the sumacs; *also* : this tree
¹**ca·shier** \ka-'shir\ *vb* : to dismiss from service; *esp* : to dismiss in disgrace
²**cash·ier** \ka-'shir\ *n* **1** : a bank official responsible for moneys received and paid out **2** : a person who receives and records payments
cashier's check *n* : a check drawn by a bank upon its own funds and signed by its cashier
cash in *vb* **1** : to convert into cash ⟨*cash in* bonds⟩ **2** : to settle accounts and withdraw from a gambling game or business deal **3** : to obtain financial profit or advantage
cash·less \\'kash-ləs\ *adj* : relying on monetary transactions that use electronic means rather than cash
cash·mere \\'kazh-ˌmir, 'kash-\ *n* : fine wool from the undercoat of an Indian goat (**cashmere goat**) or a yarn spun of this; *also* : a soft twilled fabric orig. woven from this yarn
cash out *vb* : to convert noncash assets into cash
cash register *n* : a business machine that usu. has a money drawer, indicates each sale, and records the money received
cash-strapped \\'kash-ˌstrapt\ *adj* : lacking sufficient money
cas·ing \\'kā-siŋ\ *n* **1** : something that encases **2** : the frame of a door or window
ca·si·no \kə-'sē-nō\ *n, pl* **-nos** [It, fr. *casa* house] **1** : a building or room for social amusements; *esp* : one used for gambling **2** *also* **cas·si·no** : a card game in which players win cards by matching those on the table
cask \\'kask\ *n* : a barrel-shaped container usu. for liquids; *also* : the quantity held by such a container
cas·ket \\'kas-kət\ *n* **1** : a small box (as for jewels) **2** : COFFIN
casque \\'kask\ *n* : HELMET
cas·sa·va \kə-'sä-və\ *n* : any of several tropical spurges with rootstocks yielding a nutritious starch from which tapioca is prepared; *also* : the rootstock or its starch
cas·se·role \\'ka-sə-ˌrōl\ *n* **1** : a dish in which food may be baked and served **2** : food cooked and served in a casserole
cas·sette *also* **ca·sette** \kə-'set\ *n* **1** : a lightproof con-

tainer for photographic plates or film **2** : a plastic case containing magnetic tape

cas·sia \'ka-shə\ *n* **1** : a dried coarse cinnamon bark **2** : any of a genus of leguminous herbs, shrubs, and trees of warm regions including several which yield senna

cas·sit·er·ite \kə-'si-tə-ˌrīt\ *n* : a dark mineral that is the chief tin ore

cas·sock \'ka-sək\ *n* : an ankle-length garment worn esp. by Roman Catholic and Anglican clergy

cas·so·wary \'ka-sə-ˌwer-ē\ *n, pl* **-war·ies** : any of a genus of large flightless birds closely related to the emu

¹cast \'kast\ *vb* **cast; cast·ing** **1** : THROW, FLING **2** : DIRECT ⟨~ a glance⟩ **3** : to deposit (a ballot) formally **4** : to throw off, out, or away : DISCARD, SHED **5** : COMPUTE; *esp* : to add up **6** : to assign the parts of (a play) to actors; *also* : to assign to a role or part **7** : to shape (a substance) by pouring in liquid or plastic form into a mold and letting harden without pressure **8** : to make (as a knot or stitch) by looping or catching up

²cast *n* **1** : THROW, FLING **2** : a throw of dice **3** : the set of actors in a dramatic production **4** : something formed in or as if in a mold; *also* : a rigid surgical casing (as for protecting and supporting a fractured bone) **5** : TINGE, HUE **6** : APPEARANCE, LOOK ⟨features of delicate ~⟩ **7** : something thrown out or off, shed, or expelled ⟨worm ~s⟩

cas·ta·net \ˌkas-tə-'net\ *n* [Sp *castañeta*, fr. *castaña* chestnut, fr. L *castanea*] : a rhythm instrument consisting of two small wooden, ivory, or plastic shells held in the hand and clicked together

cast·away \'kas-tə-ˌwā\ *adj* **1** : thrown away : REJECTED **2** : cast adrift or ashore as a survivor of a shipwreck — **castaway** *n*

caste \'kast\ *n* [Pg *casta*, lit., race, lineage, fr. fem. of *casto* pure, chaste, fr. L *castus*] **1** : one of the hereditary social classes in Hinduism **2** : a division of a society based on wealth, inherited rank, or occupation **3** : social position : PRESTIGE **4** : a system of rigid social stratification

cas·tel·lat·ed \'kas-tə-ˌlā-təd\ *adj* : having battlements like a castle

cast·er \'kas-tər\ *n* **1** *or* **cas·tor** : a small container to hold salt or pepper at the table **2** : a small wheel that turns freely and is used to support and move furniture, trucks, and equipment

cas·ti·gate \'kas-tə-ˌgāt\ *vb* **-gat·ed; -gat·ing** : to punish or criticize severely — **cas·ti·ga·tion** \ˌkas-tə-'gā-shən\ *n* — **cas·ti·ga·tor** \'kas-tə-ˌgā-tər\ *n*

cast·ing \'kas-tiŋ\ *n* **1** : CAST 7 **2** : something cast in a mold

casting vote *n* : a deciding vote cast by a presiding officer to break a tie

cast iron *n* : a hard brittle alloy of iron, carbon, and silicon cast in a mold

cas·tle \'ka-səl\ *n* **1** : a large fortified building or set of buildings **2** : a large or imposing house **3** : ³ROOK

castle in the air : an impracticable project

cast–off \'kast-ˌóf\ *adj* : thrown away or aside — **cast·off** *n*

cas·tor oil \'kas-tər-\ *n* : a thick yellowish oil extracted from the poisonous seeds of an herb (**castor–oil plant**) and used as a lubricant and purgative

cas·trate \'kas-ˌtrāt\ *vb* **cas·trat·ed; cas·trat·ing** : to deprive of sex glands and esp. testes — **cas·tra·tion** \kas-'trā-shən\ *n* — **cas·tra·tor** \-ˌtor-\ *n*

ca·su·al \'ka-zhə-wəl\ *adj* **1** : resulting from or occurring by chance **2** : OCCASIONAL, INCIDENTAL ⟨~ employment⟩ **3** : OFFHAND, NONCHALANT ⟨a ~ approach to cooking⟩ **4** : designed for informal use ⟨~ clothing⟩ — **ca·su·al·ly** *adv* — **ca·su·al·ness** *n*

ca·su·al·ty \'ka-zhəl-tē, 'ka-zhə-wəl-\ *n, pl* **-ties** **1** : serious or fatal accident **2** : a military person lost through death, injury, sickness, or capture or through being missing in action **3** : a person or thing injured, lost, or destroyed

ca·su·ist·ry \'ka-zhə-wə-strē\ *n, pl* **-ries** : specious argument : RATIONALIZATION — **ca·su·ist** \-wist\ *n* — **ca·su·is·tic** \ˌka-zhə-'wis-tik\ *or* **ca·su·is·ti·cal** \-ti-kəl\ *adj*

ca·sus bel·li \ˌkä-səs-'be-ˌlē, ˌkä-səs-'be-ˌlī\ *n, pl* **ca·sus belli** \ˌkä-ˌsüs-, ˌkä-\ [NL, occasion of war] : a cause or pretext for a declaration of war

¹cat \'kat\ *n* **1** : a carnivorous mammal long domesticated as a pet and for catching rats and mice **2** : any of a family of animals (as the lion, lynx, or leopard) including the domestic cat **3** : a malicious woman **4** : GUY

²cat *abbr* catalog

ca·tab·o·lism \kə-'ta-bə-ˌli-zəm\ *n* : destructive metabolism involving the release of energy and resulting in the breakdown of complex materials — **cat·a·bol·ic** \ˌka-tə-'bä-lik\ *adj*

cat·a·clysm \'ka-tə-ˌkli-zəm\ *n* : a violent change or upheaval — **cat·a·clys·mal** \ˌka-tə-'kliz-məl\ *or* **cat·a·clys·mic** \-'kliz-mik\ *adj*

cat·a·comb \'ka-tə-ˌkōm\ *n* : an underground burial place with galleries and recesses for tombs

cat·a·falque \'ka-tə-ˌfalk, -ˌfólk, -ˌfók\ *n* : an ornamental structure sometimes used in solemn funerals to hold the body

cat·a·lep·sy \'ka-tə-ˌlep-sē\ *n, pl* **-sies** : a trancelike state characterized esp. by loss of voluntary motion — **cat·a·lep·tic** \ˌka-tə-'lep-tik\ *adj or n*

¹cat·a·log *or* **cat·a·logue** \'ka-tə-ˌlóg\ *n* **1** : LIST, REGISTER **2** : a systematic list of items with descriptive details; *also* : a book containing such a list

²catalog *or* **catalogue** *vb* **-loged** *or* **-logued; -log·ing** *or* **-logu·ing** **1** : to make a catalog of **2** : to enter in a catalog — **cat·a·log·er** *or* **cat·a·logu·er** *n*

ca·tal·pa \kə-'tal-pə\ *n* : any of a genus of broad-leaved trees with showy flowers and long slim pods

ca·tal·y·sis \kə-'ta-lə-səs\ *n, pl* **-y·ses** \-ˌsēz\ : a change and esp. increase in the rate of a chemical reaction brought about by a substance (**cat·a·lyst** \'ka-tə-list\) that is itself unchanged at the end of the reaction — **cat·a·lyt·ic** \ˌka-tə-'li-tik\ *adj* — **cat·a·lyt·i·cal·ly** \-ti-k(ə-)lē\ *adv*

catalytic converter *n* : an automobile exhaust-system component in which a catalyst changes harmful gases into mostly harmless products

cat·a·lyze \'ka-tə-ˌlīz\ *vb* **-lyzed; -lyz·ing** : to bring about the catalysis of (a chemical reaction)

cat·a·ma·ran \ˌka-tə-mə-'ran\ *n* [Tamil (a language of southern India) *kaṭṭumaram*, fr. *kaṭṭu* to tie + *maram* tree] : a boat with twin hulls

cat·a·mount \'ka-tə-ˌmaùnt\ *n* : COUGAR; *also* : LYNX

cat·a·pult \'ka-tə-ˌpəlt, -ˌpùlt\ *n* **1** : an ancient military machine for hurling missiles **2** : a device for launching an airplane (as from an aircraft carrier) — **catapult** *vb*

cat·a·ract \'ka-tə-ˌrakt\ *n* **1** : a cloudiness of the lens of the eye obstructing vision **2** : a large waterfall; *also* : steep rapids in a river

ca·tarrh \kə-'tär\ *n* : inflammation of a mucous membrane esp. of the nose and throat — **ca·tarrh·al** \-əl\ *adj*

ca·tas·tro·phe \kə-'tas-trə-(ˌ)fē\ *n* [Gk *katastrophē*, fr. *katastrephein* to overturn, fr. *kata-* down + *strephein* to turn] **1** : a great disaster or misfortune **2** : utter failure — **cat·a·stroph·ic** \ˌka-tə-'strä-fik\ *adj* — **cat·a·stroph·i·cal·ly** \-fi-k(ə-)lē\ *adv*

cat·a·ton·ic \ˌka-tə-'tä-nik\ *adj* : of, relating to, or marked by schizophrenia characterized esp. by stupor, negativism, rigidity, purposeless excitement, and bizarre posturing — **catatonic** *n*

cat·bird \'kat-ˌbərd\ *n* : an American songbird with a catlike mewing call

cat·boat \'kat-ˌbōt\ *n* : a single-masted sailboat with a single large sail extended by a long boom

cat·call \-ˌkól\ *n* : a loud cry made esp. to express disapproval — **catcall** *vb*

¹catch \'kach, 'kech\ *vb* **caught** \'kót\; **catch·ing** [ME *cacchen*, fr. AF *cacher, chacher, chacer* to hunt, ultim. fr. L *captare* to chase] **1** : to capture esp. after pursuit **2** : TRAP **3** : to discover unexpectedly ⟨*caught* in the act⟩ **4** : to become suddenly aware of **5** : to take hold of : SNATCH ⟨~ at a straw⟩ **6** : INTERCEPT **7** : to get entangled **8** : to become affected with or by ⟨~ fire⟩ ⟨~ cold⟩ **9** : to seize and hold firmly; *also* : FASTEN **10** : OVERTAKE **11** : to be in time for ⟨~ a train⟩ **12** : to take in and retain **13** : to watch or see ⟨~ a TV show⟩

²catch *n* **1** : something caught **2** : the act of catching; *also* : a game consisting of throwing and catching a ball **3** : something that catches or checks or holds immovable ⟨a door ~⟩ **4** : one worth catching esp. as a mate **5** : FRAGMENT, SNATCH **6** : a concealed difficulty or complication

catch·all \'kach-ˌȯl, 'kech-\ n : something to hold a variety of odds and ends

catch–as–catch–can adj : using any means available

catch·er \'ka-chər, 'ke-\ n : one that catches; esp : a player positioned behind home plate in baseball

catch·ing adj 1 : INFECTIOUS, CONTAGIOUS 2 : ALLUR-ING, CATCHY

catch·ment \'kach-mənt, 'kech-\ n 1 : something that catches water 2 : the action of catching water

catch on vb 1 : UNDERSTAND 2 : to become popular

catch·pen·ny \'kach-ˌpe-nē, 'kech-\ adj : using sensationalism or cheapness for appeal ⟨a ∼ newspaper⟩

catch·phrase \-ˌfrāz\ n : a word or expression frequently used to represent or characterize a person, group, idea, or point of view

catch–22 \-ˌtwen-tē-'tü\ n, pl **catch–22's** or **catch–22s** often cap C [fr. Catch-22, a paradoxical rule found in the novel Catch-22 (1961) by Joseph Heller] : a problematic situation for which the only solution is denied by a circumstance inherent in the problem or by a rule; also : the circumstance or rule that denies a solution

catchup var of KETCHUP

catch up vb : to travel or work fast enough to overtake or complete

catch·word \'kach-ˌwərd, 'kech-\ n 1 : GUIDE WORD 2 : CATCHPHRASE

catchy \'ka-chē, 'ke-\ adj **catch·i·er; -est** 1 : likely to catch the interest or attention 2 : TRICKY ⟨a ∼ question⟩

cat·e·chism \'ka-tə-ˌki-zəm\ n : a summary or test (as of religious doctrine) usu. in the form of questions and answers — **cat·e·chist** \-ˌkist\ n — **cat·e·chize** \-ˌkīz\ vb

cat·e·chu·men \ˌka-tə-'kyü-mən\ n : a religious convert receiving training before baptism

cat·e·gor·i·cal \ˌka-tə-'gȯr-i-kal\ adj 1 : ABSOLUTE, UN-QUALIFIED ⟨a ∼ denial⟩ 2 : of, relating to, or constituting a category — **cat·e·gor·i·cal·ly** \-i-k(ə-)lē\ adv

cat·e·go·rise Brit var of CATEGORIZE

cat·e·go·rize \'ka-ti-gə-ˌrīz\ vb **-rized; -riz·ing** : to put into a category : CLASSIFY — **cat·e·go·ri·za·tion** \ˌka-ti-gə-rə-'zā-shən\ n

cat·e·go·ry \'ka-tə-ˌgȯr-ē\ n, pl **-ries** : a division used in classification; also : CLASS, GROUP, KIND

ca·ter \'kā-tər\ vb [obs. cater buyer of provisions, fr. ME catour, short for acatour, fr. AF, fr. acater, achater to buy] 1 : to provide a supply of food 2 : to supply what is wanted — **ca·ter·er** n

catercorner or **cater–cornered** var of KITTY-CORNER

cat·er·pil·lar \'ka-tər-ˌpi-lər\ n [ME catyrpel, fr. OF cate-pelose, lit., hairy cat] : a wormlike often hairy insect larva esp. of a butterfly or moth

cat·er·waul \'ka-tər-ˌwȯl\ vb : to make a harsh cry — **cat-erwaul** n

cat·fish \'kat-ˌfish\ n : any of an order of chiefly freshwater stout-bodied fishes with slender tactile processes around the mouth

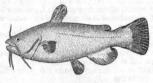

catfish

cat·gut \-ˌgət\ n : a tough cord made usu. from sheep intestines

ca·thar·sis \kə-'thär-səs\ n, pl **ca·thar·ses** \-ˌsēz\ 1 : an act of purging or purification 2 : elimination of a complex by bringing it to consciousness and affording it expression

¹**ca·thar·tic** \kə-'thär-tik\ adj : of, relating to, or producing catharsis

²**cathartic** n : PURGATIVE

ca·the·dral \kə-'thē-drəl\ n : the principal church of a diocese

cath·e·ter \'ka-thə-tər\ n : a tube for insertion into a bodily passage or cavity usu. for injecting or drawing off material or for keeping a passage open

cath·e·ter·i·za·tion \ˌka-thə-tə-rə-'zā-shən\ n : the use of

or introduction of a catheter — **cath·e·ter·ize** \'ka-thə-tə-ˌrīz\ vb

cath·ode \'ka-ˌthōd\ n 1 : the negative electrode of an electrolytic cell 2 : the positive terminal of a battery 3 : the electron-emitting electrode of an electron tube — **cath·od·al** \'ka-ˌthō-dᵊl\ adj — **ca·thod·ic** \ka-'thä-dik\ adj

cathode–ray tube n : a vacuum tube in which a beam of electrons is projected on a phosphor-coated screen to produce a luminous spot

cath·o·lic \'kath-lik, 'ka-thə-\ adj [ME catholik relating to the church universal, ultim. fr. Gk katholikos universal, general, fr. katholou in general] 1 cap : of or relating to Catholics and esp. Roman Catholics 2 : GENERAL, UNIVERSAL

Cath·o·lic \'kath-lik, 'ka-thə-\ n : a member of a church claiming historical continuity from the ancient undivided Christian church; esp : a member of the Roman Catholic Church — **Ca·thol·i·cism** \kə-'thä-lə-ˌsi-zəm\ n

cath·o·lic·i·ty \ˌka-thə-'li-sə-tē\ n, pl **-ties** 1 cap : the character of being in conformity with a Catholic church 2 : liberality of sentiments or views 3 : comprehensive range

cat·ion \'kat-ˌī-ən\ n : the ion in an electrolyte that migrates to the cathode; also : a positively charged ion

cat·kin \'kat-kən\ n : a long flower cluster (as of a willow) bearing crowded flowers and prominent bracts

cat·like \-ˌlīk\ adj : resembling a cat or its behavior; esp : STEALTHY

cat·nap \-ˌnap\ n : a very short light nap — **catnap** vb

cat·nip \-ˌnip\ n : an aromatic mint that is esp. attractive to cats

cat–o'–nine–tails \ˌka-tə-'nīn-ˌtālz\ n, pl **cat–o'–nine-tails** : a whip made of usu. nine knotted cords fastened to a handle

CAT scan \'kat-\ n [computerized axial tomography] : an image made by computed tomography

CAT scanner n : a medical instrument consisting of integrated X-ray and computing equipment that is used to make CAT scans

cat's cradle n : a game played with a string looped on the fingers in such a way as to resemble a small cradle

cat's–eye \'kats-ˌī\ n, pl **cat's–eyes** : any of various iridescent gems

cat's–paw \-ˌpȯ\ n, pl **cat's–paws** : a person used by another as a tool

cat·suit \'kat-ˌsüt\ n : a close-fitting one-piece garment that covers the torso and the legs

catsup var of KETCHUP

cat·tail \'kat-ˌtāl\ n : any of a genus of tall reedlike marsh plants with furry brown spikes of tiny flowers

cat·tle \'ka-tᵊl\ n pl : LIVESTOCK; esp : domestic bovines (as cows, bulls, or calves) — **cat·tle·man** \-mən, -ˌman\ n

cat·ty \'ka-tē\ adj **cat·ti·er; -est** : slyly spiteful ⟨∼ comments⟩ — **cat·ti·ly** \'ka-tə-lē\ adv — **cat·ti·ness** n

catty–corner or **catty–cornered** var of KITTY-CORNER

CATV abbr community antenna television

cat·walk \'kat-ˌwȯk\ n : a narrow walk (as along a bridge)

Cau·ca·sian \kȯ-'kā-zhən\ adj : of or relating to the white race of humankind — **Caucasian** n — **Cau·ca·soid** \'kȯ-kə-ˌsȯid\ adj or n

cau·cus \'kȯ-kəs\ n : a meeting of a group of persons belonging to the same political party or faction usu. to decide upon policies and candidates — **caucus** vb

cau·dal \'kȯ-dᵊl\ adj : of, relating to, or located near the tail or the hind end of the body — **cau·dal·ly** adv

cau·dil·lo \kaú-'thē-(ˌ)yō, -'thēl-\ n, pl **-llos** : a Spanish or Latin-American military dictator

caught \'kȯt\ past and past part of CATCH

caul \'kȯl\ n : the inner fetal membrane of higher vertebrates esp. when covering the head at birth

caul·dron \'kȯl-drən\ n : a large kettle

cau·li·flow·er \'kȯ-li-ˌflaú(-ə)r\ n [It cavolfiore, fr. cavolo cabbage + fiore flower] : a garden plant closely related to cabbage and grown for its compact edible head of undeveloped flowers; also : this head used as a vegetable

cauliflower ear n : an ear deformed from injury and excessive growth of scar tissue

¹**caulk** or **calk** \'kȯk\ vb [ME, fr. AF cauker, calcher to trample, fr. L calcare, fr. calx heel] : to stop up and make tight against leakage (as a boat or its seams) — **caulk·er** n

caulk • celery

²caulk or **calk** also **caulk·ing** or **calk·ing** n : material used to caulk

caus·al \'kȯ-zəl\ adj **1** : expressing or indicating cause **2** : relating to or acting as a cause — **cau·sal·i·ty** \kȯ-'za-lə-tē\ n — **caus·al·ly** adv

cau·sa·tion \kȯ-'zā-shən\ n **1** : the act or process of causing **2** : the means by which an effect is produced

¹cause \'kȯz\ n **1** : REASON, MOTIVE **2** : something that brings about a result; esp : a person or thing that is the agent of bringing something about **3** : a suit or action in court : CASE **4** : a question or matter to be decided **5** : a principle or movement earnestly supported — **cause·less** adj

²cause vb **caused; caus·ing** : to be the cause or occasion of — **caus·a·tive** \'kȯ-zə-tiv\ adj — **caus·er** n

cause cé·lè·bre \ˌkȯz-sā-'lebrᵃ, ˌkȯz-\ n, pl **causes cé·lèbres** \same\ [F, lit., celebrated case] **1** : a legal case that excites widespread interest **2** : a notorious person, thing, incident, or episode

cau·se·rie \ˌkȯz-'rē, ˌkō-zə-\ n [F] **1** : an informal conversation : CHAT **2** : a short informal essay

cause·way \'kȯz-ˌwā\ n : a raised way or road across wet ground or water

¹caus·tic \'kȯ-stik\ adj **1** : CORROSIVE **2** : SHARP, INCISIVE 〈~ wit〉

²caustic n **1** : a substance that burns or destroys organic tissue by chemical action **2** : SODIUM HYDROXIDE

cau·ter·ize \'kȯ-tə-ˌrīz\ vb **-ized; -iz·ing** : to burn or sear usu. to prevent infection or bleeding — **cau·ter·i·za·tion** \ˌkȯ-tə-rə-'zā-shən\ n

¹cau·tion \'kȯ-shən\ n **1** : ADMONITION, WARNING **2** : prudent forethought to minimize risk **3** : one that astonishes — **cau·tion·ary** \-shə-ˌner-ē\ adj

²caution vb : to advise caution to

cau·tious \'kȯ-shəs\ adj : marked by or given to caution : CAREFUL — **cau·tious·ly** adv — **cau·tious·ness** n

cav abbr **1** cavalry **2** cavity

cav·al·cade \ˌka-vəl-'kād\ n **1** : a procession of riders or carriages; also : a procession of vehicles **2** : a dramatic sequence or procession 〈a ~ of films〉

¹cav·a·lier \ˌka-və-'lir\ n [MF, fr. It cavaliere, fr. Old Occitan cavalier, fr. LL caballarius horseman, fr. L caballus horse] **1** : a mounted soldier : KNIGHT **2** cap : an adherent of Charles I of England **3** : GALLANT

²cavalier adj **1** : DEBONAIR **2** : DISDAINFUL, HAUGHTY 〈a ~ attitude toward money〉 — **cav·a·lier·ly** adv

cav·al·ry \'ka-vəl-rē\ n, pl **-ries** : troops mounted on horseback or moving in motor vehicles — **cav·al·ry·man** \-mən, -ˌman\ n

¹cave \'kāv\ n : a natural underground chamber open to the surface

²cave vb **caved; cav·ing** **1** : to collapse or cause to collapse **2** : to cease to resist : SUBMIT — usu. used with in

ca·ve·at \'ka-vē-ˌät, -ˌat; 'kä-vē-ˌät\ n [L, let him beware] : WARNING

caveat emp·tor \-'emp-tər, -ˌtȯr\ n [NL, let the buyer beware] : a principle in commerce: without a warranty the buyer takes a risk

cave–in \'kā-ˌvin\ n **1** : the action of caving in **2** : a place where earth has caved in

cave·man \'kāv-ˌman\ n **1** : a cave dweller esp. of the Stone Age **2** : a man who acts in a rough or crude manner

cav·ern \'ka-vərn\ n : CAVE; esp : one of large or unknown size — **cav·ern·ous** adj — **cav·ern·ous·ly** adv

cav·i·ar also **cav·i·are** \'ka-vē-ˌär, 'kä-\ n : the salted roe of a large fish (as sturgeon) used as an appetizer

cav·il \'ka-vəl\ vb **-iled** or **-illed; -il·ing** or **-il·ling** : to make frivolous objections or raise trivial objections to — **cavil** n — **cav·il·er** or **cav·il·ler** n

cav·ing \'kā-viŋ\ n : the sport of exploring caves : SPELUNKING

cav·i·ta·tion \ˌka-və-'tā-shən\ n : the formation of partial vacuums in a liquid by a swiftly moving solid body (as a propeller) or by high-intensity sound waves

cav·i·ty \'ka-və-tē\ n, pl **-ties** **1** : an unfilled space within a mass : a hollow place **2** : an area of decay in a tooth

ca·vort \kə-'vȯrt\ vb : PRANCE, CAPER

ca·vy \'kā-vē\ n, pl **cavies** : GUINEA PIG 1

caw \'kȯ\ vb : to utter the harsh call of the crow or a similar cry — **caw** n

cay \'kē, 'kā\ n : ⁴KEY

cay·enne pepper \ˌkī-'en-, ˌkā-\ n : a condiment consisting of ground dried fruits or seeds of a hot pepper

cayman var of CAIMAN

Ca·yu·ga \kā-'ü-gə, kī-\ n, pl **Cayuga** or **Cayugas** : a member of an American Indian people of New York

Cay·use \'kī-ˌyüs, kī-'\ n **1** pl **Cayuse** or **Cayuses** : a member of an American Indian people of Oregon and Washington **2** pl **cayuses, not cap, West** : a native range horse

Cb symbol columbium

CB \'sē-'bē\ n : CITIZENS BAND; also : the radio set used for citizens-band communications

CBC abbr Canadian Broadcasting Corporation

CBD abbr cash before delivery

CBS abbr Columbia Broadcasting System

CBW abbr chemical and biological warfare

¹cc \ˌsē-'sē\ vb **cc'd; cc'ing** : to send a copy of an e-mail, letter, etc., to someone 〈~ an e-mail to a coworker〉 〈~ me on your reply〉

²cc abbr **1** carbon copy **2** cubic centimeter

CC abbr **1** community college **2** country club

CCD \ˌsē-ˌsē-'dē\ n : CHARGE-COUPLED DEVICE

CCTV abbr closed-circuit television

CCU abbr **1** cardiac care unit **2** coronary care unit **3** critical care unit

ccw abbr counterclockwise

cd abbr cord

Cd symbol cadmium

¹CD \ˌsē-'dē\ n : CERTIFICATE OF DEPOSIT

²CD n : a small optical disk usu. containing recorded music or computer data; also : the content of a CD

³CD abbr Civil Defense

CDR abbr commander

CD–ROM \ˌsē-ˌdē-'räm\ n : a CD containing computer data that cannot be altered

CDT abbr central daylight (saving) time

Ce symbol cerium

CE abbr **1** chemical engineer **2** civil engineer **3** Corps of Engineers

cease \'sēs\ vb **ceased; ceas·ing** : to come or bring to an end : STOP

cease–fire \'sēs-'fī(-ə)r\ n : a suspension of active hostilities

cease·less \'sēs-ləs\ adj : being without pause or stop : CONTINUOUS — **cease·less·ly** adv — **cease·less·ness** n

ce·cum also **cae·cum** \'sē-kəm\ n, pl **ce·ca** \-kə\ : the blind pouch at the beginning of the large intestine into which the small intestine opens — **ce·cal** also **cae·cal** \-kəl\ adj

ce·dar \'sē-dər\ n : any of numerous coniferous trees (as a juniper) noted for their fragrant durable wood; also : this wood

cede \'sēd\ vb **ced·ed; ced·ing** **1** : to yield or give up esp. by treaty **2** : ASSIGN, TRANSFER — **ced·er** n

ce·di \'sā-dē\ n — see MONEY table

ce·dil·la \si-'di-lə\ n : a mark placed under the letter c (as ç) to show that the c is to be pronounced like s

ceil·ing \'sē-liŋ\ n **1** : the overhead inside lining of a room **2** : the height above the ground of the base of the lowest layer of clouds when over half of the sky is obscured **3** : the greatest height at which an airplane can operate efficiently **4** : a prescribed upper limit 〈price ~〉

cel·an·dine \'se-lən-ˌdīn, -ˌdēn\ n : a yellow-flowered herb related to the poppies

cel·e·brant \'se-lə-brənt\ n : one who celebrates; esp : a priest officiating at the Eucharist

cel·e·brate \'se-lə-ˌbrāt\ vb **-brat·ed; -brat·ing** **1** : to perform (as a sacrament) with appropriate rites **2** : to honor (as a holiday) by solemn ceremonies or by refraining from ordinary business **3** : to observe a notable occasion with festivities **4** : EXTOL — **cel·e·bra·tion** \ˌse-lə-'brā-shən\ n — **cel·e·bra·tor** \'se-lə-brā-tər\ n — **cel·e·bra·to·ry** \-brə-ˌtȯr-ē, ˌse-lə-'brā-tə-rē\ adj

celebrated adj : widely known and often referred to 〈a ~ author〉 ♦ **Synonyms** DISTINGUISHED, RENOWNED, NOTED, FAMOUS, ILLUSTRIOUS, NOTORIOUS

ce·leb·ri·ty \sə-'le-brə-tē\ n, pl **-ties** **1** : the state of being celebrated : RENOWN **2** : a celebrated person

ce·ler·i·ty \sə-'ler-ə-tē\ n : SPEED, RAPIDITY

cel·ery \'se-lə-rē\ n, pl **-er·ies** : a European herb related

to the carrot and widely grown for the crisp edible stems of its leaves
celery cabbage *n* : CHINESE CABBAGE 2
ce·les·ta \sə-'les-tə\ *or* **ce·leste** \sə-'lest\ *n* : a keyboard instrument with hammers that strike steel plates
ce·les·tial \sə-'les-chəl\ *adj* **1** : HEAVENLY, DIVINE **2** : of or relating to the sky ⟨~ bodies⟩ — **ce·les·tial·ly** *adv*
celestial navigation *n* : navigation by observation of the positions of stars
celestial sphere *n* : an imaginary sphere of infinite radius against which the celestial bodies appear to be projected
cel·i·ba·cy \'se-lə-bə-sē\ *n* **1** : the state of being unmarried; *esp* : abstention by vow from marriage **2** : abstention from sexual intercourse
cel·i·bate \'se-lə-bət\ *n* : one who lives in celibacy — **celibate** *adj*
cell \'sel\ *n* **1** : a small room (as in a convent or prison) usu. for one person; *also* : a small compartment, cavity, or bounded space **2** : a tiny mass of protoplasm that usu. contains a nucleus, is enclosed by a membrane, and forms the smallest structural unit of living matter capable of functioning independently **3** : a container holding an electrolyte either for generating electricity or for use in electrolysis **4** : a single unit in a device for converting radiant energy into electrical energy — **celled** \'seld\ *adj*
cel·lar \'se-lər\ *n* **1** : BASEMENT 1 **2** : the lowest place in the standings (as in an athletic league) **3** : a stock of wines
cel·lar·ette *or* **cel·lar·et** \se-lə-'ret\ *n* : a case or cabinet for a few bottles of wine or liquor
cell body *n* : the nucleus-containing central part of a neuron exclusive of its processes
cel·lo \'che-lō\ *n, pl* **cellos** : a bass member of the violin family tuned an octave below the viola — **cel·list** \-list\ *n*
cel·lo·phane \'se-lə-ˌfān\ *n* : a thin transparent material made from cellulose and used as a wrapping
cell phone *n* : a portable cordless telephone for use in a cellular system
cel·lu·lar \'sel-yə-lər\ *adj* **1** : of, relating to, or consisting of cells ⟨~ proteins⟩ **2** : of, relating to, or being a radiotelephone system in which a geographical area is divided into small sections each served by a transmitter of limited range
cel·lu·lite \'sel-yə-ˌlīt\ *n* : deposits of lumpy fat within connective tissue (as in the thighs, hips, and buttocks)
cel·lu·lose \'sel-yə-ˌlōs\ *n* : a complex carbohydrate of the cell walls of plants used esp. in making paper or rayon — **cel·lu·los·ic** \ˌsel-yə-'lō-sik\ *adj or n*
Cel·si·us \'sel-sē-əs\ *adj* : relating to or having a scale for measuring temperature on which the interval between the triple point and the boiling point of water is divided into 99.99 degrees with 0.01° being the triple point and 100.00° the boiling point; *also* : CENTIGRADE
Celt \'kelt, 'selt\ *n* : a member of any of a group of peoples (as the Irish or Welsh) of western Europe — **Celt·ic** *adj*
cem·ba·lo \'chem-bə-ˌlō\ *n, pl* **-ba·li** \-ˌlē\ *or* **-balos** [It] : HARPSICHORD
¹ce·ment \si-'ment\ *n* **1** : CONCRETE; *also* : a powder that is produced from a burned mixture chiefly of clay and limestone and that is used in mortar and concrete **2** : a binding element or agency **3** : CEMENTUM; *also* : a substance for filling cavities in teeth
²cement *vb* **1** : to unite by or as if by cement **2** : to cover with concrete — **ce·ment·er** *n*
ce·men·tum \si-'men-təm\ *n* : a specialized external bony layer covering the dentin of the part of a tooth normally within the gum
cem·e·tery \'se-mə-ˌter-ē\ *n, pl* **-ter·ies** [ME *cimitery*, fr. AF *cimiterie*, fr. LL *coemeterium*, fr. Gk *koimētērion* sleeping chamber, burial place, fr. *koiman* to put to sleep] : a burial ground : GRAVEYARD
cen·o·bite \'se-nə-ˌbīt\ *n* : a member of a religious group living together in a monastic community — **cen·o·bit·ic** \ˌse-nə-'bi-tik\ *adj*
ceno·taph \'se-nə-ˌtaf\ *n* [F *cénotaphe*, fr. L *cenotaphium*, fr. Gk *kenotaphion*, fr. *kenos* empty + *taphos* tomb] : a tomb or a monument erected in honor of a person whose body is elsewhere

Ce·no·zo·ic \ˌsē-nə-'zō-ik, ˌse-\ *adj* : of, relating to, or being the era of geologic history that extends from about 65 million years ago to the present — **Cenozoic** *n*
cen·ser \'sen-sər\ *n* : a vessel for burning incense (as in a religious ritual)
¹cen·sor \'sen-sər\ *n* **1** : a person who inspects printed matter or films with power to suppress anything objectionable **2** : one of two early Roman magistrates whose duties included taking the census — **cen·so·ri·al** \sen-'sōr-ē-əl\ *adj*
²censor *vb* : to subject to censorship
cen·so·ri·ous \sen-'sōr-ē-əs\ *adj* : marked by or given to censure : CRITICAL — **cen·so·ri·ous·ly** *adv* — **cen·so·ri·ous·ness** *n*
cen·sor·ship \'sen-sər-ˌship\ *n* **1** : the action of a censor esp. in stopping the transmission or publication of matter considered objectionable **2** : the office of a Roman censor
¹cen·sure \'sen-chər\ *n* **1** : the act of blaming or condemning sternly **2** : an official reprimand
²censure *vb* **cen·sured; cen·sur·ing** : to find fault with and criticize as blameworthy — **cen·sur·able** *adj* — **cen·sur·er** *n*
cen·sus \'sen-səs\ *n* **1** : a periodic governmental count of population **2** : COUNT, TALLY — **census** *vb*
¹cent \'sent\ *n* [F, hundred, fr. L *centum*] **1** — see *birr, dollar, euro, leone, lilangeni, nakfa, rand, rupee, shilling* at MONEY table **2** : a coin, token, or note representing one cent **3** : a monetary unit formerly used in Suriname (¹⁄₁₀₀ gulden), Malta (¹⁄₁₀₀ lira), and Cyprus (¹⁄₁₀₀ pound)
²cent *abbr* **1** centigrade **2** central **3** century
cen·tas \'sen-ˌtäs\ *n, pl* **cen·tai** \-ˌtī\ *or* **cen·tu** \-ˌtü\ : a monetary unit equal to ¹⁄₁₀₀ litas formerly used in Lithuania
cen·taur \'sen-ˌtȯr\ *n* : any of a race of creatures in Greek mythology half human and half horse
¹cen·ta·vo \sen-'tä-(ˌ)vō\ *n, pl* **-vos 1** — see *boliviano, cordoba, lempira, peso, quetzal* at MONEY table **2** : a monetary unit equal to ¹⁄₁₀₀ sucre formerly used in Ecuador
²cen·ta·vo \-'tä-(ˌ)vü, -(ˌ)vō\ *n, pl* **-vos 1** — see *escudo, metical, real* at MONEY table **2** : a former monetary unit equal to ¹⁄₁₀₀ Portuguese escudo
cen·te·nar·i·an \ˌsen-tə-'ner-ē-ən\ *n* : a person who is 100 or more years old
cen·te·na·ry \sen-'te-nə-rē, 'sen-tə-ˌner-ē\ *n, pl* **-ries** : CENTENNIAL — **centenary** *adj*
cen·ten·ni·al \sen-'te-nē-əl\ *n* : a 100th anniversary or its celebration — **centennial** *adj*
¹cen·ter \'sen-tər\ *n* **1** : the point that is equally distant from all points on the circumference of a circle or surface of a sphere; *also* : MIDDLE 1 **2** : the point about which an activity concentrates or from which something originates **3** : a region of concentrated population **4** : a middle part **5** *often cap* : political figures holding moderate views esp. between those of conservatives and liberals **6** : a player occupying a middle position (as in football or basketball)
²center *vb* **1** : to place or fix at or around a center or central area **2** : to give a central focus or basis : CONCENTRATE **3** : to have a center : FOCUS
cen·ter·board \'sen-tər-ˌbȯrd\ *n* : a retractable keel used esp. in sailboats
cen·ter·piece \-ˌpēs\ *n* **1** : an object in a central position; *esp* : an adornment in the center of a table **2** : one that is of central importance or interest in a larger whole ⟨the ~ of his speech⟩
cen·tes·i·mal \sen-'te-sə-məl\ *adj* : marked by or relating to division into hundredths
¹cen·tes·i·mo \chen-'te-zə-ˌmō\ *n, pl* **-mi** \-(ˌ)mē\ : a former monetary unit equal to ¹⁄₁₀₀ Italian lira
²cen·tes·i·mo \sen-'te-sə-ˌmō\ *n, pl* **-mos** — see *balboa, peso* at MONEY table
cen·ti·grade \'sen-tə-ˌgrād, 'sän-\ *adj* : relating to, conforming to, or having a thermometer scale on which the interval between the freezing and boiling points of water is divided into 100 degrees with 0° representing the freezing point and 100° the boiling point ⟨10° ~⟩ — compare CELSIUS
cen·ti·gram \-ˌgram\ *n* — see METRIC SYSTEM table
cen·ti·li·ter \'sen-ti-ˌlē-tər\ *n* — see METRIC SYSTEM table

cen·time \'sän-ˌtēm\ *n* **1** : a former monetary unit of any of several countries (as Belgium, France, and Luxembourg) equal to ¹/₁₀₀ franc **2** — see *dinar, dirham, franc, gourde* at MONEY table

cen·ti·me·ter \'sen-tə-ˌmē-tər, 'sän-\ *n* — see METRIC SYSTEM table

centimeter–gram–second *adj* : of, relating to, or being a system of units based on the centimeter as the unit of length, the gram as the unit of mass, and the second as the unit of time

cen·ti·mo \'sen-tə-ˌmō\ *n, pl* **-mos** **1** — see *bolivar, colón, dobra, guarani, sol* at MONEY table **2** : a former monetary unit equal to ¹/₁₀₀ peseta

cên·ti·mo \'sen-tə-ˌmō\ *n, plural* **-mos** — see *kwanza* at MONEY table

cen·ti·pede \'sen-tə-ˌpēd\ *n* [L *centipeda*, fr. *centum* hundred + *pes* foot] : any of a class of long flattened segmented arthropods with one pair of legs on each segment except the first which has a pair of poison fangs

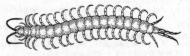

centipede

¹cen·tral \'sen-trəl\ *adj* **1** : constituting a center **2** : ESSENTIAL, PRINCIPAL ⟨the novel's ∼ character⟩ **3** : situated at, in, or near the center **4** : centrally placed and superseding separate units ⟨∼ heating⟩ — **cen·tral·ly** *adv*

²central *n* : a central controlling office

cen·tral·ise *Brit var of* CENTRALIZE

cen·tral·ize \'sen-trə-ˌlīz\ *vb* **-ized; -iz·ing** : to bring to a central point or under central control — **cen·tral·i·za·tion** \ˌsen-trə-lə-'zā-shən\ *n* — **cen·tral·iz·er** \'sen-trə-ˌlī-zər\ *n*

central nervous system *n* : the part of the nervous system which integrates nervous function and activity and which in vertebrates consists of the brain and spinal cord

cen·tre *chiefly Brit var of* CENTER

cen·trif·u·gal \sen-'tri-fyə-gəl, -fi-\ *adj* [NL *centrifugus*, fr. *centr-* center + L *fugere* to flee] **1** : proceeding or acting in a direction away from a center or axis **2** : using or acting by centrifugal force

centrifugal force *n* : the apparent force felt by an object moving in a curved path and acting outward from a center of rotation

cen·tri·fuge \'sen-trə-ˌfyüj\ *n* : a machine using centrifugal force (as for separating substances of different densities or for removing moisture)

cen·trip·e·tal \sen-'tri-pə-tᵊl\ *adj* [NL *centripetus*, fr. *centr-* center + L *petere* to seek] : proceeding or acting in a direction toward a center or axis

centripetal force *n* : the force needed to keep an object revolving about a point moving in a circular path

cen·trist \'sen-trist\ *n* **1** *often cap* : a member of a center party **2** : one who holds moderate views

cen·tu·ri·on \sen-'tür-ē-ən, -'tyür-\ *n* : an officer commanding a Roman century

cen·tu·ry \'sen-chə-rē\ *n, pl* **-ries** **1** : a subdivision of a Roman legion **2** : a group or sequence of 100 like things **3** : a period of 100 years

century plant *n* : a Mexican agave maturing and flowering only once in many years and then dying

CEO \ˌsē-(ˌ)ē-'ō\ *n* : the executive with the chief decision-making authority in an organization or business

ce·phal·ic \sə-'fa-lik\ *adj* **1** : of or relating to the head **2** : directed toward or situated on or in or near the head

ce·ram·ic \sə-'ra-mik\ *n* **1** *pl* : the art or process of making articles from a nonmetallic mineral (as clay) by firing **2** : a product produced by ceramics — **ceramic** *adj*

ce·ra·mist \sə-'ra-mist\ *or* **ce·ram·i·cist** \sə-'ra-mə-sist\ *n* : one who engages in ceramics

¹ce·re·al \'sir-ē-əl\ *adj* [L *cerealis*, fr. *Ceres*, the Roman goddess of agriculture] : relating to grain or to the plants that produce it; *also* : made of grain

²cereal *n* **1** : a grass (as wheat) yielding grain suitable for food; *also* : its grain **2** : a food and esp. a breakfast food prepared from the grain of a cereal

cer·e·bel·lum \ˌser-ə-'be-ləm\ *n, pl* **-bellums** *or* **-bel·la**

\-lə\ [ML, fr. L, dim. of *cerebrum* brain] : a part of the brain that projects over the medulla and is concerned esp. with coordination of muscular action and with bodily balance — **cer·e·bel·lar** \-lər\ *adj*

ce·re·bral \sə-'rē-brəl, 'ser-ə-\ *adj* **1** : of or relating to the brain, intellect, or cerebrum **2** : appealing to or involving the intellect — **ce·re·bral·ly** *adv*

cerebral cortex *n* : the surface layer of gray matter of the cerebrum that functions chiefly in coordination of sensory and motor information

cerebral palsy *n* : a disorder caused by brain damage usu. before, during, or shortly after birth and marked esp. by defective muscle control

cer·e·brate \'ser-ə-ˌbrāt\ *vb* **-brat·ed; -brat·ing** : THINK — **cer·e·bra·tion** \ˌser-ə-'brā-shən\ *n*

ce·re·brum \sə-'rē-brəm, 'ser-ə-\ *n, pl* **-brums** *or* **-bra** \-brə\ [L, brain] : the enlarged front and upper part of the brain that contains the higher nervous centers

cere·ment \'ser-ə-mənt, 'sir-mənt\ *n* : a shroud for the dead

¹cer·e·mo·ni·al \ˌser-ə-'mō-nē-əl\ *adj* : of, relating to, or forming a ceremony; *also* : stressing careful attention to form and detail — **cer·e·mo·ni·al·ly** *adv*

²ceremonial *n* : a ceremonial act or system : RITUAL, FORM

²cer·e·mo·ni·ous \ˌser-ə-'mō-nē-əs\ *adj* **1** : devoted to forms and ceremony **2** : CEREMONIAL **3** : according to formal usage or procedure **4** : marked by ceremony — **cer·e·mo·ni·ous·ly** *adv* — **cer·e·mo·ni·ous·ness** *n*

cer·e·mo·ny \'ser-ə-ˌmō-nē\ *n, pl* **-nies** **1** : a formal act or series of acts prescribed by law, ritual, or convention **2** : a conventional act of politeness **3** : a mere outward form with no deeper significance **4** : FORMALITY

ce·re·us \'sir-ē-əs\ *n* : any of various cacti of the western U.S. and tropical America

ce·rise \sə-'rēs\ *n* [F, lit., cherry] : a moderate red color

ce·ri·um \'sir-ē-əm\ *n* : a malleable metallic chemical element used esp. in alloys

cer·met \'sər-ˌmet\ *n* : a strong alloy of a heat-resistant compound and a metal used esp. for turbine blades

cert *abbr* certificate; certification; certified; certify

¹cer·tain \'sər-tᵊn\ *adj* **1** : FIXED, SETTLED **2** : of a specific but unspecified character ⟨∼ people in authority⟩ **3** : DEPENDABLE, RELIABLE **4** : INDISPUTABLE, UNDENIABLE ⟨it is ∼ that we exist⟩ **5** : assured in mind or action ⟨I am ∼ that they are right⟩ — **cer·tain·ly** *adv*

²certain *pron* : certain ones

cer·tain·ty \-tē\ *n, pl* **-ties** **1** : something that is certain **2** : the quality or state of being certain

cer·tif·i·cate \sər-'ti-fi-kət\ *n* **1** : a document testifying to the truth of a fact **2** : a document testifying that one has fulfilled certain requirements (as of a course) **3** : a document giving evidence of ownership or debt ⟨a stock ∼⟩

certificate of deposit : a money-market bond redeemable without penalty only on maturity

cer·ti·fi·ca·tion \ˌsər-tə-fə-'kā-shən\ *n* **1** : the act of certifying : the state of being certified **2** : a certified statement

certified mail *n* : first class mail for which proof of delivery may be secured but no indemnity value is claimed

certified public accountant *n* : an accountant who has met the requirements of a state law and has been granted a certificate

cer·ti·fy \'sər-tə-ˌfī\ *vb* **-fied; -fy·ing** **1** : VERIFY, CONFIRM **2** : to endorse officially **3** : to guarantee (a bank check) as good by a statement to that effect stamped on its face **4** : to recognize as having met specific qualifications within a field ⟨*certified* teachers⟩ ♦ **Synonyms** ACCREDIT, APPROVE, SANCTION, ENDORSE — **cer·ti·fi·able** \-ə-bəl\ *adj* — **cer·ti·fi·ably** \-blē\ *adv* — **cer·ti·fi·er** *n*

cer·ti·tude \'sər-tə-ˌtüd, -ˌtyüd\ *n* : the state of being or feeling certain

ce·ru·le·an \sə-'rü-lē-ən\ *adj* : AZURE

ce·ru·men \sə-'rü-mən\ *n* : EARWAX

cer·vi·cal \'sər-vi-kəl\ *adj* : of or relating to a neck or cervix

cervical cap *n* : a contraceptive device in the form of a thimble-shaped molded cap that fits snugly over the uterine cervix and blocks sperm from entering the uterus

cer·vix \'sər-viks\ *n, pl* **cer·vi·ces** \-və-ˌsēz\ *or* **cer·vix·es** **1** : NECK; *esp* : the back part of the neck **2** : a constricted portion of an organ or part; *esp* : the narrow outer end of the uterus

ce·sar·e·an or cae·sar·e·an also ce·sar·i·an or cae·sar·i·an \si-'zer-ē-ən\ n, often cap : CESAREAN SECTION — cesarean or caesarean also cesarian or caesarian adj

cesarean section also caesarean section n, often cap C [fr. the legendary association of such a delivery with the Roman cognomen Caesar] : surgical incision of the walls of the abdomen and uterus for delivery of offspring

ce·si·um \'sē-zē-əm\ n : a silver-white soft ductile chemical element

ces·sa·tion \se-'sā-shən\ n : a temporary or final ceasing (as of action)

ces·sion \'se-shən\ n : a yielding (as of rights) to another

cess·pool \'ses-,pül\ n 1 : an underground pit or tank for receiving household sewage 2 : a filthy or corrupt situation

ce·ta·cean \si-'tā-shən\ n : any of an order of aquatic mostly marine mammals that includes whales, porpoises, dolphins, and related forms — cetacean adj

cf abbr [L confer] compare

Cf symbol californium

CF abbr cystic fibrosis

CFC abbr chlorofluorocarbon

CFL abbr compact fluorescent lamp; compact fluorescent light bulb

CFO abbr chief financial officer

cg abbr centigram

CG abbr 1 coast guard 2 commanding general

cgs abbr centimeter-gram-second

ch abbr 1 chain 2 champion 3 chapter 4 church

CH abbr 1 clearinghouse 2 courthouse 3 customhouse

Cha·blis \sha-'blē, shə-, shä-; 'sha-,blē\ n, pl Cha·blis \-'blēz, -(,)blē\ 1 : a dry sharp white Burgundy wine 2 : a white California wine

cha–cha \'chä-,chä\ n : a fast rhythmic ballroom dance of Latin American origin

chafe \'chāf\ vb chafed; chaf·ing 1 : IRRITATE, VEX 2 : FRET 3 : to warm by rubbing 4 : to rub so as to wear away; also : to make sore by rubbing

cha·fer \'chā-fər\ n : any of various scarab beetles

¹chaff \'chaf\ n 1 : debris (as husks) separated from grain in threshing 2 : something relatively worthless — chaffy adj

²chaff n : light jesting talk : BANTER

³chaff vb : to tease good-naturedly

chaf·fer \'cha-fər\ vb : BARGAIN, HAGGLE — chaf·fer·er n

chaf·finch \'cha-,finch\ n : a common European finch with a cheerful song

chaf·ing dish \'chā-fiŋ-\ n : a utensil for cooking food at the table

¹cha·grin \shə-'grin\ n : mental uneasiness or annoyance caused by failure, disappointment, or humiliation

²chagrin vb cha·grined \-'grind\; cha·grin·ing : to cause to feel chagrin

¹chain \'chān\ n [ME cheyne, fr. AF chaene, fr. L catena] 1 : a flexible series of connected links 2 : a chainlike surveying instrument; also : a unit of length equal to 66 feet (about 20 meters) 3 pl : BONDS, FETTERS 4 : a series of things linked together ⟨mountain ∼s⟩; also : a group of usu. identical enterprises with a single owner ⟨fast-food ∼s⟩ ♦ Synonyms TRAIN, STRING, SEQUENCE, SUCCESSION, SERIES

²chain vb : to fasten, bind, or connect with a chain; also : FETTER

chain gang n : a gang of convicts chained together

chain letter n : a letter sent to several persons with a request that each send copies to an equal number of persons

chain mail n : flexible armor of interlocking metal rings

chain reaction n 1 : a series of events in which each event initiates the succeeding one 2 : a chemical or nuclear reaction yielding products that cause further reactions of the same kind

chain saw n : a portable power saw that has teeth linked together to form an endless chain — chain·saw \'chān-,sȯ\ vb

chain–smoke \'chān-'smōk\ vb : to smoke esp. cigarettes continuously

¹chair \'cher\ n [ME chaiere, fr. AF, fr. L cathedra, fr. Gk kathedra, fr. kata- down + hedra seat] 1 : a seat with a back for one person 2 : ELECTRIC CHAIR 3 : an official seat; also : an office or position of authority or dignity 4 : CHAIRMAN

²chair vb : to act as chairman of

chair·lift \'cher-,lift\ n : a motor-driven conveyor for skiers consisting of seats hung from a moving cable

chair·man \-mən\ n : the presiding officer of a meeting, committee, or event — chair·man·ship n

chair·per·son \-,pər-sən\ n : CHAIRMAN

chair·wom·an \-,wu̇-mən\ n : a woman who serves as chairman

chaise \'shāz\ n : a 2-wheeled horse-drawn carriage with a folding top

chaise longue \'shāz-'lȯŋ\ n, pl chaise longues \same or -'lȯŋz\ [F, lit., long chair] : a long reclining chair

chaise lounge \-'lau̇nj\ n : CHAISE LONGUE

chal·ced·o·ny \kal-'se-dⁿn-ē\ n, pl -nies : a translucent quartz of various colors

chal·co·py·rite \,kal-kə-'pī-,rīt\ n : a yellow mineral constituting an important copper ore

cha·let \sha-'lā\ n 1 : a herdsman's cabin in the Swiss mountains 2 : a building in the style of a Swiss cottage with a wide roof overhang

chal·ice \'cha-ləs\ n : a drinking cup; esp : the eucharistic cup

¹chalk \'chȯk\ n 1 : a soft limestone 2 : chalk or chalky material esp. when used as a crayon — chalky adj

²chalk vb 1 : to rub or mark with chalk 2 : to record with or as if with chalk — usu. used with up

chalk·board \'chȯk-,bȯrd\ n : BLACKBOARD

chalk up vb 1 : ASCRIBE, CREDIT 2 : ATTAIN, ACHIEVE ⟨chalk up a victory⟩

¹chal·lenge \'cha-lənj\ vb chal·lenged; chal·leng·ing [ME chalengen to accuse, fr. AF chalenger, fr. L calumniari to accuse falsely, fr. calumnia calumny] 1 : to order to halt and prove identity 2 : to take exception to : DISPUTE ⟨∼ a ruling⟩ 3 : to issue an invitation to compete ⟨challenged me to another game⟩ 4 : to stimulate by presenting difficulties ⟨a job that ∼s her⟩ — chal·leng·er n

²challenge n 1 : a summons to a duel 2 : an invitation to compete in a sport 3 : a calling into question 4 : an exception taken to a juror 5 : a sentry's command to halt and prove identity 6 : a stimulating or interesting task or problem

challenged adj : presented with difficulties (as by a disability)

chal·lis \'sha-lē\ n, pl chal·lises \-lēz\ : a lightweight clothing fabric of wool, cotton, or synthetic yarns

cham·ber \'chām-bər\ n 1 : ROOM; esp : BEDROOM 2 : an enclosed space or cavity 3 : a hall for meetings of a legislative body 4 : a judge's consultation room — usu. used in pl. 5 : a legislative or judicial body; also : a council for a business purpose 6 : the part of a firearm that holds the cartridge or powder charge during firing — cham·bered \-bərd\ adj

cham·ber·lain \'chām-bər-lən\ n 1 : a chief officer in the household of a king or nobleman 2 : TREASURER

cham·ber·maid \-,mād\ n : a maid who takes care of bedrooms

chamber music n : music intended for performance by a few musicians before a small audience

chamber of commerce : an association of businesspeople for promoting commercial and industrial interests in the community

cham·bray \'sham-,brā\ n : a lightweight clothing fabric of white and colored threads

cha·me·leon \kə-'mēl-yən\ n [ME camelion, fr. MF, L chamaeleon, fr. Gk chamaileōn, fr. chamai on the ground + leōn lion] : a small lizard whose skin changes color esp. according to its surroundings

chameleon

¹**cham·fer** \'cham-fər\ *vb* **1** : to cut a furrow in (as a column) : GROOVE **2** : to make a chamfer on : BEVEL
²**chamfer** *n* : a beveled edge
cham·ois \'sha-mē\ *n, pl* **cham·ois** *same or* -mēz\ **1** : a small goatlike ruminant mammal of Europe and the Caucasus region of Russia **2** *also* **cham·my** \'sha-mē\ : a soft leather made esp. from the skin of the sheep or goat **3** : a cotton fabric made in imitation of chamois leather
cham·o·mile *or* **cam·o·mile** \'ka-mə-ˌmī(-ə)l, -ˌmēl\ *n* : any of a genus of strong-scented herbs related to the daisies and having flower heads that yield a bitter substance used esp. in tonics and teas
¹**champ** \'champ, 'chämp\ *vb* **1** : to chew noisily **2** : to show impatience of delay or restraint
²**champ** \'champ\ *n* : CHAMPION
cham·pagne \sham-'pān\ *n* : a white effervescent wine
¹**cham·pi·on** \'cham-pē-ən\ *n* **1** : a militant advocate or defender **2** : one that wins first prize or place in a contest **3** : one that is acknowledged to be better than all others
²**champion** *vb* : to protect or fight for as a champion
✦ *Synonyms* BACK, ADVOCATE, UPHOLD, SUPPORT
cham·pi·on·ship \-ˌship\ *n* **1** : the position or title of a champion **2** : the act of championing : DEFENSE **3** : a contest held to determine a champion
¹**chance** \'chans\ *n* **1** : something that happens without apparent cause **2** : the unpredictable element in existence : LUCK, FORTUNE **3** : OPPORTUNITY **4** : the likelihood of a particular outcome in an uncertain situation : PROBABILITY **5** : RISK **6** : a raffle ticket — **chance** *adj* — **by chance** : in the haphazard course of events
²**chance** *vb* **chanced; chanc·ing** **1** : to take place by chance : HAPPEN **2** : to come casually and unexpectedly — used with *upon* **3** : to leave to chance **4** : to accept the risk of
chan·cel \'chan-səl\ *n* : the part of a church including the altar and choir
chan·cel·lery *or* **chan·cel·lory** \'chan-sə-lə-rē\ *n, pl* **-ler·ies** *or* **-lor·ies** **1** : the position or office of a chancellor **2** : the building or room where a chancellor works **3** : the office or staff of an embassy or consulate
chan·cel·lor \'chan-sə-lər\ *n* **1** : a high state official in various countries **2** : the head of a university **3** : a judge in the equity court in various states of the U.S. **4** : the chief minister of state in some European countries — **chan·cel·lor·ship** *n*
chan·cery \'chan-sə-rē\ *n, pl* **-cer·ies** **1** : a record office for public or diplomatic archives **2** : any of various courts of equity in the U.S. and Britain **3** : a chancellor's court or office **4** : the office of an embassy **5** : the business office of a diocese
chan·cre \'shaŋ-kər\ *n* [F, fr. OF, fr. L *cancer*] : a primary sore or ulcer at the site of entry of an infective agent (as of syphilis)
chan·croid \'chaŋ-ˌkròid\ *n* : a sexually transmitted disease caused by a bacterium and characterized by chancres that differ from those of syphilis in lacking hardened margins
chancy \'chan-sē\ *adj* **chanc·i·er; -est** **1** *Scot* : AUSPICIOUS **2** : RISKY
chan·de·lier \ˌshan-də-'lir\ *n* : a branched lighting fixture suspended from a ceiling
chan·dler \'chand-lər\ *n* [ME *chandeler* a maker or seller of candles, fr. AF, fr. *chandele* candle, fr. L *candela*] : a dealer in provisions and supplies of a specified kind ⟨ship's ∼⟩ — **chan·dlery** *n*
¹**change** \'chānj\ *vb* **changed; chang·ing** **1** : to make or become different : ALTER **2** : to replace with another **3** : to give or receive an equivalent sum in notes or coins of usu. smaller denominations or of another currency **4** : to put fresh clothes or covering on ⟨∼ a bed⟩ **5** : to put on different clothes **6** : EXCHANGE — **change·able** *adj* — **chang·er** *n*
²**change** *n* **1** : the act, process, or result of changing **2** : a fresh set of clothes **3** : money given in exchange for other money of higher denomination **4** : money returned when a payment exceeds the sum due **5** : coins esp. of small denominations — **change·ful** *adj*
change·ling \'chānj-liŋ\ *n* : a child secretly exchanged for another in infancy
change of life : MENOPAUSE
change·over \'chānj-ˌō-vər\ *n* : CONVERSION, TRANSITION

change ringing *n* : the art or practice of ringing a set of tuned bells in continually varying order
¹**chan·nel** \'cha-nᵊl\ *n* **1** : the bed of a stream **2** : the deeper part of a waterway **3** : STRAIT **4** : a means of passage or transmission **5** : a range of frequencies of sufficient width for a single radio or television transmission **6** : a usu. tubular enclosed passage : CONDUIT **7** : a long gutter, groove, or furrow
²**channel** *vb* **-neled** *or* **-nelled; -neling** *or* **-nel·ling** **1** : to make a channel in **2** : to direct into or through a channel
chan·nel·ize \'cha-nə-ˌlīz\ *vb* **-ized; -iz·ing** : CHANNEL — **chan·nel·i·za·tion** \ˌcha-nə-lə-'zā-shən\ *n*
chan·son \shäⁿ-'sōⁿ\ *n, pl* **chan·sons** *same or* -'sōⁿz\ : SONG; *esp* : a cabaret song
¹**chant** \'chant\ *vb* **1** : SING; *esp* : to sing a chant **2** : to utter or recite in the manner of a chant **3** : to celebrate or praise in song — **chant·er** *n*
²**chant** *n* **1** : a repetitive melody in which several words are sung to one tone : SONG; *esp* : a liturgical melody **2** : a manner of singing or speaking in musical monotones
chan·te·relle \ˌshan-tə-'rel\ *n* : a fragrant edible mushroom
chan·teuse \shäⁿ-'tərz, shan-'tüz\ *n; pl* **chan·teuses** *same or* -'tər-zəz, -'tü-zəz\ [F] : a woman who is a concert or nightclub singer
chan·tey *or* **chan·ty** \'shan-tē, 'chan-\ *n, pl* **chanteys** *or* **chanties** : a song sung by sailors in rhythm with their work
chan·ti·cleer \ˌchan-tə-'klir, ˌshan-\ *n* : ROOSTER
Chanukah *var of* HANUKKAH
cha·os \'kā-ˌäs\ *n* **1** *often cap* : the confused unorganized state existing before the creation of distinct forms **2** : the inherent unpredictability in the behavior of a complex natural system (as the atmosphere or the beating heart) **3** : complete disorder ✦ *Synonyms* CONFUSION, JUMBLE, SNARL, MUDDLE, DISARRAY — **cha·ot·ic** \kā-'ä-tik\ *adj* — **cha·ot·i·cal·ly** \-ti-k(ə-)lē\ *adv*
chaos theory *n* : a branch of mathematical and physical theory concerned with chaotic systems
¹**chap** \'chap\ *vb* **chapped; chap·ping** : to dry and crack open usu. from wind and cold ⟨*chapped* lips⟩
²**chap** *n* : a jaw with its fleshy covering — usu. used in pl.
³**chap** *n, chiefly Brit* : FELLOW
⁴**chap** *abbr* chapter
chap·ar·ral \ˌsha-pə-'ral\ *n* **1** : a dense impenetrable thicket of shrubs or dwarf trees **2** : an ecological community esp. of southern California composed of shrubby plants
chap·book \'chap-ˌbùk\ *n* : a small book of ballads, tales, or tracts
cha·peau \sha-'pō\ *n, pl* **cha·peaus** \-'pōz\ *or* **cha·peaux** \-'pō, -'pōz\ [MF] : HAT
cha·pel \'cha-pəl\ *n* [ME, fr. AF *chapele*, fr. ML *cappella*, fr. LL *cappa* cloak; fr. the cloak of St. Martin of Tours preserved as a sacred relic in a chapel built for that purpose] **1** : a private or subordinate place of worship **2** : an assembly at an educational institution usu. including devotional exercises **3** : a place of worship used by a Christian group other than an established church
¹**chap·er·one** *or* **chap·er·on** \'sha-pə-ˌrōn\ *n* [F *chaperon*, lit., hood, fr. MF, head covering, fr. *chape* cape, fr. LL *cappa*] **1** : a person (as a matron) who accompanies young unmarried women in public for propriety **2** : an older person who accompanies young people at a social gathering to ensure proper behavior
²**chaperone** *or* **chaperon** *vb* **-oned; -on·ing** **1** : ESCORT, GUIDE **2** : to act as a chaperone to or for ⟨∼ a dance⟩ ⟨∼ teens⟩ — **chap·er·on·age** \-ˌrō-nij\ *n*
chap·fall·en \'chap-ˌfò-lən, 'chäp-\ *adj* **1** : having the lower jaw hanging loosely **2** : DEJECTED, DEPRESSED
chap·lain \'cha-plən\ *n* **1** : a member of the clergy officially attached to a special group (as the army) **2** : a person chosen to conduct religious exercises (as for a club) — **chap·lain·cy** \-sē\ *n*
chap·let \'cha-plət\ *n* **1** : a wreath for the head **2** : a string of beads : NECKLACE
chap·man \'chap-mən\ *n, Brit* : an itinerant dealer : PEDDLER
chaps \'shaps, 'chaps\ *n pl* [MexSp *chaparreras*] : leather leggings resembling pants without a seat that are worn esp. by western ranch hands

chap·ter \'chap-tər\ *n* 1 : a main division of a book 2 : a body of canons (as of a cathedral) 3 : a local branch of a society or fraternity

¹char \'chär\ *n, pl* **char** *or* **chars** : any of a genus of trouts (as the common brook trout) with small scales

²char *vb* **charred; char·ring** 1 : to burn or become burned to charcoal 2 : SCORCH

³char *vb* **charred; char·ring** : to work as a cleaning woman

char·ac·ter \'ker-ik-tər\ *n* [ME *caracter*, fr. L *character* mark, distinctive quality, fr. Gk *charaktēr*, fr. *charassein* to scratch, engrave] 1 : a graphic symbol (as a letter) used in writing or printing 2 : a symbol that represents information; *also* : a representation of such a character that may be accepted by a computer 3 : a distinguishing feature : ATTRIBUTE 4 : the complex of mental and ethical traits marking a person or a group 5 : a person marked by conspicuous often peculiar traits 6 : one of the persons in a novel or play 7 : REPUTATION ⟨an attack on his ~⟩ 8 : moral excellence

¹char·ac·ter·is·tic \ˌker-ik-tə-'ris-tik\ *n* : a distinguishing trait, quality, or property

²characteristic *adj* : serving to mark individual character ◆ **Synonyms** INDIVIDUAL, PECULIAR, DISTINCTIVE — **char·ac·ter·is·ti·cal·ly** \-ti-k(ə-)lē\ *adv*

char·ac·ter·ize \'ker-ik-tə-ˌrīz\ *vb* **-ized; -iz·ing** 1 : to describe the character of 2 : to be characteristic of — **char·ac·ter·i·za·tion** \ˌker-ik-tə-rə-'zā-shən\ *n*

cha·rades \shə-'rādz\ *n sing or pl* : a game in which some of the players try to guess a word or phrase from the actions of another player who may not speak

char·coal \'chär-ˌkōl\ *n* 1 : a porous carbon prepared from vegetable or animal substances 2 : a piece of fine charcoal used in drawing; *also* : a drawing made with charcoal

chard \'chärd\ *n* : SWISS CHARD

char·don·nay \ˌshar-d°n-'ā\ *n, often cap* [F] : a dry white wine made from a single variety of white grape

¹charge \'chärj\ *n* 1 : a quantity (as of fuel or ammunition) required to fill something to capacity 2 : a store or accumulation of force 3 : an excess or deficiency of electrons in a body 4 : THRILL, KICK 5 : a task or duty imposed 6 : CARE, RESPONSIBILITY 7 : one given into another's care 8 : instructions from a judge to a jury 9 : COST, EXPENSE, PRICE; *also* : a debit to an account 10 : ACCUSATION, INDICTMENT 11 : ATTACK, ASSAULT

²charge *vb* **charged; charg·ing** 1 : to load or fill to capacity 2 : to give an electric charge to; *also* : to restore the activity of (a storage battery) by means of an electric current 3 : to impose a task or responsibility on 4 : COMMAND, ORDER 5 : ACCUSE 6 : to rush against : rush forward in assault 7 : to make liable for payment; *also* : to record a debt or liability against 8 : to fix as a price — **charge·able** *adj*

charge–coupled device *n* : a semiconductor device used esp. as an optical sensor

char·gé d'af·faires \shär-ˌzhā-də-'fer\ *n, pl* **chargés d'affaires** \-ˌzhā-, -ˌzhāz-\ [F] : a diplomat who substitutes for an ambassador or minister

¹char·ger \'chär-jər\ *n* : a large platter

²charger *n* 1 : a device or a worker that charges something 2 : WARHORSE 1

char·i·ot \'cher-ē-ət\ *n* : a 2-wheeled horse-drawn vehicle of ancient times used esp. in war and in races — **char·i·o·teer** \ˌcher-ē-ə-'tir\ *n*

cha·ris·ma \kə-'riz-mə\ *n* : a personal quality of leadership arousing popular loyalty or enthusiasm — **char·is·mat·ic** \ˌkar-əz-'ma-tik\ *adj*

char·i·ta·ble \'cher-ə-tə-bəl\ *adj* 1 : liberal in giving to needy people 2 : merciful or lenient in judging others ◆ **Synonyms** BENEVOLENT, PHILANTHROPIC, ALTRUISTIC, HUMANITARIAN — **char·i·ta·ble·ness** *n* — **char·i·ta·bly** \-blē\ *adv*

char·i·ty \'cher-ə-tē\ *n, pl* **-ties** 1 : goodwill toward or love of humanity 2 : an act or feeling of generosity 3 : the giving of aid to the poor; *also* : ALMS 4 : an institution engaged in relief of the poor 5 : leniency in judging others ◆ **Synonyms** MERCY, CLEMENCY, LENITY

char·la·tan \'shär-lə-tən\ *n* : a person making usu. showy pretenses to knowledge or ability : FRAUD, FAKER

Charles·ton \'chärl-stən\ *n* : a lively dance in which the

knees are swung in and out and the heels are turned sharply outward on each step

char·ley horse \'chär-lē-ˌhórs\ *n* : a muscular pain, cramping, or stiffness from a strain or bruise

¹charm \'chärm\ *n* [ME *charme*, fr. AF, fr. L *carmen* song, fr. *canere* to sing] 1 : a practice or expression believed to have magic power 2 : something worn about the person to ward off evil or bring good fortune : AMULET 3 : a trait that fascinates or allures 4 : physical grace or attraction 5 : a small ornament worn on a bracelet or chain 6 : a quark with a charge of +⅔ and a measured energy of approximately 1.5 billion electron volts

²charm *vb* 1 : to affect by or as if by a magic spell 2 : to protect by or as if by charms 3 : FASCINATE, ENCHANT ◆ **Synonyms** ALLURE, CAPTIVATE, BEWITCH, ATTRACT — **charm·er** *n*

charmed \'chärmd\ *adj* : extremely lucky or prosperous ⟨a ~ life⟩

charm·ing \'chär-min\ *adj* : PLEASING, DELIGHTFUL — **charm·ing·ly** *adv*

char·nel house \'chär-n°l-\ *n* : a building or chamber in which bodies or bones are deposited

¹chart \'chärt\ *n* 1 : MAP 2 : a sheet giving information in the form of a table, list, or diagram; *also* : GRAPH

²chart *vb* 1 : PLAN ⟨~ a course⟩ 2 : to make a chart of 3 : CHRONICLE ⟨~ed his adventures⟩

¹char·ter \'chär-tər\ *n* 1 : an official document granting rights or privileges (as to a colony, town, or college) from a sovereign or a governing body 2 : CONSTITUTION 3 : a written instrument from a society creating a branch 4 : a mercantile lease of a ship

²charter *vb* 1 : to grant a charter to 2 *Brit* : CERTIFY ⟨~ed engineer⟩ 3 : to hire, rent, or lease for temporary use ⟨~ a bus⟩ — **char·ter·er** *n*

charter member *n* : an original member of an organization

char·treuse \shär-'trüz, -'trüs\ *n* : a brilliant yellow green

char·wom·an \'chär-ˌwù-mən\ *n* : a cleaning woman esp. in large buildings

chary \'cher-ē\ *adj* **chari·er; -est** [ME, sorrowful, dear, fr. OE *cearig* sorrowful, fr. *caru* sorrow] 1 : CAUTIOUS, CIRCUMSPECT 2 : SPARING — **char·i·ly** \-ə-lē\ *adv*

¹chase \'chās\ *n* 1 : PURSUIT; *also* : HUNTING 2 : QUARRY 3 : a tract of unenclosed land used as a game preserve

²chase *vb* **chased; chas·ing** 1 : to follow rapidly : PURSUE 2 : HUNT 3 : to seek out ⟨*chasing* down clues⟩ 4 : to cause to depart or flee : drive away 5 : RUSH, HASTEN

³chase *vb* **chased; chas·ing** : to decorate (a metal surface) by embossing or engraving

⁴chase *n* : FURROW, GROOVE

chas·er \'chā-sər\ *n* 1 : one that chases 2 : a mild drink (as beer) taken after hard liquor

chasm \'ka-zəm\ *n* : GORGE 2

chas·sis \'cha-sē, 'sha-sē\ *n, pl* **chas·sis** \-sēz\ : the supporting frame of a structure (as an automobile or television set)

chaste \'chāst\ *adj* **chast·er; chast·est** 1 : innocent of unlawful sexual intercourse : VIRTUOUS, PURE 2 : CELIBATE 3 : pure in thought : MODEST 4 : severe or simple in design — **chaste·ly** *adv* — **chaste·ness** *n*

chas·ten \'chā-s°n\ *vb* : to correct through punishment or suffering : DISCIPLINE; *also* : PURIFY — **chas·ten·er** *n*

chas·tise \chas-'tīz\ *vb* **chas·tised; chas·tis·ing** [ME *chastisen*, alter. of *chasten*] 1 : to punish esp. bodily 2 : to censure severely : CASTIGATE — **chas·tise·ment** \-mənt, 'chas-təz-\ *n*

chas·ti·ty \'chas-tə-tē\ *n* : the quality or state of being chaste; *esp* : sexual purity

cha·su·ble \'cha-zə-bəl, -sə-\ *n* : the outer vestment of the priest at mass

chat \'chat\ *n* 1 : light familiar informal talk 2 : online discussion in a chat room — **chat** *vb*

châ·teau \sha-'tō\ *n, pl* **châ·teaus** \-'tōz\ *or* **châ·teaux** \-'tō, -'tōz\ [F, fr. OF *chastel*, fr. L *castellum* castle, dim. of *castra* camp] 1 : a feudal castle in France 2 : a large country house 3 : a French vineyard estate

chat·e·laine \'shat-tə-ˌlān\ *n* 1 : the mistress of a chateau 2 : a clasp or hook for a watch, purse, or keys

chat room *n* : a real-time online interactive discussion group

chat·tel \'cha-t⁹l\ *n* 1 : an item of tangible property other than real estate 2 : SLAVE, BONDMAN
chat·ter \'cha-tər\ *vb* 1 : to utter speechlike but meaningless sounds 2 : to talk idly, incessantly, or fast 3 : to click repeatedly or uncontrollably — **chatter** *n* —
chat·ter·er *n*
chat·ter·box \'cha-tər-ˌbäks\ *n* : one who talks incessantly
chat·ty \'cha-tē\ *adj* **chat·ti·er; -est** : TALKATIVE — **chat·ti·ly** \-tə-lē\ *adv* — **chat·ti·ness** \-tē-nəs\ *n*
¹chauf·feur \'shō-fər, shō-'fər\ *n* [F, lit., stoker, fr. *chauffer* to heat] : a person employed to drive an automobile
²chauffeur *vb* 1 : to do the work of a chauffeur 2 : to transport in the manner of a chauffeur ⟨~ed the kids to school⟩
chaunt *var of* CHANT
chau·vin·ism \'shō-və-ˌni-zəm\ *n* [F *chauvinisme*, fr. Nicolas *Chauvin*, fictional soldier of excessive patriotism and devotion to Napoleon] 1 : excessive or blind patriotism 2 : an attitude of superiority toward members of the opposite sex — **chau·vin·ist** \-nist\ *n or adj* — **chau·vin·is·tic** \ˌshō-və-'nis-tik\ *adj* — **chau·vin·is·ti·cal·ly** \-ti-k(ə-)lē\ *adv*
cheap \'chēp\ *adj* 1 : INEXPENSIVE 2 : costing little effort to obtain ⟨~ tickets⟩ 3 : worth little : SHODDY, TAWDRY ⟨~ workmanship⟩ 4 : worthy of scorn 5 : STINGY — **cheap** *adv* — **cheap·ly** *adv* — **cheap·ness** *n*
cheap·en \'chē-pən\ *vb* 1 : to make or become cheap or cheaper in price or value 2 : to make tawdry
cheap·skate \'chēp-ˌskāt\ *n* : a miserly or stingy person; *esp* : one who tries to avoid paying a fair share of costs
¹cheat \'chēt\ *vb* 1 : to deprive of something through fraud or deceit ⟨~ed workers of their pay⟩ 2 : to practice fraud or trickery 3 : to violate rules dishonestly ⟨~ at cards⟩ 4 : to be sexually unfaithful — **cheat·er** *n*
²cheat *n* 1 : the act of deceiving : FRAUD, DECEPTION 2 : one that cheats : a dishonest person
¹check \'chek\ *n* 1 : exposure of a chess king to an attack 2 : a sudden stoppage of progress 3 : a sudden pause or break 4 : something that stops or restrains 5 : a standard for testing or evaluation 6 : EXAMINATION, INVESTIGATION 7 : the act of testing or verifying 8 : a written order to a bank to pay money 9 : a ticket or token showing ownership or identity 10 : a slip indicating an amount due 11 : a pattern in squares; *also* : a fabric in such a pattern 12 : a mark typically ✓ placed beside an item to show that it has been noted 13 : CRACK, SPLIT
²check *vb* 1 : to put (a chess king) in check 2 : to slow down or stop : BRAKE 3 : to restrain the action or force of : CURB 4 : to compare with a source, original, or authority : VERIFY 5 : to inspect or test for satisfactory condition 6 : to mark with a check as examined 7 : to consign for shipment for one holding a passenger ticket 8 : to mark into squares 9 : to leave or accept for safekeeping in a checkroom 10 : to prove to be consistent or truthful 11 : CRACK, SPLIT
check·book \'chek-ˌbùk\ *n* : a book containing blank checks
¹check·er \'che-kər\ *n* : a piece in the game of checkers
²checker *vb* 1 : to variegate with different colors or shades 2 : to vary with contrasting elements ⟨a ~ed career⟩ 3 : to mark into squares
³checker *n* : one that checks; *esp* : an employee who checks out purchases in a store
check·er·ber·ry \'che-kər-ˌber-ē\ *n* : WINTERGREEN 1; *also* : the spicy red fruit of this plant
check·er·board \-ˌbórd\ *n* : a board of 64 squares of alternate colors used in various games
check·ered \'che-kərd\ *adj* : marked by inconsistent fortune or recurring problems ⟨his ~ past⟩
check·ers \'che-kərz\ *n* : a checkerboard game for 2 players each with 12 pieces
check in *vb* : to report one's presence or arrival (as at a hotel)
check·list \'chek-ˌlist\ *n* : a list of things to be checked or done; *also* : a comprehensive list
check·mate \'chek-ˌmāt\ *vb* [ME *chekmaten*, fr. *chekmate*, interj. used to announce checkmate, fr. AF *eschec mat*, fr. Ar *shāh māt*, fr. Pers, lit., the king is left unable to escape] 1 : to thwart completely : DEFEAT, FRUSTRATE 2 : to attack (an opponent's king) in chess so that escape is impossible — **checkmate** *n*

check·off \'chek-ˌòf\ *n* : the deduction of union dues from a worker's paycheck by the employer
check·out \'chek-ˌaùt\ *n* 1 : the action or an instance of checking out 2 : a counter at which checking out is done 3 : the process of examining and testing something as to readiness for intended use
check out *vb* 1 : to settle one's account (as at a hotel) and leave 2 : to total or have totaled the cost of purchases in a store and to make or receive payment for them
check·point \'chek-ˌpóint\ *n* : a point at which a check is performed
check·room \-ˌrüm, -ˌrùm\ *n* : a room at which baggage, parcels, or clothing is left for safekeeping
checks and balances *n pl* : a system allowing each branch of a government to restrict the actions of another branch (as by a veto)
check·up \'chek-ˌəp\ *n* : EXAMINATION; *esp* : a general physical examination
ched·dar \'che-dər\ *n*, *often cap* : a hard mild to sharp white or yellow cheese of smooth texture
cheek \'chēk\ *n* 1 : the fleshy side part of the face 2 : IMPUDENCE, BOLDNESS, AUDACITY 3 : BUTTOCK 1 — **cheeked** \'chēkt\ *adj*
cheek·bone \'chēk-ˌbōn\ *n* : the bone or bony ridge below the eye
cheeky \'chē-kē\ *adj* **cheek·i·er; -est** : IMPUDENT, SAUCY — **cheek·i·ly** \-kə-lē\ *adv* — **cheek·i·ness** \-kē-nəs\ *n*
cheep \'chēp\ *vb* : to utter faint shrill sounds : PEEP — **cheep** *n*
¹cheer \'chir\ *n* [ME *chere* face, cheer, fr. AF, face, fr. ML *cara*, prob. fr. Gk *kara* head, face] 1 : state of mind or heart : SPIRIT 2 : ANIMATION, GAIETY 3 : hospitable entertainment : WELCOME 4 : food and drink for a feast 5 : something that gladdens 6 : a shout of applause or encouragement
²cheer *vb* 1 : to give hope or courage to : COMFORT 2 : to make glad 3 : to urge on esp. by shouts 4 : to applaud with shouts 5 : to grow or be cheerful — usu. used with *up* — **cheer·er** *n*
cheer·ful \'chir-fəl\ *adj* 1 : having or showing good spirits 2 : conducive to good spirits : pleasant and bright — **cheer·ful·ly** *adv* — **cheer·ful·ness** *n*
cheer·lead·er \'chir-ˌlē-dər\ *n* : a person who directs organized cheering esp. at a sports event — **cheer·lead·ing** *n*
cheer·less \'chir-ləs\ *adj* : BLEAK, DISPIRITING ⟨a ~ office⟩ — **cheer·less·ly** *adv* — **cheer·less·ness** *n*
cheery \'chir-ē\ *adj* **cheer·i·er; -est** : CHEERFUL ⟨~ music⟩ — **cheer·i·ly** \-ə-lē\ *adv* — **cheer·i·ness** \-ē-nəs\ *n*
cheese \'chēz\ *n* : the curd of milk usu. pressed into cakes and cured for use as food
cheese·burg·er \-ˌbər-gər\ *n* : a hamburger topped with cheese
cheese·cake \-ˌkāk\ *n* 1 : a dessert consisting of a creamy filling usu. containing cheese baked in a shell 2 : photographs of shapely scantily clad women
cheese·cloth \-ˌklóth\ *n* : a lightweight coarse cotton gauze
cheese·par·ing \-ˌper-iŋ\ *n* : miserly economizing — **cheeseparing** *adj*
cheese·steak \-ˌstāk\ *n* : a sandwich of thinly sliced beef topped with melted cheese
cheesy \'chē-zē\ *adj* **chees·i·er; -est** 1 : resembling, suggesting, or containing cheese 2 : CHEAP 3 ⟨~ motels⟩
chee·tah \'chē-tə\ *n* [Hindi *cītā* leopard, fr. Skt *citraka*, fr. *citra* bright, variegated] : a large long-legged swift-moving spotted cat of Africa and formerly Asia
chef \'shef\ *n* : COOK; *esp* : one who manages a kitchen (as of a restaurant)
chef d'oeu·vre \shā-'dœvr⁹\ *n*, *pl* **chefs d'oeuvre** *same*\ : MASTERPIECE
chem *abbr* chemical; chemist; chemistry
¹chem·i·cal \'ke-mi-kəl\ *adj* 1 : of, relating to, used in, or produced by chemistry ⟨~ reactions⟩ 2 : acting or operated or produced by chemicals — **chem·i·cal·ly** \-k(ə-)lē\ *adv*
²chemical *n* 1 : a substance obtained by a chemical process or producing a chemical effect 2 : DRUG
chemical engineering *n* : engineering dealing with the industrial application of chemistry — **chemical engineer** *n*

chemical warfare *n* : warfare using incendiary mixtures, smokes, or irritant, burning, or asphyxiating gases

chemical weapon *n* : a weapon used in chemical warfare

che·mise \shə-ˈmēz\ *n* 1 : a woman's one-piece undergarment 2 : a loose straight-hanging dress

chem·ist \ˈke-mist\ *n* 1 : one trained in chemistry 2 *Brit* : PHARMACIST

chem·is·try \ˈke-mə-strē\ *n, pl* **-tries** 1 : the science that deals with the composition, structure, and properties of substances and of the changes they undergo 2 : chemical composition or properties ⟨the ~ of gasoline⟩ 3 : a strong mutual attraction; *also* : harmonious interaction among people (as on a team)

che·mo \ˈkē-mō\ *n* : CHEMOTHERAPY

che·mo·ther·a·py \ˌkē-mō-ˈther-ə-pē\ *n* : the use of chemicals in the treatment or control of disease — **che·mo·ther·a·peu·tic** \-ˌther-ə-ˈpyü-tik\ *adj*

che·nille \shə-ˈnēl\ *n* [F, lit., caterpillar, fr. OF, fr. L *canicula*, dim. of *canis* dog] : a fabric with a deep fuzzy pile often used for bedspreads and rugs

cheque *chiefly Brit var of* ¹CHECK 7

che·quer *chiefly Brit var of* CHECKER

cher·ish \ˈcher-ish\ *vb* 1 : to hold dear : treat with care and affection 2 : to keep deeply in mind ⟨~ a memory⟩ — **cher·ish·able** *adj* — **cher·ish·er** *n*

Cher·o·kee \ˈcher-ə-ˌ(ˌ)kē\ *n, pl* **Cherokee** or **Cherokees** : a member of an American Indian people orig. of Tennessee and No. Carolina; *also* : their language

che·root \shə-ˈrüt\ *n* : a cigar cut square at both ends

cher·ry \ˈcher-ē\ *n, pl* **cherries** [ME *chery*, fr. AF *cherise, cirice* (taken as a plural), fr. LL *ceresia*, fr. L *cerasus* cherry tree, fr. Gk *kerasos*] 1 : the small fleshy pale yellow to deep blackish red fruit of a tree related to the roses; *also* : the tree or its wood 2 : a moderate red

chert \ˈchərt, ˈchat\ *n* : a rock resembling flint and consisting essentially of fine crystalline quartz and fibrous chalcedony — **cherty** *adj*

cher·ub \ˈcher-əb\ *n* 1 *pl* **cher·u·bim** \ˈcher-ə-ˌbim\ : an angel of the 2d highest rank 2 *pl* **cherubs** : a chubby rosy person — **che·ru·bic** \chə-ˈrü-bik\ *adj*

chess \ˈches\ *n* : a game for 2 played on a chessboard with each player having 16 pieces — **chess·man** \-ˌman, -mən\ *n*

chess·board \ˈches-ˌbȯrd\ *n* : a checkerboard used in the game of chess

chest \ˈchest\ *n* 1 : a box, case, or boxlike receptacle for storage or shipping 2 : the part of the body enclosed by the ribs and sternum — **chest·ed** \ˈches-təd\ *adj* — **chest·ful** \ˈchest-ˌful\ *n*

ches·ter·field \ˈches-tər-ˌfēld\ *n* : an overcoat with a velvet collar

chest·nut \ˈches-(ˌ)nət\ *n* 1 : the edible nut of any of a genus of trees related to the beeches and oaks; *also* : this tree or its wood 2 : a grayish to reddish brown 3 : an old joke or story

chet·rum \ˈche-trəm\ *n, pl* **chetrums** or **chetrum** — see *ngultrum* at MONEY table

che·val glass \shə-ˈval-\ *n* : a full-length mirror that may be tilted in a frame

che·va·lier \ˌshe-və-ˈlir, shə-ˈval-ˌyā\ *n* : a member of one of various orders of knighthood or of merit

chev·i·ot \ˈshe-vē-ət\ *n, often cap* 1 : a twilled fabric with a rough nap 2 : a sturdy soft-finished cotton fabric

chev·ron \ˈshe-vrən\ *n* : a sleeve badge of one or more V-shaped or inverted V-shaped stripes worn to indicate rank or service (as in the armed forces)

¹**chew** \ˈchü\ *vb* 1 : to crush or grind with the teeth — **chew·able** *adj* — **chew·er** *n* — **chewy** \ˈchü-ē\ *adj* — **chew on** : to think about : PONDER ⟨*chew* on the proposals⟩ — **chew the fat** : to make conversation : CHAT

²**chew** *n* 1 : an act of chewing 2 : something for chewing

Chey·enne \shī-ˈan, -ˈen\ *n, pl* **Cheyenne** or **Cheyennes** [AmerF, fr. Dakota *šahíyena*] : a member of an American Indian people of the western plains of the U.S.; *also* : their language

chg *abbr* 1 change 2 charge

chi \ˈkī\ *n* : the 22d letter of the Greek alphabet — X or χ

Chi·an·ti \kē-ˈän-tē, -ˈan-\ *n* : a dry usu. red wine

chiar·oscu·ro \kē-ˌär-ə-ˈskür-ō, -ˈskyür-\ *n, pl* **-ros** [It, fr. *chiaro* clear, light + *oscuro* obscure, dark] 1 : pictorial representation in terms of light and shade without regard

to color 2 : the arrangement or treatment of light and dark parts in a pictorial work of art

¹**chic** \ˈshēk\ *n* : STYLISHNESS

²**chic** *adj* : cleverly stylish : SMART; *also* : currently fashionable

Chi·ca·na \chi-ˈkä-nə *also* shi-\ *n* : an American woman or girl of Mexican descent — **Chicana** *adj*

chi·cane \shi-ˈkān\ *n* : CHICANERY

chi·ca·nery \-ˈka-nə-rē\ *n, pl* **-ner·ies** : TRICKERY, DECEPTION

Chi·ca·no \chi-ˈkä-nō\ *n, pl* **-nos** : a usu. male American of Mexican descent — **Chicano** *adj*

chi-chi \ˈshē-(ˌ)shē, ˈchē-(ˌ)chē\ *adj* [F] 1 : SHOWY, FRILLY 2 : ARTY, PRECIOUS ⟨~ poetry⟩ 3 : CHIC ⟨~ nightclubs⟩ — **chichi** *n*

chick \ˈchik\ *n* 1 : a young chicken; *also* : a young bird 2 *sometimes offensive* : GIRL, WOMAN

chick·a·dee \ˈchi-kə-(ˌ)dē\ *n* : any of several small grayish American birds with black or brown caps

Chick·a·saw \ˈchi-kə-ˌsȯ\ *n, pl* **Chickasaw** or **Chickasaws** : a member of an American Indian people of Mississippi and Alabama

¹**chick·en** \ˈchi-kən\ *n* 1 : a common domestic fowl esp. when young; *also* : its flesh used as food 2 : COWARD

²**chicken** *adj* 1 : COWARDLY 2 *slang* : insistent on petty esp. military discipline

chicken feed *n, slang* : an insignificant sum of money

chick·en-heart·ed \ˌchi-kən-ˈhär-təd\ *adj* : TIMID, COWARDLY

chicken out *vb* : to lose one's courage

chicken pox *n* : an acute contagious viral disease esp. of children characterized by a low fever and blisters

chicken wire *n* : a light wire netting of hexagonal mesh

chick·pea \ˈchik-ˌpē\ *n* : an Asian herb of the legume family cultivated for its short pods with one or two edible seeds; *also* : its seed

chick·weed \ˈchik-ˌwēd\ *n* : any of several low-growing small-leaved weeds related to the pinks

chi·cle \ˈchi-kəl\ *n* : a gum from the latex of a tropical tree used as the chief ingredient of chewing gum

chic·o·ry \ˈchi-kə-rē\ *n, pl* **-ries** : a usu. blue-flowered herb related to the daisies and grown for its root and for use in salads; *also* : its dried ground root used to flavor or adulterate coffee

chide \ˈchīd\ *vb* **chid** \ˈchid\ or **chid·ed** \ˈchī-dəd\; **chid** or **chid·den** \ˈchi-ᵊn\ or **chided**; **chid·ing** : to speak disapprovingly to ◆ **Synonyms** REPROACH, REPROVE, REPRIMAND, ADMONISH, SCOLD, REBUKE

¹**chief** \ˈchēf\ *adj* 1 : highest in rank ⟨the ~ executive⟩ 2 : most important ⟨the ~ complaint⟩ ◆ **Synonyms** PRINCIPAL, MAIN, LEADING, MAJOR — **chief·ly** *adv*

²**chief** *n* 1 : the leader of a body or organization : HEAD 2 : the principal or most valuable part — **chief·dom** *n*

chief master sergeant *n* : a noncommissioned officer of the highest rank in the air force

chief of staff 1 : the ranking officer of a staff in the armed forces 2 : the ranking office of the army or air force

chief of state : the formal head of a national state as distinguished from the head of the government

chief petty officer *n* : an enlisted person in the navy ranking next below a senior chief petty officer

chief·tain \ˈchēf-tən\ *n* : a leader of a band, tribe, or clan — **chief·tain·cy** \-sē\ *n* — **chief·tain·ship** *n*

chief warrant officer *n* : a warrant officer of senior rank

chif·fon \shi-ˈfän, ˈshi-ˌ\ *n* [F, lit., rag, fr. *chiffe* old rag] : a sheer fabric esp. of silk

chif·fo·nier \ˌshi-fə-ˈnir\ *n* : a high narrow chest of drawers

chig·ger \ˈchi-gər\ *n* : a bloodsucking larval mite that causes intense itching

chi·gnon \ˈshēn-ˌyän\ *n* [F, fr. MF *chaignon* chain, collar, nape] : a knot of hair worn at the back of the head

Chi·hua·hua \chə-ˈwä-ˌwä\ *n* : any of a breed of very small large-eared dogs that originated in Mexico

chil·blain \ˈchil-ˌblān\ *n* : a sore or inflamed swelling (as on the feet or hands) caused by exposure to cold

child \ˈchī(-ə)ld\ *n, pl* **chil·dren** \ˈchil-drən\ 1 : an unborn or recently born person 2 : a young person between the periods of infancy and youth 3 : a male or female offspring : SON, DAUGHTER 4 : one strongly influenced by another or by a place or state of affairs — **child·ish** *adj* — **child·ish·ly** *adv* — **child·ish·ness** *n* — **child·less** *adj* — **child·less·ness** *n* — **child·like** *adj*

Chihuahua

child·bear·ing \'chīld-,ber-iŋ\ *n* : CHILDBIRTH — **childbearing** *adj*
child·birth \-,bərth\ *n* : the act or process of giving birth to offspring
child·hood \-,hůd\ *n* : the state or time of being a child
¹child·proof \-,prüf\ *adj* **1** : made to prevent opening or use by children ⟨~ lighters⟩ **2** : made safe for children
²childproof *vb* : to make childproof ⟨~ a house⟩
child's play *n* : a simple task or act
chili *also* **chile** *or* **chil·li** \'chi-lē\ *n, pl* **chil·ies** *also* **chil·es** *or* **chilis** *or* **chil·lies** **1** : any of various pungent peppers related to the tomato **2** : a thick sauce of meat and chilies **3** : CHILI CON CARNE
chili con car·ne \,chi-lē-,kän-'kär-nē\ *n* [AmerSp *chile con carne* chili with meat] : a spiced stew of ground beef and chili peppers or chili powder usu. with beans
chili powder *n* : a seasoning made of ground chili peppers and other spices
chili sauce *n* : a spiced tomato sauce usu. made with red and green peppers
¹chill \'chil\ *n* **1** : a feeling of coldness accompanied by shivering **2** : moderate coldness **3** : a check to enthusiasm or warmth of feeling
²chill *adj* **1** : moderately cold **2** : COLD, RAW **3** : DISTANT, FORMAL ⟨a ~ reception⟩ **4** : DEPRESSING, DISPIRITING
³chill *vb* **1** : to make or become cold or chilly **2** : to make cool esp. without freezing **3** : RELAX — **chill·er** *n*
chill·ing \'chi-liŋ\ *adj* : gravely disturbing or frightening ⟨a ~ scene⟩
chilly \'chi-lē\ *adj* **chill·i·er; -est** **1** : noticeably cold **2** : unpleasantly affected by cold **3** : lacking warmth of feeling ⟨a ~ reception⟩ — **chill·i·ness** *n*
chimaera *chiefly Brit var of* CHIMERA
¹chime \'chīm\ *n* **1** : a set of bells musically tuned **2** : the sound of a set of bells — usu. used in pl. **3** : a musical sound suggesting bells
²chime *vb* **chimed; chim·ing** **1** : to make bell-like sounds **2** : to indicate (as the time of day) by chiming **3** : to be or act in accord : be in harmony
chime in *vb* : to break into or join in a conversation
chi·me·ra \kī-'mir-ə, kə-\ *n* [L *chimaera*, fr. Gk *chimaira* she-goat, chimera] **1** : an imaginary monster made up of incongruous parts **2** : an illusion or fabrication of the mind; *esp* : an impossible dream
chi·me·ri·cal \ki-'mer-i-kəl\ *also* **chi·me·ric** \-ik\ *adj* **1** : FANTASTIC, IMAGINARY **2** : inclined to fantastic schemes
chim·ney \'chim-nē\ *n, pl* **chimneys** **1** : a vertical structure extending above the roof of a building for carrying off smoke **2** : a glass tube around a lamp flame
chimp \'chimp\ *n* : CHIMPANZEE
chim·pan·zee \,chim-,pan-'zē, chim-'pan-zē\ *n* : an African ape related to the much larger gorilla
¹chin \'chin\ *n* : the part of the face below the lower lip including the prominence of the lower jaw — **chin·less** *adj*
²chin *vb* **chinned; chin·ning** : to raise (oneself) while hanging by the hands until the chin is level with the support
chi·na \'chī-nə\ *n* : porcelain ware; *also* : domestic pottery in general
Chi·na·town \-,taůn\ *n* : the Chinese quarter of a city
chinch bug \'chinch-\ *n* : a small black and white bug destructive to cereal grasses

chin·chil·la \chin-'chi-lə\ *n* **1** : either of two small So. American rodents with soft pearl-gray fur; *also* : this fur **2** : a heavy long-napped woolen cloth
chine \'chīn\ *n* : BACKBONE, SPINE; *also* : a cut of meat including all or part of the backbone
Chi·nese \chī-'nēz, -'nēs\ *n, pl* **Chinese** **1** : a native or inhabitant of China **2** : any of a group of related languages of China — **Chinese** *adj*
Chinese cabbage *n* **1** : BOK CHOY **2** : an Asian garden plant related to the cabbage and widely grown in the U.S. for its tight elongate cylindrical heads of pale green to cream-colored leaves
Chinese checkers *n* : a game in which each player in turn transfers a set of marbles from a home point to the opposite point of a pitted 6-pointed star
Chinese gooseberry *n* : a subtropical vine that bears kiwifruit; *also* : KIWIFRUIT
Chinese lantern *n* : a collapsible translucent cover for a light
¹chink \'chiŋk\ *n* : a small crack or fissure
²chink *vb* : to fill the chinks of : stop up
³chink *n* : a slight sharp metallic sound
⁴chink *vb* : to make a slight sharp metallic sound
chi·no \'chē-nō\ *n, pl* **chinos** **1** : a usu. khaki cotton twill **2** *pl* : an article of clothing made of chino
Chi·nook \shə-'nůk, chə-, -'nük\ *n, pl* **Chinook** *or* **Chinooks** : a member of an American Indian people of Oregon
chintz \'chints\ *n* : a usu. glazed printed cotton cloth
chintzy \'chint-sē\ *adj* **chintz·i·er; -est** **1** : decorated with or as if with chintz **2** : GAUDY, CHEAP ⟨a ~ low-budget film⟩ **3** : STINGY — **chintz·i·ness** *n*
chin–up \'chin-,əp\ *n* : the act of chinning oneself
¹chip \'chip\ *n* **1** : a small usu. thin and flat piece (as of wood) cut or broken off **2** : a thin crisp morsel of food **3** : a counter used in games (as poker) **4** *pl, slang* : MONEY **5** : a flaw left after a chip is broken off **6** : INTEGRATED CIRCUIT **7** : a very small slice of silicon containing electronic circuits — **chip off the old block** : a child that resembles his or her parent
²chip *vb* **chipped; chip·ping** **1** : to cut or break chips from **2** : to break off in small pieces at the edges **3** : to play a chip shot
chip in *vb* : CONTRIBUTE
chip·munk \'chip-,məŋk\ *n* [earlier *chitmunk*, prob. fr. Ojibwa *ačitamo·n?* red squirrel] : any of a genus of small striped No. American and Asian rodents closely related to the squirrels and marmots
chi·pot·le \chə-'pōt-lā\ *n* : a smoked and usu. dried jalapeño pepper
chipped beef \'chipt-\ *n* : smoked dried beef sliced thin
¹chip·per \'chi-pər\ *n* : one that chips
²chipper *adj* : LIVELY, CHEERFUL
Chip·pe·wa \'chi-pə-,wó, -,wä, -,wä, -wə\ *n, pl* **Chippewa** *or* **Chippewas** : OJIBWA
chip shot *n* : a short usu. low shot to the green in golf
chi·rog·ra·phy \kī-'rä-grə-fē\ *n* : HANDWRITING, PENMANSHIP — **chi·ro·graph·ic** \,kī-rə-'gra-fik\ *adj*
chi·rop·o·dy \kə-'rä-pə-dē, shə-\ *n* : PODIATRY — **chi·rop·o·dist** \-dist\ *n*
chi·ro·prac·tic \'kī-rə-,prak-tik\ *n* : a system of therapy based esp. on manipulation of body structures — **chi·ro·prac·tor** \-tər\ *n*
chirp \'chərp\ *n* : a short sharp sound characteristic of a small bird or cricket — **chirp** *vb* — **chirpy** \'chər-pē\ *adj*
¹chis·el \'chi-zəl\ *n* : a metal tool with a sharpened edge at one end used to chip, carve, or cut into a solid material (as wood or stone)
²chisel *vb* **-eled** *or* **-elled; -el·ing** *or* **-el·ling** **1** : to work with or as if with a chisel **2** : to obtain by shrewd often unfair methods; *also* : CHEAT — **chis·el·er** *n*
¹chit \'chit\ *n* [ME *chitte* kitten, cub] **1** : CHILD **2** : a pert young woman
²chit *n* [Hindi *ciṭṭhī* letter, note] : a signed voucher for a small debt
chit·chat \'chit-,chat\ *n* : casual or trifling conversation — **chitchat** *vb*
chi·tin \'kī-t°n\ *n* : a sugar polymer that forms part of the hard outer integument esp. of insects — **chi·tin·ous** *adj*
chit·ter·lings *or* **chit·lins** \'chit-lənz\ *n pl* : the intestines of hogs esp. when prepared as food

chi·val·ric \shə-'val-rik\ *adj* : relating to chivalry : CHIV-ALROUS

chiv·al·rous \'shi-vəl-rəs\ *adj* 1 : of or relating to chivalry 2 : marked by honor, courtesy, and generosity 3 : marked by courtesy esp. to women — **chiv·al·rous·ly** *adv* — **chiv·al·rous·ness** *n*

chiv·al·ry \'shi-vəl-rē\ *n, pl* **-ries** 1 : mounted men-at-arms 2 : the system or practices of knighthood 3 : the spirit or character of the ideal knight

chive \'chīv\ *n* : an herb related to the onion that has slender leaves used for flavoring; *also* : its leaves

chla·myd·ia \klə-'mi-dē-ə\ *n, pl* **-i·ae** \-dē-,ē\ 1 : any of a genus of bacteria that cause various diseases of the eye and urogenital tract 2 : a disease or infection caused by chlamydiae

chlo·ral hydrate \'klȯr-əl-\ *n* : a white crystalline compound used as a hypnotic and sedative

chlor·dane \'klȯr-,dān\ *n* : a highly chlorinated persistent insecticide

chlo·ride \'klȯr-,īd\ *n* : a compound of chlorine with another element or group

chlo·ri·nate \'klȯr-ə-,nāt\ *vb* **-nat·ed; -nat·ing** : to treat or combine with chlorine or a chlorine compound — **chlo·ri·na·tion** \,klȯr-ə-'nā-shən\ *n* — **chlo·ri·na·tor** \'klȯr-ə-,nā-tər\ *n*

chlo·rine \'klȯr-,ēn\ *n* : a nonmetallic chemical element that is found alone as a strong-smelling greenish-yellow irritating gas and is used as a bleach, oxidizing agent, and disinfectant

chlorine monoxide *n* : a reactive radical that plays a major role in stratospheric ozone depletion

chlo·rite \'klȯr-,īt\ *n* : a usu. green mineral found with and resembling mica

chlo·ro·flu·o·ro·car·bon \,klȯr-ə-'flȯr-ə-,kär-bən, -'flu̇r-\ *n* : any of several gaseous compounds that contain carbon, chlorine, fluorine, and sometimes hydrogen and are used esp. as solvents, refrigerants, and aerosol propellants

¹chlo·ro·form \'klȯr-ə-,fȯrm\ *n* : a colorless heavy fluid with etherlike odor used as a solvent

²chloroform *vb* : to treat with chloroform to produce anesthesia or death

chlo·ro·phyll \-,fil\ *n* : the green coloring matter of plants that functions in photosynthesis

chlo·ro·plast \'klȯr-ə-,plast\ *n* : a cytoplasmic organelle that contains chlorophyll and is the site of photosynthesis

chm *abbr* chairman

chock \'chäk\ *n* : a wedge for steadying something or for blocking the movement of a wheel — **chock** *vb*

chock-a-block \'chäk-ə-,bläk\ *adj* : very full : CROWDED

chock–full \'chək-'fu̇l, 'chäk-\ *adj* : full to the limit : CRAMMED

choc·o·late \'chä-k(ə-)lət, 'chȯ-\ *n* [Sp, fr. Nahuatl *chocolātl*] 1 : a food prepared from ground roasted cacao beans; *also* : a drink prepared from this 2 : a candy made of or with a coating of chocolate 3 : a dark brown color — **choc·o·laty** *or* **choc·o·lat·ey** \-k(ə-)lə-tē\ *adj*

Choc·taw \'chäk-,tȯ\ *n, pl* **Choctaw** *or* **Choctaws** : a member of an American Indian people of Mississippi, Alabama, and Louisiana; *also* : their language

¹choice \'chȯis\ *n* 1 : the act of choosing : SELECTION 2 : the power or opportunity of choosing : OPTION 3 : the best part 4 : a person or thing selected 5 : a variety offered for selection

²choice *adj* **choic·er; choic·est** 1 : worthy of being chosen 2 : selected with care 3 : of high quality

choir \'kwī(-ə)r\ *n* 1 : an organized company of singers (as in a church service) 2 : the part of the church occupied by the singers or by the clergy

choir·boy \'kwī(-ə)r-,bȯi\ *n* : a boy member of a choir

choir·mas·ter \-,mas-tər\ *n* : the director of a choir (as in a church)

¹choke \'chōk\ *vb* **choked; chok·ing** 1 : to hinder breathing (as by obstructing the trachea) : STRANGLE 2 : to check the growth or action of 3 : CLOG, OBSTRUCT 4 : to enrich the fuel mixture of (a motor) by restricting the carburetor air intake 5 : to perform badly in a critical situation

²choke *n* 1 : the act of choking 2 : a narrowing in size toward the muzzle in the bore of a gun 3 : a valve for choking a gasoline engine

choke hold *n* 1 : a hold that involves strong choking pressure 2 : absolute control

chok·er \'chō-kər\ *n* : something (as a necklace) worn tightly around the neck

cho·ler \'kä-lər, 'kō-\ *n* : a tendency toward anger : IRASCIBILITY

chol·era \'kä-lə-rə\ *n* : any of several bacterial diseases usu. marked by severe vomiting and dysentery

cho·ler·ic \'kä-lə-rik, kə-'ler-ik\ *adj* 1 : IRASCIBLE 2 : ANGRY, IRATE

cho·les·ter·ol \kə-'les-tə-,rȯl\ *n* : a physiologically important waxy steroid alcohol found in animal tissues and in high concentrations implicated as a cause of arteriosclerosis

chomp \'chämp, 'chȯmp\ *vb* : to chew or bite on something heavily

chon \'chän\ *n, pl* **chon** 1 — see **won** at MONEY table 2 : the jeon of South Korea

choose \'chüz\ *vb* **chose** \chōz\; **cho·sen** \'chō-zᵊn\; **choos·ing** \'chü-ziŋ\ 1 : to select esp. after consideration 2 : DECIDE 3 : to have a preference for — **choos·er** *n*

choosy *or* **choos·ey** \'chü-zē\ *adj* **choos·i·er; -est** : very particular in making choices

¹chop \'chäp\ *vb* **chopped; chop·ping** 1 : to cut by repeated blows 2 : to cut into small pieces : MINCE 3 : to strike (a ball) with a short quick downward stroke

²chop *n* 1 : a sharp downward blow or stroke 2 : a small cut of meat often including part of a rib 3 : a short abrupt motion (as of a wave)

³chop *n* 1 : an official seal or stamp 2 : a mark on goods to indicate quality or kind; *also* : QUALITY, GRADE

chop·house \'chäp-,hau̇s\ *n* : RESTAURANT

chop·per \'chä-pər\ *n* 1 : one that chops 2 *pl, slang* : TEETH 3 : HELICOPTER

chop·pi·ness \'chä-pē-nəs\ *n* : the quality or state of being choppy

¹chop·py \'chä-pē\ *adj* **chop·pi·er; -est** 1 : rough with small waves ⟨a ~ sea⟩ 2 : JERKY, DISCONNECTED ⟨short ~ sentences⟩ — **chop·pi·ly** \-pə-lē\ *adv*

²choppy *adj* **chop·pi·er; -est** : CHANGEABLE, VARIABLE ⟨a ~ wind⟩

chops \'chäps\ *n pl* 1 : the fleshy covering of the jaws 2 : expertise in a particular field or activity ⟨acting ~⟩

chop·stick \'chäp-,stik\ *n* : one of a pair of sticks used chiefly in Asian countries for lifting food to the mouth

chop su·ey \chäp-'sü-ē\ *n, pl* **chop sueys** : a dish made of vegetables (as bean sprouts, bamboo shoots, water chestnuts, onions, mushrooms) and meat or fish and served with rice

cho·ral \'kȯr-əl\ *adj* : of, relating to, or sung by a choir or chorus or in chorus — **cho·ral·ly** *adv*

cho·rale \kə-'ral, -'räl\ *n* 1 : a hymn or psalm sung in church; *also* : a harmonization of a traditional melody 2 : CHORUS, CHOIR

¹chord \'kȯrd\ *n* [alter. of ME *cord*, short for *accord*] : three or more musical tones sounded simultaneously

²chord *n* 1 : CORD 2 2 : a straight line joining two points on a curve

chore \'chȯr\ *n* [ME *char* turn, piece of work, fr. OE *cierr*] 1 *pl* : the daily light work of a household or farm 2 : a routine task or job 3 : a difficult or disagreeable task

cho·rea \kə-'rē-ə\ *n* : any of various nervous disorders marked by spasmodic uncontrolled movements

cho·re·og·ra·phy \,kȯr-ē-'ä-grə-fē\ *n, pl* **-phies** : the art of composing and arranging dances and esp. ballets — **cho·reo·graph** \'kȯr-ē-ə-,graf\ *vb* — **cho·re·og·ra·pher** \,kȯr-ē-'ä-grə-fər\ *n* — **cho·reo·graph·ic** \,kȯr-ē-ə-'gra-fik\ *adj* — **cho·reo·graph·i·cal·ly** \-fi-k(ə-)lē\ *adv*

cho·ris·ter \'kȯr-ə-stər\ *n* : a singer in a choir

chor·tle \'chȯr-tᵊl\ *vb* **chor·tled; chor·tling** : to laugh or chuckle esp. in satisfaction or exultation — **chortle** *n*

¹cho·rus \'kȯr-əs\ *n* 1 : an organized company of singers : CHOIR 2 : a group of dancers and singers (as in a musical comedy) 3 : a part of a song repeated at intervals 4 : a composition to be sung by a chorus; *also* : group singing 5 : sounds uttered by a number of persons or animals together ⟨a ~ of boos⟩

²chorus *vb* : to sing or utter in chorus

chose *past of* CHOOSE

cho·sen \'chō-zᵊn\ *adj* : selected or marked for special favor or privilege

chou·croute \shü-'krüt\ *n* **1** : SAUERKRAUT **2** *or* **choucroute gar·nie** \-gär-'nē\ : sauerkraut cooked and served with meat

¹chow \'chaù\ *n* : FOOD

²chow *vb* : EAT — often used with *down*

³chow *n* : CHOW CHOW

chow·chow \'chaù-,chaù\ *n* : chopped mixed pickles in mustard sauce

chow chow \'chaù-,chaù\ *n* : any of a breed of thick= coated muscular dogs of Chinese origin with a blue= black tongue and a short tail curled close to the back

chow·der \'chaù-dər\ *n* : a soup or stew made from seafood or vegetables and containing milk or tomatoes

chow mein \'chaù-'mān\ *n* : a seasoned stew of shredded or diced meat, mushrooms, and vegetables that is usu. served with fried noodles

chrism \'kri-zəm\ *n* : consecrated oil used esp. in baptism, confirmation, and ordination

Christ \'krīst\ *n* [ME *Crist*, fr. OE, fr. L *Christus*, fr. Gk *Christos*, lit., anointed] : Jesus esp. as the Messiah — **Christ·like** *adj* — **Christ·ly** *adj*

chris·ten \'kri-sⁿn\ *vb* **1** : BAPTIZE **2** : to name at baptism **3** : to name or dedicate (as a ship) by a ceremony suggestive of baptism — **chris·ten·ing** *n*

Chris·ten·dom \'kri-sⁿn-dəm\ *n* **1** : CHRISTIANITY **2** : the part of the world in which Christianity prevails

¹Chris·tian \'kris-chən\ *n* : an adherent of Christianity

²Christian *adj* **1** : of or relating to Christianity **2** : based on or conforming with Christianity **3** : of or relating to a Christian **4** : professing Christianity

Chris·ti·an·i·ty \,kris-chē-'a-nə-tē\ *n* : the religion derived from Jesus Christ, based on the Bible as sacred scripture, and professed by Christians

Chris·tian·ize \'kris-chə-,nīz\ *vb* **-ized; -iz·ing** : to make Christian

Christian name *n* : GIVEN NAME

Christian Science *n* : a religion and system of healing founded by Mary Baker Eddy and taught by the Church of Christ, Scientist — **Christian Scientist** *n*

chris·tie *or* **chris·ty** \'kris-tē\ *n, pl* **christies** : a skiing turn made by shifting body weight forward and skidding into a turn with parallel skis

Christ·mas \'kris-məs\ *n* : December 25 celebrated as a church festival in commemoration of the birth of Christ and observed as a legal holiday

Christmas club *n* : a savings account in which regular deposits are made to provide money for Christmas shopping

Christ·mas·tide \'kris-məs-,tīd\ *n* : the season of Christmas

chro·mat·ic \krō-'ma-tik\ *adj* **1** : of or relating to color **2** : proceeding by half steps of the musical scale — **chro·mat·i·cism** \-tə-,si-zəm\ *n*

chro·mato·graph \krō-'ma-tə-,graf\ *n* : an instrument used in chromatography

chro·ma·tog·ra·phy \,krō-mə-'tä-grə-fē\ *n* : the separation of a complex mixture into its component compounds as a result of the different rates at which the compounds travel through or over a stationary substance due to differing affinities for the substance — **chro·mato·graph·ic** \krō-,ma-tə-'gra-fik\ *adj* — **chro·mato·graph·i·cal·ly** \-fi-k(ə-)lē\ *adv*

chrome \'krōm\ *n* **1** : CHROMIUM **2** : a chromium pigment **3** : something plated with an alloy of chromium

chro·mi·um \'krō-mē-əm\ *n* : a bluish white metallic element used esp. in alloys and chrome plating

chro·mo·some \'krō-mə-,sōm, -,zōm\ *n* [G *Chromosom*, fr. Gk *chrōma* color, pigment + *sōma* body] : any of the rod-shaped or threadlike DNA-containing structures of cellular organisms that contain most or all of the genes of the organism — **chro·mo·som·al** \,krō-mə-'sō-məl, -'zō-\ *adj*

chro·mo·sphere \'krō-mə-,sfir\ *n* : the lower part of a star's atmosphere

chron *abbr* **1** chronicle **2** chronological; chronology

Chron *abbr* Chronicles

chron·ic \'krä-nik\ *adj* : marked by long duration or frequent recurrence ⟨a ~ disease⟩; *also* : HABITUAL ⟨a ~ grumbler⟩ — **chron·i·cal·ly** \-ni-k(ə-)lē\ *adv*

chronic fatigue syndrome *n* : a disorder of unknown cause that is characterized by persistent profound fatigue

¹chron·i·cle \'krä-ni-kəl\ *n* : HISTORY, NARRATIVE

²chronicle *vb* **-cled; -cling** : to record in or as if in a chronicle — **chron·i·cler** *n*

Chronicles *n* — see BIBLE table

chro·no·graph \'krä-nə-,graf\ *n* : an instrument for measuring and recording time intervals with accuracy — **chro·no·graph·ic** \,krä-nə-'gra-fik\ *adj* — **chro·nog·ra·phy** \krə-'nä-grə-fē\ *n*

chro·nol·o·gy \krə-'nä-lə-jē\ *n, pl* **-gies** **1** : the science that deals with measuring time and dating events **2** : a chronological list or table **3** : arrangement of events in the order of their occurrence — **chron·o·log·i·cal** \,krän-ºl-'ä-ji-kəl\ *adj* — **chron·o·log·i·cal·ly** \-k(ə-)lē\ *adv* — **chro·nol·o·gist** \krə-'nä-lə-jist\ *n*

chro·nom·e·ter \krə-'nä-mə-tər\ *n* : a very accurate timepiece

chrys·a·lid \'kri-sə-ləd\ *n* : CHRYSALIS

chrys·a·lis \'kri-sə-ləs\ *n, pl* **chry·sal·i·des** \kri-'sa-lə-,dēz\ *or* **chrys·a·lis·es** : an insect pupa in a firm case without a cocoon

chry·san·the·mum \kri-'san-thə-məm\ *n* [L, fr. Gk *chrysanthemon*, fr. *chrysos* gold + *anthemon* flower] : any of various plants related to the daisies including some grown for their showy brightly colored flowers or for medicinal products or insecticides; *also* : a flower of a chrysanthemum

chub \'chəb\ *n, pl* **chub** *or* **chubs** : any of various small freshwater fishes related to the carp

chub·by \'chə-bē\ *adj* **chub·bi·er; -est** : PLUMP ⟨a ~ child⟩ — **chub·bi·ness** *n*

¹chuck \'chək\ *vb* **1** : to give a pat or tap **2** : TOSS **3** : DISCARD; *also* : EJECT **4** : to have done with ⟨~ed his job⟩

²chuck *n* **1** : a light pat under the chin **2** : TOSS

³chuck *n* **1** : a cut of beef including most of the neck and the parts around the shoulder blade and the first three ribs **2** : a device for holding work or a tool in a machine (as a lathe)

chuck·hole \'chək-,hōl\ *n* : POTHOLE

chuck·le \'chə-kəl\ *vb* **chuck·led; chuck·ling** : to laugh in a quiet hardly audible manner — **chuckle** *n*

chuck wagon *n* : a wagon equipped with a stove and food supplies

¹chug \'chəg\ *n* : a dull explosive sound made by or as if by a laboring engine

²chug *vb* **chugged; chug·ging** : to move or go with chugs

chuk·ka \'chə-kə\ *n* : a usu. ankle-length leather boot

chuk·ker \'chə-kər\ *also* **chuk·ka** \'chə-kə\ *n* : a playing period of a polo game

¹chum \'chəm\ *n* : a close friend

²chum *vb* **chummed; chum·ming** **1** : to room together **2** : to be a close friend

chum·my \'chə-mē\ *adj* **chum·mi·er; -est** : quite friendly — **chum·mi·ly** \-mə-lē\ *adv* — **chum·mi·ness** \-mē-nəs\ *n*

chump \'chəmp\ *n* : FOOL, BLOCKHEAD

chunk \'chəŋk\ *n* **1** : a short thick piece ⟨a ~ of meat⟩ **2** : a sizable amount

chunky \'chəŋ-kē\ *adj* **chunk·i·er; -est** **1** : STOCKY **2** : containing chunks

church \'chərch\ *n* [ME *chirche*, fr. OE *cirice*, ultim. fr. LGk *kyriakon*, fr. Gk, neut. of *kyriakos* of the lord, fr. *kyrios* lord, master] **1** : a building esp. for Christian public worship **2** *often cap* : the whole body of Christians **3** : DENOMINATION **4** : CONGREGATION **5** : public divine worship

church·go·er \'chərch-,gō-ər\ *n* : one who habitually attends church — **church·go·ing** *adj or n*

church·less \'chərch-ləs\ *adj* : not affiliated with a church

church·man \'chərch-mən\ *n* **1** : CLERGYMAN **2** : a member of a church

church·war·den \'chərch-,wòr-dⁿn\ *n* : WARDEN 5

church·yard \-,yärd\ *n* : a yard that belongs to a church and is often used as a burial ground

churl \'chərl\ *n* **1** : a medieval peasant **2** : RUSTIC **3** : a rude ill-bred person — **churl·ish** *adj* — **churl·ish·ly** *adv* — **churl·ish·ness** *n*

¹churn \'chərn\ *n* : a container in which milk or cream is agitated in making butter

²churn *vb* **1** : to stir in a churn; *also* : to make (butter) by such stirring **2** : to shake around violently

churn out *vb* : to produce mechanically or in large quantity

chute \'shüt\ *n* **1** : an inclined surface, trough, or passage down or through which something may pass ⟨a coal ∼⟩ ⟨a mail ∼⟩ **2** : PARACHUTE

chut·ney \'chət-nē\ *n, pl* **chutneys** : a thick sauce containing fruits, vinegar, sugar, and spices

chutz·pah \'huṫ-spə, 'k̇uṫ-, -(ˌ)spä\ *n* : supreme self-confidence

CIA *abbr* Central Intelligence Agency

cía *abbr* [Sp *compañía*] company

cia·bat·ta \chə-'bä-tə\ *n* [It, lit., slipper] : a flat bread with a moist interior and a crispy crust

ciao \'chaù\ *interj* — used to express greeting or farewell

ci·ca·da \sə-'kā-də\ *n* : any of a family of stout-bodied insects related to the aphids and having wide blunt heads and large transparent wings

ci·ca·trix \'si-kə-ˌtriks\ *n, pl* **ci·ca·tri·ces** \ˌsi-kə-'trī-ˌsēz\ [L] : a scar resulting from formation and contraction of fibrous tissue in a wound

ci·ce·ro·ne \ˌsi-sə-'rō-nē, ˌchē-chə-\ *n, pl* **-ni** \-(ˌ)nē\ : a guide who conducts sightseers

CID *abbr* Criminal Investigation Department

ci·der \'sī-dər\ *n* : juice pressed from fruit (as apples) and used as a beverage, vinegar, or flavoring

cie *abbr* [F *compagnie*] company

ci·gar \si-'gär\ *n* [Sp *cigarro*] : a roll of tobacco for smoking

cig·a·rette \ˌsi-gə-'ret, 'si-gə-ˌret\ *n* [F, dim. of *cigare* cigar] : a slender roll of cut tobacco enclosed in paper for smoking

cig·a·ril·lo \ˌsi-gə-'ri-lō, -'rē-ō\ *n, pl* **-los** [Sp] **1** : a very small cigar **2** : a cigarette wrapped in tobacco rather than paper

ci·lan·tro \si-'län-trō, -'lan-\ *n* : leaves of coriander used as a flavoring or garnish; *also* : the coriander plant

cil·i·ate \'si-lē-ˌāt\ *n* : any of a group of protozoans characterized by cilia

cil·i·um \'si-lē-əm\ *n, pl* **cil·ia** \-lē-ə\ **1** : a minute short hairlike process; *esp* : one of a cell **2** : EYELASH

C in C *abbr* commander in chief

cinch \'sinch\ *n* **1** : a girth for a pack or saddle **2** : a sure or an easy thing — **cinch** *vb*

cin·cho·na \siŋ-'kō-nə\ *n* : any of a genus of So. American trees related to the madder; *also* : the bitter quinine-containing bark of a cinchona

cinc·ture \'siŋk-chər\ *n* : BELT, SASH

cin·der \'sin-dər\ *n* **1** : SLAG **2** *pl* : ASHES **3** : a hot piece of partly burned wood or coal **4** : a fragment of lava from an erupting volcano — **cin·dery** *adj*

cinder block *n* : a building block made of cement and coal cinders

cin·e·ma \'si-nə-mə\ *n* **1** : a motion-picture theater **2** : MOVIES — **cin·e·mat·ic** \ˌsi-nə-'ma-tik\ *adj*

cin·e·ma·theque \ˌsi-nə-mə-'tek\ *n* : a small movie house specializing in avant-garde films

cin·e·ma·tog·ra·phy \ˌsi-nə-mə-'tä-grə-fē\ *n* : motion-picture photography — **cin·e·ma·tog·ra·pher** *n* — **cin·e·mat·o·graph·ic** \-ˌma-tə-'gra-fik\ *adj*

cine·phile \'si-nə-ˌfī(-ə)l\ *n* : a lover of motion pictures

cin·e·plex \'si-nə-ˌpleks\ *n* : a complex that houses several movie theaters

cin·er·ar·i·um \ˌsi-nə-'rer-ē-əm\ *n, pl* **-ia** \-ē-ə\ : a place to receive the ashes of the cremated dead — **cin·er·ary** \'si-nə-ˌrer-ē\ *adj*

cin·na·bar \'si-nə-ˌbär\ *n* **1** : a red mineral that is the only important ore of mercury **2** : a deep vivid red

cin·na·mon \'si-nə-mən\ *n* : a spice prepared from the highly aromatic bark of any of several Asian trees related to the true laurel; *also* : a tree that yields cinnamon

cinque·foil \'siŋk-ˌfói(-ə)l, 'saŋk-\ *n* : any of a genus of plants related to the roses with leaves having five lobes

¹ci·pher \'sī-fər\ *n* [ME, fr. ML *cifra*, fr. Ar *ṣifr* empty, zero] **1** : ZERO, NAUGHT **2** : a method of secret writing

²cipher *vb* : to compute arithmetically

cir *or* **circ** *abbr* circular

cir·ca \'sər-kə\ *prep* : ABOUT ⟨∼ 1600⟩

cir·ca·di·an \ˌsər-'kā-dē-ən\ *adj* : being, having, characterized by, or occurring in approximately 24-hour intervals (as of biological activity)

¹cir·cle \'sər-kəl\ *n* **1** : a closed curve every point of which

is equally distant from a fixed point within it **2** : something circular **3** : an area of action or influence **4** : CYCLE **5** : a group bound by a common tie ⟨sewing ∼⟩

²circle *vb* **cir·cled; cir·cling** **1** : to enclose in a circle **2** : to move or revolve around; *also* : to move in a circle

cir·clet \'sər-klət\ *n* : a small circle; *esp* : a circular ornament

cir·cuit \'sər-kət\ *n* **1** : a boundary around an enclosed space **2** : a course around a periphery **3** : a regular tour (as by a judge) around an assigned territory **4** : the complete path of an electric current; *also* : an assemblage of electronic components **5** : LEAGUE; *also* : a chain of theaters

circuit board *n* : BOARD 7

circuit breaker *n* : a switch that automatically interrupts the current of an overloaded circuit

circuit court *n* : a court that sits at two or more places within one judicial district

cir·cu·i·tous \ˌsər-'kyü-ə-təs\ *adj* **1** : having a circular or winding course ⟨a ∼ route⟩ **2** : not being forthright or direct in language or action ⟨a ∼ explanation⟩

cir·cuit·ry \'sər-kə-trē\ *n, pl* **-ries** : the plan or the components of an electric circuit

cir·cu·ity \ˌsər-'kyü-ə-tē\ *n, pl* **-ities** : INDIRECTION

¹cir·cu·lar \'sər-kyə-lər\ *adj* **1** : having the form of a circle : ROUND **2** : moving in or around a circle **3** : CIRCUITOUS **4** : intended for circulation ⟨a ∼ letter⟩ — **cir·cu·lar·i·ty** \ˌsər-kyə-'ler-ə-tē\ *n*

²circular *n* : a paper (as a leaflet) intended for wide distribution

cir·cu·lar·ise *Brit var of* CIRCULARIZE

cir·cu·lar·ize \'sər-kyə-lə-ˌrīz\ *vb* **-ized; -iz·ing** **1** : to send circulars to **2** : to poll by questionnaire **3** : to make circular

circular saw *n* : a power saw with a round cutting blade

cir·cu·late \'sər-kyə-ˌlāt\ *vb* **-lat·ed; -lat·ing** **1** : to move or cause to move in a circle, circuit, or orbit **2** : to pass from place to place or from person to person — **cir·cu·la·tion** \ˌsər-kyə-'lā-shən\ *n*

cir·cu·la·to·ry \'sər-kyə-lə-ˌtór-ē\ *adj* : of or relating to circulation or the circulatory system

circulatory system *n* : the system of blood, blood vessels, lymphatic vessels, and heart concerned with the circulation of the blood and lymph

cir·cum·am·bu·late \ˌsər-kəm-'am-byə-ˌlāt\ *vb* **-lat·ed; -lat·ing** : to circle on foot esp. as part of a ritual

cir·cum·cise \'sər-kəm-ˌsīz\ *vb* **-cised; -cis·ing** [ME, fr. L *circumcisus*, pp. of *circumcidere*, lit., to cut around, fr. *circum* around + *caedere* to cut] : to cut off the foreskin of — **cir·cum·ci·sion** \ˌsər-kəm-'si-zhən\ *n*

cir·cum·fer·ence \sər-'kəm-f(ə-)rəns\ *n* **1** : the perimeter of a circle **2** : the external boundary or surface of a figure or object

cir·cum·flex \'sər-kəm-ˌfleks\ *n* : the mark ˆ over a vowel

cir·cum·lo·cu·tion \ˌsər-kəm-lō-'kyü-shən\ *n* : the use of unnecessary words in expressing an idea

cir·cum·lu·nar \-'lü-nər\ *adj* : revolving about or surrounding the moon

cir·cum·nav·i·gate \-'na-və-ˌgāt\ *vb* : to go completely around (as the earth) esp. by water — **cir·cum·nav·i·ga·tion** \-ˌna-və-'gā-shən\ *n*

cir·cum·po·lar \-'pō-lər\ *adj* **1** : continually visible above the horizon ⟨a ∼ star⟩ **2** : surrounding or found near a pole of the earth ⟨a ∼ current⟩

cir·cum·scribe \'sər-kəm-ˌskrīb\ *vb* **1** : to constrict the range or activity of **2** : to draw a line around — **cir·cum·scrip·tion** \ˌsər-kəm-'skrip-shən\ *n*

cir·cum·spect \'sər-kəm-ˌspekt\ *adj* : careful to consider all circumstances and consequences : PRUDENT — **cir·cum·spec·tion** \ˌsər-kəm-'spek-shən\ *n*

cir·cum·stance \'sər-kəm-ˌstans\ *n* **1** : a fact or event that must be considered along with another fact or event **2** : surrounding conditions **3** : CHANCE, FATE **4** *pl* : situation with regard to wealth **5** : CEREMONY ⟨pomp and ∼⟩

cir·cum·stan·tial \ˌsər-kəm-'stan-chəl\ *adj* **1** : consisting of or depending on circumstances **2** : INCIDENTAL **3** : containing full details — **cir·cum·stan·tial·ly** *adv*

cir·cum·vent \ˌsər-kəm-'vent\ *vb* : to check or defeat esp. by stratagem — **cir·cum·ven·tion** \-'vent-shən\ *n*

cir·cus \'sər-kəs\ *n* **1** : a usu. traveling show that features feats of physical skill, wild animal acts, and performances by clowns **2** : a circus performance; *also* : the equipment, livestock, and personnel of a circus

cirque \'sərk\ *n* : a deep steep-walled mountain basin usu. forming the blunt end of a valley

cir·rho·sis \sə-'rō-səs\ *n, pl* **-rho·ses** \-,sēz\ [NL, fr. Gk *kirrhos* orange-colored] : fibrosis of the liver — **cir·rhot·ic** \-'rä-tik\ *adj or n*

cir·rus \'sir-əs\ *n, pl* **cir·ri** \'sir-,ī\ : a wispy white cloud usu. of minute ice crystals at high altitudes

cis \'sis\ *adj* : CISGENDER

cis·gen·der \(,)sis-'jen-dər\ *also* **cis·gen·dered** \-dərd\ *adj* : of, relating to, or being a person whose gender identity corresponds with the sex the person had or was identified as having at birth

cis·lu·nar \(,)sis-'lü-nər\ *adj* : lying between the earth and the moon or the moon's orbit

cis·sy *Brit var of* SISSY

cis·tern \'sis-tərn\ *n* : an often underground tank for storing water

cit *abbr* **1** citation; cited **2** citizen

cit·a·del \'si-tə-dəl, -,del\ *n* **1** : a fortress commanding a city **2** : STRONGHOLD

ci·ta·tion \sī-'tā-shən\ *n* **1** : an official summons to appear (as before a court) **2** : QUOTATION **3** : a formal statement of the achievements of a person; *also* : a specific reference in a military dispatch to meritorious performance of duty

cite \'sīt\ *vb* **cit·ed; cit·ing** **1** : to summon to appear before a court **2** : QUOTE **3** : to refer to esp. in commendation or praise

cit·i·fied \'si-ti-,fīd\ *adj* : of, relating to, or characterized by an urban style of living

cit·i·zen \'si-tə-zən\ *n* **1** : an inhabitant of a city or town **2** : a person who owes allegiance to a government and is entitled to its protection — **cit·i·zen·ship** *n*

cit·i·zen·ry \-rē\ *n, pl* **-ries** : a whole body of citizens

citizens band *n* : a range of radio frequencies set aside for private radio communications

cit·ric acid \'si-trik-\ *n* : a sour organic acid obtained from lemon and lime juices or by fermentation of sugars and used chiefly as a flavoring

cit·ron \'si-trən\ *n* **1** : the oval lemonlike fruit of a citrus tree; *also* : the tree **2** : a small hard-fleshed watermelon used esp. in pickles and preserves

cit·ro·nel·la \,si-trə-'ne-lə\ *n* : a lemon-scented oil obtained from a fragrant grass of southern Asia and used in perfumes and as an insect repellent

cit·rus \'si-trəs\ *n, pl* **citrus** *or* **cit·rus·es** : any of a genus of often thorny evergreen trees or shrubs grown in warm regions for their fruits (as the orange, lemon, lime, and grapefruit); *also* : the fruit

city \'si-tē\ *n, pl* **cit·ies** [ME *citie* large or small town, fr. AF *cité*, fr. ML *civitas*, fr. L, citizenship, state, city of Rome, fr. *civis* citizen] **1** : an inhabited place larger or more important than a town **2** : a municipality in the U.S. governed under a charter granted by the state; *also* : an incorporated municipal unit of the highest class in Canada

city manager *n* : an official employed by an elected council to direct the administration of a city government

city–state \'si-tē-,stāt\ *n* : an autonomous state consisting of a city and surrounding territory

civ *abbr* **1** civil; civilian **2** civilization

civ·et \'si-vət\ *n* : a yellowish strong-smelling substance obtained from a catlike Old World mammal (**civet cat**) and used in making perfumes

civ·ic \'si-vik\ *adj* : of or relating to a city, citizenship, or civil affairs

civ·ics \-viks\ *n* : a social science dealing with the rights and duties of citizens

civ·il \'si-vəl\ *adj* **1** : of or relating to citizens or to the state as a political body **2** : COURTEOUS, POLITE **3** : of or relating to legal proceedings in connection with private rights and obligations ⟨the ∼ code⟩ **4** : of or relating to the general population : not military or ecclesiastical

civil defense *n* : protective measures and emergency relief activities conducted by civilians in case of enemy attack or natural disaster

civil disobedience *n* : refusal to obey governmental commands esp. as a nonviolent means of protest

civil engineer *n* : an engineer whose training or occupation is in the design and construction esp. of public works (as roads or harbors) — **civil engineering** *n*

ci·vil·ian \sə-'vil-yən\ *n* : a person not on active duty in a military, police, or fire-fighting force

civ·i·li·sa·tion, civ·i·lise *chiefly Brit var of* CIVILIZATION, CIVILIZE

ci·vil·i·ty \sə-'vi-lə-tē\ *n, pl* **-ties** **1** : POLITENESS, COURTESY **2** : a polite act or expression

civ·i·li·za·tion \,si-və-lə-'zā-shən\ *n* **1** : a relatively high level of cultural and technological development **2** : the culture characteristic of a time or place — **civ·i·li·za·tion·al** \-shə-nᵊl\ *adj*

civ·i·lize \'si-və-,līz\ *vb* **-lized; -liz·ing** **1** : to raise from a primitive state to an advanced and ordered stage of cultural development **2** : REFINE — **civ·i·lized** *adj*

civil liberty *n* : freedom from arbitrary governmental interference specifically by denial of governmental power — usu. used in pl.

civ·il·ly \'si-vəl-lē\ *adv* **1** : in terms of civil rights, matters, or law ⟨∼ dead⟩ **2** : in a civil manner : POLITELY

civil rights *n pl* : the nonpolitical rights of a citizen; *esp* : those guaranteed by the 13th and 14th amendments to the Constitution and by acts of Congress

civil servant *n* : a member of a civil service

civil service *n* : the administrative service of a government

civil war *n* : a war between opposing groups of citizens of the same country

civ·vies \'si-vēz\ *n pl* : civilian clothes as distinguished from a military uniform

CJ *abbr* chief justice

ck *abbr* **1** cask **2** check

cl *abbr* **1** centiliter **2** class

Cl *symbol* chlorine

¹clack \'klak\ *vb* **1** : CHATTER, PRATTLE **2** : to make or cause to make a clatter

²clack *n* **1** : rapid continuous talk : CHATTER **2** : a sound of clacking ⟨the ∼ of a typewriter⟩

clad \'klad\ *adj* **1** : CLOTHED, COVERED **2** : being or consisting of coins made of outer layers of one metal bonded to a core of a different metal

¹claim \'klām\ *vb* [ME, fr. AF *claimer, clamer*, fr. L *clamare* to cry out, shout] **1** : to ask for as one's own; *also* : to take as the rightful owner **2** : to call for : REQUIRE **3** : to state as a fact : MAINTAIN

²claim *n* **1** : a demand for something due ⟨an insurance ∼⟩ **2** : a right to something usu. in another's possession **3** : an assertion open to challenge **4** : something claimed (as a tract of land)

claim·ant \'klā-mənt\ *n* : a person making a claim

clair·voy·ant \klar-'vȯi-ənt\ *adj* [F, fr. *clair* clear + *voyant* seeing] **1** : able to see beyond the range of ordinary perception **2** : having the power of discerning objects not present to the senses — **clair·voy·ance** \-əns\ *n* — **clairvoyant** *n*

clam \'klam\ *n* **1** : any of numerous bivalve mollusks including many that are edible **2** : DOLLAR

clam 1

clam·bake \-,bāk\ *n* : a party or gathering (as at the seashore) at which food is cooked usu. on heated rocks covered by seaweed

clam·ber \'klam-bər\ *vb* : to climb awkwardly — **clam·ber·er** *n*

clam·my \'kla-mē\ *adj* **clam·mi·er; -est** : being damp, soft, sticky, and usu. cool — **clam·mi·ness** *n*

clam·or \'kla-mər\ *n* **1** : a noisy shouting **2** : a loud continuous noise **3** : insistent public expression (as of support or protest) — **clamor** *vb* — **clam·or·ous** *adj*

clam·our *chiefly Brit var of* CLAMOR

¹clamp \'klamp\ *n* : a device that holds or presses parts together firmly

²clamp *vb* : to fasten with or as if with a clamp

clamp down *vb* : to impose restrictions : become repressive — **clamp-down** \'klamp-,daún\ *n*

clam-shell \'klam-,shel\ *n* 1 : the shell of a clam 2 : a bucket or grapnel (as on a dredge) having two hinged jaws

clam up *vb* : to become silent

clan \'klan\ *n* [ME, fr. ScGael *clann* offspring, clan, fr. Old Irish *cland* plant, offspring, fr. L *planta* plant] : a group (as in the Scottish Highlands) made up of households whose heads claim descent from a common ancestor — **clan-nish** *adj* — **clan-nish-ness** *n*

clan-des-tine \klan-'des-tən\ *adj* : held in or conducted with secrecy

clang \'klaŋ\ *n* : a loud metallic ringing sound — **clang** *vb*

clan-gor \'klaŋ-ər, -gər\ *n* : a resounding clang or medley of clangs

clan-gour *chiefly Brit var of* CLANGOR

clank \'klaŋk\ *n* : a sharp brief metallic ringing sound — **clank** *vb*

¹clap \'klap\ *vb* **clapped; clap-ping** 1 : to strike noisily 2 : APPLAUD

²clap *n* 1 : a loud noisy crash 2 : the noise made by clapping the hands

³clap *n* : GONORRHEA

clap-board \'kla-bərd, -,bórd; 'klap-,bórd\ *n* : a narrow board thicker at one edge than the other used for siding — **clap-board** *vb*

clap-per \'kla-pər\ *n* : one that claps; *esp* : the tongue of a bell

clap-trap \'klap-,trap\ *n* : pretentious nonsense

claque \'klak\ *n* [F, fr. *claquer* to clap] 1 : a group hired to applaud at a performance 2 : a group of sycophants

clar-et \'kler-ət\ *n* [ME, fr. AF (*vin*) *claret* clear wine] : a dry red wine

clar-i-fy \'kler-ə-,fī\ *vb* **-fied; -fy-ing** : to make or become clear — **clar-i-fi-ca-tion** \,kler-ə-fə-'kā-shən\ *n*

clar-i-net \,kler-ə-'net\ *n* : a single-reed woodwind instrument in the form of a cylindrical tube with a moderately flaring end — **clar-i-net-ist** *or* **clar-i-net-tist** \-'ne-tist\ *n*

clar-i-on \'kler-ē-ən\ *adj* : brilliantly clear ⟨a ~ call⟩

clar-i-ty \'kler-ə-tē\ *n* : CLEARNESS

¹clash \'klash\ *vb* 1 : to make or cause to make a clash 2 : CONFLICT, COLLIDE

²clash *n* 1 : a noisy usu. metallic sound of collision 2 : a hostile encounter 3 : a sharp conflict ⟨a ~ of opinions⟩

clasp \'klasp\ *n* : a device (as a hook) for holding objects or parts together 2 : EMBRACE, GRASP — **clasp** *vb*

¹class \'klas\ *n* [F *classe*, fr. L *classis* group called to military service, fleet, class] 1 : a group of students meeting regularly in a course; *also* : a group graduating together 2 : a course of instruction; *also* : the period when such a course is taught 3 : social rank; *also* : high quality 4 : a group of the same general status or nature; *esp* : a major category in biological classification that is above the order and below the phylum 5 : a division or rating based on grade or quality — **class-less** *adj*

²class *vb* : CLASSIFY

class action *n* : a legal action undertaken in behalf of the plaintiffs and all others having an identical interest in the alleged wrong

¹clas-sic \'kla-sik\ *adj* 1 : serving as a standard of excellence ⟨a ~ novel⟩; *also* : TRADITIONAL 2 : CLASSICAL 2 3 : notable esp. as the best example ⟨his winning goal was ~⟩ 4 : AUTHENTIC ⟨a ~ folk dance⟩

²classic *n* 1 : a work of enduring excellence and esp. of ancient Greece or Rome; *also* : its author 2 : a traditional event ⟨a football ~⟩

clas-si-cal \'kla-si-kəl\ *adj* 1 : CLASSIC 2 : of or relating to the ancient Greek and Roman classics 3 : of or relating to a form or system of primary significance before modern times ⟨~ economics⟩ 4 : concerned with a general study of the arts and sciences — **clas-si-cal-ly** \-k(ə-)lē\ *adv*

clas-si-cism \'kla-sə-,si-zəm\ *n* 1 : the principles or style of the literature or art of ancient Greece and Rome 2 : adherence to traditional standards believed to be universally valid — **clas-si-cist** \-sist\ *n*

clas-si-fied \'kla-sə-,fīd\ *adj* : withheld from general circulation for reasons of national security

clas-si-fieds \-,fīdz\ *n pl* : advertisements grouped by subject

clas-si-fy \'kla-sə-,fī\ *vb* **-fied; -fy-ing** : to arrange in or assign to classes — **clas-si-fi-able** *adj* — **clas-si-fi-ca-tion** \,kla-sə-fə-'kā-shən\ *n* — **clas-si-fi-er** *n*

class-mate \'klas-,māt\ *n* : a member of the same class (as in a college)

class-room \-,rüm-, -,rùm\ *n* : a place where classes meet

classy \'kla-sē\ *adj* **class-i-er; -est** : ELEGANT, STYLISH ⟨a ~ clientele⟩ — **class-i-ness** *n*

clat-ter \'kla-tər\ *n* : a rattling sound ⟨the ~ of dishes⟩ — **clatter** *vb*

clause \'klóz\ *n* 1 : a group of words having its own subject and predicate but forming only part of a compound or complex sentence 2 : a separate part of an article or document

claus-tro-pho-bia \,kló-strə-'fō-bē-ə\ *n* : abnormal dread of being in closed or narrow spaces — **claus-tro-pho-bic** \-bik\ *adj*

clav-i-chord \'kla-və-,kórd\ *n* : an early keyboard instrument in use before the piano

clav-i-cle \'kla-vi-kəl\ *n* [F *clavicule*, fr. NL *clavicula*, fr. L, dim. of L *clavis* key] : COLLARBONE

cla-vier \klə-'vir; 'klā-vē-ər\ *n* 1 : the keyboard of a musical instrument 2 : an early keyboard instrument

¹claw \'kló\ *n* 1 : a sharp usu. curved nail on the toe of an animal 2 : a sharp curved process (as on the foot of an insect); *also* : a pincerlike organ at the end of a limb of some arthropods (as a lobster) — **clawed** \'klód\ *adj*

²claw *vb* : to rake, seize, or dig with or as if with claws

clay \'klā\ *n* 1 : an earthy material that is plastic when moist but hard when fired and is used in making pottery; *also* : finely divided soil consisting largely of such clay 2 : EARTH, MUD 3 : a plastic substance used for modeling 4 : the mortal human body — **clay-ey** \'klā-ē\ *adj*

clay-more \'klā-,mór\ *n* : a large 2-edged sword formerly used by Scottish Highlanders

clay pigeon *n* : a saucer-shaped target thrown from a trap in trapshooting

¹clean \'klēn\ *adj* 1 : free from dirt, disease, or pollution ⟨~ air⟩ 2 : PURE ⟨the ~ thrill of one's first flight⟩; *also* : HONORABLE 3 : THOROUGH ⟨made a ~ sweep⟩ 4 : TRIM ⟨a ~ edge⟩ ⟨a ship with ~ lines⟩; *also* : EVEN 5 : habitually neat ⟨~ clean⟩ — **clean** *adv* — **clean-ly** \'klēn-lē\ *adv* — **clean-ness** \'klēn-nəs\ *n*

²clean *vb* : to make or become clean — **clean-able** \'klē-nə-bəl\ *adj* — **clean-er** *n*

clean-cut \'klēn-'kət\ *adj* 1 : cut so that the surface or edge is smooth and even 2 : sharply defined or outlined 3 : giving an effect of wholesomeness

clean-ly \'klen-lē\ *adj* **clean-li-er; -est** 1 : careful to keep clean 2 : habitually kept clean — **clean-li-ness** *n*

clean room \'klēn-,rüm, -,rùm\ *n* : an uncontaminated room maintained for the manufacture or assembly of objects (as precision parts)

cleanse \'klenz\ *vb* **cleansed; cleans-ing** : to make clean — **cleans-er** *n*

¹cleanup \'klēn-,əp\ *n* 1 : an act or instance of cleaning 2 : a very large profit

²cleanup *adj* : being 4th in the batting order of a baseball team — **cleanup** *adv*

clean up *vb* : to make up a profit business profit

¹clear \'klir\ *adj* [ME *clere*, fr. AF *cler*, fr. L *clarus*] 1 : BRIGHT, LUMINOUS; *also* : UNTROUBLED, SERENE 2 : CLOUDLESS 3 : CLEAN, PURE; *also* : TRANSPARENT 4 : easily heard, seen, or understood 5 : capable of sharp discernment; *also* : free from doubt 6 : INNOCENT ⟨~ conscience⟩ 7 : free from restriction, obstruction, or entanglement — **clear** *adv* — **clear-ness** *n*

²clear *vb* 1 : to make or become clear 2 : to go away : DISPERSE 3 : to free from accusation or blame; *also* : to certify as trustworthy 4 : EXPLAIN 5 : to get free from obstruction 6 : SETTLE ⟨~ a debt⟩ 7 : NET ⟨~ed a profit⟩ 8 : to get rid of : REMOVE ⟨~ the snow off the driveway⟩ 9 : to jump or go by without touching; *also* : PASS ⟨the bill ~ed the legislature⟩

³clear *n* : a clear space or part

clear-ance \'klir-əns\ *n* 1 : an act or process of clearing

2 : the distance by which one object clears another **3** : AUTHORIZATION

clear–cut \'klir-'kət\ *adj* **1** : sharply outlined **2** : DEFINITE, UNEQUIVOCAL ⟨a ∼ victory⟩

clear–cut·ting \-,kə-tiŋ\ *n* : removal of all the trees in a stand of timber — **clear–cut** \-,kət\ *vb*

clear·head·ed \-'he-dəd\ *adj* : having a clear understanding : PERCEPTIVE

clear·ing \'klir-iŋ\ *n* **1** : a tract of land cleared of wood and brush **2** : the passage of checks and claims through a clearinghouse

clear·ing·house \-,haús\ *n* : an institution maintained by banks for making an exchange of checks and claims held by each bank against other banks; *also* : an informal channel for information or assistance

clear·ly \'klir-lē\ *adv* **1** : in a clear manner **2** : it is clear

cleat \'klēt\ *n* : a piece of wood or metal fastened on or projecting from something to give strength, provide a grip, or prevent slipping

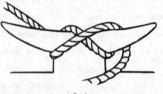

cleat

cleav·age \'klē-vij\ *n* **1** : a splitting apart : SPLIT **2** : the depression between a woman's breasts esp. when exposed by a low-cut neckline

¹cleave \'klēv\ *vb* **cleaved** \'klēvd\ *or* **clove** \'klōv\; **cleaved; cleav·ing** : ADHERE, CLING ⟨the child *cleaved* to her mother⟩

²cleave *vb* **cleaved** \'klēvd\ *also* **cleft** \'kleft\ *or* **clove** \'klōv\; **cleaved** *also* **cleft** *or* **clo·ven** \'klō-vən\; **cleav·ing 1** : to divide by force : split asunder ⟨∼ logs⟩ **2** : DIVIDE

cleav·er \'klē-vər\ *n* : a heavy chopping knife for cutting meat

clef \'klef\ *n* : a sign placed on the staff in music to show what pitch is represented by each line and space

cleft \'kleft\ *n* : FISSURE, CRACK

cleft lip *n* : a birth defect in which the upper lip is vertically split

cleft palate *n* : a split in the roof of the mouth that appears as a birth defect

clem·a·tis \'kle-mə-təs; kli-'ma-təs\ *n* : any of a genus of vines or herbs related to the buttercups that have showy usu. white or purple flowers

clem·en·cy \'kle-mən-sē\ *n, pl* **-cies 1** : disposition to be merciful **2** : mildness of weather

clem·ent \'kle-mənt\ *adj* **1** : MERCIFUL, LENIENT ⟨a ∼ judge⟩ **2** : TEMPERATE, MILD ⟨∼ weather for this time of year⟩

clem·en·tine \'kle-mən-,tēn\ *n* : a small citrus fruit that is probably a hybrid between a tangerine and an orange

clench \'klench\ *vb* **1** : CLINCH 1 **2** : to hold fast **3** : to set or close tightly

clere·sto·ry \'klir-,stór-ē\ *n* : an outside wall of a room or building that rises above an adjoining roof and contains windows

cler·gy \'klər-jē\ *n* : a body of religious officials authorized to conduct services

cler·gy·man \-mən\ *n* : a member of the clergy

cler·gy·per·son \-,pər-s°n\ *n* : a member of the clergy

cler·ic \'kler-ik\ *n* : a member of the clergy

cler·i·cal \'kler-i-kəl\ *adj* **1** : of or relating to the clergy ⟨∼ vestments⟩ **2** : of or relating to a clerk

cler·i·cal·ism \'kler-i-kə-,li-zəm\ *n* : a policy of maintaining or increasing the power of a religious hierarchy

clerk \'klərk, *Brit* 'klärk\ *n* **1** : CLERIC **2** : an official responsible for correspondence, records, and accounts; *also* : a person employed to perform general office work **3** : a store salesperson — **clerk** *vb* — **clerk·ship** *n*

clev·er \'kle-vər\ *adj* **1** : showing skill or resourcefulness **2** : marked by wit or ingenuity — **clev·er·ly** *adv* — **clev·er·ness** *n*

clev·is \'kle-vəs\ *n* : a U-shaped shackle used for fastening

¹clew \'klü\ *n* **1** : CLUE **2** : a metal loop on a lower corner of a sail

²clew *vb* : to haul (a sail) up or down by ropes through the clews

cli·ché \kli-'shā\ *n* [F] : a trite phrase or expression — **cli·chéd** \-'shād\ *adj*

¹click \'klik\ *vb* **1** : to make or cause to make a click **2** : to fit or work together smoothly **3** : to select or make a selection on a computer by pressing a button on a control device (as a mouse) — **click·able** \'kli-kə-bəl\ *adj*

²click *n* **1** : a slight sharp noise **2** : an instance of clicking ⟨a mouse ∼⟩

click·er \'kli-kər\ *n* : REMOTE CONTROL 2

cli·ent \'klī-ənt\ *n* **1** : DEPENDENT **2** : a person who engages the professional services of another; *also* : PATRON, CUSTOMER **3** : a computer in a network that uses the services (as access to files) provided by a server

cli·en·tele \,klī-ən-'tel, ,klē-\ *n* : a body of clients and esp. customers

cliff \'klif\ *n* : a high steep face of rock, earth. or ice

cliff–hang·er \-,haŋ-ər\ *n* **1** : an adventure serial or melodrama usu. presented in installments each of which ends in suspense **2** : a contest whose outcome is in doubt up to the very end

cli·mac·ter·ic \klī-'mak-tə-rik\ *n* **1** : a major turning point or critical stage **2** : MENOPAUSE; *also* : a corresponding period in the male

cli·mate \'klī-mət\ *n* [ME *climat*, fr. MF, fr. LL *clima*, fr. Gk *klima* inclination, latitude, climate, fr. *klinein* to lean] **1** : a region having specific climatic conditions **2** : the average weather conditions at a place over a period of years **3** : the prevailing set of conditions (as temperature and humidity) indoors **4** : a prevailing atmosphere or environment ⟨the ∼ of opinion⟩ — **cli·mat·ic** \klī-'ma-tik\ *adj* — **cli·mat·i·cal·ly** \-ti-k(ə-)lē\ *adv*

cli·ma·tol·o·gy \,klī-mə-'tä-lə-jē\ *n* : the science that deals with climates — **cli·ma·to·log·i·cal** \-mə-tə-'lä-ji-kəl\ *adj* — **cli·ma·to·log·i·cal·ly** \-k(ə-)lē\ *adv* — **cli·ma·tol·o·gist** \-mə-'tä-lə-jist\ *n*

¹cli·max \'klī-,maks\ *n* [L, fr. Gk *klimax*, lit., ladder, fr. *klinein* to lean] **1** : a series of ideas or statements so arranged that they increase in force and power from the first to the last; *also* : the last member of such a series **2** : the highest point ⟨the ∼ of her career⟩ **3** : ORGASM — **cli·mac·tic** \klī-'mak-tik\ *adj*

²climax *vb* : to come or bring to a climax

¹climb \'klīm\ *vb* **1** : to rise to a higher point **2** : to go up or down esp. by use of hands and feet; *also* : to ascend in growing — **climb·er** *n*

²climb *n* **1** : a place where climbing is necessary **2** : the act of climbing : ascent by climbing

clime \'klīm\ *n* : CLIMATE ⟨warmer ∼s⟩

¹clinch \'klinch\ *vb* **1** : to turn over or flatten the end of something sticking out ⟨∼ a nail⟩; *also* : to fasten by clinching **2** : to make final : SETTLE ⟨∼ a deal⟩ **3** : to hold a boxing opponent **4** : to hold fast or firmly

²clinch *n* **1** : a fastening by means of a clinched nail, rivet, or bolt **2** : an act or instance of clinching in boxing

clinch·er \'klin-chər\ *n* : one that clinches; *esp* : a decisive fact, argument, act, or remark

cling \'kliŋ\ *vb* **clung** \'kləŋ\; **cling·ing 1** : to adhere as if glued; *also* : to hold or hold on tightly **2** : to have a strong emotional attachment — **clingy** \'kliŋ-ē\ *adj*

cling·stone \'kliŋ-,stōn\ *n* : any of various fruits (as some peaches) whose flesh adheres strongly to the pit

clin·ic \'kli-nik\ *n* **1** : a medical class in which patients are examined and discussed **2** : a group meeting for teaching a certain skill and working on individual problems ⟨a reading ∼⟩ **3** : a facility (as of a hospital) for diagnosis and treatment of outpatients

clin·i·cal \'kli-ni-kəl\ *adj* **1** : of, relating to, or typical of a clinic; *esp* : involving direct observation of the patient ⟨∼ studies⟩ **2** : scientifically dispassionate — **clin·i·cal·ly** \-k(ə-)lē\ *adv*

cli·ni·cian \kli-'ni-shən\ *n* : a person qualified in the clinical practice of medicine, psychiatry, or psychology as distinguished from one specializing in laboratory or research techniques or in theory

¹clink \'kliŋk\ *vb* : to make or cause to make a sharp short metallic sound

²**clink** n : a clinking sound

clin·ker \'kliŋ-kər\ n : stony matter fused together : SLAG

¹**clip** \'klip\ vb **clipped; clip·ping** : to fasten with a clip

²**clip** n 1 : a device that grips, clasps, or hooks 2 : a cartridge holder for a rifle

³**clip** vb **clipped; clip·ping** 1 : to cut or cut off with shears ⟨*clipped* a recipe from the magazine⟩ 2 : CURTAIL, DIMINISH 3 : HIT, PUNCH 4 : to illegally block (an opponent) in football

⁴**clip** n 1 : a 2-bladed instrument for cutting esp. the nails 2 : a sharp blow 3 : a rapid pace ⟨moving at a good ∼⟩

clip art n : ready-made usu. copyright-free illustrations

clip·board \'klip-ˌbȯrd\ n 1 : a small writing board with a spring clip at the top for holding papers 2 : a section of computer memory that temporarily stores data esp. to facilitate its movement or duplication

clip joint n, slang : an establishment (as a nightclub) that makes a practice of defrauding its customers

clip·per \'kli-pər\ n 1 : an implement for clipping esp. the hair or nails — usu. used in pl. 2 : a fast sailing ship

clip·ping \'kli-piŋ\ n : a piece clipped from something (as a newspaper)

clique \'klēk, 'klik\ n [F] : a small exclusive group of people : COTERIE ⟨high school ∼s⟩ — **cliqu·ey** \'klē-kē, 'kli-\ adj — **cliqu·ish** \-kish\ adj

cli·to·ris \'kli-tə-rəs\ n, pl **cli·to·ris·es** : a small erectile organ at the anterior or ventral part of the vulva homologous to the penis — **cli·to·ral** \-rəl\ adj

clk abbr clerk

clo abbr clothing

¹**cloak** \'klōk\ n 1 : a loose outer garment 2 : something that conceals

²**cloak** vb : to cover or hide with a cloak

cloak–and–dagger adj : involving or suggestive of espionage

clob·ber \'klä-bər\ vb 1 : to pound mercilessly; also : to hit with force : SMASH 2 : to defeat overwhelmingly

cloche \'klōsh\ n [F, lit., bell] : a woman's small close-fitting hat

¹**clock** \'kläk\ n : a timepiece not intended to be carried on the person

²**clock** vb 1 : to time (a person or a performance) by a timing device 2 : to register (as speed) on a mechanical recording device — **clock·er** n

³**clock** n : an ornamental figure on a stocking or sock

clock·wise \'kläk-ˌwīz\ adv : in the direction in which the hands of a clock move — **clockwise** adj

clock·work \-ˌwərk\ n 1 : the machinery that runs a mechanical device (as a clock or toy) 2 : the precision or regularity associated with a clock

clod \'kläd\ n 1 : a lump esp. of earth or clay 2 : a dull or insensitive person

clod·hop·per \-ˌhä-pər\ n 1 : an uncouth rustic 2 : a large heavy shoe

¹**clog** \'kläg\ n 1 : a weight attached esp. to an animal to impede motion 2 : a thick-soled shoe

²**clog** vb **clogged; clog·ging** 1 : to impede with a clog : HINDER 2 : to obstruct passage through 3 : to become filled with extraneous matter

cloi·son·né \ˌklȯi-zə-'nā\ adj : a colored decoration made of enamels poured into the divided areas in a design outlined with wire or metal strips

¹**clois·ter** \'klȯi-stər\ n [ME cloistre, fr. AF, fr. ML claustrum, fr. L, bar, bolt, fr. claudere to close] 1 : a monastic establishment 2 : a covered usu. colonnaded passage on the side of a court — **clois·tral** \-strəl\ adj

²**cloister** vb : to shut away from the world

clone \'klōn\ n [Gk klōn twig, slip] 1 : the collection of genetically identical cells or organisms produced asexually from a single ancestral cell or organism; also : an individual grown from a single cell and genetically identical to it ⟨a sheep ∼⟩ 2 : a group of replicas of a biological molecule (as DNA) 3 : one that appears to be a copy of an original form — **clon·al** \'klō-nᵊl\ adj — **clone** vb

clop \'kläp\ n : a sound made by or as if by a hoof or wooden shoe against pavement — **clop** vb

¹**close** \'klōz\ vb **closed; clos·ing** 1 : to bar passage through : SHUT 2 : to suspend the operations (as of a school) 3 : END, TERMINATE 4 : to bring together the

parts or edges of; also : to fill up 5 : GRAPPLE ⟨∼ with the enemy⟩ 6 : to enter into an agreement — **clos·able** or **close·able** adj

²**close** \'klōz\ n : CONCLUSION, END

³**close** \'klōs\ adj **clos·er; clos·est** 1 : having no openings 2 : narrowly restricting or restricted 3 : limited to a privileged class 4 : SECLUDED; also : SECRETIVE 5 : RIGOROUS ⟨keep ∼ watch⟩ 6 : SULTRY, STUFFY 7 : STINGY 8 : having little space between items or units 9 : fitting tightly; also : SHORT ⟨∼ haircut⟩ 10 : NEAR ⟨at ∼ range⟩ 11 : INTIMATE ⟨∼ friends⟩ 12 : ACCURATE 13 : decided by a narrow margin ⟨a ∼ game⟩ — **close** adv — **close·ly** adv — **close·ness** n

closed–circuit \'klōzd-'sər-kət\ adj : used in, shown on, or being a television installation in which the signal is transmitted by wire to a limited number of receivers

closed shop n : an establishment having only members of a labor union on the payroll

close-fist·ed \'klōz-'fis-təd, 'klōs-\ adj : STINGY

close–knit \'klōs-'nit\ adj : closely bound together by social, cultural, economic, or political ties

close-mouthed \'klōz-'mau̇t̲h̲d, 'klōs-'mau̇tht\ adj : cautious or reticent in speaking

close-out \'klōz-ˌau̇t\ n : a sale of a business's entire stock at low prices

close out vb 1 : to dispose of by a closeout 2 : to dispose of a business : SELL OUT

clos·er \'klō-zər\ n : one that closes; esp : a relief pitcher who specializes in finishing games

¹**clos·et** \'klä-zət, 'klȯ-\ n 1 : a small room for privacy 2 : a small compartment for household utensils or clothing 3 : a state or condition of secrecy ⟨came out of the ∼⟩

²**closet** vb : to take into a private room for an interview

close–up \'klōs-ˌəp\ n 1 : a photograph or movie shot taken at close range 2 : an intimate view or examination

clo·sure \'klō-zhər\ n 1 : an act of closing : the condition of being closed 2 : something that closes 3 : CLOTURE

clot \'klät\ n : a mass formed by a portion of liquid (as blood) thickening and sticking together — **clot** vb

cloth \'klȯth\ n, pl **cloths** \'klȯt̲h̲z, 'klȯths\ 1 : a pliable fabric made usu. by weaving or knitting natural or synthetic fibers and filaments 2 : TABLECLOTH 3 : distinctive dress of the clergy; also : CLERGY

clothe \'klōt̲h̲\ vb **clothed** or **clad** \'klad\; **cloth·ing** 1 : DRESS; also : to provide with clothes 2 : to express by suitably significant language ⟨policies clothed in rhetoric⟩

clothes \'klōt̲h̲z, 'klōz\ n pl 1 : CLOTHING 2 : BEDCLOTHES

clothes·horse \-ˌhȯrs\ n 1 : a frame on which to hang clothes 2 : a conspicuously dressy person

¹**clothes·line** \-ˌlīn\ n : a rope or cord on which clothes are hung to dry

²**clothesline** vb : to knock down by catching by the neck with one's outstretched arm

clothes moth n : any of several small pale moths whose larvae eat wool, fur, and feathers

clothes·pin \'klōt̲h̲z-ˌpin, 'klōz-\ n : a device for fastening clothes on a line

clothes·press \-ˌpres\ n : a receptacle for clothes

cloth·ier \'klōt̲h̲-yər, 'klō-t̲h̲ē-ər\ n : a maker or seller of clothing

cloth·ing \'klō-t̲h̲iŋ\ n : garments in general

clo·ture \'klō-chər\ n : the closing or limitation (as by calling for a vote) of debate in a legislative body

¹**cloud** \'klau̇d\ n [ME, rock, cloud, fr. OE clūd] 1 : a visible mass of particles of condensed vapor (as water or ice) suspended in the atmosphere 2 : usu. visible mass of minute airborne particles; also : a mass of obscuring matter in interstellar space 3 : CROWD, SWARM ⟨a ∼ of mosquitoes⟩ 4 : something having a dark or threatening aspect ⟨a ∼ of suspicion⟩ 5 : something that obscures or blemishes ⟨a ∼ of ambiguity⟩ 6 : the computers and networks that support cloud computing — **cloud·i·ness** \'klau̇-dē-nəs\ n — **cloud·less** adj — **cloudy** adj

²**cloud** vb 1 : to darken or hide with or as if with a cloud 2 : OBSCURE ⟨∼ed in mystery⟩ 3 : TAINT, SULLY ⟨a ∼ed reputation⟩

cloud·burst \-ˌbərst\ n : a sudden heavy rainfall

cloud computing n : the practice of storing regularly

used computer data on multiple servers that can be accessed through the Internet

cloud·let \-lət\ *n* : a small cloud

cloud nine *n* : a feeling of extreme well-being or elation — usu. used with *on*

¹clout \'klaut\ *n* **1** : a blow esp. with the hand **2** : PULL, INFLUENCE

²clout *vb* : to hit forcefully

¹clove \'klōv\ *n* : one of the small bulbs that grows at the base of the scales of a large bulb ⟨a ∼ of garlic⟩

²clove *past of* CLEAVE

³clove *n* [ME *clowe*, fr. AF *clou* (*de girofle*), lit., nail of clove, fr. L *clavus* nail] : the dried flower bud of a tropical tree used esp. as a spice

clo·ven \'klō-vən\ *past part of* CLEAVE

cloven foot *n* : CLOVEN HOOF — **cloven–foot·ed** \-'fu-təd\ *adj*

cloven hoof *n* : a foot (as of a sheep) with the front part divided into two parts — **cloven–hoofed** \-'huft, -'huvd\ *adj*

clo·ver \'klō-vər\ *n* : any of a genus of leguminous herbs with usu. 3-parted leaves and dense flower heads

clo·ver·leaf \-,lēf\ *n, pl* **cloverleafs** \-,lēfs\ *or* **clo·ver·leaves** \-,lēvz\ : an interchange between two major highways that from above resembles a 4-leaf clover

¹clown \'klaun\ *n* **1** : BOOR **2** : a fool or comedian in an entertainment (as a circus) **3** : a person given to joking and buffoonery — **clown·ish** *adj* — **clown·ish·ly** *adv* — **clown·ish·ness** *n*

²clown *vb* : to act like a clown

cloy \'klȯi\ *vb* : to disgust or nauseate with excess of something orig. pleasing — **cloy·ing·ly** *adv*

clr *abbr* clear

¹club \'kləb\ *n* **1** : a heavy wooden stick or staff used as a weapon; *also* : BAT **2** : any of a suit of playing cards marked with a black figure resembling a clover leaf **3** : a group of persons associated for a common purpose; *also* : the meeting place of such a group **4** : CLUB SANDWICH

²club *vb* **clubbed; club·bing 1** : to strike with a club **2** : to unite or combine for a common cause **3** : to patronize nightclubs

club·foot \'kləb-'fut\ *n* : a misshapen foot twisted out of position from birth; *also* : this deformed condition — **club·foot·ed** \-'fu-təd\ *adj*

club·house \'kləb-,haus\ *n* **1** : a house occupied by a club **2** : locker rooms used by an athletic team **3** : a building at a golf course with locker rooms and usu. a pro shop and a restaurant

club sandwich *n* : a sandwich of three slices of bread with two layers of meat (as turkey) and lettuce, tomato, and mayonnaise

club soda *n* : SODA WATER

cluck \'klək\ *n* : the call of a hen esp. to her chicks — **cluck** *vb*

¹clue \'klü\ *n* **1** : something that guides through an intricate procedure or maze; *esp* : a piece of evidence leading to the solution of a problem **2** : IDEA, NOTION ⟨has no ∼ what he's doing⟩

²clue *vb* **clued; clue·ing** *or* **clu·ing** : to provide with a clue; *also* : to give information to ⟨∼ me in⟩

¹clump \'kləmp\ *n* **1** : a group of things clustered together **2** : a heavy tramping sound

²clump *vb* : to tread clumsily and noisily

clum·sy \'kləm-zē\ *adj* **clum·si·er; -est 1** : lacking dexterity, nimbleness, or grace **2** : not tactful or subtle ⟨a ∼ attempt at a joke⟩ — **clum·si·ly** \-zə-lē\ *adv* — **clum·si·ness** \-zē-nəs\ *n*

clung *past and past part of* CLING

clunk·er \'kləŋ-kər\ *n* **1** : a dilapidated automobile **2** : a notable failure

¹clus·ter \'kləs-tər\ *n* : GROUP, BUNCH

²cluster *vb* : to grow or gather in a cluster

¹clutch \'kləch\ *vb* : to grasp with or as if with the hand

²clutch *n* **1** : the claws or a hand in the act of grasping; *also* : CONTROL, POWER **2** : a device for gripping an object **3** : a coupling used to connect and disconnect a driving and a driven part of a mechanism; *also* : a lever or pedal operating such a coupling **4** : a crucial situation

³clutch *adj* : made, done, or successful in a crucial situation

⁴clutch *n* **1** : a nest or batch of eggs; *also* : a brood of chicks **2** : GROUP, BUNCH

¹clut·ter \'klə-tər\ *vb* : to fill or cover with a disorderly scattering of things

²clutter *n* : a crowded mass

cm *abbr* centimeter

Cm *symbol* curium

CM *abbr* [Commonwealth of the Northern Mariana Islands] Northern Mariana Islands

cmdr *abbr* commander

cml *abbr* commercial

CMSgt *abbr* chief master sergeant

Cn *symbol* copernicium

CNO *abbr* chief of naval operations

CNS *abbr* central nervous system

co *abbr* **1** company **2** county

Co *symbol* cobalt

CO *abbr* **1** Colorado **2** commanding officer **3** conscientious objector

c/o *abbr* care of

¹coach \'kōch\ *n* [MF *coche*, ultim. fr. Hung *kocsi* (*szekér*), lit., (wagon) of Kocs (town in Hungary)] **1** : a large closed 4-wheeled carriage with an elevated outside front seat for the driver **2** : a railroad passenger car esp. for day travel **3** : BUS **4** : a private tutor; *also* : one who instructs or trains ⟨a soccer ∼⟩

²coach *vb* : to instruct, direct, or prompt as a coach

coach·man \-mən\ *n* : a man who drives a coach or carriage

co·ad·ju·tor \,kō-ə-'jü-tər, kō-'a-jə-tər\ *n* : ASSISTANT; *esp* : an assistant bishop having the right of succession

co·ag·u·lant \kō-'a-gyə-lənt\ *n* : something that produces coagulation

co·ag·u·late \-,lāt\ *vb* **-lat·ed; -lat·ing** : CLOT — **co·ag·u·la·tion** \kō-,a-gyə-'lā-shən\ *n*

¹coal \'kōl\ *n* **1** : EMBER **2** : a black solid combustible mineral used as fuel

²coal *vb* **1** : to supply with coal **2** : to take in coal

co·a·lesce \,kō-ə-'les\ *vb* **co·a·lesced; co·a·lesc·ing** : to grow together; *also* : FUSE ✦ **Synonyms** MERGE, BLEND, MINGLE, MIX — **co·a·les·cence** \-ᵊns\ *n*

coal·field \'kōl-,fēld\ *n* : a region rich in coal deposits

coal gas *n* : gas from coal; *esp* : gas distilled from bituminous coal and used for heating

co·a·li·tion \,kō-ə-'li-shən\ *n* : UNION; *esp* : a temporary union for a common purpose — **co·a·li·tion·ist** *n*

coal oil *n* : KEROSENE

coal tar *n* : tar distilled from bituminous coal and used in dyes and drugs

co·an·chor \'kō-'aŋ-kər\ *n* : a newscaster who shares the duties of head broadcaster

coarse \'kȯrs\ *adj* **coars·er; coars·est 1** : of ordinary or inferior quality **2** : composed of large parts or particles ⟨∼ sand⟩ **3** : CRUDE ⟨∼ manners⟩ **4** : ROUGH, HARSH — **coarse·ly** *adv* — **coarse·ness** *n*

coars·en \'kȯr-sᵊn\ *vb* : to make or become coarse

¹coast \'kōst\ *n* [ME *cost*, fr. AF *coste*, fr. L *costa* rib, side] **1** : SEASHORE **2** : a slide down a slope **3** : the immediate area of view — used in the phrase *the coast is clear* — **coast·al** *adj*

²coast *vb* **1** : to sail along the shore **2** : to move (as downhill on a sled) without effort

coast·er *n* **1** : one that coasts **2** : a shallow container or a plate or mat to protect a surface

coaster brake *n* : a brake in the hub of the rear wheel of a bicycle

coast guard *n* : a military force employed in guarding or patrolling a coast — **coast·guards·man** \'kōst-,gärdz-mən\ *n*

coast·line \'kōst-,līn\ *n* : the outline or shape of a coast

¹coat \'kōt\ *n* **1** : an outer garment for the upper part of the body **2** : an external growth (as of fur or feathers) on an animal **3** : a covering layer ⟨a ∼ of paint⟩ — **coat·ed** \'kō-təd\ *adj*

²coat *vb* : to cover usu. with a finishing or protective coat

coat·ing \'kō-tiŋ\ *n* : COAT, COVERING

coat of arms : the heraldic bearings (as of a person) usu. depicted on an escutcheon

coat of mail : a garment of metal scales or rings worn as armor

co·au·thor \'kō-'ȯ-thər\ *n* : a joint or associate author — **coauthor** *vb*

coax \'kōks\ *vb* : WHEEDLE; *also* : to gain by gentle urging or flattery

co·ax·i·al \'kō-'ak-sē-əl\ *adj* : having coincident axes — **co·ax·i·al·ly** *adv*

coaxial cable *n* : a cable that consists of a tube of electrically conducting material surrounding a central conductor

cob \'käb\ *n* 1 : a male swan 2 : CORN-COB 3 : a short-legged stocky horse

co·balt \'kō-,bȯlt\ *n* [G *Kobalt*, alter. of *Kobold*, lit., goblin; fr. its occurrence in silver ore, believed to be due to goblins] : a tough shiny silver-white magnetic metallic chemical element found with iron and nickel

cob·ble \'kä-bəl\ *vb* **cob·bled**; **cob·bling** : to make or put together roughly or hastily ⟨~ together a solution⟩

cob·bler \'kä-blər\ *n* 1 : a mender or maker of shoes 2 : a deep-dish fruit pie with a thick crust

cob·ble·stone \'kä-bəl-,stōn\ *n* : a naturally rounded stone larger than a pebble and smaller than a boulder

co·bra \'kō-brə\ *n* [Pg *cobra (de capello)*, lit., hooded snake] : any of several venomous snakes of Asia and Africa that when excited expand the skin of the neck into a broad hood

cob·web \'käb-,web\ *n* [ME *coppeweb*, fr. *coppe* spider, fr. OE ātor*coppe*] 1 : SPIDERWEB; *also* : a thread spun by a spider or insect larva 2 : something flimsy or entangling — **co·web·by** \-,we-bē\ *adj*

co·caine \kō-'kān, 'kō-,kān\ *n* : a drug obtained from the leaves of a So. American shrub (**co·ca** \'kō-kə\) that can result in severe psychological dependence and is sometimes used in medicine as a local anesthetic and illegally as a stimulant of the central nervous system

coc·cus \'kä-kəs\ *n, pl* **coc·ci** \'käk-,sī\ : a spherical bacterium

coc·cyx \'käk-siks\ *n, pl* **coc·cy·ges** \'käk-sə-,jēz\ *also* **coc·cyx·es** \'käk-sik-səz\ : the end of the spinal column beyond the sacrum esp. in humans

co·chi·neal \'kä-chə-,nēl\ *n* : a red dye made from the dried bodies of females of a tropical American insect (**cochineal insect**)

co·chlea \'kō-klē-ə, 'kä-\ *n, pl* **co·chle·as** *or* **co·chle·ae** \-klē-,ē, -,ī\ : the usu. spiral part of the inner ear containing nerve endings which carry information about sound to the brain — **co·chle·ar** \-klē-ər\ *adj*

¹cock \'käk\ *n* 1 : the adult male of a bird and esp. of the common domestic chicken 2 : VALVE, FAUCET 3 : LEADER 4 : the hammer of a firearm; *also* : the position of the hammer when ready for firing

²cock *vb* 1 : to draw back the hammer of a firearm 2 : to set or draw back in readiness for some action ⟨~ your arm to throw⟩ 3 : to turn or tilt usu. to one side ⟨~ one's head⟩

³cock *n* : a small pile (as of hay)

cock·ade \kä-'kād\ *n* : an ornament worn on the hat as a badge

cock·a·tiel \'kä-kə-'tēl\ *n* : a small crested gray parrot often kept as a cage bird

cock·a·too \'kä-kə-,tü\ *n, pl* **-toos** [D *kaketoe*, fr. Malay *kakatua*] : any of various large noisy crested parrots chiefly of Australia

cock·a·trice \'kä-kə-trəs, -,trīs\ *n* : a legendary serpent with a deadly glance

cock·crow \'käk-,krō\ *n* : DAWN

cocked hat \'käkt-\ *n* : a hat with the brim turned up on two or three sides

cock·er·el \'kä-kə-rəl\ *n* : a young male domestic chicken

cock·er spaniel \'kä-kər-\ *n* [*cocking* woodcock hunting] : any of a breed of small spaniels with long ears, square muzzle, and silky coat

cock·eyed \'kä-'kīd\ *adj* 1 : turned or tilted to one side 2 : slightly crazy : FOOLISH

cock·fight \'käk-,fīt\ *n* : a contest of gamecocks usu. fitted with metal spurs

¹cock·le \'kä-kəl\ *n* : any of several weedy plants related to the pinks

²cockle *n* : a bivalve mollusk with a heart-shaped shell

cock·le·shell \-,shel\ *n* 1 : the shell of a cockle 2 : a light flimsy boat

cock·ney \'käk-nē\ *n, pl* **cockneys** : a native of London and esp. of the East End of London; *also* : the dialect of a cockney

cock·pit \'käk-,pit\ *n* 1 : a pit for cockfights 2 : a space or compartment in a vehicle from which it is steered, piloted, or driven

cock·roach \'käk-,rōch\ *n* [Sp *cucaracha*] : any of an order or suborder of active nocturnal insects including some which infest houses and ships

cock·sure \'käk-'shùr\ *adj* 1 : perfectly sure : CERTAIN 2 : COCKY

cock·tail \'käk-,tāl\ *n* 1 : an iced drink made of liquor and flavoring ingredients 2 : an appetizer (as tomato juice) served as a first course of a meal

cocky \'kä-kē\ *adj* **cock·i·er; -est** : marked by overconfidence : PERT, CONCEITED — **cock·i·ly** \-kə-lē\ *adv* — **cock·i·ness** \-kē-nəs\ *n*

co·coa \'kō-kō\ *n* 1 : CACAO 2 : chocolate deprived of some of its fat and powdered; *also* : a drink made of this heated with water or milk

cocoa butter *n* : a pale vegetable fat obtained from cacao beans

co·co·nut \'kō-kə-(,)nət\ *n* : a large edible hard-shelled fruit produced by a tall tropical palm (**coconut palm**)

co·coon \kə-'kün\ *n* 1 : a case usu. of silk formed by some insect larvae for protection during the pupal stage 2 : something that offers protection or isolation

cod \'käd\ *n, pl* **cod** *also* **cods** : a bottom-dwelling bony fish of the North Atlantic that is an important food fish; *also* : a related fish of the Pacific Ocean

COD *abbr* 1 cash on delivery 2 collect on delivery

co·da \'kō-də\ *n* : a closing section in a musical composition that is formally distinct from the main structure

cod·dle \'kä-d°l\ *vb* **cod·dled; cod·dling** 1 : to cook slowly in water below the boiling point 2 : PAMPER

¹code \'kōd\ *n* [ME, fr. MF, fr. L *caudex, codex* trunk of a tree, document formed orig. from wooden tablets] 1 : a systematic statement of a body of law 2 : a system of principles or rules ⟨moral ~⟩ 3 : a system of signals 4 : a system of symbols (as in secret communication) with special meanings 5 : GENETIC CODE

²code *vb* **cod·ed; cod·ing** : to put into the form or symbols of a code

co·deine \'kō-,dēn\ *n* : a narcotic drug obtained from opium and used esp. as an analgesic and cough suppressant

co·dex \'kō-,deks\ *n, pl* **co·di·ces** \'kō-də-,sēz, 'kä-\ : a manuscript book (as of the Scriptures or classics)

cod·fish \'käd-,fish\ *n* : COD

cod·ger \'kä-jər\ *n* : an odd or cranky and usu. elderly fellow

cod·i·cil \'kä-də-səl, -,sil\ *n* : a legal instrument modifying an earlier will

cod·i·fy \'kä-də-,fī, 'kō-\ *vb* **-fied; -fy·ing** : to arrange in a systematic form — **cod·i·fi·ca·tion** \,kä-də-fə-'kā-shən, ,kō-\ *n*

co·ed \'kō-,ed\ *n* : a female student in a coeducational institution — **coed** *adj*

co·ed·u·ca·tion \,kō-,e-jə-'kā-shən\ *n* : the education of male and female students at the same institution — **co·ed·u·ca·tion·al** \-shə-nəl\ *adj* — **co·ed·u·ca·tion·al·ly** *adv*

co·ef·fi·cient \,kō-ə-'fi-shənt\ *n* 1 : a constant factor as distinguished from a variable in a mathematical term 2 : a number that serves as a measure of some property (as of a substance, device, or process)

coe·len·ter·ate \si-'len-tə-,rāt, -rət\ *n* : any of a phylum of radially symmetrical invertebrate animals including the corals, sea anemones, and jellyfishes

co·equal \kō-'ē-kwəl\ *adj* : equal with another — **coequal** *n* — **co·equal·i·ty** \,kō-ē-'kwä-lə-tē\ *n* — **co·equal·ly** *adv*

co·erce \kō-'ərs\ *vb* **co·erced; co·erc·ing** 1 : RESTRAIN, REPRESS 2 : COMPEL 3 : ENFORCE — **co·er·cion** \-'ər-zhən, -shən\ *n* — **co·er·cive** \-'ər-siv\ *adj*

co·e·val \kō-'ē-vəl\ *adj* : of the same age — **coeval** *n*

co·ex·ist \,kō-ig-'zist\ *vb* 1 : to exist together or at the same time 2 : to live in peace with each other — **co·ex·is·tence** \-'zis-təns\ *n*

co·ex·ten·sive \,kō-ik-'sten-siv\ *adj* : having the same scope or extent in space or time

C of C *abbr* Chamber of Commerce

cof·fee \'kȯ-fē\ *n* [It & Turk; It *caffè*, fr. Turk *kahve*, fr.

Ar *qahwa*] : a drink made from the roasted and ground seeds of a fruit of a tropical shrub or tree; *also* : these seeds (**coffee beans**) or a plant producing them
cof·fee·house \-ˌhaůs\ *n* : a place where refreshments (as coffee) are sold
coffee klatch \-ˌklach\ *n* : KAFFEE-KLATSCH
cof·fee·pot \-ˌpät\ *n* : a pot for brewing or serving coffee
coffee shop *n* : a small restaurant
coffee table *n* : a low table customarily placed in front of a sofa
cof·fer \ˈkȯ-fər\ *n* : a chest or box used esp. for valuables
cof·fer·dam \-ˌdam\ *n* : a watertight enclosure from which water is pumped to expose the bottom of a body of water and permit construction
cof·fin \ˈkȯ-fən\ *n* : a box or chest for burying a corpse
C of S *abbr* chief of staff
¹**cog** \ˈkäg\ *n* : a tooth on the rim of a wheel or gear — **cogged** \ˈkägd\ *adj*
²**cog** *abbr* cognate
co·gen·e·ra·tion \ˌkō-je-nə-ˈrä-shən\ *n* : the simultaneous generation of electricity and heat from the same fuel
co·gent \ˈkō-jənt\ *adj* : having power to compel or constrain : CONVINCING ⟨a ~ argument⟩ — **co·gen·cy** \-jən-sē\ *n*
cog·i·tate \ˈkä-jə-ˌtāt\ *vb* **-tat·ed; -tat·ing** : THINK, PONDER ⟨*cogitated* about his future⟩ — **cog·i·ta·tion** \ˌkä-jə-ˈtä-shən\ *n* — **cog·i·ta·tive** \ˈkä-jə-ˌtä-tiv\ *adj*
co·gnac \ˈkōn-ˌyak\ *n* : a French brandy
cog·nate \ˈkäg-ˌnāt\ *adj* **1** : of the same or similar nature **2** : RELATED; *esp* : related by descent from the same ancestral language — **cognate** *n*
cog·ni·tive \ˈkäg-nə-tiv\ *adj* : of, relating to, or being conscious intellectual activity (as thinking, remembering, reasoning, or using language) — **cog·ni·tion** \käg-ˈni-shən\ *n* — **cog·ni·tive·ly** *adv*
cog·ni·zance \ˈkäg-nə-zəns\ *n* **1** : apprehension by the mind : AWARENESS ⟨had no ~ of the crime⟩ **2** : NOTICE, HEED — **cog·ni·zant** \ˈkäg-nə-zənt\ *adj*
cog·no·men \käg-ˈnō-mən, ˈkäg-nə-\ *n, pl* **cognomens** or **cog·no·mi·na** \käg-ˈnä-mə-nə, -ˈnō-\ : NAME; *esp* : NICKNAME
co·gno·scen·te \ˌkän-yə-ˈshen-tē\ *n, pl* **-scen·ti** \-tē\ [obs. It] : CONNOISSEUR
cog·wheel \ˈkäg-ˌhwēl\ *n* : a wheel with cogs or teeth
co·hab·it \kō-ˈha-bət\ *vb* : to live together as a couple — **co·hab·i·ta·tion** \-ˌha-bə-ˈtä-shən\ *n*
co·here \kō-ˈhir\ *vb* **co·hered; co·her·ing** : to stick together
co·her·ent \kō-ˈhir-ənt\ *adj* **1** : having the quality of cohering **2** : logically consistent ⟨a ~ explanation⟩ — **co·her·ence** \-əns\ *n* — **co·her·ent·ly** *adv*
co·he·sion \kō-ˈhē-zhən\ *n* **1** : a sticking together **2** : molecular attraction by which the particles of a body are united — **co·he·sive** \-siv\ *adj* — **co·he·sive·ly** *adv* — **co·he·sive·ness** *n*
co·ho \ˈkō-ˌhō\ *n, pl* **cohos** or **coho** : a rather small Pacific salmon with light-colored flesh
co·hort \ˈkō-ˌhȯrt\ *n* **1** : a group of warriors or followers **2** : COMPANION, ACCOMPLICE
coif \ˈkȯif; **2** *usu* ˈkwäf\ *n* **1** : a close-fitting hat **2** : COIFFURE
coif·feur \kwä-ˈfər\ *n* [F] : HAIRDRESSER
coif·feuse \kwä-ˈfərz, -ˈfəz, -ˈfüz, -ˈfyüz\ *n* : a female hairdresser
coif·fure \kwä-ˈfyůr\ *n* : a manner of arranging the hair
¹**coil** \ˈkȯi(-ə)l\ *vb* : to wind in a spiral shape
²**coil** *n* : a series of rings or loops (as of coiled rope, wire, or pipe) : RING, LOOP
¹**coin** \ˈkȯin\ *n* [ME, wedge, corner, image on a coin, fr. AF *coing*, fr. L *cuneus* wedge] **1** : a piece of metal issued by government authority as money **2** : metal money
²**coin** *vb* **1** : to make (a coin) esp. by stamping : MINT **2** : CREATE, INVENT ⟨~ a phrase⟩ — **coin·er** *n*
coin·age \ˈkȯi-nij\ *n* **1** : the act or process of coining **2** : COINS
co·in·cide \ˌkō-ən-ˈsīd, ˈkō-ən-ˌsīd\ *vb* **-cid·ed; -cid·ing** **1** : to occupy the same place in space or time **2** : to correspond or agree exactly
co·in·ci·dence \kō-ˈin-sə-dəns\ *n* **1** : exact agreement **2** : occurrence together apparently without reason; *also* : an event that so occurs

co·in·ci·dent \-sə-dənt\ *adj* **1** : of similar nature **2** : occupying the same space or time — **co·in·ci·den·tal** \kō-ˌin-sə-ˈden-tᵊl\ *adj*
co·i·tus \ˈkō-ə-təs\ *n* [L, fr. *coire* to come together] : SEXUAL INTERCOURSE **1** — **co·i·tal** \-tᵊl\ *adj*
¹**coke** \ˈkōk\ *n* : a hard gray porous fuel made by heating soft coal to drive off most of its volatile material
²**coke** *n* : COCAINE
¹**col** *abbr* **1** colonial; colony **2** column
²**col** *or* **coll** *abbr* **1** collect, collected, collection **2** college, collegiate
Col *abbr* **1** colonel **2** Colorado **3** Colossians
COL *abbr* **1** colonel **2** cost of living
co·la \ˈkō-lə\ *n* : a carbonated soft drink usu. containing sugar, caffeine, caramel, and special flavoring
col·an·der \ˈkə-lən-dər, ˈkä-\ *n* : a perforated utensil for draining food
¹**cold** \ˈkōld\ *adj* **1** : having a low or decidedly subnormal temperature **2** : lacking warmth of feeling **3** : suffering or uncomfortable from lack of warmth — **cold·ly** *adv* — **cold·ness** *n* — **in cold blood** : with premeditation : DELIBERATELY ⟨murdered her *in cold blood*⟩
²**cold** *n* **1** : a condition marked by low temperature; *also* : cold weather **2** : a chilly feeling **3** : a bodily disorder popularly associated with chilling; *esp* : COMMON COLD
³**cold** *adv* **1** : TOTALLY, FINALLY ⟨stopped them ~⟩ **2** : without notice or preparation ⟨performed the part ~⟩
cold–blood·ed \ˈkōld-ˈblə-dəd\ *adj* **1** : lacking normal human feelings **2** : having a body temperature not internally regulated but close to that of the environment **3** : sensitive to cold
cold cuts *n pl* : sliced assorted cold cooked meats
cold feet *n pl* : doubt or fear that prevents action
cold front *n* : an advancing edge of a cold air mass
cold shoulder *n* : cold or unsympathetic behavior — **cold–shoul·der** *vb*
cold sore *n* : a group of fluid-filled blisters appearing in or about the mouth in the oral form of herpes simplex
cold sweat *n* : concurrent perspiration and chill usu. associated with fear, pain, or shock
¹**cold turkey** *n* : abrupt complete cessation of the use of an addictive drug
²**cold turkey** *adv* **1** : without a period of adjustment **2** : without preparation
cold war *n* : a conflict characterized by the use of means short of sustained overt military action
cole·slaw \ˈkōl-ˌslȯ\ *n* [D *koolsla*, fr. *kool* cabbage + *sla* salad] : a salad made of raw cabbage
col·ic \ˈkä-lik\ *n* **1** : sharp sudden abdominal pain **2** : a condition marked by recurrent episodes of crying and irritability in an otherwise healthy infant — **col·icky** \ˈkä-li-kē\ *adj*
col·i·se·um \ˌkä-lə-ˈsē-əm\ *n* : a large structure esp. for athletic contests
co·li·tis \kō-ˈlī-təs\ *n* : inflammation of the colon
col·lab·o·rate \kə-ˈla-bə-ˌrāt\ *vb* **-rat·ed; -rat·ing** **1** : to work jointly with others (as in writing a book) **2** : to cooperate with an enemy force occupying one's country — **col·lab·o·ra·tion** \-ˌla-bə-ˈrä-shən\ *n* — **col·lab·o·ra·tive** \-ˈla-bə-ˌrā-tiv, -b(ə-)rə-\ *adj* — **col·lab·o·ra·tor** \-ˈla-bə-ˌrā-tər\ *n*
col·lage \kə-ˈläzh\ *n* [F, lit., gluing] : an artistic composition of fragments (as of printed matter) pasted on a surface; *also* : a work that combines various elements into a cohesive whole
col·la·gen \ˈkä-lə-jən\ *n* : any of a group of fibrous proteins widely found in vertebrate connective tissue
¹**col·lapse** \kə-ˈlaps\ *vb* **col·lapsed; col·laps·ing** **1** : to shrink together abruptly : DISINTEGRATE; *also* : to fall in : give way **3** : to break down physically or mentally; *esp* : to fall helpless or unconscious **4** : to fold down compactly — **col·laps·ible** *adj*
²**collapse** *n* : BREAKDOWN
¹**col·lar** \ˈkä-lər\ *n* **1** : a band, strip, or chain worn around the neck or the neckline of a garment **2** : something resembling a collar — **col·lar·less** *adj*
²**collar** *vb* : to seize by the collar; *also* : ARREST, GRAB ⟨~ a fugitive⟩
col·lar·bone \-ˌbōn\ *n* : the bone of the shoulder that joins the breastbone and the shoulder blade

col·lard \'kä-lərd\ *n* : a stalked smooth-leaved kale — usu. used in pl.

col·late \kə-'lāt; 'kä-ˌlāt, 'kō-\ *vb* **col·lat·ed; col·lat·ing** **1** : to compare (as two texts) carefully and critically **2** : to assemble in proper order

¹col·lat·er·al \kə-'la-tə-rəl\ *adj* **1** : associated but of secondary importance **2** : descended from the same ancestors but not in the same line **3** : PARALLEL **4** : of, relating to, or being collateral used as security; *also* : secured by collateral

²collateral *n* : property (as stocks) used as security for the repayment of a loan

col·la·tion \kä-'lā-shən, kō-\ *n* **1** : a light meal **2** : the act, process, or result of collating

col·league \'kä-ˌlēg\ *n* : an associate esp. in a profession

¹col·lect \'kä-likt, -ˌlekt\ *n* : a short prayer comprising an invocation, petition, and conclusion

²col·lect \kə-'lekt\ *vb* **1** : to bring or come together into one body or place : GATHER **2** : to accumulate (as coins) as a hobby **3** : to gain control of ⟨∼ his thoughts⟩ **4** : to receive payment of — **col·lect·ible** *or* **col·lect·able** *adj or n* — **col·lec·tor** \-'lek-tər\ *n*

³col·lect \kə-'lekt\ *adv or adj* : to be paid for by the receiver

col·lect·ed \kə-'lek-təd\ *adj* **1** : gathered together ⟨his ∼ poems⟩ **2** : SELF-POSSESSED, CALM

col·lec·tion \kə-'lek-shən\ *n* **1** : the act or process of collecting ⟨garbage ∼⟩ **2** : something collected ⟨a stamp ∼⟩ **3** : GROUP, AGGREGATE

¹col·lec·tive \kə-'lek-tiv\ *adj* **1** : of, relating to, or denoting a group of individuals considered as a whole **2** : involving all members of a group as distinct from its individuals ⟨∼ action⟩ **3** : shared or assumed by all members of the group ⟨a ∼ groan⟩ — **col·lec·tive·ly** *adv*

²collective *n* **1** : GROUP **2** : a cooperative unit or organization

collective bargaining *n* : negotiation between an employer and a labor union

col·lec·tiv·ise *chiefly Brit var of* COLLECTIVIZE

col·lec·tiv·ism \kə-'lek-ti-ˌvi-zəm\ *n* : a political or economic theory advocating collective control esp. over production and distribution

col·lec·tiv·ize \-ˌvīz\ *vb* **-ized; -iz·ing** : to organize under collective control — **col·lec·tiv·i·za·tion** \-ˌlek-ti-və-'zā-shən\ *n*

col·leen \kä-'lēn, 'kä-ˌlēn\ *n* : an Irish girl

col·lege \'kä-lij\ *n* [ME, endowed body of clergy or scholars, fr. AF, fr. L *collegium* society, fr. *collega* colleague, fr. *com-* with + *legare* to depute] **1** : a building used for an educational or religious purpose **2** : an institution of higher learning or division of a university granting a bachelor's degree; *also* : an institution offering instruction esp. in a vocational or technical field ⟨barber ∼⟩ **3** : an organized body of persons having common interests or duties ⟨∼ of cardinals⟩ — **col·le·giate** \kə-'lē-jət\ *adj*

col·le·gi·al·i·ty \kə-ˌlē-jē-'a-lə-tē\ *n* : the relationship of colleagues

col·le·gian \kə-'lē-jən\ *n* : a college student or recent college graduate

col·le·gi·um \kə-'le-gē-əm, -'lā-\ *n, pl* **-gia** \-gē-ə\ *or* **-giums** : a group in which each member has approximately equal power

col·lide \kə-'līd\ *vb* **col·lid·ed; col·lid·ing** **1** : to come together with solid impact **2** : to come into conflict : CLASH

col·lid·er \kə-'lī-dər\ *n* : a particle accelerator in which two beams of particles are made to collide

col·lie \'kä-lē\ *n* : any of a breed of large dogs developed in Scotland for herding sheep that occur in rough-coated and smooth-coated varieties

col·lier \'käl-yər\ *n* **1** : a coal miner **2** : a ship for carrying coal

col·liery \'käl-yə-rē\ *n, pl* **-lier·ies** : a coal mine and its associated buildings

col·li·mate \'kä-lə-ˌmāt\ *vb* **-mat·ed; -mat·ing** : to make (as light rays) parallel

col·li·sion \kə-'li-zhən\ *n* : an act or instance of colliding

col·lo·ca·tion \ˌkä-lə-'kā-shən\ *n* : the act or result of placing or arranging together; *esp* : a noticeable arrangement or conjoining of linguistic elements (as words)

col·loid \'kä-ˌlóid\ *n* : a substance in the form of submi- croscopic particles that when in solution or suspension do not settle out; *also* : such a substance together with the medium in which it is dispersed — **col·loi·dal** \kə-'lói-dᵊl\ *adj*

colloq *abbr* colloquial

col·lo·qui·al \kə-'lō-kwē-əl\ *adj* : of, relating to, or characteristic of conversation and esp. of familiar and informal conversation

col·lo·qui·al·ism \-'lō-kwē-ə-ˌli-zəm\ *n* : a colloquial expression

col·lo·qui·um \kə-'lō-kwē-əm\ *n, pl* **-qui·ums** *or* **-quia** \-ə\ : CONFERENCE, SEMINAR

col·lo·quy \'kä-lə-kwē\ *n, pl* **-quies** : a usu. formal conversation or conference

col·lu·sion \kə-'lü-zhən\ *n* : secret agreement or cooperation for an illegal or deceitful purpose — **col·lu·sive** \-siv\ *adj*

Colo *abbr* Colorado

co·logne \kə-'lōn\ *n* [*Cologne*, Germany] : a perfumed liquid — **co·logned** \-'lōnd\ *adj*

Co·lom·bi·an \kə-'ləm-bē-ən\ *n* : a native or inhabitant of Colombia — **Colombian** *adj*

¹co·lon \'kō-lən\ *n, pl* **colons** *or* **co·la** \-lə\ : the part of the large intestine extending from the cecum to the rectum — **co·lon·ic** \kō-'lä-nik\ *adj*

²colon *n, pl* **colons** : a punctuation mark : used esp. to direct attention to following matter (as a list)

co·lón *also* **co·lone** \kə-'lōn\ *n, pl* **co·lo·nes** \-'lō-ˌnäs\ — see MONEY table

col·o·nel \'kər-nᵊl\ *n* [alter. of *coronel,* fr. MF, fr. It *colonnello* column of soldiers, colonel, ultim. fr. L *columna* column] : a commissioned officer (as in the army) ranking next below a brigadier general

¹co·lo·nial \kə-'lō-nē-əl\ *adj* **1** : of, relating to, or characteristic of a colony; *also* : possessing or composed of colonies **2** *often cap* : of or relating to the original 13 colonies forming the U.S.

²colonial *n* **1** : a member or inhabitant of a colony **2** : a house built in the style of the American colonial period

co·lo·nial·ism \-ˌli-zəm\ *n* : control by one power over a dependent area or people; *also* : a policy advocating or based on such control — **co·lo·nial·ist** \-list\ *n or adj*

col·o·nise *Brit var of* COLONIZE

col·o·nist \'kä-lə-nist\ *n* **1** : COLONIAL **2** : one that colonizes or settles in a new country

col·o·nize \'kä-lə-ˌnīz\ *vb* **-nized; -niz·ing** **1** : to establish a colony in or on **2** : SETTLE — **col·o·ni·za·tion** \ˌkä-lə-nə-'zā-shən\ *n* — **col·o·niz·er** *n*

col·on·nade \ˌkä-lə-'nād\ *n* : an evenly spaced row of columns usu. supporting the base of a roof structure

colonnade

co·lo·nos·co·py \ˌkō-lə-'näs-kə-pē\ *n, pl* **-pies** : endoscopic examination of the colon — **co·lon·o·scope** \kō-'lä-nə-ˌskōp\ *n*

col·o·ny \'kä-lə-nē\ *n, pl* **-nies** **1** : a body of people living in a new territory; *also* : the territory inhabited by these people **2** : a localized population of organisms ⟨a ∼ of bees⟩ **3** : a group with common interests situated in close association ⟨a writers' ∼⟩; *also* : the area occupied by such a group

col·o·phon \'kä-lə-fən, -ˌfän\ *n* **1** : an inscription placed at the end of a book with facts relative to its production **2** : an identifying mark used by a printer or publisher

¹col·or \'kə-lər\ *n* **1** : a phenomenon of light (as red or blue) or visual perception that enables one to differentiate otherwise identical objects; *also* : a hue as contrasted with black, white, or gray **2** : APPEARANCE **3** : complexion tint **4** *pl* : FLAG; *also* : military service ⟨a call to the ∼*s*⟩ **5** : VIVIDNESS, INTEREST — **col·or·ful** *adj* — **col·or·less** *adj*

²**color** \vb\ **1** : to give color to; *also* : to change the color of **2** : BLUSH

Col·o·ra·do potato beetle \ˌkä-lə-ˈra-dō-, -ˈrä-\ n : a black=and-yellow striped beetle that feeds on the leaves of the potato

col·or·ation \ˌkə-lə-ˈrā-shən\ n : use or arrangement of colors

col·or·a·tu·ra \ˌkə-lə-rə-ˈtur-ə, -ˈtyur-\ n **1** : elaborate ornamentation in vocal music **2** : a soprano specializing in coloratura

col·or-blind \ˈkə-lər-ˌblīnd\ adj **1** : partially or totally unable to distinguish one or more chromatic colors **2** : not influenced by differences of race — **color blind·ness** n

co·lo·rec·tal \ˌkō-lō-ˈrek-tᵊl\ adj : relating to or affecting the colon and rectum ⟨∼ cancer⟩

col·ored \ˈkə-lərd\ adj **1** : having color **2** : SLANTED, BIASED

col·or·fast \ˈkə-lər-ˌfast\ adj : having color that does not fade or run — **col·or·fast·ness** n

col·or·ize \ˈkə-lə-ˌrīz\ vb **-ized; -iz·ing** : to add color to by means of a computer — **col·or·i·za·tion** \ˌkə-lə-rə-ˈzā-shən\ n

co·los·sal \kə-ˈlä-səl\ adj : of very great size or degree ⟨a ∼ feat⟩

Co·los·sians \kə-ˈlä-shənz\ n — see BIBLE table

co·los·sus \kə-ˈlä-səs\ n, pl **co·los·si** \-ˌsī\ [L] : a gigantic statue; *also* : something of immense size or power

col·our chiefly Brit var of COLOR

col·por·teur \ˈkäl-ˌpór-tər\ n [F] : a peddler of religious books

colt \ˈkōlt\ n : FOAL; *also* : a young male horse, ass, or zebra — **colt·ish** adj

col·um·bine \ˈkä-ləm-ˌbīn\ n [ME, fr. AF, fr. ML columbina, fr. L, fem. of columbinus dovelike, fr. columba dove] : any of a genus of plants with showy spurred flowers that are related to the buttercups

co·lum·bi·um \kə-ˈləm-bē-əm\ n : NIOBIUM

Columbus Day \kə-ˈləm-bəs-\ n : the 2d Monday in October or formerly October 12 observed as a legal holiday in many states in commemoration of the landing of Columbus in the Bahamas in 1492

col·umn \ˈkä-ləm\ n **1** : one of two or more vertical sections of a printed page; *also* : one in a usu. regular series of articles (as in a newspaper) **2** : a supporting pillar; *esp* : one consisting of a usu. round shaft, a capital, and a base **3** : something resembling a column ⟨a ∼ of water⟩ **4** : a long row (as of soldiers) **5** : a statistical category tracked vertically (as on a spreadsheet) — **co·lum·nar** \kə-ˈləm-nər\ adj

col·um·nist \ˈkä-ləm-nist\ n : a person who writes a newspaper or magazine column

com abbr **1** comedy; comic **2** comma **3** commercial organization

co·ma \ˈkō-mə\ n : a state of deep unconsciousness caused by disease, injury, or poison — **co·ma·tose** \ˈkō-mə-ˌtōs, ˈkä-\ adj

Co·man·che \kə-ˈman-chē\ n, pl **Comanche** or **Comanches** : a member of an American Indian people ranging from Wyoming and Nebraska south into New Mexico and Texas

¹**comb** \ˈkōm\ n **1** : a toothed instrument for arranging the hair or for separating and cleaning textile fibers **2** : a fleshy crest on the head of a fowl **3** : HONEYCOMB

²**comb** vb **1** : to pass a comb through **2** : to search through systematically

³**comb** abbr combination; combining

com·bat \kəm-ˈbat, ˈkäm-ˌbat\ vb **-bat·ed** or **-bat·ted; -bat·ing** or **-bat·ting** **1** : FIGHT, CONTEND **2** : to struggle against : OPPOSE — **com·bat** \ˈkäm-ˌbat\ n — **com·bat·ant** \kəm-ˈba-tᵊnt, ˈkäm-bə-tənt\ n — **com·bat·ive** \kəm-ˈba-tiv\ adj

combat fatigue n : a traumatic psychological reaction occurring under wartime conditions (as combat) that cause intense stress

comb·er \ˈkō-mər\ n **1** : one that combs **2** : a long curling wave of the sea

com·bi·na·tion \ˌkäm-bə-ˈnā-shən\ n **1** : a result or product of combining **2** : a sequence of letters or numbers chosen in setting a lock **3** : the act or process of combining; *also* : the quality or state of being combined

¹**com·bine** \kəm-ˈbīn\ vb **com·bined; com·bin·ing** : to become one : UNITE

²**com·bine** \ˈkäm-ˌbīn\ n **1** : a combination esp. of business or political interests **2** : a machine that harvests and threshes grain while moving over a field

comb·ings \ˈkō-miŋz\ n pl : loose hairs or fibers removed by a comb

combining form n : a linguistic form that occurs only in compounds or derivatives

com·bo \ˈkäm-bō\ n, pl **combos** : a small jazz or dance band

comb-over \ˈkōm-ˌō-vər\ n : a hairstyle in which hair from the side of the head is combed over a bald spot

com·bus·ti·ble \kəm-ˈbəs-tə-bəl\ adj **1** : capable of being burned **2** : easily excited — **com·bus·ti·bil·i·ty** \-ˌbəs-tə-ˈbi-lə-tē\ n — **combustible** n

com·bus·tion \kəm-ˈbəs-chən\ n **1** : an act or instance of burning **2** : slow oxidation (as in the animal body)

comdg abbr commanding

comdr abbr commander

comdt abbr commandant

come \ˈkəm\ vb **came** \ˈkäm\; **come; com·ing** \ˈkə-miŋ\ **1** : APPROACH **2** : ARRIVE **3** : to reach the point of being or becoming ⟨∼ to a boil⟩ **4** : AMOUNT ⟨the bill came to $10⟩ **5** : to take place **6** : ORIGINATE, ARISE ⟨wine ∼s from grapes⟩ **7** : to be available ⟨∼s in three sizes⟩ **8** : REACH, EXTEND ⟨grass that ∼s to our knees⟩ — **come across** **1** : to make a specified impression ⟨came across as rude⟩ **2** : to find esp. by chance ⟨came across an intriguing story⟩ — **come clean** : CONFESS — **come into** : ACQUIRE, ACHIEVE — **come of age** : MATURE — **come to grips with** : to meet or deal with frankly — **come to pass** : HAPPEN — **come to terms** : to reach an agreement

come·back \ˈkəm-ˌbak\ n **1** : RETORT **2** : a return to a former position or condition — **come back** vb

co·me·di·an \kə-ˈmē-dē-ən\ n **1** : an actor in comedy **2** : a comic person; *esp* : an entertainer specializing in comedy

co·me·di·enne \-ˌmē-dē-ˈen\ n : a woman who is a comedian

come·down \ˈkəm-ˌdaun\ n : a descent in rank or dignity

com·e·dy \ˈkä-mə-dē\ n, pl **-dies** [ME, narrative that ends happily, fr. ML comoedia, fr. L, play with a happy ending, fr. Gk kōmōidia, fr. kōmos revel + aeidein to sing] **1** : a light amusing play with a happy ending **2** : a literary work treating a comic theme or written in a comic style **3** : humorous entertainment — **co·me·dic** \kə-ˈmē-dik\ adj

come·ly \ˈkəm-lē\ adj **come·li·er; -est** : ATTRACTIVE, HANDSOME — **come·li·ness** n

come off vb **1** : APPEAR, SEEM ⟨comes off as crass⟩ **2** : SUCCEED **3** : to have recently ended ⟨is coming off surgery⟩

come-on \ˈkə-ˌmón, -ˌmän\ n : INDUCEMENT, LURE

come out vb **1** : to come into public view **2** : to declare oneself **3** : TURN OUT **6** ⟨everything came out all right⟩ — **come out with** : SAY 1

com·er \ˈkə-mər\ n **1** : one that comes ⟨all ∼s⟩ **2** : a promising beginner

¹**co·mes·ti·ble** \kə-ˈmes-tə-bəl\ adj : EDIBLE

²**comestible** n : FOOD — usu. used in pl.

com·et \ˈkä-mət\ n [ME comete, fr. OE cometa, fr. L, fr. Gk komētēs, lit., long-haired, fr. komē hair] : a small bright celestial body that develops a long tail when near the sun

come to vb : to regain consciousness

come·up·pance \kə-ˈmə-pəns\ n : a deserved rebuke or penalty

com·fit \ˈkəm-fət\ n : a candied fruit or nut

¹**com·fort** \ˈkəm-fərt\ vb **1** : to give strength and hope to **2** : CONSOLE

²**comfort** n **1** : CONSOLATION **2** : freedom from pain, trouble, or anxiety; *also* : something that gives such freedom

com·fort·able \ˈkəm-fər-tə-bəl, ˈkəmf-tər-\ adj **1** : providing comfort or security **2** : feeling at ease — **com·fort·ably** \-blē\ adv

com·fort·er \ˈkəm-fər-tər\ n **1** : one that comforts **2** : QUILT

com·frey \ˈkəm-frē\ n, pl **comfreys** : any of a genus of perennial herbs that have coarse hairy leaves and are often used in herbal remedies

com·fy \'kəm-fē\ adj : COMFORTABLE

¹com·ic \'kä-mik\ adj 1 : relating to comedy or comic strips 2 : provoking laughter or amusement ✦ Synonyms LAUGHABLE, FUNNY, FARCICAL — com·i·cal adj

²comic n 1 : COMEDIAN 2 pl : the part of a newspaper devoted to comic strips

comic book n : a magazine containing sequences of comic strips

comic strip n : a group of cartoons in narrative sequence

coming adj 1 : APPROACHING, NEXT 2 : gaining importance ⟨the ~ trend⟩

co·mi·ty \'kä-mə-tē, 'kō-\ n, pl -ties : friendly civility : COURTESY

coml abbr commercial

comm abbr 1 command; commander 2 commerce; commercial 3 commission; commissioner 4 committee 5 common 6 commonwealth

com·ma \'kä-mə\ n : a punctuation mark , used esp. as a mark of separation within the sentence

¹com·mand \kə-'mand\ vb 1 : to direct authoritatively : ORDER 2 : DOMINATE, CONTROL, GOVERN 3 : to overlook from a strategic position

²command n 1 : an order given 2 : ability to control : MASTERY 3 : the act of commanding 4 : a signal that actuates a device (as a computer); also : the activation of a device by means of a signal 5 : a body of troops under a commander; also : an area or position that one commands 6 : a position of highest authority

com·man·dant \'kä-mən-ˌdant, -ˌdänt\ n : an officer in command

com·man·deer \ˌkä-mən-'dir\ vb : to take possession of by force

com·mand·er \kə-'man-dər\ n 1 : LEADER, CHIEF; esp : an officer commanding an army or subdivision of an army 2 : a commissioned officer in the navy ranking next below a captain

commander in chief : the supreme commander of the armed forces

com·mand·ment \kə-'mand-mənt\ n : COMMAND, ORDER; esp : any of the Ten Commandments

command module n : a space vehicle module designed to carry the crew and reentry equipment

com·man·do \kə-'man-dō\ n, pl -dos or -does : a member of a military unit trained for surprise raids

command sergeant major n : a noncommissioned officer in the army ranking above a sergeant major

com·mem·o·rate \kə-'me-mə-ˌrāt\ vb -rat·ed; -rat·ing 1 : to call or recall to mind 2 : to serve as a memorial of — com·mem·o·ra·tion \-ˌme-mə-'rā-shən\ n

com·mem·o·ra·tive \kə-'mem-rə-tiv, -'me-mə-ˌrā-tiv\ adj : intended to commemorate an event ⟨a ~ stamp⟩

com·mence \kə-'mens\ vb com·menced; com·menc·ing : BEGIN, START ⟨~ the festivities⟩

com·mence·ment \-mənt\ n 1 : the act or time of a beginning 2 : the graduation exercises of a school or college

com·mend \kə-'mend\ vb 1 : to commit to one's care 2 : RECOMMEND 3 : PRAISE — com·mend·able \-'men-də-bəl\ adj — com·mend·ably \-blē\ adv — com·men·da·tion \ˌkä-mən-'dā-shən, -ˌmen-\ n — com·mend·er n

com·men·su·ra·ble \kə-'men-sə-rə-bəl\ adj : having a common measure or a common divisor

com·men·su·rate \kə-'men-sə-rət, -men-chə-\ adj : equal in measure or extent; also : PROPORTIONAL, CORRESPONDING ⟨a job ~ with her abilities⟩

com·ment \'kä-ˌment\ n 1 : an expression of opinion 2 : an explanatory, illustrative, or critical note or observation : REMARK — comment vb

com·men·tary \'kä-mən-ˌter-ē\ n, pl -tar·ies : a systematic series of comments

com·men·ta·tor \-ˌtā-tər\ n : one who comments; esp : a person who discusses news events on radio or television

com·merce \'kä-(ˌ)mərs\ n : the buying and selling of commodities : TRADE

¹com·mer·cial \kə-'mər-shəl\ adj : having to do with commerce; also : designed for profit or for mass appeal — com·mer·cial·ly adv

²commercial n : an advertisement broadcast on radio or television

com·mer·cial·ise Brit var of COMMERCIALIZE

com·mer·cial·ism \kə-'mər-shə-ˌli-zəm\ n 1 : a spirit, method, or practice characteristic of business 2 : excessive emphasis on profit

com·mer·cial·ize \-ˌliz\ vb -ized; -iz·ing 1 : to manage on a business basis for profit 2 : to exploit for profit

com·mi·na·tion \ˌkä-mə-'nā-shən\ n : DENUNCIATION — com·mi·na·to·ry \'kä-mə-nə-ˌtȯr-ē\ adj

com·min·gle \kə-'miŋ-gəl\ vb : MINGLE, BLEND

com·mis·er·ate \kə-'mi-zə-ˌrāt\ vb -at·ed; -at·ing : to feel or express pity : SYMPATHIZE — com·mis·er·a·tion \-ˌmi-zə-'rā-shən\ n

com·mis·sar \'kä-mə-ˌsär\ n [Russ komissar] : a Communist party official

com·mis·sar·i·at \ˌkä-mə-'ser-ē-ət\ n 1 : a system for supplying troops with food 2 : a department headed by a commissar

com·mis·sary \'kä-mə-ˌser-ē\ n, pl -sar·ies : a store for equipment and provisions esp. for military personnel

¹com·mis·sion \kə-'mi-shən\ n 1 : a warrant granting certain powers and imposing certain duties 2 : a certificate conferring military rank and authority 3 : authority to act as agent for another; also : something to be done by an agent 4 : a body of persons charged with performing a duty 5 : the doing of some act ⟨~ of a crime⟩; also : the thing done 6 : the allowance made to an agent for transacting business for another

²commission vb 1 : to give a commission to 2 : to order to be made ⟨~ a portrait⟩ 3 : to put (a ship) into a state of readiness for service

commissioned officer n : an officer of the armed forces holding rank by a commission from the president

com·mis·sion·er \kə-'mi-shə-nər\ n 1 : a member of a commission 2 : an official in charge of a department of public service ⟨a police ~⟩ 3 : the administrative head of a professional sport — com·mis·sion·er·ship n

com·mit \kə-'mit\ vb com·mit·ted; com·mit·ting 1 : to put into charge or trust : ENTRUST 2 : to put in a prison or mental institution 3 : TRANSFER, CONSIGN 4 : to carry into action : PERPETRATE ⟨~ a crime⟩ 5 : to pledge or assign to some particular course or use — com·mit·ment n — com·mit·tal n

com·mit·tee \kə-'mi-tē\ n : a body of persons selected to consider and act or report on some matter — com·mit·tee·man \-mən\ n — com·mit·tee·wom·an \-ˌwu̇-mən\ n

commo abbr commodore

com·mode \kə-'mōd\ n [F, fr. commode, adj., suitable, convenient, fr. L commodus, fr. com- with + modus measure] 1 : a movable washstand with cupboard below 2 : TOILET 3

com·mo·di·ous \kə-'mō-dē-əs\ adj : comfortably spacious : ROOMY

com·mod·i·ty \kə-'mä-də-tē\ n, pl -ties 1 : a product of agriculture or mining 2 : an article of commerce 3 : something useful or valued ⟨that valuable ~ patience⟩

com·mo·dore \'kä-mə-ˌdȯr\ n 1 : a commissioned officer in the navy ranking next below a rear admiral 2 : an officer commanding a group of merchant ships 3 : the chief officer of a yacht club

¹com·mon \'kä-mən\ adj 1 : belonging to or serving the community : PUBLIC 2 : shared by a number in a group 3 : widely or generally known, found, or observed : FAMILIAR ⟨~ knowledge⟩ 4 : VERNACULAR 3 ⟨~ names of plants⟩ 5 : not above the average esp. in social status ✦ Synonyms UNIVERSAL, GENERAL, GENERIC — com·mon·ly adv

²common n 1 pl : the common people 2 pl : a dining hall 3 pl, cap : the lower house of the British and Canadian parliaments 4 : a piece of land subject to common use — in common : shared together

com·mon·al·ty \'kä-mə-nᵊl-tē\ n, pl -ties : the common people

common cold n : a contagious respiratory disease caused by a virus and characterized by a sore, swollen, and inflamed nose and throat, usu. by much mucus, and by coughing and sneezing

common denominator n 1 : a common multiple of the denominators of a group of fractions 2 : a common trait or theme

common divisor n : a number or expression that divides two or more numbers or expressions without remainder

com·mon·er \'kä-mə-nər\ *n* : one of the common people : a person having no rank of nobility

common fraction *n* : a fraction (as ½ or ¾) in which the numerator and denominator are both integers and are separated by a horizontal or slanted line

common law *n* : a group of legal practices and traditions based on judges' decisions and social customs and usu. having the same force as laws passed by legislative bodies

common logarithm *n* : a logarithm whose base is 10

common market *n* : an economic association formed to remove trade barriers among members

common multiple *n* : a multiple of each of two or more numbers or expressions

¹**com·mon·place** \'kä-mən-ˌplās\ *n* : something that is ordinary or trite

²**commonplace** *adj* : ORDINARY

common sense *n* : ordinary good sense and judgment — **com·mon·sen·si·cal** \'kä-mən-'sen-si-kəl\ *adj*

com·mon·weal \'kä-mən-ˌwēl\ *n* 1 *archaic* : COMMONWEALTH 2 : the general welfare

com·mon·wealth \-ˌwelth\ *n* 1 : the body of people politically organized into a state 2 : STATE; *also* : an association or federation of autonomous states

com·mo·tion \kə-'mō-shən\ *n* 1 : DISTURBANCE, UPRISING 2 : AGITATION

com·mu·nal \kə-'myü-n³l, 'käm-yə-n³l\ *adj* 1 : of or relating to a commune or community 2 : marked by collective ownership and use of property 3 : shared or used in common

¹**com·mune** \kə-'myün\ *vb* **com·muned**; **com·mun·ing** : to communicate intimately ⟨~ with nature⟩

²**com·mune** \'käm-ˌyün; kə-'myün\ *n* 1 : the smallest administrative district in some European countries 2 : a community organized on a communal basis

com·mu·ni·ca·ble \kə-'myü-ni-kə-bəl\ *adj* : capable of being communicated ⟨~ diseases⟩ — **com·mu·ni·ca·bil·i·ty** \-ˌmyü-ni-kə-'bi-lə-tē\ *n*

com·mu·ni·cant \-'myü-ni-kənt\ *n* 1 : a church member entitled to receive Communion 2 : one that communicates; *esp* : INFORMANT

com·mu·ni·cate \kə-'myü-nə-ˌkāt\ *vb* **-cat·ed**; **-cat·ing** 1 : to make known 2 : to pass from one to another : TRANSMIT 3 : to receive Communion 4 : to be in communication 5 : JOIN, CONNECT — **com·mu·ni·cat·or** \-ˌkā-tər\ *n*

com·mu·ni·ca·tion \kə-ˌmyü-nə-'kā-shən\ *n* 1 : an act of transmitting 2 : MESSAGE 3 : exchange of information or opinions 4 : a means of communicating — **com·mu·ni·ca·tive** \-'myü-nə-ˌkā-tiv, -ni-kə-tiv\ *adj*

com·mu·nion \kə-'myü-nyən\ *n* 1 : a sharing of something with others 2 *cap* : a Christian sacrament in which bread and wine are consumed as the substance or symbols of Christ's body and blood in commemoration of the death of Christ 3 : intimate fellowship or rapport 4 : a body of Christians having a common faith and discipline ⟨the Anglican ~⟩

com·mu·ni·qué \kə-'myü-nə-ˌkā, -ˌmyü-nə-'kā\ *n* : BULLETIN 1

com·mu·nism \'käm-yə-ˌni-zəm\ *n* 1 : social organization in which goods are held in common 2 : a theory of social organization advocating common ownership of means of production and a distribution of products of industry based on need 3 *cap* : a political doctrine based on revolutionary Marxist socialism that was the official ideology of the U.S.S.R. and some other countries; *also* : a system of government in which one party controls state-owned means of production — **com·mu·nist** \-nist\ *n or adj, often cap* — **com·mu·nis·tic** \ˌkäm-yə-'nis-tik\ *adj, often cap*

com·mu·ni·ty \kə-'myü-nə-tē\ *n, pl* **-ties** 1 : a body of people living in the same place under the same laws; *also* : a natural population of plants and animals that interact ecologically and live in one place (as a pond) 2 : society at large 3 : joint ownership ⟨~ of goods⟩ 4 : SIMILARITY, LIKENESS ⟨~ of interests⟩

community college *n* : a 2-year government-supported college that offers an associate degree

community property *n* : property held jointly by a married couple

com·mu·ta·tion \ˌkäm-yə-'tā-shən\ *n* : substitution of one form of payment or penalty for another

com·mu·ta·tive \'käm-yə-ˌtā-tiv, kə-'myü-tə-\ *adj* : of, having, or being the property that the result obtained using a mathematical operation on any two elements of a set does not differ with the order in which the elements are used ⟨*a* x *b* = *b* x *a* because multiplication is ~⟩ — **com·mu·ta·tiv·i·ty** \kə-ˌmyü-tə-'ti-və-tē, ˌkäm-yə-tə-\ *n*

com·mu·ta·tor \'käm-yə-ˌtā-tər\ *n* : a device (as on a generator or motor) for changing the direction of electric current

¹**com·mute** \kə-'myüt\ *vb* **com·mut·ed**; **com·mut·ing** 1 : EXCHANGE 2 : to revoke (a sentence) and impose a milder penalty 3 : to travel back and forth regularly — **com·mut·er** *n*

²**commute** *n* : a trip made in commuting

comp *abbr* 1 comparative; compare 2 compensation 3 compiled; compiler 4 composition; compositor 5 compound 6 comprehensive 7 comptroller

¹**com·pact** \kəm-'pakt, 'käm-ˌpakt\ *adj* 1 : SOLID, DENSE 2 : BRIEF, SUCCINCT 3 : occupying a small volume by efficient use of space ⟨~ camera⟩ — **com·pact·ly** *adv* — **com·pact·ness** *n*

²**compact** *vb* : to pack together : COMPRESS — **com·pac·tor** \kəm-'pak-tər, 'käm-ˌpak-\ *n*

³**com·pact** \'käm-ˌpakt\ *n* 1 : a small case for cosmetics 2 : a small automobile

⁴**com·pact** \'käm-ˌpakt\ *n* : AGREEMENT, COVENANT

compact disc \'käm-ˌpakt-\ *n* : CD

com·pa·dre \kəm-'pä-drā\ *n* : a close friend : BUDDY

¹**com·pan·ion** \kəm-'pan-yən\ *n* [ME *compainoun*, fr. AF *cumpaing, cumpaignun*, fr. LL *companion-, companio*, fr. L *com-* together + *panis* bread] 1 : an intimate friend or associate : COMRADE 2 : one that is closely connected with something similar 3 : a celestial body that appears close to another but that may not be associated with it in space — **com·pan·ion·able** *adj* — **com·pan·ion·ship** *n*

²**companion** *n* : COMPANIONWAY

com·pan·ion·way \-ˌwā\ *n* : a ship's stairway from one deck to another

com·pa·ny \'kəm-pə-nē\ *n, pl* **-nies** 1 : association with others : FELLOWSHIP; *also* : COMPANIONS 2 : GUESTS 3 : a group of persons or things 4 : an infantry unit consisting of two or more platoons and normally commanded by a captain 5 : a group of musical or dramatic performers 6 : the officers and crew of a ship 7 : an association of persons for carrying on a business ◆ *Synonyms* PARTY, BAND, TROOP, TROUPE, CORPS, OUTFIT

com·pa·ra·ble \'käm-pə-rə-bəl, -prə-\ *adj* : capable of being compared ⟨singers of ~ talent⟩ ◆ *Synonyms* PARALLEL, SIMILAR, LIKE, ALIKE, CORRESPONDING — **com·pa·ra·bil·i·ty** \ˌkäm-pə-rə-'bi-lə-tē\ *n*

¹**com·par·a·tive** \kəm-'per-ə-tiv\ *adj* 1 : of, relating to, or constituting the degree of grammatical comparison that denotes increase in quality, quantity, or relation 2 : RELATIVE ⟨a ~ stranger⟩ — **com·par·a·tive·ly** *adv*

²**comparative** *n* : the comparative degree or form in a language

¹**com·pare** \kəm-'per\ *vb* **com·pared**; **com·par·ing** 1 : to represent as similar : LIKEN 2 : to examine for likenesses and differences 3 : to inflect or modify (an adjective or adverb) according to the degrees of comparison

²**compare** *n* : the possibility of comparing ⟨beauty beyond ~⟩

com·par·i·son \kəm-'per-ə-sən\ *n* 1 : the act of comparing 2 : change in the form of an adjective or adverb to show different levels of quality, quantity, or relation

com·part·ment \kəm-'pärt-mənt\ *n* 1 : a separate division 2 : a section of an enclosed space : ROOM

com·part·men·tal·ise *Brit var of* COMPARTMENTALIZE

com·part·men·tal·ize \kəm-ˌpärt-'men-t³l-ˌīz\ *vb* **-ized**; **-iz·ing** : to separate into compartments

¹**com·pass** \'kəm-pəs, 'käm-\ *vb* [ME, fr. AF *cumpasser* to measure, fr. VL **compassare* to pace off, fr. L *com-* + *passus* pace] 1 : CONTRIVE, PLOT 2 : ENCIRCLE, ENCOMPASS 3 : BRING ABOUT, ACHIEVE

²**compass** *n* 1 : BOUNDARY, CIRCUMFERENCE 2 : an enclosed space 3 : RANGE, SCOPE 4 : a device for determining direction by means of a magnetic needle swinging freely and pointing to the magnetic north; *also* : a nonmagnetic device that indicates direction 5 : an instrument for drawing circles or transferring measurements consisting of two legs joined by a pivot

compassion • compound

com·pas·sion \kəm-'pa-shən\ n : sympathetic feeling : PITY, MERCY — **com·pas·sion·ate** \-shə-nət\ adj — **com·pas·sion·ate·ly** adv

com·pat·i·ble \kəm-'pa-tə-bəl\ adj : able to exist or act together harmoniously ⟨~ colors⟩ ⟨~ drugs⟩ ◆ *Synonyms* CONSONANT, CONGENIAL, SYMPATHETIC — **com·pat·i·bil·i·ty** \-,pa-tə-'bi-lə-tē\ n

com·pa·tri·ot \kəm-'pā-trē-ət, -,ät\ n : a fellow countryman

com·peer \'käm-,pir\ n : EQUAL, PEER

com·pel \kəm-'pel\ vb **com·pelled; com·pel·ling** : to drive or urge with force

com·pen·di·ous \kəm-'pen-dē-əs\ adj : concise and comprehensive; also : COMPREHENSIVE ⟨a ~ almanac⟩

com·pen·di·um \kəm-'pen-dē-əm\ n, pl **-di·ums** or **-dia** \-ə\ 1 : a brief summary of a larger work or of a field of knowledge 2 : COLLECTION

com·pen·sate \'käm-pən-,sāt\ vb **-sat·ed; -sat·ing** 1 : to be equivalent to : make up for 2 : PAY, REMUNERATE ◆ *Synonyms* BALANCE, OFFSET, COUNTERBALANCE, COUNTERPOISE — **com·pen·sa·tion** \,käm-pən-'sā-shən\ n — **com·pen·sa·to·ry** \kəm-'pen-sə-,tȯr-ē\ adj

com·pete \kəm-'pēt\ vb **com·pet·ed; com·pet·ing** : CONTEND, VIE ⟨~ for the title⟩ ⟨~ for customers⟩

com·pe·tence \'käm-pə-təns\ n 1 : adequate means for subsistence 2 : FITNESS, ABILITY ⟨trusted his doctor's ~⟩

com·pe·ten·cy \-tən-sē\ n, pl **-cies** : COMPETENCE

com·pe·tent \-tənt\ adj : CAPABLE, FIT, QUALIFIED ⟨a ~ mechanic⟩ ⟨a ~ juror⟩

com·pe·ti·tion \,käm-pə-'ti-shən\ n 1 : the act of competing : RIVALRY 2 : CONTEST, MATCH; also : one's competitors — **com·pet·i·tive** \kəm-'pe-tə-tiv\ adj — **com·pet·i·tive·ly** adv — **com·pet·i·tive·ness** n

com·pet·i·tor \kəm-'pe-tə-tər\ n : one that competes : RIVAL

com·pile \kəm-'pī(-ə)l\ vb **com·piled; com·pil·ing** [ME, fr. AF compiler, fr. L compilare to plunder] 1 : to compose out of materials from other documents 2 : to collect and edit into a volume 3 : to translate (a computer program) with a compiler 4 : to build up gradually ⟨~ a record of four wins and two losses⟩ — **com·pi·la·tion** \,käm-pə-'lā-shən\ n

com·pil·er \kəm-'pī-lər\ n 1 : one that compiles 2 : a computer program that translates any program correctly written in a specific programming language into machine language

com·pla·cence \kəm-'plā-sᵊns\ n : COMPLACENCY — **com·pla·cent** \-sᵊnt\ adj — **com·pla·cent·ly** adv

com·pla·cen·cy \-sᵊn-sē\ n, pl **-cies** : SATISFACTION; esp : SELF-SATISFACTION

com·plain \kəm-'plān\ vb 1 : to express grief, pain, or discontent 2 : to make a formal accusation — **com·plain·ant** n — **com·plain·er** n

com·plaint \kəm-'plānt\ n 1 : expression of grief, pain, or dissatisfaction 2 : a bodily ailment or disease 3 : a formal accusation against a person

com·plai·sance \kəm-'plā-sᵊns, ,käm-plā-'zans\ n [F] : disposition to please — **com·plai·sant** \-sᵊnt, -'zant\ adj — **com·plai·sant·ly** adv

com·pleat \kəm-'plēt\ adj : PROFICIENT

com·plect·ed \kəm-'plek-təd\ adj : having a specified facial complexion ⟨dark-complected⟩

¹**com·ple·ment** \'käm-plə-mənt\ n 1 : something that fills up or completes; also : the full quantity, number, or amount that makes a thing complete 2 : an added word by which a predicate is made complete 3 : a group of proteins in blood that combines with antibodies to destroy antigens — **com·ple·men·ta·ry** \,käm-plə-'men-t(ə-)rē\ adj

²**com·ple·ment** \-,ment\ vb : to be complementary to : fill out

complementary medicine n : ALTERNATIVE MEDICINE

¹**com·plete** \kəm-'plēt\ adj **com·plet·er; -est** 1 : having all parts or elements 2 : brought to an end 3 : fully carried out; also : ABSOLUTE 2 ⟨~ silence⟩ — **com·plete·ly** adv — **com·plete·ness** n — **com·ple·tion** \-'plē-shən\ n

²**complete** vb **com·plet·ed; com·plet·ing** 1 : FINISH, CONCLUDE 2 : to make whole or perfect ⟨the hat ~s the outfit⟩

com·plet·ist \kəm-'plē-tist\ n : one who wants to make something (as a collection) complete

¹**com·plex** \'käm-,pleks\ n 1 : a whole made up of or involving intricately interrelated elements 2 : a group of repressed desires and memories that exert a dominating influence on one's personality and behavior ⟨a guilt ~⟩

²**com·plex** \käm-'pleks, 'käm-,pleks\ adj 1 : composed of two or more parts 2 : consisting of a main clause and one or more subordinate clauses ⟨~ sentence⟩ 3 : hard to separate, analyze, or solve — **com·plex·i·ty** \käm-'plek-sə-tē\ n — **com·plex·ly** adv

complex fraction n : a fraction with a fraction or mixed number in the numerator or denominator or both

com·plex·ion \kəm-'plek-shən\ n 1 : the hue or appearance of the skin esp. of the face 2 : overall appearance — **com·plex·ioned** \-shənd\ adj

complex number n : a number of the form $a + b \sqrt{-1}$ where a and b are real numbers

com·pli·ance \kəm-'plī-əns\ n 1 : the act of complying to a demand or proposal 2 : a disposition to yield — **com·pli·ant** \-ənt\ adj

com·pli·cate \'käm-plə-,kāt\ vb **-cat·ed; -cat·ing** : to make or become complex or intricate

com·pli·cat·ed \'käm-plə-,kā-təd\ adj 1 : consisting of parts intricately combined 2 : difficult to analyze, understand, or explain ⟨a ~ issue⟩ — **com·pli·cat·ed·ly** adv

com·pli·ca·tion \,käm-plə-'kā-shən\ n 1 : the quality or state of being complicated; also : a complex feature 2 : a disease or condition that develops during and affects the course of a primary disease or condition

com·plic·i·ty \kəm-'pli-sə-tē\ n, pl **-ties** : the state of being an accomplice

¹**com·pli·ment** \'käm-plə-mənt\ n 1 : an expression of approval or admiration; esp : a flattering remark 2 pl : best wishes : REGARDS

²**com·pli·ment** \-,ment\ vb : to pay a compliment to

com·pli·men·ta·ry \,käm-plə-'men-t(ə-)rē\ adj 1 : containing or expressing a compliment 2 : given free as a courtesy ⟨~ ticket⟩

com·ply \kəm-'plī\ vb **com·plied; com·ply·ing** : CONFORM, YIELD

¹**com·po·nent** \kəm-'pō-nənt, 'käm-,pō-\ n : a component part ◆ *Synonyms* INGREDIENT, ELEMENT, FACTOR, CONSTITUENT

²**component** adj : serving to form a part of : CONSTITUENT

com·port \kəm-'pȯrt\ vb 1 : AGREE, ACCORD ⟨actions that ~ with policy⟩ 2 : CONDUCT ⟨~ oneself with dignity⟩ ◆ *Synonyms* BEHAVE, ACQUIT, DEPORT — **com·port·ment** n

com·pose \kəm-'pōz\ vb **com·posed; com·pos·ing** 1 : to form by putting together : FASHION 2 : to produce (as pages of type) by composition 3 : ADJUST, ARRANGE 4 : CALM, QUIET ⟨~ yourself before acting⟩ 5 : to practice composition ⟨~ music⟩ — **com·pos·er** n

¹**com·pos·ite** \käm-'pä-zət\ adj 1 : made up of distinct parts or elements 2 : of, relating to, or being a large family of flowering plants (as a daisy or aster) that bear many small flowers united into compact heads resembling single flowers

²**composite** n 1 : something composite 2 : a plant of the composite family ◆ *Synonyms* BLEND, COMPOUND, MIXTURE, AMALGAMATION

com·po·si·tion \,käm-pə-'zi-shən\ n 1 : the act or process of composing; esp : arrangement esp. in artistic form 2 : the arrangement or production of type for printing 3 : general makeup 4 : a product of mixing various elements or ingredients 5 : a literary, musical, or artistic product; esp : ESSAY

com·po·si·tion·ist \-'zi-shə-nist\ n : a teacher of writing

com·pos·i·tor \kəm-'pä-zə-tər\ n : one who sets type

com·post \'käm-,pōst\ n : a fertilizing material consisting largely of decayed organic matter — **compost** vb

com·po·sure \kəm-'pō-zhər\ n : CALMNESS, SELF-POSSESSION

com·pote \'käm-,pōt\ n 1 : fruits cooked in syrup 2 : a bowl (as of glass) usu. with a base and stem for serving esp. fruit or compote

¹**com·pound** \käm-'paund, 'käm-,\ vb [ME compounen, fr. AF *cumpundre, fr. L componere, fr. com- together + ponere to put] 1 : COMBINE 2 : to form by combining

parts ⟨∼ a medicine⟩ 3 : SETTLE ⟨∼ a dispute⟩; *also* : to refrain from prosecuting (an offense) in return for a consideration 4 : to increase (as interest) by an amount that can itself vary; *also* : to add to
²com·pound \'käm-ˌpau̇nd\ *adj* 1 : made up of individual parts 2 : composed of united similar parts esp. of a kind usu. independent ⟨a ∼ plant ovary⟩ 3 : formed by the combination of two or more otherwise independent elements ⟨∼ sentence⟩
³com·pound \'käm-ˌpau̇nd\ *n* 1 : a word consisting of parts that are words 2 : something formed from a union of elements or parts; *esp* : a distinct substance formed by the union of two or more chemical elements ♦ Synonyms MIXTURE, COMPOSITE, BLEND, ADMIXTURE, ALLOY
⁴com·pound \'käm-ˌpau̇nd\ *n* [by folk etymology fr. Malay *kampung* group of buildings, village] : an enclosure containing buildings
compound interest *n* : interest computed on the sum of an original principal and accrued interest
com·pre·hend \ˌkäm-pri-'hend\ *vb* 1 : UNDERSTAND 2 : INCLUDE — com·pre·hen·si·ble \-'hen-sə-bəl\ *adj* — com·pre·hen·sion \-'hen-chən\ *n*
com·pre·hen·sive \ˌkäm-pri-'hen-siv\ *adj* : covering completely or broadly ⟨∼ insurance⟩ — com·pre·hen·sive·ly *adv* — com·pre·hen·sive·ness *n*
¹com·press \kəm-'pres\ *vb* 1 : to squeeze together 2 : to reduce in size as if by squeezing ♦ Synonyms CONSTRICT, CONTRACT, SHRINK — com·pres·sor \-'pre-sər\ *n*
²com·press \'käm-ˌpres\ *n* : a folded pad or cloth used to press upon a body part
compressed air *n* : air under pressure greater than that of the atmosphere
com·pres·sion \kəm-'pre-shən\ *n* 1 : the act or process of compressing 2 : the process of compressing the fuel mixture in an internal combustion engine 3 : conversion (as of data) in order to reduce the space occupied or the bandwidth required
com·prise \kəm-'prīz\ *vb* com·prised; com·pris·ing 1 : INCLUDE, CONTAIN 2 : to be made up of ⟨the play ∼s three acts⟩ 3 : COMPOSE, CONSTITUTE
¹com·pro·mise \'käm-prə-ˌmīz\ *n* : a settlement of differences reached by mutual concessions
²compromise *vb* -mised; -mis·ing 1 : to settle by compromise 2 : to expose to suspicion or loss of reputation
comp·trol·ler \kən-'trō-lər, 'kämp-ˌtrō-\ *n* : an official who audits and supervises expenditures and accounts
com·pul·sion \kəm-'pəl-shən\ *n* 1 : an act of compelling 2 : a force that compels 3 : an irresistible persistent impulse to perform an act ♦ Synonyms CONSTRAINT, FORCE, VIOLENCE, DURESS — com·pul·sive \-siv\ *adj* — com·pul·sive·ly *adv* — com·pul·so·ry \-sə-rē\ *adj*
com·punc·tion \kəm-'pəŋk-shən\ *n* : anxiety arising from guilt : REMORSE
com·pute \kəm-'pyüt\ *vb* com·put·ed; com·put·ing : CALCULATE, RECKON — com·pu·ta·tion \ˌkäm-pyü-'tä-shən\ *n* — com·pu·ta·tion·al *adj*
computed tomography *n* : radiography in which a three-dimensional image of a body structure is constructed by computer from a series of plane cross-sectional images made along an axis
com·put·er \kəm-'pyü-tər\ *n* : a programmable electronic device that can store, retrieve, and process data
com·put·er·ise chiefly Brit var of COMPUTERIZE
com·put·er·ize \kəm-'pyü-tə-ˌrīz\ *vb* -ized; -iz·ing 1 : to carry out, control, or produce by means of a computer 2 : to provide with computers 3 : to store in a computer; *also* : put into a form that a computer can use — com·put·er·i·za·tion \-ˌpyü-tə-rə-'zä-shən\ *n*
computerized axial tomography *n* : COMPUTED TOMOGRAPHY
com·rade \'käm-ˌrad\ *n* [MF *camarade* group sleeping in one room, roommate, companion, fr. Sp *camarada*, fr. *cámara* room, fr. LL *camera*] : COMPANION, ASSOCIATE — com·rade·ly *adj* — com·rade·ship *n*
¹con \'kän\ *vb* conned; con·ning 1 : MEMORIZE 2 : STUDY
²con *adv* : in opposition : AGAINST
³con *n* : an opposing argument, person, or position ⟨pros and ∼s⟩

⁴con *vb* conned; con·ning 1 : SWINDLE 2 : PERSUADE, CAJOLE
⁵con *n* : CONVICT
conc *abbr* concentrated
con·cat·e·nate \kän-'ka-tə-ˌnāt\ *vb* -nat·ed; -nat·ing : to link together in a series or chain — con·cat·e·na·tion \(ˌ)kän-ˌka-tə-'nā-shən\ *n*
con·cave \kän-'kāv, 'kän-ˌ\ *adj* : curved or rounded inward like the inside of a bowl — con·cav·i·ty \kän-'ka-və-tē\ *n*
con·ceal \kən-'sēl\ *vb* : to place out of sight : HIDE ⟨∼ evidence⟩ — con·ceal·er *n* — con·ceal·ment *n*
con·cede \kən-'sēd\ *vb* con·ced·ed; con·ced·ing 1 : to admit to be true 2 : GRANT, YIELD ♦ Synonyms ALLOW, ACKNOWLEDGE, AVOW, CONFESS
con·ceit \kən-'sēt\ *n* 1 : excessively high opinion of one's self or ability : VANITY 2 : an elaborate or strained metaphor — con·ceit·ed *adj* — con·ceit·ed·ly *adv* — con·ceit·ed·ness *n*
con·ceive \kən-'sēv\ *vb* con·ceived; con·ceiv·ing 1 : to become pregnant or pregnant with ⟨∼ a child⟩ 2 : to form an idea of : THINK, IMAGINE ⟨∼ a plan⟩ — con·ceiv·able \-'sē-və-bəl\ *adj* — con·ceiv·ably \-blē\ *adv*
con·cel·e·brant \kən-'se-lə-brənt\ *n* : one that jointly participates in celebrating the Eucharist
¹con·cen·trate \'kän-sən-ˌträt\ *vb* -trat·ed; -trat·ing 1 : to gather into one body, mass, or force 2 : to make less dilute 3 : to fix one's powers, efforts, or attentions
²concentrate *n* : something concentrated
con·cen·tra·tion \ˌkän-sən-'trä-shən\ *n* 1 : the act or process of concentrating : the state of being concentrated; *esp* : direction of attention on a single object 2 : the amount of a component in a given area or volume
concentration camp *n* : a camp where persons (as prisoners of war or political prisoners) are confined
con·cen·tric \kən-'sen-trik\ *adj* 1 : having a common center ⟨∼ circles⟩ 2 : COAXIAL
¹con·cept \'kän-ˌsept\ *n* : THOUGHT, NOTION, IDEA — con·cep·tu·al \kən-'sep-chə-wəl\ *adj* — con·cep·tu·al·ly *adv*
²concept *adj* 1 : organized around a main idea or theme ⟨a ∼ album⟩ 2 : created to illustrate a concept ⟨a ∼ car⟩
con·cep·tion \kən-'sep-shən\ *n* 1 : the process of conceiving or being conceived 2 : the power to form or understand ideas or concepts 3 : IDEA, CONCEPT 4 : the originating of something
con·cep·tu·al·ise Brit var of CONCEPTUALIZE
con·cep·tu·al·ize \-'sep-chə-wə-ˌlīz\ *vb* -ized; -iz·ing : to form a conception of
¹con·cern \kən-'sərn\ *vb* 1 : to relate to 2 : to be the business of : INVOLVE 3 : ENGAGE, OCCUPY
²concern *n* 1 : INTEREST, ANXIETY 2 : AFFAIR, MATTER 3 : a business organization ♦ Synonyms CARE, WORRY, DISQUIET, UNEASE
con·cerned \-'sərnd\ *adj* 1 : ANXIOUS, UNEASY ⟨∼ for their safety⟩ 2 : INVOLVED ⟨is ∼ed with films⟩
con·cern·ing \-'sər-niŋ\ *prep* : relating to : REGARDING ⟨news ∼ his business⟩
con·cern·ment \-'sərn-mənt\ *n* 1 : something in which one is concerned 2 : IMPORTANCE, CONSEQUENCE
¹con·cert \'kän-(ˌ)sərt\ *n* 1 : agreement in a plan or design 2 : a public performance (as of music)
²con·cert \kən-'sərt\ *vb* : to plan together
con·cert·ed \kən-'sər-təd\ *adj* : mutually agreed on; *also* : performed in unison
con·cer·ti·na \ˌkän-sər-'tē-nə\ *n* : an instrument of the accordion family
concertina wire *n* : a coiled wire with sharp points for use as an obstacle
con·cert·mas·ter \'kän-sərt-ˌmas-tər\ *or* con·cert·meis·ter \-ˌmī-stər\ *n* : the leader of the first violins of an orchestra and assistant to the conductor
con·cer·to \kən-'cher-tō\ *n, pl* -ti \-(ˌ)tē\ *or* -tos [It] : a piece for one or more solo instruments and orchestra in three movements
con·ces·sion \kən-'se-shən\ *n* 1 : an act of conceding or yielding 2 : something yielded 3 : a grant by a government of land or of a right to use it 4 : a grant of a

portion of premises for some specific purpose; *also* : the activities or enterprise carried on — **con·ces·sion·ary** \-'se-shə-ˌner-ē\ *adj*

con·ces·sion·aire \kən-ˌse-shə-'ner\ *n* : one that owns or operates a concession

conch \'käŋk, 'känch\ *n, pl* **conchs** \'käŋks\ *or* **conch·es** \'kän-chəz\ : a large spiral-shelled marine gastropod mollusk; *also* : its shell

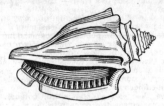

conch

con·cierge \kōⁿ-'syerzh\ *n, pl* **con·cierges** *same or* -'syerzhəz\ [F] **1** : a resident in an apartment building who performs services for the tenants **2** : a usu. multilingual hotel staff member who usu. handles mail and reservations

con·cil·i·ate \kən-'si-lē-ˌāt\ *vb* **-at·ed; -at·ing 1** : to bring into agreement : RECONCILE **2** : to gain the goodwill of — **con·cil·i·a·tion** \-ˌsi-lē-'ā-shən\ *n* — **con·cil·i·a·tor** \-'si-lē-ˌā-tər\ *n* — **con·cil·ia·to·ry** \-'si-lē-ə-ˌtȯr-ē\ *adj*

con·cise \kən-'sīs\ *adj* : expressing much in few words : BRIEF ⟨a ~ history⟩ — **con·cise·ly** *adv* — **con·cise·ness** *n*

con·clave \'kän-ˌklāv\ *n* [ME, fr. ML, fr. L, room that can be locked, fr. *com-* together + *clavis* key] : a private gathering; *also* : CONVENTION

con·clude \kən-'klüd\ *vb* **con·clud·ed; con·clud·ing 1** : to bring to a close : END **2** : DECIDE, JUDGE **3** : to bring about as a result ✦ *Synonyms* CLOSE, FINISH, TERMINATE, COMPLETE, HALT

con·clu·sion \kən-'klü-zhən\ *n* **1** : the logical consequence of a reasoning process **2** : TERMINATION, END **3** : OUTCOME, RESULT — **con·clu·sive** \-siv\ *adj* — **con·clu·sive·ly** *adv* — **con·clu·sive·ness** *n*

con·coct \kən-'käkt, kän-\ *vb* **1** : to prepare by combining raw materials **2** : DEVISE — **con·coc·tion** \-'käkshən\ *n*

con·com·i·tant \-'kä-mə-tənt\ *adj* : ACCOMPANYING, ATTENDING — **concomitant** *n*

con·cord \'kän-ˌkȯrd, 'käŋ-\ *n* : AGREEMENT, HARMONY

con·cor·dance \kən-'kȯr-dᵊns\ *n* **1** : an alphabetical index of words in a book or in an author's works with the passages in which they occur **2** : AGREEMENT, COVENANT

con·cor·dant \-dᵊnt\ *adj* : HARMONIOUS, AGREEING

con·cor·dat \kən-'kȯr-ˌdat\ *n* : CONCORDANCE 2

con·course \'kän-ˌkȯrs\ *n* **1** : a spontaneous coming together : GATHERING **2** : an open space or hall (as in a bus terminal) where crowds gather

¹con·crete \'kän-ˌkrēt, 'kän-ˌkrēt\ *adj* **1** : naming a real thing or class of things : not abstract **2** : not theoretical : ACTUAL **3** : made of or relating to concrete

²con·crete \'kän-ˌkrēt, kän-'krēt\ *vb* **con·cret·ed; con·cret·ing 1** : SOLIDIFY **2** : to cover with concrete

³con·crete \'kän-ˌkrēt, kän-'krēt\ *n* : a hard building material made by mixing cement, sand, and gravel with water

con·cre·tion \kän-'krē-shən\ *n* : a hard mass esp. when formed abnormally in the body

con·cu·bine \'käŋ-kyu-ˌbīn\ *n* [ME, fr. AF, fr. L *concubina*, fr. *com-* with + *cubare* to lie] : a woman who is not legally a wife but lives with a man and sometimes has a recognized position in his household; *also* : MISTRESS — **con·cu·bi·nage** \kän-'kyü-bə-nij\ *n*

con·cu·pis·cence \kän-'kyü-pə-səns\ *n* : ardent sexual desire : LUST

con·cur \kən-'kər\ *vb* **con·curred; con·cur·ring 1** : to act together **2** : AGREE **3** : COINCIDE ✦ *Synonyms* UNITE, COMBINE, COOPERATE, BAND, JOIN

con·cur·rence \-'kər-əns\ *n* **1** : agreement in action or opinion **2** : occurrence together : CONJUNCTION

con·cur·rent \-'kər-ənt\ *adj* **1** : happening or operating at the same time **2** : joint and equal in authority

con·cus·sion \kən-'kə-shən\ *n* **1** : a hard blow or collision; *also* : bodily injury (as to the brain) resulting from a sudden jar **2** : AGITATION, SHAKING

con·demn \kən-'dem\ *vb* **1** : to declare to be wrong **2** : to convict of guilt **3** : to sentence judicially **4** : to pronounce unfit for use ⟨~ a building⟩ **5** : to declare forfeited or taken for public use ✦ *Synonyms* DENOUNCE, CENSURE, BLAME, CRITICIZE, REPREHEND — **con·dem·na·tion** \ˌkän-ˌdem-'nä-shən\ *n* — **con·dem·na·to·ry** \kən-'dem-nə-ˌtȯr-ē\ *adj*

con·den·sate \'kän-dən-ˌsāt, kən-'den-\ *n* : a product of condensation

con·dense \kən-'dens\ *vb* **con·densed; con·dens·ing 1** : to make or become more compact or dense : CONCENTRATE **2** : to change from vapor to liquid ✦ *Synonyms* CONTRACT, SHRINK, COMPRESS, CONSTRICT — **con·den·sa·tion** \ˌkän-den-'sā-shən\ *n*

con·dens·er \kən-'den-sər\ *n* **1** : one that condenses **2** : CAPACITOR

con·de·scend \ˌkän-di-'send\ *vb* : to assume an air of superiority — **con·de·scend·ing·ly** \-'sen-diŋ-lē\ *adv* — **con·de·scen·sion** \-'sen-chən\ *n*

con·dign \kən-'dīn, 'kän-ˌdīn\ *adj* : DESERVED, APPROPRIATE ⟨~ punishment⟩

con·di·ment \'kän-də-mənt\ *n* : something used to make food savory; *esp* : a pungent seasoning (as pepper)

¹con·di·tion \kən-'di-shən\ *n* **1** : something essential to the occurrence of some other thing **2** : state of being **3** : social status **4** *pl* : state of affairs : CIRCUMSTANCES **5** : a bodily state in which something is wrong ⟨a heart ~⟩ **6** : a state of health, fitness, or working order ⟨in good ~⟩

²condition *vb* **1** : to put into proper condition for action or use **2** : to adapt, modify, or mold to respond in a particular way **3** : to modify so that an act or response previously associated with one stimulus becomes associated with another

con·di·tion·al \kən-'di-shə-nəl\ *adj* : containing, implying, or depending on a condition — **con·di·tion·al·ly** *adv*

con·di·tioned \-'di-shənd\ *adj* : determined or established by conditioning

con·di·tion·er \-'di-shə-nər\ *n* : a preparation used to improve the condition of hair

con·do \'kän-ˌdō\ *n* : CONDOMINIUM 3

con·dole \kən-'dōl\ *vb* **con·doled; con·dol·ing** : to express sympathetic sorrow — **con·do·lence** \kən-'dō-ləns\ *n*

con·dom \'kän-dəm, 'kən-\ *n* : a usu. rubber sheath worn over the penis (as to prevent pregnancy or venereal infection during sexual intercourse)

con·do·min·i·um \ˌkän-də-'mi-nē-əm\ *n, pl* **-ums 1** : joint sovereignty (as by two or more nations) **2** : a politically dependent territory under condominium **3** : individual ownership of a unit (as an apartment) in a multiunit structure; *also* : a unit so owned

con·done \kən-'dōn\ *vb* **con·doned; con·don·ing** : to overlook or forgive esp. by treating (an offense) as harmless or trivial ✦ *Synonyms* EXCUSE, PARDON, FORGIVE, REMIT — **con·do·na·tion** \ˌkän-dō-'nā-shən\ *n*

con·dor \'kän-dər, -ˌdȯr\ *n* [Sp *cóndor*, fr. Quechua *kuntur*] : a very large American vulture of the high Andes; *also* : a related nearly extinct vulture of southern California now resident only in captivity

con·duce \kən-'düs, -'dyüs\ *vb* **con·duced; con·duc·ing** : to lead or contribute to a particular result — **con·du·cive** *adj*

¹con·duct \'kän-(ˌ)dəkt\ *n* **1** : MANAGEMENT, DIRECTION **2** : BEHAVIOR

²con·duct \kən-'dəkt\ *vb* **1** : GUIDE, ESCORT **2** : MANAGE, DIRECT **3** : to act as a medium for conveying or transmitting **4** : BEHAVE — **con·duc·tion** \-'dək-shən\ *n*

con·duc·tance \kən-'dək-təns\ *n* : the readiness with which a conductor transmits an electric current

con·duc·tive \kən-'dək-tiv\ *adj* : having the power to conduct (as heat or electricity) — **con·duc·tiv·i·ty** \ˌkän-ˌdək-'ti-və-tē\ *n*

con·duc·tor \kən-'dək-tər\ *n* **1** : one that conducts; *esp* : a material that permits an electric current to flow easily **2** : a collector of fares in a public conveyance **3** : the leader of a musical ensemble

con·duit \'kän-ˌdü-ət, ˌdyü-, -dwət\ *n* 1 : a channel for conveying fluid 2 : a tube or trough for protecting electric wires or cables 3 : a means of transmitting or distributing

con·dyle \'kän-ˌdī(-ə)l, -dᵊl\ *n* : an articular prominence of a bone — **con·dy·lar** \-də-lər\ *adj*

cone \'kōn\ *n* 1 : the scaly usu. ovate fruit of trees of most conifers 2 : a solid figure formed by rotating a right triangle about one of its legs 3 : a solid figure that slopes evenly to a point from a usu. circular base 4 : any of the conical light-sensitive receptor cells of the retina that function in color vision 5 : something shaped like a cone

cone·flow·er \'kōn-ˌflau̇(-ə)r\ *n* : any of several composite plants having cone-shaped flower disks

Con·es·to·ga wagon \ˌkä-nə-'stō-gə-\ *n* : a broad-wheeled covered wagon used esp. for transporting freight across the prairies

co·ney *or* **co·ny** \'kō-nē\ *n, pl* **coneys** *or* **conies** 1 : RABBIT; *also* : its fur 2 : PIKA

conf *abbr* 1 conference 2 confidential

con·fab \'kän-ˌfab, kən-'fab\ *n* : CONFABULATION 1

con·fab·u·la·tion \kən-ˌfab-yə-'lā-shən\ *n* 1 : CHAT; *also* : CONFERENCE 2 : a filling in of gaps in memory by fabrication — **con·fab·u·late** \-'fa-byə-ˌlāt\ *vb*

con·fec·tion \kən-'fek-shən\ *n* 1 : something put together from varied material 2 : a fancy dish or sweet; *also* : CANDY — **con·fect** \kən-'fekt\ *vb*

con·fec·tion·er \-sh(ə-)nər\ *n* : a maker of or dealer in confections

con·fec·tion·ery \-shə-ˌner-ē\ *n, pl* **-er·ies** 1 : sweet foods 2 : a confectioner's place of business

Confed *abbr* Confederate

con·fed·er·a·cy \kən-'fe-də-rə-sē\ *n, pl* **-cies** 1 : LEAGUE, ALLIANCE 2 *cap* : the 11 southern states that seceded from the U.S. in 1860 and 1861

¹con·fed·er·ate \kən-'fe-də-rət\ *adj* 1 : united in a league : ALLIED 2 *cap* : of or relating to the Confederacy

²confederate *n* 1 : ALLY, ACCOMPLICE 2 *cap* : an adherent of the Confederacy

³con·fed·er·ate \-'fe-də-ˌrāt\ *vb* **-at·ed; -at·ing** : to unite in a confederacy

con·fed·er·a·tion \kən-ˌfe-də-'rā-shən\ *n* 1 : an act of confederating : ALLIANCE 2 : LEAGUE

con·fer \kən-'fər\ *vb* **con·ferred; con·fer·ring** 1 : GRANT, BESTOW ⟨~ an award⟩ 2 : to exchange views : CONSULT — **con·fer·ee** \ˌkän-fə-'rē\ *n*

con·fer·ence \'kän-f(ə-)rəns\ *n* 1 : an interchange of views; *also* : a meeting for this purpose 2 : an association of athletic teams

con·fer·enc·ing \'kän-f(ə-)rən-siŋ\ *n* : the holding of conferences esp. by means of electronic devices

con·fess \kən-'fes\ *vb* 1 : to acknowledge or disclose one's misdeed, fault, or sin 2 : to acknowledge one's sins to God or to a priest 3 : to receive the confession of (a penitent) ♦ *Synonyms* ADMIT, OWN, AVOW, CONCEDE, GRANT

con·fessed·ly \-'fe-səd-lē\ *adv* : by confession : ADMITTEDLY

con·fes·sion \-'fe-shən\ *n* 1 : an act of confessing (as in the sacrament of penance) 2 : an acknowledgment of guilt 3 : a formal statement of religious beliefs 4 : a religious body having a common creed — **con·fes·sion·al** *adj*

con·fes·sion·al \-'fe-shə-nəl\ *n* : a place where a priest hears confessions

con·fes·sor \kən-'fe-sər\ *n* 1 : one that confesses 2 : a priest who hears confessions

con·fet·ti \kən-'fe-tē\ *n* [It, pl. of *confetto* sweetmeat, fr. ML *confectum*, fr. L, neut. of *confectus*, pp. of *conficere* to prepare] : bits of colored paper or ribbon for throwing (as at weddings)

con·fi·dant \'kän-fə-ˌdänt, -ˌdant\ *n* : one to whom secrets are confided

con·fi·dante \-ˌdänt, -ˌdant\ *n* : CONFIDANT; *esp* : one who is a woman

con·fide \kən-'fīd\ *vb* **con·fid·ed; con·fid·ing** 1 : to have or show faith : TRUST ⟨~ in a friend⟩ 2 : to tell confidentially ⟨~ a secret⟩ 3 : ENTRUST

¹con·fi·dence \'kän-fə-dəns\ *n* 1 : TRUST, RELIANCE 2 : SELF-ASSURANCE, BOLDNESS 3 : a state of trust or intimacy 4 : SECRET 2 — **con·fi·dent** \-dənt\ *adj* — **con·fi·dent·ly** *adv*

²confidence *adj* : of or relating to swindling by false promises ⟨a ~ game⟩

con·fi·den·tial \ˌkän-fə-'den-shəl\ *adj* 1 : SECRET, PRIVATE ⟨~ information⟩ 2 : entrusted with confidences ⟨~ clerk⟩ — **con·fi·den·ti·al·i·ty** \-ˌden-shē-'a-lə-tē\ *n* — **con·fi·den·tial·ly** \-'den-shə-lē\ *adv*

con·fig·u·ra·tion \kən-ˌfi-gyə-'rä-shən\ *n* : structural arrangement of parts : SHAPE

con·fig·ure \kən-'fi-gyər\ *vb* **-ured; -ur·ing** : to set up for operation esp. in a particular way

con·fine \kən-'fīn\ *vb* **con·fined; con·fin·ing** 1 : to hold within a location; *also* : IMPRISON 2 : to keep within limits ⟨will ~ my remarks to one subject⟩ — **con·fine·ment** *n* — **con·fin·er** *n*

con·fines \'kän-ˌfīnz\ *n pl* : BOUNDS, BORDERS

con·firm \kən-'fərm\ *vb* 1 : to give approval to : RATIFY 2 : to make firm or firmer 3 : to administer the rite of confirmation to 4 : VERIFY, CORROBORATE — **con·fir·ma·to·ry** \-'fər-mə-ˌtȯr-ē\ *adj*

con·fir·ma·tion \ˌkän-fər-'mä-shən\ *n* 1 : a religious ceremony admitting a person to full membership in a church or synagogue 2 : an act of ratifying or corroborating; *also* : PROOF

con·fis·cate \'kän-fə-ˌskāt\ *vb* **-cat·ed; -cat·ing** [L *confiscare*, fr. *com-* with + *fiscus* treasury] : to take possession of by or as if by public authority — **con·fis·ca·tion** \ˌkän-fə-'skä-shən\ *n* — **con·fis·ca·to·ry** \kən-'fis-kə-ˌtȯr-ē\ *adj*

con·fit \kōn-'fē\ *n* : a garnish of fruit or vegetables cooked in a seasoned liquid

con·fla·gra·tion \ˌkän-flə-'grä-shən\ *n* : FIRE; *esp* : a large disastrous fire

¹con·flict \'kän-ˌflikt\ *n* 1 : WAR 2 : a clash between hostile or opposing elements, ideas, or forces

²con·flict \kən-'flikt\ *vb* : to show opposition or irreconcilability : CLASH

con·flu·ence \'kän-ˌflü-əns, kən-'flü-\ *n* 1 : a coming together at one point 2 : the meeting or place of meeting of two or more streams — **con·flu·ent** \-ənt\ *adj*

con·flux \'kän-ˌfləks\ *n* : CONFLUENCE

con·form \kən-'fȯrm\ *vb* 1 : to be similar or identical; *also* : AGREE 2 : to obey customs or standards; *also* : COMPLY ⟨~ to regulations⟩ — **con·form·able** *adj* — **con·form·ist** \-'fȯr-mist\ *adj*

con·for·mance \kən-'fȯr-məns\ *n* : CONFORMITY

con·for·ma·tion \ˌkän-fȯr-'mä-shən\ *n* : a forming into a whole by arranging parts

con·for·mi·ty \kən-'fȯr-mə-tē\ *n, pl* **-ties** 1 : HARMONY, AGREEMENT 2 : COMPLIANCE, OBEDIENCE

con·found \kən-'fau̇nd, kän-\ *vb* 1 : to throw into disorder or confusion 2 : CONFUSE 2 ♦ *Synonyms* BEWILDER, PUZZLE, PERPLEX, BEFOG

con·fra·ter·ni·ty \ˌkän-frə-'tər-nə-tē\ *n* : a society devoted to a religious or charitable cause

con·frere \'kän-ˌfrer, 'kōⁿ-\ *n* : COLLEAGUE, COMRADE

con·front \kən-'frənt\ *vb* 1 : to face esp. in challenge : OPPOSE; *also* : to deal unflinchingly with ⟨~ed the issue⟩ 2 : to cause to face or meet — **con·fron·ta·tion** \ˌkän-frən-'tä-shən\ *n* — **con·fron·ta·tion·al** \-shə-nᵊl\ *adj*

Con·fu·cian \kən-'fyü-shən\ *adj* : of or relating to the Chinese philosopher Confucius or his teachings — **Con·fu·cian·ism** \-shə-ˌni-zəm\ *n*

con·fuse \kən-'fyüz\ *vb* **con·fused; con·fus·ing** 1 : to make mentally unclear or uncertain; *also* : to disturb the composure of 2 : to mix up : JUMBLE ♦ *Synonyms* MUDDLE, BEFUDDLE, ADDLE, FLUSTER — **con·fus·ed·ly** \-'fyü-zəd-lē\ *adv* — **con·fus·ing·ly** \-'fyü-ziŋ-lē\ *adv*

con·fu·sion \-'fyü-zhən\ *n* 1 : an act or instance of confusing 2 : the quality or state of being confused

con·fute \kən-'fyüt\ *vb* **con·fut·ed; con·fut·ing** : to overwhelm by argument : REFUTE ⟨~ a proposition⟩ — **con·fu·ta·tion** \ˌkän-fyü-'tä-shən\ *n*

cong *abbr* congress; congressional

con·ga \'käŋ-gə\ *n* : a Cuban dance of African origin performed by a group usu. in single file

con·geal \kən-'jēl\ *vb* 1 : FREEZE 2 : to make or become hard or thick

con·gee \'kän-jē\ *n* : porridge made from rice

con·ge·ner \'kän-jə-nər\ *n* : one related to another; *esp* : a plant or animal of the same taxonomic genus as another — **con·ge·ner·ic** \ˌkän-jə-'ner-ik\ *adj*

con·ge·nial \kən-'jē-nyəl\ *adj* **1** : KINDRED, SYMPATHETIC ⟨~ companions⟩ **2** : suited to one's taste or nature : AGREEABLE — **con·ge·ni·al·i·ty** \-ˌjē-nē-'a-lə-tē\ *n* — **con·ge·nial·ly** *adv*

con·gen·i·tal \kən-'je-nə-t°l\ *adj* : existing at or dating from birth ⟨~ deafness⟩ ♦ **Synonyms** INBORN, INNATE, NATURAL

con·ger eel \'käŋ-gər-\ *n* : a large edible marine eel of the Atlantic

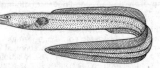

conger eel

con·ge·ries \'kän-jə-(ˌ)rēz\ *n, pl* **congeries** : AGGREGATION, COLLECTION

con·gest \kən-'jest\ *vb* **1** : to cause excessive fullness of the blood vessels of (as a lung) **2** : to obstruct by overcrowding — **con·ges·tion** \-'jes-chən\ *n* — **con·ges·tive** \-'jes-tiv\ *adj*

congestive heart failure *n* : heart failure in which the heart is unable to keep enough blood circulating in the tissues or is unable to pump out the blood returned to it by the veins

¹con·glom·er·ate \kən-'glä-mə-rət\ *adj* [L *conglomerare* to roll together, fr. *com-* together + *glomerare* to wind into a ball, fr. *glomer-, glomus* ball] : made up of parts from various sources

²con·glom·er·ate \-ˌrāt\ *vb* **-at·ed; -at·ing** : to form into a mass — **con·glom·er·a·tion** \-ˌglä-mə-'rā-shən\ *n*

³con·glom·er·ate \-rət\ *n* **1** : a mass formed of fragments from various sources; *esp* : a rock composed of fragments varying from pebbles to boulders held together by a cementing material **2** : a widely diversified corporation

con·grat·u·late \kən-'gra-chə-ˌlāt\ *vb* **-lat·ed; -lat·ing** : to express sympathetic pleasure to on account of success or good fortune : FELICITATE — **con·grat·u·la·tion** \-ˌgra-chə-'lā-shən\ *n* — **con·grat·u·la·to·ry** \-'gra-chə-lə-ˌtōr-ē\ *adj*

con·gre·gate \'käŋ-gri-ˌgāt\ *vb* **-gat·ed; -gat·ing** [ME, fr. L *congregatus*, pp. of *congregare*, fr. *com-* together + *greg-, grex* flock] : ASSEMBLE

con·gre·ga·tion \ˌkäŋ-gri-'gā-shən\ *n* **1** : an assembly of persons met esp. for worship; *also* : a group that habitually so meets **2** : a religious community or order **3** : the act or an instance of congregating

con·gre·ga·tion·al \-shə-nəl\ *adj* **1** : of or relating to a congregation **2** *cap* : observing the faith and practice of certain Protestant churches which recognize the independence of each congregation in church matters — **con·gre·ga·tion·al·ism** \-nə-ˌli-zəm\ *n, often cap* — **con·gre·ga·tion·al·ist** \-list\ *n, often cap*

con·gress \'käŋ-grəs\ *n* **1** : an assembly esp. of delegates for discussion and usu. action on some question **2** : the body of senators and representatives constituting a nation's legislature — **con·gres·sio·nal** \kən-'gre-shə-nəl\ *adj*

con·gress·man \'käŋ-grəs-mən\ *n* : a member of a congress

con·gress·wom·an \-ˌwu̇-mən\ *n* : a woman who is a member of a congress

con·gru·ence \kən-'grü-əns, 'käŋ-grü-\ *n* : the quality of agreeing or coinciding : CONGRUITY — **con·gru·ent** \kən-'grü-ənt, 'käŋ-grü-\ *adj*

con·gru·en·cy \-sē\ *n, pl* **-cies** : CONGRUENCE

con·gru·ity \kän-'grü-ə-tē\ *n, pl* **-ities** : correspondence between things — **con·gru·ous** \'käŋ-grü-əs\ *adj*

con·ic \'kä-nik\ *adj* **1** : of or relating to a cone **2** : CONICAL

con·i·cal \'kä-ni-kəl\ *adj* : resembling a cone esp. in shape

co·ni·fer \'kä-nə-fər, 'kō-\ *n* : any of an order of shrubs or trees (as the pines) that usu. are evergreen and bear cones — **co·nif·er·ous** \kō-'ni-fə-rəs\ *adj*

conj *abbr* conjunction

con·jec·ture \kən-'jek-chər\ *n* : GUESS, SURMISE — **con·jec·tur·al** \-chə-rəl\ *adj* — **conjecture** *vb*

con·join \kən-'jȯin\ *vb* : to join together — **con·joint** \-'jȯint\ *adj*

con·ju·gal \'kän-ji-gəl\ *adj* : of or relating to marriage : MATRIMONIAL

¹con·ju·gate \'kän-ji-gət, -jə-ˌgāt\ *adj* **1** : united esp. in pairs : COUPLED **2** : of kindred origin and meaning ⟨*sing* and *song* are ~⟩ — **con·ju·gate·ly** *adv*

²con·ju·gate \-jə-ˌgāt\ *vb* **-gat·ed; -gat·ing** **1** : INFLECT ⟨~ a verb⟩ **2** : to join together : COUPLE

con·ju·ga·tion \ˌkän-jə-'gā-shən\ *n* **1** : an arrangement of the inflectional forms of a verb **2** : the act of conjugating : the state of being conjugated

con·junct \kän-'jəŋkt\ *adj* : JOINED, UNITED

con·junc·tion \kən-'jəŋk-shən\ *n* **1** : COMBINATION **2** : occurrence at the same time **3** : a word that joins together sentences, clauses, phrases, or words

con·junc·ti·va \ˌkän-jəŋk-'tī-və\ *n, pl* **-vas** *or* **-vae** \-(ˌ)vē\ : the mucous membrane lining the inner surface of the eyelids and continuing over the forepart of the eyeball

con·junc·tive \kən-'jəŋk-tiv\ *adj* **1** : CONNECTIVE **2** : CONJUNCT ⟨the ~ operation of different factors⟩ **3** : being or functioning like a conjunction

con·junc·ti·vi·tis \kən-ˌjəŋk-ti-'vī-təs\ *n* : inflammation of the conjunctiva

con·junc·ture \kən-'jəŋk-chər\ *n* **1** : CONJUNCTION, UNION **2** : JUNCTURE 3

con·jun·to \kȯn-'hün-tō\ *n* : Mexican-American music influenced by the music of German immigrants to Texas

con·jure \'kän-jər, 'kən-, *for 1, 2*; kən-'ju̇r *for 3*\ *vb* **con·jured; con·jur·ing** **1** : to implore earnestly or solemnly **2** : to practice magic; *esp* : to summon (as a devil) by sorcery **3** : to practice sleight of hand — **con·ju·ra·tion** \ˌkän-jù-'rā-shən, ˌkən-\ *n* — **con·jur·er** *or* **con·ju·ror** \'kän-jər-ər, 'kən-\ *n*

conk \'käŋk\ *vb* : BREAK DOWN; *esp* : STALL ⟨the motor ~ed out⟩

Conn *abbr* Connecticut

con·nect \kə-'nekt\ *vb* **1** : JOIN, LINK **2** : to associate in one's mind **3** : to establish a communications connection ⟨~ to the Internet⟩ — **con·nect·able** *adj* — **con·nec·tor** *n*

con·nec·tion \kə-'nek-shən\ *n* **1** : JUNCTION, UNION **2** : logical relationship : COHERENCE; *esp* : relation of a word to other words in a sentence **3** : family relationship **4** : BOND, LINK **5** : a person related by blood or marriage **6** : relationship in social affairs or in business **7** : an association of persons; *esp* : a religious denomination **8** : a means of communication or transport ⟨a telephone ~⟩

¹con·nec·tive \kə-'nek-tiv\ *adj* : serving to connect — **con·nec·tiv·i·ty** \ˌkä-ˌnek-'ti-və-tē\ *n*

²connective *n* : a word (as a conjunction) that connects words or word groups

connective tissue *n* : a tissue (as bone or cartilage) that forms a supporting framework for the body or its parts

con·nex·ion *chiefly Brit var of* CONNECTION

con·ning tower \'kä-niŋ-\ *n* : a raised structure on the deck of a submarine

con·nip·tion \kə-'nip-shən\ *n* : a fit of rage, hysteria, or alarm

con·nive \kə-'nīv\ *vb* **con·nived; con·niv·ing** [F *or* L; F *conniver*, fr. L *conivēre* to close the eyes, connive] **1** : to pretend ignorance of something one ought to oppose as wrong **2** : to cooperate secretly : give secret aid — **con·niv·ance** *n* — **con·niv·er** *n*

con·nois·seur \ˌkä-nə-'sər\ *n* : a critical judge in matters of art or taste

con·no·ta·tion \ˌkä-nə-'tā-shən\ *n* : a meaning in addition to or apart from the thing explicitly named or described by a word

con·no·ta·tive \'kä-nə-ˌtā-tiv, kə-'nō-tə-\ *adj* **1** : connoting or tending to connote **2** : relating to connotation

con·note \kə-'nōt\ *vb* **con·not·ed; con·not·ing** : to suggest or mean as a connotation

con·nu·bi·al \kə-'nü-bē-əl, -'nyü-\ *adj* : of or relating to marriage : CONJUGAL

con·quer \'käŋ-kər\ *vb* **1** : to gain by force of arms : WIN **2** : to get the better of : OVERCOME ♦ **Synonyms** DEFEAT, SUBJUGATE, SUBDUE, OVERTHROW, VANQUISH — **con·quer·or** \-ər\ *n*

con·quest \'kän-ˌkwest, 'käŋ-\ *n* **1** : an act of conquering : VICTORY **2** : something conquered
con·quis·ta·dor \kȯn-'kēs-tə-ˌdȯr, kän-'kwis-\ *n, pl* **-dores** \-ˌkēs-tə-'dȯr-ēz, -ˌkwis-\ *or* **-dors** : CONQUEROR; *esp* : a leader in the Spanish conquest of the Americas in the 16th century
cons *abbr* consonant
con·san·guin·i·ty \ˌkän-ˌsan-'gwi-nə-tē, -ˌsaŋ-\ *n, pl* **-ties** : blood relationship — **con·san·guin·e·ous** \-nē-əs\ *adj*
con·science \'kän-chəns\ *n* : consciousness of the moral right and wrong of one's own acts or motives — **con·science·less** *adj*
con·sci·en·tious \ˌkän-chē-'en-chəs\ *adj* : guided by one's own sense of right and wrong ✦ *Synonyms* SCRUPULOUS, HONORABLE, HONEST, UPRIGHT, JUST — **con·sci·en·tious·ly** *adv*
conscientious objector *n* : a person who refuses to serve in the armed forces or to bear arms on moral or religious grounds
¹con·scious \'kän-chəs\ *adj* **1** : AWARE **2** : known or felt by one's inner self **3** : mentally awake or alert : not asleep or unconscious **4** : done with awareness or purpose ⟨a ∼ decision⟩ — **con·scious·ly** *adv* — **con·scious·ness** *n*
²conscious *n* : the upper level of mental life of which a person is aware : CONSCIOUSNESS
con·script \kən-'skript\ *vb* : to enroll by compulsion for military or naval service — **conscript** \'kän-ˌskript\ *n* — **con·scrip·tion** \kən-'skrip-shən\ *n*
con·se·crate \'kän-sə-ˌkrāt\ *vb* **-crat·ed; -crat·ing** [ME, fr. L *consecratus,* pp. of *consecrare,* fr. *com-* together + *sacrare* to set aside as sacred, fr. *sacer* sacred] **1** : to induct (as a bishop) into an office with a religious rite **2** : to make or declare sacred ⟨∼ a church⟩ **3** : to devote solemnly to a purpose — **con·se·cra·tion** \ˌkän-sə-'krā-shən\ *n*
con·sec·u·tive \kən-'se-kyə-tiv\ *adj* : following in regular order : SUCCESSIVE — **con·sec·u·tive·ly** *adv*
con·sen·su·al \kən-'sen-chə-wəl\ *adj* : involving or based on mutual consent
con·sen·sus \kən-'sen-səs\ *n* **1** : agreement in opinion, testimony, or belief **2** : collective opinion
¹con·sent \kən-'sent\ *vb* : to give assent or approval ⟨∼ed to the marriage⟩
²consent *n* : approval or acceptance of something done or proposed by another
con·se·quence \'kän-sə-ˌkwens\ *n* **1** : RESULT **2** : IMPORTANCE ✦ *Synonyms* EFFECT, OUTCOME, AFTERMATH, UPSHOT
con·se·quent \-kwənt, -ˌkwent\ *adj* : following as a result or effect
con·se·quen·tial \ˌkän-sə-'kwen-chəl\ *adj* **1** : having significant consequences **2** : showing self-importance
con·se·quent·ly \'kän-sə-ˌkwent-lē, -kwənt-\ *adv* : as a result : ACCORDINGLY
con·ser·van·cy \kən-'sər-vən-sē\ *n, pl* **-cies** : an organization or area designated to conserve natural resources
con·ser·va·tion \ˌkän-sər-'vā-shən\ *n* : PRESERVATION; *esp* : planned management of natural resources
con·ser·va·tion·ist \-shə-nist\ *n* : a person who advocates conservation esp. of natural resources
con·ser·va·tism \kən-'sər-və-ˌti-zəm\ *n* : disposition to keep to established ways : opposition to change
¹con·ser·va·tive \kən-'sər-və-tiv\ *adj* **1** : PRESERVATIVE **2** : disposed to maintain existing views, conditions, or institutions **3** : MODERATE, CAUTIOUS ⟨a ∼ investment⟩ — **con·ser·va·tive·ly** *adv*
²conservative *n* : a person who is conservative esp. in politics
con·ser·va·tor \kən-'sər-və-tər, 'kän-sər-ˌvā-\ *n* **1** : PROTECTOR, GUARDIAN **2** : one named by a court to protect the interests of an incompetent (as a child)
con·ser·va·to·ry \kən-'sər-və-ˌtȯr-ē\ *n, pl* **-ries** **1** : GREENHOUSE **2** : a place of instruction in one of the fine arts (as music)
¹con·serve \kən-'sȯrv\ *vb* **con·served; con·serv·ing** : to keep from losing or wasting : PRESERVE ⟨∼ energy⟩
²con·serve \'kän-ˌsȯrv\ *n* **1** : CONFECTION **2**; *esp* : a candied fruit **2** : PRESERVE; *esp* : one prepared from a mixture of fruits
con·sid·er \kən-'si-dər\ *vb* [ME, fr. AF *considerer,* fr. L

considerare to observe, think about, fr. *com-* together + *sider-, sidus* heavenly body] **1** : THINK, PONDER **2** : HEED, REGARD **3** : JUDGE, BELIEVE — **con·sid·ered** *adj*
con·sid·er·able \-'si-dər-ə-bəl, -'si-drə-bəl\ *adj* **1** : IMPORTANT **2** : large in extent, amount, or degree — **con·sid·er·ably** \-blē\ *adv*
con·sid·er·ate \kən-'si-də-rət\ *adj* : observant of the rights and feelings of others ✦ *Synonyms* THOUGHTFUL, ATTENTIVE
con·sid·er·ation \kən-ˌsi-də-'rā-shən\ *n* **1** : careful thought : DELIBERATION **2** : a matter taken into account **3** : thoughtful attention **4** : JUDGMENT, OPINION **5** : RECOMPENSE
con·sid·er·ing \-'si-d(ə-)riŋ\ *prep* : in view of : taking into account ⟨did well ∼ his limitations⟩
con·sign \kən-'sīn\ *vb* **1** : ENTRUST, COMMIT **2** : to deliver formally **3** : to send (goods) to an agent for sale — **con·sign·ee** \ˌkän-sə-'nē, -ˌsī-; kən-ˌsī-\ *n* — **con·sign·or** \ˌkän-sə-'nȯr, -ˌsī-; kən-ˌsī-\ *n*
con·sign·ment \kən-'sīn-mənt\ *n* : something consigned esp. in a single shipment
con·sil·ience \kən-'sil-yəns\ *n* : the linking together of principles from different disciplines when forming a comprehensive theory
con·sist \kən-'sist\ *vb* **1** : to be inherent : LIE — usu. used with *in* **2** : to be composed or made up — usu. used with *of*
con·sis·tence \kən-'sis-təns\ *n* : CONSISTENCY
con·sis·ten·cy \-tən-sē\ *n, pl* **-cies** **1** : COHESIVENESS, FIRMNESS **2** : agreement or harmony in parts or of different things **3** : UNIFORMITY ⟨∼ of behavior⟩ — **con·sis·tent** \-tənt\ *adj* — **con·sis·tent·ly** *adv*
con·sis·to·ry \kən-'sis-tə-rē\ *n, pl* **-ries** : a solemn assembly (as of Roman Catholic cardinals)
consol *abbr* consolidated
¹con·sole \'kän-ˌsōl\ *n* [F] **1** : the desklike part of an organ at which the organist sits **2** : the combination of displays and controls of a device or system **3** : a cabinet for a radio or television set resting directly on the floor **4** : a small storage cabinet set between bucket seats in an automobile
²con·sole \kən-'sōl\ *vb* **con·soled; con·sol·ing** : to soothe the grief of : COMFORT, SOLACE — **con·so·la·tion** \ˌkän-sə-'lā-shən\ *n* — **con·so·la·to·ry** \kən-'sō-lə-ˌtȯr-ē, -'sä-\ *adj*
con·sol·i·date \kən-'sä-lə-ˌdāt\ *vb* **-dat·ed; -dat·ing** **1** : to unite or become united into one whole : COMBINE **2** : to make firm or secure **3** : to form into a compact mass — **con·sol·i·da·tion** \-ˌsä-lə-'dā-shən\ *n* — **con·sol·i·da·tor** \-'sä-lə-ˌdā-tər\ *n*
con·som·mé \ˌkän-sə-'mā\ *n* [F] : a clear soup made from well-seasoned stock
con·so·nance \'kän-sə-nəns\ *n* **1** : AGREEMENT, HARMONY **2** : repetition of consonants esp. as an alternative to rhyme in verse
¹con·so·nant \-nənt\ *adj* : having consonance, harmony, or agreement ✦ *Synonyms* CONSISTENT, COMPATIBLE, CONGRUOUS, CONGENIAL, SYMPATHETIC — **con·so·nant·ly** *adv*
²consonant *n* **1** : a speech sound (as \p\, \g\, \n\, \l\, \s\, \r\) characterized by constriction or closure at one or more points in the breath channel **2** : a letter other than *a, e, i, o,* and *u* — **con·so·nan·tal** \ˌkän-sə-'nan-t°l\ *adj*
¹con·sort \'kän-ˌsȯrt\ *n* **1** : a ship accompanying another **2** : SPOUSE, MATE
²con·sort \kən-'sȯrt\ *vb* **1** : to keep company **2** : ACCORD, HARMONIZE
con·sor·tium \kən-'sȯr-shəm; -shē-əm, -tē-\ *n, pl* **-sor·tia** \-shə-; -shē-ə, -tē-\ [L, fellowship] : an agreement or combination (as of companies) formed to undertake a large enterprise
con·spec·tus \kən-'spek-təs\ *n* **1** : a brief survey or summary **2** : SUMMARY
con·spic·u·ous \kən-'spi-kyə-wəs\ *adj* : attracting attention : PROMINENT, STRIKING ✦ *Synonyms* NOTICEABLE, REMARKABLE, OUTSTANDING — **con·spic·u·ous·ly** *adv*
con·spir·a·cy \kən-'spir-ə-sē\ *n, pl* **-cies** : an agreement among conspirators : PLOT
con·spir·a·tor \kən-'spir-ə-tər\ *n* : one who conspires — **con·spir·a·to·ri·al** \-ˌspir-ə-'tȯr-ē-əl\ *adj*

con·spire \kən-'spī(-ə)r\ vb conspired; con·spir·ing [ME, fr. AF conspirer, fr. L conspirare to be in harmony, conspire, fr. com- together + spirare to breathe] : to plan secretly an unlawful act : PLOT

const abbr 1 constant 2 constitution; constitutional

con·sta·ble \'kän-stə-bəl, 'kən-\ n [ME conestable, fr. AF, fr. LL comes stabuli, lit., officer of the stable] : a public officer responsible for keeping the peace

con·stab·u·lary \kən-'sta-byə-ˌler-ē\ n, pl -lar·ies 1 : the police of a particular district or country 2 : a police force organized like the military

con·stan·cy \'kän-stən-sē\ n, pl -cies 1 : firmness of mind 2 : STABILITY

¹con·stant \-stənt\ adj 1 : STEADFAST, FAITHFUL ⟨∼ friends⟩ 2 : FIXED, UNCHANGING ⟨a ∼ flow⟩ 3 : continually recurring : REGULAR ⟨a ∼ annoyance⟩ — con·stant·ly adv

²constant n : something unchanging

con·stel·la·tion \ˌkän-stə-'lā-shən\ n 1 : any of 88 groups of stars forming patterns 2 : a group of usu. related persons, qualities, or things

con·ster·na·tion \ˌkän-stər-'nā-shən\ n : amazed dismay and confusion

con·sti·pa·tion \ˌkän-stə-'pā-shən\ n : abnormally difficult or infrequent bowel movements — con·sti·pate \'kän-stə-ˌpāt\ vb

con·stit·u·en·cy \kən-'sti-chə-wən-sē\ n, pl -cies : a body of constituents; also : an electoral district

¹con·stit·u·ent \-wənt\ n 1 : a person entitled to vote for a representative for a district 2 : a component part

²constituent adj 1 : COMPONENT ⟨∼ parts⟩ 2 : having power to create a government or frame or amend a constitution

con·sti·tute \'kän-stə-ˌtüt, -ˌtyüt\ vb -tut·ed; -tut·ing 1 : to appoint to an office or duty 2 : SET UP, ESTABLISH ⟨∼ a law⟩ 3 : MAKE UP, COMPOSE

con·sti·tu·tion \ˌkän-stə-'tü-shən, -'tyü-\ n 1 : an established law or custom 2 : the physical makeup of the individual 3 : the structure, composition, or makeup of something ⟨∼ of the sun⟩ 4 : the basic law in a politically organized body; also : a document containing such law

¹con·sti·tu·tion·al \-shə-nəl\ adj 1 : of or relating to the constitution of body or mind 2 : being in accord with the constitution of a state or society; also : of or relating to such a constitution — con·sti·tu·tion·al·ly adv

²constitutional n : an exercise (as a walk) taken for one's health

con·sti·tu·tion·al·i·ty \-ˌtü-shə-'na-lə-tē, -ˌtyü-\ n : the quality or state of being constitutional

con·sti·tu·tive \'kän-stə-ˌtü-tiv, -ˌtyü-, kən-'sti-chə-tiv\ adj 1 : CONSTRUCTIVE 2 : CONSTITUENT, ESSENTIAL

constr abbr construction

con·strain \kən-'strān\ vb 1 : COMPEL, FORCE 2 : CONFINE 3 : RESTRAIN

con·straint \-'strānt\ n 1 : COMPULSION; also : RESTRAINT 2 : repression of one's natural feelings

con·strict \kən-'strikt\ vb : to draw together : SQUEEZE — con·stric·tion \-'strik-shən\ n — con·stric·tive \-'strik-tiv\ adj

con·stric·tor \kən-'strik-tər\ n : a snake that coils around and compresses its prey

con·struct \kən-'strəkt\ vb : BUILD, MAKE — con·struc·tor \-'strək-tər\ n

con·struc·tion \kən-'strək-shən\ n 1 : INTERPRETATION 2 : the art, process, or manner of building; also : something built, created, or established : STRUCTURE 3 : syntactical arrangement of words in a sentence — con·struc·tive \-tiv\ adj

con·struc·tion·ist \-shə-nist\ n : a person who construes a legal document (as the U.S. Constitution) in a specific way ⟨a strict ∼⟩

con·strue \kən-'strü\ vb con·strued; con·stru·ing 1 : to analyze the mutual relations of words in a sentence; also : TRANSLATE 2 : EXPLAIN, INTERPRET ⟨construed the act as hostile⟩ — con·stru·able adj — con·stru·al \-'strü-əl\ n

con·sub·stan·ti·a·tion \ˌkän-səb-ˌstan-chē-'ā-shən\ n : the actual substantial presence and combination of the body and blood of Christ with the eucharistic bread and wine

con·sul \'kän-səl\ n 1 : a chief magistrate of the Roman

republic 2 : a government official who resides in a foreign country to care for the commercial interests of the appointing government's citizens — con·sul·ar \-sə-lər\ adj — con·sul·ate \-lət\ n — con·sul·ship n

con·sult \kən-'səlt\ vb 1 : to ask the advice or opinion of 2 : CONFER — con·sul·tant \-'səl-tᵊnt\ n — con·sul·ta·tion \ˌkän-səl-'tā-shən\ n

con·sume \kən-'süm\ vb con·sumed; con·sum·ing 1 : DESTROY ⟨consumed by fire⟩ 2 : to spend wastefully 3 : to eat up : DEVOUR 4 : to absorb the attention of : ENGROSS ⟨consumed with jealousy⟩ 5 : to utilize as a customer — con·sum·able adj — con·sum·er n

con·sum·er·ism \kən-'sü-mə-ˌri-zəm\ n : the promotion of consumers' interests (as against false advertising)

consumer price index n : an index measuring the change in the cost of widely purchased goods and services from the cost in some base period

¹con·sum·mate \'kän-sə-mət, kən-'sə\ adj : PERFECT ⟨a ∼ team player⟩ ♦ Synonyms FINISHED, ACCOMPLISHED

²con·sum·mate \'kän-sə-ˌmāt\ vb -mat·ed; -mat·ing : to make complete : FINISH, ACHIEVE — con·sum·ma·tion \ˌkän-sə-'mā-shən\ n

con·sump·tion \kən-'səmp-shən\ n 1 : progressive bodily wasting away; also : TUBERCULOSIS 2 : the act of consuming or using up 3 : the use of economic goods

¹con·sump·tive \-'səmp-tiv\ adj 1 : tending to consume 2 : relating to or affected with consumption

²consumptive n : a person who has consumption

cont abbr 1 containing 2 contents 3 continent; continental 4 continued 5 control

¹con·tact \'kän-ˌtakt\ n 1 : a touching or meeting of bodies 2 : ASSOCIATION, RELATIONSHIP; also : CONNECTION, COMMUNICATION 3 : a person serving as a go-between or source of information 4 : CONTACT LENS

²contact vb 1 : to come or bring into contact : TOUCH 2 : to get in communication with ⟨∼ed his lawyer⟩

contact lens n : a thin lens fitting over the cornea usu. to correct vision

con·ta·gion \kən-'tā-jən\ n [ME, fr. L contagio, fr. contingere to have contact with, pollute, fr. com- together + tangere to touch] 1 : a contagious disease; also : the transmission of such a disease 2 : a disease-producing agent (as a virus) 3 : transmission of an influence on the mind or emotions

con·ta·gious \-jəs\ adj 1 : able to be passed by contact between individuals ⟨colds are ∼⟩ ⟨∼ disease⟩; also : capable of passing on a contagious disease 2 : communicated or transmitted like a contagious disease; esp : exciting similar emotion or conduct in others

con·tain \kən-'tān\ vb 1 : RESTRAIN 2 : to have within : HOLD 3 : COMPRISE, INCLUDE — con·tain·able \-'tā-nə-bəl\ adj — con·tain·ment \-'tān-mənt\ n

con·tain·er \kən-'tā-nər\ n : RECEPTACLE

con·tam·i·nant \kən-'ta-mə-nənt\ n : something that contaminates

con·tam·i·nate \kən-'ta-mə-ˌnāt\ vb -nat·ed; -nat·ing : to soil, stain, or infect by contact or association — con·tam·i·na·tion \-ˌta-mə-'nā-shən\ n

contd abbr continued

con·temn \kən-'tem\ vb : to view or treat with contempt : DESPISE

con·tem·plate \'kän-təm-ˌplāt\ vb -plat·ed; -plat·ing [L contemplari, fr. com- with + templum space marked out for observation of auguries] 1 : to view or consider with continued attention 2 : INTEND — con·tem·pla·tion \ˌkän-təm-'plā-shən\ n — con·tem·pla·tive \kən-'tem-plə-tiv, 'kän-təm-ˌplā-\ adj

con·tem·po·ra·ne·ous \kən-ˌtem-pə-'rā-nē-əs\ adj : CONTEMPORARY 1

con·tem·po·rary \kən-'tem-pə-ˌrer-ē\ adj 1 : occurring or existing at the same time 2 : marked by characteristics of the present period — contemporary n

con·tempt \kən-'tempt\ n 1 : the act of despising : the state of mind of one who despises 2 : the state of being despised 3 : disobedience to or open disrespect of a court or legislature

con·tempt·ible \kən-'temp-tə-bəl\ adj : deserving contempt : DESPICABLE — con·tempt·ibly \-blē\ adv

con·temp·tu·ous \-'temp-chə-wəs\ adj : feeling or expressing contempt — con·temp·tu·ous·ly adv

con·tend \kən-'tend\ *vb* 1 : to strive against rivals or difficulties 2 : ARGUE 3 : MAINTAIN, ASSERT — **con·tend·er** *n*

¹**con·tent** \kən-'tent\ *adj* : SATISFIED

²**content** *vb* : SATISFY; *esp* : to limit (oneself) in requirements or actions

³**content** *n* : CONTENTMENT ⟨ate to his heart's ~⟩

⁴**con·tent** \'kän-₁tent\ *n* 1 : something contained ⟨~s of a room⟩ 2 : subject matter or topics treated (as in a book) 3 : material (as text or music) offered by a website 4 : MEANING, SIGNIFICANCE 5 : the amount of material contained

con·tent·ed \kən-'ten-təd\ *adj* : SATISFIED — **con·tent·ed·ly** *adv* — **con·tent·ed·ness** *n*

con·ten·tion \kən-'ten-chən\ *n* 1 : CONTEST, STRIFE 2 : an idea or point for which a person argues — **con·ten·tious** \-chəs\ *adj* — **con·ten·tious·ly** *adv*

con·tent·ment \kən-'tent-mənt\ *n* : ease of mind : SATISFACTION

con·ter·mi·nous \kän-'tər-mə-nəs\ *adj* : having the same or a common boundary — **con·ter·mi·nous·ly** *adv*

¹**con·test** \kən-'test\ *vb* 1 : to engage in a struggle or competition : COMPETE, VIE 2 : CHALLENGE, DISPUTE ⟨~ the accusations⟩ — **con·tes·tant** \-'tes-tənt\ *n*

²**con·test** \'kän-₁test\ *n* : STRUGGLE, COMPETITION

con·text \'kän-₁tekst\ *n* [ME, fr. L *contextus* connection of words, coherence, fr. *contexere* to weave together] : the parts of a discourse that surround a word or passage and help to explain its meaning; *also* : the circumstances surrounding an act or event ⟨the ~ of the war⟩ — **con·tex·tu·al·ly** *adv*

con·tig·u·ous \kən-'ti-gyə-wəs\ *adj* : being in contact : TOUCHING ⟨the 48 ~ states⟩; *also* : NEXT, ADJOINING — **con·ti·gu·i·ty** \₁kän-tə-'gyü-ə-tē\ *n*

con·ti·nence \'kän-tə-nəns\ *n* 1 : SELF-RESTRAINT; *esp* : a refraining from sexual intercourse 2 : the ability to retain urine or feces voluntarily

¹**con·ti·nent** \'kän-tə-nənt\ *adj* : exercising continence

²**continent** *n* 1 : any of the great divisions of land on the globe 2 *cap* : the continent of Europe

¹**con·ti·nen·tal** \₁kän-tə-'nen-t°l\ *adj* 1 : of or relating to a continent; *esp*, *often cap* : of or relating to the continent of Europe 2 *often cap* : of or relating to the colonies later forming the U.S. 3 : of or relating to cuisine based on classical European cooking

²**continental** *n* 1 *often cap* : a soldier in the Continental army 2 : EUROPEAN

continental drift *n* : a slow movement of the continents over a fluid layer deep within the earth

continental shelf *n* : a shallow submarine plain forming a border to a continent

continental slope *n* : a comparatively steep slope from a continental shelf to the ocean floor

con·tin·gen·cy \kən-'tin-jən-sē\ *n*, *pl* **-cies** : a chance or possible event

¹**con·tin·gent** \-jənt\ *adj* 1 : liable but not certain to happen : POSSIBLE 2 : happening by chance : not planned 3 : dependent on something that may or may not occur 4 : CONDITIONAL ♦ *Synonyms* ACCIDENTAL, CASUAL, INCIDENTAL, ODD

²**contingent** *n* : a quota (as of troops) supplied from an area or group

con·tin·u·al \kən-'tin-yə-wəl\ *adj* 1 : CONTINUOUS, UNBROKEN 2 : steadily recurring — **con·tin·u·al·ly** *adv*

con·tin·u·ance \-yə-wəns\ *n* 1 : unbroken succession 2 : the extent of continuing : DURATION 3 : adjournment of legal proceedings

con·tin·u·a·tion \kən-₁tin-yə-'wā-shən\ *n* 1 : extension or prolongation of a state or activity 2 : resumption after an interruption; *also* : something that carries on after a pause or break

con·tin·ue \kən-'tin-yü\ *vb* **-tin·ued; -tinu·ing** 1 : to maintain without interruption 2 : ENDURE, LAST ⟨the tradition ~s⟩ 3 : to remain in a place or condition ⟨~ at this job⟩ 4 : to resume (as a story) after an intermission 5 : EXTEND ⟨~ a subscription⟩; *also* : to persist in ⟨will ~ to remind you⟩ 6 : to allow to remain 7 : to keep (a legal case) on the calendar or undecided

con·ti·nu·i·ty \₁kän-tə-'nü-ə-tē, -'nyü-\ *n*, *pl* **-ties** 1 : the state of being continuous 2 : something (as a film script) that has or provides continuity

con·tin·u·ous \kən-'tin-yə-wəs\ *adj* : continuing without interruption — **con·tin·u·ous·ly** *adv*

con·tin·u·um \-yə-wəm\ *n*, *pl* **-ua** \-yə-wə\ *also* **-u·ums** : something that is the same throughout or consists of a series of variations or of a sequence of things in regular order

con·tort \kən-'tórt\ *vb* : to twist out of shape ⟨a ~ed face⟩ ⟨~ the truth⟩ — **con·tor·tion** \-'tór-shən\ *n*

con·tor·tion·ist \-'tór-shə-nist\ *n* : an acrobat able to twist the body into unusual postures

con·tour \'kän-₁túr\ *n* [F, fr. It *contorno* fr. *contornare* to round off, fr. ML, to turn around, fr. L *com-* together + *tornare* to turn on a lathe, fr. *tornus* lathe] 1 : OUTLINE 2 : SHAPE, FORM — often used in pl. ⟨the ~s of a statue⟩

contr *abbr* contract; contraction

con·tra·band \'kän-trə-₁band\ *n* : goods legally prohibited in trade; *also* : smuggled goods

con·tra·cep·tion \₁kän-trə-'sep-shən\ *n* : intentional prevention of conception and pregnancy — **con·tra·cep·tive** \-'sep-tive\ *adj or n*

¹**con·tract** \'kän-₁trakt\ *n* 1 : a binding agreement; *also* : a document stating its terms 2 : an undertaking to win a specified number of tricks in bridge — **contract** *adj* — **con·trac·tu·al** \kən-'trak-chə-wəl\ *adj* — **con·trac·tu·al·ly** *adv*

²**con·tract** \kən-'trakt, 2 *usu* 'kän-₁trakt\ *vb* 1 : to become affected with ⟨~ a disease⟩ 2 : to establish or undertake by contract 3 : SHRINK, LESSEN; *esp* : to draw together esp. so as to shorten ⟨~ a muscle⟩ 4 : to shorten (a word) by omitting letters or sounds in the middle — **con·tract·ible** \kən-'trak-tə-bəl, 'kän-₁\ *adj* — **con·trac·tion** \kən-'trak-shən\ *n* — **con·trac·tor** \'kän-₁trak-tər, kən-'trak-\ *n*

con·trac·tile \kən-'trak-t°l\ *adj* : able to contract — **con·trac·til·i·ty** \₁kän-₁trak-'ti-lə-tē\ *n*

con·tra·dict \₁kän-trə-'dikt\ *vb* : to assert the contrary of : deny the truth of ⟨~ a rumor⟩ — **con·tra·dic·tion** \-'dik-shən\ *n* — **con·tra·dic·to·ry** \-'dik-tə-rē\ *adj*

con·tra·dis·tinc·tion \₁kän-trə-dis-'tiŋk-shən\ *n* : distinction by contrast

con·trail \'kän-₁trāl\ *n* : a streak of condensed water vapor created by an airplane or rocket at high altitudes

con·tra·in·di·cate \₁kän-trə-'in-də-₁kāt\ *vb* : to make (a treatment or procedure) inadvisable — **con·tra·in·di·ca·tion** \-₁in-də-'kā-shən\ *n*

con·tral·to \kən-'tral-tō\ *n*, *pl* **-tos** : the lowest female voice; *also* : a singer having such a voice

con·trap·tion \kən-'trap-shən\ *n* : CONTRIVANCE, DEVICE

con·tra·pun·tal \₁kän-trə-'pən-t°l\ *adj* : of or relating to counterpoint

con·tra·ri·ety \₁kän-trə-'rī-ə-tē\ *n*, *pl* **-eties** : the state of being contrary : DISAGREEMENT, INCONSISTENCY

con·trari·wise \'kän-₁trer-ē-₁wīz, kən-'trer-\ *adv* 1 : on the contrary 2 : VICE VERSA

con·trary \'kän-₁trer-ē; 4 *often* kən-'trer-ē\ *adj* 1 : opposite in nature or position 2 : COUNTER, OPPOSED 3 : UNFAVORABLE — used of wind or weather 4 : unwilling to accept control or advice — **con·trar·i·an** \'trer-ē-ən, kän-\ *n or adj* — **con·trari·ly** \'kän-₁trer-ə-lē, kən-'trer-\ *adv* — **con·trary** \'n *is* 'kän-₁trer-ē, *adv is like adj*\ *n or adv*

¹**con·trast** \kən-'trast\ *vb* [F *contraster*, fr. MF, to oppose, resist, fr. VL **contrastare*, fr. L *contra-* against + *stare* to stand] 1 : to show differences when compared 2 : to compare in such a way as to show differences

²**con·trast** \'kän-₁trast\ *n* 1 : diversity of adjacent parts in color, emotion, tone, or brightness ⟨the ~ of a photograph⟩ 2 : unlikeness as shown when things are compared : DIFFERENCE

con·tra·vene \₁kän-trə-'vēn\ *vb* **-vened; -ven·ing** 1 : to go or act contrary to ⟨~ a law⟩ 2 : CONTRADICT ⟨~ a claim⟩

con·tre·temps \'kän-trə-₁tä^n, kō^n-trə-'tä^n\ *n*, *pl* **con·tre·temps** \-₁tä^n-, -₁tä^nz\ [F] : an inopportune or embarrassing occurrence

contrib *abbr* contribution; contributor

con·trib·ute \kən-'tri-byət\ *vb* **-ut·ed; -ut·ing** : to give along with others (as to a fund); *also* : HELP, ASSIST — **con·tri·bu·tion** \₁kän-trə-'byü-shən\ *n* — **con·trib·u·tor** \kən-'tri-byə-tər\ *n* — **con·trib·u·to·ry** \-byə-₁tór-ē\ *adj*

contrite • cookie

110

con·trite \'kän-ˌtrīt, kən-'trīt\ *adj* : PENITENT, REPEN-
TANT — **con·trite·ly** *adv* — **con·tri·tion** \kən-'tri-shən\ *n*
con·triv·ance \kən-'trī-vəns\ *n* 1 : a mechanical device
2 : SCHEME, PLAN
con·trive \kən-'trīv\ *vb* **con·trived; con·triv·ing** 1 : PLAN,
DEVISE 2 : FRAME, MAKE 3 : to bring about with difficulty — **con·triv·er** *n*
con·trived \-'trīvd\ *adj* : lacking in natural quality ⟨a ~
plot⟩
¹con·trol \kən-'trōl\ *vb* **con·trolled; con·trol·ling** [ME
countrollen to verify, fr. AF *countrerouler*, fr. *countre-
roule* copy of an account, audit, fr. ML *contrarotulus*,
fr. L *contra* against + ML *rotulus* roll] 1 : to exercise
restraining or directing influence over : REGULATE 2
: DOMINATE, RULE — **con·trol·la·ble** \-'trō-lə-bəl\ *adj*
²control *n* 1 : power to direct or regulate 2 : RESERVE,
RESTRAINT 3 : a device for regulating a mechanism
con·trol·ler \kən-'trō-lər, 'kän-ˌtrō-lər\ *n* 1 : COMPTROL-
LER 2 : a person or thing that controls ⟨an air traffic
~⟩ ⟨a game ~⟩
con·tro·ver·sy \'kän-trə-ˌvər-sē\ *n, pl* **-sies** : a clash of
opposing views : DISPUTE — **con·tro·ver·sial** \ˌkän-trə-
ˌvər-shəl, -sē-əl\ *adj*
con·tro·vert \'kän-trə-ˌvərt, ˌkän-trə-'vərt\ *vb* : DENY,
CONTRADICT ⟨~ an allegation⟩ — **con·tro·vert·ible** *adj*
con·tu·ma·cious \ˌkän-tü-'mā-shəs, -tyü-\ *adj* : stubbornly disobedient ♦ **Synonyms** REBELLIOUS, INSUB-
ORDINATE, SEDITIOUS — **con·tu·ma·cy** \kən-'tü-mə-sē,
-'tyü-\ *n* — **con·tu·ma·cious·ly** *adv*
con·tu·me·ly \kən-'tü-mə-lē, -'tyü-; 'kän-tə-ˌmē-lē, -tyə-\
n, pl **-lies** : contemptuous treatment : INSULT
con·tu·sion \kən-'tü-zhən, -'tyü-\ *n* : BRUISE — **con·tuse**
\-'tüz, -'tyüz\ *vb*
co·nun·drum \kə-'nən-drəm\ *n* : RIDDLE
conv *abbr* 1 convention 2 convertible
con·va·lesce \ˌkän-və-'les\ *vb* **-lesced; -lesc·ing** : to recover health gradually — **con·va·les·cence** \-'le-sᵊns\ *n*
— **con·va·les·cent** \-sᵊnt\ *adj or n*
con·vec·tion \kən-'vek-shən\ *n* : circulatory motion in
a fluid due to warmer portions rising and cooler denser
portions sinking; *also* : the transfer of heat by such motion — **con·vec·tion·al** \-shə-nəl\ *adj* — **con·vec·tive**
\-'vek-tiv\ *adj*
convection oven *n* : an oven with a fan that circulates
hot air uniformly and continuously around the food
con·vene \kən-'vēn\ *vb* **con·vened; con·ven·ing** : AS-
SEMBLE, MEET
con·ve·nience \kən-'vē-nyəns\ *n* 1 : SUITABLENESS 2
: a laborsaving device 3 : a suitable time ⟨at your ~⟩
4 : personal comfort : EASE
convenience store *n* : a small market that is open long
hours
con·ve·nient \-nyənt\ *adj* : suited to personal comfort
or ease 2 : placed near at hand — **con·ve·nient·ly** *adv*
con·vent \'kän-vənt, -ˌvent\ *n* [ME *covent*, fr. AF, fr. ML
conventus, fr. L, assembly, fr. *convenire* to come together]
: a local community or house of a religious order esp. of
nuns — **con·ven·tu·al** \kän-'ven-chə-wəl\ *adj*
con·ven·ti·cle \kən-'ven-ti-kəl\ *n* : MEETING; *esp* : a secret meeting for worship
con·ven·tion \kən-'ven-chən\ *n* 1 : an agreement esp.
between states on a matter of common concern 2
: MEETING, ASSEMBLY 3 : an assembly of persons con-
vened for some purpose 4 : generally accepted custom,
practice, or belief
con·ven·tion·al \-chə-nəl\ *adj* 1 : sanctioned by general custom 2 : COMMONPLACE, ORDINARY — **con-
ven·tion·al·i·ty** \-ˌven-chə-'na-lə-tē\ *n* — **con·ven-
tion·al·ize** \-'ven-chə-nə-ˌlīz\ *vb* — **con·ven·tion·al·ly**
adv
con·verge \kən-'vərj\ *vb* **con·verged; con·verg·ing**
: to approach one common center or single point ⟨con-
verging paths⟩ — **con·ver·gence** \kən-'vər-jəns\ *n* —
con·ver·gent \-jənt\ *adj*
con·ver·sant \kən-'vər-sᵊnt\ *adj* : having knowledge and
experience — used with *with*
con·ver·sa·tion \ˌkän-vər-'sā-shən\ *n* : an informal talking together — **con·ver·sa·tion·al** \-shə-nᵊl\ *adj* —
con·ver·sa·tion·al·ly *adv*
con·ver·sa·tion·al·ist \-shə-nᵊl-ist\ *n* : a person who con-
verses a great deal or who excels in conversation

¹con·verse \'kän-ˌvərs\ *n* : CONVERSATION
²con·verse \kən-'vərs\ *vb* **con·versed; con·vers·ing** : to
engage in conversation
³con·verse \'kän-ˌvərs\ *n* : a statement related to another
statement by having its hypothesis and conclusion or its
subject and predicate reversed or interchanged
⁴con·verse \kən-'vərs, 'kän-ˌvers\ *adj* : reversed in order
or relation — **con·verse·ly** *adv*
con·ver·sion \kən-'vər-zhən\ *n* 1 : a change in nature or
form 2 : an experience associated with a decisive adoption of religion
¹con·vert \kən-'vərt\ *vb* 1 : to turn from one belief
or party to another 2 : TRANSFORM, CHANGE 3
: MISAPPROPRIATE 4 : EXCHANGE — **con·vert·er** or
con·ver·tor \-'vər-tər\ *n*
²con·vert \'kän-ˌvərt\ *n* : a person who has undergone religious conversion
¹con·vert·ible \kən-'vər-tə-bəl\ *adj* : capable of being converted
²convertible *n* : an automobile with a top that may be
lowered or removed
con·vex \kän-'veks, 'kän-ˌveks\ *adj* : curved or rounded
outward like the exterior of a sphere or circle —
con·vex·i·ty \kän-'vek-sə-tē\ *n*
con·vey \kən-'vā\ *vb* 1 : CARRY, TRANSPORT ⟨a river
~ing logs⟩ 2 : TRANSFER, COMMUNICATE ⟨~ a mes-
sage⟩ — **con·vey·or** *also* **con·vey·er** \-ər\ *n*
con·vey·ance \-'vā-əns\ *n* 1 : the act of conveying 2 : a
legal paper transferring ownership of property 3 : VE-
HICLE
¹con·vict \kən-'vikt\ *vb* : to prove or find guilty
²con·vict \'kän-ˌvikt\ *n* : a person serving a prison sentence
con·vic·tion \kən-'vik-shən\ *n* 1 : the act of convicting
esp. in a court 2 : the state of being convinced : BELIEF
con·vince \kən-'vins\ *vb* **con·vinced; con·vinc·ing**
: to bring (as by argument) to belief or action —
con·vinc·ing *adj* — **con·vinc·ing·ly** *adv*
con·viv·ial \kən-'vi-vē-əl\ *adj* [LL *convivialis*, fr. L *con-
vivium* banquet, fr. *com-* together + *vivere* to live] : enjoying companionship and the pleasures of feasting
and drinking : JOVIAL, FESTIVE ⟨a ~ gathering⟩ —
con·viv·i·al·i·ty \-ˌvi-vē-'a-lə-tē\ *n* — **con·viv·ial·ly** *adv*
con·vo·ca·tion \ˌkän-və-'kā-shən\ *n* 1 : a ceremonial assembly (as of the clergy) 2 : the act of convoking
con·voke \kən-'vōk\ *vb* **con·voked; con·vok·ing** : to call
together to a meeting ⟨convoked a meeting of the del-
egates⟩
con·vo·lut·ed \'kän-və-ˌlü-təd\ *adj* 1 : folded in curved or
tortuous windings 2 : INVOLVED, INTRICATE ⟨~ logic⟩
con·vo·lu·tion \ˌkän-və-'lü-shən\ *n* : a tortuous or winding structure; *esp* : one of the ridges of the brain
¹con·voy \'kän-ˌvȯi, kən-'vȯi\ *vb* : to accompany for protection
²con·voy \'kän-ˌvȯi\ *n* 1 : one that convoys; *esp* : a protective escort (as for ships) 2 : the act of convoying 3
: a group of moving vehicles
con·vulse \kən-'vəls\ *vb* **con·vulsed; con·vuls·ing** : to
agitate violently
con·vul·sion \kən-'vəl-shən\ *n* 1 : an abnormal and violent involuntary contraction or series of contractions of
muscle 2 : a violent disturbance — **con·vul·sive** \-siv\
adj — **con·vul·sive·ly** *adv*
cony *var of* CONEY
coo \'kü\ *n* : a soft low sound made by doves or pigeons;
also : a sound like this — **coo** *vb*
COO *abbr* chief operating officer
¹cook \'kuk\ *n* : a person who prepares food for eating
²cook *vb* 1 : to prepare food for eating 2 : to subject
to heat or fire 3 : CONCOCT, FABRICATE — usu. used
with *up* ⟨~ up a scheme⟩ — **cook·er** *n* — **cook·ware**
\-ˌwer\ *n*
cook·book \-ˌbuk\ *n* : a book of cooking directions and
recipes
cook·ery \'ku-kə-rē\ *n, pl* **-er·ies** : the art or practice of
cooking
cook·ie *or* **cooky** \'ku-kē\ *n, pl* **cook·ies** [D *koekje*, dim.
of *koek* cake] 1 : a small sweet flat cake 2 *cookie* : a
file containing information about a website user created
and read by a website server and stored on the user's
computer

cookie–cutter *adj* : marked by a lack of originality or distinction ⟨~ malls⟩

cook·out \'kŭk-ˌaut\ *n* : an outing at which a meal is cooked and served in the open

¹**cool** \'kül\ *adj* 1 : moderately cold 2 : not excited : CALM 3 : not friendly 4 : IMPUDENT 5 : protecting from heat 6 *slang* : very good 7 *slang* : FASHIONABLE ✦ **Synonyms** UNFLAPPABLE, COMPOSED, COLLECTED, UNRUFFLED, NONCHALANT — **cool·ly** *adv* — **cool·ness** *n*

²**cool** *vb* : to make or become cool

³**cool** *n* 1 : a cool time or place 2 : INDIFFERENCE; *also* : SELF-ASSURANCE, COMPOSURE ⟨kept his ~⟩

cool·ant \'kü-lənt\ *n* : a usu. fluid cooling agent

cool·er \'kü-lər\ *n* 1 : a container for keeping food or drink cool 2 : JAIL, PRISON 3 : a tall iced drink

coo·lie \'kü-lē\ *n* [Hindi & Urdu *qulī*] *usu offensive* : an unskilled laborer usu. in or from the Far East

coon \'kün\ *n* : RACCOON

coon·hound \-ˌhaund\ *n* : a sporting dog trained to hunt raccoons

coon·skin \-ˌskin\ *n* : the pelt of a raccoon; *also* : something (as a cap) made of this

¹**coop** \'küp, 'kúp\ *n* : a small enclosure or building usu. for poultry

²**coop** *vb* : to confine in or as if in a coop — usu. used with *up*

co–op \'kō-ˌäp\ *n* : COOPERATIVE

coo·per \'kü-pər, 'kú-\ *n* : one who makes or repairs barrels or casks — **cooper** *vb* — **coo·per·age** \-pə-rij\ *n*

co·op·er·ate \kō-'ä-pə-ˌrāt\ *vb* : to act jointly or in compliance with others — **co·op·er·a·tion** \-ˌä-pə-'rā-shən\ *n* — **co·op·er·a·tor** \-'ä-pə-ˌrā-tər\ *n*

¹**co·op·er·a·tive** \kō-'ä-prə-tiv, -'ä-pə-ˌrā-\ *adj* 1 : willing to work with others 2 : of or relating to an association formed to enable its members to buy or sell to better advantage by eliminating middlemen's profits

²**cooperative** *n* : a cooperative association

co–opt \kō-'äpt\ *vb* 1 : to choose or elect as a colleague 2 : ABSORB, ASSIMILATE; *also* : TAKE OVER ⟨a style ~ed by advertisers⟩

¹**co·or·di·nate** \kō-'ȯr-də-nət\ *adj* 1 : equal in rank or order 2 : of equal rank in a compound sentence ⟨~ clause⟩ 3 : joining words or word groups of the same rank — **co·or·di·nate·ly** *adv*

²**co·or·di·nate** \-'ȯr-də-ˌnāt\ *vb* **-nat·ed; -nat·ing** 1 : to make or become coordinate ⟨~ our schedules⟩ 2 : to work or act together harmoniously ⟨a *coordinated* wardrobe⟩ — **co·or·di·na·tion** \-ˌȯr-də-'nā-shən\ *n* — **co·or·di·na·tor** \-'ȯr-də-ˌnā-tər\ *n*

³**co·or·di·nate** \-'ȯr-də-nət\ *n* 1 : one of a set of numbers used in specifying the location of a point on a surface or in space 2 *pl* : articles (as of clothing) designed to be used together and to attain their effect through pleasing contrast

coot \'küt\ *n* 1 : a dark-colored ducklike bird related to the rails 2 : any of several No. American sea ducks 3 : a harmless simple person

coo·tie \'kü-tē\ *n* : a body louse

¹**cop** \'käp\ *n* : POLICE OFFICER

²**cop** *vb* 1 *slang* : STEAL ⟨~ a glance⟩ 2 *slang* : ADMIT — used with *to* ⟨~ to the charges⟩ 3 : ADOPT ⟨~ an attitude⟩

co–pay \'kō-ˌpā\ *n* : CO-PAYMENT

co–pay·ment \'kō-ˌpā-mənt, ˌkō-'\ *n* : a fixed fee required of a patient by a health insurer (as an HMO) at the time of each outpatient service or filling of a prescription

¹**cope** \'kōp\ *n* : a long cloaklike ecclesiastical vestment

²**cope** *vb* **coped; cop·ing** : to struggle to overcome problems or difficulties ⟨~ with tragedy⟩

co·per·nic·i·um \ˌkō-pər-'ni-sē-əm\ *n* [NL, fr. Nikolaus *Copernicus*] : a short-lived artificially produced radioactive element

copi·er \'kä-pē-ər\ *n* : one that copies; *esp* : a machine for making copies

co·pi·lot \'kō-ˌpī-lət\ *n* : an assistant pilot of an aircraft or spacecraft

cop·ing \'kō-piŋ\ *n* : the top layer of a wall

co·pi·ous \'kō-pē-əs\ *adj* : LAVISH, ABUNDANT ⟨a ~ harvest⟩ — **co·pi·ous·ly** *adv* — **co·pi·ous·ness** *n*

cop–out \'käp-ˌaut\ *n* : an excuse for copping out; *also* : an act of copping out

cop out *vb* : to back out (as of an unwanted responsibility)

cop·per \'kä-pər\ *n* 1 : a malleable reddish metallic chemical element that is one of the best conductors of heat and electricity 2 : a coin or token made of copper — **cop·pery** *adj*

cop·per·head \'kä-pər-ˌhed\ *n* : a largely coppery brown pit viper esp. of the eastern and central U.S.

cop·pice \'kä-pəs\ *n* : THICKET

co·pra \'kō-prə\ *n* : dried coconut meat yielding coconut oil

copse \'käps\ *n* : THICKET

cop·ter \'käp-tər\ *n* : HELICOPTER

cop·u·la \'kä-pyə-lə\ *n* : LINKING VERB — **cop·u·la·tive** \-lə-tiv, -ˌlā-\ *adj*

cop·u·late \'kä-pyə-ˌlāt\ *vb* **-lat·ed; -lat·ing** : to engage in sexual intercourse — **cop·u·la·tion** \ˌkä-pyə-'lā-shən\ *n* — **cop·u·la·to·ry** \'kä-pyə-lə-ˌtȯr-ē\ *adj*

¹**copy** \'kä-pē\ *n, pl* **cop·ies** 1 : an imitation or reproduction of an original work 2 : material to be set in type 3 : DUPLICATE ✦ **Synonyms** DUPLICATE, REPRODUCTION, FACSIMILE, REPLICA

²**copy** *vb* **cop·ied; copy·ing** 1 : to make a copy of 2 : IMITATE — **copy·ist** *n*

copy·book \'kä-pē-ˌbúk\ *n* : a book formerly used to teach handwriting containing examples to be copied

copy·boy \-ˌbȯi\ *n* : a person who carries copy and runs errands (as in a newspaper office)

copy·cat \-ˌkat\ *n* : a slavish imitator

copy·desk \-ˌdesk\ *n* : the desk at which newspaper copy is edited

copy editor *n* : one who edits or prepares copy (as headlines) esp. for a newspaper

copy·read·er \-ˌrē-dər\ *n* : COPY EDITOR

¹**copy·right** \-ˌrīt\ *n* : the sole right to reproduce, publish, sell, or distribute a literary or artistic work

²**copyright** *vb* : to secure a copyright on

copy·writ·er \'kä-pē-ˌrī-tər\ *n* : a writer of advertising copy

co·quet *or* **co·quette** \kō-'ket\ *vb* **co·quet·ted; co·quet·ting** : FLIRT — **co·quet·ry** \'kō-kə-trē, kō-'ke-trē\ *n*

co·quette \kō-'ket\ *n* [F, fem. of *coquet*, flirtatious man, dim. of *coq* cock] : FLIRT — **co·quett·ish** *adj*

cor *abbr* corner

Cor *abbr* Corinthians

cor·a·cle \'kȯr-ə-kəl\ *n* [W *corwgl*] : a boat made of a frame covered usu. with hide or tarpaulin

cor·al \'kȯr-əl\ *n* 1 : a stony or horny material that forms the skeleton of colonies of tiny sea polyps and includes a red form used in jewelry; *also* : a coral-forming polyp or polyp colony 2 : a deep pink color — **coral** *adj*

coral snake *n* : any of several venomous chiefly tropical New World snakes brilliantly banded in red, black, and yellow or white

cor·bel \'kȯr-bəl\ *n* : a bracket-shaped architectural member that projects from a wall and supports a weight

¹**cord** \'kȯrd\ *n* 1 : a usu. heavy string consisting of several strands woven or twisted together 2 : a long slender anatomical structure (as a tendon or nerve) 3 : a small flexible insulated electrical cable used to connect an appliance with a receptacle 4 : a cubic measure used esp. for firewood and equal to a stack 4×4×8 feet 5 : a rib or ridge on cloth

²**cord** *vb* 1 : to tie or furnish with a cord 2 : to pile (wood) in cords

cord·age \'kȯr-dij\ *n* : ROPES, CORDS; *esp* : ropes in the rigging of a ship

¹**cor·dial** \'kȯr-jəl\ *adj* [ME, fr. ML *cordialis*, fr. L *cord-, cor* heart] : warmly receptive or welcoming — HEARTFELT, HEARTY — **cor·di·al·i·ty** \ˌkȯr-jē-'a-lə-tē, kȯr-'ja-\ *n* — **cor·dial·ly** *adv*

²**cordial** *n* 1 : a stimulating medicine or drink 2 : LIQUEUR

cor·dil·le·ra \ˌkȯr-dəl-'yer-ə, -də-'ler-\ *n* [Sp] : a series of parallel mountain ranges

cord·less \'kȯrd-ləs\ *adj* : having no cord; *esp* : powered by a battery ⟨a ~ phone⟩ — **cord·less** *n*

cór·do·ba \'kȯr-də-bə, -və\ *n* — see MONEY table

cor·don \'kȯr-dᵊn\ *n* 1 : an ornamental cord or ribbon 2 : an encircling line (as of troops or police) — **cordon** *vb*

cor·do·van \'kȯr-də-vən\ n : a soft fine-grained leather
cor·du·roy \'kȯr-də-ˌrȯi\ n, pl -roys : a heavy ribbed fabric; also, pl : pants of this material
cord·wain·er \'kȯrd-ˌwā-nər\ n : SHOEMAKER
¹core \'kȯr\ n 1 : the central usu. inedible part of some fruits (as the apple); also : an inmost part of something 2 : GIST, ESSENCE
²core vb cored; cor·ing : to take out the core of — cor·er n
CORE \'kȯr\ abbr Congress of Racial Equality
co·re·op·sis \ˌkȯr-ē-'äp-səs\ n, pl coreopsis : any of a genus of widely cultivated composite herbs with showy often yellow flower heads
co·re·spon·dent \ˌkō-ri-'spän-dənt\ n : a person named as guilty of adultery with the defendant in a divorce suit
co·ri·an·der \'kȯr-ē-ˌan-dər\ n : an herb related to the carrot; also : its aromatic dried fruit used as a flavoring
Cor·in·thi·ans \kə-'rin-thē-ənz\ n — see BIBLE table
¹cork \'kȯrk\ n 1 : the tough elastic bark of a European oak (cork oak) used esp. for stoppers and insulation; also : a stopper of this 2 : a tissue of a woody plant making up most of the bark — corky adj
²cork vb : to furnish with or stop up with cork or a cork ⟨~ a bottle⟩
cork·screw \'kȯrk-ˌskrü\ n : a device for drawing corks from bottles
corm \'kȯrm\ n : a solid bulblike underground part of a stem (as of the crocus or gladiolus)
cor·mo·rant \'kȯr-mə-rənt, -ˌrant\ n [ME cormeraunt, fr. MF cormorant, fr. OF cormareng, fr. corp raven + marenc of the sea, fr. L marinus] : any of various dark= colored water birds with a long neck, hooked bill, and distensible throat pouch
¹corn \'kȯrn\ n 1 Brit : the seeds of a cereal grass and esp. of the chief cereal crop of a region (as wheat in Britain); also : a cereal grass 2 a : a tall widely cultivated cereal grass grown for its large ears of starchy seeds b : the typically yellow or whitish seeds of corn used esp. as a food c : an ear of corn
²corn vb : to salt (as beef) in brine and preservatives
³corn n : a local hardening and thickening of skin (as on a toe)
¹corn·ball \'kȯrn-ˌbȯl\ n : an unsophisticated person; also : something corny
²cornball adj : CORNY ⟨~ humor⟩
corn bread n : bread made with cornmeal
corn·cob \-ˌkäb\ n : the woody core on which the kernels of corn are arranged
corn·crib \-ˌkrib\ n : a crib for storing ears of corn
cor·nea \'kȯr-nē-ə\ n : the transparent part of the coat of the eyeball covering the iris and the pupil — cor·ne·al adj
corn ear·worm \-'ir-ˌwərm\ n : a moth whose larva is destructive esp. to corn
¹cor·ner \'kȯr-nər\ n [ME, fr. AF cornere, fr. corne horn, corner, fr. L cornu horn, point] 1 : the point or angle formed by the meeting of lines, edges, or sides 2 : the place where two streets come together 3 : a quiet secluded place 4 : a position from which retreat or escape is impossible 5 : control of enough of the available supply (as of a commodity) to permit manipulation of the price — cor·nered adj — around the corner : IMMINENT ⟨has a birthday just around the corner⟩
²cor·ner vb 1 : to drive into a corner 2 : to get a corner on ⟨~ the wheat market⟩ 3 : to turn a corner
cor·ner·stone \'kȯr-nər-ˌstōn\ n 1 : a stone forming part of a corner in a wall; esp : such a stone laid at a formal ceremony 2 : something of basic importance
cor·net \kȯr-'net\ n : a brass band instrument resembling the trumpet

cornet

corn flour n, Brit : CORNSTARCH
corn·flow·er \'kȯrn-ˌflau̇(-ə)r\ n : BACHELOR'S BUTTON
cor·nice \'kȯr-nəs\ n : the horizontal projecting part crowning the wall of a building
corn·meal \'kȯrn-ˌmēl\ n : meal ground from corn
corn·row \-ˌrō\ n : a section of hair braided flat to the scalp in rows — cornrow vb
corn·stalk \-ˌstȯk\ n : a stalk of corn
corn·starch \-ˌstärch\ n : a starch made from corn and used in cookery as a thickening agent
corn syrup n : a sweet syrup obtained from cornstarch
cor·nu·co·pia \ˌkȯr-nə-'kō-pē-ə, -nyə-\ n [LL, fr. L cornu copiae horn of plenty] 1 : a horn-shaped container filled with fruits and grain emblematic of abundance 2 : ABUNDANCE
corny \'kȯr-nē\ adj corn·i·er; -est : tiresomely simple or sentimental
co·rol·la \kə-'rä-lə, -'rō-\ n : the petals of a flower
cor·ol·lary \'kȯr-ə-ˌler-ē\ n, pl -lar·ies 1 : a deduction from a proposition already proved true 2 : CONSEQUENCE, RESULT
co·ro·na \kə-'rō-nə\ n 1 : a colored circle often seen around and close to a luminous body (as the sun or moon) 2 : the outermost part of the atmosphere of a star (as the sun) — co·ro·nal \'kȯr-ə-nᵊl, kə-'rō-\ adj
cor·o·nal \'kȯr-ə-nᵊl\ n : a circlet for the head
¹cor·o·nary \'kȯr-ə-ˌner-ē\ adj : of or relating to the heart or its blood vessels
²coronary n, pl -nar·ies 1 : a coronary blood vessel 2 : CORONARY THROMBOSIS; also : HEART ATTACK
coronary thrombosis n : the blocking by a thrombus of one of the arteries supplying the heart tissues
cor·o·na·tion \ˌkȯr-ə-'nā-shən\ n : the act or ceremony of crowning a monarch
cor·o·ner \'kȯr-ə-nər\ n [ME, an officer of the crown, fr. AF, fr. corone crown, fr. L corona] : a public official who investigates causes of deaths possibly not due to natural causes
cor·o·net \ˌkȯr-ə-'net\ n 1 : a small crown 2 : an ornamental band worn around the temples
corp abbr 1 corporal 2 corporation
¹cor·po·ral \'kȯr-p(ə-)rəl\ adj : of or relating to the body ⟨~ punishment⟩
²corporal n : a noncommissioned officer (as in the army) ranking next below a sergeant
cor·po·rate \'kȯr-p(ə-)rət\ adj 1 : INCORPORATED; also : belonging to an incorporated body 2 : of or relating to large-scale business ⟨~ mergers⟩ 3 : combined into one body
cor·po·ra·tion \ˌkȯr-pə-'rā-shən\ n 1 : the municipal authorities of a town or city 2 : a legal creation authorized to act with the rights and liabilities of a person; also : COMPANY
cor·po·rat·ize \'kȯr-pə-rə-ˌtīz\ vb -ized; -iz·ing : to subject to corporate control ⟨~ education⟩
cor·po·re·al \kȯr-'pȯr-ē-əl\ adj 1 : PHYSICAL, MATERIAL 2 archaic : BODILY — cor·po·re·al·i·ty \kȯr-ˌpȯr-ē-'a-lə-tē\ n — cor·po·re·al·ly adv
corps \'kȯr\ n, pl corps \'kȯrz\ [F, fr. OF cors, fr. L corpus body] 1 : an organized subdivision of a country's military forces 2 : a group acting under common direction
corpse \'kȯrps\ n : a dead body
corps·man \'kȯr-mən, 'kȯrz-\ n : an enlisted person trained to give first aid
cor·pu·lence \'kȯr-pyə-ləns\ n : excessive fatness : OBESITY
cor·pu·lent \-lənt\ adj : OBESE
cor·pus \'kȯr-pəs\ n, pl cor·po·ra \-pə-rə\ [ME, fr. L] 1 : BODY; esp : CORPSE 2 : a body of writings or works
cor·pus·cle \'kȯr-pə-səl, -ˌpə-\ n 1 : a minute particle 2 : a living cell (as in blood or cartilage) not aggregated into continuous tissues — cor·pus·cu·lar \kȯr-'pəs-kyə-lər\ adj
cor·pus de·lic·ti \ˌkȯr-pəs-di-'lik-ˌtī, -tē\ n, pl corpora delicti [NL, lit., body of the crime] 1 : the substantial fact proving that a crime has been committed 2 : the body of a victim of murder
corr abbr 1 correct; corrected; correction 2 correspondence; correspondent; corresponding
cor·ral \kə-'ral\ n [Sp] : an enclosure for confining or

capturing animals; *also* : an enclosure of wagons for defending a camp — **corral** *vb*
¹**cor·rect** \kə-'rekt\ *vb* **1** : to make right ⟨~ an error⟩ **2** : REPROVE, CHASTISE ⟨~*ed* the child⟩ — **cor·rect·able** \-'rek-tə-bəl\ *adj* — **cor·rec·tion** \-'rek-shən\ *n* — **cor·rec·tion·al** \-'rek-sh(ə-)nəl\ *adj* — **cor·rec·tive** \-'rektiv\ *adj*
²**correct** *adj* **1** : conforming to a conventional standard ⟨~ behavior⟩ **2** : agreeing with fact or truth ⟨a ~ answer⟩ **3** : conforming to the standards of a specific ideology ⟨environmentally ~⟩ — **cor·rect·ly** *adv* — **cor·rect·ness** *n*
cor·re·late \'kor-ə-,lāt\ *vb* **-lat·ed; -lat·ing** : to connect in a systematic way : establish the mutual relations of — **cor·re·late** \-lət, -,lāt\ *n* — **cor·re·la·tion** \,kor-ə-'lāshən\ *n*
cor·rel·a·tive \kə-'rel-ə-tiv\ *adj* **1** : reciprocally related **2** : regularly used together (as *either* and *or*) — **correlative** *n* — **cor·rel·a·tive·ly** *adv*
cor·re·spond \,kor-ə-'spänd\ *vb* **1** : to be in agreement : SUIT, MATCH **2** : to communicate by letter — **cor·re·spond·ing·ly** *adv*
cor·re·spon·dence \-'spän-dəns\ *n* **1** : agreement between particular things **2** : communication by letters; *also* : the letters exchanged
¹**cor·re·spon·dent** \-dənt\ *adj* **1** : SIMILAR **2** : FITTING, CONFORMING
²**correspondent** *n* **1** : something that corresponds **2** : a person with whom one communicates by letter **3** : a person employed to contribute news regularly from a place ⟨a war ~⟩
cor·ri·dor \'kor-ə-dər, -,dor\ *n* **1** : a passageway into which compartments or rooms open (as in a hotel or school) **2** : a narrow strip of land esp. through foreign-held territory **3** : a densely populated strip of land including two or more major cities **4** : an area identified by a common characteristic or purpose ⟨a ~ of liberalism⟩
cor·ri·gen·dum \,kor-ə-'jen-dəm\ *n, pl* **-da** \-də\ [L] : an error in a printed work discovered after printing and shown with its correction on a separate sheet
cor·ri·gi·ble \'kor-ə-jə-bəl\ *adj* : CORRECTABLE
cor·rob·o·rate \kə-'rä-bə-,rāt\ *vb* **-rat·ed; -rat·ing** [L *corroborare,* fr. *robur* strength] : to support with evidence : CONFIRM — **cor·rob·o·ra·tion** \-,rä-bə-'rā-shən\ *n* — **cor·rob·o·ra·tive** \-'rä-bə-,rā-tiv, -'rä-brə-\ *adj* — **cor·rob·o·ra·to·ry** \-'rä-bə-rə-,tor-ē\ *adj*
cor·rode \kə-'rōd\ *vb* **cor·rod·ed; cor·rod·ing** : to wear or be worn away gradually (as by chemical action) — **cor·ro·sion** \-'rō-zhən\ *n* — **cor·ro·sive** \-'rō-siv\ *adj or n*
cor·ru·gate \'kor-ə-,gāt\ *vb* **-gat·ed; -gat·ing** : to form into wrinkles or ridges and grooves — **cor·ru·gat·ed** *adj* — **cor·ru·ga·tion** \,kor-ə-'gā-shən\ *n*
¹**cor·rupt** \kə-'rəpt\ *vb* **1** : to make evil : DEPRAVE; *esp* : BRIBE **2** : ROT, SPOIL — **cor·rupt·ible** *adj* — **cor·rup·tion** \-'rəp-shən\ *n*
²**corrupt** *adj* : morally degenerate; *also* : characterized by improper conduct ⟨~ officials⟩
cor·sage \kor-'säzh, -'säj\ *n* [F, bust, bodice, fr. OF, bust, fr. *cors* body, fr. L *corpus*] **1** : the waist or bodice of a dress **2** : a bouquet to be worn or carried
cor·sair \'kor-,ser\ *n* : PIRATE
cor·set \'kor-sət\ *n* : a stiffened undergarment worn for support or to give shape to the waist and hips
cor·tege *also* **cor·tège** \kor-'tezh, 'kor-,tezh\ *n* [F] : PROCESSION; *esp* : a funeral procession
cor·tex \'kor-,teks\ *n, pl* **cor·ti·ces** \'kor-tə-,sēz\ *or* **cor·tex·es** : an outer or covering layer of an organism or one of its parts ⟨the adrenal ~⟩ ⟨~ of a plant stem⟩; *esp* : CEREBRAL CORTEX — **cor·ti·cal** \'kor-ti-kəl\ *adj*
cor·ti·co·ste·roid \,kor-ti-kō-'stir-,oid, -'ster-\ *n* : any of various steroids made in the adrenal cortex and used medically as anti-inflammatory agents
cor·ti·sone \'kor-tə-,sōn, -,zōn\ *n* : a corticosteroid used esp. in treating rheumatoid arthritis
co·run·dum \kə-'rən-dəm\ *n* : a very hard aluminum-containing mineral used as an abrasive or as a gem
cor·us·cate \'kor-ə-,skāt\ *vb* **-cat·ed; -cat·ing** : FLASH, SPARKLE — **cor·us·ca·tion** \,kor-ə-'skā-shən\ *n*
cor·vette \kor-'vet\ *n* **1** : a naval sailing ship smaller

than a frigate **2** : an armed escort ship smaller than a destroyer
co·ry·za \kə-'rī-zə\ *n* : an inflammatory disorder of the upper respiratory tract; *esp* : COMMON COLD
cos *abbr* cosine
COS *abbr* **1** cash on shipment **2** chief of staff
co·sig·na·to·ry \kō-'sig-nə-,tor-ē\ *n* : a joint signer
co·sign·er \'kō-,sī-nər\ *n* : COSIGNATORY; *esp* : a joint signer of a promissory note
co·sine \'kō-,sīn\ *n* : the trigonometric function that is the ratio between the side next to an acute angle in a right triangle and the hypotenuse
¹**cos·met·ic** \käz-'me-tik\ *adj* [Gk *kosmētikos* skilled in adornment, fr. *kosmein* to arrange, adorn, fr. *kosmos* order, ornament, universe] **1** : intended to beautify the hair or complexion **2** : correcting physical defects esp. to improve appearance ⟨~ dentistry⟩ **3** : SUPERFICIAL ⟨~ changes⟩ — **cos·met·i·cal·ly** \-ti-k(ə-)lē\ *adv*
²**cosmetic** *n* : a cosmetic preparation
cos·me·tol·o·gist \,käz-mə-'tä-lə-jist\ *n* : one who gives beauty treatments — **cos·me·tol·o·gy** \-jē\ *n*
cos·mic \'käz-mik\ *also* **cos·mi·cal** \-mi-kəl\ *adj* **1** : of or relating to the cosmos **2** : VAST, GRAND **3** : of or relating to spiritual or metaphysical ideas ⟨a ~ thinker⟩ — **cos·mi·cal·ly** *adv*
cosmic ray *n* : a stream of very penetrating atomic nuclei that enter the earth's atmosphere from outer space
cos·mog·o·ny \käz-'mä-gə-nē\ *n, pl* **-nies** : the origin or creation of the world or universe
cos·mol·o·gy \-'mä-lə-jē\ *n, pl* **-gies** : a branch of astronomy dealing with the origin and structure of the universe — **cos·mo·log·i·cal** \,käz-mə-'lä-ji-kəl\ *adj* — **cos·mol·o·gist** \käz-'mä-lə-jist\ *n*
cos·mo·naut \'käz-mə-,nȯt\ *n* : a Soviet or Russian astronaut
cos·mo·pol·i·tan \,käz-mə-'pä-lə-tən\ *adj* : belonging to all the world : not local ✦ *Synonyms* UNIVERSAL, GLOBAL, CATHOLIC — **cosmopolitan** *n*
cos·mos \'käz-məs, *1 also* -,mōs, -,mäs\ *n* **1** : UNIVERSE **2** : a tall garden herb related to the daisies
co·spon·sor \'kō-,spän-sər, -'spän-\ *n* : a joint sponsor — **cosponsor** *vb*
Cos·sack \'kä-,sak, -sək\ *n* [Pol & Ukrainian *kozak,* of Turkic origin] : a member of one of several autonomous communities drawn from various ethnic groups in southern Russia; *also* : a mounted soldier from one of these communities
¹**cost** \'kost\ *n* **1** : the amount paid or charged for something : PRICE **2** : the loss or penalty incurred in gaining something **3** *pl* : expenses incurred in a lawsuit — **at all costs** : regardless of consequences ⟨win *at all costs*⟩
²**cost** *vb* **cost; cost·ing** **1** : to require a specified amount in payment **2** : to cause to pay, suffer, or lose
co·star \'kō-,stär\ *n* : one of two leading players in a motion picture or play — **co·star** *vb*
cos·tive \'käs-tiv\ *adj* : affected with or causing constipation
cost·ly \'kost-lē\ *adj* **cost·li·er; -est** **1** : of great cost or value ⟨~ gems⟩ **2** : done at great expense or sacrifice ⟨a ~ error⟩ ✦ *Synonyms* DEAR, VALUABLE, EXPENSIVE — **cost·li·ness** *n*
cos·tume \'käs-,tüm, -,tyüm\ *n* [F, fr. It, custom, dress, fr. L *consuetudo* custom] **1** : the style of attire characteristic of a period or country **2** : a special or fancy dress ⟨Halloween ~s⟩ — **cos·tum·er** \'käs-,tü-mər, -,tyü-\ *n*
costume jewelry *n* : inexpensive jewelry
co·sy *chiefly Brit var of* COZY
¹**cot** \'kät\ *n* : a small house : COTTAGE
²**cot** *n* : a small often collapsible bed
cote \'kōt, 'kät\ *n* : a small shed or coop (as for sheep or doves)
co·te·rie \'kō-tə-,rē, ,kō-tə-'rē\ *n* [F] : an intimate often exclusive group of persons with a common interest
co·ter·mi·nous \kō-'tər-mə-nəs\ *adj* : having the same scope or duration
co·til·lion \kō-'til-yən, kə-\ *n* : a formal ball
cot·tage \'kä-tij\ *n* : a small house — **cot·tag·er** *n*
cottage cheese *n* : a soft uncured cheese made from soured skim milk
cot·tar *or* **cot·ter** \'kä-tər\ *n* : a peasant or farm laborer occupying a cottage and often a small holding

cotter pin *n* : a metal strip bent into a pin whose ends can be spread apart after insertion through a hole or slot

cot·ton \'kä-tᵊn\ *n* [ME *coton*, fr. AF *cotun*, fr. Ar *quṭun*] **1** : a soft fibrous usu. white substance composed of hairs attached to the seeds of various tropical plants related to the mallow; *also* : this plant **2** : thread or cloth made of cotton — **cot·tony** *adj*

cotton candy *n* : a candy made of spun sugar

cot·ton·mouth \'kä-tᵊn-ˌmau̇th\ *n* : WATER MOCCASIN

cot·ton·seed \-ˌsēd\ *n* : the seed of the cotton plant yielding a protein-rich meal and a fatty oil (**cottonseed oil**) used esp. in cooking

cot·ton·tail \-ˌtāl\ *n* : a No. American rabbit with a white-tufted tail

cot·ton·wood \-ˌwu̇d\ *n* : a poplar having seeds with cottony hairs

cot·y·le·don \ˌkä-tə-'lē-dᵊn\ *n* : the first leaf or one of the first pair or whorl of leaves developed by a seed plant

¹couch \'kau̇ch\ *vb* **1** : to lie or place on a couch **2** : to phrase in a specified manner ⟨proposals *∼ed* in jargon⟩

²couch *n* : a piece of furniture (as a bed or sofa) that one can sit or lie on

couch·ant \'kau̇-chənt\ *adj* : lying down with the head raised ⟨coat of arms with lion *∼*⟩

couch potato *n* : one who spends a great deal of time watching television

cou·gar \'kü-gər\ *n, pl* **cougars** *also* **cougar** [F *couguar*, fr. NL *cuguacuarana*, modif. of Tupi (a Brazilian Indian language) *stwasuarána*, fr. *siwásu* deer + *-ran* resembling] : a large powerful tawny brown wild American cat

cougar

cough \'kȯf\ *vb* : to force air from the lungs with short sharp noises; *also* : to expel by coughing — **cough** *n*

could \kəd, 'ku̇d\ *past of* CAN — used as an auxiliary in the past or as a polite or less forceful alternative to *can* in the present

cou·lee \'kü-lē\ *n* **1** : a small stream **2** : a dry streambed **3** : GULLY

cou·lomb \'kü-ˌläm, -ˌlōm\ *n* : a unit of electric charge equal to the electricity transferred by a current of one ampere in one second

coun·cil \'kau̇n-səl\ *n* **1** : ASSEMBLY, MEETING **2** : an official body of lawmakers ⟨city *∼*⟩ — **coun·cil·lor** *or* **coun·cil·or** \-sə-lər\ *n* — **coun·cil·man** \-səl-mən\ *n* — **coun·cil·wom·an** \-ˌwu̇-mən\ *n*

¹coun·sel \'kau̇n-səl\ *n* **1** : ADVICE **2** : a plan of action **3** : deliberation together **4** *pl* **counsel** : LAWYER

²counsel *vb* **-seled** *or* **-selled; -sel·ing** *or* **-sel·ling** **1** : ADVISE **2** : CONSULT

coun·sel·or *or* **coun·sel·lor** \'kau̇n-sə-lər\ *n* **1** : ADVISER **2** : LAWYER **3** : one who has supervisory duties at a summer camp

¹count \'kau̇nt\ *vb* [ME, fr. AF *cunter, counter*, fr. L *computare*, fr. *com-* with + *putare* to consider] **1** : to name or indicate one by one in order to find the total number **2** : to recite numbers in order **3** : CONSIDER, ACCOUNT **4** : RELY ⟨you can *∼* on me⟩ **5** : to be of value or account ⟨*∼s* toward your grade⟩ — **count·able** *adj*

²count *n* **1** : the act of counting; *also* : the total obtained by counting **2** : a particular charge in an indictment or legal declaration ⟨two *∼s* of murder⟩

³count *n* [ME, fr. AF *cunte*, fr. LL *comes*, fr. L, companion, one of the imperial court, fr. *com-* with + *ire* to go] : a European nobleman whose rank corresponds to that of a British earl

count·down \'kau̇nt-ˌdau̇n\ *n* : a backward counting in

fixed units (as secoᵈs) to indicate the time remaining before an event (as the launching of a rocket) — **count down** *vb*

¹coun·te·nance \'kau̇n-tᵊn-əns\ *n* **1** : the human face **2** : FAVOR, APPROVAL

²countenance *vb* **-nanced; -nanc·ing** : SANCTION, TOLERATE

¹count·er \'kau̇n-tər\ *n* **1** : a piece (as of metal or plastic) used in reckoning or in games **2** : a level surface over which business is transacted, food is served, or work is conducted

²count·er *n* : a device for recording a number or amount

³coun·ter *vb* : to act in opposition to

⁴coun·ter *adv* : in an opposite direction : CONTRARY

⁵coun·ter *n* **1** : OPPOSITE, CONTRARY **2** : an answering or offsetting force or blow

⁶coun·ter *adj* : CONTRARY, OPPOSITE

coun·ter·act \ˌkau̇n-tər-'akt\ *vb* : to lessen the force of : OFFSET — **coun·ter·ac·tive** \-'ak-tiv\ *adj*

coun·ter·at·tack \'kau̇n-tər-ə-ˌtak\ *n* : an attack made to oppose an enemy's attack — **counterattack** *vb*

¹coun·ter·bal·ance \'kau̇n-tər-ˌba-ləns\ *n* : a weight or influence that balances another

²counterbalance \ˌkau̇n-tər-'ba-ləns\ *vb* : to oppose with equal weight or influence

coun·ter·claim \'kau̇n-tər-ˌklām\ *n* : an opposing claim esp. in law

coun·ter·clock·wise \ˌkau̇n-tər-'kläk-ˌwīz\ *adv* : in a direction opposite to that in which the hands of a clock rotate — **counterclockwise** *adj*

coun·ter·cul·ture \'kau̇n-tər-ˌkəl-chər\ *n* : a culture with values and mores that run counter to those of established society

coun·ter·es·pi·o·nage \ˌkau̇n-tər-'es-pē-ə-ˌnäzh, -nij\ *n* : activities intended to discover and defeat enemy espionage

¹coun·ter·feit \'kau̇n-tər-ˌfit\ *adj* : SHAM, SPURIOUS; *also* : FORGED ⟨*∼* money⟩

²counterfeit *vb* **1** : to copy or imitate in order to deceive **2** : PRETEND, FEIGN — **coun·ter·feit·er** *n*

³counterfeit *n* : something counterfeit : FORGERY ♦ *Synonyms* FRAUD, SHAM, FAKE, IMPOSTURE, DECEIT, DECEPTION

coun·ter·in·sur·gen·cy \ˌkau̇n-tər-in-'sər-jən-sē\ *n* : military activity designed to deal with insurgents

coun·ter·in·tel·li·gence \-in-'te-lə-jəns\ *n* : organized activities of an intelligence service designed to counter the activities of an enemy's intelligence service

coun·ter·in·tu·i·tive \-in-'tü-ə-tiv, -'tyü-\ *adj* : contrary to what would intuitively be expected

count·er·man \'kau̇n-tər-ˌman, -mən\ *n* : one who tends a counter

coun·ter·mand \'kau̇nt-ər-ˌmand\ *vb* : to withdraw (an order already given) by a contrary order

coun·ter·mea·sure \-ˌme-zhər\ *n* : an action or device designed to counter another

coun·ter·of·fen·sive \-ə-ˌfen-siv\ *n* : a large-scale counterattack

coun·ter·pane \-ˌpān\ *n* : BEDSPREAD

coun·ter·part \-ˌpärt\ *n* : a person or thing very closely like or corresponding to another person or thing

coun·ter·point \-ˌpȯint\ *n* : music in which one melody is accompanied by one or more other melodies all woven into a harmonious whole

coun·ter·poise \-ˌpȯiz\ *n* : COUNTERBALANCE

coun·ter·rev·o·lu·tion \ˌkau̇n-tər-ˌre-və-'lü-shən\ *n* : a revolution opposed to a current or earlier one — **coun·ter·rev·o·lu·tion·ary** \-ˌsha-ˌner-ē\ *adj or n*

coun·ter·sign \'kau̇n-tər-ˌsīn\ *n* **1** : a confirmatory signature added to a writing already signed by another person **2** : a military secret signal that must be given by a person who wishes to pass a guard — **countersign** *vb*

coun·ter·sink \-ˌsiŋk\ *vb* **-sunk** \-ˌsəŋk\; **-sink·ing** **1** : to form a funnel-shaped enlargement at the outer end of a drilled hole **2** : to set the head of (as a screw) at or below the surface — **countersink** *n*

coun·ter·spy \-ˌspī\ *n* : a spy engaged in counterespionage

coun·ter·ten·or \-ˌte-nər\ *n* : a tenor with an unusually high range

coun·ter·vail \ˌkau̇n-tər-'vāl\ *vb* : COUNTERACT

coun·ter·weight \'kaùn-tər-ˌwāt\ *n* : COUNTERBALANCE
count·ess \'kaùn-təs\ *n* 1 : the wife or widow of a count or an earl 2 : a woman holding the rank of a count or an earl in her own right
count·ing·house \'kaùn-tiŋ-ˌhaùs\ *n* : a building or office for keeping books and conducting business
count·less \'kaùnt-ləs\ *adj* : INNUMERABLE
coun·tri·fied *also* **coun·try·fied** \'kən-tri-ˌfīd\ *adj* 1 : RURAL, RUSTIC 2 : UNSOPHISTICATED 3 : played or sung in the manner of country music
¹**coun·try** \'kən-trē\ *n, pl* **countries** [ME *contree,* fr. AF *cuntree, contré,* fr. ML *contrata,* fr. L *contra* against, on the opposite side] 1 : REGION, DISTRICT 2 : FATHERLAND 3 : a nation or its territory 4 : rural regions as opposed to towns and cities 5 : COUNTRY MUSIC
²**country** *adj* 1 : RURAL 2 : of or relating to country music ⟨a ∼ singer⟩
country and western *n* : COUNTRY MUSIC
country club *n* : a suburban club for social life and recreation; *esp* : one having a golf course — **country–club** *adj*
coun·try–dance \'kən-trē-ˌdans\ *n* : an English dance in which partners face each other esp. in rows
coun·try·man \'kən-trē-mən, 2 often -ˌman\ *n* 1 : an inhabitant of a specified country 2 : COMPATRIOT 3 : one raised or living in the country : RUSTIC
country music *n* : music derived from or imitating the folk style of the southern U.S. or of the Western cowboy
coun·try·side \'kən-trē-ˌsīd\ *n* : a rural area or its people
coun·ty \'kaùn-tē\ *n, pl* **counties** 1 : the domain of a count 2 : a territorial division of a country or state for purposes of local government
coup \'kü\ *n, pl* **coups** \'küz\ [F, blow, stroke] 1 : a brilliant sudden stroke or stratagem 2 : COUP D'ÉTAT
coup de grace \ˌkü-də-'gräs\ *n, pl* **coups de grace** *same*\ [F *coup de grâce,* lit., stroke of mercy] : DEATHBLOW; *also* : a final decisive stroke or event
coup d'état \ˌkü-də-'tä\ *n, pl* **coups d'état** *same*\ [F, lit., stroke of state] : a sudden violent overthrow of a government by a small group
cou·pé *or* **coupe** \kü-'pā, 2 often 'küp\ *n* [F *coupé,* fr. *couper* to cut] 1 : a closed horse-drawn carriage for two persons inside with an outside seat for the driver 2 *usu* **coupe** : a 2-door automobile with an enclosed body
¹**cou·ple** \'kə-pəl\ *n* 1 : two persons married, engaged, or otherwise romantically paired 2 : PAIR 3 : BOND, TIE 4 : an indefinite small number : FEW ⟨a ∼ of days ago⟩
²**couple** *vb* **cou·pled; cou·pling** : to link together
cou·plet \'kə-plət\ *n* : two successive rhyming lines of verse
cou·pling \'kə-pliŋ (*usual for 2*), -pə-liŋ\ *n* 1 : CONNECTION 2 : a device for connecting two parts or things
cou·pon \'kü-ˌpän, 'kyü-\ *n* 1 : a statement attached to a bond showing interest due and designed to be cut off and presented for payment 2 : a form surrendered in order to obtain an article, service, or accommodation 3 : a printed document or slip used to submit orders or inquiries or to obtain a discount on merchandise or services
cour·age \'kər-ij\ *n* : ability to conquer fear or despair : BRAVERY, VALOR — **cou·ra·geous** \kə-'rā-jəs\ *adj* — **cou·ra·geous·ly** *adv*
cou·ri·er \'kur-ē-ər, 'kər-ē-\ *n* : one who bears messages or information esp. for the diplomatic or military services
¹**course** \'kórs\ *n* 1 : PROGRESS, PASSAGE; *also* : direction of progress 2 : the ground or path over which something moves 3 : method of procedure : CONDUCT, BEHAVIOR 4 : an ordered series of acts or proceedings : sequence of events 5 : a series of instruction periods dealing with a subject 6 : the series of studies leading to graduation from a school or college 7 : the part of a meal served at one time — **of course** : as might be expected
²**course** *vb* **coursed; cours·ing** 1 : to hunt with dogs 2 : to run or go speedily
cours·er \'kór-sər\ *n* : a swift or spirited horse
¹**court** \'kórt\ *n* [ME, fr. AF, fr. L *cohort-, cohors* enclosure, group, retinue, cohort] 1 : the residence of a sovereign or similar dignitary 2 : a sovereign's formal assembly of officials and advisers as a governing power

3 : an assembly of the retinue of a sovereign 4 : an open space enclosed by a building or buildings 5 : a space walled or marked off for playing a game (as tennis or basketball) 6 : the place where justice is administered; *also* : a judicial body or a meeting of a judicial body 7 : attention intended to win favor
²**court** *vb* 1 : to try to gain the favor of 2 : WOO 3 : ATTRACT, TEMPT
cour·te·ous \'kər-tē-əs\ *adj* : marked by respect for others : CIVIL, POLITE — **cour·te·ous·ly** *adv*
cour·te·san \'kór-tə-zən, -ˌzan\ *n* : PROSTITUTE
cour·te·sy \'kər-tə-sē\ *n, pl* **-sies** 1 : courteous behavior : POLITENESS 2 : a favor courteously performed
court·house \'kórt-ˌhaùs\ *n* : a building in which courts of law are held or county offices are located
court·ier \'kór-tē-ər\ *n* : a person in attendance at a royal court
court·ly \'kórt-lē\ *adj* **court·li·er; -est** : REFINED, ELEGANT, POLITE ♦ **Synonyms** GALLANT, GRACIOUS — **court·li·ness** *n*
court–mar·tial \'kórt-ˌmär-shəl\ *n, pl* **courts–martial** : a military or naval court for trial of offenses against military or naval law; *also* : a trial by this court — **court–martial** *vb*
court·room \-ˌrüm, -ˌrum\ *n* : a room in which a court of law is held
court·ship \-ˌship\ *n* : the act of courting : WOOING
court·yard \-ˌyärd\ *n* : an enclosure next to a building
cous·cous \'küs-ˌküs\ *n* : a No. African dish of steamed semolina usu. served with meat or vegetables; *also* : the semolina itself
cous·in \'kə-zən\ *n* [ME *cosin,* fr. AF, fr. L *consobrinus,* fr. *com-* with + *sobrinus* second cousin, fr. *soror* sister] : a child of one's uncle or aunt
cou·ture \kü-'túr, -'tuer\ *n* [F] : the business of designing fashionable custom-made women's clothing; *also* : the designers and establishments engaged in this business
cou·tu·ri·er \kü-'túr-ē-ər, -ē-ˌā\ *n* [F, dressmaker] : the owner of an establishment engaged in couture
cove \'kōv\ *n* : a small sheltered inlet or bay
co·ven \'kə-vən\ *n* : an assembly or band of witches
cov·e·nant \'kə-və-nənt\ *n* : a formal binding agreement : COMPACT — **cov·e·nant** \-nənt, -ˌnant\ *vb*
¹**cov·er** \'kə-vər\ *vb* 1 : to bring or hold within range of a firearm 2 : PROTECT, GUARD ⟨∼*ed* by insurance⟩ ⟨∼ third base⟩ 3 : HIDE, CONCEAL ⟨∼ up a crime⟩ 4 : to place something over or upon 5 : INCLUDE, COMPRISE 6 : to have as one's field of activity ⟨one salesman ∼*s* the state⟩ 7 : to buy (stocks) in order to have them for delivery on a previous short sale
²**cover** *n* 1 : something that protects or shelters 2 : LID, TOP 3 : CASE, BINDING 4 : TABLECLOTH 5 : a cloth used on a bed 6 : SCREEN, DISGUISE 7 : an envelope or wrapper for mail
cov·er·age \'kə-və-rij\ *n* 1 : the act or fact of covering 2 : the total group covered : SCOPE
cov·er·all \'kə-vər-ˌól\ *n* : a one-piece outer garment worn to protect one's clothes — usu. used in pl.
cover charge *n* : a charge made by a restaurant or nightclub in addition to the charge for food and drink
cover crop *n* : a crop planted to prevent soil erosion and to provide humus
cov·er·let \'kə-vər-lət\ *n* : BEDSPREAD
¹**co·vert** \'kō-ˌvərt, 'kə-vərt\ *adj* 1 : HIDDEN, SECRET ⟨a ∼ operation⟩ 2 : SHELTERED — **co·vert·ly** *adv*
²**co·vert** \'kō-vərt, 'kə-vərt, 'kō-\ *n* 1 : a secret or sheltered place; *esp* : a thicket sheltering game 2 : a feather covering the bases of the quills of the wings and tail of a bird
cov·er–up \'kə-vər-ˌəp\ *n* 1 : a device for masking or concealing 2 : a usu. concerted effort to keep an illegal or unethical act or situation from being made public
cov·et \'kə-vət\ *vb* : to desire enviously (what belongs to another) — **cov·et·ous** *adj* — **cov·et·ous·ness** *n*
cov·ey \'kə-vē\ *n, pl* **coveys** [ME, fr. AF *covee* sitting (of a hen), fr. *cover* to sit on, brood over, fr. L *cubare* to lie] 1 : a bird with her brood of young 2 : a small flock (as of quail) 3 : GROUP 1
¹**cow** \'kaù\ *n* 1 : the mature female of cattle or of an animal (as the moose, elephant, or whale) of which the male is called *bull* 2 : any domestic bovine animal irrespective of sex or age

²**cow** *vb* : INTIMIDATE, DAUNT, OVERAWE

cow·ard \'kaú(-ə)rd\ *n* [ME, fr. AF *cuard*, fr. *cue*, *coe* tail, fr. L *cauda*] : one who lacks courage or shows shameful fear or timidity — **coward** *adj* — **cow·ard·ice** \'kaú-ər-dəs\ *n* — **cow·ard·ly** *adv or adj*

cow·bird \'kaú-ˌbərd\ *n* : a small No. American blackbird that lays its eggs in the nests of other birds

cow·boy \-ˌbói\ *n* : one (as a mounted ranch hand) who tends cattle or horses

cow·er \'kaú(-ə)r\ *vb* : to shrink or crouch down from fear or cold : QUAIL

cow·girl \'kaú-ˌgərl\ *n* : a girl or woman who tends cattle or horses

cow·hand \'kaú-ˌhand\ *n* : COWBOY

cow·herd \-ˌhərd\ *n* : one who tends cows

cow·hide \-ˌhīd\ *n* **1** : the hide of a cow; *also* : leather made from it **2** : a coarse whip of braided rawhide

cowl \'kaú(-ə)l\ *n* : a monk's hood

cow·lick \'kaú-ˌlik\ *n* : a turned-up tuft of hair that resists control

cowl·ing \'kaú-liŋ\ *n* : a usu. metal covering for the engine or another part of an airplane

cow·man \'kaú-mən, -ˌman\ *n* : COWBOY; *also* : a cattle owner or rancher

co·work·er \'kō-ˌwər-kər\ *n* : a fellow worker

cow·poke \'kaú-ˌpōk\ *n* : COWBOY

cow pony *n* : a strong and agile horse trained for herding cattle

cow·pox \'kaú-ˌpäks\ *n* : a mild disease of the cow that when communicated to humans protects against smallpox

cow·punch·er \-ˌpən-chər\ *n* : COWBOY

cow·slip \'kaú-ˌslip\ *n* **1** : a yellow-flowered European primrose **2** : MARSH MARIGOLD

cox·comb \'käks-ˌkōm\ *n* : a conceited foolish person : FOP

cox·swain \'käk-sən, -ˌswān\ *n* : the steersman of a ship's boat or a racing shell

coy \'kói\ *adj* [ME, quiet, shy, fr. AF *quei*, *quoi*, *koi* quiet, fr. L *quietus*] **1** : BASHFUL, SHY **2** : marked by artful playfulness : COQUETTISH — **coy·ly** *adv* — **coy·ness** *n*

coy·ote \'kī-ˌōt, kī-'ō-tē\ *n*, *pl* **coyotes** *or* **coyote** : a mammal of No. America smaller than the related wolves

coy·pu \'kói-pü\ *n* : NUTRIA 2

coz·en \'kə-zᵊn\ *vb* : CHEAT, DEFRAUD — **coz·en·age** \-ij\ *n* — **coz·en·er** *n*

¹**co·zy** \'kō-zē\ *adj* **co·zi·er**; **-est** : SNUG, COMFORTABLE \a ∼ cabin\ — **co·zi·ly** \-zə-lē\ *adv* — **co·zi·ness** \-zē-nəs\ *n*

²**cozy** *n*, *pl* **co·zies** : a padded covering for a vessel (as a teapot) to keep the contents hot

cp *abbr* **1** compare **2** coupon

CP *abbr* **1** cerebral palsy **2** chemically pure **3** command post **4** communist party

CPA *abbr* certified public accountant

CPB *abbr* Corporation for Public Broadcasting

cpd *abbr* compound

CPI *abbr* consumer price index

Cpl *abbr* corporal

CPO *abbr* chief petty officer

CPOM *abbr* master chief petty officer

CPOS *abbr* senior chief petty officer

CPR *abbr* cardiopulmonary resuscitation

CPT *abbr* captain

CPU \ˌsē-ˌpē-'yü\ *n* [central processing *u*nit] : the part of a computer that performs its basic operations, manages its components, and exchanges data with memory or peripherals

CQ *abbr* charge of quarters

cr *abbr* credit; creditor

Cr *symbol* chromium

¹**crab** \'krab\ *n*, *pl* **crabs** *also* **crab** : any of various crustaceans with a short broad shell and small abdomen

²**crab** *n* : an ill-natured person

³**crab** *vb* **crabbed**; **crab·bing** : COMPLAIN, GROUSE

crab apple *n* : a small often highly colored sour apple; *also* : a tree that produces crab apples

crab·bed \'kra-bəd\ *adj* **1** : MOROSE, PEEVISH \a ∼ view of human nature\ **2** : CRAMPED, IRREGULAR \∼ handwriting\

crab·by \'kra-bē\ *adj* **crab·bi·er**; **-est** : CROSS, ILL-NATURED

crab·grass \'krab-ˌgras\ *n* : a weedy grass with creeping or sprawling stems that root freely at the nodes

crab louse *n* : a louse infesting the pubic region in humans

¹**crack** \'krak\ *vb* **1** : to break with a sharp sudden sound **2** : to break with or without completely separating into parts **3** : to fail in tone or become harsh \her voice ∼ed\ **4** : to subject (as a petroleum oil) to heat for breaking down into lighter products (as gasoline)

²**crack** *n* **1** : a sudden sharp noise **2** : a witty or sharp remark **3** : a narrow break or opening : FISSURE **4** : a sharp blow **5** : ATTEMPT, TRY **6** : a potent form of cocaine in small chips used illicitly for smoking

³**crack** *adj* : extremely proficient

crack·down \'krak-ˌdaún\ *n* : an act or instance of taking positive disciplinary action \a ∼ on gambling\ — **crack down** *vb*

crack·er \'kra-kər\ *n* **1** : FIRECRACKER **2** : a dry thin crispy baked bread product made of flour and water

crack·er·jack \-ˌjak\ *adj* : EXCELLENT, GREAT \a ∼ salesperson\ — **crackerjack** *n*

crack·le \'kra-kəl\ *vb* **crack·led**; **crack·ling** **1** : to make small sharp snapping noises **2** : to develop fine cracks in a surface — **crackle** *n* — **crack·ly** \-k(ə-)lē\ *adj*

crack·pot \'krak-ˌpät\ *n* : an eccentric person

crack–up \'krak-ˌəp\ *n* : CRASH, WRECK; *also* : BREAKDOWN

crack up *vb* **1** : PRAISE \isn't all it's *cracked up* to be\ **2** : to laugh or cause to laugh out loud **3** : to crash a vehicle

¹**cra·dle** \'krā-dᵊl\ *n* **1** : a baby's bed or cot **2** : a framework or support (as for a telephone receiver) **3** : INFANCY \from ∼ to the grave\ **4** : a place of origin

²**cradle** *vb* **cra·dled**; **cra·dling** **1** : to place in or as if in a cradle **2** : SHELTER, REAR

craft \'kraft\ *n* **1** : ART, SKILL; *also* : an occupation requiring special skill **2** : CUNNING, GUILE \used ∼ to close the deal\ **3** *pl usu* **craft** : a boat esp. of small size; *also* : AIRCRAFT, SPACECRAFT

crafts·man \'krafts-mən\ *n* : a skilled artisan — **crafts·man·ship** *n*

crafty \'kraf-tē\ *adj* **craft·i·er**; **-est** : CUNNING, DECEITFUL, SUBTLE — **craft·i·ly** \-tə-lē\ *adv* — **craft·i·ness** \-tē-nəs\ *n*

crag \'krag\ *n* : a steep rugged cliff or rock — **crag·gy** *adj*

cram \'kram\ *vb* **crammed**; **cram·ming** **1** : to pack in tight : JAM **2** : to eat greedily **3** : to study rapidly under pressure for an examination

¹**cramp** \'kramp\ *n* **1** : a sudden painful contraction of muscle **2** : sharp abdominal pain — usu. used in pl.

²**cramp** *vb* **1** : to affect with a cramp or cramps **2** : to restrain from free action : HAMPER

cran·ber·ry \'kran-ˌber-ē, -bə-rē\ *n* : the red acid berry of any of several trailing plants related to the heaths; *also* : one of these plants

¹**crane** \'krān\ *n* **1** : any of a family of tall wading birds related to the rails; *also* : any of several herons **2** : a machine for lifting and carrying heavy objects

²**crane** *vb* **craned**; **cran·ing** : to stretch one's neck to see better

crane fly *n* : any of a family of long-legged slender dipteran flies that resemble large mosquitoes but do not bite

cranial nerve *n* : any of the nerves that arise in pairs from the lower surface of the brain and pass through openings in the skull to the periphery of the body

cra·ni·um \'krā-nē-əm\ *n*, *pl* **-ni·ums** *or* **-nia** \-ə\ : SKULL; *esp* : the part enclosing the brain — **cra·ni·al** \-əl\ *adj*

¹**crank** \'kraŋk\ *n* **1** : a bent part of an axle or shaft or an arm at right angles to the end of a shaft by which circular motion is imparted to or received from it **2** : an eccentric person **3** : a bad-tempered person : GROUCH

²**crank** *vb* : to start or operate by or as if by turning a crank

crank·case \'kraŋk-ˌkās\ *n* : the housing of a crankshaft

crank out *vb* : to produce in a mechanical manner

crank·shaft \'kraŋk-ˌshaft\ *n* : a shaft turning or driven by a crank

cranky \'kraŋ-kē\ *adj* **crank·i·er**; **-est** **1** : IRRITABLE **2** : operating uncertainly or imperfectly \a ∼ old tractor\

cran·ny \'kra-nē\ *n*, *pl* **crannies** : CREVICE, CHINK

craps \'kraps\ *n* : a gambling game played with two dice
crap·shoot·er \'krap-ˌshü-tər\ *n* : a person who plays craps
¹crash \'krash\ *vb* **1** : to break noisily : SMASH **2** : to damage an airplane in landing **3** : to enter or attend without invitation or without paying ⟨~ a party⟩ **4** : to suffer a sudden major failure usu. with loss of data ⟨my computer ~ed⟩
²crash *n* **1** : a loud sound (as of things smashing) **2** : an instance of crashing ⟨a plane ~⟩; *also* : COLLISION **3** : a sudden failure (as of a business)
³crash *adj* : marked by concentrated effort over the shortest possible time ⟨a ~ diet⟩
⁴crash *n* : coarse linen fabric used for towels and draperies
crash–land \'krash-ˈland\ *vb* : to land an aircraft or spacecraft under emergency conditions usu. with damage to the craft — **crash landing** *n*
crass \'kras\ *adj* : GROSS, INSENSITIVE ⟨~ ignorance⟩ — **crass·ly** *adv* — **crass·ness** *n*
crate \'krāt\ *n* : a container often of wooden slats — **crate** *vb*
cra·ter \'krā-tər\ *n* [L, mixing bowl, crater, fr. Gk *kratēr*, fr. *kerannynai* to mix] **1** : the depression around the opening of a volcano **2** : a depression formed by the impact of a meteorite or by the explosion of a bomb or shell
cra·vat \krə-ˈvat\ *n* : NECKTIE
crave \'krāv\ *vb* **craved; crav·ing** **1** : to ask for earnestly : BEG **2** : to long for : DESIRE
cra·ven \'krā-vən\ *adj* : COWARDLY — **craven** *n* — **cra·ven·ly** *adv*
crav·ing \'krā-viŋ\ *n* : an urgent or abnormal desire
craw·fish \'krȯ-ˌfish\ *n* **1** : CRAYFISH 1 **2** : SPINY LOBSTER
¹crawl \'krȯl\ *vb* **1** : to move slowly by drawing the body along the ground **2** : to advance feebly, cautiously, or slowly **3** : to be swarming with or feel as if swarming with creeping things ⟨a place ~ing with ants⟩ ⟨her flesh ~ed⟩
²crawl *n* **1** : a very slow pace **2** : a prone speed swimming stroke
cray·fish \'krā-ˌfish\ *n* **1** : any of numerous freshwater crustaceans usu. much smaller than the related lobsters **2** : SPINY LOBSTER

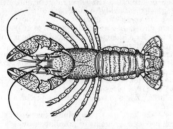

crayfish 1

cray·on \'krā-ˌän, -ən\ *n* : a stick of chalk or wax used for writing, drawing, or coloring; *also* : a drawing made with such material — **crayon** *vb*
¹craze \'krāz\ *vb* **crazed; craz·ing** [ME *crasen* to crush, craze, of Scand origin] : to make or become insane
²craze *n* : FAD, MANIA
cra·zy \'krā-zē\ *adj* **cra·zi·er; -est** **1** : mentally disordered : INSANE **2** : wildly impractical ⟨a ~ plan⟩; *also* : ERRATIC ⟨~ drivers⟩ — **cra·zi·ly** \-zə-lē\ *adv* — **cra·zi·ness** \-zē-nəs\ *n*
CRC *abbr* Civil Rights Commission
creak \'krēk\ *vb* : to make a prolonged squeaking or grating sound — **creak** *n* — **creaky** *adj*
¹cream \'krēm\ *n* **1** : the yellowish fat-rich part of milk **2** : a thick smooth sauce, confection, or cosmetic **3** : the choicest part **4** : a pale yellow color — **creamy** *adj*
²cream *vb* **1** : to prepare with a cream sauce **2** : to beat or blend into creamy consistency **3** : to defeat decisively
cream cheese *n* : a cheese made from whole milk enriched with cream

cream·ery \'krē-mə-rē\ *n, pl* **-er·ies** : an establishment where butter and cheese are made or milk and cream are prepared for sale
crease \'krēs\ *n* : a mark or line made by or as if by folding — **crease** *vb*
cre·ate \krē-ˈāt\ *vb* **cre·at·ed; cre·at·ing** : to bring into being : cause to exist : MAKE, PRODUCE — **cre·a·tive** \-ˈā-tiv\ *adj* — **cre·a·tive·ness** *n* — **cre·a·tiv·i·ty** \ˌkrē-(ˌ)ā-ˈti-və-tē\ *n*
cre·a·tion \krē-ˈā-shən\ *n* **1** : the act of creating or producing ⟨~ of the world⟩ **2** : something that is created **3** : all created things : WORLD
cre·a·tion·ism \krē-ˈā-shə-ˌni-zəm\ *n* : a doctrine or theory holding that matter, the various forms of life, and the world were created by God out of nothing — **cre·a·tion·ist** \-nist\ *n or adj*
cre·a·tor \krē-ˈā-tər\ *n* **1** : one that creates : MAKER, AUTHOR **2** *cap* : GOD 1
crea·ture \'krē-chər\ *n* : a lower animal; *also* : a human being
crèche \'kresh\ *n* [F, manger, crib, fr. OF *creche*, of Gmc origin] : a representation of the Nativity scene
cre·dence \'krē-dᵊns\ *n* : mental acceptance as true or real
cre·den·tial \kri-ˈden-chəl\ *n* : something that gives a basis for credit or confidence
cre·den·za \kri-ˈden-zə\ *n* [It, lit., belief, confidence] : a sideboard, buffet, or bookcase usu. without legs
cred·i·ble \'kre-də-bəl\ *adj* : TRUSTWORTHY, BELIEVABLE — **cred·i·bil·i·ty** \ˌkre-də-ˈbi-lə-tē\ *n* — **cred·i·bly** \'kre-də-blē\ *adv*
¹cred·it \'kre-dət\ *n* [MF, fr. It *credito*, fr. L *creditum* something entrusted to another, loan, fr. *credere* to believe, entrust] **1** : the balance (as in a bank) in a person's favor **2** : time given for payment for goods sold on trust **3** : an accounting entry of payment received **4** : BELIEF, FAITH **5** : financial trustworthiness **6** : ESTEEM **7** : a source of honor or distinction **8** : a unit of academic work
²credit *vb* **1** : BELIEVE **2** : to give credit to ⟨the players all ~ed their coach⟩
cred·it·able \'kre-də-tə-bəl\ *adj* : worthy of esteem or praise ⟨did a ~ job⟩ — **cred·it·ably** \-blē\ *adv*
credit card *n* : a card authorizing purchases on credit
cred·i·tor \'kre-də-tər\ *n* : a person to whom money is owed
cre·do \'krē-dō, 'krā-\ *n, pl* **credos** [ME, fr. L, I believe] : CREED
cred·u·lous \'kre-jə-ləs\ *adj* : inclined to believe esp. on slight evidence — **cre·du·li·ty** \kri-ˈdü-lə-tē, -ˈdyü-\ *n* — **cred·u·lous·ly** *adv*
Cree \'krē\ *n, pl* **Cree** *or* **Crees** : a member of an American Indian people of Canada
creed \'krēd\ *n* [ME *crede*, fr. OE *crēda*, fr. L *credo* I believe, first word of the Apostles' and Nicene Creeds] : a statement of the essential beliefs of a religious faith
creek \'krēk, 'krik\ *n* **1** *chiefly Brit* : a small inlet **2** : a stream smaller than a river and larger than a brook
Creek \'krēk\ *n* : a member of an American Indian people of Alabama, Georgia, and Florida
creel \'krēl\ *n* : a wicker basket esp. for carrying fish
creep \'krēp\ *vb* **crept** \'krept\; **creep·ing** **1** : CRAWL **2** : to feel as though insects were crawling on the skin **3** : to spread or grow over a surface like ivy — **creep** *n* — **creep·er** *n*
creep·ing \'krē-piŋ\ *adj* : developing or advancing by imperceptible degrees
creepy \'krē-pē\ *adj* **creep·i·er; -est** : having or producing a nervous shivery fear
cre·mate \'krē-ˌmāt\ *vb* **cre·mat·ed; cre·mat·ing** : to reduce (a dead body) to ashes with fire — **cre·ma·tion** \kri-ˈmā-shən\ *n*
cre·ma·to·ry \'krē-mə-ˌtȯr-ē, 'kre-\ *n, pl* **-ries** : a furnace for cremating; *also* : a structure containing such a furnace
crème *or* **creme** \'krem, 'krēm\ *n, pl* **crèmes** *or* **cremes** \same *or* 'kremz, 'krēmz\ [F, lit., cream] : a sweet liqueur
cren·el·lat·ed *or* **cren·el·at·ed** \'kre-nə-ˌlā-təd\ *adj* : having battlements — **cren·el·la·tion** \ˌkre-nə-ˈlā-shən\ *n*
Cre·ole \'krē-ˌōl\ *n* **1** : a descendant of early French or Spanish settlers of the U.S. Gulf states preserving their

speech and culture; *also* : a person of mixed French or Spanish and black descent speaking a dialect of French or Spanish 2 *not cap* : a language that has evolved from a pidgin but serves as the native language of a speech community

cre·o·sote \'krē-ə-ˌsōt\ *n* : an oily liquid obtained by distillation of coal tar and used in preserving wood

crepe *or* crêpe \'krāp\ *n* : a light crinkled fabric of any of various fibers

crêpe su·zette \ˌkrāp-sü-'zet\ *n, pl* crêpes suzette *same or* ˌkrāps-\ *or* crêpe suzettes \-sü-'zets\ *often cap S* : a thin folded or rolled pancake in a hot orange-butter sauce that is sprinkled with a liqueur and set ablaze for serving

cre·pus·cu·lar \kri-'pəs-kyə-lər\ *adj* 1 : of, relating to, or resembling twilight 2 : occurring or active during twilight ⟨∼ insects⟩

cre·scen·do \krə-'shen-dō\ *adv or adj* [It] : increasing in loudness — used as a direction in music — crescendo *n*

cres·cent \'kre-sᵊnt\ *n* [ME *cressant*, fr. AF fr. prp. of *crestre* to grow, increase, fr. L *crescere*] : the moon at any stage between new moon and first quarter and between last quarter and new moon; *also* : something shaped like the figure of the crescent moon with a convex and a concave edge — cres·cen·tic \kre-'sen-tik\ *adj*

cress \'kres\ *n* : any of several salad plants related to the mustards

¹crest \'krest\ *n* 1 : a tuft or process on the head of an animal (as a bird) 2 : a heraldic device 3 : an upper part, edge, or limit ⟨the ∼ of a hill⟩ — crest·ed \'kres-təd\ *adj* — crest·less *adj*

²crest *vb* 1 : CROWN 2 : to reach the crest of 3 : to rise to a crest

crest·fall·en \'krest-ˌfȯ-lən\ *adj* : DISPIRITED, DEJECTED

Cre·ta·ceous \kri-'tā-shəs\ *adj* : of, relating to, or being the latest period of the Mesozoic era marked by great increase in flowering plants, diversification of mammals, and extinction of the dinosaurs — Cretaceous *n*

cre·tin \'krē-tᵊn\ *n* [F *crétin*, fr. F dial. *cretin*, lit., wretch, innocent victim, fr. L *christianus* Christian] 1 : one affected with cretinism 2 : a stupid person

cre·tin·ism \-ˌi-zəm\ *n* : a usu. congenital abnormal condition characterized by physical stunting and mental retardation

cre·tonne \'krē-ˌtän\ *n* : a strong unglazed cotton cloth for curtains and upholstery

cre·vasse \kri-'vas\ *n* : a deep fissure esp. in a glacier

crev·ice \'kre-vəs\ *n* : a narrow fissure

¹crew \'krü\ *chiefly Brit past of* CROW

²crew *n* [ME *crue*, fr. MF, a reinforcement, lit., increase, fr. *croistre* to grow, fr. L *crescere*] 1 : a body of people trained to work together for certain purposes 2 : a group of people who operate a ship, train, aircraft, or spacecraft 3 : the rowers and coxswain of a racing shell; *also* : the sport of rowing engaged in by a crew — crew·man \-mən\ *n*

crew cut *n* : a very short bristly haircut

crew·el \'krü-əl\ *n* : slackly twisted worsted yarn used for embroidery — crew·el·work \-ˌwərk\ *n*

¹crib \'krib\ *n* 1 : a manger for feeding animals 2 : a child's bedstead with high sides 3 : a building or bin for storage (as of grain) 4 : something used for cheating in an exam

²crib *vb* cribbed; crib·bing 1 : to put in a crib 2 : STEAL, PLAGIARIZE — crib·ber *n*

crib·bage \'kri-bij\ *n* : a card game usu. played by two players and scored on a board (cribbage board)

crib death *n* : SUDDEN INFANT DEATH SYNDROME

crick \'krik\ *n* : a painful spasm of muscles (as of the neck)

¹crick·et \'kri-kət\ *n* [ME *criket*, fr. AF, of imit. origin] : any of a family of leaping insects related to the grasshoppers and noted for the chirping noises of the male

²cricket *n* [MF *criquet* goal stake in a bowling game] : a game played with a bat and ball by two teams on a field centering upon two wickets each defended by a batsman

cri·er \'krī(-ə)r\ *n* : one who calls out proclamations and announcements

crime \'krīm\ *n* : a serious offense against the public law

¹crim·i·nal \'kri-mə-nᵊl\ *adj* 1 : involving or being a crime 2 : relating to crime or its punishment — crim·i·nal·i·ty \ˌkri-mə-'na-lə-tē\ *n* — crim·i·nal·ly *adv*

²criminal *n* : one who has committed a crime

crim·i·nol·o·gy \ˌkri-mə-'nä-lə-jē\ *n* : the scientific study of crime and criminals — crim·i·no·log·i·cal \-mə-nə-'lä-ji-kəl\ *adj* — crim·i·nol·o·gist \ˌkri-mə-'nä-lə-jist\ *n*

¹crimp \'krimp\ *vb* : to cause to become crinkled, wavy, or bent

²crimp *n* : something (as a curl in hair) produced by or as if by crimping

crim·son \'krim-zən\ *n* : a deep purplish red color — crimson *adj*

cringe \'krinj\ *vb* cringed; cring·ing : to shrink in fear : WINCE, COWER

crin·kle \'krin-kəl\ *vb* crin·kled; crin·kling : to form many short bends or curves; *also* : WRINKLE — crinkle *n* — crin·kly \-kə-lē\ *adj*

crin·o·line \'kri-nə-lən\ *n* 1 : an open-weave cloth used for stiffening and lining 2 : a full stiff skirt or underskirt made of crinoline

¹crip·ple \'kri-pəl\ *n* : one that is disabled or deficient in a specified manner ⟨a social ∼⟩

²cripple *vb* crip·pled; crip·pling 1 : to make lame 2 : to make useless or imperfect — crip·pler \'kri-p(ə-)lər\ *n*

cri·sis \'krī-səs\ *n, pl* cri·ses \-ˌsēz\ [ME, fr. L, fr. Gk *krisis*, lit., decision, fr. *krinein* to decide] 1 : the turning point for better or worse in an acute disease or fever 2 : a decisive or critical moment

crisp \'krisp\ *adj* 1 : CURLY, WAVY 2 : BRITTLE ⟨a ∼ potato chip⟩ 3 : FIRM, FRESH ⟨∼ lettuce⟩ 4 : being sharp and clear ⟨a ∼ photo⟩ 5 : LIVELY, SPARKLING 6 : FROSTY, SNAPPY; *also* : INVIGORATING — crisp *vb* — crisp·ly *adv* — crisp·ness *n* — crispy *adj*

¹criss·cross \'kris-ˌkrȯs\ *vb* 1 : to mark with crossed lines 2 : to go or pass back and forth

²crisscross *adj* : marked or characterized by crisscrossing — crisscross *adv*

³crisscross *n* : a pattern formed by crossed lines

crit *abbr* critical; criticism

cri·te·ri·on \krī-'tir-ē-ən\ *n, pl* -ria \-ē-ə\ : a standard on which a judgment may be based

crit·ic \'kri-tik\ *n* 1 : a person who judges literary or artistic works 2 : one inclined to find fault

crit·i·cal \'kri-ti-kəl\ *adj* 1 : being or relating to a condition or disease involving danger of death ⟨∼ care⟩ 2 : being a crisis 3 : inclined to criticize 4 : relating to criticism or critics 5 : requiring careful judgment ⟨∼ thinking⟩ — crit·i·cal·ly \-k(ə-)lē\ *adv*

crit·i·cise *Brit var of* CRITICIZE

crit·i·cism \'kri-tə-ˌsi-zəm\ *n* 1 : the act of criticizing; *esp* : CENSURE 2 : a judgment or review 3 : the art of judging works of literature or art

crit·i·cize \'kri-tə-ˌsīz\ *vb* -cized; -ciz·ing 1 : to judge as a critic : EVALUATE 2 : to find fault : express criticism
   ◆ Synonyms BLAME, CENSURE, CONDEMN

cri·tique \krə-'tēk\ *n* : a critical estimate or discussion

crit·ter \'kri-tər\ *n* : CREATURE

croak \'krōk\ *n* : a hoarse harsh cry (as of a frog) — croak *vb*

croak·er \'krō-kər\ *n* 1 : an animal that croaks 2 : a fish that produces croaking or grunting noises

Croat \'krō-ˌat\ *n* : CROATIAN

Cro·atian \krō-'ā-shən\ *n* 1 : a native or inhabitant of Croatia 2 : a Slavic language spoken by Croatians — Croatian *adj*

cro·chet \krō-'shā\ *n* : needlework done with a single thread and hooked needle — crochet *vb*

crock \'kräk\ *n* : a thick earthenware pot or jar

crock·ery \'krä-kə-rē\ *n* : EARTHENWARE

croc·o·dile \'krä-kə-ˌdī(-ə)l\ *n* [ME & L; ME *cocodrille*, fr. AF, fr. ML *cocodrillus*, alter. of L *crocodilus*, fr. Gk *krokodilos* lizard, crocodile, fr. *krokē* shingle, pebble + *drillos* worm] : any of several thick-skinned long-bodied carnivorous reptiles of tropical and subtropical waters

cro·cus \'krō-kəs\ *n, pl* cro·cus·es *also* crocus *or* cro·ci \-ˌkī\ : any of a large genus of low herbs related to the irises and having brightly colored flowers borne singly in early spring

Crohn's disease \'krōnz\ *n* : a chronic inflammatory disease of the gastrointestinal tract and esp. the ileum

crois·sant \krȯ-'sänt, krwä-'säⁿ\ *n, pl* croissants *same or* -'sänts, -'säⁿz\ : a rich crescent-shaped roll

Cro·Ma·gnon \krō-ˈmag-nən, -ˈman-yən\ *n* : a hominid of a tall erect race known from skeletal remains found in southern France and usu. classified as the same species as present-day humans — **Cro–Magnon** *adj*
crone \ˈkrōn\ *n* : HAG
cro·ny \ˈkrō-nē\ *n, pl* **cronies** : a close friend esp. of long standing
¹**crook** \ˈkru̇k\ *vb* : to curve or bend sharply
²**crook** *n* 1 : a bent or curved implement 2 : a bent or curved part; *also* : BEND, CURVE 3 : SWINDLER, THIEF
crook·ed \ˈkru̇k-kəd\ *adj* 1 : having a crook : BENT, CURVED 2 : DISHONEST — **crook·ed·ly** *adv* — **crook·ed·ness** *n*
croon \ˈkrün\ *vb* : to sing or hum in a gentle murmuring voice — **croon·er** *n*
¹**crop** \ˈkräp\ *n* 1 : the handle of a whip; *also* : a short riding whip 2 : a pouch in the throat of many birds and insects where food is received 3 : something (as a plant product) that can be harvested; *also* : the yield at harvest
²**crop** *vb* **cropped; crop·ping** 1 : to remove the tips of : cut off short; *also* : TRIM 2 : to feed on by cropping 3 : to devote (land) to crops 4 : to appear unexpectedly ⟨problems have *cropped* up⟩
crop duster *n* : a person who uses an airplane to spray crops with insecticidal dusts; *also* : an airplane so used
crop·land \-ˌland\ *n* : land devoted to the production of plant crops
crop·per \ˈkrä-pər\ *n* : a raiser of crops; *esp* : SHARECROPPER
cro·quet \krō-ˈkā\ *n* : a game in which mallets are used to drive wooden balls through a series of wickets set out on a lawn
cro·quette \krō-ˈket\ *n* [F] : a small often rounded mass of minced meat, fish, or vegetables fried in deep fat
cro·sier *or* **cro·zier** \ˈkrō-zhər\ *n* : a staff carried by bishops and abbots
¹**cross** \ˈkròs\ *n* 1 : a structure consisting of an upright beam and a crossbar used esp. by the ancient Romans for execution 2 : a figure of the cross on which Christ was crucified used as a Christian symbol 3 : a hybridizing of unlike individuals or strains; *also* : a product of this 4 : a punch delivered with a circular motion over an opponent's lead
²**cross** *vb* 1 : to lie or place across; *also* : INTERSECT 2 : to cancel by marking a cross on or by lining through 3 : THWART, OBSTRUCT 4 : to go or extend across : TRAVERSE 5 : HYBRIDIZE 6 : to meet and pass on the way ⟨our letters ∼*ed* in the mail⟩
³**cross** *adj* 1 : lying across 2 : CONTRARY, OPPOSED 3 : marked by bad temper 4 : HYBRID — **cross·ly** *adv*
cross·bar \ˈkròs-ˌbär\ *n* : a transverse bar or piece
cross·bow \-ˌbō\ *n* : a short bow mounted crosswise at the end of a wooden stock that shoots short arrows
cross·breed \ˈkròs-ˌbrēd, -ˈbrēd\ *vb* **-bred** \-ˈbred\; **-breed·ing** : HYBRIDIZE
cross–coun·try \-ˈkən-trē\ *adj* 1 : extending or moving across a country 2 : proceeding over the countryside (as fields and woods) and not by roads 3 : of or relating to racing or skiing over the countryside instead of over a track or run — **cross–country** *adv*
cross–cur·rent \-ˈkər-ənt\ *n* 1 : a current running counter to another 2 : a conflicting tendency — usu. used in pl.
¹**cross–cut** \-ˌkət\ *vb* : to cut or saw crosswise esp. of the grain of wood
²**crosscut** *adj* 1 : made or used for crosscutting ⟨a ∼ saw⟩ 2 : cut across the grain
³**crosscut** *n* : something that cuts through transversely
cross–ex·am·ine \ˌkròs-sig-ˈza-mən\ *vb* : to examine with questions to check the answers to previous questions — **cross–ex·am·i·na·tion** \-ˌza-mə-ˈnā-shən\ *n* — **cross–ex·am·in·er** *n*
cross–eyed \ˈkròs-ˌsīd\ *adj* : having one or both eyes turned inward toward the nose
cross–fer·til·i·za·tion \-ˌfər-tə-lə-ˈzā-shən\ *n* 1 : fertilization between sex cells produced by separate individuals or sometimes by individuals of different kinds; *also* : CROSS-POLLINATION 2 : a broadening or productive interchange (as between cultures) — **cross–fer·til·ize** \-ˈfərt-lə-ˌīz\ *vb*
cross fire *n* 1 : crossing lines of fire in combat 2 : rapid or angry interchange

cross·hair \ˈkròs-ˌher\ *n* : a fine wire or thread in the eyepiece of an optical instrument used as a reference line
cross·hatch \ˈkròs-ˌhach\ *vb* : to mark with two series of parallel lines that intersect — **cross–hatch·ing** *n*
cross·ing \ˈkrò-siŋ\ *n* 1 : a place or structure for crossing something (as a river) 2 : a point of intersection (as of a street and a railroad track)
cross·over \ˈkròs-ˌō-vər\ *n* 1 : CROSSING 2 : a member of a political party who votes in the primary of the other party 3 : a broadening of the popular appeal of an artist (as a musician) by a change in the artist's style, genre, or medium 4 : an instance of breaking into another category
cross over *vb* : to achieve broader popularity by a change of medium or style
cross·piece \ˈkròs-ˌpēs\ *n* : a horizontal member
cross–pol·li·na·tion \ˌkròs-ˌpä-lə-ˈnā-shən\ *n* : transfer of pollen from one flower to the stigma of another — **cross–pol·li·nate** \ˈkròs-ˈpä-lə-ˌnāt\ *vb*
cross–pur·pose \ˈkròs-ˈpər-pəs\ *n* : a purpose contrary to another purpose ⟨working at ∼*s*⟩
cross–ques·tion \-ˈkwes-chən\ *vb* : CROSS-EXAMINE — **cross–question** *n*
cross–re·fer \ˌkròs-ri-ˈfər\ *vb* : to refer by a notation or direction from one place to another (as in a book or list) — **cross–ref·er·ence** \ˈkròs-ˈre-frəns\ *n*
cross·road \ˈkròs-ˌrōd\ *n* 1 : a road that crosses a main road or runs between main roads 2 : a place where roads meet — usu. used in pl. 3 : a crucial point where a decision must be made — usu. used in pl.
cross section *n* 1 : a section cut across something; *also* : a representation made by or as if by such cutting 2 : a number of persons or things selected from a group that show the general nature of the whole group — **cross–sec·tion·al** *adj*
cross·walk \ˈkròs-ˌwòk\ *n* : a marked path for pedestrians crossing a street
cross·ways \-ˌwāz\ *adv* : CROSSWISE
cross·wind \-ˌwind\ *n* : a wind not parallel to a course (as of an airplane)
cross·wise \-ˌwīz\ *adv* : so as to cross something : ACROSS — **crosswise** *adj*
cross·word \ˈkròs-ˌwərd\ *n* : a puzzle in which words are put into a pattern of numbered squares in answer to clues
cros·ti·ni \krò-ˈstē-nē\ *n pl* : small slices of toasted bread served with a topping
crotch \ˈkräch\ *n* : an angle or area formed by the parting of two legs, branches, or members
crotch·et \ˈkrä-chət\ *n* : an odd notion : WHIM — **crotch·ety** *adj*
crouch \ˈkrau̇ch\ *vb* 1 : to stoop or bend low 2 : CRINGE, COWER — **crouch** *n*
croup \ˈkrüp\ *n* : laryngitis esp. of infants marked by a hoarse ringing cough and difficult breathing — **croupy** *adj*
crou·pi·er \ˈkrü-pē-ər, -pē-ˌā\ *n* [F, lit., rider on the rump of a horse, fr. *croupe* rump] : an employee of a gambling casino who collects and pays bets at a gaming table
crou·ton \ˈkrü-ˌtän\ *n* [F *croûton*, dim. of *croûte* crust] : a small cube of bread toasted or fried crisp
¹**crow** \ˈkrō\ *n* 1 : any of various large glossy black birds related to the jays 2 *cap* : a member of an American Indian people of a region in Montana and Wyoming; *also* : the language of the Crow people
²**crow** *vb* 1 : to make the loud shrill sound characteristic of the cock 2 : to utter a sound expressive of pleasure 3 : EXULT, GLOAT; *also* : BRAG, BOAST
³**crow** *n* : the cry of the cock
crow·bar \ˈkrō-ˌbär\ *n* : a metal bar usu. wedge-shaped at the end for use as a pry or lever
¹**crowd** \ˈkrau̇d\ *vb* 1 : to press close 2 : to collect in numbers : THRONG 3 : CRAM, STUFF ⟨a box ∼*ed* with toys⟩
²**crowd** *n* : a large number of people gathered together at random : THRONG
¹**crown** \ˈkrau̇n\ *n* 1 : a mark of victory or honor; *esp* : the title of a champion in a sport 2 : a royal headdress 3 : the top of the head; *also* : the part of a hat that covers the top of the head 4 : the highest part (as of a tree or tooth) 5 *often cap* : sovereign power; *also* : MONARCH 6 : a formerly used British silver coin — **crowned** \ˈkrau̇nd\ *adj*

²**crown** *vb* **1 :** to place a crown on **2 :** HONOR **3 :** TOP, SURMOUNT **4 :** to fit (a tooth) with an artificial crown

crown vetch *n* **:** a Eurasian leguminous herb with umbels of pink-and-white flowers and sharp-angled pods

crow's-foot \'krōz-ₐfut\ *n, pl* **crow's-feet** \-ₐfēt\ **:** any of the wrinkles around the outer corners of the eyes — usu. used in pl.

crow's nest *n* **:** a partly enclosed platform high on a ship's mast for use as a lookout

crozier *var of* CROSIER

¹**CRT** \ₐsē-(ₐ)är-'tē\ *n, pl* **CRTs** *or* **CRT's :** CATHODE-RAY TUBE; *also* **:** a display device incorporating a cathode-ray tube

²**CRT** *abbr* carrier route

cru·cial \'krü-shəl\ *adj* **:** DECISIVE ⟨a ∼ step⟩; *also* **:** IMPORTANT, SIGNIFICANT ⟨a ∼ question⟩

cru·ci·ate \'krü-shē-ₐāt\ *adj* **:** CRUCIFORM

cru·ci·ble \'krü-sə-bəl\ *n* **:** a heat-resistant container in which material can be subjected to great heat

cru·ci·fix \'krü-sə-ₐfiks\ *n* **:** a representation of Christ on the cross

cru·ci·fix·ion \ₐkrü-sə-'fik-shən\ *n* **1** *cap* **:** the crucifying of Christ **2 :** the act of crucifying

cru·ci·form \'krü-sə-ₐfòrm\ *adj* **:** shaped like a cross

cru·ci·fy \'krü-sə-ₐfī\ *vb* **-fied; -fy·ing 1 :** to put to death by nailing or binding the hands and feet to a cross **2 :** MORTIFY **1 :** TORTURE, PERSECUTE

¹**crude** \'krüd\ *adj* **crud·er; crud·est 1 :** not refined **:** RAW ⟨∼ oil⟩ ⟨∼ statistics⟩ **2 :** lacking grace, taste, tact, or polish **:** RUDE — **crude·ly** *adv* — **crude·ness** *n* — **cru·di·ty** \'krü-də-tē\ *n*

²**crude** *n* **:** unrefined petroleum

cru·el \'krü-əl\ *adj* **cru·el·er** *or* **cru·el·ler; cru·el·est** *or* **cru·el·lest** [ME, fr. AF, fr. L *crudelis*, fr. *crudus* crude] **:** causing pain and suffering to others **:** MERCILESS — **cru·el·ly** *adv* — **cru·el·ty** \-tē\ *n*

cru·et \'krü-ət\ *n* **:** a small usu. glass bottle for vinegar, oil, or sauce

cruise \'krüz\ *vb* **cruised; cruis·ing** [D *kruisen* to make a cross, cruise] **1 :** to sail about touching at a series of ports **2 :** to travel for pleasure **3 :** to travel about the streets at random **4 :** to travel at the most efficient operating speed ⟨the plane's *cruising* speed⟩ **5 :** SURF 2 — **cruise** *n*

cruis·er \'krü-zər\ *n* **1 :** SQUAD CAR **2 :** a large fast moderately armored and gunned warship **3 :** a motorboat equipped for living aboard

cruis·er·weight \-ₐwāt\ *n* **:** a boxer weighing no more than 190 pounds

crul·ler \'krə-lər\ *n* **1 :** a small sweet cake in the form of a twisted strip fried in deep fat **2** *Northern & Midland* **:** an unraised doughnut

¹**crumb** \'krəm\ *n* **:** a small fragment

²**crumb** *vb* **1 :** to break into crumbs **2 :** to cover with crumbs

crum·ble \'krəm-bəl\ *vb* **crum·bled; crum·bling :** to break into small pieces **:** DISINTEGRATE — **crum·bly** *adj*

crum·my *also* **crumby** \'krə-mē\ *adj* **crum·mi·er** *also* **crumb·i·er; -est :** very poor or inferior **:** LOUSY

crum·pet \'krəm-pət\ *n* **:** a small round unsweetened bread cooked on a griddle

crum·ple \'krəm-pəl\ *vb* **crum·pled; crum·pling 1 :** to crush together **:** RUMPLE **2 :** COLLAPSE

¹**crunch** \'krənch\ *vb* **1 :** to chew with a grinding noise; *also* **:** to grind or press with a crushing noise

²**crunch** *n* **1 :** an act of or a sound made by crunching **2 :** a tight or critical situation — **crunchy** *adj*

cru·sade \krü-'sād\ *n* **1** *cap* **:** any of the expeditions in the 11th, 12th, and 13th centuries undertaken by Christian countries to take the Holy Land from the Muslims **2 :** a reforming enterprise undertaken with zeal — **cru·sade** *vb* — **cru·sad·er** *n*

cruse \'krüz, 'krüs\ *n* **:** a jar for water or oil

¹**crush** \'krəsh\ *vb* **1 :** to squeeze out of shape **2 :** HUG, EMBRACE **3 :** to grind or pound to small bits **4 :** OVERWHELM, SUPPRESS

²**crush** *n* **1 :** an act of crushing **2 :** a violent crowding **3 :** INFATUATION

crust \'krəst\ *n* **1 :** the outside part of bread; *also* **:** a piece of old dry bread **2 :** the cover of a pie **3 :** a hard or brittle surface layer — **crust·al** *adj*

crus·ta·cean \ₐkrəs-'tā-shən\ *n* **:** any of a large class of

mostly aquatic arthropods (as lobsters or crabs) having a firm crustlike shell — **crustacean** *adj*

crusty \'krəs-tē\ *adj* **crust·i·er; -est 1 :** having or being a crust **2 :** CROSS, GRUMPY

crutch \'krəch\ *n* **:** a supporting device; *esp* **:** a support fitting under the armpit for use by the disabled in walking

crux \'krəks, 'krùks\ *n, pl* **crux·es** [L, cross, torture] **1 :** a puzzling or difficult problem **2 :** a crucial point

¹**cry** \'krī\ *vb* **cried; cry·ing 1 :** to call out **:** SHOUT **2 :** to proclaim publicly **:** ADVERTISE **3 :** WEEP

²**cry** *n, pl* **cries 1 :** a loud outcry **2 :** APPEAL, ENTREATY **3 :** a fit of weeping **4 :** the characteristic sound uttered by an animal **5 :** DISTANCE — usu. used in the phrase *a far cry*

cry·ba·by \'krī-ₐbā-bē\ *n* **:** one who cries easily or often

cryo·gen·ic \ₐkrī-ə-'je-nik\ *adj* **:** of or relating to the production of very low temperatures; *also* **:** involving the use of a very low temperature — **cryo·gen·i·cal·ly** \-ni-k(ə-)lē\ *adv*

cryo·gen·ics \-niks\ *n* **:** a branch of physics that relates to the production and effects of very low temperatures

cryo·lite \'krī-ə-ₐlīt\ *n* **:** a usu. white mineral formerly used in making aluminum

crypt \'kript\ *n* **:** a chamber wholly or partly underground

cryp·tic \'krip-tik\ *adj* **:** meant to be puzzling or mysterious ⟨∼ messages⟩

cryp·to·gram \'krip-tə-ₐgram\ *n* **:** a communication in cipher or code

cryp·tog·ra·phy \krip-'tä-grə-fē\ *n* **:** the coding and decoding of secret messages — **cryp·tog·ra·pher** \-fər\ *n*

cryp·to·sys·tem \ₐkrip-tō-'sis-təm\ *n* **:** a method for coding and decoding messages

crys·tal \'kris-tᵊl\ *n* [ME *cristal*, fr. AF, fr. L *crystallum*, fr. Gk *krystallos* ice, crystal] **1 :** transparent quartz **2 :** something resembling crystal (as in transparency); *esp* **:** a clear colorless glass of superior quality **3 :** a body that is formed by solidification of a substance and has a regular repeating arrangement of atoms and often of external plane faces ⟨a salt ∼⟩ **4 :** the transparent cover of a watch dial

crystal 3: snowflake crystals

crystal clear *adj* **:** perfectly or transparently clear

crys·tal·line \'kris-tə-lən\ *adj* **1 :** made of or resembling crystal **2 :** very clear or sparkling

crys·tal·lise *Brit var of* CRYSTALLIZE

crys·tal·lize \'kris-tə-ₐlīz\ *vb* **-lized; -liz·ing 1 :** to assume or cause to assume a crystalline form **2 :** to take or cause to take a definite form ⟨publicity can ∼ public opinion⟩ — **crys·tal·li·za·tion** \ₐkris-tə-lə-'zā-shən\ *n*

crys·tal·log·ra·phy \ₐkris-tə-'lä-grə-fē\ *n* **:** the science dealing with the forms and structures of crystals — **crys·tal·log·ra·pher** *n*

cs *abbr* case; cases

Cs *symbol* cesium

CS *abbr* **1** civil service **2** county seat

CSA *abbr* Confederate States of America

C–section \'sē-ₐsek-shən\ *n* **:** CESAREAN SECTION

CSM *abbr* command sergeant major

CST *abbr* central standard time

ct *abbr* **1** carat **2** cent **3** count **4** county **5** court

CT *abbr* **1** central time **2** Connecticut

ctn *abbr* carton

ctr *abbr* **1** center **2** counter

CT scan \ₐsē-'tē-\ *n* **:** CAT SCAN

cu *abbr* cubic

Cu *symbol* [L *cuprum*] copper

cub \'kəb\ *n* **:** a young individual of some animals (as a fox, bear, or lion)

Cu·ban sandwich \'kyü-bən-\ *n* **:** a usu. grilled and pressed sandwich served on a long split roll

cub·by·hole \'kə-bē-ₐhōl\ *n* **:** a snug place (as for storing things)

¹**cube** \'kyüb\ *n* **1 :** a solid having 6 equal square sides **2**

: the result of raising a number to the third power ⟨the ~ of 3 is 27⟩

²**cube** *vb* **cubed; cub·ing 1** : to raise to the third power **2** : to form into a cube **3** : to cut into cubes

cube root *n* : a number whose cube is a given number

cu·bic \'kyü-bik\ *also* **cu·bi·cal** *adj* **1** : having the form of a cube **2** : being the volume of a cube whose edge is a specified unit **3** : having length, width, and height

cu·bi·cle \'kyü-bi-kəl\ *n* : a small separate space (as for sleeping, studying, or working)

cubic measure *n* : a unit (as cubic inch) for measuring volume — see METRIC SYSTEM table, WEIGHT table

cubic zir·co·nia \-,zər-'kō-nē-ə\ *also* **cubic zirconium** *n* : a synthetic gemstone resembling a diamond made from an oxide of zirconium

cub·ism \'kyü-,bi-zəm\ *n* : a style of art characterized by the abstraction of natural forms into fragmented geometric shapes — **cub·ist** \-bist\ *n or adj*

cu·bit \'kyü-bət\ *n* : an ancient unit of length equal to about 18 inches (46 centimeters)

Cub Scout *n* : a member of the program of the Boy Scouts for boys in the first through fifth grades in school

cuck·old \'kə-kəld, 'kú-\ *n* : a man whose wife is unfaithful — **cuckold** *vb*

¹**cuck·oo** \'kü-kü, 'kú-\ *n, pl* **cuckoos** : a largely grayish brown European bird that lays its eggs in the nests of other birds for them to hatch

²**cuckoo** *adj* : SILLY, FOOLISH

cu·cum·ber \'kyü-(,)kəm-bər\ *n* : the long fleshy many‑seeded fruit of a vine of the gourd family that is grown as a garden vegetable; *also* : this vine

cud \'kəd\ *n* : food brought up into the mouth by some animals (as cows) from the rumen to be chewed again

cud·dle \'kə-d°l\ *vb* **cud·dled; cud·dling** : to lie close : SNUGGLE

cud·gel \'kə-jəl\ *n* : a short heavy club — **cudgel** *vb*

¹**cue** \'kyü\ *n* **1** : a word, phrase, or action in a play serving as a signal for the next actor to speak or act **2** : HINT — **cue** *vb*

²**cue** *n* : a tapered rod for striking the balls in billiards or pool

cue ball *n* : the ball a player strikes with a cue in billiards or pool

¹**cuff** \'kəf\ *n* **1** : a part (as of a sleeve or glove) encircling the wrist **2** : the folded hem of a trouser leg

²**cuff** *vb* : to strike esp. with the open hand : SLAP

³**cuff** *n* : a blow with the hand esp. when open

cui·sine \kwi-'zēn\ *n* : style of cooking; *also* : the food prepared

cuke \'kyük\ *n* : CUCUMBER

cul–de–sac \,kəl-di-'sak, ,kúl-\ *n, pl* **culs–de–sac** *same or* ,kəlz-, ,kúlz-\ *also* **cul–de–sacs** \,kəl-də-'saks, ,kúl-\ [F, lit., bottom of the bag] : a street or passage closed at one end

cu·li·nary \'kə-lə-,ner-ē, 'kyü-\ *adj* : of or relating to the kitchen or cookery

¹**cull** \'kəl\ *vb* : to pick out from a group

²**cull** *n* : something rejected from a group or lot as worthless or inferior

cul·mi·nate \'kəl-mə-,nāt\ *vb* **-nat·ed; -nat·ing** : to reach the highest point — **cul·mi·na·tion** \,kəl-mə-'nā-shən\ *n*

cu·lotte \'kü-,lät, ,kyü-, kü-,lät, kyü-\ *n* [F, breeches, fr. dim. of *cul* backside] : a divided skirt; *also* : a garment having a divided skirt — often used in pl.

cul·pa·ble \'kəl-pə-bəl\ *adj* : deserving blame — **cul·pa·bil·i·ty** \,kəl-pə-'bi-lə-tē\ *n*

cul·prit \'kəl-prət\ *n* [AF *cul.* (abbr. of *culpable* guilty) + *prest, prit* ready (i.e., to prove it), fr. L *praestus*] : one accused or guilty of a crime

cult \'kəlt\ *n* **1** : formal religious veneration **2** : a religious system; *also* : its adherents **3** : faddish devotion; *also* : a group of persons showing such devotion — **cult·ish** \'kəl-tish\ *adj* — **cult·ist** \-tist\ *n*

cul·ti·va·ble \'kəl-tə-və-bəl\ *adj* : capable of being cultivated

cul·ti·var \'kəl-tə-,vär, -ver\ *n* : a plant variety originating and persisting under cultivation

cul·ti·vate \'kəl-tə-,vāt\ *vb* **-vat·ed; -vat·ing 1** : to prepare for the raising of crops **2** : to foster the growth of by tilling or by labor and care ⟨~ vegetables⟩ **3** : REFINE, IMPROVE ⟨~ the mind⟩ **4** : ENCOURAGE, FURTHER ⟨~

the arts⟩ **5** : to seek the friendship of — **cul·ti·va·tion** \,kəl-tə-'vā-shən\ *n* — **cul·ti·va·tor** \'kəl-tə-,vā-tər\ *n*

cul·ture \'kəl-chər\ *n* **1** : TILLAGE, CULTIVATION **2** : the act of developing by education and training **3** : refinement of intellectual and artistic taste **4** : the customary beliefs, social forms, and material traits of a racial, religious, or social group — **cul·tur·al** \'kəl-chə-rəl\ *adj* — **cul·tur·al·ly** *adv* — **cul·tured** \-chərd\ *adj*

cul·vert \'kəl-vərt\ *n* : a drain crossing under a road or railroad

cum *abbr* cumulative

cum·ber \'kəm-bər\ *vb* : to weigh down : BURDEN, HINDER

cum·ber·some \'kəm-bər-səm\ *adj* : hard to handle or manage because of size or weight — **cum·ber·some·ly** *adv*

cum·brous \'kəm-brəs\ *adj* : CUMBERSOME — **cum·brous·ly** *adv* — **cum·brous·ness** *n*

cum·in \'kə-mən, 'kyü-\ *n* : the seedlike fruit of a small annual herb related to the carrot that is used as a spice; *also* : this herb

cum·mer·bund \'kə-mər-,bənd, 'kəm-bər-\ *n* [Hindi & Urdu *kamarband*, fr. Pers. fr. *kamar* waist + *band* band] : a broad sash worn as a waistband

cu·mu·la·tive \'kyü-myə-lə-tiv, -,lā-\ *adj* : increasing in force or value by successive additions

cu·mu·lo·nim·bus \,kyü-myə-lō-'nim-bəs\ *n* : an anvil‑shaped cumulus cloud extending to great heights

cu·mu·lus \'kyü-myə-ləs\ *n, pl* **-li** \-,lī, -,lē\ : a dense puffy cloud having a flat base and rounded outlines

cu·ne·i·form \kyü-'nē-ə-,fȯrm\ *adj* **1** : wedge-shaped **2** : composed of wedge-shaped characters

cun·ni·lin·gus \,kə-ni-'liŋ-gəs\ *also* **cun·ni·linc·tus** \-'liŋk-təs\ *n* : oral stimulation of the vulva or clitoris

¹**cun·ning** \'kə-niŋ\ *adj* **1** : SKILLFUL, DEXTEROUS **2** : marked by wiliness and trickery ⟨~ schemes⟩ **3** : CUTE ⟨a ~ kitten⟩ — **cun·ning·ly** *adv*

²**cunning** *n* **1** : SKILL **2** : SLYNESS

¹**cup** \'kəp\ *n* **1** : a small bowl-shaped drinking vessel **2** : the contents of a cup **3** : the consecrated wine of the Communion **4** : something resembling a cup : a small bowl or hollow **5** : a half pint — **cup·ful** *n* — **cup·like** \-,līk\ *adj*

²**cup** *vb* **cupped; cup·ping** : to curve into the shape of a cup

cup·board \'kə-bərd\ *n* : a small closet with shelves for food or dishes

cup·cake \'kəp-,kāk\ *n* : a small cake baked in a cuplike mold

cu·pid \'kyü-pəd\ *n* : a winged naked figure of an infant often with a bow and arrow that represents the god Cupid

cu·pid·i·ty \kyü-'pi-də-tē\ *n, pl* **-ties** : excessive desire for money

cu·po·la \'kyü-pə-lə, -,lō\ *n* : a small structure on top of a roof or building

¹**cur** \'kər\ *n* : a mongrel dog

²**cur** *abbr* **1** currency **2** current

cu·rate \'kyùr-ət\ *n* **1** : a member of the clergy who is in charge of a parish **2** : a member of the clergy who assists a rector or vicar — **cu·ra·cy** \-ə-sē\ *n*

cu·ra·tive \-ə-tiv\ *adj* : relating to or used in the cure of diseases ⟨~ therapy⟩ ⟨~ powers⟩ — **curative** *n*

cu·ra·tor \'kyùr-,ā-tər, kyù-'rā-\ *n* : CUSTODIAN; *esp* : one in charge of a place of exhibit (as a museum or zoo)

¹**curb** \'kərb\ *n* **1** : a bit that exerts pressure on a horse's jaws **2** : CHECK, RESTRAINT **3** : a raised edging (as of stone or concrete) along a paved street

²**curb** *vb* : to hold in or back : RESTRAIN

curb·ing \'kər-biŋ\ *n* **1** : the material for a curb **2** : CURB

curd \'kərd\ *n* : the thick protein-rich part of coagulated milk

cur·dle \'kər-d°l\ *vb* **cur·dled; cur·dling** : to form curds; *also* : SPOIL, SOUR

¹**cure** \'kyùr\ *n* **1** : spiritual care **2** : recovery or relief from disease **3** : a curative agent : REMEDY **4** : a course or period of treatment

²**cure** *vb* **cured; cur·ing 1** : to restore to health : HEAL, REMEDY; *also* : to become cured **2** : to process for storage or use ⟨~ bacon⟩ — **cur·able** *adj*

cu·ré \kyù-'rā\ *n* [F] : a parish priest

cure–all \'kyùr-,ȯl\ *n* : a remedy for all ills : PANACEA

cu·ret·tage \,kyùr-ə-'tàzh\ *n* : a surgical scraping or cleaning of a body part (as the uterus)

cur·few \'kər-,fyü\ *n* [ME, fr. AF *covrefeu*, signal given to bank the hearth fire, curfew, fr. *coverir* to cover + *fu, feu* fire, fr. L *focus* hearth] : a regulation that specified persons (as children) be off the streets at a set hour of the evening; *also* : the sounding of a signal (as a bell) at this hour

cu·ria \'kyür-ē-ə, 'kür-\ *n, pl* **cu·ri·ae** \'kyür-ē-ˌē, 'kür-ē-ˌī\ *often cap* : the body of congregations, tribunals, and offices through which the pope governs the Roman Catholic Church

cu·rie \'kyür-ē\ *n* : a unit of radioactivity equal to 37 billion disintegrations per second

cu·rio \'kyür-ē-ˌō\ *n, pl* **cu·ri·os** : an object or article valued because it is strange or rare

cu·ri·ous \'kyür-ē-əs\ *adj* 1 : having a desire to investigate and learn 2 : STRANGE, UNUSUAL, ODD ⟨a ~ coincidence⟩ — **cu·ri·os·i·ty** \ˌkyür-ē-'ä-sə-tē\ *n* — **cu·ri·ous·ness**

cu·ri·ous·ly *adv* 1 : in a curious manner 2 : as is curious

cu·ri·um \'kyür-ē-əm\ *n* : a metallic radioactive element produced artificially

¹**curl** \'kərl\ *vb* 1 : to form into ringlets 2 : CURVE, COIL — **curl·er** *n*

²**curl** *n* 1 : a lock of hair that coils : RINGLET 2 : something having a spiral or twisted form — **curly** *adj*

cur·lew \'kər-lü, 'kərl-yü\ *n, pl* **curlews** or **curlew** : any of various long-legged brownish birds that have a down= curved bill and are related to the sandpipers and snipes

curli·cue \'kər-li-ˌkyü\ *n* : a fancifully curved or spiral figure

cur·rant \'kər-ənt\ *n* 1 : a small seedless raisin 2 : the acid berry of various shrubs related to the gooseberry; *also* : this plant

cur·ren·cy \'kər-ən-sē\ *n, pl* **-cies** 1 : general use or acceptance 2 : something that is in circulation as a medium of exchange : MONEY

¹**cur·rent** \'kər-ənt\ *adj* 1 : occurring in or belonging to the present ⟨the ~ crisis⟩ 2 : used as a medium of exchange 3 : generally accepted or practiced

²**current** *n* 1 : the part of a body of fluid moving continuously in a certain direction; *also* : the swiftest part of a stream 2 : a flow of electric charge; *also* : the rate of such flow

cur·ric·u·lum \kə-'ri-kyə-ləm\ *n, pl* **-la** \-lə\ *also* **-lums** [L, running, course, fr. *currere* to run] : the courses offered by an educational institution

¹**cur·ry** \'kər-ē\ *vb* **cur·ried; cur·ry·ing** 1 : to clean the coat of (a horse) with a currycomb 2 : to treat (tanned leather) esp. by incorporating oil or grease — **curry favor** : to seek to gain favor by flattery or attention

²**cur·ry** *n, pl* **cur·ries** : a powder of pungent spices used in cooking; *also* : a food seasoned with curry

cur·ry·comb \-ˌkōm\ *n* : a comb used esp. to curry horses — **currycomb** *vb*

¹**curse** \'kərs\ *n* 1 : a prayer for harm to come upon one 2 : something that is cursed 3 : evil or misfortune coming as if in response to a curse

²**curse** *vb* **cursed; curs·ing** 1 : to call on divine power to send injury upon 2 : BLASPHEME 3 : AFFLICT ♦ *Synonyms* EXECRATE, DAMN, ANATHEMATIZE, OBJURGATE

cur·sive \'kər-siv\ *adj* : written with the strokes of the letters joined together and the angles rounded

cur·sor \'kər-sər\ *n* : a visual cue (as a pointer) on a computer screen that indicates position (as for data entry)

cur·so·ry \'kər-sə-rē\ *adj* : rapidly and often superficially done : HASTY ⟨a ~ reading of the report⟩ — **cur·so·ri·ly** \-rə-lē\ *adv*

curt \'kərt\ *adj* : rudely short or abrupt — **curt·ly** *adv* — **curt·ness** *n*

cur·tail \(ˌ)kər-'tāl\ *vb* : to cut off the end of : SHORTEN — **cur·tail·ment** *n*

cur·tain \'kər-tᵊn\ *n* 1 : a hanging screen that can be drawn back esp. at a window 2 : the screen between the stage and auditorium of a theater — **curtain** *vb*

curt·sy *also* **curt·sey** \'kərt-sē\ *n, pl* **curtsies** or **curtseys** : a courteous bow made by women chiefly by bending the knees — **curtsy** *also* **curtsey** *vb*

cur·va·ceous *also* **cur·va·cious** \ˌkər-'vā-shəs\ *adj* : having curves suggestive of a well-proportioned feminine figure

cur·va·ture \'kər-və-ˌchür\ *n* : a measure or amount of curving : BEND

¹**curve** \'kərv\ *vb* **curved; curv·ing** : to bend from a straight line or course

²**curve** *n* 1 : a line esp. when curved 2 : something that

bends or curves without angles ⟨a ~ in the road⟩ 3 : a baseball pitch thrown so that it swerves esp. downward and to one side

cur·vet \(ˌ)kər-'vet\ *n* : a prancing leap of a horse — **curvet** *vb*

¹**cush·ion** \'kü-shən\ *n* [ME *cusshin*, fr. AF *cussin, quissin*, fr. VL **coxinus*, fr. L *coxa* hip] 1 : a soft pillow or pad to rest on or against 2 : the springy pad inside the rim of a billiard table 3 : something soft that prevents discomfort or protects against injury

²**cushion** *vb* 1 : to provide (as a seat) with a cushion 2 : to soften or lessen the force or shock of

cusp \'kəsp\ *n* : a pointed end or part (as of a tooth)

cus·pid \'kəs-pəd\ *n* : a canine tooth

cus·pi·dor \'kəs-pə-ˌdȯr\ *n* : SPITTOON

cus·tard \'kəs-tərd\ *n* : a sweetened cooked mixture of milk and eggs

cus·to·di·al \ˌkəs-'tō-dē-əl\ *adj* : marked by watching and protecting rather than seeking to cure ⟨~ care⟩

cus·to·di·an \ˌkəs-'tō-dē-ən\ *n* : one who has custody (as of a building)

cus·to·dy \'kəs-tə-dē\ *n, pl* **-dies** : immediate charge and control

¹**cus·tom** \'kəs-təm\ *n* 1 : habitual course of action : recognized usage 2 *pl* : taxes levied on imports 3 : business patronage

²**custom** *adj* 1 : made to personal order 2 : doing work only on order

cus·tom·ary \'kəs-tə-ˌmer-ē\ *adj* 1 : based on or established by custom 2 : commonly practiced or observed : HABITUAL — **cus·tom·ar·i·ly** *adv*

cus·tom–built \'kəs-təm-'bilt\ *adj* : built to individual order

cus·tom·er \'kəs-tə-mər\ *n* : BUYER, PURCHASER; *esp* : a regular or frequent buyer

cus·tom·house \'kəs-təm-ˌhaüs\ *n* : the building where customs are paid

cus·tom·ise *Brit var of* CUSTOMIZE

cus·tom·ize \'kəs-tə-ˌmīz\ *vb* **-ized; -iz·ing** : to build, fit, or alter according to individual specifications

cus·tom–made \'kəs-təm-'mād\ *adj* : made to individual order

¹**cut** \'kət\ *vb* **cut; cut·ting** 1 : to penetrate or divide with a sharp edge : CLEAVE, GASH; *also* : to experience the growth of (a tooth) through the gum 2 : to hurt the feelings of 3 : to strike sharply 4 : SHORTEN, REDUCE 5 : to remove by severing or paring 6 : INTERSECT, CROSS 7 : to divide into parts 8 : to go quickly or change direction abruptly 9 : to cause to stop 10 : to remove (text, etc.) from a computer document for pasting elsewhere

²**cut** *n* 1 : something made by cutting : GASH, CLEFT 2 : SHARE 3 : a segment or section of a meat carcass 4 : an excavated channel or roadway 5 : BAND 4 6 : a sharp stroke or blow 7 : REDUCTION ⟨a ~ in wages⟩ 8 : the shape or manner in which a thing is cut

cut–and–dried \ˌkət-ᵊn-'drīd\ *also* **cut–and–dry** \-'drī\ *adj* : according to a plan, set procedure, or formula

cu·ta·ne·ous \kyü-'tā-nē-əs\ *adj* : of, relating to, or affecting the skin

cut·back \'kət-ˌbak\ *n* 1 : something cut back 2 : REDUCTION

cute \'kyüt\ *adj* **cut·er; cut·est** [short for *acute*] 1 : CLEVER, SHREWD 2 : daintily attractive : PRETTY

cu·ti·cle \'kyü-ti-kəl\ *n* 1 : an outer layer (as of skin or a leaf) 2 : dead or horny epidermis esp. around a fingernail — **cu·tic·u·lar** \kyü-'ti-kyə-lər\ *adj*

cut in *vb* 1 : to thrust oneself between others 2 : to interrupt a dancing couple and take one as one's partner

cut·lass \'kət-ləs\ *n* : a short heavy curved sword

cut·ler \'kət-lər\ *n* [ME, fr. AF *cuteler*, fr. LL *cultellarius*, fr. L *cultellus* knife] : one who makes, deals in, or repairs cutlery

cut·lery \'kət-lə-rē\ *n* : edged or cutting tools; *esp* : implements for cutting and eating food

cut·let \'kət-lət\ *n* : a slice of meat (as veal) for broiling or frying

cut·off \'kət-ˌȯf\ *n* 1 : the channel formed when a stream cuts through the neck of an oxbow; *also* : SHORTCUT 2 : a device for cutting off 3 *pl* : shorts orig. made from jeans with the legs cut off at the knees or higher

cut·out \'kət-ˌaüt\ *n* : something cut out or prepared for cutting out from something else

cut out *vb* 1 : to determine or assign through necessity

⟨had her work *cut out* for her⟩ **2 :** DISCONNECT **3 :** to cease operating ⟨the engine *cut out*⟩ **4 :** ELIMINATE ⟨*cut out* unnecessary expense⟩
cut–rate \'kət-'rāt\ *adj* **:** relating to or dealing in goods sold at reduced rates
cut·ter \'kə-tər\ *n* **1 :** a tool or a machine for cutting **2 :** a ship's boat for carrying stores and passengers **3 :** a small armed vessel in government service **4 :** a light sleigh
¹cut·throat \'kət-,thrōt\ *n* **:** MURDERER
²cutthroat *adj* **1 :** MURDEROUS, CRUEL **2 :** RUTHLESS ⟨~ competition⟩
cutthroat trout *n* **:** a large American trout with a red mark under the jaw
¹cut·ting \'kə-tiŋ\ *n* **:** a piece of a plant able to grow into a new plant
²cutting *adj* **1 :** SHARP, EDGED **2 :** marked by piercing cold **3 :** likely to hurt the feelings **:** SARCASTIC ⟨a ~ remark⟩
cut·tle·fish \'kə-t³l-,fish\ *n* **:** any of various marine mollusks having eight arms and two usu. longer tentacles and an internal shell (**cut·tle·bone** \-,bōn\) composed of calcium compounds
cut·up \'kət-,əp\ *n* **:** a person who clowns or acts boisterously — **cut up** *vb*
cut·worm \-,wərm\ *n* **:** any of various smooth-bodied moth larvae that feed on plants at night
cw *abbr* clockwise
CWO *abbr* **1** cash with order **2** chief warrant officer
cwt *abbr* hundredweight
-cy \sē\ *n suffix* **1 :** action **:** practice ⟨mendicancy⟩ **2 :** rank **:** office ⟨chaplaincy⟩ **3 :** body **:** class ⟨constituency⟩ **4 :** state **:** quality ⟨accuracy⟩
cy·an \'sī-,an, -ən\ *n* **:** a greenish blue color
cy·a·nide \'sī-ə-,nīd, -nəd\ *n* **:** a poisonous compound of carbon and nitrogen with another element (as potassium)
cy·ber \'sī-bər\ *adj* **:** of, relating to, or involving computers or computer networks
cyber- *comb form* **:** computer **:** computer network
cy·ber·at·tack \'sī-bər-ə-,tak\ *n* **:** an attempt to gain illegal access to a computer or computer system for the purpose of causing damage or harm
cy·ber·bul·ly·ing \'sī-bər-,bù-lē-iŋ, -,bə-\ *n* **:** the electronic posting of mean-spirited messages about a person
cy·ber·ca·fe \'sī-bər-ka-'fā\ *n* **:** a small restaurant offering use of computers with Internet access
cy·ber·net·ics \,sī-bər-'ne-tiks\ *n* **:** the science of communication and control theory that is concerned esp. with the comparative study of automatic control systems — **cy·ber·net·ic** *adj*
cy·ber·punk \'sī-bər-,pəŋk\ *n* **1 :** science fiction dealing with computer-dominated future societies **2 :** HACKER **3**
cy·ber·sex \'sī-bər-,seks\ *n* **1 :** online sex-oriented conversations **2 :** sex-oriented material available on a computer
cy·ber·space \'sī-bər-,spās\ *n* **:** the online world of the Internet
cy·ber·ter·ror·ism \-,ter-ər-,i-zəm\ *n* **:** terrorist activities intended to damage or disrupt computer systems
cy·cla·men \'sī-klə-mən\ *n* **:** any of a genus of plants related to the primroses and having showy nodding flowers
¹cy·cle \'sī-kəl\ *n* **1 :** a period of time occupied by a se-

ries of events that repeat themselves regularly and in the same order **2 :** a recurring round of operations or events **3 :** one complete occurrence of a periodic process (as a vibration or current alternation) **4 :** a circular or spiral arrangement **5 :** a long period of time **:** AGE **6 :** BICYCLE **7 :** MOTORCYCLE — **cy·clic** \'sī-klik, 'si-\ *or* **cy·cli·cal** \-kli-kəl\ *adj* — **cy·cli·cal·ly** \-k(ə-)lē\ *also* **cy·clic·ly** *adv*
²cycle *vb* **cy·cled; cy·cling :** to ride a cycle — **cy·clist** \'sī-klist, -klə-list\ *n*
cy·clone \'sī-,klōn\ *n* **1 :** a storm or system of winds that rotates about a center of low atmospheric pressure and advances at 20 to 30 miles (about 30 to 50 kilometers) an hour **2 :** TORNADO — **cy·clon·ic** \sī-'klä-nik\ *adj*
cy·clo·pe·dia *also* **cy·clo·pae·dia** \,sī-klə-'pē-dē-ə\ *n* **:** ENCYCLOPEDIA
cy·clo·tron \'sī-klə-,trän\ *n* **:** a device for giving high speed to charged particles by magnetic and electric fields
cy·der *Brit var of* CIDER
cyg·net \'sig-nət\ *n* **:** a young swan
cyl *abbr* cylinder
cyl·in·der \'si-lən-dər\ *n* **:** the solid figure formed by turning a rectangle about one side as an axis; *also* **:** a body or space of this form ⟨an engine ~⟩ ⟨a bullet in the ~ of a revolver⟩ — **cy·lin·dri·cal** \sə-'lin-dri-kəl\ *adj*
cym·bal \'sim-bəl\ *n* **:** a concave brass plate that produces a brilliant clashing sound
cyn·ic \'si-nik\ *n* **:** one who attributes all actions to selfish motives — **cyn·i·cal** \-ni-kəl\ *adj* — **cyn·i·cal·ly** \-k(ə-)lē\ *adv* — **cyn·i·cism** \si-nə-,si-zəm\ *n*
cy·no·sure \'sī-nə-,shùr, 'si-\ *n* [MF & L; MF, Ursa Minor, guide, fr. L *cynosura* Ursa Minor, fr. Gk *kynosoura*, fr. *kynos oura*, lit., dog's tail] **:** a center of attraction
CYO *abbr* Catholic Youth Organization
cy·pher *chiefly Brit var of* CIPHER
cy·press \'sī-prəs\ *n* **1 :** any of a genus of scaly-leaved evergreen trees and shrubs **2 :** BALD CYPRESS **3 :** the wood of a cypress
cyst \'sist\ *n* **:** an abnormal closed bodily sac usu. containing liquid — **cys·tic** \'sis-tik\ *adj*
cystic fibrosis *n* **:** a common hereditary disease marked esp. by deficiency of pancreatic enzymes, by respiratory symptoms, and by excessive loss of salt in the sweat
cy·tol·o·gy \sī-'tä-lə-jē\ *n* **:** a branch of biology dealing with cells — **cy·to·log·i·cal** \,sī-tə-'lä-ji-kəl\ *or* **cy·to·log·ic** \-jik\ *adj* — **cy·tol·o·gist** \sī-'tä-lə-jist\ *n*
cy·to·plasm \'sī-tə-,pla-zəm\ *n* **:** the protoplasm of a cell that lies external to the nucleus — **cy·to·plas·mic** \,sī-tə-'plaz-mik\ *adj*
cy·to·sine \'sī-tə-,sēn\ *n* **:** a chemical base that is a pyrimidine coding genetic information in DNA and RNA
CZ *abbr* **1** Canal Zone **2** cubic zirconia
czar *also* **tsar** *or* **tzar** \'zär, 'tsär\ *n* [NL, fr. Russ *tsar'*, ultim. fr. L *Caesar* Caesar] **:** the ruler of Russia until 1917; *also* **:** one having great authority — **czar·ist** *also* **tsar·ist** \-ist\ *n or adj*
cza·ri·na \zä-'rē-nə\ *n* **:** the wife of a czar
Czech \'chek\ *n* **1 :** a native or inhabitant of Czechoslovakia or the Czech Republic **2 :** the language of the Czechs — **Czech** *adj*

D

¹d \'dē\ *n, pl* **d's** *or* **ds** \'dēz\ *often cap* **1 :** the 4th letter of the English alphabet **2 :** a grade rating a student's work as poor **3 :** DEFENSE
²d *abbr, often cap* **1** date **2** daughter **3** day **4** dead **5** deceased **6** degree **7** Democrat **8** [L *denarius, denarii*] penny; pence **9** depart; departure **10** diameter
D *symbol* deuterium
DA *abbr* **1** deposit account **2** district attorney **3** don't answer
¹dab \'dab\ *n* **1 :** a sudden blow or thrust **:** POKE; *also* **:** PECK **2 :** a gentle touch or stroke **:** PAT

²dab *vb* **dabbed; dab·bing 1 :** to strike or touch gently **:** PAT **2 :** to apply lightly or irregularly **:** DAUB — **dab·ber** *n*
³dab *n* **1 :** DAUB **2 :** a small amount
dab·ble \'da-bəl\ *vb* **dab·bled; dab·bling 1 :** to wet by splashing **:** SPATTER **2 :** to paddle or play in or as if in water **3 :** to work or involve oneself without serious effort — **dab·bler** *n*
da ca·po \dä-'kä-(,)pō\ *adv or adj* [It] **:** from the beginning — used as a direction in music to repeat
dace \'dās\ *n, pl* **dace :** any of various small No. American freshwater fishes related to the carp

da·cha \'dä-chə\ *n* [Russ] : a Russian country house
dachs·hund \'däks-ˌhûnt\ *n* [G, fr. *Dachs* badger + *Hund* dog] : any of a breed of long-bodied short-legged dogs of German origin

dachshund

dac·tyl \'dak-tᵊl\ *n* [ME *dactile*, fr. L *dactylus*, fr. Gk *daktylos*, lit., finger; fr. the fact that the three syllables have the first one longest like the joints of the finger] : a metrical foot of one accented syllable followed by two unaccented syllables — **dac·tyl·ic** \dak-'ti-lik\ *adj or n*
dad \'dad\ *n* : FATHER 1
Da·da \'dä-(ˌ)dä\ *n* : a movement in art and literature based on deliberate irrationality and negation of traditional artistic values — **da·da·ism** \-ˌi-zəm\ *n, often cap* — **da·da·ist** \-ˌist\ *n or adj, often cap*
dad·dy \'da-dē\ *n, pl* **daddies** : FATHER 1
dad·dy long·legs \ˌda-dē-'lȯn-ˌlegz\ *n, pl* **daddy longlegs** : any of an order of arachnids resembling the true spiders but having small rounded bodies and long slender legs
daemon *var of* DEMON
daf·fo·dil \'da-fə-ˌdil\ *n* : any of various bulbous herbs with usu. large flowers having a trumpetlike center
daf·fy \'da-fē\ *adj* **daf·fi·er; -est** : DAFT
daft \'daft\ *adj* : FOOLISH; *also* : INSANE — **daft·ness** *n*
dag *abbr* dekagram
dag·ger \'da-gər\ *n* 1 : a sharp pointed knife for stabbing 2 : a character † used as a reference mark or to indicate a death date
da·guerre·o·type \də-'ger-(ē-)ə-ˌtīp\ *n* : an early photograph produced on a silver or a silver-covered copper plate
dahl·ia \'dal-yə, 'däl-\ *n* : any of a genus of tuberous herbs related to the daisies and having showy flowers
¹dai·ly \'dā-lē\ *adj* 1 : occurring, done, or used every day or every weekday 2 : of or relating to every day ⟨∼ visitors⟩ 3 : computed in terms of one day ⟨∼ wages⟩ ✦ **Synonyms** DIURNAL, QUOTIDIAN — **dai·li·ness** \-lē-nəs\ *n* — **daily** *adv*
²daily *n, pl* **dailies** : a newspaper published every weekday
daily double *n* : a system of betting on races in which the bettor must pick the winners of two stipulated races in order to win
¹dain·ty \'dān-tē\ *n, pl* **dainties** [ME *deinte* high esteem, delight, fr. AF *deinté*, fr. L *dignitas* dignity, worth] : something delicious or pleasing to the taste : DELICACY
²dainty *adj* **dain·ti·er; -est** 1 : pleasing to the taste 2 : delicately pretty 3 : having or showing delicate taste; *also* : FASTIDIOUS ✦ **Synonyms** CHOICE, DELICATE, EXQUISITE, RARE, RECHERCHÉ — **dain·ti·ly** \-ti-lē\ *adv* — **dain·ti·ness** \-tē-nəs\ *n*
dai·qui·ri \'da-kə-rē, 'dī-\ *n* [*Daiquirí*, Cuba] : a cocktail made usu. of rum, lime juice, and sugar
dairy \'der-ē\ *n, pl* **dair·ies** [ME *deyerie*, fr. *deye* dairymaid, fr. OE *dæge* kneader of bread] 1 : CREAMERY 2 : a farm specializing in milk production 3 : food made primarily of or from milk
dairy·ing \'der-ē-iŋ\ *n* : the business of operating a dairy
dairy·maid \-ˌmād\ *n* : a woman employed in a dairy
dairy·man \-mən, -ˌman\ *n* : a person who operates a dairy farm or works in a dairy
da·is \'dā-əs\ *n* : a raised platform usu. above the floor of a hall or large room
dai·sy \'dā-zē\ *n, pl* **daisies** [ME *dayeseye*, fr. OE *dægeséage*, fr. *dæg* day + *éage* eye] : any of numerous composite plants having flower heads in which the marginal flowers resemble petals

dai·sy–chain \-ˌchān\ *vb* : to link (as computer components) together in series — **daisy chain** *n*
daisy wheel *n* : a disk with spokes bearing type that serves as the printing element of an electric typewriter or printer; *also* : a printer that uses such a disk
Da·ko·ta \də-'kō-tə\ *n, pl* **Dakotas** *also* **Dakota** : a member of an American Indian people of the northern Mississippi valley; *also* : their language
dal *abbr* dekaliter
da·la·si \dä-'lä-sē\ *n, pl* **dalasi** *or* **dalasis** — see MONEY table
dale \'dāl\ *n* : VALLEY
dal·ly \'da-lē\ *vb* **dal·lied; dal·ly·ing** 1 : to act playfully; *esp* : to play amorously 2 : to waste time 3 : LINGER, DAWDLE ✦ **Synonyms** FLIRT, COQUET, TOY, TRIFLE — **dal·li·ance** \-lē-əns\ *n*
dal·ma·tian \dal-'mā-shən\ *n, often cap* : any of a breed of medium-sized dogs having a white short-haired coat with many black or brown spots
¹dam \'dam\ *n* : the female parent of an animal and esp. of a domestic animal
²dam *n* : a barrier (as across a stream) to stop the flow of water — **dam** *vb*
³dam *abbr* dekameter
¹dam·age \'da-mij\ *n* 1 : loss or harm due to injury to persons, property, or reputation 2 *pl* : compensation in money imposed by law for loss or injury ⟨bring a suit for ∼s⟩
²damage *vb* **dam·aged; dam·ag·ing** : to cause damage to ⟨∼ the furniture⟩
dam·a·scene \'da-mə-ˌsēn\ *vb* **-scened; -scen·ing** : to ornament (as iron or steel) with wavy patterns or with inlaid work of precious metals
dam·ask \'da-məsk\ *n* 1 : a firm lustrous reversible figured fabric used for household linen 2 : a tough steel having decorative wavy lines
dame \'dām\ *n* 1 : a woman of rank, station, or authority 2 : an elderly woman 3 : WOMAN
damn \'dam\ *vb* [ME *dampnen*, fr. AF *dampner*, fr. L *damnare*, fr. *damnum* damage, loss, fine] 1 : to condemn esp. to hell 2 : CURSE — **damned** *adj*
dam·na·ble \'dam-nə-bəl\ *adj* 1 : liable to or deserving punishment 2 : DETESTABLE ⟨∼ weather⟩ — **dam·na·bly** \-blē\ *adv*
dam·na·tion \dam-'nā-shən\ *n* 1 : the act of damning 2 : the state of being damned
¹damp \'damp\ *n* 1 : a noxious gas 2 : MOISTURE
²damp *vb* : DAMPEN
³damp *adj* : MOIST — **damp·ness** *n*
damp·en \'dam-pən\ *vb* 1 : to check or diminish in activity or vigor ⟨∼ enthusiasm⟩ 2 : to make or become damp ⟨∼ a sponge⟩
damp·er \'dam-pər\ *n* 1 : a dulling or deadening influence ⟨put a ∼ on the party⟩ 2 : one that damps; *esp* : a valve or movable plate (as in the flue of a stove, furnace, or fireplace) to regulate the draft
dam·sel \'dam-zəl\ *n* : MAIDEN, GIRL
dam·sel·fly \-ˌflī\ *n* : any of a group of insects that are closely related to the dragonflies but fold their wings above the body when at rest
dam·son \'dam-zən\ *n* : a plum with acid purple fruit; *also* : its fruit
Dan *abbr* Daniel
¹dance \'dans\ *vb* **danced; danc·ing** 1 : to glide, step, or move through a set series of movements usu. to music 2 : to move quickly up and down or about 3 : to perform or take part in as a dancer — **danc·er** *n*
²dance *n* 1 : an act or instance of dancing 2 : a social gathering for dancing 3 : a piece of music (as a waltz) by which dancing may be guided 4 : the art of dancing
D & C *n* [dilation *and* curettage] : a surgical procedure that involves stretching the cervix and scraping the inside walls of the uterus (as to test for cancer or to perform an abortion)
dan·de·li·on \'dan-də-ˌlī-ən, -dē-\ *n* [ME *dendelyoun*, fr. AF *dent de lion*, lit., lion's tooth] : any of a genus of common yellow-flowered composite herbs
dan·der \'dan-dər\ *n* : ANGER, TEMPER
dan·di·fy \'dan-di-ˌfī\ *vb* **-fied; -fy·ing** : to cause to resemble a dandy
dan·dle \'dan-dᵊl\ *vb* **dan·dled; dan·dling** : to move up

and down in one's arms or on one's knee in affectionate play ◆ *Synonyms* CARESS, FONDLE, LOVE, PET

dan·druff \'dan-drəf\ *n* : scaly white or grayish flakes of dead skin cells that come off the scalp — **dan·druffy** \-drə-fē\ *adj*

¹dan·dy \'dan-dē\ *n, pl* **dandies** **1** : a man unduly attentive to personal appearance **2** : something excellent in its class ◆ *Synonyms* FOP, COXCOMB, POPINJAY

²dandy *adj* **dan·di·er; -est** : very good : FIRST-RATE

Dane \'dān\ *n* **1** : a native or inhabitant of Denmark **2** : GREAT DANE

dan·ger \'dān-jər\ *n* [ME *daunger* control, resistance, peril, fr. AF *dangier,* fr. VL **dominiarium,* fr. L *dominium* ownership] **1** : exposure or liability to injury, harm, or evil **2** : something that may cause injury or harm ◆ *Synonyms* PERIL, HAZARD, RISK, JEOPARDY

dan·ger·ous \'dān-jə-rəs\ *adj* **1** : HAZARDOUS, PERILOUS ⟨a ∼ slope⟩ **2** : able or likely to inflict injury ⟨a ∼ man⟩ — **dan·ger·ous·ly** *adv*

dan·gle \'daŋ-gəl\ *vb* **dan·gled; dan·gling** **1** : to hang loosely esp. with a swinging motion : SWING **2** : to be a hanger-on or dependent **3** : to be left without proper grammatical connection in a sentence ⟨a *dangling* participle⟩ **4** : to keep hanging uncertainly **5** : to offer as an inducement

Dan·iel \'dan-yəl\ *n* — see BIBLE table

Dan·ish \'dā-nish\ *n* : the language of the Danes — **Danish** *adj*

Danish pastry *n* : a pastry made of a rich yeast-raised dough

dank \'daŋk\ *adj* : disagreeably wet or moist : DAMP — **dank·ness** *n*

dan·seuse \däⁿ-'sərz, -'səz; dän-'süz\ *n* [F] : a female ballet dancer

dap·per \'da-pər\ *adj* **1** : SPRUCE, TRIM **2** : being alert and lively in movement and manners : JAUNTY

dap·ple \'da-pəl\ *vb* **dap·pled; dap·pling** : to mark with different-colored spots

DAR *abbr* Daughters of the American Revolution

¹dare \'der\ *vb* **dared; dar·ing** **1** : to have sufficient courage : be bold enough to **2** : CHALLENGE ⟨*dared* him to jump⟩ **3** : to confront boldly

²dare *n* : an act or instance of daring : CHALLENGE

dare·dev·il \-,de-vəl\ *n* : a recklessly bold person — **daredevil** *adj*

dar·ing \'der-iŋ\ *n* : venturesome boldness — **daring** *adj* — **dar·ing·ly** *adv*

¹dark \'därk\ *adj* **1** : being without light or without much light **2** : not light in color ⟨a ∼ suit⟩ **3** : GLOOMY ⟨a ∼ outlook⟩ **4** *often cap* : being a period of stagnation or decline ⟨the *Dark* Ages⟩ **5** : SECRETIVE ⟨∼ dealings⟩ ◆ *Synonyms* DIM, DUSKY, MURKY, TENEBROUS — **dark·ly** *adv* — **dark·ness** *n*

²dark *n* **1** : absence of light : DARKNESS; *esp* : NIGHT **2** : a dark or deep color — **in the dark** **1** : in secrecy **2** : in ignorance ⟨kept *in the dark* about the plans⟩

dark·en \'där-kən\ *vb* **1** : to make or grow dark or darker **2** : DIM **3** : BESMIRCH, TARNISH **4** : to make or become gloomy or forbidding

dark horse *n* : a contestant or a political figure whose abilities and chances as a contender are not known

dark·ling \'där-kliŋ\ *adj* **1** : DARK ⟨a ∼ plain⟩ **2** : MYSTERIOUS

dark·room \'därk-,rüm, -,rùm\ *n* : a lightproof room in which photographic materials are processed

¹dar·ling \'där-liŋ\ *n* **1** : a dearly loved person **2** : FAVORITE

²darling *adj* **1** : dearly loved : FAVORITE **2** : very pleasing : CHARMING

darm·stadt·i·um \,därm-'sta-tē-əm\ *n* : a short-lived radioactive chemical element produced artificially

¹darn \'därn\ *vb* : to mend with interlacing stitches — **darn·er** *n*

²darn *or* **darned** *adv* : VERY, EXTREMELY ⟨a ∼ good job⟩

darning needle *n* **1** : a needle for darning **2** : DRAGONFLY

¹dart \'därt\ *n* **1** : a small missile with a point on one end and feathers on the other; *also, pl* : a game in which darts are thrown at a target **2** : something causing a sudden pain **3** : a stitched tapering fold in a garment **4** : a quick movement

²dart *vb* **1** : to throw with a sudden movement **2** : to thrust or move suddenly or rapidly ⟨∼ed across the street⟩ **3** : to shoot with a dart containing a usu. tranquilizing drug

dart·er \'där-tər\ *n* : any of numerous small No. American freshwater fishes related to the perches

Dar·win·ism \'där-wə-,ni-zəm\ *n* : a theory explaining the origin and continued existence of new species of plants and animals by means of natural selection acting on chance variations — **Dar·win·ist** \-nist\ *n or adj*

¹dash \'dash\ *vb* **1** : SMASH **2** : to knock, hurl, or thrust violently **3** : SPLASH, SPATTER **4** : RUIN **5** : DEPRESS, SADDEN **6** : to perform or finish hastily ⟨∼ off a letter⟩ **7** : to move with sudden speed ⟨∼ed down the hall⟩

²dash *n* **1** : a sudden burst or splash **2** : a stroke of a pen **3** : a punctuation mark — that is used esp. to indicate a break in the thought or structure of a sentence **4** : a small addition ⟨a ∼ of salt⟩ **5** : flashy showiness **6** : animation in style and action **7** : a sudden rush or attempt ⟨made a ∼ for the door⟩ **8** : a short foot race **9** : DASHBOARD

dash·board \-,bȯrd\ *n* : a panel in an automobile or aircraft below the windshield usu. containing dials and controls

dash·er \'da-shər\ *n* : a device (as in a churn) for agitating something

da·shi·ki \də-'shē-kē\ *also* **dai·shi·ki** \dī-\ *n* [modif. of Yoruba (an African language) *dànṣíkí*] : a usu. brightly colored loose-fitting pullover garment

dash·ing \'da-shin\ *adj* **1** : marked by vigorous action **2** : marked by smartness esp. in dress and manners ◆ *Synonyms* STYLISH, CHIC, FASHIONABLE, MODISH, SMART, SWANK

das·tard \'das-tərd\ *n* **1** : COWARD **2** : a person who acts treacherously — **das·tard·ly** *adj*

dat *abbr* dative

da·ta \'dā-tə, 'da-, 'dä-\ *n sing or pl* [L, pl. of *datum*] : factual information (as measurements or statistics) used as a basis for reasoning, discussion, or calculation

da·ta·base \-,bās\ *n* : a usu. large collection of data organized esp. for rapid search and retrieval (as by a computer) — **database** *vb*

data processing *n* : the action or process of supplying a computer with information and having the computer use it to produce a desired result

¹date \'dāt\ *n* [ME, fr. AF, ultim. fr. L *dactylus,* fr. Gk *daktylos,* lit., finger] : the oblong edible fruit of a tall palm; *also* : this palm

²date *n* [ME, fr. AF, fr. LL *data,* fr. *data* (as in *data Romae* given at Rome), fem. of L *datus,* pp. of *dare* to give] **1** : the day, month, or year of an event **2** : a statement giving the time of execution or making (as of a coin or check) **3** : the period to which something belongs **4** : APPOINTMENT; *esp* : a social engagement between two persons that often has a romantic character **5** : a person with whom one has a usu. romantic date — **to date** : up to the present moment

³date *vb* **dat·ed; dat·ing** **1** : to record the date of or on **2** : to determine, mark, or reveal the date, age, or period of **3** : go on a date or dates with ⟨∼ed her for a year⟩ **4** : ORIGINATE ⟨∼s from ancient times⟩ **5** : EXTEND ⟨*dating* back to childhood⟩ **6** : to show qualities typical of a past period

dat·ed \'dā-təd\ *adj* **1** : provided with a date **2** : OLD-FASHIONED ⟨a ∼ custom⟩ ◆ *Synonyms* ANTIQUATED, ARCHAIC, OLD HAT, OUTDATED, OUTMODED, PASSÉ

date·less \'dāt-ləs\ *adj* **1** : ENDLESS **2** : having no date **3** : too ancient to be dated **4** : TIMELESS

date·line \'dāt-,līn\ *n* : a line in a publication giving the date and place of composition or issue — **dateline** *vb*

date rape *n* : rape committed by the victim's date

da·tive \'dā-tiv\ *adj* : of, relating to, or constituting a grammatical case marking typically the indirect object of a verb — **dative** *n*

da·tum \'dā-təm, 'da-, 'dä-\ *n, pl* **da·ta** \-tə\ *or* **datums** : a single piece of data : FACT

dau *abbr* daughter

¹daub \'dȯb\ *vb* **1** : to cover with soft adhesive matter **2** : SMEAR, SMUDGE **3** : to paint crudely — **daub·er** *n*

²daub *n* **1** : something daubed on : SMEAR **2** : a crude picture

daugh·ter \'dȯ-tər\ *n* **1** : a female offspring esp. of human beings **2** : a female adopted child **3** : a human female descendant — **daughter** *adj* — **daugh·ter·less** \-ləs\ *adj*

daugh·ter–in–law \'dȯ-tə-rən-ˌlȯ\ *n, pl* **daugh·ters–in–law** \-tər-zən-\ : the wife of one's son or daughter

daunt \'dȯnt\ *vb* [ME, fr. AF *danter, daunter,* fr. L *domitare* to tame] : to lessen the courage of : INTIMIDATE, OVERWHELM

daunt·ing \'dȯn-tiŋ\ *adj* : tending to overwhelm or intimidate ⟨a ~ task⟩

daunt·less \-ləs\ *adj* : FEARLESS, UNDAUNTED ♦ *Synonyms* BRAVE, BOLD, COURAGEOUS, LIONHEARTED — **daunt·less·ly** *adv*

dau·phin \'dȯ-fən\ *n, often cap* : the eldest son of a king of France

DAV *abbr* Disabled American Veterans

dav·en·port \'da-vən-ˌpȯrt\ *n* : a large upholstered sofa

da·vit \'dā-vət, 'da-\ *n* : a small crane on a ship used in pairs esp. to raise or lower boats

daw·dle \'dȯ-dᵊl\ *vb* **daw·dled; daw·dling 1** : to spend time wastefully or idly **2** : LOITER — **daw·dler** *n*

¹dawn \'dȯn\ *vb* **1** : to begin to grow light as the sun rises **2** : to begin to appear or develop **3** : to begin to be understood ⟨the solution ~ed on him⟩

²dawn *n* **1** : the first appearance of light in the morning **2** : a first appearance : BEGINNING ⟨the ~ of a new era⟩

day \'dā\ *n* **1** : the period of light between one night and the next; *also* : DAYLIGHT, DAYTIME **2** : the period of rotation of a planet (as earth) or a moon on its axis **3** : a period of 24 hours beginning at midnight **4** : a specified day or date ⟨wedding ~⟩ **5** : a specified time or period : AGE ⟨in olden ~s⟩ **6** : the conflict or contention of the day **7** : the time set apart by usage or law for work ⟨the 8-hour ~⟩

day·bed \'dā-ˌbed\ *n* : a couch that can be converted into a bed

day·book \-ˌbu̇k\ *n* : DIARY, JOURNAL

day·break \-ˌbrāk\ *n* : DAWN

day care *n* : supervision of and care for children or disabled adults provided during the day; *also* : a program offering day care

day·dream \'dā-ˌdrēm\ *n* : a pleasant reverie — **daydream** *vb*

day·light \'dā-ˌlīt\ *n* **1** : the light of day **2** : DAYTIME **3** : DAWN **4** : understanding of something that has been obscure **5** *pl* : CONSCIOUSNESS; *also* : WITS **6** : a perceptible space, gap, or difference

daylight saving time *n* : time usu. one hour ahead of standard time

Day of Atonement *n* : YOM KIPPUR

day school *n* : a private school without boarding facilities

day student *n* : a student who attends regular classes at a college or preparatory school but does not live there

day·time \'dā-ˌtīm\ *n* : the period of daylight

daze \'dāz\ *vb* **dazed; daz·ing 1** : to stupefy esp. by a blow **2** : DAZZLE — **daze** *n* — **da·zed·ly** \'dā-zəd-lē\ *adv*

daz·zle \'da-zəl\ *vb* **daz·zled; daz·zling 1** : to overpower with light **2** : to impress greatly or confound with brilliance ⟨*dazzled* by her wit⟩ — **dazzle** *n*

dB *abbr* decibel

Db *symbol* dubnium

d/b/a *abbr* doing business as

dbl *or* **dble** *abbr* double

DC *abbr* **1** [It *da capo*] from the beginning **2** direct current **3** District of Columbia **4** doctor of chiropractic

DD *abbr* **1** days after date **2** demand draft **3** dishonorable discharge **4** doctor of divinity

D–day *n* [*D,* abbr. for *day*] : a day set for launching an operation (as an invasion)

DDS *abbr* doctor of dental surgery

DDT \ˌdē-(ˌ)dē-'tē\ *n* : a persistent insecticide poisonous to many higher animals

DE *abbr* Delaware

dea·con \'dē-kən\ *n* [ME *dekene,* fr. OE *dēacon,* fr. LL *diaconus,* fr. Gk *diakonos,* lit., servant] : a subordinate officer in a Christian church

dea·con·ess \'dē-kə-nəs\ *n* : a woman chosen to assist in the church ministry

de·ac·ti·vate \dē-'ak-tə-ˌvāt\ *vb* : to make inactive or ineffective

¹dead \'ded\ *adj* **1** : LIFELESS **2** : DEATHLIKE, DEADLY ⟨in a ~ faint⟩ **3** : NUMB **4** : very tired **5** : UNRESPONSIVE **6** : EXTINGUISHED ⟨~ coals⟩ **7** : INANIMATE, INERT **8** : no longer active or functioning ⟨a ~ battery⟩ **9** : lacking power, significance, or effect ⟨a ~ custom⟩ **10** : OBSOLETE ⟨a ~ language⟩ **11** : lacking in gaiety or animation ⟨a ~ party⟩ **12** : QUIET, DULL, UNPRODUCTIVE ⟨~ capital⟩ **13** : lacking elasticity ⟨a ~ tennis ball⟩ **14** : not circulating : STAGNANT ⟨~ air⟩ **15** : lacking warmth, vigor, or taste ⟨~ wine⟩ **16** : absolutely uniform ⟨~ level⟩ **17** : UNERRING, EXACT ⟨a ~ shot⟩ **18** : ABRUPT ⟨a ~ stop⟩ **19** : COMPLETE ⟨a ~ loss⟩

²dead *n, pl* **dead 1** : one that is dead — usu. used collectively ⟨the living and the ~⟩ **2** : the time of greatest quiet ⟨the ~ of the night⟩

³dead *adv* **1** : UTTERLY ⟨~ right⟩ **2** : in a sudden and complete manner ⟨stopped ~⟩ **3** : DIRECTLY ⟨~ ahead⟩

dead·beat \-ˌbēt\ *n* : a person who persistently fails to pay personal debts or expenses

dead duck *n* : GONER

dead·en \'de-dᵊn\ *vb* **1** : to impair in vigor or sensation : BLUNT ⟨~ pain⟩ **2** : to lessen the luster or spirit of **3** : to make (as a wall) soundproof

dead end *n* **1** : an end (as of a street) without an exit **2** : a position, situation, or course of action that leads to nothing further — **dead–end** \ˌded-ˌend\ *adj*

dead heat *n* : a contest in which two or more contestants tie (as by crossing the finish line simultaneously)

dead horse *n* : an exhausted topic or issue

dead letter *n* **1** : something that has lost its force or authority without being formally abolished **2** : a letter that cannot be delivered or returned

dead·line \'ded-ˌlīn\ *n* : a date or time before which something must be done

dead·lock \'ded-ˌläk\ *n* **1** : a stoppage of action because neither faction in a struggle will give in **2** : a tie score — **deadlock** *vb*

¹dead·ly \'ded-lē\ *adj* **dead·li·er; -est 1** : likely to cause or capable of causing death **2** : HOSTILE, IMPLACABLE **3** : very accurate : UNERRING **4** : tending to deprive of force or vitality ⟨a ~ habit⟩ **5** : suggestive of death **6** : very great : EXTREME — **dead·li·ness** *n*

²deadly *adv* **1** : suggesting death ⟨~ pale⟩ **2** : EXTREMELY ⟨~ dull⟩

deadly sin *n* : one of seven sins of pride, covetousness, lust, anger, gluttony, envy, and sloth held to be fatal to spiritual progress

dead meat *n* : one that is doomed

¹dead·pan \'ded-ˌpan\ *adj* : marked by an impassive manner or expression ⟨~ humor⟩ — **deadpan** *vb* — **deadpan** *adv*

²deadpan *n* : a completely expressionless face

dead reckoning *n* : the determination of the position of a ship or aircraft solely from the record of the direction and distance of its course

dead·weight \'ded-'wāt\ *n* **1** : the unrelieved weight of an inert mass **2** : a ship's load including the weight of cargo, fuel, crew, and passengers

dead·wood \-ˌwu̇d\ *n* **1** : wood dead on the tree **2** : useless personnel or material

deaf \'def\ *adj* **1** : unable to hear **2** : unwilling to hear or listen ⟨~ to all suggestions⟩ — **deaf·ness** *n*

deaf·en \'de-fən\ *vb* : to make deaf

¹deal \'dēl\ *n* **1** : a usu. large or indefinite quantity or degree ⟨a great ~ of support⟩ **2** : the act or right of distributing cards to players in a card game; *also* : HAND

²deal *vb* **dealt; deal·ing 1** : DISTRIBUTE; *esp* : to distribute playing cards to players in a game **2** : ADMINISTER, DELIVER ⟨*dealt* him a blow⟩ **3** : to concern itself : TREAT ⟨the book ~s with crime⟩ **4** : to take action in regard to something ⟨~ with offenders⟩ **5** : TRADE; *also* : to sell or distribute something as a business ⟨~ in used cars⟩ **6** : to reach a state of acceptance ⟨~ with her child's death⟩ — **deal·er** *n*

³deal *n* **1** : BARGAINING, NEGOTIATION **2** : TRANSACTION; *esp* : an agreement by contract **3** : treatment received ⟨a raw ~⟩ **4** : an often secret agreement or arrangement for mutual advantage **5** : BARGAIN

⁴deal *n* : wood or a board of fir or pine

deal·er·ship \'dē-lər-,ship\ *n* : an authorized sales agency ⟨an auto ~⟩

deal·ing \'dē-liŋ\ *n* **1** : a way of acting or of doing business **2** *pl* : friendly or business transactions

dean \'dēn\ *n* [ME *deen,* fr. AF *deien,* fr. LL *decanus,* lit., chief of ten, fr. Gk *dekanos,* fr. *deka* ten] **1** : a clergyman who is head of a group of canons or of joint pastors of a church **2** : the head of a division, faculty, college, or school of a university **3** : a college or secondary school administrator in charge of counseling and disciplining students **4** : DOYEN ⟨the ~ of a diplomatic corps⟩ — **dean·ship** *n*

dean·ery \'dē-nə-rē\ *n, pl* **-er·ies** : the office, jurisdiction, or official residence of a clerical dean

¹dear \'dir\ *adj* **1** : highly valued : PRECIOUS **2** : AFFECTIONATE, FOND **3** : EXPENSIVE **4** : HEARTFELT — **dear·ly** *adv* — **dear·ness** *n*

²dear *n* : a loved one : DARLING

Dear John \-'jän\ *n* : a letter (as to a soldier) in which a woman breaks off a marital or romantic relationship

dearth \'dərth\ *n* **1** : SCARCITY, FAMINE **2** : an inadequate supply : LACK ⟨a ~ of jobs⟩

death \'deth\ *n* **1** : the end of life **2** : the cause of loss of life **3** : a cause of ruin **4** : the state of being dead **5** : DESTRUCTION, EXTINCTION **6** : SLAUGHTER — **death·like** *adj*

death·bed \-,bed\ *n* **1** : the bed in which a person dies **2** : the last hours of life

death·blow \-,blō\ *n* : a destructive or killing stroke or event

death grip *n* : an extremely tight grip or hold

death·less \-ləs\ *adj* : IMMORTAL, IMPERISHABLE ⟨~ fame⟩

death·ly \-lē\ *adj* **1** : FATAL **2** : of, relating to, or suggestive of death ⟨a ~ pallor⟩ — **deathly** *adv*

death rattle *n* : a sound produced by air passing through mucus in the lungs and air passages of a dying person

death's-head \'deths-,hed\ *n* : a human skull emblematic of death

death·watch \'deth-,wäch\ *n* : a vigil kept over the dead or dying

deb \'deb\ *n* : DEBUTANTE

de·ba·cle \di-'bä-kəl, -'ba-\ *also* **dé·bâ·cle** *same or* dā-'bäk\ *n* [F *débâcle*] : DISASTER, FAILURE, ROUT ⟨a financial ~⟩

de·bar \di-'bär\ *vb* : to bar from having or doing something : PRECLUDE

de·bark \di-'bärk\ *vb* : DISEMBARK — **de·bar·ka·tion** \,dē-,bär-'kā-shən\ *n*

de·base \di-'bäs\ *vb* : to lower in character, quality, or value ✦ *Synonyms* DEGRADE, CORRUPT, DEPRAVE — **de·base·ment** *n*

de·bate \di-'bāt\ *vb* **de·bat·ed; de·bat·ing 1** : to discuss a question by considering opposed arguments **2** : to take part in a debate — **de·bat·able** *adj* — **debate** *n* — **de·bat·er** *n*

de·bauch \di-'bóch\ *vb* : SEDUCE, CORRUPT ✦ *Synonyms* DEBASE, DEMORALIZE, DEPRAVE, PERVERT — **de·bauch·ery** \-'bó-chə-rē\ *n*

de·ben·ture \di-'ben-chər\ *n* : BOND; *esp* : one secured by the general credit of the issuer rather than a lien on particular assets

de·bil·i·tate \di-'bi-lə-,tāt\ *vb* **-tat·ed; -tat·ing** : to impair the health or strength of ✦ *Synonyms* WEAKEN, DISABLE, ENFEEBLE, UNDERMINE

de·bil·i·ty \di-'bi-lə-tē\ *n, pl* **-ties** : an infirm or weakened state

¹deb·it \'de-bət\ *vb* : to enter as a debit : charge with or as a debit

²debit *n* **1** : an entry in an account showing money paid out or owed **2** : DISADVANTAGE, SHORTCOMING

debit card *n* : a card by which money may be withdrawn or the cost of purchases paid directly from the holder's bank account

deb·o·nair \,de-bə-'ner\ *adj* [ME *debonere,* fr. AF *debonaire,* fr. *de bon aire* of good family or nature] : SUAVE, URBANE; *also* : LIGHTHEARTED

de·bouch \di-'bauch, -'büsh\ *vb* [F *déboucher,* fr. *dé-* out of + *bouche* mouth] : to come out into an open area : EMERGE

de·brief \di-'brēf\ *vb* **1** : to question (as a pilot back from a mission) in order to obtain useful information **2** : to review carefully upon completion

de·bris \də-'brē, dā-; 'dā-,brē\ *n, pl* **debris** \-'brēz, -,brēz\ **1** : the remains of something broken down or destroyed **2** : an accumulation of rock fragments **3** : RUBBISH

debt \'det\ *n* **1** : SIN, TRESPASS **2** : something owed : OBLIGATION **3** : a condition of owing

debt·or \'de-tər\ *n* **1** : one guilty of neglect or violation of duty **2** : one that owes a debt

de·bug \(,)dē-'bəg\ *vb* : to eliminate errors in ⟨~ a computer program⟩

de·bunk \dē-'bəŋk\ *vb* : to expose the sham or falseness of ⟨~ a legend⟩

¹de·but \'dā-,byü, dā-'byü\ *n* **1** : a first appearance **2** : a formal entrance into society

²debut *vb* : to make a debut; *also* : INTRODUCE

deb·u·tante \'de-byü-,tänt\ *n* : a young woman making her formal entrance into society

dec *abbr* **1** deceased **2** decrease

Dec *abbr* December

de·cade \'de-,kād, de-'kād\ *n* : a period of 10 years

dec·a·dence \'de-kə-dəns, di-'kā-d°ns\ *n* : DETERIORATION, DECLINE — **dec·a·dent** \'de-kə-dənt, di-'kā-d°nt\ *adj or n*

de·caf \'dē-,kaf\ *n* : decaffeinated coffee

de·caf·fein·at·ed \(,)dē-'ka-fə-nā-təd\ *adj* : having the caffeine removed ⟨~ coffee⟩

deca·gon \'de-kə-,gän\ *n* : a plane polygon of 10 angles and 10 sides

de·cal \'dē-,kal\ *n* : a picture, design, or label made to be transferred (as to glass) from specially prepared paper

de·cal·co·ma·nia \di-,kal-kə-'mā-nē-ə\ *n* [F *décalcomanie,* fr. *décalquer* to copy by tracing (fr. *calquer* to trace, fr. It *calcare,* lit., to tread, fr. L) + *manie* mania, fr. LL *mania*] : the process of making decals; *also* : DECAL

Deca·logue \'de-kə-,lóg\ *n* : TEN COMMANDMENTS

de·camp \di-'kamp\ *vb* **1** : to break up a camp **2** : to depart suddenly ✦ *Synonyms* ESCAPE, ABSCOND, FLEE

de·cant \di-'kant\ *vb* : to pour (as wine) from one vessel into another

de·cant·er \di-'kan-tər\ *n* : an ornamental glass bottle for serving wine

de·cap·i·tate \di-'ka-pə-,tāt\ *vb* **-tat·ed; -tat·ing** : BEHEAD — **de·cap·i·ta·tion** \-,ka-pə-'tā-shən\ *n* — **de·cap·i·ta·tor** \-'ka-pə-,tā-tər\ *n*

deca·syl·lab·ic \,de-kə-sə-'la-bik\ *adj* : having or composed of verses having 10 syllables — **decasyllabic** *n*

de·cath·lon \di-'kath-lən, -,län\ *n* : a 10-event athletic contest

de·cay \di-'kā\ *vb* **1** : to decline from a sound or prosperous condition ⟨a ~*ing* town⟩ **2** : to cause or undergo decomposition ⟨radium ~*s* slowly⟩; *esp* : to break down while spoiling ⟨ROT ⟨~*ing* teeth⟩ — **decay** *n*

decd *abbr* deceased

de·cease \di-'sēs\ *n* : DEATH

¹de·ceased \-'sēst\ *adj* : no longer living; *esp* : recently dead

²deceased *n, pl* **deceased** : a dead person

de·ce·dent \di-'sē-d°nt\ *n* : a deceased person

de·ceit \di-'sēt\ *n* **1** : DECEPTION **2** : TRICK **3** : DECEITFULNESS ✦ *Synonyms* DISSIMULATION, DUPLICITY, GUILE

de·ceit·ful \-fəl\ *adj* : practicing or tending to practice deceit **2** : MISLEADING, DECEPTIVE ⟨a ~ answer⟩ — **de·ceit·ful·ly** *adv* — **de·ceit·ful·ness** *n*

de·ceive \di-'sēv\ *vb* **de·ceived; de·ceiv·ing 1** : to cause to believe an untruth **2** : to use or practice deceit ✦ *Synonyms* BEGUILE, BETRAY, DELUDE, MISLEAD — **de·ceiv·er** *n*

de·cel·er·ate \dē-'se-lə-,rāt\ *vb* **-at·ed; -at·ing** : to slow down

De·cem·ber \di-'sem-bər\ *n* [ME *Decembre,* fr. OE or AF, both fr. L *December* (tenth month), fr. *decem* ten] : the 12th month of the year

de·cen·cy \'dē-s°n-sē\ *n, pl* **-cies 1** : PROPRIETY **2** : conformity to standards of taste, propriety, or quality **3** : standard of propriety — usu. used in pl.

de·cen·ni·al \di-'se-nē-əl\ *adj* **1** : consisting of 10 years **2** : happening every 10 years ⟨~ census⟩

de·cent \'dē-s°nt\ *adj* **1** : conforming to standards of propriety, good taste, or morality **2** : modestly clothed **3** : free from immodesty or obscenity **4** : ADEQUATE ⟨~ housing⟩ — **de·cent·ly** *adv*

de·cen·tral·i·za·tion \dē-ˌsen-trə-lə-ˈzā-shən\ *n* **1** : the distribution of powers from a central authority to regional and local authorities **2** : the redistribution of population and industry from urban centers to outlying areas — **de·cen·tral·ize** \-ˈsen-trə-ˌlīz\ *vb*

de·cep·tion \di-ˈsep-shən\ *n* **1** : the act of deceiving **2** : the fact or condition of being deceived **3** : FRAUD, TRICK — **de·cep·tive** \-ˈsep-tiv\ *adj* — **de·cep·tive·ly** *adv* — **de·cep·tive·ness** *n*

deci·bel \ˈde-sə-ˌbel, -bəl\ *n* : a unit for measuring the relative loudness of sounds

de·cide \di-ˈsīd\ *vb* **de·cid·ed; de·cid·ing** [ME, fr. L *decidere*, lit., to cut off, fr. *de-* off + *caedere* to cut] **1** : make a final choice or judgment **2** : to bring to a definite end ⟨one blow *decided* the fight⟩ **3** : to induce to come to a choice

de·cid·ed \di-ˈsī-dəd\ *adj* **1** : UNQUESTIONABLE ⟨a ~ advantage⟩ **2** : FIRM, DETERMINED — **de·cid·ed·ly** *adv*

de·cid·u·ous \di-ˈsi-jə-wəs\ *adj* **1** : falling off or out usu. at the end of a period of growth or function ⟨~ leaves⟩ ⟨a ~ tooth⟩ **2** : having deciduous parts ⟨~ trees⟩

deci·gram \ˈde-sə-ˌgram\ *n* — see METRIC SYSTEM table

deci·li·ter \-ˌlē-tər\ *n* — see METRIC SYSTEM table

¹dec·i·mal \ˈde-sə-məl\ *adj* : based on the number 10 : reckoning by tens

²decimal *n* : any number expressed in base 10; *esp* : DECIMAL FRACTION

decimal fraction *n* : a fraction or mixed number in which the denominator is a power of 10 and that is usu. expressed with a decimal point ⟨the *decimal fraction* .25 is equivalent to the common fraction ²⁵/₁₀₀⟩

decimal place *n* : the position of a digit as counted to the right of the decimal point in a decimal fraction

decimal point *n* : a period, centered dot, or in some countries a comma at the left of a decimal fraction (as .678) less than one or between a whole number and a decimal fraction in a mixed number (as 3.678)

dec·i·mate \ˈde-sə-ˌmāt\ *vb* **-mat·ed; -mat·ing** **1** : to take or destroy the 10th part of **2** : to cause great destruction or harm to ⟨factories *decimated* by fire⟩

dec·i·me·ter \ˈde-sə-ˌmē-tər\ *n* — see METRIC SYSTEM table

de·ci·pher \di-ˈsī-fər\ *vb* **1** : DECODE **2** : to make out the meaning of despite indistinctness — **de·ci·pher·able** *adj*

de·ci·sion \di-ˈsi-zhən\ *n* **1** : the act or result of deciding **2** : promptness and firmness in deciding : DETERMINATION

de·ci·sive \-ˈsī-siv\ *adj* **1** : having the power to decide ⟨the ~ vote⟩ **2** : RESOLUTE, DETERMINED **3** : CONCLUSIVE ⟨a ~ victory⟩ — **de·ci·sive·ly** *adv* — **de·ci·sive·ness** *n*

¹deck \ˈdek\ *n* **1** : a floorlike platform of a ship; *also* : something resembling the deck of a ship **2** : a pack of playing cards

²deck *vb* **1** : ARRAY ⟨men ~*ed* out in suits⟩ **2** : DECORATE **3** : to furnish with a deck **4** : KNOCK DOWN, FLOOR

deck·hand \ˈdek-ˌhand\ *n* : a sailor who performs manual duties

de·claim \di-ˈklām\ *vb* : to speak or deliver in the manner of a formal speech ⟨an actor ~*ing* his lines⟩ — **dec·la·ma·tion** \ˌde-klə-ˈmā-shən\ *n* — **de·clam·a·to·ry** \di-ˈkla-mə-ˌtȯr-ē\ *adj*

de·clar·a·tive \di-ˈkler-ə-tiv\ *adj* : making a declaration ⟨~ sentence⟩

de·clare \di-ˈkler\ *vb* **de·clared; de·clar·ing** **1** : to make known formally, officially, or explicitly : ANNOUNCE ⟨~ war⟩ **2** : to state emphatically : AFFIRM **3** : to make a full statement of ✦ *Synonyms* BLAZON, BROADCAST, PROCLAIM, PUBLISH — **dec·la·ra·tion** \ˌde-klə-ˈrā-shən\ *n* — **de·clar·a·to·ry** \di-ˈkler-ə-ˌtȯr-ē\ *adj* — **de·clar·er** *n*

de·clas·si·fy \dē-ˈkla-sə-ˌfī\ *vb* : to remove the security classification of ⟨~ documents⟩ — **de·clas·si·fi·ca·tion** \-ˌkla-sə-fə-ˈkā-shən\ *n*

de·clen·sion \di-ˈklen-chən\ *n* **1** : the inflectional forms of a noun, pronoun, or adjective **2** : DECLINE, DETERIORATION **3** : DESCENT, SLOPE

¹de·cline \di-ˈklīn\ *vb* **de·clined; de·clin·ing** **1** : to slope downward : DESCEND **2** : DROOP **3** : RECEDE ⟨morale *declined*⟩ **4** : WANE **5** : to withhold consent; *also* : REFUSE, REJECT ⟨~ an invitation⟩ ⟨~ to answer⟩

6 : INFLECT **2** ⟨~ a noun⟩ — **de·clin·able** *adj* — **dec·li·na·tion** \ˌde-klə-ˈnā-shən\ *n*

²decline *n* **1** : a gradual sinking and wasting away **2** : a change to a lower state or level **3** : the time when something is approaching its end ⟨an empire in ~⟩ **4** : a descending slope

de·cliv·i·ty \di-ˈkli-və-tē\ *n, pl* **-ties** : a steep downward slope

de·code \dē-ˈkōd\ *vb* : to convert (a coded message) into ordinary language — **de·cod·er** *n*

dé·col·le·tage \dā-ˌkä-lə-ˈtäzh\ *n* : the low-cut neckline of a dress

dé·col·le·té \dā-ˌkäl-ˈtā\ *adj* [F] **1** : wearing a strapless or low-necked gown **2** : having a low-cut neckline

de·com·mis·sion \ˌdē-kə-ˈmi-shən\ *vb* : to remove from service

de·com·pose \ˌdē-kəm-ˈpōz\ *vb* **1** : to separate into constituent parts **2** : to break down in decay : ROT — **de·com·po·si·tion** \ˌdē-ˌkäm-pə-ˈzi-shən\ *n*

de·com·press \ˌdē-kəm-ˈpres\ *vb* : to release from pressure or compression — **de·com·pres·sion** \-ˈpre-shən\ *n*

decompression sickness *n* : ²BEND 3

de·con·ges·tant \ˌdē-kən-ˈjes-tənt\ *n* : an agent that relieves congestion (as of mucous membranes)

de·con·struc·tion \ˌdē-kən-ˈstrək-shən\ *n* : the analysis of something (as language or literature) by the separation and individual examination of its basic elements — **de·con·struct** \-ˈstrəkt\ *vb*

de·con·tam·i·nate \ˌdē-kən-ˈta-mə-ˌnāt\ *vb* : to rid of contamination (as radioactive material) — **de·con·tam·i·na·tion** \-ˌta-mə-ˈnā-shən\ *n*

de·con·trol \ˌdē-kən-ˈtrōl\ *vb* : to end control of ⟨~ prices⟩ — **decontrol** *n*

de·cor *or* **dé·cor** \dā-ˈkȯr, ˈdā-ˌkȯr\ *n* : DECORATION; *esp* : the style and layout of interior furnishings

dec·o·rate \ˈde-kə-ˌrāt\ *vb* **-rat·ed; -rat·ing** **1** : to furnish with something ornamental ⟨~ a room⟩ **2** : to award a mark of honor (as a medal) to ⟨*decorated* soldiers⟩ ✦ *Synonyms* ADORN, BEAUTIFY, BEDECK, GARNISH, ORNAMENT

dec·o·ra·tion \ˌde-kə-ˈrā-shən\ *n* **1** : the act or process of decorating **2** : ORNAMENT **3** : a badge of honor

dec·o·ra·tive \ˈde-kə-rə-tiv\ *adj* : ORNAMENTAL

dec·o·ra·tor \ˈde-kə-ˌrā-tər\ *n* : one that decorates; *esp* : a person who designs or executes interiors and their furnishings

dec·o·rous \ˈde-kə-rəs, di-ˈkȯr-əs\ *adj* : PROPER, SEEMLY, CORRECT

de·co·rum \di-ˈkȯr-əm\ *n* [L] **1** : conformity to accepted standards of conduct **2** : ORDERLINESS, PROPRIETY

¹de·coy \ˈdē-ˌkȯi, di-ˈkȯi\ *n* [prob. fr. D *de kooi*, lit., the cage] **1** : something that lures or entices; *esp* : an artificial bird used to attract live birds within shot **2** : something used to draw attention away from another

²de·coy \di-ˈkȯi, ˈdē-ˌkȯi\ *vb* : to lure by or as if by a decoy : ENTICE

¹de·crease \di-ˈkrēs\ *vb* **de·creased; de·creas·ing** : to grow or cause to grow less : DIMINISH

²de·crease \ˈdē-ˌkrēs\ *n* **1** : the process of decreasing **2** : REDUCTION

¹de·cree \di-ˈkrē\ *n* **1** : ORDER, EDICT **2** : a judicial decision

²decree *vb* **de·creed; de·cree·ing** **1** : COMMAND **2** : to determine or order judicially ✦ *Synonyms* DICTATE, ORDAIN, PRESCRIBE

dec·re·ment \ˈde-krə-mənt\ *n* **1** : gradual decrease **2** : the quantity lost by diminution or waste

de·crep·it \di-ˈkre-pət\ *adj* : broken down with age : WORN-OUT — **de·crep·i·tude** \-pə-ˌtüd, -ˌtyüd\ *n*

de·cre·scen·do \ˌdā-krə-ˈshen-dō\ *adv or adj* : with a decrease in volume — used as a direction in music

de·crim·i·nal·ize \dē-ˈkri-mə-nə-ˌlīz\ *vb* : to remove or reduce the criminal status of

de·cry \di-ˈkrī\ *vb* : to express strong disapproval of ⟨~ welfare policies⟩

ded·i·cate \ˈde-di-ˌkāt\ *vb* **-cat·ed; -cat·ing** **1** : to devote to the worship of a divine being esp. with sacred rites **2** : to set apart for a definite purpose **3** : to inscribe or address as a compliment ⟨~ a novel⟩ — **ded·i·ca·tion** \ˌde-di-ˈkā-shən\ *n* — **ded·i·ca·tor** \ˈde-di-ˌkā-tər\ *n* — **ded·i·ca·to·ry** \-kə-ˌtȯr-ē\ *adj*

de·duce \di-'düs, -'dyüs\ vb **de·duced; de·duc·ing** 1 : to derive by reasoning : INFER 2 : to trace the course of — **de·duc·ible** adj

de·duct \di-'dəkt\ vb : SUBTRACT — **de·duct·ible** adj

de·duc·tion \di-'dək-shən\ n 1 : SUBTRACTION 2 : something that is or may be subtracted 3 : the deriving of a conclusion by reasoning : the conclusion so reached — **de·duc·tive** \-'dək-tiv\ adj — **de·duc·tive·ly** adv

¹deed \'dēd\ n 1 : something done 2 : FEAT, EXPLOIT 3 : a document containing some legal transfer, bargain, or contract

²deed vb : to convey or transfer by deed

dee·jay \'dē-jā\ n : DISC JOCKEY

deem \'dēm\ vb : THINK, JUDGE ♦ **Synonyms** CONSIDER, ACCOUNT, RECKON, REGARD, VIEW

de–em·pha·size \dē-'em-fə-ˌsīz\ vb : to reduce in relative importance; also : to attach little importance to — **de–em·pha·sis** \-səs\ n

¹deep \'dēp\ adj 1 : extending far down, back, within, or outward ⟨a ~ well⟩ 2 : having a specified extension downward or backward ⟨3 feet ~⟩ 3 : difficult to understand; also : MYSTERIOUS, OBSCURE ⟨a ~ dark secret⟩ 4 : WISE 5 : ENGROSSED, INVOLVED ⟨~ in thought⟩ 6 : INTENSE, PROFOUND ⟨~ sleep⟩ 7 : dark and rich in color ⟨a ~ red⟩ 8 : having a low musical pitch or range ⟨a ~ voice⟩ 9 : situated well within 10 : covered, enclosed, or filled often to a specified degree — **deep·ly** adv

²deep adv 1 : DEEPLY 2 : far on : LATE ⟨~ in the night⟩

³deep n 1 : an extremely deep place or part; esp : OCEAN 2 : the middle or most intense part ⟨the ~ of winter⟩

deep·en \'dē-pən\ vb : to make or become deep or deeper

deep–freeze \'dēp-'frēz\ vb **-froze** \-'frōz\; **-fro·zen** \-'frō-zᵊn\ : QUICK-FREEZE

deep–fry vb : to cook in enough oil to cover the food being fried

deep pocket n 1 : one having substantial financial resources 2 pl : substantial financial resources

deep–root·ed \'dēp-'rü-təd, -'rü-\ adj : deeply implanted or established

deep–sea \'dēp-'sē\ adj : of, relating to, or occurring in the deeper parts of the sea ⟨~ fishing⟩

deep–seat·ed \'dēp-'sē-təd\ adj 1 : situated far below the surface 2 : firmly established ⟨~ convictions⟩

deer \'dir\ n, pl **deer** [ME, deer, animal, fr. OE dēor beast] : any of numerous ruminant mammals with cloven hoofs and usu. antlers esp. in the males

deer·fly \-ˌflī\ n : any of numerous small horseflies

deer·skin \-ˌskin\ n : leather made from the skin of a deer; also : a garment of such leather

deer tick n : a tick that transmits the bacterium causing Lyme disease

de–es·ca·late \dē-'es-kə-ˌlāt\ vb : to decrease in extent, volume, or scope : LIMIT — **de–es·ca·la·tion** \-ˌes-kə-'lā-shən\ n

deet \'dēt\ n, often all cap : a colorless oily liquid insect and tick repellent

¹def \'def\ adj def·fer; def·fest slang : very good : COOL

²def abbr 1 defendant 2 definite 3 definition

de·face \di-'fās\ vb : to destroy or mar the face or surface of ⟨~ a desk⟩ — **de·face·ment** n — **de·fac·er** n

de fac·to \di-'fak-tō, dā-\ adj or adv 1 : existing though not formally recognized ⟨a de facto recession⟩ 2 : actually exercising power ⟨de facto government⟩

de·fal·ca·tion \ˌdē-ˌfal-'kā-shən, -ˌfȯl-; ˌde-fəl-\ n : EMBEZZLEMENT

de·fame \di-'fām\ vb **de·famed; de·fam·ing** : to injure or destroy the reputation of by libel or slander ♦ **Synonyms** CALUMNIATE, DENIGRATE, LIBEL, MALIGN, SLANDER, VILIFY — **def·a·ma·tion** \ˌde-fə-'mā-shən\ n — **de·fam·a·to·ry** \di-'fa-mə-ˌtȯr-ē\ adj

de·fault \di-'fȯlt\ n 1 : failure to do something required by duty or law; also : failure to appear for a legal proceeding 2 : failure to compete in or to finish an appointed contest ⟨lose a race by ~⟩ 3 : a choice made without active consideration due to lack of viable alternatives 4 : a selection made automatically by a computer in the absence of a choice by the user — **default** vb — **de·fault·er** n

¹de·feat \di-'fēt\ vb 1 : FRUSTRATE, NULLIFY 2 : to win victory over : BEAT — **de·feat·able** \-'fē-tə-bəl\ adj

²defeat n 1 : FRUSTRATION 2 : an overthrow of an army in battle 3 : loss of a contest

de·feat·ism \-'fē-ˌti-zəm\ n : acceptance of or resignation to defeat — **de·feat·ist** \-tist\ n or adj

def·e·cate \'de-fi-ˌkāt\ vb **-cat·ed; -cat·ing** 1 : to free from impurity or corruption 2 : to discharge feces from the bowels — **def·e·ca·tion** \ˌde-fi-'kā-shən\ n

¹de·fect \'dē-ˌfekt, di-'fekt\ n : BLEMISH, FAULT, IMPERFECTION

²de·fect \di-'fekt\ vb : to desert a cause, party, or nation esp. in order to espouse another — **de·fec·tion** \-'fek-shən\ n — **de·fec·tor** \-'fek-tər\ n

de·fec·tive \di-'fek-tiv\ adj : FAULTY, DEFICIENT — **defective** n

de·fence chiefly Brit var of DEFENSE

de·fend \di-'fend\ vb [ME, fr. AF defendre, fr. L defendere, fr. de- from + -fendere to strike] 1 : to repel danger or attack from ⟨~ the fort⟩ 2 : to act as attorney for 3 : to oppose the claim of another in a lawsuit : CONTEST 4 : to maintain against opposition ⟨~ an idea⟩ 5 : to try to retain against a challenge ⟨~ed his title⟩ — **de·fend·er** n

de·fen·dant \di-'fen-dənt\ n : a person required to make answer in a legal action or suit

de·fense \di-'fens\ n 1 : the act of defending : resistance against attack 2 : means, method, or capability of defending 3 : an argument in support 4 : the answer made by the defendant in a legal action 5 : a defending party, group, or team — **de·fense·less** adj — **de·fen·si·ble** adj

defense mechanism n : an often unconscious mental process (as repression) that assists in reaching compromise solutions to personal problems

¹de·fen·sive \di-'fen-siv\ adj 1 : serving or intended to defend or protect 2 : of or relating to the attempt to keep an opponent from scoring (as in a game) — **de·fen·sive·ly** adv — **de·fen·sive·ness** n

²defensive n : a defensive position

¹de·fer \di-'fər\ vb **de·ferred; de·fer·ring** [ME deferren, differren, fr. MF differer, fr. L differre to postpone, be different] : POSTPONE, PUT OFF

²defer vb **deferred; deferring** [ME deferren, differren, fr. MF deferer, defferer, fr. LL deferre, fr. L, to bring down, bring, fr. de- down + ferre to carry] : to submit or yield to the opinion or wishes of another — **de·fer·ral** \-əl\ n

def·er·ence \'de-fər-əns\ n : courteous, respectful, or ingratiating regard for another's wishes ♦ **Synonyms** HONOR, HOMAGE, OBEISANCE, REVERENCE — **def·er·en·tial** \ˌde-fə-'ren-chəl\ adj

de·fer·ment \di-'fər-mənt\ n : the act of delaying; esp : official postponement of military service

de·fi·ance \di-'fī-əns\ n 1 : CHALLENGE 2 : disposition to resist or contend

de·fi·ant \-ənt\ adj : full of defiance : BOLD, IMPUDENT — **de·fi·ant·ly** adv

de·fi·bril·la·tor \dē-'fi-brə-ˌlā-tər\ n : an electronic device that applies an electric shock to restore the rhythm of a fibrillating heart — **de·fi·bril·late** \-ˌlāt\ vb — **de·fi·bril·la·tion** \-ˌfi-brə-'lā-shən\ n

deficiency disease n : a disease (as scurvy or beriberi) caused by a lack of essential dietary elements and esp. a vitamin or mineral

de·fi·cient \di-'fi-shənt\ adj : lacking in something necessary; also : not up to a normal standard — **de·fi·cien·cy** \-shən-sē\ n

def·i·cit \'de-fə-sət\ n : a deficiency in amount; esp : an excess of expenditures over revenue

¹de·file \di-'fī(-ə)l\ vb **de·filed; de·fil·ing** 1 : to make filthy 2 : CORRUPT 3 : to violate the chastity of 4 : to violate the sanctity of : DESECRATE 5 : DISHONOR ♦ **Synonyms** CONTAMINATE, POLLUTE, SOIL, TAINT — **de·file·ment** n

²de·file \di-'fī(-ə)l, 'dē-ˌfī(-ə)l\ n : a narrow passage or gorge

de·fine \di-'fīn\ vb **de·fined; de·fin·ing** 1 : to set forth the meaning of ⟨~ a word⟩ 2 : to fix or mark the limits of 3 : to clarify in outline or character — **de·fin·able** adj — **de·fin·er** n

def·i·nite \'de-fə-nət\ adj 1 : having distinct limits : FIXED 2 : clear in meaning 3 : typically designating an identified or immediately identifiable person or thing ⟨a ~ article⟩ — **def·i·nite·ly** adv — **def·i·nite·ness** n

def·i·ni·tion \ˌde-fə-'ni-shən\ n 1 : an act of determining or settling 2 : a statement of the meaning of a word or word group; *also* : the action or process of defining **3** : the action or the power of making definite and clear : CLARITY, DISTINCTNESS

de·fin·i·tive \di-'fi-nə-tiv\ *adj* **1** : DECISIVE, CONCLUSIVE **2** : authoritative and apparently exhaustive ⟨a ~ edition⟩ **3** : serving to define or specify precisely ⟨~ laws⟩

de·flate \di-'flāt\ *vb* **de·flat·ed; de·flat·ing 1** : to release air or gas from **2** : to reduce in size, importance, or effectiveness; *also* : to reduce from a state of inflation **3** : to become deflated

de·fla·tion \-'flā-shən\ *n* **1** : an act or instance of deflating : the state of being deflated **2** : reduction in the volume of available money or credit resulting in a decline of the general price level

de·flect \di-'flekt\ *vb* : to turn aside — **de·flec·tion** \-'flek-shən\ *n*

de·flo·ra·tion \₁de-flə-'rā-shən\ *n* : rupture of the hymen

de·flow·er \dē-'flaú(-ə)r\ *vb* : to deprive of virginity

de·fog \dē-'fóg, -'fäg\ *vb* : to remove fog or condensed moisture from ⟨~ a windshield⟩ — **de·fog·ger** *n*

de·fo·li·ant \dē-'fō-lē-ənt\ *n* : a chemical spray or dust used to defoliate plants

de·fo·li·ate \-,āt\ *vb* : to deprive of leaves esp. prematurely — **de·fo·li·a·tion** \dē-,fō-lē-'ā-shən\ *n* — **de·fo·li·a·tor** \dē-'fō-lē-,ā-tər\ *n*

de·for·es·ta·tion \dē-,fòr-ə-'stā-shən\ *n* : the action or process of clearing an area of forests; *also* : the state of having been cleared of forests — **de·for·est** \(,)dē-'fòr-əst, -'fär-\ *vb*

de·form \di-'fòrm\ *vb* **1** : DISFIGURE, DEFACE **2** : to make or become misshapen or changed in shape — **de·for·ma·tion** \dē-,fòr-'mā-shən, ,de-fər-\ *n*

de·for·mi·ty \di-'fòr-mə-tē\ *n, pl* **-ties 1** : the state of being deformed **2** : a physical blemish or distortion

de·fraud \di-'fród\ *vb* : CHEAT

de·fray \di-'frā\ *vb* : to provide for the payment of : PAY — **de·fray·al** *n*

de·frock \(,)dē-'fräk\ *vb* : to deprive (as a priest) of the right to exercise the functions of office

de·frost \di-'fróst\ *vb* **1** : to thaw out **2** : to free from ice — **de·frost·er** *n*

deft \'deft\ *adj* : quick and neat in action — **deft·ly** *adv* — **deft·ness** *n*

de·funct \di-'fəŋkt\ *adj* : DEAD, EXTINCT ⟨a ~ language⟩

de·fuse \dē-'fyüz\ *vb* **1** : to remove the fuse from (as a bomb) **2** : to make less harmful, potent, or tense

de·fy \di-'fī\ *vb* **de·fied; de·fy·ing** [ME, to renounce faith in, challenge, fr. AF *desfier, defier,* fr. *de-* from + *fier* to entrust, ultim. fr. L *fidere* to trust] **1** : CHALLENGE, DARE **2** : to refuse boldly to obey or to yield to : DISREGARD ⟨~ the law⟩ **3** : WITHSTAND, BAFFLE ⟨a scene that *defies* description⟩

deg *abbr* degree

de·gas \dē-'gas\ *vb* : to remove gas from

de·gen·er·a·cy \di-'je-nə-rə-sē\ *n, pl* **-cies 1** : the state of being degenerate **2** : the process of becoming degenerate **3** : PERVERSION

¹de·gen·er·ate \di-'je-nə-rət\ *adj* : fallen or deteriorated from a former, higher, or normal condition — **de·gen·er·a·tion** \-,je-nə-'rā-shən\ *n* — **de·gen·er·a·tive** \-'je-nə-,rā-tiv\ *adj*

²de·gen·er·ate \di-'je-nə-,rāt\ *vb* : to undergo deterioration (as in morality, intelligence, structure, or function)

³de·gen·er·ate \-rət\ *n* : a degenerate person; *esp* : a sexual pervert

de·grad·able \di-'grā-də-bəl\ *adj* : capable of being chemically degraded

de·grade \di-'grād\ *vb* **1** : to reduce from a higher to a lower rank or degree **2** : DEBASE, CORRUPT **3** : DECOMPOSE — **deg·ra·da·tion** \₁de-grə-'dā-shən\ *n*

de·gree \di-'grē\ *n* [ME, fr. AF *degré,* fr. VL **degradus,* fr. L *de-* down + *gradus* step, grade] **1** : a step in a series **2** : a rank or grade of official, ecclesiastical, or social position; *also* : the civil condition of a person **3** : the extent, intensity, or scope of something esp. as measured by a graded series **4** : one of the forms or sets of forms used in the comparison of an adjective or adverb **5** : a title conferred upon students by a college, university, or professional school on completion of a program of study **6** : a line or space of the musical staff; *also* : a note or tone of a musical scale **7** : a unit of measure for angles

that is equal to an angle with its vertex at the center of a circle and its sides cutting off ¹⁄₃₆₀ of the circumference; *also* : a unit of measure for arcs of a circle that is equal to the amount of arc extending ¹⁄₃₆₀ of the circumference **8** : any of various units for measuring temperature

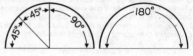

degree 7

de·horn \dē-'hórn\ *vb* : to deprive of horns

de·hu·man·ize \dē-'hyü-mə-,nīz\ *vb* : to deprive of human qualities, personality, or spirit — **de·hu·man·i·za·tion** \,dē-,hyü-mə-nə-'zā-shən\ *n*

de·hu·mid·i·fy \,dē-hyü-'mi-də-,fī\ *vb* : to remove moisture from (as the air) — **de·hu·mid·i·fi·er** *n*

de·hy·drate \dē-'hī-,drāt\ *vb* : to remove water from; *also* : to lose liquid — **de·hy·dra·tion** \,dē-hī-'drā-shən\ *n*

de·hy·dro·ge·na·tion \,dē-(,)hī-,drä-jə-'nā-shən, -drə-\ *n* : the removal of hydrogen from a chemical compound — **de·hy·dro·ge·nate** \,dē-(,)hī-'drä-jə-,nāt, dē-'hī-drə-jə-\ *vb*

de·ice \dē-'īs\ *vb* : to keep free or rid of ice ⟨~ a plane⟩ — **de·ic·er** *n*

de·i·fy \'dē-ə-,fī, 'dā-\ *vb* **-fied; -fy·ing 1** : to make a god of **2** : WORSHIP, GLORIFY — **de·i·fi·ca·tion** \,dē-ə-fə-'kā-shən, ,dā-\ *n*

deign \'dān\ *vb* [ME, fr. AF *deigner,* fr. L *dignare, dignari,* fr. *dignus* worthy] : CONDESCEND

de·ion·ize \dē-'ī-ə-,nīz\ *vb* : to remove ions from

de·ism \'dē-,i-zəm, 'dā-\ *n, often cap* : a system of thought advocating natural religion based on human morality and reason rather than divine revelation — **de·ist** \-ist\ *n, often cap* — **de·is·tic** \dē-'is-tik, dā-\ *adj*

de·i·ty \'dē-ə-tē, 'dā-\ *n, pl* **-ties 1** : DIVINITY **2** **2** *cap* : GOD **3** : a god or goddess

dé·jà vu \,dā-,zhä-'vü\ *n* [F, adj., already seen] : the feeling that one has seen or heard something before

de·ject·ed \di-'jek-təd\ *adj* : low in spirits : SAD — **de·ject·ed·ly** *adv*

de·jec·tion \di-'jek-shən\ *n* : lowness of spirits

de ju·re \dē-'jùr-ē\ *adv or adj* [ML] : by legal right

deka·gram \'de-kə-,gram\ *n* — see METRIC SYSTEM table

deka·li·ter \-,lē-tər\ *n* — see METRIC SYSTEM table

deka·me·ter \-,mē-tər\ *n* — see METRIC SYSTEM table

del *abbr* delegate; delegation

Del *abbr* Delaware

Del·a·ware \'de-lə-,wer\ *n, pl* **Delaware** *or* **Delawares** : a member of an American Indian people orig. of the Delaware valley; *also* : their language

¹de·lay \di-'lā\ *n* **1** : the act of delaying : the state of being delayed **2** : the time for which something is delayed

²delay *vb* **1** : POSTPONE, PUT OFF **2** : to stop, detain, or hinder for a time **3** : to move or act slowly

de·lec·ta·ble \di-'lek-tə-bəl\ *adj* **1** : highly pleasing : DELIGHTFUL **2** : DELICIOUS

de·lec·ta·tion \,dē-,lek-'tā-shən\ *n* **1** : DELIGHT, PLEASURE, DIVERSION

¹del·e·gate \'de-li-gət, -,gāt\ *n* **1** : DEPUTY, REPRESENTATIVE **2** : a member of the lower house of the legislature of Maryland, Virginia, or West Virginia

²del·e·gate \-,gāt\ *vb* **1** : to entrust to another ⟨~ authority⟩ **2** : to appoint as one's delegate

del·e·ga·tion \,de-li-'gā-shən\ *n* **1** : the act of delegating **2** : one or more persons chosen to represent others

de·le·git·i·mize \,dē-lə-'ji-tə-,mīz\ *vb* : to diminish or destroy the legitimacy, prestige, or authority of

de·lete \di-'lēt\ *vb* **de·let·ed; de·let·ing** [L *deletus,* fr. *delēre* to wipe out, destroy] : to eliminate esp. by blotting out, cutting out, or erasing ⟨~ a computer file⟩ — **de·le·tion** \-'lē-shən\ *n*

del·e·te·ri·ous \,de-lə-'tir-ē-əs\ *adj* : HARMFUL, NOXIOUS

delft \'delft\ *n* **1** : a Dutch pottery with an opaque white glaze and predominantly blue decoration **2** : glazed pottery esp. when blue and white

delft·ware \-,wer\ *n* : DELFT

deli \'de-lē\ *n, pl* **del·is** : DELICATESSEN

¹de·lib·er·ate \di-ˈli-bə-ˌrāt\ vb -at·ed; -at·ing : to consider carefully — de·lib·er·a·tion \-ˌli-bə-ˈrā-shən\ n — de·lib·er·a·tive \-ˈli-bə-ˌrā-tiv, -brə-tiv\ adj — de·lib·er·a·tive·ly adv

²de·lib·er·ate \di-ˈli-bə-rət, -ˈli-brət\ adj 1 : determined after careful thought 2 : done or said intentionally 3 : UNHURRIED, SLOW — de·lib·er·ate·ly adv — de·lib·er·ate·ness n

del·i·ca·cy \ˈde-li-kə-sē\ n, pl -cies 1 : something pleasing to eat and considered rare or luxurious 2 : FINENESS, DAINTINESS; also : FRAILTY 3 : nicety or expressiveness of touch 4 : precise perception and discrimination : SENSITIVITY 5 : sensibility in feeling or conduct; also : SQUEAMISHNESS 6 : the quality or state of requiring delicate handling

del·i·cate \ˈde-li-kət\ adj 1 : pleasing to the senses of taste or smell esp. in a mild or subtle way 2 : marked by daintiness or charm : EXQUISITE 3 : FASTIDIOUS, SQUEAMISH ⟨a person of ∼ tastes⟩ 4 : easily damaged : FRAGILE; also : SICKLY 5 : requiring skill or tact 6 : marked by care, skill, or tact 7 : marked by minute precision : very sensitive ⟨a ∼ instrument⟩ — del·i·cate·ly adv

del·i·ca·tes·sen \ˌde-li-kə-ˈte-sⁿn\ n pl [G, pl. of Delicatesse delicacy, fr. F délicatesse] 1 : ready-to-eat food products (as cooked meats and prepared salads) 2 sing, pl delicatessens : a store where delicatessen are sold

de·li·cious \di-ˈli-shəs\ adj : affording great pleasure : DELIGHTFUL; esp : very pleasing to the taste or smell — de·li·cious·ly adv — de·li·cious·ness n

¹de·light \di-ˈlīt\ n 1 : great pleasure or satisfaction : JOY 2 : something that gives great pleasure — de·light·ful \-fəl\ adj — de·light·ful·ly adv

²delight vb 1 : to take great pleasure 2 : to satisfy greatly : PLEASE

de·light·ed adj : highly pleased : GRATIFIED — de·light·ed·ly adv

de·lim·it \di-ˈli-mət\ vb : to fix the limits of

de·lin·eate \di-ˈli-nē-ˌāt\ vb -eat·ed; -eat·ing 1 : SKETCH, PORTRAY 2 : to picture in words : DESCRIBE — de·lin·ea·tion \-ˌli-nē-ˈā-shən\ n

de·lin·quen·cy \di-ˈliŋ-kwən-sē\ n, pl -cies : the quality or state of being delinquent

¹de·lin·quent \-kwənt\ n : a delinquent person

²delinquent adj 1 : offending by neglect or violation of duty or of law 2 : being overdue in payment

del·i·quesce \ˌde-li-ˈkwes\ vb -quesced; -quesc·ing : MELT, DISSOLVE — del·i·ques·cent \-ˈkwe-sⁿnt\ adj

de·lir·i·um \di-ˈlir-ē-əm\ n [L, fr. delirare to be crazy, lit., to leave the furrow (in plowing), fr. de- from + lira furrow] : mental disturbance marked by confusion, disordered speech, and hallucinations; also : frenzied excitement — de·lir·i·ous \-ē-əs\ adj — de·lir·i·ous·ly adv

delirium tre·mens \-ˈtrē-mənz, -ˈtre-\ n : a violent delirium with tremors that is induced by excessive and prolonged use of alcoholic liquors

de·liv·er \di-ˈli-vər\ vb -ered; -er·ing 1 : to set free : SAVE 2 : CONVEY, TRANSFER ⟨∼ a letter⟩ 3 : to assist in giving birth or at the birth of; also : to give birth to 4 : UTTER, COMMUNICATE 5 : to send to an intended target or destination — de·liv·er·able \-ˈli-v(ə-)rə-bəl\ adj — de·liv·er·er n

de·liv·er·ance \-v(ə-)rəns\ n — de·liv·er·er n

de·liv·ery \di-ˈli-və-rē\ n, pl -er·ies : the act of delivering something; also : something delivered — de·liv·ery·man \-ˌman\ n

dell \ˈdel\ n : a small secluded valley

de·louse \dē-ˈlaús\ vb : to remove lice from

del·phin·i·um \del-ˈfi-nē-əm\ n : any of a genus of mostly perennial herbs related to the buttercups with tall branching spikes of irregular flowers

del·ta \ˈdel-tə\ n 1 : the 4th letter of the Greek alphabet — Δ or δ 2 : something shaped like a capital Δ; esp : the triangular silt-formed land at the mouth of a river — del·ta·ic \del-ˈtā-ik\ adj

del·toid \ˈdel-ˌtóid\ n : a large triangular muscle that covers the shoulder joint and raises the arm laterally

de·lude \di-ˈlüd\ vb de·lud·ed; de·lud·ing : MISLEAD, DECEIVE, TRICK

¹del·uge \ˈdel-yüj\ n 1 : a flooding of land by water 2 : a drenching rain 3 : a great amount or number ⟨a ∼ of mail⟩

²deluge vb del·uged; del·ug·ing 1 : INUNDATE, FLOOD

2 : to overwhelm as if with a deluge ⟨deluged with e-mails⟩

de·lu·sion \di-ˈlü-zhən\ n : a deluding or being deluded; esp : a persistent false psychotic belief — de·lu·sion·al \-ˈlü-zhə-nəl\ adj — de·lu·sive \-ˈlü-siv\ adj

de·luxe \di-ˈlúks, -ˈləks, -ˈlüks\ adj : notably luxurious or elegant

delve \ˈdelv\ vb delved; delv·ing 1 : DIG 2 : to seek laboriously for information

dely abbr delivery

Dem abbr Democrat; Democratic

de·mag·ne·tize \dē-ˈmag-nə-ˌtīz\ vb : to cause to lose magnetic properties — de·mag·ne·ti·za·tion \dē-ˌmag-nə-tə-ˈzā-shən\ n

dem·a·gogue also dem·a·gog \ˈde-mə-ˌgäg\ n [Gk dēmagōgos, fr. dēmos people + agōgos leading, fr. agein to lead] : a person who appeals to the emotions and prejudices of people esp. in order to gain political power — dem·a·gogu·ery \-ˌgä-gə-rē\ n — dem·a·gogy \-ˌgä-gē, -ˌgä-jē\ n

¹de·mand \di-ˈmand\ n 1 : an act of demanding; also : something claimed as due or just 2 : the ability and desire to buy goods or services; also : the quantity of goods wanted at a stated price 3 : a seeking or being sought after : urgent need 4 : a pressing need or requirement

²demand vb 1 : to ask for with authority : claim as due or just 2 : to ask earnestly or in the manner of a command 3 : REQUIRE, NEED ⟨a patient who ∼s constant care⟩

de·mar·cate \di-ˈmär-ˌkāt, ˈdē-ˌmär-\ vb -cat·ed; -cat·ing 1 : DELIMIT 2 : to set apart : DISTINGUISH — de·mar·ca·tion \ˌdē-ˌmär-ˈkā-shən\ n

dé·marche or de·marche \dā-ˈmärsh\ n : a course of action : MANEUVER

¹de·mean \di-ˈmēn\ vb de·meaned; de·mean·ing : to behave or conduct (oneself) usu. in a proper manner

²demean vb de·meaned; de·mean·ing : DEGRADE, DEBASE

de·mean·or \di-ˈmē-nər\ n : CONDUCT, BEARING

de·mean·our Brit var of DEMEANOR

de·ment·ed \di-ˈmen-təd\ adj : MAD, INSANE — de·ment·ed·ly adv

de·men·tia \di-ˈmen-chə\ n 1 : deterioration of cognitive functioning (as in Alzheimer's disease) 2 : INSANITY

de·mer·it \di-ˈmer-ət\ n 1 : FAULT 2 : a mark placed against a person's record for some fault or offense

de·mesne \di-ˈmān, -ˈmēn\ n 1 : REALM 2 : manorial land actually possessed by the lord and not held by free tenants 3 : ESTATE 4 : REGION

demi·god \ˈde-mi-ˌgäd\ n : a mythological being with more power than a mortal but less than a god

demi·john \ˈde-mi-ˌjän\ n [F dame-jeanne, lit., Lady Jane] : a large narrow-necked bottle usu. enclosed in wickerwork

de·mil·i·ta·rize \dē-ˈmi-lə-tə-ˌrīz\ vb : to strip of military forces, weapons, or fortifications — de·mil·i·tar·i·za·tion \dē-ˌmi-lə-tə-rə-ˈzā-shən\ n

demi·mon·daine \ˌde-mi-ˌmän-ˈdän\ n : a woman of the demimonde

demi·monde \ˈde-mi-ˌmänd\ n [F demi-monde, fr. demi-half + monde world] 1 : a class of women on the fringes of respectable society supported by wealthy lovers 2 : a distinct isolated group having low reputation or prestige

de·min·er·al·ize \dē-ˈmi-nə-rə-ˌlīz\ vb : to remove the mineral matter from — de·min·er·al·i·za·tion \-ˌmi-nə-rə-lə-ˈzā-shən\ n

de·mise \di-ˈmīz\ n 1 : LEASE 2 : transfer of sovereignty to a successor ⟨∼ of the crown⟩ 3 : DEATH 4 : loss of status

demi·tasse \ˈde-mi-ˌtas\ n : a small cup of black coffee; also : the cup used to serve it

demo \ˈde-mō\ n, pl dem·os 1 : DEMONSTRATION 2 : a product used to show performance or merits to prospective buyers 3 : a recording used to show off a song or performer

de·mo·bi·lize \di-ˈmō-bə-ˌlīz, dē-\ vb 1 : DISBAND 2 : to discharge from military service — de·mo·bi·li·za·tion \di-ˌmō-bə-lə-ˈzā-shən, dē-\ n

de·moc·ra·cy \di-ˈmä-krə-sē\ n, pl -cies [MF democratie, fr. LL democratia, fr. Gk dēmokratia, fr. dēmos people + kratos strength, power] 1 : government by the people;

esp : rule of the majority **2** : a government in which the supreme power is held by the people **3** : a political unit that has a democratic government **4** *cap* : the principles and policies of the Democratic party in the U.S. **5** : the common people esp. when constituting the source of political authority **6** : the absence of hereditary or arbitrary class distinctions or privileges

dem·o·crat \'de-mə-ˌkrat\ *n* **1** : one who believes in or practices democracy **2** *cap* : a member of the Democratic party of the U.S.

dem·o·crat·ic \ˌde-mə-'kra-tik\ *adj* **1** : of, relating to, or favoring democracy **2** *often cap* : of or relating to one of the two major political parties in the U.S. associated in modern times with policies of broad social reform and internationalism **3** : relating to or appealing to the common people ⟨~ art⟩ **4** : not snobbish — **dem·o·crat·i·cal·ly** \-ti-k(ə-)lē\ *adv*

de·moc·ra·tize \di-'mä-krə-ˌtīz\ *vb* **-tized; -tiz·ing** : to make democratic

dé·mo·dé \ˌdā-mō-'dā\ *adj* [F] : no longer fashionable : OUT-OF-DATE

de·mo·graph·ics \ˌde-mə-'gra-fiks, ˌdē-\ *n pl* : the statistical characteristics of human populations

de·mog·ra·phy \di-'mä-grə-fē\ *n* : the statistical study of human populations and esp. their size and distribution and the number of births and deaths — **de·mog·ra·pher** \-fər\ *n* — **de·mo·graph·ic** \ˌde-mə-'gra-fik, ˌdē-\ *adj* — **de·mo·graph·i·cal·ly** \-fi-k(ə-)lē\ *adv*

dem·oi·selle \ˌdem-wə-'zel\ *n* [F] : a young woman

de·mol·ish \di-'mä-lish\ *vb* **1** : to destroy by breaking apart : RAZE **2** : SMASH **3** : to put an end to ⟨~ a theory⟩

de·mo·li·tion \ˌde-mə-'li-shən, ˌdē-\ *n* : the act of demolishing; *esp* : destruction by means of explosives

de·mon *or* **dae·mon** \'dē-mən\ *n* **1** : an evil spirit : DEVIL **2** *usu daemon* : an attendant power or spirit **3** : one that has unusual drive or effectiveness ⟨a ~ for work⟩

de·mon·e·tize \dē-'mä-nə-ˌtīz, -'mə-\ *vb* : to stop using as money or as a monetary standard ⟨~ silver⟩ — **de·mon·e·ti·za·tion** \dē-ˌmä-nə-tə-'zā-shən, -ˌmə-\ *n*

de·mo·ni·ac \di-'mō-nē-ˌak\ *also* **de·mo·ni·a·cal** \ˌdē-mə-'nī-ə-kəl\ *adj* **1** : possessed or influenced by a demon **2** : DEMONIC

de·mon·ic \di-'mä-nik\ *also* **de·mon·i·cal** \-ni-kəl\ *adj* : DEVILISH, FIENDISH ⟨~ cruelty⟩

de·mon·ize \'dē-mə-ˌnīz\ *vb* **-ized; -iz·ing** **1** : to convert into a demon **2** : to characterize or treat as evil or harmful

de·mon·ol·o·gy \ˌdē-mə-'nä-lə-jē\ *n* **1** : the study of demons **2** : belief in demons

de·mon·stra·ble \di-'män-strə-bəl\ *adj* **1** : capable of being demonstrated **2** : APPARENT, EVIDENT — **de·mon·stra·bly** \-blē\ *adv*

dem·on·strate \'de-mən-ˌstrāt\ *vb* **-strat·ed; -strat·ing** **1** : to show clearly **2** : to prove or make clear by reasoning or evidence **3** : to explain esp. with many examples **4** : to show publicly ⟨~ a new car⟩ **5** : to make a public display ⟨~ in protest⟩ — **dem·on·stra·tion** \ˌde-mən-'strā-shən\ *n* — **dem·on·stra·tor** \'de-mən-ˌstrā-tər\ *n*

¹de·mon·stra·tive \di-'män-strə-tiv\ *adj* **1** : demonstrating as real or true **2** : characterized by demonstration **3** : pointing out the one referred to and distinguishing it from others of the same class ⟨~ pronoun⟩ **4** : marked by display of feeling : EFFUSIVE — **de·mon·stra·tive·ly** *adv* — **de·mon·stra·tive·ness** *n*

²demonstrative *n* : a demonstrative word and esp. a pronoun

de·mor·al·ize \di-'mȯr-ə-ˌlīz\ *vb* **1** : to corrupt in morals **2** : to weaken in discipline or spirit : DISORGANIZE — **de·mor·al·i·za·tion** \di-ˌmȯr-ə-lə-'zā-shən\ *n*

de·mote \di-'mōt\ *vb* **de·mot·ed; de·mot·ing** : to reduce to a lower grade or rank — **de·mo·tion** \-'mō-shən\ *n*

de·mot·ic \di-'mä-tik\ *adj* : COMMON, POPULAR ⟨~ idiom⟩

de·mur \di-'mər\ *vb* **de·murred; de·mur·ring** [ME *demuren, demeren* to linger, fr. AF *demurer, demoerer,* fr. L *demorari,* fr. *morari* to linger, fr. *mora* delay] : to take exception : OBJECT — **de·mur** *n*

de·mure \di-'myu̇r\ *adj* **1** : quietly modest : DECOROUS **2** : affectedly modest, reserved, or serious : PRIM ♦ **Syn-**

onyms SHY, BASHFUL, COY, DIFFICULT, RETIRING, UNASSERTIVE — **de·mure·ly** *adv*

de·mur·rer \di-'mər-ər\ *n* : a claim by the defendant in a legal action that the plaintiff does not have sufficient grounds to proceed

den \'den\ *n* **1** : LAIR 1 **2** : HIDEOUT ⟨a robber's ~⟩; *also* : a place like a hideout or a center of secret activity ⟨opium ~⟩ ⟨a ~ of iniquity⟩ **3** : a cozy private little room

Den *abbr* Denmark

de·nar \'de-ˌnär, 'dā-\ — see MONEY table

de·na·ture \dē-'nā-chər\ *vb* **de·na·tured; de·na·tur·ing** : to remove or change the natural qualities of; *esp* : to make (alcohol) unfit for drinking

den·drol·o·gy \den-'drä-lə-jē\ *n* : the study of trees — **den·drol·o·gist** \-jist\ *n*

den·gue \'deŋ-gē, -gā\ *n* [Sp] : an acute infectious disease characterized by headache, severe joint pain, and rash

de·ni \'de-ˌnē, 'dā-\ *n pl* — see *denar* at MONEY table

de·ni·al \di-'nī(-ə)l\ *n* **1** : rejection of a request **2** : refusal to admit the truth of a statement or charge; *also* : assertion that something alleged is false **3** : DISAVOWAL **4** : restriction on one's own activity or desires

de·nier \'den-yər\ *n* : a unit of fineness for yarn

den·i·grate \'de-ni-ˌgrāt\ *vb* **-grat·ed; -grat·ing** [L *denigrare,* fr. *nigrare* to blacken, fr. *niger* black] : to cast aspersions on : DEFAME — **den·i·gra·tion** \ˌde-ni-'grā-shən\ *n*

den·im \'de-nəm\ *n* [F *(serge) de Nîmes* serge of Nîmes, France] **1** : a firm durable twilled usu. cotton fabric woven with colored warp and white filling threads **2** *pl* : overalls or pants of usu. blue denim

den·i·zen \'de-nə-zən\ *n* : INHABITANT

de·nom·i·nate \di-'nä-mə-ˌnāt\ *vb* : to give a name to : DESIGNATE

de·nom·i·na·tion \di-ˌnä-mə-'nā-shən\ *n* **1** : an act of denominating **2** : a value or size of a series of related values (as of money) **3** : NAME, DESIGNATION; *esp* : a general name for a category **4** : a religious organization uniting local congregations in a single body — **de·nom·i·na·tion·al** \-shə-nəl\ *adj*

de·nom·i·na·tor \di-'nä-mə-ˌnā-tər\ *n* : the part of a fraction that is below the line indicating division

de·no·ta·tive \'dē-nō-ˌtā-tiv, di-'nō-tə-tiv\ *adj* **1** : denoting or tending to denote **2** : relating to denotation

de·note \di-'nōt\ *vb* **1** : to mark out plainly : INDICATE **2** : to make known **3** : MEAN, NAME — **de·no·ta·tion** \ˌdē-nō-'tā-shən\ *n*

de·noue·ment \ˌdā-ˌnü-'mäⁿ\ *n* [F *dénouement,* lit., untying] : the final outcome of the dramatic complications in a literary work

de·nounce \di-'nau̇ns\ *vb* **de·nounced; de·nounc·ing** **1** : to pronounce esp. publicly to be blameworthy or evil **2** : to inform against : ACCUSE **3** : to announce formally the termination of (as a treaty) — **de·nounce·ment** *n*

de no·vo \di-'nō-vō\ *adv or adj* [L] : over again : ANEW ⟨a case tried ~⟩

dense \'dens\ *adj* **dens·er; dens·est** **1** : marked by compactness or crowding together of parts : THICK ⟨~ forest⟩ ⟨a ~ fog⟩ **2** : DULL, STUPID — **dense·ly** *adv* — **dense·ness** *n*

den·si·ty \'den-sə-tē\ *n, pl* **-ties** **1** : the quality or state of being dense **2** : the quantity of something per unit volume, unit area, or unit length

dent \'dent\ *n* **1** : a small depressed place made by a blow or by pressure **2** : an impression or weakening effect made usu. against resistance **3** : initial progress — **dent** *vb*

den·tal \'den-t³l\ *adj* : of or relating to teeth or dentistry — **den·tal·ly** *adv*

dental floss *n* : a thread used to clean between the teeth

dental hygienist *n* : a person licensed to clean and examine teeth

den·tate \'den-ˌtāt\ *adj* : having pointed projections : NOTCHED

den·ti·frice \'den-tə-frəs\ *n* [ME *dentifricie,* fr. L *dentifricium,* fr. *dent-, dens* tooth + *fricare* to rub] : a powder, paste, or liquid for cleaning the teeth

den·tin \'den-t³n\ *or* **den·tine** \'den-ˌtēn, den-'tēn\ *n* : a calcareous material like bone but harder and denser that composes the principal mass of a tooth

den·tist \'den-tist\ *n* : a person licensed in the care, treatment, and replacement of teeth — **den·tist·ry** *n*

den·ti·tion \den-'ti-shən\ *n* : the number, kind, and arrangement of teeth (as of a person or animal); *also* : TEETH

den·ture \'den-chər\ *n* : a set of teeth; *esp* : a partial or complete set of false teeth

de·nude \di-'nüd, -'nyüd\ *vb* **de·nud·ed; de·nud·ing** : to strip the covering from — **de·nu·da·tion** \ˌdē-nü-'dā-shən, -nyü-\ *n*

de·nun·ci·a·tion \di-ˌnən-sē-'ā-shən\ *n* : the act of denouncing; *esp* : a public condemnation — **de·nun·ci·a·to·ry** \-'nən-sē-ə-ˌtȯr-ē\ *adj*

de·ny \di-'nī\ *vb* **de·nied; de·ny·ing** **1** : to declare untrue **2** : to refuse to recognize or acknowledge : DISAVOW **3** : to refuse to grant ⟨∼ a request⟩ **4** : to reject as false ⟨∼ a theory⟩

de·o·dar \'dē-ə-ˌdär\ *n* [Hindi & Urdu *devadār, deodār,* fr. Skt *devadāru,* fr. *deva* god + *dāru* wood] : a Himalayan cedar

de·odor·ant \dē-'ō-də-rənt\ *n* : a preparation that destroys or masks unpleasant odors

de·odor·ize \dē-'ō-də-ˌrīz\ *vb* : to eliminate the offensive odor of

de·ox·i·dize \dē-'äk-sə-ˌdīz\ *vb* : to remove esp. elemental oxygen from

de·oxy·ri·bo·nu·cle·ic acid \dē-ˌäk-si-ˌrī-bō-nü-ˌklē-ik-, -nyü-\ *n* : DNA

de·oxy·ri·bose \dē-ˌäk-si-'rī-ˌbōs\ *n* : a sugar with five carbon and four oxygen atoms in each molecule that is part of DNA

dep *abbr* **1** depart; departure **2** deposit **3** deputy

de·part \di-'pärt\ *vb* **1** : to go away : go away from : LEAVE **2** : DIE **3** : to turn aside : DEVIATE

de·part·ee \di-pär-'tē\ *n* : a person who is departing or who has departed

de·part·ment \di-'pärt-mənt\ *n* **1** : a distinct sphere or category esp. of an activity or attribute **2** : a functional or territorial division (as of a government, business, or college) — **de·part·men·tal** \di-ˌpärt-'men-tᵊl, ˌdē-\ *adj* — **de·part·men·tal·ly** *adv*

department store *n* : a store having separate sections for a wide variety of goods

de·par·ture \di-'pär-chər\ *n* **1** : the act of going away **2** : a starting out (as on a journey) **3** : DIVERGENCE ⟨a ∼ from tradition⟩

de·pend \di-'pend\ *vb* **1** : to be determined, based, or contingent ⟨life ∼s on food⟩ **2** : TRUST, RELY ⟨you can ∼ on me⟩ **3** : to be dependent esp. for financial support **4** : to hang down ⟨a vine ∼ing from a tree⟩

de·pend·able \di-'pen-də-bəl\ *adj* : TRUSTWORTHY, RELIABLE — **de·pend·abil·i·ty** \-ˌpen-də-'bi-lə-tē\ *n*

de·pen·dence *also* **de·pen·dance** \di-'pen-dəns\ *n* **1** : the quality or state of being dependent; *esp* : the quality or state of being influenced by or subject to another **2** : RELIANCE, TRUST **3** : something on which one relies **4** : drug addiction; *also* : HABITUATION **2**

de·pen·den·cy \-dən-sē\ *n, pl* **-cies** **1** : DEPENDENCE **2** : a territory under the jurisdiction of a nation but not formally annexed by it

¹de·pen·dent \-dənt\ *adj* **1** : hanging down **2** : determined or conditioned by another; *also* : affected with drug dependence **3** : relying on another for support **4** : subject to another's jurisdiction **5** : SUBORDINATE **4** ⟨∼ clauses⟩

²dependent *also* **de·pen·dant** \-dənt\ *n* : one that is dependent; *esp* : a person who relies on another for support

dependent variable *n* : a variable whose value is determined by that of one or more other variables in a function

de·pict \di-'pikt\ *vb* **1** : to represent by a picture **2** : to describe in words — **de·pic·tion** \-'pik-shən\ *n*

de·pil·a·to·ry \di-'pi-lə-ˌtȯr-ē\ *n, pl* **-ries** : a preparation for removing hair, wool, or bristles

de·plane \dē-'plān\ *vb* : to get out of an airplane

de·plete \di-'plēt\ *vb* **de·plet·ed; de·plet·ing** : to exhaust esp. of strength or resources — **de·ple·tion** \-'plē-shən\ *n*

de·plor·able \di-'plȯr-ə-bəl\ *adj* **1** : LAMENTABLE ⟨a ∼ death⟩ **2** : WRETCHED — **de·plor·ably** *adv*

de·plore \-'plȯr\ *vb* **de·plored; de·plor·ing** **1** : to feel or express grief for **2** : to regret strongly **3** : to consider unfortunate or deserving of disapproval

de·ploy \di-'plȯi\ *vb* : to spread out (as troops or ships) in order for battle — **de·ploy·ment** \-mənt\ *n*

de·po·nent \di-'pō-nənt\ *n* : one who gives evidence

de·pop·u·late \dē-'pä-pyə-ˌlāt\ *vb* : to reduce greatly the population of — **de·pop·u·la·tion** \-ˌpä-pyə-'lā-shən\ *n*

de·port \di-'pȯrt\ *vb* **1** : CONDUCT, BEHAVE **2** : BANISH, EXILE — **de·por·ta·tion** \ˌdē-ˌpȯr-'tā-shən\ *n*

de·port·ment \di-'pȯrt-mənt\ *n* : BEHAVIOR, BEARING

de·pose \di-'pōz\ *vb* **de·posed; de·pos·ing** **1** : to remove from high office (as of king) **2** : to testify under oath or by affidavit

¹de·pos·it \di-'pä-zət\ *vb* **de·pos·it·ed** \-zə-təd\; **de·pos·it·ing** **1** : to place for safekeeping or as a pledge; *esp* : to put money in a bank **2** : to lay down : PLACE **3** : to let fall or sink ⟨silt ∼*ed* by a flood⟩ — **de·pos·i·tor** \-zə-tər\ *n*

²deposit *n* **1** : the state of being deposited ⟨money on ∼⟩ **2** : something placed for safekeeping; *esp* : money deposited in a bank **3** : money given as a pledge **4** : an act of depositing **5** : something laid down ⟨a ∼ of silt⟩ **6** : a natural accumulation (as of a mineral)

de·po·si·tion \ˌde-pə-'zi-shən, ˌdē-\ *n* **1** : an act of removing from a position of authority **2** : TESTIMONY **3** : the process of depositing **4** : DEPOSIT

de·pos·i·to·ry \di-'pä-zə-ˌtȯr-ē\ *n, pl* **-ries** : a place where something is deposited esp. for safekeeping

de·pot *1, 2 usu* 'de-pō, *3 usu* 'dē-\ *n* **1** : a place for storing goods or vehicles **2** : a place where military supplies or replacements are kept or assembled **3** : a building for railroad or bus passengers

depr *abbr* depreciation

de·prave \di-'prāv\ *vb* **de·praved; de·prav·ing** [ME, fr. AF *depraver,* fr. L *depravare* to pervert, fr. *pravus* crooked, bad] : CORRUPT, PERVERT — **de·praved** *adj* — **de·prav·i·ty** \-'pra-və-tē\ *n*

dep·re·cate \'de-pri-ˌkāt\ *vb* **-cat·ed; -cat·ing** [L *deprecari* to avert by prayer, fr. *precari* to pray] **1** : to express disapproval of **2** : BELITTLE — **dep·re·ca·tion** \ˌde-pri-'kā-shən\ *n*

dep·re·ca·to·ry \'de-pri-kə-ˌtȯr-ē\ *adj* **1** : APOLOGETIC **2** : serving to deprecate : DISAPPROVING

de·pre·ci·ate \di-'prē-shē-ˌāt\ *vb* **-at·ed; -at·ing** [ME, fr. LL *depreciatus,* pp. of *depretiare,* fr. L *pretium* price] **1** : BELITTLE, DISPARAGE **2** : to lessen in price or value — **de·pre·cia·ble** \-shə-bəl\ *adj* — **de·pre·ci·a·tion** \-ˌprē-shē-'ā-shən\ *n*

dep·re·da·tion \ˌde-prə-'dā-shən\ *n* : a laying waste or plundering — **dep·re·date** \'de-prə-ˌdāt\ *vb*

de·press \di-'pres\ *vb* **1** : to press down : cause to sink to a lower position **2** : to lessen the activity or force of **3** : SADDEN, DISCOURAGE **4** : to lessen in price or value — **de·pres·sor** \-'pre-sər\ *n*

de·pres·sant \di-'pre-sᵊnt\ *n* : one that depresses; *esp* : a chemical substance (as a drug) that reduces bodily functional activity — **depressant** *adj*

de·pressed \-'prest\ *adj* **1** : low in spirits; *also* : affected with psychological depression **2** : suffering from economic depression

de·pres·sion \di-'pre-shən\ *n* **1** : an act of depressing : a state of being depressed **2** : a pressing down : LOWERING **3** : a state of feeling sad **4** : a psychological disorder marked esp. by sadness, inactivity, difficulty in thinking and concentration, and feelings of dejection **5** : a depressed area or part **6** : a period of low general economic activity with widespread unemployment

¹de·pres·sive \di-'pre-siv\ *adj* **1** : tending to depress **2** : characterized or affected by psychological depression

²depressive *n* : a person affected with or prone to psychological depression

de·pres·sur·ize \(ˌ)dē-'pre-shə-ˌrīz\ *vb* : to release pressure from

dep·ri·va·tion \ˌde-prə-'vā-shən\ *n* **1** : an act or instance of depriving : LOSS **2** : PRIVATION **2**

de·prive \di-'prīv\ *vb* **de·prived; de·priv·ing** **1** : to take something away from **2** : to stop from having something

deprived *adj* : marked by deprivation esp. of the necessities of life

de·pro·gram \(ˌ)dē-'prō-ˌgram, -grəm\ *vb* : to dissuade from convictions usu. of a religious nature often by coercive means

dept *abbr* department

depth \'depth\ *n, pl* **depths** \'depths\ **1** : something that is deep; *esp* : the deep part of a body of water **2** : a part that is far from the outside or surface; *also* : the middle or innermost part **3** : ABYSS **4** : a profound or intense state ⟨the ∼*s* of reflection⟩; *also* : the worst part ⟨during the ∼*s* of the depression⟩ **5** : a reprehensibly low condition **6** : the distance from top to bottom or from front to back **7** : the quality of being deep **8** : the degree of intensity
depth charge *n* : an explosive device for use underwater esp. against submarines
dep·u·ta·tion \,de-pyə-'tā-shən\ *n* **1** : the act of appointing a deputy **2** : DELEGATION
de·pute \di-'pyüt\ *vb* **de·put·ed; de·put·ing** : DELEGATE
dep·u·tize \'de-pyə-,tīz\ *vb* **-tized; -tiz·ing** : to appoint or act as deputy
dep·u·ty \'de-pyə-tē\ *n, pl* **-ties** **1** : a person appointed to act for or in place of another **2** : an assistant empowered to act as a substitute in the absence of a superior **3** : a member of a lower house of a legislative assembly
der *or* **deriv** *abbr* derivation; derivative
de·rail \di-'rāl\ *vb* : to leave or cause to leave the rails — **de·rail·ment** *n*
de·rail·leur \di-'rā-lər\ *n* [F *dérailleur*] : a device for shifting gears on a bicycle by moving the chain from one set of exposed gears to another
de·range \di-'rānj\ *vb* **de·ranged; de·rang·ing** **1** : DISARRANGE, UPSET **2** : to make insane — **de·range·ment** *n*
der·by \'dər-bē, *Brit* 'där-\ *n, pl* **derbies** **1** : a horse race usu. for three-year-olds held annually **2** : a race or contest open to all **3** : a stiff felt hat with dome-shaped crown and narrow brim

derby 3

de·re·cho \də-'rā-(,)chō\ *n, pl* **-chos** [Sp, straight (contrasted with *tornado*, taken to mean "turned")] : a complex of thunderstorms with powerful winds
de·reg·u·la·tion \(,)dē-,re-gyù-'lā-shən\ *n* : the act of removing restrictions or regulations — **de·reg·u·late** \-'re-gyù-,lāt\ *vb*
¹**der·e·lict** \'der-ə-,likt\ *adj* **1** : abandoned by the owner or occupant **2** : NEGLIGENT ⟨∼ in his duty⟩
²**derelict** *n* **1** : something voluntarily abandoned; *esp* : a ship abandoned on the high seas **2** : a destitute homeless social misfit : VAGRANT, BUM
der·e·lic·tion \,der-ə-'lik-shən\ *n* **1** : the act of abandoning : the state of being abandoned **2** : intentional neglect ⟨∼ of duty⟩
de·ride \di-'rīd\ *vb* **de·rid·ed; de·rid·ing** : to laugh at scornfully : RIDICULE
de ri·gueur \də-rē-'gər\ *adj* [F] : prescribed or required by fashion, etiquette, or custom : PROPER
de·ri·sion \də-'ri-zhən\ *n* : RIDICULE — **de·ri·sive** \-'rī-siv\ *adj* — **de·ri·sive·ly** *adv* — **de·ri·sive·ness** *n* — **de·ri·so·ry** \-'rī-sə-rē\ *adj*
der·i·va·tion \,der-ə-'vā-shən\ *n* **1** : the formation of a word from an earlier word or root; *also* : an act of ascertaining or stating the derivation of a word **2** : ETYMOLOGY **3** : SOURCE, ORIGIN; *also* : DESCENT **4** : an act or process of deriving
de·riv·a·tive \di-'ri-və-tiv\ *n* **1** : a word formed by derivation **2** : something derived **3** : the limit of the ratio of the change of a function's value to the change in its independent variable as the latter change approaches zero — **derivative** *adj*
de·rive \di-'rīv\ *vb* **de·rived; de·riv·ing** [ME, fr. AF *deriver*, fr. L *derivare*, lit., to draw off (water), fr. *de-* from + *rivus* stream] **1** : to receive or obtain from a source **2** : to obtain from a parent substance **3** : INFER, DEDUCE

4 : to trace the derivation of **5** : to come from a certain source
der·mal \'dər-məl\ *adj* : of or relating to the skin : CUTANEOUS
der·ma·ti·tis \,dər-mə-'tī-təs\ *n, pl* **-tit·i·des** \-'ti-tə-,dēz\ *or* **-ti·tis·es** : inflammation of the skin
der·ma·tol·o·gy \-'tä-lə-jē\ *n* : a branch of medical science dealing with the structure, functions, and diseases of the skin — **der·ma·tol·o·gist** \-jist\ *n*
der·mis \'dər-məs\ *n* : the sensitive vascular inner layer of the skin
der·o·gate \'der-ə-,gāt\ *vb* **-gat·ed; -gat·ing** **1** : to cause to seem inferior : DISPARAGE **2** : DETRACT — **der·o·ga·tion** \,der-ə-'gā-shən\ *n* — **de·ro·ga·tive** \di-'rä-gə-tiv\ *adj*
de·rog·a·to·ry \di-'rä-gə-,tòr-ē\ *adj* : intended to lower the reputation of a person or thing : DISPARAGING — **de·rog·a·to·ri·ly** \-,rä-gə-'tòr-ə-lē\ *adv*
der·rick \'der-ik\ *n* [obs. *derrick* hangman, gallows, fr. *Derick*, name of 17th cent. Eng. hangman] **1** : a hoisting apparatus : CRANE **2** : a framework over a drill hole (as for oil) for supporting machinery
der·ri·ere *or* **der·ri·ère** \,der-ē-'er\ *n* : BUTTOCKS
der·ring–do \,der-iŋ-'dü\ *n* : DARING
der·rin·ger \'der-ən-jər\ *n* : a short-barreled pocket pistol
der·vish \'dər-vish\ *n* [Turk *derviş*, lit., beggar, fr. Pers *darvīsh*] : a member of a Muslim religious order noted for devotional exercises (as bodily movements leading to a trance)
de·sal·i·nate \dē-'sa-lə-,nāt\ *vb* **-nat·ed; -nat·ing** : DESALT — **de·sal·i·na·tion** \-,sa-lə-'nā-shən\ *n*
de·sal·i·nize \dē-'sa-lə-,nīz\ *vb* **-nized; -niz·ing** : DESALT — **de·sal·i·ni·za·tion** \-,sa-lə-nə-'zā-shən\ *n*
de·salt \dē-'sòlt\ *vb* : to remove salt from ⟨∼ seawater⟩ — **de·salt·er** *n*
des·cant \'des-,kant\ *vb* **1** : to sing or play part music : SING **2** : to discourse or write at length
de·scend \di-'send\ *vb* **1** : to pass from a higher to a lower place or level ; pass, move, or climb down or down along **2** : DERIVE ⟨∼ed from royalty⟩ **3** : to pass by inheritance or transmission **4** : to incline, lead, or extend downward **5** : to swoop down or appear suddenly (as in an attack)
¹**de·scen·dant** *also* **de·scen·dent** \di-'sen-dənt\ *adj* **1** : DESCENDING **2** : proceeding from an ancestor or source
²**descendant** *also* **descendent** *n* **1** : one descended from another or from a common stock **2** : one deriving directly from a precursor or prototype
de·scent \di-'sent\ *n* **1** : ANCESTRY, BIRTH, LINEAGE **2** : the act or process of descending **3** : SLOPE **4** : a descending way (as a downgrade) **5** : a sudden hostile raid or assault **6** : a downward step (as in station or value) : DECLINE
de·scram·ble \dē-'skram-bəl\ *vb* : UNSCRAMBLE **2** ⟨∼ satellite transmissions⟩ — **de·scram·bler** \-b(ə-)lər\ *n*
de·scribe \di-'skrīb\ *vb* **de·scribed; de·scrib·ing** **1** : to represent or give an account of in words **2** : to trace the outline of — **de·scrib·able** *adj*
de·scrip·tion \di-'skrip-shən\ *n* **1** : an account of something; *esp* : an account that presents a picture to a person who reads or hears it **2** : KIND, SORT — **de·scrip·tive** \-'skrip-tiv\ *adj*
de·scry \di-'skrī\ *vb* **de·scried; de·scry·ing** **1** : to catch sight of **2** : to discover by observation or investigation
des·e·crate \'de-si-,krāt\ *vb* **-crat·ed; -crat·ing** : PROFANE — **des·e·cra·tion** \,de-si-'krā-shən\ *n*
de·seg·re·gate \dē-'se-gri-,gāt\ *vb* : to eliminate segregation in; *esp* : to free of any law or practice requiring isolation on the basis of race — **de·seg·re·ga·tion** \-,se-gri-'gā-shən\ *n*
de·sen·si·tize \dē-'sen-sə-,tīz\ *vb* : to make (a sensitized or hypersensitive individual) insensitive or nonreactive to a sensitizing agent — **de·sen·si·ti·za·tion** \-,sen-sə-tə-'zā-shən\ *n*
¹**des·ert** \'de-zərt\ *n* : dry land with few plants and little rainfall
²**des·ert** \'de-zərt\ *adj* : of, relating to, or resembling a desert; *esp* : being barren and without life ⟨a ∼ island⟩
³**de·sert** \di-'zərt\ *n* **1** : the quality or fact of deserving reward or punishment **2** : a just reward or punishment
⁴**de·sert** \di-'zərt\ *vb* **1** : to withdraw from **2** : ABANDON, FORSAKE — **de·sert·er** *n* — **de·ser·tion** \-'zər-shən\ *n*

de·serve \di-'zərv\ *vb* **de·served; de·serv·ing** : to be worthy of : MERIT — **de·serv·ing** *adj*

de·serv·ed·ly \-'zər-vəd-lē\ *adv* : according to merit : JUSTLY

deshabille *var of* DISHABILLE

des·ic·cate \'de-si-ˌkāt\ *vb* **-cat·ed; -cat·ing** : DRY, DEHYDRATE — **des·ic·ca·tion** \ˌde-si-'kā-shən\ *n* — **des·ic·ca·tor** \'de-si-ˌkā-tər\ *n*

de·sid·er·a·tum \di-ˌsi-də-'rä-təm, -ˌzi-, -'rā-\ *n, pl* **-ta** \-tə\ [L] : something desired as essential

1de·sign \di-'zīn\ *vb* **1** : to conceive and plan out in the mind **2** : INTEND **3** : to devise for a specific function or end **4** : to make a pattern or sketch of **5** : to conceive and draw the plans for

2design *n* **1** : a particular purpose : deliberate planning **2** : a mental project or scheme : PLAN **3** : a secret project or scheme : PLOT **4** *pl* : aggressive or evil intent — used with *on* or *against* **5** : a preliminary sketch or plan **6** : an underlying scheme that governs functioning, developing, or unfolding : MOTIF ⟨the general ∼ of the epic⟩ **7** : the arrangement of elements or details in a product or a work of art **8** : a decorative pattern ⟨a floral ∼⟩ **9** : the art of executing designs

1des·ig·nate \'de-zig-ˌnāt, -nət\ *adj* : chosen but not yet installed ⟨ambassador ∼⟩

2des·ig·nate \-ˌnāt\ *vb* **-nat·ed; -nat·ing** **1** : to appoint and set apart for a special purpose **2** : to mark or point out : INDICATE; *also* : SPECIFY, STIPULATE **3** : to call by a name or title — **des·ig·na·tion** \ˌde-zig-'nā-shən\ *n*

designated driver *n* : a person chosen to abstain from alcohol so as to transport others safely

designated hitter *n* : a baseball player designated at the start of the game to bat in place of the pitcher without causing the pitcher to be removed from the game

de·sign·er \di-'zī-nər\ *n* **1** : one who creates plans for a project or structure **2** : one who designs and manufactures high-fashion clothing — **designer** *adj*

designer drug *n* : a synthetic version of an illicit drug that has been chemically altered to avoid its prohibition

de·sign·ing \di-'zī-niŋ\ *adj* : CRAFTY, SCHEMING

de·sir·able \di-'zī-rə-bəl\ *adj* **1** : PLEASING, ATTRACTIVE **2** : ADVISABLE ⟨∼ legislation⟩ — **de·sir·abil·i·ty** \-ˌzī-rə-'bi-lə-tē\ *n* — **de·sir·able·ness** *n* — **de·sir·ably** \-'zī-rə-blē\ *adv*

1de·sire \di-'zī(-ə)r\ *vb* **de·sired; de·sir·ing** [ME, fr. AF *desirer*, fr. L *desiderare*, fr. *sider-, sidus* heavenly body] **1** : to long or hope for : exhibit or feel desire for **2** : REQUEST

2desire *n* **1** : a strong wish : LONGING, CRAVING **2** : sexual urge or appetite **3** : a usu. formal request for action **4** : something desired

de·sir·ous \di-'zī(ə)r-əs\ *adj* : eagerly wishing : DESIRING ⟨∼ of fame⟩

de·sist \di-'zist, -'sist\ *vb* : to cease to proceed or act

desk \'desk\ *n* [ME *deske*, fr. ML *desca*, fr. It *desco* table, fr. L *discus* dish, disc] **1** : a table, frame, or case esp. for writing and reading **2** : a counter, stand, or booth at which a person performs duties **3** : a specialized division of an organization (as a newspaper) ⟨city ∼⟩

desk·top publishing \'desk-ˌtäp-\ *n* : the production of printed matter by means of a microcomputer

1des·o·late \'de-sə-lət, -zə-\ *adj* **1** : DESERTED, ABANDONED **2** : FORSAKEN, LONELY **3** : DILAPIDATED **4** : BARREN, LIFELESS ⟨a ∼ landscape⟩ **5** : CHEERLESS, GLOOMY ⟨∼ memories⟩ — **des·o·late·ly** *adv* — **des·o·late·ness** *n*

2des·o·late \-ˌlāt\ *vb* **-lat·ed; -lat·ing** : to make desolate : lay waste : make wretched

des·o·la·tion \ˌde-sə-'lā-shən, -zə-\ *n* **1** : the action of desolating **2** : GRIEF, SADNESS **3** : LONELINESS **4** : DEVASTATION, RUIN **5** : barren wasteland

des·oxy·ri·bo·nu·cle·ic acid \de-ˌzäk-sē-'rī-bō-nù-ˌklē-ik-, -nyù-\ *n* : DNA

1de·spair \di-'sper\ *vb* : to lose all hope or confidence — **de·spair·ing** \-iŋ\ *adj* — **de·spair·ing·ly** *adv*

2despair *n* **1** : utter loss of hope **2** : a cause of hopelessness

des·patch *chiefly Brit var of* DISPATCH

des·per·a·do \ˌdes-pə-'rä-dō, -'rā-\ *n, pl* **-does** or **-dos** : a bold or reckless criminal

des·per·ate \'des-pə-rət, -prət\ *adj* **1** : being beyond or almost beyond hope : causing despair **2** : RASH ⟨a ∼

attempt⟩ **3** : extremely intense — **des·per·ate·ly** *adv* — **des·per·ate·ness** *n*

des·per·a·tion \ˌdes-pə-'rā-shən\ *n* **1** : a loss of hope and surrender to despair **2** : a state of hopelessness leading to rashness

de·spi·ca·ble \di-'spi-kə-bəl, 'des-pi-\ *adj* : deserving to be despised — **de·spi·ca·bly** \-blē\ *adv*

de·spise \di-'spīz\ *vb* **de·spised; de·spis·ing** **1** : to look down on with contempt or aversion : DISDAIN, DETEST **2** : to regard as negligible, worthless, or distasteful

de·spite \di-'spīt\ *prep* : in spite of

de·spoil \di-'spói(-ə)l\ *vb* : to strip of belongings, possessions, or value — **de·spoil·er** *n* — **de·spoil·ment** *n*

de·spo·li·a·tion \di-ˌspō-lē-'ā-shən\ *n* : the act of plundering : the state of being despoiled

1de·spond \di-'spänd\ *vb* : to become discouraged or disheartened

2despond *n* : DESPONDENCY

de·spon·den·cy \-'spän-dən-sē\ *n* : DEJECTION, HOPELESSNESS — **de·spon·dent** \-dənt\ *adj* — **de·spon·dent·ly** *adv*

des·pot \'des-pət, -ˌpät\ *n* [MF *despote*, fr. Gk *despotēs* master, lord, autocrat] **1** : a ruler with absolute power and authority **2** : a person exercising power tyrannically — **des·pot·ic** \des-'pä-tik\ *adj* — **des·po·tism** \'des-pə-ˌti-zəm\ *n*

des·sert \di-'zərt\ *n* : a course of sweet food, fruit, or cheese served at the close of a meal

de·stig·ma·tize \dē-'stig-mə-ˌtīz\ *vb* : to remove associations of shame or disgrace from

des·ti·na·tion \ˌdes-tə-'nā-shən\ *n* **1** : a purpose for which something is destined **2** : an act of appointing, setting aside for a purpose, or predetermining **3** : a place to which one is journeying or to which something is sent

des·tine \'des-tən\ *vb* **des·tined; des·tin·ing** **1** : to settle in advance **2** : to designate, assign, or dedicate in advance **3** : to direct or set apart for a specific purpose or place

des·ti·ny \'des-tə-nē\ *n, pl* **-nies** **1** : something to which a person or thing is destined : FATE, FORTUNE **2** : a predetermined course of events

des·ti·tute \'des-tə-ˌtüt, -ˌtyüt\ *adj* **1** : lacking something needed or desirable **2** : suffering extreme poverty — **des·ti·tu·tion** \ˌdes-tə-'tü-shən, -'tyü-\ *n*

de·stroy \di-'strói\ *vb* **1** : to put an end to : RUIN **2** : KILL

de·stroy·er \di-'strói-ər\ *n* **1** : one that destroys **2** : a small speedy warship

de·struc·ti·ble \di-'strək-tə-bəl\ *adj* : capable of being destroyed — **de·struc·ti·bil·i·ty** \-ˌstrək-tə-'bi-lə-tē\ *n*

de·struc·tion \di-'strək-shən\ *n* **1** : RUIN **2** : the action or process of destroying something **3** : a destroying agency

de·struc·tive \di-'strək-tiv\ *adj* **1** : causing destruction : RUINOUS **2** : designed or tending to hurt or destroy — **de·struc·tive·ly** *adv* — **de·struc·tive·ness** *n*

de·sue·tude \'de-swi-ˌtüd, -ˌtyüd\ *n* : DISUSE

des·ul·to·ry \'de-səl-ˌtór-ē\ *adj* : passing aimlessly from one thing or subject to another : DISCONNECTED

det *abbr* **1** detached; detachment **2** detail

de·tach \di-'tach\ *vb* **1** : to separate esp. from a larger mass **2** : DISENGAGE, WITHDRAW — **de·tach·able** *adj*

de·tached \di-'tacht\ *adj* **1** : not joined or connected : SEPARATE **2** : ALOOF, IMPARTIAL ⟨a ∼ attitude⟩

de·tach·ment \di-'tach-mənt\ *n* **1** : SEPARATION **2** : the dispatching of a body of troops or part of a fleet from the main body for special service; *also* : the portion so dispatched **3** : a small permanent military unit of special composition **4** : indifference to worldly concerns : ALOOFNESS **5** : IMPARTIALITY

1de·tail \di-'tāl, 'dē-ˌtāl\ *n* [F *détail*, fr. OF *detail* slice, piece, fr. *detaillier* to cut in pieces, fr. *taillier* to cut] **1** : a dealing with something item by item ⟨go into ∼⟩; *also* : ITEM, PARTICULAR ⟨the ∼s of a story⟩ **2** : selection (as of soldiers) for special duty; *also* : the persons thus selected

2detail *vb* **1** : to report in particulars : SPECIFY **2** : to assign to a special duty

de·tailed \di-'tāld, 'dē-ˌtāld\ *adj* : marked by abundant detail

de·tail·ing \'dē-ˌtāl-iŋ\ *n* : the meticulous cleaning and refurbishing of an automobile

de·tain \di-'tān\ *vb* **1** : to hold in or as if in custody **2** : STOP, DELAY

de·tect \di-'tekt\ *vb* : to discover the nature, existence, presence, or fact of — **de·tect·able** *adj* — **de·tec·tion** \-'tek-shən\ *n* — **de·tec·tor** \-'tek-tər\ *n*

1de·tec·tive \di-'tek-tiv\ *adj* **1** : fitted or used for detection **2** : of or relating to detectives

2detective *n* : a person employed or engaged in detecting lawbreakers or getting information that is not readily accessible

dé·tente *or* **de·tente** \dā-'tänt\ *n* [F] : a relaxation of strained relations or tensions (as between nations)

de·ten·tion \di-'ten-chən\ *n* **1** : the act or fact of detaining : CONFINEMENT; *esp* : a period of temporary custody prior to disposition by a court **2** : a forced delay

de·ter \di-'tər\ *vb* **de·terred; de·ter·ring** [L *deterrēre*, fr. *terrēre* to frighten] **1** : to turn aside, discourage, or prevent from acting (as by fear) **2** : INHIBIT

de·ter·gent \di-'tər-jənt\ *n* : a cleansing agent; *esp* : a chemical product similar to soap in its cleaning ability

de·te·ri·o·rate \di-'tir-ē-ə-,rāt\ *vb* **-rat·ed; -rat·ing** : to make or become worse in quality or condition — **de·te·ri·o·ra·tion** \-,tir-ē-ə-'rā-shən\ *n*

de·ter·min·able \-'tər-mə-nə-bəl\ *adj* : capable of being determined; *esp* : ASCERTAINABLE

de·ter·mi·nant \-mə-nənt\ *n* **1** : something that determines or conditions **2** : GENE

de·ter·mi·nate \di-'tər-mə-nət\ *adj* **1** : having fixed limits : DEFINITE ⟨a ~ period of time⟩ **2** : definitely settled ⟨in ~ order⟩ — **de·ter·mi·nate·ness** *n*

de·ter·mi·na·tion \di-,tər-mə-'nā-shən\ *n* **1** : the act of coming to a decision; *also* : the decision or conclusion reached **2** : a fixing of the extent, position, or character of something **3** : accurate measurement (as of length or volume) **4** : firm or fixed purpose — **de·ter·mi·na·tive** \-'tər-mə-,nā-tiv, -'tər-mə-nə-\ *adj*

de·ter·mine \di-'tər-mən\ *vb* **-mined; -min·ing** **1** : to fix conclusively or authoritatively **2** : to come to a decision : SETTLE, RESOLVE **3** : to fix the form or character of beforehand : ORDAIN; *also* : REGULATE **4** : to find out the limits, nature, dimensions, or scope of ⟨~ a position at sea⟩ **5** : to bring about as a result

de·ter·mined \-'tər-mənd\ *adj* **1** : firmly resolved **2** : characterized by or showing determination — **de·ter·mined·ly** \-mənd-lē, -mə-nəd-lē\ *adv* — **de·ter·mined·ness** *n*

de·ter·min·ism \di-'tər-mə-,ni-zəm\ *n* : a doctrine that acts of the will, natural events, or social changes are determined by preceding events or natural causes — **de·ter·min·ist** \-nist\ *n or adj*

de·ter·rence \di-'tər-əns\ *n* : the inhibition of criminal behavior by fear esp. of punishment

de·ter·rent \-ənt\ *adj* **1** : serving to deter ⟨the law's ~ effect⟩ **2** : relating to deterrence — **deterrent** *n*

de·test \di-'test\ *vb* [L *detestari*, lit., to curse while calling a deity to witness, fr. *de-* from + *testari* to call to witness, fr. *testis* witness] : LOATHE, HATE — **de·test·able** *adj* — **de·tes·ta·tion** \,dē-,tes-'tā-shən\ *n*

de·throne \di-'thrōn\ *vb* : to remove from a throne : DEPOSE — **de·throne·ment** *n*

det·o·nate \'de-t²n-,āt\ *vb* **-nat·ed; -nat·ing** : to explode or cause to explode with violence — **det·o·na·tion** \,de-t²n-'ā-shən\ *n*

det·o·na·tor \'de-t²n-,ā-tər\ *n* : a device for detonating an explosive

1de·tour \'dē-,tùr\ *n* : an indirect way replacing part of a route

2detour *vb* : to go by detour

de·tox \'dē-,täks, di-'täks\ *n* : detoxification from an intoxicating or addictive substance — **detox** *vb*

de·tox·i·fy \dē-'täk-sə-,fī\ *vb* **-fied; -fy·ing** **1** : to remove a poison or toxin or the effect of such from **2** : to free (someone) from an intoxicating or addictive substance or from dependence on it — **de·tox·i·fi·ca·tion** \dē-,täk-sə-fə-'kā-shən\ *n*

de·tract \di-'trakt\ *vb* **1** : to take away or diminish the value or effect of something **2** : DIVERT ⟨~s attention from the real issue⟩ — **de·trac·tion** \-'trak-shən\ *n* — **de·trac·tor** \-'trak-tər\ *n*

de·train \dē-'trān\ *vb* : to leave or cause to leave a railroad train

det·ri·ment \'de-trə-mənt\ *n* : INJURY, DAMAGE; *also* : a cause of injury or damage — **det·ri·men·tal** \,de-trə-'ment-²l\ *adj* — **det·ri·men·tal·ly** *adv*

de·tri·tus \di-'trī-təs\ *n, pl* **de·tri·tus** : fragments resulting from disintegration (as of rocks) : DEBRIS

deuce \'düs, 'dyüs\ *n* **1** : a two in cards or dice **2** : a tie in a tennis game with both sides at 40 **3** : DEVIL — used chiefly as a mild oath

Deut *abbr* Deuteronomy

deu·te·ri·um \dü-'tir-ē-əm, dyü-\ *n* : an isotope of hydrogen that has twice the mass of ordinary hydrogen

Deu·ter·on·o·my \,dü-tə-'rä-nə-mē, ,dyü-\ *n* — see BIBLE table

deut·sche mark \'dòi-chə-,märk\ *n* : a former basic monetary unit of Germany

dev *abbr* deviation

de·val·ue \dē-'val-yü\ *vb* : to reduce the international exchange value of ⟨~ a currency⟩ — **de·val·u·a·tion** \-,val-yə-'wā-shən\ *n*

dev·as·tate \'de-və-,stāt\ *vb* **-tat·ed; -tat·ing** **1** : to bring to ruin **2** : to reduce to chaos or helplessness — **dev·as·tat·ing·ly** *adv* — **dev·as·ta·tion** \,de-və-'stā-shən\ *n*

de·vel·op \di-'ve-ləp\ *vb* **1** : to unfold gradually or in detail **2** : to place (exposed photographic material) in chemicals to produce a visible image **3** : to bring out the possibilities of **4** : to make more available or usable ⟨~ land⟩ **5** : to acquire gradually ⟨~ a taste for olives⟩ **6** : to go through a natural process of growth, differentiation, or evolution **7** : to come into being gradually — **de·vel·op·er** *n* — **de·vel·op·ment** *n* — **de·vel·op·men·tal** \-,ve-ləp-'men-t²l\ *adj* — **de·vel·op·men·tal·ly** \-'t²l-ē\ *adv*

de·vi·ant \'dē-vē-ənt\ *adj* : deviating esp. from some accepted norm ⟨~ behavior⟩ — **de·vi·ance** \-əns\ *n* — **de·vi·an·cy** \-ən-sē\ *n* — **deviant** *n*

de·vi·ate \'dē-vē-,āt\ *vb* **-at·ed; -at·ing** [LL *deviare*, fr. L *de-* from + *via* way] : to turn aside from a course, standard, principle, or topic — **de·vi·ate** \-vē-ət, -vē-,āt\ *n* — **de·vi·a·tion** \,dē-vē-'ā-shən\ *n*

de·vice \di-'vīs\ *n* **1** : SCHEME, STRATAGEM **2** : a piece of equipment or a mechanism for a special purpose **3** : DESIRE, INCLINATION ⟨left to my own ~s⟩ **4** : an emblematic design

1dev·il \'de-vəl\ *n* [ME *devel*, fr. OE *dēofol*, fr. LL *diabolus*, fr. Gk *diabolos*, lit., slanderer, fr. *diaballein* to throw across, slander, fr. *dia-* across + *ballein* to throw] **1** *often cap* : the personal supreme spirit of evil **2** : DEMON **3** : a wicked person **4** : an energetic, reckless, or dashing person **5** : FELLOW ⟨poor ~⟩ ⟨lucky ~⟩

2devil *vb* **-iled** *or* **-illed; -il·ing** *or* **-il·ling** **1** : to season highly ⟨~ed eggs⟩ **2** : TEASE, ANNOY

dev·il·ish \'de-və-lish\ *adj* **1** : befitting a devil : EVIL; *also* : MISCHIEVOUS **2** : EXTREME ⟨in a ~ hurry⟩ — **dev·il·ish·ly** *adv* — **dev·il·ish·ness** *n*

dev·il·ment \'de-vəl-mənt, -,ment\ *n* : MISCHIEF

dev·il·ry \-rē\ *or* **dev·il·try** \-trē\ *n, pl* **-il·ries** *or* **-il·tries** **1** : action performed with the help of the devil **2** : MISCHIEF

de·vi·ous \'dē-vē-əs\ *adj* **1** : deviating from a straight line : ROUNDABOUT **2** : ERRANT **3** : TRICKY, CUNNING

1de·vise \di-'vīz\ *vb* **de·vised; de·vis·ing** [ME, fr. AF *deviser* to divide, distinguish, invent, fr. VL **divisare*, fr. L *dividere* to divide] **1** : INVENT **2** : PLOT **3** : to give (real estate) by will

2devise *n* **1** : a disposing of real property by will **2** : a will or clause of a will disposing of real property **3** : property given by will

de·vi·tal·ize \dē-'vī-tə-,līz\ *vb* : to deprive of life or vitality

de·void \di-'vòid\ *adj* : being without : VOID ⟨a book ~ of interest⟩

de·voir \də-'vwär\ *n* **1** : DUTY **2** : a formal act of civility or respect

de·volve \di-'välv\ *vb* **de·volved; de·volv·ing** : to pass (as rights or responsibility) from one to another usu. by succession or transmission — **dev·o·lu·tion** \,de-və-'lü-shən, ,dē-\ *n*

De·vo·ni·an \di-'vō-nē-ən\ *adj* : of, relating to, or being the period of the Paleozoic era between the Silurian and the Mississippian — **Devonian** *n*

de·vote \di-'vōt\ *vb* **de·vot·ed; de·vot·ing** **1** : to commit to wholly or chiefly ⟨~s herself to serving the poor⟩ **2** : to set apart for a special purpose : DEDICATE de·vot·ed \-'vō-təd\ adj : characterized by loyalty and devotion : FAITHFUL ⟨~ fans⟩

dev·o·tee \ˌde-və-'tē, -'tā\ n : an ardent follower, supporter, or enthusiast

de·vo·tion \di-'vō-shən\ n 1 : religious fervor 2 : an act of prayer or private worship — usu. used in pl. 3 : a religious exercise for private use 4 : the fact or state of being dedicated and loyal ⟨~ to music⟩; also : the act of devoting — de·vo·tion·al \-shə-nəl\ adj

de·vour \di-'vaù(-ə)r\ vb 1 : to eat up greedily or ravenously 2 : WASTE, ANNIHILATE ⟨the forest was ~ed by fire⟩ 3 : to enjoy avidly ⟨~ a book⟩ — de·vour·er n

de·vout \di-'vaùt\ adj 1 : devoted to religion : PIOUS 2 : expressing devotion or piety 3 : EARNEST, SERIOUS ⟨a ~ baseball fan⟩ — de·vout·ly adv — de·vout·ness n

dew \'dü, 'dyü\ n : moisture that condenses on the surfaces of cool bodies at night — dewy adj

dew·ber·ry \'dü-ˌber-ē, 'dyü-\ n : any of several sweet edible berries related to and resembling blackberries; also : a trailing bramble bearing these

dew·claw \-ˌklö\ n : a digit on the foot of a mammal that does not reach the ground; also : its claw or hoof

dew·lap \-ˌlap\ n : loose skin hanging under the neck of an animal

dew point n : the temperature at which the moisture in the air begins to condense

dex·ter·i·ty \dek-'ster-ə-tē\ n, pl -ties 1 : mental skill or quickness 2 : readiness and grace in physical activity; esp : skill and ease in using the hands

dex·ter·ous \'dek-strəs\ adj 1 : CLEVER 2 : done with skillfulness 3 : skillful and competent with the hands — dex·ter·ous·ly adv

dex·trose \'dek-ˌstrōs\ n : the naturally occurring form of glucose found in plants and blood

DFC abbr Distinguished Flying Cross

dg abbr decigram

DG abbr 1 [LL Dei gratia] by the grace of God 2 director general

DH \ˌdē-'āch\ n : DESIGNATED HITTER

dhow \'daù\ n : an Arab sailing ship usu. having a long overhang forward and a high poop

DI abbr drill instructor

dia abbr diameter

di·a·be·tes \ˌdī-ə-'bē-tēz, -təs\ n : an abnormal state marked by passage of excessive amounts of urine; esp : one (diabetes mel·li·tus \-'me-lə-təs\) characterized by deficient insulin, by excess sugar in the blood and urine, and by thirst, hunger, and loss of weight — di·a·bet·ic \-'be-tik\ adj or n

di·a·bol·i·cal \ˌdī-ə-'bä-li-kəl\ or di·a·bol·ic \-'bä-lik\ adj : DEVILISH ⟨a ~ plot⟩ — di·a·bol·i·cal·ly \-k(ə-)lē\ adv

di·a·crit·ic \ˌdī-ə-'kri-tik\ n : a mark accompanying a letter and indicating a sound value different from that of the same letter when unmarked — di·a·crit·i·cal \-ti-kəl\ adj

di·a·dem \'dī-ə-ˌdem\ n : CROWN; esp : a royal headband

di·aer·e·sis or di·er·e·sis \dī-'er-ə-səs\ n, pl -e·ses \-ˌsēz\ : a mark ¨ placed over a vowel to show that it is pronounced in a separate syllable (as in naïve)

diag abbr 1 diagonal 2 diagram

di·ag·no·sis \ˌdī-ig-'nō-səs\ n, pl -no·ses \-ˌsēz\ : the art or act of identifying a disease from its signs and symptoms; also : the decision reached by diagnosis — di·ag·nose \'dī-ig-ˌnōs\ vb — di·ag·nos·tic \ˌdī-ig-'näs-tik\ adj — di·ag·nos·ti·cian \-ˌnäs-'ti-shən\ n

¹di·ag·o·nal \dī-'a-gə-nəl\ adj 1 : extending from one corner to the opposite corner in a 4-sided figure 2 : running in a slanting direction ⟨~ stripes⟩ 3 : having slanting markings or parts ⟨a ~ weave⟩ — di·ag·o·nal·ly adv

²diagonal n 1 : a diagonal line 2 : a diagonal row, pattern, or direction 3 : SLASH 3

¹di·a·gram \'dī-ə-ˌgram\ n : a design and esp. a drawing that makes something easier to understand — di·a·gram·ma·ble \-ˌgra-mə-bəl\ adj — di·a·gram·mat·ic \ˌdī-ə-grə-'ma-tik\ adj — di·a·gram·mat·i·cal·ly \-ti-k(ə-)lē\ adv

²diagram vb -grammed or -gramed \-ˌgramd\; -gram·ming or -gram·ing : to represent by a diagram

¹di·al \'dī(-ə)l\ n [ME dyal, fr. ML dialis clock wheel revolving daily, fr. L dies day] 1 : the face of a sundial 2 : the face of a timepiece 3 : a face with a pointer and numbers that indicate something ⟨the ~ of a gauge⟩ 4

: a device used for making electrical connections or for regulating operation (as of a radio)

²dial vb di·aled or di·alled; di·al·ing or di·al·ling 1 : to manipulate a dial so as to operate or select 2 : to make a telephone call or connection

³dial abbr dialect

di·a·lect \'dī-ə-ˌlekt\ n : a regional variety of a language

di·a·lec·tic \ˌdī-ə-'lek-tik\ n : the process or art of reasoning by discussion of conflicting ideas; also : the tension between opposing elements — di·a·lec·ti·cal \-ti-kəl\ adj

dialog box n : a window on a computer screen for choosing options or inputting information

di·a·logue \'dī-ə-ˌlóg\ n 1 : a conversation between two or more parties 2 : the parts of a literary or dramatic work that represent conversation

di·al·y·sis \dī-'a-lə-səs\ n, pl -y·ses \-ˌsēz\ 1 : the separation of substances from solution by means of their unequal diffusion through semipermeable membranes 2 : the medical procedure of removing blood from an artery, purifying it by dialysis, and returning it to a vein

diam abbr diameter

di·am·e·ter \dī-'a-mə-tər\ n [ME diametre, fr. MF, fr. L diametros, fr. Gk, fr. dia- through + metron measure] 1 : a straight line passing through the center of a figure or body; esp : one that divides a circle in half 2 : the length of a diameter

di·a·met·ric \ˌdī-ə-'me-trik\ or di·a·met·ri·cal \-tri-kəl\ adj 1 : of, relating to, or constituting a diameter 2 : completely opposed or opposite — di·a·met·ri·cal·ly \-k(ə-)lē\ adv

di·a·mond \'dī-mənd, 'dī-ə-\ n 1 : a hard brilliant mineral that consists of crystalline carbon and is used as a gem 2 : a flat figure having four equal sides, two acute angles, and two obtuse angles 3 : any of a suit of playing cards marked with a red diamond 4 : INFIELD; also : the entire playing field in baseball

di·a·mond·back rattlesnake \-ˌbak-\ n : either of two large and deadly rattlesnakes of the southern U.S.

di·an·thus \dī-'an-thəs\ n : ¹PINK 1

di·a·pa·son \ˌdī-ə-'pā-z²n, -s²n\ n 1 : the organ stop governing the flue pipes that form the primary basis of organ tone 2 : the entire range of musical tones

¹di·a·per \'dī-pər, 'dī-ə-\ n 1 : a cotton or linen fabric woven in a simple geometric pattern 2 : a garment for a baby drawn up between the legs and fastened about the waist

²diaper vb 1 : to ornament with diaper designs 2 : to put a diaper on

di·aph·a·nous \dī-'a-fə-nəs\ adj : of so fine a texture as to be transparent

di·a·pho·ret·ic \ˌdī-ə-fə-'re-tik\ adj : having the power to increase perspiration — diaphoretic n

di·a·phragm \'dī-ə-ˌfram\ n 1 : a sheet of muscle between the chest and abdominal cavities of a mammal 2 : a vibrating disk (as in a microphone) 3 : a cup-shaped device usu. of thin rubber fitted over the uterine cervix to act as a mechanical contraceptive barrier — di·a·phrag·mat·ic \ˌdī-ə-frag-'ma-tik, -ˌfrag-\ adj

di·a·rist \'dī-ə-rist\ n : one who keeps a diary

di·a·ris·tic \ˌdī-ə-'ris-tik\ adj : of, relating to, or characteristic of a diary

di·ar·rhea \ˌdī-ə-'rē-ə\ n [ME diaria, fr. LL diarrhoea, fr. Gk diarrhoia, fr. diarhein to flow through, fr. dia- through + rhein to flow] : abnormally frequent and watery bowel movements — di·ar·rhe·al \-'rē-əl\ adj

di·ar·rhoea chiefly Brit var of DIARRHEA

di·a·ry \'dī-ə-rē\ n, pl -ries : a daily record esp. of personal experiences; also : a book used as a diary

di·as·po·ra \dī-'as-pə-rə\ n 1 cap : the settling of scattered colonies of Jews outside Palestine after the Babylonian exile 2 cap : the Jews living outside Palestine or modern Israel 3 : the migration or scattering of a people away from an ancestral homeland

di·as·to·le \dī-'as-tə-(ˌ)lē\ n : the stretching of the chambers of the heart during which they fill with blood — di·a·stol·ic \ˌdī-ə-'stä-lik\ adj

dia·ther·my \'dī-ə-ˌthər-mē\ n : the generation of heat in tissue by electric currents for medical purposes

di·a·tom \'dī-ə-ˌtäm\ n : any of a class of planktonic one-celled or colonial algae with skeletons of silica

di·atom·ic \ˌdī-ə-'tä-mik\ adj : having two atoms in the molecule

di·a·tribe \'dī-ə-ˌtrīb\ *n* : biting or abusive speech or writing

di·az·e·pam \dī-'a-zə-ˌpam\ *n* : a tranquilizer used esp. to relieve anxiety, tension, and muscle spasms

dib·ble \'di-bəl\ *n* : a pointed hand tool for making holes (as for planting bulbs) in the ground — **dibble** *vb*

¹dice \'dīs\ *n, pl* **dice** : DIE 1

²dice *vb* **diced; dic·ing 1** : to cut into small cubes ⟨~ carrots⟩ **2** : to play games with dice

di·chot·o·my \dī-'kä-tə-mē\ *n, pl* **-mies** : a division or the process of dividing into two esp. mutually exclusive or contradictory groups — **di·chot·o·mous** \-məs\ *adj*

dick·er \'di-kər\ *vb* : BARGAIN, HAGGLE

dick·ey *or* **dicky** \'di-kē\ *n, pl* **dickeys** *or* **dick·ies** : a small fabric insert worn to fill in the neckline

di·cot·y·le·don \ˌdī-ˌkä-tə-'lēd-ᵊn\ *n* : any of a group of seed plants having an embryo with two cotyledons — **di·cot·y·le·don·ous** *adj*

dict *abbr* dictionary

¹dic·tate \'dik-ˌtāt\ *vb* **dic·tat·ed; dic·tat·ing 1** : to speak or read for a person to transcribe or for a machine to record **2** : COMMAND, ORDER — **dic·ta·tion** \dik-'tā-shən\ *n*

²dic·tate \'dik-ˌtāt\ *n* : an authoritative rule, prescription, or injunction : COMMAND ⟨the ~s of conscience⟩

dic·ta·tor \'dik-ˌtā-tər\ *n* **1** : a person ruling absolutely and often brutally and oppressively **2** : one that dictates

dic·ta·to·ri·al \ˌdik-tə-'tȯr-ē-əl\ *adj* : of, relating to, or characteristic of a dictator or a dictatorship

dic·ta·tor·ship \dik-'tā-tər-ˌship, 'dik-ˌtā-\ *n* **1** : the office of a dictator **2** : autocratic rule, control, or leadership **3** : a government or country in which absolute power is held by a dictator or a small clique

dic·tion \'dik-shən\ *n* **1** : choice of words esp. with regard to correctness, clearness, or effectiveness : WORDING **2** : ENUNCIATION

dic·tio·nary \'dik-shə-ˌner-ē\ *n, pl* **-nar·ies** : a reference book containing words usu. alphabetically arranged along with information about their forms, pronunciations, functions, etymologies, meanings, and syntactical and idiomatic uses

dic·tum \'dik-təm\ *n, pl* **dic·ta** \-tə\ *also* **dictums** : a noteworthy, formal, or authoritative statement or observation

did *past of* DO

di·dac·tic \dī-'dak-tik\ *adj* **1** : intended to instruct, inform, or teach a moral lesson **2** : making moral observations

di·do \'dī-dō\ *n, pl* **didoes** *or* **didos** : a mischievous act : PRANK

¹die \'dī\ *vb* **died; dy·ing** \'dī-iŋ\ [ME *dien*, fr. or akin to ON *deyja* to die] **1** : to stop living : EXPIRE **2** : to pass out of existence ⟨a *dying* race⟩ **3** : SUBSIDE **4** ⟨the wind *died* down⟩ **4** : to long keenly ⟨*dying* to go⟩ **5** : STOP ⟨the motor *died*⟩

²die \'dī\ *n* [ME *dee*, fr. AF *dé*] **1** *pl* **dice** \'dīs\ : a small cube marked on each face with one to six spots and used usu. in pairs in games and gambling **2** *pl* **dies** \'dīz\ : a device used to shape, finish, or impress an object

die·hard \'dī-ˌhärd\ *n* : one who is strongly devoted to or determined — **die–hard** *adj*

dieresis *var of* DIAERESIS

die·sel \'dē-zəl, -səl\ *n* **1** : DIESEL ENGINE **2** : a vehicle driven by a diesel engine **3** : DIESEL FUEL

diesel engine *n* : an internal combustion engine in whose cylinders air is compressed to a temperature sufficiently high to ignite the fuel

diesel fuel *n* : a heavy mineral oil used as fuel in diesel engines

die·sel·ing \'dē-zə-liŋ\ *n* : the continued operation of an internal combustion engine after the ignition has been turned off

¹di·et \'dī-ət\ *n* [ME *diete*, fr. AF, fr. L *diaeta*, fr. Gk *diaita*, lit., manner of living, fr. *diaitasthai* to lead one's life] **1** : food and drink regularly consumed : FARE **2** : an allowance of food prescribed for a special reason (as to lose weight) — **di·e·tary** \-ə-ˌter-ē\ *adj or n*

²diet *vb* : to eat or cause to eat or drink less or according to a prescribed rule — **di·et·er** *n*

dietary supplement *n* : a product taken orally that contains ingredients (as vitamins or amino acids) intended to supplement one's diet

di·e·tet·ics \ˌdī-ə-'te-tiks\ *n sing or pl* : the science or art of applying the principles of nutrition to diet — **di·e·tet·ic** *adj*

di·e·ti·tian *or* **di·e·ti·cian** \ˌdī-ə-'ti-shən\ *n* : a specialist in dietetics

dif *or* **diff** *abbr* difference

dif·fer \'di-fər\ *vb* **dif·fered; dif·fer·ing 1** : to be unlike **2** : VARY **3** : DISAGREE

dif·fer·ence \'di-frəns, 'di-fə-rəns\ *n* **1** : UNLIKENESS ⟨~ in their looks⟩ **2** : distinction or discrimination in preference **3** : DISAGREEMENT; *also* : an instance or cause of disagreement ⟨unable to settle their ~s⟩ **4** : the amount by which one number or quantity differs from another

dif·fer·ent \'di-frənt, 'di-fə-rənt\ *adj* **1** : unlike in nature or quality **2** : DISTINCT ⟨~ age groups⟩; *also* : VARIOUS ⟨~ members of the club⟩ **3** : ANOTHER ⟨try a ~ channel⟩ **4** : UNUSUAL, SPECIAL ⟨a quite ~ style⟩ — **dif·fer·ent·ly** *adv*

¹dif·fer·en·tial \ˌdi-fə-'ren-chəl\ *adj* : showing, creating, or relating to a difference

²differential *n* **1** : the amount or degree by which things differ **2** : an arrangement of gears in an automobile that allows one wheel to turn faster than another (as in rounding curves)

differential gear *n* : DIFFERENTIAL 2

dif·fer·en·ti·ate \ˌdi-fə-'ren-chē-ˌāt\ *vb* **-at·ed; -at·ing 1** : to make or become different **2** : to attain a specialized adult form and function during development **3** : to recognize or state the difference ⟨~ between them⟩ — **dif·fer·en·ti·a·tion** \-ˌren-chē-'ā-shən\ *n*

dif·fi·cult \'di-fi-(ˌ)kəlt\ *adj* **1** : hard to do or make ⟨a ~ climb⟩ **2** : hard to understand or deal with ⟨~ reading⟩ ⟨a ~ child⟩

dif·fi·cul·ty \-(ˌ)kəl-tē\ *n, pl* **-ties** [ME *difficulte*, fr. AF *difficulté*, fr. L *difficilis* not easy, fr. *dis-* not + *facilis* easy] **1** : difficult nature ⟨the ~ of a task⟩ **2** : DISAGREEMENT ⟨settled their *difficulties*⟩ **3** : OBSTACLE ⟨overcome *difficulties*⟩ **4** : TROUBLE ⟨in financial *difficulties*⟩ ♦ **Synonyms** HARDSHIP, RIGOR, VICISSITUDE

dif·fi·dent \'di-fə-dənt\ *adj* **1** : lacking confidence **2** : RESERVED 1 — **dif·fi·dence** \-dəns\ *n* — **dif·fi·dent·ly** *adv*

dif·frac·tion \di-'frak-shən\ *n* : the bending or spreading of waves (as of light) esp. when passing through narrow slits

¹dif·fuse \di-'fyüs\ *adj* **1** : VERBOSE, WORDY ⟨~ writing⟩ **2** : not concentrated or localized ⟨~ light⟩

²dif·fuse \di-'fyüz\ *vb* **dif·fused; dif·fus·ing 1** : to pour out or spread widely **2** : to undergo or cause to undergo diffusion **3** : to break up light by diffusion

dif·fu·sion \di-'fyü-zhən\ *n* **1** : a diffusing or a being diffused **2** : movement of particles (as of a gas) from a region of high to one of lower concentration **3** : the reflection of light from a rough surface or the passage of light through a translucent material

¹dig \'dig\ *vb* **dug** \'dəg\; **dig·ging 1** : to turn up the soil (as with a spade) **2** : to hollow out or form by removing earth ⟨~ a hole⟩ **3** : to uncover or seek by turning up earth ⟨~ potatoes⟩ **4** : DISCOVER ⟨~ up information⟩ **5** : POKE, THRUST ⟨~ a person in the ribs⟩ **6** : to work hard **7** : UNDERSTAND, APPRECIATE; *also* : LIKE, ADMIRE

²dig *n* **1** : THRUST, POKE; *also* : a cutting remark : GIBE **2** *pl* : living or working accommodations

³dig *abbr* digest

¹di·gest \'dī-ˌjest\ *n* : a summarized or shortened version esp. of a literary work

²di·gest \dī-'jest, də-\ *vb* **1** : to think over and arrange in the mind **2** : to convert (food) into simpler forms that can be absorbed by the body **3** : to compress into a short summary — **di·gest·ibil·i·ty** \-ˌjes-tə-'bi-lə-tē\ *n* — **di·gest·ible** *adj* — **di·ges·tion** \-'jes-chən\ *n* — **di·ges·tive** \-'jes-tiv\ *adj*

di·ges·tif \ˌdē-zhes-'tēf\ *n* : an alcoholic drink taken after a meal

dig in *vb* **1** : to take a defensive stand esp. by digging trenches **2** : to firmly set to work **3** : to begin eating

dig·it \'di-jət\ *n* [ME, fr. L *digitus* finger, toe] **1** : any of the Arabic numerals 1 to 9 and usu. the symbol 0 **2** : FINGER, TOE

dig·i·tal \'di-jə-t³l\ *adj* **1** : of, relating to, or done with a finger or toe **2** : of, relating to, or using calculation by numerical methods or by discrete units **3** : relating to or employing communications signals in the form of binary digits ⟨a ∼ broadcast⟩ **4** : providing a readout in numerical digits ⟨a ∼ watch⟩ **5** : ELECTRONIC; *also* : characterized by computerized technology ⟨the ∼ age⟩ — **dig·i·tal·ly** *adv*

digital camera *n* : a camera that records images as digital data instead of on film

dig·i·tal·is \ˌdi-jə-'ta-ləs\ *n* : a drug from the common foxglove that is a powerful heart stimulant; *also* : FOXGLOVE

digital versatile disc *n* : DVD

digital video disc *n* : DVD

dig·ni·fied \'dig-nə-ˌfīd\ *adj* : showing or expressing dignity

dig·ni·fy \-ˌfī\ *vb* -**fied;** -**fy·ing** : to give dignity, distinction, or attention to

dig·ni·tary \'dig-nə-ˌter-ē\ *n, pl* -**tar·ies** : a person of high position or honor

dig·ni·ty \'dig-nə-tē\ *n, pl* -**ties** **1** : the quality or state of being worthy, honored, or esteemed **2** : high rank, office, or position **3** : formal reserve of manner, language, or appearance

di·graph \'dī-ˌgraf\ *n* : a group of two successive letters whose phonetic value is a single sound (as *ea* in *bread*)

di·gress \dī-'gres, də-\ *vb* : to turn aside esp. from the main subject or argument — **di·gres·sion** \-'gre-shən\ *n* — **di·gres·sive** \-'gre-siv\ *adj*

Di·jon mustard \'dē-ˌzhän-, di-'zhän-\ *n* : a mustard made from dark mustard seeds, white wine, and spices

dike \'dīk\ *n* : a bank of earth constructed to control water : LEVEE

dil *abbr* dilute

di·lap·i·dat·ed \də-'la-pə-ˌdā-təd\ *adj* : fallen into partial ruin or decay — **di·lap·i·da·tion** \-ˌla-pə-'dā-shən\ *n*

di·late \dī-'lāt, 'dī-ˌlāt\ *vb* **di·lat·ed; di·lat·ing** : SWELL, DISTEND, EXPAND ⟨her pupils were *dilated*⟩ — **dil·a·ta·tion** \ˌdi-lə-'tā-shən\ *n* — **di·la·tion** \dī-'lā-shən\ *n*

dil·a·to·ry \'di-lə-ˌtōr-ē\ *adj* **1** : DELAYING **2** : TARDY, SLOW

di·lem·ma \də-'le-mə\ *n* **1** : a usu. undesirable or unpleasant choice; *also* : a situation involving such a choice **2** : PREDICAMENT

dil·et·tante \ˌdi-lə-'tänt, -'tant\ *n, pl* -**tantes** *or* -**tan·ti** \-'tän-tē, -'tan-\ [It, fr. prp. of *dilettare* to delight, fr. L *dilectare*] : a person having a superficial interest in an art or a branch of knowledge

dil·i·gent \'di-lə-jənt\ *adj* : characterized by steady, earnest, and energetic effort : PAINSTAKING — **dil·i·gence** \-jəns\ *n* — **dil·i·gent·ly** *adv*

dill \'dil\ *n* : an herb related to the carrot with aromatic leaves and seeds used as a seasoning and in pickles

dil·ly \'di-lē\ *n, pl* **dil·lies** : one that is remarkable or outstanding

dil·ly·dal·ly \'di-lē-ˌda-lē\ *vb* : to waste time by loitering or delaying

¹di·lute \dī-'lüt, də-\ *vb* **di·lut·ed; di·lut·ing** : to lessen the consistency or strength of by mixing with something else — **di·lu·tion** \-'lü-shən\ *n*

²dilute *adj* : DILUTED, WEAK

¹dim \'dim\ *adj* **dim·mer; dim·mest** **1** : LUSTERLESS, DULL ⟨∼ colors⟩ **2** : not bright or distinct : OBSCURE, FAINT **3** : not seeing or understanding clearly — **dim·ly** *adv* — **dim·ness** *n*

²dim *vb* **dimmed; dim·ming** **1** : to make or become dim or lusterless **2** : to reduce the light from

³dim *abbr* **1** dimension **2** diminished **3** diminutive

dime \'dīm\ *n* [ME, tenth part, tithe, fr. AF *disme, dime,* fr. L *decima,* fr. fem. of *decimus* tenth, fr. *decem* ten] : a U.S. coin worth ¹/₁₀ dollar

di·men·sion \də-'men-chən, dī-\ *n* **1** : the physical property of length, breadth, or thickness; *also* : a measure of this **2** : EXTENT, SCOPE, PROPORTIONS — usu. used in pl. ⟨the ∼s of this problem⟩ — **di·men·sion·al** \-'men-chə-nəl\ *adj* — **di·men·sion·al·i·ty** \-ˌmen-chə-'na-lə-tē\ *n*

di·min·ish \də-'mi-nish\ *vb* **1** : to make less or cause to appear less **2** : BELITTLE **3** : DWINDLE **4** : TAPER — **dim·i·nu·tion** \ˌdi-mə-'nü-shən, -'nyü-\ *n*

di·min·u·en·do \də-ˌmin-yə-'wen-dō\ *adv or adj* : DECRESCENDO

¹di·min·u·tive \də-'min-yə-tiv\ *n* **1** : a diminutive word or affix ⟨the word "kitchenette" is a ∼⟩ **2** : a diminutive individual

²diminutive *adj* **1** : indicating small size and sometimes the state or quality of being lovable, pitiable, or contemptible ⟨the ∼ suffixes -*ette* and -*ling*⟩ **2** : extremely small : TINY

dim·i·ty \'di-mə-tē\ *n, pl* -**ties** : a thin usu. corded cotton fabric

dim·mer \'di-mər\ *n* : a device for controlling the amount of light from an electric lighting unit

di·mor·phic \(ˌ)dī-'mȯr-fik\ *adj* : occurring in two distinct forms — **di·mor·phism** \-ˌfi-zəm\ *n*

dim·ple \'dim-pəl\ *n* : a small depression esp. in the cheek or chin

²dimple *vb* **dim·pled; dim·pling** : to form dimples (as in smiling)

din \'din\ *n* : a loud confused mixture of noises

di·nar \di-'när\ *n* **1** — see MONEY table **2** — see *rial* at MONEY table

dine \'dīn\ *vb* **dined; din·ing** [ME, fr. AF *disner, diner* to eat, have a meal, fr. VL **disjejunare* to break one's fast, ultim. fr. L *jejunus* fasting] **1** : to eat dinner **2** : to give a dinner to

din·er \'dī-nər\ *n* **1** : one that dines **2** : a railroad dining car **3** : a restaurant usu. resembling a dining car

di·nette \dī-'net\ *n* : an alcove or small room used for dining

ding \'diŋ\ *vb* : to cause minor damage to a surface — **ding** *n*

din·ghy \'diŋ-ē\ *n, pl* **dinghies** **1** : a small boat **2** : LIFE RAFT

din·gle \'diŋ-gəl\ *n* : a small wooded valley

din·go \'diŋ-gō\ *n, pl* **dingoes** : a reddish brown wild dog of Australia

din·gus \'diŋ-gəs, -əs\ *n* : DOODAD

din·gy \'din-jē\ *adj* **din·gi·er; -est** : DIRTY, UNCLEAN; *also* : SHABBY — **din·gi·ness** *n*

dink \'diŋk\ *n, often all cap* [*double income, no kids*] : a couple with two incomes and no children; *also* : a member of such a couple

din·ky \'diŋ-kē\ *adj* **din·ki·er; -est** : overly small ⟨a ∼ apartment⟩

din·ner \'di-nər\ *n* : the main meal of the day; *also* : a formal banquet

din·ner·ware \'di-nər-ˌwer\ *n* : tableware other than flatware

di·no \'dī-nō\ *n, pl* **dinos** : DINOSAUR

di·no·fla·gel·late \ˌdī-nō-'fla-jə-lət, -ˌlāt\ *n* : any of an order of planktonic plantlike unicellular flagellates of which some cause red tide

di·no·saur \'dī-nə-ˌsȯr\ *n* [ultim. fr. Gk *deinos* terrifying + *sauros* lizard] : any of a group of extinct long-tailed Mesozoic reptiles often of huge size

dint \'dint\ *n* **1** : FORCE ⟨by ∼ of sheer grit⟩ **2** : DENT

di·o·cese \'dī-ə-səs, -ˌsēz, -ˌsēs\ *n, pl* -**ces·es** \-sə-səz, -ˌsē-zəz, -ˌsē-səz\ : the territorial jurisdiction of a bishop — **di·oc·e·san** \dī-'ä-sə-sən, ˌdī-ə-'sē-z°n\ *adj or n*

di·ode \'dī-ˌōd\ *n* : an electronic device with two electrodes or terminals used esp. as a rectifier

di·ox·in \dī-'äk-sən\ *n* : a persistent toxic hydrocarbon that occurs esp. as a by-product of industrial processes and waste incineration

¹dip \'dip\ *vb* **dipped; dip·ping** **1** : to plunge temporarily or partially under the surface (as of a liquid) **2** : to thrust in a way to suggest immersion **3** : to scoop up or out : LADLE **4** : to lower and then raise quickly ⟨∼ a flag in salute⟩ **5** : to drop or slope down esp. suddenly ⟨the moon *dipped* below the crest⟩ **6** : to decrease moderately and usu. temporarily ⟨prices *dipped*⟩ **7** : to reach inside or as if inside or below a surface ⟨*dipped* into their savings⟩ **8** : to delve casually into something; *esp* : to read superficially ⟨∼ into a book⟩

²dip *n* **1** : an act of dipping; *esp* : a short swim **2** : inclination downward : DROP **3** : something obtained by or used in dipping **4** : a sauce or soft mixture into which food may be dipped **5** : a liquid into which something may be dipped (as for cleansing or coloring)

diph·the·ria \dif-'thir-ē-ə\ *n* : an acute contagious bacterial disease marked by fever and by coating of the air passages with a membrane that interferes with breathing

diph·thong \'dif-,thȯṅ, 'dip-\ *n* : two vowel sounds joined in one syllable to form one speech sound (as *ou* in *out*)
dip·loid \'di-,plȯid\ *adj* : having two haploid sets of chromosomes ⟨~ somatic cells⟩ — **diploid** *n*
di·plo·ma \də-'plō-mə\ *n* : an official record of graduation from or of a degree conferred by a school
di·plo·ma·cy \də-'plō-mə-sē\ *n* 1 : the art and practice of conducting negotiations between nations 2 : TACT
dip·lo·mat \'di-plə-,mat\ *n* : one employed or skilled in diplomacy — **dip·lo·mat·ic** \,di-plə-'ma-tik\ *adj*
di·plo·ma·tist \də-'plō-mə-tist\ *n* : DIPLOMAT
dip·per \'di-pər\ *n* 1 : any of a genus of birds that are related to the thrushes and are skilled in diving 2 : something (as a ladle or scoop) that dips or is used for dipping 3 *cap* : BIG DIPPER 4 *cap* : LITTLE DIPPER

dipper 2

dip·so·ma·nia \,dip-sə-'mā-nē-ə\ *n* : an uncontrollable craving for alcoholic liquors — **dip·so·ma·ni·ac** \-nē-,ak\ *n*
dip·stick \'dip-,stik\ *n* : a graduated rod for indicating depth
dip·ter·an \'dip-tə-rən\ *adj* : of, relating to, or being a fly (sense 2) — **dipteran** *n* — **dip·ter·ous** \-rəs\ *adj*
dir *abbr* 1 direction 2 director
di·ram \dē-'ram\ *n* — see *somoni* at MONEY table
dire \'dī(-ə)r\ *adj* **dir·er; dir·est** 1 : very horrible : DREADFUL ⟨~ suffering⟩ 2 : warning of disaster 3 : EXTREME ⟨~ poverty⟩
¹di·rect \də-'rekt, dī-\ *vb* 1 : ADDRESS ⟨~ a letter⟩; *also* : to impart orally : AIM ⟨~ a remark to the gallery⟩ 2 : to regulate the activities or course of : guide the supervision, organizing, or performance of 3 : to cause to turn, move, or point or to follow a certain course 4 : to point, extend, or project in a specified line or course 5 : to request or instruct with authority 6 : to show or point out the way
²direct *adj* 1 : stemming immediately from a source ⟨~ result⟩ 2 : being or passing in a straight line of descent : LINEAL ⟨~ ancestor⟩ 3 : leading from one point to another in time or space without turn or stop : STRAIGHT 4 : NATURAL, STRAIGHTFORWARD ⟨a ~ manner⟩ 5 : operating without an intervening agency or step ⟨~ action⟩ 6 : effected by the action of the people or the electorate and not by representatives ⟨~ democracy⟩ 7 : consisting of or reproducing the exact words of a speaker or writer — **direct** *adv* — **di·rect·ly** *adv* — **di·rect·ness** *n*
direct broadcast satellite *n* : a television broadcasting system in which satellite transmissions are received at the viewing location
direct current *n* : an electric current flowing in one direction only
direct deposit *n* : a method of payment in which money is transferred to the payee's account without the use of checks or cash
di·rec·tion \də-'rek-shən, dī-\ *n* 1 : MANAGEMENT, GUIDANCE 2 : COMMAND, ORDER, INSTRUCTION 3 : the course or line along which something moves, lies, or points 4 : TENDENCY, TREND — **di·rec·tion·al** \-shə-nəl\ *adj*
di·rec·tive \də-'rek-tiv, dī-\ *n* : something that directs and usu. impels toward an action or goal; *esp* : an order issued by a high-level body or official
direct mail *n* : printed matter used for soliciting business or contributions and mailed direct to individuals
di·rec·tor \də-'rek-tər, dī-\ *n* 1 : one that directs : MANAGER, SUPERVISOR, CONDUCTOR 2 : one of a group of persons who direct the affairs of an organized body — **di·rec·to·ri·al** \-,rek-'tȯr-ē-əl\ *adj* — **di·rec·tor·ship** *n*

di·rec·tor·ate \-tə-rət\ *n* 1 : the office or position of director 2 : a board of directors; *also* : membership on such a board 3 : an executive staff
director's cut *n* : a version of a motion picture that is edited according to the director's wishes
di·rec·to·ry \-tə-rē\ *n, pl* **-ries** 1 : an alphabetical or classified list esp. of names and addresses 2 : FOLDER 4
dire·ful \'dī(-ə)r-fəl\ *adj* : DREADFUL ⟨a ~ disease⟩; *also* : OMINOUS
dirge \'dərj\ *n* [ME *dirige* church service for the dead, fr. the first word of a LL anthem, fr. L, imper. of *dirigere* to direct] : a song of lamentation; *also* : a slow mournful piece of music
dir·ham \'dir-həm\ *n* 1 — see MONEY table 2 — see *dinar, riyal* at MONEY table
di·ri·gi·ble \'dir-ə-jə-bəl, də-'ri-jə-\ *n* : AIRSHIP
dirk \'dərk\ *n* : DAGGER 1
dirndl \'dərn-dᵊl\ *n* [short for G *Dirndlkleid*, fr. G dial. *Dirndl* girl + G *Kleid* dress] : a full skirt with a tight waistband
dirt \'dərt\ *n* 1 : a filthy or soiling substance (as mud, dust, or grime) 2 : loose or packed earth : SOIL 3 : moral uncleanness 4 : scandalous gossip 5 : embarrassing or incriminating information
¹dirty \'dər-tē\ *adj* **dirt·i·er; -est** 1 : SOILED, FILTHY 2 : INDECENT, SMUTTY ⟨~ jokes⟩ 3 : BASE, UNFAIR ⟨a ~ trick⟩ 4 : STORMY, FOGGY ⟨~ weather⟩ 5 : not clear in color : DULL ⟨a ~ red⟩ — **dirt·i·ness** *n* — **dirty** *adv*
²dirty *vb* **dirt·ied; dirty·ing** : to make or become dirty
dis·able \di-'sā-bəl\ *vb* **dis·abled; dis·abling** 1 : to disqualify legally 2 : to make unable to perform by or as if by illness, injury, or malfunction — **dis·abil·i·ty** \,di-sə-'bi-lə-tē\ *n*
dis·abled *adj* : incapacitated by illness or injury; *also* : physically or mentally impaired
dis·abuse \,di-sə-'byüz\ *vb* : to free from error, fallacy, or misconception
dis·ad·van·tage \,di-sad-'van-tij\ *n* 1 : loss or damage esp. to reputation or finances 2 : an unfavorable, inferior, or prejudicial condition, quality, or circumstance — **dis·ad·van·ta·geous** \di-,sad-,van-'tā-jəs, -vən-\ *adj*
dis·ad·van·taged \-tijd\ *adj* : lacking in basic resources or conditions believed necessary for an equal position in society
dis·af·fect \,di-sə-'fekt\ *vb* : to alienate the affection or loyalty of — **dis·af·fec·tion** \-'fek-shən\ *n*
dis·agree \,di-sə-'grē\ *vb* 1 : to fail to agree 2 : to differ in opinion 3 : to cause discomfort or distress ⟨fried foods ~ with her⟩ — **dis·agree·ment** *n*
dis·agree·able \-ə-bəl\ *adj* 1 : causing discomfort : UNPLEASANT, OFFENSIVE ⟨a ~ odor⟩ 2 : ILL-TEMPERED, PEEVISH — **dis·agree·able·ness** *n* — **dis·agree·ably** \-blē\ *adv*
dis·al·low \,dis-ə-'laů\ *vb* : to refuse to admit or recognize : REJECT ⟨~ a claim⟩ — **dis·al·low·ance** *n*
dis·ap·pear \,dis-ə-'pir\ *vb* 1 : to pass out of sight 2 : to cease to be : become lost — **dis·ap·pear·ance** *n*
dis·ap·point \,dis-ə-'pȯint\ *vb* : to fail to fulfill the expectation or hope of — **dis·ap·point·ment** *n*
dis·ap·pro·ba·tion \dis-,a-prə-'bā-shən\ *n* : DISAPPROVAL
dis·ap·prov·al \,dis-ə-'prü-vəl\ *n* : adverse judgment : CENSURE
dis·ap·prove \-'prüv\ *vb* 1 : CONDEMN 2 : to feel or express disapproval ⟨~s of smoking⟩ 3 : REJECT — **dis·ap·prov·ing·ly** \-'prü-viṅ-lē\ *adv*
dis·arm \dis-'ärm\ *vb* 1 : to take arms or weapons from 2 : to reduce the size and strength of the armed forces of a country 3 : to make harmless, peaceable, or friendly : win over ⟨a ~ing smile⟩ — **dis·ar·ma·ment** \-'är-mə-mənt\ *n*
dis·ar·range \,dis-ə-'rānj\ *vb* : to disturb the arrangement or order of — **dis·ar·range·ment** *n*
dis·ar·ray \-'rā\ *n* 1 : DISORDER, CONFUSION 2 : disorderly or careless dress
dis·as·sem·ble \,dis-ə-'sem-bəl\ *vb* : to take apart
dis·as·so·ci·ate \-'sō-shē-,āt, -sē-\ *vb* : to detach from association
dis·as·ter \di-'zas-tər, -'sas-\ *n* [MF *desastre*, fr. It *disastro*, fr. *astro* star, fr. L *astrum*] : a sudden or great misfortune — **dis·as·trous** \-'zas-trəs\ *adj* — **dis·as·trous·ly** *adv*
dis·avow \,dis-ə-'vaů\ *vb* : to deny responsibility for : REPUDIATE — **dis·avow·al** \-'vaů-(ə)l\ *n*

dis·band \dis-'band\ *vb* : to break up the organization of : DISPERSE

dis·bar \dis-'bär\ *vb* : to expel from the legal profession — **dis·bar·ment** *n*

dis·be·lieve \ˌdis-bə-'lēv\ *vb* 1 : to hold not worthy of belief : not believe 2 : to withhold or reject belief — **dis·be·lief** \-'lēf\ *n* — **dis·be·liev·er** *n*

dis·bur·den \dis-'bər-dᵊn\ *vb* : to rid of a burden

dis·burse \dis-'bərs\ *vb* **dis·bursed; dis·burs·ing** 1 : to pay out : EXPEND 2 : DISTRIBUTE — **dis·burse·ment** *n*

¹disc *var of* DISK

²disc *abbr* discount

dis·card \dis-'kärd, 'dis-ˌkärd\ *vb* 1 : to let go a playing card from one's hand; *also* : to play (a card) from a suit other than a trump but different from the one led 2 : to get rid of as unwanted — **dis·card** \'dis-ˌkärd\ *n*

disc brake *n* : a brake that operates by the friction of a pair of plates pressing against the sides of a rotating disc

dis·cern \di-'sərn, -'zərn\ *vb* 1 : to detect with the eyes : DISTINGUISH 2 : DISCRIMINATE 3 : to come to know or recognize mentally ⟨~ right from wrong⟩ — **dis·cern·ible** *adj* — **dis·cern·ment** *n*

dis·cern·ing *adj* : revealing insight and understanding ⟨a ~ critic⟩

¹dis·charge \dis-'chärj, 'dis-ˌchärj\ *vb* 1 : to relieve of a charge, load, or burden : UNLOAD; *esp* : to remove the electrical energy from ⟨~ a storage battery⟩ 2 : to let or put off ⟨~ passengers⟩ 3 : SHOOT ⟨~ an arrow⟩ 4 : to set free ⟨~ a prisoner⟩ 5 : to dismiss from service or employment ⟨~ a soldier⟩ 6 : to get rid of by paying or doing ⟨~ a debt⟩ 7 : to give forth fluid ⟨the river ~s into the ocean⟩

²dis·charge \'dis-ˌchärj, dis-'chärj\ *n* 1 : the act of discharging, unloading, or releasing 2 : something that discharges; *esp* : a certification of release or payment 3 : a firing off (as of a gun) 4 : a flowing out (as of blood from a wound); *also* : something that is emitted ⟨a purulent ~⟩ 5 : release or dismissal esp. from an office or employment; *also* : complete separation from military service 6 : a flow of electricity (as through a gas)

dis·ci·ple \di-'sī-pəl\ *n* [ultim. fr. LL *discipulus* follower of Jesus in his lifetime, fr. L, pupil] 1 : one who accepts and helps to spread the teachings of another; *also* : a convinced adherent 2 *cap* : a member of the Disciples of Christ

dis·ci·pli·nar·i·an \ˌdi-sə-plə-'ner-ē-ən\ *n* : one who enforces order

dis·ci·plin·ary \'di-sə-plə-ˌner-ē\ *adj* : of or relating to discipline; *also* : CORRECTIVE ⟨take ~ action⟩

¹dis·ci·pline \'di-sə-plən\ *n* 1 : PUNISHMENT 2 : a field of study : SUBJECT 3 : training that corrects, molds, or perfects 4 : control gained by obedience or training : orderly conduct 5 : a system of rules governing conduct

²discipline *vb* **-plined; -plin·ing** 1 : PUNISH 2 : to train or develop by instruction and exercise esp. in self-control 3 : to bring under control ⟨~ troops⟩; *also* : to impose order upon

disc jockey *or* **disk jockey** *n* : an announcer of a radio show of popular recorded music

dis·claim \dis-'klām\ *vb* : DENY, DISAVOW — **dis·claim·er** *n*

dis·close \dis-'klōz\ *vb* : to expose to view — **dis·clo·sure** \-'klō-zhər\ *n*

dis·co \'dis-kō\ *n, pl* **discos** 1 : a nightclub for dancing to live or recorded music 2 : popular dance music characterized by hypnotic rhythm, repetitive lyrics, and electronically produced sounds

dis·col·or \dis-'kə-lər\ *vb* : to alter or change in hue or color esp. for the worse — **dis·col·or·a·tion** \-ˌkə-lə-'rā-shən\ *n*

dis·com·bob·u·late \ˌdis-kəm-'bä-byù-ˌlāt\ *vb* **-lat·ed; -lat·ing** : UPSET, CONFUSE

dis·com·fit \dis-'kəm-fət, *esp Southern* ˌdis-kəm-'fit\ *vb* : UPSET, FRUSTRATE — **dis·com·fi·ture** \dis-'kəm-fə-ˌchùr\ *n*

¹dis·com·fort \dis-'kəm-fərt\ *vb* : to make uncomfortable or uneasy

²discomfort *n* : mental or physical uneasiness

dis·com·mode \ˌdis-kə-'mōd\ *vb* **-mod·ed; -mod·ing** : INCONVENIENCE, TROUBLE

dis·com·pose \-kəm-'pōz\ *vb* 1 : to destroy the calmness or peace of 2 : DISARRANGE — **dis·com·po·sure** \-'pō-zhər\ *n*

dis·con·cert \ˌdis-kən-'sərt\ *vb* : CONFUSE, UPSET ⟨the bad news ~ed her⟩

dis·con·nect \ˌdis-kə-'nekt\ *vb* : to undo the connection of — **dis·con·nec·tion** \-'nek-shən\ *n*

dis·con·nect·ed *adj* : not connected; *also* : INCOHERENT — **dis·con·nect·ed·ly** *adv* — **dis·con·nect·ed·ness** *n*

dis·con·so·late \dis-'kän-sə-lət\ *adj* 1 : CHEERLESS 2 : hopelessly sad — **dis·con·so·late·ly** *adv*

dis·con·tent \ˌdis-kən-'tent\ *n* : uneasiness of mind : DISSATISFACTION — **dis·con·tent·ed** *adj*

dis·con·tin·ue \ˌdis-kən-'tin-yü\ *vb* 1 : to break the continuity of : cease to operate, use, or take 2 : END — **dis·con·tin·u·ance** \-yə-wəns\ *n* — **dis·con·ti·nu·i·ty** \dis-ˌkän-tə-'nü-ə-tē, -'nyü-\ *n* — **dis·con·tin·u·ous** \ˌdis-kən-'tin-yə-wəs\ *adj*

dis·cord \'dis-ˌkòrd\ *n* 1 : lack of agreement or harmony : DISSENSION, CONFLICT 2 : a harsh combination of musical sounds 3 : a harsh or unpleasant sound — **dis·cor·dant** \dis-'kòr-dᵊnt\ *adj* — **dis·cor·dant·ly** *adv*

dis·co·theque *or* **discothèque** \'dis-kə-ˌtek\ *n* : DISCO 1

¹dis·count \'dis-ˌkaùnt\ *n* 1 : a reduction made from a regular or list price 2 : a deduction of interest in advance when lending money

²dis·count \'dis-ˌkaùnt, dis-'kaùnt\ *vb* 1 : to deduct from the amount of a bill, debt, or charge usu. for cash or prompt payment; *also* : to sell or offer for sale at a discount 2 : to lend money after deducting the discount ⟨~ a note⟩ 3 : DISREGARD; *also* : MINIMIZE 4 : to make allowance for bias or exaggeration 5 : to take into account (as a future event) in present calculations — **dis·count·able** *adj* — **dis·count·er** *n*

³dis·count \'dis-ˌkaùnt\ *adj* : selling goods or services at a discount; *also* : sold at or reflecting a discount

dis·coun·te·nance \dis-'kaùn-tə-nənts\ *vb* 1 : EMBARRASS, DISCONCERT 2 : to look with disfavor on

dis·cour·age \dis-'kər-ij\ *vb* **-aged; -ag·ing** 1 : to deprive of courage or confidence : DISHEARTEN 2 : to hinder by disfavoring 3 : to attempt to dissuade — **dis·cour·age·ment** *n* — **dis·cour·ag·ing·ly** *adv*

¹dis·course \'dis-ˌkòrs\ *n* [ME *discours*, fr. ML & LL *discursus*; ML, argument, fr. LL, conversation, fr. L, act of running about, fr. *discurrere* to run about, fr. *currere* to run] 1 : CONVERSATION 2 : formal and usu. extended expression of thought on a subject

²dis·course \dis-'kòrs\ *vb* **dis·coursed; dis·cours·ing** 1 : to express oneself in esp. oral discourse 2 : TALK, CONVERSE

dis·cour·te·ous \(ˌ)dis-'kər-tē-əs\ *adj* : lacking courtesy : UNCIVIL, RUDE — **dis·cour·te·ous·ly** *adv*

dis·cour·te·sy \-'kər-tə-sē\ *n* : RUDENESS; *also* : a rude act

dis·cov·er \dis-'kə-vər\ *vb* 1 : to make known or visible 2 : to obtain sight or knowledge of for the first time; *also* : FIND OUT — **dis·cov·er·er** *n*

dis·cov·ery \dis-'kə-və-rē\ *n, pl* **-er·ies** 1 : the act or process of discovering 2 : something discovered 3 : the disclosure usu. before a civil trial of pertinent facts or documents

¹dis·cred·it \(ˌ)dis-'kre-dət\ *vb* 1 : DISBELIEVE 2 : to cause disbelief in the accuracy or authority of 3 : DISGRACE — **dis·cred·it·able** *adj*

²discredit *n* 1 : loss of reputation 2 : lack or loss of belief or confidence

dis·creet \dis-'krēt\ *adj* : showing good judgment; *esp* : capable of observing prudent silence — **dis·creet·ly** *adv*

dis·crep·an·cy \dis-'kre-pən-sē\ *n, pl* **-cies** 1 : DIFFERENCE, DISAGREEMENT 2 : an instance of being discrepant

dis·crep·ant \-pənt\ *adj* [ME *discrepaunt*, fr. L *discrepans*, prp. of *discrepare* to sound discordantly, fr. *crepare* to rattle, creak] : being at variance : DISAGREEING ⟨~ conclusions⟩

dis·crete \dis-'krēt, 'dis-ˌkrēt\ *adj* 1 : individually distinct ⟨several ~ sections⟩ 2 : NONCONTINUOUS

dis·cre·tion \dis-'kre-shən\ *n* 1 : the quality of being discreet : PRUDENCE 2 : individual choice or judgment ⟨left the decision to his ~⟩ 3 : power of free decision or latitude of choice — **dis·cre·tion·ary** *adj* dis·crim·i·nate \dis-'kri-mə-ˌnāt\ vb -nat·ed; -nat·ing 1 : DISTINGUISH, DIFFERENTIATE 2 : to make a difference in treatment on a basis other than individual merit — dis·crim·i·na·tion \-ˌkri-mə-'nā-shən\ n

dis·crim·i·nat·ing adj : marked by discrimination; esp : DISCERNING, JUDICIOUS — dis·crim·i·nat·ing·ly adv

dis·crim·i·na·to·ry \dis-'kri-mə-nə-ˌtór-ē\ adj : marked by esp. unjust discrimination ⟨~ treatment⟩

dis·cur·sive \dis-'kər-siv\ adj : passing from one topic to another : RAMBLING ⟨a ~ speech⟩ — dis·cur·sive·ly adv — dis·cur·sive·ness n

dis·cus \'dis-kəs\ n, pl dis·cus·es : a heavy disk that is hurled for distance in a track-and-field contest

dis·cuss \di-'skəs\ vb [ME, fr. AF discusser, fr. L discussus, pp. of discutere to disperse, fr. dis- apart + quatere to shake] 1 : to argue or consider carefully by presenting the various sides 2 : to talk about — dis·cus·sion \-'skə-shən\ n

dis·cus·sant \di-'skə-sᵊnt\ n : one who takes part in a formal discussion

¹dis·dain \dis-'dān\ n : CONTEMPT, SCORN ⟨a look of ~⟩ — dis·dain·ful \-fəl\ adj — dis·dain·ful·ly adv

²disdain vb 1 : to look on with scorn 2 : to reject or refrain from because of disdain ⟨~ed gambling⟩

dis·ease \di-'zēz\ n : an abnormal bodily condition that impairs normal functioning and can usu. be recognized by signs and symptoms : SICKNESS — dis·eased \-'zēzd\ adj

dis·em·bark \ˌdi-səm-'bärk\ vb : to go or put ashore from a ship — dis·em·bar·ka·tion \di-ˌsem-ˌbär-'kā-shən\ n

dis·em·body \ˌdi-səm-'bä-dē\ vb : to deprive of bodily existence

dis·em·bow·el \-'baú(-ə)l\ vb : EVISCERATE 1 — dis·em·bow·el·ment n

dis·em·power \ˌdis-im-'paù(-ə)r\ vb : to deprive of power, authority, or influence

dis·en·chant \ˌdis-in-'chant\ vb : DISILLUSION — dis·en·chant·ment \-mənt\ n

dis·en·chant·ed \-'chan-təd\ adj : DISAPPOINTED, DISSATISFIED

dis·en·cum·ber \ˌdis-ᵊn-'kəm-bər\ vb : to free from something that burdens

dis·en·fran·chise \ˌdis-in-'fran-ˌchīz\ vb : to deprive of a franchise, a legal right, or a privilege; esp : to deprive of the right to vote — dis·en·fran·chise·ment n

dis·en·gage \ˌdis-ᵊn-'gāj\ vb : RELEASE, EXTRICATE, DISENTANGLE ⟨~ from a harness⟩ — dis·en·gage·ment n

dis·en·gaged \-'gājd\ adj : IMPARTIAL, DETACHED ⟨a ~ observer⟩

dis·en·tan·gle \ˌdis-in-'taŋ-gəl\ vb : to free from entanglement : UNRAVEL

dis·equi·lib·ri·um \dis-ˌē-kwə-'li-brē-əm\ n : loss or lack of equilibrium

dis·es·tab·lish \ˌdis-ə-'sta-blish\ vb : to end the establishment of; esp : to deprive of the status of an established church — dis·es·tab·lish·ment n

dis·es·teem \ˌdis-ə-'stēm\ n : lack of esteem : DISFAVOR, DISREPUTE

dis·fa·vor \(ˌ)dis-'fā-vər\ n 1 : DISAPPROVAL, DISLIKE 2 : the state or fact of being no longer favored

dis·fig·ure \dis-'fi-gyər\ vb : to spoil the appearance of ⟨disfigured by a scar⟩ — dis·fig·ure·ment n

dis·fran·chise \dis-'fran-ˌchīz\ vb : DISENFRANCHISE — dis·fran·chise·ment n

disfunction var of DYSFUNCTION

dis·gorge \dis-'górj\ vb : VOMIT; also : to discharge forcefully or confusedly

¹dis·grace \di-'skrās, dis-'grās\ vb : to bring reproach or shame to

²disgrace n 1 : SHAME, DISHONOR; also : a cause of shame 2 : the condition of being out of favor : loss of respect — dis·grace·ful \-fəl\ adj — dis·grace·ful·ly adv

dis·grun·tle \dis-'grən-tᵊl\ vb dis·grun·tled; dis·grun·tling : to put in bad humor ⟨disgruntled employees⟩

¹dis·guise \dis-'gīz\ vb dis·guised; dis·guis·ing 1 : to change the appearance of so as to conceal the identity or to resemble another 2 : HIDE, CONCEAL

²disguise n 1 : clothing put on to conceal one's identity or counterfeit another's 2 : an outward appearance that hides what something really is

¹dis·gust \dis-'gəst\ n : AVERSION, REPUGNANCE — dis·gust·ful \-fəl\ adj

²disgust vb : to provoke to loathing, repugnance, or aversion : be offensive to — dis·gust·ed·ly adv — dis·gust·ing \-'gəs-tin\ adj — dis·gust·ing·ly adv

¹dish \'dish\ n [ME, fr. OE disc plate, fr. L discus quoit, disk, dish, fr. Gk diskos, fr. dikein to throw] 1 : a vessel used for serving food 2 : the food served in a dish ⟨a ~ of berries⟩ 3 : food prepared in a particular way 4 : something resembling a dish esp. in being shallow and concave 5 : SATELLITE DISH 6 : GOSSIP 2

²dish vb 1 : to put into a dish 2 : to make concave like a dish 3 : GOSSIP

dis·ha·bille \ˌdis-ə-'bēl\ or des·ha·bille \ˌde-\ n [F déshabillé] : the state of being dressed in a casual or careless manner

dis·har·mo·ny \(ˌ)dis-'här-mə-nē\ n : lack of harmony — dis·har·mo·ni·ous \ˌdis-(ˌ)här-'mō-nē-əs\ adj

dish·cloth \'dish-ˌklóth\ n : a cloth for washing dishes

dis·heart·en \dis-'här-tᵊn\ vb : DISCOURAGE, DEJECT

dished \'disht\ adj : CONCAVE

di·shev·el \di-'she-vəl\ vb -shev·eled or -shev·elled; -shev·el·ing or -shev·el·ling [ME dischevele barehead·ed, with disordered hair, fr. AF descheveleé, fr. des- apart + chevoil hair, fr. L capillus] : to throw into disorder or disarray — di·shev·eled or di·shev·elled adj — di·shev·el·ment \-mənt\ n

dis·hon·est \di-'sä-nəst\ adj : not honest : UNTRUSTWORTHY, DECEITFUL — dis·hon·est·ly adv — dis·hon·es·ty \-nə-stē\ n

¹dis·hon·or \dis-'ä-nər\ n 1 : lack or loss of honor 2 : SHAME, DISGRACE 3 : a cause of disgrace 4 : the act of dishonoring a negotiable instrument when presented for payment — dis·hon·or·able \dis-'ä-nə-rə-bəl\ adj — dis·hon·or·ably \-blē\ adv

²dishonor vb 1 : DISGRACE 2 : to refuse to accept or pay ⟨~ a check⟩

dish out vb : to give freely

dish·rag \'dish-ˌrag\ n : DISHCLOTH

dish·wash·er \-ˌwó-shər, -ˌwä-\ n : a person or machine that washes dishes

dish·wa·ter \-ˌwó-tər, -ˌwä-\ n : water used for washing dishes

dis·il·lu·sion \ˌdis-ə-'lü-zhən\ vb : to free from illusion — dis·il·lu·sion·ment n

dis·il·lu·sioned adj : DISAPPOINTED, DISSATISFIED

dis·in·cli·na·tion \dis-ˌin-klə-'nā-shən\ n : a preference for avoiding something : slight aversion

dis·in·cline \ˌdis-in-'klīn\ vb : to make unwilling

dis·in·clined adj : unwilling because of dislike or disapproval

dis·in·fect \ˌdis-in-'fekt\ vb : to cleanse of infection-causing germs — dis·in·fec·tant \-'fek-tənt\ n — dis·in·fec·tion \-'fek-shən\ n

dis·in·for·ma·tion \ˌin-fər-'mä-shən\ n : false information deliberately and often covertly spread

dis·in·gen·u·ous \ˌdis-in-'jen-yə-wəs\ adj : lacking in candor; also : giving a false appearance of simple frankness

dis·in·her·it \ˌdis-in-'her-ət\ vb : to deprive of the right to inherit

dis·in·te·grate \dis-'in-tə-ˌgrāt\ vb 1 : to break or decompose into constituent parts or small particles 2 : to destroy the unity or integrity of — dis·in·te·gra·tion \-ˌin-tə-'grā-shən\ n

dis·in·ter \ˌdis-in-'tər\ vb 1 : to take from the grave or tomb 2 : UNEARTH

dis·in·ter·est·ed \(ˌ)dis-'in-tə-rəs-təd, -ˌres-\ adj 1 : not interested 2 : free from selfish motive or interest : UNBIASED — dis·in·ter·est·ed·ness n

dis·join \(ˌ)dis-'jóin\ vb : SEPARATE

dis·joint \(ˌ)dis-'jóint\ vb : to disturb the orderly arrangement of; also : to separate at the joints

dis·joint·ed adj 1 : INCOHERENT ⟨~ conversation⟩ 2 : separated at or as if at the joint

disk or disc \'disk\ n 1 : something round and flat; esp : a flat rounded anatomical structure (as the central part of the flower head of a composite plant or a pad of cartilage between vertebrae) 2 usu disc : a phonograph record 3 : a round flat plate coated with a magnetic substance on which data for a computer is stored 4 usu disc : OPTICAL DISK

disk drive n : a device for accessing or storing data on a magnetic disk
dis·kette \dis-'ket\ n : FLOPPY DISK
disk jockey var of DISC JOCKEY
[1]dis·like \(,)dis-'līk\ n : a feeling of aversion or disapproval
[2]dislike vb : to regard with dislike : DISAPPROVE
dis·lo·cate \'dis-lō-,kāt, dis-'lō-\ vb 1 : to put out of place; esp : to displace (a bone or joint) from normal connections ⟨~ a shoulder⟩ 2 : DISRUPT — **dis·lo·ca·tion** \,dis-(,)lō-'kā-shən\ n
dis·lodge \(,)dis-'läj\ vb : to force out of a place esp. of rest, hiding, or defense
dis·loy·al \(,)dis-'lói-(ə)l\ adj : lacking in loyalty — **dis·loy·al·ty** n
dis·mal \'diz-məl\ adj [ME, fr. dismal, n., days marked as unlucky in medieval calendars, fr. AF, fr. ML dies mali, lit., evil days] 1 : showing or causing gloom or depression 2 : lacking merit ⟨a ~ performance⟩ — **dis·mal·ly** adv
dis·man·tle \(,)dis-'man-t²l\ vb -tled; -tling 1 : to take apart 2 : to strip of furniture and equipment — **dis·man·tle·ment** n
dis·may \dis-'mā\ vb : to cause to lose courage or resolution from alarm or fear : DAUNT — **dismay** n — **dis·may·ing·ly** adv
dis·mem·ber \dis-'mem-bər\ vb 1 : to cut off or separate the limbs or parts of 2 : to break up or tear into pieces — **dis·mem·ber·ment** n
dis·miss \dis-'mis\ vb 1 : to send away 2 : DISCHARGE 5 3 : to put aside or out of mind 4 : to put out of judicial consideration ⟨~ed all charges⟩ — **dis·miss·al** n — **dis·mis·sive** \-'mi-siv\ adj — **dis·mis·sive·ly** adv
dis·mount \dis-'maùnt\ vb 1 : to get down from something (as a horse or bicycle) 2 : UNHORSE 3 : DISASSEMBLE
dis·obe·di·ence \,dis-ə-'bē-dē-əns\ n : neglect or refusal to obey — **dis·obe·di·ent** \-ənt\ adj
dis·obey \,dis-ə-'bā\ vb : to fail to obey : be disobedient
dis·oblige \,dis-ə-'blīj\ vb 1 : to go counter to the wishes of 2 : INCONVENIENCE
[1]dis·or·der \dis-'ór-dər\ vb 1 : to disturb the order of 2 : to disturb the regular or normal functions of
[2]disorder n 1 : lack of order : CONFUSION 2 : breach of the peace or public order : TUMULT 3 : an abnormal physical or mental condition : AILMENT
dis·or·der·ly \-lē\ adj 1 : offensive to public order 2 : marked by disorder ⟨a ~ desk⟩ — **dis·or·der·li·ness** n
dis·or·ga·nize \dis-'ór-gə-,nīz\ vb : to break up the regular system of : throw into disorder — **dis·or·ga·ni·za·tion** \dis-,ór-gə-nə-'zā-shən\ n
dis·ori·ent \dis-'ór-ē-,ent\ vb : to cause to be confused or lost — **dis·ori·en·ta·tion** \dis-,ór-ē-ən-'tā-shən\ n
dis·own \dis-'ōn\ vb : REPUDIATE, RENOUNCE, DISCLAIM ⟨her parents ~ed her⟩
dis·par·age \di-'sper-ij\ vb -aged; -ag·ing [ME, to degrade by marriage below one's class, disparage, fr. AF desparager to marry below one's class, fr. parage equality, lineage, fr. per peer] 1 : to lower in rank or reputation : DEGRADE 2 : BELITTLE — **dis·par·age·ment** n — **dis·par·ag·ing·ly** adv
dis·pa·rate \'dis-pə-rət, di-'sper-ət\ adj : distinct in quality or character — **dis·par·i·ty** \di-'sper-ə-tē\ n
dis·pas·sion·ate \(,)dis-'pa-shə-nət\ adj : not influenced by strong feeling : CALM, IMPARTIAL — **dis·pas·sion** \-'pa-shən\ n — **dis·pas·sion·ate·ly** adv
[1]dis·patch \di-'spach\ vb 1 : to send off or away with promptness or speed esp. on official business 2 : to put to death 3 : to attend to rapidly or efficiently 4 : DEFEAT — **dis·patch·er** n
[2]dis·patch \di-'spach, 'dis-,pach\ n 1 : MESSAGE 2 : a news item sent in by a correspondent to a newspaper 3 : the act of dispatching; esp : SHIPMENT 4 : the act of putting to death 5 : promptness and efficiency in performing a task
dis·pel \di-'spel\ vb **dis·pelled; dis·pel·ling** : to drive away by scattering : DISSIPATE ⟨~ a rumor⟩
dis·pens·able \di-'spen-sə-bəl\ adj : capable of being dispensed with
dis·pen·sa·ry \di-'spen-sə-rē\ n, pl -ries : a place where medicine or medical or dental aid is dispensed
dis·pen·sa·tion \,dis-pən-'sā-shən\ n 1 : a system of rules

for ordering affairs 2 : a particular arrangement or provision esp. of nature 3 : an exemption from a rule or from a vow or oath 4 : the act of dispensing 5 : something dispensed or distributed
dis·pense \di-'spens\ vb **dis·pensed; dis·pens·ing** 1 : to portion out 2 : ADMINISTER ⟨~ justice⟩ 3 : EXEMPT 4 : to make up and give out (remedies) — **dis·pens·er** n — **dispense with** 1 : SUSPEND 2 : to do without
dis·perse \di-'spərs\ vb **dis·persed; dis·pers·ing** 1 : to break up and scatter about : SPREAD — **dis·per·sal** \-'spər-səl\ n — **dis·per·sion** \-'spər-zhən\ n
dis·pir·it \dis-'pir-ət\ vb : DEPRESS, DISCOURAGE, DISHEARTEN
dis·place \dis-'plās\ vb 1 : to remove from the usual or proper place; esp : to expel or force to flee from home or native land ⟨displaced persons⟩ 2 : to move out of position ⟨water displaced by a floating object⟩ 3 : to take the place of : REPLACE
dis·place·ment \-mənt\ n 1 : the act of displacing : the state of being displaced 2 : the volume or weight of a fluid (as water) displaced by a floating body (as a ship) 3 : the difference between the initial position of an object and a later position
[1]dis·play \dis-'splā\ vb [ME, fr. AF desplaier, desploier, lit., to unfold, fr. des- un- + ploier, plier to fold, fr. L plicare] : to present to view : make evident
[2]display n 1 : a displaying of something 2 : an electronic device (as a cathode-ray tube) that gives information in visual form; also : the visual information
dis·please \(,)dis-'plēz\ vb 1 : to arouse the disapproval and dislike of 2 : to be offensive to : give displeasure
dis·plea·sure \-'ple-zhər\ n : a feeling of dislike and irritation
dis·port \di-'spórt\ vb 1 : DIVERT, AMUSE 2 : FROLIC 3 : DISPLAY
dis·pos·able \di-'spō-zə-bəl\ adj 1 : remaining after deduction of taxes ⟨~ income⟩ 2 : designed to be used once and then thrown away ⟨~ diapers⟩ — **disposable** n
dis·pos·al \di-'spō-zəl\ n 1 : CONTROL, COMMAND 2 : an orderly arrangement 3 : a getting rid of 4 : MANAGEMENT, ADMINISTRATION 5 : presenting or bestowing something ⟨~ of favors⟩ 6 : a device used to reduce waste matter (as by grinding)
dis·pose \di-'spōz\ vb **dis·posed; dis·pos·ing** 1 : to give a tendency to : INCLINE ⟨disposed to accept⟩ 2 : to put in place : ARRANGE ⟨troops disposed for withdrawal⟩ 3 : SETTLE — **dis·pos·er** n — **dispose of** 1 : to transfer to the control of another 2 : to get rid of 3 : to deal with conclusively
dis·po·si·tion \,dis-pə-'zi-shən\ n 1 : the act or power of disposing : DISPOSAL 2 : RELINQUISHMENT 3 : ARRANGEMENT 4 : TENDENCY, INCLINATION 5 : natural attitude toward things ⟨a cheerful ~⟩
dis·pos·sess \,dis-pə-'zes\ vb 1 : to put out of possession or occupancy — **dis·pos·ses·sion** \-'ze-shən\ n
dis·praise \(,)dis-'prāz\ vb : DISPARAGE — **dispraise** n — **dis·prais·er** n
dis·pro·por·tion \,dis-prə-'pór-shən\ n : lack of proportion, symmetry, or proper relation — **dis·pro·por·tion·ate** \-shə-nət\ adj
dis·prove \(,)dis-'prüv\ vb : to prove to be false — **dis·proof** \-'prüf\ n
dis·pu·tant \di-'spyü-t²nt, 'dis-pyə-tənt\ n : one that is engaged in a dispute
dis·pu·ta·tion \,dis-pyü-'tā-shən\ n 1 : DEBATE 2 : an oral defense of an academic thesis
dis·pu·ta·tious \-shəs\ adj : inclined to dispute : ARGUMENTATIVE
[1]dis·pute \di-'spyüt\ vb **dis·put·ed; dis·put·ing** 1 : ARGUE, DEBATE 2 : WRANGLE 3 : to deny the truth or rightness of 4 : to struggle against or over : OPPOSE — **dis·put·able** \di-'spyü-tə-bəl, 'dis-pyə-tə-bəl\ adj — **dis·put·er** n
[2]dis·pute n 1 : DEBATE 2 : QUARREL
dis·qual·i·fy \(,)dis-'kwä-lə-,fī\ vb : to make or declare unfit or not qualified — **dis·qual·i·fi·ca·tion** \-,kwä-lə-fə-'kā-shən\ n
[1]dis·qui·et \(,)dis-'kwī-ət\ vb : to make uneasy or restless : DISTURB ⟨was ~ed by the news⟩ — **dis·qui·et·ing** adj
[2]disquiet n : lack of peace or tranquillity : ANXIETY

dis·qui·etude \(ˌ)dis-'kwī-ə-ˌtüd, -ˌtyüd\ *n* : AGITATION, ANXIETY

dis·qui·si·tion \ˌdis-kwə-'zi-shən\ *n* : a formal inquiry or discussion

¹**dis·re·gard** \ˌdis-ri-'gärd\ *vb* : to pay no attention to : treat as unworthy of notice or regard

²**disregard** *n* : the act of disregarding : the state of being disregarded — **dis·re·gard·ful** *adj*

dis·re·pair \ˌdis-ri-'per\ *n* : the state of being in need of repair

dis·rep·u·ta·ble \dis-'re-pyü-tə-bəl\ *adj* : having a bad reputation

dis·re·pute \ˌdis-ri-'pyüt\ *n* : lack or decline of reputation : low esteem

dis·re·spect \ˌdis-ri-'spekt\ *n* : DISCOURTESY — **dis·re·spect·ful** *adj*

dis·robe \dis-'rōb\ *vb* : UNDRESS

dis·rupt \dis-'rəpt\ *vb* **1** : to break apart **2** : to throw into disorder **3** : INTERRUPT — **dis·rup·tion** \-'rəp-shən\ *n* — **dis·rup·tive** \-'rəp-tiv\ *adj*

dis·sat·is·fac·tion \di-ˌsa-təs-'fak-shən\ *n* : DISCONTENT

dis·sat·is·fy \di-'sa-təs-ˌfī\ *vb* : to fail to satisfy : DISPLEASE

dis·sect \dī-'sekt, di-\ *vb* **1** : to divide into parts esp. for examination and study **2** : ANALYZE — **dis·sec·tion** \-'sek-shən\ *n* — **dis·sec·tor** \-'sek-tər\ *n*

dis·sect·ed *adj* : cut deeply into narrow lobes ⟨a ~ leaf⟩

dis·sem·ble \di-'sem-bəl\ *vb* **-bled; -bling** **1** : to hide under or put on a false appearance : conceal facts, intentions, or feelings under some pretense **2** : SIMULATE — **dis·sem·bler** *n*

dis·sem·i·nate \di-'se-mə-ˌnāt\ *vb* **-nat·ed; -nat·ing** : to spread abroad as if sowing seed ⟨~ ideas⟩ — **dis·sem·i·na·tion** \-ˌse-mə-'nā-shən\ *n*

dis·sen·sion \di-'sen-chən\ *n* : disagreement in opinion : DISCORD

¹**dis·sent** \di-'sent\ *vb* **1** : to withhold assent **2** : to differ in opinion

²**dissent** *n* **1** : difference of opinion; *esp* : religious nonconformity **2** : a written statement in which a justice disagrees with the opinion of the majority

dis·sent·er \di-'sen-tər\ *n* **1** : one that dissents **2** *cap* : an English Nonconformist

dis·ser·ta·tion \ˌdi-sər-'tā-shən\ *n* : an extended usu. written treatment of a subject; *esp* : one submitted for a doctorate

dis·ser·vice \di-'sər-vəs\ *n* : INJURY, HARM, MISCHIEF

dis·sev·er \di-'se-vər\ *vb* : SEPARATE, DISUNITE

dis·si·dent \'di-sə-dənt\ *adj* [L *dissidens*, prp. of *dissidēre* to sit apart, disagree, fr. *dis-* apart + *sedēre* to sit] : disagreeing esp. with an established religious or political system, organization, or belief — **dis·si·dence** \-dəns\ *n* — **dissident** *n*

dis·sim·i·lar \di-'si-mə-lər\ *adj* : UNLIKE — **dis·sim·i·lar·i·ty** \di-ˌsi-mə-'ler-ə-tē\ *n*

dis·sim·u·late \di-'si-myə-ˌlāt\ *vb* : to hide under a false appearance : DISSEMBLE — **dis·sim·u·la·tion** \di-ˌsi-myə-'lā-shən\ *n*

dis·si·pate \'di-sə-ˌpāt\ *vb* **-pat·ed; -pat·ing** **1** : to break up and drive off : DISPERSE, SCATTER ⟨the breeze *dissipated* the fog⟩ **2** : SQUANDER **3** : to break up and vanish **4** : to be dissolute; *esp* : to drink alcoholic beverages to excess — **dis·si·pat·ed** *adj* — **dis·si·pa·tion** \di-sə-'pā-shən\ *n*

dis·so·ci·ate \di-'sō-shē-ˌāt\ *vb* **-at·ed; -at·ing** : DISCONNECT, DISUNITE — **dis·so·ci·a·tion** \di-ˌsō-shē-'ā-shən\ *n* — **dis·so·cia·tive** \di-'sō-shē-ˌā-tiv\ *adj*

dis·so·lute \'di-sə-ˌlüt\ *adj* : loose in morals or conduct — **dis·so·lute·ly** *adv* — **dis·so·lute·ness** *n*

dis·so·lu·tion \ˌdi-sə-'lü-shən\ *n* **1** : the action or process of dissolving **2** : separation of a thing into its parts **3** : DECAY; *also* : DEATH **4** : the termination or breaking up of (as an assembly)

dis·solve \di-'zälv\ *vb* **1** : to separate into component parts **2** : to pass or cause to pass into solution ⟨sugar ~s in water⟩ **3** : TERMINATE, DISPERSE ⟨~ parliament⟩ **4** : to waste or fade away ⟨his courage *dissolved*⟩ **5** : to be overcome emotionally ⟨~ in tears⟩ **6** : to resolve itself as if by dissolution

dis·so·nance \'di-sə-nəns\ *n* : DISCORD — **dis·so·nant** \-nənt\ *adj*

dis·suade \di-'swād\ *vb* **dis·suad·ed; dis·suad·ing** : to advise against a course of action : persuade or try to persuade not to do something — **dis·sua·sion** \-'swā-zhən\ *n* — **dis·sua·sive** \-'swā-siv\ *adj*

dist *abbr* **1** distance **2** district

¹**dis·taff** \'dis-ˌtaf\ *n, pl* **distaffs** \-ˌtafs, -ˌtavz\ [ME *distaf*, fr. OE *distæf*, fr. *dis-* bunch of flax + *stæf* stick, staff] **1** : a staff for holding the flax, tow, or wool in spinning **2** : a woman's work or domain **3** : the female branch or side of a family

²**distaff** *adj* **1** : MATERNAL **2** ⟨the ~ side of the family⟩ **2** : FEMALE 1 ⟨~ executives⟩

dis·tal \'dis-t°l\ *adj* **1** : situated away from the point of attachment or origin esp. on the body **2** : of, relating to, or being the surface of a tooth that is farthest from the middle of the front of the jaw — **dis·tal·ly** *adv*

¹**dis·tance** \'dis-təns\ *n* **1** : measure of separation in space or time **2** : EXPANSE **3** : the full length ⟨go the ~⟩ **4** : spatial remoteness **5** : COLDNESS, RESERVE **6** : DIFFERENCE, DISPARITY **7** : a distant point

²**distance** *vb* **dis·tanced; dis·tanc·ing** : to leave far behind : OUTSTRIP

³**distance** *adj* : taking place via electronic media linking instructors and students ⟨~ learning⟩

dis·tant \'dis-tənt\ *adj* **1** : separate in space : AWAY **2** : FAR-OFF ⟨a ~ galaxy⟩ **3** : far apart or behind **4** : not close in relationship ⟨a ~ cousin⟩ **5** : different in kind **6** : RESERVED, ALOOF, COLD ⟨~ politeness⟩ **7** : going a long distance ⟨~ voyages⟩ — **dis·tant·ly** *adv* — **dis·tant·ness** *n*

dis·taste \(ˌ)dis-'tāst\ *n* : DISINCLINATION, DISLIKE — **dis·taste·ful** *adj*

dis·tem·per \(ˌ)dis-'tem-pər\ *n* : a bodily disorder usu. of a domestic animal; *esp* : a contagious often fatal virus disease of dogs

dis·tend \di-'stend\ *vb* : EXPAND, SWELL — **dis·ten·si·ble** \-'sten-sə-bəl\ *adj* — **dis·ten·sion** *or* **dis·ten·tion** \-chən\ *n*

dis·tich \'dis-(ˌ)tik\ *n* : a unit of two lines of poetry

dis·till *also* **dis·til** \di-'stil\ *vb* **dis·tilled; dis·till·ing** **1** : to fall or let fall in drops **2** : to obtain or purify by distillation — **dis·till·er** *n* — **dis·till·ery** \-'sti-lə-rē\ *n*

dis·til·late \'dis-tə-ˌlāt, -lət\ *n* : a liquid product condensed from vapor during distillation

dis·til·la·tion \ˌdis-tə-'lā-shən\ *n* : the process of purifying a liquid by successive evaporation and condensation

dis·tinct \di-'stiŋkt\ *adj* **1** : SEPARATE, INDIVIDUAL ⟨a ~ cultural group⟩ **2** : presenting a clear unmistakable impression — **dis·tinct·ly** *adv* — **dis·tinct·ness** *n*

dis·tinc·tion \di-'stiŋk-shən\ *n* **1** : the distinguishing of a difference; *also* : the difference distinguished **2** : something that distinguishes **3** : special honor or recognition

dis·tinc·tive \di-'stiŋk-tiv\ *adj* **1** : serving to distinguish ⟨the ~ flight of the crane⟩ **2** : having or giving style or distinction — **dis·tinc·tive·ly** *adv* — **dis·tinc·tive·ness** *n*

dis·tin·guish \di-'stiŋ-gwish\ *vb* [alter. of ME *distinguen*, fr. AF *distinguer*, fr. L *distinguere*, lit., to separate by pricking] **1** : to recognize by some mark or characteristic **2** : to hear or see clearly : DISCERN **3** : to make distinctions ⟨~ between right and wrong⟩ **4** : to give prominence or distinction to; *also* : to take special notice of — **dis·tin·guish·able** *adj*

dis·tin·guished \-gwisht\ *adj* **1** : marked by eminence or excellence **2** : befitting an eminent person

dis·tort \di-'stȯrt\ *vb* **1** : to twist out of the true meaning **2** : to twist out of a natural, normal, or original shape or condition **3** : to cause to be perceived unnaturally — **dis·tor·tion** \-'stȯr-shən\ *n*

distr *abbr* distribute; distribution

dis·tract \di-'strakt\ *vb* **1** : to draw (the attention or mind) to a different object : DIVERT **2** : to stir up or confuse with conflicting emotions or motives — **dis·trac·tion** \-'strak-shən\ *n*

dis·trait \di-'strā\ *adj* : DISTRAUGHT 1

dis·traught \di-'strȯt\ *adj* **1** : agitated with doubt or mental conflict or pain **2** : INSANE

¹**dis·tress** \di-'stres\ *n* **1** : suffering of body or mind : PAIN, ANGUISH **2** : TROUBLE, MISFORTUNE **3** : a condition of danger or desperate need — **dis·tress·ful** *adj*

²**distress** *vb* **1** : to subject to great strain or difficulties **2** : UPSET

dis·tress·ed \-'strest\ *adj* : experiencing economic decline or difficulty

dis·trib·ute \di-'stri-byüt\ *vb* **-ut·ed; -ut·ing** **1** : to divide among several or many **2** : to spread out : SCATTER; *also* : DELIVER **3** : CLASSIFY — **dis·tri·bu·tion** \ˌdis-trə-'byü-shən\ *n*

dis·trib·u·tive \di-'stri-byù-tiv\ *adj* **1** : of or relating to distribution **2** : of, having, or being the property of producing the same value when an operation is carried out on a whole expression and when it is carried out on each part of an expression with the results then collected together ⟨a(b + c) = ab + ac because multiplication is ∼⟩ — **dis·trib·u·tive·ly** *adv*

dis·trib·u·tor \di-'stri-byù-tər\ *n* **1** : one that distributes **2** : one that markets goods **3** : a device for directing current to the spark plugs of an engine

dis·trict \'dis-(ˌ)trikt\ *n* **1** : a fixed territorial division (as for administrative or electoral purposes) **2** : an area, region, or section with a distinguishing character

district attorney *n* : the prosecuting attorney of a judicial district

¹**dis·trust** \dis-'trəst\ *n* : a lack or absence of trust — **dis·trust·ful** \-fəl\ *adj* — **dis·trust·ful·ly** *adv*

²**distrust** *vb* : to have no trust or confidence in

dis·turb \di-'stərb\ *vb* **1** : to interfere with : INTERRUPT **2** : to alter the position or arrangement of; *also* : to upset the natural and esp. the ecological balance of **3** : to destroy the tranquillity or composure of : make uneasy **4** : to throw into disorder **5** : INCONVENIENCE — **dis·tur·bance** \-'stər-bəns\ *n* — **dis·turb·er** *n* — **dis·turb·ing·ly** \-'stər-biŋ-lē\ *adv*

dis·turbed \-'stərbd\ *adj* : showing symptoms of emotional illness

dis·unite \ˌdis-yü-'nīt\ *vb* : DIVIDE, SEPARATE

dis·uni·ty \dis-'yü-nə-tē\ *n* : lack of unity; *esp* : DISSENSION

dis·use \-'yüs\ *n* : a cessation of use or practice

dis·used \-'yüzd\ *adj* : no longer used or occupied

¹**ditch** \'dich\ *n* : a long narrow channel or trench dug in the earth

²**ditch** *vb* **1** : to enclose with a ditch; *also* : to dig a ditch in **2** : to get rid of : DISCARD **3** : to make a forced landing of an airplane on water

dith·er \'di-thər\ *n* : a highly nervous, excited, or agitated state

dit·to \'di-tō\ *n, pl* **dittos** [It *ditto, detto,* pp. of *dire* to say, fr. L *dicere*] **1** : a thing mentioned previously or above — used to avoid repeating a word **2** : a mark " or " used as a symbol for the word *ditto*

dit·ty \'di-tē\ *n, pl* **ditties** : a short simple song

dit·zy *or* **dit·sy** \'dit-sē\ *adj* **ditz·i·er** *or* **dits·i·er; -est** : eccentrically silly, giddy, or inane

di·uret·ic \ˌdī-yə-'re-tik\ *adj* : tending to increase urine flow — **diuretic** *n*

di·ur·nal \dī-'ər-nᵊl\ *adj* **1** : DAILY ⟨a ∼ chore⟩ **2** : of, relating to, occurring, or active in the daytime ⟨∼ animals⟩

div *abbr* **1** divided **2** dividend **3** division **4** divorced

di·va \'dē-və\ *n, pl* **divas** *or* **di·ve** \-ˌvä\ [It, lit., goddess, fr. L, fem. of *divus* divine, god] **1** : PRIMA DONNA **2** : a usu. glamorous and successful female performer or personality

di·va·gate \'dī-və-ˌgāt\ *vb* **-gat·ed; -gat·ing** : to wander or stray from a course or subject : DIVERGE — **di·va·ga·tion** \ˌdī-və-'gā-shən\ *n*

di·van \'dī-ˌvan, di-'van\ *n* : COUCH, SOFA

¹**dive** \'dīv\ *vb* **dived** \'dīvd\ *or* **dove** \'dōv\; **dived; div·ing** **1** : to plunge into water headfirst **2** : SUBMERGE **3** : to come or drop down precipitously **4** : to descend in an airplane at a steep angle **5** : to plunge into some matter or activity **6** : DART, LUNGE — **div·er** *n*

²**dive** *n* **1** : the act or an instance of diving **2** : a sharp decline **3** : a disreputable bar or place of amusement

di·verge \də-'vərj, dī-\ *vb* **di·verged; di·verg·ing** **1** : to move or extend in different directions from a common point : draw apart **2** : to differ in character, form, or opinion **3** : DEVIATE **4** : DEFLECT — **di·ver·gence** \-'vər-jəns\ *n* — **di·ver·gent** \-jənt\ *adj*

di·vers \'dī-vərz\ *adj* : VARIOUS

di·verse \dī-'vərs, də-, 'dī-ˌvərs\ *adj* **1** : UNLIKE **2** : composed of distinct forms or qualities — **di·verse·ly** *adv*

di·ver·si·fy \də-'vər-sə-ˌfī, dī-\ *vb* **-fied; -fy·ing** : to make different or various in form or quality — **di·ver·si·fi·ca·tion** \-ˌvər-sə-fə-'kā-shən\ *n*

di·ver·sion \də-'vər-zhən, dī-\ *n* **1** : a turning aside from a course, activity, or use : DEVIATION **2** : something that diverts or amuses : PASTIME

di·ver·si·ty \də-'vər-sə-tē, dī-\ *n, pl* **-ties** **1** : the condition of being diverse : VARIETY **2** : an instance of being diverse

di·vert \də-'vərt, dī-\ *vb* **1** : to turn from a course or purpose : DEFLECT **2** : DISTRACT **3** : ENTERTAIN, AMUSE

di·vert·ing \-'vər-tiŋ\ *adj* : providing amusement or entertainment

di·vest \dī-'vest, də-\ *vb* **1** : to deprive or dispossess esp. of property, authority, or rights **2** : to strip esp. of clothing, ornament, or equipment

¹**di·vide** \də-'vīd\ *vb* **di·vid·ed; di·vid·ing** **1** : SEPARATE; *also* : CLASSIFY **2** : CLEAVE, PART ⟨a ship *dividing* the waves⟩ **3** : DISTRIBUTE, APPORTION **4** : to possess or make use of in common : share in **5** : to cause to be separate, distinct, or apart from one another **6** : to separate into opposing sides or parties **7** : to mark divisions on **8** : to subject to or use in mathematical division; *also* : to be used as a divisor with respect to **9** : to branch out

²**divide** *n* : WATERSHED 1

div·i·dend \'di-və-ˌdend\ *n* **1** : an individual share of something distributed **2** : BONUS **3** : a number to be divided **4** : a sum or fund to be divided or distributed

di·vid·er \də-'vī-dər\ *n* **1** : one that divides (as a partition) ⟨room ∼⟩ **2** *pl* : COMPASS 5

div·i·na·tion \ˌdi-və-'nā-shən\ *n* **1** : the art or practice of using omens or magic powers to foretell the future **2** : unusual insight or intuitive perception

¹**di·vine** \də-'vīn\ *adj* **di·vin·er; -est** **1** : of, relating to, or being God or a god **2** : supremely good : SUPERB; *also* : HEAVENLY — **di·vine·ly** *adv*

²**divine** *n* **1** : CLERGYMAN **2** : THEOLOGIAN

³**divine** *vb* **di·vined; di·vin·ing** **1** : INFER, CONJECTURE **2** : PROPHESY **3** : DOWSE — **di·vin·er** *n*

divining rod *n* : a forked rod believed to reveal the presence of water or minerals by dipping downward when held over a vein

di·vin·i·ty \də-'vi-nə-tē\ *n, pl* **-ties** **1** : THEOLOGY **2** : the quality or state of being divine **3** : a divine being; *esp* : GOD 1

di·vis·i·ble \də-'vi-zə-bəl\ *adj* : capable of being divided ⟨9 is ∼ by 3⟩ — **di·vis·i·bil·i·ty** \-ˌvi-zə-'bi-lə-tē\ *n*

di·vi·sion \də-'vi-zhən\ *n* **1** : DISTRIBUTION, SEPARATION **2** : one of the parts or groupings into which a whole is divided **3** : DISAGREEMENT, DISUNITY **4** : something that divides or separates **5** : the mathematical operation of finding how many times one number is contained in another **6** : a large self-contained military unit **7** : an administrative or operating unit of a governmental, business, or educational organization — **di·vi·sion·al** \-'vizh-nəl\ *adj*

di·vi·sive \də-'vī-siv, -'vi-ziv\ *adj* : creating disunity or dissension — **di·vi·sive·ly** *adv* — **di·vi·sive·ness** *n*

di·vi·sor \də-'vī-zər\ *n* : the number by which a dividend is divided

di·vorce \də-'vȯrs\ *n* **1** : an act or instance of legally dissolving a marriage **2** : SEPARATION, SEVERANCE — **divorce** *vb* — **di·vorce·ment** *n*

di·vor·cé \də-ˌvȯr-'sā\ *n* [F] : a divorced man

di·vor·cée \də-ˌvȯr-'sā, -'sē\ *n* : a divorced woman

div·ot \'di-vət\ *n* : a piece of turf dug from a golf fairway in making a stroke

di·vulge \də-'vəlj, dī-\ *vb* **di·vulged; di·vulg·ing** : REVEAL, DISCLOSE

Dix·ie·land \'dik-sē-ˌland\ *n* : jazz music in duple time played in a style developed in New Orleans

diz·zy \'di-zē\ *adj* **diz·zi·er; -est** [ME *disy,* fr. OE *dysig* stupid] **1** : FOOLISH, SILLY **2** : having a sensation of whirling : GIDDY **3** : causing or caused by giddiness — **diz·zi·ly** \-zə-lē\ *adv* — **diz·zi·ness** \-zē-nəs\ *n*

DJ *n, often not cap* : DISC JOCKEY

dk *abbr* **1** dark **2** deck **3** dock

dl *abbr* deciliter

DLitt *or* **DLit** *abbr* [NL *doctor litterarum*] doctor of letters; doctor of literature

DLO *abbr* dead letter office

dm *abbr* decimeter

DMD *abbr* [NL *dentariae medicinae doctor*] doctor of dental medicine

DMZ *abbr* demilitarized zone

dn *abbr* down

DNA \ˌdē-(ˌ)en-ˈā\ *n* : any of various nucleic acids that are usu. the molecular basis of heredity and are localized esp. in cell nuclei

DNR *abbr* do not resuscitate

¹**do** \ˈdü\ *vb* did \ˈdid\; **done** \ˈdən\; **do·ing; does** \ˈdəz\ **1** : to bring to pass : ACCOMPLISH **2** : ACT, BEHAVE ⟨~ as I say⟩ **3** : to be active or busy ⟨up and ~*ing*⟩ **4** : HAPPEN ⟨what's ~*ing*?⟩ **5** : to be engaged in the study or practice of : work at ⟨he *does* tailoring⟩ **6** : COOK ⟨steak *done* rare⟩ **7** : to put in order (as by cleaning or arranging) ⟨~ the dishes⟩ **8** : DECORATE ⟨*did* the hall in blue⟩ **9** : GET ALONG ⟨~ well in school⟩ **10** : CARRY ON, MANAGE **11** : RENDER ⟨sleep will ~ you good⟩ **12** : FINISH ⟨when he had *done*⟩ **13** : EXERT ⟨*did* my best⟩ **14** : PRODUCE ⟨*did* a poem⟩ **15** : to play the part of **16** : CHEAT ⟨*did* him out of his share⟩ **17** : TRAVERSE, TOUR **18** : TRAVEL **19** : to spend or serve out a period of time ⟨*did* ten years in prison⟩ **20** : SUFFICE, SUIT **21** : to be fitting or proper **22** : USE ⟨doesn't ~ drugs⟩ **23** — used as an auxiliary verb (1) before the subject in an interrogative sentence ⟨*does* he work?⟩ and after some adverbs ⟨never *did* she say so⟩, (2) in a negative statement ⟨I *don't* know⟩, (3) for emphasis ⟨you ~ know⟩, and (4) as a substitute for a preceding predicate ⟨he works harder than I ~⟩ — **do·able** \ˈdü-ə-bəl\ *adj* — **do away with 1** : to put an end to **2** : DESTROY, KILL — **do by** : to deal with : TREAT ⟨*did* right *by* her⟩ — **do for** *chiefly Brit* : to bring about the death or ruin of — **do the trick** : to produce a desired result

²**do** *n* **1** : AFFAIR, PARTY **2** : a command or entreaty to do something ⟨list of ~s and don'ts⟩ **3** : HAIRSTYLE

³**do** *abbr* ditto

DOA *abbr* dead on arrival

DOB *abbr* date of birth

dob·bin \ˈdä-bən\ *n* [*Dobbin*, nickname for *Robert*] **1** : a farm horse **2** : a quiet plodding horse

Do·ber·man pin·scher \ˈdō-bər-mən-ˈpin-chər\ *n* : any of a German breed of short-haired medium-sized dogs

do·bra \ˈdō-brə\ *n* — see MONEY table

¹**doc** \ˈdäk\ *n* : DOCTOR

²**doc** *abbr* document

do·cent \ˈdō-sᵊnt, dōt-ˈsent\ *n* [obs. G (now *Dozent*), fr. L *docens*, prp. of *docēre* to teach] : TEACHER, LECTURER; *also* : a person who leads a guided tour

doc·ile \ˈdä-səl\ *adj* [L *docilis*, fr. *docēre* to teach] : easily taught, led, or managed : TRACTABLE — **do·cil·i·ty** \dä-ˈsi-lə-tē\ *n*

¹**dock** \ˈdäk\ *n* : any of a genus of coarse weedy herbs related to buckwheat

²**dock** *vb* **1** : to cut off the end of : cut short **2** : to take away a part of : deduct from ⟨~ a worker's wages⟩

³**dock** *n* **1** : an artificial basin to receive ships **2** : ²SLIP 2 **3** : a wharf or platform for loading or unloading materials or for mooring a boat

⁴**dock** *vb* **1** : to bring or come into dock **2** : to join (as two spacecraft) mechanically in space

⁵**dock** *n* : the place in a court where a prisoner stands or sits during trial

dock·age \ˈdä-kij\ *n* : docking facilities

dock·et \ˈdä-kət\ *n* **1** : a formal abridged record of the proceedings in a legal action; *also* : a register of such records **2** : a list of legal causes to be tried **3** : a calendar of matters to be acted on : AGENDA **4** : a label attached to a document containing identification or directions — **docket** *vb*

dock·hand \ˈdäk-ˌhand\ *n* : LONGSHOREMAN

dock·work·er \-ˌwər-kər\ *n* : LONGSHOREMAN

dock·yard \-ˌyärd\ *n* : SHIPYARD

¹**doc·tor** \ˈdäk-tər\ *n* [ME *doctour* teacher, doctor, fr. AF & ML; AF, fr. ML *doctor*, fr. L, teacher, fr. *docēre* to teach] **1** : a person holding one of the highest academic degrees (as a PhD) conferred by a university **2** : a person skilled in healing arts; *esp* : one (as a physician, dentist, or veterinarian) academically and legally qualified to practice **3** : a person who restores or repairs things — **doc·tor·al** \-tə-rəl\ *adj*

²**doctor** *vb* **1** : to give medical treatment to **2** : to prac-

tice medicine **3** : REPAIR **4** : to adapt or modify for a desired end **5** : to alter deceptively

doc·tor·ate \ˈdäk-tə-rət\ *n* : the degree, title, or rank of a doctor

doc·tri·naire \ˌdäk-trə-ˈner\ *n* [F] : one who attempts to put an abstract theory into effect without regard to practical difficulties — **doctrinaire** *adj*

doc·trine \ˈdäk-trən\ *n* **1** : something that is taught **2** : DOGMA, TENET — **doc·tri·nal** \-trə-nᵊl\ *adj*

docu·dra·ma \ˈdä-kyə-ˌdrä-mə, -ˌdra-\ *n* : a drama made for television, motion pictures, or theater that deals freely with historical events

doc·u·ment \ˈdä-kyə-mənt\ *n* **1** : a paper that furnishes information, proof, or support of something else **2** : a computer file containing information input by a computer user usu. via a word processor — **doc·u·ment** \-ˌment\ *vb* — **doc·u·men·ta·tion** \ˌdä-kyə-mən-ˈtā-shən\ *n* — **doc·u·ment·er** *n*

doc·u·men·ta·ry \ˌdä-kyə-ˈmen-tə-rē\ *adj* **1** : consisting of documents; *also* : being in writing ⟨~ proof⟩ **2** : giving a factual presentation in artistic form ⟨a ~ movie⟩ — **documentary** *n*

DOD *abbr* Department of Defense

¹**dod·der** \ˈdä-dər\ *n* : any of a genus of leafless parasitic twining vines that are highly deficient in chlorophyll

²**dodder** *vb* **dod·dered; dod·der·ing 1** : to tremble or shake usu. from age **2** : to progress feebly and unsteadily

¹**dodge** \ˈdäj\ *n* **1** : an act of evading by sudden bodily movement **2** : an artful device to evade, deceive, or trick **3** : EXPEDIENT

²**dodge** *vb* **dodged; dodg·ing 1** : to evade usu. by trickery **2** : to move suddenly aside; *also* : to avoid or evade by so doing — **dodg·er** *n*

do·do \ˈdō-dō\ *n, pl* **dodoes** *or* **dodos** [Pg *doudo*, fr. *doudo* silly, stupid] **1** : an extinct heavy flightless bird of the island of Mauritius related to the pigeons and larger than a turkey **2** : one hopelessly behind the times; *also* : a stupid person

doe \ˈdō\ *n, pl* **does** *or* **doe** : an adult female of various mammals (as a deer, rabbit, or kangaroo) of which the male is called *buck*

DOE *abbr* Department of Energy

do·er \ˈdü-ər\ *n* : one that does

does *pres 3d sing of* DO; *pl of* DOE

doff \ˈdäf\ *vb* [ME, fr. *don* to do + *of* off] **1** : to take off (the hat) in greeting or as a sign of respect **2** : to rid oneself of

¹**dog** \ˈdȯg\ *n* **1** : a flesh-eating domestic mammal related to the wolves; *esp* : a male of this animal **2** : a worthless or contemptible person **3** : FELLOW, CHAP ⟨you lucky ~⟩ **4** : a mechanical device for holding something **5** : uncharacteristic or affected stylishness or dignity ⟨put on the ~⟩ **6** *pl* : RUIN ⟨gone to the ~s⟩

²**dog** *vb* **dogged; dog·ging 1** : to hunt or track like a hound **2** : to worry as if by pursuit with dogs : PLAGUE

dog·bane \ˈdȯg-ˌbān\ *n* : any of a genus of mostly poisonous herbs with milky juice and often showy flowers

dog·cart \-ˌkärt\ *n* : a light one-horse carriage with two seats back to back

dog·catch·er \-ˌka-chər, -ˌke-\ *n* : a community official assigned to catch and dispose of stray dogs

dog·ear \ˈdȯg-ˌir\ *n* : the turned-down corner of a leaf of a book — **dog-ear** *vb* — **dog-eared** \-ˌird\ *adj*

dog·fight \ˈdȯg-ˌfīt\ *n* : a fight between fighter planes at close range

dog·fish \-ˌfish\ *n* : any of various small usu. bottom-dwelling sharks

dog·ged \ˈdȯ-gəd\ *adj* : stubbornly determined : TENACIOUS — **dog·ged·ly** *adv* — **dog·ged·ness** *n*

dog·ger·el \ˈdȯ-gə-rəl\ *n* : verse that is loosely styled and irregular in measure esp. for comic effect

dog·gie bag *or* **doggy bag** \ˈdȯ-gē-\ *n* : a container for carrying home leftover food from a restaurant meal

¹**dog·gy** *or* **dog·gie** \ˈdȯ-gē\ *n, pl* **doggies** : a small dog

²**dog·gy** *adj* **dog·gi·er; -est** : of or resembling a dog ⟨a ~ odor⟩

dog·house \ˈdȯg-ˌhau̇s\ *n* : a shelter for a dog — **in the doghouse** : in a state of disfavor

do·gie \ˈdō-gē\ *n, chiefly West* : a motherless calf in a range herd

dog·leg \\'dȯg-ˌleg\ *n* : a sharp bend or angle (as in a road or golf fairway) — **dogleg** *vb*

dog·ma \\'dȯg-mə\ *n, pl* **dogmas** *also* **dog·ma·ta** \-mə-tə\ [L, fr. Gk, fr. *dokein* to think, have an opinion] **1** : a tenet or code of tenets **2** : a doctrine or body of doctrines formally proclaimed by a church

dog·ma·tism \\'dȯg-mə-ˌti-zəm\ *n* : positiveness in stating matters of opinion esp. when unwarranted or arrogant — **dog·mat·ic** \dȯg-'ma-tik\ *adj* — **dog·mat·i·cal·ly** \-ti-k(ə-)lē\ *adv*

do–good·er \\'dü-ˌgu̇-dər\ *n* : an earnest often naive humanitarian or reformer

dog·tooth violet \\'dȯg-ˌtüth-\ *n* : any of a genus of small spring-flowering bulbous herbs related to the lilies

dog·trot \\'dȯg-ˌträt\ *n* : a gentle trot — **dogtrot** *vb*

dog·wood \\'dȯg-ˌwu̇d\ *n* : any of a genus of trees and shrubs having heads of small flowers often with showy white, pink, or red bracts

doi·ly \\'dȯi-lē\ *n, pl* **doilies** : a small often decorative mat

do in *vb* **1** : RUIN **2** : KILL **3** : TIRE, EXHAUST ⟨the climb *did* him *in*⟩ **4** : CHEAT

do·ings \\'dü-iŋz\ *n pl* : GOINGS-ON

do–it–yourself *n* : the activity of doing or making something without professional training or help — **do–it–your·self·er** *n*

dol *abbr* dollar

dol·drums \\'dōl-drəmz, 'däl-\ *n pl* **1** : a spell of listlessness or despondency **2** *often cap* : a part of the ocean near the equator known for calms **3** : a state or period of inactivity, stagnation, or slump

¹dole \\'dōl\ *n* **1** : a distribution esp. of food, money, or clothing to the needy; *also* : something so distributed **2** : a grant of government funds to the unemployed

²dole *vb* **doled; dol·ing** : to give or distribute as a charity — usu. used with *out*

dole·ful \\'dōl-fəl\ *adj* : full of grief : SAD — **dole·ful·ly** *adv*

dole out *vb* **1** : to give or deliver in small portions **2** : DISH OUT

doll \\'däl, 'dȯl\ *n* **1** : a small figure of a human being used esp. as a child's plaything **2** : a pretty woman **3** : an attractive person — **doll·ish** \\'dä-lish, 'dȯ-\ *adj*

dol·lar \\'dä-lər\ *n* [Dutch or LG *daler*, fr. G *Taler*, short for *Joachimstaler*, fr. Sankt *Joachimsthal*, Bohemia, where talers were first made] **1** : any of various basic monetary units (as in the U.S. and Canada) — see MONEY table **2** : a coin, note, or token representing one dollar **3** : RINGGIT

dol·lop \\'dä-ləp\ *n* **1** : LUMP, GLOB **2** : PORTION **1** — **dollop** *vb*

doll up *vb* **1** : to dress elegantly or extravagantly **2** : to make more attractive **3** : to get dolled up

dol·ly \\'dä-lē\ *n, pl* **dollies** : a small cart or wheeled platform (as for a television or movie camera)

dol·men \\'dōl-mən, 'däl-\ *n* : a prehistoric monument consisting of two or more upright stones supporting a horizontal stone slab

dolmen

do·lo·mite \\'dō-lə-ˌmīt, 'dä-\ *n* : a mineral found in broad layers as a compact limestone

do·lor \\'dō-lər, 'dä-\ *n* : mental suffering or anguish : SORROW — **do·lor·ous** *adj* — **do·lor·ous·ly** *adv*

do·lour *chiefly Brit var of* DOLOR

dol·phin \\'däl-fən\ *n* **1** : any of various small whales with conical teeth and an elongated beaklike snout **2** : either of two active food fishes of tropical and temperate seas

dolt \\'dōlt\ *n* : a stupid person — **dolt·ish** \\'dōl-tish\ *adj* — **dolt·ish·ness** *n*

dom *n* **1** domestic **2** dominant **3** dominion

-dom *n suffix* **1** : dignity : office ⟨duke*dom*⟩ **2** : realm : jurisdiction ⟨king*dom*⟩ **3** : state or fact of being ⟨free*dom*⟩ **4** : those having a (specified) office, occupation, interest, or character ⟨official*dom*⟩

do·main \dō-'mān\ *n* **1** : complete and absolute owner-

ship of land **2** : land completely owned **3** : a territory over which dominion is exercised **4** : a sphere of knowledge, influence, or activity ⟨the ∼ of science⟩ **5** : a subdivision of the Internet made up of computers whose URLs share a characteristic abbreviation (as *com* or *gov*)

domain name *n* : a sequence of characters (as Merriam-Webster.com) that specifies a group of online resources and forms part of its URL

dome \\'dōm\ *n* **1** : a large hemispherical roof or ceiling **2** : a structure or natural formation that resembles the dome of a building **3** : a roofed sports stadium — **dome** *vb*

¹do·mes·tic \də-'mes-tik\ *adj* **1** : living near or about human habitations **2** : TAME, DOMESTICATED **3** : relating and limited to one's own country or the country under consideration **4** : of or relating to the household or the family **5** : devoted to home duties and pleasures **6** : INDIGENOUS — **do·mes·ti·cal·ly** \-ti-k(ə-)lē\ *adv*

²domestic *n* : a household servant

do·mes·ti·cate \də-'mes-ti-ˌkāt\ *vb* **-cat·ed; -cat·ing** : to adapt to life in association with and to the use of humans — **do·mes·ti·ca·tion** \-ˌmes-ti-'kā-shən\ *n*

do·mes·tic·i·ty \ˌdō-ˌmes-'ti-sə-tē, də-\ *n, pl* **-ties** **1** : the quality or state of being domestic or domesticated **2** : domestic activities or life

domestic violence *n* : the inflicting of injury by one family or household member on another

do·mi·cile \\'dä-mə-ˌsi(-ə)l, 'dō-; 'dä-mə-səl\ *n* : a dwelling place : HOME — **domicile** *vb* — **dom·i·cil·i·ary** \ˌdä-mə-'si-lē-ˌer-ē, ˌdō-\ *adj*

dom·i·nance \\'dä-mə-nəns\ *n* **1** : AUTHORITY, CONTROL **2** : the property of one of a pair of alleles or traits that suppresses expression of the other when both are present

¹dom·i·nant \-nənt\ *adj* **1** : controlling or prevailing over all others **2** : overlooking from a high position **3** : exhibiting genetic dominance

²dominant *n* : a dominant gene or trait

dom·i·nate \\'dä-mə-ˌnāt\ *vb* **-nat·ed; -nat·ing** **1** : RULE, CONTROL **2** : to have a commanding position or controlling power over **3** : to rise high above in a position suggesting power to dominate — **dom·i·na·tor** \-ˌnā-tər\ *n*

dom·i·na·tion \ˌdä-mə-'nā-shən\ *n* **1** : supremacy or preeminence over another **2** : exercise of mastery, ruling power, or preponderant influence

do·mi·na·trix \ˌdä-mə-'nā-triks\ *n, pl* **-tri·ces** \-'nā-trə-ˌsēz, -nə-'trī-sēz\ : a woman who dominates her partner in a sadomasochistic encounter; *broadly* : a dominating woman

dom·i·neer \ˌdä-mə-'nir\ *vb* **1** : to rule in an arrogant manner **2** : to be overbearing

do·mi·nie *1 usu* 'dä-mə-nē, *2 usu* 'dō-\ *n* **1** *chiefly Scot* : SCHOOLMASTER **2** : CLERGYMAN

do·min·ion \də-'min-yən\ *n* **1** : DOMAIN **2** : supreme authority : SOVEREIGNTY **3** *often cap* : a self-governing nation of the Commonwealth

dom·i·no \\'dä-mə-ˌnō\ *n, pl* **-noes** *or* **-nos** **1** : a long loose hooded cloak usu. worn with a half mask as a masquerade costume **2** : a flat rectangular block used as a piece in a game (**dominoes**)

¹don \\'dän\ *vb* **donned; don·ning** [ME, fr. *don* to do + *on*] : to put on (as clothes)

²don *n* [Sp, fr. L *dominus* lord, master] **1** : a Spanish nobleman or gentleman — used as a title prefixed to the Christian name **2** : a head, tutor, or fellow in an English university

do·ña \\'dō-nya\ *n* : a Spanish woman of rank — used as a title prefixed to the Christian name

do·nate \\'dō-ˌnāt\ *vb* **do·nat·ed; do·nat·ing** **1** : to make a gift of : CONTRIBUTE **2** : to make a donation

do·na·tion \dō-'nā-shən\ *n* **1** : the making of a gift esp. to a charity **2** : a free contribution : GIFT

¹done \\'dən\ *past part of* DO

²done *adj* **1** : doomed to failure, defeat, or death **2** : gone by : OVER ⟨when day is ∼⟩ **3** : cooked sufficiently **4** : conformable to social convention

done deal *n* : FAIT ACCOMPLI

dong \\'dȯŋ, 'däŋ\ *n* — see MONEY table

don·key \\'däŋ-kē, 'dəŋ-\ *n, pl* **donkeys** **1** : a sturdy and patient domestic mammal classified with the asses **2** : a stupid or obstinate person

don·ny·brook \'dä-nē-₁brúk\ *n, often cap* [*Donnybrook Fair*, annual Irish event known for its brawls] : an uproarious brawl

do·nor \'dō-nər\ *n* : one that gives, donates, or presents

donut *var of* DOUGHNUT

doo·dad \'dü-₁dad\ *n* : an often small article whose common name is unknown or forgotten

doo·dle \'dü-dᵊl\ *vb* **doo·dled; doo·dling** : to draw or scribble aimlessly while occupied with something else — **doodle** *n* — **doo·dler** *n*

doom \'düm\ *n* **1** : JUDGMENT; *esp* : a judicial condemnation or sentence **2** : DESTINY **3** : RUIN, DEATH — **doom** *vb*

dooms·day \'dümz-₁dā\ *n* : JUDGMENT DAY

door \'dōr\ *n* **1** : a barrier by which an entry is closed and opened; *also* : a similar part of a piece of furniture **2** : DOORWAY **3** : a means of access or participation : OPPORTUNITY

door·keep·er \-₁kē-pər\ *n* : a person who tends a door

door·knob \-₁näb\ *n* : a knob that when turned releases a door latch

door·man \-₁man, -mən\ *n* : a usu. uniformed attendant at the door of a building (as a hotel)

door·mat \-₁mat\ *n* : a mat placed before or inside a door for wiping dirt from the shoes

door·plate \-₁plāt\ *n* : a nameplate on a door

door·step \-₁step\ *n* : a step or series of steps before an outer door

door·way \-₁wā\ *n* **1** : the opening that a door closes **2** : DOOR 3

do·pa \'dō-pə\ *n* : a form of an amino acid that is used esp. in the treatment of Parkinson's disease

do·pa·mine \'dō-pə-₁mēn\ *n* : an organic compound that occurs esp. as a neurotransmitter in the brain

¹dope \'dōp\ *n* **1** : a preparation for giving a desired quality **2** : an illicit, habit-forming, or narcotic drug; *esp* : MARIJUANA **3** : a stupid person **4** : INFORMATION

²dope *vb* **doped; dop·ing 1** : to treat with dope; *esp* : to give a narcotic to **2** : FIGURE OUT — usu. used with *out* **3** : to take dope — **dop·er** *n*

dop·ey *also* **dopy** \'dō-pē\ *adj* **dop·i·er; -est 1** : dulled by alcohol or a narcotic **2** : SLUGGISH **3** : STUPID — **dop·i·ness** *n*

doping *n* : the use of a substance or technique to illegally improve athletic performance

Dopp·ler effect \'dä-plər-\ *n* : a change in the frequency at which waves (as of sound) reach an observer from a source in motion with respect to the observer

do·rag \'dü-₁rag\ *n* : a kerchief worn esp. to cover the hair

dork \'dórk\ *n, slang* : NERD; *also* : JERK 2

dorm \'dórm\ *n* : DORMITORY

dor·mant \'dór-mənt\ *adj* : INACTIVE; *esp* : not actively growing or functioning 〈~ buds〉 — **dor·man·cy** \-mən-sē\ *n*

dor·mer \'dór-mər\ *n* [MF *dormeor* dormitory, fr. L *dormitorium*, fr. *dormire* to sleep] : a window built upright in a sloping roof; *also* : the roofed structure containing such a window

dor·mi·to·ry \'dór-mə-₁tór-ē\ *n, pl* **-ries 1** : a room for sleeping; *esp* : a large room containing a number of beds **2** : a residence hall providing sleeping rooms

dor·mouse \'dór-₁maús\ *n* : any of numerous Old World rodents that resemble small squirrels

dor·sal \'dór-səl\ *adj* : of, relating to, or located near or on the surface of the body that in humans is the back but in most other animals is the upper surface — **dor·sal·ly** *adv*

do·ry \'dór-ē\ *n, pl* **dories** : a flat-bottomed boat with high flaring sides and a sharp bow

DOS *abbr* disk operating system

¹dose \'dōs\ *n* [ME, fr. MF, fr. LL *dosis*, fr. Gk, lit., act of giving, fr. *didonai* to give] **1** : a measured quantity (as of medicine) to be taken or administered at one time **2** : the quantity of radiation administered or absorbed — **dos·age** \'dō-sij\ *n*

²dose *vb* **dosed; dos·ing 1** : to give in doses **2** : to give medicine to

do·sim·e·ter \dō-'si-mə-tər\ *n* : a device for measuring doses of radiations (as X-rays) — **do·sim·e·try** \-mə-trē\ *n*

dos·sier \'dós-₁yā, 'dó-sē-₁ā\ *n* [F, bundle of documents labeled on the back, dossier, fr. *dos* back, fr. OF, fr. L *dorsum*] : a file containing detailed records on a particular person or subject

¹dot \'dät\ *n* **1** : a small spot : SPECK **2** : a small round mark **3** : a precise point esp. in time 〈be here on the ~〉

²dot *vb* **dot·ted; dot·ting 1** : to mark with a dot 〈~ an *i*〉 **2** : to cover with or as if with dots — **dot·ter** *n*

DOT *abbr* Department of Transportation

dot·age \'dō-tij\ *n* : feebleness of mind esp. in old age : SENILITY

dot·ard \-tərd\ *n* : a person in dotage

dot·com \'dät-₁käm\ *n* : a company that markets its products or services usu. exclusively via a website

dote \'dōt\ *vb* **dot·ed; dot·ing 1** : to be feebleminded esp. from old age **2** : to be lavish or excessive in one's attention, affection, or fondness 〈*doted* on her niece〉

dot matrix *n* : a rectangular arrangement of dots from which alphanumeric characters can be formed (as by a computer printer)

Dou·ay Version \dü-'ā-\ *n* : an English translation of the Vulgate used by Roman Catholics

¹dou·ble \'də-bəl\ *adj* [ME, fr. AF, fr. L *duplus*, fr. *duo* two + *-plus* multiplied by] **1** : TWOFOLD, DUAL 〈serving a ~ function〉 **2** : consisting of two members or parts **3** : being twice as great or as many **4** : folded in two **5** : having more than one whorl of petals 〈~ roses〉

²double *vb* **dou·bled; dou·bling 1** : to make, be, or become twice as great or as many **2** : to make a call in bridge that increases the trick values and penalties of (an opponent's bid) **3** : FOLD **4** : CLENCH **5** : to be or cause to be bent over **6** : to take the place of another **7** : to hit a double **8** : to turn sharply and suddenly; *esp* : to turn back on one's course

³double *adv* **1** : DOUBLY **2** : two together 〈sleep ~〉

⁴double *n* **1** : something twice another in size, strength, speed, quantity, or value **2** : a base hit that enables the batter to reach second base **3** : COUNTERPART, DUPLICATE; *esp* : a person who closely resembles another **4** : UNDERSTUDY, SUBSTITUTE **5** : a sharp turn : REVERSAL **6** : FOLD **7** : a combined bet placed on two different contests **8** *pl* : a game between two pairs of players **9** : an act of doubling in a card game

double bond *n* : a chemical bond in which two atoms in a molecule share two pairs of electrons

double cross *n* : an act of betraying or cheating esp. an associate — **dou·ble–cross** \₁də-bəl-'krós\ *vb* — **double–cross·er** *n*

dou·ble–deal·ing \₁də-bəl-'dē-liŋ\ *n* : DUPLICITY — **dou·ble–deal·er** \-'dē-lər\ *n* — **double–dealing** *adj*

dou·ble–deck·er \-'de-kər\ *n* : something having two decks, levels, or layers — **dou·ble–deck** \-₁dek\ *or* **dou·ble–decked** \-₁dekt\ *adj*

dou·ble–dig·it \₁də-bəl-'di-jət\ *adj* : amounting to 10 percent or more

double down *vb* : to become more tenacious, zealous, or resolute

dou·ble en·ten·dre \₁düb-ᵊl-äⁿ-'täⁿd, ₁də-bəl-, -'tänd-rᵊ\ *n, pl* **double entendres** 〈*same or* -'tän-drəz〉 [obs. F, lit., double meaning] : a word or expression capable of two interpretations with one usu. risqué

dou·ble–head·er \₁də-bəl-'he-dər\ *n* : two games played consecutively on the same day

double helix *n* : a helix or spiral consisting of two strands (as of DNA) in the surface of a cylinder which coil around its axis

dou·ble–hung \₁də-bəl-'həŋ\ *adj, of a window* : having an upper and a lower sash that can slide past each other

dou·ble–joint·ed \-'jóin-təd\ *adj* : having a joint that permits an exceptional degree of freedom of motion of the parts joined 〈a ~ finger〉

dou·ble–park \₁də-bəl-'pärk\ *vb* : to park a vehicle beside a row of vehicles already parked parallel to the curb

double play *n* : a play in baseball by which two players are put out

double pneumonia *n* : pneumonia affecting both lungs

double standard *n* : a set of principles that applies differently and usu. more rigorously to one group of people or circumstances than to another

dou·blet \'də-blət\ *n* **1** : a man's close-fitting jacket worn in Europe esp. in the 16th century   **2** : one of two similar or identical things

dou·ble take \'də-bəl-ˌtāk\ *n* : a delayed reaction to a surprising or significant situation after an initial failure to notice anything unusual

dou·ble–talk \-ˌtók\ *n* : language that appears to be meaningful but in fact is a mixture of sense and nonsense

double up *vb* : to share accommodations designed for one

double whammy *n* : a combination of two usu. adverse forces, circumstances, or effects

dou·bloon \ˌdə-'blün\ *n* : a former gold coin of Spain and Spanish America

dou·bly \'də-blē\ *adv*   **1** : in a twofold manner   **2** : to twice the degree ⟨~ glad⟩

¹doubt \'daút\ *vb*   **1** : to be uncertain about   **2** : to lack confidence in   **3** : to consider unlikely — **doubt·able** *adj* — **doubt·er** *n*

²doubt *n*   **1** : uncertainty of belief or opinion   **2** : a condition causing uncertainty, hesitation, or suspense ⟨the outcome was in ~⟩   **3** : DISTRUST   **4** : an inclination not to believe or accept

doubt·ful \'daút-fəl\ *adj*   **1** : QUESTIONABLE ⟨~ they knew what happened⟩   **2** : UNDECIDED ⟨the outcome of the election is ~⟩ — **doubt·ful·ly** *adv* — **doubt·ful·ness** *n*

¹doubt·less \'daút-ləs\ *adv*   **1** : without doubt   **2** : PROBABLY

²doubtless *adj* : free from doubt : CERTAIN — **doubt·less·ly** *adv*

douche \'düsh\ *n* [F]   **1** : a jet of fluid (as water) directed against a part or into a cavity of the body; *also* : a cleansing with a douche   **2** : a device for giving douches — **douche** *vb*

dough \'dō\ *n*   **1** : a mixture that consists of flour or meal and a liquid (as milk or water) and is stiff enough to knead or roll   **2** : something resembling dough esp. in consistency   **3** : MONEY — **doughy** \'dō-ē\ *adj*

dough·boy \-ˌbói\ *n* : an American infantryman esp. in World War I

dough·nut *also* **do·nut** \-(ˌ)nət\ *n* : a small usu. ring-shaped cake fried in fat

dough·ty \'daú-tē\ *adj* **dough·ti·er; -est** : ABLE, VALIANT ⟨a ~ warrior⟩

Doug·las fir \'də-gləs-\ *n* : a tall evergreen timber tree of the western U.S.

dou·la \'dü-lə\ *n* : a woman who provides assistance to a mother before, during, and just after childbirth

do up *vb*   **1** : to prepare (as by cleaning) for use   **2** : to wrap up   **3** : CLOTHE, DECORATE   **4** : FASTEN

dour \'daú-(ə)r, 'dúr\ *adj* [ME, fr. L *durus* hard]   **1** : STERN, HARSH   **2** : OBSTINATE   **3** : SULLEN — **dour·ly** *adv*

douse \'daús, 'daúz\ *vb* **doused; dous·ing**   **1** : to plunge into water   **2** : DRENCH   **3** : EXTINGUISH ⟨~ a match⟩

¹dove \'dəv\ *n*   **1** : any of numerous pigeons; *esp* : a small wild pigeon   **2** : an advocate of peace or of a peaceful policy — **dov·ish** \'də-vish\ *adj*

²dove \'dōv\ *past of* DIVE

¹dove·tail \'dəv-ˌtāl\ *n* : something that resembles a dove's tail; *esp* : a flaring tenon and a mortise into which it fits tightly

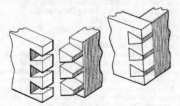

dovetail: with mortises and tenons

²dovetail *vb*   **1** : to join by means of dovetails   **2** : to fit skillfully together to form a whole ⟨our plans ~ nicely⟩

dow·a·ger \'daú-i-jər\ *n*   **1** : a widow owning property or a title from her deceased husband   **2** : a dignified elderly woman

dowdy \'daú-dē\ *adj* **dowd·i·er; -est** : lacking neatness and charm : SHABBY, UNTIDY; *also* : lacking smartness

dow·el \'daú(-ə)l\ *n*   **1** : a pin used for fastening together two pieces of wood   **2** : a round rod (as of wood) — **dowel** *vb*

¹dow·er \'daú(-ə)r\ *n* [ME *dowere*, fr. AF *dower*, *douaire*, fr. ML *dotarium*, fr. L *dot*, *dos* gift, marriage portion]   **1** : the part of a deceased husband's real estate which the law gives for life to his widow   **2** : DOWRY

²dower *vb* : to supply with a dower or dowry : ENDOW

dow·itch·er \'daú-i-chər\ *n* : any of several long-billed wading birds related to the sandpipers

¹down \'daún\ *adv* [ME *doun*, fr. OE *dūne*, short for *adūne*, of *dūne*, lit., from (the) hill]   **1** : toward or in a lower physical position   **2** : to a lying or sitting position   **3** : toward or to the ground, floor, or bottom   **4** : as a down payment ⟨paid $5 ~⟩   **5** : on paper ⟨put ~ what he says⟩   **6** : in a direction that is the opposite of up   **7** : SOUTH   **8** : to or in a lower or worse condition or status   **9** : from a past time   **10** : to or in a state of less activity   **11** : into defeat ⟨voted the motion ~⟩

²down *prep* : down in, on, along, or through : toward the bottom of ⟨fell ~ a hole⟩ ⟨lives ~ the road⟩

³down *vb*   **1** : to go or cause to go or come down ⟨~ed a warplane⟩   **2** : DEFEAT   **3** : to cause (a football) to be out of play   **4** : CONSUME 3 ⟨~ed two beers⟩

⁴down *adj*   **1** : occupying a low position; *esp* : lying on the ground   **2** : directed or going downward   **3** : being in a state of reduced or low activity   **4** : DEPRESSED, DEJECTED   **5** : SICK ⟨~ with a cold⟩   **6** : FINISHED, DONE   **7** : completely mastered ⟨got her lines ~⟩   **8** : being on record ⟨you're ~ for two tickets⟩

⁵down *n*   **1** : a low or falling period (as in activity, emotional life, or fortunes)   **2** : one of a series of attempts to advance a football   **3** : a quark with a charge of -⅓ that is one of the constituents of the proton and neutron

⁶down *n* : a rolling usu. treeless upland with sparse soil — usu. used in pl.

⁷down *n*   **1** : a covering of soft fluffy feathers; *also* : such feathers   **2** : a downlike covering or material

down·beat \'daún-ˌbēt\ *n* : the downward stroke of a conductor indicating the principally accented note of a measure of music

down·burst \-ˌbərst\ *n* : a powerful downdraft usu. associated with a thunderstorm that is a hazard for low-flying aircraft; *also* : MICROBURST

down·cast \-ˌkast\ *adj*   **1** : DEJECTED   **2** : directed down ⟨a ~ glance⟩

down·draft \-ˌdraft\ *n* : a downward current of gas (as air)

down·er \'daú-nər\ *n*   **1** : a depressant drug; *esp* : BARBITURATE   **2** : someone or something depressing

down·fall \'daún-ˌfól\ *n*   **1** : a sudden fall (as from high rank)   **2** : something that causes a downfall — **down·fall·en** \-ˌfó-lən\ *adj*

¹down·grade \'daún-ˌgrād\ *n*   **1** : a downward slope (as of a road)   **2** : a decline toward a worse condition

²downgrade *vb* : to lower in quality, value, extent, or status

down·heart·ed \-'här-təd\ *adj* : DEJECTED

¹down·hill \'daún-'hil\ *adv* : toward the bottom of a hill — **downhill** \-ˌhil\ *adj*

²down·hill \-ˌhil\ *n* : the sport of skiing downhill usu. in a race against time

¹down·load \'daún-ˌlōd\ *n* : an act or instance of downloading something; *also* : the item downloaded

²download *vb* : to transfer (data) from a computer to another device — **down·load·able** \-ˌlō-də-bəl\ *adj*

down payment *n* : a part of the full price paid at the time of purchase or delivery with the balance to be paid later

down·play \'daún-ˌplā\ *vb* : DE-EMPHASIZE ⟨~ed the allegations⟩

down·pour \'daún-ˌpór\ *n* : a heavy rain

down·range \-'rānj\ *adv* : away from a launching site

¹down·right \-ˌrīt\ *adv* : THOROUGHLY

²downright *adj*   **1** : ABSOLUTE, UTTER ⟨a ~ lie⟩   **2** : PLAIN, BLUNT ⟨a ~ man⟩

down·shift \-ˌshift\ *vb* : to shift an automotive vehicle into a lower gear

down·size \-ˌsīz\ *vb* : to reduce or undergo reduction in size or numbers

down·spout \-ˌspaút\ *n* : a vertical pipe used to drain rainwater from a roof

Down syndrome \'daún-\ or **Down's syndrome** \'daúnz-\ n : a birth defect characterized by mental retardation, slanting eyes, a broad short skull, broad hands with short fingers, and the presence of an extra chromosome

down·stage \'daún-'stāj\ adv or adj : toward or at the front of a theatrical stage — **down·stage** \-ˌstāj\ n

down·stairs \-'sterz\ adv : on or to a lower floor and esp. the main or ground floor — **down·stairs** \-ˌsterz\ adj or n

down·stream \-'strēm\ adv or adj : in the direction of flow of a stream

down·stroke \-ˌstrōk\ n : a downward stroke

down·swing \-ˌswiŋ\ n 1 : a swing downward 2 : DOWNTURN

down–to–earth adj : PRACTICAL, REALISTIC

down·town \'daún-ˌtaún\ n : the main business district of a town or city — **downtown** \'daún-'taún\ adj or adv

down·trod·den \'daún-'trä-dᵊn\ adj : suffering oppression

down·turn \-ˌtərn\ n : a downward turn esp. in economic activity

¹**down·ward** \'daún-wərd\ or **down·wards** \-wərdz\ adv 1 : from a higher to a lower place or condition 2 : from an earlier time 3 : from an ancestor or predecessor

²**downward** adj : directed toward or situated in a lower place or condition

down·wind \'daún-'wind\ adv or adj : in the direction that the wind is blowing

downy \'daú-nē\ adj **down·i·er; -est** : resembling or covered with down

downy mildew n : any of various parasitic fungi producing whitish masses esp. on the underside of plant leaves; also : a plant disease caused by downy mildew

downy woodpecker n : a small black-and-white woodpecker of No. America

dow·ry \'daú(-ə)r-ē\ n, pl **dowries** [ME dowarie, fr. AF, alter. of dower, douaire dower] : the property that a woman brings to her husband in marriage

dowse \'daúz\ vb **dowsed; dows·ing** : to use a divining rod esp. to find water — **dows·er** n

dox·ol·o·gy \däk-'sä-lə-jē\ n, pl **-gies** : a usu. short hymn of praise to God

doy·en \'dòi-ən, 'dwä-ˌyaⁿ\ n : the senior or most experienced person in a group

doy·enne \dòi-'yen, dwä-'yen\ n : a woman who is a doyen

doy·ley chiefly Brit var of DOILY

doz abbr dozen

doze \'dōz\ vb **dozed; doz·ing** : to sleep lightly — **doze** n

doz·en \'də-zᵊn\ n, pl **dozens** or **dozen** [ME dozeine, fr. AF duzeine, fr. duze twelve, fr. L duodecim, fr. duo two + decem ten] : a group of twelve — **doz·enth** \-zᵊnth\ adj

¹**DP** \ˌdē-'pē\ n, pl **DP's** or **DPs** 1 : a displaced person 2 : DOUBLE PLAY

²**DP** abbr data processing

dpt abbr department

DPT abbr diphtheria-pertussis-tetanus (vaccines)

dr abbr 1 debtor 2 dram 3 drive 4 drum

Dr abbr doctor

DR abbr 1 dead reckoning 2 dining room

drab \'drab\ adj **drab·ber; drab·best** 1 : being of a light olive-brown color 2 : DULL, MONOTONOUS, CHEERLESS — **drab·ly** adv — **drab·ness** n

drach·ma \'drak-mə\ n, pl **drach·mas** or **drach·mai** \-ˌmī\ or **drach·mae** \-(ˌ)mē\ : the former basic monetary unit of Greece

dra·co·ni·an \drā-'kō-nē-ən, drə-\ adj, often cap : CRUEL; also : SEVERE

¹**draft** \'draft, 'dräft\ n 1 : the act of drawing or hauling 2 : the act or an instance of drinking or inhaling; also : the portion drunk or inhaled in one such act 3 : DOSE, POTION 4 : DELINEATION, PLAN, DESIGN; also : a preliminary sketch, outline, or version ⟨a rough ∼ of a speech⟩ 5 : the act of drawing (as from a cask); also : a portion of liquid so drawn 6 : the depth of water a ship draws esp. when loaded 7 : a system for or act of selecting persons (as for sports teams or compulsory military service); also : the persons so selected 8 : an order for the payment of money drawn by one person or bank on another 9 : a heavy demand : STRAIN 10 : a current of air; also : a device to regulate air supply (as in a stove) — **on draft** : ready to be drawn from a receptacle ⟨beer on draft⟩

²**draft** adj 1 : used or adapted for drawing loads ⟨∼ horses⟩ 2 : being or having been on draft ⟨∼ beer⟩

³**draft** vb 1 : to select usu. on a compulsory basis; esp : to conscript for military service 2 : to draw the preliminary sketch, version, or plan of 3 : COMPOSE, PREPARE 4 : to draw off or away

draft·ee \draf-'tē, dräf-\ n : a person who is drafted

drafts·man \'draft-smən, 'dräft-\ n : a person who draws plans (as for buildings or machinery) — **drafts·man·ly** \-lē\ adj

drafty \'draf-tē, 'dräf-\ adj **draft·i·er; -est** : exposed to or abounding in drafts of air ⟨a ∼ room⟩

¹**drag** \'drag\ n 1 : a device pulled along under water for detecting or gathering 2 : something (as a harrow or sledge) that is dragged along over a surface 3 : the act or an instance of dragging 4 : something that hinders progress; also : something boring ⟨thinks school is a ∼⟩ 5 : STREET ⟨the main ∼⟩ 6 : clothing typical of one sex worn by a member of the opposite sex

²**drag** vb **dragged; drag·ging** 1 : HAUL 2 : to move or proceed with slowness or difficulty ⟨dragged himself out of bed⟩ ⟨the lecture dragged on⟩ 3 : to force into or out of some situation, condition, or course of action 4 : PROTRACT ⟨∼ a story out⟩ 5 : to hang or lag behind 6 : to explore, search, or fish with a drag 7 : to trail along on the ground 8 : DRAW, PUFF ⟨∼ on a cigarette⟩ 9 : to move (items on a computer screen) esp. by using a mouse — **drag·ger** n — **drag one's feet** also **drag one's heels** : to act slowly or with hesitation

drag·net \-ˌnet\ n 1 : NET, TRAWL 2 : a network of planned actions for pursuing and catching ⟨a police ∼⟩

drag·o·man \'dra-gə-mən\ n, pl **-mans** or **-men** \-mən\ : an interpreter employed esp. in the Near East

drag·on \'dra-gən\ n [ME, fr. AF dragun, fr. L dracon-, draco serpent, dragon, fr. Gk drakōn serpent] : a fabulous animal usu. represented as a huge winged scaly serpent with a crested head and large claws

drag·on·fly \-ˌflī\ n : any of a group of large harmless 4-winged insects that hold the wings horizontal and unfolded in repose

¹**dra·goon** \drə-'gün, dra-\ n [F dragon dragon, dragoon, fr. MF] 1 : a heavily armed mounted soldier 2 : CAVALRYMAN

²**dragoon** vb : to force or attempt to force into submission : COERCE

drag race n : an acceleration contest between vehicles — **drag racer** n

drag·ster \'drag-stər\ n : a usu. high-powered vehicle used in a drag race

drag strip n : a site for drag races

¹**drain** \'drān\ vb 1 : to draw off or flow off gradually or completely 2 : to exhaust physically or emotionally ⟨∼ed by the work⟩ 3 : to make or become gradually dry or empty ⟨∼ a swamp⟩ 4 : to carry away the surface water of : discharge surface or surplus water 5 : EMPTY, EXHAUST ⟨∼ed our savings⟩ — **drain·er** n

²**drain** n 1 : a means (as a channel or sewer) of draining 2 : the act of draining 3 : a gradual outflow; also : something causing an outflow ⟨a ∼ on our savings⟩

drain·age \'drā-nij\ n 1 : the act or process of draining; also : something that is drained off 2 : a means for draining : DRAIN, SEWER 3 : an area drained

drain·pipe \'drān-ˌpīp\ n : a pipe for drainage

drake \'drāk\ n : a male duck

¹**dram** \'dram\ n 1 — see WEIGHT table 2 : FLUID DRAM 3 : a small drink

²**dram** \'dram\ n — see MONEY table

dra·ma \'drä-mə, 'dra-\ n [LL, fr. Gk, deed, drama, fr. dran to do, act] 1 : a literary composition designed for theatrical presentation; also : a production (as a film) with a serious tone or subject 2 : dramatic art, literature, or affairs 3 : a series of events involving conflicting forces — **dra·mat·ic** \drə-'ma-tik\ adj — **dra·mat·i·cal·ly** \-ti-k(ə-)lē\ adv — **dra·ma·tist** \'drä-mə-tist, 'dra-\ n

dram·a·ti·sa·tion, dram·a·tise Brit var of DRAMATIZATION, DRAMATIZE

dra·ma·tize \'dra-mə-ˌtīz, 'drä-\ vb **-tized; -tiz·ing** 1 : to adapt for or be suitable for theatrical presentation 2 : to present or represent in a dramatic manner — **dram·a·ti·za·tion** \ˌdra-mə-tə-'zā-shən, ˌdrä-\ n

dra·me·dy \'drä-mə-ˌdē, 'dra-\ n : a comedy having dramatic moments

drank past and past part of DRINK

¹**drape** \'drāp\ *vb* **draped; drap·ing** **1** : to cover or adorn with or as if with folds of cloth ⟨kings *draped* in robes⟩ **2** : to cause to hang or stretch out loosely or carelessly **3** : to arrange or become arranged in flowing lines or folds

²**drape** *n* **1** : CURTAIN **2** : arrangement in or of folds **3** : the cut or hang of clothing

drap·er \'drā-pər\ *n, chiefly Brit* : a dealer in cloth and sometimes in clothing and dry goods

drap·ery \'drā-pə-rē\ *n, pl* **-er·ies** **1** *Brit* : DRY GOODS **2** : a decorative fabric esp. when hung loosely and in folds; *also* : hangings of heavy fabric used as a curtain

dras·tic \'dras-tik\ *adj* : HARSH, RIGOROUS, SEVERE ⟨~ punishment⟩ — **dras·ti·cal·ly** \-ti-k(ə-)lē\ *adv*

draught \'dráft\, **draughty** \'dráf-tē\ *chiefly Brit var of* DRAFT, DRAFTY

draughts \'dráfts\ *n, Brit* : CHECKERS

draughts·man *chiefly Brit var of* DRAFTSMAN

Dra·vid·i·an \drə-'vi-dē-ən\ *n* : a language family of south Asia that includes the major literary languages of southern India

¹**draw** \'dró\ *vb* **drew** \'drü\; **drawn** \'drón\; **draw·ing** **1** : to cause to move toward a force exerted **2** : to cause to go in a certain direction ⟨*drew* him aside⟩ **3** : to move or go steadily or gradually ⟨night ~s near⟩ **4** : ATTRACT, ENTICE **5** : PROVOKE, ROUSE ⟨*drew* enemy fire⟩ **6** : INHALE ⟨~ a deep breath⟩ **7** : to bring or pull out ⟨*drew* a gun⟩ **8** : to cause to come out of a container or source ⟨~ blood⟩ ⟨~ water for a bath⟩ **9** : EVISCERATE **10** : to require (a specified depth) to float in **11** : ACCUMULATE, GAIN ⟨~ing interest⟩ **12** : to take money from a place of deposit : WITHDRAW **13** : to receive regularly ⟨~ a salary⟩ **14** : to take (cards) from a stack or the dealer **15** : to receive or take at random ⟨~ a winning number⟩ **16** : to bend (a bow) by pulling back the string **17** : WRINKLE, SHRINK **18** : to change shape by or as if by pulling or stretching ⟨a face *drawn* with sorrow⟩ **19** : to leave (a contest) undecided : TIE **20** : DELINEATE, SKETCH **21** : to write out in due form : DRAFT ⟨~ up a will⟩ **22** : FORMULATE ⟨~ comparisons⟩ **23** : INFER ⟨~ a conclusion⟩ **24** : to spread or elongate (metal) by hammering or by pulling through dies **25** : to produce or allow a draft or current of air ⟨the chimney ~s well⟩ **26** : to swell out in a wind ⟨all sails ~ing⟩ — **draw a blank** : to be unable to think of something — **draw the line** *or* **draw a line** : to fix an arbitrary boundary usu. between two things

²**draw** *n* **1** : the act, process, or result of drawing **2** : a lot or chance drawn at random **3** : a contest left undecided or deadlocked : TIE **4** : one that draws attention or patronage : ATTRACTION

draw·back \'dró-ˌbak\ *n* : DISADVANTAGE **2** ⟨the ~s of rural living⟩

draw·bridge \-ˌbrij\ *n* : a bridge made to be raised, lowered, or turned to permit or deny passage

draw·er \'drór, 'dró-ər\ *n* **1** : one that draws **2** *pl* : an undergarment for the lower part of the body **3** : a sliding boxlike compartment (as in a table or desk)

draw·ing \'dró-iŋ\ *n* **1** : an act or instance of drawing; *esp* : an occasion when something is decided by drawing lots ⟨tonight's lottery ~⟩ **2** : the act or art of making a figure, plan, or sketch by means of lines **3** : a representation made by drawing : SKETCH

drawing card *n* : DRAW **4**

drawing room *n* : a formal reception room

drawl \'dról\ *vb* : to speak or utter slowly with vowels greatly prolonged — **drawl** *n*

draw on *vb* : APPROACH ⟨night *draws on*⟩

draw out *vb* **1** : PROLONG **2** : to cause to speak freely

draw·string \'dró-ˌstriŋ\ *n* : a string, cord, or tape for use in closing a bag or controlling fullness in garments or curtains

draw up *vb* **1** : to prepare a draft or version of **2** : to pull oneself erect **3** : to bring or come to a stop

dray \'drā\ *n* : a strong low cart for carrying heavy loads

¹**dread** \'dred\ *vb* **1** : to fear greatly **2** : to feel extreme reluctance to meet or face

²**dread** *n* : great fear esp. of some harm to come

³**dread** *adj* **1** : causing great fear or anxiety ⟨a ~ disease⟩ **2** : inspiring awe

dread·ful \'dred-fəl\ *adj* **1** : inspiring dread or awe

2 : extremely distasteful, unpleasant, or shocking ⟨a ~ accident⟩ — **dread·ful·ly** *adv*

dread·locks \'dred-ˌläks\ *n pl* : long braids of hair over the entire head

dread·nought \'dred-ˌnòt\ *n* : BATTLESHIP

¹**dream** \'drēm\ *n* [ME *dreem*, fr. OE *drēam* noise, joy, and ON *draumr* dream] **1** : a series of thoughts, images, or emotions occurring during sleep **2** : a dreamlike vision : DAYDREAM, REVERIE **3** : something notable for its beauty, excellence, or enjoyable quality **4** : IDEAL — **dream·like** \-ˌlīk\ *adj* — **dreamy** *adj*

²**dream** \'drēm\ *vb* **dreamed** \'dremt, 'drēmd\ *or* **dreamt** \'dremt\; **dream·ing** **1** : to have a dream of **2** : to indulge in daydreams or fantasies : pass (time) in reverie or inaction **3** : IMAGINE — **dream·er** *n*

dream·boat \'drēm-ˌbōt\ *n, slang* : something highly desirable; *esp* : a very attractive person

dream·land \'drēm-ˌland\ *n* : an unreal delightful country that exists in imagination or in dreams

dream up *vb* : INVENT, CONCOCT

dream·world \-ˌwərld\ *n* : a world of illusion or fantasy

drear \'drir\ *adj* : DREARY

drea·ry \'drir-ē\ *adj* **drea·ri·er; -est** [ME *drery*, fr. OE *drēorig* sad, bloody, fr. *drēor* gore] **1** : DOLEFUL, SAD **2** : DISMAL, GLOOMY — **drea·ri·ly** \-ə-lē\ *adv*

¹**dredge** \'drej\ *vb* **dredged; dredg·ing** : to gather or search with or as if with a dredge — **dredg·er** *n*

²**dredge** *n* : a machine or barge for removing earth or silt

³**dredge** *vb* **dredged; dredg·ing** : to coat (food) by sprinkling (as with flour)

dregs \'dregz\ *n pl* **1** : SEDIMENT 1 **2** : the most undesirable part ⟨the ~ of humanity⟩

drench \'drench\ *vb* : to wet thoroughly

¹**dress** \'dres\ *vb* [ME, fr. AF *drescer* to direct, put right, fr. VL **directiare*, fr. L *directus* direct] **1** : to make or set straight : ALIGN **2** : to prepare for use; *esp* : BUTCHER **3** : TRIM, EMBELLISH ⟨~ a store window⟩ **4** : to put clothes on : CLOTHE; *also* : to put on or wear formal or fancy clothes **5** : to apply dressings or medicine to ⟨~ a wound⟩ **6** : to arrange (the hair) by combing, brushing, or curling **7** : to apply fertilizer to ⟨~ a field⟩ **8** : SMOOTH, FINISH ⟨~ leather⟩

²**dress** *n* **1** : APPAREL, CLOTHING ⟨casual ~⟩ **2** : a garment usu. consisting of a one-piece bodice and skirt — **dress·mak·er** \-ˌmā-kər\ *n* — **dress·mak·ing** \-ˌmā-kiŋ\ *n*

³**dress** *adj* : suitable for a formal occasion; *also* : requiring formal dress

dres·sage \drə-'säzh\ *n* [F] : the execution by a trained horse of complex movements in response to barely perceptible signals from its rider

dress down *vb* : to scold severely

¹**dress·er** \'dre-sər\ *n* : a chest of drawers or bureau with a mirror

²**dresser** *n* : one that dresses

dress·ing \'dre-siŋ\ *n* **1** : the act or process of one who dresses **2** : a sauce for adding to a dish (as a salad) **3** : a seasoned mixture usu. used as stuffing **4** : material used to cover an injury (as a wound)

dressing gown *n* : a loose robe worn esp. while dressing or resting

dressy \'dre-sē\ *adj* **dress·i·er; -est** **1** : showy in dress **2** : STYLISH, SMART

drew *past of* DRAW

¹**drib·ble** \'dri-bəl\ *vb* **drib·bled; drib·bling** **1** : to fall or flow in drops : TRICKLE **2** : DROOL **3** : to propel by successive slight taps or bounces

²**dribble** *n* **1** : a small trickling stream or flow **2** : a drizzling shower **3** : the dribbling of a ball or puck

drib·let \'dri-blət\ *n* **1** : a trifling amount **2** : a drop of liquid

dri·er *or* **dry·er** \'drī-ər\ *n* **1** : a substance that speeds drying (as of paint or ink) **2** *usu* **dryer** : a device for drying

¹**drift** \'drift\ *n* **1** : the motion or course of something drifting; *also* : a gradual shift of position **2** : a mass of matter (as snow or sand) piled up esp. by wind **3** : earth, gravel, and rock deposited by a glacier **4** : a general underlying design or tendency : MEANING ⟨catch my ~⟩

²**drift** *vb* **1** : to float or be driven along by or as if by a current of water or air ⟨~ing logs⟩ **2** : to become piled up by wind or water ⟨~ing snow⟩

drift·er \'drif-tər\ *n* : a person who moves about aimlessly

drift net *n* : a fishing net often miles in extent arranged to drift with the tide or current

drift·wood \'drift-,wùd\ *n* : wood drifted or floated by water

1drill \'dril\ *n* 1 : a tool for boring holes 2 : the training of soldiers in marching and the handling of arms 3 : a regularly practiced exercise ⟨a shooting ∼⟩

2drill *vb* 1 : to instruct and exercise by repetition 2 : to train in or practice military drill 3 : to bore with a drill ⟨∼ a hole⟩ — **drill·er** *n*

3drill *n* 1 : a shallow furrow or trench in which seed is sown 2 : an agricultural implement for making furrows and dropping seed into them

4drill *n* : a firm cotton twilled fabric

drill·mas·ter \'dril-,mas-tər\ *n* : an instructor in military drill

drill press *n* : an upright drilling machine in which the drill is pressed to the work usu. by a hand lever

drily *var of* DRYLY

1drink \'driŋk\ *vb* **drank** \'draŋk\; **drunk** \'drəŋk\ *or* **drank**; **drink·ing** 1 : to swallow liquid : IMBIBE 2 : ABSORB 3 : to take in through the senses ⟨∼ in the beautiful scenery⟩ 4 : to give or join in a toast 5 : to drink alcoholic beverages esp. to excess — **drink·able** *adj* — **drink·er** *n*

2drink *n* 1 : BEVERAGE; *also* : an alcoholic beverage 2 : a draft or portion of liquid 3 : excessive consumption of alcoholic beverages

1drip \'drip\ *vb* **dripped; drip·ping** 1 : to fall or let fall in drops 2 : to let fall drops of moisture or liquid ⟨a *dripping* faucet⟩ 3 : to overflow with or as if with moisture ⟨clothes *dripping* with sweat⟩ ⟨stories *dripping* with irony⟩

2drip *n* 1 : a falling in drops 2 : liquid that falls, overflows, or is extruded in drops 3 : the sound made by or as if by falling drops

1drive \'drīv\ *vb* **drove** \'drōv\; **driv·en** \'dri-vən\; **driv·ing** 1 : to urge, push, or force onward 2 : to carry through strongly ⟨∼ a bargain⟩ 3 : to set or keep in motion or operation 4 : to direct the movement or course of 5 : to convey in a vehicle ⟨*drove* her to school⟩ 6 : to bring into a specified condition ⟨the noise ∼*s* me crazy⟩ 7 : FORCE, COMPEL ⟨*driven* by hunger to steal⟩ 8 : to project, inject, or impress forcefully ⟨*drove* the lesson home⟩ 9 : to produce by opening a way ⟨∼ a well⟩ 10 : to progress with strong momentum ⟨a *driving* rain⟩ 11 : to propel an object of play (as a golf ball) by a hard blow — **driv·er** *n*

2drive *n* 1 : a trip in a carriage or automobile : a driving or collecting of animals ⟨a cattle ∼⟩ 3 : the guiding of logs downstream to a mill 4 : the act of driving a ball; *also* : the flight of a ball 5 : DRIVEWAY 6 : a public road for driving (as in a park) 7 : the state of being hurried and under pressure 8 : an intensive campaign ⟨membership ∼⟩ 9 : the apparatus by which motion is imparted to a machine 10 : an offensive or aggressive move : a military attack 11 : NEED, LONGING ⟨the ∼ to succeed⟩ 12 : dynamic quality 13 : a device for reading and writing on magnetic media (as magnetic tape or disks)

drive–in \'drī-,vin\ *adj* : accommodating patrons while they remain in their automobiles — **drive–in** *n*

1driv·el \'dri-vəl\ *vb* **-eled** *or* **-elled; -el·ing** *or* **-el·ling** 1 : DROOL, SLAVER 2 : to talk or utter stupidly, carelessly, or in an infantile way — **driv·el·er** *n*

2drivel *n* : NONSENSE

drive·shaft \'drīv-,shaft\ *n* : a shaft that transmits mechanical power

drive–through *also* **drive–thru** \'drīv-,thrü\ *adj* : designed for the service of patrons remaining in their automobiles — **drive–through** *also* **drive–thru** *n*

drive·way \-,wā\ *n* : a short private road leading from the street to a house, garage, or parking lot

1driz·zle \'dri-zəl\ *n* : a fine misty rain

2drizzle *vb* **driz·zled; driz·zling** : to rain in very small drops

drogue \'drōg\ *n* : a small parachute for slowing down or stabilizing something (as a space capsule)

droid \'dròid\ *n* : ANDROID

droll \'drōl\ *adj* [F *drôle*, fr. *drôle* scamp, fr. MF *drolle*, fr. MD, imp] : having a humorous, whimsical, or odd quality ⟨a ∼ expression⟩ — **droll·ery** \'drō-lə-rē\ *n* — **drol·ly** *adv*

drom·e·dary \'drä-mə-,der-ē\ *n, pl* **-dar·ies** [ME *dromedarie*, fr. MF *dromedaire*, fr. LL *dromedarius*, fr. L *dromad-, dromas*, fr. Gk, running] : CAMEL; *esp* : a domesticated one-humped camel of western Asia and northern Africa

1drone \'drōn\ *n* 1 : a male honeybee 2 : one that lives on the labors of others : PARASITE 3 : an unmanned aircraft or ship guided by remote control 4 : one whose work is menial or monotonous

2drone *vb* **droned; dron·ing** : to sound with a low dull monotonous murmuring sound : speak monotonously

3drone *n* : a deep monotonous sound ⟨the ∼ of engines⟩

drool \'drül\ *vb* 1 : to let liquid flow from the mouth 2 : to talk foolishly — **drool** *n*

droop \'drüp\ *vb* 1 : to hang or incline downward 2 : to sink gradually 3 : LANGUISH — **droop** *n* — **droopy** *adj*

1drop \'dräp\ *n* 1 : the quantity of fluid that falls in one spherical mass 2 *pl* : a dose of medicine measured by drops 3 : a small quantity of drink 4 : the smallest practical unit of liquid measure 5 : something (as a pendant or a small round candy) that resembles a liquid drop 6 : FALL 7 : a decline in quantity or quality 8 : a descent by parachute 9 : the distance through which something drops 10 : a slot into which something is to be dropped 11 : something that drops or has dropped

2drop *vb* **dropped; drop·ping** 1 : to fall or let fall in drops 2 : to let fall : LOWER ⟨∼ a glove⟩ ⟨*dropped* his voice⟩ 3 : SEND ⟨∼ me a note⟩ 4 : to let go : DISMISS ⟨∼ the subject⟩ 5 : MENTION ⟨∼ a suggestion⟩ 6 : to knock down : cause to fall 7 : to go lower : become less ⟨prices *dropped*⟩ 8 : SPEND, LOSE ⟨∼ $20⟩ ⟨*dropped* ten pounds⟩ 9 : to come or go unexpectedly or informally ⟨a friend *dropped* in⟩ 10 : to pass from one state into a less active one ⟨∼ off to sleep⟩ 11 : to move downward or with a current 12 : QUIT ⟨*dropped* out of the race⟩ — **drop back** : to move toward the rear — **drop behind** : to fail to keep up

drop–down \'dräp-,daùn\ *adj* : PULL-DOWN

drop–kick \-'kik\ *n* : a kick made by dropping a ball to the ground and kicking it at the moment it starts to rebound — **drop–kick** *vb*

drop·let \'drä-plət\ *n* : a tiny drop

drop–off \'dräp-,òf\ *n* 1 : a steep or perpendicular descent 2 : a marked decline ⟨a ∼ in attendance⟩ 3 : an act or instance of delivering or depositing something ⟨∼ points along the route⟩

drop off *vb* : to fall asleep

drop out *vb* : to withdraw from participation or membership; *esp* : to leave school before graduation — **drop·out** \'dräp-,aùt\ *n*

drop·per \'drä-pər\ *n* 1 : one that drops 2 : a short glass tube with a rubber bulb used to measure out liquids by drops

drop·pings *n pl* : MANURE, DUNG

drop·sy \'dräp-sē\ *n* [ME *dropesie*, short for *ydropesie*, fr. AF, fr. L *hydropisis*, fr. Gk *hydrōps*, fr. *hydōr* water] : EDEMA — **drop·si·cal** \-si-kəl\ *adj*

drop–top \'dräp-,täp\ *n* : CONVERTIBLE

dross \'dräs\ *n* 1 : the scum that forms on the surface of a molten metal 2 : waste matter : REFUSE

drought \'draùt\ *also* **drouth** \'draùth\ *n* : a long spell of dry weather

1drove \'drōv\ *n* 1 : a group of animals driven or moving in a body 2 : a large number : CROWD — usu. used in pl. ⟨tourists arriving in ∼*s*⟩

2drove *past of* DRIVE

drov·er \'drō-vər\ *n* : one who drives domestic animals usu. to market

drown \'draùn\ *vb* **drowned** \'draùnd\; **drown·ing** 1 : to suffocate by submersion esp. in water 2 : to become drowned 3 : to cover with water 4 : to cause to be muted (as a sound) by a loud noise 5 : OVERPOWER, OVERWHELM

drowse \'draùz\ *vb* **drowsed; drows·ing** : DOZE — **drowse** *n*

drowsy \'draù-zē\ *adj* **drows·i·er; -est** 1 : ready to fall asleep 2 : making one sleepy ⟨∼ music⟩ — **drows·i·ly** \-zə-lē\ *adv* — **drows·i·ness** \-zē-nəs\ *n*

drub \'drəb\ *vb* **drubbed; drub·bing** 1 : to beat severely 2 : to berate critically 3 : to defeat decisively

drudge \'drəj\ *vb* **drudged; drudg·ing** : to do hard, menial, or monotonous work — **drudge** *n* — **drudg·ery** \'drə-jə-rē\ *n*

¹drug \'drəg\ *n* **1** : a substance used as a medicine or in making medicine **2** : a substance (as heroin or marijuana) that can cause addiction, habituation, or a marked change in mental status

²drug *vb* **drugged; drug·ging** : to affect with or as if with drugs; *esp* : to stupefy with a narcotic

drug·gist \'drə-gist\ *n* : a dealer in drugs and medicines; *also* : PHARMACIST

drug·store \'drəg-,stȯr\ *n* : a retail shop where medicines and miscellaneous articles are sold

dru·id \'drü-əd\ *n, often cap* : one of an ancient Celtic priesthood appearing in Irish, Welsh, and Christian legends as magicians and wizards

¹drum \'drəm\ *n* **1** : a percussion instrument usu. consisting of a hollow cylinder with a skin or plastic head stretched over one or both ends that is beaten with the hands or with a stick **2** : the sound of a drum; *also* : a similar sound **3** : a drum-shaped object (as a structure or container)

²drum *vb* **drummed; drum·ming** **1** : to beat a drum **2** : to sound rhythmically : THROB, BEAT **3** : to summon or enlist by or as if by beating a drum ⟨*drummed* into service⟩ **4** : EXPEL — usu. used with *out* **5** : to drive or force by steady effort ⟨~ the facts into memory⟩ **6** : to strike or tap repeatedly so as to produce rhythmic sounds

drum·beat \'drəm-,bēt\ *n* : a stroke on a drum or its sound

drum major *n* : the leader of a marching band

drum ma·jor·ette \-,mā-jə-'ret\ *n* : a girl or woman who leads a marching band; *also* : a baton twirler who accompanies a marching band

drum·mer \'drə-mər\ *n* **1** : one that plays a drum **2** : a traveling salesman

drum·stick \'drəm-,stik\ *n* **1** : a stick for beating a drum **2** : the lower segment of a fowl's leg

drum up *vb* **1** : to bring about by persistent effort ⟨*drum up* business⟩ **2** : INVENT, ORIGINATE ⟨*drum up* a new method⟩

¹drunk *past part of* DRINK

²drunk \'drəŋk\ *adj* **1** : having the faculties impaired by alcohol ⟨~ drivers⟩ **2** : dominated by an intense feeling ⟨~ with power⟩ **3** : of, relating to, caused by, or characterized by intoxication

³drunk *n* **1** : a period of excessive drinking **2** : a drunken person

drunk·ard \'drəŋ-kərd\ *n* : one who is habitually drunk

drunk·en \'drəŋ-kən\ *adj* **1** : DRUNK **2** : given to habitual excessive use of alcohol **3** : of, relating to, or resulting from intoxication ⟨a ~ brawl⟩ **4** : unsteady or lurching as if from intoxication ⟨walked with a ~ shuffle⟩ — **drunk·en·ly** *adv* — **drunk·en·ness** *n*

drupe \'drüp\ *n* : a partly fleshy fruit (as a plum or cherry) having one seed enclosed in a hard inner shell

¹dry \'drī\ *adj* **dri·er** \'drī-ər\; **dri·est** \-əst\ **1** : free or freed from water or liquid ⟨~ fruits⟩; *also* : not being in or under water **2** : characterized by lack of water or moisture ⟨~ climate⟩ **3** : lacking freshness : STALE **4** : devoid of natural moisture; *also* : THIRSTY **5** : no longer liquid or sticky ⟨the ink is ~⟩ **6** : not giving milk ⟨a ~ cow⟩ **7** : marked by the absence of alcoholic beverages ⟨a ~ dormitory⟩ **8** : prohibiting the making or distributing of alcoholic beverages **9** : not sweet ⟨~ wine⟩ **10** : solid as opposed to liquid ⟨~ groceries⟩ **11** : containing or employing no liquid **12** : SEVERE; *also* : UNINTERESTING, WEARISOME **13** : not productive ⟨a writer's ~ spell⟩ **14** : marked by a matter-of-fact, ironic, or terse manner of expression ⟨~ humor⟩ — **dri·ly** *or* **dry·ly** *adv* — **dry·ness** *n*

²dry *vb* **dried; dry·ing** : to make or become dry

³dry *n, pl* **drys** : PROHIBITIONIST

dry·ad \'drī-əd, -,ad\ *n* : WOOD NYMPH

dry cell *n* : a battery whose contents are not spillable

dry-clean \'drī-,klēn\ *vb* : to clean (fabrics) chiefly with solvents other than water — **dry cleaning** *n*

dry dock \'drī-,däk\ *n* : a dock that can be kept dry during ship construction or repair

dryer *var of* DRIER

dry farm·ing *n* : farming without irrigation in areas of limited rainfall — **dry-farm** *vb* — **dry farm·er** *n*

dry goods \'drī-,gu̇dz\ *n pl* : cloth goods (as fabrics, ribbon, and ready-to-wear clothing)

dry ice *n* : solid carbon dioxide

dry measure *n* : a series of units of capacity for dry commodities — see METRIC SYSTEM table, WEIGHT table

dry rot *n* : decay of timber in which fungi consume the wood's cellulose

dry run *n* : REHEARSAL, TRIAL

dry·wall \'drī-,wȯl\ *n* : a wallboard consisting of fiberboard, paper, or felt over a plaster core

Ds *symbol* darmstadtium

DSC *abbr* **1** Distinguished Service Cross **2** doctor of surgical chiropody

DSM *abbr* Distinguished Service Medal

DST *abbr* daylight saving time

DTP *abbr* diphtheria, tetanus, pertussis (vaccines)

d.t.'s \dē-'tēz\ *n pl, often cap D&T* : DELIRIUM TREMENS

du·al \'dü-əl, 'dyü-\ *adj* **1** : TWOFOLD, DOUBLE **2** : having a double character or nature — **du·al·ism** \-ə-,li-zəm\ *n* — **du·al·i·ty** \dü-'a-lə-tē, dyü-\ *n*

du·ath·lon \dü-'ath-lən, -,län\ *n* : a long-distance race involving running and bicycling — **du·ath·lete** *n*

¹dub \'dəb\ *vb* **dubbed; dub·bing** **1** : to confer knighthood upon **2** : NAME, NICKNAME

²dub *n* : a clumsy person : DUFFER

³dub *vb* **dubbed; dub·bing** : to add (sound effects) to a motion picture or to a radio or television production

du·bi·ety \dü-'bī-ə-tē, dyü-\ *n, pl* **-eties** **1** : UNCERTAINTY **2** : a matter of doubt

du·bi·ous \'dü-bē-əs, 'dyü-\ *adj* **1** : UNCERTAIN **2** : QUESTIONABLE ⟨a ~ choice⟩ **3** : feeling doubt : UNDECIDED — **du·bi·ous·ly** *adv* — **du·bi·ous·ness** *n*

dub·ni·um \'dü̇b-nē-əm, 'dəb-\ *n* : a short-lived radioactive chemical element produced artificially

du·cal \'dü-kəl, 'dyü-\ *adj* : of or relating to a duke or dukedom

duc·at \'də-kət\ *n* : a gold coin formerly used in various European countries

duch·ess \'də-chəs\ *n* **1** : the wife or widow of a duke **2** : a woman holding the rank of duke in her own right

duchy \'də-chē\ *n, pl* **duch·ies** : the territory of a duke or duchess : DUKEDOM

¹duck \'dək\ *n, pl* **ducks** : any of various swimming birds related to but smaller than geese and swans

¹duck

²duck *vb* **1** : to thrust or plunge under water **2** : to lower the head or body suddenly : BOW; *also* : DODGE **3** : to evade a duty, question, or responsibility ⟨~ the issue⟩

³duck *n* **1** : a durable closely woven usu. cotton fabric **2** *pl* : light clothes made of duck

duck·bill \'dək-,bil\ *n* : PLATYPUS

duck·ling \-liŋ\ *n* : a young duck

duck·pin \-,pin\ *n* **1** : a small bowling pin shorter and wider in the middle than a tenpin **2** *pl but sing in constr* : a bowling game using duckpins

duck sauce *n* : a thick sweet sauce made with fruits and seasonings and used in Chinese cuisine

duct \'dəkt\ *n* **1** : a tube or canal for conveying a bodily fluid **2** : a pipe or tube through which a fluid (as air) flows — **duct·less** *adj*

duc·tile \'dək-t⁰l\ *adj* **1** : capable of being drawn out into wire or thread **2** : easily led : DOCILE — **duc·til·i·ty** \dək-'ti-lə-tē\ *n*

ductless gland *n* : an endocrine gland

duct tape *n* : a cloth adhesive tape orig. designed for sealing certain ducts and joints — **duct-tape** *vb*

dud \'dəd\ *n* **1** *pl* : CLOTHING **2** : one that fails completely; *also* : a bomb or missile that fails to explode

dude \'düd, 'dyüd\ *n* **1** : DANDY 1 **2** : a city dweller; *esp*

: an Easterner in the West **3** : FELLOW, GUY — sometimes used as an informal form of address

dude ranch *n* : a vacation resort offering activities (as horseback riding) typical of western ranches

dud·geon \'də-jən\ *n* : a fit or state of indignation ⟨in high ∼⟩

¹**due** \'dü, 'dyü\ *adj* [ME, fr. AF *deu*, pp. of *dever* to owe, fr. L *debēre*] **1** : owed or owing as a debt **2** : owed or owing as a right ⟨is ∼ a fair trial⟩ **3** : APPROPRIATE, FITTING ⟨with all ∼ respect⟩ **4** : SUFFICIENT, ADEQUATE **5** : REGULAR, LAWFUL ⟨∼ process of law⟩ **6** : ATTRIBUTABLE, ASCRIBABLE ⟨∼ to negligence⟩ **7** : PAYABLE ⟨a bill ∼ today⟩ **8** : SCHEDULED ⟨∼ to arrive soon⟩

²**due** *n* **1** : something that rightfully belongs to one ⟨give everyone their ∼⟩ **2** : DEBT **3** *pl* : FEES, CHARGES

³**due** *adv* : DIRECTLY, EXACTLY ⟨∼ north⟩

du·el \'dü-əl, 'dyü-\ *n* : a combat between two persons; *esp* : one fought with weapons in front of witnesses — **duel** *vb* — **du·el·ist** \-ə-list\ *n*

du·en·de \dü-'en-dā\ *n* [Sp dial., charm, fr. Sp, ghost, goblin, fr. *duen de casa*, prob. fr. *dueño de casa* owner of a house] : the power to attract through personal magnetism and charm

du·en·na \dü-'e-nə, dyü-\ *n* **1** : an elderly woman in charge of the younger ladies in a Spanish or Portuguese family **2** : CHAPERONE

du·et \dü-'et, dyü-\ *n* : a musical composition for two performers

due to *prep* : BECAUSE OF

duf·fel bag \'də-fəl-\ *n* : a soft oblong bag for personal belongings

duf·fer \'də-fər\ *n* : an incompetent or clumsy person

dug *past and past part of* DIG

dug·out \'dəg-,aùt\ *n* **1** : a boat made by hollowing out a log **2** : a shelter dug in the ground **3** : a low shelter facing a baseball diamond that contains the players' bench

DUI *n* : the act or crime of driving while under the influence of alcohol

duke \'dük, 'dyük\ *n* **1** : a sovereign ruler of a continental European duchy **2** : a nobleman of the highest rank; *esp* : a member of the highest grade of the British peerage **3** *slang* : FIST 1 ⟨put up your ∼s⟩ — **duke·dom** *n*

dul·cet \'dəl-sət\ *adj* **1** : pleasing to the ear **2** : AGREEABLE, SOOTHING

dul·ci·mer \'dəl-sə-mər\ *n* **1** : a stringed instrument of trapezoidal shape played with light hammers held in the hands **2** *or* **dul·ci·more** \-,mōr\ : an American folk instrument with three or four strings that is held on the lap and played by plucking or strumming

¹**dull** \'dəl\ *adj* **1** : mentally slow : STUPID **2** : slow in perception or sensibility **3** : LISTLESS **4** : slow in action : SLUGGISH ⟨a ∼ market⟩ **5** : lacking intensity ⟨a ∼ pain⟩; *also* : not resonant or ringing **6** : BLUNT **7** : lacking brilliance or luster ⟨a ∼ finish⟩ **8** : low in saturation and lightness ⟨∼ color⟩ **9** : CLOUDY, OVERCAST ⟨∼ weather⟩ **10** : TEDIOUS, UNINTERESTING ⟨a ∼ lecture⟩ — **dull·ness** *also* **dul·ness** *n* — **dul·ly** *adv*

²**dull** *vb* : to make or become dull

dull·ard \'də-lərd\ *n* : a stupid person

du·ly \'dü-lē, 'dyü-\ *adv* : in a due manner or time

dumb \'dəm\ *adj* **1** *often offensive* : lacking the power of speech **2** : SILENT **3** : STUPID — **dumb·ly** *adv*

dumb·bell \'dəm-,bel\ *n* **1** : a bar with weights at the end used for exercise **2** : one who is stupid

dumb down *vb* : to lower the level of intelligence or intellectual content of

dumb·found *also* **dum·found** \,dəm-'faùnd\ *vb* : ASTONISH, AMAZE — **dumb·found·ing·ly** \-'faùn-diŋ-lē\ *adv*

dumb·wait·er \'dəm-,wā-tər\ *n* : a small elevator for conveying food and dishes from one floor to another

dum·my \'də-mē\ *n, pl* **dummies** **1** : a stupid person **2** *dated, offensive* : a person who cannot speak **3** : the exposed hand in bridge played by the declarer in addition to that player's own hand; *also* : a bridge player whose hand is a dummy **4** : an imitative substitute for something; *also* : MANNEQUIN **5** : one seeming to act alone but really acting for another **6** : a mock-up of matter to be reproduced esp. by printing

¹**dump** \'dəmp\ *vb* **1** : to let fall in a pile ⟨∼ laundry on the floor⟩; *also* : to get rid of carelessly ⟨∼ed her boyfriend⟩

²**dump** *n* **1** : a place for dumping something (as refuse) **2**

: a reserve supply; *also* : a place where such supplies are kept ⟨an ammunition ∼⟩ **3** : a messy or objectionable place

dump·ing \'dəm-piŋ\ *n* : the selling of goods in quantity at below market price

dump·ling \'dəm-pliŋ\ *n* **1** : a small mass of boiled or steamed dough **2** : a dessert of fruit baked in biscuit dough

dumps \'dəmps\ *n pl* : a gloomy state of mind : low spirits ⟨in the ∼⟩

dump·ster \'dəm(p)-stər\ *n, often cap* : a large trash receptacle

dump truck *n* : a truck for transporting and dumping bulk material

dumpy \'dəm-pē\ *adj* **dump·i·er; -est** **1** : short and thick in build **2** : SHABBY

¹**dun** \'dən\ *n* : a brownish dark gray

²**dun** *vb* **dunned; dun·ning** **1** : to make persistent demands for payment **2** : PLAGUE, PESTER — **dun** *n*

dunce \'dəns\ *n* [John *Duns* Scotus, whose once accepted writings were ridiculed in the 16th cent.] : a slow stupid person

dun·der·head \'dən-dər-,hed\ *n* : DUNCE, BLOCKHEAD

dune \'dün, 'dyün\ *n* : a hill or ridge of sand piled up by the wind

dune buggy *n* : a motor vehicle with oversize tires for use on sand

¹**dung** \'dəŋ\ *n* : MANURE

²**dung** *vb* : to dress (land) with dung

dun·ga·ree \,dəŋ-gə-'rē\ *n* **1** : a heavy coarse cotton twill; *esp* : blue denim **2** *pl* : clothes made of blue denim

dun·geon \'dən-jən\ *n* [ME *dongeoun* fortress, prison, fr. AF *donjun*, fr. VL *domnion-, *domnio keep, mastery, fr. L *dominus* lord] : a dark prison commonly underground

dung·hill \'dəŋ-,hil\ *n* : a manure pile

dunk \'dəŋk\ *vb* **1** : to dip or submerge temporarily in liquid **2** : to submerge oneself in water **3** : to shoot a basketball into the basket from above the rim

duo \'dü-(,)ō, 'dyü-\ *n, pl* **du·os** **1** : DUET **2** : PAIR 3

duo·dec·i·mal \,dü-ə-'de-sə-məl, ,dyü-\ *adj* : of, relating to, or being a system of numbers with a base of 12

du·o·de·num \,dü-ə-'dē-nəm, ,dyü-, dü-'ä-də-nəm, dyü-\ *n, pl* **-de·na** \-'dē-nə, -də-nə\ *or* **-denums** : the first part of the small intestine extending from the stomach to the jejunum — **du·o·de·nal** \-'dē-nᵊl, -də-nəl\ *adj*

dup *abbr* **1** duplex **2** duplicate

¹**dupe** \'düp, 'dyüp\ *n* : one who is easily deceived or cheated : FOOL

²**dupe** *vb* **duped; dup·ing** : to make a dupe of : DECEIVE, FOOL

du·ple \'dü-pəl, 'dyü-\ *adj* : having two beats or a multiple of two beats to the measure ⟨∼ time⟩

¹**du·plex** \'dü-,pleks, 'dyü-\ *adj* : DOUBLE

²**duplex** *n* : something duplex; *esp* : a 2-family house

¹**du·pli·cate** \'dü-pli-kət, 'dyü-\ *adj* **1** : consisting of or existing in two corresponding or identical parts or examples **2** : being the same as another

²**du·pli·cate** \'dü-pli-,kāt, 'dyü-\ *vb* **-cat·ed; -cat·ing** **1** : to make double or twofold **2** : to make a copy of — **du·pli·ca·tion** \,dü-pli-'kā-shən, ,dyü-\ *n*

³**du·pli·cate** \-kət\ *n* : a thing that exactly resembles another in appearance, pattern, or content : COPY

du·pli·ca·tor \'dü-pli-,kā-tər, 'dyü-\ *n* : COPIER

du·plic·i·ty \dü-'pli-sə-tē, dyü-\ *n, pl* **-ties** : the disguising of true intentions by deceptive words or action — **du·plic·i·tous** \-təs\ *adj* — **du·plic·i·tous·ly** *adv*

du·ra·ble \'dur-ə-bəl, 'dyur-\ *adj* : able to exist for a long time without significant deterioration ⟨∼ goods⟩ — **du·ra·bil·i·ty** \,dur-ə-'bi-lə-tē, ,dyur-\ *n*

du·rance \'dur-əns, 'dyur-\ *n* : restraint by or as if by physical force ⟨held in ∼ vile⟩

du·ra·tion \dù-'rā-shən, dyù-\ *n* : the time during which something exists or lasts

du·ress \dù-'res, dyù-\ *n* : compulsion by threat ⟨confession made under ∼⟩

dur·ing \'dur-iŋ, 'dyur-\ *prep* **1** : THROUGHOUT ⟨swims every day ∼ the summer⟩ **2** : at some point in ⟨broke in ∼ the night⟩

dusk \'dəsk\ *n* **1** : the darker part of twilight esp. at night **2** : partial darkness

dusky \'dəs-kē\ *adj* **dusk·i·er; -est** **1** : somewhat dark in color **2** : SHADOWY — **dusk·i·ly** \-kə-lē\ *adv* — **dusk·i·ness** *n*

¹dust \'dəst\ *n* **1** : fine particles of matter **2** : the particles into which something disintegrates **3** : something worthless **4** : the surface of the ground — **dust·less** *adj* — **dusty** *adj*

²dust *vb* **1** : to make free of or remove dust ⟨~ the furniture⟩ **2** : to sprinkle with fine particles ⟨popcorn ~ed with salt⟩ **3** : to sprinkle in the form of dust **4** : to defeat badly

dust bowl *n* : a region suffering from long droughts and dust storms

dust devil *n* : a small whirlwind containing sand or dust

dust·er \'dəs-tər\ *n* **1** : one that removes dust **2** : a dress-length housecoat **3** : one that scatters fine particles; *esp* : a device for applying insecticides to crops

dust·pan \'dəst-ˌpan\ *n* : a flat-ended pan for sweepings

dust storm *n* : a violent wind carrying dust across a dry region

dutch \'dəch\ *adv, often cap* : with each person paying his or her own way ⟨go ~⟩

Dutch \'dəch\ *n* **1 Dutch** *pl* : the people of the Netherlands **2** : the language of the Netherlands — **Dutch** *adj* — **Dutch·man** \-mən\ *n*

Dutch elm disease *n* : a fungus disease of elms characterized by yellowing of the foliage, defoliation, and death

dutch treat *n, often cap D* : an entertainment (as a meal) for which each person pays his or her own way — **dutch treat** *adv, often cap D*

du·te·ous \'dü-tē-əs, 'dyü-\ *adj* : DUTIFUL, OBEDIENT

du·ti·able \'dü-tē-ə-bəl, 'dyü-\ *adj* : subject to a duty ⟨~ imports⟩

du·ti·ful \'dü-ti-fəl, 'dyü-\ *adj* **1** : motivated by a sense of duty ⟨a ~ son⟩ **2** : coming from or showing a sense of duty ⟨~ affection⟩ — **du·ti·ful·ly** *adv* — **du·ti·ful·ness** *n*

du·ty \'dü-tē, 'dyü-\ *n, pl* **duties 1** : conduct or action required by one's occupation or position **2** : assigned service or business; *esp* : active military service **3** : a moral or legal obligation **4** : TAX **5** : the service required (as of a machine) : USE ⟨a heavy-*duty* tire⟩

DV *abbr* **1** [L *Deo volente*] God willing **2** Douay Version

DVD \ˌdē-ˌvē-'dē\ *n* [*d*igital *v*ideo *d*isk] : a high-capacity optical disk format; *also* : an optical disk using such a format

DVM *abbr* doctor of veterinary medicine

DVR \ˌdē-ˌvē-'är\ *n* [*d*igital *v*ideo *r*ecorder] : a device that records and plays back television programs

¹dwarf \'dwȯrf\ *n, pl* **dwarfs** \'dwȯrfs\ *also* **dwarves** \'dwȯrvz\ **1** : a person of unusually small stature **2** : an animal or plant that is much below normal size — **dwarf·ish** *adj* — **dwarf·ism** \'dwȯr-ˌfi-zəm\ *n*

²dwarf *vb* **1** : to restrict the growth or development of : STUNT **2** : to cause to appear smaller ⟨*dwarfed* by comparison⟩

dwarf planet *n* : a spherical celestial body that orbits the sun but is too small to disturb other objects from its orbit

dwell \'dwel\ *vb* **dwelt** \'dwelt\ *or* **dwelled** \'dweld,

'dwelt\; **dwell·ing** [ME, fr. OE *dwellan* to go astray, hinder] **1** : ABIDE, REMAIN **2** : RESIDE, EXIST **3** : to keep the attention directed **4** : to write or speak insistently — used with *on* or *upon* — **dwell·er** *n*

dwell·ing \'dwe-liŋ\ *n* : RESIDENCE

DWI \ˌdē-ˌdəb-əl-(ˌ)yü-'ī\ *n* [*d*riving *w*hile *i*ntoxicated] : DUI

dwin·dle \'dwin-dᵊl\ *vb* **dwin·dled; dwin·dling** : to make or become steadily less : DIMINISH

dwt *abbr* pennyweight

Dy *symbol* dysprosium

dyb·buk \'di-bək\ *n, pl* **dyb·bu·kim** \ˌdi-bù-'kēm\ *also* **dybbuks** : a wandering soul believed in Jewish folklore to enter and possess a person

¹dye \'dī\ *n* **1** : color produced by dyeing **2** : material used for coloring or staining

²dye *vb* **dyed; dye·ing 1** : to impart a new color to esp. by impregnating with a dye **2** : to take up or impart color in dyeing — **dy·er** \'dī(-ə)r\ *n*

dye·stuff \'dī-ˌstəf\ *n* : DYE 2

dying *pres part of* DIE

dyke *chiefly Brit var of* DIKE

dy·nam·ic \dī-'na-mik\ *also* **dy·nam·i·cal** \-mi-kəl\ *adj* : of or relating to physical force producing motion : ENERGETIC, FORCEFUL

¹dy·na·mite \'dī-nə-ˌmīt\ *n* : an explosive made of nitroglycerin absorbed in a porous material; *also* : an explosive made without nitroglycerin

²dynamite *vb* **-mit·ed; -mit·ing** : to blow up with dynamite

³dynamite *adj* : TERRIFIC, WONDERFUL

dy·na·mo \'dī-nə-ˌmō\ *n, pl* **-mos 1** : an electrical generator **2** : a forceful energetic individual

dy·na·mom·e·ter \ˌdī-nə-'mä-mə-tər\ *n* : an instrument for measuring mechanical power (as of an engine)

dy·nas·ty \'dī-nəs-tē, -ˌnas-\ *n, pl* **-ties 1** : a succession of rulers of the same family **2** : a powerful group or family that maintains its position for a long time — **dy·nas·tic** \dī-'nas-tik\ *adj*

dys·en·tery \'di-sᵊn-ˌter-ē\ *n, pl* **-ter·ies** : a disease marked by diarrhea with blood and mucus in the feces; *also* : DIARRHEA

dys·func·tion *also* **dis·func·tion** \dis-'fəŋk-shən\ *n* **1** : impaired or abnormal functioning ⟨liver ~⟩ **2** : abnormal or unhealthy behavior within a group ⟨family ~⟩ — **dys·func·tion·al** \-shə-nəl\ *adj*

dys·lex·ia \dis-'lek-sē-ə\ *n* : a learning disability marked by difficulty in reading, writing, and spelling — **dys·lex·ic** \-sik\ *adj or n*

dys·pep·sia \dis-'pep-shə, -sē-ə\ *n* : INDIGESTION — **dys·pep·tic** \-'pep-tik\ *adj or n*

dys·pla·sia \dis-'plā-zh(ē-)ə\ *n* : abnormal growth or development

dys·pro·si·um \dis-'prō-zē-əm\ *n* : a metallic chemical element that forms highly magnetic compounds

dys·tro·phy \'dis-trə-fē\ *n, pl* **-phies** : a disorder involving atrophy of muscular tissue; *esp* : MUSCULAR DYSTROPHY

dz *abbr* dozen

¹e \'ē\ *n, pl* **e's** *or* **es** \'ēz\ *often cap* **1** : the 5th letter of the English alphabet **2** : the base of the system of natural logarithms having the approximate value 2.71828 **3** : a grade rating a student's work as poor or failing

²e *abbr, often cap* **1** east; eastern **2** error **3** excellent

e- *comb form* : electronic ⟨*e*-commerce⟩

ea *abbr* each

¹each \'ēch\ *adj* : being one of the class named ⟨~ player⟩

²each *pron* : every individual one

³each *adv* : APIECE ⟨cost five cents ~⟩

each other *pron* : each of two or more in reciprocal action or relation ⟨looked at *each other*⟩

ea·ger \'ē-gər\ *adj* : marked by urgent or enthusiastic de-

sire or interest ⟨~ to learn⟩ ♦ **Synonyms** AVID, ANXIOUS, ARDENT, KEEN — **ea·ger·ly** *adv* — **ea·ger·ness** *n*

¹ea·gle \'ē-gəl\ *n* **1** : a large bird of prey related to the hawks **2** : a score of two under par on a hole in golf

²eagle *vb* **ea·gled; ea·gling** : to score an eagle in golf

ea·glet \'ē-glət\ *n* : a young eagle

-ean — see -AN

E and OE *abbr* errors and omissions excepted

¹ear \'ir\ *n* **1** : the organ of hearing; *also* : the outer part of this in a vertebrate **2** : something resembling a mammal's ear in shape, position, or function **3** : an ability to understand and appreciate something heard ⟨a good ~ for music⟩ **4** : sympathetic attention

²**ear** *n* : the fruiting spike of a cereal (as wheat or corn)
ear·ache \-ˌāk\ *n* : an ache or pain in the ear
ear·drum \-ˌdrəm\ *n* : a thin membrane that receives and transmits sound waves in the ear
eared \ˈird\ *adj* : having ears esp. of a specified kind or number ⟨a long-*eared* dog⟩
ear·ful \ˈir-ˌfu̇l\ *n* : a verbal outpouring (as of news, gossip, or complaint)
earl \ˈərl\ *n* [ME *erl*, fr. OE *eorl* warrior, nobleman] : a member of the British peerage ranking below a marquess and above a viscount — **earl·dom** \-dəm\ *n*
ear·lobe \ˈir-ˌlōb\ *n* : the pendent part of the ear
¹**ear·ly** \ˈər-lē\ *adv* **ear·li·er; -est** : at an early time (as in a period or series)
²**early** *adj* **ear·li·er; -est** **1** : of, relating to, or occurring near the beginning **2** : ANCIENT, PRIMITIVE ⟨~ tools⟩ **3** : occurring before the usual time ⟨an ~ breakfast⟩; *also* : occurring in the near future
¹**ear·mark** \ˈir-ˌmärk\ *n* : an identification mark (as on the ear of an animal); *also* : a distinguishing mark ⟨~s of poverty⟩
²**earmark** *vb* **1** : to mark with an earmark **2** : to designate for a specific purpose ⟨money ~*ed* for education⟩
ear·muff \-ˌməf\ *n* : one of a pair of ear coverings worn to protect against cold
earn \ˈərn\ *vb* **1** : to receive as a return for service **2** : DESERVE, MERIT ♦ **Synonyms** GAIN, SECURE, GET, OBTAIN, ACQUIRE, WIN — **earn·er** *n*
earned run *n* : a run in baseball that scores without benefit of an error before the fielding team has had a chance to make the third putout of the inning
earned run average *n* : the average number of earned runs per game scored against a pitcher in baseball
¹**ear·nest** \ˈər-nəst\ *n* : an intensely serious state of mind ⟨spoke in ~⟩
²**earnest** *adj* **1** : seriously intent and sober ⟨an ~ face⟩ ⟨an ~ attempt⟩ **2** : GRAVE, IMPORTANT ♦ **Synonyms** SOLEMN, SEDATE, STAID — **ear·nest·ly** *adv* — **ear·nest·ness** *n*
³**earnest** *n* **1** : something of value given by a buyer to a seller to bind a bargain **2** : PLEDGE
earn·ings \ˈər-niŋz\ *n pl* **1** : something (as wages) earned **2** : the balance of revenue after deduction of costs and expenses
ear·phone \ˈir-ˌfōn\ *n* : a device that reproduces sound and is worn over or in the ear
ear·piece \-ˌpēs\ *n* : a part of an instrument which is placed against or in the ear; *esp* : EARPHONE
ear·plug \-ˌpləg\ *n* : a protective device for insertion into the opening of the ear
ear·ring \-ˌriŋ\ *n* : an ornament for the earlobe
ear·shot \-ˌshät\ *n* : range of hearing
ear·split·ting \-ˌspli-tiŋ\ *adj* : intolerably loud or shrill
earth \ˈərth\ *n* **1** : SOIL, DIRT **2** : LAND, GROUND **3** *often cap* : the planet on which we live that is 3d in order from the sun
earth·en \ˈər-thən\ *adj* : made of earth or baked clay
earth·en·ware \-ˌwer\ *n* : slightly porous opaque pottery fired at low heat
earth·ling \ˈərth-liŋ\ *n* : an inhabitant of the earth
earth·ly \ˈərth-lē\ *adj* : having to do with the earth esp. as distinguished from heaven — **earth·li·ness** *n*
earth·quake \-ˌkwāk\ *n* : a shaking or trembling of a portion of the earth
earth science *n* : any of the sciences (as geology or meteorology) that deal with the earth or one of its parts
earth·shak·ing \ˈərth-ˌshā-kiŋ\ *adj* : of great importance : MOMENTOUS
earth·ward \-wərd\ *also* **earth·wards** \-wərdz\ *adv* : toward the earth
earth·work \ˈərth-ˌwərk\ *n* : an embankment or fortification of earth
earth·worm \-ˌwərm\ *n* : a long segmented worm found in damp soil
earthy \ˈər-thē\ *adj* **earth·i·er; -est** **1** : of, relating to, or consisting of earth; *also* : suggesting earth ⟨~ flavors⟩ **2** : PRACTICAL **4 3** : COARSE, GROSS ⟨~ humor⟩ — **earth·i·ness** *n*
ear·wax \ˈir-ˌwaks\ *n* : the yellow waxy secretion from the ear
ear·wig \-ˌwig\ *n* : any of numerous insects with slender

antennae and a pair of appendages resembling forceps at the end of the body
¹**ease** \ˈēz\ *n* **1** : comfort of body or mind **2** : naturalness of manner **3** : freedom from difficulty or effort ♦ **Synonyms** RELAXATION, REST, REPOSE, LEISURE
²**ease** *vb* **eased; eas·ing** **1** : to relieve from distress **2** : to lessen the pressure or tension of **3** : to make or become less difficult ⟨~ credit⟩
ea·sel \ˈē-zəl\ *n* [Dutch *ezel*, lit., ass] : a frame for supporting something (as an artist's canvas)
¹**east** \ˈēst\ *adv* : to or toward the east
²**east** *adj* **1** : situated toward or at the east ⟨an ~ window⟩ **2** : coming from the east ⟨an ~ wind⟩
³**east** *n* **1** : the general direction of sunrise **2** : the compass point directly opposite to west **3** *cap* : regions or countries east of a specified or implied point — **east·er·ly** \ˈē-stər-lē\ *adv* or *adj* — **east·ward** *adv* or *adj* — **east·wards** *adv*
Eas·ter \ˈē-stər\ *n* : a church feast observed on a Sunday in March or April in commemoration of Christ's resurrection
east·ern \ˈē-stərn\ *adj* **1** *often cap* : of, relating to, or characteristic of a region designated East **2** *cap* : of, relating to, or being the Christian churches originating in the Church of the Eastern Roman Empire **3** : lying toward or coming from the east — **East·ern·er** *n*
easy \ˈē-zē\ *adj* **eas·i·er; -est** **1** : marked by ease ⟨an ~ life⟩; *esp* : not causing distress or difficulty ⟨~ tasks⟩ **2** : MILD, LENIENT ⟨be ~ on him⟩ **3** : GRADUAL ⟨an ~ slope⟩ **4** : LEISURELY ⟨an ~ pace⟩ **5** : free from pain, trouble, or worry **6** : COMFORTABLE ⟨an ~ chair⟩ **7** : showing ease : NATURAL ⟨an ~ manner⟩ — **eas·i·ly** \ˈē-zə-lē\ *adv* — **eas·i·ness** \-zē-nəs\ *n*
easy·go·ing \ˌē-zē-ˈgō-iŋ\ *adj* : relaxed and casual in style or manner
eat \ˈēt\ *vb* **ate** \ˈāt\; **eat·en** \ˈēt-ᵊn\; **eat·ing** **1** : to take in as food : take food **2** : to use up : DEVOUR **3** : CORRODE — **eat·able** *adj or n* — **eat·er** *n*
eat·ery \ˈē-tə-rē\ *n, pl* **-er·ies** : LUNCHEONETTE, RESTAURANT
eaves \ˈēvz\ *n pl* : the overhanging lower edge of a roof
eaves·drop \ˈēvz-ˌdräp\ *vb* : to listen secretly — **eaves·drop·per** *n*
¹**ebb** \ˈeb\ *n* **1** : the flowing back from shore of water brought in by the tide **2** : a point or state of decline
²**ebb** *vb* **1** : to recede from the flood **2** : DECLINE ⟨his fortunes ~*ed*⟩
EBCDIC \ˈeb-sə-ˌdik\ *n* [extended binary coded decimal interchange code] : a computer code for representing alphanumeric information
Ebo·la \ē-ˈbō-lə\ *n* : an often fatal hemorrhagic fever caused by a virus (**Ebola virus**) of African origin
¹**eb·o·ny** \ˈe-bə-nē\ *n, pl* **-nies** : a hard heavy blackish wood of various tropical trees related to the persimmon
²**ebony** *adj* **1** : made of or resembling ebony **2** : BLACK, DARK
e-book \ˈē-ˌbu̇k\ *n* : a book in digital form for display on a computer screen or a handheld device
ebul·lient \i-ˈbu̇l-yənt, -ˈbəl-\ *adj* **1** : BOILING, AGITATED **2** : EXUBERANT — **ebul·lience** \-yəns\ *n*
EC *abbr* European Community
ec·cen·tric \ik-ˈsen-trik\ *adj* **1** : deviating from a usual or accepted pattern **2** : deviating from a circular path ⟨~ orbits⟩ **3** : set with axis or support off center ⟨an ~ cam⟩; *also* : being off center ♦ **Synonyms** ERRATIC, QUEER, SINGULAR, CURIOUS, ODD — **eccentric** *n* — **ec·cen·tri·cal·ly** \-tri-k(ə-)lē\ *adv* — **ec·cen·tric·i·ty** \ˌek-ˌsen-ˈtri-sə-tē\ *n*
Eccles *abbr* Ecclesiastes
Ec·cle·si·as·tes \i-ˌklē-zē-ˈas-tēz\ *n* — see BIBLE table
ec·cle·si·as·tic \i-ˌklē-zē-ˈas-tik\ *n* : CLERGYMAN
ec·cle·si·as·ti·cal \-ti-kəl\ *or* **ec·cle·si·as·tic** \-tik\ *adj* : of or relating to a church esp. as an institution ⟨~ art⟩ — **ec·cle·si·as·ti·cal·ly** \-ti-k(ə-)lē\ *adv*
Ec·cle·si·as·ti·cus \i-ˌklē-zē-ˈas-ti-kəs\ *n* — see BIBLE table
Ecclus *abbr* Ecclesiasticus
ECG *abbr* electrocardiogram
ech·e·lon \ˈe-shə-ˌlän\ *n* [F *échelon*, lit., rung of a ladder] **1** : a steplike arrangement (as of troops or airplanes) **2** : a level (as of authority or responsibility) within an organization

ech·i·na·cea \ˌe-ki-ˈnā-sē-ə, -shə\ *n* : the dried root of three composite herbs that is used primarily in herbal remedies to boost the immune system; *also* : any of these herbs

echi·no·derm \i-ˈkī-nə-ˌdərm\ *n* : any of a phylum of marine animals (as starfishes and sea urchins) having similar body parts (as the arms of a starfish) arranged around a central axis and often having a calcium-containing outer skeleton

echo \ˈe-kō\ *n, pl* **ech·oes** *also* **ech·os** : repetition of a sound caused by a reflection of the sound waves; *also* : the reflection of a radar signal by an object — **echo** *vb* — **echo·ic** \e-ˈkō-ik\ *adj*

echo·lo·ca·tion \ˌe-kō-lō-ˈkā-shən\ *n* : a process for locating distant or invisible objects by sound waves reflected back to the sender (as a bat) from the objects

echt \ˈekt\ *adj* [G] : TRUE, GENUINE ⟨an ∼ New Yorker⟩

éclair \ā-ˈkler\ *n* [F, lit., lightning] : an oblong shell of light pastry with whipped cream or custard filling

éclat \ā-ˈklä\ *n* [F] **1** : a dazzling effect or success **2** : ACCLAIM

eclec·tic \e-ˈklek-tik\ *adj* : selecting or made up of what seems best of varied sources — **eclectic** *n* — **eclec·ti·cism** \-ˈklek-tə-ˌsi-zəm\ *n*

¹eclipse \i-ˈklips\ *n* **1** : the total or partial obscuring of one heavenly body by another; *also* : a passing into the shadow of a heavenly body **2** : a falling into obscurity or decline ⟨a career in ∼⟩

²eclipse *vb* **eclipsed; eclips·ing** : to cause an eclipse of; *also* : SURPASS

eclip·tic \i-ˈklip-tik\ *n* : the great circle of the celestial sphere that is the apparent path of the sun

ec·logue \ˈek-ˌlog, -ˌläg\ *n* : a pastoral poem

ECM *abbr* European Common Market

ecol *abbr* ecological; ecology

E. coli \ˌē-ˈkō-ˌlī\ *n, pl* **E. coli** : a rod-shaped bacterium that sometimes causes intestinal illness

ecol·o·gy \i-ˈkä-lə-jē, e-\ *n, pl* **-gies** [G *Ökologie*, fr. Gk *oikos* house + *logos* word] **1** : a branch of science concerned with the relationships between organisms and their environment **2** : the pattern of relations between one or more organisms and the environment — **eco·log·i·cal** \ˌē-kə-ˈlä-ji-kəl, ˌe-\ *also* **eco·log·ic** \-jik\ *adj* — **eco·log·i·cal·ly** \-ji-k(ə-)lē\ *adv* — **ecol·o·gist** \i-ˈkä-lə-jist, e-\ *n*

e–com·merce \ˈē-ˌkä-(ˌ)mərs\ *n* : commerce conducted via the Internet

econ *abbr* economics; economist; economy

eco·nom·ic \ˌe-kə-ˈnä-mik, ˌē-\ *adj* : of or relating to the production, distribution, and consumption of goods and services

eco·nom·i·cal \-ˈnä-mi-kəl\ *adj* **1** : THRIFTY **2** : operating with little waste or at a saving ✦ *Synonyms* FRUGAL, SPARING, PROVIDENT — **ec·o·nom·i·cal·ly** \-k(ə-)lē\ *adv*

eco·nom·ics \ˌe-kə-ˈnä-miks, ˌē-\ *n sing or pl* : a social science dealing with the production, distribution, and consumption of goods and services — **econ·o·mist** \i-ˈkä-nə-mist\ *n*

econ·o·mise *Brit var of* ECONOMIZE

econ·o·mize \i-ˈkä-nə-ˌmīz\ *vb* **-mized; -miz·ing** : to practice economy : be frugal — **econ·o·miz·er** *n*

¹econ·o·my \i-ˈkä-nə-mē\ *n, pl* **-mies** [MF *yconomie*, fr. ML *oeconomia*, fr. Gk *oikonomia*, fr. *oikonomos* household manager, fr. *oikos* house + *nemein* to manage] **1** : thrifty and efficient use of resources; *also* : an instance of this **2** : manner of arrangement or functioning : ORGANIZATION **3** : an economic system ⟨a money ∼⟩

²economy *adj* : ECONOMICAL ⟨∼ cars⟩

eco·sys·tem \ˈē-kō-ˌsis-təm, ˈe-\ *n* : the complex of an ecological community and its environment functioning as a unit in nature

eco·tour·ism \ˌē-kō-ˈtùr-ˌi-zəm, ˌe-\ *n* : the touring of natural habitats in a manner meant to minimize ecological impact — **eco·tour·ist** \-ˈtùr-ist\ *n*

ecru \ˈe-krü, ˈā-\ *n* [F *écru*, lit., unbleached] : BEIGE — **ecru** *adj*

ec·sta·sy \ˈek-stə-sē\ *n, pl* **-sies** **1** : extreme and usu. rapturous emotional excitement **2** *often cap* : an illicit drug with hallucinogenic properties that is chemically related to amphetamine — **ec·stat·ic** \ek-ˈsta-tik, ik-\ *adj* — **ec·stat·i·cal·ly** \-ti-k(ə-)lē\ *adv*

Ecua *abbr* Ecuador

ec·u·men·i·cal \ˌe-kyù-ˈme-ni-kəl\ *adj* **1** : general in extent or influence **2** : promoting or tending toward worldwide Christian unity — **ec·u·men·i·cal·ly** \-k(ə-)lē\ *adv*

ec·ze·ma \ig-ˈzē-mə, ˈeg-zə-mə, ˈek-sə-\ *n* : an itching skin inflammation with oozing and then crusted lesions — **ec·zem·a·tous** \ig-ˈze-mə-təs\ *adj*

ed *abbr* **1** edited; edition; editor **2** education

¹-ed \d *after a vowel or* b, g, j, l, m, n, ŋ, r, th, v, z, zh; əd, id *after* d, t; t *after other sounds*\ *vb suffix or adj suffix* **1** — used to form the past participle of regular weak verbs ⟨ended⟩ ⟨faded⟩ ⟨tried⟩ ⟨patted⟩ **2** : having : characterized by ⟨cultured⟩ ⟨2-legged⟩; *also* : having the characteristics of ⟨bigoted⟩

²-ed *vb suffix* — used to form the past tense of regular weak verbs ⟨judged⟩ ⟨denied⟩ ⟨dropped⟩

Edam \ˈē-dəm, -ˌdam\ *n* : a yellow Dutch pressed cheese made in balls

ed·a·ma·me \ˌe-də-ˈmä-mā\ *n* [Jp, fr. *eda* branch + *mame* beans] : immature green soybeans usu. in the pod

ed·dy \ˈe-dē\ *n, pl* **eddies** : WHIRLPOOL — **eddy** *vb*

edel·weiss \ˈā-dᵊl-ˌwīs, -ˌvīs\ *n* [G, fr. *edel* noble + *weiss* white] : a small perennial woolly composite herb that grows high in the Alps

ede·ma \i-ˈdē-mə\ *n* : abnormal accumulation of watery fluid in connective tissue or in a serous cavity — **edem·a·tous** \-ˈde-mə-təs\ *adj*

Eden \ˈē-dᵊn\ *n* : PARADISE 2

¹edge \ˈej\ *n* **1** : the cutting side of a blade **2** : SHARPNESS; *also* : FORCE, EFFECTIVENESS **3** : the line where something begins or ends; *also* : the area adjoining such an edge **4** : ADVANTAGE ⟨has an ∼ on the competition⟩ — **edged** \ˈejd\ *adj*

²edge *vb* **edged; edg·ing** **1** : to give or form an edge **2** : to move or force gradually ⟨∼ into a crowd⟩ **3** : to defeat by a small margin ⟨edged out her opponent⟩ — **edg·er** *n*

edge·wise \ˈej-ˌwīz\ *adv* : SIDEWAYS

edg·ing \ˈe-jiŋ\ *n* : something that forms an edge or border ⟨a lace ∼⟩

edgy \ˈe-jē\ *adj* **edg·i·er; -est** **1** : SHARP ⟨an ∼ tone⟩ **2** : TENSE, NERVOUS **3** : having a bold, provocative, or unconventional quality — **edg·i·ness** *n*

ed·i·ble \ˈe-də-bəl\ *adj* : fit or safe to be eaten — **ed·i·bil·i·ty** \ˌe-də-ˈbi-lə-tē\ *n* — **edible** *n*

edict \ˈē-ˌdikt\ *n* : ORDER, DECREE

ed·i·fi·ca·tion \ˌe-də-fə-ˈkā-shən\ *n* : instruction and improvement esp. in morality — **ed·i·fy** \ˈe-də-ˌfī\ *vb*

ed·i·fice \ˈe-də-fəs\ *n* : a usu. large building

ed·it \ˈe-dət\ *vb* **1** : to revise, assemble, or prepare for publication or release (as a motion picture) **2** : to direct the publication and policies of (as a newspaper) **3** : DELETE — **ed·i·tor** \ˈe-də-tər\ *n* — **ed·i·tor·ship** *n* — **edi·tress** \-trəs\ *n*

edi·tion \i-ˈdi-shən\ *n* **1** : the form in which a text is published **2** : the total number of copies (as of a book) published at one time **3** : VERSION

¹ed·i·to·ri·al \ˌe-də-ˈtòr-ē-əl\ *adj* **1** : of or relating to an editor or editing **2** : being or resembling an editorial — **ed·i·to·ri·al·ly** *adv*

²editorial *n* : an article (as in a newspaper) giving the views of the editors or publishers; *also* : an expression of opinion resembling an editorial ⟨a television ∼⟩

ed·i·to·ri·al·ize \ˌe-də-ˈtòr-ē-ə-ˌlīz\ *vb* **-ized; -iz·ing** **1** : to express an opinion in an editorial **2** : to introduce opinions into factual reporting **3** : to express an opinion — **ed·i·to·ri·al·i·za·tion** \-ˌtòr-ē-ə-lə-ˈzā-shən\ *n* — **ed·i·to·ri·al·iz·er** *n*

EDP *abbr* electronic data processing

EDT *abbr* Eastern daylight (saving) time

educ *abbr* education; educational

ed·u·ca·ble \ˈe-jə-kə-bəl\ *adj* : capable of being educated

ed·u·cate \ˈe-jə-ˌkāt\ *vb* **-cat·ed; -cat·ing** [ME, to rear, fr. L *educatus*, pp. of *educare*, fr. *educere* to lead forth, draw out] **1** : to provide with schooling **2** : to develop mentally and morally; *also* : to provide with information ✦ *Synonyms* TRAIN, DISCIPLINE, SCHOOL, INSTRUCT, TEACH — **ed·u·ca·tor** \-ˌkā-tər\ *n*

ed·u·ca·tion \ˌe-jə-ˈkā-shən\ *n* **1** : the action or process of educating or being educated **2** : a field of study dealing with methods of teaching and learning — **ed·u·ca·tion·al** \-shə-nəl\ *adj* — **ed·u·ca·tion·al·ly** *adv*

educational television *n* **1** : television that provides educational programming (as for students) **2** : television (as public television) that receives support from contributions rather than from commercials

educe \i-'düs, -'dyüs\ *vb* **educed; educ·ing 1** : ELICIT, EVOKE **2** : DEDUCE ✦ *Synonyms* EXTRACT, EVINCE, EXTORT

ed·u·tain·ment \ͺe-jə-'tān-mənt\ *n* : entertainment that is designed to be educational

¹-ee \'ē, ͺͺ)ē\ *n suffix* **1** : one that receives or benefits from (a specified action or thing) ⟨grant*ee*⟩ ⟨patent*ee*⟩ **2** : a person who does (a specified action) ⟨escap*ee*⟩

²-ee *n suffix* **1** : a particular esp. small kind of ⟨boot*ee*⟩ **2** : one resembling or suggestive of ⟨goat*ee*⟩

EE *abbr* electrical engineer

EEC *abbr* European Economic Community

EEG *abbr* **1** electroencephalogram **2** electroencephalograph

eel \'ēl\ *n* : any of numerous snakelike bony fishes with a smooth slimy skin

EEO *abbr* equal employment opportunity

ee·rie *also* **ee·ry** \'ir-ē\ *adj* **ee·ri·er; -est** : WEIRD, UNCANNY — **ee·ri·ly** \'ir-ə-lē\ *adv*

eff *abbr* efficiency

ef·face \i-'fās, e-\ *vb* **ef·faced; ef·fac·ing** : to obliterate or obscure by or as if by rubbing out ✦ *Synonyms* ERASE, DELETE, ANNUL, CANCEL, EXPUNGE — **ef·face·able** *adj* — **ef·face·ment** *n*

¹ef·fect \i-'fekt\ *n* **1** : MEANING, INTENT **2** : RESULT **3** : APPEARANCE **4** : INFLUENCE **5** *pl* : GOODS, POSSESSIONS **6** : the quality or state of being operative : OPERATION ✦ *Synonyms* CONSEQUENCE, OUTCOME, UPSHOT, AFTERMATH, ISSUE

²effect *vb* : to cause to happen ⟨~ repairs⟩ ⟨~ changes⟩

ef·fec·tive \i-'fek-tiv\ *adj* **1** : producing a decisive or desired effect **2** : IMPRESSIVE, STRIKING **3** : ready for service or action ⟨~ manpower⟩ **4** : being in effect — **ef·fec·tive·ly** *adv* — **ef·fec·tive·ness** *n*

ef·fec·tu·al \i-'fek-chə-wəl\ *adj* : producing an intended effect : ADEQUATE — **ef·fec·tu·al·ly** *adv*

ef·fec·tu·ate \i-'fek-chə-ͺwāt\ *vb* **-at·ed; -at·ing** : BRING ABOUT, EFFECT

ef·fem·i·nate \ə-'fe-mə-nət\ *adj* : marked by qualities more typical of women than men — **ef·fem·i·na·cy** \-nə-sē\ *n*

ef·fen·di \e-'fen-dē\ *n* [Turk *efendi* master, fr. ModGk *authentēs*] : a man of property, authority, or education in an eastern Mediterranean country

ef·fer·ent \'e-fə-rənt\ *adj* : bearing or conducting outward from a more central part ⟨~ nerves⟩

ef·fer·vesce \ͺe-fər-'ves\ *vb* **-vesced; -vesc·ing 1** : to bubble and hiss as gas escapes **2** : to show liveliness or exhilaration — **ef·fer·ves·cence** \-'ve-sᵊns\ *n* — **ef·fer·ves·cent** \-sᵊnt\ *adj* — **ef·fer·ves·cent·ly** *adv*

ef·fete \e-'fēt\ *adj* **1** : having lost character, vitality, or strength; *also* : DECADENT **2** : EFFEMINATE

ef·fi·ca·cious \ͺe-fə-'kā-shəs\ *adj* : producing an intended effect ⟨~ remedies⟩ ✦ *Synonyms* EFFECTUAL, EFFECTIVE, EFFICIENT — **ef·fi·ca·cy** \'e-fi-kə-sē\ *n*

ef·fi·cient \i-'fi-shənt\ *adj* : productive of desired effects esp. without waste — **ef·fi·cien·cy** \-shən-sē\ *n* — **ef·fi·cient·ly** *adv*

ef·fi·gy \'e-fə-jē\ *n, pl* **-gies** : IMAGE; *esp* : a crude figure of a hated person

ef·flo·res·cence \ͺe-flə-'re-sᵊns\ *n* **1** : the period or state of flowering **2** : the action or process of developing **3** : fullness of development : FLOWERING

ef·flu·ence \'e-ͺflü-əns\ *n* : something that flows out

ef·flu·ent \'e-ͺflü-ənt\ *n* : something that flows out; *esp* : a fluid (as sewage) discharged as waste — **effluent** *adj*

ef·flu·vi·um \e-'flü-vē-əm\ *n, pl* **-via** \-vē-ə\ *also* **-vi·ums** [L, outflow] **1** : a usu. unpleasant emanation **2** : a byproduct usu. in the form of waste

ef·fort \'e-fərt\ *n* **1** : EXERTION, ENDEAVOR; *also* : a product of effort **2** : active or applied force — **ef·fort·less** *adj* — **ef·fort·less·ly** *adv*

ef·fron·tery \i-'frən-tə-rē\ *n, pl* **-ter·ies** : shameless boldness : IMPUDENCE ✦ *Synonyms* TEMERITY, AUDACITY, BRASS, GALL, NERVE, CHUTZPAH

ef·ful·gence \i-'fül-jəns, -'fəl-\ *n* : radiant splendor : BRILLIANCE ⟨the ~ of its golden age⟩ — **ef·ful·gent** \-jənt\ *adj*

ef·fu·sion \i-'fyü-zhən, e-\ *n* : a gushing forth; *also* : unrestrained utterance — **ef·fuse** \-'fyüz, e-\ *vb* — **ef·fu·sive** \i-'fyü-siv, e-\ *adj* — **ef·fu·sive·ly** *adv*

eft \'eft\ *n* : NEWT

EFT *or* **EFTS** *abbr* electronic funds transfer (system)

e.g. *abbr* [L *exempli gratia*] for example

Eg *abbr* Egypt; Egyptian

egal·i·tar·i·an·ism \i-ͺga-lə-'ter-ē-ə-ͺni-zəm\ *n* : a belief in human equality esp. in social, political, and economic affairs — **egal·i·tar·i·an** *adj or n*

¹egg \'eg\ *vb* [ME, fr. ON *eggia;* akin to OE *ecg* edge] : to urge to action — usu. used with *on*

²egg *n* [ME *egge*, fr. ON *egg;* akin to OE *ǣg* egg, L *ovum*] **1** : a rounded usu. hard-shelled reproductive body esp. of birds and reptiles from which the young hatches; *also* : the egg of the common domestic chicken as an article of food **2** : a germ cell produced by a female

egg·beat·er \'eg-ͺbē-tər\ *n* : a hand-operated kitchen utensil for beating, stirring, or whipping

egg cell *n* : EGG 2

egg foo yong *or* **egg foo young** *or* **egg foo yung** \-'fü-'yəŋ\ : a fried egg patty

egg·head \-ͺhed\ *n, often disparaging* : INTELLECTUAL, HIGHBROW

egg·nog \-ͺnäg\ *n* : a drink consisting of eggs beaten with sugar, milk or cream, and often alcoholic liquor

egg·plant \-ͺplant\ *n* : the edible usu. large and dark purplish fruit of a plant related to the potato; *also* : the plant

egg roll *n* : a thin egg-dough casing filled with minced vegetables and often bits of meat and usu. deep-fried

egg·shell \'eg-ͺshel\ *n* : the hard exterior covering of an egg

egis *var of* AEGIS

eg·lan·tine \'e-glən-ͺtīn, -ͺtēn\ *n* : SWEETBRIAR

ego \'ē-gō\ *n, pl* **egos** [L, I] **1** : the self as distinguished from others **2** : the one of the three divisions of the psyche in psychoanalytic theory that is the organized conscious mediator between the person and reality

ego·cen·tric \ͺē-gō-'sen-trik\ *adj* : concerned or overly concerned with the self; *esp* : SELF-CENTERED

ego·ism \'ē-gō-ͺi-zəm\ *n* **1** : a doctrine holding self-interest to be the motive or the valid end of action **2** : excessive concern for oneself with or without exaggerated feelings of self-importance — **ego·ist** \-ist\ *n* — **ego·is·tic** \ͺē-gō-'is-tik\ *adj* — **ego·is·ti·cal·ly** *adv*

ego·tism \'ē-gə-ͺti-zəm\ *n* **1** : the practice of talking about oneself too much **2** : an exaggerated sense of self-importance : CONCEIT — **ego·tist** \-tist\ *n* — **ego·tis·tic** \ͺē-gə-'tis-tik\ *or* **ego·tis·ti·cal** \-ti-kəl\ *adj* — **ego·tis·ti·cal·ly** *adv*

ego trip *n* : an act that enhances and satisfies one's ego

egre·gious \i-'grē-jəs\ *adj* [L *egregius* outstanding, fr. *ex, e* out of + *greg-, grex* flock, herd] : notably bad : FLAGRANT ⟨~ errors⟩ — **egre·gious·ly** *adv* — **egre·gious·ness** *n*

egress \'ē-ͺgres\ *n* : a way out : EXIT

egret \'ē-grət, i-'gret\ *n* : any of various herons that bear long plumes during the breeding season

egret

Egyp·tian \i-'jip-shən\ *n* **1** : a native or inhabitant of Egypt **2** : the language of the ancient Egyptians from earliest times to about the 3d century A.D. — **Egyptian** *adj*

ei·der \'ī-dər\ *n* : any of several northern sea ducks that yield a soft down

ei·der·down \-ˌdau̇n\ *n* **1** : the down of the eider **2** : a comforter filled with eiderdown

ei·do·lon \ī-ˈdō-lən\ *n, pl* **-lons** *or* **-la** \-lə\ **1** : PHANTOM **2** : IDEAL

eight \ˈāt\ *n* **1** : one more than seven **2** : the 8th in a set or series **3** : something having eight units — **eight** *adj or pron* — **eighth** \ˈātth\ *adj or adv or n*

eight ball *n* : a black pool ball numbered 8 — **behind the eight ball** : in a highly disadvantageous position

eigh·teen \ˈāt-ˈtēn\ *n* : one more than 17 — **eighteen** *adj or pron* — **eigh·teenth** \-ˈtēnth\ *adj or n*

eighty \ˈā-tē\ *n, pl* **eight·ies** : eight times 10 — **eight·i·eth** \ˈā-tē-əth\ *adj or n* — **eighty** *adj or pron*

ein·stei·ni·um \īn-ˈstī-nē-əm\ *n* : an artificially produced radioactive element

ei·re·nic *chiefly Brit var of* IRENIC

¹ei·ther \ˈē-thər, ˈī-\ *adj* **1** : being the one and the other of two : EACH ⟨trees on ~ side⟩ **2** : being the one or the other of two ⟨take ~ road⟩

²either *pron* : the one or the other

³either *conj* — used as a function word before the first of two or more words or word groups of which the last is preceded by *or* to indicate that they represent alternatives ⟨a statement is ~ true or false⟩

ejac·u·late \i-ˈja-kyə-ˌlāt\ *vb* **-lat·ed; -lat·ing** **1** : to eject a fluid (as semen) **2** : to utter suddenly : EXCLAIM — **ejac·u·la·tion** \-ˌja-kyə-ˈlā-shən\ *n* — **ejac·u·la·to·ry** \-ˈja-kyə-lə-ˌtȯr-ē\ *adj*

eject \i-ˈjekt\ *vb* : to drive or throw out or off ♦ *Synonyms* EXPEL, OUST, EVICT, DISMISS — **ejec·tion** \-ˈjek-shən\ *n*

eke \ˈēk\ *vb* **eked; ek·ing** : to gain, supplement, or extend usu. with effort — usu. used with *out* ⟨~ out a living⟩

EKG *abbr* [G *Elektrokardiogramm*] electrocardiogram; electrocardiograph

el *abbr* elevation

¹elab·o·rate \i-ˈla-bə-rət, -ˈla-brət\ *adj* **1** : planned or carried out with great care **2** : being complex and usu. ornate — **elab·o·rate·ly** *adv* — **elab·o·rate·ness** *n*

²elab·o·rate \i-ˈla-bə-ˌrāt\ *vb* **-rat·ed; -rat·ing** **1** : to build up from simpler ingredients **2** : to work out in detail : develop fully — **elab·o·ra·tion** \-ˌla-bə-ˈrā-shən\ *n*

élan \ā-ˈlä⁽ⁿ⁾\ *n* [F] : ARDOR, SPIRIT

eland \ˈē-lənd, -ˌland\ *n, pl* **eland** *also* **elands** [Afrikaans] : either of two large African antelopes with spirally twisted horns in both sexes

elapse \i-ˈlaps\ *vb* **elapsed; elaps·ing** : to slip by : PASS

¹elas·tic \i-ˈlas-tik\ *adj* **1** : SPRINGY **2** : FLEXIBLE, PLIABLE ⟨an ~ bandage⟩ **3** : ADAPTABLE ⟨an ~ plan⟩ ♦ *Synonyms* RESILIENT, SUPPLE, STRETCH — **elas·tic·i·ty** \-ˌlas-ˈti-sə-tē, ˌē-ˌlas-\ *n*

²elastic *n* **1** : elastic material **2** : a rubber band

elate \i-ˈlāt\ *vb* **elat·ed; elat·ing** : to fill with joy — **ela·tion** \-ˈlā-shən\ *n*

¹el·bow \ˈel-ˌbō\ *n* [ME *elbowe*, fr. OE *elboga*, fr. *el-* (akin to *eln* ell) + *boga* bow] **1** : the joint of the arm; *also* : the outer curve of the bent arm **2** : a bend or joint resembling an elbow in shape

²elbow *vb* : to push aside with the elbow; *also* : to make one's way by elbowing

el·bow room \ˈel-ˌbō-ˌrüm, -ˌru̇m\ *n* : enough space for work or operation

¹el·der \ˈel-dər\ *n* : ELDERBERRY 2

²elder *adj* **1** : OLDER **2** : EARLIER, FORMER **3** : of higher rank : SENIOR

³elder *n* **1** : an older individual : SENIOR **2** : one having authority by reason of age and experience **3** : a church officer

el·der·ber·ry \ˈel-dər-ˌber-ē\ *n* **1** : the edible black or red fruit of a shrub or tree related to the honeysuckle and bearing flat clusters of small white or pink flowers **2** : a tree or shrub bearing elderberries

el·der·ly \ˈel-dər-lē\ *adj* **1** : rather old; *esp* : past middle age **2** : of, relating to, or characteristic of later life

el·dest \ˈel-dəst\ *adj* : of the greatest age

El Do·ra·do \ˌel-də-ˈrä-dō, -ˈrā-\ *n* [Sp, lit., the gilded one] : a place of vast riches, abundance, or opportunity

elec *abbr* electric; electrical; electricity

¹elect \i-ˈlekt\ *adj* **1** : CHOSEN, SELECT **2** : elected but not yet installed in office ⟨the president-*elect*⟩

²elect *n, pl* **elect** **1** : a selected person **2** *pl* : a select or exclusive group

³elect *vb* **1** : to select by vote (as for office or membership) **2** : CHOOSE, PICK

elec·tion \i-ˈlek-shən\ *n* **1** : an act or process of electing **2** : the fact of being elected

elec·tion·eer \i-ˌlek-shə-ˈnir\ *vb* : to work for the election of a candidate or party

¹elec·tive \i-ˈlek-tiv\ *adj* **1** : chosen or filled by election **2** : permitting a choice : OPTIONAL

²elective *n* : an elective course or subject of study

elec·tor \i-ˈlek-tər\ *n* **1** : one qualified to vote in an election **2** : one elected to an electoral college — **elec·tor·al** \i-ˈlek-tə-rəl\ *adj*

electoral college *n* : a body of electors who elect the president and vice president of the U.S.

elec·tor·ate \i-ˈlek-tə-rət\ *n* : a body of persons entitled to vote

elec·tric \i-ˈlek-trik\ *adj* [NL *electricus* produced from amber by friction, electric, fr. ML, of amber, fr. L *electrum* amber, fr. Gk *ēlektron*] **1** *or* **elec·tri·cal** \-tri-kəl\ : of, relating to, operated by, or produced by electricity **2** : ELECTRIFYING, THRILLING ⟨an ~ performance⟩ — **elec·tri·cal·ly** *adv*

electrical storm *n* : THUNDERSTORM

electric chair *n* : a chair used to carry out the death penalty by electrocution

electric eye *n* : PHOTOELECTRIC CELL

elec·tri·cian \i-ˌlek-ˈtri-shən\ *n* : a person who installs, operates, or repairs electrical equipment

elec·tric·i·ty \i-ˌlek-ˈtri-sə-tē\ *n, pl* **-ties** **1** : a form of energy that occurs naturally (as in lightning) or is produced (as in a generator) and that is expressed in terms of the movement and interaction of electrons **2** : electric current

elec·tri·fy \i-ˈlek-trə-ˌfī\ *vb* **-fied; -fy·ing** **1** : to charge with electricity **2** : to equip for use of electric power **3** : THRILL — **elec·tri·fi·ca·tion** \i-ˌlek-trə-fə-ˈkā-shən\ *n*

elec·tro·car·dio·gram \i-ˌlek-trō-ˈkär-dē-ə-ˌgram\ *n* : the tracing made by an electrocardiograph

elec·tro·car·dio·graph \-ˌgraf\ *n* : a device for recording the changes of electrical potential occurring during the heartbeat — **elec·tro·car·dio·graph·ic** \-ˌkär-dē-ə-ˈgrafik\ *adj* — **elec·tro·car·di·og·ra·phy** \-dē-ˈä-grə-fē\ *n*

elec·tro·chem·is·try \-ˈke-mə-strē\ *n* : a branch of chemistry that deals with the relation of electricity to chemical changes — **elec·tro·chem·i·cal** \-ˈke-mi-kəl\ *adj*

elec·tro·cute \i-ˈlek-trə-ˌkyüt\ *vb* **-cut·ed; -cut·ing** **1** : to kill (a criminal) by electricity **2** : to kill by electric shock — **elec·tro·cu·tion** \-ˌlek-trə-ˈkyü-shən\ *n*

elec·trode \i-ˈlek-ˌtrōd\ *n* : a conductor used to establish electrical contact with a nonmetallic part of a circuit

elec·tro·en·ceph·a·lo·gram \i-ˌlek-trō-in-ˈse-fə-lə-ˌgram\ *n* : the tracing made by an electroencephalograph

elec·tro·en·ceph·a·lo·graph \-ˌgraf\ *n* : an apparatus for detecting and recording brain waves — **elec·tro·en·cepha·lo·graph·ic** \-ˌse-fə-lə-ˈgra-fik\ *adj* — **elec·tro·en·ceph·a·log·ra·phy** \-ˈlä-grə-fē\ *n*

elec·trol·o·gist \i-ˌlek-ˈträ-lə-jist\ *n* : one that uses electrical means to remove hair, warts, moles, and birthmarks from the body

elec·trol·y·sis \i-ˌlek-ˈträ-lə-səs\ *n* **1** : the production of chemical changes by passage of an electric current through an electrolyte **2** : the destruction of hair roots with an electric current — **elec·tro·lyt·ic** \-trə-ˈli-tik\ *adj*

elec·tro·lyte \i-ˈlek-trə-ˌlīt\ *n* : a nonmetallic electric conductor in which current is carried by the movement of ions; *also* : a substance whose solution or molten form is such a conductor

elec·tro·mag·net \i-ˌlek-trō-ˈmag-nət\ *n* : a core of magnetic material (as iron) surrounded by a coil of wire through which an electric current is passed to magnetize the core

elec·tro·mag·net·ic \-mag-ˈne-tik\ *adj* : of, relating to, or produced by electromagnetism — **elec·tro·mag·net·i·cal·ly** *adv*

electromagnetic radiation *n* : energy in the form of electromagnetic waves; *also* : a series of electromagnetic waves

electromagnetic wave *n* : a wave (as a radio wave, an X-ray, or a wave of visible light) that consists of associated electric and magnetic effects and that travels at the speed of light

elec·tro·mag·ne·tism \i-ˌlek-trō-'mag-nə-ˌti-zəm\ *n* 1 : magnetism developed by a current of electricity 2 : a natural force responsible for interactions between charged particles which result from their charge

elec·tro·mo·tive force \i-ˌlek-trə-'mō-tiv-\ *n* : the potential difference derived from an electrical source per unit quantity of electricity passing through the source

elec·tron \i-'lek-ˌträn\ *n* : a negatively charged elementary particle

elec·tron·ic \i-ˌlek-'trä-nik\ *adj* 1 : of or relating to electrons or electronics 2 : involving a computer — **elec·tron·i·cal·ly** \-ni-k(ə-)lē\ *adv*

electronic mail *n* : E-MAIL

elec·tron·ics \i-ˌlek-'trä-niks\ *n* 1 : the physics of electrons and electronic devices 2 : electronic components, devices, or equipment

electron microscope *n* : an instrument in which a beam of electrons is used to produce an enlarged image of a minute object

electron tube *n* : a device in which electrical conduction by electrons takes place within a sealed container and which is used for the controlled flow of electrons

electron volt *n* : a unit of energy equal to 1.60×10^{-19} joule

elec·tro·pho·re·sis \i-ˌlek-trə-fə-'rē-səs\ *n* : the movement of suspended particles through a medium (as paper or gel) by an electromotive force — **elec·tro·pho·ret·ic** \-'re-tik\ *adj*

elec·tro·plate \i-'lek-trə-ˌplāt\ *vb* : to coat (as with metal) by electrolysis

elec·tro·shock therapy \i-'lek-trō-ˌshäk-\ *n* : the treatment of mental illness by applying electric current to the head and inducing convulsions

elec·tro·stat·ics \i-ˌlek-trə-'sta-tiks\ *n* : physics dealing with the interactions of stationary electric charges

el·ee·mos·y·nary \e-li-'mäs-sə-ˌner-ē\ *adj* : CHARITABLE

el·e·gance \'e-li-gəns\ *n* 1 : refined gracefulness; *also* : tasteful richness (as of design) 2 : something marked by elegance — **el·e·gant** \-gənt\ *adj* — **el·e·gant·ly** *adv*

ele·gi·ac \ˌe-lə-'jī-ək, -ˌak\ *adj* : of or relating to an elegy

el·e·gy \'e-lə-jē\ *n, pl* **-gies** : a song, poem, or speech expressing grief for one who is dead; *also* : a reflective poem usu. melancholy in tone

elem *abbr* elementary

el·e·ment \'e-lə-mənt\ *n* 1 *pl* : weather conditions; *esp* : severe weather ⟨boards exposed to the ∼s⟩ 2 : natural environment ⟨in her ∼⟩ 3 : a constituent part 4 *pl* : the simplest principles (as of an art or science) : RUDIMENTS 5 : a member of a mathematical set 6 : any of the fundamental substances that consist of atoms of only one kind ♦ **Synonyms** COMPONENT, INGREDIENT, CONSTITUENT — **el·e·men·tal** \ˌe-lə-'ment-ᵊl\ *adj*

el·e·men·ta·ry \ˌe-lə-'men-trē, -tə-rē\ *adj* : SIMPLE, RUDIMENTARY; *also* : of, relating to, or teaching the basic subjects of education

elementary particle *n* : a subatomic particle of matter and energy that does not appear to be made up of other smaller particles

elementary school *n* : a school usu. including the first six or the first eight grades

el·e·phant \'e-lə-fənt\ *n, pl* **elephants** *also* **elephant** : any of a family of huge thickset nearly hairless mammals that have the snout lengthened into a trunk and two long curving pointed ivory tusks

el·e·phan·ti·a·sis \ˌe-lə-fən-'tī-ə-səs\ *n, pl* **-a·ses** \-ˌsēz\ : enlargement and thickening of tissues in response esp. to infection by minute parasitic worms

el·e·phan·tine \ˌe-lə-'fan-ˌtēn, -ˌtīn, 'e-lə-fən-\ *adj* 1 : of great size or strength 2 : CLUMSY, PONDEROUS ⟨∼ verse⟩

elev *abbr* elevation

el·e·vate \'e-lə-ˌvāt\ *vb* **-vat·ed; -vat·ing** 1 : to lift up : RAISE 2 : EXALT, ENNOBLE ⟨great books that ∼ their readers⟩ 3 : ELATE

el·e·va·tion \ˌe-lə-'vā-shən\ *n* 1 : the height to which something is raised (as above sea level) 2 : a lifting up 3 : something (as a hill) that is elevated

el·e·va·tor \'e-lə-ˌvā-tər\ *n* 1 : a cage or platform for conveying people or things from one level to another 2 : a building for storing and discharging grain 3 : a movable surface on an airplane to produce motion up or down

elev·en \i-'le-vən\ *n* 1 : one more than 10 2 : the 11th in a set or series 3 : something having 11 units; *esp* : a football team — **eleven** *adj or pron* — **elev·enth** \-vənth\ *adj or n*

elf \'elf\ *n, pl* **elves** \'elvz\ : a mischievous fairy — **elf·ish** \'el-fish\ *adj*

ELF *abbr* extremely low frequency

elf·in \'el-fən\ *adj* : of, relating to, or resembling an elf

elic·it \i-'li-sət\ *vb* : to draw out or forth ♦ **Synonyms** EVOKE, EDUCE, EXTRACT, EXTORT

elide \i-'līd\ *vb* **elid·ed; elid·ing** : to suppress or alter by elision

el·i·gi·ble \'e-lə-jə-bəl\ *adj* : qualified to participate or to be chosen — **el·i·gi·bil·i·ty** \ˌe-lə-jə-'bi-lə-tē\ *n* — **eligible** *n*

elim·i·nate \i-'li-mə-ˌnāt\ *vb* **-nat·ed; -nat·ing** [L *eliminatus,* pp. of *eliminare,* fr. *limen* threshold] 1 : REMOVE, ERADICATE 2 : to pass (wastes) from the body 3 : to leave out : IGNORE — **elim·i·na·tion** \-ˌli-mə-'nā-shən\ *n*

eli·sion \i-'li-zhən\ *n* : the omission of a final or initial sound or of a word; *esp* : the omission of an unstressed vowel or syllable in a verse to achieve a uniform rhythm

elite \ā-'lēt, ē-\ *n* [F *élite*] 1 : the choice part; *also* : a superior group 2 : a typewriter type providing 12 characters to the inch — **elite** *adj*

elit·ism \-'lē-ˌti-zəm\ *n* : leadership or rule by an elite; *also* : advocacy of such elitism — **elit·ist** \-tist\ *n or adj*

elix·ir \i-'lik-sər\ *n* [ME, fr. ML, fr. Ar *al-iksīr* the elixir, fr. *al* the + *iksīr* elixir] 1 : a substance held capable of prolonging life indefinitely; *also* : PANACEA 2 : a sweetened alcoholic medicinal solution

Eliz·a·be·than \i-ˌli-zə-'bē-thən\ *adj* : of, relating to, or characteristic of Elizabeth I of England or her times

elk \'elk\ *n, pl* **elk** *or* **elks** 1 : MOOSE — used for one of the Old World 2 : a large gregarious deer of No. America, Europe, Asia, and northwestern Africa with curved antlers having many branches

elk

¹**ell** \'el\ *n* [ME *eln,* fr. OE; akin to L *ulna* forearm, Gk *ōlenē* elbow] : a former English cloth measure of 45 inches

²**ell** *n* : an extension at right angles to a building

el·lipse \i-'lips, e-\ *n* : a closed curve of oval shape

el·lip·sis \i-'lip-səs, e-\ *n, pl* **el·lip·ses** \-ˌsēz\ 1 : omission from an expression of a word clearly implied 2 : marks (as . . .) to show omission

el·lip·soid \i-'lip-ˌsóid, e-\ *n* : a surface all plane sections of which are circles or ellipses — **el·lip·soi·dal** \-ˌlip-'sói-dᵊl\ *also* **ellipsoid** *adj*

el·lip·ti·cal \i-'lip-ti-kəl, e-\ *or* **el·lip·tic** \-tik\ *adj* 1 : of, relating to, or shaped like an ellipse 2 : of, relating to, or marked by ellipsis — **el·lip·ti·cal·ly** \-ti-k(ə-)lē\ *adv*

elm \'elm\ *n* : any of a genus of large trees that have toothed leaves and nearly circular one-seeded winged fruits and are often grown as shade trees; *also* : the wood of an elm

El Ni·ño \el-'nēn-yō\ *n* : a flow of unusually warm Pacific Ocean water moving toward and along the west coast of So. America

CHEMICAL ELEMENTS

ELEMENT NAME	SYMBOL & ATOMIC NUMBER	ATOMIC WEIGHT[1]	ELEMENT NAME	SYMBOL & ATOMIC NUMBER	ATOMIC WEIGHT[1]
actinium	(Ac = 89)	(227)	mendelevium	(Md = 101)	(258)
aluminum	(Al = 13)	26.98154	mercury	(Hg = 80)	200.59
americium	(Am = 95)	(243)	molybdenum	(Mo = 42)	95.94
antimony	(Sb = 51)	121.760	moscovium	(Mc = 115)	(289)
argon	(Ar = 18)	39.948	neodymium	(Nd = 60)	144.242
arsenic	(As = 33)	74.92160	neon	(Ne = 10)	20.180
astatine	(At = 85)	(210)	neptunium	(Np = 93)	(237)
barium	(Ba = 56)	137.33	nickel	(Ni = 28)	58.6934
berkelium	(Bk = 97)	(247)	nihonium	(Nh = 113)	(286)
beryllium	(Be = 4)	9.012182	niobium	(Nb = 41)	92.90638
bismuth	(Bi = 83)	208.98040	nitrogen	(N = 7)	14.0067
bohrium	(Bh = 107)	(264)	nobelium	(No = 102)	(259)
boron	(B = 5)	10.81	oganesson	(Og = 118)	(294)
bromine	(Br = 35)	79.904	osmium	(Os = 76)	190.23
cadmium	(Cd = 48)	112.41	oxygen	(O = 8)	15.9994
calcium	(Ca = 20)	40.078	palladium	(Pd = 46)	106.42
californium	(Cf = 98)	(251)	phosphorus	(P = 15)	30.973762
carbon	(C = 6)	12.011	platinum	(Pt = 78)	195.084
cerium	(Ce = 58)	140.116	plutonium	(Pu = 94)	(244)
cesium	(Cs = 55)	132.90545	polonium	(Po = 84)	(209)
chlorine	(Cl = 17)	35.453	potassium	(K = 19)	39.0983
chromium	(Cr = 24)	51.996	praseodymium	(Pr = 59)	140.90765
cobalt	(Co = 27)	58.93320	promethium	(Pm = 61)	(145)
copernicium	(Cn = 112)	(285)	protactinium	(Pa = 91)	(231)
copper	(Cu = 29)	63.546	radium	(Ra = 88)	(226)
curium	(Cm = 96)	(247)	radon	(Rn = 86)	(222)
darmstadtium	(Ds = 110)	(269)	rhenium	(Re = 75)	186.207
dubnium	(Db = 105)	(262)	rhodium	(Rh = 45)	102.90550
dysprosium	(Dy = 66)	162.50	roentgenium	(Rg = 111)	(280)
einsteinium	(Es = 99)	(252)	rubidium	(Rb = 37)	85.4678
erbium	(Er = 68)	167.259	ruthenium	(Ru = 44)	101.07
europium	(Eu = 63)	151.964	rutherfordium	(Rf = 104)	(261)
fermium	(Fm = 100)	(257)	samarium	(Sm = 62)	150.36
flerovium	(Fl = 114)	(289)	scandium	(Sc = 21)	44.95591
fluorine	(F = 9)	18.998403	seaborgium	(Sg = 106)	(266)
francium	(Fr = 87)	(223)	selenium	(Se = 34)	78.96
gadolinium	(Gd = 64)	157.25	silicon	(Si = 14)	28.0855
gallium	(Ga = 31)	69.723	silver	(Ag = 47)	107.8682
germanium	(Ge = 32)	72.64	sodium	(Na = 11)	22.989769
gold	(Au = 79)	196.96657	strontium	(Sr = 38)	87.62
hafnium	(Hf = 72)	178.49	sulfur	(S = 16)	32.07
hassium	(Hs = 108)	(277)	tantalum	(Ta = 73)	180.9479
helium	(He = 2)	4.002602	technetium	(Tc = 43)	(98)
holmium	(Ho = 67)	164.93032	tellurium	(Te = 52)	127.60
hydrogen	(H = 1)	1.0079	tennessine	(Ts = 117)	(293)
indium	(In = 49)	114.818	terbium	(Tb = 65)	158.92535
iodine	(I = 53)	126.90447	thallium	(Tl = 81)	204.3833
iridium	(Ir = 77)	192.217	thorium	(Th = 90)	(232)
iron	(Fe = 26)	55.845	thulium	(Tm = 69)	168.93421
krypton	(Kr = 36)	83.80	tin	(Sn = 50)	118.71
lanthanum	(La = 57)	138.90547	titanium	(Ti = 22)	47.867
lawrencium	(Lr = 103)	(262)	tungsten	(W = 74)	183.84
lead	(Pb = 82)	207.2	uranium	(U = 92)	(238)
lithium	(Li = 3)	6.941	vanadium	(V = 23)	50.9415
livermorium	(Lv = 116)	(293)	xenon	(Xe = 54)	131.29
lutetium	(Lu = 71)	174.967	ytterbium	(Yb = 70)	173.04
magnesium	(Mg = 12)	24.305	yttrium	(Y = 39)	88.90585
manganese	(Mn = 25)	54.93805	zinc	(Zn = 30)	65.39
meitnerium	(Mt = 109)	(268)	zirconium	(Zr = 40)	91.224

[1]Weights are based on the naturally occurring isotope compositions and scaled to $^{12}C = 12$. For elements lacking stable isotopes, the mass number of the longest-lived one is shown in parentheses.

el·o·cu·tion \ˌe-lə-ˈkyü-shən\ *n* : the art of effective public speaking — **el·o·cu·tion·ist** \-shə-nist\ *n*

elon·gate \i-ˈlȯṇ-ˌgāt\ *vb* **-gat·ed; -gat·ing** : to make or grow longer ♦ *Synonyms* EXTEND, LENGTHEN, PROLONG, PROTRACT — **elon·ga·tion** \(ˌ)ē-ˌlȯṇ-ˈgā-shən\ *n*

elope \i-ˈlōp\ *vb* **eloped; elop·ing** : to run away esp. to be married — **elope·ment** *n* — **elop·er** *n*

el·o·quent \ˈe-lə-kwənt\ *adj* 1 : having or showing clear and forceful expression ⟨an ~ speaker⟩ 2 : clearly showing some feeling or meaning — **el·o·quence** \-kwəns\ *n* — **el·o·quent·ly** *adv*

¹**else** \ˈels\ *adv* 1 : in a different or additional manner or place or at a different or additional time ⟨where ~ can we meet⟩ 2 : OTHERWISE ⟨obey or ~ you'll be sorry⟩

²**else** *adj* : OTHER; *esp* : being in addition ⟨what ~ do you want⟩

else·where \-ˌhwer\ *adv* : in or to another place ⟨took my business ~⟩

elu·ci·date \i-ˈlü-sə-ˌdāt\ *vb* **-dat·ed; -dat·ing** : to make clear usu. by explanation ♦ *Synonyms* CLARIFY, EXPLAIN, ILLUMINATE — **elu·ci·da·tion** \-ˌlü-sə-ˈdā-shən\ *n*

elude \ē-ˈlüd\ *vb* **elud·ed; elud·ing** 1 : EVADE 2 : to escape the notice of

elu·sive \ē-ˈlü-siv\ *adj* : tending to elude : EVASIVE ⟨the solution remains ~⟩ — **elu·sive·ly** *adv* — **elu·sive·ness** *n*

el·ver \ˈel-vər\ *n* [alter. of *eelfare* migration of eels] : a young eel

elves *pl of* ELF

Ely·si·um \i-ˈli-zhē-əm, -zē-\ *n, pl* **-si·ums** *or* **-sia** \-zhē-ə, -zē-\ : PARADISE 2 — **Ely·sian** \-ˈli-zhən\ *adj*

em \ˈem\ *n* : a length approximately the width of the letter *M*

EM *abbr* 1 electromagnetic 2 electron microscope 3 enlisted man

ema·ci·ate \i-ˈmā-shē-ˌāt\ *vb* **-at·ed; -at·ing** : to become or cause to become very thin — **ema·ci·a·tion** \-ˌmā-shē-ˈā-shən, -sē-\ *n*

e–mail \ˈē-ˌmāl\ *or* **email** *n* 1 : a system for transmitting messages between computers on a network 2 : a message or messages sent and received through an e-mail system — **e–mail** *or* **email** *vb*

emalangeni *pl of* LILANGENI

em·a·nate \ˈe-mə-ˌnāt\ *vb* **-nat·ed; -nat·ing** : to come out from a source ♦ *Synonyms* PROCEED, SPRING, RISE, ARISE, ORIGINATE — **em·a·na·tion** \ˌe-mə-ˈnā-shən\ *n*

eman·ci·pate \i-ˈman-sə-ˌpāt\ *vb* **-pat·ed; -pat·ing** : to set free ♦ *Synonyms* LIBERATE, RELEASE, DELIVER, DISCHARGE — **eman·ci·pa·tion** \-ˌman-sə-ˈpā-shən\ *n* — **eman·ci·pa·tor** \-ˈman-sə-ˌpā-tər\ *n*

emas·cu·late \i-ˈmas-kyü-ˌlāt\ *vb* **-lat·ed; -lat·ing** : to deprive of virility : CASTRATE; *also* : WEAKEN — **emas·cu·la·tion** \i-ˌmas-kyü-ˈlā-shən\ *n*

em·balm \im-ˈbäm, -ˈbälm\ *vb* : to treat (a corpse) so as to protect from decay — **em·balm·er** *n*

em·bank·ment \im-ˈbaŋk-mənt\ *n* : a raised structure (as of earth) to hold back water or carry a roadway

em·bar·go \im-ˈbär-gō\ *n, pl* **-goes** [Sp, fr. *embargar* to bar] : a prohibition on commerce — **embargo** *vb*

em·bark \im-ˈbärk\ *vb* 1 : to put or go on board a ship or airplane 2 : to make a start — **em·bar·ka·tion** \ˌem-ˌbär-ˈkā-shən\ *n*

em·bar·rass \im-ˈber-əs\ *vb* 1 : CONFUSE, DISCONCERT 2 : to involve in financial difficulties 3 : to cause to experience self-conscious distress 4 : HINDER, IMPEDE — **em·bar·rass·ing·ly** *adv* — **em·bar·rass·ment** *n*

em·bas·sy \ˈem-bə-sē\ *n, pl* **-sies** 1 : a group of representatives headed by an ambassador 2 : the function, position, or mission of an ambassador 3 : the official residence and offices of an ambassador

em·bat·tle \im-ˈba-tᵊl\ *vb* 1 : to arrange in order for battle; *also* : FORTIFY

em·bat·tled *adj* 1 : engaged in battle, conflict, or controversy 2 : being a site of battle, conflict, or controversy 3 : characterized by conflict or controversy ⟨an ~ presidency⟩

em·bed \im-ˈbed\ *vb* **em·bed·ded; em·bed·ding** 1 : to enclose closely in a surrounding mass 2 : to make something an integral part of

em·bel·lish \im-ˈbe-lish\ *vb* 1 : ADORN, DECORATE 2 : to add ornamental details to ♦ *Synonyms* BEAU-

TIFY, DECK, BEDECK, GARNISH, ORNAMENT, DRESS — **em·bel·lish·er** *n* — **em·bel·lish·ment** *n*

em·ber \ˈem-bər\ *n* 1 : a glowing or smoldering fragment from a fire 2 *pl* : the smoldering remains of a fire

em·bez·zle \im-ˈbe-zəl\ *vb* **-zled; -zling** : to steal (as money) by falsifying records — **em·bez·zle·ment** *n* — **em·bez·zler** *n*

em·bit·ter \im-ˈbi-tər\ *vb* 1 : to arouse bitter feelings in 2 : to make bitter

em·bla·zon \im-ˈblā-zᵊn\ *vb* 1 : to adorn with heraldic devices 2 : to display conspicuously

em·blem \ˈem-bləm\ *n* : something (as an object or picture) suggesting another object or an idea : SYMBOL — **em·blem·at·ic** \ˌem-blə-ˈma-tik\ *also* **em·blem·at·i·cal** \-ti-kəl\ *adj*

em·body \im-ˈbä-dē\ *vb* **em·bod·ied; em·body·ing** 1 : INCARNATE 2 : to express in definite form 3 : to incorporate into a system or body 4 : PERSONIFY ♦ *Synonyms* COMBINE, INTEGRATE — **em·bodi·ment** \-di-mənt\ *n*

em·bold·en \im-ˈbōl-dən\ *vb* : to inspire with courage ⟨his speech ~ed the soldiers⟩

em·bo·lism \ˈem-bə-ˌli-zəm\ *n* : the obstruction of a blood vessel by a foreign or abnormal particle

em·bon·point \äⁿ-bōⁿ-ˈpwaⁿ\ *n* [F] : plumpness of person : STOUTNESS

em·boss \im-ˈbäs, -ˈbȯs\ *vb* : to ornament with raised work

em·bou·chure \ˈäm-bu̇-ˌshu̇r, ˌäm-bu̇-ˈshu̇r\ *n* [F, ultim. fr. *bouche* mouth] : the position and use of the lips, tongue, and teeth in playing a wind instrument

em·bow·er \im-ˈbau̇(-ə)r\ *vb* : to shelter or enclose in a bower

¹**em·brace** \im-ˈbrās\ *vb* **em·braced; em·brac·ing** 1 : to clasp in the arms; *also* : CHERISH, LOVE 2 : ENCIRCLE 3 : TAKE UP, ADOPT ⟨embraced the cause⟩; *also* : WELCOME ⟨embraced the opportunity⟩ 4 : INCLUDE 5 : to participate in an embrace ♦ *Synonyms* COMPREHEND, INVOLVE, ENCOMPASS, EMBODY

²**embrace** *n* : an encircling with the arms

em·bra·sure \im-ˈbrā-zhər\ *n* 1 : an opening in a wall through which a cannon is fired 2 : a recess of a door or window

em·bro·ca·tion \ˌem-brə-ˈkā-shən\ *n* : LINIMENT

em·broi·der \im-ˈbrȯi-dər\ *vb* 1 : to ornament with or do needlework 2 : to elaborate with exaggerated detail

em·broi·dery \im-ˈbrȯi-də-rē\ *n, pl* **-der·ies** 1 : the forming of decorative designs with needlework 2 : something embroidered

em·broil \im-ˈbrȯi(-ə)l\ *vb* 1 : to throw into confusion or disorder 2 : to involve in conflict or difficulties ⟨~ed in a dispute⟩ — **em·broil·ment** *n*

em·bryo \ˈem-brē-ˌō\ *n, pl* **embryos** : a living thing in its earliest stages of development — **em·bry·on·ic** \ˌem-brē-ˈä-nik\ *adj*

em·bry·ol·o·gy \ˌem-brē-ˈä-lə-jē\ *n* : a branch of biology dealing with embryos and their development — **em·bry·o·log·i·cal** \-brē-ə-ˈlä-ji-kəl\ *adj* — **em·bry·ol·o·gist** \-brē-ˈä-lə-jist\ *n*

em·cee \ˈem-ˈsē\ *n* : MASTER OF CEREMONIES — **emcee** *vb*

emend \ē-ˈmend\ *vb* : to correct usu. by altering the text of ♦ *Synonyms* RECTIFY, REVISE, AMEND — **emen·da·tion** \ˌē-ˌmen-ˈdā-shən\ *n*

emer *abbr* emeritus

¹**em·er·ald** \ˈem-rəld, ˈe-mə-\ *n* : a green beryl prized as a gem

²**emerald** *adj* : brightly or richly green

emerge \i-ˈmərj\ *vb* **emerged; emerg·ing** : to rise, come forth, or come out into view — **emer·gence** \-ˈmər-jəns\ *n* — **emer·gent** \-jənt\ *adj*

emer·gen·cy \i-ˈmər-jən-sē\ *n, pl* **-cies** : an unforeseen event or condition requiring prompt action ♦ *Synonyms* EXIGENCY, CONTINGENCY, CRISIS, JUNCTURE

emergency room *n* : a hospital room for receiving and treating persons needing immediate medical care

emer·i·ta \i-ˈmer-ə-tə\ *adj* : EMERITUS — used of a woman

emer·i·tus \i-ˈmer-ə-təs\ *adj* [L] : retired from active duty ⟨professor ~⟩

em·ery \ˈe-mə-rē\ *n, pl* **em·er·ies** : a dark granular mineral consisting primarily of corundum and used as an abrasive

emet·ic \i-'me-tik\ *n* : an agent that induces vomiting — **emetic** *adj*

emf *n* [electromotive *force*] : POTENTIAL DIFFERENCE

em·i·grate \'e-mə-ˌgrāt\ *vb* **-grat·ed; -grat·ing** : to leave a place (as a country) to settle elsewhere — **em·i·grant** \-mi-grənt\ *n* — **em·i·gra·tion** \ˌe-mə-'grā-shən\ *n*

émi·gré *also* **emi·gré** \'e-mi-ˌgrā, ˌe-mi-'grā\ *n* [F] : a person who emigrates esp. because of political conditions

em·i·nence \'e-mə-nəns\ *n* **1** : high rank or position; *also* : a person of high rank or attainment **2** : a lofty place

em·i·nent \'e-mə-nənt\ *adj* **1** : CONSPICUOUS, EVIDENT **2** : DISTINGUISHED, PROMINENT ⟨an ∼ physician⟩ — **em·i·nent·ly** *adv*

eminent domain *n* : a right of a government to take private property for public use

emir *or* **amir** \ə-'mir, ā-\ *n* [Ar *amīr* commander] : a ruler, chief, or commander in Islamic countries — **emir·ate** \'e-mər-ət\ *n*

em·is·sary \'e-mə-ˌser-ē\ *n, pl* **-sar·ies** : AGENT; *esp* : a secret agent

emis·sion \ē-'mi-shən\ *n* : something emitted; *esp* : substances discharged into the air

emit \ē-'mit\ *vb* **emit·ted; emit·ting** **1** : to give off or out ⟨∼ light⟩; *also* : EJECT **2** : EXPRESS, UTTER ⟨emitted a groan⟩ — **emit·ter** *n*

emo·ji \ē-'mō-jē\ *n, pl* **emoji** *or* **emo·jis** [Jp, fr. *e*- picture, drawing + *moji* character] : any of various small images, symbols, or icons used in text fields in electronic communications to express something (as an emotion) without using words

emol·lient \i-'mäl-yənt\ *adj* : making soft or supple; *also* : soothing esp. to the skin or mucous membrane ⟨an ∼ hand lotion⟩ — **emol·lient** *n*

emol·u·ment \i-'mäl-yə-mənt\ *n* [ME, fr. L *emolumentum* advantage, fr. *emolere* to produce by grinding] : the product (as salary or fees) of an employment

emote \i-'mōt\ *vb* **emot·ed; emot·ing** : to give expression to emotion in or as if in a play

emo·ti·con \i-'mō-ti-ˌkän\ *n* : a group of keyboard characters (as :)) that often represents a facial expression and that is used especially in electronic communications

emo·tion \i-'mō-shən\ *n* : a usu. intense feeling (as of love, hate, or despair) — **emo·tion·al** \-shə-nəl\ *adj* — **emo·tion·al·ly** *adv*

emot·ive \i-'mō-tiv\ *adj* **1** : of or relating to the emotions **2** : appealing to or expressing emotion

emp *abbr* emperor; empress

empanel *var of* IMPANEL

em·pa·thy \'em-pə-thē\ *n* : the experiencing as one's own of the feelings of another; *also* : the capacity for this — **em·path·ic** \em-'pa-thik\ *adj*

em·pen·nage \ˌäm-pə-'näzh, ˌem-\ *n* [F] : the tail assembly of an airplane

em·per·or \'em-pər-ər\ *n* : the sovereign male ruler of an empire

em·pha·sis \'em-fə-səs\ *n, pl* **-pha·ses** \-ˌsēz\ : particular prominence given (as to a syllable in speaking or to a phase of action)

em·pha·sise *Brit var of* EMPHASIZE

em·pha·size \-ˌsīz\ *vb* **-sized; -siz·ing** : to place emphasis on : STRESS

em·phat·ic \im-'fa-tik, em-\ *adj* : uttered with emphasis : STRESSED ⟨an ∼ refusal⟩ — **em·phat·i·cal·ly** \-'ti-k(ə-)lē\ *adv*

em·phy·se·ma \ˌem-fə-'zē-mə, -'sē-\ *n* : a condition marked esp. by abnormal expansion of the air spaces of the lungs resulting in severe breathlessness

em·pire \'em-ˌpī(-ə)r\ *n* **1** : a large state or a group of states under a single sovereign who is usu. an emperor; *also* : something resembling a political empire **2** : imperial sovereignty or dominion

em·pir·i·cal \im-'pir-i-kəl\ *also* **em·pir·ic** \-ik\ *adj* : based on observation; *also* : subject to verification by observation or experiment ⟨∼ laws⟩ — **em·pir·i·cal·ly** \-i-k(ə-)lē\ *adv*

em·pir·i·cism \im-'pir-ə-ˌsi-zəm, em-\ *n* : the practice of relying on observation and experiment esp. in the natural sciences — **em·pir·i·cist** \-sist\ *n*

em·place·ment \im-'plās-mənt\ *n* **1** : a prepared position for weapons or military equipment **2** : PLACEMENT

¹**em·ploy** \im-'plói\ *vb* **1** : to make use of **2** : to use the services of **3** : OCCUPY, DEVOTE — **em·ploy·er** *n*

²**em·ploy** \im-'plói; 'im-ˌplói, 'em-\ *n* : EMPLOYMENT

em·ploy·ee *also* **em·ploye** \im-ˌplói-'ē, ˌem-; im-'plói-ˌē, em-\ *n* : a person who works for another

em·ploy·ment \im-'plói-mənt\ *n* **1** : OCCUPATION, ACTIVITY **2** : the act of employing : the condition of being employed

em·po·ri·um \im-'pór-ē-əm, em-\ *n, pl* **-ri·ums** *also* **-ria** \-ē-ə\ [L, fr. Gk *emporion*, fr. *emporos* traveler, trader] : a commercial center; *esp* : a store carrying varied articles

em·pow·er \im-'paú(-ə)r\ *vb* : to give authority or power to; *also* : ENABLE — **em·pow·er·ment** \-mənt\ *n*

em·press \'em-prəs\ *n* **1** : the wife or widow of an emperor **2** : a woman who is the sovereign ruler of an empire

¹**emp·ty** \'emp-tē\ *adj* **emp·ti·er; -est** [ME, fr. OE ǣmettig unoccupied, fr. ǣmetta leisure] **1** : containing nothing ⟨∼ shelves⟩ **2** : UNOCCUPIED, UNINHABITED ⟨an ∼ building⟩ **3** : lacking value, force, sense, or purpose
♦ Synonyms VACANT, BLANK, VOID, STARK, VACUOUS — **emp·ti·ness** *n*

²**empty** *vb* **emp·tied; emp·ty·ing** **1** : to make or become empty **2** : to discharge contents; *also* : to remove from what holds or encloses

³**empty** *n, pl* **empties** : an empty bottle or can

emp·ty–hand·ed \ˌemp-tē-'han-dəd\ *adj* **1** : having or bringing nothing **2** : having acquired or gained nothing

em·py·re·an \ˌem-ˌpī-'rē-ən, -pə-\ *n* **1** : the highest heaven; *also* : FIRMAMENT **2** : an ideal place or state

EMT \ˌē-(ˌ)em-'tē\ *n* [emergency *m*edical *t*echnician] : a specially trained medical technician certified to provide basic medical services before and during transport to a hospital

¹**emu** \'ē-myü, -mü\ *n* : a swift-running flightless Australian bird smaller than the related ostrich

²**emu** *abbr* electromagnetic unit

em·u·late \'em-yü-ˌlāt\ *vb* **-lat·ed; -lat·ing** : to strive to equal or excel : IMITATE — **em·u·la·tion** \ˌem-yü-'lā-shən\ *n* — **em·u·lous** \'em-yü-ləs\ *adj*

emul·si·fi·er \i-'məl-sə-ˌfī(-ə)r\ *n* : a substance (as a soap) that helps to form and stabilize an emulsion

emul·si·fy \-ˌfī\ *vb* **-fied; -fy·ing** : to disperse (as an oil) in an emulsion — **emul·si·fi·ca·tion** \i-ˌməl-sə-fə-'kā-shən\ *n*

emul·sion \i-'məl-shən\ *n* **1** : a mixture of mutually insoluble liquids in which one is dispersed in droplets throughout the other ⟨an ∼ of oil in water⟩ **2** : a light-sensitive coating on photographic film or paper

en \'en\ *n* : a length approximately half the width of the letter *M*

¹**-en** *also* **-n** *adj suffix* : made of : consisting of ⟨earthen⟩

²**-en** *vb suffix* **1** : become or cause to be ⟨sharpen⟩ **2** : cause or come to have ⟨lengthen⟩

en·able \i-'nā-bəl\ *vb* **en·abled; en·abling** **1** : to make able or feasible ⟨wings that ∼ one to fly⟩ **2** : to give legal power, capacity, or sanction to

en·act \i-'nakt\ *vb* **1** : to make into law **2** : to act out — **en·act·ment** *n*

enam·el \i-'na-məl\ *n* **1** : a glasslike substance used to coat the surface of metal or pottery **2** : the hard outer layer of a tooth **3** : a usu. glossy paint that forms a hard coat — **enamel** *vb*

enam·el·ware \-ˌwer\ *n* : metal utensils coated with enamel

en·am·or \i-'na-mər\ *vb* : to inflame with love

en·am·our *chiefly Brit var of* ENAMOR

en bloc \äⁿ-'bläk\ *adv or adj* : as a whole : in a mass

enc *or* **encl** *abbr* enclosure

en·camp \in-'kamp\ *vb* : to make camp — **en·camp·ment** *n*

en·cap·su·late \in-'kap-sə-ˌlāt\ *vb* **-lat·ed; -lat·ing** **1** : to encase or become encased in a capsule **2** : SUMMARIZE — **en·cap·su·la·tion** \-ˌkap-sə-'lā-shən\ *n*

en·case \in-'kās\ *vb* : to enclose in or as if in a case — **en·case·ment** \-'kā-smənt\ *n*

-ence *n suffix* **1** : action or process ⟨emergence⟩ : instance of an action or process ⟨reference⟩ **2** : quality or state ⟨dependence⟩

en·ceinte \äⁿ-'sant\ *adj* : PREGNANT 1

en·ceph·a·li·tis \in-ˌse-fə-'lī-təs\ *n, pl* **-lit·i·des** \-'li-tə-ˌdēz\ : inflammation of the brain — **en·ceph·a·lit·ic** \-'li-tik\ *adj*

en·ceph·a·lop·a·thy \in-ˌse-fə-'lä-pə-thē\ *n, pl* **-thies** : a disease of the brain

enchain • enfeeble

164

en·chain \in-ˈchān\ vb : FETTER, CHAIN
en·chant \in-ˈchant\ vb 1 : BEWITCH 2 : ENRAPTURE, FASCINATE ⟨was ~ed by his poetry⟩ — en·chant·er n — en·chant·ing·ly adv — en·chant·ment n — en·chant·ress \-ˈchan-trəs\ n
en·chi·la·da \ˌen-chə-ˈlä-də\ n : a tortilla rolled around a filling, covered with chili sauce, and usu. baked
en·ci·pher \in-ˈsī-fər, en-\ vb : ENCODE
en·cir·cle \in-ˈsər-kəl\ vb : to pass completely around : SURROUND — en·cir·cle·ment n
en·clave \ˈen-ˌklāv; ˈän-ˌkläv\ n : a distinct territorial, cultural, or social unit enclosed within or as if within foreign territory
en·close \in-ˈklōz\ vb 1 : to shut up or in; esp : to surround with a fence 2 : to include along with something else in a parcel or envelope ⟨~ a check⟩ — en·clo·sure \-ˈklō-zhər\ n
en·code \in-ˈkōd, en-\ vb : to convert (a message) into code
en·co·mi·um \en-ˈkō-mē-əm\ n, pl -mi·ums also -mia \-mē-ə\ : high or glowing praise
en·com·pass \in-ˈkəm-pəs\ vb 1 : ENCIRCLE 2 : ENVELOP, INCLUDE
en·core \ˈän-ˌkȯr\ n 1 : a demand for repetition or reappearance 2 : a further performance or appearance demanded by an audience 3 : a second achievement that usu. surpasses the first — encore vb
¹en·coun·ter \in-ˈkaůn-tər\ vb 1 : to meet as an enemy : FIGHT 2 : to meet usu. unexpectedly ⟨~ problems⟩
²encounter n 1 : a hostile usu. violent meeting 2 : a chance meeting 3 : an experience shared with another ⟨a romantic ~⟩
en·cour·age \in-ˈkər-ij\ vb -aged; -ag·ing 1 : to inspire with courage and hope 2 : STIMULATE, INCITE ⟨tax cuts to ~ spending⟩ 3 : FOSTER — en·cour·age·ment n — en·cour·ag·ing·ly adv
en·croach \in-ˈkrōch\ vb [ME encrochen to seize, fr. AF encrocher, fr. croche hook] : to enter gradually or stealthily upon another's property or rights — en·croach·er n — en·croach·ment n
en·crust also in·crust \in-ˈkrəst\ vb : to provide with or form a crust
en·crus·ta·tion \(ˌ)in-ˌkrəs-ˈtā-shən, ˌen-\ var of INCRUSTATION
en·crypt \in-ˈkript, en-\ vb : to change (information) from one form to another esp. to hide its meaning
en·cum·ber \in-ˈkəm-bər\ vb 1 : to weigh down : BURDEN 2 : to hinder the function or activity of ⟨relations ~ed by mistrust⟩ — en·cum·brance \-brəns\ n
ency or encyc abbr encyclopedia
-en·cy n suffix : quality or state ⟨despondency⟩
¹en·cyc·li·cal \in-ˈsi-kli-kəl, en-\ adj : addressed to all the individuals of a group
²encyclical n : an encyclical letter; esp : a papal letter to the bishops of the church
en·cy·clo·pae·dia, en·cy·clo·pae·dic chiefly Brit var of ENCYCLOPEDIA, ENCYCLOPEDIC
en·cy·clo·pe·dia \in-ˌsī-klə-ˈpē-dē-ə\ n [ML encyclopaedia course of general education, fr. Gk enkyklios paideia general education] : a work treating the various branches of learning — en·cy·clo·pe·dic \-ˈpē-dik\ adj
en·cyst \in-ˈsist, en-\ vb : to form or become enclosed in a cyst — en·cyst·ment n
¹end \ˈend\ n 1 : the part of an area that lies at the boundary; also : a point which marks the extent or limit of something or at which something ceases to exist 2 : a ceasing of a course (as of action or activity); also : DEATH 3 : the ultimate state; also : RESULT, ISSUE 4 : REMNANT 5 : PURPOSE, OBJECTIVE 6 : a player stationed at the extremity of a line (as in football) 7 : a share, operation, or aspect of an undertaking
²end vb 1 : to bring or come to an end 2 : DESTROY; also : DIE 3 : to form or be at the end of ♦ Synonyms CLOSE, CONCLUDE, TERMINATE, FINISH, COMPLETE
en·dan·ger \in-ˈdān-jər\ vb : to bring into danger; also : to create danger
en·dan·gered adj : being or relating to an endangered species
endangered species : a species threatened with extinction
en·dear \in-ˈdir\ vb : to cause to become beloved or admired

en·dear·ment \-mənt\ n : a sign of affection : CARESS
en·deav·or \in-ˈde-vər\ vb : TRY, ATTEMPT — endeavor n
en·deav·our chiefly Brit var of ENDEAVOR
en·dem·ic \en-ˈde-mik, in-\ adj : restricted to a particular place ⟨~ plants⟩ ⟨an ~ disease⟩ — endemic n
end·ing \ˈen-diŋ\ n : something that forms an end; esp : SUFFIX
en·dive \ˈen-ˌdīv\ n 1 : an herb related to chicory and grown as a salad plant 2 : the blanched shoot of chicory
end·less \ˈend-ləs\ adj 1 : having or seeming to have no end : ETERNAL ⟨~ debates⟩ 2 : united at the ends : CONTINUOUS ⟨an ~ belt⟩ ♦ Synonyms INTERMINABLE, EVERLASTING, UNCEASING, CEASELESS, UNENDING — end·less·ly adv
end·most \-ˌmōst\ adj : situated at the very end
end·note \-ˌnōt\ n : a note placed at the end of a text
en·do·crine \ˈen-də-krən, -ˌkrīn, -ˌkrēn\ adj : producing secretions that are distributed by way of the bloodstream ⟨~ glands⟩ — endocrine n — en·do·cri·nol·o·gist \-kri-ˈnä-lə-jist\ n — en·do·cri·nol·o·gy \-jē\ n
en·dog·e·nous \en-ˈdä-jə-nəs\ adj : caused or produced by factors inside the organism or system ⟨~ depression⟩ — en·dog·e·nous·ly adv
en·do·me·tri·um \ˌen-dō-ˈmē-trē-əm\ n, pl -tria \-trē-ə\ : the mucous membrane lining the uterus — en·do·me·tri·al \-trē-əl\ adj
en·dor·phin \en-ˈdȯr-fən\ n : any of a group of endogenous morphinelike proteins found esp. in the brain
en·dorse also in·dorse \in-ˈdȯrs\ vb en·dorsed; en·dors·ing [ME endosen, fr. AF endosser to put on, don, write on the back of, fr. dos back, fr. L dorsum] 1 : to sign one's name on the back of (as a check) 2 : APPROVE, SANCTION 3 : to recommend (as a product) usu. for financial compensation — en·dorse·ment also in·dorse·ment n
en·do·scope \ˈen-də-ˌskōp\ n : an illuminated usu. fiberoptic instrument for visualizing the interior of a hollow organ or part (as the colon or esophagus) — en·do·scop·ic \ˌen-də-ˈskä-pik\ adj — en·dos·co·py \en-ˈdäs-kə-pē\ n
en·do·ther·mic \ˌen-də-ˈthər-mik\ adj : characterized by or formed with absorption of heat
en·dow \in-ˈdaů\ vb 1 : to furnish with funds for support ⟨~ a school⟩ 2 : to furnish with something freely or naturally ⟨~ed with intellect⟩ — en·dow·ment n
en·due \in-ˈdü, -ˈdyü\ vb en·dued; en·du·ing : PROVIDE, ENDOW
en·dur·ance \in-ˈdůr-əns, -ˈdyůr-\ n 1 : DURATION 2 : the ability to withstand hardship or stress : FORTITUDE
en·dure \in-ˈdůr, -ˈdyůr\ vb en·dured; en·dur·ing 1 : LAST, PERSIST 2 : to suffer firmly or patiently : BEAR 3 : TOLERATE — en·dur·able adj
end·ways \ˈend-ˌwāz\ adv or adj 1 : LENGTHWISE 2 : with the end forward 3 : on end
end·wise \-ˌwīz\ adv or adj : ENDWAYS
ENE abbr east-northeast
en·e·ma \ˈe-nə-mə\ n, pl enemas also ene·ma·ta \ˌe-nə-ˈmä-tə, ˈe-nə-mə-tə\ : injection of liquid into the rectum; also : material so injected
en·e·my \ˈe-nə-mē\ n, pl -mies [ME enemi, fr. AF, fr. L inimicus, fr. in- not + amicus friend] : one that attacks or tries to harm another : FOE; esp : a military opponent
en·er·get·ic \ˌe-nər-ˈje-tik\ adj : marked by energy : ACTIVE, VIGOROUS ♦ Synonyms STRENUOUS, LUSTY, DYNAMIC, VITAL — en·er·get·i·cal·ly \-ti-k(ə-)lē\ adv
en·er·gise Brit var of ENERGIZE
en·er·gize \ˈe-nər-ˌjīz\ vb -gized; -giz·ing : to give energy to
en·er·gy \ˈe-nər-jē\ n, pl -gies 1 : vigorous action : EFFORT 2 : capacity for action 3 : a fundamental entity of nature usu. regarded as the capacity for performing work 4 : usable power (as heat or electricity); also : the resources for producing such power
energy level n : one of the stable states of constant energy that may be assumed by a physical system (as the electrons in an atom)
en·er·vate \ˈe-nər-ˌvāt\ vb -vat·ed; -vat·ing : to lessen the strength or vigor of : weaken in mind or body ⟨enervated by work⟩ — en·er·vat·ing·ly \-ˌvā-tiŋ-lē\ adv — en·er·va·tion \ˌe-nər-ˈvā-shən\ n
en·fee·ble \in-ˈfē-bəl\ vb -bled; -bling : to make feeble

✦ **Synonyms** WEAKEN, DEBILITATE, SAP, UNDERMINE, CRIPPLE — **en·fee·ble·ment** *n*

en·fi·lade \'en-fə-ˌlād, -ˌläd\ *n* : gunfire directed along the length of an enemy battle line — **enfilade** *vb*

en·fold \in-'fōld\ *vb* **1** : ENVELOP ⟨darkness ~ed the city⟩ **2** : EMBRACE

en·force \in-'fȯrs\ *vb* **1** : COMPEL ⟨~ obedience by threats⟩ **2** : to execute effectively ⟨~ the law⟩ — **force·able** *adj* — **en·force·ment** *n*

en·forc·er \in-'fȯr-sər\ *n* : one that enforces; *esp* : a player (as in ice hockey) known for rough play

en·fran·chise \in-'fran-ˌchīz\ *vb* **-chised; -chis·ing 1** : to set free (as from slavery) **2** : to admit to citizenship; *also* : to grant the vote to — **en·fran·chise·ment** \-ˌchīz-mənt, -chəz-\ *n*

eng *abbr* engine; engineer; engineering

Eng *abbr* England; English

en·gage \in-'gāj\ *vb* **en·gaged; en·gag·ing 1** : PLEDGE; *esp* : to bind by a pledge to marry **2** : EMPLOY, HIRE **3** : to attract and hold esp. by interesting; *also* : to cause to participate **4** : to commence or take part in a venture ⟨*engaged* in shady deals⟩ **5** : to bring or enter into conflict ⟨~ the enemy⟩ **6** : to connect or interlock with : MESH; *also* : to cause to mesh

en·gage·ment \in-'gāj-mənt\ *n* **1** : APPOINTMENT **2** : EMPLOYMENT **3** : a mutual promise to marry : BETROTHAL **4** : a hostile encounter

en·gag·ing *adj* : ATTRACTIVE ⟨an ~ smile⟩ — **en·gag·ing·ly** *adv*

en·gen·der \in-'jen-dər\ *vb* **1** : BEGET **2** : BRING ABOUT, CREATE ⟨~ controversy⟩ ✦ **Synonyms** GENERATE, BREED, OCCASION, PRODUCE

en·gine \'en-jən\ *n* [ME *engin*, fr. AF, fr. L *ingenium* natural disposition, talent] **1** : a mechanical device **2** : a machine for converting energy into mechanical motion **3** : LOCOMOTIVE **4** : software that performs a fundamental function esp. of a larger program — **en·gine·less** *adj*

¹**en·gi·neer** \ˌen-jə-'nir\ *n* **1** : a member of a military unit specializing in engineering work **2** : a designer or builder of engines **3** : one trained in engineering **4** : one that operates an engine

²**engineer** *vb* **1** : to lay out or manage as an engineer **2** : to guide the course of ⟨~ a rally⟩ ✦ **Synonyms** PILOT, LEAD, STEER

en·gi·neer·ing *n* : the practical applications of scientific and mathematical principles

En·glish \'iŋ-glish\ *n* **1** : the language of England, the U.S., and many areas now or formerly under British rule **2 English** *pl* : the people of England **3** : spin imparted to a ball that is driven or rolled — **English** *adj* — **En·glish·man** \-mən\ *n* — **En·glish·wom·an** \-ˌwu̇-mən\ *n*

English horn *n* : a woodwind instrument longer than and having a range lower than the oboe

English horn

English setter *n* : any of a breed of hunting dogs with a flat silky coat of white or white with color

English sparrow *n* : HOUSE SPARROW

English system *n* : a system of weights and measures in which the foot is the principal unit of length and the pound is the principal unit of weight

engr *abbr* **1** engineer **2** engraved

en·gram \'en-ˌgram\ *n* : a hypothetical change in neural tissue postulated in order to account for persistence of memory

en·grave \in-'grāv\ *vb* **en·graved; en·grav·ing 1** : to produce (as letters or lines) by incising a surface **2** : to cut

figures, letters, or designs on for printing; *also* : to print from an engraved plate ⟨~ an invitation⟩ **3** : PHOTOENGRAVE — **en·grav·er** *n*

en·grav·ing \in-'grā-viŋ\ *n* **1** : the art of one who engraves **2** : an engraved plate; *also* : a print made from it

en·gross \in-'grōs\ *vb* : to take up the whole interest or attention of ✦ **Synonyms** MONOPOLIZE, ABSORB, CONSUME

en·gulf \in-'gəlf\ *vb* : to flow over and enclose : OVERWHELM ⟨~ed in flames⟩

en·hance \in-'hans\ *vb* **en·hanced; en·hanc·ing** : to increase or improve (as in value or desirability) ✦ **Synonyms** HEIGHTEN, INTENSIFY, MAGNIFY — **en·hance·ment** *n*

enig·ma \i-'nig-mə\ *n* [L *aenigma*, fr. Gk *ainigma*, fr. *ainissesthai* to speak in riddles, fr. *ainos* fable] : something obscure or hard to understand

enig·mat·ic \ˌe-nig-'ma-tik\ *adj* : resembling an enigma ✦ **Synonyms** OBSCURE, CRYPTIC, MYSTIFYING — **en·ig·mat·i·cal·ly** \-ti-k(ə-)lē\ *adv*

en·join \in-'jȯin\ *vb* **1** : COMMAND, ORDER ⟨~ed us to desist⟩ **2** : FORBID ✦ **Synonyms** DIRECT, BID, CHARGE, COMMAND, INSTRUCT

en·joy \in-'jȯi\ *vb* **1** : to have for one's benefit or use ⟨~ good health⟩ **2** : to take pleasure or satisfaction in ⟨~ed the concert⟩ — **en·joy·able** *adj* — **en·joy·ment** *n*

enl *abbr* **1** enlarged **2** enlisted

en·large \in-'lärj\ *vb* **en·larged; en·larg·ing 1** : to make or grow larger **2** : ELABORATE ✦ **Synonyms** INCREASE, AUGMENT, MULTIPLY, EXPAND — **en·large·ment** *n*

en·light·en \in-'lī-tᵊn\ *vb* **1** : INSTRUCT, INFORM **2** : to give spiritual insight to — **en·light·en·ment** *n*

en·list \in-'list\ *vb* **1** : to secure the aid or support of **2** : to engage for service in the armed forces — **en·list·ee** \-ˌlis-'tē\ *n* — **en·list·ment** \-'list-mənt\ *n*

en·list·ed \in-'lis-təd\ *adj* : of, relating to, or forming the part of a military force below commissioned or warrant officers

enlisted man *n* : a man or woman in the armed forces ranking below a commissioned or warrant officer

en·liv·en \in-'lī-vən\ *vb* : to give life, action, or spirit to : ANIMATE

en masse \äⁿ-'mas\ *adv* [F] : in a body : as a whole

en·mesh \in-'mesh\ *vb* : to catch or entangle in or as if in meshes

en·mi·ty \'en-mə-tē\ *n, pl* **-ties** : ILL WILL; *esp* : mutual hatred ✦ **Synonyms** HOSTILITY, ANTIPATHY, ANIMOSITY, RANCOR, ANTAGONISM

en·no·ble \i-'nō-bəl\ *vb* **-bled; -bling** : EXALT, ELEVATE; *esp* : to raise to noble rank — **en·no·ble·ment** *n*

en·nui \ˌän-'wē\ *n* [F] : BOREDOM

enor·mi·ty \i-'nȯr-mə-tē\ *n, pl* **-ties 1** : an outrageous, vicious, or immoral act **2** : great wickedness **3** : IMMENSITY

enor·mous \i-'nȯr-məs\ *adj* [L *enormis*, fr. *e, ex* out of + *norma* rule] **1** : exceedingly wicked **2** : great in size, number, or degree : HUGE ✦ **Synonyms** IMMENSE, VAST, GIGANTIC, COLOSSAL, MAMMOTH, ELEPHANTINE — **enor·mous·ly** *adv*

¹**enough** \i-'nəf\ *adj* : SUFFICIENT

²**enough** *adv* **1** : SUFFICIENTLY **2** : FULLY, QUITE **3** : TOLERABLY

³**enough** *pron* : a sufficient number, quantity, or amount

en·quire \in-'kwī-(ə)r\, **en·qui·ry** \'in-ˌkwī-(ə)r-ē, in-'; 'in-kwə-rē, 'in-\ *chiefly Brit var of* INQUIRE, INQUIRY

en·rage \in-'rāj\ *vb* : to fill with rage

en·rap·ture \in-'rap-chər\ *vb* **en·rap·tured; en·rap·tur·ing** : DELIGHT

en·rich \in-'rich\ *vb* **1** : to make rich or richer **2** : ORNAMENT, ADORN — **en·rich·ment** *n*

en·roll *also* **en·rol** \in-'rōl\ *vb* **en·rolled; en·roll·ing 1** : to enter or register on a roll or list **2** : to offer (oneself) for enrolling — **en·roll·ment** *n*

en route \än-'rüt, en-\ *adv* or *adj* : on or along the way ⟨while *en route* to work⟩

ENS *abbr* ensign

en·sconce \in-'skäns\ *vb* **en·sconced; en·sconc·ing 1** : SHELTER, CONCEAL **2** : to settle snugly or securely ✦ **Synonyms** SECRETE, HIDE, CACHE, STASH

en·sem·ble \än-'säm-bəl\ *n* [F, *ensemble* together, fr. L *insimul* at the same time] : a group (as of singers, dancers, or players) or a set (as of clothes) producing a single effect

en·sheathe \in-'shēth\ *vb* : to cover with or as if with a sheath

en·shrine \in-'shrīn\ *vb* **1** : to enclose in or as if in a shrine **2** : to cherish as sacred — **en·shrine·ment** \-mənt\ *n*

en·shroud \in-'shraùd\ *vb* : SHROUD, OBSCURE

en·sign \'en-sən, *1 also* 'en-ˌsīn\ *n* **1** : FLAG; *also* : BADGE, EMBLEM **2** : a commissioned officer in the navy ranking next below a lieutenant junior grade

en·slave \in-'slāv\ *vb* : to make a slave of — **en·slave·ment** *n*

en·snare \in-'sner\ *vb* : SNARE, TRAP ✦ *Synonyms* ENTRAP, BAG, CATCH, CAPTURE

en·sue \in-'sü\ *vb* **en·sued; en·su·ing** : to follow in time or as a result ⟨the birds escaped and chaos *ensued*⟩

en·sure \in-'shùr\ *vb* **en·sured; en·sur·ing** : INSURE, GUARANTEE

en·tail \in-'tāl\ *vb* **1** : to limit the inheritance of (property) to the owner's lineal descendants or to a class thereof **2** : to include or involve as a necessary step or result ⟨the sacrifices that parenting ∼*s*⟩ — **en·tail·ment** *n*

en·tan·gle \in-'taŋ-gəl\ *vb* : TANGLE, CONFUSE — **en·tan·gle·ment** *n*

en·tente \än-'tänt\ *n* [F] : an understanding providing for joint action; *also* : parties linked by such an entente

en·ter \'en-tər\ *vb* **1** : to go or come in or into **2** : to become a member of : JOIN ⟨∼ the ministry⟩ **3** : BEGIN **4** : to take part in : CONTRIBUTE **5** : to go into or upon and take possession **6** : to set down (as in a list) : REGISTER ⟨∼ the data⟩ **7** : to place (a complaint) before a court; *also* : to put on record ⟨∼ a complaint⟩

en·ter·i·tis \ˌen-tə-'rī-təs\ *n* : intestinal inflammation; *also* : a disease marked by this

en·ter·prise \'en-tər-ˌprīz\ *n* **1** : UNDERTAKING, PROJECT **2** : readiness for daring action : INITIATIVE **3** : a business organization

en·ter·pris·ing \-ˌprī-ziŋ\ *adj* : bold and vigorous in action : ENERGETIC

en·ter·tain \ˌen-tər-'tān\ *vb* **1** : to treat or receive as a guest **2** : AMUSE, DIVERT ⟨∼*ed* us with jokes⟩ **3** : to hold in mind ⟨∼*ed* thoughts of retirement⟩ ✦ *Synonyms* HARBOR, SHELTER, LODGE, HOUSE, BILLET — **en·ter·tain·er** *n* — **en·ter·tain·ment** *n*

en·thrall *or* **en·thral** \in-'thròl\ *vb* **en·thralled; en·thrall·ing 1** : ENSLAVE **2** : to hold spellbound

en·throne \in-'thrōn\ *vb* **1** : to seat on or as if on a throne **2** : EXALT

en·thuse \in-'thüz, -'thyüz\ *vb* **en·thused; en·thus·ing 1** : to make enthusiastic **2** : to show enthusiasm

en·thu·si·asm \in-'thü-zē-ˌa-zəm, -'thyü-\ *n* [Gk *enthousiasmos,* fr. *enthousiazein* to be inspired, irreg. fr. *entheos* inspired, fr. *theos* god] **1** : strong warmth of feeling : keen interest : FERVOR **2** : a cause of fervor — **en·thu·si·ast** \-ˌast, -əst\ *n* — **en·thu·si·as·tic** \in-ˌthü-zē-'as-tik, -ˌthyü-\ *adj* — **en·thu·si·as·ti·cal·ly** \-ti-k(ə-)lē\ *adv*

en·tice \in-'tīs\ *vb* **en·ticed; en·tic·ing** : ALLURE, TEMPT — **en·tice·ment** *n*

en·tire \in-'tī(-ə)r\ *adj* : COMPLETE, WHOLE ✦ *Synonyms* SOUND, PERFECT, INTACT, UNDAMAGED — **en·tire·ly** *adv*

en·tire·ty \in-'tī-rə-tē, -'tī(-ə)r-tē\ *n, pl* **-ties 1** : COMPLETENESS **2** : WHOLE, TOTALITY

en·ti·tle \in-'tī-t°l\ *vb* **en·ti·tled; en·ti·tling 1** : NAME, DESIGNATE **2** : to give a right or claim to ⟨*entitled* to a fair trial⟩

en·ti·tle·ment \in-'tī-t°l-mənt\ *n* : a government program providing benefits to members of a specified group

en·ti·ty \'en-tə-tē\ *n, pl* **-ties 1** : EXISTENCE, BEING **2** : something with separate and real existence

en·tomb \in-'tüm\ *vb* : to place in a tomb : BURY — **en·tomb·ment** *n*

en·to·mol·o·gy \ˌen-tə-'mä-lə-jē\ *n* : a branch of zoology that deals with insects — **en·to·mo·log·i·cal** \-mə-'lä-ji-kəl\ *adj* — **en·to·mol·o·gist** \-jist\ *n*

en·tou·rage \ˌän-tù-'räzh\ *n* [F] : RETINUE

en·tr'acte \'äⁿ-ˌtrakt\ *n* [F] **1** : something (as a dance) performed between two acts of a play **2** : the interval between two acts of a play

en·trails \'en-ˌtrālz\ *n pl* : VISCERA; *esp* : INTESTINES

¹en·trance \'en-trəns\ *n* **1** : permission or right to enter **2** : the act of entering **3** : a means or place of entry

²en·trance \in-'trans\ *vb* **en·tranced; en·tranc·ing** : CHARM, DELIGHT

en·trant \'en-trənt\ *n* : one that enters esp. as a competitor

en·trap \in-'trap\ *vb* : ENSNARE, TRAP — **en·trap·ment** *n*

en·treat \in-'trēt\ *vb* **1** : to ask urgently : BESEECH ✦ *Synonyms* BEG, IMPLORE, PLEAD, SUPPLICATE — **en·treaty** \-'trē-tē\ *n*

en·trée *or* **en·tree** \'än-ˌtrā\ *n* [F *entrée*] **1** : freedom of entry or access **2** : the main course of a meal in the U.S. ✦ *Synonyms* ADMISSION, ADMITTANCE, ENTRANCE

en·trench \in-'trench\ *vb* **1** : to place within or surround with a trench esp. for defense; *also* : to establish solidly ⟨∼*ed* customs⟩ **2** : ENCROACH, TRESPASS — **en·trench·ment** *n*

en·tre·pre·neur \ˌän-trə-prə-'nər, -'nùr, -'nyùr\ *n* [F, fr. OF, fr. *entreprendre* to undertake] : one who organizes and assumes the risk of a business or enterprise — **en·tre·pre·neur·ial** \-'nùr-ē-əl, -'nyùr-, -'nər-\ *adj* — **en·tre·pre·neur·ship** \-ˌship\ *n*

en·tro·py \'en-trə-pē\ *n, pl* **-pies 1** : the degree of disorder in a system **2** : an ultimate state of inert uniformity

en·trust \in-'trəst\ *vb* **1** : to commit something to as a trust **2** : to commit to another with confidence ✦ *Synonyms* CONFIDE, CONSIGN, RELEGATE, COMMEND

en·try \'en-trē\ *n, pl* **entries 1** : ENTRANCE **2** : ENTRANCE 3; *also* : VESTIBULE 1 **3** : an entering in a record; *also* : an item so entered **4** : a headword with its definition or identification; *also* : VOCABULARY ENTRY **5** : one entered in something (as a contest or market)

en·twine \in-'twīn\ *vb* : to twine together or around

enu·mer·ate \i-'nü-mə-ˌrāt, -'nyü-\ *vb* **-at·ed; -at·ing 1** : to determine the number of : COUNT **2** : LIST — **enu·mer·a·tion** \-ˌnü-mə-'rā-shən, -ˌnyü-\ *n*

enun·ci·ate \ē-'nən-sē-ˌāt\ *vb* **-at·ed; -at·ing 1** : to state definitely; *also* : ANNOUNCE, PROCLAIM **2** : PRONOUNCE, ARTICULATE ⟨∼ every syllable⟩ — **enun·ci·a·tion** \-ˌnən-sē-'ā-shən\ *n*

en·ure·sis \ˌen-yù-'rē-səs\ *n* : involuntary discharge of urine : BED-WETTING

env *abbr* envelope

en·vel·op \in-'ve-ləp\ *vb* **1** : to enclose completely with or as if with a covering — **en·vel·op·ment** *n*

en·ve·lope \'en-və-ˌlōp, 'än-\ *n* **1** : a usu. paper container for a letter **2** : WRAPPER, COVERING **3** : a conventionally accepted limit ⟨fashions that push the ∼⟩

en·ven·om \in-'ve-nəm\ *vb* **1** : to make poisonous **2** : EMBITTER

en·vi·able \'en-vē-ə-bəl\ *adj* : highly desirable — **en·vi·ably** \-blē\ *adv*

en·vi·ous \'en-vē-əs\ *adj* : feeling or showing envy — **en·vi·ous·ly** *adv* — **en·vi·ous·ness** *n*

en·vi·ron·ment \in-'vī-rən-mənt, -'vī(-ə)rn-\ *n* **1** : SURROUNDINGS **2** : the whole complex of factors (as soil, climate, and living things) that influence the form and the ability to survive of a plant or animal or ecological community — **en·vi·ron·men·tal** \-ˌvī-rən-'men-t°l, -ˌvīrn-\ *adj* — **en·vi·ron·men·tal·ly** \-t°l-ē\ *adv*

en·vi·ron·men·tal·ist \-ˌvī-rən-'men-təl-ist, -ˌvīrn-(ə)n-\ *n* : a person concerned with environmental quality esp. with respect to control of pollution — **en·vi·ron·men·tal·ism** \-ˌvī-rən-'men-tə-ˌli-zəm, -ˌvī(-ə)rn-\ *n*

en·vi·rons \in-'vī-rənz\ *n pl* **1** : SUBURBS **2** : SURROUNDINGS; *also* : VICINITY

en·vis·age \in-'vi-zij\ *vb* **-aged; -ag·ing** : to have a mental picture of

en·vi·sion \in-'vi-zhən, en-\ *vb* : to picture to oneself ⟨∼*s* world peace⟩

en·voy \'en-ˌvói, 'än-\ *n* **1** : a diplomatic agent **2** : REPRESENTATIVE, MESSENGER

¹en·vy \'en-vē\ *n, pl* **envies** [ME *envie,* fr. AF, fr. L *invidia,* fr. *invidus* envious, fr. *invidēre* to look askance at, envy, fr. *vidēre* to see] : painful or resentful awareness of another's advantages; *also* : an object of envy

²envy *vb* **en·vied; en·vy·ing** : to feel envy toward or on account of

en·zyme \'en-ˌzīm\ *n* : any of various complex proteins produced by living cells that catalyze specific biochemical reactions at body temperatures — **en·zy·mat·ic** \,en-zə-'ma-tik\ *adj*

Eo·cene \'ē-ə-,sēn\ *adj* : of, relating to, or being the epoch of the Tertiary between the Paleocene and the Oligocene — **Eocene** *n*

EOE *abbr* equal opportunity employer

eo·lian \ē-'ō-lē-ən\ *adj* : borne, deposited, or produced by the wind

EOM *abbr* end of month

eon *var of* AEON

EP *abbr* European plan

Eph *or* **Ephes** *abbr* Ephesians

EPA *abbr* Environmental Protection Agency

ep·au·let *also* **ep·au·lette** \,e-pə-'let\ *n* [F *épaulette*, dim. of *épaule* shoulder] : a shoulder ornament esp. on a coat or military uniform

épée \'e-,pā, ā-'pā\ *n* [F] : a fencing or dueling sword

ephed·rine \i-'fe-drən\ *n* : a stimulant drug used to treat asthma and nasal congestion

ephem·era \i-'fe-mər-ə\ *n pl* : paper items (as posters or tickets) of little original value collected usu. as a hobby

ephem·er·al \i-'fe-mə-rəl\ *adj* [Gk *ephēmeros* lasting a day, daily, fr. *epi-* on + *hēmera* day] : SHORT-LIVED, TRANSITORY ✦ *Synonyms* PASSING, FLEETING, TRANSIENT, EVANESCENT — **ephem·er·al·i·ty** \i-,fe-mə-'ra-lə-tē\ *n*

Ephe·sians \i-'fē-zhənz\ *n* — see BIBLE table

ep·ic \'e-pik\ *n* : a long poem in elevated style narrating the deeds of a hero — **epic** *adj*

epi·cen·ter \'e-pi-,sen-tər\ *n* : the point on the earth's surface directly above the point of origin of an earthquake

ep·i·cure \'e-pi-,kyùr\ *n* : a person with sensitive and discriminating tastes esp. in food and wine

ep·i·cu·re·an \,e-pi-kyù-'rē-ən, -'kyùr-ē-\ *n* : EPICURE — **epicurean** *adj*

¹**ep·i·dem·ic** \,e-pə-'de-mik\ *adj* : affecting many persons at one time ⟨~ disease⟩; *also* : excessively prevalent

²**epidemic** *n* : an epidemic outbreak esp. of disease

ep·i·de·mi·ol·o·gy \,ep-ə-,dē-mē-'ä-lə-jē\ *n* : the study of the incidence, distribution, and control of disease in a population — **ep·i·de·mi·o·log·i·cal** \-,dē-mē-ə-'lä-ji-kəl\ *also* **ep·i·de·mi·o·log·ic** \-jik\ — **ep·i·de·mi·ol·o·gist** \-'ä-lə-jist\ *n*

epi·der·mis \,e-pə-'dər-məs\ *n* : an outer layer esp. of skin — **epi·der·mal** \-məl\ *adj*

epi·du·ral \,e-pi-'d(y)ùr-əl\ *adj* : administered into the space outside the membrane that envelops the spinal cord ⟨~ anesthesia⟩ — **epidural** *n*

epi·glot·tis \,e-pə-'glä-təs\ *n* : a thin plate of flexible tissue protecting the tracheal opening during swallowing

ep·i·gram \'e-pə-,gram\ *n* : a short witty poem or saying — **ep·i·gram·mat·ic** \,e-pə-grə-'ma-tik\ *adj*

ep·i·lep·sy \'e-pə-,lep-sē\ *n, pl* -**sies** [ultim. fr. Gk *epilēpsia*, fr. *epilambanein* to seize] : a disorder marked by abnormal electrical discharges in the brain and typically manifested by sudden periods of diminished consciousness or by convulsions — **ep·i·lep·tic** \,e-pə-'lep-tik\ *adj or n*

ep·i·logue *also* **ep·i·log** \'e-pə-,lóg, -,läg\ *n* 1 : a concluding section of a literary work 2 : a speech addressed to the spectators by an actor at the end of a play

epi·neph·rine \,e-pə-'ne-frən\ *n* : an adrenal hormone used medicinally esp. as a heart stimulant, a muscle relaxant, and a vasoconstrictor

epiph·a·ny \i-'pi-fə-nē\ *n, pl* -**nies** 1 *cap* : January 6 observed as a church festival in commemoration of the coming of the Magi to Jesus at Bethlehem 2 : a sudden striking understanding of something

epis·co·pa·cy \i-'pis-kə-pə-sē\ *n, pl* -**cies** 1 : government of a church by bishops 2 : EPISCOPATE

epis·co·pal \i-'pis-kə-pəl\ *adj* 1 : of or relating to a bishop or episcopacy 2 *cap* : of or relating to the Protestant Episcopal Church

Epis·co·pa·lian \i-,pis-kə-'pāl-yən\ *n* : a member of the Protestant Episcopal Church

epis·co·pate \i-'pis-kə-pət, -,pāt\ *n* 1 : the rank, office, or term of a bishop 2 : a body of bishops

ep·i·sode \'e-pə-,sōd\ *n* [Gk *epeisodion*, fr. *epeisodios* coming in besides, fr. *eisodios* coming in, fr. *eis* into + *hodos* road, journey] 1 : a unit of action in a dramatic or literary work 2 : an incident in a course of events

: OCCURRENCE ⟨a feverish ~⟩ — **ep·i·sod·ic** \,e-pə-'sä-dik\ *adj*

epis·tle \i-'pi-səl\ *n* 1 *cap* : one of the letters of the New Testament 2 : LETTER — **epis·to·lary** \i-'pis-tə-,ler-ē\ *adj*

ep·i·taph \'e-pə-,taf\ *n* : an inscription in memory of a dead person

ep·i·tha·la·mi·um \,e-pə-thə-'lā-mē-əm\ *or* **ep·i·tha·la·mi·on** \-mē-ən\ *n, pl* -**mi·ums** *or* -**mia** \-mē-ə\ : a song or poem in honor of a bride and bridegroom

ep·i·the·li·um \,e-pə-'thē-lē-əm\ *n, pl* -**lia** \-lē-ə\ : a cellular membrane covering a bodily surface or lining a cavity — **ep·i·the·li·al** \-lē-əl\ *adj*

ep·i·thet \'e-pə-,thet, -thət\ *n* : a characterizing and often abusive word or phrase ⟨a racial ~⟩

epit·o·me \i-'pi-tə-mē\ *n* 1 : ABSTRACT, SUMMARY 2 : EMBODIMENT ⟨the ~ of elegance⟩ — **epit·o·mize** \-,mīz\ *vb*

ep·och \'e-pək, -,päk\ *n* : a usu. extended period : ERA, AGE — **ep·och·al** \-pə-kəl, -,pä-\ *adj*

ep·onym \'e-pə-,nim\ *n* 1 : one for whom something is or is believed to be named 2 : a name (as of a disease) based on or derived from an eponym — **epon·y·mous** \i-'pä-nə-məs\ *adj*

ep·oxy \i-'päk-sē\ *vb* **ep·ox·ied** *or* **ep·oxyed**; **ep·oxy·ing** : to glue, fill, or coat with epoxy resin

epoxy resin *n* : a synthetic resin used in coatings and adhesives

ep·si·lon \'ep-sə-län, -lən\ *n* : the 5th letter of the Greek alphabet — E or ε

Ep·som salts \'ep-səm-\ *n* : a bitter colorless or white magnesium salt with cathartic properties

eq *abbr* 1 equal 2 equation

equa·ble \'e-kwə-bəl, 'ē-\ *adj* : UNIFORM, EVEN; *esp* : free from unpleasant extremes — **eq·ua·bil·i·ty** \,e-kwə-'bi-lə-tē, ,ē-\ *n* — **equa·bly** \'e-kwə-blē, 'ē-\ *adv*

¹**equal** \'ē-kwəl\ *adj* 1 : of the same measure, quantity, value, quality, number, degree, or status as another ⟨~ opportunity⟩ 2 : IMPARTIAL ⟨~ justice⟩ 3 : free from extremes 4 : able to cope with a situation or task — **equal·i·ty** \i-'kwä-lə-tē\ *n* — **equal·ly** *adv*

²**equal** *vb* **equaled** *or* **equalled**; **equal·ing** *or* **equal·ling** : to be or become equal to; *also* : to be identical in value to

³**equal** *n* : one that is equal

equal·ise, equal·is·er *Brit var of* EQUALIZE, EQUALIZER

equal·ize \'ē-kwə-,līz\ *vb* -**ized**; -**iz·ing** : to make equal, uniform, or constant — **equal·i·za·tion** \,ē-kwə-lə-'zā-shən\ *n* — **equal·iz·er** *n*

equals sign *or* **equal sign** *n* : a sign = indicating equivalence

equa·nim·i·ty \,ē-kwə-'ni-mə-tē, ,e-\ *n, pl* -**ties** : COMPOSURE

equate \i-'kwāt\ *vb* **equat·ed**; **equat·ing** : to make, treat, or regard as equal or comparable ⟨~s liars with thieves⟩

equa·tion \i-'kwā-zhən\ *n* 1 : an act of equating : the state of being equated 2 : a usu. formal statement of equivalence esp. of mathematical expressions

equa·tor \i-'kwā-tər, 'ē-\ *n* : an imaginary circle around the earth that is everywhere equally distant from the two poles — **equa·to·ri·al** \,ē-kwə-'tór-ē-əl, ,e-\ *adj*

equer·ry \'e-kwə-rē, i-'kwer-ē\ *n, pl* -**ries** 1 : an officer in charge of the horses of a prince or noble 2 : a personal attendant of a member of the British royal family

¹**eques·tri·an** \i-'kwes-trē-ən\ *adj* : of or relating to horseback riding ⟨~ competition⟩; *also* : representing a person on horseback ⟨an ~ statue⟩

²**equestrian** *n* : one who rides a horse

eques·tri·enne \i-,kwes-trē-'en\ *n* : a female rider on horseback

equi·dis·tant \,ē-kwə-'dis-tənt\ *adj* : equally distant

equi·lat·er·al \,ē-kwə-'la-tə-rəl\ *adj* : having all sides or faces equal ⟨~ triangles⟩

equi·lib·ri·um \,ē-kwə-'li-brē-əm, ,e-\ *n, pl* -**ri·ums** *or* -**ria** \-brē-ə\ : a state of intellectual or emotional balance; *also* : a state of balance between opposing forces or actions ✦ *Synonyms* POISE, BALANCE, EQUIPOISE

equine \'ē-,kwīn, 'e-\ *adj* [L *equinus*, fr. *equus* horse] : of or relating to the horse — **equine** *n*

equi·noc·tial \,ē-kwə-'näk-shəl, ,e-\ *adj* : relating to an equinox

equi·nox \'ē-kwə-,näks, 'e-\ *n* : either of the two times each year when the sun appears directly overhead at the equator and day and night are everywhere on earth of equal length

equip \i-'kwip\ *vb* **equipped; equip·ping** [AF *eskiper* to load on board a ship, outfit, man, of Gmc origin] **1** : to supply with needed resources **2** : to make ready : PREPARE ⟨*equipped* for the challenge⟩

eq·ui·page \'e-kwə-pij\ *n* : a horse-drawn carriage usu. with its servants

equip·ment \i-'kwip-mənt\ *n* **1** : things used in equipping : SUPPLIES, OUTFIT **2** : the equipping of a person or thing : the state of being equipped

equi·poise \'e-kwə-ˌpòiz, 'ē-\ *n* **1** : BALANCE, EQUILIBRIUM **2** : COUNTERBALANCE

eq·ui·ta·ble \'e-kwə-tə-bəl\ *adj* : JUST, FAIR — **eq·ui·ta·bly** \-blē\ *adv*

eq·ui·ta·tion \ˌe-kwə-'tā-shən\ *n* : the act or art of riding on horseback

eq·ui·ty \'e-kwə-tē\ *n, pl* **-ties** **1** : JUSTNESS, IMPARTIALITY **2** : value of a property or of an interest in it in excess of claims against it

equiv *abbr* equivalent

equiv·a·lent \i-'kwi-və-lənt\ *adj* : EQUAL; *also* : virtually identical — **equiv·a·lence** \-ləns\ *n* — **equivalent** *n*

equiv·o·cal \i-'kwi-və-kəl\ *adj* **1** : AMBIGUOUS ⟨∼ answers⟩ **2** : UNCERTAIN, UNDECIDED **3** : SUSPICIOUS, DUBIOUS ⟨∼ behavior⟩ ✦ **Synonyms** OBSCURE, DARK, VAGUE, ENIGMATIC — **equiv·o·cal·ly** *adv*

equiv·o·cate \i-'kwi-və-ˌkāt\ *vb* **-cat·ed; -cat·ing** **1** : to use misleading language **2** : to avoid giving a definite answer — **equiv·o·ca·tion** \-ˌkwi-və-'kā-shən\ *n*

¹-er \ər\ *adj suffix or adv suffix* — used to form the comparative degree of adjectives and adverbs of one or two syllables ⟨hott*er*⟩ ⟨dri*er*⟩ ⟨silli*er*⟩ and sometimes of longer ones

²-er \ər\ *also* **-ier** \ē-ər, yər\ *or* **-yer** \yər\ *n suffix* **1** : a person occupationally connected with ⟨furri*er*⟩ ⟨lawy*er*⟩ **2** : a person or thing belonging to or associated with ⟨old-tim*er*⟩ **3** : a native of : resident of ⟨island*er*⟩ **4** : one that has ⟨double-deck*er*⟩ **5** : one that produces or yields ⟨pork*er*⟩ **6** : one that does or performs (a specified action) ⟨batt*er*⟩ **7** : one that is a suitable object of (a specified action) ⟨broil*er*⟩ **8** : one that is ⟨foreign*er*⟩

Er *symbol* erbium

ER *abbr* emergency room

era \'er-ə, 'e-rə, 'ir-ə\ *n* [LL *aera*, fr. L, counters, pl. of *aes* copper, money] **1** : a chronological order or system of notation reckoned from a given date as basis **2** : a period identified by some special feature ⟨the ∼ of industrialization⟩ **3** : any of the four major divisions of geologic time ✦ **Synonyms** AGE, EPOCH, PERIOD, TIME

ERA *abbr* **1** earned run average **2** Equal Rights Amendment

erad·i·cate \i-'ra-də-ˌkāt\ *vb* **-cat·ed; -cat·ing** [L *eradicatus*, pp. of *eradicare*, fr. *e-* out + *radix* root] : UPROOT, ELIMINATE ✦ **Synonyms** EXTERMINATE, ANNIHILATE, ABOLISH, EXTINGUISH — **erad·i·ca·ble** \-di-kə-bəl\ *adj* — **erad·i·ca·tion** \-ˌra-də-'kā-shən\ *n*

erase \i-'rās\ *vb* **erased; eras·ing** : to rub or scratch out (as written words); *also* : OBLITERATE ✦ **Synonyms** CANCEL, EFFACE, DELETE, EXPUNGE — **eras·er** *n* — **era·sure** \i-'rā-shər\ *n*

er·bi·um \'ər-bē-əm\ *n* : a rare metallic element found with yttrium

¹ere \'er\ *prep* : BEFORE

²ere *conj* : BEFORE

e-read·er \'ē-ˌrē-dər\ *n* : a handheld electronic device used esp. for reading e-books

¹erect \i-'rekt\ *adj* **1** : not leaning or lying down : UPRIGHT **2** : being in a state of physiological erection

²erect *vb* **1** : BUILD **2** : to fix or set in an upright position ⟨∼ an antenna⟩ **3** : SET UP; *also* : ESTABLISH, DEVELOP

erec·tile \i-'rek-t°l, -'rek-ˌtī(-ə)l\ *adj* : capable of becoming erect ⟨∼ tissue⟩ ⟨∼ feathers of a bird⟩

erec·tion \i-'rek-shən\ *n* **1** : the turgid state of a previously flaccid bodily part when it becomes dilated with blood **2** : CONSTRUCTION ⟨the ∼ of a building⟩

ere·long \er-'lòŋ\ *adv* : before long

er·e·mite \'er-ə-ˌmīt\ *n* : HERMIT

er·go \'er-gō, 'ər-\ *adv* [L] : THEREFORE

er·go·nom·ics \ˌər-gə-'nä-miks\ *n sing or pl* : an applied science concerned with designing and arranging things

people use in order to improve efficiency and safety — **er·go·nom·ic** \-mik\ *adj*

er·got \'ər-gət, -ˌgät\ *n* **1** : a disease of rye and other cereals caused by a fungus; *also* : this fungus **2** : a medicinal compound or preparation derived from an ergot fungus

er·mine \'ər-mən\ *n, pl* **ermines** **1** : any of several weasels with winter fur mostly white; *also* : this white fur **2** : a rank or office whose official robe is ornamented with ermine

ermine 1

erode \i-'rōd\ *vb* **erod·ed; erod·ing** : to diminish or destroy by degrees; *esp* : to gradually eat into or wear away ⟨soil *eroded* by wind and water⟩ — **erod·ible** \-'rō-də-bəl\ *adj*

erog·e·nous \i-'rä-jə-nəs\ *adj* **1** : sexually sensitive ⟨∼ zones⟩ **2** : of, relating to, or arousing sexual feelings

ero·sion \i-'rō-zhən\ *n* : the process or state of being eroded — **ero·sion·al** \-'rō-zhə-nəl\ *adj* — **ero·sion·al·ly** *adv*

ero·sive \i-'rō-siv\ *adj* : tending to erode — **ero·sive·ness** *n*

erot·ic \i-'rä-tik\ *adj* : relating to or dealing with sexual love : AMATORY ⟨∼ art⟩ — **erot·i·cal·ly** \-ti-k(ə-)lē\ *adv* — **erot·i·cism** \-tə-ˌsi-zəm\ *n*

err \'er, 'ər\ *vb* : to be or do wrong

er·rand \'er-ənd\ *n* : a short trip taken to do something; *also* : the object or purpose of such a trip

er·rant \'er-ənt\ *adj* **1** : WANDERING ⟨an ∼ knight⟩ **2** : straying outside proper bounds ⟨an ∼ throw⟩ **3** : behaving wrongly ⟨an ∼ child⟩

er·ra·ta \e-'rä-tə\ *n* : a list of corrigenda

er·rat·ic \i-'ra-tik\ *adj* **1** : having no fixed course **2** : INCONSISTENT ⟨∼ dieting⟩; *also* : ECCENTRIC ⟨∼ behavior⟩ — **er·rat·i·cal·ly** \-ti-k(ə-)lē\ *adv*

er·ra·tum \e-'rä-təm\ *n, pl* **-ta** \-tə\ : CORRIGENDUM

er·ro·ne·ous \i-'rō-nē-əs, e-'rō-\ *adj* : INCORRECT — **er·ro·ne·ous·ly** *adv*

er·ror \'er-ər\ *n* **1** : a usu. ignorant or unintentional deviating from accuracy or truth ⟨made an ∼ in adding⟩ **2** : a defensive misplay in baseball **3** : the state of one that errs ⟨to be in ∼⟩ **4** : a product of mistake ⟨a typographical ∼⟩ — **er·ror·less** *adj*

er·satz \'er-ˌzäts\ *adj* [G *ersatz-*, fr. *Ersatz*, n., substitute] : being usu. an artificial and inferior substitute ⟨∼ diamonds⟩

erst \'ərst\ *adv, archaic* : ERSTWHILE

¹erst·while \-ˌhwī(-ə)l\ *adv* : in the past : FORMERLY

²erstwhile *adj* : FORMER, PREVIOUS ⟨∼ friends⟩

er·u·di·tion \ˌer-ə-'di-shən, ˌer-yə-\ *n* : SCHOLARSHIP, LEARNING — **er·u·dite** \'er-ə-ˌdīt, 'er-yə-\ *adj*

erupt \i-'rəpt\ *vb* **1** : to burst forth or cause to burst forth : EXPLODE **2** : to break through a surface ⟨teeth ∼*ing* through the gum⟩ **3** : to break out with or as if with a skin rash — **erup·tion** \-'rəp-shən\ *n* — **erup·tive** \-tiv\ *adj*

-ery *n suffix* **1** : qualities collectively : character : -NESS ⟨snobb*ery*⟩ **2** : art : practice ⟨cook*ery*⟩ **3** : place of doing, keeping, producing, or selling (the thing specified) ⟨fish*ery*⟩ ⟨bak*ery*⟩ **4** : collection : aggregate ⟨fin*ery*⟩ **5** : state or condition ⟨slav*ery*⟩

ery·sip·e·las \ˌer-ə-'si-pə-ləs, ˌir-\ *n* : an acute bacterial disease marked by fever and severe skin inflammation

er·y·the·ma \ˌer-ə-'thē-mə\ *n* : abnormal redness of the skin due to capillary congestion (as in inflammation)

eryth·ro·cyte \i-'ri-thrə-ˌsīt\ *n* : RED BLOOD CELL

Es *symbol* einsteinium

¹-es \əz, iz *after* s, z, sh, ch; z *after* v *or a vowel*\ *n pl* suf-

fix — used to form the plural of most nouns that end in *s* ⟨glass*es*⟩, *z* ⟨fuzz*es*⟩, *sh* ⟨bush*es*⟩, *ch* ⟨peach*es*⟩, or a final *y* that changes to *i* ⟨lad*ies*⟩ and of some nouns ending in *f* that changes to *v* ⟨loa*ves*⟩

²-es *vb suffix* — used to form the third person singular present of most verbs that end in *s* ⟨bless*es*⟩, *z* ⟨fizz*es*⟩, *sh* ⟨hush*es*⟩, *ch* ⟨catch*es*⟩, or a final *y* that changes to *i* ⟨def*ies*⟩

es·ca·late \'es-kə-ˌlāt\ *vb* **-lat·ed; -lat·ing** : to increase in extent, volume, number, intensity, or scope ⟨the violence *escalated*⟩ — **es·ca·la·tion** \ˌes-kə-'lā-shən\ *n*

es·ca·la·tor \'es-kə-ˌlā-tər\ *n* : a moving set of stairs

escallop *var of* SCALLOP

es·ca·pade \'es-kə-ˌpād\ *n* [F, action of escaping] : a mischievous adventure

¹**es·cape** \is-'kāp\ *vb* **es·caped; es·cap·ing** [ME, fr. AF *escaper, eschaper,* fr. VL *excappare, fr. L ex-* out + LL *cappa* head covering, cloak] **1** : to get free or away **2** : to avoid a threatening evil **3** : AVOID 2 ⟨~ injury⟩ **4** : ELUDE ⟨his name ~s me⟩ **5** : to be produced or uttered involuntarily ⟨let a sob ~ him⟩

²**escape** *n* **1** : flight from or avoidance of something unpleasant **2** : LEAKAGE **3** : a means of escape

³**escape** *adj* : providing a means or way of escape

es·cap·ee \is-ˌkā-'pē, ˌes-(ˌ)kā-\ *n* : one that has escaped esp. from prison

escape velocity *n* : the minimum velocity needed by a body (as a rocket) to escape from the gravitational field of a celestial body (as the earth)

es·cap·ism \is-'kā-ˌpi-zəm\ *n* : diversion of the mind to imaginative activity as an escape from routine — **es·cap·ist** \-pist\ *adj or n*

es·car·got \ˌes-ˌkär-'gō\ *n, pl* **-gots** \-'gō(z)\ : a snail prepared for use as food

es·ca·role \'es-kə-ˌrōl\ *n* : ENDIVE 1

es·carp·ment \es-'kärp-mənt\ *n* **1** : a steep slope in front of a fortification **2** : a long cliff

es·chew \is-'chü\ *vb* : SHUN, AVOID

¹**es·cort** \'es-ˌkȯrt\ *n* : one (as a person or warship) accompanying another esp. as a protection or courtesy

²**es·cort** \is-'kȯrt, es-\ *vb* : to accompany as an escort

es·crow \'es-ˌkrō\ *n* [AF *escrowe* scroll, strip of parchment] : something (as a deed or a sum of money) delivered by one person to another to be delivered to a third party only upon the fulfillment of a condition; *also* : a fund or deposit serving as an escrow

es·cu·do \is-'kü-dō\ *n, pl* **-dos** **1** : the former basic monetary unit of Portugal **2** — see MONEY table

es·cutch·eon \is-'kə-chən\ *n* : the usu. shield-shaped surface on which a coat of arms is shown

Esd *abbr* Esdras

Es·dras \'ez-drəs\ *n* — see BIBLE table

ESE *abbr* east-southeast

Es·ki·mo \'es-kə-ˌmō\ *n* **1** *now sometimes offensive* : a member of a group of peoples of northern Canada, Greenland, Alaska, and eastern Siberia **2** : any of the languages of the Eskimo peoples

Eskimo dog *n* : a sled dog of American origin

ESL *abbr* English as a second language

esoph·a·gus \i-'sä-fə-gəs\ *n, pl* **-gi** \-ˌgī, -ˌjī\ : a muscular tube that leads from the cavity behind the mouth to the stomach — **esoph·a·geal** \-ˌsä-fə-'jē-əl\ *adj*

es·o·ter·ic \ˌe-sə-'ter-ik\ *adj* **1** : designed for or understood only by the specially initiated **2** : PRIVATE, SECRET

esp *abbr* especially

ESP \ˌē-(ˌ)es-'pē\ *n* : EXTRASENSORY PERCEPTION

es·pa·drille \'es-pə-ˌdril\ *n* [F] : a flat sandal usu. having a fabric upper and a flexible sole

es·pal·ier \is-'pal-yər, -ˌyā\ *n* : a plant (as a fruit tree) trained to grow flat against a support — **espalier** *vb*

es·pe·cial \is-'pe-shəl\ *adj* : SPECIAL, PARTICULAR — **es·pe·cial·ly** *adv*

Es·pe·ran·to \ˌes-pə-'ran-tō, -'rän-\ *n* : an artificial international language based esp. on words common to the chief European languages

es·pi·o·nage \'es-pē-ə-ˌnäzh, -nij\ *n* [F *espionnage*] : the practice of spying

es·pla·nade \'es-plə-ˌnäd\ *n* : a level open stretch or area; *esp* : one for walking or driving along a shore

es·pous·al \i-'spaú-zəl\ *n* **1** : BETROTHAL; *also* : WED-

DING **2** : a taking up (as of a cause) as a supporter ⟨~ of human rights⟩ — **es·pouse** \-'spaúz\ *vb*

espres·so \e-'spre-sō\ *n, pl* **-sos** : coffee brewed by forcing steam or hot water through finely ground darkly roasted coffee beans

es·prit \i-'sprē\ *n* : sprightly wit

es·prit de corps \i-ˌsprē-də-'kȯr\ *n* [F] : the common spirit existing in the members of a group

es·py \i-'spī\ *vb* **es·pied; es·py·ing** : to catch sight of
♦ **Synonyms** BEHOLD, SEE, VIEW, DESCRY

Esq *or* **Esqr** *abbr* esquire

es·quire \'es-ˌkwī(-ə)r\ *n* [ME, fr. AF *esquier* squire, fr. LL *scutarius,* fr. L *scutum* shield] **1** : a man of the English gentry ranking next below a knight **2** : a candidate for knighthood serving as attendant to a knight **3** — used as a title of courtesy

-ess \əs, ˌes\ *n suffix* : female ⟨author*ess*⟩

¹**es·say** \e-'sā, 'e-ˌsā\ *vb* : ATTEMPT, TRY

²**es·say** \'e-ˌsā\ *n* **1** ⟨e-'sā\ : ATTEMPT **2** \'e-ˌsā\ : a literary composition usu. dealing with a subject from a limited or personal point of view — **es·say·ist** \'e-ˌsā-ist\ *n*

es·sence \'e-sᵊns\ *n* **1** : fundamental nature or quality **2** : a substance distilled or extracted from another substance (as a plant or drug) and having the special qualities of the original substance **3** : PERFUME **4** : the most significant element or aspect of something ⟨the ~ of the issue⟩

¹**es·sen·tial** \i-'sen-chəl\ *adj* **1** : of, relating to, or constituting an essence ⟨voting is an ~ right of citizenship⟩ ⟨~ oils⟩ **2** : of the utmost importance : INDISPENSABLE ⟨water is ~ for life⟩ **3** : being a substance that must be obtained from the diet because it is not sufficiently produced by the body ⟨~ amino acids⟩ ♦ **Synonyms** IMPERATIVE, NECESSARY, NECESSITOUS — **es·sen·tial·ly** *adv*

²**essential** *n* : something essential

est *abbr* **1** established **2** estimate; estimated

EST *abbr* eastern standard time

¹**-est** \əst, ist\ *adj suffix or adv suffix* — used to form the superlative degree of adjectives and adverbs of one or two syllables ⟨fatt*est*⟩ ⟨lat*est*⟩ ⟨lucki*est*⟩ ⟨often*est*⟩ and less often of longer ones

²**-est** \əst, ist\ *or* **-st** \st\ *vb suffix* — used to form the archaic second person singular of English verbs (with *thou*) ⟨did*st*⟩

es·tab·lish \i-'sta-blish\ *vb* **1** : to institute permanently ⟨~ a law⟩ **2** : FOUND ⟨~ a settlement⟩; *also* : EFFECT **3** : to make firm or stable **4** : to put on a firm basis : SET UP ⟨~ a son in business⟩ **5** : to gain acceptance or recognition of ⟨the movie ~ed her as a star⟩; *also* : PROVE ⟨~ed his innocence⟩

es·tab·lish·ment \-mənt\ *n* **1** : something established **2** : a place of residence or business with its furnishings and staff **3** : an established ruling or controlling group ⟨the literary ~⟩ **4** : the act or state of establishing or being established

es·tate \i-'stāt\ *n* **1** : STATE, CONDITION; *also* : social standing : STATUS **2** : a social or political class ⟨the three ~s of nobility, clergy, and commons⟩ **3** : a person's possessions : FORTUNE **4** : a landed property

¹**es·teem** \i-'stēm\ *n* : high regard

²**esteem** *vb* **1** : REGARD ⟨was highly ~ed⟩ **2** : to set a high value on ♦ **Synonyms** RESPECT, ADMIRE, REVERE

es·ter \'es-tər\ *n* : an often fragrant organic compound formed by the reaction of an acid and an alcohol

Esth *abbr* Esther

Es·ther \'es-tər\ *n* — see BIBLE table

esthete, esthetic, esthetically, esthetics *var of* AESTHETE, AESTHETIC, AESTHETICALLY, AESTHETICS

es·ti·ma·ble \'es-tə-mə-bəl\ *adj* : worthy of esteem ⟨an ~ adversary⟩

¹**es·ti·mate** \'es-tə-ˌmāt\ *vb* **-mat·ed; -mat·ing** **1** : to give or form an approximation (as of value, size, or cost) **2** : JUDGE, CONCLUDE ♦ **Synonyms** EVALUATE, VALUE, RATE, APPRAISE, ASSAY, ASSESS — **es·ti·ma·tor** \-ˌmā-tər\ *n*

²**es·ti·mate** \'es-tə-mət\ *n* **1** : OPINION, JUDGMENT **2** : a rough or approximate calculation **3** : a statement of the cost of work to be done

es·ti·ma·tion \ˌes-tə-'mā-shən\ *n* **1** : JUDGMENT, OPINION **2** : ESTIMATE **3** : ESTEEM, HONOR es·ti·vate \'es-tə-ˌvāt\ vb -vat·ed; -vat·ing : to pass the summer in an inactive or resting state ⟨creatures *estivating* in the cool mud⟩ — es·ti·va·tion \ˌes-tə-'vā-shən\ n

es·trange \i-'strānj\ vb es·tranged; es·trang·ing : to alienate the affections or confidence of — es·trange·ment n

es·tro·gen \'es-trə-jən\ n : a steroid (as a sex hormone) that tends to cause estrus and the development of female secondary sex characteristics — es·tro·gen·ic \ˌes-trə-'je-nik\ adj

estrous cycle n : the cycle of changes in the endocrine and reproductive systems of a female mammal from the beginning of one period of estrus to the beginning of the next

es·trus \'es-trəs\ n : a periodic state of sexual excitability during which the female of most mammals is willing to mate with the male and is capable of becoming pregnant : HEAT — es·trous \-trəs\ adj

es·tu·ary \'es-chə-ˌwer-ē\ n, pl -ar·ies : an arm of the sea at the mouth of a river — es·tu·a·rine \-wə-ˌrīn, -ˌrēn, -rin\ adj

ET abbr eastern time

eta \'ā-tə\ n : the 7th letter of the Greek alphabet — H or η

ETA abbr estimated time of arrival

et al. \et-'al\ abbr [L et alii (masc.), et aliae (fem.), or et alia (neut.)] and others

etc. abbr et cetera

et cet·era \et-'se-tə-rə, -'se-trə\ [L] and others esp. of the same kind

etch \'ech\ vb [D etsen, fr. G ätzen to etch, corrode, fr. OHG azzen to feed] 1 : to produce (as a design) on a hard material by corroding its surface (as by acid) 2 : to delineate clearly — etch·er n

etch·ing n 1 : the action, process, or art of etching 2 : a design produced on or print made from an etched plate

ETD abbr estimated time of departure

eter·nal \i-'tər-nᵊl\ adj : EVERLASTING, PERPETUAL — eter·nal·ly adv

eter·ni·ty \i-'tər-nə-tē\ n, pl -ties 1 : infinite duration 2 : IMMORTALITY

¹-eth \əth, ith\ or -th \th\ vb suffix — used to form the archaic third person singular present of verbs ⟨doth⟩

²-eth — see ²-TH

eth·ane \'e-ˌthān\ n : a colorless odorless gaseous hydrocarbon found in natural gas and used esp. as a fuel

eth·a·nol \'e-thə-ˌnȯl\ n : ALCOHOL 1

ether \'ē-thər\ n 1 : the upper regions of space; also : the gaseous element formerly held to fill these regions 2 : a light flammable liquid used as an anesthetic and solvent

ethe·re·al \i-'thir-ē-əl\ adj 1 : CELESTIAL, HEAVENLY 2 : exceptionally delicate : AIRY, DAINTY ⟨∼ flaky pastry⟩ — ethe·re·al·ly adv — ethe·re·al·ness n

Ether·net \'ē-thər-ˌnet\ n : a computer network architecture for local area networks

eth·i·cal \'e-thi-kəl\ adj 1 : of or relating to ethics 2 : conforming to accepted and esp. professional standards of conduct ✦ Synonyms VIRTUOUS, MORAL, PRINCIPLED — eth·i·cal·ly adv

eth·ics \'e-thiks\ n sing or pl 1 : a discipline dealing with good and evil and with moral duty 2 : moral principles or practice

¹eth·nic \'eth-nik\ adj [ME, heathen, fr. LL ethnicus, fr. Gk ethnikos national, gentile, fr. ethnos nation, people] : of or relating to races or large groups of people classed according to common traits and customs — eth·ni·cal·ly adv

²ethnic n : a member of a minority ethnic group who retains its customs, language, or social views

eth·nol·o·gy \eth-'nä-lə-jē\ n : a science dealing with the races of human beings, their origin, distribution, characteristics, and relations — eth·no·log·i·cal \ˌeth-nə-'lä-ji-kəl\ adj — eth·nol·o·gist \eth-'nä-lə-jist\ n

ethol·o·gy \ē-'thä-lə-jē\ n : the scientific and objective study of animal behavior — etho·log·i·cal \ˌē-thə-'lä-ji-kəl, ˌe-\ adj — ethol·o·gist \ē-'thä-lə-jist\ n

ethos \'ē-ˌthäs\ n : the distinguishing character, sentiment, moral nature, or guiding beliefs of a person, group, or institution

ethyl alcohol n : ALCOHOL 1

eth·yl·ene \'e-thə-ˌlēn\ n : a colorless flammable gas found in coal gas or obtained from petroleum

eti·ol·o·gy \ˌē-tē-'ä-lə-jē\ n : the causes of a disease or abnormal condition; also : a branch of medicine concerned with the causes and origins of diseases — eti·o·log·ic \ˌē-tē-ə-'lä-jik\ or eti·o·log·i·cal \-ji-kəl\ adj

et·i·quette \'e-ti-kət, -ˌket\ n [F étiquette, lit., label, list] : the forms prescribed by custom or authority to be observed in social, official, or professional life ✦ Synonyms PROPRIETY, DECORUM, DECENCY, DIGNITY

Etrus·can \i-'trəs-kən\ n 1 : the language of the Etruscans 2 : an inhabitant of ancient Etruria — Etruscan adj

et seq abbr [L et sequens] and the following one; [L et sequentes (masc. & fem. pl.) or et sequentia (neut. pl.)] and the following ones

-ette \'et, ˌet, ət, it\ n suffix 1 : little one ⟨dinette⟩ 2 : female ⟨usherette⟩

étude \'ā-ˌtüd, -ˌtyüd\ n [F, lit., study] : a musical composition for practice to develop technical skill

et·y·mol·o·gy \ˌe-tə-'mä-lə-jē\ n, pl -gies 1 : the history of a linguistic form (as a word) shown by tracing its development and relationships 2 : a branch of linguistics dealing with etymologies — et·y·mo·log·i·cal \-mə-'lä-ji-kəl\ adj — et·y·mol·o·gist \-'mä-lə-jist\ n

Eu symbol europium

EU abbr European Union

eu·ca·lyp·tus \ˌyü-kə-'lip-təs\ n, pl -ti \-ˌtī\ or -tus·es : any of a genus of mostly Australian evergreen trees widely grown for shade or their wood, oils, resins, and gums

Eu·cha·rist \'yü-kə-rəst\ n : COMMUNION 2 — eu·cha·ris·tic \ˌyü-kə-'ris-tik\ adj, often cap

¹eu·chre \'yü-kər\ n : a card game in which the side naming the trump must take three of five tricks to win

²euchre vb eu·chred; eu·chring : CHEAT, TRICK

eu·clid·e·an or eu·clid·i·an \yü-'kli-dē-ən\ adj, often cap : of or relating to the geometry of Euclid or a geometry based on similar axioms

eu·gen·ics \yü-'je-niks\ n : a science dealing with the improvement (as by selective breeding) of hereditary qualities esp. of human beings — eu·gen·ic \-nik\ adj

eu·lo·gy \'yü-lə-jē\ n, pl -gies 1 : a speech in praise of some person or thing esp. in honor of a deceased person 2 : high praise — eu·lo·gis·tic \ˌyü-lə-'jis-tik\ adj — eu·lo·gize \'yü-lə-ˌjīz\ vb

eu·nuch \'yü-nək\ n : a castrated man

eu·phe·mism \'yü-fə-ˌmi-zəm\ n [Gk euphēmismos, fr. euphēmos auspicious, sounding good, fr. eu- good + phēmē speech] : the substitution of a mild or pleasant expression for one offensive or unpleasant; also : the expression substituted — eu·phe·mis·tic \ˌyü-fə-'mis-tik\ adj — eu·phe·mis·ti·cal·ly \-tī-k(ə-)lē\ adv

eu·pho·ni·ous \yü-'fō-nē-əs\ adj : pleasing to the ear — eu·pho·ni·ous·ly adv

eu·pho·ny \'yü-fə-nē\ n, pl -nies : the effect produced by words so combined as to please the ear

eu·pho·ria \yü-'fȯr-ē-ə\ n : a marked feeling of well-being or elation — eu·phor·ic \-'fȯr-ik\ adj

Eur abbr Europe; European

Eur·asian \yü-'rā-zhən, -shən\ adj 1 : of mixed European and Asian origin 2 : of or relating to Europe and Asia — Eurasian n

eu·re·ka \yü-'rē-kə\ interj [Gk heurēka I have found, fr. heuriskein to find; fr. the exclamation attributed to Archimedes on discovering a method for determining the purity of gold] — used to express triumph on a discovery

eu·ro \'yu̇r-ō\ n, pl euros : the common basic monetary unit of most countries of the European Union — see MONEY table

Eu·ro–Amer·i·can \ˌyu̇r-ō-ə-'mer-ə-kən\ n 1 : a person of mixed European and American ancestry 2 : CAUCASIAN

Eu·ro·bond \'yu̇r-ō-ˌbänd\ n : a bond of a U.S. corporation that is sold outside the U.S. but that is valued and paid for in dollars and yields interest in dollars

Eu·ro·cur·ren·cy \'yu̇r-ō-ˌkər-ən-sē\ n : moneys (as of the U.S. and Japan) held outside their countries of origin and used in the money markets of Europe

Eu·ro·dol·lar \'yu̇r-ō-ˌdä-lər\ n : a U.S. dollar held as Eurocurrency

Eu·ro·pe·an \ˌyu̇r-ə-'pē-ən\ n 1 : a native or inhabitant of Europe 2 : a person of European descent — European adj — Eu·ro·pe·an·ize \-ə-ˌnīz\ vb

European–American *n* : EURO-AMERICAN

Eu·ro·pe·an·ism \yur-,ō-'pē-ə-ni-zəm\ *n* **1** : allegiance to the traditions, interests, or ideals of Europeans **2** : advocacy of political and economic integration of Europe — **eu·ro·pe·an·ist** \-nist\ *n*

European plan *n* : a hotel plan whereby the daily rates cover only the cost of the room

eu·ro·pi·um \yu-'rō-pē-əm\ *n* : a rare metallic chemical element

eu·sta·chian tube \yu-'stā-shən-\ *n, often cap E* : a tube connecting the inner cavity of the ear with the throat and equalizing air pressure on both sides of the eardrum

eu·tha·na·sia \,yu-thə-'nā-zhə\ *n* [Gk, easy death, fr. *eu-* good + *thanatos* death] : the act or practice of killing or permitting the death of hopelessly sick or injured persons or animals with as little pain as possible for reasons of mercy

EVA *abbr* extravehicular activity

evac·u·ate \i-'va-kyə-,wāt\ *vb* **-at·ed; -at·ing** **1** : EMPTY **2** : to discharge wastes from the body **3** : to remove or withdraw from : VACATE — **evac·u·a·tion** \-,va-kyə-'wā-shən\ *n*

evac·u·ee \i-,va-kyə-'wē\ *n* : a person removed from a dangerous place

evade \i-'vād\ *vb* **evad·ed; evad·ing** : to manage to avoid esp. by dexterity or slyness : ELUDE, ESCAPE ⟨*evaded* capture⟩

eval·u·ate \i-'val-yu-,wāt\ *vb* **-at·ed; -at·ing** : APPRAISE, VALUE ⟨~ the candidates⟩ — **eval·u·a·tion** \-,val-yu-'wā-shən\ *n*

ev·a·nes·cent \,e-və-'ne-s°nt\ *adj* : tending to vanish like vapor ⟨~ pleasures⟩ ✦ *Synonyms* PASSING, TRANSIENT, TRANSITORY, MOMENTARY — **ev·a·nes·cence** \-s°ns\ *n*

evan·gel·i·cal \,ē-,van-'je-li-kəl, ,e-vən-\ *adj* [LL *evangelium* gospel, fr. Gk *evangelion*, fr. *euangelos* bringing good news, fr. *eu-* good + *angelos* messenger] **1** : of or relating to the Christian gospel esp. as presented in the four Gospels **2** : of or relating to certain Protestant churches emphasizing the authority of Scripture and the importance of preaching as contrasted with ritual **3** : ZEALOUS ⟨~ fervor⟩ — **Evangelical** *n* — **Evan·gel·i·cal·ism** \-kə-,li-zəm\ *n* — **evan·gel·i·cal·ly** *adv*

evan·ge·lism \i-'van-jə-,li-zəm\ *n* **1** : the winning or revival of personal commitments to Christ **2** : militant or crusading zeal — **evan·ge·lis·tic** \-,van-jə-'lis-tik\ *adj* — **evan·ge·lis·ti·cal·ly** *adv*

evan·ge·list \i-'van-jə-list\ *n* **1** *often cap* : the writer of any of the four Gospels **2** : a person who evangelizes; *esp* : a Protestant minister or layman who preaches at special services

evan·ge·lize \i-'van-jə-,līz\ *vb* **-lized; -liz·ing** **1** : to preach the gospel **2** : to convert to Christianity

evap *abbr* evaporate

evap·o·rate \i-'va-pə-,rāt\ *vb* **-rat·ed; -rat·ing** **1** : to pass off or cause to pass off in vapor **2** : to disappear quickly **3** : to drive out the moisture from (as by heat) — **evap·o·ra·tion** \-,va-pə-'rā-shən\ *n* — **evap·o·ra·tor** \-'rā-tər\ *n*

evap·o·rite \i-'va-pə-,rīt\ *n* : a sedimentary rock that originates by the evaporation of seawater in an enclosed basin

eva·sion \i-'vā-zhən\ *n* **1** : a means of evading **2** : an act or instance of evading ⟨arrested for tax ~⟩ — **eva·sive** \i-'vā-siv\ *adj* — **eva·sive·ness** *n*

eve \'ēv\ *n* **1** : EVENING **2** : the period just before some important event

¹even \'ē-vən\ *adj* **1** : LEVEL, FLAT ⟨~ ground⟩ **2** : REGULAR, SMOOTH **3** : EQUAL, FAIR ⟨an ~ exchange⟩ **4** : BALANCED; *also* : fully revenged **5** : divisible by two **6** : EXACT ⟨an ~ dollar⟩ — **even·ly** *adv* — **even·ness** *n*

²even *adv* **1** : EXACTLY, PRECISELY **2** : FULLY, QUITE **3** : at the very time **4** — used as an intensive to stress identity ⟨~ I know that⟩ **5** — used as an intensive to emphasize something extreme or highly unlikely ⟨so simple ~ a child can do it⟩ **6** — used as an intensive to stress the comparative degree ⟨did ~ better⟩ **7** — used as an intensive to indicate a small or minimum degree ⟨didn't ~ try⟩

³even *vb* : to make or become even

even·hand·ed \,ē-vən-'han-dəd\ *adj* : FAIR, IMPARTIAL ⟨an ~ assessment⟩ — **even·hand·ed·ly** *adv*

eve·ning \'ēv-niŋ\ *n* **1** : the end of the day and early part of the night **2** *chiefly Southern & Midland* : AFTERNOON

evening primrose *n* : a coarse biennial herb with yellow flowers that open in the evening

evening star *n* : a bright planet (as Venus) seen esp. in the western sky at or after sunset

even·song \'ē-vən-,sȯŋ\ *n, often cap* **1** : VESPERS **2** : evening prayer esp. when sung

event \i-'vent\ *n* [MF or L; MF, fr. L *eventus*, fr. *evenire* to happen, fr. *venire* to come] **1** : OCCURRENCE **2** : a noteworthy happening **3** : CONTINGENCY ⟨in the ~ of rain⟩ **4** : a contest in a program of sports — **event·ful** *adj*

even·tide \'ē-vən-,tīd\ *n* : EVENING

even·tu·al \i-'ven-chú-wəl\ *adj* : coming at some later time : ULTIMATE — **even·tu·al·ly** *adv*

even·tu·al·i·ty \i-,ven-chú-'wa-lə-tē\ *n, pl* **-ties** : a possible event or outcome

even·tu·ate \i-'ven-chú-,wāt\ *vb* **-at·ed; -at·ing** : to result finally

ev·er \'e-vər\ *adv* **1** : ALWAYS ⟨~ faithful⟩ **2** : at any time **3** : in any way : AT ALL ⟨how can I ~ thank you⟩

ev·er·glade \'e-vər-,glād\ *n* : a low-lying tract of swampy or marshy land

ev·er·green \-,grēn\ *adj* : having foliage that remains green ⟨most coniferous trees are ~⟩ — **evergreen** *n*

¹ev·er·last·ing \,e-vər-'las-tiŋ\ *adj* **1** : enduring forever : ETERNAL **2** : having or being flowers or foliage that retain form or color for a long time when dried — **ev·er·last·ing·ly** *adv*

²everlasting *n* **1** : ETERNITY ⟨from ~⟩ **2** : a plant with everlasting flowers; *also* : its flower

ev·er·more \,e-vər-'mȯr\ *adv* : FOREVER

ev·ery \'ev-rē\ *adj* [ME *everich, every*, fr. OE *æfre ælc*, fr. *æfre* ever + *ælc* each] **1** : being each one of a group **2** : all possible ⟨given ~ chance⟩; *also* : COMPLETE ⟨have ~ confidence⟩

ev·ery·body \'ev-ri-,bä-dē, -bə-\ *pron* : every person

ev·ery·day \'ev-rē-,dā\ *adj* : encountered or used routinely : ORDINARY

ev·ery·one \-(,)wən\ *pron* : EVERYBODY

ev·ery·thing \'ev-rē-,thiŋ\ *pron* **1** : all that exists **2** : all that is relevant

ev·ery·where \'ev-rē-,hwer\ *adv* : in every place or part

evg *abbr* evening

evict \i-'vikt\ *vb* **1** : to put (a person) out from a property by legal process **2** : EXPEL ✦ *Synonyms* EJECT, OUST, DISMISS — **evic·tion** \-'vik-shən\ *n*

¹ev·i·dence \'e-və-dəns\ *n* **1** : an outward sign **2** : PROOF, TESTIMONY; *esp* : matter submitted in court to determine the truth of alleged facts

²evidence *vb* : PROVE, EVINCE

ev·i·dent \-dənt\ *adj* : clear to the vision and understanding ✦ *Synonyms* MANIFEST, DISTINCT, OBVIOUS, APPARENT, PLAIN

ev·i·dent·ly \'e-və-dənt-lē, ,e-və-'dent-\ *adv* **1** : in an evident manner **2** : on the basis of available evidence

¹evil \'ē-vəl\ *adj* **evil·er** *or* **evil·ler; evil·est** *or* **evil·lest** **1** : WICKED **2** : causing or threatening distress or harm : PERNICIOUS — **evil·ly** *adv*

²evil *n* **1** : the fact of suffering, misfortune, and wrongdoing **2** : a source of sorrow, distress, or calamity

evil·do·er \,ē-vəl-'dü-ər\ *n* : one who does evil

evil–mind·ed \-'mīn-dəd\ *adj* : having an evil disposition or evil thoughts — **evil–mind·ed·ly** *adv*

evince \i-'vins\ *vb* **evinced; evinc·ing** : SHOW, REVEAL ⟨*evinced* an interest in art⟩

evis·cer·ate \i-'vi-sə-,rāt\ *vb* **-at·ed; -at·ing** **1** : to remove the entrails of **2** : to deprive of vital content or force — **evis·cer·a·tion** \-,vi-sə-'rā-shən\ *n*

evoke \i-'vōk\ *vb* **evoked; evok·ing** : to call forth or up — **evo·ca·tion** \,ē-vō-'kā-shən, ,e-və-\ *n* — **evoc·a·tive** \i-'vä-kə-tiv\ *adj*

evo·lu·tion \,e-və-'lü-shən\ *n* **1** : one of a set of prescribed movements (as in a dance) **2** : a process of change in a particular direction **3** : a theory that the various kinds of plants and animals are descended from other kinds that lived in earlier times and that the differences are due to inherited changes that occurred over

many generations — **evo·lu·tion·ary** \-shə-ˌner-ē\ *adj* — **evo·lu·tion·ist** \-shə-nist\ *n*
evolve \i-ˈvälv\ *vb* **evolved; evolv·ing** [L *evolvere* to unroll] : to develop or change by or as if by evolution
EW *abbr* enlisted woman
e–waste \ˈē-ˌwāst\ *n* : waste consisting of discarded electronic products
ewe \ˈyü\ *n* : a female sheep
ew·er \ˈyü-ər\ *n* : a water pitcher
¹ex \ˈeks\ *prep* [L] : out of : FROM
²ex *n* : a former spouse
³ex *abbr* **1** example **2** express **3** extra
Ex *abbr* Exodus
ex- \e *also occurs in this prefix where only* i *is shown below (as in "express") and* ks *sometimes occurs where only* gz *is shown (as in "exact")*\ *prefix* **1** : out of : outside **2** : former ⟨*ex*-president⟩
ex·ac·er·bate \ig-ˈza-sər-ˌbāt\ *vb* **-bat·ed; -bat·ing** : to make more violent, bitter, or severe ⟨comments that ∼ the dispute⟩ — **ex·ac·er·ba·tion** \-ˌza-sər-ˈbā-shən\ *n*
¹ex·act \ig-ˈzakt\ *vb* **1** : to compel to furnish **2** : to call for as suitable or necessary — **ex·ac·tion** \-ˈzak-shən\ *n*
²exact *adj* : precisely accurate or correct — **ex·act·ly** *adv* — **ex·act·ness** *n*
ex·act·ing \ig-ˈzak-tiŋ\ *adj* **1** : greatly demanding ⟨an ∼ taskmaster⟩ **2** : requiring close attention and precision
ex·ac·ti·tude \ig-ˈzak-tə-ˌtüd, -ˌtyüd\ *n* : the quality or state of being exact
ex·ag·ger·ate \ig-ˈza-jə-ˌrāt\ *vb* **-at·ed; -at·ing** [L *exaggeratus,* pp. of *exaggerare,* lit., to heap up, fr. *agger* heap] : to enlarge (as a statement) beyond normal : OVERSTATE — **ex·ag·ger·at·ed·ly** *adv* — **ex·ag·ger·a·tion** \-ˌza-jə-ˈrā-shən\ *n* — **ex·ag·ger·a·tor** \-ˈza-jə-ˌrā-tər\ *n*
ex·alt \ig-ˈzȯlt\ *vb* **1** : to raise up esp. in rank, power, or dignity **2** : GLORIFY ⟨the poem ∼s her beauty⟩ — **ex·al·ta·tion** \ˌeg-ˌzȯl-ˈtā-shən, ˌek-ˌsȯl-\ *n*
exam \ig-ˈzam\ *n* : EXAMINATION
ex·am·ine \ig-ˈza-mən\ *vb* **ex·am·ined; ex·am·in·ing** **1** : to inspect closely **2** : QUESTION; *esp* : to test by questioning ◆ **Synonyms** INTERROGATE, QUERY, QUIZ, CATECHIZE — **ex·am·i·na·tion** \-ˌza-mə-ˈnā-shən\ *n*
ex·am·ple \ig-ˈzam-pəl\ *n* **1** : something forming a model to be followed or avoided **2** : a representative sample **3** : a problem to be solved in order to show the application of some rule
ex·as·per·ate \ig-ˈzas-pə-ˌrāt\ *vb* **-at·ed; -at·ing** : VEX, IRRITATE — **ex·as·per·a·tion** \ig-ˌzas-pə-ˈrā-shən\ *n*
exc *abbr* **1** excellent **2** except
ex·ca·vate \ˈek-skə-ˌvāt\ *vb* **-vat·ed; -vat·ing** **1** : to hollow out; *also* : to form by hollowing out **2** : to dig out and remove (as earth) **3** : to reveal to view by digging away a covering — **ex·ca·va·tion** \ˌek-skə-ˈvā-shən\ *n* — **ex·ca·va·tor** \ˈek-skə-ˌvā-tər\ *n*
ex·ceed \ik-ˈsēd\ *vb* **1** : to go or be beyond the limit of **2** : SURPASS ⟨∼*ed* our expectations⟩ — **ex·ceed·ance** \-ˈsē-dᵊns\ *n*
ex·ceed·ing·ly \-ˈsē-diŋ-lē\ *also* **ex·ceed·ing** *adv* : EXTREMELY, VERY
ex·cel \ik-ˈsel\ *vb* **ex·celled; ex·cel·ling** : SURPASS, OUTDO
ex·cel·lence \ˈek-sə-ləns\ *n* **1** : the quality of being excellent **2** : an excellent or valuable quality : VIRTUE **3** : EXCELLENCY 2
ex·cel·len·cy \-lən-sē\ *n, pl* **-cies** **1** : EXCELLENCE **2** — used as a title of honor
ex·cel·lent \-lənt\ *adj* : very good of its kind : FIRST-CLASS — **ex·cel·lent·ly** *adv*
ex·cel·si·or \ik-ˈsel-sē-ər\ *n* : fine curled wood shavings used esp. for packing fragile items
¹ex·cept \ik-ˈsept\ *also* **ex·cept·ing** *prep* : with the exclusion or exception of ⟨daily ∼ Sundays⟩
²except *vb* **1** : to take or leave out ⟨children were ∼*ed* from the study⟩ **2** : OBJECT
³except *also* **excepting** *conj* **1** : UNLESS ⟨∼ you repent⟩ **2** : ONLY ⟨I'd go, ∼ it's too far⟩
ex·cep·tion \ik-ˈsep-shən\ *n* **1** : the act of excepting **2** : something excepted ⟨an ∼ to the rule⟩ **3** : OBJECTION
ex·cep·tion·able \ik-ˈsep-shə-nə-bəl\ *adj* : OBJECTIONABLE
ex·cep·tion·al \ik-ˈsep-shə-nəl\ *adj* **1** : UNUSUAL ⟨an ∼ number of rainy days⟩ **2** : SUPERIOR ⟨∼ skill⟩ — **ex·cep·tion·al·ly** *adv*

ex·cerpt \ˈek-ˌsərpt, ˈeg-ˌzərpt\ *n* : a passage selected or copied : EXTRACT — **excerpt** \ek-ˈsərpt, eg-ˈzərpt; ˈek-ˌsərpt, ˈeg-ˌzərpt\ *vb*
ex·cess \ik-ˈses, ˈek-ˌses\ *n* **1** : SUPERFLUITY, SURPLUS **2** : the amount by which one quantity exceeds another **3** : INTEMPERANCE; *also* : an instance of intemperance ⟨the dictator's ∼*es*⟩ — **excess** *adj* — **ex·ces·sive** \ik-ˈse-siv\ *adj* — **ex·ces·sive·ly** *adv*
exch *abbr* exchange; exchanged
¹ex·change \iks-ˈchānj\ *n* **1** : the giving or taking of one thing in return for another : TRADE **2** : a substituting of one thing for another **3** : interchange of valuables and esp. of bills of exchange or money of different countries **4** : a place where things and services are exchanged; *esp* : a marketplace for securities **5** : a central office in which telephone lines are connected for communication
²exchange *vb* **ex·changed; ex·chang·ing** : to transfer in return for some equivalent : BARTER, SWAP — **ex·change·able** \iks-ˈchān-jə-bəl\ *adj*
ex·che·quer \ˈeks-ˌche-kər\ *n* [ME *escheker,* fr. AF, chessboard, counting table, office charged with revenue collection, fr. *eschec* check (in chess), chess] : TREASURY; *esp* : a national treasury
ex·cise \ˈek-ˌsīz\ *n* : a tax on the manufacture, sale, or consumption of a commodity
ex·ci·sion \ik-ˈsi-zhən\ *n* : removal by or as if by cutting out esp. by surgical means — **ex·cise** \ik-ˈsīz\ *vb*
ex·cit·able \ik-ˈsī-tə-bəl\ *adj* : easily excited — **ex·cit·abil·i·ty** \-ˌsī-tə-ˈbi-lə-tē\ *n*
ex·cite \ik-ˈsīt\ *vb* **ex·cit·ed; ex·cit·ing** **1** : to stir up the emotions of : ROUSE **2** : to increase the activity of : STIMULATE ◆ **Synonyms** PROVOKE, PIQUE, QUICKEN — **ex·ci·ta·tion** \ˌek-ˌsī-ˈtā-shən, ˌek-sə-\ *n* — **ex·cit·ed·ly** *adv* — **ex·cit·ing·ly** *adv*
ex·cite·ment \ik-ˈsīt-mənt\ *n* : AGITATION, STIR
ex·claim \iks-ˈklām\ *vb* : to cry out, speak, or utter sharply or vehemently — **ex·cla·ma·tion** \ˌeks-klə-ˈmā-shən\ *n* — **ex·clam·a·to·ry** \iks-ˈkla-mə-ˌtȯr-ē\ *adj*
exclamation point *n* : a punctuation mark ! used esp. after an interjection or exclamation
ex·clude \iks-ˈklüd\ *vb* **ex·clud·ed; ex·clud·ing** **1** : to prevent from using or participating : BAR **2** : to put out : EXPEL — **ex·clu·sion** \-ˈklü-zhən\ *n* — **ex·clu·sion·ary** \-zhə-ˌner-ē\ *adj*
ex·clu·sive \iks-ˈklü-siv\ *adj* **1** : reserved for particular persons **2** : snobbishly aloof; *also* : STYLISH **3** : SOLE ⟨∼ rights⟩; *also* : UNDIVIDED ⟨my ∼ attention⟩ ◆ **Synonyms** CHIC, MODISH, SMART, SWANK, FASHIONABLE — **exclusive** *n* — **ex·clu·sive·ly** *adv* — **ex·clu·sive·ness** *n* — **ex·clu·siv·i·ty** \ˌeks-ˌklü-si-və-tē, iks-, -zi-\ *n*
exclusive of *prep* : not taking into account
ex·cog·i·tate \ek-ˈskä-jə-ˌtāt\ *vb* : to think out : DEVISE
ex·com·mu·ni·cate \ˌek-skə-ˈmyü-nə-ˌkāt\ *vb* **1** : to cut off officially from the rites of the church — **ex·com·mu·ni·ca·tion** \-ˌmyü-nə-ˈkā-shən\ *n*
ex·co·ri·ate \ek-ˈskȯr-ē-ˌāt\ *vb* **-at·ed; -at·ing** : to criticize severely — **ex·co·ri·a·tion** \(ˌ)ek-ˌskȯr-ē-ˈā-shən\ *n*
ex·cre·ment \ˈek-skrə-mənt\ *n* : waste discharged from the body; *esp* : FECES — **ex·cre·men·tal** \ˌek-skrə-ˈmen-tᵊl\ *adj*
ex·cres·cence \ik-ˈskre-sᵊns\ *n* : OUTGROWTH; *esp* : an abnormal outgrowth (as a wart)
ex·cre·ta \ik-ˈskrē-tə\ *n pl* : waste matter (as feces) separated or eliminated from the body
ex·crete \ik-ˈskrēt\ *vb* **ex·cret·ed; ex·cret·ing** : to separate and eliminate wastes from the body esp. in urine or sweat — **ex·cre·tion** \-ˈskrē-shən\ *n* — **ex·cre·to·ry** \ˈek-skrə-ˌtȯr-ē\ *adj*
ex·cru·ci·at·ing \ik-ˈskrü-shē-ˌā-tiŋ\ *adj* [L *excruciare* to torture, fr. *cruciare* to crucify, fr. *crux* cross] : intensely painful or distressing ◆ **Synonyms** AGONIZING, HARROWING, TORTUROUS — **ex·cru·ci·at·ing·ly** *adv*
ex·cul·pate \ˈek-(ˌ)skəl-ˌpāt\ *vb* **-pat·ed; -pat·ing** : to clear from alleged fault or guilt ◆ **Synonyms** ABSOLVE, EXONERATE, ACQUIT, VINDICATE, CLEAR
ex·cur·sion \ik-ˈskər-zhən\ *n* **1** : EXPEDITION; *esp* : a pleasure trip **2** : DIGRESSION — **ex·cur·sion·ist** \-zhə-nist\ *n*
ex·cur·sive \-ˈskər-siv\ *adj* : constituting or characterized by digression
¹ex·cuse \ik-ˈskyüz\ *vb* **ex·cused; ex·cus·ing** [ME, fr. AF

excuser, fr. L *excusare,* fr. *causa* cause, explanation] **1** : to make apology for **2** : PARDON **3** : to release from an obligation **4** : JUSTIFY — **ex·cus·able** *adj*

²**excuse** \ik-'skyüs\ *n* **1** : an act of excusing **2** : something that excuses or is a reason for excusing : JUSTIFICATION

exec *n* : EXECUTIVE

ex·e·cra·ble \'ek-si-krə-bəl\ *adj* **1** : DETESTABLE ⟨~ crimes⟩ **2** : very bad ⟨~ spelling⟩

ex·e·crate \'ek-sə-ˌkrāt\ *vb* **-crat·ed; -crat·ing** [L *exsecratus,* pp. of *exsecrari* to put under a curse, fr. *ex-* out of + *sacer* sacred] : to denounce as evil or detestable; *also* : DETEST — **ex·e·cra·tion** \ˌek-sə-'krā-shən\ *n*

ex·e·cute \'ek-si-ˌkyüt\ *vb* **-cut·ed; -cut·ing 1** : to carry out fully : put completely into effect **2** : to do what is called for (as by a law) **3** : to put to death in accordance with a legal sentence **4** : to produce by carrying out a design **5** : to do what is needed to give validity to ⟨~ a deed⟩ — **ex·e·cu·tion** \ˌek-si-'kyü-shən\ *n* — **ex·e·cu·tion·er** *n*

¹**ex·ec·u·tive** \ig-'ze-kyə-tiv\ *adj* **1** : of or relating to the enforcement of laws and the conduct of affairs **2** : designed for or related to carrying out plans or purposes

²**executive** *n* **1** : the branch of government with executive duties **2** : one having administrative or managerial responsibility

ex·ec·u·tor \ig-'ze-kyə-tər\ *n* : the person named in a will to execute it

ex·ec·u·trix \ig-'ze-kyə-ˌtriks\ *n, pl* **ex·ec·u·tri·ces** \-ˌze-kyə-'trī-ˌsēz\ *or* **ex·ec·u·trix·es** \-'ze-kyə-ˌtrik-səz\ : a woman who is an executor

ex·e·ge·sis \ˌek-sə-'jē-səs\ *n, pl* **-ge·ses** \-'jē-ˌsēz\ : explanation or critical interpretation of a text

ex·e·gete \'ek-sə-ˌjēt\ *n* : one who practices exegesis — **ex·e·get·i·cal** \ˌek-sə-'je-ti-kəl\ *adj*

ex·em·plar \ig-'zem-ˌplär, -plər\ *n* **1** : one that serves as a model or example; *esp* : an ideal model ⟨an ~ of courage⟩ **2** : a typical instance or example

ex·em·pla·ry \ig-'zem-plə-rē\ *adj* : serving as a pattern; *also* : COMMENDABLE ⟨~ courage⟩

ex·em·pli·fy \ig-'zem-plə-ˌfī\ *vb* **-fied; -fy·ing** : to illustrate by example : serve as an example of — **ex·em·pli·fi·ca·tion** \-ˌzem-plə-fə-'kā-shən\ *n*

¹**ex·empt** \ig-'zempt\ *adj* : free from some liability to which others are subject ⟨~ from taxation⟩

²**exempt** *vb* : to make exempt : EXCUSE — **ex·emp·tion** \ig-'zemp-shən\ *n*

¹**ex·er·cise** \'ek-sər-ˌsīz\ *n* **1** : EMPLOYMENT, USE ⟨~ of authority⟩ **2** : exertion made for the sake of training or physical fitness **3** : a task or problem done to develop skill **4** *pl* : a public exhibition or ceremony

²**exercise** *vb* **-cised; -cis·ing 1** : EXERT ⟨~ control⟩ **2** : to train by or engage in exercise **3** : WORRY, DISTRESS ⟨issues that ~ voters⟩ — **ex·er·cis·er** *n*

ex·ert \ig-'zərt\ *vb* : to bring or put into action ⟨~ influence⟩ ⟨~ed himself⟩ — **ex·er·tion** \-'zər-shən\ *n*

ex·fo·li·ate \eks-'fō-lē-ˌāt\ *vb* **-at·ed; -at·ing** : to cast off in scales, layers, or splinters — **ex·fo·li·a·tion** \-ˌfō-lē-'ā-shən\ *n*

ex·hale \eks-'hāl\ *vb* **ex·haled; ex·hal·ing 1** : to breathe out **2** : to give or pass off in the form of vapor — **ex·ha·la·tion** \ˌeks-hə-'lā-shən\ *n*

¹**ex·haust** \ig-'zȯst\ *vb* **1** : to use up wholly **2** : to tire or wear out **3** : to draw off or let out completely; *also* : EMPTY **4** : to develop (a subject) completely

²**exhaust** *n* **1** : the escape of used vapor or gas from an engine; *also* : the gas that escapes **2** : a system of pipes through which exhaust escapes

ex·haus·tion \ig-'zȯs-chən\ *n* : extreme weariness : FATIGUE

ex·haus·tive \ig-'zȯ-stiv\ *adj* : covering all possibilities : THOROUGH ⟨an ~ investigation⟩ — **ex·haus·tive·ly** *adv*

¹**ex·hib·it** \ig-'zi-bət\ *vb* **1** : to display esp. publicly **2** : to present to a court in legal form ✦ *Synonyms* DISPLAY, SHOW, PARADE, FLAUNT — **ex·hi·bi·tion** \ˌek-sə-'bi-shən\ *n* — **ex·hib·i·tor** \ig-'zi-bə-tər\ *n*

²**exhibit** *n* **1** : an act or instance of exhibiting; *also* : something exhibited **2** : something produced and identified in court for use as evidence

ex·hi·bi·tion·ism \ˌek-sə-'bi-shə-ˌni-zəm\ *n* **1** : a perver-

sion marked by a tendency to indecently expose one's genitals **2** : the act or practice of behaving so as to attract attention to oneself — **ex·hi·bi·tion·ist** \-nist\ *n or adj*

ex·hil·a·rate \ig-'zi-lə-ˌrāt\ *vb* **-rat·ed; -rat·ing** : ENLIVEN, STIMULATE — **ex·hil·a·ra·tion** \-ˌzi-lə-'rā-shən\ *n*

ex·hort \ig-'zȯrt\ *vb* : to urge, advise, or warn earnestly — **ex·hor·ta·tion** \ˌek-ˌsȯr-tā-shən, ˌeg-ˌzȯr-, -zər-\ *n*

ex·hume \ig-'züm, iks-'hyüm\ *vb* **ex·humed; ex·hum·ing** [ME fr. ML *exhumare,* fr. L *ex* out of + *humus* earth] : DISINTER — **ex·hu·ma·tion** \ˌeks-hyü-'mā-shən, ˌeg-zü-\ *n*

ex·i·gen·cy \'ek-sə-jən-sē, ig-'zi-jən-\ *n, pl* **-cies 1** *pl* : REQUIREMENTS **2** : urgent need — **ex·i·gent** \'ek-sə-jənt\ *adj*

ex·ig·u·ous \ig-'zi-gyə-wəs\ *adj* : scanty in amount —

¹**ex·ile** \'eg-ˌzī(-ə)l, 'ek-ˌsī(-ə)l\ *n* **1** : BANISHMENT; *also* : voluntary absence from one's country or home **2** : a person driven from his or her native place

²**exile** *vb* **ex·iled; ex·il·ing** : BANISH, EXPEL ✦ *Synonyms* EXPATRIATE, DEPORT, OSTRACIZE

ex·ist \ig-'zist\ *vb* **1** : to have being **2** : to continue to be : LIVE

ex·is·tence \ig-'zis-təns\ *n* **1** : continuance in living **2** : actual or present occurrence ⟨~ of a state of war⟩ — **ex·is·tent** \-tənt\ *adj*

ex·is·ten·tial \ˌeg-zis-'ten-chəl, ˌek-sis-\ *adj* **1** : of or relating to existence **2** : EMPIRICAL **3** : having being in time and space **4** : of or relating to existentialism or existentialists

ex·is·ten·tial·ism \ˌeg-zis-'ten-chə-ˌli-zəm\ *n* : a philosophy centered on individual existence and personal responsibility for acts of free will in the absence of certain knowledge of what is right or wrong — **ex·is·ten·tial·ist** \-list\ *adj or n*

ex·it \'eg-zət, 'ek-sət\ *n* **1** : a departure from a stage **2** : a going out or away; *also* : DEATH **3** : a way out of an enclosed space **4** : a point of departure from an expressway — **exit** *vb*

exo·bi·ol·o·gy \ˌek-sō-bī-'ä-lə-jē\ *n* : biology concerned with life originating or existing outside the earth or its atmosphere — **exo·bi·ol·o·gist** \-jist\ *n*

exo·crine gland \'ek-sə-krən-, -ˌkrīn-, -ˌkrēn-\ *n* : a gland (as a salivary gland) that releases a secretion externally by means of a canal or duct

Exod *abbr* Exodus

ex·o·dus \'ek-sə-dəs\ *n* **1** *cap* — see BIBLE table **2** : a mass departure : EMIGRATION

ex of·fi·cio \ˌek-sə-'fi-shē-ˌō\ *adv or adj* : by virtue of or because of an office ⟨*ex officio* chairman⟩

ex·og·e·nous \ek-'sä-jə-nəs\ *adj* : caused or produced by factors outside the organism or system — **ex·og·e·nous·ly** *adv*

ex·on·er·ate \ig-'zä-nə-ˌrāt\ *vb* **-at·ed; -at·ing** [ME, fr. L *exoneratus,* pp. of *exonerare* to unburden, fr. *ex-* out + *onus* load] : to free from blame ✦ *Synonyms* ACQUIT, ABSOLVE, EXCULPATE, VINDICATE — **ex·on·er·a·tion** \-ˌzä-nə-'rā-shən\ *n*

exo·plan·et \'ek-sō-ˌpla-nət\ *n* : a planet orbiting a star that is not our sun

ex·or·bi·tant \ig-'zȯr-bə-tənt\ *adj* : exceeding what is usual or proper

ex·or·cise \'ek-ˌsȯr-ˌsīz, -sər-\ *vb* **-cised; -cis·ing 1** : to get rid of by or as if by solemn command **2** : to free of an evil spirit — **ex·or·cism** \-ˌsi-zəm\ *n* — **ex·or·cist** \-ˌsist\ *n*

exo·sphere \'ek-sō-ˌsfir\ *n* : the outermost region of the atmosphere

exo·ther·mic \ˌek-sō-'thər-mik\ *adj* : characterized by or formed with evolution of heat

ex·ot·ic \ig-'zä-tik\ *adj* **1** : introduced from another country ⟨~ plants⟩ **2** : strikingly, excitingly, or mysteriously different or unusual ⟨~ flavors⟩ — **exotic** *n* — **ex·ot·i·cal·ly** \-ti-k(ə-)lē\ *adv* — **ex·ot·i·cism** \-tə-ˌsi-zəm\ *n*

exp *abbr* **1** expense **2** experiment **3** export **4** express

ex·pand \ik-'spand\ *vb* **1** : to open up : UNFOLD **2** : ENLARGE **3** : to develop in detail ✦ *Synonyms* AMPLIFY, SWELL, DISTEND, INFLATE, DILATE — **ex·pand·able** \-'span-də-bəl\ *adj* — **ex·pand·er** *n*

ex·panse \ik-'spans\ *n* : a broad extent (as of land or sea)

ex·pan·sion \ik-'span-chən\ *n* **1** : the act or process of expanding **2** : the quality or state of being expanded **3** : an expanded part or thing

expansion slot *n* : a socket on a motherboard for a circuit board (**expansion card**) offering additional capabilities

ex·pan·sive \ik-'span-siv\ *adj* **1** : tending to expand or to cause expansion **2** : warmly benevolent, generous, or ready to talk **3** : of large extent or scope — **ex·pan·sive·ly** *adv* — **ex·pan·sive·ness** *n*

ex par·te \eks-'pär-tē\ *adv or adj* [ML] : from a one-sided point of view

ex·pa·ti·ate \ek-'spā-shē-,āt\ *vb* **-at·ed; -at·ing** : to talk or write at length — **ex·pa·ti·a·tion** \ek-,spā-shē-'ā-shən\ *n*

¹ex·pa·tri·ate \ek-'spā-trē-,āt\ *vb* **-at·ed; -at·ing** : EXILE — **ex·pa·tri·a·tion** \ek-,spā-trē-'ā-shən\ *n*

²ex·pa·tri·ate \ek-'spā-trē-,āt, -trē-ət\ *adj* : living in a foreign country — **expatriate** *n*

ex·pect \ik-'spekt\ *vb* **1** : SUPPOSE, THINK **2** : to look forward to : ANTICIPATE **3** : to consider reasonable, due, or necessary **4** : to consider to be obliged

ex·pec·tan·cy \-'spek-tən-sē\ *n, pl* **-cies** **1** : EXPECTATION **2** : the expected amount (as of years of life)

ex·pec·tant \-tənt\ *adj* : marked by expectation; *esp* : expecting the birth of a child ⟨~ parents⟩ — **ex·pec·tant·ly** *adv*

ex·pec·ta·tion \ek-,spek-'tā-shən\ *n* **1** : the act or state of expecting **2** : prospect of inheritance — usu. used in pl. **3** : something expected

ex·pec·to·rant \ik-'spek-tə-rənt\ *n* : an agent that promotes the discharge or expulsion of mucus from the respiratory tract — **expectorant** *adj*

ex·pec·to·rate \-,rāt\ *vb* **-rat·ed; -rat·ing** : SPIT — **ex·pec·to·ra·tion** \-,spek-tə-'rā-shən\ *n*

ex·pe·di·ence \ik-'spē-dē-əns\ *n* : EXPEDIENCY

ex·pe·di·en·cy \-ən-sē\ *n, pl* **-cies** **1** : fitness to some end **2** : use of expedient means and methods; *also* : something expedient

¹ex·pe·di·ent \-ənt\ *adj* [ME, fr. AF or L; AF, fr. L *expediens*, prp. of *expedire* to extricate, prepare, be useful, fr. *ex-* out + *ped-, pes* foot] **1** : adapted for achieving a particular end **2** : marked by concern with what is advantageous; *esp* : governed by self-interest

²expedient *n* : something expedient; *esp* : a temporary means to an end

ex·pe·dite \'ek-spə-,dīt\ *vb* **-dit·ed; -dit·ing** : to carry out promptly; *also* : to speed up ⟨~ a lawsuit⟩

ex·pe·dit·er \-,dī-tər\ *n* : one that expedites; *esp* : one employed to ensure efficient movement of goods or supplies in a business

ex·pe·di·tion \ek-spə-'di-shən\ *n* **1** : a journey for a particular purpose; *also* : the persons making it **2** : efficient promptness

ex·pe·di·tion·ary \-'di-shə-,ner-ē\ *adj* : of, relating to, or constituting an expedition; *also* : sent on military service abroad

ex·pe·di·tious \-'di-shəs\ *adj* : marked by or acting with prompt efficiency ♦ **Synonyms** SWIFT, FAST, RAPID, SPEEDY

ex·pel \ik-'spel\ *vb* **ex·pelled; ex·pel·ling** : to drive or force out : EJECT

ex·pend \ik-'spend\ *vb* **1** : to pay out : SPEND **2** : UTILIZE ⟨~ resources⟩; *also* : USE UP — **ex·pend·able** *adj*

ex·pen·di·ture \ik-'spen-di-chər, -,chür\ *n* **1** : the act or process of expending **2** : something expended

ex·pense \ik-'spens\ *n* **1** : EXPENDITURE **2** : COST **3** : a cause of expenditure **4** : SACRIFICE ⟨had a laugh at my ~⟩

ex·pen·sive \ik-'spen-siv\ *adj* : COSTLY, DEAR — **ex·pen·sive·ly** *adv*

¹ex·pe·ri·ence \ik-'spir-ē-əns\ *n* **1** : observation of or participation in events resulting in or tending toward knowledge **2** : knowledge, practice, or skill derived from observation or participation in events; *also* : the length of such participation **3** : something encountered, undergone, or lived through (as by a person or community)

²experience *vb* **-enced; -enc·ing** **1** : FIND OUT, DISCOVER **2** : to have experience of : UNDERGO ⟨~ the loss of a pet⟩

ex·pe·ri·enced *adj* : made capable through experience ⟨an ~ pilot⟩

¹ex·per·i·ment \ik-'sper-ə-mənt\ *n* : a controlled procedure carried out to discover, test, or demonstrate something; *also* : the process of testing — **ex·per·i·men·tal** \-,sper-ə-'men-t³l\ *adj* — **ex·per·i·men·tal·ly** \-'men-t³l-ē\ *adv*

²ex·per·i·ment \-,ment\ *vb* : to make experiments — **ex·per·i·men·ta·tion** \ik-,sper-ə-mən-'tā-shən\ *n* — **ex·per·i·men·ter** *n*

¹ex·pert \'ek-,spərt\ *adj* : showing special skill or knowledge — **ex·pert·ly** *adv* — **ex·pert·ness** *n*

²ex·pert \'ek-,spərt\ *n* : an expert person : SPECIALIST ⟨a computer ~⟩

ex·per·tise \,ek-(,)spər-'tēz\ *n* : the skill of an expert ⟨~ in legal matters⟩

expert system *n* : computer software that attempts to mimic the reasoning of a human specialist

ex·pi·ate \'ek-spē-,āt\ *vb* **-at·ed; -at·ing** : to give satisfaction for : ATONE ⟨~ sin⟩ — **ex·pi·a·tion** \,ek-spē-'ā-shən\ *n*

ex·pi·a·to·ry \'ek-spē-ə-,tór-ē\ *adj* : serving to expiate

expiration date *n* **1** : the date after which something is no longer in effect **2** : the date after which a product is expected to decline in quality or effectiveness

ex·pire \ik-'spī-(ə)r, ek-\ *vb* **ex·pired; ex·pir·ing** **1** : to breathe one's last breath : DIE **2** : to come to an end **3** : to breathe out from or as if from the lungs — **ex·pi·ra·tion** \,ek-spə-'rā-shən\ *n*

ex·plain \ik-'splān\ *vb* [ME *explanen*, fr. L *explanare*, lit., to make level, fr. *planus* level, flat] **1** : to make clear **2** : to give the reason for — **ex·pla·na·tion** \,ek-splə-'nā-shən\ *n* — **ex·plan·a·to·ry** \ik-'spla-nə-,tór-ē\ *adj*

ex·ple·tive \'ek-splə-tiv\ *n* : a usu. profane exclamation

ex·pli·ca·ble \ek-'spli-kə-bəl, 'ek-(,)spli-\ *adj* : capable of being explained

ex·pli·cate \'ek-splə-,kāt\ *vb* **-cat·ed; -cat·ing** : to give a detailed explanation of — **ex·pli·ca·tion** \,ek-splə-'kā-shən\ *n*

ex·plic·it \ik-'spli-sət\ *adj* : clearly and precisely expressed ⟨~ directions⟩ — **ex·plic·it·ly** *adv* — **ex·plic·it·ness** *n*

ex·plode \ik-'splōd\ *vb* **ex·plod·ed; ex·plod·ing** [L *explodere* to drive off the stage by clapping, fr. *ex-* out + *plaudere* to clap] **1** : DISCREDIT ⟨~ a belief⟩ **2** : to burst or cause to burst violently and noisily ⟨~ a bomb⟩ ⟨the boiler *exploded*⟩ **3** : to undergo a rapid chemical or nuclear reaction with production of heat and violent expansion of gas ⟨dynamite ~s⟩ **4** : to give forth a sudden strong and noisy outburst of emotion **5** : to increase rapidly ⟨the city's population *exploded*⟩

exploded *adj* : showing the parts separated but in correct relationship to each other ⟨an ~ view of a carburetor⟩

¹ex·ploit \'ek-,splóit\ *n* : DEED; *esp* : a notable or heroic act

²ex·ploit \ik-'splóit\ *vb* **1** : to make productive use of : UTILIZE ⟨~ natural resources⟩ **2** : to use unfairly for one's own advantage ⟨~ migrant workers⟩ — **ex·ploi·ta·tion** \,ek-,splói-'tā-shən\ *n*

ex·plore \ik-'splór\ *vb* **ex·plored; ex·plor·ing** **1** : to look into or travel over thoroughly **2** : to examine carefully ⟨~ a wound⟩ — **ex·plo·ra·tion** \,ek-splə-'rā-shən\ *n* — **ex·plor·ato·ry** \ik-'splór-ə-,tór-ē\ *adj* — **ex·plor·er** *n*

ex·plo·sion \ik-'splō-zhən\ *n* : the act or an instance of exploding

ex·plo·sive \ik-'splō-siv\ *adj* **1** : relating to or able to cause explosion **2** : tending to explode ⟨an ~ temper⟩ — **explosive** *n* — **ex·plo·sive·ly** *adv*

ex·po \'ek-,spō\ *n, pl* **expos** : EXPOSITION 2

ex·po·nent \ik-'spō-nənt, 'ek-,spō-\ *n* **1** : a symbol written above and to the right of a mathematical expression (as ^{3} in a^3) to signify how many times it is to be used as a factor **2** : INTERPRETER, EXPOUNDER **3** : ADVOCATE, CHAMPION — **ex·po·nen·tial** \,ek-spə-'nen-chəl\ *adj* — **ex·po·nen·tial·ly** *adv*

ex·po·nen·ti·a·tion \,ek-spə-,nen-chē-'ā-shen\ *n* : the mathematical operation of raising a quantity to a power

¹ex·port \ek-'spórt, 'ek-,spórt\ *vb* : to send (as merchandise) to foreign countries — **ex·por·ta·tion** \,ek-,spór-'tā-shən, -spər-\ *n* — **ex·port·er** *n*

²ex·port \'ek-,spórt\ *n* **1** : something exported esp. for trade **2** : the act of exporting

ex·pose \ik-'spōz\ *vb* **ex·posed; ex·pos·ing** **1** : to deprive of shelter or protection **2** : to submit or subject to an action or influence; *esp* : to subject (as photographic

film) to radiant energy (as light) **3** : to bring to light : DISCLOSE ⟨~ a scam⟩ **4** : to cause to be open to view
ex·po·sé \‚ek-spō-'zā\ *n* : an exposure of something discreditable
ex·po·si·tion \‚ek-spə-'zi-shən\ *n* **1** : a setting forth of the meaning or purpose (as of a writing); *also* : discourse designed to convey information **2** : a public exhibition
ex·pos·i·tor \ik-'spä-zə-tər\ *n* : one who explains : COMMENTATOR
ex post fac·to \‚eks-'pōst-‚fak-tō\ *adv or adj* : after the fact
ex·pos·tu·late \ik-'späs-chə-‚lāt\ *vb* : to reason earnestly with a person esp. in dissuading : REMONSTRATE — **ex·pos·tu·la·tion** \-‚späs-chə-'lā-shən\ *n*
ex·po·sure \ik-'spō-zhər\ *n* **1** : the fact or condition of being exposed **2** : the act or an instance of exposing **3** : the length of time for which a film is exposed **4** : a section of a photographic film for one picture
ex·pound \ik-'spaúnd\ *vb* **1** : STATE **2** : INTERPRET, EXPLAIN — **ex·pound·er** *n*
¹ex·press \ik-'spres\ *adj* **1** : EXPLICIT; *also* : EXACT, PRECISE **2** : SPECIFIC ⟨this ~ purpose⟩ **3** : traveling at high speed and esp. with few stops ⟨an ~ train⟩; *also* : adapted to high-speed use ⟨~ roads⟩ — **ex·press·ly** *adv*
²express *adv* : by express ⟨ship it ~⟩
³express *n* **1** : a system for the prompt transportation of goods; *also* : a company operating such a service or the shipments so transported **2** : an express vehicle
⁴express *vb* **1** : to make known : SHOW, STATE ⟨~ regret⟩; *also* : SYMBOLIZE **2** : to squeeze out : extract by pressing **3** : to send by express **4** : to manifest or produce by a genetic process
ex·pres·sion \ik-'spre-shən\ *n* **1** : UTTERANCE **2** : something that represents or symbolizes : SIGN; *esp* : a mathematical symbol or combination of signs and symbols representing a quantity or operation **3** : the detectable effect of a gene **4** : a significant word or phrase; *also* : manner of expressing (as in writing or music) **5** : facial aspect or vocal intonation indicative of feeling — **ex·pression·less** *adj*
ex·pres·sion·ism \ik-'spre-shə-‚ni-zəm\ *n* : a theory or practice in art of seeking to depict the artist's subjective responses to objects and events — **ex·pres·sion·ist** \-nist\ *n or adj* — **ex·pres·sion·is·tic** \-‚spre-shə-'nis-tik\ *adj*
ex·pres·sive \ik-'spre-siv\ *adj* **1** : of or relating to expression **2** : serving to express ⟨an ~ gesture⟩ — **ex·pres·sive·ly** *adv* — **ex·pres·sive·ness** *n*
ex·press·way \ik-'spres-‚wā\ *n* : a divided superhighway with limited access
ex·pro·pri·ate \ek-'sprō-prē-‚āt\ *vb* **-at·ed; -at·ing** : to deprive of possession or the right to own — **ex·propri·a·tion** \(‚)ek-‚sprō-prē-'ā-shən\ *n*
expt *abbr* experiment
ex·pul·sion \ik-'spəl-shən\ *n* : an expelling or being expelled : EJECTION
ex·punge \ik-'spənj\ *vb* **ex·punged; ex·pung·ing** [L *expungere* to mark for deletion by dots, fr. *ex-* out + *pungere* to prick] : OBLITERATE, ERASE
ex·pur·gate \'ek-spər-‚gāt\ *vb* **-gat·ed; -gat·ing** : to clear (as a book) of objectionable passages — **ex·pur·ga·tion** \‚ek-spər-'gā-shən\ *n*
ex·qui·site \ek-'skwi-zət, 'ek-(‚)skwi-\ *adj* [ME *exquisit*, fr. L *exquisitus*, pp. of *exquirere* to search out, fr. *ex* out + *quaerere* to seek] **1** : marked by flawless form or workmanship **2** : keenly appreciative or sensitive **3** : pleasingly beautiful or delicate **4** : INTENSE ⟨~ pain⟩
ext *abbr* **1** extension **2** exterior **3** external **4** extra **5** extract
ex·tant \'ek-stənt; ek-'stant\ *adj* : EXISTENT; *esp* : not lost or destroyed
ex·tem·po·ra·ne·ous \ek-‚stem-pə-'rā-nē-əs\ *adj* : not planned beforehand : IMPROMPTU — **ex·tem·po·ra·ne·ous·ly** *adv*
ex·tem·po·rary \ik-'stem-pə-‚rer-ē\ *adj* : EXTEMPORANEOUS
ex·tem·po·re \ik-'stem-pə-(‚)rē\ *adv* : EXTEMPORANEOUSLY
ex·tem·po·rise *Brit var of* EXTEMPORIZE
ex·tem·po·rize \ik-'stem-pə-‚rīz\ *vb* **-rized; -riz·ing** : to do something extemporaneously ⟨~ a speech⟩

ex·tend \ik-'stend\ *vb* **1** : to spread or stretch forth or out (as in reaching) **2** : to exert or cause to exert to full capacity **3** : PROFFER ⟨~ credit⟩ **4** : PROLONG ⟨~ a note⟩ **5** : to make greater or broader ⟨~ knowledge⟩ ⟨~ a business⟩ **6** : to stretch out or reach across a distance, space, or time ♦ *Synonyms* LENGTHEN, ELONGATE, PROTRACT — **ex·tend·able** *also* **ex·tend·ible** \-'sten-də-bəl\ *adj*
ex·ten·sion \ik-'sten-chən\ *n* **1** : an extending or being extended **2** : a program that geographically extends the educational resources of an institution **3** : an additional part; *also* : an extra telephone connected to a line
ex·ten·sive \ik-'sten-siv\ *adj* : of considerable extent : FAR-REACHING, BROAD ⟨~ training⟩ — **ex·ten·sive·ly** *adv*
ex·tent \ik-'stent\ *n* **1** : the range or space over which something extends ⟨a property of large ~⟩ **2** : the point or degree to which something extends ⟨to the fullest ~ of the law⟩
ex·ten·u·ate \ik-'sten-yù-‚wāt\ *vb* **-at·ed; -at·ing** : to lessen the seriousness of — **ex·ten·u·a·tion** \-‚sten-yù-'wā-shən\ *n*
¹ex·te·ri·or \ek-'stir-ē-ər\ *adj* **1** : EXTERNAL **2** : suitable for use on an outside surface ⟨~ paint⟩
²exterior *n* : an exterior part or surface
ex·ter·mi·nate \ik-'stər-mə-‚nāt\ *vb* **-nat·ed; -nat·ing** : to get rid of completely usu. by killing off ♦ *Synonyms* EXTIRPATE, ERADICATE, ABOLISH, ANNIHILATE — **ex·ter·mi·na·tion** \-‚stər-mə-'nā-shən\ *n* — **ex·ter·mi·na·tor** \-'stər-mə-‚nā-tər\ *n*
¹ex·ter·nal \ek-'stər-n³l\ *adj* **1** : outwardly perceivable; *also* : SUPERFICIAL **2** : of, relating to, or located on the outside or an outer part **3** : arising or acting from without; *also* : FOREIGN ⟨~ affairs⟩ — **ex·ter·nal·ly** *adv*
²external *n* : an external feature
ex·tinct \ik-'stiŋkt\ *adj* **1** : EXTINGUISHED; *also* : no longer active ⟨an ~ volcano⟩ **2** : no longer existing or in use ⟨dinosaurs are ~⟩ ⟨~ languages⟩ — **ex·tinc·tion** \ik-'stiŋk-shən\ *n*
ex·tin·guish \ik-'stiŋ-gwish\ *vb* : to cause to stop burning; *also* : to bring to an end (as by destroying) — **ex·tin·guish·able** *adj* — **ex·tin·guish·er** *n*
ex·tir·pate \'ek-stər-‚pāt\ *vb* **-pat·ed; -pat·ing** [L *exstirpatus*, pp. of *exstirpare*, fr. *ex-* out + *stirps* trunk, root] **1** : to destroy completely ⟨~ a heresy⟩ **2** : UPROOT ♦ *Synonyms* EXTERMINATE, ERADICATE, ABOLISH, ANNIHILATE — **ex·tir·pa·tion** \‚ek-stər-'pā-shən\ *n*
ex·tol *also* **ex·toll** \ik-'stōl\ *vb* **ex·tolled; ex·tol·ling** : to praise highly : GLORIFY
ex·tort \ik-'stórt\ *vb* [L *extortus*, pp. of *extorquēre* to wrench out, extort, fr. *ex-* out + *torquēre* to twist] : to obtain by force or improper pressure ⟨~ a bribe⟩ — **ex·tor·tion** \-'stór-shən\ *n* — **ex·tor·tion·er** *n* — **ex·tor·tion·ist** *n*
ex·tor·tion·ate \ik-'stór-shə-nət\ *adj* : EXCESSIVE, EXORBITANT ⟨~ prices⟩ — **ex·tor·tion·ate·ly** *adv*
¹ex·tra \'ek-strə\ *adj* **1** : ADDITIONAL ⟨~ work⟩ **2** : SUPERIOR ⟨~ quality⟩
²extra *n* **1** : a special edition of a newspaper **2** : an added charge **3** : an additional worker or performer (as in a motion picture)
³extra *adv* : beyond what is usual ⟨~ large⟩
¹ex·tract \ik-'strakt, *esp for 3* 'ek-‚strakt\ *vb* **1** : to draw out; *esp* : to pull out forcibly ⟨~ a tooth⟩ **2** : to withdraw (as a juice or a constituent) by a physical or chemical process **3** : to select for citation : QUOTE — **ex·tract·able** *adj* — **ex·trac·tion** \ik-'strak-shən\ *n* — **ex·trac·tor** \-tər\ *n*
²ex·tract \'ek-‚strakt\ *n* **1** : EXCERPT, CITATION **2** : a product (as a juice or concentrate) obtained by extracting
ex·tra·cur·ric·u·lar \‚ek-strə-kə-'ri-kyə-lər\ *adj* : lying outside the regular curriculum; *esp* : of or relating to school-connected activities (as sports) usu. carrying no academic credit
ex·tra·dite \'ek-strə-‚dīt\ *vb* **-dit·ed; -dit·ing** : to obtain by or deliver up to extradition
ex·tra·di·tion \‚ek-strə-'di-shən\ *n* : the surrender of an alleged criminal to a different jurisdiction for trial
ex·tra·mar·i·tal \‚ek-strə-'ma-rə-t³l\ *adj* : of or relating to sexual intercourse by a married person with someone other than his or her spouse

ex·tra·mu·ral \-'myùr-əl\ *adj* : existing or functioning beyond the bounds of an organized unit

ex·tra·ne·ous \ek-'strā-nē-əs\ *adj* 1 : coming from without ⟨~ light⟩ 2 : not forming a vital part; *also* : IRRELEVANT — ex·tra·ne·ous·ly *adv*

ex·tra·net \'ek-strə-,net\ *n* : a network like an intranet but also allowing access by certain outside parties

ex·traor·di·nary \ik-'strór-də-,ner-ē, ,ek-strə-'ór-\ *adj* 1 : notably unusual or exceptional 2 : employed on special service ⟨an ambassador ~⟩ — ex·traor·di·nari·ly \-,strór-də-'ner-ə-lē, ,ek-strə-,ór-\ *adv*

ex·trap·o·late \ik-'stra-pə-,lāt\ *vb* -lat·ed; -lat·ing : to infer (unknown data) from known data — ex·trap·o·la·tion \-,stra-pə-'lā-shən\ *n*

ex·tra·sen·so·ry \,ek-strə-'sen-sə-rē\ *adj* : not acting or occurring through the known senses

extrasensory perception *n* : perception (as in telepathy) of events external to the self not gained through the senses and not deducible from previous experience

ex·tra·solar \-'sō-lər\ *adj* : originating or existing outside the solar system

ex·tra·ter·res·tri·al \,-tə-'res-trē-əl\ *adj* : originating or existing outside the earth or its atmosphere ⟨~ life⟩ — extraterrestrial *n*

ex·tra·ter·ri·to·ri·al \,-ter-ə-'tór-ē-əl\ *adj* : existing or taking place outside the territorial limits of a jurisdiction

ex·tra·ter·ri·to·ri·al·i·ty \,-,tór-ē-'a-lə-tē\ *n* : exemption from the application or jurisdiction of local law or tribunals ⟨diplomats enjoy ~⟩

ex·trav·a·gant \ik-'stra-vi-gənt\ *adj* 1 : EXCESSIVE ⟨~ claims⟩ 2 : unduly lavish : WASTEFUL 3 : too costly ✦ *Synonyms* IMMODERATE, EXORBITANT, EXTREME, INORDINATE, UNDUE — ex·trav·a·gance \-gəns\ *n* — ex·trav·a·gant·ly *adv*

ex·trav·a·gan·za \ik-,stra-və-'gan-zə\ *n* 1 : a literary or musical work marked by extreme freedom of style and structure 2 : a spectacular show

¹ex·treme \ik-'strēm\ *adj* 1 : very great or intense ⟨~ cold⟩ 2 : very severe or radical ⟨~ measures⟩ 3 : going to great lengths or beyond normal limits ⟨politically ~⟩ 4 : most remote ⟨the ~ end⟩ 5 : UTMOST; *also* : MAXIMUM — ex·treme·ly *adv*

²extreme *n* 1 : something located at one end or the other of a range or series 2 : EXTREMITY 4

extremely low frequency *n* : a radio frequency in the lowest range of the radio spectrum

ex·trem·ism \ik-'strē-,mi-zəm\ *n* : the quality or state of being extreme; *esp* : advocacy of extreme political measures — ex·trem·ist \-'mist\ *n or adj*

ex·trem·i·ty \ik-'stre-mə-tē\ *n, pl* -ties 1 : the most remote part or point 2 : a limb of the body; *esp* : a human hand or foot 3 : the greatest need or danger 4 : the utmost degree ⟨the *extremities* of suffering⟩ 5 : a drastic or desperate measure

ex·tri·cate \'ek-strə-,kāt\ *vb* -cat·ed; -cat·ing [L *extricatus*, pp. of *extricare*, fr. *ex-* out + *tricae* trifles, perplexities] : to free from an entanglement or difficulty ✦ *Synonyms* DISENTANGLE, UNTANGLE, DISENCUMBER — ex·tri·ca·ble \ik-'stri-kə-bəl, ek-; 'ek-(,)stri-\ *adj* — ex·tri·ca·tion \,ek-strə-'kā-shən\ *n*

ex·trin·sic \ek-'strin-zik, -sik\ *adj* 1 : not forming part of or belonging to a thing 2 : EXTERNAL — ex·trin·si·cal·ly \-zi-k(ə-)lē, -si-\ *adv*

ex·tro·vert *also* ex·tra·vert \'ek-strə-,vərt\ *n* : a gregarious and unreserved person — ex·tro·ver·sion *or* ex·tra·ver·sion \,ek-strə-'vər-zhən\ *n* — ex·tro·vert·ed *also* ex·tra·vert·ed *adj*

ex·trude \ik-'strüd\ *vb* ex·trud·ed; ex·trud·ing 1 : to force, press, or push out 2 : to shape (as plastic) by forcing through a die — ex·tru·sion \-'strü-zhən\ *n* — ex·trud·er *n*

ex·u·ber·ant \ig-'zü-bə-rənt\ *adj* 1 : unrestrained in enthusiasm or style 2 : PROFUSE ⟨~ vegetation⟩ — ex·u·ber·ance \-rəns\ *n* — ex·u·ber·ant·ly *adv*

ex·ude \ig-'züd\ *vb* ex·ud·ed; ex·ud·ing [L *exsudare*, fr. *ex-* out + *sudare* to sweat] 1 : to discharge slowly through pores or cuts ⟨~s charm⟩ — ex·u·date \'ek-sù-,dāt, -syù-\ *n* — ex·u·da·tion \,ek-sù-'dā-shən, -syù-\ *n*

ex·ult \ig-'zəlt\ *vb* : REJOICE, GLORY ⟨~ed in their victory⟩ — ex·ul·tant \-'zəl-tᵊnt\ *adj* — ex·ul·tant·ly *adv* — ex·ul·ta·tion \,ek-(,)səl-'tā-shən, ,eg-(,)zəl-\ *n*

ex·urb \'ek-,sərb, 'eg-,zərb\ *n* : a region outside a city and its suburbs inhabited chiefly by well-to-do families — ex·ur·ban \ek-'sər-bən, eg-'zər-\ *adj*

ex·ur·ban·ite \ek-'sər-bə-,nīt; eg-'zər-\ *n* : one who lives in an exurb

ex·ur·bia \ek-'sər-bē-ə, eg-'zər-\ *n* : the generalized region of exurbs

-ey — see -Y

¹eye \'ī\ *n* 1 : an organ of sight typically consisting in vertebrates of a globular structure that is located in a socket of the skull, is lined with a sensitive retina, and is normally paired 2 : VISION, PERCEPTION; *also* : faculty of discrimination ⟨an ~ for bargains⟩ 3 : POINT OF VIEW, JUDGMENT — often used in pl. ⟨in the ~s of the law⟩ 4 : something suggesting an eye (as the hole of a needle or the bud of a potato) 5 : the calm center of a cyclone — eyed \'īd\ *adj*

²eye *vb* eyed; eye·ing *or* ey·ing : to look at : WATCH

¹eye·ball \'ī-,ból\ *n* : the globular capsule of the vertebrate eye

²eyeball *vb* : to look at intently

eye·brow \-,braù\ *n* : the ridge over the eye or the hair growing on it

eye·drop·per \-,drä-pər\ *n* : DROPPER 2

eye·glass \-,glas\ *n* : a lens worn to aid vision; *also, pl* : GLASSES

eye·lash \-,lash\ *n* 1 : the fringe of hair edging the eyelid — usu. used in pl. 2 : a single hair of the eyelashes

eye·let \-lət\ *n* 1 : a small hole intended for ornament or for passage of a cord or lace 2 : a typically metal ring for reinforcing an eyelet : GROMMET

eye·lid \-,lid\ *n* : either of the movable folds of skin and muscle that can be closed over the eyeball

eye·lin·er \-,lī-nər\ *n* : makeup used to emphasize the contour of the eyes

eye·open·er \-,ō-pə-nər\ *n* : something startling or surprising — eye-open·ing *adj*

eye·piece \-,pēs\ *n* : the lens or combination of lenses at the eye end of an optical instrument

eye shadow *n* : a colored cosmetic applied to the eyelids to accent the eyes

eye·sight \-,sīt\ *n* : SIGHT, VISION

eye·sore \-,sór\ *n* : something offensive to view

eye·strain \-,strān\ *n* : weariness or a strained state of the eye

eye·tooth \-'tüth\ *n* : a canine tooth of the upper jaw

eye·wash \-,wòsh, -,wäsh\ *n* 1 : an eye lotion 2 : misleading or deceptive statements, actions, or procedures

eye·wit·ness \-'wit-nəs\ *n* : a person who actually sees something happen

ey·rie \'ā-,rir\ *chiefly Brit var of* AERIE

ey·ra \'ā-,rir\ *n, pl* au·rar \'aù-,rär\ — see *krona* at MONEY table

Ez *or* Ezr *abbr* Ezra

Ezech *abbr* Ezechiel

Eze·chiel \i-'zē-kyəl\ *n* — see BIBLE table

Ezek *abbr* Ezekiel

Eze·kiel \i-'zē-kyəl\ *n* — see BIBLE table

e-zine \'ē-,zēn\ *n* : an online magazine

Ez·ra \'ez-rə\ *n* — see BIBLE table

F

¹**f** \'ef\ *n, pl* **f's** *or* **fs** \'efs\ *often cap* **1** : the 6th letter of the English alphabet **2** : a grade rating a student's work as failing
²**f** *abbr, often cap* **1** Fahrenheit **2** false **3** family **4** farad **5** female **6** feminine **7** forte **8** French **9** frequency **10** Friday
³**f** *symbol* focal length
F *symbol* fluorine
FAA *abbr* Federal Aviation Administration
fab \'fab\ *adj* : FABULOUS
Fa·bi·an \'fā-bē-ən\ *adj* : of, relating to, or being a society of socialists organized in England in 1884 to spread socialist principles gradually — **Fabian** *n* — **Fa·bi·an·ism** *n*
fa·ble \'fā-bəl\ *n* **1** : a legendary story of supernatural happenings **2** : a narration intended to teach a lesson; *esp* : one in which animals speak and act like people **3** : FALSEHOOD
fa·bled \'fā-bəld\ *adj* **1** : FICTITIOUS **2** : told or celebrated in fable ⟨~ deeds⟩
fab·ric \'fa-brik\ *n* [MF *fabrique*, fr. L *fabrica* workshop, structure] **1** : STRUCTURE, FRAMEWORK ⟨the ~ of society⟩ **2** : CLOTH; *also* : a material that resembles cloth
fab·ri·cate \'fa-bri-ˌkāt\ *vb* **-cat·ed; -cat·ing** **1** : INVENT, CREATE **2** : to make up for the sake of deception ⟨reporters *fabricating* news stories⟩ **3** : CONSTRUCT, MANUFACTURE ⟨~ tools⟩ — **fab·ri·ca·tion** \ˌfa-bri-'kā-shən\ *n*
fab·u·lous \'fa-byə-ləs\ *adj* **1** : resembling a fable; *also* : INCREDIBLE, MARVELOUS ⟨had a ~ time⟩ **2** : told in or based on fable — **fab·u·lous·ly** *adv*
fac *abbr* **1** facsimile **2** faculty
fa·cade *also* **fa·çade** \fə-'säd\ *n* [F *façade*, fr. It *facciata*, fr. *faccia* face] **1** : the principal face or front of a building **2** : a false, superficial, or artificial appearance ✦ *Synonyms* MASK, DISGUISE, FRONT, GUISE, PRETENSE, VENEER
¹**face** \'fās\ *n* **1** : the front part of the head **2** : PRESENCE ⟨in the ~ of danger⟩ **3** : facial expression : LOOK ⟨put a sad ~ on⟩ **4** : GRIMACE ⟨made a ~⟩ **5** : outward appearance ⟨looks easy on the ~ of it⟩ **6** : CONFIDENCE; *also* : BOLDNESS **7** : DIGNITY, PRESTIGE ⟨afraid to lose ~⟩ **8** : SURFACE; *esp* : a front, principal, bounding, or contacting surface ⟨~ of a cliff⟩ ⟨the ~s of a cube⟩ ⟨the ~ of a golf club⟩ — **faced** \'fāst, 'fā-səd\ *adj*
²**face** *vb* **faced; fac·ing** **1** : to confront brazenly **2** : to line near the edge esp. with a different material; *also* : to cover the front or surface of ⟨~ a building with marble⟩ **3** : to meet or bring in direct contact or confrontation ⟨*faced* the problem⟩ **4** : to stand or sit with the face toward ⟨~ the sun⟩ **5** : to have the front oriented toward ⟨a house *facing* the park⟩ **6** : to have as or be a prospect ⟨~ a grim future⟩ **7** : to turn the face or body in a specified direction — **face the music** : to meet the unpleasant consequences of one's actions
face·down \ˌfās-'daun\ *adv* : with the face downward ⟨cards turned ~⟩
face·less \-ləs\ *n* **1** : lacking character or individuality **2** : lacking a face
face-lift \'fās-ˌlift\ *n* **1** : plastic surgery on the face and neck to remove defects (as wrinkles) typical of aging **2** : MODERNIZATION — **face-lift** *vb*
face-off \'fās-ˌóf\ *n* **1** : a method of beginning play by dropping a puck or ball (as in hockey) between two opposing players each of whom attempts to control it **2** : CONFRONTATION — **face off** *vb*
fac·et \'fa-sət\ *n* [F *facette*, dim. of *face*] **1** : a small plane surface of a cut gem **2** : ASPECT, PHASE
fa·ce·tious \fə-'sē-shəs\ *adj* **1** : joking often inappropriately ⟨~ remarks⟩ **2** : JOCULAR, JOCOSE ✦ *Synonyms* WITTY, HUMOROUS — **fa·ce·tious·ly** *adv* — **fa·ce·tious·ness** *n*
¹**fa·cial** \'fā-shəl\ *adj* **1** : of or relating to the face **2** : used to improve the appearance of the face

²**facial** *n* : a facial treatment
fac·ile \'fa-səl\ *adj* **1** : easily accomplished, handled, or attained **2** : SIMPLISTIC **3** : readily manifested and often insincere ⟨~ prose⟩ **4** : READY, FLUENT ⟨a ~ writer⟩
fa·cil·i·tate \fə-'si-lə-ˌtāt\ *vb* **-tat·ed; -tat·ing** : to make easier — **fa·cil·i·ta·tion** \-ˌsi-lə-'tā-shən\ *n* — **fa·cil·i·ta·tor** \-'si-lə-ˌtā-tər\ *n*
fa·cil·i·ty \fə-'si-lə-tē\ *n, pl* **-ties** **1** : the quality of being easily performed **2** : ease in performance : APTITUDE **3** : PLIANCY **4** : something that makes easier an action, operation, or course of conduct; *also* : REST ROOM — often used in pl. **5** : something (as a hospital) built or installed for a particular purpose
fac·ing \'fā-siŋ\ *n* **1** : a lining at the edge esp. of a garment **2** *pl* : the collar, cuffs, and trimmings of a uniform coat **3** : an ornamental or protective layer **4** : material for facing
fac·sim·i·le \fak-'si-mə-lē\ *n* [L *fac simile* make similar] **1** : an exact copy **2** : a system of transmitting and reproducing printed matter or pictures by means of signals sent over telephone lines
fact \'fakt\ *n* **1** : DEED; *esp* : CRIME ⟨accessory after the ~⟩ **2** : the quality of being actual **3** : something that exists or occurs **4** : a piece of information — **in fact** : in truth
fac·tion \'fak-shən\ *n* : a group or combination (as in a government) acting together within and usu. against a larger body : CLIQUE — **fac·tion·al·ism** \-shə-nə-ˌli-zəm\ *n*
fac·tious \'fak-shəs\ *adj* **1** : of, relating to, or caused by faction **2** : inclined to faction or the formation of factions : causing dissension ✦ *Synonyms* INSUBORDINATE, CONTUMACIOUS, INSURGENT, SEDITIOUS, REBELLIOUS
fac·ti·tious \fak-'ti-shəs\ *adj* : ARTIFICIAL, SHAM ⟨a ~ display of grief⟩
fac·toid \'fak-ˌtóid\ *n* **1** : an invented fact believed to be true because of its appearance in print **2** : a brief usu. trivial fact
¹**fac·tor** \'fak-tər\ *n* **1** : AGENT **2** : something that actively contributes to a result ⟨a ~ in her decision⟩ **3** : GENE **4** : any of the numbers or symbols in mathematics that when multiplied together form a product; *esp* : any of the integers that divide a given integer without a remainder
²**factor** *vb* **1** : to work as a factor **2** : to find the mathematical factors of and esp. the prime mathematical factors of
¹**fac·to·ri·al** \fak-'tór-ē-əl\ *adj* : of, relating to, or being a factor
²**factorial** *n* : the product of all the positive integers from 1 to a given integer *n*
fac·to·ry \'fak-trē, -tə-rē\ *n, pl* **-ries** **1** : a trading post where resident brokers trade **2** : a building or group of buildings used for manufacturing

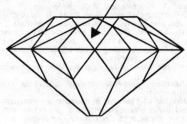

facet 1

fac·to·tum \fak-'tō-təm\ *n* [NL, lit., do everything, fr. L *fac* do + *totum* everything] : a person (as a servant) having numerous or varied duties

facts of life : the physiological processes and behavior involved in sex and reproduction

fac·tu·al \'fak-chə-wəl\ *adj* : of or relating to facts; *also* : based on fact — **fac·tu·al·ly** *adv*

fac·ul·ty \'fa-kəl-tē\ *n, pl* **-ties** **1** : ability to act or do : POWER; *also* : natural aptitude **2** : one of the powers of the mind or body ⟨the ~ of hearing⟩ **3** : the teachers in a school or college or one of its divisions

fad \'fad\ *n* : a practice or interest followed for a time with exaggerated zeal : CRAZE — **fad·dish** *adj* — **fad·dish·ly** *adv* — **fad·dist** *n*

¹fade \'fād\ *vb* **fad·ed; fad·ing** **1** : WITHER **2** : to lose or cause to lose freshness or brilliance of color **3** : VANISH ⟨a *fading* memory⟩ **4** : to grow dim or faint

²fade *n* : a short haircut in which hair on top of the head stands high

FADM *abbr* fleet admiral

fae·cal, fae·ces *chiefly Brit var of* FECAL, FECES

fa·er·ie *also* **fa·ery** \'fā-rē, 'fer-ē\ *n, pl* **fa·er·ies** **1** : FAIRYLAND **2** : FAIRY

¹fag \'fag\ *vb* **fagged; fag·ging** **1** : DRUDGE **2** : TIRE, EXHAUST ⟨*fagged* by the work⟩

²fag *n* : MENIAL, DRUDGE

³fag *n* : an English public-school boy who acts as servant to another

⁴fag *vb* : to act as a fag

⁵fag *n* : CIGARETTE

fag end *n* **1** : REMNANT **2** : the extreme end **3** : the last part or coarser end of a web of cloth **4** : the untwisted end of a rope

fag·ot *or* **fag·got** \'fa-gət\ *n* : a bundle of sticks or twigs

fag·ot·ing *or* **fag·got·ing** *n* : an embroidery produced by tying threads in hourglass-shaped clusters

Fah *or* **Fahr** *abbr* Fahrenheit

Fahr·en·heit \'fer-ən-,hīt\ *adj* : relating to, conforming to, or having a thermometer scale with the boiling point of water at 212 degrees and the freezing point at 32 degrees above zero

fa·ience *or* **fa·ïence** \fā-'äns\ *n* [F] : earthenware decorated with opaque colored glazes

¹fail \'fāl\ *vb* **1** : to become feeble; *esp* : to decline in health **2** : to die away **3** : to stop functioning **4** : to fall short ⟨~ed in his duty⟩ **5** : to be or become absent or inadequate **6** : to be unsuccessful esp. in achieving a passing grade **7** : to become bankrupt **8** : DISAPPOINT **9** : NEGLECT ⟨~ed to lock the door⟩

²fail *n* : FAILURE ⟨without ~⟩

¹fail·ing \'fā-liŋ\ *n* : WEAKNESS, SHORTCOMING

²failing *prep* : in the absence or lack of

faille \'fī(-ə)l\ *n* : a somewhat shiny closely woven ribbed fabric (as silk)

fail–safe \'fāl-,sāf\ *adj* **1** : incorporating a counteractive feature for a possible source of failure **2** : having no chance of failure — **fail–safe** *n*

fail·ure \'fāl-yər\ *n* **1** : a failing to do or perform **2** : a state of inability to perform a normal function adequately ⟨heart ~⟩; *also* : an abrupt cessation of functioning ⟨a power ~⟩ **3** : a fracturing or giving way under stress **4** : a lack of success **5** : BANKRUPTCY **6** : DEFICIENCY ⟨crop ~⟩ **7** : DETERIORATION, DECAY **8** : one that has failed

¹fain \'fān\ *adj* **1** *archaic* : GLAD; *also* : INCLINED **2** : being obliged or compelled

²fain *adv* **1** : with pleasure **2** : by preference

¹faint \'fānt\ *adj* [ME *faint, feint,* fr. AF, fr. *faindre, feindre* to feign, lose heart] **1** : COWARDLY, SPIRITLESS ⟨~ of heart⟩ **2** : weak, dizzy, and likely to faint **3** : lacking vigor or strength : FEEBLE ⟨~ praise⟩ **4** : hardly perceptible ⟨~ handwriting⟩ — **faint·ly** *adv* — **faint·ness** *n*

²faint *vb* : to lose consciousness

³faint *n* : the action of fainting; *also* : the resulting condition

faint·heart·ed \,fānt-'här-təd\ *adj* : lacking courage : TIMID

¹fair \'fer\ *adj* **1** : pleasing in appearance : BEAUTIFUL **2** : superficially pleasing : SPECIOUS **3** : CLEAN, PURE **4** : CLEAR, LEGIBLE **5** : not stormy or cloudy **6** : JUST **7** : conforming with the rules : ALLOWED; *also* : being

within the foul lines ⟨~ ball⟩ **8** : open to legitimate pursuit or attack ⟨~ game⟩ **9** : PROMISING, LIKELY ⟨a ~ chance of winning⟩ **10** : favorable to a ship's course ⟨a ~ wind⟩ **11** : light in complexion : BLOND **12** : ADEQUATE **13** : significant in size ⟨a ~ amount of traffic⟩ — **fair·ness** *n*

²fair *adv* **1** : in a fair manner ⟨play ~⟩ **2** *chiefly Brit* : FAIRLY 4

³fair *n* **1** : a gathering of buyers and sellers at a stated time and place for trade **2** : a competitive exhibition (as of farm products) **3** : a sale of assorted articles usu. for a charitable purpose ⟨a book ~⟩ **4** : an exhibition that promotes available services ⟨a job ~⟩

fair·ground \-,graund\ *n* : an area where outdoor fairs, circuses, or exhibitions are held

fair·ing \'fer-iŋ\ *n* : a structure for producing a smooth outline and reducing drag (as on an airplane)

fair·ly \'fer-lē\ *adv* **1** : HANDSOMELY **2** : in a manner of speaking ⟨~ bursting with pride⟩ **3** : without bias **4** : to a full degree or extent : PLAINLY, DISTINCTLY **5** : SOMEWHAT, RATHER ⟨a ~ easy job⟩

fair–spo·ken \'fer-'spō-kən\ *adj* : pleasant and courteous in speech

fair–trade \-'trād\ *adj* : of, relating to, or being an agreement between a producer and a seller that branded merchandise will be sold at or above a specified price — **fair–trade** *vb*

fair·way \-,wā\ *n* : the mowed part of a golf course between tee and green

fairy \'fer-ē\ *n, pl* **fair·ies** [ME *fairie* fairyland, enchantment, fr. AF *faerie,* fr. *fee* fairy, fr. L *Fata,* goddess of fate, fr. *fatum* fate] : an imaginary being of folklore and romance usu. having diminutive human form and magic powers — **fairy** *adj*

fairy·land \-,land\ *n* **1** : the land of fairies **2** : a beautiful or charming place

fairy tale *n* **1** : a children's story usu. about mythical beings (as fairies) **2** : FIB

fait ac·com·pli \'fāt-,a-,kōⁿ-'plē\ *n, pl* **faits accomplis** *same or* -'plēz\ [F, accomplished fact] : a thing accomplished and presumably irreversible

faith \'fāth\ *n, pl* **faiths** \'fāths, 'fāᵺz\ [ME *feith,* fr. AF *feid, fei,* fr. L *fides*] **1** : allegiance to duty or a person : LOYALTY **2** : belief and trust in God **3** : complete trust **4** : a system of religious beliefs — **faith·ful** \-fəl\ *adj* — **faith·ful·ly** *adv* — **faith·ful·ness** *n*

faith·less \'fāth-ləs\ *adj* **1** : DISLOYAL **2** : not to be relied on ♦ **Synonyms** FALSE, TRAITOROUS, TREACHEROUS, UNFAITHFUL — **faith·less·ly** *adv* — **faith·less·ness** *n*

fa·ji·ta \fə-'hē-tə\ *n* : a marinated strip usu. of beef or chicken grilled or broiled and served usu. with a flour tortilla and savory fillings

¹fake \'fāk\ *adj* : COUNTERFEIT, SHAM

²fake *n* **1** : IMITATION, FRAUD; *also* : IMPOSTOR **2** : a simulated move in sports (as a pretended pass)

³fake *vb* **faked; fak·ing** **1** : to treat so as to falsify **2** : COUNTERFEIT **3** : to deceive (an opponent) in a sports contest by making a fake move — **fak·er** *n*

fa·kir \fə-'kir\ *n* [Ar *faqīr,* lit., poor man] **1** : a Muslim mendicant : DERVISH **2** : a wandering Hindu ascetic

fal·con \'fal-kən, 'fȯl-\ *n* **1** : a hawk trained for use in falconry **2** : any of various swift long-winged long-tailed hawks having a notched beak and usu. inhabiting open areas

fal·con·ry \'fal-kən-rē, 'fȯl-\ *n* **1** : the art of training hawks to hunt in cooperation with a person **2** : the sport of hunting with hawks — **fal·con·er** *n*

¹fall \'fȯl\ *vb* **fell** \'fel\; **fall·en** \'fȯ-lən\; **fall·ing** **1** : to descend freely by the force of gravity **2** : to hang freely **3** : to come or go as if by falling ⟨darkness *fell*⟩ **4** : to become uttered **5** : to lower or become lowered : DROP ⟨her eyes *fell*⟩ **6** : to leave an erect position suddenly and involuntarily **7** : STUMBLE, STRAY **8** : to drop down wounded or dead esp. in battle **9** : to become captured ⟨the city *fell* to the enemy⟩ **10** : to suffer ruin, defeat, or failure **11** : to commit an immoral act **12** : to move or extend in a downward direction **13** : SUBSIDE, ABATE **14** : to decline in quality, activity, quantity, or value **15** : to assume a look of shame or dejection ⟨her face *fell*⟩ **16** : to occur at a certain time **17** : to come by chance

18 : DEVOLVE ⟨the duties *fell* to him⟩ 19 : to have the proper place or station ⟨the accent ~*s* on the first syllable⟩ 20 : to come within the scope of something 21 : to pass from one condition to another ⟨*fell* ill⟩ 22 : to set about heartily or actively ⟨~ to work⟩ — **fall all over oneself** *or* **fall over backward** : to display excessive eagerness — **fall flat** : to produce no response or result — **fall for** 1 : to fall in love with 2 : to become a victim of — **fall from grace** : BACKSLIDE — **fall into line** : to comply with a certain course of action — **fall short** 1 : to be deficient 2 : to fail to attain

²**fall** *n* 1 : the act of falling 2 : a falling out, off, or away : DROPPING 3 : AUTUMN 4 : a thing or quantity that falls ⟨a light ~ of snow⟩ 5 : COLLAPSE, DOWNFALL 6 : the surrender or capture of a besieged place 7 : departure from virtue or goodness 8 : SLOPE 9 : WATERFALL — usu. used in pl. 10 : a decrease in size, quantity, degree, or value ⟨a ~ in price⟩ 11 : the distance which something falls 12 : an act of forcing a wrestler's shoulders to the mat; *also* : a bout of wrestling

fal·la·cious \fə-'lā-shəs\ *adj* 1 : embodying a fallacy ⟨a ~ argument⟩ 2 : MISLEADING, DECEPTIVE

fal·la·cy \'fa-lə-sē\ *n, pl* **-cies** 1 : a false or mistaken idea 2 : an often plausible argument using false or illogical reasoning

fall back *vb* : RETREAT, RECEDE

fall guy *n* : SCAPEGOAT

fal·li·ble \'fa-lə-bəl\ *adj* 1 : liable to be erroneous 2 : capable of making a mistake — **fal·li·bly** \-blē\ *adv*

fall·ing–out \ˌfȯl-liŋ-'aút\ *n, pl* **fallings–out** *or* **falling–outs** : QUARREL

falling star *n* : METEOR

fal·lo·pi·an tube \fə-'lō-pē-ən-\ *n, often cap F* : either of the pair of anatomical tubes that carry the eggs from the ovary to the uterus

fall·out \'fȯl-ˌaút\ *n* 1 : the often radioactive particles that result from a nuclear explosion and descend through the air 2 : a secondary and often lingering effect or result

fall out *vb* : QUARREL

¹**fal·low** \'fa-(ˌ)lō\ *n* : fallow land; *also* : the state or period of being fallow — **fallow** *vb*

²**fallow** *adj* 1 : left without tilling or sowing after plowing 2 : DORMANT, INACTIVE ⟨a writer's ~ period⟩

false \'fȯls\ *adj* **fals·er; fals·est** 1 : not genuine : ARTIFICIAL ⟨~ teeth⟩ 2 : intentionally untrue 3 : adjusted or made so as to deceive ⟨~ scales⟩ 4 : tending to mislead : DECEPTIVE ⟨~ promises⟩ 5 : not true ⟨~ concepts⟩ 6 : not faithful or loyal : TREACHEROUS 7 : not essential or permanent ⟨~ front⟩ 8 : inaccurate in pitch 9 : based on mistaken ideas — **false·ly** *adv* — **false·ness** *n* — **fal·si·ty** \'fȯl-sə-tē\ *n*

false·hood \'fȯls-ˌhůd\ *n* 1 : LIE 2 : absence of truth or accuracy 3 : the practice of lying

fal·set·to \fȯl-'se-tō\ *n, pl* **-tos** [It, fr. dim. of *falso* false] : an artificially high voice; *esp* : an artificial singing voice that overlaps and extends above the range of the full voice esp. of a tenor

fal·si·fy \'fȯl-sə-ˌfī\ *vb* **-fied; -fy·ing** 1 : to prove to be false 2 : to alter so as to deceive 3 : LIE; *also* : MISREPRESENT — **fal·si·fi·able** \ˌfȯl-sə-'fī-ə-bəl\ *adj* — **fal·si·fi·ca·tion** \ˌfȯl-sə-fə-'kā-shən\ *n*

fal·ter \'fȯl-tər\ *vb* 1 : to move unsteadily : STUMBLE, TOTTER 2 : to hesitate in speech : STAMMER 3 : to hesitate in purpose or action : WAVER, FLINCH 4 : to lose effectiveness ⟨a ~*ing* business⟩ — **fal·ter·ing·ly** *adv*

fam *abbr* 1 familiar 2 family

fame \'fām\ *n* : public reputation : RENOWN — **famed** \'fāmd\ *adj*

fa·mil·ial \fə-'mil-yəl\ *adj* 1 : of, relating to, or suggestive of a family 2 : tending to occur in more members of a family than expected by chance alone ⟨a ~ disorder⟩

¹**fa·mil·iar** \fə-'mil-yər\ *n* 1 : COMPANION 2 : a spirit held to attend and serve or guard a person 3 : one who frequents a place

²**familiar** *adj* 1 : closely acquainted : INTIMATE 2 : of or relating to a family 3 : INFORMAL ⟨a ~ style⟩ 4 : FORWARD, PRESUMPTUOUS 5 : frequently seen or experienced ⟨a ~ face⟩ 6 : of everyday occurrence — **fa·mil·iar·ly** *adv*

fa·mil·iar·ise *Brit var of* FAMILIARIZE

fa·mil·iar·i·ty \fə-ˌmil-'yer-ə-tē, -ˌmi-lē-'er-\ *n, pl* **-ties** 1 : close friendship : INTIMACY 2 : INFORMALITY 3 : an unduly bold or forward act or expression : IMPROPRIETY 4 : close acquaintance with something ⟨~ with current software⟩

fa·mil·iar·ize \fə-'mil-yə-ˌrīz\ *vb* **-ized; -iz·ing** 1 : to make known or familiar 2 : to make thoroughly acquainted

fam·i·ly \'fam-lē, 'fa-mə-\ *n, pl* **-lies** [ME *familie*, fr. L *familia* household, fr. *famulus* servant] 1 : a group of individuals living under one roof and under one head : HOUSEHOLD 2 : a group of persons of common ancestry : CLAN 3 : a group of things having common characteristics; *esp* : a group of related plants or animals ranking in biological classification above a genus and below an order 4 : a social unit usu. consisting of one or two parents and their children

family planning *n* : planning intended to determine the number and spacing of one's children by using birth control

family tree *n* : GENEALOGY; *also* : a genealogical diagram

fam·ine \'fa-mən\ *n* 1 : an extreme scarcity of food 2 : a great shortage

fam·ish \'fa-mish\ *vb* 1 : STARVE 2 : to suffer for lack of something necessary

fa·mous \'fā-məs\ *adj* 1 : widely known 2 : honored for achievement 3 : EXCELLENT, FIRST-RATE ♦ **Synonyms** RENOWNED, CELEBRATED, NOTED, NOTORIOUS, DISTINGUISHED, EMINENT, ILLUSTRIOUS

fa·mous·ly *adv* : SPLENDIDLY, EXCELLENTLY ⟨got along ~⟩

¹**fan** \'fan\ *n* : a device (as a hand-waved triangular piece or a mechanism with blades) for producing a current of air

²**fan** *vb* **fanned; fan·ning** 1 : to drive away the chaff from grain by winnowing 2 : to move (air) with or as if with a fan 3 : to direct a current of air upon ⟨~ a fire⟩ 4 : to stir up to activity : STIMULATE 5 : to spread like a fan 6 : to strike out in baseball

³**fan** *n* : an enthusiastic follower or admirer

fa·nat·ic \fə-'na-tik\ *or* **fa·nat·i·cal** \-ti-kəl\ *adj* [L *fanaticus* inspired by a deity, frenzied, fr. *fanum* temple] : marked by excessive enthusiasm and often intense uncritical devotion — **fanatic** *n* — **fa·nat·i·cism** \-tə-ˌsi-zəm\ *n*

fan·ci·er \'fan-sē-ər\ *n* 1 : one that has a special liking or interest 2 : a person who breeds or grows some kind of animal or plant for points of excellence

fan·ci·ful \'fan-si-fəl\ *adj* 1 : marked by, existing in, or given to unrestrained imagination or whim rather than reason 2 : curiously made or shaped ⟨a ~ design⟩ — **fan·ci·ful·ly** *adv*

¹**fan·cy** \'fan-sē\ *vb* **fan·cied; fan·cy·ing** 1 : LIKE 2 : IMAGINE 3 : to believe without evidence or certainty 4 : to visualize or interpret as

²**fancy** *n, pl* **fancies** [ME *fantasie, fantsy* imagination, image, preference, fr. AF *fantasie* illusion, fr. L *phantasia*, fr. Gk, appearance, imagination] 1 : LIKING, INCLINATION; *also* : LOVE 2 : WHIM, NOTION, IDEA ⟨a passing ~⟩ 3 : IMAGINATION 4 : TASTE, JUDGMENT ♦ **Synonyms** CAPRICE, CROTCHET, VAGARY

³**fancy** *adj* **fan·ci·er; -est** 1 : WHIMSICAL 2 : not plain : ORNAMENTAL, POSH 3 : of particular excellence 4 : bred esp. for a showy appearance 5 : EXCESSIVE 6 : executed with technical skill and style — **fan·ci·ly** \'fan-sə-lē\ *adv*

fancy dress *n* : a costume (as for a masquerade) chosen to suit a fancy

fan·cy–free \ˌfan-sē-'frē\ *adj* : free from amorous attachment; *also* : free to imagine

fan·cy·work \'fan-sē-ˌwərk\ *n* : ornamental needlework (as embroidery)

fan·dan·go \fan-'daŋ-gō\ *n, pl* **-gos** 1 : a lively Spanish or Spanish-American dance 2 : TOMFOOLERY

fane \'fān\ *n* 1 : TEMPLE 2 : CHURCH

fan·fare \'fan-ˌfer\ *n* 1 : a flourish of trumpets 2 : a showy display

fan fiction *n* : stories involving fictional characters that are written by fans

fang \'faŋ\ *n* : a long sharp tooth; *esp* : a grooved or hollow tooth of a venomous snake — **fanged** \'faŋd\ *adj*

fan·light \'fan-ˌlīt\ *n* : a semicircular window with radiating bars like a fan that is set over a door or window

fan·ny \'fa-nē\ *n, pl* **fannies** : BUTTOCKS

fan·tail \'fan-ˌtāl\ *n* **1** : a fan-shaped tail or end **2** : an overhang at the stern of a ship

fan·ta·sia \fan-'tā-zhə, -zhē-ə, -zē-ə; ˌfan-tə-'zē-ə\ *n* : a musical composition free and fanciful in form

fan·ta·sise *Brit var of* FANTASIZE

fan·ta·size \'fan-tə-ˌsīz\ *vb* **-sized; -siz·ing** : IMAGINE, DAYDREAM

fan·tas·tic \fan-'tas-tik\ *also* **fan·tas·ti·cal** \-ti-kəl\ *adj* **1** : IMAGINARY, UNREAL **2** : conceived by unrestrained fancy **3** : exceedingly or unbelievably great **4** : ECCENTRIC ♦ *Synonyms* CHIMERICAL, FANCIFUL, IMAGINARY — **fan·tas·ti·cal·ly** \-ti-k(ə-)lē\ *adv*

fan·ta·sy *also* **phan·ta·sy** \'fan-tə-sē\ *n, pl* **-sies** **1** : IMAGINATION, FANCY **2** : a product of the imagination : ILLUSION **3** : FANTASIA — **fantasy** *vb*

FAQ \'fak, ˌef-ˌā-'kyü\ *n* : a document (as on a website) that provides answers to a list of typical user questions

¹**far** \'fär\ *adv* **far·ther** \-thər\ *or* **fur·ther** \'fər-\; **far·thest** *or* **fur·thest** \-thəst\ **1** : at or to a considerable distance in space or time ⟨~ from home⟩ **2** : by a broad interval : WIDELY, MUCH ⟨~ better⟩ **3** : to or at a definite distance, point, or degree ⟨as ~ as I know⟩ **4** : to an advanced point or extent ⟨go ~ in his field⟩ — **by far** : by a considerable margin — **far and away** : DECIDEDLY — **so far** : until now

²**far** *adj* **farther** *or* **further**; **farthest** *or* **furthest** **1** : remote in space or time **2** : DIFFERENT **3** : LONG ⟨a ~ journey⟩ **4** : being the more distant of two ⟨on the ~ side of the lake⟩

far·ad \'far-ˌad, -əd\ *n* : a unit of capacitance equal to the capacitance of a capacitor having a potential difference of one volt between its plates when it is charged with one coulomb of electricity

far·away \'fär-ə-ˌwā\ *adj* **1** : DISTANT, REMOTE ⟨~ lands⟩ **2** : DREAMY

farce \'färs\ *n* **1** : a broadly satirical comedy with an improbable plot **2** : the humor characteristic of farce or pretense **3** : a ridiculous or empty display — **far·ci·cal** \'fär-si-kəl\ *adj*

far cry *n* **1** : a long distance **2** : something notably different ⟨a *far cry* from what we expected⟩

¹**fare** \'fer\ *vb* **fared; far·ing** **1** : GO, TRAVEL **2** : GET ALONG, SUCCEED ⟨*fared* well in math⟩ **3** : EAT, DINE

²**fare** *n* **1** : range of food : DIET; *also* : material provided for use, consumption, or enjoyment **2** : the price charged to transport a person **3** : a person paying a fare : PASSENGER

¹**fare·well** \fer-'wel\ *vb imper* : get along well — used interjectionally to or by one departing

²**farewell** *n* **1** : a wish of well-being at parting : GOOD-BYE **2** : LEAVE-TAKING

³**fare·well** \'fer-ˌwel\ *adj* : PARTING, FINAL ⟨a ~ concert⟩

far-fetched \'fär-'fecht\ *adj* : not easily or naturally deduced or introduced : IMPROBABLE ⟨a ~ story⟩

far-flung \-'fləŋ\ *adj* : widely spread or distributed ⟨a ~ empire⟩

fa·ri·na \fə-'rē-nə\ *n* [L, meal, flour] : a fine meal (as of wheat) used in puddings or as a breakfast cereal

far·i·na·ceous \ˌfar-ə-'nā-shəs\ *adj* **1** : having a mealy texture or surface **2** : containing or rich in starch

¹**farm** \'färm\ *n* [ME *ferme* rent, lease, fr. AF, fr. *fermer* to fix, rent, fr. L *firmare* to make firm, fr. *firmus* firm] **1** : a tract of land used for raising crops or livestock **2** : a minor-league subsidiary of a major-league team

²**farm** *vb* **1** : to use (land) as a farm ⟨~*ed* 200 acres⟩; *also* : to raise crops or livestock — **farm·er** *n*

farm·hand \'färm-ˌhand\ *n* : a farm laborer

farm·house \-ˌhaůs\ *n* : a dwelling on a farm

farm·ing \'fär-miŋ\ *n* : the occupation or business of a person who farms

farm·land \'färm-ˌland\ *n* : land used or suitable for farming

farm out *vb* : to turn over (as a task) to another

farm·stead \'färm-ˌsted\ *n* : a farm with its buildings

farm·yard \-ˌyärd\ *n* : land around or enclosed by farm buildings

far-off \'fär-'óf\ *adj* : remote in time or space : DISTANT

fa·rouche \fə-'rüsh\ *adj* [F] **1** : WILD **2** : marked by shyness and lack of polish

far-out \'fär-'aůt\ *adj* : very unconventional ⟨~ clothes⟩

far·ra·go \fə-'rä-gō, -'rä-\ *n, pl* **-goes** [L, mixed fodder, mixture] : a confused collection : MIXTURE

far-reach·ing \'fär-'rē-chiŋ\ *adj* : having a wide range or effect

far·ri·er \'fer-ē-ər\ *n* [alter. of ME *ferrour*, fr. AF, blacksmith, fr. *ferrer* to shoe (horses)] : a person who shoes horses

¹**far·row** \'fer-ō\ *vb* : to give birth to a litter of pigs

²**farrow** *n* : a litter of pigs

far-see·ing \'fär-ˌsē-iŋ\ *adj* **1** : FARSIGHTED **1** **2** : FARSIGHTED **2**

far·sight·ed \'fär-ˌsī-təd\ *adj* **1** : seeing or able to see to a great distance : JUDICIOUS, WISE, SHREWD **3** : affected with an eye condition in which vision is better for distant than near objects — **far·sight·ed·ness** *n*

¹**far·ther** \'fär-thər\ *adv* **1** : at or to a greater distance or more advanced point **2** : to a greater degree or extent

²**farther** *adj* **1** : more distant **2** : ADDITIONAL

far·ther·most \-ˌmōst\ *adj* : FARTHEST

¹**far·thest** \'fär-thəst\ *adj* : most distant

²**farthest** *adv* **1** : to or at the greatest distance : REMOTEST ⟨hit the ball ~⟩ **2** : to the most advanced point **3** : by the greatest degree or extent : MOST

far·thing \'fär-thiŋ\ *n* **1** : a former British monetary unit equal to ¼ of a penny; *also* : a coin representing this unit **2** : something of small value

fas·cia *1 is usu* 'fä-sh(ē-)ə, *2 is usu* 'fa-\ *n, pl* **-ci·ae** \-shē-ˌē\ *or* **-cias** **1** : a flat usu. horizontal part (as a band or board) of or on a building **2** : a sheet of connective tissue covering body structures (as muscles)

fas·ci·cle \'fa-si-kəl\ *n* **1** : a small or slender bundle (as of pine needles or nerve fibers) **2** : one of the divisions of a book published in parts — **fas·ci·cled** \-kəld\ *adj*

fas·ci·nate \'fa-sə-ˌnāt\ *vb* **-nat·ed; -nat·ing** [L *fascinare*, fr. *fascinum* evil spell] **1** : to transfix and hold spellbound by an irresistible power **2** : ALLURE **3** : to be irresistibly attractive — **fas·ci·na·tion** \ˌfa-sə-'nā-shən\ *n*

fas·cism \'fa-ˌshi-zəm\ *n, often cap* : a political philosophy, movement, or regime that exalts nation and often race and stands for a centralized autocratic often militaristic government — **fas·cist** \-shist\ *n or adj, often cap* — **fas·cis·tic** \fa-'shis-tik\ *adj, often cap*

¹**fash·ion** \'fa-shən\ *n* **1** : the make or form of something **2** : MANNER, WAY **3** : a prevailing custom, usage, or style **4** : the prevailing style (as in dress) ♦ *Synonyms* MODE, VOGUE, RAGE, TREND

²**fashion** *vb* **1** : MOLD, CONSTRUCT ⟨~ a vase out of clay⟩ **2** : FIT, ADAPT

fash·ion·able \'fa-shə-nə-bəl\ *adj* **1** : dressing or behaving according to fashion : STYLISH **2** : of or relating to the world of fashion ⟨~ resorts⟩ ♦ *Synonyms* CHIC, MODISH, SMART, SWANK — **fash·ion·ably** \-blē\ *adv*

¹**fast** \'fast\ *adj* **1** : firmly fixed **2** : tightly shut **3** : adhering firmly **4** : STUCK **5** : STAUNCH ⟨~ friends⟩ **6** : characterized by quick motion, operation, or effect ⟨a ~ trip⟩ ⟨a ~ track⟩ **7** : indicating ahead of the correct time ⟨the clock is ~⟩ **8** : not easily disturbed : SOUND ⟨a ~ sleep⟩ **9** : permanently dyed; *also* : being proof against fading ⟨colors ~ to sunlight⟩ **10** : DISSIPATED, WILD ⟨a ~ crowd⟩ **11** : sexually promiscuous ♦ *Synonyms* RAPID, SWIFT, FLEET, QUICK, SPEEDY, HASTY

²**fast** *adv* **1** : in a firm or fixed manner ⟨stuck ~ in the mud⟩ **2** : SOUNDLY, DEEPLY ⟨~ asleep⟩ **3** : SWIFTLY **4** : RECKLESSLY

³**fast** *vb* **1** : to abstain from food **2** : to eat sparingly or abstain from some foods

⁴**fast** *n* **1** : the act or practice of fasting **2** : a time of fasting

fast·back \'fast-ˌbak\ *n* : an automobile having a roof with a long slope to the rear

fast·ball \-ˌbȯl\ *n* : a baseball pitch thrown at full speed

fas·ten \'fa-sⁿn\ *vb* **1** : to attach or join by or as if by pinning, tying, or nailing **2** : to make fast : fix securely **3** : to become fixed or joined **4** : to focus attention ⟨~*ed* onto the newest trends⟩ — **fas·ten·er** *n*

fas·ten·ing *n* : something that fastens : FASTENER

fast-food \ˌfast-'füd\ *adj* : specializing in food that is prepared and served quickly ⟨a ~ restaurant⟩

fast-for·ward \-'fȯr-wərd\ *n* **1** : a function of an electronic device that advances a recording rapidly **2** : a state of rapid advancement — **fast-forward** *vb*

fas·tid·i·ous \fa-'sti-dē-əs\ *adj* **1** : overly difficult to please **2** : showing a meticulous or demanding attitude ⟨~ workmanship⟩ ✦ *Synonyms* NICE, FINICKY, FUSSY, PARTICULAR, PERSNICKETY, SQUEAMISH — **fas·tid·i·ous·ly** *adv* — **fas·tid·i·ous·ness** *n*

fast·ness \'fast-nəs\ *n* **1** : the quality or state of being fast **2** : a fortified or secure place : STRONGHOLD

fast–talk \'fast-ˌtòk\ *vb* : to influence by persuasive and usu. deceptive talk

fast–track \'fast-ˌtrak\ *vb* : to speed up the processing or production of

fast track *n* : a course leading to rapid advancement or success

¹fat \'fat\ *adj* **fat·ter; fat·test** **1** : PLUMP, OBESE **2** : OILY, GREASY **3** : well filled out : BIG **4** : well stocked : ABUNDANT **5** : richly rewarding — **fat·ness** *n*

²fat *n* **1** : animal tissue rich in greasy or oily matter **2** : any of various energy-rich esters that occur naturally in animal fats and in plants and are soluble in organic solvents (as ether) but not in water **3** : the best or richest portion ⟨lived on the ~ of the land⟩ **4** : OBESITY **5** : excess matter ⟨trim the ~ from the budget⟩

fa·tal \'fāt-ᵊl\ *adj* **1** : FATEFUL ⟨that ~ day⟩ **2** : causing death or ruin ⟨a ~ mistake⟩ — **fa·tal·ly** *adv*

fa·tal·ism \-ˌi-zəm\ *n* : the belief that events are determined by fate — **fa·tal·ist** \-ist\ *n* — **fa·tal·is·tic** \ˌfāt-ᵊl-'is-tik\ *adj* — **fa·tal·is·ti·cal·ly** \-ti-k(ə-)lē\ *adv*

fa·tal·i·ty \fā-'ta-lə-tē, fə-\ *n, pl* **-ties** **1** : DEADLINESS **2** : FATE **3** : death resulting from a disaster or accident; *also* : one who suffers such a death

fat·back \'fat-ˌbak\ *n* : a fatty strip from the back of the hog usu. cured by salting and drying

fat cat *n* **1** : a wealthy contributor to a political campaign **2** : a wealthy privileged person

fate \'fāt\ *n* [ME, fr. MF or L; MF, fr. L *fatum*, lit., what has been spoken, fr. *fari* to speak] **1** : the cause or will that is held to determine events : DESTINY **2** : LOT, FORTUNE **3** : DISASTER; *esp* : DEATH **4** : END, OUTCOME **5** *pl, cap* : the three goddesses of classical mythology who determine the course of human life

fat·ed \'fā-təd\ *adj* : decreed, controlled, or marked by fate

fate·ful \'fāt-fəl\ *adj* **1** : OMINOUS, PROPHETIC **2** : IMPORTANT, DECISIVE **3** : DEADLY, DESTRUCTIVE **4** : determined by fate — **fate·ful·ly** *adv*

fath *abbr* fathom

fat·head \'fat-ˌhed\ *n* : a stupid person — **fat·head·ed** \-'he-dəd\ *adj*

¹fa·ther \'fä-thər\ *n* **1** : a male parent **2** *cap* : God esp. as the first person of the Trinity **3** : FOREFATHER **4** : one deserving the respect and love given to a father **5** *often cap* : an early Christian writer accepted by the church as an authoritative witness to its teaching and practice **6** : ORIGINATOR ⟨the ~ of modern radio⟩; *also* : SOURCE **7** : PRIEST — used esp. as a title **8** : one of the leading men ⟨city ~s⟩ — **fa·ther·hood** \-ˌhùd\ *n* — **fa·ther·less** *adj* — **fa·ther·ly** *adj*

²father *vb* **1** : BEGET **2** : to be the founder, producer, or author of **3** : to treat or care for as a father

father–in–law \'fä-thə-rən-ˌló\ *n, pl* **fa·thers–in–law** \-thər-zən-\ : the father of one's spouse

fa·ther·land \'fä-thər-ˌland\ *n* **1** : the native land of one's ancestors **2** : one's native land

¹fath·om \'fa-thəm\ *n* [ME *fadme*, fr. OE *fæthm* length of the outstretched arms] : a unit of length equal to 6 feet (about 1.8 meters) used esp. for measuring the depth of water

²fathom *vb* **1** : to measure by a sounding line : PROBE **3** : to penetrate and come to understand ⟨~ the problem⟩ — **fath·om·able** \'fa-thə-mə-bəl\ *adj*

fath·om·less \'fa-thəm-ləs\ *adj* : incapable of being fathomed

¹fa·tigue \fə-'tēg\ *n* [F] **1** : manual or menial work performed by military personnel **2** *pl* : the uniform or work clothing worn on fatigue and in the field **3** : weariness from labor or stress **4** : the tendency of a material to break under repeated stress

²fatigue *vb* **fa·tigued; fa·tigu·ing** : WEARY, TIRE

fat·ten \'fa-tᵊn\ *vb* : to make or grow fat

Fat Tuesday *n* : MARDI GRAS

¹fat·ty \'fa-tē\ *adj* **fat·ti·er; -est** **1** : containing fat esp. in unusual amounts **2** : GREASY

²fatty *n, pl* **fat·ties** *offensive* : an overweight person

fatty acid *n* : any of numerous acids that contain only carbon, hydrogen, and oxygen and that occur naturally in fats and various oils

fa·tu·i·ty \fa-'tü-ə-tē, -'tyü-\ *n, pl* **-ities** : FOOLISHNESS, STUPIDITY

fat·u·ous \'fa-chù-wəs\ *adj* : FOOLISH, INANE, SILLY — **fat·u·ous·ly** *adv*

fau·bourg \fō-'bùr\ *n* **1** : a suburb esp. of a French city **2** : a city quarter

fau·ces \'fò-ˌsēz\ *n pl* [L, throat] : the narrow passage located between the soft palate and the base of the tongue that joins the mouth to the pharynx

fau·cet \'fò-sət, 'fä-\ *n* : a fixture for drawing off a liquid (as from a pipe)

¹fault \'fòlt\ *n* **1** : a weakness in character : FAILING **2** : IMPERFECTION, IMPAIRMENT, DEFECT **3** : an error esp. in service in a net or racket game **4** : MISDEMEANOR; *also* : MISTAKE **5** : responsibility for something wrong **6** : a fracture in the earth's crust accompanied by a displacement of one side relative to the other — **fault·i·ly** \'fòl-tə-lē\ *adv* — **fault·less** *adj* — **fault·less·ly** *adv* — **faulty** *adj*

²fault *vb* **1** : to commit a fault : ERR **2** : to fracture so as to produce a geologic fault **3** : to find a fault in **4** : BLAME, CRITICIZE

fault·find·er \'fòlt-ˌfīn-dər\ *n* : a person who tends to find fault or complain ✦ *Synonyms* CRITIC, CARPER, CAVILER, COMPLAINER — **fault·find·ing** *n or adj*

faun \'fòn\ *n* : a Roman god similar to but gentler than a satyr

fau·na \'fò-nə\ *n, pl* **faunas** *also* **fau·nae** \-ˌnē, -ˌnī\ [NL, fr. L *Fauna*, sister of Faunus (the Roman god of animals)] : animals or animal life esp. of a region, period, or environment — **fau·nal** \-nəl\ *adj*

fau·vism \'fō-ˌvi-zəm\ *n, often cap* : a movement in painting characterized by vivid colors, free treatment of form, and a vibrant and decorative effect — **fau·vist** \-vist\ *n, often cap*

faux pas \'fō-ˌpä, fo-'\ *n, pl* **faux pas** *same or* -ˌpäz, -'päz\ [F, lit., false step] : BLUNDER; *esp* : a social blunder

fa·va bean \'fä-və-\ *n* : the large flat edible seed of an Old World vetch; *also* : this plant

¹fa·vor \'fā-vər\ *n* **1** : friendly regard shown toward another esp. by a superior **2** : APPROVAL **3** : PARTIALITY **4** : POPULARITY **5** : gracious kindness; *also* : an act of such kindness **6** *pl* : effort in one's behalf : ATTENTION **7** : a token of love (as a ribbon) usu. worn conspicuously **8** : a small gift or decorative item given out at a party **9** : a special privilege **10** : sexual privileges — usu. used in pl. **11** *archaic* : LETTER **12** : BEHALF, INTEREST ⟨acted in his own ~⟩

²favor *vb* **1** : to regard or treat with favor **2** : OBLIGE **3** : ENDOW ⟨~ed by nature⟩ **4** : to treat gently or carefully : SPARE ⟨~ a lame leg⟩ **5** : PREFER **6** : SUPPORT, SUSTAIN ⟨~ed the tax reform⟩ **7** : FACILITATE ⟨darkness ~s attack⟩ **8** : RESEMBLE ⟨he ~s his father⟩

fa·vor·able \'fā-və-rə-bəl\ *adj* **1** : APPROVING ⟨a ~ response⟩ **2** : HELPFUL, PROMISING, ADVANTAGEOUS ⟨~ weather⟩ — **fa·vor·ably** \-blē\ *adv*

fa·vor·ite \'fā-və-rət, -vrət\ *n* **1** : a person or a thing that is favored above others **2** : a competitor regarded as most likely to win — **favorite** *adj*

favorite son *n* : a candidate supported by the delegates of his state at a presidential nominating convention

fa·vor·it·ism \'fā-və-rə-ˌti-zəm\ *n* : PARTIALITY, BIAS

fa·vour *chiefly Brit var of* FAVOR

¹fawn \'fòn, 'fän\ *vb* **1** : to show affection ⟨a dog ~*ing* on its master⟩ **2** : to court favor by a cringing or flattering manner ✦ *Synonyms* GROVEL, KOWTOW, TOADY, TRUCKLE

²fawn *n* **1** : a young deer **2** : a light grayish brown — **fawny** \'fò-nē, 'fä-\ *adj*

fax \'faks\ *n* **1** : FACSIMILE 2 **2** : a device used to send or receive facsimile communications; *also* : such a communication — **fax** *vb*

fay \'fā\ *n* : FAIRY, ELF — **fay** *adj*

faze \'fāz\ *vb* **fazed; faz·ing** : to disturb the composure or courage of : DAUNT

FBI *abbr* Federal Bureau of Investigation

FCC *abbr* Federal Communications Commission

FD *abbr* fire department

FDA *abbr* Food and Drug Administration

FDIC *abbr* Federal Deposit Insurance Corporation

Fe *symbol* [L *ferrum*] iron

fe·al·ty \'fē(-ə)l-tē\ *n, pl* **-ties** : LOYALTY, ALLEGIANCE ✦ **Synonyms** FIDELITY, DEVOTION, FAITHFULNESS, PIETY

¹fear \'fir\ *vb* **1** : to have a reverent awe of ⟨~ God⟩ **2** : to be afraid of ⟨~s spiders⟩ **3** : to be apprehensive

²fear *n* **1** : an unpleasant often strong emotion caused by expectation or awareness of danger; *also* : an instance of or a state marked by this emotion **2** : anxious concern : SOLICITUDE **3** : profound reverence esp. toward God ✦ **Synonyms** DREAD, FRIGHT, ALARM, PANIC, TERROR, TREPIDATION

fear·ful \-fəl\ *adj* **1** : causing fear **2** : filled with fear **3** : showing or caused by fear **4** : extremely bad, intense, or large ⟨paid a ~ price⟩ — **fear·ful·ly** *adv*

fear·less \-ləs\ *adj* : free from fear : BRAVE — **fear·less·ly** *adv* — **fear·less·ness** *n*

fear·some \-səm\ *adj* **1** : causing fear **2** : TIMID **3** : INTENSE ⟨~ determination⟩

fea·si·ble \'fē-zə-bəl\ *adj* [ME *faisible*, fr. AF *faisable*, fr. *fais-*, stem of *faire* to make, do] **1** : capable of being done or carried out ⟨a ~ plan⟩ **2** : SUITABLE **3** : REASONABLE, LIKELY ✦ **Synonyms** POSSIBLE, PRACTICABLE, VIABLE, WORKABLE — **fea·si·bil·i·ty** \,fē-zə-'bi-lə-tē\ *n* — **fea·si·bly** \'fē-zə-blē\ *adv*

¹feast \'fēst\ *n* **1** : an elaborate meal : BANQUET **2** : ABUNDANCE ⟨a ~ of good books⟩ **3** : FESTIVAL 1

²feast *vb* **1** : to take part in a feast; *also* : to give a feast for **2** : to enjoy some unusual pleasure or delight **3** : DELIGHT, GRATIFY

feat \'fēt\ *n* : DEED, EXPLOIT, ACHIEVEMENT; *esp* : an act notable for courage, skill, endurance, or ingenuity

¹feath·er \'fe-thər\ *n* **1** : any of the light horny outgrowths that form the external covering of the body of a bird **2** : the vane of an arrow **3** : PLUMAGE **4** : KIND, NATURE ⟨birds of a ~⟩ **5** : ATTIRE, DRESS ⟨in full ~⟩ **6** : CONDITION, MOOD ⟨in fine ~⟩ — **feath·ered** \-thərd\ *adj* — **feath·er·less** *adj* — **feath·ery** *adj* — **a feather in one's cap** : a mark of distinction : HONOR

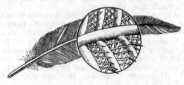

feather 1

²feather *vb* **1** : to furnish with a feather ⟨~ an arrow⟩ **2** : to cover, clothe, line, or adorn with or as if with feathers — **feather one's nest** : to provide for oneself financially esp. while exploiting a position of trust

feath·er·bed·ding \'fe-thər-,be-diŋ\ *n* : the requiring of an employer usu. under a union rule or safety statute to employ more workers than are needed

feath·er·edge \-,ej\ *n* : a very thin sharp edge

feath·er·weight \-,wāt\ *n* : one that is very light in weight; *esp* : a boxer weighing more than 118 but not over 126 pounds

¹fea·ture \'fē-chər\ *n* [ME *feture*, fr. AF, fr. L *factura* act of making, fr. *facere* to make] **1** : the shape or appearance of the face or its parts **2** : a part of the face ⟨her eyes are her best ~⟩ **3** : a prominent part or characteristic **4** : a special attraction (as in a newspaper) **5** : something offered to the public or advertised as particularly attractive ⟨a new car's ~s⟩ — **fea·ture·less** *adj*

²feature *vb* **1** : to picture in the mind : IMAGINE **2** : to give special prominence to ⟨the show ~s new artists⟩ **3** : to play an important part

Feb *abbr* February

fe·brile \'fe-,brī(-ə)l\ *adj* : FEVERISH

Feb·ru·ary \'fe-b(y)ə-,wer-ē, 'fe-brə-\ *n* [ME *Februarie*, fr. L *Februarius*, fr. *Februa*, pl., feast of purification] : the 2d month of the year

fe·ces \'fē-,sēz\ *n pl* : bodily waste discharged from the intestine : EXCREMENT — **fe·cal** \-kəl\ *adj*

feck·less \'fek-ləs\ *adj* **1** : WEAK, INEFFECTIVE **2** : WORTHLESS, IRRESPONSIBLE ⟨~ drifters⟩

fe·cund \'fe-kənd, 'fē-\ *adj* : FRUITFUL, PROLIFIC ⟨~ fields⟩ — **fe·cun·di·ty** \fi-'kən-də-tē, fe-\ *n*

fed *abbr* federal; federation

fed·er·al \'fe-də-rəl, -drəl\ *adj* **1** : formed by a compact between political units that surrender individual sovereignty to a central authority but retain certain limited powers **2** : of or constituting a form of government in which power is distributed between a central authority and constituent territorial units **3** : of or relating to the central government of a federation **4** *cap* : FEDERALIST **5** *often cap* : of, relating to, or loyal to the federal government or the Union armies of the U.S. in the American Civil War — **fed·er·al·ly** *adv*

Federal *n* : a supporter of the U.S. government in the Civil War; *esp* : a soldier in the federal armies

federal district *n* : a district (as the District of Columbia) set apart as the seat of the central government of a federation

fed·er·al·ism \'fe-də-rə-li-zəm, -drə-\ *n* **1** *often cap* : the distribution of power in an organization (as a government) between a central authority and the constituent units **2** : support or advocacy of federalism **3** *cap* : the principles of the Federalists

fed·er·al·ist \-list\ *n* **1** : an advocate of federalism **2** *often cap* : an advocate of a federal union between the American colonies after the Revolution and of adoption of the U.S. Constitution **3** *cap* : a member of a major political party in the early years of the U.S. favoring a strong centralized national government — **federalist** *adj, often cap*

fed·er·al·ize \'fe-də-rə-,līz, -drə-\ *vb* **-ized; -iz·ing 1** : to unite in or under a federal system **2** : to bring under the jurisdiction of a federal government

fed·er·ate \'fe-də-,rāt\ *vb* **-at·ed; -at·ing** : to join in a federation

fed·er·a·tion \,fe-də-'rā-shən\ *n* **1** : a political or societal entity formed by uniting smaller entities **2** : a federal government **3** : a union of organizations **4** : the forming of a federal union

fedn *abbr* federation

fe·do·ra \fi-'dòr-ə\ *n* : a low soft felt hat with the crown creased lengthwise

fed up *adj* : utterly sated, tired, or disgusted ⟨fed up with bureaucracy⟩

fee \'fē\ *n* [ME, fr. AF *fé, fief*, of Gmc origin; akin to OE *feoh* cattle, property] **1** : an estate in land held from a feudal lord **2** : an inherited or heritable estate in land **3** : a fixed charge; *also* : a charge for a service

fee·ble \'fē-bəl\ *adj* **fee·bler** \-bə-lər\; **fee·blest** \-bə-ləst\ [ME *feble*, fr. AF, fr. L *flebilis* lamentable, wretched, fr. *flēre* to weep] **1** : DECREPIT, FRAIL **2** : INEFFECTIVE, INADEQUATE ⟨a ~ protest⟩ — **fee·ble·ness** *n* — **fee·bly** \-blē\ *adv*

fee·ble·mind·ed \,fē-bəl-'mīn-dəd\ *adj* : lacking normal intelligence — **fee·ble·mind·ed·ness** *n*

¹feed \'fēd\ *vb* **fed** \'fed\; **feed·ing 1** : to give food to; *also* : to give as food **2** : EAT 1; *also* : PREY **3** : to furnish what is necessary to the development or function of ⟨used wood to ~ the fire⟩ **4** : to supply for another to use ⟨~ a pass⟩ ⟨fed the actor his lines⟩ — **feed·er** *n*

²feed *n* **1** : a usu. large meal : food for livestock **3** : a mechanism for feeding material to a machine **4** : a continuous series of electronic information updates (as to a blog or social media account)

feed·back \'fēd-,bak\ *n* **1** : the return to the input of a part of the output of a machine, system, or process **2** : response esp. to one in authority about an activity or policy **3** : sound (as whistling) resulting from the retransmission of an amplified or broadcast signal

feed·lot \'fēd-,lät\ *n* : land on which cattle are fattened for market

feed·stuff \-,stəf\ *n* : FEED 2

¹feel \'fēl\ *vb* **felt** \'felt\; **feel·ing 1** : to perceive or examine through physical contact : TOUCH, HANDLE **2** : EXPERIENCE; *also* : to suffer from **3** : to ascertain by cautious trial ⟨~ out public sentiment⟩ **4** : to be aware of **5** : to be conscious of an inward impression, state of mind, or physical condition **6** : BELIEVE, THINK **7** : to search for something with the fingers : GROPE **8** : SEEM ⟨it ~s like spring⟩ **9** : to have sympathy or pity

²feel *n* **1** : the sense of touch **2** : SENSATION, FEELING **3** : the quality of a thing as imparted through touch

feel·er \'fē-lər\ *n* **1** : one that feels; *esp* : a tactile organ (as on the head of an insect) **2** : a proposal or remark made to find out the views of other people

¹feel·ing \'fē-liŋ\ *n* **1** : the sense of touch; *also* : a sensation perceived by this **2** : a state of mind ⟨a ~ of loneliness⟩ **3** *pl* : general emotional condition : SENSIBILITIES ⟨hurt their ~s⟩ **4** : OPINION, BELIEF **5** : capacity to respond emotionally

²feeling *adj* **1** : SENSITIVE; *esp* : easily moved emotionally **2** : expressing emotion or sensitivity — **feel·ing·ly** *adv*

feet *pl of* FOOT

feign \'fān\ *vb* **1** : to give a false appearance of : SHAM ⟨~ illness⟩ **2** : to assert as if true : PRETEND

feint \'fānt\ *n* : something feigned; *esp* : a mock blow or attack intended to distract attention from the real point of attack — **feint** *vb*

feisty \'fī-stē\ *adj* **feist·i·er; -est** : having or showing a lively aggressiveness

feld·spar \'feld-ˌspär\ *n* : any of a group of crystalline minerals consisting of silicates of aluminum with another element (as potassium or sodium)

fe·lic·i·tate \fi-'li-sə-ˌtāt\ *vb* **-tat·ed; -tat·ing** : CONGRATU-LATE ⟨felicitated the winner⟩ — **fe·lic·i·ta·tion** \-ˌli-sə-'tā-shən\ *n*

fe·lic·i·tous \fi-'li-sə-təs\ *adj* **1** : well chosen : APT **2** : PLEASANT, DELIGHTFUL — **fe·lic·i·tous·ly** *adv*

fe·lic·i·ty \fi-'li-sə-tē\ *n, pl* **-ties** **1** : the quality or state of being happy; *esp* : great happiness **2** : something that causes happiness **3** : a pleasing manner or quality esp. in art or language ⟨her ~ with words⟩ **4** : an apt expression

fe·line \'fē-ˌlīn\ *adj* [L *felinus*, fr. *felis* cat] **1** : of or relating to cats or their kin **2** : sleekly graceful **3** : SLY, TREACHEROUS **4** : STEALTHY — **feline** *n*

¹fell \'fel\ *n* : SKIN, HIDE, PELT

²fell *vb* **1** : to cut, beat, or knock down; *also* : KILL **2** : to sew (a seam) by folding one raw edge under the other

³fell *past of* FALL

⁴fell *adj* : CRUEL, FIERCE; *also* : DEADLY — **in one fell swoop** *also* **at one fell swoop** : all at once : with a single effort

fel·lah \'fe-lə, fə-'lä\ *n, pl* **fel·la·hin** *or* **fel·la·heen** \ˌfe-lə-'hēn\ : a peasant or agricultural laborer in Arab countries (as Egypt or Syria)

fel·la·tio \fə-'lā-shē-ˌō\ *also* **fel·la·tion** \-shən\ *n* : oral stimulation of the penis

fel·low \'fe-lō\ *n* [ME *felawe*, fr. OE *fēolaga*, fr. ON *fēlagi*, fr. *fēlag* partnership (fr. *fē* cattle, money) + *lag* act of laying] **1** : COMRADE, ASSOCIATE **2** : EQUAL, PEER **3** : one of a pair : MATE **4** : a member of an incorporated literary or scientific society **5** : MAN, BOY **6** : BOYFRIEND **7** : a person granted a stipend for advanced study

fellow man *n* : a kindred human being

fel·low·ship \'fe-lō-ˌship\ *n* **1** : the condition of friendly relationship existing among persons : COMRADESHIP **2** : a community of interest or feeling **3** : a group with similar interests **4** : the position of a fellow (as of a university) **5** : the stipend granted a fellow

fellow traveler *n* : a sympathetic supporter of another's cause; *esp* : a person who sympathizes with and often furthers the ideals and program of an organized group (as the Communist party) without joining it

fel·on \'fe-lən\ *n* **1** : one who has committed a felony **2** : WHITLOW

fel·o·ny \'fe-lə-nē\ *n, pl* **-nies** : a serious crime punishable by a heavy sentence — **fe·lo·ni·ous** \fə-'lō-nē-əs\ *adj*

fel·spar *chiefly Brit var of* FELDSPAR

¹felt \'felt\ *n* **1** : a cloth made of wool and fur often mixed with natural or synthetic fibers **2** : a material resembling felt

²felt *past and past part of* FEEL

fem *abbr* **1** female **2** feminine

FEMA *abbr* Federal Emergency Management Agency

fe·male \'fē-ˌmāl\ *adj* [ME, alter. of *femel*, fr. AF *femele*, fr. ML *femella*, fr. L, girl, dim. of *femina* woman] **1** : of, relating to, or being the sex that typically bears young;

also : PISTILLATE **2** : characteristic of girls or women ⟨~ voices⟩ **♦ Synonyms** FEMININE, WOMANLY, WOM-ANLIKE, WOMANISH, EFFEMINATE — **female** *n*

¹fem·i·nine \'fe-mə-nən\ *adj* **1** : of the female sex; *also* : characteristic of or appropriate or unique to women **2** : of, relating to, or constituting the gender that includes most words or grammatical forms referring to females — **fem·i·nin·i·ty** \ˌfe-mə-'ni-nə-tē\ *n*

²feminine *n* : a noun, pronoun, adjective, or inflectional form or class of the feminine gender; *also* : the feminine gender

fem·i·nism \'fe-mə-ˌni-zəm\ *n* **1** : the theory of the political, economic, and social equality of the sexes **2** : organized activity on behalf of women's rights and interests — **fem·i·nist** \-nist\ *n or adj*

femme fa·tale \ˌfem-fə-'tal\ *n, pl* **femmes fa·tales** *same or* -'talz\ [F, lit., disastrous woman] : a seductive woman

fe·mur \'fē-mər\ *n, pl* **fe·murs** *or* **fem·o·ra** \'fe-mə-rə\ : the long leg bone extending from the hip to the knee — **fem·o·ral** \'fe-mə-rəl\ *adj*

¹fen \'fen\ *n* : low swampy land

²fen \'fən\ *n, pl* **fen** — see *yuan* at MONEY table

¹fence \'fens\ *n* [ME *fens*, short for *defens* defense] **1** : a barrier (as of wood or wire) to prevent escape or entry or to mark a boundary **2** : a person who receives stolen goods; *also* : a place where stolen goods are disposed of — **on the fence** : in a position of neutrality or indecision

²fence *vb* **fenced; fenc·ing** **1** : to enclose with a fence **2** : to keep in or out with a fence **3** : to practice fencing **4** : to use tactics of attack and defense esp. in debate — **fenc·er** *n*

fenc·ing *n* **1** : the art or practice of attack and defense with the foil, épée, or saber **2** : the fences of a property or region **3** : material used for building fences

fend \'fend\ *vb* **1** : to keep or ward off : REPEL **2** : SHIFT ⟨~ for yourself⟩

fend·er \'fen-dər\ *n* : a protective device (as a guard over the wheel of an automobile)

fen·es·tra·tion \ˌfe-nə-'strā-shən\ *n* : the arrangement and design of windows and doors in a building

Fe·ni·an \'fē-nē-ən\ *n* : a member of a secret 19th century Irish and Irish-American organization dedicated to overthrowing British rule in Ireland

fen·ing \'fe-niŋ\ *n, pl* **fen·inga** \'fe-niŋ-ə\ *also* **fen·ing** \'fe-niŋ\ *or* **fen·ings** — see *marka* at MONEY table

fen·nel \'fe-nᵊl\ *n* : a garden plant related to the carrot and grown for its aromatic foliage and seeds

FEPC *abbr* Fair Employment Practices Commission

fe·ral \'fir-əl, 'fer-\ *adj* **1** : SAVAGE **2** : WILD 1 **3** : having escaped from domestication and become wild

fer–de–lance \'fer-də-'lans\ *n, pl* **fer–de–lance** [F, lit., lance iron, spearhead] : a large venomous pit viper of Central and So. America

¹fer·ment \fər-'ment\ *vb* **1** : to cause or undergo fermentation **2** : to be or cause to be in a state of agitation or intense activity

²fer·ment \'fər-ˌment\ *n* **1** : a living organism (as a yeast) causing fermentation by its enzymes; *also* : ENZYME **2** : AGITATION, TUMULT

fer·men·ta·tion \ˌfər-mən-'tā-shən, -ˌmen-\ *n* **1** : chemical decomposition of an organic substance (as in the souring of milk or the formation of alcohol from sugar) by enzymatic action in the absence of oxygen often with formation of gas **2** : FERMENT 2

fer·mi·um \'fer-mē-əm, 'fər-\ *n* : an artificially produced radioactive metallic chemical element

fern \'fərn\ *n* : any of an order of vascular plants resembling seed plants in having roots, stems, and leaflike fronds but reproducing by spores instead of by flowers and seeds

fern·ery \'fər-nə-rē\ *n, pl* **-er·ies** **1** : a place for growing ferns **2** : a collection of growing ferns

fe·ro·cious \fə-'rō-shəs\ *adj* **1** : FIERCE, SAVAGE **2** : extremely intense — **fe·ro·cious·ly** *adv* — **fe·ro·cious·ness** *n*

fe·roc·i·ty \fə-'rä-sə-tē\ *n* : the quality or state of being ferocious

¹fer·ret \'fer-ət\ *n* : a partially domesticated usu. white European mammal related to the weasels

²ferret *vb* **1** : to hunt game with ferrets **2** : to drive out of a hiding place **3** : to find and bring to light by searching ⟨~ out the truth⟩

fer·ric \'fer-ik\ *adj* : of, relating to, or containing iron

ferric oxide *n* : an oxide of iron found in nature as hematite and as rust and used esp. as a pigment, for polishing, and in magnetic materials

Fer·ris wheel \'fer-əs-\ *n* : an amusement device consisting of a large upright power-driven wheel with seats that remain horizontal around its rim

fer·ro·mag·net·ic \,fer-ō-mag-'ne-tik\ *adj* : of or relating to substances that are easily magnetized

fer·rous \'fer-əs\ *adj* : of, relating to, or containing iron

fer·rule \'fer-əl\ *n* : a metal ring or cap around a slender wooden shaft to prevent splitting

¹fer·ry \'fer-ē\ *vb* **fer·ried; fer·ry·ing** [ME *ferien*, fr. OE *ferian* to carry, convey] **1** : to carry by boat across a body of water **2** : to cross by a ferry **3** : to convey from one place to another

²ferry *n, pl* **ferries** **1** : a place where persons or things are ferried **2** : FERRYBOAT

fer·ry·boat \'fer-ē-,bōt\ *n* : a boat used in ferrying

fer·tile \'fer-t⁰l\ *adj* **1** : producing plentifully : PRODUCTIVE ⟨~ soils⟩ ⟨a ~ mind⟩ **2** : capable of developing or reproducing ⟨~ seed⟩ ⟨a ~ bull⟩ ✦ *Synonyms* FRUITFUL, PROLIFIC, FECUND, PRODUCTIVE — **fer·til·i·ty** \(,)fər-'ti-lə-tē\ *n*

fer·til·ize \'fər-tə-,līz\ *vb* **-ized; -iz·ing** **1** : to unite with in the process of fertilization ⟨a sperm ~s an egg⟩ **2** : to apply fertilizer to — **fer·til·i·za·tion** \,fər-tə-lə-'zā-shən\ *n*

fer·til·iz·er \'fər-tə-,lī-zər\ *n* : material (as manure or a chemical mixture) for enriching land

fer·ule \'fer-əl\ *n* : a rod or ruler used to punish children

fer·ven·cy \'fər-vən-sē\ *n, pl* **-cies** : FERVOR

fer·vent \'fər-vənt\ *adj* **1** : very hot : GLOWING **2** : marked by great intensity of feeling ✦ *Synonyms* IMPASSIONED, ARDENT, FERVID, FIERY, PASSIONATE — **fer·vent·ly** *adv*

fer·vid \-vəd\ *adj* **1** : very hot **2** : ARDENT, ZEALOUS — **fer·vid·ly** *adv*

fer·vor \'fər-vər\ *n* **1** : intense heat **2** : intensity of feeling or expression

fer·vour *chiefly Brit var of* FERVOR

fes·cue \'fes-kyü\ *n* : any of a genus of tufted perennial grasses

fes·tal \'fes-t⁰l\ *adj* : FESTIVE

fester \'fes-tər\ *vb* **1** : to form pus **2** : PUTREFY, ROT **3** : RANKLE

fes·ti·val \'fes-tə-vəl\ *n* **1** : a time of celebration marked by special observances; *esp* : an occasion marked with religious ceremonies **2** : a periodic season or program of cultural events or entertainment ⟨a dance ~⟩

fes·tive \'fes-tiv\ *adj* **1** : of, relating to, or suitable for a feast or festival **2** : JOYFUL, GAY — **fes·tive·ly** *adv*

fes·tiv·i·ty \fes-'ti-və-tē\ *n, pl* **-ties** **1** : FESTIVAL 1 **2** : the quality or state of being festive **3** : festive activity

¹fes·toon \fes-'tün\ *n* [F *feston*, fr. It *festone*, fr. *festa* festival] **1** : a decorative chain or strip hanging between two points **2** : a carved, molded, or painted ornament representing a decorative chain

²festoon *vb* **1** : to hang or form festoons on **2** : to shape into festoons

fe·ta \'fe-tə\ *n* : a white crumbly Greek cheese made from sheep's or goat's milk

fe·tal \'fē-t⁰l\ *adj* : of, relating to, or being a fetus

fetch \'fech\ *vb* **1** : to go or come after and bring or take back ⟨teach a dog to ~ a stick⟩ **2** : to bring in (as a price) **3** : to cause to come : bring out ⟨~ed tears from the eyes⟩ **4** : to give by striking ⟨~ him a blow⟩

fetch·ing *adj* : ATTRACTIVE, PLEASING ⟨a ~ smile⟩ — **fetch·ing·ly** *adv*

¹fete *or* **fête** \'fāt, 'fet\ *n* [F *fête*, fr. OF *feste*] **1** : FESTIVAL **2** : a large elaborate entertainment or party

²fete *or* **fête** *vb* **fet·ed** *or* **fêt·ed; fet·ing** *or* **fêt·ing** **1** : to honor or commemorate with a fete **2** : to pay high honor to

fet·id \'fe-təd\ *adj* : having an offensive smell : STINKING

fe·tish *also* **fe·tich** \'fe-tish\ *n* [F & Pg; F *fétiche*, fr. Pg *feitiço*, fr. *feitiço* artificial, false, fr. L *facticius* factitious] **1** : an object (as an idol or image) believed to have magical powers (as in curing disease) **2** : an object of unreasoning devotion or concern **3** : an object whose real or fantasied presence is psychologically necessary for sexual gratification

fe·tish·ism \-ti-,shi-zəm\ *n* **1** : belief in or devotion to fetishes **2** : the pathological transfer of sexual interest and gratification to a fetish — **fe·tish·ist** \-shist\ *n* — **fe·tish·is·tic** \,fe-ti-'shis-tik\ *adj*

fe·tish·ize \-ti-,shīz\ *vb* **-ized -iz·ing** : to make a fetish of

fet·lock \'fet-,läk\ *n* : a projection on the back of a horse's leg above the hoof; *also* : a tuft of hair on this

fet·ter \'fe-tər\ *n* **1** : a chain or shackle for the feet **2** : something that confines : RESTRAINT — **fetter** *vb*

fet·tle \'fe-t⁰l\ *n* : a state of fitness or order : CONDITION ⟨in fine ~⟩

fe·tus \'fē-təs\ *n* : an unborn or unhatched vertebrate esp. after its basic structure is laid down; *esp* : a developing human in the uterus from usu. three months after conception to birth

feud \'fyüd\ *n* : a prolonged quarrel; *esp* : a lasting conflict between families or clans marked by violent attacks made for revenge — **feud** *vb*

feu·dal \'fyü-d⁰l\ *adj* **1** : of, relating to, or having the characteristics of a medieval fee **2** : of, relating to, or characteristic of feudalism

feu·dal·ism \'fyü-də-,li-zəm\ *n* : a system of political organization prevailing in medieval Europe in which a vassal renders service to a lord and receives protection and land in return; *also* : a similar political or social system — **feu·dal·is·tic** \,fyü-d⁰l-'is-tik\ *adj*

¹feu·da·to·ry \'fyü-də-,tòr-ē\ *adj* : owing feudal allegiance

²feudatory *n, pl* **-ries** **1** : FIEF **2** : a person who holds lands by feudal law or usage

fe·ver \'fē-vər\ *n* **1** : a rise in body temperature above the normal; *also* : a disease of which this is a chief symptom **2** : a state of heightened emotion or activity **3** : CRAZE ⟨football ~⟩ — **fe·ver·ish** *adj* — **fe·ver·ish·ly** *adv*

¹few \'fyü\ *pron* : not many : a small number

²few *adj* **1** : consisting of or amounting to a small number **2** : not many but some ⟨caught a ~ fish⟩ — **few·ness** *n* — **few and far between** : RARE **3**

³few *n* **1** : a small number of units or individuals ⟨a ~ of them⟩ **2** : a special limited number ⟨among the ~⟩

few·er \'fyü-ər\ *pron* : a smaller number of persons or things

fey \'fā\ *adj* **1** *chiefly Scot* : fated to die; *also* : marked by a foreboding of death or calamity **2** : able to see into the future : VISIONARY **3** : marked by an otherworldly air or attitude **4** : CRAZY, TOUCHED

fez \'fez\ *n, pl* **fez·zes** *also* **fez·es** : a round red felt hat that has a flat top and a tassel but no brim

ff *abbr* **1** folios **2** [*following*] and the following ones **3** fortissimo

FHA *abbr* Federal Housing Administration

fi·an·cé \,fē-,än-'sā\ *n* [F, fr. MF, fr. pp. of *fiancer* to promise, betroth, fr. OF *fiancier*, fr. *fiance* promise, trust, fr. *fier* to trust, ultim. fr. L *fidere*] : a man engaged to be married

fi·an·cée \,fē-,än-'sā\ *n* : a woman engaged to be married

fi·as·co \fē-'as-kō\ *n, pl* **-coes** [F] : a complete failure

fi·at \'fē-ət, -,at, -,ät; 'fī-ət, -,at\ *n* [L, let it be done] : an authoritative and often arbitrary order or decree

¹fib \'fib\ *n* : a trivial or childish lie

²fib *vb* **fibbed; fib·bing** : to tell a fib — **fib·ber** *n*

fi·ber \'fī-bər\ *n* **1** : a threadlike substance or structure (as a muscle cell or fine root); *esp* : a natural (as wool or flax) or artificial (as rayon) filament capable of being spun or woven **2** : indigestible material in food that stimulates the intestine to move its contents along **3** : an element that gives texture or substance **4** : basic toughness : STRENGTH ⟨moral ~⟩ — **fi·brous** \-brəs\ *adj*

fi·ber·board \'fī-bər-,bòrd\ *n* : a material made by compressing fibers (as of wood) into stiff sheets

fi·ber·fill \-,fil\ *n* : synthetic fibers used as a filling material (as for cushions)

fi·ber·glass \-,glas\ *n* : glass in fibrous form used in making various products (as insulation)

fiber optics *n* **1** *pl* : thin transparent fibers of glass or plastic that are enclosed by a less refractive material and that transmit light by internal reflection; *also* : a bundle of such fibers used in an instrument **2** : the technique of the use of fiber optics — **fiber–optic** *adj*

fibre *chiefly Brit var of* FIBER

fi·bril \\'fī-brəl, 'fi-\\ *n* : a small fiber
fi·bril·la·tion \\ˌfi-brə-'lā-shən, ˌfī-\\ *n* : rapid irregular contractions of the heart muscle fibers resulting in a lack of synchronism between heartbeat and pulse — **fib·ril·late** \\'fi-brə-ˌlāt, 'fī-\\ *vb*
fi·brin \\'fī-brən\\ *n* : a white insoluble fibrous protein formed in the clotting of blood
¹fi·broid \\'fī-ˌbroid, 'fi-\\ *adj* : resembling, forming, or consisting of fibrous tissue ⟨~ tumors⟩
²fibroid *n* : a benign tumor of the uterus
fi·bro·my·al·gia \\ˌfī-ˌbrō-ˌmī-'al-jə\\ *n* : any of a group of rheumatic disorders affecting soft tissues (as muscles or tendons)
fi·bro·sis \\fī-'brō-səs\\ *n* : a condition marked by abnormal increase of fiber-containing tissue
fib·u·la \\'fi-byə-lə\\ *n, pl* **-lae** \\-ˌlē, -ˌlī\\ *or* **-las** : the outer and us. the smaller of the two bones between the knee and ankle — **fib·u·lar** \\-lər\\ *adj*
FICA *abbr* Federal Insurance Contributions Act
-fication *n comb form* : making : production ⟨simpli*fication*⟩
fiche \\'fēsh\\ *n, pl* **fiche** : MICROFICHE
fi·chu \\'fi-shü\\ *n* [F] : a woman's light triangular scarf draped over the shoulders and fastened in front
fick·le \\'fi-kəl\\ *adj* : not firm or steadfast in disposition or character : INCONSTANT ⟨~ friends⟩ — **fick·le·ness** *n*
fic·tion \\'fik-shən\\ *n* 1 : something (as a story) invented by the imagination 2 : fictitious literature (as novels) — **fic·tion·al** \\-shə-nəl\\ *adj* — **fic·tion·al·ly** *adv*
fic·ti·tious \\fik-'ti-shəs\\ *adj* 1 : of, relating to, or characteristic of fiction : IMAGINARY 2 : FALSE, ASSUMED ⟨a ~ name⟩ 3 : FEIGNED ◆ *Synonyms* CHIMERICAL, FANCIFUL, FANTASTIC, UNREAL
¹fid·dle \\'fi-dᵊl\\ *n* : VIOLIN
²fiddle *vb* **fid·dled; fid·dling** 1 : to play on a fiddle 2 : to move the hands or fingers restlessly 3 : PUTTER 4 : MEDDLE, TAMPER — **fid·dler** *n*
fid·dle·head \\'fi-dᵊl-ˌhed\\ *n* : one of the young unfurling fronds of some ferns that are often eaten as greens
fiddler crab *n* : any of a genus of burrowing crabs with one claw much enlarged in the male

fiddler crab

fid·dle·stick \\'fi-dᵊl-ˌstik\\ *n* 1 : a violin bow 2 *pl* : NONSENSE — used as an interjection
fi·del·i·ty \\fə-'de-lə-tē, fī-\\ *n, pl* **-ties** 1 : the quality or state of being faithful 2 : ACCURACY ⟨~ in sound reproduction⟩ ◆ *Synonyms* ALLEGIANCE, LOYALTY, DEVOTION, FEALTY
¹fidg·et \\'fi-jət\\ *n* 1 : uneasiness or restlessness as shown by nervous movements — usu. used in pl. 2 : one that fidgets — **fidg·ety** *adj*
²fidget *vb* : to move or cause to move or act restlessly or nervously
fi·du·cia·ry \\fə-'dü-shē-ˌer-ē, -'dyü-, -shə-rē\\ *adj* 1 : involving a confidence or trust 2 : held or holding in trust for another ⟨~ accounts⟩ — **fiduciary** *n*
fie \\'fī\\ *interj* — used to express disgust or disapproval
fief \\'fēf\\ *n* [F, fr. OF] : a feudal estate : FEE
¹field \\'fēld\\ *n* 1 : open country 2 : a piece of cleared land for cultivation or pasture 3 : a piece of land yielding some special product 4 : the place where a battle is fought; *also* : BATTLE 5 : an area, division, or sphere of activity ⟨the ~ of science⟩ ⟨salesmen in the ~⟩ 6 : an area for military exercises 7 : an area for sports 8 : a background on which something is drawn or projected ⟨a flag with white stars on a ~ of blue⟩ 9 : a region or space in which a given effect (as magnetism) exists — **field** *adj*
²field *vb* 1 : to handle a batted or thrown baseball while on defense 2 : to put into the field 3 : to answer satisfactorily ⟨~ a tough question⟩ — **field·er** *n*

field day *n* 1 : a day devoted to outdoor sports and athletic competition 2 : a time of extraordinary pleasure or opportunity
field event *n* : a track-and-field event (as weight-throwing) other than a race
field glass *n* : a hand-held binocular telescope — usu. used in pl.
field guide *n* : a manual for identifying natural objects, plants, or animals
field hockey *n* : a field game played between two teams of 11 players each whose object is to knock a ball into the opponent's goal with a curved stick
field marshal *n* : an officer (as in the British army) of the highest rank
field–test \\-ˌtest\\ *vb* : to test (as a new product) in actual situations reflecting intended use — **field test** *n*
fiend \\'fēnd\\ *n* 1 : DEVIL 1 2 : DEMON 3 : an extremely wicked or cruel person 4 : a person excessively devoted to a pursuit ⟨a golf ~⟩ 5 : ADDICT ⟨a dope ~⟩ — **fiend·ish** *adj* — **fiend·ish·ly** *adv*
fierce \\'firs\\ *adj* **fierc·er; fierc·est** 1 : violently hostile or aggressive in temperament 2 : PUGNACIOUS 3 : INTENSE ⟨~ pain⟩ 4 : furiously active or determined 5 : wild or menacing in appearance ◆ *Synonyms* FEROCIOUS, BARBAROUS, SAVAGE, CRUEL — **fierce·ly** *adv* — **fierce·ness** *n*
fi·ery \\'fī-ə-rē\\ *adj* **fi·er·i·er; -est** 1 : consisting of fire 2 : BURNING, BLAZING 3 : FLAMMABLE 4 : hot like a fire : INFLAMED, FEVERISH 5 : RED ⟨a ~ sunset⟩ 6 : full of emotion or spirit 7 : IRRITABLE — **fi·eri·ness** \\-rē-nəs\\ *n*
fi·es·ta \\fē-'es-tə\\ *n* [Sp] : FESTIVAL
fife \\'fīf\\ *n* [G *Pfeife* pipe, fife] : a small flute
FIFO *abbr* first in, first out
fif·teen \\fif-'tēn\\ *n* : one more than 14 — **fifteen** *adj or pron* — **fif·teenth** \\-'tēnth\\ *adj or n*
fifth \\'fifth\\ *n* 1 : one that is number five in a countable series 2 : one of five equal parts of something 3 : a unit of measure for liquor equal to ¹/₅ U.S. gallon (0.757 liter) — **fifth** *adj or adv*
fifth column *n* : a group of secret supporters of a nation's enemy that engage in espionage or sabotage within the country — **fifth columnist** *n*
fifth wheel *n* : one that is unnecessary and often burdensome
fif·ty \\'fif-tē\\ *n, pl* **fifties** : five times 10 — **fif·ti·eth** \\-tē-əth\\ *adj or n* — **fifty** *adj or pron*
fif·ty–fif·ty \\ˌfif-tē-'fif-tē\\ *adj* 1 : shared equally ⟨a ~ proposition⟩ 2 : half favorable and half unfavorable
¹fig \\'fig\\ *n* : a soft usu. pear-shaped edible fruit of a tree related to the mulberry; *also* : a tree bearing figs
²fig *abbr* 1 figurative; figuratively 2 figure
¹fight \\'fīt\\ *vb* **fought** \\'fot\\; **fight·ing** 1 : to contend against another in battle or physical combat 2 : BOX 3 : to put forth a determined effort 4 : STRUGGLE, CONTEND 5 : to attempt to prevent the success or effectiveness of 6 : WAGE ⟨~ a war⟩ 7 : to gain by struggle
²fight *n* 1 : a hostile encounter : BATTLE 2 : a boxing match 3 : a verbal disagreement 4 : a struggle for a goal or an objective 5 : strength or disposition for fighting ⟨full of ~⟩
fight·er \\'fī-tər\\ *n* : one that fights; *esp* : WARRIOR 2 : BOXER 1 3 : a fast maneuverable warplane for destroying enemy aircraft
fig·ment \\'fig-mənt\\ *n* : something imagined or made up
fig·u·ra·tion \\ˌfi-gyə-'rā-shən, -gə-\\ *n* 1 : FORM, OUTLINE 2 : an act or instance of representation in figures and shapes
fig·u·ra·tive \\'fi-gyə-rə-tiv, -gə-\\ *adj* 1 : EMBLEMATIC 2 : SYMBOLIC, METAPHORICAL ⟨~ language⟩ — **fig·u·ra·tive·ly** *adv*
¹fig·ure \\'fi-gyər, -gər\\ *n* [ME, fr. AF, fr. L *figura*, fr. *fingere* to shape] 1 : NUMERAL 2 *pl* : arithmetical calculations 3 : a written or printed character 4 : PRICE, SUM ⟨sold at a low ~⟩ 5 : a combination of points, lines, or surfaces in geometry ⟨a circle is a closed plane ~⟩ 6 : SHAPE, FORM, OUTLINE 7 : the graphic representation of a form esp. of a person 8 : a diagram or pictorial illustration of textual matter 9 : PATTERN, DESIGN 10 : appearance made or impression produced ⟨they cut quite a ~⟩ 11 : a series of movements (as in a dance) 12 : PERSONAGE ⟨a well-known sports ~⟩
²figure *vb* **fig·ured; fig·ur·ing** 1 : to represent by or as if by a figure or outline 2 : to decorate with a pattern

3 : to indicate or represent by numerals 4 : REGARD, CONSIDER 5 : to be or appear important or conspicuous 6 : COMPUTE, CALCULATE ⟨*figured* the cost⟩
fig·ure·head \'fi-gyər-ˌhed, -gər-\ *n* 1 : a figure on the bow of a ship 2 : a head or chief in name only
figure of speech : a form of expression (as a simile or metaphor) that often compares or identifies one thing with another to convey meaning or heighten effect
figure out *vb* 1 : FIND OUT, DISCOVER 2 : SOLVE ⟨*figure out* a math problem⟩
figure skating *n* : skating that includes various jumps, spins, and dance movements
fig·u·rine \ˌfi-gyə-'rēn, -gə-\ *n* : a small carved or molded figure
fil·a·ment \'fi-lə-mənt\ *n* : a fine thread or threadlike object, part, or process — **fil·a·men·tous** \ˌfi-lə-'men-təs\ *adj*
fil·bert \'fil-bərt\ *n* : the sweet thick-shelled nut of either of two European hazels; *also* : a shrub or small tree bearing filberts
filch \'filch\ *vb* : to steal furtively
¹**file** \'fi(-ə)l\ *n* : a usu. steel tool with a ridged or toothed surface used esp. for smoothing a hard substance
²**file** *vb* **filed; fil·ing** : to rub, smooth, or cut away with a file
³**file** *vb* **filed; fil·ing** [ME, fr. ML *filare* to string documents on a string or wire, fr. *filum* file of documents, lit., thread, fr. L] 1 : to arrange in order 2 : to enter or record officially or as prescribed by law ⟨∼ a lawsuit⟩ 3 : to send (copy) to a newspaper
⁴**file** *n* 1 : a device (as a folder or cabinet) by means of which papers may be kept in order 2 : a collection of papers or publications usu. arranged or classified 3 : a collection of data (as text) treated by a computer as a unit
⁵**file** *n* : a row of persons, animals, or things arranged one behind the other
⁶**file** *vb* **filed; fil·ing** : to march or proceed in file
fi·let mi·gnon \ˌfi-(ˌ)lā-mēn-'yōⁿ, fi-ˌlā-\ *n, pl* **filets mignons** \-(ˌ)lā-mēn-'yōⁿz, -ˌlā-\ [F, lit., dainty fillet] : a thick slice of beef cut from the narrow end of a beef tenderloin
fil·ial \'fi-lē-əl, 'fil-yəl\ *adj* : of, relating to, or befitting a son or daughter
fil·i·bus·ter \'fi-lə-ˌbəs-tər\ *n* [Sp *filibustero*, lit., freebooter] 1 : a military adventurer; *esp* : an American engaged in fomenting 19th century Latin American uprisings 2 : the use of delaying tactics (as extremely long speeches) esp. in a legislative assembly; *also* : an instance of this practice — **filibuster** *vb* — **fil·i·bus·ter·er** *n*
fil·i·cide \'fi-lə-ˌsīd\ *n* : the murder of one's own daughter or son
fil·i·gree \'fi-lə-ˌgrē\ *n* [F *filigrane*] : ornamental openwork (as of fine wire) — **fil·i·greed** \-ˌgrēd\ *adj*
fil·ing \'fi-liŋ\ *n* 1 : the act or instance of using a file 2 : a small piece scraped off by a file ⟨iron ∼s⟩
Fil·i·pi·no \ˌfi-lə-'pē-nō\ *n, pl* **Filipinos** : a native or inhabitant of the Philippines — **Filipino** *adj*
¹**fill** \'fil\ *vb* 1 : to make or become full 2 : to stop up : PLUG ⟨∼ a cavity⟩ 3 : FEED, SATIATE 4 : SATISFY, FULFILL ⟨∼ all requirements⟩ 5 : to occupy fully 6 : to spread through ⟨laughter ∼ed the room⟩ 7 : OCCUPY ⟨∼ the office of president⟩ 8 : to put a person in ⟨∼ a vacancy⟩ 9 : to supply as directed ⟨∼ a prescription⟩
²**fill** *n* 1 : a full supply; *esp* : a quantity that satisfies or satiates 2 : material used esp. for filling a low place
¹**fill·er** \'fil-ər\ *n* 1 : one that fills 2 : a substance added to another substance (as to increase bulk or weight) 3 : a material used for filling cracks and pores in wood before painting
²**fill·er** \'fi-ˌler\ *n, pl* **fillers** *or* **filler** — see *forint* at MONEY table
¹**fil·let** \'fi-lət, in sense 2 fi-'lā, 'fi-(ˌ)lā\ *also* **fi·let** \fi-'lā, 'fi-(ˌ)lā\ *n* [ME *filet*, fr. AF, dim. of *fil* thread] 1 : a narrow band, strip, or ribbon 2 : a piece or slice of boneless meat or fish; *esp* : the tenderloin of beef
²**fil·let** \'fi-lət, in sense 2 also fi-'lā, 'fi-(ˌ)lā\ *vb* 1 : to bind or adorn with or as if with a fillet 2 : to cut into fillets
fill in *vb* 1 : to provide necessary or recent information 2 : to serve as a temporary substitute
fill·ing \'fi-liŋ\ *n* 1 : material used to fill something ⟨a ∼ for a tooth⟩ 2 : the yarn interlacing the warp in a fabric 3 : a food mixture used to fill pastry or sandwiches

filling station *n* : GAS STATION
fil·lip \'fi-ləp\ *n* 1 : a blow or gesture made by a flick or snap of the finger across the thumb 2 : something that serves to arouse or excite — **fillip** *vb*
fill–up \'fil-ˌəp\ *n* : an act or instance of filling something
fil·ly \'fi-lē\ *n, pl* **fillies** : a young female horse usu. less than four years old
¹**film** \'film\ *n* 1 : a thin skin or membrane 2 : a thin coating or layer 3 : a flexible strip of chemically treated material used in taking pictures 4 : MOTION PICTURE — **filmy** *adj*
²**film** *vb* 1 : to cover with a film 2 : to make a motion picture of
film·dom \'film-dəm\ *n* : the motion-picture industry
film·og·ra·phy \fil-'mä-grə-fē\ *n, pl* **-phies** : a list of motion pictures featuring the work of a film figure or a particular topic
film·strip \'film-ˌstrip\ *n* : a strip of film bearing a sequence of images for projection as still pictures
¹**fils** \'fēs\ *n* [F] : SON — used after a family name to distinguish a son from his father
²**fils** \'fils\ *n, pl* **fils** — see *dinar*, *dirham*, *rial* at MONEY table
¹**fil·ter** \'fil-tər\ *n* 1 : a porous material through which a fluid is passed to separate out matter in suspension; *also* : a device containing such material 2 : a device for suppressing waves of certain frequencies; *esp* : one (as for a camera) that absorbs light of certain colors 3 : software for sorting or blocking certain online material
²**filter** *vb* 1 : to remove by means of a filter 2 : to pass through a filter — **fil·ter·able** *also* **fil·tra·ble** \-tə-rə-bəl, -trə-\ *adj* — **fil·tra·tion** \fil-'trā-shən\ *n*
filth \'filth\ *n* [ME, fr. OE *fȳlth*, fr. *fūl* foul] 1 : foul matter; *esp* : loathsome dirt or refuse 2 : moral corruption 3 : OBSCENITY — **filth·i·ness** *n* — **filthy** \'fil-thē\ *adj*
filthy *adv* : VERY, EXTREMELY ⟨∼ dirty⟩ ⟨∼ rich⟩
fil·trate \'fil-ˌtrāt\ *n* : fluid that has passed through a filter
¹**fin** \'fin\ *n* 1 : a thin external process by which an aquatic animal (as a fish) moves through water 2 : a fin-shaped part (as on an airplane) 3 : FLIPPER 2 — **finned** \'find\ *adj*
²**fin** *abbr* 1 finance; financial 2 finish
fi·na·gle \fə-'nā-gəl\ *vb* **-gled; -gling** 1 : to obtain by indirect or dishonest means : WANGLE 2 : to use devious dishonest methods to achieve one's ends — **fi·na·gler** *n*
¹**fi·nal** \'fi-nºl\ *adj* 1 : not to be altered or undone ⟨all sales are ∼⟩ 2 : ULTIMATE 3 : relating to or occurring at the end or conclusion ⟨the ∼ results⟩ — **fi·nal·i·ty** \fī-'na-lə-tē, fə-\ *n* — **fi·nal·ly** *adv*
²**final** *n* 1 : a deciding match or game — usu. used in pl. 2 : the last examination in a course — often used in pl.
fi·na·le \fə-'na-lē, fi-'nä-\ *n* : the close or end of something; *esp* : the last section of a musical composition
fi·nal·ise *Brit var of* FINALIZE
fi·nal·ist \'fi-nə-list\ *n* : a contestant in the finals of a competition
fi·nal·ize \'fi-nə-ˌlīz\ *vb* **-ized; -iz·ing** : to put in final or finished form
¹**fi·nance** \fə-'nans, 'fī-ˌnans\ *n* [ME, ending, payment, fr. AF, fr. *finer* to end, pay, fr. *fin* end, fr. L *finis* boundary, end] 1 *pl* : money resources available esp. to a government or business 2 : management of money affairs
²**finance** *vb* **fi·nanced; fi·nanc·ing** 1 : to raise or provide funds for 2 : to furnish with necessary funds 3 : to sell or supply on credit
finance company *n* : a company that makes usu. small short-term loans usu. to individuals
fi·nan·cial \fə-'nan-chəl, fī-\ *adj* : relating to finance or financiers ⟨∼ problems⟩ — **fi·nan·cial·ly** *adv*
fi·nan·cials \-shəlz\ *n pl* : financial statistics
fi·nan·cier \ˌfi-nən-'sir, ˌfī-ˌnan-\ *n* 1 : a person skilled in managing public moneys 2 : a person who deals with large-scale finance and investment
finch \'finch\ *n* : any of numerous songbirds with strong conical bills
¹**find** \'find\ *vb* **found** \'faund\; **find·ing** 1 : to meet with either by chance or by searching or study : ENCOUNTER, DISCOVER 2 : to obtain by effort or management ⟨∼ time to read⟩ 3 : to arrive at : REACH ⟨the bullet *found* its mark⟩ 4 : EXPERIENCE, FEEL ⟨*found* happiness⟩ 5 : to gain or regain the use of ⟨*found* his voice again⟩ 6

: to determine and make a statement about ⟨~ a verdict⟩

²find *n* **1** : an act or instance of finding **2** : something found; *esp* : a valuable item of discovery

find·er \'fīn-dər\ *n* : one that finds; *esp* : VIEWFINDER

fin de siè·cle \ₑfaⁿ-də-sē-'ekl'\ *adj* [F, end of century] **1** : of, relating to, or characteristic of the close of the 19th century **2** : of or relating to the end of a century

find·ing \'fīn-diŋ\ *n* **1** : the act of finding **2** : FIND **2** **3** : the result of a judicial proceeding or inquiry

find out *vb* : to learn by study, observation, or search : DISCOVER

¹fine \'fīn\ *n* : money exacted as a penalty for an offense

²fine *vb* **fined; fin·ing** : to impose a fine on : punish by a fine

³fine *adj* **fin·er; fin·est** **1** : free from impurity **2** : very thin in gauge or texture **3** : not coarse ⟨~ sand⟩ **4** : SUBTLE, SENSITIVE ⟨a ~ distinction⟩ **5** : superior in quality or appearance **6** : ELEGANT, REFINED ⟨~ manners⟩ — **fine·ly** *adv* — **fine·ness** *n*

⁴fine *adv* **1** : very well **2** — used to express agreement

fine art *n* : art (as painting, sculpture, or music) concerned esp. with the creation of beautiful objects — usu. used in pl.

fin·ery \'fī-nə-rē\ *n, pl* **-er·ies** : ORNAMENT, DECORATION; *esp* : showy clothing and jewels

fine-spun \'fīn-'spən\ *adj* : developed with extremely or excessively fine delicacy or detail

fi·nesse \fə-'nes\ *n* **1** : refinement or delicacy of workmanship, structure, or texture **2** : CUNNING, SUBTLETY ⟨handling questions with ~⟩ — **finesse** *vb*

fine-tune \'fīn-'tün\ *vb* : to adjust so as to bring to the highest level of performance or effectiveness

fin·fish \'fin-ₑfish\ *n* : FISH 2

¹fin·ger \'fiŋ-gər\ *n* **1** : any of the five divisions at the end of the hand; *esp* : one other than the thumb **2** : something that resembles or does the work of a finger **3** : a part of a glove into which a finger is inserted

²finger *vb* **fin·gered; fin·ger·ing** **1** : to touch or feel with the fingers : HANDLE **2** : to perform with the fingers or with a certain fingering **3** : to mark the notes of a piece of music as a guide in playing **4** : to point out ⟨was ~ed as a suspect⟩

fin·ger·board \'fiŋ-gər-ₑbórd\ *n* : the part of a stringed instrument against which the fingers press the strings to vary the pitch

finger bowl *n* : a small water bowl for rinsing the fingers at the table

fin·ger·ing \'fiŋ-gə-riŋ\ *n* **1** : handling or touching with the fingers **2** : the act or method of using the fingers in playing an instrument **3** : the marking of the method of fingering

fin·ger·ling \'fiŋ-gər-liŋ\ *n* : a small fish

fin·ger·nail \'fiŋ-gər-ₑnāl\ *n* : the nail of a finger

fin·ger·print \-ₑprint\ *n* : the pattern of marks made by pressing the tip of a finger or thumb on a surface; *esp* : an ink impression of such a pattern taken for the purpose of identification — **fingerprint** *vb*

fin·ger·tip \-ₑtip\ *n* : the tip of a finger

fin·i·al \'fi-nē-əl\ *n* : an ornamental projection or end (as on a spire)

fin·ick·ing \'fi-ni-kiŋ\ *adj* : FINICKY

fin·icky \'fi-ni-kē\ *adj* : excessively particular in taste or standards ⟨a ~ eater⟩

fi·nis \'fi-nəs\ *n* : END, CONCLUSION

¹fin·ish \'fi-nish\ *vb* **1** : TERMINATE **2** : to use or dispose of entirely **3** : to bring to completion : ACCOMPLISH **4** : to put a final coat or surface on **5** : to come to the end of a course or undertaking ⟨my horse ~ed third⟩ — **fin·ish·er** *n*

²finish *n* **1** : END, CONCLUSION **2** : something that completes or perfects **3** : the final treatment or coating of a surface

fi·nite \'fī-ₑnīt\ *adj* **1** : having definite or definable limits; *also* : having a limited nature or existence **2** : being less than some positive integer in number or measure and greater than its negative **3** : showing distinction of grammatical person and number ⟨a ~ verb⟩

fink \'fiŋk\ *n* **1** : a contemptible person **2** : STRIKEBREAKER **3** : INFORMER

Finn \'fin\ *n* : a native or inhabitant of Finland

fin·nan had·die \ₑfi-nən-'ha-dē\ *n* : smoked haddock

¹Finn·ish \'fi-nish\ *adj* : of or relating to Finland, the Finns, or Finnish

²Finnish *n* : the language of the Finns

fin·ny \'fi-nē\ *adj* **1** : having or characterized by fins **2** : relating to or being fish

fiord *var of* FJORD

fir \'fər\ *n* : any of a genus of usⁿ. large evergreen trees related to the pines; *also* : the light soft wood of a fir

¹fire \'fī(-ə)r\ *n* **1** : the light or heat and esp. the flame of something burning **2** : ENTHUSIASM, ZEAL **3** : fuel that is burning (as in a stove or fireplace) **4** : destructive burning (as of a house) **5** : the firing of weapons — **fire·less** *adj*

²fire *vb* **fired; fir·ing** **1** : KINDLE, IGNITE ⟨~ a house⟩ **2** : STIR, ENLIVEN ⟨~ the imagination⟩ **3** : to dismiss from employment **4** : SHOOT ⟨~ a gun⟩ ⟨~ an arrow⟩ **5** : BAKE ⟨*firing* pottery in a kiln⟩ **6** : to apply fire or fuel to something ⟨~ a furnace⟩

fire ant *n* : either of two small fiercely stinging So. American ants introduced into the southeastern U.S. where they are agricultural pests

fire·arm \'fī(-ə)r-ₑärm\ *n* : a weapon (as a pistol) from which a shot is discharged by gunpowder

fire·ball \-ₑból\ *n* **1** : a ball of fire **2** : a very bright meteor **3** : the highly luminous cloud of vapor and dust created by a nuclear explosion **4** : a highly energetic person

fire·boat \-ₑbōt\ *n* : a boat equipped for fighting fires

fire·bomb \-ₑbäm\ *n* : an incendiary bomb — **firebomb** *vb*

fire·box \-ₑbäks\ *n* **1** : a chamber (as of a furnace) that contains a fire **2** : a box containing a fire alarm

fire·brand \-ₑbrand\ *n* **1** : a piece of burning wood **2** : a person who creates unrest or strife : AGITATOR

fire·break \-ₑbräk\ *n* : a barrier of cleared or plowed land intended to check a forest or grass fire

fire·bug \-ₑbəg\ *n* : a person who deliberately sets destructive fires

fire·crack·er \-ₑkra-kər\ *n* : a usu. paper tube containing an explosive and a fuse and set off to make a noise

fire department *n* : an organization for preventing or extinguishing fires; *also* : its members

fire engine *n* : a motor vehicle with equipment for extinguishing fires

fire escape *n* : a stairway or ladder for escape from a burning building

fire·fight·er \'fī(-ə)r-ₑfīt-ər\ *n* : a person who fights fires; *esp* : a member of a fire department

fire·fly \-ₑflī\ *n* : any of various small night-flying beetles that produce flashes of light for courtship purposes

firefly

fire·house \-ₑhaús\ *n* : FIRE STATION

fire irons *n pl* : tools for tending a fire esp. in a fireplace

fire·man \'fī(-ə)r-mən\ *n* **1** : STOKER **2** : FIREFIGHTER

fire off *vb* : to write and send

fire·place \-ₑplās\ *n* **1** : a framed opening made in a chimney to hold an open fire **2** : an outdoor structure of brick or stone for an open fire

fire·plug \-ₑpləg\ *n* : HYDRANT

fire·pow·er \-ₑpaú(-ə)r\ *n* : the ability to deliver gunfire or warheads on a target

¹fire·proof \-'prüf\ *adj* : resistant to fire

²fireproof *vb* : to make fireproof

fire-sale \-ₑsäl\ *adj* : heavily discounted ⟨~ prices⟩

fire screen *n* : a protective screen before a fireplace

¹fire·side \'fī(-ə)r-ₑsīd\ *n* **1** : a place near the fire or hearth **2** : HOME

²**fireside** *adj* : having an informal or intimate quality

fire station *n* : a building housing fire engines and usu. firefighters

fire·storm \'fī(-ə)r-ˌstȯrm\ *n* 1 : a large destructive very hot fire 2 : a sudden or violent outburst ⟨~ of criticism⟩

fire tower *n* : a tower (as in a forest) from which a watch for fires is kept

fire·trap \'fī(-ə)r-ˌtrap\ *n* : a building or place apt to catch on fire or difficult to escape from in case of fire

fire truck *n* : FIRE ENGINE

fire·wall \-ˌwȯl\ *n* : computer hardware or software for preventing unauthorized access to data

fire·wa·ter \'fī(-ə)r-ˌwȯ-tər, -ˌwä-\ *n* : intoxicating liquor

fire·wood \-ˌwu̇d\ *n* : wood used for fuel

fire·work \-ˌwərk\ *n* : a device designed to produce a striking display by the burning of explosive or flammable materials

firing line *n* 1 : a line from which fire is delivered against a target 2 : the forefront of an activity

¹**firm** \'fərm\ *adj* 1 : securely fixed in place 2 : SOLID, VIGOROUS ⟨a ~ handshake⟩ 3 : having a solid or compact texture 4 : not subject to change or fluctuation : STEADY ⟨~ prices⟩ 5 : STEADFAST 6 : indicating firmness or resolution — **firm·ly** *adv* — **firm·ness** *n*

²**firm** *vb* : to make or become firm

³**firm** *n* [G *Firma*, fr. It, signature, ultim. fr. L *firmare* to make firm, confirm] 1 : the name under which a company transacts business 2 : a business partnership of two or more persons 3 : a business enterprise

fir·ma·ment \'fər-mə-mənt\ *n* : the arch of the sky : HEAVENS

firm·ware \'firm-ˌwer\ *n* : computer programs contained permanently in a hardware device

¹**first** \'fərst\ *adj* : preceding all others as in time, order, or importance

²**first** *adv* 1 : before any other 2 : for the first time 3 : in preference to something else

³**first** *n* 1 : number one in a countable series 2 : something that is first 3 : the lowest forward gear in an automotive vehicle 4 : the winning or highest place in a competition or examination

first aid *n* : emergency care or treatment given an injured or ill person

first·born \'fərst-ˈbȯrn\ *adj* : ELDEST — **firstborn** *n*

first class *n* : the best or highest group in a classification — **first–class** *adj or adv*

first·hand \'fərst-ˈhand\ *adj* : coming from direct personal observation or experience — **firsthand** *adv*

first lady *n, often cap F&L* : the wife or hostess of the chief executive of a political unit (as a country)

first lieutenant *n* : a commissioned officer (as in the army) ranking next below a captain

first·ling \'fərst-liŋ\ *n* : one that comes or is produced first

first·ly \-lē\ *adv* : in the first place : FIRST

¹**first–rate** \-ˈrāt\ *adj* : of the first order of size, importance, or quality

²**first–rate** *adv* : very well

first sergeant *n* 1 : a noncommissioned officer serving as the chief assistant to the commander of a military unit 2 : a rank in the army below a sergeant major and in the marine corps below a master gunnery sergeant

first strike *n* : a preemptive nuclear attack

first–string \'fərst-ˈstriŋ\ *adj* : being a regular as distinguished from a substitute — **first–string·er** \-ˌstriŋ-ər\ *n*

firth \'fərth\ *n* [ME, fr. ON *fjǫrthr*] : ESTUARY

fis·cal \'fis-kəl\ *adj* [L *fiscalis*, fr. *fiscus* basket, treasury] 1 : of or relating to taxation, public revenues, or public debt 2 : of or relating to financial matters — **fis·cal·ly** *adv*

¹**fish** \'fish\ *n, pl* **fish** *or* **fish·es** 1 : a water-dwelling animal — usu. used in combination ⟨star*fish*⟩ ⟨shell*fish*⟩ 2 : any of numerous cold-blooded water-breathing vertebrates with fins, gills, and usu. scales that include the bony fishes and usu. the cartilaginous and jawless fishes 3 : the flesh of fish used as food

²**fish** *vb* 1 : to attempt to catch fish 2 : to seek something by roundabout means ⟨~ for praise⟩ 3 : to search for something underwater 4 : to engage in a search by groping 5 : to draw forth

fish–and–chips *n pl* : fried fish and french fried potatoes

fish·bowl \'fish-ˌbōl\ *n* 1 : a bowl for the keeping of live fish 2 : a place or condition that affords no privacy

fish·er \'fi-shər\ *n* 1 : one that fishes 2 : a dark brown No. American carnivorous mammal related to the weasels

fish·er·man \-mən\ *n* 1 : a person engaged in fishing 2 : a fishing boat

fish·ery \'fi-shə-rē\ *n, pl* **-er·ies** 1 : the business of catching fish 2 : a place for catching fish

fish·hook \'fish-ˌhu̇k\ *n* : a usu. barbed hook for catching fish

fish ladder *n* : an arrangement of pools in steps by which fish can pass over a dam in going upstream

fish·net \'fish-ˌnet\ *n* 1 : netting for catching fish 2 : a coarse open-mesh fabric

fish·tail \-ˌtāl\ *vb* : to have the rear end slide from side to side out of control while moving forward

fish·wife \-ˌwīf\ *n* 1 : a woman who sells fish 2 : a vulgar abusive woman

fishy \'fi-shē\ *adj* **fish·i·er; -est** 1 : of or resembling fish 2 : QUESTIONABLE ⟨the story sounds ~ to me⟩

fis·sion \'fi-shən, -zhən\ *n* [L *fissio*, fr. *findere* to split] 1 : a cleaving into parts 2 : a method of reproduction in which a living cell or body divides into two or more parts each of which grows into a whole new individual 3 : the splitting of an atomic nucleus resulting in the release of large amounts of energy — **fis·sion·able** \'fi-shə-nə-bəl, -zhə-\ *adj*

fis·sure \'fi-shər\ *n* : a narrow opening or crack

fist \'fist\ *n* 1 : the hand with fingers folded into the palm 2 : INDEX FINGER

fist bump *n* : a gesture in which two people bump their fists together — **fist–bump** *vb*

fist·ful \'fist-ˌfu̇l\ *n* : HANDFUL

fist·i·cuffs \'fis-ti-ˌkəfs\ *n pl* : a fight with the fists

fist pump *n* : a celebratory gesture in which the fist is raised and lowered quickly and vigorously — **fist–pump** *vb*

fis·tu·la \'fis-chə-lə\ *n, pl* **-las** *or* **-lae** : an abnormal passage leading from an abscess or hollow organ — **fis·tu·lous** \-ləs\ *adj*

¹**fit** \'fit\ *adj* **fit·ter; fit·test** 1 : adapted to a purpose : APPROPRIATE 2 : PROPER, RIGHT ⟨a movie ~ for children⟩ 3 : PREPARED, READY 4 : physically and mentally sound — **fit·ly** *adv* — **fit·ness** *n*

²**fit** *n* 1 : a sudden violent attack (as in epilepsy) 2 : a sudden outburst

³**fit** *vb* **fit·ted** *also* **fit; fit·ting** 1 : to be suitable for or to 2 : to be correctly adjusted to or shaped for 3 : to insert or adjust until correctly in place 4 : to make a place or room for 5 : to be in agreement or accord with 6 : PREPARE 7 : ADJUST 8 : SUPPLY, EQUIP ⟨*fitted* out with gear⟩ 9 : BELONG — **fit·ter** *n*

⁴**fit** *n* : the fact, condition, or manner of fitting or being fitted

fit·ful \'fit-fəl\ *adj* : not regular : INTERMITTENT ⟨~ sleep⟩ — **fit·ful·ly** *adv*

¹**fit·ting** \'fi-tiŋ\ *adj* : APPROPRIATE, SUITABLE ⟨a ~ tribute⟩ — **fit·ting·ly** *adv*

²**fitting** *n* 1 : the action or act of one that fits; *esp* : a trying on of clothes being made or altered 2 : a small often standardized part ⟨a plumbing ~⟩

five \'fīv\ *n* 1 : one more than four 2 : the 5th in a set or series 3 : something having five units; *esp* : a basketball team 4 : a 5-dollar bill — **five** *adj or pron*

¹**fix** \'fiks\ *vb* 1 : to make firm, stable, or fast 2 : to give a permanent or final form to 3 : AFFIX, ATTACH 4 : to hold or direct steadily ⟨~*es* his eyes on the horizon⟩ 5 : ESTABLISH, SET 6 : ASSIGN ⟨~ the blame⟩ 7 : to set in order : ADJUST 8 : PREPARE 9 : to make whole or sound again 10 : to get even with 11 : to influence by improper or illegal methods ⟨~ a race⟩ — **fix·er** *n*

²**fix** *n* 1 : PREDICAMENT 2 : a determination of position (as of a ship) 3 : an accurate determination or understanding 4 : an act of improper influence 5 : a supply or dose of something (as an addictive drug) strongly desired or craved 6 : something that fixes or restores

fix·a·tion \fik-ˈsā-shən\ *n* : an obsessive or unhealthy preoccupation or attachment — **fix·ate** \'fik-ˌsāt\ *vb*

fix·a·tive \'fik-sə-tiv\ *n* : something that stabilizes or sets

fixed \'fikst\ *adj* 1 : securely placed or fastened : STATIONARY 2 : not volatile 3 : SETTLED, FINAL 4 : IN-

TENT, CONCENTRATED ⟨a ~ stare⟩ **5** : supplied with a definite amount of something needed (as money) — **fixed·ly** \'fik-səd-lē\ *adv* — **fixed·ness** \'fik-səd-nəs\ *n*

fix·i·ty \'fik-sə-tē\ *n, pl* **-ties** : the quality or state of being fixed or stable

fix·ture \'fiks-chər\ *n* **1** : something firmly attached as a permanent part of some other thing **2** : a familiar feature in a particular setting; *esp* : a person associated with a place or activity

¹**fizz** \'fiz\ *vb* : to make a hissing or sputtering sound

²**fizz** *n* : an effervescent beverage

¹**fiz·zle** \'fi-zəl\ *vb* **fiz·zled**; **fiz·zling** **1** : FIZZ **2** : to fail after a good start — often used with *out*

²**fizzle** *n* : FAILURE

fjord \fē-'örd\ *n* [Norw] : a narrow inlet of the sea between cliffs or steep slopes

fl *abbr* **1** [L *floruit*] flourished **2** fluid

Fl *symbol* flerovium

FL *or* **Fla** *abbr* Florida

flab \'flab\ *n* : soft flabby body tissue

flab·ber·gast \'fla-bər-ˌgast\ *vb* : ASTOUND

flab·by \'fla-bē\ *adj* **flab·bi·er**; **-est** : lacking firmness : FLACCID ⟨~ muscles⟩ — **flab·bi·ness** \-bē-nəs\ *n*

flac·cid \'fla-səd\ *adj* : lacking firmness ⟨~ muscles⟩

¹**flag** \'flag\ *n* : any of various irises; *esp* : a wild iris

²**flag** *n* **1** : a usu. rectangular piece of fabric of distinctive design that is used as a symbol (as of a nation) or as a signaling device **2** : something used like a flag to signal or attract attention **3** : one of the cross strokes of a musical note less than a quarter note in value

³**flag** *vb* **flagged**; **flag·ging** **1** : to signal with or as if with a flag; *esp* : to signal to stop ⟨~ a taxi⟩ **2** : to mark or identify with or as if with a flag **3** : to call a penalty on ⟨~ a football player⟩

⁴**flag** *vb* **flagged**; **flag·ging** **1** : to hang loose or limp **2** : to become unsteady, feeble, or spiritless **3** : to decline in interest or attraction ⟨the topic *flagged*⟩

⁵**flag** *n* : a hard flat stone suitable for paving

flag·el·late \'fla-jə-ˌlāt\ *vb* **-lat·ed**; **-lat·ing** : to punish by whipping — **flag·el·la·tion** \ˌfla-jə-'lā-shən\ *n*

fla·gel·lum \flə-'je-ləm\ *n, pl* **-la** \-lə\ *also* **-lums** : a long whiplike process that is the primary organ of motion of many microorganisms — **fla·gel·lar** \-lər\ *adj*

fla·geo·let \ˌfla-jə-'let, -'lā\ *n* [F] : a small woodwind instrument belonging to the flute class

fla·gi·tious \flə-'ji-shəs\ *adj* : grossly wicked : VILLAINOUS

flag·on \'fla-gən\ *n* : a container for liquids usu. with a handle, spout, and lid

flag·pole \'flag-ˌpōl\ *n* : a pole on which to raise a flag

fla·grant \'flā-grənt\ *adj* [L *flagrans*, prp. of *flagrare* to burn] : conspicuously bad ⟨~ abuse of power⟩ — **fla·grant·ly** *adv*

fla·gran·te de·lic·to \flə-ˌgran-tē-di-'lik-tō\ *adv* : IN FLAGRANTE DELICTO

flag·ship \'flag-ˌship\ *n* **1** : the ship that carries the commander of a fleet or subdivision thereof and flies his flag **2** : the most important one of a group

flag·staff \-ˌstaf\ *n* : FLAGPOLE

flag·stone \-ˌstōn\ *n* : ⁵FLAG

¹**flail** \'flāl\ *n* : a tool for threshing grain by hand

²**flail** *vb* : to strike or swing with or as if with a flail

flair \'fler\ *n* [F, lit., sense of smell, fr. OF, odor, fr. *flairier* to give off an odor, fr. VL **flagrare*, alter. of L *fragrare*] **1** : ability to appreciate or make good use of something : BENT, TALENT **2** : a unique style

flak \'flak\ *n, pl* **flak** [G, fr. *Fliegerabwehrkanonen*, fr. *Flieger* flyer + *Abwehr* defense + *Kanonen* cannons] **1** : antiaircraft guns or bursting shells fired from them **2** : CRITICISM, OPPOSITION

¹**flake** \'flāk\ *n* **1** : a small loose mass or bit **2** : a thin flattened piece or layer : CHIP — **flaky** *adj*

²**flake** *vb* **flaked**; **flak·ing** : to form or separate into flakes

³**flake** *n* : a markedly eccentric person : ODDBALL — **flak·i·ness** \'flā-kē-nəs\ *n* — **flaky** *adj*

flam·beau \'flam-ˌbō\ *n, pl* **flambeaux** \-ˌbōz\ *or* **flambeaus** [F, fr. MF, fr. *flambe* flame] : a flaming torch

flam·boy·ant \flam-'böi-ənt\ *adj* : marked by or given to strikingly elaborate or colorful display or behavior — **flam·boy·ance** \-əns\ *n* — **flam·boy·an·cy** \-ən-sē\ *n* — **flam·boy·ant·ly** *adv*

flame \'flām\ *n* **1** : the glowing gaseous part of a fire **2**

: a state of blazing combustion **3** : a flamelike condition **4** : burning zeal or passion **5** : BRILLIANCE **6** : SWEETHEART **7** : an angry, hostile, or abusive electronic message — **flame** *vb*

fla·men·co \flə-'men-kō\ *n, pl* **-cos** [Sp, fr. *flamenco* of the Gypsies, lit., Flemish, fr. Flemish, fr. MD *Vlaminc* Fleming] : a vigorous rhythmic dance style of the Spanish Gypsies

flame·throw·er \'flām-ˌthrō-ər\ *n* : a device that expels from a nozzle a burning stream of liquid or semiliquid fuel under pressure

fla·min·go \flə-'miŋ-gō\ *n, pl* **-gos** *also* **-goes** : any of several long-legged long-necked tropical water birds with scarlet wings and a broad bill bent downward

flam·ma·ble \'fla-mə-bəl\ *adj* : easily ignited and quick-burning — **flam·ma·bil·i·ty** \ˌfla-mə-'bi-lə-tē\ *n* — **flammable** *n*

flan \'flan, 'flän\ *n* **1** : an open pie with a sweet or savory filling **2** : custard baked with a caramel glaze

flange \'flanj\ *n* : a rim used for strengthening or guiding something or for attachment to another object

¹**flank** \'flaŋk\ *n* **1** : the fleshy part of the side between the ribs and the hip; *also* : the side of a quadruped **2** : SIDE **3** : the right or left of a formation

²**flank** *vb* **1** : to be situated on the side of : BORDER **2** : to attack or threaten the flank of

flank·er \'flaŋ-kər\ *n* : a football player stationed wide of the formation slightly behind the line of scrimmage as a pass receiver

flan·nel \'fla-nᵊl\ *n* **1** : a soft twilled wool or worsted fabric with a napped surface **2** : a stout cotton fabric napped on one side **3** *pl* : flannel underwear or pants

¹**flap** \'flap\ *n* **1** : a stroke with something broad : SLAP **2** : something broad, limber, or flat and usu. thin that hangs loose **3** : the motion or sound of something broad and limber as it swings to and fro **4** : a state of excitement or confusion

²**flap** *vb* **flapped**; **flap·ping** **1** : to beat with something broad and flat **2** : FLING **3** : to move (as wings) with a beating motion **4** : to sway loosely usu. with a noise of striking

flap·jack \'flap-ˌjak\ *n* : PANCAKE

flap·per \'fla-pər\ *n* **1** : one that flaps **2** : a young woman of the 1920s who showed freedom from conventions (as in conduct)

¹**flare** \'fler\ *n* **1** : a blaze of light used esp. to signal or illuminate; *also* : a device for producing such a blaze **2** : an unsteady glaring light

²**flare** *vb* **flared**; **flar·ing** **1** : to flame with a sudden unsteady light **2** : to become suddenly excited or angry ⟨after his harangue, I *flared* up⟩ **3** : to spread outward

flare-up \-ˌəp\ *n* : a sudden outburst or intensification

¹**flash** \'flash\ *vb* **1** : to break forth in or like a sudden flame **2** : to appear or pass suddenly or with great speed **3** : to send out in or as if in flashes ⟨~ a message⟩ **4** : to make a sudden display (as of brilliance or feeling) **5** : to gleam or glow intermittently **6** : to fill by a sudden rush of water **7** : to expose to view very briefly ⟨~ a badge⟩ ♦ *Synonyms* GLANCE, GLINT, SPARKLE, TWINKLE — **flash·er** *n*

²**flash** *n* **1** : a sudden burst of light **2** : a movement of a flag or light in signaling **3** : a sudden and brilliant burst (as of wit) **4** : a brief time **5** : SHOW, DISPLAY; *esp* : ostentatious display **6** : one that attracts notice; *esp* : an outstanding athlete **7** : GLIMPSE, LOOK **8** : a first brief news report **9** : FLASHLIGHT **10** : a device for producing a brief and very bright flash of light for taking photographs **11** : a quick-spreading flame or momentary intense outburst of radiant heat

³**flash** *adj* : of sudden origin and short duration ⟨a ~ fire⟩ ⟨a ~ flood⟩

⁴**flash** *adv* : by very brief exposure to an intense agent (as heat or cold) ⟨~ fry⟩ ⟨~ freeze⟩

flash·back \'flash-ˌbak\ *n* **1** : interruption of the chronological sequence (as of a film or literary work) by an event of earlier occurrence **2** : a past event remembered vividly

flash back *vb* **1** : to vividly remember a past incident **2** : to employ a flashback

flash·bulb \-ˌbəlb\ *n* : an electric bulb that can be used only once to produce a brief and very bright flash of light for taking photographs

flash card *n* : a card bearing words, numbers, or pictures briefly displayed usu. as a learning aid

flash drive *n* : a data storage device that uses flash memory

flash·gun \-ˌgən\ *n* : a device for producing a bright flash of light for photography

flash·ing \'fla-shiŋ\ *n* : sheet metal used in waterproofing (as at the angle between a chimney and a roof)

flash·light \'flash-ˌlīt\ *n* : a battery-operated portable electric light

flash memory *n* : a computer memory chip not requiring connection to a power source to retain its data

flashy \'fla-shē\ *adj* **flash·i·er; -est** **1** : momentarily dazzling **2** : superficially attractive or impressive : SHOWY ⟨∼ clothes⟩ — **flash·i·ly** \-shə-lē\ *adv* — **flash·i·ness** \-shē-nəs\ *n*

flask \'flask\ *n* : a flattened bottle-shaped container ⟨a whiskey ∼⟩

¹flat \'flat\ *adj* **flat·ter; flat·test** **1** : spread out along a surface; *also* : being or characterized by a horizontal line **2** : having a smooth, level, or even surface **3** : having a broad smooth surface and little thickness **4** : DOWNRIGHT, POSITIVE ⟨a ∼ refusal⟩ **5** : FIXED, UNCHANGING ⟨a ∼ fee⟩ **6** : EXACT, PRECISE ⟨in four minutes ∼⟩ **7** : DULL, UNINTERESTING; *also* : INSIPID **8** : DEFLATED ⟨a ∼ tire⟩ **9** : lower than the true pitch; *also* : lower by a half step **10** : free from gloss ⟨a ∼ paint⟩ **11** : lacking depth of characterization — **flat·ly** *adv* — **flat·ness** *n*

²flat *n* **1** : a level surface of land : PLAIN **2** : a flat part or surface **3** : a character ♭ that indicates that a specified note is to be lowered by a half step; *also* : the resulting note **4** : something flat **5** : an apartment on one floor **6** : a deflated tire

³flat *adv* **1** : FLATLY **2** : COMPLETELY ⟨∼ broke⟩ **3** : below the true musical pitch

⁴flat *vb* **flat·ted; flat·ting** **1** : FLATTEN **2** : to lower in pitch by a half step

flat·bed \'flat-ˌbed\ *n* : a truck or trailer with a body in the form of a platform or shallow box

flat·boat \-ˌbōt\ *n* : a flat-bottomed boat used esp. for carrying bulky freight

flat·car \-ˌkär\ *n* : a railroad freight car without sides or roof

flat·fish \-ˌfish\ *n* : any of an order of flattened marine bony fishes with both eyes on the upper side

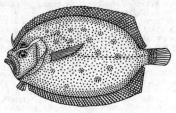

flatfish

flat·foot \-ˌfu̇t, -'fu̇t\ *n, pl* **flat·feet** \-ˌfēt, -'fēt\ : a condition in which the arch of the foot is flattened so that the entire sole rests upon the ground — **flat·foot·ed** \-'fu̇-təd\ *adj*

Flat·head \-ˌhed\ *n, pl* **Flatheads** *or* **Flathead** : a member of an American Indian people of Montana

flat·iron \-ˌī(-ə)rn\ *n* : IRON 3

flat·land \-ˌland\ *n* : land lacking significant variation in elevation

flat–out \'flat-ˌau̇t\ *adj* **1** : being or going at maximum effort or speed **2** : OUT-AND-OUT, DOWNRIGHT ⟨it was a ∼ lie⟩

flat out *adv* **1** : BLUNTLY, DIRECTLY **2** : at top speed **3** *usu* **flat–out** : to the greatest degree : COMPLETELY ⟨is just *flat-out* confusing⟩

flat–pan·el \-'pa-nᵊl\ *adj* : relating to or being a thin flat video display

flat·ten \'fla-tᵊn\ *vb* : to make or become flat

flat·ter \'fla-tər\ *vb* [ME *flateren*, fr. AF *flater* to lap, flatter] **1** : to praise too much or without sincerity **2** : to represent too favorably ⟨the portrait ∼s him⟩ **3** : to

display to advantage **4** : to judge (oneself) favorably or too favorably — **flat·ter·er** *n*

flat·tery \'fla-tə-rē\ *n, pl* **-ter·ies** : flattering speech or attentions : insincere or excessive praise

flat·top \'flat-ˌtäp\ *n* **1** : AIRCRAFT CARRIER **2** : CREW CUT

flat·u·lent \'fla-chə-lənt\ *adj* **1** : full of gas ⟨a ∼ stomach⟩ **2** : INFLATED, POMPOUS — **flat·u·lence** \-ləns\ *n*

fla·tus \'flā-təs\ *n* : gas formed in the intestine or stomach

flat·ware \'flat-ˌwer\ *n* : eating and serving utensils

flat·worm \-ˌwu̇rm\ *n* : any of a phylum of flattened mostly parasitic segmented worms (as trematodes and tapeworms)

flaunt \'flȯnt\ *vb* **1** : to display oneself to public notice **2** : to wave or flutter showily **3** : to display ostentatiously or impudently : PARADE — **flaunt** *n*

flau·ta \'flau̇-tə\ *n* : a tortilla rolled around a filling and deep-fried

flau·tist \'flȯ-tist, 'flau̇-\ *n* [It *flautista*] : FLUTIST

¹fla·vor \'flā-vər\ *n* **1** : the quality of something that affects the sense of taste or of taste and smell **2** : a substance that adds flavor **3** : characteristic or predominant quality — **fla·vored** \-vərd\ *adj* — **fla·vor·ful** *adj* — **fla·vor·less** *adj* — **fla·vor·some** *adj*

²flavor *vb* : to give or add flavor to

fla·vor·ing *n* : FLAVOR 2

fla·vour *chiefly Brit var of* FLAVOR

flaw \'flȯ\ *n* : a small often hidden defect — **flaw·less** *adj* — **flaw·less·ly** *adv* — **flaw·less·ness** *n*

flax \'flaks\ *n* : a fiber that is the source of linen; *also* : a blue-flowered plant grown for this fiber and its oily seeds

flax·en \'flak-sən\ *adj* **1** : made of flax **2** : resembling flax esp. in pale soft straw color

flay \'flā\ *vb* **1** : to strip off the skin or surface of **2** : to criticize harshly

fl dr *abbr* fluid dram

flea \'flē\ *n* : any of an order of small wingless leaping bloodsucking insects

flea·bane \'flē-ˌbān\ *n* : any of various plants of the daisy family once believed to drive away fleas

flea–bit·ten \-ˌbi-tᵊn\ *adj* : bitten by or infested with fleas

flea market *n* : a usu. open-air market for secondhand articles and antiques

¹fleck \'flek\ *vb* : STREAK, SPOT

²fleck *n* **1** : SPOT, MARK **2** : FLAKE, PARTICLE

fledge \'flej\ *vb* **fledged; fledg·ing** : to develop the feathers necessary for flying or independent activity

fledg·ling \'flej-liŋ\ *n* **1** : a young bird just fledged **2** : an immature or inexperienced person

flee \'flē\ *vb* **fled** \'fled\; **flee·ing** **1** : to run away often from danger or evil **2** : VANISH **3** : to run away from : SHUN

¹fleece \'flēs\ *n* **1** : the woolly coat of an animal and esp. a sheep **2** : a soft or woolly covering — **fleecy** *adj*

²fleece *vb* **fleeced; fleec·ing** **1** : to strip of money or property by fraud or extortion **2** : SHEAR

¹fleet \'flēt\ *vb* : to pass rapidly

²fleet *n* [ME *flete*, fr. OE *flēot* ship, fr. *flēotan* to float] **1** : a group of warships under one command **2** : a group (as of ships, planes, or trucks) under one management

³fleet *adj* **1** : SWIFT, NIMBLE **2** : not enduring : FLEETING — **fleet·ness** *n*

fleet admiral *n* : an admiral of the highest rank in the navy

fleet·ing \'flē-tiŋ\ *adj* : passing swiftly

Flem·ing \'fle-miŋ\ *n* : a member of a Germanic people inhabiting chiefly northern Belgium

Flem·ish \'fle-mish\ *n* **1** : the Dutch language as spoken by the Flemings **2 Flemish** *pl* : FLEMINGS — **Flemish** *adj*

fle·ro·vi·um \flə-'rō-vē-əm\ *n* a short-lived artificially produced radioactive chemical element

¹flesh \'flesh\ *n* **1** : the soft parts of an animal's body; *esp* : muscular tissue **2** : MEAT **3** : the physical nature of humans as distinguished from the soul **4** : human beings; *also* : living beings **5** : STOCK, KINDRED **6** : fleshy plant tissue (as fruit pulp) — **fleshed** \'flesht\ *adj*

²flesh *vb* : to make fuller or more nearly complete — usu. used with *out* ⟨*flesh out* a schedule⟩

flesh fly *n* : a dipteran fly whose maggots feed on flesh

flesh·ly \'flesh-lē\ *adj* **1** : CORPOREAL, BODILY **2** : not spiritual : WORLDLY **3** : CARNAL, SENSUAL ⟨∼ appetites⟩

flesh·pot \'flesh-ˌpät\ *n* **1** *pl* : bodily comfort : LUXURY **2** : a place of lascivious entertainment — usu. used in pl.
fleshy \'fle-shē\ *adj* **flesh·i·er; -est 1** : consisting of or resembling animal flesh **2** : PLUMP, FAT
flew *past of* ¹FLY
flex \'fleks\ *vb* : to bend esp. repeatedly — **flex** *n*
flex·i·ble \'flek-sə-bəl\ *adj* **1** : capable of being flexed : PLIANT **2** : yielding to influence : TRACTABLE **3** : readily changed or changing : ADAPTABLE ◆ *Synonyms* ELASTIC, SUPPLE, RESILIENT, SPRINGY — **flex·i·bil·i·ty** \ˌflek-sə-'bi-lə-tē\ *n*
flex·or \'flek-sər, -ˌsor\ *n* : a muscle serving to bend a body part
flex·ure \'flek-shər\ *n* : TURN, FOLD
flib·ber·ti·gib·bet \ˌfli-bər-tē-'ji-bət\ *n* : a silly flighty person
¹**flick** \'flik\ *n* **1** : a light sharp jerky stroke or movement **2** : a sound produced by a flick **3** : ²FLICKER
²**flick** *vb* **1** : to strike lightly with a quick sharp motion **2** : FLUTTER, FLIT
³**flick** *n* : MOVIE
¹**flick·er** \'fli-kər\ *vb* **1** : to move irregularly or unsteadily : FLUTTER **2** : to burn fitfully or with a fluctuating light — **flick·er·ing·ly** *adv*
²**flicker** *n* **1** : an act of flickering **2** : a sudden brief movement ⟨a ~ of an eyelid⟩ **3** : a momentary stirring ⟨a ~ of interest⟩ **4** : a slight indication : HINT **5** : a wavering light
³**flicker** *n* : a large barred and spotted No. American woodpecker with a brown back that occurs as an eastern form with yellow on the underside of the wings and tail and a western form with red in these areas
flied *past and past part of* ³FLY
fli·er \'flī(-ə)r\ *n* **1** : one that flies; *esp* : PILOT **2** : a reckless or speculative undertaking **3** *usu* **fly·er** : an advertising circular
¹**flight** \'flīt\ *n* **1** : an act or instance of flying **2** : the ability to fly **3** : a passing through air or space **4** : the distance covered in a flight **5** : swift movement **6** : a trip made by or in an airplane or spacecraft **7** : a group of similar individuals (as birds or airplanes) flying as a unit **8** : a passing (as of the imagination) beyond ordinary limits **9** : a series of stairs from one landing to another — **flight·less** *adj*
²**flight** *n* : an act or instance of running away
flight bag *n* **1** : a lightweight traveling bag with zippered outside pockets **2** : a small canvas satchel
flight line *n* : a parking and servicing area for airplanes
flighty \'flī-tē\ *adj* **flight·i·er; -est 1** : easily upset : VOLATILE **2** : easily excited : SKITTISH **3** : CAPRICIOUS, SILLY — **flight·i·ness** \-tē-nəs\ *n*
flim·flam \'flim-ˌflam\ *n* : DECEPTION, FRAUD — **flim·flam·mery** \-ˌfla-mə-re\ *n*
flim·sy \'flim-zē\ *adj* **flim·si·er; -est 1** : lacking strength or substance **2** : of inferior materials and workmanship **3** : having little worth or plausibility ⟨a ~ excuse⟩ — **flim·si·ly** \-zə-lē\ *adv* — **flim·si·ness** \-zē-nəs\ *n*
flinch \'flinch\ *vb* [MF *flenchir* to bend] : to shrink from or as if from pain : WINCE — **flinch** *n*
¹**fling** \'fliŋ\ *vb* **flung** \'fləŋ\; **fling·ing 1** : to move hastily, brusquely, or violently ⟨*flung* out of the room⟩ **2** : to kick or plunge vigorously **3** : to throw with force or recklessness; *also* : to cast as if by throwing **4** : to put suddenly into a state or condition
²**fling** *n* **1** : an act or instance of flinging **2** : a casual try : ATTEMPT **3** : a period of self-indulgence
flint \'flint\ *n* **1** : a hard dark quartz that produces a spark when struck by steel **2** : an alloy used for producing a spark in lighters — **flinty** *adj*
flint glass *n* : heavy glass containing an oxide of lead and used in lenses and prisms
flint·lock \'flint-ˌläk\ *n* **1** : a lock for a gun using a flint to ignite the charge **2** : a firearm fitted with a flintlock

flintlock pistol

¹**flip** \'flip\ *vb* **flipped; flip·ping 1** : to turn by tossing ⟨~ a coin⟩ **2** : to turn over; *also* : to leaf through **3** : FLICK, JERK ⟨~ a light switch⟩ **4** : to lose self-control — **flip** *n*
²**flip** *adj* : FLIPPANT, IMPERTINENT
flip·pant \'fli-pənt\ *adj* : lacking proper respect or seriousness — **flip·pan·cy** \'fli-pən-sē\ *n*
flip·per \'fli-pər\ *n* **1** : a broad flat limb (as of a seal) adapted for swimming **2** : a paddlelike shoe used in skin diving
flip side *n* : the reverse and usu. less popular side of a phonograph record
¹**flirt** \'flərt\ *vb* **1** : to move erratically : FLIT **2** : to behave amorously without serious intent **3** : to show casual interest ⟨~ed with the idea⟩; *also* : to come close to ⟨~ with danger⟩ — **flir·ta·tion** \ˌflər-'tā-shən\ *n* — **flir·ta·tious** \-shəs\ *adj*
²**flirt** *n* **1** : an act or instance of flirting **2** : a person who flirts
flit \'flit\ *vb* **flit·ted; flit·ting** : to pass or move quickly or abruptly from place to place : DART — **flit** *n*
flitch \'flich\ *n* : a side of cured meat; *esp* : a side of bacon
fliv·ver \'fli-vər\ *n* : a small cheap usu. old automobile
¹**float** \'flōt\ *n* **1** : something (as a raft) that floats **2** : a cork buoying up the baited end of a fishing line **3** : a hollow ball that floats at the end of a lever in a cistern or tank and regulates the liquid level **4** : a vehicle with a platform to carry an exhibit **5** : a soft drink with ice cream floating in it
²**float** *vb* **1** : to rest on the surface of or be suspended in a fluid **2** : to move gently on or through a fluid **3** : to cause to float **4** : WANDER **5** : to offer (securities) in order to finance an enterprise **6** : to finance by floating an issue of stocks or bonds **7** : to arrange for ⟨~ a loan⟩ — **float·er** *n*
floaty \'flō-tē\ *adj* **float·i·er; -est 1** : tending to float : BUOYANT **2** : light and billowy ⟨a ~ skirt⟩
¹**flock** \'fläk\ *n* **1** : a group of animals (as birds or sheep) assembled or herded together **2** : a group of people under the guidance of a leader; *esp* : CONGREGATION **3** : a large number ⟨a ~ of tourists⟩
²**flock** *vb* : to gather or move in a flock ⟨people ~ed to the beach⟩
floe \'flō\ *n* : a flat mass of floating ice
flog \'fläg\ *vb* **flogged; flog·ging 1** : to beat with or as if with a rod or whip **2** : SELL ⟨~ encyclopedias⟩ — **flog·ger** *n*
¹**flood** \'fləd\ *n* **1** : a great flow of water over the land **2** : the flowing in of the tide **3** : an overwhelming volume
²**flood** *vb* **1** : to cover or become filled with a flood **2** : to fill abundantly or excessively; *esp* : to supply an excess of fuel to **3** : to pour forth in a flood — **flood·er** *n*
flood·gate \'fləd-ˌgāt\ *n* : a gate for controlling a body of water : SLUICE
flood·light \-ˌlīt\ *n* : a lamp that throws a broad beam of light; *also* : the beam itself — **floodlight** *vb*
flood·plain \-ˌplān\ *n* : a plain along a river or stream subject to periodic flooding
flood tide *n* **1** : a rising tide **2** : an overwhelming quantity **3** : a high point
flood·wa·ter \'fləd-ˌwo-tər, -ˌwä-\ *n* : the water of a flood
¹**floor** \'flor\ *n* **1** : the bottom of a room on which one stands **2** : a ground surface **3** : a story of a building **4** : a main level space (as in a legislative chamber) distinguished from a platform or gallery **5** : AUDIENCE **6** : the right to address an assembly **7** : a lower limit ⟨put a ~ under wheat prices⟩ — **floor·ing** *n*
²**floor** *vb* **1** : to furnish with a floor **2** : to knock down **3** : AMAZE, DUMBFOUND ⟨was ~ed by the news⟩ **4** : to press (a vehicle's accelerator) to the floorboard esp. rapidly
floor·board \-ˌbord\ *n* **1** : a board in a floor **2** : the floor of an automobile
floor leader *n* : a member of a legislative body who has charge of a party's organization and strategy on the floor
floor show *n* : a series of acts presented in a nightclub
floor·walk·er \'flor-ˌwo-kər\ *n* : a person employed in a retail store to oversee the sales force and aid customers
floo·zy *or* **floo·zie** \'flü-zē\ *n, pl* **floozies** : a usu. young woman of loose morals
flop \'fläp\ *vb* **flopped; flop·ping 1** : FLAP **2** : to throw oneself down heavily, clumsily, or in a relaxed manner

⟨*flopped* into a chair⟩ 3 : FAIL ⟨the show *flopped*⟩ — **flop** *n* — **flop** *adv* — **flop·per** *n*
flop·house \'fläp-ˌhaus\ *n* : a cheap hotel
¹**flop·py** \'flä-pē\ *adj* **flop·pi·er; -est** : tending to flop; *esp* : soft and flexible — **flop·pi·ly** \-pə-lē\ *adv*
²**floppy** *n, pl* **flop·pies** : FLOPPY DISK
floppy disk *n* : a thin plastic disk with a magnetic coating on which computer data can be stored
flop sweat *n* : sweat caused by the fear of failing
flo·ra \'flōr-ə\ *n, pl* **floras** *also* **flo·rae** \-ˌē, -ˌī\ [L *Flora*, Roman goddess of flowers] : plants or plant life esp. of a region or period
flo·ral \'flōr-əl\ *adj* : of, relating to, or depicting flowers ⟨a ~ design⟩
flo·res·cence \flō-'re-sᵊns, flə-\ *n* : a state or period of being in bloom or flourishing — **flo·res·cent** \-ᵊnt\ *adj*
flor·id \'flōr-əd\ *adj* 1 : very flowery in style : ORNATE ⟨~ prose⟩ 2 : tinged with red : RUDDY 3 : marked by emotional or sexual fervor ⟨~ love letters⟩
flo·rin \'flōr-ən\ *n* 1 : an old gold coin first struck at Florence, Italy, in 1252 2 : a gold coin of a European country patterned after the florin of Florence 3 : any of several modern silver coins issued in Commonwealth countries 4 : GULDEN
flo·rist \'flōr-ist\ *n* : a person who sells flowers or ornamental plants
¹**floss** \'fläs\ *n* 1 : soft thread of silk or mercerized cotton for embroidery 2 : DENTAL FLOSS 3 : fluffy fibrous material
²**floss** *vb* : to use dental floss on (one's teeth)
flossy \'flä-sē\ *adj* **floss·i·er; -est** 1 : of, relating to, or having the characteristics of floss 2 : STYLISH, GLAMOROUS ⟨~ hotels⟩ — **floss·i·ly** \-sə-lē\ *adv*
flo·ta·tion \flō-'tā-shən\ *n* : the process or an instance of floating
flo·til·la \flō-'ti-lə\ *n* [Sp, dim. of *flota* fleet] : a fleet esp. of small ships
flot·sam \'flät-səm\ *n* : floating wreckage of a ship or its cargo
¹**flounce** \'flauns\ *vb* **flounced; flounc·ing** 1 : to move with exaggerated jerky or bouncy motions 2 : to go with sudden determination
²**flounce** *n* : an act or instance of flouncing — **flouncy** \'flaun-sē\ *adj*
³**flounce** *n* : a strip of fabric attached by one edge; *also* : a wide ruffle
¹**floun·der** \'flaun-dər\ *n, pl* **flounder** *or* **flounders** : FLATFISH; *esp* : any of various important marine food fishes
²**flounder** *vb* 1 : to struggle to move or obtain footing 2 : to proceed clumsily ⟨~ed through the speech⟩
¹**flour** \'flaù(-ə)r\ *n* [ME, flower, best of anything, flour, fr. AF *flur* flower] : finely ground and sifted meal of a grain (as wheat); *also* : a fine soft powder — **floury** *adj*
²**flour** *vb* : to coat with or as if with flour
¹**flour·ish** \'flər-ish\ *vb* 1 : THRIVE, PROSPER 2 : to be in a state of activity or production ⟨~ed about 1850⟩ 3 : to reach a height of development or influence 4 : to make bold and sweeping gestures 5 : BRANDISH ⟨~ed his sword⟩
²**flourish** *n* 1 : a florid bit of speech or writing; *also* : an ornamental touch or decorative detail 2 : FANFARE ⟨a ~ of trumpets⟩ 3 : WAVE ⟨with a ~ of his cane⟩ 4 : showiness in doing something
¹**flout** \'flaut\ *vb* : to treat with contemptuous disregard ⟨~ the law⟩ — **flout·er** *n*
²**flout** *n* : TAUNT
¹**flow** \'flō\ *vb* 1 : to issue or move in a stream 2 : RISE ⟨the tide ebbs and ~s⟩ 3 : ABOUND 4 : to proceed smoothly and readily 5 : to have a smooth continuity 6 : to hang loose and billowing 7 : COME, ARISE 8 : MENSTRUATE
²**flow** *n* 1 : an act of flowing 2 : FLOOD 1, 2 3 : a smooth uninterrupted movement 4 : STREAM; *also* : a mass of material that has flowed when molten 5 : the quantity that flows in a certain time 6 : MENSTRUATION 7 : a continuous transfer of energy — **flow·age** \'flō-ij\ *n*
flow·chart \'flō-ˌchärt\ *n* : a symbolic diagram showing step-by-step progression through a procedure
flow diagram *n* : FLOWCHART
¹**flow·er** \'flaù(-ə)r\ *n* [ME *flour*, fr. AF *flur, flour*, fr. L *flor-, flos*] 1 : a plant shoot modified for reproduction and bearing leaves specialized into floral organs; *esp* : one of

a seed plant consisting of a calyx, corolla, stamens, and carpels 2 : a plant cultivated for its blossoms 3 : the best part or example 4 : the finest most vigorous period 5 : a state of blooming or flourishing — **flow·ered** \'flaù(-ə)rd\ *adj* — **flow·er·less** *adj* — **flow·er·like** \-ˌlīk\ *adj*
²**flower** *vb* 1 : DEVELOP; *also* : FLOURISH 2 : to produce flowers : BLOOM
flower girl *n* : a little girl who carries flowers at a wedding
flower head *n* : a compact cluster of small flowers without stems suggesting a single flower
flowering plant *n* : any of a major group of vascular plants (as magnolias, grasses, or roses) that produce flowers and fruit and have the seeds enclosed in an ovary
flow·er·pot \'flaù(-ə)r-ˌpät\ *n* : a pot in which to grow plants
flow·ery \'flaù(-ə)r-ē\ *adj* 1 : of, relating to, or resembling flowers 2 : full of fine words or phrases ⟨a ~ speech⟩ — **flow·er·i·ness** \-ē-nəs\ *n*
flown \'flōn\ *past part of* ¹FLY
fl oz *abbr* fluid ounce
flu \'flü\ *n* 1 : INFLUENZA 2 : any of several virus diseases marked esp. by respiratory or intestinal symptoms — **flu–like** \-ˌlīk\ *adj*
flub \'fləb\ *vb* **flubbed; flub·bing** : BOTCH, BLUNDER — **flub** *n*
fluc·tu·ate \'flək-chə-ˌwāt\ *vb* **-at·ed; -at·ing** 1 : WAVER 2 : to move up and down or back and forth — **fluc·tu·a·tion** \ˌflək-chə-'wā-shən\ *n*
flue \'flü\ *n* : a passage (as in a chimney) for directing a current (as of smoke or gases)
flu·ent \'flü-ənt\ *adj* 1 : capable of flowing : FLUID 2 : ready or facile in speech ⟨~ in French⟩; *also* : having or showing mastery in a subject or skill 3 : effortlessly smooth and rapid ⟨~ speech⟩ — **flu·en·cy** \-ən-sē\ *n* — **flu·ent·ly** *adv*
flue pipe *n* : an organ pipe whose tone is produced by an air current striking the beveled opening of the pipe
¹**fluff** \'fləf\ *n* 1 : ²DOWN 1 ⟨~ from a pillow⟩ 2 : something fluffy 3 : something inconsequential 4 : BLUNDER; *esp* : an actor's lapse of memory
²**fluff** *vb* 1 : to make or become fluffy ⟨~ up a pillow⟩ 2 : to make a mistake
fluffy \'flə-fē\ *adj* **fluff·i·er; -est** 1 : covered with or resembling fluff 2 : being light and soft or airy ⟨a ~ omelet⟩ 3 : lacking in meaning or substance — **fluff·i·ly** \-fə-lē\ *adv*
¹**flu·id** \'flü-əd\ *adj* 1 : capable of flowing 2 : subject to change or movement 3 : showing a smooth easy style ⟨~ movements⟩ 4 : available for a different use; *esp* : LIQUID 5 ⟨~ assets⟩ — **flu·id·i·ty** \flü-'i-də-tē\ *n* — **flu·id·ly** *adv*
²**fluid** *n* : a substance (as a liquid or gas) tending to flow or take the shape of its container
fluid dram *or* **flu·i·dram** \ˌflü-ə-'dram\ *n* — see WEIGHT table
fluid ounce *n* — see WEIGHT table
¹**fluke** \'flük\ *n* : any of various trematode flatworms
²**fluke** *n* 1 : the part of an anchor that fastens in the ground 2 : a lobe of a whale's tail
³**fluke** *n* : a stroke of luck — **fluky** *also* **fluk·ey** \'flü-kē\ *adj*
flume \'flüm\ *n* 1 : an inclined channel for carrying water 2 : a ravine or gorge with a stream running through it
flung *past and past part of* FLING
flunk \'fləŋk\ *vb* : to fail esp. in an examination or course — **flunk** *n*
flun·ky *also* **flun·key** *or* **flun·kie** \'fləŋ-kē\ *n, pl* **flunkies** *also* **flunkeys** 1 : a liveried servant; *also* : one performing menial or miscellaneous duties 2 : YES-MAN
fluo·res·cence \flò-'re-sᵊns\ *n* : luminescence caused by radiation absorption that ceases almost immediately after the incident radiation has stopped; *also* : the emitted radiation — **fluo·resce** \-'res\ *vb* — **fluo·res·cent** \-'re-sᵊnt\ *adj*
fluorescent lamp *n* : a tubular electric lamp in which light is produced by the action of ultraviolet light on a fluorescent material that coats the inner surface of the lamp
fluo·ri·date \'flòr-ə-ˌdāt\ *vb* **-dat·ed; -dat·ing** : to add a fluoride to (as drinking water) to reduce tooth decay — **fluo·ri·da·tion** \ˌflòr-ə-'dā-shən\ *n*
fluo·ride \'flòr-ˌīd\ *n* : a compound of fluorine

fluo·ri·nate \\'flȯr-ə-ˌnāt\\ *vb* **-nat·ed; -nat·ing** : to treat or cause to combine with fluorine or a compound of fluorine — **fluo·ri·na·tion** \\ˌflȯr-ə-'nā-shən\\ *n*

fluo·rine \\'flȯr-ˌēn, -ən\\ *n* : a pale yellowish flammable irritating toxic gaseous chemical element

fluo·rite \\'flȯr-ˌīt\\ *n* : a mineral that consists of the fluoride of calcium used as a flux and in making glass

fluo·ro·car·bon \\ˌflȯr-ō-'kär-bən\\ *n* : a compound containing fluorine and carbon used chiefly as a lubricant, refrigerant, or nonstick coating; *also* : CHLOROFLUOROCARBON

fluo·ro·scope \\'flȯr-ə-ˌskōp\\ *n* : an instrument for observing the internal structure of an opaque object (as the living body) by means of X-rays — **fluo·ro·scop·ic** \\ˌflȯr-ə-'skä-pik\\ *adj* — **fluo·ros·co·py** \\-'ä-skə-pē\\ *n*

fluo·ro·sis \\ˌflu̇-'rō-səs, ˌflȯ-\\ *n* : an abnormal condition (as spotting of the teeth) caused by fluorine or its compounds

flu·ox·e·tine \\flü-'ak-sə-ˌtēn\\ *n* : an antidepressant drug that enhances serotonin activity

flur·ry \\'flər-ē\\ *n, pl* **flurries** **1** : a gust of wind **2** : a brief light snowfall **3** : COMMOTION, BUSTLE **4** : a brief outburst of activity ⟨a ~ of trading⟩ — **flurry** *vb*

¹flush \\'fləsh\\ *vb* : to cause (a bird) to fly away suddenly

²flush *n* : a hand of cards all of the same suit

³flush *n* **1** : a sudden flow (as of water) **2** : a surge esp. of emotion ⟨a ~ of triumph⟩ **3** : a tinge of red : BLUSH **4** : a fresh and vigorous state ⟨in the ~ of youth⟩ **5** : a passing sensation of extreme heat

⁴flush *vb* **1** : to flow and spread suddenly and freely **2** : to glow brightly **3** : BLUSH **4** : to wash out with a rush of fluid **5** : INFLAME, EXCITE ⟨was ~ed with anger⟩ **6** : to cause to blush

⁵flush *adj* **1** : of a ruddy healthy color **2** : full of life and vigor **3** : filled to overflowing **4** : AFFLUENT **5** : readily available : ABUNDANT **6** : having an unbroken or even surface **7** : directly abutting : immediately adjacent **8** : set even with an edge of a type page or column — **flush·ness** *n*

⁶flush *adv* **1** : in a flush manner **2** : SQUARELY ⟨a blow ~ on the chin⟩

⁷flush *vb* : to make flush

flus·ter \\'fləs-tər\\ *vb* : to put into a state of agitated confusion — **fluster** *n*

flute \\'flüt\\ *n* **1** : a hollow pipelike musical instrument **2** : a grooved pleat **3** : GROOVE — **flute** *vb* — **flut·ed** *adj*

flut·ing *n* : fluted decoration

flut·ist \\'flü-tist\\ *n* : a flute player

¹flut·ter \\'flə-tər\\ *vb* [ME *floteren* to float, flutter, fr. OE *floterian*, fr. *flotian* to float] **1** : to flap the wings rapidly **2** : to move with quick wavering or flapping motions **3** : to vibrate in irregular spasms **4** : to move about or behave in an agitated aimless manner — **flut·tery** \\-tə-rē\\ *adj*

²flutter *n* **1** : an act of fluttering **2** : a state of nervous confusion **3** : FLURRY

¹flux \\'fləks\\ *n* **1** : an act of flowing **2** : a state of continuous change **3** : a substance used to aid in fusing metals

²flux *vb* : ¹FUSE

¹fly \\'flī\\ *vb* **flew** \\'flü\\ **flown** \\'flōn\\; **fly·ing** **1** : to move in or pass through the air with wings **2** : to move through the air or before the wind **3** : to float or cause to float, wave, or soar in the air **4** : FLEE **5** : to fade and disappear : VANISH **6** : to move or pass swiftly ⟨time *flies*⟩ **7** : to become expended or dissipated rapidly **8** : to operate or travel in an aircraft or spacecraft **9** : to journey over by flying **10** : AVOID, SHUN **11** : to transport by flying

²fly *n, pl* **flies** **1** : the action or process of flying : FLIGHT **2** *pl* : the space over a theater stage **3** : a garment closing concealed by a fold of cloth **4** : the length of an extended flag from its staff or support **5** : a baseball hit high into the air **6** : the outer canvas of a tent with a double top — **on the fly** : while still in the air

³fly *vb* **flied; fly·ing** : to hit a fly in baseball

⁴fly *n, pl* **flies** **1** : a winged insect — usu. used in combination ⟨butter*fly*⟩ **2** : any of a large order of insects mostly with one pair of functional wings and another pair that if present are reduced to balancing organs and often with larvae without a head, eyes, or legs; *esp* : one (as a housefly) that is large and stout-bodied **3** : a fishhook dressed to suggest an insect

fly·able \\'flī-ə-bəl\\ *adj* : suitable for flying or being flown

fly ball *n* : ²FLY 5

fly·blown \\'flī-ˌblōn\\ *adj* : not pure : TAINTED, CORRUPT

fly·by \\-ˌbī\\ *n, pl* **flybys** **1** : a usu. low-altitude flight by an aircraft over a public gathering **2** : a flight of a spacecraft past a heavenly body (as Jupiter) close enough to obtain scientific data

fly-by-night \\-bī-ˌnīt\\ *adj* **1** : seeking a quick profit usu. by shady acts **2** : TRANSITORY, PASSING ⟨~ fashions⟩

fly casting *n* : the casting of artificial flies in fly-fishing or as a competitive sport

fly·catch·er \\-ˌka-chər, -ˌke-\\ *n* : any of various passerine birds that feed on insects caught in flight

flyer *var of* FLIER

fly-fish·ing \\'flī-ˌfi-shin\\ *n* : a method of fishing in which an artificial fly is used for bait

flying boat *n* : a seaplane with a hull designed for floating

flying buttress *n* : a projecting arched structure to support a wall or building

flying fish *n* : any of numerous marine bony fishes capable of long gliding flights out of water by spreading their large fins like wings

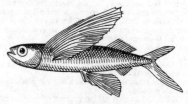

flying fish

flying saucer *n* : an unidentified flying object reported to be saucer-shaped or disk-shaped

flying squirrel *n* : either of two small nocturnal No. American squirrels with folds of skin connecting the forelegs and hind legs that enable them to make long gliding leaps

fly·leaf \\'flī-ˌlēf\\ *n, pl* **fly·leaves** \\-ˌlēvz\\ : a blank leaf at the beginning or end of a book

fly·pa·per \\-ˌpā-pər\\ *n* : paper poisoned or coated with a sticky substance for killing or catching flies

fly·speck \\-ˌspek\\ *n* **1** : a speck of fly dung **2** : something small and insignificant

fly·way \\-ˌwā\\ *n* : an established air route of migratory birds

fly·wheel \\-ˌhwēl\\ *n* : a heavy wheel for regulating the speed of machinery

fm *abbr* fathom

Fm *symbol* fermium

FM \\'ef-ˌem\\ *n* : a broadcasting system using frequency modulation; *also* : a radio receiver of such a system

fn *abbr* footnote

fo *or* **fol** *abbr* folio

FO *abbr* foreign office

¹foal \\'fōl\\ *n* : a young horse or related animal; *esp* : one under one year

²foal *vb* : to give birth to a foal

foam \\'fōm\\ *n* **1** : a mass of bubbles formed on the surface of a liquid : FROTH, SPUME **2** : material (as rubber) in a lightweight cellular form — **foamy** *adj*

²foam *vb* : to form foam : FROTH

fob \\'fäb\\ *n* **1** : a short strap, ribbon, or chain attached esp. to a pocket watch **2** : a small ornament worn on a fob

FOB *abbr* free on board

fob off *vb* **1** : to put off with a trick, excuse, or inferior substitute **2** : to pass or offer as genuine **3** : to put aside

FOC *abbr* free of charge

focal length *n* : the distance of a focus from a lens or curved mirror

fo'c'sle *var of* FORECASTLE

¹fo·cus \\'fō-kəs\\ *n, pl* **fo·ci** \\-ˌsī\\ *also* **fo·cus·es** [NL, fr. L, hearth] **1** : a point at which rays (as of light, heat, or sound) meet or diverge or appear to diverge; *esp* : the point at which an image is formed by a mirror, lens, or optical system **2** : FOCAL LENGTH **3** : adjustment (as of eyes or eyeglasses) that gives clear vision **4** : central point : CENTER — **fo·cal** \\'fō-kəl\\ *adj* — **fo·cal·ly** *adv*

²focus *vb* **-cused** *also* **-cussed; -cus·ing** *also* **-cus·sing** **1** : to bring or come to a focus ⟨~ rays of light⟩ **2** : CENTER ⟨~ attention on a problem⟩ **3** : to adjust the focus of

fod·der \\'fä-dər\ n 1 : coarse dry food (as cornstalks) for livestock 2 : available material used to supply a heavy demand

foe \\'fō\ n [ME fo, fr. OE fāh, fr. fāh hostile] : ENEMY

FOE abbr Fraternal Order of Eagles

foehn or **föhn** \\'fərn, 'fœn, 'fän\ n [G Föhn] : a warm dry wind blowing down a mountainside

foe·man \\'fō-mən\ n : FOE

foe·tal, foe·tus chiefly Brit var of FETAL, FETUS

¹**fog** \\'fȯg, 'fäg\ n 1 : fine particles of water suspended in the lower atmosphere 2 : mental confusion ⟨was in a ∼ as what to do next⟩ — **fog·gy** adj

²**fog** vb **fogged; fog·ging** : to obscure or be obscured with or as if with fog

fog·horn \\'fȯg-ˌhȯrn, 'fäg-\ n : a horn sounded in a fog to give warning

fo·gy also **fo·gey** \\'fō-gē\ n, pl **fogies** also **fogeys** : a person with old-fashioned ideas ⟨an old ∼⟩

foi·ble \\'fȯi-bəl\ n : a minor failing or weakness in character or behavior

foie gras \\'fwä-'grä\ n [F, lit., fat liver] : the fattened liver of an animal and esp. of a goose usu. served as a pâté

¹**foil** \\'fȯi(-ə)l\ vb [ME, alter. of fullen to full cloth, fr. AF foller] 1 : to prevent from attaining an end : DEFEAT 2 : to bring to naught : THWART

²**foil** n [ME, leaf, fr. AF fuille, foille, fr. L folia, pl. of folium leaf] 1 : a very thin sheet of metal ⟨aluminum ∼⟩ 2 : one that serves as a contrast to another ⟨acted as a ∼ for a comedian⟩

³**foil** n : a light fencing sword with a flexible blade tapering to a blunt point

foist \\'fȯist\ vb : to pass off (something false or worthless) as genuine

¹**fold** \\'fōld\ n 1 : an enclosure for sheep 2 : a group of people with a common faith, belief, or interest

²**fold** vb : to house (sheep) in a fold

³**fold** vb 1 : to lay one part over or against another part 2 : to lay one part over or against another part 3 : to clasp together 3 : EMBRACE 4 : to bend (as a layer of rock) into folds 5 : to incorporate into a mixture by overturning repeatedly without stirring or beating 6 : to become doubled or pleated 7 : FAIL, COLLAPSE ⟨the business ∼ed⟩

⁴**fold** n 1 : a doubling or folding over 2 : a part doubled or laid over another part

fold·away \\'fōld-ə-ˌwā\ adj : designed to fold out of the way or out of sight

fold·er \\'fōl-dər\ n 1 : one that folds 2 : a folded printed circular 3 : a folded cover or large envelope for loose papers 4 : an object in a computer operating system used to organize files or other folders

fol·de·rol \\'fäl-də-ˌräl\ n 1 : a useless trifle 2 : NONSENSE

fold·out \\'fōld-ˌaȯt\ n : a folded leaf (as in a magazine) larger in some dimension than the page

fo·liage \\'fō-lē-ij\ n : a mass of leaves (as of a plant or forest)

fo·li·at·ed \\'fō-lē-ˌā-təd\ adj : composed of or separable into layers

fo·lic acid \\'fō-lik-\ n : a vitamin of the vitamin B complex used esp. to treat nutritional anemias

fo·lio \\'fō-lē-ˌō\ n, pl **fo·li·os** 1 : a leaf of a book; also : a page number 2 : the size of a piece of paper cut two from a sheet 3 : a book printed on folio pages

¹**folk** \\'fōk\ n, pl **folk** or **folks** 1 : the largest number or most characteristic part of a group of people forming a tribe or nation 2 pl : PEOPLE, PERSONS ⟨country ∼⟩ ⟨old ∼s⟩ 3 folks pl : the persons of one's own family

²**folk** adj : of, relating to, or originating among the common people ⟨∼ music⟩

folk art n : the traditional anonymous art of usu. untrained people

folk·lore \\'fōk-ˌlȯr\ n : customs, beliefs, stories, and sayings of a people handed down from generation to generation — **folk·lor·ic** \-ˌlȯr-ik\ adj — **folk·lor·ist** \-ist\ n

folk mass n : a mass in which traditional liturgical music is replaced by folk music

folk·sing·er \\'fōk-ˌsiŋ-ər\ n : a singer of folk songs — **folk·sing·ing** n

folksy \\'fōk-sē\ adj **folks·i·er; -est** 1 : SOCIABLE, FRIENDLY 2 : informal, casual, or familiar in manner or style ⟨∼ humor⟩

folk·way \\'fōk-ˌwā\ n : a way of thinking, feeling, or acting common to a given group of people; esp : a traditional social custom

fol·li·cle \\'fä-li-kəl\ n 1 : a small anatomical cavity or gland ⟨a hair ∼⟩ 2 : a small fluid-filled cavity in the ovary of a mammal enclosing a developing egg — **fol·lic·u·lar** \fə-'li-kyə-lər\ adj

fol·low \\'fä-lō\ vb 1 : to go or come after 2 : to proceed along ⟨∼ the path⟩ 3 : to engage in as a way of life ⟨∼ the sea⟩ ⟨∼ a profession⟩ 4 : OBEY ⟨∼ instructions⟩ 5 : PURSUE 6 : to come after in order or rank or natural sequence 7 : to keep one's attention fixed on 8 : to result from 9 : to subscribe to the social media feed of ✦ **Synonyms** SUCCEED, ENSUE, SUPERVENE — **follow·er** n — **follow suit** 1 : to play a card of the same suit as the card led 2 : to follow an example set

¹**fol·low·ing** \\'fä-lə-wiŋ\ adj 1 : next after : SUCCEEDING ⟨the ∼ day⟩ 2 : that immediately follows ⟨trains will leave at the ∼ times⟩

²**following** n : a group of followers, adherents, or partisans

³**following** prep : subsequent to : AFTER ⟨∼ the lecture tea was served⟩

follow–up \\'fä-lō-ˌəp\ n : a system or instance of pursuing an initial effort by supplementary action

fol·ly \\'fä-lē\ n, pl **follies** [ME folie, fr. AF, fr. fol fool] 1 : lack of good sense 2 : a foolish act or idea : FOOLISHNESS 3 : an excessively costly or unprofitable undertaking

fo·ment \fō-'ment\ vb : INCITE

fo·men·ta·tion \ˌfō-mən-'tā-shən, -ˌmen-\ n 1 : a hot moist material (as a damp cloth) applied to the body to ease pain 2 : the act of fomenting : INSTIGATION

fond \\'fänd\ adj [ME, fr. fonne fool] 1 : FOOLISH, SILLY ⟨∼ pride⟩ 2 : prizing highly : DESIROUS ⟨∼ of praise⟩ 3 : strongly attracted or predisposed ⟨∼ of music⟩ 4 : foolishly tender : INDULGENT; also : LOVING, AFFECTIONATE 5 : CHERISHED, DEAR ⟨his ∼est hopes⟩ — **fond·ly** adv — **fond·ness** n

fon·dant \\'fän-dənt\ n : a creamy preparation of sugar used as a basis for candies or icings

fon·dle \\'fän-dᵊl\ vb **fon·dled; fon·dling** : to touch or handle lovingly : CARESS

fon·due also **fon·du** \fän-'dü, -'dyü\ n [F] : a preparation of melted cheese often flavored with white wine

¹**font** \\'fänt\ n 1 : a receptacle for baptismal or holy water 2 : FOUNTAIN, SOURCE ⟨a ∼ of information⟩

²**font** n : an assortment of printing type of one style and sometimes one size

food \\'füd\ n 1 : material taken into an organism and used for growth, repair, and vital processes and as a source of energy; also : organic material produced by green plants and used by them as food 2 : nourishment in solid form 3 : something that nourishes, sustains, or supplies ⟨∼ for thought⟩

food chain n 1 : a hierarchical arrangement of organisms in an ecological community such that each uses the next usu. lower element as a food source 2 : a hierarchy based on power or importance

food court n : an area (as within a shopping mall) set apart for food concessions

food poisoning n : a digestive illness caused by bacteria or by chemicals in food

food·stuff \\'füd-ˌstəf\ n : a substance with food value; esp : a specific nutrient (as fat or protein)

¹**fool** \\'fül\ n [ME, fr. AF fol, fr. LL follis, fr. L, bellows, bag] 1 : a person who lacks sense or judgment 2 : JESTER 3 : DUPE 4 : IDIOT

²**fool** vb 1 : to spend time idly or aimlessly 2 : to meddle or tamper thoughtlessly or ignorantly 3 : JOKE 4 : DECEIVE 5 : FRITTER ⟨∼ed away his time⟩

fool·ery \\'fü-lə-rē\ n, pl **-er·ies** 1 : a foolish act, utterance, or belief 2 : foolish behavior

fool·har·dy \\'fül-ˌhär-dē\ adj : foolishly daring : RASH — **fool·har·di·ness** \-dē-nəs\ n

fool·ish \\'fü-lish\ adj 1 : showing or arising from folly or lack of judgment 2 : ABSURD, RIDICULOUS 3 : ABASHED — **fool·ish·ly** adv — **fool·ish·ness** n

fool·proof \\'fül-ˌprüf\ adj : so simple or reliable as to leave no opportunity for error, misuse, or failure ⟨a ∼ plan⟩

fools·cap \\'fül-ˌskap\ n [fr. the watermark of a fool's cap formerly applied to such paper] : a size of paper typically 16×13 inches

fool's gold n : PYRITE

¹foot \'fut\ n, pl **feet** \'fēt\ also **foot** 1 : the end part of a leg below the ankle of a vertebrate animal 2 — see WEIGHT table 3 : a group of syllables forming the basic unit of verse meter 4 : something resembling an animal's foot in position or use 5 : the lowest part : BOTTOM 6 : the part at the opposite end from the head 7 : the part (as of a stocking) that covers the foot

²foot vb 1 : DANCE 2 : to go on foot 3 : to add up 4 : to pay or provide for paying

foot·age \'fu-tij\ n 1 : length expressed in feet 2 : the length of film used for a scene; also : the material contained on such footage

foot–and–mouth disease n : an acute contagious viral disease esp. of cattle

foot·ball \'fut-,bȯl\ n 1 : any of several games played by two teams on a rectangular field with goalposts at each end in which the object is to get the ball over the goal line or between goalposts by running, passing, or kicking 2 : the ball used in football

foot·board \-,bȯrd\ n 1 : a narrow platform on which to stand or brace the feet 2 : a board forming the foot of a bed

foot·bridge \-,brij\ n : a bridge for pedestrians

foot·ed \'fu-tǝd\ adj : having a foot or feet of a specified kind or number ⟨flat-footed⟩ ⟨four-footed⟩

-foot·er \'fu-tǝr\ comb form : one that is a specified number of feet in height, length, or breadth ⟨a six-footer⟩

foot·fall \'fut-,fȯl\ n : the sound of a footstep

foot·hill \-,hil\ n : a hill at the foot of higher hills or mountains

foot·hold \-,hōld\ n 1 : a hold for the feet : FOOTING 2 : a position usable as a base for further advance

foot·ing n 1 : the placing of one's feet in a stable position 2 : the act of moving on foot 3 : a place or space for standing : FOOTHOLD 4 : position with respect to one another : STATUS 5 : BASIS

foot·less \'fut-lǝs\ adj 1 : having no feet ⟨~ tights⟩ 2 : INEPT, INEFFECTUAL

foot·lights \-,līts\ n pl 1 : a row of lights along the front of a stage floor 2 : the stage as a profession ⟨succeeded in the ~⟩

foo·tling \'fut-lin\ adj 1 : INEPT ⟨~ amateurs⟩ 2 : TRIVIAL

foot·lock·er \'fut-,lä-kǝr\ n : a small trunk designed to be placed at the foot of a bed (as in a barracks)

foot·loose \-,lüs\ adj : having no ties : FREE, UNTRAMMELED

foot·man \-mǝn\ n : a male servant who attends a carriage or waits on table, admits visitors, and runs errands

foot·note \-,nōt\ n 1 : a note of reference, explanation, or comment placed usu. at the bottom of a page 2 : COMMENTARY

foot·pad \-,pad\ n : a round somewhat flat foot on the leg of a spacecraft for distributing weight to minimize sinking into a surface

foot·path \-,path, -,päth\ n : a narrow path for pedestrians

foot·print \-,print\ n 1 : an impression of the foot 2 : the area on a surface covered by something ⟨a tire with a wide ~⟩

foot·race \-,rās\ n : a race run on foot

foot·rest \-,rest\ n : a support for the feet

foot·sore \-,sȯr\ adj : having sore or tender feet (as from much walking)

foot·step \-,step\ n 1 : the mark of the foot : TRACK 2 : TREAD 3 : distance covered by a step : PACE 4 : a step on which to ascend or descend 5 : a way of life, conduct, or action

foot·stool \-,stül\ n : a low stool to support the feet

foot·wear \-,wer\ n : apparel (as shoes or boots) for the feet

foot·work \-,wǝrk\ n : the management of the feet (as in boxing)

fop \'fäp\ n : DANDY 1 — **fop·pery** \'fä-pǝ-rē\ n — **fop·pish** adj

¹for \fǝr, 'fȯr\ prep 1 : as a preparation toward ⟨dress ~ dinner⟩ 2 : toward the purpose or goal of ⟨need time ~ study⟩ ⟨money ~ a trip⟩ 3 : so as to reach or attain ⟨run ~ cover⟩ 4 : as being ⟨took him ~ a fool⟩ 5 : because of ⟨cry ~ joy⟩ 6 — used to indicate a recipient ⟨a letter ~ you⟩ 7 : in support of ⟨fought ~ his

country⟩ 8 : directed at : AFFECTING ⟨a cure ~ what ails you⟩ 9 — used with a noun or pronoun followed by an infinitive to form the equivalent of a noun clause ⟨~ you to go would be silly⟩ 10 : in exchange as equal to : so as to return the value of ⟨a lot of trouble ~ nothing⟩ ⟨pay $10 ~ a hat⟩ 11 : CONCERNING ⟨a stickler ~ detail⟩ 12 : CONSIDERING ⟨tall ~ her age⟩ 13 : through the period of ⟨served ~ three years⟩ 14 : in honor of ⟨named ~ her grandmother⟩

²for conj : BECAUSE

³for abbr 1 foreign 2 forestry

¹for·age \'fȯr-ij\ n [ME, fr. AF, fr. fuerre, foer fodder, straw, of Gmc origin] 1 : food for animals esp. when taken by browsing or grazing 2 : a search for food or supplies

²forage vb **for·aged**; **for·ag·ing** 1 : to collect forage from 2 : to search for food or supplies 3 : to get by foraging 4 : to make a search : RUMMAGE

for·ay \'fȯr-,ā, fȯ-'rā\ vb : to raid esp. in search of plunder : PILLAGE — **foray** n

¹for·bear \fȯr-'ber\ vb **-bore** \-'bȯr\; **-borne** \-'bȯrn\; **-bear·ing** 1 : to refrain from : ABSTAIN 2 : to be patient — **for·bear·ance** \-'ber-ǝns\ n

²forbear var of FOREBEAR

for·bid \fǝr-'bid\ vb **-bade** \-'bad, -'bād\ also **-bad** \-'bad\; **-bid·den** \-'bi-dᵃn\; **-bid·ding** 1 : to command against : PROHIBIT 2 : HINDER, PREVENT ✦ Synonyms ENJOIN, INTERDICT, INHIBIT, BAN

forbidding adj : DISAGREEABLE, REPELLENT ⟨a ~ task⟩

¹force \'fȯrs\ n 1 : strength or energy esp. of an exceptional degree : active power 2 : capacity to persuade or convince 3 : military strength; also, pl : the whole military strength (as of a nation) 4 : a body (as of persons or ships) available for a particular purpose 5 : VIOLENCE, COMPULSION 6 : an influence (as a push or pull) that causes motion or a change of motion — **force·ful** \-fǝl\ adj — **force·ful·ly** adv — **in force** 1 : in great numbers 2 : VALID, OPERATIVE ⟨the ban remains in force⟩

²force vb **forced**; **forc·ing** 1 : COMPEL, COERCE 2 : to cause through necessity ⟨forced to admit defeat⟩ 3 : to press, attain to, or effect against resistance or inertia ⟨~ your way through⟩ 4 : to raise or accelerate to the utmost ⟨~ the pace⟩ 5 : to produce with unnatural or unwilling effort ⟨forced a smile⟩ 6 : to hasten (as in growth) by artificial means

for·ceps \'fȯr-sǝps\ n, pl **forceps** [L] : a handheld instrument for grasping, holding, or pulling objects esp. for delicate operations (as by a surgeon)

forc·ible \'fȯr-sǝ-bǝl\ adj 1 : obtained or done by force 2 : showing force or energy : POWERFUL — **forc·i·bly** \-blē\ adv

¹ford \'fȯrd\ n : a place where a stream may be crossed by wading

²ford vb : to cross (a body of water) by wading

¹fore \'fȯr\ adv : in, toward, or adjacent to the front : FORWARD

²fore adj : being or coming before in time, order, or space

³fore n : something that occupies a front position

⁴fore interj — used by a golfer to warn anyone within range of the probable line of flight of the ball

fore–and–aft \,fȯr-ǝ-'naft\ adj : lying, running, or acting along the length of a structure (as a ship)

¹fore·arm \(,)fȯr-'ärm\ vb : to arm in advance : PREPARE

²fore·arm \'fȯr-,ärm\ n : the part of the arm between the elbow and the wrist

fore·bear \-,ber\ n : ANCESTOR, FOREFATHER

fore·bode also **for·bode** \fȯr-'bōd\ vb 1 : to have a premonition esp. of misfortune 2 : FORETELL, PREDICT ✦ Synonyms AUGUR, BODE, FORESHADOW, PORTEND, PROMISE — **fore·bod·ing** n or adj — **fore·bod·ing·ly** adv

fore·cast \'fȯr-,kast\ vb **-cast** also **-cast·ed**; **-cast·ing** 1 : PREDICT, CALCULATE ⟨~ weather conditions⟩ 2 : to indicate as likely to occur — **forecast** n — **fore·cast·er** n

fore·cas·tle or **fo'·c'sle** \'fōk-sǝl\ n 1 : the forward part of the upper deck of a ship 2 : the crew's quarters usu. in a ship's bow

fore·close \fȯr-'klōz\ vb 1 : to shut out : PRECLUDE 2 : to take legal measures to terminate a mortgage and take possession of the mortgaged property

foreclosure • forge

196

fore·clo·sure \-'klō-zhər\ *n* : the act of foreclosing; *esp* : the legal procedure of foreclosing a mortgage
fore·doom \fôr-'düm\ *vb* : to doom beforehand
fore·fa·ther \'fôr-ˌfä-t͟hər\ *n* 1 : ANCESTOR 2 : a person of an earlier period and common heritage
forefend *var of* FORFEND
fore·fin·ger \-ˌfiŋ-gər\ *n* : INDEX FINGER
fore·foot \-ˌfůt\ *n* : either of the front feet of a quadruped; *also* : the front part of the human foot
fore·front \-ˌfrənt\ *n* : the foremost part or place
foregather *var of* FORGATHER
¹fore·go \fôr-'gō\ *vb* **-went** \-'went\; **-gone** \-'gôn\; **-go·ing** : PRECEDE
²forego *var of* FORGO
foregoing *adj* : PRECEDING ⟨the ~ statement can be proven⟩
fore·gone \'fôr-ˌgôn\ *adj* : determined in advance ⟨a ~ conclusion⟩
fore·ground \-ˌgraůnd\ *n* 1 : the part of a scene or representation that appears nearest to and in front of the spectator 2 : a position of prominence
fore·hand \-ˌhand\ *n* : a stroke (as in tennis) made with the palm of the hand turned in the direction in which the hand is moving; *also* : the side on which such a stroke is made — **forehand** *adj*
fore·hand·ed \(ˌ)fôr-'han-dəd\ *adj* : mindful of the future : PRUDENT
fore·head \'fôr-əd, 'fôr-ˌhed\ *n* : the part of the face above the eyes
for·eign \'fôr-ən\ *adj* [ME *forein*, fr. AF, fr. LL *foranus* on the outside, fr. L *foris* outside] 1 : situated outside a place or country and esp. one's own country 2 : born in, belonging to, or characteristic of some place or country other than the one under consideration ⟨~ language⟩ 3 : not connected, pertinent, or characteristically present 4 : related to or dealing with other nations ⟨~ affairs⟩ 5 : occurring in an abnormal situation in the living body ⟨a ~ body in the eye⟩
for·eign·er \'fôr-ə-nər\ *n* : a person belonging to or owing allegiance to a foreign country
foreign minister *n* : a governmental minister for foreign affairs
fore·know \fôr-'nō\ *vb* **-knew** \-'nü, -'nyü\; **-known** \-'nōn\; **-know·ing** : to have previous knowledge of — **fore·knowl·edge** \'fôr-ˌnä-lij, ˌfôr-'nä-\ *n*
fore·la·dy \'fôr-ˌlā-dē\ *n* : FOREWOMAN
fore·leg \-ˌleg\ *n* : a front leg
fore·limb \-ˌlim\ *n* : a front or upper limb (as a wing, arm, fin, or leg)
fore·lock \-ˌläk\ *n* : a lock of hair growing from the front part of the head
fore·man \-mən\ *n* 1 : a spokesperson of a jury 2 : a person in charge of a group of workers
fore·mast \-ˌmast\ *n* : the mast nearest the bow of a ship
fore·most \-ˌmōst\ *adj* : first in time, place, or order : most important — **foremost** *adv*
fore·name \-ˌnām\ *n* : a first name
fore·named \-ˌnāmd\ *adj* : previously named : AFORESAID
fore·noon \-ˌnün\ *n* : MORNING
¹fo·ren·sic \fə-'ren-sik\ *adj* [L *forensis* public, forensic, fr. *forum* forum] 1 : belonging to, used in, or suitable to courts of law or to public speaking or debate 2 : relating to the application of scientific knowledge to legal problems ⟨~ medicine⟩
²forensic *n* 1 : an argumentative exercise 2 *pl* : the art or study of argumentative discourse 3 *pl* : scientific analysis of physical evidence (as from a crime scene)
fore·or·dain \ˌfôr-ôr-'dān\ *vb* : to ordain or decree beforehand : PREDESTINE
fore·part \'fôr-ˌpärt\ *n* 1 : the anterior part of something 2 : the earlier part of a period of time
fore·quar·ter \-ˌkwôr-tər\ *n* : the front half of a lateral half of the body or carcass of a quadruped ⟨a ~ of beef⟩
fore·run·ner \-ˌrə-nər\ *n* 1 : one that goes before to give notice of the approach of others : HARBINGER 2 : PREDECESSOR, ANCESTOR ✦ *Synonyms* PRECURSOR, HERALD
fore·sail \-ˌsāl, -səl\ *n* 1 : the lowest sail on the foremast of a square-rigged ship or schooner 2 : the principal sail forward of the foremast (as of a sloop)
fore·see \fôr-'sē\ *vb* **-saw** \-'sô\; **-seen** \-'sēn\; **-see·ing** : to see or realize beforehand : EXPECT ✦ *Synonyms*

FOREKNOW, DIVINE, APPREHEND, ANTICIPATE — **fore·see·able** *adj*
fore·shad·ow \-'sha-dō\ *vb* : to give a hint or suggestion of beforehand
fore·short·en \fôr-'shôr-t²n\ *vb* : to shorten (a detail) in a drawing or painting so that it appears to have depth
fore·sight \'fôr-ˌsīt\ *n* 1 : the act or power of foreseeing 2 : care or provision for the future : PRUDENCE 3 : an act of looking forward; *also* : a view forward — **fore·sight·ed** \-ˌsī-təd\ *adj* — **fore·sight·ed·ly** *adv* — **fore·sight·ed·ness** *n*
fore·skin \-ˌskin\ *n* : a fold of skin enclosing the end of the penis
for·est \'fôr-əst\ *n* [ME, fr. AF, fr. LL *forestis (silva)* unenclosed (woodland), fr. L *foris* outside] : a large thick growth of trees and underbrush — **for·est·ed** \'fôr-ə-stəd\ *adj* — **for·est·land** \'fôr-əst-ˌland\ *n*
fore·stall \fôr-'stôl\ *vb* : to counter, hinder, or prevent by measures taken in advance ⟨his comments ~ed the criticism⟩
forest ranger *n* : a person in charge of the management and protection of a portion of a forest
for·est·ry \'fôr-ə-strē\ *n* : the science of growing and caring for forests — **for·est·er** \'fôr-ə-stər\ *n*
foreswear *var of* FORSWEAR
¹fore·taste \'fôr-ˌtāst\ *n* : an advance indication, warning, or notion ⟨a ~ of winter⟩
²fore·taste \fôr-'tāst\ *vb* : to taste beforehand : ANTICIPATE
fore·tell \fôr-'tel\ *vb* **-told** \-'tōld\; **-tell·ing** : to tell of beforehand : PREDICT ✦ *Synonyms* FORECAST, PROPHESY, PROGNOSTICATE
fore·thought \'fôr-ˌthôt\ *n* 1 : PREMEDITATION 2 : consideration for the future
fore·to·ken \fôr-'tō-kən\ *vb* : to indicate in advance
fore·top \'fôr-ˌtäp\ *n* : a platform near the top of a ship's foremast
for·ev·er \fôr-'e-vər\ *adv* 1 : for a limitless time 2 : at all times : ALWAYS
for·ev·er·more \-ˌe-vər-'môr\ *adv* : FOREVER
fore·warn \fôr-'wôrn\ *vb* : to warn beforehand — **fore·warn·ing** \-'wôr-niŋ\ *n*
forewent *past of* FOREGO
fore·wing \'fôr-ˌwiŋ\ *n* : either of the anterior wings of a 4-winged insect
fore·wom·an \'fôr-ˌwů-mən\ *n* : a woman who is a foreman
fore·word \-ˌwərd\ *n* : PREFACE
¹for·feit \'fôr-fət\ *n* [ME *forfait*, fr. AF, fr. pp. of *forfaire, forsfaire* to commit a crime, forfeit, fr. *fors* outside + *faire* to do] 1 : something forfeited : PENALTY, FINE 2 : FORFEITURE 3 : something deposited and then redeemed on payment of a fine 4 *pl* : a game in which forfeits are exacted
²forfeit *vb* : to lose or lose the right to esp. by some error, offense, or crime
for·fei·ture \'fôr-fə-ˌchůr\ *n* 1 : the act of forfeiting 2 : something forfeited : PENALTY
for·fend \fôr-'fend\ *vb* 1 : PREVENT 2 : PROTECT, PRESERVE
for·gath·er *or* **fore·gath·er** \fôr-'ga-t͟hər\ *vb* 1 : to come together : ASSEMBLE 2 : to meet someone usu. by chance
¹forge \'fôrj\ *n* [ME, fr. AF, fr. L *fabrica*, fr. *faber* smith] : a furnace or shop with its furnace where metal is heated and worked
²forge *vb* **forged; forg·ing** 1 : to form (metal) by heating and hammering : FASHION, SHAPE ⟨~ an agreement⟩ 3 : to make or imitate falsely esp. with intent to defraud ⟨~ a signature⟩ — **forg·er** *n* — **forg·ery** \'fôr-jə-rē\ *n*

foresail 1

³**forge** *vb* **forged; forg·ing** : to move ahead steadily but gradually

for·get \fər-'get\ *vb* **-got** \-'gät\; **-got·ten** \-'gät-ᵊn\ *or* **-got; -get·ting** **1** : to be unable to think of or recall **2** : to fail to become mindful of at the proper time **3** : NEGLECT, DISREGARD ⟨*forgot* their old friends⟩ **4** : to give up hope for or expectation of — **for·get·ful** \-'get-fəl\ *adj* — **for·get·ful·ly** *adv* — **for·get·ful·ness** *n*

for·get-me-not \fər-'get-mē-₁nät\ *n* : any of a genus of small herbs with bright blue or white flowers

forg·ing *n* : a piece of forged work

for·give \fər-'giv\ *vb* **-gave** \-'gāv\; **-giv·en** \-'gi-vən\; **-giv·ing** **1** : to give up resentment of **2** : PARDON, ABSOLVE **3** : to grant relief from payment of ⟨~ a debt⟩ — **for·giv·able** *adj* — **for·give·ness** *n* — **for·giv·er** *n*

forgiving *adj* **1** : willing or able to forgive **2** : allowing room for error or weakness ⟨a ~ recipe⟩

for·go \fȯr-'gō\ *vb* **-went** \-'went\; **-gone** \-'gȯn\; **-go·ing** : to give up the enjoyment or advantage of : do without

fo·rint \'fȯr-int\ *n, pl* **forints** *also* **forint** — see MONEY table

¹**fork** \'fȯrk\ *n* **1** : an implement with two or more prongs for taking up (as in eating), pitching, or digging **2** : a forked part, tool, or piece of equipment **3** : a dividing into branches or a place where something branches; *also* : a branch of such a fork

²**fork** *vb* **1** : to divide into two or more branches **2** : to give the form of a fork to ⟨~*ing* her fingers⟩ **3** : to raise or pitch with a fork ⟨~ hay⟩ **4** : PAY, CONTRIBUTE — used with *over, out,* or *up*

forked \'fȯrkt, 'fȯr-kəd\ *adj* : having a fork : shaped like a fork ⟨~ lightning⟩

fork·lift \'fȯrk-₁lift\ *n* : a machine for lifting heavy objects by means of steel fingers inserted under the load

for·lorn \fər-'lȯrn, fȯr-\ *adj* **1** : sad and lonely because of isolation or desertion **2** : WRETCHED **3** : nearly hopeless — **for·lorn·ly** *adv* — **for·lorn·ness** *n*

¹**form** \'fȯrm\ *n* **1** : SHAPE, STRUCTURE **2** : a body esp. of a person : FIGURE **3** : the essential nature of a thing **4** : established manner of doing or saying something **5** : FORMULA **6** : a document with blank spaces for insertion of information ⟨tax ~⟩ **7** : CEREMONY **8** : manner of performing according to recognized standards **9** : a long seat : BENCH **10** : a model of the human figure used for displaying clothes **11** : MOLD ⟨a ~ for concrete⟩ **12** : type or plates in a frame ready for printing **13** : MODE, KIND, VARIETY ⟨coal is a ~ of carbon⟩ **14** : orderly method of arrangement; *also* : a particular kind or instance of such arrangement ⟨the sonnet ~ in poetry⟩ **15** : the structural element, plan, or design of a work of art **16** : a bounded surface or volume **17** : a grade in a British school or in some American private schools **18** : RACING FORM **19** : known ability to perform; *also* : condition (as of an athlete) suitable for performing **20** : one of the ways in which a word is changed to show difference in use ⟨the plural ~ of a noun⟩ — **form·less** *adj*

²**form** *vb* **1** : to give form or shape to : FASHION, MAKE **2** : TRAIN, INSTRUCT **3** : CONSTITUTE, COMPOSE **4** : DEVELOP, ACQUIRE ⟨~ a habit⟩ **5** : to arrange in order ⟨~ a battle line⟩ **6** : to take form : ARISE ⟨clouds are ~*ing*⟩ **7** : to take a definite form, shape, or arrangement

¹**for·mal** \'fȯr-məl\ *adj* **1** : according with conventional forms and rules ⟨a ~ dinner party⟩ **2** : done in due or lawful form ⟨a ~ contract⟩ **3** : CEREMONIOUS, PRIM ⟨a ~ manner⟩ **4** : NOMINAL — **for·mal·ly** *adv*

²**formal** *n* : something (as a social event) formal in character

form·al·de·hyde \fȯr-'mal-də-₁hīd\ *n* : a colorless pungent gas used in water solution as a preservative and disinfectant

for·mal·ise *Brit var of* FORMALIZE

for·mal·ism \'fȯr-mə-₁li-zəm\ *n* : strict adherence to set forms

for·mal·i·ty \fȯr-'ma-lə-tē\ *n, pl* **-ties** **1** : compliance with formal or conventional rules **2** : the quality or state of being formal **3** : an established form that is required or conventional

for·mal·ize \'fȯr-mə-₁līz\ *vb* **-ized; -iz·ing** **1** : to give a certain or definite form to **2** : to make formal; *also* : to give formal status or approval to

¹**for·mat** \'fȯr-₁mat\ *n* **1** : the general composition or style of a publication **2** : the general plan or arrangement of something **3** : a method of organizing data ⟨various file ~s⟩

²**format** *vb* **for·mat·ted; for·mat·ting** : to arrange (as material to be printed) in a particular format — **for·mat·ter** *n*

for·ma·tion \fȯr-'mā-shən\ *n* **1** : an act of giving form to something ; DEVELOPMENT **2** : something that is formed **3** : STRUCTURE, SHAPE **4** : an arrangement of persons or things in a prescribed manner or for a certain purpose

for·ma·tive \'fȯr-mə-tiv\ *adj* **1** : giving or capable of giving form : CONSTRUCTIVE **2** : of, relating to, or characterized by important growth or formation ⟨a child's ~ years⟩

for·mer \'fȯr-mər\ *adj* **1** : PREVIOUS, EARLIER **2** : FOREGOING ⟨the ~ part of the chapter⟩ **3** : being first mentioned or in order of two or more things

for·mer·ly \-lē\ *adv* : in time past : PREVIOUSLY

form·fit·ting \'fȯrm-₁fi-tiŋ\ *adj* : conforming to the outline of the body ⟨a ~ sweater⟩

for·mi·da·ble \'fȯr-mə-də-bəl, fȯr-'mi-\ *adj* **1** : exciting fear, dread, or awe ⟨a ~ foe⟩ **2** : imposing serious difficulties ⟨a ~ barrier⟩ — **for·mi·da·bly** \-blē\ *adv*

form letter *n* **1** : a letter on a frequently recurring topic that can be sent to different people at different times **2** : a letter for mass circulation sent out in many printed copies

for·mu·la \'fȯr-myə-lə\ *n, pl* **-las** *or* **-lae** \-₁lē, -₁lī\ **1** : a set form of words for ceremonial use **2** : RECIPE, PRESCRIPTION **3** : a milk mixture or substitute for a baby **4** : a group of symbols or figures joined to express information concisely **5** : a customary or set form or method

for·mu·late \-₁lāt\ *vb* **-lat·ed; -lat·ing** **1** : to express in a formula **2** : DESIGN, DEVISE ⟨~ a policy⟩ **3** : to prepare according to a formula — **for·mu·la·tion** \₁fȯr-myə-'lā-shən\ *n*

for·ni·ca·tion \₁fȯr-nə-'kā-shən\ *n* : consensual sexual intercourse between two persons not married to each other — **for·ni·cate** \'fȯr-nə-₁kāt\ *vb* — **for·ni·ca·tor** \-₁kā-tər\ *n*

for·sake \fər-'sāk, fȯr-\ *vb* **for·sook** \-'sùk\; **for·sak·en** \-'sā-kən\; **for·sak·ing** [ME, fr. OE *forsacan,* fr. *sacan* to dispute] : to renounce or turn away from entirely ⟨*forsook* teaching for a film career⟩

for·sooth \fər-'süth\ *adv* : in truth : INDEED

for·swear \fȯr-'swer\ *vb* **-swore** \-'swȯr\; **-sworn** \-'swȯrn\; **-swear·ing** **1** : to swear falsely : commit perjury **2** : to renounce earnestly or under oath **3** : to deny under oath

for·syth·ia \fər-'si-thē-ə\ *n, pl* **-ias** *also* **-ia** : any of a genus of shrubs related to the olive and having yellow bell-shaped flowers appearing before the leaves in early spring

fort \'fȯrt\ *n* [ME *forte,* fr. AF *fort,* fr. *fort* strong, fr. L *fortis*] **1** : a fortified place **2** : a permanent army post

¹**forte** \'fȯrt, 'fȯr-₁tā\ *n* [F *fort,* fr. *fort,* adj., strong] : one's strong point

²**for·te** \'fȯr-₁tā\ *adv or adj* [It, fr. *forte* strong] : LOUD — used as a direction in music

forth \'fȯrth\ *adv* **1** : FORWARD, ONWARD ⟨from that day ~⟩ **2** : out into view ⟨plants putting ~ leaves⟩

forth·com·ing \fȯrth-'kə-miŋ\ *adj* **1** : coming or available soon ⟨the ~ holidays⟩ **2** : marked by openness and candor : OUTGOING

forth·right \'fȯrth-₁rīt\ *adj* : free from ambiguity or evasiveness : going straight to the point ⟨a ~ answer⟩ — **forth·right·ly** *adv* — **forth·right·ness** *n*

forth·with \₁fȯrth-'with\ *adv* : IMMEDIATELY

for·ti·fy \'fȯr-tə-₁fī\ *vb* **-fied; -fy·ing** **1** : to strengthen by military defenses **2** : to give physical strength or endurance to **3** : ENCOURAGE **4** : to strengthen or enrich with a material ⟨~ bread with vitamins⟩ — **for·ti·fi·ca·tion** \₁fȯr-tə-fə-'kā-shən\ *n*

for·tis·si·mo \fȯr-'ti-sə-₁mō\ *adv or adj* : very loud — used as a direction in music

for·ti·tude \'fȯr-tə-₁tüd, -₁tyüd\ *n* : strength of mind that enables one to meet danger or bear pain or adversity with courage ♦ **Synonyms** GRIT, BACKBONE, PLUCK, GUTS

fort·night \'fȯrt-₁nīt\ *n* [ME *fourtenight,* alter. of *fourtene night* fourteen nights] : two weeks — **fort·night·ly** \-lē\ *adj or adv*

for·tress \'fȯr-trəs\ n : FORT 1

for·tu·itous \fȯr-'tü-ə-təs, -'tyü-\ adj 1 : happening by chance ⟨a ~ discovery⟩ 2 : FORTUNATE — **for·tu·itous·ly** adv

for·tu·ity \-ə-tē\ n, pl **-ities** 1 : the quality or state of being fortuitous 2 : a chance event or occurrence

for·tu·nate \'fȯr-chə-nət\ adj 1 : bringing some good thing not foreseen 2 : LUCKY

for·tu·nate·ly \-lē\ adv 1 : in a fortunate manner 2 : it is fortunate that

for·tune \'fȯr-chən\ n 1 : prosperity attained partly through luck; also : CHANCE, LUCK 2 : what happens to a person : good or bad luck 3 : FATE, DESTINY 4 : RICHES, WEALTH

fortune hunter n : a person who seeks wealth esp. by marriage

for·tune-tell·er \-ˌte-lər\ n : a person who professes to foretell future events — **for·tune-tell·ing** n or adj

for·ty \'fȯr-tē\ n, pl **forties** : four times 10 — **for·ti·eth** \'fȯr-tē-əth\ adj or n — **forty** adj or pron

for·ty-five \ˌfȯr-tē-'fīv\ n 1 : a .45 caliber handgun — usu. written .45 2 : a phonograph record designed to be played at 45 revolutions per minute — usu. written 45

for·ty-nin·er \-'nī-nər\ n : a person in the rush to California for gold in 1849

forty winks n sing or pl : a short sleep

fo·rum \'fȯr-əm\ n, pl **forums** also **fo·ra** \-ə\ [L] 1 : the marketplace or central meeting place of an ancient Roman city 2 : a medium (as a publication or online service) of open discussion 3 : COURT 4 : a public assembly, lecture, or program involving audience or panel discussion

¹for·ward \'fȯr-wərd\ adj 1 : being near or at or belonging to the front 2 : EAGER, READY 3 : BRASH, BOLD 4 : notably advanced or developed : PRECOCIOUS 5 : moving, tending, or leading toward a position in front 6 : EXTREME, RADICAL 7 : of, relating to, or getting ready for the future — **for·ward·ness** n

²forward adv : to or toward what is ahead or in front

³forward vb 1 : to help onward : ADVANCE 2 : to send forward : TRANSMIT 3 : to send or ship onward

⁴forward n : a player who plays at the front of a team's offensive formation near the opponent's goal

for·ward·er \-wər-dər\ n : one that forwards; esp : an agent who forwards goods

for·wards \'fȯr-wərdz\ adv : FORWARD

forwent past of FORGO

¹fos·sil \'fä-səl\ adj [L fossilis obtained by digging, fr. fodere to dig] 1 : preserved from a past geologic age ⟨~ plants⟩ 2 : of or relating to fossil fuels

²fossil n 1 : a trace or impression or the remains of a plant or animal of a past geologic age preserved in the earth's crust 2 : a person whose ideas are out-of-date — **fos·sil·ize** \'fä-sə-ˌlīz\ vb

fossil fuel n : a fuel (as coal or oil) that is formed in the earth from plant or animal remains

¹fos·ter \'fȯs-tər\ adj [ME, fr. OE fōster-, fr. fōstor food, feeding] : affording, receiving, or sharing nourishment or parental care though not related by blood or legal ties ⟨~ parent⟩ ⟨~ child⟩

²foster vb 1 : to give parental care to : NURTURE 2 : to promote the growth or development of : ENCOURAGE

foster home n : a household in which an orphaned, neglected, or delinquent child is placed for care

fos·ter·ling \-tər-liŋ\ n : a foster child

Fou·cault pendulum \ˌfü-'kō-\ n : a device that consists of a heavy weight hung by a long wire and that swings in a constant direction which appears to change showing that the earth rotates

fought past and past part of FIGHT

¹foul \'faul\ adj 1 : offensive to the senses : LOATHSOME; also : clogged with dirt 2 : ODIOUS, DETESTABLE ⟨a ~ crime⟩ 3 : OBSCENE, ABUSIVE ⟨~ language⟩ 4 : DISAGREEABLE, STORMY ⟨~ weather⟩ 5 : TREACHEROUS, DISHONORABLE, UNFAIR ⟨by fair means or ~⟩ 6 : marking the bounds of a playing field ⟨~ lines⟩; also : being outside the foul line ⟨~ ball⟩ ⟨~ territory⟩ 7 : containing marked-up corrections 8 : ENTANGLED — **foul·ly** adv — **foul·ness** n

²foul n 1 : an entanglement or collision in fishing or sailing 2 : an infraction of the rules in a game or sport; also : a baseball hit outside the foul line

³foul vb 1 : to make or become foul or filthy 2 : to entangle or become entangled 3 : OBSTRUCT, BLOCK 4 : to collide with 5 : to make or hit a foul

⁴foul adv : in a foul manner

fou·lard \fu-'lärd\ n : a lightweight silk of plain or twill weave usu. decorated with a printed pattern

foul-mouthed \'faul-(ˌ)l-'mauthd, -'mautht\ adj : given to the use of obscene, profane, or abusive language

foul of prep : AFOUL OF

foul play n : VIOLENCE; esp : MURDER

foul-up \'faul-(ˌ)l-ˌəp\ n 1 : a state of being fouled up 2 : a mechanical difficulty

foul up vb 1 : to spoil by mistakes or poor judgment 2 : to cause a foul-up : BUNGLE

¹found \'faund\ past and past part of FIND

²found vb [ME, fr. AF funder, fonder, fr. L fundare, fr. fundus bottom] 1 : to take the first steps in building 2 : to set or ground on something solid : BASE 3 : to establish (as an institution) often with provision for future maintenance — **found·er** n

foun·da·tion \faun-'dā-shən\ n 1 : the act of founding 2 : a basis upon which something stands or is supported ⟨suspicions without ~⟩ 3 : funds given for the permanent support of an institution : ENDOWMENT; also : an institution so endowed 4 : supporting structure : BASE 5 : CORSET — **foun·da·tion·al** \-shə-nəl\ adj

foun·der \'faun-dər\ vb 1 : to make or become lame ⟨the horse ~ed⟩ 2 : COLLAPSE 3 : SINK ⟨a ~ing ship⟩ 4 : FAIL

found·ling \'faund-liŋ\ n : an infant found after its unknown parents have abandoned it

found·ry \'faun-drē\ n, pl **foundries** : a building or works where metal is cast

fount \'faunt\ n : SOURCE, FOUNTAIN

foun·tain \'faun-tᵊn\ n 1 : a spring of water 2 : SOURCE 3 : an artificial jet of water 4 : a container for liquid that can be drawn off as needed

foun·tain·head \-ˌhed\ n : SOURCE

fountain pen n : a pen with a reservoir that feeds the writing point with ink

four \'fȯr\ n 1 : one more than three 2 : the 4th in a set or series 3 : something having four units — **four** adj or pron

4x4 also **four-by-four** \'fȯr-bī-ˌfȯr\ n : a four-wheel automobile with four-wheel drive

four-flush \-ˌfləsh\ vb : to make a false claim : BLUFF — **four-flush·er** n

four·fold \-ˌfōld, -'fōld\ adj 1 : being four times as great or as many 2 : having four units or members — **four·fold** \-'fōld\ adv

4-H \'fȯr-'āch\ adj [fr. the fourfold aim of improving the head, heart, hands, and health] : of or relating to a program set up by the U.S. Department of Agriculture to help young people become productive citizens — **4-H'er** n

Four Hundred or **400** n : the exclusive social set of a community — used with the

four-in-hand \'fȯr-ən-ˌhand\ n 1 : a team of four horses driven by one person; also : a vehicle drawn by such a team 2 : a necktie tied in a slipknot with long ends overlapping vertically in front

four-o'clock \'fȯr-ə-ˌkläk\ n : a garden plant with fragrant yellow, red, or white flowers without petals that open late in the afternoon

four-post·er \ˌfȯr-'pō-stər\ n : a bed with tall corner posts orig. designed to support curtains or a canopy

four·score \'fȯr-'skȯr\ adj : being four times twenty : EIGHTY

four·some \'fȯr-səm\ n 1 : a group of four persons or things 2 : a golf match between two pairs of partners

four·square \-'skwer\ adj 1 : SQUARE 2 : marked by boldness and conviction : FORTHRIGHT — **foursquare** adv

four·teen \fȯr-'tēn\ n : one more than 13 — **fourteen** adj or pron — **four·teenth** \-'tēnth\ adj or n

fourth \'fȯrth\ n 1 : one that is number four in a countable series 2 : one of four equal parts of something — **fourth** adj or adv

fourth estate n, often cap F&E : the public press

fourth wall n : an imaginary wall that keeps performers from recognizing or directly addressing their audience

4WD *abbr* four-wheel drive

four–wheel \'fȯr-ˌhwēl\ *or* **four–wheeled** \-ˌhwēld\ *adj* : acting on or by means of four wheels of a motor vehicle ⟨~ disc brakes⟩

four–wheel drive *n* : an automotive drive mechanism that acts on all four wheels of the vehicle; *also* : a vehicle with such a drive

¹**fowl** \'fau̇(-ə)l\ *n, pl* **fowl** *or* **fowls** **1** : BIRD **2** : a cock or hen of the domestic chicken; *also* : the flesh of these used as food

²**fowl** *vb* : to hunt wildfowl

¹**fox** \'fäks\ *n, pl* **fox·es** *also* **fox** **1** : any of various flesh-eating mammals related to the wolves but smaller and with shorter legs and a more pointed muzzle; *also* : the fur of a fox **2** : a clever crafty person **3** *cap* : a member of an American Indian people formerly living in what is now Wisconsin

²**fox** *vb* : TRICK, OUTWIT

fox·glove \'fäks-ˌgləv\ *n* : a common plant related to the snapdragons that is grown for its showy spikes of dotted white or purple tubular flowers and as a source of digitalis

fox·hole \-ˌhōl\ *n* : a pit dug for protection against enemy fire

fox·hound \-ˌhau̇nd\ *n* : any of various large swift powerful hounds used in hunting foxes

fox·ing \'fäk-siŋ\ *n* : brownish spots on old paper

fox terrier *n* : a small lively terrier that occurs in varieties with smooth dense coats or with harsh wiry coats

fox terrier

fox–trot \'fäks-ˌträt\ *n* **1** : a short broken slow trotting gait **2** : a ballroom dance in duple time

foxy \'fäk-sē\ *adj* **fox·i·er; -est** **1** : resembling or suggestive of a fox **2** : WILY **3** : physically attractive

foy·er \'fȯi(-ə)r, 'fȯi-ˌyā\ *n* [F, lit., fireplace, fr. OF *foier*, fr. VL **focarium*, fr. L *focus* hearth] : LOBBY; *also* : an entrance hallway

fpm *abbr* feet per minute

FPO *abbr* fleet post office

fps *abbr* feet per second

fr *abbr* **1** father **2** franc **3** friar **4** from

¹**Fr** *abbr* **1** France; French **2** Friday

²**Fr** *symbol* francium

fra·cas \'frā-kəs, 'fra-\ *n, pl* **fra·cas·es** \-kə-səz\ [F, din, row, fr. It *fracasso*, fr. *fracassare* to shatter] : BRAWL

frack·ing \'fra-kiŋ\ *n* [by shortening & alter. fr. (*hydraulic*) *fracturing*] : the injection of fluid into shale beds so as to free up petroleum — **frack** \'frak\ *vb*

frac·tal \'frak-tᵊl\ *n* : an irregular curve or shape that repeats itself at any scale on which it is examined — **fractal** *adj*

frac·tion \'frak-shən\ *n* **1** : a numerical representation (as ½, ¼, or 3.323) indicating the quotient of two numbers **2** : FRAGMENT **3** : PORTION ⟨a small ~ of voters⟩ — **frac·tion·al** \-shə-nəl\ *adj* — **frac·tion·al·ly** *adv*

frac·tious \'frak-shəs\ *adj* **1** : tending to be troublesome : hard to handle or control **2** : QUARRELSOME, IRRITABLE

frac·ture \'frak-chər\ *n* **1** : a breaking of something and esp. a bone **2** : CRACK, CLEFT — **fracture** *vb*

frag·ile \'fra-jəl, -ˌjī(-ə)l\ *adj* : easily broken : DELICATE — **fra·gil·i·ty** \frə-'ji-lə-tē\ *n*

¹**frag·ment** \'frag-mənt\ *n* : a part broken off, detached, or incomplete

²**frag·ment** \-ˌment\ *vb* : to break into fragments — **frag·men·ta·tion** \ˌfrag-mən-'tā-shən, -ˌmən-\ *n*

frag·men·tary \'frag-mən-ˌter-ē\ *adj* : made up of fragments : INCOMPLETE ⟨a ~ account⟩

fra·grant \'frā-grənt\ *adj* : sweet or agreeable in smell — **fra·grance** \-grəns\ *n* — **fra·grant·ly** *adv*

frail \'frāl\ *adj* [ME, fr. AF *fraile*, fr. L *fragilis* fragile, fr. *frangere* to break] **1** : morally or physically weak **2** : FRAGILE, DELICATE

frail·ty \'frāl-tē\ *n, pl* **frailties** **1** : the quality or state of being frail **2** : a fault due to weakness

¹**frame** \'frām\ *vb* **framed; fram·ing** **1** : PLAN, CONTRIVE **2** : SHAPE, CONSTRUCT **3** : FORMULATE **4** : DRAW UP ⟨~ a constitution⟩ **5** : to make appear guilty **6** : to fit or adjust for a purpose : ARRANGE **7** : to provide with or enclose in a frame — **fram·er** *n*

²**frame** *n* **1** : something made of parts fitted and joined together **2** : the physical makeup of the body **3** : an arrangement of structural parts that gives form or support **4** : a supporting or enclosing border or open case (as for a window or picture) **5** : one picture of a series (as on a length of film) **6** : FRAME-UP

³**frame** *adj* : having a wood frame ⟨~ houses⟩

frame of mind *n* : mental attitude or outlook : MOOD

frame–up \'frā-ˌməp\ *n* **1** : an act or series of actions in which someone is framed **2** : an action that is planned, contrived, or formulated

frame·work \'frām-ˌwərk\ *n* : a basic supporting part or structure

franc \'fraŋk\ *n* **1** : any of various former basic monetary units (as of Belgium, France, and Luxembourg) **2** — see MONEY table

fran·chise \'fran-ˌchīz\ *n* [ME, fr. AF, fr. *franchir* to free, fr. *franc* free] **1** : a right or license granted to an individual or group ⟨a ~ to operate a ferry⟩ **2** : a constitutional or statutory right or privilege; *esp* : the right to vote **3** : the right of membership in a professional sports league; *also* : a team having such membership

fran·chi·see \ˌfran-ˌchī-'zē, -chə-\ *n* : one granted a franchise

fran·chis·er \'fran-ˌchī-zər\ *n* **1** : FRANCHISEE **2** : FRANCHISOR

fran·chi·sor \ˌfran-ˌchī-'zȯr, -chə-\ *n* : one that grants a franchise

fran·ci·um \'fran-sē-əm\ *n* : a radioactive metallic chemical element

Fran·co–Amer·i·can \ˌfraŋ-kō-ə-'mer-ə-kən\ *n* : an American of French or esp. French-Canadian descent — **Franco–American** *adj*

fran·gi·ble \'fran-jə-bəl\ *adj* : BREAKABLE — **fran·gi·bil·i·ty** \ˌfran-jə-'bi-lə-tē\ *n*

¹**frank** \'fraŋk\ *adj* : marked by free, forthright, and sincere expression — **frank·ness** *n*

²**frank** *vb* : to mark (a piece of mail) with an official sign so that it can be mailed free; *also* : to mail free

³**frank** *n* **1** : the signature or mark on a piece of mail indicating free or paid postage **2** : the privilege of sending mail free

⁴**frank** *n* : FRANKFURTER

Fran·ken·stein \'fraŋ-kən-ˌstīn\ *n* **1** : a monstrous creation that usu. ruins its originator **2** : a monster in the shape of a man

frank·furt·er \'fraŋk-fər-tər, -ˌfər-\ *or* **frank·furt** \-fərt\ *n* : a seasoned sausage (as of beef or beef and pork)

frank·in·cense \'fraŋ-kən-ˌsens\ *n* : a fragrant resin burned as incense

frank·ly \'fraŋ-klē\ *adv* **1** : in a frank manner **2** : in truth : INDEED ⟨~, I don't know⟩

fran·tic \'fran-tik\ *adj* : marked by uncontrolled emotion or disordered anxious activity — **fran·ti·cal·ly** \-ti-k(ə-)lē\ *adv*

frap·pé \fra-'pā\ *or* **frappe** \same *or* 'frap\ *n* [F *frappé*, fr. pp. of *frapper* to strike, chill] **1** : an iced or frozen drink **2** : a thick milk shake — **frap·pé** \fra-'pā\ *adj*

fra·ter·nal \frə-'tər-nᵊl\ *adj* **1** : of, relating to, or involving brothers **2** : of, relating to, or being a fraternity or society **3** : derived from two ova ⟨~ twins⟩ **4** : FRIENDLY, BROTHERLY — **fra·ter·nal·ly** *adv*

fra·ter·ni·ty \frə-'tər-nə-tē\ *n, pl* **-ties** **1** : a social, honorary, or professional group; *esp* : a men's student organization **2** : BROTHERLINESS, BROTHERHOOD **3** : persons of the same class, profession, or tastes

frat·er·nize \'fra-tər-ˌnīz\ *vb* **-nized; -niz·ing 1** : to mingle as friends **2** : to associate on close terms with members of a hostile group — **frat·er·ni·za·tion** \ˌfra-tər-nə-'zā-shən\ *n*

frat·ri·cide \'fra-trə-ˌsīd\ *n* **1** : one that kills a sibling or countryman **2** : the act of a fratricide — **frat·ri·cid·al** \ˌfra-trə-'sī-dᵊl\ *adj*

fraud \'fród\ *n* **1** : DECEIT, TRICKERY **2** : TRICK **3** : IMPOSTOR, CHEAT

fraud·ster \'fród-stər\ *n, chiefly Brit* : a person who engages in fraud

fraud·u·lent \'fró-jə-lənt\ *adj* : characterized by, based on, or done by fraud : DECEITFUL — **fraud·u·lence** \-ləns\ *n* — **fraud·u·lent·ly** *adv*

fraught \'frót\ *adj* : full of or accompanied by something specified ⟨~ with danger⟩

¹fray \'frā\ *n* : FIGHT, STRUGGLE; *also* : QUARREL, DISPUTE

²fray *vb* **1** : to wear (as an edge of cloth) by rubbing **2** : to separate the threads at the edge of **3** : STRAIN, IRRITATE ⟨~ed nerves⟩

fraz·zle \'fra-zəl\ *vb* **fraz·zled; fraz·zling 1** : FRAY **2** : to put in a state of extreme physical or nervous fatigue — **frazzle** *n*

¹freak \'frēk\ *n* **1** : WHIM, CAPRICE **2** : a strange, abnormal, or unusual person or thing **3** *slang* : a person who uses an illicit drug **4** : an ardent enthusiast — **freak·ish** *adj* — **freaky** \'frē-kē\ *adj*

²freak *vb* **1** : to experience the effects (as hallucinations) of taking illicit drugs — often used with *out* **2** : to distress or become distressed — often used with *out* — **freak-out** \'frē-ˌkaüt\ *n*

freck·le \'fre-kəl\ *n* : a small brownish spot on the skin — **freckle** *vb*

¹free \'frē\ *adj* **fre·er; fre·est 1** : having liberty **2** : enjoying political or personal independence; *also* : not subject to or allowing slavery **3** : made or done voluntarily : SPONTANEOUS **4** : relieved from or lacking something unpleasant **5** : not subject to a duty, tax, or charge **6** : not obstructed : CLEAR **7** : not being used or occupied ⟨waved with my ~ hand⟩ **8** : not fastened ⟨the ~ end of the rope⟩ **9** : LAVISH **10** : OPEN, FRANK ⟨a ~ exchange of ideas⟩ **11** : given without charge **12** : not literal or exact ⟨~ translation⟩ **13** : not restricted by conventional forms ⟨~ skating⟩ — **free·ly** *adv*

²free *vb* **freed; free·ing 1** : to set free **2** : RELIEVE, RID **3** : DISENTANGLE, CLEAR ♦ **Synonyms** RELEASE, LIBERATE, DISCHARGE, EMANCIPATE, LOOSE

³free *adv* **1** : FREELY **2** : without charge

free·base \'frē-ˌbās\ *n* : purified cocaine smoked as crack or heated to produce vapors for inhalation — **freebase** *vb*

free·bie *or* **free·bee** \'frē-bē\ *n* : something given without charge

free·board \'frē-ˌbórd\ *n* : the vertical distance between the waterline and the upper edge of the side of a boat

free·boo·ter \-ˌbü-tər\ *n* [D *vrijbuiter*, fr. *vrijbuit* plunder, fr. *vrij* free + *buit* booty] : PLUNDERER, PIRATE

free·born \-'bórn\ *adj* **1** : not born in vassalage or slavery **2** : of, relating to, or befitting one that is freeborn

freed·man \'frēd-mən, -ˌman\ *n* : a person freed from slavery

free·dom \'frē-dəm\ *n* **1** : the quality or state of being free : INDEPENDENCE **2** : EXEMPTION, RELEASE **3** : EASE, FACILITY ⟨spoke the language with ~⟩ **4** : FRANKNESS **5** : unrestricted use **6** : a political right; *also* : FRANCHISE, PRIVILEGE

freedom fighter *n* : a person who takes part in a resistance movement against an oppressive political or social establishment

free enterprise *n* : freedom of private business to operate with little regulation by the government

free-for-all \'frē-fə-ˌ(r)ól\ *n* : a competition or fight open to all comers and usu. with no rules : BRAWL — **free-for-all** *adj*

free·hand \'frē-ˌhand\ *adj* : done without mechanical aids or devices ⟨~ drawing⟩

free·hold \'frē-ˌhōld\ *n* : ownership of an estate for life usu. with the right to bequeath it to one's heirs; *also* : an estate thus owned — **free·hold·er** *n*

free·lance \-ˌlans\ *n* : one who pursues a profession (as writing) without a long-term commitment to any one employer — **free·lance** *adj or vb*

free–living \'frē-'li-vin\ *adj* **1** : unrestricted in pursuing personal pleasures **2** : being neither parasitic nor symbiotic ⟨~ organisms⟩

free·load \'frē-ˌlōd\ *vb* : to impose upon another's hospitality — **free·load·er** *n*

free love *n* **1** : the practice of living openly with one of the opposite sex without marriage **2** : sexual relations without any commitments by either partner

free·man \'frē-mən, -ˌman\ *n* **1** : one who has civil or political liberty **2** : one having the full rights of a citizen

Free·ma·son \-ˌmā-sᵊn\ *n* : a member of a secret fraternal society called Free and Accepted Masons — **Free·ma·son·ry** \-rē\ *n*

free radical *n* : an esp. reactive atom or group of atoms with one or more unpaired electrons; *esp* : one that can cause bodily damage (as by altering the chemical structure of cells)

free–range \'frē-ˌrānj\ *adj* : allowed to range and forage with relative freedom ⟨~ chickens⟩; *also* : produced by free-range animals ⟨~ eggs⟩

free speech *n* : speech that is protected by the First Amendment to the U.S. Constitution

free spirit *n* : NONCONFORMIST

free·stand·ing \'frē-'stan-din\ *adj* : standing alone or on its own foundation free of support

free·stone \'frē-ˌstōn\ *n* **1** : a stone that may be cut freely without splitting **2** : a fruit stone to which the flesh does not cling; *also* : a fruit (as a peach or cherry) having such a stone

free·think·er \-'thin-kər\ *n* : one who forms opinions on the basis of reason independently of authority; *esp* : one who doubts or denies religious dogma — **free·think·ing** *n or adj*

free trade *n* : trade between nations without restrictions (as high taxes on imports)

free verse *n* : verse whose meter is irregular or whose rhythm is not metrical

free·ware \'frē-ˌwer\ *n* : software that is free or that has a small usu. optional cost

free·way \'frē-ˌwā\ *n* : an expressway without tolls

free·wheel \-'hwēl\ *vb* : to move, live, or play freely or irresponsibly

free·will \'frē-ˌwil\ *adj* : VOLUNTARY

free will *n* : voluntary choice or decision

¹freeze \'frēz\ *vb* **froze** \'frōz\; **fro·zen** \'frō-zᵊn\; **freez·ing 1** : to harden or cause to harden into a solid (as ice) by loss of heat **2** : to withstand freezing **3** : to chill or become chilled with cold **4** : to damage by frost **5** : to adhere solidly by or as if by freezing **6** : to become fixed, motionless, or incapable of speech **7** : to cause to grip tightly **8** : to become clogged with ice **9** : to fix at a certain stage or level ⟨~ wages⟩

²freeze *n* **1** : an act or instance of freezing **2** : the state of being frozen **3** : a state of weather marked by low temperature

freeze–dry \'frēz-'drī\ *vb* : to dry in a frozen state under vacuum esp. for preservation — **freeze–dried** *adj*

freez·er \'frē-zər\ *n* : a compartment, device, or room for freezing food or keeping it frozen

¹freight \'frāt\ *n* **1** : payment for carrying goods **2** : CARGO **3** : BURDEN **4** : the carrying of goods by a common carrier **5** : a train that carries freight

²freight *vb* **1** : to load with goods for transportation **2** : BURDEN, CHARGE **3** : to ship or transport by freight

freight·er \'frā-tər\ *n* : a ship or airplane used chiefly to carry freight

French \'french\ *n* **1** : the language of France **2** **French** *pl* : the people of France **3** : strong language ⟨pardon my ~⟩ — **French** *adj* — **French·man** \-mən\ *n* — **French·wom·an** \-ˌwu̇-mən\ *n*

French door *n* : a door with small panes of glass extending the full length

French dressing *n* **1** : a thin salad dressing usu. made of vinegar and oil with spices **2** : a creamy salad dressing flavored with tomatoes

french fry *n, often cap 1st F* : a strip of potato fried in deep fat until brown — **french fry** *vb, often cap 1st F*

French horn *n* : a curved brass instrument with a funnel-shaped mouthpiece and a flaring bell

French press *n* : a coffeepot in which ground beans are infused and then pressed by a plunger

French toast *n* : bread dipped in a mixture of eggs and milk and fried at a low heat

French twist *n* : a woman's hairstyle in which the hair is coiled at the rear and secured in place

fren·e·my \'fre-nə-mē\ *n, pl* **-mies** : one who pretends to be a friend but is actually an enemy

fre·net·ic \fri-'ne-tik\ *adj* : FRANTIC — **fre·net·i·cal·ly** \-ti-k(ə-)lē\ *adv*

fren·zy \'fren-zē\ *n, pl* **frenzies** **1** : temporary madness or a violently agitated state **2** : intense often disordered activity — **fren·zied** \-zēd\ *adj*

freq *abbr* frequency; frequent; frequently

fre·quen·cy \'frē-kwən-sē\ *n, pl* **-cies** **1** : the fact or condition of occurring frequently **2** : rate of occurrence **3** : the number of cycles per second of an alternating current **4** : the number of waves (as of sound or electromagnetic energy) that pass a fixed point each second

frequency modulation *n* : variation of the frequency of a carrier wave according to another signal; *also* : FM

¹fre·quent \frē-'kwent, 'frē-kwənt\ *vb* : to associate with, be in, or resort to habitually — **fre·quent·er** *n*

²fre·quent \'frē-kwənt\ *adj* **1** : happening often or at short intervals ⟨making ∼ stops⟩ **2** : HABITUAL ⟨a ∼ visitor⟩ — **fre·quent·ly** *adv*

fre·quent–fli·er \'frē-kwənt-'flī-ər\ *adj* : of, relating to, or being an airline program offering awards for specified numbers of air miles traveled

fres·co \'fres-kō\ *n, pl* **frescoes** [It, fr. *fresco* fresh] : the art of painting on fresh plaster; *also* : a painting done by this method

fresh \'fresh\ *adj* **1** : VIGOROUS, REFRESHED **2** : not stale, sour, or decayed ⟨∼ bread⟩ **3** : not faded **4** : not worn or rumpled **5** : not altered by processing (as freezing or canning) **6** : not containing salt **7** : free from taint : PURE ⟨∼ air⟩ **8** : fairly strong : BRISK ⟨∼ breeze⟩ **9** : experienced, made, or received newly or anew **10** : ADDITIONAL, ANOTHER ⟨made a ∼ start⟩ **11** : ORIGINAL, VIVID ⟨a ∼ portrayal⟩ **12** : INEXPERIENCED **13** : newly come or arrived ⟨∼ from school⟩ **14** : IMPUDENT — **fresh·ly** *adv* — **fresh·ness** *n*

fresh·en \'fre-shən\ *vb* : to make, grow, or become fresh

fresh·et \'fre-shət\ *n* : an overflowing of a stream (as by heavy rains)

fresh·man \'fresh-mən\ *n* **1** : a 1st-year student **2** : BEGINNER, NEWCOMER

fresh·wa·ter \-,wȯ-tər, -,wä-\ *n* : water that is not salty — **freshwater** *adj*

¹fret \'fret\ *vb* **fret·ted; fret·ting** [ME, to devour, fret, fr. OE *fretan* to devour] **1** : WEAR, CORRODE; *also* : FRAY **2** : RUB, CHAFE **3** : to make by wearing away **4** : to become irritated : WORRY, VEX ⟨*fretted* over his taxes⟩ **5** : GRATE; *also* : AGITATE

²fret *n* : an irritated or worried state ⟨in a ∼ about the interview⟩

³fret *n* : ornamental work esp. of straight lines in symmetrical patterns

⁴fret *n* : one of a series of ridges across the fingerboard of a stringed musical instrument — **fret·ted** *adj*

fret·ful \'fret-fəl\ *adj* : IRRITABLE — **fret·ful·ly** *adv* — **fret·ful·ness** *n*

fret·saw \-,sȯ\ *n* : a narrow-bladed handsaw used for cutting curved outlines

fret·work \-,wərk\ *n* **1** : decoration consisting of frets **2** : ornamental openwork or work in relief

Fri *abbr* Friday

fri·a·ble \'frī-ə-bəl\ *adj* : easily crumbled or pulverized ⟨∼ soil⟩

fri·ar \'frī(-ə)r\ *n* [ME *frere, fryer,* fr. AF *frere, friere,* lit., brother, fr. L *frater*] : a member of a religious order that orig. lived by alms

fri·ary \'frī(-ə)r-ē\ *n, pl* **-ar·ies** : a monastery of friars

¹fric·as·see \'fri-kə-,sē, ,fri-kə-'sē\ *n* : a dish made of meat (as chicken) cut into pieces, stewed in stock, and served in sauce

²fricassee *vb* **-seed; -see·ing** : to cook as a fricassee

fric·tion \'frik-shən\ *n* **1** : the rubbing of one body against another **2** : the force that resists motion between bodies in contact **3** : clash in opinions between persons or groups : DISAGREEMENT — **fric·tion·al** *adj*

friction tape *n* : a usu. cloth adhesive tape impregnated with insulating material and used esp. to protect and insulate electrical conductors

Fri·day \'frī-dē, -(,)dā\ *n* : the sixth day of the week

fridge \'frij\ *n* : REFRIGERATOR

fried·cake \'frīd-,kāk\ *n* : DOUGHNUT, CRULLER

fried rice *n* : a dish of boiled or steamed rice that is stir–fried with soy sauce and typically includes egg, meat, and vegetables

¹friend \'frend\ *n* **1** : one attached to another by respect or affection **2** : ACQUAINTANCE **3** : one who is not hostile **4** : one who supports or favors something ⟨a ∼ of art⟩ **5** *cap* : a member of the Society of Friends : QUAKER — **friend·less** *adj* — **friend·li·ness** \-lē-nəs\ *n* — **friend·ly** *adj* — **friend·ship** \-,ship\ *n*

²friend *vb* **1** : BEFRIEND **2** : to include (someone) in a list of designated friends on a person's social networking site

frieze \'frēz\ *n* : an ornamental often sculptured band extending around something (as a building or room)

frig·ate \'fri-gət\ *n* **1** : a square-rigged warship **2** : a warship smaller than a destroyer

fright \'frīt\ *n* **1** : sudden terror : ALARM **2** : something that is ugly or shocking

fright·en \'frī-tᵊn\ *vb* **1** : to make afraid **2** : to drive away or out by frightening **3** : to become frightened — **fright·en·ing·ly** *adv*

fright·ful \'frīt-fəl\ *adj* **1** : TERRIFYING **2** : STARTLING **3** : EXTREME ⟨∼ thirst⟩ — **fright·ful·ly** *adv* — **fright·ful·ness** *n*

frig·id \'fri-jəd\ *adj* **1** : intensely cold **2** : lacking warmth or ardor : INDIFFERENT **3** : abnormally averse to or unable to achieve orgasm during sexual intercourse — used esp. of women — **fri·gid·i·ty** \fri-'ji-də-tē\ *n*

frigid zone *n* : the area or region between the arctic circle and the north pole or between the antarctic circle and the south pole

frill \'fril\ *n* **1** : a gathered, pleated, or ruffled edging **2** : something unessential — **frilly** *adj*

fringe \'frinj\ *n* [ME *frenge,* fr. AF, fr. VL **frimbia,* alter. of L *fimbriae* (pl.)] **1** : an ornamental border consisting of short threads or strips hanging from an edge or band **2** : something that resembles a fringe : EDGE ⟨operated on the ∼s of the law⟩ **3** : something that is additional or secondary to an activity, process, or subject — **fringe** *vb*

fringe benefit *n* **1** : an employment benefit paid for by an employer without affecting basic wage rates **2** : any additional benefit

frip·pery \'fri-pə-rē\ *n, pl* **-per·ies** [MF *friperie*] **1** : FINERY **2** : pretentious display

frisk \'frisk\ *vb* **1** : to leap, skip, or dance in a lively or playful way : GAMBOL **2** : to search (a person) esp. for concealed weapons by running the hand rapidly over the clothing

frisky \'fris-kē\ *adj* **frisk·i·er; -est** : PLAYFUL — **frisk·i·ly** \-kə-lē\ *adv* — **frisk·i·ness** \-kē-nəs\ *n*

¹frit·ter \'fri-tər\ *n* : a small lump of fried batter often containing fruit or meat

²fritter *vb* **1** : to reduce or waste piecemeal **2** : to break into small fragments

fritz \'frits\ *n* : a state of disorder or disrepair — used in the phrase *on the fritz*

friv·o·lous \'fri-və-ləs\ *adj* **1** : of little importance : TRIVIAL **2** : lacking in seriousness — **fri·vol·i·ty** \fri-'vä-lə-tē\ *n* — **friv·o·lous·ly** *adv*

frizz \'friz\ *vb* : to form into small tight curls — **frizz** *n* — **frizzy** *adj*

friz·zies \'fri-zēz\ *n pl* : hair which has become difficult to manage (as due to humidity)

¹friz·zle \'fri-zəl\ *vb* **friz·zled; friz·zling** : FRIZZ, CURL — **frizzle** *n*

²frizzle *vb* **friz·zled; friz·zling** **1** : to fry until crisp and curled **2** : to cook with a sizzling noise

fro \'frō\ *adv* : BACK, AWAY — used in the phrase *to and fro*

frock \'fräk\ *n* **1** : an outer garment worn by monks and friars **2** : an outer garment worn esp. by men **3** : a woman's or girl's dress

frock coat *n* : a man's knee-length usu. double-breasted coat

frog \'frȯg, 'fräg\ *n* **1** : any of various largely aquatic smooth-skinned tailless leaping amphibians **2** : an ornamental braiding for fastening the front of a garment by a loop through which a button passes **3** : a condition in the throat causing hoarseness **4** : a small holder (as of metal, glass, or plastic) with perforations or spikes that is placed in a bowl or vase to keep cut flowers in position

frog 2

frog·man \'frȯg-ˌman, 'fräg-, -mən\ *n* : a swimmer equipped to work underwater for long periods of time
¹frol·ic \'frä-lik\ *vb* **frol·icked; frol·ick·ing** **1** : to make merry **2** : to play about happily : ROMP
²frolic *n* **1** : a playful or mischievous action **2** : FUN, MERRIMENT — **frol·ic·some** \-səm\ *adj*
from \'frəm, 'främ\ *prep* **1** — used to show a starting point ⟨a letter ~ home⟩ **2** — used to show removal or separation ⟨subtract 3 ~ 9⟩ **3** — used to show a material, source, or cause ⟨suffering ~ a cold⟩
frond \'fränd\ *n* : a usu. large divided leaf esp. of a fern or palm tree
¹front \'frənt\ *n* **1** : FOREHEAD; *also* : the whole face **2** : external and often feigned appearance **3** : a region of active fighting; *also* : a sphere of activity **4** : a political coalition **5** : the side of a building containing the main entrance **6** : the forward part or surface **7** : FRONTAGE **8** : a boundary between two dissimilar air masses **9** : a position directly before or ahead of something else **10** : a person, group, or thing used to mask the identity of the actual controlling agent
²front *vb* **1** : to have the principal side adjacent to something **2** : to serve as a front **3** : CONFRONT
front·age \'frən-tij\ *n* **1** : a piece of land lying adjacent (as to a street or the ocean) **2** : the length of a frontage **3** : the front side of a building
front·al \'frən-t°l\ *adj* **1** : of, relating to, or next to the forehead **2** : of, relating to, or directed at the front ⟨a ~ attack⟩ — **fron·tal·ly** *adv*
fron·tier \ˌfrən-'tir\ *n* **1** : a border between two countries **2** : a region that forms the margin of settled territory **3** : the outer limits of knowledge or achievement ⟨the ~s of science⟩ — **fron·tiers·man** \-'tirz-mən\ *n*
fron·tis·piece \'frən-tə-ˌspēs\ *n* : an illustration preceding and usu. facing the title page of a book
front man *n* : a person serving as a front or figurehead
front·ward \'frənt-wərd\ *or* **front·wards** \-wərdz\ *adv or adj* : toward the front
¹frost \'frȯst\ *n* **1** : freezing temperature **2** : a covering of tiny ice crystals on a cold surface — **frosty** *adj*
²frost *vb* **1** : to cover with frost **2** : to put icing on (as a cake) **3** : to produce a slightly roughened surface on (as glass) **4** : to injure or kill by frost
¹frost·bite \'frȯst-ˌbīt\ *vb* **-bit** \-ˌbit\; **-bit·ten** \-ˌbi-t°n\; **-bit·ing** : to injure by frost or frostbite
²frostbite *n* : the freezing or the local effect of a partial freezing of some part of the body
frost heave *n* : an upthrust of pavement caused by freezing of moist soil
frost·ing \'frȯs-tiŋ\ *n* **1** : ICING **2** : dull finish on metal or glass
froth \'frȯth\ *n, pl* **froths** \'frȯths, 'frȯthz\ [ME, fr. ON *frotha*] **1** : bubbles formed in or on a liquid **2** : something light or worthless — **frothy** *adj*
frou·frou \'frü-ˌfrü\ *n* [F] **1** : a rustling esp. of a woman's skirts **2** : showy or frilly ornamentation
fro·ward \'frō-wərd\ *adj* : DISOBEDIENT, WILLFUL
frown \'fraün\ *vb* **1** : to wrinkle the forehead (as in displeasure or thought) **2** : to look with disapproval **3** : to express with a frown — **frown** *n*
frow·sy *or* **frow·zy** \'fraü-zē\ *adj* **frow·si·er** *or* **frow·zi·er**; **-est** : having a slovenly or uncared-for appearance
froze *past of* FREEZE
fro·zen \'frō-z°n\ *adj* **1** : treated, affected, or crusted over by freezing **2** : subject to long and severe cold **3** : incapable of being changed, moved, or undone : FIXED ⟨~

wages⟩ **4** : not available for present use ⟨~ capital⟩ **5** : expressing or characterized by cold unfriendliness
FRS *abbr* Federal Reserve System
frt *abbr* freight
fruc·ti·fy \'frək-tə-ˌfī, 'frük-\ *vb* **-fied; -fy·ing** **1** : to bear fruit **2** : to make fruitful or productive
fruc·tose \'frək-ˌtōs, 'frük-\ *n* : a very sweet soluble sugar that occurs esp. in fruit juices and honey
fru·gal \'frü-gəl\ *adj* : ECONOMICAL, THRIFTY — **fru·gal·i·ty** \frü-'ga-lə-tē\ *n* — **fru·gal·ly** *adv*
¹fruit \'früt\ *n* [ME, fr. AF *frut, fruit*, fr. L *fructus* fruit, use, fr. *frui* to enjoy, have the use of] **1** : a product of plant growth; *esp* : a usu. edible and sweet reproductive body (as a strawberry or apple) of a seed plant **2** : a product of fertilization in a plant; *esp* : the ripe ovary of a seed plant with its contents and appendages **3** : CONSEQUENCE, RESULT — **fruit·ed** \'frü-təd\ *adj*
²fruit *vb* : to bear or cause to bear fruit
fruit·cake \'früt-ˌkāk\ *n* : a rich cake containing nuts, dried or candied fruits, and spices
fruit fly *n* : any of various small dipteran flies whose larvae feed on fruit or decaying vegetable matter
fruit·ful \'früt-fəl\ *adj* **1** : yielding or producing fruit **2** : very productive; *also* : bringing results ⟨a ~ idea⟩ — **fruit·ful·ly** *adv* — **fruit·ful·ness** *n*
fru·ition \frü-'i-shən\ *n* **1** : ENJOYMENT **2** : the state of bearing fruit **3** : REALIZATION, ACCOMPLISHMENT ⟨guided the project to ~⟩
fruit·less \'früt-ləs\ *adj* **1** : not bearing fruit **2** : UNSUCCESSFUL ⟨a ~ attempt⟩ — **fruit·less·ly** *adv*
fruity \'frü-tē\ *adj* **fruit·i·er; -est** : resembling a fruit esp. in flavor
frumpy \'frəm-pē\ *adj* **frump·i·er; -est** : DOWDY, DRAB ⟨a ~ dress⟩
frus·trate \'frəs-ˌtrāt\ *vb* **frus·trat·ed; frus·trat·ing** **1** : to balk or defeat in an endeavor **2** : to induce feelings of insecurity, discouragement, or dissatisfaction in **3** : to bring to nothing — **frus·trat·ing·ly** *adv* — **frus·tra·tion** \ˌfrəs-'trā-shən\ *n*
frus·tum \'frəs-təm\ *n, pl* **frustums** *or* **frus·ta** \-tə\ : the part of a cone or pyramid formed by cutting off the top by a plane parallel to the base
frwy *abbr* freeway
¹fry \'frī\ *vb* **fried; fry·ing** [ME *frien*, fr. AF *frire*, fr. L *frigere* to roast] **1** : to cook in a pan or on a griddle over heat esp. with the use of fat **2** : to undergo frying **3** : to damage or destroy by overheating esp. by high voltage
²fry *n, pl* **fries** **1** : a social gathering where fried food is eaten **2** : a dish of something fried; *esp, pl* : FRENCH FRIES
³fry *n, pl* **fry** [ME, fr. AF *frie*, fr. *freier, frier* to rub, spawn, fr. L *fricare* to rub] **1** : recently hatched fishes; *also* : very small adult fishes **2** : members of a group or class ⟨small ~⟩
fry·er \'frī(-ə)r\ *n* **1** : something (as a young chicken) suitable for frying **2** : a deep utensil for frying foods
FSLIC *abbr* Federal Savings and Loan Insurance Corporation
ft *abbr* **1** feet; foot **2** fort
FTC *abbr* Federal Trade Commission
FTP \ˌef-ˌtē-'pē\ *n* [file transfer protocol] : a system for transferring computer files esp. via the Internet — **FTP** *vb*
fuch·sia \'fyü-shə\ *n* **1** : any of a genus of shrubs related to the evening primrose and grown for their showy nodding often red or purple flowers **2** : a vivid reddish purple color
fud·dle \'fə-d°l\ *vb* **fud·dled; fud·dling** : MUDDLE, CONFUSE
fud·dy-dud·dy \'fə-dē-ˌdə-dē\ *n, pl* **-dies** : one that is old-fashioned, unimaginative, or conservative
¹fudge \'fəj\ *vb* **fudged; fudg·ing** **1** : to exceed the proper bounds of something **2** : CHEAT; *also* : FALSIFY ⟨*fudged* their data⟩ **3** : to fail to come to grips with
²fudge *n* **1** : NONSENSE **2** : a soft candy of milk, sugar, butter, and flavoring
¹fu·el \'fyü-əl, 'fyül\ *n* : a material used to produce heat or power by burning; *also* : a material from which nuclear energy can be liberated
²fuel *vb* **-eled** *or* **-elled; -el·ing** *or* **-el·ling** : to provide with or take in fuel
fuel cell *n* : a device that continuously changes the chemical energy of a fuel directly into electrical energy
fuel injection *n* : a system for injecting a precise amount of atomized fuel into an internal combustion engine — **fuel–in·ject·ed** \'fyül-in-ˈjek-təd\ *adj*

¹fu·gi·tive \'fyü-jə-tiv\ *adj* **1** : running away or trying to escape **2** : likely to vanish suddenly : not fixed or lasting
²fugitive *n* **1** : one who flees or tries to escape **2** : something elusive or hard to find
fugue \'fyüg\ *n* **1** : a musical composition in which different parts successively repeat the theme **2** : a disturbed state of consciousness characterized by acts that are not recalled upon recovery
füh·rer *or* **fueh·rer** \'fyùr-ər, 'fir-\ *n* [G] : LEADER; *esp* : TYRANT
¹-ful \fəl\ *adj suffix, sometimes* **-ful·ler;** *sometimes* **-ful·lest** **1** : full of ⟨pride*ful*⟩ **2** : characterized by ⟨peace*ful*⟩ **3** : having the qualities of ⟨master*ful*⟩ **4** : tending, given, or liable to ⟨help*ful*⟩
²-ful \ˌfül\ *n suffix* : number or quantity that fills or would fill ⟨*room*ful⟩
ful·crum \'fül-krəm, 'fəl-\ *n, pl* **ful·crums** *or* **ful·cra** \-krə\ [LL, fr. L, bedpost] : the support on which a lever turns
ful·fill *or* **ful·fil** \fül-'fil\ *vb* **ful·filled; ful·fill·ing** **1** : to put into effect **2** : to bring to an end **3** : SATISFY ⟨~*ed* expectations⟩ — **ful·fill·ment** *or* **ful·fil·ment** *n*
¹full \'fül\ *adj* **1** : FILLED **2** : complete esp. in detail, number, or duration **3** : having all the distinguishing characteristics ⟨a ~ member⟩ **4** : MAXIMUM ⟨~ strength⟩ **5** : rounded in outline ⟨a ~ figure⟩ **6** : possessing or containing an abundance ⟨~ of wrinkles⟩ **7** : having an abundance of material ⟨a ~ skirt⟩ **8** : satisfied esp. with food or drink **9** : having volume or depth of sound **10** : completely occupied with a thought or plan — **full·ness** *also* **ful·ness** *n*
²full *adv* **1** : VERY, EXTREMELY **2** : ENTIRELY ⟨fill a glass ~⟩ **3** : STRAIGHT, SQUARELY ⟨hit him ~ in the face⟩
³full *n* **1** : the highest or fullest state or degree **2** : the utmost extent — **in full** : to the requisite or complete amount
⁴full *vb* : to shrink and thicken (woolen cloth) by moistening, heating, and pressing — **full·er** *n*
full·back \'fül-ˌbak\ *n* : a football back stationed between the halfbacks
full–blood·ed \'fül-'blə-dəd\ *adj* : of unmixed ancestry : PUREBRED
full–blown \-'blōn\ *adj* **1** : being at the height of bloom **2** : fully mature or developed
full–bod·ied \-'bä-dēd\ *adj* : marked by richness and fullness
full dress *n* : the style of dress worn for ceremonial or formal occasions
full–fledged \'fül-'flejd\ *adj* **1** : fully developed **2** : having attained complete status ⟨a ~ lawyer⟩
full house *n* : a poker hand containing three of a kind and a pair
full moon *n* : the moon with its whole disk illuminated
full–on \-ˌȯn, -ˌän\ *adj* : COMPLETE, FULL-FLEDGED
full–scale \'fül-'skāl\ *adj* **1** : identical to an original in proportion and size ⟨~ drawing⟩ **2** : involving full use of available resources ⟨a ~ revolt⟩
full–term \-ˌtərm\ *adj* : retained in the uterus for the normal period of gestation before birth ⟨a ~ baby⟩
full tilt *adv* : at high speed
full–time \'fül-'tīm\ *adj or adv* : involving or working a normal or standard schedule
ful·ly \'fù-lē\ *adv* **1** : in a full manner or degree : COMPLETELY **2** : at least ⟨~ nine tenths of us⟩
ful·mi·nate \'fül-mə-ˌnāt, 'fəl-\ *vb* **-nat·ed; -nat·ing** [ME, fr. ML *fulminatus,* pp. of *fulminare,* fr. L, to strike (of lightning), fr. *fulmen* lightning] : to utter or send out censure or invective : condemn severely ⟨*fulminated* against the tax increase⟩ — **ful·mi·na·tion** \ˌfül-mə-'nā-shən, ˌfəl-\ *n*
ful·some \'fül-səm\ *adj* **1** : COPIOUS, ABUNDANT ⟨~ detail⟩ **2** : generous in amount or extent ⟨a ~ victory⟩ **3** : excessively flattering ⟨~ praise⟩
fu·ma·role \'fyü-mə-ˌrōl\ *n* : a hole in a volcanic region from which hot gases issue
fum·ble \'fəm-bəl\ *vb* **fum·bled; fum·bling** **1** : to grope about clumsily **2** : to fail to hold, catch, or handle properly — **fumble** *n*
¹fume \'fyüm\ *n* : a usu. irritating smoke, vapor, or gas
²fume *vb* **fumed; fum·ing** **1** : to treat with fumes **2** : to give off fumes **3** : to express anger or annoyance
fu·mi·gant \'fyü-mi-gənt\ *n* : a substance used for fumigation
fu·mi·gate \'fyü-mə-ˌgāt\ *vb* **-gat·ed; -gat·ing** : to treat with fumes to disinfect or destroy pests — **fu·mi·ga·tion** \ˌfyü-mə-'gā-shən\ *n* — **fu·mi·ga·tor** \'fyü-mə-ˌgā-tər\ *n*

¹fun \'fən\ *n* [E dial. *fun* to hoax] **1** : something that provides amusement or enjoyment **2** : ENJOYMENT
²fun *adj* : full of fun ⟨a ~ person⟩ ⟨had a ~ time⟩
¹func·tion \'fəŋk-shən\ *n* **1** : OCCUPATION **2** : special purpose **3** : the particular purpose for which a person or thing is specially fitted or used or for which a thing exists ⟨the ~ of a hammer⟩; *also* : the natural or proper action of a bodily part in a living thing ⟨the ~ of the heart⟩ **4** : a formal ceremony or social affair **5** : a mathematical relationship that assigns to each element of a set one and only one element of the same or another set **6** : a variable (as a quality, trait, or measurement) that depends on and varies with another ⟨height is a ~ of age in children⟩ **7** : a computer subroutine that performs a calculation with variables provided by a program — **func·tion·al** \-shə-nəl\ *adj* — **func·tion·al·ly** *adv*
²function *vb* : to have or carry on a function ⟨the computer ~s well⟩
func·tion·ary \'fəŋk-shə-ˌner-ē\ *n, pl* **-ar·ies** : one who performs a certain function; *esp* : OFFICIAL
function word *n* : a word (as a preposition, auxiliary verb, or conjunction) expressing the grammatical relationship between other words
¹fund \'fənd\ *n* [L *fundus* bottom, country estate] **1** : a sum of money or resources intended for a special purpose **2** : STORE, SUPPLY **3** *pl* : available money **4** : an organization administering a special fund
²fund *vb* **1** : to provide funds for ⟨~*ed* cancer research⟩ **2** : to convert (a short-term obligation) into a long-term interest-bearing debt — **fund·er** *n*
fun·da·men·tal \ˌfən-də-'men-t°l\ *adj* **1** : serving as an origin : PRIMARY **2** : BASIC, ESSENTIAL **3** : RADICAL ⟨~ change⟩ **4** : of central importance : PRINCIPAL ⟨~ purpose⟩ — **fundamental** *n* — **fun·da·men·tal·ly** *adv*
fun·da·men·tal·ism \-tə-ˌli-zəm\ *n* **1** *often cap* : a Protestant religious movement emphasizing the literal infallibility of the Bible **2** : a movement or attitude stressing strict adherence to a set of basic principles — **fun·da·men·tal·ist** \-list\ *adj or n*
¹fu·ner·al \'fyü-nə-rəl\ *adj* **1** : of, relating to, or constituting a funeral **2** : FUNEREAL 2
²funeral *n* : the ceremonies held for a dead person usu. before burial
fu·ner·ary \'fyü-nə-ˌrer-ē\ *adj* : of, used for, or associated with burial ⟨~ rites⟩
fu·ne·re·al \fyù-'nir-ē-əl\ *adj* **1** : of or relating to a funeral **2** : suggesting a funeral ⟨a ~ mood⟩
fun·gi·cide \'fən-jə-ˌsīd, 'fəŋ-gə-\ *n* : an agent that kills or checks the growth of fungi — **fun·gi·cid·al** \ˌfən-jə-'sī-d°l, ˌfəŋ-gə-\ *adj*
fun·gus \'fəŋ-gəs\ *n, pl* **fun·gi** \'fən-ˌjī, 'fəŋ-ˌgī\ *also* **fun·gus·es** \'fəŋ-gə-səz\ : any of a kingdom of parasitic spore-producing organisms (as molds, mildews, and mushrooms) formerly classified as plants — **fun·gal** \-gəl\ *adj* — **fun·gous** \-gəs\ *adj*
fu·nic·u·lar \fyù-'ni-kyə-lər, fə-\ *n* : a cable railway ascending a mountain
¹funk \'fəŋk\ *n* : a strong offensive smell
²funk *n* : a depressed state of mind
funky \'fəŋ-kē\ *adj* **funk·i·er; -est** **1** : having an earthy unsophisticated style and feeling; *esp* : having the style and feeling of older African American music **2** : odd or quaint in appearance or style ⟨a ~ little restaurant⟩ — **funk·i·ness** *n*
fun·nel \'fə-n°l\ *n* **1** : a cone-shaped utensil with a tube used for catching and directing a downward flow (as of liquid) **2** : FLUE, SMOKESTACK
²funnel *vb* **-neled** *also* **-nelled; -nel·ing** *also* **-nel·ling** **1** : to pass through or as if through a funnel **2** : to move to a central point or into a central channel
fun·nies \'fə-nēz\ *n pl* : a comic strip or a comic section (as of a newspaper) — used with *the*
fun·ny \'fə-nē\ *adj* **fun·ni·er; -est** **1** : AMUSING **2** : FACETIOUS **3** : PECULIAR **3** **4** : UNDERHANDED — **funny** *adv*
funny bone *n* : a place at the back of the elbow where a blow easily compresses a nerve and causes a painful tingling sensation
fun·plex \'fən-ˌpleks\ *n* : a center containing various entertainment facilities
¹fur \'fər\ *n* **1** : an article of clothing made of or with fur **2** : the hairy coat of a mammal esp. when fine, soft, and

thick; *also* : this coat dressed for use — **fur** *adj* — **furred** \'fərd\ *adj*

²**fur** *abbr* furlong

fur·be·low \'fər-bə-ˌlō\ *n* **1** : FLOUNCE, RUFFLE **2** : showy trimming

fur·bish \'fər-bish\ *vb* **1** : to make lustrous : POLISH **2** : to give a new look to : RENOVATE

fu·ri·ous \'fyùr-ē-əs\ *adj* **1** : FIERCE, ANGRY, VIOLENT **2** : BOISTEROUS **3** : INTENSE ⟨∼ growth⟩ — **fu·ri·ous·ly** *adv*

furl \'fərl\ *vb* **1** : to wrap or roll (as a sail or a flag) close to or around something **2** : to curl in furls — **furl** *n*

fur·long \'fər-ˌlòŋ\ *n* [ME, fr. OE *furlang*, fr. *furh* furrow + *lang* long] : a unit of distance equal to 220 yards (about 201 meters)

fur·lough \'fər-lō\ *n* [D *verlof*, lit., permission] : a leave of absence from duty granted esp. to a soldier — **furlough** *vb*

fur·nace \'fər-nəs\ *n* : an enclosed structure in which heat is produced

fur·nish \'fər-nish\ *vb* **1** : to provide with what is needed : EQUIP **2** : SUPPLY, GIVE ⟨∼ed them with food⟩

fur·nish·ings \-ni-shiŋz\ *n pl* **1** : articles or accessories of dress **2** : FURNITURE

fur·ni·ture \'fər-ni-chər\ *n* : equipment that is necessary or desirable; *esp* : movable articles (as chairs or beds) for a room

fu·ror \'fyùr-ˌòr\ *n* **1** : ANGER, RAGE **2** : a contagious excitement; *esp* : a fashionable craze **3** : UPROAR

fu·rore \-ˌòr\ *n* [It] : FUROR 2, 3

fur·ri·er \'fər-ē-ər\ *n* : one who prepares or deals in fur

fur·ring \'fər-iŋ\ *n* : wood or metal strips applied to a wall or ceiling to form a level surface or an air space

fur·row \'fər-ō\ *n* **1** : a trench in the earth made by a plow **2** : a narrow groove or wrinkle — **furrow** *vb*

fur·ry \'fər-ē\ *adj* **fur·ri·er; -est** **1** : resembling or consisting of fur **2** : covered with fur

¹**fur·ther** \'fər-thər\ *adv* **1** : FARTHER 1 **2** : in addition : MOREOVER **3** : to a greater extent or degree

²**further** *vb* : to help forward — **fur·ther·ance** \'fər-thə-rəns\ *n*

³**further** *adj* **1** : FARTHER 1 **2** : ADDITIONAL ⟨∼ education⟩

fur·ther·more \'fər-thər-ˌmór\ *adv* : in addition to what precedes : BESIDES

fur·ther·most \-ˌmōst\ *adj* : most distant : FARTHEST

fur·thest \'fər-thəst\ *adv or adj* : FARTHEST

fur·tive \'fər-tiv\ *adj* [F or L; F *furtif*, fr. L *furtivus*, fr. *furtum* theft, fr. *fur* thief] : done by stealth : SLY ⟨a ∼ glance⟩ — **fur·tive·ly** *adv* — **fur·tive·ness** *n*

fu·ry \'fyùr-ē\ *n, pl* **furies** **1** : intense and often destructive rage **2** : extreme fierceness or violence **3** : FRENZY

furze \'fərz\ *n* : GORSE

¹**fuse** \'fyüz\ *vb* **fused; fus·ing** **1** : MELT **2** : to unite by or as if by melting together — **fus·ible** *adj*

²**fuse** *n* : an electrical safety device having a metal wire or strip that melts and interrupts the circuit when the current becomes too strong

³**fuse** *n* **1** : a cord or cable that is set afire to ignite an explosive charge **2** *usu* **fuze** : a mechanical or electrical device for setting off the explosive charge of a projectile, bomb, or torpedo

⁴**fuse** *also* **fuze** \'fyüz\ *vb* **fused** *also* **fuzed; fus·ing** *also* **fuz·ing** : to equip with a fuse

fu·se·lage \'fyü-sə-ˌläzh, -zə-\ *n* : the central body portion of an aircraft

fu·sil·lade \'fyü-sə-ˌläd, -ˌlād\ *n* : a number of shots fired simultaneously or in rapid succession

fu·sion \'fyü-zhən\ *n* **1** : the act or process of melting or making plastic by heat **2** : union by or as if by melting **3** : the union of light atomic nuclei to form heavier nuclei with the release of huge quantities of energy

¹**fuss** \'fəs\ *n* **1** : needless bustle or excitement : COMMOTION **2** : effusive praise **3** : a state of agitation **4** : OBJECTION, PROTEST **5** : DISPUTE

²**fuss** *vb* : to make a fuss ⟨∼ed over the baby⟩

fuss·bud·get \'fəs-ˌbə-jət\ *n* : one who fusses or is fussy about trifles

fussy \'fə-sē\ *adj* **fuss·i·er; -est** **1** : IRRITABLE **2** : overly decorative ⟨a ∼ wallpaper pattern⟩ **3** : requiring or giving close attention or concern to details or niceties — **fuss·i·ly** \-sə-lē\ *adv* — **fuss·i·ness** \-sē-nəs\ *n*

fus·tian \'fəs-chən\ *n* **1** : a strong usu. cotton fabric **2** : pretentious writing or speech — **fustian** *adj*

fus·ty \'fəs-tē\ *adj* **fus·ti·er; -est** [prob. alter. of ME *foisted, foist* musty, fr. *foist* wine cask, fr. AF *fust, fuist* wood, tree trunk, cask] **1** : MUSTY **2** : OLD-FASHIONED ⟨∼ notions⟩

fut *abbr* future

fu·tile \'fyü-t³l, 'fyü-ˌtī(-ə)l\ *adj* **1** : USELESS, VAIN **2** : FRIVOLOUS, TRIVIAL — **fu·tile·ly** *adv* — **fu·til·i·ty** \fyü-'ti-lə-tē\ *n*

fu·ton \'fü-ˌtän\ *n* [Jp] : a usu. cotton-filled mattress used on the floor or in a frame as a bed, couch, or chair

¹**fu·ture** \'fyü-chər\ *adj* **1** : of, relating to, or constituting a verb tense that expresses time yet to come **2** : coming after the present

²**future** *n* **1** : time that is to come **2** : what is going to happen **3** : an expectation of advancement or progressive development **4** : the future tense; *also* : a verb form in it

fu·tur·ism \'fyü-chə-ˌri-zəm\ *n* : a modern movement in art, music, and literature that tries esp. to express the energy and activity of mechanical processes — **fu·tur·ist** \'fyü-chə-rist\ *n*

fu·tur·is·tic \ˌfyü-chə-'ris-tik\ *adj* : of or relating to the future or to futurism; *also* : very modern

fu·tu·ri·ty \fyù-'tùr-ə-tē, -'tyùr-\ *n, pl* **-ties** **1** : FUTURE **2** : the quality or state of being future **3** *pl* : future events or prospects

fuze *var of* FUSE

fuzz \'fəz\ *n* : fine light particles or fibers (as of down or fluff)

fuzzy \'fə-zē\ *adj* **fuzz·i·er; -est** **1** : having or resembling fuzz **2** : INDISTINCT ⟨∼ photos⟩ **3** : being or relating to pleasant usu. sentimental emotions ⟨∼ feelings⟩ — **fuzz·i·ness** \-zē-nəs\ *n*

fuzzy logic *n* : a system of logic in which a statement can be true, false, or any of a continuum of values in between

fwd *abbr* forward

FWD *abbr* front-wheel drive

FY *abbr* fiscal year

-fy *vb suffix* : make : form into ⟨dandi*fy*⟩

FYI *abbr* for your information

---

¹**g** \'jē\ *n, pl* **g's** *or* **gs** \'jēz\ *often cap* **1** : the 7th letter of the English alphabet **2** : a unit of force equal to the force exerted by gravity on a body at rest and used to indicate the force to which a body is subjected when accelerated **3** *slang* : a sum of $1000

²**g** *abbr, often cap* **1** game **2** gauge **3** good **4** gram **5** gravity

ga *abbr* gauge

¹**Ga** *abbr* Georgia

²**Ga** *symbol* gallium

GA *abbr* **1** general assembly **2** general average **3** general of the army **4** Georgia

gab \'gab\ *vb* **gabbed; gab·bing** : to talk in a rapid or thoughtless manner : CHATTER — **gab** *n*

gab·ar·dine \'ga-bər-ˌdēn\ *n* **1** : GABERDINE 1 **2** : a firm durable twilled fabric having diagonal ribs and made of various fibers; *also* : a garment of gabardine

gab·ble \'ga-bəl\ *vb* **gab·bled; gab·bling** : JABBER, BABBLE

gab·by \'ga-bē\ *adj* **gab·bi·er; -est** : TALKATIVE, GARRULOUS

gab·er·dine \'ga-bər-ˌdēn\ n 1 : a long loose outer garment worn in medieval times and associated esp. with Jews 2 : GABARDINE 2
gab·fest \'gab-ˌfest\ n 1 : an informal gathering for general talk 2 : an extended conversation
ga·ble \'gā-bəl\ n : the vertical triangular end of a building formed by the sides of the roof sloping from the ridge down to the eaves — **ga·bled** \-bəld\ adj
gad \'gad\ vb **gad·ded; gad·ding** : to be constantly active without specific purpose — usu. used with about ⟨gadded about Europe for a year⟩ — **gad·der** n
gad·about \'ga-də-ˌbaut\ n : a person who flits about in social activity
gad·fly \'gad-ˌflī\ n 1 : a fly that bites or harasses livestock 2 : a person who annoys esp. by persistent criticism
gad·get \'ga-jət\ n : DEVICE, CONTRIVANCE — **gad·get·ry** \'ga-jə-trē\ n
gad·o·lin·i·um \ˌga-də-'li-nē-əm\ n : a magnetic metallic chemical element
¹Gael \'gāl\ n : a Celtic inhabitant of Ireland or Scotland
²Gael abbr Gaelic
Gael·ic \'gā-lik\ adj : of or relating to the Gaels or their languages — **Gaelic** n
gaff \'gaf\ n 1 : a spear used in taking fish or turtles; also : a metal hook for holding or lifting heavy fish 2 : the spar supporting the top of a fore-and-aft sail 3 : rough treatment : ABUSE — **gaff** vb
gaffe \'gaf\ n : a usu. social blunder
gaf·fer \'ga-fər\ n 1 : an old man 2 : a lighting electrician on a motion-picture or television set
¹gag \'gag\ vb **gagged; gag·ging** 1 : to restrict use of the mouth of with a gag 2 : to prevent from speaking freely 3 : to retch or cause to retch 4 : OBSTRUCT, CHOKE 5 : BALK 6 : to make quips — **gag·ger** n
²gag n 1 : something thrust into the mouth esp. to prevent speech or outcry 2 : an official check or restraint on free speech 3 : a laugh-provoking remark or act 4 : PRANK, TRICK
¹gage \'gāj\ n 1 : a token of defiance; esp : a glove or cap cast on the ground as a pledge of combat 2 : SECURITY
²gage var of GAUGE
gag·gle \'ga-gəl\ n [ME gagyll, fr. gagelen to cackle] 1 : a flock of geese 2 : an unorganized group
gai·ety also **gay·ety** \'gā-ə-tē\ n, pl **-eties** 1 : festive activity : MERRYMAKING 2 : MERRIMENT 3 : FINERY ✦ **Synonyms** MIRTH, FESTIVITY, GLEE, HILARITY, JOLLITY
gai·ly also **gay·ly** \'gā-lē\ adv : in a gay manner ⟨chatting ~⟩
¹gain \'gān\ n 1 : PROFIT 2 : ACQUISITION, ACCUMULATION 3 : INCREASE
²gain vb 1 : to get possession of : EARN 2 : WIN ⟨~ a victory⟩ 3 : to increase in ⟨~ momentum⟩ 4 : PERSUADE 5 : to arrive at 6 : ACHIEVE ⟨~ strength⟩ 7 : to run fast ⟨the watch ~s a minute a day⟩ 8 : PROFIT 9 : INCREASE 10 : to improve in health ✦ **Synonyms** ACCOMPLISH, ATTAIN, REALIZE — **gain·er** n
gain·ful \'gān-fəl\ adj : PROFITABLE ⟨~ employment⟩ — **gain·ful·ly** adv
gain·say \ˌgān-'sā\ vb **-said** \-'sād, -'sed\; **-say·ing; -says** \-'sāz, -'sez\ [ME gainsayen, fr. gain- against + sayen to say] 1 : DENY, DISPUTE 2 : to speak against ✦ **Synonyms** CONTRADICT, CONTRAVENE, IMPUGN, NEGATE — **gain·say·er** n
gait \'gāt\ n : manner of moving on foot; also : a particular pattern or style of such moving — **gait·ed** adj
gai·ter \'gā-tər\ n 1 : a leg covering reaching from the instep to ankle, mid-calf, or knee 2 : an overshoe with a fabric upper 3 : an ankle-high shoe with elastic gores in the sides
¹gal \'gal\ n : GIRL
²gal abbr gallon
Gal abbr Galatians
ga·la \'gā-lə, 'ga-, 'gä-\ n : a festive celebration : FESTIVITY — **gala** adj
ga·lac·tic \gə-'lak-tik\ adj : of or relating to a galaxy
Ga·la·tians \gə-'lā-shənz\ n — see BIBLE table
gal·axy \'ga-lək-sē\ n, pl **-ax·ies** [ME galaxie, galaxias, fr. LL galaxias, fr. Gk, fr. galakt-, gala milk] 1 often cap : MILKY WAY GALAXY — used with the 2 : a very large

group of stars 3 : an assemblage of brilliant or famous persons or things
gale \'gāl\ n 1 : a strong wind 2 : an emotional outburst ⟨~s of laughter⟩
ga·le·na \gə-'lē-nə\ n : a lustrous bluish gray mineral that consists of the sulfide of lead and is the chief ore of lead
¹gall \'gol\ n 1 : BILE 2 : something bitter to endure 3 : RANCOR 4 : IMPUDENCE ✦ **Synonyms** EFFRONTERY, BRASS, CHEEK, CHUTZPAH, AUDACITY, PRESUMPTION
²gall n : a skin sore caused by chafing
³gall vb 1 : CHAFE; esp : to become sore or worn by rubbing 2 : VEX, HARASS
⁴gall n : an abnormal outgrowth of plant tissue usu. due to parasites
¹gal·lant \gə-'lant, -'länt; 'ga-lənt\ n 1 : a young man of fashion 2 : a man who shows a marked fondness for the company of women and who is esp. attentive to them 3 : SUITOR
²gal·lant \'ga-lənt (usual for 2, 3, 4); gə-'lant, -'länt (usual for 5)\ adj 1 : showy in dress or bearing : SMART 2 : SPLENDID, STATELY 3 : SPIRITED, BRAVE 4 : CHIVALROUS, NOBLE 5 : polite and attentive to women — **gal·lant·ly** adv
gal·lant·ry \'ga-lən-trē\ n, pl **-ries** 1 archaic : gallant appearance 2 : an act of marked courtesy 3 : courteous attention to a woman 4 : conspicuous bravery ✦ **Synonyms** HEROISM, VALOR, PROWESS
gall·blad·der \'gol-ˌbla-dər\ n : a membranous muscular sac attached to the liver and serving to store bile
gal·le·on \'ga-lē-ən\ n : a large square-rigged sailing ship formerly used esp. by the Spanish
gal·le·ria \ˌga-lə-'rē-ə\ n [It] : a roofed and usu. glass-enclosed promenade or court
gal·lery \'ga-lə-rē\ n, pl **-ler·ies** 1 : an outdoor balcony; also : PORCH, VERANDA 2 : a long narrow passage, apartment, or hall 3 : a narrow passage (as one made underground by a miner or through wood by an insect) 4 : a room where works of art are exhibited; also : an organization dealing in works of art 5 : a balcony in a theater, auditorium, or church; esp : the highest one in a theater 6 : the spectators at a sporting event (as a tennis or golf match) 7 : a photographer's studio — **gal·ler·ied** \-rēd\ adj
gal·ley \'ga-lē\ n, pl **galleys** 1 : a long low ship propelled esp. by oars and formerly used esp. in the Mediterranean Sea 2 : the kitchen esp. of a ship or airplane 3 : a proof of typeset matter esp. in a single column

galley 1

Gal·lic \'ga-lik\ adj : of or relating to Gaul or France
gal·li·mau·fry \ˌga-lə-'mo-frē\ n, pl **-fries** [MF galimafree stew] : HODGEPODGE
gal·li·nule \'ga-lə-ˌnül, -ˌnyül\ n : any of several aquatic birds related to the rails
gal·li·um \'ga-lē-əm\ n : a bluish-white metallic chemical element used esp. in semiconductors
gal·li·vant \'ga-lə-ˌvant\ vb : to travel, roam, or move about for pleasure
gal·lon \'ga-lən\ n — see WEIGHT table
¹gal·lop \'ga-ləp\ vb 1 : to go or cause to go at a gallop 2 : to run fast — **gal·lop·er** n
²gallop n 1 : a bounding gait of a quadruped; esp : a fast 3-beat gait of a horse 2 : a ride or run at a gallop
gal·lows \'ga-lōz\ n, pl **gallows** or **gal·lows·es** 1 : a frame usu. of two upright posts and a crosspiece from which criminals are hanged; also : the punishment of hanging
gall·stone \'gol-ˌstōn\ n : an abnormal concretion occurring in the gallbladder or bile passages

gal·lus·es \'ga-lə-səz\ *n pl* : SUSPENDERS

ga·lore \gə-'lȯr\ *adj* [Ir *go leor* enough] : ABUNDANT, PLENTIFUL

ga·losh \gə-'läsh\ *n* : a high overshoe

galv *abbr* galvanized

gal·va·nise *Brit var of* GALVANIZE

gal·va·nize \'gal-və-ˌnīz\ *vb* **-nized; -niz·ing** **1** : to stimulate as if by an electric shock ⟨~ public opinion⟩ **2** : to coat (iron or steel) with zinc — **gal·va·ni·za·tion** \ˌgal-və-nə-'zā-shən\ *n* — **gal·va·niz·er** *n*

gal·va·nom·e·ter \ˌgal-və-'nä-mə-tər\ *n* : an instrument for detecting or measuring a small electric current

gam·bit \'gam-bət\ *n* [It *gambetto*, lit., act of tripping someone, fr. *gamba* leg] **1** : a chess opening in which a player risks one or more minor pieces to gain an advantage in position **2** : a calculated move : STRATAGEM ✦ *Synonyms* TRICK, ARTIFICE, GIMMICK, MANEUVER, PLAY, RUSE

¹gam·ble \'gam-bəl\ *vb* **gam·bled; gam·bling** **1** : to play a game for money or property **2** : BET, WAGER **3** : VENTURE, HAZARD — **gam·bler** *n*

²gamble *n* : a risky undertaking

gam·bol \'gam-bəl\ *vb* **-boled** *or* **-bolled; -bol·ing** *or* **-bol·ling** : to skip about in play : FRISK — **gambol** *n*

gam·brel roof \'gam-brəl-\ *n* : a roof with a lower steeper slope and an upper flatter one on each side

¹game \'gām\ *n* **1** : AMUSEMENT, DIVERSION **2** : SPORT, FUN ⟨made ~ of the strange boy⟩ **3** : SCHEME, PROJECT **4** : a line of work : PROFESSION **5** : CONTEST **6** : animals hunted for sport or food; *also* : the flesh of a game animal

²game *vb* **gamed; gam·ing** **1** : to play for a stake **2** : to take dishonest advantage of ⟨~ the tax system⟩

³game *adj* : PLUCKY, RESOLUTE — **game·ly** *adv* — **game·ness** *n*

⁴game *adj* : LAME ⟨a ~ leg⟩

game·cock \'gām-ˌkäk\ *n* : a rooster trained for fighting

game fish *n* : SPORT FISH

game·keep·er \'gām-ˌkē-pər\ *n* : a person in charge of the breeding and protection of game animals or birds on a private preserve

game show *n* : a television program on which contestants compete usu. for prizes in a game

game·some \'gām-səm\ *adj* : MERRY ✦ *Synonyms* PLAYFUL, FROLICSOME, SPORTIVE, ANTIC

game·ster \'gām-stər\ *n* : GAMBLER

gam·ete \'ga-ˌmēt\ *n* : a mature germ cell — **ga·met·ic** \gə-'me-tik\ *adj*

game theory *n* : the analysis of a situation involving conflicting interests (as in business) in terms of gains and losses among opposing players

gam·in \'ga-mən\ *n* [F] **1** : a boy who loiters on the streets **2** : GAMINE 2

ga·mine \ga-'mēn\ *n* **1** : a girl who loiters on the streets **2** : a small playfully mischievous girl

gam·ma \'ga-mə\ *n* : the 3d letter of the Greek alphabet — Γ or γ

gamma globulin *n* : a blood protein fraction rich in antibodies; *also* : a solution of this from human blood donors that is given to provide immunity against some infectious diseases (as measles)

gamma ray *n* : a photon emitted by a radioactive substance; *also* : a photon of higher energy than that of an X-ray — usu. used in pl.

gam·mon \'ga-mən\ *n, chiefly Brit* : a cured ham or side of bacon

gam·ut \'ga-mət\ *n* : an entire range or series ✦ *Synonyms* SCALE, SPECTRUM

gamy *or* **gam·ey** \'gā-mē\ *adj* **gam·i·er; -est** **1** : GAME, PLUCKY **2** : having the flavor of game esp. when near tainting ⟨~ meat⟩ **3** : SCANDALOUS; *also* : DISREPUTABLE — **gam·i·ness** \-mē-nəs\ *n*

¹gan·der \'gan-dər\ *n* : a male goose

²gander *n* : LOOK, GLANCE

¹gang \'gaŋ\ *n* **1** : a set of implements or devices arranged to operate together **2** : a group of persons working or associated together; *esp* : a group of criminals or young delinquents

²gang *vb* **1** : to attack in a gang — usu. used with *up* **2** : to form into or move or act as a gang

gang·land \'gaŋ-ˌland\ *n* : the world of organized crime

gan·gling \'gaŋ-gliŋ\ *adj* : loosely and awkwardly built : LANKY

gan·gli·on \'gaŋ-glē-ən\ *n, pl* **-glia** \-ə\ *also* **-gli·ons** : a mass of nerve tissue containing cell bodies of neurons outside the central nervous tissue; *also* : NUCLEUS 3 — **gan·gli·on·ic** \ˌgaŋ-glē-'ä-nik\ *adj*

gan·gly \'gaŋ-glē\ *adj* : GANGLING

gang·plank \'gaŋ-ˌplaŋk\ *n* : a movable bridge from a ship to the shore

gang·plow \-ˌplau̇\ *n* : a plow that turns two or more furrows at one time

gan·grene \'gaŋ-ˌgrēn, gaŋ-'grēn\ *n* : the death of soft tissues in a local area of the body due to loss of the blood supply — **gangrene** *vb* — **gan·gre·nous** \'gaŋ-grə-nəs\ *adj*

gang·sta \'gaŋ-stə\ *n* : a member of an urban street gang

gangsta rap *n* : rap music with usu. hostile lyrics portraying urban gang life

gang·ster \'gaŋ-stər\ *n* : a member of a gang of criminals : RACKETEER

gang·way \'gaŋ-ˌwā\ *n* **1** : PASSAGEWAY; *also* : GANGPLANK **2** : clear passage through a crowd

gan·net \'ga-nət\ *n, pl* **gannets** *also* **gannet** : any of several large fish-eating usu. white and black seabirds that breed chiefly on offshore islands

gant·let *var of* GAUNTLET

gan·try \'gan-trē\ *n, pl* **gantries** : a frame structure on side supports over or around something

GAO *abbr* General Accounting Office

gaol \'jāl\, **gaol·er** \'jā-lər\ *chiefly Brit var of* JAIL, JAILER

gap \'gap\ *n* **1** : BREACH, CLEFT **2** : a mountain pass **3** : a blank space; *also* : an incomplete or deficient area **4** : a wide difference in character or attitude **5** : a problem caused by a disparity ⟨credibility ~⟩

gape \'gāp\ *vb* **gaped; gap·ing** **1** : to open the mouth wide **2** : to open or part widely **3** : to stare with mouth open **4** : YAWN — **gape** *n*

¹gar \'gär\ *n* : any of several fishes that have a long body resembling that of a pike and long narrow jaws

²gar *abbr* garage

GAR *abbr* Grand Army of the Republic

¹ga·rage \gə-'räzh, -'räj\ *n* [F, act of docking, garage, fr. *garer* to dock, fr. MF *garrer*, prob. ultim. fr. ON *vara* to beware, take care] : a shelter or repair shop for automobiles

²garage *vb* **ga·raged; ga·rag·ing** : to keep or put in a garage

garage sale *n* : a sale of used household or personal articles held on the seller's own premises

garb \'gärb\ *n* **1** : style of dress **2** : outward form : APPEARANCE — **garb** *vb*

gar·bage \'gär-bij\ *n* **1** : food waste **2** : unwanted or useless material

gar·bage·man \-ˌman\ *n* : a person who collects and removes garbage

gar·ble \'gär-bəl\ *vb* **gar·bled; gar·bling** : to distort the meaning of ⟨~ a story⟩

gar·çon \gär-'sōⁿ\ *n, pl* **garçons** *same or* gär-'sōⁿz\ [F, boy, servant] : WAITER

¹gar·den \'gär-dᵊn\ *n* **1** : a plot for growing fruits, flowers, or vegetables **2** : a public recreation area; *esp* : one for displaying plants or animals

²garden *vb* : to lay out or work in a garden — **gar·den·er** *n*

gar·de·nia \gär-'dē-nyə\ *n* [NL, genus name, fr. Alexander *Garden* †1791 Scot. naturalist] : any of a genus of tropical trees or shrubs that are related to the madder and have fragrant white or yellow flowers

garden–variety *adj* : COMMONPLACE, ORDINARY ⟨~ police dramas⟩

gar·fish \'gär-ˌfish\ *n* : GAR

gar·gan·tuan \gär-'gan-chə-wən\ *adj, often cap* : tremendous in size, volume, or degree ⟨~ waterfalls⟩ ✦ *Synonyms* HUGE, COLOSSAL, GIGANTIC, MAMMOTH, MONSTROUS, TITANIC

gar·gle \'gär-gəl\ *vb* **gar·gled; gar·gling** : to rinse the throat with liquid agitated by air forced through it from the lungs — **gargle** *n*

gar·goyle \'gär-ˌgȯi(-ə)l\ *n* **1** : a waterspout in the form of a grotesque human or animal figure projecting from the roof or eaves of a building **2** : a grotesquely carved figure

gar·ish \'ger-ish\ *adj* : FLASHY, GLARING, SHOWY, GAUDY ⟨a ~ wardrobe⟩

¹gar·land \'gär-lənd\ *n* : a decorative wreath or rope (as of leaves)

²garland *vb* : to form into or deck with a garland

gar·lic \'gär-lik\ *n* [ME *garlek,* fr. OE *gārlēac,* fr. *gār* spear + *lēac* leek] : an herb related to the lilies and grown for its pungent bulbs used in cooking; *also* : its bulb — **gar·licky** \-li-kē\ *adj*

gar·ment \'gär-mənt\ *n* : an article of clothing

gar·ner \'gär-nər\ *vb* **1** : to gather into storage **2** : to acquire by effort ⟨~ evidence⟩ **3** : ACCUMULATE, COLLECT

gar·net \'gär-nət\ *n* [ME *gernet,* fr. AF *gernete,* fr. *gernet* dark red, fr. *pume gernete* pomegranate] : a transparent deep red mineral sometimes used as a gem

gar·nish \'gär-nish\ *vb* **1** : DECORATE, EMBELLISH **2** : to add decorative or savory touches to (food) **3** : GARNISHEE — **garnish** *n*

gar·nish·ee \ˌgär-nə-'shē\ *vb* **-eed; -ee·ing** **1** : to serve with a garnishment **2** : to take (as a debtor's wages) by legal authority

gar·nish·ment \'gär-nish-mənt\ *n* **1** : GARNISH **2** : a legal warning concerning the attachment of property to satisfy a debt; *also* : the attachment of such property

gar·ni·ture \-ni-chər, -ˌchùr\ *n* : EMBELLISHMENT, TRIMMING

gar·ret \'ger-ət\ *n* : the part of a house just under the roof : ATTIC

gar·ri·son \'ger-ə-sən\ *n* [ME *garisoun* protection, fr. AF *garisun* healing, protection, fr. *garir* to heal, protect, of Gmc origin] **1** : a military post; *esp* : a permanent military installation **2** : the troops stationed at a garrison — **garrison** *vb*

garrison state *n* : a state organized on a primarily military basis

gar·rote *or* **ga·rotte** \gə-'rät, -'rōt\ *n* [Sp *garrote*] **1** : a method of execution by strangulation; *also* : the apparatus used **2** : an implement (as a wire with handles) for strangulation — **garrote** *or* **garotte** *vb*

gar·ru·lous \'ger-ə-ləs\ *adj* : TALKATIVE — **gar·ru·li·ty** \gə-'rü-lə-tē\ *n* — **gar·ru·lous·ly** *adv* — **gar·ru·lous·ness** *n*

gar·ter \'gär-tər\ *n* : a band or strap worn to hold up a stocking or sock

garter snake *n* : any of a genus of harmless American snakes with longitudinal stripes on the back

¹gas \'gas\ *n, pl* **gas·es** *also* **gas·ses** [NL, alter. of L *chaos* space, chaos] **1** : a fluid (as hydrogen or air) that tends to expand indefinitely **2** : a gas or mixture of gases used as a fuel or anesthetic **3** : a substance that can be used to produce a poisonous, asphyxiating, or irritant atmosphere **4** : GASOLINE — **gas·eous** \'ga-sē-əs, -shəs\ *adj*

²gas *vb* **gassed; gas·sing** **1** : to treat with gas; *also* : to poison with gas **2** : to fill with gasoline ⟨~ up the car⟩

gash \'gash\ *n* : a deep long cut — **gash** *vb*

gas·ket \'gas-kət\ *n* : material (as rubber) or a part used to seal a joint

gas·light \'gas-ˌlīt\ *n* **1** : light made by burning illuminating gas **2** : a gas flame; *also* : a gas lighting fixture

gas mask *n* : a mask with a chemical air filter used to protect the face and lungs against poison gas

gas·o·line \'ga-sə-ˌlēn, ˌga-sə-'lēn\ *n* : a flammable liquid mixture made from petroleum and used esp. as a motor fuel

gasp \'gasp\ *vb* **1** : to catch the breath audibly (as with shock) **2** : to breathe laboriously : PANT **3** : to utter in a gasping manner — **gasp** *n*

gas station *n* : a retail station for servicing and fueling motor vehicles

gas·tric \'gas-trik\ *adj* : of or relating to the stomach

gastric juice *n* : the acid digestive secretion of the stomach

gas·tri·tis \gas-'trī-təs\ *n* : inflammation of the lining of the stomach

gas·tro·en·ter·i·tis \ˌgas-trō-ˌen-tə-'rī-təs\ *n* : inflammation of the lining membrane of the stomach and intestines

gas·tro·en·ter·ol·o·gy \ˌgas-trō-ˌen-tə-'rä-lə-jē\ *n* : a branch of medicine concerned with the structure, functions, and diseases of the stomach and intestines — **gas·tro·en·ter·ol·o·gist** \-jist\ *n*

gas·tro·in·tes·ti·nal \ˌgas-trō-in-'tes-tə-nᵊl\ *adj* : of, relating to, affecting, or including both the stomach and intestine ⟨~ tract⟩ ⟨~ distress⟩

gas·tron·o·my \gas-'trä-nə-mē\ *n* [F *gastronomie,* fr. Gk *Gastronomia,* title of a 4th cent. B.C. poem, fr. *gastēr* belly + *-nomia* system of laws] : the art of good eating — **gas·tro·nom·ic** \ˌgas-trə-'nä-mik\ *also* **gas·tro·nom·i·cal** \-mi-kəl\ *adj* — **gas·tro·nom·i·cal·ly** \-k(ə-)lē\ *adv*

gas·tro·pod \'gas-trə-ˌpäd\ *n* : any of a large class of mollusks (as snails and slugs) with a muscular foot and a spiral shell or none — **gastropod** *adj*

gas·works \'gas-ˌwərks\ *n sing or pl* : a plant for manufacturing gas

gate \'gāt\ *n* **1** : an opening for passage in a wall or fence **2** : a city or castle entrance often with defensive structures **3** : the frame or door that closes a gate **4** : a device (as a valve) for controlling the passage of a fluid or signal **5** : the total admission receipts or the number of people at an event

-gate \ˌgāt\ *n comb form* [*Watergate,* scandal that resulted in the resignation of President Richard Nixon in 1974] : *usu.* political scandal often involving the concealment of wrongdoing

gate–crash·er \'gāt-ˌkra-shər\ *n* : a person who enters without paying admission or attends without invitation

gate·keep·er \-ˌkē-pər\ *n* : a person who tends or guards a gate

gate·post \-ˌpōst\ *n* : the post to which a gate is hung or against which it closes

gate·way \-ˌwā\ *n* **1** : an opening for a gate **2** : a means of entrance or exit

¹gath·er \'ga-thər\ *vb* **1** : to bring together : COLLECT : PICK, HARVEST **3** : to pick up little by little **4** : to scoop up from a resting place ⟨~ed up the child⟩ **5** : to gain or win by gradual increase **6** : ATTRACT, ACCUMULATE ⟨~ dust⟩ **7** : to summon up ⟨~ courage to dive⟩ **8** : to gain control of ⟨~ed his wits⟩ **9** : to draw about or close to something **10** : to pull (fabric) along a line of stitching into puckers **11** : GUESS, DEDUCE, INFER **12** : ASSEMBLE **13** : to swell out and fill with pus **14** : GROW, INCREASE ◆ *Synonyms* CONGREGATE, FORGATHER — **gath·er·er** *n*

²gather *n* : a puckering in cloth made by gathering

GATT \'gat\ *abbr* General Agreement on Tariffs and Trade

gauche \'gōsh\ *adj* [F, lit., left] **1** : lacking social experience or grace; *also* : not tactful **2** : crudely made or done ◆ *Synonyms* CLUMSY, HEAVY-HANDED, INEPT, MALADROIT

gau·che·rie \ˌgō-shə-'rē\ *n* : a tactless or awkward action

gau·cho \'gaù-chō\ *n, pl* **gauchos** : a cowboy of the So. American pampas

gaud \'gòd\ *n* : ORNAMENT, TRINKET

gaudy \'gò-dē\ *adj* **gaud·i·er; -est** **1** : ostentatiously or tastelessly ornamented **2** : marked by showiness or extravagance : OUTLANDISH **3** : EXCEPTIONAL ⟨a ~ batting average⟩ ◆ *Synonyms* GARISH, FLASHY, GLARING, TAWDRY — **gaud·i·ly** \-də-lē\ *adv* — **gaud·i·ness** \-dē-nəs\ *n*

¹gauge *also* **gage** \'gāj\ *n* **1** : measurement according to some standard or system **2** : DIMENSIONS, SIZE **3** *usu* **gage** : an instrument for measuring, testing, or registering

²gauge *also* **gage** *vb* **gauged** *also* **gaged; gaug·ing** *also* **gag·ing** **1** : MEASURE **2** : to determine the capacity or contents of **3** : ESTIMATE, JUDGE

gaunt \'gònt\ *adj* **1** : excessively thin and angular ⟨a ~ face⟩ **2** : BARREN, DESOLATE ◆ *Synonyms* BONY, LANK, LANKY, LEAN, RAWBONED, SKINNY — **gaunt·ness** *n*

¹gaunt·let *also* **gant·let** \'gònt-lət\ *n* **1** : a protective glove **2** : an open challenge (as to combat) **3** : a dress glove extending above the wrist

²gauntlet *also* **gantlet** \''\ *n* **1** : a double file of men armed with weapons (as clubs) with which to strike at an individual who is made to run between them **2** : ORDEAL **3** : a line or series of something to be greeted or managed

gauss \'gaùs\ *n* : the centimeter-gram-second unit of magnetic flux density that is equal to 1×10^4 tesla

gauze \'gòz\ *n* : a very thin often transparent fabric used esp. for draperies and surgical dressings

gauzy \'gò-zē\ *adj* **gauz·i·er; -est** **1** : made of or resembling gauze **2** : not clear : HAZY ⟨a ~ memory⟩

gave *past of* GIVE

gav·el \'ga-vəl\ *n* : a mallet used by a presiding officer or auctioneer

ga·votte \gə-'vät\ *n* : a dance of French peasant origin marked by the raising rather than sliding of the feet

gawk \'gȯk\ *vb* : to gape or stare stupidly — **gawk·er** *n*

gawky \'gȯ-kē\ *adj* **gawk·i·er; -est** : AWKWARD, CLUMSY — **gawk·i·ly** \-kə-lē\ *adv* — **gawk·i·ness** *n*

gay \'gā\ *adj* **1** : MERRY **2** : BRIGHT, LIVELY **3** : brilliant in color **4** : given to social pleasures; *also* : LICENTIOUS **5** : HOMOSEXUAL; *also* : of, relating to, or used by homosexuals ⟨a ∼ bar⟩

gayety, gayly *var of* GAIETY, GAILY

gaz *abbr* gazette

gaze \'gāz\ *vb* **gazed; gaz·ing** : to fix the eyes in a steady intent look ✦ *Synonyms* GAPE, GAWK, GLARE, GOGGLE, PEER, STARE — **gaze** *n* — **gaz·er** *n*

ga·ze·bo \gə-'zē-bō\ *n, pl* **-bos** **1** : BELVEDERE **2** : a freestanding roofed structure usu. open on the sides

ga·zelle \gə-'zel\ *n, pl* **gazelles** *also* **gazelle** : any of numerous small swift graceful antelopes

gazelle

ga·zette \gə-'zet\ *n* **1** : NEWSPAPER **2** : an official journal

gaz·et·teer \ˌga-zə-'tir\ *n* : a geographical dictionary

ga·zil·lion \gə-'zil-yən\ *n* : ZILLION — **gazillion** *adj* — **ga·zil·lionth** \-yənth\ *adj*

gaz·pa·cho \gəz-'pä-(ˌ)chō, gə-'spä-\ *n, pl* **-chos** [Sp] : a spicy soup usu. made from raw vegetables and served cold

GB *abbr* Great Britain

GCA *abbr* ground-controlled approach

gd *abbr* good

Gd *symbol* gadolinium

GDR *abbr* German Democratic Republic

Ge *symbol* germanium

gear \'gir\ *n* **1** : CLOTHING **2** : movable property : GOODS **3** : EQUIPMENT ⟨fishing ∼⟩ **4** : a mechanism that performs a specific function ⟨steering ∼⟩ **5** : a toothed wheel **6** : working order or adjustment ⟨got her career in ∼⟩ **7** : an adjustment of transmission gears (as of an automobile or bicycle) that determines speed and direction of travel — **gear** *vb*

gear·box \'gir-ˌbäks\ *n* : TRANSMISSION 3

gear·shift \-ˌshift\ *n* : a mechanism by which transmission gears are shifted

gear·wheel \-ˌhwēl\ *n* : GEAR 5

gecko \'ge-kō\ *n, pl* **geck·os** *also* **geck·oes** : any of numerous small chiefly tropical insect-eating lizards

GED *abbr* general equivalency diploma

geek \'gēk\ *n* : a person of an intellectual bent who is often disliked — **geek·i·ness** *n* — **geeky** *adj*

geese *pl of* GOOSE

gee·zer \'gē-zər\ *n* : an odd or eccentric person usu. of old age

Gei·ger counter \'gī-gər-\ *n* : an electronic instrument for detecting the presence of cosmic rays or radioactive substances

gei·sha \'gā-shə, 'gē-\ *n, pl* **geisha** *or* **geishas** [Jp, fr. *gei* art + *-sha* person] : a Japanese girl or woman who is trained to provide entertaining company for men

gel \'jel\ *n* : a solid jellylike colloid (as gelatin dessert) — **gel** *vb*

gel·a·tin *also* **gel·a·tine** \'je-lə-tən\ *n* : glutinous material and esp. protein obtained from animal tissues by boiling and used as a food, in dyeing, and in photography; *also*

: an edible jelly formed with gelatin — **ge·lat·i·nous** \jə-'la-tə-nəs\ *adj*

geld \'geld\ *vb* : CASTRATE

geld·ing *n* : a castrated male horse

gel·id \'je-ləd\ *adj* : extremely cold

gem \'jem\ *n* **1** : JEWEL **2** : a usu. valuable stone cut and polished for ornament **3** : something valued for beauty or perfection ⟨a ∼ of colonial architecture⟩

Gem·i·ni \'je-mə-(ˌ)nē, -ˌnī; 'ge-mə-ˌnē\ *n* **1** : a zodiacal constellation between Taurus and Cancer usu. pictured as twins sitting together **2** : the 3d sign of the zodiac in astrology; *also* : one born under this sign

gem·ol·o·gy *or* **gem·mol·o·gy** \je-'mä-lə-jē, jə-\ *n* : the science of gems — **gem·olog·i·cal** \ˌje-mə-'lä-ji-kəl\ *adj* — **gem·ol·o·gist** *also* **gem·mol·o·gist** \-jist\ *n*

gem·stone \'jem-ˌstōn\ *n* : a mineral or petrified material that when cut and polished can be used in jewelry

gen *abbr* **1** general **2** genitive

Gen *abbr* Genesis

Gen AF *abbr* general of the air force

gen·darme \'zhän-ˌdärm, 'jän-\ *n* [F, intended as sing. of *gensdarmes*, pl. of *gent d'armes*, lit., armed people] : a member of a body of soldiers esp. in France serving as an armed police force

gen·der \'jen-dər\ *n* [ME *gendre*, fr. AF *genre, gendre*, fr. L *gener-, genus* birth, race, kind, gender] **1** : any of two or more divisions within a grammatical class that determine agreement with and selection of other words or grammatical forms **2** : SEX 1 — **gen·der·less** *adj*

gender identity *n* : a person's internal sense of being male, female, a combination of male and female, or neither male nor female

gene \'jēn\ *n* : a part of DNA or RNA that contains chemical information needed to make a particular protein (as an enzyme) controlling or influencing an inherited bodily trait (as eye color) or activity (as metabolism) or that influences or controls the activity of another gene or genes — **gen·ic** \'jē-nik, 'je-\ *adj*

ge·ne·al·o·gy \ˌjē-nē-'ä-lə-jē, je-, -'a-\ *n, pl* **-gies** : PEDIGREE, LINEAGE; *also* : the study of family pedigrees — **ge·ne·a·log·i·cal** \ˌjē-nē-ə-'lä-ji-kəl, je-\ *adj* — **ge·ne·a·log·i·cal·ly** \-k(ə-)lē\ *adv* — **ge·ne·al·o·gist** \ˌjē-nē-'ä-lə-jist, je-, -'a-\ *n*

gene pool *n* : the total genetic information contained in a population of interbreeding organisms

genera *pl of* GENUS

¹gen·er·al \'je-nə-rəl, 'jen-rəl\ *adj* **1** : of or relating to the whole **2** : taken as a whole **3** : relating to or covering all instances **4** : not special or specialized **5** : common to many ⟨a ∼ custom⟩ **6** : not limited in meaning : not specific **7** : holding superior rank ⟨inspector ∼⟩ ✦ *Synonyms* GENERIC, UNIVERSAL

²general *n* **1** : something that involves or is applicable to the whole **2** : a commissioned officer ranking next below a general of the army or a general of the air force **3** : a commissioned officer of the highest rank in the marine corps — **in general** : for the most part

general assembly *n* **1** : a legislative assembly; *esp* : a U.S. state legislature **2** *cap G&A* : the supreme deliberative body of the United Nations

gen·er·al·i·sa·tion, gen·er·al·ise, gen·er·al·ised *Brit var of* GENERALIZATION, GENERALIZE, GENERALIZED

gen·er·a·lis·si·mo \ˌje-nə-rə-'li-sə-ˌmō\ *n, pl* **-mos** [It, fr. *generale* general] : the chief commander of an army

gen·er·al·i·ty \ˌje-nə-'ra-lə-tē\ *n, pl* **-ties** **1** : the quality or state of being general **2** : GENERALIZATION 2 **3** : a vague or inadequate statement **4** : the greatest part : BULK

gen·er·al·i·za·tion \ˌje-nə-rə-lə-'zā-shən, ˌjen-rə-\ *n* **1** : the act or process of generalizing **2** : a general statement, law, principle, or proposition

gen·er·al·ize \'je-nə-rə-ˌlīz, 'jen-rə-\ *vb* **-ized; -iz·ing** **1** : to make general **2** : to draw general conclusions from **3** : to reach a general conclusion esp. on the basis of particular instances **4** : to extend throughout the body

gen·er·al·ly \'jen-rə-lē, 'je-nə-\ *adv* **1** : in a general manner **2** : as a rule

general of the air force : a commissioned officer of the highest rank in the air force

general of the army : a commissioned officer of the highest rank in the army

general practitioner *n* : a physician or veterinarian whose practice is not limited to a specialty

gen·er·al·ship \'je-nə-rəl-,ship, 'jen-rəl-\ *n* **1** : office or tenure of office of a general **2** : LEADERSHIP **3** : military skill as a high commander

general store *n* : a retail store that carries a wide variety of goods but is not divided into departments

gen·er·ate \'je-nə-,rāt\ *vb* **-at·ed; -at·ing** : to bring into existence : PRODUCE ⟨~ electricity⟩ ◆ *Synonyms* CREATE, ORIGINATE, PROCREATE, SPAWN

gen·er·a·tion \,je-nə-'rā-shən\ *n* **1** : a body of living beings constituting a single step in the line of descent from an ancestor; *also* : the average period between generations **2** : PRODUCTION

Generation X *n* : the generation of Americans born in the 1960s and 1970s

gen·er·a·tive \'je-nə-rə-tiv, -,rā-tiv\ *adj* : having the power or function of generating, originating, producing, or reproducing ⟨~ organs⟩

gen·er·a·tor \'je-nə-,rā-tər\ *n* : one that generates; *esp* : a machine by which mechanical energy is changed into electrical energy

ge·ner·ic \jə-'ner-ik\ *adj* **1** : not specific : GENERAL **2** : not protected by a trademark ⟨a ~ drug⟩ **3** : of or relating to a biological genus **4** : having no particularly distinctive quality ⟨~ towns⟩ — **generic** *n* — **ge·ner·i·cal·ly** \-i-k(ə-)lē\ *adv*

gen·er·ous \'je-nə-rəs\ *adj* **1** : free in giving or sharing ⟨~ donors⟩ **2** : HIGH-MINDED, NOBLE **3** : ABUNDANT, AMPLE, COPIOUS ⟨a ~ salary⟩ ◆ *Synonyms* LIBERAL, BOUNTIFUL, MUNIFICENT, OPENHANDED — **gen·er·os·i·ty** \,je-nə-'rä-sə-tē\ *n* — **gen·er·ous·ly** \'je-nə-rəs-lē\ *adv* — **gen·er·ous·ness** *n*

gen·e·sis \'je-nə-səs\ *n, pl* **-e·ses** \-,sēz\ : the origin or coming into existence of something

Genesis *n* — see BIBLE table

gene–splic·ing \-,splī-siŋ\ *n* : the process of preparing recombinant DNA

gene therapy *n* : the insertion of normal or altered genes into cells esp. to replace defective genes in the treatment of genetic disorders or to provide a specialized disease-fighting function

ge·net·ic \jə-'ne-tik\ *adj* : of or relating to the origin, development, or causes of something; *also* : of, relating to, or caused by genes or genetics ⟨~ research⟩ — **ge·net·i·cal·ly** \-ti-k(ə-)lē\ *adv*

genetic code *n* : the chemical code that is the basis of genetic inheritance and consists of units of three linked chemical groups in DNA and RNA which specify particular amino acids used to make proteins or which start or stop the process of making proteins

genetic engineering *n* : the alteration of genetic material esp. by cutting up and joining together DNA from one or more species of organism and inserting the result into an organism — **genetically engineered** *adj*

ge·net·ics \jə-'ne-tiks\ *n* : a branch of biology dealing with heredity and variation — **ge·net·i·cist** \-tə-sist\ *n*

ge·nial \'jē-nyəl, 'jē-nē-əl\ *adj* **1** : favorable to growth or comfort ⟨~ sunshine⟩ **2** : CHEERFUL, KINDLY ⟨a ~ host⟩ ◆ *Synonyms* AFFABLE, CONGENIAL, CORDIAL, GRACIOUS, SOCIABLE — **ge·nial·i·ty** \jē-nē-'a-lə-tē, jēn-'ya-\ *n* — **ge·nial·ly** *adv*

-gen·ic \'je-nik\ *adj comb form* **1** : producing : forming **2** : produced by : formed from **3** : suitable for production or reproduction by (such) a medium

ge·nie \'jē-nē\ *n, pl* **ge·nies** *also* **ge·nii** \-nē-,ī\ [F *génie*, fr. Ar *jinnī*] : a supernatural spirit that often takes human form usu. serving the person who calls on it

gen·i·tal \'je-nə-t°l\ *adj* **1** : concerned with reproduction ⟨~ organs⟩ **2** : of, relating to, or characterized by the stage of psychosexual development in psychoanalytic theory in which oral and anal impulses are subordinated to adaptive interpersonal mechanisms — **gen·i·tal·ly** *adv*

gen·i·ta·lia \,je-nə-'tāl-yə\ *n pl* : reproductive organs; *esp* : the external genital organs — **gen·i·ta·lic** \-'ta-lik, -'tā-\ *adj*

gen·i·tals \'je-nə-t°lz\ *n pl* : GENITALIA

gen·i·tive \'je-nə-tiv\ *adj* : of, relating to, or constituting a grammatical case marking typically a relationship of possessor or source — **genitive** *n*

gen·i·to·uri·nary \,je-nə-tō-'yúr-ə-,ner-ē\ *adj* : of or relating to the genital and urinary organs or functions

ge·nius \'jē-nyəs\ *n, pl* **ge·nius·es** *or* **ge·nii** \-nē-,ī\ [L, tutelary spirit, natural inclinations, fr. *gignere* to beget] **1** *pl* **genii** : an attendant spirit of a person or place; *also* : a person who influences another for good or evil **2** : a strong leaning or inclination **3** : a peculiar or distinctive character or spirit (as of a nation or a language) **4** *pl usu* **genii** : SPIRIT, GENIE **5** *pl usu* **geniuses** : a single strongly marked capacity or aptitude **6** : extraordinary intellectual power; *also* : a person having such power ◆ *Synonyms* GIFT, FACULTY, FLAIR, KNACK, TALENT

genl *abbr* general

geno·cide \'je-nə-,sīd\ *n* : the deliberate and systematic destruction of a racial, political, or cultural group

ge·nome \'jē-,nōm\ *n* **1** : one haploid set of chromosomes **2** : the genetic material of an organism

ge·no·mics \jē-'nō-miks\ *n* : a branch of biotechnology concerned esp. with investigating and collecting data about the structure and function of all or part of an organism's genome

-genous \jə-nəs\ *adj comb form* **1** : producing : yielding ⟨ero*genous*⟩ **2** : having (such) an origin ⟨endo*genous*⟩

genre \'zhän-rə, 'zhä°-; 'zhä°r; 'jän-rə\ *n* **1** : a distinctive type or category esp. of literary composition **2** : a style of painting in which everyday subjects are treated realistically

gens \'jenz, 'gens\ *n, pl* **gen·tes** \'jen-,tēz, 'gen-,täs\ [L] : a Roman clan embracing the families of the same stock in the male line

gent *n* : GENTLEMAN

gen·teel \jen-'tēl\ *adj* **1** : ARISTOCRATIC **2** : ELEGANT, STYLISH **3** : POLITE, REFINED **4** : maintaining the appearance of superior social status **5** : marked by false delicacy, prudery, or affectation — **gen·teel·ly** *adv* — **gen·teel·ness** *n*

gen·tian \'jen-chən\ *n* : any of numerous herbs with opposite leaves and showy usu. blue flowers in the fall

gen·tile \'jen-,tī(-ə)l\ *n* [ME, fr. LL *gentilis* heathen, pagan, fr. L *gent-, gens* clan, nation] **1** *often cap* : a person who is not Jewish; *esp* : a Christian as distinguished from a Jew **2** : HEATHEN, PAGAN — **gentile** *adj, often cap*

gen·til·i·ty \jen-'ti-lə-tē\ *n, pl* **-ties** **1** : good birth and family **2** : the qualities characteristic of a well-bred person **3** : good manners **4** : superior social status shown in manners or mode of life

¹gen·tle \'jen-t°l\ *adj* **gen·tler** \'jent-lər, -t°l-ər\; **gen·tlest** \'jent-ləst, -t°l-əst\ **1** : belonging to a family of high social station **2** : of, relating to, or characteristic of a gentleman **3** : KIND, AMIABLE ⟨a ~ pastor⟩ **4** : TRACTABLE, DOCILE ⟨a ~ dog⟩ **5** : not harsh, stern, or violent **6** : SOFT, DELICATE **7** : MODERATE — **gen·tle·ness** *n* — **gen·tly** *adv*

²gentle *vb* **gen·tled; gen·tling** **1** : to make or become mild, docile, soft, or moderate **2** : MOLLIFY, PLACATE

gen·tle·folk \'jen-t°l-,fōk\ *also* **gen·tle·folks** \-,fōks\ *n* : persons of good family and breeding

gen·tle·man \-mən\ *n* **1** : a man of good family **2** : a well-bred man **3** : MAN — used in pl. as a form of address — **gen·tle·man·ly** *adj*

gen·tle·wom·an \-,wú-mən\ *n* **1** : a woman of good family **2** : a woman attending a lady of rank **3** : a woman with very good manners : LADY

gen·tri·fi·ca·tion \,jen-trə-fə-'kā-shən\ *n* : the process of renewal accompanying the influx of middle-class people into deteriorating areas that often displaces earlier usu. poorer residents — **gen·tri·fy** \'jen-trə-fī\ *vb*

gen·try \'jen-trē\ *n, pl* **gentries** **1** : people of good birth, breeding, and education : ARISTOCRACY **2** : the class of English people between the nobility and the yeomanry **3** : persons of a designated class

gen·u·flect \'jen-yù-,flekt\ *vb* : to bend the knee esp. in worship — **gen·u·flec·tion** \,jen-yù-'flek-shən\ *n*

gen·u·ine \'jen-yə-wən\ *adj* **1** : AUTHENTIC, REAL ⟨a ~ signature⟩ **2** : SINCERE, HONEST ⟨their love is ~⟩ ◆ *Synonyms* BONA FIDE, TRUE, VERITABLE — **gen·u·ine·ly** *adv* — **gen·u·ine·ness** *n*

ge·nus \'jē-nəs\ *n, pl* **gen·era** \'je-nə-rə\ [L, birth, race, kind] : a category of biological classification that ranks between the family and the species and contains related species

geocentric • gewgaw 210

geo·cen·tric \ˌjē-ō-ˈsen-trik\ *adj* **1** : relating to or measured from the earth's center **2** : having or relating to the earth as a center
geo·chem·is·try \-ˈke-mə-strē\ *n* : a branch of geology that deals with the chemical composition of and chemical changes in the earth — **geo·chem·i·cal** \-mi-kəl\ *adj* — **geo·chem·ist** \-mist\ *n*
ge·ode \ˈjē-ˌōd\ *n* : a nodule of stone having a cavity lined with mineral matter
¹geo·de·sic \ˌjē-ə-ˈde-sik\ *adj* : made of light straight structural elements ⟨a ~ dome⟩
²geodesic *n* : the shortest line between two points on a surface
geo·det·ic \ˌjē-ə-ˈde-tik\ *adj* : of, relating to, or being precise measurement of the earth and its features ⟨a ~ survey⟩
geog *abbr* geographic; geographical; geography
ge·og·ra·phy \jē-ˈä-grə-fē\ *n, pl* **-phies** **1** : a science that deals with the natural features of the earth and its climate, products, and inhabitants **2** : the natural features of a region — **ge·og·ra·pher** \-fər\ *n* — **geo·graph·ic** \ˌjē-ə-ˈgra-fik\ *or* **geo·graph·i·cal** \-fi-kəl\ *adj* — **geo·graph·i·cal·ly** \-fi-k(ə-)lē\ *adv*
geol *abbr* geologic; geological; geology
ge·ol·o·gy \jē-ˈä-lə-jē\ *n, pl* **-gies** **1** : a science that deals with the history of the earth and its life esp. as recorded in rocks; *also* : a study of the features of a celestial body (as the moon) **2** : the geologic features of an area — **geo·log·ic** \ˌjē-ə-ˈlä-jik\ *or* **geo·log·i·cal** \-ji-kəl\ *adj* — **geo·log·i·cal·ly** \-ji-k(ə-)lē\ *adv* — **ge·ol·o·gist** \jē-ˈä-lə-jist\ *n*
geom *abbr* geometric; geometrical; geometry
geo·mag·net·ic \ˌjē-ō-mag-ˈne-tik\ *adj* : of or relating to the magnetism of the earth — **geo·mag·ne·tism** \-ˈmag-nə-ˌti-zəm\ *n*
geometric mean *n* : the *n*th root of the product of *n* numbers; *esp* : a number that is the second term of three consecutive terms of a geometric progression ⟨the *geometric mean* of 9 and 4 is 6⟩
geometric progression *n* : a progression (as 1, ½, ¼) in which the ratio of a term to its predecessor is always the same
ge·om·e·try \jē-ˈä-mə-trē\ *n, pl* **-tries** [ultim. fr. Gk *geōmetria*, fr. *geōmetrein* to measure the earth, fr. *gē* earth + *metron* measure] : a branch of mathematics dealing with the relations, properties, and measurements of solids, surfaces, lines, points, and angles — **ge·om·e·ter** \-tər\ *n* — **geo·met·ric** \ˌjē-ə-ˈme-trik\ *or* **geo·met·ri·cal** \-tri-kəl\ *adj*
geo·phys·ics \ˌjē-ō-ˈfi-ziks\ *n* : the physics of the earth — **geo·phys·i·cal** \-zi-kəl\ *adj* — **geo·phys·i·cist** \-zə-sist\ *n*
geo·pol·i·tics \-ˈpä-lə-ˌtiks\ *n* : a combination of political and geographic factors relating to a state — **geo·po·lit·i·cal** \-pə-ˈli-ti-kəl\ *adj*
geo·ther·mal \ˌjē-ō-ˈthər-məl\ *adj* : of, relating to, or using the heat of the earth's interior ⟨~ energy⟩
ger *abbr* gerund
Ger *abbr* German; Germany
ge·ra·ni·um \jə-ˈrā-nē-əm\ *n* [L, fr. Gk *geranion*, fr. *geranos* crane] : any of a genus of herbs with usu. deeply cut leaves and typically pink, purple, or white flowers; *also* : any of a related genus of herbs that are native to southern Africa and are widely grown for their clusters of showy usu. red, pink, or white flowers
ger·bil *also* **ger·bile** \ˈjər-bəl\ *n* : any of numerous Old World burrowing desert rodents with long hind legs
ge·ri·at·ric \ˌjer-ē-ˈa-trik\ *adj* **1** : of or relating to geriatrics or the process of aging **2** : of, relating to, or appropriate for elderly people **3** : OLD
ge·ri·at·rics \-triks\ *n* : a branch of medicine dealing with the problems and diseases of old age and aging
germ \ˈjərm\ *n* **1** : a bit of living matter capable of growth and development (as into an organism) **2** : SOURCE, RUDIMENTS **3** : MICROORGANISM; *esp* : one causing disease
Ger·man \ˈjər-mən\ *n* **1** : a native or inhabitant of Germany **2** : the language of Germany, Austria, and parts of Switzerland — **German** *adj* — **Ger·man·ic** \jər-ˈma-nik\ *adj*
ger·mane \jər-ˈmān\ *adj* [ME *germain*, lit., having the same parents, fr. AF, fr. L *germanus*, fr. *germen* sprout, bud] : RELEVANT, APPROPRIATE ♦ *Synonyms* APPLICABLE, MATERIAL, PERTINENT
ger·ma·ni·um \jər-ˈmā-nē-əm\ *n* : a grayish white hard chemical element used esp. in semiconductor and optical materials and as a catalyst
German measles *n sing or pl* : an acute contagious virus disease milder than typical measles but damaging to the fetus when occurring early in pregnancy
German shepherd *n* : any of a breed of intelligent responsive working dogs of German origin often used in police work and as guide dogs for the blind
germ cell *n* : an egg or sperm or one of their antecedent cells
ger·mi·cide \ˈjər-mə-ˌsīd\ *n* : an agent that destroys germs — **ger·mi·cid·al** \ˌjər-mə-ˈsī-dᵊl\ *adj*
ger·mi·nal \ˈjər-mə-nəl\ *adj* : of or relating to a germ or germ cell; *also* : EMBRYONIC
ger·mi·nate \ˈjər-mə-ˌnāt\ *vb* **-nat·ed; -nat·ing** **1** : to cause to develop : begin to develop : SPROUT **2** : to come into being : EVOLVE — **ger·mi·na·tion** \ˌjər-mə-ˈnā-shən\ *n*
ger·on·tol·o·gy \ˌjer-ən-ˈtä-lə-jē\ *n* : a scientific study of aging and the problems of the aged — **ge·ron·to·log·i·cal** \jə-ˌrän-tə-ˈlä-ji-kəl\ *adj* — **ger·on·tol·o·gist** \ˌjer-ən-ˈtä-lə-jist\ *n*
ger·ry·man·der \ˈjer-ē-ˌman-dər\ *vb* : to divide into election districts so as to give one political party an advantage — **gerrymander** *n*
ger·und \ˈjer-ənd\ *n* : a word having the characteristics of both verb and noun
ge·sta·po \gə-ˈstä-pō\ *n, pl* **-pos** [G, fr. *Geheime Staatspolizei*, lit., secret state police] : a usu. terrorist secret-police organization operating against persons suspected of disloyalty
ges·ta·tion \je-ˈstā-shən\ *n* : PREGNANCY, INCUBATION — **ges·tate** \ˈjes-ˌtāt\ *vb*
ges·tic·u·late \je-ˈsti-kyə-ˌlāt\ *vb* **-lat·ed; -lat·ing** : to make gestures esp. when speaking — **ges·tic·u·la·tion** \-ˌsti-kyə-ˈlā-shən\ *n*
ges·ture \ˈjes-chər\ *n* **1** : a movement usu. of the body or limbs that expresses or emphasizes an idea, sentiment, or attitude **2** : something said or done by way of formality or courtesy, as a symbol or token, or for its effect on the attitudes of others — **ges·tur·al** \-chə-rəl\ *adj* — **gesture** *vb*
ge·sund·heit \gə-ˈzùnt-ˌhīt\ *interj* [G, lit., health] — used to wish good health esp. to one who has just sneezed
¹get \ˈget\ *vb* **got** \ˈgät\; **got** *or* **got·ten** \ˈgä-tᵊn\; **get·ting** **1** : to gain possession of (as by receiving, acquiring, earning, buying, or winning) : PROCURE, OBTAIN, FETCH **2** : to succeed in coming or going ⟨*got* away to the lake⟩ **3** : to cause to come or go ⟨*got* the car to the station⟩ **4** : BEGET **5** : to cause to be in a certain condition or position ⟨don't ~ wet⟩ **6** : BECOME ⟨~ sick⟩ **7** : PREPARE **8** : SEIZE **9** : to move emotionally; *also* : IRRITATE **10** : BAFFLE, PUZZLE **11** : KILL **12** : HIT **13** : to be subjected to ⟨~ the measles⟩ **14** : to receive as punishment **15** : to find out by calculation **16** : HEAR; *also* : UNDERSTAND ⟨*got* the joke⟩ **17** : PERSUADE, INDUCE **18** : HAVE ⟨he's *got* no money⟩ **19** : to have as an obligation or necessity ⟨you have *got* to come⟩ **20** : to establish communication with **21** : to be able ⟨finally *got* to go to med school⟩ **22** : to come to be ⟨*got* talking about old times⟩ **23** : to leave at once — **get ahead** : to achieve success — **get a move on** : HURRY — **get away with** : to avoid punishment for (as a crime) — **get into** : to become strongly involved or interested in ⟨*got into* music⟩ — **get over** : to reconcile oneself to ⟨*got over* the breakup⟩
²get \ˈget\ *n* : OFFSPRING, PROGENY
get along *vb* **1** : GET BY **2** : to be on friendly terms
get·away \ˈge-tə-ˌwā\ *n* **1** : ESCAPE **2** : START **3** : a usu. brief vacation
get by *vb* : to meet one's needs
get–to·geth·er \ˈget-tə-ˌge-thər\ *n* : an informal social gathering
get·up \ˈget-ˌəp\ *n* **1** : OUTFIT, COSTUME **2** : general composition or structure
get up *vb* **1** : to arise from bed **2** : to rise to one's feet **3** : PREPARE, ORGANIZE ⟨*get up* a petition⟩ **4** : to produce in oneself by effort ⟨*get up* the courage⟩
gew·gaw \ˈgü-ˌgò, ˈgyü-\ *n* : a showy trifle : BAUBLE, TRINKET

gey·ser \'gī-zər\ *n* [Icelandic *Geysir,* hot spring in Iceland] : a spring that intermittently shoots up hot water and steam

g–force \'jē-,fórs\ *n* : the force of gravity or acceleration on a body

ghast·ly \'gast-lē\ *adj* **ghast·li·er; -est** **1** : HORRIBLE, SHOCKING **2** : resembling a ghost : DEATHLIKE, PALE ✦ *Synonyms* GRUESOME, GRIM, LURID, GRISLY, MACABRE

ghat \'gót\ *n* [Hindi & Urdu *ghāṭ*] : a broad flight of steps on an Indian riverbank that provides access to the water

gher·kin \'gər-kən\ *n* **1** : a small prickly fruit of a vine related to the cucumber used to make pickles **2** : an immature cucumber

ghet·to \'ge-tō\ *n, pl* **ghettos** *or* **ghettoes** : a quarter of a city in which members of a minority group live because of social, legal, or economic pressure

¹ghost \'gōst\ *n* **1** : the seat of life : SOUL **2** : a disembodied soul; *esp* : the soul of a dead person believed to be an inhabitant of the unseen world or to appear in bodily form to living people **3** : SPIRIT, DEMON **4** : a faint trace ⟨a ∼ of a smile⟩ **5** : a false image in a photographic negative or on a television screen — **ghost·ly** *adv*

²ghost *vb* : GHOSTWRITE

ghost·write \-,rīt\ *vb* **-wrote** \-,rōt\; **-writ·ten** \-,ri-t⁹n\ : to write for and in the name of another — **ghost·writ·er** *n*

ghoul \'gül\ *n* [Ar *ghūl*] : a legendary evil being that robs graves and feeds on corpses — **ghoul·ish** *adj*

GHQ *abbr* general headquarters

gi *abbr* gill

¹GI \,jē-'ī\ *adj* [galvanized *i*ron; fr. abbr. used in listing such articles as garbage cans, but taken as abbr. for *government issue*] **1** : provided by an official U.S. military supply department ⟨∼ shoes⟩ **2** : of, relating to, or characteristic of U.S. military personnel **3** : conforming to military regulations or customs ⟨a ∼ haircut⟩

²GI *n, pl* **GIs** *or* **GI's** \-'īz\ : a member or former member of the U.S. armed forces; *esp* : an enlisted person

³GI *abbr* **1** galvanized iron **2** gastrointestinal **3** general issue **4** government issue

gi·ant \'jī-ənt\ *n* **1** : a legendary humanlike being of great size and strength **2** : a living being or thing of extraordinary size or powers — **giant** *adj*

gi·ant·ess \'jī-ən-təs\ *n* : a female giant

giant panda *n* : PANDA 2

gib·ber \'ji-bər\ *vb* : to speak rapidly, inarticulately, and often foolishly

gib·ber·ish \'ji-bə-rish\ *n* : unintelligible or confused speech or language

¹gib·bet \'ji-bət\ *n* : GALLOWS

²gibbet *vb* **1** : to hang on a gibbet **2** : to expose to public scorn **3** : to execute by hanging

gib·bon \'gi-bən\ *n* : any of several tailless apes of southeastern Asia

gib·bous \'ji-bəs, 'gi-\ *adj* **1** : rounded like the exterior of a sphere or circle **2** : seen with more than half but not all of the apparent disk illuminated ⟨∼ moon⟩ **3** : having a hump : HUMPBACKED

gibe *or* **jibe** \'jīb\ *vb* **gibed** *or* **jibed; gib·ing** *or* **jib·ing** : to utter taunting words : SNEER — **gibe** *or* **jibe** *n*

gib·lets \'jib-ləts\ *n pl* : the edible viscera of a fowl

Gib·son girl \'gib-sən-\ *adj* : of or relating to a style in women's clothing characterized by high necks, full sleeves, and slender waistlines

gid·dy \'gi-dē\ *adj* **gid·di·er; -est** **1** : DIZZY **2** : causing dizziness ⟨a ∼ height⟩ **3** : not serious : FRIVOLOUS, SILLY — **gid·di·ness** \-dē-nəs\ *n*

gid·dy·ap \,gi-dē-'ap, -'əp\ *or* **gid·dy·up** \-'əp\ *vb imper* — a command (as to a horse) to go ahead or go faster

GIF \'gif, 'jif\ *n* [graphic *i*nterchange *f*ormat] : a computer file format for digital images; *also* : the image itself

gift \'gift\ *n* **1** : a special ability : TALENT **2** : something given : PRESENT **3** : the act or power of giving

gift card *n* : a card entitling the recipient to goods or services of a specified value from the issuer

gift·ed \'gif-təd\ *adj* : TALENTED

¹gig \'gig\ *n* **1** : a long light ship's boat **2** : a light 2-wheeled one-horse carriage

²gig *n* : a pronged spear for catching fish — **gig** *vb*

³gig *n* : a job for a specified time; *esp* : an entertainer's engagement

⁴gig *n* : a military demerit — **gig** *vb*

giga·byte \'ji-gə-,bīt, 'gi-\ *n* : 1024 megabytes or 1,073,741,824 bytes; *also* : one billion bytes

gi·gan·tic \jī-'gan-tik\ *adj* : exceeding the usual (as in size or force)

gig·gle \'gi-gəl\ *vb* **gig·gled; gig·gling** : to laugh with repeated short catches of the breath — **giggle** *n* — **gig·gly** \-gə-lē\ *adj*

GIGO *abbr* garbage in, garbage out

gig·o·lo \'ji-gə-,lō\ *n, pl* **-los** **1** : a man supported by a woman usu. in return for his attentions **2** : a professional dancing partner or male escort

Gi·la monster \'hē-lə-\ *n* : a large orange and black venomous lizard of the southwestern U.S.

¹gild \'gild\ *vb* **gild·ed** *or* **gilt** \'gilt\; **gild·ing** **1** : to overlay with or as if with a thin covering of gold **2** : to give an attractive but often deceptive appearance to

²gild *var of* GUILD

¹gill \'jil\ *n* — see WEIGHT table

²gill \'gil\ *n* : an organ (as of a fish) for obtaining oxygen from water

¹gilt \'gilt\ *adj* : of the color of gold

²gilt *n* : gold or a substance resembling gold laid on the surface of an object

³gilt *n* : a young female swine

¹gim·crack \'jim-,krak\ *n* : a showy object of little use or value

²gimcrack *adj* : CHEAP, SHODDY

gim·let \'gim-lət\ *n* : a small tool with screw point and cross handle for boring holes

gim·me cap \'gi-mē-\ *n* : an adjustable visored cap featuring a corporate logo or slogan

gim·mick \'gi-mik\ *n* **1** : CONTRIVANCE, GADGET **2** : an important feature that is not immediately apparent : CATCH **3** : a new and ingenious scheme **4** : a device used to attract business or attention — **gim·micky** \-mi-kē\ *adj*

gim·mick·ry \'gi-mi-krē\ *n, pl* **-ries** : an array of or the use of gimmicks

gimpy \'gim-pē\ *adj* : LAME 1

¹gin \'jin\ *n* [ME *gin,* fr. AF, short for *engin* engine] **1** : TRAP, SNARE **2** : a machine to separate seeds from cotton — **gin** *vb*

²gin *n* [by shortening & alter. fr. *geneva,* fr. MD *genever,* alter. fr. ML *juniperus* juniper] : a liquor distilled from a grain mash and flavored with juniper berries

gin·ger \'jin-jər\ *n* : the pungent aromatic rootstock of a tropical plant used esp. as a spice and in medicine; *also* : the spice or the plant

ginger ale *n* : a carbonated soft drink flavored with ginger

gin·ger·bread \'jin-jər-,bred\ *n* **1** : a cake made with molasses and flavored with ginger **2** : lavish or superfluous ornament esp. in architecture

gin·ger·ly \'jin-jər-lē\ *adj* : very cautious or careful — **gingerly** *adv*

gin·ger·snap \-,snap\ *n* : a thin brittle molasses cookie flavored with ginger

ging·ham \'giŋ-əm\ *n* : a cotton cloth that is often marked with a pattern of colored squares

gin·gi·vi·tis \,jin-jə-'vī-təs\ *n* : inflammation of the gums

gink·go *also* **ging·ko** \'giŋ-(,)kō\ *n, pl* **ginkgoes** *or* **ginkgos** *also* **gingkos** *or* **gingkoes** **1** : a tree of eastern China with fan-shaped leaves often grown as a shade tree **2** : GINKGO BILOBA

ginkgo bi·lo·ba \-,bī-'lō-bə\ *n* : an extract of the leaves of ginkgo that is held to enhance mental functioning

¹gig 2

gin·seng \'jin-ˌseŋ\ *n* : an aromatic root of a Chinese or No. American herb used esp. in Chinese medicine; *also* : one of these herbs

Gip·sy *chiefly Brit var of* GYPSY

gi·raffe \jə-'raf\ *n, pl* **giraffes** [It *giraffa*, fr. Ar *zirāfa*] : an African ruminant mammal with a very long neck and a short coat with dark blotches

gird \'gərd\ *vb* **gird·ed** *or* **girt** \'gərt\; **gird·ing** 1 : to encircle or fasten (as a sword) with or as if with a belt 2 : to invest esp. with power or authority 3 : PREPARE, BRACE

gird·er \'gər-dər\ *n* : a horizontal main supporting beam

gir·dle \'gər-dᵊl\ *n* 1 : something (as a belt or sash) that encircles or confines 2 : a woman's supporting undergarment that extends from the waist to below the hips — **girdle** *vb*

girl \'gərl\ *n* 1 : a female child 2 : a young woman 3 : SWEETHEART — **girl·hood** \-ˌhủd\ *n* — **girl·ish** *adj*

girl Friday *n* : a female assistant (as in an office) entrusted with a wide variety of tasks

girl·friend \'gərl-ˌfrend\ *n* 1 : a female friend 2 : a regular female companion in a romantic or sexual relationship

Girl Scout *n* : a member of any of the scouting programs of the Girl Scouts of the United States of America

girth \'gərth\ *n* 1 : a band around an animal by which something (as a saddle) may be fastened on its back 2 : a measure around something

gist \'jist\ *n* [AF, it lies, fr. *gesir* to lie, ultim. fr. L *jacēre*] : the main point or part ⟨the ∼ of his speech⟩

git *dial var of* GET

¹give \'giv\ *vb* **gave** \'gāv\; **giv·en** \'gi-vən\; **giv·ing** 1 : to make a present of 2 : to bestow by formal action 3 : to accord or yield to another 4 : to yield to force, strain, or pressure 5 : to put into the possession or keeping of another 6 : PROFFER ⟨*gave* her his hand⟩ 7 : DELIVER ⟨*gave* the bride away⟩ 8 : to present in public performance or to view 9 : PROVIDE ⟨∼ a party⟩ 10 : ATTRIBUTE 11 : to make, form, or yield as a product or result ⟨cows ∼ milk⟩ 12 : PAY 13 : to deliver by some bodily action ⟨*gave* me a push⟩ 14 : to offer as a pledge ⟨I ∼ you my word⟩ 15 : DEVOTE 16 : to cause to have or receive ⟨∼ me time⟩

²give *n* 1 : capacity or tendency to yield to force or strain 2 : the quality or state of being springy

give–and–take \ˌgiv-ən-'tāk\ *n* 1 : COMPROMISE 2 : a usu. good-natured exchange (as of remarks or ideas)

give·away \'gi-və-ˌwā\ *n* 1 : an unintentional revelation or betrayal 2 : something given away free; *esp* : PREMIUM

give in *vb* : SUBMIT, SURRENDER

¹giv·en \'gi-vən\ *adj* 1 : DISPOSED, INCLINED ⟨∼ to swearing⟩ 2 : SPECIFIED, PARTICULAR ⟨at a ∼ time⟩

²given *n* : something taken for granted : a basic condition or assumption

³given *prep* : CONSIDERING

given name *n* : a name that precedes one's surname

give out *vb* 1 : EMIT 2 : BREAK DOWN 3 : to become exhausted : COLLAPSE

give up *vb* 1 : SURRENDER 2 : to abandon (oneself) to a feeling, influence, or activity 3 : QUIT ⟨*gave up* his job⟩

giz·mo *also* **gis·mo** \'giz-mō\ *n, pl* **gizmos** *also* **gismos** : GADGET

giz·zard \'gi-zərd\ *n* : the muscular usu. horny-lined enlargement of the alimentary canal of a bird used for churning and grinding up food

gla·cial \'glā-shəl\ *adj* 1 : extremely cold 2 : of or relating to glaciers 3 : being or relating to a past period of time when a large part of the earth was covered by glaciers 4 *cap* : PLEISTOCENE 5 : very slow ⟨a ∼ pace⟩ — **gla·cial·ly** *adv*

gla·ci·ate \'glā-shē-ˌāt\ *vb* **-at·ed; -at·ing** 1 : to subject to glacial action 2 : to produce glacial effects in or on — **gla·ci·a·tion** \ˌglā-shē-'ā-shən, -sē-\ *n*

gla·cier \'glā-shər\ *n* [F, fr. MF dial. (Savoy), fr. *glace* ice, fr. L *glacies*] : a large body of ice moving slowly down a slope or spreading outward on a land surface

¹glad \'glad\ *adj* **glad·der; glad·dest** 1 : experiencing pleasure, joy, or delight 2 : PLEASED 3 : very willing ⟨was ∼ to help⟩ 4 : PLEASANT, JOYFUL ⟨a ∼ morning⟩ — **glad·ly** *adv* — **glad·ness** *n*

²glad *n* : GLADIOLUS

glad·den \'gla-dᵊn\ *vb* : to make glad

glade \'glād\ *n* : a grassy open space surrounded by woods

glad·i·a·tor \'gla-dē-ˌā-tər\ *n* 1 : a person engaged in a fight to the death for public entertainment in ancient Rome 2 : a person engaging in a public fight or controversy; *also* : PRIZEFIGHTER — **glad·i·a·to·ri·al** \ˌgla-dē-ə-'tȯr-ē-əl\ *adj*

glad·i·o·lus \ˌgla-dē-'ō-ləs\ *n, pl* **-oli** \-'ō-(ˌ)lē, -ˌlī\ *or* **-olus** *also* **-o·lus·es** [L, fr. dim. of *gladius* sword] : any of a genus of chiefly African plants related to the irises and having erect sword-shaped leaves and stalks of bright-colored flowers

glad·some \'glad-səm\ *adj* : giving or showing joy : CHEERFUL

glam \'glam\ *n* : extravagantly showy glamour — **glam** *adj*

glam·or·ise *Brit var of* GLAMORIZE

glam·or·ize *also* **glam·our·ize** \'gla-mə-ˌrīz\ *vb* **-ized; -iz·ing** : to make or look upon as glamorous

glam·our *also* **glam·or** \'gla-mər\ *n* [Sc *glamour* magic spell, alter. of E *grammar*; fr. the popular association of erudition with occult practices] : an exciting and often illusory and romantic attractiveness; *esp* : alluring personal attraction — **glam·or·ous** *also* **glam·our·ous** \-mə-rəs\ *adj*

¹glance \'glans\ *vb* **glanced; glanc·ing** 1 : to strike and fly off to one side 2 : GLEAM 3 : to give a quick look

²glance *n* 1 : a quick intermittent flash or gleam 2 : a deflected impact or blow 3 : a quick look

gland \'gland\ *n* : a cell or group of cells that prepares and secretes a substance (as saliva or sweat) for further use in or discharge from the body

glan·du·lar \'glan-jə-lər\ *adj* : of, relating to, or involving glands

glans \'glanz\ *n, pl* **glan·des** \'glan-ˌdēz\ [L, lit., acorn] : a conical vascular body forming the extremity of the penis or clitoris

¹glare \'gler\ *vb* **glared; glar·ing** 1 : to shine with a harsh dazzling light 2 : to stare fiercely or angrily

²glare *n* 1 : a harsh dazzling light 2 : an angry or fierce stare

glaring *adj* : very conspicuous ⟨a ∼ error⟩ — **glar·ing·ly** *adv*

glass \'glas\ *n* 1 : a hard brittle amorphous usu. transparent or translucent material consisting typically of silica 2 : something made of glass; *esp* : TUMBLER 2 3 *pl* : a pair of lenses used to correct defects of vision : SPECTACLES 4 : the quantity held by a glass container — **glass** *adj* — **glass·ful** \-ˌfủl\ *n* — **glassy** *adj*

glass·blow·ing \-ˌblō-iŋ\ *n* : the art of shaping a mass of glass that has been softened by heat by blowing air into it through a tube — **glass·blow·er** *n*

glass·ware \-ˌwer\ *n* : articles made of glass

glau·co·ma \glaủ-'kō-mə, glȯ-\ *n* : a disease of the eye marked by increased pressure within the eyeball resulting in damage to the retina and gradual loss of vision

¹glaze \'glāz\ *vb* **glazed; glaz·ing** 1 : to furnish (as a window frame) with glass 2 : to apply glaze to

²glaze *n* : a glassy coating or surface

gla·zier \'glā-zhər\ *n* : a person who sets glass in window frames

¹gleam \'glēm\ *n* 1 : a transient subdued or partly obscured light 2 : GLINT 3 : a faint trace ⟨a ∼ of hope⟩

²gleam *vb* 1 : to shine with subdued light or moderate brightness 2 : to appear briefly or faintly ✦ **Synonyms** FLASH, GLIMMER, GLISTEN, GLITTER, SHIMMER, SPARKLE

glean \'glēn\ *vb* 1 : to gather grain left by reapers 2 : to collect little by little or with patient effort ⟨antiques ∼ed from flea markets⟩ — **glean·able** *adj* — **glean·er** *n*

glean·ings \'glē-niŋz\ *n pl* : things acquired by gleaning

glee \'glē\ *n* [ME, fr. OE *glēo* entertainment, music] 1 : JOY, HILARITY 2 : a part-song for three usu. male voices — **glee·ful** *adj* — **glee·ful·ly** *adv*

glee club *n* : a chorus organized for singing usu. short choral pieces

glen \'glen\ *n* : a narrow hidden valley

glen·gar·ry \glen-'ga-rē\ *n, pl* **-ries** *often cap* : a woolen cap of Scottish origin

glib \'glib\ *adj* **glib·ber; glib·best** : speaking or spoken with careless ease — **glib·ly** *adv*

glide \'glīd\ *vb* **glid·ed; glid·ing** 1 : to move smoothly and effortlessly 2 : to descend gradually without engine power ⟨∼ in an airplane⟩ — **glide** *n*

glid·er \'glī-dər\ *n* **1** : one that glides **2** : an aircraft resembling an airplane but having no engine **3** : a porch seat suspended from an upright frame

¹glim·mer \'gli-mər\ *vb* : to shine faintly or unsteadily

²glimmer *n* **1** : a faint unsteady light **2** : INKLING **3** : a small amount : HINT

¹glimpse \'glimps\ *vb* **glimpsed; glimps·ing** : to take a brief look : see momentarily or incompletely

²glimpse *n* **1** : a faint idea : GLIMMER **2** : a short hurried look

glint \'glint\ *vb* **1** : to shine by reflection : SPARKLE, GLITTER, GLEAM **2** : to appear briefly or faintly — **glint** *n*

glis·san·do \gli-'sän-(ˌ)dō\ *n, pl* **-di** \-(ˌ)dē\ *or* **-dos** : a rapid sliding up or down the musical scale

¹glis·ten \'gli-sᵊn\ *vb* : to shine by reflection with a soft luster or sparkle

²glisten *n* : GLITTER, SPARKLE

glis·ter \'glis-tər\ *vb* : GLITTER

glitch \'glich\ *n* : MALFUNCTION; *also* : SNAG 2

¹glit·ter \'gli-tər\ *vb* **1** : to shine with brilliant or metallic luster : SPARKLE **2** : to shine with strong emotion : FLASH ⟨eyes ∼*ing* in anger⟩ **3** : to be brilliantly attractive esp. in a superficial way

²glitter *n* **1** : sparkling brilliancy, showiness, or attractiveness **2** : small glittering objects used for ornamentation — **glit·tery** \'gli-tə-rē\ *adj*

¹glitz \'glits\ *n* : extravagant showiness — **glitzy** \'glit-sē\ *adj*

²glitz *vb* : to make flashy or extravagant in appearance — often used with *up*

gloam·ing \'glō-miŋ\ *n* : TWILIGHT, DUSK

gloat \'glōt\ *vb* : to think about something with triumphant and often malicious delight ⟨∼*ing* over their victory⟩

glob \'gläb\ *n* **1** : a small drop **2** : a large rounded mass

glob·al \'glō-bəl\ *adj* **1** : WORLDWIDE **2** : COMPREHENSIVE, GENERAL — **glob·al·ly** *adv*

glob·al·i·za·tion \ˌglō-bə-lə-'zā-shən\ *n* : the development of an increasingly integrated global economy

Global Positioning System *n* : GPS

global warming *n* : an increase in the earth's atmospheric and oceanic temperatures due to an increase in the greenhouse effect

globe \'glōb\ *n* **1** : BALL, SPHERE **2** : EARTH; *also* : a spherical representation of the earth

globe-trot·ter \'glōb-ˌträ-tər\ *n* : a person who travels widely — **globe-trot·ting** *n or adj*

glob·u·lar \'glä-byə-lər\ *adj* : having the shape of a globe or globule

glob·ule \'glä-(ˌ)byül\ *n* : a tiny globe or ball esp. of a liquid

glob·u·lin \'glä-byə-lən\ *n* : any of a class of simple proteins insoluble in pure water but soluble in dilute salt solutions that occur widely in plant and animal tissues

glock·en·spiel \'glä-kən-ˌshpēl, -ˌspēl\ *n* [G, fr. *Glocke* bell + *Spiel* play] : a percussion musical instrument consisting of a series of metal bars played with two hammers

gloom \'glüm\ *n* **1** : partial or total darkness **2** : lowness of spirits : DEJECTION **3** : an atmosphere of despondency ⟨a ∼ fell over the household⟩ — **gloom·i·ly** \'glü-mə-lē\ *adv* — **gloom·i·ness** \-mē-nəs\ *n* — **gloomy** \'glü-mē\ *adj*

Gloomy Gus \-'gəs\ *n, pl* **Gloomy Gus·es** : a person who is habitually gloomy

glop \'gläp\ *n* : a messy mass or mixture

glo·ri·fy \'glȯr-ə-ˌfī\ *vb* **-fied; -fy·ing 1** : to raise to heavenly glory **2** : to light up brilliantly **3** : EXTOL **4** : to give glory to (as in worship) — **glo·ri·fi·ca·tion** \ˌglȯr-ə-fə-'kā-shən\ *n*

glo·ri·ous \'glȯr-ē-əs\ *adj* **1** : possessing or deserving glory : PRAISEWORTHY **2** : conferring glory **3** : RESPLENDENT, MAGNIFICENT ⟨a ∼ sunset⟩ **4** : DELIGHTFUL, WONDERFUL ⟨had a ∼ weekend⟩ — **glo·ri·ous·ly** *adv*

¹glo·ry \'glȯr-ē\ *n, pl* **glories 1** : RENOWN **2** : honor and praise rendered in worship **3** : something that secures praise or renown **4** : a distinguishing quality or asset **5** : RESPLENDENCE, MAGNIFICENCE **6** : heavenly bliss **7** : a height of prosperity or achievement

²glory *vb* **glo·ried; glo·ry·ing** : to rejoice proudly : EXULT

¹gloss \'gläs, 'glȯs\ *n* **1** : LUSTER, SHEEN, BRIGHTNESS **2** : outward show

²gloss *vb* **1** : to give a false appearance of acceptableness to ⟨∼ over inadequacies⟩ **2** : to deal with too lightly or not at all ⟨∼*ed* over the problem⟩

³gloss *n* [alter. of *gloze*, fr. ME *glose*, fr. AF, fr. ML *glosa*, *glossa*, fr. Gk *glōssa*, *glōtta* tongue, language, unusual word] **1** : an explanatory note (as in the margin of a text) **2** : GLOSSARY **3** : an interlinear translation **4** : a continuous commentary accompanying a text

⁴gloss *vb* : to furnish glosses for

glos·sa·ry \'glä-sə-rē, 'glȯ-\ *n, pl* **-ries** : a collection of difficult or specialized terms with their meanings — **glos·sar·i·al** \glä-'ser-ē-əl, glȯ-\ *adj*

glos·so·la·lia \ˌglä-sə-'lā-lē-ə, ˌglȯ-\ *n* [ultim. fr. Gk *glōssa* tongue, language + *lalia* chatter] : TONGUE 6

¹glossy \'glä-sē, 'glȯ-\ *adj* **gloss·i·er; -est** : having a surface luster or brightness — **gloss·i·ly** \-sə-lē\ *adv* — **gloss·i·ness** \-sē-nəs\ *n*

²glossy *n, pl* **gloss·ies** : a photograph printed on smooth shiny paper

glot·tis \'glä-təs\ *n, pl* **glot·tis·es** *or* **glot·ti·des** \-tə-ˌdēz\ : the slitlike opening between the vocal cords in the larynx — **glot·tal** \'glä-tᵊl\ *adj*

glove \'gləv\ *n* **1** : a covering for the hand having separate sections for each finger **2** : a padded leather covering for the hand for use in a sport

¹glow \'glō\ *vb* **1** : to shine with or as if with intense heat **2** : to have a rich warm usu. ruddy color : FLUSH, BLUSH **3** : to feel hot **4** : to show exuberance or elation ⟨∼ with pride⟩

²glow *n* **1** : brightness or warmth of color; *esp* : REDNESS **2** : warmth of feeling or emotion **3** : a sensation of warmth **4** : light such as is emitted from a heated substance

glow·er \'glaů-(ə)r\ *vb* : to stare angrily : SCOWL — **glower** *n*

glow·worm \'glō-ˌwərm\ *n* : any of various insect larvae or adults that give off light

glox·in·ia \gläk-'si-nē-ə\ *n* : any of a genus of tropical herbs related to the African violets; *esp* : one with showy bell-shaped or slipper-shaped flowers

gloze \'glōz\ *vb* **glozed; gloz·ing** : to make appear right or acceptable : GLOSS

glu·cose \'glü-ˌkōs\ *n* **1** : a form of crystalline sugar; *esp* : DEXTROSE **2** : a sweet light-colored syrup made from cornstarch

glue \'glü\ *n* : a jellylike protein substance made from animal materials and used for sticking things together; *also* : any of various other strong adhesives — **glue** *vb* — **glu·ey** \'glü-ē\ *adj*

glum \'gləm\ *adj* **glum·mer; glum·mest 1** : broodingly morose : SULLEN **2** : DREARY, GLOOMY ⟨a ∼ countenance⟩ ♦ **Synonyms** CRABBED, DOUR, SATURNINE, SULKY

¹glut \'glət\ *vb* **glut·ted; glut·ting 1** : OVERSUPPLY **2** : to fill esp. with food to satiety : SATIATE

²glut *n* : an excessive supply

glu·ten \'glü-tᵊn\ *n* : a gluey protein substance that causes dough to be sticky

glu·ti·nous \'glü-tə-nəs\ *adj* : STICKY

glut·ton \'glə-tᵊn\ *n* : one that eats to excess — **glut·ton·ous** \'glə-tə-nəs\ *adj* — **glut·tony** \'glə-tə-nē\ *n*

glyc·er·in *or* **glyc·er·ine** \'gli-sə-rən\ *n* : GLYCEROL

glyc·er·ol \'gli-sə-ˌrȯl, -ˌrōl\ *n* : a sweet syrupy alcohol usu. obtained from fats and used esp. as a solvent

gly·co·gen \'glī-kə-jən\ *n* : a white tasteless substance that is the chief storage carbohydrate of animals

gm *abbr* gram

GM *abbr* **1** general manager **2** guided missile

G-man \'jē-ˌman\ *n* : a special agent of the Federal Bureau of Investigation

GMT *abbr* Greenwich mean time

gnarled \'närld\ *adj* **1** : KNOTTY ⟨∼ hands⟩ **2** : GLOOMY, SULLEN

gnash \'nash\ *vb* : to grind (as teeth) together

gnat \'nat\ *n* : any of various small usu. biting dipteran flies

gnaw \'nȯ\ *vb* **1** : to consume, wear away, or make by persistent biting or nibbling **2** : to affect as if by gnawing — **gnaw·er** *n*

gneiss \'nīs\ *n* : a layered rock similar in composition to granite

gnome \'nōm\ *n* : a dwarf of folklore who lives inside the earth and guards precious ore or treasure — **gnome-like** \-ˌlīk\ *adj* — **gnom·ish** *adj*

GNP *abbr* gross national product
gnu \'nü\ *n, pl* **gnu** *or* **gnus** : WILDEBEEST
¹**go** \'gō\ *vb* **went** \'went\; **gone** \'gȯn, 'gän\; **go·ing; goes**
\'gōz\ **1** : to move on a course : PROCEED ⟨~ slow⟩ **2**
: LEAVE, DEPART **3** : to take a certain course or follow a
certain procedure ⟨reports ~ through department chan-
nels⟩ **4** : EXTEND, RUN ⟨his land ~*es* to the river⟩; *also*
: LEAD ⟨that door ~*es* to the cellar⟩ **5** : to be habitually in a certain state ⟨~*es* barefoot⟩ **6** : to become lost,
consumed, or spent; *also* : DIE **7** : ELAPSE, PASS **8** : to
pass by sale ⟨went for a good price⟩ **9** : to become impaired or weakened ⟨his hearing started to ~⟩ **10** : to
give way under force or pressure : BREAK **11** : to move
along in a specified manner ⟨it *went* well⟩ **12** : to be in
general or on an average ⟨cheap, as yachts ~⟩ **13** : to
become esp. as the result of a contest ⟨the decision *went*
against him⟩ **14** : to put or subject oneself ⟨~ to great
expense⟩ **15** : RESORT ⟨went to court to recover dam-
ages⟩ **16** : to begin or maintain an action or motion **17**
: to function properly ⟨the clock doesn't ~⟩ **18** : to be
known ⟨~*es* by an alias⟩ **19** : to be or act in accordance
⟨a good rule to ~ by⟩ **20** : to come to be applied **21**
: to pass by award, assignment, or lot **22** : to contribute to a result ⟨qualities that ~ to make a hero⟩ **23** : to
be about, intending, or expecting something ⟨is ~*ing*
to leave town⟩ **24** : to arrive at a certain state or condition ⟨~ to sleep⟩ **25** : to come to be ⟨the tire *went*
flat⟩ **26** : to be capable of being sung or played ⟨the
tune ~*es* like this⟩ **27** : to be suitable or becoming
: HARMONIZE **28** : to be capable of passing, extending,
or being contained or inserted ⟨this coat will ~ in the
trunk⟩ **29** : to have a usual or proper place or position
: BELONG ⟨these books ~ on the top shelf⟩ **30** : to be
capable of being divided ⟨3 ~*es* into 6 twice⟩ **31** : to
have a tendency ⟨that ~*es* to show that he is honest⟩ **32**
: to be acceptable, satisfactory, or adequate ⟨any color
will ~ with black⟩ **33** : to empty the bladder or bowels **34** : to proceed along or according to : FOLLOW **35**
: TRAVERSE **36** : BET, BID ⟨willing to ~ $50⟩ **37** : to as-
sume the function or obligation of ⟨~ bail for a friend⟩
38 : to participate to the extent of ⟨~ halves⟩ **39**
: WEIGH **40** : ENDURE, TOLERATE **41** : AFFORD ⟨can't
~ the price⟩ **42** : SAY — used chiefly in oral narration
of speech **43** : to engage in ⟨don't ~ telling everyone⟩
— go at 1 : ATTACK, ATTEMPT **2** : UNDERTAKE **— go
back on 1** : ABANDON **2** : BETRAY **3** : FAIL **— go by
the board** : to be discarded **— go for 1** : to pass for or
serve as **2** : to try to secure **3** : FAVOR **— go one better**
: OUTDO, SURPASS **— go over 1** : EXAMINE **2** : REPEAT
3 : STUDY, REVIEW **— go places** : to be on the way to
success **— go steady** : to date one person exclusively **—
go to bat for** : DEFEND, CHAMPION **— go to town 1** : to
work or act efficiently **2** : to be very successful
²**go** *n, pl* **goes 1** : the act or manner of going **2** : the
height of fashion ⟨boots are all the ~⟩ **3** : a turn of affairs : OCCURRENCE **4** : ENERGY, VIGOR **5** : ATTEMPT,
TRY ⟨give it a ~⟩ **6** : a spell of activity ⟨finished the job
at one ~⟩ **— no go** : USELESS, HOPELESS **— on the go**
: constantly active
³**go** *adj* : functioning properly ⟨declared all systems ~⟩
goad \'gōd\ *n* [ME *gode,* fr. OE *gād* spear, goad] **1** : a
pointed rod used to urge on an animal **2** : something that
urges ♦ **Synonyms** STIMULUS, IMPETUS, INCENTIVE,
SPUR, STIMULANT — **goad** *vb*
go–ahead \'gō-ə-ˌhed\ *n* : authority to proceed ⟨got the
~ for the project⟩
goal \'gōl\ *n* **1** : the mark set as limit to a race; *also* : an
area to be reached safely in children's games **2** : AIM,
PURPOSE **3** : an area or object toward which play is directed to score; *also* : a successful attempt to score
goal·ie \'gō-lē\ *n* : GOALKEEPER
goal·keep·er \'gōl-ˌkē-pər\ *n* : a player who defends the
goal in various games
goal·post \-ˌpōst\ *n* : one of the two vertical posts with a
crossbar that constitute the goal in various games
goat \'gōt\ *n, pl* **goats** *or* **goat** : any of various hollow-
horned ruminant mammals related to the sheep that have
backward-curving horns, a short tail, and usu. straight
hair
goa·tee \gō-'tē\ *n* : a small trim pointed or tufted beard
on a man's chin

goat·herd \'gōt-ˌhərd\ *n* : a person who tends goats
goat·skin \-ˌskin\ *n* : the skin of a goat or a leather made
from it
¹**gob** \'gäb\ *n* : LUMP, MASS
²**gob** *n* : SAILOR
gob·bet \'gä-bət\ *n* : LUMP, MASS
¹**gob·ble** \'gä-bəl\ *vb* **gob·bled; gob·bling 1** : to swallow
or eat greedily **2** : to take eagerly : GRAB
²**gobble** *vb* **gob·bled; gob·bling** : to make the natural guttural noise of a male turkey
gob·ble·dy·gook *also* **gob·ble·de·gook** \'gä-bəl-dē-ˌgük,
-ˌgük\ *n* : generally unintelligible jargon
gob·bler \'gä-blər\ *n* : a male turkey
go–be·tween \'gō-bə-ˌtwēn\ *n* : an intermediate agent : BRO-
KER
gob·let \'gä-blət\ *n* : a drinking glass with a foot and stem
gob·lin \'gä-blən\ *n* : an ugly or grotesque sprite that is
mischievous and sometimes evil and malicious
go·by \'gō-bē\ *n, pl* **gobies** *also* **goby** : any of numerous
spiny-finned fishes usu. having the pelvic fins united to
form a ventral sucking disk
god \'gäd, 'gȯd\ *n* **1** *cap* : the supreme reality; *esp* : the
Being worshiped as the creator and ruler of the universe
2 : a being or object believed to have supernatural attributes and powers and to require worship **3** : a thing of
supreme value **4** : an extraordinarily attractive person
god·child \'gäd-ˌchī(-ə)ld, 'gȯd-\ *n* : a person for whom
another person stands as sponsor at baptism
god·daugh·ter \-ˌdȯ-tər\ *n* : a female godchild
god·dess \'gä-dəs, 'gȯ-\ *n* **1** : a female god **2** : a woman
whose charm or beauty arouses adoration
god·fa·ther \'gäd-ˌfä-t͟hər, 'gȯd-\ *n* **1** : a man who sponsors a person at baptism **2** : the leader of an organized
crime syndicate
god·head \-ˌhed\ *n* **1** : divine nature or essence **2** *cap*
: GOD 1; *also* : the nature of God esp. as existing in three
persons
god·hood \-ˌhùd\ *n* : DIVINITY
god·less \-ləs\ *adj* : not acknowledging a deity or divine
law — **god·less·ness** *n*
god·like \-ˌlīk\ *adj* : resembling or having the qualities of
God or a god
god·ly \-lē\ *adj* **god·li·er; -est 1** : DIVINE **2** : PIOUS, DE-
VOUT — **god·li·ness** *n*
god·moth·er \-ˌmə-t͟hər\ *n* : a woman who sponsors a person at baptism
god·par·ent \-ˌper-ənt\ *n* : a sponsor at baptism
god·send \-ˌsend\ *n* : a desirable or needed thing or event
that comes unexpectedly
god·son \-ˌsən\ *n* : a male godchild
God·speed \-'spēd\ *n* : a prosperous journey : SUCCESS
⟨bade him ~⟩
go·fer *or* **go·pher** \'gō-fər\ *n* [alter. of *go for*] : an employee
whose duties include running errands
go–get·ter \'gō-ˌge-tər\ *n* : an aggressively enterprising
person — **go–get·ting** *adj or n*
gog·gle \'gä-gəl\ *vb* **gog·gled; gog·gling** : to stare with
wide or protuberant eyes
gog·gles \'gä-gəlz\ *n pl* : protective glasses set in a flexible
frame that fits snugly against the face
go–go \'gō-ˌgō\ *adj* **1** : related to, being, or employed to
entertain in a disco ⟨~ dancers⟩ **2** : aggressively enterprising and energetic ⟨~ entrepreneurs⟩
go·ings–on \ˌgō-iŋ-'zȯn, -'zän\ *n pl* : ACTIONS, EVENTS
goi·ter \'gȯi-tər\ *n* : an abnormally enlarged thyroid gland
visible as a swelling at the base of the neck — **goi·trous**
\-trəs, -tə-rəs\ *adj*
goi·tre *chiefly Brit var of* GOITER
go–kart \'gō-ˌkärt\ *n* : a small motorized vehicle used esp.
for racing
gold \'gōld\ *n* **1** : a malleable yellow metallic chemical
element used esp. for coins and jewelry **2** : gold coins;
also : MONEY **3** : a yellow color
gold·brick \'gōld-ˌbrik\ *n* : a person who shirks assigned
work — **goldbrick** *vb*
gold coast *n, often cap G&C* : an exclusive residential district
gold digger *n* : a person who uses charm to extract money
or gifts from others
gold·en \'gōl-dən\ *adj* **1** : made of or relating to gold **2**
: having the color of gold; *also* : BLOND **3** : SHINING,

LUSTROUS **4** : SUPERB **5** : FLOURISHING, PROSPEROUS **6** : radiantly youthful and vigorous **7** : FAVORABLE, ADVANTAGEOUS ⟨a ∼ opportunity⟩ **8** : MELLOW, RESONANT ⟨a ∼ tenor⟩

gold·en-ag·er \'gōl-dən-'ā-jər\ *n* : an elderly and often retired person usu. engaging in club activities

golden eagle *n* : a large dark brown eagle with gold-colored feathers on the back of the head and neck

golden hamster *n* : a small tawny hamster often kept as a pet

golden handcuffs *n pl* : special benefits offered to an employee as an inducement to continue service

golden handshake *n* : a generous severance agreement given esp. as an inducement to early retirement

golden retriever *n* : any of a breed of retrievers with a flat golden coat

gold·en·rod \'gōl-dən-ˌräd\ *n* : any of numerous herbs related to the daisies that have tall slender stalks with many tiny usu. yellow flower heads

golden years *n pl* : the advanced years in a lifetime

gold·finch \-ˌfinch\ *n* **1** : a small largely red, black, and yellow Old World finch often kept in a cage **2** : any of three small related American finches of which the males usu. become bright yellow and black in summer

gold·fish \-ˌfish\ *n* : a small usu. golden-orange carp often kept as an aquarium or pond fish

gold·smith \-ˌsmith\ *n* : a person who makes or deals in articles of gold

golf \'gälf, 'gȯlf\ *n* : a game played with a small ball and various clubs on a course having 9 or 18 holes — **golf** *vb* — **golf·er** *n*

-gon \ˌgän\ *n comb form* : figure having (so many) angles ⟨hexagon⟩

go·nad \'gō-ˌnad\ *n* : a sperm- or egg-producing gland : OVARY, TESTIS — **go·nad·al** \gō-'na-dᵊl\ *adj*

go·nad·o·trop·ic \gō-ˌna-də-'trä-pik\ *also* **go·nad·o·tro·phic** \-'trō-fik, -'trä-\ *adj* : acting on or stimulating the gonads

go·nad·o·tro·pin \-'trō-pən\ *also* **go·nad·o·tro·phin** \-fən\ *n* : a gonadotropic hormone

gon·do·la \'gän-də-lə (*usual for 1*), gän-'dō-lə\ *n* [It. dial. (Venice), prob. fr. MGk *kontoura* small vessel] **1** : a long narrow boat used on the canals of Venice **2** : a railroad car used for hauling loose freight (as coal) **3** : an enclosure beneath an airship or balloon **4** : an enclosed car suspended from a cable and used esp. for transporting skiers

gon·do·lier \ˌgän-də-'lir\ *n* : a person who propels a gondola

¹gone \'gȯn\ *past part of* GO

²gone *adj* **1** : LOST, RUINED **2** : DEAD **3** : SINKING, WEAK **4** : INVOLVED, ABSORBED **5** : INFATUATED **6** : PREGNANT **7** : PAST

gon·er \'gȯ-nər\ *n* : one whose case is hopeless

gong \'gäŋ, 'gȯŋ\ *n* : a metallic disk that produces a resounding tone when struck

gono·coc·cus \ˌgä-nə-'kä-kəs\ *n, pl* **-coc·ci** \-'käk-ˌsī, -(ˌ)sē, -'kä-ˌkī, -(ˌ)kē\ : a pus-producing bacterium causing gonorrhea — **gono·coc·cal** \-'kä-kəl\ *adj*

gon·or·rhea \ˌgä-nə-'rē-ə\ *n* : a contagious sexually transmitted inflammation of the genital tract caused by the gonococcus — **gon·or·rhe·al** \-'rē-əl\ *adj*

goo \'gü\ *n* **1** : a viscid or sticky substance **2** : sentimental tripe — **goo·ey** \-ē\ *adj*

goo·ber \'gü-bər, 'gu̇-\ *n, Southern & Midland* : PEANUT

¹good \'gu̇d\ *adj* **bet·ter** \'be-tər\; **best** \'best\ **1** : of a favorable character or tendency **2** : BOUNTIFUL, FERTILE ⟨∼ land⟩ **3** : COMELY, ATTRACTIVE **4** : SUITABLE, FIT **5** : SOUND, WHOLE ⟨only one ∼ arm⟩ **6** : AGREEABLE, PLEASANT ⟨had a ∼ time⟩ **7** : SALUTARY, WHOLESOME **8** : CONSIDERABLE, AMPLE ⟨a ∼ bit of time⟩ **9** : FULL ⟨waited a ∼ hour⟩ **10** : WELL-FOUNDED **11** : TRUE ⟨holds ∼ for everybody⟩ **12** : legally valid or effectual **13** : ADEQUATE, SATISFACTORY **14** : conforming to a standard ⟨∼ English⟩ **15** : DISCRIMINATING **16** : COMMENDABLE, VIRTUOUS **17** : KIND **18** : UPPER-CLASS **19** : COMPETENT **20** : LOYAL, CLOSE ⟨a ∼ friend⟩ — **good·ish** *adj*

²good *n* **1** : something good **2** : GOODNESS **3** : BENEFIT, WELFARE ⟨for the ∼ of mankind⟩ **4** : something that has economic utility **5** *pl* : personal property **6** *pl* : CLOTH **7** *pl* : WARES, MERCHANDISE ⟨canned ∼s⟩ **8** : good persons ⟨the ∼ die young⟩ **9** *pl* : proof of wrongdoing — **for good** : FOREVER, PERMANENTLY —

to the good : in a position of net gain or profit ⟨$10 *to the good*⟩

³good *adv* : WELL

good–bye *or* **good–by** \gu̇d-'bī, gə-\ *n* : a concluding remark at parting

good cholesterol *n* : HDL

good–for–noth·ing \'gu̇d-fər-ˌnə-thiŋ\ *adj* : of no use or value — **good–for–nothing** *n*

Good Friday *n* : the Friday before Easter observed as the anniversary of the crucifixion of Christ

good–heart·ed \'gu̇d-'här-təd\ *adj* : having a kindly generous disposition — **good–heart·ed·ly** *adv* — **good–heart·ed·ness** *n*

good–look·ing \'gu̇d-'lu̇-kiŋ\ *adj* : having an attractive appearance

good·ly \'gu̇d-lē\ *adj* **good·li·er**; **-est** **1** : of pleasing appearance **2** : LARGE, CONSIDERABLE ⟨a ∼ sum of money⟩

good·man \'gu̇d-mən\ *n, archaic* : MR.

good–na·tured \'gu̇d-'nā-chərd\ *adj* : of a cheerful disposition — **good–na·tured·ly** \-chərd-lē\ *adv*

good·ness \-nəs\ *n* : EXCELLENCE, VIRTUE

good·wife \-ˌwīf\ *n, archaic* : MRS.

good·will \-'wil\ *n* **1** : BENEVOLENCE **2** : the value of the trade a business has built up over time **3** : cheerful consent **4** : willing effort

goody *or* **good·ie** \'gu̇-dē\ *n, pl* **good·ies** : something that is good esp. to eat

goody–goody \ˌgu̇-dē-'gu̇-dē\ *adj* : affectedly good — **goody–goody** *n*

goof \'güf\ *vb* **1** : to spend time idly or foolishly — usu. used with *off* **2** : BLUNDER — usu. used with *up* — **goof** *n*

goof·ball \'güf-ˌbȯl\ *n* **1** *slang* : a barbiturate sleeping pill **2** : a goofy person

go off *vb* **1** : EXPLODE **2** : to follow a course ⟨the party *went off* well⟩

goof–off \'güf-ˌȯf\ *n* : one who evades work or responsibility

goofy \'gü-fē\ *adj* **goof·i·er**; **-est** : CRAZY, SILLY — **goof·i·ness** \-fē-nəs\ *n*

goo·gle \'gü-gəl\ *vb* **goo·gled**; **goo·gling** [*Google*, trademark for a search engine] : to use the Google search engine to obtain information on the World Wide Web

goon \'gün\ *n* : a man hired to terrorize or kill opponents

go on *vb* **1** : to continue in a course of action **2** : to take place : HAPPEN

goose \'güs\ *n, pl* **geese** \'gēs\ **1** : any of numerous long-necked web-footed birds related to the swans and ducks; *also* : a female goose as distinguished from a gander **2** : a foolish person **3** *pl* **goos·es** : a tailor's smoothing iron

goose·ber·ry \'güs-ˌber-ē, 'güz-, -bə-rē\ *n* : the acid berry of any of several shrubs related to the currant and used esp. in jams and pies

goose bumps *n pl* : roughening of the skin caused usu. by cold, fear, or a sudden feeling of excitement

goose·flesh \-ˌflesh\ *n* : GOOSE BUMPS

goose pimples *n pl* : GOOSE BUMPS

go out *vb* **1** : to become extinguished **2** : to become a candidate ⟨*went out* for the football team⟩

go over *vb* : SUCCEED

GOP *abbr* Grand Old Party (Republican)

¹go·pher \'gō-fər\ *n* **1** : a burrowing American land tortoise **2** : any of a family of No. American burrowing rodents with large cheek pouches opening beside the mouth **3** : any of several small ground squirrels of the prairie region of No. America

gopher 2

²**gopher** *var of* GOFER

go·pik \gō-'pēk, -'pik\ *n, pl* **gopik** — see *manat* at MONEY table

¹**gore** \'gòr\ *n* : a tapering or triangular piece (as of cloth in a skirt)

²**gore** *vb* **gored; gor·ing** : to pierce or wound with something pointed

³**gore** *n* **1** : BLOOD **2** : gruesomeness depicted in vivid detail

¹**gorge** \'gòrj\ *n* **1** : THROAT **2** : a narrow ravine **3** : a mass of matter that chokes up a passage

²**gorge** *vb* **gorged; gorg·ing** : to eat greedily : stuff to capacity : GLUT

gor·geous \'gòr-jəs\ *adj* : resplendently beautiful

Gor·gon·zo·la \ˌgòr-gən-'zō-lə\ *n* : a pungent blue cheese of Italian origin

go·ril·la \gə-'ri-lə\ *n* [NL, fr. Gk *Gorillai*, a tribe of hairy women in an account of a voyage around Africa] : an African anthropoid ape related to but much larger than the chimpanzee

gor·man·dise *chiefly Brit var of* GORMANDIZE

gor·man·dize \'gòr-mən-ˌdīz\ *vb* **-dized; -diz·ing** : to eat ravenously — **gor·man·diz·er** *n*

gorp \'gòrp\ *n* : a snack consisting of high-calorie food (as raisins and nuts)

gorse \'gòrs\ *n* : a spiny yellow-flowered European evergreen shrub of the legume family

gory \'gòr-ē\ *adj* **gor·i·er; -est 1** : BLOODSTAINED **2** : HORRIBLE, SENSATIONAL ⟨the ∼ details⟩

gos·hawk \'gäs-ˌhòk\ *n* : any of several long-tailed hawks with short rounded wings

gos·ling \'gäz-liŋ, 'gòz-\ *n* : a young goose

¹**gos·pel** \'gäs-pəl\ *n* [ME, fr. OE *gōdspel*, fr. *gōd* good + *spell* message, news] **1** : the teachings of Christ and the apostles **2** *cap* : any of the first four books of the New Testament **3** : something accepted or promoted as infallible truth

²**gospel** *adj* **1** : of, relating to, or emphasizing the gospel **2** : relating to or being American religious songs associated with evangelism

gos·sa·mer \'gä-sə-mər\ *n* [ME *gossomer*, fr. *gos* goose + *somer* summer] **1** : a film of cobwebs floating in the air **2** : something light, delicate, or tenuous

¹**gos·sip** \'gä-səp\ *n* **1** : a person who habitually reveals personal or sensational facts **2** : rumor or report of an intimate nature **3** : an informal conversation — **gos·sipy** *adj*

²**gossip** *vb* : to spread gossip

got *past and past part of* GET

Goth \'gäth\ *n* : a member of a Germanic people that early in the Christian era overran the Roman Empire

¹**Goth·ic** \'gä-thik\ *adj* **1** : of or relating to the Goths **2** : of or relating to a style of architecture prevalent in western Europe from the middle 12th to the early 16th century

²**Gothic** *n* **1** : the Germanic language of the Goths **2** : the Gothic architectural style or decoration

gotten *past part of* GET

Gou·da \'gü-də\ *n* : a mild Dutch milk cheese shaped in balls

¹**gouge** \'gaùj\ *n* **1** : a rounded troughlike chisel **2** : a hole or groove made with or as if with a gouge

²**gouge** *vb* **gouged; goug·ing 1** : to cut holes or grooves in with or as if with a gouge **2** : DEFRAUD, CHEAT

gou·lash \'gü-ˌläsh, -ˌlash\ *n* [Hungarian *gulyás*] : a stew made with meat, assorted vegetables, and paprika

go under *vb* : to be overwhelmed, defeated, or destroyed : FAIL

gourd \'gòrd, 'gùrd\ *n* **1** : any of a family of tendril-bearing vines including the cucumber, squash, and melon **2** : the fruit of a gourd; *esp* : any of various inedible hard-shelled fruits used esp. for ornament or implements

gourde \'gùrd\ *n* — see MONEY table

gour·mand \'gùr-ˌmänd\ *n* **1** : one who is excessively fond of eating and drinking **2** : GOURMET

gour·met \'gùr-ˌmā, gùr-'mā\ *n* [F, fr. MF, alter. of *gromet* boy servant, vintner's assistant] : a connoisseur of food and drink

gout \'gaùt\ *n* : a metabolic disease marked by painful inflammation and swelling of the joints — **gouty** *adj*

gov *abbr* **1** government **2** governor **3** governmental institution — used in World Wide Web addresses

gov·ern \'gə-vərn\ *vb* [ME, fr. AF *governer*, fr. L *guber-*

nare to steer, govern, fr. Gk *kybernan*] **1** : to control and direct the making and administration of policy in : RULE **2** : CONTROL, DIRECT, INFLUENCE **3** : DETERMINE, REGULATE **4** : RESTRAIN — **gov·ern·able** \-vər-nə-bəl\ *adj* — **gov·er·nance** \-vər-nəns\ *n*

gov·ern·ess \'gə-vər-nəs\ *n* : a woman who teaches and trains a child esp. in a private home

gov·ern·ment \'gə-vərn-mənt\ *n* **1** : authoritative direction or control : RULE **2** : the making of policy **3** : the organization or agency through which a political unit exercises authority **4** : the complex of institutions, laws, and customs through which a political unit is governed **5** : the governing body — **gov·ern·men·tal** \ˌgə-vərn-'men-t°l\ *adj* — **gov·ern·men·tal·ly** \-t°l-ē\ *adv*

gov·er·nor \'gə-vər-nər\ *n* **1** : one that governs; *esp* : a ruler, chief executive, or head of a political unit (as a state) **2** : an attachment to a machine for automatic control of speed — **gov·er·nor·ship** *n*

govt *abbr* government

gown \'gaùn\ *n* **1** : a loose flowing outer garment **2** : an official robe worn esp. by a judge, clergyman, or teacher **3** : a woman's dress ⟨evening ∼s⟩ **4** : a loose robe **5** : an academic community within a town or city — **gown** *vb*

gp *abbr* group

GP *abbr* general practitioner

GPO *abbr* **1** general post office **2** Government Printing Office

GPS \ˌjē-ˌpē-'es\ *n* [*G*lobal *P*ositioning *S*ystem] : a navigation system that uses satellite signals to fix location; *also* : the signal receiver itself

GQ *abbr* general quarters

gr *abbr* **1** grade **2** grain **3** gram **4** gravity **5** gross

grab \'grab\ *vb* **grabbed; grab·bing** : to take hastily : SNATCH — **grab** *n*

¹**grace** \'grās\ *n* **1** : unmerited help given to people by God (as in overcoming temptation) **2** : freedom from sin through divine grace **3** : a virtue coming from God **4** — used as a title for a duke, a duchess, or an archbishop **5** : a short prayer at a meal **6** : a temporary respite (as from the payment of a debt) **7** : APPROVAL, ACCEPTANCE ⟨in his good ∼s⟩ **8** : CHARM **9** : ATTRACTIVENESS, BEAUTY **10** : fitness or proportion of line or expression **11** : ease of movement **12** : a musical trill or ornament — **grace·ful** \-fəl\ *adj* — **grace·ful·ly** *adv* — **grace·ful·ness** *n* — **grace·less** *adj*

²**grace** *vb* **graced; grac·ing 1** : HONOR **2** : ADORN, EMBELLISH

gra·cious \'grā-shəs\ *adj* **1** : marked by kindness and courtesy ⟨a ∼ host⟩ **2** : GRACEFUL **3** : characterized by charm and good taste **4** : MERCIFUL — **gra·cious·ly** *adv* — **gra·cious·ness** *n*

grack·le \'gra-kəl\ *n* : any of several large American blackbirds with glossy iridescent plumage

grad *abbr* graduate; graduated

gra·da·tion \grā-'dā-shən, grə-\ *n* **1** : a series forming successive stages **2** : a step, degree, or stage in a series **3** : an advance by regular degrees **4** : the act or process of grading

¹**grade** \'grād\ *n* [L *gradus* step, degree, fr. *gradi* to step, go] **1** : a position in a scale of rank, quality, or order **2** : a stage in a process or ranking **3** : a division of the school course representing one year's work; *also* : the pupils in such a division **4** : a class of persons or things of the same rank or quality **5** : a mark or rating esp. of accomplishment in school **6** : the degree of slope (as of a road); *also* : SLOPE **7** *pl* : the elementary school system

²**grade** *vb* **grad·ed; grad·ing 1** : to arrange in grades : SORT **2** : to make level or evenly sloping ⟨∼ a highway⟩ **3** : to give a grade to ⟨∼ a pupil in history⟩ **4** : to assign to a grade

grade inflation *n* : the assigning of grades higher than previously assigned for given levels of achievement

grad·er \'grā-dər\ *n* **1** : a machine for leveling earth **2** : a pupil in a school grade

grade school *n* : ELEMENTARY SCHOOL

gra·di·ent \'grā-dē-ənt\ *n* : SLOPE, GRADE

grad·u·al \'gra-jə-wəl\ *adj* : proceeding or changing by steps or degrees ⟨∼ improvements⟩ — **grad·u·al·ly** *adv*

grad·u·al·ism \-wə-ˌli-zəm\ *n* : the policy of approaching a desired end gradually

¹**grad·u·ate** \'gra-jə-wət\ *n* **1** : a holder of an academic

degree or diploma **2** : a graduated container for measuring contents

²graduate *adj* **1** : holding an academic degree or diploma **2** : of or relating to studies beyond the first or bachelor's degree 〈~ school〉

³grad·u·ate \'gra-jə-ˌwāt\ *vb* **-at·ed; -at·ing 1** : to grant or receive an academic degree or diploma **2** : to divide into grades, classes, or intervals **3** : to admit to a particular standing or grade

grad·u·a·tion \ˌgra-jə-'wā-shən\ *n* **1** : a mark that graduates something **2** : an act or process of graduating **3** : COMMENCEMENT 2

graf·fi·ti \grə-'fē-(ˌ)tē\ *n* : unauthorized writing or drawing on a public surface

graf·fi·to \gra-'fē-tō, grə-\ *n, pl* **-ti** \-(ˌ)tē\ : an inscription or drawing made on a public surface (as a wall)

¹graft \'graft\ *n* **1** : a grafted plant; *also* : the point of union in this **2** : material (as skin) used in grafting **3** : the getting of money or advantage dishonestly; *also* : the money or advantage so gained

²graft *vb* **1** : to insert a shoot from one plant into another so that they join and grow; *also* : to join one thing to another as in plant grafting 〈~ skin over a burn〉 **2** : to get (as money) dishonestly — **graft·er** *n*

gra·ham cracker \'grā-əm-, 'gram-\ *n* : a slightly sweet cracker made chiefly of whole wheat flour

Grail \'grāl\ *n* **1** : the cup or platter used according to medieval legend by Christ at the Last Supper and thereafter the object of knightly quests **2** *not cap* : the object of an extended or difficult quest

grain \'grān\ *n* **1** : a seed or fruit of a cereal grass **2** : seeds or fruits of various food plants and esp. cereal grasses; *also* : a plant (as wheat) producing grain **3** : a small hard particle **4** : a unit of weight based on the weight of a grain of wheat — see WEIGHT table **5** : TEXTURE; *also* : the arrangement of fibers in wood **6** : natural disposition 〈lying goes against my ~〉 — **grained** \'grānd\ *adj*

grain alcohol *n* : ALCOHOL 1

grainy \'grā-nē\ *adj* **grain·i·er; -est** : resembling or having some characteristic of grain : not smooth or fine **2** *of a photograph* : appearing to be composed of grain-like particles

¹gram \'gram\ *n* [F *gramme*, fr. LL *gramma*, a small weight, fr. Gk *gramma* letter, writing, a small weight, fr. *graphein* to write] : a metric unit of mass and weight equal to ¹/₁₀₀₀ kilogram — see METRIC SYSTEM table

²gram *abbr* grammar; grammatical

-gram \ˌgram\ *n comb form* : drawing : writing : record 〈telegram〉

gram·mar \'gra-mər\ *n* **1** : the study of the classes of words, their inflections, and their functions and relations in the sentence **2** : a study of what is to be preferred and what avoided in inflection and syntax **3** : speech or writing evaluated according to its conformity to grammatical rules — **gram·mar·i·an** \grə-'mer-ē-ən, -'mar-\ *n* — **gram·mat·i·cal** \-'ma-ti-kəl\ *adj* — **gram·mat·i·cal·ly** \-k(ə-)lē\ *adv*

grammar school *n* **1** : a secondary school emphasizing Latin and Greek in preparation for college; *also* : a British college preparatory school **2** : a school intermediate between the primary grades and high school **3** : ELEMENTARY SCHOOL

gramme \'gram\ *chiefly Brit var of* GRAM

gram·o·phone \'gra-mə-ˌfōn\ *n* : PHONOGRAPH

gra·na·ry \'grā-nə-rē, 'gra-\ *n, pl* **-ries 1** : a storehouse for grain **2** : a region producing grain in abundance

¹grand \'grand\ *adj* **1** : higher in rank or importance : FOREMOST, CHIEF **2** : great in size **3** : INCLUSIVE, COMPLETE 〈a ~ total〉 **4** : MAGNIFICENT, SPLENDID **5** : showing wealth or high social standing **6** : IMPRESSIVE, STATELY **7** : very good : FINE 〈had a ~ time〉 — **grand·ly** *adv* — **grand·ness** *n*

²grand *n, pl* **grand** *slang* : a thousand dollars

gran·dam \'gran-ˌdam, -dəm\ *or* **gran·dame** \-ˌdām, -dəm\ *n* : an old woman

grand·child \'grand-ˌchī(-ə)ld\ *n* : a child of one's son or daughter

grand·daugh·ter \'gran-ˌdȯ-tər\ *n* : a daughter of one's son or daughter

grande dame \'grän-'däm\ *n, pl* **grandes dames** : a usu. elderly woman of great prestige or ability

gran·dee \gran-'dē\ *n* : a high-ranking Spanish or Portuguese nobleman

gran·deur \'gran-jər\ *n* **1** : the quality or state of being grand : MAGNIFICENCE **2** : something that is grand

grand·fa·ther \'grand-ˌfä-thər\ *n* : the father of one's father or mother; *also* : ANCESTOR

grandfather clock *n* : a tall clock that stands on the floor

gran·dil·o·quence \gran-'di-lə-kwəns\ *n* : pompous eloquence — **gran·dil·o·quent** \-kwənt\ *adj*

gran·di·ose \'gran-dē-ˌōs, ˌgran-dē-'ōs\ *adj* : IMPRESSIVE, IMPOSING; *also* : affectedly splendid — **gran·di·ose·ly** *adv* — **gran·di·os·i·ty** \ˌgran-dē-'ä-sə-tē\ *n*

grand jury *n* : a jury that examines accusations of crime against persons and makes formal charges on which the persons are later tried

grand mal \'grän-ˌmäl; 'grand-ˌmal\ *n* [F, lit., great illness] : severe epilepsy

grand·moth·er \'grand-ˌmə-thər\ *n* : the mother of one's father or mother; *also* : a female ancestor

grand·par·ent \-ˌper-ənt\ *n* : a parent of one's father or mother

grand piano *n* : a piano with horizontal frame and strings

grand prix \gräⁿ-'prē\ *n, pl* **grand prix** *same or* -'prēz\ *often cap G&P* : a long-distance auto race over a road course; *also* : a high-level competition in another sport (as sailing)

grand slam *n* **1** : a total victory or success **2** : a home run hit with three runners on base

grand·son \'grand-ˌsən\ *n* : a son of one's son or daughter

grand·stand \-ˌstand\ *n* : a usu. roofed stand for spectators at a racecourse or stadium

grange \'grānj\ *n* **1** : a farm or farmhouse with its various buildings **2** *cap* : one of the lodges of a national association originally made up of farmers; *also* : the association itself — **Grang·er** \'grān-jər\ *n*

gran·ite \'gra-nət\ *n* : a hard granular igneous rock used esp. for building — **gra·nit·ic** \grə-'ni-tik\ *adj*

gran·ite·ware \'gra-nət-ˌwer\ *n* : ironware with mottled enamel

gra·no·la \grə-'nō-lə\ *n* : a cereal made of rolled oats and usu. raisins and nuts

¹grant \'grant\ *vb* **1** : to consent to : ALLOW, PERMIT **2** : GIVE, BESTOW 〈~ed land to settlers〉 **3** : to admit as true — **grant·er** *n* — **grant·or** \'gran-tər, -ˌtȯr\ *n*

²grant *n* **1** : the act of granting **2** : something granted; *esp* : a gift for a particular purpose 〈a ~ for study abroad〉 **3** : a transfer of property by deed or writing; *also* : the instrument by which such a transfer is made **4** : the property transferred by grant — **grant·ee** \gran-'tē\ *n*

gran·u·lar \'gra-nyə-lər\ *adj* : consisting of or appearing to consist of granules — **gran·u·lar·i·ty** \ˌgra-nyə-'lar-ə-tē\ *n*

gran·u·late \'gra-nyə-ˌlāt\ *vb* **-lat·ed; -lat·ing** : to form into grains or crystals — **gran·u·la·tion** \ˌgra-nyə-'lā-shən\ *n*

gran·ule \'gra-nyül\ *n* : a small grain or particle

grape \'grāp\ *n* [ME, fr. AF, grape stalk, bunch of grapes, grape, of Gmc origin] **1** : a smooth-skinned juicy edible greenish white, deep red, or purple berry that is the chief source of wine **2** : any of numerous woody vines widely grown for their bunches of grapes

grape·fruit \'grāp-ˌfrüt\ *n* **1** *pl* **grapefruit** *or* **grapefruits** : a large edible yellow-skinned citrus fruit **2** : a tree bearing grapefruit

grape hyacinth *n* : any of several small bulbous herbs related to the lilies that produce clusters of usu. blue flowers in the spring

grape·shot \'grāp-ˌshät\ *n* : a cluster of small iron balls formerly fired at people from short range by a cannon

grape·vine \-ˌvīn\ *n* **1** : GRAPE 2 **2** : RUMOR; *also* : an informal means of circulating information or gossip

graph \'graf\ *n* : a diagram that usu. by means of dots and lines shows change in one variable factor in comparison with one or more other factors — **graph** *vb*

-graph \ˌgraf\ *n comb form* **1** : something written 〈autograph〉 **2** : instrument for making or transmitting records 〈seismograph〉

¹graph·ic \'gra-fik\ *also* **graph·i·cal** \-fi-kəl\ *adj* **1** : of or relating to the arts (**graphic arts**) of representation, decoration, and printing on flat surfaces **2** : being written, drawn, or engraved **3** : vividly described 〈~ details〉 — **graph·i·cal·ly** \-fi-k(ə-)lē\ *adv*

²graphic *n* **1** : a picture, map, or graph used for illustration **2** : a pictorial image displayed on a computer screen

graphical user interface *n* : a computer program designed to allow easy user interaction esp. by having graphic menus or icons

graph·ics tablet \-fiks-\ *n* : a computer input device for entering pictorial information by drawing or tracing

graph·ite \'gra-ˌfīt\ *n* [G *Graphit*, fr. Gk *graphein* to write] : a soft black form of carbon used esp. for lead pencils and lubricants

grap·nel \'grap-nəl\ *n* : a small anchor used esp. to recover a sunken object or to anchor a small boat

¹grap·ple \'gra-pəl\ *n* : the act of grappling

²grapple *vb* **grap·pled; grap·pling** **1** : to seize or hold with or as if with a hooked implement **2** : to come to grips with : WRESTLE

¹grasp \'grasp\ *vb* **1** : to make the motion of seizing **2** : to take or seize firmly **3** : to enclose and hold with the fingers or arms **4** : COMPREHEND

²grasp *n* **1** : HANDLE **2** : EMBRACE **3** : HOLD, CONTROL **4** : the reach of the arms **5** : the power of seizing and holding or attaining **6** : COMPREHENSION

grasp·ing *adj* : GREEDY, AVARICIOUS

grass \'gras\ *n* **1** : herbage for grazing animals **2** : any of a large family of plants (as wheat, bamboo, or sugarcane) with jointed stems and narrow leaves **3** : grass-covered land **4** : MARIJUANA — **grass·like** \-ˌlīk\ *adj* — **grassy** *adj*

grass·hop·per \-ˌhä-pər\ *n* : any of numerous leaping plant-eating insects

grass·land \-ˌland\ *n* : land covered naturally or under cultivation with grasses and low-growing herbage

grass roots *n pl* : society at the local level as distinguished from the centers of political leadership

¹grate \'grāt\ *vb* **grat·ed; grat·ing** **1** : to pulverize by rubbing against something rough **2** : to grind or rub against with a rasping noise **3** : IRRITATE — **grat·er** *n* — **grat·ing·ly** *adv*

²grate *n* **1** : GRATING **2** : a frame of iron bars for holding fuel while it burns

grate·ful \'grāt-fəl\ *adj* **1** : THANKFUL, APPRECIATIVE; *also* : expressing gratitude **2** : PLEASING — **grate·ful·ly** *adv* — **grate·ful·ness** *n*

grat·i·fy \'gra-tə-ˌfī\ *vb* **-fied; -fy·ing** : to afford pleasure to — **grat·i·fi·ca·tion** \ˌgra-tə-fə-ˈkā-shən\ *n*

grat·ing \'grā-tiŋ\ *n* : a framework with parallel bars or crossbars

gra·tis \'gra-təs, 'grā-\ *adv or adj* : without charge or recompense : FREE

grat·i·tude \'gra-tə-ˌtüd, -ˌtyüd\ *n* : THANKFULNESS

gra·tu·itous \grə-ˈtü-ə-təs, -ˈtyü-\ *adj* **1** : done or provided without recompense : FREE **2** : UNWARRANTED ⟨a ∼ assumption⟩ ⟨∼ violence in movies⟩

gra·tu·ity \-ə-tē\ *n, pl* **-ities** : ¹⁰TIP

gra·va·men \grə-ˈvä-mən\ *n, pl* **-va·mens** *or* **-vam·i·na** \-ˈva-mə-nə\ [LL, burden] : the basic or significant part of a grievance or complaint

¹grave \'grāv\ *vb* **graved; grav·en** \'grā-vən\ *or* **graved; grav·ing** : SCULPTURE, ENGRAVE

²grave *n* : an excavation in the earth as a place of burial; *also* : TOMB

³grave \'grāv; 5 *also* 'gräv\ *adj* **1** : IMPORTANT **2** : threatening great harm or danger **3** : DIGNIFIED, SOLEMN **4** : drab in color : SOMBER **5** : of, marked by, or being an accent mark having the form ` — **grave·ly** *adv* — **grave·ness** *n*

grav·el \'gra-vəl\ *n* : pebbles and small pieces of rock larger than grains of sand — **grav·el·ly** *adj*

Graves' disease \'grāvz-\ *n* : hyperthyroidism characterized by goiter and often protrusion of the eyeballs

grave·stone \'grāv-ˌstōn\ *n* : a burial monument

grave·yard \-ˌyärd\ *n* : CEMETERY

grav·id \'gra-vəd\ *adj* [L *gravidus*, fr. *gravis* heavy] : PREGNANT

gra·vi·me·ter \grə-ˈvi-mə-tər, 'gra-və-ˌmē-\ *n* : a device for measuring variations in a gravitational field

grav·i·tate \'gra-və-ˌtāt\ *vb* **-tat·ed; -tat·ing** : to move or tend to move toward something

grav·i·ta·tion \ˌgra-və-ˈtā-shən\ *n* **1** : a natural force of attraction that tends to draw bodies together and that occurs because of the mass of the bodies **2** : the action or process of gravitating — **grav·i·ta·tion·al** \-shə-nəl\ *adj* — **grav·i·ta·tion·al·ly** *adv*

grav·i·ty \'gra-və-tē\ *n, pl* **-ties** **1** : IMPORTANCE; *esp* : SERIOUSNESS **2** : ²MASS **5** **3** : the gravitational attraction of the mass of a celestial object (as earth) for bodies close to it; *also* : GRAVITATION 1

gra·vure \grə-ˈvyùr\ *n* [F] : PHOTOGRAVURE

gra·vy \'grā-vē\ *n, pl* **gravies** **1** : a sauce made from the thickened and seasoned juices of cooked meat **2** : unearned or illicit gain : GRAFT

¹gray *also* **grey** \'grā\ *adj* **1** : of the color gray; *also* : dull in color **2** : having gray hair **3** : CHEERLESS, DISMAL ⟨a ∼ day⟩ **4** : intermediate in position or character ⟨an ethically ∼ area⟩ — **gray·ish** *adj* — **gray·ness** *n*

²gray *also* **grey** *n* **1** : something of a gray color **2** : a neutral color ranging between black and white

³gray *also* **grey** *vb* : to make or become gray

gray·beard \'grā-ˌbird\ *n* : an old man

gray·ling \'grā-liŋ\ *n, pl* **grayling** *also* **graylings** : any of several slender freshwater food and sport fishes related to the trouts

gray matter *n* **1** : the grayish part of nervous tissue consisting mostly of the cell bodies of neurons **2** : INTELLIGENCE

gray wolf *n* : a large wolf of northern No. America and Asia that is usu. gray

gray wolf

¹graze \'grāz\ *vb* **grazed; graz·ing** [ME *grasen*, fr. OE *grasian*, fr. *græs* grass] **1** : to feed on herbage or pasture **2** : to feed (livestock) on grass or pasture — **graz·er** *n*

²graze *vb* **grazed; graz·ing** **1** : to touch lightly in passing **2** : SCRATCH, ABRADE

¹grease \'grēs\ *n* **1** : rendered animal fat **2** : oily material **3** : a thick lubricant — **greasy** \'grē-sē, -zē\ *adj*

²grease \'grēs, 'grēz\ *vb* **greased; greas·ing** : to smear or lubricate with grease

grease·paint \'grēs-ˌpānt\ *n* : theater makeup

great \'grāt\ *adj* **1** : large in size : BIG **2** : ELABORATE, AMPLE ⟨in ∼ detail⟩ **3** : large in number : NUMEROUS **4** : being beyond the average : MIGHTY, INTENSE ⟨a ∼ weight⟩ ⟨in ∼ pain⟩ **5** : EMINENT, GRAND **6** : long continued ⟨a ∼ while⟩ **7** : MAIN, PRINCIPAL ⟨a reception in the ∼ hall⟩ **8** : more distant in a family relationship by one generation ⟨a *great*-grandfather⟩ **9** : markedly superior in character, quality, or skill ⟨∼ at bridge⟩ **10** : EXCELLENT, FINE ⟨had a ∼ time⟩ — **great·ly** *adv* — **great·ness** *n*

great ape *n* : any of a family of primates including the gorilla, orangutan, and chimpanzees

great blue heron *n* : a large crested grayish-blue American heron

great circle *n* : a circle on the surface of a sphere that has the same center as the sphere; *esp* : one on the surface of the earth an arc of which is the shortest travel distance between two points

great·coat \'grāt-ˌkōt\ *n* : a heavy overcoat

Great Dane *n* : any of a breed of very tall powerful smooth-coated dogs

great·er *adj, often cap* : consisting of a central city together with adjacent areas ⟨∼ London⟩

great·heart·ed \'grāt-ˈhär-təd\ *adj* **1** : COURAGEOUS **2** : MAGNANIMOUS

great power *n, often cap G&P* : one of the nations that figure most decisively in international affairs

great white shark *n* : a large and dangerous shark of warm seas that has large saw-edged teeth and is whitish below and bluish or brownish above

grebe \'grēb\ *n* : any of a family of lobe-toed diving birds related to the loons

Gre·cian \'grē-shən\ *adj* : GREEK

greed \'grēd\ *n* : acquisitive or selfish desire beyond reason — **greed·i·ly** \'grē-də-lē\ *adv* — **greed·i·ness** \-dē-nəs\ *n* — **greedy** \'grē-dē\ *adj*

¹**Greek** \'grēk\ *n* **1** : a native or inhabitant of Greece **2** : the ancient or modern language of Greece

²**Greek** *adj* **1** : of, relating to, or characteristic of Greece, the Greeks, or Greek **2** : ORTHODOX 3

¹**green** \'grēn\ *adj* **1** : of the color green **2** : covered with verdure; *also* : consisting of green plants or of the leafy parts of plants ⟨a ∼ salad⟩ **3** : UNRIPE; *also* : IMMATURE **4** : having a sickly appearance **5** : not fully processed or treated ⟨∼ liquor⟩ ⟨∼ hides⟩ **6** : INEXPERIENCED; *also* : NAIVE **7** : concerned with or supporting environmentalism ⟨∼ companies⟩ — **green·ish** *adj* — **green·ness** *n*

²**green** *vb* : to make or become green

³**green** *n* **1** : a color between blue and yellow in the spectrum : the color of growing fresh grass or of the emerald **2** : something of a green color **3** : green vegetation; *esp, pl* : leafy herbs or leafy parts of a vegetable ⟨collard ∼s⟩ ⟨beet ∼s⟩ **4** : a grassy plot; *esp* : a smooth grassy area around the hole into which the ball must be played in golf

green·back \'grēn-,bak\ *n* : a U.S. legal-tender note

green bean *n* : a kidney bean that is used as a snap bean when the pods are colored green

green-belt \'grēn-,belt\ *n* : a belt of parks or farmlands around a community

green card *n* : an identity card attesting the permanent resident status of an alien in the U.S.

green·ery \'grēn-ə-rē\ *n, pl* **-er·ies** : green foliage or plants

green–eyed \'grē-'nīd\ *adj* : JEALOUS

green·gro·cer \'grēn-,grō-sər\ *n, chiefly Brit* : a retailer of fresh vegetables and fruit

green·horn \-,hȯrn\ *n* : an inexperienced person; *also* : NEWCOMER

green·house \-,haus\ *n* : a glass structure for the growing of tender plants

greenhouse effect *n* : warming of a planet's atmosphere that occurs when the sun's radiation passes through the atmosphere, is absorbed by the planet, and is reradiated as radiation of longer wavelength that can be absorbed by atmospheric gases

green manure *n* : an herbaceous crop (as clover) plowed under when green to enrich the soil

green onion *n* : a young onion pulled before the bulb has enlarged and used esp. in salads : SCALLION

green pepper *n* : a sweet pepper before it turns red at maturity

green–room \'grēn-,rüm, -,rum\ *n* : a room (as in a theater or studio) where performers can relax before, between, or after appearances

green–sward \-,swȯrd\ *n* : turf that is green with growing grass

green thumb *n* : an unusual ability to make plants grow

green·wash·ing \'grēn-,wȯ-shiŋ, -,wä-\ *n* : expressions of environmentalist concerns as a cover for products, policies, or activities deleterious to the environment

Green·wich mean time \'gri-nij-, 'gre-, -nich-\ *n* [*Greenwich*, England] : the time of the meridian of Greenwich used historically as the basis of worldwide standard time

Greenwich time *n* : GREENWICH MEAN TIME

green·wood \'grēn-,wud\ *n* : a forest that is green with foliage

greet \'grēt\ *vb* **1** : to address with expressions of kind wishes **2** : to meet or react to in a specified manner **3** : to be perceived by — **greet·er** *n*

greet·ing *n* **1** : a salutation on meeting **2** *pl* : best wishes : REGARDS

greeting card *n* : a card that bears a message usu. sent on a special occasion

gre·gar·i·ous \gri-'ger-ē-əs\ *adj* [L *gregarius* of a flock or herd, fr. *greg-, grex* flock, herd] **1** : SOCIAL, COMPANIONABLE **2** : tending to flock together — **gre·gar·i·ous·ly** *adv* — **gre·gar·i·ous·ness** *n*

grem·lin \'grem-lən\ *n* : a cause of error or equipment malfunction conceived of as a small gnome

gre·nade \grə-'nād\ *n* [MF, lit., pomegranate, fr. LL *granata*, fr. L, fem. of *granatus* seedy, fr. *granum* grain] : a small bomb that is thrown by hand or launched (as by a rifle)

gren·a·dier \,gre-nə-'dir\ *n* : a member of a European regiment formerly armed with grenades

gren·a·dine \,gre-nə-'dēn, 'gre-nə-,dēn\ *n* : a syrup flavored with pomegranates and used in mixed drinks

grew *past of* GROW

grey *var of* GRAY

grey·hound \'grā-,haund\ *n* : any of a breed of tall slender dogs noted for speed and keen sight

grid \'grid\ *n* **1** : GRATING **2** : a network of conductors for distributing electric power **3** : a network of horizontal and perpendicular lines (as for locating points on a map) **4** : GRIDIRON 2; *also* : FOOTBALL

grid·dle \'gri-dᵊl\ *n* : a flat usu. metal surface for cooking food

griddle cake *n* : PANCAKE

grid·iron \'grid-,ī-(-ə)rn\ *n* **1** : a grate for broiling food **2** : a football field

grid·lock \-,läk\ *n* : a traffic jam in which an intersection is so blocked that vehicles cannot move

grief \'grēf\ *n* **1** : emotional distress caused by or as if by bereavement; *also* : a cause of such distress **2** : DISASTER ⟨the ship came to ∼⟩; *also* : MISHAP

griev·ance \'grē-vəns\ *n* **1** : a cause of distress affording reason for complaint or resistance **2** : COMPLAINT

grieve \'grēv\ *vb* **grieved; griev·ing** [ME *greven*, fr. AF *grever*, fr. L *gravare* to burden, fr. *gravis* heavy, grave] **1** : to cause grief or sorrow to : DISTRESS **2** : to feel grief : SORROW

griev·ous \'grē-vəs\ *adj* **1** : causing suffering, grief, or sorrow : SEVERE ⟨a ∼ wound⟩ **2** : OPPRESSIVE, ONEROUS ⟨∼ costs of war⟩ **3** : SERIOUS, GRAVE ⟨a ∼ fault⟩ — **griev·ous·ly** *adv*

¹**grill** \'gril\ *vb* **1** : to broil on a grill; *also* : to fry or toast on a griddle **2** : to question intensely ⟨∼ a suspect⟩

²**grill** *n* **1** : a cooking utensil of parallel bars on which food is grilled **2** : a usu. informal restaurant

grille *or* **grill** \'gril\ *n* : a grating that forms a barrier or screen

grill·work \'gril-,wərk\ *n* : work constituting or resembling a grille

grim \'grim\ *adj* **grim·mer; grim·mest** **1** : CRUEL, FIERCE **2** : harsh and forbidding in appearance **3** : ghastly or repellent in character **4** : RELENTLESS — **grim·ly** *adv* — **grim·ness** *n*

gri·mace \'gri-məs, gri-'mās\ *n* : a facial expression usu. of disgust or disapproval — **grimace** *vb*

grime \'grīm\ *n* : soot, smut, or dirt adhering to or embedded in a surface; *also* : accumulated dirtiness and disorder — **grimy** *adj*

grin \'grin\ *vb* **grinned; grin·ning** : to draw back the lips so as to show the teeth esp. in amusement — **grin** *n*

¹**grind** \'grīnd\ *vb* **ground** \'graund\; **grind·ing** **1** : to reduce to small particles **2** : to wear down, polish, or sharpen by friction **3** : OPPRESS **4** : to press with a grating noise : GRIT ⟨∼ the teeth⟩ **5** : to operate or produce by turning a crank **6** : DRUDGE; *esp* : to study hard **7** : to move with difficulty or friction ⟨gears ∼ing⟩

²**grind** *n* **1** : dreary monotonous labor, routine, or study **2** : one who works or studies excessively

grind·er \'grīn-dər\ *n* **1** : MOLAR **2** *pl* : TEETH **3** : one that grinds **4** : SUBMARINE 2 **5** : an athlete who succeeds through hard work and determination

grind·stone \'grīnd-,stōn\ *n* : a flat circular stone of natural sandstone that revolves on an axle and is used for grinding, shaping, or smoothing

¹**grip** \'grip\ *vb* **gripped; grip·ping** **1** : to seize or hold firmly **2** : to hold the interest of strongly ⟨gripped by the story⟩

²**grip** *n* **1** : GRASP; *also* : strength in gripping **2** : a firm tenacious hold **3** : UNDERSTANDING **4** : a device for gripping **5** : TRAVELING BAG

gripe \'grīp\ *vb* **griped; grip·ing** **1** : IRRITATE, VEX **2** : to cause or experience spasmodic pains in the bowels **3** : COMPLAIN — **gripe** *n*

grippe \'grip\ *n* : INFLUENZA

gris–gris \'grē-,grē\ *n, pl* **gris–gris** \-,grēz\ [F] : an amulet or incantation used chiefly by people of black African ancestry

gris·ly \'griz-lē\ *adj* **gris·li·er; -est** : HORRIBLE, GRUESOME

grist \'grist\ *n* : grain to be ground or already ground

gris·tle \'gri-səl\ *n* : CARTILAGE — **gris·tly** \'gris-lē\ *adj*

grist·mill \'grist-,mil\ *n* : a mill for grinding grain

¹**grit** \'grit\ *n* 1 : a hard sharp granule (as of sand); *also* : material composed of such granules 2 : unyielding courage ⟨the pioneers' ∼⟩ — **grit·ty** *adj*

²**grit** *vb* **grit·ted; grit·ting** : GRIND, GRATE

grits \'grits\ *n pl* : coarsely ground hulled grain ⟨hominy ∼⟩

griz·zled \'gri-zəld\ *adj* : streaked or mixed with gray; *also* : having gray hair

griz·zly \'griz-lē\ *adj* **griz·zli·er; -est** : GRIZZLED

grizzly bear *n* : a large powerful brownish bear of western No. America

gro *abbr* gross

groan \'grōn\ *vb* 1 : MOAN 2 : to make a harsh sound under sudden or prolonged strain ⟨the chair ∼ed under his weight⟩ — **groan** *n*

groat \'grōt\ *n* : an old British coin worth four pennies

gro·cer \'grō-sər\ *n* [ME, fr. AF *groser* wholesaler, fr. *gros* coarse, wholesale, fr. L *grossus* coarse] : a dealer esp. in staple foodstuffs — **gro·cery** \'grōs-rē, 'grōsh-, 'grō-sə-\ *n*

grog \'gräg\ *n* [*Old Grog*, nickname of Edward Vernon †1757 Eng. admiral responsible for diluting the sailors' rum] : alcoholic liquor; *esp* : liquor (as rum) mixed with water

grog·gy \'grä-gē\ *adj* **grog·gi·er; -est** : weak and unsteady on the feet or in action — **grog·gi·ly** \-gə-lē\ *adv* — **grog·gi·ness** \-gē-nəs\ *n*

groin \'grȯin\ *n* 1 : the juncture of the lower abdomen and inner part of the thigh; *also* : the region of this juncture 2 : the curved line or rib on a ceiling along which two vaults meet

grok \'gräk\ *vb* **grokked; grok·king** : to understand profoundly and intuitively

grom·met \'grä-mət, 'grə-\ *n* 1 : a ring of rope 2 : an eyelet of firm material to strengthen or protect an opening

¹**groom** \'grüm, 'grùm\ *n* 1 : a person responsible for the care of horses 2 : BRIDEGROOM

²**groom** *vb* 1 : to clean and care for (an animal) 2 : to make neat or attractive 3 : PREPARE

grooms·man \'grümz-mən, 'grùmz-\ *n* : a male friend who attends a bridegroom at his wedding

groove \'grüv\ *n* 1 : a long narrow channel 2 : a fixed routine — **groove** *vb*

groovy \'grü-vē\ *adj* **groov·i·er; -est** 1 : EXCELLENT 2 : HIP

grope \'grōp\ *vb* **groped; grop·ing** 1 : to feel about or search for blindly or uncertainly ⟨∼ for the right word⟩ 2 : to feel one's way by groping

gros·beak \'grōs-,bēk\ *n* : any of several finches of Europe or America with large stout conical bills

gro·schen \'grō-shən\ *n, pl* **groschen** : a former Austrian monetary unit equal to ¹/₁₀₀ schilling

gros·grain \'grō-,grān\ *n* [F *gros grain* coarse texture] : a silk or rayon fabric with crosswise cotton ribs

¹**gross** \'grōs\ *adj* 1 : glaringly noticeable 2 : OUT-AND-OUT, UTTER 3 : BIG, BULKY; *esp* : excessively fat 4 : GENERAL, BROAD 5 : consisting of an overall total exclusive of deductions ⟨∼ earnings⟩ 6 : CARNAL, EARTHY ⟨∼ pleasures⟩ 7 : UNREFINED; *also* : crudely vulgar 8 : lacking knowledge — **gross·ly** *adv* — **gross·ness** *n*

²**gross** *n* : an overall total exclusive of deductions — **gross** *vb*

³**gross** *n, pl* **gross** : a total of 12 dozen things ⟨a ∼ of pencils⟩

gross domestic product *n* : the gross national product excluding the value of net income earned abroad

gross national product *n* : the total value of the goods and services produced in a nation during a year

gro·szy \'grō-shē\ *n, pl* **groszy** — see *zloty* at MONEY table

grot \'grät\ *n* : GROTTO

gro·tesque \grō-'tesk\ *adj* 1 : FANCIFUL, BIZARRE 2 : absurdly incongruous 3 : ECCENTRIC — **gro·tesque·ly** *adv*

grot·to \'grä-tō\ *n, pl* **grottoes** *also* **grottos** 1 : CAVE 2 : an artificial cavelike structure

grouch \'graùch\ *n* 1 : a fit of bad temper 2 : a habitually irritable or complaining person — **grouch** *vb* — **grouchy** *adj*

¹**ground** \'graùnd\ *n* 1 : the bottom of a body of water 2 *pl* : sediment at the bottom of a liquid 3 : a basis for be-

lief, action, or argument 4 : BACKGROUND 5 : the surface of the earth; *also* : SOIL 6 : an area with a particular use ⟨fishing ∼s⟩ 7 *pl* : the area about and belonging to a building 8 : a conductor that makes electrical connection with the earth — **ground·less** *adj*

²**ground** *vb* 1 : to bring to or place on the ground 2 : to run or cause to run aground 3 : to provide a reason or justification for 4 : to furnish with a foundation of knowledge 5 : to connect electrically with a ground 6 : to restrict to the ground; *also* : prohibit from some activity ⟨∼ed the boy for a week⟩

³**ground** *past and past part of* GRIND

ground ball *n* : a batted baseball that rolls or bounces along the ground

ground cover *n* : low plants that grow over and cover the soil; *also* : a plant suitable for use as ground cover

ground·ed \'graùn-dəd\ *adj* : mentally and emotionally stable

ground·er \'graùn-dər\ *n* : GROUND BALL

ground·hog \'graùnd-,hȯg, -,häg\ *n* : WOODCHUCK

ground·ling \'graùnd-liŋ\ *n* : a spectator in the pit of an Elizabethan theater

ground rule *n* 1 : a sports rule adopted to modify play on a particular field, court, or course 2 : a rule of procedure

ground squirrel *n* : any of various burrowing squirrels of No. America and Eurasia that often live in colonies in open areas

ground swell *n* 1 : a broad deep ocean swell caused by an often distant gale or earthquake 2 *usu* **ground·swell** : a rapid spontaneous growth (as of political opinion)

ground·wa·ter \'graùnd-,wȯ-tər, -,wä-\ *n* : water within the earth that supplies wells and springs

ground·work \-,wərk\ *n* : FOUNDATION, BASIS

ground zero *n* 1 : the point above, below, or at which a nuclear explosion occurs 2 : the center or origin of rapid, intense, or violent activity

¹**group** \'grüp\ *n* 1 : a number of individuals related by a common factor (as physical association, community of interests, or blood) 2 : a combination of atoms commonly found together in a molecule ⟨a methyl ∼⟩

²**group** *vb* : to associate in groups : CLUSTER, AGGREGATE

grou·per \'grü-pər\ *n, pl* **groupers** *also* **grouper** : any of numerous large solitary bottom fishes of warm seas

group home *n* : a residence for persons requiring care or supervision

group·ie \'grü-pē\ *n* : a fan of a rock group who usu. follows the group around on concert tours; *also* : ENTHUSIAST, FAN

group therapy *n* : therapy in the presence of a therapist in which several patients discuss their personal problems

groupware \'grüp-,wer\ *n* : software that enables users to work jointly via a network on projects or files

¹**grouse** \'graùs\ *n, pl* **grouse** *or* **grouses** : any of various chiefly ground-dwelling game birds that have feathered legs and are usu. of reddish brown or other protective color

grouse

²**grouse** *vb* **groused; grous·ing** : COMPLAIN, GRUMBLE

grout \'graùt\ *n* : material (as mortar) used for filling spaces — **grout** *vb*

grove \'grōv\ *n* : a small wood usu. without underbrush

grov·el \'grä-vəl, 'grə-\ *vb* **-eled** *or* **-elled; -el·ing** *or* **-el·ling** 1 : to creep or lie with the body prostrate in fear or humility 2 : to abase oneself

grow \'grō\ *vb* **grew** \'grü\; **grown** \'grōn\; **grow·ing** 1 : to spring up and develop to maturity 2 : to be able to grow : THRIVE **3** : to take on some relation through or as if through growth ⟨tree limbs *grown* together⟩ **4** : INCREASE, EXPAND **5** : to develop from a parent source **6** : BECOME **7** : to have an increasing influence **8** : to cause to grow ⟨~ a business⟩ — **grow·er** *n*

growing pains *n pl* **1** : pains in the legs of growing children having no known relation to growth **2** : the stresses and strains attending a new project or development

growl \'graù(-ə)l\ *vb* **1** : RUMBLE **2** : to utter a deep throaty sound **3** : GRUMBLE — **growl** *n*

grown–up \'grō-,nəp\ *adj* : not childish : ADULT — **grown–up** *n*

growth \'grōth\ *n* **1** : stage or condition attained in growing **2** : a process of growing esp. through progressive development or increase **3** : a result or product of growing ⟨a fine ~ of hair⟩; *also* : an abnormal mass of tissue (as a tumor)

growth hormone *n* : a vertebrate hormone that is secreted by the pituitary gland and regulates growth

growth industry *n* : a business, interest, or activity that is increasingly popular, profitable, or trendy

¹**grub** \'grəb\ *vb* **grubbed**; **grub·bing** **1** : to clear or root out by digging **2** : to dig in the ground usu. for a hidden object **3** : to search about

²**grub** *n* **1** : a soft thick wormlike insect larva ⟨beetle ~*s*⟩ **2** : DRUDGE; *also* : a slovenly person **3** : FOOD

grub·by \'grə-bē\ *adj* **grub·bi·er**; **-est** : DIRTY, SLOVENLY ⟨~ clothes⟩ — **grub·bi·ness** \-bē-nəs\ *n*

grub·stake \'grəb-,stāk\ *n* : supplies or funds furnished a mining prospector in return for a share in his finds

¹**grudge** \'grəj\ *vb* **grudged**; **grudg·ing** : to be reluctant to give : BEGRUDGE

²**grudge** *n* : a feeling of deep-seated resentment or ill will

gru·el \'grü-əl\ *n* : a thin porridge

gru·el·ing *or* **gru·el·ling** \'grü-liŋ, 'grü-ə-\ *adj* : requiring extreme effort : EXHAUSTING ⟨a ~ race⟩

grue·some \'grü-səm\ *adj* [fr. earlier *growsome*, fr. E dial. *grow, grue* to shiver] : inspiring horror or repulsion — **grue·some·ly** *adv* — **grue·some·ness** *n*

gruff \'grəf\ *adj* **1** : rough in speech or manner **2** : being deep and harsh : HOARSE — **gruff·ly** *adv*

grum·ble \'grəm-bəl\ *vb* **grum·bled**; **grum·bling** **1** : to mutter in discontent **2** : GROWL, RUMBLE — **grum·bler** *n*

grumpy \'grəm-pē\ *adj* **grump·i·er**; **-est** : moodily cross : SURLY — **grump·i·ly** \-pə-lē\ *adv* — **grump·i·ness** \-pē-nəs\ *n*

grunge \'grənj\ *n* **1** : one that is grungy **2** : heavy metal rock music expressing alienation and discontent **3** : untidy or tattered clothing typically worn by grunge fans

grun·gy \'grən-jē\ *adj* **grun·gi·er**; **-est** : shabby or dirty in character or condition

grun·ion \'grən-yən\ *n* : a fish of the California coast which comes inshore to spawn at nearly full moon

grunt \'grənt\ *n* : a deep throaty sound (as that of a hog) — **grunt** *vb*

GSA *abbr* **1** General Services Administration **2** Girl Scouts of America

G suit *n* [gravity] : a suit for a pilot or astronaut designed to counteract the physiological effects of acceleration

GSUSA *abbr* Girl Scouts of the United States of America

gt *abbr* great

Gt Brit *abbr* Great Britain

gtd *abbr* guaranteed

GU *abbr* Guam

gua·ca·mo·le \,gwä-kə-'mō-lē\ *n* [MexSp, fr. Nahuatl *āhuacamōlli*, fr. *āhuacatl* avocado + *mōlli* sauce] : mashed and seasoned avocado

gua·nine \'gwä-,nēn\ *n* : a purine base that codes genetic information in the molecular chain of DNA and RNA

gua·no \'gwä-nō\ *n* [Sp, fr. Quechua *wanu* fertilizer, dung] : excrement esp. of seabirds or bats; *also* : a fertilizer composed chiefly of this excrement

gua·ra·ni \,gwär-ə-'nē\ *n, pl* **guaranies** *also* **guaranis** — see MONEY table

¹**guar·an·tee** \,ger-ən-'tē\ *n* **1** : GUARANTOR **2** : GUARANTY 1 3 : an agreement by which one person undertakes to secure another in the possession or enjoyment of something **4** : an assurance of the quality of or of the length of use to be expected from a product offered for sale **5** : GUARANTY 4

²**guarantee** *vb* **-teed**; **-tee·ing** **1** : to undertake to answer for the debt, failure to perform, or faulty performance of (another) **2** : to undertake an obligation to establish, perform, or continue **3** : to give security to

guar·an·tor \,ger-ən-'tòr\ *n* : one who gives a guarantee

¹**guar·an·ty** \'ger-ən-tē\ *n, pl* **-ties** **1** : an undertaking to answer for another's failure to pay a debt or perform a duty **2** : GUARANTEE 3 **3** : GUARANTOR **4** : PLEDGE, SECURITY

²**guaranty** *vb* **-tied**; **-ty·ing** : GUARANTEE

¹**guard** \'gärd\ *n* **1** : a person or a body of persons on sentinel duty **2** *pl* : troops assigned to protect a sovereign **3** : a defensive position (as in boxing) **4** : the act or duty of protecting or defending **5** : PROTECTION **6** : a protective or safety device **7** : a football lineman playing between center and tackle; *also* : a basketball player stationed farthest from the goal — **on guard** : WATCHFUL, ALERT

²**guard** *vb* **1** : PROTECT, DEFEND **2** : to watch over **3** : to be on guard

guard·house \'gärd-,haùs\ *n* **1** : a building occupied by a guard or used as a headquarters by soldiers on guard duty **2** : a military jail

guard·ian \'gär-dē-ən\ *n* **1** : CUSTODIAN **2** : one who has the care of the person or property of another — **guard·ian·ship** *n*

guard·room \'gärd-,rüm\ *n* **1** : a room used by a military guard while on duty **2** : a room where military prisoners are confined

guards·man \'gärdz-mən\ *n* : a member of a military body called *guard* or *guards*

gua·va \'gwä-və\ *n* : the sweet yellow or pink acid fruit of a shrubby tropical American tree used esp. for making jam and jelly; *also* : the tree

gu·ber·na·to·ri·al \,gü-bər-nə-'tòr-ē-əl\ *adj* : of or relating to a governor

guer·don \'gər-d⁺n\ *n* : REWARD, RECOMPENSE

Guern·sey \'gərn-zē\ *n, pl* **Guernseys** : any of a breed of usu. reddish-brown and white dairy cattle that produce rich yellowish milk

guer·ril·la *or* **gue·ril·la** \gə-'ri-lə\ *n* [Sp *guerrilla*, fr. dim. of *guerra* war, of Gmc origin] : one who engages in irregular warfare esp. as a member of an independent unit

guess \'ges\ *vb* **1** : to form an opinion from little or no evidence **2** : BELIEVE, SUPPOSE **3** : to conjecture correctly about : DISCOVER — **guess** *n*

guest \'gest\ *n* **1** : a person to whom hospitality (as of a house or a club) is extended **2** : a patron of a commercial establishment (as a hotel) **3** : a person not a regular member of a cast who appears on a program

guest·house \'gest-,haùs\ *n* : a house run as a boarding house or bed-and-breakfast

guf·faw \(,)gə-'fò\ *n* : a loud burst of laughter — **guf·faw** *vb*

guid·ance \'gī-d⁺ns\ *n* **1** : the act or process of guiding **2** : ADVICE, DIRECTION

¹**guide** \'gīd\ *n* **1** : one who leads or directs another's course **2** : one who shows and explains points of interest **3** : something that provides guiding information; *also* : SIGNPOST **4** : a device to direct the motion of something

²**guide** *vb* **guid·ed**; **guid·ing** **1** : to act as a guide to **2** : MANAGE, DIRECT **3** : to superintend the training of — **guid·able** \'gī-də-bəl\ *adj*

guide·book \'gīd-,bùk\ *n* : a book of information for travelers

guided missile *n* : a missile whose course may be altered during flight

guide dog *n* : a dog trained to lead the blind

guide·line \'gīd-,līn\ *n* : an indication or outline of policy or conduct

guide word *n* : a term at the head of a page of an alphabetical reference work that indicates the alphabetically first or last word on that page

gui·don \'gī-,dän, -d⁺n\ *n* : a small flag (as of a military unit)

guild \'gild\ *n* : an association of people with common aims and interests; *esp* : a medieval association of merchants or craftsmen — **guild·hall** \-,hòl\ *n*

guil·der \'gil-dər\ *n* : GULDEN

guile \'gī(-ə)l\ *n* : deceitful cunning : DUPLICITY — **guile·ful** *adj* — **guile·less** *adj* — **guile·less·ness** *n*

guil·lo·tine \'gi-lə-ˌtēn, ˌgē-ə-'tēn\ *n* [F, fr. Joseph *Guillotin* †1814 Fr. physician] : a machine for beheading persons — **guillotine** *vb*

guilt \'gilt\ *n* 1 : the fact of having committed an offense esp. against the law 2 : BLAMEWORTHINESS 3 : a feeling of responsibility for wrongdoing — **guilt·less** *adj*

guilt–trip \'gilt-ˌtrip\ *vb* : to cause feelings of guilt in

guilty \'gil-tē\ *adj* **guilt·i·er; -est** 1 : having committed a breach of conduct or a crime 2 : suggesting or involving guilt 3 : aware of or suffering from guilt — **guilt·i·ly** \-tə-lē\ *adv* — **guilt·i·ness** \-tē-nəs\ *n*

guin·ea \'gi-nē\ *n* 1 : a British gold coin no longer issued worth 21 shillings 2 : a unit of value equal to 21 shillings

guinea fowl *n* : a gray and white spotted West African bird related to the pheasants and widely raised for food; *also* : any of several related birds

guinea hen *n* : a female guinea fowl; *also* : GUINEA FOWL

guinea pig *n* 1 : a small stocky short-eared and nearly tailless So. American rodent often kept as a pet or used in lab research 2 : a subject of research or testing

guise \'gīz\ *n* 1 : a form or style of dress : COSTUME 2 : external appearance : SEMBLANCE

gui·tar \gi-'tär\ *n* : a musical instrument with usu. six strings plucked with a pick or with the fingers

gulch \'gəlch\ *n* : RAVINE

gul·den \'gùl-dən, 'gùl-\ *n, pl* **guldens** *or* **gulden** 1 : the basic monetary unit of the Netherlands until 2002 2 : the basic monetary unit of Suriname until 2004

gulf \'gəlf\ *n* [ME *goulf*, fr. MF *golfe*, fr. It *golfo*, fr. LL *colpus*, fr. Gk *kolpos* bosom, gulf] 1 : a part of an ocean or sea partly or mostly surrounded by land 2 : ABYSS, CHASM 3 : a wide separation ⟨the ~ between generations⟩

¹**gull** \'gəl\ *n* : any of numerous mostly white or gray long= winged web-footed seabirds

²**gull** *vb* : to make a dupe of : DECEIVE

³**gull** *n* : DUPE

gul·let \'gə-lət\ *n* : ESOPHAGUS; *also* : THROAT

gull·ible \'gə-lə-bəl\ *adj* : easily duped or cheated

gul·ly \'gə-lē\ *n, pl* **gullies** : a trench worn in the earth by and often filled with running water after rains

gulp \'gəlp\ *vb* 1 : to swallow hurriedly or greedily 2 : SUPPRESS ⟨~ down a sob⟩ 3 : to catch the breath as if in taking a long drink — **gulp** *n*

¹**gum** \'gəm\ *n* : the oral tissue that surrounds the necks of the teeth

²**gum** *n* [ME *gomme*, fr. MF, fr. L *cummi, gummi*, fr. Gk *kommi*, fr. Egyptian *qmy.t*] 1 : a sticky plant exudate; *esp* : one that hardens on drying 2 : a sticky substance 3 : a preparation usu. of a plant gum sweetened and flavored and used for chewing — **gum·my** *adj*

gum arabic *n* : a water-soluble gum obtained from several acacias and used esp. in making inks, adhesives, confections, and pharmaceuticals

gum·bo \'gəm-bō\ *n* [AmerF *gombo*, of Bantu origin] : a rich thick soup usu. thickened with okra

gum·drop \'gəm-ˌdräp\ *n* : a candy made usu. from corn syrup with gelatin and coated with sugar crystals

gump·tion \'gəmp-shən\ *n* 1 *chiefly dial* : shrewd common sense 2 : ENTERPRISE, INITIATIVE ⟨lacked the ~ to try⟩

gum·shoe \'gəm-ˌshü\ *n* : DETECTIVE — **gumshoe** *vb*

¹**gun** \'gən\ *n* 1 : CANNON 2 : a portable firearm 3 : a discharge of a gun 4 : something suggesting a gun in shape or function 5 : THROTTLE — **gunned** \'gənd\ *adj*

²**gun** *vb* **gunned; gun·ning** 1 : to hunt with a gun 2 : SHOOT 3 : to open up the throttle of so as to increase speed

gun·boat \'gən-ˌbōt\ *n* : a small lightly armed ship for use in shallow waters

gun·fight \-ˌfīt\ *n* : a duel with guns — **gun·fight·er** *n*

gun·fire \-ˌfī(-ə)r\ *n* : the firing of guns

gung ho \'gəŋ-'hō\ *adj* : extremely zealous or enthusiastic

gun·man \-mən\ *n* : a man armed with a gun; *esp* : a professional killer

gun·ner \'gə-nər\ *n* 1 : a soldier or airman who operates or aims a gun 2 : one who hunts with a gun

gun·nery \'gə-nə-rē\ *n* : the use of guns; *esp* : the science of the flight of projectiles and effective use of guns

gunnery sergeant *n* : a noncommissioned officer in the marine corps ranking next below a master sergeant

gun·ny·sack \'gə-nē-ˌsak\ *n* : a sack made of a coarse heavy fabric (as burlap)

gun·point \'gən-ˌpóint\ *n* : the muzzle of a gun — **at gunpoint** : under a threat of death by being shot

gun·pow·der \-ˌpaù-dər\ *n* : an explosive powder used in guns and blasting

gun·shot \-ˌshät\ *n* 1 : shot fired from a gun 2 : the range of a gun ⟨within ~⟩

gun–shy \-ˌshī\ *adj* 1 : afraid of a loud noise 2 : markedly distrustful

gun·sling·er \-ˌsliŋ-ər\ *n* : a skilled gunman esp. in the American West

gun·smith \-ˌsmith\ *n* : one who designs, makes, or repairs firearms

gun·wale *also* **gun·nel** \'gə-nᵊl\ *n* : the upper edge of a ship's or boat's side

gup·py \'gə-pē\ *n, pl* **guppies** [R.J.L. *Guppy* †1916 Trinidadian naturalist] : a small brightly colored tropical fish

gur·gle \'gər-gəl\ *vb* **gur·gled; gur·gling** : to make a sound like that of an irregularly flowing or gently splashing liquid — **gurgle** *n*

Gur·kha \'gùr-kə, 'gər-\ *n* : a soldier from Nepal in the British or Indian army

gur·ney \'gər-nē\ *n, pl* **gurneys** : a wheeled cot or stretcher

gu·ru \'gùr-ü\ *n, pl* **gurus** [ultim. fr. Sanskrit *guru*, fr. *guru*, adj., heavy, venerable] 1 : a personal religious and spiritual teacher in Hinduism 2 : a teacher in matters of fundamental concern 3 : EXPERT ⟨a fitness ~⟩

gush \'gəsh\ *vb* 1 : to issue or pour forth copiously or violently : SPOUT 2 : to make an effusive display of affection or enthusiasm

gush·er \'gə-shər\ *n* : one that gushes; *esp* : an oil well with a large natural flow

gushy \'gə-shē\ *adj* **gush·i·er; -est** : marked by effusive sentimentality

gus·set \'gə-sət\ *n* : a triangular insert (as in a seam of a sleeve) to give width or strength — **gusset** *vb*

gus·sy up \'gə-sē-\ *vb* **gus·sied up; gus·sy·ing up** 1 : to dress in best or formal clothes 2 : to make more attractive, glamorous, or fancy

¹**gust** \'gəst\ *n* 1 : a sudden brief rush of wind 2 : a sudden outburst : SURGE ⟨a ~ of emotion⟩ — **gusty** *adj*

²**gust** *vb* : to blow in gusts

gus·ta·to·ry \'gəs-tə-ˌtòr-ē\ *adj* : relating to or associated with the sense of taste

gus·to \'gəs-tō\ *n, pl* **gustoes** : enthusiastic enjoyment; *also* : VITALITY 4

¹**gut** \'gət\ *n* 1 *pl* : BOWELS, ENTRAILS 2 : the alimentary canal or a part of it (as the intestine); *also* : BELLY, ABDOMEN 3 *pl* : the inner essential parts ⟨a car's ~s⟩ 4 *pl* : COURAGE, PLUCK

²**gut** *vb* **gut·ted; gut·ting** 1 : EVISCERATE 2 : to destroy the inside of ⟨fire *gutted* the building⟩

gut check *n* : a test of courage, character, or determination

gutsy \'gət-sē\ *adj* **guts·i·er; -est** : marked by courage and determination

gut·ter \'gə-tər\ *n* : a groove or channel for carrying off esp. rainwater

gut·ter·snipe \-ˌsnīp\ *n* : a street urchin

gut·tur·al \'gə-tə-rəl\ *adj* 1 : sounded in the throat 2 : being or marked by an utterance that is strange, unpleasant, or disagreeable — **guttural** *n*

gut·ty \'gə-tē\ *adj* **gut·ti·er; -est** 1 : GUTSY 2 : having a vigorous challenging quality ⟨a ~ role in a play⟩

gut–wrench·ing \'gət-ˌren-chiŋ\ *adj* : causing emotional anguish

¹**guy** \'gī\ *n* : a rope, chain, or rod attached to something as a brace or guide

²**guy** *vb* : to steady or reinforce with a guy

³**guy** *n* : MAN, FELLOW; *also, pl* : PERSONS

⁴**guy** *vb* : to make fun of : RIDICULE

guz·zle \'gə-zəl\ *vb* **guz·zled; guz·zling** : to drink greedily

gym \'jim\ *n* : GYMNASIUM

gym·kha·na \jim-'kä-nə\ *n* : a meet featuring sports contests; *esp* : a contest of automobile-driving skill

gym·na·si·um \for 1 jim-'nā-zē-əm, -zhəm, for 2 gim-'nä-zē-əm\ *n, pl* **-na·si·ums** *or* **-na·sia** \-'nā-zē-ə, -'nä-zhə; -'nä-zē-ə\ [L, exercise ground, school, fr. Gk *gymnasion*, fr. *gymnazein* to exercise naked, fr. *gymnos* naked] 1 : a room or building for indoor sports 2 : a European secondary school that prepares students for the university

gym·nas·tics \jim-'nas-tiks\ *n* : a competitive sport developed from physical exercises designed to demonstrate strength, balance, and body control — **gym·nast** \'jim-ˌnast\ *n* — **gym·nas·tic** *adj*

gym·no·sperm \'jim-nə-ˌspərm\ *n* : any of a group of woody vascular seed plants (as conifers) that produce naked seeds not enclosed in an ovary

gyn *or* **gynecol** *abbr* gynecology

gy·nae·col·o·gy *chiefly Brit var of* GYNECOLOGY

gy·ne·col·o·gy \ˌgī-nə-'kä-lə-jē\ *n* : a branch of medicine that deals with the diseases and routine care of the reproductive system of women — **gy·ne·co·log·ic** \-ni-kə-'lä-jik\ *or* **gy·ne·co·log·i·cal** \-ji-kəl\ *adj* — **gy·ne·col·o·gist** \-nə-'kä-lə-jist\ *n*

gy·no·cen·tric \ˌgī-nə-'sen-trik\ *adj* : emphasizing feminine interests or a feminine point of view

gyp \'jip\ *n, now sometimes offensive* **1** : CHEAT, SWINDLER **2** : FRAUD, SWINDLE — **gyp** *vb, now sometimes offensive*

gyp·sum \'jip-səm\ *n* : a calcium-containing mineral used in making plaster of paris

Gyp·sy \'jip-sē\ *n, pl* **Gypsies** [by shortening & alter. fr. *Egyptian*] **1** *sometimes offensive* : a member of a traditionally traveling people coming orig. from India and living chiefly in Europe, Asia, and No. America **2** : the language of the Gypsies

gypsy moth *n* : an Old World moth that was introduced into the U.S. where its caterpillar is a destructive defoliator of many trees

gy·rate \'jī-ˌrāt\ *vb* **gy·rat·ed; gy·rat·ing 1** : to revolve around a point or axis **2** : to oscillate with or as if with a circular or spiral motion — **gy·ra·tion** \jī-'rā-shən\ *n*

gyr·fal·con \'jər-ˌfal-kən, -ˌfȯl-\ *n* : an arctic falcon with several color forms that is the largest of all falcons

¹gy·ro \'jī-rō\ *n, pl* **gyros** : GYROSCOPE

²gy·ro \'yē-ˌrō, 'zhir-ō\ *n, pl* **gyros** : a sandwich esp. of lamb and beef, tomato, onion, and yogurt sauce on pita bread

gy·ro·scope \'jī-rō-ˌskōp\ *n* : a wheel or disk mounted to spin rapidly about an axis that is free to turn in various directions

Gy Sgt *abbr* gunnery sergeant

gyve \'jīv, 'gīv\ *n* : FETTER — **gyve** *vb*

H

¹h \'āch\ *n, pl* **h's** *or* **hs** \'ā-chəz\ *often cap* : the 8th letter of the English alphabet

²h *abbr, often cap* **1** hard; hardness **2** heroin **3** hit **4** husband

H *symbol* hydrogen

¹ha \'hä\ *interj* — used esp. to express surprise or joy

²ha *abbr* hectare

Hab *abbr* Habacuc; Habakkuk

Ha·ba·cuc \'ha-bə-ˌkək, hə-'ba-kək\ *n* : HABAKKUK

Ha·bak·kuk \'ha-bə-ˌkək, hə-'ba-kək\ *n* — see BIBLE table

ha·ba·ne·ra \ˌhä-bə-'ner-ə\ *n* [Sp *(danza) habanera*, lit., dance of Havana] : a Cuban dance in slow time; *also* : the music for this dance

ha·ba·ne·ro *also* **ha·ba·ñe·ro** \ˌ(h)ä-bə-'n(y)er-ō\ *n* : a very hot chili pepper that is usu. orange when mature

ha·be·as cor·pus \'hä-bē-əs-'kȯr-pəs\ *n* [ME, fr. ML, lit., you should have the body (the opening words of the writ)] : a writ issued to bring a party before a court

hab·er·dash·er \'ha-bər-ˌda-shər\ *n* : a dealer in men's clothing and accessories

hab·er·dash·ery \-ˌda-sha-rē\ *n, pl* **-er·ies 1** : goods sold by a haberdasher **2** : a haberdasher's shop

ha·bil·i·ment \hə-'bi-lə-mənt\ *n* **1** *pl* : TRAPPINGS, EQUIPMENT **2** : DRESS; *esp* : the dress characteristic of an occupation or occasion — usu. used in pl.

hab·it \'ha-bət\ *n* **1** : DRESS, GARB **2** : BEARING, CONDUCT **3** : PHYSIQUE **4** : mental makeup **5** : a usual manner of behavior : CUSTOM **6** : a behavior pattern acquired by frequent repetition ⟨has a ~ of swearing⟩ **7** : ADDICTION ⟨a drug ~⟩ **8** : mode of growth or occurrence ⟨trees with a spreading ~⟩

hab·it·able \'ha-bə-tə-bəl\ *adj* : capable of being lived in — **hab·it·abil·i·ty** \ˌha-bə-tə-'bi-lə-tē\ *n*

hab·i·tat \'ha-bə-ˌtat\ *n* [L, it inhabits] : the place or environment where a plant or animal naturally occurs

hab·i·ta·tion \ˌha-bə-'tā-shən\ *n* **1** : OCCUPANCY **2** : a dwelling place : RESIDENCE **3** : SETTLEMENT

hab·it-form·ing \'ha-bət-ˌfȯr-miŋ\ *adj* : causing addiction : ADDICTIVE

ha·bit·u·al \hə-'bi-chə-wəl\ *adj* **1** : CUSTOMARY **2** : doing, practicing, or acting by force of habit **3** : inherent in an individual ⟨~ grace⟩ — **ha·bit·u·al·ly** *adv* — **ha·bit·u·al·ness** *n*

ha·bit·u·ate \hə-'bi-chə-ˌwāt\ *vb* **-at·ed; -at·ing 1** : ACCUSTOM **2** : to cause or undergo habituation

ha·bit·u·a·tion \hə-ˌbi-chə-'wā-shən\ *n* **1** : the process of making habitual **2** : psychological dependence on a drug after a period of use

ha·bi·tué *also* **ha·bi·tue** \hə-'bi-chə-ˌwā\ *n* [F] **1** : one who may be regularly found in or at (as a place of entertainment) **2** : DEVOTEE

ha·ci·en·da \ˌhä-sē-'en-də\ *n* **1** : a large estate in a Spanish-speaking country **2** : the main building of a farm or ranch

¹hack \'hak\ *vb* **1** : to cut or sever with repeated irregular blows **2** : to cough in a short dry manner **3** : to manage successfully; *also* : TOLERATE ⟨can't ~ the pressure⟩ **4** : to gain access to a computer or computer system illegally

²hack *n* **1** : an implement for hacking **2** : a short dry cough **3** : a hacking blow **4** : an act or instance of gaining access to a computer or computer system illegally

³hack *n* **1** : a horse hired or used for varied work **2** : a horse worn out in service **3** : a light easy often 3-gaited saddle horse **4** : HACKNEY, TAXICAB **5** : a person who works solely for mercenary reasons; *esp* : a writer working solely for commercial success — **hack** *adj*

⁴hack *vb* : to operate a taxicab

hack·er \'ha-kər\ *n* **1** : one that hacks; *also* : a person unskilled at something **2** : an expert at using a computer **3** : a person who illegally gains access to and sometimes tampers with information in a computer system

hack·ie \'ha-kē\ *n* : a taxicab driver

hack·le \'ha-kəl\ *n* **1** : one of the long feathers on the neck or back of a bird **2** *pl* : hairs (as on a dog's neck) that can be erected **3** *pl* : TEMPER, DANDER

hack·man \'hak-mən\ *n* : HACKIE

¹hack·ney \'hak-nē\ *n, pl* **hackneys 1** : a horse for riding or driving **2** : a carriage or automobile kept for hire

²hackney *vb* : to make trite

hack·neyed \'hak-nēd\ *adj* : lacking in freshness or originality ⟨~ slogans⟩

hack·saw \'hak-ˌsȯ\ *n* : a fine-tooth saw in a frame for cutting metal

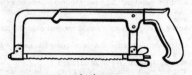

hacksaw

hack·work \-ˌwərk\ *n* : work done on order usu. according to a formula

had *past and past part of* HAVE

had·dock \\'ha-dək\\ *n, pl* **haddock** *also* **haddocks** : an Atlantic food fish usu. smaller than the related cod

Ha·des \\'hā-(ˌ)dēz\\ *n* **1** : the abode of the dead in Greek mythology **2** *often not cap* : HELL

haem *chiefly Brit var of* HEME

hae·ma·tite *Brit var of* HEMATITE

haf·ni·um \\'haf-nē-əm\\ *n* : a gray metallic chemical element

haft \\'haft\\ *n* : the handle of a weapon or tool

hag \\'hag\\ *n* **1** : an ugly or evil-looking old woman **2** : WITCH 1

Hag *abbr* Haggai

Hag·gai \\'ha-gē-ˌī, 'ha-ˌgī\\ *n* — see BIBLE table

hag·gard \\'ha-gərd\\ *adj* : having a worn or emaciated appearance ⟨~ faces⟩ ♦ **Synonyms** CAREWORN, WASTED, DRAWN — **hag·gard·ly** *adv* — **hag·gard·ness** *n*

hag·gis \\'ha-gəs\\ *n* : a traditionally Scottish dish made of the heart, liver, and lungs of a sheep or a calf minced with suet, onions, oatmeal, and seasonings

hag·gle \\'ha-gəl\\ *vb* **hag·gled; hag·gling** : to argue in bargaining — **hag·gler** *n*

Ha·gi·og·ra·pha \\ˌha-gē-'ä-grə-fə, ˌhä-jē-\\ *n pl* — see WRITINGS

ha·gi·o·graph·ic \\ˌha-gē-ə-'gra-fik, ˌhä-, -jē-\\ *adj* : of or relating to hagiography; *esp* : excessively flattering

ha·gi·og·ra·phy \\ˌha-gē-'ä-grə-fē, ˌhä-jē-\\ *n* **1** : biography of saints or venerated persons **2** : idealizing or idolizing biography — **ha·gi·og·ra·pher** \\-fər\\ *n*

hai·ku \\'hī-(ˌ)kü\\ *n, pl* **haiku** [Jp] : an unrhymed Japanese verse form of three lines containing usu. five, seven, and five syllables respectively; *also* : a poem in this form

¹**hail** \\'hāl\\ *n* **1** : precipitation in the form of small lumps of ice **2** : something that gives the effect of falling hail

²**hail** *vb* **1** : to precipitate hail **2** : to pour down and strike like hail

³**hail** *interj* [ME, fr. ON *heill*, fr. *heill* healthy] — used to express acclamation

⁴**hail** *vb* **1** : SALUTE, GREET **2** : SUMMON

⁵**hail** *n* **1** : an expression of greeting, approval, or praise **2** : hearing distance

Hail Mary *n* **1** : a salutation and prayer to the Virgin Mary **2** : a long forward pass in football thrown as a final attempt to score

hail·stone \\'hāl-ˌstōn\\ *n* : a pellet of hail

hail·storm \\-ˌstorm\\ *n* : a storm accompanied by hail

hair \\'her\\ *n* : a threadlike outgrowth esp. from the skin of a mammal; *also* : a covering or growth of hairs of an animal or a body part — **haired** \\'herd\\ *adj* — **hair·less** *adj*

hair·breadth \\'her-ˌbredth\\ *or* **hairs·breadth** \\'herz-\\ *n* : a very small distance or margin

hair·brush \\-ˌbrəsh\\ *n* : a brush for the hair

hair·cloth \\-ˌkloth\\ *n* : a stiff wiry fabric used esp. for upholstery

hair·cut \\-ˌkət\\ *n* : the act, process, or style of cutting and shaping the hair

hair·do \\-ˌdü\\ *n, pl* **hairdos** : HAIRSTYLE

hair·dress·er \\-ˌdre-sər\\ *n* : a person who dresses or cuts hair — **hair·dress·ing** *n*

hair·line \\-ˌlīn\\ *n* **1** : a very thin line **2** : the outline of the hair on the head

hair·piece \\-ˌpēs\\ *n* **1** : supplementary hair (as a switch) used in some women's hairdos **2** : TOUPEE

hair·pin \\-ˌpin\\ *n* **1** : a U-shaped pin to hold the hair in place **2** : a sharp U-shaped turn in a road — **hairpin** *adj*

hair–rais·ing \\'her-ˌrā-ziŋ\\ *adj* : causing terror or astonishment

hair·split·ter \\-ˌspli-tər\\ *n* : a person who makes excessively fine distinctions in reasoning — **hair·split·ting** \\-ˌspli-tiŋ\\ *adj or n*

hair·spray \\'her-ˌsprā\\ *n* : a liquid sprayed onto the hair to hold it in place

hair·style \\-ˌstī(-ə)l\\ *n* : a way of wearing the hair — **hair·styl·ing** *n*

hair·styl·ist \\-ˌstī-list\\ *n* : HAIRDRESSER

hair–trigger *adj* : immediately responsive to the slightest stimulus

hairy \\'her-ē\\ *adj* **hair·i·er; -est** **1** : covered with or as if with hair **2** : tending to cause nervous tension ⟨a few ~ moments⟩ **3** : difficult to deal with — **hair·i·ness** \\-ē-nəs\\ *n*

hairy woodpecker *n* : a common No. American woodpecker with a white back that is larger than the similarly marked downy woodpecker

hajj \\'haj\\ *n* : a pilgrimage to Mecca prescribed as a religious duty for Muslims

hajji \\'ha-jē\\ *n* : one who has made a pilgrimage to Mecca — often used as a title

hake \\'hāk\\ *n* : any of several marine food fishes related to the cod

ha·la·la \\hə-'lä-lə\\ *n, pl* **halala** *or* **halalas** — see *riyal* at MONEY table

hal·berd \\'hal-bərd, 'hol-\\ *also* **hal·bert** \\-bərt\\ *n* : a weapon esp. of the 15th and 16th centuries consisting of a battle-ax and pike on a long handle

hal·cy·on \\'hal-sē-ən\\ *adj* [Gk *halkyōn, alkyōn*, a mythical bird believed to nest at sea and to calm the waves] **1** : CALM, PEACEFUL ⟨a ~ lake⟩ **2** : being a time of happiness, success, or prosperity

¹**hale** \\'hāl\\ *adj* : free from defect, disease, or infirmity ♦ **Synonyms** HEALTHY, SOUND, ROBUST, WELL

²**hale** *vb* **haled; hal·ing** **1** : HAUL, PULL **2** : to compel to go

ha·ler \\'hä-lər\\ *n, pl* **ha·le·ru** \\'hä-lə-ˌrü\\ — see *koruna* at MONEY table

¹**half** \\'haf, 'häf\\ *n, pl* **halves** \\'havz, 'hävz\\ **1** : either of two equal parts into which something is divisible **2** : one of a pair

²**half** *adj* **1** : being one of two equal parts **2** : amounting to nearly half **3** : PARTIAL, INCOMPLETE — **half** *adv*

half–and–half \\ˌhaf-ᵊn-'haf, ˌhäf-ᵊn-'häf\\ *n* : something that is half one thing and half another

half·back \\'haf-ˌbak, 'häf-\\ *n* **1** : a football back stationed on or near the flank **2** : a player stationed immediately behind the forward line

half–baked \\-'bākt\\ *adj* **1** : poorly planned **2** : lacking common sense **3** : not thoroughly baked

half–breed \\-ˌbrēd\\ *n, often offensive* : one of mixed racial descent — **half–breed** *adj, often offensive*

half brother *n* : a brother related through one parent only

half–caste \\'haf-ˌkast, 'häf-\\ *n, often offensive* : HALF=BREED — **half–caste** *adj, often offensive*

half–cocked \\'haf-'käkt, 'häf-\\ *adj* : lacking adequate preparation

half–dol·lar \\-'dä-lər\\ *n* **1** : a coin representing one half of a dollar **2** : the sum of fifty cents

half–heart·ed \\-'här-təd\\ *adj* : lacking spirit or interest — **half–heart·ed·ly** *adv* — **half–heart·ed·ness** *n*

half–life \\-ˌlīf\\ *n* : the time required for half of something (as atoms or a drug) to undergo a process

half–mast \\-'mast\\ *n* : a point about halfway down from the top of a mast or staff

half note *n* : a musical note equal in time to one half that of a whole note

half·pen·ny \\'hāp-nē\\ *n, pl* **half·pence** \\'hā-pəns\\ *or* **half·pennies** : a formerly used British coin representing one half of a penny

half–pint \\'haf-ˌpīnt, 'häf-\\ *adj* : of less than average size — **half–pint** *n*

half sister *n* : a sister related through one parent only

half sole *n* : a shoe sole extending from the shank forward — **half–sole** *vb*

half–staff \\'haf-'staf, 'häf-\\ *n* : HALF-MAST

half step *n* : a musical interval equivalent to one twelfth of an octave

half·time \\'haf-ˌtīm, 'häf-\\ *n* : an intermission between halves of a game

half–track \\-ˌtrak\\ *n* : a motor vehicle propelled by an endless chain-track drive system; *esp* : such a vehicle lightly armored for military use

half–truth \\-ˌtrüth\\ *n* : a statement that is only partially true; *esp* : one that deliberately mixes truth and falsehood

half·way \\-'wā\\ *adj* **1** : midway between two points **2** : PARTIAL 1 — **halfway** *adv*

half–wit \\-ˌwit\\ *n* : a foolish or imbecilic person — **half–wit·ted** \\-'wi-təd\\ *adj* — **half–wit·ted·ness** *n*

hal·i·but \\'ha-lə-bət\\ *n, pl* **halibut** *also* **halibuts** [ME *halybutte*, fr. *haly, holy* holy + *butte* flatfish; fr. its being eaten on holy days] : any of several large edible marine flatfishes

ha·lite \\'ha-ˌlīt, 'hā-\\ *n* : ROCK SALT

hal·i·to·sis \\ˌha-lə-'tō-səs\\ *n* : the condition of having fetid breath

hall \'hȯl\ n 1 : the residence of a medieval king or noble; also : the house of a landed proprietor 2 : a large public building 3 : a college or university building; also : DORMITORY 4 : LOBBY; also : CORRIDOR 5 : AUDITORIUM

hal·le·lu·jah \ˌha-lə-'lü-yə\ interj [Heb hallĕlūyāh praise (ye) the Lord] — used to express praise, joy, or thanks

hall·mark \'hȯl-ˌmärk\ n 1 : a mark put on an article to indicate origin, purity, or genuineness 2 : a distinguishing characteristic

hal·low \'ha-lō\ vb 1 : CONSECRATE 2 : REVERE, VENERATE ⟨our ∼ed leader⟩ — **hal·lowed** \-lōd, -lə-wəd\ adj

Hal·low·een also **Hal·low·e'en** \ˌha-lə-'wēn, ˌhä-\ n : the evening of October 31 observed esp. by children in merrymaking and masquerading

hal·lu·ci·nate \hə-'lü-sə-ˌnāt\ vb **-nat·ed; -nat·ing** : to have hallucinations or experience as a hallucination

hal·lu·ci·na·tion \hə-ˌlü-sə-'nā-shən\ n : perception of objects with no reality due usu. to use of drugs (as LSD) or to disorder of the nervous system; also : something so perceived ✦ **Synonyms** DELUSION, ILLUSION, MIRAGE — **hal·lu·ci·na·to·ry** \-'lü-sə-nə-ˌtȯr-ē\ adj

hal·lu·ci·no·gen \hə-'lü-sə-nə-jən\ n : a substance that induces hallucinations — **hal·lu·ci·no·gen·ic** \-ˌlü-sə-nə-'je-nik\ adj or n

hall·way \'hȯl-ˌwā\ n 1 : an entrance hall 2 : CORRIDOR

ha·lo \'hā-lō\ n, pl **halos** or **haloes** [L halos, fr. Gk halōs threshing floor, disk, halo] 1 : a circle of light appearing to surround a shining body (as the sun) 2 : the aura of glory surrounding an idealized person or thing

¹**hal·o·gen** \'ha-lə-jən\ n : any of the five elements fluorine, chlorine, bromine, iodine, and astatine

²**halogen** adj : containing, using, or being a halogen ⟨a ∼ lamp⟩

¹**halt** \'hȯlt\ adj : LAME 1

²**halt** n : STOP

³**halt** vb 1 : to stop marching or traveling 2 : DISCONTINUE, END ⟨∼ protests⟩

¹**hal·ter** \'hȯl-tər\ n 1 : a rope or strap for leading or tying an animal; also : HEADSTALL 2 : NOOSE 3 : a brief blouse held in place by straps around the neck and across the back

²**halter** vb **hal·tered; hal·ter·ing** 1 : to catch with or as if with a halter; also : to put a halter on (as a horse) 2 : HANG 3 : IMPEDE, RESTRAIN

halt·ing \'hȯl-tiŋ\ adj : UNCERTAIN, FALTERING — **halt·ing·ly** adv

halve \'hav, 'häv\ vb **halved; halv·ing** 1 : to divide into two equal parts 2 : to reduce to one half

halv·ers \'ha-vərz, 'hä-\ n pl : half shares : HALVES

halves pl of HALF

hal·yard \'hal-yərd\ n : a rope or tackle for hoisting and lowering (as sails)

¹**ham** \'ham\ n 1 : a buttock with its associated thigh — usu. used in pl. 2 : a cut of meat and esp. pork from the thigh 3 : a showy performer 4 : an operator of an amateur radio station — **ham** adj

²**ham** vb **hammed; ham·ming** : to overplay a part : OVERACT

ham·burg·er \'ham-ˌbər-gər\ or **ham·burg** \-ˌbərg\ n [G Hamburger of Hamburg, Germany] 1 : ground beef 2 : a sandwich consisting of a ground-beef patty in a round roll

ham·let \'ham-lət\ n : a small village

¹**ham·mer** \'ha-mər\ n 1 : a hand tool used for pounding; also : something resembling a hammer in form or function 2 : the part of a gun whose striking action causes explosion of the charge 3 : a metal sphere hurled by a flexible handle for distance in a track-and-field event (**hammer throw**) 4 : ACCELERATOR 2

²**hammer** vb 1 : to beat, drive, or shape with repeated blows of a hammer : POUND 2 : to produce or bring about as if by repeated blows — usu. used with out 3 : to criticize severely

ham·mer·head \'ha-mər-ˌhed\ n 1 : the striking part of a hammer 2 : any of a family of medium-sized sharks with eyes at the ends of lateral extensions of the flattened head

ham·mer·lock \-ˌläk\ n : a wrestling hold in which an opponent's arm is held bent behind the back

ham·mer·toe \-ˌtō\ n : a toe deformed by having one or more joints permanently flexed

¹**ham·mock** \'ha-mək\ n [Sp hamaca, of AmerInd origin] : a swinging couch hung by cords at each end

²**hammock** n : a fertile elevated area of the southern U.S. and esp. Florida with hardwood vegetation and soil rich in humus

¹**ham·per** \'ham-pər\ vb : IMPEDE; also : RESTRAIN ✦ **Synonyms** TRAMMEL, CLOG, FETTER, SHACKLE

²**hamper** n : a large usu. lidded basket

ham·ster \'ham-stər\ n [G, fr. OHG hamustro, of Slavic origin] : any of a subfamily of small Old World rodents with large cheek pouches

¹**ham·string** \'ham-ˌstriŋ\ n : any of several muscles at the back of the thigh or tendons at the back of the knee

²**hamstring** vb **-strung** \-ˌstrəŋ\; **-string·ing** 1 : to make ineffective or powerless ⟨hamstrung by guilt⟩ 2 : to cripple by cutting the leg tendons

¹**hand** \'hand\ n 1 : the end of a front limb when modified (as in humans) for grasping 2 : an indicator or pointer on a dial 3 : personal possession — usu. used in pl.; also : CONTROL 4 : SIDE 5 5 : a pledge esp. of betrothal 6 : HANDWRITING 7 : SKILL, ABILITY; also : a significant part ⟨had a ∼ in the victory⟩ 8 : ASSISTANCE; also : PARTICIPATION ⟨had no ∼ in the affair⟩ 9 : an outburst of applause 10 : a single round in a card game; also : the cards held by a player after a deal 11 : WORKER, EMPLOYEE; also : a member of a ship's crew — **hand·less** adj — **at hand** : near in time or place — **on hand** : in present possession or readily available — **out of hand** : out of control

²**hand** vb 1 : to lead, guide, or assist with the hand 2 : to give, pass, or transmit with the hand ⟨∼ed her the letter⟩

hand·bag \'hand-ˌbag\ n : a bag for carrying small personal articles and money

hand·ball \-ˌbȯl\ n : a game played by striking a small rubber ball against a wall with the hand

hand·bill \-ˌbil\ n : a small printed sheet for distribution by hand

hand·book \-ˌbu̇k\ n : a concise reference book : MANUAL

hand·car \-ˌkär\ n : a small 4-wheeled railroad car propelled by hand or by a small motor

hand·clasp \-ˌklasp\ n : HANDSHAKE

hand·craft \-ˌkraft\ vb : to fashion by manual skill

¹**hand·cuff** \-ˌkəf\ n : a metal fastening that can be locked around a wrist and is usu. connected with another such fastening — usu. used in pl.

²**handcuff** vb : MANACLE

hand·ed \'han-dəd\ adj : having or using such or so many hands ⟨a left-handed person⟩ — **hand·ed·ness** n

hand·ful \'hand-ˌfu̇l\ n, pl **hand·fuls** \-ˌfu̇lz\ also **hands·ful** \'handz-ˌfu̇l\ 1 : as much or as many as the hand will grasp 2 : a small number 3 : as much as one can manage

hand·gun \-ˌgən\ n : a firearm held and fired with one hand

hand·held \-ˌheld\ adj : designed for use while being held in the hand — **handheld** n

¹**hand·i·cap** \'han-di-ˌkap\ n [obs. E handicap, a game in which forfeit money was held in a cap, fr. hand in cap] 1 : a contest in which an artificial advantage is given or disadvantage imposed on a contestant to equalize chances of winning; also : the advantage given or disadvantage imposed 2 : a disadvantage that makes achievement difficult

²**handicap** vb **-capped; -cap·ping** 1 : to give a handicap to 2 : to put at a disadvantage

hand·i·capped adj, sometimes offensive : having a physical or mental disability

hand·i·cap·per \-ˌka-pər\ n : a person who predicts the winners in a contest

hand·i·craft \'han-di-ˌkraft\ n 1 : manual skill 2 : an occupation requiring manual skill 3 : the articles fashioned by those engaged in handicraft — **hand·i·craft·er** \-ˌkraf-tər\ n — **hand·i·crafts·man** \-ˌkrafts-mən\ n

hand in glove or **hand and glove** adv : in an extremely close relationship

hand·i·work \'han-di-ˌwərk\ n : work done personally or by the hands

hand·ker·chief \'haŋ-kər-chəf, -ˌchēf\ n, pl **-chiefs** \-chəfs, -ˌchēfs\ also **-chieves** \-ˌchēvz\ : a small piece of cloth used for various personal purposes (as the wiping of the face)

¹han·dle \'han-d°l\ *n* 1 : a part (as of a tool) designed to be grasped by the hand 2 : NAME; *also* : NICKNAME — **han·dled** \-d°ld\ *adj* — **off the handle** : into a state of sudden and violent anger — usu. used with *fly*

²handle *vb* **han·dled; han·dling** 1 : to touch, hold, or manage with the hands 2 : to have responsibility for 3 : to deal or trade in 4 : to behave in a certain way when managed or directed ⟨a car that ~s well⟩ — **han·dler** *n*

han·dle·bar \'han-d°l-bär\ *n* : a usu. bent bar with a grip at each end (as for steering a bicycle) — usu. used in pl.

hand·made \'hand-'mād\ *adj* : made by hand or by a hand process

hand·maid·en \-,mā-d°n\ *also* **hand·maid** \-,mād\ *n* : a female attendant

hand·me·down \-me-,daún\ *adj* : used by one person after having been used by another — **hand·me·down** *n*

hand·out \'hand-,aút\ *n* 1 : a portion (as of food) given to a beggar 2 : a piece of printed information for free distribution; *also* : a prepared statement released to the press

hand over *vb* : to yield control of

hand·pick \'hand-'pik\ *vb* : to select personally ⟨a ~ed candidate⟩

hand·rail \-,rāl\ *n* : a narrow rail for grasping as a support

hand·saw \-,sò\ *n* : a saw designed to be used with one hand

hands down *adv* 1 : with little effort 2 : without question

hand·sel \'han-səl\ *n* 1 : a gift made as a token of good luck 2 : a first installment : earnest money

hand·set \'hand-,set\ *n* : a combined telephone transmitter and receiver mounted on a handheld device

hand·shake \-,shāk\ *n* : a clasping usu. of right hands by two people

hands·off \'handz-'òf\ *adj* : characterized by noninterference

hand·some \'han-səm\ *adj* **hand·som·er; -est** [ME *handsom* easy to manipulate] 1 : SIZABLE, AMPLE ⟨a ~ profit⟩ 2 : GENEROUS, LIBERAL 3 : pleasing and usu. impressive in appearance ♦ **Synonyms** BEAUTIFUL, LOVELY, PRETTY, COMELY, FAIR — **hand·some·ly** *adv* — **hand·some·ness** *n*

hands·on \'handz-'òn, -'än\ *adj* 1 : being or providing direct practical experience in the operation of something 2 : characterized by active personal involvement ⟨~ management⟩

hand·spring \'hand-,spriη\ *n* : an acrobatic feat in which the body turns in a full circle from a standing position and lands first on the hands and then on the feet

hand·stand \-,stand\ *n* : an act of supporting the body on the hands with the trunk and legs balanced in the air

hand·to·hand *adj* : involving physical contact or very close range ⟨~ fighting⟩ — **hand to hand** *adv*

hand·to·mouth *adj* : having or providing nothing to spare ⟨lived a ~ existence⟩ — **hand to mouth** *adv*

hand·wo·ven \'hand-,wō-vən\ *adj* : produced on a hand-operated loom

hand·writ·ing \-,rī-tiη\ *n* : writing done by hand; *also* : the form of writing peculiar to a person — **hand·writ·ten** \-,ri-t°n\ *adj*

handy \'han-dē\ *adj* **hand·i·er; -est** 1 : conveniently near 2 : easily used ⟨a ~ tool⟩ 3 : DEXTEROUS — **hand·i·ly** \-də-lē\ *adv* — **hand·i·ness** \-dē-nəs\ *n*

handy·man \-,man\ *n* 1 : one who does odd jobs 2 : one competent in a variety of small skills or repair work

¹hang \'haη\ *vb* **hung** \'həη\ *also* **hanged; hang·ing** 1 : to fasten or remain fastened to an elevated point without support from below; *also* : to fasten or be fastened so as to allow free motion on the point of suspension ⟨~ a door⟩ 2 : to suspend by the neck until dead; *also* : to die by hanging 3 : DROOP ⟨hung his head in shame⟩ 4 : to fasten to a wall ⟨~ wallpaper⟩ 5 : to prevent (a jury) from coming to a decision 6 : to display (pictures) in a gallery 7 : to remain stationary in the air 8 : to be imminent 9 : DEPEND 10 : to take hold for support 11 : to be burdensome 12 : to undergo delay 13 : to incline downward; *also* : to fall or fall from the figure in easy lines 14 : to be raptly attentive 15 : to pass time idly by relaxing or socializing ⟨~ing at the mall⟩ — often used with *around* or *out* — **hang out to dry** : to subject to ruin by abandonment

²hang *n* 1 : the manner in which a thing hangs 2 : understanding of something ⟨got the ~ of skiing⟩

han·gar \'haη-ər\ *n* [F] : a covered and usu. enclosed area for housing and repairing aircraft

hang·dog \'haη-,dòg\ *adj* 1 : SAD, DEJECTED ⟨a ~ look on his face⟩ 2 : SHEEPISH

hang·er \'haη-ər\ *n* 1 : one that hangs 2 : a device that fits inside or around a garment for hanging from a hook or rod

hang·er·on \'haη-ər-'òn, -'än\ *n, pl* **hangers·on** : one who hangs around a person or place esp. for personal gain

hang in *vb* : to persist tenaciously

hang·ing *n* 1 : an execution by strangling or snapping the neck by a suspended noose 2 : something hung

hang·man \'haη-mən\ *n* 1 : a public executioner 2 : a game in which players must identify an unknown word by guessing the letters that comprise it within a designated number of chances

hang·nail \-,nāl\ *n* : a bit of skin hanging loose at the edge of a fingernail

hang on *vb* 1 : to keep hold onto something 2 : HANG IN 3 : to await something desired

hang·out \'haη-,aút\ *n* : a favorite place for spending time

hang·over \-,ō-vər\ *n* 1 : something that remains from what is past 2 : disagreeable physical effects following heavy drinking or the use of drugs

hang·up \'haη-,əp\ *n* : a source of mental or emotional difficulty

hang up *vb* 1 : to place on a hook or hanger 2 : to end a telephone conversation by breaking the connection 3 : to keep delayed or suspended

hank \'haηk\ *n* : COIL, LOOP ⟨a ~ of rope⟩

han·ker \'haη-kər\ *vb* : to desire strongly or persistently — **han·ker·ing** *n*

han·kie *or* **han·ky** \'haη-kē\ *n, pl* **hankies** : HANDKERCHIEF

han·ky–pan·ky \,haη-kē-'paη-kē\ *n* 1 : questionable or underhanded activity 2 : sexual dalliance

hansel *var of* HANDSEL

han·som \'han-səm\ *n* : a 2-wheeled covered carriage with the driver's seat elevated at the rear

han·ta·virus \'hän-tə-,vī-rəs, 'hən-, 'han-\ *n* : any of a genus of viruses including some transmitted by rodents that cause pneumonia or hemorrhagic fevers

Ha·nuk·kah *also* **Cha·nu·kah** \'kä-nə-kə, 'hä-\ *n* [Heb *ḥănukkāh* dedication] : an 8-day Jewish holiday commemorating the rededication of the Temple of Jerusalem after its defilement by Antiochus of Syria

hap \'hap\ *n* 1 : HAPPENING 2 : CHANCE, FORTUNE

¹hap·haz·ard \hap-'ha-zərd\ *n* : CHANCE

²haphazard *adj* : marked by lack of plan or order — **hap·haz·ard·ly** *adv* — **hap·haz·ard·ness** *n*

hap·less \'hap-ləs\ *adj* : UNFORTUNATE — **hap·less·ly** *adv* — **hap·less·ness** *n*

hap·loid \'hap-,lòid\ *adj* : having the number of chromosomes characteristic of gametic cells — **haploid** *n*

hap·ly \'hap-lē\ *adv* : by chance

hap·pen \'ha-pən\ *vb* 1 : to occur by chance 2 : to take place 3 : CHANCE 2

¹hap·pen·ing *n* 1 : OCCURRENCE 2 : an event that is especially interesting, entertaining, or important

²happening *adj* 1 : very fashionable 2 : offering much stimulating activity ⟨a ~ nightclub⟩

hap·pi·ly \'ha-pə-lē\ *adv* 1 : LUCKILY 2 : in a happy manner or state ⟨lived ~ ever after⟩ 3 : APTLY, SUCCESSFULLY

hap·pi·ness \'ha-pē-nəs\ *n* 1 : a state of well-being and contentment; *also* : a pleasurable satisfaction 2 : APTNESS

hap·py \'ha-pē\ *adj* **hap·pi·er; -est** 1 : FORTUNATE 2 : APT, FELICITOUS 3 : enjoying well-being and contentment ⟨a ~ childhood⟩ 4 : PLEASANT ⟨a ~ ending⟩; *also* : PLEASED, GRATIFIED ⟨~ to meet you⟩ 5 : quick or enthusiastic to use or do something ⟨trigger-*happy*⟩ ⟨a cliché-*happy* writer⟩ ♦ **Synonyms** GLAD, CHEERFUL, LIGHTHEARTED, JOYFUL, JOYOUS

hap·py–go–lucky \,ha-pē-gō-'lə-kē\ *adj* : CAREFREE

happy hour *n* : a period of time when the price of drinks at a bar is reduced

hara–kiri \,ha-ri-'kir-ē, -'ka-rē\ *n* [Jp *harakiri*, fr. *hara* belly + *kiri* cutting] : ritual suicide by disembowelment

ha·rangue \hə-'raŋ\ *n* **1** : a ranting speech or writing **2** : LECTURE — **harangue** *vb* — **ha·rangu·er** *n*
ha·rass \hə-'ras, 'ha-rəs\ *vb* [F *harasser,* fr. MF, fr. *harer* to set a dog on, fr. OF *hare,* interj. used to incite dogs, of Gmc origin] **1** : EXHAUST, FATIGUE **2** : to worry and impede by repeated raids **3** : to annoy continually **4** : to create an unpleasant or hostile situation for esp. by one's verbal or physical conduct ✦ *Synonyms* HARRY, PLAGUE, PESTER, TEASE, BEDEVIL — **ha·rass·ment** *n*
har·bin·ger \'här-bən-jər\ *n* : one that announces or foreshadows what is coming : PRECURSOR; *also* : PORTENT
¹**har·bor** \'här-bər\ *n* **1** : a place of security and comfort **2** : a part of a body of water protected and deep enough to furnish anchorage : PORT
²**harbor** *vb* **1** : to give or take refuge : SHELTER ⟨∼ a fugitive⟩ ⟨∼ed in the barn⟩ **2** : to be the home or habitat of; *also* : LIVE **3** : to hold a thought or feeling ⟨∼ a grudge⟩
har·bor·age \'här-bə-rij\ *n* : HARBOR
har·bour *chiefly Brit var of* HARBOR
hard \'härd\ *adj* **1** : not easily penetrated : not easily yielding to pressure **2** : high in alcoholic content **3** : containing salts that prevent lathering with soap ⟨∼ water⟩ **4** : stable in value ⟨∼ currency⟩ **5** : physically fit **6** : FIRM, DEFINITE ⟨∼ agreement⟩; *also* : based on clear fact ⟨∼ evidence⟩ **7** : CLOSE, SEARCHING ⟨a ∼ look⟩ **8** : REALISTIC ⟨good ∼ sense⟩ **9** : OBDURATE, UNFEELING ⟨a ∼ heart⟩ **10** : difficult to bear ⟨∼ times⟩; *also* : HARSH, SEVERE **11** : RESENTFUL ⟨∼ feelings⟩ **12** : STRICT, UNRELENTING ⟨a ∼ bargain⟩ **13** : INCLEMENT ⟨a ∼ winter⟩ **14** : intense in force or manner ⟨a ∼ gust of wind⟩ **15** : ARDUOUS, STRENUOUS ⟨∼ work⟩ **16** : sounding as in *arcing* and *geese* respectively — used of *c* and *g* **17** : TROUBLESOME ⟨a ∼ problem⟩ **18** : having difficulty in doing something ⟨∼ of hearing⟩ **19** : addictive and gravely detrimental to health ⟨∼ drugs⟩ **20** : of or relating to the natural sciences and esp. the physical sciences — **hard** *adv* — **hard·ness** *n*
hard–and–fast *adj* : rigidly binding : STRICT ⟨a ∼ rule⟩
hard·back \'härd-,bak\ *n* : a hardcover book
hard·ball \-,böl\ *n* **1** : BASEBALL **2** : forceful uncompromising methods
hard–bit·ten \-'bi-tᵊn\ *adj* : SEASONED, TOUGH ⟨∼ campaigners⟩
hard·board \-,bòrd\ *n* : a very dense fiberboard
hard–boiled \-'bói(-ə)ld\ *adj* **1** *of an egg* : boiled until both white and yolk have solidified **2** : lacking sentiment : TOUGH; *also* : HARDHEADED 2
hard·bound \-,baùnd\ *adj* : HARDCOVER
hard copy *n* : a copy of textual or graphic information (as from computer storage) produced on paper
hard–core \'härd-'kòr\ *adj* **1** : extremely resistant to solution or improvement **2** : being the most determined or dedicated members of a specified group **3** : containing explicit depictions of sex acts — **hard core** *n*
hard·cov·er \-'kə-vər\ *adj* : having rigid boards on the sides covered in cloth or paper ⟨∼ books⟩
hard disk *n* : a sealed rigid metal disk used as a computer storage device; *also* : HARD DRIVE
hard drive *n* : a data-storage device consisting of a drive and one or more hard disks
hard·en \'här-dᵊn\ *vb* **1** : to make or become hard or harder **2** : to confirm or become confirmed in disposition or action — **hard·en·er** *n*
hard·hack \'härd-,hak\ *n* : an American spirea with dense clusters of pink or white flowers and leaves having a hairy rusty yellow underside
hard hat *n* **1** : a protective hat worn esp. by construction workers **2** : a construction worker
hard·head·ed \'härd-'he-dəd\ *adj* **1** : STUBBORN, WILLFUL **2** : SOBER, REALISTIC ⟨some ∼ advice⟩ — **hard·head·ed·ly** *adv* — **hard·head·ed·ness** *n*
hard–heart·ed \-'här-təd\ *adj* : PITILESS, CRUEL — **hard–heart·ed·ly** *adv* — **hard–heart·ed·ness** *n*
har·di·hood \'här-dē-,hùd\ *n* **1** : resolute courage and fortitude **2** : VIGOR, ROBUSTNESS
hard–line \'härd-'līn\ *adj* : advocating or involving a rigidly uncompromising course of action ⟨a ∼ conservative⟩ — **hard–lin·er** \-'lī-nər\ *n*
hard–luck \-,lək\ *adj* : marked by or relating to bad luck ⟨∼ losing teams⟩
hard·ly \'härd-lē\ *adv* **1** : with force **2** : SEVERELY **3**

: with difficulty **4** : only just : BARELY ⟨can ∼ tell the difference⟩ **5** : certainly not ⟨is ∼ a friend of mine⟩
hard–nosed \'härd-'nōzd\ *adj* : TOUGH, UNCOMPROMISING; *also* : HARDHEADED 2
hard palate *n* : the bony anterior part of the palate forming the roof of the mouth
hard·pan \'härd-,pan\ *n* : a compact layer in soil that is impenetrable by roots
hard–pressed \-'prest\ *adj* : HARD PUT; *esp* : being under financial strain
hard put *adj* **1** : barely able **2** : faced with difficulty or perplexity
hard rock *n* : rock music marked by a heavy beat, high amplification, and usu. frenzied performances
hard–shell \'härd-,shel\ *or* **hard–shelled** \-,sheld\ *adj* **1** : having a hard shell **2** : HIDEBOUND, UNCOMPROMISING ⟨a ∼ conservative⟩
hard·ship \-,ship\ *n* **1** : SUFFERING, PRIVATION **2** : something that causes suffering or privation
hard·tack \-,tak\ *n* : a saltless hard biscuit, bread, or cracker
hard·top \-,täp\ *n* : an automobile having a permanent rigid top
hard·ware \-,wer\ *n* **1** : ware (as cutlery or tools) made of metal **2** : the physical components (as electronic devices) of a vehicle (as a spacecraft) or an apparatus (as a computer)
hard·wired \-,wī(-ə)rd\ *adj* **1** : connected or incorporated by or as if by permanent electrical connections **2** : genetically or innately determined or predisposed ⟨∼ reactions⟩ ⟨is ∼ to avoid change⟩
hard·wood \-,wùd\ *n* : the wood of a broad-leaved usu. deciduous tree as distinguished from that of a conifer; *also* : such a tree — **hardwood** *adj*
hard·work·ing \-'wər-kiŋ\ *adj* : INDUSTRIOUS, DILIGENT
har·dy \'här-dē\ *adj* **har·di·er; -est 1** : BOLD, BRAVE ⟨∼ pioneers⟩ **2** : AUDACIOUS, BRAZEN **3** : ROBUST; *also* : able to withstand adverse conditions (as of weather) ⟨∼ shrubs⟩ — **har·di·ly** \-də-lē\ *adv* — **har·di·ness** \-dē-nəs\ *n*
hare \'her\ *n, pl* **hare** *or* **hares** : any of various swift timid long-eared mammals like the related rabbits but born with open eyes and fur
hare·bell \'her-,bel\ *n* : a slender herb with bright blue bell-shaped flowers
hare–brained \-'brānd\ *adj* : FOOLISH, ABSURD ⟨∼ notions⟩
hare·lip \-'lip\ *n, sometimes offensive* : CLEFT LIP
ha·rem \'her-əm\ *n* [Ar *ḥarīm,* lit., something forbidden & *ḥaram,* lit., sanctuary] **1** : a house or part of a house allotted to women in a Muslim household **2** : the women and servants occupying a harem **3** : a group of females associated with one male
hark \'härk\ *vb* : LISTEN
harken *var of* HEARKEN
har·le·quin \'här-li-kən, -kwən\ *n* **1** *cap* : a character (as in comedy) with a shaved head, masked face, variegated tights, and wooden sword **2** : CLOWN 2
har·lot \'här-lət\ *n* : PROSTITUTE
¹**harm** \'härm\ *n* **1** : physical or mental damage : INJURY **2** : MISCHIEF, HURT — **harm·ful** \-fəl\ *adj* — **harm·ful·ly** *adv* — **harm·ful·ness** *n* — **harm·less** *adj* — **harm·less·ly** *adv* — **harm·less·ness** *n*
²**harm** *vb* : to cause harm to : INJURE
¹**har·mon·ic** \här-'mä-nik\ *adj* **1** : of or relating to musical harmony or harmonics **2** : pleasing to the ear — **har·mon·i·cal·ly** \-ni-k(ə-)lē\ *adv*
²**harmonic** *n* : a musical overtone
har·mon·i·ca \här-'mä-ni-kə\ *n* : a small wind instrument in which the sound is produced by metal reeds
har·mo·ni·ous \här-'mō-nē-əs\ *adj* **1** : musically concordant **2** : CONGRUOUS **3** : marked by accord in sentiment or action ⟨a ∼ relationship⟩ — **har·mo·ni·ous·ly** *adv* — **har·mo·ni·ous·ness** *n*
har·mo·nise *Brit var of* HARMONIZE
har·mo·ni·um \här-'mō-nē-əm\ *n* : a keyboard wind instrument in which the wind acts on a set of metal reeds
har·mo·nize \'här-mə-,nīz\ *vb* **-nized; -niz·ing 1** : to play or sing in harmony **2** : to be in harmony **3** : to bring into consonance or accord — **har·mo·ni·za·tion** \,här-mə-nə-'zā-shən\ *n*

har·mo·ny \'här-mə-nē\ *n, pl* **-nies** [ME *armony*, fr. AF *armonie*, fr. L *harmonia*, fr. Gk, joint, harmony, fr. *harmos* joint] **1** : musical agreement of sounds; *esp* : the combination of tones into chords and progressions of chords **2** : a pleasing arrangement of parts; *also* : ACCORD **3** : internal calm

¹har·ness \'här-nəs\ *n* **1** : the gear other than a yoke of a draft animal **2** : something that resembles a harness

²harness *vb* **1** : to put a harness on; *also* : YOKE **2** : UTILIZE ⟨~ one's potential⟩

¹harp \'härp\ *n* : a musical instrument consisting of a triangular frame set with strings plucked by the fingers — **harp·ist** \'här-pist\ *n*

²harp **1** : to play on a harp **2** : to dwell on a subject tiresomely — **harp·er** *n*

har·poon \här-'pün\ *n* : a barbed spear used esp. in hunting whales — **harpoon** *vb* — **har·poon·er** *n*

harp·si·chord \'härp-si-ˌkȯrd\ *n* : a keyboard instrument producing tones by the plucking of its strings with quills or with leather or plastic points

har·py \'här-pē\ *n, pl* **harpies** [L *Harpyia*, a malign creature of myth having a woman's head and a bird's body, fr. Gk] **1** : a predatory person : LEECH **2** : a shrewish woman

har·ri·dan \'her-ə-dən\ *n* : SHREW 2

¹har·ri·er \'her-ē-ər\ *n* **1** : any of a breed of medium-sized foxhounds **2** : a runner on a cross-country team

²harrier *n* : a slender long-legged hawk

har·row \'her-ō\ *n* : a cultivating tool that has spikes, spring teeth, or disks and is used esp. to pulverize and smooth the soil

²harrow *vb* **1** : to cultivate with a harrow **2** : TORMENT, VEX

har·rumph \hə-'rəmf\ *vb* : to comment disapprovingly as though clearing the throat

har·ry \'her-ē\ *vb* **har·ried; har·ry·ing** **1** : RAID, PILLAGE **2** : to torment by or as if by constant attack ♦ *Synonyms* WORRY, ANNOY, PLAGUE, PESTER

harsh \'härsh\ *adj* **1** : disagreeably rough **2** : causing discomfort or pain **3** : unduly exacting : SEVERE — **harsh·ly** *adv* — **harsh·ness** *n*

harsh·en \'här-shən\ *vb* : to make or become harsh ⟨~ed his voice⟩

hart \'härt\ *n, chiefly Brit* : STAG

har·um–scar·um \ˌhar-əm-'skar-əm\ *adj* : RECKLESS, IRRESPONSIBLE

¹har·vest \'här-vəst\ *n* **1** : the season for gathering in crops; *also* : the act of gathering in a crop **2** : a mature crop **3** : the product or reward of effort

²harvest *vb* **1** : to gather in a crop : REAP **2** : to gather, hunt, or kill (as deer) for human use or population control **3** : to remove cells, tissues, or organs from a living or recently deceased body esp. for transplanting — **har·vest·er** *n*

has *pres 3d sing of* HAVE

has–been \'haz-ˌbin\ *n* : one that has passed the peak of ability, power, effectiveness, or popularity

¹hash \'hash\ *vb* [F *hacher*, fr. OF *hachier*, fr. *hache* battle-ax, of Gmc origin] **1** : to chop into small pieces **2** : to talk about — often used with *over* or *out*

²hash *n* **1** : chopped meat mixed with potatoes and browned **2** : HODGEPODGE, JUMBLE

³hash *n* : HASHISH

hash browns *n pl* : boiled potatoes that have been diced, mixed with chopped onions and shortening, and fried

hash·ish \'ha-ˌshēsh, ha-'shēsh\ *n* [Ar *ḥashīsh*] : the intoxicating concentrated resin from the flowering tops of the female hemp plant

hash·tag \'hash-ˌtag\ *n* : a word or phrase preceded by the symbol # that classifies the accompanying text

hasp \'hasp\ *n* : a fastener (as for a door) consisting of a hinged metal strap that fits over a staple and is secured by a pin or padlock

has·si·um \'ha-sē-əm\ *n* : an artificially produced radioactive metallic chemical element

has·sle \'ha-səl\ *n* **1** : WRANGLE; *also* : FIGHT **2** : an annoying or troublesome concern — **hassle** *vb*

has·sock \'ha-sək\ *n* : a cushion that serves as a seat or leg rest; *also* : a cushion to kneel on in prayer

haste \'hāst\ *n* **1** : rapidity of motion or action : SPEED **2** : rash or headlong action **3** : excessive eagerness

hast·i·ly \'hā-stə-lē\ *adv* — **hast·i·ness** \-stē-nəs\ *n* — **hasty** \'hā-stē\ *adj*

has·ten \'hā-sⁿn\ *vb* **1** : to urge on **2** : to move or act quickly : HURRY ♦ *Synonyms* SPEED, ACCELERATE, QUICKEN

hat \'hat\ *n* : a covering for the head usu. having a shaped crown and brim — **under one's hat** : SECRET ⟨kept the plans *under his hat*⟩

hat·box \'hat-ˌbäks\ *n* : a round piece of luggage esp. for carrying hats

¹hatch \'hach\ *n* **1** : a small door or opening **2** : a door or cover for access down into a compartment of a ship

²hatch *vb* **1** : to produce by incubation; *also* : INCUBATE **2** : to emerge from an egg or pupa; *also* : to give forth young **3** : ORIGINATE ⟨~ a scheme⟩ — **hatch·ery** \'ha-chə-rē\ *n*

hatch·back \'hach-ˌbak\ *n* : an automobile with a rear hatch that opens upward

hatch·et \'ha-chət\ *n* **1** : a short-handled ax with a hammerlike part opposite the blade **2** : TOMAHAWK

hatchet man *n* : a person hired for murder, coercion, or unscrupulous attack

hatch·ing \'ha-chiŋ\ *n* : the engraving or drawing of closely spaced fine lines chiefly to give an effect of shading; *also* : the pattern so created

hatch·way \'hach-ˌwā\ *n* : a hatch giving access usu. by a ladder or stairs

¹hate \'hāt\ *n* **1** : intense hostility and aversion **2** : an object of hatred — **hate·ful** \-fəl\ *adj* — **hate·ful·ly** *adv* — **hate·ful·ness** *n*

²hate *vb* **hat·ed; hat·ing** **1** : to express or feel extreme enmity **2** : to find distasteful ♦ *Synonyms* DETEST, ABHOR, ABOMINATE, LOATHE — **hat·er** *n*

ha·tred \'hā-trəd\ *n* : HATE; *also* : prejudiced hostility or animosity

hat·ter \'ha-tər\ *n* : one that makes, sells, or cleans or repairs hats

hau·berk \'hȯ-bərk\ *n* : a coat of mail

haugh·ty \'hȯ-tē\ *adj* **haugh·ti·er; -est** [obs. *haught*, fr. ME *haute*, fr. AF *halt, haut*, lit., high, fr. L *altus*] : disdainfully proud ♦ *Synonyms* INSOLENT, LORDLY, OVERBEARING, ARROGANT — **haugh·ti·ly** \-tə-lē\ *adv* — **haugh·ti·ness** \-tē-nəs\ *n*

¹haul \'hȯl\ *vb* **1** : to exert traction on : DRAW, PULL **2** : to furnish transportation : CART — **haul·er** *n*

²haul *n* **1** : PULL, TUG **2** : the result of an effort to obtain, collect, or win **3** : the length or course of a transportation route; *also* : LOAD

haul·age \'hȯ-lij\ *n* **1** : the act or process of hauling **2** : a charge for hauling

haunch \'hȯnch\ *n* **1** : ²HIP **2** : HINDQUARTER 2 — usu. used in pl. **3** : HINDQUARTER 1

¹haunt \'hȯnt\ *vb* **1** : to visit often : FREQUENT **2** : to have a disquieting effect on ⟨was ~ed by his past⟩; *also* : to reappear continually in **3** : to visit or inhabit as a ghost — **haunt·er** *n* — **haunt·ing·ly** *adv*

²haunt \'hȯnt, *2 is usu* 'hant\ *n* **1** : a place habitually frequented **2** *chiefly dial* : GHOST

haute cou·ture \ˌōt-kü-'tùr\ *n* [F] : the establishments or designers that create exclusive and often trend-setting fashions for women; *also* : the fashions created

haute cui·sine \-kwi-'zēn\ *n* : artful or elaborate cuisine

hau·teur \hō-'tər, ō-, hȯ-\ *n* : ARROGANCE, HAUGHTINESS

¹have \'hav, həv, v; *in sense 2 before "to"* usu 'haf\ *vb* **had** \'had, həd\; **hav·ing; has** \'haz, həz, *in sense 2 before "to"* usu 'has\ **1** : to hold in possession; *also* : to hold in one's use, service, or regard ⟨*has* a good job⟩ **2** : to be compelled or forced ⟨~ to go now⟩ **3** : to stand in relationship to ⟨*has* many enemies⟩ **4** : OBTAIN; *also* : RECEIVE, ACCEPT **5** : to be marked by ⟨*has* red hair⟩ **6** : SHOW; *also* : USE, EXERCISE ⟨~ mercy⟩ **7** : EXPERIENCE; *also* : TAKE ⟨~ a look⟩ **8** : to entertain in the mind ⟨~ an idea⟩ **9** : to cause to **10** : ALLOW **11** : to be competent in **12** : to hold in a disadvantageous position; *also* : TRICK **13** : BEGET **14** : to partake of **15** — used as an auxiliary with the past participle to form the present perfect, past perfect, or future perfect — **have at** : ATTACK — **have coming** : DESERVE — **have done** : to be finished with — **have had it** : to have endured all one will permit or can stand — **have to do with** : to have in the way of relation with or effect on

²**have** \'hav\ *n* : one that has material wealth
ha·ven \'hā-vən\ *n* 1 : HARBOR, PORT 2 : a place of
safety 3 : a place offering favorable conditions ⟨an artist's ∼⟩
have–not \'hav-₊nät, -'nät\ *n* : one that is poor in material wealth
hav·er·sack \'ha-vər-₊sak\ *n* [F *havresac,* fr. G *Habersack*
bag for oats] : a bag similar to a knapsack but worn over
one shoulder
hav·oc \'ha-vək\ *n* 1 : wide and general destruction 2
: great confusion and disorder
haw \'hȯ\ *n* : a hawthorn berry; *also* : HAWTHORN
Ha·wai·ian \hə-'wä-yən\ *n* 1 : a native or resident of Hawaii; *esp* : one of Polynesian ancestry 2 : the Polynesian
language of Hawaii
¹**hawk** \'hȯk\ *n* 1 : any of numerous mostly small or medium-sized day-flying birds of prey (as a falcon or kite) 2
: a supporter of a war or a warlike policy — **hawk·ish** *adj*

hawk 1

²**hawk** *vb* : to make a harsh coughing sound in or as if in
clearing the throat; *also* : to raise by hawking
³**hawk** *vb* : to offer goods for sale by calling out in the
street — **hawk·er** *n*
hawk·weed \'hȯk-₊wēd\ *n* : any of several plants related
to the daisies usu. having yellow flowers
haw·ser \'hȯ-zər\ *n* : a large rope for towing, mooring, or
securing a ship
haw·thorn \'hȯ-₊thȯrn\ *n* : any of a genus of spiny spring-
flowering shrubs or small trees related to the apple
¹**hay** \'hā\ *n* 1 : herbage (as grass) mowed and cured for
fodder 2 : REWARD 3 *slang* : BED ⟨hit the ∼⟩ 4 : a
small amount of money
²**hay** *vb* : to cut, cure, and store for hay
hay·cock \'hā-₊käk\ *n* : a small conical pile of hay
hay fever *n* : an acute allergic reaction esp. to plant pollen that resembles a cold
hay·loft \'hā-₊lȯft\ *n* : a loft for hay
hay·mow \-₊maú\ *n* : a mow of or for hay
hay·rick \-₊rik\ *n* : a large sometimes thatched outdoor
stack of hay
hay·seed \-₊sēd\ *n, pl* **hayseed** *or* **hayseeds** 1 : clinging
bits of straw or chaff from hay 2 : BUMPKIN, YOKEL
hay·stack \-₊stak\ *n* : a stack of hay
hay·wire \-₊wī(-ə)r\ *adj* : being out of order or control
: CRAZY ⟨things went ∼⟩
¹**haz·ard** \'ha-zərd\ *n* [ME, a dice game, fr. AF *hasard,* fr.
Sp *azar,* Ar *al-zahr* the die] 1 : a source of danger 2
: CHANCE; *also* : ACCIDENT 3 : an obstacle on a golf
course — **haz·ard·ous** *adj*
²**hazard** *vb* : VENTURE, RISK ⟨∼ a guess⟩
¹**haze** \'hāz\ *n* 1 : fine dust, smoke, or light vapor causing
lack of transparency in the air 2 : vagueness of mind or
perception
²**haze** *vb* **hazed; haz·ing** : to harass by abusive and humiliating tricks usu. by way of initiation
ha·zel \'hā-zəl\ *n* 1 : any of a genus of shrubs or small
trees related to the birches and bearing edible brown
nuts (**ha·zel·nuts** \-₊nəts\) 2 : a light brown color
hazy \'hā-zē\ *adj* **haz·i·er; -est** 1 : obscured or darkened by
haze 2 : VAGUE, INDEFINITE ⟨a ∼ memory⟩; *also* : UN-
CERTAIN — **haz·i·ly** \-zə-lē\ *adv* — **haz·i·ness** \-zē-nəs\ *n*
Hb *abbr* hemoglobin
HBM *abbr* Her Britannic Majesty; His Britannic Majesty
H–bomb \'āch-₊bäm\ *n* : HYDROGEN BOMB
HC *abbr* 1 Holy Communion 2 House of Commons
hd *abbr* head
HD *abbr* 1 heavy-duty 2 high definition
hdbk *abbr* handbook

hdkf *abbr* handkerchief
HDL \₊āch-(₊)dē-'el\ *n* [*high-d*ensity *l*ipoprotein] : a choles-
terol-poor protein-rich lipoprotein of blood plasma correlated with reduced risk of atherosclerosis
hdwe *abbr* hardware
he \'hē\ *pron* 1 : that male one 2 : a person : the person
⟨∼ who hesitates is lost⟩
He *symbol* helium
HE *abbr* 1 Her Excellency 2 His Eminence 3 His Excellency
¹**head** \'hed\ *n* 1 : the front or upper part of the body containing the brain, the chief sense organs, and the mouth
2 : MIND; *also* : natural aptitude ⟨has a ∼ for math⟩ 3
: POISE ⟨a level ∼⟩ 4 : the obverse of a coin 5 : INDI-
VIDUAL; *also, pl* **head** : one of a number (as of cattle) 6
: the end that is upper or higher or opposite the foot; *also*
: either end of something (as a drum) whose two ends
need not be distinguished 7 : a compact mass of plant
parts (as leaves or flowers) 8 : the source of a stream
9 : DIRECTOR, LEADER; *also* : a leading element (as of a
procession) 10 : a projecting part; *also* : the striking part
of a weapon 11 : the place of leadership or honor 12
: a separate part or topic 13 : the foam on a fermenting
or effervescing liquid 14 : a critical point ⟨events came
to a ∼⟩ — **head·ed** \'he-dəd\ *adj* — **head·less** *adj* —
over one's head : beyond one's comprehension or competence
²**head** *adj* : PRINCIPAL, CHIEF ⟨∼ chef⟩
³**head** *vb* 1 : to provide with or form a head; *also* : to
form the head of 2 : LEAD, CONDUCT ⟨∼ed the search⟩
3 : to get in front of esp. so as to stop; *also* : SURPASS 4
: to put or stand at the head 5 : to point or proceed in a
certain direction ⟨∼ed west⟩
head·ache \'he-₊dāk\ *n* 1 : pain in the head 2 : a
baffling situation or problem — **head·achy** *also*
head·achey \-₊ā-kē\ *adj*
head·band \'hed-₊band\ *n* : a band worn on or around the
head
head·bang·er \-₊baŋ-ər\ *n* : one who performs or enjoys
hard rock
head·board \-₊bȯrd\ *n* : a board forming the head (as of
a bed)
head cold *n* : a common cold centered in the nasal passages and adjacent mucous tissues
head·dress \'hed-₊dres\ *n* : an often elaborate covering
for the head
head·first \-'fərst\ *adv* : HEADLONG 1 ⟨dove ∼ into the wa-
ter⟩ — **headfirst** *adj*
head·gear \-₊gir\ *n* : a covering or protective device for
the head
head·hunt·er \-₊hən-tər\ *n* 1 : one that engages in head-
hunting 2 : a recruiter of esp. executive personnel
head–hunt·ing \-₊hən-tiŋ\ *n* : the practice of seeking out
and decapitating enemies and preserving their heads as
trophies
head·ing \'he-diŋ\ *n* 1 : the compass direction in which
the longitudinal axis of a ship or airplane points 2
: something that appears at the top or beginning of something else (as a document)
head·land \'hed-lənd, -₊land\ *n* : PROMONTORY
head·light \-₊līt\ *n* : a light mounted on the front of a vehicle to illuminate the road ahead
¹**head·line** \-₊līn\ *n* : a head of a newspaper story or article
usu. printed in large type
²**headline** *vb* 1 : to provide with a headline 2 : to publicize highly 3 : to be a leading performer in
head·lock \-₊läk\ *n* : a wrestling hold in which one encircles the opponent's head with one arm
¹**head·long** \-'lȯŋ\ *adv* 1 : with the head foremost 2
: RECKLESSLY 3 : without delay
²**head·long** \-₊lȯŋ\ *adj* 1 : PRECIPITATE, RASH ⟨∼ flight⟩
2 : plunging with the head foremost
head·man \'hed-'man, -₊man\ *n* : one who is a leader : CHIEF
head·mas·ter \-₊mas-tər\ *n* : a man who is head of a private school
head·mis·tress \-₊mis-trəs\ *n* : a woman who is head of a
private school
head of steam : strong driving force : MOMENTUM
head–on \'hed-'ȯn, -'än\ *adj* : having the front facing in
the direction of initial contact or line of sight ⟨∼ colli-
sion⟩ — **head–on** *adv*

head·phone \-ˌfōn\ *n* : an earphone held on by a band over the head
head·piece \-ˌpēs\ *n* : a covering for the head
head·pin \-ˌpin\ *n* : a bowling pin that stands foremost in the arrangement of pins
head·quar·ters \-ˌkwȯr-tərz\ *n sing or pl* 1 : a place from which a commander exercises command 2 : the administrative center of an enterprise
head·rest \-ˌrest\ *n* 1 : a support for the head 2 : a pad at the top of the back of an automobile seat
head·room \-ˌrüm, -ˌru̇m\ *n* : vertical space in which to stand, sit, or move
head–scratcher \-ˌskra-chər\ *n* : PUZZLE, MYSTERY
head·set \-ˌset\ *n* : a pair of headphones
head·ship \-ˌship\ *n* : the position, office, or dignity of a head
heads·man \'hedz-mən\ *n* : EXECUTIONER
head·stall \'hed-ˌstȯl\ *n* : a part of a bridle or halter that encircles the head
head·stone \-ˌstōn\ *n* : a memorial stone at the head of a grave
head·strong \'hed-ˌstrȯŋ\ *adj* 1 : not easily restrained 2 : directed by ungovernable will ♦ **Synonyms** UNRULY, INTRACTABLE, WILLFUL, PERTINACIOUS, REFRACTORY, STUBBORN
heads–up \'hedz-'əp\ *n* : WARNING
head·wait·er \-'wā-tər\ *n* : the head of the dining-room staff of a restaurant or hotel
head·wa·ter \-ˌwȯ-tər, -ˌwä-\ *n* : the source of a stream — usu. used in pl.
head·way \-ˌwā\ *n* : forward motion; *also* : PROGRESS
head·wind \-ˌwind\ *n* : a wind blowing in a direction opposite to a course esp. of a ship or aircraft
head·word \'hed-ˌwərd\ *n* 1 : a word or term placed at the beginning 2 : a word qualified by a modifier
head·work \-ˌwərk\ *n* : mental work or effort : THINKING
heady \'he-dē\ *adj* **head·i·er; -est** 1 : WILLFUL, RASH; *also* : IMPETUOUS 2 : INTOXICATING ⟨a ~ wine⟩ 3 : SHREWD
heal \'hēl\ *vb* 1 : to make or become healthy, sound, or whole 2 : CURE, REMEDY — **heal·er** *n*
health \'helth\ *n* 1 : sound physical or mental condition; *also* : overall condition of the body ⟨in poor ~⟩ 2 : WELL-BEING 3 : a toast to someone's health or prosperity
health care *n* : efforts made to maintain or restore health — usu. hyphenated when used attributively
health club *n* : a commercial establishment providing health and fitness facilities and equipment for members
health·ful \'helth-fəl\ *adj* 1 : beneficial to health 2 : HEALTHY — **health·ful·ly** *adv* — **health·ful·ness** *n*
health maintenance organization *n* : HMO
healthy \'hel-thē\ *adj* **health·i·er; -est** 1 : enjoying or typical of good health : WELL 2 : evincing or conducive to health 3 : PROSPEROUS ⟨a ~ economy⟩; *also* : CONSIDERABLE 2 ⟨a ~ savings⟩ — **health·i·ly** \-thə-lē\ *adv* — **health·i·ness** \-thē-nəs\ *n*
¹**heap** \'hēp\ *n* : PILE ⟨rubbish ~⟩; *also* : LOT 5 ⟨a ~ of fun⟩
²**heap** *vb* 1 : to throw or lay in a heap 2 : to give in large quantities; *also* : to load heavily
hear \'hir\ *vb* **heard** \'hərd\; **hear·ing** 1 : to perceive by the ear 2 : to gain knowledge of by hearing : LEARN 3 : HEED; *also* : ATTEND 4 : to give a legal hearing to or take testimony from — **hear·er** *n*
hear·ing *n* 1 : the process, function, or power of perceiving sound; *esp* : the special sense by which noises and tones are received as stimuli 2 : EARSHOT 3 : opportunity to be heard 4 : a listening to arguments (as in a court); *also* : a session (as of a legislative committee) in which testimony is taken from witnesses
hear·ken \'här-kən\ *vb* : to give attention : LISTEN ♦ **Synonyms** HEAR, HARK, HEED
hear·say \'hir-ˌsā\ *n* : RUMOR
hearse \'hərs\ *n* : a vehicle for carrying the dead to the grave
heart \'härt\ *n* 1 : a hollow muscular organ that by rhythmic contraction keeps up the circulation of the blood in the body; *also* : something resembling a heart in shape 2 : any of a suit of playing cards marked with a red figure of a heart; *also, pl* : a card game in which the

object is to avoid taking tricks containing hearts 3 : the whole personality; *also* : the emotional or moral as distinguished from the intellectual nature 4 : COURAGE 5 : one's innermost being ⟨knew it in his ~⟩ 6 : CENTER; *also* : the essential part 7 : the younger central part of a compact leafy cluster (as of lettuce) — **heart·ed** \'här-təd\ *adj* — **by heart** : by rote or from memory
heart·ache \-ˌāk\ *n* : anguish of mind
heart attack *n* : an acute episode of heart disease due to insufficient blood supply to the heart muscle
heart·beat \'härt-ˌbēt\ *n* : one complete pulsation of the heart
heart·break \-ˌbrāk\ *n* : crushing grief
heart·break·ing \-ˌbrā-kiŋ\ *adj* : causing extreme sorrow or distress — **heart·break·er** \-ˌbrā-kər\ *n* — **heart·break·ing·ly** *adv*
heart·bro·ken \-ˌbrō-kən\ *adj* : overcome by sorrow
heart·burn \-ˌbərn\ *n* : a burning distress behind the sternum due esp. to the backward flow of acid from the stomach to the esophagus
heart disease *n* : an abnormal organic condition of the heart or of the heart and circulation
heart·en \'härt-ᵊn\ *vb* : ENCOURAGE, CHEER ⟨were ~ed by the victory⟩
heart·felt \'härt-ˌfelt\ *adj* : deeply felt : SINCERE ⟨~ thanks⟩
hearth \'härth\ *n* 1 : an area (as of brick) in front of a fireplace; *also* : the floor of a fireplace 2 : HOME
hearth·stone \'härth-ˌstōn\ *n* 1 : stone forming a hearth 2 : HOME
heart·less \'härt-ləs\ *adj* : CRUEL
heart·rend·ing \-ˌren-diŋ\ *adj* : HEARTBREAKING
heart·sick \-ˌsik\ *adj* : very despondent — **heart·sick·ness** *n*
heart–stop·ping \-ˌstä-piŋ\ *adj* : extremely shocking or exciting
heart·strings \-ˌstriŋz\ *n pl* : the deepest emotions or affections
heart·throb \-ˌthräb\ *n* 1 : the throb of a heart 2 : sentimental emotion 3 : SWEETHEART 4 : an entertainer noted for his sex appeal
heart–to–heart *adj* : SINCERE, FRANK
heart·warm·ing \'härt-ˌwȯr-miŋ\ *adj* : inspiring sympathetic feeling
heart·wood \-ˌwu̇d\ *n* : the older harder nonliving and usu. darker wood of the central part of a tree trunk
¹**hearty** \'här-tē\ *adj* **heart·i·er; -est** 1 : giving full support; *also* : JOVIAL 2 : vigorously healthy 3 : ABUNDANT; *also* : NOURISHING ⟨~ soups⟩ ♦ **Synonyms** SINCERE, WHOLEHEARTED, UNFEIGNED, HEARTFELT — **heart·i·ly** \-tə-lē\ *adv* — **heart·i·ness** \-tē-nəs\ *n*
²**hearty** *n, pl* **heart·ies** : an enthusiastic jovial fellow; *also* : SAILOR
¹**heat** \'hēt\ *vb* 1 : to make or become warm or hot 2 : EXCITE ⟨~ed discussion⟩ — **heat·ed·ly** *adv* — **heat·er** *n*
²**heat** *n* 1 : a condition of being hot : WARMTH 2 : a form of energy that when added to a body causes the body to rise in temperature, to fuse, to evaporate, or to expand 3 : high temperature 4 : intensity of feeling; *also* : sexual excitement esp. in a female mammal 5 : a preliminary race for narrowing the competition 6 : pungency of flavor 7 *slang* : POLICE 8 : PRESSURE, COERCION; *also* : ABUSE, CRITICISM ⟨took ~ for my mistakes⟩
heat exchanger *n* : a device (as an automobile radiator) for transferring heat from one fluid to another without allowing them to mix
heat exhaustion *n* : a condition marked by weakness, nausea, dizziness, and profuse sweating resulting from physical exertion in a hot environment
heath \'hēth\ *n* 1 : a tract of wasteland 2 : any of a family of often evergreen shrubby plants (as a blueberry or heather) of wet acid soils — **heathy** *adj*
hea·then \'hē-thən\ *n, pl* **heathens** *or* **heathen** 1 : an unconverted member of a people or nation that does not acknowledge the God of the Bible 2 : an uncivilized or irreligious person — **heathen** *adj* — **hea·then·dom** *n* — **hea·then·ish** *adj* — **hea·then·ism** *n*
heath·er \'he-thər\ *n* : a northern and alpine evergreen heath with usu. lavender flowers — **heath·ery** *adj*
heat lightning *n* : flashes of light without thunder ascribed to distant lightning reflected by high clouds
heat·stroke \'hēt-ˌstrōk\ *n* : a disorder marked esp. by

high body temperature without sweating and by collapse that follows prolonged exposure to excessive heat

¹heave \'hēv\ *vb* **heaved** *or* **hove** \'hōv\; **heav·ing 1 :** to rise or lift upward **2 :** THROW **3 :** to rise and fall rhythmically; *also* : PANT **4 :** RETCH **5 :** PULL, PUSH — **heav·er** *n*

²heave *n* **1 :** an effort to lift or raise **2 :** THROW, CAST **3 :** an upward motion **4** *pl* **:** a chronic lung disease of horses marked by difficult breathing and persistent cough

heav·en \'he-vən\ *n* **1 :** FIRMAMENT — usu. used in pl. **2** *often cap* **:** the abode of the Deity and of the blessed dead; *also* : a spiritual state of everlasting communion with God **3** *cap* : GOD 1 **4 :** a place of supreme happiness — **heav·en·ly** *adj* — **heav·en·ward** *adv or adj*

¹heavy \'he-vē\ *adj* **heavi·er; -est 1 :** having great weight **2 :** hard to bear **3 :** SERIOUS **4 :** DEEP, PROFOUND ⟨a ∼ silence⟩ **5 :** burdened with something oppressive; *also* : PREGNANT **6 :** SLUGGISH **7 :** DRAB; *also* : DOLEFUL **8 :** DROWSY **9 :** greater than the average of its kind or class **10 :** very rich and hard to digest; *also* : not properly raised or leavened **11 :** producing goods (as steel) used in the production of other goods — **heavi·ly** \-və-lē\ *adv* — **heavi·ness** \-vē-nəs\ *n*

²heavy *n, pl* **heav·ies :** a theatrical role representing a dignified or imposing person; *also* : a villain esp. in a story

heavy-du·ty \,he-vē-'dü-tē, -'dyü-\ *adj* **:** able to withstand unusual strain

heavy-hand·ed \-'han-dəd\ *adj* **1 :** CLUMSY **2 :** OPPRESSIVE, HARSH

heavy-heart·ed \-'här-təd\ *adj* **:** SADDENED, DESPONDENT

heavy lifting *n* **:** a burdensome or laborious duty

heavy metal *n* **:** energetic and highly amplified electronic rock music

heavy-set \,he-vē-'set\ *adj* **:** stocky and compact in build

heavy water *n* **:** water enriched in deuterium

heavy·weight \'he-vē-,wāt\ *n* **:** one above average in weight; *esp* : a boxer in an unlimited weight division

Heb *abbr* Hebrews

He·bra·ism \'hē-brā-,i-zəm\ *n* **:** the thought, spirit, or practice characteristic of the Hebrews — **He·bra·ic** \hi-'brā-ik\ *adj*

He·bra·ist \'hē-,brā-ist\ *n* **:** a specialist in Hebrew and Hebraic studies

He·brew \'hē-brü\ *n* **1 :** the language of the Hebrews **2 :** a member of or descendant from a group of Semitic peoples; *esp* : ISRAELITE — **Hebrew** *adj*

He·brews \'hē-(,)brüz\ *n* — see BIBLE table

hec·a·tomb \'he-kə-,tōm\ *n* **:** an ancient Greek and Roman sacrifice of 100 oxen or cattle

heck·le \'he-kəl\ *vb* **heck·led; heck·ling :** to harass with questions or gibes : BADGER — **heck·ler** *n*

hect·are \'hek-,ter\ *n* — see METRIC SYSTEM table

hec·tic \'hek-tik\ *adj* **1 :** being hot and flushed **2 :** filled with excitement, activity, or confusion — **hec·ti·cal·ly** \-ti-k(ə-)lē\ *adv*

hec·to·gram \'hek-tə-,gram\ *n* — see METRIC SYSTEM table

hec·to·li·ter \'hek-tə-,lē-tər\ *n* — see METRIC SYSTEM table

hec·to·me·ter \'hek-tə-,mē-tər, hek-'tä-mə-tər\ *n* — see METRIC SYSTEM table

hec·tor \'hek-tər\ *vb* [*hector* bully, fr. *Hector*, champion of Troy in Greek legend] **1 :** SWAGGER **2 :** to intimidate by bluster or personal pressure

¹hedge \'hej\ *n* **1 :** a fence or boundary formed of shrubs or small trees **2 :** BARRIER **3 :** a means of protection (as against financial loss)

²hedge *vb* **hedged; hedg·ing 1 :** ENCIRCLE **2 :** HINDER **3 :** to protect oneself financially by a counterbalancing action **4 :** to evade the risk of commitment — **hedg·er** *n*

hedge·hog \'hej-,hog, -,häg\ *n* **:** a small Old World insect=eating mammal covered with spines; *also* : PORCUPINE

hedge·hop \-,häp\ *vb* **:** to fly an airplane very close to the ground

hedge·row \-,rō\ *n* **:** a row of shrubs or trees bounding or separating fields

he·do·nism \'hē-də-,ni-zəm\ *n* [Gk *hēdonē* pleasure] **:** the doctrine that pleasure is the chief good in life; *also* : a way of life based on this — **he·do·nist** \-nist\ *n* — **he·do·nis·tic** \,hē-də-'ni-stik\ *adj*

¹heed \'hēd\ *vb* **:** to pay attention

²heed *n* **:** ATTENTION, NOTICE — **heed·ful** \-fəl\ *adj* — **heed·ful·ly** *adv* — **heed·ful·ness** *n* — **heed·less** *adj* — **heed·less·ly** *adv* — **heed·less·ness** *n*

¹heel \'hēl\ *n* **1 :** the hind part of the foot **2 :** one of the crusty ends of a loaf of bread **3 :** a solid attachment forming the back of the sole of a shoe **4 :** a rear, low, or bottom part **5 :** a contemptible person

²heel *vb* **:** to tilt to one side : LIST

¹heft \'heft\ *n* **:** WEIGHT, HEAVINESS

²heft *vb* **:** to test the weight of by lifting

hefty \'hef-tē\ *adj* **heft·i·er; -est 1 :** marked by bigness, bulk, and usu. strength **2 :** impressively large ⟨got a ∼ raise⟩

he·ge·mo·ny \hi-'je-mə-nē\ *n* **:** preponderant influence or authority over others : DOMINATION

he·gi·ra \hi-'jī-rə\ *n* [the *Hegira*, flight of Muhammad from Mecca in A.D. 622, fr. ML, fr. Ar *hijra*, lit., departure] **:** a journey esp. when undertaken to escape a dangerous or undesirable environment

heif·er \'he-fər\ *n* **:** a young cow; *esp* : one that has not had a calf

height \'hīt\ *n* **1 :** the highest part or point **2 :** the distance from the bottom to the top of something standing upright **3 :** ALTITUDE

height·en \'hī-t³n\ *vb* **1 :** to increase in amount or degree **2 :** to make or become high or higher ♦ **Synonyms** ENHANCE, INTENSIFY, AGGRAVATE, MAGNIFY

Heim·lich maneuver \'hīm-lik-\ *n* [Henry J. *Heimlich* b1920 Am. surgeon] **:** the manual application of sudden upward pressure on the upper abdomen of a choking victim to force a foreign object from the trachea

hei·nous \'hā-nəs\ *adj* [ME, fr. AF *hainus, heinous*, fr. *haine* hate, fr. *hair* to hate] **:** hatefully or shockingly evil — **hei·nous·ly** *adv* — **hei·nous·ness** *n*

heir \'er\ *n* **:** one who inherits or is entitled to inherit property, rank, title, or office — **heir·ship** *n*

heir apparent *n, pl* **heirs apparent :** an heir whose right to succeed (as to a title) cannot be taken away if he or she survives the present holder

heir·ess \'er-əs\ *n* **:** a female heir esp. to great wealth

heir·loom \'er-,lüm\ *n* **1 :** a piece of personal property that descends by inheritance **2 :** something handed on from one generation to another

heir presumptive *n, pl* **heirs presumptive :** an heir whose present right to inherit could be lost through the birth of a nearer relative

heist \'hīst\ *vb* **:** to commit armed robbery on; *also* : STEAL — **heist** *n*

held *past and past part of* HOLD

he·li·cal \'he-li-kəl, 'hē-\ *adj* **:** SPIRAL

he·li·cop·ter \'he-lə-,käp-tər, 'hē-\ *n* [F *hélicoptère*, fr. Gk *helik-, helix* spiral + *pteron* wing] **:** an aircraft that is supported in the air by one or more rotors revolving on substantially vertical axes

he·lio·cen·tric \,hē-lē-ō-'sen-trik\ *adj* **:** having or relating to the sun as center

he·lio·sphere \'hē-lē-ə-,sfir, -ō-\ *n* **:** the region in space influenced by the sun or solar wind

he·lio·trope \'hē-lē-ə-,trōp\ *n* [L *heliotropium*, fr. Gk *hēliotropion*, fr. *hēlios* sun + *tropos* turn; fr. its flowers' turning toward the sun] **:** any of a genus of herbs or shrubs related to the forget-me-nots that have small white or purple flowers

he·li·port \'he-lə-,pòrt\ *n* **:** a landing and takeoff place for a helicopter

he·li·um \'hē-lē-əm\ *n* [NL, fr. Gk *hēlios* sun] **:** a very light inert gaseous chemical element occurring in various natural gases

he·lix \'hē-liks\ *n, pl* **he·li·ces** \'he-lə-,sēz, 'hē-\ *also* **he·lix·es** \'hē-lik-səz\ **:** something spiral in form

hell \'hel\ *n* **1 :** a nether world in which the dead continue to exist **2 :** the realm of the devil in which the damned suffer everlasting punishment **3 :** a place or state of torment or destruction — **hell·ish** *adj*

hel·la·cious \he-'lā-shəs\ *adj* **1 :** exceptionally powerful or violent ⟨∼ winds⟩ **2 :** remarkably good **3 :** extremely difficult ⟨a ∼ schedule⟩ **4 :** extraordinarily large

hell-bent \'hel-,bent\ *adj* **:** stubbornly determined ⟨∼ on revenge⟩

hell·cat \-,kat\ *n* **1 :** WITCH **2 :** a violently temperamental person; *esp* : an ill-tempered woman

hel·le·bore \'he-lə-,bór\ *n* **1 :** any of a genus of poisonous herbs related to the buttercups; *also* : the dried root of a hellebore **2 :** a poisonous plant related to the lilies; *also* : its dried roots used in medicine and insecticides

Hel·lene \'he-ˌlēn\ *n* : GREEK

Hel·le·nism \'he-lə-ˌni-zəm\ *n* : a body of humanistic and classical ideals associated with ancient Greece — **Hel·len·ic** \he-'le-nik\ *adj* — **Hel·le·nist** \'he-lə-nist\ *n*

Hel·le·nis·tic \ˌhe-lə-'nis-tik\ *adj* : of or relating to Greek history, culture, or art after Alexander the Great

hell–for–leather *adv* : at full speed

hell·gram·mite \'hel-grə-ˌmīt\ *n* : an aquatic insect larva that is used as bait in fishing

hell·hole \'hel-ˌhōl\ *n* : a place of extreme misery or squalor

hell·ion \'hel-yən\ *n* : a troublesome or mischievous person

hel·lo \hə-'lō, he-\ *n, pl* **hellos** : an expression of greeting — used interjectionally

helm \'helm\ *n* **1** : a lever or wheel for steering a ship **2** : a position of control

hel·met \'hel-mət\ *n* : a protective covering for the head

helmet: ancient battle helmets and modern football helmet

helms·man \'helmz-mən\ *n* : the person at the helm : STEERSMAN

helms·per·son \-ˌpər-sᵊn\ *n* : HELMSMAN

hel·ot \'he-lət\ *n* : SLAVE, SERF

¹help \'help\ *vb* **1** : AID, ASSIST **2** : IMPROVE, RELIEVE **3** : to be of use; *also* : PROMOTE **4** : to change for the better **5** : to refrain from; *also* : PREVENT **6** : to serve with food or drink ⟨~ yourself⟩ — **help·er** *n*

²help *n* **1** : AID, ASSISTANCE; *also* : a source of aid **2** : REMEDY, RELIEF **3** : one who assists another **4** : EMPLOYEE — **help·ful** \-fəl\ *adj* — **help·ful·ly** *adv* — **help·ful·ness** *n* — **help·less** *adj* — **help·less·ly** *adv* — **help·less·ness** *n*

helper T cell *n* : a T cell that participates in the immune response by recognizing foreign antigens and has a protein on its surface to which HIV attaches

help·ing *n* : a portion of food

help·mate \'help-ˌmāt\ *n* **1** : HELPER **2** : WIFE

help·meet \-ˌmēt\ *n* : HELPMATE

hel·ter–skel·ter \ˌhel-tər-'skel-tər\ *adv* **1** : in undue haste or disorder **2** : HAPHAZARDLY

helve \'helv\ *n* : a handle of a tool or weapon

Hel·ve·tian \hel-'vē-shən\ *adj* : SWISS — **Helvetian** *n*

¹hem \'hem\ *n* **1** : a border of an article (as of cloth) doubled back and stitched down **2** : RIM, MARGIN

²hem *vb* **hemmed; hem·ming** **1** : to make a hem in sewing; *also* : BORDER, EDGE **2** : to surround restrictively

he–man \'hē-ˌman\ *n* : a strong virile man

he·ma·tite \'hē-mə-ˌtīt\ *n* : a mineral that consists of an oxide of iron and that constitutes an important iron ore

he·ma·tol·o·gy \ˌhē-mə-'tä-lə-jē\ *n* : a branch of biology that deals with the blood and blood-forming organs — **he·ma·to·log·ic** \-tə-'lä-jik\ *also* **he·ma·to·log·i·cal** \-ji-kəl\ *adj* — **he·ma·tol·o·gist** \-'tä-lə-jist\ *n*

he·ma·to·ma \-'tō-mə\ *n, pl* **-mas** *also* **-ma·ta** \-mə-tə\ : a usu. clotted mass of blood forming as a result of a broken blood vessel

heme \'hēm\ *n* : the deep red iron-containing part of hemoglobin

hemi·sphere \'he-mə-ˌsfir\ *n* **1** : one of the halves of the earth as divided by the equator into northern and southern parts or by a meridian into eastern and western parts **2** : either of two half spheres formed by a plane through the sphere's center — **hemi·spher·ic** \ˌhe-mə-'sfir-ik, -'s-fer-\ *or* **hemi·spher·i·cal** \-'sfir-i-kəl, -'sfer-\ *adj*

hem·line \'hem-ˌlīn\ *n* : the line formed by the lower edge of a garment

hem·lock \'hem-ˌläk\ *n* **1** : any of several poisonous herbs related to the carrot **2** : an evergreen tree related to the pines; *also* : its soft light wood

he·mo·glo·bin \'hē-mə-ˌglō-bən\ *n* : an iron-containing compound found in red blood cells that carries oxygen from the lungs to the body tissues

he·mo·phil·ia \ˌhē-mə-'fi-lē-ə\ *n* : a hereditary blood defect usu. of males that slows blood clotting with resulting difficulty in stopping bleeding — **he·mo·phil·i·ac** \-lē-ˌak\ *adj or n*

hem·or·rhage \'hem-rij, 'he-mə-\ *n* : a large discharge of blood from the blood vessels — **hemorrhage** *vb* — **hem·or·rhag·ic** \ˌhe-mə-'ra-jik\ *adj*

hemorrhagic fever *n* : any of a group of virus diseases characterized chiefly by sudden onset, fever, aching, and bleeding in the internal organs

hem·or·rhoid \'hem-ˌröid, 'he-mə-\ *n* : a swollen mass of dilated veins at or just within the anus — usu. used in pl.

hemp \'hemp\ *n* : a tall widely grown Asian herb that is the source of a tough fiber used in rope and of marijuana and hashish from its flowers and leaves; *also* : the fiber — **hemp·en** \'hem-pən\ *adj*

hem·stitch \'hem-ˌstich\ *vb* : to embroider (fabric) by drawing out parallel threads and stitching the exposed threads in groups to form designs

hen \'hen\ *n* : a female chicken esp. over a year old; *also* : a female bird

hence \'hens\ *adv* **1** : AWAY **2** : from this time ⟨four years ~⟩ **3** : CONSEQUENTLY **4** : from this source or origin

hence·forth \hens-ˌfȯrth\ *adv* : from this point on

hence·for·ward \-'fȯr-wərd\ *adv* : HENCEFORTH

hench·man \'hench-mən\ *n* [ME *hengestman* groom, fr. *hengest* stallion] : a trusted follower or supporter

hen·na \'he-nə\ *n* **1** : an Old World tropical shrub with fragrant white flowers; *also* : a reddish brown dye obtained from its leaves and used esp. on hair **2** : the color of henna dye

hen·peck \'hen-ˌpek\ *vb* : to nag and boss one's husband

hep \'hep\ *adj* : HIP

hep·a·rin \'he-pə-rən\ *n* : a compound found esp. in liver that slows the clotting of blood and is used medically

he·pat·ic \hi-'pa-tik\ *adj* : of, relating to, or associated with the liver

he·pat·i·ca \hi-'pa-ti-kə\ *n* : any of a genus of herbs related to the buttercups that have lobed leaves and delicate white, pink, or bluish flowers

hep·a·ti·tis \ˌhe-pə-'tī-təs\ *n, pl* **-tit·i·des** \-'ti-tə-ˌdēz\ : inflammation of the liver; *also* : a virus disease of which this is a feature

hep·tam·e·ter \hep-'ta-mə-tər\ *n* : a line of verse containing seven metrical feet

hep·tath·lon \hep-'tath-lən, -ˌlän\ *n* : a 7-event athletic contest for women

¹her \'hər\ *adj* : of or relating to her or herself

²her *pron, objective case of* SHE

¹her·ald \'her-əld\ *n* **1** : an official crier or messenger **2** : HARBINGER **3** : ANNOUNCER **4** : ADVOCATE

²herald *vb* **1** : to give notice of **2** : HAIL, GREET; *also* : PUBLICIZE

he·ral·dic \he-'ral-dik, hə-\ *adj* : of or relating to heralds or heraldry

her·ald·ry \'her-əl-drē\ *n, pl* **-ries** **1** : the practice of devising and granting armorial insignia and of tracing genealogies **2** : INSIGNIA **3** : PAGEANTRY

herb \'ərb, 'hərb\ *n* **1** : a seed plant that lacks woody tissue and dies to the ground at the end of a growing season **2** : a plant or plant part valued for medicinal or savory qualities — **her·ba·ceous** \ˌər-'bā-shəs, ˌhər-\ *adj*

herb·age \'ər-bij, 'hər-\ *n* : green plants esp. when used or fit for grazing

her·bal \'ər-bəl, 'hər-\ *adj* : of, relating to, utilizing, or made of herbs

herb·al·ist \'ər-bə-list, 'hər-\ *n* **1** : a person who practices healing by the use of herbs **2** : a person who collects or grows herbs

her·bar·i·um \ˌər-'ber-ē-əm, ˌhər-\ *n, pl* **-ia** \-ē-ə\ **1** : a collection of dried plant specimens **2** : a place that houses an herbarium

her·bi·cide \'ər-bə-ˌsīd, 'hər-\ *n* : an agent used to destroy or inhibit plant growth — **her·bi·cid·al** \ˌər-bə-'sī-dᵊl, ˌhər-\ *adj*

her·biv·o·rous \ˌər-'bi-və-rəs, ˌhər-\ *adj* : feeding on plants — **her·bi·vore** \'ər-bə-ˌvȯr, 'hər-\ *n*

her·cu·le·an \ˌhər-kyə-'lē-ən, ˌhər-'kyü-lē-\ *adj, often cap* [*Hercules*, hero of Greek myth renowned for his strength] : of extraordinary power, size, or difficulty ⟨a ~ task⟩

¹herd \'hərd\ *n* **1** : a group of animals of one kind kept or living together   2 : a group of people with a common bond ⟨a ∼ of tourists⟩   3 : MOB

²herd *vb* : to assemble or move in a herd — **herd·er** *n*

herds·man \'hərdz-mən\ *n* : one who manages, breeds, or tends livestock

¹here \'hir\ *adv*   1 : in or at this place; *also* : NOW   2 : at or in this point, particular, or case   3 : in the present life or state   4 : to this place ⟨come ∼⟩

²here *n* : this place ⟨get away from ∼⟩

here·abouts \'hir-ə-ˌbaüts\ *or* **here·about** \-ˌbaüt\ *adv* : in this vicinity

¹here·af·ter \hir-'af-tər\ *adv*   1 : after this in sequence or in time   2 : in some future time or state

²hereafter *n, often cap*   1 : FUTURE   2 : an existence beyond earthly life

here·by \hir-'bī\ *adv* : by means of this

he·red·i·tary \hə-'re-də-ˌter-ē\ *adj*   1 : genetically passed or passable from parent to offspring   2 : passing by inheritance; *also* : having title or possession through inheritance   3 : of a kind established by tradition

he·red·i·ty \-də-tē\ *n* : the characteristics and potentialities genetically derived from one's ancestors; *also* : the passing of these from ancestor to descendant

Her·e·ford \'hər-fərd\ *n* : any of a breed of red-coated beef cattle with white faces and markings

here·in \hir-'in\ *adv* : in this

here·of \-'əv, -'äv\ *adv* : of this

here·on \-'ȯn, -'än\ *adv* : on this

her·e·sy \'her-ə-sē\ *n, pl* **-sies** [ME *heresie,* fr. AF, fr. LL *haeresis,* fr. LGk *hairesis,* fr. Gk, action of taking, choice, sect, fr. *hairein* to take]   1 : adherence to a religious opinion contrary to church dogma   2 : an opinion or doctrine contrary to church dogma   3 : dissent from a dominant theory, opinion, or practice — **her·e·tic** \-ˌtik\ *n* — **he·ret·i·cal** \hə-'re-ti-kəl\ *adj*

here·to \hir-'tü\ *adv* : to this document

here·to·fore \'hir-tə-ˌfȯr\ *adv* : up to this time

here·un·der \hir-'ən-dər\ *adv* : under this or according to this writing

here·un·to \hir-'ən-tü\ *adv* : to this

here·up·on \'hir-ə-ˌpȯn, -ˌpän\ *adv* : on this or immediately after this

here·with \'hir-'with, -'with\ *adv*   1 : with this   2 : HEREBY

her·i·ta·ble \'her-ə-tə-bəl\ *adj* : capable of being inherited

her·i·tage \'her-ə-tij\ *n*   1 : property that descends to an heir   2 : LEGACY   3 : BIRTHRIGHT

her·maph·ro·dite \(ˌ)hər-'ma-frə-ˌdīt\ *n* : an animal or plant having both male and female reproductive organs — **hermaphrodite** *adj* — **her·maph·ro·dit·ic** \(ˌ)hər-ˌma-frə-'di-tik\ *adj*

her·met·ic \hər-'me-tik\ *also* **her·met·i·cal** \-ti-kəl\ *adj* : AIRTIGHT — **her·met·i·cal·ly** \-ti-k(ə-)lē\ *adv*

her·mit \'hər-mət\ *n* [ME *heremite, eremite,* fr. AF, fr. LL *eremita,* fr. LGk *erēmitēs,* fr. Gk, adj., living in the desert, fr. *erēmia* desert, fr. *erēmos* desolate] : one who lives in solitude esp. for religious reasons

her·mit·age \-mə-tij\ *n*   1 : the dwelling of a hermit   2 : a secluded dwelling

hermit crab *n* : any of numerous crabs that occupy empty mollusk shells

her·nia \'hər-nē-ə\ *n, pl* **-ni·as** *or* **-ni·ae** \-nē-ˌē, -nē-ˌī\ : a protrusion of a bodily part (as a loop of intestine) into a pouch of the weakened wall of a cavity in which it is normally enclosed — **her·ni·ate** \-nē-ˌāt\ *vb* — **her·ni·a·tion** \ˌhər-nē-'ā-shən\ *n*

he·ro \'hē-rō\ *n, pl* **heroes**   1 : a mythological or legendary figure of great strength or ability   2 : a man admired for his achievements and qualities   3 : the chief male character in a literary or dramatic work   4 *pl usu* **heros** : SUBMARINE   2 — **he·ro·ic** \hi-'rō-ik\ *adj* — **he·ro·i·cal·ly** \-i-k(ə-)lē\ *adv*

heroic couplet *n* : a rhyming couplet in iambic pentameter

he·ro·ics \hi-'rō-iks\ *n pl* : heroic or showy behavior

her·o·in \'her-ə-wən\ *n* : an illicit addictive narcotic drug made from morphine

her·o·ine \'her-ə-wən\ *n*   1 : a woman admired for her achievements and qualities   2 : the chief female character in a literary or dramatic work

her·o·ism \'her-ə-ˌwi-zəm\ *n*   1 : heroic conduct   2 : the qualities of a hero ✦ *Synonyms* VALOR, PROWESS, GALLANTRY

her·on \'her-ən\ *n, pl* **herons** *also* **heron** : any of various long-legged long-billed wading birds with soft plumage

her·pes \'hər-pēz\ *n* : any of several virus diseases characterized by the formation of blisters on the skin or mucous membranes

herpes sim·plex \-'sim-ˌpleks\ *n* : either of two virus diseases marked in one by watery blisters above the waist (as on the mouth and lips) and in the other on the sex organs

herpes zos·ter \-'zäs-tər\ *n* : SHINGLES

her·pe·tol·o·gy \ˌhər-pə-'tä-lə-jē\ *n* : a branch of zoology dealing with reptiles and amphibians — **her·pe·tol·o·gist** \ˌhər-pə-'tä-lə-jist\ *n*

her·ring \'her-iŋ\ *n, pl* **herring** *or* **herrings** : a valuable narrow-bodied food fish of the No. Atlantic; *also* : a related fish of the No. Pacific harvested esp. for its roe

her·ring·bone \'her-iŋ-ˌbōn\ *n* : a pattern made up of rows of parallel lines with adjacent rows slanting in reverse directions; *also* : a twilled fabric with this pattern

hers \'hərz\ *pron* : one or the ones belonging to her

her·self \hər-'self\ *pron* : SHE, HER — used reflexively, for emphasis, or in absolute constructions

hertz \'hərts, 'herts\ *n, pl* **hertz** : a unit of frequency equal to one cycle per second

hes·i·tant \'he-zə-tənt\ *adj* : tending to hesitate — **hes·i·tance** \-təns\ *n* — **hes·i·tan·cy** \-tən-sē\ *n* — **hes·i·tant·ly** *adv*

hes·i·tate \'he-zə-ˌtāt\ *vb* **-tat·ed; -tat·ing**   1 : to hold back (as in doubt)   2 : PAUSE ✦ *Synonyms* WAVER, VACILLATE, FALTER, SHILLY-SHALLY — **hes·i·ta·tion** \ˌhe-zə-'tā-shən\ *n*

het·ero·dox \'he-tə-rə-ˌdäks\ *adj*   1 : differing from an acknowledged standard   2 : holding unorthodox opinions — **het·er·o·doxy** \-ˌdäk-sē\ *n*

het·er·o·ge·neous \ˌhe-tə-rə-'jē-nē-əs, -nyəs\ *adj* : consisting of dissimilar ingredients or constituents : MIXED — **het·er·o·ge·ne·i·ty** \-jə-'nē-ə-tē\ *n* — **het·er·o·ge·neous·ly** *adv*

het·ero·glos·sia \ˌhe-tə-rō-'glä-sē-ə, -'glò-\ *n* : a diversity of voices, styles of discourse, or points of view in a literary work

het·ero·sex·ism \ˌhe-tə-rō-'sek-si-zəm\ *n* : discrimination or prejudice by heterosexuals against homosexuals

het·ero·sex·u·al \ˌhe-tə-rō-'sek-shə-wəl\ *adj*   1 : of, relating to, or marked by sexual interest in the opposite sex; *also* : of, relating to, or involving sexual intercourse between members of opposite sex   2 : of or relating to different sexes — **heterosexual** *n* — **het·ero·sex·u·al·i·ty** \-ˌsek-shə-'wa-lə-tē\ *n*

hew \'hyü\ *vb* **hewed; hewed** *or* **hewn** \'hyün\; **hew·ing**   1 : to cut or fell with blows (as of an ax)   2 : to give shape to with or as if with an ax   3 : to conform strictly ⟨∼ed to the rules⟩ — **hew·er** *n*

HEW *abbr* Department of Health, Education, and Welfare

¹hex \'heks\ *vb*   1 : to practice witchcraft   2 : JINX

²hex *n* : SPELL, JINX

³hex *adj* : HEXAGONAL

⁴hex *abbr* hexagon

hexa·gon \'hek-sə-ˌgän\ *n* [ultim. fr. Gk *hex* six + *gōnia* angle] : a polygon having six angles and six sides — **hex·ag·o·nal** \hek-'sa-gən-ᵊl\ *adj*

hex·am·e·ter \hek-'sa-mə-tər\ *n* : a line of verse containing six metrical feet

hey \'hā\ *interj* — used esp. to call attention to or to express doubt, surprise, or joy

hey·day \'hā-ˌdā\ *n* : a period of greatest strength, vigor, or prosperity

hf *abbr* half

Hf *symbol* hafnium

HF *abbr* high frequency

hg *abbr* hectogram

Hg *symbol* [NL *hydrargyrum,* lit., water silver] mercury

hgt *abbr* height

hgwy *abbr* highway

HH *abbr*   1 Her Highness   2 His Highness   3 His Holiness

HHS *abbr* Department of Health and Human Services

HI *abbr*   1 Hawaii   2 humidity index

hi·a·tus \hī-'ā-təs\ *n* [L, fr. *hiare* to yawn]   1 : a break in an object : GAP   2 : a period when something is suspended or interrupted

hi·ba·chi \hi-'bä-chē\ *n* [Jp] : a charcoal brazier

hi·ber·nate \'hī-bər-ˌnāt\ vb **-nat·ed; -nat·ing** : to pass the winter in a torpid or resting state — **hi·ber·na·tion** \ˌhī-bər-'nā-shən\ n — **hi·ber·na·tor** \'hī-bər-ˌnā-tər\ n

hi·bis·cus \hī-'bis-kəs, hə-\ n : any of a genus of herbs, shrubs, and trees related to the mallows and noted for large showy flowers

hic·cup also **hic·cough** \'hi-(ˌ)kəp\ n **1** : a spasmodic breathing movement checked by sudden closing of the glottis accompanied by a peculiar sound; also, pl : an attack of hiccuping **2** : a slight irregularity, error, or malfunction **3** : a brief minor interruption or change — **hiccup** vb

hick \'hik\ n [Hick, nickname for Richard] : an unsophisticated provincial person — **hick** adj

hick·o·ry \'hi-kə-rē\ n, pl **-ries** : any of a genus of No. American hardwood trees related to the walnuts; also : the wood of a hickory — **hickory** adj

hi·dal·go \hi-'dal-gō\ n, pl **-gos** often cap [Sp, fr. earlier fijo dalgo, lit., son of something] : a member of the lower nobility of Spain

hidden tax n **1** : a tax ultimately paid by someone other than the person on whom it is formally levied **2** : an economic injustice that reduces one's income or buying power

¹hide \'hīd\ vb **hid** \'hid\; **hid·den** \'hid-ᵊn\ or **hid**; **hid·ing 1** : to put or remain out of sight **2** : to conceal for shelter or protection; also : to seek protection **3** : to keep secret **4** : to turn away in shame or anger — **hid·er** n

²hide n : the skin of an animal

hide–and–seek \ˌhīd-ᵊn-'sēk\ n : a children's game in which everyone hides from one player who tries to find them

hide·away \'hī-də-ˌwā\ n : HIDEOUT

hide·bound \'hīd-ˌbaůnd\ adj : being inflexible or conservative

hid·eous \'hi-dē-əs\ adj [ME hidous, fr. AF hidus, hisdos, fr. hisde, hide terror] **1** : offensive to one of the senses : UGLY **2** : morally offensive : SHOCKING ✦ **Synonyms** GHASTLY, GRISLY, GRUESOME, HORRIBLE, LURID, MACABRE — **hid·eous·ly** adv — **hid·eous·ness** n

hide·out \'hīd-ˌaůt\ n : a place of refuge or concealment

hie \'hī\ vb **hied; hy·ing** or **hie·ing** : HASTEN

hi·er·ar·chy \'hī-ə-ˌrär-kē\ n, pl **-chies 1** : a ruling body of clergy organized into ranks **2** : persons or things arranged in a graded series — **hi·er·ar·chi·cal** \ˌhī-ə-'rär-ki-kəl\ adj — **hi·er·ar·chi·cal·ly** \-k(ə-)lē\ adv

hi·er·o·glyph·ic \ˌhī-ə-rə-'gli-fik\ n [MF hieroglyphique, adj., ultim. fr. Gk hieroglyphikos, fr. hieros sacred + glyphein to carve] **1** : a character in a system of picture writing (as of the ancient Egyptians) **2** : a symbol or sign difficult to decipher

hieroglyphic 1

hi–fi \'hī-'fī\ n **1** : HIGH FIDELITY **2** : equipment for reproduction of sound with high fidelity

hig·gle·dy–pig·gle·dy \ˌhi-gəl-dē-'pi-gəl-dē\ adv : in confusion

¹high \'hī\ adj **1** : ELEVATED; also : TALL **2** : advanced toward fullness or culmination; also : slightly tainted **3** : advanced esp. in complexity ⟨~er mathematics⟩ **4** : long past **5** : SHRILL, SHARP **6** : far from the equator ⟨~ latitudes⟩ **7** : exalted in character **8** : of greater degree, size, or amount than average ⟨~ in cholesterol⟩ **9** : of relatively great importance **10** : FORCIBLE, STRONG ⟨~ winds⟩ **11** : showing elation or excitement **12** : INTOXICATED; also : excited or stupefied by or as if by a drug — **high·ly** adv

²high adv **1** : at or to a high place or degree **2** : LUXURIOUSLY ⟨living ~⟩

³high n **1** : an elevated place **2** : a region of high barometric pressure **3** : a high point or level **4** : the gear of a vehicle giving the highest speed **5** : an excited or stupefied state produced by or as if by a drug

high·ball \'hī-ˌból\ n : a usu. tall drink of liquor mixed with water or a carbonated beverage

high beam n : a vehicle headlight with a long-range focus

high·born \'hī-'bórn\ adj : of noble birth

high·boy \-ˌbói\ n : a high chest of drawers mounted on a base with legs

high·bred \-'bred\ adj : coming from superior stock

high·brow \-ˌbraů\ n : a person of superior learning or culture — **highbrow** adj — **high·brow·ism** \-ˌbraů-ˌi-zəm\ n

high–definition adj : being or relating to a television system with twice as many scan lines per frame as a conventional system — **high definition** n

high–density li·po·pro·tein \-ˌlī-pō-'prō-tēn, -ˌli-\ n : HDL

high·er–up \ˌhī-ər-'əp\ n : a superior officer or official

high·fa·lu·tin \ˌhī-fə-'lü-tᵊn\ adj : PRETENTIOUS, POMPOUS

high fashion n **1** : HIGH STYLE **2** : HAUTE COUTURE

high fidelity n : the reproduction of sound or image with a high degree of faithfulness to the original

high five n : a slapping of upraised right hands by two people (as in celebration) — **high–five** vb

high–flown \'hī-'flōn\ adj **1** : EXALTED **2** : BOMBASTIC

high frequency n : a radio frequency between 3 and 30 megahertz

high gear n **1** : HIGH 4 **2** : a state of intense or maximum activity

high–hand·ed \'hī-'han-dəd\ adj : OVERBEARING — **high–hand·ed·ly** adv — **high–hand·ed·ness** n

high–hat \-'hat\ adj : SUPERCILIOUS, SNOBBISH — **high–hat** vb

high·land \'hī-lənd\ n : elevated or mountainous land

high·land·er \-lən-dər\ n **1** : an inhabitant of a highland **2** cap : an inhabitant of the Scottish Highlands

high–lev·el \'hī-'le-vəl\ adj **1** : being of high importance or rank **2** : being or relating to highly concentrated and environmentally hazardous nuclear waste

¹high·light \-ˌlīt\ n : an event or detail of major importance

²highlight vb **1** : EMPHASIZE **2** : to constitute a highlight of **3** : to mark (text) with a highlighter **4** : to cause to be displayed in a way that stands out on a computer screen

high·light·er \-ˌlīt-ər\ n : a pen with transparent ink used for marking text passages

high–mind·ed \'hī-'mīn-dəd\ adj : marked by elevated principles and feelings — **high–mind·ed·ness** n

high·ness \'hī-nəs\ n **1** : the quality or state of being high **2** — used as a title (as for kings)

high–pres·sure \-'pre-shər\ adj : using or involving aggressive and insistent sales techniques

high–rise \-'rīz\ adj **1** : having several stories and being equipped with elevators ⟨~ apartments⟩ **2** : of or relating to high-rise buildings

high road n : HIGHWAY

high school n : a school usu. including grades 9 to 12 or 10 to 12

high sea n : the open sea outside territorial waters — usu. used in pl.

high–sound·ing \'hī-'saůn-diŋ\ adj : POMPOUS, IMPOSING ⟨~ rhetoric⟩

high–spir·it·ed \-'spir-ə-təd\ adj : characterized by a bold or energetic spirit

high–strung \-'strəŋ\ adj : having an extremely nervous or sensitive temperament

high style n : the newest in fashion or design

high·tail \'hī-ˌtāl\ vb : to retreat at full speed

high tech \-'tek\ n : HIGH TECHNOLOGY

high technology n : technology involving the use of advanced devices

high–ten·sion \'hī-'ten-chən\ adj : having or using a high voltage

high–test \-'test\ adj : having a high octane number

high–tick·et \-'ti-kət\ adj : EXPENSIVE

high–toned \-'tōnd\ adj **1** : high in social, moral, or intellectual quality **2** : PRETENTIOUS, POMPOUS

high·way \'hī-ˌwā\ n : a main direct road

high·way·man \'hī-ˌwā-mən\ n : a thief who robs travelers on a road

hi·jab \hē-'jäb, -'jab\ n [Ar ḥijāb cover, screen, veil] : the covering for the hair and neck that is worn by Muslim women

hi·jack also **high·jack** \'hī-ˌjak\ vb : to steal esp. by stopping a vehicle on the highway; also : to commandeer a flying airplane — **hijack** n — **hi·jack·er** n

¹hike \'hīk\ vb **hiked; hik·ing 1** : to move or raise with a sudden motion **2** : to take a long walk — **hik·er** n

²hike n **1** : a long walk **2** : RISE, INCREASE ⟨price ~⟩

hi·lar·i·ous \hi-'ler-ē-əs, hī-\ adj : marked by or providing

boisterous merriment — **hi·lar·i·ous·ly** adv — **hi·lar·i·ty**
\-ə-tē\ n
hill \'hil\ n 1 : a usu. rounded elevation of land 2 : a
little heap or mound (as of earth) — **hilly** adj
hill·bil·ly \'hil-ˌbi-lē\ n, pl **-lies** often offensive : a person
from a backwoods area
hill·ock \'hi-lək\ n : a small hill
hill·side \'hil-ˌsīd\ n : the part of a hill between the summit
and the foot
hill·top \-ˌtäp\ n : the top of a hill
hilt \'hilt\ n : a handle esp. of a sword or dagger
him \'him\ pron, objective case of HE
him·self \him-'self\ pron : HE, HIM — used reflexively,
for emphasis, or in absolute constructions
¹**hind** \'hīnd\ n, pl **hinds** also **hind** : a female of a common
Eurasian deer
²**hind** adj : REAR ⟨the dog's ~ legs⟩
¹**hin·der** \'hin-dər\ vb 1 : to impede the progress of 2 : to
hold back ◆ **Synonyms** OBSTRUCT, BLOCK, BAR, IMPEDE
²**hind·er** \'hīn-dər\ adj : HIND
Hin·di \'hin-dē\ n : a literary and official language of
northern India
hind·most \'hīnd-ˌmōst\ adj : farthest to the rear
hind·quar·ter \-ˌkwȯr-tər\ n 1 : one side of the back half of
the carcass of a quadruped 2 pl : the part of the body of
a quadruped behind the junction of hind limbs and trunk
hin·drance \'hin-drəns\ n 1 : the state of being hindered
2 : IMPEDIMENT 1 3 : the action of hindering
hind·sight \'hīnd-ˌsīt\ n : understanding of an event after
it has happened
Hindu–Arabic adj : relating to, being, or composed of
Arabic numerals
Hin·du·ism \'hin-dü-ˌi-zəm\ n : a body of religious beliefs
and practices native to India — **Hin·du** n or adj
hind wing n : either of the posterior wings of a 4-winged
insect
¹**hinge** \'hinj\ n : a jointed device on which a swinging part
(as a door, gate, or lid) turns
²**hinge** vb **hinged; hing·ing** 1 : to attach by or furnish
with hinges 2 : to be contingent on a single consideration
hint \'hint\ n 1 : an indirect or summary suggestion 2
: CLUE 3 : a very small amount ◆ **Synonyms** DASH,
SOUPÇON, SUSPICION, TINCTURE, TOUCH — **hint** vb
hin·ter·land \'hin-tər-ˌland\ n 1 : a region behind a coast
2 : a region remote from cities
¹**hip** \'hip\ n : the fruit of a rose
²**hip** n 1 : the part of the body on either side below the
waist consisting of the side of the pelvis and the upper
thigh 2 : HIP JOINT
³**hip** adj **hip·per; hip·pest** : keenly aware of or interested
in the newest developments or styles — **hip·ness** n
⁴**hip** vb **hipped; hip·ping** : TELL, INFORM
hip·bone \'hip-'bōn, -ˌbōn\ n : the large flaring bone that
makes a lateral half of the pelvis in mammals
hip-hop \'hip-ˌhäp\ n 1 : a subculture esp. of inner-city
youths who are devotees of rap music 2 : the stylized
rhythmic music that accompanies rap — **hip-hop** adj
hip-hug·gers \'hip-ˌhə-gərz\ n pl : low-slung close-fitting
pants that rest on the hips
hip joint n : the articulation between the femur and the
hipbone
hipped \'hipt\ adj : having hips esp. of a specified kind
⟨broad-hipped⟩
hip·pie or **hip·py** \'hi-pē\ n, pl **hippies** : a usu. young
person who rejects established mores and advocates non-
violence; also : a long-haired unconventionally dressed
young person
hip·po \'hi-pō\ n, pl **hippos** : HIPPOPOTAMUS
hip·po·drome \'hi-pə-ˌdrōm\ n : an arena for equestrian
performances
hip·po·pot·a·mus \ˌhi-pə-'pä-tə-məs\ n, pl **-mus·es** or **-mi**
\-ˌmī\ [L, fr. Gk hippopotamos, alter. of hippos potamios,
lit., river horse] : a large thick-skinned aquatic mammal
of sub-Saharan Africa that is related to the swine
¹**hire** \'hī(-ə)r\ n 1 : payment for labor or personal services : WAGES 2 : EMPLOYMENT 3 : one who is hired
²**hire** vb **hired; hir·ing** 1 : to employ for pay 2 : to engage
the temporary use of for pay 3 : to take employment
hire·ling \'hī(-ə)r-liŋ\ n : a hired person; esp : one with
mercenary motives

hir·sute \'hər-ˌsüt, 'hir-\ adj : HAIRY
¹**his** \'hiz\ adj : of or relating to him or himself
²**his** pron : one or the ones belonging to him
His·pan·ic \hi-'spa-nik\ adj : of, relating to, or being a
person of Latin-American descent living in the U.S. —
Hispanic n
hiss \'his\ vb : to make a sharp sibilant sound; also : to
express disapproval of by hissing — **hiss** n
hissy fit \'hi-sē-\ n : TANTRUM
hist abbr historian; historical; history
his·ta·mine \'his-tə-ˌmēn, -mən\ n : a compound widespread in animal tissues that plays a major role in allergic reactions (as hay fever)
his·to·gram \'his-tə-ˌgram\ n : a representation of statistical data by rectangles whose widths represent class intervals and whose heights usu. represent corresponding
frequencies
his·tol·o·gy \his-'tä-lə-jē\ n, pl **-gies** 1 : a branch of
anatomy dealing with tissue structure 2 : tissue structure or organization — **his·to·log·i·cal** \ˌhis-tə-'lä-ji-kəl\
or **his·to·log·ic** \-'lä-jik\ adj — **his·tol·o·gist** \-'tä-lə-jist\
n
his·to·ri·an \hi-'stȯr-ē-ən\ n : a student or writer of history
his·to·ric·i·ty \ˌhis-tə-'ri-sə-tē\ n : historical actuality
his·to·ri·og·ra·pher \hi-ˌstȯr-ē-'ä-grə-fər\ n : HISTORIAN
his·to·ry \'his-tə-rē\ n, pl **-ries** [ultim. fr. L historia, fr.
Gk, inquiry, history, fr. histōr, istōr knowing, learned]
1 : a chronological record of significant events often
with an explanation of their causes 2 : a branch of
knowledge that records and explains past events 3
: events that form the subject matter of history 4
: an established record ⟨a convict's ~ of violence⟩ —
his·tor·ic \hi-'stȯr-ik\ adj — **his·tor·i·cal** \-i-kəl\ adj —
his·tor·i·cal·ly \-k(ə-)lē\ adv
his·tri·on·ic \ˌhis-trē-'ä-nik\ adj [LL histrionicus, fr. L histrio
actor] 1 : deliberately affected 2 : of or relating to actors, acting, or the theater — **his·tri·on·i·cal·ly** \-ni-k(ə-)lē\
adv
his·tri·on·ics \-niks\ n pl 1 : theatrical performances 2
: deliberate display of emotion for effect
¹**hit** \'hit\ vb **hit; hit·ting** 1 : to reach with a blow : STRIKE;
also : to arrive with a force like a blow ⟨the storm ~⟩
2 : to make or bring into contact : COLLIDE 3 : to affect detrimentally ⟨was ~ by the flu⟩ 4 : to make a
request of 5 : to come upon 6 : to accord with : SUIT
7 : REACH, ATTAIN 8 : to indulge in often to excess —
hit·ter n
²**hit** n 1 : an act or instance of hitting or being hit 2 : a
great success 3 : BASE HIT 4 : a dose of a drug 5 : a
murder committed by a gangster 6 : an instance of connecting to a particular website 7 : a successful match in
a search (as of the Internet)
¹**hitch** \'hich\ vb 1 : to move by jerks 2 : to catch or fasten esp. by a hook or knot 3 : HITCHHIKE
²**hitch** n 1 : JERK, PULL 2 : a sudden halt 3 : a connection between something towed and its mover 4 : KNOT
hitch·hike \'hich-ˌhīk\ vb : to travel by securing free rides
from passing vehicles — **hitch·hik·er** n
¹**hith·er** \'hi-thər\ adv : to this place
²**hither** adj : being on the near or adjacent side
hith·er·to \-ˌtü\ adv : up to this time
HIV \ˌāch-(ˌ)ī-'vē\ n [human immunodeficiency virus]
: any of several retroviruses that infect and destroy
helper T cells causing the great reduction in their numbers that is diagnostic of AIDS
hive \'hīv\ n 1 : a container for housing honeybees 2
: a colony of bees 3 : a place swarming with busy occupants — **hive** vb
hives \'hīvz\ n sing or pl : an allergic disorder marked by
raised itching patches on the skin or mucous membranes
hl abbr hectoliter
HL abbr House of Lords
hm abbr hectometer
HM abbr 1 Her Majesty; Her Majesty's 2 His Majesty;
His Majesty's
HMO \ˌāch-(ˌ)em-'ō\ n [health maintenance organization]
: a comprehensive health-care organization financed by
periodic fixed payments by voluntarily enrolled individuals and families
HMS abbr 1 Her Majesty's ship 2 His Majesty's ship

Ho *symbol* holmium

hoa·gie *also* **hoa·gy** \'hō-gē\ *n, pl* **hoagies** : SUBMARINE 2

hoard \'hórd\ *n* : a hidden accumulation — **hoard** *vb* — **hoard·er** *n*

hoar·frost \'hór-,fròst\ *n* : FROST 2

hoarse \'hórs\ *adj* **hoars·er; hoars·est** 1 : rough and harsh in sound 2 : having a grating voice — **hoarse·ly** *adv* — **hoarse·ness** *n*

hoary \'hòr-ē\ *adj* **hoar·i·er; -est** 1 : gray or white with or as if with age 2 : ANCIENT — **hoar·i·ness** \'hór-ē-nəs\ *n*

hoax \'hōks\ *n* : an act intended to trick or dupe; *also* : something accepted or established by fraud — **hoax** *vb* — **hoax·er** *n*

hob \'häb\ *n* : MISCHIEF, TROUBLE ⟨raising ∼⟩

¹**hob·ble** \'hä-bəl\ *vb* **hob·bled, hob·bling** 1 : to limp along; *also* : to make lame 2 : FETTER

²**hobble** *n* 1 : a hobbling movement 2 : something used to hobble an animal

hob·by \'hä-bē\ *n, pl* **hobbies** : a pursuit or interest engaged in for relaxation — **hob·by·ist** \-ist\ *n*

hob·by·horse \'hä-bē-,hórs\ *n* 1 : a stick with a horse's head on which children pretend to ride 2 : a toy horse mounted on rockers 3 : a topic to which one constantly reverts

hob·gob·lin \'häb-,gäb-lən\ *n* 1 : a mischievous goblin 2 : BOGEY 1

hob·nail \-,nāl\ *n* : a short large-headed nail for studding shoe soles — **hob·nailed** \-,nāld\ *adj*

hob·nob \-,näb\ *vb* **hob·nobbed; hob·nob·bing** : to associate familiarly

ho·bo \'hō-bō\ *n, pl* **hoboes** *also* **hobos** : TRAMP 2

¹**hock** \'häk\ *n* : a joint or region in the hind limb of a quadruped just above the foot and corresponding to the human ankle

²**hock** *n* [D *hok* pen, prison] : ²PAWN 2 ⟨got his watch out of ∼⟩; *also* : DEBT 3 ⟨trying to get out of ∼⟩ — **hock** *vb*

hock·ey \'hä-kē\ *n* 1 : FIELD HOCKEY 2 : ICE HOCKEY

ho·cus-po·cus \,hō-kəs-'pō-kəs\ *n* 1 : SLEIGHT OF HAND 2 : nonsense or sham used to conceal deception

hod \'häd\ *n* : a long-handled carrier for mortar or bricks

hodge·podge \'häj-,päj\ *n* : a heterogeneous mixture : JUMBLE

Hodgkin's disease \'häj-kinz-\ *n* : a neoplastic disease of lymphoid tissue characterized esp. by enlargement of lymph nodes, spleen, and liver

hoe \'hō\ *n* : a long-handled implement with a thin flat blade used esp. for cultivating, weeding, or loosening the earth around plants — **hoe** *vb*

hoe·cake \'hō-,kāk\ *n* : a small cornmeal cake

hoe·down \-,daún\ *n* 1 : SQUARE DANCE 2 : a gathering featuring hoedowns

¹**hog** \'hóg, 'häg\ *n, pl* **hogs** *also* **hog** 1 : a domestic swine esp. when grown 2 : a selfish, gluttonous, or filthy person — **hog·gish** *adj*

²**hog** *vb* **hogged; hog·ging** : to take or hold selfishly ⟨*hogged* the limelight⟩

ho·gan \'hō-,gän\ *n* : a Navajo Indian dwelling usu. made of logs and mud

hogan

hog·back \'hóg-,bak, 'häg-\ *n* : a ridge with a sharp summit and steep sides

hog·nose snake \'hóg-,nōz-, 'häg-\ *or* **hog·nosed snake** \-,nōzd-\ *n* : any of a genus of rather small harmless stout-bodied No. American snakes that seldom bite but hiss wildly and often play dead when disturbed

hogs·head \'hógz-,hed, 'hägz-\ *n* 1 : a large cask or barrel 2 : a liquid measure equal to 63 U.S. gallons

hog-tie \'hóg-,tī, 'häg-\ *vb* 1 : to tie together the feet of ⟨∼ a calf⟩ 2 : to make helpless

hog·wash \-,wósh, -,wäsh\ *n* 1 : SWILL, SLOP 2 : NONSENSE, BALONEY

hog wild *adj* : lacking in restraint

hoi pol·loi \,hói-pə-'lói\ *n pl* [Gk, the many] : the general populace

hoi·sin sauce \'hói-,sin-\ *n* : a thick reddish sauce of soybeans, spices, and garlic used in Asian cookery

¹**hoist** \'hóist\ *vb* : RAISE, LIFT

²**hoist** *n* 1 : LIFT 2 : an apparatus for hoisting

hoke \'hōk\ *vb* **hoked; hok·ing** : FAKE — usu. used with *up*

hok·ey \'hō-kē\ *adj* **hok·i·er; -est** 1 : CORNY ⟨∼ songs⟩ 2 : PHONY ⟨a ∼ excuse⟩

ho·kum \'hō-kəm\ *n* : NONSENSE

¹**hold** \'hōld\ *vb* **held** \'held\; **hold·ing** 1 : POSSESS; *also* : KEEP 2 : RESTRAIN 3 : to have a grasp on 4 : to support, remain, or keep in a particular situation or position 5 : SUSTAIN; *also* : RESERVE 6 : BEAR, COMPORT 7 : to maintain in being or action : PERSIST 8 : CONTAIN, ACCOMMODATE 9 : HARBOR, ENTERTAIN; *also* : CONSIDER, REGARD 10 : to carry on by concerted action; *also* : CONVOKE 11 : to occupy esp. by appointment or election 12 : to be valid 13 : HALT, PAUSE — **hold·er** *n* — **hold forth** : to speak at length — **hold to** : to adhere to : MAINTAIN — **hold with** : to agree with or approve of

²**hold** *n* 1 : STRONGHOLD 2 : CONFINEMENT; *also* : PRISON 3 : the act or manner of holding : GRIP 4 : a restraining, dominating, or controlling influence 5 : something that may be grasped as a support 6 : an order or indication that something is to be reserved or delayed — **on hold** : in a temporary state of waiting (as during a phone call); *also* : in a state of postponement ⟨plans *on hold*⟩

³**hold** *n* 1 : the interior of a ship below decks; *esp* : a ship's cargo deck 2 : an airplane's cargo compartment

hold·ing *n* 1 : land or other property owned 2 : a ruling of a court esp. on an issue of law

holding pattern *n* : a course flown by an aircraft waiting to land

hold out *vb* 1 : to continue to fight or work 2 : to refuse to come to an agreement — **hold·out** \'hōl-,daút\ *n*

hold·over \'hōl-,dō-vər\ *n* : one that is held over

hold·up \'hōl-,dəp\ *n* 1 : DELAY 2 : robbery at the point of a gun

hole \'hōl\ *n* 1 : an opening into or through something 2 : a hollow place (as a pit or cave) 3 : DEN, BURROW 4 : a wretched or dingy place 5 : a unit of play from tee to cup in golf 6 : an awkward position — **hole** *vb*

hol·i·day \'hä-lə-,dā\ *n* [ME, fr. OE *hāligdæg*, fr. *hālig* holy + *dæg* day] 1 : a day set aside for special religious observance 2 : a day of freedom from work; *esp* : one in commemoration of an event 3 : VACATION — **holiday** *vb*

ho·li·ness \'hō-lē-nəs\ *n* : the quality or state of being holy — used as a title for various high religious officials

ho·lis·tic \hō-'lis-tik\ *adj* : relating to or concerned with integrated wholes or complete systems rather than with the analysis or treatment of separate parts ⟨∼ medicine⟩ ⟨∼ ecology⟩

hol·lan·daise \,hä-lən-'dāz\ *n* : a rich sauce made basically of butter, egg yolks, and lemon juice or vinegar

hol·ler \'hä-lər\ *vb* : to cry out : SHOUT — **holler** *n*

¹**hol·low** \'hä-lō\ *n* 1 : CAVITY, HOLE 2 : a surface depression

²**hollow** *adj* **hol·low·er** \'hä-lə-wər\; **hol·low·est** \-lə-wəst\ 1 : CONCAVE, SUNKEN 2 : having a cavity within 3 : lacking in real value, sincerity, or substance; *also* : FALSE 4 : MUFFLED ⟨a ∼ sound⟩ — **hol·low·ness** *n*

³**hollow** *vb* : to make or become hollow

hol·low·ware *or* **hol·lo·ware** \'hä-lə-,war\ *n* : vessels (as bowls or cups) with a significant depth and volume

hol·ly \'hä-lē\ *n, pl* **hollies** : either of two trees or shrubs with branches of usu. evergreen glossy spiny-margined leaves and red berries

hol·ly·hock \'hä-lē-,häk, -,hók\ *n* [ME *holihoc*, fr. *holi* holy + *hoc* mallow] : a biennial or perennial herb related to the mallows that is widely grown for its tall stalks of showy flowers

hol·mi·um \'hōl-mē-əm\ *n* : a metallic chemical element

ho·lo·caust \'hä-lə-ˌkȯst, 'hō-\ *n*   **1** : a thorough destruction esp. by fire   **2** *often cap* : the killing of European Jews by the Nazis during World War II; *also* : GENOCIDE

Ho·lo·cene \'hō-lə-ˌsēn\ *adj* : of, relating to, or being the present geologic epoch — **Holocene** *n*

ho·lo·gram \'hō-lə-ˌgram, 'hä-\ *n* : a three-dimensional image produced by an interference pattern of light (as laser light)

ho·lo·graph \'hō-lə-ˌgraf, 'hä-\ *n* : a document wholly in the handwriting of its author

ho·log·ra·phy \hō-'lä-grə-fē\ *n* : the process of making a hologram — **ho·lo·graph·ic** \ˌhō-lə-'gra-fik, ˌhä-\ *adj*

Hol·stein \'hōl-ˌstēn, -ˌstīn\ *n* : any of a breed of large black-and-white dairy cattle that produce large quantities of comparatively low-fat milk

Hol·stein–Frie·sian \-'frē-zhən\ *n* : HOLSTEIN

hol·ster \'hōl-stər\ *n* [D] : a usu. leather case for a firearm

ho·ly \'hō-lē\ *adj* **ho·li·er; -est**   **1** : worthy of absolute devotion   **2** : SACRED   **3** : having a divine quality
   ◆ *Synonyms* HALLOWED, BLESSED, SANCTIFIED, CONSECRATED — **ho·li·ly** \-lə-lē\ *adv*

Holy Spirit *n* : the third person of the Christian Trinity

ho·ly·stone \'hō-lē-ˌstōn\ *n* : a soft sandstone used to scrub a ship's wooden decks — **holystone** *vb*

hom·age \'ä-mij, 'hä-\ *n* [ME, fr. AF *homage, omage,* fr. *home* man, vassal, fr. L *homo* human being] : expression of high regard; *also* : TRIBUTE 3

hom·bre \'äm-ˌbrā, 'əm-, -brē\ *n* : GUY, FELLOW

hom·burg \'häm-ˌbərg\ *n* [*Homburg,* Germany] : a man's felt hat with a stiff curled brim and a high crown creased lengthwise

¹home \'hōm\ *n*   **1** : one's residence; *also* : HOUSE   **2** : the social unit formed by a family living together   **3** : a congenial environment; *also* : HABITAT   **4** : a place of origin   **5** : the objective in various games

²home *vb* **homed; hom·ing**   **1** : to go or return home   **2** : to proceed to or toward a source of radiated energy used as a guide

home·body \'hōm-ˌbä-dē\ *n* : one whose life centers on home

home·boy \-ˌbȯi\ *n*   **1** : a boy or man from one's neighborhood, hometown, or region   **2** : a fellow member of a youth gang   **3** : an inner-city youth

home·bred \-'bred\ *adj* : produced at home : INDIGENOUS

home·com·ing \-ˌkə-min\ *n*   **1** : a return home   **2** : an annual celebration for alumni at a college or university

home computer *n* : a small inexpensive microcomputer

home economics *n* : the theory and practice of homemaking

home·girl \'hōm-gərl\ *n*   **1** : a girl or woman from one's neighborhood, hometown, or region   **2** : a girl or woman who is a member of one's peer group   **3** : an inner-city girl or woman

home·grown \'hōm-'grōn\ *adj*   **1** : grown domestically ⟨∼ peaches⟩   **2** : LOCAL, INDIGENOUS ⟨a ∼ artist⟩

home·land \-ˌland\ *n*   **1** : native land   **2** : an area set aside to be a state for a people of a particular national, cultural, or racial origin

home·less \-ləs\ *adj* : having no home or permanent residence — **home·less·ness** *n*

home·ly \'hōm-lē\ *adj* **home·li·er; -est**   **1** : FAMILIAR   **2** : unaffectedly natural   **3** : lacking beauty or proportion — **home·li·ness** \-lē-nəs\ *n*

home·made \'hōm-ˌmād\ *adj* : made in the home, on the premises, or by one's own efforts

home·mak·er \-ˌmā-kər\ *n* : one who manages a household esp. as a wife and mother — **home·mak·ing** \-kin\ *n*

ho·me·op·a·thy \ˌhō-mē-'ä-pə-thē\ *n* : a system of medical practice that treats disease esp. with minute doses of a remedy that would in larger amounts produce symptoms in healthy persons similar to those of the disease — **ho·meo·path** \'hō-mē-ə-ˌpath\ *n* — **ho·meo·path·ic** \ˌhō-mē-ə-'pa-thik\ *adj*

ho·meo·sta·sis \ˌhō-mē-ō-'stā-səs\ *n* : the maintenance of a relatively stable state of equilibrium between interrelated physiological, psychological, or social factors char-

acteristic of an individual or group — **ho·meo·stat·ic** \-'sta-tik\ *adj*

home page *n* : the page usu. encountered first at a website that usu. contains hyperlinks to the other pages of the site

home plate *n* : a slab at the apex of a baseball diamond that a base runner must touch in order to score

hom·er \'hō-mər\ *n* : HOME RUN — **homer** *vb*

home·room \'hōm-ˌrüm, -ˌrùm\ *n* : a classroom where pupils report at the beginning of each school day

home run *n* : a hit in baseball that enables the batter to go around all the bases and score a run

home·school \'hōm-ˌskül\ *vb* : to teach school subjects to one's children at home — **home·school·er** \-ˌskü-lər\ *n*

home·sick \'hōm-ˌsik\ *adj* : longing for home and family while absent from them — **home·sick·ness** *n*

home·spun \-ˌspən\ *adj*   **1** : spun or made at home; *also* : made of a loosely woven usu. woolen or linen fabric   **2** : SIMPLE, HOMELY

¹home·stead \-ˌsted\ *n* : the home and land occupied by a family

²homestead *vb* : to acquire or settle on public land — **home·stead·er** *n*

home·stretch \-'strech\ *n*   **1** : the part of a racecourse between the last curve and the winning post   **2** : a final stage (as of a project)

home theater *n* : an entertainment system (as a television with surround sound and a DVD player) for the home

home video *n* : prerecorded videocassettes or videodiscs for home viewing

¹home·ward \-wərd\ *or* **home·wards** \-wərdz\ *adv* : toward home

²homeward *adj* : being or going toward home

home·work \-ˌwərk\ *n*   **1** : an assignment given a student to be completed outside the classroom   **2** : preparatory reading or research

¹hom·ey \'hō-mē\ *adj* **hom·i·er; -est** : characteristic of home

²homey *or* **hom·ie** \'hō-mē\ *n, pl* **homeys** *or* **homies** : HOMEBOY

ho·mi·cide \'hä-mə-ˌsīd, 'hō-\ *n* [L *homicida* murderer & *homicidium* manslaughter; both fr. *homo* human being + *caedere* to cut, kill]   **1** : a person who kills another   **2** : a killing of one human being by another — **hom·i·cid·al** \ˌhä-mə-'sī-dᵊl\ *adj*

hom·i·ly \'hä-mə-lē\ *n, pl* **-lies** : SERMON — **hom·i·let·ic** \ˌhä-mə-'le-tik\ *adj*

homing pigeon *n* : a racing pigeon trained to return home

hom·i·nid \'hä-mə-nəd, -ˌnid\ *n* : any of a family of primate mammals that comprise all living humans and extinct ancestral and related forms — **hominid** *adj*

hom·i·ny \'hä-mə-nē\ *n* : hulled corn with the germ removed

ho·mo·cys·te·ine \ˌhō-mō-'sis-tə-ˌēn\ *n* : an amino acid associated with an increased risk of heart disease when occurring at high levels in the blood

ho·mo·erot·ic \ˌhō-mō-i-'rä-tik\ *adj* : marked by or portraying homosexual desire — **ho·mo·erot·i·cism** \-'rä-tə-ˌsi-zəm\ *n*

ho·mo·ge·neous \ˌhō-mə-'jē-nē-əs, -nyəs\ *adj* : of the same or a similar kind; *also* : of uniform structure — **ho·mo·ge·ne·i·ty** \-jə-'nē-ə-tē\ *n* — **ho·mo·ge·neous·ly** *adv*

ho·mog·e·ni·sa·tion, ho·mog·e·nise *Brit var of* HOMOGENIZATION, HOMOGENIZE

ho·mog·e·nize \hō-'mä-jə-ˌnīz, hə-\ *vb* **-nized; -niz·ing**   **1** : to make homogeneous   **2** : to reduce the particles in (as milk) to uniform size and distribute them evenly throughout the liquid — **ho·mog·e·ni·za·tion** \-ˌmä-jə-nə-'zā-shən\ *n* — **ho·mog·e·niz·er** *n*

ho·mo·graph \'hä-mə-ˌgraf, 'hō-\ *n* : one of two or more words spelled alike but different in origin, meaning, or pronunciation (as the *bow* of a ship, a *bow* and arrow)

ho·mol·o·gy \hō-'mä-lə-jē, hə-\ *n, pl* **-gies**   **1** : structural likeness between corresponding parts of different plants or animals due to evolution from a common ancestor   **2** : structural likeness between different parts of the same individual — **ho·mol·o·gous** \-'mä-lə-gəs\ *adj*

hom·onym \'hä-mə-ˌnim, 'hō-\ *n*   **1** : HOMOPHONE, HOMOGRAPH   **2** : one of two or more words spelled and pronounced alike but different in meaning (as *pool* of water and *pool* the game)

ho·mo·pho·bia \ˌhō-mə-ˈfō-bē-ə\ *n* : irrational fear of, aversion to, or discrimination against homosexuality or homosexuals — **ho·mo·phobe** \ˈhō-mə-ˌfōb\ *n* — **ho·mo·pho·bic** \-ˈfō-bik\ *adj*

ho·mo·phone \ˈhä-mə-ˌfōn, ˈhō-\ *n* : one of two or more words (as *to, too, two*) pronounced alike but different in meaning or derivation or spelling

Ho·mo sa·pi·ens \ˌhō-mō-ˈsä-pē-ənz, -ˈsa-\ *n* : HUMANKIND

ho·mo·sex·u·al \ˌhō-mō-ˈsek-shə-wəl\ *adj* : of, relating to, or marked by sexual interest in the same sex as oneself : GAY; *also* : of, relating to, or involving sexual intercourse between members of the same sex — **homosexual** *n* — **ho·mo·sex·u·al·i·ty** \-ˌsek-shə-ˈwa-lə-tē\ *n*

hon *abbr* honor; honorable; honorary

hone \ˈhōn\ *n* : WHETSTONE — **hone** *vb* — **hon·er** *n*

hone in *vb* : to move toward or direct attention to an objective

¹**hon·est** \ˈä-nəst\ *adj* [ME, fr. AF, fr. L *honestus* honorable, fr. *honos, honor* honor] 1 : free from deception : TRUTHFUL; *also* : GENUINE, REAL 2 : REPUTABLE 3 : CREDITABLE ⟨an ~ day's work⟩ 4 : marked by integrity 5 : FRANK ♦ *Synonyms* UPRIGHT, JUST, CONSCIENTIOUS, HONORABLE — **hon·est·ly** *adv* — **hon·es·ty** \-nə-stē\ *n*

²**honest** *adv* : HONESTLY; *also* : with all sincerity ⟨I didn't do it, ~⟩

hon·ey \ˈhə-nē\ *n, pl* **honeys** : a sweet sticky substance made by honeybees from the nectar of flowers — **hon·eyed** \-nēd\ *adj*

hon·ey·bee \ˈhə-nē-ˌbē\ *n* : a honey-producing bee often kept in hives

¹**hon·ey·comb** \-ˌkōm\ *n* : a mass of 6-sided wax cells built by honeybees; *also* : something of similar structure or appearance

²**honeycomb** *vb* : to make or become full of cavities like a honeycomb

hon·ey·dew \-ˌdü, -ˌdyü\ *n* : a sweetish deposit secreted on plants by aphids, scale insects, or fungi

honeydew melon *n* : a smooth-skinned muskmelon with sweet green flesh

honey locust *n* : a tall usu. spiny No. American leguminous tree with hard durable wood and long twisted pods

hon·ey·moon \ˈhə-nē-ˌmün\ *n* 1 : a period of harmony esp. just after marriage 2 : a holiday taken by a newly married couple — **honeymoon** *vb* — **hon·ey·moon·er** *n*

hon·ey·suck·le \ˈhə-nē-ˌsə-kəl\ *n* : any of a genus of shrubs with fragrant tube-shaped flowers rich in nectar

honk \ˈhäŋk, ˈhȯŋk\ *n* : the cry of a goose; *also* : a similar sound (as of a horn) — **honk** *vb* — **honk·er** *n*

hon·ky–tonk \ˈhäŋ-kē-ˌtäŋk, ˈhȯŋ-kē-ˌtȯŋk\ *n* : a tawdry nightclub or dance hall — **honky–tonk** *adj*

¹**hon·or** \ˈä-nər\ *n* 1 : good name : REPUTATION; *also* : outward respect 2 : PRIVILEGE 3 : a person of superior standing — used esp. as a title 4 : one who brings respect or fame ⟨an ~ to the class⟩ 5 : an evidence or symbol of distinction ⟨CHASTITY, PURITY 7 : INTEGRITY ♦ *Synonyms* HOMAGE, REVERENCE, DEFERENCE, OBEISANCE

²**honor** *vb* 1 : to regard or treat with honor 2 : to confer honor on 3 : to fulfill the terms of; *also* : to accept as payment — **hon·or·ee** \ˌä-nə-ˈrē\ *n* — **hon·or·er** *n*

hon·or·able \ˈä-nə-rə-bəl\ *adj* 1 : deserving of honor 2 : of great renown 3 : accompanied with marks of honor 4 : doing credit to the possessor 5 : characterized by integrity — **hon·or·able·ness** *n* — **hon·or·ably** \-blē\ *adv*

hon·o·rar·i·um \ˌä-nə-ˈrer-ē-əm\ *n, pl* **-ia** \-ē-ə\ *also* **-iums** : a reward usu. for services on which custom or propriety forbids a price to be set

hon·or·ary \ˈä-nə-ˌrer-ē\ *adj* 1 : having or conferring distinction 2 : conferred in recognition of achievement without the usual prerequisites ⟨~ degree⟩ 3 : UNPAID, VOLUNTARY ⟨an ~ chairman⟩ — **hon·or·ari·ly** \ˌä-nə-ˈrer-ə-lē\ *adv*

hon·or·if·ic \ˌä-nə-ˈri-fik\ *adj* : conferring or conveying honor ⟨~ titles⟩

hon·our, hon·our·able *chiefly Brit var of* HONOR, HONORABLE

¹**hood** \ˈhu̇d\ *n* 1 : a covering for the head and neck and sometimes the face 2 : an ornamental fold (as at the back of an ecclesiastical vestment) 3 : a cover for parts of mechanisms; *esp* : the covering over an automobile engine — **hood·ed** \ˈhu̇-dəd\ *adj*

²**hood** \ˈhu̇d, ˈhüd\ *n* : HOODLUM

³**hood** \ˈhu̇d\ *n* : an inner-city neighborhood; *also* : INNER CITY

-hood \ˌhu̇d\ *n suffix* 1 : state : condition : quality : character ⟨boy*hood*⟩ ⟨hardi*hood*⟩ 2 : instance of a (specified) state or quality ⟨false*hood*⟩ 3 : individuals sharing a (specified) state or character ⟨brother*hood*⟩

hood·ie \ˈhu̇-dē\ *n* : a hooded sweatshirt

hood·lum \ˈhu̇d-ləm, ˈhüd-\ *n* 1 : THUG 2 : a young ruffian

hoo·doo \ˈhü-dü\ *n, pl* **hoodoos** 1 : a body of magical practices traditional esp. among blacks in the southern U.S. 2 : something that brings bad luck — **hoodoo** *vb*

hood·wink \ˈhu̇d-ˌwiŋk\ *vb* : to deceive by false appearance

hoo·ey \ˈhü-ē\ *n* : NONSENSE

hoof \ˈhu̇f, ˈhüf\ *n, pl* **hooves** \ˈhu̇vz, ˈhüvz\ *also* **hoofs** : a horny covering that protects the ends of the toes of ungulate mammals (as horses or cattle); *also* : a hoofed foot — **hoofed** \ˈhu̇ft, ˈhüft\ *adj*

¹**hook** \ˈhu̇k\ *n* 1 : a curved or bent device for catching, holding, or pulling 2 : something curved or bent like a hook 3 : a flight of a ball (as in golf) that curves in a direction opposite to the dominant hand of the player propelling it 4 : a short punch delivered with a circular motion and with the elbow bent and rigid

²**hook** *vb* 1 : CURVE, CROOK 2 : to seize or make fast with a hook 3 : STEAL 4 : to work as a prostitute

hoo·kah \ˈhu̇-kə, ˈhü-\ *n* [Ar *ḥuqqa* bottle of a water pipe] : WATER PIPE

hook·er \ˈhu̇-kər\ *n* 1 : one that hooks 2 : PROSTITUTE

hook·up \ˈhu̇-ˌkəp\ *n* : an assemblage (as of apparatus or circuits) used for a specific purpose (as in radio)

hook up *vb* : to become involved in a working, social, or sexual relationship

hook·worm \ˈhu̇k-ˌwərm\ *n* : any of several parasitic intestinal nematode worms having hooks or plates around the mouth; *also* : infestation with or disease caused by hookworms

hoo·li·gan \ˈhü-li-gən\ *n* : RUFFIAN, HOODLUM — **hoo·li·gan·ism** \-gə-ˌni-zəm\ *n*

hoop \ˈhu̇p, ˈhüp\ *n* 1 : a circular strip used esp. for holding together the staves of a barrel 2 : a circular figure or object : RING 3 : a circle of flexible material for expanding a woman's skirt 4 : BASKETBALL — usu. used in pl.

hoop·la \ˈhüp-ˌlä, ˈhu̇p-\ *n* [F *houp-lā,* interj.] : TO-DO; *also* : BALLYHOO

hoop·ster \ˈhüp-stər\ *n* : a basketball player

hoo·ray \hu̇-ˈrā\ *interj* — used to express joy, approval, or encouragement

hoose·gow \ˈhüs-ˌgau̇\ *n* [Sp *juzgado* panel of judges, courtroom] : JAIL

¹**hoot** \ˈhüt\ *vb* 1 : to shout or laugh usu. in contempt 2 : to make the natural throat noise of an owl — **hoot·er** *n*

²**hoot** *n* 1 : a sound of hooting 2 : the least bit ⟨don't give a ~⟩ 3 : something or someone amusing ⟨the play is a real ~⟩

hoo·te·nan·ny \ˈhü-tə-ˌna-nē\ *n, pl* **-nies** : a gathering at which folksingers entertain often with the audience joining in

¹**hop** \ˈhäp\ *vb* **hopped; hop·ping** 1 : to move by quick springy leaps 2 : to make a quick trip 3 : to ride on esp. surreptitiously and without authorization

²**hop** *n* 1 : a short brisk leap esp. on one leg 2 : DANCE 3 : a short trip by air

³**hop** *n* : a vine related to the hemp plant whose ripe dried pistillate catkins are used esp. in flavoring malt liquors; *also, pl* : its pistillate catkins

¹**hope** \ˈhōp\ *vb* **hoped; hop·ing** : to desire with expectation of fulfillment

²**hope** *n* 1 : TRUST, RELIANCE 2 : desire accompanied by expectation of fulfillment; *also* : something hoped for 3 : one that gives promise for the future — **hope·ful** \-fəl\ *adj* — **hope·ful·ness** *n* — **hope·less** *adj* — **hope·less·ly** *adv* — **hope·less·ness** *n*

HOPE *abbr* Health Opportunity for People Everywhere

hope·ful·ly \ˈhōp-fə-lē\ *adv* 1 : in a hopeful manner 2 : it is hoped

Ho·pi \ˈhō-pē\ *n, pl* **Hopi** *or* **Hopis** : a member of an

American Indian people of Arizona; *also* : the language of the Hopi people

hopped–up \'häpt-'əp\ *adj* **1** : being under the influence of a narcotic; *also* : full of enthusiasm or excitement **2** : having more than usual power ⟨a ∼ engine⟩

hop·per \'hä-pər\ *n* **1** : a usu. immature hopping insect (as a grasshopper) **2** : a usu. funnel-shaped container for delivering material (as grain) **3** : a freight car with hinged doors in a sloping bottom **4** : a box into which a bill to be considered by a legislative body is dropped **5** : a tank holding a liquid and having a device for releasing its contents through a pipe

hop·scotch \'häp-ˌskäch\ *n* : a child's game in which a player tosses an object (as a stone) into areas of a figure drawn on the ground and hops through the figure to pick up the object

hor *abbr* horizontal

horde \'hȯrd\ *n* : THRONG, SWARM

ho·ri·zon \hə-'rī-zᵊn\ *n* [ME, fr. LL, fr. Gk *horizont-*, *horizōn*, fr. prp. of *horizein* to bound, fr. *horos* limit, boundary] **1** : the apparent junction of earth and sky **2** : range of outlook or experience

hor·i·zon·tal \ˌhȯr-ə-'zän-tᵊl\ *adj* : parallel to the horizon : LEVEL — **horizontal** *n* — **hor·i·zon·tal·ly** *adv*

hor·mon·al \hȯr-'mō-nᵊl\ *adj* : of, relating to, or effected by hormones — **hor·mon·al·ly** \-nᵊl-ē\ *adv*

hor·mone \'hȯr-ˌmōn\ *n* [Gk *hormōn*, prp. of *horman* to stir up, fr. *hormē* impulse, assault] : a product of living cells that circulates in body fluids and has a specific effect on the activity of cells remote from its point of origin

horn \'hȯrn\ *n* **1** : one of the hard projections of bone or keratin on the head of many hoofed mammals **2** : something resembling or suggesting a horn **3** : a brass wind instrument **4** : a usu. electrical device that makes a noise ⟨an automobile ∼⟩ — **horned** \'hȯrnd\ *adj* — **horn·less** *adj*

horn·book \'hȯrn-ˌbůk\ *n* **1** : a child's primer consisting of a sheet of parchment or paper protected by a sheet of transparent horn **2** : a rudimentary treatise

horned toad *n* : any of several small harmless insect-eating lizards with spines on the head resembling horns and spiny scales on the body

hor·net \'hȯr-nət\ *n* : any of the larger social wasps

horn in *vb* : to participate without invitation : INTRUDE

horn·pipe \'hȯrn-ˌpīp\ *n* : a lively folk dance of the British Isles

horny \'hȯr-nē\ *adj* **horn·i·er; -est 1** : of or made of horn; *also* : HARD, CALLOUS **2** : having horns **3** : desiring sexual gratification; *also* : excited sexually

ho·rol·o·gy \hə-'rä-lə-jē\ *n* : the science of measuring time or constructing time-indicating instruments — **hor·o·log·i·cal** \ˌhȯr-ə-'lä-ji-kəl\ *adj* — **ho·rol·o·gist** \hə-'rä-lə-jist\ *n*

horo·scope \'hȯr-ə-ˌskōp\ *n* [ME *horoscopum*, fr. L *horoscopus*, fr. Gk *hōroskopos*, fr. *hōra* hour + *skopos* watcher] **1** : a diagram of the relative positions of planets and signs of the zodiac at a particular time for use by astrologers to foretell events of a person's life **2** : an astrological forecast

hor·ren·dous \hȯ-'ren-dəs\ *adj* : DREADFUL, HORRIBLE

hor·ri·ble \'hȯr-ə-bəl\ *adj* **1** : marked by or conducive to horror **2** : highly disagreeable ⟨a ∼ mistake⟩ — **hor·ri·ble·ness** *n* — **hor·ri·bly** \-blē\ *adv*

hor·rid \'hȯr-əd\ *adj* **1** : HIDEOUS **2** : REPULSIVE — **hor·rid·ly** *adv*

hor·rif·ic \hȯ-'ri-fik\ *adj* : having the power to horrify ⟨a ∼ crime⟩ — **hor·rif·i·cal·ly** \-fi-k(ə-)lē\ *adv*

hor·ri·fy \'hȯr-ə-ˌfī\ *vb* **-fied; -fy·ing** : to cause to feel horror ♦ **Synonyms** APPALL, DAUNT, DISMAY

hor·ror \'hȯr-ər\ *n* **1** : painful and intense fear, dread, or dismay **2** : intense repugnance **3** : something that horrifies

horror story *n* : an account of an unsettling or unfortunate occurrence

hors de com·bat \ˌȯr-də-kōⁿ-'bä\ *adv or adj* : in a disabled condition

hors d'oeuvre \ȯr-'dərv\ *n, pl* **hors d'oeuvres** \same or -'dərvz\ *also* **hors d'oeuvre** [F *hors-d'oeuvre*, lit., outside of the work] : any of various savory foods usu. served as appetizers

horse \'hȯrs\ *n, pl* **hors·es** *also* **horse 1** : a large solid-

hoofed herbivorous mammal domesticated as a draft and saddle animal **2** : a supporting framework usu. with legs — **horse·less** *adj*

¹horse·back \'hȯrs-ˌbak\ *n* : the back of a horse

²horseback *adv* : on horseback

horse chestnut *n* : a large tree with palmate leaves, erect conical clusters of showy flowers, and large glossy brown seeds enclosed in a prickly bur; *also* : its seed

horse-flesh \'hȯrs-ˌflesh\ *n* : horses for riding, driving, or racing

horse-fly \-ˌflī\ *n* : any of a family of large dipteran flies with bloodsucking females

horse-hair \-ˌher\ *n* **1** : the hair of a horse esp. from the mane or tail **2** : cloth made from horsehair

horse-hide \-ˌhīd\ *n* **1** : the dressed or raw hide of a horse **2** : the ball used in baseball

horse latitudes *n pl* : either of two calm regions near 30°N and 30°S latitude

horse-laugh \'hȯrs-ˌlaf, -ˌläf\ *n* : a loud boisterous laugh

horse-man \-mən\ *n* **1** : one who rides horseback; *also* : one skilled in managing horses **2** : a breeder or raiser of horses — **horse-man·ship** *n*

horse-play \-ˌplā\ *n* : rough boisterous play

horse-play·er \-ˌər\ *n* : a bettor on horse races

horse-pow·er \'hȯrs-ˌpau̇(-ə)r\ *n* : a unit of power equal in the U.S. to 746 watts

horse-rad·ish \-ˌra-dish\ *n* : a tall white-flowered herb related to the mustards whose pungent root is used as a condiment; *also* : the pungent condiment

horse-shoe \'hȯrs-ˌshü\ *n* **1** : a usu. U-shaped protective metal plate fitted to the rim of a horse's hoof **2** *pl* : a game in which horseshoes are pitched at a fixed object — **horse·shoe** *vb* — **horse·sho·er** *n*

horseshoe crab *n* : any of several marine arthropods with a broad crescent-shaped combined head and thorax

horse-tail \'hȯrs-ˌtāl\ *n* : any of a genus of primitive spore-producing plants with hollow jointed stems and leaves reduced to sheaths about the joints

horse-whip \-ˌhwip\ *vb* : to flog with a whip made to be used on a horse

horse-wom·an \-ˌwu̇-mən\ *n* **1** : a woman skilled in riding horseback or in caring for or managing horses **2** : a woman who breeds or raises horses

hors·ey *also* **horsy** \'hȯr-sē\ *adj* **hors·i·er; -est 1** : of, relating to, or suggesting a horse **2** : having to do with horses or horse racing

hort *abbr* horticultural; horticulture

hor·ta·tive \'hȯr-tə-tiv\ *adj* : giving exhortation ⟨a ∼ appeal⟩

hor·ta·to·ry \'hȯr-tə-ˌtȯr-ē\ *adj* : HORTATIVE

hor·ti·cul·ture \'hȯr-tə-ˌkəl-chər\ *n* : the science and art of growing fruits, vegetables, flowers, and ornamental plants — **hor·ti·cul·tur·al** \ˌhȯr-tə-'kəl-chə-rəl\ *adj* — **hor·ti·cul·tur·ist** \-rist\ *n*

Hos *abbr* Hosea

ho·san·na \hō-'za-nə, -'zä-\ *interj* [Gk *hōsanna*, fr. Heb *hōshī'āh-nnā* pray, save (us)!] — used as a cry of acclamation and adoration — **hosanna** *n*

¹hose \'hōz\ *n, pl* **hose** *or* **hos·es 1** *pl* **hose** : STOCKING, SOCK; *also* : a close-fitting garment covering the legs and waist **2** : a flexible tube for conveying fluids (as from a faucet)

²hose *vb* **hosed; hos·ing** : to spray, water, or wash with a hose

Ho·sea \hō-'zā-ə, -'zē-\ *n* — see BIBLE table

ho·siery \'hō-zhə-rē, -zə-\ *n* : STOCKINGS, SOCKS

hosp *abbr* hospital

hos·pice \'häs-pəs\ *n* **1** : a lodging for travelers or for young persons or the underprivileged **2** : a facility or program for caring for dying persons

hos·pi·ta·ble \hä-'spi-tə-bəl, 'häs-(ˌ)pi-\ *adj* **1** : given to generous and cordial reception of guests **2** : readily receptive — **hos·pi·ta·bly** \-blē\ *adv*

hos·pi·tal \'häs-ˌpi-tᵊl\ *n* [ME, fr. AF, fr. ML *hospitale* hospice, guest house, fr. neut. of L *hospitalis* of a guest, fr. *hospit-, hospes* guest, host] : an institution where the sick or injured receive medical or surgical care

hos·pi·tal·ise *Brit var of* HOSPITALIZE

hos·pi·tal·i·ty \ˌhäs-pə-'ta-lə-tē\ *n, pl* **-ties** : hospitable treatment, reception, or disposition

hos·pi·tal·ize \'häs-,pi-tə-,līz\ *vb* **-ized; -iz·ing** : to place in a hospital as a patient — **hos·pi·tal·i·za·tion** \,häs-,pi-t°l-ə-'zā-shən\ *n*

¹host \'hōst\ *n* [ME, fr. AF *ost*, fr. LL *hostis*, fr. L, stranger, enemy] **1** : ARMY **2** : MULTITUDE ⟨a ~ of options⟩

²host *n* [ME *hoste* host, guest, fr. AF, fr. L *hospit-, hospes*] **1** : one who receives or entertains guests **2** : one who talks to guests on a show **3** : an animal or plant on or in which a parasite lives **4** : one into which something (as an organ) is transplanted **5** : SERVER 2 — **host** *vb*

³host *n, often cap* [ultim. fr. L *hostia* sacrifice] : the eucharistic bread

hos·tage \'häs-tij\ *n* **1** : a person kept as a pledge pending the fulfillment of an agreement **2** : a person taken by force to secure the taker's demands

hos·tel \'häs-t°l\ *n* [ME, fr. AF, fr. ML *hospitale* hospice] **1** : INN **2** : a supervised lodging for youth — **hos·tel·er** *or* **hos·tel·ler** *n*

hos·tel·ry \-rē\ *n, pl* **-ries** : INN, HOTEL

host·ess \'hō-stəs\ *n* **1** : a woman who receives or entertains guests **2** : a woman who talks to guests on a show

hos·tile \'häs-t°l, -,tī(-ə)l\ *adj* : marked by usu. overt antagonism : UNFRIENDLY — **hostile** *n* — **hos·tile·ly** *adv*

hos·til·i·ty \hä-'sti-lə-tē\ *n, pl* **-ties** **1** : an unfriendly state or action **2** *pl* : overt acts of war

hos·tler \'häs-lər, 'äs-\ *n* : one who takes care of horses or mules

hot \'hät\ *adj* **hot·ter; hot·test** **1** : marked by a high temperature or an uncomfortable degree of body heat **2** : giving a sensation of heat or of burning **3** : ARDENT, FIERY **4** : sexually excited **5** : EAGER **6** : newly made or received **7** : PUNGENT **8** : unusually lucky or favorable ⟨~ dice⟩ **9** : recently and illegally obtained ⟨~ jewels⟩ — **hot** *adv* — **hot·ly** *adv* — **hot·ness** *n*

hot·bed \-,bed\ *n* **1** : a glass-covered bed of soil heated (as by fermenting manure) and used esp. for raising seedlings **2** : an environment that favors rapid growth or development

hot–blood·ed \-'blə-dəd\ *adj* : easily roused or excited ⟨~ rebels⟩

hot·box \-,bäks\ *n* : a bearing (as of a railroad car) overheated by friction

hot button *n* : an emotional issue or concern that triggers immediate intense reaction

hot·cake \-,kāk\ *n* : PANCAKE

hot dog *n* : a cooked frankfurter usu. served in a long split roll

ho·tel \hō-'tel\ *n* [F *hôtel*, fr. OF *hostel*, fr. ML *hospitale* hospice] : a building where lodging and usu. meals, entertainment, and various personal services are provided for the public

hot flash *n* : a sudden brief flushing and sensation of heat usu. associated with menopausal endocrine imbalance

hot·head·ed \'hät-'he-dəd\ *adj* : FIERY, IMPETUOUS ⟨a ~ troublemaker⟩ — **hot·head** \-,hed\ *n* — **hot·head·ed·ly** *adv* — **hot·head·ed·ness** *n*

hot·house \-,haùs\ *n* : a heated greenhouse esp. for raising tropical plants

hotline *n* : a telephone line for emergency use (as between governments or to a counseling service)

hot pants *n pl* : very short shorts

hot pepper *n* : a small usu. thin-walled pepper with a pungent taste; *also* : a plant bearing hot peppers

hot plate *n* : a simple portable appliance for heating or for cooking

hot potato *n* : an embarrassing or controversial issue

hot rod *n* : an automobile modified for high speed and fast acceleration — **hot–rod·der** \-'rä-dər\ *n*

hots \'häts\ *n pl* : strong sexual desire — usu. used with *the*

hot seat *n* : a position of anxiety or embarrassment

hot·shot \'hät-,shät\ *n* : a showily skillful person ⟨a ~ lawyer⟩

hot tub *n* : a large tub of hot water for one or more bathers

hot water *n* : TROUBLE, DIFFICULTY

hot–wire \'hät-,wī(-ə)r\ *vb* : to start (an automobile) by short-circuiting the ignition system

¹hound \'haùnd\ *n* **1** : any of various hunting dogs that track prey by scent or sight **2** : FAN, ADDICT ⟨autograph ~s⟩

²hound *vb* : to pursue relentlessly

hour \'aù(-ə)r\ *n* **1** : the 24th part of a day : 60 minutes **2** : the time of day **3** : a particular or customary time **4** : a class session — **hour·ly** *adv or adj*

hour·glass \'aù(-ə)r-,glas\ *n* : a glass vessel for measuring time in which sand runs from an upper compartment to a lower compartment in an hour

hou·ri \'hur-ē\ *n* [F, fr. Pers *hūri*, fr. Ar *ḥūrīya*] : one of the beautiful maidens of the Muslim paradise

¹house \'haùs\ *n, pl* **hous·es** \'haù-zəz\ **1** : a building for human habitation **2** : an animal shelter (as a den or nest) **3** : a building in which something is stored **4** : HOUSEHOLD; *also* : FAMILY **5** : a residence for a religious community or for students; *also* : those in residence **6** : a legislative body **7** : a place of business or entertainment **8** : a business organization **9** : the audience in a theater or concert hall — **house·ful** *n*

²house \'haùz\ *vb* **housed; hous·ing** **1** : to provide with or take shelter : LODGE **2** : STORE ⟨paintings *housed* in a gallery⟩

house·boat \'haùs-,bōt\ *n* : a pleasure boat fitted for use as a dwelling or for leisurely cruising

house·boy \-,bói\ *n* : a boy or man hired to act as a household servant

house·break \-,brāk\ *vb* **-broke; -brok·en; -break·ing** : to train (a pet) in excretory habits acceptable in indoor living

house·break·ing \-,brā-kiŋ\ *n* : the act of breaking into a dwelling with the intent of committing a felony

house·clean \-,klēn\ *vb* : to clean a house and its furniture — **house·clean·ing** *n*

house·coat \-,kōt\ *n* : a woman's often long-skirted informal garment for wear around the house

house·fly \-,flī\ *n* : a dipteran fly that is common about human habitations

¹house·hold \-,hōld\ *n* : those who dwell as a family under the same roof — **house·hold·er** *n*

²household *adj* **1** : DOMESTIC **2** : FAMILIAR, COMMON ⟨a ~ name⟩

house·keep·er \-,kē-pər\ *n* : a person employed to take care of a house

house·keep·ing \-,kē-piŋ\ *n* : the care and management of a house or institutional property

house·lights \-,līts\ *n pl* : the lights that illuminate the auditorium of a theater

house·maid \-,mād\ *n* : a girl or woman who is a servant employed to do housework

house·moth·er \-,mə-thər\ *n* : a woman acting as hostess, chaperone, and often housekeeper in a group residence

house·plant \-,plant\ *n* : a plant grown or kept indoors

house sparrow *n* : a Eurasian sparrow widely introduced in urban and agricultural areas

house·top \'haùs-,täp\ *n* : ROOF

house·wares \-,werz\ *n pl* : small articles of household equipment

house·warm·ing \-,wòr-miŋ\ *n* : a party to celebrate the taking possession of a house or premises

house·wife \-,wīf\ *n* : a married woman in charge of a household — **house·wife·ly** *adj* — **house·wif·ery** \-,wī-fə-rē\ *n*

house·work \-,wərk\ *n* : the work of housekeeping

¹hous·ing \'haù-ziŋ\ *n* **1** : SHELTER **2** : dwellings provided for people **2** : something that covers or protects

²housing *n* : CAPARISON 1

HOV *abbr* high-occupancy vehicle

hove *past and past part of* HEAVE

hov·el \'hə-vəl, 'hä-\ *n* : a small, wretched, and often dirty house : HUT

hov·er \'hə-vər, 'hä-\ *vb* **hov·ered; hov·er·ing** **1** : FLUTTER; *also* : to move to and fro **2** : to be in an uncertain state

hov·er·craft \-,kraft\ *n* : a vehicle that rides on a cushion of air over a surface

¹how \'haù\ *adv* **1** : in what way or manner ⟨~ was it done⟩ **2** : with what meaning ⟨~ do we interpret such behavior⟩ **3** : for what reason ⟨~ could you have done such a thing⟩ **4** : to what extent or degree ⟨~ deep is it⟩ **5** : in what state or condition ⟨~ are you⟩ — **how about** : what do you say to or think of ⟨*how about* coming with me⟩ — **how come** : why is it that

²how *conj* **1** : the way or manner in which ⟨remember ~ they fought⟩ **2** : HOWEVER ⟨do it ~ you like⟩

¹**how·be·it** \haů-'bē-ət\ *conj* : ALTHOUGH
²**howbeit** *adv* : NEVERTHELESS
how·dah \'haů-də\ *n* [Hindi & Urdu *hauda,* fr. Ar *haudaj*] : a seat or covered pavilion on the back of an elephant or camel
¹**how·ev·er** \haů-'e-vər\ *conj* : in whatever manner that
²**however** *adv* 1 : in whatever manner; *also* : to whatever degree 2 : in spite of that
how·it·zer \'haů-ət-sər\ *n* : a short cannon that shoots shells at a high angle
howl \'haů(-ə)l\ *vb* 1 : to emit a long doleful sound characteristic of dogs 2 : to cry loudly — **howl** *n*
howl·er \'haů-lər\ *n* 1 : one that howls 2 : a humorous and ridiculous blunder
howl·ing *adj* 1 : DESOLATE, WILD 2 : very great ⟨a ~ success⟩
how·so·ev·er \haů-sə-'we-vər\ *adv* : HOWEVER 1
hoy·den \'hȯi-dᵊn\ *n* : a girl or woman of saucy, boisterous, or carefree behavior — **hoy·den·ish** *adj*
hp *abbr* horsepower
HP *abbr* high pressure
HPF *abbr* highest possible frequency
HQ *abbr* headquarters
hr *abbr* 1 here 2 hour
HR *abbr* House of Representatives
HRH *abbr* 1 Her Royal Highness 2 His Royal Highness
hryv·nia \'(h)riv-nē-ə\ *n, pl* **hryvnia** *or* **hryvnias** — see MONEY table
hrzn *abbr* horizon
Hs *symbol* hassium
HS *abbr* high school
HST *abbr* Hawaiian standard time
ht *abbr* height
HT *abbr* 1 Hawaii time 2 high-tension
HTML \ach-tē-em-'el\ *n* [*hypertext markup language*] : a computer language used to create World Wide Web documents
http *abbr* hypertext transfer protocol
hua·ra·che \wə-'rä-chē\ *n* [MexSp] : a sandal with an upper made of interwoven leather strips
hub \'həb\ *n* 1 : the central part of a circular object (as a wheel) 2 : a center of activity; *esp* : an airport or city through which an airline routes most of its traffic
hub·bub \'hə-bəb\ *n* : UPROAR ⟨the ~ in the stadium⟩; *also* : TURMOIL ⟨the ~ following the war⟩
hub·cap \'həb-kap\ *n* : a removable metal cap over the end of an axle
hu·bris \'hyü-brəs\ *n* : exaggerated pride or self-confidence
huck·le·ber·ry \'hə-kəl-ber-ē\ *n* 1 : any of a genus of American shrubs of the heath family; *also* : its edible dark blue berry 2 : BLUEBERRY
huck·ster \'hək-stər\ *n* : PEDDLER, HAWKER — **huck·ster·ism** \-stə-ri-zəm\ *n*
HUD *abbr* Department of Housing and Urban Development
¹**hud·dle** \'hə-dᵊl\ *vb* **hud·dled; hud·dling** 1 : to crowd together 2 : CONFER
²**huddle** *n* 1 : a closely packed group 2 : MEETING, CONFERENCE
hue \'hyü\ *n* 1 : COLOR; *also* : gradation of color 2 : the attribute of colors that permits them to be classed as red, yellow, green, blue, or an intermediate color — **hued** \'hyüd\ *adj*
hue and cry *n* : a clamor of pursuit or protest
huff \'həf\ *n* : a fit of anger or pique — **huff** *vb* — **huff·i·ly** \'hə-fə-lē\ *adv* — **huffy** \'hə-fē\ *adj*
hug \'həg\ *vb* **hugged; hug·ging** 1 : EMBRACE 2 : to stay close to — **hug** *n*
huge \'hyüj\ *adj* **hug·er; hug·est** : very large or extensive — **huge·ly** *adv* — **huge·ness** *n*
hug·ger-mug·ger \'hə-gər-mə-gər\ *n* 1 : SECRECY 2 : CONFUSION, MUDDLE
Hu·gue·not \'hyü-gə-nät\ *n* : a French Protestant of the 16th and 17th centuries
hu·la \'hü-lə\ *n* : a sinuous Polynesian dance usu. accompanied by chants
hulk \'həlk\ *n* 1 : a heavy clumsy ship 2 : an old ship unfit for service 3 : a bulky or unwieldy person or thing
hulk·ing \'həl-kiŋ\ *adj* : BURLY, MASSIVE
¹**hull** \'həl\ *n* 1 : the outer covering of a fruit or seed 2 : the frame or body esp. of a ship or boat

²**hull** *vb* : to remove the hulls of — **hull·er** *n*
hul·la·ba·loo \'hə-lə-bə-lü\ *n, pl* **-loos** : a confused noise : UPROAR
hul·lo \hə-'lō\ *chiefly Brit var of* HELLO
hum \'həm\ *vb* **hummed; hum·ming** 1 : to utter a sound like that of the speech sound \m\ prolonged 2 : DRONE 3 : to be busily active 4 : to run smoothly 5 : to sing with closed lips — **hum** *n* — **hum·mer** *n*
¹**hu·man** \'hyü-mən, 'yü-\ *adj* 1 : of, relating to, being, or characteristic of humans 2 : having human form or attributes — **hu·man·ly** *adv* — **hu·man·ness** *n*
²**human** *n* : any of a species of bipedal primate mammals comprising all living persons and their recent ancestors; *also* : HOMINID — **hu·man·like** \-lik\ *adj*
hu·mane \hyü-'mān, yü-\ *adj* 1 : marked by compassion, sympathy, or consideration for others 2 : HUMANISTIC — **hu·mane·ly** *adv* — **hu·mane·ness** *n*
human immunodeficiency virus *n* : HIV
hu·man·ism \'hyü-mə-ni-zəm, 'yü-\ *n* 1 : devotion to the humanities; *also* : the revival of classical letters characteristic of the Renaissance 2 : a doctrine or way of life centered on human interests or values — **hu·man·ist** \-nist\ *n or adj* — **hu·man·is·tic** \hyü-mə-'nis-tik, yü-\ *adj*
hu·man·i·tar·i·an \hyü-ma-nə-'ter-ē-ən, yü-\ *n* : one who practices philanthropy — **humanitarian** *adj* — **hu·man·i·tar·i·an·ism** *n*
hu·man·i·ty \hyü-'ma-nə-tē, yü-\ *n, pl* **-ties** 1 : the quality or state of being human or humane 2 *pl* : the branches of learning dealing with human concerns (as philosophy) as opposed to natural processes (as physics) 3 : the human race
hu·man·ize \'hyü-mə-niz, 'yü-\ *vb* **-ized; -iz·ing** : to make human or humane — **hu·man·i·za·tion** \hyü-mə-nə-'zā-shən, yü-\ *n* — **hu·man·iz·er** *n*
hu·man·kind \'hyü-mən-kind, 'yü-\ *n* : the human race
hu·man·oid \'hyü-mə-nȯid, 'yü-\ *adj* : having human form or characteristics — **humanoid** *n*
human pap·il·lo·ma·virus \-pa-pə-'lō-mə-vī-rəs\ *n* : any of numerous DNA-containing viruses that cause various human warts
¹**hum·ble** \'həm-bəl\ *adj* **hum·bler** \-bə-lər\; **hum·blest** \-bə-ləst\ [ME, fr. AF, fr. L *humilis* low, humble, fr. *humus* earth] 1 : not proud or haughty 2 : not pretentious : UNASSUMING 3 : INSIGNIFICANT ✦ *Synonyms* MEEK, MODEST, LOWLY — **hum·ble·ness** *n* — **hum·bly** *adv*
²**humble** *vb* **hum·bled; hum·bling** 1 : to make humble 2 : to destroy the power or prestige of — **hum·bler** *n*
¹**hum·bug** \'həm-bəg\ *n* 1 : HOAX, FRAUD 2 : NONSENSE
²**humbug** *vb* **hum·bugged; hum·bug·ging** : DECEIVE
hum·ding·er \'həm-diŋ-ər\ *n* : a person or thing of striking excellence
hum·drum \'həm-drəm\ *adj* : MONOTONOUS, DULL — **humdrum** *n*
hu·mer·us \'hyü-mə-rəs\ *n, pl* **hu·meri** \'hyü-mə-rī, -rē\ : the long bone extending from shoulder to elbow
hu·mid \'hyü-məd, 'yü-\ *adj* : containing or characterized by perceptible moisture : DAMP — **hu·mid·ly** *adv*
hu·mid·i·fy \hyü-'mi-də-fī\ *vb* **-fied; -fy·ing** : to make humid — **hu·mid·i·fi·ca·tion** \-mi-də-fə-'kā-shən\ *n* — **hu·mid·i·fi·er** \-'mi-də-fī-ər\ *n*
hu·mid·i·ty \hyü-'mi-də-tē, yü-\ *n, pl* **-ties** : the amount of atmospheric moisture
hu·mi·dor \'hyü-mə-dȯr, 'yü-\ *n* : a case (as for storing cigars) in which the air is kept properly humidified
hu·mil·i·ate \hyü-'mi-lē-āt, yü-\ *vb* **-at·ed; -at·ing** : to injure the self-respect of : MORTIFY — **hu·mil·i·at·ing·ly** *adv* — **hu·mil·i·a·tion** \-mi-lē-'ā-shən\ *n*
hu·mil·i·ty \hyü-'mi-lə-tē, yü-\ *n* : the quality or state of being humble
hum·ming·bird \'hə-miŋ-bərd\ *n* : any of a family of tiny brightly colored American birds related to the swifts
hum·mock \'hə-mək\ *n* : a rounded mound : KNOLL — **hum·mocky** \-mə-kē\ *adj*
hum·mus \'hə-məs, 'hü-\ *n* [Ar *ḥummuṣ* chickpeas] : a paste of pureed chickpeas usu. mixed with sesame oil or paste
hu·mon·gous \hyü-'məŋ-gəs, -'mäŋ-\ *adj* [perh. alter. of *huge + monstrous*] : extremely large ⟨a ~ stadium⟩
¹**hu·mor** \'hyü-mər, 'yü-\ *n* 1 : TEMPERAMENT 2 : MOOD 3 : WHIM 4 : a quality that appeals to a sense of the ludicrous or incongruous; *also* : a keen perception of the

ludicrous or incongruous **5** : comical or amusing entertainment — **hu·mor·ist** \'hyü-mə-rist, 'yü-\ *n* — **hu·mor·less** \'hyü-mər-ləs, 'yü-\ *adj* — **hu·mor·less·ly** *adv* — **hu·mor·less·ness** *n* — **hu·mor·ous** \'hyü-mə-rəs, 'yü-\ *adj* — **hu·mor·ous·ly** *adv* — **hu·mor·ous·ness** *n*

²**humor** *vb* : to comply with the wishes or mood of ⟨~ed his boss⟩

hu·mour *chiefly Brit var of* HUMOR

hump \'həmp\ *n* **1** : a rounded protuberance (as on the back of a camel) **2** : a difficult phase or obstacle ⟨over the ~⟩ — **humped** *adj*

hump·back \'həmp-,bak; *1 also* -'bak\ *n* **1** : HUNCHBACK **2** : HUMPBACK WHALE — **hump·backed** *adj*

humpback whale *n* : a large baleen whale having very long flippers

hu·mus \'hyü-məs, 'yü-\ *n* : the dark organic part of soil formed from decaying matter

Hun \'hən\ *n* : a member of an Asian people that invaded Europe about A.D. 450

¹**hunch** \'hənch\ *vb* **1** : to thrust oneself forward **2** : to assume or cause to assume a bent or crooked posture

²**hunch** *n* **1** : PUSH **2** : a strong intuitive feeling about what will happen

hunch·back \'hənch-,bak\ *n* : a person with a crooked back; *also* : a back with a hump — **hunch·backed** *adj*

hun·dred \'hən-drəd\ *n, pl* **hundreds** *or* **hundred** : 10 times 10 — **hundred** *adj* — **hun·dredth** \-drədth\ *adj or n*

hun·dred·weight \-,wāt\ *n, pl* **hundredweight** *or* **hundredweights** — see WEIGHT table

¹**hung** *past and past part of* HANG

²**hung** *adj* : unable to reach a decision or verdict ⟨a ~ jury⟩

Hung *abbr* Hungarian; Hungary

Hun·gar·i·an \,hən-'ger-ē-ən\ *n* **1** : a native or inhabitant of Hungary **2** : the language of the Hungarians — **Hungarian** *adj*

hun·ger \'hən-gər\ *n* **1** : a craving or urgent need for food **2** : a strong desire — **hunger** *vb* — **hun·gri·ly** *adv* — **hun·gry** *adj*

hung·over \'hən-'ō-vər\ *adj* : having a hangover

hung up *adj* **1** : DELAYED **2** : ENTHUSIASTIC; *also* : PREOCCUPIED — usu. used with *on* ⟨hung up on winning⟩

hunk \'hənk\ *n* **1** : a large piece **2** : an attractive well-built man — **hunky** *adj*

hun·ker \'hən-kər\ *vb* **1** : CROUCH, SQUAT — usu. used with *down* **2** : to settle in for a sustained period — used with *down*

hun·ky-do·ry \,hən-kē-'dór-ē\ *adj* : quite satisfactory : FINE

¹**hunt** \'hənt\ *vb* **1** : to pursue for food or in sport; *also* : to take part in a hunt **2** : to try to find : SEEK **3** : to drive or chase esp. by harrying **4** : to traverse in search of prey — **hunt·er** *n*

²**hunt** *n* : an act, practice, or instance of hunting

Hun·ting·ton's disease \'hən-tiŋ-tənz-\ *n* : a chorea that usu. begins in middle age and leads to dementia

hunt·ress \'hən-trəs\ *n* : a woman who hunts game

hunts·man \'hənts-mən\ *n* **1** : HUNTER **2** : a person who manages a hunt and looks after the hounds

hur·dle \'hər-d⁸l\ *n* **1** : a barrier to leap over in a race **2** : OBSTACLE — **hurdle** *vb* — **hur·dler** *n*

hur·dy-gur·dy \,hər-dē-'gər-dē, 'hər-dē-,gər-dē\ *n, pl* **-gur·dies** : a musical instrument in which the sound is produced by turning a crank

hurl \'hərl\ *vb* **1** : to move or cause to move vigorously **2** : to throw down with violence **3** : FLING; *also* : PITCH — **hurl** *n* — **hurl·er** *n*

hur·ly-bur·ly \,hər-lē-'bər-lē\ *n* : UPROAR, TUMULT

Hu·ron \'hyùr-ən, 'hyùr-,än\ *n, pl* **Hurons** *or* **Huron** : a member of a confederacy of American Indian peoples formerly living between Georgian Bay and Lake Ontario

hur·rah \hù-'ró, -'rä\ *also* **hur·ray** \hù-'rä\ *interj* — used to express joy, approval, or encouragement

hur·ri·cane \'hər-ə-,kān\ *n* [Sp *huracán*, of AmerInd origin] : a tropical cyclone with winds of 74 miles (118 kilometers) per hour or greater that is usu. accompanied by rain, thunder, and lightning

¹**hur·ry** \'hər-ē\ *vb* **hur·ried; hur·ry·ing** **1** : to carry or cause to go with haste **2** : to impel to a greater speed **3** : to move or act with haste — **hurried** *adj* — **hur·ried·ly** *adv*

²**hurry** *n* : extreme haste or eagerness

¹**hurt** \'hərt\ *vb* **hurt; hurt·ing** **1** : to feel or cause to feel physical or emotional pain **2** : to do harm to : DAMAGE **3** : OFFEND **4** : HAMPER **5** : to be in need — usu. used with *for* — **hurt** *adj*

²**hurt** *n* **1** : a bodily injury or wound **2** : SUFFERING **3** : HARM, WRONG — **hurt·ful** *adj* — **hurt·ful·ness** *n*

hur·tle \'hər-t⁸l\ *vb* **hur·tled; hur·tling** **1** : to move rapidly or forcefully **2** : HURL, FLING

¹**hus·band** \'həz-bənd\ *n* [ME *husbonde*, fr. OE *hūsbonda* master of a house, fr. ON *hūsbōndi*, fr. *hūs* house + *bōndi* householder] : a male partner in a marriage

²**husband** *vb* : to manage prudently

hus·band·man \'həz-bənd-mən\ *n* : FARMER

hus·band·ry \'həz-bən-drē\ *n* **1** : the control or judicious use of resources **2** : AGRICULTURE **3** : the production and care of domestic animals

¹**hush** \'həsh\ *vb* **1** : to make or become quiet or calm **2** : SUPPRESS

²**hush** *n* : SILENCE, QUIET

hush–hush \'həsh-,həsh\ *adj* : SECRET, CONFIDENTIAL

¹**husk** \'həsk\ *n* **1** : a usu. thin dry outer covering of a seed or fruit **2** : an outer layer : SHELL

²**husk** *vb* : to strip the husk from — **husk·er** *n*

¹**hus·ky** \'həs-kē\ *adj* **hus·ki·er; -est** : HOARSE — **hus·ki·ly** \-kə-lē\ *adv* — **hus·ki·ness** \-kē-nəs\ *n*

²**husky** *n, pl* **huskies** **1** : a heavy-coated working dog of the New World Arctic **2** : SIBERIAN HUSKY

³**husky** *adj* **1** : BURLY, ROBUST **2** : LARGE

hus·sar \(,)hə-'zär\ *n* [Hung *huszár*] : a member of any of various European cavalry units

hus·sy \'hə-zē, -sē\ *n, pl* **hussies** [alter. of *housewife*] **1** : a lewd or brazen woman **2** : a pert or mischievous girl

hus·tings \'həs-tiŋz\ *n pl* : a place where political campaign speeches are made; *also* : the proceedings in an election campaign

hus·tle \'hə-səl\ *vb* **hus·tled; hus·tling** **1** : JOSTLE, SHOVE **2** : HASTEN, HURRY **3** : to work energetically — **hustle** *n* — **hus·tler** \'həs-lər\ *n*

hut \'hət\ *n* : a small and often temporary dwelling : SHACK

hutch \'həch\ *n* **1** : a chest or compartment for storage **2** : a cupboard esp. surmounted with open shelves **3** : a pen or coop for an animal **4** : HUT

huz·zah *or* **huz·za** \(,)hə-'zä\ *n* : a shout of acclaim — often used interjectionally to express joy or approbation

HV *abbr* **1** high velocity **2** high voltage

HVAC *abbr* heating, ventilating and air-conditioning

hvy *abbr* heavy

HW *abbr* hot water

hwy *abbr* highway

hy·a·cinth \'hī-ə-(,)sinth\ *n* : a bulbous Mediterranean herb related to the lilies that is widely grown for its spikes of fragrant bell-shaped flowers

hy·brid \'hī-brəd\ *n* **1** : an offspring of genetically differing parents (as members of different breeds or species) **2** : one of mixed origin or composition — **hybrid** *adj* — **hy·brid·i·za·tion** \,hī-brə-də-'zā-shən\ *n* — **hy·brid·ize** \'hī-brə-,dīz\ *vb* — **hy·brid·iz·er** *n*

hy·dra \'hī-drə\ *n* : any of numerous small tubular freshwater coelenterates that are polyps having at one end a mouth surrounded by tentacles

hy·dran·gea \hī-'drān-jə\ *n* : any of a genus of shrubs related to the currants and grown for their showy clusters of white, pink, or bluish flowers

hy·drant \'hī-drənt\ *n* : a pipe with a valve and spout at which water may be drawn from a main line

hy·drate \'hī-,drāt\ *n* : a compound formed by union of water with some other substance — **hydrate** *vb*

hy·drau·lic \hī-'dró-lik\ *adj* [ultim. fr. Gk *hydraulis* pipe organ using water pressure, fr. *hydōr* water + *aulos* reed instrument] **1** : operated, moved, or effected by means of water **2** : of or relating to hydraulics **3** : operated by the resistance offered or the pressure transmitted when a quantity of liquid is forced through a small orifice or through a tube **4** : hardening or setting under water

hy·drau·lics \-liks\ *n* : a science that deals with practical applications of liquid (as water) in motion

hydro \'hī-drō\ *n* : HYDROPOWER

hy·dro·car·bon \'hī-drō-,kär-bən\ *n* : an organic compound containing only carbon and hydrogen

hy·dro·ceph·a·lus \ˌhī-drō-'se-fə-ləs\ *n* : abnormal increase in the amount of fluid in the cranial cavity accompanied by enlargement of the skull and atrophy of the brain

hy·dro·chlo·ric acid \ˌhī-drə-'klȯr-ik-\ *n* : a sharp-smelling corrosive acid used in the laboratory and in industry and present in dilute form in gastric juice

hy·dro·dy·nam·ics \ˌhī-drō-dī-'na-miks\ *n* : a science that deals with the motion of fluids and the forces acting on moving bodies immersed in fluids — **hy·dro·dy·nam·ic** *adj*

hy·dro·elec·tric \ˌhī-drō-i-'lek-trik\ *adj* : of or relating to production of electricity by waterpower — **hy·dro·elec·tric·i·ty** \-ˌlek-'tri-sə-tē\ *n*

hy·dro·foil \'hī-drə-ˌfȯi(-ə)l\ *n* : a boat that has fins attached to the bottom by struts for lifting the hull clear of the water to allow faster speeds

hy·dro·gen \'hī-drə-jən\ *n* [F *hydrogène*, fr. Gk *hydōr* water + *-genēs* born; fr. the fact that water is generated by its combustion] : a gaseous colorless odorless highly flammable chemical element that is the lightest of the elements — **hy·drog·e·nous** \hī-'drä-jə-nəs\ *adj*

hy·dro·ge·nate \hī-'drä-jə-ˌnāt, 'hī-drə-\ *vb* **-nat·ed; -nat·ing** : to combine or treat with hydrogen; *esp* : to add hydrogen to the molecule of — **hy·dro·ge·na·tion** \hī-ˌdrä-jə-'nā-shən, ˌhī-drə-\ *n*

hydrogen bomb *n* : a bomb whose violent explosive power is due to the sudden release of atomic energy resulting from the fusion of light nuclei (as of hydrogen atoms)

hydrogen peroxide *n* : an unstable compound of hydrogen and oxygen used esp. as an oxidizing and bleaching agent, an antiseptic, and a propellant

hy·dro·graph·ic \ˌhī-drə-'gra-fik\ *adj* : of or relating to the description and study of bodies of water — **hy·drog·ra·pher** *n* — **hy·drog·ra·phy** \hī-'drä-grə-fē\ *n*

hy·drol·o·gy \hī-'drä-lə-jē\ *n* : a science dealing with the properties, distribution, and circulation of water — **hy·dro·log·ic** \ˌhī-drə-'lä-jik\ *or* **hy·dro·log·i·cal** \-ji-kəl\ *adj* — **hy·drol·o·gist** \hī-'drä-lə-jist\ *n*

hy·dro·ly·sis \hī-'drä-lə-səs\ *n* : a chemical decomposition involving the addition of the elements of water

hy·drom·e·ter \hī-'drä-mə-tər\ *n* : a floating instrument for determining specific gravities of liquids and hence the strength (as of alcoholic liquors)

hy·dro·pho·bia \ˌhī-drə-'fō-bē-ə\ *n* [LL, fr. Gk, fr. *hydōr* water + *phobos* fear] : RABIES

hy·dro·phone \'hī-drə-ˌfōn\ *n* : an underwater listening device

¹**hy·dro·plane** \'hī-drə-ˌplān\ *n* **1** : a powerboat designed for racing that skims the surface of the water **2** : SEAPLANE

²**hydroplane** *vb* : to skid on a wet road due to loss of contact between the tires and road

hy·dro·pon·ics \ˌhī-drə-'pä-niks\ *n* : the growing of plants in nutrient solutions — **hy·dro·pon·ic** *adj*

hy·dro·pow·er \'hī-drə-ˌpaů(-ə)r\ *n* : hydroelectric power

hy·dro·sphere \'hī-drə-ˌsfir\ *n* : the water (as vapor or lakes) of the earth

hy·dro·stat·ic \ˌhī-drə-'sta-tik\ *adj* : of or relating to fluids at rest or to the pressures they exert or transmit

hy·dro·ther·a·py \ˌhī-drə-'ther-ə-pē\ *n* : the use of water esp. externally in the treatment of disease or disability

hy·dro·ther·mal \ˌhī-drə-'thər-məl\ *adj* : of or relating to hot water

hy·drous \'hī-drəs\ *adj* : containing water

hy·drox·ide \hī-'dräk-ˌsīd\ *n* **1** : a negatively charged ion consisting of one atom of oxygen and one atom of hydrogen **2** : a compound of hydroxide with an element or group

hy·e·na \hī-'ē-nə\ *n* [ME *hyene*, fr. L *hyaena*, fr. Gk *hyaina*, fr. *hys* hog] : any of several large doglike carnivorous mammals of Asia and Africa

hy·giene \'hī-jēn\ *n* **1** : a science concerned with establishing and maintaining good health **2** : conditions or practices conducive to health — **hy·gien·ic** \hī-'je-nik, -'jē-\ *adj* — **hy·gien·i·cal·ly** \-ni-k(ə-)lē\ *adv* — **hy·gien·ist** \hī-'jē-nist, 'hī-ˌjē-, hī-'je-\ *n*

hy·grom·e·ter \hī-'grä-mə-tər\ *n* : any of several instruments for measuring the humidity of the atmosphere

hy·gro·scop·ic \ˌhī-grə-'skä-pik\ *adj* : readily taking up and retaining moisture

hying *pres part of* HIE

hy·men \'hī-mən\ *n* : a fold of mucous membrane partly closing the opening of the vagina

hy·me·ne·al \ˌhī-mə-'nē-əl\ *adj* : NUPTIAL

hymn \'him\ *n* : a song of praise esp. to God — **hymn** *vb*

hym·nal \'him-nəl\ *n* : a book of hymns

hyp *abbr* hypothesis; hypothetical

¹**hype** \'hīp\ *vb* **hyped; hyp·ing** **1** : STIMULATE — usu. used with *up* **2** : INCREASE — **hyped–up** *adj*

²**hype** *vb* **hyped; hyping** **1** : DECEIVE **2** : PUBLICIZE

³**hype** *n* **1** : DECEPTION, PUT-ON **2** : PUBLICITY

hy·per \'hī-pər\ *adj* **1** : HIGH-STRUNG, EXCITABLE **2** : extremely active

hy·per·acid·i·ty \ˌhī-pər-ə-'si-də-tē\ *n* : the condition of containing excessive acid esp. in the stomach — **hy·per·ac·id** \-'a-səd\ *adj*

hy·per·ac·tive \-'ak-tiv\ *adj* : excessively or pathologically active — **hy·per·ac·tiv·i·ty** \-ˌak-'ti-və-tē\ *n*

hy·per·bar·ic \ˌhī-pər-'ber-ik\ *adj* : of, relating to, or utilizing greater than normal pressure (as of oxygen)

hy·per·bo·la \hī-'pər-bə-lə\ *n, pl* **-las** *or* **-lae** \-(ˌ)lē\ : a curve formed by the intersection of a double right circular cone with a plane that cuts both halves of the cone — **hy·per·bol·ic** \ˌhī-pər-'bä-lik\ *adj*

hy·per·bo·le \hī-'pər-bə-(ˌ)lē\ *n* : extravagant exaggeration used as a figure of speech

hy·per·crit·i·cal \ˌhī-pər-'kri-ti-kəl\ *adj* : excessively critical — **hy·per·crit·i·cal·ly** \-k(ə-)lē\ *adv*

hy·per·drive \'hī-pər-ˌdrīv\ *n* : a state of extremely heightened activity

hy·per·ex·tend \ˌhī-pər-ik-'stend\ *vb* : to extend beyond the normal range of motion — **hy·per·ex·ten·sion** \-'sten-shən\ *n*

hy·per·gly·ce·mia \ˌhī-pər-glī-'sē-mē-ə\ *n* : excess of sugar in the blood — **hy·per·gly·ce·mic** \-mik\ *adj*

hy·per·ki·net·ic \-kə-'ne-tik\ *adj* : characterized by fast-paced or frenetic activity

hy·per·link \'hī-pər-ˌliŋk\ *n* : a connecting element (as highlighted text) between one place in a hypertext or hypermedia document and another

hy·per·me·dia \'hī-pər-ˌmē-dē-ə\ *n* : a database format offering direct access to text, sound, or images related to that on display

hy·per·opia \ˌhī-pə-'rō-pē-ə\ *n* : a condition in which visual images come to focus behind the retina resulting esp. in defective vision for near objects — **hy·per·opic** \-'rō-pik, -'rä-\ *adj*

hy·per·sen·si·tive \-'sen-sə-tiv\ *adj* **1** : excessively or abnormally sensitive **2** : abnormally susceptible physiologically to a specific agent (as a drug) — **hy·per·sen·si·tive·ness** *n* — **hy·per·sen·si·tiv·i·ty** \-ˌsen-sə-'ti-və-tē\ *n*

hy·per·ten·sion \'hī-pər-ˌten-chən\ *n* : high blood pressure — **hy·per·ten·sive** \ˌhī-pər-'ten-siv\ *adj or n*

hy·per·text \'hī-pər-ˌtekst\ *n* : a database format in which information related to that on display can be accessed directly from the display

hy·per·thy·roid·ism \ˌhī-pər-'thī-ˌrȯi-di-zəm\ *n* : excessive activity of the thyroid gland; *also* : the resulting bodily condition — **hy·per·thy·roid** \-'thī-ˌrȯid\ *adj*

hy·per·tro·phy \hī-'pər-trə-fē\ *n, pl* **-phies** : excessive development of a body part — **hy·per·tro·phic** \ˌhī-pər-'trō-fik\ *adj* — **hypertrophy** *vb*

hy·per·ven·ti·late \ˌhī-pər-'ven-tə-ˌlāt\ *vb* : to breathe rapidly and deeply esp. to the point of losing an abnormal amount of carbon dioxide from the blood — **hy·per·ven·ti·la·tion** \-ˌven-tə-'lā-shən\ *n*

hy·phen \'hī-fən\ *n* : a punctuation mark - used esp. to divide or to compound words or word parts — **hyphen** *vb*

hy·phen·ate \'hī-fə-ˌnāt\ *vb* **-at·ed; -at·ing** : to connect or divide with a hyphen — **hy·phen·ation** \ˌhī-fə-'nā-shən\ *n*

hyp·no·sis \hip-'nō-səs\ *n, pl* **-no·ses** \-ˌsēz\ : an induced state that resembles sleep and in which the subject is responsive to suggestions of the inducer (**hyp·no·tist** \'hip-nə-tist\) — **hyp·no·tism** \'hip-nə-ˌti-zəm\ *n* — **hyp·no·tiz·able** \'hip-nə-ˌtī-zə-bəl\ *adj* — **hyp·no·tize** \-ˌtīz\ *vb*

¹**hyp·not·ic** \hip-'nä-tik\ *adj* **1** : inducing sleep : SOPORIFIC **2** : of or relating to hypnosis or hypnotism **3** : readily holding the attention — **hyp·not·i·cal·ly** \-ti-k(ə-)lē\ *adv*

²**hypnotic** *n* : a sleep-inducing drug

hy·po \'hī-pō\ *n, pl* **hypos** : SODIUM THIOSULFATE; *also* : a solution of sodium thiosulfate

hy·po·al·ler·gen·ic \ˌhī-pō-ˌa-lər-'je-nik\ *adj* : having little likelihood of causing an allergic response

hy·po·cen·ter \'hī-pə-ˌsen-tər\ *n* : the point of origin of an earthquake

hy·po·chon·dria \ˌhī-pə-'kän-drē-ə\ *n* [NL, fr. LL, pl., upper abdomen (formerly regarded as the seat of hypochondria, fr. Gk, lit., the parts under the cartilage (of the breastbone), fr. *hypo-* under + *chondros* cartilage] : depression of mind often centered on imaginary physical ailments — **hy·po·chon·dri·ac** \-drē-ˌak\ *adj or n*

hy·poc·ri·sy \hi-'pä-krə-sē\ *n, pl* **-sies** : a feigning to be what one is not or to believe what one does not; *esp* : the false assumption of an appearance of virtue or religion — **hyp·o·crite** \'hi-pə-ˌkrit\ *n* — **hyp·o·crit·i·cal** \ˌhi-pə-'kri-ti-kəl\ *adj* — **hyp·o·crit·i·cal·ly** \-k(ə-)lē\ *adv*

¹hy·po·der·mic \ˌhī-pə-'dər-mik\ *adj* : administered by or used in making an injection beneath the skin

²hypodermic *n* : HYPODERMIC SYRINGE; *also* : an injection made with this

hypodermic needle *n* : NEEDLE 3; *also* : HYPODERMIC SYRINGE

hypodermic syringe *n* : a small syringe with a hollow needle for injecting material into or through the skin

hypodermic syringe

hy·po·gly·ce·mia \ˌhī-pō-glī-'sē-mē-ə\ *n* : abnormal decrease of sugar in the blood — **hy·po·gly·ce·mic** \-mik\ *adj*

hy·pot·e·nuse \hī-'pä-tə-ˌnüs, -ˌnyüs, -ˌnüz, -ˌnyüz\ *n* : the side of a right triangle that is opposite the right angle; *also* : its length

hy·po·thal·a·mus \ˌhī-pō-'tha-lə-məs\ *n* : a part of the brain that lies beneath the thalamus and is a control center for the autonomic nervous system

hy·poth·e·sis \hī-'pä-thə-səs\ *n, pl* **-e·ses** \-ˌsēz\ : an assumption made esp. in order to test its logical or empirical consequences — **hy·po·thet·i·cal** \ˌhī-pə-'the-ti-kəl\ *adj* — **hy·po·thet·i·cal·ly** \-k(ə-)lē\ *adv*

hy·poth·e·size \-ˌsīz\ *vb* **-sized; -siz·ing** : to adopt as a hypothesis

hy·po·thy·roid·ism \ˌhī-pō-'thī-ˌroi-di-zəm\ *n* : deficient activity of the thyroid gland; *also* : a resultant lowered metabolic rate and general loss of vigor — **hy·po·thy·roid** *adj*

hys·sop \'hi-səp\ *n* : a European mint sometimes used as a potherb

hys·ter·ec·to·my \ˌhis-tə-'rek-tə-mē\ *n, pl* **-mies** : surgical removal of the uterus

hys·te·ria \hi-'ster-ē-ə, -'stir-\ *n* [NL, fr. E *hysteric*, adj., fr. L *hystericus*, fr. Gk *hysterikos*, fr. *hystera* womb; fr. the Greek notion that hysteria was peculiar to women and caused by disturbances in the uterus] **1** : a nervous disorder marked esp. by defective emotional control **2** : unmanageable fear or outburst of emotion — **hys·ter·ic** \-'ster-ik\ *n* — **hys·ter·i·cal** \-'ster-i-kəl\ *also* **hysteric** *adj* — **hys·ter·i·cal·ly** \-k(ə-)lē\ *adv*

hys·ter·ics \-'ster-iks\ *n pl* : a fit of uncontrollable laughter or crying

Hz *abbr* hertz

I

¹i \'ī\ *n, pl* **i's** *or* **is** \'īz\ *often cap* : the 9th letter of the English alphabet

²i *abbr, often cap* island; isle

³i *symbol* imaginary unit

¹I \'ī, ə\ *pron* : the one speaking or writing

²I *abbr* interstate

³I *symbol* iodine

Ia *or* **IA** *abbr* Iowa

-ial *adj suffix* : ¹-AL ⟨manor*ial*⟩

iamb \'ī-ˌam\ *or* **iam·bus** \ī-'am-bəs\ *n, pl* **iambs** \'ī-ˌamz\ *or* **iam·bus·es** : a metrical foot of one unaccented syllable followed by one accented syllable — **iam·bic** \ī-'am-bik\ *adj or n*

-ian — see -AN

-iatric *also* **-iatrical** *adj comb form* : of or relating to (such) medical treatment or healing ⟨pedi*atric*⟩

-iatrics *n pl comb form* : medical treatment ⟨pedi*atrics*⟩

ib *or* **ibid** *abbr* ibidem

ibex \'ī-ˌbeks\ *n, pl* **ibex** *or* **ibex·es** [L] : any of several Old World wild goats with large curved horns

ibi·dem \'i-bə-ˌdem, i-'bī-dəm\ *adv* [L] : in the same place

-ibility — see -ABILITY

ibis \'ī-bəs\ *n, pl* **ibis** *or* **ibis·es** [L, fr. Gk, fr. Egypt *hbw*] : any of various wading birds related to the herons but having a downwardly curved bill

-ible — see -ABLE

ibu·pro·fen \ˌī-byü-'prō-fən\ *n* : a nonsteroidal anti-inflammatory drug used to relieve pain and fever

IC \ˌī-'sē\ *n* : INTEGRATED CIRCUIT

¹-ic *adj suffix* **1** : of, relating to, or having the form of : being ⟨panora*mic*⟩ **2** : related to, derived from, or containing ⟨alcohol*ic*⟩ **3** : in the manner of : like that of : characteristic of **4** : associated or dealing with : utilizing ⟨electron*ic*⟩ **5** : characterized by : exhibiting ⟨nostalg*ic*⟩ : affected with ⟨allerg*ic*⟩ **6** : caused by **7** : tending to produce ⟨analges*ic*⟩

²-ic *n suffix* : one having the character or nature of : one

belonging to or associated with : one exhibiting or affected by : one that produces

-ical *adj suffix* : -IC ⟨symmetr*ical*⟩ ⟨geolog*ical*⟩ — **-ically** *adv suffix*

ICBM \ˌī-ˌsē-(ˌ)bē-'em\ *n, pl* **ICBM's** *or* **ICBMs** \-'emz\ : an intercontinental ballistic missile

ICC *abbr* Interstate Commerce Commission

¹ice \'īs\ *n* **1** : frozen water **2** : a substance resembling ice **3** : a state of coldness (as from formality or reserve) **4** : a flavored frozen dessert; *esp* : one containing no milk or cream

²ice *vb* **iced; ic·ing 1** : FREEZE **2** : CHILL **3** : to cover with or as if with icing

ice age *n* : a time of widespread glaciation

ice bag *n* : a waterproof bag to hold ice for local application of cold to the body

ice·berg \'īs-ˌbərg\ *n* : a large floating mass of ice broken off from a glacier

iceberg lettuce *n* : any of various crisp light green lettuces that form a compact head like a cabbage

ice·boat \'īs-ˌbōt\ *n* : a boatlike frame on runners propelled on ice by sails

ice·bound \-ˌbau̇nd\ *adj* : surrounded, obstructed, or covered by ice

ice·box \-ˌbäks\ *n* : REFRIGERATOR

ice·break·er \-ˌbrā-kər\ *n* : a ship equipped (as with a reinforced bow) to make a channel through ice

ice cap *n* : a glacier forming on relatively level land and flowing outward from its center

ice cream *n* : a frozen food containing sweetened or flavored cream or butterfat

ice hockey *n* : a game in which two teams of ice-skating players try to shoot a puck into the opponent's goal

ice·house \'īs-ˌhau̇s\ *n* : a building in which ice is made or stored

¹Ice·lan·dic \īs-'lan-dik\ *adj* : of, relating to, or characteristic of Iceland, the Icelanders, or their language

²Icelandic *n* : the language of Iceland
ice·man \\ˈīs-ˌman\ *n* : one who sells or delivers ice
ice milk *n* : a sweetened frozen food made of skim milk
ice pick *n* : a hand tool ending in a spike for chipping ice
ice–skate \\ˈīs-ˌskāt\ *vb* : to skate on ice — **ice–skater** *n*
ice storm *n* : a storm in which falling rain freezes on contact
ice water *n* : chilled or iced water esp. for drinking
ich·thy·ol·o·gy \\ˌik-thē-ˈä-lə-jē\ *n* : a branch of zoology dealing with fishes — **ich·thy·ol·o·gist** \\-jist\ *n*
ici·cle \\ˈī-ˌsi-kəl\ *n* [ME *isikel*, fr. *is* ice + *ikel* icicle, fr. OE *gicel*] : a hanging mass of ice formed by the freezing of dripping water
ic·ing \\ˈī-siŋ\ *n* : a sweet usu. creamy mixture used to coat baked goods
ICJ *abbr* International Court of Justice
icky \\ˈi-kē\ *adj* **ick·i·er; -est** : OFFENSIVE, DISTASTEFUL — **ick·i·ness** *n*
icon *also* **ikon** \\ˈī-ˌkän\ *n* **1** : IMAGE; *esp* : a religious image painted on a wood panel **2** : a small picture on a computer display that suggests the purpose of an available function — **icon·ic** \\ī-ˈkä-nik\ *adj*
icon·o·clasm \\ī-ˈkä-nə-ˌkla-zəm\ *n* : the doctrine, practice, or attitude of an iconoclast
icon·o·clast \\-ˌklast\ *n* [ML *iconoclastes*, fr. MGk *eikonoklastēs*, lit., image destroyer, fr. Gk *eikōn* image + *klan* to break] **1** : one who destroys religious images or opposes their veneration **2** : one who attacks cherished beliefs or institutions
-ics \\iks\ *n sing or pl suffix* **1** : study : knowledge : skill : practice ⟨linguist*ics*⟩ ⟨electron*ics*⟩ **2** : characteristic actions or activities ⟨acrobat*ics*⟩ **3** : characteristic qualities, operations, or phenomena ⟨mechan*ics*⟩
ic·tus \\ˈik-təs\ *n* : the recurring stress or beat in a rhythmic or metrical series of sounds
ICU *abbr* intensive care unit
icy \\ˈī-sē\ *adj* **ic·i·er; -est** **1** : covered with, abounding in, or consisting of ice **2** : intensely cold **3** : being cold and unfriendly — **ic·i·ly** \\ˈī-sə-lē\ *adv* — **ic·i·ness** \\-sē-nəs\ *n*
¹id \\ˈid\ *n* [L, it] : the part of the psyche in psychoanalytic theory that is completely unconscious and concerned with instinctual needs and drives
²id *abbr* idem
¹ID \\ˈī-ˈdē\ *n* : a document with identifying information about an individual whose name appears on it
²ID *vb* **ID'd** *or* **IDed; ID'ing** *or* **IDing** : IDENTIFY
³ID *abbr* **1** Idaho **2** identification
idea \\ī-ˈdē-ə\ *n* **1** : a plan for action : DESIGN **2** : something imagined or pictured in the mind **3** : a central meaning or purpose ♦ *Synonyms* CONCEPT, CONCEPTION, NOTION, IMPRESSION
¹ide·al \\ī-ˈdēl\ *adj* **1** : existing only in the mind : IMAGINARY; *also* : lacking practicality **2** : of or relating to an ideal or to perfection : PERFECT
²ideal *n* **1** : a standard of excellence **2** : one regarded as a model worthy of imitation **3** : GOAL ♦ *Synonyms* ARCHETYPE, EXAMPLE, EXEMPLAR, PARADIGM, PATTERN
ide·al·ise *Brit var of* IDEALIZE
ide·al·ism \\ī-ˈdē-ə-ˌli-zəm\ *n* : the practice of forming ideals or living under their influence; *also* : an idealized representation — **ide·al·ist** \\-list\ *n* — **ide·al·is·tic** \\ī-ˌdē-ə-ˈlis-tik\ *adj* — **ide·al·is·ti·cal·ly** \\-ti-k(ə-)lē\ *adv*
ide·al·ize \\ī-ˈdē-ə-ˌlīz\ *vb* **-ized; -iz·ing** : to think of or represent as ideal — **ide·al·i·za·tion** \\-ˌdē-ə-lə-ˈzā-shən\ *n*
ide·al·ly \\ī-ˈdē-lē, -ˈdē-ə-lē\ *adv* **1** : in idea or imagination : MENTALLY **2** : in agreement with an ideal : PERFECTLY
ide·a·tion \\ˌī-dē-ˈā-shən\ *n* : the forming or entertaining of ideas — **ide·ate** \\ˈī-dē-ˌāt\ *vb* — **ide·a·tion·al** \\ˌī-dē-ˈā-shə-nəl\ *adj*
idem \\ˈī-ˌdem, ˈē-, ˈi-\ *pron* [L, same] : the same as something previously mentioned
iden·ti·cal \\ī-ˈden-ti-kəl\ *adj* **1** : being the same **2** : essentially alike ♦ *Synonyms* EQUIVALENT, EQUAL, TANTAMOUNT
iden·ti·fi·ca·tion \\ī-ˌden-tə-fə-ˈkā-shən\ *n* **1** : an act of identifying : the state of being identified **2** : evidence of identity **3** : an unconscious psychological process by which an individual models thoughts, feelings, and actions after another person or an object
iden·ti·fy \\ī-ˈden-tə-ˌfī\ *vb* **-fied; -fy·ing** **1** : to regard as

identical **2** : ASSOCIATE **3** : to establish the identity of **4** : to practice psychological identification — **iden·ti·fi·able** \\-ˌden-tə-ˈfī-ə-bəl\ *adj* — **iden·ti·fi·ably** \\-blē\ *adv* — **iden·ti·fi·er** \\-ˌfī(-ə)r\ *n*
iden·ti·ty \\ī-ˈden-tə-tē\ *n, pl* **-ties** **1** : sameness of essential character **2** : INDIVIDUALITY **3** : the fact of being the same person or thing as claimed
identity crisis *n* : psychological conflict esp. in adolescence involving confusion about one's social role and one's personality
identity theft *n* : the illegal use of someone else's personal information to obtain money or credit
ideo·gram \\ˈi-dē-ə-ˌgram, ˈī-\ *n* **1** : a picture or symbol used in a system of writing to represent a thing or an idea **2** : a character or symbol used in a system of writing to represent an entire word
ideo·logue *also* **idea·logue** \\ˈī-dē-ə-ˌlȯg\ *n* : a partisan advocate or adherent of a particular ideology
ide·ol·o·gy \\ˌī-dē-ˈä-lə-jē, ˌi-\ *also* **ide·al·o·gy** \\-ˈä-lə-jē, -ˈa-\ *n, pl* **-gies** **1** : the body of ideas characteristic of a particular individual, group, or culture **2** : the assertions, theories, and aims that constitute a political, social, and economic program — **ideo·log·i·cal** \\ˌī-dē-ə-ˈlä-ji-kəl, ˌi-\ *adj* — **ideo·log·i·cal·ly** \\-ˈlä-ji-k(ə-)lē\ *adv* — **ide·ol·o·gist** \\-ä-jist\ *n*
ides \\ˈīdz\ *n sing or pl* : the 15th day of March, May, July, or October or the 13th day of any other month in the ancient Roman calendar
id·i·o·cy \\ˈi-dē-ə-sē\ *n, pl* **-cies** **1** : something notably stupid or foolish **2** *dated, now offensive* : extreme mental retardation
id·i·om \\ˈi-dē-əm\ *n* **1** : the language peculiar to a person or group **2** : the characteristic form or structure of a language **3** : an expression that cannot be understood from the meanings of its separate words (as *give way*) — **id·i·o·mat·ic** \\ˌi-dē-ə-ˈma-tik\ *adj* — **id·i·o·mat·i·cal·ly** \\-ti-k(ə-)lē\ *adv*
id·i·o·path·ic \\ˌi-dē-ə-ˈpa-thik\ *adj* : arising spontaneously or from an obscure or unknown cause ⟨an ～ disease⟩
id·i·o·syn·cra·sy \\ˌi-dē-ə-ˈsin-krə-sē\ *n, pl* **-sies** : personal peculiarity — **id·i·o·syn·crat·ic** \\ˌi-dē-ō-sin-ˈkra-tik\ *adj* — **id·i·o·syn·crat·i·cal·ly** \\-ˈkra-ti-k(ə-)lē\ *adv*
id·i·ot \\ˈi-dē-ət\ *n* [ME, fr. AF *ydiote*, fr. L *idiota* ignorant person, fr. Gk *idiōtēs* one in a private station, layman, ignorant person, fr. *idios* one's own, private] **1** : a foolish or stupid person **2** *dated, now offensive* : a person affected with idiocy — **id·i·ot·ic** \\ˌi-dē-ˈä-tik\ *adj* — **id·i·ot·i·cal·ly** \\-ti-k(ə-)lē\ *adv*
id·i·ot-proof \\ˈi-dē-ət-ˌprüf\ *adj* : extremely easy to operate or maintain
¹idle \\ˈī-dᵊl\ *adj* **idler** \\ˈī-də-lər\; **idlest** \\ˈī-də-ləst\ **1** : GROUNDLESS, WORTHLESS, USELESS ⟨～ talk⟩ **2** : not occupied or employed : INACTIVE **3** : LAZY — **idle·ness** *n* — **idly** \\ˈīd-lē\ *adv*
²idle *vb* **idled; idling** **1** : to spend time doing nothing **2** : to make idle **3** : to run without being connected so that power is not used for useful work — **idler** *n*
idol \\ˈī-dᵊl\ *n* **1** : an image worshipped as a god; *also* : a false god **2** : an object of passionate devotion ⟨a sports ～⟩
idol·a·ter *or* **idol·a·tor** \\ī-ˈdä-lə-tər\ *n* : a worshiper of idols
idol·a·try \\-trē\ *n, pl* **-tries** **1** : the worship of a physical object as a god **2** : excessive devotion — **idol·a·trous** \\-trəs\ *adj*
idol·ize \\ˈī-də-ˌlīz\ *vb* **-ized; -iz·ing** : to make an idol of ⟨*idolized* his father⟩ — **idol·i·za·tion** \\ˌī-də-lə-ˈzā-shən\ *n*
idyll \\ˈī-dᵊl\ *n* **1** : a simple work of writing or poetry that describes country life or suggests a peaceful setting **2** : a fit subject for an idyll — **idyl·lic** \\ī-ˈdi-lik\ *adj*
i.e. \\ˈī-ˈē\ *abbr* [L *id est*] that is
IE *abbr* industrial engineer
IED *abbr* improvised explosive device
-ier — see -ER
if \\ˈif\ *conj* **1** : in the event that ⟨～ he stays, I leave⟩ **2** : WHETHER ⟨ask ～ he left⟩ **3** : — used as a function word to introduce an exclamation expressing a wish ⟨～ it would only rain⟩ **4** : even though ⟨an interesting ～ untenable argument⟩ **5** : and perhaps not even ⟨few ～ any changes are expected⟩
IF *abbr* intermediate frequency

if·fy \'i-fē\ adj : full of contingencies or unknown conditions

-i·fy \ə-ˌfī\ vb suffix : -FY

IG abbr inspector general

ig·loo \'i-glü\ n, pl **igloos** [Inuit (an Eskimo language) iglu house] : a house or hut that is often made of snow blocks and in the shape of a dome and that is associated esp. with indigenous peoples of arctic regions

ig·ne·ous \'ig-nē-əs\ adj 1 : FIERY 2 : formed by solidification of molten rock

ig·nite \ig-'nīt\ vb **ig·nit·ed; ig·nit·ing** : to set afire or catch fire — **ig·nit·able** \-'nī-tə-bəl\ adj

ig·ni·tion \ig-'ni-shən\ n 1 : a setting on fire 2 : the process or means (as an electric spark) of igniting the fuel mixture in an engine 3 : a device that activates an ignition system

ig·no·ble \ig-'nō-bəl\ adj 1 : of common birth 2 : not honorable : BASE, MEAN ✦ **Synonyms** DESPICABLE, SCURVY, SORDID, VILE, WRETCHED — **ig·no·bly** adv

ig·no·min·i·ous \ˌig-nə-'mi-nē-əs\ adj 1 : DISHONORABLE 2 : DESPICABLE 3 : HUMILIATING, DEGRADING ✦ **Synonyms** DISREPUTABLE, DISCREDITABLE, DISGRACEFUL, INGLORIOUS — **ig·no·min·i·ous·ly** adv — **ig·no·mi·ny** \'ig-nə-ˌmi-nē, ig-'nä-mə-nē\ n

ig·no·ra·mus \ˌig-nə-'rā-məs\ n, pl **-mus·es** also **-mi** \-mē\ [Ignoramus, ignorant lawyer in Ignoramus (1615), play by George Ruggle] : an utterly ignorant person

ig·no·rance \'ig-nə-rəns\ n : the state of being ignorant

ig·no·rant \'ig-nə-rənt\ adj 1 : lacking knowledge 2 : resulting from or showing lack of knowledge or intelligence 3 : UNAWARE, UNINFORMED ✦ **Synonyms** BENIGHTED, ILLITERATE, UNEDUCATED, UNLETTERED, UNTUTORED — **ig·no·rant·ly** adv

ig·nore \ig-'nór\ vb **ig·nored; ig·nor·ing** : to refuse to take notice of ✦ **Synonyms** OVERLOOK, SLIGHT, NEGLECT

igua·na \i-'gwä-nə\ n : any of various large tropical American lizards

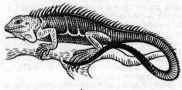

iguana

ihp abbr indicated horsepower

IHS \ˌī-ˌäch-'es\ [LL, part transliteration of Gk IHΣ, abbr. for IHΣΟΥΣ Iēsous Jesus] — used as a Christian symbol and monogram for Jesus

ikon var of ICON

IL abbr Illinois

il·e·itis \ˌi-lē-'ī-təs\ n : inflammation of the ileum

il·e·um \'i-lē-əm\ n, pl **il·ea** \-lē-ə\ : the part of the small intestine between the jejunum and the large intestine

il·i·ac \'i-lē-ˌak\ adj : of, relating to, or located near the ilium

il·i·um \'i-lē-əm\ n, pl **il·ia** \-lē-ə\ : the uppermost and largest of the three bones making up either side of the pelvis

ilk \'ilk\ n : SORT, KIND

1ill \'il\ adj **worse** \'wərs\; **worst** \'wərst\ 1 : attended or caused by an evil intent ⟨~ deeds⟩ 2 : not normal or sound ⟨~ health⟩; also : not in good health : SICK 3 : BAD, UNLUCKY ⟨an ~ omen⟩ 4 : not right or proper ⟨~ manners⟩ 5 : UNFRIENDLY, HOSTILE ⟨~ feeling⟩

2ill adv **worse; worst** 1 : with displeasure 2 : in a harsh manner 3 : HARDLY, SCARCELY ⟨can ~ afford it⟩ 4 : BADLY, UNLUCKILY 5 : in a faulty way

3ill n 1 : EVIL 2 : MISFORTUNE, DISTRESS 3 : AILMENT, SICKNESS; also : TROUBLE

4ill abbr illustrated; illustration; illustrator

Ill abbr Illinois

ill–ad·vised \ˌil-əd-'vīzd\ adj : not well counseled ⟨~ efforts⟩ — **ill–ad·vis·ed·ly** \-'vī-zəd-lē\ adv

ill–bred \-'bred\ adj : badly brought up : IMPOLITE ⟨an ~ child⟩

il·le·gal \il-'lē-gəl\ adj : not lawful; also : not sanctioned by official rules ✦ **Synonyms** UNLAWFUL, CRIMINAL, ILLEGITIMATE, ILLICIT, WRONGFUL — **il·le·gal·i·ty** \ˌi-li-'ga-lə-tē\ n — **il·le·gal·ly** adv

il·leg·i·ble \il-'le-jə-bəl\ adj : not legible — **il·leg·i·bil·i·ty** \il-ˌle-jə-'bi-lə-tē\ n — **il·leg·i·bly** \il-'le-jə-blē\ adv

il·le·git·i·mate \ˌi-li-'ji-tə-mət\ adj 1 : born of unmarried parents 2 : ILLOGICAL 3 : ILLEGAL — **il·le·git·i·ma·cy** \-'ji-tə-mə-sē\ n — **il·le·git·i·mate·ly** adv

ill–fat·ed \'il-'fā-təd\ adj : UNFORTUNATE ⟨an ~ expedition⟩

ill–fa·vored \-'fā-vərd\ adj : UGLY, UNATTRACTIVE

ill–got·ten \-'gä-t²n\ adj : acquired by improper means ⟨~ gains⟩

ill–hu·mored \-'hyü-mərd, -'yü-\ adj : SURLY, IRRITABLE

il·lib·er·al \il-'li-bə-rəl\ adj : not liberal : NARROW, BIGOTED

il·lic·it \il-'li-sət\ adj : not permitted : UNLAWFUL — **il·lic·it·ly** adv

il·lim·it·able \il-'li-mə-tə-bəl\ adj : BOUNDLESS, MEASURELESS — **il·lim·it·ably** \-blē\ adv

Il·li·nois \ˌi-lə-'nói also -'nóiz\ n, pl **Illinois** : a member of an American Indian people of Illinois, Iowa, and Wisconsin

il·lit·er·ate \il-'li-tə-rət\ adj 1 : having little or no education; esp : unable to read or write 2 : showing a lack of familiarity with the fundamentals of a particular field of knowledge — **il·lit·er·a·cy** \-'li-tə-rə-sē\ n — **illiterate** n

ill–man·nered \'il-'ma-nərd\ adj : marked by bad manners : RUDE

ill–na·tured \-'nā-chərd\ adj : CROSS, SURLY — **ill–na·tured·ly** adv

ill·ness \'il-nəs\ n : SICKNESS

il·log·i·cal \il-'lä-ji-kəl\ adj : lacking sound reasoning; also : SENSELESS — **il·log·i·cal·ly** \-ji-k(ə-)lē\ adv

ill–starred \'il-'stärd\ adj : UNLUCKY 1

ill–tem·pered \-'tem-pərd\ adj : CROSS

ill–treat \-'trēt\ vb : to treat cruelly or improperly : MALTREAT — **ill–treat·ment** n

il·lu·mi·nate \i-'lü-mə-ˌnāt\ vb **-nat·ed; -nat·ing** 1 : to supply or brighten with light : light up 2 : to make clear : ELUCIDATE; also : to bring to the fore 3 : to decorate (as a manuscript) with designs or pictures in gold or colors — **il·lu·mi·nat·ing·ly** adv — **il·lu·mi·na·tion** \-ˌlü-mə-'nā-shən\ n — **il·lu·mi·na·tor** \-'lü-mə-ˌnā-tər\ n

il·lu·mine \i-'lü-mən\ vb **-mined; -min·ing** : ILLUMINATE

ill–us·age \'il-'yü-sij\ n : harsh, unkind, or abusive treatment

ill–use \-'yüz\ vb : MALTREAT, ABUSE

il·lu·sion \i-'lü-zhən\ n [ME, fr. AF, fr. LL illusio, fr. L, action of mocking, fr. illudere to mock at, fr. ludere to play, mock] 1 : a mistaken idea : MISCONCEPTION 2 : a misleading visual image; also : HALLUCINATION

il·lu·sion·ist \i-'lü-zhə-nist\ n : one that produces illusions; esp : a sleight-of-hand performer

il·lu·sive \i-'lü-siv\ adj : DECEPTIVE

il·lu·so·ry \i-'lü-sə-rē, -zə-\ adj : DECEPTIVE ⟨~ hopes⟩

illust or **illus** abbr illustrated; illustration

il·lus·trate \'i-ləs-ˌtrāt\ vb **-trat·ed; -trat·ing** [L illustrare, fr. lustrare to purify, make bright] 1 : to explain by use of examples : CLARIFY; also : DEMONSTRATE 2 : to provide with pictures or figures that explain or decorate 3 : to serve to explain or decorate — **il·lus·tra·tor** \'i-ləs-ˌtrā-tər\ n

il·lus·tra·tion \ˌi-lə-'strā-shən\ n 1 : the act of illustrating : the condition of being illustrated 2 : an example or instance that helps make something clear 3 : a picture or diagram that explains or decorates

il·lus·tra·tive \i-'ləs-trə-tiv, 'i-ləs-ˌstrā-\ adj : serving, tending, or designed to illustrate — **il·lus·tra·tive·ly** adv

il·lus·tri·ous \i-'ləs-trē-əs\ adj : notably outstanding because of rank or achievement ✦ **Synonyms** DISTINGUISHED, EMINENT, FAMOUS, GREAT, NOTABLE, PROMINENT — **il·lus·tri·ous·ness** n

ill will n : unfriendly feeling

ILS abbr instrument landing system

1IM \'ī-'em\ vb **IM'd; IM'ing** 1 : to send an instant message to 2 : to communicate by instant message

2IM abbr instant message

1im·age \'i-mij\ n 1 : a likeness or imitation of a person or thing; esp : STATUE 2 : a picture of an object formed by a device (as a mirror or lens) 3 : a visual representation of something ⟨a computer ∼⟩ **4** a person strikingly like another person ⟨he is the ∼ of his father⟩ **5** : a mental picture or conception : IMPRESSION, IDEA, CONCEPT **6** : a vivid representation or description

²**image** *vb* **im·aged; im·ag·ing 1** : to call up a mental picture of **2** : to describe or portray in words **3** : to create a representation of **4** : REFLECT, MIRROR **5** : to make appear : PROJECT

im·ag·ery \'i-mij-rē\ *n, pl* **-er·ies 1** : IMAGES; *also* : the art of making images **2** : figurative language **3** : mental images; *esp* : the products of imagination

imag·in·able \i-'ma-jə-nə-bəl\ *adj* : capable of being imagined : CONCEIVABLE — **imag·in·ably** *adv*

imag·i·nary \i-'ma-jə-ˌner-ē\ *adj* **1** : existing only in the imagination **2** : containing or relating to a quantity (**imaginary unit**) that is the positive square root of minus 1 ($\sqrt{-1}$)

imaginary number *n* : a complex number (as $2 + 3i$) with a nonzero term (**imaginary part**) containing the imaginary unit as a factor

imag·i·na·tion \i-ˌma-jə-'nā-shən\ *n* **1** : the act or power of forming a mental image of something not present to the senses or not previously known or experienced **2** : creative ability **3** : RESOURCEFULNESS **4** : a mental image : a creation of the mind — **imag·i·na·tive** \i-'ma-jə-nə-tiv, -ˌnā-\ *adj* — **imag·i·na·tive·ly** *adv*

imag·ine \i-'ma-jən\ *vb* **imag·ined; imag·in·ing 1** : to form a mental picture of something not present **2** : THINK, GUESS ⟨I ∼ it will rain⟩

imag·in·ings \-'maj-ninz, -'ma-jə-\ *n pl* : products of the imagination

im·ag·ism \'i-mi-ˌji-zəm\ *n, often cap* : a movement in poetry advocating free verse and the expression of ideas and emotions through clear precise images — **im·ag·ist** \-jist\ *n*

ima·go \i-'mā-gō, -'mä-\ *n, pl* **imagoes** *or* **ima·gi·nes** \-'mā-gə-ˌnēz, -'mä-\ [NL, fr. L, image] : an insect in its final adult stage — **ima·gi·nal** \i-'mā-gə-nᵊl, -'mä-\ *adj*

im·bal·ance \'im-'ba-ləns\ *n* : lack of balance : the state of being out of equilibrium or out of proportion

im·be·cile \'im-bə-səl, -ˌsil\ *n* **1** : FOOL, IDIOT **2** *dated, now offensive* : a person affected with moderate mental retardation — **imbecile** *or* **im·be·cil·ic** \ˌim-bə-'si-lik\ *adj* — **im·be·cil·i·ty** \ˌim-bə-'si-lə-tē\ *n*

imbed *var of* EMBED

im·bibe \im-'bīb\ *vb* **im·bibed; im·bib·ing 1** : to receive and retain in the mind **2** : to drink alcoholic beverages **3** : to take in or up : ABSORB — **im·bib·er** *n*

im·bri·ca·tion \ˌim-brə-'kā-shən\ *n* **1** : an overlapping of edges (as of tiles) **2** : a pattern showing imbrication — **im·bri·cate** \'im-bri-kət\ *adj*

im·bro·glio \im-'brōl-yō\ *n, pl* **-glios** [It, fr. *imbrogliare* to entangle] **1** : a confused mass **2** : a complicated situation; *also* : a serious or embarrassing misunderstanding

im·brue \im-'brü\ *vb* **im·brued; im·bru·ing** : STAIN ⟨hands *imbrued* with blood⟩

im·bue \-'byü\ *vb* **im·bued; im·bu·ing 1** : to permeate or influence as if by dyeing **2** : to tinge or dye deeply

IMF *abbr* International Monetary Fund

imit *abbr* imitative

im·i·ta·ble \'i-mə-tə-bəl\ *adj* : capable or worthy of being imitated or copied

im·i·tate \'i-mə-ˌtāt\ *vb* **-tat·ed; -tat·ing 1** : to follow as a model : COPY **2** : RESEMBLE **3** : REPRODUCE **4** : MIMIC, COUNTERFEIT — **im·i·ta·tor** \-ˌtā-tər\ *n*

im·i·ta·tion \ˌi-mə-'tā-shən\ *n* **1** : an act of imitating **2** : COPY, COUNTERFEIT **3** : a literary work that reproduces the style of another author — **imitation** *adj*

im·i·ta·tive \'i-mə-ˌtā-tiv\ *adj* **1** : marked by imitation **2** : inclined to imitate **3** : COUNTERFEIT

im·mac·u·late \i-'ma-kyə-lət\ *adj* **1** : being without stain or blemish : PURE **2** : spotlessly clean ⟨∼ linen⟩ — **im·mac·u·late·ly** *adv*

im·ma·nent \'i-mə-nənt\ *adj* **1** INHERENT **2** : being within the limits of experience or knowledge — **im·ma·nence** \-nəns\ *n* — **im·ma·nen·cy** \-nən-sē\ *n*

im·ma·te·ri·al \ˌi-mə-'tir-ē-əl\ *adj* **1** : not consisting of matter : SPIRITUAL **2** : UNIMPORTANT, TRIFLING ♦ *Synonyms* BODILESS, DISEMBODIED, INCORPOREAL, INSUBSTANTIAL, NONPHYSICAL — **im·ma·te·ri·al·i·ty** \-ˌtir-ē-'a-lə-tē\ *n*

im·ma·ture \ˌi-mə-'tùr, -'tyùr\ *adj* : lacking complete development : not yet mature ⟨∼ behavior⟩ — **im·ma·tu·ri·ty** \-'tùr-ə-tē, -'tyùr-\ *n*

im·mea·sur·able \(ˌ)i-'me-zhə-rə-bəl\ *adj* : not capable of being measured : indefinitely extensive : ILLIMITABLE — **im·mea·sur·ably** \-blē\ *adv*

im·me·di·a·cy \i-'mē-dē-ə-sē\ *n, pl* **-cies 1** : the quality or state of being immediate **2** : something that is of immediate importance

im·me·di·ate \i-'mē-dē-ət\ *adj* **1** : acting directly and alone : DIRECT ⟨the ∼ cause of death⟩ **2** : being next in line or relation ⟨members of the ∼ family⟩ **3** : not distant : CLOSE **4** : made or done at once ⟨an ∼ response⟩ **5** : near to or related to the present time ⟨the ∼ future⟩ — **im·me·di·ate·ly** *adv*

im·me·mo·ri·al \ˌi-mə-'mòr-ē-əl\ *adj* : extending beyond the reach of memory, record, or tradition ⟨from time ∼⟩

im·mense \i-'mens\ *adj* [ME, fr. MF, fr. L *immensus* immeasurable, fr. *mensus*, pp. of *metiri* to measure] **1** : very great in size or degree : VAST, HUGE **2** : EXCELLENT — **im·mense·ly** *adv* — **im·men·si·ty** \-'men-sə-tē\ *n*

im·merse \i-'mərs\ *vb* **im·mersed; im·mers·ing 1** : to plunge or dip esp. into a fluid **2** : ENGROSS, ABSORB **3** : to baptize by immersing — **im·mer·sion** \-'mər-zhən\ *n*

im·mi·grant \'i-mi-grənt\ *n* **1** : a person who immigrates **2** : a plant or animal that becomes established where it did not previously occur

im·mi·grate \'i-mə-ˌgrāt\ *vb* **-grat·ed; -grat·ing** : to come into a foreign country and take up residence — **im·mi·gra·tion** \ˌi-mə-'grā-shən\ *n*

im·mi·nent \'i-mə-nənt\ *adj* : ready to take place; *esp* : hanging threateningly over one's head ⟨in ∼ danger⟩ — **im·mi·nence** \-nəns\ *n* — **im·mi·nent·ly** *adv*

im·mis·ci·ble \(ˌ)i-'mi-sə-bəl\ *adj* : incapable of mixing

im·mis·er·a·tion \(ˌ)i-ˌmi-zə-'rā-shən\ *n* : IMPOVERISHMENT

im·mo·bile \(ˌ)i-'mō-bəl\ *adj* : incapable of being moved : FIXED — **im·mo·bil·i·ty** \ˌi-mō-'bi-lə-tē\ *n*

im·mo·bi·lize \i-'mō-bə-ˌlīz\ *vb* : to make immobile — **im·mo·bi·li·za·tion** \i-ˌmō-bə-lə-'zā-shən\ *n*

im·mod·er·ate \(ˌ)i-'mä-də-rət\ *adj* : lacking in moderation : EXCESSIVE ⟨∼ drinking⟩ — **im·mod·er·a·cy** \-rə-sē\ *n* — **im·mod·er·ate·ly** *adv*

im·mod·est \(ˌ)i-'mä-dəst\ *adj* : not modest : BRAZEN, INDECENT ⟨an ∼ dress⟩ ⟨∼ conduct⟩ — **im·mod·est·ly** *adv* — **im·mod·es·ty** \-də-stē\ *n*

im·mo·late \'i-mə-ˌlāt\ *vb* **-lat·ed; -lat·ing** [L *immolare*, to sprinkle with meal before sacrificing, sacrifice, fr. *mola* sacrificial barley cake, lit., millstone] : to offer in sacrifice; *esp* : to kill as a sacrificial victim — **im·mo·la·tion** \ˌi-mə-'lā-shən\ *n*

im·mor·al \(ˌ)i-'mòr-əl\ *adj* : not moral — **im·mor·al·ly** *adv*

im·mo·ral·i·ty \ˌi-mò-'ra-lə-tē, ˌi-mə-\ *n* **1** : WICKEDNESS; *esp* : UNCHASTITY **2** : an immoral act or practice

¹**im·mor·tal** \(ˌ)i-'mòr-tᵊl\ *adj* **1** : not mortal : exempt from death ⟨∼ gods⟩ **2** : destined to be remembered forever ⟨those ∼ words⟩ — **im·mor·tal·ly** *adv*

²**immortal** *n* **1** : one exempt from death **2** *pl, often cap* : the gods in Greek and Roman mythology **3** : a person whose fame is lasting ⟨an ∼ of baseball⟩

im·mor·tal·i·ty \ˌi-ˌmòr-'ta-lə-tē\ *n* : the quality or state of being immortal; *esp* : unending existence

im·mor·tal·ize \i-'mòr-tə-ˌlīz\ *vb* **-ized; -iz·ing** : to make immortal

im·mov·able \(ˌ)i-'mü-və-bəl\ *adj* **1** : firmly fixed, settled, or fastened : FAST, STATIONARY ⟨∼ mountains⟩ **2** : STEADFAST, UNYIELDING **3** : IMPASSIVE — **im·mov·abil·i·ty** \-ˌmü-və-'bi-lə-tē\ *n* — **im·mov·ably** \-blē\ *adv*

im·mune \i-'myün\ *adj* **1** : EXEMPT **2** : having a special capacity for resistance (as to a disease) **3** : containing or producing antibodies — **im·mu·ni·ty** \-'myü-nə-tē\ *n*

immune response *n* : a response of the body to an antigen resulting in the formation of antibodies and cells designed to react with the antigen and render it harmless

immune system *n* : the bodily system that protects the body from foreign substances, cells, and tissues by producing the immune response and that includes esp. the thymus, spleen, lymph nodes, and lymphocytes

im·mu·nize \'i-myə-ˌnīz\ vb -nized; -niz·ing : to make immune — **im·mu·ni·za·tion** \ˌi-myə-nə-'zā-shən\ n
im·mu·no·de·fi·cien·cy \ˌi-myə-nō-di-'fi-shən-sē\ n : inability to produce the normal number of antibodies or immunologically sensitized cells esp. in response to specific antigens — **im·mu·no·de·fi·cient** \-'fi-shənt\ adj
im·mu·no·glob·u·lin \ˌi-myə-nō-'glä-byə-lən\ n : ANTIBODY
im·mu·nol·o·gy \ˌi-myə-'nä-lə-jē\ n : a science that deals with the immune system, immunity, and the immune response — **im·mu·no·log·ic** \-nə-'lä-jik\ or **im·mu·no·log·i·cal** \-ji-kəl\ adj — **im·mu·no·log·i·cal·ly** \-ji-k(ə-)lē\ adv — **im·mu·nol·o·gist** \-'nä-lə-jist\ n
im·mu·no·sup·pres·sion \ˌi-myə-nō-sə-'pre-shən\ n : suppression (as by drugs) of natural immune responses — **im·mu·no·sup·press** \-'pres\ vb — **im·mu·no·sup·pres·sant** \-'pre-sⁿt\ n or adj — **im·mu·no·sup·pres·sive** \-'pre-siv\ adj
im·mu·no·ther·a·py \-'ther-ə-pē\ n : the treatment or prevention of disease by attempting to induce immunity
im·mure \i-'myu̇r\ vb **im·mured; im·mur·ing** 1 : to enclose within or as if within walls 2 : to build into a wall; esp : to entomb in a wall
im·mu·ta·ble \(ˌ)i-'myü-tə-bəl\ adj : UNCHANGEABLE, UNCHANGING — **im·mu·ta·bil·i·ty** \-ˌmyü-tə-'bi-lə-tē\ n — **im·mu·ta·bly** \-'myü-tə-blē\ adv
¹**imp** \'imp\ n 1 : a small demon : FIEND 2 : a mischievous child
²**imp** abbr 1 imperative 2 imperfect 3 imperial 4 import; imported
¹**im·pact** \im-'pakt\ vb 1 : to press together 2 : to have an impact on
²**im·pact** \'im-ˌpakt\ n 1 : a forceful contact, collision, or onset; also : the impetus communicated in or as if in a collision 2 : EFFECT
im·pact·ed \im-'pak-təd\ adj 1 : packed or wedged in 2 : wedged between the jawbone and another tooth
im·pair \im-'per\ vb : to diminish in quantity, value, excellence, or strength : DAMAGE, LESSEN — **im·pair·ment** n
im·paired \-'pard\ adj : being in a less than perfect or whole condition; esp : disabled or functionally defective — often used in combination ⟨hearing-impaired⟩
im·pa·la \im-'pa-lə\ n, pl **impalas** or **impala** : a large brownish African antelope that in the male has slender curved horns with ridges
im·pale \im-'pāl\ vb **im·paled; im·pal·ing** : to pierce with or as if with something pointed — **im·pale·ment** n
im·pal·pa·ble \(ˌ)im-'pal-pə-bəl\ adj 1 : unable to be felt by touch : INTANGIBLE 2 : not easily seen or understood — **im·pal·pa·bly** \-blē\ adv
im·pan·el or **em·pan·el** \im-'pan-ᵊl\ vb : to enter in or on a panel : ENROLL ⟨~ a jury⟩
im·part \im-'pärt\ vb 1 : to give from one's store or abundance ⟨the sun ~s warmth⟩ 2 : to make known
im·par·tial \(ˌ)im-'pär-shəl\ adj : not partial : UNBIASED, JUST — **im·par·tial·i·ty** \-ˌpär-shē-'a-lə-tē\ n — **im·par·tial·ly** adv
im·pass·able \(ˌ)im-'pa-sə-bəl\ adj : incapable of being passed, traversed, or crossed ⟨~ roads⟩ — **im·pass·ably** \-blē\ adv
im·passe \'im-ˌpas\ n 1 : a predicament from which there is no obvious escape 2 : an impassable road or way
im·pas·si·ble \(ˌ)im-'pa-sə-bəl\ adj : incapable of feeling : IMPASSIVE
im·pas·sioned \im-'pa-shənd\ adj : filled with passion or zeal : showing great warmth or intensity of feeling
♦ **Synonyms** PASSIONATE, ARDENT, FERVENT, FERVID
im·pas·sive \(ˌ)im-'pa-siv\ adj : showing no signs of feeling, emotion, or interest : EXPRESSIONLESS, INDIFFERENT ♦ **Synonyms** STOIC, PHLEGMATIC, APATHETIC, STOLID — **im·pas·sive·ly** adv — **im·pas·siv·i·ty** \ˌim-ˌpa-'si-və-tē\ n
im·pas·to \im-'pas-tō, -'päs-\ n : the thick application of a pigment to a canvas or panel in painting; also : the body of pigment so applied
im·pa·tiens \im-'pā-shənz, -shənz\ n : any of a genus of herbs with usu. spurred flowers and seed capsules that readily split open
im·pa·tient \(ˌ)im-'pā-shənt\ adj 1 : not patient : restless or short of temper esp. under irritation, delay, or oppo-

sition 2 : INTOLERANT ⟨~ of poverty⟩ 3 : prompted or marked by impatience ⟨an ~ reply⟩ 4 : ANXIOUS — **im·pa·tience** \-shəns\ n — **im·pa·tient·ly** adv
im·peach \im-'pēch\ vb [ME empechen to accuse, fr. AF empecher, enpechier to ensnare, impede, prosecute, fr. LL impedicare to fetter, fr. L pedica fetter, fr. ped-, pes foot] 1 : to charge (a public official) before an authorized tribunal with misconduct in office 2 : to challenge the credibility or validity of 3 : to remove from public office for misconduct — **im·peach·ment** n
im·pec·ca·ble \(ˌ)im-'pe-kə-bəl\ adj 1 : not capable of sinning or wrongdoing 2 : FAULTLESS, IRREPROACHABLE ⟨a man of ~ character⟩ — **im·pec·ca·bil·i·ty** \-ˌpe-kə-'bi-lə-tē\ n — **im·pec·ca·bly** \-'pe-kə-blē\ adv
im·pe·cu·nious \ˌim-pi-'kyü-nyəs, -nē-əs\ adj : having little or no money — **im·pe·cu·nious·ness** n
im·ped·ance \im-'pē-dᵊns\ n : the opposition in an electrical circuit to the flow of an alternating current
im·pede \im-'pēd\ vb **im·ped·ed; im·ped·ing** [L impedire, fr. ped-, pes foot] : to interfere with the progress of
im·ped·i·ment \im-'pe-də-mənt\ n 1 : something that impedes, hinders, or obstructs 2 : a speech defect
im·ped·i·men·ta \im-ˌpe-də-'men-tə\ n pl : things that impede
im·pel \im-'pel\ vb **im·pelled; im·pel·ling** : to urge or drive forward or on : FORCE; also : PROPEL
im·pel·ler also **im·pel·lor** \im-'pe-lər\ n : a rotor esp. in a pump
im·pend \im-'pend\ vb 1 : to hover or hang over threateningly : MENACE 2 : to be about to occur
im·pen·e·tra·ble \(ˌ)im-'pe-nə-trə-bəl\ adj 1 : incapable of being penetrated or pierced ⟨an ~ jungle⟩ 2 : incapable of being comprehended : INSCRUTABLE ⟨an ~ mystery⟩ — **im·pen·e·tra·bil·i·ty** \-ˌpe-nə-trə-'bi-lə-tē\ n — **im·pen·e·tra·bly** \-'pe-nə-trə-blē\ adv
im·pen·i·tent \(ˌ)im-'pe-nə-tənt\ adj : not penitent : not repenting of sin — **im·pen·i·tence** \-təns\ n
im·per·a·tive \im-'per-ə-tiv\ adj 1 : expressing a command, request, or encouragement ⟨~ sentence⟩ 2 : having power to restrain, control, or direct 3 : NECESSARY ⟨an ~ duty⟩ — **imperative** n — **im·per·a·tive·ly** adv
im·per·cep·ti·ble \ˌim-pər-'sep-tə-bəl\ adj : not perceptible; esp : too slight to be perceived ⟨~ changes⟩ — **im·per·cep·ti·bly** \-blē\ adv
im·per·cep·tive \ˌim-pər-'sep-tiv\ adj : not perceptive ⟨an ~ reader⟩
imperf abbr imperfect
¹**im·per·fect** \(ˌ)im-'pər-fikt\ adj 1 : not perfect : DEFECTIVE, INCOMPLETE 2 : of, relating to, or being a verb tense used to designate a continuing state or an incomplete action esp. in the past — **im·per·fect·ly** adv
²**imperfect** n : the imperfect tense; also : a verb form in it
im·per·fec·tion \ˌim-pər-'fek-shən\ n : the quality or state of being imperfect; also : FAULT, BLEMISH
im·pe·ri·al \im-'pir-ē-əl\ adj 1 : of, relating to, or befitting an empire or an emperor; also : of or relating to the United Kingdom or to the Commonwealth or British Empire 2 : ROYAL, SOVEREIGN; also : REGAL, IMPERIOUS 3 : of unusual size or excellence
im·pe·ri·al·ism \im-'pir-ē-ə-ˌli-zəm\ n : the policy of seeking to extend the power, dominion, or territories of a nation — **im·pe·ri·al·ist** \-list\ n or adj — **im·pe·ri·al·is·tic** \-ˌpir-ē-ə-'lis-tik\ adj — **im·pe·ri·al·is·ti·cal·ly** \-ti-k(ə-)lē\ adv
im·per·il \im-'per-əl\ vb -iled or -illed; -il·ing or -il·ling : ENDANGER
im·pe·ri·ous \im-'pir-ē-əs\ adj 1 : COMMANDING, LORDLY 2 : ARROGANT, DOMINEERING 3 : IMPERATIVE, URGENT ⟨~ problems⟩ — **im·pe·ri·ous·ly** adv
im·per·ish·able \(ˌ)im-'per-i-shə-bəl\ adj : not perishable or subject to decay
im·per·ma·nent \(ˌ)im-'pər-mə-nənt\ adj : not permanent : TRANSIENT — **im·per·ma·nent·ly** adv
im·per·me·able \(ˌ)im-'pər-mē-ə-bəl\ adj : not permitting passage (as of a fluid) through its substance
im·per·mis·si·ble \ˌim-pər-'mi-sə-bəl\ adj : not permissible ⟨~ by law⟩
im·per·son·al \(ˌ)im-'pər-sə-nəl\ adj 1 : not referring to any particular person or thing 2 : not involving human emotions — **im·per·son·al·i·ty** \-ˌpər-sə-'na-lə-tē\ n — **im·per·son·al·ly** adv

im·per·son·ate \im-'pər-sə-ˌnāt\ vb **-at·ed; -at·ing** : to assume or act the character of — **im·per·son·a·tion** \-ˌpər-sə-'nā-shən\ n — **im·per·son·a·tor** \-'pər-sə-ˌnā-tər\ n

im·per·ti·nent \(ˌ)im-'pər-tə-nənt\ adj **1** : IRRELEVANT **2** : not restrained within due or proper bounds : RUDE, INSOLENT, SAUCY ⟨an ～ reply⟩ — **im·per·ti·nence** \-nəns\ n — **im·per·ti·nent·ly** adv

im·per·turb·able \ˌim-pər-'tər-bə-bəl\ adj : marked by extreme calm, impassivity, and steadiness : SERENE

im·per·vi·ous \(ˌ)im-'pər-vē-əs\ adj **1** : incapable of being penetrated (as by moisture) **2** : not capable of being affected or disturbed ⟨～ to criticism⟩

im·pe·ti·go \ˌim-pə-'tē-gō, -'tī-\ n : a contagious skin disease characterized by vesicles, pustules, and yellowish crusts

im·pet·u·ous \im-'pe-chə-wəs\ adj **1** : marked by impulsive vehemence ⟨～ temper⟩ **2** : marked by force and violence ⟨with ～ speed⟩ — **im·pet·u·os·i·ty** \(ˌ)im-ˌpe-chə-'wä-sə-tē\ n — **im·pet·u·ous·ly** adv

im·pe·tus \'im-pə-təs\ n [L, assault, impetus, fr. impetere to attack, fr. petere to go to, seek] **1** : a driving force : IMPULSE; also : INCENTIVE **2** : MOMENTUM

im·pi·e·ty \(ˌ)im-'pī-ə-tē\ n, pl **-ties 1** : the quality or state of being impious **2** : an impious act

im·pinge \im-'pinj\ vb **im·pinged; im·ping·ing 1** : to strike or dash esp. with a sharp collision **2** : ENCROACH, INFRINGE — **im·pinge·ment** n

im·pi·ous \'im-pē-əs, (ˌ)im-'pī-\ adj : not pious : IRREVERENT, PROFANE

imp·ish \'im-pish\ adj : of, relating to, or befitting an imp; esp : MISCHIEVOUS — **imp·ish·ly** adv — **imp·ish·ness** n

im·pla·ca·ble \(ˌ)im-'pla-kə-bəl, -'plā-\ adj : not capable of being appeased, pacified, mitigated, or changed ⟨an ～ enemy⟩ — **im·pla·ca·bil·i·ty** \-ˌpla-kə-'bi-lə-tē, -ˌplā-\ n — **im·pla·ca·bly** \-'pla-kə-blē\ adv

im·plant \im-'plant\ vb **1** : to set firmly or deeply **2** : to fix in the mind or spirit **3** : to insert in living tissue (as for growth or absorption) — **im·plant** \'im-ˌplant\ n — **im·plan·ta·tion** \ˌim-ˌplan-'tā-shən\ n

im·plau·si·ble \(ˌ)im-'plȯ-zə-bəl\ adj : not plausible — **im·plau·si·bil·i·ty** \-ˌplȯ-zə-'bi-lə-tē\ n — **im·plau·si·bly** \-'plȯ-zə-blē\ adv

¹im·ple·ment \'im-plə-mənt\ n [ME, fr. AF, fr. ML implementum item making a full complement, appurtenance, tool, fr. LL, act of filling up, fr. L implēre to fill up] : TOOL, UTENSIL, INSTRUMENT

²im·ple·ment \-ˌment\ vb **1** : CARRY OUT; esp : to put into practice ⟨～ a plan⟩ **2** : to provide implements for — **im·ple·men·ta·tion** \ˌim-plə-mən-'tā-shən\ n

im·pli·cate \'im-plə-ˌkāt\ vb **-cat·ed; -cat·ing 1** : IMPLY **2** : INVOLVE — **im·pli·ca·tion** \ˌim-plə-'kā-shən\ n

im·plic·it \im-'pli-sət\ adj **1** : understood though not directly stated or expressed : IMPLIED; also : POTENTIAL **2** : COMPLETE, UNQUESTIONING, ABSOLUTE ⟨～ faith⟩ — **im·plic·it·ly** adv

im·plode \im-'plōd\ vb **im·plod·ed; im·plod·ing 1** : to burst or collapse inward **2** : SELF-DESTRUCT — **im·plo·sion** \-'plō-zhən\ n — **im·plo·sive** \-siv\ adj

im·plore \im-'plȯr\ vb **im·plored; im·plor·ing** : BESEECH, ENTREAT ⟨implored him not to go⟩ ✦ **Synonyms** SUPPLICATE, BEG, IMPORTUNE, PLEAD

im·ply \im-'plī\ vb **im·plied; im·ply·ing 1** : to involve or indicate by inference, association, or necessary consequence rather than by direct statement ⟨war implies fighting⟩ **2** : to express indirectly ; hint at : SUGGEST

im·po·lite \ˌim-pə-'līt\ adj : not polite : RUDE, DISCOURTEOUS

im·pol·i·tic \(ˌ)im-'pä-lə-ˌtik\ adj : not politic : UNWISE

im·pon·der·a·ble \(ˌ)im-'pän-də-rə-bəl\ adj : incapable of being weighed or evaluated with exactness — **im·pon·der·able** n

¹im·port \im-'pȯrt\ vb **1** : MEAN, SIGNIFY **2** : to bring (as merchandise) into a place or country from a foreign or external source — **im·port·er** n

²im·port \'im-ˌpȯrt\ n **1** : IMPORTANCE, SIGNIFICANCE **2** : MEANING, SIGNIFICATION **3** : something (as merchandise) brought in from another country

im·por·tance \im-'pȯr-tᵊns\ n : the quality or state of being important : MOMENT, SIGNIFICANCE ✦ **Synonyms** CONSEQUENCE, IMPORT, WEIGHT

im·por·tant \im-'pȯr-tᵊnt\ adj **1** : marked by importance

: SIGNIFICANT **2** : giving an impression of importance — **im·por·tant·ly** adv

im·por·ta·tion \ˌim-ˌpȯr-'tā-shən, -pər-\ n **1** : the act or practice of importing **2** : something imported

im·por·tu·nate \im-'pȯr-chə-nət\ adj **1** : troublesomely urgent or persistent **2** : BURDENSOME, TROUBLESOME

im·por·tune \ˌim-pər-'tün, -'tyün; im-'pȯr-chən\ vb **-tuned; -tun·ing** : to urge or beg with troublesome persistence — **im·por·tu·ni·ty** \-pər-'tü-nə-tē, -'tyü-\ n

im·pose \im-'pōz\ vb **im·posed; im·pos·ing 1** : to establish or apply by authority ⟨～ a tax⟩; also : to establish by force ⟨imposed a government⟩ **2** : OBTRUDE ⟨imposed herself on others⟩ **3** : to take unwarranted advantage of something ⟨～ on her good nature⟩ — **im·po·si·tion** \ˌim-pə-'zi-shən\ n

im·pos·ing adj : impressive because of size, bearing, dignity, or grandeur — **im·pos·ing·ly** adv

im·pos·si·ble \(ˌ)im-'pä-sə-bəl\ adj **1** : incapable of being or of occurring **2** : enormously difficult **3** : extremely undesirable : UNACCEPTABLE — **im·pos·si·bil·i·ty** \-ˌpä-sə-'bi-lə-tē\ n — **im·pos·si·bly** \-'pä-sə-blē\ adv

¹im·post \'im-ˌpōst\ n : TAX, DUTY

²impost n : a block, capital, or molding from which an arch springs

im·pos·tor or **im·pos·ter** \im-'päs-tər\ n : one that assumes an identity or title not one's own in order to deceive

im·pos·ture \im-'päs-chər\ n : DECEPTION; esp : fraudulent impersonation

im·po·tent \'im-pə-tənt\ adj **1** : lacking in power or strength : HELPLESS **2** : unable to copulate; also : STERILE — **im·po·tence** \-təns\ n — **im·po·ten·cy** \-tən-sē\ n — **im·po·tent·ly** adv

im·pound \im-'paùnd\ vb **1** : CONFINE, ENCLOSE ⟨～ stray dogs⟩ **2** : to seize and hold in legal custody **3** : to collect in a reservoir ⟨～ water⟩ — **im·pound·ment** n

im·pov·er·ish \im-'pä-və-rish\ vb : to make poor; also : to deprive of strength, richness, or fertility — **im·pov·er·ish·ment** n

im·prac·ti·ca·ble \(ˌ)im-'prak-ti-kə-bəl\ adj : not practicable : incapable of being put into practice or use ⟨an ～ plan⟩

im·prac·ti·cal \(ˌ)im-'prak-ti-kəl\ adj **1** : not practical **2** : IMPRACTICABLE

im·pre·cate \'im-pri-ˌkāt\ vb **-cat·ed; -cat·ing** : CURSE — **im·pre·ca·tion** \ˌim-pri-'kā-shən\ n

im·pre·cise \ˌim-pri-'sīs\ adj : not precise — **im·pre·cise·ly** adv — **im·pre·cise·ness** n — **im·pre·ci·sion** \-'si-zhən\ n

im·preg·na·ble \im-'preg-nə-bəl\ adj : incapable of being taken by assault : UNCONQUERABLE, UNASSAILABLE — **im·preg·na·bil·i·ty** \(ˌ)im-ˌpreg-nə-'bi-lə-tē\ n

im·preg·nate \im-'preg-ˌnāt\ vb **-nat·ed; -nat·ing 1** : to fertilize or make pregnant **2** : to cause to be filled, permeated, or saturated — **im·preg·na·tion** \ˌim-ˌpreg-'nā-shən\ n

im·pre·sa·rio \ˌim-prə-'sär-ē-ˌō\ n, pl **-ri·os** [It, fr. impresa undertaking, fr. imprendere to undertake] **1** : the manager or conductor of an opera or concert company **2** : one who puts on an entertainment **3** : MANAGER, PRODUCER

¹im·press \im-'pres\ vb **1** : to apply with or produce (as a mark) by pressure : IMPRINT **2** : to press, stamp, or print in or upon **3** : to produce a vivid impression of **4** : to affect esp. forcibly or deeply — **im·press·ible** adj

²im·press \'im-ˌpres\ n **1** : a characteristic or distinctive mark **2** : IMPRESSION, EFFECT **3** : an impression or image of something formed by or as if by pressure; also : a product of pressure or influence

³im·press \im-'pres\ vb **1** : to force into naval service **2** : to get the aid or services of by forcible argument or persuasion — **im·press·ment** n

im·pres·sion \im-'pre-shən\ n **1** : a characteristic trait or feature resulting from influence : IMPRESS **2** : a stamp, form, or figure made by impressing : IMPRINT **3** : an esp. marked influence or effect on feeling, sense, or mind **4** : a single print or copy (as from type or from an engraved plate or book) **5** : all the copies of a publication (as a book) printed for one issue : PRINTING **6** : a usu. vague notion or remembrance **7** : an imitation in caricature of a noted personality as a form of entertainment

im·pres·sion·able \im-'pre-shə-nə-bəl\ adj : capable of being easily impressed : easily molded or influenced

im·pres·sion·ism \im-'pre-shə-ˌni-zəm\ *n, often cap* : a theory or practice in modern art of depicting the natural appearances of objects by dabs or strokes of primary unmixed colors in order to simulate actual reflected light — **im·pres·sion·is·tic** \-ˌpre-shə-'nis-tik\ *adj*

im·pres·sion·ist \im-'pre-shə-nist\ *n* 1 *often cap* : a painter who practices impressionism 2 : an entertainer who does impressions

im·pres·sive \im-'pre-siv\ *adj* : making or tending to make a marked impression ⟨an ~ speech⟩ — **im·pres·sive·ly** *adv* — **im·pres·sive·ness** *n*

im·pri·ma·tur \ˌim-prə-'mä-ˌtu̇r\ *n* [NL, let it be printed] 1 : a license to print or publish; *also* : official approval of a publication by a censor 2 : SANCTION, APPROVAL

¹im·print \im-'print, 'im-ˌprint\ *vb* 1 : to stamp or mark by or as if by pressure : IMPRESS 2 : to fix firmly (as on the memory)

²im·print \'im-ˌprint\ *n* 1 : something imprinted or printed 2 : a publisher's name printed at the foot of a title page 3 : an indelible distinguishing effect or influence ⟨put her ~ on the company⟩

im·pris·on \im-'pri-zᵊn\ *vb* : to put in or as if in prison : CONFINE — **im·pris·on·ment** *n*

im·prob·a·ble \(ˌ)im-'prä-bə-bəl\ *adj* : unlikely to be true or to occur — **im·prob·a·bil·i·ty** \ˌprä-bə-'bi-lə-tē\ *n* — **im·prob·a·bly** \-'prä-bə-blē\ *adv*

im·promp·tu \im-'prämp-tü, -tyü\ *adj* [F, fr. *impromptu* extemporaneously, fr. L *in promptu* in readiness] 1 : made or done on or as if on the spur of the moment 2 : EXTEMPORANEOUS, UNREHEARSED ⟨an ~ speech⟩ — **impromptu** *adv or n*

im·prop·er \(ˌ)im-'prä-pər\ *adj* 1 : not proper, fit, or suitable 2 : INCORRECT, INACCURATE 3 : not in accord with propriety, modesty, or good manners — **im·prop·er·ly** *adv*

improper fraction *n* : a fraction whose numerator is equal to or larger than the denominator

im·pro·pri·e·ty \ˌim-prə-'prī-ə-tē\ *n, pl* **-ties** 1 : an improper act or remark; *esp* : an unacceptable use of a word or of language 2 : the quality or state of being improper

im·prov \'im-ˌpräv\ *adj* : of, relating to, or being an improvised comedy routine — **improv** *n*

im·prove \im-'prüv\ *vb* **im·proved; im·prov·ing** 1 : to enhance or increase in value or quality 2 : to grow or become better ⟨your work is *improving*⟩ 3 : to make good use of ⟨~ the time by reading⟩ — **im·prov·able** \-'prü-və-bəl\ *adj*

im·prove·ment \im-'prüv-mənt\ *n* 1 : the act or process of improving 2 : increased value or excellence of something 3 : something that adds to the value or appearance of a thing

im·prov·i·dent \(ˌ)im-'prä-və-dənt\ *adj* : not providing for the future — **im·prov·i·dence** \-dəns\ *n*

im·pro·vise \'im-prə-ˌvīz\ *vb* **-vised; -vis·ing** [F *improviser*, fr. It *improvvisare*, fr. *improvviso* sudden, fr. L *improvisus*, lit., unforeseen] 1 : to compose, recite, play, or sing on the spur of the moment : EXTEMPORIZE ⟨~ on the piano⟩ 2 : to make, invent, or arrange offhand ⟨~ a sail out of shirts⟩ — **im·pro·vi·sa·tion** \im-ˌprä-və-'zā-shən, ˌim-prə-və-\ *n* — **im·pro·vis·er** *or* **im·pro·vi·sor** \ˌim-prə-'vī-zər, 'im-prə-ˌvī-\ *n*

im·pru·dent \(ˌ)im-'prü-dᵊnt\ *adj* : not prudent : lacking discretion, wisdom, or good judgment — **im·pru·dence** \-dᵊns\ *n* — **im·pru·dent·ly** *adv*

im·pu·dent \'im-pyü-dənt\ *adj* : marked by contemptuous boldness or disregard of others — **im·pu·dence** \-dəns\ *n* — **im·pu·dent·ly** *adv*

im·pugn \im-'pyün\ *vb* [ME, to assail, fr. AF *empugner*, fr. L *inpugnare*, fr. *pugnare* to fight] : to attack by words or arguments : oppose or attack as false or as lacking integrity ⟨~ed his rival's character⟩

im·pulse \'im-ˌpəls\ *n* 1 : a force that starts a body into motion; *also* : the motion produced by such a force 2 : an arousing of the mind and spirit to some usu. unpremeditated action 3 : NERVE IMPULSE

im·pul·sion \im-'pəl-shən\ *n* 1 : the act of impelling : the state of being impelled 2 : a force that impels 3 : IMPULSE 2; *also* : COMPULSION 3

im·pul·sive \im-'pəl-siv\ *adj* 1 : having the power of or actually driving or impelling 2 : arising from or prone to act on impulse — **im·pul·sive·ly** *adv* — **im·pul·sive·ness** *n*

im·pu·ni·ty \im-'pyü-nə-tē\ *n* [MF or L; MF *impunité*, fr. L *impunitas*, fr. *impune* without punishment, fr. *poena* penalty, punishment] : exemption from punishment, harm, or loss

im·pure \(ˌ)im-'pyu̇r\ *adj* 1 : not pure : UNCHASTE, OBSCENE 2 : DIRTY, FOUL ⟨~ water⟩ 3 : ADULTERATED, MIXED — **im·pu·ri·ty** \-'pyu̇r-ə-tē\ *n*

im·pute \im-'pyüt\ *vb* **im·put·ed; im·put·ing** 1 : to lay the responsibility or blame for often falsely or unjustly 2 : to credit to a person or a cause : ATTRIBUTE — **im·put·able** \-'pyü-tə-bəl\ *adj* — **im·pu·ta·tion** \ˌim-pyü-'tā-shən\ *n*

¹in \'in\ *prep* 1 — used to indicate physical surroundings ⟨swim ~ the lake⟩ 2 : INTO 1 ⟨ran ~ the house⟩ 3 : DURING ⟨~ the summer⟩ 4 : WITH ⟨written ~ pencil⟩ 5 — used to indicate one's situation or state of being ⟨~ luck⟩ ⟨~ love⟩ 6 — used to indicate manner or purpose ⟨~ a hurry⟩ ⟨said ~ reply⟩ 7 : INTO 2 ⟨broke ~ pieces⟩

²in *adv* 1 : to or toward the inside ⟨come ~⟩; *also* : to or toward some destination or place ⟨flew ~ from the South⟩ 2 : at close quarters : NEAR ⟨the enemy closed ~⟩ 3 : into the midst of something ⟨mix ~ the flour⟩ 4 : to or at its proper place ⟨fit a piece ~⟩ 5 : WITHIN ⟨locked ~⟩ 6 : in vogue or season 7 : in one's presence, possession, or control ⟨the results are ~⟩

³in *adj* 1 : located inside or within 2 : that is in position, operation, or power ⟨the ~ party⟩ 3 : directed inward : INCOMING ⟨the ~ train⟩ 4 : keenly aware of and responsive to what is new and fashionable ⟨the ~ crowd⟩; *also* : extremely fashionable ⟨the ~ thing to do⟩

⁴in *n* 1 : one who is in office or power or on the inside 2 : INFLUENCE, PULL ⟨he has an ~ with the owner⟩

⁵in *abbr* 1 inch 2 inlet

In *symbol* indium

IN *abbr* Indiana

in- \(ˌ)in\ *prefix* : not : absence of : NON-, UN-

inaccessibility	indecipherable
inaccessible	indemonstrable
inaccuracy	indestructible
inaccurate	indeterminable
inaction	indiscernible
inactive	indistinguishable
inactivity	inedible
inadmissibility	ineducable
inadmissible	ineffaceable
inadvisability	inefficacious
inadvisable	inefficacy
inapparent	inelastic
inapplicable	inelasticity
inapposite	inequitable
inapproachable	inequity
inappropriate	ineradicable
inaptitude	inerrant
inarguable	inexpedient
inartistic	inexpensive
inattentive	inexpressive
inaudible	inextinguishable
inaudibly	infeasible
inauspicious	inharmonious
inauthentic	inhospitable
incautious	injudicious
incombustible	inoffensive
incomprehension	insanitary
inconclusive	insensitive
incongruent	insensitivity
inconsistency	insignificance
inconsistent	insignificant
incoordination	insolvable
incurious	insusceptible

in·abil·i·ty \ˌi-nə-'bi-lə-tē\ *n* : the quality or state of being unable

in ab·sen·tia \ˌin-ab-'sen-chə, -chē-ə\ *adv* : in one's absence

in·ac·ti·vate \(ˌ)i-'nak-tə-ˌvāt\ *vb* : to make inactive — **in·ac·ti·va·tion** \(ˌ)i-ˌnak-tə-'vā-shən\ *n*

in·ad·e·quate \(ˌ)i-'na-di-kwət\ *adj* : not adequate : INSUFFICIENT — **in·ad·e·qua·cy** \-kwə-sē\ *n* — **in·ad·e·quate·ly** *adv* — **in·ad·e·quate·ness** *n*

in·ad·ver·tent \ˌi-nəd-'vər-tᵊnt\ *adj* 1 : HEEDLESS, INAT-

TENTIVE **2** : UNINTENTIONAL ⟨an ∼ omission⟩ — **in·ad·ver·tence** \-'t°ns\ *n* — **in·ad·ver·ten·cy** \-'t°n-sē\ *n* — **in·ad·ver·tent·ly** *adv*

in·alien·able \(ˌ)i-'nāl-yə-nə-bəl, -'nā-lē-ə-\ *adj* : incapable of being alienated, surrendered, or transferred ⟨∼ rights⟩ — **in·alien·abil·i·ty** \(ˌ)i-ˌnāl-yə-nə-'bi-lə-tē, -ˌnā-lē-ə-\ *n* — **in·alien·ably** *adv*

in·amo·ra·ta \i-ˌnä-mə-'rä-tə\ *n* : a woman with whom one is in love

inane \i-'nān\ *adj* **inan·er; -est** : EMPTY, INSUBSTANTIAL; *also* : SHALLOW, SILLY ⟨∼ comments⟩ — **inane·ly** *adv* — **inan·i·ty** \i-'na-nə-tē\ *n*

in·an·i·mate \(ˌ)i-'na-nə-mət\ *adj* : not animate or animated : lacking the qualities of living things — **in·an·i·mate·ly** *adv* — **in·an·i·mate·ness** *n*

in·ap·pre·cia·ble \ˌi-nə-'prē-shə-bəl\ *adj* : too small to be perceived — **in·ap·pre·cia·bly** \-blē\ *adv*

in·apt \(ˌ)i-'napt\ *adj* **1** : not suitable ⟨an ∼ analogy⟩ **2** : INEPT — **in·apt·ly** *adv* — **in·apt·ness** *n*

in·ar·tic·u·late \ˌi-när-'ti-kyə-lət\ *adj* **1** : not understandable as spoken words **2** : MUTE **3** : incapable of being expressed by speech ⟨∼ fear⟩; *also* : UNSPOKEN **4** : not having the power of distinct utterance or effective expression — **in·ar·tic·u·late·ly** *adv*

in·as·much as \ˌi-nəz-'məch-\ *conj* : seeing that : SINCE

in·at·ten·tion \ˌi-nə-'ten-chən\ *n* : failure to pay attention : DISREGARD — **in·at·ten·tive** \-'ten-tiv\ *adj*

¹**in·au·gu·ral** \i-'nò-gyə-rəl, -gə-\ *adj* **1** : of or relating to an inauguration **2** : marking a beginning

²**inaugural** *n* **1** : an inaugural address **2** : INAUGURATION

in·au·gu·rate \i-'nò-gyə-ˌrāt, -gə-\ *vb* **-rat·ed; -rat·ing 1** : to introduce into an office with suitable ceremonies : INSTALL **2** : to dedicate ceremoniously **3** : BEGIN, INITIATE — **in·au·gu·ra·tion** \-ˌnò-gyə-'rä-shən, -gə-\ *n*

in·board \'in-ˌbòrd\ *adv* **1** : inside the hull of a ship **2** : close or closest to the center line of a vehicle or craft — **inboard** *adj*

in·born \'in-'bòrn\ *adj* **1** : present from or as if from birth **2** : HEREDITARY, INHERITED ✦ **Synonyms** INNATE, CONGENITAL, NATIVE

in·bound \'in-ˌbaund\ *adj* : inward bound ⟨∼ traffic⟩

in·box \'in-ˌbäks\ *n* : a receptacle for incoming interoffice letters; *also* : a computer folder for incoming e-mail

in·bred \'in-'bred\ *adj* **1** : ingrained in one's nature as deeply as if by heredity **2** : subjected to or produced by inbreeding

in·breed·ing \'in-ˌbrē-diŋ\ *n* **1** : the interbreeding of closely related individuals esp. to preserve and fix desirable characters of and to eliminate unfavorable characters from a stock **2** : confinement to a narrow range or a local or limited field of choice — **in·breed** \-ˌbrēd\ *vb*

inc *abbr* **1** incomplete **2** incorporated **3** increase

In·ca \'iŋ-kə\ *n* [Sp, fr. Quechua *inka* ruler of the Inca empire] **1** : a noble or a member of the ruling family of an Indian empire of Peru, Ecuador, and Bolivia until the Spanish conquest **2** : a member of any people under Inca influence

in·cal·cu·la·ble \(ˌ)in-'kal-kyə-lə-bəl\ *adj* **1** : not capable of being calculated; *esp* : very great **2** : not predictable ⟨∼ consequences⟩ — **in·cal·cu·la·bly** \-blē\ *adv*

in·can·des·cent \ˌin-kən-'de-s°nt\ *adj* **1** : glowing with heat **2** : SHINING, BRILLIANT — **in·can·des·cence** \-s°ns\ *n*

incandescent lamp *n* : LIGHT BULB 1

in·can·ta·tion \ˌin-ˌkan-'tā-shən\ *n* : a use of spells or verbal charms spoken or sung as a part of a ritual of magic; *also* : a formula of words used in or as if in such a ritual

in·ca·pa·ble \(ˌ)in-'kā-pə-bəl\ *adj* : lacking ability or qualification for a particular purpose; *also* : UNQUALIFIED — **in·ca·pa·bil·i·ty** \-ˌkā-pə-'bi-lə-tē\ *n*

in·ca·pac·i·tate \ˌin-kə-'pa-sə-ˌtāt\ *vb* **-tat·ed; -tat·ing** : to make incapable or unfit

in·ca·pac·i·ty \ˌin-kə-'pa-sə-tē\ *n, pl* **-ties** : the quality or state of being incapable

in·car·cer·ate \in-'kär-sə-ˌrāt\ *vb* **-at·ed; -at·ing** : IMPRISON, CONFINE — **in·car·cer·a·tion** \(ˌ)in-ˌkär-sə-'rä-shən\ *n*

in·car·na·dine \in-'kär-nə-ˌdīn, -ˌdēn\ *vb* **-dined; -din·ing** : REDDEN

in·car·nate \in-'kär-nət, -ˌnāt\ *adj* **1** : having bodily and esp. human form and substance **2** : PERSONIFIED — **in·car·nate** \-ˌnāt\ *vb*

in·car·na·tion \ˌin-ˌkär-'nä-shən\ *n* **1** : the embodiment of a deity or spirit in an earthly form **2** *cap* : the union of divine and human natures in Jesus Christ **3** : a person showing a trait or typical character to a marked degree **4** : the act of incarnating : the state of being incarnate

in·cen·di·ary \in-'sen-dē-ˌer-ē\ *adj* **1** : of or relating to a deliberate burning of property **2** : tending to excite or inflame **3** : designed to start fires ⟨an ∼ bomb⟩ — **incendiary** *n*

¹**in·cense** \'in-ˌsens\ *n* **1** : material used to produce a fragrant odor when burned **2** : the perfume or smoke from some spices and gums when burned

²**in·cense** \in-'sens\ *vb* **in·censed; in·cens·ing** : to make extremely angry

in·cen·tive \in-'sen-tiv\ *n* [ME, fr. LL *incentivum*, fr. *incentivus* stimulating, fr. L, setting the tune, fr. *incinere* to play (a tune), fr. *canere* to sing] : something that incites or is likely to incite to determination or action

in·cep·tion \in-'sep-shən\ *n* : BEGINNING, COMMENCEMENT

in·cer·ti·tude \(ˌ)in-'sər-tə-ˌtüd, -ˌtyüd\ *n* **1** : UNCERTAINTY, DOUBT, INDECISION **2** : INSECURITY, INSTABILITY

in·ces·sant \(ˌ)in-'se-s°nt\ *adj* : continuing or flowing without interruption ⟨∼ rains⟩ — **in·ces·sant·ly** *adv*

in·cest \'in-ˌsest\ *n* [ME, fr. L *incestus* sexual impurity, fr. *incestus* impure, fr. *castus* pure] : sexual intercourse between persons so closely related that marriage is illegal — **in·ces·tu·ous** \in-'ses-chù-wəs\ *adj*

¹**inch** \'inch\ *n* [ME, fr. OE *ynce*, fr. L *uncia* twelfth part, inch, ounce] — see WEIGHT table

²**inch** *vb* : to move by small degrees

in·cho·ate \in-'kō-ət, 'in-kə-ˌwāt\ *adj* : being only partly in existence or operation : INCOMPLETE ⟨∼ yearnings⟩

inch·worm \'inch-ˌwərm\ *n* : LOOPER

in·ci·dence \'in-sə-dəns\ *n* : rate of occurrence or effect

¹**in·ci·dent** \-dənt\ *n* **1** : OCCURRENCE, HAPPENING **2** : an action likely to lead to grave consequences esp. in diplomatic matters

²**incident** *adj* **1** : occurring or likely to occur esp. in connection with some other happening **2** : falling or striking on something ⟨∼ light rays⟩

¹**in·ci·den·tal** \ˌin-sə-'den-t°l\ *adj* **1** : subordinate, nonessential, or attendant in position or significance ⟨∼ expenses⟩ **2** : CASUAL, CHANCE

²**incidental** *n* **1** *pl* : minor items (as of expense) that are not individually accounted for **2** : something incidental

in·ci·den·tal·ly \ˌin-sə-'den-tə-lē, -'dent-lē\ *adv* **1** : in an incidental manner **2** : by the way

in·cin·er·ate \in-'si-nə-ˌrāt\ *vb* **-at·ed; -at·ing** : to burn to ashes — **in·cin·er·a·tion** \-ˌsi-nə-'rä-shən\ *n*

in·cin·er·a·tor \in-'si-nə-ˌrā-tər\ *n* : a furnace for burning waste

in·cip·i·ent \in-'si-pē-ənt\ *adj* : beginning to be or become apparent

in·cise \in-'sīz\ *vb* **in·cised; in·cis·ing 1** : to cut into **2** : CARVE, ENGRAVE

in·ci·sion \in-'si-zhən\ *n* : CUT, GASH; *esp* : a surgical cut

in·ci·sive \in-'sī-siv\ *adj* : impressively direct and decisive — **in·ci·sive·ly** *adv*

in·ci·sor \in-'sī-zər\ *n* : a front tooth typically adapted for cutting

in·cite \in-'sīt\ *vb* **in·cit·ed; in·cit·ing** : to arouse to action : stir up — **in·cite·ment** *n* — **in·cit·er** *n*

in·ci·vil·i·ty \ˌin-sə-'vi-lə-tē\ *n* **1** : RUDENESS, DISCOURTESY **2** : a rude or discourteous act

incl *abbr* include; included; including; inclusive

in·clem·ent \(ˌ)in-'kle-mənt\ *adj* : SEVERE, STORMY ⟨∼ weather⟩ — **in·clem·en·cy** \-mən-sē\ *n*

in·cli·na·tion \ˌin-klə-'nä-shən\ *n* **1** : PROPENSITY, BENT; *esp* : LIKING **2** : BOW, NOD ⟨an ∼ of the head⟩ **3** : a tilting of something **4** : SLANT, SLOPE

¹**in·cline** \in-'klīn\ *vb* **in·clined; in·clin·ing 1** : BOW, BEND **2** : to be drawn toward an opinion or course of action **3** : to deviate from the vertical or horizontal : SLOPE **4** : INFLUENCE, PERSUADE — **in·clin·er** *n*

²**in·cline** \'in-ˌklīn\ *n* : SLOPE

inclose, inclosure *var of* ENCLOSE, ENCLOSURE

in·clude \in-'klüd\ *vb* **in·clud·ed; in·clud·ing** : to take in or comprise as a part of a whole ⟨the price ∼s tax⟩ — **in·clu·sion** \in-'klü-zhən\ *n*

in·clu·sive \in-'klü-siv\ *adj* **1** : including stated limits or extremes ⟨from Monday to Friday ∼⟩ **2** : broad in scope; *esp* : covering all items, costs, or services — **in·clu·sive·ly** *adv* — **in·clu·sive·ness** *n*

incog *abbr* incognito

¹in·cog·ni·to \,in-ˌkäg-ˈnē-to, in-ˈkäg-nə-ˌtō\ *adv or adj* [It, fr. L *incognitus* unknown, fr. *cognoscere* to know] : with one's identity concealed

²incognito *n, pl* **-tos** **1** : one appearing or living incognito **2** : the state or disguise of an incognito

in·co·her·ent \,in-kō-ˈhir-ənt, -ˈher-\ *adj* **1** : not sticking closely or compactly together : LOOSE **2** : lacking normal clarity or intelligibility in speech or thought ⟨an ~ patient⟩ — **in·co·her·ence** \-əns\ *n* — **in·co·her·ent·ly** *adv*

in·come \ˈin-ˌkəm\ *n* : a gain usu. measured in money that derives from labor, business, or property

income tax *n* : a tax on the net income of an individual or business concern

in·com·ing \ˈin-ˌkə-miŋ\ *adj* : coming in ⟨the ~ tide⟩ ⟨~ freshmen⟩

in·com·men·su·rate \,in-kə-ˈmen-sə-rət, -ˈmen-chə-\ *adj* : not commensurate; *esp* : INADEQUATE

in·com·mode \,in-kə-ˈmōd\ *vb* **-mod·ed; -mod·ing** : INCONVENIENCE, DISTURB

in·com·mu·ni·ca·ble \,in-kə-ˈmyü-ni-kə-bəl\ *adj* : not communicable or not capable of being communicated or imparted; *also* : UNCOMMUNICATIVE

in·com·mu·ni·ca·do \,in-kə-ˌmyü-ni-ˈkä-dō\ *adv or adj* : without means of communication; *also* : in solitary confinement ⟨a prisoner held ~⟩

in·com·pa·ra·ble \(ˌ)in-ˈkäm-pə-rə-bəl, -prə-\ *adj* **1** : eminent beyond comparison : MATCHLESS **2** : not suitable for comparison — **in·com·pa·ra·bly** \-blē\ *adv*

in·com·pat·i·ble \,in-kəm-ˈpa-tə-bəl\ *adj* : incapable of or unsuitable for association or use together ⟨~ colors⟩ ⟨temperamentally ~⟩ — **in·com·pat·i·bil·i·ty** \,in-kəm-ˌpa-tə-ˈbi-lə-tē\ *n*

in·com·pe·tent \(ˌ)in-ˈkäm-pə-tənt\ *adj* **1** : not legally qualified **2** : not competent : lacking sufficient knowledge, skill, or ability — **in·com·pe·tence** \-təns\ *n* — **in·com·pe·ten·cy** \-tən-sē\ *n* — **incompetent** *n*

in·com·plete \,in-kəm-ˈplēt\ *adj* : lacking a part or parts : UNFINISHED, IMPERFECT — **in·com·plete·ly** *adv* — **in·com·plete·ness** *n*

in·com·pre·hen·si·ble \,in-ˌkäm-prē-ˈhen-sə-bəl\ *adj* : impossible to comprehend : UNINTELLIGIBLE ⟨~ muttering⟩

in·con·ceiv·able \,in-kən-ˈsē-və-bəl\ *adj* **1** : impossible to comprehend **2** : UNBELIEVABLE

in·con·gru·ous \(ˌ)in-ˈkäŋ-grü-wəs\ *adj* : not consistent with or suitable to the surroundings or associations — **in·con·gru·i·ty** \,in-kən-ˈgrü-ə-tē, -ˌkän-\ *n* — **in·con·gru·ous·ly** *adv*

in·con·se·quen·tial \,in-ˌkän-sə-ˈkwen-chəl\ *adj* **1** : ILLOGICAL; *also* : IRRELEVANT **2** : of no significance : UNIMPORTANT — **in·con·se·quence** \(ˌ)in-ˈkän-sə-ˌkwens\ *n* — **in·con·se·quen·tial·ly** *adv*

in·con·sid·er·able \,in-kən-ˈsi-də-rə-bəl\ *adj* : SLIGHT, TRIVIAL ⟨the cost was not ~⟩

in·con·sid·er·ate \,in-kən-ˈsi-də-rət\ *adj* : HEEDLESS, THOUGHTLESS; *esp* : not respecting the rights or feelings of others — **in·con·sid·er·ate·ly** *adv* — **in·con·sid·er·ate·ness** *n*

in·con·sol·able \,in-kən-ˈsō-lə-bəl\ *adj* : incapable of being consoled — **in·con·sol·ably** \-blē\ *adv*

in·con·spic·u·ous \,in-kən-ˈspi-kyə-wəs\ *adj* : not readily noticeable — **in·con·spic·u·ous·ly** *adv*

in·con·stant \(ˌ)in-ˈkän-stənt\ *adj* : not constant : CHANGEABLE ✦ *Synonyms* FICKLE, CAPRICIOUS, MERCURIAL, UNSTABLE, VOLATILE — **in·con·stan·cy** \-stən-sē\ *n* — **in·con·stant·ly** *adv*

in·con·test·able \,in-kən-ˈtes-tə-bəl\ *adj* : not contestable : INDISPUTABLE — **in·con·test·ably** \-ˈtes-tə-blē\ *adv*

in·con·ti·nent \(ˌ)in-ˈkänt-ᵊn-ənt\ *adj* **1** : lacking self-restraint **2** : unable to retain urine or feces voluntarily — **in·con·ti·nence** \-əns\ *n*

in·con·tro·vert·ible \,in-ˌkän-trə-ˈvər-tə-bəl\ *adj* : not open to question : INDISPUTABLE ⟨~ evidence⟩ — **in·con·tro·vert·ibly** \-blē\ *adv*

¹in·con·ve·nience \,in-kən-ˈvē-nyəns\ *n* **1** : something that is inconvenient **2** : the quality or state of being inconvenient

²inconvenience *vb* **-nienced; -nienc·ing** : to subject to inconvenience

in·con·ve·nient \,in-kən-ˈvē-nyənt\ *adj* : not convenient : causing trouble or annoyance : INOPPORTUNE — **in·con·ve·nient·ly** *adv*

in·cor·po·rate \in-ˈkȯr-pə-ˌrāt\ *vb* **-rat·ed; -rat·ing** **1** : to unite closely or so as to form one body : BLEND **2** : to form, form into, or become a corporation **3** : to give material form to : EMBODY — **in·cor·po·ra·tion** \-ˌkȯr-pə-ˈrā-shən\ *n*

in·cor·po·re·al \,in-kȯr-ˈpȯr-ē-əl\ *adj* : having no material body or form

in·cor·rect \,in-kə-ˈrekt\ *adj* **1** : INACCURATE, FAULTY ⟨an ~ transcription⟩ **2** : not true : WRONG **3** : UNBECOMING, IMPROPER — **in·cor·rect·ly** *adv* — **in·cor·rect·ness** *n*

in·cor·ri·gi·ble \(ˌ)in-ˈkȯr-ə-jə-bəl\ *adj* : incapable of being corrected, amended, or reformed — **in·cor·ri·gi·bil·i·ty** \(ˌ)in-ˌkȯr-ə-jə-ˈbi-lə-tē\ *n* — **in·cor·ri·gi·bly** \-ˈkȯr-ə-jə-blē\ *adv*

in·cor·rupt·ible \,in-kə-ˈrəp-tə-bəl\ *adj* **1** : not subject to decay or dissolution **2** : incapable of being bribed or morally corrupted — **in·cor·rupt·ibil·i·ty** \-ˌrəp-tə-ˈbi-lə-tē\ *n* — **in·cor·rupt·ibly** \-ˈrəp-tə-blē\ *adv*

incr *abbr* increase; increased

¹in·crease \in-ˈkrēs, ˈin-ˌkrēs\ *vb* **in·creased; in·creas·ing** [ME *encresen*, fr. AF *encreistre*, fr. L *increscere*, fr. *crescere* to grow] **1** : to become greater : GROW **2** : to multiply by the production of young ⟨rabbits ~ rapidly⟩ **3** : to make greater — **increased** *adj* — **in·creas·ing·ly** \-ˈkrē-siŋ-lē\ *adv*

²in·crease \ˈin-ˌkrēs, in-ˈkrēs\ *n* **1** : addition or enlargement in size, extent, or quantity : GROWTH **2** : something that is added to an original stock or amount (as by growth)

in·cred·i·ble \(ˌ)in-ˈkre-də-bəl\ *adj* : too extraordinary and improbable to be believed; *also* : hard to believe — **in·cred·i·bil·i·ty** \(ˌ)in-ˌkre-də-ˈbi-lə-tē\ *n* — **in·cred·i·bly** \-ˈkre-də-blē\ *adv*

in·cred·u·lous \-ˈkre-jə-ləs\ *adj* **1** : SKEPTICAL **2** : expressing disbelief — **in·cre·du·li·ty** \,in-kri-ˈdü-lə-tē, -ˈdyü-\ *n* — **in·cred·u·lous·ly** *adv*

in·cre·ment \ˈiŋ-krə-mənt, ˈin-\ *n* **1** : the action or process of increasing esp. in quantity or value : ENLARGEMENT **2** : something gained or added; *esp* : one of a series of regular consecutive additions — **in·cre·men·tal** \,iŋ-krə-ˈmen-tᵊl, ,in-\ *adj* — **in·cre·men·tal·ly** *adv*

in·crim·i·nate \in-ˈkri-mə-ˌnāt\ *vb* **-nat·ed; -nat·ing** : to charge with or prove involvement in a crime or fault : ACCUSE — **in·crim·i·na·tion** \-ˌkri-mə-ˈnā-shən\ *n* — **in·crim·i·na·to·ry** \-ˈkri-mə-nə-ˌtȯr-ē\ *adj*

incrust *var of* ENCRUST

in·crus·ta·tion *also* **en·crus·ta·tion** \,in-ˌkrəs-ˈtā-shən\ *n* **1** : CRUST; *also* : an accumulation (as of habits, opinions, or customs) resembling a crust **2** : the act of encrusting : the state of being encrusted

in·cu·bate \ˈiŋ-kyù-ˌbāt, ˈin-\ *vb* **-bat·ed; -bat·ing** : to sit on (eggs) to hatch by the warmth of the body; *also* : to keep (as an embryo) under conditions favorable for development — **in·cu·ba·tion** \,iŋ-kyù-ˈbā-shən, ,in-\ *n*

in·cu·ba·tor \ˈiŋ-kyù-ˌbāt-ər, ˈin-\ *n* : one that incubates; *esp* : an apparatus providing suitable conditions (as of warmth and moisture) for incubating something (as a premature baby)

in·cu·bus \ˈiŋ-kyə-bəs, ˈin-\ *n, pl* **-bi** \-ˌbī, -ˌbē\ *also* **-bus·es** [ME, fr. LL, fr. L *incubare* to lie on] **1** : a spirit supposed to work evil on persons in their sleep **2** : NIGHTMARE 1 **3** : one that oppresses like a nightmare

in·cul·cate \in-ˈkəl-ˌkāt, ˈin-(ˌ)kəl-\ *vb* **-cat·ed; -cat·ing** [L *inculcare*, lit., to tread on, fr. *calcare* to trample, fr. *calx* heel] : to teach and impress by frequent repetitions or admonitions — **in·cul·ca·tion** \,in-(ˌ)kəl-ˈkā-shən\ *n*

in·cul·pa·ble \in-ˈkəl-pə-bəl\ *adj* : free from guilt : INNOCENT

in·cul·pate \in-ˈkəl-ˌpāt, ˈin-(ˌ)kəl-\ *vb* **-pat·ed; -pat·ing** : INCRIMINATE

in·cum·ben·cy \in-ˈkəm-bən-sē\ *n, pl* **-cies** **1** : something that is incumbent **2** : the quality or state of being incumbent **3** : the office or period of office of an incumbent

¹in·cum·bent \in-ˈkəm-bənt\ *n* : the holder of an office or position

²**incumbent** *adj* 1 : imposed as a duty 2 : occupying a specified office 3 : lying or resting on something else

in·cu·nab·u·lum \ˌin-kyə-ˈna-byə-ləm, iŋ-\ *n, pl* **-la** \-lə\ [NL, fr. L *incunabula*, pl., bands holding the baby in a cradle, fr. *cunae* cradle] : a book printed before 1501

in·cur \in-ˈkər\ *vb* **in·curred; in·cur·ring** : to become liable or subject to : bring down upon oneself

in·cur·able \(ˌ)in-ˈkyùr-ə-bəl\ *adj* 1 : not curable 2 : not likely to be changed — **incurable** *n* — **in·cur·ably** \(ˌ)in-ˈkyùr-ə-blē\ *adv*

in·cur·sion \in-ˈkər-zhən\ *n* 1 : a sudden hostile invasion : RAID 2 : an entering in or into (as an activity)

in·cus \ˈiŋ-kəs\ *n, pl* **in·cu·des** \iŋ-ˈkyü-(ˌ)dēz\ [NL, fr. L, anvil] : the middle bone of a chain of three small bones in the middle ear of a mammal

ind *abbr* 1 independent 2 index 3 industrial; industry

Ind *abbr* 1 Indian 2 Indiana

in·debt·ed \in-ˈde-təd\ *adj* 1 : owing gratitude or recognition to another 2 : owing money — **in·debt·ed·ness** *n*

in·de·cent \(ˌ)in-ˈdē-sᵊnt\ *adj* : not decent; *esp* : grossly improper or offensive — **in·de·cen·cy** \-sᵊn-sē\ *n* — **in·de·cent·ly** *adv*

in·de·ci·sion \ˌin-di-ˈsi-zhən\ *n* : a wavering between two or more possible courses of action : IRRESOLUTION

in·de·ci·sive \ˌin-di-ˈsī-siv\ *adj* 1 : INCONCLUSIVE ⟨an ~ battle⟩ 2 : marked by or prone to indecision 3 : INDEFINITE — **in·de·ci·sive·ly** *adv* — **in·de·ci·sive·ness** *n*

in·de·co·rous \(ˌ)in-ˈde-kə-rəs; ˌin-di-ˈkōr-əs\ *adj* : conflicting with accepted standards of good conduct or good taste ✦ *Synonyms* IMPROPER, UNSEEMLY, INDECENT, UNBECOMING, INDELICATE — **in·de·co·rous·ly** *adv* — **in·de·co·rous·ness** *n*

in·deed \in-ˈdēd\ *adv* 1 : without any question : TRULY — often used interjectionally to express irony, disbelief, or surprise 2 : in reality 3 : all things considered

in·de·fat·i·ga·ble \ˌin-di-ˈfa-ti-gə-bəl\ *adj* : UNTIRING ⟨an ~ worker⟩ — **in·de·fat·i·ga·bly** \-blē\ *adv*

in·de·fea·si·ble \-ˈfē-zə-bəl\ *adj* : not capable of being annulled or voided — **in·de·fea·si·bly** \-blē\ *adv*

in·de·fen·si·ble \-ˈfen-sə-bəl\ *adj* 1 : incapable of being maintained as right or valid 2 : INEXCUSABLE ⟨~ comments⟩ 3 : incapable of being protected against physical attack

in·de·fin·able \-ˈfī-nə-bəl\ *adj* : incapable of being precisely described or analyzed — **in·de·fin·ably** \-blē\ *adv*

in·def·i·nite \(ˌ)in-ˈde-fə-nət\ *adj* 1 : not defining or identifying ⟨an is an ~ article⟩ 2 : not precise : VAGUE 3 : having no fixed limits — **in·def·i·nite·ly** *adv* — **in·def·i·nite·ness** *n*

in·del·i·ble \in-ˈde-lə-bəl\ *adj* [ME, fr. ML *indelibilis*, alter. of L *indelebilis*, fr. *delēre* to delete, destroy] 1 : not capable of being removed or erased 2 : making marks that cannot be erased 3 : LASTING, UNFORGETTABLE ⟨an ~ performance⟩ — **in·del·i·bly** \in-ˈde-lə-blē\ *adv*

in·del·i·cate \(ˌ)in-ˈde-li-kət\ *adj* : not delicate; *esp* : IMPROPER, COARSE, TACTLESS ✦ *Synonyms* INDECENT, UNSEEMLY, INDECOROUS, UNBECOMING — **in·del·i·ca·cy** \in-ˈde-lə-kə-sē\ *n*

in·dem·ni·fy \in-ˈdem-nə-ˌfī\ *vb* **-fied; -fy·ing** [L *indemnis* unharmed, fr. *in-* not + *damnum* damage] 1 : to secure against hurt, loss, or damage 2 : to make compensation to for hurt, loss, or damage — **in·dem·ni·fi·ca·tion** \-ˌdem-nə-fə-ˈkā-shən\ *n*

in·dem·ni·ty \in-ˈdem-nə-tē\ *n, pl* **-ties** 1 : security against hurt, loss, or damage; *also* : exemption from incurred penalties or liabilities 2 : something that indemnifies

¹**in·dent** \in-ˈdent\ *vb* [ME, fr. AF *endenter*, fr. *dent* tooth, fr. L *dent-, dens*] 1 : to notch the edge of 2 : INDENTURE 3 : to set (as a line of a paragraph) in from the margin

²**indent** *vb* 1 : to force inward so as to form a depression 2 : to form a dent in

in·den·ta·tion \ˌin-ˌden-ˈtā-shən\ *n* 1 : NOTCH; *also* : a recess in a surface 2 : the action of indenting : the condition of being indented 3 : DENT 4 : INDENTION 2

in·den·tion \in-ˈden-chən\ *n* : INDENTATION 2 2 : the blank space produced by indenting

¹**in·den·ture** \in-ˈden-chər\ *n* 1 : a written certificate or agreement; *esp* : a contract binding one person (as an ap-

prentice) to work for another for a given period of time — often used in pl. 2 : INDENTATION 1 3 : DENT

²**indenture** *vb* **in·den·tured; in·den·tur·ing** : to bind (as an apprentice) by indentures

in·de·pen·dence \ˌin-də-ˈpen-dəns\ *n* : the quality or state of being independent : FREEDOM

Independence Day *n* : July 4 observed as a legal holiday in the U.S. in commemoration of the adoption of the Declaration of Independence in 1776

in·de·pen·dent \ˌin-də-ˈpen-dənt\ *adj* 1 : SELF-GOVERNING; *also* : not affiliated with a larger controlling unit 2 : not requiring or relying on something else or somebody else ⟨an ~ conclusion⟩ ⟨~ of her parents⟩ 3 : not easily influenced : showing self-reliance and personal freedom ⟨an ~ mind⟩ 4 : not committed to a political party ⟨an ~ voter⟩ 5 : MAIN ⟨an ~ clause⟩ — **independent** — **in·de·pen·dent·ly** *adv*

independent variable *n* : a variable whose value is not determined by that of any other variable in a function

in·de·scrib·able \ˌin-di-ˈskrī-bə-bəl\ *adj* 1 : that cannot be described 2 : being too intense or great for description — **in·de·scrib·ably** \-blē\ *adv*

in·de·ter·mi·nate \ˌin-di-ˈtər-mə-nət\ *adj* 1 : VAGUE; *also* : not known in advance 2 : not limited in advance; *also* : not leading to a definite end or result — **in·de·ter·mi·na·cy** \-nə-sē\ *n* — **in·de·ter·mi·nate·ly** *adv*

¹**in·dex** \ˈin-ˌdeks\ *n, pl* **in·dex·es** *or* **in·di·ces** \-də-ˌsēz\ 1 : POINTER 2 : SIGN, INDICATION ⟨an ~ of character⟩ 3 : a guide for facilitating references; *esp* : an alphabetical list of items treated in a printed work with the page number where each item may be found 4 : a list of restricted or prohibited material 5 *pl usu* **indices** : a number or symbol or expression (as an exponent) associated with another to indicate a mathematical operation or use or position in an arrangement or expansion 6 : a character ☞ used to direct attention (as to a note) 7 : INDEX NUMBER

²**index** *vb* 1 : to provide with or put into an index 2 : to serve as an index of 3 : to regulate by indexation

in·dex·ation \ˌin-ˌdek-ˈsā-shən\ *n* : a system of economic control in which a body of variables (as wages and interest) rise or fall at the same rate as an index of the cost of living

index finger *n* : the finger next to the thumb

in·dex·ing *n* : INDEXATION

index number *n* : a number used to indicate change in magnitude (as of cost) as compared with the magnitude at some specified time

index of refraction *n* : REFRACTIVE INDEX

in·dia ink \ˈin-dē-ə-\ *n, often cap 1st I* 1 : a solid black pigment used in drawing 2 : a fluid made from india ink

In·di·an \ˈin-dē-ən\ *n* 1 : a native or inhabitant of India or of the East Indies; *also* : a person of Indian descent 2 : AMERICAN INDIAN — **Indian** *adj*

Indian corn *n* 1 : CORN 2 2 : corn having hard kernels of various colors (as reddish-brown or purple) used esp. for ornament

Indian meal *n* : CORNMEAL

Indian paintbrush *n* : any of a genus of herbaceous plants related to the snapdragons that have brightly colored bracts

Indian pipe *n* : a waxy white leafless saprophytic herb of Asia and the U.S.

Indian summer *n* : a period of mild weather in late autumn or early winter

In·dia paper \ˈin-dē-ə-\ *n* 1 : a thin absorbent paper used esp. for taking impressions (as of steel engravings) 2 : a thin tough opaque printing paper

in·di·cate \ˈin-də-ˌkāt\ *vb* **-cat·ed; -cat·ing** 1 : to point out or to 2 : to show indirectly 3 : to state briefly — **in·di·ca·tion** \ˌin-də-ˈkā-shən\ *n* — **in·di·ca·tor** \ˈin-də-ˌkā-tər\ *n*

¹**in·dic·a·tive** \in-ˈdi-kə-tiv\ *adj* 1 : of, relating to, or being a verb form that represents an act or state as a fact ⟨~ mood⟩ 2 : serving to indicate ⟨actions ~ of fear⟩

²**indicative** *n* 1 : the indicative mood of a language 2 : a form in the indicative mood

in·di·cia \in-ˈdi-shə, -shē-ə\ *n pl* 1 : distinctive marks 2 : postal markings often imprinted on mail or mailing labels

in·dict \in-ˈdīt\ *vb* [alter. of earlier *indite*, fr. ME, fr. AF *enditer* to write, point out, indict, ultim. fr. L *indicere* to

make known formally, fr. *dicere* to say] **1** : to charge with a fault or offense **2** : to charge with a crime by the finding of a jury — **in·dict·able** *adj* — **in·dict·ment** *n*
in·die \'in-dē\ *n* **1** : one that is independent; *esp* : an unaffiliated record or motion-picture production company **2** something produced by an indie — **indie** *adj*
in·dif·fer·ent \in-'di-frənt, -fə-rənt\ *adj* **1** : UNBIASED, UNPREJUDICED **2** : of no importance one way or the other **3** : marked by no special liking for or dislike of something **4** : being neither excessive nor inadequate **5** : PASSABLE, MEDIOCRE **6** : being neither right nor wrong — **in·dif·fer·ence** \-frəns, -fə-rəns\ *n* — **in·dif·fer·ent·ly** *adv*
in·dig·e·nous \in-'di-jə-nəs\ *adj* : produced, growing, or living naturally in a particular region
in·di·gent \'in-di-jənt\ *adj* : IMPOVERISHED, NEEDY — **in·di·gence** \-jəns\ *n*
in·di·gest·ible \,in-dī-'jes-tə-bəl, -də-\ *adj* : not readily digested
in·di·ges·tion \-'jes-chən\ *n* : inadequate or difficult digestion : DYSPEPSIA
in·dig·nant \in-'dig-nənt\ *adj* : filled with or marked by indignation — **in·dig·nant·ly** *adv*
in·dig·na·tion \,in-dig-'nā-shən\ *n* : anger aroused by something unjust, unworthy, or mean
in·dig·ni·ty \in-'dig-nə-tē\ *n, pl* **-ties** : an offense against personal dignity or self-respect; *also* : humiliating treatment
in·di·go \'in-di-,gō\ *n, pl* **-gos** *or* **-goes** [It dial., fr. L *indicum*, fr. Gk *indikon*, fr. *indikos* Indic, fr. *Indos* India] **1** : a blue dye obtained from plants or synthesized **2** : a deep reddish blue color
in·di·rect \,in-də-'rekt, -dī-\ *adj* **1** : not straight ⟨an ~ route⟩ **2** : not straightforward and open ⟨~ methods⟩ **3** : not having a plainly seen connection ⟨an ~ cause⟩ **4** : not directly to the point ⟨an ~ answer⟩ — **in·di·rec·tion** \-'rek-shən\ *n* — **in·di·rect·ly** *adv* — **in·di·rect·ness** *n*
in·dis·creet \,in-di-'skrēt\ *adj* : not discreet : IMPRUDENT — **in·dis·creet·ly** *adv*
in·dis·cre·tion \,in-di-'skre-shən\ *n* **1** : IMPRUDENCE ⟨dietary ~⟩ **2** : something marked by lack of discretion; *esp* : an act deviating from accepted morality
in·dis·crim·i·nate \,in-di-'skri-mə-nət\ *adj* **1** : not careful in making choices **2** : HAPHAZARD, RANDOM ⟨an ~ application of a law⟩ **3** : UNRESTRAINED **4** : MOTLEY — **in·dis·crim·i·nate·ly** *adv*
in·dis·pens·able \,in-di-'spen-sə-bəl\ *adj* : absolutely essential : REQUISITE — **in·dis·pens·abil·i·ty** \-,spen-sə-'bi-lə-tē\ *n* — **indispensable** *n* — **in·dis·pens·ably** \-'spen-sə-blē\ *adv*
in·dis·posed \-'spōzd\ *adj* **1** : slightly ill **2** : AVERSE — **in·dis·po·si·tion** \(,)in-,dis-pə-'zi-shən\ *n*
in·dis·put·able \,in-di-'spyü-tə-bəl, (,)in-'dis-pyə-\ *adj* : not disputable : UNQUESTIONABLE ⟨~ proof⟩ — **in·dis·put·ably** \-blē\ *adv*
in·dis·sol·u·ble \,in-di-'säl-yə-bəl\ *adj* : not capable of being dissolved, undone, or broken : PERMANENT ⟨an ~ contract⟩
in·dis·tinct \,in-di-'stiŋkt\ *adj* **1** : not sharply outlined or separable : BLURRED, FAINT, DIM **2** : not readily distinguishable : UNCERTAIN — **in·dis·tinct·ly** *adv* — **in·dis·tinct·ness** *n*
in·dite \in-'dīt\ *vb* **in·dit·ed; in·dit·ing** : COMPOSE ⟨~ a poem⟩; *also* : to put in writing ⟨~ a letter⟩
in·di·um \'in-dē-əm\ *n* : a malleable silvery metallic chemical element
indiv *abbr* individual
¹in·di·vid·u·al \,in-də-'vi-jə-wəl\ *adj* **1** : of, relating to, or associated with an individual ⟨~ traits⟩ **2** : being an individual : existing as an indivisible whole **3** : intended for one person **4** : SEPARATE ⟨~ copies⟩ **5** : having marked individuality ⟨an ~ style⟩ — **in·di·vid·u·al·ly** *adv*
²individual *n* **1** : a single member of a category : a particular person, animal, or thing **2** : PERSON ⟨a disagreeable ~⟩
in·di·vid·u·al·ise *Brit var of* INDIVIDUALIZE
in·di·vid·u·al·ism \,in-də-'vi-jə-wə-,li-zəm\ *n* **1** : a doctrine that the interests of the individual are primary **2** : a doctrine holding that the individual has political or economic rights with which the state must not interfere **3** : INDIVIDUALITY

in·di·vid·u·al·ist \-list\ *n* **1** : one that pursues a markedly independent course in thought or action **2** : one that advocates or practices individualism — **individualist** *or* **in·di·vid·u·al·is·tic** \-,vi-jə-wə-'lis-tik\ *adj*
in·di·vid·u·al·i·ty \-,vi-jə-'wa-lə-tē\ *n, pl* **-ties** **1** : the sum of qualities that characterize and distinguish an individual from all others; *also* : PERSONALITY **2** : separate or distinct existence **3** : INDIVIDUAL, PERSON
in·di·vid·u·al·ize \-'vi-jə-wə-,līz\ *vb* **-ized; -iz·ing** **1** : to make individual in character **2** : to treat or notice individually : PARTICULARIZE **3** : to adapt to the needs of an individual
individual retirement account *n* : IRA
in·di·vid·u·ate \,in-də-'vi-jə-,wāt\ *vb* **-at·ed; -at·ing** : to give individuality to : form into an individual — **in·di·vid·u·a·tion** \-,vi-jə-'wā-shən\ *n*
in·di·vis·i·ble \,in-də-'vi-zə-bəl\ *adj* : impossible to divide or separate — **in·di·vis·i·bil·i·ty** \-,vi-zə-'bi-lə-tē\ *n* — **in·di·vis·i·bly** *adv*
In·do-Ar·y·an \,in-dō-'er-ē-ən\ *n* : a branch of the Indo-European language family that includes Hindi and other languages of south Asia
in·doc·tri·nate \in-'däk-trə-,nāt\ *vb* **-nat·ed; -nat·ing** **1** : to instruct esp. in fundamentals or rudiments : TEACH **2** : to teach the beliefs and doctrines of a particular group — **in·doc·tri·na·tion** \(,)in-,däk-trə-'nā-shən\ *n* — **in·doc·tri·na·tor** *n*
In·do-Eu·ro·pe·an \,in-dō-,yur-ə-'pē-ən\ *adj* : of, relating to, or constituting a family of languages comprising those spoken in most of Europe and in the parts of the world colonized by Europeans since 1500 and also in Persia, the subcontinent of India, and some other parts of Asia
in·do·lent \'in-də-lənt\ *adj* [LL *indolens* insensitive to pain, fr. L *dolēre* to feel pain] **1** : slow to develop or heal ⟨~ ulcers⟩ **2** : LAZY — **in·do·lence** \-ləns\ *n* — **in·do·lent·ly** *adv*
in·dom·i·ta·ble \in-'dä-mə-tə-bəl\ *adj* : UNCONQUERABLE ⟨~ courage⟩ — **in·dom·i·ta·bly** \-blē\ *adv*
in·door \'in-,dòr\ *adj* **1** : of or relating to the inside of a building **2** : living, located, or carried on within a building
in·doors \in-'dórz\ *adv* : in or into a building
indorse, indorsement *var of* ENDORSE, ENDORSEMENT
in·du·bi·ta·ble \(,)in-'dü-bə-tə-bəl, -'dyü-\ *adj* : UNQUESTIONABLE ⟨~ truths⟩ — **in·du·bi·ta·bly** \-blē\ *adv*
in·duce \in-'düs, -'dyüs\ *vb* **in·duced; in·duc·ing** **1** : PERSUADE, INFLUENCE **2** : BRING ABOUT **3** : to produce (as an electric current) by induction **4** : to determine by induction; *esp* : to infer from particulars — **in·duc·er** *n*
in·duce·ment \-mənt\ *n* **1** : something that induces : MOTIVE **2** : the act or process of inducing
in·duct \in-'dəkt\ *vb* **1** : to place in office **2** : to admit as a member **3** : to enroll for military training or service — **in·duct·ee** \-,dək-'tē\ *n*
in·duc·tance \in-'dək-təns\ *n* : a property of an electric circuit by which a varying current produces an electromotive force in that circuit or in a nearby circuit; *also* : the measure of this property
in·duc·tion \in-'dək-shən\ *n* **1** : the act or process of inducting; *also* : INITIATION **2** : the formality by which a civilian is inducted into military service **3** : inference of a generalized conclusion from particular instances; *also* : a conclusion so reached **4** : the act of causing or bringing on or about **5** : the process by which an electric current, an electric charge, or magnetism is produced in a body by the proximity of an electric or magnetic field
in·duc·tive \in-'dək-tiv\ *adj* : of, relating to, or employing induction
in·duc·tor \in-'dək-tər\ *n* : an electrical component that acts upon another or is itself acted upon by induction
in·dulge \in-'dəlj\ *vb* **in·dulged; in·dulg·ing** **1** : to give free rein to : GRATIFY **2** : HUMOR **3** : to gratify one's taste or desire for ⟨~ in alcohol⟩
in·dul·gence \in-'dəl-jəns\ *n* **1** : remission of temporal punishment due in Roman Catholic doctrine for sins whose eternal punishment has been remitted by reception of the sacrifice of penance **2** : the act of indulging : the state of being indulgent **3** : an indulgent act **4** : the thing indulged in **5** : SELF-INDULGENCE — **in·dul·gent** \-jənt\ *adj* — **in·dul·gent·ly** *adv*

in·du·rat·ed \'in-dyù-ˌrā-təd, -dù-\ *adj* : physically or emotionally hardened — **in·du·ra·tion** \ˌin-dyù-'rā-shən, -dù-\ *n*

in·dus·tri·al \in-'dəs-trē-əl\ *adj* 1 : of or relating to industry 2 : HEAVY-DUTY ⟨an ~ zipper⟩ 3 : characterized by highly developed industries — **in·dus·tri·al·ly** *adv*

in·dus·tri·al·ise *Brit var of* INDUSTRIALIZE

in·dus·tri·al·ist \-ə-list\ *n* : a person owning or engaged in the management of an industry

in·dus·tri·al·ize \in-'dəs-trē-ə-ˌlīz\ *vb* **-ized; -iz·ing** : to make or become industrial — **in·dus·tri·al·i·za·tion** \-ˌdəs-trē-ə-lə-'zā-shən\ *n*

in·dus·tri·ous \in-'dəs-trē-əs\ *adj* : DILIGENT, BUSY — **in·dus·tri·ous·ly** *adv* — **in·dus·tri·ous·ness** *n*

in·dus·try \'in-(ˌ)dəs-trē\ *n, pl* **-tries** 1 : DILIGENCE 2 : a department or branch of a craft, art, business, or manufacture; *esp* : one that employs a large personnel and capital 3 : a distinct group of productive enterprises 4 : manufacturing activity as a whole

in·dwell \(ˌ)in-'dwel\ *vb* : to exist within as an activating spirit or force

In·dy car \'in-dē-\ *n* : a single-seat, open-cockpit racing car with the engine in the rear

¹**in·e·bri·ate** \i-'nē-brē-ˌāt\ *vb* **-at·ed; -at·ing** : to make drunk : INTOXICATE — **in·e·bri·a·tion** \-ˌnē-brē-'ā-shən\ *n*

²**in·e·bri·ate** \-ət\ *n* : one that is drunk; *esp* : DRUNKARD

in·ef·fa·ble \(ˌ)in-'e-fə-bəl\ *adj* 1 : incapable of being expressed in words : INDESCRIBABLE ⟨~ joy⟩ 2 : UNSPEAKABLE ⟨~ disgust⟩ 3 : not to be uttered : TABOO — **in·ef·fa·bly** \-blē\ *adv*

in·ef·fec·tive \ˌi-nə-'fek-tiv\ *adj* 1 : INEFFECTUAL 2 : not able to perform efficiently or as expected : INCAPABLE — **in·ef·fec·tive·ly** *adv* — **in·ef·fec·tive·ness** *n*

in·ef·fec·tu·al \-'fek-chə-wəl\ *adj* 1 : not producing the proper or usual effect 2 : INEFFECTIVE 2 — **in·ef·fec·tu·al·ly** *adv*

in·ef·fi·cient \ˌi-nə-'fi-shənt\ *adj* 1 : not producing the desired effect 2 : wasteful of time or energy 3 : INCAPABLE, INCOMPETENT — **in·ef·fi·cien·cy** \-'fi-shən-sē\ *n* — **in·ef·fi·cient·ly** *adv*

in·el·e·gant \(ˌ)i-'ne-li-gənt\ *adj* : lacking in refinement, grace, or good taste — **in·el·e·gance** \-gəns\ *n* — **in·el·e·gant·ly** *adv*

in·el·i·gi·ble \(ˌ)i-'ne-lə-jə-bəl\ *adj* : not qualified for an office or position — **in·el·i·gi·bil·i·ty** \(ˌ)i-ˌne-lə-jə-'bi-lə-tē\ *n*

in·eluc·ta·ble \ˌi-ni-'lək-tə-bəl\ *adj* : not to be avoided, changed, or resisted ⟨an ~ conclusion⟩ — **in·eluc·ta·bly** \-blē\ *adv*

in·ept \i-'nept\ *adj* 1 : lacking in fitness or aptitude : UNFIT 2 : FOOLISH 3 : being out of place : INAPPROPRIATE 4 : generally incompetent : BUNGLING — **in·ept·ly** *adv* — **in·ept·ness** *n*

in·ep·ti·tude \(ˌ)i-'nep-ti-ˌtüd, -ˌtyüd\ *n* : the quality or state of being inept; *esp* : INCOMPETENCE

in·equal·i·ty \ˌi-ni-'kwä-lə-tē\ *n* 1 : the quality of being unequal or uneven; *esp* : UNEVENNESS, DISPARITY 2 : an instance of being unequal

in·ert \i-'nərt\ *adj* [L *inert-, iners* unskilled, idle, fr. *art-, ars* skill] 1 : powerless to move 2 : SLUGGISH 3 : lacking in active properties ⟨chemically ~⟩ — **in·ert·ly** *adv* — **in·ert·ness** *n*

in·er·tia \i-'nər-shə, -shē-ə\ *n* 1 : a property of matter whereby it remains at rest or continues in uniform motion unless acted upon by some outside force 2 : INERTNESS, SLUGGISHNESS — **in·er·tial** \-shəl\ *adj*

in·es·cap·able \ˌi-nə-'skā-pə-bəl\ *adj* : incapable of being escaped : INEVITABLE — **in·es·cap·ably** \-blē\ *adv*

in·es·ti·ma·ble \(ˌ)i-'nes-tə-mə-bəl\ *adj* 1 : incapable of being estimated or computed ⟨~ errors⟩ 2 : too valuable or excellent to be fully appreciated — **in·es·ti·ma·bly** \-blē\ *adv*

in·ev·i·ta·ble \i-'ne-və-tə-bəl\ *adj* : incapable of being avoided or evaded : bound to happen ⟨the ~ result⟩ — **in·ev·i·ta·bil·i·ty** \(ˌ)i-ˌne-və-tə-'bi-lə-tē\ *n*

in·ev·i·ta·bly \-blē\ *adv* 1 : in an inevitable way 2 : as is to be expected

in·ex·act \ˌi-nig-'zakt\ *adj* 1 : not precisely correct or true : INACCURATE 2 : not rigorous and careful — **in·ex·act·ly** *adv* — **in·ex·act·ness** *n*

in·ex·cus·able \ˌi-nik-'skyü-zə-bəl\ *adj* : impossible to excuse or justify ⟨~ rudeness⟩ — **in·ex·cus·ably** \-blē\ *adv*

in·ex·haust·ible \ˌi-nig-'zò-stə-bəl\ *adj* 1 : incapable of being used up ⟨an ~ supply⟩ 2 : UNTIRING ⟨an ~ hiker⟩ — **in·ex·haust·ibly** \-blē\ *adv*

in·ex·o·ra·ble \(ˌ)i-'nek-sə-rə-bəl\ *adj* : not to be persuaded, moved, or stopped : RELENTLESS — **in·ex·o·ra·bly** *adv*

in·ex·pe·ri·ence \ˌi-nik-'spir-ē-əns\ *n* : lack of experience or of knowledge gained by experience — **in·ex·pe·ri·enced** \-ənst\ *adj*

in·ex·pert \(ˌ)i-'nek-ˌspərt\ *adj* : not expert : UNSKILLED — **in·ex·pert·ly** *adv*

in·ex·pi·a·ble \(ˌ)i-'nek-spē-ə-bəl\ *adj* : not capable of being atoned for

in·ex·pli·ca·ble \ˌi-nik-'spli-kə-bəl, (ˌ)i-'nek-(ˌ)spli-\ *adj* : incapable of being explained or accounted for ⟨an ~ mistake⟩ — **in·ex·pli·ca·bly** \-blē\ *adv*

in·ex·press·ible \-'spre-sə-bəl\ *adj* : not capable of being expressed ⟨~ joy⟩ — **in·ex·press·ibly** \-blē\ *adv*

in ex·tre·mis \ˌin-ik-'strā-məs, -'strē-\ *adv* : in extreme circumstances; *esp* : at the point of death

in·ex·tri·ca·ble \ˌi-nik-'stri-kə-bəl, (ˌ)i-'nek-(ˌ)stri-\ *adj* 1 : forming a maze or tangle from which it is impossible to get free 2 : incapable of being disentangled or untied — **in·ex·tri·ca·bly** \-blē\ *adv*

inf *abbr* 1 infantry 2 infinitive

in·fal·li·ble \(ˌ)in-'fa-lə-bəl\ *adj* 1 : incapable of error : UNERRING ⟨an ~ marksman⟩ 2 : SURE, CERTAIN ⟨an ~ remedy⟩ — **in·fal·li·bil·i·ty** \(ˌ)in-ˌfa-lə-'bi-lə-tē\ *n* — **in·fal·li·bly** \(ˌ)in-'fa-lə-blē\ *adv*

in·fa·mous \'in-fə-məs\ *adj* 1 : having a reputation of the worst kind 2 : DISGRACEFUL — **in·fa·mous·ly** *adv*

in·fa·my \-mē\ *n, pl* **-mies** 1 : evil reputation brought about by something grossly criminal, shocking, or brutal 2 : an extreme and publicly known criminal or evil act 3 : the state of being infamous

in·fan·cy \'in-fən-sē\ *n, pl* **-cies** 1 : early childhood 2 : a beginning or early period of existence

in·fant \'in-fənt\ *n* [ME *enfaunt*, fr. AF *enfant*, fr. L *infant-, infans*, adj., incapable of speech, young, fr. *fant-, fans*, prp. of *fari* to speak] : BABY; *also* : a person who is a legal minor

in·fan·ti·cide \in-'fan-tə-ˌsīd\ *n* : the killing of an infant

in·fan·tile \'in-fən-ˌtī(-ə)l, -t⁹l, -ˌtēl\ *adj* : of or relating to infants; *also* : CHILDISH

infantile paralysis *n* : POLIOMYELITIS

in·fan·try \'in-fən-trē\ *n, pl* **-tries** [MF & It; MF *infanterie*, fr. It *infanteria*, fr. *infante* boy, foot soldier] : soldiers trained, armed, and equipped to fight on foot — **in·fan·try·man** \-mən\ *n*

in·farct \'in-ˌfärkt\ *n* [L *infarctus*, pp. of *infarcire* to stuff] : an area of dead tissue (as of the heart wall) caused by blocking of local blood circulation — **in·farc·tion** \in-'färk-shən\ *n*

in·fat·u·ate \in-'fa-chə-ˌwāt\ *vb* **-at·ed; -at·ing** : to inspire with a foolish or extravagant love or admiration — **in·fat·u·a·tion** \-ˌfa-chə-'wā-shən\ *n*

in·fect \in-'fekt\ *vb* 1 : to contaminate with disease-producing matter 2 : to communicate a pathogen or disease to 3 : to cause to share one's feelings ⟨~ed us with his enthusiasm⟩

in·fec·tion \in-'fek-shən\ *n* 1 : a disease or condition caused by a germ or parasite; *also* : such a germ or parasite 2 : an act or process of infecting — **in·fec·tious** \-shəs\ *adj* — **in·fec·tive** \-'fek-tiv\ *adj*

infectious mononucleosis *n* : an acute infectious disease characterized by fever, swelling of lymph glands, and increased numbers of lymph cells in the blood

in·fe·lic·i·tous \ˌin-fi-'li-sə-təs\ *adj* : not appropriate in application or expression ⟨~ comments⟩ — **in·fe·lic·i·ty** \-sə-tē\ *n*

in·fer \in-'fər\ *vb* **in·ferred; in·fer·ring** 1 : to derive as a conclusion from facts or premises 2 : GUESS, SURMISE 3 : to lead to as a conclusion or consequence 4 : HINT, SUGGEST ♦ *Synonyms* DEDUCE, CONCLUDE, JUDGE, GATHER — **in·fer·ence** \'in-frəns, -fə-rəns\ *n* — **in·fer·en·tial** \ˌin-fə-'ren-chəl\ *adj*

in·fe·ri·or \in-'fir-ē-ər\ *adj* 1 : situated lower down 2 : of low or lower degree or rank 3 : of lesser quality 4 : of little or less importance, value, or merit ⟨an ~ opponent⟩ — **inferior** *n* — **in·fe·ri·or·i·ty** \(ˌ)in-ˌfir-ē-'òr-ə-tē\ *n*

in·fer·nal \in-'fər-n°l\ adj **1** : of or relating to hell **2** : HELLISH, FIENDISH ⟨~ schemes⟩ **3** : DAMNABLE ⟨an ~ pest⟩ — **in·fer·nal·ly** adv

in·fer·no \in-'fər-nō\ n, pl **-nos** [It, hell, fr. LL infernus, fr. L, lower] : a place or a state that resembles or suggests hell; also : intense heat

in·fer·tile \(,)in-'fər-t°l\ adj : not fertile or productive : BARREN — **in·fer·til·i·ty** \,in-fər-'ti-lə-tē\ n

in·fest \in-'fest\ vb : to trouble by spreading or swarming in or over; also : to live in or on as a parasite — **in·fes·ta·tion** \,in-,fes-'tā-shən\ n

in·fi·del \'in-fə-d°l, -fə-,del\ n **1** : one who is not a Christian or opposes Christianity **2** : an unbeliever esp. with respect to a particular religion

in·fi·del·i·ty \,in-fə-'de-lə-tē, -fī-\ n, pl **-ties 1** : lack of belief in a religion **2** : unfaithfulness or an instance of it esp. in marriage

in·field \'in-,fēld\ n : the part of a baseball field inside the baselines — **in·field·er** n

in·fight·ing \'in-,fī-tiŋ\ n **1** : fighting at close quarters **2** : dissension or rivalry among members of a group

in·fil·trate \in-'fil-,trāt, 'in-(,)fil-\ vb **-trat·ed; -trat·ing 1** : to enter or filter into or through something **2** : to pass into or through by or as if by filtering or permeating — **in·fil·tra·tion** \,in-(,)fil-'trā-shən\ n — **in·fil·tra·tor** n

in·fi·nite \'in-fə-nət\ adj **1** : LIMITLESS, BOUNDLESS, ENDLESS ⟨~ space⟩ ⟨~ patience⟩ **2** : VAST, IMMENSE; also : INEXHAUSTIBLE ⟨~ wealth⟩ **3** : greater than any preassigned finite value however large ⟨~ number of positive integers⟩; also : extending to infinity ⟨~ plane surface⟩ — **infinite** n — **in·fi·nite·ly** adv

in·fin·i·tes·i·mal \(,)in-,fi-nə-'te-sə-məl\ adj : immeasurably or incalculably small — **in·fin·i·tes·i·mal·ly** adv

in·fin·i·tive \in-'fi-nə-tiv\ n : a verb form having the characteristics of both verb and noun and in English usu. being used with to

in·fin·i·tude \in-'fi-nə-,tüd, -,tyüd\ n **1** : the quality or state of being infinite **2** : something that is infinite esp. in extent

in·fin·i·ty \in-'fi-nə-tē\ n, pl **-ties 1** : the quality of being infinite **2** : unlimited extent of time, space, or quantity **3** : an indefinitely great number or amount

in·firm \in-'fərm\ adj **1** : deficient in vitality; esp : feeble from age **2** : weak of mind, will, or character : IRRESOLUTE **3** : not solid or stable : INSECURE

in·fir·ma·ry \in-'fər-mə-rē\ n, pl **-ries** : a place for the care of the infirm or sick

in·fir·mi·ty \in-'fər-mə-tē\ n, pl **-ties 1** : FEEBLENESS **2** : DISEASE, AILMENT **3** : a personal failing : FOIBLE

infl abbr influenced

in fla·gran·te de·lic·to \,in-flə-'grän-tē-di-'lik-tō, -'gran-\ adv **1** : in the very act of committing a misdeed **2** : in the midst of sexual activity

in·flame \in-'flām\ vb **in·flamed; in·flam·ing 1** : KINDLE **2** : to excite to excessive or uncontrollable action or feeling; also : INTENSIFY **3** : to affect or become affected with inflammation

in·flam·ma·ble \in-'fla-mə-bəl\ adj **1** : FLAMMABLE **2** : easily inflamed, excited, or angered : IRASCIBLE

in·flam·ma·tion \,in-flə-'mā-shən\ n : a bodily response to injury in which an affected area becomes red, hot, and painful and congested with blood

in·flam·ma·to·ry \in-'fla-mə-,tòr-ē\ adj **1** : tending to excite the senses or to arouse anger, disorder, or tumult : SEDITIOUS **2** : causing or accompanied by inflammation ⟨~ disease⟩

in·flate \in-'flāt\ vb **in·flat·ed; in·flat·ing 1** : to swell with air or gas ⟨~ a balloon⟩ **2** : to puff up : ELATE ⟨~ one's ego⟩ **3** : to expand or increase abnormally ⟨~ prices⟩ — **in·flat·able** adj

in·fla·tion \in-'flā-shən\ n **1** : an act of inflating : the state of being inflated **2** : empty pretentiousness : POMPOSITY **3** : a continuing rise in the general price level usu. attributed to an increase in the volume of money and credit

in·fla·tion·ary \-shə-,ner-ē\ adj : of, characterized by, or productive of inflation

in·flect \in-'flekt\ vb **1** : to turn from a direct line or course : CURVE **2** : to vary a word by inflection **3** : to change or vary the pitch of the voice

in·flec·tion \in-'flek-shən\ n **1** : the act or result of curving or bending **2** : a change in pitch or loudness of the

voice **3** : the change of form that words undergo to mark case, gender, number, tense, person, mood, or voice — **in·flec·tion·al** \-shə-nəl\ adj

in·flex·i·ble \(,)in-'flek-sə-bəl\ adj **1** : UNYIELDING **2** : RIGID **3** : incapable of change ⟨an ~ deadline⟩ — **in·flex·i·bil·i·ty** \-,flek-sə-'bi-lə-tē\ n — **in·flex·i·bly** \-'flek-sə-blē\ adv

in·flex·ion \in-'flek-shən\ chiefly Brit var of INFLECTION

in·flict \in-'flikt\ vb : AFFLICT; also : to give by or as if by striking ⟨~ pain⟩ — **in·flic·tion** \-'flik-shən\ n

in·flo·res·cence \,in-flə-'re-s°n(t)s\ n : the manner of development and arrangement of flowers on a stem; also : a flowering stem with its appendages : a flower cluster

in·flow \'in-,flō\ n : a flowing in

¹in·flu·ence \'in-,flü-əns\ n **1** : the act or power of producing an effect without apparent force or direct authority **2** : the power or capacity of causing an effect in indirect or intangible ways **3** : one that exerts influence — **in·flu·en·tial** \,in-flü-'en-chəl\ adj — **under the influence** : affected by alcohol

²influence vb **-enced; -enc·ing 1** : to affect or alter by influence : SWAY **2** : to have an effect on the condition or development of : MODIFY

in·flu·en·za \,in-flü-'en-zə\ n [It, lit., influence, fr. ML influentia; fr. the belief that epidemics were due to the influence of the stars] : an acute and highly contagious virus disease marked by fever, prostration, aches and pains, and respiratory inflammation; also : any of various feverish usu. virus diseases typically with respiratory symptoms

in·flux \'in-,fləks\ n : a coming in

in·fo \'in-(,)fō\ n : INFORMATION

in·fold \in-'fōld\ vb **1** : ENFOLD **2** : to fold inward or toward one another

in·fo·mer·cial \'in-fō-,mər-shəl\ n : a television program that is an extended advertisement often including a discussion or demonstration

in·form \in-'fòrm\ vb **1** : to communicate knowledge to : TELL **2** : to give information or knowledge **3** : to act as an informer ✦ *Synonyms* ACQUAINT, APPRISE, ADVISE, NOTIFY

in·for·mal \(,)in-'fòr-məl\ adj **1** : conducted or carried out without formality or ceremony ⟨an ~ party⟩ **2** : characteristic of or appropriate to ordinary, casual, or familiar use ⟨~ clothes⟩ — **in·for·mal·i·ty** \,in-fòr-'ma-lə-tē, -far-\ n — **in·for·mal·ly** \(,)in-'fòr-mə-lē\ adv

in·for·mant \in-'fòr-mənt\ n : a person who gives information : INFORMER

in·for·ma·tion \,in-fər-'mā-shən\ n **1** : the communication or reception of knowledge or intelligence **2** : knowledge obtained from investigation, study, or instruction : FACTS, DATA **3** : the attribute communicated by one of two or more alternative sequences of something (as nucleotides in DNA or binary digits in a computer program) — **in·for·ma·tion·al** \-shə-nəl\ adj

information superhighway n : INTERNET

information technology n : technology involving computer systems and networks for the processing and distribution of data

in·for·ma·tive \in-'fòr-mə-tiv\ adj : imparting knowledge : INSTRUCTIVE

in·formed \in-'fòrmd\ adj **1** : having or based on information ⟨an ~ decision⟩ **2** : EDUCATED, KNOWLEDGEABLE

informed consent n : consent to a medical procedure by someone who understands what is involved

in·form·er \-'for-mər\ n : one that informs; esp : a person who informs against others for illegalities esp. for financial gain

in·fo·tain·ment \,in-fō-'tān-mənt\ n : a television program that presents information (as news) in a manner intended to be entertaining

in·frac·tion \in-'frak-shən\ n [ME, fr. ML infractio, fr. L, subduing, fr. infringere to break, crush] : the act of infringing : VIOLATION

in·fra dig \,in-frə-'dig\ adj [short for L infra dignitatem] : being beneath one's dignity

in·fra·red \,in-frə-'red\ adj : being, relating to, or using radiation having wavelengths longer than those of red light — **infrared** n

in·fra·struc·ture \'in-frə-,strək-chər\ n **1** : the underlying foundation or basic framework (as of a system or organization) **2** : the system of public works of a country, state, or region; *also* : the resources (as buildings or equipment) required for an activity

in·fre·quent \(ˌ)in-ˈfrē-kwənt\ *adj* **1** : seldom happening : RARE **2** : placed or occurring at wide intervals in space or time ✦ *Synonyms* UNCOMMON, SCARCE, SPORADIC — **in·fre·quent·ly** *adv*

in·fringe \in-ˈfrinj\ *vb* **in·fringed; in·fring·ing 1** : VIOLATE, TRANSGRESS ⟨~ a patent⟩ **2** : ENCROACH, TRESPASS ⟨~ on our rights⟩ — **in·fringe·ment** *n*

in·fu·ri·ate \in-ˈfyùr-ē-ˌāt\ *vb* **-at·ed; -at·ing** : to make furious : ENRAGE — **in·fu·ri·at·ing·ly** *adv*

in·fuse \in-ˈfyüz\ *vb* **in·fused; in·fus·ing 1** : to instill a principle or quality in ⟨*infused* the team with confidence⟩ **2** : INSPIRE, ANIMATE **3** : to steep (as tea) without boiling — **in·fu·sion** \-ˈfyü-zhən\ *n*

¹-ing \iŋ\ *n suffix* **1** : action or process ⟨sleep*ing*⟩ : instance of an action or process ⟨a meet*ing*⟩ **2** : product or result of an action or process ⟨an engrav*ing*⟩ ⟨earn*ings*⟩ **3** : something used in an action or process ⟨a bed cover*ing*⟩ **4** : something connected with, consisting of, or used in making (a specified thing) ⟨scaffold*ing*⟩ **5** : something related to (a specified concept) ⟨off*ing*⟩

²-ing *n suffix* : one of a (specified) kind

³-ing *vb suffix or adj suffix* — used to form the present participle ⟨sail*ing*⟩ and sometimes to form an adjective resembling a present participle but not derived from a verb ⟨swashbuckl*ing*⟩

in·ga·ther \ˈin-ˌga-t͟hər\ *vb* : to gather in : ASSEMBLE

in·ge·nious \in-ˈjēn-yəs\ *adj* **1** : marked by special aptitude at discovering, inventing, or contriving **2** : marked by originality, resourcefulness, and cleverness in conception or execution — **in·ge·nious·ly** *adv* — **in·ge·nious·ness** *n*

in·ge·nue *or* **in·gé·nue** \ˈan-jə-ˌnü, ˈän-; ˈaⁿ-zhə-, ˈäⁿ-\ *n* : a naive girl or young woman; *esp* : an actress portraying such a person

in·ge·nu·i·ty \ˌin-jə-ˈnü-ə-tē, -ˈnyü-\ *n, pl* **-ties** : skill or cleverness in planning or inventing : INVENTIVENESS

in·gen·u·ous \in-ˈjen-yə-wəs\ *adj* [L *ingenuus* native, freeborn, fr. *gignere* to beget] **1** : innocently straightforward ⟨her ~ curiosity⟩ **2** : lacking craft or subtlety ⟨~ comments⟩ — **in·gen·u·ous·ly** *adv* — **in·gen·u·ous·ness** *n*

in·gest \in-ˈjest\ *vb* : to take in for or as if for digestion — **in·ges·tion** \-ˈjes-chən\ *n*

in·gle·nook \ˈiŋ-gəl-ˌnùk\ *n* : a nook by a large open fireplace; *also* : a bench occupying this nook

in·glo·ri·ous \(ˌ)in-ˈglòr-ē-əs\ *adj* **1** : SHAMEFUL **2** : not glorious : lacking fame or honor — **in·glo·ri·ous·ly** *adv*

in·got \ˈiŋ-gət\ *n* : a mass of metal cast in a form convenient for storage or transportation

¹in·grain \(ˌ)in-ˈgrān\ *vb* : to work indelibly into the natural texture or mental or moral constitution — **in·grained** *adj*

²in·grain \ˈin-ˌgrān\ *adj* **1** : made of fiber that is dyed before being spun into yarn **2** : made of yarn that is dyed before being woven or knitted **3** : INNATE — **in·grain** *n*

in·grate \ˈin-ˌgrāt\ *n* : an ungrateful person

in·gra·ti·ate \in-ˈgrā-shē-ˌāt\ *vb* **-at·ed; -at·ing** : to gain favor by deliberate effort

in·gra·ti·at·ing *adj* **1** : capable of winning favor : PLEASING ⟨an ~ smile⟩ **2** : FLATTERING ⟨an ~ manner⟩

in·grat·i·tude \(ˌ)in-ˈgra-tə-ˌtüd, -ˌtyüd\ *n* : lack of gratitude : UNGRATEFULNESS

in·gre·di·ent \in-ˈgrē-dē-ənt\ *n* : one of the substances that make up a mixture or compound : CONSTITUENT

in·gress \ˈin-ˌgres\ *n* : ENTRANCE, ACCESS — **in·gres·sion** \in-ˈgre-shən\ *n*

in·grow·ing \ˈin-ˌgrō-iŋ\ *adj* : growing or tending inward

in·grown \in-ˈgrōn\ *adj* : grown in; *esp* : having the free tip or edge embedded in the flesh ⟨an ~ toenail⟩

in·gui·nal \ˈiŋ-gwə-nᵊl\ *adj* : of, relating to, or situated in or near the region of the groin ⟨an ~ hernia⟩

in·hab·it \in-ˈha-bət\ *vb* : to live or dwell in ⟨spiders that ~ caves⟩ — **in·hab·it·able** *adj* — **in·hab·i·ta·tion** \in-ˌha-bə-ˈtā-shən\ *n*

in·hab·i·tant \in-ˈha-bə-tənt\ *n* : a permanent resident in a place

in·hal·ant \in-ˈhā-lənt\ *n* : something (as a medicine) that is inhaled

in·ha·la·tor \ˈin-hə-ˌlā-tər\ *n* : a device that provides a mixture of carbon dioxide and oxygen for breathing

in·hale \in-ˈhāl\ *vb* **in·haled; in·hal·ing** : to breathe in — **in·ha·la·tion** \ˌin-hə-ˈlā-shən\ *n*

in·hal·er \in-ˈhā-lər\ *n* : a device by means of which medicinal material is inhaled

in·here \in-ˈhir\ *vb* **in·hered; in·her·ing** : to be inherent

in·her·ent \in-ˈhir-ənt, -ˈher-\ *adj* : established as an essential part of something : INTRINSIC ⟨risks ~ in the venture⟩ — **in·her·ent·ly** *adv*

in·her·it \in-ˈher-ət\ *vb* **1** : to receive esp. from one's ancestors **2** : to receive by genetic transmission — **in·her·it·able** \-ə-tə-bəl\ *adj* — **in·her·i·tance** \-ə-təns\ *n* — **in·her·i·tor** \-ə-tər\ *n*

in·hib·it \in-ˈhi-bət\ *vb* **1** : PROHIBIT, FORBID **2** : to hold in check : RESTRAIN ⟨~ed by fear⟩ — **in·hib·i·tor** \-bə-tər\ *n* — **in·hib·i·to·ry** \-bə-ˌtòr-ē\ *adj*

in·hi·bi·tion \ˌin-hə-ˈbi-shən\ *n* **1** : PROHIBITION, RESTRAINT **2** : a usu. inner check on free activity, expression, or functioning

in–house \ˈin-ˌhaùs, -ˈhaùs\ *adj* : existing, originating, or carried on within a group or organization

in·hu·man \(ˌ)in-ˈhyü-mən, -ˈyü-\ *adj* **1** : lacking pity, kindness, or mercy : SAVAGE ⟨an ~ tyrant⟩ **2** : COLD, IMPERSONAL **3** : not worthy of or conforming to the needs of human beings ⟨~ living conditions⟩ **4** : of or suggesting a nonhuman class of beings — **in·hu·man·ly** *adv* — **in·hu·man·ness** *n*

in·hu·mane \ˌin-hyü-ˈmān, -yü-\ *adj* : not humane : INHUMAN 1

in·hu·man·i·ty \-ˈma-nə-tē\ *n, pl* **-ties 1** : the quality or state of being cruel or barbarous **2** : a cruel or barbarous act

in·im·i·cal \i-ˈni-mi-kəl\ *adj* **1** : being adverse often by reason of hostility ⟨forces ~ to change⟩ **2** : HOSTILE, UNFRIENDLY ⟨~ factions⟩ — **in·im·i·cal·ly** *adv*

in·im·i·ta·ble \(ˌ)i-ˈni-mə-tə-bəl\ *adj* : not capable of being imitated

in·iq·ui·ty \i-ˈni-kwə-tē\ *n, pl* **-ties** [ME *iniquite*, fr. AF *iniquité*, fr. L *iniquitas*, fr. *iniquus* uneven, fr. *aequus* equal] **1** : WICKEDNESS **2** : a wicked act — **in·iq·ui·tous** \-təs\ *adj*

¹ini·tial \i-ˈni-shəl\ *adj* **1** : of or relating to the beginning : INCIPIENT ⟨my ~ reaction⟩ **2** : being at the beginning — **ini·tial·ly** *adv*

²initial *n* : the first letter of a word or name

³initial *vb* **-tialed** *or* **-tialled; -tial·ing** *or* **-tial·ling** : to affix an initial to

¹ini·ti·ate \i-ˈni-shē-ˌāt\ *vb* **-at·ed; -at·ing 1** : START, BEGIN **2** : to induct into membership by or as if by special ceremonies **3** : to instruct in the rudiments or principles of something — **ini·ti·a·tion** \-ˌni-shē-ˈā-shən\ *n*

²ini·ti·ate \i-ˈni-shē-ət\ *n* **1** : a person who is undergoing or has passed an initiation **2** : a person who is instructed or adept in some special field

ini·tia·tive \i-ˈni-shə-tiv\ *n* **1** : an introductory step **2** : self-reliant enterprise ⟨showed great ~⟩ **3** : a process by which laws may be introduced or enacted directly by vote of the people

ini·tia·to·ry \i-ˈni-shē-ə-ˌtòr-ē\ *adj* **1** : INTRODUCTORY **2** : tending or serving to initiate ⟨~ rites⟩

in·ject \in-ˈjekt\ *vb* **1** : to force into something ⟨~ serum with a needle⟩ **2** : to introduce as an element into some situation or subject ⟨~ a note of suspicion⟩ — **in·jec·tion** \-ˈjek-shən\ *n*

in·junc·tion \in-ˈjəŋk-shən\ *n* **1** : ORDER, ADMONITION **2** : a court writ whereby one is required to do or to refrain from doing a specified act

in·jure \ˈin-jər\ *vb* **in·jured; in·jur·ing 1** : WRONG **2** : to damage or hurt esp. physically ✦ *Synonyms* HARM, IMPAIR, MAR, SPOIL

in·ju·ry \ˈin-jə-rē\ *n, pl* **-ries 1** : an act that damages or hurts : WRONG **2** : hurt, damage, or loss sustained — **in·ju·ri·ous** \in-ˈjùr-ē-əs\ *adj*

in·jus·tice \(ˌ)in-ˈjəs-təs\ *n* **1** : violation of a person's rights : UNFAIRNESS **2** : an unjust act or deed : WRONG

¹ink \ˈiŋk\ *n* [ME *enke*, fr. AF *encre, enke*, fr. LL *encaustum*, fr. L *encaustus* burned in, fr. Gk *enkaustos*, fr. *enkaiein* to burn in] : a usu. liquid and colored material for writing and printing — **inky** *adj*

²ink *vb* : to put ink on; *esp* : SIGN

ink·blot test \ˈiŋk-ˌblät-\ *n* : any of several psychological tests based on the interpretation of irregular figures

ink·horn \-ˌhòrn\ *n* : a small bottle (as of horn) for holding ink

in-kind \'in-'kīnd\ *adj* : consisting of something (as goods) other than money

ink-jet *n* : a computer printer that sprays electrically charged droplets of ink onto paper — **inkjet** *adj*

ink-ling \'iŋ-kliŋ\ *n* **1** : HINT, INTIMATION **2** : a vague idea

ink-stand \'iŋk-ˌstand\ *n* : INKWELL; *also* : a pen and ink stand

ink-well \-ˌwel\ *n* : a container for ink

in-laid \'in-'lād\ *adj* : decorated with material set into a surface

¹in-land \'in-ˌland, -lənd\ *adj* **1** *chiefly Brit* : not foreign : DOMESTIC ⟨~ revenue⟩ **2** : of or relating to the interior of a country ⟨the ~ states⟩

²inland *n* : the interior of a country

³inland *adv* : into or toward the interior

in–law \'in-ˌlȯ\ *n* : a relative by marriage

¹in-lay \(ˌ)in-'lā, 'in-ˌlā\ *vb* **in-laid** \-'lād\; **in-lay-ing** : to set (a material) into a surface or ground material esp. for decoration

²in-lay \'in-ˌlā\ *n* **1** : inlaid work **2** : a shaped filling cemented into a tooth

in-let \'in-ˌlet, -lət\ *n* **1** : a small or narrow bay **2** : an opening for intake esp. of a fluid

in-line skate *n* : a roller skate whose four wheels are set in a straight line — **in–line skater** *n* — **in–line skating** *n*

in-mate \'in-ˌmāt\ *n* : any of a group occupying a single place of residence; *esp* : a person confined (as in a hospital or prison)

in me-di-as res \in-ˌmä-dē-əs-'rās\ *adv* [L, lit., into the midst of things] : in or into the middle of a narrative or plot

in me-mo-ri-am \ˌin-mə-'mȯr-ē-əm\ *prep* [L] : in memory of

in-most \'in-ˌmōst\ *adj* : deepest within : INNERMOST

inn \'in\ *n* : HOTEL, TAVERN

in-nards \'i-nərdz\ *n pl* [alter. of *inwards*] **1** : the internal organs of a human being or animal; *esp* : VISCERA **2** : the internal parts of a structure or mechanism

in-nate \i-'nāt\ *adj* **1** : existing in, belonging to, or determined by factors present in an individual from birth : NATIVE **2** : INHERENT, INTRINSIC ⟨the ~ defects of a plan⟩ — **in-nate-ly** *adv*

in-ner \'i-nər\ *adj* **1** : situated farther in ⟨the ~ bark⟩ **2** : near a center esp. of influence ⟨the ~ circle⟩ **3** : of or relating to the mind or spirit ⟨an ~ voice⟩ **4** : being a usu. repressed part of one's psychological makeup ⟨the ~ child⟩

inner city *n* : the usu. older, poorer, and more densely populated section of a city — **inner–city** *adj*

in-ner-di-rect-ed \ˌi-nər-də-'rek-təd, -(ˌ)dī-\ *adj* : directed in thought and action by one's own scale of values as opposed to external norms

inner ear *n* : the part of the ear that is most important for hearing, is located in a cavity in the temporal bone, and contains sense organs of hearing and of awareness of position in space

in-ner-most \'i-nər-ˌmōst\ *adj* : farthest inward : INMOST

in-ner-sole \'i-nər-'sōl\ *n* : INSOLE

in-ner-spring \'i-nər-'spriŋ\ *adj* : having coil springs inside a padded casing ⟨an ~ mattress⟩

inner tube *n* : an airtight rubber tube inside a tire to hold air under pressure

in-ning \'i-niŋ\ *n* **1** *sing or pl* : a division of a cricket match **2** : a baseball team's turn at bat; *also* : a division of a baseball game consisting of a turn at bat for each team

inn-keep-er \'in-ˌkē-pər\ *n* **1** : a proprietor of an inn **2** : a hotel manager

in-no-cence \'i-nə-səns\ *n* **1** : BLAMELESSNESS; *also* : freedom from legal guilt **2** : GUILELESSNESS, SIMPLICITY; *also* : IGNORANCE

in-no-cent \-sənt\ *adj* [ME, fr. AF, fr. L *innocens*, fr. *nocens* wicked, fr. *nocēre* to harm] **1** : free from guilt or sin : BLAMELESS **2** : harmless in effect or intention; *also* : CANDID ⟨an ~ remark⟩ **3** : free from legal guilt or fault : LAWFUL **4** : INGENUOUS ⟨an ~ question⟩ **5** : UNAWARE — **innocent** *n* — **in-no-cent-ly** *adv*

in-noc-u-ous \i-'nä-kyə-wəs\ *adj* **1** : HARMLESS **2** : not offensive; *also* : INSIPID ⟨~ jokes⟩

in-nom-i-nate \i-'nä-mə-nət\ *adj* : having no name; *also* : ANONYMOUS

in-no-vate \'i-nə-ˌvāt\ *vb* **-vat-ed; -vat-ing** : to introduce as or as if new : make changes — **in-no-va-tive** \-ˌvā-tiv\ *adj* — **in-no-va-tor** \-ˌvā-tər\ *n*

in-no-va-tion \ˌi-nə-'vā-shən\ *n* **1** : the introduction of something new **2** : a new idea, method, or device

in-nu-en-do \ˌin-yə-'wen-dō\ *n, pl* **-dos** *or* **-does** [L, by nodding, fr. *innuere* to nod to, make a sign to, fr. *nuere* to nod] : HINT, INSINUATION; *esp* : a veiled reflection on character or reputation

in-nu-mer-a-ble \i-'nü-mə-rə-bəl, -'nyü-\ *adj* : too many to be numbered

in-oc-u-late \i-'nä-kyə-ˌlāt\ *vb* **-lat-ed; -lat-ing** [ME, to insert a bud in a plant, fr. L *inoculare*, fr. *oculus* eye, bud] : to introduce something into; *esp* : to introduce a serum or antibody into (an organism) to treat or prevent a disease — **in-oc-u-la-tion** \-ˌnä-kyə-'lā-shən\ *n*

in-op-er-a-ble \(ˌ)in-'ä-pə-rə-bəl\ *adj* **1** : not suitable for surgery ⟨an ~ tumor⟩ **2** : not operable ⟨~ vehicles⟩

in-op-er-a-tive \-'ä-pə-rə-tiv, -'ä-pə-ˌrā-\ *adj* : not functioning

in-op-por-tune \(ˌ)in-ˌä-pər-'tün, -'tyün\ *adj* : INCONVENIENT, INAPPROPRIATE — **in-op-por-tune-ly** *adv*

in-or-di-nate \in-'ȯr-dᵊn-ət\ *adj* : exceeding reasonable limits : IMMODERATE ⟨an ~ amount⟩ — **in-or-di-nate-ly** *adv*

in-or-gan-ic \ˌin-ȯr-'ga-nik\ *adj* : being or composed of matter of other than plant or animal origin : MINERAL

in-pa-tient \'in-ˌpā-shənt\ *n* : a hospital patient who receives lodging and food as well as treatment

in-put \'in-ˌpu̇t\ *n* **1** : something put in **2** : power or energy put into a machine or system **3** : information fed into a computer or data processing system **4** : ADVICE, OPINION — **input** *vb*

in-quest \'in-ˌkwest\ *n* **1** : an official inquiry or examination esp. before a jury **2** : INQUIRY, INVESTIGATION

in-qui-etude \(ˌ)in-'kwī-ə-ˌtüd, -ˌtyüd\ *n* : UNEASINESS, RESTLESSNESS

in-quire \in-'kwī(-ə)r\ *vb* **in-quired; in-quir-ing 1** : to ask about : ASK **2** : INVESTIGATE, EXAMINE — **in-quir-er** *n* — **in-quir-ing-ly** *adv*

in-qui-ry \'in-ˌkwī(-ə)r-ē, in-'kwī(-ə)r-ē; 'in-kwə-rē, 'iŋ-\ *n, pl* **-ries 1** : a request for information; *also* : RESEARCH **2** : a systematic investigation of a matter of public interest

in-qui-si-tion \ˌin-kwə-'zi-shən, ˌiŋ-\ *n* **1** : a judicial or official inquiry usu. before a jury **2** *cap* : a former Roman Catholic tribunal for the discovery and punishment of heresy **3** : a severe questioning — **in-quis-i-tor** \in-'kwi-zə-tər\ *n* — **in-quis-i-to-ri-al** \-ˌkwi-zə-'tȯr-ē-əl\ *adj*

in-quis-i-tive \in-'kwi-zə-tiv\ *adj* **1** : given to examination or investigation ⟨an ~ mind⟩ **2** : unduly curious — **in-quis-i-tive-ly** *adv* — **in-quis-i-tive-ness** *n*

in re \in-'rā, -'rē\ *prep* : in the matter of

INRI *abbr* [L *Iesus Nazarenus Rex Iudaeorum*] Jesus of Nazareth, King of the Jews

in-road \'in-ˌrōd\ *n* **1** : INVASION, RAID **2** : an advance made usu. at the expense of another ⟨made ~s toward getting the job⟩

in-rush \'in-ˌrəsh\ *n* : a crowding or flooding in

ins *abbr* **1** inches **2** insurance

INS *abbr* Immigration and Naturalization Service

in-sa-lu-bri-ous \ˌin-sə-'lü-brē-əs\ *adj* : UNWHOLESOME, NOXIOUS ⟨~ air⟩

ins and outs *n pl* **1** : characteristic peculiarities **2** : RAMIFICATIONS

in-sane \(ˌ)in-'sān\ *adj* **1** : exhibiting serious and debilitating mental disorder; *also* : used by or for the insane **2** : ABSURD **3** : greatly exceeding the ordinary, usual, or expected — **in-sane-ly** *adv* — **in-san-i-ty** \in-'sa-nə-tē\ *n*

in-sa-tia-ble \(ˌ)in-'sā-shə-bəl\ *adj* : incapable of being satisfied ⟨an ~ thirst⟩ — **in-sa-tia-bil-i-ty** \(ˌ)in-ˌsā-shə-'bi-lə-tē\ *n* — **in-sa-tia-bly** *adv*

in-sa-ti-ate \(ˌ)in-'sā-shē-ət, -shət\ *adj* : INSATIABLE — **in-sa-ti-ate-ly** *adv*

in-scribe \in-'skrīb\ *vb* **1** : to write, engrave, or print as a lasting record **2** : ENROLL **3** : to write, engrave, or print characters upon **4** : to dedicate to someone **5** : to draw within a figure so as to touch in as many places as possible — **in-scrip-tion** \-'skrip-shən\ *n*

in-scru-ta-ble \in-'skrü-tə-bəl\ *adj* : not readily comprehensible : MYSTERIOUS ⟨an ~ smile⟩ — **in-scru-ta-bly** \-blē\ *adv*

in-seam \'in-ˌsēm\ *n* : the seam on the inside of the leg of a pair of pants; *also* : the length of this seam

in-sect \'in-ˌsekt\ *n* [L *insectum*, fr. *insectus*, pp. of *insec-*

are to cut into, fr. *secure* to cut] : any of a class of small usu. winged arthropod animals (as flies, bees, beetles, and moths) with usu. three pairs of legs as adults

in·sec·ti·cide \in-'sek-tə-ˌsīd\ *n* : an agent for destroying insects — **in·sec·ti·cid·al** \(ˌ)in-ˌsek-tə-'sī-dᵊl\ *adj*

in·sec·tiv·o·rous \ˌin-ˌsek-'ti-və-rəs\ *adj* : feeding on insects

in·se·cure \ˌin-si-'kyûr\ 1 : UNCERTAIN 2 : not protected : UNSAFE ⟨an ~ investment⟩ 3 : LOOSE, SHAKY ⟨an ~ hinge⟩ 4 : not highly stable ⟨an ~ marriage⟩; *also* : lacking assurance : ANXIOUS, FEARFUL — **in·se·cure·ly** *adv* — **in·se·cu·ri·ty** \-'kyûr-ə-tē\ *n*

in·sem·i·nate \in-'se-mə-ˌnāt\ *vb* **-nat·ed; -nat·ing** : to introduce semen into the genital tract of (a female) — **in·sem·i·na·tion** \-ˌse-mə-'nā-shən\ *n*

in·sen·sate \(ˌ)in-'sen-ˌsāt, -sət\ *adj* 1 : lacking sense or understanding; *also* : FOOLISH 2 : INANIMATE 3 : BRUTAL, INHUMAN ⟨~ rage⟩

in·sen·si·ble \(ˌ)in-'sen-sə-bəl\ *adj* 1 : IMPERCEPTIBLE; *also* : SLIGHT, GRADUAL 2 : INANIMATE 3 : UNCONSCIOUS 4 : lacking sensory perception or ability to react ⟨~ to pain⟩ 5 : APATHETIC, INDIFFERENT; *also* : UNAWARE ⟨~ of their danger⟩ 6 : MEANINGLESS 7 : lacking delicacy or refinement — **in·sen·si·bil·i·ty** \-ˌsen-sə-'bi-lə-tē\ *n* — **in·sen·si·bly** \-'sen-sə-blē\ *adv*

in·sen·tient \(ˌ)in-'sen-chē-ənt\ *adj* : lacking perception, consciousness, or animation — **in·sen·tience** \-chē-əns\ *n*

in·sep·a·ra·ble \(ˌ)in-'se-prə-bəl, -pə-rə-\ *adj* 1 : incapable of being separated or disjoined 2 : very close or intimate ⟨~ friends⟩ — **in·sep·a·ra·bil·i·ty** \-ˌse-prə-'bi-lə-tē, -ˌpe-rə-\ *n* — **inseparable** *n* — **in·sep·a·ra·bly** \-'se-prə-blē, -pə-rə-\ *adv*

¹**in·sert** \in-'sərt\ *vb* 1 : to put or thrust in ⟨~ a key in a lock⟩ ⟨~ a comma⟩ 2 : INTERPOLATE 3 : to set in (as a piece of fabric) and make fast

²**in·sert** \'in-ˌsərt\ *n* : something that is inserted or is for insertion; *esp* : written or printed material inserted (as between the leaves of a book)

in·ser·tion \in-'sər-shən\ *n* 1 : something that is inserted 2 : the act or process of inserting

in·set \'in-ˌset\ *vb* **inset** *or* **in·set·ted; in·set·ting** : to set in : INSERT — **inset** *n*

¹**in·shore** \'in-'shôr\ *adj* 1 : situated, living, or carried on near shore 2 : moving toward shore ⟨an ~ current⟩

²**inshore** *adv* : to or toward shore

¹**in·side** \in-'sīd, 'in-ˌsīd\ *n* 1 : an inner side or surface : INTERIOR 2 : inward nature, thoughts, or feeling 3 *pl* : VISCERA, ENTRAILS 4 : a position of power, trust, or familiarity — **inside** *adj*

²**inside** *adv* 1 : on the inner side 2 : in or into the interior

³**inside** *prep* 1 : in or into the inside of ⟨~ the house⟩ 2 : WITHIN ⟨~ an hour⟩

inside of *prep* : INSIDE

inside out *adv* 1 : in such a manner that the inner surface becomes the outer ⟨turned the shirt *inside out*⟩ 2 : in a state of disarray or reorganization ⟨turned her life *inside out*⟩

in·sid·er \in-'sī-dər\ *n* : a person who is in a position of power or has access to confidential information

in·sid·i·ous \in-'si-dē-əs\ *adj* [L *insidiosus,* fr. *insidiae* ambush, fr. *insidēre* to sit in, sit on, fr. *sedēre* to sit] 1 : SLY, TREACHEROUS 2 : SEDUCTIVE 3 : having a gradual and cumulative effect : SUBTLE — **in·sid·i·ous·ly** *adv* — **in·sid·i·ous·ness** *n*

in·sight \'in-ˌsīt\ *n* : the power, act, or result of seeing into a situation : UNDERSTANDING ⟨a leader of great ~⟩ — **in·sight·ful** \'in-ˌsīt-fəl, in-'sīt-\ *adj*

in·sig·nia \in-'sig-nē-ə\ *also* **in·sig·ne** \-(ˌ)nē\ *n, pl* **-nia** *or* **-ni·as** : a distinguishing mark esp. of authority or honor : BADGE

in·sin·cere \ˌin-sin-'sir\ *adj* : not sincere : HYPOCRITICAL — **in·sin·cere·ly** *adv* — **in·sin·cer·i·ty** \-'ser-ə-tē\ *n*

in·sin·u·ate \in-'sin-yə-ˌwāt\ *vb* **-at·ed; -at·ing** [L *insinuare,* fr. *sinuare* to bend, curve, fr. *sinus* curve] 1 : to introduce gradually or in a subtle, indirect, or artful way 2 : to imply in a subtle or devious way — **in·sin·u·a·tion** \(ˌ)in-ˌsin-yə-'wā-shən\ *n*

in·sin·u·at·ing *adj* 1 : winning favor and confidence by imperceptible degrees 2 : tending gradually to cause doubt, distrust, or change of outlook

in·sip·id \in-'si-pəd\ *adj* 1 : lacking taste or savor 2

: DULL, FLAT ⟨an ~ movie⟩ — **in·si·pid·i·ty** \ˌin-sə-'pi-də-tē\ *n*

in·sist \in-'sist\ *vb* [MF or L; MF *insister,* fr. L *insistere* to stand upon, persist, fr. *sistere* to take a stand] : to take a resolute stand ⟨~ed on paying⟩

in·sis·tence \in-'sis-təns\ *n* : the act of insisting; *also* : an insistent attitude or quality : URGENCY

in·sis·tent \in-'sis-tənt\ *adj* : disposed to insist — **in·sis·tent·ly** *adv*

in si·tu \in-'sī-tü, -'sē-\ *adv or adj* [L, in position] : in the natural or original position ⟨an *in situ* cancer⟩

in·so·far as \ˌin-sə-'fär-\ *conj* : to the extent or degree that

insol *abbr* insoluble

in·so·la·tion \ˌin-(ˌ)sō-'lā-shən\ *n* : solar radiation that has been received

in·sole \'in-ˌsōl\ *n* 1 : an inside sole of a shoe 2 : a loose thin strip placed inside a shoe for warmth or comfort

in·so·lent \'in-sə-lənt\ *adj* : contemptuous, rude, disrespectful, or bold in behavior or language — **in·so·lence** \-ləns\ *n*

in·sol·u·ble \(ˌ)in-'säl-yə-bəl\ *adj* 1 : having or admitting of no solution or explanation 2 : difficult or impossible to dissolve — **in·sol·u·bil·i·ty** \-ˌsäl-yə-'bi-lə-tē\ *n*

in·sol·vent \(ˌ)in-'säl-vənt\ *adj* 1 : unable or insufficient to pay all debts ⟨an ~ estate⟩ 2 : IMPOVERISHED, DEFICIENT — **in·sol·ven·cy** \-vən-sē\ *n*

in·som·nia \in-'säm-nē-ə\ *n* : prolonged and usu. abnormal sleeplessness — **in·som·ni·ac** \-nē-ˌak\ *n*

in·so·much as \ˌin-sə-'məch-\ *conj* : INASMUCH AS

insomuch that *conj* : to such a degree that : so

in·sou·ci·ance \in-'sü-sē-əns, aⁿ-süs-'yäⁿs\ *n* [F] : lighthearted unconcern ⟨youthful ~⟩ — **in·sou·ci·ant** \in-'sü-sē-ənt, aⁿ-süs-'yäⁿ\ *adj*

insp *abbr* inspector

in·spect \in-'spekt\ *vb* : to view closely and critically : EXAMINE ⟨~ the gem for flaws⟩ — **in·spec·tion** \-'spek-shən\ *n* — **in·spec·tor** \-tər\ *n*

inspector general *n* : the head of a system of inspection (as of an army)

in·spi·ra·tion \ˌin-spə-'rā-shən\ *n* 1 : the act or power of moving the intellect or emotions 2 : INHALATION 3 : the quality or state of being inspired; *also* : something that is inspired 4 : an inspiring agent or influence — **in·spi·ra·tion·al** \-shə-nəl\ *adj*

in·spire \in-'spīr\ *vb* **in·spired; in·spir·ing** 1 : to influence, move, or guide by divine or supernatural inspiration 2 : to exert an animating, enlivening, or exalting influence upon ⟨a painter *inspired* by cubism⟩; *also* : AFFECT 3 : to communicate to an agent supernaturally; *also* : bring out or about 4 : INHALE 5 : INCITE 6 : to spread by indirect means — **in·spir·er** *n*

in·spir·it \in-'spir-ət\ *vb* : ENCOURAGE, HEARTEN ⟨~ed the team⟩

inst *abbr* 1 instant 2 institute; institution; institutional

in·sta·bil·i·ty \ˌin-stə-'bi-lə-tē\ *n* : lack of steadiness; *esp* : lack of emotional or mental stability

in·stal *chiefly Brit var of* INSTALL

in·stall \in-'stöl\ *vb* 1 : to place formally in office : induct into an office, rank, or order 2 : to establish in an indicated place, condition, or status 3 : to set up for use or service — **in·stal·la·tion** \ˌin-stə-'lā-shən\ *n*

¹**in·stall·ment** *also* **in·stal·ment** \in-'stöl-mənt\ *n* : INSTALLATION

²**installment** *also* **instalment** *n* 1 : one of the parts into which a debt or sum is divided for payment 2 : one of several parts presented at intervals

¹**in·stance** \'in-stəns\ *n* 1 : INSTIGATION, REQUEST 2 : EXAMPLE ⟨for ~⟩ 3 : an event or step that is part of a process or series ♦ **Synonyms** CASE, ILLUSTRATION, SAMPLE, SPECIMEN

²**instance** *vb* **in·stanced; in·stanc·ing** : to mention as a case or example

¹**in·stant** \'in-stənt\ *n* 1 : MOMENT ⟨the ~ we met⟩ 2 : the present or current month

²**instant** *adj* 1 : URGENT 2 : PRESENT, CURRENT 3 : IMMEDIATE ⟨~ relief⟩ 4 : premixed or precooked for easy final preparation ⟨~ cake mix⟩; *also* : immediately soluble in water ⟨~ coffee⟩

in·stan·ta·neous \ˌin-stən-'tā-nē-əs\ *adj* : done or occurring in an instant or without delay ⟨an ~ chemical reaction⟩ — **in·stan·ta·neous·ly** *adv*

in·stan·ter \in-ˈstan-tər\ *adv* : at once

in·stan·ti·ate \in-ˈstan-chē-ˌāt\ *vb* -**at·ed; -at·ing** : to represent (an abstraction) by a concrete example — **in·stan·ti·a·tion** \-ˌstan-chē-ˈā-shən\ *n*

in·stant·ly \ˈin-stənt-lē\ *adv* : at once : IMMEDIATELY

instant messaging *n* : a means or system for transmitting electronic messages instantly — **instant message** *n or vb*

in·state \in-ˈstāt\ *vb* : to establish in a rank or office : INSTALL

in·stead \in-ˈsted\ *adv* **1** : as a substitute or equivalent **2** : as an alternative

instead of *prep* : as a substitute for or alternative to ⟨use glue *instead of* paste⟩

in·step \ˈin-ˌstep\ *n* : the arched part of the human foot in front of the ankle joint; *esp* : its upper surface

in·sti·gate \ˈin-stə-ˌgāt\ *vb* -**gat·ed; -gat·ing** : to goad or urge forward : PROVOKE, INCITE ⟨∼ a revolt⟩ — **in·sti·ga·tion** \ˌin-stə-ˈgā-shən\ *n* — **in·sti·ga·tor** \ˈin-stə-ˌgā-tər\ *n*

in·stil *chiefly Brit var of* INSTILL

in·still \in-ˈstil\ *vb* **1** : to cause to enter drop by drop **2** : to impart gradually

¹in·stinct \ˈin-ˌstiŋkt\ *n* **1** : a natural aptitude **2** : a largely inheritable and unalterable tendency of an organism to make a complex and specific response to environmental stimuli without involving reason; *also* : behavior originating below the conscious level — **in·stinc·tive** \in-ˈstiŋk-tiv\ *adj* — **in·stinc·tive·ly** *adv*

²in·stinct \in-ˈstiŋkt, ˈin-ˌstiŋkt\ *adj* : IMBUED, INFUSED

in·stinc·tu·al \in-ˈstiŋk-chə-wəl\ *adj* : of, relating to, or based on instinct

¹in·sti·tute \ˈin-stə-ˌtüt, -ˌtyüt\ *vb* -**tut·ed; -tut·ing 1** : to establish in a position or office **2** : ORGANIZE **3** : INAUGURATE, INITIATE ⟨∼ a new policy⟩

²institute *n* **1** : an elementary principle recognized as authoritative; *also, pl* : a collection of such principles and precepts **2** : an organization for the promotion of a cause : ASSOCIATION **3** : an educational institution **4** : a brief course of instruction on a particular field

in·sti·tu·tion \ˌin-stə-ˈtü-shən, -ˈtyü-\ *n* **1** : an act of originating, setting up, or founding **2** : an established practice, law, or custom **3** : a society or corporation esp. of a public character ⟨a charitable ∼⟩; *also* : ASYLUM **3** — **in·sti·tu·tion·al** \-ˈtü-shə-nəl, -ˈtyü-\ *adj* — **in·sti·tu·tion·al·ize** \-nə-ˌlīz\ *vb* — **in·sti·tu·tion·al·ly** *adv*

instr *abbr* **1** instructor **2** instrument; instrumental

in·struct \in-ˈstrəkt\ *vb* [ME, fr. L *instructus*, pp. of *instruere*, fr. *struere* to build] **1** : TEACH **2** : INFORM **3** : to give an order or a command to

in·struc·tion \in-ˈstrək-shən\ *n* **1** : LESSON, PRECEPT **2** : COMMAND, ORDER **3** *pl* : DIRECTIONS **4** : the action, practice, or profession of a teacher — **in·struc·tion·al** \-shə-nəl\ *adj*

in·struc·tive \in-ˈstrək-tiv\ *adj* : carrying a lesson : ENLIGHTENING ⟨an ∼ book⟩

in·struc·tor \in-ˈstrək-tər\ *n* : one that instructs; *esp* : a college teacher below professorial rank — **in·struc·tor·ship** *n*

in·stru·ment \ˈin-strə-mənt\ *n* **1** : a device used to produce music **2** : a means by which something is done **3** : a device for doing work and esp. precision work ⟨a drafting ∼⟩ **4** : a legal document (as a deed) **5** : a device used in navigating an airplane — **in·stru·ment** \-ˌment\ *vb*

in·stru·men·tal \ˌin-strə-ˈmen-tᵊl\ *adj* **1** : acting as a crucial agent or means ⟨was ∼ in arranging the deal⟩ **2** : of, relating to, or done with an instrument **3** : relating to, composed for, or performed on a musical instrument

in·stru·men·tal·ist \-ˈmen-tə-list\ *n* : a player on a musical instrument

in·stru·men·tal·i·ty \ˌin-strə-mən-ˈta-lə-tē, -ˌmen-\ *n, pl* -**ties 1** : the quality or state of being instrumental **2** : MEANS, AGENCY

in·stru·men·ta·tion \ˌin-strə-mən-ˈtā-shən, -ˌmen-\ *n* **1** : ORCHESTRATION **2** : instruments for a particular purpose

instrument panel *n* : DASHBOARD

in·sub·or·di·nate \ˌin-sə-ˈbȯr-də-nət\ *adj* : disobedient to authority — **in·sub·or·di·na·tion** \-ˌbȯr-də-ˈnā-shən\ *n*

in·sub·stan·tial \ˌin-səb-ˈstan-chəl\ *adj* **1** : lacking substance or reality **2** : lacking firmness or solidity

in·suf·fer·able \(ˌ)in-ˈsə-fə-rə-bəl\ *adj* : not to be endured : INTOLERABLE ⟨an ∼ bore⟩ — **in·suf·fer·ably** \-blē\ *adv*

in·suf·fi·cient \ˌin-sə-ˈfi-shənt\ *adj* : not sufficient ⟨∼ funds⟩; *also* : lacking capacity — **in·suf·fi·cien·cy** \-shən-sē\ *n* — **in·suf·fi·cient·ly** *adv*

in·su·lar \ˈin-sə-lər, -syə-\ *adj* **1** : of, relating to, or forming an island **2** : dwelling or situated on an island **3** : NARROW-MINDED ⟨an ∼ perspective⟩ — **in·su·lar·i·ty** \ˌin-sə-ˈlar-ə-tē, -syə-\ *n*

in·su·late \ˈin-sə-ˌlāt\ *vb* -**lat·ed; -lat·ing** [L *insula* island] : ISOLATE; *esp* : to separate a conductor of electricity, heat, or sound from other conducting bodies by means of a nonconductor — **in·su·la·tion** \ˌin-sə-ˈlā-shən\ *n* — **in·su·la·tor** \ˈin-sə-ˌlā-tər\ *n*

in·su·lin \ˈin-sə-lən\ *n* : a pancreatic hormone essential esp. for the metabolism of carbohydrates and the regulation of glucose levels in the blood

¹in·sult \in-ˈsəlt\ *vb* [MF or L; MF *insulter*, fr. L *insultare*, lit., to spring upon, fr. *saltare* to leap] : to treat with insolence or contempt : AFFRONT ⟨were ∼ed by his rudeness⟩ — **in·sult·ing·ly** *adv*

²in·sult \ˈin-ˌsəlt\ *n* : a gross indignity

in·su·per·a·ble \(ˌ)in-ˈsü-pə-rə-bəl\ *adj* : incapable of being surmounted, overcome, passed over, or solved — **in·su·per·a·bly** \-blē\ *adv*

in·sup·port·able \ˌin-sə-ˈpȯr-tə-bəl\ *adj* **1** : UNENDURABLE **2** : UNJUSTIFIABLE

in·sur·able \in-ˈshu̇r-ə-bəl\ *adj* : capable of being or proper to be insured

in·sur·ance \in-ˈshu̇r-əns\ *n* **1** : the business of insuring persons or property **2** : coverage by contract whereby one party agrees to guarantee another against a specified loss **3** : the sum for which something is insured **4** : a means of guaranteeing protection or safety

in·sure \in-ˈshu̇r\ *vb* **in·sured; in·sur·ing 1** : to provide or obtain insurance on or for : UNDERWRITE **2** : to make certain : ENSURE

in·sured \in-ˈshu̇rd\ *n* : a person whose life or property is insured

in·sur·er \in-ˈshu̇r-ər\ *n* : one that insures; *esp* : an insurance company

in·sur·gent \in-ˈsər-jənt\ *n* **1** : a person who revolts against civil authority or an established government : REBEL **2** : a member of a political party who rebels against it — **in·sur·gence** \-jəns\ *n* — **in·sur·gen·cy** \-jən-sē\ *n* — **in·sur·gent** *adj*

in·sur·mount·able \ˌin-sər-ˈmau̇n-tə-bəl\ *adj* : INSUPERABLE ⟨∼ problems⟩ — **in·sur·mount·ably** \-blē\ *adv*

in·sur·rec·tion \ˌin-sə-ˈrek-shən\ *n* : an act or instance of revolting against civil authority or an established government — **in·sur·rec·tion·ist** \-shə-nist\ *n*

int *abbr* **1** interest **2** interior **3** intermediate **4** internal **5** international **6** intransitive

in·tact \in-ˈtakt\ *adj* : untouched esp. by anything that harms or diminishes

in·ta·glio \in-ˈtal-yō\ *n, pl* -**glios** [It] : an engraving cut deeply into the surface of a hard material (as stone)

intaglio

in·take \ˈin-ˌtāk\ *n* **1** : an opening through which fluid enters **2** : the act of taking in **3** : something taken in

¹in·tan·gi·ble \(ˌ)in-ˈtan-jə-bəl\ *adj* : incapable of being touched : IMPALPABLE ⟨∼ benefits⟩ — **in·tan·gi·bly** \-blē\ *adv*

²intangible *n* **1** : an incorporeal asset **2** : an abstract quality or attribute

in·te·ger \'in-ti-jər\ *n* [L, adj., whole, entire] : a number (as 1, 2, 3, 12, 432) that is not a fraction and does not include a fraction, is the negative of such a number, or is 0

¹**in·te·gral** \'in-ti-grəl\ *adj* 1 : essential to completeness ⟨∼ to the company⟩ 2 : formed as a unit with another part 3 : composed of parts that make up a whole 4 : ENTIRE

²**integral** *n* : the result of a mathematical integration

in·te·grate \'in-tə-ˌgrāt\ *vb* -grat·ed; -grat·ing 1 : to find a function that has a given derivative 2 : to form, coordinate, or blend into a functioning whole : UNITE 3 : to incorporate into a larger unit 4 : to end the segregation of and bring into equal membership in society or an organization; *also* : DESEGREGATE — **in·te·gra·tion** \ˌin-tə-'grā-shən\ *n*

integrated circuit *n* : a group of tiny electronic components and their connections that is produced in or on a small slice of material (as silicon)

in·teg·ri·ty \in-'te-grə-tē\ *n* 1 : adherence to a code of values : INCORRUPTIBILITY 2 : SOUNDNESS 3 : COMPLETENESS

in·teg·u·ment \in-'te-gyə-mənt\ *n* : a covering layer (as a skin or cuticle) of an organism or one of its parts

in·tel·lect \'in-tə-ˌlekt\ *n* 1 : the power of knowing : the capacity for knowledge 2 : the capacity for rational or intelligent thought esp. when highly developed 3 : a person with great intellectual powers

in·tel·lec·tu·al \ˌin-tə-'lek-chə-wəl\ *adj* 1 : of, relating to, or performed by the intellect : RATIONAL 2 : given to study, reflection, and speculation ⟨∼ games⟩ 3 : engaged in activity requiring the creative use of the intellect — **intellectual** *n* — **in·tel·lec·tu·al·ly** *adv*

intellectual disability *n* : significant impairment in intellectual ability accompanied by deficits in skills necessary for independent daily functioning : MENTAL RETARDATION

in·tel·lec·tu·al·ism \-chə-wə-ˌli-zəm\ *n* : devotion to the exercise of intellect or to intellectual pursuits

in·tel·li·gence \in-'te-lə-jəns\ *n* 1 : ability to learn and understand or to deal with new or trying situations 2 : mental acuteness 3 : INFORMATION, NEWS 4 : an agency engaged in obtaining information esp. concerning an enemy or possible enemy; *also* : the information so gained

intelligence quotient *n* : IQ

in·tel·li·gent \in-'te-lə-jənt\ *adj* [L *intelligens*, fr. *intelligere* to understand, fr. *inter* between + *legere* to select] : having or showing intelligence or intellect ⟨an ∼ decision⟩ — **in·tel·li·gent·ly** *adv*

in·tel·li·gent·sia \in-ˌte-lə-'jent-sē-ə, -'gent-\ *n* [Russ *intelligentsiya*, fr. L *intelligentia* intelligence] : intellectuals forming a vanguard or elite

in·tel·li·gi·ble \in-'te-lə-jə-bəl\ *adj* : capable of being understood or comprehended ⟨a very ∼ plan⟩ — **in·tel·li·gi·bil·i·ty** \-ˌte-lə-jə-'bi-lə-tē\ *n* — **in·tel·li·gi·bly** \-'te-lə-jə-blē\ *adv*

in·tem·per·ance \(ˌ)in-'tem-pə-rəns\ *n* : lack of moderation; *esp* : habitual or excessive drinking of intoxicants — **in·tem·per·ate** \-pə-rət\ *adj* — **in·tem·per·ate·ness** *n*

in·tend \in-'tend\ *vb* [ME *entenden*, *intenden*, fr. AF *entendre*, fr. L *intendere* to stretch out, direct, aim at, fr. *tendere* to stretch] 1 : to have in mind as a purpose or aim ⟨∼s to retire⟩ 2 : to design for a specified use or future ⟨programs ∼ed to help students⟩

in·ten·dant \in-'ten-dənt\ *n* : an official (as a governor) esp. under the French, Spanish, or Portuguese monarchies

¹**in·tend·ed** *adj* 1 : expected to be such in the future; *esp* : BETROTHED 2 : INTENTIONAL ⟨an ∼ pun⟩

²**intended** *n* : an engaged person

in·tense \in-'tens\ *adj* 1 : existing in an extreme degree ⟨∼ pain⟩ 2 : marked by great zeal, energy, or eagerness ⟨∼ effort⟩ 3 : showing strong feeling; *also* : deeply felt — **in·tense·ly** *adv*

in·ten·si·fy \in-'ten-sə-ˌfī\ *vb* -fied; -fy·ing 1 : to make or become intense or more intensive 2 : to make more acute : SHARPEN ✦ *Synonyms* AGGRAVATE, HEIGHTEN, ENHANCE, MAGNIFY — **in·ten·si·fi·ca·tion** \-ˌten-sə-fə-'kā-shən\ *n*

in·ten·si·ty \in-'ten-sə-tē\ *n, pl* -ties 1 : the quality or state of being intense; *esp* : degree of strength, energy, or force

¹**in·ten·sive** \in-'ten-siv\ *adj* 1 : highly concentrated 2 : serving to give emphasis — **in·ten·sive·ly** *adv*

²**intensive** *n* : an intensive word, particle, or prefix ⟨the word "very" is an ∼⟩

intensive care *n* : continuous monitoring and treatment of seriously ill patients; *also* : an area of a hospital providing this treatment

¹**in·tent** \in-'tent\ *n* 1 : the state of mind with which an act is done : VOLITION 2 : PURPOSE, AIM ⟨the artist's ∼⟩ 3 : MEANING, SIGNIFICANCE

²**intent** *adj* 1 : directed with keen attention ⟨an ∼ gaze⟩ 2 : ENGROSSED; *also* : DETERMINED ⟨∼ on winning⟩ — **in·tent·ly** *adv* — **in·tent·ness** *n*

in·ten·tion \in-'ten-chən\ *n* 1 : a determination to act in a certain way 2 : PURPOSE, AIM, END ✦ *Synonyms* INTENT, DESIGN, OBJECT, OBJECTIVE, GOAL

in·ten·tion·al \in-'ten-chə-nəl\ *adj* : done by intention or design : INTENDED — **in·ten·tion·al·ly** *adv*

in·ter \in-'tər\ *vb* **in·terred**; **in·ter·ring** : BURY

in·ter·ac·tion \ˌin-tər-'ak-shən\ *n* : mutual or reciprocal action or influence — **in·ter·act** \-'akt\ *vb*

in·ter·ac·tive \-'ak-tiv\ *adj* 1 : mutually or reciprocally active 2 : involving the actions or input of a user ⟨∼ exhibits⟩ 3 : allowing two-way electronic communications (as between a person and a computer) — **in·ter·ac·tive·ly** *adv* — **in·ter·ac·tiv·i·ty** \-ˌak-'ti-və-tē\ *n*

in·ter alia \ˌin-tər-'ā-lē-ə, -'ä-\ *adv* : among other things

in·ter·atom·ic \ˌin-tər-ə-'tä-mik\ *adj* : existing or acting between atoms

in·ter·breed \-'brēd\ *vb* -bred \-'bred\; -breed·ing : to breed together

in·ter·ca·la·ry \in-'tər-kə-ˌler-ē\ *adj* 1 : INTERCALATED ⟨February 29 is an ∼ day⟩ 2 : INTERPOLATED

in·ter·ca·late \-ˌlāt\ *vb* -lat·ed; -lat·ing 1 : to insert (as a day) in a calendar 2 : to insert between or among existing elements or layers — **in·ter·ca·la·tion** \-ˌtər-kə-'lā-shən\ *n*

in·ter·cede \ˌin-tər-'sēd\ *vb* -ced·ed; -ced·ing : to act between parties with a view to reconciling differences

¹**in·ter·cept** \ˌin-tər-'sept\ *vb* 1 : to stop or interrupt the progress or course of 2 : to include (as part of a curve or solid) between two points, curves, or surfaces 3 : to gain possession of (an opponent's pass) — **in·ter·cep·tion** \-'sep-shən\ *n*

²**in·ter·cept** \'in-tər-ˌsept\ *n* : INTERCEPTION; *esp* : the interception of a target by an interceptor or missile

in·ter·cep·tor \ˌin-tər-'sep-tər\ *n* : a fighter plane designed for defense against attacking bombers

in·ter·ces·sion \ˌin-tər-'se-shən\ *n* 1 : MEDIATION 2 : prayer or petition in favor of another — **in·ter·ces·sor** \-'se-sər\ *n* — **in·ter·ces·so·ry** \-'se-sə-rē\ *adj*

¹**in·ter·change** \ˌin-tər-'chānj\ *vb* 1 : to put each in the place of the other 2 : EXCHANGE 3 : to change places mutually — **in·ter·change·able** \-'chān-jə-bəl\ *adj* — **in·ter·change·ably** \-blē\ *adv*

²**in·ter·change** \'in-tər-ˌchānj\ *n* 1 : EXCHANGE 2 : a highway junction that by separated levels permits passage between highways without crossing traffic streams

in·ter·col·le·giate \ˌin-tər-kə-'lē-jət\ *adj* : existing or carried on between colleges ⟨∼ sports⟩

in·ter·com \'in-tər-ˌkäm\ *n* : a two-way system for localized communication

in·ter·con·nect \ˌin-tər-kə-'nekt\ *vb* : to connect with one another — **in·ter·con·nec·tion** \-'nek-shən\ *n*

in·ter·con·ti·nen·tal \ˌin-tər-ˌkän-tə-'nen-tᵊl\ *adj* 1 : extending among or carried on between continents ⟨∼ trade⟩ 2 : capable of traveling between continents ⟨∼ ballistic missiles⟩

in·ter·course \'in-tər-ˌkȯrs\ *n* 1 : connection or dealings between persons or nations 2 : physical sexual contact between individuals that involves the genitalia of at least one person ⟨anal ∼⟩; *esp* : SEXUAL INTERCOURSE

in·ter·de·nom·i·na·tion·al \ˌin-tər-di-ˌnä-mə-'nā-shə-nəl\ *adj* : involving different denominations

in·ter·de·part·men·tal \ˌin-tər-di-ˌpärt-'men-tᵊl, -ˌdē-\ *adj* : carried on between or involving different departments (as of a college)

in·ter·de·pen·dent \ˌin-tər-di-'pen-dənt\ *adj* : dependent upon one another — **in·ter·de·pen·dence** \-dəns\ *n*

in·ter·dict \ˌin-tər-'dikt\ *vb* 1 : to prohibit by decree 2 : to destroy, cut off, or damage (as an enemy line of supply) 3 : INTERCEPT ⟨∼ed drug shipments⟩ — **in·ter·dic·tion** \-'dik-shən\ *n* in·ter·dis·ci·plin·ary \-'di-sə-plə-,ner-ē\ adj : involving two or more academic, scientific, or artistic disciplines

¹in·ter·est \'in-trəst; 'in-tə-rəst, -,rest\ n 1 : right, title, or legal share in something 2 : a charge for borrowed money that is generally a percentage of the amount borrowed; also : the return received by capital on its investment 3 : WELFARE, BENEFIT; also : SELF-INTEREST 4 : CURIOSITY, CONCERN 5 : readiness to be concerned with or moved by an object or class of objects 6 : a quality in a thing that arouses interest

²interest vb 1 : to persuade to participate or engage 2 : to engage the attention of

in·ter·est·ing adj : holding the attention — in·ter·est·ing·ly adv

¹in·ter·face \'in-tər-,fās\ n 1 : a surface forming a common boundary of two bodies, spaces, or phases ⟨an oil-water ∼⟩ 2 : the place at which two independent systems meet and act on or communicate with each other ⟨the man-machine ∼⟩ 3 : the means by which interaction or communication is achieved at an interface — in·ter·fa·cial \,in-tər-'fā-shəl\ adj

²interface vb -faced; -fac·ing 1 : to connect by means of an interface 2 : to serve as an interface

in·ter·faith \,in-tər-'fāth\ adj : involving persons of different religious faiths

in·ter·fere \,in-tər-'fir\ vb -fered; -fer·ing [ME enterferen, fr. AF (s')entreferir to strike one another, fr. entre between, among + ferir to strike, fr. L ferire] 1 : to come in collision or be in opposition : CLASH 2 : to enter into the affairs of others 3 : to affect one another

in·ter·fer·ence \-'fir-əns\ n 1 : the act or process of interfering 2 : something that interferes : OBSTRUCTION 3 : the mutual effect on meeting of two waves resulting in areas of increased and decreased amplitude 4 : the blocking of an opponent in football to make way for the ball-carrier 5 : the illegal hindering of an opponent in sports

in·ter·om·e·ter \,in-tər-fə-'rä-mə-tər\ n : an apparatus that uses the interference of waves (as of light) for making precise measurements — in·ter·fer·om·e·try \-fə-'rä-mə-trē\ n

in·ter·fer·on \,in-tər-'fir-,än\ n : any of a group of antiviral proteins of low molecular weight produced usu. by animal cells in response to a virus, a parasite in the cell, or a chemical

in·ter·ga·lac·tic \,in-tər-gə-'lak-tik\ adj : relating to or situated in the spaces between galaxies

in·ter·gen·er·a·tion·al \-,je-nə-'rā-shə-nəl\ adj : existing or occurring between generations ⟨∼ conflicts⟩

in·ter·gla·cial \-'glā-shəl\ n : a warm period between successive glaciations

in·ter·gov·ern·men·tal \-,gə-vərn-'men-t³l\ adj : existing or occurring between two governments or levels of government

in·ter·im \'in-tə-rəm\ n [L, adv., meanwhile, fr. inter between] : a time intervening : INTERVAL — interim adj

¹in·te·ri·or \in-'tir-ē-ər\ adj 1 : lying, occurring, or functioning within the limiting boundaries : INSIDE, INNER 2 : remote from the surface, border, or shore : INLAND

²interior n 1 : the inland part (as of a country) 2 : INSIDE 3 : the internal affairs of a state or nation 4 : a scene or view of the interior of a building

interior decoration n : INTERIOR DESIGN — interior decorator n

interior design n : the art or practice of planning and supervising the design and execution of architectural interiors and their furnishings — interior designer n

interj abbr interjection

in·ter·ject \,in-tər-'jekt\ vb : to throw in between or among other things

in·ter·jec·tion \,in-tər-'jek-shən\ n : an exclamatory word (as ouch) — in·ter·jec·tion·al·ly \-shə-nə-lē\ adv

in·ter·lace \,in-tər-'lās\ vb 1 : to unite by or as if by lacing together : INTERWEAVE 2 : INTERSPERSE

in·ter·lard \,in-tər-'lärd\ vb : to vary by inserting or interjecting something ⟨a speech ∼ed with anecdotes⟩

in·ter·leave \,in-tər-'lēv\ vb -leaved; -leav·ing : to arrange in alternate layers

in·ter·leu·kin \,in-tər-'lü-kən\ n : any of several proteins of low molecular weight that are produced by cells of the body and regulate the immune system and immune responses

¹in·ter·line \,in-tər-'līn\ vb : to insert between lines already written or printed

²interline vb : to provide (as a coat) with an interlining

in·ter·lin·ear \,in-tər-'li-nē-ər\ adj : inserted between lines already written or printed ⟨an ∼ translation of a text⟩

in·ter·lin·gual \,in-tər-'liŋ-gwəl\ adj : of, relating to, or existing between two or more languages

in·ter·lin·ing \'in-tər-,lī-niŋ\ n : a lining (as of a coat) between the ordinary lining and the outside fabric

in·ter·link \,in-tər-'liŋk\ vb : to link together

in·ter·lock \,in-tər-'läk\ vb 1 : to engage or interlace together : lock together : UNITE 2 : to connect so that action of one part affects action of another part — in·ter·lock \'in-tər-,läk\ n

in·ter·loc·u·tor \,in-tər-'lä-kyə-tər\ n : one who takes part in dialogue or conversation

in·ter·loc·u·to·ry \,in-tər-'lä-kyə-,tȯr-ē\ adj : made during the progress of a legal action and not final or definite ⟨an ∼ decree⟩

in·ter·lope \,in-tər-'lōp\ vb -loped; -lop·ing 1 : to encroach on the rights (as in trade) of others 2 : INTRUDE, INTERFERE — in·ter·lop·er n

in·ter·lude \'in-tər-,lüd\ n 1 : a usu. short simple play or dramatic entertainment 2 : an intervening period, space, or event 3 : a piece of music inserted between the parts of a longer composition or a religious service

in·ter·mar·riage \,in-tər-'mer-ij\ n 1 : marriage within one's own group as required by custom 2 : marriage between members of different groups

in·ter·mar·ry \-'mer-ē\ vb 1 : to marry each other 2 : to marry within a group 3 : to become connected by intermarriage

¹in·ter·me·di·ary \,in-tər-'mē-dē-,er-ē\ adj 1 : INTERMEDIATE 2 : acting as a mediator

²intermediary n, pl -ar·ies : MEDIATOR, GO-BETWEEN

¹in·ter·me·di·ate \,in-tər-'mē-dē-ət\ adj : being or occurring at the middle place or degree or between extremes

²intermediate n 1 : one that is intermediate 2 : INTERMEDIARY

intermediate school n 1 : JUNIOR HIGH SCHOOL 2 : a school usu. comprising grades 4–6

in·ter·ment \in-'tər-mənt\ n : BURIAL

in·ter·mez·zo \,in-tər-'met-sō, -'med-zō\ n, pl -zi \-sē, -zē\ or -zos [It, ultim. fr. L intermedius intermediate] : a short movement connecting major sections of an extended musical work (as a symphony); also : a short independent instrumental composition

in·ter·mi·na·ble \(,)in-'tər-mə-nə-bəl\ adj : ENDLESS; esp : wearisomely protracted — in·ter·mi·na·bly \-blē\ adv

in·ter·min·gle \,in-tər-'miŋ-gəl\ vb : to mingle or mix together

in·ter·mis·sion \,in-tər-'mi-shən\ n 1 : INTERRUPTION, BREAK 2 : a temporary halt esp. in a public performance

in·ter·mit \-'mit\ vb -mit·ted; -mit·ting : DISCONTINUE; also : to be intermittent

in·ter·mit·tent \-'mi-t³nt\ adj : coming and going at intervals ⟨∼ rain⟩ ♦ Synonyms RECURRENT, PERIODIC, ALTERNATE — in·ter·mit·tent·ly adv

in·ter·mix \,in-tər-'miks\ vb : to mix together : INTERMINGLE — in·ter·mix·ture \-'miks-chər\ n

in·ter·mo·lec·u·lar \-mə-'le-kyə-lər\ adj : existing or acting between molecules

¹in·tern \'in-,tərn, in-'tərn\ vb : to confine or impound esp. during a war — in·tern·ee \(,)in-,tər-'nē\ n — in·tern·ment \in-'tərn-mənt\ n

²in·tern also in·terne \'in-,tərn\ n : an advanced student or recent graduate (as in medicine) gaining supervised practical experience — in·tern·ship n

³in·tern \'in-,tərn\ vb : to work as an intern

in·ter·nal \in-'tər-n³l\ adj 1 : INWARD, INTERIOR 2 : relating to or located in the inside of the body ⟨∼ pain⟩ 3 : of, relating to, or occurring within the confines of an organized structure ⟨∼ affairs⟩ 4 : of, relating to, or existing within the mind 5 : INTRINSIC, INHERENT ⟨∼ evidence⟩ — in·ter·nal·ly adv

internal combustion engine n : an engine in which the fuel is ignited within the engine cylinder

in·ter·nal·ise Brit var of INTERNALIZE

in·ter·nal·ize \in-'tər-nə-,līz\ vb -ized; -iz·ing : to incorporate (as values) within the self through learning or socialization ⟨internalized their parents' values⟩ — in·ter·nal·i·za·tion \-,tər-nə-lə-'zā-shən\ n

internal medicine *n* : a branch of medicine that deals with the diagnosis and treatment of diseases not requiring surgery

¹**in·ter·na·tion·al** \ˌin-tər-ˈna-shə-nəl\ *adj* **1** : common to or affecting two or more nations ⟨~ trade⟩ **2** : of, relating to, or constituting a group having members in two or more nations — **in·ter·na·tion·al·ly** *adv*

²**international** *n* : one that is international; *esp* : an organization of international scope

in·ter·na·tion·al·ise *Brit var of* INTERNATIONALIZE

in·ter·na·tion·al·ism \-ˈna-shə-nə-ˌli-zəm\ *n* : a policy of cooperation among nations; *also* : an attitude favoring such a policy — **in·ter·na·tion·al·ist** \-ˌlist\ *n or adj*

in·ter·na·tion·al·ize \-ˈna-shə-nə-ˌlīz\ *vb* : to make international; *esp* : to place under international control

International System of Units *n* : a system of units based on the metric system and used by international convention esp. for scientific work

in·ter·ne·cine \ˌin-tər-ˈne-ˌsēn, -ˈnē-ˌsīn\ *adj* [L *internecinus*, fr. *internecare* to destroy, kill, fr. *necare* to kill, fr. *nec-, nex* violent death] **1** : DEADLY; *esp* : mutually destructive **2** : of, relating to, or involving conflict within a group ⟨~ feuds⟩

In·ter·net \ˈin-tər-ˌnet\ *n, often not cap* : an electronic communications network that connects computer networks worldwide

Internet service provider *n* : a company that provides its customers with Internet access and related services

in·ter·nist \ˈin-ˌtər-nist\ *n* : a physician who specializes in internal medicine

in·ter·nun·cio \ˌin-tər-ˈnən-sē-ˌō, -ˈnün-\ *n* [It *internunzio*] : a papal legate of lower rank than a nuncio

in·ter·of·fice \-ˈȯ-fəs\ *adj* : functioning or communicating between the offices of an organization

in·ter·per·son·al \-ˈpər-sə-nəl\ *adj* : being, relating to, or involving relations between persons ⟨~ communication⟩ — **in·ter·per·son·al·ly** *adv*

in·ter·plan·e·tary \ˌin-tər-ˈpla-nə-ˌter-ē\ *adj* : existing, carried on, or operating between planets ⟨~ space⟩

in·ter·play \ˈin-tər-ˌplā\ *n* : INTERACTION

in·ter·po·late \in-ˈtər-pə-ˌlāt\ *vb* **-lat·ed; -lat·ing** **1** : to change (as a text) by inserting new or foreign matter **2** : to insert (as words) into a text or into a conversation **3** : to estimate values of (data or a function) between two known values — **in·ter·po·la·tion** \-ˌtər-pə-ˈlā-shən\ *n*

in·ter·pose \ˌin-tər-ˈpōz\ *vb* **-posed; -pos·ing** **1** : to place between **2** : to thrust in : INTRUDE, INTERRUPT **3** : to inject between parts of a conversation or argument **4** : to come or be between ♦ **Synonyms** INTERFERE, INTERCEDE, INTERMEDIATE, INTERVENE — **in·ter·po·si·tion** \-pə-ˈzi-shən\ *n*

in·ter·pret \in-ˈtər-prət\ *vb* **1** : to explain the meaning of; *also* : to act as an interpreter : TRANSLATE **2** : to understand according to individual belief, judgment, or interest **3** : to represent artistically — **in·ter·pret·er** *n* — **in·ter·pre·tive** \-ˈtər-prə-tiv\ *adj*

in·ter·pre·ta·tion \in-ˌtər-prə-ˈtā-shən\ *n* **1** : EXPLANATION ⟨~ of the law⟩ **2** : an instance of artistic interpretation in performance or adaptation — **in·ter·pre·ta·tive** \-ˈtər-prə-ˌtā-tiv\ *adj*

in·ter·ra·cial \-ˈrā-shəl\ *adj* : of, involving, or designed for members of different races

in·ter·reg·num \ˌin-tə-ˈreg-nəm\ *n, pl* **-nums** *or* **-na** \-nə\ **1** : the time during which a throne is vacant between two successive reigns or regimes **2** : a pause in a continuous series

in·ter·re·late \ˌin-tər-ri-ˈlāt\ *vb* : to bring into or have a mutual relationship — **in·ter·re·lat·ed·ness** \-ˈlā-təd-nəs\ *n* — **in·ter·re·la·tion** \-ˈlā-shən\ *n* — **in·ter·re·la·tion·ship** *n*

interrog *abbr* interrogative

in·ter·ro·gate \in-ˈter-ə-ˌgāt\ *vb* **-gat·ed; -gat·ing** : to question esp. formally and systematically ⟨~ a suspect⟩ — **in·ter·ro·ga·tion** \-ˌter-ə-ˈgā-shən\ *n* — **in·ter·ro·ga·tor** \-ˈter-ə-ˌgā-tər\ *n*

in·ter·rog·a·tive \ˌin-tə-ˈrä-gə-tiv\ *adj* : asking a question ⟨~ sentence⟩ — **interrogative** *n* — **in·ter·rog·a·tive·ly** *adv*

in·ter·rog·a·to·ry \ˌin-tə-ˈrä-gə-ˌtȯr-ē\ *adj* : INTERROGATIVE

in·ter·rupt \ˌin-tə-ˈrəpt\ *vb* **1** : to stop or hinder by breaking in **2** : to break the uniformity or continuity of **3**

: to break in by speaking while another is speaking — **in·ter·rupt·er** *n* — **in·ter·rup·tion** \-ˈrəp-shən\ *n* — **in·ter·rup·tive** \-ˈrəp-tiv\ *adj*

in·ter·scho·las·tic \ˌin-tər-skə-ˈlas-tik\ *adj* : existing or carried on between schools ⟨~ sports⟩

in·ter·sect \ˌin-tər-ˈsekt\ *vb* **1** : to divide by passing through or across **2** : to meet and cross (as at a point); *also* : OVERLAP — **in·ter·sec·tion** \-ˈsek-shən\ *n*

in·ter·sperse \ˌin-tər-ˈspərs\ *vb* **-spersed; -spers·ing** **1** : to place something at intervals in or among **2** : to insert at intervals among other things — **in·ter·sper·sion** \-ˈspər-zhən\ *n*

¹**in·ter·state** \ˌin-tər-ˈstāt\ *adj* : relating to, including, or connecting two or more states esp. of the U.S. ⟨~ commerce⟩

²**in·ter·state** \ˈin-tər-ˌstāt\ *n* : an interstate highway

in·ter·stel·lar \ˌin-tər-ˈste-lər\ *adj* : located or taking place among the stars

in·ter·stice \in-ˈtər-stəs\ *n, pl* **-stic·es** \-stə-ˌsēz, -stə-səz\ : a space that intervenes between things : CHINK — **in·ter·sti·tial** \ˌin-tər-ˈsti-shəl\ *adj*

in·ter·tid·al \ˌin-tər-ˈtī-dᵊl\ *adj* : of, relating to, or being the area that is above low-tide mark but exposed to tidal flooding ⟨life in the ~ mud⟩

in·ter·twine \-ˈtwīn\ *vb* : to twine or cause to twine about one another : INTERLACE

in·ter·twist \-ˈtwist\ *vb* : INTERTWINE

in·ter·ur·ban \-ˈər-bən\ *adj* : connecting cities or towns

in·ter·val \ˈin-tər-vəl\ *n* [ME *intervalle*, fr. AF & L; AF *entreval*, fr. L *intervallum* space between ramparts, interval, fr. *inter-* between + *vallum* rampart] **1** : a space of time between events or states : PAUSE **2** : a space between objects, units, or states **3** : the difference in pitch between two tones

in·ter·vene \ˌin-tər-ˈvēn\ *vb* **-vened; -ven·ing** **1** : to occur, fall, or come between points of time or between events **2** : to enter or appear as an unrelated feature or circumstance ⟨rain intervened and we postponed the trip⟩ **3** : to come in or between in order to stop, settle, or modify ⟨~ in a quarrel⟩ **4** : to occur or lie between two things — **in·ter·ven·tion** \-ˈven-chən\ *n*

in·ter·ven·tion·ism \-ˈven-chə-ˌni-zəm\ *n* : interference by one country in the political affairs of another — **in·ter·ven·tion·ist** \-ˈven-chə-nist\ *n or adj*

in·ter·view \ˈin-tər-ˌvyü\ *n* **1** : a formal consultation usu. to evaluate qualifications **2** : a meeting at which a writer or reporter obtains information from a person; *also* : the recorded or written account of such a meeting — **interview** *vb* — **in·ter·view·ee** \ˌin-tər-(ˌ)vyü-ˈē\ *n* — **in·ter·view·er** *n*

in·ter·vo·cal·ic \ˌin-tər-vō-ˈka-lik\ *adj* : immediately preceded and immediately followed by a vowel ⟨an ~ consonant⟩

in·ter·weave \ˌin-tər-ˈwēv\ *vb* **-wove** \-ˈwōv\ *also* **-weaved; -wo·ven** \-ˈwō-vən\ *also* **-weaved; -weav·ing** : to weave or blend together : INTERTWINE, INTERMINGLE — **interwoven** *adj*

in·tes·tate \in-ˈtes-ˌtāt, -tət\ *adj* **1** : having made no valid will ⟨died ~⟩ **2** : not disposed of by will ⟨~ estate⟩

in·tes·tine \in-ˈtes-tən\ *n* : the tubular part of the alimentary canal that extends from stomach to anus and consists of a long narrow upper part (**small intestine**) followed by a broader shorter lower part (**large intestine**) — **in·tes·ti·nal** \-tə-nᵊl\ *adj*

in·ti·fa·da \ˌin-tə-ˈfä-də\ *n* : an armed uprising of Palestinians against Israeli occupation of the West Bank and Gaza Strip

¹**in·ti·mate** \ˈin-tə-ˌmāt\ *vb* **-mat·ed; -mat·ing** [LL *intimare* to put in, announce, fr. L *intimus* innermost] **1** : ANNOUNCE, NOTIFY **2** : to communicate indirectly : HINT — **in·ti·ma·tion** \ˌin-tə-ˈmā-shən\ *n*

²**in·ti·mate** \ˈin-tə-mət\ *adj* **1** : INTRINSIC; *also* : INNERMOST **2** : marked by very close association, contact, or familiarity **3** : marked by a warm friendship ⟨~ friends⟩ **4** : suggesting informal warmth or privacy **5** : of a very personal or private nature ⟨~ feelings⟩ — **in·ti·ma·cy** \ˈin-tə-mə-sē\ *n* — **in·ti·mate·ly** *adv*

³**in·ti·mate** \ˈin-tə-mət\ *n* : an intimate friend, associate, or confidant

in·tim·i·date \in-ˈti-mə-ˌdāt\ *vb* **-dat·ed; -dat·ing** : to make timid or fearful : FRIGHTEN; *esp* : to compel or deter by or as if by threats ♦ **Synonyms** COW, BULLDOZE, BULLY,

BROWBEAT — **in·tim·i·dat·ing·ly** *adv* — **in·tim·i·da·tion** \-ˌti-mə-ˈdā-shən\ *n*

intl *or* **intnl** *abbr* international

in·to \ˈin-tü\ *prep* **1** : to the inside of ⟨ran ∼ the house⟩ **2** : to the state, condition, or form of ⟨got ∼ trouble⟩ **3** : AGAINST ⟨ran ∼ a wall⟩

in·tol·er·a·ble \(ˌ)in-ˈtä-lə-rə-bəl\ *adj* **1** : UNBEARABLE ⟨∼ pain⟩ **2** : EXCESSIVE — **in·tol·er·a·bly** \-blē\ *adv*

in·tol·er·ant \(ˌ)in-ˈtä-lə-rənt\ *adj* **1** : unable or unwilling to endure ⟨is lactose ∼⟩ **2** : unwilling to grant equality, freedom, or other social rights : BIGOTED — **in·tol·er·ance** \-rəns\ *n*

in·to·na·tion \ˌin-tō-ˈnā-shən\ *n* **1** : something that is intoned **2** : the act of intoning and esp. of chanting **3** : the manner of singing, playing, or uttering tones; *esp* : the rise and fall in pitch of the voice in speech

in·tone \in-ˈtōn\ *vb* **in·toned; in·ton·ing** : to utter in musical or prolonged tones : CHANT ⟨∼ a prayer⟩

in to·to \in-ˈtō-tō\ *adv* [L, on the whole] : TOTALLY, ENTIRELY

in·tox·i·cant \in-ˈtäk-si-kənt\ *n* : something that intoxicates; *esp* : an alcoholic drink — **intoxicant** *adj*

in·tox·i·cate \-sə-ˌkāt\ *vb* **-cat·ed; -cat·ing 1** : to affect by a drug (as alcohol or cocaine) esp. to the point of physical or mental impairment **2** : to excite to enthusiasm or frenzy ⟨*intoxicated* by his power⟩ — **in·tox·i·ca·tion** \-ˌtäk-sə-ˈkā-shən\ *n*

in·trac·ta·ble \(ˌ)in-ˈtrak-tə-bəl\ *adj* : not easily controlled

in·tra·mu·ral \-ˈmyùr-əl\ *adj* : being or occurring within the walls or limits (as of a city or college) ⟨∼ sports⟩

in·tra·mus·cu·lar \-ˈməs-kyə-lər\ *adj* : situated within, occurring in, or administered by entering a muscle — **in·tra·mus·cu·lar·ly** *adv*

in·tra·net \ˈin-trə-ˌnet\ *n* a network similar to the World Wide Web but having access limited to certain authorized users

intrans *abbr* intransitive

in·tran·si·gent \-jənt\ *adj* : UNCOMPROMISING ⟨an ∼ attitude⟩ — **in·tran·si·gence** \-jəns\ *n* — **intransigent** *n*

in·tran·si·tive \(ˌ)in-ˈtran-sə-tiv, -zə-\ *adj* : not transitive; *esp* : not having or containing an object ⟨an ∼ verb⟩ — **in·tran·si·tive·ly** *adv* — **in·tran·si·tive·ness** *n*

in·tra·state \ˌin-trə-ˈstāt\ *adj* : existing or occurring within a state ⟨∼ rivals⟩

in·tra·uter·ine device \-ˈyü-tə-rən-, -ˌrīn-\ *n* : a device inserted into and left in the uterus to prevent pregnancy

in·tra·ve·nous \ˌin-trə-ˈvē-nəs\ *adj* : being within or entering by way of the veins ⟨∼ feeding⟩; *also* : used in or using intravenous procedures ⟨∼ needles⟩ — **in·tra·ve·nous·ly** *adv*

intrench *var of* ENTRENCH

in·trep·id \in-ˈtre-pəd\ *adj* : characterized by resolute fearlessness, fortitude, and endurance ⟨an ∼ explorer⟩ — **in·tre·pid·i·ty** \ˌin-trə-ˈpi-də-tē\ *n*

in·tri·cate \ˈin-tri-kət\ *adj* [ME, fr. L *intricatus*, pp. of *intricare* to entangle, fr. *tricae* trifles, complications] **1** : having many complexly interrelated parts : COMPLICATED **2** : difficult to follow, understand, or solve — **in·tri·ca·cy** \-tri-kə-sē\ *n* — **in·tri·cate·ly** *adv*

¹**in·trigue** \ˈin-ˌtrēg, in-ˈtrēg\ *n* **1** : a secret scheme : PLOT **2** : a clandestine love affair

²**in·trigue** \in-ˈtrēg\ *vb* **in·trigued; in·trigu·ing 1** : to accomplish by intrigue **2** : to carry on an intrigue; *esp* : PLOT, SCHEME **3** : to arouse the interest, desire, or curiosity of — **in·trigu·ing·ly** *adv*

in·trin·sic \in-ˈtrin-zik, -sik\ *adj* : belonging to the essential nature or constitution of a thing — **in·trin·si·cal·ly** \-zi-k(ə-)lē, -si-\ *adv*

introd *abbr* introduction

in·tro·duce \ˌin-trə-ˈdüs, -ˈdyüs\ *vb* **-duced; -duc·ing 1** : to lead or bring in esp. for the first time **2** : to bring into practice or use **3** : to cause to be acquainted **4** : to present for discussion **5** : PLACE, INSERT ♦ *Synonyms* INSINUATE, INTERPOLATE, INTERPOSE, INTERJECT — **in·tro·duc·tion** \-ˈdək-shən\ *n* — **in·tro·duc·to·ry** \-ˈdək-tə-rē\ *adj*

in·troit \ˈin-ˌtròit, -ˌtrō-ət\ *n* **1** *often cap* : the first part of the traditional proper of the Mass **2** : a piece of music sung or played at the beginning of a worship service

in·tro·spec·tion \-ˈspek-shən\ *n* : a reflective looking inward : an examination of one's own thoughts or feelings

in·tro·spect \ˌin-trə-ˈspekt\ *vb* — **in·tro·spec·tive** \-ˈspek-tiv\ *adj* — **in·tro·spec·tive·ly** *adv*

in·tro·vert \ˈin-trə-ˌvərt\ *n* : a reserved or shy person — **in·tro·ver·sion** \ˌin-trə-ˈvər-zhən\ *n* — **introvert** *adj* — **in·tro·vert·ed** \ˈin-trə-ˌvər-təd\ *adj*

in·trude \in-ˈtrüd\ *vb* **in·trud·ed; in·trud·ing 1** : to thrust, enter, or force in or upon **2** : ENCROACH, TRESPASS — **in·trud·er** *n* — **in·tru·sion** \-ˈtrü-zhən\ *n* — **in·tru·sive** \-ˈtrü-siv\ *adj* — **in·tru·sive·ness** *n*

intrust *var of* ENTRUST

in·tu·it \in-ˈtü-ət, -ˈtyü-\ *vb* : to know, sense, or understand by intuition

in·tu·ition \ˌin-tü-ˈwi-shən, -tyü-\ *n* **1** : quick and ready insight **2** : the power or faculty of knowing things without conscious reasoning — **in·tu·i·tive** \in-ˈtü-ə-tiv, -ˈtyü-\ *adj* — **in·tu·i·tive·ly** *adv*

In·u·it \ˈi-nü-wət, ˈin-yü-\ *n* [Inuit *inuit*, pl. of *inuk* person] **1** *pl* **Inuit** *or* **Inuits** : a member of the indigenous people of No. America and Greenland **2** : the language of the Inuit people

in·un·date \ˈi-nən-ˌdāt\ *vb* **-dat·ed; -dat·ing** : to cover with or as if with a flood : OVERFLOW — **in·un·da·tion** \ˌi-nən-ˈdā-shən\ *n*

in·ure \i-ˈnùr, -ˈnyùr\ *vb* **in·ured; in·ur·ing** [ME *enuren*, fr. *in ure* customary, fr. *putten in ure* to use, put into practice, part trans. of AF *mettre en ovre, en uevre*] **1** : to accustom to accept something undesirable ⟨*inured* to violence⟩ **2** : to become of advantage

in utero \in-ˈyü-tə-ˌrō\ *adv or adj* [L] : in the uterus : before birth

inv *abbr* **1** inventor **2** invoice

in vac·uo \in-ˈva-kyə-ˌwō\ *adv* [L] : in a vacuum

in·vade \in-ˈvād\ *vb* **in·vad·ed; in·vad·ing 1** : to enter for conquest or plunder **2** : to encroach upon **3** : to spread through and usu. harm ⟨germs ∼ the tissues⟩ — **in·vad·er** *n*

¹**in·val·id** \(ˌ)in-ˈva-ləd\ *adj* : being without foundation or force in fact, reason, or law — **in·va·lid·i·ty** \ˌin-və-ˈli-də-tē\ *n* — **in·val·id·ly** *adv*

²**in·va·lid** \ˈin-və-ləd\ *adj* : being in ill health : SICKLY

³**invalid** \ˈin-və-ləd\ *n* : a person in usu. chronic ill health — **in·va·lid·ism** \-lə-ˌdi-zəm\ *n*

⁴**in·va·lid** \ˈin-və-ləd, -ˌlid\ *vb* **1** : to remove from active duty by reason of sickness or disability **2** : to make sickly or disabled

in·val·i·date \(ˌ)in-ˈva-lə-ˌdāt\ *vb* : to make invalid ⟨*invalidate* a contract⟩; *esp* : to weaken or make valueless — **in·val·i·da·tion** \in-ˌva-lə-ˈdā-shən\ *n*

in·valu·able \-ˈval-yə-bəl, -yə-wə-bəl\ *adj* : valuable beyond estimation

in·vari·able \-ˈver-ē-ə-bəl\ *adj* : not changing or capable of change : CONSTANT — **in·vari·ably** \-blē\ *adv*

in·va·sion \in-ˈvā-zhən\ *n* : an act or instance of invading; *esp* : entry of an army into a country for conquest

in·va·sive \in-ˈvā-siv, -ziv\ *adj* **1** : tending to spread ⟨∼ cancer cells⟩ **2** : involving entry into the living body (as by surgery)

in·vec·tive \in-ˈvek-tiv\ *n* **1** : an abusive expression or speech **2** : abusive language — **invective** *adj*

in·veigh \in-ˈvā\ *vb* : to protest or complain bitterly or vehemently : RAIL

in·vei·gle \in-ˈvā-gəl, -ˈvē-\ *vb* **in·vei·gled; in·vei·gling** [AF *enveegler, aveogler* to blind, hoodwink, fr. *avogle, enveugle* blind, fr. ML *ab oculis*, lit., lacking eyes] **1** : to win over by flattery : ENTICE **2** : to acquire by ingenuity or flattery ⟨*inveigled* his way into her confidence⟩

in·vent \in-ˈvent\ *vb* **1** : to think up **2** : to create or produce for the first time — **in·ven·tor** \-ˈven-tər\ *n*

in·ven·tion \in-ˈven-chən\ *n* **1** : INVENTIVENESS **2** : a creation of the imagination; *esp* : a false conception **3** : a device, contrivance, or process originated after study and experiment **4** : the act or process of inventing

in·ven·tive \in-ˈven-tiv\ *adj* **1** : CREATIVE, INGENIOUS ⟨an ∼ composer⟩ **2** : characterized by invention ⟨an ∼ turn of mind⟩ — **in·ven·tive·ness** *n*

in·ven·to·ry \ˈin-vən-ˌtór-ē\ *n, pl* **-ries 1** : an itemized list of current goods or assets **2** : SURVEY, SUMMARY **3** : STOCK, SUPPLY **4** : the act or process of taking an inventory — **inventory** *vb*

¹**in·verse** \(ˌ)in-ˈvərs, ˈin-ˌvərs\ *adj* : opposite in order, nature, or effect : REVERSED — **in·verse·ly** *adv*

²inverse n : something inverse or resulting in or from inversion : OPPOSITE

in·ver·sion \in-'vər-zhən\ n 1 : a reversal of position, order, or relationship; esp : an increase of temperature with altitude through a layer of air 2 : the act or process of inverting

in·vert \in-'vərt\ vb 1 : to reverse in position, order, or relationship 2 : to turn upside down or inside out 3 : to turn inward

in·ver·te·brate \(ˌ)in-'vər-tə-brət, -ˌbrāt\ adj : lacking a backbone; also : of or relating to invertebrate animals — **invertebrate** n

¹in·vest \in-'vest\ vb 1 : to install formally in an office or honor 2 : to furnish with power or authority : VEST 3 : to cover completely : ENVELOP 4 : CLOTHE, ADORN 5 : BESIEGE 6 : to endow with a quality or characteristic

²invest vb 1 : to commit (money) in order to earn a financial return ⟨~ed in real estate⟩ 2 : to expend for future benefits or advantages 3 : to make an investment — **in·ves·tor** \-'ves-tər\ n

in·ves·ti·gate \in-'ves-tə-ˌgāt\ vb **-gat·ed; -gat·ing** [L investigare to track, investigate, fr. vestigium footprint, track] : to study by close examination and systematic inquiry — **in·ves·ti·ga·tion** \-ˌves-tə-'gā-shən\ n — **in·ves·ti·ga·tive** \-'ves-tə-ˌgā-tiv\ adj — **in·ves·ti·ga·tor** \-ˌgā-tər\ n

in·ves·ti·ture \in-'ves-tə-ˌchùr, -chər\ n 1 : the act of ratifying or establishing in office 2 : something that covers or adorns

¹in·vest·ment \in-'vest-mənt\ n 1 : an outer layer : ENVELOPE 2 : INVESTITURE 1 3 : BLOCKADE, SIEGE

²investment n : the outlay of money for income or profit; also : the sum invested or the property purchased

in·vet·er·ate \in-'ve-tə-rət\ adj 1 : firmly established by age or long persistence 2 : confirmed in a habit ⟨an ~ liar⟩

in·vi·a·ble \(ˌ)in-'vī-ə-bəl\ adj : incapable of surviving

in·vid·i·ous \in-'vi-dē-əs\ adj 1 : tending to cause discontent, animosity, or envy ⟨as ~ comparison⟩ 2 : ENVIOUS 3 : OBNOXIOUS ⟨~ remarks⟩ — **in·vid·i·ous·ly** adv

in·vig·o·rate \in-'vi-gə-ˌrāt\ vb **-rat·ed; -rat·ing** : to give life and energy to : ANIMATE ⟨~ the economy⟩ — **in·vig·o·ra·tion** \-ˌvi-gə-'rā-shən\ n

in·vin·ci·ble \(ˌ)in-'vin-sə-bəl\ adj : incapable of being conquered, overcome, or subdued — **in·vin·ci·bil·i·ty** \-ˌvin-sə-'bi-lə-tē\ n — **in·vin·ci·bly** \-'vin-sə-blē\ adv

in·vi·o·la·ble \-'vī-ə-lə-bəl\ adj 1 : safe from violation or profanation 2 : UNASSAILABLE ⟨~ borders⟩ — **in·vi·o·la·bil·i·ty** \-ˌvī-ə-lə-'bi-lə-tē\ n

in·vi·o·late \-'vī-ə-lət\ adj : not violated or profaned : PURE ⟨an ~ principle⟩

in·vis·i·ble \-'vi-zə-bəl\ adj 1 : incapable of being seen ⟨~ to the naked eye⟩ 2 : HIDDEN 3 : IMPERCEPTIBLE, INCONSPICUOUS — **in·vis·i·bil·i·ty** \-ˌvi-zə-'bi-lə-tē\ n — **in·vis·i·bly** \-'vi-zə-blē\ adv

invisible hand n : a hypothetical economic force that works for the benefit of all

in·vi·ta·tion·al \in-və-'tā-shə-nəl\ adj : limited to invited participants ⟨an ~ tournament⟩ — **invitational** n

in·vite \in-'vīt\ vb **in·vit·ed; in·vit·ing** 1 : ENTICE, TEMPT 2 : to increase the likelihood of ⟨~ trouble⟩ 3 : to request the presence or participation of : ASK 4 : to request formally 5 : ENCOURAGE ⟨~ suggestions⟩ — **in·vi·ta·tion** \ˌin-və-'tā-shən\ n

in·vit·ing adj : ATTRACTIVE, TEMPTING

in vi·tro \in-'vē-trō, -'vī-, -'vi-\ adv or adj [NL, lit., in glass] : outside the living body and in an artificial environment ⟨in vitro fertilization⟩

in·vo·ca·tion \ˌin-və-'kā-shən\ n 1 : SUPPLICATION; esp : a prayer at the beginning of a service 2 : a formula for conjuring : INCANTATION

¹in·voice \'in-ˌvȯis\ n [modif. of MF envois, pl. of envoi message] : an itemized list of goods shipped usu. specifying the price and the terms of sale : BILL

²invoice vb **in·voiced; in·voic·ing** : to send an invoice to or for : BILL

in·voke \in-'vōk\ vb **in·voked; in·vok·ing** 1 : to petition for help or support 2 : to appeal to or cite as authority ⟨~ a law⟩ 3 : to call forth by incantation : CONJURE ⟨~ spirits⟩ 4 : to make an earnest request for : SOLICIT ⟨invoked mercy⟩ 5 : to put into effect or operation 6 : to bring about : CAUSE

in·vol·un·tary \(ˌ)in-'vä-lən-ˌter-ē\ adj 1 : done contrary to or without choice 2 : COMPULSORY ⟨~ servitude⟩ 3 : not controlled by the will : REFLEX ⟨~ contractions⟩ — **in·vol·un·tari·ly** \-ˌvä-lən-'ter-ə-lē\ adv

in·vo·lute \'in-və-ˌlüt\ adj : INVOLVED, INTRICATE ⟨an ~ maneuver⟩

in·vo·lu·tion \ˌin-və-'lü-shən\ n 1 : the act or an instance of enfolding or entangling 2 : COMPLEXITY, INTRICACY

in·volve \in-'välv\ vb **in·volved; in·volv·ing** 1 : to draw in as a participant 2 : ENVELOP 3 : to occupy (as oneself) absorbingly; esp : to commit oneself emotionally 4 : to relate closely : CONNECT 5 : to have as part of itself : INCLUDE 6 : ENTAIL, IMPLY ⟨the job ~s traveling⟩ 7 : ²AFFECT — **in·volve·ment** n

in·volved \-'välvd\ adj : INTRICATE, COMPLEX ⟨an ~ plot⟩

in·vul·ner·a·ble \(ˌ)in-'vəl-nə-rə-bəl\ adj 1 : incapable of being wounded, injured, or damaged 2 : immune to or proof against attack — **in·vul·ner·a·bil·i·ty** \-ˌvəl-nə-rə-'bi-lə-tē\ n — **in·vul·ner·a·bly** \-'vəl-nə-rə-blē\ adv

¹in·ward \'in-wərd\ adj 1 : situated on the inside 2 : MENTAL; also : SPIRITUAL 3 : directed toward the interior

²inward or **in·wards** \-wərdz\ adv 1 : toward the inside, center, or interior 2 : toward the inner being ⟨turned his thoughts ~⟩

in·ward·ly \'in-wərd-lē\ adv 1 : MENTALLY, SPIRITUALLY 2 : INTERNALLY ⟨bled ~⟩ 3 : to oneself ⟨cursed ~⟩

IOC abbr International Olympic Committee

io·dide \'ī-ə-ˌdīd\ n : a compound of iodine with another element or group

io·dine \'ī-ə-ˌdīn, -dᵊn\ n 1 : a nonmetallic chemical element used esp. in medicine and photography 2 : a solution of iodine used as a local antiseptic

io·dise Brit var of IODIZE

io·dize \'ī-ə-ˌdīz\ vb **io·dized; io·diz·ing** : to treat with iodine or an iodide

ion \'ī-ən, 'ī-ˌän\ n [Gk, neut. of iōn, prp. of ienai to go; so called because in electrolysis it goes to one of the two poles] : an electrically charged particle, atom, or group of atoms — **ion·ic** \ī-'ä-nik\ adj

-ion n suffix : act, process, state, or condition ⟨validation⟩

ion·ise Brit var of IONIZE

ion·ize \'ī-ə-ˌnīz\ vb **ion·ized; ion·iz·ing** 1 : to convert wholly or partly into ions 2 : to become ionized — **ion·iz·able** \ˌī-ə-'nī-zə-bəl\ adj — **ion·i·za·tion** \ˌī-ə-nə-'zā-shən\ n — **ion·iz·er** \'ī-ə-ˌnī-zər\ n

ion·o·sphere \ī-'ä-nə-ˌsfir\ n : the part of the earth's atmosphere extending from about 30 miles (50 kilometers) to the exosphere that contains ionized atmospheric gases — **ion·o·spher·ic** \ī-ˌä-nə-'sfir-ik, -'sfer-\ adj

IOOF abbr Independent Order of Odd Fellows

io·ta \ī-'ō-tə\ n [L, fr. Gk iōta] : the 9th letter of the Greek alphabet — I or ι 2 : a very small quantity : JOT

IOU \ˌī-(ˌ)ō-'yü\ n : an acknowledgement of a debt

IP abbr innings pitched

IP address \'ī-'pē-\ n [Internet protocol] : the numeric address of a computer on the Internet

ip·e·cac \'i-pi-ˌkak\ n [Pg ipecacuanha] : an emetic and expectorant drug used esp. as a syrup in treating accidental poisoning; also : either of two tropical American plants or their rhizomes and roots used to make ipecac

IPO \ˌī-ˌpē-'ō\ n, pl **IPOs** : an initial public offering of a company's stock

ip·so fac·to \ˌip-sō-'fak-tō\ adv [NL, lit., by the fact itself] : by the very nature of the case

iq abbr [L idem quod] the same as

IQ \'ī-'kyü\ n : a number used to express a person's relative intelligence as determined by a standardized test

¹Ir abbr Irish

²Ir symbol iridium

IR abbr infrared

¹IRA \ˌī-(ˌ)är-'ā; 'ī-rə\ n [individual retirement account] : a retirement savings account in which income taxes are deferred until withdrawals are made

²IRA abbr Irish Republican Army

irai·mbi·lan·ja \ē-ˌrīm-bē-'län(d)-zə\ n, pl **iraimbilanja** — see ariary at MONEY table

iras·ci·ble \i-'ra-sə-bəl\ adj : marked by hot temper and easily provoked anger ♦ **Synonyms** CHOLERIC, TESTY, TOUCHY, CRANKY, CROSS — **iras·ci·bil·i·ty** \-ˌra-sə-'bi-lə-tē\ n

irate \ī-ʹrāt\ adj **1** : roused to ire ⟨an ~ customer⟩ **2** : arising from anger — **irate·ly** adv

ire \ʹī(-ə)r\ n : ANGER, WRATH — **ire·ful** adj

Ire abbr Ireland

ire·nic \ī-ʹre-nik\ adj : favoring, conducive to, or operating toward peace or conciliation ⟨~ measures⟩

ir·i·des·cence \ˌir-ə-ʹde-sᵊns\ n : a rainbowlike play of colors — **ir·i·des·cent** \-sᵊnt\ adj

irid·i·um \ir-ʹi-dē-əm\ n : a hard brittle heavy metallic chemical element

iris \ʹī-rəs\ n, pl **iris·es** also **iri·des** \ʹī-rə-ˌdēz, ʹi-rə-\ [ME, fr. L iris rainbow, iris plant, fr. Gk, rainbow, iris plant, iris of the eye] **1** : the colored part around the pupil of the eye **2** : any of a large genus of plants with linear basal leaves and large showy flowers

Irish \ʹī-rish\ n **1 Irish** pl : the people of Ireland **2** : the Celtic language of Ireland — **Irish** adj — **Irish·man** \-mən\ n — **Irish·wom·an** \-ˌwu̇-mən\ n

Irish bull n : an incongruous statement (as "it was hereditary in his family to have no children")

Irish coffee n : hot sugared coffee with Irish whiskey and whipped cream

Irish moss n : the dried and bleached plants of a red alga that is a source of carrageenan; also : this red alga

Irish setter n : any of a breed of hunting dogs with a mahogany-red coat

irk \ʹərk\ vb : to make weary, irritated, or bored : ANNOY

irk·some \ʹərk-səm\ adj : tending to irk : ANNOYING — **irk·some·ly** adv

¹iron \ʹī(-ə)rn\ n [ME, fr. OE īsern, īren] **1** : a heavy malleable magnetic metallic chemical element that rusts easily and is vital to biological processes **2** : something made of metal and esp. iron; also : something (as handcuffs) used to bind or restrain ⟨put them in ~s⟩ **3** : a household device with a flat base that is heated and used for pressing cloth **4** : STRENGTH, HARDNESS

²iron vb **1** : to press or smooth with or as if with a heated iron **2** : to remove (as wrinkles) by ironing — **iron·er** n

¹iron·clad \-ʹklad\ adj **1** : sheathed in iron armor **2** : so firm or secure as to be unbreakable

²iron·clad \-ˌklad\ n : an armored naval vessel esp. of the 19th century

iron curtain n : a political, military, and ideological barrier that isolates an area; esp, often cap : one formerly isolating an area under Soviet control

iron·ic \ī-ʹrä-nik\ also **iron·i·cal** \-ni-kəl\ adj **1** : of, relating to, or marked by irony **2** : given to irony

iron·i·cal·ly \-ni-k(ə-)lē\ adv **1** : in an ironic manner **2** : it is ironic

iron·ing n : clothes ironed or to be ironed

iron lung n : a device for artificial respiration that encloses the chest in a chamber in which changes of pressure force air into and out of the lungs

iron out vb : to remove or lessen difficulties in or extremes of

iron oxide n : FERRIC OXIDE

iron·stone \ʹī(-ə)rn-ˌstōn\ n **1** : a hard iron-rich sedimentary rock **2** : a hard heavy durable pottery developed in England in the 19th century

iron·ware \-ˌwer\ n : articles made of iron

iron·weed \-ˌwēd\ n : any of a genus of mostly weedy plants related to the asters that have terminal heads of red, purple, or white flowers

iron·wood \-ˌwu̇d\ n : any of numerous trees or shrubs with exceptionally hard wood; also : the wood

iron·work \-ˌwərk\ n **1** : work in iron **2** pl : a mill or building where iron or steel is smelted or heavy iron or steel products are made — **iron·work·er** n

iro·ny \ʹī-rə-nē\ n, pl **-nies** [L ironia, fr. Gk eirōnia, fr. eirōn dissembler] **1** : the use of words to express the opposite of what one really means **2** : incongruity between the actual result of a sequence of events and the expected result

Ir·o·quois \ʹir-ə-ˌkwȯi\ n, pl **Iroquois** \same or -ˌkwȯiz\ **1** pl : an American Indian confederacy orig. of New York that consisted of the Cayuga, Mohawk, Oneida, Onondaga, and Seneca and later included the Tuscarora **2** : a member of any of the Iroquois peoples

ir·ra·di·ate \i-ʹrā-dē-ˌāt\ vb **-at·ed; -at·ing 1** : ILLUMINATE **2** : ENLIGHTEN **3** : to treat by exposure to radiation **4** : RADIATE — **ir·ra·di·a·tion** \-ˌrā-dē-ʹā-shən\ n

¹ir·ra·tio·nal \(ˌ)i-ʹra-shə-nəl\ adj **1** : incapable of reasoning ⟨~ beasts⟩; also : defective in mental power ⟨~ with fever⟩ **2** : not based on reason ⟨~ fears⟩ **3** : being or numerically equal to an irrational number — **ir·ra·tio·nal·i·ty** \(ˌ)i-ˌra-shə-ʹna-lə-tē\ n — **ir·ra·tio·nal·ly** adv

²irrational n : IRRATIONAL NUMBER

irrational number n : a real number that cannot be expressed as the quotient of two integers

ir·rec·on·cil·able \(ˌ)i-ˌre-kən-ʹsī-lə-bəl, -ʹre-kən-ˌsī-\ adj : impossible to reconcile, adjust, or harmonize — **ir·rec·on·cil·abil·i·ty** \(ˌ)i-ˌre-kən-ˌsī-lə-ʹbi-lə-tē\ n

ir·re·cov·er·able \ˌir-i-ʹkə-və-rə-bəl\ adj : not capable of being recovered or rectified : IRREPARABLE ⟨an ~ loss⟩ — **ir·re·cov·er·ably** \-blē\ adv

ir·re·deem·able \ˌir-i-ʹdē-mə-bəl\ adj **1** : not redeemable; esp : not terminable by payment of the principal ⟨an ~ bond⟩ **2** : not convertible into gold or silver at the will of the holder **3** : being beyond remedy : HOPELESS ⟨~ villains⟩

ir·re·den·tism \-ʹden-ˌti-zəm\ n : a principle or policy directed toward the incorporation of a territory historically or ethnically part of another into that other — **ir·re·den·tist** \-tist\ n or adj

ir·re·duc·ible \ˌir-i-ʹdü-sə-bəl, -ʹdyü-\ adj : not reducible ⟨an ~ fraction⟩ — **ir·re·duc·ibly** \-blē\ adv

ir·re·fut·able \ˌir-i-ʹfyü-tə-bəl, (ˌ)i-ʹre-fyət-\ adj : impossible to refute

irreg abbr irregular

ir·reg·u·lar \(ˌ)i-ʹre-gyə-lər\ adj **1** : not regular : not natural or uniform **2** : not conforming to the normal or usual manner of inflection ⟨~ verbs⟩ **3** : not belonging to a regular or organized army ⟨~ troops⟩ — **irregular** n — **ir·reg·u·lar·ly** adv

ir·reg·u·lar·i·ty \i-ˌre-gyə-ʹla-rə-tē\ n, pl **-ties 1** : something that is irregular **2** : the quality or state of being irregular **3** : occasional constipation

ir·rel·e·vant \(ˌ)i-ʹre-lə-vənt\ adj : not relevant — **ir·rel·e·vance** \-vəns\ n

ir·re·li·gious \ˌir-i-ʹli-jəs\ adj : lacking religious emotions, doctrines, or practices

ir·re·me·di·a·ble \ˌir-i-ʹmē-dē-ə-bəl\ adj : impossible to remedy or correct

ir·re·mov·able \-ʹmü-və-bəl\ adj : not removable

ir·rep·a·ra·ble \(ˌ)i-ʹre-pə-rə-bəl\ adj : impossible to make good, undo, repair, or remedy ⟨~ damage⟩

ir·re·place·able \ˌir-i-ʹplā-sə-bəl\ adj : not replaceable ⟨~ antiques⟩

ir·re·press·ible \-ʹpre-sə-bəl\ adj : impossible to repress or control ⟨~ curiosity⟩

ir·re·proach·able \-ʹprō-chə-bəl\ adj : not reproachable : BLAMELESS

ir·re·sist·ible \ˌir-i-ʹzis-tə-bəl\ adj : impossible to successfully resist ⟨an ~ craving⟩ — **ir·re·sist·ibly** \-blē\ adv

ir·res·o·lute \(ˌ)i-ʹre-zə-ˌlüt\ adj : uncertain how to act or proceed : VACILLATING — **ir·res·o·lute·ly** \-ˌlüt-lē; (ˌ)i-ˌre-zə-ʹlüt\ adv — **ir·res·o·lu·tion** \(ˌ)i-ˌre-zə-ʹlü-shən\ n

ir·re·spec·tive of \ˌir-i-ʹspek-tiv-\ prep : without regard to

ir·re·spon·si·ble \-ʹspän-sə-bəl\ adj : not responsible ⟨~ wastrels⟩ — **ir·re·spon·si·bil·i·ty** \-ˌspän-sə-ʹbi-lə-tē\ n — **ir·re·spon·si·bly** \-ʹspän-sə-blē\ adv

ir·re·triev·able \ˌir-i-ʹtrē-və-bəl\ adj : not retrievable : IRRECOVERABLE

ir·rev·er·ence \(ˌ)i-ʹre-və-rəns\ n **1** : lack of reverence **2** : an irreverent act or utterance — **ir·rev·er·ent** \-rənt\ adj — **ir·rev·er·ent·ly** adv

ir·re·vers·ible \ˌir-i-ʹvər-sə-bəl\ adj : incapable of being reversed ⟨an ~ loss⟩

ir·re·vo·ca·ble \(ˌ)i-ʹre-və-kə-bəl\ adj : incapable of being revoked or recalled ⟨~ change⟩ — **ir·rev·o·ca·bly** \-blē\ adv

ir·ri·gate \ʹir-ə-ˌgāt\ vb **-gat·ed; -gat·ing** : to supply (as land) with water by artificial means; also : to flush with liquid — **ir·ri·ga·tion** \ˌir-ə-ʹgā-shən\ n

ir·ri·ta·bil·i·ty \ˌir-ə-tə-ʹbi-lə-tē\ n **1** : the property of living things and of protoplasm that enables reaction to stimuli **2** : the quality or state of being irritable; esp : readiness to become annoyed or angry

ir·ri·ta·ble \ʹir-ə-tə-bəl\ adj : capable of being irritated; esp : readily or easily irritated — **ir·ri·ta·bly** \-blē\ adv

ir·ri·tate \ʹir-ə-ˌtāt\ vb **-tat·ed; -tat·ing 1** : to excite to anger

: EXASPERATE **2** : to make sore or inflamed — **ir·ri·tant** \\'ir-ə-tənt\\ *adj or n* — **ir·ri·tat·ing·ly** *adv* — **ir·ri·ta·tion** \\ˌir-ə-'tā-shən\\ *n*

ir·rupt \\(ˌ)i-'rəpt\\ *vb* **1** : to rush in forcibly or violently **2** : to increase suddenly in numbers ⟨rabbits ~ in cycles⟩ — **ir·rup·tion** \\-'rəp-shən\\ *n*

IRS *abbr* Internal Revenue Service

is *pres 3d sing of* BE

Isa *or* **Is** *abbr* Isaiah

Isa·iah \\ī-'zā-ə\\ *n* — see BIBLE table

Isa·ias \\ī-'zā-əs\\ *n* : ISAIAH

ISBN *abbr* International Standard Book Number

is·che·mia \\is-'kē-mē-ə\\ *n* : deficient supply of blood to a body part (as the brain) — **is·che·mic** \\-mik\\ *adj*

-ish *adj suffix* **1** : of, relating to, or being ⟨Finn*ish*⟩ **2** : characteristic of ⟨boy*ish*⟩ ⟨mul*ish*⟩ **3** : inclined or liable to ⟨book*ish*⟩ **4** : having a touch or trace of : somewhat ⟨purpl*ish*⟩ **5** : having the approximate age of ⟨forty*ish*⟩

isin·glass \\'ī-z³n-ˌglas, 'ī-ziŋ-\\ *n* **1** : a gelatin obtained from various fish **2** : mica esp. in thin sheets

isl *abbr* island

Is·lam \\is-'läm, iz-, -'lam, 'is-ˌ, 'iz-ˌ\\ *n* [Ar *islām* submission (to the will of God)] : the religious faith of Muslims including belief in Allah as the sole deity and in Muhammad as his prophet; *also* : the civilization built on this faith — **Is·lam·ic** \\is-'lä-mik, iz-, -'la-\\ *adj*

is·land \\'ī-lənd\\ *n* [ME *iland*, fr. OE *īgland*, fr. *īg* island + *land* land] **1** : a body of land smaller than a continent surrounded by water **2** : something resembling an island in its isolation

is·land·er \\'ī-lən-dər\\ *n* : a native or inhabitant of an island

isle \\'ī(-ə)l\\ *n* : ISLAND; *esp* : a small island

is·let \\'ī-lət\\ *n* : a small island

ism \\ˌi-zəm\\ *n* : a distinctive doctrine, cause, or theory

-ism *n suffix* **1** : act : practice : process ⟨critic*ism*⟩ **2** : manner of action or behavior characteristic of a (specified) person or thing ⟨fanatic*ism*⟩ **3** : state : condition : property ⟨dual*ism*⟩ **4** : abnormal state or condition ⟨alcohol*ism*⟩ **5** : doctrine : theory : cult ⟨Buddh*ism*⟩ **6** : adherence to a set of principles ⟨stoic*ism*⟩ **7** : prejudice or discrimination on the basis of a (specified) attribute ⟨rac*ism*⟩ ⟨sex*ism*⟩ **8** : characteristic or peculiar feature or trait ⟨colloquial*ism*⟩

iso·bar \\'ī-sə-ˌbär\\ *n* : a line on a map connecting places of equal barometric pressure — **iso·bar·ic** \\ˌī-sə-'bär-ik, -'ber-\\ *adj*

isobars

iso·late \\'ī-sə-ˌlāt\\ *vb* **-lat·ed; -lat·ing** [fr. *isolated* set apart, fr. F *isolé*, fr. It *isolato*, fr. *isola* island, fr. L *insula*] : to place or keep by itself : separate from others — **iso·la·tion** \\ˌī-sə-'lā-shən\\ *n*

isolated *adj* **1** : occurring alone or once : UNIQUE **2** : SPORADIC ⟨~ outbreaks⟩

iso·la·tion·ism \\ˌī-sə-'lā-shə-ˌni-zəm\\ *n* : a policy of national isolation by abstention from international political and economic relations — **iso·la·tion·ist** \\-shə-nist\\ *n or adj*

iso·mer \\'ī-sə-mər\\ *n* : any of two or more chemical compounds that contain the same numbers of atoms of the same elements but differ in structural arrangement and properties — **iso·mer·ic** \\ˌī-sə-'mer-ik\\ *adj* — **isom·er·ism** \\ī-'sä-mə-ˌri-zəm\\ *n*

iso·met·rics \\ˌī-sə-'me-triks\\ *n sing or pl* : exercise involving a series of brief and intense contractions of muscles against each other or against an immovable resistance — **iso·met·ric** *adj*

iso·prene \\'ī-sə-ˌprēn\\ *n* : a hydrocarbon used esp. in making synthetic rubber

isos·ce·les \\ī-'sä-sə-ˌlēz\\ *adj* : having two equal sides ⟨an ~ triangle⟩

iso·therm \\'ī-sə-ˌthərm\\ *n* : a line on a map connecting points having the same temperature

iso·ther·mal \\ˌī-sə-'thər-məl\\ *adj* : of, relating to, or marked by equality of temperature

iso·tope \\'ī-sə-ˌtōp\\ *n* [Gk *isos* equal + *topos* place] : any of the forms of a chemical element that differ chiefly in the number of neutrons in an atom — **iso·to·pic** \\ˌī-sə-'tä-pik, -'tō-\\ *adj* — **iso·to·pi·cal·ly** \\-'tä-pi-k(ə-)lē, -'tō-\\ *adv*

ISP *abbr* Internet service provider

Isr *abbr* Israel; Israeli

Is·ra·el·ite \\'iz-rē-ə-ˌlīt\\ *n* : a member of the Hebrew people descended from Jacob

is·su·ance \\'i-shü-wəns\\ *n* : the act of issuing or giving out esp. officially

¹is·sue \\'i-shü\\ *n* [ME, exit, proceeds, fr. AF, fr. *issir* to come out, go out, fr. L. *exire*, fr. *ire* to go] **1** : the action of going, coming, or flowing out : EGRESS, EMERGENCE **2** : EXIT, OUTLET, VENT **3** : OFFSPRING, PROGENY **4** : OUTCOME, RESULT **5** : a point of debate or controversy; *also* : the point at which an unsettled matter is ready for a decision **6** : a discharge (as of blood) from the body **7** : something coming forth from a specified source **8** : the act of officially giving out or printing : PUBLICATION; *also* : the quantity of things given out at one time

²issue *vb* **is·sued; is·su·ing** **1** : to go, come, or flow out **2** : to come forth or cause to come forth : EMERGE, DISCHARGE, EMIT **3** : ACCRUE **4** : to descend from a specified parent or ancestor **5** : to result in **6** : to put forth or distribute officially **7** : PUBLISH **8** : EMANATE, RESULT — **is·su·er** *n*

¹-ist *n suffix* **1** : one that performs a (specified) action ⟨cyc*list*⟩ : one that makes or produces ⟨novel*ist*⟩ **2** : one that plays a (specified) musical instrument ⟨harp*ist*⟩ **3** : one that operates a (specified) mechanical instrument or contrivance ⟨machin*ist*⟩ **4** : one that specializes in a (specified) art or science or skill ⟨geolog*ist*⟩ **5** : one that adheres to or advocates a (specified) doctrine or system or code of behavior ⟨social*ist*⟩ or that of a (specified) individual ⟨Darwin*ist*⟩

²-ist *adj suffix* : -ISTIC

isth·mus \\'is-məs\\ *n* : a narrow strip of land connecting two larger land areas

¹it \\'it, ət\\ *pron* **1** : that one — used of a lifeless thing, a plant, a person or animal, or an abstract entity ⟨~'s a big building⟩ ⟨~'s a shade tree⟩ ⟨who is ~⟩ ⟨beauty is everywhere and ~ is a source of joy⟩ **2** — used as a subject of an impersonal verb that expresses a condition or action without reference to an agent ⟨~ is raining⟩ **3** — used as an anticipatory subject or object ⟨~'s good to see you⟩

²it \\'it\\ *n* : the player in a game who performs the principal action of the game (as trying to find others in hide-and-seek)

It *abbr* Italian; Italy

ital *abbr* italic; italicized

Ital *abbr* Italian

Ital·ian \\i-'tal-yən\\ *n* **1** : a native or inhabitant of Italy **2** : the language of Italy — **Italian** *adj*

ital·ic \\i-'ta-lik, ī-\\ *adj* : relating to type in which the letters slope up toward the right (as in *"italic"*) — **italic** *n*

ital·i·cise *Brit var of* ITALICIZE

ital·i·cize \\i-'ta-lə-ˌsīz, ī-\\ *vb* **-cized; -ciz·ing** : to print in italics — **ital·i·ci·za·tion** \\-ˌta-lə-sə-'zā-shən\\ *n*

itch \\'ich\\ *n* **1** : an uneasy irritating skin sensation that evokes a desire to scratch the affected area **2** : a skin disorder accompanied by an itch **3** : a persistent desire — **itch** *vb* — **itchy** *adj*

-ite *n suffix* **1** : native : resident ⟨suburban*ite*⟩ **2** : adherent : follower ⟨Lenin*ite*⟩ **3** : product ⟨metabol*ite*⟩ **4** : mineral : rock ⟨quartz*ite*⟩

item \\'ī-təm\\ *n* [L, likewise, also] **1** : a separate particular in a list, account, or series : ARTICLE **2** : a separate piece of news (as in a newspaper)

item·ise *Brit var of* ITEMIZE

item·ize \\'ī-tə-ˌmīz\\ *vb* **-ized; -iz·ing** : to set down in detail : LIST — **item·i·za·tion** \\ˌī-tə-mə-'zā-shən\\ *n*

it·er·ate \\'i-tə-ˌrāt\\ *vb* **-at·ed; -at·ing** : REITERATE ⟨*iterated* his innocence⟩

it·er·a·tion \\ˌi-tə-'rā-shən\\ *n* **1** : REPETITION; *esp* : a computational process in which a series of operations is repeated until a condition is met **2** : one repetition of the series of operations in iteration **3** : VERSION

itin·er·ant \ī-'ti-nə-rənt, ə-\ *adj* : traveling from place to place; *esp* : covering a circuit ⟨an ~ preacher⟩

itin·er·ary \ī-'ti-nə-ˌrer-ē, ə-\ *n, pl* **-ar·ies** **1** : the route of a journey or the proposed outline of one **2** : a travel diary **3** : GUIDEBOOK

its \'its\ *adj* : of or relating to it or itself

it·self \it-'self\ *pron* : that identical one — used reflexively, for emphasis, or in absolute constructions

-ity *n suffix* : quality : state : degree ⟨alkalin*ity*⟩

IUD \ˌī-(ˌ)yü-'dē\ *n* : INTRAUTERINE DEVICE

IV \ˌī-'vē\ *n, pl* **IVs** [*intravenous*] : an apparatus used to administer a fluid (as of nutrients) intravenously; *also* : a fluid administered by IV

-ive *adj suffix* : that performs or tends toward an (indicated) action ⟨correct*ive*⟩

ivo·ry \'ī-vrē, -və-rē\ *n, pl* **-ries** [ME *ivorie*, fr. AF *ivoire, ivurie*, fr. L *eboreus* of ivory, fr. *ebur* ivory] **1** : the hard creamy-white material composing the tusks of an elephant or walrus **2** : a pale yellow color **3** : something made of ivory or of a similar substance

ivory tower *n* **1** : an impractical lack of concern with urgent problems **2** : a place of learning

ivy \'ī-vē\ *n, pl* **ivies** : a trailing woody evergreen vine with small black berries that is related to ginseng

IWW *abbr* Industrial Workers of the World

-ize *vb suffix* **1** : cause to be or conform to or resemble ⟨American*ize*⟩ : cause to be formed into ⟨union*ize*⟩ **2** : subject to a (specified) action ⟨satir*ize*⟩ **3** : saturate, treat, or combine with ⟨macadam*ize*⟩ **4** : treat like ⟨idol*ize*⟩ **5** : become : become like ⟨crystall*ize*⟩ **6** : be productive in or of : engage in a (specified) activity ⟨philosoph*ize*⟩ **7** : adopt or spread the manner of activity or the teaching of ⟨Christian*ize*⟩

J

¹j \'jā\ *n, pl* **j's** *or* **js** \'jāz\ *often cap* : the 10th letter of the English alphabet

²j *abbr, often cap* **1** jack **2** journal **3** judge **4** justice

¹jab \'jab\ *vb* **jabbed; jab·bing** : to thrust quickly or abruptly : POKE

²jab *n* : a usu. short straight punch

jab·ber \'ja-bər\ *vb* : to talk rapidly, indistinctly, or unintelligibly : CHATTER — **jabber** *n* — **jab·ber·er** *n*

jab·ber·wocky \'ja-bər-ˌwä-kē\ *n* : meaningless speech or writing

ja·bot \zha-'bō, 'ja-ˌbō\ *n* : a ruffle worn down the front of a dress or shirt

jac·a·ran·da \ˌja-kə-'ran-də\ *n* : any of a genus of pinnate-leaved tropical American trees with clusters of showy blue flowers

¹jack \'jak\ *n* **1** : a mechanical device; *esp* : one used to raise a heavy body a short distance **2** : a male donkey **3** : a small target ball in lawn bowling **4** : a small national flag flown by a ship **5** : a small 6-pointed metal object used in a game (**jacks**) **6** : a playing card bearing the figure of a soldier or servant **7** : a socket into which a plug is inserted for connecting electric circuits

²jack *vb* **1** : to raise by means of a jack **2** : INCREASE ⟨~ up prices⟩

jack·al \'ja-kəl\ *n* [Turk *çakal*, fr. Pers *shaqāl*] : any of several mammals of Asia and Africa related to the wolves

jack·a·napes \'ja-kə-ˌnāps\ *n* **1** : MONKEY, APE **2** : an impudent or conceited person

jack·ass \'jak-ˌas\ *n* **1** : DONKEY; *esp* : a male donkey **2** : a stupid person : FOOL

jack·boot \-ˌbüt\ *n* **1** : a heavy military boot of glossy black leather extending above the knee **2** : a laceless military boot reaching to the calf

jack·daw \'jak-ˌdȯ\ *n* : a black and gray Old World crow-like bird

jack·et \'ja-kət\ *n* [ME *jaket*, fr. AF *jackés*, pl., dim. of MF *jaque* short jacket, fr. *jacques* peasant, fr. the name *Jacques* James] **1** : a garment for the upper body usu. having a front opening, collar, and sleeves **2** : an outer covering or casing ⟨a book ~⟩

Jack Frost *n* : frost or frosty weather personified

jack·ham·mer \'jak-ˌha-mər\ *n* : a pneumatic percussion tool for drilling rock or breaking pavement

jack–in–the–box *n, pl* **jack–in–the–boxes** *or* **jacks–in–the–box** : a toy consisting of a small box out of which a figure springs when the lid is raised

jack–in–the–pulpit *n, pl* **jack–in–the–pulpits** *also* **jacks–in–the–pulpit** : a No. American spring-flowering woodland herb having an upright club-shaped spadix arched over by a green and purple spathe

¹jack·knife \'jak-ˌnīf\ *n* **1** : a large pocketknife **2** : a dive

in which the diver bends from the waist and touches the ankles before straightening out

²jackknife *vb* : to fold like a jackknife ⟨the trailer truck *jackknifed*⟩

jack·leg \'jak-ˌleg\ *adj* **1** : lacking skill or training **2** : MAKESHIFT

jack-of-all-trades *n, pl* **jacks-of-all-trades** : one who is able to do passable work at various tasks

jack-o'-lan·tern \'ja-kə-ˌlan-tərn\ *n* : a lantern made of a pumpkin cut to look like a human face

jack·pot \'jak-ˌpät\ *n* **1** : a large sum of money formed by the accumulation of stakes from previous play (as in poker) **2** : an impressive and often unexpected success or reward

jack·rab·bit \-ˌra-bət\ *n* : any of several large hares of western No. America with very long ears and hind legs

Jack Russell terrier \'jak-'rə-səl-\ *n* : any of a breed of small terriers having a white coat with dark markings

jack·straw \-ˌstrȯ\ *n* **1** *pl* : a game in which straws or thin sticks are let fall in a heap and each player in turn tries to remove them one at a time without disturbing the rest **2** : one of the pieces used in jackstraws

jack·tar \-'tär\ *n, often cap* : SAILOR

Ja·cob's ladder \'jā-kəbz-\ *n* : any of several perennial herbs related to phlox that have pinnate leaves and blue or white bell-shaped flowers

jac·quard \'ja-ˌkärd\ *n, often cap* : a fabric of intricate variegated weave or pattern

¹jade \'jād\ *n* **1** : a broken-down, vicious, or worthless horse **2** : a disreputable woman

²jade *vb* **jad·ed; jad·ing** **1** : to wear out by overwork or abuse **2** : to become weary ♦ **Synonyms** EXHAUST, FATIGUE, TIRE

³jade *n* [F, fr. obs. Sp (*piedra de la*) *ijada*, lit., loin stone; fr. the belief that jade cures renal colic] : a usu. green gemstone that takes a high polish

jad·ed *adj* : made dull, apathetic, or cynical by experience or by surfeit

¹jag \'jag\ *n* : a sharp projecting part

²jag *n* : SPREE ⟨a crying ~⟩

jag·ged \'ja-gəd\ *adj* : sharply notched

jag·uar \'ja-ˌgwär\ *n* : a black-spotted tropical American cat that is larger and stockier than the Old World leopard

jai alai \'hī-ˌlī\ *n* [Sp, fr. Basque, fr. *jai* festival + *alai* merry] : a court game played by usu. two or four players with a ball and a curved wicker basket strapped to the wrist

jail \'jāl\ *n* [ME *jaiole*, fr. AF *gaiole, jaiole*, fr. LL *caveola*, dim. of L *cavea* cage] : PRISON; *esp* : one for persons held in lawful custody — **jail** *vb*

jail·bird \-ˌbərd\ *n* : a habitual criminal

jail·break \-ˌbrāk\ *n* : a forcible escape from jail

jaguar

jail·er *also* **jail·or** \'jā-lər\ *n* : a keeper of a jail
jal·ap \'ja-ləp, 'jä-\ *n* : a powdered purgative drug from the root of a Mexican plant related to the morning glory; *also* : this root or plant
ja·la·pe·ño \ˌhä-lə-'pān-(ˌ)yō\ *n* : a small plump dark green chili pepper
ja·lopy \jə-'lä-pē\ *n, pl* **ja·lop·ies** : a dilapidated vehicle (as an automobile)
jal·ou·sie \'ja-lə-sē\ *n* [F, lit., jealousy] : a blind, window, or door with adjustable horizontal slats or louvers
¹**jam** \'jam\ *vb* **jammed; jam·ming** **1** : to press into a close or tight position **2** : to cause to become wedged so as to be unworkable; *also* : to make or become unworkable through the jamming of a movable part **3** : to push forcibly ⟨∼ on the brakes⟩ **4** : CRUSH, BRUISE ⟨jammed a finger in the door⟩ **5** : to make unintelligible by sending out interfering signals or messages **6** : to take part in a jam session — **jam·mer** *n*
²**jam** *n* **1** : a crowded mass that impedes or blocks ⟨traffic ∼⟩ **2** : a difficult state of affairs
³**jam** *n* : a food made by boiling fruit and sugar to a thick consistency
Jam *abbr* Jamaica
jamb \'jam\ *n* [ME *jambe*, fr. AF *jambe, gambe,* lit., leg] : an upright piece forming the side of an opening (as of a door)
jam·ba·laya \ˌjəm-bə-'lī-ə\ *n* [LaF] : rice cooked with ham, sausage, chicken, shrimp, or oysters and seasoned with herbs
jam·bo·ree \ˌjam-bə-'rē\ *n* : a large festive gathering
James \'jāmz\ *n* — see BIBLE table
jam–pack \'jam-'pak\ *vb* : to pack tightly or to excess
jam session *n* : an impromptu performance esp. by jazz musicians
Jan *abbr* January
jan·gle \'jaŋ-gəl\ *vb* **jan·gled; jan·gling** : to make a harsh or discordant sound — **jangle** *n*
jan·i·tor \'ja-nə-tər\ *n* [L, doorkeeper, fr. *janus* arch, gate] : a person who has the care of a building — **jan·i·to·ri·al** \ˌja-nə-'tȯr-ē-əl\ *adj*
Jan·u·ary \'ja-nyə-ˌwer-ē\ *n* [ME *Januarie,* fr. L *Januarius,* first month of the ancient Roman year, fr. *Janus,* two-faced god of gates and beginnings] : the 1st month of the year
¹**ja·pan** \jə-'pan\ *n* : a varnish giving a hard brilliant finish
²**japan** *vb* **ja·panned; ja·pan·ning** : to cover with a coat of japan
Jap·a·nese \ˌja-pə-'nēz, -'nēs\ *n, pl* **Japanese** **1** : a native or inhabitant of Japan **2** : the language of Japan — **Japanese** *adj*
Japanese beetle *n* : a small metallic green and brown scarab beetle introduced from Japan that is a pest on the roots of grasses as a grub and on foliage and fruits as an adult
¹**jape** \'jāp\ *vb* **japed; jap·ing** **1** : JOKE **2** : MOCK
²**jape** *n* : JEST, GIBE
¹**jar** \'jär\ *vb* **jarred; jar·ring** **1** : to make a harsh or discordant sound **2** : to have a harsh or disagreeable effect **3** : VIBRATE, SHAKE ⟨tremors *jarred* the house⟩
²**jar** *n* **1** : a state of conflict **2** : a harsh discordant sound **3** : JOLT **4** : a painful effect : SHOCK
³**jar** *n* : a widemouthed container usu. of glass or earthenware
jar·di·niere \ˌjär-də-'nir\ *n* : an ornamental stand for plants or flowers

jar·gon \'jär-gən\ *n* **1** : confused unintelligible language **2** : the special vocabulary of a particular group or activity **3** : obscure and often pretentious language
Jas *abbr* James
jas·mine \'jaz-mən\ *also* **jes·sa·mine** \'jes-mən, 'je-sə-\ *n* [MF *jasmin,* fr. Ar *yāsamīn,* fr. Pers] : any of various climbing shrubs with fragrant flowers
jas·per \'jas-pər\ *n* : a usu. red, yellow, or brown opaque quartz
jaun·dice \'jȯn-dəs\ *n* : yellowish discoloration of skin, tissues, and body fluids by bile pigments; *also* : an abnormal condition marked by jaundice
jaun·diced \-dəst\ *adj* **1** : affected with or as if with jaundice **2** : exhibiting envy, distaste, or hostility ⟨a ∼ critic⟩
jaunt \'jȯnt\ *n* : a short trip usu. for pleasure
jaun·ty \'jȯn-tē\ *adj* **jaun·ti·er; -est** : sprightly in manner or appearance : LIVELY ⟨∼ tunes⟩ — **jaun·ti·ly** \-tə-lē\ *adv* — **jaun·ti·ness** \-tē-nəs\ *n*
jav·e·lin \'jav-və-lən\ *n* **1** : a light spear **2** : a slender shaft thrown for distance in a track-and-field contest
¹**jaw** \'jȯ\ *n* **1** : either of the bony or cartilaginous structures that support the soft tissues enclosing the mouth and that usu. bear teeth **2** : the parts forming the walls of the mouth and serving to open and close it — usu. used in pl. **3** : one of a pair of movable parts for holding or crushing something — **jawed** \'jȯd\ *adj*
²**jaw** *vb* : to talk abusively, indignantly, or at length ⟨∼ing with her sister⟩
¹**jaw·bone** \-ˌbōn\ *n* : JAW 1
²**jawbone** *vb* : to talk forcefully and persuasively
jaw·break·er \-ˌbrā-kər\ *n* **1** : a word difficult to pronounce **2** : a round hard candy
jaw–drop·ping \'jȯ-ˌdra-piŋ\ *adj* : causing great surprise or astonishment
jaw·less fish \'jȯ-ləs-\ *n* : any of a group of primitive vertebrates (as lampreys) without jaws
jay \'jā\ *n* : any of various noisy brightly colored often largely blue birds smaller than the related crows
jay·bird \'jā-ˌbərd\ *n* : JAY
jay·vee \ˌjā-'vē\ *n* **1** : JUNIOR VARSITY **2** : a member of a junior varsity team
jay·walk \'jā-ˌwȯk\ *vb* : to cross a street carelessly without regard for traffic regulations — **jay·walk·er** *n*
¹**jazz** \'jaz\ *n* **1** : American music characterized by improvisation, syncopated rhythms, and contrapuntal ensemble playing **2** : empty talk **3** : similar but unspecified things : STUFF
²**jazz** *vb* : ENLIVEN ⟨∼ things up⟩
jazzy \'ja-zē\ *adj* **jazz·i·er; -est** **1** : having the characteristics of jazz **2** : marked by unrestraint, animation, or flashiness
JCS *abbr* joint chiefs of staff
jct *abbr* junction
JD *abbr* **1** [L *juris doctor*] doctor of jurisprudence; doctor of law **2** [L *jurum doctor*] doctor of laws **3** justice department **4** juvenile delinquent
jeal·ous \'je-ləs\ *adj* **1** : demanding complete devotion **2** : suspicious of a rival or of one believed to enjoy an advantage ⟨∼ of his rich friends⟩ **3** : VIGILANT — **jeal·ous·ly** *adv* — **jeal·ou·sy** \-lə-sē\ *n*
jeans \'jēnz\ *n, pl* [pl. of *jean* twilled cloth, short for *jean fustian,* fr. ME *Gene* Genoa, Italy] : pants made of durable twilled cotton cloth
jeep \'jēp\ *n* : a small four-wheel drive general-purpose motor vehicle used in World War II
¹**jeer** \'jir\ *vb* : to speak or cry out in derision : MOCK ⟨∼ed the umpire⟩
²**jeer** *n* : TAUNT ⟨∼ed by the bully⟩
Je·ho·vah \ji-'hō-və\ *n* : GOD 1
je·hu \'jē-hü, -hyü\ *n* : a driver of a coach or cab
je·june \ji-'jün\ *adj* [L *jejunus* empty of food, hungry, meager] : lacking interest or significance : DULL
je·ju·num \ji-'jü-nəm\ *n* [L] : the section of the small intestine between the duodenum and the ileum — **je·ju·nal** \-'jü-nᵊl\ *adj*
jell \'jel\ *vb* **1** : to come to the consistency of jelly **2** : to take shape ⟨my ideas began to ∼⟩
jel·ly \'je-lē\ *n, pl* **jellies** **1** : a food with a soft elastic consistency due usu. to the presence of gelatin or pectin; *esp* : a fruit product made by boiling sugar and the juice of a fruit **2** : a substance resembling jelly — **jelly** *vb* — **jel·ly·like** *adj*

jelly bean *n* : a bean-shaped candy

jel·ly·fish \'je-lē-ˌfish\ *n* : a marine coelenterate with a nearly transparent jellylike body and stinging tentacles

jen·net \'je-nət\ *n* **1** : a small Spanish horse **2** : a female donkey

jen·ny \'je-nē\ *n, pl* **jennies** : a female bird or donkey

je·on \(ˌ)jä-'ȯn\ *n, pl* **jeon** — see **won** at MONEY table

jeop·ar·dy \'je-pər-dē\ *n* [ME *jeopardie*, fr. AF *juparti, jeuparti* alternative, lit., divided game] : exposure to death, loss, or injury ♦ *Synonyms* PERIL, HAZARD, RISK, DANGER — **jeop·ar·dize** \-ˌdīz\ *vb*

Jer *abbr* Jeremiah; Jeremias

jer·e·mi·ad \ˌjer-ə-'mī-əd, -ˌad\ *n* : a prolonged lamentation or complaint; *also* : a cautionary or angry harangue

Jer·e·mi·ah \ˌjer-ə-'mī-ə\ *n* — see BIBLE table

Jer·e·mi·as \ˌjer-ə-'mī-əs\ *n* : JEREMIAH

¹jerk \'jərk\ *n* **1** : a short quick pull or twist : TWITCH **2** : an annoyingly stupid or foolish person — **jerk·i·ly** \'jər-kə-lē\ *adv* — **jerky** \'jər-kē\ *adj*

²jerk *vb* **1** : to give a sharp quick push, pull, or twist **2** : to move in short abrupt motions

jer·kin \'jər-kən\ *n* : a close-fitting usu. sleeveless jacket

jerk·wa·ter \'jərk-ˌwȯ-tər, -ˌwä-\ *adj* [fr. *jerkwater* rural train] : of minor importance : INSIGNIFICANT ⟨∼ towns⟩

jer·ry-built \'jer-ē-ˌbilt\ *adj* : built cheaply and flimsily

jer·ry-rigged \-ˌrigd\ *adj* : organized or constructed in a crude or improvised manner

jer·sey \'jər-zē\ *n, pl* **jerseys** [*Jersey*, one of the Channel islands] **1** : a plain weft-knitted fabric **2** : a close-fitting knitted shirt **3** *often cap* : any of a breed of small usu. fawn-colored dairy cattle

Jersey barrier *n* : a concrete slab that is used with others to block or reroute traffic or to divide a highway

Je·ru·sa·lem artichoke \jə-'rü-sə-ləm-\ *n* : a No. American sunflower widely grown for its edible tubers that are used as a vegetable; *also* : its tubers

jess \'jes\ *n* : a leg strap by which a captive bird of prey may be controlled

jessamine *var of* JASMINE

jest \'jest\ *n* **1** : an act intended to provoke laughter **2** : a witty remark **3** : a frivolous mood ⟨said in ∼⟩ — **jest** *vb*

jest·er \'jes-tər\ *n* : a retainer formerly kept to provide casual entertainment

¹jet \'jet\ *n* : a velvet-black coal that takes a good polish and is often used for jewelry

²jet *vb* **jet·ted; jet·ting** : to spout or emit in a stream

³jet *n* **1** : a forceful rush (as of liquid or gas) through a narrow opening; *also* : a nozzle for a jet of fluid **2** : a jet-propelled airplane

⁴jet *vb* **jet·ted; jet·ting** : to travel by jet

jet lag *n* : a condition that is marked esp. by fatigue and irritability and occurs following a long flight through several time zones — **jet-lagged** *adj*

jet·lin·er \'jet-ˌli-nər\ *n* : a jet-propelled airliner

jet·port \-ˌpȯrt\ *n* : an airport designed to handle jets

jet–pro·pelled \ˌjet-prə-'peld\ *adj* : driven by an engine (**jet engine**) that produces propulsion (**jet propulsion**) by the rearward discharge of a jet of fluid (as heated air and exhaust gases)

jet·sam \'jet-səm\ *n* : jettisoned goods; *esp* : such goods washed ashore

jet set *n* : an international group of wealthy people who frequent fashionable resorts

jet stream *n* : a long narrow high-altitude current of high-speed winds blowing generally from the west

jet·ti·son \'je-tə-sən\ *vb* **1** : to throw (goods) overboard to lighten a ship or aircraft in distress **2** : DISCARD ⟨∼ed their old computers⟩ — **jettison** *n*

jet·ty \'je-tē\ *n, pl* **jetties** **1** : a pier built to influence the current or to protect a harbor **2** : a landing wharf

jeu d'es·prit \zhœ-des-'prē\ *n, pl* **jeux d'esprit** *same*\ [F, lit., play of the mind] : a witty comment or composition

Jew \'jü\ *n* **1** : ISRAELITE **2** : one whose religion is Judaism — **Jew·ish** *adj*

¹jew·el \'jü-əl\ *n* [ME *juel*, fr. AF, dim. of *ju, jeu* game, play, fr. L *jocus* game, joke] **1** : an ornament of precious metal **2** : GEMSTONE, GEM

²jewel *vb* **-eled** *or* **-elled; -el·ing** *or* **-el·ling** : to adorn or equip with jewels

jewel box *n* : a thin plastic case for a CD or DVD

jew·el·er *or* **jew·el·ler** \'jü-ə-lər\ *n* : a person who makes or deals in jewelry and related articles

jew·el·lery *chiefly Brit var of* JEWELRY

jew·el·ry \'jü-əl-rē\ *n* : JEWELS; *esp* : objects of precious metal set with gems and worn for personal adornment

Jew·ry \'jü-rē, 'jú-ər-ē, 'jü-rē\ *n* : the Jewish people

jg *abbr* junior grade

¹jib \'jib\ *n* : a triangular sail set on a line running from the bow to the mast

²jib *vb* **jibbed; jib·bing** : to refuse to proceed further

¹jibe *var of* GIBE

²jibe \'jīb\ *vb* **jibed; jib·ing** : to be in accord : AGREE ⟨his conclusion does not ∼ with theirs⟩

ji·ca·ma \'hē-kə-mə\ *n* : an edible starchy tuber of a tropical American vine of the legume family

jif·fy \'ji-fē\ *n, pl* **jiffies** : MOMENT, INSTANT ⟨I'll be ready in a ∼⟩

¹jig \'jig\ *n* **1** : a lively dance in triple rhythm **2** : TRICK, GAME ⟨the ∼ is up⟩ **3** : a device used to hold work during manufacture or assembly

²jig *vb* **jigged; jig·ging** : to dance a jig

jig·ger \'ji-gər\ *n* : a measure usu. holding 1 to 2 ounces (30 to 60 milliliters) used in mixing drinks

jig·gle \'ji-gəl\ *vb* **jig·gled; jig·gling** : to move with quick little jerks — **jiggle** *n*

jig·saw \'jig-ˌsȯ\ *n* : SCROLL SAW 2

jigsaw puzzle *n* : a puzzle consisting of small irregularly cut pieces to be fitted together to form a picture

ji·had \ji-'häd, -'had\ *n* **1** : a Muslim holy war **2** : CRUSADE 2

ji·had·ist \ji-'hä-dist, -'ha-\ *n* : a Muslim who advocates or participates in a jihad

¹jilt \'jilt\ *vb* : to drop (as a lover) capriciously or unfeelingly

²jilt *n* : one who jilts a lover

jim crow \'jim-'krō\ *n, often cap J&C* : discrimination against blacks esp. by legal enforcement or traditional sanctions — **jim crow** *adj, often cap J&C* — **jim crow·ism** \-'krō-ˌi-zəm\ *n, often cap J&C*

jim–dan·dy \'jim-'dan-dē\ *n* : something excellent of its kind — **jim-dandy** *adj*

jim·mies \'ji-mēz\ *n pl* : tiny rod-shaped bits of usu. chocolate-flavored candy often sprinkled on ice cream

¹jim·my \'ji-mē\ *n, pl* **jimmies** : a small crowbar

²jimmy *vb* **jim·mied; jim·my·ing** : to force open with a jimmy

jim·son·weed \'jim-sən-ˌwēd\ *n, often cap* : a coarse poisonous weed related to the tomato that has large trumpet-shaped white or violet flowers

¹jin·gle \'jiŋ-gəl\ *vb* **jin·gled; jin·gling** : to make a light clinking or tinkling sound

²jingle *n* **1** : a light clinking or tinkling sound **2** : a short verse or song with catchy repetition

jin·go·ism \'jiŋ-gō-ˌi-zəm\ *n* : extreme chauvinism or nationalism marked esp. by a belligerent foreign policy — **jin·go·ist** \-ist\ *n* — **jin·go·is·tic** \ˌjiŋ-gō-'is-tik\ *adj*

jin·rik·sha \jin-'rik-ˌshȯ\ *n* : RICKSHAW

¹jinx \'jiŋks\ *n* : one that brings bad luck

²jinx *vb* : to foredoom to failure or misfortune

jit·ney \'jit-nē\ *n, pl* **jitneys** : a small bus that serves a regular route on a flexible schedule

jit·ter·bug \'ji-tər-ˌbəg\ *n* : a dance in which couples two-step, balance, and twirl vigorously in standardized patterns — **jitterbug** *vb*

jit·ters \'ji-tərz\ *n pl* : extreme nervousness — **jit·tery** \-tə-rē\ *adj*

¹jive \'jīv\ *n* **1** : swing music or dancing performed to it **2** : glib, deceptive, or foolish talk **3** : the jargon of jazz enthusiasts

²jive *vb* **jived; jiv·ing** **1** : KID, TEASE **2** : to dance to or play jive

Jn *or* **Jno** *abbr* John

Jo *abbr* Joel

¹job \'jäb\ *n* **1** : a piece of work **2** : something that has to be done : TASK **3** : a regular remunerative position — **job·less** *adj*

²job *vb* **jobbed; job·bing** **1** : to do occasional pieces of work for hire **2** : to hire or let by the job

Job \'jōb\ *n* — see BIBLE table

job action *n* : a protest action by workers to force compliance with demands

job·ber \'jä-bər\ *n* **1** : a person who buys goods and then

sells them to other dealers : MIDDLEMAN **2** : a person who does work by the job
job·hold·er \'jäb-ˌhōl-dər\ *n* : one having a regular job
jock \'jäk\ *n* [*jockstrap*] : ATHLETE; *esp* : a school or college athlete
¹**jock·ey** \'jä-kē\ *n, pl* **jockeys** : one who rides a horse esp. as a professional in a race
²**jockey** *vb* **jock·eyed; jock·ey·ing** : to maneuver or manipulate by adroit or devious means ⟨rivals ∼*ed* for power⟩
jock·strap \'jäk-ˌstrap\ *n* [E slang *jock* penis] : ATHLETIC SUPPORTER
jo·cose \jō-'kōs\ *adj* **1** : MERRY ⟨∼ partygoers⟩ **2** : HUMOROUS ✦ *Synonyms* JOCULAR, FACETIOUS, WITTY
joc·u·lar \'jä-kyə-lər\ *adj* : marked by jesting : PLAYFUL — **joc·u·lar·i·ty** \ˌjäk-yə-'lar-ə-tē\ *n* — **joc·u·lar·ly** *adv*
jo·cund \'jä-kənd\ *adj* : marked by mirth or cheerfulness ⟨a ∼ celebration⟩
jodh·pur \'jäd-pər\ *n* **1** *pl* : riding breeches loose above the knee and tight-fitting below **2** : an ankle-high boot fastened with a strap
Joe Blow \'jō-\ *n* : an average or ordinary man
Jo·el \'jō-əl\ *n* — see BIBLE table
Joe Six–Pack \'jō-\ *n* : a blue-collar worker
¹**jog** \'jäg\ *vb* **jogged; jog·ging 1** : to give a slight shake or push to **2** : to go at a slow monotonous pace **3** : to run or ride at a slow trot — **jog·ger** *n*
²**jog** *n* **1** : a slight shake **2** : a jogging movement or pace
³**jog** *n* **1** : a projecting or retreating part of a line or surface **2** : a brief abrupt change in direction
jog·gle \'jä-gəl\ *vb* **jog·gled; jog·gling** : to shake slightly — **joggle** *n*
john \'jän\ *n* **1** : TOILET **2** : a prostitute's client
John \'jän\ *n* — see BIBLE table
john·ny \'jä-nē\ *n, pl* **johnnies** : a short-sleeved gown opening in the back that is worn by hospital patients
John·ny–jump–up \ˌjä-nē-'jəmp-ˌəp\ *n* : any of various small-flowered cultivated pansies
joie de vi·vre \ˌzhwä-də-'vēvrᵊ\ *n* [F] : keen enjoyment of life
join \'jȯin\ *vb* **1** : to bring or come together so as to form a unit **2** : to come or bring into close association **3** : to become a member of **4** : ADJOIN **5** : to take part in a collective activity
join·er \'jȯi-nər\ *n* **1** : a worker who constructs articles by joining pieces of wood **2** : a gregarious person who joins many organizations
¹**joint** \'jȯint\ *n* **1** : the point of contact between bones of an animal skeleton with the parts that surround and support it **2** : a cut of meat suitable for roasting **3** : a place where two things or parts are connected **4** : ESTABLISHMENT; *esp* : a shabby or disreputable establishment **5** : a marijuana cigarette — **joint·ed** *adj*
²**joint** *adj* **1** : UNITED **2** : common to two or more — **joint·ly** *adv*
³**joint** *vb* **1** : to unite by or provide with a joint **2** : to separate the joints of
joist \'jȯist\ *n* : any of the small beams ranged parallel from wall to wall in a building to support a floor or ceiling

floor joists

¹**joke** \'jōk\ *n* : something said or done to provoke laughter; *esp* : a brief narrative with a humorous climax
²**joke** *vb* **joked; jok·ing** : to make jokes — **jok·ing·ly** *adv*
jok·er \'jō-kər\ *n* **1** : a person who jokes **2** : an extra card used in some card games **3** : a misleading part of an agreement that works to one party's disadvantage
jol·li·fi·ca·tion \ˌjä-li-fə-'kā-shən\ *n* : a festive celebration
jol·li·ty \'jä-lə-tē\ *n, pl* **-ties** : GAIETY, MERRIMENT
jol·ly \'jä-lē\ *adj* **jol·li·er; -est** : full of high spirits : MERRY

¹**jolt** \'jōlt\ *vb* **1** : to give a quick hard knock or blow to **2** : to move with a sudden jerky motion — **jolt·er** *n*
²**jolt** *n* **1** : an abrupt jerky blow or movement **2** : a sudden shock
Jon *abbr* Jonah; Jonas
Jo·nah \'jō-nə\ *n* — see BIBLE table
Jo·nas \'jō-nəs\ *n* : JONAH
¹**jones** \'jōnz\ *n* **1** *slang* : addiction to heroin **2** *slang* : HEROIN **3** *slang* : a craving for something
²**jones** *vb, slang* : to have a craving for something
jon·gleur \zhōⁿ-'glər\ *n* : an itinerant medieval minstrel
jon·quil \'jän-kwəl\ *n* [F *jonquille*, fr. Sp *junquillo*, dim. of *junco* reed, fr. L *juncus*] : a narcissus with fragrant clustered white or yellow flowers
josh \'jäsh\ *vb* : TEASE, JOKE
Josh *abbr* Joshua
Josh·ua \'jä-shə-wə\ *n* — see BIBLE table
Joshua tree *n* : a tall branched yucca of the southwestern U.S.
jos·tle \'jä-səl\ *vb* **jos·tled; jos·tling 1** : to come in contact or into collision **2** : to make one's way by pushing and shoving ⟨*jostled* his way onto the bus⟩
Jos·ue \'jä-shü-ē\ *n* : JOSHUA
¹**jot** \'jät\ *n* : the least bit : IOTA
²**jot** *vb* **jot·ted; jot·ting** : to write briefly and hurriedly
jot·ting \'jä-tiŋ\ *n* : a brief note
joule \'jül\ *n* : a unit of work or energy equal to the work done by a force of one newton acting through a distance of one meter
jounce \'jaúns\ *vb* **jounced; jounc·ing** : JOLT — **jounce** *n*
jour *abbr* **1** journal **2** journeyman
jour·nal \'jər-nᵊl\ *n* [ME, service book containing the day hours, fr. AF *jurnal*, fr. *jurnal* daily, fr. L *diurnalis*, fr. *dies* day] **1** : a brief account of daily events **2** : a record of proceedings (as of a legislative body) **3** : a periodical (as a newspaper) dealing esp. with current events **4** : the part of a rotating axle or spindle that turns in a bearing
jour·nal·ese \ˌjər-nə-'lēz, -'lēs\ *n* : a style of writing held to be characteristic of newspapers
jour·nal·ism \'jər-nə-ˌli-zəm\ *n* **1** : the business of writing for, editing, or publishing periodicals (as newspapers) **2** : writing designed for or characteristic of newspapers — **jour·nal·ist** \-list\ *n* — **jour·nal·is·tic** \ˌjər-nə-'lis-tik\ *adj*
¹**jour·ney** \'jər-nē\ *n, pl* **journeys** [ME, fr. OF *journee* day's journey, fr. *jour* day] : a traveling from one place to another
²**journey** *vb* **jour·neyed; jour·ney·ing** : to go on a journey : TRAVEL
jour·ney·man \-mən\ *n* **1** : a worker who has learned a trade and works for another person **2** : an experienced reliable worker
¹**joust** \'jaúst\ *vb* : to engage in a joust
²**joust** *n* : a combat on horseback between two knights with lances esp. as part of a tournament
jo·vial \'jō-vē-əl\ *adj* : marked by good humor ⟨in a ∼ mood⟩ — **jo·vi·al·i·ty** \ˌjō-vē-'a-lə-tē\ *n* — **jo·vi·al·ly** *adv*
¹**jowl** \'jaúl-(ə)l\ *n* : loose flesh about the lower jaw or throat
²**jowl** *n* : the lower jaw **2** : CHEEK
¹**joy** \'jȯi\ *n* [ME, fr. AF *joie*, fr. L *gaudia*] **1** : a feeling of happiness that comes from success, good fortune, or a sense of well-being **2** : a source of happiness ✦ *Synonyms* BLISS, DELIGHT, ENJOYMENT, PLEASURE — **joy·less** *adj*
²**joy** *vb* : REJOICE
joy·ful \-fəl\ *adj* : experiencing, causing, or showing joy ⟨∼ news⟩ — **joy·ful·ly** *adv*
joy·ous \'jȯi-əs\ *adj* : JOYFUL — **joy·ous·ly** *adv* — **joy·ous·ness** *n*
joy·ride \'jȯi-ˌrīd\ *n* : a ride for pleasure often marked by reckless driving — **joyride** *vb* — **joy·rid·er** *n* — **joy·rid·ing** *n*
joy·stick \-ˌstik\ *n* : a control device (as for a computer) consisting of a lever capable of motion in two or more directions
JP *abbr* **1** jet propulsion **2** justice of the peace
JPEG \'jā-ˌpeg\ *n* [*Joint Photographic Experts Group*] : a computer file format for usu. high-quality digital images
Jr *abbr* junior
jt *or* **jnt** *abbr* joint
ju·bi·lant \'jü-bə-lənt\ *adj* [L *jubilans*, prp. of *jubilare* to rejoice] : EXULTANT ⟨∼ winners⟩ — **ju·bi·lant·ly** *adv*

ju·bi·la·tion \ˌjü-bə-ˈlā-shən\ n : EXULTATION

ju·bi·lee \ˈjü-bə-ˌlē, ˌjü-bə-ˈlē\ n [ME, fr. AF & LL; AF *jubilé*, fr. LL *jubilaeus*, fr. LGk *iōbēlaios*, fr. Heb *yōbhēl* ram's horn, trumpet, jubilee] 1 : a 50th anniversary 2 : a season or occasion of celebration

ju·co \ˈjü-ˌkō\ n, pl **jucos** : JUNIOR COLLEGE; also : an athlete at a junior college

Jud abbr Judith

Ju·da·ic \jü-ˈdā-ik\ also **Ju·da·ical** \-ˈdā-ə-kəl\ adj : of, relating to, or characteristic of Jews or Judaism

Ju·da·ism \ˈjü-də-ˌi-zəm, -dā-, -dē-\ n : a religion developed among the ancient Hebrews and marked by belief in one God and by the moral and ceremonial laws of the Old Testament and the rabbinic tradition

Jude \ˈjüd\ n — see BIBLE table

Judg abbr Judges

¹judge \ˈjəj\ vb **judged; judg·ing** 1 : to form an authoritative opinion 2 : to decide as a judge : TRY 3 : to form an estimate or evaluation about something : THINK
♦ *Synonyms* CONCLUDE, DEDUCE, GATHER, INFER

²judge n 1 : a public official authorized to decide questions brought before a court 2 : UMPIRE 3 : one who gives an authoritative opinion : CRITIC — **judge·ship** n

Judges n — see BIBLE table

judg·ment or **judge·ment** \ˈjəj-mənt\ n 1 : a decision or opinion given after judging; esp : a formal decision given by a court 2 cap : the final judging of mankind by God 3 : the process of forming an opinion by discerning and comparing 4 : the capacity for judging : DISCERNMENT

judg·men·tal \ˌjəj-ˈmen-təl\ adj 1 : of, relating to, or involving judgment 2 : characterized by a tendency to judge harshly — **judg·men·tal·ly** adv

judgment call n : a subjective decision, ruling, or opinion

Judgment Day n : the day of the final judging of all human beings by God

ju·di·ca·ture \ˈjü-di-kə-ˌchu̇r\ n 1 : the administration of justice 2 : JUDICIARY 1

ju·di·cial \ju̇-ˈdi-shəl\ adj 1 : of or relating to the administration of justice or the judiciary 2 : ordered or enforced by a court 3 : CRITICAL — **ju·di·cial·ly** adv

ju·di·cia·ry \ju̇-ˈdi-shē-ˌer-ē, -shə-rē\ n 1 : a system of courts of law; also : the judges of these courts 2 : a branch of government in which judicial power is vested — **judiciary** adj

ju·di·cious \ju̇-ˈdi-shəs\ adj : having, exercising, or characterized by sound judgment ⟨a ~ decision⟩ ♦ *Synonyms* PRUDENT, SAGE, SANE, SENSIBLE, WISE — **ju·di·cious·ly** adv

Ju·dith \ˈjü-dəth\ n — see BIBLE table

ju·do \ˈjü-dō\ n [Jp, fr. *jū* weakness, gentleness + *dō* art] : a sport derived from jujitsu that emphasizes the use of quick movement and leverage to throw an opponent — **ju·do·ist** \-ist\ n

ju·do·ka \ˈjü-dō-ˌkä\ n, pl **judoka** or **judokas** : one who participates in judo

¹jug \ˈjəg\ n 1 : a large deep container with a narrow mouth and a handle 2 : JAIL, PRISON

²jug vb **jugged;** : JAIL, IMPRISON

jug–eared \ˈjəg-ˌird\ adj : having protuberant ears

jug·ger·naut \ˈjə-gər-ˌnȯt\ n [Hindi *Jagannāth*, title of Vishnu (a Hindu god), lit., lord of the world] : a massive inexorable force or object that crushes everything in its path

jug·gle \ˈjə-gəl\ vb **jug·gled; jug·gling** 1 : to keep several objects in motion in the air at the same time 2 : to manipulate esp. in order to achieve a desired and often fraudulent end — **jug·gler** \ˈjə-glər\ n

jug·u·lar \ˈjə-gyə-lər\ adj : of, relating to, or situated in or on the throat or neck ⟨the ~ veins⟩

juice \ˈjüs\ n 1 : the extractable fluid contents of cells or tissues 2 pl : the natural fluids of an animal body 3 : something that supplies power; esp : ELECTRICITY

juic·er \ˈjü-sər\ n : an appliance for extracting juice (as from fruit)

juice up vb : to give life, energy, or spirit to ⟨*juice up* the music⟩

juicy \ˈjü-sē\ adj **juic·i·er; -est** 1 : SUCCULENT 2 : rich in interest; also : RACY ⟨~ gossip⟩ — **juic·i·ly** \-sə-lē\ adv — **juic·i·ness** \-sē-nəs\ n

ju·jit·su also **ju·jut·su** or **jiu·jit·su** \jü-ˈjit-sü\ n : an art of fighting employing holds, throws, and paralyzing blows

ju·ju \ˈjü-jü\ n : a style of African music characterized by a rapid beat, use of percussion instruments, and vocal harmonies

ju·jube \ˈjü-ˌjüb, ˈjü-jü-ˌbē\ n : a fruit-flavored gumdrop or lozenge

juke·box \ˈjük-ˌbäks\ n : a coin-operated machine that automatically plays selected recordings

Jul abbr July

ju·lep \ˈjü-ləp\ n [ME, sweetened water, fr. MF, fr. Ar *julāb*, fr. Pers *gulāb*, fr. *gul* rose + *āb* water] : a drink made of bourbon, sugar, and mint served over crushed ice

Ju·ly \ju̇-ˈlī\ n [ME *Julie*, fr. OE *Julius*, fr. L, fr. Gaius *Julius* Caesar] : the 7th month of the year

¹jum·ble \ˈjəm-bəl\ vb **jum·bled; jum·bling** : to mix in a confused mass

²jumble n : a disorderly mass or pile

jum·bo \ˈjəm-bō\ n, pl **jumbos** [*Jumbo*, a huge elephant exhibited by P.T. Barnum] : a very large specimen of its kind ⟨a ~ TV screen⟩ — **jumbo** adj

¹jump \ˈjəmp\ vb 1 : to spring into the air : leap over 2 : to give a start 3 : to rise or increase suddenly or sharply 4 : to make a sudden attack 5 : to leave hurriedly and often furtively ⟨~ town⟩ 6 : to act or move before (as a signal) — **jump bail** : to abscond after being released from custody on bail — **jump ship** 1 : to leave the company of a ship without authority 2 : to desert a cause — **jump the gun** : to begin something before the proper time

²jump n 1 : a spring into the air; esp : one made for height or distance in a track meet 2 : a sharp sudden increase 3 : an initial advantage ⟨got the ~ on his rival⟩

¹jump·er \ˈjəm-pər\ n : one that jumps

²jumper n 1 : a loose blouse 2 : a sleeveless one-piece dress worn usu. with a blouse 3 pl : a child's sleeveless coverall

jumping bean n : a seed of any of several Mexican shrubs that tumbles about because of the movements of a small moth larva inside it

jumping–off place n 1 : a remote or isolated place 2 : a place from which an enterprise is launched

jump·mas·ter \ˈjəmp-ˌmas-tər\ n : a person who supervises parachutists

jump–start \ˈjəmp-ˌstärt\ vb : to start (an engine or vehicle) by connection to an external power source

jump·suit \ˈjəmp-ˌsüt\ n 1 : a coverall worn by parachutists in jumping 2 : a one-piece garment consisting of a blouse or shirt with attached pants or shorts

jumpy \ˈjəm-pē\ adj **jump·i·er; -est** : NERVOUS, JITTERY

jun abbr junior

Jun abbr June

junc abbr junction

jun·co \ˈjəŋ-kō\ n, pl **juncos** or **juncoes** : any of a genus of small common pink-billed No. American finches that are largely gray with conspicuous white tail feathers

junc·tion \ˈjəŋk-shən\ n 1 : an act of joining 2 : a place or point of meeting

junc·ture \ˈjəŋk-chər\ n 1 : JOINT, CONNECTION 2 : UNION 3 : a critical time or state of affairs

June \ˈjün\ n [ME, fr. L *Junius*] : the 6th month of the year

jun·gle \ˈjəŋ-gəl\ n [Hindi & Urdu *jangal* forest] 1 : a thick tangled mass of tropical vegetation; also : a tract overgrown with vegetation 2 : a place of ruthless struggle for survival

¹ju·nior \ˈjü-nyər\ adj 1 : YOUNGER 2 : lower in rank ⟨a ~ partner⟩ 3 : of or relating to juniors

²junior n 1 : a person who is younger or of lower rank than another 2 : a student in the next-to-last year before graduating

junior college n : a school that offers studies corresponding to those of the 1st two years of college

junior high school n : a school usu. including grades 7–9

junior varsity n : a team whose members lack the experience or qualifications required for the varsity

ju·ni·per \ˈjü-nə-pər\ n : any of numerous coniferous shrubs or trees with leaves like needles or scales and female cones like berries

¹junk \ˈjəŋk\ n 1 : old iron, glass, paper, or waste; also : discarded articles 2 : a shoddy product 3 : something of little meaning, worth, or significance 4 slang : NARCOTICS; esp : HEROIN — **junky** adj

²junk vb : DISCARD, SCRAP

³**junk** *n* : a ship of eastern Asia with a high stern and 4-cornered sails

junk·er \'jəŋ-kər\ *n* : something (as an old automobile) ready for scrapping

Jun·ker \'yůŋ-kər\ *n* [G] : a member of the Prussian landed aristocracy

jun·ket \'jəŋ-kət\ *n* 1 : a pudding of sweetened flavored milk set by rennet 2 : a trip made by an official at public expense

junk food *n* : food that is high in calories but low in nutritional content

junk·ie *also* **junky** \'jəŋ-kē\ *n, pl* **junkies** 1 : a narcotics peddler or addict 2 : one that derives inordinate pleasure from or is dependent on something ⟨a sugar ~⟩

jun·ta \'hůn-tə, 'jən-, 'hən-\ *n* [Sp, fr. *junto* joined, fr. L *junctus*, pp. of *jungere* to join] : a group of persons controlling a government esp. after a revolutionary seizure of power

Ju·pi·ter \'jü-pə-tər\ *n* : the largest of the planets and the one 5th in order of distance from the sun

Ju·ras·sic \jů-'ra-sik\ *adj* : of, relating to, or being the period of the Mesozoic era between the Triassic and the Cretaceous that is marked esp. by the presence of dinosaurs — **Jurassic** *n*

ju·rid·i·cal \jů-'ri-di-kəl\ *also* **ju·rid·ic** \-dik\ *adj* 1 : of or relating to the administration of justice 2 : LEGAL — **ju·rid·i·cal·ly** \-di-k(ə-)lē\ *adv*

ju·ris·dic·tion \,jůr-əs-'dik-shən\ *n* 1 : the power, right, or authority to interpret and apply the law 2 : the authority of a sovereign power 3 : the limits or territory within which authority may be exercised — **ju·ris·dic·tion·al** \-shə-nəl\ *adj*

ju·ris·pru·dence \-'prü-dᵊns\ *n* 1 : the science or philosophy of law 2 : a system of laws

ju·rist \'jůr-ist\ *n* : one having a thorough knowledge of law; *esp* : JUDGE

ju·ris·tic \jů-'ris-tik\ *adj* 1 : of or relating to a jurist or jurisprudence 2 : of, relating to, or recognized in law

ju·ror \'jůr-ər, -,ór\ *n* : a member of a jury

¹**ju·ry** \'jůr-ē\ *n, pl* **juries** 1 : a body of persons sworn to inquire into a matter submitted to them and to give their verdict 2 : a committee for judging and awarding prizes

²**jury** *adj* : improvised for temporary use esp. in an emergency ⟨a ~ mast⟩

jury nullification *n* : the acquitting of a defendant by a jury in disregard of the judge's instructions and contrary to the jury's findings of fact

jury-rig \'jůr-ē-,rig\ *vb* : to construct or arrange in a makeshift fashion

¹**just** \'jəst\ *adj* 1 : having a basis in or conforming to fact or reason : REASONABLE ⟨~ comment⟩ 2 : CORRECT, PROPER ⟨~ proportions⟩ 3 : morally or legally right ⟨a ~ title⟩ 4 : DESERVED, MERITED ⟨~ punishment⟩ ✦ **Synonyms** UPRIGHT, HONORABLE, CONSCIENTIOUS, HONEST — **just·ly** *adv* — **just·ness** *n*

²**just** \'jəst, 'jist\ *adv* 1 : EXACTLY ⟨~ right⟩ 2 : very recently ⟨has ~ left⟩ 3 : BARELY ⟨~ too late⟩ 4 : DIRECTLY ⟨~ west of here⟩ 5 : ONLY ⟨~ last year⟩ 6 : QUITE ⟨~ wonderful⟩ 7 : POSSIBLY ⟨it ~ might work⟩

jus·tice \'jəs-təs\ *n* 1 : the administration of what is just (as by assigning merited rewards or punishments) 2 : JUDGE 3 : the administration of law 4 : FAIRNESS; *also* : RIGHTEOUSNESS

justice of the peace : a local magistrate empowered chiefly to try minor cases, to administer oaths, and to perform marriages

jus·ti·fy \'jəs-tə-,fī\ *vb* **-fied; -fy·ing** 1 : to prove to be just, right, or reasonable 2 : to pronounce free from guilt or blame 3 : to adjust spaces in a line of printed text so the margins are even — **jus·ti·fi·able** *adj* — **jus·ti·fi·ca·tion** \,jəs-tə-fə-'kā-shən\ *n*

jut \'jət\ *vb* **jut·ted; jut·ting** : PROJECT, PROTRUDE

jute \'jüt\ *n* : a strong glossy fiber from either of two tropical plants used esp. for making sacks and twine

juv *abbr* juvenile

¹**ju·ve·nile** \'jü-və-,nī(-ə)l, -nəl\ *adj* 1 : showing incomplete development 2 : of, relating to, or characteristic of children or young people

²**juvenile** *n* 1 : a young person; *esp* : one below the legally established age of adulthood 2 : a young animal (as a fish or a bird) or plant 3 : an actor or actress who plays youthful parts

juvenile delinquency *n* : violation of the law or antisocial behavior by a juvenile — **juvenile delinquent** *n*

jux·ta·pose \'jək-stə-,pōz\ *vb* **-posed; -pos·ing** : to place side by side — **jux·ta·po·si·tion** \,jək-stə-pə-'zi-shən\ *n*

JV *abbr* junior varsity

¹**k** \'kā\ *n, pl* **k's** or **ks** \'kāz\ 1 *often cap* : the 11th letter of the English alphabet 2 *cap* : STRIKEOUT

²**k** *abbr* 1 karat 2 kitchen 3 knit 4 kosher — often enclosed in a circle

¹**K** *abbr* 1 Kelvin 2 kindergarten

²**K** *symbol* [NL *kalium*] potassium

kab·ba·lah *also* **kab·ba·la** *or* **ka·ba·la** *or* **ca·ba·la** \kə-'bä-lə, 'ka-bə-lə\ *n, often cap* 1 : a medieval Jewish mysticism marked by belief in creation through emanation and a cipher method of interpreting Scripture 2 : esoteric or mysterious doctrine

kabob *var of* KEBAB

Ka·bu·ki \kə-'bü-kē\ *n* : traditional Japanese popular drama with highly stylized singing and dancing

kad·dish \'kä-dish\ *n, often cap* : a Jewish prayer recited in the daily synagogue ritual and by mourners at public services after the death of a close relative

kaf·fee·klatsch \'kó-fē-,klach, 'kä-\ *n, often cap* [G] : an informal social gathering for coffee and conversation

kai·ser \'kī-zər\ *n* : EMPEROR; *esp* : the ruler of Germany from 1871 to 1918

Ka·lash·ni·kov \kə-'lash-nə-,kóf\ *n* [M. T. *Kalashnikov* b1919 Soviet weapons designer] : a Soviet-designed assault rifle

kale \'kāl\ *n* : a hardy cabbage with curled leaves that do not form a head

ka·lei·do·scope \kə-'lī-də-,skōp\ *n* : a tube containing loose bits of colored material (as glass) and two mirrors at one end that shows many different patterns as it is turned — **ka·lei·do·scop·ic** \-,lī-də-'skä-pik\ *adj* — **ka·lei·do·scop·i·cal·ly** \-pi-k(ə-)lē\ *adv*

ka·ma·ai·na \,kä-mə-'ī-nə\ *n* [Hawaiian *kama'āina*, fr. *kama* child + *'āina* land] : one who has lived in Hawaii for a long time

kame \'kām\ *n* [Sc, lit., comb] : a short ridge or mound of material deposited by water from a melting glacier

ka·mi·ka·ze \,kä-mi-'kä-zē\ *n* [Jp, lit., divine wind] : a member of a corps of Japanese pilots assigned to make a suicidal crash on a target; *also* : an airplane flown in such an attack

Kan *or* **Kans** *abbr* Kansas

kan·ga·roo \,kaŋ-gə-'rü\ *n, pl* **-roos** : any of various large leaping marsupial mammals of Australia and adjacent islands with powerful hind legs and a long thick tail used as a support

kangaroo court *n* : a court or an illegal self-appointed tribunal characterized by irresponsible, perverted, or irregular procedures

ka·o·lin \'kā-ə-lən\ *n* : a fine usu. white clay used in ceramics and refractories and for the treatment of diarrhea

ka·pey·ka \kä-'pā-kä\ *n, pl* **ka·pe·ek** \kä-'pā-ək\ — see *rubel* at MONEY table

kapok • key

ka·pok \'kā-ˌpäk\ *n* : silky fiber from the seeds of a tropical tree used esp. as a filling (as for life preservers)

Kap·o·si's sar·co·ma \ˈka-pə-sēz-sär-ˈkō-mə\ *n* : a neoplastic disease associated esp. with AIDS that affects esp. the skin and mucous membranes and is characterized usu. by the formation of pink to reddish-brown or bluish plaques

kap·pa \'ka-pə\ *n* : the 10th letter of the Greek alphabet — K or κ

ka·put *also* **ka·putt** \kä-ˈpu̇t, kə-, -ˈpu̇t\ *adj* [G, fr. F *capot* not having made a trick at piquet] **1** : utterly defeated or destroyed **2** : unable to function : USELESS

kar·a·kul \'ker-ə-kəl\ *n* : the usu. curly glossy black coat of a very young lamb of a hardy Asian breed of sheep

kar·a·o·ke \ˌker-ē-ˈō-kē\ *n* [Jp] : a device that plays instrumental accompaniments for songs to which the user sings along

kar·at \'ker-ət\ *n* : a unit for expressing proportion of gold in an alloy equal to 1/24 part of pure gold

kar·a·te \kə-ˈrä-tē\ *n* [Jp, lit., empty hand] : an art of self-defense in which an attacker is disabled by crippling kicks and punches

kar·ma \'kär-mə\ *n, often cap* [Skt] : the force generated by a person's actions held in Hinduism and Buddhism to perpetuate reincarnation and to determine the nature of the person's next existence — **kar·mic** \-mik\ *adj*

karst \'kärst\ *n* [G] : an irregular limestone region with sinks, underground streams, and caverns

ka·ty·did \'kä-tē-ˌdid\ *n* : any of several large green tree-dwelling American grasshoppers with long antennae

kay·ak \'kī-ˌak\ *n* : a canoe that is made of a skin-covered frame with a small opening and propelled by a double-bladed paddle and that is associated esp. with indigenous peoples of arctic regions; *also* : a similar portable boat — **kay·ak·er** *n*

kayo \(ˌ)kā-ˈō, ˈkā-ō\ *n* : KNOCKOUT — **kayo** *vb*

ka·zoo \kə-ˈzü\ *n, pl* **kazoos** : a toy musical instrument consisting of a tube with a membrane sealing one end and a side hole to sing or hum into

KB *abbr* kilobyte

kc *abbr* kilocycle

KC *abbr* **1** Kansas City **2** King's Counsel **3** Knights of Columbus

kc/s *abbr* kilocycles per second

KD *abbr* knocked down

ke·bab *or* **ke·bob** *also* **ka·bob** \kə-ˈbäb\ *n* : cubes of meat cooked with vegetables usu. on a skewer

kedge \'kej\ *n* : a small anchor

¹keel \'kēl\ *n* **1** : the chief structural member of a ship running lengthwise along the center of its bottom **2** : something (as a bird's breastbone) like a ship's keel in form or use — **keeled** \'kēld\ *adj*

²keel *vb* : FAINT, SWOON — usu. used with *over* ⟨~ed over from the heat⟩

keel·boat \'kēl-ˌbōt\ *n* : a shallow covered keeled riverboat for freight that is usu. rowed, poled, or towed

keel·haul \-ˌhȯl\ *vb* : to haul under the keel of a ship as punishment

¹keen \'kēn\ *adj* **1** : SHARP ⟨a ~ knife⟩ **2** : SEVERE ⟨a ~ wind⟩ **3** : ENTHUSIASTIC ⟨~ about swimming⟩ **4** : mentally alert ⟨a ~ mind⟩ **5** : STRONG, ACUTE ⟨~ eyesight⟩ **6** : WONDERFUL, EXCELLENT — **keen·ly** *adv* — **keen·ness** *n*

²keen *n* : a lamentation for the dead uttered in a loud wailing voice or in a wordless cry — **keen** *vb*

¹keep \'kēp\ *vb* **kept** \'kept\; **keep·ing** **1** : FULFILL, OBSERVE ⟨~ a promise⟩ ⟨~ a holiday⟩ **2** : GUARD ⟨~ us from harm⟩; *also* : to take care of ⟨~ a neighbor's children⟩ **3** : MAINTAIN ⟨~ silence⟩ **4** : to have in one's service or at one's disposal ⟨~ a horse⟩ **5** : to preserve a

record in ⟨~ a diary⟩ **6** : to have in stock for sale **7** : to retain in one's possession ⟨~ what you find⟩ **8** : to carry on (as a business) : CONDUCT **9** : HOLD, DETAIN ⟨~ him in jail⟩ **10** : to refrain from revealing ⟨~ a secret⟩ **11** : to continue in good condition ⟨meat will ~ in a freezer⟩ **12** : ABSTAIN, REFRAIN — **keep·er** *n*

²keep *n* **1** : FORTRESS **2** : the means or provisions by which one is kept — **for keeps** **1** : with the provision that one keep what one has won ⟨play marbles *for keeps*⟩ **2** : PERMANENTLY ⟨came home *for keeps*⟩

keep–away \'kēp-ə-ˌwā\ *n* : a game in which players try to keep an object from one or more other players

keeping *n* : CONFORMITY ⟨in ~ with good taste⟩

keeping room *n* : a common room used for multiple purposes

keep·sake \'kēp-ˌsāk\ *n* : MEMENTO

keep up *vb* **1** : to persevere in **2** : MAINTAIN, SUSTAIN **3** : to keep informed **4** : to continue without interruption

keg \'keg\ *n* : a small cask or barrel

keg·ger \'ke-gər\ *n* : a party featuring one or more kegs of beer

keg·ler \'ke-glər\ *n* : ¹BOWLER

kelp \'kelp\ *n* : any of various coarse brown seaweeds; *also* : a mass of these or their ashes often used as fertilizer

kel·vin \'kel-vən\ *n* : a unit of temperature equal to 1/273.16 of the Kelvin scale temperature of the triple point of water and equal to the Celsius degree

Kelvin *adj* : relating to, conforming to, or being a temperature scale according to which absolute zero is 0 K, the equivalent of −273.15°C

ken \'ken\ *n* **1** : range of vision : SIGHT **2** : range of understanding

ken·nel \'ke-nᵊl\ *n* : a shelter for a dog or cat; *also* : an establishment for the breeding or boarding of dogs or cats — **kennel** *vb*

ke·no \'kē-nō\ *n* : a game resembling bingo

ke·no·sis \kə-ˈnō-səs\ *n* : the relinquishment of divine attributes by Jesus Christ in becoming human — **ke·not·ic** \-ˈnä-tik\ *adj*

ken·te cloth \'ken-ˌtā-\ *n* : colorfully patterned cloth traditionally woven by hand in Ghana

Ken·tucky bluegrass \kən-ˈtə-kē-\ *n* : a valuable pasture and meadow grass of both Europe and America

Ke·ogh plan \'kē-(ˌ)ō-\ *n* [Eugene James *Keogh* †1989 Am. politician] : an individual retirement account for the self-employed

ke·pi \'kā-pē, 'ke-\ *n* [F] : a military cap with a round flat top and a visor

ker·a·tin \'ker-ə-tən\ *n* : any of various sulfur-containing proteins that make up hair and horny tissues

kerb \'kərb\ *n, Brit* : CURB 3

ker·chief \'kər-chəf, -ˌchēf\ *n, pl* **kerchiefs** \-chəfs, -ˌchēfs\ *also* **kerchieves** \-ˌchēvz\ [ME *courchef*, fr. AF *coverchef, cuerchief*, fr. *coverir* to cover + *chef* head] **1** : a square of cloth worn esp. as a head covering **2** : HANDKERCHIEF

kerf \'kərf\ *n* : a slit or notch made by a saw or cutting torch

ker·nel \'kər-nᵊl\ *n* **1** : the inner softer part of a seed, fruit stone, or nut **2** : a whole seed of a cereal ⟨a ~ of corn⟩ **3** : a central or essential part : CORE

ker·o·sene *also* **ker·o·sine** \'ker-ə-ˌsēn, ˌker-ə-ˈsēn\ *n* : a flammable oil produced from petroleum and used for a fuel and as a solvent

kes·trel \'kes-trəl\ *n* : any of various small falcons that usu. hover in the air while searching for prey

ketch \'kech\ *n* : a large fore-and-aft rigged boat with two masts

ketch·up *also* **catch·up** \'ke-chəp, 'ka-\ *or* **cat·sup** \'ke-chəp, 'ka-; 'kat-səp\ *n* : a seasoned tomato puree

ket·tle \'ke-tᵊl\ *n* : a metallic vessel for boiling liquids

ket·tle·drum \-ˌdrəm\ *n* : a brass, copper, or fiberglass drum with calfskin or plastic stretched across the top

¹key \'kē\ *n* **1** : a usu. metal instrument by which the bolt of a lock is turned; *also* : a device having the form or function of a key **2** : a means of gaining or preventing entrance, possession, or control **3** : EXPLANATION, SOLUTION **4** : one of the levers pressed by a finger in operating or playing an instrument **5** : a leading individual or principle **6** : a system of seven tones based on their relationship to a tonic; *also* : the tone or pitch of a voice **7** : a small switch for opening or closing an electric circuit ⟨a telegraph ~⟩

²**key** *vb* **1** : SECURE, FASTEN **2** : to regulate the musical pitch of **3** : to bring into harmony or conformity **4** : to make nervous — usu. used with *up*
³**key** *adj* : BASIC, CENTRAL ⟨∼ issues⟩
⁴**key** *n* : a low island or reef (as off the southern coast of Florida)
⁵**key** *n, slang* : a kilogram esp. of marijuana or heroin
key·board \-ˌbȯrd\ *n* **1** : a row of keys (as on a piano) **2** : an assemblage of keys for operating a machine
key club *n* : a private club serving liquor and providing entertainment
key·hole \ˈkē-ˌhōl\ *n* : a hole for receiving a key
¹**key·note** \-ˌnōt\ *n* **1** : the first and harmonically fundamental tone of a scale **2** : the central fact, idea, or mood
²**keynote** *vb* **1** : to set the keynote of **2** : to deliver the major address (as at a convention) — **key·not·er** *n*
key·punch \ˈkē-ˌpənch\ *n* : a machine with a keyboard used to cut holes or notches in punch cards — **key·punch** *vb* — **key·punch·er** *n*
key·stone \-ˌstōn\ *n* : the wedge-shaped piece at the crown of an arch that locks the other pieces in place
key·stroke \-ˌstrōk\ *n* : an act or instance of depressing a key on a keyboard
key word *n* : a word that is a key; *esp usu* **key·word** : a significant word from a title or document used esp. as an indication of the content
kg *abbr* kilogram
KGB *abbr* [Russ *Komitet gosudarstvennoĭ bezopasnosti*] (Soviet) State Security Committee
kha·ki \ˈka-kē, ˈkä-\ *n* [Hindi & Urdu *khākī* dust-colored, fr. *khāk* dust, fr. Pers] **1** : a light yellowish brown color **2** : a khaki-colored cloth; *also* : a military uniform of this cloth
khan \ˈkän, ˈkan\ *n* : a Mongol leader; *esp* : a successor of Genghis Khan
khe·dive \kə-ˈdēv\ *n* : a ruler of Egypt from 1867 to 1914 governing as a viceroy of the sultan of Turkey
khoum \ˈküm\ *n* — see *ouguiya* at MONEY table
kHz *abbr* kilohertz
KIA *abbr* killed in action
kib·ble \ˈki-bəl\ *vb* **kib·bled; kib·bling** : to grind coarsely — **kibble** *n*
kib·butz \ki-ˈbu̇ts, -ˈbüts\ *n, pl* **kib·but·zim** \-ˌbu̇t-ˈsēm, -ˌbüt-\ [ModHeb *qibbūṣ*] : a communal farm or settlement in Israel
ki·bitz·er \ˈki-bət-sər, kə-ˈbit-\ *n* : one who looks on and usu. offers unwanted advice — **kib·itz** \ˈki-bəts\ *vb*
ki·bosh \ˈkī-ˌbäsh\ *n* : something that serves as a check or stop ⟨put the ∼ on his plan⟩
¹**kick** \ˈkik\ *vb* **1** : to strike out or hit with the foot; *also* : to score by kicking a ball **2** : to object strongly **3** : to recoil when fired — **kick·er** *n*
²**kick** *n* **1** : a blow or thrust with the foot; *esp* : a propelling of a ball with the foot **2** : the recoil of a gun **3** : a feeling or expression of objection **4** : stimulating effect esp. of pleasure
kick·back \ˈkik-ˌbak\ *n* **1** : a sharp violent reaction **2** : a secret return of a part of a sum received
kick back *vb* : to assume a relaxed position or attitude
kick·box·ing \ˈkik-ˌbäk-siŋ\ *n* : boxing in which boxers are permitted to kick with bare feet — **kick·box·er** \-sər\ *n*
kick in *vb* **1** : CONTRIBUTE **2** *slang* : DIE **3** : to begin operating or having an effect ⟨the caffeine started to *kick in*⟩
kick·off \ˈkik-ˌȯf\ *n* **1** : a kick that puts the ball in play (as in football) **2** : COMMENCEMENT ⟨campaign ∼⟩
kick off *vb* **1** : to start or resume play with a placekick **2** : to begin proceedings ⟨*kick off* a campaign⟩ **3** *slang* : DIE
kick over *vb* : to begin or cause to begin to fire — used of an internal combustion engine
kick·shaw \ˈkik-ˌshȯ\ *n* [modif. of F *quelque chose* something] **1** : DELICACY **2** : TRINKET
kick·stand \ˈkik-ˌstand\ *n* : a swiveling metal bar attached to a 2-wheeled vehicle for holding it up when not in use
kick–start \ˈkik-ˌstärt\ *vb* : JUMP-START
kicky \ˈki-kē\ *adj* : providing a kick or thrill : EXCITING; *also* : excitingly fashionable
¹**kid** \ˈkid\ *n* **1** : a young goat **2** : the flesh, fur, or skin of a young goat; *also* : something made of kid **3** : CHILD, YOUNGSTER — **kid·dish** *adj*
²**kid** *vb* **kid·ded; kid·ding 1** : FOOL **2** : TEASE — **kid·der** *n* — **kid·ding·ly** *adv*

kid·do \ˈki-dō\ *n, pl* **kiddos 1** — used as a familiar form of address ⟨you're okay, ∼⟩ **2** : CHILD, KID
kid·nap \ˈkid-ˌnap\ *vb* **kid·napped** *also* **kid-naped** \-ˌnapt\; **kid·nap·ping** *also* **kid·nap·ing** \-ˌna-piŋ\ : to hold or carry a person away by unlawful force or by fraud and against one's will — **kid·nap·per** *also* **kid·nap·er** \-ˌna-pər\ *n*
kid·ney \ˈkid-nē\ *n, pl* **kidneys** : either of a pair of organs lying near the backbone that excrete waste products of the body in the form of urine
kidney bean *n* **1** : an edible seed of the common cultivated bean; *esp* : one that is large and dark red **2** : a plant bearing kidney beans
kid·skin \ˈkid-ˌskin\ *n* : the skin of a young goat used for leather
kiel·ba·sa \kēl-ˈbä-sə, kil-\ *n, pl* **-basas** *also* **-ba·sy** \-ˈbä-sē\ [Pol *kiełbasa*] : a smoked sausage of Polish origin
¹**kill** \ˈkil\ *vb* **1** : to deprive of life **2** : to put an end to ⟨∼ competition⟩; *also* : DEFEAT ⟨∼ a proposed amendment⟩ **3** : USE UP ⟨∼ time⟩ **4** : to mark for omission
♦ **Synonyms** SLAY, MURDER, ASSASSINATE, EXECUTE — **kill·er** *n*
²**kill** *n* **1** : an act of killing **2** : an animal or animals killed (as in a hunt); *also* : an aircraft, ship, or vehicle destroyed by military action
kill·deer \ˈkil-ˌdir\ *n, pl* **killdeers** *or* **killdeer** [imit.] : an American plover with a plaintive penetrating cry
killer app \-ˈap\ *n* : a component (as a computer application) that in itself makes something worth having or using
killer bee *n* : AFRICANIZED BEE
killer whale *n* : a small gregarious black and white flesh= eating whale with a white oval patch behind each eye
kill·ing *n* : a sudden notable gain or profit
killing field *n* : a scene of mass killing
kill·joy \ˈkil-ˌjȯi\ *n* : one who spoils the pleasures of others
kiln \ˈkil, ˈkiln\ *n* [ME *kilne*, fr. OE *cyln*, fr. L *culina* kitchen] : a heated enclosure (as an oven) for processing a substance by burning, firing, or drying — **kiln** *vb*
ki·lo \ˈkē-lō\ *n, pl* **kilos** : KILOGRAM
ki·lo·byte \ˈki-lə-ˌbīt, ˈkē-\ *n* : 1024 bytes
kilo·cy·cle \ˈki-lə-ˌsī-kəl\ *n* : KILOHERTZ
ki·lo·gram \ˈkē-lə-ˌgram, ˈki-\ *n* **1** : the basic metric unit of mass that is nearly equal to the mass of 1000 cubic centimeters of water at its maximum density — see METRIC SYSTEM table **2** : the weight of a kilogram mass under earth's gravity
ki·lo·hertz \ˈki-lə-ˌhərts, ˈkē-, -ˌherts\ *n* : 1000 hertz
kilo·li·ter \ˈki-lə-ˌlē-tər\ *n* — see METRIC SYSTEM table
ki·lo·me·ter \ki-ˈlä-mə-tər, ˈki-lə-ˌmē-\ *n* : a metric unit of length equal to 1000 meters — see METRIC SYSTEM table
ki·lo·ton \ˈki-lə-ˌtən, ˈkē-lō-\ *n* **1** : 1000 tons **2** : an explosive force equivalent to that of 1000 tons of TNT
ki·lo·volt \-ˌvōlt\ *n* : 1000 volts
kilo·watt \ˈki-lə-ˌwät\ *n* : 1000 watts
kilowatt–hour *n* : a unit of energy equal to that expended by one kilowatt in one hour
kilt \ˈkilt\ *n* : a knee-length pleated skirt usu. of tartan worn by men in Scotland
kil·ter \ˈkil-tər\ *n* : proper condition ⟨out of ∼⟩
ki·mo·no \kə-ˈmō-nə\ *n, pl* **-nos 1** : a loose robe with wide sleeves traditionally worn with a wide sash as an outer garment by the Japanese **2** : a loose dressing gown or jacket
kin \ˈkin\ *n* **1** : an individual's relatives **2** : KINSMAN
ki·na \ˈkē-nə\ *n, pl* **kina** — see MONEY table
ki·na·ra \kē-ˈnä-rə\ *n* : a candelabra with seven candlesticks used during Kwanzaa
¹**kind** \ˈkīnd\ *n* **1** : essential quality or character **2** : a group united by common traits or interests : CATEGORY; *also* : VARIETY **3** : goods or commodities as distinguished from money
²**kind** *adj* **1** : of a sympathetic, forbearing, or pleasant nature **2** : arising from sympathy or forbearance ⟨∼ deeds⟩
♦ **Synonyms** BENEVOLENT, BENIGN, BENIGNANT, KINDLY — **kind·ness** *n*
kin·der·gar·ten \ˈkin-dər-ˌgär-tᵊn\ *n* [G, lit., children's garden] : a school or class for children usu. from four to six years old
kin·der·gart·ner \-ˌgärt-nər\ *n* **1** : a kindergarten teacher **2** : a kindergarten pupil
kind·heart·ed \ˌkīnd-ˈhär-təd\ *adj* : marked by a sympathetic nature
kin·dle \ˈkin-dᵊl\ *vb* **kin·dled; kin·dling 1** : to set on fire : start burning **2** : to stir up : AROUSE **3** : ILLUMINATE, GLOW

kin·dling \'kind-liŋ, 'kin-lən\ *n* : easily combustible material for starting a fire

¹kind·ly \'kīnd-lē\ *adj* **kind·li·er; -est** **1** : of an agreeable or beneficial nature **2** : of a sympathetic or generous nature — **kind·li·ness** *n*

²kindly *adv* **1** : READILY ⟨does not take ~ to criticism⟩ **2** : SYMPATHETICALLY **3** : COURTEOUSLY, OBLIGINGLY

kind of *adv* : to a moderate degree ⟨it's *kind of* late to begin⟩

¹kin·dred \'kin-drəd\ *n* **1** : a group of related individuals **2** : one's relatives

²kindred *adj* : of a like nature or character

kine \'kīn\ *archaic pl of* COW

kin·e·ma \'kin-ə-mə\ *Brit var of* CINEMA

ki·ne·mat·ics \ˌki-nə-'ma-tiks\ *n* : a science that deals with motion apart from considerations of mass and force — **ki·ne·mat·ic** \-tik\ *or* **ki·ne·mat·i·cal** \-ti-kəl\ *adj*

kin·es·the·sia \ˌki-nəs-'thē-zhə, -zhē-ə\ *or* **kin·es·the·sis** \-'thē-səs\ *n, pl* **-the·sias** *or* **-the·ses** \-ˌsēz\ : a sense that perceives bodily movement, position, and weight and is mediated by sensory receptors in tendons, muscles, and joints; *also* : sensory experience derived from this sense — **kin·es·thet·ic** \-'the-tik\ *adj*

ki·net·ic \kə-'ne-tik\ *adj* : of or relating to the motion of material bodies and the forces and energy (**kinetic energy**) associated with them

ki·net·ics \-tiks\ *n sing or pl* : a science that deals with the effects of forces upon the motions of material bodies or with changes in a physical or chemical system

kin·folk \'kin-ˌfōk\ *or* **kinfolks** *n pl* : RELATIVES

king \'kiŋ\ *n* **1** : a male monarch **2** : a chief among competitors ⟨home-run ~⟩ **3** : the principal piece in the game of chess **4** : a playing card bearing the figure of a king **5** : a checker that has been crowned — **king·less** *adj* — **king·ly** *adj* — **king·ship** *n*

king crab *n* **1** : HORSESHOE CRAB **2** : a large crab of the No. Pacific caught commercially for food

king·dom \'kiŋ-dəm\ *n* **1** : a country whose head is a king or queen **2** : a realm or region in which something or someone is dominant ⟨a cattle ~⟩ **3** : one of the three primary divisions of lifeless material, plants, and animals into which natural objects are grouped; *also* : a biological category that ranks above the phylum

king·fish·er \-ˌfi-shər\ *n* : any of numerous usu. brightly colored crested birds that feed chiefly on fish

king·pin \'kiŋ-ˌpin\ *n* **1** : HEADPIN **2** : the leader in a group or undertaking

Kings *n* — see BIBLE table

king–size \'kiŋ-ˌsīz\ *or* **king–sized** \-ˌsīzd\ *adj* **1** : longer than the regular or standard size **2** : unusually large **3** : having dimensions of about 76 by 80 inches (1.9 by 2.0 meters) ⟨a ~ bed⟩; *also* : of a size that fits a king-size bed

kink \'kiŋk\ *n* **1** : a short tight twist or curl **2** : a mental peculiarity : QUIRK **3** : CRAMP ⟨a ~ in the back⟩ **4** : an imperfection likely to cause difficulties in operation — **kinky** *adj*

kin·ship \'kin-ˌship\ *n* : RELATIONSHIP

kins·man \'kinz-mən\ *n* : RELATIVE; *esp* : a male relative

kins·wom·an \-ˌwu̇-mən\ *n* : a female relative

ki·osk \'kē-ˌäsk\ *n* **1** : a small structure with one or more open sides **2** : a stand-alone device providing information and services on a computer screen ⟨interactive ~s at the museum⟩

Ki·o·wa \'kī-ə-ˌwȯ, -ˌwä, -ˌwä\ *n, pl* **Kiowa** *or* **Kiowas** : a member of an American Indian people of Colorado, Kansas, New Mexico, Oklahoma, and Texas

kip \'kip, 'gip\ *n, pl* **kip** *or* **kips** — see MONEY table

kip·per \'ki-pər\ *n* : a fish (as a herring) preserved by salting and drying or smoking — **kipper** *vb*

kirk \'kərk, 'kirk\ *n, chiefly Scot* : CHURCH

kir·tle \'kər-tᵊl\ *n* : a long gown or dress worn by women

kis·met \'kiz-ˌmet, -mət\ *n, often cap* [Turk, fr. Ar *qisma* portion, lot] : FATE

¹kiss \'kis\ *vb* **1** : to touch or caress with the lips as a mark of affection or greeting **2** : to touch gently or lightly

²kiss *n* **1** : a caress with the lips **2** : a gentle touch or contact **3** : a bite-size candy

kiss·er \'ki-sər\ *n* **1** : one that kisses **2** *slang* : MOUTH **3** *slang* : FACE

kit \'kit\ *n* **1** : a set of articles for personal use; *also* : a set of tools or implements or of parts to be assembled **2** : a container (as a case) for a kit

kitch·en \'ki-chən\ *n* **1** : a room with cooking facilities **2** : the personnel that prepares, cooks, and serves food

kitch·en·ette \ˌki-chə-'net\ *n* : a small kitchen or an alcove containing cooking facilities

kitchen police *n* **1** : KP **2** : the work of KPs

kitch·en·ware \'ki-chən-ˌwer\ *n* : utensils and appliances for kitchen use

kite \'kīt\ *n* **1** : any of various long-winged hawks often with deeply forked tails **2** : a light frame covered with paper or cloth and designed to be flown in the air at the end of a long string

kith \'kith\ *n* [ME, fr. OE *cȳthth*, fr. *cūth* known] : familiar friends, neighbors, or relatives ⟨~ and kin⟩

kitsch \'kich\ *n* [G] : something often of poor quality that appeals to popular or lowbrow taste — **kitschy** \'ki-chē\ *adj*

kit·ten \'ki-tᵊn\ *n* : a young cat — **kit·ten·ish** *adj*

¹kit·ty \'ki-tē\ *n, pl* **kitties** : CAT; *esp* : KITTEN

²kitty *n, pl* **kitties** : a fund in a poker game made up of contributions from each pot; *also* : POOL

kit·ty–cor·ner *also* **cat·ty–cor·ner** *or* **cat·er·cor·ner** \'ki-tē-ˌkȯr-nər, 'ka-; 'ka-tə-\ *or* **kit·ty–cor·nered** *or* **cat·er·cornered** \-nərd\ *adv or adj* : in a diagonal or oblique position

ki·wi \'kē-(ˌ)wē\ *n* **1** : any of a small genus of flightless New Zealand birds **2** : KIWIFRUIT

ki·wi·fruit \-ˌfrüt\ *n* : a brownish hairy egg-shaped fruit of a subtropical vine that has sweet bright green flesh and small edible black seeds

KJV *abbr* King James Version

KKK *abbr* Ku Klux Klan

kl *abbr* kiloliter

klatch *also* **klatsch** \'klach\ *n* [G *Klatsch* gossip] : a gathering marked by informal conversation

klep·toc·ra·cy \klep-'tä-krə-sē\ *n, pl* **-cies** : government by those who seek chiefly status and personal gain at the expense of the governed

klep·to·ma·nia \ˌklep-tə-'mā-nē-ə\ *n* : a persistent neurotic impulse to steal esp. without economic motive — **klep·to·ma·ni·ac** \-nē-ˌak\ *n*

klieg light *or* **kleig light** \'klēg-\ *n* : a very bright lamp used in making motion pictures

klutz \'kləts\ *n* [Yiddish *klots*, lit., wooden beam] : a clumsy person — **klutzy** *adj*

km *abbr* kilometer

kn *abbr* knot

knack \'nak\ *n* **1** : a clever way of doing something **2** : natural aptitude

knap·sack \'nap-ˌsak\ *n* : a bag (as of canvas) strapped on the back and used esp. for carrying supplies

knave \'nāv\ *n* **1** : ROGUE **2** : JACK 6 — **knav·ery** \'nā-və-rē\ *n* — **knav·ish** \'nā-vish\ *adj*

knead \'nēd\ *vb* : to work and press into a mass with the hands; *also* : MASSAGE — **knead·er** *n*

knee \'nē\ *n* : the joint in the middle part of the leg — **kneed** \'nēd\ *adj*

knee·cap \'nē-ˌkap\ *n* : a thick flat triangular movable bone forming the front of the knee

knee–hole \-ˌhōl\ *n* : a space (as under a desk) for the knees

knee–jerk \'nē-ˌjərk\ *adj* : readily predictable ⟨a ~ reaction⟩

kneel \'nēl\ *vb* **knelt** \'nelt\ *or* **kneeled; kneel·ing** : to bend the knee : fall or rest on the knees

¹knell \'nel\ *vb* **1** : to ring esp. for a death or disaster **2** : to summon, announce, or proclaim by a knell

²knell *n* **1** : a stroke of a bell esp. when tolled (as for a funeral) **2** : an indication of the end or failure of something

knew *past of* KNOW

knick·ers \'ni-kərz\ *n pl* : loose-fitting short pants gathered at the knee

knick·knack \'nik-ˌnak\ *n* : a small trivial article intended for ornament

¹knife \'nīf\ *n, pl* **knives** \'nīvz\ **1** : a cutting instrument consisting of a sharp blade fastened to a handle **2** : a sharp cutting tool in a machine

²knife *vb* **knifed; knif·ing** : to stab, slash, or wound with a knife

¹knight \'nīt\ *n* **1** : a mounted warrior of feudal times serving a king **2** : a man honored by a sovereign for merit and in Great Britain ranking below a baronet **3** : a man devoted to the service of a lady **4** : a member of an order or society **5** : a chess piece having an L-shaped move — **knight·ly** *adj*

²**knight** *vb* : to make a knight of

knight·hood \'nīt-,húd\ *n* **1** : the rank, dignity, or profession of a knight **2** : CHIVALRY **3** : knights as a class or body

knish \kǝ-'nish\ *n* [Yiddish] : a small round or square of dough stuffed with a filling (as of meat or fruit) and baked or fried

¹**knit** \'nit\ *vb* **knit** *or* **knit·ted; knit·ting** **1** : to link firmly or closely **2** : WRINKLE ⟨∼ her brows⟩ **3** : to form a fabric by interlacing yarn or thread in connected loops with needles **4** : to grow together ⟨the fractured bone *knitted* slowly⟩ — **knit·ter** *n*

²**knit** *n* **1** : a basic knitting stitch **2** : a knitted garment or fabric

knit·wear \-,wer\ *n* : knitted clothing

knob \'näb\ *n* **1** : a rounded protuberance; *also* : a small rounded ornament or handle **2** : a rounded usu. isolated hill — **knobbed** \'näbd\ *adj* — **knob·by** \'nä-bē\ *adj*

¹**knock** \'näk\ *vb* **1** : to strike with a sharp blow **2** : BUMP, COLLIDE **3** : to make a pounding noise; *esp* : to have engine knock **4** : to find fault with

²**knock** *n* **1** : a sharp blow **2** : a pounding noise; *esp* : one caused by abnormal ignition in an automobile engine

knock-down \'näk-,daún\ *n* **1** : the action of knocking down **2** : something (as a blow) that knocks down **3** : something that can be easily assembled or disassembled

knock down *vb* **1** : to strike to the ground with or as if with a sharp blow **2** : to take apart : DISASSEMBLE **3** : to receive as income or salary : EARN **4** : to make a reduction in

knock·er \'nä-kǝr\ *n* : one that knocks; *esp* : a device hinged to a door for use in knocking

knock–knee \'näk-,nē\ *n* : a condition in which the legs curve inward at the knees — **knock–kneed** \-,nēd\ *adj*

knock-off \'näk-,óf\ *n* : a copy or imitation of someone or something popular

knock off **1** : to stop doing something **2** : to do quickly, carelessly, or routinely **3** : to deduct from a price **4** : KILL **5** : ROB **6** : COPY, IMITATE

knock·out \'näk-,aút\ *n* **1** : a blow that fells and immobilizes an opponent (as in boxing) **2** : something sensationally striking or attractive

knock out *vb* **1** : to defeat by a knockout **2** : to make unconscious or inoperative **3** : to tire out : EXHAUST

knock·wurst *also* **knack·wurst** \'näk-,wǝrst, -,vǔrst\ *n* : a short thick heavily seasoned sausage

knoll \'nōl\ *n* : a small round hill

¹**knot** \'nät\ *n* **1** : an interlacing (as of string) forming a lump or knob and often used for fastening or tying together **2** : PROBLEM **3** : a bond of union; *esp* : the marriage bond **4** : a protuberant lump or swelling in tissue **5** : a rounded cross-grained area in lumber that is a section through the junction of a tree branch with the trunk; *also* : the woody tissue forming this junction in a tree **6** : GROUP, CLUSTER **7** : an ornamental bow of ribbon **8** : one nautical mile per hour; *also* : one nautical mile — **knot·ty** *adj*

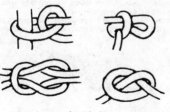

knot 1

²**knot** *vb* **knot·ted; knot·ting** **1** : to tie in or with a knot **2** : ENTANGLE

knot·hole \-,hōl\ *n* : a hole in a board or tree trunk where a knot has come out

knout \'naút, 'nüt\ *n* : a whip used for flogging

know \'nō\ *vb* **knew** \'nü, 'nyü\; **known** \'nōn\; **know·ing** **1** : to perceive directly : have understanding or direct cognition of; *also* : to recognize the nature of **2** : to be acquainted or familiar with **3** : to be aware of the truth

of **4** : to have a practical understanding of — **know·able** *adj* — **know·er** *n* — **in the know** : possessing confidential information

know–how \'nō-,haú\ *n* : knowledge of how to do something smoothly and efficiently

knowing *adj* **1** : having or reflecting knowledge, intelligence, or information **2** : shrewdly and keenly alert **3** : DELIBERATE ⟨∼ interference⟩ ✦ *Synonyms* CLEVER, BRIGHT, SMART — **know·ing·ly** *adv*

knowl·edge \'nä-lij\ *n* **1** : understanding gained by actual experience ⟨a ∼ of carpentry⟩ **2** : range of information ⟨to the best of my ∼⟩ **3** : clear perception of truth **4** : something learned and kept in the mind

knowl·edge·able \'nä-li-jǝ-bǝl\ *adj* : having or showing knowledge or intelligence

knuck·le \'nǝ-kǝl\ *n* : the rounded knob at a joint and esp. at a finger joint

knuckle down *vb* : to apply oneself earnestly ⟨*knuckled down* to the task⟩

knuckle under *vb* : SUBMIT, SURRENDER

knurl \'nǝrl\ *n* **1** : KNOB **2** : one of a series of small ridges on a metal surface to aid in gripping — **knurled** \'nǝrld\ *adj* — **knurly** *adj*

¹**KO** \(,)kā-'ō, 'kā-ō\ *n* : KNOCKOUT

²**KO** *vb* **KO'd; KO'·ing** : to knock out in boxing

ko·ala \kō-'ä-lǝ\ *n* : a gray furry Australian marsupial that has large hairy ears and feeds on eucalyptus leaves

ko·bo \'kō-(,)bō\ *n, pl* **kobo** — see naira at MONEY table

K of C *abbr* Knights of Columbus

kohl·ra·bi \kōl-'rä-bē\ *n, pl* **-bies** [G, fr. It *cavolo rapa*, lit., cabbage turnip] : a cabbage that forms no head but has a swollen fleshy edible stem

koi \'kói\ *n, pl* **koi** [Jp] : a carp bred for large size and a variety of colors and often stocked in ornamental ponds

ko·lin·sky \kǝ-'lin-skē\ *n, pl* **-skies** : the fur of various Asian minks

Ko·mo·do dragon \kǝ-'mō-dō-\ *n* [*Komodo* Island, Indonesia] : a carnivorous lizard of Indonesia that is the largest of all known lizards

kook \'kük\ *n* : SCREWBALL 2

kooky *also* **kook·ie** \'kü-kē\ *adj* **kook·i·er; -est** : having the characteristics of a kook : CRAZY, ECCENTRIC ⟨a ∼ radical⟩ — **kook·i·ness** *n*

Koo·te·nai *or* **Ku·te·nai** \'kü-tǝ-,nä\ *n, pl* **-nai** *or* **-nais** : a member of an American Indian people of the Rocky Mountains in both the U.S. and Canada; *also* : their language

ko·peck *or* **ko·pek** \'kō-,pek\ *n* [Russ *kopeĭka*] — see *ruble* at MONEY table

ko·piy·ka \,kō-'pē-kǝ\ *n* — see *hryvnia* at MONEY table

ko·ra \'kór-ǝ\ *n* : a 21-stringed African musical instrument

Ko·ran *or* **Qur·an** *also* **Qur·'an** \kǝ-'ran, -'rän\ *n* [Ar *qur'ān*] : a sacred book of Islam that contains revelations made to Muhammad by Allah

ko·ru·na \'kór-ǝ-,nä\ *n, pl* **ko·ru·ny** \-ǝ-nē\ *or* **korunas** *or* **ko·run** \-ǝn\ — see MONEY table **2** : the basic monetary unit of Slovakia from 1992 to 2009

ko·sher \'kō-shǝr\ *adj* [Yiddish, fr. Heb *kāshēr* fit, proper] **1** : ritually fit for use according to Jewish law **2** : selling or serving kosher food

kow·tow \kaú-'taú, 'kaú-,taú\ *vb* [Chin *kòutóu*, fr. *kòu* to knock + *tóu* head] **1** : to show obsequious deference **2** : to kneel and touch the forehead to the ground as a sign of homage or deep respect

KP \,kā-'pē\ *n* **1** : an enlisted person detailed to help the cooks in a military mess **2** : the work of KPs

kph *abbr* kilometers per hour

Kr *symbol* krypton

kraal \'kräl, 'król\ *n* **1** : a native village in southern Africa **2** : an enclosure for domestic animals in southern Africa

kraut \'kraút\ *n* : SAUERKRAUT

Krem·lin \'krem-lǝn\ *n* : the Russian government

Krem·lin·ol·o·gist \,krem-lǝ-'nä-lǝ-jist\ *n* : a specialist in the policies and practices of the government of the Soviet Union

¹**kro·na** \'krō-nǝ\ *n, pl* **kro·nor** \-,nór\ [Sw] — see MONEY table

²**kro·na** \'krō-nǝ\ *n, pl* **kro·nur** \-nǝr\ [Icel] — see MONEY table

kro·ne \'krō-nǝ\ *n, pl* **kro·ner** \-nǝr\ — see MONEY table

kroon \'krōn\ *n, pl* **kroo·ni** \'krō-nē\ *or* **kroons** : the basic monetary unit of Estonia from 1928 to 1940 and from 1991 to 2011

Kru·ger·rand \'krü-gər-,rand, -,ränd\ *n* : a 1-ounce gold coin of the Republic of South Africa

kryp·ton \'krip-,tän\ *n* : a gaseous chemical element used esp. in electric lamps

KS *abbr* Kansas

kt *abbr* **1** karat **2** knight

ku·do \'kü-dō, 'kyü-\ *n, pl* kudos [fr. *kudos* (taken as pl.)] **1** : AWARD, HONOR **2** : COMPLIMENT, PRAISE

ku·dos \'kü-,däs, 'kyü-\ *n* : fame and renown resulting from achievement

kud·zu \'kúd-zü, 'kəd-\ *n* [Jp *kuzu*] : a fast-growing weedy leguminous vine used for forage and erosion control

ku·lak \kü-'lak, kyü-, -'läk\ *n* [Russ, lit., fist] **1** : a wealthy peasant farmer in 19th century Russia **2** : a farmer characterized by Communists as too wealthy

kum·quat \'kəm-,kwät\ *n* : any of several small citrus fruits with sweet spongy rind and acid pulp

ku·na \'kü-,nä\ *n, pl* kuna *or* ku·ne \-nä\ — see MONEY table

kung fu \,kəŋ-'fü, ,kúŋ-\ *n* : a Chinese art of self-defense resembling karate

kung pao \'kəŋ-,paú, 'küŋ-, 'kúŋ-\ *adj* : being stir-fried or deep-fried and served in a spicy hot sauce usu. with peanuts

kur·ta \'kər-tə\ *n* : a long loose-fitting collarless shirt

ku·rus \kə-'rüsh\ *n, pl* kurus — see *lira* at MONEY table

kV *abbr* kilovolt

kvell \'kvel\ *vb* : to be extraordinarily proud

kvetch \'kvech, 'kfech\ *vb* : to complain habitually — **kvetch** *n*

kW *abbr* kilowatt

kwa·cha \'kwä-chə\ *n, pl* kwacha — see MONEY table

kwan·za \'kwän-zə\ *n, pl* kwanzas *or* kwanza — see MONEY table

Kwan·zaa *also* **Kwan·za** \'kwän-zə\ *n* [Swahili *kwanza* first] : an African American cultural festival held from December 26 to January 1

kwash·i·or·kor \,kwä-shē-'ôr-kòr, -òr-'kòr\ *n* : a disease of young children caused by deficient intake of protein

kWh *abbr* kilowatt-hour

Ky *or* **KY** *abbr* Kentucky

kyat \'chät\ *n, pl* kyats *or* kyat — see MONEY table

ky·bosh *chiefly Brit var of* KIBOSH

L

¹l \'el\ *n, pl* **l's** *or* **ls** \'elz\ *often cap* : the 12th letter of the English alphabet

²l *abbr, often cap* **1** lake **2** large **3** left **4** [L *libra*] pound **5** line **6** liter

¹La *abbr* Louisiana

²La *symbol* lanthanum

LA *abbr* **1** law agent **2** Los Angeles **3** Louisiana

laa·ri \'lä-rē\ *n, pl* laari — see *rufiyaa* at MONEY table

lab \'lab\ *n* : LABORATORY

Lab *n* : LABRADOR RETRIEVER

¹la·bel \'lä-bəl\ *n* **1** : a slip attached to something for identification or description **2** : a descriptive or identifying word or phrase **3** : BRAND 3

²label *vb* -beled *or* -belled; -bel·ing *or* -bel·ling **1** : to affix a label to **2** : to describe or name with a label

la·bi·al \'lä-bē-əl\ *adj* : of, relating to, or situated near the lips or labia

la·bia ma·jo·ra \'lä-bē-ə-mə-'jòr-ə\ *n pl* : the outer fatty folds of the vulva

labia mi·no·ra \-mə-'nòr-ə\ *n pl* : the inner highly vascular folds of the vulva

la·bile \'lä-,bī(-ə)l, -bəl\ *adj* **1** : UNSTABLE ⟨a ∼ mineral⟩ **2** : ADAPTABLE

la·bi·um \'lä-bē-əm\ *n, pl* la·bia \-ə\ [NL, fr. L, lip] : any of the folds at the margin of the vulva

¹la·bor \'lä-bər\ *n* **1** : physical or mental effort; *also* : human activity that provides the goods or services in an economy **2** : the physical efforts of giving birth; *also* : the period of such labor **3** : TASK **4** : those who do manual labor or work for wages; *also* : labor unions or their officials

²labor *vb* **1** : WORK **2** : to move with great effort **3** : to be in the labor of giving birth **4** : to suffer from some disadvantage or distress ⟨∼ under a delusion⟩ **5** : to treat or work out laboriously — **la·bor·er** *n*

lab·o·ra·to·ry \'la-brə-,tòr-ē, -bə-rə-\ *n, pl* -ries : a place equipped for making scientific experiments or tests

Labor Day *n* : the 1st Monday in September observed as a legal holiday in recognition of the working people

la·bored \'lä-bərd\ *adj* : not freely or easily done ⟨∼ breathing⟩

la·bo·ri·ous \lə-'bòr-ē-əs\ *adj* **1** : INDUSTRIOUS **2** : requiring great effort — **la·bo·ri·ous·ly** *adv*

la·bor·sav·ing \'lä-bər-,sä-viŋ\ *adj* : designed to replace or decrease labor

labor union *n* : an organization of workers formed to advance its members' interest in respect to wages and working conditions

la·bour *chiefly Brit var of* LABOR

lab·ra·dor·ite \'la-brə-,dòr-,īt\ *n* : an iridescent feldspar used in jewelry

Lab·ra·dor retriever \'la-brə-,dòr-\ *n* : any of a breed of strongly built retrievers having a short dense black, yellow, or chocolate coat

la·bur·num \lə-'bər-nəm\ *n* : any of a genus of leguminous shrubs or trees with hanging clusters of yellow flowers

lab·y·rinth \'la-bə-,rinth\ *n* : a place constructed of or filled with confusing intricate passageways : MAZE

lab·y·rin·thine \,la-bə-'rin-thən, -,thīn, -,thēn\ *adj* : INTRICATE, INVOLVED ⟨a ∼ plot⟩ ⟨∼ hallways⟩

lac \'lak\ *n* : a resinous substance secreted by a scale insect and used chiefly in the form of shellac

¹lace \'lās\ *vb* laced; lac·ing **1** : TIE **2** : to adorn with lace **3** : INTERTWINE **4** : BEAT, LASH **5** : to add something that taints (as a drug) or enhances flavor (as a spice) **6** : to criticize sharply — used with *into* ⟨laced into his opponent⟩

²lace *n* [ME, fr. AF *lace, laz,* fr. L *laqueus* snare] **1** : a cord or string used for drawing together two edges **2** : an ornamental braid **3** : a fine openwork usu. figured fabric made of thread — **lacy** \'lā-sē\ *adj*

lac·er·ate \'la-sə-,rāt\ *vb* -at·ed; -at·ing : to tear roughly — **lac·er·a·tion** \,la-sə-'rā-shən\ *n*

lace·wing \'lās-,wiŋ\ *n* : any of various insects with delicate wing veins, long antennae, and often brilliant eyes

lacewing

lach·ry·mal *or* **lac·ri·mal** \'la-krə-məl\ *adj* **1** *usu* lacrimal : of, relating to, or being glands that produce tears **2** : of, relating to, or marked by tears

lach·ry·mose \'la-krə-,mōs\ *adj* **1** : TEARFUL **2** : MOURNFUL ⟨∼ songs⟩

¹lack \'lak\ *vb* **1** : to be wanting or missing **2** : to be deficient in ⟨∼s experience⟩

²**lack** *n* : the fact or state of being wanting or deficient : NEED

lack·a·dai·si·cal \ˌla-kə-'dā-zi-kəl\ *adj* : lacking life, spirit, or zest — **lack·a·dai·si·cal·ly** \-k(ə-)lē\ *adv*

lack·ey \'la-kē\ *n, pl* **lackeys** 1 : FOOTMAN, SERVANT 2 : TOADY

lack·lus·ter \'lak-ˌləs-tər\ *adj* : DULL

la·con·ic \lə-'kä-nik\ *adj* [L *laconicus* Spartan, fr. Gk *lakōnikos;* fr. the Spartan reputation for terseness of speech] : sparing of words : TERSE ✦ **Synonyms** CONCISE, CURT, SHORT, SUCCINCT, BRUSQUE — **la·con·i·cal·ly** \-ni-k(ə-)lē\ *adv*

lac·quer \'la-kər\ *n* : a clear or colored usu. glossy and quick-drying surface coating — **lacquer** *vb*

lac·ri·ma·tion \ˌla-krə-'mā-shən\ *n* : secretion of tears

la·crosse \lə-'krós\ *n* [CanF *la crosse,* lit., the crooked stick] : a goal game in which players use a long-handled triangular-headed stick having a mesh pouch for catching, carrying, and throwing the ball

lac·tate \'lak-ˌtāt\ *vb* **lac·tat·ed; lac·tat·ing** : to secrete milk — **lac·ta·tion** \lak-'tā-shən\ *n*

lac·tic \'lak-tik\ *adj* 1 : of or relating to milk 2 : obtained from sour milk or whey

lactic acid *n* : a syrupy acid present in blood and muscle tissue and used esp. in food and medicine

lac·tose \'lak-ˌtōs\ *n* : a sugar present in milk

la·cu·na \lə-'kü-nə, -'kyü-\ *n, pl* **la·cu·nae** \-nē\ *also* **la·cu·nas** [L, pool, pit, gap, fr. *lacus* lake] : a blank space or missing part : GAP, DEFICIENCY

lad \'lad\ *n* : YOUTH; *also* : FELLOW

lad·der \'la-dər\ *n* 1 : a structure for climbing that consists of two parallel sidepieces joined at intervals by crosspieces 2 : something resembling a ladder in having ascending steps or stages ⟨a tournament ∼⟩

lad·die \'la-dē\ *n* : a young lad

lad·en \'lā-dᵉn\ *adj* : LOADED, BURDENED

lad·ing \'lā-diŋ\ *n* : CARGO, FREIGHT

la·dle \'lā-dᵉl\ *n* : a deep-bowled long-handled spoon used in taking up and conveying liquids — **ladle** *vb*

la·dy \'lā-dē\ *n, pl* **ladies** [ME, fr. OE *hlǣfdīge,* fr. *hlāf* bread + *-dīge* (akin to *dǣge* kneader of bread)] 1 : a woman of property, rank, or authority; *also* : a woman of superior social position or of refinement 2 : WOMAN 3 : WIFE

lady beetle *n* : LADYBUG

la·dy·bird \'lā-dē-ˌbərd\ *n* : LADYBUG

la·dy·bug \-ˌbəg\ *n* : any of various small nearly hemispherical and usu. brightly colored beetles that feed mostly on other insects

la·dy·fin·ger \-ˌfiŋ-gər\ *n* : a small finger-shaped sponge cake

lady–in–waiting *n, pl* **ladies–in–waiting** : a lady appointed to attend or wait on a queen or princess

la·dy·like \'lā-dē-ˌlīk\ *adj* : WELL-BRED

la·dy·ship \-ˌship\ *n* : the condition of being a lady : rank of lady

lady's slipper *also* **lady slipper** *n* : any of several No. American orchids with slipper-shaped flowers

¹**lag** \'lag\ *n* 1 : a slowing up or falling behind; *also* : the amount by which one lags 2 : INTERVAL

²**lag** *vb* **lagged; lag·ging** 1 : to fail to keep up : stay behind 2 : to slacken gradually ✦ **Synonyms** DAWDLE, DALLY, TARRY, LOITER

la·ger \'lä-gər\ *n* : a usu. dry beer slowly brewed and matured under refrigeration

lag·gard \'la-gərd\ *adj* : tending to lag ⟨∼ workers⟩ — **laggard** *n* — **lag·gard·ly** *adv or adj* — **lag·gard·ness** *n*

la·gniappe \'lan-ˌyap\ *n* : something given free esp. with a purchase

la·goon \lə-'gün\ *n* : a shallow sound, channel, or pond near or connected to a larger body of water

laid *past and past part of* LAY

laid–back \'lād-'bak\ *adj* : having a relaxed style or character ⟨∼ music⟩

lain *past part of* ¹LIE

lair \'ler\ *n* 1 : the resting or living place of a wild animal : DEN 2 : a usu. hidden refuge

laird \'lerd\ *n, chiefly Scot* : a landed proprietor

lais·ser–faire *chiefly Brit var of* LAISSEZ-FAIRE

lais·sez–faire \ˌle-ˌsā-'fer, ˌlā-, -ˌzā-\ *n* [F *laissez faire* let do] : a doctrine opposing governmental control of economic affairs beyond that necessary to maintain peace and property rights

la·ity \'lā-ə-tē\ *n* 1 : the people of a religious faith as distinct from its clergy 2 : the mass of people as distinct from those of a particular field

lake \'lāk\ *n* : an inland body of standing water of considerable size; *also* : a pool of liquid (as lava or pitch)

La·ko·ta \lə-'kō-tə\ *n, pl* **Lakota** *also* **Lakotas** : a member of a western division of the Dakota peoples; *also* : their language

¹**lam** \'lam\ *vb* **lammed; lam·ming** : to flee hastily — **lam** *n*

²**lam** *abbr* laminated

Lam *abbr* Lamentations

la·ma \'lä-mə\ *n* : a Buddhist monk of Tibet or Mongolia

la·ma·sery \'lä-mə-ˌser-ē\ *n, pl* **-ser·ies** : a monastery for lamas

¹**lamb** \'lam\ *n* 1 : a young sheep; *also* : its flesh used as food 2 : an innocent or gentle person

²**lamb** *vb* : to bring forth a lamb

lam·baste *or* **lam·bast** \lam-'bāst, -'bast\ *vb* 1 : BEAT 2 : EXCORIATE ✦ **Synonyms** CASTIGATE, FLAY, LASH

lamb·da \'lam-də\ *n* : the 11th letter of the Greek alphabet — Λ or λ

lam·bent \'lam-bənt\ *adj* [L *lambens,* prp. of *lambere* to lick] 1 : FLICKERING ⟨a ∼ flame⟩ 2 : softly radiant ⟨∼ eyes⟩ 3 : marked by lightness or brilliance ⟨∼ humor⟩ ✦ **Synonyms** EFFULGENT, INCANDESCENT, LUCENT, LUMINOUS — **lam·ben·cy** \-bən-sē\ *n* — **lam·bent·ly** *adv*

lamb·skin \'lam-ˌskin\ *n* : a lamb's skin or a small fine-grade sheepskin or the leather made from either

¹**lame** \'lām\ *adj* **lam·er; lam·est** 1 : having a body part and esp. a limb so disabled as to impair freedom of movement; *also* : marked by stiffness and soreness 2 : lacking substance : WEAK ⟨∼ excuses⟩ 3 : INFERIOR, PITIFUL ⟨a ∼ school⟩ — **lame·ly** *adv* — **lame·ness** *n*

²**lame** *vb* **lamed; lam·ing** : to make lame : DISABLE ⟨was *lamed* by a broken leg⟩

la·mé \lä-'mā, la-\ *n* [F] : a brocaded clothing fabric with tinsel filling threads (as of gold or silver)

lame·brain \'lām-ˌbrān\ *n* : DOLT

lame duck *n* : an elected official continuing to hold office between an election and the inauguration of a successor — **lame–duck** *adj*

¹**la·ment** \lə-'ment\ *vb* 1 : to mourn aloud : WAIL 2 : to express sorrow or regret for : BEWAIL — **lam·en·ta·ble** \'la-mən-tə-bəl, lə-'men-tə-\ *adj* — **lam·en·ta·bly** \-blē\ *adv* — **lam·en·ta·tion** \ˌla-mən-'tā-shən\ *n*

²**lament** *n* 1 : a crying out in grief : WAIL 2 : DIRGE, ELEGY 3 : COMPLAINT

Lamentations *n* — see BIBLE table

la·mia \'lā-mē-ə\ *n* : a female demon

lam·i·na \'la-mə-nə\ *n, pl* **-nae** \-ˌnē\ *or* **-nas** : a thin plate or scale

lam·i·nate \'la-mə-ˌnāt\ *vb* **-nat·ed; -nat·ing** : to make by uniting layers of one or more materials — **lam·i·na·tion** \ˌla-mə-'nā-shən\ *n*

²**lam·i·nate** \-nət\ *n* : a product manufactured by laminating

lamp \'lamp\ *n* 1 : a vessel with a wick for burning a flammable liquid (as oil) to produce light 2 : a device for producing light or heat

lamp·black \-ˌblak\ *n* : black soot used esp. as a pigment

lamp·light·er \-ˌlī-tər\ *n* : one that lights a lamp

lam·poon \lam-'pün\ *n* : SATIRE; *esp* : a harsh satire directed against an individual — **lampoon** *vb*

lam·prey \'lam-prē\ *n, pl* **lampreys** : any of a family of eel-shaped jawless fishes that have well-developed eyes and a large disk-shaped sucking mouth armed with horny teeth

LAN \'lan, ˌel-ˌā-'en\ *n* : LOCAL AREA NETWORK

la·nai \lə-'nī\ *n* [Hawaiian *lānai*] : PORCH, VERANDA

¹**lance** \'lans\ *n* 1 : a spear carried by mounted soldiers 2 : any of various sharp-pointed implements; *esp* : LANCET

²**lance** *vb* **lanced; lanc·ing** : to pierce or open with a lance ⟨∼ a boil⟩

lance corporal *n* : an enlisted person in the marine corps ranking above a private first class and below a corporal

lanc·er \'lan-sər\ *n* : a cavalryman of a unit formerly armed with lances

lan·cet \'lan-sət\ *n* : a sharp-pointed and usu. 2-edged surgical instrument

¹**land** \'land\ *n* **1** : the solid part of the surface of the earth; *also* : a part of the earth's surface ⟨fenced ∼⟩ ⟨marshy ∼⟩ **2** : NATION **3** : REALM, DOMAIN ⟨the ∼ of the living⟩ — **land·less** *adj*

²**land** *vb* **1** : DISEMBARK; *also* : to touch at a place on shore **2** : to alight or cause to alight on a surface ⟨∼ a punch⟩ **3** : to bring to or arrive at a destination **4** : to catch and bring in ⟨∼ a fish⟩; *also* : GAIN, SECURE ⟨∼ a job⟩

lan·dau \'lan-ˌdau̇\ *n* : a 4-wheeled carriage with a top divided into two sections that can be lowered, thrown back, or removed

land·ed *adj* : having an estate in land ⟨∼ gentry⟩

land·er \'lan-dər\ *n* : a space vehicle designed to land on a celestial body

land·fall \'land-ˌfȯl\ *n* : a sighting or making of land (as after a voyage); *also* : the land first sighted

land·fill \-ˌfil\ *n* : a low-lying area on which refuse is buried between layers of earth — **landfill** *vb*

land·form \-ˌfȯrm\ *n* : a natural feature of a land surface

land·hold·er \-ˌhōl-dər\ *n* : a holder or owner of land — **land·hold·ing** \-diŋ\ *adj or n*

land·ing \'lan-diŋ\ *n* **1** : the action of one that lands **2** : a place for discharging or taking on passengers and cargo **3** : a level part of a staircase

landing gear *n* : the part that supports the weight of an aircraft when it is on the ground

land·la·dy \'land-ˌlā-dē\ *n* : a woman who is a landlord

land·locked \-ˌläkt\ *adj* **1** : enclosed or nearly enclosed by land ⟨a ∼ country⟩ **2** : confined to fresh water by some barrier ⟨∼ salmon⟩

land·lord \-ˌlȯrd\ *n* **1** : the owner of property leased or rented to another **2** : a person who rents lodgings : INN-KEEPER

land·lub·ber \-ˌlə-bər\ *n* : one who knows little of the sea or seamanship

land·mark \-ˌmärk\ *n* **1** : an object that marks a course or boundary or serves as a guide **2** : an event that marks a turning point **3** : a structure of unusual historical and usu. aesthetic interest

land·mass \-ˌmas\ *n* : a large area of land

land mine *n* **1** : a mine placed on or just below the surface of the ground and designed to be exploded by the weight of someone or something passing over it **2** : a trap for the unwary

land·own·er \-ˌō-nər\ *n* : an owner of land

¹**land·scape** \-ˌskāp\ *n* **1** : a picture of natural inland scenery **2** : a portion of land that can be seen in one glance

²**landscape** *vb* **land·scaped; land·scap·ing** : to modify (a natural landscape) by grading, clearing, or decorative planting

land·slide \-ˌslīd\ *n* **1** : the slipping down of a mass of rocks or earth on a steep slope; *also* : the mass of material that slides **2** : an overwhelming victory esp. in a political contest

lands·man \'landz-mən\ *n* : a person who lives on land; *esp* : LANDLUBBER

land·ward \'land-wərd\ *adv or adj* : to or toward the land

lane \'lān\ *n* **1** : a narrow passageway (as between fences) **2** : a relatively narrow way or track ⟨traffic ∼⟩

lang *abbr* language

lan·guage \'laŋ-gwij\ *n* [ME, fr. AF *langage*, fr. *langue* tongue, language, fr. L *lingua*] **1** : the words, their pronunciation, and the methods of combining them used and understood by a community **2** : form or style of verbal expression ⟨legal ∼⟩ **3** : a system of signs and symbols and rules for using them that is used to carry information

lan·guid \'laŋ-gwəd\ *adj* **1** : WEAK **2** : sluggish in character or disposition : LISTLESS ⟨a ∼ summer day⟩ **3** : SLOW — **lan·guid·ly** *adv* — **lan·guid·ness** *n*

lan·guish \'laŋ-gwish\ *vb* **1** : to become languid **2** : to become dispirited : PINE **3** : to appeal for sympathy by assuming an expression of grief

lan·guor \'laŋ-gər\ *n* **1** : a languid feeling **2** : listless indolence or inertia ✦ *Synonyms* LETHARGY, LASSITUDE, TORPIDITY, TORPOR — **lan·guor·ous** *adj* — **lan·guor·ous·ly** *adv*

La Ni·ña \lä-'nē-nyə\ *n* : an upwelling of unusually cold ocean water along the west coast of So. America that often follows an El Niño

lank \'laŋk\ *adj* **1** : not well filled out **2** : hanging straight and limp ⟨∼ hair⟩

lanky \'laŋ-kē\ *adj* **lank·i·er; -est** : ungracefully tall and thin

lan·o·lin \'lan-ᵊl-ən\ *n* : the fatty coating of sheep's wool esp. when refined for use in ointments and cosmetics

lan·ta·na \lan-'tä-nə\ *n* : any of a genus of tropical shrubs related to the vervains with showy heads of small bright flowers

lan·tern \'lan-tərn\ *n* [ME *lanterne*, fr. AF, fr. L *lanterna*, fr. Gk *lamptēr*, fr. *lampein* to shine] **1** : a usu. portable light with a protective covering **2** : the chamber in a lighthouse containing the light **3** : a projector for slides

lan·tha·num \'lan-thə-nəm\ *n* : a soft malleable metallic chemical element

lan·yard \'lan-yərd\ *n* : a piece of rope for fastening something in ships; *also* : any of various cords

¹**lap** \'lap\ *n* **1** : a loose panel of a garment **2** : the clothing that lies on the knees, thighs, and lower part of the trunk when one sits; *also* : the front part of the lower trunk and thighs of a seated person **3** : an environment of nurture ⟨the ∼ of luxury⟩ **4** : CHARGE, CONTROL ⟨in the ∼ of the gods⟩

²**lap** *vb* **lapped; lap·ping** **1** : FOLD **2** : WRAP **3** : to lay over or near so as to partly cover

³**lap** *n* **1** : the amount by which an object overlaps another; *also* : the part of an object that overlaps another **2** : an act or instance of going over a course (as a track or swimming pool)

⁴**lap** *vb* **lapped; lap·ping** **1** : to scoop up food or drink with the tip of the tongue; *also* : DEVOUR — usu. used with *up* **2** : to splash gently ⟨*lapping* waves⟩

⁵**lap** *n* **1** : an act or instance of lapping **2** : a gentle splashing sound

lap·a·ros·co·py \ˌla-pə-'räs-kə-pē\ *n, pl* **-pies** **1** : visual examination of the abdomen by means of an endoscope; *also* : surgery using laparoscopy — **lap·a·ro·scope** \'la-pə-rə-ˌskōp\ *n* — **lap·a·ro·scop·ic** \ˌla-pə-rə-'skä-pik\ *adj*

lap·dog \'lap-ˌdȯg\ *n* : a small dog that may be held in the lap

la·pel \lə-'pel\ *n* : the fold of the front of a coat that is usu. a continuation of the collar

¹**lap·i·dary** \'la-pə-ˌder-ē\ *n, pl* **-dar·ies** : a person who cuts, polishes, or engraves precious stones

²**lapidary** *adj* **1** : of, relating to, or suitable for engraved inscriptions **2** : of, relating to, or suggestive of precious stones or the art of cutting them

lap·in \'la-pən\ *n* : rabbit fur usu. sheared and dyed

la·pis la·zu·li \ˌla-pəs-'la-zə-lē, -zhə-\ *n* : a usu. blue semiprecious stone often having sparkling bits of pyrite

lap·pet \'la-pət\ *n* : a fold or flap on a garment

¹**lapse** \'laps\ *n* [L *lapsus*, fr. *labi* to slip] **1** : a slight error ⟨a mental ∼⟩ **2** : a fall from a higher to a lower state **3** : the termination of a right or privilege through failure to meet requirements **4** : INTERRUPTION **5** : APOSTASY **6** : a passage of time; *also* : INTERVAL ✦ *Synonyms* BLOOPER, BLUNDER, BONER, GOOF, MISTAKE, SLIP

²**lapse** *vb* **lapsed; laps·ing** **1** : to commit apostasy **2** : SINK, SLIP ⟨*lapsed* into a coma⟩ **3** : CEASE

lap·top \'lap-ˌtäp\ *adj* : of a size that can be used conveniently on one's lap ⟨a ∼ computer⟩ — **laptop** *n*

lap·wing \'lap-ˌwiŋ\ *n* : an Old World crested plover

lar·board \'lär-bərd\ *n* : ⁵PORT

lar·ce·ny \'lär-sə-nē\ *n, pl* **-nies** [ME, fr. AF *larcin* theft, fr. L *latrocinium* robbery, fr. *latro* mercenary soldier] : THEFT — **lar·ce·nous** \-nəs\ *adj*

larch \'lärch\ *n* : any of a genus of trees related to the pines that shed their needles in the fall

¹**lard** \'lärd\ *vb* **1** : to insert strips of usu. pork fat into (meat) before cooking; *also* : GREASE **2** *obs* : ENRICH

²**lard** *n* : a soft white fat obtained by rendering fatty tissue of the hog

lar·der \'lär-dər\ *n* : a place where foods (as meat) are kept

large \'lärj\ *adj* **larg·er; larg·est** **1** : having more than usual power, capacity, or scope **2** : exceeding most other things of like kind in quantity or size ✦ *Synonyms* BIG, GREAT, OVERSIZE — **large** *adv* — **large·ness** *n* — **at large** **1** : UNCONFINED **2** : as a whole

large·ly \'lärj-lē\ *adv* : to a large extent

lar·gesse *or* **lar·gess** \lär-'zhes, -'jes\ *n* **1** : liberal giving **2** : a generous gift

¹**lar·go** \'lär-gō\ *adv or adj* [It, slow, broad, fr. L *largus* abundant] : at a very slow tempo — used as a direction in music

²**largo** *n, pl* **largos** : a largo movement
lari \'lä-rē\ *n, pl* **lari** — see MONEY table
lar·i·at \'lar-ē-ət\ *n* [AmerSp *la reata* the lasso, fr. Sp *la* the + AmerSp *reata* lasso, fr. Sp *reatar* to tie again] : a long rope used to catch or tether livestock : LASSO
¹**lark** \'lärk\ *n* : any of a family of small songbirds; *esp* : SKYLARK
²**lark** *n* : a source of or quest for fun or adventure
³**lark** *vb* : to engage in harmless fun or mischief — often used with *about*
lark·spur \'lärk-₁spər\ *n* : DELPHINIUM; *esp* : any of the widely cultivated annual delphiniums
lar·va \'lär-və\ *n, pl* **lar·vae** \-(₁)vē\ *also* **larvas** [NL, fr. L, specter, mask] : the wingless often wormlike form in which insects hatch from the egg; *also* : any young animal (as a tadpole) that is fundamentally unlike its parent — **lar·val** \-vəl\ *adj*
lar·yn·gi·tis \₁lar-ən-'jī-təs\ *n* : inflammation of the larynx
lar·ynx \'lar-iŋks\ *n, pl* **la·ryn·ges** \lə-'rin-jēz\ *or* **lar·ynx·es** : the upper part of the trachea containing the vocal cords — **la·ryn·ge·al** \lə-'rin-jəl\ *adj*
la·sa·gna \lə-'zän-yə\ *n* [It] : boiled broad flat noodles baked with a sauce usu. of tomatoes, cheese, and meat
las·car \'las-kər\ *n* : an Indian sailor
las·civ·i·ous \lə-'si-vē-əs\ *adj* : LUSTFUL, LEWD ♦ *Synonyms* LICENTIOUS, LECHEROUS, LIBIDINOUS, SALACIOUS — **las·civ·i·ous·ness** *n*
la·ser \'lā-zər\ *n* [*l*ight *a*mplification by *s*timulated *e*mission of *r*adiation] **1** : a device that produces an intense monochromatic beam of light **2** : something thrown or directed straight with high speed or intensity ⟨threw a ~ into the end zone⟩
laser disc *n* : OPTICAL DISK; *esp* : one containing a video recording
¹**lash** \'lash\ *vb* **1** : to move violently or suddenly **2** : WHIP **3** : to attack verbally
²**lash** *n* **1** : a stroke esp. with a whip; *also* : WHIP **2** : a stinging rebuke **3** : EYELASH
³**lash** *vb* : to bind with or as if with a line
lass \'las\ *n* : GIRL
lass·ie \'la-sē\ *n* : LASS
las·si·tude \'la-sə-₁tüd, -₁tyüd\ *n* **1** : WEARINESS, FATIGUE **2** : LANGUOR
las·so \'la-sō, la-'sü\ *n, pl* **lassos** *or* **lassoes** [Sp *lazo*] : a rope or long leather thong with a noose used for catching livestock — **lasso** *vb*
¹**last** \'last\ *vb* **1** : to continue in existence or operation **2** : to remain fresh or unimpaired : ENDURE **3** : to manage to continue **4** : to be enough for the needs of
²**last** *n* : a foot-shaped form on which a shoe is shaped or repaired
³**last** *vb* : to shape with a last
⁴**last** *adv* **1** : at the end **2** : most recently **3** : in conclusion
⁵**last** *adj* **1** : following all the rest : FINAL **2** : next before the present ⟨~ week⟩ **3** : most up-to-date **4** : farthest from a specified quality, attitude, or likelihood ⟨the ~ thing we want⟩ **5** : CONCLUSIVE; *also* : SUPREME — **last·ly** *adv*
⁶**last** *n* : something that is last ⟨the ~ of them⟩ — **at last** : FINALLY
last–ditch \'last-₁dich\ *adj* : made as a final effort esp. to avert disaster
last laugh *n* : an ultimate satisfaction or triumph despite previous doubt or criticism
Last Supper *n* : the supper eaten by Jesus and his disciples on the night of his betrayal
lat *abbr* latitude
Lat *abbr* Latin
¹**latch** \'lach\ *vb* : to catch or get hold
²**latch** *n* : a catch that holds a door or gate closed
³**latch** *vb* : to make fast with a latch
latch·et \'la-chət\ *n* : a strap, thong, or lace for fastening a shoe or sandal
latch·key \'lach-₁kē\ *n* : a key for opening a door latch esp. from the outside
latch·string \-₁striŋ\ *n* : a string on a latch that may be left hanging outside the door for raising the latch
¹**late** \'lāt\ *adj* **lat·er; lat·est 1** : coming or remaining after the due, usual, or proper time **2** : far advanced toward the close or end **3** : recently deceased **4** : made, appearing, or happening just previous to the present : RECENT ⟨~ news⟩ — **late·ly** *adv* — **late·ness** *n*

²**late** *adv* **lat·er; lat·est 1** : after the usual or proper time; *also* : at or to an advanced point in time **2** : RECENTLY
late·com·er \'lāt-₁kə-mər\ *n* : one who arrives late
la·teen \lə-'tēn\ *adj* : relating to or being a triangular sail extended by a long spar slung to a low mast
la·tent \'lāt-ᵊnt\ *adj* : present but not visible or active ♦ *Synonyms* DORMANT, QUIESCENT, POTENTIAL — **la·ten·cy** \-ᵊn-sē\ *n*
¹**lat·er·al** \'la-tə-rəl\ *adj* : situated on, directed toward, or coming from the side ⟨a ~ view⟩ — **lat·er·al·ly** *adv*
²**lateral** *n* **1** : a branch from the main part **2** : a football pass thrown parallel to the line of scrimmage or away from the opponent's goal
la·tex \'lā-₁teks\ *n, pl* **la·ti·ces** \'lā-tə-₁sēz, 'la-\ *or* **la·tex·es 1** : a milky juice produced by various plant cells (as of milkweeds, poppies, and the rubber tree) **2** : a water emulsion of a synthetic rubber or plastic used esp. in paint
lath \'lath, 'làth\ *n, pl* **laths** *or* **lath** : a thin narrow strip of wood used esp. as a base for plaster; *also* : a building material in sheets used for the same purpose — **lath** *vb*
lathe \'lāth\ *n* : a machine in which a piece of material is held and turned while being shaped by a tool
¹**lath·er** \'la-thər\ *n* **1** : a foam or froth formed when a detergent is agitated in water; *also* : foam from profuse sweating (as by a horse) **2** : DITHER
²**lather** *vb* : to spread lather over ⟨~ed his face before shaving⟩; *also* : to form a lather
Lat·in \'lat-ᵊn\ *n* **1** : the language of ancient Rome **2** : a member of any of the peoples whose languages derive from Latin — **Latin** *adj*
La·ti·na \lə-tē-nə\ *n* : a woman or girl who is a native or inhabitant of Latin America; *also* : a woman or girl of Latin-American origin living in the U.S.
Latin American *n* : a native or inhabitant of any of the countries of No., Central, or So. America whose official language is Spanish or Portuguese — **Latin–American** *adj*
La·ti·no \lə-'tē-nō\ *n, pl* **-nos** : a native or inhabitant of Latin America; *also* : a person of Latin-American origin living in the U.S. — **Latino** *adj*
lat·i·tude \'la-tə-₁tüd, -₁tyüd\ *n* **1** : angular distance north or south from the earth's equator measured in degrees **2** : a region marked by its latitude **3** : freedom of action or choice
lat·i·tu·di·nar·i·an \₁la-tə-₁tü-də-'ner-ē-ən, -₁tyü-\ *n* : a person who is liberal in religious belief and conduct
la·trine \lə-'trēn\ *n* : TOILET
lats \'läts\ *n, pl* **la·ti** \'lä-tē\ *or* **la·tu** \'lä-tü\ : the basic monetary unit of Latvia from 1922 to 1940 and from 1991 through 2013
lat·ter \'la-tər\ *adj* **1** : more recent; *also* : FINAL **2** : of, relating to, or being the second of two things referred to
lat·ter–day *adj* **1** : of present or recent times **2** : of a later or subsequent time
Latter–day Saint *n* : a member of a religious body founded by Joseph Smith in 1830 and accepting the Book of Mormon as divine revelation : MORMON
lat·ter·ly \'la-tər-lē\ *adv* **1** : LATER **2** : of late : RECENTLY
lat·tice \'la-təs\ *n* **1** : a framework of crossed wood or metal strips; *also* : a window, door, or gate having a lattice **2** : a regular geometrical arrangement

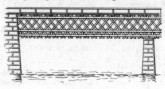

lattice 1

lat·tice·work \-₁wərk\ *n* : LATTICE; *also* : work made of lattices
Lat·vi·an \'lat-vē-ən\ *n* **1** : a native or inhabitant of Latvia **2** : the language of the Latvians — **Latvian** *adj*
¹**laud** \'lȯd\ *n* : PRAISE, ACCLAIM
²**laud** *vb* : PRAISE, EXTOL ♦ *Synonyms* CELEBRATE, EULOGIZE, GLORIFY, MAGNIFY — **laud·able** *adj* — **laud·ably** *adv*
lau·da·num \'lȯd-ᵊn-əm\ *n* : a tincture of opium

lau·da·to·ry \'lȯ-də-ˌtōr-ē\ *adj* : of, relating to, or expressive of praise

¹laugh \'laf, 'lȧf\ *vb* [ME, fr. OE *hliehhan*] : to show mirth, joy, or scorn with a chuckle or explosive vocal sound; *also* : to become amused or derisive — **laugh·able** *adj* — **laugh·ing·ly** *adv*

²laugh *n* **1** : the act of laughing **2** : JOKE; *also* : JEER **3** *pl* : SPORT 1

laughing gas *n* : NITROUS OXIDE

laugh·ing·stock \'la-fiŋ-ˌstäk, 'lȧ-\ *n* : an object of ridicule

laugh·ter \'laf-tər, 'lȧf-\ *n* : the action or sound of laughing

¹launch \'lȯnch\ *vb* **1** : THROW, HURL; *also* : to send off ⟨~ a rocket⟩ **2** : to set afloat **3** : to set in operation : START ⟨~ a business⟩ — **launch·er** *n*

²launch *n* : an act or instance of launching

³launch *n* : a small open or half-decked motorboat

launch·pad \'lȯnch-ˌpad\ *n* : a platform from which a rocket is launched

laun·der \'lȯn-dər\ *vb* **1** : to wash or wash and iron clothing and household linens **2** : to transfer (as money of an illegal origin) through an outside party to conceal the true source — **laun·der·er** *n*

laun·dress \'lȯn-drəs\ *n* : a woman who is a laundry worker

laun·dry \'lȯn-drē\ *n, pl* **laundries** [fr. obs. *launder* launderer, fr. AF *lavandere*, fr. ML *lavandarius*, fr. L *lavandus* needing to be washed, fr. *lavare* to wash] **1** : a place where laundering is done **2** : clothes or linens that have been or are to be laundered — **laun·dry·man** \-mən\ *n*

lau·re·ate \'lȯr-ē-ət\ *n* : the recipient of honor for achievement in an art or science — **lau·re·ate·ship** *n*

lau·rel \'lȯ-rəl\ *n* **1** : an evergreen tree or shrub of southern Europe that is related to the sassafras and cinnamon and has glossy aromatic leaves **2** : MOUNTAIN LAUREL **3** : a crown of laurel awarded as an honor — usu. used in pl.

lav *abbr* lavatory

la·va \'lä-və, 'la-\ *n* [It] : melted rock coming from a volcano; *also* : such rock that has cooled and hardened

la·vage \lə-'väzh\ *n* [F] : WASHING; *esp* : the washing out (as of an organ) esp. for medicinal reasons

lav·a·to·ry \'la-və-ˌtōr-ē\ *n, pl* **-ries** **1** : a fixed washbowl with running water and drainpipe **2** : BATHROOM

lave \'läv\ *vb* **laved; lav·ing** : WASH

lav·en·der \'la-vən-dər\ *n* **1** : a Mediterranean mint or its dried leaves and flowers used to perfume clothing and bed linen **2** : a pale purple color

¹lav·ish \'la-vish\ *adj* [ME *laves, lavage*, prob. fr. MF *lavasse, lavache* downpour, fr. *laver* to wash] **1** : expending or bestowing profusely **2** : expended or produced in abundance ⟨~ gifts⟩ **3** : marked by excess ⟨~ decor⟩ — **lav·ish·ly** *adv* — **lav·ish·ness** *n*

²lavish *vb* : to expend or give freely

law \'lȯ\ *n* **1** : a rule of conduct or action established by custom or laid down and enforced by a governing authority; *also* : the whole body of such rules **2** : the control brought about by enforcing rules **3** *cap* : the revelation of the divine will set forth in the Old Testament; *also* : the first part of the Jewish scriptures — see BIBLE table **4** : a rule or principle of construction or procedure **5** : the science that deals with laws and their interpretation and application **6** : the profession of a lawyer **7** : a rule or principle stating something that always works in the same way under the same conditions

law·break·er \'lȯ-ˌbrā-kər\ *n* : a person who violates the law

law·ful \'lȯ-fəl\ *adj* **1** : permitted by law **2** : RIGHTFUL — **law·ful·ly** *adv*

law·giv·er \-ˌgi-vər\ *n* : LEGISLATOR

law·less \'lȯ-ləs\ *adj* **1** : having no laws **2** : UNRULY, DISORDERLY ⟨a ~ mob⟩ — **law·less·ly** *adv* — **law·less·ness** *n*

law·mak·er \-ˌmā-kər\ *n* : LEGISLATOR

law·man \'lȯ-mən\ *n* : a law enforcement official (as a sheriff or marshal)

¹lawn \'lȯn\ *n* : ground (as around a house) covered with mowed grass

²lawn *n* : a fine sheer linen or cotton fabric

lawn bowling *n* : a bowling game played on a green with wooden balls which are rolled at a jack

law·ren·ci·um \lȯ-'ren-sē-əm\ *n* : a short-lived radioactive element

law·suit \'lȯ-ˌsüt\ *n* : a suit in law

law·yer \'lȯ-yər\ *n* : one who conducts lawsuits for clients or advises as to legal rights and obligations in other matters — **law·yer·ly** *adj*

lax \'laks\ *adj* **1** : not strict ⟨~ discipline⟩ **2** : not tense or rigid ♦ **Synonyms** REMISS, NEGLIGENT, NEGLECTFUL, DELINQUENT, DERELICT — **lax·i·ty** \'lak-sə-tē\ *n* — **lax·ly** *adv* — **lax·ness** *n*

¹lax·a·tive \'lak-sə-tiv\ *adj* : relieving constipation

²laxative *n* : a usu. mild laxative drug

¹lay \'lā\ *vb* **laid** \'lād\; **lay·ing** **1** : to beat or strike down **2** : to put on or set down : PLACE **3** : to produce and deposit eggs **4** : SETTLE; *also* : ALLAY **5** : SPREAD **6** : PREPARE, CONTRIVE **7** : WAGER **8** : to impose esp. as a duty or burden **9** : to set in order or position **10** : to bring to a specified condition ⟨*laid* waste the land⟩ **11** : to put forward : SUBMIT

²lay *n* : the way in which something lies or is laid in relation to something else

³lay *past of* ¹LIE

⁴lay *n* **1** : a simple narrative poem **2** : SONG

⁵lay *adj* **1** : of or relating to the laity **2** : not of a particular profession; *also* : lacking extensive knowledge of a particular subject

lay·away \'lā-ə-ˌwā\ *n* : a purchasing agreement by which a retailer agrees to hold merchandise secured by a deposit until the price is paid in full

lay·er \'lā-ər\ *n* **1** : one that lays **2** : one thickness, course, or fold laid or lying over or under another

lay·ette \lā-'et\ *n* [F, fr. MF, dim. of *laye* box] : an outfit of clothing and equipment for a newborn infant

lay·man \'lā-mən\ *n* : a person who is a member of the laity

lay·off \'lā-ˌȯf\ *n* **1** : a period of inactivity **2** : the act of laying off an employee

lay off *vb* **1** : to cease to employ (a worker) often temporarily **2** : to leave undisturbed **3** : to stop doing something

lay·out \'lā-ˌau̇t\ *n* : the final arrangement, plan, or design of something

lay·over \-ˌō-vər\ *n* : STOPOVER

lay·per·son \-ˌpər-sən\ *n* : a member of the laity

lay·wom·an \'lā-ˌwu̇-mən\ *n* : a woman who is a member of the laity

la·zar \'la-zər, 'lā-\ *n* : LEPER

laze \'lāz\ *vb* **lazed; laz·ing** : to pass time in idleness or relaxation

la·zy \'lā-zē\ *adj* **la·zi·er; -est** **1** : disliking activity or exertion **2** : encouraging idleness ⟨a ~ day⟩ **3** : SLUGGISH **4** : DROOPY, LAX **5** : not rigorous or strict ⟨~ work habits⟩ — **la·zi·ly** \-zə-lē\ *adv* — **la·zi·ness** \-zē-nəs\ *n*

la·zy·bones \-ˌbōnz\ *n sing or pl* : a lazy person

lazy Su·san \ˌlā-zē-'süz-ᵊn\ *n* : a revolving tray used for serving food

lb *abbr* [L *libra*] pound

lc *abbr* lowercase

LC *abbr* Library of Congress

¹LCD \ˌel-(ˌ)sē-'dē\ *n* [*l*iquid *c*rystal *d*isplay] : a display (as of the time in a digital watch) that consists of segments of a liquid crystal whose reflectivity varies with the voltage applied to them

²LCD *abbr* least common denominator; lowest common denominator

LCDR *abbr* lieutenant commander

LCM *abbr* least common multiple; lowest common multiple

LCpl *abbr* lance corporal

LCS *abbr* League Championship Series

ld *abbr* **1** load **2** lord

LD *abbr* learning disabled; learning disability

LDC *abbr* less developed country

ldg *abbr* **1** landing **2** loading

LDL \ˌel-(ˌ)dē-'el\ *n* [*l*ow-*d*ensity *l*ipoprotein] : a cholesterol-rich protein-poor lipoprotein of blood plasma correlated with increased probability of developing atherosclerosis

L–do·pa \'el-'dō-pə\ *n* : an isomer of dopa used esp. in the treatment of Parkinson's disease

LDS *abbr* Latter-day Saints

lea \'lē, 'lā\ *n* : PASTURE, MEADOW

leach \'lēch\ *vb* : to pass a liquid (as water) through to carry off the soluble components; *also* : to dissolve out by such means ⟨~ alkali from ashes⟩

¹lead \'lēd\ *vb* **led** \'led\; **lead·ing** **1** : to guide on a way **2** : LIVE ⟨∼ a quiet life⟩ **3** : to direct the operations, activity, or performance of ⟨∼ an orchestra⟩ **4** : to go at the head of : be first ⟨∼ a parade⟩ **5** : to begin play with; *also* : BEGIN, OPEN **6** : to tend toward a definite result ⟨study ∼*ing* to a degree⟩ — **lead·er** *n* — **lead·er·less** *adj* — **lead·er·ship** *n*

²lead \'lēd\ *n* **1** : a position at the front; *also* : a margin by which one leads **2** : the privilege of leading in cards; *also* : the card or suit led **3** : EXAMPLE **4** : one that leads **5** : a principal role (as in a play); *also* : one who plays such a role **6** : INDICATION, CLUE **7** : an insulated electrical conductor

³lead \'led\ *n* **1** : a heavy malleable bluish white chemical element **2** : an article made of lead; *esp* : a weight for sounding at sea **3** : a thin strip of metal used to separate lines of type in printing **4** : a thin stick of marking substance in or for a pencil

⁴lead \'led\ *vb* **1** : to cover, line, or weight with lead **2** : to fix (glass) in position with lead **3** : to treat or mix with lead or a lead compound

lead·en \'led-ᵊn\ *adj* **1** : made of lead; *also* : of the color of lead **2** : SLUGGISH, DULL ⟨a ∼ lecture⟩

lead off *vb* : OPEN, BEGIN; *esp* : to bat first in an inning — **lead·off** \'lēd-ˌof\ *n or adj*

¹leaf \'lēf\ *n, pl* **leaves** \'lēvz\ **1** : a usu. flat and green outgrowth of a plant stem that is a unit of foliage and functions esp. in photosynthesis; *also* : FOLIAGE **2** : something (as a page or a flat moving part) that is suggestive of a leaf — **leaf·less** *adj* — **leafy** *adj*

²leaf *vb* **1** : to produce leaves **2** : to turn the pages of a book

leaf·age \'lē-fij\ *n* : FOLIAGE

leafed \'lēft\ *adj* : LEAVED

leaf·hop·per \'lēf-ˌhä-pər\ *n* : any of a family of small leaping insects related to the cicadas that suck the juices of plants

leaf·let \'lē-flət\ *n* **1** : a division of a compound leaf **2** : PAMPHLET, FOLDER

leaf mold *n* : a compost or layer composed chiefly of decayed leaves

leaf·stalk \'lēf-ˌstok\ *n* : PETIOLE

league \'lēg\ *n* : a unit of distance equal to about three miles (five kilometers)

²league *n* **1** : an association or alliance (as of nations or sports teams) for a common purpose **2** : CLASS, CATEGORY — **league** *vb* — **leagu·er** \'lē-gər\ *n*

¹leak \'lēk\ *vb* **1** : to enter or escape through a leak **2** : to let a substance in or out through an opening **3** : to become or make known ⟨∼ed the news⟩

²leak *n* **1** : a crack or hole that accidentally admits a fluid or light or lets it escape; *also* : something that secretly or accidentally permits the admission or escape of something else **2** : LEAKAGE — **leaky** *adj*

leak·age \'lē-kij\ *n* **1** : the act of leaking **2** : the thing or amount that leaks

¹lean \'lēn\ *vb* **1** : to bend from a vertical position : INCLINE **2** : to cast one's weight to one side for support **3** : to rely on for support **4** : to incline in opinion, taste, or desire — **lean** *n*

²lean *adj* **1** : lacking or deficient in flesh and esp. in fat ⟨∼ meat⟩ **2** : lacking richness or productiveness ⟨∼ profits⟩ **3** : low in fuel content — **lean·ness** *n*

leant \'lent\ *chiefly Brit past of* LEAN

lean-to \'lēn-ˌtü\ *n, pl* **lean-tos** \-ˌtüz\ : a wing or extension of a building having a roof of only one slope; *also* : a rough shed or shelter with a similar roof

¹leap \'lēp\ *vb* **leapt** \'lēpt, 'lept\ *or* **leaped**; **leap·ing** : to spring free from a surface or over an obstacle : JUMP

²leap *n* : JUMP

leap·frog \'lēp-ˌfrog, -ˌfräg\ *n* : a game in which a player bends down and is vaulted over by another — **leapfrog** *vb*

leap year *n* : a year containing 366 days with February 29 as the extra day

learn \'lərn\ *vb* **learned** \'lərnd, 'lərnt\; **learn·ing** **1** : to gain knowledge, understanding, or skill by study or experience; *also* : MEMORIZE ⟨∼ the poem⟩ **2** : to find out : ASCERTAIN ⟨∼ the truth⟩ — **learn·er** *n*

learn·ed \'lər-nəd\ *adj* : SCHOLARLY, ERUDITE — **learn·ed·ly** *adv* — **learn·ed·ness** *n*

learn·ing \'lər-niŋ\ *n* : KNOWLEDGE

learning disability *n* : any of various conditions (as dyslexia) that interfere with a person's ability to learn and so result in impaired functioning (as in language) — **learning disabled** *adj*

learnt \'lərnt\ *chiefly Brit past and past part of* LEARN

¹lease \'lēs\ *n* : a contract transferring real estate for a term of years or at will usu. for a specified rent

²lease *vb* **leased**; **leas·ing** [AF *lesser, lescher* to leave, hand over, lease, fr. L *laxare* to loosen, fr. *laxus* slack] **1** : to grant by lease **2** : to hold under a lease ♦ **Synonyms** LET, CHARTER, HIRE, RENT

lease·hold \'lēs-ˌhōld\ *n* **1** : a tenure by lease **2** : land held by lease — **lease·hold·er** *n*

leash \'lēsh\ *n* [ME *lees, leshe,* fr. AF **lesche, lesse* prob. fr. *lesser* to leave, let go] **1** : a line for leading or restraining an animal **2** : a state of restraint ⟨kept spending on a tight ∼⟩ — **leash** *vb*

¹least \'lēst\ *adj* **1** : lowest in importance or position **2** : smallest in size or degree **3** : SLIGHTEST ⟨the ∼ sign of trouble⟩

²least *n* : one that is least

³least *adv* : in the smallest or lowest degree

least common denominator *n* : the least common multiple of two or more denominators

least common multiple *n* : the smallest common multiple of two or more numbers

least·wise \'lēst-ˌwīz\ *adv* : at least

leath·er \'le-thər\ *n* : animal skin dressed for use — **leath·ern** \-thərn\ *adj* — **leath·ery** *adj*

leath·er·back \-ˌbak\ *n* : the largest existing sea turtle with a flexible leathery carapace

leath·er·neck \-ˌnek\ *n* : MARINE

¹leave \'lēv\ *vb* **left** \'left\; **leav·ing** **1** : to allow or cause to remain behind **2** : to have as a remainder **3** : BEQUEATH **4** : to let stay without interference **5** : to go away : depart from **6** : GIVE UP, ABANDON ⟨left his wife for another woman⟩

²leave *n* **1** : PERMISSION; *also* : authorized absence from duty **2** : DEPARTURE

³leave *vb* **leaved**; **leav·ing** : LEAF

leaved \'lēvd\ *adj* : having leaves

¹leav·en \'le-vən\ *n* **1** : a substance (as yeast) used to produce fermentation (as in dough) **2** : something that modifies or lightens

²leaven *vb* : to raise (dough) with a leaven; *also* : to permeate with a modifying or vivifying element ⟨lectures ∼ed with humor⟩

leav·en·ing *n* : LEAVEN

leaves *pl of* LEAF

leave-tak·ing \'lēv-ˌtā-kiŋ\ *n* : DEPARTURE, FAREWELL

leav·ings \'lē-viŋz\ *n pl* : REMNANT, RESIDUE ⟨the ∼ of a meal⟩

lech·ery \'le-chə-rē\ *n* : inordinate indulgence in sexual activity — **lech·er** \'le-chər\ *n* — **lech·er·ous** \'le-chərəs\ *adj* — **lech·er·ous·ly** *adv* — **lech·er·ous·ness** *n*

lec·i·thin \'le-sə-thən\ *n* : any of several waxy phosphoruscontaining substances that are common in animals and plants, form colloidal solutions in water, and have emulsifying and wetting properties

lect *abbr* lecture; lecturer

lec·tern \'lek-tərn\ *n* : a stand to support a book for a standing reader

lec·tor \-tər\ *n* : one whose chief duty is to read the lessons in a church service

lec·ture \'lek-chər\ *n* **1** : a discourse given before an audience esp. for instruction **2** : REPRIMAND — **lec·ture** *vb* — **lec·tur·er** *n* — **lec·ture·ship** *n*

led *past and past part of* LEAD

LED \ˌel-(ˌ)ē-'dē\ *n* [*light-emitting d*iode] : a semiconductor diode that emits light when a voltage is applied to it and is used esp. for electronic displays

le·der·ho·sen \'lā-dər-ˌhōz-ᵊn\ *n pl* : leather shorts often with suspenders worn esp. in Bavaria

ledge \'lej\ *n* [ME *legge* bar of a gate] **1** : a shelflike projection from a top or an edge **2** : REEF

led·ger \'le-jər\ *n* : a book containing accounts to which debits and credits are transferred in final form

lee \'lē\ *n* **1** : a protecting shelter **2** : the side (as of a ship) that is sheltered from the wind — **lee** *adj*

leech \'lēch\ *n* **1** : any of various bloodsucking segmented usu. freshwater worms that are related to the earthworms and have a sucker at each end **2** : a hanger= on who seeks gain

leek \'lēk\ *n* : an onionlike herb grown for its mildly pungent leaves and stalk

leer \'lir\ *n* : a suggestive, knowing, or malicious look — **leer** *vb*

leery \'lir-ē\ *adj* : SUSPICIOUS, WARY

lees \'lēz\ *n pl* : DREGS ⟨∼ in the bottle⟩

¹**lee·ward** \'lē-wərd, 'lü-ərd\ *n* : the lee side

²**leeward** *adj* : situated away from the wind

lee·way \'lē-,wā\ *n* **1** : lateral movement of a ship when under way **2** : an allowable margin of freedom or variation

¹**left** \'left\ *adj* [ME, fr. OE, weak; fr. the left hand's being the weaker in most individuals] **1** : of, relating to, or being the side of the body in which the heart is mostly located; *also* : located nearer to this side than to the right **2** *often cap* : of, adhering to, or constituted by the political left — **left** *adv*

²**left** *n* **1** : the left hand; *also* : the side or part that is on or toward the left side **2** *often cap* : those professing political views marked by desire to reform the established order and usu. to give greater freedom to the common people — **left·ward** \-wərd\ *adv or adj*

³**left** *past and past part of* LEAVE

left–click \'left-'klik\ *vb* : to press the leftmost button on a computer mouse or similar input device

left–hand *adj* **1** : situated on the left **2** : LEFT-HANDED

left–hand·ed \'left-'han-dəd\ *adj* **1** : using the left hand habitually or more easily than the right **2** : designed for or done with the left hand **3** : INSINCERE, BACKHANDED ⟨a ∼ compliment⟩ **4** : COUNTERCLOCKWISE — **left-handed** *adv* — **left–hand·ed·ness** *n* — **left–hand·er** \-dər\ *n*

left·ism \'lef-,ti-zəm\ *n* **1** : the principles and views of the left **2** : advocacy of the doctrines of the left — **left·ist** \-tist\ *n or adj*

left·over \'left-,ō-vər\ *n* : something that remains unused or unconsumed

lefty \'lef-tē\ *n, pl* **left·ies 1** : a left-handed person **2** : an advocate of leftism

¹**leg** \'leg\ *n* **1** : a limb of an animal used esp. for supporting the body and in walking; *also* : the part of the vertebrate leg between knee and foot **2** : something resembling or analogous to an animal leg ⟨table ∼⟩ **3** : the part of an article of clothing that covers the leg **4** : a portion of a trip **5** *pl* : long-term appeal or interest ⟨a musical that has ∼s⟩ — **leg·ged** \'le-gəd\ *adj* — **leg·less** *adj*

²**leg** *vb* **legged; leg·ging** : to use the legs in walking or esp. in running

³**leg** *abbr* **1** legal **2** legislative; legislature

leg·a·cy \'le-gə-sē\ *n, pl* **-cies** : INHERITANCE; *also* : something that has come from a predecessor or the past

le·gal \'lē-gəl\ *adj* **1** : of or relating to law or lawyers **2** : LAWFUL; *also* : STATUTORY **3** : enforced in courts of law — **le·gal·i·ty** \li-'ga-lə-tē\ *n* — **le·gal·ize** \'lē-gə-,līz\ *vb* — **le·gal·ly** *adv*

le·gal·ese \,lē-gə-'lēz\ *n* : the specialized language of the legal profession

le·gal·ism \'lē-gə-,li-zəm\ *n* **1** : strict, literal, or excessive conformity to the law or to a religious or moral code **2** : a legal term — **le·gal·is·tic** \,lē-gə-'lis-tik\ *adj*

leg·ate \'le-gət\ *n* : an official representative

leg·a·tee \,le-gə-'tē\ *n* : a person to whom a legacy is bequeathed

le·ga·tion \li-'gā-shən\ *n* **1** : a diplomatic mission headed by a minister **2** : the official residence and office of a minister in a foreign country

le·ga·to \li-'gä-tō\ *adv or adj* [It, lit., tied] : in a smooth and connected manner (as of music)

leg·end \'le-jənd\ *n* [ME *legende*, fr. AF & ML; AF *legende*, fr. ML *legenda*, fr. L *legere* to read] **1** : a story coming down from the past; *esp* : one popularly accepted as historical though not verifiable **2** : an inscription on an object; *also* : CAPTION **3** : an explanatory list of the symbols on a map or chart

leg·end·ary \'le-jən-,der-ē\ *adj* **1** : of, relating to, or characteristic of a legend **2** : FAMOUS ⟨∼ actors⟩ — **leg·en·dari·ly** \-,der-ə-lē\ *adv*

leg·er·de·main \,le-jər-də-'mān\ *n* [ME, fr. MF *leger de main* light of hand] : SLEIGHT OF HAND

leg·ging *or* **leg·gin** \'le-gən, -gin\ *n* : a covering for the leg; *also* : TIGHTS

leg·gy \'le-gē\ *adj* **leg·gi·er; -est 1** : having unusually long legs **2** : having long and attractive legs **3** : SPINDLY — used of a plant

leg·horn \'leg-,hórn, 'le-gərn\ *n* **1** : a fine plaited straw; *also* : a hat made of this straw **2** : any of a Mediterranean breed of small hardy chickens

leg·i·ble \'le-jə-bəl\ *adj* : capable of being read : CLEAR — **leg·i·bil·i·ty** \,le-jə-'bi-lə-tē\ *n* — **leg·i·bly** \'le-jə-blē\ *adv*

¹**le·gion** \'lē-jən\ *n* **1** : a unit of the Roman army comprising 3000 to 6000 soldiers **2** : MULTITUDE ⟨∼s of fans⟩ **3** : an association of ex-servicemen — **le·gion·ary** \-jə-,ner-ē\ *n* — **le·gion·naire** \,lē-jə-'nar\ *n*

²**legion** *adj* : MANY, NUMEROUS

Legionnaires' disease *also* **Legionnaire's disease** \-'nerz-\ *n* : a lobar pneumonia caused by a bacterium

legis *abbr* legislation; legislative; legislature

leg·is·late \'le-jəs-,lāt\ *vb* **-lat·ed; -lat·ing** : to make or enact laws; *also* : to bring about by legislation — **leg·is·la·tor** \-,lā-tər\ *n*

leg·is·la·tion \,le-jəs-'lā-shən\ *n* **1** : the action of legislating **2** : laws made by a legislative body

leg·is·la·tive \'le-jəs-,lā-tiv\ *adj* **1** : having the power of legislating **2** : of or relating to a legislature or legislation

leg·is·la·ture \'le-jəs-,lā-chər\ *n* : an organized body of persons having the authority to make laws

le·git \li-'jit\ *adj, slang* : LEGITIMATE

¹**le·git·i·mate** \li-'ji-tə-mət\ *adj* **1** : lawfully begotten **2** : GENUINE **3** : LAWFUL **4** : conforming to recognized principles or accepted rules or standards — **le·git·i·ma·cy** \-mə-sē\ *n* — **le·git·i·mate·ly** *adv*

²**le·git·i·mate** \-,māt\ *vb* : to make legitimate

le·git·i·mise *Brit var of* LEGITIMIZE

le·git·i·mize \li-'ji-tə-,mīz\ *vb* **-mized; -miz·ing** : LEGITIMATE

leg·man \'leg-,man\ *n* **1** : a reporter assigned usu. to gather information **2** : an assistant who gathers information and runs errands

le·gume \'le-,gyüm, li-'gyüm\ *n* [F] **1** : any of a large family of plants having fruits that are dry pods and split when ripe and including important food and forage plants (as beans and clover); *also* : the part (as seeds or pods) of a legume used as food **2** : the pod of a legume — **le·gu·mi·nous** \li-'gyü-mə-nəs\ *adj*

legume 2

¹**lei** \'lā, 'lā-,ē\ *n* : a wreath or necklace usu. of flowers

²**lei** \'lā\ *pl of* LEU

lei·sure \'lē-zhər, 'le-, 'lā-\ *n* **1** : time free from work or duties **2** : EASE; *also* : CONVENIENCE ⟨read it at your ∼⟩ ◆ **Synonyms** RELAXATION, REST, REPOSE — **lei·sure·ly** *adj or adv*

leit·mo·tif *also* **leit·mo·tiv** \'līt-mō-,tēf\ *n* [G *Leitmotiv*, fr. *leiten* to lead + *Motiv* motive] : a dominant recurring theme

lek \'lek\ *n, pl* **leks** *or* **le·ke** *or* **lekë** \'le-kə\ — see MONEY table

lem·ming \'le-miŋ\ *n* [Norw] : any of various short-tailed rodents found mostly in northern regions and noted for recurrent mass migrations

lem·on \'le-mən\ *n* **1** : an acid yellow usu. nearly oblong citrus fruit; *also* : a citrus tree that bears lemons **2** : something (as an automobile) unsatisfactory or defective — **lem·ony** *adj*

lem·on·ade \,le-mə-'nād\ *n* : a beverage of lemon juice, sugar, and water

lemon curd *n* : a custard made with lemon juice, butter, sugar, and eggs

lem·on·grass \'le-mən-ˌgras\ *n* : a tropical Asian grass grown for its lemon-scented foliage used as a seasoning
lem·pi·ra \lem-'pir-ə\ *n* — see MONEY table
le·mur \'lē-mər\ *n* : any of various arboreal primates largely of Madagascar that have large eyes, very soft woolly fur, and a long furry tail
Len·a·pe \'le-nə-pē, lə-'nä-pē\ *n, pl* **Lenape** *or* **Lenapes** : DELAWARE
lend \'lend\ *vb* **lent** \'lent\; **lend·ing** **1** : to give for temporary use on condition that the same or its equivalent be returned **2** : AFFORD, FURNISH **3** : ACCOMMODATE — **lend·er** *n*
lend–lease \-'lēs\ *n* : the transfer of goods and services to an ally to aid in a common cause with payment made by a return of the items or their use in the cause or by a similar transfer of other goods and services
length \'leŋth\ *n* **1** : the longer or longest dimension of an object; *also* : a measured distance **2** : duration or extent in time or space **3** : the length of something taken as a unit of measure **4** : a single piece of a series of pieces that may be joined together ⟨a ∼ of pipe⟩ — **at length** **1** : in full **2** : FINALLY
length·en \'leŋ-thən\ *vb* : to make or become longer ♦ **Synonyms** EXTEND, ELONGATE, PROLONG, PROTRACT
length·wise \'leŋth-ˌwīz\ *adv* : in the direction of the length — **lengthwise** *adj*
lengthy \'leŋ-thē\ *adj* **length·i·er; -est** **1** : protracted excessively **2** : EXTENDED, LONG ⟨a ∼ journey⟩
le·nient \'lē-nē-ənt, -nyənt\ *adj* : of mild and tolerant disposition or effect ♦ **Synonyms** INDULGENT, FORBEARING, MERCIFUL, TOLERANT — **le·ni·en·cy** \'lē-nē-ən-sē, -nyən-sē\ *n* — **le·ni·ent·ly** *adv*
len·i·ty \'le-nə-tē\ *n* : LENIENCY
lens \'lenz\ *n* [L *lent-, lens* lentil; so called fr. the shape of a convex lens] **1** : a curved piece of glass or plastic used singly or combined in an optical instrument for forming an image; *also* : a device for focusing radiation other than light **2** : a transparent body in the eye that focuses light rays on receptors at the back of the eye
Lent \'lent\ *n* : a 40-day period of penitence and fasting observed from Ash Wednesday to Easter by many churches — **Lent·en** \'len-tᵊn\ *adj*
len·til \'len-tᵊl\ *n* : a Eurasian annual legume grown for its flat edible seeds and for fodder; *also* : its seed
Leo \'lē-ō\ *n* [L, lit., lion] **1** : a zodiacal constellation between Cancer and Virgo usu. pictured as a lion **2** : the 5th sign of the zodiac in astrology; *also* : one born under this sign
le·one \lē-'ōn\ *n, pl* **leones** *or* **leone** — see MONEY table
le·o·nine \'lē-ə-ˌnīn\ *adj* : of, relating to, or resembling a lion
leop·ard \'le-pərd\ *n* : a large usu. tawny and black-spotted cat of southern Asia and Africa
le·o·tard \'lē-ə-ˌtärd\ *n* : a close-fitting garment worn esp. by dancers and for exercise
lep·er \'le-pər\ *n* **1** : a person affected with leprosy **2** : OUTCAST
lep·re·chaun \'le-prə-ˌkän\ *n* : a mischievous elf of Irish folklore
lep·ro·sy \'le-prə-sē\ *n* : a chronic bacterial disease marked esp. if not treated by slow-growing swellings with deformity and loss of sensation of affected parts — **lep·rous** \-prəs\ *adj*
lep·tin \'lep-tən\ *n* : a hormone that is produced by fat-containing cells and plays a role in body weight regulation
lep·ton \lep-'tän\ *n, pl* **lep·ta** \-'tä\ : a former monetary unit equal to ¹⁄₁₀₀ drachma
les·bi·an \'lez-bē-ən\ *n* [fr. the reputed homosexual group associated with the poet Sappho of Lesbos] : a woman who is a homosexual — **lesbian** *adj* — **les·bi·an·ism** \-ə-ˌni-zəm\ *n*
lèse ma·jes·té *or* **lese maj·es·ty** \'lāz-'ma-jə-stē, 'lez-, 'lēz-\ *n* [MF *lese majesté*, fr. L *laesa majestas*, lit., injured majesty] : an offense violating the dignity of a sovereign
le·sion \'lē-zhən\ *n* : an abnormal structural change in the body due to injury or disease; *esp* : one clearly marked off from healthy tissue around it
¹less \'les\ *adj, comparative of* ¹LITTLE **1** : FEWER ⟨∼ than six⟩ **2** : of lower rank, degree, or importance **3** : SMALLER; *also* : more limited in quantity ⟨∼ than a year⟩

²less *adv, comparative of* ²LITTLE : to a lesser extent or degree
³less *n, pl* **less** **1** : a smaller portion **2** : something of less importance
⁴less *prep* : diminished by : MINUS ⟨list price ∼ the discount⟩
-less \ləs\ *adj suffix* **1** : destitute of : not having ⟨childless⟩ **2** : unable to be acted on or to act (in a specified way) ⟨dauntless⟩
les·see \le-'sē\ *n* : a tenant under a lease
less·en \'le-sᵊn\ *vb* : to make or become less ♦ **Synonyms** DECREASE, DIMINISH, DWINDLE, ABATE
less·er \'le-sər\ *adj, comparative of* ¹LITTLE : of less size, quality, or significance
les·son \'le-sᵊn\ *n* **1** : a passage from sacred writings read in a service of worship **2** : a reading or exercise to be studied by a pupil; *also* : something learned **3** : a period of instruction **4** : an instructive example
les·sor \'le-ˌsȯr, le-'sȯr\ *n* : one who conveys property by a lease
lest \'lest\ *conj* : for fear that
¹let \'let\ *n* [ME *lette*, fr. *letten* to delay, hinder, fr. OE *lettan*] **1** : HINDRANCE, OBSTACLE **2** : a shot or point in racket games that does not count
²let *vb* **let; let·ting** [ME *leten*, fr. OE *lǣtan*] **1** : to cause to : MAKE ⟨∼ it be known⟩ **2** : RENT, LEASE; *also* : to assign esp. after bids **3** : ALLOW, PERMIT ⟨∼ me go⟩
-let *n suffix* **1** : small one ⟨booklet⟩ **2** : article worn on ⟨wristlet⟩
let·down \'let-ˌdau̇n\ *n* **1** : DISAPPOINTMENT **2** : a slackening of effort
le·thal \'lē-thəl\ *adj* : DEADLY, FATAL ⟨∼ weapons⟩ — **le·thal·ly** *adv*
leth·ar·gy \'le-thər-jē\ *n* **1** : abnormal drowsiness **2** : the quality or state of being lazy or indifferent ♦ **Synonyms** LANGUOR, LASSITUDE, TORPOR — **le·thar·gic** \li-'thär-jik\ *adj*
let on *vb* **1** : REVEAL 1 ⟨knows a lot more than he *lets on*⟩ **2** : PRETEND
¹let·ter \'le-tər\ *n* **1** : a symbol that stands for a speech sound and constitutes a unit of an alphabet **2** : a written or printed communication **3** *pl* : LITERATURE; *also* : LEARNING **4** : the literal meaning ⟨the ∼ of the law⟩ **5** : a single piece of type
²letter *vb* : to mark with letters : INSCRIBE — **let·ter·er** *n*
letter bomb *n* : an explosive device concealed in an envelope and mailed to the intended victim
let·ter·boxed \'le-tər-ˌbäkst\ *adj* : being a video recording formatted to display a frame size proportional to a standard theater screen
letter carrier *n* : a person who delivers mail
let·ter·head \'le-tər-ˌhed\ *n* : stationery with a printed or engraved heading; *also* : the heading itself
let·ter–per·fect \ˌle-tər-'pər-fikt\ *adj* : correct to the smallest detail
let·ter·press \'le-tər-ˌpres\ *n* : printing done directly by impressing the paper on an inked raised surface
letters of marque \-'märk\ *n* : a license granted to a private person by a government to fit out an armed ship to capture enemy shipping
letters patent *n pl* : a written grant from a government to a person in a form readily open for inspection by all
let·tuce \'le-təs\ *n* [ME *letuse*, fr. AF, prob. fr. pl. of *letue* lettuce plant, fr. L *lactuca*, fr. *lac* milk; fr. its milky juice] : a garden composite plant with crisp leaves used esp. in salads
let·up \'let-ˌəp\ *n* : a lessening of effort
leu \'leu̇\ *n, pl* **lei** \'lā\ — see MONEY table
leu·kae·mia *chiefly Brit var of* LEUKEMIA
leu·ke·mia \lü-'kē-mē-ə\ *n* : a malignant disease characterized by an abnormal increase in the number of white blood cells in the blood-forming tissues — **leu·ke·mic** \-mik\ *adj or n*
leu·ko·cyte \'lü-kə-ˌsīt\ *n* : WHITE BLOOD CELL
lev \'lef\ *n, pl* **le·va** \'le-və\ — see MONEY table
Lev *or* **Levit** *abbr* Leviticus
¹le·vee \'le-vē; lə-'vē, -'vā\ *n* [F *lever* act of arising] : a reception held by or for a person of distinction
²lev·ee \'le-vē\ *n* : an embankment to prevent or confine flooding; *also* : a river landing place
¹lev·el \'le-vəl\ *n* **1** : a device for establishing a horizontal

line or plane **2** : horizontal condition **3** : a horizontal position, line, or surface often taken as an index of altitude; *also* : a flat area of ground **4** : height, position, rank, or size in a scale
²**level** *vb* **-eled** *or* **-elled; -el·ing** *or* **-el·ling** **1** : to make flat or level; *also* : to come to a level **2** : AIM, DIRECT **3** : EQUALIZE **4** : RAZE — **lev·el·er** *n*
³**level** *adj* **1** : having a flat even surface **2** : HORIZONTAL **3** : of the same height or rank; *also* : UNIFORM **4** : steady and cool in judgment ⟨keep a ∼ head when in danger⟩ — **lev·el·ly** *adv* — **lev·el·ness** *n*
lev·el·head·ed \‚le-vəl-'he-dəd\ *adj* : having or showing sound judgment : SENSIBLE ⟨a ∼ decision⟩
le·ver \'le-vər, 'lē-\ *n* **1** : a bar used for prying or dislodging something; *also* : a means for achieving one's purpose **2** : a rigid piece turning about an axis and used for transmitting and changing force and motion
le·ver·age \'le-vrij, 'lē-, -və-rij\ *n* : the action or mechanical effect of a lever
le·vi·a·than \li-'vī-ə-thən\ *n* **1** : a large sea animal **2** : something large or formidable ⟨the ocean liner is a ∼⟩
lev·i·tate \'le-və-‚tāt\ *vb* **-tat·ed; -tat·ing** : to rise or cause to rise in the air in seeming defiance of gravitation — **lev·i·ta·tion** \‚le-və-'tā-shən\ *n*
Le·vit·i·cus \li-'vi-tə-kəs\ *n* — see BIBLE table
lev·i·ty \'le-və-tē\ *n* : lack of seriousness ✦ **Synonyms** LIGHTNESS, FLIPPANCY, FRIVOLITY
levo·do·pa \‚le-və-'dō-pə\ *n* : L-DOPA
¹**levy** \'le-vē\ *n, pl* **lev·ies** **1** : the imposition or collection of an assessment; *also* : an amount levied **2** : the enlistment or conscription of men for military service; *also* : troops raised by levy
²**levy** *vb* **lev·ied; levy·ing** **1** : to impose or collect by legal authority ⟨∼ taxes⟩ **2** : to enlist for military service **3** : WAGE ⟨∼ war⟩ **4** : to seize property
lewd \'lüd\ *adj* [ME *lewed* vulgar, fr. OE *lǣwede* lay, ignorant] : sexually unchaste; *also* : OBSCENE, VULGAR — **lewd·ly** *adv* — **lewd·ness** *n*
lex·i·cog·ra·phy \‚lek-sə-'kä-grə-fē\ *n* **1** : the editing or making of a dictionary **2** : the principles and practices of dictionary making — **lex·i·cog·ra·pher** \-fər\ *n* — **lex·i·co·graph·i·cal** \-kō-'gra-fi-kəl\ *or* **lex·i·co·graph·ic** \-fik\ *adj*
lex·i·con \'lek-sə-‚kän\ *n, pl* **lex·i·ca** \-si-kə\ *or* **lexicons** **1** : DICTIONARY **2** : the vocabulary of a language, speaker, or subject
lg *abbr* **1** large **2** long
LGBT *abbr* lesbian, gay, bisexual, and transgender
LH *abbr* **1** left hand **2** lower half
li *abbr* link
Li *symbol* lithium
LI *abbr* Long Island
li·a·bil·i·ty \‚lī-ə-'bi-lə-tē\ *n, pl* **-ties** **1** : the quality or state of being liable **2** *pl* : DEBTS **3** : DISADVANTAGE
li·a·ble \'lī-ə-bəl\ *adj* **1** : legally obligated : RESPONSIBLE **2** : LIKELY, APT ⟨∼ to fall⟩ **3** : SUSCEPTIBLE ⟨∼ to disease⟩
li·ai·son \'lē-ə-‚zän, lē-'ā-\ *n* [F] **1** : a close bond : INTERRELATIONSHIP **2** : an illicit sexual relationship **3** : communication for mutual understanding (as between parts of an armed force); *also* : one that carries on a liaison
li·ar \'lī-(ə)r\ *n* : a person who lies
¹**lib** \'lib\ *n* : LIBERATION
²**lib** *abbr* **1** liberal **2** librarian; library
li·ba·tion \lī-'bā-shən\ *n* **1** : an act of pouring a liquid as a sacrifice (as to a god); *also* : the liquid poured **2** : DRINK
¹**li·bel** \'lī-bəl\ *n* [ME, written declaration, fr. AF, fr. L *libellus*, dim. of *liber* book] **1** : a spoken or written statement or a representation that gives an unjustly unfavorable impression of a person or thing **2** : the action or crime of publishing a libel — **li·bel·ous** *or* **li·bel·lous** \-bə-ləs\ *adj*
²**libel** *vb* **-beled** *or* **-belled; -bel·ing** *or* **-bel·ling** **1** : to make or publish a libel — **li·bel·er** *n* — **li·bel·ist** *n*
¹**lib·er·al** \'li-brəl, -bə-rəl\ *adj* [ME, fr. AF, fr. L *liberalis* suitable for a freeman, generous, fr. *liber* free] **1** : of, relating to, or based on the liberal arts **2** : GENEROUS, BOUNTIFUL ⟨a ∼ serving⟩ **3** : not literal **4** : not narrow in opinion or judgment : TOLERANT; *also* : not orthodox **5** : not conservative — **lib·er·al·ly** \-brə-lə-tē\ *n* — **lib·er·al·i·za·tion** \‚li-brə-lə-'zā-shən, -bə-rə-\ *n* — **lib·er·al·ize** \'li-brə-‚līz, -bə-rə-\ *vb* — **lib·er·al·ly** *adv*

²**liberal** *n* : a person who holds liberal views
liberal arts *n pl* : the studies (as language, philosophy, history, literature, or abstract science) in a college or university intended to provide chiefly general knowledge and to develop the general intellectual capacities
lib·er·al·ism \'li-brə-‚li-zəm, -bə-rə-\ *n* : liberal principles and theories
lib·er·ate \'li-bə-‚rāt\ *vb* **-at·ed; -at·ing** **1** : to free from bondage or restraint; *also* : to raise to equal rights and status **2** : to free (as a gas) from combination — **lib·er·a·tion** \‚li-bə-'rā-shən\ *n* — **lib·er·a·tor** \'li-bə-‚rā-tər\ *n*
liberated *adj* : freed from or opposed to traditional social and sexual attitudes or roles ⟨a ∼ marriage⟩
lib·er·tar·i·an \‚li-bər-'ter-ē-ən\ *n* **1** : an advocate of the doctrine of free will **2** : one who upholds the principles of unrestricted liberty
lib·er·tine \'li-bər-‚tēn\ *n* : a person who leads a dissolute life
lib·er·ty \'li-bər-tē\ *n, pl* **-ties** **1** : FREEDOM **2** : an action going beyond normal limits; *esp* : FAMILIARITY **3** : a short leave from naval duty
li·bid·i·nous \lə-'bi-də-nəs\ *adj* **1** : LASCIVIOUS **2** : LIBIDINAL
li·bi·do \lə-'bē-dō\ *n, pl* **-dos** [NL, fr. L, desire, lust] **1** : psychic energy derived from basic biological urges **2** : sexual drive — **li·bid·i·nal** \lə-'bi-də-nəl\ *adj*
Li·bra \'lē-brə\ *n* [L, lit., scales] **1** : a zodiacal constellation between Virgo and Scorpio usu. pictured as a balance scale **2** : the 7th sign of the zodiac in astrology; *also* : one born under this sign
li·brar·i·an \lī-'brer-ē-ən\ *n* : a specialist in the management of a library
li·brary \'lī-‚brer-ē\ *n, pl* **-brar·ies** **1** : a place in which books and related materials are kept for use but not for sale **2** : a collection of books
li·bret·to \lə-'bre-tō\ *n, pl* **-tos** *or* **-ti** \-tē\ [It, dim. of *libro* book, fr. L *liber*] : the text esp. of an opera — **li·bret·tist** \-tist\ *n*
lice *pl of* LOUSE
li·cense *or* **li·cence** \'lī-s²ns\ *n* **1** : permission to act **2** : a permission granted by authority to engage in an activity **3** : a document, plate, or tag providing proof of a license **4** : freedom used irresponsibly — **license** *vb*
licensed practical nurse *n* : a specially trained person who is licensed (as by a state) to provide routine care for the sick
li·cens·ee \‚lī-s²n-'sē\ *n* : a licensed person
licente *pl of* SENTE
li·cen·ti·ate \lī-'sen-chē-ət\ *n* : one licensed to practice a profession
li·cen·tious \lī-'sen-chəs\ *adj* : LEWD, LASCIVIOUS — **li·cen·tious·ly** *adv* — **li·cen·tious·ness** *n*
lichee *var of* LITCHI
li·chen \'lī-kən\ *n* : any of various complex plantlike organisms made up of an alga and a fungus growing as a unit on a solid surface — **li·chen·ous** *adj*
lic·it \'li-sət\ *adj* : LAWFUL
¹**lick** \'lik\ *vb* **1** : to draw the tongue over; *also* : to flicker over like a tongue **2** : THRASH; *also* : DEFEAT
²**lick** *n* **1** : a stroke of the tongue **2** : a small amount **3** : a hasty careless effort **4** : BLOW **5** : a natural deposit of salt that animals lick
lick·e·ty-split \‚li-kə-tē-'split\ *adv* : at great speed
lick·spit·tle \'lik-‚spi-t²l\ *n* : a fawning subordinate : TOADY
lic·o·rice \'li-kə-rish, -rəs\ *n* [ME, fr. AF *licoris*, fr. LL *liquiritia*, alter. of L *glycyrrhiza*, fr. Gk *glykyrrhiza*, fr. *glykys* sweet + *rhiza* root] **1** : the dried root of a European leguminous plant; *also* : an extract from it used esp. as a flavoring and in medicine **2** : a candy flavored with licorice **3** : a plant yielding licorice
lid \'lid\ *n* **1** : a movable cover **2** : EYELID **3** : something that confines or suppresses — **lid·ded** \'li-dəd\ *adj*
li·do \'lē-dō\ *n, pl* **lidos** : a fashionable beach resort
¹**lie** \'lī\ *vb* **lay** \'lā\; **lain** \'lān\; **ly·ing** \'lī-iŋ\ **1** : to be in, stay at rest in, or assume a horizontal position; *also* : to be in a helpless or defenseless state **2** : EXTEND ⟨our route *lay* to the west⟩ **3** : to occupy a certain relative position **4** : to have an effect esp. through mere presence
²**lie** *n* : the position in which something lies
³**lie** *vb* **lied; ly·ing** \'lī-iŋ\ : to tell a lie

⁴lie *n* : an untrue statement made with intent to deceive

lied \'lēt\ *n, pl* lie·der \'lē-dər\ [G] : a German song esp. of the 19th century

lie detector *n* : a polygraph for detecting physiological evidence of the tension that accompanies lying

lief \'lēv, 'lēf\ *adv* : GLADLY, WILLINGLY

¹liege \'lēj\ *adj* : LOYAL, FAITHFUL

²liege *n* 1 : VASSAL 2 : a feudal superior

lien \'lēn, 'lē-ən\ *n* : a legal claim on the property of another for the satisfaction of a debt or duty

lieu \'lü\ *n, archaic* : PLACE, STEAD — in lieu of : in the place of

lieut *abbr* lieutenant

lieu·ten·ant \lü-'te-nənt\ *n* [ME, fr. AF *lieu tenant*, fr. *liu, lieu* place + *tenant* holding, fr. *tenir* to hold, fr. L *tenēre*] 1 : a representative of another in the performance of duty 2 : FIRST LIEUTENANT; *also* : SECOND LIEUTENANT 3 : a commissioned officer in the navy ranking next below a lieutenant commander — lieu·ten·an·cy \-nən-sē\ *n*

lieutenant colonel *n* : a commissioned officer (as in the army) ranking next below a colonel

lieutenant commander *n* : a commissioned officer in the navy ranking next below a commander

lieutenant general *n* : a commissioned officer (as in the army) ranking next below a general

lieutenant governor *n* : a deputy or subordinate governor

lieutenant junior grade *n, pl* lieutenants junior grade : a commissioned officer in the navy ranking next below a lieutenant

life \'līf\ *n, pl* lives \'līvz\ 1 : the quality that distinguishes a vital and functional being from a dead body or inanimate matter; *also* : a state of an organism characterized esp. by capacity for metabolism, growth, reaction to stimuli, and reproduction 2 : the physical and mental experiences of an individual 3 : BIOGRAPHY 4 : a specific phase or period ⟨adult ∼⟩ 5 : the period from birth to death; *also* : a sentence of imprisonment for the remainder of a person's life 6 : a way of living 7 : PERSON ⟨many *lives* were lost in the fire⟩ 8 : ANIMATION, SPIRIT ⟨danced without ∼⟩ 9 : living beings ⟨forest ∼⟩ 10 : animate activity ⟨signs of ∼⟩ 11 : one providing interest and vigor ⟨∼ of the party⟩ — life·less *adj* — life·like *adj*

life·blood \'līf-ˌbləd\ *n* : a basic source of strength and vitality

life·boat \-ˌbōt\ *n* : a sturdy boat designed for use in saving lives at sea

life·guard \-ˌgärd\ *n* : a usu. expert swimmer employed to safeguard bathers

life·line \-ˌlīn\ *n* 1 : a line to which persons may cling for safety 2 : something considered vital for survival

life·long \-ˌlȯŋ\ *adj* : continuing through life

life preserver *n* : a buoyant device designed to save a person from drowning

lif·er \'lī-fər\ *n* 1 : a person sentenced to life imprisonment 2 : a person who makes a career in the armed forces

life raft *n* : a raft for use by people forced into the water

life·sav·ing \'līf-ˌsā-viŋ\ *n* : the skill or practice of saving or protecting lives esp. of drowning persons — life·sav·er \-ˌsā-vər\ *n*

life science *n* : a branch of science (as biology, medicine, and sometimes anthropology or sociology) that deals with living organisms and life processes — usu. used in pl. — life scientist *n*

¹life·style \'līf-ˌstī(-ə)l\ *n* : a way of living

²lifestyle *adj* : associated with, reflecting, or promoting an enhanced or more desirable lifestyle

life·time \-ˌtīm\ *n* : the duration of an individual's existence

life·work \-ˌwərk\ *n* : the entire or principal work of one's lifetime; *also* : a work extending over a lifetime

life·world \-ˌwər(-ə)ld\ *n* : the total of an individual's physical surroundings and everyday experiences

LIFO *abbr* last in, first out

¹lift \'lift\ *vb* 1 : RAISE, ELEVATE; *also* : RISE, ASCEND 2 : to put an end to : STOP ⟨∼ a ban⟩ 3 : to pay off ⟨∼ a mortgage⟩ — lift·er *n*

²lift *n* 1 : LOAD 2 : the action or an instance of lifting 3 : HELP; *also* : a ride along one's way 4 : RISE, ADVANCE 5 *chiefly Brit* : ELEVATOR 6 : an elevation of the spirits

7 : the upward force that is developed by a moving airfoil and that opposes the pull of gravity

lift-off \-ˌȯf\ *n* : a vertical takeoff (as by a rocket)

lift truck *n* : a small truck for lifting and transporting loads

lig·a·ment \'li-gə-mənt\ *n* : a band of tough fibrous tissue that holds bones together or supports an organ in place

li·gate \'lī-ˌgāt\ *vb* li·gat·ed; li·gat·ing : to tie with a ligature — li·ga·tion \lī-'gā-shən\ *n*

lig·a·ture \'li-gə-ˌchu̇r, -chər\ *n* 1 : something that binds or ties; *also* : a thread used in surgery esp. for tying blood vessels 2 : a printed or written character consisting of two or more letters or characters (as æ) united

¹light \'līt\ *n* 1 : something that makes vision possible : electromagnetic radiation visible to the human eye; *also* : the sensation aroused by stimulation of the visual sense organs 2 : DAYLIGHT 3 : a source of light (as a candle) 4 : ENLIGHTENMENT; *also* : TRUTH 5 : public knowledge ⟨facts brought to ∼⟩ 6 : a particular aspect presented to view ⟨saw the matter in a different ∼⟩ 7 : WINDOW 8 *pl* : STANDARDS ⟨according to his ∼s⟩ 9 : CELEBRITY 10 : LIGHTHOUSE, BEACON; *also* : TRAFFIC LIGHT 11 : a flame for lighting something

²light *adj* 1 : having light : BRIGHT 2 : PALE 2 ⟨∼ blue⟩ — light·ness *n*

³light *vb* lit \'lit\ *or* light·ed; light·ing 1 : to make or become light 2 : to cause to burn : BURN 3 : to conduct with a light 4 : ILLUMINATE

⁴light *adj* 1 : not heavy 2 : not serious ⟨∼ reading⟩ 3 : SCANTY ⟨∼ rain⟩ 4 : easily disturbed ⟨a ∼ sleeper⟩ 5 : GENTLE ⟨a ∼ blow⟩ 6 : easily endurable ⟨a ∼ cold⟩; *also* : requiring little effort ⟨∼ exercise⟩ 7 : SWIFT, NIMBLE 8 : FRIVOLOUS 9 : DIZZY 10 : made with lower calorie content or less of some ingredient than usual ⟨∼ salad dressing⟩ 11 : producing goods for direct consumption by the consumer ⟨∼ industry⟩ — light·ly *adv* — light·ness *n*

⁵light *adv* 1 : LIGHTLY 2 : with little baggage ⟨travel ∼⟩

⁶light *vb* lit \'lit\ *or* light·ed; light·ing 1 : SETTLE, ALIGHT 2 : to fall unexpectedly 3 : HAPPEN ⟨∼ed on a solution⟩

light bulb *n* 1 : a lamp in which an electrically heated filament emits light 2 : FLUORESCENT LAMP

light-emitting diode *n* : LED

¹light·en \'lī-tᵊn\ *vb* 1 : ILLUMINATE, BRIGHTEN 2 : to give out flashes of lightning

²lighten *vb* 1 : to relieve of a burden 2 : GLADDEN 3 : to become lighter

lighten up *vb* : to take things less seriously ⟨*lighten up* and relax⟩

¹light·er \'lī-tər\ *n* : a barge used esp. in loading or unloading ships

²light·er \'lī-tər\ *n* : one that lights; *esp* : a device for lighting (as a fire or cigarette)

light·face \'līt-ˌfās\ *n* : a type having light thin lines — light·faced \-ˌfāst\ *adj*

light-head·ed \'līt-ˌhe-dəd\ *adj* 1 : feeling confused or dizzy 2 : lacking maturity or seriousness

light·heart·ed \-ˌhär-təd\ *adj* : free from worry — light·heart·ed·ly *adv* — light·heart·ed·ness *n*

light·house \-ˌhau̇s\ *n* : a structure with a powerful light for guiding sailors

light meter *n* : a usu. handheld device for indicating correct photographic exposure

¹light·ning \'līt-niŋ\ *n* : the flashing of light produced by a discharge of atmospheric electricity; *also* : the discharge itself

²lightning *adj* : extremely fast

lightning bug *n* : FIREFLY

lightning rod *n* : a grounded metallic rod set up on a structure to protect it from lightning

light out *vb* : to leave in a hurry

light-proof \'līt-ˌprüf\ *adj* : impenetrable by light

lights \'līts\ *n pl* : the lungs esp. of a slaughtered animal

light·ship \'līt-ˌship\ *n* : a ship with a powerful light moored at a place dangerous to navigation

light show *n* : a kaleidoscopic display (as of colored lights)

light·some \'līt-səm\ *adj* 1 : free from care 2 : NIMBLE

¹light·weight \'līt-ˌwāt\ *n* : one of less than average weight; *esp* : a boxer weighing not over 135 pounds

²lightweight *adj* 1 : INCONSEQUENTIAL 2 : of less than average weight

light–year \'līt-,yir\ *n* **1** : an astronomical unit of distance equal to the distance that light travels in one year in a vacuum or about 5.88 trillion miles (9.46 trillion kilometers) **2** : an extremely large measure of comparison ⟨saw it ∼*s* ago⟩

lig·nin \'lig-nən\ *n* : a substance related to cellulose that occurs in the woody cell walls of plants and in the cementing material between them

lig·nite \'lig-,nīt\ *n* : brownish black soft coal

¹like \'līk\ *vb* **liked; lik·ing 1** : ENJOY ⟨∼*s* baseball⟩ **2** : WANT ⟨would ∼ a drink⟩ **3** : CHOOSE ⟨does as she ∼*s*⟩ — **lik·able** *or* **like·able** \'lī-kə-bəl\ *adj*

²like *n* : PREFERENCE

³like *adj* : SIMILAR ♦ *Synonyms* ALIKE, ANALOGOUS, COMPARABLE, PARALLEL, UNIFORM

⁴like *prep* **1** : similar or similarly to ⟨seems ∼ a dream⟩ **2** : typical of **3** : comparable to **4** : as though there would be ⟨looks ∼ rain⟩ **5** : such as ⟨a subject ∼ physics⟩

⁵like *n* **1** : COUNTERPART **2** : one that is similar to another ⟨we may never see his ∼ again⟩ — **and the like** : ET CETERA

⁶like *conj* **1** : AS IF ⟨acted ∼ they were scared⟩ **2** : in the same way that ⟨do it ∼ mom said⟩

-like *adj comb form* : resembling or characteristic of ⟨ladylike⟩ ⟨lifelike⟩

like·li·hood \'lī-klē-,húd\ *n* : PROBABILITY

¹like·ly \'lī-klē\ *adj* **like·li·er; -est 1** : very probable **2** : BELIEVABLE **3** : PROMISING ⟨a ∼ place to fish⟩

²likely *adv* : in all probability

lik·en \'lī-kən\ *vb* : COMPARE

like·ness \'līk-nəs\ *n* **1** : COPY, PORTRAIT **2** : SEMBLANCE **3** : RESEMBLANCE

like·wise \-,wīz\ *adv* **1** : in like manner **2** : in addition : ALSO

lik·ing \'lī-kiŋ\ *n* : favorable regard ⟨took a ∼ to the newcomer⟩; *also* : TASTE

li·lac \'lī-lək, -,lak, -,läk\ *n* [obs. F (now *lilas*), fr. Ar *līlak*, fr. Pers *nīlak* bluish, fr. *nīl* blue, fr. Skt *nīla* dark blue] **1** : a shrub related to the olive that produces large clusters of fragrant grayish pink, purple, or white flowers **2** : a moderate purple color

lil·an·ge·ni \,li-lən-'ge-nē\ *n, pl* **em·a·lan·ge·ni** \,e-mə-lən-'ge-nē\ — see MONEY table

lil·li·pu·tian \,li-lə-'pyü-shən\ *adj, often cap* **1** : SMALL, MINIATURE **2** : PETTY

lilt \'lilt\ *n* **1** : a cheerful lively song or tune **2** : a rhythmical swing or flow

lily \'li-lē\ *n, pl* **lil·ies** : any of a genus of tall bulbous herbs with leafy stems and usu. funnel-shaped flowers; *also* : any of various related plants

lily of the valley : a low perennial herb related to the lilies that produces a raceme of fragrant nodding bell-shaped white flowers

li·ma bean \'lī-mə-\ *n* : a bushy or tall-growing bean widely cultivated for its flat edible usu. pale green or whitish seeds; *also* : the seed

limb \'lim\ *n* **1** : one of the projecting paired appendages (as legs, arms, or wings) used by an animal esp. in moving or grasping **2** : a large branch of a tree : BOUGH — **limb·less** *adj*

¹lim·ber \'lim-bər\ *adj* **1** : FLEXIBLE, SUPPLE **2** : LITHE, NIMBLE

²limber *vb* : to make or become limber

lim·bic \'lim-bik\ *adj* : of, relating to, or being a group of structures of the brain (**limbic system**) concerned esp. with emotion and motivation

¹lim·bo \'lim-bō\ *n, pl* **limbos** [ME, fr. ML, abl. of *limbus* limbo, fr. L, border] **1** *often cap* : an abode of souls barred from heaven through no fault of their own **2** : a place or state of confinement, oblivion, or uncertainty ⟨a ∼ of forgotten things⟩

²limbo *n, pl* **limbos** : an acrobatic dance or contest that involves passing under a horizontal pole

Lim·burg·er \'lim-,bər-gər\ *n* : a pungent semisoft surface-ripened cheese

¹lime \'līm\ *n* : a caustic powdery white solid that consists of calcium and oxygen, is obtained from limestone or shells, and is used in making cement and in fertilizer — **lime** *vb* — **limy** \'lī-mē\ *adj*

²lime *n* : a small yellowish green citrus fruit with juicy acid pulp

lime·ade \,līm-'ād, 'lī-,mād\ *n* : a beverage of lime juice, sugar, and water

lime·light \'līm-,līt\ *n* **1** : a device in which flame is directed against a cylinder of lime formerly used in the theater to cast a strong white light on the stage **2** : the center of public attention

lim·er·ick \'li-mə-rik\ *n* : a light or humorous poem of 5 lines

lime·stone \'līm-,stōn\ *n* : a rock that is formed by accumulation of organic remains (as shells), is used in building, and yields lime when burned

¹lim·it \'li-mət\ *n* **1** : something that restrains or confines; *also* : the utmost extent **2** : BOUNDARY; *also, pl* : BOUNDS **3** : a prescribed maximum or minimum **4** : a number whose value becomes arbitrarily close to that of a function as its independent variable approaches a given value — **lim·it·less** *adj* — **lim·it·less·ness** *n*

²limit *vb* **1** : to set limits to **2** : to reduce in quantity or extent — **lim·i·ta·tion** \,li-mə-'tā-shən\ *n*

lim·it·ed *adj* **1** : confined within limits **2** : offering faster service esp. by making fewer stops ⟨a ∼ train⟩

limn \'lim\ *vb* **limned; limn·ing** \'li-miŋ, 'lim-niŋ\ **1** : DRAW; *also* : PAINT **2** : DELINEATE **3** : DESCRIBE

limo \'li-(,)mō\ *n, pl* **limos** : LIMOUSINE

li·mo·nite \'lī-mə-,nīt\ *n* : a ferric oxide that is a major ore of iron — **li·mo·nit·ic** \,lī-mə-'ni-tik\ *adj*

lim·ou·sine \'li-mə-,zēn, ,li-mə-'zēn\ *n* [F] **1** : a large luxurious often chauffeur-driven sedan **2** : a large vehicle for transporting passengers to and from an airport

¹limp \'limp\ *vb* : to walk lamely; *also* : to proceed with difficulty

²limp *n* : a limping movement or gait

³limp *adj* **1** : having no defined shape; *also* : not stiff or rigid **2** : lacking in strength or firmness ⟨went ∼ from fatigue⟩ — **limp·ly** *adv* — **limp·ness** *n*

lim·pet \'lim-pət\ *n* : any of numerous gastropod sea mollusks with a conical shell that clings to rocks or timbers

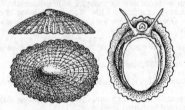

limpet: shell and bottom view

lim·pid \'lim-pəd\ *adj* : CLEAR, TRANSPARENT ⟨∼ water⟩

lin *abbr* **1** lineal **2** linear

lin·age \'lī-nij\ *n* : the number of lines of written or printed matter

linch·pin \'linch-,pin\ *n* : a locking pin inserted crosswise (as through the end of an axle)

lin·den \'lin-dən\ *n* : any of a genus of trees with large heart-shaped leaves and clustered yellowish flowers; *also* : the light white wood of a linden

¹line \'līn\ *n* **1** : CORD, ROPE, WIRE; *also* : a length of material used in measuring and leveling **2** : pipes for conveying a fluid ⟨a gas ∼⟩ **3** : a horizontal row of written or printed characters; *also* : VERSE **4** : NOTE **5** : the words making up a part in a drama — usu. used in pl. **6** : something distinct, long, and narrow; *also* : ROUTE **7** : a state of agreement **8** : a course of conduct, action, or thought; *also* : OCCUPATION **9** : LIMIT **10** : an arrangement of persons or objects of one kind in an orderly series ⟨waiting in ∼⟩ **11** : a transportation system **12 a** : the football players who are stationed on the line of scrimmage **b** : a group of three players who play together as a unit in hockey **13** : a long narrow mark; *also* : EQUATOR **14** : a geometric element that is the path of a moving point **15** : CONTOUR **16** : a general plan ⟨thinking along these ∼*s*⟩ **17** : an indication based on insight or investigation

²line *vb* **lined; lin·ing 1** : to mark with a line **2** : to place or form a line along **3** : ALIGN ⟨∼ up the sheets of paper⟩

³line *vb* **lined; lin·ing 1** : to cover the inner surface of ⟨∼ the box with paper⟩

lin·eage \'li-nē-ij\ *n* : lineal descent from a common progenitor; *also* : FAMILY

lin·eal \'li-nē-əl\ *adj* 1 : LINEAR 2 : consisting of or being in a direct line of ancestry; *also* : HEREDITARY

lin·ea·ment \'li-nē-ə-mənt\ *n* : an outline, feature, or contour of a body and esp. of a face — usu. used in pl.

lin·ear \'li-nē-ər\ *adj* 1 : of, relating to, resembling, or having a graph that is a line and esp. a straight line : STRAIGHT 2 : composed of simply drawn lines with little attempt at pictorial representation ⟨∼ script⟩ 3 : being long and uniformly narrow

line·back·er \'lin-,ba-kər\ *n* : a defensive football player who lines up just behind the line of scrimmage

line drive *n* : a batted baseball hit in a flatter path than a fly ball

line–item veto *n* : the power of a government executive to veto specific items in an appropriations bill

line·man \'lin-mən\ *n* 1 : a person who sets up or repairs communication or power lines 2 : a player in the line in football

lin·en \'li-nən\ *n* 1 : cloth made of flax; *also* : thread or yarn spun from flax 2 : clothing or household articles made of linen cloth or similar fabric

line of scrimmage : an imaginary line in football parallel to the goal lines and tangent to the nose of the ball laid on the ground before a play

¹lin·er \'li-nər\ *n* : a ship or airplane of a regular transportation line

²liner *n* : one that lines or is used as a lining — **lin·er·less** *adj*

line score *n* : a score of a baseball game giving the runs, hits, and errors made by each team

lines·man \'linz-mən\ *n* 1 : LINEMAN 1 2 : an official who assists a referee

line·up \'li-,nəp\ *n* 1 : a list of players taking part in a game (as of baseball) 2 : a line of persons arranged esp. for identification by police

ling \'liŋ\ *n* : any of various fishes related to the cod

-ling *n suffix* 1 : one associated with ⟨nestling⟩ 2 : young, small, or minor one ⟨duckling⟩

lin·ger \'liŋ-gər\ *vb* : TARRY; *also* : PROCRASTINATE — **lin·ger·er** *n*

lin·ge·rie \,län-jə-'rā, ,laⁿ-zhə-, -'rē\ *n* [F, fr. MF, fr. *linge* linen, fr. L *lineus* made of linen, fr. *linum* flax, linen] : women's intimate apparel

lin·go \'liŋ-gō\ *n, pl* **lingoes** : a usu. strange or incomprehensible language

lin·gua fran·ca \,liŋ-gwə-'fraŋ-kə\ *n, pl* **lingua francas** *or* **lin·guae fran·cae** \-gwē-'fraŋ-,kē\ [It] 1 *often cap* : a common language consisting of Italian mixed with French, Spanish, Greek, and Arabic that was formerly spoken in Mediterranean ports 2 : a common or commercial tongue among speakers of different languages

lin·gual \'liŋ-gwəl\ *adj* : of, relating to, or produced by the tongue

lin·gui·ca \liŋ-'gwē-sə\ *n* : a spicy Portuguese sausage

lin·guist \'liŋ-gwist\ *n* 1 : a person skilled in languages 2 : a person who specializes in linguistics

lin·guis·tics \liŋ-'gwis-tiks\ *n* : the study of human speech including the units, nature, structure, and modification of language — **lin·guis·tic** \-tik\ *adj*

lin·i·ment \'li-nə-mənt\ *n* : a liquid preparation rubbed on the skin esp. to relieve pain

lin·ing \'lī-niŋ\ *n* : material used to line esp. an inner surface

link \'liŋk\ *n* 1 : a connecting structure; *esp* : a single ring of a chain 2 : BOND, TIE 3 : HYPERLINK — **link** *vb* — **link·er** *n*

link·age \'liŋ-kij\ *n* 1 : the manner or style of being united 2 : the quality or state of being linked 3 : a system of links

linking verb *n* : a word or expression (as a form of *be, become, feel,* or *seem*) that links a subject with its predicate

links \'liŋks\ *n pl* : a golf course

link·up \'liŋ-,kəp\ *n* 1 : MEETING 2 : something that serves as a linking device or factor

lin·net \'li-nət\ *n* : an Old World finch

li·no·leum \lə-'nō-lē-əm\ *n* [L *linum* flax + *oleum* oil] : a floor covering with a canvas back and a surface of hardened linseed oil and a filler

lin·seed \'lin-,sēd\ *n* : the seeds of flax yielding a yellowish oil (**linseed oil**) used esp. in paints and linoleum

lin·sey–wool·sey \,lin-zē-'wúl-zē\ *n* : a coarse sturdy fabric of wool and linen or cotton

lint \'lint\ *n* 1 : linen made into a soft fleecy substance 2 : fine ravels and short fibers of yarn or fabric 3 : the fibers that surround cotton seeds and form the cotton staple

lin·tel \'lin-t²l\ *n* : a horizontal piece across the top of an opening (as of a door) that carries the weight of the structure above it

linz·er torte \'lin-sər-, -zər-\ *n, often cap L* : a baked buttery torte made with chopped almonds, sugar, and spices and filled with jam or preserves

li·on \'lī-ən\ *n, pl* **lions** : a large heavily built cat of Africa and southern Asia with a shaggy mane in the male

li·on·ess \'lī-ə-nəs\ *n* : a female lion

li·on·heart·ed \,lī-ən-'här-təd\ *adj* : COURAGEOUS, BRAVE

li·on·ise *Brit var of* LIONIZE

li·on·ize \'lī-ə-,nīz\ *vb* -**ized**; -**iz·ing** : to treat as an object of great interest or importance — **li·on·i·za·tion** \,lī-ə-nə-'zā-shən\ *n*

lion's den *n* : a place or state of extreme disadvantage, antagonism, or hostility

lip \'lip\ *n* 1 : either of the two fleshy folds that surround the mouth; *also* : the margin of the human lip 2 : a part or projection suggesting a lip 3 : the edge of a hollow vessel or cavity — **lipped** \'lipt\ *adj*

li·pa \'lē-,pä, -pə\ *n, pl* **lipa** — see *kuna* at MONEY table

lip·id \'li-pəd\ *n* : any of various substances (as fats and waxes) that with proteins and carbohydrates make up the principal structural parts of living cells

lip–lock \'lip-,läk\ *n* : a long amorous kiss

li·po·pro·tein \,lī-pō-'prō-,tēn, ,li-\ *n* : a protein that is a complex of protein and lipid

li·po·suc·tion \'li-pə-,sək-shən, 'lī-\ *n* : surgical removal of local fat deposits (as in the thighs) esp. for cosmetic purposes

lip·read·ing \'lip-,rē-diŋ\ *n* : the interpreting of a speaker's words by watching lip and facial movements without hearing the voice

lip service *n* : an avowal of allegiance that is not matched by action

lip·stick \'lip-,stik\ *n* : a waxy solid colored cosmetic in stick form for the lips — **lip-sticked** \-,stikt\ *adj*

liq *abbr* 1 liquid 2 liquor

liq·ue·fy *also* **liq·ui·fy** \'li-kwə-,fī\ *vb* -**fied**; -**fy·ing** : to make or become liquid — **liq·ue·fi·er** \-,fī(-ə)r\ *n*

li·queur \li-'kər\ *n* [F] : a distilled alcoholic liquor flavored with aromatic substances and usu. sweetened

¹liq·uid \'li-kwəd\ *adj* 1 : flowing freely like water 2 : neither solid nor gaseous 3 : shining and clear ⟨large ∼ eyes⟩ 4 : smooth and musical in tone; *also* : smooth and unconstrained in movement 5 : consisting of or capable of ready conversion into cash ⟨∼ assets⟩ — **li·quid·i·ty** \li-'kwi-də-tē\ *n*

²liquid *n* : a liquid substance

liq·ui·date \'li-kwə-,dāt\ *vb* -**dat·ed**; -**dat·ing** 1 : to settle the accounts and distribute the assets of (as a business) 2 : to pay off ⟨∼ a debt⟩ 3 : to get rid of; *esp* : KILL — **liq·ui·da·tion** \,li-kwə-'dā-shən\ *n*

liquid crystal *n* : an organic liquid that resembles a crystal in having ordered molecular arrays

liquid crystal display *n* : LCD

liquid measure *n* : a unit or series of units for measuring liquid capacity — see METRIC SYSTEM table, WEIGHT table

li·quor \'li-kər\ *n* [ME *licour*, fr. AF, fr. L *liquor*, fr. *liquēre* to be fluid] : a liquid substance; *esp* : a distilled alcoholic beverage

li·quo·rice *chiefly Brit var of* LICORICE

li·ra \'lir-ə, 'lē-rə\ *n* 1 *pl* **li·re** \'lē-rā\ : the former basic monetary unit of Italy 2 *pl* **lire** : the basic monetary unit of Turkey — see MONEY table 3 *pl* **li·ri** \'lē-rē\ : the basic monetary unit of Malta until 2008

lisente *pl of* SENTE

lisle \'līl(-ə)l\ *n* : a smooth tightly twisted thread usu. made of long-staple cotton

lisp \'lisp\ *vb* : to pronounce \s\ and \z\ imperfectly esp. by turning them into \th\ and \th\; *also* : to speak childishly — **lisp** *n* — **lisp·er** *n*

lis·some *also* **lis·som** \'li-səm\ *adj* 1 : easily flexed 2 : LITHE 2 ⟨a ∼ dancer⟩ 3 : NIMBLE — **lis·some·ly** *adv*

¹list \'list\ *vb, archaic* : PLEASE; *also* : WISH

²**list** *vb, archaic* : LISTEN
³**list** *n* : a leaning to one side : TILT
⁴**list** *vb* : TILT
⁵**list** *n* 1 : a simple series of words or numerals; *also* : an official roster 2 : CATALOG, CHECKLIST
⁶**list** *vb* : to make a list of; *also* : to include on a list — **list·ee** \li-'stē\ *n*
lis·ten \'li-sᵊn\ *vb* 1 : to pay attention in order to hear 2 : HEED — **lis·ten·er** *n*
lis·ten·er·ship \'li-sᵊn-ər-,ship\ *n* : the audience for a radio program or recording
list·ing \'lis-tiŋ\ *n* 1 : an act or instance of making or including in a list 2 : something that is listed
list·less \'list-ləs\ *adj* : SPIRITLESS, LANGUID ⟨a ∼ performance⟩ — **list·less·ly** *adv* — **list·less·ness** *n*
list price *n* : the price of an item as published in a catalog, price list, or advertisement before being discounted
lists \'lists\ *n pl* : an arena for combat (as jousting)
¹**lit** \'lit\ *past and past part of* LIGHT
²**lit** *abbr* 1 liter 2 literal; literally 3 literary 4 literature
lit·a·ny \'li-tə-nē\ *n, pl* **-nies** [ME *letanie*, fr. AF & LL; AF, fr. LL *litania*, fr. LGk *litaneia*, fr. Gk, entreaty, fr. *litanos* suppliant] 1 : a prayer consisting of a series of supplications and responses said alternately by a leader and a group 2 : a lengthy list or series ⟨a ∼ of complaints⟩
li·tas \'lē-,täs\ *n, pl* **li·tai** \-,tī\ *or* **li·tu** \-,tü\ : the basic monetary unit of Lithuania from 1923 to 1940 and from 1991 through 2014
litchi *var of* LYCHEE
lite \'līt\ *adj* 1 : ¹LIGHT 10 ⟨∼ beer⟩ 2 : lacking in substance or seriousness ⟨∼ news⟩
li·ter \'lē-tər\ *n* — see METRIC SYSTEM table
lit·er·al \'li-tə-rəl\ *adj* 1 : adhering to fact or to the ordinary or usual meaning (as of a word) 2 : UNADORNED; *also* : PROSAIC 3 : VERBATIM
lit·er·al·ism \-rə-,li-zəm\ *n* 1 : adherence to the explicit substance (as of an idea) 2 : fidelity to observable fact — **lit·er·al·ist** \-list\ *n* — **lit·er·al·is·tic** \,li-tə-rə-'lis-tik\ *adj*
lit·er·al·ly \'li-tə-rə-lē, 'li-trə-\ *adv* 1 : ACTUALLY ⟨was ∼ insane⟩ 2 : VIRTUALLY ⟨∼ poured out new ideas⟩
lit·er·ary \'li-tə-,rer-ē\ *adj* 1 : of or relating to literature 2 : WELL-READ
lit·er·ate \'li-trət, -tə-rət\ *adj* 1 : EDUCATED; *also* : able to read and write 2 : LITERARY; *also* : POLISHED, LUCID — **lit·er·a·cy** \'li-trə-sē, -tə-rə-\ *n* — **literate** *n*
li·te·ra·ti \,li-tə-'rä-tē\ *n pl* 1 : the educated class 2 : persons interested in literature or the arts
lit·er·a·ture \'li-trə-,chùr, -tə-rə-, -chər\ *n* 1 : the production of written works having excellence of form or expression and dealing with ideas of permanent interest 2 : the written works produced in a particular language, country, or age
lithe \'līth̲, 'līth\ *adj* 1 : SUPPLE 2 : characterized by effortless grace; *also* : athletically slim ⟨a ∼ body⟩
lithe·some \'līth̲-səm, 'līth\ *adj* : LISSOME
lith·i·um \'li-thē-əm\ *n* : a light silver-white metallic chemical element
li·thog·ra·phy \li-'thä-grə-fē\ *n* : the process of printing from a plane surface (as a smooth stone or metal plate) on which the image to be printed is ink-receptive and the blank area ink-repellent — **lith·o·graph** \'li-thə-,graf\ *vb* — **lithograph** *n* — **li·thog·ra·pher** \li-'thä-grə-fər, 'li-thə-,gra-fər\ *n* — **lith·o·graph·ic** \,li-thə-'gra-fik\ *adj* — **lith·o·graph·i·cal·ly** \-fi-k(ə-)lē\ *adv*
li·thol·o·gy \li-'thä-lə-jē\ *n, pl* **-gies** : the study of rocks — **lith·o·log·ic** \,li-thə-'lä-jik\ *or* **lith·o·log·i·cal** \-ji-kəl\ *adj*
lith·o·sphere \'li-thə-,sfir\ *n* : the outer part of the solid earth
Lith·u·a·nian \,li-thə-'wā-nē-ən, -thyù-\ *n* 1 : a native or inhabitant of Lithuania 2 : the language of the Lithuanians — **Lithuanian** *adj*
lit·i·gant \'li-ti-gənt\ *n* : a party to a lawsuit — **litigant** *adj*
lit·i·gate \-,gāt\ *vb* **-gat·ed; -gat·ing** : to carry on a legal contest by judicial process; *also* : to contest at law — **lit·i·ga·tion** \,li-tə-'gā-shən\ *n*
li·ti·gious \lə-'ti-jəs\ *adj* 1 : CONTENTIOUS 2 : prone to engage in lawsuits 3 : of or relating to litigation — **li·ti·gious·ly** *adv* — **li·ti·gious·ness** *n*
lit·mus \'lit-məs\ *n* : a coloring matter from lichens that turns red in acid solutions and blue in alkaline

litmus test *n* : a test in which a single factor (as an attitude) is decisive
Litt D *or* **Lit D** *abbr* [ML *litterarum doctor*] : doctor of letters; doctor of literature
¹**lit·ter** \'li-tər\ *n* [ME, fr. AF *litere*, fr. *lit* bed, fr. L *lectus*] 1 : a covered and curtained couch with shafts that is used to carry a single passenger; *also* : a device (as a stretcher) for carrying a sick or injured person 2 : material used as bedding for animals; *also* : material used to absorb the urine and feces of animals 3 : the offspring of an animal at one birth 4 : RUBBISH
²**litter** *vb* 1 : to give birth to young 2 : to strew or mark with scattered objects
lit·ter·bug \'li-tər-,bəg\ *n* : one who litters a public area
¹**lit·tle** \'li-tᵊl\ *adj* **lit·tler** \'li-tᵊl-ər\ *or* **less** \'les\ *or* **less·er** \'le-sər\; **lit·tlest** \'li-tᵊl-əst\ *or* **least** \'lēst\ 1 : not big; *also* : YOUNG 2 : not important 3 : PETTY 3 4 : not much — **lit·tle·ness** *n*
²**little** *adv* **less** \'les\; **least** \'lēst\ 1 : SLIGHTLY; *also* : not at all 2 : INFREQUENTLY
³**little** *n* 1 : a small amount or quantity 2 : a short time or distance
Little Dipper *n* : the seven bright stars of Ursa Minor arranged in a form resembling a dipper
little finger *n* : PINKIE
little theater *n* : a small theater for low-cost dramatic productions designed for a limited audience
lit·to·ral \'li-tə-rəl; ,li-tə-'ral\ *adj* : of, relating to, or growing on or near a shore esp. of the sea — **littoral** *n*
lit·ur·gy \'li-tər-jē\ *n, pl* **-gies** : a rite or body of rites prescribed for public worship — **li·tur·gi·cal** \lə-'tər-ji-kəl\ *adj* — **li·tur·gi·cal·ly** \-k(ə-)lē\ *adv* — **lit·ur·gist** \'li-tər-jist\ *n*
liv·able *also* **live·able** \'li-və-bəl\ *adj* 1 : suitable for living in or with ⟨a ∼ house⟩ ⟨∼wages⟩ 2 : ENDURABLE — **liv·a·bil·i·ty** \,li-və-'bi-lə-tē\ *n*
¹**live** \'liv\ *vb* **lived; liv·ing** 1 : to be or continue alive ⟨*lived* 80 years⟩ 2 : SUBSIST 3 : RESIDE ⟨∼s next door⟩ 4 : to conduct one's life 5 : to remain in human memory or record ⟨his legacy ∼s⟩
²**live** \'līv\ *adj* 1 : having life ⟨∼ worms⟩ 2 : ACTUAL ⟨a real ∼ celebrity⟩ 3 : BURNING, GLOWING ⟨a ∼ cigar⟩ 4 : connected to electric power ⟨a ∼ wire⟩ 5 : UNEXPLODED ⟨a ∼ bomb⟩ 6 : of continuing interest ⟨a ∼ issue⟩ 7 : of or involving the actual presence of real people ⟨∼ audience⟩; *also* : broadcast directly at the time of production 8 : being in play ⟨a ∼ ball⟩
lived–in \'livd-,in\ *adj* : of or suggesting long-term human habitation or use
live down *vb* : to live so as to wipe out the memory or effects of
live in *vb* : to live in one's place of employment — used of a servant — **live–in** \'liv-,in\ *adj*
live·li·hood \'līv-lē-,hùd\ *n* : means of support or subsistence
live·long \'liv-,lȯŋ\ *adj* [ME *lef long*, fr. *lef* dear + *long* long] : WHOLE, ENTIRE ⟨the ∼ day⟩
live·ly \'līv-lē\ *adj* **live·li·er; -est** 1 : ANIMATED ⟨∼ debate⟩ 2 : KEEN, VIVID ⟨∼ interest⟩ 3 : showing activity or vigor ⟨a ∼ manner⟩ 4 : quick to rebound ⟨a ∼ ball⟩ 5 : full of life ♦ **Synonyms** VIVACIOUS, SPRIGHTLY, GAY, SPIRITED — **live·li·ness** *n* — **live·ly** *adv*
liv·en \'lī-vən\ *vb* : ENLIVEN
live oak *n* : any of several American evergreen oaks; *esp* : one of the southeastern U.S. that is often planted as a shade tree
¹**liv·er** \'li-vər\ *n* 1 : a large glandular organ of vertebrates that secretes bile and is a center of metabolic activity 2 : the liver of an animal (as a calf or chicken) eaten as food
²**liver** *n* : one that lives esp. in a specified way ⟨a fast ∼⟩
liv·er·ish \'li-və-rish\ *adj* 1 : resembling liver esp. in color 2 : BILIOUS 3 : PEEVISH — **liv·er·ish·ness** *adj*
liv·er·mo·ri·um \,li-vər-'mȯr-ē-əm\ *n* : a short-lived artificially produced radioactive chemical element
liver spots *n pl* : AGE SPOTS
liv·er·wort \'li-vər-,wərt\ *n* : any of a class of flowerless plants resembling the related mosses
liv·er·wurst \-,wərst, -,wùrst\ *n* [part trans. of G *Leberwurst*, fr. *Leber* liver + *Wurst* sausage] : a sausage consisting chiefly of liver
liv·ery \'li-və-rē\ *n, pl* **-er·ies** 1 : a servant's uniform; *also*

: distinctive dress   **2** : the feeding, care, and stabling of horses for pay; *also* : an establishment (as a stable or business) keeping horses or vehicles for hire — **liv·er·ied** \-rēd\ *adj* — **liv·ery·man** \'li-və-rē-mən\ *n*

lives *pl of* LIFE

live·stock \'līv-ˌstäk\ *n* : farm animals kept for use and profit

live wire *n* : an alert, active, or aggressive person — **live–wire** *adj*

liv·id \'li-vəd\ *adj* [F *livide*, fr. L *lividus*, fr. *livēre* to be blue]   **1** : discolored by bruising   **2** : ASHEN, PALLID   **3** : REDDISH   **4** : ENRAGED — **li·vid·i·ty** \li-'vi-də-tē\ *n*

¹**liv·ing** \'li-vin\ *adj*   **1** : having life   **2** : NATURAL   **3** : full of life and vigor; *also* : VIVID ⟨in ∼ color⟩

²**living** *n*   **1** : the condition of being alive   **2** : LIVELIHOOD   **3** : manner of life

living room *n* : a room in a residence used for the common social activities of the occupants

living wage *n* : a wage sufficient to provide an acceptable standard of living

living will *n* : a document requesting that the signer not be kept alive by artificial means unless there is a reasonable expectation of recovery

livre \'lēvrᵊ\ *n* : the pound of Lebanon

liz·ard \'li-zərd\ *n* : any of a group of 4-legged reptiles with long tapering tails

Lk *abbr* Luke

ll *abbr* lines

lla·ma \'lä-mə\ *n* [Sp, fr. Quechua] : any of a genus of wild or domesticated So. American mammals related to the camels but smaller and without a hump

lla·no \'lä-nō\ *n, pl* **llanos** : an open grassy plain esp. of Latin America

LLD *abbr* [NL *legum doctor*] doctor of laws

LNG *abbr* liquefied natural gas

¹**load** \'lōd\ *n*   **1** : PACK; *also* : CARGO   **2** : a mass of weight supported by something   **3** : something that burdens the mind or spirits   **4** : a large quantity — usu. used in pl.   **5** : a standard, expected, or authorized burden

²**load** *vb*   **1** : to put a load in or on; *also* : to receive a load   **2** : to encumber with an obligation or something heavy or disheartening   **3** : to increase the weight of by adding something   **4** : to supply abundantly   **5** : to put a charge in (as a firearm)   **6** : to copy or transfer into a computer's memory esp. from an external source

load·ed *adj*   **1** *slang* : HIGH 12   **2** : having a large amount of money   **3** : equipped with an abundance of options ⟨a ∼ car⟩

load·stone *var of* LODESTONE

¹**loaf** \'lōf\ *n, pl* **loaves** \'lōvz\ : a shaped or molded mass esp. of bread

²**loaf** *vb* : to spend time in idleness : LOUNGE

loaf·er \'lō-fər\ *n*   **1** : one that loafs : IDLER   **2** : a low step‑ in shoe

loam \'lōm, 'lüm\ *n* : SOIL; *esp* : a loose soil of mixed clay, sand, and silt — **loamy** *adj*

¹**loan** \'lōn\ *n*   **1** : money lent at interest; *also* : something lent for the borrower's temporary use   **2** : the grant of temporary use

²**loan** *vb* : LEND

loan shark *n* : a person who lends money at excessive rates of interest — **loan·shark·ing** \'lōn-ˌshär-kiŋ\ *n*

loan·word \-ˌwərd\ *n* : a word taken from another language and at least partly naturalized

loath *also* **loth** \'lōth, 'lōth\ *or* **loathe** \'lōth, 'lōth\ *adj* : RELUCTANT

loathe \'lōth\ *vb* **loathed; loath·ing** : to dislike greatly
♦ **Synonyms** ABOMINATE, ABHOR, DETEST, HATE

loath·ing \'lō-thin\ *n* : extreme disgust

loath·some \'lōth-səm, 'lōth-\ *adj* : exciting loathing : REPULSIVE

lob \'läb\ *vb* **lobbed; lob·bing**   **1** : to throw, hit, or propel something in a high arc   **2** : to direct (as a question) so as to elicit a response — **lob** *n*

¹**lob·by** \'lä-bē\ *n, pl* **lobbies**   **1** : a corridor used esp. as a passageway or waiting room   **2** : a group of persons engaged in lobbying

²**lobby** *vb* **lob·bied; lob·by·ing** : to try to influence public officials and esp. legislators — **lob·by·ist** *n*

lobe \'lōb\ *n* : a curved or rounded part esp. of a bodily organ — **lo·bar** \'lō-bər\ *adj* — **lobed** \'lōbd\ *adj*

lo·be·lia \lō-'bēl-yə\ *n* : any of a genus of plants often grown for their clusters of showy flowers

lo·bot·o·my \lō-'bä-tə-mē\ *n, pl* **-mies** : surgical severance of certain nerve fibers in the brain used esp. formerly to relieve some mental disorders

lob·ster \'läb-stər\ *n* [ME, fr. OE *loppestre*, fr. *loppe* spider] : any of a family of edible marine crustaceans with two large pincerlike claws and four other pairs of legs; *also* : SPINY LOBSTER

¹**lo·cal** \'lō-kəl\ *adj*   **1** : of, relating to, or occupying a particular place   **2** : serving a particular limited district; *also* : making all stops ⟨a ∼ train⟩   **3** : affecting a small part of the body ⟨a ∼ infection⟩ — **lo·cal·ly** *adv*

²**local** *n* : one that is local

local area network *n* : a network of personal computers in a small area (as an office)

lo·cale \lō-'kal\ *n* : a place that is the setting for a particular event

lo·cal·ise *Brit var of* LOCALIZE

lo·cal·i·ty \lō-'ka-lə-tē\ *n, pl* **-ties** : a particular spot, situation, or location

lo·cal·ize \'lō-kə-ˌlīz\ *vb* **-ized; -iz·ing** : to fix in or confine to a definite place or locality — **lo·cal·i·za·tion** \ˌlō-kə-lə-'zā-shən\ *n*

lo·cate \'lō-ˌkāt, lō-'kāt\ *vb* **lo·cat·ed; lo·cat·ing**   **1** : STATION, SETTLE   **2** : to determine the site of   **3** : to find or fix the place of in a sequence

lo·ca·tion \lō-'kā-shən\ *n*   **1** : SITUATION, PLACE   **2** : the process of locating   **3** : a place outside a studio where a motion picture is filmed

lo·ca·vore \'lō-kə-ˌvȯr\ *n* [*local* + *-vore* (as in *carnivore*)] : one who eats foods grown locally whenever possible

loc cit *abbr* [L *loco citato*] in the place cited

loch \'läk, 'läk\ *n, Scot* : LAKE; *also* : a bay or arm of the sea esp. when nearly landlocked

¹**lock** \'läk\ *n* : a tuft, strand, or ringlet of hair; *also* : a cohering bunch (as of wool or flax)

²**lock** *n*   **1** : a fastening in which a bolt is operated   **2** : the mechanism of a firearm by which the charge is exploded   **3** : an enclosure (as in a canal) used in raising or lowering boats from level to level   **4** : AIR LOCK   **5** : a wrestling hold

³**lock** *vb*   **1** : to fasten the lock of; *also* : to make fast with a lock   **2** : to confine or exclude by means of a lock   **3** : INTERLOCK   **4** : to make or become motionless by the interlocking of parts

lock·er \'lä-kər\ *n*   **1** : a drawer, cupboard, or compartment for individual storage use   **2** : an insulated compartment for storing frozen food

lock·et \'lä-kət\ *n* : a small usu. metal case for a memento worn suspended from a chain or necklace

lock·jaw \'läk-ˌjȯ\ *n* : a symptom of tetanus marked by spasms of the jaw muscles and inability to open the jaws; *also* : TETANUS

lock·nut \-ˌnət\ *n*   **1** : a nut screwed tight on another to prevent it from slacking back   **2** : a nut designed to lock itself when screwed tight

lock·out \-ˌaut\ *n* : the suspension of work by an employer during a labor dispute in order to make employees accept the terms being offered

lock·smith \-ˌsmith\ *n* : one who makes or repairs locks

lock·step \-ˌstep\ *n* : a mode of marching in step by a body of persons moving in a very close single file

lock·up \-ˌəp\ *n* : JAIL

lo·co \'lō-kō\ *adj* [Sp] *slang* : CRAZY, FRENZIED

lo·co·mo·tion \ˌlō-kə-'mō-shən\ *n*   **1** : the act or power of moving from place to place   **2** : TRAVEL

¹**lo·co·mo·tive** \ˌlō-kə-'mō-tiv\ *adj* : of or relating to locomotion or a locomotive

²**locomotive** *n* : a self-propelled vehicle used to move railroad cars

lo·co·mo·tor \ˌlō-kə-'mō-tər\ *adj* : of or relating to locomotion or organs used in locomotion

lo·co·weed \'lō-kō-ˌwēd\ *n* : any of several leguminous plants of western No. America that are poisonous to livestock

lo·cus \'lō-kəs\ *n, pl* **lo·ci** \'lō-ˌsī\ [L]   **1** : PLACE, LOCALITY   **2** : the set of all points whose location is determined by stated conditions

lo·cust \'lō-kəst\ *n*   **1** : a usu. destructive migratory grasshopper   **2** : CICADA   **3** : any of various leguminous trees; *also* : the wood of a locust

lo·cu·tion \lō-ˈkyü-shən\ *n* : a particular form of expression; *also* : PHRASEOLOGY

lode \ˈlōd\ *n* : an ore deposit

lode·stone \-ˌstōn\ *n* : an iron-containing rock with magnetic properties

¹**lodge** \ˈläj\ *vb* **lodged; lodg·ing** **1** : to provide quarters for; *also* : to settle in a place **2** : CONTAIN **3** : to come to a rest and remain ⟨*lodged* in his throat⟩ **4** : to deposit for safekeeping **5** : to vest (as authority) in an agent **6** : FILE ⟨∼ a complaint⟩

²**lodge** *n* **1** : a house set apart for residence in a special season or by an employee on an estate; *also* : INN **2** : a den or lair esp. of gregarious animals **3** : the meeting place of a branch of a fraternal organization; *also* : the members of such a branch

lodg·er \ˈlä-jər\ *n* : a person who occupies a rented room in another's house

lodg·ing \ˈlä-jiŋ\ *n* **1** : DWELLING **2** : a room or suite of rooms in another's house rented as a dwelling place — usu. used in pl.

lodg·ment *or* **lodge·ment** \ˈläj-mənt\ *n* **1** : a lodging place **2** : the act or manner of lodging **3** : DEPOSIT

loess \ˈles, ˈləs\ *n* : a usu. yellowish brown loamy deposit believed to be chiefly deposited by the wind

lo-fi \ˈlō-ˌfī\ *n* : audio production of rough or unpolished sound quality — **lo-fi** *adj*

¹**loft** \ˈlȯft\ *n* [ME, fr. OE, air, sky, fr. ON *lopt*] **1** : ATTIC **2** : GALLERY ⟨organ ∼⟩ **3** : an upper floor (as in a warehouse or barn) esp. when not partitioned **4** : the thickness of a fabric or insulated material (as of a sleeping bag)

²**loft** *vb* : to strike or throw a ball so that it rises high in the air

lofty \ˈlȯf-tē\ *adj* **loft·i·er; -est** **1** : NOBLE; *also* : SUPERIOR ⟨∼ ideals⟩ **2** : extremely proud **3** : HIGH, TALL — **loft·i·ly** \ˈlȯf-tə-lē\ *adv* — **loft·i·ness** \-tē-nəs\ *n*

¹**log** \ˈlȯg, ˈläg\ *n* **1** : a bulky piece of a cut or fallen tree **2** : an apparatus for measuring a ship's speed **3** : the daily record of a ship's progress; *also* : a regularly kept record of performance or events ⟨a pilot's ∼⟩ ⟨a runner's ∼⟩

²**log** *vb* **logged; log·ging** **1** : to cut (trees) for lumber; *also* : to clear (land) of trees in lumbering **2** : to enter in a log **3** : to sail a ship or fly an airplane for (an indicated distance or period of time) **4** : to have (an indicated record) to one's credit : ACHIEVE — **log·ger** \ˈlȯ-gər, ˈlä-\ *n*

³**log** *n* : LOGARITHM

lo·gan·ber·ry \ˈlō-gən-ˌber-ē\ *n* : a red-fruited upright-growing dewberry; *also* : its berry

log·a·rithm \ˈlȯ-gə-ˌri-thəm, ˈlä-\ *n* : the exponent that indicates the power to which a base is raised to produce a given number ⟨the ∼ of 100 to base 10 is 2 since $10^2 = 100$⟩ — **log·a·rith·mic** \ˌlȯ-gə-ˈrith-mik, ˌlä-\ *adj*

loge \ˈlōzh\ *n* **1** : a small compartment; *also* : a box in a theater **2** : a small partitioned area; *also* : the forward section of a theater mezzanine **3** : a raised level of seats in a stadium

log·ger·head \ˈlȯ-gər-ˌhed, ˈlä-\ *n* : a large sea turtle of subtropical and temperate waters — **at loggerheads** : in a state of quarrelsome disagreement

log·gia \ˈlȯ-jē-ə, ˈlȯ-jä\ *n, pl* **loggias** \ˈlȯ-jē-əz, ˈlȯ-jäz\ : a roofed open gallery

log·ic \ˈlä-jik\ *n* **1** : a science that deals with the rules and tests of sound thinking and proof by reasoning **2** : sound reasoning **3** : the arrangement of circuit elements for arithmetical computation in a computer — **log·i·cal** \-ji-kəl\ *adj* — **log·i·cal·ly** \-jik-(ə-)lē\ *adv* — **lo·gi·cian** \lō-ˈji-shən\ *n*

log in *vb* : LOG ON

lo·gis·tics \lō-ˈjis-tiks\ *n sing or pl* : the procurement, maintenance, and transportation of matériel, facilities, and personnel — **lo·gis·tic** \-tik\ *or* **lo·gis·ti·cal** \-ti-kəl\ *adj*

log·jam \ˈlȯg-ˌjam, ˈläg-\ *n* **1** : a deadlocked jumble of logs in a watercourse **2** : DEADLOCK — **logjam** *vb*

logo \ˈlō-gō\ *n, pl* **log·os** \-gōz\ : an identifying symbol (as for advertising)

log off *vb* : to end the connection of a computer to a network or system

log on *vb* : to start the connection of a computer to a network or system

logo·type \ˈlō-gə-ˌtīp, ˈlä-\ *n* : LOGO

log·roll·ing \-ˌrō-liŋ\ *n* : the trading of votes by legislators to secure favorable action on projects of individual interest

lo·gy \ˈlō-gē\ *also* **log·gy** \ˈlȯ-gē, ˈlä-\ *adj* **lo·gi·er; -est** : deficient in vitality : SLUGGISH

loin \ˈlȯin\ *n* [ME *loyne*, fr. AF *loigne*, fr. VL **lumbea*, fr. L *lumbus*] **1** : the part of the body on each side of the spinal column and between the hip and the lower ribs; *also* : a cut of meat from this part of an animal **2** *pl* : the pubic region; *also* : the organs of reproduction

loin·cloth \-ˌklȯth\ *n* : a cloth worn about the loins often as the sole article of clothing in warm climates

loi·ter \ˈlȯi-tər\ *vb* **1** : LINGER **2** : to hang around idly
♦ **Synonyms** DAWDLE, DALLY, PROCRASTINATE, LAG, TARRY — **loi·ter·er** *n*

loll \ˈläl\ *vb* **1** : DROOP, DANGLE **2** : LOUNGE ⟨∼*ing* by the pool⟩

lol·la·pa·loo·za \ˌlä-lə-pə-ˈlü-zə\ *n* : something extraordinarily impressive or outstanding

lol·li·pop *or* **lol·ly·pop** \ˈlä-li-ˌpäp\ *n* : a lump of hard candy on a stick

lol·ly·gag \ˈlä-lē-ˌgag\ *vb* **-gagged; -gag·ging** : DAWDLE

Lond *abbr* London

lone \ˈlōn\ *adj* **1** : SOLITARY ⟨a ∼ sentinel⟩ **2** : SOLE, ONLY ⟨the ∼ theater in town⟩ **3** : ISOLATED ⟨a ∼ tree⟩

lone·ly \ˈlōn-lē\ *adj* **lone·li·er; -est** **1** : being without company **2** : UNFREQUENTED ⟨a ∼ spot⟩ **3** : LONESOME — **lone·li·ness** *n*

lon·er \ˈlō-nər\ *n* : one that avoids others

lone·some \ˈlōn-səm\ *adj* **1** : sad from lack of companionship **2** : REMOTE; *also* : SOLITARY ⟨a ∼ road⟩ — **lone·some·ly** *adv* — **lone·some·ness** *n*

¹**long** \ˈlȯŋ\ *adj* **lon·ger** \ˈlȯŋ-gər\; **lon·gest** \ˈlȯŋ-gəst\ **1** : extending for a considerable distance ⟨a ∼ corridor⟩; *also* : TALL, ELONGATED ⟨∼ legs⟩ **2** : having a specified length **3** : extending over a considerable time; *also* : TEDIOUS ⟨∼ lectures⟩ **4** : containing many items in a series ⟨a ∼ list⟩ **5** : being a syllable or speech sound of relatively great duration **6** : extending far into the future **7** : well furnished with something — used with *on* ⟨∼ on talent⟩

²**long** *adv* : for or during a long time

³**long** *n* : a long period of time

⁴**long** *vb* **longed; long·ing** \ˈlȯŋ-iŋ\ : to feel a strong desire or wish ♦ **Synonyms** YEARN, HANKER, PINE, HUNGER, THIRST

⁵**long** *abbr* longitude

long·boat \ˈlȯŋ-ˌbōt\ *n* : a large boat usu. carried by a merchant sailing ship

long·bow \-ˌbō\ *n* : a wooden bow drawn by hand and used esp. by medieval English archers

lon·gev·i·ty \län-ˈje-və-tē\ *n* [LL *longaevitas*, fr. L *longaevus* long-lived, fr. *longus* long + *aevum* age] : a long duration of individual life; *also* : length of life

long·hair \ˈlȯŋ-ˌher\ *n* **1** : a lover of classical music **2** : HIPPIE **3** : a domestic cat having long outer fur — **long–haired** \-ˌherd\ *or* **long·hair** *adj*

long·hand \-ˌhand\ *n* : HANDWRITING

long·horn \-ˌhȯrn\ *n* : any of the cattle with long horns formerly common in the southwestern U.S.

long hundredweight *n, Brit* — see WEIGHT table

long·ing \ˈlȯŋ-iŋ\ *n* : a strong desire esp. for something unattainable — **long·ing·ly** *adv*

lon·gi·tude \ˈlän-jə-ˌtüd, -ˌtyüd\ *n* : angular distance expressed usu. in degrees east or west from the prime meridian through Greenwich, England

lon·gi·tu·di·nal \ˌlän-jə-ˈtü-dᵊn-əl, -ˈtyüd-\ *adj* **1** : extending lengthwise **2** : of or relating to length — **lon·gi·tu·di·nal·ly** *adv*

long–range \ˈlȯŋ-ˈrānj\ *adj* **1** : relating to or fit for long distances **2** : involving a long period of time

long·shore·man \ˈlȯŋ-ˌshȯr-mən\ *n* : a laborer at a wharf who loads and unloads cargo

long–suf·fer·ing \-ˈsə-friŋ, -fə-riŋ\ *adj* : patiently enduring lasting offense or hardship

long–term \ˈlȯŋ-ˈtərm\ *adj* **1** : extending over or involving a long period of time **2** : constituting a financial obligation based on a term usu. of more than 10 years ⟨∼ bonds⟩

long·time \ˈlȯŋ-ˈtīm\ *adj* : of long duration ⟨∼ friends⟩

long ton *n* — see WEIGHT table

lon·gueur \lōⁿ-ˈgœr\ *n, pl* **longueurs** \same or -ˈgœrz\ [F, lit., length] : a dull tedious portion (as of a book)

long–wind·ed \ˌlȯŋ-ˈwin-dəd\ *adj* : tediously long in speaking or writing

loo·fah \ˈlü-fə\ *n* : a sponge consisting of the fibrous skeleton of a gourd

¹look \ˈlu̇k\ *vb* **1** : to exercise the power of vision : SEE ⟨∼ what I won⟩ **2** : EXPECT **3** : to have an appearance that befits ⟨∼s the part⟩ **4** : SEEM ⟨∼s thin⟩ **5** : to direct one's attention : HEED ⟨∼ at the sign⟩ **6** : POINT, FACE ⟨∼s east⟩ **7** : to show a tendency — **look after** : to take care of — **look at 1** : CONSIDER ⟨*looking at* all possibilities⟩ **2** : CONFRONT, FACE ⟨*looking at* stiff fines⟩ — **look for** : EXPECT — **look forward** : to anticipate with pleasure ⟨*look forward* to summer⟩

²look *n* **1** : the action of looking : GLANCE **2** : EXPRESSION; *also* : physical appearance **3** : ASPECT

look down *vb* : to regard with contempt — used with *on* or *upon*

looking glass *n* : MIRROR

look·out \ˈlu̇k-ˌau̇t\ *n* **1** : a person assigned to watch (as on a ship) **2** : a careful watch **3** : VIEW **4** : a matter of concern

look up *vb* **1** : IMPROVE ⟨business is *looking up*⟩ **2** : to search for in or as if in a reference work **3** : to seek out esp. for a brief visit

¹loom \ˈlüm\ *n* : a frame or machine for weaving together threads or yarns into cloth

²loom *vb* **1** : to come into sight in an unnaturally large, indistinct, or distorted form **2** : to appear in an impressively exaggerated form

loon \ˈlün\ *n* : any of several web-footed black-and-white fish-eating diving birds

loon

loo·ny *or* **loo·ney** \ˈlü-nē\ *adj* **loo·ni·er; -est** : CRAZY, FOOLISH

loony bin *n, now often offensive* : a psychiatric hospital

loop \ˈlüp\ *n* **1** : a fold or doubling of a line through which another line or hook can be passed; *also* : a loop-shaped figure or course ⟨a ∼ in a river⟩ **2** : a circular airplane maneuver executed in the vertical plane **3** : a continuously repeated segment of film, music, or sound — **loop** *vb*

loop·er \ˈlü-pər\ *n* : any of numerous rather small hairless moth caterpillars that move with a looping motion

loop·hole \ˈlüp-ˌhōl\ *n* **1** : a small opening in a wall through which firearms may be discharged **2** : a means of escape; *esp* : an ambiguity or omission that allows one to evade the intent of a law or contract

loopy \ˈlü-pē\ *adj* **loop·i·er; -est** **1** : having loops **2** : CRAZY, BIZARRE — **loop·i·ly** \-pə-lē\ *adv* — **loop·i·ness** \-pē-nəs\ *n*

¹loose \ˈlüs\ *adj* **loos·er; loos·est** **1** : not rigidly fastened **2** : free from restraint or obligation **3** : not dense or compact in structure **4** : not chaste : LEWD **5** : SLACK **6** : not precise or exact — **loose·ly** *adv* — **loose·ness** *n*

²loose *vb* **loosed; loos·ing** **1** : RELEASE **2** : UNTIE **3** : DETACH **4** : DISCHARGE **5** : RELAX, SLACKEN

³loose *adv* : LOOSELY

loos·en \ˈlü-sᵊn\ *vb* **1** : FREE **2** : to make or become loose **3** : to relax the severity of ⟨∼ rules⟩

loot \ˈlüt\ *n* [Hindi & Urdu *lūṭ*; akin to Skt *luṇṭati* he plunders] : goods taken in war or by robbery : PLUNDER — **loot** *vb* — **loot·er** *n*

¹lop \ˈläp\ *vb* **lopped; lop·ping** : to cut branches or twigs from : TRIM; *also* : to cut off

²lop *vb* **lopped; lop·ping** : to hang downward; *also* : to flop or sway loosely

lope \ˈlōp\ *n* : an easy bounding gait — **lope** *vb*

lop·sid·ed \ˈläp-ˈsī-dəd\ *adj* **1** : leaning to one side **2** : UNSYMMETRICAL — **lop·sid·ed·ly** *adv* — **lop·sid·ed·ness** *n*

lo·qua·cious \lō-ˈkwā-shəs\ *adj* : excessively talkative — **lo·quac·i·ty** \-ˈkwa-sə-tē\ *n*

¹lord \ˈlȯrd\ *n* [ME *loverd, lord,* fr. OE *hlāford,* fr. *hlāf* loaf + *weard* keeper] **1** : one having power and authority over others; *esp* : a person from whom a feudal fee or estate is held **2** *cap* : GOD **1** **3** : a man of rank or high position; *esp* : a British nobleman **4** *pl, cap* : the upper house of the British parliament **5** : a person of great power in some field

²lord *vb* : to act like a lord; *esp* : to put on airs — usu. used with *it*

lord chancellor *n, pl* **lords chancellor** : a British officer of state who presides over the House of Lords, serves as head of the British judiciary, and is usu. a leading member of the cabinet

lord·ly \-lē\ *adj* **lord·li·er; -est** **1** : DIGNIFIED; *also* : NOBLE **2** : HAUGHTY

lord·ship \-ˌship\ *n* **1** : the rank or dignity of a lord — used as a title **2** : the authority or territory of a lord

Lord's Supper *n* : COMMUNION

lore \ˈlȯr\ *n* : KNOWLEDGE; *esp* : traditional knowledge or belief

lor·gnette \lȯrn-ˈyet\ *n* [F, fr. *lorgner* to take a sidelong look at, fr. MF, fr. *lorgne* squinting] : a pair of eyeglasses or opera glasses with a handle

lorn \ˈlȯrn\ *adj* : FORSAKEN, DESOLATE

lor·ry \ˈlȯr-ē\ *n, pl* **lorries** *chiefly Brit* : MOTORTRUCK

lose \ˈlüz\ *vb* **lost** \ˈlȯst\; **los·ing** \ˈlü-ziŋ\ **1** : DESTROY **2** : to miss from a customary place : MISLAY **3** : to suffer deprivation of **4** : to fail to use : WASTE ⟨no time to ∼⟩ **5** : to fail to win or obtain ⟨∼ the game⟩ **6** : to fail to keep or maintain ⟨∼ his balance⟩ **7** : to wander from ⟨∼ her way⟩ **8** : to get rid of ⟨should ∼ the beard⟩ — **los·er** *n* — **lose it** **1** : to go crazy **2** : to fail to keep one's composure

loss \ˈlȯs\ *n* **1** : RUIN **2** : the harm resulting from losing **3** : something that is lost **4** *pl* : killed, wounded, or captured soldiers **5** : failure to win **6** : an amount by which the cost exceeds the selling price **7** : decrease in amount or degree

loss leader *n* : an article sold at a loss in order to draw customers

lost \ˈlȯst\ *adj* **1** : not used, won, or claimed **2** : no longer possessed or known **3** : ruined or destroyed physically or morally **4** : DENIED; *also* : HARDENED **5** : unable to find the way; *also* : HELPLESS **6** : ABSORBED, RAPT **7** : not appreciated or understood ⟨his jokes were ∼ on me⟩ **8** : made obscure : OVERLOOKED ⟨∼ in translation⟩ **9** : FUTILE ⟨a ∼ cause⟩

lot \ˈlät\ *n* **1** : an object used in deciding something by chance; *also* : the use of lots to decide something **2** : SHARE, PORTION; *also* : FORTUNE, FATE **3** : a plot of land **4** : a group of individuals : SET **5** : a considerable quantity ⟨a ∼ of trouble⟩

loth *var of* LOATH

lo·ti \ˈlō-tē\ *n, pl* **ma·lo·ti** \mə-ˈlō-tē\ — see MONEY table

lo·tion \ˈlō-shən\ *n* : a liquid preparation for cosmetic and external medicinal use

lot·tery \ˈlä-tə-rē\ *n, pl* **-ter·ies** **1** : a drawing of lots in which prizes are given to the winning names or numbers **2** : a matter determined by chance

lo·tus \ˈlō-təs\ *n* **1** : a fruit held in Greek legend to cause dreamy contentment and forgetfulness **2** : any of various water lilies represented esp. in ancient Egyptian and Hindu art **3** : any of several leguminous forage plants

loud \ˈlau̇d\ *adj* **1** : marked by intensity or volume of sound **2** : CLAMOROUS, NOISY **3** : obtrusive or offensive in color or pattern ⟨a ∼ tie⟩ — **loud** *adv* — **loud·ly** *adv* — **loud·ness** *n*

loud-mouthed \-ˌmau̇tht, -ˌmau̇thd\ *adj* : given to loud offensive talk

loud·speak·er \-ˌspē-kər\ *n* : a device that changes electrical signals into sound

¹lounge \ˈlau̇nj\ *vb* **lounged; loung·ing** : to act or move lazily or listlessly

²lounge *n* **1** : a room with comfortable furniture; *also* : a room (as in a theater) with lounging, smoking, and toilet facilities **2** : a long couch

lour, loury *var of* LOWER, LOWERY

louse \\'laùs\ *n, pl* **lice** \\'līs\ **1** : any of various small wingless usu. flattened insects parasitic on warm-blooded animals **2** : a plant pest (as an aphid) **3** *pl* **lous·es** \\'laù-sǝz\ : a contemptible person

lousy \\'laù-zē\ *adj* **lous·i·er; -est** **1** : infested with lice **2** : POOR, INFERIOR **3** : somewhat ill **4** : amply supplied ⟨~ with money⟩ — **lous·i·ly** \-zǝ-lē\ *adv* — **lous·i·ness** \-zē-nǝs\ *n*

lout \\'laùt\ *n* : a stupid awkward fellow — **lout·ish** *adj* — **lout·ish·ly** *adv*

lou·ver *or* **lou·vre** \\'lü-vǝr\ *n* **1** : an opening having parallel slanted slats to allow flow of air but to exclude rain or sun or to provide privacy; *also* : a slat in such an opening **2** : a device with movable slats for controlling the flow of air or light

¹love \\'lǝv\ *n* **1** : strong affection **2** : warm attachment ⟨~ of the sea⟩ **3** : attraction based on sexual desire **4** : a beloved person **5** : unselfish loyal and benevolent concern for others **6** : a score of zero in tennis — **love·less** *adj*

²love *vb* **loved; lov·ing** **1** : CHERISH **2** : to feel a passion, devotion, or tenderness for **3** : CARESS **4** : to take pleasure in ⟨~s to play bridge⟩ — **lov·able** *also* **love·able** \\'lǝ-vǝ-bǝl\ *adj* — **lov·er** *n*

love·bird \\'lǝv-ˌbǝrd\ *n* : any of various small usu. gray or green parrots that seem to show caring behavior for their mates

love·lorn \-ˌlòrn\ *adj* : deprived of love or of a lover

love·ly \\'lǝv-lē\ *adj* **love·li·er; -est** : BEAUTIFUL — **love·li·ly** \\'lǝv-lǝ-lē\ *adv* — **love·li·ness** *n* — **lovely** *adv*

love·mak·ing \-ˌmā-kiŋ\ *n* **1** : COURTSHIP **2** : sexual activity; *esp* : COPULATION

love·sick \-ˌsik\ *adj* **1** : YEARNING ⟨a ~ suitor⟩ **2** : expressing a lover's longing — **love·sick·ness** *n*

lov·ing \\'lǝ-viŋ\ *adj* **1** : AFFECTIONATE **2** : PAINSTAKING — **lov·ing·ly** *adv*

¹low \\'lō\ *vb* : MOO

²low *n* : MOO

³low *adj* **low·er** \\'lō-ǝr\; **low·est** \\'lō-ǝst\ **1** : not high or tall ⟨~ wall⟩; *also* : DÉCOLLETÉ **2** : situated or passing below the normal level or surface ⟨~ ground⟩; *also* : marking a nadir **3** : not loud ⟨~ voice⟩ **4** : being near the equator **5** : humble in status **6** : WEAK; *also* : DEPRESSED **7** : STRICKEN, PROSTRATE **8** : less than usual in number, amount, or value; *also* : of lesser degree than average **9** : falling short of a standard **10** : UNFAVORABLE — **low** *adv* — **low·ness** *n*

⁴low *n* **1** : something that is low **2** : a region of low barometric pressure **3** : the arrangement of gears in an automobile transmission that gives the slowest speed and greatest power

low·ball \\'lō-ˌbòl\ *vb* : to give a deceptively low price, cost estimate, or offer to

low beam *n* : a vehicle headlight beam with short-range focus

low blow *n* : an unprincipled attack

low·brow \\'lō-ˌbraù\ *adj* : having little taste or intellectual interest ⟨~ humor⟩ — **lowbrow** *n*

low–density lipoprotein *n* : LDL

low–down \-ˌdaùn\ *n* : pertinent and esp. guarded information

low–down \-ˌdaùn\ *adj* **1** : MEAN, CONTEMPTIBLE **2** : deeply emotional

low–end \-ˌend\ *adj* : of, relating to, or being the lowest-priced merchandise in a manufacturer's line

¹low·er *also* **lour** \\'laù-(ǝ)r\ *vb* **1** : FROWN **2** : to become dark, gloomy, and threatening — **lower** *also* **lour** *n*

²low·er \\'lō-ǝr\ *adj* **1** : relatively low (as in rank) **2** : SOUTHERN ⟨the ~ states⟩ **3** : less advanced in the scale of evolutionary development ⟨~ animals⟩ **4** : situated beneath the earth's surface **5** : constituting the popular and more representative branch of a bicameral legislative body

³low·er \\'lō-ǝr\ *vb* **1** : DROP; *also* : DIMINISH **2** : to let descend by its own weight; *also* : to reduce the height of **3** : to reduce in value, number, or amount **4** : DEGRADE; *also* : HUMBLE

low·er·case \ˌlō-ǝr-'kās\ *adj* : being a letter that belongs to or conforms to the series a, b, c, etc., rather than A, B, C, etc. — **lowercase** *n*

lower class *n* : a social class occupying a position below the middle class and having the lowest status in a society — **lower–class** \-'klas\ *adj*

low·er·most \\'lō-ǝr-ˌmōst\ *adj* : LOWEST

low·ery *also* **loury** \\'laù-(ǝ)rē\ *adj* : GLOOMY, LOWERING ⟨a ~ sky⟩

lowest common denominator *n* **1** : LEAST COMMON DENOMINATOR **2** : something designed to appeal to a low-brow audience; *also* : such an audience

lowest common multiple *n* : LEAST COMMON MULTIPLE

low–key \\'lō-'kē\ *also* **low–keyed** \-'kēd\ *adj* : of low intensity : RESTRAINED

low·land \\'lō-lǝnd, -ˌland\ *n* : low and usu. level country

low–lev·el \\'lō-'le-vǝl\ *adj* **1** : being of low importance or rank **2** : being or relating to nuclear waste of low concentration

low·life \\'lō-ˌlīf\ *n, pl* **low·lifes** \-ˌlīfs\ *also* **low·lives** \-ˌlīvz\ : a person of low social status or moral character

low·ly \\'lō-lē\ *adj* **low·li·er; -est** **1** : HUMBLE, MEEK **2** : ranking low in some hierarchy — **low·li·ness** *n*

low–rise \\'lō-'rīz\ *adj* **1** : having few stories and not equipped with elevators ⟨a ~ building⟩ **2** : of, relating to, or characterized by low-rise buildings

low–slung \\'lō-ˌslǝŋ\ *adj* : relatively low to the ground or floor ⟨a ~ building⟩ ⟨~ pants⟩

low–tech \\'lō-'tek\ *adj* : technologically simple or unsophisticated

¹lox \\'läks\ *n* : liquid oxygen

²lox *n, pl* **lox** *or* **lox·es** : salmon cured in brine and sometimes smoked

loy·al \\'lòi-(ǝ)l\ *adj* [MF, fr. OF *leial, leel*, fr. L *legalis* legal] **1** : faithful in allegiance to one's government **2** : faithful esp. to a cause or ideal : CONSTANT — **loy·al·ly** \\'lòi-ǝ-lē\ *adv* — **loy·al·ty** \\'lòi-(ǝ)l-tē\ *n*

loy·al·ist \\'lòi-ǝ-list\ *n* : one who is or remains loyal to a political party, government, or sovereign

loz·enge \\'lä-zǝnj\ *n* **1** : a diamond-shaped figure **2** : a small flat often medicated candy

LP *abbr* low pressure

LPG *abbr* liquefied petroleum gas

LPGA *abbr* Ladies Professional Golf Association

LPN \ˌel-'pē-'en\ *n* : LICENSED PRACTICAL NURSE

Lr *symbol* Lawrencium

LSD \ˌel-(ˌ)es-'dē\ *n* [G *Lysergsäure-Diäthylamid* lysergic acid diethylamide] : an illicit and highly potent hallucinogenic drug derived from ergot or produced synthetically

lt *abbr* light

Lt *abbr* lieutenant

LT *abbr* long ton

LTC *or* **Lt Col** *abbr* lieutenant colonel

Lt Comdr *abbr* lieutenant commander

ltd *abbr* limited

LTG *or* **Lt Gen** *abbr* lieutenant general

LTJG *abbr* lieutenant, junior grade

ltr *abbr* letter

Lu *symbol* lutetium

lu·au \\'lü-ˌaù\ *n* : a Hawaiian feast

lub *abbr* lubricant; lubricating

lub·ber \\'lǝ-bǝr\ *n* **1** : LOUT **2** : an unskilled seaman — **lub·ber·ly** *adj*

lube \\'lüb\ *n* : LUBRICANT; *also* : an application of a lubricant

lu·bri·cant \\'lü-bri-kǝnt\ *n* : a material capable of reducing friction when applied between moving parts

lu·bri·cate \\'lü-brǝ-ˌkāt\ *vb* **-cat·ed; -cat·ing** : to apply a lubricant to — **lu·bri·ca·tion** \ˌlü-brǝ-'kā-shǝn\ *n* — **lu·bri·ca·tor** \\'lü-brǝ-ˌkā-tǝr\ *n*

lu·bri·cious \lü-'bri-shǝs\ *or* **lu·bri·cous** \\'lü-bri-kǝs\ *adj* **1** : SMOOTH, SLIPPERY **2** : LECHEROUS; *also* : SALACIOUS — **lu·bric·i·ty** \lü-'bri-sǝ-tē\ *n*

lu·cent \\'lü-sᵊnt\ *adj* **1** : LUMINOUS **2** : CLEAR, LUCID — **lu·cent·ly** *adv*

lu·cerne \lü-'sǝrn\ *n, chiefly Brit* : ALFALFA

lu·cid \\'lü-sǝd\ *adj* **1** : SHINING **2** : mentally sound **3** : easily understood ⟨a ~ explanation⟩ — **lu·cid·i·ty** \lü-'si-dǝ-tē\ *n* — **lu·cid·ly** *adv* — **lu·cid·ness** *n*

Lu·ci·fer \\'lü-sǝ-fǝr\ *n* [ME, the morning star, a fallen rebel archangel, the Devil, fr. OE, fr. L, the morning star, fr. *lucifer* light-bearing] : DEVIL, SATAN

¹luck \\'lǝk\ *n* **1** : CHANCE, FORTUNE **2** : good fortune — **luck·less** *adj*

²luck *vb* **1** : to prosper or succeed esp. through chance or good fortune — usu. used with *out* **2** : to come upon something desirable by chance — usu. used with *out, on, onto,* or *into*

luck·i·ly \'lə-kə-lē\ *adv* **1** : in a lucky manner **2** : FORTUNATELY 2

lucky \'lə-kē\ *adj* **luck·i·er; -est 1** : favored by luck : FORTUNATE **2** : FORTUITOUS **3** : seeming to bring good luck ⟨a ~ penny⟩ — **luck·i·ness** *n*

lu·cra·tive \'lü-krə-tiv\ *adj* : PROFITABLE ⟨~ business deals⟩ — **lu·cra·tive·ly** *adv* — **lu·cra·tive·ness** *n*

lu·cre \'lü-kər\ *n* [ME, fr. AF, fr. L *lucrum*] : PROFIT; *also* : MONEY

lu·cu·bra·tion \,lü-kyə-'brā-shən, -kə-\ *n* : laborious study : MEDITATION

Lud·dite \'lə-,dīt\ *n* [perh. fr. Ned *Ludd*, 18th cent. Eng. workman who destroyed a knitting frame] : one who is opposed to technological change

lu·di·crous \'lü-də-krəs\ *adj* : LAUGHABLE, RIDICULOUS ⟨a ~ idea⟩ — **lu·di·crous·ly** *adv* — **lu·di·crous·ness** *n*

luff \'ləf\ *vb* : to turn the head of a ship toward the wind

¹lug \'ləg\ *vb* **lugged; lug·ging 1** : DRAG, PULL **2** : to carry laboriously

²lug *n* **1** : a projecting piece (as for fastening, support, or traction) **2** : a nut securing a wheel on an automobile

lug·gage \'lə-gij\ *n* : containers (as suitcases) for carrying personal belongings : BAGGAGE

lu·gu·bri·ous \lu-'gü-brē-əs\ *adj* : mournful often to an exaggerated degree ⟨~ music⟩ — **lu·gu·bri·ous·ly** *adv* — **lu·gu·bri·ous·ness** *n*

Luke \'lük\ *n* — see BIBLE table

luke·warm \'lük-'wȯrm\ *adj* **1** : moderately warm : TEPID **2** : not enthusiastic ⟨~ praise⟩ — **luke·warm·ly** *adv*

¹lull \'ləl\ *vb* **1** : SOOTHE, CALM **2** : to cause to relax vigilance

²lull *n* **1** : a temporary calm (as during a storm) **2** : a temporary drop in activity ⟨a ~ in sales⟩

lul·la·by \'lə-lə-,bī\ *n, pl* **-bies** : a song to lull children to sleep

lu·ma \,lü-'mä\ *n* — see *dram* at MONEY table

lum·ba·go \,ləm-'bā-gō\ *n* : acute or chronic pain in the lower back

lum·bar \'ləm-bər, -,bär\ *adj* : of, relating to, or constituting the loins or the vertebrae between the thoracic vertebrae and sacrum ⟨~ region⟩

¹lum·ber \'ləm-bər\ *vb* : to move heavily or clumsily ⟨an elephant ~ed along the road⟩

²lumber *n* **1** : surplus or disused articles that are stored away **2** : timber or logs esp. when dressed for use

³lumber *vb* : to cut logs; *also* : to saw logs into lumber — **lum·ber·man** \-mən\ *n*

lum·ber·jack \-,jak\ *n* : LOGGER

lum·ber·yard \-,yärd\ *n* : a place where lumber is kept for sale

lu·mi·nary \'lü-mə-,ner-ē\ *n, pl* **-nar·ies 1** : a very famous person **2** : a source of light; *esp* : a celestial body

lu·mi·nes·cence \,lü-mə-'ne-s⁸ns\ *n* : the low-temperature emission of light (as by a chemical or physiological process); *also* : such light — **lu·mi·nes·cent** \-s⁸nt\ *adj*

lu·mi·nous \'lü-mə-nəs\ *adj* **1** : emitting light; *also* : LIGHTED **2** : CLEAR, INTELLIGIBLE **3** : ILLUSTRIOUS — **lu·mi·nance** \-nəns\ *n* — **lu·mi·nos·i·ty** \,lü-mə-'nä-sə-tē\ *n* — **lu·mi·nous·ly** *adv*

lum·mox \'lə-məks\ *n* : a clumsy person

¹lump \'ləmp\ *n* **1** : a piece or mass of indefinite size and shape **2** : AGGREGATE, TOTALITY **3** : a usu. abnormal swelling — **lump·ish** *adj* — **lumpy** *adj*

²lump *vb* **1** : to heap together in a lump **2** : to form into lumps

³lump *adj* : not divided into parts ⟨a ~ sum⟩

lump·ec·to·my \,ləm-'pek-tə-mē\ *n, pl* **-mies** : excision of a breast tumor

lu·na·cy \'lü-nə-sē\ *n, pl* **-cies 1** : INSANITY **2** : extreme folly

lu·nar \'lü-nər\ *adj* : of or relating to the moon ⟨a ~ eclipse⟩

lu·na·tic \'lü-nə-,tik\ *adj* [ME *lunatik*, fr. AF & LL; AF *lunatik*, fr. LL *lunaticus*, fr. L *luna* moon; fr. the belief that lunacy fluctuated with the phases of the moon] **1** : INSANE; *also* : used for insane persons **2** : extremely foolish — **lunatic** *n*

¹lunch \'lənch\ *n* **1** : a light meal usu. eaten in the middle of the day **2** : the food prepared for a lunch

²lunch *vb* : to eat lunch

lun·cheon \'lən-chən\ *n* : a usu. formal lunch

lun·cheon·ette \,lən-chə-'net\ *n* : a small restaurant serving light lunches

lunch·room \'lənch-,rüm, -,rum\ *n* **1** : LUNCHEONETTE **2** : a room (as in a school) where lunches are sold and eaten or lunches brought from home may be eaten

lu·nette \lü-'net\ *n* : something shaped like a crescent

lung \'ləŋ\ *n* **1** : one of the usu. paired baglike breathing organs in the chest of an air-breathing vertebrate **2** : a mechanical device to promote breathing and make it easier — **lunged** \'ləŋd\ *adj*

¹lunge \'lənj\ *n* **1** : a sudden thrust or pass (as with a sword) **2** : a sudden forward stride or leap — **lunge** *vb*

lu·pine \'lü-pən\ *n* : any of a genus of leguminous plants with long upright clusters of pealike flowers

lu·pus \'lü-pəs\ *n* [ML, fr. L, wolf] : any of several diseases characterized by skin lesions; *esp* : SYSTEMIC LUPUS ERYTHEMATOSUS

lurch \'lərch\ *n* : a sudden swaying or tipping movement — **lurch** *vb*

¹lure \'lur\ *n* **1** : ENTICEMENT; *also* : APPEAL ⟨the ~ of easy money⟩ **2** : an artificial bait for catching fish

²lure *vb* **lured; lur·ing** : to draw on with a promise of pleasure or gain

lu·rid \'lur-əd\ *adj* **1** : GRUESOME; *also* : SENSATIONAL **2** : wan and ghostly pale in appearance **3** : shining with the red glow of fire seen through smoke or cloud ◆ **Synonyms** GHASTLY, GRISLY, GRIM, HORRIBLE, MACABRE — **lu·rid·ly** *adv*

lurk \'lərk\ *vb* **1** : to move furtively : SNEAK **2** : to lie concealed

lus·cious \'lə-shəs\ *adj* **1** : having a pleasingly sweet taste or smell **2** : sensually appealing ⟨a ~ voice⟩ — **lus·cious·ly** *adv* — **lus·cious·ness** *n*

¹lush \'ləsh\ *adj* : having or covered with abundant growth ⟨~ pastures⟩

²lush *n* : a habitual heavy drinker

lust \'ləst\ *n* **1** : usu. intense or unbridled sexual desire : LASCIVIOUSNESS **2** : an intense longing ⟨a ~ to succeed⟩ — **lust** *vb* — **lust·ful** *adj*

lus·ter *or* **lus·tre** \'ləs-tər\ *n* **1** : a shine or sheen esp. from reflected light **2** : BRIGHTNESS, GLITTER **3** : GLORY, SPLENDOR — **lus·ter·less** *adj* — **lus·trous** \-trəs\ *adj*

lus·tral \'ləs-trəl\ *adj* : serving or intended to purify ⟨~ water⟩

lusty \'ləs-tē\ *adj* **lust·i·er; -est 1** : full of vitality : ROBUST — **lust·i·ly** \'ləs-tə-lē\ *adv* — **lust·i·ness** \-tē-nəs\ *n*

lute \'lüt\ *n* : a stringed musical instrument with a large pear-shaped body and a fretted fingerboard — **lu·te·nist** *or* **lu·ta·nist** \'lü-tə-nist\ *n*

lu·te·tium *also* **lu·te·cium** \lü-'tē-shē-əm, -shəm\ *n* : a metallic chemical element

Lu·ther·an \'lü-thə-rən\ *n* : a member of a Protestant denomination adhering to the doctrines of Martin Luther — **Lu·ther·an·ism** \-rə-,ni-zəm\ *n*

lux·u·ri·ant \,ləg-'zhur-ē-ənt, ,lək-'shur-\ *adj* **1** : yielding or growing abundantly : LUSH, PRODUCTIVE ⟨~ vegetation⟩ **2** : abundantly rich and varied; *also* : FLORID ⟨~ fabric⟩ ◆ **Synonyms** EXUBERANT, LAVISH, OPULENT, PRODIGAL, PROFUSE, RIOTOUS — **lux·u·ri·ance** \-ē-əns\ *n* — **lux·u·ri·ant·ly** *adv*

lux·u·ri·ate \-ē-,āt\ *vb* **-at·ed; -at·ing 1** : to grow profusely **2** : REVEL

lux·u·ry \'lək-shə-rē, 'ləg-zhə-\ *n, pl* **-ries 1** : great ease and comfort **2** : something adding to pleasure or comfort but not absolutely necessary — **lux·u·ri·ous** \,ləg-'zhur-ē-əs, ,lək-'shur-\ *adj* — **lux·u·ri·ous·ly** *adv*

lv *abbr* leave

Lv *symbol* livermorium

lwei \lə-'wā\ *n, pl* **lwei** : a former monetary subunit of the kwanza

LWV *abbr* League of Women Voters

¹-ly \lē\ *adj suffix* **1** : like in appearance, manner, or nature ⟨queen*ly*⟩ **2** : characterized by regular recurrence in (specified) units of time : every ⟨hour*ly*⟩ ⟨week*ly*⟩

²-ly *adv suffix* **1** : in a (specified) manner ⟨slow*ly*⟩ **2** : from a (specified) point of view ⟨grammatical*ly*⟩

ly·ce·um \lī-'sē-əm, 'lī-sē-\ *n* **1** : a hall for public lectures **2** : an association providing public lectures, concerts, and entertainments

ly·chee or **li·tchi** \'lē-chē, 'lī-\ n [Ch(Beijing) *lìzhī*] **1** : an oval fruit with a hard scaly outer covering, a small hard seed, and edible flesh **2** : an Asian tree bearing lychees
lye \'lī\ n : a corrosive alkaline substance used esp. in making soap
ly·ing \'lī-iŋ\ adj : UNTRUTHFUL, FALSE
ly·ing–in \ˌlī-iŋ-'in\ n, pl **lyings–in** or **lying–ins** : the state during and consequent to childbirth : CONFINEMENT
Lyme disease \'līm-\ n [*Lyme*, Connecticut, where it was first reported] : an acute inflammatory disease that is caused by a spirochete transmitted by ticks, is characterized usu. by chills and fever, and if left untreated may result in joint pain, arthritis, and cardiac and neurological disorders
lymph \'limf\ n : a usu. clear fluid consisting chiefly of blood plasma and white blood cells, circulating in thin-walled tubes (**lymphatic vessels**), and bathing the body tissues — **lym·phat·ic** \lim-'fa-tik\ adj
lymph·ade·nop·a·thy \ˌlim-ˌfa-də-'nä-pə-thē\ n, pl **-thies** : abnormal enlargement of the lymph nodes
lymph node n : any of the rounded masses of lymphoid tissue surrounded by a capsule of connective tissue
lym·pho·cyte \'lim-fə-ˌsīt\ n : any of the white blood cells arising from lymphoid tissue that are typically found in lymph and blood and that include the cellular mediators (as a B cell or a T cell) of immunity — **lym·pho·cyt·ic** \ˌlim-fə-'si-tik\ adj
lym·phoid \'lim-ˌfóid\ adj **1** : of, relating to, or being tissue (as of the lymph nodes) containing lymphocytes **2** : of, relating to, or resembling lymph
lym·pho·ma \lim-'fō-mə\ n, pl **-mas** also **-ma·ta** \-mə-tə\ : a usu. malignant tumor of lymphoid tissue
lynch \'linch\ vb : to put to death by mob action without legal sanction or due process of law — **lynch·er** n
lynx \'liŋks\ n, pl **lynx** or **lynx·es** : any of several wildcats with a short tail, long legs, and usu. tufted ears
lyre \'lī(-ə)r\ n : a stringed musical instrument of the harp class having a U-shaped frame and used by the ancient Greeks
¹lyr·ic \'lir-ik\ n **1** : a lyric poem **2** pl : the words of a popular song — **lyr·i·cal** \-i-kəl\ adj
²lyric adj **1** : suitable for singing : MELODIC **2** : expressing direct and usu. intense personal emotion ⟨~ poetry⟩
ly·ser·gic acid di·eth·yl·am·ide \lə-'sər-jik . . . ˌdī-ˌe-thə-'la-ˌmīd, lī-, -'la-məd\ n : LSD
LZ abbr landing zone

¹m \'em\ n, pl **m's** or **ms** \'emz\ often cap : the 13th letter of the English alphabet
²m abbr, often cap **1** Mach **2** male **3** married **4** masculine **5** medium **6** [L *meridies*] noon **7** meter **8** mile **9** [L *mille*] thousand **10** minute **11** month **12** moon
ma \'mä, 'mȯ\ n : MOTHER
MA abbr **1** [ML *magister artium*] master of arts **2** Massachusetts **3** mental age
ma'am \'mam, after "yes" often əm\ n : MADAM
Mac abbr Machabees
Mac or **Macc** abbr Maccabees
ma·ca·bre \mə-'käb; 'kä-brə, -bər\ adj [F] **1** : having death as a subject **2** : GRUESOME **3** : HORRIBLE
mac·ad·am \mə-'ka-dəm\ n [John L. *McAdam* †1836 Brit. engineer] : a roadway or pavement of small closely packed broken stone — **mac·ad·am·ize** \-də-ˌmīz\ vb
mac·a·da·mia nut \ˌma-kə-'dā-mē-ə-\ n : a hard-shelled richly flavored nut of any of several Australian trees
ma·caque \mə-'kak, -'käk\ n : any of a genus of short-tailed chiefly Asian monkeys; esp : RHESUS MONKEY
mac·a·ro·ni \ˌma-kə-'rō-nē\ n **1** : pasta made chiefly of wheat flour and shaped in the form of slender tubes **2** pl **-nis** or **-nies** : FOP, DANDY
mac·a·roon \ˌma-kə-'rün\ n : a small cookie made chiefly of egg whites, sugar, and ground almonds or coconut
ma·caw \mə-'kȯ\ n : any of numerous parrots of Central and So. America
Mac·ca·bees \'ma-kə-ˌbēz\ n — see BIBLE table
¹mace \'mās\ n : a spice made from the fibrous coating of the nutmeg
²mace n **1** : a heavy often spiked club used as a weapon esp. in the Middle Ages **2** : an ornamental staff carried as a symbol of authority
mac·er·ate \'ma-sə-ˌrāt\ vb **-at·ed; -at·ing 1** : to cause to waste away **2** : to soften by steeping or soaking so as to separate the parts — **mac·er·a·tion** \ˌma-sə-'rā-shən\ n
Mac·Guf·fin or **Mc·Guf·fin** \mə-'gə-fən\ n : an object, event, or character whose main purpose is to advance the plot of a motion picture
mach abbr machine; machinery; machinist
Mach \'mäk\ n : a speed expressed by a Mach number
Mach·a·bees \'ma-kə-ˌbēz\ n : MACCABEES
ma·chete \mə-'she-tē\ n : a large heavy knife used for cutting sugarcane and underbrush and as a weapon
Ma·chi·a·vel·lian \ˌma-kē-ə-'ve-lē-ən\ adj [Niccolò *Machiavelli*, †1527 Ital. political philosopher] : characterized by cunning, duplicity, and bad faith — **Ma·chi·a·vel·lian·ism** n
mach·i·na·tion \ˌma-kə-'nā-shən, ˌma-shə-\ n : an act of planning esp. to do harm; esp : PLOT — **mach·i·nate** \'ma-kə-ˌnāt, 'ma-shə-\ vb
¹ma·chine \mə-'shēn\ n **1** : CONVEYANCE, VEHICLE; esp : AUTOMOBILE **2** : a combination of mechanical parts that transmit forces, motion, and energy one to another **3** : an instrument (as a lever) for transmitting or modifying force or motion **4** : an electrical, electronic, or mechanical device for performing a task ⟨a sewing ~⟩ **5** : a highly organized political group under the leadership of a boss or small clique
²machine vb **ma·chined; ma·chin·ing** : to shape or finish by machine-operated tools — **ma·chin·able** \-'shē-nə-bəl\ adj
machine gun n : an automatic gun capable of rapid continuous firing — **machine–gun** vb — **machine gunner** n
machine language n : the set of symbolic instruction codes used to represent operations and data in a machine (as a computer)
machine–readable adj : directly usable by a computer
ma·chin·ery \mə-'shē-nə-rē\ n, pl **-er·ies 1** : MACHINES; also : the working parts of a machine **2** : the means by which something is done
ma·chin·ist \mə-'shē-nist\ n : a person who makes or works on machines
ma·chis·mo \mä-'chēz-(ˌ)mō, -'chiz-\ n : a strong or exaggerated pride in one's masculinity
Mach number \'mäk-\ n : a number representing the ratio of the speed of a body (as an aircraft) to the speed of sound in the surrounding atmosphere
ma·cho \'mä-chō\ adj [Sp, lit., male, fr. L *masculus*] : characterized by machismo
mack·er·el \'ma-kə-rəl\ n, pl **mackerel** or **mackerels** : a No. Atlantic food fish greenish above and silvery below
mack·i·naw \'ma-kə-ˌnȯ\ n : a short heavy plaid coat
mack·in·tosh also **mac·in·tosh** \'ma-kən-ˌtäsh\ n **1** chiefly Brit : RAINCOAT **2** : a lightweight waterproof fabric
mac·ra·mé \'ma-krə-ˌmā\ n [ultim. fr. Ar *miqrama* coverlet] : a coarse lace or fringe made by knotting threads or cords in a geometrical pattern
¹mac·ro \'ma-(ˌ)krō\ adj : very large; also : involving large quantities or being on a large scale ⟨~ economic policies⟩
²macro n, pl **macros** : a single computer instruction that stands for a sequence of operations
mac·ro·bi·ot·ic \ˌma-krō-bī-'ä-tik, -bē-\ adj : relating to

or being a very restricted diet (as one containing chiefly whole cereals or grains)
mac·ro·cosm \'ma-krə-ˌkä-zəm\ *n* : the great world : UNIVERSE
ma·cron \'mā-ˌkrän, 'ma-\ *n* : a mark ‾ placed over a vowel (as in \māk\) to show that the vowel is long
mac·ro·scop·ic \ˌma-krə-'skä-pik\ *adj* : visible to the naked eye — **mac·ro·scop·i·cal·ly** \-pi-k(ə-)lē\ *adv*
mac·u·la \'ma-kyə-lə\ *n, pl* **-lae** \-ˌlē, -ˌlī\ *also* **-las** : an anatomical spot distinguishable from surrounding tissues — **mac·u·lar** \-lər\ *adj*
mad \'mad\ *adj* **mad·der; mad·dest** 1 : disordered in mind : INSANE 2 : being rash and foolish 3 : FURIOUS, ENRAGED 4 : carried away by enthusiasm 〈∼ about football〉 5 : RABID 6 : marked by wild gaiety and merriment 7 : FRANTIC 〈a ∼ rush〉 — **mad·ly** *adv* — **mad·ness** *n*
mad·am \'ma-dəm\ *n* 1 *pl* **mes·dames** \mā-'däm\ — used as a form of polite address to a woman 2 *pl* **mad·ams** : the female head of a house of prostitution
ma·dame \mə-'dam, *before a surname also* 'ma-dəm\ *n, pl* **mes·dames** \mā-'däm\ : MISTRESS — used as a title equivalent to *Mrs.* for a married woman not of English-speaking nationality
mad·cap \'mad-ˌkap\ *adj* : WILD, RECKLESS 〈a ∼ scheme〉 — **madcap** *n*
mad cow disease *n* : a fatal encephalopathy of cattle that affects the nervous system causing the brain tissue to resemble a porous sponge
mad·den \'ma-dᵊn\ *vb* : to make mad — **mad·den·ing·ly** *adv*
mad·der \'ma-dər\ *n* : a Eurasian herb with yellow flowers and fleshy red roots; *also* : its root or a dye prepared from it
made *past and past part of* MAKE
Ma·dei·ra \mə-'dir-ə\ *n* : an amber-colored dessert wine
ma·de·moi·selle \ˌmad-mə-mə-'zel, -mwə-, mam-'zel\ *n, pl* **ma·de·moi·selles** \-'zelz\ *or* **mes·de·moi·selles** \ˌmā-də-me-'zel, -mwə-\ : an unmarried girl or woman — used as a title for an unmarried woman not of English-speaking nationality
made–to–measure *adj* : CUSTOM-MADE
made–up \'mād-'əp\ *adj* 1 : fancifully conceived or falsely devised 2 : marked by the use of makeup
mad·house \'mad-ˌhau̇s\ *n* 1 : a place for the detention and care of the insane 2 : a place of great uproar
mad·man \'mad-ˌman, -mən\ *n* : LUNATIC
Ma·don·na \mə-'dä-nə\ *n* : a representation (as a picture or statue) of the Virgin Mary
ma·dras \'ma-drəs; ˌmə-'dras, -'dräs\ *n* [*Madras,* India] : a fine usu. cotton fabric with various designs (as plaid)
ma·dras·sa *or* **ma·dra·sa** \mə-'dra-sə, -'drä-\ *n* : a Muslim school, college, or university that is often part of a mosque
mad·ri·gal \'ma-dri-gəl\ *n* [It *madrigale*] 1 : a short lyrical poem in a strict poetic form 2 : an elaborate part-song esp. of the 16th and 17th centuries
mad·wom·an \'mad-ˌwu̇-mən\ *n* : a woman who is insane
mael·strom \'māl-strəm\ *n* 1 : a violent whirlpool 2 : TUMULT
mae·stro \'mī-strō\ *n, pl* **maestros** *or* **mae·stri** \-ˌstrē\ [It] : a master in an art; *esp* : an eminent composer, conductor, or teacher of music
Ma·fia \'mä-fē-ə\ *n* [It] : a secret criminal society of Sicily or Italy; *also* : a similar organization elsewhere
ma·fi·o·so \ˌmä-fē-'ō-(ˌ)sō\ *n, pl* **-si** \-(ˌ)sē\ : a member of the Mafia
¹mag \'mag\ *n* : MAGAZINE
²mag *abbr* 1 magnetism 2 magneto 3 magnitude
mag·a·zine \'ma-gə-ˌzēn\ *n* [MF, fr. Old Occitan, fr. Ar *makhāzin,* pl. of *makhzan* storehouse] 1 : a storehouse esp. for military supplies 2 : a place for keeping gunpowder in a fort or ship 3 : a publication usu. containing stories, articles, or poems and issued periodically 4 : a container in a gun for holding cartridges; *also* : a chamber (as on a camera) for film
ma·gen·ta \mə-'jen-tə\ *n* : a deep purplish red color
mag·got \'ma-gət\ *n* : the legless wormlike larva of a dipteran fly — **mag·goty** *adj*
ma·gi \'mā-ˌjī\ *n pl, often cap* : the three wise men from the East who paid homage to the infant Jesus
mag·ic \'ma-jik\ *n* 1 : the use of means (as charms or

spells) believed to have supernatural power over natural forces 2 : an extraordinary power or influence seemingly from a supernatural force 3 : SLEIGHT OF HAND — **magic** *adj* — **mag·i·cal** \-ji-kəl\ *adj* — **mag·i·cal·ly** \-ji-k(ə-)lē\ *adv*
ma·gi·cian \mə-'ji-shən\ *n* : a person skilled in magic
mag·is·te·ri·al \ˌma-jə-'stir-ē-əl\ *adj* 1 : AUTHORITATIVE 〈a ∼ attitude〉 2 : of or relating to a magistrate or a magistrate's office or duties
ma·gis·tral \'ma-jə-strəl\ *adj* : AUTHORITATIVE
mag·is·trate \'ma-jə-ˌstrāt\ *n* : an official entrusted with administration of the laws — **mag·is·tra·cy** \-strə-sē\ *n*
mag·lev \'mag-lev\ *n* 1 : the use of magnetic fields to float an object above a solid surface 2 : a train using maglev technology
mag·ma \'mag-mə\ *n* : molten rock material within the earth — **mag·mat·ic** \mag-'ma-tik\ *adj*
mag·nan·i·mous \mag-'na-nə-məs\ *adj* 1 : showing or suggesting a lofty and courageous spirit 2 : NOBLE, GENEROUS — **mag·na·nim·i·ty** \ˌmag-nə-'ni-mə-tē\ *n* — **mag·nan·i·mous·ly** *adv* — **mag·nan·i·mous·ness** *n*
mag·nate \'mag-ˌnāt\ *n* : a person of rank, influence, or distinction
mag·ne·sia \mag-'nē-shə, -zhə\ *n* [NL, fr. *magnes carneus,* a white earth, lit., flesh magnet] : a light white oxide of magnesium used as a laxative
mag·ne·sium \mag-'nē-zē-əm, -zhəm\ *n* : a silver-white light malleable metallic chemical element
mag·net \'mag-nət\ *n* 1 : LODESTONE 2 : a body that is able to attract iron 3 : something that attracts
mag·net·ic \mag-'ne-tik\ *adj* 1 : having an unusual ability to attract 〈a ∼ leader〉 2 : of or relating to a magnet or magnetism 3 : magnetized or capable of being magnetized — **mag·net·i·cal·ly** \-ti-k(ə-)lē\ *adv*
magnetic disk *n* : DISK 3
magnetic levitation *n* : MAGLEV 1
magnetic north *n* : the northerly direction in the earth's magnetic field indicated by the north-seeking pole of a compass needle
magnetic resonance imaging *n* : a noninvasive diagnostic technique that produces computerized images of internal body tissues based on electromagnetically induced activity of atoms within the body
magnetic tape *n* : a ribbon coated with a magnetic material on which information (as sound) may be stored
mag·ne·tise *Brit var of* MAGNETIZE
mag·ne·tism \'mag-nə-ˌti-zəm\ *n* 1 : the power (as of a magnet) to attract iron 2 : the science that deals with magnetic phenomena 3 : an ability to attract or charm
mag·ne·tite \'mag-nə-ˌtīt\ *n* : a black mineral that is an important iron ore
mag·ne·tize \'mag-nə-ˌtīz\ *vb* **-tized; -tiz·ing** 1 : to induce magnetic properties in 2 : to attract like a magnet : CHARM — **mag·ne·tiz·able** *adj* — **mag·ne·ti·za·tion** \ˌmag-nə-tə-'zā-shən\ *n*
mag·ne·to \mag-'nē-tō\ *n, pl* **-tos** : a generator used to produce sparks in an internal combustion engine
mag·ne·tom·e·ter \ˌmag-nə-'tä-mə-tər\ *n* : an instrument for measuring the strength of a magnetic field
mag·ne·to·sphere \mag-'nē-tə-ˌsfir, -'ne-\ *n* : a region around a celestial object (as the earth) in which charged particles are trapped within its magnetic field — **mag·ne·to·spher·ic** \-ˌnē-tə-'sfir-ik, -'sfer-\ *adj*
mag·ni·fi·ca·tion \ˌmag-nə-fə-'kā-shən\ *n* 1 : the act of magnifying 2 : the amount by which an optical lens or instrument magnifies
mag·nif·i·cent \mag-'ni-fə-sənt\ *adj* 1 : characterized by grandeur or beauty : SPLENDID 2 : EXALTED, NOBLE
✦ **Synonyms** IMPOSING, STATELY, GRAND, MAJESTIC — **mag·nif·i·cence** \-səns\ *n* — **mag·nif·i·cent·ly** *adv*
mag·nif·i·co \mag-'ni-fi-ˌkō\ *n, pl* **-coes** *or* **-cos** 1 : a nobleman of Venice 2 : a person of high position
mag·ni·fy \'mag-nə-ˌfī\ *vb* **-fied; -fy·ing** 1 : EXTOL, LAUD; *also* : to cause to be held in greater esteem 2 : INTENSIFY; *also* : EXAGGERATE 3 : to enlarge in fact or in appearance — **mag·ni·fi·er** \'mag-nə-ˌfī(-ə)r\ *n*
mag·nil·o·quent \mag-'ni-lə-kwənt\ *adj* : characterized by an exalted and often bombastic style or manner — **mag·nil·o·quence** \-kwəns\ *n*
mag·ni·tude \'mag-nə-ˌtüd, -ˌtyüd\ *n* 1 : greatness of size or extent 2 : SIZE 3 : QUANTITY 4 : a number representing

the brightness of a celestial body **5** : a number representing the intensity of an earthquake

mag·no·lia \mag-'nōl-yə\ *n* : any of a genus of usu. spring-flowering shrubs and trees with large often fragrant flowers

mag·num opus \'mag-nəm-'ō-pəs\ *n* [L] : the greatest achievement of an artist or writer

mag·pie \'mag-ˌpī\ *n* : any of various long-tailed often black-and-white birds related to the jays

Mag·yar \'mag-ˌyär, 'mäg-ˌ 'mä-jär\ *n* : a member of the dominant people of Hungary — **Magyar** *adj*

ma·ha·ra·ja or **ma·ha·ra·jah** \ˌmä-hə-'rä-jə\ *n* : a Hindu prince ranking above a raja

ma·ha·ra·ni or **ma·ha·ra·nee** \-'rä-nē\ *n* **1** : the wife of a maharaja **2** : a Hindu princess ranking above a rani

ma·ha·ri·shi \ˌmä-hə-'rē-shē\ *n* : a Hindu teacher of mystical knowledge

ma·hat·ma \mə-'hät-mə, -'hat-\ *n* [Skt *mahātman*, fr. *mahātman* great-souled, fr. *mahat* great + *ātman* soul] : a person revered for high-mindedness, wisdom, and selflessness

Ma·hi·can \mə-'hē-kən\ or **Mo·hi·can** \mō-, mə-\ *n, pl* **-can** or **-cans** : a member of an American Indian people of the upper Hudson River valley

ma·hog·a·ny \mə-'hä-gə-nē\ *n, pl* **-nies** : the reddish wood of any of various chiefly tropical trees that is used in furniture; *also* : a tree yielding this wood

ma·hout \mə-'haut\ *n* [Hindi & Urdu *mahāwat, mahāut*] : a keeper and driver of an elephant

maid \'mād\ *n* **1** : an unmarried girl or young woman **2** : MAIDSERVANT; *also* : a woman or girl employed to do domestic work

¹**maid·en** \'mā-dᵊn\ *n* : MAID 1 — **maid·en·ly** *adj*

²**maiden** *adj* **1** : UNMARRIED; *also* : VIRGIN **3** : FIRST ⟨a ship's ~ voyage⟩

maid·en·hair fern \-ˌher-\ *n* : any of a genus of ferns with delicate feathery fronds

maid·en·head \'mā-dᵊn-ˌhed\ *n* **1** : VIRGINITY **2** : HYMEN

maid·en·hood \-ˌhùd\ *n* : the condition or time of being a maiden

maid–in–waiting *n, pl* **maids–in–waiting** : a young woman assigned to attend a queen or princess

maid of honor : a bride's principal unmarried wedding attendant

maid·ser·vant \'mād-ˌsər-vənt\ *n* : a girl or woman who is a servant

¹**mail** \'māl\ *n* [ME *male* bag, fr. AF, of Gmc origin] **1** : material sent or carried in the postal system **2** : a nation's postal system — often used in pl. **3** : E-MAIL

²**mail** *vb* : to send by mail

³**mail** *n* [ME *maille* metal link, mail, fr. AF, fr. L *macula* spot, mesh] : armor made of metal links or plates

mail·box \'māl-ˌbäks\ *n* **1** : a public box for the collection of mail **2** : a private box for the delivery of mail

mail·man \-ˌman\ *n* : a man who delivers mail

maim \'mām\ *vb* : to mutilate, disfigure, or wound seriously

¹**main** \'mān\ *n* **1** : FORCE ⟨with might and ~⟩ **2** : MAINLAND; *also* : HIGH SEA **3** : the chief part **4** : a principal pipe, duct, or circuit of a utility system

²**main** *adj* **1** : CHIEF, PRINCIPAL ⟨the ~ idea⟩ **2** : fully exerted ⟨~ force⟩ **3** : expressing the chief predication in a complex sentence ⟨the ~ clause⟩ — **main·ly** *adv*

main·frame \'mān-ˌfrām\ *n* : a large fast computer

main·land \-ˌland, -lənd\ *n* : a continuous body of land constituting the chief part of a country or continent

main·line \-ˌlīn\ *vb, slang* : to inject a narcotic drug into a vein

main line *n* : a principal highway or railroad line

main·mast \'mān-ˌmast, -məst\ *n* : the principal mast on a sailing ship

main·sail \-ˌsāl, -səl\ *n* : the largest sail on the mainmast

main·spring \-ˌspriŋ\ *n* **1** : the chief spring in a mechanism (as of a watch) **2** : the chief motive, agent, or cause

main·stay \-ˌstā\ *n* **1** : a stay running from the head of the mainmast to the foot of the foremast **2** : a chief support

main·stream \-ˌstrēm\ *n* : a prevailing current or direction of activity or influence — **mainstream** *adj*

main·tain \mān-'tān\ *vb* [ME *mainteinen*, fr. AF *maintenir*,

maynteiner, fr. ML *manutenēre*, fr. L *manu tenēre* to hold in the hand] **1** : to keep in an existing state (as of repair) **2** : to sustain against opposition or danger **3** : to continue in : CARRY ON **4** : to provide for : SUPPORT **5** : ASSERT ⟨~ed his innocence⟩ — **main·tain·abil·i·ty** \-ˌtā-nə-'bi-lə-tē\ *n* — **main·tain·able** \-'tā-nə-bəl\ *adj* — **main·te·nance** \'mān-tə-nəns\ *n*

main·top \'mān-ˌtäp\ *n* : a platform at the head of the mainmast of a square-rigged ship

mai·son·ette \ˌmā-zə-'net\ *n* **1** : a small house **2** : an apartment often on two floors

mai tai \'mī-ˌtī\ *n* : a cocktail made with liquors and fruit juices

maî·tre d' or **mai·tre d'** \ˌmā-trə-'dē, ˌme-\ *n, pl* **maître d's** or **maitre d's** \-'dēz\ : MAÎTRE D'HÔTEL

maî·tre d'hô·tel \ˌmā-trə-dō-'tel, ˌme-\ *n, pl* **maîtres d'hôtel** *same*\ [F, lit., master of house] **1** : MAJORDOMO **2** : HEADWAITER

maize \'māz\ *n* : CORN 2

Maj *abbr* major

maj·es·ty \'ma-jə-stē\ *n, pl* **-ties** **1** : sovereign power, authority, or dignity; *also* : the person of a sovereign — used as a title **2** : GRANDEUR, SPLENDOR — **ma·jes·tic** \mə-'jes-tik\ *adj* — **ma·jes·ti·cal·ly** \-ti-k(ə-)lē\ *adv*

Maj Gen *abbr* Major General

ma·jol·i·ca \mə-'jä-li-kə\ *also* **ma·iol·i·ca** \-'yä-\ *n* : any of several faiences; *esp* : an Italian tin-glazed pottery

¹**ma·jor** \'mā-jər\ *adj* **1** : greater in number, extent, or importance ⟨a ~ poet⟩ **2** : notable or conspicuous in effect or scope ⟨a ~ improvement⟩ **3** : SERIOUS ⟨a ~ illness⟩ **4** : having half steps between the 3d and 4th and the 7th and 8th degrees ⟨~ scale⟩; *also* : based on a major scale ⟨~ key⟩ ⟨~ chord⟩

²**major** *n* **1** : a commissioned officer (as in the army) ranking next below a lieutenant colonel **2** : an academic subject chosen as a field of specialization; *also* : a student specializing in such a field ⟨a history ~⟩

³**major** *vb* : to pursue an academic major

ma·jor·do·mo \ˌmā-jər-'dō-mō\ *n, pl* **-mos** [Sp *mayordomo* or obs. It *maiordomo*, fr. ML *major domus*, lit., chief of the house] **1** : a head steward **2** : BUTLER

ma·jor·ette \ˌmā-jə-'ret\ *n* : DRUM MAJORETTE

major general *n* : a commissioned officer (as in the army) ranking next below a lieutenant general

ma·jor·i·ty \mə-'jòr-ə-tē\ *n, pl* **-ties** **1** : the age at which full civil rights are accorded; *also* : the status of one who has attained this age **2** : a number greater than half of a total; *also* : the excess of this greater number over the remainder **3** : the rank of a major

ma·jus·cule \'ma-jəs-ˌkyūl, mə-'jəs-\ *n* : a large letter (as a capital)

Ma·kah \'mä-kä\ *n, pl* **Makah** or **Makahs** : a member of an American Indian people of the northwest coast of No. America

¹**make** \'māk\ *vb* **made** \'mād\; **mak·ing** **1** : to cause to exist, occur, or appear; *also* : DESTINE ⟨was *made* to be an actor⟩ **2** : FASHION ⟨~ a dress⟩; *also* : COMPOSE **3** : to formulate in the mind ⟨~ plans⟩ **4** : CONSTITUTE ⟨house *made* of stone⟩ **5** : to compute to be **6** : to set in order : PREPARE ⟨~ a bed⟩ **7** : to cause to be or become; *also* : APPOINT **8** : ENACT; *also* : EXECUTE ⟨~ a will⟩ **9** : CONCLUDE ⟨didn't know what to ~ of it⟩ **10** : CARRY OUT, PERFORM ⟨~ a gesture⟩ **11** : COMPEL **12** : to assure the success of ⟨will ~ us or break us⟩ **13** : to amount to in significance ⟨~s no difference⟩ **14** : to be capable of developing or being fashioned into **15** : REACH, ATTAIN; *also* : GAIN **16** : to start out : GO **17** : to have weight or effect ⟨courtesy ~s for safer driving⟩ ✦ *Synonyms* FORM, SHAPE, FABRICATE, MANUFACTURE — **mak·er** *n* — **make believe** : PRETEND — **make do** : to manage with the means at hand — **make fun of** : RIDICULE, MOCK — **make good** **1** : INDEMNIFY ⟨make good the loss⟩; *also* : to carry out successfully ⟨made good his promise⟩ **2** : SUCCEED — **make way** **1** : to give room for passing, entering, or occupying **2** : to make progress

²**make** *n* **1** : the manner or style of construction; *also* : BRAND **3** : MAKEUP **3** : the action of manufacturing — **on the make** : in search of wealth, social status, or sexual adventure

¹**make–be·lieve** \'māk-bə-ˌlēv\ *n* : a pretending that what is not real is real

²make–believe *adj* : IMAGINED, PRETENDED

make–do \-ˌdü\ *adj* : MAKESHIFT

make out *vb* 1 : to draw up in writing ⟨*make out* a list⟩ 2 : to find or grasp the meaning of ⟨can you *make* that *out*⟩ 3 : to represent as being 4 : to pretend to be true 5 : DISCERN ⟨*make out* a ship in the fog⟩ 6 : GET ALONG, FARE ⟨*make out* well in life⟩ 7 : to engage in amorous kissing and caressing

make over *vb* : REMAKE, REMODEL — make·over \'mā-ˌkō-vər\ *n*

make·shift \'māk-ˌshift\ *n* : a temporary expedient — makeshift *adj*

make·up \'mā-ˌkəp\ *n* 1 : the way in which something is put together; *also* : physical, mental, and moral constitution 2 : cosmetics esp. for the face; *also* : materials (as wigs and cosmetics) used in making up

make up *vb* 1 : FORM, COMPOSE 2 : to compensate for a deficiency 3 : SETTLE ⟨*made up* my mind⟩ 4 : INVENT, IMPROVISE 5 : to become reconciled 6 : to put on makeup (as for a play)

make–work \'māk-ˌwərk\ *n* : BUSYWORK

mak·ings \'mā-kiŋz\ *n pl* : the material from which something is made

Mal *abbr* Malachi

Mal·a·chi \'ma-lə-ˌkī\ *n* — see BIBLE table

Mal·a·chi·as \ˌma-lə-'kī-əs\ *n* : MALACHI

mal·a·chite \'ma-lə-ˌkīt\ *n* : a green mineral that is a carbonate of copper used for making ornamental objects

mal·adapt·ed \ˌma-lə-'dap-təd\ *adj* : poorly suited to a particular use, purpose, or situation

mal·ad·just·ed \ˌma-lə-'jəs-təd\ *adj* : poorly or inadequately adjusted (as to one's environment) — mal·ad·just·ment \-'jəst-mənt\ *n*

mal·adroit \ˌma-lə-'droit\ *adj* : not adroit : INEPT ⟨the ~ handling of the crisis⟩

mal·a·dy \'ma-lə-dē\ *n, pl* -dies : a disease or disorder of body or mind

mal·aise \mə-'lāz, ma-\ *n* [F] : a hazy feeling of not being well

mal·a·mute \'ma-lə-ˌmyüt\ *n* : a dog often used to draw sleds esp. in northern No. America

mal·a·prop·ism \'ma-lə-ˌprä-ˌpi-zəm\ *n* : a usu. humorous misuse of a word

mal·ap·ro·pos \ˌma-ˌla-prə-'pō, ma-'la-prə-ˌpō\ *adv* : in an inappropriate or inopportune way — malapropos *adj*

ma·lar·ia \mə-'ler-ē-ə\ *n* [It, fr. *mala aria* bad air] : a disease marked by recurring chills and fever and caused by a protozoan parasite of the blood that is transmitted by anopheles mosquitoes — ma·lar·i·al \-əl\ *adj*

ma·lar·key \mə-'lär-kē\ *n* : insincere or foolish talk

mal·a·thi·on \ˌma-lə-'thī-ən, -ˌän\ *n* : an insecticide with a relatively low toxicity for mammals

Ma·lay \mə-'lā, 'mā-ˌlā\ *n* 1 : a member of a people of the Malay Peninsula and Archipelago 2 : the language of the Malays — Malay *adj* — Ma·lay·an \mə-'lā-ən, 'mā-ˌlā-\ *n or adj*

mal·con·tent \ˌmal-kən-'tent\ *adj* : marked by a dissatisfaction with the existing state of affairs : DISCONTENTED — malcontent *n*

mal de mer \ˌmal-də-'mer\ *n* [F] : SEASICKNESS

¹male \'māl\ *n* : a male individual

²male *adj* 1 : of, relating to, or being the sex that produces germ cells which fertilize the eggs of a female; *also* : STAMINATE 2 : MASCULINE — male·ness *n*

male·dic·tion \ˌma-lə-'dik-shən\ *n* : CURSE, EXECRATION

male·fac·tor \'ma-lə-ˌfak-tər\ *n* : EVILDOER; *esp* : one who commits an offense against the law — mal·e·fac·tion \ˌma-lə-'fak-shən\ *n*

ma·lef·ic \mə-'le-fik\ *adj* 1 : BALEFUL ⟨~ influences⟩ 2 : MALICIOUS

ma·lef·i·cent \-fə-sənt\ *adj* : working or productive of harm or evil

ma·lev·o·lent \mə-'le-və-lənt\ *adj* : having, showing, or arising from ill will, spite, or hatred ◆ *Synonyms* MALIGNANT, MALIGN, MALICIOUS, SPITEFUL — ma·lev·o·lence \-ləns\ *n*

mal·fea·sance \mal-'fē-zⁿns\ *n* : wrongful conduct esp. by a public official

mal·for·ma·tion \ˌmal-fȯr-'mā-shən\ *n* : irregular or faulty formation or structure; *also* : an instance of this — malformed \mal-'fȯrmd\ *adj*

mal·func·tion \mal-'fəŋk-shən\ *vb* : to fail to operate normally — malfunction *n*

mal·ice \'ma-ləs\ *n* : desire to cause injury or distress to another — ma·li·cious \mə-'li-shəs\ *adj* — ma·li·cious·ly *adv*

¹ma·lign \mə-'līn\ *adj* 1 : evil in nature, influence, or effect; *also* : MALIGNANT 2 2 : moved by ill will

²malign *vb* : to speak evil of : DEFAME

ma·lig·nant \mə-'lig-nənt\ *adj* 1 : INJURIOUS, MALIGN 2 : tending to produce death or deterioration ⟨a ~ tumor⟩ — ma·lig·nan·cy \-nən-sē\ *n* — ma·lig·nant·ly *adv* — ma·lig·ni·ty \-nə-tē\ *n*

ma·lin·ger \mə-'liŋ-gər\ *vb* [F *malingre* sickly] : to pretend illness so as to avoid duty — ma·lin·ger·er *n*

mal·i·son \'ma-lə-sən, -zən\ *n* : CURSE

mall \'mȯl, 'mal\ *n* 1 : a shaded walk : PROMENADE 2 : an urban shopping area featuring a variety of shops surrounding a concourse 3 : a usu. large enclosed suburban shopping area containing various shops

mal·lard \'ma-lərd\ *n, pl* mallard *or* mallards : a common wild duck that is the source of domestic ducks

mal·lea·ble \'ma-lē-ə-bəl\ *adj* 1 : capable of being extended or shaped by beating with a hammer or by the pressure of rollers 2 : ADAPTABLE, PLIABLE ⟨~ young minds⟩ ◆ *Synonyms* PLASTIC, PLIANT, DUCTILE, SUPPLE — mal·le·a·bil·i·ty \ˌma-lē-ə-'bi-lə-tē\ *n*

mal·let \'ma-lət\ *n* 1 : a tool with a large head for driving another tool or for striking a surface without marring it 2 : a long-handled hammerlike implement for striking a ball (as in croquet)

mal·le·us \'ma-lē-əs\ *n, pl* mal·lei \-lē-ˌī, -lē-ˌē\ [NL, fr. L, hammer] : the outermost of the three small bones of the mammalian middle ear

mal·low \'ma-lō\ *n* : any of a genus of herbs with lobed leaves, usu. showy flowers, and a disk-shaped fruit

malm·sey \'mälm-zē\ *n, often cap* : the sweetest variety of Madeira

mal·nour·ished \mal-'nər-isht\ *adj* : UNDERNOURISHED

mal·nu·tri·tion \ˌmal-nü-'tri-shən, -nyü-\ *n* : faulty and esp. inadequate nutrition

mal·oc·clu·sion \ˌma-lə-'klü-zhən\ *n* : faulty coming together of teeth in biting

mal·odor·ous \ma-'lō-də-rəs\ *adj* : ill-smelling — mal·odor·ous·ly *adv* — mal·odor·ous·ness *n*

maloti *pl of* LOTI

mal·prac·tice \mal-'prak-təs\ *n* : a dereliction of professional duty or a failure of professional skill that results in injury, loss, or damage

malt \'mȯlt\ *n* 1 : grain and esp. barley steeped in water until it has sprouted and used in brewing and distilling 2 : liquor made with malt — malty *adj*

malted milk \'mȯl-təd-\ *n* : a powder prepared from dried milk and an extract from malt; *also* : a beverage of this powder in milk or other liquid

Mal·thu·sian \mal-'thü-zhən, -'thyü-\ *adj* : of or relating to a theory that population unless checked (as by war) tends to increase faster than its means of subsistence — Malthusian *n* — Mal·thu·sian·ism \-zhə-ˌni-zəm\ *n*

malt·ose \'mȯl-ˌtōs\ *n* : a sugar formed esp. from starch by the action of enzymes

mal·treat \mal-'trēt\ *vb* : to treat cruelly or roughly : ABUSE — mal·treat·ment *n*

mal·ware \'mal-ˌwer\ *n* : software designed to interfere with a computer's normal functioning

ma·ma *or* mam·ma \'mä-mə\ *n* : MOTHER

mam·bo \'mäm-bō\ *n, pl* mambos : a dance of Cuban origin related to the rumba — mambo *vb*

mam·mal \'ma-məl\ *n* [NL *Mammalia*, fr. LL, neut. pl. of *mammalis* of the breast, fr. L *mamma* breast] : any of a class of warm-blooded vertebrates that includes humans and all other animals which nourish their young with milk and have the skin more or less covered with hair — mam·ma·li·an \mə-'mā-lē-ən, ma-\ *adj or n*

mam·ma·ry \'ma-mə-rē\ *adj* : of, relating to, or being the glands (mammary glands) that in female mammals secrete milk

mam·mo·gram \'ma-mə-ˌgram\ *n* : an X-ray photograph of the breasts

mam·mog·ra·phy \ma-'mä-grə-fē\ *n* : X-ray examination of the breasts (as for early detection of cancer)

mam·mon \'ma-mən\ *n, often cap* : material wealth having a debasing influence

¹**mam·moth** \'ma-məth\ *n* : any of a genus of large hairy extinct elephants

²**mammoth** *adj* : of very great size : GIGANTIC ✦ Syno-, nyms COLOSSAL, ENORMOUS, IMMENSE, VAST, ELEPHANTINE

¹**man** \'man\ *n, pl* **men** \'men\ **1** : a human being; *esp* : an adult male **2** : the human race : HUMANKIND **3** : one possessing in high degree the qualities considered distinctive of manhood **4** : an adult male servant or employee **5** : the individual who can fulfill one's requirements ⟨he's your ∼⟩ **6 a** : one of the pieces with which various games (as chess) are played **b** : one of the players on a team **7** *often cap* : white society or people

²**man** *vb* **manned; man·ning** **1** : to supply with people ⟨∼ a fleet⟩ **2** : FORTIFY, BRACE

³**man** *abbr* manual

Man *abbr* Manitoba

man–about–town *n, pl* **men–about–town** : a worldly and socially active man

man·a·cle \'ma-ni-kəl\ *n* **1** : a shackle for the hand or wrist **2** : something used as a restraint

man·age \'ma-nij\ *vb* **man·aged; man·ag·ing** **1** : HANDLE, CONTROL ⟨∼s her skis well⟩; *also* : to direct or carry on business or affairs **2** : to make and keep compliant **3** : to treat with care : HUSBAND **4** : to achieve one's purpose : CONTRIVE — **man·age·abil·i·ty** \,ma-ni-jə-'bi-lə-tē\ *n* — **man·age·able** \'ma-ni-jə-bəl\ *adj* — **man·age·able·ness** *n* — **man·age·ably** \-blē\ *adv*

managed care *n* : a health-care system that controls costs by limiting doctor's fees and by restricting the patient's choice of doctors

man·age·ment \'ma-nij-mənt\ *n* **1** : the act or art of managing : CONTROL **2** : judicious use of means to accomplish an end **3** : the group of those who manage or direct an enterprise

man·ag·er \'ma-ni-jər\ *n* : one that manages — **man·a·ge·ri·al** \,ma-nə-'jir-ē-əl\ *adj*

ma·ña·na \mən-'yä-nə\ *n* [Sp, lit., tomorrow] : an indefinite time in the future

ma·nat \mä-'nät\ *n, pl* **manat** *or* **manats** — see MONEY table

man–at–arms *n, pl* **men–at–arms** : SOLDIER; *esp* : one who is heavily armed and mounted

man·a·tee \'ma-nə-,tē\ *n* : any of a genus of chiefly tropical plant-eating aquatic mammals having a broad rounded tail

man·ci·ple \'man-sə-pəl\ *n* : a steward or purveyor esp. for a college or monastery

man·da·mus \man-'dā-məs\ *n* [L, we enjoin] : a writ issued by a superior court commanding that an official act or duty be performed

man·da·rin \'man-də-rən\ *n* **1** : a public official of high rank under the Chinese Empire **2** *cap* : the chief dialect group of China **3** : a yellow to reddish orange loose-skinned citrus fruit; *also* : a tree that bears mandarins

man·date \'man-,dāt\ *n* **1** : an authoritative command **2** : an authorization to act given to a representative **3** : a commission granted by the League of Nations to a member nation for governing conquered territory; *also* : a territory so governed

man·da·to·ry \'man-də-,tór-ē\ *adj* **1** : containing or constituting a command : OBLIGATORY **2** : of or relating to a League of Nations mandate

man·di·ble \'man-də-bəl\ *n* **1** : JAW; *esp* : a lower jaw **2** : either segment of a bird's bill — **man·dib·u·lar** \man-'di-byə-lər\ *adj*

man·do·lin \,man-də-'lin, 'man-də-lən\ *n* : a stringed musical instrument with a pear-shaped body and a fretted neck

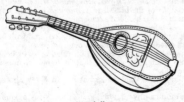

mandolin

man·drake \'man-,drāk\ *n* **1** : an Old World herb related to the nightshades or its large forked root formerly credited with magical properties **2** : MAYAPPLE

man·drel *also* **man·dril** \'man-drəl\ *n* **1** : an axle or spindle inserted into a hole in a piece of work to support it during machining **2** : a metal bar used as a core around which material may be cast, shaped, or molded

man·drill \'man-drəl\ *n* : a large baboon of western central Africa

mane \'mān\ *n* : long heavy hair growing about the neck of some mammals (as horses) — **maned** \'mānd\ *adj*

man·eat·er \'man-,ē-tər\ *n* : one (as a shark or cannibal) that has or is thought to have an appetite for human flesh — **man·eat·ing** *adj*

ma·nège \ma-'nezh, mə-\ *n* : the art of horsemanship or of training horses

ma·nes \'mä-,nās, 'mä-,nēz\ *n pl, often cap* : the spirits of the dead and gods of the lower world in ancient Roman belief

ma·neu·ver \mə-'nü-vər, -'nyü-\ *n* [F *manœuvre*, fr. OF *maneuvre* work done by hand, fr. ML *manuopera*, *manu operare* to work by hand] **1** : a military or naval movement; *also* : an armed forces training exercise — often used in pl. **2** : a procedure involving expert physical movement **3** : an evasive movement or shift of tactics; *also* : an action taken to gain a tactical end — **maneuver** *vb* — **ma·neu·ver·abil·i·ty** \-,nü-və-rə-'bi-lə-tē, -,nyü-\ *n* — **ma·neu·ver·able** \-'nü-və-rə-bəl, -'nyü-\ *adj*

man Friday *n* : an efficient and devoted aide or employee

man·ful \'man-fəl\ *adj* : having or showing courage and resolution ⟨a ∼ struggle⟩ — **man·ful·ly** *adv*

man·ga \'mäŋ-gə\ *n* [Jp, comic, cartoon, fr. *man-* involuntary, aimless + *-ga* picture] : a Japanese comic book or graphic novel

man·ga·nese \'maŋ-gə-,nēz, -,nēs\ *n* : a metallic chemical element resembling iron but not magnetic

mange \'mānj\ *n* : any of several contagious itchy skin diseases esp. of domestic animals — **mangy** \'mān-jē\ *adj*

man·ger \'mān-jər\ *n* : a trough or open box for livestock feed or fodder

¹**man·gle** \'maŋ-gəl\ *vb* **man·gled; man·gling** **1** : to cut, bruise, or hack with repeated blows **2** : to spoil or injure esp. through ineptitude — **man·gler** *n*

²**mangle** *n* : a machine with heated rollers for ironing laundry

man·go \'maŋ-gō\ *n, pl* **mangoes** *also* **mangos** [Pg *manga*, prob. fr. Malayalam (Dravidian language of India) *māṅṅa*] : an edible juicy yellowish-red fruit borne by a tropical evergreen tree related to the sumacs; *also* : this tree

man·grove \'man-,grōv\ *n* : any of a genus of tropical maritime trees that send out many prop roots and form dense thickets important in coastal land building

man·han·dle \'man-,han-dᵊl\ *vb* : to handle roughly

man·hat·tan \man-'ha-tᵊn\ *n, often cap* : a cocktail made of whiskey and vermouth

man·hole \'man-,hōl\ *n* : a hole through which a person may go esp. to gain access to an underground or enclosed structure

man·hood \-,hùd\ *n* **1** : the condition of being an adult male **2** : qualities associated with men : MANLINESS **3** : MEN ⟨the nation's ∼⟩

man–hour \-'aù(-ə)r\ *n* : a unit of one hour's work by one person

man·hunt \-,hənt\ *n* : an organized hunt for a person and esp. for one charged with a crime

ma·nia \'mā-nē-ə, -nyə\ *n* **1** : excitement manifested by mental and physical hyperactivity, disorganized behavior, and elevated mood **2** : excessive enthusiasm

ma·ni·ac \'mā-nē-,ak\ *n* : LUNATIC, MADMAN

ma·ni·a·cal \mə-'nī-ə-kəl\ *also* **ma·ni·ac** \'mā-nē-ak\ *adj* **1** : affected with or suggestive of madness **2** : FRANTIC ⟨a ∼ mob⟩

man·ic \'ma-nik\ *adj* : affected with, relating to, characterized by, or resulting from mania — **manic** *n* — **man·i·cal·ly** \-ni-k(ə-)lē\ *adv*

manic depression *n* : BIPOLAR DISORDER

man·ic–de·pres·sive \,ma-nik-di-'pre-siv\ *adj* : characterized by or affected with either mania or depression or alternating episodes of mania and depression — **manic–depressive** *n*

¹man·i·cure \'ma-nə-ˌkyu̇r\ *n* 1 : MANICURIST 2 : a treatment for the care of the hands and nails

²manicure *vb* -cured; -cur·ing 1 : to do manicure work on 2 : to trim closely and evenly

man·i·cur·ist \-ˌkyu̇r-ist\ *n* : a person who gives manicure treatments

¹man·i·fest \'ma-nə-ˌfest\ *adj* [ME, fr. AF or L; AF *manifeste*, fr. L *manifestus*, caught in the act, flagrant, obvious, perh. fr. *manus* hand + *-festus* (akin to L in*festus* hostile)] 1 : readily perceived by the senses and esp. by the sight 2 : easily understood : OBVIOUS — man·i·fest·ly *adv*

²manifest *vb* : to make evident or certain by showing or displaying ✦ **Synonyms** EVINCE, DEMONSTRATE, EXHIBIT

³manifest *n* : a list of passengers or an invoice of cargo for a ship or plane

man·i·fes·ta·tion \ˌma-nə-fə-'stā-shən\ *n* : DISPLAY, DEMONSTRATION

man·i·fes·to \ˌma-nə-'fes-tō\ *n, pl* -tos *or* -toes : a public declaration of intentions, motives, or views

¹man·i·fold \'ma-nə-ˌfōld\ *adj* 1 : marked by diversity or variety 2 : consisting of or operating many of one kind combined

²manifold *n* : a pipe fitting with several lateral outlets for connecting it with other pipes

³manifold *vb* 1 : MULTIPLY 2 : to make a number of copies of (as a letter)

man·i·kin *also* man·ni·kin \'ma-ni-kən\ *n* 1 : MANNEQUIN 2 *dated, usu disparaging* : a little man : DWARF

Ma·ni·la hemp \mə-'ni-lə-\ *n* : a tough fiber from a Philippine plant related to the banana that is used for cordage

manila paper *n, often cap M* : a tough brownish paper made orig. from Manila hemp

man·i·oc \'ma-nē-ˌäk\ *n* : CASSAVA

ma·nip·u·late \mə-'ni-pyə-ˌlāt\ *vb* -lat·ed; -lat·ing 1 : to treat or operate manually or mechanically esp. with skill 2 : to manage or use skillfully 3 : to influence esp. with intent to deceive — ma·nip·u·la·tion \mə-ni-pyə-'lā-shən\ *n* — ma·nip·u·la·tive \-'ni-pyə-ˌlā-tiv\ *adj* — ma·nip·u·la·tor \-ˌlā-tər\ *n*

ma·nip·u·la·tives \mə-'ni-pyə-ˌlā-tivz\ *n pl* : objects that a student is instructed to use in a way that teaches or reinforces a lesson

man·kind *n* 1 \'man-'kīnd\ : the human race 2 \-ˌkīnd\ : men as distinguished from women

¹man·ly \'man-lē\ *adv* : in a manly manner

²manly *adj* man·li·er; -est : having qualities appropriate to or generally associated with a man : BOLD, RESOLUTE ⟨a ~ competitor⟩ — man·li·ness *n*

man–made \'man-'mād\ *adj* : made by humans rather than nature ⟨~ systems⟩; *esp* : SYNTHETIC ⟨~ fibers⟩

man·na \'ma-nə\ *n* 1 : food miraculously supplied to the Israelites in the wilderness 2 : something of value that comes unexpectedly : WINDFALL

manned \'mand\ *adj* : carrying or performed by a person ⟨~ spaceflight⟩

man·ne·quin \'ma-ni-kən\ *n* 1 : a form representing the human figure used esp. for displaying clothes 2 : a person employed to model clothing

man·ner \'ma-nər\ *n* 1 : KIND, SORT ⟨what ~ of man is he⟩ 2 : a way of acting or proceeding ⟨worked in a brisk ~⟩; *also* : normal behavior ⟨spoke bluntly as was his ~⟩ 3 : a method of artistic execution 4 *pl* : social conduct; *also* : BEARING 5 *pl* : BEHAVIOR ⟨taught the child good ~s⟩

man·nered \'ma-nərd\ *adj* 1 : having manners of a specified kind ⟨well-*mannered*⟩ 2 : having an artificial character ⟨a highly ~ style⟩

man·ner·ism \'ma-nə-ˌri-zəm\ *n* 1 : ARTIFICIALITY, PRECIOSITY 2 : a peculiarity of action, bearing, or treatment ✦ **Synonyms** POSE, AIR, AFFECTATION

man·ner·ly \'ma-nər-lē\ *adj* : showing good manners : POLITE — man·ner·li·ness *n* — mannerly *adv*

man·nish \'ma-nish\ *adj* 1 : resembling or suggesting a man rather than a woman 2 : generally associated with or characteristic of a man ⟨a ~ voice⟩ — man·nish·ly *adv* — man·nish·ness *n*

ma·no a ma·no \ˌmä-nō-ä-'mä-nō\ *adv or adj* : in direct competition or conflict

ma·noeu·vre \mə-'nü-vər, -'nyü-\ *chiefly Brit var of* MANEUVER

man–of–war \ˌman-əv-'wȯr\ *n, pl* men–of–war \ˌmen-\ : WARSHIP

ma·nom·e·ter \mə-'nä-mə-tər\ *n* : an instrument for measuring the pressure of gases and vapors — mano·met·ric \ˌma-nə-'me-trik\ *adj*

man·or \'ma-nər\ *n* 1 : the house or hall of an estate; *also* : a landed estate 2 : an English estate of a feudal lord — ma·no·ri·al \mə-'nȯr-ē-əl\ *adj* — ma·no·ri·al·ism \-ə-ˌli-zəm\ *n*

man power *n* 1 : power available from or supplied by the physical effort of human beings 2 *usu* man·pow·er : the total supply of persons available and fitted for service

man·qué \mäⁿ-'kā\ *adj* [F, fr. pp. of *manquer* to lack, fail] : short of or frustrated in the fulfillment of one's aspirations or talents ⟨a poet ~⟩

man·sard \'man-ˌsärd, -sərd\ *n* : a roof having two slopes on all sides with the lower slope steeper than the upper one

manse \'mans\ *n* : the residence esp. of a Presbyterian minister

man·ser·vant \'man-ˌsər-vənt\ *n, pl* men·ser·vants \'men-ˌsər-vənts\ : a male servant

man·sion \'man-chən\ *n* : a large imposing residence; *also* : a separate apartment in a large structure

man–size \'man-ˌsīz\ *or* man–sized \-ˌsīzd\ *adj* : suitable for or requiring a man ⟨a ~ job⟩

man·slaugh·ter \-ˌslȯ-tər\ *n* : the unlawful killing of a human being without express or implied malice

man·ta \'man-tə\ *n* : a square piece of cloth or blanket used in southwestern U.S. and Latin America as a cloak or shawl

man·teau \'man-ˌtō\ *n* : a loose cloak, coat, or robe

man·tel \'man-tᵊl\ *n* : a beam, stone, or arch serving as a lintel to support the masonry above a fireplace; *also* : a shelf above a fireplace

man·tel·piece \'man-tᵊl-ˌpēs\ *n* : the shelf of a mantel

man·til·la \man-'tē-yə, -'ti-lə\ *n* : a light scarf worn over the head and shoulders esp. by Spanish and Latin-American women

man·tis \'man-təs\ *n, pl* man·tis·es *also* man·tes \-ˌtēz\ [NL, fr. Gk, lit., diviner, prophet] : any of a group of large usu. green insect-eating insects that hold their prey in forelimbs folded as if in prayer

man·tis·sa \man-'ti-sə\ *n* : the part of a logarithm to the right of the decimal point

¹man·tle \'man-tᵊl\ *n* 1 : a loose sleeveless garment worn over other clothes 2 : something that covers, enfolds, or envelops 3 : a lacy sheath that gives light by incandescence when placed over a flame 4 : the portion of the earth lying between the crust and the core 5 : MANTEL

²mantle *vb* man·tled; man·tling 1 : to cover with a mantle 2 : BLUSH

man·tra \'man-trə\ *n* : a mystical formula of invocation or incantation (as in Hinduism)

¹man·u·al \'man-yə-wəl\ *adj* 1 : of, relating to, or involving the hands; *also* : worked by hand ⟨a ~ pump⟩ 2 : requiring or using physical skill and energy ⟨~ labor⟩ — man·u·al·ly *adv*

²manual *n* 1 : a small book; *esp* : HANDBOOK 2 : the prescribed movements in the handling of a military item and esp. a weapon during a drill or ceremony ⟨the ~ of arms⟩ 3 : a keyboard esp. of an organ 4 : an automobile with a manual transmission

man·u·fac·to·ry \ˌman-yə-'fak-tə-rē\ *n* : FACTORY

¹man·u·fac·ture \ˌman-yə-'fak-chər\ *n* [MF, fr. ML *manufactura*, L *manu factus* made by hand] 1 : something made from raw materials 2 : the process of making wares by hand or by machinery; *also* : a productive industry using machinery

²manufacture *vb* -tured; -tur·ing 1 : to make from raw materials by hand or by machinery; *also* : to engage in manufacture 2 : INVENT, FABRICATE; *also* : CREATE — man·u·fac·tur·er *n*

man·u·mit \ˌman-yə-'mit\ *vb* -mit·ted; -mit·ting : to free from slavery — man·u·mis·sion \-'mi-shən\ *n*

¹ma·nure \mə-'nu̇r, -'nyu̇r\ *vb* ma·nured; ma·nur·ing : to fertilize land with manure

²manure *n* : FERTILIZER; *esp* : refuse from stables and barnyards — ma·nu·ri·al \-'nu̇r-ē-əl, -'nyu̇r-\ *adj*

man·u·script \'man-yə-ˌskript\ *n* [L *manu scriptus* written by hand] 1 : a written or typed composition or document;

also : a document submitted for publication **2** : writing as opposed to print

Manx \'maŋks\ *n pl* : the people of the Isle of Man — **Manx** *adj*

¹**many** \'me-nē\ *adj* **more** \'mōr\; **most** \'mōst\ : consisting of or amounting to a large but indefinite number ⟨~ years ago⟩

²**many** *pron* : a large number ⟨~ are called⟩

³**many** *n* : a large but indefinite number ⟨a good ~ of them⟩

many-fold \ˌme-nē-'fōld\ *adv* : by many times

many-sid-ed \-'sī-dəd\ *adj* **1** : having many sides or aspects **2** : VERSATILE

Mao-ism \'maù-ˌi-zəm\ *n* : the theory and practice of Communism developed in China chiefly by Mao Zedong — **Mao-ist** \'maù-ist\ *n or adj*

Mao-ri \'maù-(ə)r-ē\ *n, pl* **Maori** *or* **Maoris** : a member of a Polynesian people native to New Zealand

¹**map** \'map\ *n* [ML *mappa*, fr. L, napkin, towel] **1** : a representation usu. on a flat surface of the whole or part of an area **2** : a representation of the celestial sphere or part of it

²**map** *vb* **mapped; map-ping 1** : to make a map of **2** : to plan in detail ⟨~ out a program⟩ — **map-pa-ble** \'ma-pə-bəl\ *adj* — **map-per** *n*

MAP *abbr* modified American plan

ma-ple \'mā-pəl\ *n* : any of a genus of trees or shrubs with 2-winged dry fruit and opposite leaves; *also* : the hard light-colored wood of a maple used esp. for floors and furniture

maple sugar *n* : sugar made by boiling maple syrup

maple syrup *n* : syrup made by concentrating the sap of maple trees and esp. the sugar maple

mar \'mär\ *vb* **marred; mar-ring** : to detract from the wholeness or perfection of : SPOIL ✦ **Synonyms** INJURE, HURT, HARM, DAMAGE, IMPAIR, BLEMISH

Mar *abbr* March

ma-ra-ca \mə-'rä-kə, -'ra-\ *n* [Pg *maracá*] : a rattle usu. made from a gourd and used as a percussion instrument

mar-a-schi-no \ˌmer-ə-'skē-nō-, -'shē-\ *n, often cap* : a cherry preserved in a sweet liqueur made from the juice of a bitter wild cherry

mar-a-thon \'mer-ə-ˌthän\ *n* [*Marathon*, Greece, site of a victory of Greeks over Persians in 490 B.C. the news of which was carried to Athens by a long-distance runner] **1** : a long-distance race esp. on foot **2** : an endurance contest

mar-a-thon-er \'mer-ə-ˌthä-nər\ *n* : a person who takes part in a marathon — **mar-a-thon-ing** *n*

ma-raud \mə-'rȯd\ *vb* : to roam about and raid in search of plunder : PILLAGE — **ma-raud-er** *n*

mar-ble \'mär-bəl\ *n* **1** : a limestone that can be polished and used in fine building work **2** : something resembling marble (as in coldness) **3** : a small ball (as of glass) used in various games; *also, pl* : a children's game played with these small balls — **marble** *adj*

mar-bling \-bə-liŋ, -bliŋ\ *n* : an intermixture of fat through the lean of a cut of meat

mar-cel \mär-'sel\ *n* : a deep soft wave made in the hair by the use of a heated curling iron — **marcel** *vb*

¹**march** \'märch\ *n* : a border region : FRONTIER

²**march** *vb* **1** : to move along in or as if in military formation **2** : to walk in a direct purposeful manner; *also* : PROGRESS, ADVANCE **3** : TRAVERSE ⟨~ed 10 miles⟩ — **march-er** *n*

³**march** *n* **1** : the action of marching; *also* : the distance covered (as by a military unit) in a march **2** : a regular measured stride or rhythmic step used in marching **3** : forward movement **4** : a piece of music with marked rhythm suitable for marching to

March *n* [ME, fr. AF, fr. L *martius*, fr. *martius* of Mars, fr. *Mart-, Mars*, Roman god of war] : the 3d month of the year

mar-chio-ness \'mär-shə-nəs\ *n* **1** : the wife or widow of a marquess **2** : a woman holding the rank of a marquess in her own right

Mar-di Gras \'mär-dē-ˌgrä\ *n* [F, lit., fat Tuesday] : the Tuesday before Ash Wednesday often observed with parades and merrymaking

¹**mare** \'mer\ *n* : an adult female of the horse or a related mammal

²**ma-re** \'mär-(ˌ)ā\ *n, pl* **ma-ria** \'mär-ē-ə\ : any of several large dark areas on the surface of the moon or Mars

mar-ga-rine \'mär-jə-rən\ *n* : a food product made usu. from vegetable oils churned with skimmed milk and used as a substitute for butter

mar-ga-ri-ta \ˌmär-gə-'rē-tə\ *n* : a cocktail consisting of tequila, lime or lemon juice, and an orange-flavored liqueur

mar-gin \'mär-jən\ *n* **1** : the part of a page outside the main body of printed or written matter **2** : EDGE ⟨continental ~⟩ **3** : a spare amount, measure, or degree allowed for use if needed ⟨a safety ~⟩ **4** : measure or degree of difference ⟨a one-vote ~⟩

mar-gin-al \-jə-nəl\ *adj* **1** : written or printed in the margin **2** : of, relating to, or situated at a margin or border **3** : close to the lower limit of quality or acceptability **4** : excluded from or existing outside the mainstream of society or a group — **mar-gin-al-ly** *adv*

mar-gi-na-lia \ˌmär-jə-'nā-lē-ə\ *n pl* : marginal notes or embellishments

mar-gin-al-ize \'mär-jə-nᵊl-ˌīz\ *vb* **-ized; -iz-ing** : to relegate to an unimportant position within a society or group

mar-grave \'mär-ˌgrāv\ *n* : the military governor esp. of a medieval German border province

ma-ri-a-chi \ˌmär-ē-'ä-chē, ˌmer-\ *n* : a Mexican street band; *also* : a member of or the music of such a band

mari-gold \'mer-ə-ˌgōld\ *n* : any of a genus of tropical American herbs related to the daisies that are grown for their showy usu. yellow, orange, or maroon flower heads

mar-i-jua-na *also* **mar-i-hua-na** \ˌmer-ə-'wä-nə, -'hwä-\ *n* [MexSp *marihuana*] : the dried leaves and flowering tops of the female hemp plant smoked usu. illegally for their intoxicating effect; *also* : HEMP

ma-rim-ba \mə-'rim-bə\ *n* : a xylophone of southern Africa and Central America; *also* : a modern version of it

marimba

ma-ri-na \mə-'rē-nə\ *n* : a dock or basin providing secure moorings for pleasure boats

mar-i-nade \ˌmer-ə-'nād\ *n* : a savory usu. acidic sauce in which meat, fish, or a vegetable is soaked to enrich its flavor or to tenderize it

mar-i-na-ra \ˌmer-ə-'ner-ə\ *adj* [It (*alla*) *marinara*, lit., in sailor style] : made with tomatoes, onions, garlic, and spices; *also* : served with marinara sauce

mar-i-nate \'mer-ə-ˌnāt\ *vb* **-nat-ed; -nat-ing** : to steep (as meat or fish) in a marinade

¹**ma-rine** \mə-'rēn\ *adj* **1** : of or relating to the sea or its navigation or commerce **2** : of or relating to marines

²**marine** *n* **1** : the mercantile and naval shipping of a country **2** : any of a class of soldiers serving on shipboard or with a naval force

mar-i-ner \'mer-ə-nər\ *n* : SAILOR

mar-i-o-nette \ˌmer-ē-ə-'net\ *n* : a puppet moved by strings or by hand

mar-i-tal \'mer-ə-tᵊl\ *adj* : of or relating to marriage : CONJUGAL ✦ **Synonyms** MATRIMONIAL, CONNUBIAL, NUPTIAL

mar-i-time \'mer-ə-ˌtīm\ *adj* **1** : of, relating to, or bordering on the sea **2** : of or relating to navigation or commerce of the sea

mar-jo-ram \'mär-jə-rəm\ *n* : any of various fragrant mints often used as seasoning

¹**mark** \'märk\ *n* **1** : something (as a line or fixed object) designed to record position; *also* : the starting line or position in a track event **2** : TARGET; *also* : GOAL, OBJECT

3 : an object of abuse or ridicule **4** : the question under discussion **5** : NORM ⟨not up to the ∼⟩ **6** : a visible sign : INDICATION; *also* : CHARACTERISTIC **7** : a written or printed symbol **8** : GRADE 5 ⟨a ∼ of B+⟩ **9** : IMPORTANCE, DISTINCTION **10** : a lasting impression ⟨made his ∼ in the world⟩; *also* : a damaging impression left on a surface

²**mark** *vb* **1** : to set apart by a line or boundary **2** : to designate by a mark or make a mark on **3** : CHARACTERIZE ⟨the vehemence that ∼s his speeches⟩; *also* : SIGNALIZE ⟨this year ∼s our 50th anniversary⟩ **4** : to take notice of : OBSERVE ⟨∼ my words⟩ — **mark·er** *n*

³**mark** *n* : DEUTSCHE MARK

Mark \'märk\ *n* — see BIBLE table

mar·ka \'mär-kə\ *n, pl* **mar·a·ka** \'mär-ə-kə\ *or* **marka** *or* **mar·kas** — see MONEY table

mark·down \'märk-ˌdau̇n\ *n* **1** : a lowering of price **2** : the amount by which an original price is reduced

mark down *vb* : to put a lower price on

marked \'märkt\ *adj* : NOTICEABLE — **mark·ed·ly** \'mär-kəd-lē\ *adv*

¹**mar·ket** \'mär-kət\ *n* **1** : a meeting together of people for trade by purchase and sale; *also* : a public place where such a meeting is held **2** : the rate or price offered for a commodity or security **3** : the course of commercial activity by which the exchange of commodities is effected **4** : a geographical area of demand for commodities; *also* : extent of demand **5** : a retail establishment usu. of a specific kind

²**market** *vb* : to go to a market to buy or sell; *also* : SELL — **mar·ket·able** *adj*

mar·ket·place \'mär-kət-ˌplās\ *n* **1** : an open square in a town where markets are held **2** : the world of trade or economic activity

mark·ka \'mär-ˌkä\ *n, pl* **mark·kaa** \'mär-ˌkä\ *or* **markkas** \-ˌkäz\ : the basic monetary unit of Finland from 1917 to 2001

marks·man \'märks-mən\ *n* : a person skillful at hitting a target — **marks·man·ship** *n*

mark·up \'mär-ˌkəp\ *n* **1** : a raising of price **2** : an amount added to the cost price of an article to determine the selling price

mark up *vb* : to put a higher price on

markup language *n* : a system for marking the components and layout of a computer document

marl \'märl\ *n* : an earthy deposit rich in lime used esp. as fertilizer — **marly** \'mär-lē\ *adj*

mar·lin \'mär-lən\ *n* : any of several large oceanic sport fishes related to sailfishes

mar·line·spike *also* **mar·lin·spike** \'mär-lən-ˌspīk\ *n* : a pointed iron tool used to separate strands of rope or wire (as in splicing)

mar·ma·lade \'mär-mə-ˌlād\ *n* : a clear jelly holding in suspension pieces of fruit and fruit rind

mar·mo·re·al \mär-'mȯr-ē-əl\ *adj* : of, relating to, or suggestive of marble

mar·mo·set \'mär-mə-ˌset\ *n* : any of numerous small bushy-tailed monkeys of Central and So. America

mar·mot \'mär-mət\ *n* : any of a genus of stout short-legged burrowing No. American rodents

¹**ma·roon** \mə-'rün\ *vb* **1** : to put ashore (as on a desolate island) and leave to one's fate **2** : to leave in isolation and without hope of escape

²**maroon** *n* : a dark red color

¹**mar·quee** \mär-'kē\ *n* [modif. of F *marquise,* lit., marchioness] **1** : a large tent set up (as for an outdoor party) **2** : a usu. metal and glass canopy over an entrance (as of a theater) **3** : a sign over the entrance of a theater or arena advertising a performance

²**marquee** *adj* : having or being a great attraction : PREEMINENT ⟨∼ athletes⟩

mar·quess \'mär-kwəs\ *or* **mar·quis** \'mär-kwəs, mär-'kē\ *n* **1** : a nobleman of hereditary rank in Europe and Japan **2** : a member of the British peerage ranking below a duke and above an earl

mar·que·try \'mär-kə-trē\ *n* : inlaid work of wood, shell, or ivory (as on a table or cabinet)

mar·quise \mär-'kēz\ *n, pl* **mar·quises** *same or* -'kē-zəz\ : MARCHIONESS

mar·riage \'mer-ij\ *n* **1** : the state of being united as spouses in a consensual and contractual relationship recognized by law **2** : a wedding ceremony and attendant festivities **3** : a close union ⟨a ∼ of light and shadow⟩ — **mar·riage·able** *adj*

married name *n* : a surname acquired through marriage

mar·row \'mer-ō\ *n* : a soft vascular tissue that fills the cavities of most bones

mar·row·bone \'mer-ə-ˌbōn, 'mer-ō-\ *n* : a bone (as a shinbone) rich in marrow

mar·ry \'mer-ē\ *vb* **mar·ried; mar·ry·ing 1** : to join in marriage **2** : to take as a spouse : WED **3** : to enter into a close union **4** : COMBINE, UNITE — **mar·ried** *adj or n*

Mars \'märz\ *n* : the planet 4th from the sun and conspicuous for its red color

marsh \'märsh\ *n* : a tract of soft wet land — **marshy** *adj*

¹**mar·shal** \'mär-shəl\ *n* [ME, fr. AF *mareschal,* of Gmc origin; akin to OHG *marahscalc* marshal, fr. *marah* horse + *scalc* servant] **1** : a high official in a medieval household; *also* : a person in charge of the ceremonial aspects of a gathering **2** : a general officer of the highest military rank **3** : an administrative officer (as of a U.S. judicial district) having duties similar to a sheriff's **4** : the administrative head of a city police or fire department

²**marshal** *vb* **mar·shaled** *or* **mar·shalled; mar·shal·ing** *or* **mar·shal·ling 1** : to arrange in order, rank, or position ⟨∼ troops⟩ **2** : to bring together ⟨∼ arguments⟩ **3** : to lead with ceremony : USHER

marsh gas *n* : METHANE

marsh·mal·low \'märsh-ˌme-lō, -ˌma-\ *n* : a light spongy confection made from corn syrup, sugar, albumen, and gelatin

marsh marigold *n* : a swamp herb related to the buttercups that has bright yellow flowers

mar·su·pi·al \mär-'sü-pē-əl\ *n* : any of an order of primitive mammals (as opossums, kangaroos, or wombats) that bear very immature young which are nourished in a pouch on the abdomen of the female — **marsupial** *adj*

mart \'märt\ *n* : MARKET

mar·ten \'mär-tᵊn\ *n, pl* **marten** *or* **martens** : a slender mammal that is larger than the related weasels and has soft gray or brown fur; *also* : this fur

mar·tial \'mär-shəl\ *adj* [L *martialis* of Mars, fr. *Mart-, Mars* Mars, Roman god of war] **1** : of, relating to, or suited for war or a warrior ⟨∼ music⟩ **2** : of or relating to an army or military life **3** : WARLIKE

martial art *n* : any of several arts of combat (as karate and judo) practiced as sport

martial law *n* **1** : the law applied in occupied territory by the occupying military forces **2** : the established law of a country administered by military forces in an emergency when civilian law enforcement agencies are unable to maintain public order and safety

mar·tian \'mär-shən\ *adj, often cap* : of or relating to the planet Mars or its hypothetical inhabitants — **martian** *n, often cap*

mar·tin \'mär-tᵊn\ *n* : any of several swallows and esp. one of No. America with purplish blue plumage

mar·ti·net \ˌmär-tə-'net\ *n* : a strict disciplinarian

mar·tin·gale \'mär-tᵊn-ˌgāl\ *n* : a strap connecting a horse's girth to the bit or reins so as to hold down its head

mar·ti·ni \mär-'tē-nē\ *n* : a cocktail made of gin or vodka and dry vermouth

¹**mar·tyr** \'mär-tər\ *n* [ME, fr. OE, fr. LL, fr. Gk *martyr, martys* witness] **1** : a person who dies rather than renounce a religion; *also* : a person who makes a great sacrifice for the sake of principle **2** : a great or constant sufferer

²**martyr** *vb* **1** : to put to death for adhering to a belief **2** : TORTURE

mar·tyr·dom \'mär-tər-dəm\ *n* **1** : the suffering and death of a martyr **2** : TORTURE

¹**mar·vel** \'mär-vəl\ *n* **1** : one that causes wonder or astonishment **2** : intense surprise or interest

²**marvel** *vb* **mar·veled** *or* **mar·velled; mar·vel·ing** *or* **mar·vel·ling** : to feel surprise, wonder, or amazed curiosity ⟨∼ed at the circus act⟩

mar·vel·ous *or* **mar·vel·lous** \'mär-və-ləs\ *adj* **1** : causing wonder **2** : of the highest kind or quality — **mar·vel·ous·ly** *adv* — **mar·vel·ous·ness** *n*

Marx·ism \'märk-ˌsi-zəm\ *n* : the political, economic, and social principles and policies advocated by Karl Marx — **Marx·ist** \-sist\ *n or adj*

mar·zi·pan \'märt-sə-ˌpan, -ˌpan; 'mär-zə-ˌpan\ n [G, fr. It *marzapane*] : a confection of almond paste, sugar, and egg whites

masc abbr masculine

mas·cara \ma-'sker-ə\ n : a cosmetic esp. for darkening the eyelashes

mas·car·po·ne \ˌmas-kär-'pō-nā\ n : an Italian cream cheese

mas·cot \'mas-ˌkät, -kət\ n [F *mascotte*, fr. Occitan *mascoto*, fr. *masco* witch, fr. ML *masca*] : a person, animal, or object adopted usu. by a group to bring good luck

¹mas·cu·line \'mas-kyə-lən\ adj 1 : MALE; also : MANLY 2 : of, relating to, or constituting the gender that includes most words or grammatical forms referring to males — **mas·cu·lin·i·ty** \ˌmas-kyə-'li-nə-tē\ n

²masculine n : a noun, pronoun, adjective, or inflectional form or class of the masculine gender; also : the masculine gender

¹mash \'mash\ n 1 : a mixture of ground feeds for livestock 2 : crushed malt or grain steeped in hot water to make wort 3 : a soft pulpy mass

²mash vb 1 : to reduce to a soft pulpy state 2 : CRUSH, SMASH ⟨∼ a finger⟩ — **mash·er** n

MASH abbr mobile army surgical hospital

mash–up \'mash-ˌəp\ n : something created by combining elements from two or more sources

¹mask \'mask\ n 1 : a cover for the face usu. for disguise or protection 2 : MASQUE 3 : a figure of a head worn on the stage in antiquity 4 : a copy of a face made by means of a mold ⟨death ∼⟩ 5 : something that conceals or disguises 6 : the face of an animal

²mask vb 1 : to conceal from view : DISGUISE 2 : to cover for protection

mask·er \'mas-kər\ n : a participant in a masquerade

mas·och·ism \'ma-sə-ˌki-zəm, 'ma-zə-\ n 1 : a sexual perversion characterized by pleasure in being subjected to pain or humiliation 2 : pleasure in being abused or dominated — **mas·och·ist** \-kist\ n — **mas·och·is·tic** \ˌma-sə-'kis-tik, ˌma-zə-\ adj

ma·son \'mā-sⁿn\ n 1 : a skilled worker who builds with stone, brick, or concrete 2 cap : FREEMASON

Ma·son·ic \mə-'sä-nik\ adj : of or relating to Freemasons or Freemasonry

ma·son·ry \'mā-sⁿn-rē\ n, pl -ries 1 : something constructed of materials used by masons 2 : the art, trade, or work of a mason 3 cap : FREEMASONRY

masque \'mask\ n 1 : MASQUERADE 2 : a short allegorical dramatic performance (as of the 17th century)

¹mas·quer·ade \ˌmas-kə-'rād\ n 1 : a social gathering of persons wearing masks; also : a costume for wear at such a gathering 2 : DISGUISE

²masquerade vb -ad·ed; -ad·ing 1 : to disguise oneself : POSE 2 : to take part in a masquerade — **mas·quer·ad·er** n

¹mass \'mas\ n 1 cap : a sequence of prayers and ceremonies forming the eucharistic service of the Roman Catholic Church 2 often cap : a celebration of the Eucharist 3 : a musical setting for parts of the Mass

²mass n 1 : a quantity or aggregate of matter usu. of considerable size 2 : EXPANSE, BULK; also : MASSIVENESS 3 : the principal part 4 : AGGREGATE, WHOLE 5 : the quantity of matter that a body possesses as measured by its inertia 6 : a large quantity, amount, or number 7 : the great body of people — usu. used in pl. — **massy** adj

³mass vb : to form or collect into a mass

Mass abbr Massachusetts

mas·sa·cre \'ma-si-kər\ n 1 : the killing of many persons under cruel or atrocious circumstances 2 : a wholesale slaughter — **massacre** vb

¹mas·sage \mə-'säzh, -'säj\ n : manipulation of tissues (as by rubbing and kneading) for therapeutic purposes

²massage vb mas·saged; mas·sag·ing 1 : to subject to massage 2 : to treat flatteringly; also : MANIPULATE, DOCTOR ⟨∼ data⟩

mas·seur \ma-'sər\ n : a man who practices massage

mas·seuse \-'sərz, -'süz\ n : a woman who practices massage

mas·sif \ma-'sēf\ n : a principal mountain mass

mas·sive \'ma-siv\ adj 1 : forming or consisting of a large mass 2 : large in structure, scope, or degree — **mas·sive·ly** adv — **mas·sive·ness** n

mass·less \'mas-ləs\ adj : having no mass ⟨∼ particles⟩

mass medium n, pl **mass media** : a medium of communication (as the newspapers or television) that is designed to reach the mass of the people

mass–pro·duce \ˌmas-prə-'düs, -'dyüs\ vb : to produce in quantity usu. by machinery — **mass production** n

¹mast \'mast\ n 1 : a long pole or spar rising from the keel or deck of a ship and supporting the yards, booms, and rigging 2 : a slender vertical structure — **mast·ed** \'mas-təd\ adj

²mast n : nuts (as acorns) accumulated on the forest floor and often serving as food for animals (as hogs)

mas·tec·to·my \ma-'stek-tə-mē\ n, pl -mies : surgical removal of the breast

¹mas·ter \'mas-tər\ n 1 : a male teacher; also : a person holding an academic degree higher than a bachelor's but lower than a doctor's 2 : one highly skilled (as in an art or profession) 3 : one having authority or control 4 : VICTOR, SUPERIOR 5 : the commander of a merchant ship 6 : a youth or boy too young to be called *mister* — used as a title 7 : an original from which copies are made

²master vb 1 : to become master of : OVERCOME 2 : to become skilled or proficient in 3 : to produce a master recording of (as a musical performance)

master chief petty officer n : a petty officer of the highest rank in the navy

mas·ter·ful \'mas-tər-fəl\ adj 1 : inclined and usu. competent to act as master 2 : having or reflecting the skill of a master ⟨∼ verse⟩ — **mas·ter·ful·ly** adv — **mas·ter·ful·ness** n

master gunnery sergeant n : a noncommissioned officer in the marine corps ranking above a master sergeant

master key n : a key designed to open several different locks

mas·ter·ly \'mas-tər-lē\ adj 1 : indicating thorough knowledge or superior skill ⟨∼ performance⟩ 2 : having the skill of a master ⟨a ∼ writer⟩ — **mas·ter·ly** adv

mas·ter·mind \-ˌmīnd\ n : a person who directs or provides creative intelligence for a project — **mastermind** vb

master of ceremonies : a person who acts as host at a formal event or a program of entertainment

mas·ter·piece \'mas-tər-ˌpēs\ n : a work done with extraordinary skill

master plan n : an overall plan

mas·ter's \'mas-tərz\ n : a master's degree

master sergeant n 1 : a noncommissioned officer in the army ranking next below a sergeant major 2 : a noncommissioned officer in the air force ranking next below a senior master sergeant 3 : a noncommissioned officer in the marine corps ranking next below a master gunnery sergeant

mas·ter·stroke \'mas-tər-ˌströk\ n : a masterly performance or move

mas·ter·work \-ˌwərk\ n : MASTERPIECE

mas·tery \'mas-tə-rē\ n 1 : DOMINION; also : SUPERIORITY 2 : possession or display of great skill or knowledge

mast·head \'mast-ˌhed\ n 1 : the top of a mast 2 : the printed matter in a newspaper or periodical giving the title and details of ownership and rates of subscription or advertising

mas·tic \'mas-tik\ n : a pasty material used as a coating or cement

mas·ti·cate \'mas-tə-ˌkāt\ vb -cat·ed; -cat·ing : CHEW — **mas·ti·ca·tion** \ˌmas-tə-'kā-shən\ n

mas·tiff \'mas-təf\ n : any of a breed of large smooth-coated dogs used esp. as guard dogs

mast·odon \'mas-tə-ˌdän\ n [NL, fr. Gk *mastos* breast + *odōn, odous* tooth] : any of numerous huge extinct mammals related to the mammoths

mas·toid \'mas-ˌtòid\ n : a bony prominence behind the ear — **mastoid** adj

mas·tur·ba·tion \ˌmas-tər-'bā-shən\ n : stimulation of the genital organs apart from sexual intercourse, usu. to orgasm, and esp. by use of one's own hand — **mas·tur·bate** \'mas-tər-ˌbāt\ vb — **mas·tur·ba·to·ry** \'mas-tər-bə-ˌtòr-ē\ adj

¹mat \'mat\ n 1 : a piece of coarse woven or plaited fabric 2 : something made up of many intertwined strands 3 : a large thick pad used as a surface for wrestling and gymnastics

²**mat** *vb* **mat·ted; mat·ting 1** : to provide with a mat **2** : to form into a tangled mass ⟨dirt *matted* her hair⟩

³**mat** *vb* **mat·ted; mat·ting 1** *also* **matte** *or* **matt** : to make (as a color) matte **2** : to provide (a picture) with a mat

⁴**mat** *var of* ²MATTE

⁵**mat** *or* **matt** *or* **matte** *n* : a border going around a picture between picture and frame or serving as the frame

mat·a·dor \'ma-tə-ˌdȯr\ *n* [Sp, fr. *matar* to kill] : a bullfighter whose role is to kill the bull in a bullfight

¹**match** \'mach\ *n* **1** : a person or thing equal or similar to another; *also* : one able to cope with another : RIVAL **2** : a suitable pairing of persons or objects **3** : a contest or game between two or more individuals **4** : a marriage union; *also* : a prospective marriage partner — **match·less** *adj*

²**match** *vb* **1** : to meet as an antagonist; *also* : PIT ⟨∼ wits⟩ **2** : to provide with a worthy competitor; *also* : to set in comparison with **3** : MARRY **4** : to combine suitably or congenially ⟨∼ed the drapes with the rug⟩; *also* : ADAPT, SUIT **5** : to act in harmony ⟨his shoes and belt ∼⟩ **6** : to provide with a counterpart

³**match** *n* : a short slender piece of flammable material (as wood) tipped with a combustible mixture that ignites through friction

match·book \'mach-ˌbuk\ *n* : a small folder containing rows of paper matches

match·lock \-ˌläk\ *n* : a musket with a slow-burning cord lowered over a hole in the breech to ignite the charge

match·mak·er \-ˌmā-kər\ *n* : one who arranges a match and esp. a marriage

match·wood \-ˌwud\ *n* : small pieces of wood

¹**mate** \'māt\ *vb* **mat·ed; mat·ing** : CHECKMATE — **mate** *n*

²**mate** *n* **1** : ASSOCIATE, COMPANION; *also* : HELPER **2** : a deck officer on a merchant ship ranking below the captain **3** : one of a pair; *esp* : either member of a married couple or a breeding pair of animals

³**mate** *vb* **mat·ed; mat·ing 1** : to join or fit together **2** : to come or bring together as mates **3** : COPULATE

¹**ma·te·ri·al** \mə-'tir-ē-əl\ *adj* **1** : PHYSICAL ⟨∼ world⟩; *also* : BODILY ⟨∼ needs⟩ **2** : of or relating to matter rather than form ⟨∼ cause⟩; *also* : EMPIRICAL ⟨∼ knowledge⟩ **3** : highly important : SIGNIFICANT **4** : of a physical or worldly nature ⟨∼ progress⟩ — **ma·te·ri·al·ly** *adv*

²**material** *n* **1** : the elements or substance of which something is composed or made **2** : apparatus necessary for doing or making something

ma·te·ri·al·ise *Brit var of* MATERIALIZE

ma·te·ri·al·ism \mə-'tir-ē-ə-ˌli-zəm\ *n* **1** : a theory that everything can be explained as being or coming from matter **2** : a preoccupation with material rather than intellectual or spiritual things — **ma·te·ri·al·ist** \-list\ *n or adj* — **ma·te·ri·al·is·tic** \-ˌtir-ē-ə-'lis-tik\ *adj* — **ma·te·ri·al·is·ti·cal·ly** \-ti-k(ə-)lē\ *adv*

ma·te·ri·al·ize \mə-'tir-ē-ə-ˌlīz\ *vb* **-ized; -iz·ing 1** : to give material form to; *also* : to assume bodily form **2** : to make an often unexpected appearance — **ma·te·ri·al·i·za·tion** \-ˌtir-ē-ə-lə-'zā-shən\ *n*

ma·te·ri·el *or* **ma·te·ri·el** \mə-ˌtir-ē-'el\ *n* [F *matériel*] : equipment, apparatus, and supplies used by an organization

ma·ter·nal \mə-'tər-nᵊl\ *adj* **1** : MOTHERLY **2** : related through or inherited or derived from a female parent ⟨his ∼ grandparents⟩ — **ma·ter·nal·ly** *adv*

¹**ma·ter·ni·ty** \mə-'tər-nə-tē\ *n, pl* **-ties 1** : the quality or state of being a mother; *also* : MOTHERLINESS **2** : a hospital facility for the care of women before and during childbirth and for newborn babies

²**maternity** *adj* **1** : designed for wear during pregnancy ⟨∼ dress⟩ **2** : effective for the period close to and including childbirth ⟨∼ leave⟩

¹**math** \'math\ *n* : MATHEMATICS

²**math** *abbr* mathematical; mathematician

math·e·mat·ics \ˌma-thə-'ma-tiks\ *n* : the science of numbers and their properties, operations, and relations and in shapes in space and their structure and measurement — **math·e·mat·i·cal** \-'ma-ti-kəl\ *adj* — **math·e·mat·i·cal·ly** \-ti-k(ə-)lē\ *adv* — **math·e·ma·ti·cian** \ˌma-thə-mə-'ti-shən\ *n*

mat·i·nee *or* **mat·i·née** \ˌma-tə-'nā\ *n* [F *matinée*, lit., morning, fr. OF, fr. *matin* morning, fr. L *matutinum*, fr. neut. of *matutinus* of the morning, fr. *Matuta*, goddess

of morning] : a musical or dramatic performance in the daytime and esp. the afternoon

mat·ins \'ma-tᵊnz\ *n pl, often cap* **1** : special prayers said between midnight and 4 a.m. **2** : a morning service of liturgical prayer in Anglican churches

ma·tri·arch \'mā-trē-ˌärk\ *n* : a woman who rules or dominates a family, group, or state — **ma·tri·ar·chal** \ˌmā-trē-'är-kəl\ *adj* — **ma·tri·ar·chy** \'mā-trē-ˌär-kē\ *n*

ma·tri·cide \'ma-trə-ˌsīd, 'mā-\ *n* : the murder of a mother by her child — **ma·tri·cid·al** \ˌma-trə-'sī-dᵊl, ˌmā-\ *adj*

ma·tric·u·late \mə-'tri-kyə-ˌlāt\ *vb* **-lat·ed; -lat·ing** : to enroll as a member of a body and esp. of a college or university — **ma·tric·u·la·tion** \-ˌtri-kyə-'lā-shən\ *n*

mat·ri·mo·ny \'ma-trə-ˌmō-nē\ *n* [ME, fr. AF *matrimoignie*, fr. L *matrimonium*, fr. *mater* mother, matron] : MARRIAGE — **mat·ri·mo·nial** \ˌma-trə-'mō-nē-əl\ *adj* — **mat·ri·mo·nial·ly** *adv*

ma·trix \'mā-triks\ *n, pl* **ma·tri·ces** \'mā-trə-ˌsēz, 'ma-\ *or* **ma·trix·es** \'mā-trik-səz\ **1** : something within or from which something else originates, develops, or takes form **2** : a mold from which a relief surface (as a piece of type) is made

ma·tron \'mā-trən\ *n* **1** : a married woman usu. of dignified maturity or social distinction **2** : a woman supervisor (as in a school or police station) — **ma·tron·ly** *adj*

Matt *abbr* Matthew

¹**matte** *or* **matt** *var of* ³MAT

²**matte** *also* **matt** \'mat\ *adj* : not shiny : DULL

¹**mat·ter** \'ma-tər\ *n* **1** : a subject of interest or concern **2** *pl* : events or circumstances of a particular situation **3** : the subject of a discourse or writing **4** : TROUBLE, DIFFICULTY ⟨what's the ∼⟩ **5** : the substance of which a physical object is composed **6** : PUS **7** : an indefinite amount or quantity ⟨a ∼ of a few days⟩ **8** : something written or printed **9** : MAIL — **as a matter of fact** : ACTUALLY — **no matter** : without regard to ⟨will follow *no matter* where you go⟩ — **no matter what** : regardless of the consequences ⟨must win, *no matter what*⟩

²**matter** *vb* : to be of importance

mat·ter-of-fact \ˌma-tə-rəv-'fakt\ *adj* : adhering to fact; *also* : being plain, straightforward, or unemotional — **mat·ter-of-fact·ly** *adv* — **mat·ter-of-fact·ness** *n*

Mat·thew \'ma-thyü\ *n* — see BIBLE table

mat·tins *often cap, chiefly Brit var of* MATINS

mat·tock \'ma-tək\ *n* : a digging and grubbing tool with features of an adze and an ax or pick

mat·tress \'ma-trəs\ *n* **1** : a fabric case filled with resilient material used as or for a bed **2** : an inflatable airtight sack for use as a mattress

mat·u·rate \'ma-chə-ˌrāt\ *vb* **-rat·ed; -rat·ing** : MATURE

mat·u·ra·tion \ˌma-chə-'rā-shən\ *n* **1** : the process of becoming mature **2** : the emergence of personal and behavioral characteristics through growth processes — **mat·u·ra·tion·al** \-shə-nəl\ *adj*

¹**ma·ture** \mə-'tur, -'tyur\ *adj* **ma·tur·er; -est 1** : based on slow careful consideration **2** : having attained a final or desired state **3** : of or relating to a condition of full development **4** : suitable only for adults ⟨∼ content⟩ **5** : due for payment — **ma·ture·ly** *adv*

²**mature** *vb* **ma·tured; ma·tur·ing** : to reach or bring to maturity or completion

ma·tu·ri·ty \mə-'tur-ə-tē, -'tyur-\ *n* **1** : the quality or state of being mature; *esp* : full development **2** : the date when a note becomes due for payment

ma·tu·ti·nal \ˌma-chù-'tī-nᵊl; mə-'tü-tə-nəl, -'tyü-\ *adj* : of, relating to, or occurring in the morning : EARLY

mat·zo *or* **mat·zoh** \'mät-sə\ *n, pl* **mat·zoth** \-ˌsōt, -ˌsōth, -sōs\ *or* **mat·zos** *or* **mat·zohs** [Yiddish *matse*, fr. Heb *maṣṣāh*] : unleavened bread eaten esp. at the Passover

maud·lin \'mȯd-lən\ *adj* [alter. of Mary *Magdalene*; fr. her depiction as a weeping, penitent sinner] **1** : drunk enough to be silly **2** : weakly and effusively sentimental ⟨a ∼ love story⟩

¹**maul** \'mȯl\ *n* : a heavy hammer often with a wooden head used esp. for driving wedges

²**maul** *vb* **1** : BEAT, BRUISE; *also* : MANGLE **2** : to handle roughly

maun·der \'mȯn-dər\ *vb* **1** : to wander slowly and idly **2** : to speak indistinctly or disconnectedly

mau·so·le·um \ˌmȯ-sə-'lē-əm, ˌmȯ-zə-\ *n, pl* **-leums** *or* **-lea** \-'lē-ə\ [L, fr. Gk *mausōleion*, fr. *Mausōlos* Mausolus † *ab*

353 B.C. ruler of Caria whose tomb was one of the seven wonders of the ancient world] : a large tomb; *esp* : a usu. stone building for entombment of the dead above ground

mauve \'mōv, 'móv\ *n* : a moderate purple, violet, or lilac color

ma·ven *also* **ma·vin** \'mā-vən\ *n* [Yiddish *meyvn*, fr. LHeb *mēbhīn*] : EXPERT

mav·er·ick \'ma-vrik, -və-rik\ *n* [Samuel A. *Maverick* † 1870 Am. pioneer who did not brand his calves] 1 : an unbranded range animal 2 : NONCONFORMIST

maw \'mó\ *n* 1 : STOMACH; *also* : the crop of a bird 2 : the throat, gullet, or jaws esp. of a voracious animal

mawk·ish \'mó-kish\ *adj* : sickly sentimental ⟨~ poetry⟩ — **mawk·ish·ly** *adv* — **mawk·ish·ness** *n*

max *abbr* maximum

maxi \'mak-sē\ *n, pl* **max·is** : a long skirt, dress, or coat

maxi- *comb form* 1 : extra long ⟨*maxi*-kilt⟩ 2 : extra large ⟨*maxi*-problems⟩

max·il·la \mak-'si-lə\ *n, pl* **max·il·lae** \-'si-(,)lē\ *or* **maxillas** : JAW 1; *esp* : an upper jaw — **max·il·lary** \'mak-sə-,ler-ē\ *adj*

max·im \'mak-səm\ *n* : a proverbial saying

max·i·mal \'mak-sə-məl\ *adj* : MAXIMUM — **max·i·mal·ly** *adv*

max·i·mise *Brit var of* MAXIMIZE

max·i·mize \'mak-sə-,mīz\ *vb* **-mized; -miz·ing** 1 : to increase to a maximum 2 : to make the most of 3 : to increase the size of a computer program's window to fill an entire screen — **max·i·mi·za·tion** \,mak-sə-mə-'zā-shən\ *n*

max·i·mum \'mak-sə-məm\ *n, pl* **-ma** \-mə\ *or* **-mums** 1 : the greatest quantity, value, or degree 2 : an upper limit allowed by authority 3 : the largest of a set of numbers — **maximum** *adj*

max out *vb* 1 : to push to or reach a limit or an extreme 2 : to use up all available credit on (a credit card)

may \'mā\ *verbal auxiliary, past* **might** \'mīt\ *pres sing & pl* **may** 1 : have permission or liberty to ⟨you ~ go now⟩ 2 : be in some degree likely to ⟨you ~ be right⟩ 3 — used as an auxiliary to express a wish, purpose, contingency, or concession ⟨~ the best man win⟩

May \'mā\ *n* [ME, fr. OF *mai*, fr. L *Maius*, fr. *Maia*, Roman goddess] : the 5th month of the year

Ma·ya \'mī-ə\ *n, pl* **Maya** *or* **Mayas** : a member of a group of American Indian peoples of Yucatán, Guatemala, and adjacent areas — **Ma·yan** \'mī-ən\ *n or adj*

may·ap·ple \'mā-,a-pəl\ *n* : a No. American woodland herb related to the barberry that has a poisonous root, one or two large leaves, and an edible egg-shaped yellow fruit

may·be \'mā-bē, 'me-\ *adv* : PERHAPS

May Day \'mā-,dā\ *n* : May 1 celebrated as a springtime festival and in some countries as Labor Day

may·flow·er \'mā-,flaù(-ə)r\ *n* : any of several spring blooming herbs (as the trailing arbutus or an anemone)

may·fly \'mā-flī\ *n* : any of an order of insects with an aquatic nymph and a short-lived fragile adult having membranous wings

mayfly

may·hem \'mā-,hem, 'mā-əm\ *n* 1 : willful and permanent crippling, mutilation, or disfigurement of a person 2 : needless or willful damage

may·on·naise \'mā-ə-,nāz\ *n* [F] : a dressing made of egg yolks, vegetable oil, and vinegar or lemon juice

may·or \'mā-ər\ *n* : an official elected to act as chief executive or nominal head of a city or borough — **may·or·al** \-əl\ *adj* — **may·or·al·ty** \-əl-tē\ *n*

may·pole \'mā-,pōl\ *n, often cap* : a tall flower-wreathed pole forming a center for May Day sports and dances

maze \'māz\ *n* : a confusing intricate network of passages — **mazy** *adj*

ma·zur·ka \mə-'zər-kə\ *n* : a Polish dance in moderate triple measure

MB *abbr* Manitoba

MBA *abbr* master of business administration

mc *abbr* megacycle

Mc *symbol* moscovium

¹MC *n* : MASTER OF CEREMONIES

²MC *abbr* member of Congress

Mc- \mək\ *mə before forms beginning with* k *or* g\ *prefix* : used to indicate a convenient, low-quality version of a specified thing ⟨*Mc*Book⟩

Mc·Coy \mə-'kói\ *n* : something that is neither imitation nor substitute ⟨the real ~⟩

McGuffin *var of* MACGUFFIN

MCPO *abbr* master chief petty officer

¹Md *abbr* Maryland

²Md *symbol* mendelevium

MD *abbr* 1 [NL *medicinae doctor*] doctor of medicine 2 Maryland 3 muscular dystrophy

MDMA \,em-,dē-,em-'ā\ *n* : ECSTASY 2

mdnt *abbr* midnight

mdse *abbr* merchandise

MDT *abbr* mountain daylight (saving) time

me \'mē\ *pron, objective case of* I

Me *abbr* Maine

ME *abbr* 1 Maine 2 mechanical engineer 3 medical examiner

¹mead \'mēd\ *n* : an alcoholic beverage brewed from water and honey, malt, and yeast

²mead *n, archaic* : MEADOW

mead·ow \'me-dō\ *n* : land in or mainly in grass; *esp* : a tract of moist low-lying usu. level grassland — **mead·ow·land** \-,land\ *n* — **mead·owy** \'me-də-wē\ *adj*

mead·ow·lark \'me-dō-,lärk\ *n* : any of several American songbirds related to the orioles that are streaked brown above and in northernmost forms have a yellow breast marked with a black crescent

mead·ow·sweet \-,swēt\ *n* : a No. American native or naturalized spirea

mea·ger *or* **mea·gre** \'mē-gər\ *adj* 1 : THIN 2 : lacking richness, fertility, or strength; *also* : POOR ⟨a ~ income⟩ ◆ **Synonyms** SCANTY, SCANT, SPARE, SPARSE — **mea·ger·ly** *adv* — **mea·ger·ness** *n*

¹meal \'mēl\ *n* 1 : an act or the time of eating a portion of food 2 : the portion of food eaten at a meal

²meal *n* 1 : usu. coarsely ground seeds of a cereal 2 : a product resembling seed meal — **mealy** *adj*

meal·time \'mēl-,tīm\ *n* : the usual time at which a meal is served

mealy·bug \'mē-lē-,bəg\ *n* : any of a family of scale insects with a white cottony or waxy covering that are destructive pests esp. of fruit trees

mealy-mouthed \'mē-lē-,maủthd, -,maủth\ *adj* : not plain and straightforward : DEVIOUS ⟨a ~ politician⟩

¹mean \'mēn\ *vb* **meant** \'ment\; **mean·ing** 1 : to have in the mind as a purpose 2 : to serve to convey, show, or indicate : SIGNIFY ⟨red ~s stop⟩ 3 : to have importance to the degree of ⟨~s the world to me⟩ 4 : to direct to a particular individual ⟨a gift *meant* for me⟩

²mean *adj* 1 : HUMBLE 2 : lacking acumen : DULL 3 : SHABBY, CONTEMPTIBLE ⟨no ~ feat⟩ 4 : IGNOBLE, BASE ⟨a ~ trick⟩ 5 : STINGY 6 : pettily selfish or malicious 7 : VEXATIOUS ⟨a ~ dog⟩ 8 : EXCELLENT ⟨throws a ~ slider⟩ — **mean·ly** *adv* — **mean·ness** *n*

³mean *adj* 1 : occupying a middle position (as in space, order, or time) 2 : being a mean : AVERAGE ⟨a ~ value⟩

⁴mean *n* 1 : a middle point between extremes 2 *pl* : something helpful in achieving a desired end 3 *pl* : material resources affording a secure life 4 : ARITHMETIC MEAN

¹me·an·der \mē-'an-dər\ *n* [L *maeander*, fr. Gk *maiandros*, fr. *Maiandros* (now *Menderes*), river in Asia Minor] 1 : a winding course 2 : a winding of a stream

²meander *vb* 1 : to follow a winding course 2 : to wander aimlessly or casually

mean·ing *n* 1 : the thing one intends to convey esp. by language; *also* : the thing that is thus conveyed 2 : AIM 3 : SIGNIFICANCE; *esp* : implication of a hidden significance 4 : CONNOTATION; *also* : DENOTATION — **mean·ing·ful** \-fəl\ *adj* — **mean·ing·ful·ly** *adv* — **mean·ing·less** *adj*

¹**mean·time** \'mēn-ˌtīm\ n : the intervening time
²**meantime** adv : MEANWHILE
¹**mean·while** \-ˌhwī(-ə)l\ n : MEANTIME
²**meanwhile** adv 1 : during the intervening time 2 : at the same time
meas abbr measure
mea·sles \'mē-zəlz\ n sing or pl : an acute virus disease marked by fever and an eruption of distinct circular red spots
mea·sly \'mēz-lē, -zə-lē\ adj **mea·sli·er; -est** : contemptibly small or insignificant
¹**mea·sure** \'me-zhər, 'mā-\ n 1 : an adequate or moderate portion; also : a suitable limit 2 : the dimensions, capacity, or amount of something ascertained by measuring; also : an instrument for measuring 3 : a unit of measurement; also : a system of such units 4 : the act or process of measuring 5 : rhythmic structure or movement 6 : the part of a musical staff between two bars 7 : CRITERION 8 : a means to an end 9 : a legislative bill — **mea·sure·less** adj
²**measure** vb **mea·sured; mea·sur·ing** 1 : to mark or fix in multiples of a specific unit ⟨~ off five centimeters⟩ 2 : to find out the size, extent, or amount of 3 : to bring into comparison or competition 4 : to serve as a means of measuring 5 : to have a specified measurement — **mea·sur·able** \'me-zhə-rə-bəl, 'mā-\ adj — **mea·sur·ably** \-blē\ adv — **mea·sur·er** n
mea·sure·ment \'me-zhər-mənt, 'mā-\ n 1 : the act or process of measuring 2 : a figure, extent, or amount obtained by measuring
measure up vb 1 : to have necessary or fitting qualifications 2 : to equal esp. in ability
meat \'mēt\ n 1 : FOOD; esp : solid food as distinguished from drink 2 : animal and esp. mammal flesh considered as food 3 : the edible part inside a covering (as a shell or rind) — **meaty** adj
meat·ball \-ˌbȯl\ n : a small ball of chopped or ground meat
meat loaf n : a dish of ground meat seasoned and baked in the form of a loaf
mec·ca \'me-kə\ n, often cap [Mecca, Saudi Arabia, a destination of pilgrims in the Islamic world] : a center of a specified activity or interest ⟨a shopping ~⟩
mech abbr mechanical; mechanics
¹**me·chan·ic** \mi-'ka-nik\ adj : of or relating to manual work or skill
²**mechanic** n 1 : a manual worker 2 : MACHINIST; esp : one who repairs cars
me·chan·i·cal \mi-'ka-ni-kəl\ adj 1 : of or relating to machinery, to manual operations, or to mechanics 2 : done as if by a machine : AUTOMATIC ⟨a ~ response⟩ ◆ **Synonyms** INSTINCTIVE, IMPULSIVE, SPONTANEOUS — **me·chan·i·cal·ly** \-k(ə-)lē\ adv
mechanical drawing n : drawing done with the aid of instruments
me·chan·ics \mi-'ka-niks\ n sing or pl 1 : a branch of physics that deals with energy and forces and their effect on bodies 2 : the practical application of mechanics (as to the operation of machines) 3 : mechanical or functional details ⟨the ~ of the brain⟩
mech·a·nism \'me-kə-ˌni-zəm\ n 1 : a piece of machinery; also : a process or technique for achieving a result 2 : mechanical operation or action 3 : the fundamental processes involved in or responsible for a natural phenomenon ⟨the visual ~⟩
mech·a·nis·tic \ˌme-kə-'nis-tik\ adj 1 : mechanically determined ⟨~ universe⟩ 2 : MECHANICAL — **mech·a·nis·ti·cal·ly** \-ti-k(ə-)lē\ adv
mech·a·nize \'me-kə-ˌnīz\ vb **-nized; -niz·ing** 1 : to make mechanical 2 : to equip with machinery esp. in order to replace human or animal labor 3 : to equip with armed and armored motor vehicles — **mech·a·ni·za·tion** \ˌme-kə-nə-'zā-shən\ n — **mech·a·niz·er** n
¹**med** \'med\ adj : MEDICAL ⟨~ school⟩
²**med** n : MEDICINE 1 — usu. used in pl.
³**med** abbr 1 medical; medicine 2 medieval 3 medium
MEd abbr master of education
med·al \'me-dᵊl\ n [MF medaille, fr. OIt medaglia coin worth half a denarius, medal, fr. VL *medalis half, alter. of LL medialis middle, fr. L medius] 1 : a small usu. metal object bearing a religious emblem or picture 2 : a

piece of metal issued to commemorate a person or event or to award excellence or achievement
med·al·ist or **med·al·list** \'me-dᵊl-ist\ n 1 : a designer or maker of medals 2 : a recipient of a medal as an award
me·dal·lion \mə-'dal-yən\ n 1 : a large medal 2 : a tablet or panel bearing a portrait or an ornament
med·dle \'me-dᵊl\ vb **med·dled; med·dling** : to interfere without right or propriety — **med·dler** \'me-dᵊl-ər\ n
med·dle·some \'me-dᵊl-səm\ adj : inclined to meddle ⟨a ~ neighbor⟩
med·e·vac also **med·i·vac** \'me-də-ˌvak\ n 1 : emergency evacuation of the sick or wounded 2 : a helicopter used for medevac
me·dia \'mē-dē-ə\ n, pl **me·di·as** 1 : MEDIUM 4 2 sing or pl in constr : MASS MEDIA
me·di·al \'mē-dē-əl\ adj : occurring in or extending toward the middle
¹**me·di·an** \'mē-dē-ən\ n 1 : a value in an ordered set of values below and above which there are an equal number of values 2 : MEDIAN STRIP
²**median** adj 1 : being in the middle or in an intermediate position 2 : relating to or constituting a statistical median
median strip n : a strip dividing a highway into lanes according to the direction of travel
me·di·ate \'mē-dē-ˌāt\ vb **-at·ed; -at·ing** 1 : to act as an intermediary; esp : to work with opposing sides in order to resolve (as a dispute) or bring about (as a settlement) 2 : to bring about, influence, or transmit (as a physical process or effect) by acting as an intermediate or controlling agent or mechanism ◆ **Synonyms** INTERCEDE, INTERVENE, INTERPOSE, INTERFERE — **me·di·a·tion** \ˌmē-dē-'ā-shən\ n — **me·di·a·tor** \'mē-dē-ˌā-tər\ n
med·ic \'me-dik\ n : one engaged in medical work; esp : CORPSMAN
med·i·ca·ble \'me-di-kə-bəl\ adj : CURABLE
Med·ic·aid \'me-di-ˌkād\ n : a program of financial assistance for medical care designed for those unable to afford regular medical service and financed jointly by the state and federal governments
med·i·cal \'me-di-kəl\ adj : of or relating to the science or practice of medicine or the treatment of disease — **med·i·cal·ly** \-k(ə-)lē\ adv
medical examiner n : a public officer who performs autopsies on bodies to find the cause of death
me·di·ca·ment \mi-'di-kə-mənt, 'me-di-kə-\ n : a substance used in therapy
Medi·care \'me-di-ˌker\ n : a government program of financial assistance for medical care esp. for the aged
med·i·cate \'me-də-ˌkāt\ vb **-cat·ed; -cat·ing** : to treat with medicine
med·i·ca·tion \ˌme-də-'kā-shən\ n 1 : the act or process of medicating 2 : MEDICINE 1
me·dic·i·nal \mə-'di-sᵊn-əl\ adj : tending or used to cure disease or relieve pain — **me·dic·i·nal·ly** adv
med·i·cine \'me-də-sən\ n 1 : a substance or preparation used in treating disease 2 : a science and art dealing with the prevention, alleviation, and cure of disease
medicine ball n : a heavy stuffed leather ball used for conditioning exercises
medicine man n : a priestly healer or sorcerer esp. among the American Indians : SHAMAN
med·i·co \'me-di-ˌkō\ n, pl **-cos** : a medical practitioner or student
me·di·e·val also **me·di·ae·val** \ˌmē-dē-'ē-vəl, ˌme-, mē-'dē-vəl\ adj 1 : of, relating to, or characteristic of the Middle Ages 2 : having a quality (as cruelty) associated with the Middle Ages 3 : extremely outmoded or antiquated — **me·di·e·val·ism** \-və-ˌli-zəm\ n — **me·di·e·val·ist** \-list\ n
me·di·o·cre \ˌmē-dē-'ō-kər\ adj [MF, fr. L mediocris, fr. medius middle + ocris stony mountain] : of moderate or low quality : ORDINARY ⟨did a ~ job⟩ — **me·di·oc·ri·ty** \-'ä-krə-tē\ n
med·i·tate \'me-də-ˌtāt\ vb **-tat·ed; -tat·ing** 1 : to muse over : CONTEMPLATE, PONDER 2 : to engage in deep mental exercise directed toward a heightened level of spiritual awareness 3 : INTEND, PLAN — **med·i·ta·tion** \ˌme-də-'tā-shən\ n — **med·i·ta·tive** \'me-də-ˌtā-tiv\ adj — **med·i·ta·tive·ly** adv
Med·i·ter·ra·nean \ˌme-də-tə-'rā-nē-ən, -'rā-nyən\ adj : of or relating to the Mediterranean Sea or to the lands or people around it

¹me·di·um \'mē-dē-əm\ *n, pl* **mediums** *or* **me·dia** \-dē-ə\ [L] **1** : something in a middle position; *also* : a middle position or degree **2** : a means of effecting or conveying something **3** : a surrounding or enveloping substance **4** : a channel or system of communication, information, or entertainment **5** : a mode of artistic expression **6** : an individual held to be a channel of communication between the earthly world and a world of spirits **7** : a condition or environment in which something may function or flourish

²medium *adj* : intermediate in amount, quality, position, or degree

me·di·um·is·tic \ˌmē-dē-ə-'mis-tik\ *adj* : of, relating to, or being a spiritualistic medium

medivac *var of* MEDEVAC

med·ley \'med-lē\ *n, pl* **medleys** **1** : HODGEPODGE **2** : a musical composition made up esp. of a series of songs

me·dul·la \mə-'də-lə\ *n, pl* **-las** *or* **-lae** \-(ˌ)lē, -ˌlī\ : an inner or deep anatomical part; *also* : the posterior part (**medulla ob·lon·ga·ta** \-ˌä-ˌblȯṅ-'gä-tə\) of the vertebrate brain that is continuous with the spinal cord

meed \'mēd\ *n* : a fitting return

meek \'mēk\ *adj* **1** : enduring injury with patience and without resentment **2** : deficient in spirit and courage **3** : MODERATE — **meek·ly** *adv* — **meek·ness** *n*

meer·schaum \'mir-shəm, -ˌshȯm\ *n* [G, fr. *Meer* sea + *Schaum* foam] : a tobacco pipe made of a light white clayey mineral

¹meet \'mēt\ *vb* **met** \'met\; **meet·ing** **1** : to come upon : FIND **2** : JOIN, INTERSECT **3** : to appear to the perception of **4** : OPPOSE, FIGHT **5** : to join in conversation or discussion; *also* : ASSEMBLE **6** : to conform to ⟨~s requirements⟩ **7** : to pay fully **8** : to cope with **9** : to provide for **10** : to be introduced to

²meet *n* : an assembling esp. for a hunt or for competitive sports

³meet *adj* : SUITABLE, PROPER

meet·ing \'mē-tiŋ\ *n* **1** : an act of coming together : ASSEMBLY **2** : JUNCTION, INTERSECTION

meet·ing·house \-ˌhau̇s\ *n* : a building for public assembly and esp. for Protestant worship

meg \'meg\ *n* : MEGABYTE

mega- *or* **meg-** *comb form* **1** : great : large ⟨*mega*hit⟩ **2** : million ⟨*mega*hertz⟩

mega·byte \'me-gə-ˌbīt\ *n* : 1024 kilobytes or 1,048,576 bytes; *also* : one million bytes

mega·cy·cle \-ˌsī-kəl\ *n* : MEGAHERTZ

mega·death \-ˌdeth\ *n* : one million deaths — used as a unit in reference to nuclear warfare

mega·hertz \'me-gə-ˌhərts, -ˌherts\ *n* : a unit of frequency equal to one million hertz

mega·lith \'me-gə-ˌlith\ *n* : a large stone used in prehistoric monuments — **mega·lith·ic** \ˌme-gə-'li-thik\ *adj*

meg·a·lo·ma·nia \ˌme-gə-lō-'mā-nē-ə, -nyə\ *n* : a mental disorder marked by feelings of personal omnipotence and grandeur — **meg·a·lo·ma·ni·ac** \-'mā-nē-ˌak\ *adj or n* — **meg·a·lo·ma·ni·a·cal** \-mə-'nī-ə-kəl\ *adj*

meg·a·lop·o·lis \ˌme-gə-'lä-pə-ləs\ *n* : a very large urban unit

mega·phone \'me-gə-ˌfōn\ *n* : a cone-shaped device used to intensify or direct the voice — **megaphone** *vb*

mega·pix·el \'me-gə-ˌpik-səl\ *n* : one million pixels

mega·plex \-ˌpleks\ *n* : a cineplex having usu. at least 16 movie theaters

mega·ton \-ˌtən\ *n* : an explosive force equivalent to that of one million tons of TNT

mega·vi·ta·min \-ˌvī-tə-mən\ *adj* : relating to or consisting of very large doses of vitamins — **mega·vi·ta·mins** *n pl*

meh \'me\ *interj* — used to express indifference or mild disappointment

mei·o·sis \mī-'ō-səs\ *n* : a process of cell division in gamete-producing cells in which the number of chromosomes is reduced to one half — **mei·ot·ic** \mī-'ä-tik\ *adj*

meit·ner·i·um \mīt-'nir-ē-əm, -'ner-\ *n* : an artificially produced radioactive chemical element

mel·an·cho·lia \ˌme-lən-'kō-lē-ə\ *n* : a mental condition marked by extreme depression often with delusions

mel·an·chol·ic \ˌme-lən-'kä-lik\ *adj* **1** : DEPRESSED **2** : of or relating to melancholia

mel·an·choly \'me-lən-ˌkä-lē\ *n, pl* **-chol·ies** [ME *malencolie*, fr. AF, fr. LL *melancholia*, fr. Gk, fr. *melan-*, *melas*

black + *cholē* bile; so called fr. the former belief that it was caused by an excess of black bile] : depression of spirits : DEJECTION — **melancholy** *adj*

Mel·a·ne·sian \ˌme-lə-'nē-zhən\ *n* : a member of the dominant native group of the Pacific island grouping of Melanesia — **Melanesian** *adj*

mé·lange \mā-'lä°zh, -'länj\ *n* : a mixture esp. of incongruous elements

mel·a·nin \'me-lə-nən\ *n* : any of various dark brown pigments of animal or plant structures (as skin or hair)

mel·a·nism \'me-lə-ˌni-zəm\ *n* : an increased amount of black or nearly black pigmentation

mel·a·no·ma \ˌme-lə-'nō-mə\ *n, pl* **-mas** *also* **-ma·ta** \-mə-tə\ : a usu. malignant tumor containing dark pigment

¹meld \'meld\ *vb* : to show or announce for a score in a card game

²meld *n* : a card or combination of cards that is or can be melded

me·lee \'mā-ˌlā, mā-'lā\ *n* [F *mêlée*] : a confused struggle
♦ **Synonyms** FRACAS, ROW, BRAWL, DONNYBROOK

me·lio·rate \'mēl-yə-ˌrāt, 'mē-lē-ə-\ *vb* **-rat·ed; -rat·ing** : AMELIORATE — **me·lio·ra·tion** \ˌmēl-yə-'rā-shən, ˌmē-lē-ə-\ *n* — **me·lio·ra·tive** \'mēl-yə-ˌrā-tiv, 'mē-lē-ə-\ *adj*

mel·lif·lu·ous \me-'li-flə-wəs, mə-\ *adj* [ME *mellyfluous*, fr. LL *mellifluus*, fr. L *mel* honey + *fluere* to flow] : sweetly flowing ⟨a ~ voice⟩ — **mel·lif·lu·ous·ly** *adv* — **mel·lif·lu·ous·ness** *n*

¹mel·low \'me-lō\ *adj* **1** : soft and sweet because of ripeness; *also* : well aged and pleasingly mild ⟨~ wine⟩ **2** : made gentle by age or experience **3** : being rich and full but not garish or strident ⟨~ colors⟩ **4** : of soft loamy consistency ⟨~ soil⟩ — **mel·low·ness** *n*

²mellow *vb* : to make or become mellow — often used with *out*

me·lo·di·ous \mə-'lō-dē-əs\ *adj* : pleasing to the ear ⟨~ chimes⟩ — **me·lo·di·ous·ly** *adv* — **me·lo·di·ous·ness** *n*

melo·dra·ma \'me-lə-ˌdrä-mə, -ˌdra-\ *n* **1** : an extravagantly theatrical play in which action and plot predominate over characterization **2** : something having a sensational or theatrical quality — **melo·dra·mat·ic** \ˌme-lə-drə-'ma-tik\ *adj* — **melo·dra·mat·i·cal·ly** \-ti-k(ə-)lē\ *adv* — **melo·dra·ma·tist** \ˌme-lə-'dra-mə-tist, -'drä-\ *n*

mel·o·dy \'me-lə-dē\ *n, pl* **-dies** **1** : sweet or agreeable sound **2** : a particular succession of notes : TUNE, AIR — **me·lod·ic** \mə-'lä-dik\ *adj* — **me·lod·i·cal·ly** \-di-k(ə-)lē\ *adv*

mel·on \'me-lən\ *n* : any of various typically sweet fruits (as a muskmelon or watermelon) of the gourd family usu. eaten raw

¹melt \'melt\ *vb* **1** : to change from a solid to a liquid state usu. by heat **2** : DISSOLVE, DISINTEGRATE; *also* : to disappear or cause to disperse or disappear ⟨her anger ~ed away⟩ **3** : to make or become tender or gentle

²melt *n* : a melted substance

melt·down \'melt-ˌdau̇n\ *n* **1** : the melting of the core of a nuclear reactor **2** : a collapse of something (as one's self-control)

melting pot *n* : a place where different races, cultures, or individuals assimilate into a cohesive whole

melt·wa·ter \-ˌwȯ-tər, -ˌwä-\ *n* : water derived from the melting of ice and snow

mem *abbr* **1** member **2** memoir **3** memorial

mem·ber \'mem-bər\ *n* **1** : a part (as an arm, leg, leaf, or branch) of an animal or plant **2** : one of the individuals composing a group **3** : a part of a whole ⟨~s of a set⟩

mem·ber·ship \-ˌship\ *n* **1** : the state or status of being a member **2** : the body of members

mem·brane \'mem-ˌbrān\ *n* : a thin pliable layer esp. of animal or plant origin — **mem·bra·nous** \-brə-nəs\ *adj*

me·men·to \mə-'men-tō\ *n, pl* **-tos** *or* **-toes** [ME, fr. L, remember, imper. of *meminisse* to remember] : something that serves to warn or remind; *also* : SOUVENIR

memo \'me-mō\ *n, pl* **mem·os** : MEMORANDUM

mem·oir \'mem-ˌwär\ *n* **1** : MEMORANDUM **2** : AUTOBIOGRAPHY — usu. used in pl. **3** : an account of something noteworthy; *also, pl* : the record of the proceedings of a learned society

mem·o·ra·bil·ia \ˌme-mə-rə-'bi-lē-ə, -'bil-yə\ *n pl* [L] **1** : things worthy of remembrance **2** : things associated with a particular interest and that are usu. collected : MEMENTOS

mem·o·ra·ble \'me-mə-rə-bəl\ *adj* : worth remembering : NOTABLE ⟨a ~ quotation⟩ — **mem·o·ra·bil·i·ty** \‚me-mə-rə-'bi-lə-tē\ *n* — **mem·o·ra·ble·ness** *n* — **mem·o·ra·bly** \-blē\ *adv*

mem·o·ran·dum \‚me-mə-'ran-dəm\ *n, pl* **-dums** *or* **-da** \-də\ **1** : an informal record; *also* : a written reminder **2** : an informal written note

¹**me·mo·ri·al** \mə-'mór-ē-əl\ *adj* : serving to preserve remembrance

²**memorial** *n* **1** : something designed to keep remembrance alive; *esp* : MONUMENT **2** : a statement of facts often accompanied with a petition — **me·mo·ri·al·ize** *vb*

Memorial Day *n* : the last Monday in May or formerly May 30 observed as a legal holiday in honor of those who died in war

mem·o·rise *Brit var of* MEMORIZE

mem·o·rize \'me-mə-‚rīz\ *vb* **-rized; -riz·ing** : to learn by heart — **mem·o·ri·za·tion** \‚me-mə-rə-'zā-shən\ *n* — **mem·o·riz·er** *n*

mem·o·ry \'me-mə-rē\ *n, pl* **-ries** **1** : the power or process of remembering **2** : the store of things remembered **3** : COMMEMORATION **4** : something remembered **5** : the time within which past events are remembered **6** : a device (as in a computer) in which information can be stored; *esp* : RAM **7** : capacity for storing information ⟨512 megabytes of ~⟩ ♦ *Synonyms* REMEMBRANCE, RECOLLECTION, REMINISCENCE

men *pl of* MAN

¹**men·ace** \'me-nəs\ *n* **1** : THREAT **2** : DANGER ⟨those dogs are a ~⟩; *also* : NUISANCE

²**menace** *vb* **men·aced; men·ac·ing** **1** : THREATEN **2** : ENDANGER — **men·ac·ing·ly** *adv*

mé·nage \mā-'näzh\ *n* [F] : HOUSEHOLD

ménage à trois \-à-'trwä\ *n* : an arrangement in which three persons share sexual relations esp. while living together

me·nag·er·ie \mə-'na-jə-rē\ *n* : a collection of wild animals esp. for exhibition

¹**mend** \'mend\ *vb* **1** : to improve in manners or morals **2** : to put into good shape : REPAIR **3** : to improve in or restore to health : HEAL — **mend·er** *n*

²**mend** *n* **1** : an act of mending **2** : a mended place

men·da·cious \men-'dā-shəs\ *adj* : given to deception or falsehood : UNTRUTHFUL ♦ *Synonyms* DISHONEST, DECEITFUL — **men·da·cious·ly** *adv* — **men·dac·i·ty** \-'da-sə-tē\ *n*

men·de·le·vi·um \‚men-də-'lē-vē-əm, -'lā-\ *n* : a radioactive metallic chemical element artificially produced

men·di·cant \'men-di-kənt\ *n* **1** : BEGGAR **2** *often cap* : FRIAR — **men·di·can·cy** \-kən-sē\ *n* — **mendicant** *adj*

men·folk \'men-‚fōk\ *or* **men·folks** \-‚fōks\ *n pl* **1** : men in general **2** : the men of a family or community

men·ha·den \men-'hā-dᵊn, mən-\ *n, pl* **-den** *also* **-dens** : a marine fish related to the herring that is abundant along the Atlantic coast of the U.S.

¹**me·nial** \'mē-nē-əl, -nyəl\ *n* : a domestic servant

²**menial** *adj* **1** : of or relating to servants **2** : HUMBLE, SERVILE ⟨answered in ~ tones⟩ — **me·ni·al·ly** *adv*

men·in·gi·tis \‚me-nən-'jī-təs\ *n, pl* **-git·i·des** \-'ji-tə-‚dēz\ : inflammation of the membranes enclosing the brain and spinal cord; *also* : a usu. bacterial disease marked by this

me·ninx \'mē-niŋks, 'me-\ *n, pl* **me·nin·ges** \mə-'nin-(‚)jēz\ : any of the three membranes that envelop the brain and spinal cord — **men·in·ge·al** \‚me-nən-'jē-əl\ *adj*

me·nis·cus \mə-'nis-kəs\ *n, pl* **me·nis·ci** \-'nis-‚kī, -‚kē\ *also* **me·nis·cus·es** **1** : CRESCENT **2** : the curved upper surface of a column of liquid

men·o·pause \'me-nə-‚póz\ *n* : the period of life when menstruation stops naturally — **men·o·paus·al** \‚me-nə-'pó-zəl\ *adj*

me·no·rah \mə-'nór-ə\ *n* [Heb *měnōrāh* candlestick] : a candelabrum that is used in Jewish worship

men·ses \'men-‚sēz\ *n sing or pl* : the menstrual flow

menstrual cycle *n* : the complete cycle of physiological changes from the beginning of one menstrual period to the beginning of the next

men·stru·a·tion \‚men-strə-'wā-shən, men-'strā-\ *n* : a discharging of bloody matter at approximately monthly intervals from the uterus of breeding-age nonpregnant primate females; *also* : PERIOD 6 — **men·stru·al** \'men-strə-wəl\ *adj* — **men·stru·ate** \'men-strə-‚wāt, -‚strāt\ *vb*

men·su·ra·ble \'men-sə-rə-bəl, '-chə-\ *adj* : MEASURABLE

men·su·ra·tion \‚men-sə-'rā-shən, ‚men-chə-\ *n* : MEASUREMENT

-ment *n suffix* **1** : concrete result, object, or agent of a (specified) action ⟨embank*ment*⟩ ⟨entangle*ment*⟩ **2** : concrete means or instrument of a (specified) action ⟨entertain*ment*⟩ **3** : action : process ⟨encircle*ment*⟩ ⟨develop*ment*⟩ **4** : place of a (specified) action ⟨encamp*ment*⟩ **5** : state : condition ⟨amaze*ment*⟩

men·tal \'men-tᵊl\ *adj* **1** : of or relating to the mind **2** : of, relating to, or affected with a disorder of the mind ⟨~ illness⟩ — **men·tal·ly** *adv*

mental age *n* : a measure of a child's mental development in terms of the number of years it takes an average child to reach the same level

mental deficiency *n* : MENTAL RETARDATION

men·tal·i·ty \men-'ta-lə-tē\ *n, pl* **-ties** **1** : mental power or capacity **2** : mode or way of thought

mental retardation *n* : subaverage intellectual ability present from infancy that is characterized by an IQ of 70 or less and problems in development, learning, and social adjustment — **mentally retarded** *adj*

men·tee \men-'tē\ *n* : PROTÉGÉ

men·thol \'men-‚thól, -‚thōl\ *n* : an alcohol occurring esp. in mint oils that has the odor and cooling properties of peppermint — **men·tho·lat·ed** \-thə-‚lā-təd\ *adj*

¹**men·tion** \'men-chən\ *n* **1** : a brief or casual reference **2** : a formal citation for outstanding achievement

²**mention** *vb* **1** : to refer to : CITE **2** : to cite for superior achievement — **not to mention** : not even yet counting or considering

men·tor \'men-‚tór, -tər\ *n* : a trusted counselor or guide; *also* : TUTOR, COACH — **mentor** *vb*

menu \'men-yü, 'mān-\ *n, pl* **menus** [F, fr. *menu* small, detailed, fr. OF, fr. L *minutus* minute (adj.)] **1** : a list of the dishes available (as in a restaurant) for a meal; *also* : the dishes served **2** : a list of offerings or options

me·ow \mē-'aú\ *vb* : to make the characteristic cry of a cat — **meow** *n*

mer *abbr* meridian

mer·can·tile \'mər-kən-‚tēl, -‚tī(-ə)l\ *adj* : of or relating to merchants or trading

¹**mer·ce·nary** \'mər-sə-‚ner-ē\ *n, pl* **-nar·ies** : a person who serves merely for wages; *esp* : a soldier hired into foreign service

²**mercenary** *adj* **1** : serving merely for pay or gain **2** : hired to serve in a foreign army

mer·cer \'mər-sər\ *n, Brit* : a dealer in usu. expensive fabrics

mer·cer·ise *Brit var of* MERCERIZE

mer·cer·ize \'mər-sə-‚rīz\ *vb* **-ized; -iz·ing** : to treat cotton yarn or cloth with alkali so that it looks silky or takes a better dye

¹**mer·chan·dise** \'mər-chən-‚dīz, -‚dīs\ *n* : the commodities or goods that are bought and sold in business

²**mer·chan·dise** \-‚dīz\ *vb* **-dised; -dis·ing** : to buy and sell in business : TRADE — **mer·chan·dis·er** *n*

mer·chant \'mər-chənt\ *n* **1** : a buyer and seller of commodities for profit **2** : STOREKEEPER

mer·chant·able \'mər-chən-tə-bəl\ *adj* : acceptable to buyers : MARKETABLE

mer·chant·man \'mər-chənt-mən\ *n* : a ship used in commerce

merchant marine *n* : the commercial ships of a nation

merchant ship *n* : MERCHANTMAN

mer·ci·ful·ly \'mər-si-fə-lē\ *adv* **1** : in a merciful manner **2** : FORTUNATELY 2 ⟨~ we didn't have to attend⟩

mer·cu·ri·al \‚mər-'kyúr-ē-əl\ *adj* **1** : unpredictably changeable ⟨a ~ personality⟩ **2** : MERCURIC — **mer·cu·ri·al·ly** *adv* — **mer·cu·ri·al·ness** *n*

mer·cu·ric \‚mər-'kyúr-ik\ *adj* : of, relating to, or containing mercury

mercuric chloride *n* : a poisonous compound of mercury and chlorine used as an antiseptic and fungicide

mer·cu·ry \'mər-kyə-rē\ *n, pl* **-ries** **1** : a heavy silver-white liquid metallic chemical element used esp. in scientific instruments **2** *cap* : the planet nearest the sun

mer·cy \'mər-sē\ *n, pl* **mercies** [ME, fr. AF *merci*, fr. ML *merced-, merces*, fr. L, price paid, wages, fr. *merc-, merx* merchandise] **1** : compassion shown to an offender; *also* : imprisonment rather than death for first-degree murder **2**

: a blessing resulting from divine favor or compassion; *also*
: a fortunate circumstance **3** : compassion shown to victims of misfortune — **mer·ci·ful** \-si-fəl\ *adj* — **mer·ci·less**
\-si-ləs\ *adj* — **mer·ci·less·ly** *adv* — **mercy** *adj*
mercy killing *n* : EUTHANASIA
¹**mere** \'mir\ *n* : LAKE, POOL
²**mere** *adj, superlative* **mer·est** **1** : not diluted : PURE **2**
: being nothing more than ⟨a ∼ child⟩ — **mere·ly** *adv*
mer·e·tri·cious \ˌmer-ə-'tri-shəs\ *adj* [L *meretricius,* fr.
meretrix prostitute, fr. *merēre* to earn] : tawdrily attractive ⟨∼ trinkets⟩; *also* : SPECIOUS — **mer·e·tri·cious·ly**
adv — **mer·e·tri·cious·ness** *n*
mer·gan·ser \(ˌ)mər-'gan-sər\ *n* : any of various fish-eating wild ducks with a usu. crested head and a slender bill hooked at the end and serrated along the margins

merganser

merge \'mərj\ *vb* **merged; merg·ing** **1** : to blend gradually **2** : to combine, unite, or coalesce into one ✦ *Syn-onyms* MINGLE, AMALGAMATE, FUSE, INTERFUSE, INTERMINGLE
merg·er \'mər-jər\ *n* **1** : the act or process of merging **2**
: absorption by a corporation of one or more others
me·rid·i·an \mə-'ri-dē-ən\ *n* [ME, fr. AF *meridien,* fr. *me-ridien* of noon, fr. L *meridianus,* fr. *meridies* noon, south, irreg. fr. *medius* mid + *dies* day] **1** : the highest point
: CULMINATION **2** : any of the imaginary circles on the earth's surface passing through the north and south poles
3 : any of the pathways along which the body's vital energy flows according to the theory behind acupuncture
— **meridian** *adj*
me·ringue \mə-'raŋ\ *n* [F] : a baked dessert topping of stiffly beaten egg whites and powdered sugar
me·ri·no \mə-'rē-nō\ *n, pl* **-nos** [Sp] **1** : any of a breed of sheep noted for fine soft wool **2** : a fine soft fabric or yarn of wool or wool and cotton
¹**mer·it** \'mer-ət\ *n* **1** : laudable or blameworthy traits or actions **2** : a praiseworthy quality; *also* : character or conduct deserving reward or honor **3** *pl* : the intrinsic nature of a legal case; *also* : legal significance
²**merit** *vb* : EARN, DESERVE
mer·i·toc·ra·cy \ˌmer-ə-'tä-krə-sē\ *n, pl* **-cies** : a system in which the talented are chosen and moved ahead based on their achievement; *also* : leadership by the talented
mer·i·to·ri·ous \ˌmer-ə-'tȯr-ē-əs\ *adj* : deserving honor or esteem — **mer·i·to·ri·ous·ly** *adv* — **mer·i·to·ri·ous·ness**
n
mer·lin \'mər-lən\ *n* : a small compact falcon of the northern hemisphere
mer·lot \mer-'lō, mər-\ *n* : a dry red wine made from a widely grown grape; *also* : the grape itself
mer·maid \'mər-ˌmād\ *n* : a legendary sea creature with a woman's upper body and a fish's tail
mer·man \-ˌman, -mən\ *n* : a legendary sea creature with a man's upper body and a fish's tail
mer·ri·ment \'mer-i-mənt\ *n* **1** : HILARITY **2** : FESTIVITY
mer·ry \'mer-ē\ *adj* **mer·ri·er; -est** **1** : full of gaiety or high spirits **2** : marked by festivity **3** : BRISK ⟨a ∼pace⟩
✦ *Synonyms* BLITHE, JOCUND, JOVIAL, JOLLY, MIRTH-
FUL — **mer·ri·ly** \'mer-ə-lē\ *adv*
mer·ry-go-round \'mer-ē-gō-ˌraůnd\ *n* **1** : a circular revolving platform with benches and figures of animals on which people sit for a ride **2** : a busy round of activities
mer·ry·mak·ing \'mer-ē-ˌmā-kiŋ\ *n* **1** : jovial or festive activity **2** : a festive occasion — **mer·ry·mak·er** \-ˌmā-kər\
n
me·sa \'mā-sə\ *n* [Sp, lit., table, fr. L *mensa*] : a flat-topped hill with steep sides

mes·cal \me-'skal, mə-\ *n* **1** : PEYOTE **2** **2** : a usu. colorless liquor distilled from the leaves of an agave; *also*
: this agave
mes·ca·line \'mes-kə-lən, -ˌlēn\ *n* : a hallucinatory alkaloid from the peyote cactus
mes·clun \'mes-klən\ *n* : a mixture of young tender greens; *also* : a salad made with mesclun
mesdames *pl of* MADAM *or of* MADAME *or of* MRS.
mesdemoiselles *pl of* MADEMOISELLE
¹**mesh** \'mesh\ *n* **1** : one of the openings between the threads or cords of a net; *also* : one of the similar spaces in a network **2** : the fabric of a net **3** : NETWORK **4**
: working contact (as of the teeth of gears) ⟨in ∼⟩ —
meshed \'mesht\ *adj*
²**mesh** *vb* **1** : to catch in or as if in a mesh **2** : to be in or come into mesh : ENGAGE **3** : to fit together properly
mesh·work \'mesh-ˌwərk\ *n* : NETWORK
me·si·al \'mē-zē-əl, -sē-\ *adj* : of, relating to, or being the surface of a tooth that is closest to the middle of the front of the jaw
mes·mer·ise *Brit var of* MESMERIZE
mes·mer·ize \'mez-mə-ˌrīz\ *vb* **-ized; -iz·ing** : HYPNOTIZE
— **mes·mer·ic** \mez-'mer-ik\ *adj* — **mes·mer·ism** \'mez-mə-ˌri-zəm\ *n*
Me·so·lith·ic \ˌme-zə-'li-thik\ *adj* : of, relating to, or being a transitional period of the Stone Age between the Paleolithic and the Neolithic periods
me·so·sphere \'me-zə-ˌsfir\ *n* : a layer of the atmosphere between the stratosphere and the thermosphere
Me·so·zo·ic \ˌme-zə-'zō-ik, ˌmē-\ *adj* : of, relating to, or being the era of geologic history between the Paleozoic and the Cenozoic and extending from about 245 million years ago to about 65 million years ago — **Mesozoic** *n*
mes·quite \mə-'skēt, me-\ *n* : any of several spiny leguminous trees and shrubs chiefly of the southwestern U.S. with sugar-rich pods important as fodder; *also* : mesquite wood used esp. in grilling food
¹**mess** \'mes\ *n* [ME *mes,* fr. AF, fr. LL *missus* course at a meal, fr. *missus,* pp. of *mittere* to put, fr. L, to send] **1** : a quantity of food; *also* : enough food of a specified kind for a dish or meal ⟨a ∼ of beans⟩ **2** : a group of persons who regularly eat together; *also* : a meal eaten by such a group **3** : a place where meals are regularly served to a group **4** : a confused, dirty, or offensive state — **messy** *adj*
²**mess** *vb* **1** : to supply with meals; *also* : to take meals with a mess **2** : to make dirty or untidy; *also* : BUNGLE
3 : INTERFERE, MEDDLE ⟨don't ∼ with me⟩ **4** : PUTTER, TRIFLE
mes·sage \'me-sij\ *n* : a communication sent by one person to another — **message** *vb*
message board *n* : BULLETIN BOARD **2**
messeigneurs *pl of* MONSEIGNEUR
mes·sen·ger \'me-sᵊn-jər\ *n* : one who carries a message or does an errand
messenger RNA *n* : an RNA that carries the code for a particular protein from DNA in the nucleus to a ribosome in the cytoplasm and acts as a template for the formation of that protein
Mes·si·ah \mə-'sī-ə\ *n* **1** : the expected king and deliverer of the Jews **2** : Jesus **3** *not cap* : a professed or accepted leader of a cause — **mes·si·an·ic** \ˌme-sē-'a-nik\
adj
messieurs *pl of* MONSIEUR
mess·mate \'mes-ˌmāt\ *n* : a member of a group who eat regularly together
Messrs. \'me-sərz\ *pl of* MR.
mes·ti·zo \me-'stē-zō\ *n, pl* **-zos** [Sp] : a person of mixed blood
¹**met** *past and past part of* MEET
²**met** *abbr* metropolitan
me·tab·o·lism \mə-'ta-bə-ˌli-zəm\ *n* : the processes by which the substance of plants and animals incidental to life is built up and broken down; *also* : the processes by which a substance is handled in the living body ⟨the ∼ of sugar⟩ — **met·a·bol·ic** \ˌme-tə-'bä-lik\ *adj* —
me·tab·o·lize \mə-'ta-bə-ˌlīz\ *vb*
me·tab·o·lite \-ˌlīt\ *n* **1** : a product of metabolism **2** : a substance essential to the metabolism of a particular organism or to a metabolic process
meta·car·pal \ˌme-tə-'kär-pəl\ *n* : any of usu. five more or

less elongated bones of the part of the hand or forefoot between the wrist and the bones of the digits — **meta-carpal** *adj*

meta·car·pus \-'kär-pəs\ *n* : the part of the hand or forefoot that contains the metacarpals

met·al \'me-t⁹l\ *n* 1 : any of various opaque, fusible, ductile, and typically lustrous substances that are good conductors of electricity and heat 2 : METTLE; *also* : the material out of which a person or thing is made — **me·tal·lic** \mə-'ta-lik\ *adj*

met·al·lur·gy \'me-t⁹l-,ər-jē\ *n* : the science and technology of metals — **met·al·lur·gi·cal** \,me-t⁹l-'ər-ji-kəl\ *adj* — **met·al·lur·gist** \'me-t⁹l-,ər-jist\ *n*

met·al·ware \'me-t⁹l-,wer\ *n* : metal utensils for household use

met·al·work \-,wərk\ *n* : work and esp. artistic work made of metal — **met·al·work·er** \-,wər-kər\ *n* — **met·al·work·ing** *n*

meta·mor·phism \,me-tə-'mòr-,fi-zəm\ *n* : a change in the structure of rock; *esp* : a change to a more compact and more highly crystalline form produced by pressure, heat, and water — **meta·mor·phic** \-'mòr-fik\ *adj*

meta·mor·pho·sis \,me-tə-'mòr-fə-səs\ *n, pl* **-pho·ses** \-,sēz\ 1 : a change of physical form, structure, or substance esp. by supernatural means; *also* : a striking alteration (as in appearance or character) 2 : a fundamental change in form and often habits of an animal accompanying the transformation of a larva into an adult — **meta·mor·phose** \-,fōz, -,fōs\ *vb*

met·a·phor \'me-tə-,fòr\ *n* : a figure of speech in which a word for one idea or thing is used in place of another to suggest a likeness between them (as in "the ship plows the sea") — **met·a·phor·ic** \,me-tə-'fòr-ik\ *or* **met·a·phor·i·cal** \,me-tə-'fòr-i-kəl\ *adj* — **met·a·phor·i·cal·ly** \-i-k(ə-)lē\ *adv*

meta·phys·ics \,me-tə-'fi-ziks\ *n* [ML *Metaphysica*, title of Aristotle's treatise on the subject, fr. Gk (*ta*) *meta* (*ta*) *physika*, lit., the (works) after the physical (works); fr. its position in his collected works] : the philosophical study of the ultimate causes and underlying nature of things — **meta·phys·i·cal** \-'fi-zi-kəl\ *adj* — **meta·phy·si·cian** \-fə-'zi-shən\ *n*

me·tas·ta·sis \mə-'tas-tə-səs\ *n, pl* **-ta·ses** \-,sēz\ : the spread of a health-impairing agency (as cancer cells) from the initial or primary site of disease to another part of the body; *also* : a secondary growth of a malignant tumor — **me·tas·ta·size** \-tə-,sīz\ *vb* — **met·a·stat·ic** \,me-tə-'sta-tik\ *adj*

meta·tar·sal \,me-tə-'tär-səl\ *n* : any of the bones of the foot between the tarsus and the bones of the digits that in humans include five elongated bones — **metatarsal** *adj*

meta·tar·sus \-'tär-səs\ *n* : the part of the human foot or the hind foot in quadrupeds that contains the metatarsals

¹mete \'mēt\ *vb* **met·ed; met·ing** 1 *archaic* : MEASURE 2 : ALLOT — usu. used with *out* ⟨∼ out punishment⟩

²mete *n* : BOUNDARY ⟨∼s and bounds⟩

me·te·or \'mē-tē-ər, -,òr\ *n* 1 : a small particle of matter in the solar system directly observable only by its glow from frictional heating on falling into the earth's atmosphere 2 : the streak of light produced by a meteor

me·te·or·ic \,mē-tē-'òr-ik\ *adj* 1 : of, relating to, or resembling a meteor 2 : transiently brilliant ⟨a ∼ career⟩ — **me·te·or·i·cal·ly** \-i-k(ə-)lē\ *adv*

me·te·or·ite \'mē-tē-ə-,rīt\ *n* : a meteor that reaches the surface of the earth

me·te·or·oid \'mē-tē-ə-,ròid\ *n* : a small particle of matter in the solar system

me·te·o·rol·o·gy \,mē-tē-ə-'rä-lə-jē\ *n* : a science that deals with the atmosphere and its phenomena and esp. with weather forecasting — **me·te·o·ro·log·ic** \,mē-tē-,òr-ə-'lä-jik\ *or* **me·te·o·ro·log·i·cal** \-'lä-ji-kəl\ *adj* — **me·te·o·ro·log·ist** \,mē-tē-ə-'rä-lə-jist\ *n*

¹me·ter \'mē-tər\ *n* : rhythm in verse or music
²meter *n* : the basic metric unit of length — see METRIC SYSTEM table
³meter *n* : a measuring and sometimes recording instrument
⁴meter *vb* 1 : to measure by means of a meter 2 : to print postal indicia on by means of a postage meter

meter–kilogram–second *adj* : of, relating to, or being a

system of units based on the meter, the kilogram, and the second

meter maid *n* : a woman assigned to write tickets for parking violations

meth·a·done \'me-thə-,dōn\ *also* **meth·a·don** \-,dän\ *n* : a synthetic addictive narcotic drug used esp. as a substitute narcotic in the treatment of heroin addiction

meth·am·phet·amine \,me-tham-'fe-tə-,mēn, -thəm-, -mən\ *n* : a drug used medically in the form of its hydrochloride in the treatment of obesity and often illicitly as a stimulant

meth·ane \'me-,thān\ *n* : a colorless odorless flammable gas produced by decomposition of organic matter or from coal and used esp. as a fuel

meth·a·nol \'me-thə-,nòl, -,nōl\ *n* : a volatile flammable poisonous liquid alcohol used esp. as a solvent and as an antifreeze

meth·aqua·lone \me-'tha-kwə-,lōn\ *n* : a sedative and hypnotic habit-forming drug that is not a barbiturate

meth·od \'me-thəd\ *n* [ME, prescribed treatment, fr. L *methodus*, fr. Gk *methodos*, fr. *meta* with + *hodos* way] 1 : a procedure or process for achieving an end 2 : orderly arrangement : PLAN ♦ **Synonyms** MODE, MANNER, WAY, FASHION, SYSTEM — **me·thod·i·cal** \mə-'thä-di-kəl\ *adj* — **me·thod·i·cal·ly** \-k(ə-)lē\ *adv* — **me·thod·i·cal·ness** *n*

meth·od·ise *Brit var of* METHODIZE

Meth·od·ist \'me-thə-dist\ *n* : a member of a Protestant denomination adhering to the doctrines of John Wesley — **Meth·od·ism** \-,di-zəm\ *n*

meth·od·ize \'me-thə-,dīz\ *vb* **-ized; -iz·ing** : SYSTEMATIZE

meth·od·ol·o·gy \,me-thə-'dä-lə-jē\ *n, pl* **-gies** 1 : a body of methods and rules followed in a science or discipline 2 : the study of the principles or procedures of inquiry in a particular field

meth·yl \'me-thəl\ *n* : a chemical radical consisting of carbon and hydrogen

methyl alcohol *n* : METHANOL

meth·yl·mer·cury \,me-thəl-'mər-kyə-rē\ *n* : any of various toxic compounds of mercury that often occur as pollutants which accumulate in animals esp. at the top of a food chain

met·i·cal \'me-ti-kəl\ *n, pl* **met·i·cais** \-kī\ *also* **meticals** — see MONEY table

me·tic·u·lous \mə-'ti-kyə-ləs\ *adj* [L *meticulosus* fearful, fr. *metus* fear] : extremely careful in attending to details — **me·tic·u·lous·ly** *adv* — **me·tic·u·lous·ness** *n*

mé·tier \'me-,tyā, me-'tyā\ *n* : an area of activity in which one is expert or successful

me·tre \'mē-tər\ *chiefly Brit var of* METER

met·ric \'me-trik\ *adj* 1 : of or relating to measurement; *esp* : of or relating to the metric system 2 : METRICAL 1

met·ri·cal \'me-tri-kəl\ *adj* 1 : of, relating to, or composed in meter 2 : METRIC 1 — **met·ri·cal·ly** \-k(ə-)lē\ *adv*

met·ri·ca·tion \,me-tri-'kā-shən\ *n* : the act or process of converting into or expressing in the metric system

met·ri·cize \'me-trə-,sīz\ *vb* **-cized; -ciz·ing** : to change into or express in the metric system

metric system *n* : a decimal system of weights and measures based on the meter and on the kilogram
☞ the METRIC SYSTEM table is on page 312

metric ton *n* — see METRIC SYSTEM table

¹met·ro \'me-trō\ *n, pl* **metros** : SUBWAY
²metro *adj* : of, relating to, or characteristic of a metropolis and sometimes including its suburbs

met·ro·nome \'me-trə-,nōm\ *n* : an instrument for marking exact time by a regularly repeated tick

me·trop·o·lis \mə-'trä-pə-ləs\ *n* [ME, fr. LL, fr. Gk *mētropolis*, fr. *mētēr* mother + *polis* city] : the chief or capital city of a country, state, or region — **met·ro·pol·i·tan** \,me-trə-'pä-lə-tən\ *adj*

met·tle \'me-t⁹l\ *n* 1 : SPIRIT, COURAGE 2 : quality of temperament

met·tle·some \'me-t⁹l-səm\ *adj* : full of mettle ⟨COURAGEOUS ⟨a ∼ opponent⟩

MeV *abbr* million electron volts

¹mew \'myü\ *vb* : MEOW — **mew** *n*
²mew *vb* : CONFINE

mews \'myüz\ *n sing or pl, chiefly Brit* : stables usu. with living quarters built around a court; *also* : a narrow street with dwellings converted from stables

METRIC SYSTEM

LENGTH

UNIT (SYMBOL)	METRIC EQUIVALENT	U.S. EQUIVALENT
kilometer (km)	1,000 meters	0.62 mile
hectometer (hm)	100 meters	328.08 feet
dekameter (dam)	10 meters	32.81 feet
meter (m)	1 meter	39.37 inches
decimeter (dm)	0.1 meter	3.94 inches
centimeter (cm)	0.01 meter	0.39 inch
millimeter (mm)	0.001 meter	0.039 inch
micrometer (μm)	0.000001 meter	0.000039 inch

AREA

UNIT (SYMBOL)	METRIC EQUIVALENT	U.S. EQUIVALENT
square kilometer (sq km or km²)	1,000,000 square meters	0.39 square miles
hectare (ha)	10,000 square meters	2.47 acres
are (a)	100 square meters	119.60 square yards
square centimeter (sq cm or cm²)	0.0001 square meter	0.16 square inch

VOLUME

UNIT (SYMBOL)	METRIC EQUIVALENT	U.S. EQUIVALENT
cubic meter (m³)		1.31 cubic yards
cubic decimeter (dm³)	0.001 cubic meter	61.02 cubic inches
cubic centimeter (cu cm or cm³ also cc)	0.000001 cubic meter	0.061 cubic inch

MASS AND WEIGHT

UNIT (SYMBOL)	METRIC EQUIVALENT	U.S. EQUIVALENT
metric ton (t)	1,000,000 grams	1.10 short tons
kilogram (kg)	1,000 grams	2.20 pounds
hectogram (hg)	100 grams	3.53 ounces
dekagram (dag)	10 grams	0.35 ounce
gram (g)		0.035 ounce
decigram (dg)	0.1 gram	1.54 grains
centigram (cg)	0.01 gram	0.15 grain
milligram (mg)	0.001 gram	0.015 grain
microgram (μg or mcg)	0.000001 gram	0.000015 grain

CAPACITY

UNIT (SYMBOL)	METRIC EQUIVALENT	U.S. EQUIVALENT		
		CUBIC	DRY	LIQUID
kiloliter (kl)	1,000 liters	1.31 cubic yards	28.38 bushels	264.17 gallons
hectoliter (hl)	100 liters	3.53 cubic feet	2.84 bushels	26.42 gallons
dekaliter (dal)	10 liters	0.35 cubic foot	1.14 pecks	2.64 gallons
liter (l)		61.02 cubic inches	0.91 quart	1.06 quarts
deciliter (dl)	0.1 liter	6.10 cubic inches	0.18 pint	0.21 pint
centiliter (cl)	0.01 liter	0.61 cubic inch		0.34 fluid ounce
milliliter (ml)	0.001 liter	0.061 cubic inch		0.27 fluid dram
microliter (μl)	0.000001 liter	0.000061 cubic inch		0.00027 fluid dram

For metric system equivalents of U.S. system units, see WEIGHTS AND MEASURES table.

Mex *abbr* Mexican; Mexico

mez·za·nine \'me-zə-ˌnēn, ˌme-zə-'\ *n* **1** : a low-ceilinged story between two main stories of a building **2** : the lowest balcony in a theater; *also* : the first few rows of such a balcony

mez·zo for·te \ˌmet-(ˌ)sō-'fȯr-ˌtā, ˌmed-(ˌ)zō-, -tē\ *adj or adv* [It] : moderately loud — used as a direction in music

mez·zo pia·no \-pē-'ä-(ˌ)nō\ *adj or adv* [It] : moderately soft — used as a direction in music

mez·zo-so·pra·no \-sə-'pra-nō, -'prä-\ *n* : a woman's voice having a range between that of the soprano and contralto; *also* : a singer having such a voice

MFA *abbr* master of fine arts

mfr *abbr* manufacture; manufacturer

mg *abbr* milligram

Mg *symbol* magnesium

MG *abbr* **1** machine gun **2** major general **3** military government

mgr *abbr* **1** manager **2** monseigneur **3** monsignor

mgt *or* **mgmt** *abbr* management

MGy Sgt *abbr* master gunnery sergeant

MHz *abbr* megahertz

mi *abbr* **1** mile; mileage **2** mill

MI *abbr* **1** Michigan **2** military intelligence

MIA \ˌem-(ˌ)ī-'ā\ *n* [*missing in action*] : a member of the armed forces whose whereabouts following a combat mission are unknown

Mi·ami \mī-'a-mē, -mə\ *n, pl* **Mi·ami** *or* **Mi·am·is** : a member of an American Indian people orig. of Wisconsin and Indiana

mi·as·ma \mī-'az-mə, mē-\ *n, pl* **-mas** *also* **-ma·ta** \-mə-tə\ **1** : a vapor from a swamp formerly believed to cause disease **2** : a harmful influence or atmosphere ⟨a ∼ of smog⟩ — **mi·as·mal** \-məl\ *adj* — **mi·as·mic** \-mik\ *adj*

mic \'mīk\ *n* : MICROPHONE

Mic *abbr* Micah

mi·ca \'mī-kə\ *n* [NL, fr. L, grain, crumb] : any of various mineral silicates readily separable into thin transparent sheets

Mi·cah \'mī-kə\ *n* — see BIBLE table

mice *pl of* MOUSE

Mich *abbr* Michigan

Mi·che·as \'mī-kē-əs, mī-'kē-əs\ *n* : MICAH

Mic·mac \'mik-ˌmak\ *n, pl* **Micmac** *or* **Micmacs** : a member of an American Indian people of eastern Canada

micr- *or* **micro-** *comb form* **1** : small : minute ⟨*micro*capsule⟩ **2** : one millionth part of a specified unit ⟨*micro*second⟩

¹mi·cro \'mī-krō\ *adj* **1** : very small; *esp* : MICROSCOPIC **2** : involving minute quantities or variations

²micro *n, pl* **micros** : MICROCOMPUTER

mi·crobe \'mī-ˌkrōb\ *n* : MICROORGANISM; *esp* : one causing disease — **mi·cro·bi·al** \mī-'krō-bē-əl\ *adj*

mi·cro·bi·ol·o·gy \ˌmī-krō-bī-'ä-lə-jē\ *n* : a branch of biology dealing esp. with microscopic forms of life — **mi·cro·bi·o·log·i·cal** \-ˌbī-ə-'lä-ji-kəl\ *adj* — **mi·cro·bi·ol·o·gist** \-bī-'ä-lə-jist\ *n*

mi·cro·brew·ery \'mī-krō-ˌbrü-ə-rē\ *n* : a small brewery making specialty beer in limited quantities

mi·cro·burst \-ˌbərst\ *n* : a violent short-lived localized downdraft that creates extreme wind shears at low altitudes

mi·cro·cap·sule \'mī-krō-ˌkap-səl, -ˌsül\ *n* : a tiny capsule containing material (as a medicine) released when the capsule is broken, melted, or dissolved

mi·cro·chip \-ˌchip\ *n* : INTEGRATED CIRCUIT

mi·cro·cir·cuit \-ˌsər-kət\ *n* : a compact electronic circuit

mi·cro·com·put·er \-kəm-ˌpyü-tər\ *n* : a small computer that uses a microprocessor; *esp* : PERSONAL COMPUTER

mi·cro·cosm \'mī-krə-ˌkäzm\ *n* : an individual or community thought of as a miniature world or universe

mi·cro·elec·tron·ics \ˌmī-krō-i-ˌlek-'trä-niks\ *n* : a branch of electronics that deals with the miniaturization of electronic circuits and components — **mi·cro·elec·tron·ic** \-nik\ *adj*

mi·cro·en·cap·su·late \ˌmī-krō-in-'kap-sə-ˌlāt\ *vb* : to enclose (as a drug) in a microcapsule

mi·cro·fi·ber \'mī-krō-ˌfī-bər\ *n* : a fine usu. soft polyester fiber; *also* : fabric made from such fibers

mi·cro·fiche \'mī-krō-ˌfēsh, -ˌfish\ *n, pl* **-fiche** *or* **-fiches** \same *or* -ˌfē-shəz, -ˌfi-\ : a sheet of microfilm containing rows of images of pages of printed matter

mi·cro·film \-ˌfilm\ *n* : a film bearing a photographic record (as of print) on a reduced scale — **microfilm** *vb*

mi·cro·graph \'mī-krə-ˌgraf\ *n* : a graphic reproduction of the image of an object formed by a microscope

mi·cro·man·age \ˌmī-krō-'ma-nij\ *vb* : to manage esp. with excessive control or attention to details — **mi·cro·man·age·ment** \-mənt\ *n* — **mi·cro·man·ag·er** \-ni-jər\ *n*

mi·cro·me·te·or·ite \ˌmī-krō-'mē-tē-ə-ˌrīt\ *n* : a very small particle in interplanetary space

mi·crom·e·ter \mī-'krä-mə-tər\ *n* : an instrument used with a telescope or microscope for measuring minute distances

mi·cro·min·ia·tur·i·za·tion \ˌmī-kro-ˌmi-nē-ə-ˌchùr-ə-'zā-shən, -ˌmi-ni-ˌchùr-, -chər-\ *n* : the process of producing things in a very small size and esp. in a size smaller than one considered miniature — **mi·cro·min·ia·tur·ized** \-'mi-nē-ə-chə-ˌrīzd, -'mi-ni-chə-\ *adj*

mi·cron \'mī-ˌkrän\ *n* : one millionth of a meter

mi·cro·or·gan·ism \ˌmī-krō-'ȯr-gə-ˌni-zəm\ *n* : an organism (as a bacterium) too tiny to be seen by the unaided eye

mi·cro·phone \'mī-krə-ˌfōn\ *n* : an instrument for converting sound waves into variations of an electric current for transmitting or recording sound

mi·cro·pho·to·graph \ˌmī-krə-'fō-tə-ˌgraf\ *n* : PHOTOMICROGRAPH

mi·cro·pro·ces·sor \ˌmī-krō-'prä-ˌse-sər\ *n* : a computer processor contained on a microchip

mi·cro·scope \'mī-krə-ˌskōp\ *n* : an instrument for making magnified images of minute objects usu. using light — **mi·cros·co·py** \mī-'kräs-kə-pē\ *n*

mi·cro·scop·ic \ˌmī-krə-'skä-pik\ *also* **mi·cro·scop·i·cal** \-pi-kəl\ *adj* **1** : of, relating to, or involving the use of the microscope **2** : too tiny to be seen without the use of a microscope : very small — **mi·cro·scop·i·cal·ly** \-pi-k(ə-)lē\ *adv*

mi·cro·sec·ond \'mī-krō-ˌse-kənd\ *n* : one millionth of a second

mi·cro·sur·gery \ˌmī-krō-'sər-jə-rē\ *n* : minute dissection or manipulation (as by a laser beam) of living structures or tissue — **mi·cro·sur·gi·cal** \-'sər-ji-kəl\ *adj*

mi·cro·tech·nol·o·gy \-tek-'nä-lə-jē\ *n* : technology on a small or microscopic scale

¹mi·cro·wave \'mī-krə-ˌwāv\ *n* **1** : a radio wave between one millimeter and one meter in wavelength **2** : MICROWAVE OVEN

²microwave *vb* : to heat or cook in a microwave oven — **mi·cro·wav·able** *or* **mi·cro·wave·able** \ˌmī-krə-'wā-və-bəl\ *adj*

microwave oven *n* : an oven in which food is cooked by the absorption of microwave energy by water molecules in the food

¹mid \'mid\ *adj* : MIDDLE

²mid *abbr* middle

mid·air \'mid-'er\ *n* : a point or region in the air well above the ground

mid·day \'mid-ˌdā, -'dā\ *n* : NOON

mid·den \'mid-dᵊn\ *n* : a refuse heap

¹mid·dle \'mid-dᵊl\ *adj* **1** : equally distant from the extremes : MEDIAL, CENTRAL **2** : being at neither extreme : INTERMEDIATE **3** *cap* : constituting an intermediate period

²middle *n* **1** : a middle part, point, or position **2** : WAIST

middle age *n* : the period of life from about 45 to about 64 — **mid·dle-aged** \ˌmid-dᵊl-'ājd\ *adj*

Middle Ages *n pl* : the period of European history from about A.D. 500 to about 1500

mid·dle·brow \'mid-dᵊl-ˌbrau̇\ *n* : a person who is moderately but not highly cultivated — **middlebrow** *adj*

middle class *n* : a social class holding a position between the upper class and the lower class — **middle-class** *adj*

middle ear *n* : a small membrane-lined cavity of the ear through which sound waves are transmitted by a chain of tiny bones

middle finger *n* : the midmost of the five digits of the hand

mid·dle·man \'mid-dᵊl-ˌman\ *n* : INTERMEDIARY; *esp* : one intermediate between the producer of goods and the retailer or consumer

middle-of-the-road *adj* : standing for or following a course of action midway between extremes; *esp* : being neither liberal nor conservative in politics — **mid·dle–of–the–road·er** \-'rō-dər\ *n* — **mid·dle–of–the–road·ism** \-'rō-,di-zəm\ *n*

middle school *n* : a school usu. including grades 5 to 8 or 6 to 8

mid·dle·weight \'mi-d°l-,wāt\ *n* : one of average weight; *esp* : a boxer weighing not over 160 pounds

mid·dling \'mid-liŋ, -lən\ *adj* 1 : of middle, medium, or moderate size, degree, or quality 2 : MEDIOCRE

mid·dy \'mi-dē\ *n, pl* **middies** : MIDSHIPMAN

midge \'mij\ *n* : a very small fly : GNAT

midg·et \'mi-jət\ *n* 1 : something (as an animal) very small for its kind 2 *sometimes offensive* : a very small person

midi \'mi-dē\ *n* : a calf-length dress, coat, or skirt

MIDI \'mi-dē\ *n* [*musical instrument digital interface*] : a proctocol for the transmission of digitally encoded music

mid·land \'mid-lənd, -,land\ *n* : the interior or central region of a country

mid·life \'mid-'līf\ *n* : MIDDLE AGE

midlife crisis *n* : a period of emotional turmoil in middle age characterized esp. by a strong desire for change

mid·most \-,mōst\ *adj* : being in or near the exact middle — **midmost** *adv*

mid·night \-,nīt\ *n* : 12 o'clock at night

mid–ocean ridge \'mid-'ō-shən-\ *n* : an elevation on an ocean floor at the boundary of diverging tectonic plates

mid·point \'mid-,pȯint, -'pȯint\ *n* : a point at or near the center or middle

mid·riff \'mi-,drif\ *n* [ME *midrif*, fr. OE *midhrif*, fr. *midde* mid + *hrif* belly] 1 : DIAPHRAGM 1 2 : the mid-region of the human torso

mid·sec·tion \-,sek-shən\ *n* : a section midway between the extremes; *esp* : MIDRIFF 2

mid·ship·man \'mid-,ship-mən, (,)mid-'ship-\ *n* : a student in a naval academy

mid·ships \-,ships\ *adv* : AMIDSHIPS

midst \'midst\ *n* 1 : the interior or central part or point 2 : a position of proximity to the members of a group ⟨in our ~⟩ 3 : the condition of being surrounded or beset — **midst** *prep*

mid·stream \'mid-'strēm, -,strēm\ *n* : the middle of a stream

mid·sum·mer \-'sə-mər, -,sə-\ *n* 1 : the middle of summer 2 : the summer solstice

mid·town \'mid-,taùn, -'taùn\ *n* : a central section of a city; *esp* : one situated between sections called *downtown* and *uptown* — **midtown** *adj*

¹**mid·way** \'mid-,wā, -'wā\ *adv* : in the middle of the way or distance

²**mid·way** \-,wā\ *n* : an avenue (as at a carnival) for concessions and amusements

mid·week \-,wēk\ *n* : the middle of the week — **mid·week·ly** \-,wē-klē, -'wē-\ *adj or adv*

mid·wife \'mid-,wīf\ *n* : a person who helps women in childbirth — **mid·wife·ry** \-,wī-fə-rē\ *n*

mid·win·ter \'mid-'win-tər, -,win-\ *n* 1 : the winter solstice 2 : the middle of winter

mid·year \-,yir\ *n* 1 : the middle of a year 2 : a midyear examination — **midyear** *adj*

mien \'mēn\ *n* 1 : air or bearing esp. as expressive of mood or personality : DEMEANOR 2 : APPEARANCE, ASPECT ⟨dresses of formal ~⟩

miff \'mif\ *vb* : to put into an ill humor

¹**might** \'mīt\ *verbal auxiliary, past of* MAY — used as an auxiliary to express permission or possibility in the past, a present condition contrary to fact, less probability or possibility than *may*, or as a polite alternative to *may*, *ought*, or *should*

²**might** *n* : the power, authority, or resources of an individual or a group

mighty \'mī-tē\ *adj* **might·i·er; -est** 1 : very strong : POWERFUL 2 : GREAT, NOTABLE — **might·i·ly** \'mī-tə-lē\ *adv* — **might·i·ness** \-tē-nəs\ *n* — **mighty** *adv*

mi·gnon·ette \,min-yə-'net\ *n* : an annual garden herb with spikes of tiny fragrant flowers

mi·graine \'mī-,grān\ *n* [ME *mygreyn*, fr. MF *migraine*, fr. LL *hemicrania* pain in one side of the head, fr. Gk *hēmikrania*, fr. *hēmi-* half + *kranion* cranium] : a condition marked by recurrent severe headache and often nausea; *also* : an attack of migraine

mi·grant \'mī-grənt\ *n* : one that migrates; *esp* : a person

who moves in order to find work (as picking crops) — **migrant** *adj*

mi·grate \'mī-,grāt\ *vb* **mi·grat·ed; mi·grat·ing** 1 : to move from one country or place to another 2 : to pass usu. periodically from one region or climate to another for feeding or breeding — **mi·gra·tion** \mī-'grā-shən\ *n* — **mi·gra·to·ry** \'mī-grə-,tȯr-ē\ *adj*

mi·ka·do \mə-'kä-dō\ *n, pl* **-dos** : an emperor of Japan

mike \'mīk\ *n* : MICROPHONE

¹**mil** \'mil\ *n* : a unit of length equal to ¹⁄₁₀₀₀ inch

²**mil** *abbr* military

milch \'milk, 'milch\ *adj* : giving milk ⟨~ cow⟩

mild \'mī(-ə)ld\ *adj* 1 : gentle in nature or behavior 2 : moderate in action or effect 3 : TEMPERATE ⟨~ weather⟩ ✦ **Synonyms** EASY, COMPLAISANT, AMIABLE, LENIENT — **mild·ly** *adv* — **mild·ness** *n*

mil·dew \'mil-,dü, -,dyü\ *n* : a superficial usu. whitish growth produced on organic matter and on plants by a fungus; *also* : a fungus producing this growth — **mildew** *vb*

mile \'mī(-ə)l\ *n* [ME, fr. OE *mīl*, fr. L *milia* miles, fr. *milia passuum*, lit., thousands of paces] 1 — see WEIGHT table 2 : NAUTICAL MILE

mile·age \'mī-lij\ *n* 1 : an allowance for traveling expenses at a certain rate per mile 2 : distance in miles traveled (as in a day) 3 : the amount of service yielded (as by a tire) expressed in terms of miles of travel 4 : the average number of miles a motor vehicle will travel on a gallon of gasoline

mile·post \'mī(-ə)l-,pōst\ *n* : a post indicating the distance in miles from a given point

mile·stone \-,stōn\ *n* 1 : a stone serving as a milepost 2 : a significant point in development

mi·lieu \mēl-'yər, -'yü, -'yœ\ *n, pl* **mi·lieus** *or* **mi·lieux** *same or* -'yərz, -'yüz, -'yœz\ [F] : ENVIRONMENT, SETTING

mil·i·tant \'mi-lə-tənt\ *adj* 1 : engaged in warfare 2 : aggressively active esp. in a cause — **mil·i·tance** \-təns\ *n* — **mil·i·tan·cy** \-tən-sē\ *n* — **militant** *n* — **mil·i·tant·ly** *adv*

mil·i·ta·rise *Brit var of* MILITARIZE

mil·i·ta·rism \'mi-lə-tə-,ri-zəm\ *n* 1 : predominance of the military class or its ideals 2 : a policy of aggressive military preparedness — **mil·i·ta·rist** \-rist\ *n* — **mil·i·ta·ris·tic** \,mi-lə-tə-'ris-tik\ *adj*

mil·i·ta·rize \'mi-lə-tə-,rīz\ *vb* **-rized; -riz·ing** 1 : to equip with military forces and defenses ⟨~ a region⟩ 2 : to give a military character to

¹**mil·i·tary** \'mi-lə-,ter-ē\ *adj* 1 : of or relating to soldiers, arms, war, or the army 2 : performed by armed forces; *also* : supported by armed force ✦ **Synonyms** MARTIAL, WARLIKE — **mil·i·tar·i·ly** \,mi-lə-'ter-ə-lē\ *adv*

²**military** *n, pl* **military** *also* **mil·i·tar·ies** 1 : the military, naval, and air forces of a nation 2 : military persons

military police *n* : a branch of an army that exercises guard and police functions

mil·i·tate \'mi-lə-,tāt\ *vb* **-tat·ed; -tat·ing** : to have weight or effect ⟨disagreements ~ against an alliance⟩

mi·li·tia \mə-'li-shə\ *n* : a part of the organized armed forces of a country liable to call only in emergency — **mi·li·tia·man** \-mən\ *n*

¹**milk** \'milk\ *n* 1 : a nutritive usu. whitish fluid secreted by female mammals for feeding their young 2 : a milk-like liquid (as a plant juice) — **milk·i·ness** \'mil-kē-nəs\ *n* — **milky** *adj*

²**milk** *vb* 1 : to draw off the milk of ⟨~ a cow⟩ 2 : to draw something from as if by milking

milk·maid \'milk-,mād\ *n* : DAIRYMAID

milk·man \-,man, -mən\ *n* : a person who sells or delivers milk

milk of magnesia : a milk-white mixture of hydroxide of magnesium and water used as an antacid and laxative

milk shake *n* : a thoroughly blended drink made of milk, a flavoring syrup, and often ice cream

milk·sop \'milk-,säp\ *n* : an unmanly man

milk·weed \-,wēd\ *n* : any of a genus of herbs with milky juice and clustered flowers

Milky Way *n* 1 : a broad irregular band of light that stretches across the sky and is caused by the light of a very great number of faint stars 2 : MILKY WAY GALAXY

Milky Way galaxy *n* : the galaxy of which the sun is a

member and which includes the stars that create the light of the Milky Way

¹mill \'mil\ *n* 1 : a building with machinery for grinding grain into flour 2 : a machine used in processing (as by grinding, stamping, cutting, or finishing) raw material 3 : FACTORY

²mill *vb* 1 : to process in a mill 2 : to move in a circle or in an eddying mass

³mill *n* : one tenth of a cent

mill·age \'mi-lij\ *n* : a rate (as of taxation) expressed in mills

¹mil·len·ni·al \mə-'le-nē-əl\ *adj* : of or relating to a millennium

²millennial *n* : a person born in the 1980s or 1990s — usually pl.

mil·len·ni·um \mə-'le-nē-əm\ *n, pl* **-nia** \-nē-ə\ *or* **-niums** 1 : a period of 1000 years; *also* : a 1000th anniversary or its celebration 2 : the 1000 years mentioned in Revelation 20 when holiness is to prevail and Christ is to reign on earth 3 : a period of great happiness or human perfection

mill·er \'mi-lər\ *n* 1 : one that operates a mill and esp. a flour mill 2 : any of various moths having powdery wings

mil·let \'mi-lət\ *n* : any of several small-seeded cereal and forage grasses cultivated for grain or hay; *also* : the grain of a millet

milli- *comb form* : one thousandth part of

mil·li·am·pere \ˌmi-lē-'am-ˌpir\ *n* : one thousandth of an ampere

mil·liard \'mil-ˌyärd, 'mi-lē-ˌärd\ *n, Brit* : a thousand millions

mil·li·bar \'mi-lə-ˌbär\ *n* : a unit of atmospheric pressure

mil·li·gram \-ˌgram\ *n* — see METRIC SYSTEM table

mil·li·li·ter \-ˌlē-tər\ *n* — see METRIC SYSTEM table

mil·lime \mə-'lēm\ *n* — see *dinar* at MONEY table

mil·li·me·ter \'mi-lə-ˌmē-tər\ *n* — see METRIC SYSTEM table

mil·li·ner \'mi-lə-nər\ *n* [irreg. fr. *Milan*, Italy; fr. the importation of women's finery from Italy in the 16th century] : a person who designs, makes, trims, or sells women's hats

mil·li·nery \'mi-lə-ˌner-ē\ *n* 1 : women's apparel for the head 2 : the business or work of a milliner

mill·ing \'mi-liŋ\ *n* : a corrugated edge on a coin

mil·lion \'mil-yən\ *n, pl* **millions** *or* **million** : a thousand thousands — **million** *adj* — **mil·lionth** \-yənth\ *adj or n*

mil·lion·aire \ˌmil-yə-'ner, 'mil-yə-ˌner\ *n* : one whose wealth is estimated at a million or more (as of dollars or pounds)

mil·li·pede \'mi-lə-ˌpēd\ *n* : any of a class of arthropods related to the centipedes and having a long segmented body with a hard covering, two pairs of legs on most segments, and no poison fangs

mil·li·sec·ond \-ˌse-kənd\ *n* : one thousandth of a second

mil·li·volt \-ˌvōlt\ *n* : one thousandth of a volt

mill·pond \'mil-ˌpänd\ *n* : a pond made by damming a stream to produce a fall of water for operating a mill

mill·race \-ˌrās\ *n* : a canal in which water flows to and from a mill wheel

mill·stone \-ˌstōn\ *n* : either of two round flat stones used for grinding grain

mill·stream \-ˌstrēm\ *n* : a stream whose flow is used to run a mill; *also* : the stream in a millrace

mill wheel *n* : a waterwheel that drives a mill

mill·wright \'mil-ˌrīt\ *n* : a person who builds mills or sets up or maintains their machinery

milt \'milt\ *n* : the sperm-containing fluid of a male fish

mime \'mīm\ *n* 1 : MIMIC 2 : PANTOMIME — **mime** *vb*

mim·eo·graph \'mi-mē-ə-ˌgraf\ *n* : a machine for making many copies by means of a stencil through which ink is pressed — **mimeograph** *vb*

mi·me·sis \mə-'mē-səs, mī-\ *n* : IMITATION, MIMICRY

mi·met·ic \-'me-tik\ *adj* 1 : IMITATIVE 2 : relating to, characterized by, or exhibiting mimicry

¹mim·ic \'mi-mik\ *n* : one that mimics

²mimic *vb* **mim·icked** \-mikt\; **mim·ick·ing** 1 : to imitate closely 2 : to ridicule by imitation 3 : to resemble by biological mimicry

mim·ic·ry \'mi-mi-krē\ *n, pl* **-ries** 1 : an instance of mimicking 2 : a superficial resemblance of one organism to another or to natural objects among which it lives that gives it an advantage (as protection from predation)

mi·mo·sa \mə-'mō-sə, mī-, -zə\ *n* : any of a genus of trees, shrubs, and herbs of the legume family that occur in warm

regions and have ball-shaped heads of small white or pink flowers

min *abbr* 1 minim 2 minimum 3 mining 4 minister 5 minor 6 minute

min·a·ret \ˌmi-nə-'ret\ *n* [F, fr. Turk *minare*, fr. Ar *manāra* lighthouse] : a tall slender tower of a mosque from which a muezzin calls the faithful to prayer

1 minaret

mi·na·to·ry \'mi-nə-ˌtȯr-ē, 'mī-\ *adj* : THREATENING, MENACING

mince \'mins\ *vb* **minced; minc·ing** [ME, fr. AF *mincer*, fr. VL **minutiare*, fr. L *minutia* smallness, fr. *minutus* small, fr. pp. of *minuere* to lessen] 1 : to cut into very small pieces 2 : to restrain (words) within the bounds of decorum 3 : to walk in a prim affected manner

mince·meat \'mins-ˌmēt\ *n* : a finely chopped mixture esp. of raisins, apples, spices, and often meat used as a filling for a pie

¹mind \'mīnd\ *n* 1 : MEMORY 2 : the part of an individual that feels, perceives, thinks, wills, and esp. reasons 3 : INTENTION, DESIRE 4 : normal mental condition 5 : OPINION, VIEW ⟨changed her ∼⟩ 6 : MOOD 7 : mental qualities of a person or group 8 : intellectual ability 9 : ATTENTION ⟨pay him no ∼⟩

²mind *vb* 1 *chiefly dial* : REMEMBER 2 : to attend to closely 3 : HEED, OBEY 4 : to be concerned about; *also* : DISLIKE 5 : to be careful or cautious ⟨∼ the broken stair⟩ 6 : to take charge of 7 : to regard with attention

mind–bend·ing \'mīnd-ˌben-diŋ\ *adj* : MIND-BLOWING — **mind–bend·ing·ly** *adv*

mind–blow·ing \-ˌblō-iŋ\ *adj* : PSYCHEDELIC 1; *also* : MIND-BOGGLING — **mind–blow·er** \-ˌblō-ər\ *n* — **mind–blow·ing·ly** *adv*

mind–bog·gling \-ˌbä-gə-liŋ\ *adj* : mentally or emotionally exciting or overwhelming ⟨∼ special effects⟩

mind·ed \'mīn-dəd\ *adj* 1 : INCLINED, DISPOSED 2 : having a mind of a specified kind or concerned with a specific thing — usu. used in combination ⟨narrow-*minded*⟩ ⟨health-*minded*⟩

mind·ful \'mīnd-fəl\ *adj* : bearing in mind : AWARE ⟨∼ of their needs⟩ — **mind·ful·ly** *adv* — **mind·ful·ness** *n*

mind·less \-ləs\ *adj* 1 : marked by a lack of mind or consciousness; *esp* : marked by no use of the intellect 2 : not mindful : HEEDLESS — **mind·less·ly** *adv* — **mind·less·ness** *n*

¹mine \'mīn\ *pron* : that which belongs to me

²mine *n* 1 : an excavation in the earth from which minerals are taken; *also* : an ore deposit 2 : an underground passage beneath an enemy position 3 : an explosive device for destroying enemy personnel, vehicles, or ships 4 : a rich source of supply

³mine *vb* **mined; min·ing** 1 : to dig a mine 2 : UNDERMINE 3 : to get ore from the earth 4 : to place military mines in — **min·er** *n*

mine·field \'mīn-ˌfēld\ *n* 1 : an area set with mines 2 : something resembling a minefield esp. in having many dangers ⟨a political ∼⟩

mine·lay·er \-ˌlā-ər\ *n* : a naval vessel for laying underwater mines

min·er·al \'mi-nə-rəl\ *n* 1 : a crystalline substance (as diamond or quartz) of inorganic origin 2 : a naturally occurring substance (as coal, salt, or water) obtained usu. from the ground — **mineral** *adj*

min·er·al·ise *Brit var of* MINERALIZE

min·er·al·ize \'mi-nə-rə-ˌlīz\ *vb* **-ized; -iz·ing** **1** : to impregnate or supply with minerals **2** : to change into mineral form — **min·er·al·i·za·tion** \-rə-lə-'zā-shən\ *n*

min·er·al·o·gy \ˌmi-nə-'rä-lə-jē, -'ra-\ *n* : a science dealing with minerals — **min·er·al·og·i·cal** \ˌmi-nə-rə-'lä-ji-kəl\ *adj* — **min·er·al·o·gist** \ˌmi-nə-'rä-lə-jist, -'ra-\ *n*

mineral oil *n* : an oil of mineral origin; *esp* : a refined petroleum oil used as a laxative

mineral water *n* : water infused with mineral salts or gases

min·e·stro·ne \ˌmi-nə-'strō-nē, -'strōn\ *n* [It, fr. *minestra,* fr. *minestrare* to serve, dish up, fr. L *ministrare,* fr. *minister* servant] : a rich thick vegetable soup

mine·sweep·er \'mīn-ˌswē-pər\ *n* : a warship for removing or neutralizing underwater mines

min·gle \'miŋ-gəl\ *vb* **min·gled; min·gling** **1** : to bring or combine together : MIX ⟨*mingling* odors⟩ **2** : ASSOCIATE; *also* : to move about socially ⟨*mingled* with the guests⟩

ming tree \'miŋ-\ *n* : a dwarfed usu. evergreen tree grown as bonsai; *also* : an artificial plant resembling this

mini \'mi-nē\ *n, pl* **min·is** : something small of its kind — **mini** *adj*

mini- *comb form* : smaller or briefer than usual, normal, or standard

min·ia·ture \'mi-nē-ə-ˌchúr, 'mi-ni-ˌchúr, -chər\ *n* [It *miniatura* art of illuminating a manuscript, fr. ML, fr. L *miniare* to color with red lead, fr. *minium* red lead] **1** : a copy on a much reduced scale; *also* : something small of its kind **2** : a small painting — **miniature** *adj* — **min·ia·tur·ist** \-ˌchùr-ist, -chər-\ *n*

min·ia·tur·ize \'mi-nē-ə-ˌchə-ˌrīz, 'mi-ni-\ *vb* **-ized; -iz·ing** : to design or construct in small size — **min·ia·tur·i·za·tion** \ˌmi-nē-ə-ˌchúr-ə-'zā-shən, ˌmi-ni-, -chər-\ *n*

mini·bar \'mi-nē-ˌbär\ *n* : a small refrigerator in a hotel room that is stocked with beverages and snacks

mini·bike \'mi-nē-ˌbīk\ *n* : a small one-passenger motorcycle

mini·bus \-ˌbəs\ *n* : a small bus or van

mini·com·put·er \-kəm-ˌpyü-tər\ *n* : a computer between a mainframe and a microcomputer in size and speed

mini·disc \'mi-nē-ˌdisk\ *n* : a miniature optical disk

min·im \'mi-nəm\ *n* — see WEIGHT table

min·i·mal \'mi-nə-məl\ *adj* **1** : relating to or being a minimum : LEAST **2** : of or relating to minimalism or minimal art — **min·i·mal·ly** *adv*

minimal art *n* : abstract art consisting primarily of simple geometric forms executed in an impersonal style — **minimal artist** *n*

min·i·mal·ism \'mi-nə-mə-ˌli-zəm\ *n* : MINIMAL ART; *also* : a style (as in music or literature) marked by extreme spareness or simplicity — **min·i·mal·ist** \-list\ *n*

mini·mart \'mi-nē-ˌmärt\ *n* : CONVENIENCE STORE

min·i·mise *Brit var of* MINIMIZE

min·i·mize \'mi-nə-ˌmīz\ *vb* **-mized; -miz·ing** **1** : to reduce or keep to a minimum **2** : to underestimate intentionally ⟨~ the defects⟩ **3** : to replace (a window) on a computer display with a small button or icon which will restore the window when selected ♦ *Synonyms* DEPRECIATE, DECRY, DISPARAGE

min·i·mum \'mi-nə-məm\ *n, pl* **-ma** \-mə\ *or* **-mums** **1** : the least quantity assignable, admissible, or possible **2** : the least of a set of numbers **3** : the lowest degree or amount of variation (as of temperature) reached or recorded — **minimum** *adj*

min·ion \'min-yən\ *n* [MF *mignon* darling] **1** : a servile dependent, follower, or underling **2** : one highly favored **3** : a subordinate official

min·is·cule \'mi-nəs-ˌkyül\ *var of* MINUSCULE

mini·se·ries \'mi-nē-ˌsir-ēz\ *n* : a television story presented in sequential episodes

mini·skirt \-ˌskərt\ *n* : a skirt with the hemline several inches above the knee

¹min·is·ter \'mi-nə-stər\ *n* **1** : AGENT **2** : a member of the clergy esp. of a Protestant communion **3** : a high officer of state who heads a division of governmental activities **4** : a diplomatic representative to a foreign state — **min·is·te·ri·al** \ˌmi-nə-'stir-ē-əl\ *adj*

²minister *vb* **1** : to perform the functions of a minister of religion **2** : to give aid or service — **min·is·tra·tion** \ˌmi-nə-'strā-shən\ *n*

³min·is·trant \'mi-nə-strənt\ *adj, archaic* : performing service as a minister

²ministrant *n* : one that ministers

min·is·try \'mi-nə-strē\ *n, pl* **-tries** **1** : MINISTRATION **2** : the office, duties, or functions of a minister; *also* : the period of service or office **3** : CLERGY **4** : AGENCY **5** *often cap* : the body of ministers governing a nation or state; *also* : a government department headed by a minister

mini·tower \'mi-nē-ˌtaú(-ə)r\ *n* : a computer tower of intermediate size

mini·van \'mi-nē-ˌvan\ *n* : a small van

mink \'miŋk\ *n, pl* **mink** *or* **minks** : either of two slender flesh-eating mammals resembling the related weasels; *also* : the soft lustrous typically dark brown fur of a mink

min·ke whale \'miŋ-kə-\ *n* : a small grayish baleen whale with a whitish underside

Minn *abbr* Minnesota

min·ne·sing·er \'mi-ni-ˌsiŋ-ər, -ˌziŋ-\ *n* [G, fr. Middle High German, fr. *minne* love + *singer* singer] : any of a class of German lyric poets and musicians of the 12th to the 14th centuries

min·now \'mi-nō\ *n, pl* **minnows** *also* **minnow** : any of numerous small freshwater fishes

¹mi·nor \'mī-nər\ *adj* **1** : inferior in importance, size, or degree **2** : not having reached majority **3** : having the third, sixth, and sometimes the seventh degrees lowered by a half step ⟨~ scale⟩; *also* : based on a minor scale ⟨~ key⟩ **4** : not serious ⟨~ illness⟩

²minor *n* **1** : a person who has not attained majority **2** : a subject of academic study chosen as a secondary field of specialization

³minor *vb* : to pursue an academic minor ⟨~ed in philosophy⟩

mi·nor·i·ty \mə-'nȯr-ə-tē, mī-\ *n, pl* **-ties** **1** : the period or state of being a minor **2** : the smaller in number of two groups; *esp* : a group having less than the number of votes necessary for control **3** : a part of a population differing from others (as in race); *also* : a member of a minority

mi·nox·i·dil \mə-'näk-sə-ˌdil\ *n* : a drug used orally to treat hypertension and topically in solution to promote hair regrowth in some forms of baldness

min·ster \'min-stər\ *n* : a large or important church

min·strel \'min-strəl\ *n* **1** : a medieval singer of verses; *also* : MUSICIAN, POET **2** : any of a group of performers usu. with blackened faces in a program of black American songs, jokes, and impersonations ⟨a ~ show⟩

min·strel·sy \-sē\ *n* : the singing and playing of a minstrel; *also* : a body of minstrels

¹mint \'mint\ *n* **1** : any of a large family of aromatic square-stemmed herbs and shrubs; *esp* : one (as spearmint) that is fragrant and is the source of a flavoring oil **2** : a mint-flavored piece of candy — **minty** *adj*

²mint *n* **1** : a place where coins are made **2** : a vast sum ⟨worth a ~⟩

³mint *vb* **1** : to make (as coins) out of metal **2** : CREATE; *also* : to give a certain status to ⟨newly ~ed lawyers⟩ — **mint·age** \-ij\ *n* — **mint·er** *n*

⁴mint *adj* : unmarred as if fresh from a mint ⟨in ~ condition⟩

min·u·end \'min-yə-ˌwend\ *n* : a number from which another is to be subtracted

min·u·et \ˌmin-yə-'wet\ *n* : a slow graceful dance

¹mi·nus \'mī-nəs\ *prep* **1** : diminished by : LESS ⟨seven ~ three equals four⟩ **2** : LACKING, WITHOUT ⟨~ his hat⟩

²minus *n* : a negative quantity or quality

³minus *adj* **1** : algebraically negative ⟨~ quantity⟩ **2** : having a negative quality

¹mi·nus·cule \'mi-nəs-ˌkyül\ *n* : a lowercase letter

²minuscule *also* **min·is·cule** *adj* : very small

minus sign *n* : a sign – used in mathematics to indicate subtraction or a negative quantity

¹min·ute \'mi-nət\ *n* **1** : the 60th part of an hour or of a degree : 60 seconds **2** : a short space of time **3** *pl* : the official record of the proceedings of a meeting

²mi·nute \mī-'nüt, mə-, -'nyüt\ *adj* **mi·nut·er; -est** **1** : very small **2** : of little importance : TRIFLING **3** : marked by close attention to details ♦ *Synonyms* DIMINUTIVE, TINY, MINIATURE, WEE — **mi·nute·ly** *adv* — **mi·nute·ness** *n*

min·ute·man \'mi-nət-ˌman\ *n* : a member of a group of

armed men pledged to take the field at a minute's notice during and immediately before the American Revolution

mi·nu·tia \mə-'nü-shə, -'nyü-, -shē-ə\ *n, pl* **-ti·ae** \-shē-ˌē\ [L] : a minute or minor detail — usu. used in pl.

minx \'miŋks\ *n* : a pert girl

Mio·cene \'mī-ə-ˌsēn\ *adj* : of, relating to, or being the epoch of the Tertiary between the Oligocene and the Pliocene — **Miocene** *n*

mir·a·cle \'mir-i-kəl\ *n* **1** : an extraordinary event manifesting divine intervention in human affairs **2** : an unusual event, thing, or accomplishment : WONDER, MARVEL — **mi·rac·u·lous** \mə-'ra-kyə-ləs\ *adj* — **mi·rac·u·lous·ly** *adv*

miracle drug *n* : a usu. newly discovered drug that elicits a dramatic response in a patient's condition

mi·rage \mə-'räzh\ *n* **1** : an illusion that often appears as a pool of water or a mirror in which distant objects are seen inverted, is sometimes seen at sea, in the desert, or over a hot pavement, and results from atmospheric conditions **2** : something illusory and unattainable

¹mire \'mī(-ə)r\ *n* : heavy and often deep mud or slush — **miry** *adj*

²mire *vb* **mired; mir·ing** : to stick or sink in or as if in mire

mire·poix \mir-'pwä\ *n, pl* **mirepoix** : a mixture of diced vegetables and sometimes meats used in soups, stews, and sauces

¹mir·ror \'mir-ər\ *n* **1** : a polished or smooth surface (as of glass) that forms images by reflection **2** : a true representation

²mirror *vb* **1** : to reflect in or as if in a mirror **2** : RESEMBLE ⟨her mood ~s the gloomy weather⟩

mirth \'mərth\ *n* : gladness or gaiety accompanied with laughter ♦ **Synonyms** GLEE, JOLLITY, HILARITY, MERRIMENT — **mirth·ful** \-fəl\ *adj* — **mirth·ful·ly** *adv* — **mirth·ful·ness** *n* — **mirth·less** *adj*

MIRV \'mərv\ *n* [*multiple independently targeted reentry vehicle*] : an ICBM with multiple warheads that have different targets — **MIRV** *vb*

mis·ad·ven·ture \ˌmi-səd-'ven-chər\ *n* : MISFORTUNE, MISHAP

mis·aligned \ˌmi-sə-'līnd\ *adj* : not properly aligned — **mis·align·ment** \-'līn-mənt\ *n*

mis·al·li·ance \ˌmi-sə-'lī-əns\ *n* : an improper or unsuitable marriage

mis·al·lo·ca·tion \ˌmi-ˌsa-lə-'kā-shən\ *n* : faulty or improper allocation

mis·an·dry \'mi-ˌsan-drē\ *n* : a hatred of men — **mis·an·drist** \-drist\ *n or adj*

mis·an·thrope \'mi-sᵊn-ˌthrōp\ *n* : one who hates humankind — **mis·an·throp·ic** \ˌmi-sᵊn-'thrä-pik\ *adj* — **mis·an·throp·i·cal·ly** \-pi-k(ə-)lē\ *adv* — **mis·an·thro·py** \mi-'san-thrə-pē\ *n*

mis·ap·ply \ˌmi-sə-'plī\ *vb* : to apply wrongly — **mis·ap·pli·ca·tion** \ˌmi-ˌsa-plə-'kā-shən\ *n*

mis·ap·pre·hend \ˌmi-ˌsa-pri-'hend\ *vb* : MISUNDERSTAND — **mis·ap·pre·hen·sion** \-'hen-chən\ *n*

mis·ap·pro·pri·ate \ˌmi-sə-'prō-prē-ˌāt\ *vb* : to appropriate wrongly (as by embezzlement) — **mis·ap·pro·pri·a·tion** \-ˌprō-prē-'ā-shən\ *n*

mis·be·got·ten \-bi-'gä-tᵊn\ *adj* : ILLEGITIMATE; *also* : ill-conceived

mis·be·have \ˌmis-bi-'hāv\ *vb* : to behave improperly — **mis·be·hav·er** *n* — **mis·be·hav·ior** \-'hā-vyər\ *n*

mis·be·liev·er \-bə-'lē-vər\ *n* : one who holds a false or unorthodox belief

mis·brand \mis-'brand\ *vb* : to brand falsely or in a misleading manner

misc *abbr* miscellaneous

mis·cal·cu·late \mis-'kal-kyə-ˌlāt\ *vb* : to calculate wrongly — **mis·cal·cu·la·tion** \ˌmis-ˌkal-kyə-'lā-shən\ *n*

mis·call \mis-'kol\ *vb* : MISNAME

mis·car·riage \-'ker-ij\ *n* **1** : failure in the administration of justice **2** : spontaneous expulsion of a fetus before it is capable of independent life

mis·car·ry \-'ker-ē\ *vb* **1** : to have a miscarriage of a fetus **2** : to go wrong; *also* : to be unsuccessful

mis·ce·ge·na·tion \mi-se-jə-'nā-shən, ˌmi-si-jə-'nā-\ *n* [L *miscēre* to mix + *genus* race] : marriage, cohabitation, or sexual intercourse between persons of different races

mis·cel·la·neous \ˌmi-sə-'lā-nē-əs\ *adj* **1** : consisting of diverse things or members **2** : having various traits;

also : dealing with or interested in diverse subjects — **mis·cel·la·neous·ly** *adv* — **mis·cel·la·neous·ness** *n*

mis·cel·la·ny \'mi-sə-ˌlā-nē\ *n, pl* **-nies** **1** : a collection of writings on various subjects **2** : HODGEPODGE

mis·chance \mis-'chans\ *n* : bad luck; *also* : MISHAP

mis·chief \'mis-chəf\ *n* [ME *meschief*, fr. AF, misfortune, hardship, fr. OF *meschever* to come out badly, fr. *mes-* badly + *chief* head, end] **1** : injury caused by a particular agent **2** : a source of harm or irritation **3** : action that annoys; *also* : MISCHIEVOUSNESS

mis·chie·vous \'mis-chə-vəs\ *adj* **1** : HARMFUL, INJURIOUS **2** : causing annoyance or minor injury **3** : irresponsibly playful ⟨~ children⟩ — **mis·chie·vous·ly** *adv* — **mis·chie·vous·ness** *n*

mis·ci·ble \'mi-sə-bəl\ *adj* : capable of being mixed

mis·com·mu·ni·ca·tion \ˌmis-kə-ˌmyü-nə-'kā-shən\ *n* : failure to communicate clearly

mis·con·ceive \ˌmis-kən-'sēv\ *vb* : to interpret incorrectly — **mis·con·cep·tion** \-'sep-shən\ *n*

mis·con·duct \mis-'kän-(ˌ)dəkt\ *n* **1** : MISMANAGEMENT **2** : intentional wrongdoing **3** : improper behavior; *also* : a penalty in a sport for improper behavior

mis·con·strue \ˌmis-kən-'strü\ *vb* : MISINTERPRET — **mis·con·struc·tion** \-'strək-shən\ *n*

mis·count \mis-'kaúnt\ *vb* : to count incorrectly : MISCALCULATE

mis·cre·ant \'mis-krē-ənt\ *n* : one who behaves criminally or viciously — **miscreant** *adj*

mis·cue \mis-'kyü\ *n* : MISTAKE, ERROR — **miscue** *vb*

mis·deed \mis-'dēd\ *n* : a wrong deed

mis·de·mean·or \ˌmis-di-'mē-nər\ *n* **1** : a crime less serious than a felony **2** : MISDEED

mis·di·rect \ˌmis-də-'rekt, -dī-\ *vb* : to give a wrong direction to — **mis·di·rec·tion** \-'rek-shən\ *n*

mis·do·ing \mis-'dü-iŋ\ *n* : WRONGDOING — **mis·do** \-'dü\ *vb* — **mis·do·er** \-'dü-ər\ *n*

mise-en-scène \ˌmē-ˌzäⁿ-'sen, -'sän\ *n, pl* **mise-en-scènes** *same or* -'senz, -'sänz\ [F] **1** : the arrangement of the scenery, property, and actors on a stage **2** : SETTING; *also* : ENVIRONMENT

mi·ser \'mī-zər\ *n* [L *miser* miserable] : a person who hoards and is stingy with money — **mi·ser·li·ness** \-lē-nəs\ *n* — **mi·ser·ly** *adj*

mis·er·a·ble \'mi-zə-rə-bəl, 'miz-rə-\ *adj* **1** : wretchedly deficient; *also* : causing extreme discomfort **2** : being in a state of distress **3** : SHAMEFUL — **mis·er·a·ble·ness** *n* — **mis·er·a·bly** \-blē\ *adv*

mis·ery \'mi-zə-rē\ *n, pl* **-er·ies** **1** : suffering and want caused by poverty or affliction **2** : a cause of suffering or discomfort **3** : emotional distress

mis·fea·sance \mis-'fē-zᵊns\ *n* : the performance of a lawful action in an illegal or improper manner

mis·file \-'fī(-ə)l\ *vb* : to file in the wrong place

mis·fire \-'fī(-ə)r\ *vb* **1** : to fail to fire **2** : to miss an intended effect — **misfire** *n*

mis·fit \'mis-ˌfit, *sense 1 also* mis-'fit\ *n* **1** : something that fits badly **2** : a person who is poorly adjusted to a situation or environment

mis·for·tune \mis-'for-chən\ *n* **1** : bad luck **2** : an unfortunate condition or event

mis·giv·ing \-'gi-viŋ\ *n* : a feeling of doubt or suspicion esp. concerning a future event

mis·gov·ern \-'gə-vərn\ *vb* : to govern badly — **mis·gov·ern·ment** *n*

mis·guid·ance \mis-'gī-dᵊns\ *n* : faulty guidance — **mis·guide** \-'gīd\ *vb*

mis·guid·ed \-'gī-dəd\ *adj* : led or prompted by wrong or inappropriate motives or ideals — **mis·guid·ed·ly** *adv*

mis·han·dle \-'han-dᵊl\ *vb* **1** : MALTREAT **2** : to manage wrongly

mis·hap \'mis-ˌhap\ *n* : an unfortunate accident

mish·mash \'mish-ˌmash, -ˌmäsh\ *n* : HODGEPODGE, JUMBLE

mis·in·form \ˌmi-sᵊn-'form\ *vb* : to give false or misleading information to — **mis·in·for·ma·tion** \ˌmi-ˌsin-fər-'mä-shən\ *n*

mis·in·ter·pret \ˌmi-sᵊn-'tər-prət\ *vb* : to understand or explain wrongly — **mis·in·ter·pre·ta·tion** \-ˌtər-prə-'tā-shən\ *n*

mis·judge \mis-'jəj\ *vb* **1** : to estimate wrongly **2** : to have an unjust opinion of — **mis·judg·ment** \mis-'jəj-mənt\ *n* mis·la·bel \-ˈlā-bəl\ vb : to label incorrectly or falsely ⟨was ∼ed a liar⟩

mis·lay \mis-ˈlā\ vb -laid \-ˈlād\; -lay·ing : MISPLACE, LOSE ⟨mislaid his keys⟩

mis·lead \mis-ˈlēd\ vb -led \-ˈled\; -lead·ing : to lead in a wrong direction or into a mistaken action or belief — mis·lead·ing·ly adv

mis·like \-ˈlīk\ vb : DISLIKE — mis·like n

mis·man·age \-ˈma-nij\ vb : to manage badly — mis·man·age·ment n

mis·match \-ˈmach\ vb : to match unsuitably or badly — mis·match \mis-ˈmach, ˈmis-ˌmach\ n

mis·name \-ˈnām\ vb : to name incorrectly : MISCALL

mis·no·mer \mis-ˈnō-mər\ n : a wrong or inappropriate name or designation

mi·so \ˈmē-sō\ n : a high-protein fermented food paste consisting chiefly of soybeans, salt, and usu. grain

mi·sog·y·ny \mə-ˈsä-jə-nē\ n [Gk misogynia, fr. misein to hate + gynē woman] : a hatred of women — mi·sog·y·nist \-nist\ n or adj — mi·sog·y·nis·tic \mə-ˌsä-jə-ˈnis-tik\ adj

mis·ori·ent \mi-ˈsór-ē-ˌent\ vb : to orient improperly or incorrectly — mis·ori·en·ta·tion \mi-ˌsór-ē-ən-ˈtā-shən\ n

mis·place \mis-ˈplās\ vb 1 : to put in a wrong or unremembered place 2 : to set on a wrong object ⟨∼ trust⟩

mis·play \-ˈplā\ n : a wrong or unskillful play — mis·play \mis-ˈplā, ˈmis-ˌplā\ vb

mis·print \ˈmis-ˌprint\ n : a mistake in printed matter — mis·print \mis-ˈprint\ vb

mis·pro·nounce \ˌmis-prə-ˈnaůns\ vb : to pronounce incorrectly — mis·pro·nun·ci·a·tion \-prə-ˌnən-sē-ˈā-shən\ n

mis·quote \-ˈkwōt\ vb : to quote incorrectly — mis·quo·ta·tion \ˌmis-kwō-ˈtā-shən\ n

mis·read \-ˈrēd\ vb -read \-ˈred\; -read·ing : \-ˈrē-diŋ\ : to read or interpret incorrectly ⟨∼ her expression⟩

mis·rep·re·sent \ˌmis-ˌre-pri-ˈzent\ vb : to represent falsely or unfairly ⟨∼ the facts⟩ — mis·rep·re·sen·ta·tion \-ˌzen-ˈtā-shən\ n

¹mis·rule \mis-ˈrül\ vb : MISGOVERN

²misrule n 1 : MISGOVERNMENT 2 : DISORDER

¹miss \ˈmis\ vb 1 : to fail to hit, reach, or contact 2 : to feel the absence of 3 : to fail to obtain 4 : AVOID ⟨just ∼ed hitting the other car⟩ 5 : OMIT 6 : to fail to understand ⟨∼ the point⟩ 7 : to fail to perform or attend; also : MISFIRE

²miss n 1 : a failure to hit or to attain a result 2 : MISFIRE

³miss n 1 cap — used as a title prefixed to the name of an unmarried woman or girl 2 : a young unmarried woman or girl

Miss abbr Mississippi

mis·sal \ˈmi-səl\ n : a book containing all that is said or sung at mass during the entire year

mis·send \mis-ˈsend\ vb : to send incorrectly (as to a wrong destination)

mis·shap·en \-ˈshā-pən\ adj : badly shaped : having an ugly shape

mis·sile \ˈmi-səl\ n [L, fr. neut. of missilis capable of being thrown, fr. mittere to let go, send] : an object (as a stone, bullet, or rocket) thrown or projected usu. so as to strike a target

miss·ing \ˈmi-siŋ\ adj : ABSENT; also : LOST ⟨∼ in action⟩

mis·sion \ˈmi-shən\ n 1 : a group of missionaries; also : a place where missionaries work 2 : a group of envoys to a foreign country; also : a team of specialists or cultural leaders sent to a foreign country 3 : TASK, OBJECTIVE

¹mis·sion·ary \ˈmi-shə-ˌner-ē\ adj : of, relating to, or engaged in missions

²missionary n, pl -ar·ies : a person commissioned by a church to spread its faith or carry on humanitarian work

mis·sion·er \ˈmi-shə-nər\ n : MISSIONARY

Mis·sis·sip·pi·an \ˌmi-sə-ˈsi-pē-ən\ adj 1 : of or relating to Mississippi, its people, or the Mississippi River 2 : of, relating to, or being the period of the Paleozoic era between the Devonian and the Pennsylvanian — Mississippian n

mis·sive \ˈmi-siv\ n : LETTER

mis·speak \mis-ˈspēk\ vb : to say imperfectly or incorrectly

mis·spell \-ˈspel\ vb : to spell incorrectly — mis·spell·ing n

mis·spend \-ˈspend\ vb -spent \-ˈspent\; -spend·ing : WASTE, SQUANDER ⟨my misspent youth⟩

mis·state \mis-ˈstāt\ vb : to state incorrectly — mis·state·ment n

mis·step \-ˈstep\ n 1 : a wrong step 2 : MISTAKE, BLUNDER

mist \ˈmist\ n 1 : water in the form of particles suspended or falling in the air 2 : something that obscures understanding — mist vb

mis·tak·able \mə-ˈstā-kə-bəl\ adj : capable of being misunderstood or mistaken

¹mis·take \mi-ˈstāk\ vb -took \-ˈstůk\; -tak·en \-ˈstā-kən\; -tak·ing 1 : to blunder in the choice of 2 : MISINTERPRET 3 : to make a wrong judgment of the character or ability of 4 : to confuse with another — mis·tak·en·ly adv — mis·tak·er n

²mistake n 1 : a wrong judgment : MISUNDERSTANDING 2 : a wrong action or statement : ERROR

¹mis·ter \ˈmis-tər\ n 1 cap — used sometimes instead of Mr. 2 : SIR — used without a name in addressing a man

²mist·er \ˈmis-tər\ n : a device for spraying mist

mis·tle·toe \ˈmi-səl-ˌtō\ n : a European parasitic green shrub that grows on trees and has yellowish flowers and waxy white berries

mis·tral \ˈmis-trəl, mi-ˈsträl\ n [F, fr. Occitan, fr. mistral masterful, fr. LL magistralis of a teacher, fr. L magister master] : a strong cold dry northerly wind of southern France

mis·treat \mis-ˈtrēt\ vb : to treat badly : ABUSE — mis·treat·ment n

mis·tress \ˈmis-trəs\ n 1 : a woman who has power, authority, or ownership ⟨∼ of the house⟩ 2 : something personified as female that rules or dominates ⟨when Rome was ∼ of the world⟩ 3 : a woman other than his wife with whom a married man has sexual relations; also, archaic : SWEETHEART 4 — used archaically as a title prefixed to the name of a married or unmarried woman

mis·tri·al \ˈmis-ˌtrī(-ə)l\ n : a trial that has no legal effect

¹mis·trust \ˈmis-ˈtrəst\ n : a lack of confidence : DISTRUST — mis·trust·ful \-fəl\ adj — mis·trust·ful·ly adv — mis·trust·ful·ness n

²mistrust vb : to have no trust or confidence in : SUSPECT

misty \ˈmis-tē\ adj mist·i·er; -est 1 : obscured by or as if by mist : INDISTINCT ⟨a ∼ memory⟩ 2 : TEARFUL — mist·i·ly \-tə-lē\ adv — mist·i·ness \-tē-nəs\ n

mis·un·der·stand \ˌmi-ˌsən-dər-ˈstand\ vb -stood \-ˈstůd\; -stand·ing 1 : to fail to understand 2 : to interpret incorrectly

mis·un·der·stand·ing \-ˈstan-diŋ\ n 1 : MISINTERPRETATION 2 : DISAGREEMENT, QUARREL

mis·us·age \mis-ˈyü-sij\ n 1 : bad treatment : ABUSE 2 : wrong or improper use

mis·use \mis-ˈyüz\ vb 1 : to use incorrectly 2 : ABUSE, MISTREAT — mis·use \-ˈyüs\ n

¹mite \ˈmīt\ n : any of numerous tiny arthropod animals related to the spiders that often live and feed on animals or plants

²mite n 1 : a small coin or sum of money 2 : a small amount : BIT

¹mi·ter or mi·tre \ˈmī-tər\ n [ME mitre, fr. AF, fr. L mitra headband, turban, fr. Gk] 1 : a headdress worn by bishops and abbots 2 : MITER JOINT

²miter or mitre vb mi·tered or mi·tred; mi·ter·ing or mi·tring \ˈmī-tə-riŋ\ 1 : to match or fit together in a miter joint 2 : to bevel the ends of for making a miter joint

miter joint n : a usu. perpendicular joint made by fitting together two parts with the ends cut at an angle

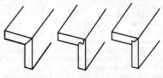

miter joints

mit·i·gate \ˈmi-tə-ˌgāt\ vb -gat·ed; -gat·ing 1 : to make less harsh or hostile 2 : to make less severe or painful — mit·i·ga·tion \ˌmi-tə-ˈgā-shən\ n — mit·i·ga·tive \ˈmi-tə-ˌgā-tiv\ adj

mi·to·chon·dri·on \ˌmī-tə-ˈkän-drē-ən\ n, pl -dria \-drē-ə\ : any of various round or long cellular organelles that produce energy for the cell — **mi·to·chon·dri·al** \-drē-əl\ adj

mi·to·sis \mī-ˈtō-səs\ n, pl -to·ses \ˌsēz\ : a process that takes place in the nucleus of a dividing cell and results in the formation of two new nuclei each of which has the same number of chromosomes as the parent nucleus; also : cell division in which mitosis occurs — **mi·tot·ic** \-ˈtä-tik\ adj

mitt \ˈmit\ n 1 : a baseball catcher's or first baseman's glove 2 slang : HAND

mit·ten \ˈmi-tⁿn\ n : a covering for the hand having a separate section for the thumb only — **mit·tened** \-tⁿnd\ adj

¹mix \ˈmiks\ vb 1 : to combine into one mass 2 : ASSOCIATE 3 : to form by mingling components 4 : to produce (a recording) by electronically combining sounds from different sources 5 : HYBRIDIZE 6 : CONFUSE ⟨∼es up the facts⟩ 7 : to become involved ♦ **Synonyms** BLEND, MERGE, COALESCE, AMALGAMATE, FUSE — **mix·able** adj — **mix it up** : to engage in a fight, contest, or dispute

²mix n : a product of mixing; esp : a commercially prepared mixture of food ingredients

mixed \ˈmikst\ adj 1 : combining features of more than one kind 2 : made up of or involving individuals or items of more than one kind 3 : including or accompanied by different or opposing elements ⟨a ∼ blessing⟩ 4 : resulting from the crossing or breeding of individuals of different races or breeds ⟨a stallion of ∼ blood⟩

mixed number n : a number (as 5²/₃) composed of an integer and a fraction

mixed–up \ˈmikst-ˈəp\ adj : CONFUSED

mix·er \ˈmik-sər\ n 1 : one that mixes; esp : a machine or device for mixing 2 : an event (as a dance) that encourages meeting and socializing 3 : a nonalcoholic beverage used in a cocktail

mixt abbr mixture

mix·ture \ˈmiks-chər\ n 1 : the act or process of mixing; also : the state of being mixed 2 : a product of mixing

mix–up \ˈmiks-ˌəp\ n 1 : an instance of confusion 2 : CONFLICT, FIGHT

miz·zen also **miz·en** \ˈmi-zⁿn\ n 1 : a fore-and-aft sail set on the mizzenmast 2 : MIZZENMAST — **mizzen** also **mizen** adj

miz·zen·mast \-ˌmast, -məst\ n : the mast aft or next aft of the mainmast

mk abbr 1 mark 2 markka

Mk abbr Mark

mks abbr meter-kilogram-second

mkt abbr market

mktg abbr marketing

ml abbr milliliter

Mlle abbr [F] mademoiselle

Mlles abbr [F] mesdemoiselles

mm abbr millimeter

MM abbr [F] messieurs

Mme abbr [F] madame

Mmes abbr [F] mesdames

Mn symbol manganese

MN abbr Minnesota

mne·mon·ic \nə-ˈmä-nik\ adj : assisting or designed to assist memory; also : of or relating to memory

mo abbr month

¹Mo abbr 1 Missouri 2 Monday

²Mo symbol molybdenum

MO abbr 1 mail order 2 medical officer 3 Missouri 4 modus operandi 5 money order

moan \ˈmōn\ n : a low prolonged sound indicative of pain or grief — **moan** vb

moat \ˈmōt\ n : a deep wide usu. water-filled trench around a castle

¹mob \ˈmäb\ n [L mobile vulgus vacillating crowd] 1 : MASSES, RABBLE 2 : a disorderly crowd 3 : a criminal gang

²mob vb **mobbed; mob·bing** 1 : to crowd about and attack or annoy ⟨mobbed by fans⟩ 2 : to crowd into or around ⟨shoppers mobbed the stores⟩

¹mo·bile \ˈmō-bəl, -ˌbī(-ə)l, -ˌbēl\ adj 1 : capable of moving or being moved 2 : changeable in appearance, mood, or purpose; also : ADAPTABLE 3 : having the opportunity for or undergoing a shift in social status 4

: using vehicles for transportation ⟨∼ warfare⟩ 5 : CELLULAR 2 — **mo·bil·i·ty** \mō-ˈbi-lə-tē\ n

²mo·bile \ˈmō-ˌbēl\ n : a construction or sculpture (as of wire and sheet metal) with parts that can be set in motion by air currents; also : a similar structure suspended so that it is moved by a current of air

mobile home n : a trailer used as a permanent dwelling

mobile phone n : CELL PHONE

mo·bi·lise chiefly Brit var of MOBILIZE

mo·bi·lize \ˈmō-bə-ˌlīz\ vb **-lized; -liz·ing** 1 : to put into movement or circulation 2 : to assemble and make ready for action ⟨∼ army reserves⟩ — **mo·bi·li·za·tion** \ˌmō-bə-lə-ˈzā-shən\ n — **mo·bi·liz·er** \ˈmō-bə-ˌlī-zər\ n

mob·ster \ˈmäb-stər\ n : a member of a criminal gang

moc·ca·sin \ˈmä-kə-sən\ n 1 : a soft leather heelless shoe 2 : WATER MOCCASIN

mo·cha \ˈmō-kə\ n [Mocha, port in Yemen] 1 : choice coffee grown in Arabia 2 : a mixture of coffee and chocolate or cocoa 3 : a dark chocolate-brown color

¹mock \ˈmäk, ˈmȯk\ vb 1 : to treat with contempt or ridicule 2 : DELUDE 3 : DEFY 4 : to mimic in sport or derision — **mock·er** n — **mock·ery** \ˈmä-kə-rē, ˈmȯ-\ n — **mock·ing·ly** adv

²mock adj : SIMULATED ⟨a ∼ trial⟩

mock–he·ro·ic \ˌmäk-hi-ˈrō-ik, ˌmȯk-\ adj : ridiculing or burlesquing heroic style, character, or action ⟨a ∼ poem⟩

mock·ing·bird \ˈmä-kiŋ-ˌbərd, ˈmȯ-\ n : a grayish No. American songbird related to the catbirds and thrashers that mimics the calls of other birds

mock–up \ˈmä-ˌkəp, ˈmȯ-\ n 1 : a full-sized structural model built for study, testing, or display ⟨a ∼ of a car⟩ 2 : a working sample (as of a magazine) for review

¹mod \ˈmäd\ adj 1 : of, relating to, or being the style of the 1960s British youth culture 2 : HIP, TRENDY

²mod abbr 1 moderate 2 modern 3 modification; modified

mode \ˈmōd\ n 1 : a particular form or variety of something; also : STYLE 2 : a manner of doing something 3 : the most frequent value of a set of data — **mod·al** \ˈmō-dⁿl\ adj

¹mod·el \ˈmä-dⁿl\ n 1 : structural design 2 : a miniature representation; also : a pattern of something to be made 3 : an example for imitation or emulation 4 : one who poses (as for an artist or to display clothes) 5 : TYPE, DESIGN ⟨a new car ∼⟩

²model vb **mod·eled** or **mod·elled; mod·el·ing** or **mod·el·ling** 1 : SHAPE, FASHION, CONSTRUCT ⟨∼ed in clay⟩ 2 : to work as a fashion model

³model adj 1 : serving as or worthy of being a pattern ⟨a ∼ student⟩ 2 : being a miniature representation of something ⟨a ∼ airplane⟩

mo·dem \ˈmō-dəm, -ˌdem\ n : a device that converts signals from one device (as a computer) to a form compatible with another (as a telephone)

¹mod·er·ate \ˈmä-də-rət\ adj 1 : avoiding extremes; also : TEMPERATE 2 : AVERAGE; also : MEDIOCRE 3 : limited in scope or effect 4 : not expensive — **moderate** n — **mod·er·ate·ly** adv — **mod·er·ate·ness** n

²mod·er·ate \ˈmä-də-ˌrāt\ vb **-at·ed; -at·ing** 1 : to lessen the intensity of : TEMPER 2 : to act as a moderator — **mod·er·a·tion** \ˌmä-də-ˈrā-shən\ n

mod·er·a·tor \ˈmä-də-ˌrā-tər\ n 1 : MEDIATOR 2 : one who presides over an assembly, meeting, or discussion

mod·ern \ˈmä-dərn\ adj [LL modernus, fr. L modo just now, fr. modus measure] : of, relating to, or characteristic of the present or the immediate past : CONTEMPORARY ⟨∼ art⟩ — **modern** n — **mo·der·ni·ty** \mə-ˈdər-nə-tē\ n — **mod·ern·ly** adv — **mod·ern·ness** n

mod·ern·ise, mod·ern·i·sa·tion Brit var of MODERNIZE, MODERNIZATION

mod·ern·ism \ˈmä-dər-ˌni-zəm\ n : a practice, movement, or belief peculiar to modern times

mod·ern·ize \ˈmä-dər-ˌnīz\ vb **-ized; -iz·ing** 1 : to make or become modern — **mod·ern·i·za·tion** \ˌmä-dər-nə-ˈzā-shən\ n — **mod·ern·iz·er** n

mod·est \ˈmä-dəst\ adj 1 : having a moderate estimate of oneself; also : DIFFIDENT 2 : observing the proprieties of dress and behavior 3 : limited in size, amount, or scope ⟨a ∼ income⟩ — **mod·est·ly** adv — **mod·es·ty** \-də-stē\ n

mod·i·cum \ˈmä-di-kəm\ n : a small amount ⟨a ∼ of privacy⟩

modif *abbr* modification

mod·i·fy \'mä-də-ˌfī\ *vb* **-fied; -fy·ing** 1 : MODERATE 2 : to limit the meaning of esp. in a grammatical construction 3 : CHANGE, ALTER — **mod·i·fi·ca·tion** \ˌmä-də-fə-'kā-shən\ *n* — **mod·i·fi·er** \'mä-də-ˌfī-ər\ *n*

mod·ish \'mō-dish\ *adj* : FASHIONABLE, STYLISH ⟨∼ decor⟩ — **mod·ish·ly** *adv* — **mod·ish·ness** *n*

mo·diste \mō-'dēst\ *n* : a maker of fashionable dresses and hats

mod·u·lar \'mä-jə-lər\ *adj* : constructed with standardized units ⟨∼ homes⟩

mod·u·lar·ized \'mä-jə-lə-ˌrīzd\ *adj* : containing or consisting of modules

mod·u·late \'mä-jə-ˌlāt\ *vb* **-lat·ed; -lat·ing** 1 : to tune to a key or pitch 2 : to keep in proper measure or proportion : TEMPER 3 : to vary the amplitude or frequency of a carrier wave for the transmission of information (as in radio or television) — **mod·u·la·tion** \ˌmä-jə-'lā-shən\ *n* — **mod·u·la·tor** \'mä-jə-ˌlā-tər\ *n* — **mod·u·la·to·ry** \-lə-ˌtor-ē\ *adj*

mod·ule \'mä-jül\ *n* 1 : any in a series of standardized units for use together 2 : an assembly of wired electronic parts for use with other such assemblies 3 : an independent unit that constitutes a part of the total structure of a space vehicle ⟨a propulsion ∼⟩

mo·dus ope·ran·di \ˌmō-dəs-ˌä-pə-'ran-dē, -ˌdī\ *n, pl* **mo·di operandi** \ˌmō-ˌdē-, ˌmō-ˌdī-\ [NL] : a method of procedure

¹mo·gul \'mō-gəl, mō-'gəl\ *n* [fr. *Mogul*, member of a Muslim dynasty ruling northern India] : an important person : MAGNATE ⟨a media ∼⟩

²mogul \'mō-gəl\ *n* : a bump in a ski run

mo·hair \'mō-ˌher\ *n* [modif. of obs. It *mocaiarro*, fr. Ar *mukhayyar*, lit., choice] : a fabric or yarn made wholly or in part from the long silky hair of the Angora goat; *also* : this goat hair

Mo·ham·med·an *also* **Mu·ham·mad·an** \mō-'ha-mə-dən, -'hä-, mü-\ *n* : MUSLIM

Mo·hawk \'mō-ˌhȯk\ *n, pl* **Mohawk** *or* **Mohawks** 1 : a member of an American Indian people of the Mohawk River valley, New York; *also* : the language of the Mohawk people 2 : a hairstyle with a narrow strip of upright hair down the center and the sides shaved

Mo·he·gan \mō-'hē-gən, mə-\ *or* **Mo·hi·can** \-'hē-kən\ *n, pl* **Mohegan** *or* **Mohegans** *or* **Mohican** *or* **Mohicans** : a member of an American Indian people of southeastern Connecticut

mo·hel \'mō-(h)el, 'mȯi(-ə)l\ *n, pl* **mohels** *also* **mo·hal·im** \ˌmō-hä-'lēm\ *also* **mo·hel·im** \-(h)e-'lēm\ : a person who performs Jewish circumcisions

Mohican *var of* MAHICAN

moi·e·ty \'mȯi-ə-tē\ *n, pl* **-ties** : one of two equal or approximately equal parts

moil \'mȯi(-ə)l\ *vb* : to work hard : DRUDGE — **moil** *n* — **moil·er** *n*

moi·ré \mȯ-'rā, mwä-\ *or* **moire** *same or* 'mȯir, 'mwär\ *n* : a fabric (as silk) having a watered appearance

moist \'mȯist\ *adj* : slightly or moderately wet — **moist·ly** *adv* — **moist·ness** *n*

moist·en \'mȯi-sᵊn\ *vb* : to make or become moist — **moist·en·er** *n*

mois·ture \'mȯis-chər\ *n* : the small amount of liquid that causes dampness

mois·tur·ise *Brit var of* MOISTURIZE

mois·tur·ize \'mȯis-chə-ˌrīz\ *vb* **-ized; -iz·ing** : to add moisture to ⟨∼ the skin⟩ — **mois·tur·iz·er** *n*

mo·ji·to \mō-'hē-tō\ *n, pl* **-tos** [AmerSp, dim. of *moje, mojo* citrus marinade, fr. Sp *mojar* to moisten] : a cocktail made of rum, sugar, mint, lime juice and soda water

mol *abbr* molecular; molecule

mo·lar \'mō-lər\ *n* [ME *molares*, pl., fr. L *molaris*, fr. *molaris* of a mill, fr. *mola* millstone] : any of the broad teeth adapted to grinding food and located in the back of the jaw — **molar** *adj*

mo·las·ses \mə-'la-səz\ *n* : the thick brown syrup that is separated from raw sugar in sugar manufacture

¹mold \'mōld\ *n* : crumbly soil rich in organic matter

²mold *n* 1 : distinctive nature or character 2 : the frame on or around which something is constructed 3 : a cavity in which something is shaped; *also* : an object so shaped 4 : MOLDING

³mold *vb* 1 : to shape in or as if in a mold 2 : to ornament with molding — **mold·er** *n*

⁴mold *n* : a surface growth of fungus esp. on damp or decaying matter; *also* : a fungus that produces mold — **mold·i·ness** \'mōl-dē-nəs\ *n* — **moldy** *adj*

⁵mold *vb* : to become moldy

mold·board \'mōld-ˌbȯrd\ *n* : a curved iron plate attached above the plowshare to lift and turn the soil

mold·er \'mōl-dər\ *vb* : to crumble into small pieces

mold·ing \'mōl-diŋ\ *n* 1 : an act or process of shaping in a mold; *also* : an object so shaped 2 : a decorative surface, plane, or curved strip

¹mole \'mōl\ *n* : a small often pigmented spot or protuberance on the skin

²mole *n* 1 : any of numerous small burrowing insect-eating mammals related to the shrews and hedgehogs 2 : a spy embedded within an organization

³mole *n* : a massive breakwater or jetty

molecular biology *n* : a branch of biology dealing with the ultimate physical and chemical organization of living matter and esp. with the molecular basis of inheritance and protein synthesis — **molecular biologist** *n*

molecular weight *n* : the mass of a molecule that is equal to the sum of the masses of all atoms contained in the molecule's formula

mol·e·cule \'mä-li-ˌkyül\ *n* : the smallest particle of matter that is the same chemically as the whole mass — **mo·lec·u·lar** \mə-'le-kyə-lər\ *adj*

mole·hill \'mōl-ˌhil\ *n* : a little ridge of earth thrown up by a mole

mole·skin \-ˌskin\ *n* 1 : the skin of the mole used as fur 2 : a heavy durable cotton fabric

mo·lest \mə-'lest\ *vb* 1 : ANNOY, DISTURB 2 : to make annoying sexual advances to; *esp* : to force physical and usu. sexual contact on — **mo·les·ta·tion** \ˌmō-ˌles-'tā-shən\ *n* — **mo·lest·er** *n*

moll \'mäl\ *n* : a gangster's girlfriend

mol·li·fy \'mä-lə-ˌfī\ *vb* **-fied; -fy·ing** 1 : to soothe in temper : APPEASE 2 : SOFTEN 3 : to reduce in intensity : ASSUAGE ⟨∼ ill feelings⟩ — **mol·li·fi·ca·tion** \ˌmä-lə-fə-'kā-shən\ *n*

mol·lusk *or* **mol·lusc** \'mä-ləsk\ *n* : any of a large phylum of usu. shelled and aquatic invertebrate animals (as snails, clams, and squids) — **mol·lus·can** *also* **mol·lus·kan** \mə-'ləs-kən\ *adj*

¹mol·ly·cod·dle \'mä-lē-ˌkä-dᵊl\ *n* : a pampered man or boy

²mollycoddle *vb* **mol·ly·cod·dled; mol·ly·cod·dling** : PAMPER

Mo·lo·tov cocktail \'mä-lə-ˌtȯf-, 'mȯ-\ *n* [Vyacheslav M. *Molotov* †1986 Soviet foreign minister] : a crude bomb made of a bottle filled usu. with gasoline and fitted with a wick (as a saturated rag) that is ignited just prior to hurling

¹molt \'mōlt\ *vb* : to shed hair, feathers, outer skin, or horns periodically with the cast-off parts being replaced by new growth — **molt·er** *n*

²molt *n* : the act or process of molting

mol·ten \'mōl-tᵊn\ *adj* 1 : fused or liquefied by heat 2 : GLOWING

mo·ly \'mō-lē\ *n* : a mythical herb with black root, white flowers, and magic powers

mo·lyb·de·num \mə-'lib-də-nəm\ *n* : a metallic chemical element used in strengthening and hardening steel

mom \'mäm, 'mȯm\ *n* : MOTHER

mom–and–pop *adj* : being a small owner-operated business

mo·ment \'mō-mənt\ *n* 1 : a minute portion of time : INSTANT 2 : a time of excellence ⟨he has his ∼s⟩ 3 : IMPORTANCE ⟨an event of great ∼⟩ ♦ **Synonyms** CONSEQUENCE, SIGNIFICANCE, WEIGHT, IMPORT

mo·men·tar·i·ly \ˌmō-mən-'ter-ə-lē\ *adv* 1 : for a moment 2 *archaic* : INSTANTLY 3 : at any moment : SOON

mo·men·tary \'mō-mən-ˌter-ē\ *adj* 1 : continuing only a moment ⟨a ∼ pause⟩; *also* : EPHEMERAL 2 : recurring at every moment — **mo·men·tar·i·ness** \-ˌter-ē-nəs\ *n*

mo·men·tous \mō-'men-təs\ *adj* : very important ⟨a ∼ decision⟩ — **mo·men·tous·ly** *adv* — **mo·men·tous·ness** *n*

mo·men·tum \mō-'men-təm\ *n, pl* **mo·men·ta** \-'men-tə\ *or* **momentums** : a property that a moving body has due to its mass and motion; *also* : IMPETUS

mom·my \'mä-mē, 'mə-\ *n, pl* **mom·mies** : MOTHER
Mon *abbr* Monday
mon·arch \'mä-nərk, -ₙnärk\ *n* **1** : a person who reigns over a kingdom or an empire **2** : one holding preeminent position or power **3** : MONARCH BUTTERFLY — **mo·nar·chi·cal** \mə-'när-ki-kəl\ *also* **mo·nar·chic** \-'när-kik\ *adj*
monarch butterfly *n* : a large orange and black migratory American butterfly whose larva feeds on milkweed
mon·ar·chist \'mä-nər-kist\ *n* : a believer in monarchical government — **mon·ar·chism** \-ₙki-zəm\ *n*
mon·ar·chy \'mä-nər-kē\ *n, pl* **-chies** : a nation or state governed by a monarch
mon·as·tery \'mä-nə-ₙster-ē\ *n, pl* **-ter·ies** : a house for persons under religious vows (as monks)
mo·nas·tic \mə-'nas-tik\ *adj* : of or relating to monasteries or to monks or nuns — **monastic** *n* — **mo·nas·ti·cal·ly** \-ti-k(ə-)lē\ *adv* — **mo·nas·ti·cism** \-tə-ₙsi-zəm\ *n*
mon·au·ral \mä-'nȯr-əl\ *adj* : MONOPHONIC — **mon·au·ral·ly** *adv*
Mon·day \'mən-dē, -ₙdā\ *n* : the second day of the week
mon·e·tary \'mä-nə-ₙter-ē, 'mə-\ *adj* : of or relating to money or to the mechanisms by which it is supplied and circulated in the economy
mon·ey \'mə-nē\ *n, pl* **moneys** *or* **mon·ies** \'mə-nēz\ **1** : something (as metal currency) accepted as a medium of exchange **2** : wealth reckoned in monetary terms **3** : the 1st, 2d, and 3d places in a horse or dog race ☞ the MONEY table is on pages 322–323
mon·eyed \'mə-nēd\ *adj* **1** : having money : WEALTHY **2** : consisting in or derived from money
mon·ey·lend·er \'mə-nē-ₙlen-dər\ *n* : one (as a bank or pawnbroker) whose business is lending money
money market *n* : the trade in short-term negotiable financial instruments
money of account : a denominator of value or basis of exchange used in keeping accounts
money order *n* : an order purchased at a post office, bank, or telegraph office directing another office to pay a sum of money to a party named on it
mon·ger \'məŋ-gər, 'mäŋ-\ *n* **1** : DEALER **2** : one who tries to stir up or spread something — usu. used in combination ⟨war*monger*⟩
mon·go \'mäŋ-(ₙ)gō\ *n, pl* **mongo** — see *tugrik* at MONEY table
Mon·gol \'mäŋ-gəl, 'mäŋ-ₙgōl\ *n* : a member of any of several traditionally pastoral peoples of Mongolia — **Mongol** *adj*
Mon·go·lian \män-'gōl-yən, mäŋ-, -'gō-lē-ən\ *n* **1** : a native or inhabitant of Mongolia **2** : a member of the Mongoloid racial stock — **Mongolian** *adj*
Mon·gol·oid \'mäŋ-gə-ₙlȯid\ *adj* : of, constituting, or characteristic of a race of humankind native to Asia and classified according to physical features — **Mongoloid** *n*
mon·goose \'män-ₙgüs, 'mäŋ-\ *n, pl* **mon·goos·es** *also* **mon·geese** \-ₙgēs\ : any of a group of small agile Old World mammals that are related to the civet cats and feed chiefly on small animals and fruits
mon·grel \'mäŋ-grəl, 'mäŋ-\ *n* : an offspring of parents of different breeds; *esp* : one of uncertain ancestry
mon·i·ker \'mä-ni-kər\ *n* : NAME, NICKNAME
mo·nism \'mō-ₙni-zəm, 'mä-\ *n* : a view that reality is basically one unitary organic whole — **mo·nist** \'mō-nist, 'mä-\ *n*
mo·ni·tion \mō-'ni-shən, mə-\ *n* : WARNING, CAUTION
¹mon·i·tor \'mä-nə-tər\ *n* **1** : a student appointed to assist a teacher **2** : one that monitors; *esp* : a video display screen (as for a computer)
²monitor *vb* : to watch, check, or observe for a special purpose
mon·i·to·ry \'mä-nə-ₙtȯr-ē\ *adj* : giving admonition : WARNING
¹monk \'məŋk\ *n* [ME, fr. OE *munuc*, fr. LL *monachus*, fr. LGk *monachos*, fr. Gk, adj., single, fr. *monos* single, alone] : a man belonging to a religious order and living in a monastery — **monk·ish** *adj*
²monk *n* : MONKEY
¹mon·key \'məŋ-kē\ *n, pl* **monkeys** : a nonhuman primate mammal; *esp* : one of the smaller, longer-tailed, and usu. more arboreal primates as contrasted with the apes

²monkey *vb* **mon·keyed; mon·key·ing** **1** : FOOL, TRIFLE — often used with *around* **2** : TAMPER — usu. used with *with* ⟨don't ∼ around with the controls⟩
monkey bars *n pl* : a framework of bars on which children can play
mon·key·shine \'məŋ-kē-ₙshīn\ *n* : PRANK — usu. used in pl.
monkey wrench *n* : a wrench with one fixed and one adjustable jaw at right angles to a handle

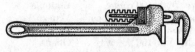

monkey wrench

monk·fish \'məŋk-ₙfish\ *n* : either of two marine bony fishes that have a large flattened head and are used for food
monks·hood \'məŋks-ₙhùd\ *n* : any of a genus of poisonous plants related to the buttercups; *esp* : a tall Eurasian herb with white or purplish flowers
¹mono \'mä-nō\ *adj* : MONOPHONIC
²mono *n* : INFECTIOUS MONONUCLEOSIS
mono·chro·mat·ic \ₙmä-nə-krō-'ma-tik\ *adj* **1** : having or consisting of one color **2** : consisting of radiation (as light) of a single wavelength
mono·chrome \'mä-nə-ₙkrōm\ *adj* : involving or producing visual images in a single color or in varying tones of a single color ⟨∼ television⟩
mon·o·cle \'mä-ni-kəl\ *n* : an eyeglass for one eye
mono·clo·nal \ₙmä-nə-'klō-nəl\ *adj* : produced by, being, or composed of cells derived from a single cell ⟨∼ antibodies⟩
mono·cot·y·le·don \ₙmä-nə-ₙkät-tə-'lē-dᵊn\ *n* : any of a class or subclass of chiefly herbaceous seed plants having an embryo with a single cotyledon and usu. parallel-veined leaves
mon·o·dy \'mä-nə-dē\ *n, pl* **-dies** : ELEGY, DIRGE — **mo·nod·ic** \mə-'nä-dik\ *or* **mo·nod·i·cal** \-di-kəl\ *adj* — **mon·o·dist** \'mä-nə-dist\ *n*
mo·nog·a·my \mə-'nä-gə-mē\ *n* **1** : marriage with but one person at a time **2** : the practice of having a single mate during a period of time — **mo·nog·a·mist** \-mist\ *n* — **mo·nog·a·mous** \-məs\ *adj*
mono·gram \'mä-nə-ₙgram\ *n* : a sign of identity composed of the combined initials of a name — **monogram** *vb*
mono·graph \'mä-nə-ₙgraf\ *n* : a learned treatise on a small area of learning
mono·lin·gual \ₙmä-nə-'liŋ-gwəl\ *adj* : knowing or using only one language
mono·lith \'mä-nə-ₙlith\ *n* **1** : a single great stone often in the form of a monument or column **2** : something large and powerful that acts as a single unified force ⟨a bureaucratic ∼⟩ — **mono·lith·ic** \ₙmä-nə-'li-thik\ *adj*
mono·logue *also* **mono·log** \'mä-nə-ₙlȯg\ *n* **1** : a dramatic soliloquy; *also* : a long speech monopolizing conversation **2** : the routine of a stand-up comic — **mono·logu·ist** \-ₙlȯg-ist\ *or* **mo·no·lo·gist** \mə-'nä-lə-jist; 'mä-nə-ₙlō-gist\ *n*
mono·ma·nia \ₙmä-nə-'mā-nē-ə, -nyə\ *n* **1** : mental disorder limited in expression to one area of thought **2** : excessive concentration on a single object or idea — **mono·ma·ni·ac** \-nē-ₙak\ *n or adj*
mono·mer \'mä-nə-mər\ *n* : a simple chemical compound that can be polymerized
mono·nu·cle·o·sis \ₙmä-nō-ₙnü-klē-'ō-səs, -ₙnyü-\ *n* : INFECTIOUS MONONUCLEOSIS
mono·phon·ic \ₙmä-nə-'fä-nik\ *adj* : of or relating to sound recording or reproduction involving a single transmission path
mono·plane \'mä-nə-ₙplān\ *n* : an airplane with only one set of wings
mo·nop·o·ly \mə-'nä-pə-lē\ *n, pl* **-lies** [L *monopolium*, fr. Gk *monopōlion*, fr. *monos* alone, single + *pōlein* to sell] **1** : exclusive ownership (as through command of supply) **2** : a commodity controlled by one party **3** : one that has a monopoly — **mo·nop·o·list** \-list\ *n* — **mo·nop·o·lis·tic** \mə-ₙnä-pə-'lis-tik\ *adj* — **mo·nop·o·li·za·tion** \-lə-'zā-shən\ *n* — **mo·nop·o·lize** \mə-'nä-pə-ₙlīz\ *vb*

MONEY — WORLD CURRENCIES

NAME	SUBDIVISION	COUNTRY	NAME	SUBDIVISION	COUNTRY
afghani	100 puls	Afghanistan	dram	100 luma	Armenia
ariary	5 iraimbilanja	Madagascar	escudo	100 centavos	Cape Verde
baht	100 satang	Thailand	euro[4]	100 cents	Austria,
balboa[1]	100 centesimos	Panama		Belgium, Cyprus, Estonia, Finland,	
birr	100 cents	Ethiopia		France, Germany, Greece, Ireland,	
bolivar	100 centimos	Venezuela		Italy, Latvia, Lithuania,	
boliviano	100 centavos	Bolivia		Luxembourg, Malta, Netherlands,	
cedi	100 pesewas	Ghana		Portugal, Slovakia, Slovenia,	
colón	100 centimos	Costa Rica		Spain	
córdoba	100 centavos	Nicaragua	forint	100 fillers[2]	Hungary
dalasi	100 bututs	Gambia	franc[5]	100 centimes	Cameroon,
denar	100 deni[2]	Macedonia		Central African Republic, Chad,	
dinar	100 centimes	Algeria		Republic of the Congo, Equatorial	
dinar	1000 fils	Bahrain		Guinea[6], Gabon	
dinar	1000 fils	Iraq	franc[7]	100 centimes	Benin,
dinar	1000 fils	Jordan		Burkina Faso, Guinea-Bissau,	
dinar	1000 fils	Kuwait		Ivory Coast, Mali, Niger, Senegal,	
dinar	1000 dirhams	Libya		Togo	
dinar	100 paras	Serbia	franc	100 centimes	Burundi
dinar	1000 millimes	Tunisia	franc	100 centimes	Comoros
dirham	100 centimes	Morocco	franc	100 centimes	Democratic
dirham	100 fils	United Arab			Republic of
		Emirates			the Congo
dobra	100 centimos	São Tomé and	franc	100 centimes	Djibouti
		Príncipe	franc	100 centimes[8]	Guinea
dollar[3]	100 cents	Antigua and	franc	100 centimes[8]	Rwanda
	Barbuda, Dominica, Grenada, St.		franc	100 centimes	Switzerland
	Kitts-Nevis, St. Lucia, St. Vincent			*or* rappen	
	and the Grenadines		gourde	100 centimes	Haiti
dollar	100 cents	Australia	guarani	100 centimos[2]	Paraguay
dollar	100 cents	Bahamas	hryvnia	100 kopiykas	Ukraine
dollar	100 cents	Barbados	kina	100 toea	Papua New
dollar	100 cents	Belize			Guinea
dollar	100 cents	Bermuda	kip	100 at *or* att[2]	Laos
dollar	100 cents	Brunei	koruna	100 haleru	Czech
dollar	100 cents	Canada			Republic
dollar	100 cents	Fiji	krona	100 aurar[2]	Iceland
dollar	100 cents	Guyana		(*sing* eyrir)	
dollar	100 cents	Hong Kong	krona	100 ore[2]	Sweden
dollar	100 cents	Jamaica	krone	100 øre	Denmark
dollar	100 cents	Liberia	krone	100 ore	Norway
dollar	100 cents	Namibia	kuna	100 lipa	Croatia
dollar	100 cents	New Zealand	kwacha	100 tambala	Malawi
dollar	100 cents	Singapore	kwacha	100 ngwee	Zambia
dollar	100 cents	Solomon	kwanza	100 cêntimos	Angola
		Islands	kyat	100 pyas	Myanmar
dollar	100 cents	Suriname	lari	100 tetri	Republic of
dollar	100 cents	Taiwan			Georgia
dollar	100 cents	Trinidad and	lek	100 qindarka[2]	Albania
		Tobago		(*sing* qindar)	
dollar	100 cents	United States	lempira	100 centavos	Honduras
dollar — see RINGGIT, below			leone	100 cents	Sierra Leone
dong	100 xu	Vietnam	leu	100 bani	Moldova
				(*sing* ban)	

MONEY — WORLD CURRENCIES

NAME	SUBDIVISION	COUNTRY	NAME	SUBDIVISION	COUNTRY
leu	100 bani (*sing* ban)	Romania	rial	1000 baiza	Oman
			rial	100 fils	Yemen
lev	100 stotinki	Bulgaria	*also* riyal		
lilangeni (*pl* emalangeni)	100 cents	Eswatini	rial — see RIYAL, below		
			riel	100 sen	Cambodia
lira *or* pound	100 kuruş	Turkey	ringgit *or* dollar	100 sen	Malaysia
livre — see POUND, below			riyal *also* rial	100 dirhams	Qatar
loti (*pl* maloti)	100 lisente (*sing* sente)	Lesotho	riyal *also* rial	100 halala	Saudi Arabia
manat	100 gopik	Azerbaijan	riyal — see RIAL, above		
manat	100 tenesi (*sing* tenne)	Turkmenistan	ruble *also* rouble	100 kapeek (*sing* kapeyka)	Belarus
marka	100 feninga (*sing* fening)	Bosnia and Herzegovina	ruble *also* rouble	100 kopecks	Russia
metical	100 centavos	Mozambique	rufiyaa	100 laari	Maldives
naira	100 kobo	Nigeria	rupee	100 paise	India
nakfa	100 cents	Eritrea	rupee	100 cents	Mauritius
ngultrum	100 chetrums	Bhutan	rupee	100 paisa	Nepal
ouguiya	5 khoums	Mauritania	rupee	100 paisa	Pakistan
pa'anga	100 seniti	Tonga	rupee	100 cents	Seychelles
pataca	100 avos	Macao	rupee	100 cents	Sri Lanka
peso	100 centavos	Argentina	rupiah	100 sen	Indonesia
peso	100 centavos	Chile	shekel *also* sheqel	100 agorot	Israel
peso	100 centavos	Colombia	shilling	100 cents	Kenya
peso	100 centavos	Cuba	shilling	100 cents	Somalia
peso	100 centavos	Dominican Republic	shilling	100 cents	Tanzania
peso	100 centavos	Mexico	shilling	100 cents[2]	Uganda
peso *or* piso	100 sentimos *or* centavos	Philippines	sol	100 centimos	Peru
			som	100 tyiyn	Kyrgyzstan
peso	100 centesimos	Uruguay	somoni	100 dirams	Tajikistan
pound	100 piastres	Egypt	sum *or* som	100 tiyin	Uzbekistan
pound *or* livre	100 piastres	Lebanon	taka	100 paisa *or* poisha	Bangladesh
pound	100 piastres	South Sudan	tala	100 sene	Samoa
pound	100 piastres	Sudan	tenge	100 tiyns	Kazakhstan
pound	100 piastres	Syria	tugrik	100 mongo	Mongolia
pound	100 pence (*sing* penny)	United Kingdom	vatu		Vanuatu
pound — see LIRA, above			won	100 chon	North Korea
pula	100 thebe	Botswana	won	100 jeon[2]	South Korea
quetzal	100 centavos	Guatemala	yen	100 sen[8]	Japan
rand	100 cents	South Africa	yuan	100 fen	China
real	100 centavos	Brazil	zloty	100 groszy	Poland
rial	100 dinars	Iran			

[1]Used along with the U.S. dollar.
[2]No longer in circulation.
[3]Issued by the Eastern Caribbean Central Bank.
[4]Replaced the individual monetary units of participating European Union countries.
[5]Issued by the Bank of Central African States.
[6]The franc of Equatorial Guinea is also called the *franco*.
[7]Issued by the West African Economic and Monetary Union.
[8]A subdivision in name only.

mono·rail \'mä-nə-ˌrāl\ *n* : a single rail serving as a track for a vehicle; *also* : a vehicle traveling on such a track

monorail

mono·so·di·um glu·ta·mate \ˌmä-nə-ˌsō-dē-əm-'glü-tə-ˌmāt\ *n* : a crystalline salt used to enhance the flavor of food

mono·syl·la·ble \'mä-nə-ˌsi-lə-bəl\ *n* : a word of one syllable — **mono·syl·lab·ic** \ˌmä-nə-sə-'la-bik\ *adj* — **mono·syl·lab·i·cal·ly** \-bi-k(ə-)lē\ *adv*

mono·the·ism \'mä-nə-(ˌ)thē-ˌi-zəm\ *n* : a doctrine or belief that there is only one deity — **mono·the·ist** \-ˌthē-ist\ *n* — **mono·the·is·tic** \-thē-'is-tik\ *adj*

mono·tone \'mä-nə-ˌtōn\ *n* : a succession of syllables, words, or sentences in one unvaried key or pitch

mo·not·o·nous \mə-'nä-tə-nəs\ *adj* 1 : uttered or sounded in one unvarying tone 2 : tediously uniform — **mo·not·o·nous·ly** *adv* — **mo·not·o·nous·ness** *n*

mo·not·o·ny \mə-'nä-tə-nē\ *n* : tedious sameness or uniformity

mono·un·sat·u·rat·ed \ˌmä-nō-ˌən-'sa-chə-ˌrā-təd\ *adj* : containing one double or triple bond per molecule — used esp. of an oil, fat, or fatty acid

mon·ox·ide \mə-'näk-ˌsīd\ *n* : an oxide containing one atom of oxygen in a molecule

mon·sei·gneur \ˌmōⁿ-ˌsän-'yər\ *n, pl* **mes·sei·gneurs** \ˌmā-ˌsän-'yər, -'yərz\ : a French dignitary — used as a title

mon·sieur \məs-'yər\ *n, pl* **mes·sieurs** *same or* -'yərz\ : a Frenchman of high rank or station — used as a title equivalent to *Mister*

mon·si·gnor \män-'sē-nyər\ *n, pl* **monsignors** *or* **mon·si·gno·ri** \ˌmän-ˌsēn-'yór-ē\ [It *monsignore*] : a Roman Catholic prelate — used as a title

mon·soon \män-'sün\ *n* [obs. Dutch *monssoen,* fr. Pg *monção,* fr. Ar *mawsim* time, season] 1 : a periodic wind esp. in the Indian Ocean and southern Asia 2 : the season of the southwest monsoon esp. in India 3 : rainfall associated with the monsoon

¹mon·ster \'män-stər\ *n* 1 : an abnormally developed plant or animal 2 : an animal of strange or terrifying shape; *also* : one unusually large of its kind 3 : an extremely ugly, wicked, or cruel person — **mon·stros·i·ty** \män-'strä-sə-tē\ *n* — **mon·strous** \'män-strəs\ *adj* — **mon·strous·ly** *adv*

²monster *adj* : very large : ENORMOUS

mon·strance \'män-strəns\ *n* : a vessel in which the consecrated Host is exposed for the adoration of the faithful

Mont *abbr* Montana

mon·tage \män-'täzh\ *n* [F] 1 : a composite photograph made by combining several separate pictures 2 : an artistic composition made up of several different kinds of elements 3 : a varied mixture : JUMBLE

month \'mənth\ *n, pl* **months** \'mən(t)s, 'mən(t)hs\ : one of the 12 parts into which the year is divided — **month·ly** *adv or adj or n*

month·long \'mənth-'lóŋ\ *adj* : lasting a month

mon·u·ment \'män-yə-mənt\ *n* 1 : a lasting reminder; *esp* : a structure erected in remembrance of a person or event 2 : NATIONAL MONUMENT

mon·u·men·tal \ˌmän-yə-'men-t³l\ *adj* 1 : of or relating to a monument 2 : MASSIVE; *also* : OUTSTANDING ⟨a ∼ achievement⟩ 3 : very great ⟨a ∼ task⟩ — **mon·u·men·tal·ly** *adv*

moo \'mü\ *vb* : to make the natural throat noise of a cow — **moo** *n*

¹mood \'müd\ *n* 1 : a conscious state of mind or predominant emotion : FEELING 2 : a prevailing attitude : DISPOSITION 3 : a distinctive atmosphere

²mood *n* : distinction of form of a verb to express whether its action or state is conceived as fact or in some other manner (as wish)

moody \'mü-dē\ *adj* **mood·i·er; -est** 1 : GLOOMY 2 : subject to moods : TEMPERAMENTAL — **mood·i·ly** \-də-lē\ *adv* — **mood·i·ness** \-dē-nəs\ *n*

¹moon \'mün\ *n* 1 : the earth's natural satellite 2 : SATELLITE 2

²moon *vb* : to engage in idle reverie

moon·beam \'mün-ˌbēm\ *n* : a ray of light from the moon

¹moon·light \-ˌlīt\ *n* : the light of the moon — **moon·lit** \-ˌlit\ *adj*

²moonlight *vb* **moon·light·ed; moon·light·ing** : to hold a second job in addition to a regular one — **moon·light·er** *n*

moon·roof \-ˌrüf, -ˌrúf\ *n* : a glass sunroof

moon·scape \-ˌskāp\ *n* : the surface of the moon as seen or as pictured

moon·shine \-ˌshīn\ *n* 1 : MOONLIGHT 2 : empty talk 3 : intoxicating liquor usu. illegally distilled

moon·stone \-ˌstōn\ *n* : a transparent or translucent feldspar of pearly luster used as a gem

moon·struck \-ˌstrək\ *adj* 1 : mentally unbalanced 2 : romantically sentimental 3 : lost in fantasy

¹moor \'múr\ *n* 1 *chiefly Brit* : an expanse of open rolling infertile land 2 : a boggy area; *esp* : one that is peaty and dominated by grasses and sedges

²moor *vb* : to make fast with or as if with cables, lines, or anchors

Moor \'múr\ *n* : one of the Arab and Berber conquerors of Spain — **Moor·ish** *adj*

moor·ing \'múr-iŋ\ *n* 1 : a place where or an object to which a craft can be made fast 2 : an established practice or stabilizing influence — usu. used in pl.

moor·land \-lənd, -ˌland\ *n* : land consisting of moors

moose \'müs\ *n, pl* **moose** : a large heavy-antlered ruminant mammal related to the deer that has humped shoulders and long legs and inhabits northern forested areas

¹moot \'müt\ *vb* : to bring up for discussion; *also* : DEBATE

²moot *adj* 1 : open to question; *also* : DISPUTED ⟨a ∼ assertion⟩ 2 : having no practical significance ⟨the issue is now ∼⟩

¹mop \'mäp\ *n* : an implement made of absorbent material fastened to a handle and used esp. for cleaning floors

²mop *vb* **mopped; mop·ping** : to use a mop on : clean with a mop

mope \'mōp\ *vb* **moped; mop·ing** 1 : to become dull, dejected, or listless 2 : DAWDLE

mo·ped \'mō-ˌped\ *n* : a light low-powered motorbike that can be pedaled

mop·pet \'mä-pət\ *n* [obs. E *mop* fool, child] : CHILD

mo·raine \mə-'rān\ *n* : an accumulation of earth and stones left by a glacier

¹mor·al \'mór-əl\ *adj* 1 : of or relating to principles of right and wrong 2 : conforming to a standard of right behavior; *also* : capable of right and wrong action 3 : probable but not proved ⟨a ∼ certainty⟩ 4 : perceptual or psychological rather than tangible or practical in nature or effect ⟨a ∼ victory⟩ ✦ **Synonyms** VIRTUOUS, RIGHTEOUS, NOBLE, ETHICAL, PRINCIPLED — **mor·al·ly** *adv*

²moral *n* 1 : the practical meaning (as of a story) 2 *pl* : moral practices or teachings ⟨protecting the public ∼s⟩

mo·rale \mə-'ral\ *n* 1 : MORALITY 2 : the mental and emotional attitudes of an individual to the tasks at hand; *also* : ESPRIT DE CORPS

mor·al·ise *Brit var of* MORALIZE

mor·al·ist \'mór-ə-list\ *n* 1 : one who leads a moral life 2 : a thinker or writer concerned with morals 3 : one concerned with regulating the morals of others — **mor·al·is·tic** \ˌmór-ə-'lis-tik\ *adj* — **mor·al·is·ti·cal·ly** \-ti-k(ə-)lē\ *adv*

mo·ral·i·ty \mə-'ra-lə-tē\ *n, pl* **-ties** : moral conduct : VIRTUE

mor·al·ize \'mór-ə-ˌlīz\ *vb* **-ized; -iz·ing** : to make moral reflections — **mor·al·i·za·tion** \ˌmór-ə-lə-'zā-shən\ *n* — **mor·al·iz·er** \'mór-ə-ˌlī-zər\ *n*

mo·rass \mə-'ras\ *n* [D *moeras,* fr. OF *maresc,* of Gmc origin; akin to OE *mersc* marsh] : SWAMP; *also* : something that entangles, impedes, or confuses

mor·a·to·ri·um \ˌmȯr-ə-ˈtȯr-ē-əm\ *n, pl* **-ri·ums** *or* **-ria** \-ē-ə\ [ultim. fr. L *mora* delay] : a suspension of activity

mo·ray eel \mə-ˈrā-, ˈmȯr-ˌā-\ *n* : any of numerous often brightly colored biting eels of warm seas

mor·bid \ˈmȯr-bəd\ *adj* **1** : of, relating to, or typical of disease; *also* : DISEASED, SICKLY **2** : characterized by gloomy or unwholesome ideas or feelings **3** : GRISLY, GRUESOME ⟨~ details⟩ — **mor·bid·i·ty** \mȯr-ˈbi-də-tē\ *n* — **mor·bid·ly** *adv* — **mor·bid·ness** *n*

mor·dant \ˈmȯr-dᵊnt\ *adj* **1** : biting or caustic in manner or style **2** : BURNING, PUNGENT — **mor·dant·ly** *adv*

¹more \ˈmȯr\ *adj* **1** : GREATER ⟨something ~ than I expected⟩ **2** : ADDITIONAL ⟨wanted ~ coffee⟩

²more *adv* **1** : in addition **2** : to a greater or higher degree ⟨~ evenly matched⟩

³more *n* **1** : a greater quantity, number, or amount ⟨the ~ the merrier⟩ **2** : an additional amount ⟨costs a little ~⟩

⁴more *pron* : additional persons or things or a greater amount

mo·rel \mə-ˈrel\ *n* : any of several pitted edible fungi

more·over \mȯr-ˈō-vər\ *adv* : in addition : FURTHER

mo·res \ˈmȯr-ˌāz\ *n pl* [L, pl. of *mor-, mos* custom] **1** : the fixed morally binding customs of a group **2** : HABITS, MANNERS ⟨cultural ~⟩

Mor·gan \ˈmȯr-gən\ *n* : any of an American breed of lightly built horses

morgue \ˈmȯrg\ *n* : a place where the bodies of dead persons are kept until claimed for burial or autopsy

mor·i·bund \ˈmȯr-ə-(ˌ)bənd\ *adj* : being in a dying condition

Mor·mon \ˈmȯr-mən\ *n* : a member of the Church of Jesus Christ of Latter-day Saints — **Mor·mon·ism** \-mə-ˌni-zəm\ *n*

morn \ˈmȯrn\ *n* : MORNING

morn·ing \ˈmȯr-niŋ\ *n* **1** : the early part of the day; *esp* : the time from the sunrise to noon **2** : BEGINNING

morn·ing-after pill \ˌmȯr-niŋ-ˈaf-tər-\ *n* : a contraceptive drug taken up to usu. three days after sexual intercourse

morning glory *n* : any of various twining plants related to the sweet potato that have often showy bell-shaped or funnel-shaped flowers

morning sickness *n* : nausea and vomiting that typically occur in the morning esp. during early pregnancy

morning star *n* : a bright planet (as Venus) seen in the eastern sky before or at sunrise

mo·roc·co \mə-ˈrä-kō\ *n* : a fine leather made of goatskins tanned with sumac

mo·ron \ˈmȯr-ˌän\ *n* **1** : a very stupid person **2** *dated, now offensive* : a person affected with mild mental retardation — **mo·ron·ic** \mə-ˈrä-nik\ *adj* — **mo·ron·i·cal·ly** \-ni-k(ə-)lē\ *adv*

mo·rose \mə-ˈrōs\ *adj* [L *morosus* hard to please, exacting, fr. *mor-, mos* custom, disposition] : having a sullen disposition; *also* : GLOOMY — **mo·rose·ly** *adv* — **mo·rose·ness** *n*

morph \ˈmȯrf\ *vb* : to change the form or character of : TRANSFORM

mor·pheme \ˈmȯr-ˌfēm\ *n* : a meaningful linguistic unit that contains no smaller meaningful parts — **mor·phe·mic** \mȯr-ˈfē-mik\ *adj*

mor·phia \ˈmȯr-fē-ə\ *n* : MORPHINE

mor·phine \ˈmȯr-ˌfēn\ *n* [F, fr. Gk *Morpheus*, Greek god of dreams] : an addictive drug obtained from opium and used to ease pain or induce sleep

mor·phol·o·gy \mȯr-ˈfä-lə-jē\ *n* **1** : a branch of biology dealing with the form and structure of organisms **2** : a study and description of word formation in a language — **mor·pho·log·i·cal** \ˌmȯr-fə-ˈlä-ji-kəl\ *adj* — **mor·phol·o·gist** \mȯr-ˈfä-lə-jist\ *n*

mor·ris \ˈmȯr-əs\ *n* : a vigorous English dance traditionally performed by men wearing costumes and bells

mor·row \ˈmär-ō\ *n* : the next day

Morse code \ˈmȯrs-\ *n* : either of two codes consisting of dots and dashes or long and short sounds used for transmitting messages

mor·sel \ˈmȯr-səl\ *n* [ME, fr. AF, dim. of *mors* bite, fr. L *morsus*, fr. *mordēre* to bite] **1** : a small piece or quantity ⟨chocolate ~s⟩ **2** : a tasty dish

mor·tal \ˈmȯr-tᵊl\ *adj* **1** : causing death : FATAL; *also* : leading to eternal punishment ⟨~ sin⟩ **2** : subject to

death ⟨~ man⟩ **3** : implacably hostile ⟨~ foe⟩ **4** : very great : EXTREME ⟨~ fear⟩ **5** : HUMAN ⟨~ limitations⟩ — **mortal** *n* — **mor·tal·i·ty** \mȯr-ˈta-lə-tē\ *n* — **mor·tal·ly** \ˈmȯr-tᵊl-ē\ *adv*

¹mor·tar \ˈmȯr-tər\ *n* **1** : a strong bowl in which substances are pounded or crushed with a pestle **2** : a short-barreled cannon used to fire shells at high angles

²mortar *n* : a building material (as a mixture of lime and cement with sand and water) that is spread between bricks or stones to bind them together as it hardens — **mortar** *vb*

mor·tar·board \ˈmȯr-tər-ˌbȯrd\ *n* **1** : a square board for holding mortar **2** : an academic cap with a flat square top

mort·gage \ˈmȯr-gij\ *n* [ME *morgage*, fr. AF *mortgage*, fr. *mort* dead + *gage* pledge] : a transfer of rights to a piece of property usu. as security for the payment of a loan or debt that becomes void when the debt is paid — **mortgage** *vb* — **mort·gag·ee** \ˌmȯr-gi-ˈjē\ *n* — **mort·gag·or** \ˌmȯr-gi-ˈjȯr\ *n*

mor·ti·cian \mȯr-ˈti-shən\ *n* [L *mort-, mors* death + E *-ician* (as in *physician*)] : UNDERTAKER

mor·ti·fy \ˈmȯr-tə-ˌfī\ *vb* **-fied; -fy·ing** **1** : to subdue (as the body) esp. by abstinence or self-inflicted pain **2** : HUMILIATE ⟨her behavior *mortified* her parents⟩ **3** : to become necrotic or gangrenous — **mor·ti·fi·ca·tion** \ˌmȯr-tə-fə-ˈkā-shən\ *n*

mor·tise *also* **mor·tice** \ˈmȯr-təs\ *n* : a hole cut in a piece of wood into which another piece fits to form a joint

mor·tu·ary \ˈmȯr-chə-ˌwer-ē\ *n, pl* **-ar·ies** : a place in which dead bodies are kept until burial

mos *abbr* months

mo·sa·ic \mō-ˈzā-ik\ *n* : a surface decoration made by inlaying small pieces (as of colored glass or stone) to form figures or patterns; *also* : a design made in mosaic — **mosaic** *adj*

mos·co·vi·um \mä-ˈskō-vē-əm\ *n* : a short-lived artificially produced radioactive chemical element

mo·sey \ˈmō-zē\ *vb* **mo·seyed; mo·sey·ing** : SAUNTER ⟨*moseyed* through the park⟩

mosh \ˈmäsh\ *vb* : to engage in rough uninhibited dancing near the stage at a rock concert

mosh pit *n* : an area in front of a stage where rough dancing takes place at a rock concert

Mos·lem \ˈmäz-ləm\ *var of* MUSLIM

mosque \ˈmäsk\ *n* : a building used for public worship by Muslims

mos·qui·to \mə-ˈskē-tō\ *n, pl* **-toes** *also* **-tos** : any of a family of dipteran flies the female of which sucks the blood of animals

mosquito net *n* : a net or screen for keeping out mosquitoes

moss \ˈmȯs\ *n* : any of a class of green plants that lack flowers but have small leafy stems and often grow in clumps — **mossy** *adj*

moss·back \ˈmȯs-ˌbak\ *n* : an extremely conservative person : FOGY

¹most \ˈmōst\ *adj* **1** : GREATEST ⟨the ~ ability⟩ **2** : the majority of ⟨~ people⟩

²most *adv* **1** : to the greatest or highest degree ⟨~ beautiful⟩ **2** : to a very great degree ⟨a ~ careful driver⟩

³most *n* : the greatest amount ⟨the ~ I can do⟩

⁴most *pron* : the greatest number or part ⟨~ became discouraged⟩

-most *adj suffix* : most ⟨inner*most*⟩ : most toward ⟨end*most*⟩

most·ly \ˈmōst-lē\ *adv* : MAINLY

mot \ˈmō\ *n, pl* **mots** \same or ˈmōz\ [F, word, saying, fr. LL *muttum* grunt] : a witty saying

mote \ˈmōt\ *n* : a small particle

mo·tel \mō-ˈtel\ *n* [blend of *motor* and *hotel*] : a hotel in which the rooms are accessible from the parking area

mo·tet \mō-ˈtet\ *n* : a choral work on a sacred text for several voices usu. without instrumental accompaniment

moth \ˈmȯth\ *n, pl* **moths** \ˈmȯthz, ˈmȯths\ : any of various insects belonging to the same order as the butterflies but usu. night-flying and with a stouter body and smaller wings

moth·ball \ˈmȯth-ˌbȯl\ *n* **1** : a ball (as of naphthalene) used to keep moths out of clothing **2** *pl* : protective storage ⟨many ships were put in ~s⟩

¹moth·er \'mə-thər\ n 1 : a female parent 2 : the superior of a religious community of women 3 : SOURCE, ORIGIN ⟨necessity is the ~ of invention⟩ — moth·er·hood \-,hüd\ n — moth·er·less adj — moth·er·li·ness \-lē-nəs\ n — moth·er·ly adj

²mother vb 1 : to give birth to; also : PRODUCE 2 : to care for or protect like a mother

moth·er·board \'mə-thər-,bórd\ n : the main circuit board esp. of a microcomputer

moth·er–in–law \'mə-thər-ən-,ló\ n, pl mothers–in–law \'mə-thərz-\ : the mother of one's spouse

moth·er·land \'mə-thər-,land\ n 1 : the land of origin of something 2 : the native land of one's ancestors

moth·er–of–pearl \,mə-thər-əv-'pərl\ n : the hard pearly matter forming the inner layer of a mollusk shell

mother ship n : a ship serving smaller craft

mo·tif \mō-'tēf\ n [F, motive, motif] : a dominant idea or central theme (as in a work of art)

mo·tile \'mō-t³l, 'mō-,tī(-ə)l\ adj : capable of spontaneous movement ⟨~ cells⟩ — mo·til·i·ty \mō-'til-ə-tē\ n

¹mo·tion \'mō-shən\ n 1 : an act, process, or instance of moving 2 : a proposal for action (as by a deliberative body) 3 pl : ACTIVITIES, MOVEMENTS — mo·tion·less adj — mo·tion·less·ly adv — mo·tion·less·ness n

²motion vb : to direct or signal by a movement

motion picture n : a series of pictures projected on a screen so rapidly that they produce a continuous picture in which persons and objects seem to move

motion sickness n : sickness induced by motion and characterized by nausea

mo·ti·vate \'mō-tə-,vāt\ vb -vat·ed; -vat·ing : to provide with a motive : IMPEL — mo·ti·va·tion \,mō-tə-'vā-shən\ n — mo·ti·va·tion·al \-shə-nəl\ adj — mo·ti·va·tor \'mō-tə-,vā-tər\ n

¹mo·tive \'mō-tiv, 2 also mō-'tēv\ n 1 : something (as a need or desire) that causes a person to act 2 : a recurrent theme in a musical composition 3 : MOTIF — mo·tive·less adj

²mo·tive \'mō-tiv\ adj 1 : moving to action 2 : of or relating to motion

mot·ley \'mät-lē\ adj 1 : variegated in color 2 : made up of diverse often incongruous elements ✦ Synonyms HETEROGENEOUS, MISCELLANEOUS, ASSORTED, MIXED, VARIED

¹mo·tor \'mō-tər\ n [L, fr. movēre to move] 1 : one that imparts motion 2 : a machine that produces motion or power for doing work 3 : AUTOMOBILE

²motor vb : to travel or transport by automobile : DRIVE — mo·tor·ist n

mo·tor·bike \'mō-tər-,bīk\ n : a small lightweight motorcycle

mo·tor·boat \-,bōt\ n : a boat propelled by a motor

mo·tor·cade \-,kād\ n : a procession of motor vehicles

mo·tor·car \-,kär\ n : AUTOMOBILE

mo·tor·cy·cle \'mō-tər-,sī-kəl\ n : a 2-wheeled automotive vehicle — mo·tor·cy·clist \-k(ə-)list\ n

motor home n : a large motor vehicle equipped as living quarters

motor inn n : MOTEL

mo·tor·ise Brit var of MOTORIZE

mo·tor·ize \'mō-tə-,rīz\ vb -ized; -iz·ing 1 : to equip with a motor 2 : to equip with automobiles

mo·tor·man \'mō-tər-mən\ n : an operator of a motor-driven vehicle (as a streetcar or subway train)

motor scooter n : a low 2- or 3-wheeled automotive vehicle resembling a child's scooter but having a seat

mo·tor·truck \'mō-tər-,trək\ n : an automotive truck

motor vehicle n : an automotive vehicle (as an automobile) not operated on rails

mot·tle \'mä-t³l\ vb mot·tled; mot·tling : to mark with spots of different color : BLOTCH

mot·to \'mä-tō\ n, pl mottoes also mottos [It, fr. LL muttum grunt, fr. L muttire to mutter] 1 : a sentence, phrase, or word inscribed on something to indicate its character or use 2 : a short expression of a guiding rule of conduct

moue \'mü\ n : a little grimace

mould chiefly Brit var of MOLD

moult chiefly Brit var of MOLT

mound \'maùnd\ n 1 : an artificial bank or hill of earth or stones 2 : KNOLL 3 : HEAP, PILE ⟨a ~ of work⟩

¹mount \'maùnt\ n : a high hill

²mount vb 1 : to increase in amount or extent; also : RISE, ASCEND 2 : to get up on something; esp : to seat oneself on (as a horse) for riding 3 : to put in position ⟨~ artillery⟩ 4 : to set on something that elevates 5 : to attach to a support 6 : to prepare esp. for examination or display — mount·able adj — mount·er n

³mount n 1 : FRAME, SUPPORT 2 : a means of conveyance; esp : SADDLE HORSE

moun·tain \'maùn-t³n\ n : a landmass higher than a hill — moun·tain·ous \-tə-nəs\ adj — moun·tainy \-t³n-ē\ adj

mountain ash n : any of various trees related to the roses that have pinnate leaves and red or orange-red fruits

mountain bike n : a bicycle with wide knobby tires, straight handlebars, and 18 or 21 gears that is designed to operate esp. on unpaved terrain

moun·tain·eer \,maùn-tə-'nir\ n 1 : a native or inhabitant of a mountainous region 2 : one who climbs mountains for sport

mountain goat n : a ruminant mammal of mountainous northwestern No. America that resembles a goat

mountain laurel n : a No. American evergreen shrub or small tree of the heath family with glossy leaves and clusters of rose-colored or white flowers

mountain lion n : COUGAR

moun·tain·side \'maùn-t³n-,sīd\ n : the side of a mountain

moun·tain·top \-,täp\ n : the summit of a mountain

moun·te·bank \'maùn-ti-,baŋk\ n [It montimbanco, fr. montare to mount + in in, on + banco, banca bench] : QUACK, CHARLATAN

Mount·ie \'maùn-tē\ n : a member of the Royal Canadian Mounted Police

mount·ing \'maùn-tiŋ\ n : something that serves as a frame or support

mourn \'mórn\ vb : to feel or express grief or sorrow — mourn·er n

mourn·ful \-fəl\ adj : expressing, feeling, or causing sorrow ⟨a ~ song⟩ — mourn·ful·ly adv — mourn·ful·ness n

mourn·ing \'mór-niŋ\ n 1 : an outward sign (as black clothes) of grief for a person's death 2 : a period of time during which signs of grief are shown

mouse \'maùs\ n, pl mice \'mīs\ 1 : any of numerous small rodents with pointed snout, long body, and slender tail 2 : a small manual device that controls cursor movement on a computer display

mouse pad n : a thin flat pad on which a computer mouse is used

mous·er \'maù-sər\ n : a cat proficient at catching mice

mouse·trap \'maùs-,trap\ n 1 : a trap for catching mice 2 : a stratagem that lures one to defeat or destruction — mousetrap vb

mousse \'müs\ n [F, lit., froth, moss] 1 : a molded chilled dessert made with sweetened and flavored whipped cream or egg whites and gelatin 2 : a foamy preparation used in styling hair — mousse vb

moustache var of MUSTACHE

mousy or mous·ey \'maù-sē, -zē\ adj mous·i·er; -est 1 : QUIET, STEALTHY 2 : TIMID 3 : grayish brown — mous·i·ness \'maù-sē-nəs, -zē-\ n

¹mouth \'maùth\ n, pl mouths \'maùthz, 'maùths\ 1 : the opening through which an animal takes in food; also : the cavity that encloses the tongue, lips, and teeth in the typical vertebrate 2 : something resembling a mouth (as in affording entrance) — mouthed \'maùthd, 'maùtht\ adj — mouth·ful n

²mouth \'maùth\ vb 1 : SPEAK; also : DECLAIM 2 : to repeat without comprehension or sincerity ⟨~ed platitudes⟩ 3 : to form soundlessly with the lips

mouth harp n : HARMONICA

mouth·part \'maùth-,pärt\ n : a structure or appendage near the mouth (as of an insect) esp. when adapted for eating

mouth·piece \-,pēs\ n 1 : a part (as of a musical instrument) that goes in the mouth or to which the mouth is applied 2 : SPOKESMAN

mouth–to–mouth adj : of, relating to, or being a method of artificial respiration in which air from a rescuer's mouth is forced into a victim's lungs

mouth·wash \-,wòsh, -,wäsh\ n : a usu. antiseptic liquid preparation for cleaning the mouth and teeth

mou·ton \'mü-ˌtän\ *n* : processed sheepskin that has been sheared or dyed to resemble beaver or seal

¹move \'müv\ *vb* **moved; mov·ing** **1** : to change or cause to change position or posture **2** : to go or cause to go from one point to another; *also* : DEPART **3** : to take or cause to take action **4** : to show marked activity **5** : to stir the emotions **6** : to make a formal request, application, or appeal **7** : to change one's residence **8** : EVACUATE **2** — **mov·able** *or* **move·able** \'mü-və-bəl\ *adj*

²move *n* **1** : an act of moving **2** : a calculated step taken to gain an objective **3** : a change of location **4** : an agile action esp. in sports

move·ment \'müv-mənt\ *n* **1** : the act or process of moving : MOVE **2** : a series of organized activities working toward an objective **3** : the moving parts of a mechanism (as of a watch) **4** : RHYTHM **5** : a section of an extended musical composition **6** : BOWEL MOVEMENT; *also* : STOOL 4

mov·er \'mü-vər\ *n* : one that moves; *esp* : one that moves the belongings of others from one location to another

mov·ie \'mü-vē\ *n* **1** : MOTION PICTURE **2** *pl* : a showing of a motion picture **3** *pl* : the motion-picture industry

¹mow \'maü\ *n* : the part of a barn where hay or straw is stored

²mow \'mō\ *vb* **mowed; mowed** *or* **mown** \'mōn\; **mow·ing** **1** : to cut (as grass) with a scythe or machine **2** : to cut the standing herbage of ⟨~ the lawn⟩ — **mow·er** *n*

mox·ie \'mäk-sē\ *n* **1** : ENERGY, PEP **2** : COURAGE, DETERMINATION

moz·za·rel·la \ˌmät-sə-ˈre-lə\ *n* [It] : a moist white unsalted unripened mild cheese of a smooth rubbery texture

¹MP \'em-'pē\ *n* **1** : a member of the military police **2** : an elected member of a parliament

²MP *abbr* **1** melting point **2** metropolitan police

MPEG \'em-ˌpeg\ *n* : any of a group of computer file formats for the compression and storage of digital video and audio data; *also* : a computer file (as of a movie) in an MPEG format

mpg *abbr* miles per gallon

mph *abbr* miles per hour

MP3 \ˌem-(ˌ)pē-'thrē\ *n* : a computer file format for the compression and storage of digital audio data; *also* : a computer file (as of a song) in the MP3 format

Mr. \'mis-tər\ *n, pl* **Messrs.** \'me-sərz\ — used as a conventional title of courtesy before a man's surname or his title of office

MRI *n* : MAGNETIC RESONANCE IMAGING; *also* : the procedure in which magnetic resonance imaging is used

Mr. Right *n* : a man who would make the perfect husband

Mrs. \'mi-səz, -səs, *esp Southern* 'mi-zəz, -zəs\ *n, pl* **Mes·dames** \mā-'däm, -'dam\ — used as a conventional title of courtesy before a married woman's surname

Ms. \'miz\ *n, pl* **Mss.** *or* **Mses.** \'mi-zez\ — used as a conventional title of courtesy before a woman's surname.

MS *abbr* **1** manuscript **2** master of science **3** military science **4** Mississippi **5** motor ship **6** multiple sclerosis

msec *abbr* millisecond

msg *abbr* message

MSG *abbr* **1** master sergeant **2** monosodium glutamate

msgr *abbr* **1** monseigneur **2** monsignor

MSgt *abbr* master sergeant

MSS *abbr* manuscripts

MST *abbr* mountain standard time

mt *abbr* mount; mountain

¹Mt *abbr* Matthew

²Mt *symbol* meitnerium

MT *abbr* **1** metric ton **2** Montana **3** mountain time

mtg *abbr* **1** meeting **2** mortgage

mtge *abbr* mortgage

mu \'myü, 'mü\ *n* : the 12th letter of the Greek alphabet — M or μ

¹much \'məch\ *adj* **more** \'mȯr\; **most** \'mōst\ : great in quantity, amount, extent, or degree ⟨~ money⟩

²much *adv* **more; most** **1** : to a great degree or extent ⟨~ happier⟩ **2** : ALMOST, NEARLY ⟨looks ~ as he did before⟩

³much *n* **1** : a great quantity, amount, extent, or degree **2** : something considerable or impressive

mu·ci·lage \'myü-sə-lij\ *n* : a watery sticky solution (as of a gum) used esp. as an adhesive — **mu·ci·lag·i·nous** \ˌmyü-sə-'la-jə-nəs\ *adj*

muck \'mək\ *n* **1** : soft moist barnyard manure **2** : FILTH, DIRT **3** : a dark richly organic soil; *also* : MUD, MIRE — **mucky** *adj*

muck·rake \-ˌrāk\ *vb* : to expose publicly real or apparent misconduct of a prominent individual or business — **muck·rak·er** *n*

mu·cus \'myü-kəs\ *n* : a slimy slippery protective secretion of membranes (**mucous membranes**) lining some body cavities — **mu·cous** \-kəs\ *adj*

mud \'məd\ *n* : soft wet earth : MIRE

mud·dle \'mə-dᵊl\ *vb* **mud·dled; mud·dling** **1** : to make muddy **2** : to confuse esp. with liquor **3** : to mix up or make a mess of ⟨*muddled* the household accounts⟩ **4** : to think or act in a confused way

mud·dle·head·ed \ˌmə-dᵊl-'he-dəd\ *adj* **1** : mentally confused **2** : INEPT

¹mud·dy \'mə-dē\ *adj* **mud·di·er; -est** **1** : full of or covered with mud **2** : suggestive of mud **3** : CLOUDY, OBSCURE — **mud·di·ness** *n*

²muddy *vb* **mud·died; mud·dy·ing** **1** : to soil or stain with or as if with mud **2** : to make cloudy or obscure **3** : CONFUSE

mud·flat \'məd-ˌflat\ *n* : a level tract alternately covered and left bare by the tide

mud·guard \'məd-ˌgärd\ *n* : a guard over or a flap behind a wheel of a vehicle to catch or deflect mud

mud·room \-ˌrüm, -ˌrùm\ *n* : a room in a house for removing dirty or wet footwear and clothing

mud·sling·er \-ˌsliŋ-ər\ *n* : one who uses invective esp. against a political opponent — **mud·sling·ing** \-ˌsliŋ-iŋ\ *n*

Muen·ster \'mən-stər, 'mün-, 'mùn-\ *n* : a semisoft bland cheese

mu·ez·zin \mü-'e-zᵊn, myü-\ *n* : a Muslim crier who calls the hour of daily prayer

¹muff \'məf\ *n* : a warm tubular covering for the hands

²muff *n* : a bungling performance; *esp* : a failure to hold a ball in attempting a catch — **muff** *vb*

muf·fin \'mə-fən\ *n* : a small soft cake baked in a cup-shaped container

muf·fle \'mə-fəl\ *vb* **muf·fled; muf·fling** **1** : to wrap up so as to conceal or protect **2** : to wrap or pad with something to dull the sound of **3** : to keep down : SUPPRESS ⟨*muffled* his feelings⟩

muf·fler \'mə-flər\ *n* **1** : a scarf worn around the neck **2** : a device (as on a car's exhaust) to deaden noise

muf·ti \'məf-tē\ *n* : civilian clothes

¹mug \'məg\ *n* : a usu. metal or earthenware cylindrical drinking cup

²mug *vb* **mugged; mug·ging** **1** : to pose or make faces esp. to attract attention or for a camera **2** : PHOTOGRAPH

³mug *vb* **mugged; mug·ging** : to assault usu. with intent to rob — **mug·ger** *n*

mug·gy \'mə-gē\ *adj* **mug·gi·er; -est** : being warm and humid — **mug·gi·ness** \-gē-nəs\ *n*

mug·wump \'məg-ˌwəmp\ *n* [obs. slang *mugwump* kingpin, fr. Massachusett (Algonquian language of New England) *mugquomp* war leader] : an independent in politics

Muhammadan *var of* MOHAMMEDAN

mu·ja·hid·een *or* **mu·ja·hed·in** \ˌmü-jä-hi-'dēn, -jä-\ *n pl* [Ar *mujāhidīn*, pl. of *mujāhid*, lit., person who wages jihad] : Islamic guerrilla fighters esp. in the Middle East

muk·luk \'mək-ˌlək\ *n* **1** : a boot of sealskin or reindeer skin typically worn by indigenous peoples of usually arctic regions **2** : a boot with a soft leather sole worn over several pairs of socks

mu·lat·to \mü-'la-tō, myü-, -'lä-\ *n, pl* **-toes** *or* **-tos** [Sp *mulato*, fr. *mulo* mule, fr. L *mulus*] **1** *now sometimes offensive* : the first-generation offspring of a black person and a white person **2** *now sometimes offensive* : a person of mixed white and black ancestry

mul·ber·ry \'məl-ˌber-ē\ *n* : any of a genus of trees with edible berrylike fruit and leaves used as food for silkworms; *also* : the fruit

mulch \'məlch\ *n* : a protective covering (as of straw or leaves) spread on the ground esp. to reduce evaporation or control weeds — **mulch** *vb*

¹mulct \'məlkt\ *n* : FINE, PENALTY

²mulct *vb* **1** : FINE **2** : CHEAT, DEFRAUD

¹mule \'myül\ *n* **1** : a hybrid offspring of a male donkey and a female horse **2** : a very stubborn person — **mul·ish** \'myü-lish\ *adj* — **mul·ish·ly** *adv* — **mu·lish·ness** *n*

²**mule** *n* : a slipper whose upper does not extend around the heel of the foot

mule deer *n* : a long-eared deer of western No. America

mu·le·teer \ˌmyü-lə-ˈtir\ *n* : one who drives mules

¹**mull** \ˈməl\ *vb* : PONDER, MEDITATE

²**mull** *vb* : to heat, sweeten, and flavor (as wine) with spices

mul·lein \ˈmə-lən\ *n* : a tall herb related to the snapdragons that has coarse woolly leaves and flowers in spikes

mul·let \ˈmə-lət\ *n, pl* **mullet** *or* **mullets** : any of a family of largely gray chiefly marine bony fishes including valuable food fishes

mul·li·gan stew \ˈmə-li-gən-\ *n* : a stew made from whatever ingredients are available

mul·li·ga·taw·ny \ˌmə-li-gə-ˈtó-nē\ *n* : a soup usu. of chicken stock seasoned with curry

mul·lion \ˈməl-yən\ *n* : a vertical strip separating windowpanes

multi- *comb form* **1** : many : multiple ⟨*multi*unit⟩ **2** : many times over ⟨*multi*millionaire⟩

mul·ti·col·ored \ˌməl-ti-ˈkə-lərd\ *adj* : having many colors

mul·ti·cul·tur·al \ˌməl-ti-ˈkəl-chə-rəl, -ˌtī-\ *adj* : of, relating to, reflecting, or adapted to diverse cultures ⟨a ∼ society⟩ — **mul·ti·cul·tur·al·ism** \-rə-ˌli-zəm\ *n* — **mul·ti·cul·tur·al·ist** \-rə-list\ *n or adj*

mul·ti·di·men·sion·al \-ti-də-ˈmen-chə-nəl, -ˌtī-, -dī-\ *adj* : of, relating to, or having many facets or dimensions ⟨a ∼ problem⟩ ⟨∼ space⟩

mul·ti·eth·nic \-ˈeth-nik\ *adj* : including, involving, or made up of people of various ethnic groups

mul·ti·fac·et·ed \-ˈfa-sə-təd\ *adj* : having many facets or aspects ⟨a ∼ concept⟩

mul·ti·fam·i·ly \-ˈfam-lē, -ˈfa-mə-\ *adj* : designed for use by several families

mul·ti·far·i·ous \ˌməl-tə-ˈfer-ē-əs\ *adj* : having great variety : DIVERSE ⟨∼ activities⟩ — **mul·ti·far·i·ous·ness** *n*

mul·ti·form \ˈməl-ti-ˌfòrm\ *adj* : having many forms or appearances — **mul·ti·for·mi·ty** \ˌməl-ti-ˈfór-mə-tē\ *n*

mul·ti·lat·er·al \ˌməl-ti-ˈla-tə-rəl, -ˌtī-, -ˈla-trəl\ *adj* : having many sides or participants ⟨∼ treaty⟩ — **mul·ti·lat·er·al·ism** \-ˈla-tə-rə-ˌli-zəm\ *n* — **mul·ti·lat·er·al·ly** *adv*

mul·ti·lay·ered \-ˈlā-ərd, -ˈlerd\ *or* **mul·ti·lay·er** \-ˈlā-ər, -ˈler\ *adj* : having or involving several distinct layers or levels

mul·ti·lev·el \-ˈle-vəl\ *adj* : having several levels

mul·ti·lin·gual \-ˈliŋ-gwəl\ *adj* : knowing or using several languages — **mul·ti·lin·gual·ism** \-gwə-ˌli-zəm\ *n*

¹**mul·ti·me·dia** \-ˈmē-dē-ə\ *adj* : using, involving, or encompassing several media ⟨a ∼ advertising campaign⟩

²**multimedia** *n sing or pl* : the technique of using several media (as in art); *also* : something (as software) that uses or facilitates it

mul·ti·mil·lion·aire \ˌməl-ti-ˌmil-yə-ˈnar, -ˌtī-, -ˈmil-yə-ˌnar\ *n* : a person worth several million dollars

mul·ti·na·tion·al \-ˈna-shə-nəl\ *adj* **1** : of or relating to several nationalities **2** : relating to or involving several nations **3** : having divisions in several countries ⟨a ∼ corporation⟩ — **multinational** *n*

mul·ti·pack \ˈməl-tē-ˌpak\ *n* : a package of several individually packed items sold as a unit

¹**mul·ti·ple** \ˈməl-tə-pəl\ *adj* : more than one; *also* : MANY ⟨∼ achievements⟩ **2** : VARIOUS

²**multiple** *n* : the product of a quantity by an integer ⟨35 is a ∼ of 7⟩

multiple–choice *adj* : having several answers given from which the correct one is to be chosen ⟨a ∼ question⟩

multiple personality disorder *n* : a neurosis in which the personality becomes separated into two or more parts each of which controls behavior part of the time

multiple sclerosis *n* : a disease marked by patches of hardened tissue in the brain or spinal cord and associated esp. with partial or complete paralysis and muscular tremor

mul·ti·plex \ˈməl-tə-ˌpleks\ *n* : CINEPLEX

mul·ti·pli·cand \ˌməl-tə-pli-ˈkand\ *n* : the number that is to be multiplied by another

mul·ti·pli·ca·tion \ˌməl-tə-plə-ˈkā-shən\ *n* **1** : INCREASE **2** : a short method of finding the result of adding a figure the number of times indicated by another figure

multiplication sign *n* **1** : TIMES SIGN **2** : a centered dot indicating multiplication

mul·ti·plic·i·ty \ˌməl-tə-ˈpli-sə-tē\ *n, pl* **-ties** : a great number or variety

mul·ti·pli·er \ˈməl-tə-ˌplī(-ə)r\ *n* : one that multiplies; *esp* : a number by which another number is multiplied

mul·ti·ply \ˈməl-tə-ˌplī\ *vb* **-plied; -ply·ing 1** : to increase in number (as by breeding) **2** : to find the product of by multiplication; *also* : to perform multiplication

mul·ti·pur·pose \ˌməl-ti-ˈpər-pəs, -ˌtī-\ *adj* : having or serving several purposes

mul·ti·ra·cial \-ˈrā-shəl\ *adj* : composed of, involving, or representing various races

mul·ti·sense \-ˌsens\ *adj* : having several meanings ⟨∼ words⟩

mul·ti·sto·ry \-ˌstòr-ē\ *adj* : having several stories ⟨∼ buildings⟩

mul·ti·task·ing \ˈməl-tē-ˌtas-kiŋ, -ˌtī-\ *n* **1** : the concurrent performance of several jobs by a computer **2** : the performance of multiple tasks at one time — **mul·ti·task** \-ˌtask\ *vb* — **mul·ti·task·er** \-ˌtas-kər\ *n*

mul·ti·tude \ˈməl-tə-ˌtüd, -ˌtyüd\ *n* : a great number — **mul·ti·tu·di·nous** \ˌməl-tə-ˈtü-dᵊn-əs, -ˈtyüd-\ *adj*

mul·ti·unit \ˌməl-ti-ˈyü-nət, -ˌtī-\ *adj* : having several units

mul·ti·vi·ta·min \-ˈvī-tə-mən\ *adj* : containing several vitamins and esp. all known to be essential to health — **multivitamin** *n*

¹**mum** \ˈməm\ *adj* : SILENT

²**mum** *chiefly Brit var of* MOM

³**mum** *n* : CHRYSANTHEMUM

mum·ble \ˈməm-bəl\ *vb* **mum·bled; mum·bling** : to speak in a low indistinct manner — **mumble** *n* — **mum·bler** *n* — **mum·bly** *adj*

mum·ble·ty–peg \ˈməm-bəl-tē-ˌpeg\ *also* **mum·ble–the–peg** \ˈməm-bəl-thə-\ *n* : a game in which the players try to flip a knife from various positions so that the blade will stick into the ground

mum·bo jum·bo \ˌməm-bō-ˈjəm-bō\ *n* **1** : a complicated ritual with elaborate trappings **2** : GIBBERISH, NONSENSE

mum·mer \ˈmə-mər\ *n* **1** : an actor esp. in a pantomime **2** : a person who goes merrymaking in disguise during festivals — **mum·mery** *n*

mum·my \ˈmə-mē\ *n, pl* **mummies** [ME *mummie* powdered parts of a mummified body used as a drug, fr. AF *mumie*, fr. ML *mumia*, fr. Ar *mūmiya* bitumen, mummy, fr. Per *mūm* wax] : a body embalmed for burial in the manner of the ancient Egyptians — **mum·mi·fi·ca·tion** \ˌmə-mi-fə-ˈkā-shən\ *n* — **mum·mi·fy** \ˈmə-mi-ˌfī\ *vb*

mumps \ˈməmps\ *n sing or pl* [fr. pl. of obs. *mump* grimace] : a virus disease marked by fever and swelling esp. of the salivary glands

mun *or* **munic** *abbr* municipal

munch \ˈmənch\ *vb* : to eat with a chewing action; *also* : to snack on

munch·ies \ˈmən-chēz\ *n pl* **1** : hunger pangs **2** : light snack foods

mun·dane \ˌmən-ˈdān, ˈmən-ˌdān\ *adj* **1** : of or relating to the world **2** : concerned with the practical details of everyday life — **mun·dane·ly** *adv*

mung bean \ˈməŋ-\ *n* : an erect bushy bean widely grown in warm regions for its edible seeds and as the chief source of bean sprouts; *also* : its seed

mu·nic·i·pal \myü-ˈni-sə-pəl\ *adj* **1** : of, relating to, or characteristic of a municipality **2** : restricted to one locality — **mu·nic·i·pal·ly** *adv*

mu·nic·i·pal·i·ty \myü-ˌni-sə-ˈpa-lə-tē\ *n, pl* **-ties** : an urban political unit with corporate status and usu. powers of self-government

mu·nif·i·cent \myü-ˈni-fə-sənt\ *adj* : liberal in giving : GENEROUS — **mu·nif·i·cence** \-səns\ *n*

mu·ni·tion \myü-ˈni-shən\ *n* : ARMAMENT, AMMUNITION

¹**mu·ral** \ˈmyùr-əl\ *adj* **1** : of or relating to a wall **2** : applied to and made part of a wall or ceiling surface

²**mural** *n* : a mural painting — **mu·ral·ist** *n*

¹**mur·der** \ˈmər-dər\ *n* **1** : the crime of unlawfully killing a person esp. with malice aforethought **2** : something unusually difficult or dangerous

²**murder** *vb* **1** : to commit a murder; *also* : to kill brutally **2** : to put an end to **3** : to spoil by performing poorly ⟨∼ a song⟩ — **mur·der·er** *n*

mur·der·ess \ˈmər-də-rəs\ *n* : a woman who murders

mur·der·ous \ˈmər-də-rəs\ *adj* **1** : having or appearing to have the purpose of murder ⟨∼ impulses⟩ **2** : marked by or causing murder or bloodshed ⟨∼ gunfire⟩ — **mur·der·ous·ly** *adv* murk \'mərk\ *n* : DARKNESS, GLOOM — **murk·i·ly** \'mər-kə-lē\ *adv* — **murk·i·ness** \-kē-nəs\ *n* — **murky** *adj*

mur·mur \'mər-mər\ *n* **1** : a muttered complaint **2** : a low indistinct often continuous sound — **murmur** *vb* — **mur·mur·er** *n* — **mur·mur·ous** *adj*

mus *abbr* **1** museum **2** music; musical; musician

mus·ca·tel \ˌməs-kə-'tel\ *n* : a sweet fortified wine

¹**mus·cle** \'mə-səl\ *n* [ME, fr. L *musculus*, fr. dim. of *mus* mouse] **1** : a body tissue consisting of long cells that contract when stimulated and produce motion; *also* : an organ consisting of this tissue and functioning in moving a body part **2** : STRENGTH, BRAWN — **mus·cled** \'mə-səld\ *adj* — **mus·cu·lar** \'məs-kyə-lər\ *adj* — **mus·cu·lar·i·ty** \ˌməs-kyə-'ler-ə-tē\ *n*

²**muscle** *vb* **mus·cled; mus·cling** : to force one's way

mus·cle-bound \'mə-səl-ˌbaůnd\ *adj* : having some of the muscles abnormally enlarged and lacking in elasticity (as from excessive exercise)

mus·cle·man \-ˌman\ *n* : a man with a muscular physique

muscular dystrophy *n* : any of a group of diseases characterized by progressive wasting of muscles

mus·cu·la·ture \'məs-kyə-lə-ˌchůr\ *n* : the muscles of the body or its parts

muscu·lo·skel·e·tal \ˌməs-kyə-lō-'ske-lə-tᵊl\ *adj* : of, relating to, or involving both musculature and skeleton

¹**muse** \'myüz\ *vb* **mused; mus·ing** [ME, fr. AF *muser* to gape, idle, muse, fr. OF **mus* mouth of an animal, fr. ML *musus*] : to become absorbed in thought 〈*mused* about what might have been〉 — **mus·ing·ly** *adv*

²**muse** *n* [fr. *Muse* any of the nine sister goddesses of learning and the arts in Greek myth, fr. ME, fr. MF, fr. L *Musa*, fr. Gk *Mousa*] : a source of inspiration

mu·se·um \myü-'zē-əm\ *n* : an institution devoted to the procurement, care, and display of objects of lasting interest or value

¹**mush** \'məsh\ *n* **1** : cornmeal boiled in water **2** : sentimental drivel

²**mush** *vb* : to travel esp. over snow with a sled drawn by dogs

¹**mush·room** \'məsh-ˌrüm, -ˌrům\ *n* : the fleshy usu. caplike spore-bearing organ of various fungi esp. when edible; *also* : such a fungus

²**mushroom** *vb* **1** : to spread out : EXPAND **2** : to collect wild mushrooms **3** : to grow rapidly 〈the population ∼ed〉

mushy \'mə-shē\ *adj* **mush·i·er; -est** **1** : soft like mush **2** : excessively sentimental 〈a ∼ movie〉

mu·sic \'myü-zik\ *n* **1** : the science or art of combining tones into a composition having structure and continuity; *also* : vocal or instrumental sounds having rhythm, melody, or harmony **2** : an agreeable sound

¹**mu·si·cal** \'myü-zi-kəl\ *adj* **1** : of or relating to music or musicians **2** : having the pleasing tonal qualities of music **3** : fond of or gifted in music 〈a ∼ family〉 — **mu·si·cal·ly** \-k(ə-)lē\ *adv*

²**musical** *n* : a film or theatrical production consisting of musical numbers and dialogue based on a unifying plot

mu·si·cale \ˌmyü-zi-'kal\ *n* : a usu. private social gathering featuring music

mu·si·cian \myü-'zi-shən\ *n* : a composer, conductor, or performer of music — **mu·si·cian·ly** *adj* — **mu·si·cian·ship** *n*

mu·si·col·o·gy \ˌmyü-zi-'kä-lə-jē\ *n* : the study of music as a field of knowledge or research — **mu·si·co·log·i·cal** \-kə-'lä-ji-kəl\ *adj* — **mu·si·col·o·gist** \-'kä-lə-jist\ *n*

musk \'məsk\ *n* : a substance obtained esp. from a small Asian deer (**musk deer**) and used as a perfume fixative — **musk·i·ness** \'məs-kē-nəs\ *n* — **musky** *adj*

mus·keg \'məs-ˌkeg\ *n* : BOG; *esp* : a mossy bog in northern No. America

mus·kel·lunge \'məs-kə-ˌlənj\ *n, pl* **muskellunge** : a large No. American pike that is a valuable sport fish

mus·ket \'məs-kət\ *n* [MF *mousquet*, fr. It *moschetto* small artillery piece, kind of small hawk, fr. dim. of *mosca* fly, fr. L *musca*] : a heavy large-caliber muzzle-loading shoulder firearm — **mus·ke·teer** \ˌməs-kə-'tir\ *n*

mus·ket·ry \'məs-kə-trē\ *n* **1** : MUSKETS **2** : MUSKETEERS **3** : musket fire

musk·mel·on \'məsk-ˌme-lən\ *n* : a small round to oval melon that has usu. a sweet edible green or orange flesh and a musky odor

musk ox *n* : a heavyset shaggy-coated wild ox of Greenland and the arctic tundra of northern No. America

musk·rat \'məs-ˌkrat\ *n, pl* **muskrat** *or* **muskrats** : a large No. American aquatic rodent with webbed feet and dark brown fur; *also* : its fur

Mus·lim \'məz-ləm\ *n* : an adherent of Islam — **Muslim** *adj*

mus·lin \'məz-lən\ *n* : a plain-woven sheer to coarse cotton fabric

¹**muss** \'məs\ *n* : a state of disorder — **muss·i·ly** \'mə-sə-lē\ *adv* — **muss·i·ness** \-sē-nəs\ *n* — **mussy** *adj*

²**muss** *vb* : to make untidy : DISARRANGE

mus·sel \'mə-səl\ *n* **1** : a dark edible saltwater bivalve mollusk **2** : any of various freshwater bivalve mollusks of the central U.S. having shells with a pearly lining

¹**must** \'məst\ *vb* — used as an auxiliary esp. to express a command, requirement, obligation, or necessity

²**must** *n* **1** : an imperative duty **2** : an indispensable item

mus·tache *also* **mous·tache** \'məs-ˌtash, (ˌ)məs-'tash\ *n* : the hair growing on the human upper lip — **mustached** *also* **moustached** \-ˌtasht, -'tasht\ *adj*

mus·tang \'məs-ˌtaŋ\ *n* [MexSp *mestengo*, fr. Sp, stray, fr. *mesteño* strayed, fr. *mesta* annual roundup of cattle that disposed of strays, fr. ML *(animalia) mixta* mixed animals] : a small hardy naturalized horse of the western plains of America; *also* : BRONC

mus·tard \'məs-tərd\ *n* **1** : a pungent yellow powder of the seeds of an herb related to the cabbage and used as a condiment or in medicine **2** : a plant that yields mustard; *also* : a closely related plant — **mus·tardy** *adj*

mustard gas *n* : a poison gas used in warfare that has violent irritating and blistering effects

¹**mus·ter** \'məs-tər\ *n* **1** : an act of assembling (as for military inspection); *also* : critical examination **2** : an assembled group

²**muster** *vb* [ME *mustren* to show, muster, fr. AF *mustrer, monstrer*, fr. L *monstrare* to show, fr. *monstrum* evil omen, monster] **1** : CONVENE, ASSEMBLE 〈∼ an army〉; *also* : to call the roll of **2** : ACCUMULATE **3** : to call forth : ROUSE 〈∼ed support〉 **4** : to amount to : COMPRISE

muster out *vb* : to discharge from military service

musty \'məs-tē\ *adj* **mus·ti·er; -est** : MOLDY, STALE; *also* : tasting or smelling of damp or decay — **must·i·ly** \-tə-lē\ *adv* — **must·i·ness** \-tē-nəs\ *n*

mu·ta·ble \'myü-tə-bəl\ *adj* **1** : prone to change : FICKLE **2** : capable of or liable to mutation : VARIABLE — **mu·ta·bil·i·ty** \ˌmyü-tə-'bi-lə-tē\ *n*

mu·tant \'myü-tᵊnt\ *adj* : of, relating to, or produced by mutation — **mutant** *n*

mu·tate \'myü-ˌtāt\ *vb* **mu·tat·ed; mu·tat·ing** : to undergo or cause to undergo mutation — **mu·ta·tive** \'myü-ˌtā-tiv, -tə-tiv\ *adj*

mu·ta·tion \myü-'tā-shən\ *n* **1** : CHANGE **2** : an inherited physical or biochemical change in genetic material; *also* : the process of producing a mutation **3** : an individual, strain, or trait resulting from mutation — **mu·ta·tion·al** *adj*

¹**mute** \'myüt\ *adj* **mut·er; mut·est** **1** : unable to speak **2** : SILENT — **mute·ly** *adv* — **mute·ness** *n*

²**mute** *n* **1** *sometimes offensive* : a person who cannot speak **2** : a device on a musical instrument that reduces, softens, or muffles the tone

³**mute** *vb* **mut·ed; mut·ing** : to muffle, reduce, or eliminate the sound of

mu·ti·late \'myü-tə-ˌlāt\ *vb* **-lat·ed; -lat·ing** **1** : to cut up or alter radically so as to make imperfect **2** : MAIM, CRIPPLE — **mu·ti·la·tion** \ˌmyü-tə-'lā-shən\ *n* — **mu·ti·la·tor** \'myü-tə-ˌlā-tər\ *n*

mu·ti·ny \'myü-tə-nē\ *n, pl* **-nies** : willful refusal to obey constituted authority; *esp* : revolt against a superior officer — **mu·ti·neer** \ˌmyü-tə-'nir\ *n* — **mu·ti·nous** \'myü-tə-nəs\ *adj* — **mu·ti·nous·ly** *adv* — **mutiny** *vb*

mutt \'mət\ *n* : MONGREL, CUR

mut·ter \'mə-tər\ *vb* **1** : to speak indistinctly or with a low voice and lips partly closed **2** : GRUMBLE — **mutter** *n*

mut·ton \'mə-tᵊn\ *n* [ME *motoun* mutton, sheep, fr. AF *mutun* ram, sheep, mutton] : the flesh of a mature sheep used for food — **mut·tony** *adj*

mut·ton·chops \\'mə-tⁿn-ˌchäps\ *n pl* : whiskers on the side of the face that are narrow at the temple and broad and round by the lower jaws

mu·tu·al \\'myü-chə-wəl\ *adj* **1** : given and received in equal amount ⟨~ trust⟩ **2** : having the same feelings one for the other ⟨~ enemies⟩ **3** : COMMON, JOINT ⟨a ~ friend⟩ — **mu·tu·al·ly** *adv*

mutual fund *n* : an investment company that invests money of its shareholders in a usu. diversified group of securities of other corporations

muu·muu \\'mü-ˌmü\ *n* : a loose dress of Hawaiian origin

¹**muz·zle** \\'mə-zəl\ *n* **1** : the nose and jaws of an animal; *also* : a covering for the muzzle to prevent biting or eating **2** : the mouth of a gun

²**muzzle** *vb* **muz·zled; muz·zling 1** : to put a muzzle on **2** : to restrain from expression : GAG ⟨tried to ~ the press⟩

mV *abbr* millivolt

MV *abbr* motor vessel

MVP *abbr* most valuable player

MW *abbr* megawatt

my \\'mī\ *adj* **1** : of or relating to me or myself **2** — used interjectionally esp. to express surprise

my·col·o·gy \mī-'kä-lə-jē\ *n* : a branch of biology dealing with fungi — **my·co·log·i·cal** \ˌmī-kə-'lä-ji-kəl\ *adj* — **my·col·o·gist** \mī-'kä-lə-jist\ *n*

my·elo·ma \ˌmī-ə-'lō-mə\ *n, pl* **-mas** *or* **-ma·ta** \-mə-tə\ : a primary tumor of the bone marrow

my·nah *or* **my·na** \\'mī-nə\ *n* : any of several Asian starlings; *esp* : a dark brown slightly crested bird sometimes taught to mimic speech

my·o·pia \mī-'ō-pē-ə\ *n* : a condition in which visual images come to a focus in front of the retina resulting esp. in defective vision of distant objects — **my·o·pic** \-'ō-pik, -'ä-\ *adj* — **my·o·pi·cal·ly** \-pi-k(ə-)lē\ *adv*

¹**myr·i·ad** \\'mir-ē-əd\ *n* [Gk *myriad-, myrias,* fr. *myrioi* countless, ten thousand] : an indefinitely large number

²**myriad** *adj* : consisting of a very great but indefinite number

myr·mi·don \\'mər-mə-ˌdän\ *n* : a loyal follower; *esp* : one who executes orders without protest or pity

myrrh \\'mər\ *n* : a fragrant aromatic plant gum used in perfumes and formerly for incense

myr·tle \\'mər-tⁿl\ *n* : an evergreen shrub of southern Europe with shiny leaves, fragrant flowers, and black berries; *also* : PERIWINKLE

my·self \mī-'self, mə-\ *pron* : I, ME — used reflexively, for emphasis, or in absolute constructions ⟨I hurt ~⟩ ⟨I ~ did it⟩ ⟨~ busy, I sent him instead⟩

mys·tery \\'mis-tə-rē\ *n, pl* **-ter·ies 1** : a religious truth known by revelation alone **2** : something not understood or beyond understanding **3** : enigmatic quality or character **4** : a work of fiction dealing with the solution of a mysterious crime — **mys·te·ri·ous** \mis-'tir-ē-əs\ *adj* — **mys·te·ri·ous·ly** *adv* — **mys·te·ri·ous·ness** *n*

¹**mys·tic** \\'mis-tik\ *adj* **1** : of or relating to mystics or mysticism **2** : MYSTERIOUS; *also* : MYSTIFYING

²**mystic** *n* : a person who follows, advocates, or experiences mysticism

mys·ti·cal \\'mis-ti-kəl\ *adj* **1** : SPIRITUAL, SYMBOLIC **2** : of or relating to an intimate knowledge of or direct communion with God (as through contemplation or visions)

mys·ti·cism \\'mis-tə-ˌsi-zəm\ *n* : the belief that direct knowledge of God or ultimate reality is attainable through immediate intuition or insight

mys·ti·fy \\'mis-tə-ˌfī\ *vb* **-fied; -fy·ing 1** : to perplex the mind of **2** : to make mysterious — **mys·ti·fi·ca·tion** \ˌmis-tə-fə-'kā-shən\ *n*

mys·tique \mi-'stēk\ *n* [F] **1** : an air or attitude of mystery and reverence developing around something or someone **2** : the special esoteric skill essential in a calling or activity

myth \\'mith\ *n* **1** : a usu. legendary narrative that presents part of the beliefs of a people or explains a practice or natural phenomenon **2** : an imaginary or unverifiable person or thing — **myth·i·cal** \\'mi-thi-kəl\ *or* **myth·ic** \-thik\ *adj*

my·thol·o·gy \mi-'thä-lə-jē\ *n, pl* **-gies** : a body of myths and esp. of those dealing with the gods and heroes of a people — **myth·o·log·i·cal** \ˌmi-thə-'lä-ji-kəl\ *adj* — **my·thol·o·gist** \mi-'thä-lə-jist\ *n* — **my·thol·o·gize** \-ˌjīz\ *vb*

¹**n** \\'en\ *n, pl* **n's** *or* **ns** \\'enz\ *often cap* **1** : the 14th letter of the English alphabet **2** : an unspecified quantity

²**n** *abbr, often cap* **1** net **2** neuter **3** noon **4** normal **5** north; northern **6** note **7** noun **8** number

N *symbol* nitrogen

-n — see -EN

Na *symbol* [NL *natrium*] sodium

NA *abbr* **1** no account **2** North America **3** not applicable **4** not available

NAACP \ˌen-ˌdə-bəl-ˌā-ˌsē-'pē, ˌen-ˌā-ˌā-ˌsē-\ *abbr* National Association for the Advancement of Colored People

nab \\'nab\ *vb* **nabbed; nab·bing** : SEIZE; *esp* : ARREST

NAB *abbr* New American Bible

na·bob \\'nā-ˌbäb\ *n* [Hindi *navāb* & Urdu *nawāb,* provincial governor (in the Mogul empire), fr. Ar *nuwwāb,* pl. of *nā'ib* governor] : a person of great wealth or prominence

na·celle \nə-'sel\ *n* : an enclosure (as for an engine) on an aircraft

na·cho \\'nä-chō\ *n, pl* **nachos** [AmerSp] : a tortilla chip topped with melted cheese and often additional savory toppings

na·cre \\'nā-kər\ *n* : MOTHER-OF-PEARL — **na·cre·ous** \\'nā-krē-əs\ *adj*

na·dir \\'nā-ˌdir, -dər\ *n* [ME, fr. MF, fr. Ar *naḍhīr* opposite] **1** : the point of the celestial sphere that is directly opposite the zenith and directly beneath the observer **2** : the lowest point

¹**nag** \\'nag\ *n* : HORSE; *esp* : an old or decrepit horse

²**nag** *vb* **nagged; nag·ging 1** : to find fault incessantly : COMPLAIN **2** : to irritate by constant scolding or urging **3** : to be a continuing source of annoyance ⟨a *nagging* backache⟩

³**nag** *n* : one who nags habitually

Nah *abbr* Nahum

Na·huatl \\'nä-ˌwä-tⁿl\ *n* : a group of American Indian languages of central and southern Mexico

Na·hum \\'nä-həm, -əm\ *n* — see BIBLE table

NAIA *abbr* National Association of Intercollegiate Athletes

na·iad \\'nā-əd, 'nī-, -ˌad\ *n, pl* **naiads** *or* **na·ia·des** \-ə-ˌdēz\ **1** : one of the nymphs in ancient mythology living in lakes, rivers, springs, and fountains **2** : an aquatic young of some insects (as a dragonfly)

¹**na·if** *or* **na·if** \nä-'ēf\ *adj* : NAIVE

²**naïf** *or* **naif** *n* : a naive person

¹**nail** \\'nāl\ *n* **1** : a horny sheath protecting the end of each finger and toe in humans and related primates **2** : a slender pointed fastener with a head designed to be pounded in

²**nail** *vb* : to fasten with or as if with a nail — **nail·er** *n*

nail down *vb* : to settle or establish clearly and unmistakably ⟨*nailed down* the victory⟩

nain·sook \\'nān-ˌsůk\ *n* : a soft lightweight muslin

nai·ra \\'nī-rə\ *n* — see MONEY table

na·ive *or* **na·ïve** \nä-'ēv\ *adj* **na·iv·er; -est** [F *naïve,* fem. of *naïf,* fr. OF, inborn, natural, fr. L *nativus* native] **1** : marked by unaffected simplicity : ARTLESS, INGENUOUS **2** : CREDULOUS ◆ *Synonyms* NATURAL, INNOCENT, SIMPLE, UNAFFECTED, UNSOPHISTICATED, UNSTUDIED — **na·ive·ly** *adv* — **na·ive·ness** *n* na·ive·te *or* na·ïve·té *also* na·ive·té \‚nä-‚ē-və-'tā, nä-'ē-və-‚tä\ *n* 1 : a naive remark or action 2 : the quality or state of being naive

na·ive·ty *also* na·ïve·ty \nä-'ē-və-tē\ *n*, *pl* -ties : NAÏVETÉ

na·ked \'nā-kəd\ *adj* 1 : having no clothes on : NUDE 2 : UNSHEATHED ⟨a ∼ sword⟩ 3 : lacking a usual or natural covering (as of foliage or feathers) 4 : PLAIN, UNADORNED ⟨the ∼ truth⟩ 5 : not aided by artificial means ⟨seen by the ∼ eye⟩ — na·ked·ly *adv* — na·ked·ness *n*

nak·fa \'näk-‚fä\ *n*, *pl* nakfa — see MONEY table

nam·by–pam·by \‚nam-bē-'pam-bē\ *adj* 1 : INSIPID 2 : WEAK, INDECISIVE ✦ *Synonyms* BLAND, FLAT, INANE, JEJUNE, VAPID, WISHY-WASHY

¹name \'nām\ *n* 1 : a word or words by which a person or thing is known 2 : a disparaging epithet ⟨call him ∼s⟩ 3 : REPUTATION; *esp* : distinguished reputation ⟨made a ∼ for herself⟩ 4 : FAMILY, CLAN ⟨was a disgrace to their ∼⟩ 5 : appearance as opposed to reality ⟨a friend in ∼ only⟩

²name *vb* named; nam·ing 1 : to give a name to : CALL 2 : to mention or identify by name 3 : NOMINATE, APPOINT 4 : to decide on : CHOOSE ⟨*named* the wedding date⟩ 5 : to mention explicitly : SPECIFY ⟨∼ a price⟩ — name·able *adj*

³name *adj* 1 : of, relating to, or bearing a name ⟨∼ tag⟩ 2 : having an established reputation ⟨∼ brands⟩

name day *n* : the church feast day of the saint after whom one is named

name·less \'nām-ləs\ *adj* 1 : having no name 2 : not marked with a name ⟨a ∼ grave⟩ 3 : not known by name ⟨a ∼ hero⟩ 4 : too distressing to be described ⟨∼ fears⟩ — name·less·ly *adv*

name·ly \-lē\ *adv* : that is to say : AS ⟨the cat family, ∼, lions, tigers, and similar animals⟩

name·plate \-‚plāt\ *n* : a plate or plaque bearing a name (as of a resident)

name·sake \‚sāk\ *n* : one that has the same name as another; *esp* : one named after another

nan·keen \nan-'kēn\ *n* : a durable brownish yellow cotton fabric orig. woven by hand in China

nan·ny \'na-nē\ *also* nan·nie *n*, *pl* -nies : a child's nurse or caregiver

nan·ny goat \'na-nē-\ *n* : a female domestic goat

nano·me·ter \'na-nə-‚mē-tər\ *n* : one billionth of a meter

nano·scale \-‚skāl\ *adj* : having dimensions measured in nanometers

nano·sec·ond \-‚se-kənd\ *n* : one billionth of a second

nano·tech \'na-nō-‚tek\ *n* : NANOTECHNOLOGY

nano·tech·nol·o·gy \‚na-nō-tek-'nä-lə-jē\ *n* : the science of manipulating materials on an atomic or molecular scale esp. to build microscopic objects or devices

nano·tube \'na-nō-‚tüb\ *n* : a microscopic tube (as of carbon) whose diameter is measured in nanometers

¹nap \'nap\ *vb* napped; nap·ping 1 : to sleep briefly esp. during the day : DOZE 2 : to be off guard ⟨was caught *napping*⟩

²nap *n* : a short sleep esp. during the day

³nap *n* : a soft downy fibrous surface (as on yarn and cloth) — nap·less *adj* — napped \'napt\ *adj*

na·palm \'nä-‚päm, -‚päm\ *n* [*naphthalene* + *palm*itate, salt of a fatty acid] 1 : a thickener used in jelling gasoline (as for incendiary bombs) 2 : fuel jelled with napalm

nape \'nāp, 'nap\ *n* : the back of the neck

na·pery \'nā-pə-rē\ *n* : household linen esp. for the table

naph·tha \'naf-thə, 'nap-\ *n* : any of various liquid hydrocarbon mixtures used chiefly as solvents

naph·tha·lene \-‚lēn\ *n* : a crystalline substance used esp. in organic synthesis and as a moth repellent

nap·kin \'nap-kən\ *n* 1 : a piece of material (as cloth) used at table to wipe the lips or fingers and protect the clothes 2 : a small cloth or towel

na·po·leon \nə-'pōl-yən, -'pō-lē-ən\ *n* : an oblong pastry with a filling of cream, custard, or jelly

Na·po·le·on·ic \nə-‚pō-lē-'ä-nik\ *adj* : of, relating to, or characteristic of Napoleon I or his family

narc *also* nark \'närk\ *n*, *slang* : a person (as a government agent) who investigates narcotics violations

nar·cis·sism \'när-sə-‚si-zəm\ *n* [G *Narzissismus*, fr. *Narziss* Narcissus, character of Greek mythology who fell in love with his own image] 1 : undue dwelling on one's own self or attainments 2 : love of or sexual

desire for one's own body — nar·cis·sist \-sist\ *n or adj* — nar·cis·sis·tic \‚när-sə-'sis-tik\ *adj*

nar·cis·sus \när-'si-səs\ *n*, *pl* nar·cis·si \-‚sī, -‚sē\ *or* nar·cis·sus·es *or* narcissus : DAFFODIL; *esp* : one with short-tubed flowers usu. borne separately

nar·co·lep·sy \'när-kə-‚lep-sē\ *n*, *pl* -sies : a condition characterized by brief attacks of deep sleep — nar·co·lep·tic \‚när-kə-'lep-tik\ *adj or n*

nar·co·sis \när-'kō-səs\ *n*, *pl* -co·ses \-‚sēz\ : a state of stupor, unconsciousness, or arrested activity produced by the influence of chemicals (as narcotics)

nar·co·ter·ror·ism \'när-kō-'ter-ər-‚i-zəm\ *n* : terrorism financed by profits from illegal drug trafficking

nar·cot·ic \när-'kä-tik\ *n* [ME *narkotik*, fr. MF *narcotique*, fr. *narcotique*, adj., fr. ML *narcoticus*, fr. Gk *narkōtikos*, fr. *narkoun* to benumb, fr. *narkē* numbness] 1 : a drug (as opium) that dulls the senses, relieves pain, and induces sleep 2 : an illegal drug (as marijuana or LSD) — narcotic *adj*

nar·co·tize \'när-kə-‚tīz\ *vb* -tized; -tiz·ing 1 : to treat with or subject to a narcotic; *also* : to put into a state of narcosis 2 : to soothe to unconsciousness or unawareness

nard \'närd\ *n* : a fragrant ointment of the ancients

na·res \'ner-(‚)ēz\ *n pl* [L] : the pair of openings of the nose

Nar·ra·gan·sett \‚na-rə-'gan-sət\ *n*, *pl* -sett *or* -setts 1 : a member of an American Indian people of Rhode Island 2 : the Algonquian language of the Narragansett people

nar·rate \'ner-‚āt\ *vb* nar·rat·ed; nar·rat·ing 1 : to recite the details of (as a story) : RELATE, TELL — nar·ra·tion \na-'rā-shən\ *n* — nar·ra·tor \'ner-‚ā-tər\ *n*

nar·ra·tive \'ner-ə-tiv\ *n* 1 : something that is narrated : STORY 2 : the art or practice of narrating

¹nar·row \'ner-ō\ *adj* 1 : of slender or less than standard width 2 : limited in size or scope : RESTRICTED 3 : not liberal in views : PREJUDICED 4 : interpreted or interpreting strictly 5 : CLOSE ⟨won by a ∼ margin⟩; *also* : barely successful ⟨a ∼ escape⟩ — nar·row·ly *adv* — nar·row·ness *n*

²narrow *vb* : to lessen in width or extent

³narrow *n* : a narrow passage : STRAIT — usu. used in pl.

nar·row–mind·ed \‚ner-ō-'mīn-dəd\ *adj* : not liberal or broad-minded ✦ *Synonyms* ILLIBERAL, BIGOTED, HIDEBOUND, INTOLERANT

nar·whal \'när-‚hwäl, 'när-wəl\ *n* : an arctic sea mammal about 20 feet (6 meters) long that is related to the dolphins and in the male has a long twisted ivory tusk

narwhal

NAS *abbr* naval air station

NASA \'na-sə\ *abbr* National Aeronautics and Space Administration

¹na·sal \'nā-zəl\ *n* 1 : a nasal part 2 : a nasal consonant or vowel

²nasal *adj* 1 : of or relating to the nose 2 : uttered through the nose — na·sal·ly *adv*

na·sal·ize \'nā-zə-‚līz\ *vb* -ized; -iz·ing : to make nasal or pronounce as a nasal sound

na·scent \'na-sᵊnt, 'nā-\ *adj* : coming into existence : beginning to grow or develop — na·scence \-sᵊns\ *n*

nas·tur·tium \nə-'stər-shəm, na-\ *n* : either of two widely cultivated watery-stemmed herbs with showy spurred flowers and pungent edible seeds

nas·ty \'nas-tē\ *adj* nas·ti·er; -est 1 : FILTHY 2 : INDECENT, OBSCENE 3 : HARMFUL, DANGEROUS ⟨took a ∼ fall⟩ 4 : DISAGREEABLE ⟨∼ weather⟩ 5 : MEAN, ILL-NATURED ⟨a ∼ temper⟩ 6 : DIFFICULT, VEXATIOUS ⟨a ∼ problem⟩ 7 : UNFAIR, DIRTY ⟨a ∼ trick⟩ — nas·ti·ly \'nas-tə-lē\ *adv* — nas·ti·ness \-tē-nəs\ *n*

nat *abbr* 1 national 2 native 3 natural

na·tal \'nā-tᵊl\ *adj* 1 : NATIVE 2 : of, relating to, or present at birth

na·ta·to·ri·um \ˌnā-tə-'tȯr-ē-əm, ˌna-\ *n* : a swimming pool esp. indoors

na·tion \'nā-shən\ *n* [ME *nacioun*, fr. AF *naciun* fr. L *nation-, natio* birth, race, nation, fr. *nasci* to be born] **1** : NATIONALITY 5; *also* : a politically organized nationality **2** : a community of people composed of one or more nationalities with its own territory and government **3** : the territory of a nation **4** : a federation of tribes (as of American Indians) — **na·tion·hood** *n*

¹na·tion·al \'na-shə-nəl\ *adj* **1** : of or relating to a nation **2** : comprising or characteristic of a nationality **3** : FEDERAL **3** — **na·tion·al·ly** *adv*

²national *n* **1** : one who owes allegiance to a nation **2** : a competition that is national in scope — usu. used in pl.

national guard *n* **1** : a military force serving as a national constabulary and defense force **2** *cap N&G* : a militia force recruited by each state of the U.S., equipped by the federal government, and jointly maintained subject to the call of either — **national guardsman** *n, often cap*

na·tion·al·ise *chiefly Brit var of* NATIONALIZE

na·tion·al·ism \'na-shə-nə-ˌli-zəm\ *n* : devotion to national interests, unity, and independence

na·tion·al·ist \-list\ *n* **1** : an advocate of or believer in nationalism **2** : a member of a political party or group advocating national independence or strong national government — **nationalist** *adj* — **na·tion·al·is·tic** \ˌna-shə-nə-'lis-tik\ *adj*

na·tion·al·i·ty \ˌna-shə-'na-lə-tē\ *n, pl* **-ties** **1** : national character **2** : a legal relationship involving allegiance of an individual and protection on the part of the state **3** : membership in a particular nation **4** : political independence or existence as a separate nation **5** : a people having a common origin, tradition, and language and capable of forming a state **6** : an ethnic group within a larger unit (as a nation)

na·tion·al·ize \'na-shə-nə-ˌlīz\ *vb* **-ized; -iz·ing** **1** : to make national : make a nation of **2** : to remove from private ownership and place under government control — **na·tion·al·i·za·tion** \ˌna-shə-nə-lə-'zā-shən\ *n*

national monument *n* : a place of historic, scenic, or scientific interest set aside for preservation usu. by presidential proclamation

national park *n* : an area of special scenic, historical, or scientific importance set aside and maintained by a national government esp. for recreation or study

national seashore *n* : a recreational area adjacent to a seacoast and maintained by the federal government

na·tion·wide \ˌnā-shən-'wīd\ *adj* : extending throughout a nation

¹na·tive \'nā-tiv\ *adj* **1** : INBORN, NATURAL ⟨∼ talents⟩ **2** : born in a particular place or country **3** : belonging to a person because of the place or circumstances of birth ⟨her ∼ language⟩ **4** : grown, produced, or originating in a particular place : INDIGENOUS **5** *cap* : NATIVE AMERICAN ♦ *Synonyms* ABORIGINAL, AUTOCHTHONOUS, ENDEMIC

²native *n* : one that is native; *esp* : a person who belongs to a particular country by birth

Native American *n* : a member of any of the aboriginal peoples of No. America and esp. the U.S.

na·tiv·ism \'nā-ti-ˌvi-zəm\ *n* **1** : a policy of favoring native inhabitants over immigrants **2** : the revival or perpetuation of a native culture esp. in opposition to acculturation

na·tiv·i·ty \nə-'ti-və-tē, nā-\ *n, pl* **-ties** **1** : the process or circumstances of being born : BIRTH **2** *cap* : the birth of Christ

natl *abbr* national

NATO \'nā-(ˌ)tō\ *abbr* North Atlantic Treaty Organization

nat·ty \'na-tē\ *adj* **nat·ti·er; -est** : trimly neat and tidy : SMART — **nat·ti·ly** \-tə-lē\ *adv* — **nat·ti·ness** \-tē-nəs\ *n*

¹nat·u·ral \'na-chə-rəl\ *adj* **1** : determined by nature : INBORN, INNATE ⟨∼ ability⟩ **2** : BORN ⟨a ∼ fool⟩ **3** : ILLEGITIMATE ⟨a ∼ child⟩ **4** : HUMAN **5** : of or relating to nature **6** : not artificial **7** : being simple and sincere : not affected **8** : LIFELIKE **9** : being neither sharp nor flat ♦ *Synonyms* INGENUOUS, NAIVE, UNSOPHISTICATED, ARTLESS, GUILELESS — **nat·u·ral·ness** *n*

²natural *n* **1** : IDIOT **2** : a character ♮ placed on a line or space of the musical staff to nullify the effect of a preceding sharp or flat **3** : one obviously suitable for a purpose **4** : AFRO

natural childbirth *n* : a system of managing childbirth in which the mother prepares to remain conscious and assist in delivery with little or no use of drugs

natural gas *n* : a combustible gaseous mixture of hydrocarbons coming from the earth's crust and used chiefly as a fuel and raw material

natural history *n* **1** : a treatise on some aspect of nature **2** : the study of natural objects esp. from an amateur or popular point of view

nat·u·ral·ise *Brit var of* NATURALIZE

nat·u·ral·ism \'na-chə-rə-ˌli-zəm\ *n* **1** : action or thought based only on natural desires and instincts **2** : a doctrine that denies a supernatural explanation of the origin or development of the universe and holds that scientific laws account for all of nature **3** : realism in art and literature — **nat·u·ral·is·tic** \ˌna-chə-rə-'lis-tik\ *adj*

nat·u·ral·ist \-list\ *n* **1** : one that advocates or practices naturalism **2** : a student of animals or plants esp. in the field

nat·u·ral·ize \-ˌīz\ *vb* **-ized; -iz·ing** **1** : to confer the rights of a citizen on **2** : to become or cause to become established as if native ⟨∼ new forage crops⟩ — **nat·u·ral·i·za·tion** \ˌna-chə-rə-lə-'zā-shən\ *n*

nat·u·ral·ly \'na-chə-rə-lē, 'nach-rə-\ *adv* **1** : by nature : by natural character or ability **2** : as might be expected **3** : without artificial aid; *also* : without affectation **4** : REALISTICALLY

natural science *n* : a science (as physics, chemistry, or biology) that deals with matter, energy, and their interrelations and transformations or with objectively measurable phenomena — **natural scientist** *n*

natural selection *n* : the natural process that results in the survival of individuals or groups best adjusted to their environment

na·ture \'nā-chər\ *n* [ME, fr. MF, fr. L *natura*, fr. *natus*, pp. of *nasci* to be born] **1** : the inherent quality or basic constitution of a person or thing; *also* : DISPOSITION, TEMPERAMENT **2** : KIND, SORT ⟨letters of a personal ∼⟩ **3** : the physical universe **4** : one's natural instincts or way of life ⟨quirks of human ∼⟩; *also* : primitive state ⟨a return to ∼⟩ **5** : natural scenery or environment

¹naught *also* **nought** \'nȯt, 'nät\ *pron* : NOTHING ⟨efforts came to ∼⟩

²naught *also* **nought** *n* **1** : NOTHINGNESS, NONEXISTENCE **2** : the arithmetical symbol 0 : ZERO

naugh·ty \'nȯ-tē, 'nä-\ *adj* **naugh·ti·er; -est** **1** : guilty of disobedience or misbehavior **2** : lacking in taste or propriety ⟨∼ jokes⟩ — **naugh·ti·ly** \-tə-lē\ *adv* — **naugh·ti·ness** \-tē-nəs\ *n*

nau·sea \'nȯ-zē-ə, -sē-; 'nȯ-zhə, -shə\ *n* [L, seasickness, nausea, fr. Gk *nautia, nausia*, fr. *nautēs* sailor] **1** : sickness of the stomach with a desire to vomit **2** : extreme disgust

nau·se·ate \'nȯ-zē-ˌāt, -sē-, -zhē-, -shē-\ *vb* **-at·ed; -at·ing** : to affect or become affected with nausea — **nau·se·at·ing·ly** *adv*

nau·seous \'nȯ-shəs, -zē-əs\ *adj* **1** : causing nausea or disgust **2** : affected with nausea or disgust

naut *abbr* nautical

nau·ti·cal \'nȯ-ti-kəl\ *adj* : of or relating to sailors, navigation, or ships ⟨∼ terms⟩ — **nau·ti·cal·ly** \-k(ə-)lē\ *adv*

nautical mile *n* : a unit of distance equal to about 6080 feet (1852 meters)

nau·ti·lus \'nȯ-tə-ləs\ *n, pl* **-lus·es** *or* **-li** \ˌlī, -ˌlē\ : any of a genus of sea mollusks related to the octopuses but having a spiral chambered shell

nav *abbr* **1** naval **2** navigable; navigation

Na·va·jo *also* **Na·va·ho** \'na-və-ˌhō, 'nä-\ *n, pl* **-jo** *or* **-jos** *also* **-ho** *or* **-hos** : a member of an American Indian people of northern New Mexico and Arizona; *also* : their language

na·val \'nā-vəl\ *adj* : of, relating to, or possessing a navy ⟨a ∼ power⟩

naval stores *n pl* : products (as pitch, turpentine, or rosin) obtained from resinous conifers (as pines)

nave \'nāv\ *n* [ML *navis*, fr. L, ship] : the central part of a church running lengthwise

na·vel \'nā-vəl\ *n* : a depression in the middle of the abdomen that marks the point of attachment of fetus and mother

navel-gaz·ing \'nā-vəl-'gā-ziŋ\ *n* : useless or excessive self-contemplation

navel orange *n* : a seedless orange having a pit at the blossom end where the fruit encloses a small secondary fruit

nav·i·ga·ble \'na-vi-gə-bəl\ *adj* 1 : capable of being navigated ⟨a ~ river⟩ 2 : capable of being steered — **nav·i·ga·bil·i·ty** \,na-vi-gə-'bi-lə-tē\ *n*

nav·i·gate \'na-və-,gāt\ *vb* **-gat·ed; -gat·ing** 1 : to sail on or through ⟨~ the Atlantic Ocean⟩ 2 : to steer or direct the course of a ship or aircraft 3 : MOVE; *esp* : WALK ⟨could hardly ~⟩ — **nav·i·ga·tion** \,na-və-'gā-shən\ *n* — **nav·i·ga·tor** \'na-və-,gā-tər\ *n*

na·vy \'nā-vē\ *n, pl* **navies** 1 : FLEET; *also* : the warships belonging to a nation 2 *often cap* : a nation's organization for naval warfare

navy yard *n* : a yard where naval vessels are built or repaired

¹**nay** \'nā\ *adv* : NO

²**nay** *n* : a negative vote; *also* : a person casting such a vote

³**nay** *conj* : not merely this but also : not only so but ⟨he was happy, ~, ecstatic⟩

nay·say·er \'nā-,sā-ər\ *n* : one who denies, refuses, or opposes something

Na·zi \'nät-sē, 'nat-\ *n* [G, fr. *Nationalsozialist*, lit., national socialist] : a member of a German fascist party controlling Germany from 1933 to 1945 under Adolf Hitler — **Nazi** *adj* — **Na·zism** \'nät-,si-zəm, 'nat-\ *also* **Na·zi·ism** \-sē-,i-zəm\ *n*

Nb *symbol* niobium

NB *abbr* 1 New Brunswick 2 nota bene

NBA *abbr* 1 National Basketball Association 2 National Boxing Association

NBC *abbr* National Broadcasting Company

NBS *abbr* National Bureau of Standards

NC *abbr* 1 no charge 2 North Carolina

NCAA *abbr* National Collegiate Athletic Association

NCO \,en-,sē-'ō\ *n* : NONCOMMISSIONED OFFICER

nd *abbr* no date

Nd *symbol* neodymium

ND *abbr* North Dakota

N Dak *abbr* North Dakota

Ne *symbol* neon

NE *abbr* 1 Nebraska 2 New England 3 northeast

Ne·an·der·thal \nē-'an-dər-,thôl, nā-'än-dər-,täl\ *n* 1 *or* **Ne·an·der·tal** \-,täl\ : an extinct Old World hominid that lived from about 30,000 to 200,000 years ago 2 : a person who resembles or suggests a caveman — **Neanderthal** *or* **Neandertal** *adj*

neap tide \'nēp-\ *n* : a tide of minimum range occurring at the first and third quarters of the moon

¹**near** \'nir\ *adv* 1 : at, within, or to a short distance or time 2 : ALMOST ⟨was ~ dead⟩

²**near** *prep* : close to

³**near** *adj* 1 : closely related or associated; *also* : INTIMATE 2 : not far away; *also* : being the closer or left-hand member of a pair ⟨the ~ side of the lake⟩ 3 : barely avoided ⟨a ~ accident⟩ 4 : DIRECT, SHORT ⟨by the ~*est* route⟩ 5 : STINGY 6 : not real but very like ⟨~ silk⟩ — **near·ly** *adv* — **near·ness** *n*

⁴**near** *vb* : APPROACH

near beer *n* : any of various malt liquors low in alcohol

near·by \nir-'bī, 'nir-,bī\ *adv or adj* : close at hand

near·sight·ed \'nir-'sī-təd\ *adj* : able to see near things more clearly than distant ones : MYOPIC — **near·sight·ed·ly** *adv* — **near·sight·ed·ness** *n*

neat \'nēt\ *adj* [MF *net*, fr. L *nitidus* bright, neat, fr. *nitēre* to shine] 1 : being orderly and clean 2 : not mixed or diluted ⟨~ brandy⟩ 3 : marked by tasteful simplicity 4 : PRECISE, SYSTEMATIC 5 : SKILLFUL, ADROIT 6 : FINE, ADMIRABLE ♦ *Synonyms* SHIPSHAPE, TIDY, TRIG, TRIM — **neat** *adv* — **neat·ly** *adv* — **neat·ness** *n*

neath \'nēth\ *prep, dial* : BENEATH

neat·nik \'nēt-nik\ *n* : a person who is compulsively neat

neb \'neb\ *n* 1 : the beak of a bird or tortoise; *also* : NOSE, SNOUT 2 : NIB

Neb *or* **Nebr** *abbr* Nebraska

NEB *abbr* New English Bible

neb·u·la \'ne-byə-lə\ *n, pl* **-lae** \-,lē, -,lī\ *also* **-las** [NL, fr. L, mist, cloud] 1 : any of numerous clouds of gas or dust in interstellar space 2 : GALAXY — **neb·u·lar** \-lər\ *adj*

neb·u·liz·er \'ne-byə-,lī-zər\ *n* : ATOMIZER

neb·u·lous \'ne-byə-ləs\ *adj* 1 : of or relating to a nebula 2 : HAZY, INDISTINCT

¹**nec·es·sary** \'ne-sə-,ser-ē\ *adj* 1 : INEVITABLE, INESCAPABLE; *also* : CERTAIN 2 : PREDETERMINED 3 : COMPULSORY 4 : positively needed : INDISPENSABLE ⟨~ supplies⟩ ♦ *Synonyms* IMPERATIVE, NECESSITOUS, ESSENTIAL — **nec·es·sar·i·ly** \,ne-sə-'ser-ə-lē\ *adv*

²**necessary** *n, pl* **-sar·ies** : an indispensable item

ne·ces·si·tate \ni-'se-sə-,tāt\ *vb* **-tat·ed; -tat·ing** : to make necessary

ne·ces·si·tous \ni-'se-sə-təs\ *adj* 1 : NEEDY, IMPOVERISHED 2 : URGENT 3 : NECESSARY ⟨~ bargaining⟩

ne·ces·si·ty \ni-'se-sə-tē\ *n, pl* **-ties** 1 : conditions that cannot be changed 2 : WANT, POVERTY 3 : something that is necessary ⟨water is a ~⟩ 4 : very great need

¹**neck** \'nek\ *n* 1 : the part of the body connecting the head and the trunk 2 : the part of a garment covering or near to the neck 3 : a relatively narrow part suggestive of a neck ⟨~ of a bottle⟩ ⟨~ of land⟩ 4 : a narrow margin esp. of victory ⟨won by a ~⟩ — **necked** \'nekt\ *adj*

²**neck** *vb* : to kiss and caress amorously

neck and neck *adv or adj* : very close (as in a race)

neck·er·chief \'ne-kər-chəf, -,chēf\ *n, pl* **-chiefs** \-chəfs, -,chēfs\ *also* **-chieves** \-,chēvz\ : a square of cloth worn folded about the neck like a scarf

neck·lace \'ne-kləs\ *n* : an ornament worn around the neck

neck·line \'nek-,līn\ *n* : the outline of the neck opening of a garment

neck·tie \-,tī\ *n* : a strip of cloth worn around the neck and tied in front

ne·crol·o·gy \nə-'krä-lə-jē\ *n, pl* **-gies** 1 : OBITUARY 2 : a list of the recently dead

nec·ro·man·cy \'ne-krə-,man-sē\ *n* 1 : the art or practice of conjuring up the spirits of the dead for purposes of magically revealing the future 2 : MAGIC, SORCERY — **nec·ro·man·cer** \-sər\ *n*

ne·crop·o·lis \nə-'krä-pə-ləs, ne-\ *n, pl* **-lis·es** *or* **-les** \-,lēz\ *or* **-leis** \-,lās\ *or* **-li** \-,lī, -,lē\ [LL, fr. Gk *nekropolis*, fr. *nekros* dead body + *polis* city] : CEMETERY; *esp* : a large elaborate cemetery of an ancient city

nec·rop·sy \'ne-,kräp-sē\ *n, pl* **-sies** : AUTOPSY; *esp* : an autopsy performed on an animal

ne·cro·sis \nə-'krō-səs, ne-\ *n, pl* **ne·cro·ses** \-,sēz\ : usu. local death of body tissue — **ne·crot·ic** \-'krä-tik\ *adj*

nec·tar \'nek-tər\ *n* 1 : the drink of the Greek and Roman gods; *also* : any delicious drink 2 : a sweet plant secretion that is the raw material of honey

nec·tar·ine \,nek-tə-'rēn\ *n* : a smooth-skinned peach

née *or* **nee** \'nā\ *adj* [F, lit., born] — used to identify a woman by her maiden family name

¹**need** \'nēd\ *n* 1 : OBLIGATION ⟨no ~ to hurry⟩ 2 : a lack of something requisite, desirable, or useful 3 : a condition requiring supply or relief ⟨when the ~ arises⟩ 4 : POVERTY ♦ *Synonyms* NECESSITY, EXIGENCY

²**need** *vb* 1 : to be in want 2 : to have cause or occasion for : REQUIRE ⟨he ~s advice⟩ 3 : to be under obligation or necessity ⟨we ~ to know the truth⟩

need·ful \'nēd-fəl\ *adj* : NECESSARY, REQUISITE ⟨bought only what was ~⟩

¹**nee·dle** \'nē-d°l\ *n* 1 : a slender pointed usu. steel implement used in sewing 2 : a slender rod (as for knitting, controlling a small opening, or transmitting vibrations to or from a recording) ⟨a phonograph ~⟩ 3 : a slender hollow instrument by which material is introduced into or withdrawn from the body 4 : a slender indicator on a dial 5 : a needle-shaped leaf (as of a pine)

²**needle** *vb* **nee·dled; nee·dling** : PROD, GOAD; *esp* : to incite to action by repeated gibes ⟨*needled* him into a fight⟩

nee·dle·nose pliers \'nē-d°l-,nōz-\ *n pl* : pliers with long slender jaws for grasping small or thin objects

nee·dle·point \'nē-d°l-,pòint\ *n* 1 : lace worked with a needle over a paper pattern 2 : embroidery done on canvas across counted threads — **needlepoint** *adj*

need·less \'nēd-ləs\ *adj* : UNNECESSARY ⟨~ waste⟩ — **need·less·ly** *adv* — **need·less·ness** *n*

nee·dle·wom·an \'nē-d°l-,wù-mən\ *n* : a woman who does needlework; *esp* : SEAMSTRESS

nee·dle·work \-,wərk\ *n* : work done with a needle; *esp* : work (as embroidery) other than plain sewing

needs \'nēdz\ *adv* : of necessity : NECESSARILY ⟨must ~ be recognized⟩

needy \'nē-dē\ *adj* **need·i·er; -est** : being in want : POVERTY-STRICKEN ne'er \'ner\ adv : NEVER

ne'er–do–well \'ner-dú-ˌwel\ n : an idle worthless person — ne'er–do–well adj

ne·far·i·ous \ni-'fer-ē-əs\ adj [L nefarius, fr. nefas crime, fr. ne- not + fas right, divine law] : very wicked : EVIL ✦ Synonyms BAD, IMMORAL, INIQUITOUS, SINFUL, VICIOUS — ne·far·i·ous·ly adv

neg abbr negative

ne·gate \ni-'gāt\ vb ne·gat·ed; ne·gat·ing 1 : to deny the existence or truth of 2 : to cause to be ineffective or invalid : NULLIFY ⟨~ a contract⟩

ne·ga·tion \ni-'gā-shən\ n 1 : the action or operation of negating or making negative 2 : a negative doctrine or statement

¹neg·a·tive \'ne-gə-tiv\ adj 1 : marked by denial, prohibition, or refusal ⟨a ~ reply⟩ 2 : not positive or constructive; esp : not affirming the presence of what is sought or suspected to be present ⟨test results were ~⟩ 3 : less than zero ⟨a ~ number⟩ 4 : being, relating to, or charged with electricity of which the electron is the elementary unit 5 : having the light and dark parts opposite to what they were in the original photographic subject — neg·a·tive·ly adv — neg·a·tive·ness n — neg·a·tiv·i·ty \ˌne-gə-'ti-və-tē\ n

²negative n 1 : a negative word or statement 2 : a negative vote or reply; also : REFUSAL 3 : something that is the opposite or negation of something else 4 : a negative number 5 : the side that votes or argues for the opposition (as in a debate) 6 : a negative photographic image on transparent material

³negative vb -tived; -tiv·ing 1 : to refuse to accept or approve 2 : to vote against 3 : DISPROVE

negative income tax n : a system of federal subsidy payments to families with incomes below a stipulated level

neg·a·tiv·ism \'ne-gə-ti-ˌvi-zəm\ n : an attitude of skepticism and denial of nearly everything affirmed or suggested by others

¹ne·glect \ni-'glekt\ vb [L neglectus, pp. of neglegere, neclegere, fr. nec- not + legere to gather] 1 : DISREGARD 2 : to leave undone or unattended to esp. through carelessness ✦ Synonyms OMIT, IGNORE, OVERLOOK, SLIGHT, FORGET, MISS

²neglect n 1 : an act or instance of neglecting something 2 : the condition of being neglected — ne·glect·ful adj

neg·li·gee also neg·li·gé \ˌne-glə-'zhā\ n : a woman's long flowing dressing gown

neg·li·gent \'ne-gli-jənt\ adj : marked by neglect ✦ Synonyms NEGLECTFUL, REMISS, DELINQUENT, DERELICT — neg·li·gence \-jəns\ n — neg·li·gent·ly adv

neg·li·gi·ble \'ne-gli-jə-bəl\ adj : so small as to be neglected or disregarded

ne·go·tiant \ni-'gō-shē-ənt\ n : NEGOTIATOR

ne·go·ti·ate \ni-'gō-shē-ˌāt\ vb -at·ed; -at·ing [L negotiari to carry on business, fr. negotium business, fr. neg- not + otium leisure] 1 : to confer with another so as to arrive at the settlement of some matter; also : to arrange for or bring about by such conferences ⟨~ a treaty⟩ 2 : to transfer to another by delivery or endorsement in return for equivalent value ⟨~ a check⟩ 3 : to get through, around, or over successfully ⟨~ a turn⟩ — ne·go·tia·ble \-shə-bəl, -shē-ə-\ adj — ne·go·ti·a·tion \ni-ˌgō-sē-'ā-shən, -shē-\ n — ne·go·ti·a·tor \-'gō-shē-ˌā-tər\ n

ne·gri·tude \'ne-grə-ˌtüd, -ˌtyüd, 'nē-\ n : a consciousness of and pride in one's African heritage

Ne·gro \'nē-grō\ n, pl Negroes [Sp or Pg, fr. negro black] dated, now sometimes offensive : a member of a race of humankind native to Africa and classified according to physical features (as dark skin pigmentation) — Negro adj, dated, sometimes offensive — Ne·groid \'nē-ˌgrȯid\ n or adj, often not cap, dated, sometimes offensive

Neh abbr Nehemiah

Ne·he·mi·ah \ˌnē-ə-'mī-ə\ n — see BIBLE table

neigh \'nā\ n : a loud prolonged cry of a horse — neigh vb

¹neigh·bor \'nā-bər\ n 1 : one living or located near another 2 : FELLOW MAN

²neighbor vb : to be next to or near to : border on

neigh·bor·hood \'nā-bər-ˌhùd\ n 1 : NEARNESS 2 : a place or region near : VICINITY; also : a number or amount near ⟨costs in the ~ of $10⟩ 3 : the people living near one another 4 : a section lived in by neighbors and usu. having distinguishing characteristics

neigh·bor·ly \-lē\ adj : befitting congenial neighbors; esp : FRIENDLY ⟨a ~ welcome⟩ — neigh·bor·li·ness n

neigh·bour chiefly Brit var of NEIGHBOR

¹nei·ther \'nē-thər, 'nī-\ conj 1 : not either ⟨~ good nor bad⟩ 2 : NOR ⟨~ did I⟩

²neither pron : neither one : not the one and not the other ⟨~ of the two⟩

³neither adj : not either ⟨~ hand⟩

nel·son \'nel-sən\ n : a wrestling hold in which one applies leverage against an opponent's arm, neck, and head

nem·a·tode \'ne-mə-ˌtōd\ n : any of a phylum of elongated cylindrical worms parasitic in animals or plants or free-living in soil or water

nem·e·sis \'ne-mə-səs\ n, pl -e·ses \-ˌsēz\ [L Nemesis, goddess of divine retribution, fr. Gk] 1 : one that inflicts retribution or vengeance 2 : a formidable and usu. victorious rival 3 : an act or effect of retribution; also : CURSE

neo·clas·sic \ˌnē-ō-'kla-sik\ or neo·clas·si·cal \-si-kəl\ adj : of or relating to a revival or adaptation of the classical style esp. in literature, art, or music

neo·co·lo·nial·ism \ˌnē-ō-kə-'lō-nē-ə-ˌli-zəm\ n : the economic and political policies by which a nation indirectly maintains or extends its influence over other areas or peoples — neo·co·lo·nial adj — neo·co·lo·nial·ist \-list\ n or adj

neo·con \'nē-ō-ˌkän\ n : NEOCONSERVATIVE

neo·con·ser·va·tive \-kən-'sər-və-tiv\ n : a former liberal espousing political conservatism — neo·con·ser·va·tism \-və-ˌti-zəm\ n — neoconservative adj

neo·dym·i·um \ˌnē-ō-'di-mē-əm\ n : a silver-white to yellow metallic chemical element

neo·im·pres·sion·ism \ˌnē-ō-im-'pre-shə-ˌni-zəm\ n, often cap N&I : a late 19th century French art movement that attempted to make impressionism more precise and to use a pointillist painting technique

Neo·lith·ic \ˌnē-ə-'li-thik\ adj : of or relating to the latest period of the Stone Age characterized by polished stone implements

ne·ol·o·gism \nē-'ä-lə-ˌji-zəm\ n : a new word or expression

ne·on \'nē-ˌän\ n [Gk, neut. of neos new] 1 : a gaseous colorless chemical element used in electric lamps 2 : a lamp in which a discharge through neon gives a reddish glow — neon adj

neo·na·tal \ˌnē-ō-'nā-tᵊl\ adj : of, relating to, or affecting the newborn ⟨a ~ infection⟩ — neo·na·tal·ly adv

ne·o·nate \'nē-ə-ˌnāt\ n : a newborn child

neo·pa·gan \ˌnē-ō-'pā-gən\ n : a person who practices a contemporary form of paganism — neo·pagan adj

neo·phyte \'nē-ə-ˌfīt\ n 1 : a new convert : PROSELYTE 2 : NOVICE 3 : BEGINNER ✦ Synonyms APPRENTICE, FRESHMAN, NEWCOMER, ROOKIE, TENDERFOOT, TYRO

neo·plasm \'nē-ə-ˌpla-zəm\ n : a new growth of tissue serving no useful purpose in the body : TUMOR — neo·plas·tic \ˌnē-ə-'plas-tik\ adj

neo·prene \'nē-ə-ˌprēn\ n : a synthetic rubber used esp. for special-purpose clothing (as wet suits)

neo·trop·i·cal \ˌnē-ō-'trä-pi-kəl\ adj, often cap : of or relating to a zoogeographic region of America that extends south from the central plateau of Mexico

ne·pen·the \nə-'pen-thē\ n 1 : a potion used by the ancients to dull pain and sorrow 2 : something capable of making one forget grief or suffering

neph·ew \'ne-fyü, chiefly Brit -vyü\ n [ME nevew, fr. AF neveu, fr. L nepot-, nepos, fr. L, grandson, descendant] : a son of one's brother, sister, brother-in-law, or sister-in-law

ne·phrit·ic \ni-'fri-tik\ adj 1 : RENAL 2 : of, relating to, or affected with nephritis

ne·phri·tis \ni-'frī-təs\ n, pl ne·phrit·i·des \-'fri-tə-ˌdēz\ : kidney inflammation

ne plus ul·tra \ˌnē-ˌpləs-'əl-trə\ n [NL, (go) no more beyond] : the highest point capable of being attained

nep·o·tism \'ne-pə-ˌti-zəm\ n [F népotisme, fr. It nepotismo, fr. nepote nephew, fr. LL nepot-, nepos] : favoritism shown to a relative (as in the granting of jobs)

Nep·tune \'nep-ˌtün, -ˌtyün\ n : the planet 8th in order from the sun — Nep·tu·ni·an \nep-'tü-nē-ən, -'tyü-\ adj

nep·tu·ni·um \nep-'tü-nē-əm, -'tyü-\ n : a short-lived radioactive element

nerd \'nərd\ *n* : an unstylish or socially inept person; *esp* : one slavishly devoted to intellectual pursuits — **nerdy** *adj*

Ne·re·id \'nir-ē-əd\ *n* : a sea nymph in Greek mythology

¹nerve \'nərv\ *n* 1 : SINEW, TENDON ⟨strain every ∼⟩ 2 : any of the strands of nervous tissue that carry nerve impulses between the brain and spinal cord and every part of the body 3 : power of endurance or control : FORTITUDE; *also* : BOLDNESS, DARING 4 *pl* : NERVOUSNESS 5 : a vein of a leaf or insect wing — **nerved** \'nərvd\ *adj* — **nerve·less** *adj*

nerve 2: cell body at left and nerve ending at right

²nerve *vb* **nerved; nerv·ing** : to give strength or courage to

nerve cell *n* : NEURON; *also* : CELL BODY

nerve gas *n* : a chemical weapon damaging esp. to the nervous and respiratory systems

nerve impulse *n* : a physical and chemical change that moves along a process of a neuron after stimulation and carries a record of sensation or an instruction to act

nerve–rack·ing *or* **nerve–wrack·ing** \'nərv-,ra-kiŋ\ *adj* : extremely trying on the nerves ⟨∼ noise⟩

ner·vous \'nər-vəs\ *adj* 1 : FORCIBLE, SPIRITED 2 : of, relating to, or made up of neurons or nerves 3 : easily excited or annoyed : JUMPY ⟨a ∼ horse⟩ 4 : TIMID, APPREHENSIVE ⟨a ∼ smile⟩ 5 : UNEASY, UNSTEADY — **ner·vous·ly** *adv* — **ner·vous·ness** *n*

nervous breakdown *n* : an attack of mental or emotional disorder of sufficient severity to be incapacitating esp. when requiring hospitalization

nervous system *n* : a bodily system that in vertebrates is made up of the brain and spinal cord, nerves, ganglia, and parts of the sense organs and that receives and interprets stimuli and transmits nerve impulses

nervy \'nər-vē\ *adj* **nerv·i·er; -est** 1 : showing calm courage ⟨a ∼ performer⟩ 2 : marked by impudence or presumption ⟨a ∼ salesperson⟩ 3 : EXCITABLE, NERVOUS ◆ **Synonyms** BOLD, CHEEKY, FORWARD, FRESH, IMPUDENT, SAUCY

-ness \nəs\ *n suffix* : state : condition : quality : degree ⟨goodness⟩

¹nest \'nest\ *n* 1 : the shelter prepared by a bird for its eggs and young 2 : a place where eggs (as of insects or fish) are laid and hatched 3 : a place of rest, retreat, or lodging 4 : DEN, HANGOUT ⟨a ∼ of thieves⟩ 5 : the occupants of a nest 6 : a series of objects (as bowls or tables) fitting inside or under one another

²nest *vb* 1 : to build or occupy a nest 2 : to fit compactly together or within one another

nest egg *n* : a fund of money accumulated as a reserve

nes·tle \'ne-səl\ *vb* **nes·tled; nes·tling** 1 : to settle snugly or comfortably 2 : to press closely and affectionately : CUDDLE 3 : to settle, shelter, or house as if in a nest

nest·ling \'nest-liŋ\ *n* : a bird too young to leave its nest

¹net \'net\ *n* 1 : a meshed fabric twisted, knotted, or woven together at regular intervals 2 : a device made all or partly of net and used esp. to catch birds, fish, or insects 3 : something made of net used esp. for protecting, confining, carrying, or dividing ⟨a tennis ∼⟩ 4 : SNARE, TRAP 5 *often cap* : INTERNET

²net *vb* **net·ted; net·ting** 1 : to cover or enclose with or as if with a net 2 : to catch in or as if in a net

³net *adj* : free from all charges or deductions ⟨∼ profit⟩ ⟨∼ weight⟩

⁴net *vb* **net·ted; net·ting** : to gain or produce as profit : CLEAR, YIELD ⟨his business *netted* $50,000 a year⟩

⁵net *n* : a net amount, profit, weight, or price

Neth *abbr* Netherlands

neth·er \'ne-thər\ *adj* : situated down or below ⟨the ∼ regions of the earth⟩

neth·er·most \-,mōst\ *adj* : LOWEST

neth·er·world \-,wərld\ *n* 1 : the world of the dead 2 : UNDERWORLD

net·i·quette \'ne-ti-kət, -,ket\ *n* : etiquette governing communication on the Internet

net·roots \'net-,rüts, -,ruts\ *n pl* : the grass-roots political activists who communicate via the Internet

nett *Brit var of* NET

net·ting *n* 1 : NETWORK 2 : the act or process of making a net or network

¹net·tle \'ne-tᵊl\ *n* : any of a genus of coarse herbs with stinging hairs

²nettle *vb* **net·tled; net·tling** : PROVOKE, VEX, IRRITATE

net·tle·some \'ne-tᵊl-səm\ *adj* : causing vexation : IRRITATING

net·work \'net-,wərk\ *n* 1 : NET 2 : a system of elements (as lines or channels) that cross in the manner of the threads in a net 3 : a group or system of related or connected parts; *esp* : a chain of radio or television stations 4 : a system of computers that are connected (as by telephone wires)

net·work·ing \'net-,wər-kiŋ\ *n* 1 : the exchange of information or services among individuals, groups, or institutions 2 : the cultivation of productive business relationships

neu·ral \'nur-əl, 'nyur-\ *adj* : of, relating to, or involving a nerve or the nervous system ⟨∼ pathways⟩

neu·ral·gia \nu-'ral-jə, nyu-\ *n* : acute pain that follows the course of a nerve — **neu·ral·gic** \-jik\ *adj*

neur·as·the·nia \,nur-əs-'thē-nē-ə, ,nyur-\ *n* [NL, fr. Gk *neuron* nerve + *asthenia* weakness, fr. *asthenēs* weak, fr. *a-* not + *sthenos* strength] : a psychological disorder marked esp. by fatiguing easily, lack of motivation, feelings of inadequacy, and psychosomatic symptoms — **neur·as·then·ic** \-the-nik, -'thē-\ *adj or n*

neu·ri·tis \nu-'rī-təs, nyu-\ *n, pl* **-rit·i·des** \-'ri-tə-,dēz\ *or* **-ri·tis·es** : inflammation of a nerve — **neu·rit·ic** \-'ri-tik\ *adj or n*

neu·ro·bi·ol·o·gy \,nur-ō-bī-'ä-lə-jē\ *n* : a branch of biology that deals with the nervous system — **neu·ro·bi·o·log·i·cal** \-,bī-ə-'lä-ji-kəl\ *adj* — **neu·ro·bi·ol·o·gist** \-bī-'ä-lə-jist\ *n*

neu·rol·o·gy \nu-'rä-lə-jē, nyu-\ *n* : the scientific study of the nervous system — **neu·ro·log·i·cal** \,nur-ə-'lä-ji-kəl, ,nyur-\ *or* **neu·ro·log·ic** \-jik\ *adj* — **neu·ro·log·i·cal·ly** \-ji-k(ə-)lē\ *adv* — **neu·rol·o·gist** \nu-'rä-lə-jist, nyu-\ *n*

neu·ro·mus·cu·lar \,nur-ō-'məs-kyə-lər, ,nyur-\ *adj* : of, relating to, or affecting nerves and muscles ⟨a ∼ disease⟩

neu·ron \'nü-,rän, 'nyü-\ *n* : a cell with specialized processes that is the fundamental functional unit of nervous tissue — **neu·ro·nal** \'nur-ə-nᵊl, 'nyur-\ *adj*

neu·rone \-,rōn\ *chiefly Brit var of* NEURON

neu·ro·sci·ence \,nur-ō-'sī-əns, ,nyur-\ *n* : a branch of the life sciences that deals with the anatomy, physiology, biochemistry, or molecular biology of nerves and nervous tissue and esp. with their relation to behavior and learning — **neu·ro·sci·en·tist** \-ən-tist\ *n*

neu·ro·sis \nu-'rō-səs, nyu-\ *n, pl* **-ro·ses** \-,sēz\ : a mental and emotional disorder that is less serious than a psychosis, is not characterized by disturbance of the use of language, and is accompanied by various bodily and mental disturbances (as visceral symptoms, anxieties, or phobias)

neu·ro·sur·gery \,nur-ō-'sər-jə-rē, ,nyur-\ *n* : surgery of nervous structures (as nerves, the brain, or the spinal cord) — **neu·ro·sur·geon** \-'sər-jən\ *n*

¹neu·rot·ic \nu-'rä-tik, nyu-\ *adj* : of, relating to, being, or affected with a neurosis — **neu·rot·i·cal·ly** \-ti-k(ə-)lē\ *adv*

²neurotic *n* : an emotionally unstable or neurotic person

neu·ro·trans·mit·ter \,nur-ō-trans-'mi-tər, ,nyur-, -tranz-\ *n* : a substance (as acetylcholine) that transmits nerve impulses across a synapse

neut *abbr* neuter

¹neu·ter \'nü-tər, 'nyü-\ *adj* [ME *neutre*, fr. MF & L; MF *neutre*, fr. L *neuter*, lit., neither, fr. *ne- not + uter* which of two] 1 : of, relating to, or constituting the gender that includes most words or grammatical forms referring to things classed as neither masculine nor feminine 2 : lacking or having imperfectly developed sex organs

²neuter *n* 1 : a noun, pronoun, adjective, or inflectional form or class of the neuter gender; *also* : the neuter gender 2 : WORKER 2; *also* : a spayed or castrated animal

³**neuter** *vb* **1** : CASTRATE, SPAY **2** : to remove the force or effectiveness of

¹**neu·tral** \'nü-trəl, 'nyü-\ *n* **1** : one that is neutral **2** : a neutral color **3** : a position of disengagement (as of gears)

²**neutral** *adj* **1** : not favoring either side in a quarrel, contest, or war **2** : of or relating to a neutral state or power **3** : MIDDLING, INDIFFERENT **4** : having no hue : GRAY; *also* : not decided in color **5** : neither acid nor basic ⟨a ∼ solution⟩ **6** : not electrically charged

neu·tral·ise *Brit var of* NEUTRALIZE

neu·tral·ism \'nü-trə-ˌli-zəm, 'nyü-\ *n* : a policy or the advocacy of neutrality esp. in international affairs

neu·tral·i·ty \nü-'tra-lə-tē, nyü-\ *n* : the quality or state of being neutral; *esp* : refusal to take part in a war between other powers

neu·tral·ize \'nü-trə-ˌlīz, 'nyü-\ *vb* **-ized; -iz·ing** : to make neutral; *esp* : COUNTERACT — **neu·tral·i·za·tion** \ˌnü-trə-lə-'zā-shən, ˌnyü-\ *n*

neu·tri·no \nü-'trē-nō, nyü-\ *n, pl* **-nos** : an uncharged elementary particle held to be massless or very light

neu·tron \'nü-ˌträn, 'nyü-\ *n* : an uncharged atomic particle that is nearly equal in mass to the proton

neutron bomb *n* : a nuclear bomb designed to produce lethal neutrons but less blast and fire damage than other nuclear bombs

neutron star *n* : a dense celestial object that results from the collapse of a large star

Nev *abbr* Nevada

nev·er \'ne-vər\ *adv* **1** : not ever **2** : not in any degree, way, or condition

nev·er·more \ˌne-vər-'mȯr\ *adv* : never again

nev·er–nev·er land \ˌne-vər-'ne-vər-\ *n* : an ideal or imaginary place

nev·er·the·less \ˌne-vər-thə-'les\ *adv* : in spite of that : HOWEVER

ne·vus \'nē-vəs\ *n, pl* **ne·vi** \-ˌvī\ : a usu. pigmented area on the skin : MOLE

¹**new** \'nü, 'nyü\ *adj* **1** : not old : RECENT, MODERN **2** : recently discovered, recognized, or learned about ⟨∼ drugs⟩ **3** : UNFAMILIAR ⟨visit ∼ places⟩ **4** : different from the former **5** : not accustomed ⟨∼ to the work⟩ **6** : beginning as a repetition of a previous act or thing ⟨a ∼ year⟩ **7** : REFRESHED, REGENERATED ⟨awoke a ∼ person⟩ **8** : being in a position or place for the first time ⟨a ∼ member⟩ **9** *cap* : having been in use after medieval times : MODERN ⟨*New* Latin⟩ **♦ Synonyms** NOVEL, NEWFANGLED, FRESH — **new·ish** *adj* — **new·ness** *n*

²**new** *adv* : NEWLY ⟨*new*-mown hay⟩

¹**new age** *adj, often cap N&A* **1** : of, relating to, or being New Age **2** : CONTEMPORARY, MODERN

²**new age** *n* **1** *cap* : a group of late 20th century social attitudes adapted from a variety of ancient and modern beliefs relating to spirituality, right living, and health **2** : a soft soothing form of instrumental music

new·bie \'nü-bē, 'nyü-\ *n* : a newcomer esp. to cyberspace

new blood *n* : persons accepted into a group or organization and expected to provide fresh ideas and vitality

¹**new·born** \-ˌbȯrn\ *adj* **1** : recently born **2** : born anew ⟨∼ hope⟩

²**newborn** *n, pl* **newborn** *or* **newborns** : a newborn individual

new·com·er \-ˌkə-mər\ *n* **1** : one recently arrived **2** : BEGINNER

New Deal *n* : the legislative and administrative program of President F. D. Roosevelt to promote economic recovery and social reform during the 1930s — **New Dealer** *n*

new·el \'nü-əl, 'nyü-\ *n* : a post about which the steps of a circular staircase wind; *also* : a post at the foot of a stairway or one at a landing

new·fan·gled \'nü-'faŋ-gəld, 'nyü-\ *adj* **1** : attracted to novelty **2** : of the newest style : NOVEL ⟨∼ gadgets⟩

new–fash·ioned \-'fa-shənd\ *adj* **1** : made in a new fashion or form ⟨∼ automobiles⟩ **2** : UP-TO-DATE

new·found \-'faund\ *adj* : newly found

New Left *n* : a radical political movement originating in the 1960s

new·ly \'nü-lē, 'nyü-\ *adv* **1** : LATELY, RECENTLY ⟨a ∼ married couple⟩ **2** : ANEW, AFRESH ⟨∼ painted⟩

new·ly·wed \-ˌwed\ *n* : a person recently married

new moon *n* : the phase of the moon with its dark side

toward the earth; *also* : the thin crescent moon seen for a few days after the new moon phase

news \'nüz, 'nyüz\ *n* **1** : a report of recent events : TIDINGS **2** : material reported in a newspaper or news periodical or on a newscast

news·boy \'nüz-ˌbȯi, 'nyüz-\ *n* : one who delivers or sells newspapers

news·cast \-ˌkast\ *n* : a radio or television broadcast of news — **news·cast·er** \-ˌkas-tər\ *n*

news·group \-ˌgrüp\ : an Internet bulletin devoted to a certain topic

news·let·ter \'nüz-ˌle-tər, 'nyüz-\ *n* : a small newspaper containing news or information of interest chiefly to a special group

news·mag·a·zine \-ˌma-gə-ˌzēn\ *n* : a usu. weekly magazine devoted chiefly to summarizing and analyzing news

news·man \-mən, -ˌman\ *n* : a person who gathers, reports, or comments on the news : REPORTER

news·pa·per \-ˌpā-pər\ *n* : a paper that is published at regular intervals and contains news, articles of opinion, features, and advertising

news·pa·per·man \-ˌpā-pər-ˌman\ *n* : a person who owns or is employed by a newspaper

news·print \-ˌprint\ *n* : paper made chiefly from wood pulp and used mostly for newspapers

news·reel \-ˌrēl\ *n* : a short motion picture portraying current events

news·stand \-ˌstand\ *n* : a place where newspapers and periodicals are sold

news·week·ly \-ˌwēk-lē\ *n* : a weekly newspaper or newsmagazine

news·wire \-ˌwī(-ə)r\ *n* : WIRE SERVICE

news·wom·an \-ˌwu̇-mən\ *n* : a woman who is a reporter

news·wor·thy \-ˌwər-ˌthē\ *adj* : sufficiently interesting to the general public to warrant reporting

newsy \'nü-zē, 'nyü-\ *adj* **news·i·er; -est** : filled with news; *esp* : TALKATIVE

newt \'nüt, 'nyüt\ *n* [ME, alter. (from misdivision of *an ewte*) of *ewt, evete,* fr. OE *efete*] : any of various small chiefly aquatic salamanders

New Testament *n* : the second of the two chief divisions of the Christian Bible — see BIBLE table

new·ton \'nü-t³n, 'nyü-\ *n* : the unit of force in the metric system equal to the force required to impart an acceleration of one meter per second per second to a mass of one kilogram

new wave *n, often cap N&W* : the latest and esp. the most outrageous style — **new–wave** *adj*

New Year *n* **1** : NEW YEAR'S DAY; *also* : the first days of the year **2** : ROSH HASHANAH

New Year's Day *n* : January 1 observed as a legal holiday

¹**next** \'nekst\ *adj* : immediately preceding or following : NEAREST

²**next** *prep* : nearest or adjacent to

³**next** *adv* **1** : in the time, place, or order nearest or immediately succeeding **2** : on the first occasion to come

⁴**next** *n* : one that is next

nex·us \'nek-səs\ *n, pl* **nex·us·es** \-sə-səz\ *or* **nex·us** \-səs, -ˌsüs\ : CONNECTION, LINK

Nez Percé \'nez-'pərs\ *n* : a member of an American Indian people of Idaho, Washington, and Oregon; *also* : the language of the Nez Percé

NF *abbr* Newfoundland

NFC *abbr* National Football Conference

NFL *abbr* National Football League

Nfld *abbr* Newfoundland

NG *abbr* **1** National Guard **2** no good

ngul·trum \eŋ-'gu̇l-trəm\ *n* — see MONEY table

ngwee \eŋ-'gwē\ *n, pl* **ngwee** — see *kwacha* at MONEY table

Nh *symbol* nihonium

NH *abbr* New Hampshire

NHL *abbr* National Hockey League

Ni *symbol* nickel

ni·a·cin \'nī-ə-sən\ *n* : an organic acid of the vitamin B complex found widely in plants and animals and used esp. against pellagra

nib \'nib\ *n* : POINT; *esp* : a pen point

¹**nib·ble** \'ni-bəl\ *vb* **nib·bled; nib·bling** : to bite gently or bit by bit

²**nibble** *n* : a small or cautious bite

ni·cad \'nī-ˌkad\ *n* : a rechargeable dry cell that has a nickel cathode and a cadmium anode

nice \'nīs\ *adj* **nic·er; nic·est** [ME, foolish, wanton, fr. AF, silly, simple, fr. L *nescius* ignorant, fr. *nescire* to not know] **1** : FASTIDIOUS, DISCRIMINATING **2** : marked by delicate discrimination or treatment ⟨a ~ distinction between those two words⟩ **3** : PLEASING, AGREEABLE ⟨had a ~ time⟩; *also* : well-executed ⟨a ~ shot⟩ **4** : WELL-BRED ⟨~ people⟩ **5** : VIRTUOUS, RESPECTABLE ♦ **Synonyms** CHOOSY, FINICKY, PARTICULAR, PERSNICKETY, PICKY — **nice·ly** *adv* — **nice·ness** *n*

nice–nel·ly \'nīs-'ne-lē\ *adj, often cap 2d N* **1** : marked by euphemism **2** : PRUDISH ⟨his ~ sweetheart⟩ — **nice nelly** *n, often cap 2d N* — **nice–nel·ly·ism** \-ˌi-zəm\ *n, often cap 2d N*

nice·ty \'nī-sə-tē\ *n, pl* **-ties** **1** : a dainty, delicate, or elegant thing ⟨enjoy the *niceties* of life⟩ **2** : a fine point or distinction ⟨*niceties* of workmanship⟩ **3** : EXACTNESS, PRECISION, ACCURACY

niche \'nich\ *n* [F] **1** : a recess in a wall esp. for a statue **2** : a place, employment, or activity for which a person or thing is best fitted **3** : the living space or role of an organism in an ecological community esp. with regard to food consumption

¹nick \'nik\ *n* **1** : a small notch, groove, or chip **2** : the final critical moment ⟨in the ~ of time⟩

²nick *vb* : NOTCH, CHIP

nick·el \'ni-kəl\ *n* **1** : a hard silver-white metallic chemical element capable of a high polish and used in alloys **2** : the U.S. 5-cent piece made of copper and nickel; *also* : the Canadian 5-cent piece

nick·el·ode·on \ˌni-kə-'lō-dē-ən\ *n* **1** : an early movie theater to which admission cost five cents **2** : JUKEBOX

nick·er \'ni-kər\ *vb* : NEIGH, WHINNY — **nicker** *n*

nick·name \'nik-ˌnām\ *n* [ME *nekename* additional name, alter. (from misdivision of *an ekename*) of *ekename*, fr. *eke* also + *name*] **1** : a usu. descriptive name given instead of or in addition to the one belonging to a person, place, or thing **2** : a familiar form of a proper name — **nickname** *vb*

nic·o·tine \'ni-kə-ˌtēn\ *n* : a poisonous and addictive substance in tobacco that is used as an insecticide

nic·o·tin·ic acid \ˌni-kə-ˌtē-nik-, -'ti-\ *n* : NIACIN

niece \'nēs\ *n* : a daughter of one's brother, sister, brother-in-law, or sister-in-law

nif·ty \'nif-tē\ *adj* **nif·ti·er; -est** : very good : very attractive

nig·gard \'ni-gərd\ *n* : a stingy person : MISER — **nig·gard·li·ness** \-lē-nəs\ *n* — **nig·gard·ly** *adj or adv*

nig·gling \'ni-gə-liŋ\ *adj* **1** : PETTY ⟨~ details⟩ **2** : bothersome in a petty way ♦ **Synonyms** INCONSEQUENTIAL, MEASLY, PICAYUNE, PIDDLING, TRIFLING, TRIVIAL

¹nigh \'nī\ *adv* **1** : near in place, time, or relationship **2** : NEARLY, ALMOST

²nigh *adj* : CLOSE, NEAR

³nigh *prep* : NEAR

night \'nīt\ *n* **1** : the period between dusk and dawn **2** : the darkness of night **3** : a period of misery or unhappiness **4** : NIGHTFALL — **night** *adj*

night blindness *n* : reduced visual capacity in faint light (as at night)

night·cap \'nīt-ˌkap\ *n* **1** : a cloth cap worn with nightclothes **2** : a usu. alcoholic drink taken at bedtime

night·clothes \-ˌklōᵗhz, -ˌklōz\ *n pl* : garments worn in bed

night·club \-ˌkləb\ *n* : a place of entertainment open at night usu. serving food and liquor and providing music for dancing

night crawl·er \-ˌkrȯ-lər\ *n* : EARTHWORM; *esp* : a large earthworm found on the soil surface at night

night·dress \'nīt-ˌdres\ *n* : NIGHTGOWN

night·fall \-ˌfȯl\ *n* : the coming of night

night·gown \-ˌgau̇n\ *n* : a loose garment for wear in bed

night·hawk \-ˌhȯk\ *n* : any of a genus of American birds related to and resembling the whip-poor-will

night·in·gale \'nī-tᵊn-ˌgāl, 'nī-tiŋ-\ *n* [ME, fr. OE *nihtegale*, fr. *niht* night + *galan* to sing] : any of several Old World thrushes noted for the sweet usu. nocturnal song of the male

night·life \'nīt-ˌlīf\ *n* : the activity of pleasure-seekers at night

night·ly \'nīt-lē\ *adj* **1** : happening, done, or produced by night or every night **2** : of or relating to the night or every night — **nightly** *adv*

night·mare \'nīt-ˌmer\ *n* **1** : a frightening dream **2** : a frightening or horrible experience — **nightmare** *adj* — **night·mar·ish** *adj*

night rider *n* : a member of a secret band who ride masked at night doing violence to punish or terrorize

night·shade \'nīt-ˌshād\ *n* : any of a large genus of herbs, shrubs, and trees that includes poisonous forms (as the belladonna), ornamentals (as the petunias), and important food plants (as the potato and eggplant)

night·shirt \-ˌshərt\ *n* : a nightgown resembling a shirt

night soil *n* : human feces used esp. for fertilizing the soil

night·stick \'nīt-ˌstik\ *n* : a police officer's club

night·time \-ˌtīm\ *n* : the time from dusk to dawn

night·walk·er \-ˌwȯ-kər\ *n* : a person who roves about at night esp. with criminal or immoral intent

ni·hil·ism \'nī-ə-ˌli-zəm, 'nē-hə-\ *n* **1** : a viewpoint that traditional values and beliefs are unfounded and that existence is senseless and useless **2** : ANARCHISM — **ni·hil·ist** \-list\ *n or adj* — **ni·hil·is·tic** \ˌnī-ə-'lis-tik, ˌnē-hə-\ *adj*

ni·ho·ni·um \ni-'hō-nē-əm\ *n* : a short-lived artificially produced radioactive chemical element

nil \'nil\ *n* : ZERO, NOTHING

nim·ble \'nim-bəl\ *adj* **nim·bler; nim·blest** [ME *nimel*, fr. OE *numol* holding much, fr. *niman* to take] **1** : quick and light in motion : AGILE ⟨a ~ dancer⟩ **2** : quick in understanding and learning : CLEVER ⟨a ~ mind⟩ ♦ **Synonyms** ACTIVE, BRISK, SPRIGHTLY, SPRY, ZIPPY — **nim·ble·ness** *n* — **nim·bly** \-blē\ *adv*

nim·bus \'nim-bəs\ *n, pl* **nim·bi** \-ˌbī, -bē\ *or* **nim·bus·es** **1** : a figure (as a disk) in an art work suggesting radiant light about the head of a divinity, saint, or sovereign **2** : a rain cloud; *also* : THUNDERHEAD

NIMBY \'nim-bē\ *n* [*not in my backyard*] : opposition to the placement of something undesirable (as a prison) in one's neighborhood

nim·rod \'nim-ˌräd\ *n* **1** : HUNTER **2** : IDIOT, JERK

nin·com·poop \'nin-kəm-ˌpüp\ *n* : FOOL, SIMPLETON

nine \'nīn\ *n* **1** : one more than eight **2** : the 9th in a set or series **3** : something having nine units; *esp* : a baseball team — **nine** *adj or pron* — **ninth** \'nīnth\ *adj or adv or n* — **to the nines 1** : to perfection **2** : in an elaborate manner ⟨dressed *to the nines*⟩

nine days' wonder *n* : something that creates a short-lived sensation

nine·pins \'nīn-ˌpinz\ *n* : a bowling game using nine pins arranged usu. in a diamond-shaped configuration

nine·teen \'nīn-'tēn\ *n* : one more than 18 — **nineteen** *adj or pron* — **nine·teenth** \-'tēnth\ *adj or n*

nine·ty \'nīn-tē\ *n, pl* **nineties** : nine times 10 — **nine·ti·eth** \-tē-əth\ *adj or n* — **ninety** *adj or pron*

nin·ja \'nin-jə, -(ˌ)jä\ *n, pl* **ninja** *or* **ninjas** [Jp] : a person trained in ancient Japanese martial arts and employed esp. for espionage and assassinations

nin·ny \'ni-nē\ *n, pl* **ninnies** : FOOL

ni·o·bi·um \nī-'ō-bē-əm\ *n* : a gray metallic chemical element used in alloys

¹nip \'nip\ *vb* **nipped; nip·ping 1** : to catch hold of and squeeze tightly between two surfaces, edges, or points **2** : ³CLIP **3** : to destroy the growth, progress, or fulfillment of ⟨*nipped* in the bud⟩ **4** : to injure or make numb with cold : CHILL **5** : SNATCH, STEAL

²nip *n* **1** : a sharp stinging cold **2** : a biting or pungent flavor **3** : PINCH, BITE **4** : a small portion : BIT

³nip *n* : a small quantity of liquor : SIP

⁴nip *vb* **nipped; nip·ping** : to take liquor in nips : TIPPLE

nip and tuck *adj or adv* : so close that the lead shifts rapidly from one contestant to another

nip·per \'ni-pər\ *n* **1** : one that nips **2** *pl* : PINCERS **3** : CHILD; *esp* : a small boy

nip·ple \'ni-pəl\ *n* : the protuberance of a mammary gland through which milk is drawn off : TEAT; *also* : something resembling a nipple

nip·py \'ni-pē\ *adj* **nip·pi·er; -est 1** : PUNGENT, SHARP **2** : CHILLY

nir·va·na \nər-'vä-nə\ *n, often cap* [Skt *nirvāṇa*, lit., act of extinguishing, fr. *nis*- out + *vāti* it blows] : the final freeing of a soul from all that enslaves it; *esp* : the supreme happiness that according to Buddhism comes when all passion, hatred, and delusion die out and the soul is released from the necessity of further purification 2 : OBLIVION; *also* : PARADISE

ni·sei \nē-'sā, 'nē-ˌsā\ *n, pl* **nisei** *often cap* : a son or daughter of immigrant Japanese parents who is born and educated in America

ni·si \'nī-ˌsī\ *adj* [L, unless, fr. *ne-* not + *si* if] : taking effect at a specified time unless previously modified or voided ⟨a divorce decree ∼⟩

nit \'nit\ *n* **1** : the egg of a parasitic insect (as a louse); *also* : the young insect **2** : a minor shortcoming

nite *var of* NIGHT

ni·ter \'nī-tər\ *n* : POTASSIUM NITRATE

nit·pick·ing \'nit-ˌpi-kiŋ\ *n* : minute and usu. unjustified criticism — **nit·pick·er** *n*

¹**ni·trate** \'nī-ˌtrāt, -trət\ *n* **1** : a salt or ester of nitric acid **2** : sodium nitrate or potassium nitrate used as a fertilizer

²**ni·trate** \-ˌtrāt\ *vb* **ni·trat·ed; ni·trat·ing** : to treat or combine with nitric acid or a nitrate — **ni·tra·tion** \nī-'trā-shən\ *n*

ni·tre *chiefly Brit var of* NITER

ni·tric acid \'nī-trik-\ *n* : a corrosive liquid acid used esp. in making dyes, explosives, and fertilizers

ni·tri·fi·ca·tion \ˌnī-trə-fə-'kā-shən\ *n* : the oxidation (as by bacteria) of ammonium salts to nitrites and then to nitrates — **ni·tri·fy·ing** \'nī-trə-fī-iŋ\ *adj*

ni·trite \'nī-ˌtrīt\ *n* : a salt of nitrous acid

ni·tro \'nī-trō\ *n, pl* **nitros** : any of various nitrated products; *esp* : NITROGLYCERIN

ni·tro·gen \'nī-trə-jən\ *n* : a tasteless odorless gaseous chemical element constituting 78 percent of the atmosphere by volume — **ni·trog·e·nous** \nī-'trä-jə-nəs\ *adj*

nitrogen narcosis *n* : a state of euphoria and confusion caused by nitrogen forced into a diver's bloodstream from atmospheric air under pressure

ni·tro·glyc·er·in *or* **ni·tro·glyc·er·ine** \ˌnī-trə-'gli-sə-rən\ *n* : an oily explosive liquid used to make dynamite and in medicine to dilate blood vessels

ni·trous acid \'nī-trəs-\ *n* : an unstable nitrogen-containing acid known only in solution or in the form of its salts

nitrous oxide *n* : a colorless gas used esp. as an anesthetic in dentistry

nit·ty-grit·ty \'ni-tē-ˌgri-tē, ˌni-tē-'gri-tē\ *n* : what is essential and basic : specific practical details

nit·wit \'nit-ˌwit\ *n* : a scatterbrained or stupid person

¹**nix** \'niks\ *n* : NOTHING

²**nix** *vb* : VETO, REJECT

³**nix** *adv* : NO

NJ *abbr* New Jersey

NL *abbr* National League

NLRB *abbr* National Labor Relations Board

NM *abbr* **1** nautical mile **2** New Mexico

N Mex *abbr* New Mexico

NMI *abbr* no middle initial

NNE *abbr* north-northeast

NNW *abbr* north-northwest

¹**no** \'nō\ *adv* **1** — used to express the negative of an alternative ⟨shall we continue or ∼⟩ **2** : in no respect or degree ⟨he is ∼ better than the others⟩ **3** : not so ⟨∼, I'm not ready⟩ **4** — used with an adjective to imply a meaning opposite to the positive statement ⟨in ∼ uncertain terms⟩ **5** — used to introduce a more emphatic or explicit statement ⟨has the right, ∼, the duty to continue⟩ **6** — used as an interjection to express surprise or doubt ⟨∼ — you don't say⟩ **7** — used in combination with a verb to form a compound adjective ⟨*no*-bake pie⟩ **8** : in negation ⟨shook his head ∼⟩

²**no** *adj* **1** : not any; *also* : hardly any **2** : not a ⟨she's ∼ expert⟩

³**no** \'nō\ *n, pl* **noes** *or* **nos** \'nōz\ **1** : REFUSAL, DENIAL ⟨got a ∼ in reply⟩ **2** : a negative vote or decision; *also*, *pl* : persons voting in the negative

⁴**no** *abbr* **1** north; northern **2** [L *numero*, abl. of *numerus*] number

¹**No** *var of* NOH

²**No** *symbol* nobelium

No·bel·ist \nō-'be-list\ *n* : a winner of a Nobel prize

no·bel·i·um \nō-'be-lē-əm\ *n* : a radioactive metallic chemical element produced artificially

No·bel prize \nō-'bel-, 'nō-ˌbel-\ *n* : any of various annual prizes (as in peace, literature, or medicine) established

by the will of Alfred Nobel for the encouragement of persons who work for the interests of humanity

no·bil·i·ty \nō-'bi-lə-tē\ *n* **1** : the quality or state of being noble **2** : nobles considered as forming a class

¹**no·ble** \'nō-bəl\ *adj* **no·bler; no·blest** [ME, fr. AF, fr. L *nobilis* well known, noble, fr. *noscere* to come to know] **1** : ILLUSTRIOUS; *also* : FAMOUS, NOTABLE **2** : of high birth, rank, or station : ARISTOCRATIC **3** : EXCELLENT **4** : STATELY, IMPOSING ⟨a ∼ edifice⟩ **5** : of a superior nature ♦ *Synonyms* AUGUST, BARONIAL, GRAND, GRANDIOSE, MAGNIFICENT, MAJESTIC — **no·ble·ness** *n* — **no·bly** \-blē\ *adv*

²**noble** *n* : a person of noble rank or birth

no·ble·man \'nō-bəl-mən\ *n* : a member of the nobility : PEER

no·blesse oblige \nō-ˌbles-ə-'blēzh\ *n* [F, lit., nobility obligates] : the obligation of honorable, generous, and responsible behavior associated with high rank or birth

no·ble·wom·an \'nō-bəl-ˌwù-mən\ *n* : a woman of noble rank : PEERESS

¹**no·body** \'nō-ˌbä-dē, -bə-\ *pron* : no person

²**nobody** *n, pl* **no·bod·ies** : a person of no influence or importance

no–brain·er \'nō-'brā-nər\ *n* : something that requires a minimum of thought

noc·tur·nal \näk-'tər-n²l\ *adj* **1** : of, relating to, or occurring in the night **2** : active at night ⟨a ∼ bird⟩

noc·turne \'näk-ˌtərn\ *n* : a work of art dealing with night; *esp* : a dreamy pensive composition for the piano

noc·u·ous \'nä-kyə-wəs\ *adj* : HARMFUL — **noc·u·ous·ly** *adv*

nod \'näd\ *vb* **nod·ded; nod·ding 1** : to bend the head downward or forward (as in bowing, going to sleep, or giving assent) **2** : to move up and down ⟨tulips *nodding* in the breeze⟩ **3** : to show by a nod of the head ⟨∼ agreement⟩ **4** : to make a slip or error in a moment of abstraction ⟨did many good things, but sometimes he *nodded*⟩ — **nod** *n*

nod·dle \'nä-d²l\ *n* : HEAD

nod·dy \'nä-dē\ *n, pl* **noddies 1** : FOOL **2** : a stout-bodied tropical tern

node \'nōd\ *n* : a thickened, swollen, or differentiated area (as of tissue); *esp* : the part of a stem from which a leaf arises — **nod·al** \-²l\ *adj*

nod·ule \'nä-jül\ *n* : a small lump or swelling — **nod·u·lar** \'nä-jə-lər\ *adj*

no·el \nō-'el\ *n* [F *noël* Christmas, carol, fr. OF *Nael* (*Deu*), *Noel* Christmas, fr. L *natalis* birthday] **1** : a Christmas carol **2** *cap* : the Christmas season

noes *pl of* NO

no–fault \'nō-ˌfȯlt\ *adj* **1** : of, relating to, or being a motor vehicle insurance plan under which someone involved in an accident is compensated usu. up to a stipulated limit for actual losses by that person's own insurance company regardless of who is responsible **2** : of, relating to, or being a divorce law under which neither party is held responsible for the breakup of the marriage

nog·gin \'nä-gən\ *n* **1** : a small mug or cup; *also* : a small quantity of drink **2** : a person's head

no–good \'nō-'gùd\ *adj* : having no worth, virtue, use, or chance of success — **no–good** \'nō-ˌgùd\ *n*

Noh *also* **No** \'nō\ *n, pl* **Noh** *also* **No** : classic Japanese dance-drama having a heroic theme, a chorus, and highly stylized action, costuming, and scenery

no–hit·ter \(ˌ)nō-'hi-tər\ *n* : a baseball game or part of a game in which a pitcher allows no base hits

no·how \'nō-ˌhaù\ *adv* : in no manner

¹**noise** \'nȯiz\ *n* [ME, fr. AF, disturbance, noise, fr. L *nausea* nausea] **1** : loud, confused, or senseless shouting or outcry **2** : SOUND; *esp* : one that lacks agreeable musical quality or is noticeably unpleasant **3** : unwanted electronic signal or disturbance — **noise·less** *adj* — **noise·less·ly** *adv*

²**noise** *vb* **noised; nois·ing** : to spread by rumor or report ⟨the story was *noised* abroad⟩

noise·mak·er \'nȯiz-ˌmā-kər\ *n* : one that makes noise; *esp* : a device used to make noise at parties

noise pollution *n* : annoying or harmful noise in an environment

noi·some \'nȯi-səm\ *adj* **1** : HARMFUL, UNWHOLESOME **2** : offensive to the senses (as smell) : DISGUSTING ⟨∼

habits⟩ ✦ **Synonyms** INSALUBRIOUS, NOXIOUS, SICKLY, UNHEALTHFUL, UNHEALTHY
noisy \'nȯi-zē\ *adj* **nois·i·er; -est 1 :** making loud noises **2 :** full of noises : LOUD — **nois·i·ly** \-zə-lē\ *adv* — **nois·i·ness** \-zē-nəs\ *n*
nol·le pro·se·qui \ˌnä-lē-'prä-sə-ˌkwī\ *n* [L, to be unwilling to pursue] : an entry on the record of a legal action that the prosecutor or plaintiff will proceed no further in an action or suit or in some aspect of it
no·lo con·ten·de·re \ˌnō-lō-kən-'ten-də-rē\ *n* [L, I do not wish to contend] : a plea in a criminal prosecution that subjects the defendant to conviction but does not admit guilt or preclude denying the charges in another proceeding
nol–pros \'näl-'präs\ *vb* **nol–prossed; nol–pros·sing :** to discontinue by entering a nolle prosequi
nom *abbr* nominative
no·mad \'nō-ˌmad\ *n* **1 :** a member of a people who have no fixed residence but move from place to place **2 :** an individual who roams about aimlessly — **nomad** *adj* — **no·mad·ic** \nō-'ma-dik\ *adj*
no–man's–land \'nō-ˌmanz-ˌland\ *n* **1 :** an area of unowned, unclaimed, or uninhabited land **2 :** an unoccupied area between opposing troops
nom de guerre \ˌnäm-di-'ger\ *n, pl* **noms de guerre** *same or* ˌnämz-\ [F, lit., war name] : PSEUDONYM
nom de plume \-'plüm\ *n, pl* **noms de plume** *same or* ˌnämz-\ [F, pen name; prob. coined in E] : PEN NAME
no·men·cla·ture \'nō-mən-ˌklā-chər\ *n* **1 :** NAME, DESIGNATION **2 :** a system of terms used in a science or art
nom·i·nal \'nä-mə-nᵊl\ *adj* **1 :** being something in name or form only ⟨~ head of a party⟩ **2 :** TRIFLING ⟨a ~ price⟩ — **nom·i·nal·ly** *adv*
nom·i·nate \'nä-mə-ˌnāt\ *vb* **-nat·ed; -nat·ing :** to choose as a candidate for election, appointment, or honor ✦ **Synonyms** APPOINT, DESIGNATE, NAME, TAP — **nom·i·na·tion** \ˌnä-mə-'nā-shən\ *n*
nom·i·na·tive \'nä-mə-nə-tiv\ *adj* : of, relating to, or constituting a grammatical case marking typically the subject of a verb — **nominative** *n*
nom·i·nee \ˌnä-mə-'nē\ *n* : a person nominated for an office, duty, or position
non- \(')nän *or* ˌnän *before stressed syllables;* ˌnän *elsewhere*\ *prefix* **1 :** not : reverse of : absence of **2 :** having no importance

nonabrasive
nonabsorbent
nonacademic
nonacceptance
nonaccredited
nonacid
nonactivated
nonadaptive
nonaddictive
nonadhesive
nonadjacent
nonadjustable
nonaggression
nonalcoholic
nonappearance
nonaromatic
nonathletic
nonattendance
nonbeliever
nonbelligerent
nonbiodegradable
nonbreakable
noncaloric
noncancerous
noncandidate
noncellular
noncitizen
nonclerical
noncoital
noncombat
noncombative
noncombustible
noncommercial
noncommunist
noncompeting
noncompetitive
noncompliance
noncomplying
nonconducting
nonconfidence
nonconflicting
nonconformance
nonconforming
nonconsensual
nonconstructive
noncontagious
noncontinuous
noncorroding
noncorrosive
noncriminal
noncritical
noncrystalline
nondeductible
nondelivery
nondemocratic
nondenominational
nondepartmental
nondestructive
nondevelopment
nondiscrimination
nondiscriminatory
nondistinctive
nondurable
noneconomic
noneducational
nonelastic
nonelection
nonelective
nonelectric
nonelectrical
nonemotional
nonenforcement
nonethical
non-euclidean
nonexclusive
nonexempt
nonexistence
nonexistent
nonexplosive
nonfarm
nonfatal
nonfattening
nonfederated
nonferrous
nonfiction
nonfictional
nonfilamentous
nonfilterable
nonflammable
nonflowering
nonfood
nonfreezing
nonfulfillment
nonfunctional
nonglare
nongraded
nonhazardous
nonhereditary
nonhomogeneous
nonhomologous
nonhuman
nonidentical
nonimportation
nonindustrial
noninfectious
noninflammable
nonintellectual
nonintercourse
noninterference
nonintoxicant
nonintoxicating
noninvasive
nonionizing
nonirritating
nonlegal
nonlethal
nonlife
nonlinear
nonliterary
nonliterate
nonliving
nonlogical
nonmagnetic
nonmalignant
nonmaterial
nonmember
nonmembership
nonmigratory
nonmilitary
nonmoral
nonmotile
nonmoving
nonnegotiable
nonobservance
nonoccurrence
nonofficial
nonoily
nonorthodox
nonparallel
nonparasitic
nonparticipant
nonparticipating
nonpathogenic
nonpaying
nonpayment
nonperformance
nonperishable
nonphysical
nonpoisonous
nonpolar
nonpolitical
nonporous
nonpregnant
nonproductive
nonprofessional
nonprotein
nonradioactive
nonrandom
nonrated
nonreactive
nonreciprocal
nonrecognition
nonrecurrent
nonrecurring
nonrefillable
nonreligious
nonrenewable
nonresidential
nonrestricted
nonreturnable
nonreusable
nonreversible
nonrigid
nonruminant
nonsalable
nonscientific
nonscientist
nonseasonal
nonsectarian
nonsegregated
nonselective
non-self-governing
nonsexist
nonsexual
nonshrinkable
nonsinkable
nonsmoker
nonsmoking
nonsocial
nonspeaking
nonspecialist
nonspecific
nonsteroidal
nonstudent
nonsuccess
nonsurgical
nontaxable
nonteaching
nontechnical
nontemporal
nontenured
nontheistic
nonthreatening
nontoxic
nontraditional
nontransferable
nontypical
nonuniform
nonvascular
nonvenomous
nonverbal
nonveteran
nonviable
nonvisual
nonvocal
nonvolatile
nonvoter
nonvoting
nonworker
nonworking
nonzero

non·age \'nä-nij, 'nō-\ *n* **1 :** legal minority **2 :** a period of youth **3 :** IMMATURITY
no·na·ge·nar·i·an \ˌnō-nə-jə-'ner-ē-ən, ˌnä-\ *n* : a person whose age is in the nineties

non·aligned \ˌnän-ə-ˈlīnd\ *adj* : not allied with other nations

no–name \ˈnō-ˌnām\ *adj* : not having a readily recognizable name ⟨~ brands⟩

non·book \ˈnän-ˌbuk\ *n* : a book of little literary merit that is often a compilation (as of pictures or speeches)

¹nonce \ˈnäns\ *n* : the one, particular, or present occasion or purpose ⟨for the ~⟩

²nonce *adj* : occurring, used, or made only once or for a special occasion ⟨a ~ word⟩

non·cha·lant \ˌnän-shə-ˈlänt\ *adj* [F, fr. OF, fr. prp. of *nonchaloir* to disregard, fr. *non-* not + *chaloir* to concern, fr. L *calēre* to be warm] : giving an effect of unconcern or indifference ♦ *Synonyms* COLLECTED, COMPOSED, COOL, IMPERTURBABLE, UNFLAPPABLE, UNRUFFLED — **non·cha·lance** \-ˈläns\ *n* — **non·cha·lant·ly** *adv*

non·com \ˈnän-ˌkäm\ *n* : NONCOMMISSIONED OFFICER

non·com·ba·tant \ˌnän-kəm-ˈba-tᵊnt, nän-ˈkäm-bə-tənt\ *n* : a member (as a chaplain) of the armed forces whose duties do not include fighting; *also* : CIVILIAN — **noncombatant** *adj*

non·com·mis·sioned officer \ˌnän-kə-ˈmi-shənd-\ *n* : a subordinate officer in the armed forces appointed from enlisted personnel

non·com·mit·tal \ˌnän-kə-ˈmi-tᵊl\ *adj* : indicating neither consent nor dissent ⟨a ~ reply⟩

non com·pos men·tis \ˌnän-ˌkäm-pəs-ˈmen-təs\ *adj* : not of sound mind

non·con·duc·tor \ˌnän-kən-ˈdək-tər\ *n* : a substance that is a very poor conductor of heat, electricity, or sound

non·con·form·ist \-kən-ˈfȯr-mist\ *n* **1** *often cap* : a person who does not conform to an established church and esp. the Church of England **2** : a person who does not conform to a generally accepted pattern of thought or action ♦ *Synonyms* DISSENTER, DISSIDENT, HERETIC, SCHISMATIC, SEPARATIST — **non·con·for·mi·ty** \-ˈfȯr-mə-tē\ *n*

non·co·op·er·a·tion \ˌnän-kō-ˌä-pə-ˈrā-shən\ *n* : failure or refusal to cooperate; *esp* : refusal through civil disobedience of a people to cooperate with the government of a country

non·cred·it \(ˌ)nän-ˈkre-dət\ *adj* : not offering credit toward a degree

non·cus·to·di·al \ˌnän-kə-ˈstō-dē-əl\ *adj* : of or being a parent who does not have legal custody of a child

non·dairy \ˈnän-ˈder-ē\ *adj* : containing no milk or milk products ⟨~ margarine⟩

non·de·script \ˌnän-di-ˈskript\ *adj* **1** : not belonging to any particular class or kind **2** : lacking distinctive qualities ⟨a ~ building⟩

non·drink·er \-ˈdriŋ-kər\ *n* : a person who abstains from alcohol

¹none \ˈnən\ *pron* **1** : not any ⟨~ of them went⟩ **2** : not one ⟨~ of the family⟩ **3** : not any such thing or person ⟨half a loaf is better than ~⟩

²none *adj, archaic* : not any : NO

³none *adv* : by no means : not at all ⟨he got there ~ too soon⟩

non·en·ti·ty \ˌnän-ˈen-tə-tē\ *n* **1** : something that does not exist or exists only in the imagination **2** : one of no consequence or significance ♦ *Synonyms* NOBODY, NOTHING, NONPARTICIPANT

nones \ˈnōnz\ *n sing or pl* : the 7th day of March, May, July, or October or the 5th day of any other month in the ancient Roman calendar

non·es·sen·tial \ˌnän-i-ˈsen-shəl\ *adj* **1** : not essential **2** : being a substance synthesized by the body in sufficient quantity to satisfy dietary needs

none·such \ˈnən-ˌsəch\ *n* : one without an equal — **none·such** *adj*

none·the·less \ˌnən-thə-ˈles\ *adv* : NEVERTHELESS

non·event \ˈnän-i-ˌvent\ *n* **1** : an event that fails to take place or to satisfy expectations **2** : a highly promoted event of little intrinsic interest

non·fat \-ˈfat\ *adj* : lacking fat solids : having fat solids removed ⟨~ milk⟩

non·gono·coc·cal \ˌnän-ˌgä-nə-ˈkä-kəl\ *adj* : not caused by a gonococcus

non·he·ro \ˈnän-ˈhē-rō\ *n* : ANTIHERO

non–Hodg·kin's lymphoma \ˈnän-ˈhäj-kənz-\ *n* : any of numerous malignant lymphomas not classified as Hodgkin's disease

non·in·ter·ven·tion \ˌnän-ˌin-tər-ˈven-chən\ *n* : refusal or failure to intervene (as in the affairs of other countries)

non·is·sue \ˈnän-ˈi-shü\ *n* : an issue of little importance or concern

non·met·al \ˈnän-ˈme-tᵊl\ *n* : a chemical element (as carbon) that lacks the characteristics of a metal — **non·me·tal·lic** \ˌnän-mə-ˈta-lik\ *adj*

non·neg·a·tive \-ˈne-gə-tiv\ *adj* : not negative : being either positive or zero

non·nu·cle·ar \ˈnän-ˈnü-klē-ər\ *adj* **1** : not nuclear **2** : not having, using, or involving nuclear weapons

non·ob·jec·tive \ˌnän-əb-ˈjek-tiv\ *adj* **1** : not objective **2** : representing no natural or actual object, figure, or scene ⟨~ art⟩

¹non·pa·reil \-pə-ˈrel\ *adj* : having no equal : PEERLESS ⟨a ~ performer⟩

²nonpareil *n* **1** : an individual of unequaled excellence : PARAGON **2** : a small flat disk of chocolate covered with white sugar pellets

non·par·ti·san \ˈnän-ˈpär-tə-zən\ *adj* : not partisan; *esp* : not influenced by political party spirit or interests

non·per·son \-ˈpər-sᵊn\ *n* **1** : UNPERSON **2** : a person having no social or legal status

non·plus \ˈnän-ˈpləs\ *vb* -plussed *also* -plused \-ˈpləst\; -plus·sing *also* -plus·ing : PUZZLE, PERPLEX

non·pre·scrip·tion \ˌnän-pri-ˈskrip-shən\ *adj* : available for sale legally without a doctor's prescription

non·prof·it \ˈnän-ˈprä-fət\ *adj* : not conducted or maintained for the purpose of making a profit ⟨a ~ organization⟩

non·pro·lif·er·a·tion \ˌnän-prə-ˌli-fə-ˈrā-shən\ *adj* : providing for the stoppage of proliferation (as of nuclear arms) ⟨a ~ treaty⟩

non·read·er \ˈnän-ˈrē-dər\ *n* : one who does not read or has difficulty reading

non·rep·re·sen·ta·tion·al \ˌnän-ˌre-pri-ˌzen-ˈtä-shə-nəl\ *adj* : NONOBJECTIVE 2

non·res·i·dent \ˈnän-ˈre-zə-dənt\ *adj* : not living in a particular place — **non·res·i·dence** \-dəns\ *n* — **nonresident** *n*

non·re·sis·tance \ˌnän-ri-ˈzis-təns\ *n* : the principles or practice of passive submission to authority even when unjust or oppressive

non·re·stric·tive \-ri-ˈstrik-tiv\ *adj* **1** : not serving or tending to restrict **2** : not limiting the reference of the word or phrase modified ⟨a ~ clause⟩

non·sched·uled \ˈnän-ˈske-jüld\ *adj* : licensed to carry passengers or freight by air without a regular schedule

non·sense \ˈnän-ˌsens, -səns\ *n* **1** : foolish or meaningless words or actions **2** : things of no importance or value — **non·sen·si·cal** \nän-ˈsen-si-kəl\ *adj* — **non·sen·si·cal·ly** \-k(ə-)lē\ *adv*

non se·qui·tur \nän-ˈse-kwə-tər\ *n* [L, it does not follow] : an inference that does not follow from the premises

non·skid \ˈnän-ˈskid\ *adj* : designed to prevent skidding ⟨a ~ surface⟩

non·slip \-ˈslip\ *adj* : designed to prevent slipping ⟨a ~ handle⟩

non·stan·dard \ˌnän-ˈstan-dərd\ *adj* **1** : not standard **2** : not conforming to the usage characteristic of educated native speakers of a language

non·start·er \ˈnän-ˈstär-tər\ *n* **1** : one that does not start **2** : one that is not productive or effective

non·stick \-ˈstik\ *adj* : allowing easy removal of cooked food particles

¹non·stop \-ˈstäp\ *adj* : done or made without a stop ⟨~ action⟩ — **nonstop** *adv*

²nonstop *n* : a nonstop airplane flight

non·sup·port \ˌnän-sə-ˈpȯrt\ *n* : failure to support; *esp* : failure on the part of one under obligation to provide maintenance

non·threat·en·ing \-ˈthret-niŋ, -ˈthre-tᵊn-iŋ\ *adj* : not likely to cause danger or anxiety ⟨a ~ illness⟩ ⟨a ~ environment⟩

non–U \ˈnän-ˈyü\ *adj* : not characteristic of the upper classes ⟨~ speech⟩

non·union \ˈnän-ˈyü-nyən\ *adj* **1** : not belonging to a trade union ⟨~ carpenters⟩ **2** : not recognizing or favoring trade unions or their members ⟨~ employers⟩

non·us·er \-ˈyü-zər\ *n* : one who does not make use of something (as drugs)

non·vi·o·lence \ˈnän-ˈvī-ə-ləns\ *n* **1** : abstention from violence as a matter of principle **2** : avoidance of violence **3** : nonviolent political demonstrations — **non·vi·o·lent** \-lənt\ *adj*

non·white \ˌnän-ʰhwīt, -ʰwīt\ *n* : a person whose features and esp. skin color are different from those of peoples of northwestern Europe — **nonwhite** *adj*

non·wo·ven \ˈnän-ʰwō-vən\ *adj* : made of fibers held together by interlocking or bonding (as by chemical or thermal means) — **nonwoven** *n*

noo·dle \ˈnü-dᵊl\ *n* [G *Nudel*] : a food paste made usu. with egg and shaped typically in ribbon form

nook \ˈnu̇k\ *n* **1** : an interior angle or corner formed usu. by two walls ⟨a chimney ∼⟩ **2** : a sheltered or hidden place ⟨searched every ∼ and cranny⟩ **3** : a usu. recessed section of a larger room ⟨a breakfast ∼⟩

noon \ˈnün\ *n* : the middle of the day : 12 o'clock in the daytime — **noon** *adj*

noon·day \ˈnün-ˌdā\ *n* : NOON, MIDDAY

no one *pron* : NOBODY

noon·tide \ˈnün-ˌtīd\ *n* : NOON

noon·time \-ˌtīm\ *n* : NOON

noose \ˈnüs\ *n* : a loop with a slipknot that binds closer the more it is drawn

nope \ˈnōp\ *adv* : NO

nor \ˈnȯr\ *conj* : and not ⟨not for you ∼ for me⟩ — used esp. to introduce and negate the second member and each later member of a series of items preceded by *neither* ⟨neither here ∼ there⟩

Nor·dic \ˈnȯr-dik\ *adj* **1** : of or relating to the Germanic peoples of northern Europe and esp. of Scandinavia **2** : of or relating to competitive ski events involving cross= country racing, ski jumping, or biathlon — **Nordic** *n*

nor·epi·neph·rine \ˌnȯr-ˌe-pə-ʰne-frən\ *n* : a nitrogen-containing neurotransmitter in parts of the sympathetic and central nervous systems

norm \ˈnȯrm\ *n* [L *norma*, lit., carpenter's square] **1** : an authoritative standard or model; *esp* : a set standard of development or achievement usu. derived from the average or median achievement of a large group **2** : a typical or widespread practice, procedure, or custom ✦ *Synonyms* AVERAGE, MEAN, MEDIAN, PAR

¹nor·mal \ˈnȯr-məl\ *adj* **1** : REGULAR, STANDARD, NATURAL **2** : of average intelligence; *also* : sound in mind and body — **nor·mal·cy** \-sē\ *n* — **nor·mal·i·ty** \nȯr-ʰma-lə-tē\ *n* — **nor·mal·ly** *adv*

²normal *n* **1** : one that is normal **2** : the usual condition, level, or quantity

nor·mal·ise *Brit var of* NORMALIZE

nor·mal·ize \ˈnȯr-mə-ˌlīz\ *vb* **-ized; -iz·ing** : to make or restore to normal ⟨*normalizing* relations⟩ — **nor·mal·i·za·tion** \ˌnȯr-mə-lə-ʰzā-shən\ *n*

Nor·man \ˈnȯr-mən\ *n* **1** : a native or inhabitant of Normandy **2** : one of the 10th century Scandinavian conquerors of Normandy **3** : one of the Norman-French conquerors of England in 1066 — **Norman** *adj*

nor·ma·tive \ˈnȯr-mə-tiv\ *adj* : of, relating to, or determining norms — **nor·ma·tive·ly** *adv* — **nor·ma·tive·ness** *n*

Norse \ˈnȯrs\ *n, pl* **Norse 1** : NORWEGIAN; *also* : any of the western Scandinavian dialects or languages **2** *pl* : SCANDINAVIANS; *also* : NORWEGIANS

Norse·man \-mən\ *n* : any of the ancient Scandinavians

¹north \ˈnȯrth\ *adv* : to, toward, or in the north

²north *adj* **1** : situated toward or at the north **2** : coming from the north

³north *n* **1** : the direction to the left of one facing east **2** : the compass point directly opposite to south **3** *cap* : regions or countries north of a specified or implied point — **north·er·ly** \ˈnȯr-thər-lē\ *adv or adj* — **north·ern** \-thərn\ *adj* — **North·ern·er** \-thər-nər\ *n* — **north·ern·most** \-thərn-ˌmōst\ *adj* — **north·ward** \ˈnȯrth-wərd\ *adv or adj* — **north·wards** \-wərdz\ *adv*

north·east \nȯrth-ʰēst\ *n* **1** : the general direction between north and east **2** : the compass point midway between north and east **3** *cap* : regions or countries northeast of a specified or implied point — **northeast** *adj or adv* — **north·east·er·ly** \-ʰthē-stər-lē\ *adv or adj* — **north·east·ern** \-stərn\ *adj*

north·east·er \-ʰē-stər\ *n* **1** : a strong northeast wind **2** : a storm with northeast winds

north·er \ˈnȯr-thər\ *n* **1** : a strong north wind **2** : a storm with north winds

northern lights *n pl* : AURORA BOREALIS

north pole *n, often cap N&P* : the northernmost point of the earth

North Star *n* : the star toward which the northern end of the earth's axis points

north·west \nȯrth-ʰwest\ *n* **1** : the general direction between north and west **2** : the compass point midway between north and west **3** *cap* : regions or countries northwest of a specified or implied point — **northwest** *adj or adv* — **north·west·er·ly** \-ʰwe-stər-lē\ *adv or adj* — **north·west·ern** \-ʰwe-stərn\ *adj*

Norw *abbr* Norway; Norwegian

Nor·we·gian \nȯr-ʰwē-jən\ *n* **1** : a native or inhabitant of Norway **2** : the language of Norway — **Norwegian** *adj*

nos *abbr* numbers

¹nose \ˈnōz\ *n* **1** : the part of the face or head containing the nostrils and covering the front of the nasal cavity **2** : the sense of smell **3** : something (as a point, edge, or projecting front part) that resembles a nose ⟨the ∼ of a plane⟩ — **nosed** \ˈnōzd\ *adj* — **on the nose** : on target : ACCURATE — **under one's nose** : extremely near : in one's presence

²nose *vb* **nosed; nos·ing 1** : to detect by or as if by smell : SCENT **2** : to push or move with the nose **3** : to touch or rub with the nose : NUZZLE **4** : PRY **5** : to move ahead slowly ⟨the ship *nosed* into her berth⟩

nose·bleed \ˈnōz-ˌblēd\ *n* : a bleeding from the nose

nose cone *n* : a protective cone constituting the forward end of an aerospace vehicle

nose·dive \ˈnōz-ˌdīv\ *n* **1** : a downward nose-first plunge (as of an airplane) **2** : a sudden extreme drop (as in prices)

nose·gay \ˈnōz-ˌgā\ *n* : a small bunch of flowers : POSY

nose out *vb* **1** : to discover often by prying **2** : to defeat by a narrow margin

nose·piece \-ˌpēs\ *n* **1** : a fitting at the lower end of a microscope tube to which the objectives are attached **2** : the bridge of a pair of eyeglasses

no-show \ˈnō-ʰshō\ *n* : a person who does not show up for an event as expected

nos·tal·gia \nä-ʰstal-jə\ *n* [NL, fr. Gk *nostos* return home + *algos* pain, grief] **1** : HOMESICKNESS **2** : a wistful yearning for something past or irrecoverable — **nos·tal·gic** \-jik\ *adj* — **nos·tal·gist** \-jist\ *n*

nos·tril \ˈnäs-trəl\ *n* [ME *nosethirl*, fr. OE *nosthyrl*, fr. *nosu* nose + *thyrel* hole] **1** : either of the nares usu. with the adjoining nasal wall and passage **2** : either fleshy lateral wall of the nose

nos·trum \ˈnäs-trəm\ *n* [L, neut. of *noster* our, ours, fr. *nos* we] : a questionable medicine or remedy

nosy *or* **nos·ey** \ˈnō-zē\ *adj* **nos·i·er; -est** : INQUISITIVE, PRYING ⟨∼ neighbors⟩

not \ˈnät\ *adv* **1** — used to make negative a group of words or a word ⟨the boys are ∼ here⟩ **2** — used to stand for the negative of a preceding group of words ⟨sometimes easy and sometimes ∼⟩

no·ta be·ne \ˌnō-tə-ʰbē-nē, -ʰbe-\ [L, mark well] — used to call attention to something important

no·ta·bil·i·ty \ˌnō-tə-ʰbi-lə-tē\ *n, pl* **-ties 1** : the quality or state of being notable **2** : NOTABLE

¹no·ta·ble \ˈnō-tə-bəl\ *adj* **1** : NOTEWORTHY, REMARKABLE ⟨a ∼ achievement⟩ **2** : DISTINGUISHED, PROMINENT ⟨two ∼ politicians made speeches⟩

²notable *n* : a person of note ✦ *Synonyms* BIGWIG, EMINENCE, NABOB, PERSONAGE, SOMEBODY, VIP

no·ta·bly \ˈnō-tə-blē\ *adv* **1** : in a notable manner **2** : ESPECIALLY, PARTICULARLY

no·tar·i·al \nō-ʰter-ē-əl\ *adj* : of, relating to, or done by a notary public

no·ta·rize \ˈnō-tə-ˌrīz\ *vb* **-rized; -riz·ing** : to acknowledge or make legally authentic as a notary public

no·ta·ry public \ˈnō-tə-rē-\ *n, pl* **notaries public** *or* **notary publics** : a public official who attests or certifies writings (as deeds) to make them legally authentic

no·ta·tion \nō-ʰtā-shən\ *n* **1** : ANNOTATION, NOTE **2** : the act, process, or method of representing data by marks, signs, figures, or characters; *also* : a system of symbols (as letters, numerals, or musical notes) used in such notation

¹notch \ˈnäch\ *n* **1** : a V-shaped hollow in an edge or surface **2** : a narrow pass between two mountains

²**notch** *vb* **1** : to cut or make notches in **2** : to score or record by or as if by cutting a series of notches ⟨~ed 20 points for the team⟩

notch·back \'näch-ˌbak\ *n* : an automobile with a trunk whose lid forms a distinct deck

¹**note** \'nōt\ *vb* **not·ed; not·ing 1** : to notice or observe with care ⟨noted her reaction⟩; *also* : to record or preserve in writing **2** : to make special mention of : REMARK

²**note** *n* **1** : a musical sound **2** : a cry, call, or sound esp. of a bird **3** : a special tone in a person's words or voice ⟨a ~ of fear⟩ **4** : a character in music used to indicate duration of a tone by its shape and pitch by its position on the staff **5** : a characteristic feature : MOOD, QUALITY ⟨a ~ of optimism⟩ **6** : MEMORANDUM **7** : a brief and informal record; *also* : a written or printed comment or explanation **8** : a written promise to pay a debt **9** : a piece of paper money **10** : a short informal letter **11** : a formal diplomatic or official communication **12** : DISTINCTION, REPUTATION ⟨an artist of ~⟩ **13** : OBSERVATION, NOTICE, HEED ⟨take ~ of the time⟩

note·book \'nōt-ˌbůk\ *n* **1** : a book for notes or memoranda **2** : a portable microcomputer smaller than a laptop computer

not·ed \'nō-təd\ *adj* : well known by reputation : EMINENT ⟨a ~ violinist⟩

note·wor·thy \'nōt-ˌwər-thē\ *adj* : worthy of note : REMARKABLE

¹**noth·ing** \'nə-thiŋ\ *pron* **1** : no thing ⟨leaves ~ to the imagination⟩ **2** : no part **3** : one of no interest, value, or importance ⟨she's ~ to me⟩ **4** : a light playful remark ⟨sweet ~s⟩

²**nothing** *adv* : not at all : in no degree

³**nothing** *n* **1** : something that does not exist **2** : ZERO **3** : a person or thing of little or no value or importance

⁴**nothing** *adj* : of no account : WORTHLESS

noth·ing·ness \'nə-thiŋ-nəs\ *n* **1** : the quality or state of being nothing **2** : NONEXISTENCE; *also* : utter insignificance **3** : something insignificant or valueless

¹**no·tice** \'nō-təs\ *n* **1** : WARNING, ANNOUNCEMENT **2** : notification of the termination of an agreement or contract at a specified time **3** : ATTENTION, HEED ⟨bring the matter to my ~⟩ **4** : a written or printed announcement **5** : a short critical account or examination (as of a play) : REVIEW

²**notice** *vb* **no·ticed; no·tic·ing 1** : to make mention of : remark on : NOTE **2** : to take notice of : OBSERVE, MARK

no·tice·able \'nō-tə-sə-bəl\ *adj* **1** : worthy of notice **2** : likely to be noticed ⟨a ~ scar⟩ — **no·tice·ably** \-blē\ *adv*

no·ti·fy \'nō-tə-ˌfī\ *vb* **-fied; -fy·ing 1** : to give notice of : report the occurrence of **2** : to give notice to — **no·ti·fi·ca·tion** \ˌnō-tə-fə-'kā-shən\ *n*

no·tion \'nō-shən\ *n* **1** : IDEA, CONCEPTION ⟨have a ~ of what he means⟩ **2** : a belief held : OPINION, VIEW **3** : WHIM, FANCY ⟨a sudden ~ to go⟩ **4** *pl* : small useful articles (as pins, needles, or thread)

no·tion·al \'nō-shə-nəl\ *adj* **1** : existing in the mind only : IMAGINARY, UNREAL **2** : given to foolish or fanciful moods or ideas : WHIMSICAL

no·to·ri·ous \nō-'tōr-ē-əs\ *adj* : generally known and talked of; *esp* : widely and unfavorably known — **no·to·ri·ety** \ˌnō-tə-'rī-ə-tē\ *n* — **no·to·ri·ous·ly** \nō-'tōr-ē-əs-lē\ *adv*

¹**not·with·stand·ing** \ˌnät-with-'stan-diŋ, -with-\ *prep* : in spite of

²**notwithstanding** *adv* : NEVERTHELESS

³**notwithstanding** *conj* : ALTHOUGH

nou·gat \'nü-gət\ *n* [F, fr. Occitan, fr. Old Occitan, *nogat*, fr. *noga* nut, ultim. fr. L *nuc-, nux*] : a confection of nuts or fruit pieces in a sugar paste

nought *var of* NAUGHT

noun \'naůn\ *n* : a word that is the name of a subject of discourse (as a person or place)

nour·ish \'nər-ish\ *vb* : to promote the growth or development of

nour·ish·ing *adj* : giving nourishment

nour·ish·ment \'nər-ish-mənt\ *n* **1** : FOOD, NUTRIENT **2** : the action or process of nourishing

nou·veau riche \ˌnü-ˌvō-'rēsh\ *n, pl* **nou·veaux riches** *same*\ [F] : a person newly rich : PARVENU

Nov *abbr* November

no·va \'nō-və\ *n, pl* **novas** *or* **no·vae** \-ˌ)vē, -ˌvī\ [NL, fem. of L *novus* new] : a star that suddenly increases greatly in brightness and then within a few months or years grows dim again

¹**nov·el** \'nä-vəl\ *adj* **1** : having no precedent : NEW **2** : STRANGE, UNUSUAL

²**novel** *n* : a long invented prose narrative dealing with human experience through a connected sequence of events — **nov·el·ist** \-və-list\ *n*

nov·el·ette \ˌnä-və-'let\ *n* : a brief novel or long short story

nov·el·ize \'nä-və-ˌlīz\ *vb* **-ized; -iz·ing** : to convert into the form of a novel — **nov·el·i·za·tion** \ˌnä-və-lə-'zā-shən\ *n*

no·vel·la \nō-'ve-lə\ *n, pl* **novellas** *or* **no·vel·le** \-'ve-lē\ : NOVELETTE

nov·el·ty \'nä-vəl-tē\ *n, pl* **-ties 1** : something new or unusual **2** : NEWNESS **3** : a small manufactured article intended mainly for personal or household adornment — usu. used in pl.

No·vem·ber \nō-'vem-bər\ *n* [ME *Novembre*, fr. AF, fr. L *November* ninth month of the early Roman calendar, fr. *novem* nine] : the 11th month of the year

no·ve·na \nō-'vē-nə\ *n* : a Roman Catholic nine-day period of prayer

nov·ice \'nä-vəs\ *n* **1** : a new member of a religious order who is preparing to take the vows of religion **2** : one who is inexperienced or untrained

no·vi·tiate \nō-'vi-shət\ *n* **1** : the period or state of being a novice **2** : a house where novices are trained **3** : NOVICE

¹**now** \'naů\ *adv* **1** : at the present time or moment **2** : in the time immediately before the present **3** : IMMEDIATELY, FORTHWITH **4** — used with the sense of present time weakened or lost (as to express command, introduce an important point, or indicate a transition) ⟨~ hear this⟩ **5** : SOMETIMES ⟨~ one and ~ another⟩ **6** : under the present circumstances **7** : at the time referred to **8** : by this time

²**now** *conj* : in view of the fact ⟨~ that you're here, we'll start⟩

³**now** *n* : the present time or moment : PRESENT

⁴**now** *adj* **1** : of or relating to the present time ⟨the ~ president⟩ **2** : excitingly new ⟨~ clothes⟩; *also* : constantly aware of what is new ⟨~ people⟩

NOW *abbr* **1** National Organization for Women **2** negotiable order of withdrawal

now·a·days \'naů-ə-ˌdāz\ *adv* : at the present time

no·way \'nō-ˌwā\ *or* **no·ways** \-ˌwāz\ *adv* : NOWISE

no·where \-ˌhwer\ *adv* **1** : not anywhere **2** : not at all — usu. used with *near* ⟨~ near enough⟩ — **nowhere** *n*

no·wise \'nō-ˌwīz\ *adv* : in no way

nox·ious \'näk-shəs\ *adj* : harmful esp. to health or morals

noz·zle \'nä-zəl\ *n* : a short tube constricted in the middle or at one end and used (as on a hose) to speed up or direct a flow of fluid

np *abbr* **1** no pagination **2** no place (of publication)

Np *symbol* neptunium

NP *abbr* notary public

NR *abbr* not rated

NRA *abbr* National Rifle Association

NS *abbr* **1** not specified **2** Nova Scotia

NSA *abbr* National Security Agency

NSC *abbr* National Security Council

NSF *abbr* **1** National Science Foundation **2** not sufficient funds

NSW *abbr* New South Wales

NT *abbr* **1** New Testament **2** Northern Territory **3** Northwest Territories

nth \'enth\ *adj* **1** : numbered with an unspecified or indefinitely large ordinal number ⟨for the ~ time⟩ **2** : EXTREME, UTMOST ⟨to the ~ degree⟩

NTP *abbr* normal temperature and pressure

nt wt *or* **n wt** *abbr* net weight

nu \'nü, 'nyü\ *n* : the 13th letter of the Greek alphabet — N or ν

NU *abbr* name unknown

nu·ance \'nü-ˌäns, 'nyü-, nü-'äns, nyü-\ *n* [F] : a shade of difference : a delicate variation (as in tone or meaning)

nub \'nəb\ *n* **1** : KNOB, LUMP **2** : GIST, POINT ⟨the ~ of the story⟩
nub·bin \'nə-bən\ *n* **1** : something (as an ear of corn) that is small for its kind, stunted, undeveloped, or imperfect **2** : a small projecting bit
nu·bile \'nü-,bī(-ə)l, 'nyü-, -bəl\ *adj* **1** : of marriageable condition or age **2** : sexually attractive — used of a young woman
nu·cle·ar \'nü-klē-ər, 'nyü-\ *adj* **1** : of, relating to, or constituting a nucleus **2** : of, relating to, or using the atomic nucleus or energy derived from it **3** : of, relating to, or being a weapon whose destructive power results from an uncontrolled nuclear reaction
nu·cle·ate \'nü-klē-,āt, 'nyü-\ *vb* **-at·ed; -at·ing** : to form, act as, or have a nucleus — **nu·cle·ation** \,nü-klē-'ā-shən, ,nyü-\ *n*
nu·cle·ic acid \nú-'klē-ik-, nyü-, -'klā-\ *n* : any of various complex organic acids (as DNA or RNA) found esp. in cell nuclei
nu·cle·o·tide \'nü-klē-ə-,tīd, 'nyü-\ *n* : any of several compounds that are the basic structural units of nucleic acids
nu·cle·us \'nü-klē-əs, 'nyü-\ *n, pl* **nu·clei** \-klē-,ī\ *also* **nu·cle·us·es** [NL, fr. L, kernel, dim. of *nuc-, nux* nut] **1** : a central mass or part about which matter gathers or is collected : CORE **2** : a cell part that is characteristic of all living things except viruses, bacteria, and certain algae, that is necessary for heredity and for making proteins, that contains the chromosomes with their genes, and that is enclosed in a membrane **3** : a mass of gray matter or group of cell bodies of neurons in the central nervous system **4** : the central part of an atom that comprises nearly all of the atomic mass **5** : a basic or essential part
¹nude \'nüd, 'nyüd\ *adj* **nud·er; nud·est 1** : BARE, NAKED, UNCLOTHED **2** : featuring or catering to naked people ⟨a ~ beach⟩ — **nu·di·ty** \'nü-də-tē, 'nyü-\ *n*
²nude *n* **1** : a nude human figure esp. as depicted in art **2** : the condition of being nude ⟨in the ~⟩
nudge \'nəj\ *vb* **nudged; nudg·ing** : to touch or push gently (as with the elbow) usu. in order to seek attention — **nudge** *n*
nud·ism \'nü-,di-zəm, 'nyü-\ *n* : the practice of going nude esp. in mixed groups at specially secluded places — **nud·ist** \-dist\ *n*
nu·ga·to·ry \'nü-gə-,tór-ē\ *adj* **1** : INCONSEQUENTIAL, WORTHLESS ⟨his efforts were rendered ~⟩ **2** : having no force : INEFFECTUAL
nug·get \'nə-gət\ *n* **1** : a lump of precious metal (as gold) **2** : TIDBIT
nui·sance \'nü-s°ns, 'nyü-\ *n* : an annoying or troublesome person or thing
nuisance tax *n* : an excise tax collected in small amounts directly from the consumer
¹nuke \'nük, 'nyük\ *n* **1** : a nuclear weapon **2** : a nuclear power plant
²nuke *vb* **nuked; nuk·ing 1** : to attack with nuclear weapons **2** : MICROWAVE
null \'nəl\ *adj* **1** : having no legal or binding force : INVALID, VOID **2** : amounting to nothing **3** : INSIGNIFICANT — **nul·li·ty** \'nə-lə-tē\ *n*
null and void *adj* : having no force, binding power, or validity
nul·li·fy \'nə-lə-,fī\ *vb* **-fied; -fy·ing** : to make null or valueless; *also* : ANNUL — **nul·li·fi·ca·tion** \,nə-lə-fə-'kā-shən\ *n*
num *abbr* numeral
Num *or* **Numb** *abbr* Numbers
numb \'nəm\ *adj* : lacking sensation or emotion : BENUMBED — **numb** *vb* — **numb·ly** *adv* — **numb·ness** *n*
¹num·ber \'nəm-bər\ *n* **1** : the total of individuals or units taken together **2** : an indefinite total ⟨a small ~ of tickets remain unsold⟩ **3** : an ascertainable total ⟨the sands of the desert are without ~⟩ **4** : a distinction of word form to denote reference to one or more than one **5** : a unit belonging to a mathematical system and subject to its laws; *also, pl* : ARITHMETIC **6** : a symbol used to represent a mathematical number; *also* : such a number used to identify or designate ⟨a phone ~⟩ **7** : one in a series of musical or theatrical performances ⟨tripped and did a ~ on her knee⟩ **8** : an act of transforming or impairing
☞ the NUMBER table is on page 344
²number *vb* **1** : COUNT, ENUMERATE **2** : to include with or

be one of a group **3** : to restrict to a small or definite number **4** : to assign a number to **5** : to comprise in number : TOTAL
num·ber·less \-ləs\ *adj* : INNUMERABLE, COUNTLESS ⟨~ stars in the sky⟩
Numbers *n* — see BIBLE table
numb·ing \'nə-min\ *adj* : tending to make numb ⟨a ~ lecture⟩ ⟨a ~ realization⟩
numbskull *var of* NUMSKULL
nu·mer·acy \'nü-mə-rə-sē, 'nyü-\ *n* : the capacity for quantitative thought or expression
nu·mer·al \'nü-mə-rəl, 'nyü-\ *n* : a conventional symbol representing a number — **numeral** *adj*
nu·mer·ate \'nü-mə-,rāt, 'nyü-\ *vb* **-at·ed; -at·ing** : ENUMERATE
nu·mer·a·tor \-,rā-tər\ *n* : the part of a fraction above the line
nu·mer·ic \nú-'mer-ik, nyü-\ *adj* : NUMERICAL; *esp* : denoting a number or a system of numbers
nu·mer·i·cal \-'mer-i-kəl\ *adj* **1** : of or relating to numbers ⟨in ~ order⟩ **2** : expressed in or involving numbers — **nu·mer·i·cal·ly** \-k(ə-)lē\ *adv*
nu·mer·ol·o·gy \,nü-mə-'rä-lə-jē, ,nyü-\ *n* : the study of the occult significance of numbers — **nu·mer·ol·o·gist** \-jist\ *n*
nu·mer·ous \'nü-mə-rəs, 'nyü-\ *adj* : consisting of, including, or relating to a great number : MANY
nu·mis·mat·ics \,nü-məz-'ma-tiks, ,nyü-\ *n* : the study or collection of monetary objects — **nu·mis·mat·ic** \-tik\ *adj* — **nu·mis·ma·tist** \nü-'miz-mə-tist, nyü-\ *n*
num·skull *also* **numb·skull** \'nəm-,skəl\ *n* : a stupid person : DUNCE
nun \'nən\ *n* : a woman belonging to a religious order; *esp* : one under solemn vows of poverty, chastity, and obedience
nun·cio \'nən-sē-,ō, 'nún-\ *n, pl* **-ci·os** [It, fr. L *nuntius* messenger] : a permanent high-ranking papal representative to a civil government
nun·nery \'nə-nə-rē\ *n, pl* **-ner·ies** : a convent of nuns
¹nup·tial \'nəp-shəl\ *adj* : of or relating to marriage or a wedding ⟨~ vows⟩
²nuptial *n* : MARRIAGE, WEDDING — usu. used in pl.
¹nurse \'nərs\ *n* [ME *norice, nurse*, fr. AF *nurice*, fr. LL *nutricia*, fr. L, fem. of *nutricius* nourishing] **1** : a girl or woman employed to take care of children **2** : a person trained to care for sick people
²nurse *vb* **nursed; nurs·ing 1** : SUCKLE **2** : to take charge of and watch over **3** : TEND ⟨~ an invalid⟩ **4** : to treat with special care ⟨~ a headache⟩ **5** : to hold in one's mind or consideration ⟨~ a grudge⟩ **6** : to act or serve as a nurse
nurse·maid \'nərs-,mād\ *n* : NURSE 1
nurse-prac·ti·tion·er \-prak-'ti-shə-nər\ *n* : a registered nurse who is qualified to assume some of the duties formerly assumed only by a physician
nurs·ery \'nər-sə-rē\ *n, pl* **-er·ies 1** : a room for children **2** : a place where children are temporarily cared for in their parents' absence **3** : a place where young plants are grown usu. for transplanting
nurs·ery·man \-mən\ *n* : a man who keeps or works in a plant nursery
nursery school *n* : a school for children under kindergarten age
nursing home *n* : a private establishment providing care for persons (as the aged or the chronically ill) who are unable to care for themselves
nurs·ling \'nərs-liŋ\ *n* **1** : one that is solicitously cared for **2** : a nursing child
¹nur·ture \'nər-chər\ *n* **1** : TRAINING, UPBRINGING; *also* : the influences that modify the expression of an individual's heredity **2** : FOOD, NOURISHMENT
²nurture *vb* **nur·tured; nur·tur·ing 1** : to care for : FEED, NOURISH **2** : EDUCATE, TRAIN ⟨~ students⟩ **3** : FOSTER ⟨~ creativity⟩
nut \'nət\ *n* **1** : a dry fruit or seed with a hard shell and a firm inner kernel; *also* : its kernel **2** : a metal block with a hole through it that is fastened to a bolt or screw by means of a screw thread within the hole **3** : the ridge on the upper end of the fingerboard in a stringed musical instrument over which the strings pass **4** : a foolish, eccentric, or crazy person **5** : ENTHUSIAST

NUMBER TABLE

CARDINAL NUMBERS[1]

ORDINAL NUMBERS[4]

NAME[2]	SYMBOL		NAME[5]	SYMBOL[6]
	Arabic	*Roman*[3]		
zero *or* naught *or* cipher	0			
one	1	I	first	1st
two	2	II	second	2d *or* 2nd
three	3	III	third	3d *or* 3rd
four	4	IV	fourth	4th
five	5	V	fifth	5th
six	6	VI	sixth	6th
seven	7	VII	seventh	7th
eight	8	VIII	eighth	8th
nine	9	IX	ninth	9th
ten	10	X	tenth	10th
eleven	11	XI	eleventh	11th
twelve	12	XII	twelfth	12th
thirteen	13	XIII	thirteenth	13th
fourteen	14	XIV	fourteenth	14th
fifteen	15	XV	fifteenth	15th
sixteen	16	XVI	sixteenth	16th
seventeen	17	XVII	seventeenth	17th
eighteen	18	XVIII	eighteenth	18th
nineteen	19	XIX	nineteenth	19th
twenty	20	XX	twentieth	20th
twenty-one	21	XXI	twenty-first	21st
twenty-two	22	XXII	twenty-second	22d *or* 22nd
twenty-three	23	XXIII	twenty-third	23d *or* 23rd
twenty-four	24	XXIV	twenty-fourth	24th
twenty-five	25	XXV	twenty-fifth	25th
twenty-six	26	XXVI	twenty-sixth	26th
twenty-seven	27	XVII	twenty-seventh	27th
twenty-eight	28	XVIII	twenty-eighth	28th
twenty-nine	29	XXIX	twenty-ninth	29th
thirty	30	XXX	thirtieth	30th
thirty-one	31	XXXI	thirty-first	31st
thirty-two *etc*	32	XXXII	thirty-second *etc*	32d *or* 32nd
forty	40	XL	fortieth	40th
forty-one	41	XLI	forty-first	41st
forty-two *etc*	42	XLII	forty-second *etc*	42d *or* 42nd
fifty	50	L	fifty	50th
sixty	60	LX	sixty	60th
seventy	70	LXX	seventieth	70th
eighty	80	LXXX	eightieth	80th
ninety	90	XC	ninetieth	90th
one hundred	100	C	one hundredth	100th
one hundred and one	101	CI	one hundred and first	101st
one hundred and two *etc*	102	CII	one hundred and second *etc*	102d *or* 102nd
two hundred	200	CC	two hundredth	200th
three hundred	300	CCC	three hundredth	300th
four hundred	400	CD	four hundredth	400th
five hundred	500	D	five hundredth	500th
six hundred	600	DC	six hundredth	600th
seven hundred	700	DCC	seven hundredth	700th
eight hundred	800	DCCC	eight hundredth	800th
nine hundred	900	CM	nine hundredth	900th
one thousand	1,000	M	one thousandth	1,000th
two thousand *etc*	2,000	MM	two thousandth *etc*	2,000th
five thousand	5,000	V̄	five thousandth	5,000th
ten thousand	10,000	X̄	ten thousandth	10,000th
one hundred thousand	100,000	C̄	hundred thousandth *or* one hundred thousandth	100,000th
one million	1,000,000	M̄	millionth *or* one millionth	1,000,000th

[1] The cardinal numbers are used in simple counting or in answer to "how many?" The words for these numbers may be used as nouns (he counted to *twelve*), as pronouns (*twelve* were found), or as adjectives (*twelve* girls).

[2] In formal contexts the numbers one to one hundred and in less formal contexts the numbers one to nine are commonly written out in words, while larger numbers are given in numerals. In nearly all contexts a number occurring at the beginning of a sentence is usually written out. Except in very formal contexts numerals are invariably used for dates. Arabic numbers from 1,000 to 9,999 are often written without commas or spaces (1000, 9999). Year numbers are always written without commas (1783).

[3] The Roman numerals are written either in capitals or in lowercase letters.

[4] The ordinal numbers are used to show the order of succession in which such items as names, objects, and periods of time are considered (the *twelfth* month; the *fourth* row of seats; the *18th* century).

[5] Each of the terms for the ordinal numbers excepting *first* and *second* is used in designating one of a number of parts into which a whole may be divided (a *fourth*; a *sixth*; a *tenth*) and as the denominator in fractions designating the number of such parts constituting a certain portion of a whole *one fourth*; *three fifths*). When used as nouns the fractions are usually written as two words, although they are regularly hyphenated as adjectives (a *two-thirds* majority). When fractions are written in numerals, the cardinal symbols are used ($1/4$, $3/5$, $5/6$).

[6] The Arabic symbols for the cardinal numbers may be read as ordinals in certain contexts (January 1 = January first; 2 Samuel = Second Samuel). The Roman numerals are sometimes read as ordinals (Henry IV = Henry the Fourth); sometimes they are written with the ordinal suffixes (XIXth Dynasty).

nut·crack·er \'nət-ˌkra-kər\ *n* : an instrument for cracking nuts

nut·hatch \-ˌhach\ *n* : any of various small tree-climbing chiefly insect-eating birds

nuthatch

nut·meg \-ˌmeg, -ˌmãg\ *n* [ME *notemuge*, ultim. fr. Old Occitan *noz muscada*, lit., musky nut] : a spice made by grinding the nutlike aromatic seed of a tropical tree; *also* : the seed or tree

nu·tria \'nü-trē-ə, 'nyü-\ *n* [Sp] 1 : the durable usu. light brown fur of a nutria 2 : a large So. American aquatic rodent with webbed hind feet

¹**nu·tri·ent** \'nü-trē-ənt, 'nyü-\ *adj* : NOURISHING ⟨∼ deficiencies⟩

²**nutrient** *n* : a nutritive substance or ingredient ⟨fruits and vegetables are important ∼s⟩

nu·tri·ment \-trə-mənt\ *n* : NUTRIENT

nu·tri·tion \nủ-'tri-shən, nyủ-\ *n* : the act or process of nourishing; *esp* : the processes by which an individual takes in and utilizes food material — **nu·tri·tion·al** \-shə-nəl\ *adj* — **nu·tri·tion·al·ly** *adv* — **nu·tri·tion·ist** \-shə-nist\ *n* — **nu·tri·tive** \'nü-trə-tiv, 'nyü-\ *adj*

nu·tri·tious \-shəs\ *adj* : NOURISHING — **nu·tri·tious·ly** *adv*

nuts \'nəts\ *adj* 1 : ENTHUSIASTIC, KEEN 2 : CRAZY, DEMENTED

nut·shell \'nət-ˌshel\ *n* : the shell of a nut — **in a nutshell** : in a few words ⟨that's the story *in a nutshell*⟩

nut·ty \'nə-tē\ *adj* **nut·ti·er; -est** 1 : containing or suggesting nuts ⟨a ∼ flavor⟩ 2 : mentally unbalanced

nuz·zle \'nə-zəl\ *vb* **nuz·zled; nuz·zling** 1 : to root around, push, or touch with or as if with the nose 2 : NESTLE, SNUGGLE

NV *abbr* Nevada

NW *abbr* northwest

NWT *abbr* Northwest Territories

NY *abbr* New York

NYC *abbr* New York City

ny·lon \'nī-ˌlän\ *n* 1 : any of numerous strong tough elastic synthetic materials used esp. in textiles and plastics 2 *pl* : stockings made of nylon

nymph \'nimf\ *n* 1 : any of the lesser goddesses in ancient mythology represented as maidens living in the mountains, forests, meadows, and waters 2 : GIRL 3 : an immature insect resembling the adult but smaller, less differentiated, and usu. lacking developed wings

nym·pho·ma·nia \ˌnim-fə-'mā-nē-ə, -nyə\ *n* : excessive sexual desire by a female — **nym·pho·ma·ni·ac** \-nē-ˌak\ *n or adj*

NZ *abbr* New Zealand

O

¹**o** \'ō\ *n, pl* **o's** *or* **os** \'ōz\ *often cap* 1 : the 15th letter of the English alphabet 2 : ZERO

²**o** *abbr, often cap* 1 ocean 2 Ohio 3 ohm

¹**O** *var of* OH

²**O** *symbol* oxygen

o/a *abbr* on or about

oaf \'ōf\ *n* : a stupid or awkward person — **oaf·ish** *adj*

oak \'ōk\ *n, pl* **oaks** *or* **oak** : any of a genus of trees or shrubs related to the beech and chestnut and bearing a rounded thin-shelled nut surrounded at the base by a hardened cup; *also* : the usu. tough hard durable wood of an oak — **oak·en** \'ō-kən\ *adj*

oa·kum \'ō-kəm\ *n* [ME *okum*, fr. OE *ācumba* flax fiber, from *ā*- out + *-cumba* (akin to OE *camb* comb)] : loosely twisted hemp or jute fiber impregnated with tar and used esp. in caulking ships

oar \'ȯr\ *n* : a long pole with a broad blade at one end used for propelling or steering a boat

oar·lock \'ȯr-ˌläk\ *n* : a U-shaped device for holding an oar in place

oars·man \'ȯrz-mən\ *n* : one who rows esp. in a racing crew

OAS *abbr* Organization of American States

oa·sis \ō-'ā-səs\ *n, pl* **oa·ses** \-ˌsēz\ : a fertile or green area in an arid region

oat \'ōt\ *n* : a cereal grass widely grown for its edible seed; *also* : this seed — **oat·en** \'ō-tᵊn\ *adj*

oat·cake \'ōt-ˌkāk\ *n* : a thin flat oatmeal cake

oath \'ōth\ *n, pl* **oaths** \'ōthz, 'ōths\ 1 : a solemn appeal to God to witness to the truth of a statement or the sacredness of a promise 2 : an irreverent or careless use of a sacred name

oat·meal \'ōt-ˌmēl\ *n* 1 : ground or rolled oats 2 : porridge made from ground or rolled oatmeal

Ob *or* **Obad** *abbr* Obadiah

Oba·di·ah \ˌō-bə-'dī-ə\ *n* — see BIBLE table

ob·bli·ga·to \ˌä-blə-'gä-tō\ *n, pl* **-tos** *also* **-ti** \-'gä-tē\ [It] : an accompanying part usu. played by a solo instrument

ob·du·rate \'äb-də-rət, -dyə-\ *adj* : stubbornly resistant

: UNYIELDING ⟨an ∼ denial⟩ ♦ *Synonyms* INFLEXIBLE, ADAMANT, RIGID, UNCOMPROMISING — **ob·du·ra·cy** \-rə-sē\ *n*

obe·di·ent \ō-'bē-dē-ənt\ *adj* : submissive to the restraint or command of authority ♦ *Synonyms* DOCILE, TRACTABLE, AMENABLE, BIDDABLE — **obe·di·ence** \-əns\ *n* — **obe·di·ent·ly** *adv*

obei·sance \ō-'bē-səns, -'bā-\ *n* 1 : a bow made to show respect or submission 2 : DEFERENCE, HOMAGE ⟨makes ∼ to her mentors⟩

obe·lisk \'ä-bə-ˌlisk\ *n* [MF *obelisque*, fr. L *obeliscus*, fr. Gk *obeliskos*, fr. dim. of *obelos* spit, pointed pillar] : a 4-sided pillar that tapers toward the top and ends in a pyramid

obese \ō-'bēs\ *adj* [L *obesus*, fr. *ob*- against + *esus*, pp. of *edere* to eat] : having excessive body fat ♦ *Synonyms* CORPULENT, FLESHY, GROSS, OVERWEIGHT, PORTLY, STOUT — **obe·si·ty** \-'bē-sə-tē\ *n*

obey \ō-'bā\ *vb* **obeyed; obey·ing** 1 : to follow the commands or guidance of : behave obediently 2 : to comply with ⟨∼ orders⟩ ♦ *Synonyms* CONFORM, KEEP, MIND, OBSERVE

ob·fus·cate \'äb-fə-ˌskāt\ *vb* **-cat·ed; -cat·ing** 1 : to make dark or obscure 2 : to make difficult to understand — **ob·fus·ca·tion** \ˌäb-fəs-'kā-shən\ *n*

OB-GYN *abbr* obstetrician gynecologist; obstetrics gynecology

obi \'ō-bē\ *n* [Jp] : a broad sash worn esp. with a Japanese kimono

obit \ō-'bit, 'ō-bət\ *n* : OBITUARY

obi·ter dic·tum \ˌō-bə-tər-'dik-təm\ *n, pl* **obiter dic·ta** \-tə\ [LL, lit., something said in passing] : an incidental remark or observation

obit·u·ary \ə-'bi-chə-ˌwer-ē\ *n, pl* **-ar·ies** : a notice of a person's death usu. with a short biographical account

obj *abbr* object; objective

¹**ob·ject** \'äb-jikt\ *n* 1 : something that may be seen or felt; *also* : something that may be perceived or examined men-

tally **2** : something that arouses an emotional response (as of affection or pity) **3** : AIM, PURPOSE ⟨the ~ is to raise money⟩ **4** : a word or word group denoting that which the action of the verb is directed on or toward; *also* : a noun or noun equivalent in a prepositional phrase

²**ob·ject** \äb-'jekt\ *vb* **1** : to offer in opposition **2** : to oppose something; *also* : DISAPPROVE ♦ *Synonyms* PROTEST, REMONSTRATE, EXPOSTULATE — **ob·jec·tor** \-'jek-tər\ *n*

object code *n* : a computer program after translation from source code

ob·jec·ti·fy \əb-'jek-tə-ˌfī\ *vb* **-fied; -fy·ing** : to make objective

ob·jec·tion \əb-'jek-shən\ *n* **1** : the act of objecting **2** : a reason for or a feeling of disapproval

ob·jec·tion·able \əb-'jek-shə-nə-bəl\ *adj* : UNDESIRABLE, OFFENSIVE — **ob·jec·tion·ably** \-blē\ *adv*

¹**ob·jec·tive** \äb-'jek-tiv\ *adj* **1** : of or relating to an object or end **2** : existing outside and independent of the mind **3** : of, relating to, or constituting a grammatical case marking typically the object of a verb or preposition **4** : treating or dealing with facts without distortion by personal feelings or prejudices — **ob·jec·tive·ly** *adv* — **ob·jec·tive·ness** *n* — **ob·jec·tiv·i·ty** \ˌäb-jek-'ti-və-tē\ *n*

²**objective** *n* **1** : the lens (as in a microscope) nearest the object and forming an image of it **2** : an aim, goal, or end of action

ob·jet d'art \ˌōb-ˌzhä-'där\ *n, pl* **ob·jets d'art** *same*\ [F] **1** : an article of artistic worth **2** : CURIO ♦ *Synonyms* KNICKKNACK, BAUBLE, BIBELOT, GEWGAW, NOVELTY, TRINKET

ob·jet trou·vé \ˌōb-ˌzhä-trü-'vā\ *n, pl* **objets trouvés** *same*\ [F, lit., found object] : a found natural or discarded object (as a piece of driftwood or an old bathtub) held to have aesthetic value

ob·jur·ga·tion \ˌäb-jər-'gā-shən\ *n* : a harsh rebuke — **ob·jur·gate** \'äb-jər-ˌgāt\ *vb*

obl *abbr* **1** oblique **2** oblong

ob·late \ä-'blāt\ *adj* : flattened or depressed at the poles ⟨an ~ spheroid⟩

ob·la·tion \ə-'blā-shən\ *n* : a religious offering

ob·li·gate \'ä-blə-ˌgāt\ *vb* **-gat·ed; -gat·ing** : to bind legally or morally

ob·li·ga·tion \ˌä-blə-'gā-shən\ *n* **1** : an act of obligating oneself to a course of action **2** : something (as a promise or a contract) that binds one to a course of action **3** : INDEBTEDNESS; *also* : LIABILITY **4** : DUTY — **oblig·a·to·ry** \ə-'bli-gə-ˌtōr-ē\ *adj*

oblige \ə-'blīj\ *vb* **obliged; oblig·ing** [ME, fr. AF *obliger*, fr. L *obligare*, lit., to bind to, fr. *ob-* toward + *ligare* to bind] **1** : FORCE, COMPEL ⟨the soldiers were *obliged* to retreat⟩ **2** : to bind by a favor; *also* : to do a favor for or do something as a favor

oblig·ing *adj* : willing to do favors — **oblig·ing·ly** *adv*

oblique \ō-'blēk\ *adj* **1** : neither perpendicular nor parallel : SLANTING **2** : not straightforward : INDIRECT — **oblique·ly** *adv* — **oblique·ness** *n* — **obliq·ui·ty** \-'bli-kwə-tē\ *n*

oblique case *n* : a grammatical case other than the nominative or vocative

oblit·er·ate \ə-'bli-tə-ˌrāt\ *vb* **-at·ed; -at·ing** [L *oblitterare*, fr. *ob* in the way of + *littera* letter] **1** : to remove from recognition or memory **2** : to make undecipherable by wiping out or covering over **3** : CANCEL — **oblit·er·a·tion** \-ˌbli-tə-'rā-shən\ *n*

obliv·i·on \ə-'bli-vē-ən\ *n* **1** : the condition of being oblivious **2** : the condition or state of being forgotten

obliv·i·ous \ə-'bli-ve-əs\ *adj* **1** : lacking memory or mindful attention **2** : UNAWARE ⟨~ of the risks⟩ — **obliv·i·ous·ly** *adv* — **obliv·i·ous·ness** *n*

ob·long \'ä-ˌblȯŋ\ *adj* : deviating from a square, circular, or spherical form by elongation in one dimension — **oblong** *n*

ob·lo·quy \'ä-blə-kwē\ *n, pl* **-quies** **1** : strongly condemnatory utterance or language **2** : bad repute : DISGRACE ♦ *Synonyms* DISHONOR, SHAME, INFAMY, DISREPUTE, IGNOMINY

ob·nox·ious \äb-'näk-shəs\ *adj* : REPUGNANT, OFFENSIVE ⟨~ behavior⟩ — **ob·nox·ious·ly** *adv* — **ob·nox·ious·ness** *n*

oboe \'ō-bō\ *n* [It, fr. F *hautbois*, fr. *haut* high + *bois* wood] : a woodwind instrument with a slender conical

tube and a double reed mouthpiece — **obo·ist** \'ō-ˌbō-ist\ *n*

ob·scene \äb-'sēn\ *adj* **1** : REPULSIVE **2** : deeply offensive to morality or decency; *esp* : designed to incite to lust or depravity ♦ *Synonyms* GROSS, VULGAR, COARSE, CRUDE, INDECENT — **ob·scene·ly** *adv* — **ob·scen·i·ty** \-'se-nə-tē\ *n*

ob·scu·ran·tism \äb-'skyu̇r-ən-ˌti-zəm, ˌäb-skyu̇-'ran-\ *n* **1** : opposition to the spread of knowledge **2** : deliberate vagueness or abstruseness — **ob·scu·ran·tist** \-tist\ *n or adj*

¹**ob·scure** \äb-'skyu̇r\ *adj* **1** : DIM, GLOOMY **2** : not readily understood : VAGUE **3** : REMOTE; *also* : HUMBLE ♦ *Synonyms* DARK, DUSKY, MURKY, TENEBROUS — **ob·scure·ly** *adv* — **ob·scu·ri·ty** \-'skyu̇r-ə-tē\ *n*

²**obscure** *vb* **ob·scured; ob·scur·ing** **1** : to make dark, dim, or indistinct **2** : to conceal or hide by or as if by covering

ob·se·qui·ous \əb-'sē-kwē-əs\ *adj* : humbly or excessively attentive (as to a person in authority) : FAWNING, SYCOPHANTIC ♦ *Synonyms* MENIAL, SERVILE, SLAVISH, SUBSERVIENT — **ob·se·qui·ous·ly** *adv* — **ob·se·qui·ous·ness** *n*

ob·se·quy \'äb-sə-kwē\ *n, pl* **-quies** : a funeral or burial rite — usu. used in pl.

ob·serv·able \əb-'zər-və-bəl\ *adj* **1** : NOTEWORTHY **2** : capable of being observed — **ob·serv·abil·i·ty** \-'bi-lə-tē\ *n*

ob·ser·vance \əb-'zər-vəns\ *n* **1** : a customary practice or ceremony **2** : an act or instance of following a custom, rule, or law **3** : OBSERVATION

ob·ser·vant \-vənt\ *adj* **1** : WATCHFUL ⟨~ spectators⟩ **2** : KEEN, PERCEPTIVE **3** : MINDFUL ⟨~ of the amenities⟩

¹**ob·ser·va·tion** \ˌäb-sər-'vā-shən, -zər-\ *n* **1** : an act or instance of observing **2** : the gathering of information (as for scientific studies) by noting facts or occurrences **3** : a conclusion drawn from observing; *also* : REMARK, STATEMENT **4** : the fact of being observed — **ob·ser·va·tion·al** \-shə-nəl\ *adj*

²**observation** *adj* : designed for use in viewing or in making observations

ob·ser·va·to·ry \əb-'zər-və-ˌtōr-ē\ *n, pl* **-ries** : a place or institution equipped for observation of natural phenomena (as in astronomy)

ob·serve \əb-'zərv\ *vb* **ob·served; ob·serv·ing** **1** : to conform one's action or practice to **2** : CELEBRATE **3** : to make a scientific observation of **4** : to see or sense esp. through careful attention **5** : to come to realize esp. through consideration of noted facts **6** : REMARK — **ob·serv·er** *n*

ob·sess \äb-'ses\ *vb* : to preoccupy intensely or abnormally

ob·ses·sion \äb-'se-shən\ *n* : a persistent disturbing preoccupation with an idea or feeling; *also* : an emotion or idea causing such a preoccupation — **ob·ses·sive** \-'se-siv\ *adj or n* — **ob·ses·sive·ly** *adv*

obsessive–compulsive *adj* : relating to, characterized by, or affected with recurring obsessions and compulsions esp. as symptoms of a neurotic state

ob·sid·i·an \äb-'si-dē-ən\ *n* : a dark natural glass formed by the cooling of molten lava

ob·so·les·cent \ˌäb-sə-'le-sᵊnt\ *adj* : going out of use : becoming obsolete ⟨~ computers⟩ — **ob·so·les·cence** \-sᵊns\ *n*

ob·so·lete \ˌäb-sə-'lēt, 'äb-sə-ˌlēt\ *adj* : no longer in use; *also* : OLD-FASHIONED ⟨an ~ technology⟩ ♦ *Synonyms* EXTINCT, OUTWORN, PASSÉ, SUPERSEDED

ob·sta·cle \'äb-sti-kəl\ *n* : something that stands in the way or opposes

ob·stet·rics \əb-'ste-triks\ *n sing or pl* : a branch of medicine that deals with birth and with its antecedents and sequels — **ob·stet·ric** \-trik\ *or* **ob·stet·ri·cal** \-tri-kəl\ *adj* — **ob·ste·tri·cian** \ˌäb-stə-'tri-shən\ *n*

ob·sti·nate \'äb-stə-nət\ *adj* : fixed and unyielding (as in an opinion or course) despite reason or persuasion : STUBBORN ⟨~ opposition⟩ — **ob·sti·na·cy** \-nə-sē\ *n* — **ob·sti·nate·ly** *adv*

ob·strep·er·ous \əb-'stre-pə-rəs\ *adj* **1** : uncontrollably noisy **2** : stubbornly resistant to control : UNRULY — **ob·strep·er·ous·ness** *n*

ob·struct \əb-'strəkt\ *vb* **1** : to block by an obstacle **2** : to impede the passage, action, or operation of **3** : to cut off from sight — **ob·struc·tive** \-'strək-tiv\ *adj* — **ob·struc·tor** \-tər\ *n*

ob·struc·tion \əb-'strək-shən\ *n* **1** : an act of obstructing : the state of being obstructed **2** : something that obstructs : HINDRANCE

ob·struc·tion·ist \-shə-nist\ *n* : a person who hinders progress or business esp. in a legislative body — **ob·struc·tion·ism** \-shə-,ni-zəm\ *n*

ob·tain \əb-'tān\ *vb* **1** : to gain or attain usu. by planning or effort **2** : to be generally recognized or established ✦ **Synonyms** PROCURE, SECURE, WIN, EARN, ACQUIRE — **ob·tain·able** *adj*

ob·trude \əb-'trüd\ *vb* **ob·trud·ed; ob·trud·ing 1** : to thrust out **2** : to thrust forward without warrant or request **3** : INTRUDE — **ob·tru·sion** \-'trü-zhən\ *n* — **ob·tru·sive** \-'trü-siv\ *adj* — **ob·tru·sive·ly** *adv* — **ob·tru·sive·ness** *n*

ob·tuse \əb-'tüs, -'tyüs\ *adj* **ob·tus·er; -est 1** : exceeding 90 degrees but less than 180 degrees ⟨~ angle⟩ **2** : not pointed or acute : BLUNT **3** : not sharp or quick of wit ⟨is too ~ to take a hint⟩ — **ob·tuse·ly** *adv* — **ob·tuse·ness** *n*

obv *abbr* obverse

¹ob·verse \äb-'vərs, 'äb-,vərs\ *adj* **1** : facing the observer or opponent **2** : being a counterpart or complement — **ob·verse·ly** *adv*

²ob·verse \'äb-,vərs, äb-'vərs\ *n* **1** : the side (as of a coin) bearing the principal design and lettering **2** : a front or principal surface **3** : a counterpart having the opposite orientation or force

ob·vi·ate \'äb-vē-,āt\ *vb* **-at·ed; -at·ing** : to anticipate and prevent (as a situation) or make unnecessary (as an action) ✦ **Synonyms** PREVENT, AVERT, FORESTALL, FORFEND, PRECLUDE — **ob·vi·a·tion** \,äb-vē-'ā-shən\ *n*

ob·vi·ous \'äb-vē-əs\ *adj* [L *obvius,* fr. *obviam* in the way, fr. *ob* in the way of + *viam,* acc. of *via* way] : easily found, seen, or understood : PLAIN ✦ **Synonyms** EVIDENT, MANIFEST, PATENT, CLEAR — **ob·vi·ous·ly** *adv* — **ob·vi·ous·ness** *n*

OC *abbr* officer candidate

oc·a·ri·na \,ä-kə-'rē-nə\ *n* [It] : a wind instrument typically having an oval body with finger holes and a projecting mouthpiece

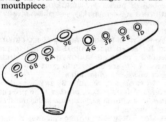

ocarina

occas *abbr* occasionally

¹oc·ca·sion \ə-'kā-zhən\ *n* **1** : a favorable opportunity **2** : a direct or indirect cause **3** : the time of an event **4** : EXIGENCY **5** *pl* : AFFAIRS, BUSINESS **6** : a special event : CELEBRATION

²occasion *vb* : BRING ABOUT, CAUSE

oc·ca·sion·al \ə-'kā-zhə-nəl\ *adj* **1** : happening or met with now and then ⟨~ visits⟩ **2** : used or designed for a special occasion ⟨~ verse⟩ ✦ **Synonyms** INFREQUENT, RARE, SPORADIC — **oc·ca·sion·al·ly** *adv*

oc·ci·den·tal \,äk-sə-'den-tᵊl\ *adj, often cap* [fr. *Occident* West, fr. ME, fr. AF, fr. L *occident-, occidens,* fr. prp. of *occidere* to fall, set (of the sun)] : WESTERN — **Occidental** *n*

Oc·ci·tan \'äk-sə-,tan\ *n* [F, fr. ML *occitanus,* fr. Old Occitan *oc* yes (contrasted with OF *oïl* yes)] : a Romance language spoken in southern France

oc·clude \ə-'klüd\ *vb* **oc·clud·ed; oc·clud·ing 1** : OBSTRUCT ⟨an *occluded* artery⟩ **2** : to come together with opposing surfaces in contact — used of teeth — **oc·clu·sion** \-'klü-zhən\ *n* — **oc·clu·sive** \-'klü-siv\ *adj*

¹oc·cult \ə-'kəlt\ *adj* **1** : not revealed : SECRET **2** : ABSTRUSE, MYSTERIOUS **3** : of or relating to supernatural agencies, their effects, or knowledge of them ⟨the ~

arts⟩ — **oc·cult·ism** \-'kəl-,ti-zəm\ *n* — **oc·cult·ist** \-tist\ *n*

²occult *n* : occult matters — used with *the*

oc·cu·pan·cy \'ä-kyə-pən-sē\ *n, pl* **-cies 1** : the act of occupying : the state of being occupied **2** : an occupied building or part of a building

oc·cu·pant \-pənt\ *n* : one who occupies something; *esp* : RESIDENT

oc·cu·pa·tion \,ä-kyə-'pā-shən\ *n* **1** : an activity in which one engages; *esp* : VOCATION **2** : the taking possession of property; *also* : the taking possession of an area by a foreign military force — **oc·cu·pa·tion·al** \-shə-nəl\ *adj* — **oc·cu·pa·tion·al·ly** *adv*

occupational therapy *n* : therapy by means of activity; *esp* : creative activity prescribed for its effect in promoting recovery or rehabilitation — **occupational therapist** *n*

oc·cu·py \'ä-kyə-,pī\ *vb* **-pied; -py·ing 1** : to engage the attention or energies of **2** : to fill up (an extent in space or time) **3** : to take or hold possession of **4** : to reside in as owner or tenant — **oc·cu·pi·er** *n*

oc·cur \ə-'kər\ *vb* **oc·curred; oc·cur·ring** [L *occurrere,* fr. *ob-* in the way + *currere* to run] **1** : to be found or met with : APPEAR **2** : HAPPEN ⟨the event will ~ at noon⟩ **3** : to come to mind

oc·cur·rence \ə-'kər-əns\ *n* **1** : something that takes place **2** : the action or process of occurring

ocean \'ō-shən\ *n* **1** : the whole body of salt water that covers nearly three fourths of the surface of the earth **2** : any of the large bodies of water into which the great ocean is divided — **oce·an·ic** \,ō-shē-'a-nik\ *adj*

ocean·ar·i·um \,ō-shə-'nar-ē-əm\ *n, pl* **-iums** *or* **-ia** \-ē-ə\ : a large marine aquarium

ocean·front \'ō-shən-,frənt\ *n* : a shore area on the ocean

ocean·go·ing \-,gō-iŋ\ *adj* : of, relating to, or suitable for travel on the ocean

ocean·og·ra·phy \,ō-shə-'nä-grə-fē\ *n* : a science dealing with the ocean and its phenomena — **ocean·og·ra·pher** \-fər\ *n* — **ocean·o·graph·ic** \-nə-'gra-fik\ *adj*

oce·lot \'ä-sə-,lät, 'ō-\ *n* : a medium-sized American wildcat ranging southward from Texas to northern Argentina and having a tawny yellow or gray coat with black markings

ocher *or* **ochre** \'ō-kər\ *n* : an earthy usu. red or yellow iron ore used as a pigment; *also* : the color esp. of yellow ocher

o'·clock \ə-'kläk\ *adv* : according to the clock

OCR *abbr* optical character reader; optical character recognition

OCS *abbr* officer candidate school

oct *abbr* octavo

Oct *abbr* October

oc·ta·gon \'äk-tə-,gän\ *n* : a polygon of eight angles and eight sides — **oc·tag·o·nal** \äk-'ta-gə-nᵊl\ *adj*

oc·tane \'äk-,tān\ *n* : OCTANE NUMBER

octane number *n* : a number used to measure the antiknock properties of gasoline that increases as the likelihood of knocking decreases

oc·tave \'äk-tiv\ *n* **1** : a musical interval embracing eight degrees; *also* : a tone or note at this interval or the whole series of notes, tones, or keys within this interval **2** : a group of eight

oc·ta·vo \äk-'tā-vō, -'tä-\ *n, pl* **-vos 1** : the size of a piece of paper cut eight from a sheet **2** : a book printed on octavo pages

oc·tet \äk-'tet\ *n* **1** : a musical composition for eight voices or eight instruments; *also* : the performers of such a composition **2** : a group or set of eight

Oc·to·ber \äk-'tō-bər\ *n* [ME *Octobre,* fr. OE *October,* fr. L, eighth month of the early Roman calendar, fr. *octo* eight] : the 10th month of the year

oc·to·ge·nar·i·an \,äk-tə-jə-'ner-ē-ən\ *n* : a person whose age is in the eighties

oc·to·pus \'äk-tə-pəs\ *n, pl* **-pus·es** *or* **-pi** \-,pī\ : any of various sea mollusks with eight long muscular arms furnished with suckers

oc·to·syl·lab·ic \,äk-tə-sə-'la-bik\ *adj* : composed of verses having eight syllables — **octosyllabic** *n*

¹oc·u·lar \'ä-kyə-lər\ *adj* **1** : VISUAL **2** : of or relating to the eye or the eyesight

²ocular *n* : EYEPIECE

oc·u·list \'ä-kyə-list\ *n* **1** : OPHTHALMOLOGIST **2** : OP-TOMETRIST

¹OD \ō-'dē\ *n* : an overdose of a drug and esp. a narcotic

²OD *vb* **OD'd** *or* **ODed; OD'ing; OD's** : to become ill or die from an OD

³OD *abbr* **1** doctor of optometry **2** [L *oculus dexter*] right eye **3** officer of the day **4** olive drab **5** overdraft **6** overdrawn

odd \'äd\ *adj* [ME *odde*, fr. ON *oddi* point of land, triangle, odd number] **1** : being only one of a pair or set ⟨an ~ shoe⟩ **2** : somewhat more than the number mentioned ⟨forty ~ years ago⟩ **3** : being an integer (as 1, 3, or 5) not divisible by two without leaving a remainder **4** : additional to what is usual ⟨~ jobs⟩ **5** : STRANGE ⟨an ~ way of behaving⟩ — **odd·ness** *n*

odd·ball \'äd-,bȯl\ *n* : one that is eccentric — **oddball** *adj*

odd·i·ty \'ä-də-tē\ *n, pl* **-ties 1** : one that is odd **2** : the quality or state of being odd

odd·ly \'äd-lē\ *adv* **1** : in an odd manner ⟨an ~ shaped roof⟩ **2** : as is odd

odd·ment \'äd-mənt\ *n* : something left over : REMNANT

odds \'ädz\ *n pl* **1** : a difference by which one thing is favored over another **2** : DISAGREEMENT — usu. used with *at* **3** : the ratio between the amount to be paid for a winning bet and the amount of the bet ⟨the horse went off at ~ of 6–1⟩

odds and ends *n pl* : miscellaneous things or matters

odds–on \'ädz-'ȯn, -'än\ *adj* : having a better than even chance to win

ode \'ōd\ *n* : a lyric poem that expresses a noble feeling with dignity

odi·ous \'ō-dē-əs\ *adj* : arousing or deserving hatred or repugnance — **odi·ous·ly** *adv* — **odi·ous·ness** *n*

odi·um \'ō-dē-əm\ *n* **1** : merited loathing : HATRED **2** : DISGRACE ⟨the ~ of defeat⟩

odom·e·ter \ō-'dä-mə-tər\ *n* [F *odomètre*, fr. Gk *hodometron*, fr. *hodos* way, road + *metron* measure] : an instrument for measuring distance traveled (as by a vehicle)

odor \'ō-dər\ *n* **1** : the quality of something that stimulates the sense of smell; *also* : a sensation resulting from such stimulation **2** : REPUTE, ESTIMATION — **odored** \'ō-dərd\ *adj* — **odor·less** *adj* — **odor·ous** *adj*

odor·if·er·ous \,ō-də-'ri-fə-rəs\ *adj* : having or yielding an odor

odour *chiefly Brit var of* ODOR

od·ys·sey \'ä-də-sē\ *n, pl* **-seys** [the *Odyssey*, epic poem attributed to Homer recounting the long wanderings of Odysseus] : a long wandering marked usu. by many changes of fortune

oe·cu·men·i·cal *esp Brit* ,ē-\ *chiefly Brit var of* ECUMENICAL

OED *abbr* Oxford English Dictionary

oe·de·ma *chiefly Brit var of* EDEMA

oe·di·pal \'e-də-pəl, 'ē-\ *adj, often cap* : of, relating to, or resulting from the Oedipus complex

Oe·di·pus complex \-pəs-\ *n* : the positive sexual feelings of a child toward the parent of the opposite sex and hostile or jealous feelings toward the parent of the same sex that may be a source of adult personality disorder when unresolved

OEO *abbr* Office of Economic Opportunity

o'er \'ȯr\ *adv or prep* : OVER

OES *abbr* Order of the Eastern Star

oe·soph·a·gus *chiefly Brit var of* ESOPHAGUS

oeu·vre \'ər-vrə, 'œvr°\ *n, pl* **oeuvres** *same*\ : a substantial body of work constituting the lifework of a writer, an artist, or a composer

¹of \'əv, 'äv\ *prep* **1** : FROM ⟨a man ~ the West⟩ **2** : having as a significant background or character element ⟨a man ~ noble birth⟩ ⟨a woman ~ ability⟩ **3** : owing to ⟨died ~ flu⟩ **4** : BY ⟨the plays ~ Shakespeare⟩ **5** : having as component parts or material, contents, or members ⟨a house ~ brick⟩ ⟨a glass ~ water⟩ ⟨a pack ~ fools⟩ **6** : belonging to or included by ⟨the front ~ the house⟩ ⟨a time ~ life⟩ ⟨one ~ you⟩ ⟨the best ~ its kind⟩ ⟨the son ~ a doctor⟩ **7** : ABOUT ⟨tales ~ the West⟩ **8** : connected with : OVER ⟨the queen ~ England⟩ **9** : that is : signified as ⟨the city ~ Rome⟩ **10** — used to indicate apposition of the words it joins ⟨that fool ~ a husband⟩ **11** : as concerns : FOR ⟨love ~ nature⟩ **12** — used to indicate the application of an adjective ⟨fond ~ candy⟩ **13** : BEFORE ⟨quarter ~ ten⟩

OF *abbr* outfield

¹off \'ȯf\ *adv* **1** : from a place or position ⟨drove ~ in a new car⟩; *also* : ASIDE ⟨turned ~ into a side road⟩ **2** : at a distance in time or space ⟨stood ~ a few yards⟩ ⟨several years ~⟩ **3** : so as to be unattached or removed ⟨the lid blew ~⟩ **4** : to a state of discontinuance, exhaustion, or completion ⟨shut the radio ~⟩ **5** : away from regular work ⟨took time ~ for lunch⟩

²off *prep* **1** : away from ⟨just ~ the highway⟩ ⟨take it ~ the table⟩ **2** : to seaward of ⟨two miles ~ the coast⟩ **3** : FROM ⟨borrowed a dollar ~ me⟩ **4** : at the expense of ⟨lives ~ his parents⟩ **5** : not now engaged in ⟨~ duty⟩ **6** : abstaining from ⟨~ liquor⟩ **7** : below the usual level of ⟨~ his game⟩

³off *adj* **1** : more removed or distant **2** : started on the way **3** : not operating **4** : not correct **5** : REMOTE, SLIGHT ⟨an ~ chance⟩ **6** : INFERIOR ⟨~ grade of oil⟩ **7** : provided for ⟨well ~⟩

⁴off *abbr* office; officer; official

of·fal \'ȯ-fəl\ *n* [ME, fr. *of* off + *fall* fall] : the waste or byproduct of a process; *esp* : the viscera and trimmings of a butchered animal removed in dressing

off and on *adv* : INTERMITTENTLY ⟨rained *off and on*⟩

¹off·beat \'ȯf-,bēt\ *n* : the unaccented part of a musical measure

²offbeat *adj* : ECCENTRIC, UNCONVENTIONAL ⟨an ~ style⟩

off–col·or \'ȯf-'kə-lər\ *or* **off–col·ored** \-lərd\ *adj* **1** : not having the right or standard color **2** : of doubtful propriety : verging on indecency ⟨~ stories⟩

of·fend \ə-'fend\ *vb* **1** : SIN, TRANSGRESS **2** : to cause discomfort or pain : HURT **3** : to cause dislike or vexation : ANNOY **♦** *Synonyms* AFFRONT, INSULT, OUTRAGE — **of·fend·er** *n*

of·fense *or* **of·fence** \ə-'fens, *esp for 2 & 3* 'ä-,fens\ *n* **1** : something that outrages the senses **2** : ATTACK, ASSAULT **3** : the offensive team or members of a team playing offensive positions **3** : DISPLEASURE **5** : SIN, MISDEED **6** : an infraction of law : CRIME

¹of·fen·sive \ə-'fen-siv, *esp for 1 & 2* 'ä-,fen-\ *adj* **1** : AGGRESSIVE **2** : of or relating to an attempt to score in a game; *also* : of or relating to a team in possession of the ball or puck **3** : OBNOXIOUS ⟨an ~ odor⟩ **4** : INSULTING ⟨~ remarks⟩ — **of·fen·sive·ly** *adv* — **of·fen·sive·ness** *n*

²offensive *n* : ATTACK

¹of·fer \'ȯ-fər\ *vb* **of·fered; of·fer·ing 1** : SACRIFICE **2** : to present for acceptance : TENDER; *also* : to propose as payment **3** : PROPOSE, SUGGEST; *also* : to declare one's readiness **4** : to try or begin to exert ⟨~ resistance⟩ **5** : to place on sale — **of·fer·ing** *n*

²offer *n* **1** : PROPOSAL **2** : BID **3** : TRY

of·fer·to·ry \'ȯ-fər-,tȯr-ē\ *n, pl* **-ries** : the presentation of offerings at a church service; *also* : the musical accompaniment during it

off–gas·sing \'ȯf-,ga-siŋ\ *n* : the emission of esp. noxious gases (as from a building material)

off–hand \'ȯf-'hand\ *adv or adj* : without previous thought or preparation

off–hour \-,au̇(-ə)r\ *n* : a period of time other than a rush hour; *also* : a period of time other than business hours

of·fice \'ȯ-fəs\ *n* **1** : a special duty or position; *esp* : a position of authority in government ⟨run for ~⟩ **2** : a prescribed form or service of worship; *also* : RITE **3** : an assigned or assumed duty or role **4** : a place where a business is transacted or a service is supplied

of·fice–hold·er \'ȯ-fəs-,hōl-dər\ *n* : one holding a public office

of·fi·cer \'ȯ-fə-sər\ *n* **1** : one charged with the enforcement of law **2** : one who holds an office of trust or authority **3** : a person who holds a position of authority or command in the armed forces; *esp* : COMMISSIONED OFFICER

¹of·fi·cial \ə-'fi-shəl\ *n* : OFFICER 2

²official *adj* **1** : of or relating to an office or to officers **2** : AUTHORIZED, AUTHORITATIVE ⟨~ statement⟩ **3** : befitting or characteristic of a person in office — **of·fi·cial·ly** *adv*

of·fi·cial·dom \ə-'fi-shəl-dəm\ *n* : officials as a class

of·fi·cial·ism \ə-'fi-shə-,li-zəm\ *n* : lack of flexibility and initiative combined with excessive adherence to regulations

of·fi·ci·ant \ə-'fi-shē-ənt\ *n* : one (as a priest) who officiates at a religious rite

of·fi·ci·ate \ə-'fi-shē-ˌāt\ vb **-at·ed; -at·ing 1** : to perform a ceremony, function, or duty **2** : to act in an official capacity

of·fi·cious \ə-'fi-shəs\ adj : volunteering one's services where they are neither asked for nor needed ⟨an ~ busybody⟩ — **of·fi·cious·ly** adv — **of·fi·cious·ness** n

off·ing \'ȯ-fiŋ\ n : the near or foreseeable future

off–line \'ȯf-'līn\ adj or adv : not connected to or controlled directly by a computer

off of prep : OFF

off·print \'ȯf-ˌprint\ n : a separately printed excerpt (as from a magazine)

off–road \-'rōd\ adj : of, relating to, or being a vehicle designed for use away from public roads — **off–road·er** \-'rō-dər\ n

off–sea·son \-ˌsē-z⁰n\ n : a time of suspended or reduced activity

¹off·set \-ˌset\ n **1** : a sharp bend (as in a pipe) by which one part is turned aside out of line **2** : a printing process in which an inked impression is first made on a rubber= blanketed cylinder and then transferred to the paper

²off·set vb **off·set; off·set·ting 1** : to place over against : BALANCE **2** : to compensate for **3** : to form an offset in (~ a wall)

off·shoot \'ȯf-ˌshüt\ n **1** : a collateral or derived branch, descendant, or member **2** : a branch of a main stem (as of a plant)

¹off·shore \'ȯf-'shòr\ adv **1** : at a distance from the shore **2** : outside the country : ABROAD

²off·shore \'ȯf-'shòr\ adj **1** : moving away from the shore **2** : situated off the shore but within waters under a country's control

off·side \-'sīd\ adv or adj : illegally in advance of the ball or puck

off·spring \-ˌspriŋ\ n, pl **offspring** also **offsprings** : PROGENY, YOUNG

off·stage \'ȯf-'stāj, -ˌstāj\ adv or adj **1** : off or away from the stage **2** : out of the public view ⟨deals made ~⟩

off–the–record adj : given or made in confidence and not for publication

off–the–shelf adj : available as a stock item : not specially designed or made

off–the–wall adj : highly unusual : BIZARRE ⟨an ~ sense of humor⟩

off·track \'ȯf-'trak\ adv or adj : away from a racetrack

off–white \'ȯf-'hwīt\ n : a yellowish or grayish white color

off year n **1** : a year in which no major election is held **2** : a year of diminished activity or production

oft \'ȯft\ adv : OFTEN

of·ten \'ȯ-fən\ adv : many times : FREQUENTLY

of·ten·times \-ˌtīmz\ or **oft·times** \'ȯft-ˌtīmz, 'ȯft-\ adv : OFTEN

Og symbol oganesson

oga·nes·son \ˌō-gə-'ne-ˌsän, ˌä-\ n a short-lived artificially produced radioactive chemical element

ogle \'ō-gəl\ vb **ogled; ogling** : to look at in a flirtatious way — **ogle** n — **ogler** n

ogre \'ō-gər\ n **1** : a monster of fairy tales and folklore that eats people **2** : a dreaded person or object

ogress \'ō-grəs\ n : a female ogre

oh also **O** \'ō\ interj **1** — used to express an emotion or in response to physical stimuli **2** — used in direct address

OH abbr Ohio

ohm \'ōm\ n : a unit of electrical resistance equal to the resistance of a circuit in which a potential difference of one volt produces a current of one ampere — **ohm·ic** \'ō-mik\ adj

ohm·me·ter \'ōm-ˌmē-tər\ n : an instrument for indicating resistance in ohms directly

¹oil \'ȯi(-ə)l\ n [ME oile, fr. AF, fr. L oleum olive oil, fr. Gk elaion, fr. elaia olive] **1** : any of numerous fatty or greasy liquid substances obtained from plants, animals, or minerals and used for fuel, food, medicines, and manufacturing **2** : PETROLEUM **3** : artists' colors made with oil; also : a painting in such colors — **oil·i·ness** \'ȯi-lē-nəs\ n — **oily** \'ȯi-lē\ adj

²oil vb : to put oil in or on — **oil·er** n

oil·cloth \'ȯi(-ə)l-ˌklȯth\ n : cloth treated with oil or paint and used for table and shelf coverings

oil pan n : the lower section of a crankcase used as an oil reservoir

oil shale n : a rock (as shale) from which oil can be recovered

oil·skin \'ȯi(-ə)l-ˌskin\ n **1** : an oiled waterproof cloth **2** : an oilskin raincoat **3** pl : an oilskin coat and pants

oink \'ȯiŋk\ n : the natural noise of a hog — **oink** vb

oint·ment \'ȯint-mənt\ n : a salve for use on the skin

OJ abbr orange juice

Ojib·wa or **Ojib·way** or **Ojibwe** \ō-'jib-ˌwä\ n, pl **Ojibwa** or **Ojibwas** or **Ojibway** or **Ojibways** or **Ojibwe** or **Ojibwes 1** : a member of an American Indian people of the region around Lake Superior and westward **2** : the Algonquian language of the Ojibwa people

OJT abbr on-the-job training

¹OK or **okay** \ō-'kā\ adv or adj : all right

²OK or **okay** vb **OK'd** or **okayed; OK'·ing** or **okay·ing** : APPROVE, AUTHORIZE — **OK** or **okay** n

³OK abbr Oklahoma

Okla abbr Oklahoma

okra \'ō-krə\ n : a tall annual plant related to the mallows that has edible green pods; also : these pods

¹old \'ōld\ adj **1** : ANCIENT; also : of long standing **2** cap : belonging to an early period ⟨Old Irish⟩ **3** : having existed for a specified period of time **4** : of or relating to a past era **5** : advanced in years **6** : showing the effects of age or use **7** : no longer in use — **old·ish** \'ōl-dish\ adj

²old n : old or earlier time ⟨days of ~⟩

old·en \'ōl-dən\ adj : of or relating to a bygone era

¹old–fash·ioned \'ōld-'fa-shənd\ adj **1** : OUT-OF-DATE, ANTIQUATED **2** : CONSERVATIVE

²old–fashioned n : a cocktail usu. made with whiskey, bitters, sugar, a twist of lemon peel, and water or soda water

old–growth \'ōld-'grōth\ adj : of, relating to, or being a forest with large old trees, numerous snags and woody debris, and a multilayered canopy

old guard n, often cap O&G : the conservative members of an organization

old hat adj **1** : OLD-FASHIONED ⟨equipment that is now old hat⟩ **2** : STALE, TRITE

old·ie \'ōl-dē\ n : something old; esp : a popular song from the past

old–line \'ōld-'līn\ adj **1** : ORIGINAL, ESTABLISHED ⟨an ~ business⟩ **2** : adhering to old policies or practices

old maid n **1** : SPINSTER **2** : a prim fussy person — **old–maid·ish** \'ōld-'mā-dish\ adj

old man n **1** : HUSBAND **2** : FATHER

old–school adj : adhering to traditional policies or practices ⟨an ~ politician⟩

old·ster \'ōld-stər\ n : an old or elderly person

Old Testament n : the first of the two chief divisions of the Christian Bible — see BIBLE table

old–time \'ōld-'tīm\ adj **1** : of, relating to, or characteristic of an earlier period **2** : of long standing

old–tim·er \'ōld-'tī-mər\ n : VETERAN; also : OLDSTER

old–world \-'wərld\ adj : having old-fashioned charm ⟨an ~ hotel⟩

ole·ag·i·nous \ˌō-lē-'a-jə-nəs\ adj : OILY

ole·an·der \'ō-lē-ˌan-dər\ n : a poisonous evergreen shrub often grown for its fragrant white to red flowers

oleo \'ō-lē-ˌō\ n, pl **ole·os** : MARGARINE

oleo·mar·ga·rine \ˌō-lē-ō-'mär-jə-rən\ n : MARGARINE

ol·fac·to·ry \äl-'fak-tə-rē, ōl-\ adj : of or relating to the sense of smell

oli·gar·chy \'ä-lə-ˌgär-kē, 'ō-\ n, pl **-chies 1** : a government in which power is in the hands of a few **2** : a state having an oligarchy; also : the group holding power in such a state — **ol·i·garch** \-ˌgärk\ n — **oli·gar·chic** \ˌä-lə-'gär-kik, ˌō-\ or **oli·gar·chi·cal** \-ki-kəl\ adj

Oli·go·cene \'ä-li-gō-ˌsēn, ə-'li-gə-ˌsēn\ adj : of, relating to, or being the epoch of the Tertiary between the Eocene and the Miocene — **Oligocene** n

olio \'ō-lē-ˌō\ n, pl **oli·os** : HODGEPODGE, MEDLEY

ol·ive \'ä-liv\ n **1** : an Old World evergreen tree grown in warm regions for its fruit that is a food and the source of an edible oil (olive oil); also : the fruit **2** : a dull yellowish green color

olive drab n **1** : a grayish olive color **2** : an olive drab wool or cotton fabric; also : a uniform of this fabric

ol·iv·ine \'ä-lə-ˌvēn\ n : a usu. greenish mineral that is a complex silicate of magnesium and iron

Olym·pic Games \ō-'lim-pik-\ n pl : a modified revival of an ancient Greek festival consisting of international athletic contests that are held at separate winter and summer gatherings at four-year intervals

om \'ōm\ *n* : a mantra consisting of the sound "om" used in contemplating ultimate reality

Oma·ha \'ō-mə-ˌhä, -ˌhó\ *n, pl* **Omaha** *or* **Omahas** : a member of an American Indian people of northeastern Nebraska

om·buds·man \'äm-ˌbùdz-mən, äm-'bùdz-\ *n, pl* **-men** \-mən\ **1** : a government official appointed to investigate complaints made by individuals against abuses or capricious acts of public officials **2** : one that investigates reported complaints (as from students or consumers)

ome·ga \ō-'mā-gə\ *n* : the 24th and last letter of the Greek alphabet — Ω or ω

om·elet *or* **om·elette** \'äm-lət, 'ä-mə-\ *n* [F *omelette*, alter. of MF *amelette, alemette*, alter. of *alemelle* thin plate, ultim. fr. L *lamella*, dim. of *lamina*] : eggs beaten with milk or water, cooked without stirring until set, and folded over

omen \'ō-mən\ *n* : an event or phenomenon believed to be a sign or warning of a future occurrence

omi·cron \'ä-mə-ˌkrän, 'ō-\ *n* : the 15th letter of the Greek alphabet — O or o

om·i·nous \'ä-mə-nəs\ *adj* : foretelling evil : THREATENING — **om·i·nous·ly** *adv* — **om·i·nous·ness** *n*

omis·si·ble \ō-'mi-sə-bəl\ *adj* : that may be omitted ⟨~ details⟩

omis·sion \ō-'mi-shən\ *n* **1** : something neglected or left undone **2** : the act of omitting : the state of being omitted

omit \ō-'mit\ *vb* **omit·ted; omit·ting 1** : to leave out or leave unmentioned **2** : to leave undone: FAIL

¹om·ni·bus \'äm-ni-(ˌ)bəs\ *n* : BUS

²omnibus *adj* : of, relating to, or providing for many things at once ⟨an ~ bill⟩

om·nip·o·tent \äm-'ni-pə-tənt\ *adj* **1** *often cap* : ALMIGHTY **1 2** : having unlimited authority or influence ⟨an ~ ruler⟩ — **om·nip·o·tence** \-təns\ *n* — **om·nip·o·tent·ly** *adv*

om·ni·pres·ent \ˌäm-ni-'pre-zᵊnt\ *adj* : present in all places at all times ⟨an ~ problem⟩ — **om·ni·pres·ence** \-zᵊns\ *n*

om·ni·scient \äm-'ni-shənt\ *adj* : having infinite awareness, understanding, and insight — **om·ni·science** \-shəns\ *n* — **om·ni·scient·ly** *adv*

om·ni·um-gath·er·um \ˌäm-nē-əm-'ga-thə-rəm\ *n, pl* **omnium-gatherums** : a miscellaneous collection

om·niv·o·rous \äm-'ni-və-rəs\ *adj* **1** : feeding on both animal and vegetable substances **2** : AVID ⟨an ~ reader⟩ — **om·ni·vore** \'äm-ni-ˌvȯr\ *n* — **om·niv·o·rous·ly** *adv*

¹on \'ȯn, 'än\ *prep* **1** : in or to a position over and in contact with ⟨jumped ~ his horse⟩ **2** : touching the surface of ⟨shadows ~ the wall⟩ **3** : AT, TO ⟨~ the right were the mountains⟩ **4** : IN, ABOARD ⟨went ~ the train⟩ **5** : during or at the time of ⟨came ~ Monday⟩ ⟨every hour ~ the hour⟩ **6** : through the agency of ⟨was cut ~ a tin can⟩ **7** : in a state or process of ⟨~ fire⟩ ⟨~ the wane⟩ **8** : connected with as a member or participant ⟨~ a committee⟩ ⟨~ tour⟩ **9** — used to indicate a basis, source, or standard of computation ⟨has it ~ good authority⟩ ⟨10 cents ~ the dollar⟩ **10** : with regard to ⟨a monopoly ~ wheat⟩ **11** : at or toward as an object ⟨crept up ~ her⟩ **12** : ABOUT, CONCERNING ⟨a book ~ minerals⟩

²on *adv* **1** : in or into a position of contact with or attachment to a surface **2** : FORWARD **3** : into operation

³on *adj* : being in operation or in progress

ON *abbr* Ontario

¹once \'wəns\ *adv* [ME *ones*, fr. genitive of *on* one] **1** : one time only **2** : at any one time ⟨didn't ~ thank me⟩ **3** : FORMERLY ⟨was ~ young⟩ **4** : by one degree of relationship ⟨first cousin ~ removed⟩

²once *n* : one single time — **at once 1** : at the same time **2** : IMMEDIATELY

³once *adj* : FORMER ⟨a ~ successful actor⟩

⁴once *conj* : AS SOON AS ⟨~ we're finished, we can leave⟩

once–over \'wəns-ˌō-vər\ *n* : a swift examination or survey

on·co·gene \'äŋ-kō-ˌjēn\ *n* : a gene having the potential to cause a normal cell to become cancerous

on·col·o·gy \än-'kä-lə-jē\ *n* : the study of tumors — **on·co·log·i·cal** \ˌäŋ-kə-'lä-ji-kəl\ *also* **on·co·log·ic** \-jik\ *adj* — **on·col·o·gist** \än-'kä-lə-jist\ *n*

on·com·ing \'ȯn-ˌkə-miŋ, 'än-\ *adj* : APPROACHING ⟨~ traffic⟩

¹one \'wən\ *adj* **1** : being a single unit or thing ⟨~ person went⟩ **2** : being one in particular ⟨early ~ morning⟩ **3** : being the same in kind or quality ⟨members of ~ race⟩; *also* : UNITED **4** : being not specified or fixed ⟨~ day soon⟩

²one *n* **1** : the number denoting unity **2** : the 1st in a set or series **3** : a single person or thing — **one·ness** \'wən-nəs\ *n*

³one *pron* **1** : a certain indefinitely indicated person or thing ⟨saw ~ of his friends⟩ **2** : a person in general ⟨~ never knows⟩ **3** — used in place of a first-person pronoun

Onei·da \ō-'nī-də\ *n, pl* **Oneida** *or* **Oneidas** : a member of an American Indian people orig. of New York

one–man band *n* **1** : a musician who plays several instruments during a solo performance **2** : a person who alone undertakes or is responsible for several tasks

oner·ous \'ä-nə-rəs, 'ō-\ *adj* : imposing or constituting a burden : TROUBLESOME ⟨an ~ task⟩ ♦ **Synonyms** OPPRESSIVE, EXACTING, BURDENSOME, WEIGHTY

one·self \(ˌ)wən-'self\ *also* **one's self** *pron* : one's own self — usu. used reflexively or for emphasis

one–sid·ed \'wən-'sī-dəd\ *adj* **1** : having or occurring on one side only; *also* : having one side prominent or more developed **2** : PARTIAL ⟨a ~ interpretation⟩

one·time \-ˌtīm\ *adj* : FORMER ⟨a ~ actor⟩

one–to–one \ˌwən-tə-'wən\ *adj* : pairing each element of a set uniquely with an element of another set

one up *adj* : being in a position of advantage ⟨was *one up* on the others⟩

one–way *adj* : moving, allowing movement, or functioning in only one direction ⟨~ streets⟩

on·go·ing \'ȯn-ˌgō-iŋ, 'än-\ *adj* : continuously moving forward

on·ion \'ən-yən\ *n* : the pungent edible bulb of a widely cultivated plant related to the lilies; *also* : this plant

on·ion·skin \-ˌskin\ *n* : a thin strong translucent paper of very light weight

on–line \'ȯn-'līn, 'än-\ *adj or adv* : connected to, served by, or available through a computer network (as the Internet); *also* : done while online ⟨~ shopping⟩ — **online** *adv*

on·look·er \'ȯn-ˌlù-kər, 'än-\ *n* : SPECTATOR

¹on·ly \'ȯn-lē\ *adj* **1** : unquestionably the best **2** : SOLE ⟨the ~ one left⟩

²only *adv* **1** : MERELY, JUST ⟨~ $2⟩ **2** : SOLELY ⟨known ~ to me⟩ **3** : at the very least ⟨was ~ too true⟩ **4** : as a final result ⟨will ~ make you sick⟩

³only *conj* : except that

on·o·mato·poe·ia \ˌä-nə-ˌmä-tə-'pē-ə\ *n* [LL, fr. Gk *onomatopoiia*, fr. *onoma* name + *poiein* to make] **1** : formation of words in imitation of natural sounds (as *buzz* or *hiss*) **2** : the use of words whose sound suggests the sense — **on·o·mato·poe·ic** \-ˌpē-ik\ *or* **on·o·mato·po·et·ic** \-pō-'e-tik\ *adj* — **on·o·mato·poe·i·cal·ly** \-ˌpē-ə-k(ə-)lē\ *or* **on·o·mato·po·et·i·cal·ly** \-pō-'e-ti-k(ə-)lē\ *adv*

On·on·da·ga \ˌä-nən-'dȯ-gə, -'dä-, -'dä-\ *n, pl* **-ga** *or* **-gas** : a member of an American Indian people of New York and Canada

on·rush \'ȯn-ˌrəsh, 'än-\ *n* : a rushing onward — **on·rush·ing** *adj*

on–screen \'ȯn-'skrēn, 'än-\ *adv or adj* : on a computer or television screen

on·set \-ˌset\ *n* **1** : ATTACK **2** : BEGINNING ⟨the ~ of winter⟩

on·shore \-ˌshȯr\ *adj* **1** : moving toward the shore **2** : situated on or near the shore — **on·shore** \-'shȯr\ *adv*

on·slaught \'ȯn-ˌslȯt, 'än-\ *n* : a fierce attack; *also* : something resembling such an attack ⟨an ~ of questions⟩

Ont *abbr* Ontario

on·to \'ȯn-tü, 'än-\ *prep* : to a position or point on

onus \'ō-nəs\ *n* **1** : BURDEN **2** : OBLIGATION **3** : BLAME

¹on·ward \'ȯn-wərd, 'än-\ *also* **on·wards** \-wərdz\ *adv* : FORWARD ⟨kept moving ~⟩

²onward *adj* : directed or moving onward : FORWARD

on·yx \'ä-niks\ *n* [ME *oniche, onyx*, fr. AF & L; AF, fr. L *onyx*, fr. Gk, lit., claw, nail] : a translucent chalcedony in parallel layers of different colors

oo·dles \'ü-dᵊlz\ *n pl* : a great quantity

oo·lite \'ō-ə-ˌlīt\ *n* : a rock consisting of small round grains cemented together — **oo·lit·ic** \ˌō-ə-'li-tik\ *adj*

¹**ooze** \'üz\ *n* [ME *wose*, fr. OE *wāse* mire] **1** : a soft deposit (as of mud) on the bottom of a body of water **2** : soft wet ground — MUD — **oozy** \'ü-zē\ *adj*

²**ooze** *vb* **oozed; ooz·ing** **1** : to flow or leak out slowly or imperceptibly **2** : EXUDE ⟨~ confidence⟩

³**ooze** *n* : something that oozes

op *abbr* **1** operation; operative; operator **2** opportunity **3** opus

OP *abbr* **1** observation post **2** out of print

opac·i·ty \ō-'pa-sə-tē\ *n, pl* **-ties** **1** : obscurity of meaning **2** : mental dullness **3** : the quality or state of being opaque **4** : an opaque spot in a normally transparent structure

opal \'ō-pəl\ *n* : a mineral with iridescent colors that is used as a gem

opal·es·cent \ˌō-pə-'le-s°nt\ *adj* : IRIDESCENT — **opal·es·cence** \-s°ns\ *n*

opaque \ō-'pāk\ *adj* **1** : blocking the passage of radiant energy and esp. light **2** : not easily understood; *also* : OBTUSE — **opaque·ly** *adv* — **opaque·ness** *n*

op art \'äp-\ *n* : OPTICAL ART — **op artist** *n*

op cit *abbr* [L *opere citato*] in the work cited

ope \'ōp\ *vb* **oped; op·ing** *archaic* : OPEN

OPEC *abbr* Organization of Petroleum Exporting Countries

op-ed \'äp-'ed\ *n, often cap O&E* : a page of special features usu. opposite the editorial page of a newspaper

¹**open** \'ō-pən\ *adj* **open·er; open·est** **1** : not shut or shut up ⟨an ~ door⟩ **2** : not secret or hidden; *also* : FRANK **3** : not enclosed or covered ⟨an ~ fire⟩; *also* : not protected **4** : free to be entered or used ⟨an ~ tournament⟩ **5** : easy to get through or see ⟨~ country⟩ **6** : spread out : EXTENDED **7** : not decided ⟨an ~ question⟩ **8** : readily accessible and cooperative; *also* : GENEROUS **9** : having openings, interruptions, or spaces ⟨an ~ mesh⟩; *also* : having components separated by a space in writing and printing ⟨the name *Spanish moss* is an ~ compound⟩ **10** : ready to consider ⟨stores are ~⟩ **11** : free from restraints or controls ⟨~ season⟩ — **open·ly** *adv* — **open·ness** *n*

²**open** \'ō-pən\ *vb* **opened; open·ing** **1** : to change or move from a shut position; *also* : to make open by clearing away obstacles **2** : to make accessible **3** : to make openings in **4** : to make or become functional ⟨~ a store⟩ **5** : REVEAL; *also* : ENLIGHTEN **6** : BEGIN ⟨~ talks⟩ — **open·er** *n*

³**open** *n* **1** : OUTDOORS **2** : a contest or tournament open to all

open–air *adj* : OUTDOOR ⟨~ theaters⟩

open arms *n pl* : an eager or warm welcome

open–faced \-'fāst\ *also* **open–face** \-'fās\ *adj* : served without a covering layer of bread ⟨an ~ sandwich⟩

open·hand·ed \ˌō-pən-'han-dəd\ *adj* : GENEROUS — **open·hand·ed·ly** *adv*

open–heart *adj* : of, relating to, or performed on a heart temporarily relieved of circulatory function and laid open for repair of defects or damage

open–hearth *adj* : of, relating to, or being a process of making steel in a furnace that reflects the heat from the roof onto the material

opening *n* **1** : an act or instance of making or becoming open **2** : BEGINNING **3** : something that is open **4** : OCCASION; *also* : an opportunity for employment

open mike *n* : an event in which amateurs may perform

open–mind·ed \ˌō-pən-'mīn-dəd\ *adj* : free from rigidly fixed preconceptions — **open–mind·ed·ness** *n*

open sentence *n* : a statement (as in mathematics) containing at least one blank or unknown so that when the blank is filled or a quantity substituted for the unknown the statement becomes a complete statement that is either true or false

open shop *n* : an establishment having members and nonmembers of a labor union on the payroll

open·work \'ō-pən-ˌwərk\ *n* : work so made as to show openings through its substance ⟨a railing of wrought-iron ~⟩ — **open–worked** \-ˌwərkt\ *adj*

¹**opera** *pl of* OPUS

²**op·era** \'ä-prə, -pə-rə\ *n* : a drama set to music — **op·er·at·ic** \ˌä-pə-'ra-tik\ *adj*

op·er·a·ble \'ä-pə-rə-bəl\ *adj* **1** : fit, possible, or desirable to use **2** : likely to result in a favorable outcome upon surgical treatment

opera glasses *n pl* : small binoculars for use in a theater

op·er·ate \'ä-pə-ˌrāt\ *vb* **-at·ed; -at·ing** **1** : to perform work : FUNCTION **2** : to produce an effect **3** : to put or keep in operation **4** : to perform or subject to an operation — **op·er·a·tor** \-ˌrā-tər\ *n*

operating system *n* : software that controls the operation of a computer

op·er·a·tion \ˌä-pə-'rā-shən\ *n* **1** : a doing or performing of a practical work **2** : an exertion of power or influence; *also* : method or manner of functioning **3** : a surgical procedure **4** : a process of deriving one mathematical expression from others according to a rule **5** : a military action or mission **6** : a usu. small business — **op·er·a·tion·al** \-shə-nəl\ *adj*

¹**op·er·a·tive** \'ä-pə-rə-tiv, -ˌrā-\ *adj* **1** : producing an appropriate effect; *also* : most significant or essential **2** : OPERATING ⟨an ~ force⟩ **3** : having to do with physical operations; *also* : WORKING ⟨an ~ craftsman⟩ **4** : based on or consisting of an operation ⟨~ dentistry⟩

²**operative** *n* **1** : OPERATOR; *esp* : a secret agent **2** : a person who works toward achieving the objectives of a larger interest

op·er·et·ta \ˌä-pə-'re-tə\ *n* [It, dim. of *opera* opera] : a light musical-dramatic work with a romantic plot, spoken dialogue, and dancing scenes

oph·thal·mic \äf-'thal-mik, äp-\ *adj* [Gk *ophthalmikos*, fr. *ophthalmos* eye] : of, relating to, or located near the eye

oph·thal·mol·o·gy \ˌäf-ˌthal-'mä-lə-jē, ˌäp-\ *n* : a branch of medicine dealing with the structure, functions, and diseases of the eye — **oph·thal·mol·o·gist** \-jist\ *n*

oph·thal·mo·scope \äf-'thal-mə-ˌskōp, äp-\ *n* : an instrument for use in viewing the interior of the eye and esp. the retina

opi·ate \'ō-pē-ət, -pē-ˌāt\ *n* : a preparation or derivative of opium; *also* : a narcotic or a substance with similar activity — **opiate** *adj*

opine \ō-'pīn\ *vb* **opined; opin·ing** : to express an opinion : STATE

opin·ion \ə-'pin-yən\ *n* **1** : JUDGMENT **2** : a belief stronger than impression and less strong than positive knowledge **3** : a formal statement by an expert after careful study

opin·ion·at·ed \ə-'pin-yə-ˌnā-təd\ *adj* : obstinately adhering to personal opinions

opi·um \'ō-pē-əm\ *n* [ME, fr. L, fr. Gk *opion*, fr. dim. of *opos* sap] : an addictive narcotic drug that is the dried latex of a Eurasian poppy

opos·sum \ə-'pä-səm\ *n, pl* **opossums** *also* **opossum** : an omnivorous tree-dwelling No. American marsupial that is active chiefly at night and has a pointed snout and a prehensile tail

opossum

opp *abbr* opposite

op·po·nent \ə-'pō-nənt\ *n* : one that opposes : ADVERSARY

op·por·tune \ˌä-pər-'tün, -'tyün\ *adj* [ME, fr. MF *opportun*, fr. L *opportunus*, fr. *ob-* toward + *portus* port, harbor] : SUITABLE ⟨an ~ moment⟩ — **op·por·tune·ly** *adv*

op·por·tun·ism \ˌä-pər-'tü-ˌni-zəm, -'tyü-\ *n* : a taking advantage of opportunities or circumstances esp. with little regard for principles or ultimate consequences —

op·por·tun·ist \-nist\ *n* — **op·por·tu·nis·tic** \-tü-'nis-tik, -tyü-\ *adj*

op·por·tu·ni·ty \ˌä-pər-'tü-nə-tē, -'tyü-\ *n, pl* **-ties** **1** : a favorable combination of circumstances, time, and place **2** : a chance for advancement

op·pose \ə-'pōz\ *vb* **op·posed**; **op·pos·ing** **1** : to place opposite or against something (as to provide resistance or contrast) **2** : to strive against : RESIST — **op·po·si·tion** \ˌä-pə-'zi-shən\ *n*

¹op·po·site \'ä-pə-zət\ *adj* **1** : set over against something that is at the other end or side **2** : OPPOSED, HOSTILE; *also* : CONTRARY **3** : contrarily turned or moving **4** : being the other of a matching or contrasting pair (the ~ sex) — **op·po·site·ly** *adv* — **op·po·site·ness** *n*

²opposite *n* : one that is opposed or contrary

³opposite *adv* : on or to an opposite side

⁴opposite *prep* : across from and usu. facing (the house ~ ours)

op·press \ə-'pres\ *vb* **1** : to crush by abuse of power or authority (~ed minorities) **2** : to weigh down : BURDEN ♦ *Synonyms* AGGRIEVE, WRONG, PERSECUTE — **op·pres·sive** \-'pre-siv\ *adj* — **op·pres·sive·ly** *adv* — **op·pres·sor** \-'pre-sər\ *n*

op·pres·sion \ə-'pre-shən\ *n* **1** : unjust or cruel exercise of power or authority **2** : DEPRESSION

op·pro·bri·ous \ə-'prō-brē-əs\ *adj* : expressing or deserving opprobrium — **op·pro·bri·ous·ly** *adv*

op·pro·bri·um \-brē-əm\ *n* **1** : something that brings disgrace **2** : public disgrace or ill fame

¹opt \'äpt\ *vb* : to make a choice; *esp* : to decide in favor of something

²opt *abbr* **1** optical; optician; optics **2** option; optional

op·tic \'äp-tik\ *adj* : of or relating to vision or the eye

op·ti·cal \'äp-ti-kəl\ *adj* **1** : relating to optics **2** : OPTIC **3** : of, relating to, or using light

optical art *n* : nonobjective art characterized by the use of geometric patterns often for an illusory effect

optical disk *n* : a disk on which information has been recorded digitally and which is read using a laser

optical fiber *n* : a single fiber-optic strand

op·ti·cian \äp-'ti-shən\ *n* **1** : a maker of or dealer in optical items and instruments **2** : a person who makes or orders eyeglasses and contact lenses to prescription and sells them

op·tics \'äp-tiks\ *n* **1** : a science that deals with the nature and properties of light **2** : the aspects of an action, policy, or decision that relate to public perceptions

op·ti·mal \'äp-tə-məl\ *adj* : most desirable or satisfactory — **op·ti·mal·ly** *adv*

op·ti·mism \'äp-tə-ˌmi-zəm\ *n* [F *optimisme*, fr. L *optimum*, n., best, fr. neut. of *optimus* best] **1** : a doctrine that this world is the best possible world **2** : an inclination to anticipate the best possible outcome of actions or events — **op·ti·mist** \-mist\ *n* — **op·ti·mis·tic** \ˌäp-tə-'mis-tik\ *adj* — **op·ti·mis·ti·cal·ly** \-ti-k(ə-)lē\ *adv*

op·ti·mize \'äp-tə-ˌmīz\ *vb* **-mized**; **-miz·ing** : to make as perfect, effective, or functional as possible — **op·ti·mi·za·tion** \ˌäp-tə-mə-'zā-shən\ *n*

op·ti·mum \'äp-tə-məm\ *n, pl* **-ma** \-mə\ *also* **-mums** [L] : the amount or degree of something most favorable to an end; *also* : greatest degree attained under implied or specified conditions

op·tion \'äp-shən\ *n* **1** : the power or right to choose **2** : a right to buy or sell something at a specified price during a specified period **3** : something offered for choice — **op·tion·al** \-shə-nəl\ *adj*

op·tom·e·try \äp-'tä-mə-trē\ *n* : the health-care profession concerned esp. with examining the eyes for defects of vision and with prescribing corrective lenses or eye exercises — **op·to·met·ric** \ˌäp-tə-'me-trik\ *adj* — **op·tom·e·trist** \äp-'tä-mə-trist\ *n*

opt out *vb* : to choose not to participate

op·u·lence \'ä-pyə-ləns\ *n* **1** : WEALTH **2** : ABUNDANCE

op·u·lent \'ä-pyə-lənt\ *adj* **1** : WEALTHY **2** : richly abundant — **op·u·lent·ly** *adv*

opus \'ō-pəs\ *n, pl* **opera** \'ō-pə-rə, 'ä-\ *also* **opus·es** \'ō-pə-səz\ : WORK; *esp* : a musical composition

or \'ȯr\ *conj* — used as a function word to indicate an alternative (sink ~ swim)

OR *abbr* **1** operating room **2** Oregon

-or *n suffix* : one that does a (specified) thing (calculat*or*)

or·a·cle \'ȯr-ə-kəl\ *n* **1** : one held to give divinely inspired answers or revelations **2** : an authoritative or wise utterance; *also* : a person of great authority or wisdom — **orac·u·lar** \ȯ-'ra-kyə-lər\ *adj*

¹oral \'ȯr-əl\ *adj* **1** : SPOKEN (an ~ report) **2** : of, given through, or involving the mouth (an ~ vaccine) **3** : of, relating to, or characterized by the first stage of psychosexual development in psychoanalytic theory in which libidinal gratification is derived from intake (as of food), by sucking, and later by biting **4** : relating to or characterized by personality traits of passive dependency and aggressiveness — **oral·ly** *adv*

²oral *n* : an oral examination — usu. used in pl.

oral sex *n* : oral stimulation of the genitals : CUNNILINGUS, FELLATIO

orang \ə-'raŋ\ *n* : ORANGUTAN

or·ange \'är-inj, 'ȯr-\ *n* **1** : a juicy citrus fruit with reddish yellow rind; *also* : an evergreen tree that bears this fruit **2** : a color between red and yellow — **or·ang·ey** *or* **or·angy** \'är-in-jē, 'ȯr-\ *adj*

or·ange·ade \ˌär-in-'jād, ˌȯr-\ *n* : a beverage of orange juice, sugar, and water

orange hawkweed *n* : a weedy herb related to the daisies with bright orange-red flower heads

or·ange·ry \'är-inj-rē, 'ȯr-\ *n, pl* **-ries** : a protected place (as a greenhouse) for raising oranges in cool climates

orang·utan \ə-'raŋ-ə-ˌtaŋ, -ˌtan\ *n* [Bazaar Malay (Malay-based pidgin), fr. Malay *orang* man + *hutan* forest] : a large reddish brown tree-living anthropoid ape of Borneo and Sumatra

orate \ȯ-'rāt\ *vb* **orat·ed**; **orat·ing** : to speak in a declamatory manner

ora·tion \ə-'rā-shən\ *n* : an elaborate discourse delivered in a formal and dignified manner

or·a·tor \'ȯr-ə-tər\ *n* : one noted for skill and power as a public speaker

or·a·tor·i·cal \ˌȯr-ə-'tȯr-i-kəl\ *adj* : of, relating to, or characteristic of an orator or oratory — **or·a·tor·i·cal·ly** \-'tȯr-i-k(ə-)lē\ *adv*

or·a·to·rio \ˌȯr-ə-'tȯr-ē-ˌō\ *n, pl* **-rios** : a lengthy choral work usu. on a scriptural subject

¹or·a·to·ry \'ȯr-ə-ˌtȯr-ē\ *n, pl* **-ries** : a private or institutional chapel

²oratory *n* : the art of speaking eloquently and effectively in public ♦ *Synonyms* RHETORIC, ELOCUTION

orb \'ȯrb\ *n* : a spherical body; *also* : EYE

¹or·bit \'ȯr-bət\ *n* [L *orbita*, lit., path, rut] **1** : a path described by one body in its revolution about another **2** : range or sphere of activity — **or·bit·al** \-bə-tᵊl\ *adj*

²orbit *vb* **1** : CIRCLE **2** : to send up and make revolve in an orbit (~ a satellite) — **or·bit·er** *n*

or·ca \'ȯr-kə\ *n* : KILLER WHALE

orch *abbr* orchestra

or·chard \'ȯr-chərd\ *n* [ME, fr. OE *ortgeard*, fr. *ort-* (fr. L *hortus* garden) + *geard* yard] : a place where fruit trees, sugar maples, or nut trees are grown; *also* : the trees of such a place — **or·chard·ist** \-chər-dist\ *n*

or·ches·tra \'ȯr-kə-strə\ *n* **1** : the front section of seats on the main floor of a theater **2** : a group of instrumentalists organized to perform ensemble music — **or·ches·tral** \ȯr-'kes-trəl\ *adj* — **or·ches·tral·ly** *adv*

or·ches·trate \'ȯr-kə-ˌstrāt\ *vb* **-trat·ed**; **-trat·ing** **1** : to compose or arrange for an orchestra **2** : to arrange so as to achieve a desired effect (~ a campaign) — **or·ches·tra·tion** \ˌȯr-kə-'strā-shən\ *n*

or·chid \'ȯr-kəd\ *n* : any of a large family of plants having often showy flowers with three petals of which the middle one is enlarged into a lip; *also* : a flower of an orchid

ord *abbr* **1** order **2** ordnance

or·dain \ȯr-'dān\ *vb* **1** : to admit to the ministry or priesthood by the ritual of a church **2** : DECREE, ENACT; *also* : DESTINE — **or·dain·ment** *n*

or·deal \ȯr-'dēl, 'ȯr-ˌdēl\ *n* : a severe trial or experience

¹or·der \'ȯr-dər\ *vb* **1** : ARRANGE, REGULATE **2** : COMMAND **3** : to place an order

²order *n* **1** : a group of people formally united; *also* : a badge or medal of such a group **2** : any of the several grades of the Christian ministry; *also, pl* : ORDINATION **3** : a rank, class, or special group of persons or things **4** : a category of biological classification ranking above the family and below the class **5** : ARRANGEMENT, SEQUENCE; *also* : the prevailing state of things **6** : a customary mode of procedure; *also* : the rule of law or proper authority **7** : a specific rule, regulation, or authoritative direction **8** : a style of building; *also* : an architectural column forming the unit of a style **9** : condition esp. with regard to repair **10** : a direction to pay money or to buy or sell goods; *also* : goods bought or sold — **in order** : APPROPRIATE, DESIRABLE ⟨apologies are *in order*⟩ — **in order to** : for the purpose of

¹**or·der·ly** \'ȯr-dər-lē\ *adj* **1** : arranged according to some order; *also* : NEAT, TIDY **2** : well behaved ⟨an ∼ crowd⟩ ✦ **Synonyms** METHODICAL, SYSTEMATIC, REGULAR — **or·der·li·ness** *n*

²**orderly** *n, pl* **-lies 1** : a soldier who attends a superior officer **2** : a hospital attendant who does general work

or·di·nal \'ȯr-də-nəl\ *adj* : indicating order or rank (as sixth) in a series

ordinal number *n* : a number (as first, second, or third) that designates the place of an item in an ordered sequence — compare CARDINAL NUMBER

or·di·nance \'ȯr-də-nəns\ *n* : an authoritative decree or law; *esp* : a municipal regulation

or·di·nary \'ȯr-də-ˌner-ē\ *adj* **1** : to be expected : USUAL **2** : of common quality, rank, or ability ⟨∼ kids⟩; *also* : POOR, INFERIOR ⟨∼ wine⟩ ✦ **Synonyms** CUSTOMARY, ROUTINE, NORMAL, EVERYDAY — **or·di·nar·i·ly** \ˌȯr-də-ner-ə-lē\ *adv* — **or·di·nar·i·ness** \'ȯr-də-ˌner-ē-nəs\ *n*

or·di·nate \'ȯr-də-nət, -ˌnāt\ *n* : the vertical coordinate of a point in a plane coordinate system obtained by measuring parallel to the y-axis

or·di·na·tion \ˌȯr-də-'nā-shən\ *n* : the act or ceremony by which a person is ordained

ord·nance \'ȯrd-nəns\ *n* **1** : military supplies **2** : CANNON, ARTILLERY

Or·do·vi·cian \ˌȯr-də-'vi-shən\ *adj* : of, relating to, or being the period of the Paleozoic era between the Cambrian and the Silurian — **Ordovician** *n*

or·dure \'ȯr-jər\ *n* : EXCREMENT

ore \'ȯr\ *n* : a naturally occurring mineral mined to obtain a substance that it contains

øre \'ər-ə\ *n, pl* **ore** — see *krona, krone* at MONEY table

Ore *or* **Oreg** *abbr* Oregon

oreg·a·no \ə-'re-gə-ˌnō\ *n* : a bushy perennial mint used as a seasoning and a source of oil

org *abbr* organization; organized

or·gan \'ȯr-gən\ *n* **1** : a musical instrument having sets of pipes sounded by compressed air and controlled by keyboards; *also* : an electronic keyboard instrument that approximates the sounds of the pipe organ **2** : a differentiated animal or plant structure (as a heart or a leaf) made up of cells and tissues and performing some bodily function **3** : a group that performs a specialized function ⟨the various ∼s of government⟩ **4** : PERIODICAL ⟨the official ∼ of the party⟩

or·gan·dy *also* **or·gan·die** \'ȯr-gən-dē\ *n, pl* **-dies** [F *organdi*] : a fine transparent muslin with a stiff finish

or·gan·elle \ˌȯr-gə-'nel\ *n* : a specialized cell part that resembles an organ in having a special function

or·gan·ic \ȯr-'ga-nik\ *adj* **1** : of, relating to, or arising in a bodily organ **2** : of, relating to, or derived from living things **3** : of, relating to, or containing carbon compounds **4** : of or relating to a branch of chemistry dealing with carbon compounds **5** : involving, producing, or dealing in foods produced without the use of laboratory-made fertilizers, growth substances, antibiotics, or pesticides ⟨∼ farming⟩ **6** : ORGANIZED ⟨an ∼ whole⟩ — **or·gan·i·cal·ly** \-ni-k(ə-)lē\ *adv*

or·ga·ni·sa·tion, **or·ga·nise** *Brit var of* ORGANIZATION, ORGANIZE

or·gan·ism \'ȯr-gə-ˌni-zəm\ *n* : an individual living thing (as a person, animal, or plant) — **or·gan·is·mic** \ˌȯr-gə-'niz-mik\ *adj*

or·gan·ist \'ȯr-gə-nist\ *n* : a person who plays an organ

or·ga·ni·za·tion \ˌȯr-gə-nə-'zā-shən\ *n* **1** : the act or process of organizing or of being organized; *also* : the condition or manner of being organized **2** : ASSOCIATION, SOCIETY **3** : an administrative structure (as a business or a political party) — **or·ga·ni·za·tion·al** \-shə-nəl\ *adj*

or·ga·nize \'ȯr-gə-ˌnīz\ *vb* **-nized**; **-niz·ing 1** : to develop an organic structure **2** : to form into a complete and functioning whole **3** : to set up an administrative structure for **4** : to arrange by systematic planning and united effort **5** : to join in a union; *also* : UNIONIZE ✦ **Synonyms** INSTITUTE, FOUND, ESTABLISH, CONSTITUTE — **or·ga·niz·er** *n*

or·gano·chlo·rine \ȯr-ˌga-nə-'klȯr-ˌēn\ *adj* : of, relating to, or being a chlorinated hydrocarbon pesticide (as DDT) — **organochlorine** *n*

or·gano·phos·phate \-'fäs-ˌfāt\ *n* : an organophosphorus pesticide — **organophosphate** *adj*

or·gano·phos·pho·rus \-'fäs-fə-rəs\ *also* **or·gano·phos·pho·rous** \-fäs-'fȯr-əs\ *adj* : of, relating to, or being a phosphorus-containing organic pesticide (as malathion)

or·gan·za \ȯr-'gan-zə\ *n* : a sheer dress fabric resembling organdy and usu. made of silk, rayon, or nylon

or·gasm \'ȯr-ˌga-zəm\ *n* : the climax of sexual excitement — **or·gas·mic** \ȯr-'gaz-mik\ *adj*

or·gi·as·tic \ˌȯr-jē-'as-tik\ *adj* : of, relating to, or marked by orgies

or·gu·lous \'ȯr-gyə-ləs, -gə-\ *adj* : PROUD

or·gy \'ȯr-jē\ *n, pl* **orgies** : a gathering marked by unrestrained indulgence (as in sexual activity, alcohol, or drugs)

ori·el \'ȯr-ē-əl\ *n* : a window built out from a wall and usu. supported by a bracket

ori·ent \'ȯr-ē-ˌent\ *vb* **1** : to set in a definite position esp. in relation to the points of the compass **2** : to acquaint with an existing situation or environment **3** : to direct toward the interests of a particular group

Orient *n* : EAST **3**; *esp* : the countries of eastern Asia

ori·en·tal \ˌȯr-ē-'en-tᵊl\ *adj, often cap* [fr. *Orient* East, fr. ME, fr. AF, fr. L *orient-, oriens*, fr. prp. of *oriri* to rise] : of or situated in Asia

ori·en·tate \'ȯr-ē-ən-ˌtāt\ *vb* **-tat·ed**; **-tat·ing 1** : ORIENT **2** : to face east

ori·en·ta·tion \ˌȯr-ē-ən-tā-shən\ *n* **1** : the act or state of being oriented **2** : a person's sexual identity as bisexual, heterosexual, homosexual, pansexual, etc.

or·i·fice \'ȯr-ə-fəs\ *n* : OPENING, MOUTH

ori·flamme \'ȯr-ə-ˌflam\ *n* : a brightly colored banner used as a standard or ensign in battle

orig *abbr* original; originally

ori·ga·mi \ˌȯr-ə-'gä-mē\ *n* : the Japanese art or process of paper folding

or·i·gin \'ȯr-ə-jən\ *n* **1** : ANCESTRY **2** : rise, beginning, or derivation from a source; *also* : CAUSE **3** : the intersection of coordinate axes

¹**orig·i·nal** \ə-'ri-jə-nəl\ *n* : something from which a copy, reproduction, or translation is made : PROTOTYPE

²**original** *adj* **1** : FIRST, INITIAL **2** : not copied from something else : FRESH **3** : INVENTIVE — **orig·i·nal·i·ty** \-ˌri-jə-'na-lə-tē\ *n* — **orig·i·nal·ly** \-'ri-jə-nᵊl-ē\ *adv*

orig·i·nate \ə-'ri-jə-ˌnāt\ *vb* **-nat·ed**; **-nat·ing 1** : to give rise to : INITIATE **2** : to come into existence : BEGIN — **orig·i·na·tor** \-ˌnā-tər\ *n*

ori·ole \'ȯr-ē-ˌōl\ *n* : any of various New World birds of which the males are usu. black and yellow or black and orange

or·i·son \'ȯr-ə-sən\ *n* : PRAYER

or·mo·lu \'ȯr-mə-ˌlü\ *n* : a golden or gilded brass used for decorative purposes

¹**or·na·ment** \'ȯr-nə-mənt\ *n* : something that lends grace or beauty — **or·na·men·tal** \ˌȯr-nə-'men-tᵊl\ *adj*

²**or·na·ment** \-ˌment\ *vb* : to provide with ornament : ADORN — **or·na·men·ta·tion** \ˌȯr-nə-mən-'tā-shən\ *n*

or·nate \ȯr-'nāt\ *adj* : elaborately decorated ⟨an ∼ mantel⟩ — **or·nate·ly** *adv* — **or·nate·ness** *n*

or·nery \'ȯr-nə-rē, 'ä-nə-\ *adj* : having an irritable disposition

or·ni·thol·o·gy \ˌȯr-nə-'thä-lə-jē\ *n, pl* **-gies** : a branch of zoology dealing with birds — **or·ni·tho·log·i·cal** \-thə-'lä-ji-kəl\ *adj* — **or·ni·thol·o·gist** \-'thä-lə-jist\ *n*

oro·tund \'ȯr-ə-ˌtənd\ *adj* **1** : SONOROUS ⟨an ∼ voice⟩ **2** : POMPOUS ⟨an ∼ speech⟩ — **oro·tun·di·ty** \ȯr-ə-'tən-di-tē\ *n*

or·phan \'ȯr-fən\ *n* : a child deprived by death of one or usu. both parents — **orphan** *vb*

or·phan·age \'ȯr-fə-nij\ *n* : an institution for the care of orphans

or·tho·don·tia \ˌȯr-thə-'dän-chə, -chē-ə\ *n* : ORTHODONTICS

or·tho·don·tics \ˌȯr-thə-'dän-tiks\ *n* : a branch of dentistry concerned with the correction of faults in the arrangement and placing of the teeth — **or·tho·don·tic** \-tik\ *adj* — **or·tho·don·tist** \-'dän-tist\ *n*

or·tho·dox \'òr-thə-ˌdäks\ *adj* [ME *orthodoxe*, fr. MF or LL; MF *orthodoxe*, fr. LL *orthodoxus*, fr. LGk *orthodoxos*, fr. Gk *orthos* right + *doxa* opinion] **1** : conforming to established doctrine esp. in religion **2** : CONVENTIONAL **3** *cap* : of or relating to a Christian church originating in the church of the Eastern Roman Empire — **or·tho·doxy** \-ˌdäk-sē\ *n*

or·thog·ra·phy \òr-'thä-grə-fē\ *n* : SPELLING — **or·tho·graph·ic** \ˌòr-thə-'gra-fik\ *adj*

or·tho·pe·dics *also* **or·tho·pae·dics** \ˌòr-thə-'pē-diks\ *n sing or pl* : a branch of medicine concerned with the correction or prevention of skeletal injuries or disorders — **or·tho·pe·dic** *also* **or·tho·pae·dic** \-dik\ *adj* — **or·tho·pe·dist** \-dist\ *n*

-ory *adj suffix* **1** : of, relating to, or characterized by ⟨anticipat*ory*⟩ **2** : serving for, producing, or maintaining ⟨illus*ory*⟩

Os *symbol* osmium

OS *abbr* **1** [L *oculus sinister*] left eye **2** ordinary seaman **3** out of stock

Osage \ō-'sāj\ *n, pl* **Osag·es** *or* **Osage** : a member of an American Indian people orig. of Missouri

os·cil·late \'ä-sə-ˌlāt\ *vb* **-lat·ed; -lat·ing 1** : to swing backward and forward like a pendulum **2** : to move or travel back and forth between two points **3** : VARY, FLUCTUATE — **os·cil·la·tion** \ˌä-sə-'lā-shən\ *n* — **os·cil·la·tor** \'ä-sə-ˌlā-tər\ *n* — **os·cil·la·to·ry** \'ä-sə-lə-ˌtòr-ē\ *adj*

os·cil·lo·scope \ä-'si-lə-ˌskōp\ *n* : an instrument in which variations in current or voltage appear as a visible wave form on a fluorescent screen

os·cu·late \'äs-kyə-ˌlāt\ *vb* **-lat·ed; -lat·ing** : KISS — **os·cu·la·tion** \ˌäs-kyə-'lā-shən\ *n* — **os·cu·la·to·ry** \'äs-kyə-lə-ˌtòr-ē\ *adj*

Osee \'ō-ˌzē, ō-'zā-ə\ *n* : HOSEA

OSHA \'ō-shə\ *abbr* Occupational Safety and Health Administration

osier \'ō-zhər\ *n* : any of various willows with pliable twigs used esp. in making baskets and furniture; *also* : a twig from an osier

os·mi·um \'äz-mē-əm\ *n* : a very heavy hard brittle metallic chemical element used esp. as a catalyst and in alloys

os·mo·sis \äz-'mō-səs, äs-\ *n* : movement of a solvent through a semipermeable membrane into a solution of higher concentration that tends to equalize the concentrations of the solutions on either side of the membrane — **os·mot·ic** \-'mä-tik\ *adj*

os·prey \'äs-prē, -ˌprā\ *n, pl* **ospreys** : a large dark brown and white fish-eating hawk

os·si·fy \'ä-sə-ˌfī\ *vb* **-fied; -fy·ing** : to make or become hardened or set in one's ways ⟨an *ossified* regime⟩ — **os·si·fi·ca·tion** \ˌä-sə-fə-'kā-shən\ *n*

os·su·ary \'ä-shə-ˌwer-ē, -syə-\ *n, pl* **-ar·ies** : a depository for the bones of the dead

os·ten·si·ble \ä-'sten-sə-bəl\ *adj* : shown outwardly : PROFESSED, APPARENT — **os·ten·si·bly** \-blē\ *adv*

os·ten·ta·tion \ˌäs-tən-'tā-shən\ *n* : pretentious or excessive display — **os·ten·ta·tious** \-shəs\ *adj* — **os·ten·ta·tious·ly** *adv*

os·te·o·ar·thri·tis \ˌäs-tē-ō-är-'thrī-təs\ *n* : arthritis marked by degeneration of the cartilage and bone of joints

os·teo·path \'äs-tē-ə-ˌpath\ *n* : a practitioner of osteopathy

os·te·op·a·thy \ˌäs-tē-'ä-pə-thē\ *n* : a system of treating diseases emphasizing manipulation (as of joints) but not excluding other agencies (as the use of medicine and surgery) — **os·teo·path·ic** \ˌäs-tē-ə-'pa-thik\ *adj*

os·teo·po·ro·sis \ˌäs-tē-ō-pə-'rō-səs\ *n, pl* **-ro·ses** \-ˌsēz\ : a condition affecting esp. older women and characterized by fragile and porous bones

os·tra·cize *Brit var of* OSTRACIZE

os·tra·cize \'äs-trə-ˌsīz\ *vb* **-cized; -ciz·ing** [Gk *ostrakizein* to banish by voting with potsherds, fr. *ostrakon* shell, potsherd] : to exclude from a group by common consent — **os·tra·cism** \-ˌsi-zəm\ *n*

os·trich \'äs-trich, 'òs-\ *n* : a very large swift-footed flightless bird of Africa

Os·we·go tea \ä-ˌswē-gō-\ *n* : a No. American mint with showy scarlet flowers

OT *abbr* **1** occupational therapy **2** Old Testament **3** overtime

¹oth·er \'ə-thər\ *adj* **1** : being the one left; *also* : being the ones distinct from those first mentioned **2** : ALTERNATE ⟨every ~ day⟩ **3** : DIFFERENT **4** : ADDITIONAL **5** : recently past ⟨the ~ night⟩

²other *pron* **1** : remaining one or ones **2** : a different or additional one ⟨something or ~⟩

oth·er·wise \'ə-thər-ˌwīz\ *adv* **1** : in a different way **2** : in different circumstances **3** : in other respects **4** : if not **5** : NOT — **otherwise** *adj*

oth·er·world \-ˌwərld\ *n* : a world beyond death or beyond present reality

oth·er·world·ly \ˌə-thər-'wərld-lē\ *adj* : not worldly : concerned with spiritual, intellectual, or imaginative matters

oti·ose \'ō-shē-ˌōs, 'ō-tē-\ *adj* **1** : FUTILE **2** : IDLE **3** : USELESS ⟨~ details⟩

oto·lar·yn·gol·o·gy \ˌō-tō-ˌla-rən-'gä-lə-jē\ *n* : a medical specialty concerned esp. with the ear, nose, and throat — **oto·lar·yn·gol·o·gist** \-jist\ *n*

oto·rhi·no·lar·yn·gol·o·gy \ˌō-tō-ˌrī-nō-ˌla-rən-'gä-lə-jē\ *n* : OTOLARYNGOLOGY — **oto·rhi·no·lar·yn·gol·o·gist** \-jist\ *n*

OTS *abbr* officers' training school

Ot·ta·wa \'ä-tə-wə, -ˌwä, -ˌwò\ *n, pl* **Ottawas** *or* **Ottawa** : a member of an American Indian people of Michigan and southern Ontario

ot·ter \'ä-tər\ *n, pl* **otters** *also* **otter** : any of various webfooted fish-eating mammals with dark brown fur that are related to the weasels; *also* : the fur

otter

ot·to·man \'ä-tə-mən\ *n* : an upholstered seat or couch usu. without a back; *also* : an overstuffed footstool

ou·bli·ette \ˌü-blē-'et\ *n* [F, fr. MF, fr. *oublier* to forget, ultim. fr. L *oblivisci*] : a dungeon with an opening at the top

ought \'òt\ *verbal auxiliary* — used to express moral obligation, advisability, natural expectation, or logical consequence ⟨you ~ to apologize⟩

ou·gui·ya \ü-'gwē-ə, -'gē-\ *n, pl* **ouguiya** — see MONEY table

ounce \'aùns\ *n* [ME, fr. AF *unce*, fr. L *uncia* twelfth part, ounce, fr. *unus* one] **1** : a unit of avoirdupois, troy, and apothecaries' weight — see WEIGHT table **2** : FLUID OUNCE

our \är, 'aù(-ə)r\ *adj* : of or relating to us or ourselves

ours \'aùr(-ə)z, 'ärz\ *pron* : that which belongs to us

our·selves \är-'selvz, aù(-ə)r-\ *pron* : our own selves — used reflexively, for emphasis, or in absolute constructions ⟨we pleased ~⟩ ⟨we'll do it ~⟩ ⟨we were tourists ~⟩

-ous *adj suffix* : full of : abounding in : having : possessing the qualities of ⟨clamor*ous*⟩ ⟨poison*ous*⟩

oust \'aùst\ *vb* : to eject from or deprive of property or position : EXPEL ♦ **Synonyms** EVICT, DISMISS, BANISH, DEPORT

oust·er \'aùs-tər\ *n* : EXPULSION

¹out \'aùt\ *adv* **1** : in a direction away from the inside or center **2** : beyond control **3** : to extinction, exhaustion, or completion **4** : in or into the open **5** : so as to retire a batter or base runner; *also* : so as to be retired

²out *vb* : to become known ⟨the truth will ~⟩

³out *prep* **1** : out through ⟨looked ~ the window⟩ **2** : outward on or along ⟨drive ~ the river road⟩

⁴out *adj* **1** : situated outside or at a distance **2** : not in : ABSENT; *also* : not being in power **3** : removed from play as a batter or base runner **4** : not being in vogue or fashion : not up-to-date **5** : attempting a particular activity ⟨won his first time ~⟩

⁵out *n* **1** : one who is out of office **2** : the retiring of a batter or base runner

out·age \'aù-tij\ *n* : a period or instance of interruption esp. of electricity

out–and–out *adj* : COMPLETE, THOROUGHGOING ⟨an ~ fraud⟩

out·bid \ˌaut-'bid\ *vb* : to make a higher bid than

¹out·board \'aut-ˌbȯrd\ *adj* **1** : situated outboard **2** : having or using an outboard motor

²outboard *adv* **1** : outside a ship's hull : away from the long axis of a ship **2** : in a position closer to the wing tip of an airplane

outboard motor *n* : a small internal combustion engine with propeller attached for mounting at the stern of a small boat

out·bound \'aut-ˌbaund\ *adj* : outward bound ⟨~ traffic⟩

out·break \-ˌbrāk\ *n* **1** : a sudden increase in activity, incidence, or numbers **2** : INSURRECTION, REVOLT

out·build·ing \-ˌbil-diŋ\ *n* : a building separate from but accessory to a main house

out·burst \-ˌbərst\ *n* **1** : ERUPTION; *esp* : a violent expression of feeling

out·cast \-ˌkast\ *n* : one that is cast out by society

out·class \aut-'klas\ *vb* : SURPASS

out·come \'aut-ˌkəm\ *n* : a final consequence : RESULT

out·crop \-ˌkräp\ *n* : a coming out of bedrock to the surface of the ground; *also* : the part of a rock formation that thus appears — **outcrop** *vb*

out·cry \-ˌkrī\ *n* : a loud cry : CLAMOR

out·dat·ed \aut-'dā-təd\ *adj* : OUTMODED

out·dis·tance \-'dis-təns\ *vb* : to go far ahead of (as in a race) : OUTSTRIP

out·do \-'dü\ *vb* **-did** \-'did\; **-done** \-'dən\; **-do·ing**; **-does** \-'dəz\ : to go beyond in action or performance

out·door \'aut-ˌdȯr, -'dȯr\ *also* **out·doors** \-ˌdȯrz, -'dȯrz\ *adj* **1** : of or relating to the outdoors **2** : performed outdoors **3** : not enclosed (as by a roof)

¹out·doors \aut-'dȯrz, -'dȯrz\ *adv* : in or into the open air

²outdoors *n* **1** : the open air **2** : the world away from human habitation — **out·doorsy** \ˌaut-'dȯr-zē\ *adj*

out·draw \aut-'drȯ\ *vb* **-drew** \-'drü\; **-drawn** \-'drȯn\; **-draw·ing 1** : to attract a larger audience than **2** : to draw a handgun more quickly than

out·er \'au-tər\ *adj* **1** : EXTERNAL **2** : situated farther out; *also* : being away from a center

outer ear *n* : the outer visible portion of the ear that collects and directs sound waves toward the eardrum

out·er·most \-ˌmōst\ *adj* : farthest out

outer space *n* : SPACE 5

out·er·wear \'au-tər-ˌwer\ *n* **1** : clothing for outdoor wear **2** : outer clothing as opposed to underwear

out·face \aut-'fās\ *vb* **1** : to cause to waver or submit **2** : DEFY

out·field \'aut-ˌfēld\ *n* : the part of a baseball field beyond the infield and within the foul lines; *also* : players in the outfield — **out·field·er** \-ˌfēl-dər\ *n*

out·fight \aut-'fīt\ *vb* : to surpass in fighting : DEFEAT

¹out·fit \'aut-ˌfit\ *n* **1** : the equipment or apparel for a special purpose or occasion **2** : GROUP ⟨an insurance ~⟩

²outfit *vb* **out·fit·ted; out·fit·ting** : EQUIP — **out·fit·ter** *n*

out·flank \aut-'flaŋk\ *vb* : to get around the flank of (an opposing force)

out·flow \'aut-ˌflō\ *n* **1** : a flowing out **2** : something that flows out

out·fox \aut-'fäks\ *vb* : OUTWIT

out·go \'aut-ˌgō\ *n, pl* **outgoes** : EXPENDITURES, OUTLAY

out·go·ing \-ˌgō-iŋ\ *adj* **1** : going out ⟨~ tide⟩ **2** : retiring from a place or position **3** : FRIENDLY

out·grow \aut-'grō\ *vb* **-grew** \-'grü\; **-grown** \-'grōn\; **-grow·ing 1** : to grow faster than **2** : to grow too large for

out·growth \'aut-ˌgrōth\ *n* **1** : a product of growing out : OFFSHOOT; *also* : CONSEQUENCE, RESULT

out·guess \aut-'ges\ *vb* : OUTWIT

out·gun \-'gən\ *vb* : to surpass in firepower

out·house \'aut-ˌhaus\ *n* **1** : OUTBUILDING; *esp* : an outdoor toilet

out·ing \'au-tiŋ\ *n* : a brief stay or trip in the open ⟨a family ~⟩

out·land·ish \aut-'lan-dish\ *adj* **1** : of foreign appearance or manner; *also* : BIZARRE **2** : remote from civilization — **out·land·ish·ly** *adv*

out·last \-'last\ *vb* : to last longer than

¹out·law \'aut-ˌlȯ\ *n* **1** : a person excluded from the protection of the law **2** : a lawless person

²outlaw *vb* **1** : to deprive of the protection of the law **2** : to make illegal — **out·law·ry** \'aut-ˌlȯr-ē\ *n*

out·lay \'aut-ˌlā\ *n* **1** : the act of spending **2** : EXPENDITURE

out·let \'aut-ˌlet, -lət\ *n* **1** : EXIT, VENT **2** : a means of release (as for an emotion) **3** : a medium for usu. public expression : a media organization **4** : a market for a commodity **5** : a receptacle for the plug of an electrical device

¹out·line \'aut-ˌlīn\ *n* **1** : a line marking the outer limits of an object or figure **2** : a drawing in which only contours are marked **3** : SUMMARY, SYNOPSIS ⟨an ~ of the novel⟩ **4** : PLAN

²outline *vb* **1** : to draw the outline of **2** : to indicate the chief features or parts of

out·live \aut-'liv\ *vb* : to live longer than ◆ *Synonyms* OUTLAST, SURVIVE

out·look \'aut-ˌlúk\ *n* **1** : a place offering a view; *also* : VIEW **2** : STANDPOINT **3** : the prospect for the future

out·ly·ing \-ˌlī-iŋ\ *adj* : distant from a center or main body

out·ma·neu·ver \ˌaut-mə-'nü-vər, -'nyü-\ *vb* : to defeat by more skillful maneuvering

out·mod·ed \aut-'mō-dəd\ *adj* **1** : no longer in style **2** : no longer acceptable or current ⟨~ technology⟩

out·num·ber \-'nəm-bər\ *vb* : to exceed in number

out of *prep* **1** : out from within or behind ⟨walk *out of* the room⟩ ⟨look *out of* the window⟩ **2** : from a state of ⟨wake up *out of* a deep sleep⟩ **3** : beyond the limits of ⟨*out of* sight⟩ **4** : BECAUSE OF ⟨asked *out of* curiosity⟩ **5** : FROM, WITH ⟨built it *out of* scrap⟩ **6** : in or into a state of loss or not having ⟨cheated him *out of* $5000⟩ ⟨we're *out of* matches⟩ **7** : from among ⟨one *out of* four⟩ — **out of it** : SQUARE, OLD-FASHIONED

out–of–bounds *adv or adj* : outside the prescribed boundaries or limits

out–of–date *adj* : no longer in fashion or in use : OUTMODED

out–of–door *or* **out–of–doors** *adj* : OUTDOOR

out–of–the–way *adj* **1** : UNUSUAL **2** : being off the beaten track

out·pa·tient \'aut-ˌpā-shənt\ *n* : a patient who visits a hospital or clinic for diagnosis or treatment without staying overnight

out·per·form \ˌaut-pər-'fȯrm\ *vb* : to perform better than

out·play \aut-'plā\ *vb* : to play more skillfully than

out·point \-'pȯint\ *vb* : to win more points than

out·post \'aut-ˌpōst\ *n* **1** : a security detachment dispatched by a main body of troops to protect it from enemy surprise; *also* : a military base established (as by treaty) in a foreign country **2** : an outlying or frontier settlement

out·pour·ing \-ˌpȯr-iŋ\ *n* : something that pours out or is poured out

out·pull \aut-'púl\ *vb* : OUTDRAW 1

¹out·put \'aut-ˌpút\ *n* **1** : the amount produced (as by a machine or factory) : PRODUCTION **2** : the information produced by a computer

²output *vb* **out·put·ted** *or* **output; out·put·ting** : to produce as output

¹out·rage \'aut-ˌrāj\ *n* [ME, fr. AF *utrage, outrage* insult, excess, fr. *utre, outre* beyond, fr. L *ultra*] **1** : a violent or shameful act **2** : INJURY, INSULT **3** : the anger or resentment aroused by injury or insult

²outrage *vb* **out·raged; out·rag·ing 1** : RAPE **2** : to subject to violent injury or gross insult **3** : to arouse to extreme resentment

out·ra·geous \aut-'rā-jəs\ *adj* : extremely offensive, insulting, or shameful : SHOCKING — **out·ra·geous·ly** *adv*

out·rank \-'raŋk\ *vb* : to rank higher than

ou·tré \ü-'trā\ *adj* [F] : violating convention or propriety : BIZARRE ⟨~ creations⟩

¹out·reach \aut-'rēch\ *vb* **1** : to surpass in reach **2** : to get the better of by trickery

²out·reach \'aut-ˌrēch\ *n* **1** : the act of reaching out **2** : the extent of reach **3** : the extending of services beyond usual limits

out·rid·er \-ˌrī-dər\ *n* : a mounted attendant

out·rig·ger \-ˌri-gər\ *n* **1** : a frame attached to the side of a boat to prevent capsizing **2** : a craft equipped with an outrigger

¹**out·right** \aút-'rīt\ adv 1 : COMPLETELY 2 : INSTANTANEOUSLY

²**out·right** \'aút-ˌrīt\ adj 1 : being exactly what is stated ⟨an ~ lie⟩ 2 : given or made without reservation or encumbrance ⟨an ~ sale⟩

out·run \aút-'rən\ vb **-ran** \-'ran\; **-run**; **-run·ning** : to run faster than; also : EXCEED

out·sell \-'sel\ vb **-sold** \-'sōld\; **-sell·ing** : to exceed in sales

out·set \'aút-ˌset\ n : BEGINNING, START

out·shine \aút-'shīn\ vb **-shone** \-'shōn\ or **-shined**; **-shin·ing** 1 : to shine brighter than 2 : SURPASS

¹**out·side** \aút-'sīd, 'aút-ˌsīd\ n 1 : a place or region beyond an enclosure or boundary 2 : EXTERIOR 3 : the utmost limit or extent

²**outside** adj 1 : OUTER 2 : coming from without ⟨~ influences⟩ 3 : being apart from one's regular duties ⟨~ activities⟩ 4 : REMOTE ⟨an ~ chance⟩

³**outside** adv : on or to the outside

⁴**outside** prep 1 : on or to the outside of 2 : beyond the limits of 3 : EXCEPT

outside of prep 1 : OUTSIDE 2 : BESIDES

out·sid·er \aút-'sī-dər\ n : a person who does not belong to a group

out·size \'aút-ˌsīz\ also **out·sized** \-ˌsīzd\ adj : unusually large : extravagant in size or degree

out·skirts \-ˌskərts\ n pl : the outlying parts (as of a city) : BORDERS

out·smart \aút-'smärt\ vb : OUTWIT

out·source \'aút-ˌsòrs\ vb **-sourced**; **-sourcing** : to obtain (goods or services) from an outside supplier

out·spend \-'spend\ vb 1 : to exceed the limits of in spending ⟨~s his income⟩ 2 : to spend more than

out·spo·ken \aút-'spō-kən\ adj : direct and open in speech or expression — **out·spo·ken·ly** adv — **out·spo·ken·ness** n

out·spread \-'spred\ vb **-spread**; **-spread·ing** : to spread out

out·stand·ing \-'stan-diŋ\ adj 1 : PROJECTING 2 : UNPAID; also : UNRESOLVED ⟨~ warrants⟩ 3 : publicly issued and sold 4 : CONSPICUOUS; also : DISTINGUISHED — **out·stand·ing·ly** adv

out·stay \-'stā\ vb 1 : OVERSTAY 2 : to surpass in endurance

out·stretch \aút-'strech\ vb : to stretch out : EXTEND

out·strip \-'strip\ vb 1 : to go faster than 2 : EXCEL, SURPASS

out·take \'aút-ˌtāk\ n : something taken out; esp : a take that is not used in an edited version of a film or videotape

out·vote \-'vōt\ vb : to defeat by a majority of votes

¹**out·ward** \'aút-wərd\ adj 1 : moving or directed toward the outside 2 : showing outwardly

²**outward** or **out·wards** \-wərdz\ adv : toward the outside

out·ward·ly \-wərd-lē\ adv : on the outside : EXTERNALLY

out·wear \aút-'wer\ vb **-wore** \-'wòr\; **-worn** \-'wòrn\; **-wear·ing** : to wear longer than : OUTLAST

out·weigh \-'wā\ vb : to exceed in weight, value, or importance

out·wit \-'wit\ vb : to get the better of by superior cleverness

¹**out·work** \-'wərk\ vb : to outdo in working

²**out·work** \'aút-ˌwərk\ n : a minor defensive position outside a fortified area

out·worn \aút-'wòrn\ adj : OUTMODED

ou·zo \'ü-(ˌ)zō\ n : a colorless anise-flavored unsweetened Greek liqueur

ova pl of OVUM

oval \'ō-vəl\ adj [ML ovalis, fr. LL, of an egg, fr. L ovum egg] : egg-shaped; also : broadly elliptical — **oval** n

ova·ry \'ō-və-rē\ n, pl **-ries** 1 : one of the usu. paired female reproductive organs producing eggs and in vertebrates sex hormones 2 : the part of a flower in which seeds are produced — **ovar·i·an** \ō-'ver-ē-ən\ adj

ovate \'ō-ˌvāt\ adj : egg-shaped

ova·tion \ō-'vā-shən\ n [L ovation-, ovatio, fr. ovare to exult] : an enthusiastic popular tribute

ov·en \'ə-vən\ n : a chamber (as in a stove) for baking, heating, or drying

oven·bird \-ˌbərd\ n : a large olive-green American warbler that builds its dome-shaped nest on the ground

¹**over** \'ō-vər\ adv 1 : across a barrier or intervening space 2 : across the brim ⟨boil ~⟩ 3 : so as to bring the under-

side up 4 : out of a vertical position 5 : beyond some quantity, limit, or norm 6 : ABOVE 7 : at an end 8 : THROUGH ⟨read it ~⟩; also : THOROUGHLY ⟨still thinking it ~⟩ 9 : AGAIN ⟨do it ~⟩

²**over** prep 1 : above in position, authority, or scope ⟨towered ~ her⟩ ⟨obeyed those ~ him⟩ 2 : more than ⟨cost ~ $100⟩ 3 : ON, UPON ⟨a cape ~ her shoulders⟩ 4 : along the length of ⟨~ the road⟩ 5 : through the medium of : ON ⟨spoke ~ TV⟩ 6 : all through ⟨showed me ~ the house⟩ 7 : on or to the other side or beyond ⟨jump ~ a ditch⟩ 8 : DURING ⟨~ the past 25 years⟩ 9 : on account of ⟨trouble ~ money⟩

³**over** adj 1 : UPPER, HIGHER 2 : REMAINING 3 : ENDED ⟨those days are ~⟩

over- prefix 1 : so as to exceed or surpass 2 : excessive; excessively

overabundance	overhasty
overabundant	overheat
overachiever	overhype
overactive	overindulge
overaggressive	overindulgence
overambitious	overindulgent
overanxious	overinflate
overbid	overlarge
overbold	overlearn
overbuild	overload
overburden	overlong
overbuy	overmodest
overcapacity	overnice
overcapitalize	overoptimism
overcareful	overoptimistic
overcautious	overpay
overcompensation	overpraise
overconfidence	overproduce
overconfident	overproduction
overconscientious	overprotect
overcook	overprotective
overcritical	overrate
overcrowd	overreact
overdecorated	overreaction
overdependence	overrefinement
overdetermined	overregulate
overdevelop	overreliance
overdress	overrepresented
overeager	overripe
overeat	oversensitive
overeducated	oversensitiveness
overemphasis	oversimple
overemphasize	oversimplification
overenthusiastic	oversimplify
overestimate	overspecialization
overexcite	overspecialize
overexcited	overspend
overexert	overstimulation
overexertion	overstock
overextend	oversubtle
overfatigued	oversupply
overfeed	overtax
overfill	overtired
overgeneralization	overtrain
overgeneralize	overuse
overgenerous	overvalue
overgraze	overzealous

over·act \ˌō-vər-'akt\ vb : to exaggerate in acting

¹**over·age** \ˌō-vər-'āj\ adj 1 : too old to be useful 2 : older than is normal for one's position, function, or grade

²**over·age** \'ō-və-rij\ n : SURPLUS

over·all \ˌō-vər-'òl\ adj : including everything ⟨~ expenses⟩

over·alls \'ō-vər-ˌòlz\ n pl : pants of strong material usu. with a piece extending up to cover the chest

over·arm \-ˌärm\ adj : done with the arm raised above the shoulder

over·awe \ˌō-vər-'ò\ vb : to restrain or subdue by awe

over·bal·ance \-'ba-ləns\ vb 1 : OUTWEIGH 2 : to cause to lose balance

over·bear·ing \-'ber-iŋ\ adj : ARROGANT, DOMINEERING

over·bite \'ō-vər-ˌbīt\ n : the projection of the upper front teeth over the lower

over·blown \-ˈblōn\ *adj* 1 : PORTLY 2 : INFLATED, PRETENTIOUS

over·board \ˈō-vər-ˌbȯrd\ *adv* 1 : over the side of a ship into the water 2 : to extremes of enthusiasm

¹**overcast** \ˈō-vər-ˌkast\ *adj* : clouded over : GLOOMY

²**overcast** *n* : COVERING; *esp* : a covering of clouds

over·charge \ˌō-vər-ˈchärj\ *vb* 1 : to charge too much 2 : to fill or load too full — **over·charge** \ˈō-vər-ˌchärj\ *n*

over·coat \ˈō-vər-ˌkōt\ *n* : a warm coat worn over indoor clothing

over·come \ˌō-vər-ˈkəm\ *vb* **-came** \-ˈkām\; **-come; -com·ing** 1 : CONQUER 2 : to make helpless or exhausted

over·do \ˌō-vər-ˈdü\ *vb* **-did** \-ˈdid\; **-done** \-ˈdən\; **-do·ing; -does** \-ˈdəz\ 1 : to do too much; *also* : to tire oneself 2 : EXAGGERATE 3 : to cook too long

over·dose \ˈō-vər-ˌdōs\ *n* : too great a dose (as of medicine); *also* : a lethal or toxic amount (as of a drug) — **over·dose** \ˌō-vər-ˈdōs\ *vb*

over·draft \ˈō-vər-ˌdraft\ *n* : an overdrawing of a bank account; *also* : the sum overdrawn

over·draw \ˌō-vər-ˈdrȯ\ *vb* **-drew** \-ˈdrü\; **-drawn** \-ˈdrȯn\; **-draw·ing** 1 : to draw checks on a bank account for more than the balance 2 : EXAGGERATE

over·drive \ˈō-vər-ˌdrīv\ *n* : an automotive transmission gear that transmits to the driveshaft a speed greater than the engine speed

over·dub \ˌō-vər-ˈdəb\ *vb* : to transfer (recorded sound) onto an earlier recording for a combined effect — **over·dub** \ˌō-vər-ˈdəb\ *n*

over·due \-ˈdü, -ˈdyü\ *adj* 1 : unpaid when due ⟨an ∼ bill⟩; *also* : not appearing or presented on time ⟨an ∼ train⟩ 2 : more than ready

over·ex·pose \ˌō-vər-ik-ˈspōz\ *vb* : to expose (as film) for more time than is needed — **over·ex·po·sure** \-ˈspō-zhər\ *n*

¹**over·flow** \-ˈflō\ *vb* 1 : INUNDATE; *also* : to pour forth in a flood 2 : to flow over the brim or top of

²**over·flow** \ˈō-vər-ˌflō\ *n* 1 : FLOOD; *also* : SURPLUS 2 : an outlet for surplus liquid

over·fly \ˌō-vər-ˈflī\ *vb* **-flew** \-ˈflü\; **-flown** \-ˈflōn\; **-fly·ing** : to fly over in an aircraft or spacecraft — **over·flight** \ˈō-vər-ˌflīt\ *n*

over·grow \ˌō-vər-ˈgrō\ *vb* **-grew** \-ˈgrü\; **-grown** \-ˈgrōn\; **-grow·ing** 1 : to grow over so as to cover 2 : OUTGROW 3 : to grow excessively — **over·growth** \ˈō-vər-ˌgrōth\ *n*

over·hand \ˈō-vər-ˌhand\ *adj* : made with the hand brought down from above — **overhand** *adv* — **over·hand·ed** \-ˌhan-dəd\ *adv or adj*

¹**over·hang** \ˈō-vər-ˌhaŋ, ˌō-vər-ˈhaŋ\ *vb* **-hung** \-ˌhəŋ, -ˈhəŋ\; **-hang·ing** 1 : to project over : jut out 2 : to hang over threateningly

²**over·hang** \ˈō-vər-ˌhaŋ\ *n* : a part (as of a roof) that overhangs

over·haul \ˌō-vər-ˈhȯl\ *vb* 1 : to examine thoroughly and make necessary repairs and adjustments 2 : OVERTAKE

¹**over·head** \ˌō-vər-ˈhed\ *adv* : ALOFT

²**over·head** \ˈō-vər-ˌhed\ *adj* : operating or lying above ⟨∼ storage bins⟩

³**over·head** \ˈō-vər-ˌhed\ *n* : business expenses not chargeable to a particular part of the work

over·hear \ˌō-vər-ˈhir\ *vb* **-heard** \-ˈhərd\; **-hear·ing** : to hear without the speaker's knowledge or intention

over·joyed \ˌō-vər-ˈjȯid\ *adj* : filled with great joy

over·kill \ˈō-vər-ˌkil\ *n* 1 : destructive capacity greatly exceeding that required for a target 2 : a large excess

over·land \ˈō-vər-ˌland, -lənd\ *adv or adj* : by, on, or across land

over·lap \ˌō-vər-ˈlap\ *vb* 1 : to lap over 2 : to have something in common — **over·lap** \ˈō-vər-ˌlap\ *n*

over·lay \ˌō-vər-ˈlā\ *vb* **-laid** \-ˈlād\; **-lay·ing** : to lay or spread over or across — **over·lay** \ˈō-vər-ˌlā\ *n*

over·leap \ˌō-vər-ˈlēp\ *vb* **-leaped** *or* **-leapt** \-ˈlēpt, -ˈlept\; **-leap·ing** 1 : to leap over or across 2 : to defeat (oneself) by going too far

over·lie \ˌō-vər-ˈlī\ *vb* **-lay** \-ˈlā\; **-lain** \-ˈlān\; **-ly·ing** : to lie over or upon

¹**over·look** \ˌō-vər-ˈlük\ *vb* 1 : INSPECT 2 : to look down on from above 3 : to fail to see 4 : IGNORE ⟨∼ed his faults⟩; *also* : EXCUSE 5 : SUPERINTEND

²**over·look** \ˈō-vər-ˌlük\ *n* : a place from which to look upon a scene below

over·lord \-ˌlȯrd\ *n* : a lord who has supremacy over other lords

over·ly \ˈō-vər-lē\ *adv* : EXCESSIVELY

over·match \ˌō-vər-ˈmach\ *vb* : to be more than a match for : DEFEAT

over·much \-ˈməch\ *adj or adv* : too much

¹**over·night** \-ˈnīt\ *adv* 1 : on or during the night 2 : SUDDENLY ⟨became famous ∼⟩

²**overnight** *adj* : of, lasting, or staying the night ⟨∼ guests⟩

over·pass \ˈō-vər-ˌpas\ *n* 1 : a crossing (as of two highways) at different levels by means of a bridge 2 : the upper level of an overpass

over·play \ˌō-vər-ˈplā\ *vb* 1 : EXAGGERATE; *also* : OVEREMPHASIZE 2 : to rely too much on the strength of

over·pop·u·la·tion \ˌō-vər-ˌpä-pyə-ˈlā-shən\ *n* : the condition of having a population so dense as to cause a decline in population or in living conditions — **over·pop·u·la·ted** \-ˈpä-pyə-ˌlā-təd\ *adj*

over·pow·er \-ˈpau̇-(ə)r\ *vb* : to overcome by superior force

over·price \ˌō-vər-ˈprīs\ *vb* : to price too high

over·print \-ˈprint\ *vb* : to print over with something additional — **over·print** \ˈō-vər-ˌprint\ *n*

over·qual·i·fied \-ˈkwä-lə-ˌfīd\ *adj* : having more education, training, or experience than a job calls for

over·reach \ˌō-vər-ˈrēch\ *vb* : to defeat (oneself) by too great an effort

over·ride \-ˈrīd\ *vb* **-rode** \-ˈrōd\; **-rid·den** \-ˈri-dᵊn\; **-rid·ing** 1 : to ride over or across 2 : to prevail over; *also* : to set aside ⟨∼ a veto⟩

over·rule \-ˈrül\ *vb* 1 : to prevail over 2 : to rule against 3 : to set aside

¹**over·run** \-ˈrən\ *vb* **-ran** \-ˈran\; **-run; -run·ning** 1 : to defeat and occupy the positions of 2 : OVERSPREAD; *also* : INFEST 3 : to go beyond 4 : to flow over

²**over·run** \ˈō-vər-ˌrən\ *n* 1 : an act or instance of overrunning; *esp* : an exceeding of estimated costs 2 : the amount by which something overruns

over·sea \ˌō-vər-ˈsē, ˈō-vər-ˌsē\ *adj or adv* : OVERSEAS

over·seas \ˌō-vər-ˈsēz, -ˌsēz\ *adv or adj* : beyond or across the sea : ABROAD

over·see \ˌō-vər-ˈsē\ *vb* **-saw** \-ˈsȯ\; **-seen** \-ˈsēn\; **-see·ing** 1 : OVERLOOK 2 : INSPECT; *also* : SUPERVISE ⟨∼ the project⟩ — **over·seer** \ˈō-vər-ˌsir\ *n*

over·sell \ˌō-vər-ˈsel\ *vb* **-sold**; **-sel·ling** : to sell too much to or too much of

over·sexed \ˌō-vər-ˈsekst\ *adj* : exhibiting excessive sexual drive or interest

over·shad·ow \-ˈsha-dō\ *vb* 1 : to cast a shadow over 2 : to exceed in importance

over·shoe \ˈō-vər-ˌshü\ *n* : a protective outer shoe; *esp* : GALOSH

over·shoot \ˌō-vər-ˈshüt\ *vb* **-shot** \-ˈshät\; **-shoot·ing** 1 : to pass swiftly beyond 2 : to shoot over or beyond

over·sight \ˈō-vər-ˌsīt\ *n* 1 : SUPERVISION 2 : an inadvertent omission or error

over·size \ˌō-vər-ˈsīz\ *or* **over·sized** \-ˈsīzd\ *adj* : of more than ordinary size

over·sleep \ˌō-vər-ˈslēp\ *vb* **-slept** \-ˈslept\; **-sleep·ing** : to sleep beyond the time for waking

over·spread \-ˈspred\ *vb* **-spread**; **-spread·ing** : to spread over or above

over·state \-ˈstāt\ *vb* : EXAGGERATE — **over·state·ment** *n*

over·stay \-ˈstā\ *vb* : to stay beyond the time or limits of ⟨∼ed her welcome⟩

over·step \-ˈstep\ *vb* : EXCEED

over·sub·scribe \-səb-ˈskrīb\ *vb* : to subscribe for more of than is available, asked for, or offered for sale

overt \ō-ˈvərt, ˈō-ˌvərt\ *adj* [ME, fr. AF, fr. pp. of *ovrir* to open] : not secret ⟨∼ hostility⟩ — **overt·ly** *adv*

over·take \ˌō-vər-ˈtāk\ *vb* **-took** \-ˈtük\; **-tak·en** \-ˈtā-kən\; **-tak·ing** : to catch up with; *also* : to catch up with and pass by ⟨∼ the lead runner⟩

over-the-counter *adj* : sold lawfully without a prescription ⟨∼ drugs⟩

over-the-hill *adj* 1 : past one's prime 2 : advanced in age

over-the-top *adj* : extremely flamboyant or outrageous ⟨an ∼ performance⟩

over·throw \ˌō-vər-ˈthrō\ *vb* **-threw** \-ˈthrü\; **-thrown** \-ˈthrōn\; **-throw·ing** 1 : UPSET 2 : to bring down : DE-

FEAT ⟨~ a government⟩ **3** : to throw over or past — **over·throw** \ˈō-vər-ˌthrō\ n

over·time \ˈō-vər-ˌtīm\ n : time beyond a set limit; *esp* : working time in excess of a standard day or week — **overtime** *adv*

over·tone \-ˌtōn\ n **1** : one of the higher tones in a complex musical tone **2** : IMPLICATION, SUGGESTION ⟨political ~s⟩

over·trick \ˈō-vər-ˌtrik\ n : a card trick won in excess of the number bid

over·ture \ˈō-vər-ˌchur, -chər\ n [ME, lit., opening, fr. AF, fr. VL *opertura*, alter. of L *apertura*] **1** : an opening offer **2** : an orchestral introduction to a musical dramatic work

over·turn \ˌō-vər-ˈtərn\ vb **1** : to turn over : UPSET ⟨~ a vase⟩ **2** : INVALIDATE ⟨~ a court ruling⟩

over·view \ˈō-vər-ˌvyü\ n : a general survey : SUMMARY

over·ween·ing \ˌō-vər-ˈwē-niŋ\ adj **1** : ARROGANT ⟨~ pride⟩ **2** : IMMODERATE

over·weight \ˈō-vər-ˌwāt\ n **1** : weight above what is required or allowed **2** : bodily weight greater than normal — **overweight** adj

over·whelm \ˌō-vər-ˈhwelm\ vb **1** : OVERTHROW **2** : SUBMERGE **3** : to overcome completely

over·whelm·ing adj : EXTREME, GREAT ⟨~ joy⟩ — **over·whelm·ing·ly** adv

over·win·ter \-ˈwin-tər\ vb : to survive or pass the winter

over·work \-ˈwərk\ vb **1** : to work or cause to work too hard or long **2** : to use too much — **overwork** n

over·wrought \ˌō-vər-ˈrȯt\ adj **1** : extremely excited **2** : elaborated to excess

ovi·duct \ˈō-və-ˌdəkt\ n : a tube that serves for the passage of eggs from an ovary

ovip·a·rous \ō-ˈvi-pə-rəs\ adj : reproducing by eggs that hatch outside the parent's body

ovoid \ˈō-ˌvȯid\ or **ovoi·dal** \ō-ˈvȯi-dᵊl\ adj : egg-shaped : OVAL

ovu·la·tion \ˌäv-yə-ˈlā-shən, ˌōv-\ n : the discharge of a mature egg from the ovary — **ovu·late** \ˈäv-yə-ˌlāt, ˈōv-\ vb

ovule \ˈäv-yül, ˈōv-\ n : any of the bodies in a plant ovary that after fertilization become seeds

ovum \ˈō-vəm\ n, pl **ova** \-və\ : EGG 2

ow \ˈau̇\ interj — used esp. to express sudden pain

owe \ˈō\ vb **owed; ow·ing 1** : to be under obligation to pay or render **2** : to be indebted to or for; *also* : to be in debt

owing to prep : BECAUSE OF

owl \ˈau̇(-ə)l\ n : any of an order of chiefly nocturnal birds of prey with a large head and eyes and strong talons — **owl·ish** adj — **owl·ish·ly** adv

owl·et \ˈau̇-lət\ n : a young or small owl

¹own \ˈōn\ adj : belonging to oneself — used as an intensive after a possessive adjective ⟨her ~ car⟩

²own vb **1** : to have or hold as property **2** : to have

power or mastery over **3** : ACKNOWLEDGE ⟨would not ~ up to his mistake⟩; *also* : CONFESS — **own·er** n — **own·er·ship** n

³own pron : one or ones belonging to oneself — **on one's own** : for or by oneself : left to one's own resources

ox \ˈäks\ n, pl **ox·en** \ˈäk-sən\ also **ox** : any of the large domestic bovine mammals kept for milk, draft, and meat; *esp* : an adult castrated male ox

ox·blood \ˈäks-ˌbləd\ n : a moderate reddish brown

ox·bow \-ˌbō\ n **1** : a U-shaped collar worn by a draft ox **2** : a U-shaped bend in a river — **oxbow** adj

ox·ford \ˈäks-fərd\ n : a low shoe laced or tied over the instep

ox·i·dant \ˈäk-sə-dənt\ n : OXIDIZING AGENT — **oxidant** adj

ox·i·da·tion \ˌäk-sə-ˈdā-shən\ n : the act or process of oxidizing; *also* : the condition of being oxidized — **ox·i·da·tive** \ˈäk-sə-ˌdā-tiv\ adj

ox·ide \ˈäk-ˌsīd\ n : a compound of oxygen with another element or group

ox·i·dize \ˈäk-sə-ˌdīz\ vb **-dized; -diz·ing** : to combine with oxygen ⟨iron rusts because it is *oxidized* by exposure to the air⟩ — **ox·i·diz·er** n

oxidizing agent n : a substance (as oxygen or nitric acid) that oxidizes by taking up electrons

ox·y·gen \ˈäk-si-jən\ n [F *oxygène*, fr. Gk *oxys* acidic, lit., sharp + *-genēs* giving rise to; so called because it was once thought to be an essential element of all acids] : a colorless odorless gaseous chemical element that is found in the air, is essential to life, and is involved in combustion

ox·y·gen·ate \ˈäk-si-jə-ˌnāt\ vb **-at·ed; -at·ing** : to impregnate, combine, or supply with oxygen — **ox·y·gen·a·tion** \ˌäk-si-jə-ˈnā-shən\ n

oxygen mask n : a device worn over the nose and mouth through which oxygen is supplied

oxygen tent n : a canopy which can be placed over a bedridden person and within which a flow of oxygen can be maintained

ox·y·mo·ron \ˌäk-sē-ˈmȯr-ˌän\ n : a combination of contradictory words (as *cruel kindness*) — **ox·y·mo·ron·ic** \-mə-ˈrä-nik\ adj

oys·ter \ˈȯis-tər\ n : any of various marine mollusks with an irregular 2-valved shell that include commercially important edible shellfish and pearl producers — **oys·ter·ing** n — **oys·ter·man** \-mən\ n

oz abbr [obs. It *onza* (now *oncia*)] ounce; ounces

ozone \ˈō-ˌzōn\ n **1** : a bluish gaseous reactive form of oxygen that is formed naturally in the atmosphere and is used for disinfecting, deodorizing, and bleaching **2** : pure and refreshing air

ozone layer n : an atmospheric layer at heights of about 25 miles (40 kilometers) with high ozone content which blocks most solar ultraviolet radiation

P

¹p \ˈpē\ n, pl **p's** or **ps** \ˈpēz\ often cap : the 16th letter of the English alphabet

²p abbr, often cap **1** page **2** participle **3** past **4** pawn **5** pence; penny **6** per **7** petite **8** pint **9** pressure **10** purl

P symbol phosphorus

pa \ˈpä, ˈpȯ\ n : FATHER

¹Pa abbr **1** pascal **2** Pennsylvania

²Pa symbol protactinium

¹PA \ˌ(ˌ)pē-ˈā\ n : PHYSICIAN'S ASSISTANT

²PA abbr **1** Pennsylvania **2** per annum **3** power of attorney **4** press agent **5** private account **6** professional association **7** public address **8** purchasing agent

pa·an·ga \pä-ˈäŋ-gə\ n — see MONEY table

pab·u·lum \ˈpa-byə-ləm\ n [L, food, fodder] n : usu. soft digestible food

Pac abbr Pacific

PAC abbr political action committee

¹pace \ˈpās\ n **1** : rate of movement or progress (as in walking or working) **2** : a step in walking; *also* : a measure of length based on such a step **3** : GAIT; *esp* : a horse's gait in which the legs on the same side move together

²pace vb **paced; pac·ing 1** : to go or cover at a pace or with slow steps **2** : to measure off by paces ⟨~ off a 15-yard penalty⟩ **3** : to set or regulate the pace of

³pace \ˈpä-sē; ˈpä-ˌkä, -ˌchä\ prep : contrary to the opinion of

pace·mak·er \ˈpās-ˌmā-kər\ n **1** : one that sets the pace for another **2** : a body part (as of the heart) that serves to establish and maintain a rhythmic activity **3** : an electrical device for stimulating or steadying the heartbeat

pac·er \ˈpā-sər\ n **1** : a horse that paces **2** : PACEMAKER

pachy·derm \'pa-ki-,dərm\ n [F pachyderme, fr. Gk pachydermos thick-skinned, fr. pachys thick + derma skin] : any of various thick-skinned hoofed mammals (as an elephant)

pach·ys·an·dra \,pa-ki-'san-drə\ n : any of a genus of low perennial evergreen plants used as a ground cover

pa·cif·ic \pə-'si-fik\ adj 1 : tending to lessen conflict 2 : CALM, PEACEFUL

pac·i·fi·er \'pa-sə-,fī(-ə)r\ n : one that pacifies; esp : a device for a baby to chew or suck on

pac·i·fism \'pa-sə-,fi-zəm\ n : opposition to war or violence as a means of settling disputes — **pac·i·fist** \-fist\ n or adj — **pac·i·fis·tic** \,pa-sə-'fis-tik\ adj

pac·i·fy \'pa-sə-,fī\ vb **-fied; -fy·ing** 1 : to allay anger or agitation in : SOOTHE 2 : SETTLE; also : SUBDUE — **pac·i·fi·ca·tion** \,pa-sə-fə-'kā-shən\ n

¹**pack** \'pak\ n 1 : a compact bundle; also : a flexible container for carrying a bundle esp. on the back 2 : a large amount : HEAP 3 : a set of playing cards 4 : a group or band of people or animals 5 : wet absorbent material for application to the body

²**pack** vb 1 : to stow goods in transportation 2 : to fill in or surround so as to prevent passage of air, steam, or water 3 : to put into a protective container 4 : to load with a pack ⟨~ a mule⟩ 5 : to crowd in 6 : to make into a pack 7 : to cause to go without ceremony ⟨~ them off to school⟩ 8 : WEAR, CARRY ⟨~ a gun⟩

³**pack** vb : to make up fraudulently so as to secure a desired result ⟨~ a jury⟩

¹**pack·age** \'pa-kij\ n 1 : BUNDLE, PARCEL 2 : a group of related things offered as a whole

²**package** vb **pack·aged; pack·ag·ing** : to make into or enclose in a package

package deal n : an offer containing several items all or none of which must be accepted

package store n : a store that sells alcoholic beverages in sealed containers for consumption off the premises

pack·er \'pa-kər\ n : one that packs; esp : a wholesale food dealer

pack·et \'pa-kət\ n 1 : a small bundle or package 2 : a passenger boat carrying mail and cargo on a regular schedule

pack·horse \'pak-,hórs\ n : a horse used to carry goods or supplies

pack·ing \'pa-kiŋ\ n : material used to pack something

pack·ing·house \-,haús\ n : an establishment for processing and packing food and esp. meat and its by-products

pack rat n 1 : a bushy-tailed rodent of western No. America that hoards food and miscellaneous objects; also : any of several rodents of similar habit 2 : a person who collects or saves many esp. unneeded items

pack·sad·dle \'pak-,sa-dᵊl\ n : a saddle for supporting loads on the back of an animal

pack·thread \-,thred\ n : strong thread for tying

pact \'pakt\ n : AGREEMENT, TREATY

¹**pad** \'pad\ n 1 : a cushioning part or thing : CUSHION 2 : the cushioned underside of the foot or toes of some mammals 3 : the floating leaf of a water plant 4 : a writing tablet 5 : LAUNCHPAD 6 : living quarters; also : BED

²**pad** vb **pad·ded; pad·ding** 1 : to furnish with a pad or padding 2 : to expand with needless or fraudulent matter

pad·ding n : the material with which something is padded

¹**pad·dle** \'pa-dᵊl\ vb **pad·dled; pad·dling** : to move the hands and feet about in shallow water

²**paddle** n 1 : an implement with a flat blade used in propelling and steering a small craft (as a canoe) 2 : an implement used for stirring, mixing, or beating 3 : a broad board on the outer rim of a waterwheel or a paddle wheel

³**paddle** vb **pad·dled; pad·dling** 1 : to move on or through water by or as if by using a paddle 2 : to beat or stir with a paddle

paddle wheel n : a wheel with paddles around its outer edge used to move a boat

paddle wheeler n : a steam-driven vessel propelled by a paddle wheel

pad·dock \'pa-dək\ n 1 : a usu. enclosed area for pasturing or exercising animals; esp : one where racehorses are saddled and paraded before a race 2 : an area at a racecourse where racing cars are parked

pad·dy \'pa-dē\ n, pl **paddies** : wet land where rice is grown

paddy wagon n : an enclosed motortruck for carrying prisoners

pad·lock \'pad-,läk\ n : a removable lock with a curved piece that snaps into a catch — **padlock** vb

pa·dre \'pä-drā\ n [Sp or It or Pg, lit., father, fr. L pater] 1 : PRIEST 2 : a military chaplain

pad thai \'päd-'tī\ n, often cap T : a Thai dish of rice noodles stir-fried with additional ingredients

pae·an \'pē-ən\ n : an exultant song of praise or thanksgiving

pae·di·at·ric, pae·di·a·tri·cian, pae·di·at·rics chiefly Brit var of PEDIATRIC, PEDIATRICIAN, PEDIATRICS

pa·el·la \pä-'e-lə; -'äl-yə, -'ā-yə\ n : a saffron-flavored dish of rice, meat, seafood, and vegetables

pa·gan \'pā-gən\ n [ME, fr. LL paganus, fr. L, civilian, country dweller, fr. pagus country district] : HEATHEN — **pagan** adj — **pa·gan·ism** \-gə-,ni-zəm\ n

¹**page** \'pāj\ n : ATTENDANT; esp : one employed to deliver messages

²**page** vb **paged; pag·ing** 1 : to summon by repeatedly calling out the name of 2 : to send a message to via a pager

³**page** n 1 : a single leaf (as of a book); also : a single side of such a leaf 2 : the information at a single World Wide Web address

⁴**page** vb **paged; pag·ing** : to mark or number the pages of

pag·eant \'pa-jənt\ n [ME pagyn, padgeant, lit., scene of a play, fr. AF pagine, pagent, fr. ML pagina, perh. fr. L, page] : an elaborate spectacle, show, or procession esp. with tableaux or floats — **pag·eant·ry** \-jən-trē\ n

page·boy \'pāj-,bói\ n [¹page] : an often shoulder-length hairdo with the ends of the hair turned smoothly under

pag·er \'pā-jər\ n : one that pages; esp : a small radio receiver that alerts its user to incoming messages

pag·i·nate \'pa-jə-,nāt\ vb **-nat·ed; -nat·ing** : ⁴PAGE

pag·i·na·tion \,pa-jə-'nä-shən\ n 1 : the paging of written or printed matter 2 : the number and arrangement of pages (as of a book)

pa·go·da \pə-'gō-də\ n : a tower with roofs curving upward at the division of each of several stories

paid past and past part of PAY

pail \'pāl\ n : a usu. cylindrical vessel with a handle — **pail·ful** \-,fúl\ n

¹**pain** \'pān\ n 1 : PUNISHMENT, PENALTY 2 : suffering or distress of body or mind; also : a basic bodily sensation marked by discomfort (as throbbing or aching) 3 pl : great care 4 : one that irks or annoys — **pain·ful** \-fəl\ adj — **pain·ful·ly** adv — **pain·less** adj — **pain·less·ly** adv

²**pain** vb : to cause or experience pain

pain·kill·er \'pān-,ki-lər\ n : something (as a drug) that relieves pain — **pain·kill·ing** adj

pains·tak·ing \-,stā-kiŋ\ adj : taking pains : showing care — **pains·taking** n — **pains·tak·ing·ly** adv

¹**paint** \'pānt\ vb 1 : to apply color, pigment, or paint to 2 : to produce or portray in lines or colors on a surface; also : to practice the art of painting 3 : to decorate with colors 4 : to use cosmetics 5 : to describe vividly 6 : SWAB — **paint·er** n

²**paint** n 1 : something produced by painting 2 : MAKEUP 3 : a mixture of a pigment and a liquid that forms a thin adherent coating when spread on a surface; also : the dry pigment used in making this mixture 4 : an applied coating of paint

paint·ball \'pānt-,ból\ n : a game in which two teams try to capture each other's flag using guns that shoot paint-filled pellets

paint·brush \'pānt-,brəsh\ n : a brush for applying paint

painted lady n : a migratory butterfly with wings mottled in brown, orange, black, and white

painting n 1 : a work (as a picture) produced by painting 2 : the art or occupation of painting

¹**pair** \'per\ n, pl **pairs** also **pair** [ME paire, fr. AF, fr. L paria equal things, fr. neut. pl. of par equal] 1 : two things of a kind designed for use together 2 : something made up of two corresponding pieces ⟨a ~ of pants⟩ 3 : a set of two people or animals

²**pair** vb 1 : to arrange in pairs 2 : to form a pair : MATCH 3 : to become associated with another

pai·sa \pī-'sä\ n 1 pl **pai·se** \-'sā\ — see rupee at MONEY table 2 pl **paisa** — see rupee, taka at MONEY table

pais·ley \'pāz-lē\ adj, often cap : decorated with colorful curved abstract figures ⟨a ~ fabric⟩

Pai·ute \'pī-,üt, -,yüt\ n : a member of an American Indian people orig. of Utah, Arizona, Nevada, and California

pa·ja·mas \pə-'jä-məz, -'ja-\ n pl : a loose suit for sleeping or lounging

pal \'pal\ n : a close friend

pal·ace \'pa-ləs\ n [ME palais, fr. AF, fr. L palatium, fr. Palatium, the Palatine Hill in Rome where the emperors' residences were built] 1 : the official residence of a chief of state 2 : MANSION

pal·a·din \'pa-lə-dən\ n 1 : a trusted military leader (as for a medieval prince) 2 : a leading champion of a cause

pa·laes·tra \pə-'les-trə\ n, pl -trae \-(,)trē\ : a school in ancient Greece or Rome for sports (as wrestling)

pa·lan·quin \,pa-lən-'kēn\ n : an enclosed couch for one person borne on the shoulders of men by means of poles

pal·at·able \'pa-lə-tə-bəl\ adj : agreeable to the taste ✦ **Synonyms** APPETIZING, SAVORY, TASTY, TOOTHSOME

pal·a·tal \'pa-lə-tᵊl\ adj 1 : of or relating to the palate 2 : pronounced with some part of the tongue near or touching the hard palate ⟨the \y\ in yeast and the \sh\ in she are ~ sounds⟩

pal·a·tal·ize \'pa-lə-tə-,līz\ vb -ized; -iz·ing : to pronounce as or change into a palatal sound — **pal·a·tal·i·za·tion** \,pa-lə-tə-lə-'zā-shən\ n

pal·ate \'pa-lət\ n 1 : the roof of the mouth separating the mouth from the nasal cavity 2 : TASTE

pa·la·tial \pə-'lā-shəl\ adj 1 : of, relating to, or being a palace 2 : MAGNIFICENT

pa·lat·i·nate \pə-'la-tə-nət\ n : the territory of a palatine

¹pal·a·tine \'pa-lə-,tīn\ adj 1 : possessing royal privileges; also : of or relating to a palatine or a palatinate 2 : of or relating to a palace : PALATIAL

²palatine n 1 : a feudal lord having sovereign power within his domains 2 : a high officer of an imperial palace

pa·la·ver \pə-'la-vər, -'lä-\ n [Pg palavra word, speech, fr. LL parabola parable, speech] 1 : a long parley 2 : idle talk — palaver vb

¹pale \'pāl\ n 1 : a stake or picket of a fence 2 : an enclosed place; also : a district or territory within certain bounds or under a particular jurisdiction 3 : LIMITS, BOUNDS ⟨conduct beyond the ~⟩

²pale vb paled; pal·ing : to enclose with or as if with pales : FENCE

³pale adj pal·er; pal·est 1 : deficient in color or intensity : WAN ⟨a ~ face⟩ 2 : lacking in brightness : DIM ⟨a ~ star⟩ 3 : not dark or intense in hue ⟨a ~ blue⟩ — paleness n

⁴pale vb paled; pal·ing : to make or become pale

pale ale n : a medium-colored very dry ale

pale-face \'pāl-,fās\ n : a white person

Pa·leo·cene \'pā-lē-ə-,sēn\ adj : of, relating to, or being the earliest epoch of the Tertiary — **Paleocene** n

pa·leo·con·ser·va·tive \,pā-lē-ō-kən-'sər-və-tiv\ n : a conservative espousing traditional principles and policies

pa·le·og·ra·phy \,pā-lē-'ä-grə-fē\ n [NL palaeographia, fr. Gk palaios ancient + graphein to write] : the study of ancient writings and inscriptions — **pa·le·og·ra·pher** n

Pa·leo·lith·ic \,pā-lē-ə-'li-thik\ adj : of or relating to the earliest period of the Stone Age characterized by rough or chipped stone implements

pa·le·on·tol·o·gy \,pā-lē-,än-'tä-lə-jē\ n : a science dealing with the life of past geologic periods as known from fossil remains — **pa·le·on·to·log·i·cal** \-,än-tə-'lä-ji-kəl\ adj — **pa·le·on·tol·o·gist** \-,än-'tä-lə-jist, -ən-\ n

Pa·leo·zo·ic \,pā-lē-ə-'zō-ik\ adj : of, relating to, or being the era of geologic history extending from about 570 million years ago to about 245 million years ago — **Paleozoic** n

pal·ette \'pa-lət\ n : a thin often oval board that a painter holds and mixes colors on; also : the colors on a palette

pal·frey \'pol-frē\ n, pl palfreys archaic : a saddle horse that is not a warhorse; esp : one suitable for a woman

pa·limp·sest \'pa-ləmp-,sest\ n [L palimpsestus, fr. Gk palimpsēstos scraped again] : writing material (as a parchment) used after the erasure of earlier writing

pal·in·drome \'pa-lən-,drōm\ n : a word, verse, or sentence (as "Able was I ere I saw Elba") or a number (as 1881) that reads the same backward or forward

pal·ing \'pā-liŋ\ n 1 : a fence of pales 2 : material for pales 3 : PALE, PICKET

pal·i·sade \,pa-lə-'sād\ n 1 : a high fence of stakes esp. for defense 2 : a line of steep cliffs

¹pall \'pol\ vb 1 : to lose in interest or attraction 2 : SATIATE, CLOY

²pall n 1 : a heavy cloth draped over a coffin 2 : something that produces a gloomy atmosphere

pal·la·di·um \pə-'lā-dē-əm\ n : a silver-white metallic chemical element used esp. as a catalyst and in alloys

pall·bear·er \'pol-,ber-ər\ n : a person who attends the coffin at a funeral

¹pal·let \'pa-lət\ n : a small, hard, or makeshift bed

²pallet n : a portable platform for transporting and storing materials

pal·li·ate \'pa-lē-,āt\ vb -at·ed; -at·ing 1 : to ease (as a disease) without curing 2 : to cover by excuses and apologies ⟨~ faults⟩ — **pal·li·a·tion** \,pa-lē-'ā-shən\ n — **pal·li·a·tive** \'pa-lē-,ā-tiv\ adj or n

pal·lid \'pa-ləd\ adj : PALE, WAN

pal·lor \'pa-lər\ n : PALENESS

¹palm \'päm, 'pälm\ n [ME, fr. OE, fr. L palma palm of the hand, palm tree; fr. the resemblance of the tree's leaves to the outstretched hand] 1 : any of a family of mostly tropical trees, shrubs, or vines usu. with a tall unbranched stem topped by a crown of large leaves 2 : a symbol of victory; also : VICTORY

²palm n : the underpart of the hand between the fingers and the wrist

³palm vb 1 : to conceal in or with the hand ⟨~ a card⟩ 2 : to impose by fraud

pal·mate \'pal-,māt, 'päl-\ also pal·mat·ed \-,mā-təd\ adj : resembling a hand with the fingers spread

pal·met·to \pal-'me-tō\ n, pl -tos or -toes : any of several usu. small palms with fan-shaped leaves

palm·is·try \'pä-mə-strē, 'päl-\ n : the practice of reading a person's character or future from the markings on the palms — **palm·ist** \'pä-mist, 'päl-\ n

Palm Sunday n : the Sunday preceding Easter and commemorating Christ's triumphal entry into Jerusalem

palm·top \'päm-,täp, 'pälm-\ n : a portable computer small enough to hold in the hand

palmy \'pä-mē, 'päl-\ adj palm·i·er; -est 1 : abounding in or bearing palms 2 : FLOURISHING, PROSPEROUS

pal·o·mi·no \,pa-lə-'mē-nō\ n, pl -nos [AmerSp, fr. Sp, like a dove, fr. L palumbinus, fr. palumbes, a species of dove] : a horse with a pale cream to golden coat and cream or white mane and tail

pal·pa·ble \'pal-pə-bəl\ adj 1 : capable of being touched or felt : TANGIBLE 2 : OBVIOUS, PLAIN ⟨the resentment was ~⟩ ✦ **Synonyms** PERCEPTIBLE, SENSIBLE, APPRECIABLE, TANGIBLE, DETECTABLE — **pal·pa·bly** \-blē\ adv

pal·pate \'pal-,pāt\ vb pal·pat·ed; pal·pat·ing : to examine by touch esp. medically — **pal·pa·tion** \pal-'pā-shən\ n

pal·pi·tate \'pal-pə-,tāt\ vb -tat·ed; -tat·ing : to beat rapidly and strongly : THROB — **pal·pi·ta·tion** \,pal-pə-'tā-shən\ n

pal·sy \'pol-zē\ n, pl palsies 1 : PARALYSIS 2 : a condition marked by tremor — **pal·sied** \-zēd\ adj

pal·ter \'pol-tər\ vb pal·tered; pal·ter·ing 1 : to act insincerely : EQUIVOCATE 2 : HAGGLE

pal·try \'pol-trē\ adj pal·tri·er; -est 1 : TRASHY ⟨a ~ pamphlet⟩ 2 : MEAN, DESPICABLE ⟨a ~ trick⟩ 3 : TRIVIAL ⟨~ excuses⟩ 4 : MEAGER, MEASLY ⟨a ~ sum⟩

pam·pas \'pam-pəz, 'päm-, -pəs\ n pl : wide grassy So. American plains

pam·per \'pam-pər\ vb : to treat with excessive attention : INDULGE ✦ **Synonyms** CODDLE, HUMOR, BABY, SPOIL

pam·phlet \'pam-flət\ n [ME pamflet unbound booklet, fr. Pamphilus seu De Amore Pamphilus or On Love, popular Latin love poem of the 12th cent.] : an unbound printed publication

pam·phle·teer \,pam-flə-'tir\ n : a writer of pamphlets attacking something or urging a cause

¹pan \'pan\ n 1 : a usu. broad, shallow, and open container for domestic use; also : something resembling such a container 2 : a basin or depression in land 3 : HARDPAN

²pan vb panned; pan·ning 1 : to wash earth or gravel in a pan in searching for gold 2 : to criticize severely

Pan abbr Panama

pan·a·cea \ˌpa-nə-'sē-ə\ n : a remedy for all ills or difficulties : CURE-ALL

pa·nache \pə-'nash, -'näsh\ n [MF *pennache*, ultim. fr. LL *pinnaculum* small wing] **1** : an ornamental tuft (as of feathers) esp. on a helmet **2** : dash or flamboyance in style and action

pan·a·ma \'pa-nə-ˌmä, -ˌmȯ\ n, *often cap* : a handmade hat braided from strips of the leaves from a tropical American tree

pan·cake \'pan-ˌkāk\ n : a flat cake made of thin batter and fried on both sides

pan·chro·mat·ic \ˌpan-krō-'ma-tik\ adj : sensitive to all colors of visible light ⟨∼ film⟩

pan·cre·as \'paŋ-krē-əs, 'pan-\ n : a large compound gland of vertebrates that produces insulin and discharges enzymes into the intestine — **pan·cre·at·ic** \ˌpaŋ-krē-'a-tik, ˌpan-\ adj

pan·da \'pan-də\ n **1** : a long-tailed reddish brown Himalayan mammal related to and resembling the raccoon **2** : a large black-and-white mammal of China usu. classified with the bears

panda: *A* panda 1, *B* panda 2

pan·dem·ic \pan-'de-mik\ n : a widespread outbreak of disease — **pandemic** adj

pan·de·mo·ni·um \ˌpan-də-'mō-nē-əm\ n : a wild uproar : TUMULT

¹pan·der \'pan-dər\ vb : to act as a pander ⟨∼s to the public's taste for violence⟩

²pander n **1** : a go-between in love intrigues; *also* : PIMP **2** : a person who caters to or exploits others' desires or weaknesses

P & I abbr principal and interest

P & L abbr profit and loss

Pan·do·ra's box \pan-'dȯr-əz-\ n : a prolific source of troubles

pan·dow·dy \pan-'daú-dē\ n, pl **-dies** : a deep-dish apple dessert spiced, sweetened, and covered with a crust

pane \'pān\ n : a sheet of glass (as in a door or window)

pan·e·gy·ric \ˌpa-nə-'jir-ik\ n : a eulogistic oration or writing ⟨a ∼ on war heroes⟩ — **pan·e·gyr·ist** \-'jir-ist\ n

¹pan·el \'pa-nᵊl\ n [ME, piece of cloth, jury list on a piece of parchment, fr. AF, fr. VL *pannellus*, dim. of L *pannus* cloth, rag] **1** : a list of persons appointed for special duty ⟨a jury ∼⟩; *also* : a group of people taking part in a discussion or quiz program **2** : a section of something (as a wall or door) often sunk below the level of the frame; *also* : a flat piece of construction material **3** : a flat piece of wood on which a picture is painted **4** : a mount for controls or dials

²panel vb **-eled** or **-elled; -el·ing** or **-el·ling** : to decorate with panels

paneling n : decorative panels

pan·el·ist \'pa-nᵊl-ist\ n : a member of a discussion or quiz panel

panel truck n : a small motortruck with a fully enclosed body

pang \'paŋ\ n : a sudden sharp spasm (as of pain) or attack (as of remorse)

pan·han·dle \'pan-ˌhan-dᵊl\ n : a narrow projection of a larger territory (as a state) ⟨the Texas ∼⟩

²panhandle vb **-dled; -dling** : to ask for money on the street — **pan·han·dler** n

¹pan·ic \'pa-nik\ n : a sudden overpowering fright; *also* : extreme anxiety ⟨a ∼ disorder⟩ ⟨∼ attacks⟩ ♦ **Synonyms** TERROR, CONSTERNATION, DISMAY, ALARM, DREAD, FEAR — **pan·icky** \-ni-kē\ adj

²panic vb **pan·icked** \-nikt\; **pan·ick·ing** : to affect or be affected with panic

pan·i·cle \'pa-ni-kəl\ n : a branched flower cluster (as of a lilac) in which each branch from the main stem has one or more flowers

pa·ni·ni \pə-'nē-nē\ also **pa·ni·no** \pə-'nē-nō\ n, pl **panini** or **pa·ni·nis** : a usually grilled sandwich made with Italian bread

pan·jan·drum \pan-'jan-drəm\ n, pl **-drums** also **-dra** \-drə\ : a powerful personage or pretentious official

pan·nier also **pan·ier** \'pan-yər\ n : a large basket esp. for bearing on the back

pan·o·ply \'pa-nə-plē\ n, pl **-plies 1** : a full suit of armor **2** : a protective covering **3** : an impressive array

pan·ora·ma \ˌpa-nə-'ra-mə, -'rä-\ n **1** : a picture unrolled before one's eyes **2** : a complete view in every direction — **pan·oram·ic** \-'ra-mik\ adj

pan out vb : TURN OUT; esp : SUCCEED

pan·sex·u·al \pan-'sek-sh(ə-)wəl, -shəl\ adj : of, relating to, or characterized by sexual desire or attraction that is not limited to people of a particular gender identity or sexual orientation; *also* : not solely homosexual or heterosexual

pan·sy \'pan-zē\ n, pl **pansies** [ME *pancy, pensee*, fr. MF *pensée*, fr. *pensée* thought, fr. *penser* to think, fr. L *pensare* to ponder] : a low-growing garden herb related to the violet; *also* : its showy flower

¹pant \'pant\ vb [ME, fr. AF *panteiser*, fr. VL **phantasiare* to have hallucinations, fr. Gk *phantasioun*, fr. *phantasia* appearance, imagination] **1** : to breathe in a labored manner **2** : YEARN **3** : THROB

²pant n : a panting breath or sound

³pant n **1** : an outer garment covering each leg separately and usu. extending from the waist to the ankle — usu. used in pl. **2** pl : PANTIE

pan·ta·loons \ˌpan-tə-'lünz\ n pl **1** : close-fitting pants of the 19th century usu. having straps passing under the instep **2** : loose-fitting usu. shorter than ankle-length trousers

pan·the·ism \'pan-thē-ˌi-zəm\ n : a doctrine that equates God with the forces and laws of the universe — **pan·the·ist** \-ist\ n — **pan·the·is·tic** \ˌpan-thē-'is-tik\ adj

pan·the·on \'pan-thē-ˌän, -ən\ n **1** : a temple dedicated to all the gods; *also* : the gods of a people **2** : a group of illustrious people ⟨a ∼ of great writers⟩

pan·ther \'pan-thər\ n, pl **panthers** also **panther 1** : LEOPARD; esp : a black one **2** : COUGAR **3** : JAGUAR

pant·ie or **panty** \'pan-tē\ n, pl **pant·ies** : a woman's or child's short underpants — usu. used in pl.

pan·to·mime \'pan-tə-ˌmīm\ n **1** : a play in which the actors use no words **2** : expression of something by bodily or facial movements only — **pantomime** vb — **pan·to·mim·ic** \ˌpan-tə-'mi-mik\ adj

pan·try \'pan-trē\ n, pl **pantries** : a storage room for food or dishes

pant·suit \'pant-ˌsüt\ n : a woman's outfit consisting usu. of a long jacket and pants of the same material

panty hose n pl : a one-piece undergarment for women consisting of hosiery combined with a pantie

panty·waist \'pan-tē-ˌwāst\ n : SISSY

pap \'pap\ n : soft food for infants or invalids

pa·pa \'pä-pə\ n : FATHER

pa·pa·cy \'pā-pə-sē\ n, pl **-cies 1** : the office of pope **2** : a succession of popes **3** : the term of a pope's reign **4** cap : the system of government of the Roman Catholic Church

pa·pa·in \pə-'pā-ən, -'pī-ən\ n : an enzyme in papaya juice used esp. as a meat tenderizer and in medicine

pa·pal \'pā-pəl\ adj : of or relating to the pope or to the Roman Catholic Church

papaw var of PAWPAW

pa·pa·ya \pə-'pī-ə\ n : a tropical American tree with large yellow black-seeded edible fruit; *also* : its fruit

pa·per \'pā-pər\ n [ME *papir*, fr. AF, fr. L *papyrus* papyrus, paper, fr. Gk *papyros* papyrus] **1** : a pliable substance made usu. of vegetable matter and used to write or print on, to wrap things in, or to cover walls; *also* : a single sheet of this substance **2** : a printed or written document **3** : NEWSPAPER **4** : WALLPAPER 1 — **paper** *adj or vb* — **pa·pery** \'pā-pə-rē\ *adj*

pa·per·back \-,bak\ *n* : a paper-covered book

pa·per·board \-,bórd\ *n* : CARDBOARD

pa·per·hang·er \'pā-pər-,haŋ-ər\ *n* : one that applies wallpaper — **pa·per·hang·ing** *n*

pa·per·weight \-,wāt\ *n* : an object used to hold down loose papers by its weight

pa·pier-mâ·ché \,pā-pər-mə-'shā, ,pa-,pyā-mə-, -ma-\ *n* [F, lit., chewed paper] : a molding material of wastepaper and additives (as glue) — **papier-mâché** *adj*

pa·pil·la \pə-'pi-lə\ *n, pl* **-lae** \-(,)lē, -,lī\ [L, nipple] : a small projecting bodily part (as one of the nubs on the surface of the tongue) that resembles a tiny nipple in form — **pap·il·lary** \'pa-pə-,ler-ē, pə-'pi-lə-rē\ *adj*

pa·poose \pa-'püs, pə-\ *n* [Narragansett *papoòs*] *dated, now often offensive* : a young child of American Indian parents

pa·pri·ka \pə-'prē-kə, pa-\ *n* [Hung] : a mild red spice made from the fruit of various cultivated sweet peppers

Pap smear \'pap-\ *n* : a method for the early detection of cancer esp. of the uterine cervix

Pap test *n* : PAP SMEAR

pap·ule \'pa-pyül\ *n* : a small solid usu. conical elevation of the skin — **pap·u·lar** \-pyə-lər\ *adj*

pa·py·rus \pə-'pī-rəs\ *n, pl* **-ri** \-,rī\ *or* **-rus·es** **1** : a tall grassy sedge of the Nile valley **2** : paper made from papyrus pith

¹par \'pär\ *n* **1** : a stated value (as of a security) **2** : a common level : EQUALITY **3** : an accepted standard or normal condition **4** : the score standard set for each hole of a golf course — **par** *adj*

²par *abbr* **1** paragraph **2** parallel **3** parish

par·a·ble \'pa-rə-bəl\ *n* : a simple story told to illustrate a moral truth

pa·rab·o·la \pə-'ra-bə-lə\ *n* : a plane curve formed by a point moving so that its distance from a fixed point is equal to its distance from a fixed line — **par·a·bol·ic** \,par-ə-'bä-lik\ *adj*

para·chute \'pa-rə-,shüt\ *n* [F, fr. *para-* (as in *parasol*) + *chute* fall] : a device for slowing the descent of a person or object through the air that consists of a usu. hemispherical canopy beneath which the person or object is suspended — **parachute** *vb* — **para·chut·ist** \-'shü-tist\ *n*

parachute pants *n pl* : baggy casual pants of lightweight fabric

¹pa·rade \pə-'rād\ *n* **1** : a pompous display : EXHIBITION **2** : MARCH, PROCESSION; *esp* : a ceremonial formation and march **3** : a place for strolling

²parade *vb* **pa·rad·ed; pa·rad·ing** **1** : to march in a parade **2** : PROMENADE **3** : SHOW OFF ⟨*paraded* her knowledge⟩ **4** : MASQUERADE

par·a·digm \'pa-rə-,dīm, -,dim\ *n* **1** : MODEL, PATTERN **2** : a systematic inflection of a verb or noun showing a complete conjugation or declension — **par·a·dig·mat·ic** \,pa-rə-dig-'ma-tik\ *adj*

par·a·dise \'pa-rə-,dīs, -,dīz\ *n* [ME *paradis*, fr. AF, fr. LL *paradisus*, fr. Gk *paradeisos*, lit., enclosed park, of Iranian origin] **1** : HEAVEN **2** : a place or state of bliss

par·a·di·si·a·cal \,pa-rə-də-'sī-ə-kəl\ *or* **par·a·dis·i·ac** \-'di-zē-,ak, -sē-\ *adj* : of, relating to, or resembling paradise

par·a·dox \'pa-rə-,däks\ *n* : a statement that seems contrary to common sense and yet is perhaps true — **par·a·dox·i·cal** \,pa-rə-'däk-si-kəl\ *adj* — **par·a·dox·i·cal·ly** \-k(ə-)lē\ *adv*

par·af·fin \'pa-rə-fən\ *n* : a waxy substance used esp. for making candles and sealing foods

para·glid·ing \'pa-rə-,glī-diŋ\ *n* : the sport of soaring from a slope or cliff using a modified parachute

par·a·gon \'pa-rə-,gän, -gən\ *n* : a model of perfection : PATTERN ⟨a ~ of virtue⟩

¹para·graph \'pa-rə-,graf\ *n* : a subdivision of a written composition that deals with one point or gives the words of one speaker; *also* : a character (as ¶) marking the beginning of a paragraph

²paragraph *vb* : to divide into paragraphs

par·a·keet \'pa-rə-,kēt\ *n* : any of numerous usu. small slender parrots with a long graduated tail

para·le·gal \,pa-rə-'lē-gəl\ *adj* : of, relating to, or being a paraprofessional who assists a lawyer — **paralegal** *n*

Par·a·li·pom·e·non \,pa-rə-lə-'pä-mə-,nän\ *n* : CHRONICLES

par·al·lax \'pa-rə-,laks\ *n* : the difference in apparent direction of an object as seen from two different points

¹par·al·lel \'pa-rə-,lel\ *adj* [L *parallelus*, fr. Gk *parallēlos*, fr. *para* beside + *allēlōn* of one another, fr. *allos* . . . *allos* one . . . another, fr. *allos* other] **1** : lying or moving in the same direction but always the same distance apart **2** : similar in essential parts — **par·al·lel·ism** \-,le-,li-zəm\ *n*

²parallel *n* **1** : a parallel line, curve, or surface **2** : one of the imaginary circles on the earth's surface that parallel the equator and mark the latitude **3** : something essentially similar to another **4** : SIMILARITY, LIKENESS

³parallel *vb* **1** : COMPARE **2** : to correspond to **3** : to extend in a parallel direction with

par·al·lel·o·gram \,pa-rə-'le-lə-,gram\ *n* : a 4-sided geometric figure with opposite sides equal and parallel

par·a·lyse *Brit var of* PARALYZE

pa·ral·y·sis \pə-'ra-lə-səs\ *n, pl* **-y·ses** \-,sēz\ : complete or partial loss of function esp. when involving the motion or sensation in a part of the body — **par·a·lyt·ic** \,pa-rə-'li-tik\ *adj or n*

par·a·lyze \'pa-rə-,līz\ *vb* **-lyzed; -lyz·ing** **1** : to affect with paralysis **2** : to make powerless or inactive ⟨*paralyzed* by fear⟩ — **par·a·lyz·ing·ly** *adv*

par·a·me·cium \,pa-rə-'mē-shəm, -shē-əm, -sē-əm\ *n, pl* **-cia** \-shə, -shē-ə, -sē-ə\ *also* **-ci·ums** : any of a genus of slipper-shaped protozoans that move by cilia

para·med·ic \,pa-rə-'me-dik\ *also* **para·med·i·cal** \-di-kəl\ *n* **1** : a person who assists a physician in a paramedical capacity **2** : a specially trained medical technician licensed to provide a wide range of emergency services before or during transportation to a hospital

para·med·i·cal \,pa-rə-'me-di-kəl\ *also* **para·med·ic** \-'me-dik\ *adj* : concerned with supplementing the work of trained medical professionals

pa·ram·e·ter \pə-'ra-mə-tər\ *n* **1** : a quantity whose value characterizes a statistical population or a member of a system (as a family of curves) **2** : a physical property whose value determines the characteristics or behavior of a system **3** : a characteristic element : FACTOR

para·mil·i·tary \,pa-rə-'mi-lə-,ter-ē\ *adj* : formed on a military pattern esp. as an auxiliary military force

par·a·mount \'pa-rə-,maùnt\ *adj* : superior to all others : SUPREME ♦ **Synonyms** PREPONDERANT, PREDOMINANT, DOMINANT, CHIEF, SOVEREIGN

par·amour \'pa-rə-,mùr\ *n* : an illicit lover

para·noia \,pa-rə-'nói-ə\ *n* : a psychosis marked by delusions and irrational suspicion usu. without hallucinations — **para·noid** \'pa-rə-,nóid\ *adj or n*

para·nor·mal \,pa-rə-'nòr-məl\ *adj* : not scientifically explainable : SUPERNATURAL ⟨~ phenomena⟩

par·a·pet \'pa-rə-pət, -,pet\ *n* **1** : a protecting rampart **2** : a low wall or railing (as at the edge of a bridge)

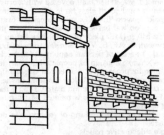

parapet 1

par·a·pher·na·lia \,pa-rə-fə-'nāl-yə, -fər-\ *n sing or pl* **1** : personal belongings **2** : EQUIPMENT, APPARATUS

para·phrase \'pa-rə-,frāz\ *n* : a restatement of a text giving the meaning in different words — **paraphrase** *vb*

para·ple·gia \,pa-rə-'plē-jə, -jē-ə\ *n* : paralysis of the lower trunk and legs — **para·ple·gic** \-jik\ *adj or n*

para·pro·fes·sion·al \-prə-'fe-shə-nəl\ *n* : a trained aide who assists a professional — **paraprofessional** *adj*

para·psy·chol·o·gy \ˌpa-rə-sī-'kä-lə-jē\ *n* : a field of study concerned with investigating paranormal psychological phenomena (as extrasensory perception) — **para·psy·chol·o·gist** \-jist\ *n*

par·a·site \'pa-rə-ˌsīt\ *n* [MF, fr. L *parasitus*, fr. Gk *parasitos*, fr. *para-* beside + *sitos* grain, food] 1 : a plant or animal living in, with, or on another organism its host. to its harm 2 : one depending on another and not making adequate return — **par·a·sit·ic** \ˌpa-rə-'si-tik\ *adj* — **par·a·sit·ism** \'pa-rə-sə-ˌti-zəm, -ˌsī-ˌti-\ *n* — **par·a·sit·ize** \-sə-ˌtīz\ *vb*

par·a·si·tol·o·gy \ˌpa-rə-sə-'tä-lə-jē\ *n* : a branch of biology dealing with parasites and parasitism esp. among animals — **par·a·si·tol·o·gist** \-jist\ *n*

para·sol \'pa-rə-ˌsȯl\ *n* [F, fr. It *parasole*, fr. *parare* to shield + *sole* sun, fr. L *sol*] : a lightweight umbrella used as a shield against the sun

para·sym·pa·thet·ic nervous system \ˌpa-rə-ˌsim-pə-'the-tik-\ *n* : the part of the autonomic nervous system that tends to induce secretion, to increase the tone and contractility of smooth muscle, and to slow heart rate

para·thi·on \ˌpa-rə-'thī-ˌän, -ˌän\ *n* : an extremely toxic insecticide

para·thy·roid \-'thī-ˌrȯid\ *n* : PARATHYROID GLAND — **parathyroid** *adj*

parathyroid gland *n* : any of usu. four small endocrine glands adjacent to or embedded in the thyroid gland that produce a hormone (**parathyroid hormone**) concerned with calcium and phosphorus metabolism

para·tran·sit \ˌpa-rə-'tran-sət, -zət\ *n* : transportation service that provides individualized rules without fixed routes or timetables

para·troop·er \'pa-rə-ˌtrü-pər\ *n* : a member of the paratroops

para·troops \-ˌtrüps\ *n pl* : troops trained to parachute from an airplane

para·ty·phoid \ˌpa-rə-'tī-ˌfȯid\ *n* : a bacterial food poisoning resembling typhoid fever

par·boil \'pär-ˌbȯi(-ə)l\ *vb* : to boil briefly

¹**par·cel** \'pär-səl\ *n* 1 : a tract or plot of land 2 : COLLECTION, LOT ⟨the story was a ∼ of lies⟩ 3 : a wrapped bundle : PACKAGE

²**parcel** *vb* **-celed** *or* **-celled; -cel·ing** *or* **-cel·ling** : to divide into portions

parcel post *n* 1 : a mail service handling parcels 2 : packages handled by parcel post

parch \'pärch\ *vb* 1 : to toast under dry heat 2 : to shrivel with heat

parch·ment \'pärch-mənt\ *n* : the skin of an animal prepared for writing on; *also* : a writing on such material

pard \'pärd\ *n* : LEOPARD

¹**par·don** \'pär-dⁿn\ *n* : excuse of an offense without penalty; *esp* : an official release from legal punishment

²**pardon** *vb* : to free from penalty : EXCUSE, FORGIVE ⟨∼ a criminal⟩ ⟨∼ a debt⟩ — **par·don·able** \'pär-dⁿn-ə-bəl\ *adj*

par·don·er \'pär-dⁿn-ər\ *n* 1 : a medieval preacher delegated to raise money for religious works by soliciting offerings and granting indulgences 2 : one that pardons

pare \'per\ *vb* **pared; par·ing** 1 : to trim off an outside part (as the skin or rind) of 2 : to reduce as if by paring ⟨∼ expenses⟩ — **par·er** *n*

par·e·gor·ic \ˌper-ə-'gȯr-ik\ *n* : an alcoholic preparation of opium and camphor used esp. to relieve pain

par·ent \'per-ənt\ *n* 1 : one that begets or brings forth offspring : FATHER, MOTHER 2 : one who brings up and cares for another 3 : SOURCE, ORIGIN — **par·ent·age** \-ən-tij\ *n* — **pa·ren·tal** \pə-'ren-tⁿl\ *adj* — **par·ent·hood** *n*

pa·ren·the·sis \pə-'ren-thə-səs\ *n, pl* **-the·ses** \-ˌsēz\ 1 : a word, phrase, or sentence inserted in a passage to explain or modify the thought 2 : one of a pair of punctuation marks ( ) used esp. to enclose parenthetic matter — **par·en·thet·ic** \ˌper-ən-'the-tik\ *or* **par·en·thet·i·cal** \-ti-kəl\ *adj* — **par·en·thet·i·cal·ly** \-k(ə-)lē\ *adv*

pa·ren·the·size \pə-'ren-thə-ˌsīz\ *vb* **-sized; -siz·ing** : to make a parenthesis of

par·ent·ing \'per-ən-tiŋ\ *n* : the raising of a child by its parents

pa·re·sis \pə-'rē-səs, 'pa-rə-\ *n, pl* **pa·re·ses** \-ˌsēz\ : a usu.

incomplete paralysis; *also* : insanity caused by syphilitic alteration of the brain that leads to dementia and paralysis

par ex·cel·lence \ˌpär-ˌek-sə-'läⁿs\ *adj* [F, lit., by excellence] : being the best of a kind : PREEMINENT

par·fait \pär-'fā\ *n* [F, lit., something perfect] : a cold dessert made of layers of fruit, syrup, ice cream, and whipped cream

pa·ri·ah \pə-'rī-ə\ *n* : OUTCAST

pa·ri·etal \pə-'rī-ə-tⁿl\ *adj* 1 : of, relating to, or forming the walls of an anatomical structure 2 : of or relating to college living or its regulation

pari–mu·tu·el \ˌper-i-'myü-chə-wəl\ *n* : a betting system in which winners share the total stakes minus a percentage for the management

paring *n* : a pared-off piece

pa·ri pas·su \ˌpa-ri-'pa-sü\ *adv or adj* [L, with equal step] : at an equal rate or pace

par·ish \'per-ish\ *n* 1 : a church district in the care of one pastor; *also* : the residents of such an area 2 : a local church community 3 : a civil division of the state of Louisiana : COUNTY

pa·rish·io·ner \pə-'ri-shə-nər\ *n* : a member or resident of a parish

par·i·ty \'per-ə-tē\ *n, pl* **-ties** : EQUALITY, EQUIVALENCE

¹**park** \'pärk\ *n* 1 : a tract of ground kept as a game preserve or recreation area 2 : a place where vehicles (as automobiles) are parked 3 : an enclosed stadium used esp. for ball games

²**park** *vb* 1 : to leave a vehicle temporarily (as in a parking lot or garage) 2 : to set and leave temporarily

par·ka \'pär-kə\ *n* : a very warm jacket with a hood

Par·kin·son's disease \'pär-kən-sənz-\ *n* : a chronic progressive neurological disease chiefly of later life marked esp. by tremor and weakness of resting muscles and by a shuffling gait

Parkinson's Law *n* : an observation in office organization: work expands so as to fill the time available for its completion

par·kour \pär-'kȯr, 'pär-ˌkȯr\ *n* [F, alter. of *parcours* course, route, fr. ML *percursus*, fr. L *percurrere* to run through] : the sport of traversing environmental obstacles by running, climbing, or leaping rapidly

park·way \'pärk-ˌwā\ *n* : a broad landscaped thoroughfare

par·lance \'pär-ləns\ *n* 1 : SPEECH 2 : manner of speaking ⟨military ∼⟩

¹**par·lay** \'pär-ˌlā, -lē\ *vb* : to increase or change into something of much greater value ⟨∼ed a $1000 loan into a fortune⟩

²**parlay** *n* : a series of bets in which the original stake plus its winnings are risked on successive wagers

par·ley \'pär-lē\ *n, pl* **parleys** : a conference usu. over matters in dispute : DISCUSSION — **parley** *vb*

par·lia·ment \'pär-lə-mənt\ *n* [ME, fr. AF *parlement*, fr. *parler* to speak, fr. ML *parabolare*, fr. LL *parabola* speech, parable] 1 : a formal governmental conference 2 *cap* : an assembly that constitutes the supreme legislative body of a country (as the United Kingdom) — **par·lia·men·ta·ry** \ˌpär-lə-'men-tə-rē\ *adj*

par·lia·men·tar·i·an \ˌpär-lə-ˌmen-'ter-ē-ən\ *n* 1 *often cap* : an adherent of the parliament during the English Civil War 2 : an expert in parliamentary procedure

par·lor \'pär-lər\ *n* 1 : a room for conversation or the reception of guests 2 : a place of business ⟨beauty ∼⟩

par·lour \'pär-lər\ *chiefly Brit var of* PARLOR

par·lous \'pär-ləs\ *adj* : full of danger or risk : PRECARIOUS — **par·lous·ly** *adv*

Par·me·san \'pär-mə-ˌzän, -ˌzhän, -ˌzan\ *n* : a hard dry cheese with a sharp flavor

par·mi·gia·na \ˌpär-mi-'jä-nə, ˌpär-mi-'zhän\ *or* **par·mi·gia·no** \-'jä-(ˌ)nō\ *adj* : made or covered with Parmesan cheese ⟨veal ∼⟩

pa·ro·chi·al \pə-'rō-kē-əl\ *adj* 1 : of or relating to a church parish 2 : limited in scope : NARROW, PROVINCIAL — **pa·ro·chi·al·ism** \-ə-ˌli-zəm\ *n*

parochial school *n* : a school maintained by a religious body

par·o·dy \'per-ə-dē\ *n, pl* **-dies** [L *parodia*, fr. Gk *parōidia*, fr. *para-* beside + *aidein* to sing] : a humorous or satirical imitation — **parody** *vb*

pa·role \pə-'rōl\ *n* : a conditional release of a prisoner whose sentence has not expired — **parole** vb — **pa·rol·ee** \-ˌrō-ˈlē, -ˈrō-ˌlē\ n

par·ox·ysm \ˈpa-rək-ˌsi-zəm, pə-ˈräk-\ n : a sudden sharp attack (as of pain or coughing) : CONVULSION — **par·ox·ys·mal** \ˌpa-rək-ˈsiz-məl, pə-ˌräk-\ adj

par·quet \ˈpär-ˌkā, pär-ˈkā\ n [F] 1 : a flooring of parquetry 2 : the lower floor of a theater; esp : the forward part of the orchestra

par·que·try \ˈpär-kə-trē\ n, pl **-tries** : fine woodwork inlaid in patterns

par·ri·cide \ˈpa-rə-ˌsīd\ n 1 : one that murders a parent or a close relative 2 : the act of a parricide

par·rot \ˈper-ət\ n : any of numerous bright-colored tropical birds that have a stout hooked bill

parrot fever n : PSITTACOSIS

par·ry \ˈper-ē\ vb **par·ried; par·ry·ing** 1 : to ward off a weapon or blow 2 : to evade esp. by an adroit answer — **parry** n

parse \ˈpärs also ˈpärz\ vb **parsed; pars·ing** : to give a grammatical description of a word or a group of words

par·sec \ˈpär-ˌsek\ n : a unit of measure for interstellar space equal to 3.26 light-years

par·si·mo·ny \ˈpär-sə-ˌmō-nē\ n : extreme or excessive frugality — **par·si·mo·ni·ous** \ˌpär-sə-ˈmō-nē-əs\ adj — **par·si·mo·ni·ous·ly** adv

pars·ley \ˈpär-slē\ n : a garden plant related to the carrot that has finely divided leaves used as a seasoning or garnish; also : the leaves

pars·nip \ˈpär-snəp\ n : a garden plant related to the carrot that has a long edible usu. whitish root which is cooked as a vegetable; also : the root

par·son \ˈpär-sⁿn\ n [ME persone, fr. AF, fr. ML persona, lit., person, fr. L] : MINISTER 2, PASTOR

par·son·age \ˈpär-sə-nij\ n : a house provided by a church for its pastor

¹**part** \ˈpärt\ n 1 : a division or portion of a whole 2 : the melody or score for a particular voice or instrument 3 : a spare piece for a machine 4 : DUTY, FUNCTION 5 : one of the sides in a dispute 6 : ROLE; also : an actor's lines in a play 7 pl : TALENTS, ABILITY ⟨a man of many ∼s⟩ 8 : the line where one's hair divides (as in combing)

²**part** vb 1 : to take leave of someone 2 : to divide or break into parts : SEPARATE 3 : to go away : DEPART; also : DIE 4 : to give up possession ⟨∼ed with her jewels⟩ 5 : APPORTION, SHARE

³**part** abbr 1 participial; participle 2 particular

par·take \pär-ˈtāk\ vb **-took** \-ˈtuk\; **-tak·en** \-ˈtā-kən\; **-tak·ing** 1 : to have a share or part 2 : to take a portion (as of food) — **par·tak·er** n

par·terre \pär-ˈter\ n [F, fr. MF, fr. par terre on the ground] 1 : an ornamental garden with paths between the flower beds 2 : the part of a theater floor behind the orchestra

par·the·no·gen·e·sis \ˌpär-thə-nō-ˈje-nə-səs\ n [NL, fr. Gk parthenos virgin + L genesis genesis] : development of a new individual from an unfertilized usu. female sex cell — **par·the·no·ge·net·ic** \-jə-ˈne-tik\ adj

par·tial \ˈpär-shəl\ adj 1 : not total or general : affecting a part only 2 : favoring one party over the other : BIASED 3 : markedly fond — used with to — **par·tial·i·ty** \ˌpär-shē-ˈa-lə-tē\ n — **par·tial·ly** adv

par·tic·i·pate \pär-ˈti-sə-ˌpāt\ vb **-pat·ed; -pat·ing** 1 : to take part in something ⟨∼ in a game⟩ 2 : SHARE — **par·tic·i·pant** \-pənt\ adj or n — **par·tic·i·pa·tion** \-ˌti-sə-ˈpā-shən\ n — **par·tic·i·pa·tor** \-ˈti-sə-ˌpā-tər\ n — **par·tic·i·pa·to·ry** \-ˈti-sə-pə-ˌtōr-ē\ adj

par·ti·ci·ple \ˈpär-tə-ˌsi-pəl\ n : a word having the characteristics of both verb and adjective — **par·ti·cip·i·al** \ˌpär-tə-ˈsi-pē-əl\ adj

par·ti·cle \ˈpär-ti-kəl\ n 1 : a very small bit of matter 2 : a unit of speech (as an article, preposition, or conjunction) expressing some general aspect of meaning or some connective or limiting relation

par·ti·cle·board \-ˌbȯrd\ n : a board made of very small pieces of wood bonded together

par·ti·col·or \ˌpär-tē-ˈkə-lər\ or **par·ti·col·ored** \-lərd\ adj : showing different colors or tints; esp : having one main color broken by patches of one or more other colors

¹**par·tic·u·lar** \pər-ˈti-kyə-lər\ adj 1 : of or relating to a specific person or thing ⟨the laws of a ∼ state⟩ 2 : DISTINCTIVE, SPECIAL ⟨the ∼ point of his talk⟩ 3 : SEPARATE, INDIVIDUAL ⟨each ∼ hair⟩ 4 : attentive to details : PRECISE 5 : hard to please : EXACTING ⟨is ∼ about her clothes⟩ — **par·tic·u·lar·i·ty** \-ˌti-kyə-ˈlar-ə-tē\ n — **par·tic·u·lar·ly** adv

²**particular** n : an individual fact or detail

par·tic·u·lar·ise Brit var of PARTICULARIZE

par·tic·u·lar·ize \pər-ˈti-kyə-lə-ˌrīz\ vb **-ized; -iz·ing** 1 : to state in detail : SPECIFY 2 : to go into details

par·tic·u·late \pər-ˈti-kyə-lət, pär-, -ˌlāt\ adj : relating to or existing as minute separate particles — **particulate** n

¹**part·ing** n : a place or point of separation or divergence

²**parting** adj : given, taken, or done at parting ⟨a ∼ kiss⟩

par·ti·san also **par·ti·zan** \ˈpär-tə-zən, -sən\ n 1 : one that takes the part of another : ADHERENT 2 : GUERRILLA — **partisan** adj — **par·ti·san·ship** n

par·tite \ˈpär-ˌtīt\ adj : divided into a usu. specified number of parts

par·ti·tion \pär-ˈti-shən\ n 1 : DIVISION 2 : something that divides or separates; esp : an interior dividing wall — **partition** vb

par·ti·tive \ˈpär-tə-tiv\ adj : of, relating to, or denoting a part

part·ly \ˈpärt-lē\ adv : in part : in some measure or degree

part·ner \ˈpärt-nər\ n 1 : ASSOCIATE, COLLEAGUE 2 : either of two persons who dance together 3 : one who plays on the same team with another 4 : SPOUSE 5 : one of two or more persons contractually associated as joint principals in a business — **part·ner·ship** n

part of speech : a class of words (as nouns or verbs) distinguished according to the kind of idea denoted and the function performed in a sentence

par·tridge \ˈpär-trij\ n, pl **partridge** or **par·tridg·es** : any of various stout-bodied Old World game birds

part–song \ˈpärt-ˌsȯŋ\ n : a song with two or more voice parts

part–time \-ˈtīm\ adj or adv : involving or working less than a full or regular schedule — **part–tim·er** \-ˌtī-mər\ n

par·tu·ri·tion \ˌpär-tə-ˈri-shən, ˌpär-chə-, ˌpär-tyu̇-\ n : CHILDBIRTH

part·way \ˈpärt-ˈwā\ adv : to some extent : PARTLY

par·ty \ˈpär-tē\ n, pl **parties** 1 : a person or group taking one side of a question; esp : a group of persons organized for the purpose of directing the policies of a government 2 : a person or group concerned in an action or affair : PARTICIPANT 3 : a group of persons detailed for a common task 4 : a social gathering

party animal n : a person known for frequent attendance at parties

par·ty·go·er \ˈpär-tē-ˌgō-ər\ n : a person who attends a party or who attends parties frequently

par·ve·nu \ˈpär-və-ˌnü, -ˌnyü\ n [F, fr. pp. of parvenir to arrive, fr. L pervenire, fr. per through + venire to come] : one who has recently or suddenly risen to wealth or power but has not yet secured the social position associated with it

pas \ˈpä\ n, pl **pas** \same or ˈpäz\ : a dance step or combination of steps

pas·cal \pas-ˈkal\ n : a unit of pressure in the metric system equal to one newton per square meter

pas·chal \ˈpas-kəl\ adj : of, relating to, appropriate for, or used during Passover or Easter ceremonies

pa·sha \ˈpä-shə, ˈpa-; pə-ˈshä\ n : a man (as formerly a governor in Turkey) of high rank

pash·mi·na \pəsh-ˈmē-nə\ n : a fine wool from the undercoat of domestic Himalayan goats; also : a shawl made from this wool

¹**pass** \ˈpas\ vb 1 : MOVE, PROCEED 2 : to go away; also : DIE 3 : to move past, beyond, or over 4 : to allow to elapse : SPEND 5 : to go or make way through 6 : to go or allow to go unchallenged 7 : to undergo transfer 8 : to render a legal judgment 9 : OCCUR 10 : to secure the approval of (as a legislature) 11 : to go or cause to go through an inspection, test, or course of study successfully 12 : to be regarded 13 : CIRCULATE ⟨∼ a note⟩ 14 : VOID 2 15 : to transfer the ball or puck to another player 16 : to decline to bid or bet on one's hand in a card game 17 : to give a base on balls 18 : to let something go by without accepting ⟨∼ed on his offer⟩ — **pass·er** n

²**pass** n : a gap in a mountain range

³**pass** n 1 : the act or an instance of passing 2 : REAL-

IZATION, ACCOMPLISHMENT **3** : a state of affairs **4** : a written authorization to leave, enter, or move about freely **5** : a transfer of a ball or puck from one player to another **6** : BASE ON BALLS **7** : EFFORT, TRY **8** : a sexually inviting gesture or approach

⁴pass *abbr* **1** passenger **2** passive

pass·able \'pa-sə-bəl\ *adj* **1** : capable of being passed or traveled on **2** : just good enough : TOLERABLE ⟨did a ∼ job⟩ — **pass·ably** \-blē\ *adv*

pas·sage \'pa-sij\ *n* **1** : a means (as a road or corridor) of passing **2** : the action or process of passing **3** : a voyage esp. by sea or air **4** : a right or permission to pass **5** : ENACTMENT **6** : a usu. brief portion or section (as of a book)

pas·sage·way \-ˌwā\ *n* : a way that allows passage

pass·book \'pas-ˌbu̇k\ *n* : BANKBOOK

pas·sé \pa-'sā\ *adj* **1** : past one's prime **2** : not up-to-date : OUTMODED

pas·sel \'pa-səl\ *n* : a large number ⟨a ∼ of children⟩

pas·sen·ger \'pa-sⁿn-jər\ *n* : a traveler in a public or private conveyance

pass·er·by \'pa-sər-ˌbī\ *n, pl* **pass·ers·by** : one who passes by

pas·ser·ine \'pa-sə-ˌrīn\ *adj* : of or relating to the large order of birds comprising singing birds that perch

pas·sim \'pa-səm\ *adv* [L, fr. *passus* scattered, fr. pp. of *pandere* to spread] : here and there : THROUGHOUT

pass·ing *n* : the act of one that passes or causes to pass; *esp* : DEATH

pas·sion \'pa-shən\ *n* **1** *often cap* : the sufferings of Christ between the night of the Last Supper and his death **2** : strong feeling; *also, pl* : the emotions as distinguished from reason **3** : RAGE, ANGER **4** : LOVE; *also* : an object of affection or enthusiasm **5** : sexual desire — **pas·sion·ate** \'pa-shə-nət\ *adj* — **pas·sion·ate·ly** *adv* — **pas·sion·less** *adj*

pas·sion·flow·er \'pa-shən-ˌflau̇-(ə)r\ *n* [fr. the fancied resemblance of parts of the flower to the instruments of Christ's crucifixion] : any of a genus of chiefly tropical woody climbing vines or erect herbs with showy flowers and pulpy often edible berries (**passion fruit**)

pas·sive \'pa-siv\ *adj* **1** : not active : acted upon **2** : asserting that the grammatical subject is subjected to or affected by the action represented by the verb ⟨∼ voice⟩ **3** : making use of the sun's heat usu. without the aid of mechanical devices **4** : SUBMISSIVE, PATIENT — **passive** *n* — **pas·sive·ly** *adv* — **pas·siv·i·ty** \pa-'si-və-tē\ *n*

pas·sive-ma·trix \-'mā-triks\ *adj* : of, relating to, or being on LCD in which pixels are controlled in groups

pass·key \'pas-ˌkē\ *n* : a key for opening two or more locks

pass out *vb* : to lose consciousness

Pass·over \'pas-ˌō-vər\ *n* [fr. the exemption of the Israelites from the slaughter of the firstborn in Egypt (Exod 12:23–27)] : a Jewish holiday celebrated in March or April in commemoration of the Hebrews' liberation from slavery in Egypt

pass·port \'pas-ˌpȯrt\ *n* : an official document issued by a country upon request to a citizen requesting protection during travel abroad

pass up *vb* : DECLINE, REJECT

pass·word \'pas-ˌwərd\ *n* **1** : a word or phrase that must be spoken by a person before being allowed to pass a guard **2** : a sequence of characters required for access to a computer system

¹past \'past\ *adj* **1** : AGO ⟨10 years ∼⟩ **2** : just gone or elapsed ⟨the ∼ month⟩ **3** : having existed or taken place in a period before the present : BYGONE **4** : of, relating to, or constituting a verb tense that expresses time gone by

²past *prep or adv* : BEYOND

³past *n* **1** : time gone by **2** : something that happened or was done in a former time **3** : the past tense; *also* : a verb form in it **4** : a secret past life

pas·ta \'päs-tə\ *n* [It] **1** : a paste in processed form (as macaroni) or in the form of fresh dough (as ravioli) **2** : a dish of cooked pasta

¹paste \'pāst\ *n* [ME, fr. AF, fr. LL *pasta* dough, paste] **1** : DOUGH **2** : a smooth food product made by evaporation or grinding ⟨tomato ∼⟩ **3** : a shaped dough (as spaghetti or ravioli) **4** : a preparation (as of flour and

water) for sticking things together **5** : a brilliant glass used for artificial gems

²paste *vb* **past·ed; past·ing** **1** : to cause to adhere by paste : STICK **2** : to put (something copied or cut from a computer document) into another place

paste·board \'pāst-ˌbȯrd\ *n* : CARDBOARD

¹pas·tel \pas-'tel\ *n* **1** : a paste made of powdered pigment; *also* : a crayon of such paste **2** : a drawing in pastel **3** : a pale or light color

²pastel *adj* **1** : of or relating to a pastel **2** : pale in color

pas·tern \'pas-tərn\ *n* : the part of a horse's foot extending from the fetlock to the top of the hoof

pas·teur·i·za·tion \ˌpas-chə-rə-'zā-shən, ˌpas-tə-\ *n* : partial sterilization of a substance (as milk) by heat or radiation — **pas·teur·ize** \'pas-chə-ˌrīz, 'pas-tə-\ *vb* — **pas·teur·iz·er** *n*

pas·tiche \pas-'tēsh\ *n* : a composition (as in literature or music) made up of selections from different works

pas·tille \pas-'tēl\ *n* : LOZENGE 2

pas·time \'pas-ˌtīm\ *n* : DIVERSION; *esp* : something that serves to make time pass agreeably

pas·tor \'pas-tər\ *n* [ME *pastour*, fr. AF, fr. L *pastor*, herdsman, fr. *pascere* to feed, pasture, nurture] : a minister or priest serving a local church or parish — **pas·tor·ate** \-tə-rət\ *n*

¹pas·to·ral \'pas-tə-rəl\ *adj* **1** : of or relating to shepherds or to rural life **2** : of or relating to spiritual guidance esp. of a congregation **3** : of or relating to the pastor of a church

²pastoral *n* : a literary work dealing with shepherds or rural life

pas·to·rale \ˌpas-tə-'räl, -'ral\ *n* [It] : a musical composition having a pastoral theme

past participle *n* : a participle that typically expresses completed action, that is one of the principal parts of the verb, and that is used in the formation of perfect tenses in the active voice and of all tenses in the passive voice

pas·tra·mi \pə-'strä-mē\ *n* [Yiddish *pastrame*] : a highly seasoned smoked beef prepared esp. from shoulder cuts

pas·try \'pā-strē\ *n, pl* **pastries** : sweet baked goods made of dough or with a crust made of enriched dough

pas·tur·age \'pas-chə-rij\ *n* : PASTURE

¹pas·ture \'pas-chər\ *n* **1** : plants (as grass) for the feeding esp. of grazing livestock **2** : land or a plot of land used for grazing

²pasture *vb* **pas·tured; pas·tur·ing** **1** : GRAZE **2** : to use as pasture

pasty \'pā-stē\ *adj* **past·i·er; -est** : resembling paste; *esp* : pallid and unhealthy in appearance

¹pat \'pat\ *n* **1** : a light tap esp. with the hand or a flat instrument; *also* : the sound made by it **2** : something (as butter) shaped into a small flat usu. square individual portion

²pat *adv* : in a pat manner : PERFECTLY

³pat *vb* **pat·ted; pat·ting** **1** : to strike lightly with a flat instrument **2** : to flatten, smooth, or put into place or shape with a pat **3** : to tap gently or lovingly with the hand

⁴pat *adj* **1** : exactly suited to the occasion : APT **2** : memorized exactly **3** : UNYIELDING ⟨stood ∼ on the issue⟩

PAT *abbr* point after touchdown

pa·ta·ca \pə-'tä-kə\ *n* — see MONEY table

¹patch \'pach\ *n* **1** : a piece used to cover a torn or worn place; *also* : one worn on a garment as an ornament or insignia **2** : a small area distinct from that about it **3** : a shield worn over the socket of an injured or missing eye

²patch *vb* **1** : to mend or cover with a patch **2** : to make of fragments **3** : to repair usu. in hasty fashion

patch·ou·li \'pa-chə-lē, pə-'chü-lē\ *n* : a heavy perfume made from the fragrant essential oil of an Asian mint; *also* : the plant itself

patch test *n* : a test for allergic sensitivity made by applying to the unbroken skin small pads soaked with the allergen to be tested

patch·work \'pach-ˌwərk\ *n* : something made of pieces of different materials, shapes, or colors

patchy \'pa-chē\ *adj* **patch·i·er; -est** : marked by or consisting of patches; *also* : irregular in appearance or quality — **patch·i·ness** \-chē-nəs\ *n*

pate \'pāt\ *n* : HEAD; *esp* : the crown of the head

pâ·té *also* **pate** \pä-'tā\ *n* [F] **1** : a meat or fish pie or patty **2** : a spread of finely chopped or pureed seasoned meat

pa·tel·la \pə-'te-lə\ n, pl -lae \-'te-(ₐ)lē, -ₐlī\ or -las [L] : KNEECAP — pa·tel·lar \-'te-lər\ adj

pat·en \'pa-tᵊn\ n 1 : PLATE; esp : one of precious metal for the eucharistic bread 2 : a thin disk

¹pa·tent \I & 4 are 'pa-tᵊnt, Brit also 'pā-, 2 & 3 are 'pa-tᵊnt, 'pā-\ adj 1 : open to public inspection — used chiefly in the phrase letters patent 2 : free from obstruction 3 : EVIDENT, OBVIOUS 4 : protected by a patent ♦ **Synonyms** MANIFEST, DISTINCT, APPARENT, PALPABLE, PLAIN, CLEAR — pat·ent·ly adv

²pat·ent \'pa-tᵊnt, Brit also 'pā-\ n 1 : an official document conferring a right or privilege 2 : a document securing to an inventor for a term of years exclusive right to his or her invention 3 : something patented

³pat·ent vb : to secure by patent

pat·en·tee \ₐpa-tᵊn-'tē, Brit also ₐpā-\ n : one to whom a grant is made or a privilege secured by patent

pat·ent medicine \'pa-tᵊnt-\ n : a packaged nonprescription drug protected by a trademark; also : any proprietary drug

pa·ter·fa·mil·i·as \ₐpā-tər-fə-'mi-lē-əs\ n, pl pa·tres·fa·mil·i·as \ₐpā-ₐtrēz-\ [L] : the father of a family : the male head of a household

pa·ter·nal \pə-'tər-nᵊl\ adj 1 : FATHERLY 2 : related through or inherited or derived from a father — pa·ter·nal·ly adv

pa·ter·nal·ism \-nə-ₐli-zəm\ n : a system under which an authority treats those under its control paternally (as by regulating their conduct and supplying their needs)

¹pa·ter·ni·ty \pə-'tər-nə-tē\ n 1 : FATHERHOOD 2 : descent from a father

²paternity adj 1 : granted to a father ⟨~ leave⟩ 2 : of or relating to the determination of paternity ⟨a ~ suit⟩

¹path \'path, 'päth\ n, pl paths \'pathz, 'paths, 'päthz, 'päths\ 1 : a trodden way : ROUTE, COURSE — path·less adj

²path or pathol abbr pathology

path·break·ing \'path-ₐbrā-kiŋ\ adj : TRAILBLAZING

pa·thet·ic \pə-'the-tik\ adj 1 : evoking tenderness, pity, or sorrow 2 : pitifully inadequate ⟨a ~ performance⟩ ♦ **Synonyms** PITIFUL, PITEOUS, PITIABLE, POOR — pa·thet·i·cal·ly \-ti-k(ə-)lē\ adv

path·find·er \'path-ₐfīn-dər, 'päth-\ n : one that discovers a way; esp : one that explores untraveled regions to mark out a new route

patho·gen \'pa-thə-jən\ n : a specific agent (as a bacterium) causing disease — patho·gen·ic \ₐpa-thə-'je-nik\ adj — patho·ge·nic·i·ty \-jə-'ni-sə-tē\ n

pa·thog·ra·phy \pa-'thä-grə-fē\ n : biography focusing on a person's flaws and misfortunes

pa·thol·o·gy \pə-'thä-lə-jē\ n, pl -gies 1 : the study of the essential nature of disease 2 : the abnormality of structure and function characteristic of a disease 3 : deviation giving rise to social ills — path·o·log·i·cal \ₐpa-thə-'lä-ji-kəl\ adj — pa·thol·o·gist \pə-'thä-lə-jist\ n

pa·thos \'pa-ₐthäs, -ₐthōs\ n : an element in experience or artistic representation evoking pity or compassion

path·way \'path-ₐwā, 'päth-\ n : PATH

pa·tience \'pā-shəns\ n 1 : the capacity, habit, or fact of being patient 2 chiefly Brit : SOLITAIRE 2

¹pa·tient \'pā-shənt\ adj 1 : bearing pain or trials without complaint 2 : showing self-control : CALM 3 : STEADFAST, PERSEVERING — pa·tient·ly adv

²patient n : one under medical care

pa·ti·na \'pa-tə-nə, pə-'tē-\ n, pl pa·ti·nas \-nəz\ or pa·ti·nae \'pa-tə-ₐnē, -ₐnī\ 1 : a green film formed on copper and bronze by exposure to moist air 2 : a superficial covering or exterior

pa·tio \'pa-tē-ₐō, 'pä-\ n, pl pa·ti·os 1 : COURTYARD 2 : an often paved area near a dwelling used esp. for outdoor dining

pa·tois \'pa-ₐtwä\ n, pl pa·tois \-ₐtwäz\ [F] 1 : a dialect other than the standard dialect; esp : uneducated or provincial speech 2 : JARGON 2

pa·tri·arch \'pā-trē-ₐärk\ n 1 : a man who is father or founder (as of a tribe) 2 : a venerable old man 3 : an ecclesiastical dignitary (as the bishop of an Eastern Orthodox see) — pa·tri·ar·chal \ₐpā-trē-'är-kəl\ adj — pa·tri·arch·ate \'pā-trē-ₐär-kət, -ₐkät\ n — pa·tri·ar·chy \-ₐär-kē\ n

pa·tri·cian \pə-'tri-shən\ n : a person of high birth : ARISTOCRAT — patrician adj

pat·ri·cide \'pa-trə-ₐsīd\ n 1 : one who murders his or her own father 2 : the murder of one's own father

pat·ri·mo·ny \'pa-trə-ₐmō-nē\ n : something (as an estate) inherited or derived esp. from one's father : HERITAGE — pat·ri·mo·ni·al \ₐpa-trə-'mō-nē-əl\ adj

pa·tri·ot \'pā-trē-ət, -ₐät\ n [MF patriote compatriot, fr. LL patriota, fr. Gk patriōtēs, fr. patria lineage, fr. patr-, patēr father] : one who loves his or her country — pa·tri·ot·ic \ₐpā-trē-'ä-tik\ adj — pa·tri·ot·i·cal·ly \-ti-k(ə-)lē\ adv — pa·tri·o·tism \'pā-trē-ə-ₐti-zəm\ n

pa·tris·tic \pə-'tris-tik\ adj : of or relating to the church fathers or their writings

¹pa·trol \pə-'trōl\ n : the action of going the rounds (as of an area) for observation or the maintenance of security; also : a person or group performing such an action

²patrol vb pa·trolled; pa·trol·ling : to carry out a patrol

pa·trol·man \pə-'trōl-mən\ n : a police officer assigned to a beat

patrol wagon n : PADDY WAGON

pa·tron \'pā-trən\ n [ME, fr. AF, fr. ML & L; ML patronus patron saint, patron of a benefice, pattern, fr. L, defender, fr. patr-, pater father] 1 : a person chosen or named as special protector 2 : a wealthy or influential supporter ⟨~ of poets⟩; also : BENEFACTOR 3 : a regular client or customer ⟨diner ~s⟩

pa·tron·age \'pa-trə-nij, 'pā-\ n 1 : the support or influence of a patron 2 : the trade of customers 3 : control of appointment to government jobs

pa·tron·ess \'pā-trə-nəs\ n : a woman who is a patron

pa·tron·ise Brit var of PATRONIZE

pa·tron·ize \'pā-trə-ₐnīz, 'pa-\ vb -ized; -iz·ing 1 : to be a customer of 2 : to treat condescendingly, haughtily, or coolly ⟨rich people who ~ the poor⟩

pat·ro·nym·ic \ₐpa-trə-'ni-mik\ n : a name derived from the name of one's father or a paternal ancestor usu. by the addition of an affix

pa·troon \pə-'trün\ n : the proprietor of a manorial estate esp. in New York under Dutch rule

pat·sy \'pat-sē\ n, pl pat·sies : a person who is easily duped or victimized

¹pat·ter \'pa-tər\ vb : to talk glibly or mechanically ♦ **Synonyms** CHATTER, PRATE, CHAT, PRATTLE, BABBLE

²patter n 1 : a specialized lingo 2 : extremely rapid talk ⟨a comedian's ~⟩

³patter vb : to strike, pat, or tap rapidly

⁴patter n : a quick succession of taps or pats ⟨the ~ of rain⟩

¹pat·tern \'pa-tərn\ n [ME patron, fr. AF, fr. ML patronus, fr. L, defender, fr. patr-, pater father] 1 : an ideal model 2 : something used as a model for making things ⟨a dressmaker's ~⟩ 3 : SAMPLE 4 : an artistic design 5 : CONFIGURATION 6 : a sample of a person's behaviors or characteristics ⟨a ~ of violence⟩

²pattern vb : to form according to a pattern

pat·ty also pat·tie \'pa-tē\ n, pl patties 1 : a little pie 2 : a small flat cake esp. of chopped food ⟨hamburger patties⟩

pau·ci·ty \'pȯ-sə-tē\ n : smallness of number or quantity

paunch \'pȯnch\ n : a usu. large belly : POTBELLY — paunchy adj

pau·per \'pȯ-pər\ n : a person without means of support except from charity — pau·per·ism \-pə-ₐri-zəm\ n — pau·per·ize \-pə-ₐrīz\ vb

¹pause \'pȯz\ n 1 : a temporary stop; also : a period of inaction 2 : a brief suspension of the voice 3 : a sign ⌒ or ⌣ above or below a musical note or rest to show it is to be prolonged 4 : a reason for pausing 5 : a function of an electronic device that pauses a recording

²pause vb paused; paus·ing : to stop, rest, or linger for a time

pave \'pāv\ vb paved; pav·ing : to cover (as a road) with hard material in order to smooth or firm the surface

pave·ment \'pāv-mənt\ n 1 : a paved surface 2 : the material with which something is paved

pa·vil·ion \pə-'vil-yən\ n [ME pavilloun, pavillioun, fr. AF, fr. L papilion-, papilio butterfly] 1 : a large tent 2 : a usu. open structure (as in a park) used for entertainment or shelter

pav·ing \'pā-viŋ\ n : PAVEMENT

¹paw \'pȯ\ n : the foot of a quadruped (as a dog or lion) having claws

²paw vb 1 : to touch or strike with a paw; also : to scrape

with a hoof **2** : to feel or handle clumsily or rudely **3** : to flail about or grab for with the hands

pawl \'pȯl\ *n* : a pivoted tongue or sliding bolt designed to fall into notches on another machine part to permit motion in one direction only

¹pawn \'pȯn\ *n* [ME *pown*, fr. AF *peoun, paun*, fr. ML *pedon-, pedo* foot soldier, fr. LL, one with broad feet, fr. L *ped-, pes* foot] **1** : a chess piece of the least value **2** : one used for the purposes of another

²pawn *n* **1** : something deposited as security for a loan; *also* : HOSTAGE **2** : the state of being pledged

³pawn *vb* : to deposit as a pledge

pawn·bro·ker \'pȯn-ˌbrō-kər\ *n* : one who lends money on goods pledged

Paw·nee \pȯ-'nē\ *n, pl* **Pawnee** *or* **Pawnees** : a member of an American Indian people orig. of Kansas and Nebraska

pawn·shop \'pȯn-ˌshäp\ *n* : a pawnbroker's place of business

paw·paw *also* **pa·paw 1** \pə-'pȯ\ : PAPAYA **2** \'pä-pȯ, 'pȯ-\ : a No. American tree with green-skinned edible fruit; *also* : its fruit

¹pay \'pā\ *vb* **paid** \'pād\ *also in sense 7* **payed; pay·ing** [ME, fr. AF *paier*, fr. L *pacare* to pacify, fr. *pac-, pax* peace] **1** : to make due return to for goods or services **2** : to discharge indebtedness for : SETTLE ⟨∼ a bill⟩ **3** : to give in forfeit ⟨∼ the penalty⟩ **4** : REQUITE **5** : to give, offer, or make freely or as fitting ⟨∼ attention⟩ **6** : to be profitable to : RETURN **7** : to make slack and allow to run out ⟨∼ out a rope⟩ — **pay·able** *adj* — **pay·ee** \pā-'ē\ *n* — **pay·er** *n*

²pay *n* **1** : something paid; *esp* : WAGES **2** : the status of being paid by an employer : EMPLOY

³pay *adj* **1** : containing something valuable (as gold) ⟨∼ dirt⟩ **2** : equipped to receive a fee for use ⟨∼ telephone⟩ **3** : requiring payment

pay·back \'pā-ˌbak\ *n* **1** : a return on an investment equal to the original capital outlay **2** : something given in return, compensation, or retaliation

pay·check \'pā-ˌchek\ *n* **1** : a check in payment of wages or salary **2** : WAGES, SALARY

pay·load \-ˌlōd\ *n* : the load carried by a vehicle in addition to what is necessary for its operation; *also* : the weight of such a load

pay·mas·ter \-ˌmas-tər\ *n* : one who distributes the payroll

pay·ment \'pā-mənt\ *n* **1** : the act of paying **2** : something paid

pay·off \-ˌȯf\ *n* **1** : PROFIT, REWARD; *also* : RETRIBUTION **2** : the climax of an incident or enterprise ⟨the ∼ of a story⟩

pay–per–view *n* : a cable television service by which customers can order access to a single airing of a TV feature

pay·roll \-ˌrōl\ *n* : a list of persons entitled to receive pay; *also* : the money to pay those on such a list

payt *abbr* payment

pay up *vb* : to pay what is due; *also* : to pay in full

Pb *symbol* [L *plumbum*] lead

PBS *abbr* Public Broadcasting Service

PBX \ˌpē-(ˌ)bē-'eks\ *n* [*private branch exchange*] : a private telephone switchboard

¹PC \ˌpē-'sē\ *n, pl* **PCs** *or* **PC's** [*personal computer*] : MICROCOMPUTER

²PC *abbr* **1** Peace Corps **2** percent; percentage **3** politically correct **4** postcard **5** [L *post cibum*] after meals **6** professional corporation

PCB \ˌpē-ˌsē-'bē\ *n* : POLYCHLORINATED BIPHENYL

PCP \ˌpē-ˌsē-'pē\ *n* : PHENCYCLIDINE

pct *abbr* percent; percentage

pd *abbr* paid

Pd *symbol* palladium

PD *abbr* **1** per diem **2** police department **3** potential difference

PDA \ˌpē-ˌdē-'ā\ *n* [*personal digital assistant*] : a small microprocessor device for storing and organizing personal information

PDQ \ˌpē-ˌdē-'kyü\ *adv, often not cap* [abbr. of *pretty damned quick*] : IMMEDIATELY

PDT *abbr* Pacific daylight (saving) time

PE *abbr* **1** physical education **2** printer's error **3** professional engineer

pea \'pē\ *n, pl* **peas** *also* **pease** \'pēz\ **1** : the round edible protein-rich seed borne in the pod of a widely grown leguminous vine; *also* : this vine **2** : any of various plants resembling or related to the pea

peace \'pēs\ *n* **1** : a state of calm and quiet; *esp* : public security under law **2** : freedom from disturbing thoughts or emotions **3** : a state of concord (as between persons or governments); *also* : an agreement to end hostilities — **peace·able** \'pē-sə-bəl\ *adj* — **peace·ably** \-blē\ *adv* — **peace·ful** *adj* — **peace·ful·ly** *adv*

peace·keep·ing \'pēs-ˌkē-piŋ\ *n* : the preserving of peace; *esp* : international enforcement and supervision of a truce — **peace·keep·er** *n*

peace·mak·er \-ˌmā-kər\ *n* : one who settles an argument or stops a fight

peace·time \-ˌtīm\ *n* : a time when a nation is not at war

peach \'pēch\ *n* [ME *peche*, fr. AF *pesche, peche,*, fr. LL *persica*, fr. L (*malum*) *Persicum*, lit., Persian fruit] : a sweet juicy fuzzy-skinned fruit of a small usu. pink-flowered tree related to the cherry and plums; *also* : this tree — **peachy** *adj*

pea·cock \'pē-ˌkäk\ *n* [ME *pecok*, fr. *pe-* (fr. OE *pēa* peafowl, fr. L *pavo* peacock) + *cok* cock] : the male peafowl that can spread its long tail feathers to make a colorful display

pea·fowl \-ˌfau̇(-ə)l\ *n* : either of two large domesticated Asian pheasants

pea·hen \-ˌhen\ *n* : the female peafowl

¹peak \'pēk\ *n* **1** : a pointed or projecting part **2** : the top of a hill or mountain; *also* : MOUNTAIN **3** : the front projecting part of a cap **4** : the narrow part of a ship's bow or stern **5** : the highest level or greatest degree — **peak** *adj*

²peak *vb* : to bring to or reach a maximum

peak·ed \'pē-kəd\ *adj* : THIN, SICKLY

¹peal \'pēl\ *n* **1** : the loud ringing of bells **2** : a set of tuned bells **3** : a loud sound or succession of sounds

²peal *vb* : to give out peals : RESOUND

pea·nut \'pē-(ˌ)nət\ *n* **1** : an annual herb related to the pea but having pods that ripen underground; *also* : this pod or one of the edible seeds it bears **2** *pl* : a very small amount **3** : a pellet of polystyrene foam

pear \'per\ *n* : the fleshy fruit of a tree related to the apple; *also* : this tree

pearl \'pərl\ *n* **1** : a small hard often lustrous body formed within the shell of some mollusks and used as a gem **2** : one that is choice or precious ⟨∼s of wisdom⟩ **3** : a slightly bluish medium gray color — **pearly** \'pər-lē\ *adj*

peas·ant \'pe-zᵊnt\ *n* **1** : any of a class of small landowners or laborers tilling the soil **2** : a usu. uneducated person of low social status — **peas·ant·ry** \-zᵊn-trē\ *n*

pea·shoot·er \'pē-ˌshü-tər\ *n* : a toy blowgun for shooting peas

peat \'pēt\ *n* : a dark substance formed by partial decay of plants (as mosses) in water — **peaty** *adj*

peat moss *n* : SPHAGNUM

¹peb·ble \'pe-bəl\ *n* : a small usu. round stone — **peb·bly** \-b(ə-)lē\ *adj*

²pebble *vb* **peb·bled; peb·bling** : to produce a rough surface texture in ⟨∼ leather⟩

pec \'pek\ *n* : PECTORAL MUSCLE

pe·can \pi-'kän, -'kan; 'pē-ˌkan\ *n* : the smooth thin-shelled edible nut of a large American hickory; *also* : this tree

pec·ca·dil·lo \ˌpe-kə-'di-lō\ *n, pl* **-loes** *or* **-los** : a slight offense

pec·ca·ry \'pe-kə-rē\ *n, pl* **-ries** : any of several American chiefly tropical mammals resembling but smaller than the related pigs

peccary

pec·ca·vi \pe-'kä-ˌvē\ *n* [L, I have sinned, fr. *peccare* to sin] : an acknowledgment of sin

¹**peck** \'pek\ *n* — see WEIGHT table

²**peck** *vb* **1** : to strike or pierce with or as if with the bill **2** : to make (as a hole) by pecking **3** : to pick up with or as if with the bill

³**peck** *n* **1** : an impression made by pecking **2** : a quick sharp stroke

pecking order *also* **peck order** *n* : a basic pattern of social organization within a flock of poultry in which each bird pecks another lower in the scale without being pecked in return and submits to pecking by one of higher rank; *also* : a social hierarchy

pec·tin \'pek-tən\ *n* : any of various water-soluble plant substances that cause fruit jellies to set — **pec·tic** \-tik\ *adj*

pec·to·ral \'pek-tə-rəl\ *adj* : of or relating to the breast or chest

pectoral muscle *n* : either of two muscles on each side of the body which connect the front walls of the chest with the bones of the upper arm and shoulder

pe·cu·liar \pi-'kyül-yər\ *adj* [ME *peculier*, fr. L *peculiaris* of private property, special, fr. *peculium* private property, fr. *pecus* cattle] **1** : belonging exclusively to one person or group **2** : CHARACTERISTIC, DISTINCTIVE **3** : QUEER, ODD ⟨her ~ behavior⟩ ✦ **Synonyms** IDIOSYNCRATIC, ECCENTRIC, SINGULAR, STRANGE, WEIRD — **pe·cu·liar·i·ty** \-ˌkyül-'ya-rə-tē, -ˌkyü-lē-'a-\ *n* — **pe·cu·liar·ly** *adv*

pe·cu·ni·ary \pi-'kyü-nē-ˌer-ē\ *adj* : of or relating to money : MONETARY

ped·a·gogue *also* **ped·a·gog** \'pe-də-ˌgäg\ *n* : TEACHER, SCHOOLMASTER

ped·a·go·gy \'pe-də-ˌgō-jē, -ˌgä-\ *n* : the art or profession of teaching; *esp* : EDUCATION **2** — **ped·a·gog·ic** \ˌpe-də-'gä-jik, -'gō-\ *or* **ped·a·gog·i·cal** \-ji-kəl\ *adj*

¹**ped·al** \'pe-dᵊl\ *n* : a lever worked by the foot

²**pedal** *adj* : of or relating to the foot

³**pedal** *vb* **ped·aled** *also* **ped·alled; ped·al·ing** *also* **ped·al·ling 1** : to use or work a pedal (as of a piano or bicycle) **2** : to ride a bicycle

ped·ant \'pe-dᵊnt\ *n* **1** : a person who makes a show of knowledge **2** : a formal uninspired teacher ⟨his piano teacher was a ~⟩ — **pe·dan·tic** \pi-'dan-tik\ *adj* — **ped·ant·ry** \'pe-dᵊn-trē\ *n*

ped·dle \'pe-dᵊl\ *vb* **ped·dled; ped·dling** : to sell or offer for sale from place to place — **ped·dler** *also* **ped·lar** \'ped-lər\ *n*

ped·er·ast \'pe-də-ˌrast\ *n* [Gk *paiderastēs*, lit., lover of boys] : a man who desires or engages in sexual activity with a boy — **ped·er·as·ty** \'pe-də-ˌras-tē\ *n*

ped·es·tal \'pe-dəs-tᵊl\ *n* **1** : the support or foot of something (as a column, statue, or vase) that is upright **2** : a position of high regard

¹**pe·des·tri·an** \pə-'des-trē-ən\ *adj* **1** : ORDINARY **2** : going on foot

²**pedestrian** *n* : WALKER

pe·di·at·rics \ˌpē-dē-'a-triks\ *n* : a branch of medicine dealing with the development, care, and diseases of children — **pe·di·at·ric** \-trik\ *adj* — **pe·di·a·tri·cian** \ˌpē-dē-ə-'tri-shən\ *n*

pedi·cab \'pe-di-ˌkab\ *n* : a pedal-driven tricycle with seats for a driver and two passengers

ped·i·cure \'pe-di-ˌkyür\ *n* : care of the feet, toes, and nails; *also* : a single treatment of these parts — **ped·i·cur·ist** \-ˌkyür-ist\ *n*

ped·i·gree \'pe-də-ˌgrē\ *n* [ME *pedegru*, fr. AF *pé de grue*, lit., crane's foot; fr. the shape made by the lines of a genealogical chart] **1** : a record of a line of ancestors **2** : an ancestral line — **ped·i·greed** \-ˌgrēd\ *adj*

ped·i·ment \'pe-də-mənt\ *n* : a low triangular gablelike decoration (as over a door or window) on a building

pe·dom·e·ter \pi-'dä-mə-tər\ *n* : an instrument that measures the distance one walks

pe·do·phile \'pe-də-ˌfī(-ə)l, 'pē-\ *n* : one affected with pedophilia

pe·do·phil·ia \ˌpe-də-'fi-lē-ə, ˌpē-\ *n* : sexual perversion in which children are the preferred sexual object

pe·dun·cle \'pē-ˌdəŋ-kəl\ *n* : a narrow supporting stalk

peek \'pēk\ *vb* **1** : to look furtively **2** : to peer from a place of concealment **3** : GLANCE — **peek** *n*

¹**peel** \'pēl\ *vb* [ME *pelen*, fr. AF *peler*, fr. L *pilare* to remove the hair from, fr. *pilus* hair] **1** : to strip the skin, bark, or rind from **2** : to strip off (as a coat); *also* : to come off **3** : to lose the skin, bark, or rind

²**peel** *n* : a skin or rind esp. of a fruit

peel·ing \'pē-liŋ\ *n* : a peeled-off piece or strip (as of skin or rind)

peen \'pēn\ *n* : the usu. hemispherical or wedge-shaped end of the head of a hammer opposite the face

¹**peep** \'pēp\ *vb* : to utter a feeble shrill sound or the slightest sound

²**peep** *n* : a feeble shrill sound

³**peep** *vb* **1** : to look slyly esp. through an aperture : PEEK **2** : to begin to emerge **3** : to look at : WATCH — **peep·er** *n*

⁴**peep** *n* **1** : a first faint appearance **2** : a brief or furtive look

peep·hole \'pēp-ˌhōl\ *n* : a hole to peep through

¹**peer** \'pir\ *n* **1** : one of equal standing with another : EQUAL **2** : NOBLE — **peer·age** \-ij\ *n*

²**peer** *vb* **1** : to look intently or curiously **2** : to come slightly into view

peer·ess \'pir-əs\ *n* : a woman who is a peer

peer·less \'pir-ləs\ *adj* : having no equal : MATCHLESS ⟨~ cellist⟩ ✦ **Synonyms** SUPREME, UNEQUALED, UNPARALLELED, INCOMPARABLE

¹**peeve** \'pēv\ *vb* **peeved; peev·ing** : to make resentful : ANNOY

²**peeve** *n* **1** : a feeling or mood of resentment **2** : a particular grievance

pee·vish \'pē-vish\ *adj* : querulous in temperament : FRETFUL ✦ **Synonyms** IRRITABLE, PETULANT, HUFFY — **pee·vish·ly** *adv* — **pee·vish·ness** *n*

pee·wee \'pē-(ˌ)wē\ *n* **1** : one that is diminutive or tiny **2** : a level of sports usu. for young children — **peewee** *adj*

¹**peg** \'peg\ *n* **1** : a small pointed piece (as of wood) used to pin down or fasten things or to fit into holes **2** : a projecting piece used as a support or boundary marker **3** : SUPPORT, PRETEXT **4** : STEP, DEGREE **5** : THROW

²**peg** *vb* **pegged; peg·ging 1** : to put a peg into : fasten, pin down, or attach with or as if with pegs **2** : to work hard and steadily : PLUG **3** : HUSTLE **4** : to mark by pegs **5** : to hold (as prices) at a set level or rate **6** : IDENTIFY ⟨was *pegged* as an intellectual⟩ **7** : THROW

PEI *abbr* Prince Edward Island

pei·gnoir \pān-'wär, pen-\ *n* [F, lit., garment worn while combing the hair, fr. MF, fr. *peigner* to comb the hair, fr. L *pectinare*, fr. *pectin-, pecten* comb] : NEGLIGEE

¹**pe·jo·ra·tive** \pi-'jȯr-ə-tiv\ *n* : a pejorative word or phrase

²**pejorative** *adj* : having negative connotations : DISPARAGING — **pe·jo·ra·tive·ly** *adv*

peke \'pēk\ *n, often cap* : PEKINGESE

Pe·king·ese *or* **Pe·kin·ese** \ˌpē-kə-'nēz, -'nēs; -kiŋ-'ēz, -'ēs\ *n, pl* **Pekingese** *or* **Pekinese** : any of a breed of Chinese origin of small short-legged long-haired dogs

pe·koe \'pē-(ˌ)kō\ *n* : a black tea made from young tea leaves

pel·age \'pe-lij\ *n* : the hairy covering of a mammal

pe·lag·ic \pə-'la-jik\ *adj* : OCEANIC

pelf \'pelf\ *n* : MONEY, RICHES

pel·i·can \'pe-li-kən\ *n* : any of a genus of large web-footed birds having a pouched lower bill used to scoop in fish

pel·la·gra \pə-'la-grə, -'lä-\ *n* : a disease caused by a diet with too little niacin and protein and marked by a skin rash, disease of the digestive system, and mental disturbances

pel·let \'pe-lət\ *n* **1** : a little ball (as of medicine) **2** : BULLET — **pel·let·al** \-lə-tᵊl\ *adj* — **pel·let·ize** \-ˌtīz\ *vb*

pell–mell \'pel-'mel\ *adv* **1** : in mingled confusion ⟨papers strewn ~ on the desk⟩ **2** : HEADLONG ⟨ran ~ for the door⟩

pel·lu·cid \pə-'lü-səd\ *adj* : extremely clear : LIMPID, TRANSPARENT ⟨a ~ stream⟩ ✦ **Synonyms** TRANSLUCENT, LUCID, LUCENT

pe·lo·ton \ˌpe-lə-'tän\ *n* : the main body of riders in a bicycle race

¹**pelt** \'pelt\ *n* : a skin esp. of a fur-bearing animal

²**pelt** *vb* : to strike with a succession of blows or missiles

pel·vis \'pel-vəs\ *n, pl* **pel·vis·es** \-və-səz\ *or* **pel·ves** \-ˌvēz\ : a basin-shaped part of the vertebrate skeleton consisting of the large bone of each hip and the nearby bones of the spine — **pel·vic** \-vik\ *adj*

pem·mi·can *also* **pem·i·can** \'pe-mi-kən\ *n* : dried meat pounded fine and mixed with melted fat

¹pen \'pen\ *vb* **penned; pen·ning** : to shut in or as if in a pen

²pen *n* **1** : a small enclosure for animals **2** : a small place of confinement or storage

³pen *n* **1** : an implement for writing or drawing with ink or a similar fluid **2** : a writing instrument regarded as a means of expression **3** : STYLUS 3

⁴pen *vb* **penned; pen·ning** : WRITE

⁵pen *n* : PENITENTIARY

⁶pen *abbr* peninsula

PEN *abbr* International Association of Poets, Playwrights, Editors, Essayists and Novelists

pe·nal \'pēn°l\ *adj* : of or relating to punishment

pe·nal·ise *Brit var of* PENALIZE

pe·nal·ize \'pēn-ə-ˌlīz, 'pe-\ *vb* **-ized; -iz·ing** : to put a penalty on

pen·al·ty \'pen-°l-tē\ *n, pl* **-ties** **1** : punishment for crime or offense **2** : something forfeited when a person fails to do something agreed to **3** : disadvantage, loss, or hardship (as to a competitor) due to some action

pen·ance \'pe-nəns\ *n* **1** : an act performed to show sorrow or repentance for sin **2** : a sacrament (as in the Roman Catholic Church) consisting of confession, absolution, and a penance directed by the confessor

pence \'pens\ *pl of* PENNY

pen·chant \'pen-chənt\ *n* [F, fr. prp. of *pencher* to incline, fr. VL *pendicare*, fr. L *pendere* to weigh] : a strong inclination : LIKING ⟨a ∼ for taking risks⟩ ✦ *Synonyms* LEANING, PROPENSITY, PREDILECTION, PREDISPOSITION

¹pen·cil \'pen-səl\ *n* : a writing or drawing tool consisting of or containing a slender cylinder of a solid marking substance

²pencil *vb* **-ciled** *or* **-cilled; -cil·ing** *or* **-cil·ling** **1** : to draw or write with a pencil **2** : to plan or designate tentatively ⟨∼ed in the appointment⟩

pen·dant *also* **pen·dent** \'pen-dənt\ *n* : a hanging ornament (as on a necklace)

pen·dent *or* **pen·dant** \'pen-dənt\ *adj* : SUSPENDED, OVERHANGING

¹pend·ing \'pen-diŋ\ *prep* **1** : DURING **2** : while awaiting ⟨∼ approval⟩

²pending *adj* **1** : not yet decided ⟨a ∼ application⟩ **2** : IMMINENT

pen·du·lous \'pen-jə-ləs, -də-\ *adj* : hanging loosely : DROOPING ⟨∼ earrings⟩

pen·du·lum \-ləm\ *n* : a body that swings freely from a fixed point

pe·ne·plain *also* **pe·ne·plane** \'pē-ni-ˌplān\ *n* : a large almost flat land surface shaped by erosion

pen·e·trate \'pe-nə-ˌtrāt\ *vb* **-trat·ed; -trat·ing** **1** : to enter into : PIERCE **2** : PERMEATE **3** : to see into : UNDERSTAND **4** : to affect deeply — **pen·e·tra·ble** \-trə-bəl\ *adj* — **pen·e·tra·tion** \ˌpe-nə-'trā-shən\ *n* — **pen·e·tra·tive** \'pe-nə-ˌtrā-tiv\ *adj*

penetrating *adj* **1** : having the power of entering, piercing, or pervading ⟨a ∼ shriek⟩ ⟨a ∼ odor⟩ **2** : ACUTE, DISCERNING ⟨a ∼ look⟩

pen·guin \'pen-gwən, 'peŋ-\ *n* : any of various erect short-legged flightless seabirds of the southern hemisphere

pen·i·cil·lin \ˌpe-nə-'si-lən\ *n* : any of several antibiotics produced by molds or synthetically and used against various bacteria

pen·in·su·la \pə-'nin-sə-lə\ *n* [L *paeninsula*, fr. *paene* almost + *insula* island] : a long narrow portion of land extending out into the water — **pen·in·su·lar** \-lər\ *adj*

pe·nis \'pē-nəs\ *n, pl* **pe·nis·es** *also* **penes** \-ˌnēz\ : a male organ of copulation that in the human male also functions as the channel by which urine leaves the body

¹pen·i·tent \'pe-nə-tənt\ *adj* : feeling sorrow for sins or offenses : REPENTANT — **pen·i·tence** \-təns\ *n* — **pen·i·ten·tial** \ˌpe-nə-'ten-chəl\ *adj*

²penitent *n* : a penitent person

¹pen·i·ten·tia·ry \ˌpe-nə-'ten-chə-rē\ *n, pl* **-ries** : a state or federal prison

²penitentiary *adj* : of, relating to, or incurring confinement in a penitentiary

pen·knife \'pen-ˌnīf\ *n* : a small pocketknife

pen·light *also* **pen·lite** \-ˌlīt\ *n* : a small flashlight resembling a fountain pen in size or shape

pen·man \'pen-mən\ *n* **1** : COPYIST **2** : one skilled in penmanship **3** : AUTHOR

pen·man·ship \-ˌship\ *n* : the art or practice of writing with the pen

Penn *or* **Penna** *abbr* Pennsylvania

pen name *n* : an author's pseudonym

pen·nant \'pe-nənt\ *n* **1** : a tapering flag used esp. for signaling **2** : a flag symbolic of championship

pen·ne \'pe-nā\ *n* : short diagonally cut tubular pasta

pen·ni \'pe-nē\ *n, pl* **pen·nia** \-nē-ə\ *or* **pen·nis** \-nēz\ : a former monetary unit equal to ¹/₁₀₀ markka

pen·non \'pe-nən\ *n* **1** : a long narrow ribbonlike flag borne on a lance **2** : WING

Penn·syl·va·nian \ˌpen-səl-'vā-nyən\ *adj* **1** : of or relating to Pennsylvania or its people **2** : of, relating to, or being the period of the Paleozoic era between the Mississippian and the Permian — **Pennsylvanian** *n*

pen·ny \'pe-nē\ *n, pl* **pennies** \-nēz\ *or* **pence** \'pens\ **1** *pl usu* **pence** : a British monetary unit formerly equal to ¹/₁₂ shilling but now equal to ¹/₁₀₀ pound; *also* : a coin of this value — see *pound* at MONEY table **2** *pl* **pennies** : a cent of the U.S. or Canada **3** : a former monetary unit equal to ¹/₁₀₀ Irish pound — **pen·ni·less** \'pe-ni-ləs\ *adj*

pen·ny–pinch·ing \'pe-nē-ˌpin-chiŋ\ *n* : PARSIMONY — **pen·ny–pinch·er** *n* — **penny–pinching** *adj*

pen·ny·weight \-ˌwāt\ *n* — see WEIGHT table

pen·ny–wise \-ˌwīz\ *adj* : wise or prudent only in small matters

pe·nol·o·gy \pi-'nä-lə-jē\ *n* : a branch of criminology dealing with prisons and the treatment of offenders

¹pen·sion \'pen-chən\ *n* : a fixed sum paid regularly esp. to a person retired from service

²pension *vb* : to pay a pension to — **pen·sion·er** *n*

pen·sive \'pen-siv\ *adj* : musingly, dreamily, or sadly thoughtful ✦ *Synonyms* REFLECTIVE, SPECULATIVE, CONTEMPLATIVE, MEDITATIVE — **pen·sive·ly** *adv*

pen·stock \'pen-ˌstäk\ *n* **1** : a sluice or gate for regulating a flow **2** : a pipe for carrying water

pent \'pent\ *adj* : shut up : CONFINED

pen·ta·gon \'pen-tə-ˌgän\ *n* : a polygon of five angles and five sides — **pen·tag·o·nal** \pen-'ta-gə-n°l\ *adj*

pen·tam·e·ter \pen-'ta-mə-tər\ *n* : a line of verse containing five metrical feet

pen·tath·lon \pen-'tath-lən\ *n* : a composite athletic contest consisting of five events

Pen·te·cost \'pen-ti-ˌkȯst\ *n* : the 7th Sunday after Easter observed as a church festival commemorating the descent of the Holy Spirit on the apostles — **Pen·te·cos·tal** \ˌpen-ti-'käs-t°l\ *adj*

Pentecostal *n* : a member of a Christian religious body that stresses expressive worship, evangelism, and spiritual gifts — **Pen·te·cos·tal·ism** \pen-ti-'käs-tə-ˌli-zəm\

pent·house \'pent-ˌhau̇s\ *n* [alter. of ME *pentis*, fr. AF *apentiz*, fr. *apent*, pp. of *apendre* to attach, hang against] **1** : a shed or sloping roof attached to a wall or building **2** : an apartment built on the top floor or roof of a building

pen·ul·ti·mate \pi-'nəl-tə-mət\ *adj* : next to the last ⟨∼ syllable⟩

pen·um·bra \pə-'nəm-brə\ *n, pl* **-brae** \-ˌ(ˌ)brē\ *or* **-bras** **1** : the partial shadow surrounding a complete shadow (as in an eclipse) **2** : something that covers or obscures ⟨a ∼ of secrecy⟩

pe·nu·ri·ous \pə-'nu̇r-ē-əs, -'nyu̇r-\ *adj* **1** : marked by penury **2** : MISERLY ✦ *Synonyms* STINGY, CLOSE, TIGHTFISTED, PARSIMONIOUS

pen·u·ry \'pe-nyə-rē\ *n* **1** : extreme poverty **2** : extreme frugality

pe·on \'pē-ˌän, -ən\ *n, pl* **peons** *or* **pe·o·nes** \pā-'ō-nēz\ **1** : a member of the landless laboring class in Spanish America **2** : one bound to service for payment of a debt — **pe·on·age** \-ə-nij\ *n*

pe·o·ny \'pē-ə-nē\ *n, pl* **-nies** : any of a genus of chiefly Eurasian plants with large often double red, pink, or white flowers; *also* : the flower

¹peo·ple \'pē-pəl\ *n, pl* **people** [ME *peple*, fr. AF *peple, peuple*, fr. L *populus*] **1** *pl* : human beings making up a group or linked by a common characteristic or interest **2** *pl* : human beings — often used in compounds instead of *persons* ⟨sales*people*⟩ or attributively ⟨∼ skills⟩ **3** *pl* : the mass of persons in a community : POPULACE; *also* : ELECTORATE ⟨the ∼'s choice⟩ **4** *pl* **peoples** : a body of persons (as a tribe, nation, or race) united by a common culture, sense of kinship, or political organization

²**people** *vb* **peo·pled; peo·pling** : to supply or fill with or as if with people

¹**pep** \'pep\ *n* : brisk energy or initiative — **pep·py** *adj*

²**pep** *vb* **pepped; pep·ping** : to put pep into : STIMULATE ⟨~ the team up⟩

¹**pep·per** \'pe-pər\ *n* **1** : either of two pungent condiments from the berry (**pep·per·corn** \-,kórn\) of an Indian climbing plant : BLACK PEPPER, WHITE PEPPER; *also* : this plant **2** : a plant related to the tomato and widely grown for its hot or mild sweet fruit; *also* : this fruit

²**pepper** *vb* **pep·pered; pep·per·ing 1** : to shower with missiles or rapid blows **2** : to sprinkle or season with or as if with pepper **3** : to deliver something in rapid succession ⟨~ed him with questions⟩

pep·per·mint \-,mint, -mənt\ *n* : a pungent aromatic mint; *also* : candy flavored with its oil

pep·per·o·ni \,pe-pə-'rō-nē\ *n* : a highly seasoned beef and pork sausage

pepper spray *n* : a temporarily disabling aerosol that causes irritation and blinding of the eyes and inflammation of the nose, throat, and skin

pep·pery \'pe-pə-rē\ *adj* **1** : having the qualities of pepper : PUNGENT, HOT **2** : having a hot temper **3** : FIERY

pep·sin \'pep-sən\ *n* : an enzyme of the stomach that promotes digestion by breaking down proteins; *also* : a preparation of this used medicinally

pep·tic \'pep-tik\ *adj* [L *pepticus*, fr. Gk *peptikos*, fr. *peptos* cooked, *peptein* to cook, digest] **1** : relating to or promoting digestion **2** : caused by digestive juices ⟨a ~ ulcer⟩

pep·tide \'pep-,tīd\ *n* : any of various organic compounds composed of two or more amino acids bonded together

Pe·quot \'pē-,kwät\ *n* : a member of an American Indian people of eastern Connecticut

¹**per** \'pər\ *prep* **1** : by means of **2** : to or for each **3** : ACCORDING TO

²**per** *adv* : for each : APIECE

³**per** *abbr* **1** period **2** person

¹**per·ad·ven·ture** \'pər-əd-,ven-chər\ *adv, archaic* : PERHAPS

²**peradventure** *n* **1** : DOUBT **2** : CHANCE 4

per·am·bu·late \pə-'ram-byə-,lāt\ *vb* **-lat·ed; -lat·ing** : to travel over esp. on foot — **per·am·bu·la·tion** \-,ram-byə-'lā-shən\ *n*

per·am·bu·la·tor \pə-'ram-byə-,lā-tər\ *n, chiefly Brit* : a baby carriage

per an·num \(,)pər-'a-nəm\ *adv* [ML] : in or for each year : ANNUALLY

per·cale \(,)pər-'kāl, 'pər-,; (,)pər-'kal\ *n* : a fine woven cotton cloth

per cap·i·ta \(,)pər-'ka-pə-tə\ *adv or adj* [ML, by heads] : by or for each person

per·ceive \pər-'sēv\ *vb* **per·ceived; per·ceiv·ing 1** : to attain awareness : REALIZE **2** : to become aware of through the senses — **per·ceiv·able** *adj*

¹**per·cent** \pər-'sent\ *adv* [*per* + L *centum* hundred] : in each hundred

²**percent** *n, pl* **percent** *or* **percents 1** : one part in a hundred : HUNDREDTH **2** : PERCENTAGE

per·cent·age \pər-'sen-tij\ *n* **1** : a part of a whole expressed in hundredths **2** : the result obtained by multiplying a number by a percent **3** : ADVANTAGE, PROFIT **4** : PROBABILITY; *also* : favorable odds

percentage point *n* : one hundredth of a whole ⟨rates rose one *percentage point* from 6.5 to 7.5 percent⟩

per·cen·tile \pər-'sen-,tī(-ə)l\ *n* : a value on a scale of one hundred indicating the standing of a score or grade in terms of the percentage of scores or grades falling within or below it

per·cept \'pər-,sept\ *n* : an impression of an object obtained by use of the senses

per·cep·ti·ble \pər-'sep-tə-bəl\ *adj* : capable of being perceived ⟨a barely ~ light⟩ — **per·cep·ti·bly** \-blē\ *adv*

per·cep·tion \pər-'sep-shən\ *n* **1** : an act or result of perceiving **2** : awareness of one's environment through physical sensation **3** : ability to understand : INSIGHT, COMPREHENSION ✦ *Synonyms* PENETRATION, DISCERNMENT, DISCRIMINATION

per·cep·tive \pər-'sep-tiv\ *adj* : capable of or exhibiting keen perception : OBSERVANT — **per·cep·tive·ly** *adv*

per·cep·tu·al \pər-'sep-chə-wəl\ *adj* : of, relating to, or involving sensory stimulus as opposed to abstract concept ⟨~ stimulation⟩ — **per·cep·tu·al·ly** *adv*

¹**perch** \'pərch\ *n* **1** : a roost for a bird **2** : a high station or vantage point

²**perch** *vb* : ROOST

³**perch** *n, pl* **perch** *or* **perch·es** : either of two small freshwater bony fishes used for food; *also* : any of various fishes resembling or related to these

per·chance \pər-'chans\ *adv* : PERHAPS

per·cip·i·ent \pər-'si-pē-ənt\ *adj* : capable of or characterized by perception — **per·cip·i·ence** \-əns\ *n*

per·co·late \'pər-kə-,lāt\ *vb* **-lat·ed; -lat·ing 1** : to trickle or filter through a permeable substance **2** : to filter hot water through to extract the essence ⟨~ coffee⟩ — **per·co·la·tor** \-,lā-tər\ *n*

per con·tra \(,)pər-'kän-trə\ *adv* [It, by the opposite side (of the ledger)] **1** : on the contrary **2** : by way of contrast

per·cus·sion \pər-'kə-shən\ *n* **1** : a sharp blow : IMPACT; *esp* : a blow upon a cap (**percussion cap**) designed to explode the charge in a firearm **2** : the beating or striking of a musical instrument; *also* : instruments sounded by striking, shaking, or scraping

per di·em \pər-'dē-əm, -'dī-\ *adv* [ML] : by the day — **per diem** *adj or n*

per·di·tion \pər-'di-shən\ *n* **1** : eternal damnation **2** : HELL

per·du·ra·ble \(,)pər-'dur-ə-bəl, -'dyur-\ *adj* : very durable — **per·du·ra·bil·i·ty** \-,dur-ə-'bi-lə-tē, -,dyur-\ *n*

père \'per\ *n* [F, fr. OF *paire, perre*, fr. L *pater*] : FATHER — used after a name to distinguish a father from a son

per·e·gri·na·tion \,per-ə-grə-'nā-shən\ *n* : a traveling about esp. on foot

per·e·grine falcon \'per-ə-grən, -grēn\ *n* : a swift nearly cosmopolitan falcon that often nests in cities and is often used in falconry

pe·remp·to·ry \pə-'remp-tə-rē\ *adj* **1** : barring a right of action or delay **2** : expressive of urgency or command : IMPERATIVE **3** : marked by arrogant self-assurance ✦ *Synonyms* IMPERIOUS, MASTERFUL, DOMINEERING, MAGISTERIAL — **pe·remp·to·ri·ly** \-tə-rə-lē\ *adv*

pe·ren·ni·al \pə-'re-nē-əl\ *adj* **1** : present at all seasons of the year ⟨~ streams⟩ **2** : continuing to live from year to year ⟨~ plants⟩ **3** : recurring regularly : PERMANENT ⟨~ problems⟩ ✦ *Synonyms* LASTING, PERPETUAL, ENDURING, EVERLASTING — **pe·ren·ni·al·ly** *adv*

²**perennial** *n* : a perennial plant

perf *abbr* **1** perfect **2** perforated

¹**per·fect** \'pər-fikt\ *adj* **1** : being without fault or defect **2** : EXACT, PRECISE **3** : COMPLETE **4** : relating to or being a verb tense that expresses an action or state completed at the time of speaking or at a time spoken of — **per·fect·ly** *adv* — **per·fect·ness** *n*

²**perfect** \pər-'fekt\ *vb* : to make perfect

³**perfect** \'pər-fikt\ *n* : the perfect tense; *also* : a verb form in it

per·fect·ible \pər-'fek-tə-bəl, 'pər-fik-\ *adj* : capable of improvement or perfection — **per·fect·ibil·i·ty** \pər-,fek-tə-'bi-lə-tē, ,pər-fik-\ *n*

per·fec·tion \pər-'fek-shən\ *n* **1** : the quality or state of being perfect **2** : the highest degree of excellence **3** : the act or process of perfecting

per·fec·tion·ist \-shə-nist\ *n* : a person who will not accept or be content with anything less than perfection

per·fec·to \pər-'fek-tō\ *n, pl* **-tos** : a cigar that is thick in the middle and tapers almost to a point at each end

per·fi·dy \'pər-fə-dē\ *n, pl* **-dies** [L *perfidia*, fr. *perfidus* faithless, fr. *per-* detrimental to + *fides* faith] : violation of faith or loyalty : TREACHERY — **per·fid·i·ous** \pər-'fi-dē-əs\ *adj* — **per·fid·i·ous·ly** *adv*

per·fo·rate \'pər-fə-,rāt\ *vb* **-rat·ed; -rat·ing** : to bore through : PIERCE; *esp* : to make a line of holes in to facilitate separation — **per·fo·ra·tion** \,pər-fə-'rā-shən\ *n*

per·force \pər-'fórs\ *adv* : of necessity ⟨we attended ~⟩

per·form \pər-'fórm\ *vb* **1** : FULFILL **2** : CARRY OUT, DO **3** : FUNCTION **4** : to do in a set manner **5** : to give a performance — **per·form·er** *n*

per·for·mance \pər-'fór-məns\ *n* **1** : the act or process of performing **2** : DEED, FEAT **3** : a public presentation

¹**per·fume** \pər-'fyüm, 'pər-,fyüm\ *n* **1** : a usu. pleasant odor : FRAGRANCE **2** : a preparation used for scenting

²**perfume** *vb* **per·fumed; per·fum·ing** : SCENT

per·fum·ery \,pər-'fyü-mə-rē\ *n, pl* **-er·ies 1** : the art or process of making perfume 2 : PERFUMES 3 : an establishment where perfumes are made

per·func·to·ry \pər-'fəŋk-tə-rē\ adj : done merely as a duty — **per·func·to·ri·ly** adv

per·go·la \'pər-gə-lə\ n [It] : a structure consisting of posts supporting an open roof in the form of a trellis

perh abbr perhaps

per·haps \pər-'haps\ adv : possibly but not certainly

per·i·gee \'per-ə-jē\ n [MF, fr. NL perigeum, fr. Gk perigeion, fr. peri around, near + gē earth] : the point at which an orbiting object is nearest the body (as the earth) being orbited

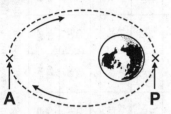

perigee: P perigee, A apogee

peri·he·lion \per-ə-'hēl-yən\ n, pl **-he·lia** \-'hēl-yə\ : the point in the path of a celestial body (as a planet) that is nearest to the sun

per·il \'per-əl\ n : DANGER; also : a source of danger : RISK — **per·il·ous** adj — **per·il·ous·ly** adv

pe·rim·e·ter \pə-'ri-mə-tər\ n 1 : the boundary of a closed plane figure; also : its length 2 : a line bounding or protecting an area

peri·na·tal \per-ə-'nā-t°l\ adj : occurring in, concerned with, or being in the period around the time of birth

¹**pe·ri·od** \'pir-ē-əd\ n [ultim. fr. Gk periodos circuit, period of time, rhetorical period, fr. peri around + hodos way] 1 : SENTENCE; also : the full pause closing the utterance of a sentence 2 : END, STOP 3 : a punctuation mark . used esp. to mark the end of a declarative sentence or an abbreviation 4 : an extent of time; esp : one regarded as a stage or division in a process or development 5 : a portion of time in which a recurring phenomenon completes one cycle and is ready to begin again 6 : a single cyclic occurrence of menstruation

²**period** adj : of or relating to a particular historical period ⟨~ furniture⟩

pe·ri·od·ic \pir-ē-'ä-dik\ adj 1 : occurring at regular intervals of time 2 : happening repeatedly 3 : of or relating to a sentence that has no trailing elements following full grammatical statement of the essential idea

¹**pe·ri·od·i·cal** \pir-ē-'ä-di-kəl\ adj 1 : PERIODIC 2 : published at regular intervals 3 : of or relating to a periodical — **pe·ri·od·i·cal·ly** \-k(ə-)lē\ adv

²**periodical** n : a periodical publication

periodic table n : an arrangement of chemical elements based on their atomic structure and on their properties ☞ the PERIODIC TABLE is on page 372

peri·odon·tal \per-ē-ō-'dän-t°l\ adj 1 : surrounding a tooth 2 : of or affecting periodontal tissues or regions

per·i·pa·tet·ic \per-ə-pə-'te-tik\ adj : performed or performing while moving about : ITINERANT ⟨~ salesmen⟩

pe·riph·er·al \pə-'ri-fər-əl\ n : a device connected to a computer to provide communication or auxiliary functions

peripheral nervous system n : the part of the nervous system that is outside the central nervous system and comprises the spinal nerves, the cranial nerves except the one supplying the retina, and the autonomic nervous system

pe·riph·ery \pə-'ri-fə-rē\ n, pl **-er·ies** 1 : the boundary of a rounded figure 2 : outward bounds : border area — **pe·riph·er·al** \-fə-rəl\ adj

pe·riph·ra·sis \pə-'ri-frə-səs\ n, pl **-ra·ses** \-ˌsēz\ : CIRCUMLOCUTION

peri·scope \'per-ə-ˌskōp\ n : a tubular optical instrument enabling an observer to see an otherwise blocked field of view

per·ish \'per-ish\ vb : to become destroyed or ruined : cease to exist

per·ish·able \'per-i-shə-bəl\ adj : easily spoiled ⟨~ foods⟩ — **perishable** n

peri·stal·sis \per-ə-'stȯl-səs, -'stal-\ n, pl **-stal·ses** : waves of contraction passing along the walls of a hollow muscular organ (as the intestine) and forcing its contents onward — **peri·stal·tic** \-'stȯl-tik, -'stal-\ adj

peri·style \'per-ə-ˌstīl\ n : a row of columns surrounding a building or court

peri·to·ne·um \per-ə-tə-'nē-əm\ n, pl **-ne·ums** or **-nea** : the smooth transparent serous membrane that lines the cavity of the abdomen — **peri·to·ne·al** \-'nē-əl\ adj

peri·to·ni·tis \per-ə-tə-'nī-təs\ n : inflammation of the peritoneum

peri·wig \'per-i-ˌwig\ n : WIG

¹**per·i·win·kle** \'per-i-ˌwiŋ-kəl\ n : a usu. blue-flowered creeping plant cultivated as a ground cover

²**periwinkle** n : any of various small edible seashore snails

per·ju·ry \'pər-jə-rē\ n : the voluntary violation of an oath to tell the truth : lying under oath — **per·jure** \'pər-jər\ vb — **per·jur·er** n

¹**perk** \'pərk\ vb 1 : to thrust (as the head) up impudently or jauntily 2 : to regain vigor or spirit 3 : to make trim or brisk : FRESHEN — **perky** adj

²**perk** vb : PERCOLATE

³**perk** n : PERQUISITE — usu. used in pl.

per·lite \'pər-ˌlīt\ n : volcanic glass that when expanded by heat forms a lightweight material used esp. in concrete and plaster and for potting plants

¹**perm** \'pərm\ n : PERMANENT

²**perm** vb : to give (hair) a permanent

³**perm** abbr permanent

per·ma·frost \'pər-mə-ˌfrȯst\ n : a permanently frozen layer below the surface in frigid regions of a planet

¹**per·ma·nent** \'pər-mə-nənt\ adj : LASTING, STABLE — **per·ma·nence** \-nəns\ n — **per·ma·nen·cy** \-nən-sē\ n — **per·ma·nent·ly** adv

²**permanent** n : a long-lasting hair wave or straightening

permanent press n : the process of treating fabrics with chemicals (as resin) and heat for setting the shape and for aiding wrinkle resistance

per·me·able \'pər-mē-ə-bəl\ adj : having small openings that permit liquids or gases to seep through — **per·me·a·bil·i·ty** \pər-mē-ə-'bi-lə-tē\ n

per·me·ate \'pər-mē-ˌāt\ vb **-at·ed; -at·ing** 1 : PERVADE 2 : to seep through the pores of : PENETRATE — **per·me·ation** \pər-mē-'ā-shən\ n

Perm·ian \'pər-mē-ən\ adj : of, relating to, or being the latest period of the Paleozoic era — **Permian** n

per·mis·si·ble \pər-'mi-sə-bəl\ adj : that may be permitted : ALLOWABLE

per·mis·sion \pər-'mi-shən\ n : formal consent : AUTHORIZATION

per·mis·sive \pər-'mi-siv\ adj : granting permission; esp : INDULGENT — **per·mis·sive·ly** adv — **per·mis·sive·ness** n

¹**per·mit** \pər-'mit\ vb **per·mit·ted; per·mit·ting** 1 : to consent to : ALLOW 2 : to make possible

²**per·mit** \'pər-ˌmit, pər-'mit\ n : a written permission : LICENSE ⟨a fishing ~⟩

per·mu·ta·tion \pər-myü-'tā-shən\ n 1 : a major or fundamental change 2 : the act or process of changing the order of an ordered set of objects ✦ **Synonyms** INNOVATION, MUTATION, VICISSITUDE

per·ni·cious \pər-'ni-shəs\ adj [ME, fr. AF, fr. L perniciosus, fr. pernicies destruction, fr. per- through + nec-, nex violent death] : very destructive or injurious ⟨a ~ influence⟩ — **per·ni·cious·ly** adv

per·o·ra·tion \'per-ə-ˌrā-shən, 'pər-\ n : the concluding part of a speech

¹**per·ox·ide** \pə-'räk-ˌsīd\ n : an oxide containing a large proportion of oxygen; esp : HYDROGEN PEROXIDE

²**peroxide** vb **-id·ed; -id·ing** : to bleach with hydrogen peroxide

perp abbr 1 perpendicular 2 perpetrator

per·pen·dic·u·lar \pər-pən-'di-kyə-lər\ adj 1 : standing at right angles to the plane of the horizon 2 : forming a right angle with each other or with a given line or plane — **perpendicular** n — **per·pen·dic·u·lar·i·ty** \-ˌdi-kyə-'la-rə-tē\ n — **per·pen·dic·u·lar·ly** adv

per·pe·trate \'pər-pə-ˌtrāt\ vb **-trat·ed; -trat·ing** : to carry out (as a crime) : COMMIT — **per·pe·tra·tion** \pər-pə-'trā-shən\ n — **per·pe·tra·tor** \'pər-pə-ˌtrā-tər\ n

PERIODIC TABLE

This is the common long form of the table, with atomic numbers given along with the symbols. Roman numerals and letters heading the vertical columns indicate the groups. (There are differences of opinion regarding the letter designations, but those given here are probably the most generally used. International standards favor numbering the groups 1-18 from left to right using Arabic numerals, but the designations shown below remain quite common.) Horizontal rows represent the periods, with two series removed from the two very long periods and represented below the main table.

IA[1]	IIA[2]	IIIB	IVB	VB	VIB	VIIB		VIII		IB	IIB	IIIA	IVA	VA	VIA	VIIA[3]	VIIIA[4]
1 H																1 H	2 He
3 Li	4 Be											5 B	6 C	7 N	8 O	9 F	10 Ne
11 Na	12 Mg											13 Al	14 Si	15 P	16 S	17 Cl	18 Ar
19 K	20 Ca	21 Sc	22 Ti	23 V	24 Cr	25 Mn	26 Fe	27 Co	28 Ni	29 Cu	30 Zn	31 Ga	32 Ge	33 As	34 Se	35 Br	36 Kr
37 Rb	38 Sr	39 Y	40 Zr	41 Nb	42 Mo	43 Tc	44 Ru	45 Rh	46 Pd	47 Ag	48 Cd	49 In	50 Sn	51 Sb	52 Te	53 I	54 Xe
55 Cs	56 Ba	57 *La	72 Hf	73 Ta	74 W	75 Re	76 Os	77 Ir	78 Pt	79 Au	80 Hg	81 Tl	82 Pb	83 Bi	84 Po	85 At	86 Rn
87 Fr	88 Ra	89 #Ac	104 Rf	105 Db	106 Sg	107 Bh	108 Hs	109 Mt	110 Ds	111 Rg	112 Cn	113 Nh	114 Fl	115 Mc	116 Lv	117 Ts	118 Og

*LANTHANIDE SERIES	58 Ce	59 Pr	60 Nd	61 Pm	62 Sm	63 Eu	64 Gd	65 Tb	66 Dy	67 Ho	68 Er	69 Tm	70 Yb	71 Lu
#ACTINIDE SERIES	90 Th	91 Pa	92 U	93 Np	94 Pu	95 Am	96 Cm	97 Bk	98 Cf	99 Es	100 Fm	101 Md	102 No	103 Lr

[1] Group IA (excluding hydrogen) comprises the alkali metals.
[2] Group IIA comprises the alkaline earth metals.
[3] Group VIIA (excluding hydrogen) comprises the halogens.
[4] Group VIIIA (also called group Zero) comprises the noble gases.

per·pet·u·al \pər-ˈpe-chə-wəl\ adj 1 : continuing forever : EVERLASTING 2 : occurring continually : CONSTANT ✦ **Synonyms** CEASELESS, UNCEASING, CONTINUAL, CONTINUOUS, INCESSANT, UNREMITTING — **per·pet·u·al·ly** adv

per·pet·u·ate \pər-ˈpe-chə-ˌwāt\ vb -at·ed; -at·ing : to make perpetual : cause to last indefinitely ⟨∼ a belief⟩ — **per·pet·u·a·tion** \-ˌpe-chə-ˈwā-shən\ n

per·pe·tu·i·ty \ˌpər-pə-ˈtü-ə-tē, -ˈtyü-\ n, pl -ties 1 : ETERNITY 1 2 : the quality or state of being perpetual

per·plex \pər-ˈpleks\ vb : to disturb mentally; esp : CONFUSE — **per·plex·i·ty** \-ˈplek-sə-tē\ n

per·plexed \-ˈplekst\ adj 1 : filled with uncertainty : PUZZLED ⟨a ∼ look⟩ 2 : full of difficulty : COMPLICATED — **per·plexed·ly** \-ˈplek-səd-lē\ adv

per·qui·site \ˈpər-kwə-zət\ n : a privilege or profit beyond regular pay

pers abbr person; personal

¹per se \(ˌ)pər-ˈsā\ adv [L] : by, of, or in itself : as such

²per se adj : being such inherently, clearly, or as a matter of law

per·se·cute \ˈpər-si-ˌkyüt\ vb -cut·ed; -cut·ing : to pursue in such a way as to injure or afflict : HARASS; esp : to cause to suffer because of belief — **per·se·cu·tion** \ˌpər-si-ˈkyü-shən\ n — **per·se·cu·tor** \ˈpər-si-ˌkyü-tər\ n

per·se·vere \ˌpər-sə-ˈvir\ vb -vered; -ver·ing : to persist (as in an undertaking) in spite of difficulties — **per·se·ver·ance** \-ˈvir-əns\ n

Per·sian \ˈpər-zhən\ n 1 : a native or inhabitant of ancient Persia 2 : a member of one of the peoples of modern Iran 3 : the language of the Persians

Persian cat n : any of a breed of stocky round-headed domestic cats that have a long silky coat

Persian lamb n : a pelt with very silky tightly curled fur that is obtained from newborn lambs which are older than those yielding broadtail

per·si·flage \ˈpər-si-ˌfläzh, ˈper-\ n [F, fr. persifler to banter, fr. per- thoroughly + siffler to whistle, hiss, boo, ultim. fr. L sibilare] : lightly jesting or mocking talk

per·sim·mon \pər-ˈsi-mən\ n : either of two trees related to the ebony; also : the edible usu. orange or red plumlike fruit of a persimmon

per·sist \pər-ˈsist, -ˈzist\ vb 1 : to go on resolutely or stubbornly in spite of difficulties 2 : to continue to exist — **per·sis·tence** \-ˈsis-təns, -ˈzis-\ n — **per·sis·ten·cy** \-tən-sē\ n — **per·sis·tent** \-tənt\ adj — **per·sis·tent·ly** adv

per·snick·e·ty \pər-ˈsni-kə-tē\ adj : fussy about small details

per·son \ˈpər-sən\ n [ME, fr. AF persone, fr. L persona actor's mask, character in a play, person, prob. fr. Etruscan phersu mask, fr. Gk prosōpa, pl. of prosōpon face, mask] 1 : a human being : INDIVIDUAL — used in combination esp. by those who prefer to avoid man in compounds applicable to both sexes ⟨chairperson⟩ 2 : one of the three modes of being in the Godhead as understood by Trinitarians 3 : the body of a human being 4 : the individual personality of a human being : SELF 5 : reference of a segment of discourse to the speaker, to one spoken to, or to one spoken of esp. as indicated by certain pronouns

per·so·na \pər-ˈsō-nə\ n, pl -nae \-nē\ or -nas : the personality that a person projects in public

per·son·able \ˈpər-sə-nə-bəl\ adj : pleasant in person : ATTRACTIVE

per·son·age \ˈpər-sə-nij\ n : a person of rank, note, or distinction

¹per·son·al \ˈpər-sə-nəl\ adj 1 : of, relating to, or affecting a person : PRIVATE ⟨∼ correspondence⟩ 2 : done in person ⟨a ∼ inquiry⟩ 3 : relating to the person or body ⟨∼ injuries⟩ 4 : relating to an individual esp. in an offensive way ⟨resented such ∼ remarks⟩ 5 : of or relating to temporary or movable property as distinguished from real estate 6 : denoting grammatical person 7 : intended for use by one person ⟨a ∼ stereo⟩

²personal n 1 : a short newspaper paragraph relating to a person or group or to personal matters 2 : a short personal or private communication in the classified ads section of a newspaper

personal computer n : a computer with a microprocessor designed for an individual user to run esp. commercial software

personal digital assistant n : PDA

per·son·al·ise Brit var of PERSONALIZE

per·son·al·i·ty \ˌpər-sə-ˈna-lə-tē\ n, pl -ties 1 : an offensively personal remark ⟨indulges in personalities⟩ 2 : the collection of emotional and behavioral traits that characterize a person 3 : distinction of personal and social traits 4 : a well-known person ⟨a TV ∼⟩ ✦ **Synonyms** INDIVIDUALITY, TEMPERAMENT, DISPOSITION, MAKEUP

per·son·al·ize \ˈpər-sə-nə-ˌlīz\ vb -ized; -iz·ing : to make personal or individual; esp : to mark as belonging to a particular person ⟨personalized stationery⟩

per·son·al·ly \-nə-lē\ adv 1 : in person 2 : as a person 3 : as far as oneself is concerned ⟨∼, I don't want to go⟩

per·son·al·ty \ˈpər-sə-nəl-tē\ n, pl -ties : personal property

per·so·na non gra·ta \pər-ˈsō-nə-ˌnän-ˈgra-tə, -ˈgrä-\ adj [L] : personally unacceptable or unwelcome

per·son·ate \ˈpər-sə-ˌnāt\ vb -at·ed; -at·ing : IMPERSONATE, REPRESENT

per·son·i·fy \pər-ˈsä-nə-ˌfī\ vb -fied; -fy·ing 1 : to think of or represent as a person 2 : to be the embodiment of : INCARNATE ⟨∼ the law⟩ — **per·son·i·fi·ca·tion** \-ˌsä-nə-fə-ˈkā-shən\ n

per·son·nel \ˌpər-sə-ˈnel\ n : a body of persons employed

per·spec·tive \pər-ˈspek-tiv\ n 1 : the science of painting and drawing so that objects represented have apparent depth and distance 2 : the aspect in which a subject or its parts are mentally viewed; esp : a view of things (as objects or events) in their true relationship or relative importance

per·spi·ca·cious \ˌpər-spə-ˈkā-shəs\ adj : having or showing keen understanding or discernment ⟨a ∼ observation⟩ — **per·spi·cac·i·ty** \-ˈka-sə-tē\ n

per·spic·u·ous \pər-ˈspi-kyə-wəs\ adj : plain to the understanding ⟨a ∼ argument⟩ — **per·spi·cu·i·ty** \ˌpər-spə-ˈkyü-ə-tē\ n

per·spire \pər-ˈspī(-ə)r\ vb per·spired; per·spir·ing : SWEAT — **per·spi·ra·tion** \ˌpər-spə-ˈrā-shən\ n

per·suade \pər-ˈswäd\ vb per·suad·ed; per·suad·ing : to win over to a belief or course of action by argument or entreaty — **per·sua·sive** \-ˈswā-siv, -ziv\ adj — **per·sua·sive·ly** adv — **per·sua·sive·ness** n

per·sua·sion \pər-ˈswā-zhən\ n 1 : the act or process of persuading 2 : a system of religious beliefs; also : a group holding such beliefs

pert \ˈpərt\ adj [ME, evident, attractive, saucy, short for apert evident, fr. AF, fr. L apertus open, fr. pp. of aperire to open] 1 : saucily free and forward : IMPUDENT 2 : stylishly trim : JAUNTY 3 : LIVELY

per·tain \pər-ˈtān\ vb 1 : to belong to as a part, quality, or function ⟨duties ∼ing to the office⟩ 2 : to have reference : RELATE ⟨books ∼ing to birds⟩

per·ti·na·cious \ˌpər-tə-ˈnā-shəs\ adj 1 : holding resolutely to an opinion or purpose 2 : obstinately persistent ⟨a ∼ bill collector⟩ ✦ **Synonyms** DOGGED, MULISH, HEADSTRONG, PERVERSE — **per·ti·nac·i·ty** \-ˈna-sə-tē\ n

per·ti·nent \ˈpər-tə-nənt\ adj : relating to the matter under consideration ✦ **Synonyms** RELEVANT, GERMANE, APPLICABLE, APROPOS — **per·ti·nence** \-əns\ n

per·turb \pər-ˈtərb\ vb : to disturb greatly esp. in mind : UPSET — **per·tur·ba·tion** \ˌpər-tər-ˈbā-shən\ n

per·tus·sis \pər-ˈtə-səs\ n : WHOOPING COUGH

pe·ruke \pə-ˈrük\ n : WIG

pe·ruse \pə-ˈrüz\ vb pe·rused; pe·rus·ing : READ; esp : to read over attentively or leisurely — **pe·rus·al** \-ˈrü-zəl\ n

per·vade \pər-ˈvād\ vb per·vad·ed; per·vad·ing : to spread through every part of : PERMEATE ⟨excitement pervaded the room⟩ — **per·va·sive** \-ˈvā-siv, -ziv\ adj

per·verse \pər-ˈvərs\ adj 1 : turned away from what is right or good : CORRUPT 2 : obstinate in opposing what is reasonable or accepted 3 : marked by perversion — **per·verse·ly** adv — **per·verse·ness** n — **per·ver·si·ty** \-ˈvər-sə-tē\ n

per·ver·sion \pər-ˈvər-zhən\ n 1 : the action of perverting : the condition of being perverted 2 : a perverted form of something; esp : aberrant sexual behavior

¹per·vert \pər-ˈvərt\ vb 1 : to lead astray : CORRUPT ⟨∼ the young⟩ 2 : to divert to a wrong purpose : MISAPPLY ⟨∼ evidence⟩ ✦ **Synonyms** DEPRAVE, DEBASE, DEBAUCH, DEMORALIZE — **per·ver·ter** n

²**per·vert** \'pər-ˌvərt\ *n* : one that is perverted; *esp* : one given to sexual perversion

pe·se·ta \pə-'sā-tə\ *n* : the former basic monetary unit of Spain

pe·se·wa \pə-'sā-wə\ *n* — see *cedi* at MONEY table

pes·ky \'pes-kē\ *adj* **pes·ki·er; -est** : causing annoyance : TROUBLESOME

pe·so \'pā-sō\ *n, pl* **pesos** — see MONEY table

pes·si·mism \'pe-sə-ˌmi-zəm\ *n* [F *pessimisme*, fr. L *pessimus* worst] : an inclination to take the least favorable view (as of events) or to expect the worst — **pes·si·mist** \-mist\ *n* — **pes·si·mis·tic** \ˌpe-sə-'mis-tik\ *adj*

pest \'pest\ *n* **1** : a destructive epidemic disease : PLAGUE **2** : a plant or animal detrimental to humans **3** : one that pesters : NUISANCE — **pesty** *adj*

pes·ter \'pes-tər\ *vb* : to harass with petty irritations : ANNOY

pes·ti·cide \'pes-tə-ˌsīd\ *n* : an agent used to destroy pests

pes·tif·er·ous \pes-'ti-fə-rəs\ *adj* **1** : PESTILENT ⟨~ vermin⟩ **2** : ANNOYING

pes·ti·lence \'pes-tə-ləns\ *n* : a destructive infectious swiftly spreading disease; *esp* : BUBONIC PLAGUE

pes·ti·lent \-lənt\ *adj* **1** : dangerous to life : DEADLY **2** : PERNICIOUS, HARMFUL **3** : TROUBLESOME **4** : INFECTIOUS, CONTAGIOUS ⟨a ~ disease⟩

pes·ti·len·tial \ˌpes-tə-'len-chəl\ *adj* **1** : causing or tending to cause pestilence : DEADLY **2** : morally harmful

pes·tle \'pes-əl, 'pes-t²l\ *n* : an implement for grinding substances in a mortar — **pestle** *vb*

¹**pet** \'pet\ *n* **1** : FAVORITE, DARLING **2** : a domesticated animal kept for pleasure rather than utility

²**pet** *adj* **1** : kept or treated as a pet ⟨~ dog⟩ **2** : expressing fondness ⟨~ name⟩ **3** : particularly liked or favored

³**pet** *vb* **pet·ted; pet·ting** **1** : to stroke gently or lovingly **2** : to make a pet of : PAMPER **3** : to engage in amorous kissing and caressing

⁴**pet** *n* : a fit of peevishness, sulkiness, or anger — **pet·tish** *adj*

Pet *abbr* Peter

pet·al \'pe-t²l\ *n* : one of the modified leaves of a flower's corolla

pe·tard \pə-'tärd, -'tär\ *n* : a case containing an explosive to break down a door or gate or breach a wall

pe·ter \'pē-tər\ *vb* : to diminish gradually and come to an end ⟨his energy ~ed out⟩

Pe·ter \'pē-tər\ *n* — see BIBLE table

pet·i·ole \'pe-tē-ˌōl\ *n* : a slender stem that supports a leaf

pe·tite \pə-'tēt\ *adj* [F] : having a small trim figure — usu. used of a woman — **petite** *n*

pe·tit four \ˌpe-tē-'fȯr\ *n, pl* **petits fours** *or* **petit fours** \-'fȯrz\ [F, lit., small oven] : a small cake cut from pound or sponge cake and frosted

¹**pe·ti·tion** \pə-'ti-shən\ *n* : an earnest request : ENTREATY; *esp* : a formal written request made to an authority

²**petition** *vb* : to make a request to or for — **pe·ti·tion·er** *n*

pe·trel \'pe-trəl\ *n* : any of numerous seabirds that fly far from land

pe·tri dish \'pē-trē-\ *n* **1** : a small shallow dish used esp. for growing bacteria **2** : something fostering development or innovation

pet·ri·fy \'pe-trə-ˌfī\ *vb* **-fied; -fy·ing** **1** : to convert (organic matter) into stone or stony material **2** : to make rigid or inactive (as from fear or awe) — **pet·ri·fac·tion** \ˌpe-trə-'fak-shən\ *n*

pet·ro·chem·i·cal \ˌpe-trō-'ke-mi-kəl\ *n* : a chemical isolated or derived from petroleum or natural gas — **pet·ro·chem·is·try** \-'ke-mə-strē\ *n*

pet·rol \'pe-trəl\ *n, chiefly Brit* : GASOLINE

pet·ro·la·tum \ˌpe-trə-'lā-təm\ *n* : PETROLEUM JELLY

pe·tro·leum \pə-'trō-lē-əm\ *n* [ML, fr. Gk *petra* rock + L *oleum* oil] : an oily flammable liquid obtained from wells drilled in the ground and refined into gasoline, fuel oils, and other products

petroleum jelly *n* : a tasteless, odorless, and oily or greasy substance from petroleum that is used esp. in ointments and dressings

¹**pet·ti·coat** \'pe-tē-ˌkōt\ *n* **1** : a skirt worn under a dress **2** : an outer skirt

²**petticoat** *adj* : of, relating to, or exercised by women : FEMALE

pet·ti·fog·ger \'pe-tē-ˌfȯ-gər, -ˌfä-\ *n* **1** : a lawyer whose

methods are petty, underhanded, or disreputable **2** : one given to quibbling over trifles — **pet·ti·fog·ging** \-giŋ\ *adj or n*

pet·ty \'pe-tē\ *adj* **pet·ti·er; -est** [ME *pety* small, minor, alter. of *petit*, fr. AF, small] **1** : having secondary rank : MINOR ⟨~ prince⟩ **2** : of little importance : TRIFLING ⟨~ faults⟩ **3** : marked by narrowness or meanness — **pet·ti·ly** \'pe-tə-lē\ *adv* — **pet·ti·ness** \-tē-nəs\ *n*

petty officer *n* : a subordinate officer in the navy or coast guard appointed from among the enlisted personnel

petty officer first class *n* : a petty officer ranking below a chief petty officer

petty officer second class *n* : a petty officer ranking below a petty officer first class

petty officer third class *n* : a petty officer ranking below a petty officer second class

pet·u·lant \'pe-chə-lənt\ *adj* : marked by capricious ill humor ♦ *Synonyms* IRRITABLE, PEEVISH, FRETFUL, FRACTIOUS, QUERULOUS — **pet·u·lance** \-ləns\ *n* — **pet·u·lant·ly** *adv*

pe·tu·nia \pi-'tün-yə, -'tyün-\ *n* : any of a genus of tropical So. American herbs related to the potato and having bright funnel-shaped flowers

pew \'pyü\ *n* [ME *pewe*, fr. MF *puie* balustrade, fr. L *podia*, pl. of *podium* parapet, podium, fr. Gk *podion* base, dim. of *pod-, pous* foot] : any of the benches with backs fixed in rows in a church

pe·wee \'pē-(ˌ)wē\ *n* : any of various small American flycatchers

pew·ter \'pyü-tər\ *n* **1** : an alloy of tin used esp. for household utensils **2** : a bluish gray color — **pewter** *adj* — **pew·ter·er** *n*

pey·o·te \pā-'ō-tē\ *also* **pey·otl** \-'ō-t²l\ *n* **1** : a hallucinogenic drug derived from the peyote cactus and containing mescaline **2** : a small cactus of the southwestern U.S. and Mexico

pf *abbr* **1** pfennig **2** preferred

PFC *or* **Pfc** *abbr* private first class

pfd *abbr* preferred

pfen·nig \'fe-nig\ *n, pl* **pfennig** *also* **pfennigs** *or* **pfen·ni·ge** \'fe-ni-gə\ : a former monetary unit equal to ¹/₁₀₀ deutsche mark

PFLAG *abbr* parents, families, and friends of lesbians and gays

pg *abbr* page

PG *abbr* postgraduate

PGA *abbr* Professional Golfers' Association

pH \(ˌ)pē-'āch\ *n* : a value used to express acidity and alkalinity; *also* : the condition represented by such a value

PH *abbr* **1** pinch hit **2** public health

pha·eton \'fā-ə-t²n\ *n* [F *phaéton*, fr. Gk *Phaethōn*, son of the sun god who persuaded his father to let him drive the chariot of the sun but who lost control of the horses with disastrous consequences] **1** : a light 4-wheeled horse-drawn vehicle **2** : an open automobile with two cross seats

phage \'fāj\ *n* : BACTERIOPHAGE

pha·lanx \'fā-ˌlaŋks\ *n, pl* **pha·lanx·es** *or* **pha·lan·ges** \fə-'lan-ˌjēz\ **1** : a group or body (as of troops) in compact formation **2** *pl* **phalanges** : one of the digital bones of the hand or foot of a vertebrate

phal·a·rope \'fa-lə-ˌrōp\ *n, pl* **-ropes** *also* **-rope** : any of a genus of small shorebirds related to sandpipers

phal·lic \'fa-lik\ *adj* **1** : of, relating to, or resembling a phallus **2** : relating to or being the stage of psychosexual development in psychoanalytic theory during which children become interested in their own sexual organs

phal·lus \'fa-ləs\ *n, pl* **phal·li** \'fa-ˌlī\ *or* **phal·lus·es** : PENIS; *also* : a symbolic representation of the penis

Phan·er·o·zo·ic \ˌfa-nə-rə-'zō-ik\ *adj* : of, relating to, or being an eon of geologic history comprising the Paleozoic, Mesozoic, and Cenozoic

phan·tasm \'fan-ˌta-zəm\ *n* : a product of the imagination : ILLUSION — **phan·tas·mal** \fan-'taz-məl\ *adj*

phan·tas·ma·go·ria \fan-ˌtaz-mə-'gȯr-ē-ə\ *n* : a constantly shifting complex succession of things seen or imagined; *also* : a scene that constantly changes or fluctuates

phantasy *var of* FANTASY

phan·tom \'fan-təm\ *n* **1** : something (as a specter) that is apparent to sense but has no substantial existence **2** : a mere show : SHADOW — **phantom** *adj*

pha·raoh \'fer-ō, 'fā-rō\ *n, often cap* : a ruler of ancient Egypt
phar·i·sa·ical \,fa-rə-'sā-ə-kəl\ *adj* : hypocritically self-righteous
phar·i·see \'fa-rə-,sē\ *n* **1** *cap* : a member of an ancient Jewish sect noted for strict observance of rites and ceremonies of the traditional law **2** : a self-righteous or hypocritical person — **phar·i·sa·ic** \,fa-rə-'sā-ik\ *adj*
pharm *abbr* pharmaceutical; pharmacist; pharmacy
phar·ma·ceu·ti·cal \,fär-mə-'sü-ti-kəl\ *adj* : of, relating to, or engaged in pharmacy or the manufacture and sale of medicinal drugs — **pharmaceutical** *n*
phar·ma·col·o·gy \,fär-mə-'kä-lə-jē\ *n* **1** : the science of drugs esp. as related to medicinal uses **2** : the reactions and properties of one or more drugs — **phar·ma·co·log·i·cal** \-kə-'lä-ji-kəl\ *also* **phar·ma·co·log·ic** \-kə-'lä-jik\ *adj* — **phar·ma·col·o·gist** \-'kä-lə-jist\ *n*
phar·ma·co·poe·ia *also* **phar·ma·co·pe·ia** \-kə-'pē-ə\ *n* **1** : a book describing drugs and medicinal preparations **2** : a stock of drugs
phar·ma·cy \'fär-mə-sē\ *n, pl* **-cies** **1** : the art, practice, or profession of preparing and dispensing medical drugs **2** : DRUGSTORE — **phar·ma·cist** \-sist\ *n*
phar·ynx \'fa-riŋks\ *n, pl* **pha·ryn·ges** \fə-'rin-jēz\ *also* **phar·ynx·es** : the muscular tubular passage extending from the back of the nasal cavity and mouth to the esophagus — **pha·ryn·ge·al** \fə-'rin-jəl, ,fa-rən-'jē-əl\ *adj*
phase \'fāz\ *n* **1** : a particular appearance in a recurring series of changes ⟨∼s of the moon⟩ **2** : a stage or interval in a process or cycle ⟨first ∼ of an experiment⟩ **3** : an aspect or part under consideration — **pha·sic** \'fā-zik\ *adj*
phase down *vb* : to reduce the size or amount of by phases
phase in *vb* : to introduce in stages
phase·out \'fāz-,aůt\ *n* : a gradual stopping of operations or production
phase out *vb* : to stop production or use of in stages ⟨*phase out* old equipment*⟩
PhD *abbr* [L *philosophiae doctor*] doctor of philosophy
pheas·ant \'fe-z°nt\ *n, pl* **pheasant** *or* **pheasants** : any of numerous long-tailed brilliantly colored game birds related to the domestic chicken

pheasant

phen·cy·cli·dine \,fen-'sī-klə-,dēn\ *n* : a drug used esp. as a veterinary anesthetic and sometimes illicitly as a hallucinogenic drug
phe·no·bar·bi·tal \,fē-nō-'bär-bə-,tȯl\ *n* : a crystalline drug used as a hypnotic and sedative
phe·nol \'fē-,nȯl\ *n* : a corrosive poisonous acidic compound present in coal and wood tars and used in solution as a disinfectant
phe·nom·e·non \fi-'nä-mə-,nän, -nən\ *n, pl* **-na** \-nə\ *or* **-nons** [LL *phaenomenon*, fr. Gk *phainomenon*, fr. neut. of *phainomenos*, prp. of *phainesthai* to appear] **1** *pl* **-na** : an observable fact or event **2** : an outward sign of the working of a law of nature **3** *pl* **-nons** : an extraordinary person or thing : PRODIGY — **phe·nom·e·nal** \-'nä-mə-n°l\ *adj* — **phe·nom·e·non·al·ly** *adv*
pher·o·mone \'fer-ə-,mōn\ *n* : a chemical substance that usu. produced by an animal and serves to stimulate a behavioral response in other individuals of the same species — **pher·o·mon·al** \,fer-ə-'mō-n°l\ *adj*
phi \'fī\ *n* : the 21st letter of the Greek alphabet — Φ or φ
phi·al \'fī(-ə)l\ *n* : VIAL
Phil *abbr* Philippians
phi·lan·der \fə-'lan-dər\ *vb* : to have casual or illicit sexual relations with many women — **phi·lan·der·er** *n*

phi·lan·thro·py \fə-'lan-thrə-pē\ *n, pl* **-pies** **1** : goodwill toward all people; *esp* : effort to promote human welfare **2** : a charitable act or gift; *also* : an organization that distributes or is supported by donated funds — **phil·an·throp·ic** \,fi-lən-'thrä-pik\ *adj* — **phil·an·throp·i·cal·ly** \-pi-k(ə-)lē\ *adv* — **phi·lan·thro·pist** \fə-'lan-thrə-pist\ *n*
phi·lat·e·ly \fə-'la-tə-lē\ *n* : the collection and study of postage and imprinted stamps — **phil·a·tel·ic** \,fi-lə-'te-lik\ *adj* — **phi·lat·e·list** \fə-'la-tə-list\ *n*
Phi·le·mon \fə-'lē-mən, fī-\ *n* — see BIBLE table
Phi·lip·pi·ans \fə-'li-pē-ənz\ *n* — see BIBLE table
phi·lip·pic \fə-'li-pik\ *n* : TIRADE
phi·lis·tine \'fi-lə-,stēn; fə-'lis-tən\ *n, often cap* [*Philistine*, inhabitant of ancient Philistia (Palestine)] : a person who is smugly insensitive or indifferent to intellectual or artistic values — **philistine** *adj, often cap*
Phil·lips \'fi-ləps\ *adj* : of, relating to, or being a screw having a head with a cross slot or its corresponding screwdriver
phi·lo·den·dron \,fi-lə-'den-drən\ *n, pl* **-drons** *also* **-dra** \-drə\ [NL, fr. Gk, neut. of *philodendros* loving trees, fr. *philos* dear, friendly + *dendron* tree] : any of various plants of the arum family grown for their showy foliage
phi·lol·o·gy \fə-'lä-lə-jē\ *n* **1** : the study of literature and relevant fields **2** : LINGUISTICS; *esp* : historical and comparative linguistics — **phil·o·log·i·cal** \,fi-lə-'lä-ji-kəl\ *adj* — **phi·lol·o·gist** \fə-'lä-lə-jist\ *n*
philos *abbr* philosopher; philosophy
phi·los·o·pher \fə-'lä-sə-fər\ *n* **1** : a reflective thinker : SCHOLAR **2** : a student of or specialist in philosophy **3** : a person whose philosophical perspective makes it possible to meet trouble calmly
phi·los·o·phise *Brit var of* PHILOSOPHIZE
phi·los·o·phize \fə-'lä-sə-,fīz\ *vb* **-phized; -phiz·ing** **1** : to reason like a philosopher : THEORIZE **2** : to expound a philosophy esp. superficially
phi·los·o·phy \fə-'lä-sə-fē\ *n, pl* **-phies** **1** : sciences and liberal arts exclusive of medicine, law, and theology ⟨doctor of ∼⟩ **2** : a critical study of fundamental beliefs and the grounds for them **3** : a system of philosophical concepts ⟨Aristotelian ∼⟩ **4** : a basic theory concerning a particular subject or sphere of activity **5** : the sum of the ideas and convictions of an individual or group ⟨her ∼ of life⟩ **6** : calmness of temper and judgment — **phil·o·soph·i·cal** \-fi-kəl\ *also* **phil·o·soph·ic** \,fi-lə-'sä-fik\ *adj* — **phil·o·soph·i·cal·ly** \-k(ə-)lē\ *adv*
phil·ter \'fil-tər\ *n* **1** : a magic potion **2** : a potion, drug, or charm held to arouse sexual passion
phil·tre *chiefly Brit var of* PHILTER
phish·ing \'fi-shiŋ\ *n* [alteration of *fishing*] : a scam by which an e-mail user is fooled into revealing personal or confidential information which can be used illegally — **phish·er** \'fi-shər\ *n*
phle·bi·tis \fli-'bī-təs\ *n* : inflammation of a vein
phle·bot·o·my \fli-'bä-tə-mē\ *n, pl* **-mies** : the opening of a vein esp. for removing or releasing blood
phlegm \'flem\ *n* [ME *fleume*, fr. AF, fr. LL *phlegma*, fr. Gk, flame, inflammation, phlegm, fr. *phlegein* to burn] : thick mucus secreted in abnormal quantity esp. in the nose and throat
phleg·mat·ic \fleg-'ma-tik\ *adj* : having or showing a slow and stolid temperament ⟨was ∼ during the crisis⟩ ♦ **Synonyms** IMPASSIVE, APATHETIC, STOIC
phlo·em \'flō-,em\ *n* : a vascular plant tissue external to the xylem that carries dissolved food material and functions in support and storage
phlox \'fläks\ *n, pl* **phlox** *or* **phlox·es** : any of a genus of American herbs that have tall stalks with showy spreading terminal clusters of flowers
pho·bia \'fō-bē-ə\ *n* : an irrational persistent fear or dread — **pho·bic** \'fō-bik\ *adj*
phoe·be \'fē-(,)bē\ *n* : a flycatcher of the eastern U.S. that has a slight crest and is grayish brown above and yellowish white below
phoe·nix \'fē-niks\ *n* : a legendary bird held to live for centuries and then to burn itself to death and rise fresh and young from its ashes
¹phone \'fōn\ *n* **1** : TELEPHONE **2** : EARPHONE
²phone *vb* **phoned; phon·ing** : TELEPHONE
phone card *n* : a prepaid card used in paying for telephone calls

pho·neme \'fō-ˌnēm\ *n* : one of the elementary units of speech that distinguish one utterance from another — **pho·ne·mic** \fō-'nē-mik\ *adj*

pho·net·ics \fə-'ne-tiks\ *n* : the study and systematic classification of the sounds made in spoken utterance — **pho·net·ic** \-tik\ *adj* — **pho·ne·ti·cian** \ˌfō-nə-'ti-shən\ *n*

pho·nic \'fä-nik\ *adj* **1** : of, relating to, or producing sound **2** : of or relating to the sounds of speech or to phonics — **pho·ni·cal·ly** \-ni-k(ə-)lē\ *adv*

pho·nics \'fä-niks\ *n* : a method of teaching people to read and pronounce words by learning the phonetic value of letters, letter groups, and esp. syllables

pho·no·graph \'fō-nə-ˌgraf\ *n* : an instrument for reproducing sounds by means of the vibration of a needle following a spiral groove on a revolving disc

pho·nol·o·gy \fə-'nä-lə-jē\ *n* : a study and description of the sound changes in a language — **pho·no·log·i·cal** \ˌfō-nə-'lä-ji-kəl\ *adj* — **pho·nol·o·gist** \fə-'nä-lə-jist\ *n*

pho·ny *also* **pho·ney** \'fō-nē\ *adj* **pho·ni·er; -est** : not genuine or real : FAKE ⟨a ∼ name⟩ — **phony** *n*

phos·phate \'fäs-ˌfāt\ *n* : a salt of a phosphoric acid — **phos·phat·ic** \fäs-'fa-tik\ *adj*

phos·phor \'fäs-fər\ *n* : a phosphorescent substance

phos·pho·res·cence \ˌfäs-fə-'re-sᵊns\ *n* **1** : luminescence caused by the absorption of radiations (as light or electrons) and continuing after these radiations stop **2** : an enduring luminescence without sensible heat — **phos·pho·res·cent** \-sᵊnt\ *adj* — **phos·pho·res·cent·ly** *adv*

phosphoric acid \fäs-'fȯr-ik-, -'fär-\ *n* : any of several oxygen-containing acids of phosphorus

phos·pho·rus *also* **phos·pho·rous** \'fäs-fə-rəs\ *n* [NL, fr. Gk *phōsphoros* light-bearing, fr. *phōs* light + *pherein* to carry, bring] : a nonmetallic chemical element that has characteristics similar to nitrogen and occurs widely esp. as phosphates — **phos·pho·ric** \fäs-'fȯr-ik, -'fär-\ *adj* — **phos·pho·rous** \'fäs-fə-rəs; fäs-'fȯr-əs\ *adj*

phot- *or* **photo-** *comb form* **1** : light ⟨*photo*graphy⟩ **2** : photograph : photographic ⟨*photo*engraving⟩ **3** : photoelectric ⟨*photo*cell⟩

pho·to \'fō-tō\ *n, pl* **photos** : PHOTOGRAPH — **photo** *vb or adj*

pho·to·cell \'fō-tə-ˌsel\ *n* : PHOTOELECTRIC CELL

pho·to·chem·i·cal \ˌfō-tō-'ke-mi-kəl\ *adj* : of, relating to, or resulting from the chemical action of radiant energy

pho·to·com·pose \-kəm-'pōz\ *vb* : to compose reading matter for reproduction by means of characters photographed on film — **pho·to·com·po·si·tion** \-ˌkäm-pə-'zi-shən\ *n*

pho·to·copy \'fō-tə-ˌkä-pē\ *n* : a photographic reproduction of graphic matter — **photocopy** *vb*

pho·to·elec·tric \ˌfō-tō-i-'lek-trik\ *adj* : relating to an electrical effect due to the interaction of light with matter — **pho·to·elec·tri·cal·ly** \-tri-k(ə-)lē\ *adv*

photoelectric cell *n* : a device whose electrical properties are modified by the action of light

pho·to·en·grave \ˌfō-tō-in-'grāv\ *vb* : to make a photoengraving of

pho·to·en·grav·ing *n* : a process by which an etched printing plate is made from a photograph or drawing; *also* : a print made from such a plate

photo finish *n* : a race finish so close that a photograph of the finish is used to determine the winner

pho·tog \fə-'täg\ *n* : PHOTOGRAPHER

pho·to·ge·nic \ˌfō-tə-'je-nik\ *adj* : eminently suitable esp. aesthetically for being photographed

pho·to·graph \'fō-tə-ˌgraf\ *n* : a picture taken by photography — **photograph** *vb* — **pho·tog·ra·pher** \fə-'tä-grə-fər\ *n*

pho·tog·ra·phy \fə-'tä-grə-fē\ *n* : the art or process of producing images on a sensitive surface (as film or a CCD chip) by the action of light — **pho·to·graph·ic** \ˌfō-tə-'gra-fik\ *adj* — **pho·to·graph·i·cal·ly** \-fi-k(ə-)lē\ *adv*

pho·to·gra·vure \ˌfō-tə-grə-'vyu̇r\ *n* : a process for making prints from an intaglio plate prepared by photographic methods

pho·to·li·thog·ra·phy \ˌfō-tō-li-'thä-grə-fē\ *n* : the process of photographically transferring a pattern to a surface for etching (as in making an integrated circuit)

pho·tom·e·ter \fō-'tä-mə-tər\ *n* : an instrument for measuring the intensity of light — **pho·to·met·ric** \ˌfō-tə-'me-trik\ *adj* — **pho·tom·e·try** \fō-'tä-mə-trē\ *n*

pho·to·mi·cro·graph \ˌfō-tə-'mī-krə-ˌgraf\ *n* : a photograph of a microscope image — **pho·to·mi·crog·ra·phy** \-mī-'krä-grə-fē\ *n*

pho·ton \'fō-ˌtän\ *n* : a quantum of electromagnetic radiation

photo op *n* : a situation or event that lends itself to the taking of pictures which favor the individuals photographed

pho·to·play \'fō-tō-ˌplā\ *n* : MOTION PICTURE

pho·to·sen·si·tive \ˌfō-tō-'sen-sə-tiv\ *adj* : sensitive or sensitized to the action of radiant energy

pho·to·shop \'fō-(ˌ)tō-ˌshäp\ *vb, often cap* : to alter a digital image with image-editing software

pho·to·sphere \'fō-tə-ˌsfir\ *n* : the luminous surface of a star — **pho·to·spher·ic** \ˌfō-tə-'sfir-ik, -'sfer-\ *adj*

pho·to·syn·the·sis \ˌfō-tō-'sin-thə-səs\ *n* : the process by which chlorophyll-containing plants make carbohydrates from water and from carbon dioxide in the air in the presence of light — **pho·to·syn·the·size** \-ˌsīz\ *vb* — **pho·to·syn·thet·ic** \-sin-'the-tik\ *adj*

phr *abbr* phrase

¹phrase \'frāz\ *n* **1** : a brief expression **2** : a group of two or more grammatically related words that form a sense unit expressing a thought

²phrase *vb* **phrased; phras·ing** : to express in words

phrase·ol·o·gy \ˌfrā-zē-'ä-lə-jē\ *n, pl* **-gies** : a manner of phrasing : STYLE

phras·ing *n* : style of expression

phre·net·ic *archaic var of* FRENETIC

phren·ic \'fre-nik\ *adj* : of or relating to the diaphragm ⟨∼ nerves⟩

phre·nol·o·gy \fri-'nä-lə-jē\ *n* : the study of the conformation of the skull based on the belief that it indicates mental faculties and character traits

phy·lac·tery \fə-'lak-tə-rē\ *n, pl* **-ter·ies** **1** : one of two small square leather boxes containing slips inscribed with scripture passages and traditionally worn on the left arm and forehead by Jewish men during morning weekday prayers **2** : AMULET

phy·lum \'fī-ləm\ *n, pl* **phy·la** \-lə\ [NL, fr. Gk *phylon* tribe, race] : a major category in biological classification esp. of animals that ranks above the class and below the kingdom; *also* : a group (as of people) apparently of common origin

phys *abbr* **1** physical **2** physics

¹phys·ic \'fi-zik\ *n* **1** : the profession of medicine **2** : MEDICINE; *esp* : PURGATIVE

²physic *vb* **phys·icked; phys·ick·ing** : PURGE 2

¹phys·i·cal \'fi-zi-kəl\ *adj* **1** : of or relating to nature or the laws of nature **2** : material as opposed to mental or spiritual **3** : of, relating to, or produced by the forces and operations of physics **4** : of or relating to the body — **phys·i·cal·ly** \-k(ə-)lē\ *adv*

²physical *n* : PHYSICAL EXAMINATION

physical education *n* : instruction in the development and care of the body ranging from simple calisthenics to training in hygiene, gymnastics, and the performance and management of athletic games

physical examination *n* : an examination of the bodily functions and condition of an individual

phys·i·cal·ize \'fi-zə-kə-ˌlīz\ *vb* **-ized; -iz·ing** : to give physical form or expression to

physical science *n* : any of the sciences (as physics and astronomy) that deal primarily with nonliving materials — **physical scientist** *n*

physical therapy *n* : the treatment of disease by physical and mechanical means (as massage, exercise, water, or heat) — **physical therapist** *n*

phy·si·cian \fə-'zi-shən\ *n* : a doctor of medicine

physician's assistant *n* : a person certified to provide basic medical care usu. under a licensed physician's supervision

phys·i·cist \'fi-zə-sist\ *n* : a scientist who specializes in physics

phys·ics \'fi-ziks\ *n* [L *physica*, pl., natural sciences, fr. Gk *physika*, fr. *physis* growth, nature, fr. *phyein* to bring forth] **1** : the science of matter and energy and their interactions **2** : the physical properties and composition of something

phys·i·og·no·my \ˌfi-zē-'äg-nə-mē\ *n, pl* **-mies** : facial appearance esp. as a reflection of inner character

phys·i·og·ra·phy \ˌfi-zē-'ä-grə-fē\ *n* : geography dealing with physical features of the earth — **phys·io·graph·ic** \ˌfi-zē-ō-ˈgra-fik\ *adj*

phys·i·ol·o·gy \ˌfi-zē-ˈä-lə-jē\ *n* **1** : a branch of biology dealing with the functions and functioning of living matter and organisms **2** : functional processes in an organism or any of its parts — **phys·i·o·log·i·cal** \-zē-ə-ˈlä-ji-kəl\ *or* **phys·i·o·log·ic** \-jik\ *adj* — **phys·i·o·log·i·cal·ly** \-ji-k(ə-)lē\ *adv* — **phys·i·ol·o·gist** \-zē-ˈä-lə-jist\ *n*

phys·io·ther·a·py \ˌfi-zē-ō-ˈther-ə-pē\ *n* : PHYSICAL THERAPY — **phys·io·ther·a·pist** \-pist\ *n*

phy·sique \fə-ˈzēk\ *n* : the build of a person's body : bodily constitution

phy·to·chem·i·cal \ˌfī-tō-ˈke-mi-kəl\ *n* : a chemical compound occurring naturally in plants

phy·to·plank·ton \ˈfī-tō-ˌplaŋk-tən\ *n* : plant life of the plankton

pi \ˈpī\ *n, pl* **pis** \ˈpīz\ **1** : the 16th letter of the Greek alphabet — Π or π **2** : the symbol π denoting the ratio of the circumference of a circle to its diameter; *also* : the ratio itself equal to approximately 3.1416

PI *abbr* private investigator

pi·a·nis·si·mo \ˌpē-ə-ˈni-sə-ˌmō\ *adv or adj* : very softly — used as a direction in music

pi·a·nist \pē-ˈa-nist, ˈpē-ə-\ *n* : a person who plays the piano

¹pi·a·no \pē-ˈä-nō\ *adv or adj* : SOFTLY — used as a direction in music

²piano \pē-ˈa-nō\ *n, pl* **pianos** [It, short for *pianoforte*, fr. *gravicembalo col piano e forte*, lit., harpsichord with soft and loud; fr. the fact that its tones could be varied in loudness] : a musical instrument having steel strings sounded by felt-covered hammers operated by a keyboard

pi·ano·forte \pē-ˌa-nō-ˈfȯr-ˌtā, -tē; pē-ˈa-nə-ˌfȯrt\ *n* : PIANO

pi·as·tre *also* **pi·as·ter** \pē-ˈas-tər\ *n* — see *pound* at MONEY table

pi·az·za \pē-ˈa-zə, *esp for 1* -ˈat-sə\ *n, pl* **piazzas** *or* **pi·az·ze** \-ˈat-(ˌ)sā, -ˈät-\ [It, fr. L *platea* broad street] **1** : an open square esp. in an Italian town **2** : a long hall with an arched roof **3** *dial* : VERANDA, PORCH

pi·broch \ˈpē-ˌbräk\ *n* : a set of variations for the bagpipe

pic \ˈpik\ *n, pl* **pics** *or* **pix** \ˈpiks\ **1** : PHOTOGRAPH **2** : MOTION PICTURE

pi·ca \ˈpī-kə\ *n* : a typewriter type with 10 characters to the inch

pi·ca·resque \ˌpi-kə-ˈresk, ˌpē-\ *adj* : of or relating to rogues ⟨∼ fiction⟩

pic·a·yune \ˌpi-kē-ˈyün\ *adj* : of little value : TRIVIAL; *also* : PETTY

pic·ca·lil·li \ˌpi-kə-ˈli-lē\ *n* : a relish of chopped vegetables and spices

pic·co·lo \ˈpi-kə-ˌlō\ *n, pl* **-los** [It, short for *piccolo flauto* small flute] : a small shrill flute pitched an octave higher than the ordinary flute

pice \ˈpīs\ *n, pl* **pice** : PAISA

¹pick \ˈpik\ *vb* **1** : to pierce or break up with a pointed instrument **2** : to remove bit by bit; *also* : to remove covering matter from **3** : to gather by plucking ⟨∼ apples⟩ **4** : CULL, SELECT **5** : ROB ⟨∼ a pocket⟩ **6** : PROVOKE ⟨∼ a quarrel⟩ **7** : to dig into or pull lightly at **8** : to pluck with fingers or a pick ⟨∼ a guitar⟩ **9** : to loosen or pull apart with a sharp point ⟨∼ wool⟩ **10** : to unlock with a wire **11** : to eat sparingly ⟨∼ at a salad⟩ — **pick·er** *n* — **pick on** : to single out for criticism, teasing, or bullying

²pick *n* **1** : the act or privilege of choosing **2** : the best or choicest one **3** : the part of a crop gathered at one time

³pick *n* **1** : a heavy wooden-handled tool pointed at one or both ends **2** : a pointed implement used for picking **3** : a small thin piece (as of plastic) used to pluck the strings of a stringed instrument

pick·a·back \ˈpi-gē-ˌbak, ˈpik-\ *var of* PIGGYBACK

pick·ax \ˈpik-ˌaks\ *n* : ³PICK 1

pick·er·el \ˈpi-kə-rəl\ *n, pl* **pickerel** *or* **pickerels** : either of two bony fishes related to the pikes; *also* : WALLEYE 2

pickerel

pick·er·el·weed \-ˌwēd\ *n* : a No. American shallow-water herb that bears spikes of purplish blue flowers

¹pick·et \ˈpi-kət\ *n* **1** : a pointed stake (as for a fence) **2** : a detached body of soldiers on outpost duty; *also* : SENTINEL **3** : a person posted by a labor union where workers are on strike; *also* : a person posted for a protest

²picket *vb* **1** : to guard with pickets **2** : TETHER ⟨∼ a horse⟩ **3** : to post pickets at ⟨∼ a factory⟩ **4** : to serve as a picket

pick·ings \ˈpi-kiŋz, -kənz\ *n pl* **1** : gleanable or eatable fragments : SCRAPS **2** : yield for effort expended : RETURN

pick·le \ˈpi-kəl\ *n* **1** : a brine or vinegar solution for preserving foods; *also* : a food (as a cucumber) preserved in a pickle **2** : a difficult situation : PLIGHT — **pickle** *vb*

pick·lock \ˈpik-ˌläk\ *n* **1** : BURGLAR, THIEF **2** : a tool for picking locks

pick·pock·et \ˈpik-ˌpä-kət\ *n* : one who steals from pockets

¹pick·up \ˈpik-ˌəp\ *n* **1** : a hitchhiker who is given a ride **2** : a temporary chance acquaintance **3** : a picking up **4** : revival of business activity **5** : ACCELERATION **6** : the conversion of mechanical movements into electrical impulses in the reproduction of sound; *also* : a device for making such conversion **7** : a light truck having an enclosed cab and an open body with low sides and a tailgate **8** : a pickup game **9** : a player acquired from another team

²pickup *adj* : using or comprising local or available personnel ⟨a ∼ game⟩

pick up *vb* **1** : to take hold of and lift **2** : IMPROVE **3** : to put in order

picky \ˈpi-kē\ *adj* **pick·i·er; -est** : FUSSY, FINICKY ⟨a ∼ eater⟩

¹pic·nic \ˈpik-ˌnik\ *n* : an outing with food usu. provided by members of the group and eaten in the open

²picnic *vb* **pic·nicked; pic·nick·ing** : to go on a picnic : eat in picnic fashion

pi·cot \ˈpē-ˌkō\ *n* : one of a series of small loops forming an edging on ribbon or lace

pic·to·ri·al \pik-ˈtȯr-ē-əl\ *adj* : of, relating to, or consisting of pictures

¹pic·ture \ˈpik-chər\ *n* **1** : a representation made by painting, drawing, or photography **2** : a vivid description in words **3** : IMAGE, COPY ⟨was the ∼ of his father⟩ **4** : a transitory visual image (as on a TV screen) **5** : MOTION PICTURE **6** : SITUATION ⟨a bleak economic ∼⟩

²picture *vb* **pic·tured; pic·tur·ing** **1** : to paint or draw a picture of **2** : to describe vividly in words **3** : to form a mental image of

pic·tur·esque \ˌpik-chə-ˈresk\ *adj* **1** : resembling a picture ⟨a ∼ landscape⟩ **2** : CHARMING, QUAINT ⟨a ∼ character⟩ **3** : GRAPHIC 3, VIVID ⟨a ∼ account⟩ — **pic·tur·esque·ness** *n*

picture tube *n* : a cathode-ray tube on which the picture appears in a television

pid·dle \ˈpi-dᵊl\ *vb* **pid·dled; pid·dling** : to act or work idly : DAWDLE

pid·dling \ˈpi-dᵊl-ən, -iŋ\ *adj* : TRIVIAL, PALTRY ⟨spent a ∼ sum⟩

pid·dly \ˈpid-lē\ *adj* : TRIVIAL, PIDDLING

pid·gin \ˈpi-jən\ *n* [fr. *pidgin English*, fr. Chinese Pidgin English *pidgin* business] : a simplified speech used for communication between people with different languages

pie \ˈpī\ *n* : a dish consisting of a pastry crust and a filling (as of fruit or meat)

¹pie·bald \ˈpī-ˌbȯld\ *adj* : of different colors; *esp* : blotched with white and black ⟨a ∼ horse⟩

²piebald *n* : a piebald animal

¹piece \ˈpēs\ *n* **1** : a part of a whole : FRAGMENT, PORTION **2** : one of a group, set, or mass ⟨∼s of flatware⟩; *also* : a single item or instance ⟨a ∼ of nonsense⟩ ⟨a ∼ of news⟩ **3** : a movable object used in a board game **4** : a length, weight, or size in which something is made or sold **5** : a product (as an essay) of creative work **6** : FIREARM **7** : COIN

²piece *vb* **pieced; piec·ing** **1** : to repair or complete by adding pieces : PATCH **2** : to join into a whole

pièce de ré·sis·tance \pē-ˌes-də-rā-ˌzē-ˈstäns\ *n, pl* **pièces de ré·sis·tance** *same*\ [F] **1** : the chief dish of a meal **2** : an outstanding item

piece·meal \'pēs-ˌmēl\ *adv or adj* : one piece at a time : GRADUALLY

piece·work \-ˌwərk\ *n* : work done and paid for by the piece — **piece·work·er** *n*

pie chart *n* : a circular chart that shows quantities or frequencies by parts of a circle shaped like pieces of pie

pied \'pīd\ *adj* : of two or more colors in blotches : VARIEGATED

pied-à-terre \pē-ˌā-də-'ter\ *n, pl* **pieds-à-terre** *same*\ [F, lit., foot to the ground] : a temporary or second lodging

pier \'pir\ *n* 1 : a support for a bridge span 2 : a structure built out into the water for use as a landing place or a promenade or to protect or form a harbor 3 : an upright supporting part (as a pillar) of a building or structure

pierce \'pirs\ *vb* **pierced; pierc·ing** 1 : to enter or thrust into sharply or painfully : STAB 2 : to make a hole in or through : PERFORATE ⟨*pierced* ears⟩ 3 : to force or make a way into or through : PENETRATE 4 : to see through : DISCERN — **pierc·er** *n*

piercing *n* : a piece of jewelry attached to pierced flesh

pies *pl of* PI *or of* PIE

pi·ety \'pī-ə-tē\ *n, pl* **pi·et·ies** 1 : fidelity to natural obligations (as to parents) 2 : dutifulness in religion : DEVOUTNESS 3 : a pious act

pif·fle \'pi-fəl\ *n* : trifling talk or action

pig \'pig\ *n* 1 : SWINE; *esp* : a young domesticated swine 2 : PORK 3 : a dirty, gluttonous, or repulsive person 4 : a crude casting of metal (as iron)

pi·geon \'pi-jən\ *n* : any of numerous stout-bodied short=legged birds with smooth thick plumage

¹pi·geon·hole \'pi-jən-ˌhōl\ *n* : a small open compartment (as in a desk) for keeping letters or documents

²pigeonhole *vb* 1 : to place in or as if in a pigeonhole : FILE 2 : to lay aside 3 : to assign to a usu. restrictive category

pi·geon–toed \-ˌtōd\ *adj* : having the toes and forefoot turned inward

pig·gish \'pi-gish\ *adj* 1 : GREEDY 2 : STUBBORN

pig·gy·back \'pi-gē-ˌbak\ *also* **pick·a·back** \'pi-gē-, 'pi-kə-\ *adv or adj* 1 : up on the back and shoulders 2 : on a railroad flatcar

pig·head·ed \'pig-'he-dəd\ *adj* : OBSTINATE, STUBBORN

pig latin *n, often cap L* : a jargon that is made by systematic alteration of English

pig·let \'pi-glət\ *n* : a small usu. young swine

pig·ment \'pig-mənt\ *n* 1 : coloring matter 2 : a powder mixed with a liquid to give color (as in paints) — **pig·ment·ed** \-mən-təd\ *adj*

pig·men·ta·tion \ˌpig-mən-'tā-shən\ *n* : coloration with or deposition of pigment; *esp* : an excessive deposition of bodily pigment

pigmy *var of* PYGMY

pig·nut \'pig-ˌnət\ *n* : the bitter nut of any of several hickory trees; *also* : any of these trees

pig·pen \-ˌpen\ *n* 1 : a pen for pigs 2 : a dirty place

pig·skin \-ˌskin\ *n* 1 : the skin of a swine or leather made of it 2 : FOOTBALL 2

pig·sty \-ˌstī\ *n* : PIGPEN

pig·tail \-ˌtāl\ *n* : a tight braid of hair

pi·ka \'pē-kə, 'pī-\ *n* : any of various small short-eared mammals related to the rabbits and occurring in rocky uplands of Asia and western No. America

¹pike \'pīk\ *n* : a sharp point or spike

²pike *n, pl* **pike** *or* **pikes** : a large slender long-snouted freshwater bony fish valued for food; *also* : any of various related fishes

³pike *n* : a long wooden shaft with a pointed steel head formerly used as a foot soldier's weapon

⁴pike *n* : TURNPIKE

pik·er \'pī-kər\ *n* 1 : one who does things in a small way or on a small scale 2 : TIGHTWAD, CHEAPSKATE

pike·staff \'pīk-ˌstaf\ *n* : the staff of a foot soldier's pike

pi·laf *also* **pi·laff** \pi-'läf, 'pē-ˌläf\ *or* **pi·lau** \pi-'lō, -'lo, 'pē-lō, -lō\ *n* : a dish made of seasoned rice often with meat

pi·las·ter \pi-'las-tər, 'pī-ˌlas-tər\ *n* : an architectural support that looks like a rectangular column and projects slightly from a wall

pil·chard \'pil-chərd\ *n* : a small European marine fish related to the herrings and often packed as a sardine

¹pile \'pī(-ə)l\ *n* : a long slender column (as of wood or steel) driven into the ground to support a vertical load

²pile *n* 1 : a quantity of things heaped together 2 : PYRE 3 : a great number or quantity : LOT ⟨∼s of money⟩

³pile *vb* **piled; pil·ing** 1 : to lay in a pile : STACK 2 : to heap up : ACCUMULATE 3 : to press forward in a mass : CROWD

⁴pile *n* : a velvety surface of fine short hairs or threads (as on cloth) — **piled** \'pī(-ə)ld\ *adj* — **pile·less** *adj*

piles \'pī(-ə)lz\ *n pl* : HEMORRHOIDS

pil·fer \'pil-fər\ *vb* : to steal in small quantities ⟨∼ pens from work⟩

pil·grim \'pil-grəm\ *n* [ME, fr. AF *pelerin, pilegrin,* fr. LL *pelegrinus,* alter. of L *peregrinus* foreigner, fr. *peregrinus* foreign, fr. *peregri* abroad, fr. *per* through + *ager* land] 1 : one who journeys in foreign lands : WAYFARER 2 : one who travels to a shrine or holy place as an act of devotion 3 *cap* : one of the English settlers founding Plymouth colony in 1620

pil·grim·age \-grə-mij\ *n* : a journey of a pilgrim esp. to a shrine or holy place

pil·ing \'pī-liŋ\ *n* : a structure of piles

pill \'pil\ *n* 1 : a small rounded mass usu. of medicine that is swallowed whole 2 : a disagreeable or tiresome person 3 *often cap* : an oral contraceptive — usu. used with *the*

pil·lage \'pi-lij\ *vb* **pil·laged; pil·lag·ing** : to take booty : LOOT, PLUNDER — **pillage** *n* — **pil·lag·er** *n*

pil·lar \'pi-lər\ *n* 1 : a strong upright support (as for a roof) 2 : a column or shaft standing alone esp. as a monument 3 : an integral or upstanding member or part 4 : a fundamental tenet ⟨the five ∼s of Islam⟩ — **pil·lared** \-lərd\ *adj*

pill·box \'pil-ˌbäks\ *n* 1 : a shallow round box for pills 2 : a low concrete emplacement esp. for machine guns

pil·lion \'pil-yən\ *n* 1 : a pad or cushion placed behind a saddle for an extra rider 2 *chiefly Brit* : a motorcycle or bicycle saddle for a passenger

¹pil·lo·ry \'pi-lə-rē\ *n, pl* **-ries** : a wooden frame for public punishment having holes in which the head and hands can be locked

²pillory *vb* **-ried; -ry·ing** 1 : to set in a pillory 2 : to expose to public scorn

¹pil·low \'pi-lō\ *n* : a case filled with springy material (as feathers) and used to support the head of a resting person

²pillow *vb* : to rest or place on or as if on a pillow; *also* : to serve as a pillow for

pil·low·case \-ˌkās\ *n* : a removable covering for a pillow

¹pi·lot \'pī-lət\ *n* 1 : HELMSMAN, STEERSMAN 2 : a person qualified and licensed to take ships into and out of a port 3 : GUIDE, LEADER 4 : one that flies an aircraft or spacecraft 5 : a television show filmed or taped as a sample of a proposed series — **pi·lot·less** *adj*

²pilot *vb* : CONDUCT, GUIDE; *esp* : to act as pilot of ⟨∼ a ship⟩

³pilot *adj* : serving as a guiding or activating device or as a testing or trial unit ⟨a ∼ light⟩ ⟨a ∼ factory⟩

pi·lot·house \'pī-lət-ˌhaús\ *n* : a shelter on the upper deck of a ship for the steering gear and the helmsman

pilot whale *n* : either of two mostly black medium-sized whales

pil·sner *also* **pil·sen·er** \'pilz-nər, 'pil-zə-\ *n* [G, lit., of Pilsen (Plzeň), a city in the Czech Republic] 1 : a light beer with a strong flavor of hops 2 : a tall slender footed glass for beer

pi·men·to \pə-'men-tō\ *n, pl* **pimentos** *or* **pimento** [Sp *pimienta* allspice, pepper, fr. LL *pigmenta,* pl. of *pigmentum* plant juice, fr. L, pigment] 1 : ALLSPICE 2 : PIMIENTO

pi·mien·to \pə-'men-tō\ *n, pl* **-tos** : any of various mild red sweet pepper fruits used esp. to stuff olives and to make paprika

pimp \'pimp\ *n* : a criminal who lives off the earnings of and usu. exerts control over one or more prostitutes — **pimp** *vb*

pim·per·nel \'pim-pər-ˌnel, -nəl\ *n* : any of a genus of herbs related to the primroses

pim·ple \'pim-pəl\ *n* : a small inflamed swelling on the skin often containing pus — **pim·ply** \-p(ə-)lē\ *adj*

¹pin \'pin\ *n* 1 : a piece of wood or metal used esp. for fastening things together or as a support by which one thing may be suspended from another; *esp* : a small pointed piece of wire with a head used for fastening clothes or attaching papers **2** : an ornament or emblem fastened to clothing with a pin **3** : one of the pieces constituting the target (as in bowling); *also* : the staff of the flag marking a hole on a golf course **4** : LEG

²**pin** *vb* **pinned; pin·ning 1** : to fasten, join, or secure with a pin **2** : to hold fast or immobile **3** : ATTACH, HANG ⟨*pinned* their hopes on a miracle⟩ **4** : to assign the blame for ⟨~ a crime on someone⟩ **5** : to define clearly : ESTABLISH ⟨~ down an idea⟩

PIN *abbr* personal identification number

pi·ña co·la·da \ˌpēn-yə-kō-ˈlä-də, ˌpē-nə-\ *n* [Sp, lit., strained pineapple] : a tall drink made of rum, cream of coconut, and pineapple juice mixed with ice

pin·afore \ˈpi-nə-ˌfōr\ *n* : a sleeveless dress or apron fastened at the back

pin·ball machine \ˈpin-ˌbȯl-\ *n* : an amusement device in which a ball is maneuvered along a slanted surface among a series of targets for points

pince–nez \paⁿs-ˈnā, *same or* -ˈnāz\ [F, fr. *pincer* to pinch + *nez* nose] : eyeglasses clipped to the nose by a spring

pin·cer \ˈpin-sər\ *n* **1** *pl* : a gripping instrument with two handles and two grasping jaws **2** : a claw (as of a lobster) resembling pincers

¹**pinch** \ˈpinch\ *vb* [ME, fr. AF *pincher, pincer, fr. VL *pinctiare, *punctiare, fr. L punctum puncture] **1** : to squeeze between the finger and thumb or between the jaws of an instrument **2** : to compress painfully **3** : CONTRACT, SHRIVEL **4** : to be miserly; *also* : to subject to strict economy **5** : to confine or limit narrowly **6** : STEAL **7** : ARREST

²**pinch** *n* **1** : a critical point : EMERGENCY **2** : painful effect **3** : an act of pinching **4** : a very small quantity **5** : ARREST

³**pinch** *adj* : SUBSTITUTE ⟨a ~ runner⟩

pinch–hit \ˌpinch-ˈhit\ *vb* **1** : to bat in the place of another player esp. when a hit is particularly needed **2** : to act or serve in place of another — **pinch hit** *n* — **pinch hitter** *n*

pin curl *n* : a curl made usu. by dampening a strand of hair, coiling it, and securing it by a hairpin or clip

pin·cush·ion \ˈpin-ˌku̇-shən\ *n* : a cushion for pins not in use

¹**pine** \ˈpīn\ *n* : any of a genus of evergreen cone-bearing trees; *also* : the light durable resinous wood of a pine

²**pine** *vb* **pined; pin·ing 1** : to lose vigor or health through distress **2** : to long for something intensely ⟨*pined* for home⟩

pi·ne·al \ˈpī-nē-əl, pī-ˈnē-əl\ *n* : PINEAL GLAND — **pineal** *adj*

pineal gland *n* : a small usu. conical appendage of the brain of all vertebrates with a cranium that functions primarily as an endocrine organ

pine·ap·ple \ˈpīn-ˌa-pəl\ *n* : a tropical plant bearing a large edible juicy fruit; *also* : its fruit

pin·feath·er \ˈpin-ˌfe-thər\ *n* : a new feather just coming through the skin

ping \ˈpiŋ\ *n* **1** : a sharp sound like that of a bullet striking **2** : engine knock

pin·hole \ˈpin-ˌhōl\ *n* : a small hole made by, for, or as if by a pin

¹**pin·ion** \ˈpin-yən\ *n* : the end section of a bird's wing; *also* : WING

²**pinion** *vb* : to restrain by binding the arms; *also* : SHACKLE

³**pinion** *n* : a gear with a small number of teeth designed to mesh with a larger wheel or rack

¹**pink** \ˈpiŋk\ *n* **1** : any of a genus of plants with narrow leaves often grown for their showy flowers **2** : the highest degree ⟨HEIGHT ⟨the ~ of condition⟩

²**pink** *n* : a light tint of red

³**pink** *adj* **1** : of the color pink **2** : holding socialistic views — **pink·ish** *adj*

⁴**pink** *vb* **1** : to perforate in an ornamental pattern **2** : PIERCE, STAB **3** : to cut a saw-toothed edge on

pink·eye \ˈpiŋk-ˌī\ *n* : an acute contagious eye inflammation

pin·kie *or* **pin·ky** \ˈpiŋ-kē\ *n, pl* **pinkies** : the smallest finger of the hand

pin·nace \ˈpi-nəs\ *n* **1** : a light sailing ship **2** : a ship's boat

pin·na·cle \ˈpi-ni-kəl\ *n* [ME *pinacle*, fr. AF, fr. LL *pinnaculum* small wing, gable, fr. L *pinna* wing, battlement]

1 : a turret ending in a small spire **2** : a lofty peak **3** : ACME

pin·nate \ˈpi-ˌnāt\ *adj* : resembling a feather esp. in having similar parts arranged on each side of an axis ⟨a ~ leaf⟩

pi·noch·le \ˈpē-nə-kəl\ *n* : a card game played with a 48-card deck

pi·ñon *or* **pin·yon** \ˈpin-ˌyȯn, -ˌyän\ *n, pl* **pi·ñons** *or* **pin·yons** *or* **pi·ño·nes** \pin-ˈyō-nēz\ [AmerSp *piñón*] : any of various small pines of western No. America with edible seeds; *also* : the edible seed of a piñon

pin·point \ˈpin-ˌpȯint\ *vb* : to locate, hit, or aim with great precision

pin·prick \-ˌprik\ *n* **1** : a small puncture made by or as if by a pin **2** : a petty irritation or annoyance

pins and needles *n pl* : a pricking tingling sensation in a limb growing numb or recovering from numbness — **on pins and needles** : in a nervous or jumpy state of anticipation

pin·stripe \ˈpin-ˌstrīp\ *n* : a narrow stripe on a fabric; *also* : a suit with such stripes — **pin–striped** \-ˌstrīpt\ *adj*

pint \ˈpīnt\ *n* — see WEIGHT table

pin·to \ˈpin-ˌtō\ *n, pl* **pintos** *also* **pintoes** : a spotted horse or pony

pinto bean *n* : a spotted seed produced by a kind of kidney bean and used for food

pin·up \ˈpin-ˌəp\ *adj* : suitable or designed for hanging on a wall; *also* : suited (as by beauty) to be the subject of a pinup photograph

pin·wheel \-ˌhwēl, -ˌwēl\ *n* **1** : a fireworks device in the form of a revolving wheel of colored fire **2** : a toy consisting of lightweight vanes that revolve at the end of a stick

pin·worm \-ˌwərm\ *n* : a nematode worm parasitic in the human intestine

pin·yin \ˈpin-ˈyin\ *n, often cap* : a system for writing Chinese ideograms by using Roman letters to represent the sounds

¹**pi·o·neer** \ˌpī-ə-ˈnir\ *n* **1** : one that originates or helps open up a new line of thought or activity **2** : an early settler in a territory

²**pioneer** *vb* **1** : to act as a pioneer **2** : to open or prepare for others to follow ⟨~ed a new treatment⟩; *also* : SETTLE

pi·ous \ˈpī-əs\ *adj* **1** : marked by reverence for deity : DEVOUT **2** : excessively or affectedly religious **3** : SACRED, DEVOTIONAL **4** : showing loyal reverence for a person or thing : DUTIFUL **5** : marked by sham or hypocrisy ⟨~ hypocrites⟩ — **pi·ous·ly** *adv*

¹**pip** \ˈpip\ *n* : one of the dots used on dice and dominoes to indicate numerical value

²**pip** *n* : a small fruit seed (as of an apple)

¹**pipe** \ˈpīp\ *n* **1** : a tubular musical instrument played by forcing air through it **2** : BAGPIPE **3** : a tube designed to conduct something (as water, steam, or oil) **4** : a device for smoking having a tube with a bowl at one end and a mouthpiece at the other **5** : a means of transmission (as of computer data)

²**pipe** *vb* **piped; pip·ing 1** : to play on a pipe **2** : to speak in a high or shrill voice **3** : to convey by or as if by pipes — **pip·er** *n*

pipe down *vb* : to stop talking or making noise

pipe dream *n* : an illusory or fantastic hope

pipe·line \ˈpīp-ˌlīn\ *n* **1** : a line of pipe with pumps, valves, and control devices for conveying fluids **2** : a channel for information **3** : PIPE 5

pi·pette *or* **pi·pet** \pī-ˈpet\ *n* : a device for measuring and transferring small volumes of liquid

pipe up *vb* : to speak loudly and distinctly; *also* : to express an opinion freely

pip·ing \ˈpī-piŋ\ *n* **1** : the music of pipes **2** : a narrow fold of material used to decorate edges or seams

piping hot *adj* : very hot

pip·pin \ˈpi-pən\ *n* : a crisp tart usu. yellowish apple

pip–squeak \ˈpip-ˌskwēk\ *n* : one that is small or insignificant

pi·quant \ˈpē-kənt\ *adj* **1** : pleasantly savory : PUNGENT ⟨a ~ sauce⟩ **2** : engagingly provocative; *also* : having a lively charm — **pi·quan·cy** \-kən-sē\ *n*

¹**pique** \ˈpēk\ *n* [F] : a passing feeling of wounded vanity : RESENTMENT

²**pique** *vb* **piqued; piqu·ing 1** : IRRITATE 1 **2** : to arouse by a provocation or challenge : GOAD

pi·qué *or* **pi·que** \pi-'kā\ *n* : a durable ribbed clothing fabric

pi·quet \pi-'kā\ *n* : a 2-handed card game played with 32 cards

pi·ra·cy \'pī-rə-sē\ *n, pl* **-cies** 1 : robbery on the high seas; *also* : an act resembling such robbery 2 : the unauthorized use of another's production or invention

pi·ra·nha \pə-'rä-nə, -'rän-yə\ *n* [Pg, fr. Tupi (So. American Indian language) *pirája*, fr. *pirá* fish + *ája* tooth] : any of various usu. small So. American fishes with sharp teeth that include some known to attack humans and large animals

pi·rate \'pī-rət\ *n* [ME, fr. MF or L; MF, fr. L *pirata*, fr. Gk *peiratēs*, fr. *peiran* to attempt, test] : one who commits piracy — **pirate** *vb* — **pi·rat·i·cal** \pə-'ra-ti-kəl, pī-\ *adj*

pir·ou·ette \pir-ə-'wet\ *n* [F] : a rapid whirling about of the body; *esp* : a full turn on the toe or ball of one foot in ballet — **pirouette** *vb*

pis *pl of* PI

pis·ca·to·ri·al \pis-kə-'tòr-ē-əl\ *adj* : of or relating to fishing

Pi·sces \'pī-sēz\ *n* [ME, fr. L, lit., fishes] 1 : a zodiacal constellation between Aquarius and Aries usu. pictured as a fish 2 : the 12th sign of the zodiac in astrology; *also* : one born under this sign

pis·mire \'pis-,mī(-ə)r\ *n* : ANT

pi·so \'pē-(,)sō\ *n* : the peso of the Philippines

pis·ta·chio \pə-'sta-shē-,ō, -'stä-\ *n, pl* **-chios** : the greenish edible seed of a small Asian tree related to the sumacs; *also* : the tree

pis·til \'pis-t°l\ *n* : the female reproductive organ in a flower — **pis·til·late** \'pis-tə-,lāt\ *adj*

pis·tol \'pis-t°l\ *n* : a handgun whose chamber is integral with the barrel

pis·tol-whip \-,hwip\ *vb* : to beat with a pistol

pis·ton \'pis-tən\ *n* : a sliding piece that receives and transmits motion and that usu. consists of a short cylinder inside a large cylinder

¹pit \'pit\ *n* 1 : a hole, shaft, or cavity in the ground 2 : an often sunken area designed for a particular use; *also* : an enclosed place (as for cockfights) 3 : HELL; *also*, *pl* : WORST ⟨it's the ∼*s*⟩ 4 : a natural hollow or indentation in a surface 5 : a small indented mark or scar (as from disease or corrosion) 6 : an area beside a racecourse where cars are fueled and repaired during a race

²pit *vb* **pit·ted; pit·ting** 1 : to form pits in or become marred with pits 2 : to match for fighting

³pit *n* : the stony seed of some fruits (as the cherry, peach, and date)

⁴pit *vb* **pit·ted; pit·ting** : to remove the pit from

pi·ta \'pē-tə\ *n* [ModGk] : a thin flat bread

pit-a-pat \,pi-ti-'pat\ *n* : PITTER-PATTER — **pit-a-pat** *adv or adj*

pit bull *n* : a powerful compact short-haired dog developed for fighting

¹pitch \'pich\ *n* 1 : a dark sticky substance left over esp. from distilling tar or petroleum 2 : resin from various conifers — **pitchy** *adj*

²pitch *vb* 1 : to erect and fix firmly in place ⟨∼ a tent⟩ 2 : THROW, FLING 3 : to deliver a baseball to a batter 4 : to toss (as coins) toward a mark 5 : to set at a particular level ⟨∼ the voice low⟩ 6 : to fall headlong 7 : to have the front end (as of a ship) alternately plunge and rise 8 : to incline downward : SLOPE

³pitch *n* 1 : the action or a manner of pitching 2 : degree of slope ⟨∼ of a roof⟩ 3 : the relative level of some quality or state ⟨a high ∼ of excitement⟩ 4 : highness or lowness of sound; *also* : a standard frequency for tuning instruments 5 : a presentation delivered to sell or promote something 6 : the delivery of a baseball to a batter; *also* : the baseball delivered

pitch·blende \'pich-,blend\ *n* : a dark mineral that is the chief source of uranium

¹pitch·er \'pi-chər\ *n* : a container for liquids that usu. has a lip and a handle

²pitcher *n* : one that pitches esp. in a baseball game

pitcher plant *n* : any of various plants with leaves modified to resemble pitchers in which insects are trapped and digested

pitch·fork \'pich-,fòrk\ *n* : a long-handled fork used esp. in pitching hay

pitch in *vb* 1 : to begin to work 2 : to contribute to a common effort

pitch·man \'pich-mən\ *n* : SALESMAN; *esp* : one who sells merchandise on the streets or from a concession

pitch-per·fect \'pich-'pər-fikt\ *adj* : having just the right tone or style ⟨a ∼ translation⟩

pit·e·ous \'pi-tē-əs\ *adj* : arousing pity : PITIFUL — **pit·e·ous·ly** *adv*

pit·fall \'pit-,fòl\ *n* 1 : TRAP, SNARE; *esp* : a covered pit used for capturing animals 2 : a hidden danger or difficulty

pith \'pith\ *n* 1 : loose spongy tissue esp. in the center of the stem of vascular plants 2 : the essential part : CORE

pithy \'pi-thē\ *adj* **pith·i·er; -est** 1 : consisting of or filled with pith 2 : having substance and point : CONCISE

piti·able \'pi-tē-ə-bəl\ *adj* : PITIFUL

piti·ful \'pi-ti-fəl\ *adj* 1 : arousing or deserving pity ⟨a ∼ sight⟩ 2 : lamentably inadequate : MEAGER — **piti·ful·ly** *adv*

piti·less \'pi-ti-ləs\ *adj* : devoid of pity : HARSH, CRUEL — **piti·less·ly** *adv*

pi·ton \'pē-,tän\ *n* [F] : a spike, wedge, or peg that can be driven into a rock or ice surface as a support

pit·tance \'pi-t°ns\ *n* : a small portion, amount, or allowance

pit·ted \'pi-təd\ *adj* : marked with pits

pit·ter-pat·ter \'pi-tər-,pa-tər, 'pi-tē-\ *n* : a rapid succession of light taps or sounds ⟨the ∼ of rain⟩ — **pitter-patter** \'pi-tər-'pa-tər, ,pi-tē-\ *adv or adj* — **pitter-patter** *same as adv*\ *vb*

pi·tu·i·tary \pə-'tü-ə-,ter-ē, -'tyü-\ *n, pl* **-itar·ies** : PITUITARY GLAND — **pituitary** *adj*

pituitary gland *n* : a small oval endocrine gland located at the base of the brain that produces various hormones that affect most basic bodily functions (as growth and reproduction)

pit viper *n* : any of various mostly New World venomous snakes with a sensory pit on each side of the head and hollow perforated fangs

¹pity \'pi-tē\ *n, pl* **pit·ies** [ME *pite*, fr. AF *pité*, fr. L *pietas* piety, pity, fr. *pius* pious] 1 : sympathetic sorrow : COMPASSION 2 : something to be regretted

²pity *vb* **pit·ied; pity·ing** : to feel pity for

¹piv·ot \'pi-vət\ *n* : a fixed pin on which something turns — **pivot** *adj*

²pivot *vb* : to turn on or as if on a pivot

piv·ot·al \'pi-və-t°l\ *adj* 1 : of or relating to a pivot 2 : vitally important : CRITICAL ⟨a ∼ decision⟩

pix *pl of* PIC

pix·el \'pik-səl, -,sel\ *n* 1 : any of the small elements that together make up an image (as on a television screen) 2 : any of the detecting elements of a charge-coupled device used as an optical sensor

pix·ie *also* **pixy** \'pik-sē\ *n, pl* **pix·ies** : FAIRY; *esp* : a mischievous sprite

piz·za \'pēt-sə\ *n* [It] : an open pie made of rolled bread dough spread with a spiced mixture (as of tomatoes, cheese, and ground meat) and baked

piz·zazz *or* **pi·zazz** \pə-'zaz\ *n* 1 : GLAMOUR 2 : VITALITY

piz·ze·ria \,pēt-sə-'rē-ə\ *n* : an establishment where pizzas are made and sold

piz·zi·ca·to \,pit-si-'kä-tō\ *adv or adj* [It] : by means of plucking instead of bowing — used as a direction in music

pj's \'pē-,jāz\ *n pl* : PAJAMAS

pk *abbr* 1 park 2 peak 3 peck 4 pike

pkg *abbr* package

pkt *abbr* 1 packet 2 pocket

pkwy *abbr* parkway

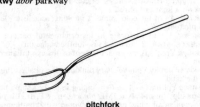

pitchfork

pl *abbr* **1** place **2** plate **3** plural

¹plac·ard \'pla-kərd, -ˌkärd\ *n* : a notice posted in a public place : POSTER

²plac·ard \-ˌkärd, -kərd\ *vb* **1** : to cover with or as if with placards **2** : to announce by or as if by posting

pla·cate \'plā-ˌkāt, 'pla-\ *vb* **pla·cat·ed; pla·cat·ing** : to soothe esp. by concessions : APPEASE — **pla·ca·ble** \'pla-kə-bəl, 'plā-\ *adj*

¹place \'plās\ *n* [ME, fr. AF, open space, fr. L *platea* broad street, fr. Gk *plateia* (*hodos*), fr. fem. of *platys* broad, flat] **1** : SPACE, ROOM **2** : an indefinite region : AREA **3** : a building or locality used for a special purpose **4** : a center of population **5** : a particular part of a surface : SPOT **6** : relative position in a scale or sequence; *also* : position at the end of a competition ⟨last ∼⟩ **7** : ACCOMMODATION; *esp* : SEAT **8** : the position of a figure within a numeral ⟨12 is a two ∼ number⟩ **9** : JOB; *esp* : public office **10** : a public square **11** : 2d place at the finish (as of a horse race) — **in place of** : INSTEAD OF — **out of place** : not in the proper location : INAPPROPRIATE

²place *vb* **placed; plac·ing** **1** : to put in a particular place : SET **2** : to distribute in an orderly manner : ARRANGE **3** : IDENTIFY **4** : to give an order for ⟨∼ a bet⟩ **5** : to earn a given spot in a competition; *esp* : to come in 2d

pla·ce·bo \plə-'sē-bō\ *n, pl* **-bos** [L, I shall please] : an inert medication used for its psychological effect or for purposes of comparison in an experiment

place·hold·er \'plās-ˌhōl-dər\ *n* : a symbol in a mathematical or logical expression that may be replaced by the name of any element of a set

place·kick \-ˌkik\ *n* : the kicking of a ball placed or held on the ground — **placekick** *vb* — **place·kick·er** *n*

place·ment \'plās-mənt\ *n* : an act or instance of placing

place–name \-ˌnām\ *n* : the name of a geographical locality

pla·cen·ta \plə-'sen-tə\ *n, pl* **-tas** *or* **-tae** \-(ˌ)tē\ [NL, fr. L, flat cake] : the organ in most mammals by which the fetus is joined to the maternal uterus and is nourished — **pla·cen·tal** \-'sen-tᵊl\ *adj or n*

plac·er \'pla-sər\ *n* : a deposit of sand or gravel containing particles of valuable mineral (as gold)

plac·id \'pla-səd\ *adj* : UNDISTURBED, PEACEFUL ♦ **Synonyms** TRANQUIL, SERENE, CALM — **pla·cid·i·ty** \pla-'si-də-tē\ *n* — **plac·id·ly** *adv*

plack·et \'pla-kət\ *n* : a slit in a garment

pla·gia·rise *Brit var of* PLAGIARIZE

pla·gia·rize \'plā-jə-ˌrīz\ *vb* **-rized; -riz·ing** : to present the ideas or words of another as one's own — **pla·gia·rism** \-ˌri-zəm\ *n* — **pla·gia·rist** \-rist\ *n*

¹plague \'plāg\ *n* **1** : a disastrous evil or influx; *also* : NUISANCE **2** : PESTILENCE; *esp* : a destructive contagious bacterial disease (as bubonic plague)

²plague *vb* **plagued; plagu·ing** **1** : to afflict with or as if with disease or disaster **2** : TEASE, TORMENT ⟨*plagued* by guilt⟩

plaid \'plad\ *n* [ScGael *plaide*] **1** : a rectangular length of tartan worn esp. over the left shoulder as part of the Scottish national costume **2** : a twilled woolen fabric with a tartan pattern **3** : a pattern of unevenly spaced repeated stripes crossing at right angles — **plaid** *adj*

¹plain \'plān\ *n* : an extensive area of level or rolling treeless country

²plain *adj* **1** : lacking ornament ⟨a ∼ dress⟩ **2** : free of extraneous matter **3** : OPEN, UNOBSTRUCTED ⟨∼ view⟩ **4** : EVIDENT, OBVIOUS **5** : easily understood : CLEAR **6** : CANDID, BLUNT **7** : SIMPLE, UNCOMPLICATED ⟨∼ cooking⟩ **8** : lacking beauty or ugliness — **plain·ly** *adv* — **plain·ness** *n*

plain-clothes·man \'plān-'klōthz-mən, -'klōz-, -ˌman\ *n* : a police officer who wears civilian clothes instead of a uniform while on duty : DETECTIVE

plain-spo·ken \-'spō-kən\ *adj* : FRANK

plaint \'plānt\ *n* **1** : LAMENTATION, WAIL **2** : PROTEST, COMPLAINT

plain·tiff \'plān-təf\ *n* : the complaining party in a lawsuit

plain·tive \'plān-tiv\ *adj* : expressive of suffering or woe : MELANCHOLY ⟨a ∼ sigh⟩ — **plain·tive·ly** *adv*

plait \'plāt, 'plat\ *n* **1** : PLEAT **2** : a braid esp. of hair or straw — **plait** *vb*

¹plan \'plan\ *n* **1** : a drawing or diagram showing the parts or details of something **2** : a method for accomplishing an objective; *also* : GOAL, AIM

²plan *vb* **planned; plan·ning** **1** : to form a plan of ⟨∼ a new city⟩ **2** : INTEND ⟨*planned* to go⟩ — **plan·ner** *n*

¹plane \'plān\ *vb* **planed; plan·ing** : to smooth or level off with or as if with a plane — **plan·er** *n*

²plane *n* : PLANE TREE

³plane *n* : a tool for smoothing or shaping a wood surface

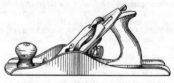

³plane

⁴plane *n* **1** : a level or flat surface **2** : a level of existence, consciousness, or development **3** : AIRPLANE

⁵plane *adj* **1** : FLAT, LEVEL **2** : dealing with flat surfaces or figures ⟨∼ geometry⟩

plane-load \'plān-ˌlōd\ *n* : a load that fills an airplane

plan·et \'pla-nət\ *n* [ME *planete*, fr. AF, fr. LL *planeta*, fr. Gk *planēt-, planēs*, lit., wanderer, fr. *planasthai* to wander] : any of the large bodies in the solar system that revolve around the sun — **plan·e·tary** \-nə-ˌter-ē\ *adj*

plan·e·tar·i·um \ˌpla-nə-'ter-ē-əm\ *n, pl* **-i·ums** *or* **-ia** \-ē-ə\ : a building or room housing a device to project images of celestial bodies

plan·e·tes·i·mal \ˌpla-nə-'tes-ə-məl\ *n* : any of numerous small solid celestial bodies which may have existed during the formation of the solar system

plan·e·toid \'pla-nə-ˌtoid\ *n* : a body resembling a planet; *esp* : ASTEROID

plane tree *n* : any of a genus of trees (as a sycamore) with large lobed leaves and globe-shaped fruit

PLANETS

NAME	SYMBOL	MEAN DISTANCE FROM THE SUN		PERIOD OF REVOLUTION IN DAYS OR YEARS	EQUATORIAL DIAMETER	
		million miles	million kilometers		miles	kilometers
Mercury	☿	35.99	57.91	87.97 d.	3,033	4,879
Venus	♀	67.25	108.21	224.70 d.	7,522	12,104
Earth	♁	92.98	149.60	365.26 d.	7,928	12,756
Mars	♂	141.67	227.94	686.99 d.	4,222	6,794
Jupiter	♃	483.78	778.41	11.86 y.	88,865	142,984
Saturn	♄	886.72	1,426.73	29.47 y.	74,914	120,536
Uranus	♅	1,784.32	2,870.97	84.02 y.	31,770	51,118
Neptune	♆	2,795.68	4,498.25	164.79 y.	30,782	49,528

plan·gent \'plan-jənt\ *adj* 1 : having a loud reverberating sound ⟨a ~ roar⟩ 2 : having an expressive esp. plaintive quality ⟨~ lyrics⟩ — **plan·gen·cy** \-jən-sē\ *n*

¹**plank** \'plaŋk\ *n* 1 : a heavy thick board 2 : an article in the platform of a political party

²**plank** *vb* 1 : to cover with planks 2 : to set or lay down forcibly 3 : to cook and serve on a board

plank·ing \'plaŋ-kiŋ\ *n* : a quantity or covering of planks

plank·ton \'plaŋk-tən\ *n* [G, fr. Gk. neut. of *planktos* drifting] : the passively floating or weakly swimming animal and plant life of a body of water — **plank·ton·ic** \plaŋk-'tä-nik\ *adj*

¹**plant** \'plant\ *vb* 1 : to set in the ground to grow 2 : ESTABLISH, SETTLE 3 : to stock or provide with something 4 : to place firmly or forcibly 5 : to hide or arrange with intent to deceive

²**plant** *n* 1 : any of a kingdom of living things that usu. have no locomotor ability or obvious sense organs and have cellulose cell walls and usu. capacity for indefinite growth 2 : the land, buildings, and machinery used in carrying on a trade or business

¹**plan·tain** \'plan-tᵊn\ *n* [ME, fr. AF, fr. L *plantagin-, plantago*, fr. *planta* sole of the foot; fr. its broad leaves] : any of a genus of weedy herbs with spikes of tiny greenish flowers

²**plantain** *n* [Sp *plántano, plátano* plane tree, banana tree, fr. ML *plantanus* plane tree, alter. of L *platanus*] : a banana plant with starchy greenish fruit that is eaten cooked; *also* : its fruit

plan·tar \'plan-tər, -ˌtär\ *adj* : of or relating to the sole of the foot

plan·ta·tion \plan-'tā-shən\ *n* 1 : a large group of plants and esp. trees under cultivation 2 : an agricultural estate usu. worked by resident laborers

plant·er \'plan-tər\ *n* 1 : one that plants or sows; *esp* : an owner or operator of a plantation 2 : a container for plants

plant louse *n* : APHID

plaque \'plak\ *n* [F] 1 : an ornamental brooch 2 : a flat thin piece (as of metal) used for decoration; *also* : a commemorative tablet 3 : a bacteria-containing film on a tooth

plash \'plash\ *n* : SPLASH — **plash** *vb*

plas·ma \'plaz-mə\ *n* 1 : the fluid part of blood, lymph, or milk 2 : a gas composed of ionized particles 3 : a display (as a television screen) in which cells of plasma emit light upon receiving an electric current — **plas·mat·ic** \plaz-'ma-tik\ *adj*

¹**plas·ter** \'plas-tər\ *n* 1 : a dressing consisting of a backing spread with an often medicated substance that clings to the skin ⟨adhesive ~⟩ 2 : a paste that hardens as it dries and is used for coating walls and ceilings

²**plaster** *vb* : to cover with or as if with plaster — **plas·ter·er** *n*

plas·ter·board \'plas-tər-ˌbȯrd\ *n* : DRYWALL

plaster of par·is \-'pa-rəs\ *often cap 2d P* : a white powder made from gypsum and used as a quick-setting paste with water for casts and molds

¹**plas·tic** \'plas-tik\ *adj* [L *plasticus* of molding, fr. Gk *plastikos*, fr. *plassein* to mold, form] 1 : capable of being molded ⟨~ clay⟩ 2 : characterized by or using modeling ⟨~ arts⟩ 3 : made or consisting of a plastic ♦ **Synonyms** PLIABLE, PLIANT, DUCTILE, MALLEABLE, ADAPTABLE — **plas·tic·i·ty** \plas-'ti-sə-tē\ *n*

²**plastic** *n* : a plastic substance; *esp* : a synthetic or processed material that can be formed into rigid objects or into films or filaments

plastic surgery *n* : surgery to repair, restore, or improve lost, injured, defective, or misshapen body parts — **plastic surgeon** *n*

¹**plat** \'plat\ *n* 1 : a small plot of ground 2 : a plan of a piece of land with actual or proposed features (as lots)

²**plat** *vb* **plat·ted; plat·ting** : to make a plat of

¹**plate** \'plāt\ *n* 1 : a flat thin piece of material 2 : domestic hollowware made of or plated with gold, silver, or base metals 3 : DISH 4 : HOME PLATE 5 : the molded metal or plastic cast of a page of type to be printed from 6 : a sheet of glass or plastic coated with a chemical sensitive to light and used in photography 7 : the part of a denture that fits to the mouth; *also* : DENTURE 8 : something printed from an engraving 9 : a huge mobile segment of the earth's crust

²**plate** *vb* **plat·ed; plat·ing** 1 : to overlay with metal (as gold or silver) 2 : to make a printing plate of

pla·teau \pla-'tō\ *n, pl* **plateaus** *or* **pla·teaux** \-'tōz\ [F] : a large level area of high land

plate glass *n* : rolled, ground, and polished sheet glass

plate·let \'plāt-lət\ *n* : a minute flattened body; *esp* : a minute colorless disklike body of mammalian blood that assists in blood clotting

plat·en \'pla-tᵊn\ *n* 1 : a flat plate; *esp* : one that exerts or receives pressure (as in a printing press) 2 : the roller of a typewriter or printer

plate tectonics *n* : a theory in geology that the lithosphere is divided into plates at the boundaries of which much of earth's seismic activity occurs 2 : the process and dynamics of tectonic plate movement — **plate–tectonic** *adj*

plat·form \'plat-ˌfȯrm\ *n* 1 : a raised flooring or stage for speakers, performers, or workers 2 : a declaration of the principles on which a group of persons (as a political party) stands 3 : OPERATING SYSTEM

plat·ing \'plā-tiŋ\ *n* : a coating of metal plates or plate ⟨the ~ of a ship⟩

plat·i·num \'pla-tə-nəm\ *n* : a heavy grayish white metallic chemical element

plat·i·tude \'pla-tə-ˌtüd, -ˌtyüd\ *n* : a flat or trite remark — **plat·i·tu·di·nous** \-'tü-də-nəs, -'tyü-\ *adj*

pla·ton·ic love \plə-'tä-nik-, plā-\ *n, often cap P* : a close relationship between two persons without sexual desire

pla·toon \plə-'tün\ *n* [F *peloton* small detachment, lit., ball, fr. *pelote* little ball] 1 : a subdivision of a company-size military unit usu. consisting of two or more squads or sections 2 : a group of football players trained either for offense or for defense and sent into the game as a body

platoon sergeant *n* : a noncommissioned officer in the army ranking below a first sergeant

plat·ter \'pla-tər\ *n* 1 : a large serving plate 2 : a phonograph record

platy \'pla-tē\ *n, pl* **platy** *or* **plat·ys** *or* **plat·ies** : either of two small stocky usu. brilliantly colored bony fishes often kept in tropical aquariums

platy·pus \'pla-ti-pəs\ *n, pl* **platy·pus·es** *also* **platy·pi** \-ˌpī\ [NL, fr. Gk *platypous* flat-footed, fr. *platys* broad, flat + *pous* foot] : a small aquatic egg-laying marsupial mammal of Australia with webbed feet and a fleshy bill like a duck's

plau·dit \'plȯ-dət\ *n* : an act of applause

plau·si·ble \'plȯ-zə-bəl\ *adj* [L *plausibilis* worthy of applause, fr. *plausus*, pp. of *plaudere* to applaud] : seemingly worthy of belief — **plau·si·bil·i·ty** \ˌplȯ-zə-'bi-lə-tē\ *n* — **plau·si·bly** \'plȯ-zə-blē\ *adv*

¹**play** \'plā\ *n* 1 : brisk handling of something (as a weapon) 2 : the course of a game; *also* : a particular act or maneuver in a game 3 : recreational activity; *esp* : the spontaneous activity of children ⟨ ~ JEST ⟨said in ~⟩ 5 : the act or an instance of punning 6 : GAMBLING 7 : OPERATION ⟨bring extra force into ~⟩ 8 : a brisk or light movement 9 : free motion (as of part of a machine) 10 : scope for action 11 : PUBLICITY 12 : an effort to arouse liking ⟨made a ~ for her⟩ 13 : a stage representation of a drama; *also* : a dramatic composition 14 : a function of an electronic device that causes a recording to play — **play·ful** \-fəl\ *adj* — **play·ful·ly** *adv* — **play·ful·ness** *n* — **in play** : in condition or position to be played

²**play** *vb* 1 : to engage in recreation : FROLIC 2 : to handle or behave lightly or absentmindedly 3 : to make a pun ⟨~ on words⟩ 4 : to take advantage ⟨~ on fears⟩ 5 : to move or operate in a brisk or irregular manner ⟨a flashlight ~ed over the wall⟩ 6 : to perform music ⟨~ on a violin⟩; *also* : to perform (music) on an instrument ⟨~ a waltz⟩ 7 : to perform music upon ⟨~ the piano⟩; *also* : to sound in performance ⟨the organ is ~ing⟩ 8 : to cause to emit sounds ⟨~ a radio⟩; *also* : to cause to reproduce recorded material ⟨~ a DVD⟩ 9 : to act in a dramatic medium; *also* : to act in the character of ⟨~ the hero⟩ 10 : GAMBLE 11 : to produce a specified impression in performance ⟨~s like a comedy⟩ 12 : to behave in a specified way ⟨~ safe⟩; *also* : COOPERATE ⟨going along with him⟩ 13 : to deal with; *also* : EMPHASIZE ⟨~ up her good qualities⟩ 14 : to perform for amusement ⟨~ a

trick⟩ **15** : WREAK **16** : to use as an esp. political strategy **17** : to contend with in a game; *also* : to fill (a certain position) on a team **18** : to make wagers on ⟨~ the races⟩ **19** : WIELD, PLY **20** : to keep in action — **play·er** *n*
play·act·ing \'plā-₁ak-tiŋ\ *n* **1** : performance in theatrical productions **2** : insincere or artificial behavior
play·back \-₁bak\ *n* : an act of reproducing recorded sound or pictures — **play back** *vb*
play·bill \-₁bil\ *n* : a poster advertising the performance of a play
play·book \-₁bůk\ *n* **1** : a notebook containing diagrammed football plays **2** : a stock of usual tactics or methods
play·boy \-₁bȯi\ *n* : a man whose chief interest is the pursuit of pleasure
play·date \-₁dāt\ *n* : a usu. prearranged play session for small children
play·go·er \-₁gō-ər\ *n* : a person who frequently attends plays
play·ground \-₁graůnd\ *n* : an area used for games and play esp. by children
play·house \-₁haůs\ *n* **1** : THEATER **2** : a small house for children to play in
playing card *n* : any of a set of 24 to 78 cards marked to show its rank and suit and used to play a game of cards
play·let \'plā-lət\ *n* : a short play
play·mate \-₁māt\ *n* : a companion in play
play–off \-₁ȯf\ *n* : a contest or series of contests to break a tie or determine a championship
play out *vb* : DEVELOP, UNFOLD ⟨see how things *play out*⟩
play·pen \-₁pen\ *n* : a portable enclosure in which a young child may play
play·suit \-₁süt\ *n* : a sports and play outfit for women and children
play·thing \-₁thiŋ\ *n* : TOY
play·wright \-₁rīt\ *n* : a writer of plays
pla·za \'pla-zə, 'plä-\ *n* [Sp, fr. L *platea* broad street] **1** : a public square in a city or town **2** : a shopping center
PLC *abbr, Brit* public limited company
plea \'plē\ *n* **1** : a defendant's answer in law to a charge or indictment **2** : something alleged as an excuse **3** : ENTREATY, APPEAL
plead \'plēd\ *vb* **plead·ed** *or* **pled** \'pled\; **plead·ing** **1** : to argue before a court or authority ⟨~ a case⟩ **2** : to answer to a charge or indictment ⟨~ guilty⟩ **3** : to argue for or against something ⟨~ for acquittal⟩ **4** : to appeal earnestly ⟨~s for help⟩ **5** : to offer as a plea (as in defense) ⟨~ed illness⟩ — **plead·er** *n*
pleas·ant \'ple-zᵊnt\ *adj* **1** : giving pleasure : AGREEABLE ⟨a ~ experience⟩ **2** : marked by pleasing behavior or appearance ⟨a ~ person⟩ — **pleas·ant·ly** *adv* — **pleas·ant·ness** *n*
pleas·ant·ry \-zᵊn-trē\ *n, pl* **-ries** : a pleasant and casual act or speech
¹please \'plēz\ *vb* **pleased; pleas·ing** **1** : to give pleasure or satisfaction to **2** : LIKE ⟨do as you ~⟩ **3** : to be the will or pleasure of ⟨may it ~ his Majesty⟩
²please *adv* — used as a function word to express politeness or emphasis in a request ⟨~ come in⟩
pleasing *adj* : giving pleasure ⟨a ~ fragrance⟩ — **pleas·ing·ly** *adv*
plea·sur·able \'ple-zhə-rə-bəl\ *adj* : PLEASANT, GRATIFYING ⟨a ~ cruise⟩ — **plea·sur·ably** \-blē\ *adv*
plea·sure \'ple-zhər\ *n* **1** : DESIRE, INCLINATION ⟨await your ~⟩ **2** : a state of gratification : ENJOYMENT **3** : a source of delight or joy ⟨a ~ to see you dance⟩
¹pleat \'plēt\ *vb* **1** : FOLD; *esp* : to arrange in pleats **2** : BRAID
²pleat *n* : a fold (as in cloth) made by doubling material over on itself
plebe \'plēb\ *n* : a freshman at a military or naval academy
¹ple·be·ian \pli-'bē-ən\ *n* **1** : a member of the Roman plebs **2** : one of the common people
²plebeian *adj* **1** : of or relating to plebeians **2** : COMMON, VULGAR ⟨~ tastes⟩
pleb·i·scite \'ple-bə-₁sīt, -sət\ *n* : a vote of the people (as of a country) on a proposal submitted to them
plebs \'plebz\ *n, pl* **ple·bes** \'plē-bēz\ **1** : the general populace **2** : the common people of ancient Rome

plec·trum \'plek-trəm\ *n, pl* **plec·tra** \-trə\ *or* **plec·trums** [L] : ³PICK 3
¹pledge \'plej\ *n* [ME *plegge* security, fr. AF *plege*, fr. LL *plebium*, fr. *plebere* to pledge, prob. of Gmc origin] **1** : something given as security for the performance of an act **2** : the state of being held as a security or guaranty **3** : TOAST 3 **4** : PROMISE, VOW
²pledge *vb* **pledged; pledg·ing** **1** : to deposit as a pledge **2** : TOAST **3** : to bind by a pledge : PLIGHT **4** : PROMISE
Pleis·to·cene \'plī-stə-₁sēn\ *adj* : of, relating to, or being the earlier epoch of the Quaternary — **Pleistocene** *n*
ple·na·ry \'plē-nə-rē, 'ple-\ *adj* **1** : FULL ⟨~ power⟩ **2** : including all entitled to attend ⟨~ session⟩
pleni·po·ten·tia·ry \₁ple-nə-pə-'ten-chə-rē, -'ten-chē-₁er-ē\ *n, pl* **-ries** : a diplomatic agent having full authority — **plenipotentiary** *adj*
plen·i·tude \'ple-nə-₁tüd, -₁tyüd\ *n* **1** : COMPLETENESS **2** : ABUNDANCE
plen·te·ous \'plen-tē-əs\ *adj* **1** : FRUITFUL **2** : existing in plenty
plen·ti·ful \'plen-ti-fəl\ *adj* **1** : containing or yielding plenty ⟨a ~ harvest⟩ **2** : ABUNDANT — **plen·ti·ful·ly** *adv*
plen·ty \'plen-tē\ *n* : a more than adequate number or amount
ple·num \'ple-nəm, 'plē-\ *n, pl* **-nums** *or* **-na** \-nə\ : a general assembly of all members esp. of a legislative body
pleth·o·ra \'ple-thə-rə\ *n* : an excessive quantity or fullness; *also* : PROFUSION
pleu·ri·sy \'plůr-ə-sē\ *n* : inflammation of the membrane that lines the chest and covers the lungs
plex·i·glass \'plek-si-₁glas\ *n* [alter. of *Plexiglas*, a trademark] : a transparent acrylic plastic often used in place of glass
plex·us \'plek-səs\ *n, pl* **plex·us·es** \-sə-səz\ : an interlacing network esp. of blood vessels or nerves
pli·able \'plī-ə-bəl\ *adj* **1** : FLEXIBLE **2** : yielding easily to others ⟨a ~ child⟩ **♦ Synonyms** PLASTIC, PLIANT, DUCTILE, MALLEABLE, ADAPTABLE — **pli·abil·i·ty** \₁plī-ə-'bi-lə-tē\ *n*
pli·ant \'plī-ənt\ *adj* **1** : FLEXIBLE **2** : easily influenced : PLIABLE ⟨a ~ senator⟩ — **pli·an·cy** \-ən-sē\ *n*
pli·ers \'plī-ərz\ *n pl* : small pincers for bending or cutting wire or handling small objects
¹plight \'plīt\ *vb* : to put or give in pledge : ENGAGE
²plight *n* : an unfortunate, difficult, or precarious situation
plinth \'plinth\ *n* : the lowest part of the base of an architectural column
Plio·cene \'plī-ə-₁sēn\ *adj* : of, relating to, or being the latest epoch of the Tertiary — **Pliocene** *n*
PLO *abbr* Palestine Liberation Organization
plod \'pläd\ *vb* **plod·ded; plod·ding** **1** : to walk heavily or slowly : TRUDGE **2** : to work laboriously and monotonously : DRUDGE — **plod·der** *n* — **plod·ding·ly** *adv*
plonk *var of* PLUNK
plop \'pläp\ *vb* **plopped; plop·ping** **1** : to fall or move with a sound like that of something dropping into water **2** : to set, drop, or throw heavily or hastily ⟨*plopped* down on the couch⟩ ⟨~ down $20⟩ — **plop** *n*
¹plot \'plät\ *n* **1** : a small area of ground **2** : a ground plan (as of an area) **3** : the main story (as of a book or movie) **4** : a secret scheme : INTRIGUE
²plot *vb* **plot·ted; plot·ting** **1** : to make a plot or plan of **2** : to mark on or as if on a chart **3** : to plan or contrive esp. secretly — **plot·ter** *n*
plo·ver \'plə-vər, 'plō-\ *n, pl* **plover** *or* **plovers** [ME, fr. AF, fr. VL *pluviarius*, fr. L *pluvia* rain] : any of a family of shorebirds that differ from the sandpipers in having shorter stouter bills
¹plow *or* **plough** \'plaů\ *n* **1** : an implement used to cut, lift, turn over, and partly break up soil **2** : a device (as a snowplow) operating like a plow
²plow *or* **plough** *vb* **1** : to open, break up, or work with a plow **2** : to move through like a plow ⟨a ship ~ing the waves⟩ **3** : to proceed laboriously ⟨~ed through his work⟩ — **plow·able** *adj* — **plow·er** *n*
plow·boy \'plaů-₁bȯi\ *n* : a boy who leads the horse drawing a plow
plow·man \-mən, -₁man\ *n* **1** : a man who guides a plow **2** : a farm laborer
plow·share \-₁sher\ *n* : a part of a plow that cuts the earth

ploy \'plȯi\ *n* : a tactic intended to embarrass or frustrate an opponent

¹**pluck** \'plək\ *vb* **1** : to pull off or out : PICK; *also* : to pull something from **2** : to play (an instrument) by pulling the strings **3** : TUG, TWITCH

²**pluck** *n* **1** : an act or instance of plucking **2** : SPIRIT, COURAGE

plucky \'plə-kē\ *adj* **pluck·i·er; -est** : COURAGEOUS, SPIRITED ⟨~ recruits⟩

¹**plug** \'pləg\ *n* **1** : STOPPER; *also* : an obstructing mass **2** : a cake of tobacco **3** : a poor or worn-out horse **4** : SPARK PLUG **5** : a lure with several hooks used in fishing **6** : a device on the end of a cord for making an electrical connection **7** : a piece of favorable publicity

²**plug** *vb* **plugged; plug·ging 1** : to stop, make tight, or secure by inserting a plug **2** : HIT, SHOOT **3** : to publicize insistently **4** : PLOD, DRUDGE

plug and play *n* : a computer feature enabling the operating system to automatically detect and configure peripherals — **plug-and-play** *adj*

plugged-in \'pləgd-'in\ *adj* : technologically or socially informed and connected

plug-in \'pləg-ˌin\ *n* : a small piece of software that supplements a larger program

plum \'pləm\ *n* [ME, fr. OE *plūme,* modif. of L *prunum* plum, fr. Gk *proumnon*] **1** : a smooth-skinned juicy fruit borne by trees related to the peach and cherry; *also* : a tree bearing plums **2** : a raisin when used in desserts (as puddings) **3** : something excellent; *esp* : something desirable given in return for a favor

plum·age \'plü-mij\ *n* : the feathers of a bird — **plumaged** \-mijd\ *adj*

¹**plumb** \'pləm\ *n* : a weight on the end of a line (**plumb line**) used esp. by builders to show vertical direction

²**plumb** *adv* **1** : VERTICALLY **2** : COMPLETELY ⟨~ tired out⟩ **3** : EXACTLY; *also* : IMMEDIATELY

³**plumb** *vb* : to sound, adjust, or test with a plumb ⟨~ the depth of a well⟩

⁴**plumb** *adj* **1** : VERTICAL **2** : COMPLETE

plumb·er \'plə-mər\ *n* : a worker who fits or repairs pipes and fixtures

plumb·ing \'plə-miŋ\ *n* : a system of pipes in a building for supplying and carrying off water

¹**plume** \'plüm\ *n* : FEATHER; *esp* : a large, conspicuous, or showy feather — **plumed** \'plümd\ *adj* — **plumy** \'plü-mē\ *adj*

²**plume** *vb* **plumed; plum·ing 1** : to provide or deck with feathers **2** : to indulge (oneself) in pride

plum·met \'plə-mət\ *n* : PLUMB; *also* : PLUMB LINE

plummet *vb* : to drop or plunge straight down

¹**plump** \'pləmp\ *vb* **1** : to drop or fall suddenly or heavily **2** : to favor something strongly ⟨~*ing* for change⟩

²**plump** *n* : a sudden heavy fall or blow; *also* : the sound made by it

³**plump** *adv* **1** : straight down; *also* : straight ahead **2** : UNQUALIFIEDLY ⟨came out ~ for free trade⟩

⁴**plump** *adj* : having a full rounded usu. pleasing form
♦ **Synonyms** FLESHY, STOUT, ROLY-POLY, ROTUND — **plump·ness** *n*

¹**plun·der** \'plən-dər\ *vb* : to take the goods of by force or wrongfully : PILLAGE — **plun·der·er** *n*

²**plunder** *n* : something taken by force or theft : LOOT

¹**plunge** \'plənj\ *vb* **plunged; plung·ing 1** : IMMERSE, SUBMERGE **2** : to enter or cause to enter a state or course of action suddenly or violently ⟨~ into war⟩ **3** : to cast oneself into or as if into water **4** : to gamble heavily and recklessly **5** : to descend suddenly

²**plunge** *n* : a sudden dive, leap, or rush

plung·er \'plən-jər\ *n* **1** : one that plunges **2** : a sliding piece driven by or against fluid pressure : PISTON **3** : a rubber cup on a handle pushed against an opening to free a waste outlet of an obstruction

plunk \'pləŋk\ *or* **plonk** \'pläŋk, 'plȯŋk\ *vb* **1** : to make or cause to make a hollow metallic sound **2** : to drop heavily or suddenly — **plunk** *n*

plu·per·fect \(ˌ)plü-'pər-fikt\ *adj* [ME *pluperfyth,* modif. of LL *plusquamperfectus,* lit., more than perfect] : of, relating to, or constituting a verb tense that denotes an action or state as completed at or before a past time spoken of — **pluperfect** *n*

¹**plu·ral** \'plur-əl\ *adj* [ME, fr. AF & L; AF *plurel,* fr. L *plu-*

ralis, fr. *plur-, plus* more] : of, relating to, or constituting a word form used to denote more than one — **plural** *n*

plu·ral·i·ty \plu-'ra-lə-tē\ *n, pl* **-ties 1** : the state of being plural **2** : an excess of votes over those cast for an opposing candidate **3** : the greatest number of votes cast when not a majority

plu·ral·ize \'plur-ə-ˌlīz\ *vb* **-ized; -iz·ing** : to make plural or express in the plural form — **plu·ral·i·za·tion** \ˌplur-ə-lə-'zā-shən\ *n*

¹**plus** \'pləs\ *adj* [L, more] **1** : mathematically positive **2** : having or being in addition to what is anticipated **3** : falling high in a specified range ⟨a grade of B ~⟩

²**plus** *n, pl* **plus·es** \'plə-səz\ *also* **plus·ses 1** : a sign + (**plus sign**) used in mathematics to indicate addition or a positive quantity **2** : an added quantity; *also* : a positive quality **3** : SURPLUS

³**plus** *prep* **1** : increased by : with the addition of ⟨3 ~ 4⟩ **2** : BESIDES

⁴**plus** *conj* : AND ⟨soup ~ salad and bread⟩

¹**plush** \'pləsh\ *n* : a fabric with a pile longer and less dense than velvet pile — **plushy** *adj*

²**plush** *adj* : notably luxurious ⟨a ~ suite⟩ — **plush·ly** *adv* — **plush·ness** *n*

plus/minus sign *n* : the sign ± used to indicate a quantity taking on both a positive value and its negative or to indicate a plus or minus quantity

plus or minus *adj* : indicating a quantity whose positive and negative values bracket a range of values ⟨*plus or minus* 3 inches⟩

plus-size \'pləs-ˌsīz\ *also* **plus-sized** \-'sīzd\ *adj* : extra large ⟨~ clothing⟩ ⟨~ shoppers⟩

Plu·to \'plü-tō\ *n* : a dwarf planet whose orbit crosses the orbit of Neptune — see PLANET table

plu·toc·ra·cy \plü-'tä-krə-sē\ *n, pl* **-cies 1** : government by the wealthy **2** : a controlling class of the wealthy — **plu·to·crat** \'plü-tə-ˌkrat\ *n* — **plu·to·crat·ic** \ˌplü-tə-'kra-tik\ *adj*

plu·to·ni·um \plü-'tō-nē-əm\ *n* : a radioactive chemical element formed by the decay of neptunium

plu·vi·al \'plü-vē-əl\ *adj* **1** : of or relating to rain **2** : characterized by abundant rain

¹**ply** \'plī\ *vb* **plied; ply·ing 1** : to use, practice, or work diligently ⟨~ a trade⟩ **2** : to keep supplying something to ⟨*plied* them with liquor⟩ **3** : to go or travel regularly esp. by sea

²**ply** *n, pl* **plies** : one of the folds, thicknesses, or strands of which something (as plywood or yarn) is made

³**ply** *vb* **plied; ply·ing** : to twist together ⟨~ yarns⟩

ply·wood \'plī-ˌwu̇d\ *n* : material made of thin sheets of wood glued and pressed together

pm *abbr* premium

Pm *symbol* promethium

PM *abbr* **1** paymaster **2** police magistrate **3** postmaster **4** post meridiem — often not cap. and often punctuated **5** postmortem **6** prime minister **7** provost marshal

pmk *abbr* postmark

PMS \ˌpē-ˌem-'es\ *n* : PREMENSTRUAL SYNDROME

pmt *abbr* payment

pneu·mat·ic \nu̇-'ma-tik, nyu̇-\ *adj* **1** : of, relating to, or using air or wind **2** : moved by air pressure **3** : filled with compressed air ⟨~ tires⟩ — **pneu·mat·i·cal·ly** \-ti-k(ə-)lē\ *adv*

pneu·mo·coc·cus \ˌnü-mə-'kä-kəs, ˌnyü-\ *n, pl* **-coc·ci** \-'käk-ˌsī, -ˌsē; -'kä-ˌkī, -ˌkē\ : a bacterium that causes pneumonia — **pneu·mo·coc·cal** \-'kä-kəl\ *adj*

pneu·mo·co·ni·o·sis \ˌnü-mō-ˌkō-nē-'ō-səs, ˌnyü-\ *n* : a disease of the lungs caused by habitual inhalation of irritant mineral or metallic particles

pneu·mo·nia \nu̇-'mō-nyə, nyu̇-\ *n* : an inflammatory disease of the lungs

Po *symbol* polonium

PO *abbr* **1** petty officer **2** post office

¹**poach** \'pōch\ *vb* [ME *pocchen,* fr. MF *pocher,* fr. OF *poché* poached, lit., bagged, fr. *poche* bag, pouch, of Gmc origin] : to cook (as an egg or fish) in simmering liquid

²**poach** *vb* : to hunt or fish unlawfully — **poach·er** *n*

POB *abbr* post office box

po·bla·no \pō-'blä-nō\ *n, pl* **-nos** : a heart-shaped usu. mild chili pepper esp. when fresh and dark green

po'·boy \'pō-ˌbȯi\ *also* **poor boy** *n* : SUBMARINE 2

pock \'päk\ *n* : a small swelling on the skin (as in smallpox); *also* : a spot suggesting this

¹**pock·et** \'pä-kət\ *n* **1** : a small bag open at the top or side inserted in a garment **2** : supply of money : MEANS **3** : RECEPTACLE, CONTAINER **4** : a small isolated area or group ⟨~s of fog⟩ **5** : a small body of ore — **pock·et·ful** *n*

²**pocket** *vb* **1** : to put in or as if in a pocket **2** : STEAL ⟨~ed the profits⟩

³**pocket** *adj* **1** : small enough to fit in a pocket; *also* : SMALL, MINIATURE ⟨a ~ park⟩ **2** : carried in or paid from one's own pocket

¹**pock·et·book** \-ˌbu̇k\ *n* **1** : PURSE; *also* : HANDBAG **2** : financial resources

²**pocketbook** *adj* : relating to money

pocket gopher *n* : GOPHER 2

pock·et·knife \'pä-kət-ˌnīf\ *n* : a knife with a folding blade to be carried in the pocket

pocket veto *n* : an indirect veto of a legislative bill by an executive through retention of the bill unsigned until after adjournment of the legislature

pock·mark \'päk-ˌmärk\ *n* : a pit or scar caused by smallpox or acne — **pock–marked** \-ˌmärkt\ *adj*

po·co \'pō-kō, ˌpȯ-\ *adv* [It, little, fr. L *paucus*] : SOMEWHAT — used to qualify a direction in music ⟨~ allegro⟩

po·co a po·co \ˌpō-kō-ä-'pō-kō, ˌpȯ-kō-ä-'pȯ-\ *adv* : little by little : GRADUALLY — used as a direction in music

pod \'päd\ *n* **1** : a dry fruit (as of a pea) that splits open when ripe **2** : an external streamlined compartment (as for a jet engine) on an airplane **3** : a compartment (as for personnel, a power unit, or an instrument) on a ship or craft

POD *abbr* pay on delivery

pod·cast \'päd-ˌkast\ *n* [*iPod*, trademark for a portable media player + broad*cast*] : a program made available in digital format for download over the Internet — **podcast** *vb* — **pod·cast·er** *n*

po·di·a·try \pə-'dī-ə-trē, pō-\ *n* : the medical care and treatment of the human foot — **po·di·at·ric** \ˌpō-dē-'a-trik\ *adj* — **po·di·a·trist** \pə-'dī-ə-trist, pō-\ *n*

po·di·um \'pō-dē-əm\ *n, pl* **podiums** *or* **po·dia** \-dē-ə\ **1** : a dais esp. for an orchestral conductor **2** : LECTERN

POE *abbr* port of entry

po·em \'pō-əm\ *n* : a composition in verse

po·esy \'pō-ə-zē\ *n* : POETRY

po·et \'pō-ət\ *n* [ME, fr. AF *poete*, fr. L *poeta*, fr. Gk *poiētēs* maker, poet, fr. *poiein* to make] : a writer of poetry; *also* : a creative artist of great sensitivity

po·et·as·ter \'pō-ə-ˌtas-tər\ *n* : an inferior poet

po·et·ess \'pō-ə-təs\ *n* : a girl or woman who is a poet

poetic justice *n* : an outcome in which vice is punished and virtue rewarded usu. in a manner peculiarly or ironically appropriate

po·et·ry \'pō-ə-trē\ *n* **1** : metrical writing **2** : POEMS — **po·et·ic** \pō-'e-tik\ *or* **po·et·i·cal** \-ti-kəl\ *adj*

po·grom \'pō-grəm, pō-'gräm\ *n* [Yiddish, fr. Russ, lit., devastation] : an organized massacre of helpless people and esp. of Jews

poi \'pȯi\ *n, pl* **poi** *or* **pois** : a food prepared from the cooked corms of taro that are mashed with water to the consistency of a paste or thick liquid

poi·gnant \'pȯi-nyənt\ *adj* **1** : painfully affecting the feelings ⟨~ grief⟩ **2** : deeply moving ⟨~ scene⟩ — **poignan·cy** \-nyən-sē\ *n*

poin·ci·ana \ˌpȯin-sē-'a-nə\ *n* : any of several ornamental tropical leguminous trees or shrubs with bright orange or red flowers

poin·set·tia \pȯin-'se-tē-ə\ *n* : a showy tropical American spurge with usu. scarlet bracts that suggest petals and surround small yellow flowers

¹**point** \'pȯint\ *n* **1** : an individual detail; *also* : the most important essential **2** : PURPOSE ⟨no ~ in continuing⟩ **3** : a geometric element that has position but no size **4** : a particular place : LOCALITY **5** : a particular stage or degree **6** : a sharp end : TIP **7** : a projecting piece of land **8** : a punctuation mark; *esp* : PERIOD **9** : DECIMAL POINT **10** : one of the divisions of the compass **11** : a unit of counting (as in a game score) — **point·less** *adj* — **pointy** \'pȯin-tē\ *adj* — **beside the point** : IRRELEVANT — **to the point** : RELEVANT, PERTINENT ⟨her remark was *to the point*⟩

²**point** *vb* **1** : to furnish with a point : SHARPEN **2**

: PUNCTUATE **3** : to separate (a decimal fraction) from an integer by a decimal point — usu. used with *off* **4** : to indicate the position of esp. by extending a finger **5** : to direct attention to ⟨~ out an error⟩ **6** : AIM, DIRECT **7** : to lie extended, aimed, or turned in a particular direction : FACE, LOOK

point–and–click *adj* : relating to or being a computer interface that allows the activation of a file by selection with a pointing device (as a mouse)

point–and–shoot *adj* : having or using preset or automatically adjusted controls ⟨a ~ camera⟩

point–blank \'pȯint-'blaŋk\ *adj* **1** : so close to the target that a missile fired will travel in a straight line to the mark **2** : DIRECT, BLUNT ⟨a ~ refusal⟩ — **point–blank** *adv*

point·ed \'pȯin-təd\ *adj* **1** : having a point **2** : being to the point : DIRECT **3** : aimed at a particular person or group; *also* : CONSPICUOUS, MARKED ⟨~ indifference⟩ — **point·ed·ly** *adv*

point·er \'pȯin-tər\ *n* **1** : one that points out : INDICATOR **2** : a large short-haired hunting dog **3** : HINT, TIP ⟨gave me some ~s on how to play⟩

poin·til·lism \'pwan-tē-ˌyi-zəm, 'pȯin-tə-ˌli-zəm\ *n* [F *pointillisme*, fr. *pointiller* to stipple, fr. *point* spot, point] : the theory or practice in painting of applying small strokes or dots of color to a surface so that from a distance they blend together — **poin·til·list** \ˌpwan-tē-'yēst, 'pȯin-tə-list\ *n or adj*

point man *n* : a principal spokesman or advocate

point of no return : a critical point at which turning back or reversal is not possible

point of view : a position from which something is considered or evaluated

point spread *n* : the number of points by which a favorite is expected to defeat an underdog

¹**poise** \'pȯiz\ *vb* **poised; pois·ing** : BALANCE

²**poise** *n* **1** : BALANCE **2** : self-possessed calmness ⟨kept her ~ even under attack⟩; *also* : a particular way of carrying oneself

poi·sha \'pȯi-shə\ *n, pl* **poisha** : the paisa of Bangladesh

¹**poi·son** \'pȯi-z²n\ *n* [ME, fr. AF *poisun* drink, potion, poison, fr. L *potion-, potio* drink] : a substance that through its chemical action can injure or kill — **poi·son·ous** \-z²n-əs\ *adj*

²**poison** *vb* **1** : to injure or kill with poison **2** : to treat or taint with poison **3** : to affect destructively : CORRUPT ⟨~ed her mind⟩ — **poi·son·er** *n*

poison hemlock *n* : a large branching poisonous herb with finely divided leaves and white flowers that is related to the carrot

poison ivy *n* **1** : a usu. climbing plant related to the sumacs that has leaves composed of three shiny leaflets and produces an irritating oil causing a usu. intensely itching skin rash; *also* : any of several related plants **2** : a skin rash caused by poison ivy

poison oak *n* : any of several shrubby plants closely related to poison ivy and having similar properties

poison sumac *n* : a No. American swamp shrub with pinnate leaves, greenish flowers, greenish white berries, and irritating properties

¹**poke** \'pōk\ *n, chiefly Southern & Midland* : BAG, SACK

²**poke** *vb* **poked; pok·ing** **1** : PROD; *also* : to stir up by prodding **2** : to make a prodding or jabbing movement esp. repeatedly **3** : HIT, PUNCH **4** : to thrust forward obtrusively **5** : RUMMAGE ⟨*poking* around the attic⟩ **6** : MEDDLE, PRY **7** : DAWDLE ⟨*poking* along toward home⟩ — **poke fun at** : RIDICULE, MOCK

³**poke** *n* : a quick thrust; *also* : PUNCH

¹**pok·er** \'pō-kər\ *n* : a metal rod for stirring a fire

²**pok·er** \'pō-kər\ *n* : any of several card games in which the player with the highest hand at the end of the betting wins

poke·weed \'pōk-ˌwēd\ *n* : a coarse American perennial herb with clusters of white flowers and dark purple juicy berries

poky *or* **pok·ey** \'pō-kē\ *adj* **pok·i·er; -est** **1** : small and cramped **2** : SHABBY, DULL **3** : annoyingly slow

pol \'päl\ *n* : POLITICIAN

po·lar \'pō-lər\ *adj* **1** : of or relating to a geographical pole **2** : of or relating to a pole (as of a magnet)

polar bear *n* : a large creamy-white bear that inhabits arctic regions

Po·lar·is \pə-'ler-əs\ *n* : NORTH STAR

po·lar·ise *Brit var of* POLARIZE

po·lar·i·ty \pō-'ler-ə-tē\ *n, pl* **-ties** : the condition of having poles and esp. magnetic or electrical poles

po·lar·i·za·tion \ˌpō-lə-rə-'zā-shən\ *n* **1** : the action of polarizing : the state of being polarized **2** : concentration about opposing extremes

po·lar·ize \'pō-lə-ˌrīz\ *vb* **-ized; -iz·ing 1** : to cause (light waves) to vibrate in a definite way **2** : to give physical polarity to **3** : to break up into opposing groups

pol·der \'pōl-dər, 'päl-\ *n* [D] : a tract of low land reclaimed from the sea

¹pole \'pōl\ *n* : a long slender piece of wood or metal ⟨telephone ~⟩

²pole *vb* **poled; pol·ing** : to impel or push with a pole ⟨~ a boat⟩

³pole *n* **1** : either end of an axis esp. of the earth **2** : either of the terminals of an electric device (as a battery or generator) **3** : one of two or more regions in a magnetized body at which the magnetism is concentrated — **pole·ward** \'pōl-wərd\ *adj or adv*

¹pole·ax \'pōl-ˌaks\ *n* : a battle-ax with a short handle

²poleax *vb* : to attack or fell with or as if with a poleax

pole·cat \'pōl-ˌkat\ *n, pl* **polecats** *or* **polecat 1** : a European carnivorous mammal of which the ferret is considered a domesticated variety **2** : SKUNK

polecat 1

po·lem·ic \pə-'le-mik\ *n* : the art or practice of disputation — usu. used in pl. — **po·lem·i·cal** \-mi-kəl\ *also* **po·lem·ic** \-mik\ *adj* — **po·lem·i·cist** \-sist\ *n*

pole·star \'pōl-ˌstär\ *n* **1** : NORTH STAR **2** : a directing principle : GUIDE

pole vault *n* : a field contest in which each contestant uses a pole to vault for height over a crossbar — **pole–vault** *vb* — **pole–vault·er** *n*

¹po·lice \pə-'lēs\ *vb* **po·liced; po·lic·ing 1** : to control, regulate, or keep in order esp. by use of police ⟨~ a highway⟩ **2** : to make clean and put in order ⟨*policed* up the concert site⟩

²police *n, pl* **police** [F, government, fr. OF, fr. LL *politia*, fr. Gk *politeia*, fr. *politēs* citizen, fr. *polis* city, state] **1** : the department of government that keeps public order and safety and enforces the laws; *also* : the members of this department **2** : a private organization resembling a police force; *also* : its members **3** : military personnel detailed to clean and put in order

po·lice·man \-mən\ *n* : POLICE OFFICER

police officer *n* : a member of a police force

police state *n* : a state characterized by repressive, arbitrary, totalitarian rule by means of secret police

po·lice·wom·an \pə-'lēs-ˌwu-mən\ *n* : a woman who is a police officer

¹pol·i·cy \'pä-lə-sē\ *n, pl* **-cies** : a definite course or method of action selected to guide and determine present and future decisions

²policy *n, pl* **-cies** : a writing whereby a contract of insurance is made

pol·i·cy·hold·er \'pä-lə-sē-ˌhōl-dər\ *n* : one granted an insurance policy

po·lio \'pō-lē-ˌō\ *n* : POLIOMYELITIS — **polio** *adj*

po·lio·my·eli·tis \-ˌmī-ə-'lī-təs\ *n* : an acute virus disease marked by inflammation of the gray matter of the spinal cord leading usu. to paralysis

¹pol·ish \'pä-lish\ *vb* **1** : to make smooth and glossy usu. by rubbing **2** : to refine or improve in manners, condition, or style

²polish *n* **1** : a smooth glossy surface : LUSTER **2** : REFINEMENT, CULTURE **3** : the action or process of polishing **4** : a preparation used to produce a gloss

Pol·ish \'pō-lish\ *n* : the Slavic language of the Poles — **Polish** *adj*

polit *abbr* political; politician

po·lit·bu·ro \'pä-lət-ˌbyur-ō, 'pō-, pə-'lit-\ *n* [Russ *politbyuro*] : the principal policy-making committee of a Communist party

po·lite \pə-'līt\ *adj* **po·lit·er; -est 1** : REFINED, CULTIVATED ⟨~ society⟩ **2** : marked by correct social conduct : COURTEOUS; *also* : CONSIDERATE, TACTFUL — **po·lite·ly** *adv* — **po·lite·ness** *n*

po·li·tesse \ˌpä-li-'tes\ *n* [F] : formal politeness

pol·i·tic \'pä-lə-ˌtik\ *adj* **1** : wise in promoting a policy ⟨a ~ statesman⟩ **2** : shrewdly tactful ⟨a ~ move⟩

po·lit·i·cal \pə-'li-ti-kəl\ *adj* **1** : of or relating to government or politics **2** : involving or charged or concerned with acts against a government or a political system ⟨~ prisoners⟩ — **po·lit·i·cal·ly** \-k(ə-)lē\ *adv*

politically correct *adj* : conforming to a belief that language and practices which could offend sensibilities (as in matters of sex or race) should be eliminated — **political correctness** *n*

pol·i·ti·cian \ˌpä-lə-'ti-shən\ *n* : a person actively engaged in government or politics

pol·i·tick \'pä-lə-ˌtik\ *vb* : to engage in political discussion or activity

po·lit·i·co \pə-'li-ti-ˌkō\ *n, pl* **-cos** *also* **-coes** : POLITICIAN

pol·i·tics \'pä-lə-ˌtiks\ *n sing or pl* **1** : the art or science of government, of guiding or influencing governmental policy, or of winning and holding control over a government **2** : political affairs or business; *esp* : competition between groups or individuals for power and leadership **3** : political opinions

pol·i·ty \'pä-lə-tē\ *n, pl* **-ties** : a politically organized unit; *also* : the form or constitution of such a unit

pol·ka \'pōl-kə, 'pō-kə\ *n* [Czech, fr. *Polka* Polish woman, fem. of *Polák* Pole] : a lively couple dance of Bohemian origin; *also* : music for this dance — **polka** *vb*

pol·ka dot \'pō-kə-ˌdät\ *n* : a dot in a pattern of regularly distributed dots — **polka–dot** *or* **polka–dot·ted** \-ˌdä-təd\ *adj*

¹poll \'pōl\ *n* **1** : HEAD **2** : the casting and recording of votes; *also* : the total vote cast **3** : the place where votes are cast — usu. used in pl. **4** : a questioning of persons to obtain information or opinions to be analyzed

²poll *vb* **1** : to cut off or shorten a growth or part of : CLIP, SHEAR **2** : to receive and record the votes of **3** : to receive (as votes) in an election **4** : to question in a poll

pol·lack *or* **pol·lock** \'pä-lək\ *n, pl* **pollack** *or* **pollock** : an important No. Atlantic food fish that is related to the cods; *also* : a related food fish of the No. Pacific

pol·len \'pä-lən\ *n* [NL, fr. L, fine flour] : a mass of male spores of a seed plant usu. appearing as a yellow dust

pol·li·na·tion \ˌpä-lə-'nā-shən\ *n* : the carrying of pollen to the female part of a plant to fertilize the seed — **pol·li·nate** \'pä-lə-ˌnāt\ *vb* — **pol·li·na·tor** \-ˌnā-tər\ *n*

poll·ster \'pōl-stər\ *n* : one that conducts a poll or compiles data obtained by a poll

poll tax *n* : a tax of a fixed amount per person levied on adults and often linked to the right to vote

pol·lute \pə-'lüt\ *vb* **pol·lut·ed; pol·lut·ing** : to make impure; *esp* : to contaminate (an environment) esp. with man-made waste — **pol·lut·ant** \-'lü-t³nt\ *n* — **pol·lut·er** *n* — **pol·lu·tion** \-'lü-shən\ *n*

pol·ly·wog *or* **pol·li·wog** \'pä-lē-ˌwäg\ *n* : TADPOLE

po·lo \'pō-lō\ *n* [Balti (Tibetan language of northern Kashmir), ball] : a game played by two teams on horseback using long-handled mallets to drive a wooden ball

po·lo·ni·um \pə-'lō-nē-əm\ *n* : a radioactive metallic chemical element

pol·ter·geist \'pōl-tər-ˌgīst\ *n* [G, fr. *poltern* to knock + *Geist* spirit] : a noisy usu. mischievous ghost held to be responsible for unexplained noises

pol·troon \päl-'trün\ *n* : COWARD

poly- *comb form* [Gk, fr. *polys* many] **1** : many : several ⟨*poly*syllabic⟩ **2** : polymeric ⟨*poly*ester⟩

poly·chlo·ri·nat·ed bi·phe·nyl \ˌpä-li-'klōr-ə-ˌnā-təd-ˌbī-'fen-ᵊl, -'fēn-\ *n* : any of several industrial compounds that are toxic environmental pollutants

poly·clin·ic \ˌpä-li-'kli-nik\ *n* : a clinic or hospital treating diseases of many sorts

poly·es·ter \'pä-lē-ˌes-tər\ *n* : a polymer composed of ester groups used esp. in making fibers or plastics; *also* : a product (as fabric) composed of polyester

poly·eth·yl·ene \ˌpä-lē-'e-thə-ˌlēn\ *n* : a lightweight plastic resistant to chemicals and moisture and used chiefly in packaging

po·lyg·a·my \pə-'li-gə-mē\ *n* : marriage in which a spouse of either sex may have more than one mate at the same time — **po·lyg·a·mist** \-mist\ *n* — **po·lyg·a·mous** \-məs\ *adj*

poly·glot \'pä-li-ˌglät\ *adj* 1 : speaking or writing several languages 2 : containing or made up of several languages — **polyglot** *n*

poly·gon \'pä-li-ˌgän\ *n* : a closed plane figure bounded by straight lines — **po·lyg·o·nal** \pə-'li-gə-nᵊl\ *adj*

poly·graph \'pä-li-ˌgraf\ *n* : an instrument (as a lie detector) for recording variations of several bodily functions (as blood pressure) simultaneously — **po·lyg·ra·pher** \pə-'li-grə-fər, 'pä-li-ˌgra-fər\ *n*

poly·he·dron \ˌpä-li-'hē-drən\ *n* : a solid formed by plane faces that are polygons — **poly·he·dral** \-drəl\ *adj*

poly·math \'pä-li-ˌmath\ *n* : a person of encyclopedic learning

poly·mer \'pä-lə-mər\ *n* : a chemical compound formed by union of small molecules and usu. consisting of repeating structural units — **poly·mer·ic** \ˌpä-lə-'mer-ik\ *adj*

po·lym·er·i·za·tion \pə-ˌli-mə-rə-'zā-shən\ *n* : a chemical reaction in which two or more small molecules combine to form polymers — **po·lym·er·ize** \pə-'li-mə-ˌrīz\ *vb*

Poly·ne·sian \ˌpä-lə-'nē-zhən\ *n* 1 : a member of any of the indigenous peoples of Polynesia 2 : a group of Austronesian languages spoken in Polynesia — **Polynesian** *adj*

poly·no·mi·al \ˌpä-lə-'nō-mē-əl\ *n* : an algebraic expression having one or more terms each of which consists of a constant multiplied by one or more variables raised to a nonnegative integral power — **polynomial** *adj*

pol·yp \'pä-ləp\ *n* 1 : an invertebrate animal (as a coral) that is a coelenterate having a hollow cylindrical body closed at one end 2 : a growth projecting from a mucous membrane (as of the colon or vocal cords)

po·lyph·o·ny \pə-'li-fə-nē\ *n* : music consisting of two or more melodically independent but harmonizing voice parts — **poly·phon·ic** \ˌpä-li-'fä-nik\ *adj*

poly·pro·pyl·ene \ˌpä-lē-'prō-pə-ˌlēn\ *n* : any of various polymer plastics or fibers

poly·sty·rene \ˌpä-li-'stī-ˌrēn\ *n* : a rigid transparent nonconducting thermoplastic used esp. in molded products and foams

poly·syl·lab·ic \-sə-'la-bik\ *adj* 1 : having more than three syllables 2 : characterized by polysyllabic words

poly·syl·la·ble \'pä-li-ˌsi-bəl\ *n* : a polysyllabic word

poly·tech·nic \ˌpä-li-'tek-nik\ *adj* : of, relating to, or instructing in many technical arts or applied sciences

poly·the·ism \'pä-li-thē-ˌi-zəm\ *n* : belief in or worship of many gods — **poly·the·ist** \-ˌthē-ist\ *adj or n* — **poly·the·is·tic** \ˌpä-li-thē-'is-tik\ *adj*

poly·un·sat·u·rat·ed \ˌpä-lē-ˌən-'sa-chə-ˌrā-təd\ *adj* : having many double or triple bonds in a molecule — used esp. of an oil or fatty acid

poly·ure·thane \ˌpä-lē-'yùr-ə-ˌthān\ *n* : any of various polymers used esp. in foams and in resins (as for coatings)

poly·vi·nyl \ˌpä-li-'vī-nᵊl\ *adj* : of, relating to, or being a polymerized vinyl compound, resin, or plastic — often used in combination

pome·gran·ate \'pä-mə-ˌgra-nət\ *n* [ME *poumgrenet*, fr. AF *pome garnette*, lit., seedy fruit] : a many-seeded reddish fruit that has an edible crimson pulp and is borne by a tropical Asian tree; *also* : the tree

¹**pom·mel** \'pə-məl, 'pä-\ *n* 1 : the knob on the hilt of a sword 2 : the knoblike bulge at the front and top of a saddlebow

²**pom·mel** \'pə-məl\ *vb* **-meled** *or* **-melled**; **-mel·ing** *or* **-mel·ling** : PUMMEL

pomp \'pämp\ *n* 1 : brilliant display : SPLENDOR 2 : OSTENTATION

pom·pa·dour \'päm-pə-ˌdȯr\ *n* : a style of dressing the hair high over the forehead

pom·pa·no \'päm-pə-ˌnō, 'päm-\ *n, pl* **-no** *or* **-nos** : a narrow silvery fish of coastal waters of the western Atlantic

pom–pom \'päm-ˌpäm\ *n* 1 : an ornamental ball or tuft used on a cap or costume 2 : a fluffy ball flourished by cheerleaders

pom·pon \'päm-ˌpän\ *n* 1 : POM-POM 2 : a chrysanthemum or dahlia with small rounded flower heads

pomp·ous \'päm-pəs\ *adj* 1 : suggestive of pomp; *esp* : OSTENTATIOUS 2 : pretentiously dignified ⟨~ politicians⟩ 3 : excessively elevated or ornate ✦ **Synonyms** ARROGANT, MAGISTERIAL, SELF-IMPORTANT — **pom·pos·i·ty** \päm-'pä-sə-tē\ *n* — **pomp·ous·ly** *adv*

pon·cho \'pän-chō\ *n, pl* **ponchos** [AmerSp, fr. Mapuche (American Indian language of Chile)] 1 : a blanket with a slit in the middle for the head so that it can be worn as a garment 2 : a waterproof garment resembling a poncho

pond \'pänd\ *n* : a small body of water

pon·der \'pän-dər\ *vb* **pon·dered**; **pon·der·ing** 1 : to weigh in the mind 2 : to consider carefully

pon·der·o·sa pine \ˌpän-də-ˌrō-sə-, -zə-\ *n* : a tall pine of western No. America with long needles; *also* : its strong reddish wood

pon·der·ous \'pän-də-rəs\ *adj* 1 : of very great weight 2 : UNWIELDY, CLUMSY ⟨a ~ weapon⟩ 3 : oppressively dull ⟨a ~ speech⟩ ✦ **Synonyms** CUMBROUS, CUMBERSOME, WEIGHTY

pone \'pōn\ *n, Southern & Midland* : an oval-shaped cornmeal cake; *also* : corn bread in the form of pones

pon·iard \'pän-yərd\ *n* : DAGGER

pon·tiff \'pän-təf\ *n* : POPE — **pon·tif·i·cal** \pän-'ti-fi-kəl\ *adj*

¹**pon·tif·i·cate** \pän-'ti-fi-kət, -fə-ˌkāt\ *n* : the state, office, or term of office of a pontiff

²**pon·tif·i·cate** \pän-'ti-fə-ˌkāt\ *vb* **-cat·ed**; **-cat·ing** : to deliver dogmatic opinions

pon·toon \pän-'tün\ *n* 1 : a flat-bottomed boat 2 : a boat or float used in building a floating temporary bridge 3 : a float of a seaplane

po·ny \'pō-nē\ *n, pl* **ponies** : a small horse

po·ny·tail \-ˌtāl\ *n* : a style of arranging hair to resemble the tail of a pony

pooch \'püch\ *n* : DOG

poo·dle \'pü-dᵊl\ *n* [G *Pudel*, short for *Pudelhund*, fr. *pudeln* to splash + *Hund* dog] : any of a breed of active intelligent dogs with a dense curly solid-colored coat

pooh–pooh \'pü-'pü\ *also* **pooh** \'pü\ *vb* 1 : to express contempt or impatience 2 : DERIDE, SCORN ⟨~ed my idea⟩

¹**pool** \'pül\ *n* 1 : a small deep body of usu. fresh water 2 : a small body of standing liquid 3 : SWIMMING POOL

²**pool** *vb* : to form a pool

³**pool** *n* 1 : all the money bet on the result of a particular event 2 : any of several games of billiards played on a table having six pockets 3 : the amount contributed by the participants in a joint venture 4 : a combination between competing firms for mutual profit 5 : a readily available supply

⁴**pool** *vb* : to combine (as resources) in a common fund or effort

¹**poop** \'püp\ *n* : an enclosed superstructure at the stern of a ship

²**poop** *n, slang* : INFORMATION

poop deck *n* : a partial deck above a ship's main afterdeck

poor \'pùr\ *adj* 1 : lacking material possessions ⟨~ people⟩ 2 : less than adequate : MEAGER ⟨a ~ crop⟩ 3 : arousing pity ⟨you ~ thing⟩ 4 : inferior in quality or value 5 : UNPRODUCTIVE, BARREN ⟨~ soil⟩ 6 : fairly unsatisfactory ⟨~ prospects⟩; *also* : UNFAVORABLE ⟨~ opinion⟩ — **poor·ly** *adv*

poor boy *var of* PO'BOY

poor·house \'pùr-ˌhaùs\ *n* : a publicly supported home for needy or dependent persons

poor-mouth \-ˌmaùth, -ˌmaùth\ *vb* : to plead poverty as a defense or excuse

¹**pop** \'päp\ *vb* **popped**; **pop·ping** 1 : to go, come, enter, or issue forth suddenly or quickly ⟨~ into bed⟩ 2 : to put or thrust suddenly ⟨~ questions⟩ 3 : to burst or cause to burst with a sharp sound; *also* : to make a sharp sound 4 : to protrude from the sockets 5 : SHOOT 6 : to hit a pop-up

²**pop** n 1 : a sharp explosive sound 2 : SHOT 3 : SODA POP
³**pop** n : FATHER
⁴**pop** adj 1 : POPULAR ⟨∼ music⟩ 2 : of or relating to pop music ⟨∼ singer⟩ 3 : of or relating to the popular culture disseminated through the mass media ⟨∼ psychology⟩ 4 : of, relating to, or imitating pop art ⟨∼ painter⟩
⁵**pop** n : pop music or culture; also : POP ART
⁶**pop** abbr population
pop art n, often cap P&A : art in which commonplace objects (as comic strips or soup cans) are used as subject matter — **pop artist** n
¹**pop·corn** \'päp-ˌkȯrn\ n : a corn whose kernels burst open into a white starchy mass when heated; also : the burst kernels
²**popcorn** adj : having widespread appeal but little artistic merit ⟨∼ movies⟩
pope \'pōp\ n, often cap : the head of the Roman Catholic Church
pop–eyed \'päp-ˌīd\ adj : having eyes that bulge (as from disease)
pop fly n : POP-UP
pop·gun \'päp-ˌgən\ n : a toy gun for shooting pellets with compressed air
pop·in·jay \'pä-pən-ˌjā\ n [ME papejay parrot, fr. MF papegai, papejai, fr. Ar babghāʾ] : a strutting supercilious person
pop·lar \'pä-plər\ n 1 : any of a genus of slender quick-growing trees (as a cottonwood) related to the willows 2 : the wood of a poplar
pop·lin \'pä-plən\ n : a strong plain-woven fabric with crosswise ribs
pop·over \'päp-ˌō-vər\ n : a hollow muffin made from a thin batter rich in egg
pop·per \'pä-pər\ n : a utensil for popping corn
pop·py \'pä-pē\ n, pl **poppies** : any of a genus of herbs with showy flowers including one that yields opium
pop·py·cock \-ˌkäk\ n : empty talk or writing : NONSENSE
pop·u·lace \'pä-pyə-ləs\ n 1 : the common people 2 : POPULATION
pop·u·lar \'pä-pyə-lər\ adj 1 : of or relating to the general public ⟨∼ government⟩ 2 : suited to the tastes of the general public ⟨∼ style⟩ 3 : INEXPENSIVE ⟨∼ rates⟩ 4 : frequently encountered or widely accepted ⟨∼ notion⟩ 5 : commonly liked or approved ⟨a ∼ teacher⟩ — **pop·u·lar·i·ty** \ˌpä-pyə-ˈla-rə-tē\ n — **pop·u·lar·ize** \'pä-pyə-lə-ˌrīz\ vb — **pop·u·lar·ly** adv
pop·u·late \'pä-pyə-ˌlāt\ vb **-lat·ed; -lat·ing** 1 : to have a place in : INHABIT 2 : PEOPLE
pop·u·la·tion \ˌpä-pyə-ˈlā-shən\ n 1 : the people or number of people in an area 2 : the organisms inhabiting a particular locality 3 : a group of individuals or items from which samples are taken for statistical measurement
population explosion n : a pyramiding of numbers of a biological population; esp : the recent great increase in human numbers resulting from increased survival and exponential population growth
pop·u·list \'pä-pyə-list\ n : a believer in or advocate of the rights, wisdom, or virtues of the common people — **pop·u·lism** \-ˌli-zəm\ n
pop·u·lous \'pä-pyə-ləs\ adj 1 : densely populated; also : having a large population 2 : CROWDED — **pop·u·lous·ness** n
¹**pop–up** \'päp-ˌəp\ n : a short high fly in baseball
²**pop–up** adj : of, relating to, or having a component or device that pops up
por·ce·lain \'pȯr-sə-lən\ n : a fine-grained translucent ceramic ware
porch \'pȯrch\ n : a covered entrance usu. with a separate roof
por·cine \'pȯr-ˌsīn\ adj : of, relating to, or suggesting swine
por·ci·ni \pȯr-ˈchē-nē\ n, pl **porcini** [It] : a large edible brownish mushroom
por·ci·no \pȯr-ˈchē-nō\ n, pl **-ni** : PORCINI
por·cu·pine \'pȯr-kyə-ˌpīn\ n [ME porke despyne, fr. MF porc espin, fr. It porcospino, fr. L porcus pig + spina spine, prickle] : any of various mammals having stiff sharp spines mingled with their hair
¹**pore** \'pȯr\ vb **pored; por·ing** 1 : to read studiously or attentively ⟨∼ over a book⟩ 2 : PONDER, REFLECT
²**pore** n : a tiny hole or space (as in the skin or soil) — **pored** \'pȯrd\ adj

pork \'pȯrk\ n : the flesh of swine dressed for use as food
pork barrel n : government projects or appropriations yielding rich patronage benefits
pork·er \'pȯr-kər\ n : HOG; esp : a young pig suitable for use as fresh pork
por·nog·ra·phy \pȯr-ˈnä-grə-fē\ n : the depiction of erotic behavior intended to cause sexual excitement — **por·no·graph·ic** \ˌpȯr-nə-ˈgra-fik\ adj
po·rous \'pȯr-əs\ adj 1 : full of pores 2 : permeable to fluids : ABSORPTIVE — **po·ros·i·ty** \pə-ˈrä-sə-tē\ n
por·phy·ry \'pȯr-fə-rē\ n, pl **-ries** : a rock consisting of feldspar crystals embedded in a compact fine-grained base material — **por·phy·rit·ic** \ˌpȯr-fə-ˈri-tik\ adj
por·poise \'pȯr-pəs\ n [ME porpoys, fr. AF porpeis, fr. ML porcopiscis, fr. L porcus pig + piscis fish] : any of a family of small gregarious blunt-snouted whales with spadelike teeth; also : DOLPHIN 1

porpoise

por·ridge \'pȯr-ij\ n : a soft food made by boiling meal of grains or legumes in milk or water
por·rin·ger \'pȯr-ən-jər\ n : a low one-handled metal bowl or cup
¹**port** \'pȯrt\ n 1 : HARBOR 2 : a city with a harbor 3 : AIRPORT
²**port** n 1 : an inlet or outlet (as in an engine) for a fluid 2 : PORTHOLE 3 : JACK 7
³**port** vb : to turn or put a helm to the left
⁴**port** n : the left side of a ship or airplane looking forward — **port** adj
⁵**port** n : a sweet fortified wine
portabella or **portabello** var of PORTOBELLO
por·ta·bil·i·ty \ˌpȯr-tə-ˈbil-ə-tē\ n, pl **-ties** 1 : the quality or state of being portable 2 : the ability to transfer benefits from one pension fund to another when a worker changes jobs
por·ta·ble \'pȯr-tə-bəl\ adj : capable of being carried — **portable** n
¹**por·tage** \'pȯr-tij, pȯr-ˈtäzh\ n [ME, fr. AF, fr. porter to carry] : the carrying of boats and goods overland between navigable bodies of water; also : a route for such carrying
²**portage** vb **por·taged; por·tag·ing** : to carry gear over a portage
por·tal \'pȯr-tᵊl\ n : DOOR, ENTRANCE; esp : a grand or imposing one
portal–to–portal adj : of or relating to the time spent by a worker in traveling from the entrance to an employer's property to the worker's actual job site (as in a mine)
port·cul·lis \pȯrt-ˈkə-ləs\ n : a grating at the gateway of a castle or fortress that can be let down to stop entrance
porte co·chere \ˌpȯrt-kō-ˈsher\ n [F porte cochère, lit., coach door] : a roofed structure extending from the entrance of a building over an adjacent driveway and sheltering those getting in or out of vehicles
por·tend \pȯr-ˈtend\ vb 1 : to give a sign or warning of beforehand 2 : INDICATE, SIGNIFY ♦ *Synonyms* AUGUR, PROGNOSTICATE, FORETELL, PREDICT, FORECAST, PROPHESY
por·tent \'pȯr-ˌtent\ n 1 : something that foreshadows a coming event : OMEN 2 : MARVEL, PRODIGY
por·ten·tous \pȯr-ˈten-təs\ adj 1 : of, relating to, or constituting a portent 2 : PRODIGIOUS 3 : self-consciously solemn : POMPOUS
¹**por·ter** \'pȯr-tər\ n, chiefly Brit : DOORKEEPER
²**porter** n 1 : a person who carries burdens; esp : one employed (as at a terminal) to carry baggage 2 : an attendant in a railroad car 3 : a dark heavy ale
por·ter·house \'pȯr-tər-ˌhau̇s\ n : a choice beefsteak with a large tenderloin

port·fo·lio \pòrt-'fō-lē-ˌō\ *n, pl* **-li·os** **1** : a portable case for papers or drawings **2** : the office and functions of a minister of state **3** : the securities held by an investor
port·hole \'pòrt-ˌhōl\ *n* : an opening (as a window) in the side of a ship or aircraft
por·ti·co \'pòr-ti-ˌkō\ *n, pl* **-coes** *or* **-cos** [It] : a row of columns supporting a roof around or at the entrance of a building
¹**por·tion** \'pòr-shən\ *n* **1** : one's part or share ⟨a ∼ of food⟩ **2** : DOWRY **3** : an individual's lot **4** : a part of a whole ⟨a ∼ of the sky⟩
²**portion** *vb* **1** : to divide into portions **2** : to allot to as a portion
port·land cement \'pòrt-lənd-\ *n* : a cement made by calcining and grinding a mixture of clay and limestone
port·ly \'pòrt-lē\ *adj* **port·li·er; -est** : somewhat stout
port·man·teau \pòrt-'man-ˌtō\ *n, pl* **-teaus** *or* **-teaux** \-ˌtōz\ [MF *portemanteau,* fr. *porter* to carry + *manteau* mantle, fr. L *mantellum*] : a large traveling bag
por·to·bel·lo \pòr-tə-'be-lō\ *also* **por·ta·bel·la** \-lə\ *or* **por·ta·bel·lo** \-lō\ *n, pl* **-los** *also* **-las** : a large dark mature mushroom noted for its meaty texture
port of call : an intermediate port where ships customarily stop for supplies, repairs, or transshipment of cargo
port of entry **1** : a place where foreign goods may be cleared through a customhouse **2** : a place where an alien may enter a country
por·trait \'pòr-trət, -ˌträt\ *n* : a picture (as a painting or photograph) of a person usu. showing the face — **por·trait·ist** \-trə-tist\ *n*
por·trai·ture \'pòr-trə-ˌchùr\ *n* : the practice or art of making portraits
por·tray \pòr-'trā\ *vb* **1** : to make a picture of : DEPICT **2** : to describe in words **3** : to play the role of — **por·tray·al** *n*
Por·tu·guese \'pòr-chə-ˌgēz, -ˌgēs; ˌpòr-chə-'gēz, -'gēs\ *n, pl* **Portuguese** **1** : a native or inhabitant of Portugal **2** : the language of Portugal and Brazil — **Portuguese** *adj*
Portuguese man–of–war *n* : any of several large colonial marine invertebrate animals related to the jellyfishes and having a large sac by which the colony floats at the surface
por·tu·la·ca \ˌpòr-chə-'la-kə\ *n* : any of a genus of succulent herbs cultivated for their showy flowers
pos *abbr* **1** position **2** positive
¹**pose** \'pōz\ *vb* **posed; pos·ing** **1** : to assume or cause to assume a posture usu. for artistic purposes **2** : to set forth : PROPOSE ⟨∼ a question⟩ **3** : to affect an attitude or character
²**pose** *n* **1** : a sustained posture; *esp* : one assumed by a model **2** : an attitude assumed for effect : PRETENSE
¹**pos·er** \'pō-zər\ *n* : a puzzling question
²**poser** *n* : a person who poses
po·seur \pō-'zər\ *n* [F, lit., poser] : an affected or insincere person
posh \'päsh\ *adj* : FASHIONABLE ⟨a ∼ restaurant⟩
pos·it \'pä-zət\ *vb* : to assume the existence of : POSTULATE
po·si·tion \pə-'zi-shən\ *n* **1** : an arranging in order **2** : the stand taken on a question **3** : the point or area occupied by something : SITUATION **4** : a certain arrangement of bodily parts ⟨exercise in a sitting ∼⟩ **5** : RANK, STATUS **6** : EMPLOYMENT, JOB — **position** *vb* — **po·si·tion·al** \-shə-nəl\ *adj*
¹**pos·i·tive** \'pä-zə-tiv\ *adj* **1** : expressed definitely ⟨her answer was a ∼ no⟩ **2** : CONFIDENT, CERTAIN ⟨∼ it was my book⟩ **3** : of, relating to, or constituting the degree of grammatical comparison that denotes no increase in quality, quantity, or relation **4** : not fictitious : REAL **5** : active and effective in function ⟨∼ leadership⟩ **6** : having the light and shade as existing in the original subject ⟨a ∼ photograph⟩ **7** : numerically greater than zero ⟨a ∼ number⟩ **8** : being, relating to, or charged with electricity of which the proton is the elementary unit **9** : AFFIRMATIVE ⟨a ∼ response⟩ **10** : FAVORABLE; *also* : marked by optimism ⟨a ∼ attitude⟩ — **pos·i·tive·ly** *adv* — **pos·i·tive·ness** *n*
²**positive** *n* **1** : the positive degree or a positive form in a language **2** : a positive photograph
pos·i·tron \'pä-zə-ˌträn\ *n* : a positively charged particle having the same mass and magnitude of charge as the electron

po·so·le *or* **po·zo·le** \pō-'sō-lā\ *n* : a thick Mexican soup made with pork, hominy, garlic, and chili
poss *abbr* possessive
pos·se \'pä-sē\ *n* [ML *posse comitatus,* lit., power or authority of the county] **1** : a body of persons organized to assist a sheriff in an emergency **2** : a body of attendants or followers
pos·sess \pə-'zes\ *vb* **1** : to have as property : OWN **2** : to have as an attribute, knowledge, or skill **3** : to enter into and control firmly ⟨∼ed by a devil⟩ — **pos·ses·sor** \-'ze-sər\ *n*
pos·ses·sion \-'ze-shən\ *n* **1** : control or occupancy of property **2** : OWNERSHIP **3** : something owned : PROPERTY **4** : domination by something (as an evil spirit, a passion, or an idea) **5** : SELF-CONTROL
pos·ses·sive \pə-'ze-siv\ *adj* **1** : of, relating to, or constituting a grammatical case denoting ownership **2** : showing the desire to possess ⟨a ∼ nature⟩ — **possessive** *n* — **pos·ses·sive·ness** *n*
pos·si·ble \'pä-sə-bəl\ *adj* **1** : being within the limits of ability, capacity, or realization **2** : being something that may or may not occur ⟨∼ dangers⟩ **3** : able or fitted to become ⟨a ∼ site for a bridge⟩ — **pos·si·bil·i·ty** \ˌpä-sə-'bi-lə-tē\ *n* — **pos·si·bly** \'pä-sə-blē\ *adv*
pos·sum \'pä-səm\ *n* : OPOSSUM
¹**post** \'pōst\ *n* **1** : an upright piece of timber or metal serving esp. as a support : PILLAR **2** : a pole or stake set up as a mark or indicator
²**post** *vb* **1** : to affix to a usual place (as a wall) for public notices **2** : to publish or announce by or as if by a public notice ⟨∼ grades⟩ **3** : to forbid (property) to trespassers by putting up a notice **4** : SCORE **4** ⟨∼ed a 70 in the final round⟩ **5** : to publish in an online forum
³**post** *n* **1** *obs* : COURIER **2** *chiefly Brit* : ¹MAIL; *also* : POST OFFICE **3** : something that is published online
⁴**post** *vb* **1** : to ride or travel with haste : HURRY **2** : MAIL ⟨∼ a letter⟩ **3** : to enter in a ledger **4** : INFORM ⟨kept him ∼ed on new developments⟩
⁵**post** *n* **1** : the place at which a soldier is stationed; *esp* : a sentry's beat or station **2** : a station or task to which a person is assigned **3** : the place at which a body of troops is stationed : CAMP **4** : OFFICE, POSITION **5** : a trading settlement or station
⁶**post** *vb* **1** : to station in a given place **2** : to put up (as bond)
post·age \'pōs-tij\ *n* : the fee for postal service; *also* : stamps representing this fee
post·al \'pōs-t⁸l\ *adj* : of or relating to the mails or the post office
postal card *n* : POSTCARD
postal service *n* : a government agency or department handling the transmission of mail
¹**post·card** \'pōst-ˌkärd\ *n* : a card on which a message may be written for mailing without an envelope
²**postcard** *adj* : PICTURESQUE
post chaise *n* : a 4-wheeled closed carriage for two to four persons
post·con·sum·er \ˌpōst-kən-'sü-mər\ *adj* **1** : discarded by a consumer **2** : having been used and recycled for reuse in another product
post·date \pōst-'dāt\ *vb* : to date with a date later than that of execution ⟨∼ a check⟩
post·doc·tor·al \-'däk-tə-rəl\ *also* **post·doc·tor·ate** \-tə-rət\ *adj* : of, relating to, or engaged in advanced academic or professional work beyond a doctor's degree
post·er \'pō-stər\ *n* : a bill or placard for posting often in a public place
¹**pos·te·ri·or** \pō-'stir-ē-ər, pä-\ *adj* **1** : later in time **2** : situated behind
²**pos·te·ri·or** \pä-'stir-ē-ər, pō-\ *n* : the hinder bodily parts; *esp* : BUTTOCKS
pos·ter·i·ty \pä-'ster-ə-tē\ *n* **1** : the descendants from one ancestor **2** : all future generations
pos·tern \'pōs-tərn, 'päs-\ *n* **1** : a back door or gate **2** : a private or side entrance
post exchange *n* : a store at a military post that sells to military personnel and authorized civilians
post·grad \'pōst-ˌgrad\ *adj* : POSTGRADUATE
post·grad·u·ate \(ˌ)pōst-'gra-jə-wət\ *adj* : of or relating to studies beyond the bachelor's degree — **postgraduate** *n*
post·haste \'pōst-'hāst\ *adv* : with all possible speed

post·hole \-ˌhōl\ *n* : a hole for a post and esp. a fence post

post·hu·mous \'päs-chə-məs\ *adj* [L *posthumus*, alter. of *postumus* last-born, posthumous, fr. superl. of *posterus* coming after] **1** : born after the death of the father **2** : published after the death of the author — **post·hu·mous·ly** *adv*

post·hyp·not·ic \ˌpōst-hip-'nä-tik\ *adj* : of, relating to, or characteristic of the period following a hypnotic trance

pos·til·ion *or* **pos·til·lion** \pō-'stil-yən\ *n* : a rider on the left-hand horse of a pair drawing a coach

Post·im·pres·sion·ism \ˌpōst-im-'pre-shə-ˌni-zəm\ *n* : a late 19th century French theory or practice of art that stresses variously volume, picture structure, or expressionism

post·lude \'pōst-ˌlüd\ *n* : an organ solo played at the end of a church service

post·man \-mən, -ˌman\ *n* : MAILMAN

post·mark \-ˌmärk\ *n* : an official postal marking on a piece of mail; *esp* : the mark canceling the postage stamp — **postmark** *vb*

post·mas·ter \-ˌmas-tər\ *n* : a person who has charge of a post office

postmaster general *n, pl* **postmasters general** : an official in charge of a national postal service

post·men·o·paus·al \ˌpōst-ˌme-nə-'pò-zəl\ *adj* **1** : having undergone menopause **2** : occurring or administered after menopause

post me·ri·di·em \ˌpōst-mə-'ri-dē-əm\ *adj* [L] : being after noon

post·mis·tress \'pōst-ˌmis-trəs\ *n* : a woman who is a postmaster

post·mod·ern \ˌpōst-'mä-dərn\ *adj* : of, relating to, or being any of various movements in reaction to modernism

¹post·mor·tem \ˌpōst-'mòr-təm\ *adj* [L *post mortem* after death] **1** : done, occurring, or collected after death ⟨a ∼ examination⟩ **2** : following the event

²postmortem *n* **1** : AUTOPSY **2** : an analysis or discussion of an event after it is over ⟨a ∼ of the election⟩

post·na·sal drip \'pōst-ˌnā-zəl-\ *n* : flow of mucous secretion from the posterior part of the nasal cavity onto the wall of the pharynx

post·na·tal \(ˌ)pōst-'nā-t⁰l\ *adj* : occurring or being after birth; *esp* : of or relating to a newborn infant

post office *n* **1** : POSTAL SERVICE **2** : a local branch of a post office department

post·op·er·a·tive \(ˌ)pōst-'ä-prə-tiv, -pə-ˌrā-\ *adj* : following or having undergone a surgical operation ⟨∼ care⟩

post·paid \'pōst-'pād\ *adj* : having the postage paid by the sender and not chargeable to the receiver

post·par·tum \(ˌ)pōst-'pär-təm\ *adj* [NL *post partum* after birth] : following parturition — **postpartum** *adv*

post·pone \pōst-'pōn\ *vb* **post·poned; post·pon·ing** : to put off to a later time — **post·pone·ment** *n*

post road *n* : a road over which mail is carried

post·script \'pōst-ˌskript\ *n* : a note added esp. to a completed letter

post time *n* : the designated time for the start of a horse race

post–traumatic *adj* : occurring after or as a result of trauma ⟨∼ stress⟩

pos·tu·lant \'päs-chə-lənt\ *n* : a probationary candidate for membership in a religious order

¹pos·tu·late \'päs-chə-ˌlāt\ *vb* **-lat·ed; -lat·ing** : to assume as true

²pos·tu·late \'päs-chə-lət, -ˌlāt\ *n* : a proposition taken for granted as true esp. as a basis for a chain of reasoning

¹pos·ture \'päs-chər\ *n* **1** : the position or bearing of the body or one of its parts **2** : STATE, CONDITION **3** : ATTITUDE ⟨a ∼ of arrogance⟩

²posture *vb* **pos·tured; pos·tur·ing** : to strike a pose esp. for effect

post·war \'pōst-'wòr\ *adj* : occurring or existing after a war

po·sy \'pō-zē\ *n, pl* **posies 1** : a brief sentiment : MOTTO **2** : a bunch of flowers; *also* : FLOWER

¹pot \'pät\ *n* **1** : a rounded container used chiefly for domestic purposes **2** : the total of the bets at stake at one time **3** : RUIN ⟨go to ∼⟩ — **pot·ful** *n*

²pot *vb* **pot·ted; pot·ting 1** : to preserve or place in a pot **2** : SHOOT

³pot *n* : MARIJUANA

po·ta·ble \'pō-tə-bəl\ *adj* : suitable for drinking — **po·ta·bil·i·ty** \ˌpō-tə-'bi-lə-tē\ *n*

po·tage \pò-'täzh\ *n* : a thick soup

pot·ash \'pät-ˌash\ *n* [sing. of *pot ashes*] : potassium or any of its various compounds esp. as used in agriculture

po·tas·si·um \pə-'ta-sē-əm\ *n* : a silver-white soft metallic chemical element that occurs abundantly in nature

potassium bromide *n* : a crystalline salt used as a sedative and in photography

potassium carbonate *n* : a white salt used in making glass and soap

potassium nitrate *n* : a soluble salt used in making gunpowder, as a fertilizer, and in medicine

po·ta·tion \pō-'tā-shən\ *n* : a usu. alcoholic drink; *also* : the act of drinking

po·ta·to \pə-'tā-tō\ *n, pl* **-toes** : the edible starchy tuber of a plant related to the tomato; *also* : this plant

potato beetle *n* : COLORADO POTATO BEETLE

potato bug *n* : COLORADO POTATO BEETLE

potbellied pig *n* : any of an Asian breed of small pigs having a straight tail, potbelly, and black, white, or black and white coat

pot·bel·ly \'pät-ˌbe-lē\ *n* : a protruding abdomen — **pot·bel·lied** \-lēd\ *adj*

pot·boil·er \-ˌbòi-lər\ *n* : a usu. inferior work of art or literature produced chiefly for profit

po·tent \'pō-t⁰nt\ *adj* **1** : having authority or influence : POWERFUL **2** : chemically or medicinally effective **3** : able to copulate — used esp. of the male ♦ *Synonyms* FORCEFUL, FORCIBLE, MIGHTY, PUISSANT — **po·ten·cy** \-t⁰n-sē\ *n*

po·ten·tate \'pō-t⁰n-ˌtāt\ *n* : one who wields controlling power : RULER

¹po·ten·tial \pə-'ten-chəl\ *adj* : existing in possibility : capable of becoming actual ⟨a ∼ champion⟩ ♦ *Synonyms* DORMANT, LATENT, QUIESCENT — **po·ten·ti·al·i·ty** \pə-ˌten-chē-'a-lə-tē\ *n* — **po·ten·tial·ly** \-'ten-chə-lē\ *adv*

²potential *n* **1** : something that can develop or become actual ⟨a ∼ for violence⟩ **2** : the work required to move a unit positive charge from infinity to a point in question; *also* : POTENTIAL DIFFERENCE

potential difference *n* : the difference in potential between two points that represents the work involved in the transfer of a unit quantity of electricity from one point to the other

potential energy *n* : the energy an object has because of its position or nature or the arrangement of its parts

po·ten·ti·ate \pə-'ten-chē-ˌāt\ *vb* **-at·ed; -at·ing** : to make potent; *esp* : to augment the activity of (as a drug) synergistically — **po·ten·ti·a·tion** \-ˌten-chē-'ā-shən\ *n*

pot·head \'pät-ˌhed\ *n* : a person who frequently smokes marijuana

poth·er \'pä-thər\ *n* : a noisy disturbance; *also* : FUSS

pot·herb \'pät-ˌərb, -ˌhərb\ *n* : an herb whose leaves or stems are boiled for greens or used to season food

pot·hole \'pät-ˌhōl\ *n* : a large pit or hole (as in a road surface)

pot·hook \-ˌhùk\ *n* : an S-shaped hook for hanging pots and kettles over an open fire

po·tion \'pō-shən\ *n* : a mixture of liquids (as liquor or medicine)

pot·luck \'pät-'lək\ *n* : the regular meal available to a guest for whom no special preparations have been made

pot·pie \-'pī\ *n* : pastry-covered meat and vegetables cooked in a deep dish

pot·pour·ri \ˌpō-pù-'rē\ *n* [F *pot pourri*, lit., rotten pot] **1** : a mixture of flowers, herbs, and spices used for scent **2** : a miscellaneous collection

pot·sherd \'pät-ˌshərd\ *n* : a pottery fragment

pot·shot \-ˌshät\ *n* **1** : a shot taken from ambush or at a random or easy target **2** : a critical remark made in a random or sporadic manner

pot sticker *n* : a crescent-shaped dumpling that is steamed and fried

pot·tage \'pä-tij\ *n* : a thick soup of vegetables and often meat

¹pot·ter \'pä-tər\ *n* : one that makes pottery

²potter *vb* : PUTTER

pot·tery \'pä-tə-rē\ *n, pl* **-ter·ies 1** : a place where earthen pots and dishes are made **2** : the art of the potter **3** : dishes, pots, and vases made from clay

pot·ty–mouthed \'pä-tē-ˌmau̇th̲d, -ˌmau̇tht\ *adj* : given to the use of vulgar language

¹pouch \'pau̇ch\ *n* [ME *pouche*, fr. AF, of Gmc origin; akin to OE *pocca* bag] **1** : a small bag (as for tobacco) carried on the person **2** : a bag for storing or transporting goods ⟨mail ∼⟩ ⟨diplomatic ∼⟩ **3** : an anatomical sac; *esp* : one for carrying the young on the abdomen of a female marsupial (as a kangaroo)

²pouch *vb* : to put or form into or as if into a pouch

poult \'pōlt\ *n* : a young fowl; *esp* : a young turkey

poul·ter·er \'pōl-tər-ər\ *n* : one that deals in poultry

poul·tice \'pōl-təs\ *n* : a soft usu. heated and medicated mass spread on cloth and applied to a sore or injury — **poultice** *vb*

poul·try \'pōl-trē\ *n* : domesticated birds kept for eggs or meat — **poul·try·man** \-mən\ *n*

pounce \'pau̇ns\ *vb* **pounced; pounc·ing** : to spring or swoop upon and seize something

¹pound \'pau̇nd\ *n, pl* **pounds** *also* **pound 1** : a unit of avoirdupois, troy, and apothecaries' weight — see WEIGHT table **2** — see MONEY table **3** : the former basic monetary unit of Ireland **4** : LIRA 3

²pound *n* : a public enclosure where stray animals are kept

³pound *vb* **1** : to crush to a powder or pulp by beating **2** : to strike or beat heavily or repeatedly **3** : DRILL 1 **4** : to move or move along heavily

pound·age \'pau̇n-dij\ *n* : POUNDS; *also* : weight in pounds

pound cake *n* : a rich cake made with a large proportion of eggs and shortening

pound–fool·ish \'pau̇nd-'fü-lish\ *adj* : imprudent in dealing with large sums or large matters

pour \'pȯr\ *vb* **1** : to flow or cause to flow in a stream or flood **2** : to rain hard **3** : to supply freely and copiously

pout \'pau̇t\ *vb* : to show displeasure by thrusting out the lips; *also* : to look sullen — **pout** *n*

pov·er·ty \'pä-vər-tē\ *n* [ME *poverte*, fr. AF *poverté*, fr. L *paupertat-, paupertas*, fr. *pauper* poor] **1** : lack of money or material possessions : WANT **2** : poor quality (as of soil)

poverty line *n* : a level of personal or family income below which one is classified as poor according to government standards

pov·er·ty–strick·en \'pä-vər-tē-ˌstri-kən\ *adj* : very poor : DESTITUTE

POW \ˌpē-(ˌ)ō-'də-bəl-(ˌ)yü\ *n* : PRISONER OF WAR

¹pow·der \'pau̇-dər\ *vb* **1** : to sprinkle or cover with or as if with powder **2** : to reduce to powder

²powder *n* [ME *poudre*, fr. AF *pudre, podre*, fr. L *pulver-, pulvis* dust] **1** : dry material made up of fine particles; *also* : a usu. medicinal or cosmetic preparation in this form **2** : a solid explosive (as gunpowder) — **pow·dery** *adj*

powder room *n* : a rest room for women

¹pow·er \'pau̇(-ə)r\ *n* **1** : the ability to act or produce an effect **2** : a position of ascendancy over others : AUTHORITY **3** : one that has control or authority; *esp* : a sovereign state **4** : physical might; *also* : mental or moral vigor **5** : the number of times as indicated by an exponent that a number occurs as a factor in a product ⟨5 to the third ∼ is 125⟩; *also* : the product itself ⟨8 is a ∼ of 2⟩ **6** : force or energy used to do work; *also* : the time rate at which work is done or energy transferred **7** : MAGNIFICATION 2 — **pow·er·ful** \-fəl\ *adj* — **pow·er·ful·ly** *adv* — **pow·er·less** *adj*

²power *vb* : to supply with power and esp. motive power

³power *adj* **1** : operated mechanically or electrically rather than manually **2** : of, relating to, or utilizing strength

pow·er·boat \-'bōt\ *n* : MOTORBOAT

pow·er·house \'pau̇(-ə)r-ˌhau̇s\ *n* **1** : POWER PLANT 1 **2** : one having great drive, energy, or ability

power plant *n* **1** : a building in which electric power is generated **2** : an engine and related parts supplying the motive power of a self-propelled vehicle

pow·wow \'pau̇-ˌwau̇\ *n* **1** : a No. American Indian ceremony (as for victory in war) **2** : a meeting for discussion : CONFERENCE

pox \'päks\ *n, pl* **pox** *or* **pox·es** : any of various diseases (as smallpox or syphilis) marked by a rash on the skin

pozole *var of* POSOLE

pp *abbr* **1** pages **2** pianissimo

PP *abbr* **1** parcel post **2** past participle **3** postpaid **4** prepaid

ppd *abbr* **1** postpaid **2** prepaid

PPO \ˌpē-ˌpē-'ō\ *n, pl* **PPOs** [*p*referred *p*rovider *o*rganization] : a health-care organization that gives economic incentives to enrolled individuals who use certain health-care providers

PPS *abbr* [L *post postscriptum*] an additional postscript

ppt *abbr* precipitate

PQ *abbr* Province of Quebec

pr *abbr* **1** pair **2** price

Pr *symbol* praseodymium

¹PR *or* **p.r.** \'pē-'är\ *n* : PUBLIC RELATIONS

²PR *abbr* **1** payroll **2** public relations **3** Puerto Rico

prac·ti·ca·ble \'prak-ti-kə-bəl\ *adj* : capable of being put into practice, done, or accomplished ⟨a ∼ method⟩ — **prac·ti·ca·bil·i·ty** \ˌprak-ti-kə-'bi-lə-tē\ *n*

prac·ti·cal \'prak-ti-kəl\ *adj* **1** : of, relating to, or shown in practice ⟨∼ questions⟩ **2** : VIRTUAL ⟨∼ control⟩ **3** : capable of being put to use ⟨a ∼ knowledge of French⟩ **4** : inclined to action as opposed to speculation ⟨a ∼ person⟩ **5** : qualified by practice ⟨a good ∼ mechanic⟩ — **prac·ti·cal·i·ty** \ˌprak-ti-'ka-lə-tē\ *n* — **prac·ti·cal·ly** \-k(ə-)lē\ *adv*

practical joke *n* : a prank intended to trick or embarrass someone or cause physical discomfort

practical nurse *n* : a professional nurse without all of the qualifications of a registered nurse; *esp* : LICENSED PRACTICAL NURSE

¹prac·tice *also* **prac·tise** \'prak-təs\ *vb* **prac·ticed** *also* **prac·tised; prac·tic·ing** *also* **prac·tis·ing 1** : CARRY OUT, APPLY ⟨∼ what you preach⟩ **2** : to perform or work at repeatedly so as to become proficient ⟨∼ tennis strokes⟩ **3** : to do or perform customarily ⟨∼ politeness⟩ **4** : to be professionally engaged in ⟨∼ law⟩

²practice *also* **practise** *n* **1** : actual performance or application **2** : customary action : HABIT **3** : systematic exercise for proficiency **4** : the exercise of a profession; *also* : a professional business

prac·ti·tion·er \prak-'ti-shə-nər\ *n* : one who practices a profession

prae·tor \'prē-tər\ *n* : an ancient Roman magistrate ranking below a consul — **prae·to·ri·an** \prē-'tȯr-ē-ən\ *adj*

prag·mat·ic \prag-'ma-tik\ *also* **prag·mat·i·cal** \-ti-kəl\ *adj* **1** : of or relating to practical affairs **2** : concerned with the practical consequences of actions or beliefs ⟨a ∼ leader⟩ — **pragmatic** *n* — **prag·mat·i·cal·ly** \-ti-k(ə-)lē\ *adv*

prag·ma·tism \'prag-mə-ˌti-zəm\ *n* : a practical approach to problems and affairs

prai·rie \'prer-ē\ *n* [F, fr. OF *prairie*, fr. VL **prataria*, fr. L *pratum* meadow] : a broad tract of level or rolling grassland

prairie dog *n* : an American burrowing black-tailed rodent related to the squirrels and living in colonies

prairie schooner *n* : a covered wagon used by pioneers in cross-country travel

praise \'prāz\ *vb* **praised; prais·ing 1** : to express approval of : COMMEND **2** : to glorify (a divinity or a saint) esp. in song — **praise** *n*

praise·wor·thy \-ˌwər-th̲ē\ *adj* : LAUDABLE ⟨a ∼ effort⟩

pra·line \'prä-ˌlēn, 'prā-\ *n* [F] : a confection of nuts and sugar

pram \'pram\ *n, chiefly Brit* : PERAMBULATOR

prance \'prans\ *vb* **pranced; pranc·ing 1** : to spring from the hind legs ⟨a *prancing* horse⟩ **2** : SWAGGER; *also* : CAPER — **prance** *n* — **pranc·er** *n*

prank \'prank\ *n* : a playful or mildly mischievous act : TRICK

prank·ster \'prank-stər\ *n* : a person who plays pranks

pra·seo·dym·i·um \ˌprä-zē-ō-'di-mē-əm\ *n* : a yellowish white metallic chemical element

prate \'prāt\ *vb* **prat·ed; prat·ing** : to talk long and idly : chatter foolishly

prat·fall \'prat-ˌfȯl\ *n* **1** : a fall on the buttocks **2** : a humiliating blunder

¹prat·tle \'pra-tᵊl\ *vb* **prat·tled; prat·tling** : PRATE, BABBLE

²prattle *n* : trifling or childish talk

prawn \'prȯn\ *n* : any of various edible shrimplike crustaceans; *also* : SHRIMP 1 pray \'prā\ vb 1 : ENTREAT, IMPLORE 2 : to ask earnestly for something 3 : to address God or a god esp. with supplication

prayer \'prer\ n 1 : a supplication or expression addressed to God or a god; also : a set order of words used in praying 2 : an earnest request or wish 3 : the act or practice of praying to God or a god 4 : a religious service consisting chiefly of prayers — often used in pl. 5 : something prayed for 6 : a slight chance

prayer book n : a book containing prayers and often directions for worship

prayer·ful \'prer-fəl\ adj 1 : DEVOUT 2 : EARNEST — prayer·ful·ly adv

praying mantis n : MANTIS

PRC abbr People's Republic of China

preach \'prēch\ vb 1 : to deliver a sermon 2 : to set forth in a sermon 3 : to advocate earnestly ⟨~ed tolerance⟩ — preach·er n — preach·ment n

pre·ad·o·les·cence \'prē-,a-də-'le-sᵊns\ n : the period of human development just preceding adolescence — pre·ad·o·les·cent \-sᵊnt\ adj or n

pre·am·ble \'prē-,am-bəl\ n [ME, fr. MF preambule, fr. ML preambulum, fr. LL, neut. of praeambulus walking in front of, fr. L prae in front of + ambulare to walk] : an introductory part ⟨the ~ to a constitution⟩

pre·ap·prove \,prē-ə-'prüv\ vb : to approve in advance — pre·ap·prov·al \,prē-ə-'prü-vəl\ n

pre·ar·range \,prē-ə-'rānj\ vb : to arrange beforehand — pre·ar·range·ment n

pre·as·sign \,prē-ə-'sīn\ vb : to assign beforehand

pre·bake \,prē-'bāk\ vb : to bake in advance

Pre·cam·bri·an \'prē-'kam-brē-ən, -'käm-\ adj : of, relating to, or being the era that is earliest in geologic history and is characterized esp. by the appearance of single-celled organisms — Precambrian n

pre·can·cel \,(,)prē-'kan-səl\ vb : to cancel (a postage stamp) in advance of use — precancel n — pre·can·cel·la·tion \,prē-,kan-sə-'lā-shən\ n

pre·can·cer·ous \(,)prē-'kan-sə-rəs\ adj : likely to become cancerous

pre·car·i·ous \pri-'ker-ē-əs\ adj : dependent on uncertain conditions : dangerously insecure : UNSTABLE ⟨a ~ foothold⟩ ⟨~ prosperity⟩ ♦ Synonyms DELICATE, SENSITIVE, TICKLISH, TOUCHY, TRICKY — pre·car·i·ous·ly adv — pre·car·i·ous·ness n

pre·cau·tion \pri-'ko-shən\ n : a measure taken beforehand to prevent harm or secure good — pre·cau·tion·ary \-sha-,ner-ē\ adj

pre·cede \pri-'sēd\ vb pre·ced·ed; pre·ced·ing : to be, go, or come ahead or in front of (as in rank or time)

pre·ce·dence \'pre-sə-dəns, pri-'sēd-ᵊns\ n 1 : the act or fact of preceding 2 : consideration based on order of importance : PRIORITY

¹prec·e·dent \pri-'sē-dᵊnt, 'pre-sə-dənt\ adj : prior in time, order, or significance

²prec·e·dent \'pre-sə-dənt\ n : something said or done that may serve to authorize or justify further words or acts of the same or a similar kind

pre·ced·ing \pri-'sē-diŋ\ adj : that precedes ♦ Synonyms ANTECEDENT, FOREGOING, PRIOR, FORMER, ANTERIOR

pre·cen·tor \pri-'sen-tər\ n : a leader of the singing of a choir or congregation

pre·cept \'prē-,sept\ n : a command or principle intended as a general rule of action or conduct

pre·cep·tor \'prē-'sep-tər, pri-'sep-\ n : TUTOR

pre·ces·sion \prē-'se-shən\ n : a slow gyration of the rotation axis of a spinning body (as the earth) — pre·cess \prē-'ses\ vb — pre·ces·sion·al \-'sə-shə-nəl\ adj

pre·cinct \'prē-,siŋkt\ n 1 : an administrative subdivision (as of a city) : DISTRICT ⟨police ~⟩ ⟨electoral ~⟩ 2 : an enclosure bounded by the limits of a building or place — often used in pl. 3 pl : ENVIRONS

pre·ci·os·i·ty \,pre-shē-'ä-sə-tē\ n, pl -ties : fastidious refinement

pre·cious \'pre-shəs\ adj 1 : of great value ⟨~ jewels⟩ 2 : greatly cherished : DEAR ⟨~ memories⟩ 3 : AFFECTED ⟨~ language⟩

prec·i·pice \'pre-sə-pəs\ n : a steep cliff

pre·cip·i·tan·cy \pri-'si-pə-tən-sē\ n : undue hastiness or suddenness

¹pre·cip·i·tate \pri-'si-pə-,tāt\ vb -tat·ed; -tat·ing [L praecipitare, fr. praecipit-, praeceps headlong, fr. prae in front of + caput head] 1 : to throw violently 2 : to throw down 3 : to cause to happen quickly or abruptly ⟨~ a quarrel⟩ 4 : to cause to separate from solution or suspension 5 : to fall as rain, snow, or hail ♦ Synonyms SPEED, ACCELERATE, QUICKEN, HASTEN, HURRY

²pre·cip·i·tate \pri-'si-pə-tət, -,tāt\ n : the solid matter that separates from a solution or suspension

³pre·cip·i·tate \pri-'si-pə-tət\ adj 1 : showing extreme or unwise haste : RASH 2 : falling with steep descent; also : PRECIPITOUS — pre·cip·i·tate·ly adv — pre·cip·i·tate·ness n

pre·cip·i·ta·tion \pri-,si-pə-'tā-shən\ n 1 : rash haste 2 : the process of precipitating or forming a precipitate 3 : water that falls to earth esp. as rain or snow; also : the quantity of this water

pre·cip·i·tous \pri-'si-pə-təs\ adj 1 : PRECIPITATE 2 : having the character of a precipice : very steep ⟨a ~ slope⟩; also : containing precipices ⟨~ trails⟩ — pre·cip·i·tous·ly adv

pré·cis \prā-'sē\ n, pl pré·cis \-'sēz\ [F] : a concise summary of essentials

pre·cise \pri-'sīs\ adj 1 : exactly defined or stated : DEFINITE 2 : highly accurate : EXACT 3 : conforming strictly to a standard : SCRUPULOUS ⟨a ~ teacher⟩ — pre·cise·ly adv — pre·cise·ness n

pre·ci·sion \pri-'si-zhən\ n : the quality or state of being precise

pre·clude \pri-'klüd\ vb pre·clud·ed; pre·clud·ing : to make impossible : BAR, PREVENT

pre·co·cious \pri-'kō-shəs\ adj [L praecoc-, praecox, lit., ripening early, fr. prae- ahead + coquere to cook] : early in development and esp. in mental development — pre·co·cious·ly adv — pre·coc·i·ty \pri-'kä-sə-tē\ n

pre·con·ceive \,prē-kən-'sēv\ vb : to form an opinion of beforehand — pre·con·cep·tion \-'sep-shən\ n

pre·con·di·tion \-'di-shən\ vb : to put in proper or desired condition or frame of mind in advance

pre·cook \,prē-'kúk\ vb : to cook partially or entirely before final cooking or reheating

pre·cur·sor \pri-'kər-sər\ n : one that precedes and indicates the approach of another : FORERUNNER

pred abbr predicate

pre·da·ceous or pre·da·cious \pri-'dā-shəs\ adj : living by preying on others : PREDATORY

pre·date \'prē-'dāt\ vb : ANTEDATE

pre·da·tion \pri-'dā-shən\ n 1 : the act of preying or plundering 2 : a mode of life in which food is primarily obtained by killing and consuming animals

pred·a·tor \'pre-də-tər\ n : an animal that lives by predation

pred·a·to·ry \'pre-də-,tór-ē\ adj 1 : of or relating to plunder ⟨~ warfare⟩ 2 : disposed to exploit others 3 : preying upon other animals

pre·dawn \(,)prē-'dón\ adj : of or relating to the time just before dawn

pre·de·cease \,prē-di-'sēs\ vb -ceased; -ceas·ing : to die before another person

pre·de·ces·sor \'pre-də-,se-sər, 'prē-\ n : a previous holder of a position to which another has succeeded

pre·des·ig·nate \(,)prē-'de-zig-,nāt\ vb : to designate beforehand

pre·des·ti·na·tion \,prē-,des-tə-'nā-shən\ n : the act of foreordaining to an earthly lot or eternal destiny by divine decree; also : the state of being so foreordained — pre·des·ti·nate \prē-'des-tə-,nāt\ vb

pre·des·tine \prē-'des-tən\ vb : to settle beforehand : FOREORDAIN

pre·de·ter·mine \,prē-di-'tər-mən\ vb : to determine beforehand

pre·dic·a·ment \pri-'di-kə-mənt\ n : a difficult or trying situation ♦ Synonyms DILEMMA, PICKLE, QUAGMIRE, JAM

¹pred·i·cate \'pre-di-kət\ n : the part of a sentence or clause that expresses what is said of the subject

²pred·i·cate \'pre-də-,kāt\ vb -cat·ed; -cat·ing 1 : AFFIRM 2 : to assert to be a quality or attribute 3 : FOUND, BASE — usu. used with on — pred·i·ca·tion \,pre-də-'kā-shən\ n

pre·dict \pri-'dikt\ vb : to declare in advance — pre·dict·abil·i·ty \-,dik-tə-'bi-lə-tē\ n — pre·dict·able \-'dik-tə-bəl\ *adj* — **pre·dict·ably** \-blē\ *adv* — **pre·dic·tion** \-'dik-shən\ *n*

pre·di·gest \ˌprē-dī-'jest\ *vb* : to simplify for easy use; *also* : to subject to artificial or natural partial digestion

pre·di·lec·tion \ˌpre-də-'lek-shən, ˌprē-\ *n* : an established preference for something

pre·dis·pose \ˌprē-di-'spōz\ *vb* : to incline in advance : make susceptible ⟨was *predisposed* to infection⟩ — **pre·dis·po·si·tion** \ˌprē-ˌdis-pə-'zi-shən\ *n*

pre·dom·i·nant \pri-'dä-mə-nənt\ *adj* : greater in importance, strength, influence, or authority — **pre·dom·i·nance** \-nəns\ *n*

pre·dom·i·nant·ly \-nənt-lē\ *adv* : for the most part : MAINLY

pre·dom·i·nate \pri-'dä-mə-ˌnāt\ *vb* : to be superior esp. in power or numbers : PREVAIL

pre·dom·i·nate·ly \pri-'dä-mə-nət-lē\ *adv* : PREDOMINANTLY

pree·mie \'prē-mē\ *n* : a premature baby

pre·em·i·nent \prē-'e-mə-nənt\ *adj* : having highest rank : OUTSTANDING — **pre·em·i·nence** \-nəns\ *n* — **pre·em·i·nent·ly** *adv*

pre·empt \prē-'empt\ *vb* **1** : to settle upon (public land) with the right to purchase before others; *also* : to take by such right **2** : to seize upon before someone else can **3** : to take the place of ♦ **Synonyms** USURP, CONFISCATE, APPROPRIATE, EXPROPRIATE — **pre·emp·tion** \-'emp-shən\ *n*

pre·emp·tive \prē-'emp-tiv\ *adj* : marked by the seizing of the initiative : initiated by oneself ⟨~ attack⟩

preen \'prēn\ *vb* [ME *prenen*, alter. of *proynen, prunen*, fr. AF *puroindre, proindre*, fr. *pur-* thoroughly + *oindre* to anoint, rub, fr. L *unguere*] **1** : to groom with the bill — used of a bird **2** : to dress or smooth up : PRIMP **3** : to pride (oneself) for achievement

pre·ex·ist \ˌprē-ig-'zist\ *vb* : to exist before — **pre·ex·is·tence** \-'zis-təns\ *n* — **pre·ex·is·tent** \-tənt\ *adj*

pref *abbr* **1** preface **2** preference **3** preferred **4** prefix

¹pre·fab \ˌprē-'fab, 'prē-ˌfab\ *adj* : produced by prefabrication ⟨a ~ house⟩

²prefab *n* : a prefabricated structure

pre·fab·ri·cate \ˌprē-'fa-brə-ˌkāt\ *vb* : to manufacture the parts of (a structure) beforehand for later assembly — **pre·fab·ri·ca·tion** \ˌprē-ˌfa-bri-'kā-shən\ *n*

¹pref·ace \'pre-fəs\ *n* : the introductory remarks of a speaker or writer — **pref·a·to·ry** \'pre-fə-ˌtȯr-ē\ *adj*

²preface *vb* **pref·aced; pref·ac·ing** : to introduce with a preface

pre·fect \'prē-ˌfekt\ *n* **1** : a high official; *esp* : a chief officer or magistrate **2** : a student monitor

pre·fec·ture \'prē-ˌfek-chər\ *n* : the office, term, or residence of a prefect

pre·fer \pri-'fər\ *vb* **pre·ferred; pre·fer·ring** **1** : PROMOTE **2** : to like better **3** : to bring (as a charge) against a person — **pref·er·a·ble** \'pre-fə-rə-bəl\ *adj* — **pref·er·a·bly** \-blē\ *adv*

pref·er·ence \'pre-frəns, -fə-rəns\ *n* **1** : a special liking for one thing over another **2** : CHOICE, SELECTION — **pref·er·en·tial** \ˌpre-fə-'ren-chəl\ *adj*

pre·fer·ment \pri-'fər-mənt\ *n* : PROMOTION, ADVANCEMENT

preferred provider organization *n* : PPO

pre·fig·ure \prē-'fi-gyər\ *vb* **1** : FORESHADOW **2** : to imagine beforehand

¹pre·fix \'prē-ˌfiks, prē-'fiks\ *vb* : to place before ⟨~ a title to a name⟩

²pre·fix \'prē-ˌfiks\ *n* : an affix occurring at the beginning of a word

pre·flight \ˌprē-'flīt\ *adj* : preparing for or preliminary to flight

pre·form \ˌprē-'fȯrm, 'prē-ˌfȯrm\ *vb* : to form or shape beforehand

preg·na·ble \'preg-nə-bəl\ *adj* : vulnerable to capture ⟨a ~ fort⟩

preg·nant \'preg-nənt\ *adj* **1** : containing unborn offspring within the body **2** : rich in significance : MEANINGFUL — **preg·nan·cy** \-nən-sē\ *n*

pre·heat \ˌprē-'hēt\ *vb* : to heat beforehand; *esp* : to heat (an oven) to a designated temperature before using

pre·hen·sile \prē-'hen-səl, -ˌsī(-ə)l\ *adj* : adapted for grasping esp. by wrapping around ⟨a monkey with a ~ tail⟩

pre·his·tor·ic \ˌprē-his-'tȯr-ik\ *also* **pre·his·tor·i·cal** \-i-kəl\ *adj* : of, relating to, or existing in the period before written history began

pre·judge \ˌ(ˌ)prē-'jəj\ *vb* : to judge before full hearing or examination

¹prej·u·dice \'pre-jə-dəs\ *n* **1** : DAMAGE; *esp* : detriment to one's rights or claims **2** : an opinion made without adequate basis ⟨racial ~⟩ — **prej·u·di·cial** \ˌpre-jə-'di-shəl\ *adj*

²prejudice *vb* **-diced; -dic·ing** **1** : to damage by a judgment or action esp. at law **2** : to cause to have prejudice

pre·kin·der·gar·ten \ˌ(ˌ)prē-'kin-dər-ˌgär-tᵊn\ *n* **1** : NURSERY SCHOOL **2** : a class or program preceding kindergarten

prel·ate \'pre-lət\ *n* : an ecclesiastic (as a bishop) of high rank — **prel·a·cy** \-lə-sē\ *n*

pre·launch \ˌprē-'lȯnch\ *adj* : preparing for or preliminary to launch

pre·lim \'prē-ˌlim, pri-'lim\ *n or adj* : PRELIMINARY

¹pre·lim·i·nary \pri-'li-mə-ˌner-ē\ *n, pl* **-nar·ies** : something that precedes or introduces the main business or event

²preliminary *adj* : preceding the main discourse or business

pre·lude \'prel-ˌyüd; 'pre-ˌlüd, 'prā-\ *n* **1** : an introductory performance or event **2** : a musical section or movement introducing the main theme; *also* : an organ solo played at the beginning of a church service

pre·mar·i·tal \ˌ(ˌ)prē-'mer-ə-tᵊl\ *adj* : existing or occurring before marriage

pre·ma·ture \ˌprē-mə-'tur, -'tyur, -'chur\ *adj* : happening, coming, born, or done before the usual or proper time ⟨a ~ birth⟩ — **pre·ma·ture·ly** *adv*

¹pre·med \ˌprē-'med\ *n* : a premedical student or course of study

²premed *adj* : PREMEDICAL

pre·med·i·cal \ˌ(ˌ)prē-'me-di-kəl\ *adj* : preceding and preparing for the professional study of medicine

pre·med·i·tate \pri-'me-də-ˌtāt\ *vb* : to consider and plan beforehand — **pre·med·i·ta·tion** \-ˌme-də-'tā-shən\ *n*

pre·men·o·paus·al \ˌ(ˌ)prē-ˌme-nə-'pȯ-zəl\ *adj* : of, relating to, or being in the period preceding menopause

pre·men·stru·al \ˌ(ˌ)prē-'men-strə-wəl\ *adj* : of, relating to, or occurring in the period just before menstruation

premenstrual syndrome *n* : a varying group of symptoms manifested by some women prior to menstruation

premie *var of* PREEMIE

¹pre·mier \pri-'mir, -'myir, 'prē-mē-ər\ *adj* [ME *primer, primier*, fr. AF, first, chief, fr. L *primarius* of the first rank] **1** : first in rank or importance : CHIEF; *also* : first in time : EARLIEST

²premier *n* : PRIME MINISTER — **pre·mier·ship** *n*

¹pre·miere \pri-'myer, -'mir\ *n* : a first performance

²premiere *also* **pre·mier** *same as* ¹PREMIERE\ *vb* **pre·miered; pre·mier·ing** : to give or receive a first public performance

¹prem·ise \'pre-məs\ *n* **1** : a statement of fact or a supposition made or implied as a basis of argument **2** *pl* : a piece of land with the structures on it; *also* : the place of business of an enterprise

²premise *vb* **prem·ised; prem·is·ing** : to base on certain assumptions

pre·mi·um \'prē-mē-əm\ *n* [L *praemium* booty, profit, reward, fr. *prae* before + *emere* to take, buy] **1** : REWARD, PRIZE **2** : a sum over and above the stated value **3** : something paid over and above a fixed wage or price **4** : something given with a purchase **5** : the sum paid for a contract of insurance **6** : an unusually high value

pre·mix \ˌprē-'miks\ *vb* : to mix before use

pre·mo·lar \ˌ(ˌ)prē-'mō-lər\ *adj* : situated in front of or preceding the molar teeth; *esp* : being or relating to those teeth of a mammal in front of the true molars and behind the canines — **premolar** *n*

pre·mo·ni·tion \ˌprē-mə-'ni-shən, ˌpre-\ *n* **1** : previous warning **2** : PRESENTIMENT ⟨had a ~ of disaster⟩ — **pre·mon·i·to·ry** \pri-'mä-nə-ˌtȯr-ē\ *adj*

pre·na·tal \'prē-'nā-tᵊl\ *adj* : occurring, existing, or taking place before birth

pre·nup·tial \prē-'nəp-shəl\ *adj* : made or occurring before marriage

prenuptial agreement *n* : an agreement between a couple before marrying in which they give up future rights to each other's property in the event of divorce or death

pre·oc·cu·pa·tion \prē-ˌä-kyə-'pā-shən\ *n* : complete absorption of the mind or interests; *also* : something that causes such absorption

pre·oc·cu·pied \prē-'ä-kyə-ˌpīd\ *adj* **1** : lost in thought; *also* : absorbed in some preoccupation **2** : already occupied ◆ *Synonyms* ABSTRACTED, ABSENT, ABSENTMINDED

pre·oc·cu·py \-ˌpī\ *vb* **1** : to occupy the attention of beforehand **2** : to take possession of before another

pre·op·er·a·tive \(ˌ)prē-'ä-prə-tiv, -pə-ˌrā-\ *adj* : occurring before a surgical operation

pre·or·dain \prē-ȯr-'dān\ *vb* : FOREORDAIN

pre–owned \(ˌ)prē-'ōnd\ *adj* : SECONDHAND ⟨~ vehicles⟩

prep *abbr* **1** preparatory **2** preposition

pre·pack·age \(ˌ)prē-'pa-kij\ *vb* : to package (as food) before offering for sale to the customer

preparatory school *n* **1** : a usu. private school preparing students primarily for college **2** *Brit* : a private elementary school preparing students primarily for British public schools

pre·pare \pri-'per\ *vb* **pre·pared; pre·par·ing 1** : to make or get ready ⟨~ dinner⟩ ⟨~ a student for college⟩ **2** : to get ready beforehand **3** : to put together : COMPOUND ⟨~ a prescription⟩ — **prep·a·ra·tion** \ˌpre-pə-'rā-shən\ *n* — **pre·pa·ra·to·ry** \pri-'per-ə-ˌtȯr-ē\ *adj*

pre·pared·ness \pri-'per-əd-nəs\ *n* : a state of adequate preparation

pre·pay \(ˌ)prē-'pā\ *vb* **-paid** \-'pād\; **-pay·ing** : to pay or pay the charge on in advance

pre·pon·der·ant \pri-'pän-də-rənt\ *adj* : having greater weight, force, influence, or frequency — **pre·pon·der·ance** \-rəns\ *n* — **pre·pon·der·ant·ly** *adv*

pre·pon·der·ate \pri-'pän-də-ˌrāt\ *vb* **-at·ed; -at·ing** [L *praeponderare*, fr. *prae-* ahead + *ponder-, pondus* weight] : to exceed in weight, force, influence, or frequency : PREDOMINATE

prep·o·si·tion \ˌpre-pə-'zi-shən\ *n* : a word that combines with a noun or pronoun to form a phrase — **prep·o·si·tion·al** \-'zi-shə-nəl\ *adj*

pre·pos·sess \ˌprē-pə-'zes\ *vb* **1** : to cause to be preoccupied **2** : to influence beforehand esp. favorably

pre·pos·sess·ing *adj* : tending to create a favorable impression ⟨a ~ manner⟩

pre·pos·ses·sion \-'ze-shən\ *n* **1** : PREJUDICE **2** : an exclusive concern with one idea or object

pre·pos·ter·ous \pri-'päs-tə-rəs\ *adj* : contrary to nature or reason : ABSURD

prep·py *or* **prep·pie** \'pre-pē\ *n, pl* **preppies 1** : a student at or a graduate of a preparatory school **2** : a person deemed to dress or behave like a preppy

pre·puce \'prē-ˌpyüs\ *n* : FORESKIN

pre·quel \'prē-kwəl\ *n* : a literary or dramatic work whose story precedes that of an earlier work

pre·re·cord·ed \(ˌ)prē-ri-'kȯr-dəd\ *adj* : recorded for later broadcast or play

pre·req·ui·site \prē-'re-kwə-zət\ *n* : something required beforehand or for the end in view — **prerequisite** *adj*

pre·rog·a·tive \pri-'rä-gə-tiv\ *n* : an exclusive or special right, power, or privilege ⟨presidential ~s⟩

pres *abbr* **1** present **2** president

¹pres·age \'pre-sij\ *n* [ME, fr. L *praesagium*, fr. *praesagus* having a foreboding, fr. *prae* before + *sagus* prophetic] **1** : something that foreshadows a future event : OMEN **2** : FOREBODING

²pres·age \'pre-sij, pri-'sāj\ *vb* **pre·saged; pre·sag·ing 1** : to give an omen or warning of : FORESHADOW **2** : FORETELL, PREDICT

pres·by·o·pia \ˌprez-bē-'ō-pē-ə\ *n* : a visual condition in which loss of elasticity of the lens of the eye causes defective accommodation and inability to focus sharply for near vision — **pres·by·o·pic** \-'ō-pik, -'ä-\ *adj or n*

pres·by·ter \'prez-bə-tər\ *n* [LL, elder, priest, fr. Gk *presbyteros*, compar. of *presbys* elder, old man] **1** : PRIEST, MINISTER **2** : an elder in a Presbyterian church

¹Pres·by·te·ri·an \ˌprez-bə-'tir-ē-ən\ *n* : a member of a Presbyterian church

²Presbyterian *adj* **1** *often not cap* : characterized by a graded system of representative ecclesiastical bodies (as presbyteries) exercising legislative and judicial powers **2** : of or relating to a group of Protestant Christian bodies that are presbyterian in government — **Pres·by·te·ri·an·ism** \-ə-ˌni-zəm\ *n*

pres·by·tery \'prez-bə-ˌter-ē\ *n, pl* **-ter·ies 1** : the part of a church reserved for the officiating clergy **2** : a ruling body in Presbyterian churches consisting of the ministers and representative elders of a district

¹pre·school \'prē-ˌskül\ *adj* : of or relating to the period in a child's life from infancy to the age of five or six — **pre·school·er** \-ˌskü-lər\ *n*

²preschool *n* : NURSERY SCHOOL

pre·science \'pre-shəns, 'prē-\ *n* : foreknowledge of events; *also* : FORESIGHT — **pre·scient** \-shənt, -shē-ənt\ *adj*

pre·scribe \pri-'skrīb\ *vb* **pre·scribed; pre·scrib·ing 1** : to lay down as a guide or rule of action **2** : to direct the use of (as a medicine) as a remedy

pre·scrip·tion \pri-'skrip-shən\ *n* **1** : the action of prescribing rules or directions **2** : a written direction for the preparation and use of a medicine; *also* : a medicine prescribed

pre·scrip·tive \pri-'skrip-tiv\ *adj* **1** : serving to prescribe ⟨~ rules⟩ **2** : acquired by, based on, or determined by prescription or by custom

pres·ence \'pre-z²ns\ *n* **1** : the fact or condition of being present **2** : the space immediately around a person **3** : one that is present **4** : the bearing of a person; *esp* : stately bearing

¹pres·ent \'pre-z²nt\ *n* : something presented : GIFT

²pre·sent \pri-'zent\ *vb* **1** : to bring into the presence or acquaintance of : INTRODUCE **2** : to bring before the public ⟨~ a play⟩ **3** : to make a gift to **4** : to give formally **5** : to lay (as a charge) before a court for inquiry **6** : to aim or direct (as a weapon) so as to face in a particular direction — **pre·sent·able** *adj* — **pre·sen·ta·tion** \ˌprē-ˌzen-'tā-shən, ˌpre-z²n-\ *n* — **pre·sent·ment** \pri-'zent-mənt\ *n*

³pres·ent \'pre-z²nt\ *adj* **1** : now existing or in progress ⟨~ conditions⟩ **2** : being in view or at hand ⟨~ at the meeting⟩ **3** : under consideration ⟨the ~ problem⟩ **4** : of, relating to, or constituting a verb tense that expresses present time or the time of speaking

⁴pres·ent \'pre-z²nt\ *n* **1** *pl* : the present legal document **2** : the present tense; *also* : a verb form in it **3** : the present time

pres·ent–day \'pre-z²nt-'dā\ *adj* : now existing or occurring : CURRENT

pre·sen·ti·ment \pri-'zen-tə-mənt\ *n* : a feeling that something is about to happen : PREMONITION ⟨a ~ of danger⟩

pres·ent·ly \'pre-z²nt-lē\ *adv* **1** : SOON ⟨~ they arrived⟩ **2** : NOW ⟨~ busy⟩

present participle *n* : a participle that typically expresses present action and that in English is formed with the suffix *-ing* and is used in the formation of the progressive tenses

¹pre·serve \pri-'zərv\ *vb* **pre·served; pre·serv·ing 1** : to keep safe : GUARD, PROTECT **2** : to keep from decaying; *esp* : to process food (as by canning or pickling) to prevent spoilage **3** : MAINTAIN ⟨~ silence⟩ — **pres·er·va·tion** \ˌpre-zər-'vā-shən\ *n* — **pre·ser·va·tive** \pri-'zər-və-tiv\ *adj or n* — **pre·serv·er** *n*

²preserve *n* **1** : preserved fruit — often used in pl. **2** : an area for the protection of natural resources (as animals)

pre·set \'prē-ˌset\ *vb* **-set; -set·ting** : to set beforehand — **preset** *n*

pre·shrink \prē-'shriŋk\ *vb* **-shrank** \-'shraŋk\; **-shrunk** \-'shrəŋk\ : to shrink (as a fabric) before making into a garment

pre·side \pri-'zīd\ *vb* **pre·sid·ed; pre·sid·ing** [L *praesidēre* to guard, preside over, fr. *prae* in front of + *sedēre* to sit] **1** : to exercise guidance or control **2** : to occupy the place of authority; *esp* : to act as chairman

pres·i·dent \'pre-zə-dənt\ *n* **1** : one chosen to preside ⟨~ of the assembly⟩ **2** : the chief officer of an organization (as a corporation or society) **3** : an elected official serving as both chief of state and chief political executive; *also* : a chief of state other than a monarch with only minimal political powers — **pres·i·den·cy** \-dən-sē\ *n* — **pres·i·den·tial** \ˌpre-zə-'den-chəl\ *adj*

pre·si·dio \pri-'sē-dē-ˌō, -'si-\ *n, pl* **-di·os** [Sp] : a military post or fortified settlement in an area currently or orig. under Spanish control

pre·sid·i·um \pri-'si-dē-əm\ *n, pl* **-ia** \-dē-ə\ *or* **-iums** [Russ *prezidium*, fr. L *praesidium* garrison] : a permanent executive committee that acts for a larger body in a Communist country

¹pre·soak \(ˌ)prē-ˈsōk\ *vb* : to soak beforehand

²pre·soak \ˈprē-ˌsōk\ *n* **1** : an instance of presoaking **2** : a preparation used in presoaking clothes

pre·sort \(ˌ)prē-ˈsȯrt\ *vb* : to sort (mail) by zip code usu. before delivery to a post office

¹press \ˈpres\ *n* **1** : a crowded condition : THRONG **2** : a machine for exerting pressure **3** : CLOSET, CUPBOARD **4** : PRESSURE **5** : the properly creased condition of a freshly pressed garment **6** : PRINTING PRESS; *also* : the act or the process of printing **7** : a printing or publishing establishment **8** : the media (as newspapers and magazines) of public news and comment; *also* : persons (as reporters) employed in these media **9** : comment in newspapers and periodicals

²press *vb* **1** : to bear down upon : push steadily against **2** : ASSAIL, COMPEL **3** : to squeeze out the juice or contents of ⟨~ grapes⟩ **4** : to squeeze to a desired density, shape, or smoothness; *esp* : IRON **5** : to try hard to persuade : URGE **6** : to follow through : PROSECUTE **7** : CROWD ⟨reporters ~ed around the players⟩ **8** : to force one's way **9** : to require haste or speed in action — **press·er** *n*

press agent *n* : an agent employed to establish and maintain good public relations through publicity

press·ing *adj* : URGENT ⟨a ~ need⟩

press·man \ˈpres-mən, -ˌman\ *n* : the operator of a press and esp. a printing press

press·room \-ˌrüm, -ˌrum\ *n* **1** : a room in a printing plant containing the printing presses **2** : a room for the use of reporters

¹pres·sure \ˈpre-shər\ *n* **1** : the burden of physical or mental distress **2** : the action of pressing; *esp* : the application of force to something by something else in direct contact with it **3** : the force exerted over a surface divided by its area **4** : the stress or urgency of matters demanding attention

²pressure *vb* **pres·sured; pres·sur·ing** : to apply pressure to

pressure group *n* : a group that seeks to influence governmental policy but not to elect candidates to office

pressure suit *n* : an inflatable suit for high-altitude flight or spaceflight to protect the body from low pressure

pres·sur·ise *Brit var of* PRESSURIZE

pres·sur·ize \ˈpre-shə-ˌrīz\ *vb* **-ized; -iz·ing** **1** : to maintain higher pressure within than without; *esp* : to maintain normal atmospheric pressure within (as an airplane cabin) during high-altitude flight or spaceflight **2** : to apply pressure to **3** : to design to withstand pressure — **pres·sur·i·za·tion** \ˌpre-shə-rə-ˈzā-shən\ *n*

pres·ti·dig·i·ta·tion \ˌpres-tə-ˌdi-jə-ˈtā-shən\ *n* : SLEIGHT OF HAND

pres·tige \pres-ˈtēzh, -ˈtēj\ *n* [F, fr. MF, conjuror's trick, illusion, fr. LL *praestigium*, fr. L *praestigiae*, pl., conjuror's tricks, fr. *praestringere* to graze, blunt, constrict, fr. *prae-* in front of + *stringere* to bind tight] : standing or estimation in the eyes of people : REPUTATION ♦ **Synonyms** INFLUENCE, AUTHORITY, WEIGHT, CACHET — **pres·ti·gious** \-ˈti-jəs, -ˈtē-\ *adj*

¹pres·to \ˈpres-tō\ *interj* [It, quick, quickly] — used to indicate the sudden appearance or occurrence of something

²presto *adv or adj* **1** : suddenly as if by magic : IMMEDIATELY **2** : at a rapid tempo — used as a direction in music

pre·stress \(ˌ)prē-ˈstres\ *vb* : to introduce internal stresses into (as a structural beam) to counteract later load stresses

pre·sum·ably \pri-ˈzü-mə-blē\ *adv* : by reasonable assumption

pre·sume \pri-ˈzüm\ *vb* **pre·sumed; pre·sum·ing** **1** : to take upon oneself without leave or warrant : DARE **2** : to take for granted : ASSUME **3** : to act or behave with undue boldness — **pre·sum·able** \-ˈzü-mə-bəl\ *adj*

pre·sump·tion \pri-ˈzəmp-shən\ *n* **1** : presumptuous attitude or conduct : AUDACITY **2** : an attitude or belief dictated by probability; *also* : the grounds lending probability to a belief — **pre·sump·tive** \-tiv\ *adj*

pre·sump·tu·ous \pri-ˈzəmp-chə-wəs\ *adj* : overstepping due bounds : taking liberties — **pre·sump·tu·ous·ly** *adv*

pre·sup·pose \ˌprē-sə-ˈpōz\ *vb* **1** : to suppose before-

hand **2** : to require beforehand as a necessary condition — **pre·sup·po·si·tion** \(ˌ)prē-ˌsə-pə-ˈzi-shən\ *n*

pre·teen \ˈprē-ˈtēn\ *n* : a boy or girl not yet 13 years old — **preteen** *adj*

pre·tend \pri-ˈtend\ *vb* **1** : PROFESS ⟨doesn't ~ to be scientific⟩ **2** : FEIGN ⟨~ to be angry⟩ **3** : to lay claim ⟨~ to a throne⟩ — **pre·tend·er** *n*

pre·tense *or* **pre·tence** \ˈprē-ˌtens, pri-ˈtens\ *n* **1** : CLAIM; *esp* : one not supported by fact **2** : mere display : SHOW **3** : an attempt to attain a certain condition ⟨made a ~ at discipline⟩ **4** : false show : PRETEXT ⟨a ~ of objectivity⟩ — **pre·ten·sion** \pri-ˈten-chən\ *n*

pre·ten·tious \pri-ˈten-chəs\ *adj* **1** : making or possessing usu. unjustified claims (as to excellence) ⟨a ~ literary style⟩ **2** : making demands on one's ability or means : AMBITIOUS ⟨too ~ an undertaking⟩ — **pre·ten·tious·ly** *adv* — **pre·ten·tious·ness** *n*

pret·er·it *or* **pret·er·ite** \ˈpre-tə-rət\ *n* : a verb form expressing action in the past

pre·term \(ˌ)prē-ˈtərm, ˈprē-ˌ\ *adj* : of, relating to, being, or brought forth by premature birth ⟨a ~ infant⟩

pre·ter·nat·u·ral \ˌprē-tər-ˈna-chə-rəl\ *adj* **1** : exceeding what is natural ⟨his ~ stamina⟩ **2** : inexplicable by ordinary means — **pre·ter·nat·u·ral·ly** *adv*

pre·text \ˈprē-ˌtekst\ *n* : a purpose stated or assumed to cloak the real intention or state of affairs

pret·ti·fy \ˈpri-ti-ˌfī\ *vb* **-fied; -fy·ing** : to make pretty — **pret·ti·fi·ca·tion** \ˌpri-ti-fə-ˈkā-shən\ *n*

¹pret·ty \ˈpri-tē\ *adj* **pret·ti·er; -est** [ME *praty, prety, prety*, fr. OE *prættig* tricky, fr. *prætt* trick] **1** : pleasing by delicacy or grace : having conventionally accepted elements of beauty ⟨~ flowers⟩ **2** : MISERABLE, TERRIBLE ⟨a ~ state of affairs⟩ **3** : moderately large ⟨a ~ profit⟩ **4** : PLEASANT — usu. used in negative constructions ⟨the truth was not so ~⟩ ♦ **Synonyms** COMELY, FAIR, BEAUTIFUL, ATTRACTIVE, LOVELY — **pret·ti·ly** \-tə-lē\ *adv* — **pret·ti·ness** \-tē-nəs\ *n*

²pretty *adv* : in some degree : MODERATELY; *also* : QUITE, MAINLY

³pretty *vb* **pret·tied; pret·ty·ing** : to make pretty — usu. used with *up*

pretty boy *n, usu disparaging* : a man who is notably good-looking

pret·zel \ˈpret-səl\ *n* [G *Brezel*, ultim. fr. L *brachiatus* having branches like arms, fr. *brachium* arm] : a brittle or chewy glazed usu. salted slender bread often shaped like a loose knot

prev *abbr* previous; previously

pre·vail \pri-ˈvāl\ *vb* **1** : to win mastery : TRIUMPH **2** : to be or become effective : SUCCEED **3** : to urge successfully ⟨~ed upon her to sing⟩ **4** : to be frequent : PREDOMINATE — **pre·vail·ing·ly** *adv*

prev·a·lent \ˈpre-və-lənt\ *adj* : generally or widely existent : WIDESPREAD — **prev·a·lence** \-ləns\ *n*

pre·var·i·cate \pri-ˈver-ə-ˌkāt\ *vb* **-cat·ed; -cat·ing** [L *praevaricari* to act in collusion, lit., to straddle, fr. *prae* in front of + *varicare* to straddle, fr. *varus* bowlegged] : to deviate from the truth : EQUIVOCATE — **pre·var·i·ca·tion** \-ˌver-ə-ˈkā-shən\ *n* — **pre·var·i·ca·tor** \-ˈver-ə-ˌkā-tər\ *n*

pre·vent \pri-ˈvent\ *vb* **1** : to keep from happening or existing ⟨steps to ~ war⟩ **2** : to hold back : HINDER, STOP ⟨~ us from going⟩ — **pre·vent·able** *also* **pre·vent·ible** \-ˈven-tə-bəl\ *adj* — **pre·ven·ta·tive** \-ˈven-tə-tiv\ *adj or n* — **pre·ven·tion** \-ˈven-chən\ *n* — **pre·ven·tive** \-ˈven-tiv\ *adj or n*

pre·ver·bal \ˌprē-ˈvər-bəl\ *adj* : having not yet acquired the faculty of speech

¹pre·view \ˈprē-ˌvyü\ *vb* : to see or discuss beforehand; *esp* : to view or show in advance of public presentation

²preview *n* **1** : FORETASTE **2** : an advance showing or viewing **3** *also* **pre·vue** \-ˌvyü\ : a showing of snatches from a motion picture advertised for future appearance

pre·vi·ous \ˈprē-vē-əs\ *adj* : going before : EARLIER, FORMER ♦ **Synonyms** FOREGOING, PRIOR, PRECEDING, ANTECEDENT — **pre·vi·ous·ly** *adv*

pre·vi·sion \prē-ˈvi-zhən\ *n* **1** : FORESIGHT, PRESCIENCE **2** : FORECAST, PREDICTION ⟨a ~ of success⟩

pre·war \ˈprē-ˈwȯr\ *adj* : occurring or existing before a war

¹prey \ˈprā\ *n, pl* **prey** *also* **preys** **1** : an animal taken for

food by a predator; *also* : VICTIM **2** : the act or habit of preying
²**prey** *vb* **1** : to raid for booty **2** : to seize and devour prey **3** : to have a harmful or wearing effect
prf *abbr* proof
¹**price** \'prīs\ *n* **1** *archaic* : VALUE **2** : the amount of money paid or asked for the sale of a specified thing; *also* : the cost at which something is obtained
²**price** *vb* **priced; pric·ing** **1** : to set a price on **2** : to ask the price of **3** : to drive by raising prices ⟨*priced* themselves out of the market⟩
price–fix·ing \'prīs,fik-siŋ\ *n* : the setting of prices artificially (as by producers or government)
price·less \-ləs\ *adj* : having a value beyond any price : INVALUABLE ✦ *Synonyms* PRECIOUS, COSTLY, EXPENSIVE
price support *n* : artificial maintenance of prices of a commodity at a level usu. fixed through government action
price war *n* : a period of commercial competition in which prices are repeatedly cut by the competitors
pric·ey *also* **pricy** \'prī-sē\ *adj* **pric·i·er; -est** : EXPENSIVE ⟨a ∼ restaurant⟩
¹**prick** \'prik\ *n* **1** : a mark or small wound made by a pointed instrument **2** : something sharp or pointed **3** : an instance of pricking; *also* : a sensation of being pricked
²**prick** *vb* **1** : to pierce slightly with a sharp point; *also* : to have or cause a pricking sensation **2** : to affect with anguish or remorse ⟨∼s his conscience⟩ **3** : to outline with punctures ⟨∼ out a pattern⟩ **4** : to stand or cause to stand erect ⟨the dog's ears ∼ed up at the sound⟩ ✦ *Synonyms* PUNCH, PUNCTURE, PERFORATE, BORE, DRILL
prick·er \'pri-kər\ *n* : BRIAR; *also* : THORN
¹**prick·le** \'pri-kəl\ *n* **1** : a small sharp process (as on a plant) **2** : a slight stinging pain — **prick·ly** \'pri-klē\ *adj*
²**prickle** *vb* **prick·led; prick·ling** **1** : to prick lightly **2** : TINGLE
prickly heat *n* : a red cutaneous eruption with intense itching and tingling caused by inflammation around the ducts of the sweat glands
prickly pear *n* : any of numerous cacti with usu. yellow flowers and prickly flat or rounded joints; *also* : the sweet pulpy pear-shaped edible fruit of various prickly pears
¹**pride** \'prīd\ *n* **1** : CONCEIT **2** : justifiable self-respect **3** : elation over an act or possession ⟨took ∼ in her work⟩ **4** : haughty behavior : DISDAIN **5** : ostentatious display — **pride·ful** *adj*
²**pride** *vb* **prid·ed; prid·ing** : to indulge (as oneself) in pride
priest \'prēst\ *n* [ME *preist*, fr. OE *prēost*, ultim. fr. LL *presbyter* elder, priest, fr. Gk *presbyteros*, fr. compar. of *presbys* old man, elder] : a person having authority to perform the sacred rites of a religion; *esp* : a member of the Anglican, Eastern, or Roman Catholic clergy ranking below a bishop and above a deacon — **priest·hood** *n* — **priest·li·ness** *n* — **priest·ly** *adj*
priest·ess \'prēs-təs\ *n* : a woman authorized to perform the sacred rites of a religion
prig \'prig\ *n* : one who irritates by rigid or pointed observance of proprieties — **prig·gish** \'pri-gish\ *adj* — **prig·gish·ly** *adv*
¹**prim** \'prim\ *adj* **prim·mer; prim·mest** : stiffly formal and precise — **prim·ly** *adv* — **prim·ness** *n*
²**prim** *abbr* **1** primary **2** primitive
pri·ma·cy \'prī-mə-sē\ *n* **1** : the state of being first (as in rank) **2** : the office, rank, or character of an ecclesiastical primate
pri·ma don·na \,pri-mə-'dä-nə\ *n, pl* **prima donnas** [It, lit., first lady] **1** : a principal female singer (as in an opera company) **2** : a vain undisciplined usu. uncooperative person
pri·ma fa·cie \'prī-mə-'fā-shə, -sē, -shē\ *adj or adv* [L, at first view] **1** : based on immediate impression : APPARENT **2** : SELF-EVIDENT
pri·mal \'prī-məl\ *adj* **1** : ORIGINAL, PRIMITIVE **2** : first in importance
pri·mar·i·ly \prī-'mer-ə-lē\ *adv* **1** : FUNDAMENTALLY **2** : ORIGINALLY
¹**pri·ma·ry** \'prī-,mer-ē, -mə-rē\ *adj* **1** : first in order of

time or development; *also* : PREPARATORY **2** : of first rank or importance; *also* : FUNDAMENTAL **3** : not derived from or dependent on something else ⟨∼ sources⟩
²**primary** *n, pl* **-ries** : a preliminary election in which voters nominate or express a preference among candidates usu. of their own party
primary care *n* : health care provided by a medical professional with whom a patient has initial contact
primary color *n* : any of a set of colors from which all other colors may be derived
primary school *n* **1** : a school usu. including grades 1-3 and sometimes kindergarten **2** : ELEMENTARY SCHOOL
pri·mate \'prī-,māt *or esp for 1* -mət\ *n* **1** *often cap* : the highest-ranking bishop of a province or nation **2** : any of an order of mammals including humans, apes, and monkeys
¹**prime** \'prīm\ *n* **1** : the earliest stage of something; *esp* : SPRINGTIME **2** : the most active, thriving, or successful stage or period (as of one's life) **3** : the best individual; *also* : the best part of something **4** : any integer other than 0, +1, or −1 that is not divisible without remainder by any integer except +1, −1, and plus or minus itself; *esp* : any such integer that is positive
²**prime** *adj* **1** : standing first (as in time, rank, significance, or quality) ⟨∼ requisite⟩ **2** : of, relating to, or being a number that is prime
³**prime** *vb* **primed; prim·ing** **1** : FILL, LOAD **2** : to lay a preparatory coating upon (as in painting) **3** : to put in working condition **4** : to instruct beforehand : COACH ⟨*primed* the witness⟩
prime meridian *n* : the meridian of 0° longitude which runs through Greenwich, England, and from which other longitudes are reckoned east and west
prime minister *n* **1** : the chief minister of a ruler or state **2** : the chief executive of a parliamentary government
¹**prim·er** \'pri-mər\ *n* [ME, layperson's prayer book, fr. AF, fr. ML *primarium*, fr. LL, neut. of *primarius* primary] **1** : a small book for teaching children to read **2** : a small introductory book on a subject ⟨a ∼ of modern art⟩ **3** : a short informative piece of writing
²**prim·er** \'prī-mər\ *n* **1** : one that primes **2** : a device for igniting an explosive **3** : material for priming a surface
prime rate *n* : an interest rate announced by a bank to be the lowest available to its most credit-worthy customers
prime time *n* **1** : the time period when the television or radio audience is largest; *also* : television shows aired in prime time **2** : the choicest or busiest time
pri·me·val \prī-'mē-vəl\ *adj* : of or relating to the earliest ages : PRIMITIVE
¹**prim·i·tive** \'pri-mə-tiv\ *adj* **1** : ORIGINAL, PRIMARY **2** : of, relating to, or characteristic of an early stage of development or evolution **3** : ELEMENTAL, NATURAL **4** *now sometimes offensive* : of, relating to, or produced by a people or culture that is nonindustrial and often nonliterate and tribal **5** : SELF-TAUGHT; *also* : produced by a self-taught artist — **prim·i·tive·ly** *adv* — **prim·i·tive·ness** *n* — **prim·i·tiv·i·ty** \,pri-mə-'ti-və-tē\ *n*
²**primitive** *n* **1** : something primitive **2** : a primitive artist **3** : a member of a primitive people
prim·i·tiv·ism \'pri-mə-ti-,vi-zəm\ *n* **1** : primitive practices or procedures; *also* : a primitive quality or state **2** : belief in the superiority of a simple way of life close to nature **3** : the style of art of primitive peoples or primitive artists
pri·mo·gen·i·tor \,prī-mō-'je-nə-tər\ *n* : ANCESTOR, FOREFATHER
pri·mo·gen·i·ture \-'je-nə-,chùr\ *n* **1** : the state of being the firstborn of a family **2** : an exclusive right of inheritance belonging to the eldest son
pri·mor·di·al \prī-'mòr-dē-əl\ *adj* : first created or developed : existing in its original state : PRIMEVAL
primp \'primp\ *vb* : to dress in a careful or finicky manner
prim·rose \'prim-,rōz\ *n* : any of a genus of perennial herbs with large leaves arranged at the base of the stem and clusters of showy flowers
prin *abbr* **1** principal **2** principle
prince \'prins\ *n* [ME, fr. AF, fr. L *princeps* leader, initiator, fr. *primus* first + *capere* to take] **1** : MONARCH, KING **2** : a male member of a royal family; *esp* : a son of

the monarch **3** : a person of high standing (as in a class) ⟨a ~ of poets⟩ — **prince·dom** \-dəm\ *n* — **prince·ly** *adj*

prince·ling \-liŋ\ *n* : a petty prince

prin·cess \'prin-səs, -₁ses\ *n* **1** : a female member of a royal family **2** : the consort of a prince

¹prin·ci·pal \'prin-sə-pəl\ *adj* : most important — **prin·ci·pal·ly** *adv*

²principal *n* **1** : a leading person (as in a play) **2** : the chief officer of an educational institution **3** : the person from whom an agent's authority derives **4** : a capital sum earning interest or used as a fund

prin·ci·pal·i·ty \₁prin-sə-'pa-lə-tē\ *n, pl* **-ties** : the position, territory, or jurisdiction of a prince

principal parts *n pl* : the inflected forms of a verb

prin·ci·ple \'prin-sə-pəl\ *n* **1** : a general or fundamental law, doctrine, or assumption **2** : a rule or code of conduct; *also* : devotion to such a code **3** : the laws or facts of nature underlying the working of an artificial device **4** : a primary source : ORIGIN; *also* : an underlying faculty or endowment **5** : the active part (as of a drug)

prin·ci·pled \-pəld\ *adj* : exhibiting, based on, or characterized by principle ⟨high-*principled*⟩

prink \'priŋk\ *vb* : PRIMP

¹print \'print\ *n* [ME *prente*, fr. AF, fr. *preint, prient*, pp. of *priendre* to press, fr. L, *premere*] **1** : a mark made by pressure **2** : something stamped with an impression **3** : printed state or form **4** : printed matter **5** : a copy made by printing **6** : cloth with a pattern applied by printing

²print *vb* **1** : to stamp (as a mark) in or on something **2** : to produce impressions of (as from type) **3** : to write in letters like those of printer's type **4** : to make (a positive picture) from a photographic negative

print·able \'prin-tə-bəl\ *adj* **1** : capable of being printed or of being printed from **2** : worthy or fit to be published

print·er \'prin-tər\ *n* : one that prints; *esp* : a device that produces printout

print·ing *n* **1** : reproduction in printed form **2** : the art, practice, or business of a printer **3** : IMPRESSION 5

printing press *n* : a machine that produces printed copies

print·out \'print-₁aut\ *n* : a printed output produced by a computer — **print out** *vb*

¹pri·or \'prī-(ə)r\ *n* : the superior ranking next to the abbot or abbess of a religious house

²prior *adj* **1** : earlier in time or order **2** : taking precedence logically or in importance — **pri·or·i·ty** \prī-'or-ə-tē\ *n*

pri·or·ess \'prī-ə-rəs\ *n* : a nun corresponding in rank to a prior

pri·or·i·tize \prī-'or-ə-₁tīz, 'prī-ə-rə-₁tīz\ *vb* **-tized; -tiz·ing** : to list or rate in order of priority

prior to *prep* : in advance of : BEFORE

pri·o·ry \'prī-ə-rē\ *n, pl* **-ries** : a religious house under a prior or prioress

prise *chiefly Brit var of* ⁵PRIZE

prism \'pri-zəm\ *n* [LL *prisma*, fr. Gk, lit., something sawed, fr. *priein* to saw] **1** : a solid whose sides are parallelograms and whose ends are parallel and alike in shape and size **2** : a usu. 3-sided transparent object that refracts light so that it breaks up into rainbow colors — **pris·mat·ic** \priz-'ma-tik\ *adj*

pris·on \'pri-z°n\ *n* : a place or state of confinement esp. for criminals

pris·on·er \'pri-z°n-ər\ *n* : a person deprived of liberty; *esp* : one on trial or in prison

prisoner of war *n* : a person captured in war

pris·sy \'pri-sē\ *adj* **pris·si·er; -est** : being overly prim and precise : PRIGGISH — **pris·si·ness** \-sē-nəs\ *n*

pris·tine \'pris-₁tēn, pri-'stēn\ *adj* **1** : PRIMITIVE **2** : having the purity of its original state : UNSPOILED

prith·ee \'pri-thē\ *interj, archaic* — used to express a wish or request

pri·va·cy \'prī-və-sē\ *n, pl* **-cies** **1** : the quality or state of being apart from others **2** : SECRECY

¹pri·vate \'prī-vət\ *adj* **1** : belonging to or intended for a particular individual or group ⟨~ property⟩ **2** : restricted to the individual : PERSONAL ⟨~ opinion⟩ **3** : carried on by the individual independently ⟨~ study⟩ **4** : not holding public office ⟨a ~ citizen⟩ **5** : withdrawn from company or observation ⟨a ~ place⟩ **6** : not known publicly ⟨~ dealings⟩ — **pri·vate·ly** *adv*

²private *n* : an enlisted person of the lowest rank in the marine corps or of one of the two lowest ranks in the army — **in private** : not openly or in public

pri·va·teer \₁prī-və-'tir\ *n* : an armed private ship licensed to attack enemy shipping; *also* : a sailor on such a ship

private first class *n* : an enlisted person ranking next below a corporal in the army and next below a lance corporal in the marine corps

pri·va·tion \prī-'vā-shən\ *n* **1** : DEPRIVATION 1 **2** : the state of being deprived; *esp* : lack of what is needed for existence

priv·et \'pri-vət\ *n* : a nearly evergreen shrub related to the olive and widely used for hedges

privet: branch and hedge

¹priv·i·lege \'priv-lij, 'pri-və-\ *n* [ME, fr. AF, fr. L *privilegium* law for or against a private person, fr. *privus* private + *leg-, lex* law] : a right or immunity granted as an advantage or favor esp. to some and not others

²privilege *vb* **-leged; -leg·ing** **1** : to grant a privilege to **2** : to accord a higher value to : FAVOR

privileged *adj* **1** : having or enjoying one or more privileges ⟨~ classes⟩ **2** : not subject to disclosure in a court of law ⟨a ~ communication⟩

¹privy \'pri-vē\ *adj* **1** : PERSONAL, PRIVATE **2** : SECRET **3** : admitted as one sharing in a secret ⟨~ to the conspiracy⟩ — **priv·i·ly** \'pri-və-lē\ *adv*

²privy *n, pl* **priv·ies** : TOILET; *esp* : OUTHOUSE

¹prize \'prīz\ *n* **1** : something offered or striven for in competition or in contests of chance **2** : something exceptionally desirable

²prize *adj* **1** : awarded or worthy of a prize ⟨a ~ essay⟩; *also* : awarded as a prize ⟨a ~ medal⟩ **2** : OUTSTANDING

³prize *vb* **prized; priz·ing** : to value highly : ESTEEM ⟨a *prized* possession⟩

⁴prize *n* : property (as a ship) lawfully captured in time of war

⁵prize *vb* **prized; priz·ing** : PRY

prize·fight \'prīz-₁fīt\ *n* : a professional boxing match — **prize·fight·er** *n* — **prize·fight·ing** *n*

prize·win·ner \-₁wi-nər\ *n* : a winner of a prize — **prize·win·ning** *adj*

¹pro \'prō\ *n, pl* **pros** : a favorable argument, person, or position

²pro *adv* : in favor : FOR

³pro *n or adj* : PROFESSIONAL

PRO *abbr* public relations officer

pro·ac·tive \prō-'ak-tiv\ *adj* : acting in anticipation of future problems or needs — **pro·ac·tive·ly** *adv*

pro–am \'prō-'am\ *adj* : involving professionals competing alongside or against amateurs ⟨a ~ tournament⟩ — **pro–am** *n*

prob *abbr* **1** probable; probably **2** problem

prob·a·bil·i·ty \₁prä-bə-'bi-lə-tē\ *n, pl* **-ties** **1** : the quality or state of being probable **2** : something probable **3** : a measure of how often a particular event will occur if something (as tossing a coin) is done repeatedly which results in any of a number of possible events

prob·a·ble \'prä-bə-bəl\ *adj* **1** : apparently or presumably true ⟨a ~ hypothesis⟩ **2** : likely to be or become true or real ⟨a ~ result⟩ — **prob·a·bly** \-blē\ *adv*

¹pro·bate \'prō-₁bāt\ *n* : the judicial determination of the validity of a will

²pro·bate *vb* **pro·bat·ed; pro·bat·ing** : to establish (a will) by probate as genuine and valid

pro·ba·tion \prō-'bā-shən\ n 1 : subjection of an individual to a period of testing and trial to ascertain fitness (as for a job) 2 : the action of giving a convicted offender freedom during good behavior under the supervision of a probation officer — **pro·ba·tion·ary** \-shə-ˌner-ē\ adj

pro·ba·tion·er \-shə-nər\ n 1 : a person (as a newly admitted student nurse) whose fitness is being tested during a trial period 2 : a convicted offender on probation

pro·ba·tive \'prō-bə-tiv\ adj 1 : serving to test or try 2 : serving to prove

¹probe \'prōb\ n 1 : a slender instrument for examining a cavity (as a wound) 2 : an information-gathering device sent into outer space 3 : a penetrating investigation ✦ **Synonyms** INQUIRY, INQUEST, RESEARCH, INQUISITION

²probe vb **probed; prob·ing** 1 : to examine with a probe 2 : to investigate thoroughly

pro·bi·ty \'prō-bə-tē\ n : UPRIGHTNESS, HONESTY

prob·lem \'prä-bləm\ n 1 : a question raised for consideration or solution 2 : an intricate unsettled question 3 : a source of perplexity or vexation — **problem** adj

prob·lem·at·ic \ˌprä-blə-'ma-tik\ also **prob·lem·at·i·cal** \-ti-kəl\ adj 1 : difficult to solve or decide : PUZZLING 2 : DUBIOUS, QUESTIONABLE

pro·bos·cis \prə-'bä-səs, -'bäs-kəs\ n, pl **-bos·cis·es** also **-bos·ci·des** \-'bä-sə-ˌdēz\ [L, fr. Gk proboskis, fr. pro- before + boskein to feed] : a long flexible snout (as the trunk of an elephant)

proc abbr proceedings

pro·caine \'prō-ˌkān\ n : a drug used esp. as a local anesthetic

pro·ce·dure \prə-'sē-jər\ n 1 : a particular way of doing something ⟨democratic ∼⟩ 2 : a series of steps followed in a regular order ⟨a surgical ∼⟩ — **pro·ce·dur·al** \-'sē-jə-rəl\ adj

pro·ceed \prō-'sēd\ vb 1 : to come forth : ISSUE 2 : to go on in an orderly way; also : CONTINUE 3 : to begin and carry on an action 4 : to take legal action 5 : to go forward : ADVANCE

pro·ceed·ing n 1 : PROCEDURE 2 pl : DOINGS 3 pl : legal action 4 : TRANSACTION 5 pl : an official record of things said or done

pro·ceeds \'prō-ˌsēdz\ n pl : the total amount or the profit arising from a business deal : RETURN

¹pro·cess \'prä-ˌses, 'prō-\ n, pl **pro·cess·es** \-ˌse-səz, -sə-səz, -sə-ˌsēz\ 1 : PROGRESS, ADVANCE 2 : something going on : PROCEEDING 3 : a natural phenomenon marked by gradual changes that lead toward a particular result ⟨the ∼ of growth⟩ 4 : a series of actions or operations directed toward a particular result ⟨a manufacturing ∼⟩ 5 : legal action 6 : a mandate issued by a court; esp : SUMMONS 7 : a projecting part of an organism or organic structure

²process vb : to subject to a special process

pro·ces·sion \prə-'se-shən\ n : a group of individuals moving along in an orderly often ceremonial way

pro·ces·sion·al \-'se-shə-nəl\ n 1 : music for a procession 2 : a ceremonial procession

pro·ces·sor \'prä-ˌse-sər, 'prō-\ n 1 : one that processes 2 : CPU

pro–choice \(ˌ)prō-'chȯis\ adj : favoring the legalization of abortion

pro·claim \prō-'klām\ vb : to make known publicly : DECLARE

proc·la·ma·tion \ˌprä-klə-'mā-shən\ n : an official public announcement

pro·cliv·i·ty \prō-'kli-və-tē\ n, pl **-ties** : an inherent inclination esp. toward something objectionable

pro·con·sul \-'kän-səl\ n 1 : a governor or military commander of an ancient Roman province 2 : an administrator in a modern colony or occupied area — **pro·con·su·lar** \-sə-lər\ adj

pro·cras·ti·nate \prə-'kras-tə-ˌnāt, prō-\ vb **-nat·ed; -nat·ing** [L procrastinare, fr. pro- forward + crastinus of tomorrow, fr. cras tomorrow] : to put off usu. habitually doing something that should be done ✦ **Synonyms** DAWDLE, DELAY — **pro·cras·ti·na·tion** \-ˌkras-tə-'nā-shən\ n — **pro·cras·ti·na·tor** \-'kras-tə-ˌnā-tər\ n

pro·cre·ate \'prō-krē-ˌāt\ vb **-at·ed; -at·ing** : to beget or bring forth offspring ✦ **Synonyms** REPRODUCE,

BREED, GENERATE, PROPAGATE — **pro·cre·ation** \ˌprō-krē-'ā-shən\ n — **pro·cre·ative** \'prō-krē-ˌā-tiv\ adj — **pro·cre·ator** \-ˌā-tər\ n

pro·crus·te·an \prə-'krəs-tē-ən\ adj, often cap [fr. Procrustes, villain of Greek mythology who made victims fit his bed by stretching them or cutting off their legs] : marked by arbitrary often ruthless disregard of individual differences or special circumstances

proc·tor \'präk-tər\ n : one appointed to supervise students (as at an examination) — **proctor** vb — **proc·to·ri·al** \präk-'tȯr-ē-əl\ adj

proc·u·ra·tor \'prä-kyə-ˌrā-tər\ n : a Roman provincial administrator

pro·cure \prə-'kyu̇r\ vb **pro·cured; pro·cur·ing** 1 : to get possession of : OBTAIN 2 : to obtain (someone) to be employed for sexual intercourse 3 : ACHIEVE ✦ **Synonyms** SECURE, ACQUIRE, GAIN, WIN, EARN — **pro·cur·able** \-'kyu̇r-ə-bəl\ adj — **pro·cure·ment** n — **pro·cur·er** n

¹prod \'präd\ vb **prod·ded; prod·ding** 1 : to thrust a pointed instrument into : GOAD 2 : INCITE, STIR — **prod** n

²prod abbr product; production

prod·i·gal \'prä-di-gəl\ adj 1 : recklessly extravagant; also : LUXURIANT 2 : WASTEFUL, LAVISH ✦ **Synonyms** PROFUSE, LUSH, OPULENT — **prodigal** n — **prod·i·gal·i·ty** \ˌprä-də-'ga-lə-tē\ n

pro·di·gious \prə-'di-jəs\ adj 1 : exciting wonder 2 : extraordinary in size or degree : ENORMOUS ✦ **Synonyms** MONSTROUS, TREMENDOUS, STUPENDOUS, MONUMENTAL — **pro·di·gious·ly** adv

prod·i·gy \'prä-də-jē\ n, pl **-gies** 1 : something extraordinary : WONDER 2 : a highly talented child

¹pro·duce \prə-'düs, -'dyüs\ vb **pro·duced; pro·duc·ing** 1 : to present to view : EXHIBIT 2 : to give birth or rise to : YIELD 3 : EXTEND, PROLONG 4 : to give being or form to : BRING ABOUT, MAKE; esp : MANUFACTURE 5 : to sponsor or oversee the making of 6 : to cause to accrue ⟨∼ a profit⟩ — **pro·duc·er** n

²pro·duce \'prä-ˌdüs, 'prō- also -(ˌ)dyüs\ n : PRODUCT 2; also : agricultural products and esp. fresh fruits and vegetables

prod·uct \'prä-(ˌ)dəkt\ n 1 : the number resulting from multiplication 2 : something produced

pro·duc·tion \prə-'dək-shən\ n 1 : something produced : PRODUCT 2 : the act or process of producing — **pro·duc·tive** \-'dək-tiv\ adj — **pro·duc·tive·ness** n — **pro·duc·tiv·i·ty** \(ˌ)prō-ˌdək-'ti-və-tē, ˌprä-(ˌ)dək-\ n

product placement n : the inclusion of a product in a television program or film as a means of advertising

pro·em \'prō-ˌem\ n 1 : preliminary comment : PREFACE 2 : PRELUDE

¹prof \'präf\ n : PROFESSOR

²prof abbr professional

¹pro·fane \prō-'fān\ vb **pro·faned; pro·fan·ing** 1 : to treat (something sacred) with irreverence or contempt 2 : to debase by an unworthy use — **prof·a·na·tion** \ˌprä-fə-'nā-shən\ n

²profane adj [ME prophane, fr. MF, fr. L profanus, fr. pro- before + fanum temple] 1 : not concerned with religion : SECULAR 2 : not holy because unconsecrated, impure, or defiled 3 : serving to debase what is holy : IRREVERENT 4 : OBSCENE, VULGAR — **pro·fane·ly** adv — **pro·fane·ness** n

pro·fan·i·ty \prō-'fa-nə-tē\ n, pl **-ties** 1 : the quality or state of being profane 2 : the use of profane language 3 : profane language

pro·fess \prə-'fes\ vb 1 : to declare or admit openly : AFFIRM 2 : to declare in words only : PRETEND 3 : to confess one's faith in 4 : to practice or claim to be versed in (a calling or occupation) — **pro·fess·ed·ly** \-'fe-səd-lē\ adv

pro·fes·sion \prə-'fe-shən\ n 1 : an open declaration or avowal of a belief or opinion 2 : a calling requiring specialized knowledge and often long academic preparation 3 : the whole body of persons engaged in a calling

¹pro·fes·sion·al \prə-'fe-shə-nəl\ adj 1 : of, relating to, or characteristic of a profession 2 : engaged in one of the professions 3 : participating for gain in an activity often engaged in by amateurs — **pro·fes·sion·al·ly** adv

²professional n : one that engages in an activity professionally

pro·fes·sion·al·ism \-nə-ˌli-zəm\ *n* **1** : the conduct, aims, or qualities that characterize or mark a profession or a professional person **2** : the following of a profession (as athletics) for gain or livelihood

pro·fes·sion·al·ize \-nə-ˌlīz\ *vb* **-ized; -iz·ing** : to give a professional nature to

pro·fes·sor \prə-ˈfe-sər\ *n* : a teacher at a university or college; *esp* : a faculty member of the highest academic rank — **pro·fes·so·ri·al** \ˌprō-fə-ˈsȯr-ē-əl, ˌprä-\ *adj* — **pro·fes·sor·ship** *n*

prof·fer \ˈprä-fər\ *vb* **prof·fered; prof·fer·ing** : to present for acceptance : OFFER — **proffer** *n*

pro·fi·cient \prə-ˈfi-shənt\ *adj* : well advanced in an art, occupation, or branch of knowledge ♦ **Synonyms** ADEPT, SKILLFUL, EXPERT, MASTERFUL, MASTERLY — **pro·fi·cien·cy** \-shən-sē\ *n* — **proficient** *n* — **pro·fi·cient·ly** *adv*

¹**pro·file** \ˈprō-ˌfī(-ə)l\ *n* [It *profilo*, fr. *profilare* to draw in outline, fr. *pro-* forward (fr. L) + *filare* to spin, fr. LL, fr. L *filum* thread] **1** : a representation of something in outline; *esp* : a human head seen in side view **2** : a concise biographical sketch **3** : degree or level of public exposure ⟨keep a low ∼⟩

²**profile** *vb* **pro·filed; pro·fil·ing** : to write or draw a profile of

profiling *n* : the act of suspecting or targeting a person solely on the basis of observed characteristics or behavior ⟨racial ∼⟩

¹**prof·it** \ˈprä-fət\ *n* **1** : a valuable return : GAIN **2** : the excess of the selling price of goods over their cost — **prof·it·less** *adj*

²**profit** *vb* **1** : to be of use : BENEFIT **2** : to derive benefit : GAIN ⟨∼ed from his mistakes⟩ — **prof·it·able** \ˈprä-fə-tə-bəl\ *adj* — **prof·it·ably** \-blē\ *adv*

prof·i·teer \ˌprä-fə-ˈtir\ *n* : one who makes what is considered an unreasonable profit — **profiteer** *vb*

prof·li·gate \ˈprä-fli-gət, -flə-ˌgāt\ *adj* **1** : completely given up to dissipation and licentiousness **2** : wildly extravagant — **prof·li·ga·cy** \-gə-sē\ *n* — **profligate** *n* — **prof·li·gate·ly** *adv*

pro for·ma \(ˌ)prō-ˈfȯr-mə\ *adj* : done or existing as a matter of form

pro·found \prə-ˈfau̇nd, prō-\ *adj* **1** : marked by intellectual depth or insight ⟨a ∼ thought⟩ **2** : coming from or reaching to a depth ⟨a ∼ sigh⟩ **3** : deeply felt : INTENSE ⟨∼ sympathy⟩ — **pro·found·ly** *adv* — **pro·fun·di·ty** \-ˈfən-də-tē\ *n*

pro·fuse \prə-ˈfyüs, prō-\ *adj* : pouring forth liberally : ABUNDANT ⟨∼ bleeding⟩ ♦ **Synonyms** LAVISH, PRODIGAL, LUXURIANT, EXUBERANT — **pro·fuse·ly** *adv* — **pro·fu·sion** \-ˈfyü-zhən\ *n*

prog *abbr* program

pro·gen·i·tor \prō-ˈje-nə-tər\ *n* **1** : a direct ancestor : FOREFATHER **2** : ORIGINATOR, PRECURSOR

prog·e·ny \ˈprä-jə-nē\ *n, pl* **-nies** : OFFSPRING, CHILDREN, DESCENDANTS

pro·ges·ter·one \prō-ˈjes-tə-ˌrōn\ *n* : a female hormone that causes the uterus to undergo changes so as to provide a suitable environment for a fertilized egg

prog·na·thous \ˈpräg-nə-thəs\ *adj* : having the lower jaw projecting beyond the upper part of the face

prog·no·sis \präg-ˈnō-səs\ *n, pl* **-no·ses** \-ˌsēz\ **1** : the prospect of recovery from disease **2** : FORECAST

¹**prog·nos·tic** \präg-ˈnäs-tik\ *n* **1** : PORTENT **2** : PROPHECY

²**prognostic** *adj* : of, relating to, or serving as ground for prognostication or a prognosis

prog·nos·ti·cate \präg-ˈnäs-tə-ˌkāt\ *vb* **-cat·ed; -cat·ing** : to foretell from signs or symptoms — **prog·nos·ti·ca·tion** \-ˌnäs-tə-ˈkā-shən\ *n* — **prog·nos·ti·ca·tor** \-ˈnäs-tə-ˌkā-tər\ *n*

¹**pro·gram** \ˈprō-ˌgram, -grəm\ *n* [F *programme* agenda, public notice, fr. Gk *programma*, fr. *prographein* to write in advance, fr. *pro-* before + *graphein* to write] **1** : a brief outline of the order to be pursued or the subjects included (as in a public entertainment); *also* : PERFORMANCE **2** : a plan of procedure esp. toward a goal **3** : coded instructions for a computer — **pro·gram·mat·ic** \ˌprō-grə-ˈma-tik\ *adj*

²**program** *also* **programme** *vb* **-grammed** *or* **-gramed; -gram·ming** *or* **-gram·ing** **1** : to arrange or furnish a program of or for **2** : to enter in a program **3** : to provide (as a computer) with a program — **pro·gram·ma·bil·i·ty**

\(ˌ)prō-ˌgra-mə-ˈbi-lə-tē\ *n* — **pro·gram·ma·ble** \ˈprō-ˌgra-mə-bəl\ *adj* — **pro·gram·mer** *also* **pro·gram·er** \ˈprō-ˌgra-mər, -grə-\ *n*

programme *chiefly Brit var of* PROGRAM

programmed instruction *n* : instruction through information given in small steps with each requiring a correct response by the learner before going on to the next step

pro·gram·ming *also* **pro·gram·ing** *n* **1** : the planning, scheduling, or performing of a program **2** : the process of instructing or learning by means of an instruction program **3** : the process of preparing an instruction program

¹**prog·ress** \ˈprä-grəs, -ˌgres\ *n* **1** : a forward movement : ADVANCE **2** : a gradual betterment ⟨the ∼ of science⟩

²**pro·gress** \prə-ˈgres\ *vb* **1** : to move forward : PROCEED **2** : to develop to a more advanced stage : IMPROVE

pro·gres·sion \prə-ˈgre-shən\ *n* **1** : an act of progressing : ADVANCE **2** : a continuous and connected series

¹**pro·gres·sive** \prə-ˈgre-siv\ *adj* **1** : of, relating to, or characterized by progress ⟨a ∼ city⟩ **2** : moving forward or onward : ADVANCING **3** : increasing in extent or severity ⟨a ∼ disease⟩ **4** *often cap* : of or relating to political Progressives **5** : of, relating to, or constituting a verb form that expresses action in progress at the time of speaking or a time spoken of — **pro·gres·sive·ly** *adv*

²**progressive** *n* **1** : one that is progressive **2** : a person believing in moderate political change and social improvement by government action; *esp, cap* : a member of a Progressive Party in the U.S.

pro·hib·it \prō-ˈhi-bət\ *vb* **1** : to forbid by authority **2** : to prevent from doing something

pro·hi·bi·tion \ˌprō-ə-ˈbi-shən\ *n* **1** : the act of prohibiting **2** : the forbidding by law of the sale or manufacture of alcoholic beverages — **pro·hi·bi·tion·ist** \-ˈbi-shə-nist\ *n* — **pro·hib·i·tive** \prō-ˈhi-bə-tiv\ *adj* — **pro·hib·i·tive·ly** *adv* — **pro·hib·i·to·ry** \-ˈhi-bə-ˌtȯr-ē\ *adj*

¹**proj·ect** \ˈprä-ˌjekt, -jikt\ *n* **1** : a specific plan or design : SCHEME **2** : a planned undertaking ⟨a research ∼⟩

²**pro·ject** \prə-ˈjekt\ *vb* **1** : to devise in the mind : DESIGN **2** : to throw forward **3** : PROTRUDE **4** : to cause (light or shadow) to fall into space or (an image) to fall on a surface ⟨∼ a beam of light⟩ **5** : to attribute (a thought, feeling, or personal characteristic) to a person, group, or object **6** : to display outwardly — **pro·jec·tion** \-ˈjek-shən\ *n*

pro·jec·tile \prə-ˈjek-tᵊl, -ˌjek-ti(-ə)l\ *n* **1** : a body hurled or projected by external force; *esp* : a missile for a firearm **2** : a self-propelling weapon

pro·jec·tion·ist \prə-ˈjek-shə-nist\ *n* : one that operates a motion-picture projector or television equipment

pro·jec·tor \-ˈjek-tər\ *n* : one that projects; *esp* : a device for projecting pictures on a screen

pro·lapse \prō-ˈlaps, ˈprō-ˌ\ *n* : the falling down or slipping of a body part from its usual position

pro·le·gom·e·non \ˌprō-li-ˈgä-mə-ˌnän, -nən\ *n, pl* **-e·na** \-nə\ : prefatory remarks

pro·le·tar·i·an \ˌprō-lə-ˈter-ē-ən\ *n* [L *proletarius* belonging to the lowest class of citizens, fr. *proles* progeny, fr. *pro-* forth + *-oles* (akin to *alere* to nourish)] : a member of the proletariat — **proletarian** *adj*

pro·le·tar·i·at \-ē-ət\ *n* : the laboring class; *esp* : industrial workers who sell their labor to live

pro–life \(ˌ)prō-ˈlīf\ *n* : ANTIABORTION

pro·lif·er·ate \prə-ˈli-fə-ˌrāt\ *vb* **-at·ed; -at·ing** : to grow or increase by rapid production of new units (as cells, offspring, or nuclear weapons) — **pro·lif·er·a·tion** \-ˌli-fə-ˈrā-shən\ *n*

pro·lif·ic \prə-ˈli-fik\ *adj* **1** : producing young or fruit abundantly **2** : marked by abundant inventiveness or productivity ⟨a ∼ writer⟩ — **pro·lif·i·cal·ly** \-fi-k(ə-)lē\ *adv*

pro·lix \prō-ˈliks, ˈprō-ˌliks\ *adj* : VERBOSE ♦ **Synonyms** WORDY, DIFFUSE, REDUNDANT — **pro·lix·i·ty** \prō-ˈlik-sə-tē\ *n*

pro·logue *also* **pro·log** \ˈprō-ˌlȯg, -ˌläg\ *n* : PREFACE ⟨∼ of a play⟩

pro·long \prə-ˈlȯŋ\ *vb* **1** : to lengthen in time : CONTINUE ⟨∼ a meeting⟩ **2** : to lengthen in extent or range ⟨∼ an airport runway⟩ ♦ **Synonyms** PROTRACT, EXTEND, ELONGATE, STRETCH — **pro·lon·ga·tion** \ˌprō-ˌlȯŋ-ˈgā-shən\ *n*

prom \ˈpräm\ *n* : a formal dance given by a high school or college class

promenade • Prophets

¹prom·e·nade \ˌprä-mə-ˈnäd, -ˈnäd\ vb -nad·ed; -nad·ing 1 : to take a promenade 2 : to walk about in or on ²promenade n [F, fr. promener to take for a walk, fr. MF, alter. of OF pourmener, fr. pour- completely (fr. L pro-) + mener to lead, fr. LL minare to drive, fr. L minari to threaten] 1 : a place for strolling 2 : a leisurely walk for pleasure or display 3 : an opening grand march at a formal ball

pro·me·thi·um \prə-ˈmē-thē-əm\ n : a metallic chemical element obtained from uranium or neodymium

prom·i·nence \ˈprä-mə-nəns\ n 1 : something prominent 2 : the quality, state, or fact of being prominent or conspicuous 3 : a mass of cloudlike gas that arises from the sun's chromosphere

prom·i·nent \-nənt\ adj 1 : jutting out : PROJECTING 2 : readily noticeable : CONSPICUOUS 3 : DISTINGUISHED, EMINENT ⟨a ~ lawyer⟩ ◆ Synonyms REMARKABLE, OUTSTANDING, STRIKING, SALIENT — prom·i·nent·ly adv

pro·mis·cu·ous \prə-ˈmis-kyə-wəs\ adj 1 : consisting of various sorts and kinds : MIXED 2 : not restricted to one class or person 3 : having a number of sexual partners ◆ Synonyms MISCELLANEOUS, ASSORTED, HETEROGENEOUS, MOTLEY, VARIED — pro·mis·cu·i·ty \ˌprä-mis-ˈkyü-ə-tē, ˌprō-ˌmis-\ n — pro·mis·cu·ous·ly adv — pro·mis·cu·ous·ness n

¹prom·ise \ˈprä-məs\ n 1 : a pledge to do or not to do something specified 2 : ground for expectation of success or improvement 3 : something promised

²promise vb prom·ised; prom·is·ing 1 : to engage to do, bring about, or provide ⟨~ help⟩ 2 : to suggest beforehand ⟨dark clouds ~ rain⟩ 3 : to give ground for expectation ⟨it ~s to be fun⟩

promising adj : likely to succeed or yield good results ⟨a ~ new medicine⟩ — prom·is·ing·ly adv

prom·is·so·ry \ˈprä-mə-ˌsòr-ē\ adj : containing a promise

prom·on·to·ry \ˈprä-mən-ˌtòr-ē\ n, pl -ries : a point of land jutting into the sea : HEADLAND

pro·mote \prə-ˈmōt\ vb pro·mot·ed; pro·mot·ing 1 : to advance in station, rank, or honor 2 : to contribute to the growth or prosperity of : FURTHER 3 : LAUNCH — pro·mo·tion \-ˈmō-shən\ n — pro·mo·tion·al \-shə-nəl\ adj

pro·mot·er \-ˈmō-tər\ n : one that promotes; esp : one that assumes the financial responsibilities of a sports event

¹prompt \ˈprämpt\ vb 1 : INCITE 2 : to assist (one acting or reciting) by suggesting the next words 3 : INSPIRE, URGE — prompt·er n

²prompt adj 1 : being ready and quick to act; also : PUNCTUAL 2 : performed readily or immediately ⟨~ service⟩ — prompt·ly adv — prompt·ness n

prompt·book \-ˌbùk\ n : a copy of a play with directions for performance used by a theater prompter

promp·ti·tude \ˈprämp-tə-ˌtüd, -ˌtyüd\ n : the quality or habit of being prompt : PROMPTNESS

pro·mul·gate \ˈprä-məl-ˌgāt; prō-ˈməl-\ vb -gat·ed; -gat·ing : to make known or put into force by open declaration — prom·ul·ga·tion \ˌprä-məl-ˈgā-shən, ˌprō-(ˌ)məl-\ n

pron abbr 1 pronoun 2 pronounced 3 pronunciation

prone \ˈprōn\ adj 1 : having a tendency or inclination : DISPOSED 2 : lying face downward; also : lying flat or prostrate ◆ Synonyms SUBJECT, EXPOSED, OPEN, LIABLE, SUSCEPTIBLE — prone·ness n

prong \ˈpròŋ\ n : one of the sharp points of a fork : TINE; also : a slender projecting part (as of an antler) — pronged \ˈpròŋd\ adj

prong·horn \ˈpròŋ-ˌhòrn\ n, pl pronghorn or pronghorns : a swift horned ruminant mammal chiefly of grasslands of western No. America that resembles an antelope

pro·noun \ˈprō-ˌnaún\ n : a word used as a substitute for a noun

pro·nounce \prə-ˈnaúns\ vb pro·nounced; pro·nounc·ing 1 : to utter officially or as an opinion ⟨~ sentence⟩ 2 : to employ the organs of speech in order to produce ⟨~ a word⟩; esp : to say or speak correctly ⟨she can't ~ his name⟩ — pro·nounce·able adj — pro·nun·ci·a·tion \-ˌnən-sē-ˈā-shən\ n

pro·nounced adj : strongly marked : DECIDED ⟨a ~ dislike⟩

pro·nounce·ment \prə-ˈnaúns-mənt\ n : a formal declaration of opinion; also : ANNOUNCEMENT

pron·to \ˈprän-ˌtō\ adv [Sp, fr. L promptus prompt] : QUICKLY

pro·nu·clear \ˈprō-ˈnü-klē-ər, -ˈnyü-\ adj : supporting the use of nuclear-powered electric generating stations

pro·nun·ci·a·men·to \prō-ˌnən-sē-ə-ˈmen-tō\ n, pl -tos or -toes : PROCLAMATION, MANIFESTO

¹proof \ˈprüf\ n [ME prof, prove, alter. of preve, fr. AF preove, fr. LL proba, fr. L probare to test, prove, fr. probus good, honest] 1 : the evidence that compels acceptance by the mind of a truth or fact 2 : a process or operation that establishes validity or truth : TEST 3 : a trial impression (as from type) 4 : a trial print from a photographic negative 5 : alcoholic content (as of a beverage) indicated by a number that is twice the percent by volume of alcohol present ⟨whiskey of 90 ~ is 45% alcohol⟩

²proof adj 1 : successful in resisting or repelling ⟨~ against tampering⟩ ⟨waterproof⟩ 2 : of standard strength or quality or alcoholic content

proof·read \-ˌrēd\ vb : to read and mark corrections in — proof·read·er n

¹prop \ˈpräp\ n : something that props

²prop vb propped; prop·ping 1 : to support by placing something under or against 2 : SUSTAIN, STRENGTHEN

³prop n : PROPERTY 4

⁴prop n : PROPELLER

⁵prop abbr 1 property 2 proposition 3 proprietor

pro·pa·gan·da \ˌprä-pə-ˈgan-də, ˌprō-\ n [NL, fr. Congregatio de propaganda fide Congregation for propagating the faith, organization established by Pope Gregory XV] : the spreading of ideas or information to further or damage a cause; also : ideas or allegations spread for such a purpose — pro·pa·gan·dist \-dist\ n

pro·pa·gan·dize \-ˌdīz\ vb -dized; -diz·ing : to subject to or carry on propaganda

prop·a·gate \ˈprä-pə-ˌgāt\ vb -gat·ed; -gat·ing 1 : to reproduce or cause to reproduce biologically : MULTIPLY 2 : to cause to spread ⟨propagating the faith⟩ — prop·a·ga·tion \ˌprä-pə-ˈgā-shən\ n

pro·pane \ˈprō-ˌpān\ n : a heavy flammable gas found in petroleum and natural gas and used esp. as a fuel

pro·pel \prə-ˈpel\ vb -pelled; -pel·ling : to drive forward or onward ◆ Synonyms PUSH, SHOVE, THRUST

pro·pel·lant also pro·pel·lent \-ˈpe-lənt\ n : something (as a fuel) that propels — propellant also propellent adj

pro·pel·ler \prə-ˈpe-lər\ n : a device consisting of a hub fitted with blades that is used to propel a vehicle (as a motorboat or an airplane)

pro·pen·si·ty \prə-ˈpen-sə-tē\ n, pl -ties : an often intense natural inclination or preference

¹prop·er \ˈprä-pər\ adj 1 : referring to one individual only ⟨~ noun⟩ 2 : belonging characteristically to a species or individual : PECULIAR 3 : very satisfactory : EXCELLENT 4 : strictly limited to a specified thing ⟨the city ~⟩ 5 : CORRECT ⟨the ~ way to proceed⟩ 6 : strictly decorous : GENTEEL 7 : marked by suitability or rightness ⟨~ punishment⟩ ◆ Synonyms MEET, APPROPRIATE, FITTING, SEEMLY — prop·er·ly adv

²proper n : the parts of the Mass that vary according to the liturgical calendar

prop·er·tied \ˈprä-pər-tēd\ adj : owning property and esp. much property

prop·er·ty \ˈprä-pər-tē\ n, pl -ties 1 : a quality peculiar to an individual or thing 2 : something owned; esp : a piece of real estate 3 : OWNERSHIP 4 : an article or object used in a play or motion picture other than painted scenery and actor's costumes

proph·e·cy also proph·e·sy \ˈprä-fə-sē\ n, pl -cies also -sies 1 : an inspired utterance of a prophet 2 : PREDICTION

proph·e·sy \-ˌsī\ vb -sied; -sy·ing 1 : to speak or utter by divine inspiration 2 : PREDICT — proph·e·si·er n

proph·et \ˈprä-fət\ n [ME prophete, fr. AF, fr. L propheta, fr. Gk prophētēs, fr. pro for + phanai to speak] 1 : one who utters divinely inspired revelations 2 : one who foretells future events

proph·et·ess \ˈprä-fə-təs\ n : a woman who is a prophet

pro·phet·ic \prə-ˈfe-tik\ or pro·phet·i·cal \-ti-kəl\ adj : of, relating to, or characteristic of a prophet or prophecy — pro·phet·i·cal·ly \-ti-k(ə-)lē\ adv

Proph·ets \ˈprä-fəts\ n pl — see BIBLE table

¹**pro·phy·lac·tic** \ˌprō-fə-ˈlak-tik, ˌprä-\ *adj* 1 : preventing or guarding from the spread or occurrence of disease or infection 2 : PREVENTIVE

²**prophylactic** *n* : something prophylactic; *esp* : a device (as a condom) for preventing venereal infection or conception

pro·phy·lax·is \-ˈlak-səs\ *n, pl* **-lax·es** \-ˈlak-ˌsēz\ : measures designed to preserve health and prevent the spread of disease

pro·pin·qui·ty \prə-ˈpiŋ-kwə-tē\ *n* 1 : KINSHIP 2 : nearness in place or time : PROXIMITY

pro·pi·ti·ate \prō-ˈpi-shē-ˌāt\ *vb* **-at·ed; -at·ing** : to gain or regain the favor of : APPEASE ⟨∼ the angry gods⟩ — **pro·pi·ti·a·tion** \-ˌpi-shē-ˈā-shən\ *n* — **pro·pi·tia·to·ry** \-ˈpi-shē-ə-ˌtȯr-ē\ *adj*

pro·pi·tious \prə-ˈpi-shəs\ *adj* 1 : favorably disposed ⟨∼ deities⟩ 2 : being of good omen ⟨∼ circumstances⟩

prop·man \ˈpräp-ˌman\ *n* : one who is in charge of stage properties

pro·po·nent \prə-ˈpō-nənt\ *n* : one who argues in favor of something

¹**pro·por·tion** \prə-ˈpȯr-shən\ *n* 1 : BALANCE, SYMMETRY 2 : SHARE, QUOTA 3 : the relation of one part to another or to the whole with respect to magnitude, quantity, or degree : RATIO 4 : SIZE, DEGREE — **in proportion** : PROPORTIONAL

²**proportion** *vb* **-tioned; -tion·ing** 1 : to adjust (a part or thing) in size relative to other parts or things 2 : to make the parts of harmonious

pro·por·tion·al \prə-ˈpȯr-shə-nəl\ *adj* : corresponding in size, degree, or intensity; *also* : having the same or a constant ratio — **pro·por·tion·al·ly** *adv*

pro·por·tion·ate \prə-ˈpȯr-shə-nət\ *adj* : PROPORTIONAL — **pro·por·tion·ate·ly** *adv*

pro·pose \prə-ˈpōz\ *vb* **pro·posed; pro·pos·ing** 1 : PLAN, INTEND ⟨∼s to buy a house⟩ 2 : to make an offer of marriage 3 : to offer for consideration : SUGGEST ⟨∼ a policy⟩ — **pro·pos·al** \-ˈpō-zəl\ *n* — **pro·pos·er** *n*

¹**prop·o·si·tion** \ˌprä-pə-ˈzi-shən\ *n* 1 : something proposed for consideration : PROPOSAL 2 : a request for sexual intercourse 3 : a statement of something to be discussed, proved, or explained 4 : SITUATION, AFFAIR ⟨a tough ∼⟩ — **prop·o·si·tion·al** \-ˈzi-shə-nəl\ *adj*

²**proposition** *vb* **-tioned; -tion·ing** : to make a proposal to; *esp* : to suggest sexual intercourse to

pro·pound \prə-ˈpau̇nd\ *vb* : to set forth for consideration ⟨∼ a doctrine⟩

pro·pri·e·tary \prə-ˈprī-ə-ˌter-ē\ *adj* 1 : of, relating to, or characteristic of a proprietor ⟨∼ rights⟩ 2 : made and sold by one with the sole right to do so ⟨∼ medicines⟩ ⟨∼ software⟩

pro·pri·e·tor \prə-ˈprī-ə-tər\ *n* : OWNER — **pro·pri·e·tor·ship** *n*

pro·pri·e·tress \-ˈprī-ə-trəs\ *n* : a woman who is a proprietor

pro·pri·e·ty \prə-ˈprī-ə-tē\ *n, pl* **-ties** 1 : the standard of what is socially acceptable in conduct or speech 2 *pl* : the customs of polite society

props \ˈpräps\ *n sing or pl* 1 *slang* : DUE 1 ⟨gave him his ∼⟩ 2 *slang* : RESPECT 2 ⟨earned the ∼ of his peers⟩ 3 *slang* : ACKNOWLEDGMENT ⟨deserves ∼ for the effort⟩

pro·pul·sion \prə-ˈpəl-shən\ *n* 1 : the action or process of propelling 2 : something that propels — **pro·pul·sive** \-siv\ *adj*

pro ra·ta \(ˌ)prō-ˈrä-tə, -ˈrā-\ *adv* : in proportion to the share of each : PROPORTIONALLY

pro·rate \(ˌ)prō-ˈrāt\ *vb* **pro·rat·ed; pro·rat·ing** : to divide, distribute, or assess proportionately

pro·rogue \prə-ˈrōg\ *vb* **pro·rogued; pro·rogu·ing** : to suspend or end a session of (a legislative body) — **pro·ro·ga·tion** \ˌprō-rō-ˈgā-shən\ *n*

pros *pl of* PRO

pro·sa·ic \prō-ˈzā-ik\ *adj* : lacking imagination or excitement : DULL

pro·sce·ni·um \prō-ˈsē-nē-əm\ *n* 1 : the part of a stage in front of the curtain 2 : the wall containing the arch that frames the stage

pro·scribe \prō-ˈskrīb\ *vb* **pro·scribed; pro·scrib·ing** 1 : OUTLAW 2 : to condemn or forbid as harmful — **pro·scrip·tion** \-ˈskrip-shən\ *n*

prose \ˈprōz\ *n* [ME, fr. AF, fr. L *prosa*, fr. fem. of *pror-*

sus, prosus, straightforward, being in prose, alter. of *proversus,* pp. of *provertere* to turn forward] : the ordinary language people use in speaking or writing

pros·e·cute \ˈprä-si-ˌkyüt\ *vb* **-cut·ed; -cut·ing** 1 : to follow to the end ⟨∼ an investigation⟩ 2 : to seek legal punishment of ⟨∼ a forger⟩ — **pros·e·cu·tion** \ˌprä-si-ˈkyü-shən\ *n* — **pros·e·cu·tor** \ˈprä-si-ˌkyü-tər\ *n* — **pros·e·cu·to·ri·al** \ˌprä-si-kyü-ˈtȯr-ē-əl\ *adj*

¹**pros·e·lyte** \ˈprä-sə-ˌlīt\ *n* : a new convert to a religion, belief, or party — **pros·e·ly·tism** \-ˌlī-ˌti-zəm\ *n*

²**proselyte** *vb* **-lyt·ed; -lyt·ing** : PROSELYTIZE

pros·e·ly·tise *Brit var of* PROSELYTIZE

pros·e·ly·tize \ˈprä-sə-lə-ˌtīz\ *vb* **-tized; -tiz·ing** 1 : to induce someone to convert to one's faith 2 : to recruit someone to join one's party, institution, or cause

pros·o·dy \ˈprä-sə-dē, -zə-\ *n, pl* **-dies** : the study of versification and esp. of metrical structure — **pro·sod·ic** \prə-ˈsä-dik\ *adj*

¹**pros·pect** \ˈprä-ˌspekt\ *n* 1 : an extensive view; *also* : OUTLOOK 2 : the act of looking forward 3 : a mental vision of something to come 4 : something that is awaited or expected : POSSIBILITY 5 : a potential buyer or customer; *also* : a likely candidate (as for a job) — **pro·spec·tive** \prə-ˈspek-tiv, ˈprä-ˌspek-\ *adj* — **pro·spec·tive·ly** *adv*

²**pros·pect** \ˈprä-ˌspekt\ *vb* : to explore esp. for mineral deposits — **pros·pec·tor** \-ˌspek-tər, prä-ˈspek-\ *n*

pro·spec·tus \prə-ˈspek-təs\ *n* : a preliminary statement that describes an enterprise and is distributed to prospective buyers or participants

pros·per \ˈpräs-pər\ *vb* **pros·pered; pros·per·ing** : SUCCEED; *esp* : to achieve economic success

pros·per·i·ty \präs-ˈper-ə-tē\ *n* : thriving condition : SUCCESS; *esp* : economic well-being

pros·per·ous \ˈpräs-pə-rəs\ *adj* 1 : FAVORABLE ⟨∼ winds⟩ 2 : marked by success or economic well-being ⟨a ∼ business⟩

pros·ta·glan·din \ˌpräs-tə-ˈglan-dən\ *n* : any of various oxygenated unsaturated fatty acids of animals that perform a variety of hormonelike actions

pros·tate \ˈpräs-ˌtāt\ *n* [NL *prostata,* fr. Gk *prostatēs,* fr. *proïstanai* to put in front] : PROSTATE GLAND — **pros·tat·ic** \prä-ˈsta-tik\ *adj*

prostate gland *n* : a glandular body about the base of the male urethra that produces a secretion which is a major part of the fluid ejaculated during an orgasm

pros·ta·ti·tis \ˌpräs-tə-ˈtī-təs\ *n* : inflammation of the prostate gland

pros·the·sis \präs-ˈthē-səs, ˈpräs-thə-\ *n, pl* **-the·ses** \-ˌsēz\ : an artificial replacement for a missing body part — **pros·thet·ic** \präs-ˈthe-tik\ *adj*

pros·thet·ics \-ˈthe-tiks\ *n pl* : the surgical or dental specialty concerned with the design, construction, and fitting of prostheses

¹**pros·ti·tute** \ˈpräs-tə-ˌtüt, -ˌtyüt\ *vb* **-tut·ed; -tut·ing** 1 : to offer indiscriminately for sexual activity esp. for money 2 : to devote to corrupt or unworthy purposes — **pros·ti·tu·tion** \ˌpräs-tə-ˈtü-shən, -ˈtyü-\ *n*

²**prostitute** *n* : one who engages in sexual activities for money

¹**pros·trate** \ˈprä-ˌsträt\ *adj* 1 : stretched out with face on the ground in adoration or submission 2 : lying flat 3 : completely overcome ⟨∼ with a cold⟩

²**prostrate** *vb* **pros·trat·ed; pros·trat·ing** 1 : to throw or put into a prostrate position 2 : to reduce to a weak or powerless condition — **pros·tra·tion** \prä-ˈsträ-shən\ *n*

prosy \ˈprō-zē\ *adj* **pros·i·er; -est** 1 : PROSAIC, ORDINARY 2 : TEDIOUS

Prot *abbr* Protestant

prot·ac·tin·i·um \ˌprō-ˌtak-ˈti-nē-əm\ *n* : a metallic radioactive chemical element of relatively short life

pro·tag·o·nist \prō-ˈta-gə-nist\ *n* 1 : the principal character in a drama or story 2 : a leader or supporter of a cause

pro·te·an \ˈprō-tē-ən\ *adj* : able to assume different shapes or roles

pro·tect \prə-ˈtekt\ *vb* : to shield from injury : GUARD

pro·tec·tion \prə-ˈtek-shən\ *n* 1 : the act of protecting 2 : one that protects ⟨wear a helmet as a ∼⟩ 3 : the supervision or support of one that is smaller and weaker 4 : the freeing of producers from foreign competition in their home market by high duties on foreign competitive goods — **pro·tec·tive** \-'tek-tiv\ *adj*

pro·tec·tion·ist \-shə-nist\ *n* : an advocate of government economic protection for domestic producers through restrictions on foreign competitors — **pro·tec·tion·ism** \-shə-ˌni-zəm\ *n*

pro·tec·tor \prə-'tek-tər\ *n* **1** : one that protects : GUARDIAN **2** : a device used to prevent injury : GUARD **3** : REGENT 1

pro·tec·tor·ate \-tə-rət\ *n* **1** : government by a protector **2** : the relationship of superior authority assumed by one state over a dependent one; *also* : the dependent political unit in such a relationship

pro·té·gé \'prō-tə-ˌzhā\ *n* [F] : one who is protected, trained, or guided by an influential person

pro·tein \'prō-ˌtēn\ *n* [F *protéine*, fr. LGk *prōteios* primary, fr. Gk *prōtos* first] : any of various complex nitrogen-containing substances that consist of chains of amino acids, are present in all living cells, and are an essential part of the human diet

pro tem \prō-'tem\ *adv* : PRO TEMPORE

pro tem·po·re \prō-'tem-pə-rē\ *adv* [L] : for the time being

Pro·te·ro·zo·ic \ˌprä-tə-rə-'zō-ik, ˌprō-\ *adj* : of, relating to, or being the eon of geologic history between the Archean and the Phanerozoic — **Proterozoic** *n*

¹pro·test \'prō-ˌtest\ *n* **1** : the act of protesting : *esp* : an organized public demonstration of disapproval **2** : a complaint or objection against an idea, an act, or a course of action

²pro·test \prō-'test\ *vb* **1** : to assert positively : make solemn declaration of ⟨~s his innocence⟩ **2** : to object strongly : make a protest against ⟨~ a ruling⟩ — **pro·tes·ta·tion** \ˌprä-təs-'tā-shən\ *n* — **pro·test·er** *or* **pro·tes·tor** \-tər\ *n*

Prot·es·tant \'prä-təs-tənt, *3 also* prə-'tes-\ *n* **1** : a member or adherent of one of the Christian churches deriving from the Reformation **2** : a Christian not of a Catholic or Orthodox church **3** *not cap* : one who makes a protest — **Prot·es·tant·ism** \'prä-təs-tən-ˌti-zəm\ *n*

pro·tha·la·mi·on \ˌprō-thə-'lā-mē-ən\ *or* **pro·tha·la·mi·um** \-mē-əm\ *n, pl* **-mia** \-mē-ə\ : a song in celebration of a marriage

pro·to·col \'prō-tə-ˌkȯl\ *n* [MF *prothocole*, fr. ML *protocollum*, fr. LGk *prōtokollon* first sheet of a papyrus roll bearing data of manufacture, fr. Gk *prōtos* first + *kollan* to glue together, fr. *kolla* glue] **1** : an original draft or record **2** : a preliminary memorandum of diplomatic negotiation **3** : a code of diplomatic or military etiquette **4** : a set of conventions for formatting data in an electronic communications system

pro·ton \'prō-ˌtän\ *n* [Gk *prōton*, neut. of *prōtos* first] : a positively charged atomic particle present in all atomic nuclei — **pro·ton·ic** \-'tä-nik\ *adj*

pro·to·plasm \'prō-tə-ˌpla-zəm\ *n* : the complex colloidal largely protein substance of living plant and animal cells — **pro·to·plas·mic** \ˌprō-tə-'plaz-mik\ *adj*

pro·to·type \'prō-tə-ˌtīp\ *n* : an original model : ARCHETYPE

pro·to·zo·an \ˌprō-tə-'zō-ən\ *n* : any of a phylum or subkingdom of unicellular lower invertebrate animals that include some pathogenic parasites of humans and domestic animals — **protozoan** *adj*

pro·tract \prō-'trakt\ *vb* : to prolong in time or space ♦ **Synonyms** EXTEND, LENGTHEN, ELONGATE, STRETCH

pro·trac·tor \-'trak-tər\ *n* : an instrument for drawing and measuring angles

pro·trude \prō-'trüd\ *vb* **pro·trud·ed; pro·trud·ing** : to stick out or cause to stick out : jut out — **pro·tru·sion** \-'trü-zhən\ *n*

pro·tu·ber·ance \prō-'tü-bə-rəns, -'tyü-\ *n* : something that protrudes

pro·tu·ber·ant \-rənt\ *adj* : extending beyond the surrounding surface in a bulge

proud \'praúd\ *adj* **1** : having or showing excessive self-esteem : HAUGHTY **2** : highly pleased : EXULTANT **3** : having proper self-respect ⟨too ~ to beg⟩ **4** : GLORIOUS ⟨a ~ occasion⟩ **5** : SPIRITED ⟨a ~ steed⟩ ♦ **Synonyms** ARROGANT, INSOLENT, OVERBEARING, DISDAINFUL — **proud·ly** *adv*

prov *abbr* **1** province; provincial **2** provisional

Prov *abbr* Proverbs

prove \'prüv\ *vb* **proved; proved** *or* **prov·en** \'prü-vən\; **prov·ing 1** : to test by experiment or by a standard **2** : to establish the truth of by argument or evidence **3** : to show to be correct, valid, or genuine **4** : to turn out esp. after trial or test ⟨the car *proved* to be a good choice⟩ — **prov·able** \'prü-və-bəl\ *adj*

prov·e·nance \'prä-və-nəns\ *n* : ORIGIN, SOURCE

Pro·ven·çal \ˌprō-vän-'säl, ˌprä-vən-\ *n* **1** : a native or inhabitant of Provence **2** : OCCITAN — **Provençal** *adj*

prov·en·der \'prä-vən-dər\ *n* **1** : dry food for domestic animals : FEED **2** : FOOD, VICTUALS

pro·ve·nience \prə-'vē-nyəns\ *n* : ORIGIN, SOURCE

prov·erb \'prä-ˌvərb\ *n* : a pithy popular saying : ADAGE

pro·ver·bi·al \prə-'vər-bē-əl\ *adj* **1** : of, relating to, or resembling a proverb **2** : commonly spoken of

Proverbs *n* — see BIBLE table

pro·vide \prə-'vīd\ *vb* **pro·vid·ed; pro·vid·ing** [ME, fr. L *providēre*, lit., to see ahead, fr. *pro-* forward + *vidēre* to see] **1** : to take measures beforehand ⟨~ against inflation⟩ **2** : to make a proviso or stipulation **3** : to supply what is needed ⟨~ for a family⟩ **4** : EQUIP **5** : to supply for use : YIELD — **pro·vid·er** *n*

pro·vid·ed *conj* : on condition that : IF

prov·i·dence \'prä-və-dəns\ *n* **1** *often cap* : divine guidance or care **2** *cap* : GOD **1 3** : the quality or state of being provident

prov·i·dent \-dənt\ *adj* **1** : making provision for the future : PRUDENT **2** : FRUGAL — **prov·i·dent·ly** *adv*

prov·i·den·tial \ˌprä-və-'den-chəl\ *adj* **1** : of, relating to, or determined by Providence **2** : OPPORTUNE, LUCKY

providing *conj* : PROVIDED

prov·ince \'prä-vəns\ *n* **1** : an administrative district or division of a country **2** *pl* : all of a country except the metropolises **3** : proper business or scope : SPHERE ⟨the ~ of the jury⟩

pro·vin·cial \prə-'vin-chəl\ *adj* **1** : of or relating to a province **2** : limited in outlook : NARROW ⟨~ ideas⟩ — **pro·vin·cial·ism** \-chə-ˌli-zəm\ *n*

proving ground *n* : a place for scientific experimentation or testing

¹pro·vi·sion \prə-'vi-zhən\ *n* **1** : the act or process of providing; *also* : a measure taken beforehand **2** : a stock of needed supplies; *esp* : a stock of food — usu. used in pl. **3** : PROVISO

²provision *vb* : to supply with provisions

pro·vi·sion·al \-'vi-zhə-nəl\ *adj* : provided for a temporary need : CONDITIONAL — **pro·vi·sion·al·ly** *adv*

pro·vi·so \prə-'vī-zō\ *n, pl* **-sos** *also* **-soes** [ME, fr. ML *proviso quod* provided that] : an article or clause that introduces a condition : STIPULATION

pro·vo·ca·teur \prō-ˌvä-kə-'tər\ *n* : one who provokes

prov·o·ca·tion \ˌprä-və-'kā-shən\ *n* **1** : the act of provoking **2** : something that provokes

pro·voc·a·tive \prə-'vä-kə-tiv\ *adj* : serving to provoke or excite

pro·voke \prə-'vōk\ *vb* **pro·voked; pro·vok·ing 1** : to incite to anger : INCENSE **2** : to call forth : EVOKE ⟨a remark that *provoked* laughter⟩ **3** : to stir up on purpose ⟨~ an argument⟩ ♦ **Synonyms** IRRITATE, EXASPERATE, AGGRAVATE, INFLAME, RILE, PIQUE — **pro·vok·er** *n*

pro·vo·lo·ne \ˌprō-və-'lō-nē\ *n* : a usu. firm pliant often smoked Italian cheese

pro·vost \'prō-ˌvōst, 'prä-vəst\ *n* : a high official : DIGNITARY; *esp* : a high-ranking university administrative officer

pro·vost mar·shal \ˌprō-ˌvō-'mär-shəl\ *n* : an officer who supervises the military police of a command

prow \'praú\ *n* : the bow of a ship

prow·ess \'praú-əs\ *n* **1** : military valor and skill **2** : extraordinary ability

prowl \'praú(-ə)l\ *vb* : to roam about stealthily — **prowl** *n* — **prowl·er** *n*

prox·i·mal \'präk-sə-məl\ *adj* **1** : next to or nearest the point of attachment or origin; *esp* : located toward the center of the body **2** : of, relating to, or being the mesial and distal surfaces of a tooth — **prox·i·mal·ly** *adv*

prox·i·mate \'präk-sə-mət\ *adj* **1** : DIRECT ⟨the ~ cause⟩ **2** : very near

prox·im·i·ty \präk-'si-mə-tē\ *n* : NEARNESS ⟨lives in ~ to a bus stop⟩

prox·i·mo \'präk-sə-ˌmō\ *adj* [L *proximo mense* in the next month] : of or occurring in the next month after the present

proxy \'präk-sē\ *n, pl* **prox·ies** [ME *proxi, procucie,* alter. of *procuracie,* fr. AF, fr. ML *procuratia,* alter. of L *procuratio* appointment of another as an agent, fr. *procurare* to take care of] : the authority or power to act for another; *also* : a document giving such authorization — **proxy** *adj*

prude \'prüd\ *n* : a person who shows or affects extreme modesty — **prud·ery** \'prü-də-rē\ *n* — **prud·ish** *adj* — **prud·ish·ly** *adv*

pru·dent \'prü-dᵊnt\ *adj* **1** : shrewd in the management of practical affairs **2** : CAUTIOUS, DISCREET **3** : PROVIDENT, FRUGAL ✦ *Synonyms* JUDICIOUS, FORESIGHTED, SENSIBLE, SANE — **pru·dence** \-dᵊns\ *n* — **pru·den·tial** \prü-'den-chəl\ *adj* — **pru·dent·ly** *adv*

¹prune \'prün\ *n* : a dried plum

²prune *vb* **pruned; prun·ing** : to cut off unwanted parts (as of a tree)

pru·ri·ent \'prur-ē-ənt\ *adj* : LASCIVIOUS; *also* : exciting to lasciviousness — **pru·ri·ence** \-ē-əns\ *n*

¹pry \'prī\ *vb* **pried; pry·ing** : to look closely or inquisitively; *esp* : SNOOP

²pry *vb* **pried; pry·ing** **1** : to raise, move, or pull apart with a pry or lever **2** : to detach or open with difficulty

³pry *n* : a tool for prying

Ps *or* **Psa** *abbr* Psalms

PS *abbr* **1** [L *postscriptum*] postscript **2** public school

PSA *abbr* public service announcement

psalm \'säm, 'sälm\ *n, often cap* [ME, fr. OE *psealm,* fr. LL *psalmus,* fr. Gk *psalmos,* lit., twanging of a harp, fr. *psallein* to pluck, play a stringed instrument] : a sacred song or poem; *esp* : one of the hymns collected in the Book of Psalms — **psalm·ist** *n*

Psalms *n* — see BIBLE table

Psal·ter \'sȯl-tər\ *n* : the Book of Psalms; *also* : a collection of the Psalms arranged for devotional use

pseud *abbr* pseudonym; pseudonymous

pseu·do \'sü-dō\ *adj* : SPURIOUS, SHAM

pseu·do·nym \'sü-də-ˌnim\ *n* : a fictitious name — **pseu·don·y·mous** \sü-'dä-nə-məs\ *adj*

pseu·do·sci·ence \ˌsü-dō-'sī-əns\ *n* : a system of theories, assumptions, and methods erroneously regarded as scientific — **pseu·do·sci·en·tif·ic** \-ˌsī-ən-'ti-fik\ *adj*

PSG *abbr* platoon sergeant

¹psi \'sī, 'psī\ *n* : the 23d letter of the Greek alphabet — Ψ or ψ

²psi *abbr* pounds per square inch

psit·ta·co·sis \ˌsi-tə-'kō-səs\ *n* : an infectious disease of birds marked by diarrhea and wasting and transmissible to humans

pso·ri·a·sis \sə-'rī-ə-səs\ *n* : a chronic skin disease characterized by red patches covered with white scales

PST *abbr* Pacific standard time

¹psych *or* **psyche** \'sīk\ *vb* **psyched; psych·ing** **1** : OUTWIT, OUTGUESS; *also* : to analyze beforehand **2** : INTIMIDATE; *also* : to prepare oneself psychologically ⟨get *psyched* up for the game⟩

²psych *abbr* psychology

psy·che \'sī-kē\ *n* : SOUL, PERSONALITY; *also* : MIND

psy·che·del·ic \ˌsī-kə-'de-lik\ *adj* **1** : of, relating to, or causing abnormal psychic effects ⟨~ drugs⟩ **2** : relating to the taking of psychedelic drugs ⟨~ experience⟩ **3** : imitating, suggestive of, or reproducing the effects of psychedelic drugs ⟨~ art⟩ ⟨~ colors⟩ — **psychedelic** *n* — **psy·che·del·i·cal·ly** \-li-k(ə-)lē\ *adv*

psy·chi·a·try \sə-'kī-ə-trē, sī-\ *n* [prob. fr. F *psychiatrie,* fr. *psychiatre* psychiatrist, fr. Gk *psychē* breath, soul + *iatros* physician] : a branch of medicine dealing with mental, emotional, and behavioral disorders — **psy·chi·at·ric** \ˌsī-kē-'a-trik\ *adj* — **psy·chi·a·trist** \sə-'kī-ə-trist, sī-\ *n*

¹psy·chic \'sī-kik\ *also* **psy·chi·cal** \-ki-kəl\ *adj* **1** : of or relating to the psyche **2** : lying outside the sphere of physical science **3** : sensitive to nonphysical or supernatural forces — **psy·chi·cal·ly** \-k(ə-)lē\ *adv*

²psychic *n* : a person apparently sensitive to nonphysical forces; *also* : MEDIUM 6

psy·cho \'sī-kō\ *n, pl* **psychos** : a mentally disturbed person — **psycho** *adj*

psy·cho·ac·tive \ˌsī-kō-'ak-tiv\ *adj* : affecting the mind or behavior

psy·cho·anal·y·sis \ˌsī-kō-ə-'na-lə-səs\ *n* : a method of dealing with psychic disorders by having the patient talk freely about personal experiences and esp. about early childhood and dreams — **psy·cho·an·a·lyst** \-'a-nə-list\ *n* — **psy·cho·an·a·lyt·ic** \-ˌa-nə-'li-tik\ *adj* — **psy·cho·an·a·lyze** \-'a-nə-ˌlīz\ *vb*

psy·cho·bab·ble \'sī-kō-ˌba-bəl\ *n* : psychological jargon esp. when used in a trite or simplistic manner

psy·cho·dra·ma \ˌsī-kō-'drä-mə, -'dra-\ *n* **1** : an extemporized dramatization designed to afford catharsis for one or more of the participants from whose life the plot is taken **2** : a dramatic event or story with psychological overtones

psy·cho·gen·ic \-'je-nik\ *adj* : originating in the mind or in mental or emotional conflict

psy·cho·graph·ics \ˌsī-kə-'gra-fiks\ *n sing or pl* : market research or statistics classifying population groups according to psychological variables

psychol *abbr* psychologist; psychology

psy·chol·o·gy \sī-'kä-lə-jē\ *n, pl* **-gies** **1** : the science of mind and behavior **2** : the mental and behavioral characteristics of an individual or group — **psy·cho·log·i·cal** \ˌsī-kə-'lä-ji-kəl\ *adj* — **psy·cho·log·i·cal·ly** \-ji-k(ə-)lē\ *adv* — **psy·chol·o·gist** \sī-'kä-lə-jist\ *n*

psy·cho·path \'sī-kō-ˌpath\ *n* : a mentally ill or unstable person; *esp* : a person who engages in antisocial behavior and exhibits a pervasive disregard for the rights, feelings, and safety of others — **psy·cho·path·ic** \ˌsī-kə-'pa-thik\ *adj*

psy·cho·sex·u·al \ˌsī-kō-'sek-shə-wəl\ *adj* **1** : of or relating to the mental, emotional, and behavioral aspects of sexual development **2** : of or relating to the physiological psychology of sex

psy·cho·sis \sī-'kō-səs\ *n, pl* **-cho·ses** \-ˌsēz\ : a serious mental illness (as schizophrenia) marked by loss of or greatly lessened ability to test whether what one is thinking and feeling about the real world is really true

psy·cho·so·cial \ˌsī-kō-'sō-shəl\ *adj* **1** : involving both psychological and social aspects **2** : relating social conditions to mental health

psy·cho·so·mat·ic \ˌsī-kō-sə-'ma-tik\ *adj* : of, relating to, involving, or concerned with bodily symptoms caused by mental or emotional disturbance

psy·cho·ther·a·py \ˌsī-kō-'ther-ə-pē\ *n* : treatment of mental or emotional disorder or of related bodily ills by psychological means — **psy·cho·ther·a·pist** \-pist\ *n*

psy·chot·ic \sī-'kä-tik\ *adj* : of or relating to psychosis ⟨~ behavior⟩ ⟨a ~ patient⟩ — **psychotic** *n*

psy·cho·tro·pic \ˌsī-kə-'trō-pik\ *adj* : acting on the mind ⟨~ drugs⟩

pt *abbr* **1** part **2** payment **3** pint **4** point **5** port

Pt *symbol* platinum

PT *abbr* **1** Pacific time **2** part-time **3** physical therapy **4** physical training

PTA *abbr* Parent-Teacher Association

ptar·mi·gan \'tär-mi-gən\ *n, pl* **-gan** *or* **-gans** : any of various grouses of northern regions with completely feathered feet

PT boat \(ˌ)pē-'tē-\ *n* [*patrol torpedo*] : a small fast patrol craft usu. armed with torpedos

pte *abbr, Brit* private

ptg *abbr* printing

PTO *abbr* **1** Parent-Teacher Organization **2** please turn over

pto·maine \'tō-ˌmān\ *n* : any of various chemical substances formed by bacteria in decaying matter (as meat) and including a few poisonous ones

Pu *symbol* plutonium

¹pub \'pəb\ *n* **1** *chiefly Brit* : PUBLIC HOUSE 2 **2** : TAVERN

²pub *abbr* **1** public **2** publication **3** published; publisher; publishing

pu·ber·ty \'pyü-bər-tē\ *n* : the condition of being or period of becoming first capable of reproducing sexually — **pu·ber·tal** \-bər-tᵊl\ *adj*

pu·bes \'pyü-bēz\ *n, pl* **pubes** [NL, fr. L, manhood, body hair, pubic region] **1** : the hair that appears upon the lower middle region of the abdomen at puberty **2** : the pubic region

pu·bes·cence \pyü-'be-sᵊns\ *n* **1** : the quality or state of being pubescent **2** : a pubescent covering or surface

pu·bes·cent \-sᵊnt\ *adj* **1** : arriving at or having reached puberty **2** : covered with fine soft short hairs

pu·bic \'pyü-bik\ *adj* : of, relating to, or situated near the pubes or the pubis

pu·bis \'pyü-bəs\ *n, pl* **pu·bes** \-bēz\ : the ventral and anterior of the three principal bones composing either half of the pelvis

publ *abbr* 1 publication 2 published; publisher

¹**pub·lic** \'pə-blik\ *adj* 1 : exposed to general view ⟨the story became ∼⟩ 2 : of, relating to, or affecting the people as a whole ⟨∼ opinion⟩ 3 : CIVIC, GOVERNMENTAL ⟨∼ expenditures⟩ 4 : of, relating to, or serving the community ⟨∼ officials⟩ 5 : not private : SOCIAL ⟨∼ morality⟩ 6 : open to all ⟨∼ library⟩ 7 : well known : PROMINENT ⟨∼ figures⟩ 8 : supported by public funds and private contributions rather than by income from commercials — **pub·lic·ly** *adv*

²**public** *n* 1 : the people as a whole : POPULACE 2 : a group of people having common interests ⟨the movie-going ∼⟩

pub·li·can \'pə-bli-kən\ *n* 1 : a Jewish tax collector for the ancient Romans 2 *chiefly Brit* : the licensee of a pub

pub·li·ca·tion \ˌpə-blə-'kā-shən\ *n* 1 : the act or process of publishing 2 : a published work

public house *n* 1 : INN 2 *chiefly Brit* : a licensed saloon or bar

pub·li·cise *Brit var of* PUBLICIZE

pub·li·cist \'pə-blə-sist\ *n* : one that publicizes; *esp* : PRESS AGENT

pub·lic·i·ty \(ˌ)pə-'bli-sə-tē\ *n* 1 : information with news value issued to gain public attention or support 2 : public attention or acclaim

pub·li·cize \'pə-blə-ˌsīz\ *vb* **-cized; -ciz·ing** : to bring to public attention : ADVERTISE ⟨*publicizing* his book⟩

pub·lic–key \'pə-blik-'kē\ *n* : the publicly shared element of a code usable only to encode messages

public relations *n sing or pl* : the business of fostering public goodwill toward a person, firm, or institution; *also* : the degree of goodwill and understanding achieved

public school *n* 1 : an endowed secondary boarding school in Great Britain offering a classical curriculum and preparation for the universities or public service 2 : a free tax-supported school controlled by a local governmental authority

public–spirited *adj* : motivated by devotion to the general or national welfare

public works *n pl* : works (as schools or highways) constructed with public funds for public use

pub·lish \'pə-blish\ *vb* 1 : to make generally known : announce publicly 2 : to produce or release literature, information, musical scores or sometimes recordings, or art for sale to the public — **pub·lish·er** *n*

¹**puck** \'pək\ *n* : a mischievous sprite — **puck·ish** *adj* — **puck·ish·ly** *adv*

²**puck** *n* : a disk used in ice hockey

¹**puck·er** \'pə-kər\ *vb* : to contract into folds or wrinkles

²**pucker** *n* : FOLD, WRINKLE

pud·ding \'pu̇-diŋ\ *n* : a soft, spongy, or thick creamy dessert

pud·dle \'pə-dᵊl\ *n* : a very small pool of usu. dirty or muddy water

pu·den·dum \pyu̇-'den-dəm\ *n, pl* **-da** \-də\ [NL, fr. L *pudēre* to be ashamed] : the human external genital organs esp. of a woman

pudgy \'pə-jē\ *adj* **pudg·i·er; -est** : being short and plump : CHUBBY

pueb·lo \'pwe-blō, pü-'e-\ *n, pl* **-los** [Sp, village, lit., people, fr. L *populus*] 1 : an American Indian village of Arizona or New Mexico that consists of flat-roofed stone or adobe houses joined in groups sometimes several stories high 2 *cap* : a member of a group of American Indian peoples of the southwestern U.S.

pu·er·ile \'pyu̇-ə-rəl\ *adj* : CHILDISH, SILLY ⟨∼ remarks⟩ — **pu·er·il·i·ty** \ˌpyü-ə-'ri-lə-tē\ *n*

pu·er·per·al \pyü-'ər-pə-rəl\ *adj* : of, relating to, or occurring during childbirth or the period immediately following ⟨∼ infection⟩ ⟨∼ depression⟩

puerperal fever *n* : an abnormal condition that results from infection of the placental site following childbirth or abortion

¹**puff** \'pəf\ *vb* 1 : to blow in short gusts 2 : PANT 3 : to emit small whiffs or clouds 4 : BLUSTER, BRAG 5 : INFLATE, SWELL 6 : to make proud or conceited 7 : to praise extravagantly

²**puff** *n* 1 : a short discharge (as of air or smoke); *also* : a slight explosive sound accompanying it 2 : a light fluffy pastry 3 : a slight swelling 4 : a fluffy mass; *also* : a small pad for applying cosmetic powder 5 : a laudatory notice or review — **puffy** *adj*

³**puff** *adj* : of, relating to, or designed for promotion or flattery ⟨∼ articles on the new TV series⟩

puff·ball \'pəf-ˌbȯl\ *n* : any of various globe-shaped and often edible fungi

puf·fin \'pə-fən\ *n* : any of several seabirds having a short neck and a deep grooved parti-colored bill

¹**pug** \'pəg\ *n* 1 : any of a breed of small stocky short-haired dogs with a wrinkled face 2 : a close coil of hair

²**pug** *n* : ¹BOXER

pu·gi·lism \'pyü-jə-ˌli-zəm\ *n* : BOXING — **pu·gi·list** \-list\ *n* — **pu·gi·lis·tic** \ˌpyü-jə-'lis-tik\ *adj*

pug·na·cious \ˌpəg-'nā-shəs\ *adj* : having a quarrelsome or combative nature ♦ *Synonyms* BELLIGERENT, BELLICOSE, CONTENTIOUS, TRUCULENT — **pug·nac·i·ty** \-'na-sə-tē\ *n*

puis·sance \'pwi-səns, 'pyü-ə-\ *n* : POWER, STRENGTH ⟨the ∼ of the king⟩ — **puis·sant** \-sənt\ *adj*

puke \'pyük\ *vb* **puked; puk·ing** : VOMIT — **puke** *n*

puk·ka \'pə-kə\ *adj* [Hindi *pakkā* cooked, ripe, solid, fr. Skt *pakva*] : GENUINE, AUTHENTIC; *also* : FIRST-CLASS, COMPLETE

pul \'pül\ *n, pl* **puls** \'pülz\ *or* **pul** — see *afghani* at MONEY table

pu·la \'pü-lə, 'pyü-\ *n, pl* **pula** — see MONEY table

pul·chri·tude \'pəl-krə-ˌtüd, -ˌtyüd\ *n* : BEAUTY — **pul·chri·tu·di·nous** \ˌpəl-krə-'tü-dᵊn-əs, -'tyü-\ *adj*

¹**pull** \'pu̇l\ *vb* 1 : to exert force so as to draw (something) toward the force; *also* : MOVE ⟨∼ out of a driveway⟩ 2 : PLUCK; *also* : EXTRACT ⟨∼ a tooth⟩ 3 : STRETCH, STRAIN ⟨∼ a tendon⟩ 4 : to draw apart : TEAR 5 : to make (as a proof) by printing 6 : REMOVE ⟨∼ed the pitcher in the third inning⟩ 7 : DRAW ⟨∼ a gun⟩ 8 : to carry out esp. with daring ⟨∼ a robbery⟩ 9 : PERPETRATE, COMMIT 10 : ATTRACT 11 : to express strong sympathy — **pull·er** *n*

²**pull** *n* 1 : the act or an instance of pulling 2 : the effort expended in moving 3 : ADVANTAGE ⟨had the ∼ of a respected family name⟩; *esp* : special influence 4 : a device for pulling something or for operating by pulling 5 : a force that attracts or compels 6 : an injury from abnormal straining or stretching ⟨a muscle ∼⟩

pull·back \'pu̇l-ˌbak\ *n* : an orderly withdrawal of troops

pull–down *adj* : appearing below a selected item (as a menu title) on a computer display ⟨a ∼ menu⟩

pul·let \'pu̇-lət\ *n* : a young hen esp. of the domestic chicken when less than a year old

pul·ley \'pu̇-lē\ *n, pl* **pulleys** : a wheel used to transmit power by means of a belt, rope, or chain; *esp* : one with a grooved rim that forms part of a tackle for hoisting or for changing the direction of a force

Pull·man \'pu̇l-mən\ *n* : a railroad passenger car with comfortable furnishings esp. for night travel

pull off *vb* : to accomplish successfully

pull·out \'pu̇l-ˌau̇t\ *n* : PULLBACK

pull·over \'pu̇l-ˌō-vər\ *adj* : put on by being pulled over the head ⟨∼ sweater⟩ — **pull·over** *n*

pull–up \'pu̇l-ˌəp\ *n* : CHIN-UP

pull up *vb* : to bring or come to an often abrupt halt : STOP

pul·mo·nary \'pu̇l-mə-ˌner-ē, 'pəl-\ *adj* : of, relating to, or carried on by the lungs ⟨the ∼ circulation⟩

pulp \'pəlp\ *n* 1 : the soft juicy or fleshy part of a fruit or vegetable 2 : a soft moist mass 3 : the soft sensitive tissue that fills the central cavity of a tooth 4 : a material (as from wood) used in making paper 5 : a magazine using cheap paper and often dealing with sensational material — **pulpy** *adj*

pul·pit \'pu̇l-ˌpit\ *n* : a raised platform or high reading desk used in preaching or conducting a worship service

pulp·wood \'pəlp-ˌwu̇d\ *n* : wood used in making pulp for paper

pul·sar \'pəl-ˌsär\ *n* : a celestial source of pulsating electromagnetic radiation (as radio waves)

pul·sate \'pəl-ˌsāt\ *vb* **pul·sat·ed; pul·sat·ing** : to expand and contract rhythmically : BEAT ⟨an artery ∼s⟩ — **pul·sa·tion** \ˌpəl-'sā-shən\ *n*

pulse \\'pəls\\ *n* 1 : the regular throbbing in the arteries caused by the contractions of the heart 2 : rhythmical beating, vibrating, or sounding 3 : a brief change in electrical current or voltage — **pulse** *vb*

pul·ver·ise *Brit var of* PULVERIZE

pul·ver·ize \\'pəl-və-ˌrīz\\ *vb* **-ized; -iz·ing** 1 : to reduce (as by crushing or grinding) or be reduced to very small particles 2 : DEMOLISH

pu·ma \\'pü-mə, 'pyü-\\ *n, pl* **pumas** *also* **puma** [Sp, fr. Quechua] : COUGAR

pum·ice \\'pə-məs\\ *n* : a light porous volcanic glass used esp. for smoothing and polishing

pum·mel \\'pə-məl\\ *vb* **-meled** *also* **-melled; -mel·ing** *also* **-mel·ling** : POUND, BEAT ⟨∼*ed* the intruder⟩

¹**pump** \\'pəmp\\ *n* : a device for raising, transferring, or compressing fluids esp. by suction or pressure

²**pump** *vb* 1 : to raise (as water) with a pump 2 : to draw fluid from with a pump; *also* : to fill by means of a pump ⟨∼ up a tire⟩ 3 : to force or propel in the manner of a pump — **pump·er** *n*

³**pump** *n* : a low shoe that grips the foot chiefly at the toe and heel

pumped \\'pəmpt\\ *adj* : filled with energetic excitement and enthusiasm

pum·per·nick·el \\'pəm-pər-ˌni-kəl\\ *n* : a dark rye bread

pump·kin \\'pəmp-kən, 'pəŋ-kən\\ *n* : the large usu. orange fruit of a vine of the gourd family that is widely used as food; *also* : this vine

pun \\'pən\\ *n* : the humorous use of a word in a way that suggests two or more interpretations — **pun** *vb*

¹**punch** \\'pənch\\ *n* : a tool for piercing, stamping, cutting, or forming

²**punch** *vb* 1 : PROD, POKE; *also* : DRIVE, HERD ⟨∼*ing* cattle⟩ 2 : to strike with the fist 3 : to emboss, perforate, or make with a punch 4 : to operate, produce, or enter (as data) by or as if by punching — **punch·er** *n*

³**punch** *n* 1 : a quick blow with or as if with the fist 2 : effective energy or forcefulness

⁴**punch** *n* [perh. fr. Hindi *pãc* five, fr. Skt *pañca;* fr. the number of ingredients] : a drink usu. composed of wine or alcoholic liquor and nonalcoholic beverages; *also* : a drink composed of nonalcoholic beverages

punch card *n* : a card with holes punched in particular positions to represent data

punch–drunk \\'pənch-ˌdrəŋk\\ *adj* 1 : suffering from brain injury resulting from repeated head blows received in boxing 2 : DAZED, CONFUSED

pun·cheon \\'pən-chən\\ *n* : a large cask

punch line *n* : the sentence or phrase in a joke that makes the point

punch list *n* : a list of tasks to be completed at the end of a project

punchy \\'pən-chē\\ *adj* **punch·i·er; -est** 1 : having punch : FORCEFUL 2 : DAZED, CONFUSED ⟨a ∼ boxer⟩ 3 : VIVID, VIBRANT ⟨∼ graphics⟩

punc·til·io \\ˌpəŋk-'ti-lē-ˌō\\ *n, pl* **-i·os** : a nice detail of conduct in a ceremony or in observance of a code 2 : careful observance of forms (as in social conduct)

punc·til·i·ous \\ˌpəŋk-'ti-lē-əs\\ *adj* : marked by precise accordance with codes or conventions ✦ *Synonyms* METICULOUS, SCRUPULOUS, CAREFUL, PUNCTUAL

punc·tu·al \\'pəŋk-chə-wəl\\ *adj* : being on time : PROMPT — **punc·tu·al·i·ty** \\ˌpəŋk-chə-'wa-lə-tē\\ *n* — **punc·tu·al·ly** *adv*

punc·tu·ate \\'pəŋk-chə-ˌwāt\\ *vb* **-at·ed; -at·ing** 1 : to mark or divide (written matter) with punctuation marks 2 : to break into at intervals 3 : EMPHASIZE

punc·tu·a·tion \\ˌpəŋk-chə-'wā-shən\\ *n* : the act, practice, or system of inserting standardized marks in written matter to clarify the meaning and separate structural units

¹**punc·ture** \\'pəŋk-chər\\ *n* 1 : an act of puncturing 2 : a small hole or wound made by puncturing

²**puncture** *vb* **punc·tured; punc·tur·ing** 1 : to make a hole in : PIERCE 2 : to make useless as if by a puncture

pun·dit \\'pən-dət\\ *n* [Hindi *paṇḍit,* fr. Skt *paṇḍita, paṇḍita* learned] 1 : a learned person : TEACHER 2 : AUTHORITY, CRITIC

pun·dit·oc·ra·cy \\ˌpən-dət-'ä-krə-sē\\ *n, pl* **-cies** : a group of powerful and influential political commentators

pun·gent \\'pən-jənt\\ *adj* 1 : having a sharp incisive quality : CAUSTIC ⟨a ∼ editorial⟩ 2 : causing a sharp,

intense, or irritating sensation (as of taste or smell); *esp* : ACRID ⟨a ∼ odor⟩ — **pun·gen·cy** \\-jən-sē\\ *n* — **pun·gent·ly** *adv*

pun·ish \\'pə-nish\\ *vb* 1 : to impose a penalty on for a fault or crime ⟨∼ an offender⟩ 2 : to inflict a penalty for ⟨∼ treason with death⟩ 3 : to inflict injury on : HURT ✦ *Synonyms* CHASTISE, CASTIGATE, CHASTEN, DISCIPLINE, CORRECT — **pun·ish·able** *adj*

pun·ish·ment *n* 1 : retributive suffering, pain, or loss : PENALTY 2 : rough treatment

pu·ni·tive \\'pyü-nə-tiv\\ *adj* : inflicting, involving, or aiming at punishment

¹**punk** \\'pəŋk\\ *n* 1 : a young inexperienced person 2 : a petty hoodlum

²**punk** *adj* : very poor : INFERIOR

³**punk** *n* : dry crumbly wood useful for tinder; *also* : a substance made from fungi for use as tinder

pun·ster \\'pən-stər\\ *n* : one who is given to punning

¹**punt** \\'pənt\\ *n* : a long narrow flat-bottomed boat with square ends

¹**punt**

²**punt** *vb* : to propel (as a punt) with a pole

³**punt** *vb* : to kick a football or soccer ball dropped from the hands before it touches the ground

⁴**punt** *n* : the act or an instance of punting a ball

pu·ny \\'pyü-nē\\ *adj* **pu·ni·er; -est** [AF *puisné* younger, weakly, lit., born afterward, fr. *puis* afterward (fr. L *post*) + *né* born, fr. L *natus*] : slight in power, size, or importance : WEAK ⟨a ∼ body⟩ ⟨∼ sales⟩

pup \\'pəp\\ *n* : a young dog; *also* : one of the young of some other animals

pu·pa \\'pyü-pə\\ *n, pl* **pu·pae** \\-(ˌ)pē\\ *or* **pupas** [NL, fr. L *pupa* doll] : a form of some insects (as a bee, moth, or beetle) between the larva and the adult that usu. has a protective covering (as a cocoon) — **pu·pal** \\-pəl\\ *adj*

¹**pu·pil** \\'pyü-pəl\\ *n* 1 : a child or young person in school or in the charge of a tutor 2 : DISCIPLE

²**pupil** *n* : the dark central opening of the iris of the eye

pup·pet \\'pə-pət\\ *n* [ME *popet* youth, doll, fr. MF *poupette,* ultim. fr. L *pupa* doll] 1 : a small figure of a person or animal moved by hand or by strings or wires 2 : DOLL 3 : one whose acts are controlled by an outside force or influence

pup·pe·teer \\ˌpə-pə-'tir\\ *n* : one who manipulates puppets

pup·py \\'pə-pē\\ *n, pl* **puppies** : a young domestic dog

pu·pu \\'pü-ˌpü\\ *n* : an Asian dish consisting of a variety of foods

pur·blind \\'pər-ˌblīnd\\ *adj* 1 : partly blind 2 : lacking in insight : OBTUSE

¹**pur·chase** \\'pər-chəs\\ *vb* **pur·chased; pur·chas·ing** : to obtain by paying money or its equivalent : BUY — **pur·chas·able** \\-chə-sə-bəl\\ *adj* — **pur·chas·er** *n*

²**purchase** *n* 1 : an act or instance of purchasing 2 : something purchased 3 : a secure hold or grasp; *also* : advantageous leverage

pur·dah \\'pər-də\\ *n* : seclusion of women from public observation among Muslims and some Hindus esp. in India; *also* : a state of seclusion

pure \\'pyùr\\ *adj* **pur·er; pur·est** 1 : unmixed with any other matter : free from taint ⟨∼ gold⟩ ⟨∼ water⟩ 2 : SHEER, ABSOLUTE ⟨∼ nonsense⟩ 3 : ABSTRACT, THEORETICAL ⟨∼ mathematics⟩ 4 : free from what vitiates, weakens, or pollutes ⟨speaks a ∼ French⟩ 5 : free from moral fault : INNOCENT 6 : CHASTE, CONTINENT — **pure·ly** *adv*

pure–blood·ed \-ˌblə-dəd\ *or* **pure–blood** \-ˌbləd\ *adj* : FULL-BLOODED — **pure·blood** *n*
pure·bred \-ˈbred\ *adj* : bred from members of a recognized breed, strain, or kind without crossbreeding over many generations — **pure·bred** \-ˌbred\ *n*
¹**pu·ree** \pyu̇-ˈrā, -ˈrē\ *n* [F *purée*, fr. MF, fr. fem. of *puré*, pp. of *purer* to purify, strain, fr. L *purare* to purify] : a paste or thick liquid suspension usu. made from finely ground cooked food; *also* : a thick soup made of pureed vegetables
²**puree** *vb* **pu·reed; pu·ree·ing** : to make a puree of
pur·ga·tion \ˌpər-ˈgā-shən\ *n* : the act or result of purging
¹**pur·ga·tive** \ˈpər-gə-tiv\ *adj* : purging or tending to purge
²**purgative** *n* : a strong laxative : CATHARTIC
pur·ga·to·ry \ˈpər-gə-ˌtȯr-ē\ *n, pl* **-ries** 1 : an intermediate state after death for expiatory purification 2 : a place or state of temporary punishment — **pur·ga·tor·i·al** \ˌpər-gə-ˈtȯr-ē-əl\ *adj*
¹**purge** \ˈpərj\ *vb* **purged; purg·ing** 1 : to cleanse or purify esp. from sin 2 : to have or cause strong and usu. repeated emptying of the bowels 3 : to get rid of ⟨the leaders had been *purged*⟩
²**purge** *n* 1 : something that purges; *esp* : PURGATIVE 2 : an act or result of purging; *esp* : a ridding of persons regarded as treacherous or disloyal
pu·ri·fy \ˈpyu̇r-ə-ˌfī\ *vb* **-fied; -fy·ing** : to make or become pure ⟨∼ water⟩ ⟨∼ the mind⟩ — **pu·ri·fi·ca·tion** \ˌpyu̇r-ə-fə-ˈkā-shən\ *n* — **pu·ri·fi·ca·to·ry** \pyu̇-ˈri-fi-kə-ˌtȯr-ē\ *adj* — **pu·ri·fi·er** *n*
Pu·rim \ˈpu̇r-(ˌ)im\ *n* : a Jewish holiday celebrated in February or March in commemoration of the deliverance of the Jews from the massacre plotted by Haman
pu·rine \ˈpyu̇r-ˌēn\ *n* : any of a group of bases including several (as adenine or guanine) that are constituents of DNA or RNA
pur·ism \ˈpyu̇r-ˌi-zəm\ *n* : rigid adherence to or insistence on purity or nicety esp. in use of words — **pur·ist** \-ist\ *n* — **pu·ris·tic** \pyu̇-ˈris-tik\ *adj*
pu·ri·tan \ˈpyu̇r-ə-tən\ *n* 1 *cap* : a member of a 16th and 17th century Protestant group in England and New England opposing the ceremonies and government of the Church of England 2 : one who practices or preaches a stricter or professedly purer moral code than that which prevails — **pu·ri·tan·i·cal** \ˌpyu̇r-ə-ˈta-ni-kəl\ *adj* — **pu·ri·tan·i·cal·ly** *adv*
pu·ri·ty \ˈpyu̇r-ə-tē\ *n* : the quality or state of being pure
¹**purl** \ˈpərl\ *n* : a stitch in knitting
²**purl** *vb* : to knit in purl stitch
³**purl** *n* : a gentle murmur or movement (as of purling water)
⁴**purl** *vb* 1 : EDDY, SWIRL 2 : to make a soft murmuring sound
pur·lieu \ˈpər-lü, ˈpərl-yü\ *n* 1 : an outlying district : SUBURB 2 *pl* : ENVIRONS
pur·loin \(ˌ)pər-ˈlȯin, ˈpər-ˌlȯin\ *vb* : STEAL, FILCH
¹**pur·ple** \ˈpər-pəl\ *adj* **pur·pler; pur·plest** 1 : of the color purple 2 : highly rhetorical ⟨a ∼ passage⟩ 3 : PROFANE ⟨∼ language⟩ — **pur·plish** *adj*
²**purple** *n* 1 : a bluish red color 2 : a purple robe emblematic esp. of regal rank or authority
¹**pur·port** \ˈpər-ˌpȯrt\ *n* [ME, fr. AF, content, tenor, fr. *purporter* to carry, mean, purport, fr. *pur-* thoroughly + *porter* to carry] : meaning conveyed or implied; *also* : GIST ⟨the ∼ of her letter⟩
²**pur·port** \(ˌ)pər-ˈpȯrt\ *vb* : to convey or profess outwardly as the meaning or intention : CLAIM ⟨∼s to be objective⟩ — **pur·port·ed·ly** \-ˈpȯr-təd-lē\ *adv*
¹**pur·pose** \ˈpər-pəs\ *n* 1 : an object or result aimed at : INTENTION 2 : RESOLUTION, DETERMINATION — **pur·pose·ful** \-fəl\ *adj* — **pur·pose·ful·ly** *adv* — **pur·pose·less** *adj* — **pur·pose·ly** *adv*
²**purpose** *vb* **pur·posed; pur·pos·ing** : to propose as an aim to oneself
purr \ˈpər\ *n* : a low murmur typical of a contented cat — **purr** *vb*
¹**purse** \ˈpərs\ *n* 1 : a receptacle (as a pouch) to carry money and often other small objects in 2 : RESOURCES 3 : a sum of money offered as a prize or present
²**purse** *vb* **pursed; purs·ing** : PUCKER
purs·er \ˈpər-sər\ *n* : an official on a ship who keeps accounts and attends to the comfort of passengers
purs·lane \ˈpər-slən, -ˌslān\ *n* : a fleshy-leaved weedy

trailing plant with tiny yellow flowers that is sometimes used in salads
pur·su·ance \pər-ˈsü-əns\ *n* : the act of carrying out or into effect
pur·su·ant to \-ˈsü-ənt-\ *prep* : in carrying out : ACCORDING TO
pur·sue \pər-ˈsü\ *vb* **pur·sued; pur·su·ing** 1 : to follow in order to overtake or overcome : CHASE 2 : to seek to accomplish ⟨∼ a goal⟩ 3 : to proceed along ⟨∼ a course⟩ 4 : to engage in ⟨∼ a career⟩ — **pur·su·er** *n*
pur·suit \pər-ˈsüt\ *n* 1 : the act of pursuing 2 : OCCUPATION, BUSINESS
pu·ru·lent \ˈpyu̇r-ə-lənt, -yə-\ *adj* : containing or accompanied by pus ⟨a ∼ discharge⟩ — **pu·ru·lence** \-ləns\ *n*
pur·vey \(ˌ)pər-ˈvā\ *vb* **pur·veyed; pur·vey·ing** : to supply (as provisions) usu. as a business — **pur·vey·ance** \-əns\ *n* — **pur·vey·or** \-ər\ *n*
pur·view \ˈpər-ˌvyü\ *n* 1 : the range or limit esp. of authority, responsibility, or intention 2 : range of vision, understanding, or cognizance
pus \ˈpəs\ *n* : thick yellowish white fluid matter (as in a boil) formed at a place of inflammation and infection (as an abscess) and containing germs, white blood cells, and tissue debris
¹**push** \ˈpu̇sh\ *vb* [ME *possen, pusshen*, prob. fr. OF *pousser* to exert pressure, fr. L *pulsare*, fr. *pellere* to drive, strike] 1 : to press against with force in order to drive or impel 2 : to thrust forward, downward, or outward 3 : to urge on : press forward 4 : to cause to increase ⟨∼ prices to record levels⟩ 5 : to urge or press the advancement, adoption, or practice of; *esp* : to make aggressive efforts to sell 6 : to engage in the illicit sale of narcotics
²**push** *n* 1 : a vigorous effort : DRIVE ⟨a ∼ for higher wages⟩ 2 : an act of pushing 3 : vigorous enterprise : ENERGY
push–button *adj* 1 : operated or done by means of push buttons 2 : using or dependent on complex and more or less automatic mechanisms ⟨∼ warfare⟩
push button *n* : a small button or knob that when pushed operates something esp. by closing an electric circuit
push·cart \ˈpu̇sh-ˌkärt\ *n* : a cart or barrow pushed by hand
push·er \ˈpu̇-shər\ *n* : one that pushes; *esp* : one that pushes illegal drugs
push·over \-ˌō-vər\ *n* 1 : something easily accomplished 2 : an opponent easy to defeat 3 : SUCKER ⟨she's nobody's ∼⟩
push–up \-ˌəp\ *n* : a conditioning exercise performed in a prone position by raising and lowering the body with the straightening and bending of the arms while keeping the back straight and supporting the body on the hands and toes
pushy \ˈpu̇-shē\ *adj* **push·i·er; -est** : aggressive often to an objectionable degree
pu·sil·lan·i·mous \ˌpyü-sə-ˈla-nə-məs\ *adj* [LL *pusillanimis*, fr. L *pusillus* very small (dim. of *pusus* boy) + *animus* spirit] : contemptibly timid : COWARDLY — **pu·sil·la·nim·i·ty** \ˌpyü-sə-lə-ˈni-mə-tē\ *n*
¹**puss** \ˈpu̇s\ *n* : CAT
²**puss** *n, slang* : FACE
¹**pussy** \ˈpu̇-sē\ *n, pl* **puss·ies** : CAT
²**pus·sy** \ˈpə-sē\ *adj* **pus·si·er; -est** : full of or resembling pus
pussy·cat \ˈpu̇-sē-ˌkat\ *n* : CAT
pussy·foot \-ˌfu̇t\ *vb* 1 : to tread or move warily or stealthily 2 : to refrain from committing oneself
pussy willow \ˈpu̇-sē-\ *n* : a willow having large silky catkins
pus·tule \ˈpəs-chül\ *n* : a pus-filled pimple
put \ˈpu̇t\ *vb* **put; put·ting** 1 : to bring into a specified position : PLACE ⟨∼ the book on the table⟩ 2 : SEND, THRUST 3 : to throw with an upward pushing motion ⟨∼ the shot⟩ 4 : to bring into a specified state ⟨∼ the plan into effect⟩ 5 : SUBJECT ⟨∼ traitors to death⟩ 6 : IMPOSE 7 : to set before one for decision ⟨∼ the question⟩ 8 : EXPRESS, STATE ⟨∼ my feelings into words⟩ 9 : TRANSLATE, ADAPT 10 : APPLY, ASSIGN ⟨∼ them to work⟩ 11 : ESTIMATE ⟨∼ the number at 20⟩ 12 : ATTACH, ATTRIBUTE ⟨∼ a high value on it⟩ 13 : to take a specified course ⟨the ship ∼ out to sea⟩
pu·ta·tive \ˈpyü-tə-tiv\ *adj* 1 : commonly accepted ⟨∼ expert⟩ 2 : assumed to exist or to have existed

put–down \'pùt-ˌdaùn\ *n* : a belittling remark

put in *vb* **1** : to come in with : INTERPOSE ⟨*put in* a good word for me⟩ **2** : to spend time at some occupation or job ⟨*put in* eight hours at the office⟩

put off *vb* : POSTPONE, DELAY ⟨*put off* my visit⟩

¹put–on \'pùt-ˌón, -ˌän\ *adj* : PRETENDED, ASSUMED ⟨a ∼ accent⟩

²put–on *n* **1** : a deliberate act of misleading someone **2** : PARODY, SPOOF

put·out \'pùt-ˌaùt\ *n* : the retiring of a base runner or batter in baseball

put out *vb* **1** : EXTINGUISH **2** : ANNOY; *also* : INCONVENIENCE **3** : to cause to be out (as in baseball)

pu·tre·fy \'pyü-trə-ˌfī\ *vb* **-fied; -fy·ing** : to make or become putrid : ROT ⟨*putrefied* meat⟩ — **pu·tre·fac·tion** \ˌpyü-trə-'fak-shən\ *n* — **pu·tre·fac·tive** \-tiv\ *adj*

pu·tres·cent \pyü-'tre-s²nt\ *adj* : becoming putrid : ROTTING ⟨∼ carcasses⟩ — **pu·tres·cence** \-s²ns\ *n*

pu·trid \'pyü-trəd\ *adj* **1** : ROTTEN, DECAYED ⟨∼ meat⟩ **2** : VILE, CORRUPT — **pu·trid·i·ty** \pyü-'tri-də-tē\ *n*

putsch \'pùch\ *n* [G] : a secretly plotted and suddenly executed attempt to overthrow a government

putt \'pət\ *n* : a golf stroke made on the green to cause the ball to roll into the hole — **putt** *vb*

put·ta·nes·ca \ˌpü-tä-'nes-kä\ *adj* : served with or being a pungent tomato sauce

¹put·ter \'pù-tər\ *n* : one that puts

²putt·er \'pə-tər\ *n* **1** : a golf club used in putting **2** : one that putts

³put·ter \'pə-tər\ *vb* **1** : to move or act aimlessly or idly **2** : TINKER

put·ty \'pə-tē\ *n, pl* **putties** [F *potée* potter's glaze, lit., potful, fr. OF, fr. *pot* pot] **1** : a doughlike cement used esp. to fasten glass in sashes **2** : one who is easily manipulated — **putty** *vb*

put up *vb* **1** : SHEATHE **2** : to prepare so as to preserve for later use **3** : to offer for public sale ⟨*put* the house *up* for auction⟩ **4** : ACCOMMODATE, LODGE ⟨*put* us *up* for the night⟩ **5** : BUILD **6** : to engage in ⟨*put up* a struggle⟩ **7** : CONTRIBUTE, PAY — **put up with** : TOLERATE 2

¹puz·zle \'pə-zəl\ *vb* **puz·zled; puz·zling** **1** : to bewilder mentally : PERPLEX **2** : to solve with difficulty or ingenuity ⟨∼ out a riddle⟩ **3** : to be in a quandary ⟨∼ over what to do⟩ **4** : to attempt a solution of a puzzle ⟨∼ over a person's words⟩ **♦ Synonyms** MYSTIFY, BEWILDER, NONPLUS, CONFOUND — **puz·zle·ment** *n* — **puz·zler** *n*

²puzzle *n* **1** : something that puzzles **2** : a question, problem, or contrivance designed for testing ingenuity

PVC *abbr* polyvinyl chloride

pvt *abbr* private

PW *abbr* prisoner of war

pwt *abbr* pennyweight

PX *abbr* post exchange

pya \pē-'ä\ *n* — see *kyat* at MONEY table

pyg·my *also* **pig·my** \'pig-mē\ *n, pl* **pygmies** *also* **pigmies** [ME *pigmei,* fr. L *pygmaeus* of a pygmy, dwarfish, fr. Gk *pygmaios,* fr. *pygmē* fist, measure of length] **1** *cap* : any of a small people of equatorial Africa **2** : an unusually small person; *also* : an insignificant or unimpressive person — **pygmy** *adj*

py·ja·mas \pə-'jä-məz\ *chiefly Brit var of* PAJAMAS

py·lon \'pī-ˌlän, -lən\ *n* **1** : a usu. massive gateway; *esp* : an Egyptian one flanked by flat-topped pyramids **2** : a tower that supports wires over a long span **3** : a post or tower marking the course in an airplane race

py·or·rhea \ˌpī-ə-'rē-ə\ *n* : an inflammation with pus of the sockets of the teeth

¹pyr·a·mid \'pir-ə-ˌmid\ *n* **1** : a massive structure with a square base and four triangular faces meeting at a point **2** : a geometrical solid having a polygon for its base and three or more triangles for its sides that meet at a point to form the top — **py·ra·mi·dal** \pə-'ra-mə-d²l, ˌpir-ə-'mid-\ *adj*

²pyramid *vb* **1** : to build up in the form of a pyramid : heap up **2** : to increase rapidly on a broadening base

pyramid scheme *n* : a usu. illegal operation in which participants pay to join and profit from payments made by subsequent participants

pyre \'pī(-ə)r\ *n* : a combustible heap for burning a dead body as a funeral rite

py·re·thrum \pī-'rē-thrəm\ *n* : an insecticide made from the dried heads of any of several Old World chrysanthemums

py·rim·i·dine \pī-'ri-mə-ˌdēn\ *n* : any of a group of bases including several (as cytosine, thymine, or uracil) that are constituents of DNA or RNA

py·rite \'pī-ˌrīt\ *n* : a mineral containing sulfur and iron that is brass-yellow in color

py·rol·y·sis \pī-'rä-lə-səs\ *n* : chemical change caused by the action of heat

py·ro·ma·nia \ˌpī-rō-'mä-nē-ə\ *n* : an irresistible impulse to start fires — **py·ro·ma·ni·ac** \-nē-ˌak\ *n*

py·ro·tech·nics \ˌpī-rə-'tek-niks\ *n pl* **1** : a display of fireworks **2** : a spectacular display (as of extreme virtuosity) ⟨musical ∼⟩ — **py·ro·tech·nic** \-nik\ *also* **py·ro·tech·ni·cal** \-ni-kəl\ *adj*

Pyr·rhic \'pir-ik\ *adj* : achieved at excessive cost ⟨a ∼ victory⟩; *also* : costly to the point of outweighing expected benefits

Py·thag·o·re·an theorem \pī-ˌtha-gə-'rē-ən-\ *n* : a theorem in geometry: the square of the length of the hypotenuse of a right triangle equals the sum of the squares of the lengths of the other two sides

py·thon \'pī-ˌthän, -thən\ *n* [L, monstrous serpent killed by the god Apollo, fr. Gk *Pythōn*] : a large snake (as a boa) that squeezes and suffocates its prey; *esp* : any of the large Old World snakes that include the largest snakes living at the present time

pyx \'piks\ *n* : a small case used to carry the Eucharist to the sick

¹q \'kyü\ *n, pl* **q's** *or* **qs** \'kyüz\ *often cap* : the 17th letter of the English alphabet

²q *abbr, often cap* **1** quart **2** quarto **3** queen **4** query **5** question

QB *abbr* quarterback

QED *abbr* [L *quod erat demonstrandum*] which was to be demonstrated

qin·dar \k(y)in-'där\ *n, pl* **qin·dar·ka** \-'där-kə\ — see *lek* at MONEY table

qi·vi·ut \'kē-vē-ˌüt\ *n* [Inuit] : the wool of the undercoat of the musk ox

Qld *abbr* Queensland

QM *abbr* quartermaster

QMC *abbr* quartermaster corps

QMG *abbr* quartermaster general

qq v *abbr* [L *quae vide*] which (*pl*) see

qr *abbr* quarter

Q rating *n* [*q*uotient] : a scale measuring popularity based on dividing an assessment of familiarity or recognition by an assessment of favorable opinion; *also* : position on such a scale

qt *abbr* **1** quantity **2** quart

q.t. \ˌkyü-'tē\ *n, often cap Q&T* : QUIET — usu. used in the phrase *on the q.t.*

qto *abbr* quarto

qty *abbr* quantity

qu *or* **ques** *abbr* question

¹quack \'kwak\ *vb* : to make the characteristic cry of a duck

²quack *n* : a sound made by quacking

³quack *n* **1** : CHARLATAN **2** : a pretender to medical skill **♦ Synonyms** FAKER, IMPOSTOR, MOUNTEBANK — **quack** *adj* — **quack·ery** \'kwa-kə-rē\ *n* — **quack·ish** *adj*

¹quad \'kwäd\ *n* : QUADRANGLE

²quad *n* **1** : QUADRUPLET **2** : a ski lift that accommodates four people

³quad *abbr* quadrant

quad·ran·gle \'kwä-,draŋ-gəl\ *n* **1** : QUADRILATERAL **2** : a 4-sided courtyard or enclosure — **quad·ran·gu·lar** \kwä-'draŋ-gyə-lər\ *adj*

quad·rant \'kwä-drənt\ *n* **1** : one quarter of a circle : an arc of 90° **2** : any of the four quarters into which something is divided by two lines intersecting each other at right angles

qua·drat·ic \kwä-'dra-tik\ *adj* : having or being a term in which the variable (as *x*) is squared but containing no term in which the variable is raised to a higher power than a square ⟨a ∼ equation⟩ — **quadratic** *n*

qua·dren·ni·al \kwä-'dre-nē-əl\ *adj* **1** : consisting of or lasting for four years **2** : occurring every four years

qua·dren·ni·um \-nē-əm\ *n, pl* **-ni·ums** *or* **-nia** \-nē-ə\ : a period of four years

quad·ri·ceps \'kwä-drə-,seps\ *n* : a muscle of the front of the thigh that is divided into four parts

¹quad·ri·lat·er·al \,kwä-drə-'la-tə-rəl\ *n* : a polygon of four sides

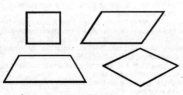

quadrilaterals

²quadrilateral *adj* : having four sides

qua·drille \kwä-'dril, kə-\ *n* : a square dance made up of five or six figures in various rhythms

quad·ri·par·tite \,kwä-drə-'pär-,tīt\ *adj* **1** : consisting of four parts **2** : shared by four parties or persons

quad·ri·ple·gia \,kwä-drə-'plē-jə, -jē-ə\ *n* : paralysis of both arms and both legs — **quad·ri·ple·gic** \-jik\ *adj or n*

qua·driv·i·um \kwä-'dri-vē-əm\ *n* : the four liberal arts of arithmetic, music, geometry, and astronomy in a medieval university

quad·ru·ped \'kwä-drə-,ped\ *n* : an animal having four feet — **qua·dru·pe·dal** \kwä-'drü-pə-d³l, ,kwä-drə-'pe-\ *adj*

¹qua·dru·ple \kwä-'drü-pəl, -'drə-; 'kwä-drə-\ *vb* **qua·dru·pled; qua·dru·pling** : to make or become four times as great or as many

²quadruple *adj* : FOURFOLD

qua·dru·plet \kwä-'drə-plət, -'drü-; 'kwä-drə-\ *n* **1** : a combination of four of a kind **2** : one of four offspring born at one birth

¹qua·dru·pli·cate \kwä-'drü-pli-kət\ *adj* **1** : repeated four times **2** : FOURTH

²qua·dru·pli·cate \-plə-,kāt\ *vb* **-cat·ed; -cat·ing 1** : QUADRUPLE **2** : to prepare in quadruplicate — **qua·dru·pli·ca·tion** \-,drü-plə-'kā-shən\ *n*

³qua·dru·pli·cate \-'drü-pli-kət\ *n* **1** : four copies all alike ⟨typed in ∼⟩ **2** : one of four like things

quaff \'kwäf, 'kwaf\ *vb* : to drink deeply or repeatedly — **quaff** *n*

quag·mire \'kwag-,mī(-ə)r, 'kwäg-\ *n* **1** : soft miry land that yields underneath the foot **2** : PREDICAMENT

qua·hog \'kō-,hȯg, 'kwȯ-, 'kwō-, -,häg\ *n* [modif. of Narragansett *poquaûhock*] : a round thick-shelled edible clam of the U.S.

quai \'kā\ *n* : QUAY

¹quail \'kwāl\ *n, pl* **quail** *or* **quails** [ME *quaile*, fr. AF, fr. ML *quaccula*, of imit. origin] : any of numerous small short-winged plump game birds (as a bobwhite) related to the domestic chicken

²quail *vb* [ME, to grow feeble, fr. MD *quelen*] : to lose heart : COWER ⟨∼*ed* at the daunting task⟩ ✦ *Synonyms* RECOIL, SHRINK, FLINCH, WINCE, BLANCH

quaint \'kwānt\ *adj* : unusual or different in character or appearance; *esp* : pleasingly old-fashioned or unfamiliar ✦ *Synonyms* ODD, QUEER, CURIOUS, STRANGE — **quaint·ly** *adv* — **quaint·ness** *n*

¹quake \'kwāk\ *vb* **quaked; quak·ing 1** : to shake usu. from shock or instability **2** : to tremble usu. from cold or fear

²quake *n* : a shaking or trembling; *esp* : EARTHQUAKE

Quak·er \'kwā-kər\ *n* : FRIEND 5

qual *abbr* quality

qual·i·fi·ca·tion \,kwä-lə-fə-'kā-shən\ *n* **1** : LIMITATION, MODIFICATION ⟨her statement stands without ∼⟩ **2** : a special skill that fits a person for some work or position **3** : REQUIREMENT ⟨a ∼ for membership⟩

qual·i·fied \'kwä-lə-,fīd\ *adj* **1** : fitted for a given purpose or job **2** : limited in some way ⟨∼ approval⟩

qual·i·fi·er \'kwä-lə-,fī(-ə)r\ *n* **1** : one that satisfies requirements **2** : a word or word group that limits the meaning of another word or word group

qual·i·fy \'kwä-lə-,fī\ *vb* **-fied; -fy·ing 1** : to reduce from a general to a particular form : MODIFY **2** : to make less harsh **3** : to limit the meaning of (as a noun) **4** : to fit by skill or training for some purpose **5** : to give or have a legal right to do something **6** : to demonstrate the necessary ability ⟨∼ for the finals⟩ ✦ *Synonyms* MODERATE, TEMPER

qual·i·ta·tive \'kwä-lə-,tā-tiv\ *adj* : of, relating to, or involving quality — **qual·i·ta·tive·ly** *adv*

¹qual·i·ty \'kwä-lə-tē\ *n, pl* **-ties 1** : peculiar and essential character : NATURE **2** : degree of excellence **3** : high social status **4** : a distinguishing attribute

²quality *adj* : being of high quality

qualm \'kwäm, 'kwälm\ *n* **1** : a sudden attack (as of nausea) **2** : a sudden feeling of doubt, fear, or uneasiness esp. in not following one's conscience or better judgment

qualm·ish \'kwä-mish, 'kwäl-\ *adj* **1** : feeling qualms : NAUSEATED **2** : overly scrupulous : SQUEAMISH **3** : of, relating to, or producing qualms

quan·da·ry \'kwän-drē\ *n, pl* **-ries** : a state of perplexity or doubt

quan·ti·fy \'kwän-tə-,fī\ *vb* **-fied; -fy·ing** : to determine, express, or measure the quantity of — **quan·ti·fi·able** \,kwän-tə-'fī-ə-bəl\ *adj*

quan·ti·ta·tive \'kwän-tə-,tā-tiv\ *adj* : of, relating to, or involving quantity — **quan·ti·ta·tive·ly** *adv*

quan·ti·ty \'kwän-tə-tē\ *n, pl* **-ties 1** : AMOUNT, NUMBER **2** : a considerable amount ⟨buys food in ∼⟩

quan·tize \'kwän-,tīz\ *vb* **quan·tized; quan·tiz·ing** : to subdivide (as energy) into small units

¹quan·tum \'kwän-təm\ *n, pl* **quan·ta** \-tə\ [L, neut. of *quantus* how much] **1** : QUANTITY, AMOUNT **2** : an elemental unit of energy

²quantum *adj* **1** : LARGE, SIGNIFICANT **2** : relating to or employing the principles of quantum mechanics

quantum mechanics *n sing or pl* : a theory of matter based on the concept of possession of wave properties by elementary particles — **quantum mechanical** *adj* — **quantum mechanically** *adv*

quantum theory *n* **1** : a theory in physics based on the idea that radiant energy (as light) is composed of small separate packets of energy **2** : QUANTUM MECHANICS

quar *abbr* quarterly

quar·an·tine \'kwȯr-ən-,tēn\ *n* [modif. of It *quarantena*, lit., period of forty days, fr. *quaranta* forty, fr. L *quadraginta*] **1** : a period during which a ship suspected of carrying contagious disease is forbidden contact with the shore **2** : a restraint on the movements of persons or goods to prevent the spread of pests or disease **3** : a place or period of quarantine **4** : a state of enforced isolation — **quarantine** *vb*

quark \'kwȯrk, 'kwärk\ *n* : a hypothetical elementary particle that carries a fractional charge and is held to be a constituent of heavier particles (as protons and neutrons)

¹quar·rel \'kwȯr-əl\ *n* **1** : a ground of dispute **2** : a verbal clash : CONFLICT — **quar·rel·some** \-səm\ *adj*

²quarrel *vb* **-reled** *or* **-relled; -rel·ing** *or* **-rel·ling 1** : to find fault **2** : to dispute angrily : WRANGLE

¹quar·ry \'kwȯr-ē\ *n, pl* **quarries** [ME *querre* entrails of game given to the hounds, fr. AF *cureie*, *quereie*, fr. *quir*, *cuir* skin, hide (on which the entrails were placed), fr. L *corium*] **1** : game hunted with hawks **2** : PREY

²quarry *n, pl* **quarries** [ME *quarey*, alter. of *quarrere*, fr. AF, fr. VL **quadraria*, fr. LL *quadraria*, fr. L *quadrus* hewn (lit., squared) stone, fr. L *quadrum* square] : an open excavation usu. for obtaining building stone or limestone — **quarry** *vb*

quart \'kwȯrt\ *n* — see WEIGHT table

¹**quar·ter** \'kwȯr-tər\ *n* **1** : one of four equal parts **2** : a fourth of a dollar; *also* : a coin of this value **3** : a district of a city **4** *pl* : LODGINGS ⟨moved into new ∼s⟩ **5** : MERCY, CLEMENCY ⟨gave no ∼⟩ **6** : a fourth part of the moon's period

²**quarter** *vb* **1** : to divide into four equal parts **2** : to provide with shelter

¹**quar·ter·back** \-ˌbak\ *n* : a football player who calls the signals and directs the offensive play for the team

²**quarterback** *vb* **1** : to direct the offensive play of a football team **2** : LEAD, BOSS

quar·ter·deck \-ˌdek\ *n* : the stern area of a ship's upper deck

quarter horse *n* : any of a breed of compact muscular saddle horses characterized by great endurance and by high speed for short distances

¹**quar·ter·ly** \'kwȯr-tər-lē\ *adv* : at 3-month intervals

²**quarterly** *adj* : occurring, issued, or payable at 3-month intervals

³**quarterly** *n, pl* **-lies** : a periodical published four times a year

quar·ter·mas·ter \-ˌmas-tər\ *n* **1** : a petty officer who attends to a ship's helm, binnacle, and signals **2** : an army officer who provides clothing and subsistence for troops

quar·ter·staff \-ˌstaf\ *n, pl* **-staves** \-ˌstavz, -ˌstāvz\ : a long stout staff formerly used as a weapon

quar·tet *also* **quar·tette** \kwȯr-'tet\ *n* **1** : a musical composition for four instruments or voices **2** : a group of four and esp. of four musicians

quar·to \'kwȯr-tō\ *n, pl* **quartos** **1** : the size of a piece of paper cut four from a sheet **2** : a book printed on quarto pages

quartz \'kwȯrts\ *n* : a common often transparent crystalline mineral that is a form of silica

quartz·ite \'kwȯrt-ˌsīt\ *n* : a compact granular rock composed of quartz and derived from sandstone

qua·sar \'kwā-ˌzär, -ˌsär\ *n* : any of a class of extremely distant starlike celestial objects

¹**quash** \'kwäsh, 'kwȯsh\ *vb* : to suppress or extinguish summarily and completely : QUELL

²**quash** *vb* : to nullify by judicial action

qua·si \'kwā-ˌzī, -ˌsī; 'kwä-zē, -sē\ *adj* : being in some sense or degree ⟨a ∼ corporation⟩

quasi- *comb form* [L, as if, as it were, approximately, fr. *quam* as + *si* if] : in some sense or degree ⟨*quasi*-historical⟩

qua·si-gov·ern·men·tal \-ˌgə-vərn-'men-t°l\ *adj* : supported by the government but managed privately

Qua·ter·na·ry \'kwä-tər-ˌner-ē, kwə-'tər-nə-rē\ *adj* : of, relating to, or being the geologic period from the end of the Tertiary to the present — **Quaternary** *n*

qua·train \'kwä-ˌtrān\ *n* : a unit of four lines of verse

qua·tre·foil \'ka-tər-ˌfȯi(-ə)l, 'ka-trə-\ *n* : a stylized figure often of a flower with four petals

qua·ver \'kwā-vər\ *vb* **1** : TREMBLE, SHAKE ⟨∼ed with nervousness⟩ **2** : TRILL **3** : to speak in tremulous tones ♦ **Synonyms** SHUDDER, QUAKE, TWITTER, QUIVER, SHIVER — **quaver** *n*

quay \'kē, 'kwā, 'kā\ *n* : WHARF

Que *abbr* Quebec

quean \'kwēn\ *n* : PROSTITUTE

quea·sy \'kwē-zē\ *adj* **quea·si·er; -est** : NAUSEATED — **quea·si·ly** \-zə-lē\ *adv* — **quea·si·ness** \-zē-nəs\ *n*

Que·chua \'ke-chə-wə, 'kech-wə\ *n* : a family of languages spoken in Peru and adjacent countries of the So. American Andes

queen \'kwēn\ *n* [ME *quene*, fr. OE *cwēn* woman, wife, queen] **1** : the wife or widow of a king **2** : a female monarch **3** : a woman notable in rank, power, or attractiveness **4** : the most powerful piece in the game of chess **5** : a playing card bearing the figure of a queen **6** : a fertile female of a social insect (as a bee or termite) — **queen·ly** *adj*

Queen Anne's lace \-'anz-\ *n* : a widely naturalized Eurasian herb from which the cultivated carrot originated

queen consort *n, pl* **queens consort** : the wife of a reigning king

queen mother *n* : a dowager queen who is mother of the reigning sovereign

queen–size *adj* : having dimensions of approximately 60 inches by 80 inches ⟨a ∼ bed⟩; *also* : of a size that fits a queen-size bed

¹**queer** \'kwir\ *adj* **1** : COUNTERFEIT ⟨∼ money⟩ **2** : differing from the usual or normal : PECULIAR, STRANGE **3** *often offensive* : HOMOSEXUAL; *also, often offensive* : of, relating to, or used by homosexuals ♦ **Synonyms** WEIRD, BIZARRE, ECCENTRIC, CURIOUS — **queer** *n* — **queer·ly** *adv* — **queer·ness** *n*

²**queer** *vb* : to spoil the effect of : DISRUPT ⟨∼ed our plans⟩

queer theory *n* : an approach to literary and cultural study that rejects traditional categories of gender and sexuality

quell \'kwel\ *vb* **1** : to put an end to by force ⟨∼ a riot⟩ **2** : CALM, PACIFY ⟨∼ fears⟩

quench \'kwench\ *vb* **1** : PUT OUT, EXTINGUISH **2** : SUBDUE **3** : SLAKE, SATISFY ⟨∼ed his thirst⟩ — **quench·able** *adj* — **quench·er** *n* — **quench·less** *adj*

quer·u·lous \'kwer-ə-ləs, -yə-\ *adj* **1** : constantly complaining **2** : FRETFUL, WHINING ⟨a ∼ voice⟩ ♦ **Synonyms** PETULANT, PETTISH, IRRITABLE, PEEVISH, HUFFY — **quer·u·lous·ly** *adv* — **quer·u·lous·ness** *n*

que·ry \'kwir-ē, 'kwer-\ *n, pl* **queries** : QUESTION — **query** *vb*

que·sa·dil·la \ˌkā-sə-'dē-ə\ *n* : a tortilla filled with a savory mixture, folded, and usu. fried

quest \'kwest\ *n* : SEARCH ⟨in ∼ of game⟩ — **quest** *vb*

¹**ques·tion** \'kwes-chən\ *n* **1** : an interrogative expression **2** : a subject for debate; *also* : a proposition to be voted on **3** : INQUIRY **4** : DISPUTE ⟨true beyond ∼⟩

²**question** *vb* **1** : to ask questions **2** : DOUBT, DISPUTE ⟨∼ed the verdict⟩ **3** : to subject to analysis : EXAMINE ♦ **Synonyms** INTERROGATE, QUIZ, QUERY — **question·er** *n*

ques·tion·able \'kwes-chə-nə-bəl\ *adj* **1** : not certain or exact : DOUBTFUL **2** : not believed to be true, sound, or moral ♦ **Synonyms** DUBIOUS, PROBLEMATICAL, MOOT, DEBATABLE — **ques·tion·ably** \-blē\ *adv*

question mark *n* : a punctuation mark ? used esp. at the end of a sentence to indicate a direct question

ques·tion·naire \ˌkwes-chə-'ner\ *n* : a set of questions for obtaining information

quet·zal \ket-'säl, -'sal\ *n, pl* **quetzals** *or* **quet·za·les** \-'sä-lās, -'sa-\ **1** : a Central American bird with brilliant plumage **2** *pl* **quetzales** — see MONEY table

¹**queue** \'kyü\ *n* [F, lit., tail, fr. OF *cue, coe,* fr. L *cauda, coda*] **1** : a braid of hair usu. worn hanging at the back of the head **2** : a waiting line (as of persons)

²**queue** *vb* **queued; queu·ing** *or* **queue·ing** : to line up in a queue

quib·ble \'kwi-bəl\ *n* **1** : an evasion of or shifting from the point at issue **2** : a minor objection or criticism — **quibble** *vb* — **quib·bler** *n*

¹**quick** \'kwik\ *adj* **1** : LIVING **2** : RAPID, SPEEDY ⟨∼ steps⟩ **3** : prompt to understand, think, or perceive : ALERT **4** : easily aroused ⟨a ∼ temper⟩ **5** : turning or bending sharply ⟨a ∼ turn in the road⟩ ♦ **Synonyms** FLEET, FAST, HASTY, EXPEDITIOUS — **quick** *adv* — **quick·ly** *adv* — **quick·ness** *n*

²**quick** *n* **1** : a sensitive area of living flesh **2** : a vital part : HEART

quick bread *n* : a bread made with a leavening agent that permits immediate baking of the dough or batter

quick·en \'kwi-kən\ *vb* **1** : to come to life : REVIVE **2** : AROUSE, STIMULATE ⟨curiosity ∼ed my interest⟩ **3** : to increase in speed : HASTEN **4** : to show vitality (as by growing or moving) ♦ **Synonyms** ANIMATE, ENLIVEN, LIVEN, VIVIFY

quick–freeze \'kwik-'frēz\ *vb* **-froze** \-'frōz\; **-fro·zen** \-'frō-z°n\; **-freez·ing** : to freeze (food) for preservation so rapidly that the natural juices and flavor are not lost

quick·ie \'kwi-kē\ *n* : something hurriedly done or made

quick·lime \'kwik-ˌlīm\ *n* : ¹LIME

quick·sand \-ˌsand\ *n* : a deep mass of loose sand mixed with water

quick·sil·ver \-ˌsil-vər\ *n* : MERCURY 1

quick·step \-ˌstep\ *n* : a spirited march tune or dance

quick–wit·ted \'kwik-'wi-təd\ *adj* : mentally alert ♦ **Synonyms** CLEVER, BRIGHT, SMART, INTELLIGENT

quid \'kwid\ *n* : a lump of something chewable ⟨a ∼ of tobacco⟩

quid pro quo \ˌkwid-ˌprō-ˈkwō\ n [NL, something for something] : something given or received for something else

qui·es·cent \kwī-ˈe-sᵊnt\ adj : being at rest : QUIET ⟨a ~ state⟩ ♦ **Synonyms** LATENT, DORMANT, POTENTIAL — **qui·es·cence** \-sᵊns\ n

¹qui·et \ˈkwī-ət\ n : REPOSE

²quiet adj **1** : marked by little motion or activity : CALM **2** : GENTLE, MILD ⟨a ~ disposition⟩ **3** : enjoyed in peace and relaxation ⟨a ~ cup of tea⟩ **4** : free from noise or uproar **5** : not showy : MODEST ⟨~ clothes⟩ **6** : SECLUDED ⟨a ~ nook⟩ — **quiet** adv — **qui·et·ly** adv — **qui·et·ness** n

³quiet vb **1** : CALM, PACIFY **2** : to become quiet — usu. used with *down*

qui·etude \ˈkwī-ə-ˌtüd, -ˌtyüd\ n : QUIETNESS, REPOSE

qui·etus \kwī-ˈē-təs\ n [ME *quietus est,* fr. ML, he is quit, formula of discharge from obligation] **1** : final settlement (as of a debt) **2** : DEATH

quill \ˈkwil\ n **1** : a large stiff feather; *also* : the hollow tubular part of a feather **2** : one of the hollow sharp spines of a hedgehog or porcupine **3** : a pen made from a feather

¹quilt \ˈkwilt\ n : a padded bed coverlet

²quilt vb **1** : to fill, pad, or line like a quilt **2** : to stitch or sew in layers with padding in between **3** : to make quilts

quince \ˈkwins\ n : a hard yellow applelike fruit; *also* : a tree related to the roses that bears this fruit

qui·nine \ˈkwī-ˌnīn\ n : a bitter white drug obtained from cinchona bark and used esp. in treating malaria

qui·noa \ˈkēn-ˌwä, kē-ˈnō-ə\ n [Sp, fr. Quechua *kinua*] : the starchy seeds of an annual herb related to spinach which are used as food and ground into flour; *also* : this herb

quint \ˈkwint\ n : QUINTUPLET

quin·tal \ˈkwin-tᵊl, ˈkan-\ n : HUNDREDWEIGHT

quin·tes·sence \kwin-ˈte-sᵊns\ n **1** : the purest essence of something **2** : the most typical example ⟨the ~ of self-control⟩ — **quin·tes·sen·tial** \ˌkwin-tə-ˈsen-chəl\ adj — **quin·tes·sen·tial·ly** adv

quin·tet \kwin-ˈtet\ n **1** : a musical composition for five instruments or voices **2** : a group of five and esp. of five musicians

¹quin·tu·ple \kwin-ˈtü-pəl, -ˈtyü-, -ˈtə-\ adj **1** : having five units or members **2** : being five times as great or as many — **quintuple** n

²quintuple vb **quin·tu·pled; quin·tu·pling** : to make or become five times as great or as many

quin·tu·plet \kwin-ˈtə-plət, -ˈtü-, -ˈtyü-\ n **1** : a group of five of a kind **2** : one of five offspring born at one birth

¹quin·tu·pli·cate \kwin-ˈtü-pli-kət, -ˈtyü-\ adj **1** : repeated five times **2** : FIFTH ⟨file the ~ copy⟩

²quintuplicate n **1** : one of five like things **2** : five copies all alike ⟨typed in ~⟩

³quin·tu·pli·cate \-plə-ˌkāt\ vb **-cat·ed; -cat·ing 1** : QUINTUPLE **2** : to provide in quintuplicate

¹quip \ˈkwip\ n : a clever remark : GIBE

²quip vb **quipped; quip·ping 1** : to make quips : GIBE **2** : to jest or gibe at

quire \ˈkwī(-ə)r\ n : a set of 24 or sometimes 25 sheets of paper of the same size and quality

quirk \ˈkwərk\ n : a peculiarity of action or behavior — **quirky** adj

quirt \ˈkwərt\ n : a riding whip with a short handle and a rawhide lash

quis·ling \ˈkwiz-liŋ\ n [Vidkun *Quisling* †1945 Norw. politician who collaborated with the Nazis] : one who helps the invaders of one's own country

quit \ˈkwit\ vb **quit** *also* **quit·ted; quit·ting 1** : CONDUCT, BEHAVE ⟨~ themselves well⟩ **2** : to depart from : LEAVE; *also* : to bring to an end **3** : to give up for good ⟨~ smoking⟩ ⟨~ my job⟩ ♦ **Synonyms** ACQUIT, COMPORT, DEPORT, DEMEAN — **quit·ter** n

quite \ˈkwīt\ adv **1** : COMPLETELY, WHOLLY ⟨not ~ finished⟩ **2** : to an extreme : POSITIVELY **3** : to a considerable extent : RATHER ⟨~ rich⟩

quits \ˈkwits\ adj : even or equal with another

quit·tance \ˈkwi-tᵊns\ n : REQUITAL

¹quiv·er \ˈkwi-vər\ n : a case for carrying arrows

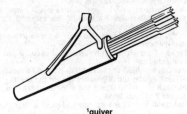

¹quiver

²quiver vb **quiv·ered; quiv·er·ing** : to shake with a slight trembling motion ⟨~ed with rage⟩ ♦ **Synonyms** SHIVER, SHUDDER, QUAVER, QUAKE, TREMBLE — **quiv·er·ing·ly** adv

³quiver n : the act or action of quivering : TREMOR

qui vive \kē-ˈvēv\ n [F *qui-vive,* fr. *qui vive?* long live who?, challenge of a French sentry] : ALERT ⟨on the *qui vive* for prowlers⟩

quix·ot·ic \kwik-ˈsä-tik\ adj [fr. Don *Quixote,* hero of the novel *Don Quixote de la Mancha* by Cervantes] : foolishly impractical esp. in the pursuit of ideals — **quix·ot·i·cal·ly** \-ti-kə-lē\ adv

¹quiz \ˈkwiz\ n, pl **quiz·zes 1** : an eccentric person **2** : PRACTICAL JOKE **3** : a short oral or written test

²quiz vb **quizzed; quiz·zing 1** : MOCK **2** : to look at inquisitively **3** : to question closely ♦ **Synonyms** ASK, INTERROGATE, QUERY

quiz·zi·cal \ˈkwi-zi-kəl\ adj **1** : comically quaint **2** : mildly teasing or mocking **3** : expressive of puzzlement, curiosity, or disbelief ⟨gave me a ~ look⟩

quoit \ˈkwät, ˈkwȯit, ˈkȯit\ n **1** : a flattened ring of iron or circle of rope used in a throwing game **2** pl : a game in which quoits are thrown at an upright pin in an attempt to ring the pin

quon·dam \ˈkwän-dəm, -ˌdam\ adj [L, at one time, formerly, fr. *quom, cum* when] : FORMER ⟨a ~ friend⟩

quo·rum \ˈkwȯr-əm\ n : the number of members required to be present for business to be legally transacted

quot abbr quotation

quo·ta \ˈkwō-tə\ n : a proportional part esp. when assigned : SHARE

quot·able \ˈkwō-tə-bəl\ adj : fit for or worth quoting ⟨a ~ comment⟩ — **quot·abil·i·ty** \-ˌbi-lə-tē\ n

quo·ta·tion \kwō-ˈtā-shən\ n **1** : the act or process of quoting **2** : the price currently bid or offered for something **3** : something that is quoted

quotation mark n : one of a pair of punctuation marks " " or ' ' used esp. to indicate the beginning and end of a quotation in which exact phraseology is directly cited

quote \ˈkwōt\ vb **quot·ed; quot·ing** [ML *quotare* to mark the number of, number references, fr. L *quotus* of what number or quantity, fr. *quot* how many, (as) many as] **1** : to speak or write a passage from another usu. with acknowledgment; *also* : to repeat a passage in substantiation or illustration **2** : to state the market price of a commodity, stock, or bond **3** : to inform a hearer or reader that matter following is quoted — **quote** n

quoth \ˈkwōth\ vb past [ME, past of *quethen* to say, fr. OE *cwethan*] archaic : SAID — usu. used in the 1st and 3d persons with the subject following

quo·tid·i·an \kwō-ˈti-dē-ən\ adj **1** : DAILY **2** : COMMONPLACE, ORDINARY ⟨~ concerns⟩

quo·tient \ˈkwō-shənt\ n : the number obtained by dividing one number by another

Quran *also* **Qur'an** *var of* KORAN

qv abbr [L *quod vide*] which see

qy abbr query

¹**r** \'är\ *n, pl* **r's** *or* **rs** \'ärz\ *often cap* : the 18th letter of the English alphabet
²**r** *abbr, often cap* **1** rabbi **2** radius **3** rare **4** Republican **5** rerun **6** resistance **7** right **8** river **9** roentgen **10** rook **11** run
Ra *symbol* radium
RA *abbr* **1** regular army **2** Royal Academy **3** research assistant
¹**rab·bet** \'ra-bət\ *n* : a groove in the edge or face of a surface (as a board) esp. to receive another piece
²**rabbet** *vb* : to cut a rabbet in; *also* : to join by means of a rabbet
rab·bi \'ra-ˌbī\ *n* [ME, fr. OE, fr. LL, fr. Gk *rhabbi*, fr. Heb *rabbī* my master, fr. *rabh* master + -*ī* my] **1** : MASTER, TEACHER — used by Jews as a term of address **2** : a Jew trained and ordained for professional religious leadership — **rab·bin·ic** \rə-'bi-nik\ *or* **rab·bin·i·cal** \-ni-kəl\ *adj*
rab·bin·ate \'ra-bə-nət, -ˌnāt\ *n* **1** : the office of a rabbi **2** : the whole body of rabbis
rab·bit \'ra-bət\ *n, pl* **rabbit** *or* **rabbits** : any of various long-eared short-tailed burrowing mammals distinguished from the related hares by being blind, furless, and helpless at birth; *also* : the pelt of a rabbit
rabbit ears *n pl* : an indoor V-shaped television antenna
rabble \'ra-bəl\ *n* **1** : MOB **2** : the lowest class of people
rab·ble–rous·er \'ra-bəl-ˌraû-zər\ *n* : one that stirs up (as to hatred or violence) the masses of the people
ra·bid \'ra-bəd\ *adj* **1** : VIOLENT, FURIOUS **2** : being fanatical or extreme ⟨~ supporters⟩ **3** : affected with rabies — **ra·bid·ly** *adv*
ra·bies \'rā-bēz\ *n, pl* **rabies** [NL, fr. L, madness] : an acute deadly virus disease of the nervous system transmitted by the bite of an affected animal
rac·coon \ra-'kün\ *n, pl* **raccoon** *or* **raccoons** : a gray No. American chiefly tree-dwelling mammal with a black mask, a bushy ringed tail, and nocturnal habits; *also* : its pelt
¹**race** \'rās\ *n* **1** : a strong current of running water; *also* : its channel **2** : an onward course (as of time or life) **3** : a contest of speed **4** : a contest for a desired end (as election to office)
²**race** *vb* **raced; rac·ing** **1** : to run in a race **2** : to run swiftly : RUSH **3** : to engage in a race with **4** : to drive or ride at high speed — **rac·er** *n*
³**race** *n* **1** : a family, tribe, people, or nation of the same stock **2** : a group of individuals within a biological species able to breed together **3** : a category of humankind that shares certain distinctive physical traits — **ra·cial** \'rā-shəl\ *adj* — **ra·cial·ly** *adv*
race·course \'rās-ˌkórs\ *n* : a course for racing
race·horse \-ˌhórs\ *n* : a horse bred or kept for racing
ra·ceme \rā-'sēm\ *n* [L *racemus* bunch of grapes] : a flower cluster with flowers borne along a stem and blooming from the base toward the tip — **rac·e·mose** \'ra-sə-ˌmōs\ *adj*
race·track \'rās-ˌtrak\ *n* : a usu. oval course on which races are run
race·way \-ˌwā\ *n* **1** : a channel for a current of water **2** : RACECOURSE
ra·cial·ism \'rā-shə-ˌli-zəm\ *n* : a theory that race determines human traits and capacities; *also* : RACISM — **ra·cial·ist** \-list\ *n* — **ra·cial·is·tic** \ˌrā-shə-'lis-tik\ *adj*
ra·cial·ize \'rā-shə-ˌlīz\ *vb* **-ized; -iz·ing** : to give a racial character to
racing form *n* : a paper giving data about racehorses for use by bettors
rac·ism \'ra-ˌsi-zəm\ *n* : a belief that some races are by nature superior to others; *also* : discrimination based on such belief — **rac·ist** \-sist\ *n*
¹**rack** \'rak\ *n* **1** : an instrument of torture on which a body is stretched **2** : a framework on or in which some-

thing may be placed (as for display or storage) **3** : a bar with teeth on one side to mesh with a pinion or worm gear

rack 3: with pinion gear

²**rack** *vb* **1** : to torture on or as if on a rack **2** : to stretch or strain by force **3** : TORMENT **4** : to place on or in a rack
¹**rack·et** *or* **rac·quet** \'ra-kət\ *n* [MF *raquette*, ultim. fr. ML *rasceta* wrist, carpus, fr. Ar *rusgh* wrist] : a light bat made of netting stretched in an oval open frame having a handle and used for striking a ball or shuttlecock
²**racket** *n* **1** : confused noise : DIN **2** : a fraudulent or dishonest scheme or activity ⟨a criminal ~⟩
³**racket** *vb* : to make a racket
rack·e·teer \ˌra-kə-'tir\ *n* : a person who obtains money by an illegal enterprise usu. involving intimidation — **rack·e·teer·ing** *n*
rack up *vb* : ACHIEVE, GAIN ⟨*racked up* their 10th victory⟩
ra·con·teur \ˌra-ˌkän-'tər\ *n* : one good at telling anecdotes
rac·quet·ball \'ra-kət-ˌból\ *n* : a game similar to handball that is played on a 4-walled court with a short-handled racket
racy \'rā-sē\ *adj* **rac·i·er; -est** **1** : full of zest **2** : PUNGENT, SPICY **3** : RISQUÉ, SUGGESTIVE ⟨~ jokes⟩ — **rac·i·ly** \'rā-sə-lē\ *adv* — **rac·i·ness** \-sē-nəs\ *n*
rad *abbr* **1** radical **2** radio **3** radius
ra·dar \'rā-ˌdär\ *n* [*ra*dio *d*etecting *a*nd *r*anging] : a device that emits radio waves for detecting and locating an object by the reflection of the radio waves and that may use this reflection to determine the object's direction and speed
radar gun *n* : a handheld device that uses radar to measure the speed of a moving object
ra·dar·scope \'rā-ˌdär-ˌskōp\ *n* : a visual display for a radar receiver
¹**ra·di·al** \'rā-dē-əl\ *adj* : arranged or having parts arranged like rays around a common center ⟨the ~ form of a starfish⟩ — **ra·di·al·ly** *adv*
²**radial** *n* : a pneumatic tire with cords laid perpendicular to the center line
radial engine *n* : an internal combustion engine with cylinders arranged radially like the spokes of a wheel
ra·di·an \'rā-dē-ən\ *n* : a unit of measure for angles that is equal to approximately 57.3 degrees
ra·di·ant \'rā-dē-ənt\ *adj* **1** : SHINING, GLOWING **2** : beaming with happiness ⟨a ~ smile⟩ **3** : transmitted by radiation ◆ *Synonyms* BRILLIANT, BRIGHT, LUMINOUS, LUSTROUS — **ra·di·ance** \-əns\ *n* — **ra·di·ant·ly** *adv*
radiant energy *n* : energy traveling as electromagnetic waves
ra·di·ate \'rā-dē-ˌāt\ *vb* **-at·ed; -at·ing** **1** : to send out rays : SHINE, GLOW **2** : to issue in or as if in rays ⟨light ~s⟩ **3** : to spread around as from a center
ra·di·a·tion \ˌrā-dē-'ā-shən\ *n* **1** : the action or process of radiating **2** : the process of emitting radiant energy in the form of waves or particles; *also* : something (as an X-ray beam) that is radiated
radiation sickness *n* : sickness that results from exposure to radiation and is commonly marked by fatigue, nausea, vomiting, loss of teeth and hair, and in more severe cases by damage to blood-forming tissue

radiation therapy *n* : RADIOTHERAPY

ra·di·a·tor \'rā-dē-ˌā-tər\ *n* : any of various devices (as a set of pipes or tubes) for transferring heat from a fluid within to an area or object outside

¹**rad·i·cal** \'ra-di-kəl\ *adj* [ME, fr. LL *radicalis*, fr. L *radic-, radix* root] **1** : FUNDAMENTAL, EXTREME, THOROUGHGOING **2** : of or relating to radicals in politics — **rad·i·cal·ism** \-kə-ˌli-zəm\ *n* — **rad·i·cal·ly** *adv*

²**radical** *n* **1** : a person who favors rapid and sweeping changes in laws and methods of government **2** : FREE RADICAL; *also* : a group of atoms considered as a unit in certain reactions or as a subunit of a larger molecule **3** : a mathematical expression indicating a root by means of a radical sign; *also* : RADICAL SIGN

rad·i·cal·ise *Brit var of* RADICALIZE

rad·i·cal·ize \-kə-ˌlīz\ *vb* **-ized; -iz·ing** : to make radical esp. in politics — **rad·i·cal·i·za·tion** \ˌra-di-kə-lə-'zā-shən\ *n*

radical sign *n* : the sign √ placed before a mathematical expression to indicate that its root is to be taken

ra·dic·chio \ra-'di-kē-ō\ *n, pl* **-chios** : a chicory with reddish variegated leaves

radii *pl of* RADIUS

¹**ra·dio** \'rā-dē-ˌō\ *n, pl* **ra·di·os** **1** : the wireless transmission or reception of signals using electromagnetic waves **2** : a radio receiving set **3** : the radio broadcasting industry — **radio** *adj*

²**radio** *vb* : to communicate or send a message to by radio

ra·dio·ac·tiv·i·ty \ˌrā-dē-ō-ˌak-'ti-və-tē\ *n* : the property that some elements or isotopes have of spontaneously emitting energetic particles by the disintegration of their atomic nuclei — **ra·dio·ac·tive** \-'ak-tiv\ *adj*

radio astronomy *n* : astronomy dealing with radio waves received from outside the earth's atmosphere

ra·dio·car·bon \ˌrā-dē-ō-'kär-bən\ *n* : CARBON 14

radio frequency *n* : an electromagnetic wave frequency intermediate between audio frequencies and infrared frequencies used esp. for communication and radar signals

ra·dio·gram \'rā-dē-ō-ˌgram\ *n* : a message transmitted by radio

ra·dio·graph \-ˌgraf\ *n* : a photograph made by some form of radiation other than light; *esp* : an X-ray photograph — **radiograph** *vb* — **ra·dio·graph·ic** \ˌrā-dē-ō-'gra-fik\ *adj* — **ra·dio·graph·i·cal·ly** \-fi-k(ə-)lē\ *adv* — **ra·di·og·ra·phy** \ˌrā-dē-'ä-grə-fē\ *n*

ra·dio·iso·tope \ˌrā-dē-ō-'ī-sə-ˌtōp\ *n* : a radioactive isotope

ra·di·ol·o·gy \ˌrā-dē-'ä-lə-jē\ *n* : the use of radiant energy (as X-rays and radium radiations) in medicine — **ra·di·ol·o·gist** \-jist\ *n*

ra·dio·man \'rā-dē-ō-ˌman\ *n* : a radio operator or technician

ra·di·om·e·ter \ˌrā-dē-'ä-mə-tər\ *n* : an instrument for measuring the intensity of radiant energy — **ra·dio·met·ric** \ˌrā-dē-ō-'me-trik\ *adj* — **ra·di·om·e·try** \-mə-trē\ *n*

ra·dio·phone \'rā-dē-ə-ˌfōn\ *n* : RADIOTELEPHONE

ra·dio·sonde \'rā-dē-ō-ˌsänd\ *n* : a small radio transmitter carried aloft (as by balloon) and used to transmit meteorological data

ra·dio·tele·phone \ˌrā-dē-ō-'te-lə-ˌfōn\ *n* : a telephone that uses radio waves wholly or partly instead of connecting wires — **ra·dio·te·le·pho·ny** \-tə-'le-fə-nē, -'te-lə-ˌfō-nē\ *n*

radio telescope *n* : a radio receiver-antenna combination used for observation in radio astronomy

ra·dio·ther·a·py \ˌrā-dē-ō-'ther-ə-pē\ *n* : the treatment of disease by means of radiation (as X-rays) — **ra·dio·ther·a·pist** \-pist\ *n*

rad·ish \'ra-dish\ *n* [ME, alter. of OE *rædic*, fr. L *radic-, radix* root, radish] : a pungent fleshy root usu. eaten raw; *also* : a plant related to the mustards that produces this root

ra·di·um \'rā-dē-əm\ *n* [NL, fr. L *radius* ray] : a very radioactive metallic chemical element that is used in the treatment of cancer

ra·di·us \'rā-dē-əs\ *n, pl* **ra·dii** \-ē-ˌī\ *also* **ra·di·us·es** **1** : a straight line extending from the center of a circle or a sphere to the circumference or surface; *also* : the length of a radius **2** : the bone on the thumb side of the human forearm **3** : a circular area defined by the length of its radius ✦ *Synonyms* RANGE, REACH, SCOPE, COMPASS

RADM *abbr* rear admiral

ra·don \'rā-ˌdän\ *n* : a heavy radioactive gaseous chemical element

RAF *abbr* Royal Air Force

raf·fia \'ra-fē-ə\ *n* : fiber used esp. for making baskets and hats that is obtained from the stalks of the leaves of a tropical African palm **(raffia palm)**

raff·ish \'ra-fish\ *adj* : jaunty or sporty esp. in a flashy or vulgar manner — **raff·ish·ly** *adv* — **raff·ish·ness** *n*

¹**raf·fle** \'ra-fəl\ *vb* **raf·fled; raf·fling** : to dispose of by a raffle

²**raffle** *n* : a lottery in which the prize is won by one of a number of persons buying chances

¹**raft** \'raft\ *n* **1** : a number of logs or timbers fastened together to form a float **2** : a flat structure for support or transportation on water

²**raft** *vb* **1** : to travel or transport by raft **2** : to make into a raft

³**raft** *n* : a large amount or number

raf·ter \'raf-tər\ *n* : any of the parallel beams that support a roof

¹**rag** \'rag\ *n* **1** : a waste piece of cloth **2** : a sleazy newspaper

²**rag** *n* : a composition in ragtime

ra·ga \'rä-gə\ *n* **1** : a traditional melodic pattern or mode in Indian music **2** : an improvisation based on a raga

rag·a·muf·fin \'ra-gə-ˌmə-fən\ *n* [ME *Ragamuffyn*, name for a ragged, oafish person] : a ragged dirty person; *esp* : a poorly clothed often dirty child

¹**rage** \'rāj\ *n* **1** : violent and uncontrolled anger **2** : VOGUE, FASHION

²**rage** *vb* **raged; rag·ing** **1** : to be furiously angry : RAVE **2** : to continue out of control ⟨the fire *raged*⟩

rag·ged \'ra-gəd\ *adj* **1** : TORN, TATTERED ⟨a ~ dress⟩; *also* : wearing tattered clothes **2** : done in an uneven way ⟨a ~ performance⟩ — **rag·ged·ly** *adv* — **rag·ged·ness** *n*

rag·lan \'ra-glən\ *n* : an overcoat with sleeves **(raglan sleeves)** sewn in with seams slanting from neck to underarm

ra·gout \ra-'gü\ *n* [F *ragoût*, fr. *ragoûter* to revive the taste, fr. MF *ragouster*, fr. *re-* + *a-* to (fr. L *ad-*) + *goust* taste, fr. L *gustus*] : a highly seasoned meat stew with vegetables

rag·pick·er \'rag-ˌpi-kər\ *n* : one who collects rags and refuse for a living

rag·time \-ˌtīm\ *n* : music in which there is more or less continuous syncopation in the melody

rag·top \'rag-ˌtäp\ *n* : CONVERTIBLE

rag·weed \-ˌwēd\ *n* : any of several chiefly No. American weedy composite herbs with allergenic pollen

¹**raid** \'rād\ *n* : a sudden usu. surprise attack or invasion : FORAY

²**raid** *vb* : to make a raid on — **raid·er** *n*

¹**rail** \'rāl\ *n* [ME *raile*, fr. AF *raille, reille* bar, rule, fr. L *regula* straightedge, rule, fr. *regere* to keep straight, direct] **1** : a bar extending from one support to another as a guard or barrier **2** : a bar of steel forming a track for wheeled vehicles : RAILROAD

²**rail** *vb* : to provide with a railing

³**rail** *n, pl* **rail** *or* **rails** : any of numerous small wading birds often hunted as game

⁴**rail** *vb* [ME, fr. MF *railler* to mock, prob. fr. OF *reillier* to growl, mutter, fr. VL **ragulare* to bray, fr. LL *ragere* to neigh] : to complain angrily : SCOLD, REVILE — **rail·er** *n*

rail·ing \'rā-lip\ *n* : a barrier of rails

rail·lery \'rā-lə-rē\ *n, pl* **-ler·ies** : good-natured ridicule : BANTER

¹**rail·road** \'rāl-ˌrōd\ *n* : a permanent road with rails fixed to ties providing a track for cars; *also* : such a road and its assets constituting a property

²**railroad** *vb* **1** : to put through (as a law) too hastily **2** : to convict hastily or with insufficient or improper evidence **3** : to send by rail **4** : to work on a railroad — **rail·road·er** *n* — **rail·road·ing** *n*

rail·way \-ˌwā\ *n* : RAILROAD

rai·ment \'rā-mənt\ *n* : CLOTHING

¹**rain** \'rān\ *n* **1** : water falling in drops from the clouds **2** : a shower of objects ⟨a ~ of bullets⟩ — **rainy** *adj*

²**rain** *vb* **1** : to send down rain **2** : to fall as or like rain **3** : to pour down

¹**rain·bow** \-ˌbō\ *n* : an arc or circle of colors formed by

the refraction and reflection of the sun's rays in rain, spray, or mist

²**rainbow** *adj* **1** : having many colors **2** : of, relating to, or made up of people of different races or cultural backgrounds

rainbow trout *n* : a large stout-bodied fish of western No. America closely related to the salmons of the Pacific and usu. having red or pink stripes with black dots along its sides

rain check *n* **1** : a ticket stub good for a later performance when the scheduled one is rained out **2** : an assurance of a deferred extension of an offer

rain·coat \'rān-ˌkōt\ *n* : a waterproof or water-repellent coat

rain date *n* : an alternative date for an event postponed due to rain

rain·drop \-ˌdräp\ *n* : a drop of rain

rain·fall \-ˌfȯl\ *n* **1** : amount of precipitation measured by depth **2** : a fall of rain

rain forest *n* : a tropical woodland having an annual rainfall of at least 100 inches (254 centimeters) and marked by lofty broad-leaved evergreen trees forming a continuous canopy

rain·mak·ing \'rān-ˌmā-kiŋ\ *n* : the action or process of producing or attempting to produce rain by artificial means — **rain·mak·er** *n*

rain out *vb* : to interrupt or prevent by rain

rain·storm \'rān-ˌstȯrm\ *n* : a storm of or with rain

rain·wa·ter \-ˌwȯ-tər, -ˌwä-\ *n* : water fallen as rain

¹**raise** \'rāz\ *vb* **raised; rais·ing** **1** : to cause or help to rise : LIFT ⟨~ a window⟩ **2** : AWAKEN, AROUSE ⟨enough to ~ the dead⟩ **3** : BUILD, ERECT ⟨~ a monument⟩ **4** : PROMOTE ⟨was *raised* to captain⟩ **5** : END ⟨~ a siege⟩ **6** : COLLECT ⟨~ money⟩ **7** : BREED, GROW ⟨~ cattle⟩ ⟨~ corn⟩; *also* : BRING UP ⟨~ a family⟩ **8** : PROVOKE ⟨~ a laugh⟩ **9** : to bring to notice ⟨~ an objection⟩ **10** : INCREASE ⟨~ prices⟩; *also* : to bet more than **11** : to make light and spongy ⟨~ dough⟩ **12** : to multiply a quantity by itself a specified number of times ⟨~ 2 to the third power⟩ **13** : to cause to form ⟨~ a blister⟩ ♦ **Synonyms** LIFT, HOIST, BOOST, ELEVATE, — **rais·er** *n* — **raise the bar** : to set a higher standard

²**raise** *n* : an increase in amount (as of a bid or bet); *also* : an increase in pay

rai·sin \'rā-zⁿn\ *n* [ME, fr. AF, grape, raisin, fr. L *racemus* cluster of grapes or berries] : a grape dried for food

rai·son d'être \ˌrā-ˌzōⁿ-'detrⁿ\ *n*, *pl* **rai·sons d'être** \-ˌzōⁿz-\ : reason or justification for existence

ra·ja *or* **ra·jah** \'rä-jə\ *n* [Hindi *rājā*, fr. Skt *rājan* king] : an Indian prince

¹**rake** \'rāk\ *n* : a long-handled garden tool having a crossbar with prongs

²**rake** *vb* **raked; rak·ing** **1** : to gather, loosen, or smooth with or as if with a rake **2** : to sweep the length of (as a trench or ship) with gunfire

³**rake** *n* : inclination from either perpendicular or horizontal : SLANT

⁴**rake** *n* : a dissolute person : LIBERTINE

rake–off \'rāk-ˌȯf\ *n* : a percentage or cut taken

¹**rak·ish** \'rā-kish\ *adj* : DISSOLUTE — **rak·ish·ly** *adv* — **rak·ish·ness** *n*

²**rakish** *adj* **1** : having a trim appearance indicative of speed ⟨a ~ sloop⟩ **2** : JAUNTY, SPORTY ⟨~ clothes⟩ — **rak·ish·ly** *adv* — **rak·ish·ness** *n*

¹**ral·ly** \'ra-lē\ *vb* **ral·lied; ral·ly·ing** **1** : to bring together for a common purpose; *also* : to bring back to order ⟨a leader ~*ing* his forces⟩ **2** : to arouse to activity or from depression or weakness **3** : to make a comeback ♦ **Synonyms** STIR, ROUSE, AWAKEN, WAKEN, KINDLE

²**rally** *n*, *pl* **rallies** **1** : an act of rallying **2** : a mass meeting to arouse enthusiasm **3** : a competitive automobile event run over public roads

³**rally** *vb* **ral·lied; ral·ly·ing** : BANTER

rallying cry *n* : WAR CRY 2

¹**ram** \'ram\ *n* **1** : a male sheep **2** : BATTERING RAM

²**ram** *vb* **rammed; ram·ming** **1** : to force or drive in or through **2** : CRAM, CROWD **3** : to strike against violently

RAM \'ram\ *n* : a computer memory that provides the main internal storage for programs and data

Ram·a·dan \'rä-mə-ˌdän, ˌrä-mə-'dän\ *n* : the ninth month

of the Islamic year observed as sacred with daily fasting from dawn to sunset

¹**ram·ble** \'ram-bəl\ *vb* **ram·bled; ram·bling** : to go about aimlessly : ROAM, WANDER

²**ramble** *n* : a leisurely excursion; *esp* : an aimless walk

ram·bler \'ram-blər\ *n* **1** : a person who rambles **2** : any of various climbing roses with large clusters of small often double flowers

ram·bunc·tious \ram-'bəŋk-shəs\ *adj* : UNRULY

ra·mie \'rā-mē, 'ra-\ *n* : a strong lustrous bast fiber from an Asian nettle

ram·i·fi·ca·tion \ˌra-mə-fə-'kā-shən\ *n* **1** : the act or process of branching **2** : CONSEQUENCE, OUTGROWTH ⟨the ~*s* of the decision⟩

ram·i·fy \'ra-mə-ˌfī\ *vb* **-fied; -fy·ing** : to branch out

ramp \'ramp\ *n* : a sloping passage or roadway connecting different levels

¹**ram·page** \'ram-ˌpāj, (ˌ)ram-'pāj\ *vb* **ram·paged; ram·pag·ing** : to rush about wildly ⟨*rampaging* soccer fans⟩

²**ram·page** \'ram-ˌpāj\ *n* : a course of violent or riotous action or behavior — **ram·pa·geous** \ram-'pā-jəs\ *adj*

ram·pant \'ram-pənt\ *adj* : unchecked in growth or spread : RIFE ⟨fear was ~ in the town⟩ — **ram·pan·cy** \-pən-sē\ *n* — **ram·pant·ly** *adv*

ram·part \'ram-ˌpärt\ *n* **1** : a protective barrier **2** : a broad embankment raised as a fortification

¹**ram·rod** \'ram-ˌräd\ *n* **1** : a rod used to ram a charge into a muzzle-loading gun **2** : a cleaning rod for small arms **3** : BOSS, OVERSEER

²**ramrod** *adj* : marked by rigidity or severity ⟨his ~ posture⟩

³**ramrod** *vb* : to direct, supervise, and control ⟨*ramrodded* the project forward⟩

ram·shack·le \'ram-ˌsha-kəl\ *adj* : RICKETY, TUMBLEDOWN

ran *past of* RUN

¹**ranch** \'ranch\ *n* [MexSp *rancho* small ranch, fr. Sp, camp, hut & Sp dial., small farm, fr. Old Spanish *ranchear* (se) to take up quarters, fr. MF (se) *ranger* to take up a position, fr. *ranger* to set in a row] **1** : an establishment for the raising and grazing of livestock (as cattle, sheep, or horses) **2** : a large farm devoted to a specialty **3** : RANCH HOUSE 2

²**ranch** *vb* : to live or work on a ranch — **ranch·er** *n*

ranch house *n* **1** : the main house on a ranch **2** : a one-story house typically with a low-pitched roof

ran·cho \'ran-chō, 'rän-\ *n*, *pl* **ranchos** : RANCH 1

ran·cid \'ran-səd\ *adj* **1** : having a rank smell or taste **2** : OFFENSIVE — **ran·cid·i·ty** \ran-'si-də-tē\ *n*

ran·cor \'raŋ-kər\ *n* : bitter deep-seated ill will ♦ **Synonyms** ANTAGONISM, ANIMOSITY, ANTIPATHY, ENMITY, HOSTILITY — **ran·cor·ous** *adj*

ran·cour *Brit var of* RANCOR

rand \'rand, 'ränd, 'ränt\ *n*, *pl* **rand** — see MONEY table

R & B *abbr* rhythm and blues

R & D *abbr* research and development

ran·dom \'ran-dəm\ *adj* : CHANCE, HAPHAZARD — **ran·dom·ly** *adv* — **ran·dom·ness** *n*

random–access *adj* : allowing access to stored data in any order the user desires

random–access memory *n* : RAM

ran·dom·ize \'ran-də-ˌmīz\ *vb* **-ized; -iz·ing** : to select, assign, or arrange in a random way — **ran·dom·i·za·tion** \ˌran-də-mə-'zā-shən\ *n*

R & R *abbr* rest and recreation; rest and recuperation

rang *past of* RING

¹**range** \'rānj\ *n* **1** : a series of things in a row **2** : a cooking stove having an oven and a flat top with burners **3** : open land where animals (as livestock) may roam and graze **4** : the region throughout which an organism occurs **5** : the act of ranging about **6** : the distance a weapon will shoot or is to be shot **7** : a place where shooting is practiced **8** : the space or extent included, covered, or used : SCOPE **9** : a variation within limits ♦ **Synonyms** REACH, COMPASS, RADIUS, CIRCLE

²**range** *vb* **ranged; rang·ing** [ME, fr. AF *renger*, fr. *renc*, *reng* line, place, row, of Gmc origin] **1** : to set in a row or in proper order **2** : to set in place among others of the same kind **3** : to roam over or through : EXPLORE **4** : to roam at large or freely **5** : to correspond in di-

rection or line **6** : to vary within limits **7** : to find the range of an object by instrument (as radar)

rang·er \'rān-jər\ n **1** : FOREST RANGER **2** : a member of a body of troops who range over a region **3** : an expert in close-range fighting and raiding tactics

rangy \'rān-jē\ adj **rang·i·er; -est** : being long-limbed and slender ⟨a ∼ teenager⟩ — **rang·i·ness** \'rān-jē-nəs\ n

ra·ni or **ra·nee** \rä-'nē, 'rä-,nē\ n : a Hindu queen : a raja's wife

¹rank \'raŋk\ adj **1** : strong and vigorous and usu. coarse in growth **2** : unpleasantly strong-smelling — **rank·ly** adv — **rank·ness** n

²rank n **1** : ROW ⟨∼s of houses⟩ **2** : a line of soldiers ranged side by side **3** pl : the body of enlisted personnel ⟨rose from the ∼s⟩ **4** : position in a group **5** : superior position **6** : a grade of official standing (as in an army) **7** : an orderly arrangement **8** : CLASS, DIVISION — usu. used in pl.

³rank vb **1** : to arrange in lines or in regular formation **2** : RATE **3** : to rate above (as in official standing) **4** : to take or have a relative position

rank and file n : the general membership of a body as contrasted with its leaders

rank·ing \'raŋ-kiŋ\ adj **1** : having a high position : of the highest rank **2** : being next to the chairman in seniority

ran·kle \'raŋ-kəl\ vb **ran·kled; ran·kling** [ME ranclen to fester, fr. AF rancler, fr. OF draoncler, raoncler, fr. draoncle, raoncle festering sore, fr. ML dracunculus, fr. L, dim. of draco serpent] : to cause anger, irritation, or bitterness

ran·sack \'ran-,sak\ vb : to search thoroughly; esp : to search through and rob

¹ran·som \'ran-səm\ n [ME ransoun, fr. OF rançun, fr. L redemption-, redemptio act of buying back, fr. redimere to buy back, redeem] **1** : something paid or demanded for the freedom of a captive **2** : the act of ransoming

²ransom vb : to free from captivity or punishment by paying a price — **ran·som·er** n

ran·som·ware \'ran(t)-səm-,wer\ n : malware that requires the victim to pay a ransom to access encrypted files

rant \'rant\ vb **1** : to talk loudly and wildly **2** : to scold violently ⟨∼ed against his opponent⟩ — **rant·er** n — **rant·ing·ly** adv

¹rap \'rap\ n **1** : a sharp blow **2** : a sharp rebuke **3** : a negative often undeserved reputation ⟨a bum ∼⟩ **4** : responsibility for or consequences of an action ⟨take the ∼⟩

²rap vb **rapped; rap·ping** **1** : to strike sharply : KNOCK **2** : to utter sharply **3** : to criticize sharply

³rap vb **rapped; rap·ping** **1** : to talk freely and frankly **2** : to perform rap music — **rap·per** n

⁴rap n **1** : TALK, CONVERSATION **2** : a rhythmic chanting of usu. rhymed couplets to a musical accompaniment; also : a piece so performed

ra·pa·cious \rə-'pā-shəs\ adj **1** : excessively greedy or covetous **2** : living on prey **3** : RAVENOUS 2 ⟨a ∼ appetite⟩ — **ra·pa·cious·ly** adv — **ra·pa·cious·ness** n — **ra·pac·i·ty** \-'pa-sə-tē\ n

¹rape \'rāp\ n : an Old World herb related to the mustards that is grown as a forage crop and for its seeds (**rapeseed** \-,sēd\)

²rape vb **raped; rap·ing** : to commit rape on — **rap·er** n — **rap·ist** \'rā-pist\ n

³rape n **1** : a carrying away by force **2** : unlawful sexual activity and usu. sexual intercourse carried out forcibly or under threat of injury

¹rap·id \'ra-pəd\ adj [L rapidus strong-flowing, rapid, fr. rapere to seize, carry away] : very fast : SWIFT ♦ **Synonyms** FLEET, QUICK, SPEEDY — **ra·pid·i·ty** \rə-'pi-də-tē\ n — **rap·id·ly** adv

²rapid n : a place in a stream where the current flows very fast usu. over obstructions — usu. used in pl.

rapid eye movement n : rapid conjugate movement of the eyes associated with REM sleep

rapid transit n : fast passenger transportation (as by subway) in cities

¹ra·pi·er \'rā-pē-ər\ n : a straight 2-edged sword with a narrow pointed blade

²rapier adj : extremely sharp or keen ⟨∼ wit⟩

rap·ine \'ra-pən, -,pīn\ n : PILLAGE, PLUNDER

rap·pel \ra-'pel, ra-\ vb **-pelled; -pel·ling** : to descend (as from a cliff) by sliding down a rope

rap·pen \'rä-pən\ n, pl **rappen** : the centime of Switzerland

rap·port \ra-'pór\ n : RELATION; esp : relation characterized by harmony

rap·proche·ment \,ra-,prōsh-'mäⁿ, ra-'prōsh-,mäⁿ\ n : the establishment of or a state of having cordial relations

rap·scal·lion \rap-'skal-yən\ n : RASCAL, SCAMP

rapt \'rapt\ adj **1** : carried away with emotion **2** : ABSORBED, ENGROSSED ⟨listened with ∼ attention⟩ — **rapt·ly** \'rapt-lē\ adv — **rapt·ness** n

rap·tor \'rap-tər, -,tór\ n **1** : BIRD OF PREY **2** : a usu. small-to-medium-sized predatory dinosaur

rap·ture \'rap-chər\ n : spiritual or emotional ecstasy — **rap·tur·ous** \-chə-rəs\ adj — **rap·tur·ous·ly** adv

rapture of the deep : NITROGEN NARCOSIS

ra·ra avis \,rär-ə-'ä-vəs, ,rär-ə-'ä-wəs\ n, pl **ra·ra avis·es** \-'ä-və-səz\ or **ra·rae aves** \,rär-,ī-'ä-,wās\ [L, rare bird] : a rare person or thing : RARITY

¹rare \'rer\ adj **rar·er; rar·est** **1** : not thick or dense : THIN ⟨∼ air⟩ **2** : unusually fine : EXCELLENT, SPLENDID **3** : seldom met with — **rare·ly** adv — **rare·ness** n — **rar·i·ty** \'rar-ə-tē\ n

²rare adj **rar·er; rar·est** : cooked so that the inside is still red ⟨∼ beef⟩

rare·bit \'rer-bət\ n : WELSH RABBIT

rar·efac·tion \,rer-ə-'fak-shən\ n **1** : the action or process of rarefying **2** : the state of being rarefied

rar·e·fy also **rar·i·fy** \'rer-ə-,fī\ vb **-fied; -fy·ing** : to make or become rare, thin, or less dense

rar·ing \'rer-ən, -iŋ\ adj : full of enthusiasm or eagerness ⟨∼ to go⟩

ras·cal \'ras-kəl\ n [ME rascaile foot soldiers, commoners, worthless person, fr. AF rascaille, fr. OF dial. *rasquer to scrape, clean off, ultim. fr. L radere to scrape, shave] **1** : a mean or dishonest person **2** : a mischievous person — **ras·cal·i·ty** \ra-'ska-lə-tē\ n — **ras·cal·ly** \'ras-kə-lē\ adj

¹rash \'rash\ adj : having or showing little regard for consequences : too hasty in decision, action, or speech : RECKLESS ♦ **Synonyms** DARING, FOOLHARDY, ADVENTUROUS, VENTURESOME — **rash·ly** adv — **rash·ness** n

²rash n : an eruption on the body

rash·er \'ra-shər\ n : a thin slice of bacon or ham broiled or fried; also : a portion consisting of several such slices

¹rasp \'rasp\ vb **1** : to rub with or as if with a rough file **2** : to grate harshly on (as one's nerves) **3** : to speak in a grating tone ⟨"Don't touch me," she ∼ed⟩

²rasp n : a coarse file with cutting points instead of ridges

rasp·ber·ry \'raz-,ber-ē, -bə-rē\ n **1** : any of various edible usu. black or red berries produced by some brambles; also : such a bramble **2** : a sound of contempt made by protruding the tongue through the lips and expelling air forcibly

¹rat \'rat\ n **1** : any of numerous rodents larger than the related mice **2** : a contemptible person; esp : one that betrays friends or associates

²rat vb **rat·ted; rat·ting** **1** : to betray or inform on one's associates **2** : to hunt or catch rats

rat cheese n : CHEDDAR

ratch·et \'ra-chət\ n : a device that consists of a bar or wheel having slanted teeth into which a pawl drops so as to allow motion in only one direction

ratchet

¹rate \'rāt\ vb **rat·ed; rat·ing** : to scold violently

²rate n **1** : quantity, amount, or degree measured by some standard **2** : an amount (as of payment) measured by its relation to some other amount (as of time) **3** : a charge, payment, or price fixed according to a ratio, scale, or standard ⟨tax ∼⟩ **4** : RANK, CLASS

³rate *vb* **rat·ed; rat·ing 1** : ESTIMATE **2** : CONSIDER, REGARD ⟨*rated* as a good pianist⟩ **3** : to settle the relative rank or class of **4** : to be classed : RANK **5** : to have a right to : DESERVE ⟨the new museum ∼*s* a visit⟩ **6** : to be of consequence — **rat·er** *n*

rath·er \'ra-ᵗhər, 'rä-, 'rə-\ *adv* [ME, fr. OE *hrathor*, compar. of *hrathe* quickly] **1** : more properly **2** : PREFERABLY ⟨I'd ∼ not go⟩ **3** : more correctly speaking **4** : to the contrary : INSTEAD **5** : SOMEWHAT ⟨∼ warm⟩

rather than *prep* : INSTEAD OF

rat·i·fy \'ra-tə-ˌfī\ *vb* **-fied; -fy·ing** : to approve and accept formally — **rat·i·fi·ca·tion** \ˌra-tə-fə-'kā-shən\ *n*

rat·ing \'rā-tiŋ\ *n* **1** : a classification according to grade : RANK **2** *Brit* : an enlisted person in the navy **3** : an estimate of the credit standing and business responsibility of a person or firm

ra·tio \'rā-shō, -shē-ō\ *n, pl* **ra·tios 1** : the indicated quotient of two numbers or mathematical expressions **2** : the relationship in number, quantity, or degree between two or more things

ra·ti·o·ci·na·tion \ˌra-tē-ˌō-sə-'nā-shən, -ˌä-\ *n* : exact thinking : REASONING — **ra·ti·o·ci·nate** \-'ō-sə-ˌnāt, -'ä-\ *vb* — **ra·ti·o·ci·na·tive** \-'ō-sə-ˌnā-tiv, -'ä-\ *adj* — **ra·ti·o·ci·na·tor** \-'ō-sə-ˌnā-tər, -'ä-sə-\ *n*

¹ra·tion \'ra-shən, 'rā-\ *n* **1** : a food allowance for one day **2** : FOOD, PROVISIONS, DIET — usu. used in pl. **3** : SHARE, ALLOTMENT

²ration *vb* **1** : to supply with or allot as rations **2** : to use or allot sparingly ✦ *Synonyms* APPORTION, PORTION, PRORATE, PARCEL

¹ra·tio·nal \'ra-shə-nəl\ *adj* **1** : having reason or understanding **2** : of or relating to reason **3** : relating to, consisting of, or being one or more rational numbers — **ra·tio·nal·ly** *adv*

²rational *n* : RATIONAL NUMBER

ra·tio·nale \ˌra-shə-'nal\ *n* **1** : an explanation of principles controlling belief or practice **2** : an underlying reason

ra·tio·nal·ise *Brit var of* RATIONALIZE

ra·tio·nal·ism \'ra-shə-nə-ˌli-zəm\ *n* : the practice of guiding one's actions and opinions solely by what seems reasonable — **ra·tio·nal·ist** \-list\ *n* — **rationalist** *or* **ra·tio·nal·is·tic** \ˌra-shə-nə-'lis-tik\ *adj* — **ra·tio·nal·is·ti·cal·ly** \-ti-k(ə-)lē\ *adv*

ra·tio·nal·i·ty \ˌra-shə-'na-lə-tē\ *n, pl* **-ties** : the quality or state of being rational

ra·tio·nal·ize \'ra-shə-nə-ˌlīz\ *vb* **-ized; -iz·ing 1** : to make (something irrational) appear rational or reasonable **2** : to provide a natural explanation of (as a myth) **3** : to justify (as one's behavior or weaknesses) esp. to oneself **4** : to find plausible but untrue reasons for conduct — **ra·tio·nal·i·za·tion** \ˌra-shə-nə-lə-'zā-shən\ *n*

rational number *n* : a number that can be expressed as an integer or the quotient of an integer divided by a nonzero integer

rat race *n* : strenuous, tiresome, and usu. competitive activity or rush

rat·tan \ra-'tan, rə-\ *n* : a cane or switch made from one of the long stems of an Asian climbing palm; *also* : this palm

rat·ter \'ra-tər\ *n* : a rat-catching dog or cat

¹rat·tle \'ra-tᵊl\ *vb* **rat·tled; rat·tling 1** : to make or cause to make a series of clattering sounds **2** : to move with a clattering sound **3** : to say or do in a brisk lively fashion ⟨∼ off the answers⟩ **4** : CONFUSE, UPSET ⟨∼ a witness⟩

²rattle *n* **1** : a toy that produces a rattle when shaken **2** : a series of clattering and knocking sounds **3** : a rattling organ at the end of a rattlesnake's tail

rat·tler \'rat-lər\ *n* : RATTLESNAKE

rat·tle·snake \'ra-tᵊl-ˌsnāk\ *n* : any of various American pit vipers with a rattle at the end of the tail

rat·tle·trap \'ra-tᵊl-ˌtrap\ *n* : something (as an old car) rickety and full of rattles

rat·tling \'rat-liŋ\ *adj* **1** : LIVELY, BRISK ⟨moved at a ∼ pace⟩ **2** : FIRST-RATE, SPLENDID

rat·trap \'rat-ˌtrap\ *n* **1** : a trap for rats **2** : a dilapidated building

rat·ty \'ra-tē\ *adj* **rat·ti·er; -est 1** : infested with rats **2** : of, relating to, or suggestive of rats **3** : SHABBY ⟨a ∼ old coat⟩

rau·cous \'ro-kəs\ *adj* **1** : HARSH, HOARSE, STRIDENT ⟨∼ voices⟩ **2** : boisterously disorderly — **rau·cous·ly** *adv* — **rau·cous·ness** *n*

raun·chy \'ron-chē, 'rän-\ *adj* **raun·chi·er; -est 1** : SLOVENLY, DIRTY **2** : OBSCENE, SMUTTY ⟨∼ jokes⟩ — **raun·chi·ness** \-chē-nəs\ *n*

rav·age \'ra-vij\ *n* [F] : an act or result of ravaging : DEVASTATION

²ravage *vb* **rav·aged; rav·ag·ing** : to lay waste : DEVASTATE — **rav·ag·er** *n*

¹rave \'rāv\ *vb* **raved; rav·ing 1** : to talk wildly in or as if in delirium : STORM, RAGE **2** : to talk with extreme enthusiasm ⟨*raved* about the show⟩ — **rav·er** *n*

²rave *n* **1** : an act or instance of raving **2** : an extravagantly favorable criticism

¹rav·el \'ra-vəl\ *vb* **-eled** *or* **-elled; -el·ing** *or* **-el·ling 1** : UNRAVEL, UNTWIST **2** : TANGLE, CONFUSE

²ravel *n* **1** : something tangled **2** : something raveled out; *esp* : a loose thread

¹ra·ven \'rā-vən\ *n* : a large black bird related to the crow

²raven *adj* : black and glossy like a raven's feathers

³rav·en \'ra-vən\ *vb* **1** : to devour greedily **2** : DESPOIL, PLUNDER **3** : PREY

rav·en·ous \'ra-və-nəs\ *adj* **1** : RAPACIOUS, VORACIOUS ⟨∼ wolves⟩ **2** : eager for food : very hungry — **rav·en·ous·ly** *adv* — **rav·en·ous·ness** *n*

ra·vine \rə-'vēn\ *n* : a small narrow steep-sided valley larger than a gully

rav·i·o·li \ˌra-vē-'ō-lē\ *n, pl* **ravioli** *also* **raviolis** [It, fr. It dial., pl. of *raviolo*, lit., little turnip, dim. of *rava* turnip, fr. L *rapa*] : small cases of dough with a savory filling (as of meat or cheese)

rav·ish \'ra-vish\ *vb* **1** : to seize and take away by violence **2** : to overcome with emotion and esp. with joy or delight ⟨∼ed by her beauty⟩ **3** : RAPE — **rav·ish·er** *n* — **rav·ish·ment** *n*

¹raw \'ro\ *adj* **raw·er** \'ro-ər\; **raw·est** \'ro-əst\ **1** : not cooked **2** : changed little from the original form : not processed ⟨∼ materials⟩ **3** : having the surface abraded or irritated ⟨a ∼ sore⟩ **4** : not trained or experienced ⟨∼ recruits⟩ **5** : VULGAR, COARSE ⟨∼ language⟩ **6** : disagreeably cold and damp ⟨a ∼ day⟩ **7** : UNFAIR ⟨∼ deal⟩ — **raw·ness** *n*

²raw *n* : a raw place or state — **in the raw** : NAKED

raw·boned \'ro-ˌbōnd\ *adj* : LEAN, GAUNT; *also* : having a heavy frame that seems to have little flesh

raw·hide \'ro-ˌhīd\ *n* : the untanned skin of cattle; *also* : a whip made of this

¹ray \'rā\ *n* : any of an order of large flat cartilaginous fishes that have the eyes on the upper surface and the hind end of the body slender and taillike

²ray *n* [ME, fr. AF *rai*, fr. L *radius* rod, ray] **1** : any of the lines of light that appear to radiate from a bright object **2** : a thin beam of radiant energy (as light) **3** : light from a beam **4** : a thin line like a beam of light **5** : an animal or plant structure resembling a ray **6** : a tiny bit : PARTICLE ⟨a ∼ of hope⟩

ray·on \'rā-ˌän\ *n* : a fiber made from cellulose; *also* : a yarn, thread, or fabric made from such fibers

raze \'rāz\ *vb* **razed; raz·ing 1** : to scrape, cut, or shave off **2** : to destroy to the ground : DEMOLISH

ra·zor \'rā-zər\ *n* : a sharp cutting instrument used to shave off hair

ra·zor–backed \'rā-zər-ˌbakt\ *or* **ra·zor·back** \-ˌbak\ *adj* : having a sharp narrow back ⟨a ∼ horse⟩

razor clam *n* : any of a family of marine bivalve mollusks having a long narrow curved thin shell

razor wire *n* : coiled wire fitted with sharp edges and used as an obstacle or barrier

¹razz \'raz\ *n* : RASPBERRY 2

²razz *vb* : RIDICULE, TEASE

Rb *symbol* rubidium

RBC *abbr* red blood cells

RBI \ˌär-(ˌ)bē-'ī, 'ri-bē\ *n, pl* **RBIs** *or* **RBI** [run batted in] : a run in baseball that is driven in by a batter

RC *abbr* **1** Red Cross **2** Roman Catholic

RCAF *abbr* Royal Canadian Air Force

RCMP *abbr* Royal Canadian Mounted Police

RCN *abbr* Royal Canadian Navy

rct *abbr* recruit

rd *abbr* **1** road **2** rod **3** round

RD *abbr* rural delivery
RDA *abbr* recommended daily allowance; recommended dietary allowance
re \'rā, 'rē\ *prep* : with regard to
Re *symbol* rhenium
re- \rē̠, ˌrē, 'rē\ *prefix* 1 : again : for a second time 2 : anew : in a new or different form 3 : back : backward

reabsorb	recolonize	reevaluation	reorient
reacquire	recolor	reexamination	reorientation
reactivate	recombine	reexamine	repack
reactivation	recommence	reexport	repaint
readdress	recommission	refashion	repass
readjust	recommit	refight	repeople
readjustment	recompile	refigure	rephotograph
readmission	recompose	refinish	rephrase
readmit	recomputation	refit	replant
reaffirm	recompute	refix	repopulate
reaffirmation	reconceive	refloat	reprice
realign	reconcentrate	refold	reprocess
realignment	reconception	reforge	reprogram
reallocate	recondensation	reformulate	republication
reallocation	recondense	reformulation	republish
reanalysis	reconfirm	refortify	repurchase
reanalyze	reconfirmation	refound	reradiate
reanimate	reconnect	refreeze	reread
reanimation	reconquer	refuel	rereading
reannex	reconquest	refurnish	rerecord
reannexation	reconsecrate	regain	reroute
reappear	reconsecration	regather	reschedule
reappearance	recontact	regild	rescore
reapplication	recontaminate	regive	rescreen
reapply	recontamination	regrade	reseal
reappoint	reconvene	regrind	reseed
reappointment	reconvert	regrow	resell
reapportion	recook	regrowth	reset
reapportionment	recopy	rehandle	resettle
reappraisal	recross	rehear	resettlement
reappraise	recrystallize	reheat	resew
rearm	recut	rehouse	reshow
rearmament	redecorate	reimpose	resocialization
rearouse	redecoration	reimposition	resow
rearrange	rededicate	reincorporate	respell
rearrangement	rededication	reinsert	restaff
rearrest	redefine	reinsertion	restart
reascend	redefinition	reintegrate	restate
reassemble	redeposit	reinterpret	restatement
reassembly	redesign	reinterpretation	restock
reassert	redetermination	reintroduce	restrengthen
reassess	redetermine	reintroduction	restructure
reassessment	redevelop	reinvention	restudy
reassign	redevelopment	reinvest	restuff
reassignment	redirect	reinvestment	restyle
reassume	rediscount	reinvigorate	resubmit
reattach	rediscover	reinvigoration	resummon
reattachment	rediscovery	reissue	resupply
reattain	redissolve	rejudge	resurface
reattempt	redistill	rekindle	resurvey
reauthorization	redistillation	reknit	resynthesis
reauthorize	redraft	relaunch	resynthesize
reawaken	redraw	relearn	retaste
rebaptism	reecho	relight	retell
rebaptize	reedit	reline	retest
rebid	reelect	reload	retrain
rebind	reelection	remanufacture	retransmission
reboil	reemerge	remap	retransmit
rebroadcast	reemergence	remarriage	retrial
reburial	reemphasis	remarry	reunification
rebury	reemphasize	rematch	reunify
recalculate	reemploy	remelt	reunite
recalculation	reemployment	remigration	reusable
rechannel	reenact	remold	reuse
recharge	reenactment	rename	revaluate
rechargeable	reenergize	renegotiate	revaluation
recharter	reenlist	renegotiation	revalue
recheck	reenlistment	renominate	revisit
rechristen	reenter	renomination	rewarm
reclassification	reequip	renumber	rewash
reclassify	reestablish	reoccupy	reweave
recoin	reestablishment	reoccur	rewed
recolonization	reevaluate	reopen	reweigh
		reorder	rewire
		reorganization	rezone
		reorganize	

[1]reach \'rēch\ *vb* 1 : to stretch out 2 : to touch or attempt to touch or seize 3 : to extend to 4 : to communicate with 5 : to arrive at ◆ *Synonyms* GAIN, REALIZE, ACHIEVE, ATTAIN — reach·able *adj* — reach·er *n*

²**reach** *n* **1** : an unbroken stretch of a river **2** : the act of reaching **3** : a reachable distance; *also* : ability to reach **4** : a range of knowledge or comprehension

re·act \rē-'akt\ *vb* **1** : to exert a return or counteracting influence **2** : to have or show a reaction **3** : to act in opposition to a force or influence **4** : to move or tend in a reverse direction **5** : to undergo chemical reaction

re·ac·tant \rē-'ak-tənt\ *n* : a chemically reacting substance

re·ac·tion \rē-'ak-shən\ *n* **1** : the act or process of reacting **2** : a counter tendency; *esp* : a tendency toward a former esp. outmoded political or social order or policy **3** : bodily, mental, or emotional response to a stimulus **4** : chemical change **5** : a process involving change in atomic nuclei

re·ac·tion·ary \rē-'ak-shə-ˌner-ē\ *adj* : relating to, marked by, or favoring esp. political reaction — **reactionary** *n*

re·ac·tive \rē-'ak-tiv\ *adj* : reacting or tending to react ⟨a ~ chemical⟩

re·ac·tor \rē-'ak-tər\ *n* **1** : one that reacts **2** : a device for the controlled release of nuclear energy

¹**read** \'rēd\ *vb* **read** \'red\; **read·ing** [ME *reden* to advise, interpret, read, fr. OE *rǣdan*] **1** : to understand language by interpreting written symbols for speech sounds **2** : to utter aloud written or printed words **3** : to learn by observing ⟨~ nature's signs⟩ **4** : to study by a course of reading ⟨~s law⟩ **5** : to discover the meaning of ⟨~ the clues⟩ **6** : to recognize or interpret as if by reading **7** : to attribute (a meaning) to something ⟨~ guilt in his manner⟩ **8** : INDICATE ⟨thermometer ~s 10°⟩ **9** : to consist in phrasing or meaning ⟨the two versions ~ differently⟩ — **read·abil·i·ty** \ˌrē-də-'bi-lə-tē\ *n* — **read·able** \'rē-də-bəl\ *adj* — **read·ably** \-blē\ *adv* — **read·er** *n*

²**read** \'red\ *adj* : informed by reading ⟨widely ~⟩

read·er·ship \'rē-dər-ˌship\ *n* : the mass or a particular group of readers

read·ing *n* **1** : something read or for reading **2** : a particular version **3** : data indicated by an instrument ⟨thermometer ~⟩ **4** : a particular interpretation (as of a law) **5** : a particular performance (as of a musical work) **6** : an indication of a certain state of affairs

read–only memory *n* : ROM

read·out \'rēd-ˌaút\ *n* **1** : the process of removing information from an automatic device (as a computer) and displaying it in an understandable form; *also* : the information removed from such a device **2** : an electronic device that presents information in visual form

read out *vb* **1** : to read aloud **2** : to expel from an organization

¹**ready** \'re-dē\ *adj* **read·i·er; -est** **1** : prepared for use or action **2** : likely to do something indicated; *also* : willingly disposed : INCLINED **3** : spontaneously prompt ⟨her ~ wit⟩ **4** : immediately available ⟨~ cash⟩ — **read·i·ly** \'re-də-lē\ *adv* — **read·i·ness** \-dē-nəs\ *n* — **at the ready** : ready for immediate use

²**ready** *vb* **read·ied; ready·ing** : to make ready : PREPARE

ready–made \ˌre-dē-'mād\ *adj* : already made up for general sale : not specially made — **ready–made** *n*

ready room *n* : a room in which pilots are briefed and await orders

re·agent \rē-'ā-jənt\ *n* : a substance that takes part in or brings about a particular chemical reaction

¹**re·al** \'rēl\ *adj* [ME, real, relating to things (in law), fr. AF, fr. ML & LL; ML *realis* relating to things (in law), fr. LL, real, fr. L *res* thing, fact] **1** : of or relating to fixed or immovable things (as land) ⟨~ property⟩ **2** : not artificial : GENUINE; *also* : not imaginary — **re·al·ness** *n* — **for real** **1** : in earnest **2** : GENUINE ⟨the threat was *for real*⟩

²**real** *adv* : VERY ⟨had a ~ good time⟩

³**re·al** \rā-'äl\ *n* — see MONEY table

real estate *n* : property in buildings and land

re·al·ism \'rē-ə-ˌli-zəm\ *n* **1** : the disposition to face facts and to deal with them practically **2** : true and faithful portrayal of nature and of people in art or literature — **re·al·ist** \-list\ *adj or n* — **re·al·is·tic** \ˌrē-ə-'lis-tik\ *adj* — **re·al·is·ti·cal·ly** \-ti-k(ə-)lē\ *adv*

re·al·i·ty \rē-'a-lə-tē\ *n, pl* **-ties** **1** : the quality or state of being real **2** : something real **3** : the totality of real things and events

re·al·ize \'rē-ə-ˌlīz\ *vb* **-ized; -iz·ing** **1** : to make actual : ACCOMPLISH **2** : to convert into money ⟨~ assets⟩

3 : OBTAIN, GAIN ⟨~ a profit⟩ **4** : to be aware of : UNDERSTAND — **re·al·iz·able** *adj* — **re·al·i·za·tion** \ˌrē-ə-lə-'zā-shən\ *n*

re·al·ly \'rē-lē, 'ri-\ *adv* : in truth : in fact : ACTUALLY

realm \'relm\ *n* **1** : KINGDOM **2** : SPHERE, DOMAIN ⟨within the ~ of possibility⟩

real number *n* : a number that has no imaginary part ⟨the set of all *real numbers* comprises the rationals and the irrationals⟩

re·al·po·li·tik \rā-'äl-ˌpō-li-ˌtēk\ *n, often cap* [G] : politics based on practical and material factors rather than on theoretical or ethical objectives

real time *n* : the actual time during which something takes place — **real–time** *adj*

re·al·ty \'rēl-tē\ *n* : REAL ESTATE

¹**ream** \'rēm\ *n* [ME *reme*, fr. AF, ultim. fr. Ar *rizma*, lit., bundle] : a quantity of paper that is variously 480, 500, or 516 sheets

²**ream** *vb* : to enlarge, shape, or clear with a reamer

ream·er \'rē-mər\ *n* : a tool with cutting edges that is used to enlarge or shape a hole

reap \'rēp\ *vb* **1** : to cut or clear with a scythe, sickle, or machine **2** : to gather by or as if by cutting : HARVEST ⟨~ a reward⟩ — **reap·er** *n*

¹**rear** \'rir\ *vb* **1** : to erect by building **2** : to set or raise upright **3** : to breed and raise for use or market ⟨~ livestock⟩ **4** : BRING UP, FOSTER **5** : to lift or rise up; *esp* : to rise on the hind legs

²**rear** *n* **1** : the unit (as of an army) or area farthest from the enemy **2** : BACK; *also* : the position at the back of something

³**rear** *adj* : being at the back

rear admiral *n* : a commissioned officer in the navy or coast guard ranking next below a vice admiral

¹**rear·ward** \'rir-wərd\ *adj* **1** : being at or toward the rear **2** : directed toward the rear ⟨a ~ glance⟩

²**rear·ward** *also* **rear·wards** \-wərdz\ *adv* : at or toward the rear ⟨looking ~⟩

reas *abbr* reasonable

¹**rea·son** \'rē-zᵊn\ *n* [ME *resoun*, fr. AF *raisun*, fr. L *ration-*, *ratio* reason, computation] **1** : a statement offered in explanation or justification **2** : GROUND, CAUSE **3** : the power to think : INTELLECT **4** : a sane or sound mind **5** : due exercise of the faculty of logical thought

²**reason** *vb* **1** : to talk with another to cause a change of mind **2** : to use the faculty of reason : THINK **3** : to discover or formulate by the use of reason — **rea·son·er** *n* — **rea·son·ing** *n*

rea·son·able \'rē-zᵊn-ə-bəl\ *adj* **1** : being within the bounds of reason : not extreme **2** : INEXPENSIVE **3** : able to reason : RATIONAL — **rea·son·able·ness** *n* — **rea·son·ably** \-blē\ *adv*

re·as·sure \ˌrē-ə-'shùr\ *vb* **1** : to assure again **2** : to restore confidence to : free from fear — **re·as·sur·ance** \-'shùr-əns\ *n* — **re·as·sur·ing·ly** *adv*

¹**re·bate** \'rē-ˌbāt\ *vb* **re·bat·ed; re·bat·ing** : to make or give a rebate

²**rebate** *n* : a return of part of a payment ♦ **Synonyms** DEDUCTION, ABATEMENT, DISCOUNT

¹**reb·el** \'re-bəl\ *adj* [ME, fr. AF, fr. L *rebellis*, fr. *re-* + *bellum* war] : of or relating to rebels

²**rebel** *n* : one that rebels against authority

³**re·bel** \ri-'bel\ *vb* **re·belled; re·bel·ling** **1** : to resist the authority of one's government **2** : to act in or show disobedience **3** : to feel or exhibit anger or revulsion

re·bel·lion \ri-'bel-yən\ *n* : resistance to authority; *esp* : defiance against a government through uprising or revolt

re·bel·lious \-yəs\ *adj* **1** : given to or engaged in rebellion **2** : inclined to resist authority — **re·bel·lious·ly** *adv* — **re·bel·lious·ness** *n*

re·birth \ˌrē-'bərth\ *n* **1** : a new or second birth **2** : RENAISSANCE, REVIVAL

re·born \-'bòrn\ *adj* : born again : REGENERATED, REVIVED

¹**re·bound** \ˌrē-'baúnd, 'rē-ˌbaúnd\ *vb* **1** : to spring back on or as if on striking another body **2** : to recover from a setback or frustration ⟨~ed quickly from the loss⟩

²**re·bound** \'rē-ˌbaúnd\ *n* **1** : the action of rebounding **2** : a rebounding ball **3** : a reaction to setback or frustration

re·buff \ri-ˈbəf\ *vb* : to reject or criticize sharply : SNUB — **rebuff** *n*

re·build \(ˌ)rē-ˈbild\ *vb* **-built** \-ˈbilt\; **-build·ing** 1 : REPAIR, RECONSTRUCT; *also* : REMODEL 2 : to build again

¹**re·buke** \ri-ˈbyük\ *vb* **re·buked; re·buk·ing** : to reprimand sharply : REPROVE

²**rebuke** *n* : a sharp reprimand

re·bus \ˈrē-bəs\ *n* [L, by things, abl. pl. of *res* thing] : a representation of syllables or words by means of pictures; *also* : a riddle composed of such pictures

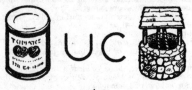

rebus

re·but \ri-ˈbət\ *vb* **re·but·ted; re·but·ting** : to refute esp. formally (as in debate) by evidence and arguments ♦ *Synonyms* DISPROVE, CONTROVERT, CONFUTE — **re·but·ter** *n*

re·but·tal \ri-ˈbə-tᵊl\ *n* : the act of rebutting

rec *abbr* 1 receipt 2 record; recording 3 recreation

re·cal·ci·trant \ri-ˈkal-sə-trənt\ *adj* [LL *recalcitrant-, recalcitrans,* prp. of *recalcitrare* to be stubbornly disobedient, fr. L, to kick back, fr. *re-* back, again + *calcitrare* to kick, fr. *calc-, calx* heel] 1 : stubbornly resisting authority ⟨a ~ prisoner⟩ 2 : resistant to handling or treatment ♦ *Synonyms* REFRACTORY, HEADSTRONG, WILLFUL, UNRULY, UNGOVERNABLE — **re·cal·ci·trance** \-trəns\ *n*

¹**re·call** \ri-ˈkȯl\ *vb* 1 : REVOKE, CANCEL 2 : to call back 3 : REMEMBER, RECOLLECT ⟨~ed their last meeting⟩

²**re·call** \ri-ˈkȯl, ˈrē-ˌkȯl\ *n* 1 : a summons to return 2 : the procedure of removing an official by popular vote 3 : remembrance of things learned or experienced 4 : the act of revoking 5 : a call by a manufacturer for the return of a product that may be defective or contaminated

re·cant \ri-ˈkant\ *vb* : to take back (something one has said) publicly : make an open confession of error — **re·can·ta·tion** \ˌrē-ˌkan-ˈtā-shən\ *n*

¹**re·cap** \ˈrē-ˌkap, rē-ˈkap\ *vb* **re·capped; re·cap·ping** : RECAPITULATE — **re·cap** \ˈrē-ˌkap\ *n*

²**recap** *vb* **re·capped; re·cap·ping** : RETREAD — **re·cap** \ˈrē-ˌkap\ *n*

re·ca·pit·u·late \ˌrē-kə-ˈpi-chə-ˌlāt\ *vb* **-lat·ed; -lat·ing** : to restate briefly : SUMMARIZE ⟨~ recent news stories⟩ — **re·ca·pit·u·la·tion** \-ˌpi-chə-ˈlā-shən\ *n*

re·cap·ture \(ˌ)rē-ˈkap-chər\ *vb* 1 : to capture again 2 : to experience again ⟨~ happy times⟩

re·cast \(ˌ)rē-ˈkast\ *vb* 1 : to cast again 2 : REVISE, REMODEL ⟨~ a sentence⟩

recd *abbr* received

re·cede \ri-ˈsēd\ *vb* **re·ced·ed; re·ced·ing** 1 : to move back or away ⟨a *receding* hairline⟩ 2 : to slant backward 3 : DIMINISH, CONTRACT ⟨a *receding* deficit⟩

¹**re·ceipt** \ri-ˈsēt\ *n* 1 : RECIPE 2 : the act of receiving 3 : something received — usu. used in pl. 4 : a written acknowledgment of something received

²**receipt** *vb* 1 : to give a receipt for 2 : to mark as paid

re·ceiv·able \ri-ˈsē-və-bəl\ *adj* 1 : capable of being received; *esp* : acceptable as legal ⟨~ certificates⟩ 2 : subject to call for payment ⟨notes ~⟩

re·ceive \ri-ˈsēv\ *vb* **re·ceived; re·ceiv·ing** 1 : to take in or accept (as something sent or paid) : come into possession of : GET 2 : CONTAIN, HOLD 3 : to permit to enter : GREET, WELCOME 4 : to be at home to visitors 5 : to accept as true or authoritative 6 : to be the subject of : UNDERGO, EXPERIENCE ⟨~ a shock⟩ 7 : to change incoming radio waves into sounds or pictures ⟨~ a broadcast⟩

re·ceiv·er \ri-ˈsē-vər\ *n* 1 : one that receives 2 : a person legally appointed to receive and have charge of property or money involved in a lawsuit 3 : a device for converting electromagnetic waves or signals into audio or visual form ⟨telephone ~⟩

re·ceiv·er·ship \-ˌship\ *n* 1 : the office or function of a receiver 2 : the condition of being in the hands of a receiver

re·cen·cy \ˈrē-sᵊn-sē\ *n* : RECENTNESS

re·cent \ˈrē-sᵊnt\ *adj* 1 : of the present time or time just past ⟨~ history⟩ 2 : having lately come into existence : NEW, FRESH ⟨~ buds⟩ 3 *cap* : HOLOCENE — **re·cent·ly** *adv* — **re·cent·ness** *n*

re·cep·ta·cle \ri-ˈsep-ti-kəl\ *n* 1 : something used to receive and hold something else : CONTAINER 2 : the enlarged end of a flower stalk upon which the parts of the flower grow 3 : an electrical fitting containing the live parts of a circuit

re·cep·tion \ri-ˈsep-shən\ *n* 1 : the act of receiving 2 : a social gathering at which guests are formally welcomed

re·cep·tion·ist \ri-ˈsep-shə-nist\ *n* : a person employed to greet callers

re·cep·tive \ri-ˈsep-tiv\ *adj* : able or inclined to receive; *esp* : open and responsive to ideas, impressions, or suggestions ⟨a ~ audience⟩ — **re·cep·tive·ly** *adv* — **re·cep·tive·ness** *n* — **re·cep·tiv·i·ty** \ˌrē-ˌsep-ti-və-tē\ *n*

re·cep·tor \ri-ˈsep-tər\ *n* 1 : one that receives stimuli : SENSE ORGAN 2 : a chemical group or molecule in the outer cell membrane or in the cell interior that has an affinity for a specific chemical group, molecule, or virus

¹**re·cess** \ˈrē-ˌses, ri-ˈses\ *n* 1 : a secret or secluded place 2 : an indentation in a line or surface (as an alcove in a room) 3 : a suspension of business or procedure for rest or relaxation

²**recess** *vb* 1 : to put into a recess 2 : to make a recess in 3 : to interrupt for a recess 4 : to take a recess

re·ces·sion \ri-ˈse-shən\ *n* 1 : the act of receding : WITHDRAWAL 2 : a departing procession (as at the end of a church service) 3 : a period of reduced economic activity

re·ces·sion·al \ri-ˈse-shə-nəl\ *n* 1 : a hymn or musical piece at the conclusion of a service or program 2 : RECESSION 2

¹**re·ces·sive** \ri-ˈse-siv\ *adj* 1 : tending to recede 2 : producing or being a bodily characteristic that is masked or not expressed when a contrasting dominant gene or trait is present ⟨~ genes⟩ ⟨~ traits⟩

²**recessive** *n* : a recessive characteristic or gene; *also* : an individual that has one or more recessive characteristics

re·cher·ché \rə-ˌsher-ˈshā, -ˈsher-ˌshā\ *adj* [F] 1 : CHOICE, RARE 2 : excessively refined ⟨~ poetry⟩

re·cid·i·vism \ri-ˈsi-də-ˌvi-zəm\ *n* : a tendency to relapse into a previous condition; *esp* : relapse into criminal behavior — **re·cid·i·vist** \-vist\ *n*

rec·i·pe \ˈre-sə-(ˌ)pē\ *n* [L, take, imperative of *recipere* to take, receive, fr. *re-* back + *capere* to take] 1 : a set of instructions for making something from various ingredients 2 : a method of procedure : FORMULA

re·cip·i·ent \ri-ˈsi-pē-ənt\ *n* : one that receives

¹**re·cip·ro·cal** \ri-ˈsi-prə-kəl\ *adj* 1 : inversely related 2 : MUTUAL, SHARED 3 : serving to reciprocate 4 : mutually corresponding — **re·cip·ro·cal·ly** *adv*

²**reciprocal** *n* 1 : something in a reciprocal relationship to another 2 : one of a pair of numbers (as ²⁄₃ and ³⁄₂) whose product is one

re·cip·ro·cate \-ˌkāt\ *vb* **-cat·ed; -cat·ing** 1 : to move backward and forward alternately 2 : to give and take mutually 3 : to make a return for something done or given — **re·cip·ro·ca·tion** \-ˌsi-prə-ˈkā-shən\ *n*

rec·i·proc·i·ty \ˌre-sə-ˈprä-sə-tē\ *n, pl* **-ties** 1 : the quality or state of being reciprocal 2 : mutual exchange of privileges (as trade advantages between countries)

re·cit·al \ri-ˈsī-tᵊl\ *n* 1 : an act or instance of reciting : ACCOUNT 2 : a public reading or recitation ⟨a poetry ~⟩ 3 : a concert given by a musician, dancer, or dance troupe 4 : a public exhibition of skill given by music or dance pupils — **re·cit·al·ist** \-tᵊl-ist\ *n*

rec·i·ta·tion \ˌre-sə-ˈtā-shən\ *n* 1 : RECITING, RECITAL 2 : delivery before an audience usu. of something memorized ⟨~ of a poem⟩ 3 : a classroom exercise in which pupils answer questions on a lesson they have studied

re·cite \ri-ˈsīt\ *vb* **re·cit·ed; re·cit·ing** 1 : to repeat verbatim (as something memorized) 2 : to recount in some detail : RELATE 3 : to reply to a teacher's questions on a lesson — **re·cit·er** *n*

reck·less \ˈre-kləs\ *adj* : lacking caution ⟨a ~ driver⟩ ♦ *Synonyms* HASTY, BRASH, HOTHEADED, THOUGHTLESS — **reck·less·ly** *adv* — **reck·less·ness** *n*

reck·on \\'re-kən\\ vb 1 : COUNT, CALCULATE, COMPUTE 2 : CONSIDER, REGARD ⟨was ∼ed as the leader⟩ 3 chiefly dial : THINK, SUPPOSE, GUESS
reck·on·ing n 1 : an act or instance of reckoning 2 : a settling of accounts ⟨day of ∼⟩
re·claim \\ri-'klām\\ vb 1 : to recall from wrong conduct : REFORM 2 : to change from an undesirable to a desired condition ⟨∼ marshy land⟩ 3 : to obtain from a waste product or by-product ⟨∼ed plastic⟩ 4 : to demand or obtain the return of — **re·claim·able** adj — **rec·la·ma·tion** \\.re-klə-'mā-shən\\ n
re·cline \\ri-'klīn\\ vb **re·clined; re·clin·ing** 1 : to lean or incline backward 2 : to lie down : REST
re·clin·er \\ri-'klī-nər\\ n : a chair with an adjustable back and footrest
re·cluse \\'re-,klüs, ri-'klüs\\ n : a person who leads a secluded or solitary life : HERMIT — **re·clu·sive** \\ri-'klü-siv\\ adj
rec·og·nise chiefly Brit var of RECOGNIZE
rec·og·ni·tion \\.re-kəg-'ni-shən\\ n 1 : the act of recognizing : the state of being recognized : ACKNOWLEDGMENT ⟨in ∼ of their achievements⟩ 2 : special notice or attention
re·cog·ni·zance \\ri-'käg-nə-zəns\\ n : a promise recorded before a court or magistrate to do something (as to appear in court or to keep the peace) usu. under penalty of a money forfeiture
rec·og·nize \\'re-kəg-,nīz\\ vb **-nized; -niz·ing** 1 : to acknowledge (as a speaker in a meeting) as one entitled to be heard at the time 2 : to acknowledge the existence or the independence of (a country or government) 3 : to take notice of 4 : to acknowledge with appreciation 5 : to acknowledge acquaintance with 6 : to identify as previously known 7 : to perceive clearly : REALIZE — **rec·og·niz·able** \\'re-kəg-,nī-zə-bəl\\ adj — **rec·og·niz·ably** \\-blē\\ adv
¹**re·coil** \\ri-'köi(-ə)l\\ vb [ME reculen, recoilen, fr. AF reculer, reculier, fr. re- back + cul backside, fr. L culus] 1 : to draw back : RETREAT 2 : to spring back to or as if to a starting point ✦ **Synonyms** SHRINK, FLINCH, WINCE, QUAIL, BLENCH
²**re·coil** \\'rē-,köi(-ə)l, ri-'köil\\ n : the action of recoiling (as by a gun or spring)
rec·ol·lect \\.re-kə-'lekt\\ vb : to recall to mind : REMEMBER ✦ **Synonyms** RECALL, REMIND, REMINISCE, BETHINK
rec·ol·lec·tion \\.re-kə-'lek-shən\\ n 1 : the act or power of recollecting 2 : something recollected
re·com·bi·nant \\(,)rē-'käm-bə-nənt\\ adj 1 : relating to genetic recombination 2 : containing or produced by recombinant DNA ⟨∼ vaccines⟩
recombinant DNA n : genetically engineered DNA prepared in vitro by joining together DNA usu. from more than one species of organism
re·com·bi·na·tion \\.rē-,käm-bə-'nā-shən\\ n : the formation of new combinations of genes
rec·om·mend \\.re-kə-'mend\\ vb 1 : to present as deserving of acceptance or trial 2 : to give in charge : COMMIT 3 : to make acceptable 4 : ADVISE, COUNSEL — **rec·om·mend·able** \\-'men-də-bəl\\ adj
rec·om·men·da·tion \\.re-kə-mən-'dā-shən\\ n 1 : the act of recommending 2 : something recommended 3 : something that recommends
¹**rec·om·pense** \\'re-kəm-,pens\\ vb **-pensed; -pens·ing** 1 : to give compensation to : pay for ⟨was recompensed for their losses⟩ 2 : to return in kind : REQUITE ✦ **Synonyms** REIMBURSE, INDEMNIFY, REPAY, COMPENSATE
²**recompense** n : COMPENSATION
rec·on·cile \\'re-kən-,sī(-ə)l\\ vb **-ciled; -cil·ing** 1 : to cause to be friendly or harmonious again 2 : ADJUST, SETTLE ⟨∼ differences⟩ 3 : to bring to submission or acceptance ✦ **Synonyms** CONFORM, ACCOMMODATE, HARMONIZE, COORDINATE — **rec·on·cil·able** adj — **rec·on·cil·er** n — **rec·on·cil·er** n
rec·on·cil·i·a·tion \\.re-kən-,si-lē-'ā-shən\\ n 1 : the action of reconciling 2 : the Roman Catholic sacrament of penance
re·con·dite \\'re-kən-,dīt\\ adj 1 : hard to understand : ABSTRUSE ⟨∼ terminology⟩ 2 : little known : OBSCURE
re·con·di·tion \\.rē-kən-'di-shən\\ vb 1 : to restore to good condition (as by replacing parts) 2 : to condition anew

re·con·nais·sance \\ri-'kä-nə-zəns, -səns\\ n [F, lit., recognition] : a preliminary survey of an area; esp : an exploratory military survey of enemy territory
re·con·noi·ter or **re·con·noi·tre** \\.rē-kə-'nöi-tər, ,re-\\ vb **-noi·tered** or **-noi·tred; -noi·ter·ing** or **-noi·tring** : to make a reconnaissance of : engage in reconnaissance ⟨∼ed to locate enemy positions⟩
re·con·sid·er \\.rē-kən-'si-dər\\ vb : to consider again with a view to changing or reversing ⟨∼ed his decision⟩ — **re·con·sid·er·a·tion** \\-,si-də-'rā-shən\\ n
re·con·sti·tute \\.rē-'kän-stə-,tüt, -,tyüt\\ vb : to restore to a former condition by adding water ⟨∼ powdered milk⟩
re·con·struct \\.rē-kən-'strəkt\\ vb : to construct again : REBUILD
re·con·struc·tion \\.rē-kən-'strək-shən\\ n 1 : the action of reconstructing : the state of being reconstructed 2 often cap : the reorganization and reestablishment of the seceded states in the Union after the American Civil War 3 : something reconstructed
¹**re·cord** \\ri-'körd\\ vb [ME, lit., to recall, fr. AF recorder, fr. L recordari, fr. re- back, again + cord-, cors heart] 1 : to set down in writing ⟨∼ed her observations⟩ 2 : to register permanently 3 : INDICATE, READ 4 : to give evidence of 5 : to cause (as sound or visual images) to be registered (as on a disc or a magnetic tape) in a form that permits reproduction
²**rec·ord** \\'re-kərd\\ n 1 : the act of being recorded 2 : a written account of proceedings 3 : known facts about a person; also : a collection of items of information (as in a database) treated as a unit 4 : an attested top performance 5 : something on which sound or visual images have been recorded
³**re·cord** \\ri-'körd\\ n : a function of an electronic device that causes it to record
re·cord·er \\ri-'kör-dər\\ n 1 : a judge in some city courts 2 : one who records transactions officially 3 : a recording device 4 : a wind instrument with a whistle mouthpiece and eight fingerholes
re·cord·ing n : RECORD 5
re·cord·ist \\ri-'kör-dist\\ n : one who records sound esp. on film
¹**re·count** \\ri-'kaunt\\ vb : to relate in detail : TELL ✦ **Synonyms** RECITE, REHEARSE, NARRATE, DESCRIBE, STATE, REPORT
²**re·count** \\'rē-,kaunt, (,)rē-'kaunt\\ vb : to count again
³**re·count** \\'rē-,kaunt, (,)rē-'kaunt\\ n : a second or fresh count
re·coup \\ri-'küp\\ vb : to get an equivalent or compensation for : make up for something lost ⟨∼ed their costs⟩
re·course \\'rē-,kórs, ri-'kórs\\ n 1 : a turning to someone or something for assistance or protection 2 : a source of aid : RESORT
re·cov·er \\ri-'kə-vər\\ vb 1 : to get back again : REGAIN, RETRIEVE 2 : to regain normal health, poise, or status 3 : to make up for : RECOUP ⟨∼ed all his losses⟩ 4 : RECLAIM ⟨∼ land from the sea⟩ 5 : to obtain a legal judgment in one's favor — **re·cov·er·able** adj
re–cov·er \\.rē-'kə-vər\\ vb : to cover again
recovering adj : being in the process of overcoming a shortcoming or problem ⟨a ∼ alcoholic⟩
re·cov·ery \\ri-'kə-və-rē\\ n 1 : an act or instance of recovering; esp : an economic upturn 2 : the process of combating a disorder or problem
¹**rec·re·ant** \\'re-krē-ənt\\ adj [ME, fr. AF, fr. prp. of (se) recreire to give up, yield, fr. ML (se) recredere to resign oneself (to a judgment), fr. L re- back + credere to believe] 1 : COWARDLY 2 : UNFAITHFUL ⟨were ∼ to their duties⟩
²**recreant** n 1 : COWARD 2 : DESERTER
rec·re·ate \\'re-krē-,āt\\ vb **-at·ed; -at·ing** 1 : to give new life or freshness to 2 : to take recreation ⟨recreated at the beach⟩ — **rec·re·ative** \\-,ā-tiv\\ adj
re–cre·ate \\.rē-krē-'āt\\ vb : to create again ⟨re-created the battle scene⟩ — **re–cre·ation** \\-'ā-shən\\ n — **re–cre·ative** \\-'ā-tiv\\ adj
rec·re·ation \\.re-krē-'ā-shən\\ n : a refreshing of strength or spirits after work; also : a means of refreshment ✦ **Synonyms** DIVERSION, ENTERTAINMENT, AMUSEMENT — **rec·re·ation·al** \\-shə-nəl\\ adj
recreational vehicle n : a vehicle designed for recreational use (as camping)

re·crim·i·na·tion \ri-ˌkri-mə-ˈnā-shən\ n : a retaliatory accusation — **re·crim·i·nate** \-ˈkri-mə-nāt\ vb — **re·crim·i·na·tory** \-ˈkri-mə-nə-ˌtȯr-ē\ adj

re·cru·des·cence \ˌrē-krü-ˈde-sᵊns\ n : a renewal or breaking out again esp. of something unhealthful or dangerous

¹**re·cruit** \ri-ˈkrüt\ vb 1 : to form or strengthen with new members ⟨∼ an army⟩ 2 : to enlist as a member of an armed service 3 : to secure the services of 4 : to seek to enroll 5 : to restore or increase in health or vigor ⟨resting to ∼ his strength⟩ — **re·cruit·er** n — **re·cruit·ment** n

²**recruit** n [F recrute, recrue fresh growth, new levy of soldiers, fr. MF, fr. recroistre to grow up again, fr. L recrescere] : a newcomer to an activity or field; esp : a newly enlisted member of the armed forces

rec·tal \ˈrek-tᵊl\ adj : of or relating to the rectum — **rec·tal·ly** adv

rect·an·gle \ˈrek-ˌtaŋ-gəl\ n : a 4-sided figure with four right angles; esp : one with adjacent sides of unequal length — **rect·an·gu·lar** \rek-ˈtaŋ-gyə-lər\ adj

rec·ti·fi·er \ˈrek-tə-ˌfī(-ə)r\ n : one that rectifies; esp : a device for converting alternating current into direct current

rec·ti·fy \ˈrek-tə-ˌfī\ vb -fied; -fy·ing : to make or set right : CORRECT ♦ **Synonyms** EMEND, AMEND, MEND, RIGHT — **rec·ti·fi·ca·tion** \ˌrek-tə-fə-ˈkā-shən\ n

rec·ti·lin·ear \ˌrek-tə-ˈli-nē-ər\ adj 1 : moving in a straight line ⟨∼ motion⟩ 2 : characterized by straight lines

rec·ti·tude \ˈrek-tə-ˌtüd, -ˌtyüd\ n 1 : moral integrity 2 : correctness of procedure ♦ **Synonyms** VIRTUE, GOODNESS, MORALITY, PROBITY

rec·to \ˈrek-tō\ n, pl **rectos** : a right-hand page

rec·tor \ˈrek-tər\ n 1 : a priest or minister in charge of a parish 2 : the head of a university or school — **rec·to·ri·al** \rek-ˈtȯr-ē-əl\ adj

rec·to·ry \ˈrek-tə-rē\ n, pl **-ries** : the residence of a rector or a parish priest

rec·tum \ˈrek-təm\ n, pl **rectums** or **rec·ta** \-tə\ [ME, fr. ML, fr. rectum intestinum, lit., straight intestine] : the last part of the intestine joining the colon and anus

re·cum·bent \ri-ˈkəm-bənt\ adj : lying down : RECLINING

re·cu·per·ate \ri-ˈkü-pə-ˌrāt, -ˈkyü-\ vb -at·ed; -at·ing : to get back (as health or strength) : RECOVER — **re·cu·per·a·tion** \-ˌkü-pə-ˈrā-shən, -ˌkyü-\ n — **re·cu·per·a·tive** \-ˈkü-pə-ˌrā-tiv, -ˈkyü-\ adj

re·cur \ri-ˈkər\ vb **re·curred**; **re·cur·ring** 1 : to go or come back in thought or discussion 2 : to occur or appear again esp. after an interval : occur time after time ⟨recurring headaches⟩ — **re·cur·rence** \-ˈkər-əns\ n — **re·cur·rent** \-ənt\ adj

re·cy·cle \rē-ˈsī-kəl\ vb 1 : to pass again through a cycle of changes or treatment 2 : to process (as liquid body waste, glass, or cans) in order to regain materials for human use — **re·cy·cla·bil·i·ty** \-ˌsī-klə-ˈbil-ə-tē\ n — **re·cy·cla·ble** \-k(ə)lə-bəl\ adj — **recycle** n

¹**red** \ˈred\ adj **red·der**; **red·dest** 1 : of the color red 2 : endorsing radical social or political change esp. by force 3 often cap : of or relating to the former U.S.S.R. or its allies 4 : tending to support Republican candidates ⟨∼ states⟩ — **red·ly** adv — **red·ness** n

²**red** n 1 : the color of blood or of the ruby 2 : a revolutionary in politics 3 cap : COMMUNIST 4 : the condition of showing a loss ⟨in the ∼⟩

re·dact \ri-ˈdakt\ vb 1 : to put in writing : FRAME ⟨∼ed the proclamation⟩ 2 : EDIT — **re·dac·tor** \-ˈdak-tər\ n

re·dac·tion \-ˈdak-shən\ n 1 : an act or instance of redacting 2 : EDITION

red alga n : any of a group of reddish usu. marine algae

red blood cell n : any of the hemoglobin-containing cells that carry oxygen from the lungs to the tissues and are responsible for the red color of vertebrate blood

red·breast \ˈred-ˌbrest\ n : ROBIN

red–carpet adj : marked by ceremonial courtesy ⟨was given the ∼ treatment⟩

red cedar n : an American juniper with scalelike leaves and fragrant close-grained red wood; also : its wood

red clover n : a European clover that has globe-shaped heads of reddish flowers and is widely cultivated for hay and forage

red·coat \ˈred-ˌkōt\ n : a British soldier esp. during the Revolutionary War

red·den \ˈre-dᵊn\ vb : to make or become red or reddish : FLUSH, BLUSH

red·dish \ˈre-dish\ adj : tinged with red — **red·dish·ness** n

red dwarf n : a star with lower temperature and less mass than the sun

re·deem \ri-ˈdēm\ vb [ME redemen, fr. AF redemer, modif. of L redimere, fr. re-, red- back, again + emere to take, buy] 1 : to recover (property) by discharging an obligation 2 : to ransom, free, or rescue by paying a price 3 : to free from the consequences of sin 4 : to remove the obligation of by payment ⟨the government ∼s savings bonds⟩; also : to convert into something of value 5 : to make good (a promise) by performing : FULFILL 6 : to atone for — **re·deem·able** adj — **re·deem·er** n

re·demp·tion \ri-ˈdemp-shən\ n : the act of redeeming : the state of being redeemed — **re·demp·tive** \-tiv\ adj — **re·demp·to·ry** \-tə-rē\ adj

re·de·ploy \ˌrē-di-ˈplȯi\ vb 1 : to transfer from one area or activity to another 2 : to relocate personnel or equipment — **re·de·ploy·ment** n

red–eye \ˈred-ˌī\ n 1 : cheap whiskey 2 : a late night or overnight flight

red·fish \ˈred-ˌfish\ n : any of various reddish marine fishes of the Atlantic including some used for food

red fox n : a fox with orange-red to reddish brown fur

red giant n : a very large star with a relatively low surface temperature

red–hand·ed \ˈred-ˈhan-dəd\ adv or adj : in the act of committing a misdeed

red·head \-ˌhed\ n : a person having red hair — **red·head·ed** \-ˌhe-dəd\ adj

red herring n : a diversion intended to distract attention from the real issue

red–hot \ˈred-ˈhät\ adj 1 : extremely hot; esp : glowing with heat 2 : EXCITED, FURIOUS 3 : very new ⟨∼ news⟩

re·dial \ˈrē-ˌdī(-ə)l\ n : a telephone function that automatically repeats the dialing of the last number called — **redial** vb

re·dis·trib·ute \ˌrē-də-ˈstri-byüt\ vb 1 : to alter the distribution of 2 : to spread to other areas — **re·dis·tri·bu·tion** \(ˌ)rē-ˌdis-trə-ˈbyü-shən\ n

re·dis·trict \ˌrē-ˈdis-(ˌ)trikt\ vb : to organize into new territorial and esp. political divisions

red–let·ter \ˈred-ˌle-tər\ adj : of special significance : MEMORABLE ⟨a ∼ day⟩

red–light adj : having many houses of prostitution ⟨a ∼ district⟩

re·do \(ˌ)rē-ˈdü\ vb : to do over or again; esp : REDECORATE

red oak n : any of various No. American oaks with leaves usu. having spiny-tipped lobes and acorns that take two years to mature; also : the wood of a red oak

red·o·lent \ˈre-də-lənt\ adj 1 : FRAGRANT, AROMATIC 2 : having a specified fragrance ⟨a room ∼ of cooked cabbage⟩ 3 : REMINISCENT, SUGGESTIVE ⟨a tavern ∼ of colonial times⟩ — **red·o·lence** \-ləns\ n — **red·o·lent·ly** adv

re·dou·ble \(ˌ)rē-ˈdə-bəl\ vb : to make twice as great in size or amount; also : INTENSIFY

re·doubt \ri-ˈdaut\ n [F redoute, fr. It ridotto, fr. ML reductus secret place, fr. L, withdrawn, fr. reducere to lead back, fr. re- back + ducere to lead] : a small usu. temporary fortification

re·doubt·able \ri-ˈdau-tə-bəl\ adj [ME redoutable, fr. AF, fr. reduter to dread, fr. re- back, again + duter to doubt] : arousing dread or fear : FORMIDABLE

re·dound \ri-ˈdaund\ vb 1 : to have an effect ⟨the change may ∼ to her benefit⟩ 2 : to become added or transferred : ACCRUE

red pepper n 1 : CAYENNE PEPPER 2 : a mature red hot pepper or sweet pepper

¹**re·dress** \ri-ˈdres\ vb 1 : to set right : REMEDY ⟨∼ injustice⟩ 2 : COMPENSATE 3 : to remove the cause of (a grievance) 4 : AVENGE

²**re·dress** n 1 : relief from distress 2 : means or possibility of seeking a remedy 3 : compensation for loss or injury 4 : an act or instance of redressing

red·shift \ˈred-ˈshift\ n : displacement of the spectrum of a heavenly body toward longer wavelengths; also : a measure of this displacement

red snapper *n* : any of various reddish fishes including several food fishes

red spider *n* : SPIDER MITE

red squirrel *n* : a common No. American squirrel with the upper parts chiefly red

red–tailed hawk \'red-,tāld-\ *n* : a rodent-eating No. American hawk with a rather short typically reddish tail

red tape *n* [fr. the red tape formerly used to bind legal documents in England] : official routine or procedure marked by excessive complexity which results in delay or inaction

red tide *n* : seawater discolored by the presence of large numbers of dinoflagellates which produce a toxin that renders infected shellfish poisonous

re·duce \ri-'düs, -'dyüs\ *vb* **re·duced; re·duc·ing** **1** : LESSEN **2** : to bring to a specified state or condition ⟨*reduced* them to tears⟩ **3** : to put in a lower rank or grade **4** : CONQUER ⟨~ a fort⟩ **5** : to bring into a certain order or classification **6** : to correct (as a fracture) by restoration of displaced parts **7** : to lessen one's weight ✦ *Synonyms* DECREASE, DIMINISH, ABATE, DWINDLE, RECEDE — **re·duc·er** *n* — **re·duc·ible** \-'dü-sə-bəl, -'dyü-\ *adj*

re·duc·tion \ri-'dək-shən\ *n* **1** : the act of reducing : the state of being reduced **2** : something made by reducing **3** : the amount taken off in reducing something

re·dun·dan·cy \ri-'dən-dən-sē\ *n, pl* **-cies** **1** : the quality or state of being redundant : SUPERFLUITY **2** : something redundant or in excess **3** : the use of surplus words

re·dun·dant \-dənt\ *adj* **1** : exceeding what is needed or normal : SUPERFLUOUS; *esp* : using more words than necessary **2** : marked by repetition — **re·dun·dant·ly** *adv*

red–winged blackbird \'red-,wiŋd-\ *n* : a No. American blackbird of which the adult male is black with a patch of bright scarlet on the wings

red·wood \'red-,wùd\ *n* : a tall coniferous timber tree esp. of coastal California; *also* : its durable wood

reed \'rēd\ *n* **1** : any of various tall slender grasses of wet areas; *also* : a stem or growth of reed **2** : a musical instrument made from the hollow stem of a reed **3** : an elastic tongue of cane, wood, or metal by which tones are produced in organ pipes and certain other wind instruments — **reedy** *adj*

re·ed·u·cate \(,)rē-'e-jə-,kāt\ *vb* : to train again; *esp* : to rehabilitate through education — **re·ed·u·ca·tion** *n*

¹reef \'rēf\ *n* **1** : a part of a sail taken in or let out in regulating the sail's size **2** : reduction in sail area by reefing

²reef *vb* : to reduce the area of a sail by rolling or folding part of it

³reef *n* : a ridge of rocks, sand or coral at or near the surface of the water

reef·er \'rē-fər\ *n* : a marijuana cigarette

¹reek \'rēk\ *n* : a strong or disagreeable fume or odor

²reek *vb* **1** : to give off or become permeated with a strong or offensive odor **2** : to give a strong impression of some constituent quality ⟨an excuse that ~ed of falsehood⟩ — **reek·er** *n* — **reeky** \'rē-kē\ *adj*

¹reel \'rēl\ *n* : a revolvable device on which something flexible (as film or tape) is wound; *also* : a quantity of something wound on such a device

²reel *vb* **1** : to wind on or as if on a reel **2** : to pull or draw (as a fish) by reeling in a line — **reel·able** *adj* — **reel·er** *n*

³reel *vb* **1** : WHIRL; *also* : to be giddy **2** : to waver or fall back (as from a blow) **3** : to walk or move unsteadily

⁴reel *n* : a reeling motion

⁵reel *n* : a lively Scottish dance or its music

reel off *vb* **1** : to tell or recite rapidly and easily ⟨*reeled off* the right answers⟩ **2** : to achieve usu. consecutively ⟨*reeled off* six straight wins⟩

re·en·try \rē-'en-trē\ *n* **1** : a second or new entry **2** : the action of reentering the earth's atmosphere from space

reeve \'rēv\ *vb* **rove** \'rōv\ *or* **reeved; reev·ing** : to pass (as a rope) through a hole in a block or cleat

¹ref \'ref\ *n* : REFEREE 2

²ref *abbr* **1** reference **2** referred **3** reformed **4** refunding

re·fec·tion \ri-'fek-shən\ *n* **1** : refreshment esp. after hunger or fatigue **2** : food and drink together : REPAST

re·fec·to·ry \ri-'fek-tə-rē\ *n, pl* **-ries** : a dining hall (as in a monastery or college)

re·fer \ri-'fər\ *vb* **re·ferred; re·fer·ring** [ME *referren*, fr. AF *referer, referir*, fr. L *referre* to bring back, report, refer, fr. *re-* back + *ferre* to carry] **1** : to assign to a cer-

tain source, cause, or relationship **2** : to direct or send to some person or place (as for information or help) **3** : to submit to someone else for consideration or action **4** : to have recourse (as for information or aid) **5** : to have connection : RELATE **6** : to direct attention : speak of : MENTION, ALLUDE ✦ *Synonyms* RECUR, REPAIR, RESORT, APPLY, GO, TURN — **re·fer·able** \'re-fə-rə-bəl, ri-'fər-ə-\ *adj*

¹ref·er·ee \,re-fə-'rē\ *n* **1** : a person to whom an issue esp. in law is referred for investigation or settlement **2** : an umpire in certain games

²referee *vb* **-eed; -ee·ing** : to act as referee

ref·er·ence \'re-frəns, -fə-rəns\ *n* **1** : the act of referring **2** : RELATION, RESPECT **3** : ALLUSION, MENTION **4** : something that refers a reader to another passage or book **5** : consultation esp. for obtaining information ⟨books for ~⟩ **6** : a person of whom inquiries as to character or ability can be made **7** : a written recommendation of a person for employment

ref·er·en·dum \,re-fə-'ren-dəm\ *n, pl* **-da** \-də\ *or* **-dums** : the submitting of legislative measures to the voters for approval or rejection; *also* : a vote on a measure so submitted

ref·er·ent \'re-frənt, -fə-rənt\ *n* : one that refers or is referred to; *esp* : the thing a word stands for — **referent** *adj*

re·fer·ral \ri-'fər-əl\ *n* **1** : the act or an instance of referring **2** : one that is referred

¹re·fill \,rē-'fil\ *vb* : to fill again : REPLENISH — **re·fill·able** *adj*

²re·fill \'rē-,fil\ *n* : a new or fresh supply of something

re·fi·nance \,rē-fə-'nans, (,)rē-'fī-nans\ *vb* : to renew or reorganize the financing of

re·fine \ri-'fīn\ *vb* **re·fined; re·fin·ing** **1** : to free from impurities or waste matter **2** : IMPROVE, PERFECT **3** : to free or become free of what is coarse or uncouth **4** : to make improvements by introducing subtle changes — **re·fin·er** *n*

re·fined \ri-'fīnd\ *adj* **1** : freed from impurities **2** : CULTURED, CULTIVATED **3** : PRECISE, EXACT

re·fine·ment \ri-'fīn-mənt\ *n* **1** : the action of refining **2** : the quality or state of being refined **3** : a refined feature or method; *also* : something intended to improve or perfect

re·fin·ery \ri-'fī-nə-rē\ *n, pl* **-er·ies** : a building and equipment for refining metals, oil, or sugar

re·flect \ri-'flekt\ *vb* [ME, fr. L *reflectere* to bend back, fr. *re-* back + *flectere* to bend] **1** : to bend or cast back (as light, heat, or sound) **2** : to give back a likeness or image of as a mirror does **3** : to bring as a result ⟨~ed credit on him⟩ **4** : to make apparent : SHOW ⟨figures that ~ economic growth⟩ **5** : to cast reproach or blame ⟨their bad conduct ~ed on their training⟩ **6** : PONDER, MEDITATE — **re·flec·tion** \-'flek-shən\ *n* — **re·flec·tive** \-tiv\ *adj* — **re·flec·tiv·i·ty** \(,)rē-,flek-'ti-və-tē\ *n*

re·flec·tor \ri-'flek-tər\ *n* : one that reflects; *esp* : a polished surface for reflecting radiation (as light)

¹re·flex \'rē-,fleks\ *n* **1** : an automatic and usu. inborn response to a stimulus not involving higher mental centers **2** *pl* : the power of acting or responding with enough speed ⟨an athlete with great ~es⟩

²reflex *adj* **1** : bent or directed back **2** : of, relating to, or produced by a reflex ⟨a ~ action⟩ — **re·flex·ly** *adv*

¹re·flex·ive \ri-'flek-siv\ *adj* : of or relating to an action directed back upon the doer or the grammatical subject ⟨a ~ verb⟩ ⟨the ~ pronoun *himself*⟩ — **re·flex·ive·ly** *adv* — **re·flex·ive·ness** *n*

²reflexive *n* : a reflexive verb or pronoun

re·flex·ol·o·gy \,rē-,flek-'sä-lə-jē\ *n* : massage in which pressure is applied to specific points on the hands or feet

re·flux \'rē-,fləks\ *n* : a flowing back

re·fo·cus \(,)rē-'fō-kəs\ *vb* **1** : to focus again **2** : to change the emphasis or direction of ⟨~ed her life⟩

re·for·es·ta·tion \,rē-,fór-ə-'stā-shən\ *n* : the action of renewing forest cover by planting seeds or young trees — **re·for·est** \rē-'fór-əst\ *vb*

¹re·form \ri-'form\ *vb* **1** : to make better or improve by removal of faults **2** : to correct or improve one's own character or habits ✦ *Synonyms* CORRECT, RECTIFY, EMEND, REMEDY, REDRESS, REVISE — **re·form·able** *adj* — **re·for·ma·tive** \-'fór-mə-tiv\ *adj*

²reform *n* : improvement or correction of what is corrupt or defective

re–form \ˌrē-ˈfȯrm\ *vb* : to form again

ref·or·ma·tion \ˌre-fər-ˈmā-shən\ *n* 1 : the act of reforming : the state of being reformed 2 *cap* : a 16th century religious movement marked by the establishment of the Protestant churches

¹re·for·ma·to·ry \ri-ˈfȯr-mə-ˌtȯr-ē\ *adj* : aiming at or tending toward reformation : REFORMATIVE

²reformatory *n, pl* **-ries** : a penal institution for reforming esp. young or first offenders

re·form·er \ri-ˈfȯr-mər\ *n* 1 : one that works for or urges reform 2 *cap* : a leader of the Protestant Reformation

refr *abbr* refraction

re·fract \ri-ˈfrakt\ *vb* [L *refractus,* pp. of *refringere* to break open, break up, fr. *re-* back + *frangere* to break] : to subject to refraction

re·frac·tion \ri-ˈfrak-shən\ *n* : the bending of a ray (as of light) when it passes obliquely from one medium into another in which its speed is different — **re·frac·tive** \-tiv\ *adj*

refractive index *n* : the ratio of the speed of radiation in one medium to that in another medium

re·frac·to·ry \ri-ˈfrak-tə-rē\ *adj* 1 : OBSTINATE, STUBBORN, UNMANAGEABLE 2 : capable of enduring high temperature ⟨∼ bricks⟩ ♦ *Synonyms* RECALCITRANT, INTRACTABLE, UNGOVERNABLE, UNRULY, HEADSTRONG, WILLFUL — **re·frac·to·ri·ness** \ri-ˈfrak-tə-rē-nəs\ *n* — **refractory** *n*

¹re·frain \ri-ˈfrān\ *vb* : to hold oneself back : FORBEAR ⟨∼ from interfering⟩ — **re·frain·ment** *n*

²refrain *n* : a phrase or verse recurring regularly in a poem or song

re·fresh \ri-ˈfresh\ *vb* 1 : to make or become fresh or fresher 2 : to revive by or as if by renewal of supplies ⟨∼ one's memory⟩ 3 : to freshen up 4 : to supply or take refreshment 5 : to update or renew esp. by sending a new signal ⟨∼ the Web page⟩ ♦ *Synonyms* RESTORE, REJUVENATE, RENOVATE, REFURBISH — **re·fresh·er** *n* — **re·fresh·ing·ly** *adv*

re·fresh·ment \-mənt\ *n* 1 : the act of refreshing : the state of being refreshed 2 : something that refreshes 3 *pl* : a light meal; *also* : assorted light foods

re-fried beans \ˈrē-ˌfrīd-\ *n pl* : beans cooked with seasonings, fried, then mashed and fried again

refrig *abbr* refrigerating; refrigeration

re·frig·er·ate \ri-ˈfri-jə-ˌrāt\ *vb* **-at·ed; -at·ing** : to make cool; *esp* : to chill or freeze (food) for preservation — **re·frig·er·ant** \-jə-rənt\ *adj or n* — **re·frig·er·a·tion** \-ˌfri-jə-ˈrā-shən\ *n* — **re·frig·er·a·tor** \-ˈfri-jə-ˌrā-tər\ *n*

ref·uge \ˈre-ˌfyüj\ *n* 1 : shelter or protection from danger or distress 2 : a place that provides protection

ref·u·gee \ˌre-fyü-ˈjē\ *n* : one who flees for safety esp. to a foreign country

re·ful·gence \ri-ˈful-jəns, -ˈfəl-\ *n* : a radiant or resplendent quality or state — **re·ful·gent** \-jənt\ *adj*

¹re·fund \ri-ˈfənd, ˈrē-ˌfənd\ *vb* : to give or put back (money) : REPAY — **re·fund·able** *adj*

²refund \ˈrē-ˌfənd\ *n* 1 : the act of refunding 2 : a sum refunded

re·fur·bish \ri-ˈfər-bish\ *vb* : to brighten or freshen up : RENOVATE

¹re·fuse \ri-ˈfyüz\ *vb* **re·fused; re·fus·ing** 1 : to decline to accept : REJECT 2 : to decline to do, give, or grant : DENY — **re·fus·al** \-ˈfyü-zəl\ *n*

²ref·use \ˈre-ˌfyüs, -ˌfyüz\ *n* : rejected or worthless matter : RUBBISH, TRASH

re·fute \ri-ˈfyüt\ *vb* **re·fut·ed; re·fut·ing** [L *refutare* to check, suppress, refute] : to prove to be false by argument or evidence — **ref·u·ta·tion** \ˌre-fyü-ˈtā-shən\ *n* — **re·fut·er** *n*

¹reg \ˈreg\ *n* : REGULATION

²reg *abbr* 1 region 2 register; registered; registration 3 regular

re·gal \ˈrē-gəl\ *adj* 1 : of, relating to, or befitting a king : ROYAL 2 : STATELY, SPLENDID — **re·gal·ly** *adv*

re·gale \ri-ˈgāl\ *vb* **re·galed; re·gal·ing** 1 : to entertain richly or agreeably 2 : to give pleasure or amusement to ⟨*regaled* us with stories⟩ ♦ *Synonyms* GRATIFY, DELIGHT, PLEASE, REJOICE, GLADDEN

re·ga·lia \ri-ˈgāl-yə\ *n pl* 1 : the emblems, symbols, or

paraphernalia of royalty (as the crown and scepter) 2 : the insignia of an office or order 3 : special costume : FINERY

¹re·gard \ri-ˈgärd\ *n* 1 : CONSIDERATION, HEED; *also* : CARE, CONCERN 2 : GAZE, GLANCE, LOOK 3 : RESPECT, ESTEEM ⟨held in high ∼⟩ 4 *pl* : friendly greetings implying respect and esteem 5 : an aspect to be considered : PARTICULAR — **re·gard·ful** *adj* — **re·gard·less** *adj*

²regard *vb* 1 : to think of : CONSIDER 2 : to pay attention to 3 : to show respect for : HEED ⟨∼s his elders⟩ 4 : to hold in high esteem : care for 5 : to look at : gaze upon ⟨∼ed the landscape⟩ 6 *archaic* : to relate to

re·gard·ing *prep* : CONCERNING

regardless of \ri-ˈgärd-ləs-\ *prep* : in spite of

re·gat·ta \ri-ˈgä-tə, -ˈga-\ *n* : a boat race or a series of boat races

re·gen·cy \ˈrē-jən-sē\ *n, pl* **-cies** 1 : the office or government of a regent or body of regents 2 : a body of regents 3 : the period during which a regent governs

re·gen·er·a·cy \ri-ˈje-nə-rə-sē\ *n* : the state of being regenerated

¹re·gen·er·ate \ri-ˈje-nə-rət\ *adj* 1 : formed or created again 2 : spiritually reborn or converted

²re·gen·er·ate \ri-ˈje-nə-ˌrāt\ *vb* 1 : to subject to spiritual renewal 2 : to reform completely 3 : to replace (a body part) by a new growth of tissue 4 : to give new life to : REVIVE — **re·gen·er·a·tion** \-ˌje-nə-ˈrā-shən\ *n* — **re·gen·er·a·tive** \-ˈje-nə-ˌrā-tiv\ *adj* — **re·gen·er·a·tor** \-ˌrā-tər\ *n*

re·gent \ˈrē-jənt\ *n* 1 : a person who rules during the childhood, absence, or incapacity of the sovereign 2 : a member of a governing board (as of a state university) — **regent** *adj*

reg·gae \ˈre-ˌgā\ *n* : popular music of Jamaican origin that combines native styles with elements of rock and soul music

reg·i·cide \ˈre-jə-ˌsīd\ *n* 1 : one who murders a king : murder of a king

re·gift \(ˌ)rē-ˈgift\ *vb* : to give a previously received gift to someone else

re·gime *also* **ré·gime** \rā-ˈzhēm, ri-\ *n* 1 : REGIMEN 2 : a form or system of government 3 : a government in power; *also* : a period of rule

reg·i·men \ˈre-jə-mən\ *n* [ME, fr. ML, position of authority, direction, set of rules, fr. L, steering, control, fr. *regere* to direct] 1 : a systematic course of treatment or training ⟨a strict dietary ∼⟩ 2 : GOVERNMENT

¹reg·i·ment \ˈre-jə-mənt\ *n* : a military unit consisting usu. of a number of battalions — **reg·i·men·tal** \ˌre-jə-ˈmen-təl\ *adj*

²reg·i·ment \ˈre-jə-ˌment\ *vb* : to organize rigidly esp. for regulation or central control; *also* : to subject to order or uniformity — **reg·i·men·ta·tion** \ˌre-jə-mən-ˈtā-shən\ *n*

reg·i·men·tals \ˌre-jə-ˈmen-təlz\ *n pl* 1 : a regimental uniform 2 : military dress

re·gion \ˈrē-jən\ *n* [ME, fr. AF *regiun,* fr. L *region-, regio,* line, direction, area, fr. *regere* to rule] : an often indefinitely defined part or area

re·gion·al \ˈrē-jə-nəl\ *adj* 1 : affecting a particular region : LOCALIZED 2 : of, relating to, characteristic of, or serving a region — **re·gion·al·ly** *adv*

¹reg·is·ter \ˈre-jə-stər\ *n* 1 : a record of items or details; *also* : a book or system for keeping such a record 2 : the range of a voice or instrument 3 : a device to regulate ventilation or heating 4 : an automatic device recording a number or quantity 5 : CASH REGISTER

²register *vb* **-tered; -ter·ing** 1 : to enter in a register (as in a list of guests) 2 : to record automatically 3 : to secure special care for (mail matter) by paying additional postage 4 : to convey an impression of : EXPRESS 5 : to make or adjust so as to correspond exactly

registered nurse *n* : a graduate trained nurse who has been licensed to practice by a state authority after passing qualifying examinations

reg·is·trant \ˈre-jə-strənt\ *n* : one that registers or is registered

reg·is·trar \-ˌsträr\ *n* : an official recorder or keeper of records (as at an educational institution)

reg·is·tra·tion \ˌre-jə-ˈstrā-shən\ *n* 1 : the act of registering 2 : an entry in a register 3 : the number of persons registered : ENROLLMENT   **4** : a document certifying an act of registering

reg·is·try \\'re-jə-strē\ *n, pl* **-tries**   **1** : ENROLLMENT, REGISTRATION   **2** : a place of registration   **3** : an official record book or an entry in one

reg·nant \\'reg-nənt\ *adj*   **1** : REIGNING   **2** : DOMINANT   **3** : of common or widespread occurrence

¹re·gress \\'rē-ˌgres\ *n*   **1** : an act or the privilege of going or coming back   **2** : RETROGRESSION

²re·gress \ri-'gres\ *vb* : to go or cause to go back or to a lower level — **re·gres·sive** *adj* — **re·gres·sor** \-'gre-sər\ *n*

re·gres·sion \ri-'gre-shən\ *n* : the act or an instance of regressing; *esp* : reversion to an earlier mental or behavioral level

¹re·gret \ri-'gret\ *vb* **re·gret·ted; re·gret·ting**   **1** : to mourn the loss or death of   **2** : to be very sorry for   **3** : to experience regret — **re·gret·ta·ble** \-'gre-tə-bəl\ *adj* — **re·gret·ter** *n*

²regret *n*   **1** : sorrow caused by something beyond one's power to remedy   **2** : an expression of sorrow   **3** *pl* : a note politely declining an invitation — **re·gret·ful** \-fəl\ *adj* — **re·gret·ful·ly** *adv*

re·gret·ta·bly \-'gre-tə-blē\ *adv*   **1** : to a regrettable extent   **2** : it is to be regretted

re·group \(ˌ)rē-'grüp\ *vb* : to form into a new grouping

regt *abbr* regiment

¹reg·u·lar \\'re-gyə-lər\ *adj* [ME *reguler*, fr. AF, fr. LL *regularis* regular, fr. L, of a bar, fr. *regula* rule, straightedge, fr. *regere* to keep straight, direct]   **1** : belonging to a religious order   **2** : made, built, or arranged according to a rule, standard, or type; *also* : even or symmetrical in form or structure   **3** : ORDERLY, METHODICAL ⟨~ habits⟩; *also* : not varying : STEADY ⟨a ~ pace⟩   **4** : made, selected, or conducted according to rule or custom   **5** : properly qualified ⟨not a ~ lawyer⟩   **6** : conforming to the normal or usual manner or inflection   **7** : of, relating to, or constituting the permanent standing military force of a state — **reg·u·lar·i·ty** \ˌre-gyə-'la-rə-tē\ *n* — **reg·u·lar·ize** \\'re-gyə-lə-ˌrīz\ *vb* — **reg·u·lar·ly** *adv*

²regular *n*   **1** : one that is regular (as in attendance)   **2** : a member of the regular clergy   **3** : a soldier in a regular army   **4** : a player on an athletic team who is usu. in the starting lineup

reg·u·late \\'re-gyə-ˌlāt\ *vb* **-lat·ed; -lat·ing**   **1** : to govern or direct according to rule : CONTROL   **2** : to bring under the control of law or authority   **3** : to put in good order   **4** : to fix or adjust the time, amount, degree, or rate of — **reg·u·la·tive** \-ˌlā-tiv\ *adj* — **reg·u·la·tor** \-ˌlā-tər\ *n* — **reg·u·la·to·ry** \-lə-ˌtòr-ē\ *adj*

reg·u·la·tion \ˌre-gyə-'lā-shən\ *n*   **1** : the act of regulating : the state of being regulated   **2** : a rule dealing with details of procedure   **3** : an order issued by an executive authority of a government and having the force of law

re·gur·gi·tate \rē-'gər-jə-ˌtāt\ *vb* **-tat·ed; -tat·ing** [ML *regurgitare*, fr. L *re-* re- + LL *gurgitare* to engulf, fr. L *gurgit-, gurges* whirlpool] : to throw or be thrown back, up, or out ⟨~ food⟩ — **re·gur·gi·ta·tion** \-ˌgər-jə-'tā-shən\ *n*

re·hab \\'rē-ˌhab\ *n*   **1** : REHABILITATION   **2** : a rehabilitated building — **rehab** *vb*

re·ha·bil·i·tate \ˌrē-hə-'bi-lə-ˌtāt, ˌrē-ə-\ *vb* **-tat·ed; -tat·ing**   **1** : to restore to a former capacity, rank, or right : REINSTATE   **2** : to restore to good condition or health — **re·ha·bil·i·ta·tion** \-ˌbi-lə-'tā-shən\ *n* — **re·ha·bil·i·ta·tive** \-ˌtā-tiv\ *adj*

re·hash \ˌrē-'hash\ *vb* : to present again in another form without real change or improvement — **rehash** *n*

re·hear·ing \ˌrē-'hir-iŋ\ *n* : a second or new hearing by the same tribunal

re·hears·al \ri-'hər-səl\ *n*   **1** : something told again : RECITAL   **2** : a private performance or practice session preparatory to a public appearance

re·hearse \ri-'hərs\ *vb* **re·hearsed; re·hears·ing**   **1** : to say again : REPEAT   **2** : to recount in order : ENUMERATE; *also* : RELATE 1   **3** : to give a rehearsal of   **4** : to train by rehearsal   **5** : to engage in a rehearsal — **re·hears·er** *n*

¹reign \\'rān\ *n*   **1** : the authority or rule of a sovereign   **2** : the time during which a sovereign rules

²reign *vb*   **1** : to rule as a sovereign   **2** : to be predominant or prevalent

re·im·burse \ˌrē-əm-'bərs\ *vb* **-bursed; -burs·ing** [*re-* re- + obs. E *imburse* to put in the pocket, pay, fr. ML

imbursare to put into a purse, fr. L *in-* in- + ML *bursa* purse, fr. LL, hide of an ox, fr. Gk *byrsa*] : to pay back : make restitution : REPAY ⟨was *reimbursed* for her travel expenses⟩ ✦ **Synonyms** INDEMNIFY, RECOMPENSE, REQUITE, COMPENSATE — **re·im·burs·able** *adj* — **re·im·burse·ment** *n*

¹rein \\'rān\ *n*   **1** : a strap fastened to a bit by which a rider or driver controls an animal   **2** : a restraining influence : CHECK   **3** : controlling or guiding power   **4** : complete freedom — usu. used in the phrase *give rein to*

²rein *vb* : to check or direct by reins

re·in·car·na·tion \ˌrē-(ˌ)in-(ˌ)kär-'nā-shən\ *n* : rebirth of the soul in a new body — **re·in·car·nate** \ˌrē-in-'kär-ˌnāt\ *vb*

rein·deer \\'rān-ˌdir\ *n* [ME *reindere*, fr. ON *hreinn* reindeer + ME *deer* animal, deer] : CARIBOU — used esp. for one of the Old World

reindeer moss *n* : a gray, erect, tufted, and much-branched edible lichen of northern regions that is an important food of reindeer

re·in·fec·tion \ˌrē-in-'fek-shən\ *n* : infection following another infection of the same type

re·in·force \ˌrē-ən-'fòrs\ *vb*   **1** : to strengthen with additional forces ⟨~ our troops⟩   **2** : to strengthen with new force, aid, material, or support — **re·in·force·ment** *n* — **re·in·forc·er** *n*

re·in·scribe \ˌrē-ən-'skrīb\ *vb* : to reestablish or rename in a new and esp. stronger form or context

re·in·state \ˌrē-in-'stāt\ *vb* **-stat·ed; -stat·ing** : to restore to a former position, condition, or capacity — **re·in·state·ment** *n*

re·in·vent \ˌrē-in-'vent\ *vb*   **1** : to make as if for the first time something already invented ⟨~ the wheel⟩   **2** : to remake completely

re·it·er·ate \rē-'i-tə-ˌrāt\ *vb* **-at·ed; -at·ing** : to state or do over again or repeatedly — **re·it·er·a·tion** \-ˌi-tə-'rā-shən\ *n*

¹re·ject \ri-'jekt\ *vb*   **1** : to refuse to accept, consider, use, or submit to   **2** : to refuse to hear, receive, or admit : REPEL   **3** : to rebuff or withhold love from   **4** : to throw out esp. as useless or unsatisfactory   **5** : to subject (a transplanted tissue) to an attack by immune system components of the recipient organism — **re·jec·tion** \-'jek-shən\ *n*

²re·ject \\'rē-ˌjekt\ *n* : a rejected person or thing

re·joice \ri-'jòis\ *vb* **re·joiced; re·joic·ing**   **1** : to give joy to : GLADDEN   **2** : to feel joy or great delight — **re·joic·er** *n*

re·join \(ˌ)rē-'jòin *for 1,* ri- *for 2*\ *vb*   **1** : to join again   **2** : to say in answer (as to a plaintiff's plea in court) : REPLY

re·join·der \ri-'jòin-dər\ *n* : REPLY; *esp* : an answer to a reply

re·ju·ve·nate \ri-'jü-və-ˌnāt\ *vb* **-nat·ed; -nat·ing** : to make young or youthful again : give new vigor to ✦ **Synonyms** RENEW, REFRESH, RENOVATE, RESTORE — **re·ju·ve·na·tion** \-ˌjü-və-'nā-shən\ *n*

rel *abbr*   **1** relating; relative   **2** religion; religious

¹re·lapse \ri-'laps, 'rē-ˌlaps\ *n* [ME, fr. ML *relapsus*, fr. L *relabi* to slide back]   **1** : the act or process of backsliding or worsening   **2** : a recurrence of illness after a period of improvement

²re·lapse \ri-'laps\ *vb* **re·lapsed; re·laps·ing** : to slip or fall back into a former worse state (as of illness)

re·late \ri-'lāt\ *vb* **re·lat·ed; re·lat·ing**   **1** : to give an account of : TELL, NARRATE   **2** : to show or establish logical or causal connection between   **3** : to have relationship or connection   **4** : to have or establish relationship ⟨the way a child ~*s* to a teacher⟩   **5** : to respond favorably ⟨can't ~ to that kind of music⟩ — **re·lat·able** *adj* — **re·lat·er** *or* **re·la·tor** \-'lā-tər\ *n*

re·lat·ed *adj*   **1** : connected by some understood relationship   **2** : connected through membership in the same family — **re·lat·ed·ness** *n*

re·la·tion \ri-'lā-shən\ *n*   **1** : NARRATION, ACCOUNT   **2** : CONNECTION, RELATIONSHIP   **3** : connection by blood or marriage : KINSHIP; *also* : RELATIVE   **4** : REFERENCE, RESPECT ⟨in ~ to⟩   **5** : the state of being mutually interested or involved (as in social or commercial matters)   **6** *pl* : DEALINGS, AFFAIRS ⟨foreign ~*s*⟩   **7** *pl* : SEXUAL INTERCOURSE — **re·la·tion·al** \-shə-nəl\ *adj*

re·la·tion·ship \-ˌship\ *n* : the state of being related or interrelated

¹**rel·a·tive** \'re-lə-tiv\ n 1 : a word referring grammatically to an antecedent 2 : a thing having a relation to or a dependence upon another thing 3 : a person connected with another by blood or marriage

²**relative** adj 1 : introducing a subordinate clause qualifying an expressed or implied antecedent ⟨∼ pronoun⟩; also : introduced by such a connective ⟨∼ clause⟩ 2 : PERTINENT, RELEVANT ⟨matters ∼ to world peace⟩ 3 : not absolute or independent : COMPARATIVE 4 : expressed as the ratio of the specified quantity to the total magnitude or to the mean of all quantities involved ♦ **Synonyms** DEPENDENT, CONTINGENT, CONDITIONAL — **rel·a·tive·ly** adv — **rel·a·tive·ness** n

relative humidity n : the ratio of the amount of water vapor actually present in the air to the greatest amount possible at the same temperature

rel·a·tiv·is·tic \ˌre-lə-ti-'vis-tik\ adj 1 : of, relating to, or characterized by relativity 2 : moving at a velocity that is a significant fraction of the speed of light so that effects predicted by the theory of relativity become evident ⟨a ∼ electron⟩ — **rel·a·tiv·is·ti·cal·ly** \-ti-k(ə-)lē\ adv

rel·a·tiv·i·ty \ˌre-lə-'ti-və-tē\ n, pl **-ties** 1 : the quality or state of being relative 2 : a theory in physics that considers mass and energy to be equivalent and that predicts changes in mass, dimension, and time which are related to speed but are noticeable esp. at speeds approaching that of light; also : an extension of the theory to include gravitation and related acceleration phenomena

re·lax \ri-'laks\ vb 1 : to make or become less firm, tense, or rigid 2 : to make less severe or strict 3 : to seek rest or recreation — **re·lax·er** n

¹**re·lax·ant** \ri-'lak-sənt\ adj : of, relating to, or producing relaxation

²**relaxant** n : a relaxing agent; esp : a drug that induces muscular relaxation

re·lax·ation \ˌrē-ˌlak-'sā-shən\ n 1 : the act of relaxing or state of being relaxed : a lessening of tension 2 : DIVERSION, RECREATION

¹**re·lay** \'rē-ˌlā\ n [ME, set of fresh hounds, fr. relayen to release fresh hounds, take a fresh horse, fr. MF relaier, fr. re- again + laier to let go, leave] 1 : a fresh supply (as of horses) arranged beforehand to relieve others 2 : a race between teams in which each team member covers a specified part of a course 3 : an electromagnetic device in which the opening or closing of one circuit activates another device (as a switch in another circuit) 4 : the act of passing along by stages

²**re·lay** \'rē-ˌlā, ri-'lā\ vb **re·layed; re·lay·ing** 1 : to place in or provide with relays 2 : to pass along by relays 3 : to control or operate by a relay

³**re·lay** \(ˌ)rē-'lā\ vb **-laid** \-'lād\; **-lay·ing** : to lay again

¹**re·lease** \ri-'lēs\ vb **re·leased; re·leas·ing** 1 : to set free from confinement or restraint; also : DISMISS ⟨released from her job⟩ 2 : to relieve from something that oppresses, confines, or burdens 3 : RELINQUISH ⟨∼ a claim⟩ 4 : to permit publication, performance, exhibition, or sale of; also : to make available to the public ♦ **Synonyms** EMANCIPATE, DISCHARGE, FREE, LIBERATE

²**release** n 1 : relief or deliverance from sorrow, suffering, or trouble 2 : discharge from an obligation or responsibility 3 : an act of setting free : the state of being freed 4 : a document effecting a legal release 5 : a releasing for performance or publication; also : the matter released (as to the press) 6 : a device for holding or releasing a mechanism as required

rel·e·gate \'re-lə-ˌgāt\ vb **-gat·ed; -gat·ing** 1 : to send into exile : BANISH 2 : to remove or dismiss to some less prominent position 3 : to assign to a particular class or sphere 4 : to submit to someone or something for appropriate action : DELEGATE ♦ **Synonyms** COMMIT, ENTRUST, CONSIGN, COMMEND — **rel·e·ga·tion** \ˌre-lə-'gā-shən\ n

re·lent \ri-'lent\ vb 1 : to become less stern, severe, or harsh 2 : SLACKEN

re·lent·less \-ləs\ adj : showing or promising no abatement of severity, intensity, or pace ⟨∼ pressure⟩ — **re·lent·less·ly** adv — **re·lent·less·ness** n

rel·e·vance \'re-lə-vəns\ n : relation to the matter at hand; also : practical and esp. social applicability

rel·e·van·cy \-vən-sē\ n : RELEVANCE

rel·e·vant \'re-lə-vənt\ adj : bearing on the matter at hand : PERTINENT ♦ **Synonyms** GERMANE, MATERIAL, APPLICABLE, APROPOS — **rel·e·vant·ly** adv

re·li·able \ri-'lī-ə-bəl\ adj : fit to be trusted or relied on : DEPENDABLE, TRUSTWORTHY — **re·li·abil·i·ty** \-ˌlī-ə-'bi-lə-tē\ n — **re·li·able·ness** n — **re·li·ably** \-'lī-ə-blē\ adv

re·li·ance \ri-'lī-əns\ n 1 : the act of relying 2 : the state of being reliant 3 : one relied on

re·li·ant \ri-'lī-ənt\ adj : having reliance on someone or something : DEPENDENT

rel·ic \'re-lik\ n 1 : an object venerated because of its association with a saint or martyr 2 : SOUVENIR, MEMENTO 3 pl : REMAINS, RUINS 4 : a remaining trace : VESTIGE

re·lict \'re-likt\ n : WIDOW

re·lief \ri-'lēf\ n 1 : removal or lightening of something oppressive, painful, or distressing 2 : WELFARE 2 3 : military assistance to an endangered post or force 4 : release from a post or from performance of a duty; also : one that takes the place of another on duty 5 : legal remedy or redress 6 : projection of figures or ornaments from the background (as in sculpture) 7 : the state of being distinguished by contrast 8 : the elevations of a land surface

relief pitcher n : a baseball pitcher who takes over for another during a game

re·lieve \ri-'lēv\ vb **re·lieved; re·liev·ing** 1 : to free partly or wholly from a burden or from distress 2 : to bring about the removal or alleviation of : MITIGATE 3 : to release from a post or duty; also : to take the place of 4 : to break the monotony of 5 : to discharge the bladder or bowels of (oneself) ♦ **Synonyms** ALLEVIATE, LIGHTEN, ASSUAGE, ALLAY — **re·liev·er** n

relig abbr religion

re·li·gion \ri-'li-jən\ n 1 : the service and worship of God or the supernatural 2 : devotion to a religious faith 3 : a personal set or institutionalized system of religious beliefs, attitudes, and practices 4 : a cause, principle, or belief held to with faith and ardor — **re·li·gion·ist** n

¹**re·li·gious** \ri-'li-jəs\ adj 1 : relating or devoted to an acknowledged ultimate reality or deity 2 : of or relating to religious beliefs or observances 3 : scrupulously and conscientiously faithful 4 : FERVENT, ZEALOUS ⟨∼ about football⟩ — **re·li·gious·ly** adv

²**religious** n, pl **religious** : a member of a religious order under monastic vows

re·lin·quish \ri-'liŋ-kwish, -'lin-\ vb 1 : to withdraw or retreat from : ABANDON, QUIT 2 : GIVE UP ⟨∼ a title⟩ 3 : to let go of : RELEASE ♦ **Synonyms** YIELD, LEAVE, RESIGN, SURRENDER, CEDE, WAIVE — **re·lin·quish·ment** n

rel·i·quary \'re-lə-ˌkwer-ē\ n, pl **-quar·ies** : a container for religious relics

¹**rel·ish** \'re-lish\ n [ME reles taste, fr. OF, something left behind, release, fr. relessier to relax, release, fr. L relaxare] 1 : characteristic flavor : SAVOR 2 : keen enjoyment of or delight in something : GUSTO 3 : APPETITE, INCLINATION ⟨has no ∼ for sports⟩ 4 : a highly seasoned sauce (as of pickles) eaten with other food to add flavor

²**relish** vb 1 : to add relish to 2 : to take pleasure in : ENJOY 3 : to eat with pleasure — **rel·ish·able** adj

re·live \(ˌ)rē-'liv\ vb : to live again or over again; esp : to experience again in the imagination

re·lo·cate \(ˌ)rē-'lō-ˌkāt, ˌrē-lō-'kāt\ vb 1 : to locate again 2 : to move to a new location — **re·lo·ca·tion** \ˌrē-lō-'kā-shən\ n

re·luc·tant \ri-'lək-tənt\ adj : feeling or showing aversion, hesitation, or unwillingness ⟨∼ to get involved⟩ ♦ **Synonyms** DISINCLINED, INDISPOSED, HESITANT, LOATH, AVERSE — **re·luc·tance** \-təns\ n — **re·luc·tant·ly** adv

re·ly \ri-'lī\ vb **re·lied; re·ly·ing** [ME relien to rally, fr. AF relier to retie, gather, rally, fr. L religare to tie out of the way, fr. re- back + ligare to tie] : to place faith or confidence in : DEPEND

REM \'rem\ n : RAPID EYE MOVEMENT

re·main \ri-'mān\ vb 1 : to be left after others have been removed, subtracted, or destroyed 2 : to be something yet to be shown, done, or treated ⟨it ∼s to be seen⟩ 3 : to stay after others have gone 4 : to continue unchanged

re·main·der \ri-'mān-dər\ n 1 : that which is left over : a remaining group, part, or trace 2 : the number left after a subtraction 3 : the number that is left over from the dividend after division and that is less than the divisor **4** : a book sold at a reduced price by the publisher after sales have slowed ♦ *Synonyms* LEAVINGS, REST, BALANCE, REMNANT, RESIDUE

re·mains \-'mānz\ *n pl* **1** : a remaining part or trace ⟨the ∼ of a meal⟩ **2** : a dead body

¹re·make \(,)rē-'māk\ *vb* **-made** \-'mād\; **-mak·ing** : to make anew or in a different form

²re·make \'rē-,māk\ *n* : one that is remade; *esp* : a new version of a motion picture

re·mand \ri-'mand\ *vb* : to order back; *esp* : to return to custody pending trial or for further detention

¹re·mark \ri-'märk\ *n* **1** : the act of remarking : OBSERVATION, NOTICE **2** : a passing observation or comment

²remark *vb* **1** : to take notice of : OBSERVE **2** : to express as an observation or comment : SAY

re·mark·able \ri-'mär-kə-bəl\ *adj* : worthy of being or likely to be noticed : UNUSUAL, EXTRAORDINARY, NOTEWORTHY — **re·mark·able·ness** *n*

re·mark·ably \ri-'mär-kə-blē\ *adv* **1** : in a remarkable manner **2** : as is remarkable ⟨∼, no one was hurt⟩

re·me·di·a·ble \ri-'mē-dē-ə-bəl\ *adj* : capable of being remedied

re·me·di·al \ri-'mē-dē-əl\ *adj* : intended to remedy or improve ⟨a class in ∼ math⟩

¹rem·e·dy \'re-mə-dē\ *n, pl* **-dies** [ME *remedie*, fr. AF, fr. L *remedium*, fr. *re-* back, again + *mederi* to heal] **1** : a medicine or treatment that cures or relieves a disease or condition **2** : something that corrects or counteracts an evil or compensates for a loss

²remedy *vb* **-died; -dy·ing** : to provide or serve as a remedy for

re·mem·ber \ri-'mem-bər\ *vb* **-bered; -ber·ing** **1** : to bring to mind or think of again : RECOLLECT **2** : to keep from forgetting : keep in mind **3** : to convey greetings from : COMMEMORATE

re·mem·brance \-brəns\ *n* **1** : an act of remembering : RECOLLECTION **2** : the ability to remember : MEMORY **3** : the period over which one's memory extends **4** : a memory of a person, thing, or event **5** : something that serves to bring to mind : REMINDER **6** : a greeting or gift recalling or expressing friendship or affection

re·mind \ri-'mīnd\ *vb* : to put in mind of something : cause to remember — **re·mind·er** *n*

rem·i·nisce \,re-mə-'nis\ *vb* **-nisced; -nisc·ing** : to indulge in reminiscence

rem·i·nis·cence \-'ni-s³ns\ *n* **1** : a recalling or telling of a past experience **2** : an account of a memorable experience

rem·i·nis·cent \-s³nt\ *adj* **1** : of or relating to reminiscence **2** : marked by or given to reminiscence **3** : serving to remind : SUGGESTIVE — **rem·i·nis·cent·ly** *adv*

re·miss \ri-'mis\ *adj* **1** : negligent or careless in the performance of work or duty **2** : showing neglect or inattention ♦ *Synonyms* LAX, NEGLECTFUL, DELINQUENT, DERELICT — **re·miss·ness** *n*

re·mis·sion \ri-'mi-shən\ *n* **1** : the act or process of remitting **2** : a state or period during which something is remitted

re·mit \ri-'mit\ *vb* **re·mit·ted; re·mit·ting** **1** : FORGIVE, PARDON ⟨∼ sins⟩ **2** : to give or gain relief from (as pain) **3** : to refer for consideration, report, or decision **4** : to refrain from exacting or enforcing (as a penalty) **5** : to send (money) in payment of a bill

re·mit·tal \ri-'mi-t³l\ *n* : REMISSION

re·mit·tance \ri-'mi-t³ns\ *n* **1** : a sum of money remitted **2** : transmittal of money (as to a distant place)

rem·nant \'rem-nənt\ *n* **1** : a usu. small part or trace remaining **2** : an unsold or unused end of a fabric that is sold by the yard

re·mod·el \rē-'mä-d³l\ *vb* : to alter the structure of : MAKE OVER

re·mon·strance \ri-'män-strəns\ *n* : an act or instance of remonstrating

re·mon·strant \-strənt\ *adj* : vigorously objecting or opposing — **remonstrant** *n* — **re·mon·strant·ly** *adv*

re·mon·strate \ri-'män-,strāt\ *vb* **-strat·ed; -strat·ing** : to plead in opposition to something : speak in protest or reproof ♦ *Synonyms* EXPOSTULATE, OBJECT, PROTEST — **re·mon·stra·tion** \ri-,män-'strā-shən, ,re-mən-\ *n* — **re·mon·stra·tor** \ri-'män-,strā-tər\ *n*

rem·o·ra \'re-mə-rə\ *n* : any of a family of marine bony fishes with sucking organs on the head by which they cling esp. to other fishes

remora: on a shark

re·morse \ri-'mȯrs\ *n* [ME, fr. AF *remors*, fr. ML *remorsus*, fr. LL, act of biting again, fr. L *remordēre* to bite again, fr. *re-* again + *mordēre* to bite] : a gnawing distress arising from a sense of guilt for past wrongs ♦ *Synonyms* PENITENCE, REPENTANCE, CONTRITION — **re·morse·ful** *adj*

re·morse·less \-ləs\ *adj* **1** : MERCILESS **2** : PERSISTENT, RELENTLESS

¹re·mote \ri-'mōt\ *adj* **re·mot·er; -est** **1** : far off in place or time : not near **2** : not closely related : DISTANT **3** : located out of the way : SECLUDED **4** : acting, acted on, or controlled indirectly or from a distance **5** : small in degree : SLIGHT ⟨a ∼ chance⟩ **6** : distant in manner ⟨became ∼ in her old age⟩ — **re·mote·ly** *adv* — **re·mote·ness** *n*

²remote *n* **1** : a radio or television program or a portion of a program originating outside the studio **2** : REMOTE CONTROL 2

remote control *n* **1** : control (as by radio signal) of operation from a point at some distance removed **2** : a device or mechanism for controlling something from a distance

¹re·mount \(,)rē-'maunt\ *vb* **1** : to mount again **2** : to furnish remounts to

²re·mount \'rē-,maunt\ *n* : a fresh horse to replace one no longer available

¹re·move \ri-'müv\ *vb* **re·moved; re·mov·ing** **1** : to move from one place to another : TRANSFER **2** : to move by lifting or taking off or away **3** : DISMISS, DISCHARGE **4** : to get rid of : ELIMINATE ⟨∼ a fire hazard⟩ **5** : to change one's residence or location **6** : to go away : DEPART **7** : to be capable of being removed — **re·mov·able** *adj* — **re·mov·al** \-'mü-vəl\ *n* — **re·mov·er** *n*

²remove *n* **1** : a transfer from one location to another : MOVE **2** : a degree or stage of separation

REM sleep *n* : a state of sleep that recurs cyclically several times during normal sleep and is associated with rapid eye movements and dreaming

re·mu·ner·ate \ri-'myü-nə-,rāt\ *vb* **-at·ed; -at·ing** : to pay an equivalent for or to : RECOMPENSE ⟨their services were *remunerated*⟩ — **re·mu·ner·a·tor** \-,rā-tər\ *n*

re·mu·ner·a·tion \ri-,myü-nə-'rā-shən\ *n* : COMPENSATION, PAYMENT

re·mu·ner·a·tive \ri-'myü-nə-rə-tiv, -,rā-\ *adj* : serving to remunerate : GAINFUL

re·nais·sance \,re-nə-'säns, -'zäns\ *n* **1** *cap* : the cultural revival and beginnings of modern science in Europe in the 14th–17th centuries; *also* : the period of the Renaissance **2** *often cap* : a movement or period of vigorous artistic and intellectual activity **3** : REBIRTH, REVIVAL

re·nal \'rē-n³l\ *adj* : of, relating to, or located in or near the kidneys

re·na·scence \ri-'na-s³ns, -'nä-\ *n, often cap* : RENAISSANCE

rend \'rend\ *vb* **rent** \'rent\; **rend·ing** **1** : to remove by violence : WREST **2** : to tear forcibly apart : SPLIT

ren·der \'ren-dər\ *vb* **1** : to extract (as lard) by heating **2** : to give to another; *also* : YIELD **3** : to give in return **4** : to do (a service) for another ⟨∼ aid⟩ **5** : to cause to be or become : MAKE **6** : to reproduce or represent by artistic or verbal means **7** : TRANSLATE ⟨∼ into English⟩

¹ren·dez·vous \'rän-di-‚vü, -dā-\ *n, pl* ren·dez·vous \-‚vüz\ [MF, fr. *rendez vous* present yourselves] 1 : a place appointed for a meeting; *also* : a meeting at an appointed place 2 : a place of popular resort 3 : the process of bringing two spacecraft together

²rendezvous *vb* -voused \-‚vüd\; -vous·ing \-‚vü-iŋ\; -vouses \-‚vüz\ : to come or bring together at a rendezvous

ren·di·tion \ren-'di-shən\ *n* : an act or a result of rendering ⟨first ∼ of the work into English⟩

ren·e·gade \'re-ni-‚gād\ *n* [Sp *renegado,* fr. ML *renegatus,* fr. pp. of *renegare* to deny, fr. L *re-* re- + *negare* to deny] : a deserter from one faith, cause, principle, or party for another

re·nege \ri-'neg\ *vb* re·neged; re·neg·ing 1 : to go back on a promise or commitment 2 : to fail to follow suit when able in a card game in violation of the rules — re·neg·er *n*

re·new \ri-'nü, -'nyü\ *vb* 1 : to make or become new, fresh, or strong again 2 : to restore to existence : REC-REATE, REVIVE 3 : to make or do again : REPEAT ⟨∼ a complaint⟩ 4 : to begin again : RESUME ⟨∼ed his efforts⟩ 5 : REPLACE ⟨∼ the lining of a coat⟩ 6 : to grant or obtain an extension of or on ⟨∼ a lease⟩ ⟨∼ a subscription⟩ — re·new·er *n*

re·new·able \ri-'nü-ə-bəl, -'nyü-\ *adj* 1 : capable of being renewed 2 : capable of being replaced by natural ecological cycles or sound management procedures ⟨∼ resources⟩

re·new·al \ri-'nü-əl, -'nyü-\ *n* 1 : the act of renewing : the state of being renewed 2 : something renewed

ren·net \'re-nət\ *n* 1 : the contents of the stomach of an unweaned animal (as a calf) or the lining membrane of the stomach used for curdling milk 2 : rennin or a substitute used to curdle milk

ren·nin \'re-nən\ *n* : a stomach enzyme that coagulates casein and is used commercially to curdle milk in the making of cheese

re·nounce \ri-'naůns\ *vb* re·nounced; re·nounc·ing 1 : to give up, refuse, or resign usu. by formal declaration 2 : to refuse further to follow, obey, or recognize : REPU-DIATE — re·nounce·ment *n*

ren·o·vate \'re-nə-‚vāt\ *vb* -vat·ed; -vat·ing : to make like new again : put in good condition : REPAIR ⟨*renovated* the kitchen⟩ 2 : to restore to vigor or activity — ren·o·va·tion \‚re-nə-'vā-shən\ *n* — ren·o·va·tor \'re-nə-‚vā-tər\ *n*

re·nown \ri-'naůn\ *n* : a state of being widely acclaimed and honored : FAME, CELEBRITY ⟨writers of ∼⟩ ♦ **Synonyms** HONOR, GLORY, REPUTATION, REPUTE — re·nowned \-'naůnd\ *adj*

¹rent \'rent\ *n* 1 : money or the amount of money paid or due at intervals for the use of another's property 2 : property rented or for rent

²rent *vb* 1 : to give possession and use of in return for rent 2 : to take and hold under an agreement to pay rent 3 : to be for rent ⟨∼s for $100 a month⟩ — rent·er *n*

³rent *n* 1 : a tear made by or as if by rending 2 : a split in a party or organized group : SCHISM

¹rent·al \'ren-təl\ *n* 1 : an amount paid or collected as rent 2 : something that is rented 3 : an act of renting

²rental *adj* : of or relating to rent

re·nun·ci·a·tion \ri-‚nən-sē-'ā-shən\ *n* : the act of renouncing : REPUDIATION

¹rep \'rep\ *n* : REPRESENTATIVE ⟨sales ∼s⟩

²rep *abbr* 1 repair 2 repeat 3 report; reporter 4 republic

Rep *abbr* Republican

re·pack·age \(‚)rē-'pa-kij\ *vb* : to package again or anew; *esp* : to put into a more attractive form

¹re·pair \ri-'per\ *vb* [ME, fr. AF *repairer* to go back, return, fr. LL *repatriare* to go home again, fr. L *re-* back + *patria* native country] : to make one's way : GO ⟨∼ed to the drawing room⟩

²repair *vb* [ME, fr. AF *reparer,* fr. L *reparare,* fr. *re-* back + *parare* to prepare] 1 : to restore to good condition : FIX 2 : to restore to a healthy state 3 : REMEDY ⟨∼ a wrong⟩ — re·pair·er *n* — re·pair·man \-‚man\ *n*

³repair *n* 1 : a result of repairing 2 : an act of repairing 3 : condition with respect to need of repairing ⟨in bad ∼⟩

rep·a·ra·tion \‚re-pə-'rā-shən\ *n* 1 : the act of making

amends for a wrong 2 : amends made for a wrong; *esp* : money paid by a defeated nation in compensation for damages caused during hostilities — usu. used in pl. ♦ **Synonyms** REDRESS, RESTITUTION, INDEMNITY

re·par·a·tive \ri-'pa-rə-tiv\ *adj* 1 : of, relating to, or effecting repairs 2 : serving to make amends

rep·ar·tee \‚re-pər-'tē\ *n* 1 : a witty reply 2 : a succession of clever replies; *also* : skill in making such replies

re·past \ri-'past, 're-‚past\ *n* : a supply of food and drink served as a meal

re·pa·tri·ate \rē-'pā-trē-‚āt\ *vb* -at·ed; -at·ing : to send or bring back to the country of origin or citizenship ⟨∼ prisoners of war⟩ — re·pa·tri·ate \-trē-ət, -trē-‚āt\ *n* — re·pa·tri·a·tion \-‚pā-trē-'ā-shən\ *n*

re·pay \rē-'pā\ *vb* -paid \-'pād\; -pay·ing 1 : to pay back : REFUND 2 : to give or do in return or requital 3 : to make a return payment to : RECOMPENSE, REQUITE ♦ **Synonyms** REMUNERATE, COMPENSATE, REIMBURSE, INDEMNIFY — re·pay·able *adj* — re·pay·ment *n*

re·peal \ri-'pēl\ *vb* [ME *repelen,* fr. AF *repeler,* lit., to call back, fr. *re-* back + *apeler* to appeal, call] : to annul by authoritative and esp. legislative action ⟨∼ a law⟩ — re·peal *n* — re·peal·er *n*

¹re·peat \ri-'pēt\ *vb* 1 : to say again 2 : to do again 3 : to say over from memory — re·peat·able *adj* — re·peat·er *n*

²re·peat \ri-'pēt, 'rē-‚pēt\ *n* 1 : the act of repeating 2 : something repeated or to be repeated (as a radio or television program)

³re·peat \ri-'pēt\ *adj* : of, relating to, or being one that repeats an offense, achievement, or action

re·peat·ed \ri-'pē-təd\ *adj* : done or recurring again and again : FREQUENT ⟨∼ requests⟩ — re·peat·ed·ly *adv*

re·pel \ri-'pel\ *vb* re·pelled; re·pel·ling 1 : to drive away : REPULSE 2 : to fight against : RESIST 3 : to turn away : REJECT 4 : to cause aversion in : DISGUST

¹re·pel·lent *also* re·pel·lant \ri-'pe-lənt\ *adj* 1 : tending to drive away ⟨a mosquito-*repellent* spray⟩ 2 : causing disgust

²repellent *also* repellant *n* : something that repels; *esp* : a substance that repels insects

re·pent \ri-'pent\ *vb* 1 : to turn from sin and resolve to reform one's life 2 : to feel sorry for (something done) : REGRET ⟨∼ed his decision⟩ — re·pen·tance \ri-'pen-tᵊns\ *n* — re·pen·tant \-'tᵊnt\ *adj*

re·per·cus·sion \‚rē-pər-'kə-shən, ‚re-\ *n* 1 : REVER-BERATION 2 : a reciprocal action or effect 3 : a widespread, indirect, or unforeseen effect of something done or said

rep·er·toire \'re-pər-‚twär\ *n* [F] 1 : a list of plays, operas, pieces, or parts which a company or performer is prepared to present 2 : a list of the skills or devices possessed by a person or needed in a person's occupation

rep·er·to·ry \'re-pər-‚tȯr-ē\ *n, pl* -ries 1 : REPOSITORY 2 : REPERTOIRE 3 : a company that presents its repertoire in the course of one season at one theater

rep·e·ti·tion \‚re-pə-'ti-shən\ *n* 1 : the act or an instance of repeating 2 : the fact of being repeated

rep·e·ti·tious \-'ti-shəs\ *adj* : marked by repetition; *esp* : tediously repeating ⟨∼ work⟩ — rep·e·ti·tious·ly *adv* — rep·e·ti·tious·ness *n*

re·pet·i·tive \ri-'pe-tə-tiv\ *adj* : REPETITIOUS — re·pet·i·tive·ly *adv* — re·pet·i·tive·ness *n*

re·pine \ri-'pīn\ *vb* re·pined; re·pin·ing 1 : to feel or express discontent or dejection 2 : to long for something

repl *abbr* replace; replacement

re·place \ri-'plās\ *vb* 1 : to restore to a former place or position 2 : to take the place of : SUPPLANT 3 : to put something new in the place of — re·place·able *adj* — re·plac·er *n*

re·place·ment \ri-'plās-mənt\ *n* 1 : the act of replacing : the state of being replaced 2 : one that replaces another esp. in a job or function

¹re·play \(‚)rē-'plā\ *vb* : to play again or over

²re·play \'rē-‚plā\ *n* 1 : an act or instance of replaying 2 : the playing of a tape (as a videotape)

re·plen·ish \ri-'ple-nish\ *vb* : to fill or build up again : stock or supply anew — re·plen·ish·ment *n*

re·plete \ri-'plēt\ *adj* 1 : fully provided ⟨a kit ∼ with instructions⟩ 2 : FULL; *esp* : full of food — re·plete·ness *n* — re·ple·tion \ri-'plē-shən\ *n*

rep·li·ca \'re-pli-kə\ *n* [It, repetition, fr. *replicare* to repeat, fr. LL, fr. L, to fold back, fr. *re-* back + *plicare* to fold] 1 : an exact reproduction (as of a painting) executed by the original artist 2 : a copy exact in all details : DUPLICATE

¹rep·li·cate \'re-plə-ˌkāt\ *vb* -cat·ed; -cat·ing : DUPLICATE, REPEAT

²rep·li·cate \-pli-kət\ *n* : one of several identical experiments or procedures

rep·li·ca·tion \ˌre-plə-'kā-shən\ *n* 1 : ANSWER, REPLY 2 : precise copying or reproduction; *also* : an act or process of this ⟨~ of DNA⟩

¹re·ply \ri-'plī\ *vb* re·plied; re·ply·ing : to say or do in answer : RESPOND

²reply *n, pl* replies : ANSWER, RESPONSE

repo \'rē-ˌpō\ *adj* : of, relating to, or being in the business of repossessing property (as a car)

¹re·port \ri-'pȯrt\ *n* [ME, fr. AF, fr. *reporter* to bring back, report, fr. L *reportare*, fr. *re-* back + *portare* to carry] 1 : common talk : RUMOR 2 : FAME, REPUTATION ⟨a person of good ~⟩ 3 : a usu. detailed account or statement 4 : an explosive noise

²report *vb* 1 : to give an account of : RELATE, TELL 2 : to serve as carrier of (a message) 3 : to prepare or present (as an account of an event) for a newspaper or a broadcast 4 : to make a charge of misconduct against 5 : to present oneself (as for work) 6 : to make known to the authorities ⟨~ a fire⟩ 7 : to return or present (as a matter referred to a committee) with conclusions and recommendations 8 : to work as a subordinate ⟨~s to the vice president⟩ — **re·port·able** *adj*

re·port·age \ri-'pȯr-tij, *esp for 2* ˌre-pər-'täzh, ˌre-ˌpȯr-'\ *n* [F] 1 : the act or process of reporting news 2 : writing intended to give an account of observed or documented events

report card *n* : a periodic report on a student's grades

re·port·ed·ly \ri-'pȯr-təd-lē\ *adv* : according to report ⟨is ~ about to be fired⟩

re·port·er \ri-'pȯr-tər\ *n* : one that reports; *esp* : a person who gathers and reports news for a news medium — **re·por·to·ri·al** \ˌre-pər-'tȯr-ē-əl\ *adj*

¹re·pose \ri-'pōz\ *vb* re·posed; re·pos·ing 1 : to lay at rest 2 : to lie at rest 3 : to lie dead 4 : to take a rest 5 : to rest for support : LIE

²repose *n* 1 : a state of resting (as after exertion); *esp* : SLEEP 2 : eternal or heavenly rest 3 : CALM, PEACE ⟨the ~ of the bayous⟩ 4 : cessation or absence of activity, movement, or animation 5 : composure of manner : POISE — **re·pose·ful** *adj*

³repose *vb* re·posed; re·pos·ing 1 : to place (as trust) in someone or something 2 : to place for control, management, or use

re·pos·i·to·ry \ri-'pä-zə-ˌtȯr-ē\ *n, pl* -ries 1 : a place where something is deposited or stored 2 : a person to whom something is entrusted

re·pos·sess \ˌrē-pə-'zes\ *vb* 1 : to regain possession of 2 : to take possession of in default of the payment of installments due — **re·pos·ses·sion** \-'ze-shən\ *n*

re·post \ˌ(ˌ)rē-'pōst\ *vb* : to post again ⟨~ a message⟩

rep·re·hend \ˌre-pri-'hend\ *vb* : to express disapproval of : CENSURE ♦ *Synonyms* CRITICIZE, CONDEMN, DENOUNCE, BLAME, PAN — **rep·re·hen·sion** \-'hen-chən\ *n*

rep·re·hen·si·ble \-'hen-sə-bəl\ *adj* : deserving blame or censure : CULPABLE — **rep·re·hen·si·bly** \-blē\ *adv*

rep·re·sent \ˌre-pri-'zent\ *vb* 1 : to present a picture or a likeness of : PORTRAY, DEPICT 2 : to serve as a sign or symbol of 3 : to act the role of 4 : to stand in the place of : act or speak for; *also* : to manage the legal and business affairs of 5 : to be a member or example of : TYPIFY 6 : to serve as an elected representative of 7 : to describe as having a specified quality or character 8 : to state with the purpose of affecting judgment or action

rep·re·sen·ta·tion \ˌre-pri-ˌzen-'tā-shən\ *n* 1 : the act of representing 2 : one (as a picture or image) that represents something else 3 : the state of being represented in a legislative body; *also* : the body of persons representing a constituency 4 : a usu. formal statement made to effect a change

¹rep·re·sen·ta·tive \ˌre-pri-'zen-tə-tiv\ *adj* 1 : serving to represent 2 : standing or acting for another 3 : founded on the principle of representation : carried on by elected representatives ⟨~ government⟩ — **rep·re·sen·ta·tive·ly** *adv* — **rep·re·sen·ta·tive·ness** *n*

²representative *n* 1 : one that represents another; *esp* : one representing a district in a legislative body usu. as a member of a lower house 2 : a typical example of a group, class, or quality

re·press \ri-'pres\ *vb* 1 : CURB, SUBDUE 2 : RESTRAIN, SUPPRESS 3 : to exclude from consciousness ⟨~ a painful memory⟩ — **re·pres·sion** \-'pre-shən\ *n* — **re·pres·sive** \-'pre-siv\ *adj*

¹re·prieve \ri-'prēv\ *vb* re·prieved; re·priev·ing 1 : to delay the punishment or execution of 2 : to give temporary relief to

²reprieve *n* 1 : the act of reprieving : the state of being reprieved 2 : a formal temporary suspension of a sentence esp. of death 3 : a temporary respite

¹rep·ri·mand \'re-prə-ˌmand\ *n* : a severe or formal reproof

²reprimand *vb* : to reprove severely or formally ⟨~ed the sergeant⟩

¹re·print \ˌ(ˌ)rē-'print\ *vb* : to print again

²re·print \'rē-ˌprint\ *n* : a reproduction of printed matter

re·pri·sal \ri-'prī-zəl\ *n* : an act in retaliation for something done by another

re·prise \ri-'prēz\ *n* : a recurrence, renewal, or resumption of an action; *also* : a musical repetition

¹re·proach \ri-'prōch\ *n* 1 : an expression of disapproval 2 : DISGRACE, DISCREDIT 3 : the act of reproaching : REBUKE 4 : a cause or occasion of blame or disgrace — **re·proach·ful** \-fəl\ *adj* — **re·proach·ful·ly** *adv* — **re·proach·ful·ness** *n*

²reproach *vb* 1 : CENSURE, REBUKE 2 : to cast discredit on ♦ *Synonyms* CHIDE, ADMONISH, REPROVE, REPRIMAND — **re·proach·able** *adj*

rep·ro·bate \'re-prə-ˌbāt\ *n* 1 : a person foreordained to damnation 2 : a thoroughly bad person : SCOUNDREL — **reprobate** *adj*

rep·ro·ba·tion \ˌre-prə-'bā-shən\ *n* : strong disapproval : CONDEMNATION

re·pro·duce \ˌrē-prə-'düs, -'dyüs\ *vb* 1 : to produce again or anew 2 : to produce offspring — **re·pro·duc·ible** \-'dü-sə-bəl, -'dyü-\ *adj* — **re·pro·duc·tion** \-'dək-shən\ *n* — **re·pro·duc·tive** \-'dək-tiv\ *adj*

re·proof \ri-'prüf\ *n* : blame or censure for a fault

re·prove \ri-'prüv\ *vb* re·proved; re·prov·ing 1 : to administer a rebuke to 2 : to express disapproval of ♦ *Synonyms* REPRIMAND, ADMONISH, REPROACH, CHIDE — **re·prov·er** *n*

rept *abbr* report

rep·tile \'rep-tī(-ə)l, -t³l\ *n* [ME *reptil*, fr. MF or LL; MF *reptile*, fr. LL *reptile*, fr. L *repere* to crawl] : any of a large class of air-breathing scaly vertebrates including snakes, lizards, alligators, turtles, and extinct related forms (as dinosaurs) — **rep·til·i·an** \rep-'ti-lē-ən\ *adj or n*

re·pub·lic \ri-'pə-blik\ *n* [F *république*, fr. MF *republique*, fr. L *respublica*, fr. *res* thing, wealth + *publica*, fem. of *publicus* public] 1 : a government having a chief of state who is not a monarch and is usu. a president; *also* : a nation or other political unit having such a government 2 : a government in which supreme power is held by the citizens entitled to vote and is exercised by elected officers and representatives governing according to law; *also* : a nation or other political unit having such a form of government 3 : a constituent political and territorial unit of the former nations of Czechoslovakia, the U.S.S.R., or Yugoslavia

¹re·pub·li·can \-bli-kən\ *n* 1 : one that favors or supports a republican form of government 2 *cap* : a member of a republican party and esp. of the Republican party of the U.S.

²republican *adj* 1 : of, relating to, or resembling a republic 2 : favoring or supporting a republic 3 *cap* : of, relating to, or constituting one of the two major political parties in the U.S. evolving in the mid-19th century — **re·pub·li·can·ism** *n, often cap*

re·pu·di·ate \ri-'pyü-dē-ˌāt\ *vb* -at·ed; -at·ing [L *repudiare* to cast off, divorce, fr. *repudium* rejection of a prospective spouse, divorce] 1 : to cast off : DISOWN 2 : to refuse to have anything to do with : refuse to acknowledge, accept, or pay ⟨~ a charge⟩ ⟨~ a debt⟩ ♦ *Synonyms*

SPURN, REJECT, DECLINE — **re·pu·di·a·tion** \-ˌpyü-dē-'ā-shən\ n — **re·pu·di·a·tor** \-'pyü-dē-ˌā-tər\ n

re·pug·nance \ri-'pəg-nəns\ n 1 : the quality or fact of being contradictory or inconsistent 2 : strong dislike, distaste, or antagonism

re·pug·nant \-nənt\ adj 1 : marked by repugnance 2 : contrary to a person's tastes or principles : exciting distaste or aversion ✦ **Synonyms** REPELLENT, ABHORRENT, DISTASTEFUL, OBNOXIOUS, REVOLTING, LOATHSOME — **re·pug·nant·ly** adv

¹**re·pulse** \ri-'pəls\ vb **re·pulsed; re·puls·ing** 1 : to drive or beat back : REPEL 2 : to repel by discourtesy or denial : REBUFF 3 : to cause a feeling of repulsion in : DISGUST ⟨repulsed by the violence⟩

²**repulse** n 1 : REBUFF, REJECTION 2 : the action of repelling an attacker : the fact of being repelled

re·pul·sion \ri-'pəl-shən\ n 1 : the action of repulsing : the state of being repulsed 2 : the force with which bodies, particles, or like forces repel one another 3 : a feeling of aversion

re·pul·sive \-siv\ adj 1 : serving or tending to repel or reject 2 : arousing aversion or disgust ✦ **Synonyms** REPUGNANT, REVOLTING, LOATHSOME, NOISOME — **re·pul·sive·ly** adv — **re·pul·sive·ness** n

re·pur·pose \(ˌ)rē-'pər-pəs\ vb : to give a new purpose or use to

rep·u·ta·ble \'re-pyə-tə-bəl\ adj : having a good reputation : ESTIMABLE ⟨a ~ lawyer⟩ — **rep·u·ta·bly** \-blē\ adv

rep·u·ta·tion \ˌre-pyù-'tā-shən\ n 1 : overall quality or character as seen or judged by people in general 2 : place in public esteem or regard

¹**re·pute** \ri-'pyüt\ vb **re·put·ed; re·put·ing** : BELIEVE, CONSIDER ⟨reputed to be a millionaire⟩

²**repute** n 1 : REPUTATION ⟨knew her by ~⟩ 2 : the state of being favorably known or spoken of

re·put·ed \ri-'pyü-təd\ adj 1 : REPUTABLE 2 : according to reputation : SUPPOSED — **re·put·ed·ly** adv

req abbr 1 request 2 require; required 3 requisition

¹**re·quest** \ri-'kwest\ n 1 : an act or instance of asking for something 2 : a thing asked for 3 : the condition of being asked for ⟨available on ~⟩

²**request** vb 1 : to make a request to or of 2 : to ask for — **re·quest·er** or **re·quest·or** n

re·qui·em \'re-kwē-əm, 'rā-\ n [ME, fr. L (first word of the requiem mass), acc. of requies rest, fr. quies quiet, rest] 1 : a mass for a dead person; also : a musical setting for this 2 : a musical service or hymn in honor of the dead

re·quire \ri-'kwī(-ə)r\ vb **re·quired; re·quir·ing** 1 : to demand as necessary or essential 2 : COMMAND, ORDER ⟨the law ~s that everyone pay the tax⟩

re·quire·ment \-mənt\ n 1 : something (as a condition or quality) required ⟨entrance ~s⟩ 2 : NECESSITY ⟨production was sufficient to satisfy military ~s⟩

req·ui·site \'re-kwə-zət\ adj : REQUIRED, NECESSARY — **requisite** n

req·ui·si·tion \ˌre-kwə-'zi-shən\ n 1 : formal application or demand (as for supplies) 2 : the state of being in demand or use — **requisition** vb

re·quite \ri-'kwīt\ vb **re·quit·ed; re·quit·ing** 1 : to make return for : REPAY 2 : to make retaliation for : AVENGE 3 : to make return to — **re·quit·al** \-'kwī-tᵊl\ n

rere·dos \'rer-ə-ˌdäs\ n : a usu. ornamental wood or stone screen or partition wall behind an altar

re·run \'rē-ˌrən, (ˌ)rē-'rən\ n : the act or an instance of running again or anew; esp : a showing of a motion picture or television program after its first run — **re·run** \(ˌ)rē-'rən\ vb

res abbr 1 research 2 reservation; reserve 3 reservoir 4 residence; resident 5 resolution

re·sale \'rē-ˌsāl, (ˌ)rē-'sāl\ n : the act of selling again usu. to a new party — **re·sal·able** \(ˌ)rē-'sā-lə-bəl\ adj

re·scind \ri-'sind\ vb : REPEAL, CANCEL, ANNUL — **re·scis·sion** \-'si-zhən\ n

re·script \'rē-ˌskript\ n : an official or authoritative order or decree

res·cue \'res-kyü\ vb **res·cued; res·cu·ing** [ME rescouen, rescuen, fr. AF rescoure, fr. re- back, again + escure to shake off, fr. L excutere] : to free from danger, harm, or confinement — **rescue** n — **res·cu·er** n

re·search \ri-'sərch, 'rē-ˌsərch\ n 1 : careful or diligent

search 2 : studious inquiry or examination aimed at the discovery and interpretation of new knowledge 3 : the collecting of information about a particular subject — **research** vb — **re·search·er** n

re·sec·tion \ri-'sek-shən\ n : the surgical removal of part of an organ or structure

re·sem·blance \ri-'zem-bləns\ n : the quality or state of resembling

re·sem·ble \ri-'zem-bəl\ vb **-bled; -bling** : to be like or similar to

re·sent \ri-'zent\ vb : to feel or exhibit annoyance or indignation at ⟨~ed his interference⟩ — **re·sent·ful** \-fəl\ adj — **re·sent·ful·ly** adv — **re·sent·ment** n

re·ser·pine \ri-'sər-ˌpēn, -pən\ n : a drug used in treating high blood pressure and nervous tension

res·er·va·tion \ˌre-zər-'vā-shən\ n 1 : an act of reserving 2 : something (as a room in a hotel) arranged for in advance 3 : something reserved; esp : a tract of public land set aside for special use 4 : a limiting condition

¹**re·serve** \ri-'zərv\ vb **re·served; re·serv·ing** 1 : to store for future or special use 2 : to hold back for oneself 3 : to set aside or arrange to have set aside or held for special use

²**reserve** n 1 : something reserved : STOCK, STORE 2 : a military force withheld from action for later use — usu. used in pl. 3 : the military forces of a country not part of the regular services; also : RESERVIST 4 : a tract set apart : RESERVATION 5 : an act of reserving 6 : restraint or caution in one's words or bearing 7 : money or its equivalent kept in hand or set apart to meet liabilities

re·served \ri-'zərvd\ adj 1 : restrained in words and actions 2 : set aside for future or special use — **re·serv·ed·ly** \-'zər-vəd-lē\ adv — **re·serv·ed·ness** \-vəd-nəs\ n

re·serv·ist \ri-'zər-vist\ n : a member of a military reserve

res·er·voir \'re-zə-ˌvwär, -zər-, -ˌvwȯr\ n [F] : a place where something is kept in store; esp : an artificial lake where water is collected and kept for use

re·shuf·fle \rē-'shə-fəl\ vb 1 : to shuffle again 2 : to reorganize usu. by redistribution of existing elements ⟨reshuffled our schedule⟩ — **reshuffle** n

re·side \ri-'zīd\ vb **re·sid·ed; re·sid·ing** 1 : to make one's home : DWELL 2 : to be present as a quality or vested as a right

res·i·dence \'re-zə-dəns\ n 1 : the act or fact of residing in a place as a dweller or in discharge of a duty or an obligation 2 : the place where one actually lives 3 : a building used as a home : DWELLING 4 : the period of living in a place

res·i·den·cy \'re-zə-dən-sē\ n, pl **-cies** 1 : the residence of or the territory under a diplomatic resident 2 : a period of advanced training in a medical specialty

¹**res·i·dent** \-dənt\ adj 1 : RESIDING 2 : being in residence 3 : not migratory

²**resident** n 1 : one who resides in a place 2 : a diplomatic representative with governing powers (as in a protectorate) 3 : a physician serving a residency

res·i·den·tial \ˌre-zə-'den-chəl\ adj 1 : used as a residence or by residents 2 : occupied by or restricted to residences — **res·i·den·tial·ly** adv

¹**re·sid·u·al** \ri-'zi-jə-wəl\ n 1 : a residual product or substance 2 : a payment (as to an actor or writer) for each rerun after an initial showing (as of a taped TV show)

²**residual** adj : being a residue or remainder

re·sid·u·ary \ri-'zi-jə-ˌwer-ē\ adj : of, relating to, or constituting a residue esp. of an estate

res·i·due \'re-zə-ˌdü, -ˌdyü\ n : a part remaining after another part has been taken away : REMAINDER

re·sid·u·um \ri-'zi-jə-wəm\ n, pl **re·sid·ua** \-jə-wə\ [L] 1 : something remaining or residual after certain deductions are made 2 : a residual product

re·sign \ri-'zīn\ vb [ME, fr. AF resigner, fr. L resignare, lit., to unseal, cancel, fr. signare to sign, seal] 1 : to give up deliberately (as one's position) esp. by a formal act 2 : to give (oneself) over (as to grief or despair) without resistance — **re·sign·ed·ly** \-'zī-nəd-lē\ adv

re–sign \(ˌ)rē-'sīn\ vb : to sign again

res·ig·na·tion \ˌre-zig-'nā-shən\ n 1 : an act or instance of resigning; also : a formal notification of such an act 2 : the quality or state of being resigned

re·sil·ience \ri-'zil-yəns\ n : the ability of a body to re-

gain its original size and shape after being compressed, bent, or stretched **2** : an ability to recover from or adjust easily to change or misfortune
re·sil·ien·cy \-yən-sē\ *n* : RESILIENCE
re·sil·ient \-yənt\ *adj* : marked by resilience ⟨∼ players⟩
res·in \'re-z°n\ *n* : any of various substances obtained from the gum or sap of some trees and used esp. in varnishes, plastics, and medicine; *also* : a comparable synthetic product — **res·in·ous** *adj*
¹**re·sist** \ri-'zist\ *vb* **1** : to fight against : OPPOSE ⟨∼ aggression⟩ **2** : to withstand the force or effect of ⟨∼ed temptation⟩ ⟨∼ disease⟩ ✦ *Synonyms* COMBAT, REPEL — **re·sist·ible** \-'zis-tə-bəl\ *adj* — **re·sist·less** *adj*
²**resist** *n* : something (as a coating) that resists or prevents a particular action
re·sis·tance \ri-'zis-təns\ *n* **1** : the act or an instance of resisting : OPPOSITION **2** : the power or capacity to resist; *esp* : the inherent ability of an organism to resist harmful influences (as disease or infection) **3** : the opposition offered by a body to the passage through it of a steady electric current
re·sis·tant \-tənt\ *adj* : giving, capable of, or exhibiting resistance
re·sis·tor \ri-'zis-tər\ *n* : a device used to provide resistance to the flow of an electric current in a circuit
res·o·lute \'re-zə-ˌlüt\ *adj* : firmly determined in purpose : RESOLVED ⟨a ∼ leader⟩ ✦ *Synonyms* STEADFAST, STAUNCH, FAITHFUL, TRUE, LOYAL — **res·o·lute·ly** *adv* — **res·o·lute·ness** *n*
res·o·lu·tion \ˌre-zə-'lü-shən\ *n* **1** : the act or process of resolving **2** : the action of solving; *also* : SOLUTION **3** : the quality of being resolute : FIRMNESS, DETERMINATION **4** : a formal statement expressing the opinion, will, or intent of a body of persons **5** : a measure of the sharpness of an image or of the fineness with which a device can produce or record such an image
¹**re·solve** \ri-'zälv\ *vb* **re·solved; re·solv·ing 1** : to break up into constituent parts : ANALYZE **2** : to distinguish between or make visible adjacent parts of **3** : to find an answer to : SOLVE ⟨∼ a dispute⟩ **4** : DETERMINE, DECIDE **5** : to make or pass a formal resolution — **re·solv·able** *adj*
²**resolve** *n* **1** : fixity of purpose **2** : something resolved
res·o·nance \'re-zə-nəns\ *n* **1** : the quality or state of being resonant **2** : a reinforcement of sound in a vibrating body caused by waves from another body vibrating at nearly the same rate
res·o·nant \-nənt\ *adj* **1** : continuing to sound : RESOUNDING **2** : relating to or exhibiting resonance **3** : intensified and enriched by or as if by resonance — **res·o·nant·ly** *adv*
res·o·nate \-ˌnāt\ *vb* **-nat·ed; -nat·ing 1** : to produce or exhibit resonance **2** : REVERBERATE, RESOUND **3** : to relate harmoniously ⟨∼ with voters⟩
res·o·na·tor \-ˌnā-tər\ *n* : something that resounds or exhibits resonance
re·sorp·tion \rē-'sȯrp-shən, -'zȯrp-\ *n* : the action or process of breaking down and assimilating something (as a tooth or an embryo)
¹**re·sort** \ri-'zȯrt\ *n* [ME, return, source of aid, fr. AF, fr. *resortir* to rebound, resort, fr. *sortir* to go out, leave] **1** : one looked to for help : REFUGE **2** : RECOURSE **3** : frequent or general visiting ⟨place of ∼⟩ **4** : a frequently visited place : HAUNT **5** : a place providing recreation esp. to vacationers
²**resort** *vb* **1** : to go often or habitually **2** : to have recourse ⟨∼ed to violence⟩
re·sound \ri-'zau̇nd\ *vb* **1** : to become filled with sound : REVERBERATE, RING **2** : to sound loudly
re·sound·ing *adj* **1** : RESONATING, RESONANT **2** : impressively sonorous ⟨∼ name⟩ **3** : EMPHATIC, UNEQUIVOCAL ⟨a ∼ success⟩ — **re·sound·ing·ly** *adv*
re·source \'rē-ˌsȯrs, ri-'sȯrs\ *n* [F *ressource*, fr. OF *ressourse* relief, resource, fr. *resourdre* to relieve, lit., to rise again, fr. L *resurgere*, fr. *re-* again + *surgere* to rise] **1** : a source of supply or support — usu. used in pl. **2** : a natural feature or phenomenon that enhances the quality of human life **3** *pl* : available funds **4** : a possibility of relief or recovery **5** : a means of spending leisure time **6** : ability to meet and handle situations — **re·source·ful** \ri-'sȯrs-fəl\ *adj* — **re·source·ful·ness** *n*

¹**re·spect** \ri-'spekt\ *n* **1** : relation to something usu. specified : REGARD ⟨in ∼ to⟩ **2** : high or special regard : ESTEEM **3** *pl* : an expression of respect or deference **4** : DETAIL, PARTICULAR — **re·spect·ful** \-fəl\ *adj* — **re·spect·ful·ly** *adv* — **re·spect·ful·ness** *n*
²**respect** *vb* **1** : to consider deserving of high regard : ESTEEM **2** : to refrain from interfering with ⟨∼ another's privacy⟩ **3** : to have reference to : CONCERN — **re·spect·er** *n*
re·spect·able \ri-'spek-tə-bəl\ *adj* **1** : worthy of respect : ESTIMABLE **2** : decent or correct in conduct : PROPER **3** : fair in size, quantity, or quality ⟨a ∼ score⟩ : MODERATE, TOLERABLE **4** : fit to be seen : PRESENTABLE — **re·spect·a·bil·i·ty** \-ˌspek-tə-'bi-lə-tē\ *n* — **re·spect·ably** \-'spek-tə-blē\ *adv*
re·spect·ing *prep* : with regard to
re·spec·tive \-tiv\ *adj* : PARTICULAR, SEPARATE ⟨returned to their ∼ homes⟩
re·spec·tive·ly \-lē\ *adv* **1** : as relating to each **2** : each in the order given
res·pi·ra·tion \ˌres-pə-'rā-shən\ *n* **1** : an act or the process of breathing **2** : the physical and chemical processes (as breathing and oxidation) by which a living thing obtains oxygen and eliminates waste gases (as carbon dioxide) — **re·spi·ra·to·ry** \'res-pə-rə-ˌtȯr-ē, ri-'spī-rə-\ *adj* — **re·spire** \ri-'spī(-ə)r\ *vb*
res·pi·ra·tor \'res-pə-ˌrā-tər\ *n* **1** : a device covering the mouth and nose esp. to prevent inhaling harmful vapors **2** : a device for artificial respiration
re·spite \'res-pət\ *n* [ME *respit*, fr. AF, fr. ML *respectus*, fr. L, act of looking back] **1** : a temporary delay **2** : an interval of rest or relief
re·splen·dent \ri-'splen-dənt\ *adj* : shining brilliantly : gloriously bright : SPLENDID ⟨∼ uniforms⟩ — **re·splen·dence** \-dəns\ *n* — **re·splen·dent·ly** *adv*
re·spond \ri-'spänd\ *vb* **1** : ANSWER, REPLY **2** : REACT ⟨∼ed to a call for help⟩ **3** : to show favorable reaction ⟨∼ to medication⟩ — **re·spond·er** *n*
re·spon·dent \ri-'spän-dənt\ *n* : one who responds; *esp* : one who answers in various legal proceedings — **respondent** *adj*
re·sponse \ri-'späns\ *n* **1** : an act of responding **2** : something constituting a reply or a reaction
re·spon·si·bil·i·ty \ri-ˌspän-sə-'bi-lə-tē\ *n, pl* **-ties 1** : the quality or state of being responsible **2** : something for which one is responsible
re·spon·si·ble \ri-'spän-sə-bəl\ *adj* **1** : liable to be called upon to answer for one's acts or decisions : ANSWERABLE **2** : able to fulfill one's obligations : RELIABLE, TRUSTWORTHY **3** : able to choose for oneself between right and wrong **4** : involving accountability or important duties ⟨∼ position⟩ — **re·spon·si·ble·ness** *n* — **re·spon·si·bly** \-blē\ *adv*
re·spon·sive \-siv\ *adj* **1** : RESPONDING **2** : quick to respond : SENSITIVE **3** : using responses ⟨∼ readings⟩ — **re·spon·sive·ly** *adv* — **re·spon·sive·ness** *n*
¹**rest** \'rest\ *n* **1** : REPOSE, SLEEP **2** : freedom from work or activity **3** : a state of motionlessness or inactivity **4** : a place of shelter or lodging **5** : a silence in music equivalent in duration to a note of the same value; *also* : a character indicating this **6** : something used as a support — **rest·ful** \-fəl\ *adj* — **rest·ful·ly** *adv*

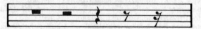

¹**rest 5: symbols for five kinds**

²**rest** *vb* **1** : to get rest by lying down; *esp* : SLEEP **2** : to cease from action or motion **3** : to give rest to : set at rest **4** : to sit or lie fixed or supported **5** : to place on or against a support **6** : to remain based or founded **7** : to cause to be firmly fixed : GROUND **8** : to remain for action : DEPEND
³**rest** *n* : something left over
res·tau·rant \'res-trənt, -tə-ˌ ränt\ *n* [F, fr. prp. of *restaurer* to restore, fr. L *restaurare*] : a public eating place
res·tau·ra·teur \ˌres-tə-rə-'tər\ *also* **res·tau·ran·teur** \-ˌrän-\ *n* : the operator or proprietor of a restaurant
rest home *n* : an establishment that gives care for the aged or convalescent

res·ti·tu·tion \,res-tə-'tü-shən, -'tyü-\ *n* : the act of restoring : the state of being restored ; *esp* : restoration of something to its rightful owner ♦ *Synonyms* AMENDS, REDRESS, REPARATION, INDEMNITY, COMPENSATION

res·tive \'res-tiv\ *adj* [ME *restyf*, fr. AF *restif*, fr. *rester* to stop, resist, remain, fr. L *restare*, fr. *re*- back + *stare* to stand] **1** : BALKY **2** : UNEASY, FIDGETY ♦ *Synonyms* RESTLESS, IMPATIENT, NERVOUS — **res·tive·ly** *adv* — **res·tive·ness** *n*

rest·less \'rest-ləs\ *adj* **1** : lacking or denying rest ⟨a ~ night⟩ **2** : never resting or settled : always moving ⟨the ~ sea⟩ **3** : marked by or showing unrest ⟨~ of mind⟩ ⟨~ pacing back and forth⟩ ♦ *Synonyms* RESTIVE, IMPATIENT, NERVOUS, FIDGETY — **rest·less·ly** *adv* — **rest·less·ness** *n*

re·stor·able \ri-'stȯr-ə-bəl\ *adj* : fit for restoring or reclaiming

res·to·ra·tion \,res-tə-'rā-shən\ *n* **1** : an act of restoring : the state of being restored **2** : something (as a building) that has been restored

re·stor·ative \ri-'stȯr-ə-tiv\ *n* : something that restores esp. to consciousness or health — **restorative** *adj*

re·store \ri-'stȯr\ *vb* **re·stored**; **re·stor·ing** **1** : to give back : RETURN **2** : to put back into use or service **3** : to put or bring back into a former or original state **4** : to put again in possession of something — **re·stor·er** *n*

re·strain \ri-'strān\ *vb* **1** : to prevent from doing something **2** : to limit, restrict, or keep under control : CURB **3** : to place under restraint or arrest — **re·strain·able** *adj* — **re·strain·er** *n*

re·strained \ri-'strānd\ *adj* : marked by restraint : DISCIPLINED — **re·strain·ed·ly** \-'strā-nəd-lē\ *adv*

restraining order *n* : a legal order directing one person to stay away from another

re·straint \ri-'strānt\ *n* **1** : an act of restraining : the state of being restrained **2** : a restraining force, agency, or device **3** : deprivation or limitation of liberty : CONFINEMENT **4** : control over one's feelings : RESERVE

re·strict \ri-'strikt\ *vb* **1** : to confine within bounds : LIMIT **2** : to place under restriction as to use — **re·stric·tive** *adj* — **re·stric·tive·ly** *adv*

re·stric·tion \ri-'strik-shən\ *n* **1** : something (as a law or rule) that restricts **2** : an act of restricting : the state of being restricted

rest room *n* : a room or suite of rooms that includes sinks and toilets

¹re·sult \ri-'zəlt\ *vb* [ME, fr. ML *resultare*, fr. L, to rebound, fr. *re*- re- + *saltare* to leap] : to come about as an effect or consequence ⟨an injury ~*ing* from a fall⟩ — **re·sul·tant** \-'zəl-tᵊnt\ *adj or n*

²result *n* **1** : something that results : EFFECT, CONSEQUENCE **2** : beneficial or discernible effect **3** : something obtained by calculation or investigation

re·sume \ri-'züm\ *vb* **re·sumed**; **re·sum·ing** **1** : to take or assume again **2** : to return to or begin again after interruption **3** : to take back to oneself — **re·sump·tion** \-'zəmp-shən\ *n*

ré·su·mé *or* **re·su·me** *or* **re·su·mé** \'re-zə-,mā, ,re-zə-'mā\ *n* [F *résumé*] **1** : SUMMARY; *esp* : a short account of one's career and qualifications usu. prepared by a job applicant **2** : a set of accomplishments ⟨a musical ~⟩

re·sur·gence \ri-'sər-jəns\ *n* : a rising again into life, activity, or prominence — **re·sur·gent** \-jənt\ *adj*

res·ur·rect \,re-zə-'rekt\ *vb* **1** : to raise from the dead **2** : to bring to attention or use again

res·ur·rec·tion \,re-zə-'rek-shən\ *n* **1** *cap* : the rising of Christ from the dead **2** *often cap* : the rising to life of all human dead before the final judgment **3** : REVIVAL ⟨the ~ of her career⟩

re·sus·ci·tate \ri-'sə-sə-,tāt\ *vb* **-tat·ed**; **-tat·ing** : to revive from apparent death or unconsciousness; *also* : REVITALIZE — **re·sus·ci·ta·tion** \ri-,sə-sə-'tā-shən, ,rē-\ *n* — **re·sus·ci·ta·tor** \ri-'sə-sə-,tā-tər\ *n*

ret *abbr* retired

¹re·tail \'rē-,tāl, *esp for 2 also* ri-'tāl\ *vb* **1** : to sell in small quantities directly to the ultimate consumer **2** : to tell in detail or to one person after another — **re·tail·er** *n*

²re·tail \'rē-,tāl\ *n* : the sale of goods in small amounts to ultimate consumers — **retail** *adj or adv*

re·tain \ri-'tān\ *vb* **1** : to hold in possession or use **2** : to engage (as a lawyer) by paying a fee in advance **3** : to

keep in a fixed place or position ♦ *Synonyms* DETAIN, WITHHOLD, RESERVE

¹re·tain·er \ri-'tā-nər\ *n* **1** : one that retains **2** : a servant in a wealthy household; *also* : EMPLOYEE **3** : a device that holds something (as teeth) in place

²retainer *n* : a fee paid to secure services (as of a lawyer)

¹re·take \(,)rē-'tāk\ *vb* **-took** \-'tu̇k\; **-tak·en** \-'tā-kən\; **-tak·ing** **1** : to take or seize again **2** : to photograph again

²re·take \'rē-,tāk\ *n* : a second photographing of a motion-picture scene

re·tal·i·ate \ri-'ta-lē-,āt\ *vb* **-at·ed**; **-at·ing** : to return like for like; *esp* : to get revenge — **re·tal·i·a·tion** \-,ta-lē-'ā-shən\ *n* — **re·tal·ia·to·ry** \-'tal-yə-,tȯr-ē\ *adj*

re·tard \ri-'tärd\ *vb* : to hold back : delay the progress of ♦ *Synonyms* SLOW, SLACKEN, DETAIN — **re·tar·da·tion** \,rē-,tär-'dā-shən, ri-\ *n* — **re·tard·er** *n*

re·tar·dant \ri-'tär-dᵊnt\ *adj* : serving or tending to retard — **retardant** *n*

re·tard·ed *adj, sometimes offensive* : slow or limited in intellectual, emotional, or academic progress

retch \'rech\ *vb* : to try to vomit; *also* : VOMIT

re·ten·tion \ri-'ten-chən\ *n* **1** : the act of retaining : the state of being retained **2** : the power of retaining esp. in the mind : RETENTIVENESS

re·ten·tive \-'ten-tiv\ *adj* : having the power of retaining; *esp* : retaining knowledge easily — **re·ten·tive·ness** *n*

re·think \(,)rē-'think\ *vb* **-thought** \-'thȯt\; **-think·ing** : to think about again : RECONSIDER

ret·i·cent \'re-tə-sənt\ *adj* **1** : tending not to talk or give out information **2** : RELUCTANT ♦ *Synonyms* RESERVED, TACITURN, CLOSEMOUTHED — **ret·i·cence** \-səns\ *n* — **ret·i·cent·ly** *adv*

ret·i·na \'re-tə-nə\ *n, pl* **retinas** *or* **ret·i·nae** \-,nē\ : the sensory membrane lining the eye that receives the image formed by the lens — **ret·i·nal** \'re-tə-nəl\ *adj*

ret·i·nue \'re-tə-,nü, -,nyü\ *n* : the body of attendants or followers of a distinguished person

re·tire \ri-'tī(-ə)r\ *vb* **re·tired**; **re·tir·ing** **1** : RETREAT **2** : to withdraw esp. for privacy **3** : to withdraw from one's occupation or position : conclude one's career **4** : to withdraw from use or service **5** : to go to bed **6** : to cause to be out in baseball — **re·tire·ment** *n*

re·tired \ri-'tī(-ə)rd\ *adj* **1** : SECLUDED, QUIET **2** : withdrawn from active duty or from one's career

re·tir·ee \ri-,tī-'rē\ *n* : a person who has retired from a career

re·tir·ing *adj* : SHY, RESERVED

re·tool \(,)rē-'tül\ *vb* **1** : to reequip with tools **2** : to modify with usu. minor improvements ⟨~ed the team for next year⟩

¹re·tort \ri-'tȯrt\ *vb* [L *retortus*, pp. of *retorquēre*, lit., to twist back, hurl back, fr. *re*- back + *torquēre* to twist] **1** : to say in reply : answer back usu. sharply **2** : to answer (an argument) by a counter argument **3** : RETALIATE

²retort *n* : a quick, witty, or cutting reply

³re·tort \ri-'tȯrt, 'rē-,tȯrt\ *n* [MF *retorte*, fr. ML *retorta*, fr. L, fem. of *retortus*, pp. of *retorquēre* to twist back; fr. its shape] : a vessel in which substances are distilled or broken up by heat

re·touch \(,)rē-'təch\ *vb* : TOUCH UP; *esp* : to change (as a photographic negative) in order to produce a more desirable appearance

re·trace \(,)rē-'trās\ *vb* : to go over again or in a reverse direction ⟨*retraced* his steps⟩

re·tract \ri-'trakt\ *vb* **1** : to draw back or in **2** : to withdraw (as a charge or promise) : DISAVOW — **re·tract·able** *adj* — **re·trac·tion** \-'trak-shən\ *n*

re·trac·tile \ri-'trak-tᵊl, -'trak-,tī(-ə)l\ *adj* : capable of being drawn back or in ⟨~ claws⟩

¹re·tread \(,)rē-'tred\ *vb* **re·tread·ed**; **re·tread·ing** : to put a new tread on (a worn tire)

²re·tread \'rē-,tred\ *n* **1** : a retreaded tire **2** : one pressed into service again; *also* : REMAKE

¹re·treat \ri-'trēt\ *n* **1** : an act of withdrawing esp. from something dangerous, difficult, or disagreeable **2** : a military signal for withdrawal; *also* : a military flag-lowering ceremony **3** : a place of privacy or safety : REFUGE **4** : a group withdrawal for prayer, meditation, or study

²retreat *vb* **1** : to make a retreat : WITHDRAW **2** : to slope backward

re·trench \ri-'trench\ *vb* [obs. F *retrencher* (now *retrancher*), fr. MF *retrenchier*, fr. *re-* + *trenchier* to cut] **1** : to cut down or pare away : REDUCE, CURTAIL **2** : to cut down expenses : ECONOMIZE ⟨the company had to ∼⟩ — **re·trench·ment** *n*

ret·ri·bu·tion \ˌre-trə-'byü-shən\ *n* : something administered or exacted in recompense; *esp* : PUNISHMENT ✦ **Synonyms** REPRISAL, VENGEANCE, REVENGE, RETALIATION — **re·trib·u·tive** \ri-'tri-byə-tiv\ *adj* — **re·trib·u·to·ry** \-byə-ˌtȯr-ē\ *adj*

re·trieve \ri-'trēv\ *vb* **re·trieved; re·triev·ing** **1** : to search about for and bring in (killed or wounded game) **2** : RECOVER, RESTORE — **re·triev·able** *adj* — **re·triev·al** \-'trē-vəl\ *n*

re·triev·er \ri-'trē-vər\ *n* : one that retrieves; *esp* : a dog of any of several breeds used esp. for retrieving game

ret·ro \'re-trō\ *adj* : relating to or being the styles and fashions of the past ⟨∼ clothing⟩

ret·ro·ac·tive \ˌre-trō-'ak-tiv\ *adj* : made effective as of a date prior to enactment ⟨a ∼ pay raise⟩ — **ret·ro·ac·tive·ly** *adv*

ret·ro·fit \'re-trō-ˌfit, ˌre-trō-'fit\ *vb* **1** : to furnish (as an aircraft) with newly available equipment **2** : to adapt to a new purpose or need : MODIFY — **ret·ro·fit** \'re-trō-ˌfit\ *n*

¹ret·ro·grade \'re-trə-ˌgrād\ *adj* **1** : moving or tending backward **2** : tending toward or resulting in a worse condition

²retrograde *vb* **1** : RETREAT **2** : DETERIORATE, DEGENERATE

ret·ro·gres·sion \ˌre-trə-'gre-shən\ *n* : return to a former and less complex level of development or organization — **ret·ro·gress** \ˌre-trə-'gres\ *vb* — **ret·ro·gres·sive** \ˌre-trə-'gre-siv\ *adj*

ret·ro·rock·et \'re-trō-ˌrä-kət\ *n* : an auxiliary rocket engine (as on a spacecraft) used to slow forward motion

ret·ro·spect \'re-trə-ˌspekt\ *n* : a review of past events — **ret·ro·spec·tion** \ˌre-trə-'spek-shən\ *n*

ret·ro·spec·tive \ˌre-trə-'spek-tiv\ *adj* **1** : a comprehensive examination of an artist's work over many years **2** : REVIEW ⟨a war ∼⟩ — **retrospective** *adj* — **ret·ro·spec·tive·ly** *adv*

ret·ro·vi·rus \'re-trō-ˌvī-rəs\ *n* : any of a group of RNA-containing viruses (as HIV) that make DNA using RNA instead of the reverse — **re·tro·vi·ral** \-rəl\ *adj*

¹re·turn \ri-'tərn\ *vb* **1** : to go or come back **2** : to pass, give, or send back to an earlier possessor **3** : to put back to or in a former place or state **4** : REPLY, ANSWER **5** : to report esp. officially **6** : to elect to office **7** : to bring in (as profit) : YIELD **8** : to give or perform in return ⟨∼ a favor⟩ — **re·turn·er** *n*

²return *n* **1** : an act of coming or going back to or into a former place or state **2** : RECURRENCE **3** : a report of the results of balloting **4** : a formal statement of taxable income **5** : the profit from labor, investment, or business : YIELD **6** : the act of returning something **7** : something that returns or is returned; *also* : a means for conveying something (as water) back to its starting point **8** : something given in repayment or reciprocation; *also* : ANSWER, RETORT **9** : an answering play — **return** *adj*

¹re·turn·able \ri-'tər-nə-bəl\ *adj* : capable of being returned (as for reuse); *also* : permitted to be returned

²returnable *n* : a returnable beverage container

re·turn·ee \ri-ˌtər-'nē\ *n* : one who returns

re·tweet \(ˌ)rē-'twēt\ *vb* : to repost to the Twitter online message service ⟨fans ∼ed her tweet⟩

re·union \rē-'yün-yən\ *n* **1** : an act of reuniting : the state of being reunited **2** : a meeting of persons after separation

¹rev \'rev\ *n* : a revolution of a motor

²rev *vb* **revved; rev·ving** **1** : to increase the revolutions per minute of (a motor) **2** : STIMULATE, EXCITE

³rev *abbr* **1** revenue **2** reverse **3** review; reviewed **4** revised; revision **5** revolution

Rev *abbr* **1** Revelation **2** Reverend

re·vamp \(ˌ)rē-'vamp\ *vb* : RECONSTRUCT, REVISE; *also* : RENOVATE

re·vanche \rə-'vä⁽ⁿ⁾sh\ *n* [F] : REVENGE; *esp* : a usu. political policy designed to recover lost territory or status

re·veal \ri-'vēl\ *vb* **1** : to make known **2** : to show plainly : open up to view

rev·eil·le \'re-və-lē\ *n* [modif. of F *réveillez*, imper. pl. of *réveiller* to awaken, fr. MF *eveiller* to awaken, fr. VL **ex-*

vigilare, fr. L *vigilare* to keep watch, stay awake] : a military signal sounded at about sunrise

¹rev·el \'re-vəl\ *vb* **-eled** *or* **-elled; -el·ing** *or* **-el·ling** **1** : to take part in a revel **2** : to take great pleasure or satisfaction ⟨∼ed in the quiet⟩ — **rev·el·er** *or* **rev·el·ler** *n* — **rev·el·ry** \-vəl-rē\ *n*

²revel *n* : a usu. wild party or celebration

rev·e·la·tion \ˌre-və-'lā-shən\ *n* **1** : an act of revealing **2** : something revealed; *esp* : an enlightening or astonishing disclosure

Revelation *n* — see BIBLE table

¹re·venge \ri-'venj\ *vb* **re·venged; re·veng·ing** : to inflict harm or injury in return for (a wrong) : AVENGE — **re·veng·er** *n*

²revenge *n* **1** : a desire for revenge **2** : an act or instance of retaliation to get even **3** : an opportunity for getting satisfaction ✦ **Synonyms** VENGEANCE, RETRIBUTION, REPRISAL — **re·venge·ful** *adj*

rev·e·nue \'re-və-ˌnü, -ˌnyü\ *n* [ME, return, revenue, fr. AF, fr. *revenir* to return, fr. L *revenire*, fr. *re-* back + *venire* to come] **1** : investment income **2** : money collected by a government (as through taxes)

re·verb \ri-'vərb, 'rē-ˌvərb\ *n* : an electronically produced echo effect in recorded music; *also* : a device for producing reverb

re·ver·ber·ate \ri-'vər-bə-ˌrāt\ *vb* **-at·ed; -at·ing** **1** : REFLECT ⟨∼ light or heat⟩ **2** : to resound in or as if in a series of echoes — **re·ver·ber·a·tion** \-ˌvər-bə-'rā-shən\ *n*

re·vere \ri-'vir\ *vb* **re·vered; re·ver·ing** : to show honor and devotion to : VENERATE ⟨a teacher *revered* by students⟩ ✦ **Synonyms** REVERENCE, WORSHIP, ADORE

¹rev·er·ence \'re-vrəns, -və-rəns\ *n* **1** : honor or respect felt or shown **2** : a gesture (as a bow or curtsy) of respect

²reverence *vb* **-enced; -enc·ing** : to regard or treat with reverence

¹rev·er·end \'re-vrənd, -və-rənd\ *adj* **1** : worthy of reverence : REVERED **2** : being a member of the clergy — used as a title

²reverend *n* : a member of the clergy

rev·er·ent \'re-vrənt, -və-rənt\ *adj* : expressing reverence — **rev·er·ent·ly** *adv*

rev·er·en·tial \ˌre-və-'ren-chəl\ *adj* : REVERENT

rev·er·ie *also* **rev·ery** \'re-və-rē\ *n, pl* **-er·ies** [F *rêverie*, fr. MF, delirium, fr. *resver, rever* to wander, be delirious] **1** : DAYDREAM **2** : the state of being lost in thought

re·ver·sal \ri-'vər-səl\ *n* : an act or process of reversing

¹re·verse \ri-'vərs\ *adj* **1** : opposite to a previous or normal condition ⟨in ∼ order⟩ **2** : acting or working in a manner opposite the usual **3** : bringing about reverse movement ⟨∼ gear⟩ — **re·verse·ly** *adv*

²reverse *vb* **re·versed; re·vers·ing** **1** : to turn upside down or completely about in position or direction **2** : to set aside or change (as a legal decision) **3** : to change to the contrary ⟨∼ a policy⟩ **4** : to go or cause to go in the opposite direction **5** : to put (as a car) in reverse — **re·vers·ible** \-'vər-sə-bəl\ *adj*

³reverse *n* **1** : something contrary to something else : OPPOSITE **2** : an act or instance of reversing; *esp* : a change for the worse **3** : the back side of something (as a coin or card) **4** : a gear that reverses something

reverse engineer *vb* : to disassemble or analyze in detail in order to discover concepts involved in manufacture — **reverse engineering** *n*

re·ver·sion \ri-'vər-zhən\ *n* **1** : the right of succession or future possession (as to a title or property) **2** : return toward some former or ancestral condition; *also* : a product of this — **re·ver·sion·ary** \-zhə-ˌner-ē\ *adj*

re·vert \ri-'vərt\ *vb* **1** : to come or go back ⟨∼ed to savagery⟩ **2** : to return to a proprietor or his or her heirs **3** : to return to an ancestral type

¹re·view \ri-'vyü\ *n* **1** : an act of revising **2** : a formal military inspection **3** : a general survey **4** : INSPECTION, EXAMINATION; *esp* : REEXAMINATION **5** : a critical evaluation (as of a book) **6** : a magazine devoted to reviews and essays **7** : a renewed study of previously studied material **8** : REVUE

²review \ri-'vyü, *1 also* 'rē-\ *vb* **1** : to examine or study again; *esp* : to reexamine judicially **2** : to hold a review of ⟨∼ troops⟩ **3** : to write a critical examination of ⟨∼ a novel⟩ **4** : to look back over ⟨∼ed her accomplishments⟩ **5** : to study material again re·view·er \ri-'vyü-ər\ n : one that reviews; esp : a writer of critical reviews

re·vile \ri-'vī(-ə)l\ vb re·viled; re·vil·ing : to abuse verbally : rail at ✦ Synonyms VITUPERATE, BERATE, RATE, UPBRAID, SCOLD — re·vile·ment n — re·vil·er n

re·vise \ri-'vīz\ vb re·vised; re·vis·ing 1 : to look over something written in order to correct or improve ⟨∼ an essay⟩ 2 : to make a new version of ⟨∼ an almanac⟩ — re·vis·able adj — re·vise n — re·vis·er or re·vi·sor \-'vī-zər\ n — re·vi·sion \-'vi-zhən\ n

re·vi·tal·ise Brit var of REVITALIZE

re·vi·tal·ize \,rē-'vīt-tə-,līz\ vb -ized; -iz·ing : to give new life or vigor to ⟨∼ the shopping district⟩ — re·vi·tal·i·za·tion \(,)rē-,vī-tə-lə-'zā-shən\ n

re·viv·al \ri-'vī-vəl\ n 1 : an act of reviving : the state of being revived 2 : a new publication or presentation (as of a book or play) 3 : an evangelistic meeting or series of meetings

re·vive \ri-'vīv\ vb re·vived; re·viv·ing 1 : to bring back to life, consciousness, or activity : make or become fresh or strong again 2 : to bring back into use ⟨revived its native language⟩ — re·viv·er n

re·viv·i·fy \rē-'vi-və-,fī\ vb : REVIVE — re·viv·i·fi·ca·tion \-,vi-və-fə-'kā-shən\ n

re·vo·ca·ble \'re-və-kə-bəl\ also ri-'vō-kə-bəl\ adj : capable of being revoked

re·vo·ca·tion \,re-və-'kā-shən\ n : an act or instance of revoking

re·voke \ri-'vōk\ vb re·voked; re·vok·ing 1 : to annul by recalling or taking back : REPEAL, RESCIND ⟨∼ a license⟩ 2 : RENEGE 2 — re·vok·er n

¹re·volt \ri-'vōlt\ vb [MF revolter, fr. It rivoltare to overthrow, fr. VL *revolvitare, fr. L revolvere to revolve, roll back] 1 : to throw off allegiance to a ruler or government : REBEL 2 : to experience disgust or shock 3 : to turn or cause to turn away with disgust or abhorrence ⟨violence ∼ed her⟩ — re·volt·er n

²revolt n : REBELLION, INSURRECTION

re·volt·ing adj : extremely offensive ⟨a ∼ odor⟩ — re·volt·ing·ly adv

rev·o·lu·tion \,re-və-'lü-shən\ n 1 : the action by a heavenly body of going round in an orbit 2 : ROTATION 3 : a sudden, radical, or complete change; esp : the overthrow or renunciation of one ruler or government and substitution of another by the governed

¹rev·o·lu·tion·ary \-shə-,ner-ē\ adj 1 : of or relating to revolution 2 : tending to or promoting revolution 3 : constituting or bringing about a major change

²revolutionary n, pl -ar·ies : one who takes part in a revolution or who advocates revolutionary doctrines

rev·o·lu·tion·ise Brit var of REVOLUTIONIZE

rev·o·lu·tion·ist \,re-və-'lü-shə-nist\ n : REVOLUTIONARY — revolutionist adj

rev·o·lu·tion·ize \-,nīz\ vb -ized; -iz·ing : to change fundamentally or completely ⟨∼ an industry⟩ — rev·o·lu·tion·iz·er n

re·volve \ri-'välv\ vb re·volved; re·volv·ing 1 : to turn over in the mind : reflect upon : PONDER 2 : to move in an orbit; also : ROTATE 3 : to have a specified focus ⟨the debate revolved around taxes⟩ — re·volv·able adj

re·volv·er \ri-'väl-vər\ n : a pistol with a revolving cylinder of several chambers

re·vue \ri-'vyü\ n : a theatrical production consisting typically of brief often satirical sketches and songs

re·vul·sion \ri-'vəl-shən\ n 1 : a strong sudden reaction or change of feeling 2 : a feeling of complete distaste or repugnance

revved past and past part of REV

revving pres part of REV

¹re·ward \ri-'word\ vb 1 : to give a reward to or for 2 : RECOMPENSE

²reward n 1 : something given in return for good or evil done or received or for some service or attainment 2 : a stimulus that is administered to an organism after a response and that increases the probability of occurrence of the response ✦ Synonyms PREMIUM, PRIZE, AWARD

re·warm \(,)rē-'worm\ vb : to make warm again ⟨∼ food⟩ ⟨∼ed herself by the fire⟩

¹re·wind \(,)rē-'wīnd\ vb -wound; -wind·ing 1 : to wind again 2 : to reverse the winding of (as film)

²re·wind \'rē-,wīnd\ n 1 : something that rewinds 2 : an act of rewinding 3 : a function of an electronic device that reverses a recording to a previous portion

re·work \(,)rē-'wərk\ vb 1 : REVISE 2 : to reprocess for further use

¹re·write \(,)rē-'rīt\ vb -wrote; -writ·ten; -writ·ing : to make a revision of : REVISE

²re·write \'rē-,rīt\ n : an instance or a piece of rewriting

RF abbr radio frequency

RFD abbr rural free delivery

Rg abbr roentgenium

Rh symbol rhodium

RH abbr right hand

rhap·so·dy \'rap-sə-dē\ n, pl -dies [L rhapsodia portion of an epic poem adapted for recitation, fr. Gk rhapsōidia recitation of selections from epic poetry, ultim. fr. rhaptein to sew, stitch together + aidein to sing] 1 : an expression of extravagant praise or ecstasy 2 : a musical composition of irregular form — rhap·sod·ic \rap-'sä-dik\ adj — rhap·sod·i·cal·ly \-di-k(ə-)lē\ adv — rhap·so·dize \'rap-sə-,dīz\ vb

rhea \'rē-ə\ n : either of two large flightless 3-toed So. American birds that resemble but are smaller than the African ostrich

rhe·ni·um \'rē-nē-əm\ n : a rare heavy metallic chemical element

rheo·stat \'rē-ə-,stat\ n : a resistor for regulating an electric current by means of variable resistances — rheo·stat·ic \,rē-ə-'sta-tik\ adj

rhe·sus monkey \'rē-səs-\ n : a pale brown Asian monkey often used in medical research

rhet·o·ric \'re-tə-rik\ n [ME rethorik, fr. AF rethorique, fr. L rhetorica, fr. Gk rhētorikē, lit., art of oratory, fr. rhētōr public speaker, fr. eirein to speak] : the art of speaking or writing effectively — rhet·o·ri·cian \,re-tə-'ri-shən\ n

rhe·tor·i·cal \ri-'tòr-i-kəl\ adj 1 : of or relating to rhetoric 2 : asked merely for effect with no answer expected ⟨a ∼ question⟩

rheum \'rüm\ n : a watery discharge from the mucous membranes esp. of the eyes or nose — rheumy adj

rheu·mat·ic fever \rù-'ma-tik-\ n : an acute disease chiefly of children and young adults that is characterized by fever, by inflammation and pain in and around the joints, and by inflammation of the membranes surrounding the heart and the heart valves

rheu·ma·tism \'rü-mə-,ti-zəm, 'rù-\ n 1 : any of various conditions marked by stiffness, pain, or swelling in muscles or joints 2 : RHEUMATOID ARTHRITIS — rheu·mat·ic \rù-'ma-tik\ adj

rheu·ma·toid arthritis \-,tòid-\ n : a usu. chronic progressive autoimmune disease characterized by inflammation and swelling of joint structures

rheu·ma·tol·o·gy \,rü-mə-'tä-lə-jē, ,rù-\ n : a medical science dealing with rheumatic diseases — rheu·ma·tol·o·gist \-jist\ n

Rh factor \,är-'āch-\ n [rhesus monkey (in which it was first detected)] : any of one or more inherited substances in red blood cells that may cause dangerous reactions in some infants or in transfusions

rhine·stone \'rīn-,stōn\ n : a colorless imitation stone of high luster made of glass, paste, or gem quartz

rhi·no \'rī-nō\ n, pl rhinos also rhino : RHINOCEROS

rhi·noc·er·os \rī-'nä-sə-rəs\ n, pl -noc·er·os·es also -noc·er·os or -noc·eri \'nä-sə-,rī\ [ME rinoceros, fr. AF, fr. L rhinoceros, fr. Gk rhinokerōs, fr. rhin-, rhis nose + keras horn] : any of a family of large thick-skinned mammals of Africa and Asia with one or two upright horns of keratin on the snout and three toes on each foot

rhinoceros

rhi·zome \'rī-ˌzōm\ *n* : a fleshy, rootlike, and usu. horizontal underground plant stem that forms shoots above and roots below — **rhi·zom·a·tous** \rī-'zā-mə-təs\ *adj*

Rh–neg·a·tive \ˌär-ˌāch-'ne-gə-tiv\ *adj* : lacking Rh factors in the red blood cells

rho \'rō\ *n* : the 17th letter of the Greek alphabet — P or ρ

rho·di·um \'rō-dē-əm\ *n* : a rare hard ductile metallic chemical element

rho·do·den·dron \ˌrō-də-'den-drən\ *n* : any of a genus of shrubs or trees of the heath family with clusters of large bright flowers

rhom·boid \'räm-ˌbȯid\ *n* : a parallelogram with unequal adjacent sides and angles that are not right angles — **rhomboid** *or* **rhom·boi·dal** \räm-'bȯi-dᵊl\ *adj*

rhom·bus \'räm-bəs\ *n, pl* **rhom·bus·es** *or* **rhom·bi** \-ˌbī\ : a parallelogram having all four sides equal

Rh–pos·i·tive \ˌär-ˌäch-'pä-zə-tiv\ *adj* : containing one or more Rh factors in the red blood cells

rhu·barb \'rü-ˌbärb\ *n* [ME *rubarbe*, fr. AF *reubarbe*, fr. ML *reubarbarum*, alter. of *rha barbarum*, lit., barbarian rhubarb] : a garden plant related to the buckwheat having leaves with thick juicy edible pink and red stems

¹rhyme *also* **rime** \'rīm\ *n* 1 : a composition in verse that rhymes; *also* : POETRY 2 : correspondence in terminal sounds (as of two lines of verse)

²rhyme *also* **rime** *vb* **rhymed** *also* **rimed; rhym·ing** *also* **rim·ing** 1 : to make rhymes; *also* : to write poetry 2 : to have rhymes : be in rhyme

rhythm \'ri-t̠həm\ *n* 1 : regular rise and fall in the flow of sound in speech 2 : a movement or activity in which some action or element recurs regularly — **rhyth·mic** \'rith-mik\ *or* **rhyth·mi·cal** \-mi-kəl\ *adj* — **rhyth·mi·cal·ly** \-k(ə-)lē\ *adv*

rhythm and blues *n* : popular music based on blues and African American folk music

rhythm method *n* : birth control by refraining from sexual intercourse during the time when ovulation is most likely to occur

RI *abbr* Rhode Island

ri·al \rē-'ȯl, -'äl\ *n* — see MONEY table

¹rib \'rib\ *n* 1 : any of the series of curved bones of the chest of most vertebrates that are joined to the backbone in pairs and help to support the body wall and protect the organs inside 2 : something resembling a rib in shape or function 3 : an elongated ridge (as in fabric)

²rib *vb* **ribbed; rib·bing** 1 : to furnish or strengthen with ribs 2 : to knit so as to form ridges

³rib *vb* **ribbed; rib·bing** : to poke fun at : TEASE — **rib·ber** *n*

rib·ald \'ri-bəld\ *adj* : coarse or indecent esp. in language ⟨~ jokes⟩ — **rib·ald·ry** \-bəl-drē\ *n*

rib·and \'ri-bənd\ *n* : RIBBON

rib·bon \'ri-bən\ *n* 1 : a narrow fabric typically of silk or velvet used for trimming and for badges 2 : a strip of inked cloth (as in a typewriter) 3 : TATTER, SHRED ⟨torn to ~s⟩

ri·bo·fla·vin \ˌrī-bə-'flā-vən, 'rī-bə-ˌflā-vən\ *n* : a growth-promoting vitamin of the vitamin B complex occurring esp. in milk and liver

ri·bo·nu·cle·ic acid \ˌrī-bō-nü-ˌklē-ik-, -nyü-, -ˌklā-\ *n* : RNA

ri·bose \'rī-ˌbōs\ *n* : a sugar with five carbon atoms and five oxygen atoms in each molecule that is part of RNA

ri·bo·some \'rī-bə-ˌsōm\ *n* : any of the RNA-rich cytoplasmic granules in a cell that are sites of protein synthesis — **ri·bo·som·al** \ˌrī-bə-'sō-məl\ *adj*

rice \'rīs\ *n* : the starchy seeds of an annual grass that are cooked and used for food; *also* : this widely cultivated grass of warm wet areas

rich \'rich\ *adj* 1 : possessing or controlling great wealth : WEALTHY 2 : COSTLY, VALUABLE 3 : deep and pleasing in color or tone 4 : ABUNDANT 5 : containing much sugar, fat, or seasoning; *also* : high in combustible content 6 : FRUITFUL, FERTILE — **rich·ly** *adv* — **rich·ness** *n*

rich·es \'ri-chəz\ *n pl* [ME, sing. or pl., fr. *richesse* wealth, fr. AF *richesce*, fr. *riche* rich] : things that make one rich : WEALTH

Rich·ter scale \'rik-tər-\ *n* : a scale for expressing the magnitude of a seismic disturbance (as an earthquake) in terms of the energy dissipated in it

rick \'rik\ *n* : a large stack (as of hay) in the open air

rick·ets \'ri-kəts\ *n* : a childhood deficiency disease marked esp. by soft deformed bones and caused by lack of vitamin D

rick·ett·sia \ri-'ket-sē-ə\ *n, pl* **-si·as** *or* **-si·ae** \-sē-ˌē\ : any of a group of usu. rod-shaped bacteria that cause various diseases (as typhus)

rick·ety \'ri-kə-tē\ *adj* 1 : affected with rickets 2 : SHAKY; *also* : in unsound physical condition ⟨~ stairs⟩

rick·shaw *also* **rick·sha** \'rik-ˌshȯ\ *n* : a small covered 2-wheeled carriage pulled by one person and used orig. in Japan

rickshaw

¹ric·o·chet \'ri-kə-ˌshā, *Brit also* -ˌshet\ *n* [F] : a bouncing off at an angle (as of a bullet off a wall); *also* : an object that ricochets

²ricochet *vb* **-cheted** \-ˌshād\ *also* **-chet·ted** \-ˌshe-təd\; **-chet·ing** \-ˌshā-iŋ\ *or* **-chet·ting** \-ˌshe-tiŋ\ : to bounce or skip with or as if with a glancing rebound

ri·cot·ta \ri-'kä-tə, -'kȯ-\ *n* : a white unripened whey cheese of Italy that resembles cottage cheese

rid \'rid\ *vb* **rid** *also* **rid·ded; rid·ding** : to make free : CLEAR, RELIEVE ⟨~ the house of mice⟩ — **rid·dance** \'ri-dᵊns\ *n*

rid·den \'ri-dᵊn\ *adj* 1 : harassed, oppressed, or obsessed by ⟨debt-*ridden*⟩ 2 : excessively full of or supplied with ⟨slum-*ridden*⟩

¹rid·dle \'ri-dᵊl\ *n* : a puzzling question to be solved or answered by guessing

²riddle *vb* **rid·dled; rid·dling** 1 : EXPLAIN, SOLVE 2 : to speak in riddles

³riddle *n* : a coarse sieve

⁴riddle *vb* **rid·dled; rid·dling** 1 : to sift with a riddle 2 : to pierce with many holes 3 : PERMEATE

¹ride \'rīd\ *vb* **rode** \'rōd\; **rid·den** \'ri-dᵊn\; **rid·ing** 1 : to go on an animal's back or in a conveyance (as a boat, car, or airplane); *also* : to sit on and control so as to be carried along ⟨~ a bicycle⟩ 2 : to float or move on water ⟨~ at anchor⟩; *also* : to move like a floating object 3 : to bear along : CARRY ⟨*rode* her on their shoulders⟩ 4 : to travel over a surface ⟨the car ~s well⟩ 5 : to proceed over on horseback 6 : to torment by nagging or teasing

²ride *n* 1 : an act of riding; *esp* : a trip on horseback or by vehicle 2 : a way (as a road or path) suitable for riding 3 : a mechanical device (as a merry-go-round) for riding on 4 : a means of transportation

rid·er \'rī-dər\ *n* 1 : one that rides 2 : an addition to a document often attached on a separate piece of paper 3 : a clause dealing with an unrelated matter attached to a legislative bill during passage — **rid·er·less** *adj*

¹ridge \'rij\ *n* [ME *rigge*, fr. OE *hrycg*] 1 : an elevated body part or structure 2 : a range of hills 3 : a raised line or strip 4 : the line made where two sloping surfaces (as of a roof) meet — **ridgy** *adj*

²ridge *vb* **ridged; ridg·ing** 1 : to form into a ridge 2 : to extend in ridges

¹rid·i·cule \'ri-də-ˌkyül\ *n* : the act of ridiculing : DERISION, MOCKERY

²ridicule *vb* **-culed; -cul·ing** : to laugh at or make fun of mockingly or contemptuously ⟨was *ridiculed* by his peers⟩ ✦ **Synonyms** DERIDE, TAUNT, TWIT, MOCK

ri·dic·u·lous \rə-'di-kyə-ləs\ *adj* : arousing or deserving ridicule : ABSURD, PREPOSTEROUS ✦ **Synonyms** LAUGHABLE, LUDICROUS, FARCICAL, RISIBLE — **ri·dic·u·lous·ly** *adv* — **ri·dic·u·lous·ness** *n*

rid·ley \'rid-lē\ *n* : either of two relatively small sea turtles

ri·el \rē-'el\ *n* — see MONEY table

Ries·ling \'rēz-liŋ, 'rēs-\ *n* : a sweet to very dry white wine made from a single variety of grape orig. grown in Germany

RIF *abbr* reduction in force

rife \'rīf\ *adj* : WIDESPREAD, PREVALENT, ABOUNDING — **rife** *adv* — **rife·ly** *adv*

¹riff \'rif\ *n* 1 : a repeated phrase in jazz typically supporting a solo improvisation; *also* : a piece based on such a phrase 2 : a usu. witty or improvised remark or outpouring 3 : a distinct variation : TAKE — **riff** *vb*

riff·raff \'rif-ˌraf\ *n* [ME *riffe raffe*, fr. *rif and raf* every single one, fr. AF *rif et raf* altogether] 1 : RABBLE ⟨did not associate with the ∼⟩ 2 : REFUSE, RUBBISH

¹ri·fle \'rī-fəl\ *vb* **ri·fled; ri·fling** : to ransack esp. with the intent to steal — **ri·fler** *n*

²rifle *vb* **ri·fled; ri·fling** : to cut spiral grooves into the bore of ⟨*rifled* pipe⟩ — **rifling** *n*

³rifle *n* 1 : a shoulder weapon with a rifled bore 2 *pl* : soldiers armed with rifles — **ri·fle·man** \-fəl-mən\ *n*

rift \'rift\ *n* 1 : CLEFT, FISSURE 2 : FAULT 6 3 : ESTRANGEMENT, SEPARATION ⟨a ∼ between spouses⟩ — **rift** *vb*

¹rig \'rig\ *vb* **rigged; rig·ging** 1 : to fit out (as a ship) with rigging 2 : CLOTHE, DRESS 3 : EQUIP 4 : to set up esp. as a makeshift ⟨∼ up a shelter⟩

²rig *n* 1 : the distinctive shape, number, and arrangement of sails and masts of a ship 2 : a carriage with its horse 3 : CLOTHING, DRESS 4 : EQUIPMENT

³rig *vb* **rigged; rig·ging** 1 : to manipulate or control esp. by deceptive or dishonest means 2 : to fix in advance for a desired result — **rig·ger** *n*

rig·ging \'ri-giŋ, -gən\ *n* 1 : the ropes and chains that hold and move masts, sails, and spars of a ship 2 : a network (as in theater scenery) used for support and manipulation

¹right \'rīt\ *adj* 1 : RIGHTEOUS, UPRIGHT 2 : JUST, PROPER 3 : conforming to truth or fact : CORRECT 4 : APPROPRIATE, SUITABLE 5 : STRAIGHT ⟨a ∼ line⟩ 6 : GENUINE, REAL 7 : of, relating to, or being the side of the body which is away from the side on which the heart is mostly located 8 : located nearer to the right hand; *esp* : being on the right when facing in the same direction as the observer 9 : made to be placed or worn outward ⟨∼ side of a rug⟩ 10 : NORMAL, SOUND ⟨not in her ∼ mind⟩ ✦ *Synonyms* CORRECT, ACCURATE, EXACT, PRECISE, NICE — **right·ness** *n*

²right *n* 1 : qualities that constitute what is correct, just, proper, or honorable 2 : something (as a power or privilege) to which one has a just or lawful claim 3 : just action or decision : the cause of justice 4 : the side or part that is on or toward the right side 5 *cap* : political conservatives 6 *often cap* : a conservative position — **right·ward** \-wərd\ *adj or adv*

³right *adv* 1 : according to what is right ⟨live ∼⟩ 2 : EXACTLY, PRECISELY ⟨∼ here and now⟩ 3 : DIRECTLY ⟨went ∼ home⟩ 4 : according to fact or truth ⟨guess ∼⟩ 5 : all the way : COMPLETELY ⟨∼ to the end⟩ 6 : IMMEDIATELY ⟨∼ after lunch⟩ 7 : QUITE, VERY ⟨∼ nice weather⟩ 8 : on or to the right ⟨looked ∼ and left⟩

⁴right *vb* 1 : to relieve from wrong 2 : to adjust or restore to a proper state or position 3 : to bring or restore to an upright position 4 : to become upright — **right·er** *n*

right angle *n* : an angle whose measure is 90° : an angle whose sides are perpendicular to each other — **right-an·gled** \'rīt-'aŋ-gəld\ *or* **right-an·gle** \-gəl\ *adj*

right circular cone *n* : CONE 2

right–click \'rīt-'klik\ *vb* : to press the rightmost button on a computer mouse or similar input device

righ·teous \'rī-chəs\ *adj* : acting or being in accordance with what is just, honorable, and free from guilt or wrong : UPRIGHT ✦ *Synonyms* VIRTUOUS, NOBLE, MORAL, ETHICAL — **righ·teous·ly** *adv* — **righ·teous·ness** *n*

right·ful \'rīt-fəl\ *adj* 1 : JUST; *also* : FITTING 2 : having or held by a legally just claim — **right·ful·ly** *adv* — **right·ful·ness** *n*

right–hand \'rīt-ˌhand\ *adj* 1 : situated on the right 2 : RIGHT-HANDED 3 : chiefly relied on ⟨his ∼ man⟩

right–hand·ed \-'han-dəd\ *adj* 1 : using the right hand habitually or better than the left 2 : designed for or done with the right hand 3 : CLOCKWISE ⟨a ∼ twist⟩ — **right–handed** *adv* — **right–hand·ed·ly** *adv* — **right–hand·ed·ness** *n*

right·ly \'rīt-lē\ *adv* 1 : FAIRLY, JUSTLY 2 : PROPERLY 3 : CORRECTLY, EXACTLY

right–of–way *n, pl* **rights–of–way** 1 : a legal right of passage over another person's ground 2 : the area over which a right-of-way exists 3 : the land on which a public road is built 4 : the land occupied by a railroad 5 : the land used by a public utility 6 : the right of traffic to take precedence over other traffic

right on *interj* — used to express agreement or give encouragement

right–to–life *adj* : ANTIABORTION — **right–to–lifer** *n*

right triangle *n* : a triangle having one right angle

right whale *n* : any of a family of large baleen whales having a very large head on a stocky body

rig·id \'ri-jəd\ *adj* 1 : lacking flexibility 2 : strictly observed ✦ *Synonyms* SEVERE, STERN, RIGOROUS, STRINGENT — **ri·gid·i·ty** \rə-'ji-də-tē\ *n* — **rig·id·ly** *adv*

rig·ma·role \'ri-gə-mə-ˌrōl\ *n* [alter. of obs. *ragman roll* long list, catalog] 1 : confused or senseless talk 2 : a complex and ritualistic procedure

rig·or \'ri-gər\ *n* 1 : the quality of being inflexible or unyielding : STRICTNESS 2 : HARSHNESS, SEVERITY 3 : a tremor caused by a chill 4 : strict precision : EXACTNESS ⟨scientific ∼⟩ — **rig·or·ous** *adj* — **rig·or·ous·ly** *adv*

rig·or mor·tis \ˌri-gər-'mȯr-təs\ *n* [NL, stiffness of death] : temporary rigidity of muscles occurring after death

rig·our *chiefly Brit var of* RIGOR

rile \'rī(-ə)l\ *vb* **riled; ril·ing** 1 : to make angry 2 : ROIL 1

rill \'ril\ *n* : a very small brook

¹rim \'rim\ *n* 1 : the outer part of a wheel 2 : an outer edge esp. of something curved : BORDER, MARGIN

²rim *vb* **rimmed; rim·ming** 1 : to serve as a rim for : BORDER 2 : to run around the rim of

¹rime \'rīm\ *n* : FROST 2 — **rimy** \'rī-mē\ *adj*

²rime *var of* RHYME

rind \'rīnd\ *n* : a usu. hard or tough outer layer ⟨lemon ∼⟩

¹ring \'riŋ\ *n* 1 : a circular band worn as an ornament or token or used for holding or fastening ⟨wedding ∼⟩ ⟨key ∼⟩ 2 : something circular in shape ⟨smoke ∼⟩ 3 : a place for contest or display ⟨boxing ∼⟩; *also* : PRIZEFIGHTING 4 : ANNUAL RING 5 : a group of people who work together for selfish or dishonest purposes ⟨a ∼ of smugglers⟩ — **ringed** *adj* — **ring·like** \'riŋ-ˌlīk\ *adj*

²ring *vb* **ringed; ring·ing** \'riŋ-iŋ\ 1 : ENCIRCLE 2 : to throw a ring over (a mark) in a game (as quoits) 3 : to move in a ring or spirally

³ring *vb* **rang** \'raŋ\; **rung** \'rəŋ\; **ring·ing** \'riŋ-iŋ\ 1 : to sound resonantly when struck; *also* : to feel as if filled with such sound 2 : to cause to make a clear metallic sound by striking 3 : to announce or call by or as if by striking a bell ⟨∼ an alarm⟩ 4 : to repeat loudly and persistently 5 : to summon esp. by a bell ⟨∼ for the butler⟩ — **ring a bell** : to arouse a response ⟨that name *rings a bell*⟩

⁴ring *n* 1 : a set of bells 2 : the clear resonant sound of vibrating metal 3 : resonant tone : SONORITY 4 : a sound or character expressive of a particular quality 5 : an act or instance of ringing; *esp* : a telephone call

¹ring·er \'riŋ-ər\ *n* 1 : one that sounds by ringing 2 : one that enters a competition under false representations 3 : one that closely resembles another

²ringer *n* : one that encircles or puts a ring around

ring finger *n* : the third finger of the left hand counting the index finger as the first

ring·git \'riŋ-git\ *n* — see MONEY table

ring·lead·er \'riŋ-ˌlē-dər\ *n* : a leader esp. of a group of troublemakers

ring·let \-lət\ *n* : a long curl

ring·mas·ter \-ˌmas-tər\ *n* : one in charge of performances in a circus ring

ring·tone \'riŋ-ˌtōn\ *n* : the sound made by a cell phone to signal an incoming call

ring up *vb* 1 : to total and record esp. by means of a cash register 2 : ACHIEVE ⟨*rang up* many triumphs⟩

ring·worm \'riŋ-ˌwərm\ *n* : any of several contagious skin diseases caused by fungi and marked by ring-shaped discolored patches

rink \'riŋk\ *n* : a level extent of ice marked off for skating or various games; *also* : a similar surface (as of wood) marked off or enclosed for a sport or game ⟨roller-skating ~⟩

¹**rinse** \'rins\ *vb* **rinsed; rins·ing** [ME *rincen*, AF *rincer*, alter. of OF *recincier*, fr. VL **recentiare*, fr. L *recent-*, *recens* fresh, recent] **1** : to wash lightly or in water only **2** : to cleanse (as of soap) with clear water **3** : to treat (hair) with a rinse — **rins·er** *n*

²**rinse** *n* **1** : an act of rinsing **2** : a liquid used for rinsing **3** : a solution that temporarily tints hair

ri·ot \'rī-ət\ *n* **1** *archaic* : disorderly behavior **2** : disturbance of the public peace; *esp* : a violent public disorder **3** : random or disorderly profusion ⟨a ~ of color⟩ **4** : one that is wildly amusing ⟨the comedy is a ~⟩ — **riot** *vb* — **ri·ot·er** *n* — **ri·ot·ous** *adj*

¹**rip** \'rip\ *vb* **ripped; rip·ping** **1** : to cut or tear open **2** : to saw or split (wood) with the grain **3** : CRITICIZE, DISPARAGE ⟨*ripped* into the team⟩ — **rip·per** *n*

²**rip** *n* : a rent made by ripping

RIP *abbr* [L *requiescat in pace*] may he rest in peace, may she rest in peace; [L *requiescant in pace*] may they rest in peace

ri·par·i·an \rə-'per-ē-ən\ *adj* : of or relating to the bank of a stream, river, or lake ⟨~ trees⟩

rip cord *n* : a cord that is pulled to release a parachute out of its container

ripe \'rīp\ *adj* **rip·er; rip·est** **1** : fully grown and developed : MATURE ⟨~ fruit⟩ **2** : fully prepared : READY ⟨slaves ~ for a revolt⟩ — **ripe·ly** *adv* — **ripe·ness** *n*

rip·en \'rī-pən\ *vb* **rip·ened; rip·en·ing** **1** : to grow or make ripe **2** : to bring to completeness or perfection; *also* : to age or cure (cheese) to develop characteristic flavor, odor, body, texture, and color

rip–off \'rip-ˌȯf\ *n* **1** : an act of stealing : THEFT **2** : a cheap imitation — **rip off** *vb*

ri·poste \ri-'pōst\ *n* [F, modif. of It *risposta*, lit., answer] **1** : a fencer's return thrust after a parry **2** : a retaliatory maneuver or response; *esp* : a quick retort — **riposte** *vb*

ripped \'ript\ *adj* : having high muscle definition ⟨a ~ body⟩

rip·ple \'ri-pəl\ *vb* **rip·pled; rip·pling** **1** : to become lightly ruffled on the surface **2** : to make a sound like that of rippling water — **ripple** *n*

rip·saw \'rip-ˌsȯ\ *n* : a coarse-toothed saw used to cut wood in the direction of the grain

rip·stop \-ˌstäp\ *adj* : being a fabric woven in such a way that small tears do not spread ⟨~ nylon⟩ — **ripstop** *n*

¹**rise** \'rīz\ *vb* **rose** \'rōz\; **ris·en** \'ri-zᵊn\; **ris·ing** **1** : to get up from sitting, kneeling, or lying **2** : to get up from sleep or from one's bed **3** : to return from death **4** : to take up arms **5** : to end a session : ADJOURN **6** : to appear above the horizon **7** : to move upward : ASCEND **8** : to extend above other objects **9** : to attain a higher level or rank **10** : to increase in quantity, intensity, or pitch **11** : to come into being : HAPPEN, BEGIN, ORIGINATE

²**rise** *n* **1** : a spot higher than surrounding ground **2** : an upward slope **3** : an act of rising : a state of being risen **4** : BEGINNING, ORIGIN **5** : the elevation of one point above another **6** : an increase in amount, number, or volume **7** : an angry reaction ⟨tried to get a ~ out of me⟩

ris·er \'rī-zər\ *n* **1** : one that rises **2** : the upright part between stair treads

ris·i·bil·i·ty \ˌri-zə-'bi-lə-tē\ *n, pl* **-ties** : the ability or inclination to laugh — often used in pl.

ris·i·ble \'ri-zə-bəl\ *adj* **1** : able or inclined to laugh **2** : arousing laughter; *esp* : amusingly ridiculous

¹**risk** \'risk\ *n* **1** : exposure to possible loss or injury : DANGER, PERIL ⟨health ~s⟩ **2** : the chance that an investment will lose value — **risk·i·ness** \'ris-kē-nəs\ *n* — **risky** *adj*

²**risk** *vb* **1** : to expose to danger ⟨~*ed* his life⟩ **2** : to incur the danger of

ri·sot·to \ri-'sȯ-tō, -'zȯ-\ *n, pl* **-tos** : rice cooked usu. in meat or seafood stock and seasoned

ris·qué \ris-'kā\ *adj* [F] : verging on impropriety or indecency ⟨~ jokes⟩

ri·tard \ri-'tärd\ *adv or adj* : with a gradual slackening in tempo — used as a direction in music

rite \'rīt\ *n* **1** : a set form for conducting a ceremony **2** : the liturgy of a church **3** : a ceremonial act or action

rit·u·al \'ri-chə-wəl\ *n* **1** : the established form esp. for a religious ceremony **2** : a system of rites **3** : a ceremonial act or action **4** : an act or series of acts regularly repeated in a precise manner — **ritual** *adj* — **rit·u·al·ism**

\-wə-ˌli-zəm\ *n* — **rit·u·al·is·tic** \ˌri-chə-wə-'lis-tik\ *adj* — **rit·u·al·is·ti·cal·ly** \-ti-k(ə-)lē\ *adv* — **rit·u·al·ly** *adv*

ritzy \'rit-sē\ *adj* **ritz·i·er; -est** : showily elegant : POSH

riv *abbr* river

¹**ri·val** \'rī-vəl\ *n* [MF or L; MF, fr. L *rivalis* one using the same stream as another, rival in love, fr. *rivalis* of a stream, fr. *rivus* stream] **1** : one of two or more trying to get what only one can have **2** : one striving for competitive advantage **3** : one that equals most esp. in desired qualities : MATCH, PEER

²**rival** *adj* : COMPETING

³**rival** *vb* **-valed** *or* **-valled; -val·ing** *or* **-val·ling** **1** : to be in competition with **2** : to try to equal or excel **3** : to have qualities that approach or equal another's

ri·val·ry \'rī-vəl-rē\ *n, pl* **-ries** : COMPETITION

rive \'rīv\ *vb* **rived** \'rīvd\; **riv·en** \'ri-vən\ *also* **rived; riv·ing** **1** : SPLIT, REND **2** : SHATTER ⟨nations *riven* by war⟩

riv·er \'ri-vər\ *n* **1** : a natural stream larger than a brook **2** : a large stream or flow

riv·er·bank \-ˌbaŋk\ *n* : the bank of a river

riv·er·bed \-ˌbed\ *n* : the channel occupied by a river

riv·er·boat \-ˌbōt\ *n* : a boat for use on a river

riv·er·front \-ˌfrənt\ *n* : the land or area along a river

riv·er·side \-ˌsīd\ *n* : the side or bank of a river

¹**riv·et** \'ri-vət\ *n* : a metal bolt with a head at one end used to join parts by being put through holes in them and then being flattened on the plain end to make another head

²**rivet** *vb* : to fasten with or as if with a rivet — **riv·et·er** *n*

riv·u·let \'ri-vyə-lət, -və-\ *n* : a small stream

ri·yal *also* **ri·al** \rē-'äl, -'al\ *n* — see MONEY table

rm *abbr* room

Rn *symbol* radon

¹**RN** \ˌär-'en\ *n* : REGISTERED NURSE

²**RN** *abbr* Royal Navy

RNA \ˌär-(ˌ)en-'ä\ *n* : any of various nucleic acids (as messenger RNA) that are found esp. in the cytoplasm of cells, have ribose as the 5-carbon sugar, and are associated with the control of cellular chemical activities

rnd *abbr* round

¹**roach** \'rōch\ *n, pl* **roach** *also* **roach·es** : any of various bony fishes related to the carp; *also* : any of several sunfishes

²**roach** *n* **1** : COCKROACH **2** : the butt of a marijuana cigarette

road \'rōd\ *n* [ME *rode*, fr. OE *rād* ride, journey] **1** : ROADSTEAD — often used in pl. **2** : an open way for vehicles, persons, and animals : HIGHWAY **3** : a way to a conclusion or end ⟨the ~ to success⟩ **4** : a series of scheduled visits (as games or performances) in several locations or the travel necessary to make these visits ⟨the team is on the ~⟩

road·bed \'rōd-ˌbed\ *n* **1** : the foundation of a road or railroad **2** : the part of the surface of a road on which vehicles travel

road·block \-ˌbläk\ *n* **1** : a barricade on the road ⟨a police ~⟩ **2** : an obstruction to progress

road·ie \'rō-dē\ *n* : a person who works for traveling entertainers

road·kill \'rōd-ˌkil\ *n* **1** : the remains of an animal that has been killed on a road by a motor vehicle **2** : one that falls victim to intense competition ⟨political ~⟩

road·run·ner \-ˌrə-nər\ *n* : a largely terrestrial bird of the southwestern U.S. and Mexico that is a speedy runner

roadrunner

roadside • roll

road·side \'rōd-ˌsīd\ *n* : the strip of land along a road — **roadside** *adj*
road·stead \-ˌsted\ *n* : an anchorage for ships usu. less sheltered than a harbor
road·ster \'rōd-stər\ *n* **1** : a driving horse **2** : an open automobile that seats two often with a storage compartment or rumble seat in the rear
road·way \-ˌwā\ *n* : ROAD; *esp* : ROADBED
road·work \-ˌwərk\ *n* **1** : work done in constructing or repairing roads **2** : conditioning for an athletic contest (as a boxing match) consisting mainly of long runs
roam \'rōm\ *vb* **1** : WANDER, ROVE **2** : to range or wander over or about **3** : to use a cell phone outside one's local calling area
¹roan \'rōn\ *adj* : of dark color (as black, red, or brown) sprinkled with white ⟨a ~ horse⟩
²roan *n* : an animal (as a horse) with a roan coat; *also* : its color
¹roar \'rȯr\ *vb* **1** : to utter a full loud prolonged sound **2** : to make a loud confused sound (as of wind or waves) — **roar·er** *n*
²roar *n* : a sound of roaring
¹roast \'rōst\ *vb* **1** : to cook by exposure to dry heat or an open flame **2** : to criticize severely or kiddingly
²roast *n* **1** : a piece of meat suitable for roasting **2** : an outing at which food is roasted ⟨corn ~⟩ **3** : severe criticism or kidding
³roast *adj* : ROASTED
roast·er \'rō-stər\ *n* **1** : one that roasts **2** : a device for roasting **3** : something (as a young chicken) fit for roasting
rob \'räb\ *vb* **robbed**; **rob·bing** **1** : to steal from **2** : to deprive of something due or expected **3** : to commit robbery — **rob·ber** *n*
robber fly *n* : any of a family of predaceous flies resembling bumblebees
rob·bery \'rä-bə-rē\ *n, pl* **-ber·ies** : the act or practice of robbing; *esp* : theft of something from a person by use of violence or threat
¹robe \'rōb\ *n* **1** : a long flowing outer garment; *esp* : one used for ceremonial occasions **2** : a wrap or covering for the lower body (as for sitting outdoors)
²robe *vb* **robed**; **rob·ing** **1** : to clothe with or as if with a robe **2** : DRESS
rob·in \'rä-bən\ *n* **1** : a small chiefly European thrush with a somewhat orange face and breast **2** : a large No. American thrush with a grayish back, a streaked throat, and a chiefly dull reddish breast
ro·bo·call \'rō-bō-ˌkȯl\ *n* : a telephone call from an automated source that delivers a message to a large number of people
ro·bot \'rō-ˌbät, -bət\ *n* [Czech, fr. *robota* compulsory labor] **1** : a machine that looks and acts like a human being **2** : an efficient but insensitive person **3** : a device that automatically performs esp. repetitive tasks **4** : something guided by automatic controls — **ro·bot·ic** \rō-'bä-tik\ *adj*
ro·bot·ics \rō-'bä-tiks\ *n* : technology dealing with the design, construction, and operation of robots
ro·bust \rō-'bəst, 'rō-ˌbəst\ *adj* [L *robustus* oaken, strong, fr. *robur* oak, strength] **1** : strong and vigorously healthy **2** : capable of performing without failure under a wide range of conditions ⟨~ software⟩ — **ro·bust·ly** *adv* — **ro·bust·ness** *n*
ROC *abbr* Republic of China (Taiwan)
¹rock \'räk\ *vb* **1** : to move back and forth in or as if in a cradle **2** : to sway or cause to sway back and forth **3** : to arouse to excitement (as with rock music) ⟨~ed the crowd⟩ **4** *slang* : to be extremely enjoyable or effective ⟨this car ~s⟩
²rock *n* **1** : a rocking movement **2** : popular music usu. played on electric instruments and characterized by a strong beat and much repetition
³rock *n* **1** : a mass of stony material; *also* : broken pieces of stone **2** : solid mineral deposits **3** : something like a rock in firmness **4** : GEM; *esp* : DIAMOND — **rock** *adj* — **rock·like** *adj* — **rocky** *adj* — **on the rocks 1** : in a state of ruin ⟨a marriage *on the rocks*⟩ **2** : on ice cubes ⟨bourbon *on the rocks*⟩
rock and roll *n* : ²ROCK 2
rock·bound \'räk-ˌbau̇nd\ *adj* : fringed or covered with rocks

rock·er \'rä-kər\ *n* **1** : one of the curved pieces on which something (as a chair or cradle) rocks **2** : a chair that rocks on rockers **3** : a device that works with a rocking motion **4** : a rock performer, song, or enthusiast
¹rock·et \'rä-kət\ *n* [It *rocchetta*, lit., small distaff] **1** : a firework that is propelled through the air by the discharge of gases produced by a burning substance **2** : a jet engine that operates on the same principle as a firework rocket but carries the oxygen needed for burning its fuel **3** : a rocket-propelled bomb or missile
²rocket *vb* **1** : to convey by means of a rocket **2** : to rise abruptly and rapidly
rock·et·ry \'rä-kə-trē\ *n* : the study or use of rockets
rocket ship *n* : a rocket-propelled spacecraft
rock·fall \'räk-ˌfȯl\ *n* : a mass of falling or fallen rocks
rock·fish \-ˌfish\ *n* : any of various bony fishes that live among rocks or on rocky bottoms
rock salt *n* : common salt in rocklike masses or large crystals
Rocky Mountain sheep *n* : BIGHORN
ro·co·co \rə-'kō-kō\ *adj* [F, irreg. fr. *rocaille* style of ornament, lit., stone debris] : of or relating to an artistic style esp. of the 18th century marked by fanciful curved forms and elaborate ornamentation — **rococo** *n*
rod \'räd\ *n* **1** : a straight slender stick **2** : a stick or bundle of twigs used in punishing a person; *also* : PUNISHMENT **3** : a staff borne to show rank **4** — see WEIGHT table **5** : any of the rod-shaped receptor cells of the retina that are sensitive to faint light **6** *slang* : HANDGUN
rode *past of* RIDE
ro·dent \'rō-dᵊnt\ *n* [ultim. fr. L *rodent-, rodens*, prp. of *rodere* to gnaw] : any of an order of relatively small mammals (as mice, squirrels, and beavers) with sharp front teeth used for gnawing
ro·deo \'rō-dē-ˌō, rə-'dā-ō\ *n, pl* **ro·de·os** [Sp, fr. *rodear* to surround, fr. *rueda* wheel, fr. L *rota*] **1** : ROUNDUP 1 **2** : a public performance featuring cowboy skills (as riding and roping)
¹roe \'rō\ *n, pl* **roe** *or* **roes** : DOE
²roe *n* : the eggs of a fish esp. while bound together in a mass
roe·buck \'rō-ˌbək\ *n, pl* **roebuck** *or* **roebucks** : a male roe deer
roe deer *n* : either of two small nimble European or Asian deers
roent·gen \'rent-gən, 'rənt-, -jən\ *n* : the international unit of measurement for X-rays and gamma rays
roent·gen·i·um \rent-'ge-nē-əm, rənt-, -'je-\ *n* : a short-lived radioactive chemical element
rog·er \'rä-jər\ *interj* — used esp. in radio and signaling to indicate that a message has been received and understood
¹rogue \'rōg\ *n* **1** : a dishonest person : SCOUNDREL **2** : a mischievous person : SCAMP — **rogu·ery** \'rō-gə-rē\ *n* — **rogu·ish** *adj* — **rogu·ish·ly** *adv* — **rogu·ish·ness** *n*
²rogue *adj* **1** : CORRUPT, DISHONEST ⟨~ cops⟩ **2** : of or being a nation whose leaders defy international law or norms
roil \'rȯi(-ə)l, *for 2 also* 'rī(-ə)l\ *vb* **1** : to make cloudy or muddy by stirring up **2** : RILE 1 — **roily** \'rȯi-lē\ *adj*
rois·ter \'rȯi-stər\ *vb* **rois·tered**; **rois·ter·ing** : to engage in noisy revelry : CAROUSE — **rois·ter·er** *n* — **rois·ter·ous** \-stə-rəs\ *adj*
ROK *abbr* Republic of Korea (South Korea)
role *also* **rôle** \'rōl\ *n* **1** : an assigned or assumed character; *also* : a part played (as by an actor) **2** : FUNCTION
role model *n* : a person whose behavior in a particular role is imitated by others
¹roll \'rōl\ *n* [ME *rolle* scroll, fr. AF, fr. ML *rolla*, alter. of *rotula*, fr. L, dim. of *rota* wheel] **1** : a document containing an official record **2** : an official list of names **3** : bread baked in a small rounded mass **4** : something that rolls : ROLLER
²roll *vb* **1** : to move by causing to tumble or swivel ⟨~ dice⟩ ⟨~ed her eyes⟩ **2** : to press with a roller ⟨~ dough⟩ **3** : to move on wheels **4** : to sound with a full reverberating tone **5** : to make a continuous beating sound (as on a drum) **6** : to utter with a trill **7** : to move onward as if by completing a revolution ⟨years ~ed by⟩ **8** : to flow or seem to flow in a continuous stream or with a rising and falling motion ⟨the river ~ed on⟩ **9** : to swing or sway from side to side **10** : to shape or become shaped

in rounded form ⟨∼ up the paper⟩ **11** : to move by or as if by turning a crank ⟨∼down the window⟩

³roll *n* **1** : a sound produced by rapid strokes on a drum **2** : a heavy reverberating sound **3** : a rolling movement or action **4** : a swaying movement (as of a ship) **5** : a somersault made in contact with the ground

roll·back \'rōl-ˌbak\ *n* : the act or an instance of rolling back

roll back *vb* **1** : to reduce (as a commodity price) on a national scale **2** : to cause to withdraw : push back

roll bar *n* : an overhead metal bar on an automobile designed to protect riders in case the automobile overturns

roll call *n* : the act or an instance of calling off a list of names (as of soldiers); *also* : a time for a roll call

roll·er \'rō-lər\ *n* **1** : a revolving cylinder used for moving, pressing, shaping, applying, or smoothing something **2** : a rod on which something is rolled up **3** : a long heavy ocean wave

roll·er coast·er \'rō-lər-ˌkō-stər\ *n* : an amusement ride consisting of an elevated railway having sharp curves and steep slopes

roller skate *n* : a skate with wheels instead of a runner — **roller–skate** *vb* — **roller skater** *n*

rol·lick \'rä-lik\ *vb* : ROMP, FROLIC

rol·lick·ing *adj* : full of fun and high spirits ⟨a ∼ good time⟩

roly–poly \ˌrō-lē-'pō-lē\ *adj* : ROTUND

Rom *abbr* **1** Roman **2** Romance **3** Romania; Romanian **4** Romans

ROM \'räm\ *n* : a computer memory that contains special-purpose information (as a program) which cannot be altered

ro·maine \rō-'mān\ *n* [F, lit., Roman] : a garden lettuce with a tall loose head of long crisp leaves

¹Ro·man \'rō-mən\ *n* **1** : a native or resident of Rome **2** *not cap* : roman letters or type

²Roman *adj* **1** : of or relating to Rome or the Romans and esp. the ancient Romans **2** *not cap* : relating to type in which the letters are upright **3** : of or relating to the Roman Catholic Church

Roman candle *n* : a cylindrical firework that discharges balls of fire

Roman Catholic *adj* : of, relating to, or being a Christian church led by the pope and having a liturgy centered in the Mass — **Roman Catholicism** *n*

¹ro·mance \rō-'mans, 'rō-ˌmans\ *n* [ME *romauns*, fr. AF *romanz* French, something written in French, tale in verse, fr. ML *Romanice* in a vernacular language, ultim. fr. L *Romanus* Roman] **1** : a medieval tale of knightly adventure **2** : a prose narrative dealing with heroic or mysterious events set in a remote time or place **3** : a love story **4** : a romantic attachment or episode between lovers — **ro·manc·er** *n*

²romance *vb* **ro·manced**; **ro·manc·ing** **1** : to exaggerate or invent detail or incident **2** : to have romantic fancies **3** : to carry on a romantic episode with

Ro·mance \rō-'mans, 'rō-ˌmans\ *adj* : of or relating to any of several languages developed from Latin

Ro·ma·nian \rū-'mā-nē-ən, rō-, -nyən\ *also* **Ru·ma·nian** \rū-\ *n* **1** : a native or inhabitant of Romania **2** : the language of the Romanians

Roman numeral *n* : a numeral in a system of notation that is based on the ancient Roman system

Ro·ma·no \rō-'mä-nō\ *n* : a hard Italian cheese that is sharper than Parmesan

Ro·mans \'rō-mənz\ *n* — see BIBLE table

¹ro·man·tic \rō-'man-tik\ *adj* **1** : IMAGINARY **2** : VISIONARY **3** : having an imaginative or emotional appeal **4** : of, relating to, or having the characteristics of romanticism — **ro·man·ti·cal·ly** \-ti-k(ə-)lē\ *adv*

²romantic *n* : a romantic person; *esp* : a romantic writer, composer, or artist

ro·man·ti·cism \rō-'man-tə-ˌsi-zəm\ *n, often cap* : a literary movement (as in early 19th century England) marked esp. by emphasis on the imagination and the emotions and by the use of autobiographical material — **ro·man·ti·cist** \-sist\ *n, often cap*

ro·man·ti·cize \-'man-tə-ˌsīz\ *vb* **-cized**; **-ciz·ing** **1** : to make romantic **2** : to have romantic ideas

romp \'rämp\ *vb* **1** : to play actively and noisily **2** : to win a contest easily — **romp** *n*

romp·er \'räm-pər\ *n* **1** : one that romps **2** : a jumpsuit usu. for infants — usu. used in pl.

rood \'rüd\ *n* : CROSS, CRUCIFIX

¹roof \'rüf, 'rů̇f\ *n, pl* **roofs** \'rüfs, 'rů̇fs; 'rüvz, 'rů̇vz\ **1** : the upper covering part of a building **2** : something suggesting a roof of a building — **roofed** \'rüft, 'rů̇ft\ *adj* — **roof·ing** *n* — **roof·less** *adj* — **through the roof** : to an extremely high level ⟨prices went *through the roof*⟩

²roof *vb* : to cover with a roof

roof·top \-ˌtäp\ *n* : a roof esp. of a house

¹rook \'ru̇k\ *n* : a crow that nests and roosts in usu. treetop colonies

²rook *vb* : CHEAT, SWINDLE

³rook *n* : a chess piece that can move parallel to the sides of the board across any number of unoccupied squares

rook·ery \'ru̇-kə-rē\ *n, pl* **-er·ies** : a breeding ground or haunt of gregarious birds or mammals; *also* : a colony of such birds or mammals

rook·ie \'ru̇-kē\ *n* : BEGINNER, RECRUIT; *esp* : a first-year player in a professional sport

¹room \'rüm, 'ru̇m\ *n* **1** : an extent of space occupied by or sufficient or available for something **2** : a partitioned part of a building : CHAMBER; *also* : the people in a room **3** : OPPORTUNITY, CHANCE ⟨∼ to develop his talents⟩ — **room·ful** *n* — **roomy** *adj*

²room *vb* : to occupy or share lodgings : LODGE — **room·er** *n*

room·ette \rü-'met, ru̇-\ *n* : a small private room on a railroad sleeping car

room·ie \'rü-mē, 'ru̇-\ *n* : ROOMMATE

room·mate \'rüm-ˌmāt, 'ru̇m-\ *n* : one of two or more persons sharing the same room or dwelling

¹roost \'rüst\ *n* : a support on which or a place where birds perch

²roost *vb* : to settle on or as if on a roost

roost·er \'rüs-tər, 'ru̇s-\ *n* : an adult male domestic chicken : COCK

¹root \'rüt, 'ru̇t\ *n* **1** : the leafless usu. underground part of a seed plant that functions in absorption, aeration, and storage or as a means of anchorage; *also* : an underground plant part esp. when fleshy and edible **2** : something (as the basal part of a tooth or hair) resembling a root **3** : SOURCE, ORIGIN; *esp* : ANCESTRY — usu. used in pl. **4** : the essential core : HEART ⟨get to the ∼ of the matter⟩ **5** : a number that when taken as a factor an indicated number of times gives a specified number **6** : the lower part — **root·less** *adj* — **root·like** *adj*

²root *vb* **1** : to form roots **2** : to fix or become fixed by or as if by roots : ESTABLISH **2** : UPROOT

³root *vb* **1** : to turn up or dig with the snout ⟨pigs ∼*ing*⟩ **2** : to poke or dig around (as in search of something)

⁴root \'rüt\ *vb* **1** : to applaud or encourage noisily : CHEER **2** : to wish success or lend support to — **root·er** *n*

root beer *n* : a sweetened carbonated beverage flavored with extracts of roots and herbs

root canal *n* : a dental operation to save a tooth by removing the pulp in the root of the tooth and filling the cavity with a protective substance

root·let \'rüt-lət, 'ru̇t-\ *n* : a small root

root·stock \-ˌstäk\ *n* : an underground part of a plant that resembles a rhizome

¹rope \'rōp\ *n* **1** : a large strong cord made of strands of fiber **2** : a hangman's noose **3** : a thick string (as of pearls) made by twisting or braiding

²rope *vb* **roped**; **rop·ing** **1** : to bind, tie, or fasten together with a rope **2** : to separate or divide by means of a rope **3** : LASSO

Ror·schach test \'rȯr-ˌshäk-\ *n* : a psychological test in which a subject interprets ink-blot designs in terms that reveal intellectual and emotional factors

ro·sa·ry \'rō-zə-rē\ *n, pl* **-ries** **1** *often cap* : a Roman Catholic devotion consisting of meditation on sacred mysteries during recitation of Hail Marys **2** : a string of beads used in praying

¹rose *past of* RISE

²rose \'rōz\ *n* **1** : any of a genus of usu. prickly often climbing shrubs with divided leaves and bright often fragrant flowers; *also* : one of these flowers **2** : something resembling a rose in form **3** : a moderate purplish red color — **rose** *adj*

rosé • roustabout

ro·sé \rō-ˈzā\ *n* [F] : a light pink wine

ro·se·ate \ˈrō-zē-ət, -zē-ˌāt\ *adj* 1 : resembling a rose esp. in color 2 : OPTIMISTIC ⟨a ~ view of the future⟩

rose·bud \ˈrōz-ˌbəd\ *n* : the flower of a rose when it is at most partly open

rose·bush \-ˌbu̇sh\ *n* : a shrubby rose

rose·mary \ˈrōz-ˌmer-ē\ *n, pl* **-mar·ies** [ME *rosmarine*, fr. AF *rosmarin*, fr. L *rosmarinus*, fr. *ros* dew + *marinus* of the sea, fr. *mare* sea] : a fragrant shrubby Mediterranean mint; *also* : its leaves used as a seasoning

ro·sette \rō-ˈzet\ *n* [F] 1 : a usu. small badge or ornament of ribbon gathered in the shape of a rose 2 : a circular ornament filled with representations of leaves

rose wa·ter \ˈrōz-ˌwȯ-tər, -ˌwä-\ *n* : a watery solution of the fragrant constituents of the rose used as a perfume

rose·wood \-ˌwu̇d\ *n* : any of various tropical trees with dark red wood streaked with black; *also* : this wood

Rosh Ha·sha·nah \ˌräsh-hə-ˈshä-nə, ˌrōsh-, -ˈshō-\ *n* [Heb *rōsh hashshānāh*, lit., beginning of the year] : the Jewish New Year observed as a religious holiday in September or October

ros·in \ˈrä-zᵊn\ *n* : a brittle resin obtained esp. from pine trees and used esp. in varnishes and on violin bows

ros·ter \ˈräs-tər\ *n* 1 : a list of personnel; *also* : the persons listed on a roster 2 : an itemized list

ros·trum \ˈräs-trəm\ *n, pl* **rostrums** *or* **ros·tra** \-trə\ [L *Rostra*, pl., a platform for speakers in the Roman Forum decorated with the beaks of captured ships, fr. pl. of *rostrum* beak, ship's beak, fr. *rodere* to gnaw] : a stage or platform for public speaking

rosy \ˈrō-zē\ *adj* **ros·i·er; -est** 1 : of the color rose 2 : HOPEFUL, PROMISING ⟨a ~ outlook⟩ — **ros·i·ly** \ˈrō-zə-lē\ *adv* — **ros·i·ness** \-zē-nəs\ *n*

¹rot \ˈrät\ *vb* **rot·ted; rot·ting** : to undergo decomposition : DECAY

²rot *n* 1 : DECAY 2 : any of various diseases of plants or animals in which tissue breaks down 3 : NONSENSE

¹ro·ta·ry \ˈrō-tə-rē\ *adj* 1 : turning on an axis like a wheel 2 : having a rotating part ⟨a ~ telephone⟩

²rotary *n, pl* **-ries** 1 : a rotary machine 2 : a one-way circular road junction

ro·tate \ˈrō-ˌtāt\ *vb* **ro·tat·ed; ro·tat·ing** 1 : to turn or cause to turn about an axis or a center : REVOLVE 2 : to alternate in a series ♦ *Synonyms* TURN, CIRCLE, SPIN, WHIRL, TWIRL — **ro·ta·tion** \rō-ˈtā-shən\ *n* — **ro·ta·tor** \ˈrō-ˌtā-tər\ *n* — **ro·ta·to·ry** \ˈrō-tə-ˌtȯr-ē\ *adj*

ROTC *abbr* Reserve Officers' Training Corps

rote \ˈrōt\ *n* 1 : repetition from memory often without attention to meaning ⟨learn by ~⟩ 2 : mechanical or unthinking routine or repetition — **rote** *adj*

ro·tis·ser·ie \rō-ˈti-sə-rē\ *n* [F] 1 : a restaurant specializing in broiled and barbecued meats 2 : an appliance fitted with a spit on which food is rotated before or over a source of heat

ro·tor \ˈrō-tər\ *n* 1 : a part that rotates; *esp* : the rotating part of an electrical machine 2 : a system of rotating horizontal blades for supporting a helicopter

ro·to·till·er \ˈrō-tō-ˌti-lər\ *n* : an engine-powered machine with rotating blades used to lift and turn over soil

rot·ten \ˈrä-tᵊn\ *adj* 1 : having rotted 2 : CORRUPT 3 : extremely unpleasant or inferior — **rot·ten·ness** *n*

rot·ten·stone \ˈrä-tᵊn-ˌstōn\ *n* : a decomposed siliceous limestone used for polishing

rott·wei·ler \ˈrät-ˌwī-lər\ *n, often cap* : any of a breed of tall powerful black-and-tan short-haired dogs

ro·tund \rō-ˈtənd\ *adj* : rounded out ♦ *Synonyms* PLUMP, CHUBBY, PORTLY, STOUT — **ro·tun·di·ty** \-ˈtən-də-tē\ *n*

ro·tun·da \rō-ˈtən-də\ *n* 1 : a round building; *esp* : one covered by a dome 2 : a large round room

rouble *var of* RUBLE

roué \rü-ˈā\ *n* [F, lit., broken on the wheel, fr. pp. of *rouer* to break on the wheel, fr. ML *rotare*, fr. L, to rotate; fr. the feeling that such a person deserves this punishment] : a man devoted to a life of sensual pleasure : RAKE

rouge \ˈrüzh, ˈrüj\ *n* [F, lit., red] : a cosmetic used to give a red color to cheeks and lips — **rouge** *vb*

¹rough \ˈrəf\ *adj* **rough·er; rough·est** 1 : uneven in surface : not smooth 2 : SHAGGY 3 : not calm : TURBULENT, TEMPESTUOUS 4 : marked by harshness or violence 5 : DIFFICULT, TRYING 6 : coarse or rugged in character or appearance 7 : marked by lack of refinement 8 : CRUDE, UNFINISHED 9 : done or made hastily or tentatively ⟨a ~ estimate⟩ — **rough·ly** *adv* — **rough·ness** *n*

²rough *n* 1 : uneven ground covered with high grass esp. along a golf fairway 2 : a crude, unfinished, or preliminary state; *also* : something in such a state 3 : ROWDY, TOUGH

³rough *vb* 1 : ROUGHEN 2 : MANHANDLE 3 : to make or shape roughly esp. in a preliminary way — **rough·er** *n*

rough·age \ˈrə-fij\ *n* : FIBER 2; *also* : food containing much indigestible material acting as fiber

rough–and–ready \ˌrə-fən-ˈre-dē\ *adj* : rude or unpolished in nature, method, or manner but effective in action or use ⟨a ~ solution⟩

rough–and–tum·ble \-ˈtəm-bəl\ *n* : rough unrestrained fighting or struggling — **rough–and–tumble** *adj*

rough·en \ˈrə-fən\ *vb* **rough·ened; rough·en·ing** : to make or become rough

rough–hewn \ˈrəf-ˈhyün\ *adj* 1 : being rough and unfinished ⟨~ beams⟩ 2 : lacking smooth manners or social grace — **rough–hew** \-ˈhyü\ *vb*

rough·house \ˈrəf-ˌhau̇s\ *vb* **rough·housed; rough·housing** : to participate in rough noisy behavior — **roughhouse** *n*

rough·neck \ˈrəf-ˌnek\ *n* 1 : ROWDY, TOUGH 2 : a worker on a crew drilling oil wells

rough·shod \ˈrəf-ˌshäd\ *adv* : in a roughly forceful manner ⟨rode ~ over the opposition⟩

rou·lette \rü-ˈlet\ *n* [F, lit., small wheel] 1 : a gambling game in which a whirling wheel is used 2 : a wheel or disk with teeth around the outside

¹round \ˈrau̇nd\ *adj* 1 : having every part of the surface or circumference the same distance from the center 2 : CYLINDRICAL 3 : COMPLETE, FULL 4 : approximately correct; *esp* : exact only to a specific decimal or place ⟨~ numbers⟩ 5 : liberal or ample in size or amount 6 : BLUNT, OUTSPOKEN 7 : moving in or forming a circle 8 : having curves rather than angles — **round·ish** *adj* — **round·ness** *n*

²round *prep or adv* : AROUND

³round *n* 1 : something round (as a circle, globe, or ring) 2 : a curved or rounded part (as a rung of a ladder) 3 : an indirect path or course; *also* : a regularly covered route (as of a security guard) 4 : a series or cycle of recurring actions or events 5 : one shot fired by a soldier or a gun; *also* : ammunition for one shot 6 : a period of time or a unit of play in a game or contest 7 : a cut of meat (as beef) esp. between the rump and the lower leg — **in the round** 1 : FREESTANDING 2 : with a center stage surrounded by an audience ⟨theater *in the round*⟩

⁴round *vb* 1 : to make or become round 2 : to go or pass around or part way around 3 : COMPLETE, FINISH 4 : to become plump or shapely 5 : to express as a round number — often used with *off* 6 : to follow a winding course : BEND

¹round·about \ˈrau̇n-də-ˌbau̇t\ *adj* : INDIRECT, CIRCUITOUS ⟨a ~ explanation⟩

²roundabout *n* 1 *Brit* : MERRY-GO-ROUND 2 *Brit* : ROTARY 2

roun·de·lay \ˈrau̇n-də-ˌlā\ *n* 1 : a simple song with a refrain 2 : a poem with a recurring refrain

round·house \ˈrau̇nd-ˌhau̇s\ *n* 1 : a circular building for housing and repairing locomotives 2 : a blow with the hand made with a wide swing — **roundhouse** *adj*

round·ly \ˈrau̇nd-lē\ *adv* 1 : in a complete manner; *also* : WIDELY 2 : in a blunt way 3 : with vigor

round–rob·in \ˈrau̇nd-ˌrä-bən\ *n* : a tournament in which each contestant meets every other contestant in turn

round–shoul·dered \-ˌshōl-dərd\ *adj* : having the shoulders stooping or rounded

round–trip *n* : a trip to a place and back

round·up \ˈrau̇nd-ˌəp\ *n* 1 : the gathering together of cattle on the range by riding around them and driving them in; *also* : the ranch hands and horses engaged in a roundup 2 : a gathering in of scattered persons or things 3 : SUMMARY ⟨news ~⟩ — **round up** *vb*

round·worm \-ˌwərm\ *n* : NEMATODE

rouse \ˈrau̇z\ *vb* **roused; rous·ing** 1 : to excite to activity : stir up 2 : to wake from sleep — **rous·er** *n*

roust·about \ˈrau̇s-tə-ˌbau̇t\ *n* 1 : one who does heavy unskilled labor (as on a dock or in an oil field) **2** : a laborer at a circus **3** : a person with no established home or occupation

¹rout \ˈraut\ *n* **1** : MOB 1, 2 **2** : DISTURBANCE **3** : a fashionable gathering

²rout *vb* **1** : RUMMAGE **2** : to gouge out **3** : to expel by force ⟨~*ed* out of their homes⟩

³rout *n* **1** : a state of wild confusion or disorderly retreat **2** : a disastrous defeat

⁴rout *vb* **1** : to put to flight **2** : to defeat decisively

¹route \ˈrüt, ˈraut\ *n* [ME, fr. AF *rute*, fr. VL **rupta* (*via*), lit., broken way] **1** : a traveled way **2** : CHANNEL **3** : a line of travel

²route *vb* **rout·ed; rout·ing** : to send by a selected route : DIRECT

¹rout·er \ˈrau-tər\ *n* : a machine with a revolving spindle and cutter for shaping a surface (as of wood)

²rout·er \ˈrü-tər, ˈrau-\ *n* : a device that sends data from one place to another within a computer network or between computer networks

rou·tine \rü-ˈtēn\ *n* [F, fr. MF, fr. *route* traveled way] **1** : a regular course of procedure **2** : an often repeated speech or formula **3** : a part fully worked out ⟨a comedy ~⟩ **4** : a set of computer instructions that will perform a certain task — **routine** *adj* — **rou·tine·ly** *adv* — **rou·tin·ize** \-ˈtē-ˌnīz\ *vb*

¹rove \ˈrōv\ *vb* **roved; rov·ing** : to wander over or through — **rov·er** *n*

²rove *past and past part of* REEVE

¹row \ˈrō\ *vb* **1** : to propel a boat with oars **2** : to transport in a rowboat **3** : to pull an oar in a crew — **row·er** \ˈrō-ər\ *n*

²row *n* : an act or instance of rowing

³row *n* **1** : a number of objects in an orderly sequence **2** : WAY, STREET

⁴row \ˈrau\ *n* : a noisy quarrel

⁵row \ˈrau\ *vb* : to engage in a row

row·boat \ˈrō-ˌbōt\ *n* : a small boat designed to be rowed

row·dy \ˈrau-dē\ *adj* **row·di·er; -est** : coarse or boisterous in behavior : ROUGH ⟨a ~ crowd⟩ — **row·di·ness** \ˈrau-dē-nəs\ *n* — **rowdy** *n* — **row·dy·ish** *adj* — **row·dy·ism** *n*

row·el \ˈrau-(ə)l\ *n* : a small pointed wheel on a rider's spur — **rowel** *vb*

¹roy·al \ˈrȯi-(ə)l\ *adj* [ME *roial*, fr. AF *real, roial*, fr. L *regalis*, fr. *reg-, rex* king] **1** : of or relating to a sovereign : REGAL **2** : fit for a king or queen ⟨a ~ welcome⟩ — **roy·al·ly** *adv*

²royal *n* : a person of royal blood

royal flush *n* : a straight flush having an ace as the highest card

roy·al·ist \ˈrȯi-ə-list\ *n* : an adherent of a king or of monarchical government

roy·al·ty \ˈrȯi-əl-tē\ *n, pl* **-ties** **1** : the state of being royal **2** : royal persons **3** : a share of a product or profit (as of a mine or oil well) claimed by the owner for allowing another person to use the property **4** : a payment made to an author or composer for each copy of a work sold or to an inventor for each article sold under a patent

RP *abbr* **1** relief pitcher **2** Republic of the Philippines

rpm *abbr* revolutions per minute

rps *abbr* revolutions per second

rpt *abbr* **1** repeat **2** report

RR *abbr* **1** railroad **2** rural route

RS *abbr* **1** recording secretary **2** revised statutes **3** Royal Society

RSV *abbr* Revised Standard Version

RSVP *abbr* [F *répondez s'il vous plaît*] please reply

rt *abbr* **1** right **2** route

RT *abbr* round-trip

rte *abbr* route

Ru *symbol* ruthenium

¹rub \ˈrəb\ *vb* **rubbed; rub·bing** **1** : to use pressure and friction on a body or object **2** : to fret or chafe with friction **3** : to scour, polish, erase, or smear by pressure and friction

²rub *n* **1** : DIFFICULTY, OBSTRUCTION **2** : something grating to the feelings

¹rub·ber \ˈrə-bər\ *n* **1** : one that rubs **2** : ERASER **3** : a flexible waterproof elastic substance made from the milky juice of various tropical plants or made synthetically; *also* : something made of this material **4** : CON-

DOM — **rubber** *adj* — **rub·ber·ize** \ˈrə-bə-ˌrīz\ *vb* — **rub·bery** *adj*

²rubber *n* **1** : a contest that consists of an odd number of games and is won by the side that takes a majority **2** : an extra game played to decide a tie

¹rub·ber·neck \-ˌnek\ *n* **1** : an idly or overly inquisitive person **2** : a person on a guided tour

²rubberneck *vb* : to look about, stare, or listen with excessive curiosity ⟨~*ing* drivers⟩ — **rub·ber·neck·er** *n*

rub·bish \ˈrə-bish\ *n* **1** : useless waste or rejected matter : TRASH **2** : something worthless or nonsensical

rub·ble \ˈrə-bəl\ *n* : broken fragments esp. of a destroyed building

ru·bel·la \rü-ˈbe-lə\ *n* : GERMAN MEASLES

ru·bi·cund \ˈrü-bi-(ˌ)kənd\ *adj* : RED, RUDDY ⟨a ~ face⟩

ru·bid·i·um \rü-ˈbi-dē-əm\ *n* : a soft silvery metallic chemical element

ru·ble *also* **rou·ble** \ˈrü-bəl\ *n* — see MONEY table

ru·bric \ˈrü-brik\ *n* [ME *rubrike* red ocher, heading in red letters of part of a book, fr. AF, fr. L *rubrica*, fr. *ruber* red] **1** : HEADING, TITLE; *also* : CLASS, CATEGORY **2** : a rule esp. for the conduct of a religious service

ru·by \ˈrü-bē\ *n, pl* **rubies** : a clear red precious stone — **ruby** *adj*

ru·by-throat·ed hummingbird \ˈrü-bē-ˌthrō-təd-\ *n* : a bright green and whitish hummingbird of eastern No. America with a red throat in the male

ruck·us \ˈrə-kəs\ *n* : ROW, DISTURBANCE

rud·der \ˈrə-dər\ *n* : a movable flat piece attached at the rear of a ship or aircraft for steering

rud·dy \ˈrə-dē\ *adj* **rud·di·er, -est** : REDDISH; *esp* : of a healthy reddish complexion — **rud·di·ness** \ˈrə-dē-nəs\ *n*

rude \ˈrüd\ *adj* **rud·er; rud·est** **1** : roughly made : CRUDE **2** : UNDEVELOPED, PRIMITIVE **3** : IMPOLITE **4** : UNSKILLED — **rude·ly** *adv* — **rude·ness** *n*

ru·di·ment \ˈrü-də-mənt\ *n* **1** : an elementary principle or basic skill — usu. used in pl. ⟨the ~s of mathematics⟩ **2** : something not fully developed — usu. used in pl. ⟨the ~s of a plan⟩ — **ru·di·men·ta·ry** \ˌrü-də-ˈmen-tə-rē\ *adj*

¹rue \ˈrü\ *n* : REGRET, SORROW — **rue·ful** \-fəl\ *adj* — **rue·ful·ly** *adv* — **rue·ful·ness** *n*

²rue *vb* **rued; ru·ing** : to feel regret, remorse, or penitence for ⟨~s his decision now⟩

³rue *n* : a European strong-scented woody herb with bitter-tasting leaves

ruff \ˈrəf\ *n* **1** : a large round pleated collar worn about 1600 **2** : a fringe of long hair or feathers around the neck of an animal — **ruffed** \ˈrəft\ *adj*

ruf·fi·an \ˈrə-fē-ən\ *n* : a brutal person — **ruf·fi·an·ly** *adj*

¹ruf·fle \ˈrə-fəl\ *vb* **ruf·fled; ruf·fling** **1** : to roughen the surface of **2** : IRRITATE, VEX **3** : to erect (as hair or feathers) in or like a ruff **4** : to flip through (as pages) **5** : to draw into or provide with plaits or folds

²ruffle *n* **1** : a strip of fabric gathered or pleated on one edge **2** : RUFF 2 **3** : RIPPLE — **ruf·fly** \ˈrə-fə-lē, -flē\ *adj*

ru·fi·yaa \ˈrü-fē-ˌyä\ *n, pl* **rufiyaa** — see MONEY table

RU–486 \ˈär-ˌyü-ˌfȯr-ˌä-tē-ˈsiks\ *n* : a drug taken orally to induce abortion esp. early in pregnancy

rug \ˈrəg\ *n* **1** : a covering for the legs, lap, and feet **2** : a piece of heavy fabric usu. with a nap or pile used as a floor covering

rug·by \ˈrəg-bē\ *n, often cap* [*Rugby* School, Rugby, England, where it was first played] : a football game in which play is continuous and interference and forward passing are not permitted

rug·ged \ˈrə-gəd\ *adj* **1** : having a rough uneven surface **2** : TURBULENT, STORMY **3** : HARSH, STERN **4** : ROBUST, STURDY — **rug·ged·ize** \ˈrə-gə-ˌdīz\ *vb* — **rug·ged·ly** *adv* — **rug·ged·ness** *n*

¹ru·in \ˈrü-ən\ *n* **1** : complete collapse or destruction **2** : the remains of something destroyed — usu. used in pl. **3** : a cause of destruction **4** : the action of destroying

²ruin *vb* **1** : DESTROY **2** : to damage beyond repair **3** : BANKRUPT

ru·in·ation \ˌrü-ə-ˈnā-shən\ *n* : RUIN, DESTRUCTION

ru·in·ous \ˈrü-ə-nəs\ *adj* **1** : RUINED, DILAPIDATED **2** : causing ruin ⟨~ conflicts⟩ — **ru·in·ous·ly** *adv*

¹rule \ˈrül\ *n* [ME *reule*, fr. AF, fr. L *regula* straightedge, rule, fr. *regere* to keep straight, direct] **1** : a guide or principle for governing action : REGULATION **2** : the

usual way of doing something **3** : the exercise of authority or control : GOVERNMENT **4** : RULER 2
²**rule** *vb* **ruled; rul·ing 1** : CONTROL; *also* : GOVERN **2** : to be supreme or outstanding in **3** : to give or state as a considered decision **4** : to mark on paper with or as if with a ruler **5** *slang* : to be extremely cool or popular
rul·er \'rü-lər\ *n* **1** : SOVEREIGN **2** : a straight strip of material (as wood or metal) marked off in units and used for measuring or as a straightedge
rum \'rəm\ *n* **1** : an alcoholic liquor made from sugarcane products (as molasses) **2** : alcoholic liquor
Ru·ma·nian *var of* ROMANIAN
rum·ba \'rəm-bə, 'rùm-\ *n* : a dance of Cuban origin marked by strong rhythmic movements
¹**rum·ble** \'rəm-bəl\ *vb* **rum·bled; rum·bling** : to make a low heavy rolling sound; *also* : to move along with such a sound — **rum·bler** *n*
²**rumble** *n* **1** : a low heavy rolling sound **2** : a street fight esp. among gangs
rumble seat *n* : a folding seat in the back of an automobile that is not covered by the top
rum·bling \'rəm-blin\ *n* **1** : RUMBLE **2** : widespread talk or complaints — usu. used in pl.
ru·men \'rü-mən\ *n, pl* **ru·mi·na** \-mə-nə\ *or* **rumens** : the large first compartment of the stomach of a ruminant (as a cow)
¹**ru·mi·nant** \'rü-mə-nənt\ *n* : a ruminant mammal
²**ruminant** *adj* **1** : chewing the cud; *also* : of or relating to a group of hoofed mammals (as cattle, deer, and camels) that chew the cud and have a complex 3- or 4-chambered stomach **2** : MEDITATIVE
ru·mi·nate \'rü-mə-ˌnāt\ *vb* **-nat·ed; -nat·ing** [L *ruminari* to chew the cud, muse upon, fr. *rumin-, rumen* first stomach chamber of a ruminant] **1** : MEDITATE, MUSE **2** : to chew the cud — **ru·mi·na·tion** \ˌrü-mə-ˈnā-shən\ *n*
¹**rum·mage** \'rə-mij\ *vb* **rum·maged; rum·mag·ing** : to search thoroughly ⟨*rummaged* the room for his key⟩ — **rum·mag·er** *n*
²**rummage** *n* **1** : a miscellaneous collection **2** : an act of rummaging
rum·my \'rə-mē\ *n* : any of several card games for two or more players
ru·mor \'rü-mər\ *n* **1** : common talk **2** : a statement or report current but not authenticated — **rumor** *vb*
ru·mour *chiefly Brit var of* RUMOR
rump \'rəmp\ *n* **1** : the rear part of an animal; *also* : a cut of meat (as beef) behind the upper sirloin **2** : a small or inferior remnant (as of a group)
rum·ple \'rəm-pəl\ *vb* **rum·pled; rum·pling** : TOUSLE, MUSS, WRINKLE — **rumple** *n* — **rum·ply** \'rəm-pə-lē\ *adj*
rum·pus \'rəm-pəs\ *n* **1** : DISTURBANCE, RUCKUS
rumpus room *n* : a room usu. in the basement of a home that is used for games, parties, and recreation
¹**run** \'rən\ *vb* **ran** \'ran\; **run; run·ning 1** : to go faster than a walk **2** : to take to flight : FLEE **3** : to go without restraint ⟨let chickens ～ loose⟩ **4** : to go rapidly or hurriedly : HASTEN, RUSH **5** : to make a quick or casual trip or visit **6** : to contend in a race; *esp* : to enter an election ⟨～ for mayor⟩ **7** : to put forward as a candidate for office **8** : to move on or as if on wheels : pass or slide freely **9** : to go back and forth : PLY **10** : to move in large numbers esp. to a spawning ground ⟨shad are *running*⟩ **11** : FUNCTION, OPERATE ⟨～s on gasoline⟩ ⟨software that ～s on her computer⟩ **12** : to continue in force ⟨two years to ～⟩ **13** : to flow rapidly or under pressure : MELT, FUSE, DISSOLVE; *also* : DISCHARGE **7** ⟨my nose is *running*⟩ **14** : to tend to produce or to recur ⟨family ～s to blonds⟩ ⟨stubbornness ～s in the family⟩ **15** : to take a certain direction **16** : to be worded or written **17** : to be current ⟨rumors *running* wild⟩ **18** : to cause to produce a flow ⟨*ran* the faucet⟩ **19** : TRACE ⟨～ down a rumor⟩ **20** : to perform or bring about by running **21** : to cause to pass ⟨～ a wire from the antenna⟩ **22** : to cause to collide **23** : SMUGGLE **24** : MANAGE, CONDUCT, OPERATE ⟨～ a business⟩ **25** : INCUR ⟨～ a risk⟩ **26** : to permit to accumulate before settling ⟨～ up a bill⟩ **27** : PRINT, PUBLISH ⟨～ a news story⟩
²**run** *n* **1** : an act or the action of running **2** : a migration of fish; *also* : the migrating fish **3** : a score in baseball **4** : BROOK, CREEK **5** : a continuous series esp. of similar things **6** : persistent heavy demands from depositors,

creditors, or customers **7** : the quantity of work turned out in a continuous operation; *also* : a period of operation (as of a machine or plant) **8** : the usual or normal kind ⟨the ordinary ～ of students⟩ **9** : the distance covered in continuous travel or sailing **10** : a regular course or trip **11** : freedom of movement in a place or area ⟨has the ～ of the house⟩ **12** : an enclosure for animals **13** : an inclined course (as for skiing) **14** : a lengthwise ravel (as in a stocking) — **run·less** *adj*
run·about \'rə-nə-ˌbaút\ *n* : a light wagon, automobile, or motorboat
run·around \'rə-nə-ˌraúnd\ *n* : evasive or delaying action esp. in response to a request
¹**run·away** \'rə-nə-ˌwā\ *n* **1** : one that runs away : FUGITIVE **2** : the act of running away out of control; *also* : something (as a horse) that is running out of control
²**runaway** *adj* **1** : FUGITIVE **2** : won by a long lead; *also* : extremely successful **3** : subject to uncontrolled changes ⟨～ inflation⟩ **4** : operating out of control ⟨a ～ locomotive⟩
run·down \'rən-ˌdaún\ *n* : an item-by-item report or review : SUMMARY
run–down \'rən-ˈdaún\ *adj* **1** : EXHAUSTED, WORN–OUT ⟨that ～ feeling⟩ **2** : being in poor repair ⟨a ～ farm⟩
run down *vb* **1** : to collide with and knock down **2** : to chase until exhausted or captured **3** : to find by search **4** : DISPARAGE **5** : to cease to operate for lack of motive power **6** : to decline in physical condition
rune \'rün\ *n* **1** : any of the characters of any of several alphabets formerly used by the Germanic peoples **2** : MYSTERY, MAGIC **3** : a poem esp. in Finnish or Old Norse — **ru·nic** \'rü-nik\ *adj*

rune 1

¹**rung** *past part of* RING
²**rung** \'rən\ *n* **1** : a rounded crosspiece between the legs of a chair **2** : one of the crosspieces of a ladder
run–in \'rən-ˌin\ *n* **1** : ALTERCATION, QUARREL **2** : something run in
run in *vb* **1** : to insert as additional matter **2** : to arrest esp. for a minor offense **3** : to pay a casual visit
run·nel \'rə-nᵊl\ *n* : BROOK, STREAMLET
run·ner \'rə-nər\ *n* **1** : one that runs **2** : BASE RUNNER **3** : BALLCARRIER **4** : a thin piece or part on which something (as a sled or an ice skate) slides **5** : the support of a drawer or a sliding door **6** : a horizontal branch from the base of a plant that produces new plants **7** : a plant producing runners **8** : a long narrow carpet **9** : a narrow decorative cloth cover for a table or dresser top
run·ner–up \'rə-nər-ˌəp\ *n, pl* **runners–up** *also* **runner–ups** : the competitor in a contest who finishes second
¹**run·ning** *adj* **1** : FLOWING **2** : FLUID, RUNNY **3** : CONTINUOUS, INCESSANT **4** : measured in a straight line ⟨cost per ～ foot⟩ **5** : of or relating to an act of running **6** : made or trained for running ⟨～ horse⟩ ⟨～ shoes⟩
²**running** *adv* : in succession
running light *n* : any of the lights carried by a vehicle (as a ship) at night
run·ny \'rə-nē\ *adj* : having a tendency to run ⟨a ～ dough⟩ ⟨a ～ nose⟩
run·off \'rən-ˌóf\ *n* : a final contest (as an election) to decide a previous indecisive contest
run–of–the–mill *adj* : not outstanding : AVERAGE ⟨a ～ performance⟩
run on *vb* **1** : to talk at length **2** : to continue (matter in type) without a break or a new paragraph **3** : to place or add (as an entry in a dictionary) at the end of a paragraphed item — **run–on** \'rən-ˌón, -ˌän\ *n*
run out *vb* **1** : to use up or exhaust a supply ⟨*ran out* of gas⟩
runt \'rənt\ *n* **1** : an animal unusually small of its kind **2** *usu disparaging* : a person of small stature — **runty** *adj*
run·way \'rən-ˌwā\ *n* **1** : a beaten path made by animals; *also* : a passage for animals **2** : a paved strip of ground for the landing and takeoff of aircraft **3** : a narrow platform from a stage into an auditorium **4** : a support (as a track) on which something runs

ru·pee \rü-'pē, 'rü-₁pē\ *n* — see MONEY table
ru·pi·ah \rü-'pē-ə\ *n, pl* **rupiah** *or* **rupiahs** — see MONEY table
¹**rup·ture** \'rəp-chər\ *n* : a breaking or tearing apart; *also* : HERNIA
²**rupture** *vb* **rup·tured; rup·tur·ing** : to cause or undergo rupture
ru·ral \'rûr-əl\ *adj* : of or relating to the country, country people, or agriculture
ruse \'rüs, 'rüz\ *n* : a wily subterfuge : TRICK, ARTIFICE
¹**rush** \'rəsh\ *n* : any of various often tufted and hollow-stemmed grasslike marsh plants — **rushy** *adj*
²**rush** *vb* [ME *russhen*, fr. AF *reuser, ruser, russher* to drive back, repulse, fr. L *recusare* to oppose] **1** : to move forward or act with too great haste or eagerness or without preparation **2** : to perform in a short time or at high speed **3** : ATTACK, CHARGE **4** : to advance a football by running — **rush·er** *n*
³**rush** *n* **1** : a violent forward motion **2** : unusual demand or activity **3** : a crowding of people to one place **4** : a running play in football **5** : a sudden feeling of pleasure
⁴**rush** *adj* : requiring or marked by special speed or urgency ⟨~ orders⟩
rush hour *n* : a time when the amount of traffic or business is at a peak
rusk \'rəsk\ *n* : a sweet or plain bread baked, sliced, and baked again until dry and crisp
rus·set \'rə-sət\ *n* **1** : a coarse reddish brown cloth **2** : a reddish brown **3** : a baking potato — **russet** *adj*
Rus·sian \'rə-shən\ *n* **1** : a native or inhabitant of Russia **2** : a Slavic language of the Russian people — **Russian** *adj*
rust \'rəst\ *n* **1** : a reddish coating formed on iron when it is exposed to esp. moist air **2** : any of numerous plant diseases characterized by usu. reddish spots; *also* : a fungus causing rust **3** : a strong reddish brown — **rust** *vb* — **rusty** *adj*

¹**rus·tic** \'rəs-tik\ *adj* : of, relating to, or suitable for the country or country people ⟨a ~ inn⟩ — **rus·ti·cal·ly** \-ti-k(ə-)lē\ *adv* — **rus·tic·i·ty** \₁rəs-'ti-sə-tē\ *n*
²**rustic** *n* : a rustic person
rus·ti·cate \'rəs-ti-₁kāt\ *vb* **-cat·ed; -cat·ing** : to go into or reside in the country — **rus·ti·ca·tion** \₁rəs-ti-'kā-shən\ *n*
¹**rus·tle** \'rə-səl\ *vb* **rus·tled; rus·tling** **1** : to make or cause a rustle **2** : to cause to rustle ⟨~ a newspaper⟩ **3** : to act or move with energy or speed; *also* : to procure in this way **4** : to forage food **5** : to steal cattle from the range — **rus·tler** *n*
²**rustle** *n* : a quick series of small sounds ⟨~ of leaves⟩
¹**rut** \'rət\ *n* : state or period of sexual excitement esp. in male deer — **rut** *vb*
²**rut** *n* **1** : a track worn by wheels or by habitual passage of something **2** : a usual or fixed routine
ru·ta·ba·ga \₁rü-tə-'bā-gə, ₁rü-\ *n* : a turnip with a large yellowish root
Ruth \'rüth\ *n* — see BIBLE table
ru·the·ni·um \rü-'thē-nē-əm\ *n* : a rare hard metallic chemical element
ruth·er·ford·ium \₁rə-thər-'fôr-dē-əm\ *n* : an artificially produced radioactive chemical element
ruth·less \'rüth-ləs\ *adj* [fr. *ruth* compassion, pity, fr. ME *ruthe*, fr. *ruen* to rue, fr. OE *hrēowan*] : having no pity : MERCILESS, CRUEL ⟨a ~ tyrant⟩ — **ruth·less·ly** *adv* — **ruth·less·ness** *n*
¹**RV** \₁är-'vē\ *n* : RECREATIONAL VEHICLE
²**RV** *abbr* Revised Version
R–value \'är-₁val-yü\ *n* : a measure of resistance to the flow of heat through a substance (as insulation)
RW *abbr* **1** right worshipful **2** right worthy
rwy *or* **ry** *abbr* railway
-ry *n suffix* : -ERY ⟨bigotry⟩
rye \'rī\ *n* **1** : a hardy annual grass grown for grain or as a cover crop; *also* : its seed **2** : a whiskey distilled from a rye mash

S

¹**s** \'es\ *n, pl* **s's** *or* **ss** \'e-səz\ *often cap* : the 19th letter of the English alphabet
²**s** *abbr, often cap* **1** saint **2** second **3** senate **4** series **5** shilling **6** singular **7** small **8** son **9** south; southern
¹**-s** \s *after sounds* f, k, k̲, p, t, th; əz *after sounds* ch, j, s, sh, z, zh; z *after other sounds*\ *n pl suffix* — used to form the plural of most nouns that do not end in *s, z, sh,* or *ch* or *y* following a consonant ⟨heads⟩ ⟨books⟩ ⟨boys⟩ ⟨beliefs⟩, to form the plural of proper nouns that end in *y* following a consonant ⟨Marys⟩, and with or without a preceding apostrophe to form the plural of abbreviations, numbers, letters, and symbols used as nouns ⟨MCs⟩ ⟨4s⟩ ⟨#s⟩ ⟨B's⟩
²**-s** *adv suffix* — used to form adverbs denoting usual or repeated action or state ⟨works nights⟩
³**-s** *vb suffix* — used to form the third person singular present of most verbs that do not end in *s, z, sh,* or *ch* or *y* following a consonant ⟨falls⟩ ⟨takes⟩ ⟨plays⟩
S *symbol* sulfur
SA *abbr* **1** Salvation Army **2** seaman apprentice **3** sex appeal **4** [L *sine anno* without year] without date **5** South Africa **6** South America **7** subject to approval
Saami *var of* SAMI
Sab·bath \'sa-bəth\ *n* [ME *sabat,* fr. AF & OE, fr. L *sabbatum,* fr. Gk *sabbaton,* fr. Heb *shabbāth,* lit., rest] **1** : the 7th day of the week observed as a day of worship by Jews and some Christians **2** : Sunday observed among Christians as a day of worship
sab·bat·i·cal \sə-'ba-ti-kəl\ *n* : a leave often with pay granted (as to a college professor) usu. every 7th year for rest, travel, or research
sa·ber *or* **sa·bre** \'sā-bər\ *n* [F *sabre*] : a cavalry sword with a curved blade and thick back

saber saw *n* : a portable electric saw with a pointed reciprocating blade; *esp* : JIGSAW
sa·ble \'sā-bəl\ *n, pl* **sables** **1** : the color black **2** *pl* : mourning garments **3** : a dark brown mammal chiefly of northern Asia related to the weasels; *also* : its fur or pelt
¹**sab·o·tage** \'sa-bə-₁täzh\ *n* [F] **1** : deliberate destruction of an employer's property or hindering of production by workers **2** : destructive or hampering action by enemy agents or sympathizers in time of war
²**sabotage** *vb* **-taged; -tag·ing** : to practice sabotage on : WRECK
sab·o·teur \₁sa-bə-'tər\ *n* : a person who practices sabotage
sac \'sak\ *n* : a pouch in an animal or plant often containing a fluid
SAC *abbr* Strategic Air Command
sac·cha·rin \'sa-kə-rən\ *n* : a white crystalline compound used as an artificial calorie-free sweetener
sac·cha·rine \'sa-kə-rən\ *adj* : nauseatingly sweet ⟨~ poetry⟩
sac·er·do·tal \₁sa-sər-'dō-t°l, -kər-\ *adj* : PRIESTLY
sac·er·do·tal·ism \-t°-₁li-zəm\ *n* : a religious belief emphasizing the powers of priests as essential mediators between God and humankind
sa·chem \'sā-chəm\ *n* [Narragansett *sâchim*] : a No. American Indian chief

saber

sa·chet \sa-'shā\ *n* [MF, fr. OF, dim. of *sac* bag] : a small bag filled with perfumed powder for scenting clothes

¹sack \'sak\ *n* **1** : a usu. rectangular-shaped bag (as of paper or burlap) **2** : a loose jacket or short coat

²sack *vb* : DISMISS, FIRE

³sack *n* [modif. of MF *sec* dry, fr. L *siccus*] : a white wine popular in England in the 16th and 17th centuries

⁴sack *vb* : to plunder a captured town

sack·cloth \-ˌklȯth\ *n* : a rough garment worn as a sign of penitence

sac·ra·ment \'sa-krə-mənt\ *n* **1** : a formal religious act or rite; *esp* : one (as baptism or the Eucharist) held to have been instituted by Christ **2** : the elements of the Eucharist — **sac·ra·men·tal** \ˌsa-krə-'men-t⁰l\ *adj*

sa·cred \'sā-krəd\ *adj* **1** : set apart for the service or worship of deity **2** : devoted exclusively to one service or use **3** : worthy of veneration or reverence **4** : of or relating to religion : RELIGIOUS **♦ Synonyms** BLESSED, DIVINE, HALLOWED, HOLY, SANCTIFIED — **sa·cred·ly** *adv* — **sa·cred·ness** *n*

sacred cow *n* : one that is often unreasonably immune from criticism

¹sac·ri·fice \'sa-krə-ˌfīs\ *n* **1** : the offering of something precious to deity **2** : something offered in sacrifice **3** : LOSS, DEPRIVATION **4** : a bunt allowing a base runner to advance while the batter is put out; *also* : a fly ball allowing a runner to score after the catch — **sac·ri·fi·cial** \ˌsa-krə-'fi-shəl\ *adj* — **sac·ri·fi·cial·ly** *adv*

²sac·ri·fice *vb* **-ficed; -fic·ing** **1** : to offer up or kill as a sacrifice **2** : to accept the loss or destruction of for an end, cause, or ideal **3** : to make a sacrifice in baseball

sac·ri·lege \'sa-krə-lij\ *n* [ME, fr. AF, fr. L *sacrilegium*, fr. *sacrilegus* one who robs sacred property fr. *sacr-, sacer* sacred + *legere* to gather, steal] **1** : violation of something consecrated to God **2** : gross irreverence toward a hallowed person, place, or thing — **sac·ri·le·gious** \ˌsa-krə-'li-jəs, -'lē-\ *adj* — **sac·ri·le·gious·ly** *adv*

sac·ris·tan \'sa-krə-stən\ *n* **1** : a church officer in charge of the sacristy **2** : SEXTON

sac·ris·ty \'sa-krə-stē\ *n, pl* **-ties** : VESTRY

sac·ro·il·i·ac \ˌsa-krō-'i-lē-ˌak\ *n* : the joint between the upper part of the hipbone and the sacrum

sac·ro·sanct \'sa-krō-ˌsaŋkt\ *adj* : SACRED, INVIOLABLE

sa·crum \'sā-krəm, 'sa-\ *n, pl* **sa·cra** \-krə, 'sā-\ : the part of the vertebral column that is directly connected with or forms a part of the pelvis and in humans consists of five fused vertebrae

sad \'sad\ *adj* **sad·der; sad·dest** **1** : GRIEVING, MOURNFUL, DOWNCAST **2** : causing sorrow **3** : DULL, SOMBER — **sad·ly** *adv* — **sad·ness** *n*

sad·den \'sa-d⁰n\ *vb* : to make sad

¹sad·dle \'sa-d⁰l\ *n* : a usu. padded leather-covered seat (as for a rider on horseback)

²saddle *vb* **sad·dled; sad·dling** **1** : to put a saddle on **2** : OPPRESS, BURDEN

sad·dle·bow \'sa-d⁰l-ˌbō\ *n* : the arch in the front of a saddle

saddle horse *n* : a horse suited for or trained for riding

Sad·du·cee \'sa-jə-ˌsē, 'sa-dyə-\ *n* : a member of an ancient Jewish sect consisting of a ruling class of priests and rejecting certain doctrines — **Sad·du·ce·an** \ˌsa-jə-'sē-ən, ˌsa-dyə-\ *adj*

sa·dism \'sā-ˌdi-zəm, 'sa-\ *n* : a sexual perversion in which gratification is obtained by inflicting physical or mental pain on others — **sa·dist** \'sā-dist, 'sa-\ *n* — **sa·dis·tic** \sə-'dis-tik\ *adj* — **sa·dis·ti·cal·ly** \-ti-k(ə-)lē\ *adv*

sa·do·mas·och·ism \ˌsā-(ˌ)dō-'ma-sə-ˌki-zəm, ˌsa-, -'ma-zə-\ *n* : the derivation of pleasure from the infliction of physical or mental pain either on others or on oneself — **sa·do·mas·och·is·tic** \-ˌma-sə-'kis-tik, -ˌma-zə-\ *adj*

SAE *abbr* **1** self-addressed envelope **2** Society of Automotive Engineers **3** stamped addressed envelope

sa·fa·ri \sə-'fär-ē\ *n* [Swahili, trip, fr. Ar *safarī* of a trip] **1** : a hunting expedition esp. in eastern Africa **2** : JOURNEY, TRIP

¹safe \'sāf\ *adj* **saf·er; saf·est** **1** : free from harm or risk **2** : affording safety; *also* : secure from danger or loss **3** : RELIABLE — **safe·ly** *adv*

²safe *n* : a container for keeping articles (as valuables) safe

safe–con·duct \-'kän-(ˌ)dəkt\ *n* : a pass permitting a person to go through enemy lines

¹safe·guard \-ˌgärd\ *n* : a measure or device for preventing accident

²safeguard *vb* : to provide a safeguard for : PROTECT ⟨∼ your valuables⟩

safe·keep·ing \'sāf-'kē-piŋ\ *n* : a keeping or being kept in safety

safer sex *n* : SAFE SEX

safe sex *n* : sexual activity and esp. sexual intercourse in which various measures (as the use of latex condoms) are taken to avoid disease (as AIDS) transmitted by sexual contact

safe·ty \'sāf-tē\ *n, pl* **safeties** **1** : freedom from danger : SECURITY **2** : a protective device **3** : a football play in which the ball is downed by the offensive team behind its own goal line **4** : a defensive football back in the deepest position — **safety** *adj*

safety glass *n* : shatter-resistant material formed of two sheets of glass with a sheet of clear plastic between them

safety match *n* : a match that ignites only when struck on a special surface

saf·flow·er \'sa-ˌflaù(-ə)r\ *n* : a widely grown Old World herb related to the daisies that has large orange or red flower heads yielding a dyestuff and seeds rich in edible oil

saf·fron \'sa-frən\ *n* : a deep orange powder from the flower of a crocus used to color and flavor foods

sag \'sag\ *vb* **sagged; sag·ging** **1** : to droop or settle from or as if from pressure ⟨a *sagging* mattress⟩ **2** : to lose firmness or vigor — **sag** *n*

sa·ga \'sä-gə\ *n* [ON] : a narrative of heroic deeds; *esp* : one recorded in Iceland in the 12th and 13th centuries

sa·ga·cious \sə-'gā-shəs\ *adj* : of keen mind : SHREWD ⟨a ∼ counselor⟩ — **sa·gac·i·ty** \-'ga-sə-tē\ *n*

sag·a·more \'sa-gə-ˌmór\ *n* : a subordinate No. American Indian chief

¹sage \'sāj\ *adj* [ME, fr. AF, fr. VL *sapius*, fr. L *sapere* to taste, have good taste, be wise] : WISE, PRUDENT — **sage·ly** *adv*

²sage *n* : one who is distinguished for wisdom

³sage *n* [ME, fr. AF *sage, salge*, fr. L *salvia*, fr. *salvus* healthy; fr. its use as a medicinal herb] **1** : a perennial mint with aromatic leaves used in flavoring; *also* : its leaves **2** : SAGEBRUSH **3** : a light grayish green

sage·brush \'sāj-ˌbrəsh\ *n* : any of several low shrubby No. American composite plants; *esp* : one of the western U.S. with a sagelike odor

Sag·it·tar·i·us \ˌsa-jə-'ter-ē-əs\ *n* [L, lit., archer] **1** : a zodiacal constellation between Scorpio and Capricorn usu. pictured as a centaur archer **2** : the 9th sign of the zodiac in astrology; *also* : one born under this sign

sa·go \'sā-gō\ *n, pl* **sagos** : a dry granulated starch esp. from the pith of various tropical palms (**sago palm**)

sa·gua·ro \sə-'wär-ə, -'gwär-, -ō\ *n, pl* **-ros** [MexSp] : a tall columnar usu. sparsely-branched cactus of dry areas of the southwestern U.S. and Mexico that may attain a height of up to 50 feet (16 meters)

said *past and past part of* SAY

¹sail \'sāl\ *n* **1** : a piece of fabric by means of which the wind is used to propel a ship **2** : a sailing ship **3** : something resembling a sail **4** : a trip on a sailboat

²sail *vb* **1** : to travel on a sailing ship **2** : to pass over in a ship **3** : to manage or direct the course of a ship **4** : to move with ease, grace, or nonchalance

sail·board \'sāl-ˌbórd\ *n* : a modified surfboard having a mast and sailed by a standing person

sail·boat \-ˌbōt\ *n* : a boat propelled primarily by sail

sail·cloth \-ˌklȯth\ *n* : a heavy canvas used for sails, tents, or upholstery

sail·fish \-ˌfish\ *n* : any of a genus of large marine bony fishes with a large dorsal fin that are related to marlins

sail·ing *n* : the sport of handling or riding in a sailboat

sail·or \'sā-lər\ *n* : one that sails; *esp* : a member of a ship's crew

sail·plane \'sāl-ˌplān\ *n* : a glider designed to rise in an upward air current

saint \'sānt, *before a name* (ˌ)sānt *or* sənt\ *n* **1** : one officially recognized as preeminent for holiness **2** : one of the spirits of the departed in heaven **3** : a holy or godly person — **saint·ed** \'sān-təd\ *adj* — **saint·hood** \-ˌhùd\ *n*

Saint Ber·nard \-bər-'närd\ *n* : any of a Swiss alpine breed of tall powerful working dogs used esp. formerly in aiding lost travelers

Saint–John's–wort \'sānt-'jänz-ˌwərt, -ˌwȯrt\ *n* **1** : any of a genus of herbs and shrubs with showy yellow flowers **2** : the dried aerial parts of a Saint-John's-wort used esp. in herbal remedies

saint·ly \'sānt-lē\ *adj* : relating to, resembling, or befitting a saint ⟨∼ zeal⟩ — **saint·li·ness** \-lē-nəs\ *n*

Saint Val·en·tine's Day \-'va-lən-ˌtīnz-\ *n* : VALENTINE'S DAY

¹**sake** \'sāk\ *n* **1** : END, PURPOSE **2** : personal or social welfare, safety, or well-being

²**sa·ke** *or* **sa·ki** \'sä-kē\ *n* : a Japanese alcoholic beverage of fermented rice

sa·laam \sə-'läm\ *n* [Ar *salām*, lit., peace] **1** : a salutation or ceremonial greeting in the East **2** : an obeisance performed by bowing very low and placing the right palm on the forehead — **salaam** *vb*

sa·la·cious \sə-'lā-shəs\ *adj* **1** : arousing sexual desire or imagination **2** : LUSTFUL — **sa·la·cious·ly** *adv* — **sa·la·cious·ness** *n*

sal·ad \'sa-ləd\ *n* : a cold dish (as of lettuce, vegetables, fish, eggs, or fruit) served with dressing

sal·a·man·der \'sa-lə-ˌman-dər\ *n* : any of numerous amphibians that look like lizards but have scaleless usu. smooth moist skin

sa·la·mi \sə-'lä-mē\ *n* [It] : a highly seasoned sausage of pork and beef

sal·a·ry \'sa-lə-rē\ *n, pl* **-ries** [ME *salarie*, fr. AF, fr. L *salarium* pension, salary, fr. neut. of *salarius* of salt, fr. *sal* salt] : payment made at regular intervals for services

sale \'sāl\ *n* **1** : transfer of ownership of property from one person to another in return for money **2** : ready market : DEMAND **3** : AUCTION **4** : a selling of goods at bargain prices — **sal·able** *or* **sale·able** \'sā-lə-bəl\ *adj*

sales·girl \'sālz-ˌgərl\ *n* : SALESWOMAN

sales·man \-mən\ *n* : one who sells in a given territory, in a store, or by telephone — **sales·man·ship** *n*

sales·per·son \-ˌpər-sən\ *n* : a salesman or saleswoman

sales·wom·an \-ˌwu̇-mən\ *n* : a woman who sells in a given territory, in a store, or by telephone

sal·i·cyl·ic acid \ˌsa-lə-'si-lik-\ *n* : a crystalline organic acid used in making aspirin and other medicinal preparations (as skin lotions)

¹**sa·lient** \'sā-lyənt, 'sā-lē-ənt\ *adj* : jutting forward beyond a line; *also* : PROMINENT ⟨a ∼ feature⟩ ✦ *Synonyms* CONSPICUOUS, STRIKING, NOTICEABLE

²**salient** *n* : a projecting part in a line of defense

¹**sa·line** \'sā-ˌlēn, -ˌlīn\ *adj* : consisting of or containing salt : SALTY — **sa·lin·i·ty** \sā-'li-nə-tē, sə-\ *n*

²**saline** *n* **1** : a metallic salt esp. with a purgative action **2** : a saline solution

sa·li·va \sə-'lī-və\ *n* : a liquid secreted into the mouth that helps digestion — **sal·i·vary** \'sa-lə-ˌver-ē\ *adj*

sal·i·vate \'sa-lə-ˌvāt\ *vb* **-vat·ed; -vat·ing** : to produce saliva esp. in excess — **sal·i·va·tion** \ˌsa-lə-'vā-shən\ *n*

sal·low \'sa-lō\ *adj* : of a yellowish sickly color ⟨a ∼ face⟩

sal·ly \'sa-lē\ *n, pl* **sallies** **1** : a rushing attack on besiegers by troops of a besieged place **2** : a witty remark or retort **3** : a brief excursion — **sally** *vb*

salm·on \'sa-mən\ *n, pl* **salmon** *also* **salmons** **1** : any of several bony fishes with pinkish flesh that are used for food and are related to the trouts **2** : a strong yellowish pink color

sal·mo·nel·la \ˌsal-mə-'ne-lə\ *n, pl* **-nel·lae** \-'ne-(ˌ)lē, -ˌlī\ *or* **-nellas** *or* **-nella** : any of a genus of rod-shaped bacteria that cause various illnesses (as food poisoning)

sa·lon \sə-'län, 'sa-ˌlän, sa-'lōⁿ\ *n* [F] : an elegant drawing room; *also* : a fashionable shop ⟨beauty ∼⟩

sa·loon \sə-'lün\ *n* **1** : a large public cabin on a ship **2** : a place where liquors are sold and drunk : BARROOM **3** *Brit* : SEDAN 2

sal·sa \'sȯl-sə, 'säl-\ *n* : a spicy sauce of tomatoes, onions, and hot peppers

¹**salt** \'sȯlt\ *n* **1** : a white crystalline substance that consists of sodium and chlorine and is used in seasoning foods **2** : a saltlike cathartic substance (as Epsom salts) **3** : a compound formed usu. by action of an acid on metal **4** : SAILOR — **salt·i·ness** \'sȯl-tē-nəs\ *n* — **salty** \'sȯl-tē\ *adj*

²**salt** *vb* : to preserve, season, or feed with salt

³**salt** *adj* : preserved or treated with salt ⟨∼ pork⟩; *also* : SALTY

SALT *abbr* Strategic Arms Limitation Talks

salt away *vb* : to lay away safely : SAVE

salt·box \'sȯlt-ˌbäks\ *n* : a frame dwelling with two stories in front and one behind and a long sloping roof

salt·cel·lar \-ˌse-lər\ *n* : a small container for holding salt at the table

sal·tine \sȯl-'tēn\ *n* : a thin crisp cracker sprinkled with salt

salt lick *n* : LICK 5

salt·pe·ter \'sȯlt-'pē-tər\ *n* [ME *salt petre*, alter. of *salpetre*, fr. ML *sal petrae*, lit., salt of the rock] **1** : POTASSIUM NITRATE **2** : SODIUM NITRATE

salt·wa·ter \-ˌwȯ-tər, -ˌwä-\ *adj* : of, relating to, or living in salt water

sa·lu·bri·ous \sə-'lü-brē-əs\ *adj* : favorable to health ⟨a ∼ climate⟩

sal·u·tary \'sal-yə-ˌter-ē\ *adj* : health-giving; *also* : BENEFICIAL ⟨∼ effects⟩

sal·u·ta·tion \ˌsal-yə-'tā-shən\ *n* : an expression of greeting, goodwill, or courtesy usu. by word or gesture

sa·lu·ta·to·ri·an \sə-ˌlü-tə-'tȯr-ē-ən\ *n* : the student having the 2d highest rank in a graduating class who delivers the salutatory address

sa·lu·ta·to·ry \sə-'lü-tə-ˌtȯr-ē\ *adj* : relating to or being the welcoming oration delivered at an academic commencement

¹**sa·lute** \sə-'lüt\ *vb* **sa·lut·ed; sa·lut·ing** **1** : GREET **2** : to honor by special ceremonies **3** : to show respect to (a superior officer) by a formal position of hand, rifle, or sword

²**salute** *n* **1** : GREETING **2** : the formal position assumed in saluting a superior

¹**sal·vage** \'sal-vij\ *n* **1** : money paid for saving a ship, its cargo, or passengers when the ship is wrecked or in danger **2** : the saving of a ship **3** : the saving of possessions in danger of being lost **4** : things saved from loss or destruction (as by a wreck or fire)

²**salvage** *vb* **sal·vaged; sal·vag·ing** : to rescue from destruction

sal·va·tion \sal-'vā-shən\ *n* **1** : the saving of a person from sin or its consequences esp. in the life after death **2** : the saving from danger, difficulty, or evil **3** : something that saves ⟨tourism has been the island's ∼⟩

¹**salve** \'sav, 'säv\ *n* **1** : a medicinal substance applied to the skin **2** : a soothing influence

²**salve** *vb* **salved; salv·ing** : EASE, SOOTHE

sal·ver \'sal-vər\ *n* [F *salve*, fr. Sp *salva* sampling of food to detect poison, tray, fr. *salvar* to save, sample food to detect poison, fr. LL *salvare* to save, fr. L *salvus* safe] : a small serving tray

sal·vo \'sal-vō\ *n, pl* **salvos** *or* **salvoes** : a simultaneous discharge of guns

Sam *or* **Saml** *abbr* Samuel

SAM \'sam, ˌes-ˌā-'em\ *n* [surface-to-*air m*issile] : a guided missile for use against aircraft by ground units

Sa·mar·i·tan \sə-'mer-ə-tən\ *n* **1** : a native or inhabitant of Samaria **2** : a person who is generous in helping those in distress

sa·mar·i·um \sə-'mer-ē-əm\ *n* : a silvery-white lustrous rare metallic chemical element

¹**same** \'sām\ *adj* **1** : being the one referred to : not different **2** : SIMILAR — **same·ness** *n*

²**same** *pron* : the same one or ones

³**same** *adv* : in the same manner

same–sex \'sām-'seks\ *adj* : of, relating to, or involving members of the same sex

Sa·mi *also* **Sa·mi** \'sä-mē\ *n, pl* **Sami** *or* **Samis** *also* **Saami** *or* **Saamis** : a member of a people of northern Scandinavia, Finland, and the Kola Peninsula of Russia

Sa·mo·an \sə-'mō-ən\ *n* : a native or inhabitant of Samoa — **Samoan** *adj*

sa·mo·sa \sə-'mō-sə\ *n* : a small triangular pastry filled with spiced meat or vegetables and fried

sam·o·var \'sa-mə-ˌvär\ *n* [Russ, fr. *samo-* self + *varit'* to boil] : an urn with a spigot at the base used esp. in Russia to boil water for tea

sam·pan \'sam-ˌpan\ *n* : a flat-bottomed skiff of eastern Asia usu. propelled by two short oars

¹**sam·ple** \'sam-pəl\ *n* : a representative piece, item, or set of individuals that shows the quality or nature of the whole from which it was taken : EXAMPLE, SPECIMEN

²**sample** *vb* **sam·pled; sam·pling** : to judge the quality of by a sample

sam·pler \'sam-plər\ *n* **1** : a piece of needlework; *esp* : one testing skill in embroidering **2** : a collection of various examples of something ⟨a chocolate ∼⟩

Sam·u·el \'sam-yə-wəl\ *n* — see BIBLE table

sam·u·rai \'sa-mə-ˌrī, 'sam-yə-\ *n, pl* **samurai** : a military retainer of a Japanese feudal lord who adhered to strict principles of honor and duty

san·a·to·ri·um \ˌsa-nə-'tōr-ē-əm\ *n, pl* **-ri·ums** *or* **-ria** \-ē-ə\ **1** : a health resort **2** : an establishment for the care esp. of convalescents or the chronically ill

sanc·ti·fy \'saŋk-tə-ˌfī\ *vb* **-fied; -fy·ing** **1** : to make holy : CONSECRATE **2** : to free from sin — **sanc·ti·fi·ca·tion** \ˌsaŋk-tə-fə-'kā-shən\ *n*

sanc·ti·mo·nious \ˌsaŋk-tə-'mō-nē-əs\ *adj* : hypocritically pious ⟨∼ politicians⟩ — **sanc·ti·mo·nious·ly** *adv*

¹**sanc·tion** \'saŋk-shən\ *n* **1** : authoritative approval **2** : a measure (as a threat or fine) designed to enforce a law or standard ⟨economic ∼s⟩

²**sanction** *vb* : to give approval to : RATIFY ♦ *Synonyms* ENDORSE, ACCREDIT, CERTIFY, APPROVE

sanc·ti·ty \'saŋk-tə-tē\ *n, pl* **-ties** **1** : GODLINESS **2** : SACREDNESS

sanc·tu·ary \'saŋk-chə-ˌwer-ē\ *n, pl* **-ar·ies** **1** : a consecrated place (as the part of a church in which the altar is placed) **2** : a place of refuge ⟨bird ∼⟩

sanc·tum \'saŋk-təm\ *n, pl* **sanctums** *also* **sanc·ta** \-tə\ : a private office or study : DEN ⟨an editor's ∼⟩

¹**sand** \'sand\ *n* : loose particles of hard broken rock — **sandy** *adj*

²**sand** *vb* **1** : to cover or fill with sand **2** : to scour, smooth, or polish with an abrasive (as sandpaper) — **sand·er** *n*

san·dal \'san-dᵊl\ *n* : a shoe consisting of a sole strapped to the foot; *also* : a low or open slipper or rubber overshoe

san·dal·wood \-ˌwùd\ *n* : the fragrant yellowish heartwood of a parasitic tree of southern Asia that is much used in ornamental carving and cabinetwork; *also* : the tree

sand·bag \'sand-ˌbag\ *n* : a bag filled with sand and used in fortifications, as ballast, or as a weapon

sand·bank \-ˌbaŋk\ *n* : a deposit of sand (as in a bar or shoal)

sand·bar \-ˌbär\ *n* : a ridge of sand formed in water by tides or currents

sand·blast \-ˌblast\ *vb* : to treat with a stream of sand blown (as for cleaning stone) by compressed air — **sand·blast·er** *n*

sand dollar *n* : any of numerous flat circular sea urchins living chiefly on sandy bottoms in shallow water

S & H *abbr* shipping and handling

sand·hog \'sand-ˌhòg, -ˌhäg\ *n* : a laborer who builds underwater tunnels

sand·lot \-ˌlät\ *n* : a vacant lot esp. when used for the unorganized sports of children — **sand·lot** *adj* — **sand·lot·ter** *n*

sand·man \-ˌman\ *n* : the genie of folklore who makes children sleepy

sand·pa·per \-ˌpā-pər\ *n* : paper with abrasive (as sand) glued on one side used in smoothing and polishing surfaces — **sandpaper** *vb*

sand·pip·er \-ˌpī-pər\ *n* : any of various shorebirds with a soft-tipped bill longer than that of the related plovers

sand·stone \-ˌstōn\ *n* : rock made of sand united by a natural cement

sand·storm \-ˌstòrm\ *n* : a windstorm that drives clouds of sand

sand trap *n* : a hazard on a golf course consisting of a hollow containing sand

¹**sand·wich** \'sand-(ˌ)wich\ *n* [after John Montagu, 4th Earl of *Sandwich* †1792 Eng. diplomat] **1** : two or more slices of bread with a layer (as of meat or cheese) spread between them **2** : something resembling a sandwich

²**sandwich** *vb* : to squeeze or crowd in

sane \'sān\ *adj* **san·er; san·est** : mentally sound and healthy; *also* : SENSIBLE, RATIONAL — **sane·ly** *adv*

sang *past of* SING

sang·froid \'sän-'frwä\ *n* [F *sang-froid*, lit., cold blood] : self-possession or an imperturbable state esp. under strain

san·gui·nary \'saŋ-gwə-ˌner-ē\ *adj* : BLOODY ⟨∼ battle⟩

san·guine \'saŋ-gwən\ *adj* **1** : RUDDY **2** : CHEERFUL, HOPEFUL ⟨a ∼ disposition⟩

sanit *abbr* sanitary; sanitation

san·i·tar·i·an \ˌsa-nə-'ter-ē-ən\ *n* : a specialist in sanitation and public health

san·i·tar·i·um \ˌsa-nə-'ter-ē-əm\ *n, pl* **-i·ums** *or* **-ia** \-ē-ə\ : SANATORIUM

san·i·tary \'sa-nə-ˌter-ē\ *adj* **1** : of or relating to health : HYGIENIC **2** : free from filth or infective matter

sanitary napkin *n* : a disposable absorbent pad used to absorb uterine flow (as during menstruation)

san·i·ta·tion \ˌsa-nə-'tā-shən\ *n* : the act or process of making sanitary; *also* : protection of health by maintenance of sanitary conditions

san·i·tize \'sa-nə-ˌtīz\ *vb* **-tized; -tiz·ing** **1** : to make sanitary **2** : to make more acceptable by removing unpleasant features

san·i·ty \'sa-nə-tē\ *n* : soundness of mind

sank *past of* SINK

sans \'sanz\ *prep* : WITHOUT

San·skrit \'san-ˌskrit\ *n* : an ancient language that is the classical language of India and of Hinduism — **Sanskrit** *adj*

San·ta Ana \ˌsan-tə-'a-nə\ *n* [*Santa Ana* Mountains in southern Calif.] : a hot dry wind from the north, northeast, or east in southern California

san·tims \'sän-ˌtims\ *n, pl* **san·ti·mi** \-ti-mē\ : a monetary unit equal to ¹/₁₀₀ lats formerly used in Latvia

¹**sap** \'sap\ *n* **1** : a vital fluid; *esp* : a watery fluid that circulates through a vascular plant **2** : a foolish gullible person — **sap·less** *adj*

²**sap** *vb* **sapped; sap·ping** **1** : UNDERMINE **2** : to weaken gradually

sa·pi·ent \'sā-pē-ənt, 'sa-\ *adj* : WISE, DISCERNING — **sa·pi·ence** \-əns\ *n*

sap·ling \'sa-pliŋ\ *n* : a young tree

sap·phire \'sa-ˌfī(-ə)r\ *n* : a hard transparent usu. rich blue gem

sap·py \'sa-pē\ *adj* **sap·pi·er; -est** **1** : full of sap **2** : overly sentimental ⟨a ∼ movie⟩ **3** : SILLY, FOOLISH

sap·ro·phyte \'sa-prə-ˌfīt\ *n* : a living thing and esp. a plant living on dead or decaying organic matter — **sap·ro·phyt·ic** \ˌsa-prə-'fi-tik\ *adj*

sap·suck·er \'sap-ˌsə-kər\ *n* : any of a genus of No. American woodpeckers

sap·wood \-ˌwùd\ *n* : the younger active and usu. lighter and softer outer layer of wood (as of a tree trunk)

sar·casm \'sär-ˌka-zəm\ *n* **1** : a cutting or contemptuous remark **2** : ironic criticism or reproach — **sar·cas·tic** \sär-'kas-tik\ *adj* — **sar·cas·ti·cal·ly** \-ti-k(ə-)lē\ *adv*

sar·co·ma \sär-'kō-mə\ *n, pl* **-mas** *also* **-ma·ta** \-mə-tə\ : a malignant tumor esp. of connective tissue, bone, cartilage, or striated muscle

sar·coph·a·gus \sär-'kä-fə-gəs\ *n, pl* **-gi** \-ˌgī, -ˌjī\ *also* **-gus·es** [L *sarcophagus* (*lapis*) limestone used for coffins, fr. Gk (*lithos*) *sarkophagos*, lit., flesh-eating stone, fr. *sark-, sarx* flesh + *phagein* to eat] : a large stone coffin

sar·dine \sär-'dēn\ *n, pl* **sardines** *also* **sardine** : a young or small fish preserved for use as food

sar·don·ic \sär-'dä-nik\ *adj* : disdainfully or skeptically humorous : derisively mocking ♦ *Synonyms* IRONIC, SATIRIC, SARCASTIC — **sar·don·i·cal·ly** \-ni-k(ə-)lē\ *adv*

sa·ri *also* **sa·ree** \'sär-ē\ *n* [Hindi *sārī*] : a garment worn by women in southern Asia that consists of a long cloth draped around the body and head or shoulder

sa·rin \'sär-ən, zä-'rēn\ *n* : an extremely toxic chemical weapon used as a lethal nerve gas

sa·rong \sə-'ròŋ, -'räŋ\ *n* : a loose garment wrapped around the body and worn by men and women of the Malay Archipelago and the Pacific islands

sar·sa·pa·ril·la \ˌsas-pə-'ri-lə, ˌsärs-\ *n* **1** : the dried roots of a tropical American smilax used esp. for flavoring; *also* : the plant **2** : a sweetened carbonated beverage flavored with sassafras and an oil from a birch

sar·to·ri·al \sär-'tōr-ē-əl\ *adj* : of or relating to a tailor or tailored clothes — **sar·to·ri·al·ly** *adv*

SASE *abbr* self-addressed stamped envelope

¹**sash** \'sash\ *n* : a broad band worn around the waist or over the shoulder

²**sash** *n, pl* **sash** *also* **sash·es** : a frame for panes of glass in a door or window; *also* : the movable part of a window

sa·shay \sa-'shā\ *vb* 1 : WALK, GLIDE, GO 2 : to strut or move about in an ostentatious manner 3 : to proceed in a diagonal or sideways manner

Sask *abbr* Saskatchewan

Sas·quatch \'sas-ˌkwach, -ˌkwäch\ *n* [Halkomelem (American Indian language of British Columbia) *sésqॉac*] : a large hairy humanlike creature reported to exist in the northwestern U.S. and western Canada

sas·sa·fras \'sa-sə-ˌfras\ *n* [Sp *sasafrás*] : an aromatic No. American tree related to the laurel; *also* : its carcinogenic dried root bark

sassy \'sa-sē\ *adj* **sass·i·er; -est** : SAUCY

¹**sat** *past and past part of* SIT

²**sat** *abbr* 1 satellite 2 saturated

Sat *abbr* Saturday

Sa·tan \'sā-t²n\ *n* : DEVIL

sa·tang \sə-'täŋ\ *n, pl* **satang** *or* **satangs** — see *baht* at MONEY table

sa·tan·ic \sə-'ta-nik, sā-\ *adj* 1 : of or characteristic of Satan 2 : extremely malicious or wicked — **sa·tan·i·cal·ly** \-ni-k(ə-)lē\ *adv*

satch·el \'sa-chəl\ *n* : SUITCASE

sate \'sāt\ *vb* **sat·ed; sat·ing** : to satisfy to the full; *also* : SURFEIT, GLUT

sa·teen \sa-'tēn, sə-\ *n* : a cotton cloth finished to resemble satin

sat·el·lite \'sa-tə-ˌlīt\ *n* [MF, fr. L *satelles* attendant] 1 : an obsequious follower of a distinguished person : TOADY 2 : a celestial body that orbits a larger body 3 : a manufactured object that orbits a celestial body

satellite dish *n* : a microwave dish for receiving usu. television transmissions from an orbiting satellite

sa·ti·ate \'sā-shē-ˌāt\ *vb* **-at·ed; -at·ing** : to satisfy fully or to excess

sa·ti·ety \sə-'tī-ə-tē\ *n* : fullness to the point of excess

sat·in \'sa-t²n\ *n* : a fabric (as of silk) with a glossy surface — **sat·iny** *adj*

sat·in·wood \'sa-t²n-ˌwùd\ *n* : a hard yellowish brown wood of satiny luster; *also* : a tree yielding this wood

sat·ire \'sa-ˌtī(-ə)r\ *n* : biting wit, irony, or sarcasm used to expose vice or folly; *also* : a literary work having these qualities — **sa·tir·ic** \sə-'tir-ik\ *or* **sa·tir·i·cal** \-i-kəl\ *adj* — **sa·tir·i·cal·ly** *adv* — **sat·i·rist** \'sa-tə-rist\ *n* — **sat·i·rize** \-tə-ˌrīz\ *vb*

sat·is·fac·tion \ˌsa-təs-'fak-shən\ *n* 1 : payment through penance of punishment incurred by sin 2 : CONTENTMENT, GRATIFICATION 3 : reparation for an insult 4 : settlement of a claim

sat·is·fac·to·ry \-'fak-tə-rē\ *adj* : giving satisfaction : ADEQUATE — **sat·is·fac·to·ri·ly** \-'fak-tə-rə-lē\ *adv*

sat·is·fy \'sa-təs-ˌfī\ *vb* **-fied; -fy·ing** 1 : to answer or discharge (a claim) in full 2 : to make happy : GRATIFY 3 : to pay what is due to 4 : CONVINCE 5 : to meet the requirements of — **sat·is·fy·ing·ly** *adv*

sa·trap \'sā-ˌtrap, 'sa-\ *n* [ME, fr. L *satrapes*, fr. Gk *satrapēs*, fr. OPers *khshathrapāvan*, lit., protector of the dominion] : a petty prince : a subordinate ruler

sat·u·rate \'sa-chə-ˌrāt\ *vb* **-rat·ed; -rat·ing** : to soak thoroughly 2 : to treat or charge with something to the point where no more can be absorbed, dissolved, or retained — **sat·u·ra·ble** \'sa-chə-rə-bəl\ *adj* — **sat·u·ra·tion** \ˌsa-chə-'rā-shən\ *n*

saturated *adj* 1 : full of moisture 2 : having no double or triple bonds between carbon atoms ⟨~ fats⟩

Sat·ur·day \'sa-tər-dē, -ˌdā\ *n* : the 7th day of the week

Saturday night special *n* : a cheap easily concealed handgun

Sat·urn \'sa-tərn\ *n* : the planet 6th in order from the sun

sat·ur·nine \'sa-tər-ˌnīn\ *adj* : SULLEN, SARDONIC

sa·tyr \'sā-tər\ *n* 1 *often cap* : a woodland deity in Greek mythology having certain characteristics of a horse or goat 2 : a lecherous man

¹**sauce** \'sȯs, 3 *usu* 'sas\ *n* 1 : a fluid dressing or topping for food 2 : stewed fruit 3 : IMPUDENCE

²**sauce** \'sȯs, 2 *usu* 'sas\ *vb* **sauced; sauc·ing** 1 : to put sauce on; *also* : to add zest to 2 : to be impudent to

sauce·pan \'sȯs-ˌpan\ *n* : a small deep cooking pan with a handle

sau·cer \'sȯ-sər\ *n* : a rounded shallow dish for use under a cup

saucy \'sa-sē, 'sȯ-\ *adj* **sauc·i·er; -est** : IMPUDENT, PERT — **sauc·i·ly** \-sə-lē\ *adv* — **sauc·i·ness** \-sē-nəs\ *n*

Sau·di \'saü-dē, 'sȯ-; sä-'ü-dē\ *n* : SAUDI ARABIAN — Saudi *adj*

Saudi Arabian *n* : a native or inhabitant of Saudi Arabia — Saudi Arabian *adj*

sau·er·kraut \'saü(-ə)r-ˌkraüt\ *n* [G, fr. *sauer* sour + *Kraut* greens] : finely cut cabbage fermented in brine

Sauk \'sȯk\ *or* **Sac** \'sak, 'sȯk\ *n, pl* **Sauk** *or* **Sauks** *or* **Sac** *or* **Sacs** : a member of an American Indian people formerly living in what is now Wisconsin

sau·na \'sȯ-nə, 'saü-nə\ *n* 1 : a Finnish steam bath in which the steam is provided by water thrown on hot stones 2 : a dry heat bath; *also* : a room or cabinet used for such a bath

saun·ter \'sȯn-tər, 'sän-\ *vb* : STROLL

sau·ro·pod \'sȯr-ə-ˌpäd\ *n* : any of a suborder of plant‑eating dinosaurs (as a brontosaurus) with a long neck and tail and a small head — **sauropod** *adj*

sau·sage \'sȯ-sij\ *n* [ME *sausige*, fr. AF *sauseche*, fr. LL *salsicia*, fr. L *salsus* salted] : minced and highly seasoned meat (as pork) usu. enclosed in a tubular casing

S Aust *abbr* South Australia

sau·té \sȯ-'tā, sō-\ *vb* **sau·téed** *or* **sau·téd; sau·té·ing** [F] : to fry lightly in a little fat — **sauté** *n*

sau·terne \sō-'tərn, sȯ-\ *n, often cap* : a usu. semisweet American white wine

¹**sav·age** \'sa-vij\ *adj* [ME, fr. AF *salvage, savage*, fr. LL *salvaticus*, alter. of L *silvaticus* of the woods, wild, fr. *silva* forest] 1 : WILD, UNTAMED 2 : UNCIVILIZED, BARBAROUS 3 : CRUEL, FIERCE — **sav·age·ly** *adv* — **sav·age·ness** *n* — **sav·age·ry** \-rē\ *n*

²**savage** *n* 1 : a member of a primitive human society 2 : a rude, unmannerly, or brutal person

sa·van·na *or* **sa·van·nah** \sə-'va-nə\ *n* [Sp *zavana*] : grassland containing scattered trees

sa·vant \sa-'vänt, sə-, 'sa-vənt\ *n* : a learned person : SCHOLAR

¹**save** \'sāv\ *vb* **saved; sav·ing** 1 : to redeem from sin 2 : to rescue from danger 3 : to preserve or guard from destruction or loss; *also* : to store (data) in a computer or on a storage device 4 : to put aside as a store or reserve — **sav·er** *n*

²**save** *n* : a play that prevents an opponent from scoring or winning

³**save** *prep* : EXCEPT

⁴**save** *conj* : BUT

savings and loan association *n* : a cooperative association that holds savings of members in the form of dividend‑bearing shares and that invests chiefly in mortgage loans

savings bank *n* : a bank that holds funds of individual depositors in interest-bearing accounts and makes long-term investments (as mortgage loans)

savings bond *n* : a registered U.S. bond issued in denominations of $50 to $10,000

sav·ior *or* **sav·iour** \'sāv-yər\ *n* 1 : one who saves 2 *cap* : Jesus Christ

sa·voir faire \ˌsav-ˌwär-'fer\ *n* [F *savoir-faire*, lit., knowing how to do] : sureness in social behavior

¹**sa·vor** *also* **sa·vour** \'sā-vər\ *n* 1 : the taste and odor of something 2 : a special flavor or quality — **sa·vory** *adj*

²**savor** *also* **savour** *vb* 1 : to have a specified taste, smell, or quality 2 : to taste with pleasure ⟨~ed every morsel⟩

sa·vo·ry \'sā-və-rē\ *n, pl* **-ries** : either of two aromatic mints used in cooking

¹**sav·vy** \'sa-vē\ *vb* **sav·vied; sav·vy·ing** : UNDERSTAND, COMPREHEND

²**savvy** *n* : practical know-how ⟨political ~⟩ — **savvy** *adj*

¹**saw** *past of* SEE

²**saw** \'sȯ\ *n* : a cutting tool with a blade having a line of teeth along its edge

³**saw** *vb* **sawed** \'sȯd\; **sawed** *or* **sawn** \'sȯn\; **saw·ing** : to cut or shape with or as if with a saw

⁴**saw** *n* : a common saying : MAXIM

saw·dust \'sȯ-(ˌ)dəst\ *n* : fine particles made by a saw in cutting

saw·fly \-ˌflī\ *n* : any of numerous insects belonging to the same order as bees and wasps and including many whose larvae are plant-feeding pests

saw·horse \-ˌhȯrs\ *n* : a rack on which wood is rested while being sawed by hand

saw·mill \-ˌmil\ *n* : a mill for sawing logs

saw palmetto *n* **1** : any of several shrubby palms with spiny-toothed petioles **2** : the fruit of a saw palmetto used esp. in herbal remedies

saw·yer \ˈsȯ-yər\ *n* : a person who saws timber

sax \ˈsaks\ *n* : SAXOPHONE

sax·i·frage \ˈsak-sə-frij, -ˌfrāj\ *n* [ME, fr. AF, fr. LL *saxifraga*, fr. L, fem. of *saxifragus*, breaking rocks] : any of a genus of plants with showy flowers and usu. with leaves growing in tufts close to the ground

sax·o·phone \ˈsak-sə-ˌfōn\ *n* : a musical instrument having a conical metal tube with a reed mouthpiece and finger keys — **sax·o·phon·ist** \-ˌfō-nist\ *n*

¹say \ˈsā\ *vb* **said** \ˈsed\; **say·ing; says** \ˈsez\ **1** : to express in words ⟨∼ what you mean⟩ **2** : to state as opinion or belief **3** : PRONOUNCE; *also* : RECITE, REPEAT ⟨∼ your prayers⟩ **4** : INDICATE ⟨the clock ∼s noon⟩

²say *n*, *pl* **says** \ˈsāz\ **1** : an expression of opinion **2** : power of decision

say·ing *n* : a commonly repeated statement

say–so \ˈsā-(ˌ)sō\ *n* : an esp. authoritative assertion or decision; *also* : the right to decide ⟨he has the ∼ on this matter⟩

sb *abbr* substantive

Sb *symbol* [L *stibium*] antimony

SB *abbr* [NL *scientiae baccalaureus*] bachelor of science

SBA *abbr* Small Business Administration

sc *abbr* **1** scene **2** science

Sc *symbol* scandium

SC *abbr* **1** South Carolina **2** supreme court

¹scab \ˈskab\ *n* **1** : scabies of domestic animals **2** : a crust of hardened blood forming over a wound **3** : a worker who replaces a striker or works under conditions not authorized by a union **4** : any of various bacterial or fungus plant diseases marked by crusted spots on stems or leaves — **scab·by** *adj*

²scab *vb* **scabbed; scab·bing 1** : to become covered with a scab **2** : to work as a scab

scab·bard \ˈska-bərd\ *n* : a sheath for the blade of a weapon (as a sword)

sca·bies \ˈskā-bēz\ *n* [L] : contagious itch or mange caused by mites living as parasites under the skin

sca·brous \ˈska-brəs, ˈskā-\ *adj* **1** : DIFFICULT, KNOTTY **2** : rough to the touch : SCALY, SCURFY ⟨a ∼ leaf⟩ **3** : dealing with suggestive, indecent, or scandalous themes ⟨∼ lyrics⟩; *also* : SQUALID

scad \ˈskad\ *n* : a large number or quantity — usu. used in pl.

scaf·fold \ˈska-fəld, -ˌfōld\ *n* **1** : a raised platform for workers to sit or stand on **2** : a platform on which a criminal is executed (as by hanging)

scaf·fold·ing *n* : a system of scaffolds; *also* : materials for scaffolds

scal·a·wag *or* **scal·ly·wag** \ˈska-li-ˌwag\ *n* : RASCAL

¹scald \ˈskȯld\ *vb* **1** : to burn with or as if with hot liquid or steam **2** : to heat to just below the boiling point

²scald *n* : a burn caused by scalding

¹scale \ˈskāl\ *n* **1** : either pan of a balance **2** : BALANCE — usu. used in pl. **3** : a weighing instrument

²scale *vb* **scaled; scal·ing** : WEIGH

³scale *n* **1** : one of the small thin plates that cover the body esp. of a fish or reptile **2** : a thin plate or flake **3** : a thin coating, layer, or incrustation **4** : SCALE INSECT — **scaled** \ˈskāld\ *adj* — **scale·less** \ˈskāl-ləs\ *adj* — **scaly** *adj*

⁴scale *vb* **scaled; scal·ing** : to strip of scales

⁵scale *n* [ME, fr. LL *scala* ladder, staircase, fr. L *scalae*, pl., stairs, rungs, ladder] **1** : something divided into regular spaces as a help in drawing or measuring **2** : a graduated series **3** : the size of a sample (as a model) in proportion to the size of the actual thing **4** : a standard of estimation or judgment **5** : a series of musical tones going up or down in pitch according to a specified scheme

⁶scale *vb* **scaled; scal·ing 1** : to climb by or as if by a ladder **2** : to arrange in a graded series

scale insect *n* : any of numerous small insects with wingless scale-covered females that are related to aphids and feed on and are often pests of plants

scale-pan \ˈskāl-ˌpan\ *n* : SCALE 1

scal·lion \ˈskal-yən\ *n* [ultim. fr. L *ascalonia* (*caepa*) on-

ion of Ascalon (seaport in Palestine)] : an onion without an enlarged bulb; *also* : GREEN ONION

¹scal·lop \ˈskä-ləp, ˈska-\ *n* **1** : any of numerous marine bivalve mollusks with radially ridged shells; *also* : a large edible muscle of this mollusk **2** : one of a continuous series of rounded projections forming an edge

²scallop *vb* **1** : to bake in a casserole ⟨∼ed potatoes⟩ **2** : to shape, cut, or finish in scallops ⟨∼ed edges⟩

¹scalp \ˈskalp\ *n* : the part of the skin and flesh of the head usu. covered with hair

²scalp *vb* **1** : to remove the scalp from **2** : to resell at greatly increased prices ⟨∼ tickets⟩ — **scalp·er** *n*

scal·pel \ˈskal-pəl\ *n* : a small straight knife with a thin blade used esp. in surgery

scam \ˈskam\ *n* : a fraudulent or deceptive act or operation

scamp \ˈskamp\ *n* : RASCAL

scam·per \ˈskam-pər\ *vb* : to run nimbly and playfully — **scamper** *n*

scam·pi \ˈskam-pē\ *n*, *pl* **scampi** [It] : a usu. large shrimp; *also* : large shrimp prepared with a garlic-flavored sauce

¹scan \ˈskan\ *vb* **scanned; scan·ning 1** : to read (verses) so as to show metrical structure **2** : to examine closely **3** : to input or examine systematically in order to obtain data esp. for display or storage **4** : to make a scan of (as the human body) — **scan·ner** *n*

²scan *n* **1** : the act or process of scanning **2** : a picture of the distribution of radioactive material in something; *also* : an image of a bodily part produced (as by computer) by combining radiographic data obtained from several angles or sections

Scand *abbr* Scandinavia

scan·dal \ˈskan-dᵊl\ *n* [ME, fr. LL *scandalum* stumbling block, offense, fr. Gk *skandalon*] **1** : DISGRACE, DISHONOR **2** : malicious gossip : SLANDER — **scan·dal·ize** *vb* — **scan·dal·ous** *adj* — **scan·dal·ous·ly** *adv*

scan·dal·mon·ger \-ˌmən-gər, -ˌmän-\ *n* : a person who circulates scandal

Scan·di·na·vian \ˌskan-də-ˈnā-vē-ən\ *n* : a native or inhabitant of Scandinavia — **Scandinavian** *adj*

scan·di·um \ˈskan-dē-əm\ *n* : a silvery-white metallic chemical element

scan·ner \ˈska-nər\ *n* **1** : a radio receiver that sequentially scans a range of frequencies for a signal **2** : a device that scans an image or document esp. for use or storage on a computer

¹scant \ˈskant\ *adj* **1** : barely sufficient ⟨food is in ∼ supply⟩ **2** : having scarcely enough ♦ **Synonyms** SCANTY, SKIMPY, MEAGER, SPARSE, EXIGUOUS

²scant *vb* **1** : SKIMP **2** : STINT

scant·ling \ˈskant-liŋ\ *n* : a small piece of lumber (as an upright in a house)

scanty \ˈskan-tē\ *adj* **scant·i·er; -est** : barely sufficient : SCANT ⟨wore ∼ outfits⟩ — **scant·i·ly** \ˈskan-tə-lē\ *adv* — **scant·i·ness** \-tē-nəs\ *n*

scape·goat \ˈskāp-ˌgōt\ *n* : one that bears the blame for others

scape·grace \-ˌgrās\ *n* [*scape* (escape)] : an incorrigible rascal

scap·u·la \ˈska-pyə-lə\ *n*, *pl* **-lae** \-ˌlē\ *or* **-las** [L] : SHOULDER BLADE

scap·u·lar \-lər\ *n* : a pair of small cloth squares worn on the breast and back under the clothing esp. for religious purposes

scar \ˈskär\ *n* : a mark left after injured tissue has healed — **scar** *vb*

scar·ab \ˈska-rəb\ *n* [MF *scarabee*, fr. L *scarabaeus*] : any of a family of large stout beetles; *also* : an ornament (as a gem) representing such a beetle

scarce \ˈskers\ *adj* **scarc·er; scarc·est 1** : deficient in quantity or number : not plentiful **2** : intentionally absent ⟨made himself ∼ at inspection time⟩ — **scar·ci·ty** \ˈsker-sə-tē\ *n*

scarce·ly \-lē\ *adv* **1** : BARELY ⟨can ∼ see them⟩ **2** : almost not **3** : very probably not

¹scare \ˈsker\ *vb* **scared; scar·ing** : FRIGHTEN, STARTLE

²scare *n* **1** : FRIGHT **2** : a widespread state of alarm

scare·crow \ˈsker-ˌkrō\ *n* : a crude figure set up to scare birds away from crops

¹scarf \ˈskärf\ *n*, *pl* **scarves** \ˈskärvz\ *or* **scarfs 1** : a broad band (as of cloth) worn about the shoulders, around the neck, over the head, or about the waist **2** : a long narrow cloth cover for a table or dresser top

²scarf *vb* [alter. of earlier *scoff* eat greedily] : to eat greedily ⟨~*ed* down his lunch⟩

scar·i·fy \'sker-ə-ˌfī\ *vb* **-fied; -fy·ing 1** : to make scratches or small cuts in ⟨~ skin for vaccination⟩ ⟨~ seeds to help them germinate⟩ **2** : to lacerate the feelings of **3** : to break up and loosen the surface of (as a road) — **scar·i·fi·ca·tion** \ˌskar-ə-fə-'kā-shən\ *n*

scar·let \'skär-lət\ *n* : a bright red color — **scarlet** *adj*

scarlet fever *n* : an acute contagious disease marked by fever, sore throat, and red rash and caused by certain streptococci

scarp \'skärp\ *n* : a line of cliffs produced by faulting or erosion

scath·ing \'skā-thin\ *adj* : bitterly severe ⟨a ~ condemnation⟩

scat·o·log·i·cal \ˌska-tə-'lä-ji-kəl\ *adj* : concerned with obscene matters

scat·ter \'ska-tər\ *vb* **1** : to distribute or strew about irregularly **2** : DISPERSE

scat·ter·brain \'ska-tər-ˌbrān\ *n* : a silly careless person — **scat·ter·brained** \-ˌbrānd\ *adj*

scav·enge \'ska-vənj\ *vb* **scav·enged; scav·eng·ing** : to work or function as a scavenger

scav·en·ger \'ska-vən-jər\ *n* [alter. of earlier *scavager*, fr. AF *scawageour* collector of scavage (duty imposed on nonresident street merchants), fr. *skawage* scavage, fr. MF dial. (Flanders) *escauver* to inspect, fr. MD *scouwen*] : a person or animal that collects, eats, or disposes of refuse or waste

sce·nar·io \sə-'ner-ē-ˌō\ *n, pl* **-i·os** : the plot or outline of a dramatic work; *also* : an account of a possible action

scene \'sēn\ *n* [MF, stage, fr. L *scena, scaena* stage, scene, prob. fr. Etruscan, fr. Gk *skēnē* temporary shelter, tent, building forming the background for a dramatic performance, stage] **1** : a division of one act of a play **2** : a single situation or sequence in a play or motion picture **3** : a stage setting **4** : VIEW, PROSPECT **5** : the place of an occurrence or action **6** : a display of strong feeling and esp. anger **7** : a sphere of activity ⟨the fashion ~⟩ — **sce·nic** \'sē-nik\ *adj*

scen·ery \'sē-nə-rē\ *n, pl* **-er·ies 1** : the painted scenes or hangings and accessories used on a theater stage **2** : a picturesque view or landscape

¹scent \'sent\ *n* **1** : ODOR, SMELL **2** : sense of smell **3** : course of pursuit : TRACK **4** : PERFUME **2** — **scent·ed** \'sen-təd\ *adj* — **scent·less** *adj*

²scent *vb* **1** : SMELL **2** : to imbue or fill with odor

scep·ter \'sep-tər\ *n* : a staff borne by a sovereign as an emblem of authority

sceptic *var of* SKEPTIC

scep·tre *Brit var of* SCEPTER

sch *abbr* school

¹sched·ule \'ske-jül, *esp Brit* 'she-dyül\ *n* **1** : a list of items or details **2** : TIMETABLE

²schedule *vb* **sched·uled; sched·ul·ing 1** : to appoint, assign, or designate for a fixed time **2** : to make a schedule of; *also* : to enter on a schedule

sche·ma \'skē-mə\ *n, pl* **sche·ma·ta** \-mə-tə\ *also* **schemas** : a diagrammatic presentation or plan : OUTLINE

sche·mat·ic \ski-'ma-tik\ *adj* : of or relating to a scheme or diagram : DIAGRAMMATIC — **schematic** *n* — **sche·mat·i·cal·ly** \-ti-k(ə-)lē\ *adv*

¹scheme \'skēm\ *n* **1** : a plan for doing something; *esp* : a crafty plot **2** : a systematic design ⟨a color ~⟩

²scheme *vb* **schemed; schem·ing** : to form a plot : INTRIGUE — **schem·er** *n*

schil·ling \'shi-liŋ\ *n* : a former basic monetary unit of Austria

schism \'si-zəm, 'ski-\ *n* **1** : DIVISION, SPLIT; *also* : DISCORD, DISSENSION **2** : a formal division in or separation from a religious body

schis·mat·ic \siz-'ma-tik, ski-\ *n* : one who creates or takes part in schism — **schismatic** *adj*

schist \'shist\ *n* : a metamorphic crystalline rock

schizo·phre·nia \ˌskit-sə-'frē-nē-ə\ *n* [NL, fr. Gk *schizein* to split + *phrēn* diaphragm, mind] : a psychotic mental illness that is characterized by a distorted view of the real world, by a greatly reduced ability to carry out

one's daily tasks, and by abnormal ways of thinking, feeling, perceiving, and behaving — **schiz·oid** \'skit-ˌsóid\ *adj or n* — **schizo·phren·ic** \ˌskit-sə-'fre-nik\ *adj or n*

schle·miel *also* **shle·miel** \shlə-'mēl\ *n* : an unlucky bungler : CHUMP

schlep *or* **schlepp** \'shlep\ *vb* [Yiddish *shlepn*] **1** : DRAG, HAUL **2** : to move slowly or awkwardly

schlock \'shläk\ *or* **schlocky** \'shlä-kē\ *adj* : of low quality or value — **schlock** *n*

schlub *also* **shlub** \'shləb\ *n* [Yiddish *zhlob, zhlub* yokel, boor] *slang* : a stupid, ineffectual, or unattractive person

schmaltz *also* **schmalz** \'shmólts, 'shmälts\ *n* [Yiddish *shmalts*, lit., rendered fat] : sentimental or florid music or art — **schmaltzy** *adj*

schmooze *or* **shmooze** \'shmüz\ *vb* : to chat informally esp. to gain favor — **schmooze** *n*

schnapps \'shnaps\ *n, pl* **schnapps** : a liquor (as gin) of high alcoholic content

schnau·zer \'shnaü-zər, 'shnaüt-sər\ *n* [G, fr. *Schnauze* snout] : a dog of any of three breeds that are characterized by a wiry coat, long head, pointed ears, heavy eyebrows, and long hair on the muzzle

schol·ar \'skä-lər\ *n* **1** : STUDENT, PUPIL **2** : a learned person : SAVANT — **schol·ar·ly** *adj*

schol·ar·ship \-ˌship\ *n* **1** : the qualities or learning of a scholar **2** : money awarded to a student to help pay for further education

scho·las·tic \skə-'las-tik\ *adj* : of or relating to schools, scholars, or scholarship

¹school \'skül\ *n* **1** : an institution for teaching and learning; *also* : the pupils in attendance **2** : a body of persons of like opinions or beliefs ⟨the radical ~⟩

²school *vb* : TEACH, TRAIN, DRILL

³school *n* : a large number of one kind of water animal swimming and feeding together

school·boy \-ˌbói\ *n* : a boy attending school

school·fel·low \-ˌfe-lō\ *n* : SCHOOLMATE

school·girl \-ˌgərl\ *n* : a girl attending school

school·house \-ˌhaüs\ *n* : a building used as a school

school·marm \-ˌmärm\ *or* **school·ma'am** \-ˌmäm, -ˌmam\ *n* **1** : a woman who is a schoolteacher **2** : a person who exhibits characteristics popularly attributed to schoolteachers

school·mas·ter \-ˌmas-tər\ *n* : a man who is a schoolteacher

school·mate \-ˌmāt\ *n* : a school companion

school·mis·tress \-ˌmis-trəs\ *n* : a woman who is a schoolteacher

school·room \-ˌrüm, -ˌrùm\ *n* : CLASSROOM

school·teach·er \-ˌtē-chər\ *n* : one who teaches in a school

schoo·ner \'skü-nər\ *n* : a fore-and-aft rigged sailing ship

schtick *var of* SHTICK

schuss \'shùs, 'shüs\ *vb* [G *Schuss*, n., lit., shot] : to ski down a slope at high speed — **schuss** *n*

sci *abbr* science; scientific

sci·at·i·ca \sī-'a-ti-kə\ *n* : pain in the region of the hips or along the course of the nerve at the back of the thigh

sci·ence \'sī-əns\ *n* [ME, fr. AF, fr. L *scientia*, fr. *scient-, sciens* having knowledge, fr. prp. of *scire* to know] **1** : an area of knowledge that is an object of study; *esp* : NATURAL SCIENCE **2** : knowledge covering general truths or the operation of general laws especially as obtained and tested through the scientific method — **sci·en·tif·ic** \ˌsī-ən-'ti-fik\ *adj* — **sci·en·tif·i·cal·ly** \-fi-k(ə-)lē\ *adv* — **sci·en·tist** \'sī-ən-tist\ *n*

science fiction *n* : fiction dealing principally with the impact of actual or imagined science on society or individuals

scientific method *n* : the rules and methods for the pursuit of knowledge involving the finding and stating of a problem, the collection of facts through observation and experiment, and the making and testing of ideas that need to be proven right or wrong

scim·i·tar \'si-mə-tər\ *n* : a curved sword used chiefly by Arabs and Turks

scin·til·la \sin-'ti-lə\ *n* : SPARK, TRACE ⟨isn't a ~ of evidence⟩

scin·til·late \'sin-tə-ˌlāt\ *vb* **-lat·ed; -lat·ing** : SPARKLE, GLEAM — **scin·til·la·tion** \ˌsin-tə-'lä-shən\ *n*

sci·on \'sī-ən\ n 1 : a shoot of a plant joined to a stock in grafting 2 : DESCENDANT ⟨a ~ of a powerful family⟩

scis·sors \'si-zərz\ n pl : a cutting instrument like shears but usu. smaller

scissors kick n : a swimming kick in which the legs move like scissors

sclero·der·ma \ˌskler-ə-'dər-mə\ n : a chronic disease characterized by the usu. progressive hardening and thickening of the skin

scle·ro·sis \sklə-'rō-səs\ n : abnormal hardening of tissue (as of an artery); also : a disease characterized by this — **scle·rot·ic** \-'rä-tik\ adj

scoff \'skäf\ vb : MOCK, JEER ⟨~ed at his proposal⟩ — **scoff·er** n

scoff·law \-ˌló\ n : a contemptuous law violator

¹scold \'skōld\ n : a person who scolds

²scold vb : to censure severely or angrily

sconce \'skäns\ n : a candlestick or an electric light fixture fastened to a wall

scone \'skōn, 'skän\ n : a biscuit (as of oatmeal) baked on a griddle

¹scoop \'sküp\ n 1 : a large shovel; also : a utensil with a shovellike or rounded end 2 : the amount contained by a scoop 3 : an act of scooping 4 : information of immediate interest

²scoop vb 1 : to take out or up or empty with or as if with a scoop 2 : to make hollow 3 : to report a news item in advance of ⟨~ed the other newspapers⟩

scoot \'sküt\ vb : to move swiftly

scoot·er \'skü-tər\ n 1 : a child's vehicle consisting of a narrow board mounted between two wheels tandem with an upright steering handle attached to the front wheel 2 : MOTOR SCOOTER

¹scope \'skōp\ n [It scopo purpose, goal, fr. Gk skopos] 1 : space or opportunity for action or thought 2 : extent covered : RANGE ⟨is beyond the ~ of this essay⟩

²scope n : an instrument (as a microscope or telescope) for viewing

scorch \'skórch\ vb : to burn the surface of; also : to dry or shrivel with heat

¹score \'skór\ n, pl **scores** 1 or pl **score** : TWENTY 2 : CUT, SCRATCH, SLASH 3 : a record of points made (as in a game) 4 : DEBT 5 : REASON, GROUND 6 : the music of a composition or arrangement with different parts indicated 7 : success in obtaining something (as drugs) esp. illegally

²score vb **scored; scor·ing** 1 : RECORD 2 : to keep score in a game 3 : to mark with lines, grooves, scratches, or notches 4 : to gain or tally in or as if in a game ⟨scored a point⟩ 5 : to assign a grade or score to ⟨~ the tests⟩ 6 : to compose a score for 7 : SUCCEED 8 : ACQUIRE ⟨scored tickets to the game⟩ — **score·less** adj — **scor·er** n

¹scorn \'skórn\ n : an emotion involving both anger and disgust : CONTEMPT — **scorn·ful** \-fəl\ adj — **scorn·ful·ly** adv

²scorn vb : to hold in contempt : DISDAIN ⟨were ~ed as fanatics⟩ — **scorn·er** n

Scor·pio \'skór-pē-ˌō\ n [L, lit., scorpion] 1 : a zodiacal constellation between Libra and Sagittarius usu. pictured as a scorpion 2 : the 8th sign of the zodiac in astrology; also : one born under this sign

scor·pi·on \'skór-pē-ən\ n : any of an order of arthropods related to the spiders that have a poisonous stinger at the tip of a long jointed tail

¹Scot \'skät\ n : a native or inhabitant of Scotland

²Scot abbr Scotland; Scottish

Scotch \'skäch\ n 1 : SCOTS 2 **Scotch** pl : the people of Scotland 3 : a whiskey distilled in Scotland esp. from malted barley — **Scotch** adj — **Scotch·man** \-mən\ n — **Scotch·wom·an** \-ˌwu̇-mən\ n

Scotch bonnet n : a small roundish very hot chili pepper esp. of the Caribbean

Scotch pine n : a pine that is naturalized in the U.S. from northern Europe and Asia and is a valuable timber tree

Scotch terrier n : SCOTTISH TERRIER

scot–free \'skät-'frē\ adj : free from obligation, harm, or penalty

Scots \'skäts\ n : the English language of Scotland

Scots·man \'skäts-mən\ n : SCOT

Scots·wom·an \-ˌwu̇-mən\ n : a woman who is a Scot

Scot·tie \'skä-tē\ n : SCOTTISH TERRIER

Scot·tish \'skä-tish\ adj : of, relating to, or characteristic of Scotland, Scots, or the Scots

Scottish terrier n : any of an old Scottish breed of terrier with short legs, a long head with small erect ears, a broad deep chest, and a thick rough coat

scoun·drel \'skau̇n-drəl\ n : a disreputable person : VILLAIN

¹scour \'skau̇(-ə)r\ vb 1 : to rub (as with a gritty substance) in order to clean 2 : to cleanse by or as if by rubbing

²scour vb 1 : to move rapidly through : RUSH 2 : to examine or observe to obtain information

¹scourge \'skərj\ n 1 : LASH, WHIP 2 : PUNISHMENT; also : a cause of affliction (as a plague)

²scourge vb **scourged; scourg·ing** 1 : LASH, FLOG 2 : to punish severely

¹scout \'skau̇t\ vb [ME, fr. AF escuter to listen, fr. L auscultare] 1 : to look around : RECONNOITER 2 : to inspect or observe to get information

²scout n 1 : a person sent out to get information; also : a soldier, airplane, or ship sent out to reconnoiter 2 : BOY SCOUT 3 : GIRL SCOUT — **scout·mas·ter** \-ˌmas-tər\ n

³scout vb : SCORN, SCOFF

scow \'skau̇\ n : a large flat-bottomed boat with square ends

scowl \'skau̇(-ə)l\ vb : to make a frowning expression of displeasure — **scowl** n

SCPO abbr senior chief petty officer

scrab·ble \'skra-bəl\ vb **scrab·bled; scrab·bling** 1 : SCRAPE, SCRATCH 2 : CLAMBER, SCRAMBLE ⟨scrabbled on the slippery rocks⟩ 3 : to work hard and long 4 : SCRIBBLE — **scrabble** n — **scrab·bler** n

scrag·gly \'skra-glē\ adj : IRREGULAR; also : RAGGED, UNKEMPT ⟨a ~ beard⟩

scram \'skram\ vb **scrammed; scram·ming** : to go away at once

scram·ble \'skram-bəl\ vb **scram·bled; scram·bling** 1 : to clamber clumsily around 2 : to struggle for or as if for possession of something 3 : to spread irregularly 4 : to mix together 5 : to cook (eggs) by stirring during frying — **scramble** n

¹scrap \'skrap\ n 1 : FRAGMENT, PIECE 2 : discarded material : REFUSE

²scrap vb **scrapped; scrap·ping** 1 : to make into scrap ⟨~ a battleship⟩ 2 : to get rid of as useless ⟨scrapped the plans⟩

³scrap n : FIGHT

⁴scrap vb **scrapped; scrap·ping** : FIGHT, QUARREL — **scrap·per** n

scrap·book \'skrap-ˌbu̇k\ n : a blank book in which mementos are kept

¹scrape \'skrāp\ vb **scraped; scrap·ing** 1 : to remove by drawing a knife over; also : to clean or smooth by rubbing off the covering 2 : to damage or injure the surface of by contact with something rough 3 : to draw across a surface with a grating sound 4 : to get together (money) by strict economy 5 : to get along with difficulty ⟨barely scraping by on her income⟩ — **scrap·er** n

²scrape n 1 : the act or the effect of scraping 2 : a bow accompanied by a drawing back of the foot 3 : an unpleasant predicament

scra·pie \'skrā-pē\ n : a usu. fatal degenerative disease of the brain esp. of sheep that is related to mad cow disease

¹scrap·py \'skra-pē\ adj **scrap·pi·er; -est** : DISCONNECTED, FRAGMENTARY

²scrappy adj **scrap·pi·er; -est** 1 : QUARRELSOME 2 : having an aggressive and determined spirit ⟨a ~ competitor⟩

¹scratch \'skrach\ vb 1 : to scrape, dig, or rub with or as if with claws or nails ⟨a dog ~ing at the door⟩ ⟨~ed my arm⟩ 2 : SCRAPE 3 ⟨~ed his nails across the blackboard⟩ 3 : SCRAPE 4 4 : to cancel or erase by or as if by drawing a line through 5 : to withdraw from a contest — **scratchy** adj — **scratch one's head** : to become confused or perplexed

²scratch n 1 : a mark or injury made by or as if by scratching; also : a sound so made 2 : the starting line in a race — **from scratch** : with no steps completed or ingredients prepared ahead of time ⟨built from ~⟩

³scratch adj 1 : made or done by chance ⟨a ~ hit⟩ 2 : made as or used for a trial attempt ⟨~ paper⟩

scratch card *n* : a card with a small area covered by an opaque coating which may be scraped away to reveal hidden information

scrawl \\'skrȯl\ *vb* : to write hastily and carelessly — **scrawl** *n*

scraw·ny \\'skrȯ-nē\ *adj* **scraw·ni·er; -est** : very thin : SKINNY

¹**scream** \\'skrēm\ *vb* : to cry out loudly and shrilly

²**scream** *n* : a loud shrill cry

scream·ing \\'skrē-miŋ\ *adj* : so striking as to attract notice as if by screaming ⟨~ headlines⟩

screech \\'skrēch\ *vb* : SHRIEK — **screech** *n* — **screechy** \\'skrē-chē\ *adj*

screech·ing \\'skrē-chiŋ\ *adj* : ABRUPT ⟨came to a ~ halt⟩

¹**screen** \\'skrēn\ *n* **1** : a device or partition used to hide, restrain, protect, or decorate ⟨a window ~⟩; *also* : something that shelters, protects, or conceals **2** : a sieve or perforated material for separating finer from coarser parts (as of sand) **3** : a surface on which an image is made to appear (as in television); *also* : the information displayed on a computer screen at one time **4** : the motion-picture industry

²**screen** *vb* **1** : to shield with or as if with a screen **2** : to separate with a screen; *also* : to select or categorize methodically ⟨~ contestants⟩ **3** : to present (as a motion picture) on the screen

screen·ing \\'skrē-niŋ\ *n* **1** : metal or plastic mesh (as for window screens) **2** : a showing of a motion picture

screen saver *n* : a computer program that displays something (as images) on the screen of a computer that is on but not in use

¹**screw** \\'skrü\ *n* [ME, fr. MF *escroe* female screw, nut, fr. ML *scrofa*, fr. L, sow] **1** : a machine consisting of a solid cylinder with a spiral groove around it and a corresponding hollow cylinder into which it fits **2** : a naillike metal piece with a spiral groove and a head with a slot that is inserted into material by rotating and is used to fasten pieces of solid material together **3** : PROPELLER

²**screw** *vb* **1** : to fasten or close by means of a screw **2** : to operate or adjust by means of a screw **3** : to move or cause to move spirally; *also* : to close or set in position by such an action

screw·ball \\'skrü-ˌbȯl\ *n* **1** : a baseball pitch breaking in a direction opposite to a curve **2** : a whimsical, eccentric, or crazy person

screw·driv·er \-ˌdrī-vər\ *n* **1** : a tool for turning screws **2** : a drink made of vodka and orange juice

screw-worm \\'skrü-ˌwərm\ *n* : an American blowfly of warm regions whose larva matures in wounds or sores of mammals and may cause disease or death; *esp* : its larva

screwy \\'skrü-ē\ *adj* **screw·i·er; -est 1** : crazily absurd, eccentric, or unusual ⟨a ~ idea⟩ **2** : CRAZY, INSANE

scrib·ble \\'skri-bəl\ *vb* **scrib·bled; scrib·bling** : to write hastily or carelessly — **scribble** *n* — **scrib·bler** *n*

scribe \\'skrīb\ *n* **1** : a scholar of Jewish law in New Testament times **2** : a person whose business is the copying of writing **3** : JOURNALIST

scrim \\'skrim\ *n* : a light loosely woven cotton or linen cloth

scrim·mage \\'skri-mij\ *n* : the play between two football teams beginning with the snap of the ball; *also* : practice play between two teams — **scrimmage** *vb*

scrimp \\'skrimp\ *vb* : to economize greatly ⟨~ and save⟩

scrim·shaw \\'skrim-ˌshȯ\ *n* : carved or engraved articles made orig. by American whalers usu. from baleen or whale ivory — **scrimshaw** *vb*

scrip \\'skrip\ *n* **1** : a certificate showing its holder is entitled to something (as stock or land) **2** : paper money issued for temporary use in an emergency

¹**script** \\'skript\ *n* **1** : written matter (as lines for a play or broadcast) **2** : HANDWRITING

²**script** *abbr* scripture

scrip·ture \\'skrip-chər\ *n* **1** *cap* : the books of the Bible — often used in pl. **2** : the sacred writings of a religion — **scrip·tur·al** \\'skrip-chə-rəl\ *adj* — **scrip·tur·al·ly** *adv*

scriv·en·er \\'skri-və-nər\ *n* : SCRIBE, COPYIST, WRITER

scrod \\'skräd\ *n* [prob. fr. Brit. dial. (Cornwall) *scrawed*, pp. of *scraw, scrawl* to split, salt, and dry (young fish)] : a young fish (as a cod or haddock); *esp* : one split and boned for cooking

scrof·u·la \\'skrȯ-fyə-lə\ *n* : tuberculosis of lymph nodes esp. in the neck

¹**scroll** \\'skrōl\ *n* : a roll of paper or parchment for writing a document; *also* : a spiral or coiled ornamental form suggesting a loosely or partly rolled scroll

²**scroll** *vb* : to move or cause to move text or graphics up, down, or across a display screen

scroll saw *n* **1** : FRETSAW **2** : a machine saw with a narrow vertically reciprocating blade for cutting curved lines or openwork

scro·tum \\'skrō-təm\ *n, pl* **scro·ta** \-tə\ *or* **scrotums** [L] : a pouch that in most male mammals contains the testes

scrounge \\'skraünj\ *vb* **scrounged; scroung·ing** : to collect by or as if by foraging

¹**scrub** \\'skrəb\ *n* **1** : a thick growth of stunted trees or shrubs; *also* : an area of land covered with scrub **2** : an inferior domestic animal **3** : a person of insignificant size or standing **4** : a player not on the first team — **scrub** *adj* — **scrub·by** *adj*

²**scrub** *vb* **scrubbed; scrub·bing 1** : to clean or wash by rubbing ⟨~ clothes⟩ ⟨~ out a spot⟩ **2** : CANCEL

³**scrub** *n* **1** : an act or instance of scrubbing ⟨gave the clothes a good ~⟩ **2** *pl* : loose-fitting clothing worn by hospital staff ⟨surgical ~s⟩

scrub·ber \\'skrə-bər\ *n* : one that scrubs; *esp* : an apparatus for removing impurities esp. from gases

scruff \\'skrəf\ *n* : the loose skin of the back of the neck : NAPE

scruffy \\'skrə-fē\ *adj* **scruff·i·er; -est** : UNKEMPT, SLOVENLY ⟨a ~ tramp⟩

scrump·tious \\'skrəmp-shəs\ *adj* : DELIGHTFUL, EXCELLENT; *esp* : DELICIOUS ⟨a ~ cake⟩ — **scrump·tious·ly** *adv*

scrunch·ie *or* **scrunchy** \\'skrən-chē, 'skrun-\ *n* : a fabric-covered elastic for the hair

¹**scru·ple** \\'skrü-pəl\ *n* [ME *scrupil, scriple*, fr. AF *scruble*, fr. L *scrupulus*, dim. of *scrupus* source of uneasiness, lit., sharp stone] **1** : a point of conscience or honor **2** : hesitation due to ethical considerations

²**scruple** *vb* **scru·pled; scru·pling** : to be reluctant on grounds of conscience : HESITATE

scru·pu·lous \\'skrü-pyə-ləs\ *adj* **1** : having moral integrity **2** : PAINSTAKING ⟨was ~ about her work⟩ — **scru·pu·lous·ly** *adv* — **scru·pu·lous·ness** *n*

scru·ti·nise *Brit var of* SCRUTINIZE

scru·ti·nize \\'skrü-tə-ˌnīz\ *vb* **-nized; -niz·ing** : to examine closely

scru·ti·ny \\'skrü-tə-nē\ *n, pl* **-nies** [L *scrutinium*, fr. *scrutari* to search, examine, prob. fr. *scruta* trash] : a careful looking over ✦ *Synonyms* INSPECTION, EXAMINATION, ANALYSIS

scu·ba \\'skü-bə\ *n* [*self*-contained *u*nderwater *b*reathing *a*pparatus] : an apparatus for breathing while swimming underwater

scuba diver *n* : one who swims underwater with the aid of scuba gear

¹**scud** \\'skəd\ *vb* **scud·ded; scud·ding** : to move speedily

²**scud** *n* : light clouds driven by the wind

¹**scuff** \\'skəf\ *vb* **1** : to scrape the feet while walking : SHUFFLE **2** : to scratch or become scratched or worn away

²**scuff** *n* **1** : a mark or injury caused by scuffing **2** : a flat-soled slipper without heel strap

scuf·fle \\'skə-fəl\ *vb* **scuf·fled; scuf·fling 1** : to struggle confusedly at close quarters ⟨*scuffled* with the police⟩ **2** : to shuffle one's feet — **scuffle** *n*

¹**scull** \\'skəl\ *n* **1** : an oar for use in sculling; *also* : one of a pair of short oars for a single oarsman **2** : a racing shell propelled by one or two persons using sculls

²**scull** *vb* : to propel (a boat) by an oar over the stern

scul·lery \\'skə-lə-rē\ *n, pl* **-ler·ies** [ME *squilerie, sculerie* department of household in charge of dishes, fr. AF *esquilerie*, fr. *escuele* bowl, fr. L *scutella* drinking bowl] : a small room near the kitchen used for cleaning dishes, cooking utensils, and vegetables

scul·lion \\'skəl-yən\ *n* : a kitchen helper

sculpt \\'skəlpt\ *vb* : CARVE, SCULPTURE

sculp·tor \\'skəlp-tər\ *n* : a person who produces works of sculpture

¹**sculp·ture** \\'skəlp-chər\ *n* : the act, process, or art of carving or molding material (as stone, wood, or plastic); *also* : work produced this way — **sculp·tur·al** \\'skəlp-chə-rəl\ *adj*

²**sculpture** *vb* **sculp·tured; sculp·tur·ing** : to form or alter as or as if a work of sculpture ⟨*sculptured* hedges⟩

scum \'skəm\ *n* **1** : a slimy or filmy covering on the surface of a liquid **2** : waste matter **3** : RABBLE
scup·per \'skə-pər\ *n* [ME *skopper-*, perh. fr. AF **escopoir*, fr. *escopir* to spit out] : an opening in the side of a ship through which water on deck is drained overboard
scurf \'skərf\ *n* : thin dry scales of skin (as dandruff); *also* : a scaly deposit or covering — **scurfy** \'skər-fē\ *adj*
scur·ri·lous \'skər-ə-ləs\ *adj* : coarsely jesting : OBSCENE, VULGAR
scur·ry \'skər-ē\ *vb* **scur·ried; scur·ry·ing** : SCAMPER ⟨*scurried* for cover⟩
¹**scur·vy** \'skər-vē\ *n* : a disease caused by a lack of vitamin C and characterized by spongy gums, loosened teeth, and bleeding under the skin
²**scurvy** *adj* : MEAN, CONTEMPTIBLE — **scur·vi·ly** \'skər-və-lē\ *adv*
scutch·eon \'skə-chən\ *n* : ESCUTCHEON
¹**scut·tle** \'skə-t³l\ *n* : a pail for carrying coal

¹scuttle

²**scuttle** *n* : a small opening with a lid esp. in the deck, side, or bottom of a ship
³**scuttle** *vb* **scut·tled; scut·tling** : to cut a hole in the deck, side, or bottom of (a ship) in order to sink
⁴**scuttle** *vb* **scut·tled; scut·tling** : SCURRY, SCAMPER
scut·tle·butt \'skə-t³l-,bət\ *n* : GOSSIP
scythe \'sīth\ *n* : an implement for mowing (as grass or grain) by hand — **scythe** *vb*
SD *abbr* **1** South Dakota **2** special delivery
S Dak *abbr* South Dakota
SDI *abbr* Strategic Defense Initiative
Se *symbol* selenium
SE *abbr* southeast
¹**sea** \'sē\ *n* **1** : a large body of salt water **2** : OCEAN **3** : rough water; *also* : a large wave **4** : something likened to the sea esp. in vastness ⟨a ~ of wheat⟩ — **sea** *adj* — **at sea** : LOST, BEWILDERED
sea anemone *n* : any of numerous coelenterate polyps whose form, bright and varied colors, and cluster of tentacles superficially resemble a flower
sea·bird \'sē-,bərd\ *n* : a bird (as a gull) frequenting the open ocean
sea·board \-,bord\ *n* : SEACOAST; *also* : the land bordering a coast
sea·borg·i·um \sē-'bor-gē-əm\ *n* : a short-lived radioactive chemical element produced artificially
sea·coast \-,kōst\ *n* : the shore of the sea
sea·far·er \-,fer-ər\ *n* : SEAMAN 1
sea·far·ing \-,fer-iŋ\ *n* : the use of the sea for travel or transportation — **seafaring** *adj*
sea·food \-,füd\ *n* : edible marine fish and shellfish
sea·go·ing \-,gō-iŋ\ *adj* : OCEANGOING
sea·gull \'sē-,gəl\ : GULL
sea horse *n* : any of a genus of small marine fishes with the head and forepart of the body sharply flexed like the head and neck of a horse
¹**seal** \'sēl\ *n, pl* **seals** *also* **seal** [ME *sele*, fr. OE *seolh*] : any of numerous large carnivorous sea mammals occurring chiefly in cold regions and having limbs adapted for swimming **2** : the pelt of a seal
²**seal** *vb* : to hunt seals
³**seal** *n* [ME *sele, seel*, fr. AF *seal, sel*, fr. L *sigillum*, fr. dim. of *signum* sign, seal] **1** : GUARANTEE, PLEDGE **2** : a device having a raised design that can be stamped on clay or wax; *also* : the impression made by stamping with such a device **3** : something that seals or closes up ⟨safety ~⟩
⁴**seal** *vb* **1** : to affix a seal to; *also* : AUTHENTICATE **2** : to fasten with or as if with a seal to prevent tampering **3**

: to close or make secure against access, leakage, or passage **4** : to determine irrevocably ⟨~ed his fate⟩
sea·lane \'sē-,lān\ *n* : an established sea route
seal·ant \'sē-lənt\ *n* : a sealing agent
seal·er \'sē-lər\ *n* : a coat applied to prevent subsequent coats of paint or varnish from sinking in
sea level *n* : the level of the surface of the sea esp. at its mean midway between mean high and low water
sea·lift \'sē-,lift\ *n* : transport of military personnel and equipment by ship
sea lion *n* : any of several large Pacific seals with small external ears
seal·skin \'sēl-,skin\ *n* **1** : ¹SEAL 2 **2** : a garment of sealskin
¹**seam** \'sēm\ *n* **1** : the line of junction of two edges and esp. of edges of fabric sewn together **2** : a layer of mineral matter **3** : WRINKLE
²**seam** *vb* **1** : to join by or as if by sewing **2** : WRINKLE, FURROW
sea·man \'sē-mən\ *n* **1** : one who assists in the handling of ships : MARINER **2** : an enlisted person in the navy ranking next below a petty officer third class
seaman apprentice *n* : an enlisted person in the navy ranking next below a seaman
seaman recruit *n* : an enlisted person of the lowest rank in the navy
sea·man·ship \'sē-mən-,ship\ *n* : the art or skill of handling a ship
seam·less \'sēm-ləs\ *adj* : having no flaws or interruptions ⟨a ~ transition⟩ — **seam·less·ly** *adv*
sea·mount \'sē-,maunt\ *n* : an underwater mountain
seam·stress \'sēm-strəs\ *n* : a woman whose occupation is sewing
seamy \'sē-mē\ *adj* **seam·i·er; -est** **1** : UNPLEASANT **2** : DEGRADED, SORDID ⟨the ~ part of town⟩
sé·ance \'sā-,äns\ *n* [F] : a meeting to receive communications from spirits
sea·plane \'sē-,plān\ *n* : an airplane that can take off from and land on water
sea·port \-,port\ *n* : a port for oceangoing ships
sear \'sir\ *vb* **1** : WITHER **2** : to cook, burn, or scorch esp. on the surface; *also* : BRAND — **sear** *n*
¹**search** \'sərch\ *vb* [ME *cerchen*, fr. AF *cercher* to travel about, investigate, search, fr. LL *circare* to go about, fr. L *circum* round about] **1** : to look through in trying to find something **2** : SEEK **3** : PROBE — **search·er** *n*
²**search** *n* : the act of searching
search engine *n* : computer software or a website used to search data (as text or other websites) for specified information
search·light \-,līt\ *n* : an apparatus for projecting a powerful beam of light; *also* : the light projected
sear·ing \'sir-iŋ\ *adj* : very sharp, harsh or intense ⟨~ pain⟩ ⟨a ~ review⟩
sea scallop *n* : a large scallop of the Atlantic coast of No. America that is harvested for food
sea·scape \'sē-,skāp\ *n* **1** : a view of the sea **2** : a picture representing a scene at or of the sea
sea·shell \'sē-,shel\ *n* : the shell of a marine animal and esp. a mollusk
sea·shore \-,shor\ *n* : the shore of a sea
sea·sick \-,sik\ *adj* : nauseated by or as if by the motion of a ship — **sea·sick·ness** *n*
sea·side \'sē-,sīd\ *n* : SEASHORE
¹**sea·son** \'sē-zən\ *n* [ME *sesoun*, fr. AF *seison* natural season, appropriate time, fr. L *sation-, satio* action of sowing, fr. *serere* to sow] **1** : one of the divisions of the year (as spring or summer) **2** : a period of the year associated with a particular activity, event, or holiday ⟨the Easter ~⟩ ⟨hunting ~⟩ — **sea·son·al** \-zə-nəl\ *adj* — **sea·son·al·ly** *adv*
²**season** *vb* **1** : to make pleasant to the taste by use of salt, pepper, or spices **2** : to make (as by aging or drying) suitable for use **3** : to accustom or habituate to something (as hardship) ♦ **Synonyms** HARDEN, INURE, ACCLIMATE, TOUGHEN — **sea·son·er** *n*
sea·son·able \'sē-zə-nə-bəl\ *adj* : occurring at a good or proper time ⟨~ weather⟩ ♦ **Synonyms** TIMELY, PROPITIOUS, OPPORTUNE — **sea·son·ably** \-blē\ *adv*
seasonal affective disorder *n* : depression that recurs as the days grow shorter during the fall and winter

sea·son·ing *n* : something that seasons : CONDIMENT
¹seat \'sēt\ *n* **1** : a chair, bench, or stool for sitting on **2** : a place which serves as a capital or center
²seat *vb* **1** : to place in or on a seat **2** : to provide seats for
seat belt *n* : straps designed to hold a person in a seat
SEATO \'sē-ˌtō\ *abbr* Southeast Asia Treaty Organization
seat-of-the-pants *adj* : employing or based on personal experience, judgment, and effort rather than technological aids ⟨~ navigation⟩
sea turtle *n* : any of two families of marine turtles that have the feet modified into paddles
sea urchin *n* : any of numerous spiny marine echinoderms having thin brittle globular shells
sea·wall \'sē-ˌwȯl\ *n* : an embankment to protect the shore from erosion
¹sea·ward \'sē-wərd\ *n* : the direction or side away from land and toward the open sea
²seaward *also* **sea·wards** \-wərdz\ *adv* : toward the sea
³seaward *adj* **1** : directed or situated toward the sea **2** : coming from the sea
sea·wa·ter \'sē-ˌwȯ-tər, -ˌwä-\ *n* : water in or from the sea
sea·way \-ˌwā\ *n* : an inland waterway that admits ocean shipping
sea·weed \-ˌwēd\ *n* : a marine alga (as a kelp); *also* : a mass of marine algae
sea·wor·thy \-ˌwər-t͟hē\ *adj* : fit for a sea voyage ⟨a ~ ship⟩
se·ba·ceous \si-'bā-shəs\ *adj* : of, relating to, or secreting fatty material
sec *abbr* **1** second; secondary **2** secretary **3** section **4** [L *secundum*] according to
SEC *abbr* Securities and Exchange Commission
se·cede \si-'sēd\ *vb* **se·ced·ed; se·ced·ing** : to withdraw from an organized body and esp. from a political body
se·ces·sion \si-'se-shən\ *n* : the act of seceding — **se·ces·sion·ist** *n*
se·clude \si-'klüd\ *vb* **se·clud·ed; se·clud·ing** : to keep or shut away from others ⟨*secluded* herself in her room⟩
se·clu·sion \si-'klü-zhən\ *n* : the act of secluding : the state of being secluded — **se·clu·sive** \-siv\ *adj*
¹sec·ond \'se-kənd\ *adj* [ME, fr. AF *second*, fr. L *secundus* second, following, favorable, fr. *sequi* to follow] **1** : being number two in a countable series **2** : next after the first **3** : ALTERNATE ⟨every ~ year⟩ — **second** *or* **sec·ond·ly** *adv*
²second *n* **1** : one that is second **2** : one who assists another (as in a duel) **3** : an inferior or flawed article **4** : the second forward gear in a motor vehicle
³second *n* [ME *secounde*, fr. ML *secunda*, fr. L, fem. of *secundus* second; fr. its being the second division of a unit into 60 parts, as a minute is the first] **1** : the 60th part of a minute of time or angular measure **2** : an instant of time
⁴second *vb* **1** : to encourage or give support to **2** : to act as a second to **3** : to support (a motion) by adding one's voice to that of a proposer
¹sec·ond·ary \'se-kən-ˌder-ē\ *adj* **1** : second in rank, value, or occurrence : LESSER **2** : belonging to a second or later stage of development **3** : coming after the primary or elementary ⟨~ schools⟩ ◆ **Synonyms** SUBORDINATE, COLLATERAL, DEPENDENT
²secondary *n, pl* **-ar·ies** : the defensive backfield of a football team
secondary sex characteristic *n* : a physical characteristic that appears in members of one sex at puberty or in seasonal breeders at breeding season and is not directly concerned with reproduction
second fiddle *n* : one that plays a supporting or subservient role
sec·ond–guess \ˌse-kənd-'ges\ *vb* **1** : to think out other strategies or explanations for after the event **2** : to seek to anticipate or predict ⟨~ the stock market⟩
sec·ond·hand \-'hand\ *adj* **1** : not original **2** : not new : USED ⟨~ clothes⟩ **3** : dealing in used goods
secondhand smoke *n* : tobacco smoke that is exhaled by smokers or is given off by burning tobacco and is inhaled by persons nearby
second lieutenant *n* : a commissioned officer (as in the army) ranking next below a first lieutenant
sec·ond–rate \ˌse-kənd-'rāt\ *adj* : INFERIOR ⟨~ hotels⟩
sec·ond–string \'se-kənd-'striŋ\ *adj* : being a substitute (as on a team)

se·cre·cy \'sē-krə-sē\ *n, pl* **-cies** **1** : the habit or practice of being secretive **2** : the condition of being hidden or concealed
¹se·cret \'sē-krət\ *adj* **1** : HIDDEN, CONCEALED ⟨a ~ staircase⟩ **2** : COVERT, STEALTHY; *also* : engaged in detecting or spying ⟨a ~ agent⟩ **3** : kept from general knowledge — **se·cret·ly** *adv*
²secret *n* **1** : MYSTERY **2** : something kept from the knowledge of others
sec·re·tar·i·at \ˌse-krə-'ter-ē-ət\ *n* **1** : the office of a secretary **2** : the secretarial staff in an office **3** : the administrative department of a governmental organization ⟨the UN ~⟩
sec·re·tary \'se-krə-ˌter-ē\ *n, pl* **-tar·ies** **1** : a person employed to handle records, correspondence, and routine work for another person **2** : an officer of a corporation or business who is in charge of correspondence and records **3** : an official at the head of a department of government **4** : a writing desk — **sec·re·tari·al** \ˌse-krə-'ter-ē-əl\ *adj* — **sec·re·tary·ship** \'se-krə-ˌter-ē-ˌship\ *n*
¹se·crete \si-'krēt\ *vb* **se·cret·ed; se·cret·ing** : to form and give off (a secretion)
²se·crete \si-'krēt, 'sē-krət\ *vb* **se·cret·ed; se·cret·ing** : HIDE, CONCEAL
se·cre·tion \si-'krē-shən\ *n* **1** : the process of secreting something **2** : a product of glandular activity; *esp* : one (as a hormone) useful in the organism **3** : the act of hiding something — **se·cre·to·ry** \'sē-krə-ˌtȯr-ē\ *adj*
se·cre·tive \'sē-krə-tiv, si-'krē-\ *adj* : tending to keep secrets or to act secretly ⟨~ about his work⟩ — **se·cre·tive·ly** *adv* — **se·cre·tive·ness** *n*
¹sect \'sekt\ *n* **1** : a dissenting religious body **2** : a religious denomination **3** : a group adhering to a distinctive doctrine or to a leader
²sect *abbr* section; sectional
¹sec·tar·i·an \sek-'ter-ē-ən\ *adj* **1** : of or relating to a sect or sectarian **2** : limited in character or scope — **sec·tar·i·an·ism** *n*
²sectarian *n* : an adherent of a sect **2** : a narrow or bigoted person
¹sec·tion \'sek-shən\ *n* **1** : a part cut off or separated **2** : a distinct part **3** : the appearance that a thing has or would have if cut straight through
²section *vb* **1** : to separate or become separated into sections ⟨~ an orange⟩ **2** : to represent in sections
sec·tion·al \'sek-shə-nəl\ *adj* **1** : of, relating to, or characteristic of a section **2** : local or regional rather than general in character **3** : divided into sections — **sec·tion·al·ism** *n*
sec·tor \'sek-tər\ *n* **1** : a part of a circle between two radii **2** : an area assigned to a military leader to defend **3** : a subdivision of society
sec·u·lar \'se-kyə-lər\ *adj* **1** : not sacred or ecclesiastical **2** : not bound by monastic vows ⟨a ~ priest⟩
sec·u·lar·ise *Brit var of* SECULARIZE
sec·u·lar·ism \'se-kyə-lə-ˌri-zəm\ *n* : indifference to or exclusion of religion — **sec·u·lar·ist** \-rist\ *n* — **secularist** *also* **sec·u·lar·is·tic** \ˌse-kyə-lə-'ris-tik\ *adj*
sec·u·lar·ize \'se-kyə-lə-ˌrīz\ *vb* **-ized; -iz·ing** **1** : to make secular **2** : to transfer from ecclesiastical to civil or lay use, possession, or control — **sec·u·lar·i·za·tion** \ˌse-kyə-lə-rə-'zā-shən\ *n*
¹se·cure \si-'kyu̇r\ *adj* **se·cur·er; -est** [L *securus* safe, secure, fr. *se* without + *cura* care] **1** : easy in mind : free from fear **2** : free from danger or risk of loss : SAFE **3** : CERTAIN, SURE — **se·cure·ly** *adv*
²secure *vb* **se·cured; se·cur·ing** **1** : to make safe : GUARD **2** : to assure payment of by giving a pledge or collateral **3** : to fasten safely ⟨~ a door⟩ **4** : GET, ACQUIRE ⟨~ permission⟩
se·cu·ri·ty \si-'kyu̇r-ə-tē\ *n, pl* **-ties** **1** : SAFETY **2** : freedom from worry **3** : something given as pledge of payment ⟨a ~ deposit⟩ **4** *pl* : bond or stock certificates **5** : PROTECTION
secy *abbr* secretary
se·dan \si-'dan\ *n* **1** : a covered chair borne on poles by two people **2** : an automobile seating four or more people and usu. having a permanent top
¹se·date \si-'dāt\ *adj* : quiet and dignified in behavior ◆ **Synonyms** STAID, SOBER, SERIOUS, SOLEMN — **se·date·ly** *adv*

²**sedate** *vb* **se·dat·ed; se·dat·ing** : to dose with sedatives — **se·da·tion** \si-'dā-shən\ *n*

¹**sed·a·tive** \'se-də-tiv\ *adj* : serving or tending to relieve tension

²**sedative** *n* : a sedative drug

sed·en·tary \'se-dⁿn-ˌter-ē\ *adj* : characterized by or requiring much sitting

sedge \'sej\ *n* : any of a family of plants esp. of marshy areas that differ from the related grasses esp. in having solid stems — **sedgy** \'se-jē\ *adj*

sed·i·ment \'se-də-mənt\ *n* 1 : the material that settles to the bottom of a liquid 2 : material (as stones and sand) deposited by water, wind, or a glacier — **sed·i·men·ta·ry** \ˌse-də-'men-tə-rē\ *adj* — **sed·i·men·ta·tion** \-mən-'tā-shən, -ˌmen-\ *n*

se·di·tion \si-'di-shən\ *n* : the causing of discontent, insurrection, or resistance against a government — **se·di·tious** \-shəs\ *adj*

se·duce \si-'düs, -'dyüs\ *vb* **se·duced; se·duc·ing** 1 : to persuade to disobedience or disloyalty 2 : to lead astray 3 : to entice to sexual intercourse ✦ *Synonyms* TEMPT, ENTICE, INVEIGLE, LURE — **se·duc·er** *n* — **se·duc·tion** \-'dək-shən\ *n* — **se·duc·tive** \-tiv\ *adj*

sed·u·lous \'se-jə-ləs\ *adj* [L *sedulus,* fr. *sedulo* sincerely, diligently, fr. *se* without + *dolus* guile] : DILIGENT

¹**see** \'sē\ *vb* **saw** \'sȯ\; **seen** \'sēn\; **see·ing** 1 : to perceive by the eye; *also* 2 : to have the power of sight 2 : EXPERIENCE 3 : UNDERSTAND 4 : to make sure ⟨that order is kept⟩ 5 : to meet with 6 : to keep company with esp. in dating 7 : ACCOMPANY, ESCORT ⟨the guests to the door⟩ ✦ *Synonyms* BEHOLD, DESCRY, ESPY, VIEW, OBSERVE, NOTE, DISCERN — **see red** : to become very angry — **see the light** : to realize an obscured truth

²**see** *n* : the authority or jurisdiction of a bishop

¹**seed** \'sēd\ *n, pl* **seed** *or* **seeds** 1 : the grains of plants used for sowing 2 : a ripened ovule of a flowering plant that may develop into a new plant; *also* : a plant structure (as a spore or small dry fruit) capable of producing a new plant 3 : DESCENDANTS 4 : SOURCE, ORIGIN 5 : a competitor seeded in a tournament — **seed·less** *adj* — **go to seed** *or* **run to seed** 1 : to develop seed 2 : DECAY, DETERIORATE

²**seed** *vb* 1 : SOW, PLANT ⟨~ land with grass⟩ 2 : to bear or shed seeds 3 : to remove seeds from 4 : to rank or schedule (contestants) in a tournament — **seed·er** *n*

seed·bed \-ˌbed\ *n* : soil or a bed of soil prepared for planting seed

seed·ling \'sēd-liŋ\ *n* 1 : a young plant grown from seed 2 : a young tree before it becomes a sapling

seed·time \'sēd-ˌtīm\ *n* : the season for sowing

seedy \'sē-dē\ *adj* **seed·i·er; -est** 1 : containing or full of seeds 2 : SHABBY

seek \'sēk\ *vb* **sought** \'sȯt\; **seek·ing** 1 : to search for 2 : to try to reach or obtain 3 : ATTEMPT — **seek·er** *n*

seem \'sēm\ *vb* 1 : to appear to the observation or understanding 2 : to give the impression of being : APPEAR

seem·ing *adj* : outwardly apparent ⟨~ indifference⟩ — **seem·ing·ly** *adv*

seem·ly \'sēm-lē\ *adj* **seem·li·er; -est** 1 : conventionally proper 2 : FIT

seep \'sēp\ *vb* : to flow or pass slowly through fine pores or cracks — **seep·age** \'sē-pij\ *n*

seer \'sir\ *n* : a person who foresees or predicts events : PROPHET

seer·suck·er \'sir-ˌsə-kər\ *n* [Hindi *śīrsakar,* fr. Pers *shīro-shakar,* lit., milk and sugar] : a light fabric of linen, cotton, or rayon usu. striped and slightly puckered

see·saw \'sē-ˌsȯ\ *n* 1 : a contest in which each side assumes then relinquishes the lead 2 : a children's sport of riding up and down on the ends of a plank supported in the middle; *also* : the plank so used — **seesaw** *vb*

seethe \'sēt͟h\ *vb* **seethed; seeth·ing** [archaic *seethe* boil] : to become violently agitated ⟨~ with jealousy⟩

seg·ment \'seg-mənt\ *n* 1 : a part cut off from a geometrical figure (as a circle) by one or more points, lines, or planes 2 : a division of a thing : SECTION — **seg·men·tal** \seg-'men-tⁿl\ *adj* — **seg·men·ta·tion** \ˌseg-mən-'tā-shən\ *n* — **seg·ment·ed** \'seg-ˌmen-təd\ *adj*

seg·re·gate \'se-gri-ˌgāt\ *vb* **-gat·ed; -gat·ing** [L *segregare,* fr. *se-* apart + *greg-, grex* herd, flock] : to cut off from others; *esp* : to separate esp. by races or ethnic groups — **seg·re·ga·tion** \ˌse-gri-'gā-shən\ *n*

seg·re·ga·tion·ist \ˌse-gri-'gā-shə-nist\ *n* : one who believes in or practices the segregation of races

¹**se·gue** \'se-(ˌ)gwā, 'sā-\ *vb* **se·gued; se·gue·ing** 1 : to proceed without pause from one musical number to another 2 : to make a transition without interruption from one activity, topic, scene, or part to another

²**segue** *n* : the act or an instance of segueing

sei·gneur \sān-'yər\ *n, often cap* [MF, fr. ML *senior,* fr. L, adj., elder] : a feudal lord

¹**seine** \'sān\ *n* : a large weighted fishing net

²**seine** *vb* **seined; sein·ing** : to fish or catch with a seine — **sein·er** *n*

seis·mic \'sīz-mik, 'sīs-\ *adj* : of, relating to, resembling, or caused by an earthquake — **seis·mi·cal·ly** \-mi-k(ə-)lē\ *adv* — **seis·mic·i·ty** \sīz-'mi-sə-tē, sīs-\ *n*

seis·mo·gram \'sīz-mə-ˌgram, 'sīs-\ *n* : the record of an earth tremor made by a seismograph

seis·mo·graph \-ˌgraf\ *n* : an apparatus to measure and record seismic vibrations — **seis·mo·graph·ic** \ˌsīz-mə-'gra-fik, ˌsīs-\ *adj* — **seis·mog·ra·phy** \sīz-'mä-grə-fē, sīs-\ *n*

seis·mol·o·gy \sīz-'mä-lə-jē, sīs-\ *n* : a science that deals with earthquakes — **seis·mo·log·i·cal** \ˌsīz-mə-'lä-ji-kəl, ˌsīs-\ *adj* — **seis·mol·o·gist** \sīz-'mä-lə-jist, sīs-\ *n*

seis·mom·e·ter \sīz-'mä-mə-tər, sīs-\ *n* : a seismograph measuring the actual movement of the ground

seize \'sēz\ *vb* **seized; seiz·ing** 1 : to lay hold of or take possession of by force 2 : ARREST 3 : UNDERSTAND 4 : to attack or overwhelm physically : AFFLICT ⟨*seized* by panic⟩ ✦ *Synonyms* TAKE, GRASP, CLUTCH, SNATCH, GRAB

sei·zure \'sē-zhər\ *n* 1 : the act of seizing : the state of being seized 2 : a sudden attack (as of disease)

sel *abbr* select; selected; selection

sel·dom \'sel-dəm\ *adv* : not often : RARELY

¹**se·lect** \sə-'lekt\ *adj* 1 : CHOSEN, PICKED; *also* : CHOICE 2 : judicious or restrictive in choice : DISCRIMINATING

²**select** *vb* : to choose from a number or group : pick out

se·lec·tion \sə-'lek-shən\ *n* 1 : the act or process of selecting 2 : something selected : CHOICE 3 : a natural or artificial process that tends to favor the survival and reproduction of individuals with certain traits but not those with others

se·lec·tive \sə-'lek-tiv\ *adj* : of or relating to selection : selecting or tending to select ⟨~ shoppers⟩

selective service *n* : a system for calling men up for military service : DRAFT

se·lect·man \si-'lekt-ˌman, -mən\ *n* : one of a board of officials elected in towns of most New England states to administer town affairs

se·le·ni·um \sə-'lē-nē-əm\ *n* : a photosensitive chemical element

self \'self\ *n, pl* **selves** \'selvz\ 1 : the essential person distinct from all other persons in identity 2 : a particular side of a person's character 3 : personal interest : SELFISHNESS

self- *comb form* 1 : oneself : itself 2 : of oneself or itself 3 : by oneself or itself; *also* : automatic 4 : to, for, or toward oneself

self-abasement	self-assurance
self-absorbed	self-assured
self-absorption	self-awareness
self-acceptance	self-betrayal
self-accusation	self-cleaning
self-acting	self-closing
self-addressed	self-complacent
self-adjusting	self-conceit
self-administer	self-concern
self-advancement	self-condemned
self-aggrandizement	self-confessed
self-aggrandizing	self-confidence
self-analysis	self-confident
self-anointed	self-congratulation
self-appointed	self-congratulatory
self-appraisal	self-constituted
self-asserting	self-contempt
self-assertion	self-contradiction
self-assertive	self-contradictory

self-control	self-inflicted
self-correcting	self-instruction
self-created	self-interest
self-criticism	self-knowledge
self-cultivation	self-limiting
self-deceit	self-love
self-deception	self-lubricating
self-defeating	self-luminous
self-definition	self-operating
self-delusion	self-perception
self-denial	self-perpetuating
self-denying	self-pity
self-deprecating	self-portrait
self-deprecation	self-possessed
self-depreciation	self-possession
self-described	self-preservation
self-despair	self-proclaimed
self-destruct	self-professed
self-destruction	self-promotion
self-destructive	self-propelled
self-determination	self-propelling
self-directed	self-protection
self-discipline	self-realization
self-distrust	self-referential
self-doubt	self-regard
self-educated	self-reliance
self-employed	self-reliant
self-employment	self-renewing
self-enhancement	self-reproach
self-esteem	self-respect
self-examination	self-respecting
self-explaining	self-restraint
self-explanatory	self-revelation
self-expression	self-rule
self-forgetful	self-sacrifice
self-giving	self-sacrificing
self-governing	self-satisfaction
self-government	self-satisfied
self-hate	self-service
self-hypnosis	self-serving
self-identity	self-starting
self-image	self-styled
self-importance	self-sufficiency
self-important	self-sufficient
self-imposed	self-supporting
self-improvement	self-sustaining
self-incrimination	self-taught
self-induced	self-torment
self-indulgence	self-winding
self-indulgent	self-worth

self-cen·tered \'self-'sen-tərd\ *adj* : concerned only with one's own self — **self-cen·tered·ness** *n*

self-com·posed \ˌself-kəm-'pōzd\ *adj* : having control over one's emotions

self-con·scious \'self-'kän-chəs\ *adj* : uncomfortably conscious of oneself as an object of observation by others — **self-con·scious·ly** *adv* — **self-con·scious·ness** *n*

self-con·tained \ˌself-kən-'tānd\ *adj* 1 : complete in itself 2 : showing self-control; *also* : reserved in manner

self-de·fense \'self-di-'fens\ *n* 1 : a plea of justification for the use of force or for homicide 2 : the act of defending oneself, one's property, or a close relative

self-ef·fac·ing \-ə-'fā-siŋ\ *adj* : RETIRING, SHY ⟨is quiet and ∼⟩

self-ev·i·dent \ˌself-'e-və-dənt\ *adj* : evident without proof or reasoning

self-fer·til·i·za·tion \ˌself-ˌfər-tə-lə-'zā-shən\ *n* : fertilization of a plant or animal by its own pollen or sperm

self-ful·fill·ing \ˌself-fül-'fi-liŋ\ *adj* : becoming real or true by virtue of having been predicted or expected ⟨a ∼ prophecy⟩

self-help \'self-'help\ *n* : the process of bettering oneself or coping with one's problems without the aid of others — **self-help** *adj*

self-ie \'sel-fē\ *n* : a digital image of oneself taken by oneself ⟨post a ∼⟩

self-ish \'sel-fish\ *adj* : concerned with one's own welfare excessively or without regard for others — **self-ish·ly** *adv* — **self-ish·ness** *n*

self-less \'self-ləs\ *adj* : UNSELFISH ⟨∼ dedication⟩ — **self-less·ness** *n*

self-made \'self-'mād\ *adj* : having achieved success or prominance by one's own efforts ⟨a ∼ millionaire⟩

self-pol·li·na·tion \ˌself-ˌpä-lə-'nā-shən\ *n* : pollination of a flower by its own pollen or sometimes by pollen from another flower on the same plant

self-reg·u·lat·ing \'self-'re-gyə-ˌlā-tiŋ\ *adj* : AUTOMATIC

self-righ·teous \-'rī-chəs\ *adj* : strongly convinced of one's own righteousness — **self-righ·teous·ly** *adv*

self·same \'self-ˌsām\ *adj* : precisely the same : IDENTICAL

self-seal·ing \'self-'sē-liŋ\ *adj* : capable of sealing itself (as after puncture)

self-seek·ing \'self-'sē-kiŋ\ *adj* : seeking only to further one's own interests — **self-seeking** *n*

self-start·er \-'stär-tər\ *n* : a person who has initiative

self-will \'self-'wil\ *n* : OBSTINACY

sell \'sel\ *vb* **sold** \'sōld\; **sell·ing** 1 : to transfer (property) in return for money or something else of value 2 : to deal in as a business 3 : to be sold ⟨cars are ∼*ing* well⟩ — **sell·er** *n*

sell out *vb* 1 : to dispose of entirely by sale; *esp* : to sell one's business 2 : BETRAY — **sell·out** \'sel-ˌaût\ *n*

selt·zer \'selt-sər\ *n* [modif. of G *Selterser (Wasser)* water of Selters, fr. Nieder *Selters*, Germany] : artificially carbonated water

sel·vage *or* **sel·vedge** \'sel-vij\ *n* : the edge of a woven fabric so formed as to prevent raveling

selves *pl of* SELF

sem *abbr* 1 semicolon 2 seminar 3 seminary

se·man·tic \si-'man-tik\ *also* **se·man·ti·cal** \-ti-kəl\ *adj* : of or relating to meaning in language ⟨∼ change⟩

se·man·tics \si-'man-tiks\ *n sing or pl* : the study of meanings in language

sema·phore \'se-mə-ˌfȯr\ *n* 1 : a visual signaling apparatus with movable arms 2 : signaling by hand-held flags

sem·blance \'sem-bləns\ *n* 1 : outward appearance 2 : IMAGE, LIKENESS

se·men \'sē-mən\ *n* [NL, fr. L, seed] : a sticky whitish fluid of the male reproductive tract that contains the sperm

se·mes·ter \sə-'mes-tər\ *n* [G, fr. L *semestris* half-yearly, fr. *sex* six + *mensis* month] 1 : half a year 2 : one of the two terms into which many colleges divide the school year

semi \'se-ˌmī\ *n, pl* **sem·is** : SEMITRAILER

semi- \'se-mi, -ˌmī\ *prefix* 1 : precisely half of 2 : half in quantity or value; *also* : half of or occurring halfway through a specified period 3 : partly : incompletely 4 : partial : incomplete 5 : having some of the characteristics of

semiannual	semiofficial
semiarid	semipermanent
semicentennial	semipolitical
semicircle	semiprecious
semicircular	semiprivate
semicivilized	semiprofessional
semiclassical	semireligious
semiconscious	semiretired
semidarkness	semiskilled
semidivine	semisoft
semiformal	semisolid
semigloss	semisweet
semi-independent	semitransparent
semiliquid	semiweekly
semiliterate	semiyearly
semimonthly	

semi·au·to·mat·ic \ˌse-mē-ˌȯ-tə-'ma-tik\ *adj, of a firearm* : able to fire repeatedly but requiring release and another press of the trigger for each successive shot

semi·co·lon \'se-mi-ˌkō-lən\ *n* : a punctuation mark ; used esp. to separate major sentence elements

semi·con·duc·tor \ˌse-mi-kən-'dək-tər\ *n* : a substance whose electrical conductivity is between that of a conductor and an insulator — **semi·con·duct·ing** *adj*

[1]**semi·fi·nal** \ˌse-mi-'fī-nᵊl\ *adj* : being next to the last in an elimination tournament

[2]**semi·fi·nal** \'se-mi-ˌfī-nᵊl\ *n* : a semifinal round or match — **semi·fi·nal·ist** \-ist\ *n*

sem·i·nal \'se-mə-nᵊl\ *adj* 1 : of, relating to, or consisting of seed or semen **2** : containing or contributing the seeds of later development : CREATIVE, ORIGINAL — **sem·i·nal·ly** *adv*

sem·i·nar \'se-mə-ˌnär\ *n* **1** : a course of study pursued by a group of advanced students doing original research under a professor **2** : CONFERENCE

sem·i·nary \'se-mə-ˌner-ē\ *n, pl* **-nar·ies** [ME, seedbed, nursery, fr. L *seminarium*, fr. *semen* seed] : an educational institution; *esp* : one that gives theological training — **sem·i·nar·i·an** \ˌse-mə-'ner-ē-ən\ *n*

Sem·i·nole \'se-mə-ˌnōl\ *n, pl* **Semi·noles** *or* **Seminole** : a member of an American Indian people of Florida

semi·per·me·able \ˌse-mi-'pər-mē-ə-bəl\ *adj* : partially but not freely or wholly permeable; *esp* : permeable to some usu. small molecules but not to other usu. larger particles ⟨a ∼ membrane⟩ — **semi·per·me·abil·i·ty** \-ˌpər-mē-ə-'bi-lə-tē\ *n*

Sem·ite \'se-ˌmīt\ *n* : a member of any of a group of peoples (as the Hebrews or Arabs) of southwestern Asia — **Se·mit·ic** \sə-'mi-tik\ *adj*

semi·trail·er \'se-mi-ˌtrā-lər, -ˌmī-\ *n* : a freight trailer that when attached is supported at its forward end by the truck tractor; *also* : a semitrailer with attached tractor

sem·o·li·na \ˌse-mə-'lē-nə\ *n* : the purified hard grains produced from the milling of wheat and used esp. for pasta

¹sen \'sen\ *n, pl* **sen** — see *yen* at MONEY table

²sen *n, pl* **sen** — see *ringgit, rupiah* at MONEY table

³sen *n, pl* **sen** — see *riel* at MONEY table

⁴sen *abbr* **1** senate; senator **2** senior

sen·ate \'se-nət\ *n* : the second of two chambers of a legislature

sen·a·tor \'se-nə-tər\ *n* : a member of a senate — **sen·a·to·ri·al** \ˌse-nə-'tòr-ē-əl\ *adj*

send \'send\ *vb* **sent** \'sent\; **send·ing** **1** : to cause to go **2** : EMIT **3** : to propel or drive esp. with force **4** : to put or bring into a certain condition ⟨*sent* them into a rage⟩ **5** : to convey or transmit by an agent — **send·er** *n*

send–off \'send-ˌòf\ *n* : a demonstration of goodwill and enthusiasm at the start of a new venture (as a trip)

send–up \'send-ˌəp\ *n* : PARODY

se·ne \'sā-(ˌ)nā\ *n, pl* **sene** — see *tala* at MONEY table

Sen·e·ca \'se-ni-kə\ *n, pl* **Seneca** *or* **Senecas** : a member of an American Indian people of western New York

Sen·e·ga·lese \ˌse-ni-gə-'lēz, -'lēs\ *n, pl* **Senegalese** : a native or inhabitant of Senegal — **Senegalese** *adj*

se·nes·cence \si-'ne-sᵊns\ *n* : the state of being old; *also* : the process of becoming old — **se·nes·cent** \-ᵊnt\ *adj*

se·nile \'sē-ˌnī(-ə)l, 'se-\ *adj* : OLD, AGED; *esp* : exhibiting a loss of cognitive abilities associated with old age — **se·nil·i·ty** \si-'ni-lə-tē\ *n*

¹se·nior \'sē-nyər\ *n* **1** : a person older or of higher rank than another **2** : a member of the graduating class of a high school or college

²senior *adj* [ME, fr. L, older, elder, compar. of *senex* old] **1** : ELDER **2** : more advanced in dignity or rank **3** : belonging to the final year of a school or college course

senior airman *n* : an enlisted person in the air force ranking next below a staff sergeant

senior chief petty officer *n* : a petty officer in the navy or coast guard ranking next below a master chief petty officer

senior citizen *n* : an elderly person; *esp* : one who has retired

senior high school *n* : a school usu. including grades 10 to 12

se·nior·i·ty \sēn-'yòr-ə-tē\ *n* **1** : the quality or state of being senior **2** : a privileged status owing to length of continuous service

senior master sergeant *n* : a noncommissioned officer in the air force ranking next below a chief master sergeant

sen·i·ti \'se-nə-tē\ *n, pl* **seniti** — see *pa'anga* at MONEY table

sen·na \'se-nə\ *n* **1** : CASSIA 2; *esp* : one used medicinally **2** : the dried leaflets or pods of a cassia used as a purgative

sen·sa·tion \sen-'sā-shən\ *n* **1** : awareness (as of noise or heat) or a mental process (as seeing or hearing) due to stimulation of a sense organ; *also* : an indefinite bodily feeling **2** : a condition of excitement; *also* : the thing that causes this condition

sen·sa·tion·al \-shə-nəl\ *adj* **1** : of or relating to sensation or the senses **2** : arousing an intense and usu. superficial interest or emotional reaction — **sen·sa·tion·al·ly** *adv*

sen·sa·tion·al·ise *Brit var of* SENSATIONALIZE

sen·sa·tion·al·ism \-ˌi-zəm\ *n* : the use or effect of sensational subject matter or treatment — **sen·sa·tion·al·ist** \-nə-list\ *adj or n* — **sen·sa·tion·al·is·tic** \-ˌsā-shə-nə-'lis-tik\ *adj*

sen·sa·tion·al·ize \-nə-ˌlīz\ *vb* **-ized; -iz·ing** : to present in a sensational manner

¹sense \'sens\ *n* **1** : semantic content : MEANING **2** : the faculty of perceiving by means of sense organs; *also* : a bodily function or mechanism (as sight, hearing, or smell) involving the action and effect of a stimulus on a sense organ **3** : SENSATION, AWARENESS **4** : INTELLIGENCE, JUDGMENT **5** : OPINION ⟨the ∼ of the meeting⟩ — **sense·less** *adj* — **sense·less·ly** *adv* — **sense·less·ness** *n*

²sense *vb* **sensed; sens·ing** **1** : to be or become aware of ⟨∼ danger⟩; *also* : to perceive by the senses **2** : to detect (as radiation) automatically

sense organ *n* : a bodily structure (as an eye or ear) that receives stimuli (as heat or light) which excite neurons to send information to the brain

sen·si·bil·i·ty \ˌsen-sə-'bi-lə-tē\ *n, pl* **-ties** : delicacy of feeling : SENSITIVITY

sen·si·ble \'sen-sə-bəl\ *adj* **1** : capable of being perceived by the senses or the mind; *also* : capable of receiving sense impressions **2** : AWARE, CONSCIOUS **3** : REASONABLE, RATIONAL ⟨a ∼ decision⟩ — **sen·si·bly** \-blē\ *adv*

sen·si·tive \'sen-sə-tiv\ *adj* **1** : subject to excitation by or responsive to stimuli **2** : having power of feeling **3** : of such a nature as to be easily affected **4** : TOUCHY ⟨a ∼ issue⟩ — **sen·si·tive·ly** *adv* — **sen·si·tive·ness** *n* — **sen·si·tiv·i·ty** \ˌsen-sə-'ti-və-tē\ *n*

sensitive plant *n* : any of several mimosas with leaves that fold or droop when touched

sen·si·tize \'sen-sə-ˌtīz\ *vb* **-tized; -tiz·ing** : to make or become sensitive or hypersensitive — **sen·si·ti·za·tion** \ˌsen-sə-tə-'zā-shən\ *n*

sen·sor \'sen-ˌsòr, -sər\ *n* : a device that responds to a physical stimulus

sen·so·ry \'sen-sə-rē\ *adj* **1** : of or relating to sensation or the senses ⟨∼ perception⟩ **2** : AFFERENT

sen·su·al \'sen-shə-wəl\ *adj* **1** : relating to gratification of the senses **2** : devoted to the pleasures of the senses — **sen·su·al·ist** *n* — **sen·su·al·i·ty** \ˌsen-shə-'wa-lə-tē\ *n* — **sen·su·al·ly** *adv*

sen·su·ous \'sen-shə-wəs\ *adj* **1** : relating to the senses or to things that can be perceived by the senses **2** : VOLUPTUOUS ⟨∼ lips⟩ — **sen·su·ous·ly** *adv* — **sen·su·ous·ness** *n*

¹sent *past and past part of* SEND

²sent \'sent\ *n, pl* **sen·ti** \'sen-tē\ : a monetary unit equal to ¹⁄₁₀₀ kroon formerly used in Estonia

sen·te \'sen-tē\ *n, pl* **li·cen·te** *or* **li·sen·te** \li-'sen-tē\ — see *loti* at MONEY table

¹sen·tence \'sen-tᵊns, -tᵊnz\ *n* [ME, fr. AF, fr. L *sententia*, lit., feeling, opinion, fr. *sentire* to feel] **1** : the punishment set by a court **2** : a grammatically self-contained speech unit that expresses an assertion, a question, a command, a wish, or an exclamation

²sentence *vb* **sen·tenced; sen·tenc·ing** : to impose a sentence on

sen·ten·tious \sen-'ten-chəs\ *adj* : using wise sayings or proverbs; *also* : using pompous language — **sen·ten·tious·ly** *adv* — **sen·ten·tious·ness** *n*

sen·tient \'sen-chənt, -chē-ənt\ *adj* : capable of feeling : having perception

sen·ti·ment \'sen-tə-mənt\ *n* **1** : FEELING; *also* : thought and judgment influenced by feeling : emotional attitude **2** : OPINION, NOTION

sen·ti·men·tal \ˌsen-tə-'men-tᵊl\ *adj* **1** : influenced by tender feelings **2** : affecting the emotions ♦ *Synonyms* BATHETIC, MAUDLIN, MAWKISH, MUSHY — **sen·ti·men·tal·ism** *n* — **sen·ti·men·tal·ist** *n* — **sen·ti·men·tal·i·ty** \-ˌmen-'ta-lə-tē, -mən-\ *n* — **sen·ti·men·tal·ly** *adv*

sen·ti·men·tal·ise *Brit var of* SENTIMENTALIZE

sen·ti·men·tal·ize \-'men-tə-ˌlīz\ *vb* **-ized; -iz·ing** **1** : to indulge in sentiment **2** : to look upon or imbue with sentiment ⟨∼s the past⟩ — **sen·ti·men·tal·i·za·tion** \-ˌmen-tə-lə-'zā-shən\ *n*

sen·ti·mo \sen-'tē-(ˌ)mō\ *n, pl* **-mos** — see *peso* at MONEY table

sen·ti·nel \'sen-tᵊn-əl\ *n* [MF *sentinelle,* fr. It *sentinella,* fr. *sentina* vigilance, fr. *sentire* to perceive, fr. L] : SENTRY

sen·try \'sen-trē\ *n, pl* **sentries** : a guard at a point of passage

sep *abbr* separate, separated

Sep *abbr* September

SEP *abbr* simplified employee pension

se·pal \'sē-pəl, 'se-\ *n* : one of the modified leaves comprising a flower calyx

sep·a·ra·ble \'se-pə-rə-bəl\ *adj* : capable of being separated — **sep·a·ra·bil·i·ty** \ˌse-pə-rə-'bi-lə-tē\ *n*

¹sep·a·rate \'se-pə-ˌrāt\ *vb* **-rat·ed; -rat·ing** **1** : to set or keep apart : DISCONNECT, SEVER **2** : to keep apart by something intervening **3** : to cease to be together : PART ⟨the couple decided to ∼⟩

²sep·a·rate \'se-prət, -pə-rət\ *adj* **1** : not connected **2** : divided from each other **3** : SINGLE, PARTICULAR ⟨the ∼ pieces of the puzzle⟩ — **sep·a·rate·ly** *adv*

³sep·a·rate \'se-prət, -pə-rət\ *n* : an article of dress designed to be worn interchangeably with others to form various combinations

sep·a·ra·tion \ˌse-pə-'rā-shən\ *n* **1** : the act or process of separating : the state of being separated **2** : a point, line, means, or area of division **3** : a formal separating of a married couple by agreement but without divorce

sep·a·rat·ist \'se-prə-tist, 'se-pə-ˌrā-\ *n* : an advocate of separation (as from a political body) — **sep·a·rat·ism** \'se-prə-ˌti-zəm\ *n*

sep·a·ra·tive \'se-pə-ˌrā-tiv, 'se-prə-tiv\ *adj* : tending toward, causing, or expressing separation ⟨∼ influences⟩

sep·a·ra·tor \'se-pə-ˌrā-tər\ *n* : one that separates; *esp* : a device for separating cream from milk

se·pia \'sē-pē-ə\ *n* : a brownish gray to dark brown color

sep·sis \'sep-səs\ *n, pl* **sep·ses** \'sep-ˌsēz\ : a toxic condition due to spread of bacteria or their toxic products in the body

Sept *abbr* September

Sep·tem·ber \sep-'tem-bər\ *n* [ME *Septembre,* fr. AF & OE, both fr. L *September* (seventh month), fr. *septem* seven] : the 9th month of the year having 30 days

sep·tic \'sep-tik\ *adj* **1** : PUTREFACTIVE **2** : relating to or involving sepsis **3** : of, relating to, or used for sewage treatment and disposal

sep·ti·ce·mia \ˌsep-tə-'sē-mē-ə\ *n* : BLOOD POISONING

septic tank *n* : a tank in which sewage is disintegrated by bacteria

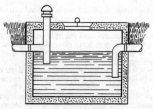

septic tank

sep·tu·a·ge·nar·i·an \ˌsep-tə-jə-'ner-ē-ən, -ˌtyü-\ *n* : a person whose age is in the seventies — **septuagenarian** *adj*

Sep·tu·a·gint \sep-'tü-ə-jənt, -'tyü-\ *n* : a Greek version of the Old Testament prepared in the 3d and 2d centuries B.C. by Jewish scholars

sep·tum \'sep-təm\ *n, pl* **sep·ta** \-tə\ : a dividing wall or membrane esp. between bodily spaces or masses of soft tissue

se·pul·chral \sə-'pəl-krəl\ *adj* **1** : relating to burial or the grave **2** : GLOOMY

¹sep·ul·chre *or* **sep·ul·cher** \'se-pəl-kər\ *n* : a burial vault : TOMB

²sepulchre *or* **sepulcher** *vb* **-chred** *or* **-chered; -chring** *or* **-cher·ing** : BURY, ENTOMB

sep·ul·ture \'se-pəl-ˌchùr\ *n* **1** : BURIAL **2** : SEPULCHRE

se·quel \'sē-kwəl\ *n* **1** : logical consequence **2** : a literary or cinematic work continuing a story begun in a preceding one

¹se·quence \'sē-kwəns\ *n* **1** : SERIES **2** : chronological order of events **3** : RESULT, SEQUEL ◆ **Synonyms** SUCCESSION, CHAIN, PROGRESSION, TRAIN — **se·quen·tial** \si-'kwen-chəl\ *adj* — **se·quen·tial·ly** *adv*

²sequence *vb* **se·quenced; se·quenc·ing** **1** : to arrange in a sequence **2** : to determine the sequence of chemical constituents in ⟨∼ DNA⟩

se·quent \'sē-kwənt\ *adj* **1** : SUCCEEDING, CONSECUTIVE **2** : RESULTANT

se·ques·ter \si-'kwes-tər\ *vb* : to set apart : SEGREGATE ⟨∼ a jury⟩

se·ques·trate \'sē-kwəs-ˌtrāt, si-'kwes-\ *vb* **-trat·ed; -trat·ing** : SEQUESTER — **se·ques·tra·tion** \ˌsē-kwəs-'trā-shən, ˌse-\ *n*

se·quin \'sē-kwən\ *n* **1** : an old gold coin of Turkey and Italy **2** : a small metal or plastic plate used for ornamentation esp. on clothing — **se·quined** *or* **se·quinned** \-kwənd\ *adj*

se·quoia \si-'kwòi-ə\ *n* : either of two huge California coniferous trees

ser *abbr* **1** serial **2** series **3** service

sera *pl of* SERUM

se·ra·glio \sə-'ral-yō\ *n, pl* **-glios** [It *serraglio*] : HAREM

se·ra·pe \sə-'rä-pē\ *n* : a colorful woolen shawl worn over the shoulders esp. by Mexican men

ser·aph \'ser-əf\ *n, pl* **ser·a·phim** \-ə-ˌfim, -ˌfēm\ *or* **ser·aphs** : one of the 6-winged angels standing in the presence of God

ser·a·phim \'ser-ə-ˌfim, -ˌfēm\ *n pl* **1** : the highest order of angels **2** *sing, pl* **seraphim** : SERAPH — **se·raph·ic** \sə-'ra-fik\ *adj*

Ser·bi·an \'sər-bē-ən\ *n* **1** : SERB **2** : a south Slavic language spoken by the Serbian people — **Serbian** *adj*

Ser·bo-Cro·a·tian \ˌsər-(ˌ)bō-krō-'ā-shən\ *n* : the Serbian and Croatian languages together with the Slavic speech of Bosnia, Herzegovina, and Montenegro taken as a single language with regional variants

sere \'sir\ *adj* : DRY, WITHERED

¹ser·e·nade \ˌser-ə-'nād\ *n* [F, fr. It *serenata,* fr. *sereno* clear, calm (of weather) fr. L *serenus*] : music sung or played as a compliment esp. outdoors at night for a woman being courted

²serenade *vb* **-nad·ed; -nad·ing** : to entertain with or perform a serenade

ser·en·dip·i·ty \ˌser-ən-'di-pə-tē\ *n* [fr. its possession by the heroes of the Persian fairy tale *The Three Princes of Serendip*] : the gift of finding valuable or agreeable things not sought for — **ser·en·dip·i·tous** \-təs\ *adj* — **ser·en·dip·i·tous·ly** *adv*

se·rene \sə-'rēn\ *adj* **1** : CLEAR ⟨∼ skies⟩ **2** : QUIET, CALM ◆ **Synonyms** TRANQUIL, PEACEFUL, PLACID — **se·rene·ly** *adv* — **se·ren·i·ty** \sə-'re-nə-tē\ *n*

serf \'sərf\ *n* : a member of a servile class bound to the land and subject to the will of the landowner — **serf·dom** \-dəm\ *n*

serge \'sərj\ *n* : a twilled woolen cloth

ser·geant \'sär-jənt\ *n* [ME, servant, attendant, sergeant, fr. AF *sergant, serjant,* fr. L *servient-, serviens,* prp. of *servire* to serve] **1** : a noncommissioned officer (as in the army) ranking next below a staff sergeant **2** : an officer in a police force

sergeant at arms : an officer of an organization who preserves order and executes commands

sergeant first class *n* : a noncommissioned officer in the army ranking next below a master sergeant

sergeant major *n, pl* **sergeants major** *or* **sergeant majors** **1** : a noncommissioned officer in the army or marine corps serving as chief administrative assistant in a headquarters **2** : a noncommissioned officer in the marine corps ranking above a first sergeant

¹se·ri·al \'sir-ē-əl\ *adj* **1** : appearing in parts that follow regularly ⟨a ∼ story⟩ **2** : performing a series of similar acts over a period of time ⟨a ∼ killer⟩; *also* : occurring in such a series — **se·ri·al·ly** *adv*

²serial *n* : a serial story or other writing — **se·ri·al·ist** \-ə-list\ *n*

se·ries \'sir-ēz\ *n, pl* **series** : a number of things or events arranged in order and connected by being alike in some way ♦ **Synonyms** SUCCESSION, PROGRESSION, SEQUENCE, CHAIN, TRAIN, STRING

seri·graph \'ser-ə-ˌgraf\ n : an original silk-screen print — **se·rig·ra·pher** \sə-'ri-grə-fər\ n — **se·rig·ra·phy** \-fē\ n

se·ri·ous \'sir-ē-əs\ adj 1 : thoughtful or subdued in appearance or manner : SOBER 2 : requiring much thought or work 3 : EARNEST, DEVOTED 4 : DANGEROUS, HARMFUL ⟨a ~ illness⟩ 5 : excessive or impressive in quantity or degree ⟨making ~ money⟩ ♦ **Synonyms** GRAVE, SEDATE, STAID — **se·ri·ous·ly** adv — **se·ri·ous·ness** n

ser·mon \'sər-mən\ n [ME, fr. AF sermun, fr. ML sermon, sermo, fr. L, speech, conversation, fr. serere to link together] 1 : a religious discourse esp. as part of a worship service 2 : a lecture on conduct or duty

ser·mon·ize \'sər-mə-ˌnīz\ vb -ized; -iz·ing 1 : to compose or deliver a sermon 2 : to preach to or on at length

se·rol·o·gy \sə-'rä-lə-jē\ n : a science dealing with serums and esp. their reactions and properties — **se·ro·log·i·cal** \ˌsir-ə-'lä-ji-kəl\ or **se·ro·log·ic** \-jik\ adj — **se·ro·log·i·cal·ly** \-ji-k(ə-)lē\ adv

se·ro·to·nin \ˌsir-ə-'tō-nən, ˌser-\ n : a neurotransmitter that is a powerful vasoconstrictor

se·rous \'sir-əs\ adj : of, relating to, resembling, or producing serum; esp : of thin watery constitution

ser·pent \'sər-pənt\ n : SNAKE

¹**ser·pen·tine** \'sər-pən-ˌtēn, -ˌtīn\ adj 1 : SLY, CRAFTY 2 : WINDING, TURNING

²**ser·pen·tine** \-ˌtēn\ n : a dull-green mineral having a mottled appearance

ser·rate \'ser-ˌāt\ adj : having a saw-toothed edge ⟨a ~ leaf⟩

ser·ried \'ser-ēd\ adj : crowded together

se·rum \'sir-əm\ n, pl serums or se·ra \-ə\ [L, whey, wheylike fluid] : the clear yellowish antibody-containing fluid that can be separated from blood when it clots; also : a preparation of animal serum containing specific antibodies and used to prevent or cure disease

serv abbr service

ser·vant \'sər-vənt\ n : one that serves others; esp : a person employed for domestic or personal work

¹**serve** \'sərv\ vb served; serv·ing 1 : to work as a servant 2 : to render obedience and worship to (God) 3 : to comply with the commands or demands of 4 : to work through or perform a term of service (as in the army) 5 : PUT IN ⟨served five years in jail⟩ 6 : to be of use : ANSWER ⟨pine boughs served for a bed⟩ 7 : BENEFIT 8 : to prove adequate or satisfactory for ⟨a pie that ~s eight people⟩ 9 : to make ready and pass out ⟨~ drinks⟩ 10 : to furnish or supply with something ⟨one power company serving the whole state⟩ 11 : to wait on ⟨~ a customer⟩ 12 : to treat or act toward in a specified way ⟨served as her maid⟩ 13 : to put the ball in play (as in tennis)

²**serve** n : the act of serving a ball (as in tennis)

ser·ver \'sər-vər\ n 1 : one that serves 2 : a computer in a network that is used to provide services (as access to files) to other computers in the network

¹**ser·vice** \'sər-vəs\ n 1 : the occupation of a servant 2 : HELP, BENEFIT 3 : a meeting for worship; also : a form followed in worship or in a ceremony ⟨burial ~⟩ 4 : the act, fact, or means of serving 5 : performance of official or professional duties 6 : SERVE 7 : a set of dishes or silverware 8 : a branch of public employment; also : the persons in it ⟨civil ~⟩ 9 : military or naval duty

²**service** vb ser·viced; ser·vic·ing : to do maintenance or repair work on or for

ser·vice·able \'sər-və-sə-bəl\ adj : prepared for service : USEFUL, USABLE

ser·vice·man \'sər-vəs-ˌman, -mən\ n 1 : a man who is a member of the armed forces 2 : a man employed to repair or maintain equipment

service mark n : a mark or device used to identify a service (as transportation or insurance) offered to customers

service station n : GAS STATION

ser·vice·wom·an \'sər-vəs-ˌwu̇-mən\ n : a woman who is a member of the armed forces

ser·vile \'sər-vəl, -ˌvī(-ə)l\ adj 1 : befitting a slave or servant 2 : behaving like a slave : SUBMISSIVE — **ser·vile·ly** adv — **ser·vil·i·ty** \ˌsər-'vi-lə-tē\ n

serv·ing \'sər-viŋ\ n : HELPING

ser·vi·tor \'sər-və-tər\ n : a male servant

ser·vi·tude \'sər-və-ˌtüd, -ˌtyüd\ n : SLAVERY, BONDAGE

ser·vo \'sər-vō\ n, pl servos 1 : SERVOMOTOR 2 : SERVOMECHANISM

ser·vo·mech·a·nism \'sər-vō-ˌme-kə-ˌni-zəm\ n : a device for automatically correcting the performance of a mechanism

ser·vo·mo·tor \-ˌmō-tər\ n : a mechanism that supplements a primary control

ses·a·me \'se-sə-mē\ n : a widely cultivated annual herb of warm regions; also : its seeds that yield an edible oil (**sesame oil**) and are used in flavoring

ses·qui·cen·ten·ni·al \ˌses-kwi-sen-'te-nē-əl\ n [L sesquione and a half, half again] : a 150th anniversary or its celebration — **sesquicentennial** adj

ses·qui·pe·da·lian \ˌses-kwə-pə-'dāl-yən\ adj 1 : having many syllables : LONG 2 : using long words

ses·sile \'se-sī(-ə)l, -səl\ adj : permanently attached and not free to move about

ses·sion \'se-shən\ n 1 : a meeting or series of meetings of a body (as a court or legislature) for the transaction of business 2 : a meeting or period devoted to a particular activity

¹**set** \'set\ vb set; set·ting 1 : to cause to sit 2 : PLACE 3 : ARRANGE, ADJUST 4 : to cause to be or do 5 : SETTLE, DECREE 6 : to fix in a frame 7 : to fix at a certain amount 8 : WAGER, STAKE 9 : to make or become fast or rigid 10 : to adapt (as words) to something (as music) 11 : to become fixed or firm or solid 12 : to be suitable : FIT 13 : BROOD 14 : to have a certain direction 15 : to pass below the horizon 16 : to defeat in bridge — **set about** : to begin to do — **set forth** : to begin a trip — **set off** 1 : to start out on a course or a trip 2 : to cause to explode — **set out** : to begin a trip or undertaking — **set sail** : to begin a voyage — **set upon** : to attack usu. with violence

²**set** n 1 : a setting or a being set 2 : DIRECTION, COURSE; also : TENDENCY 3 : FORM, BUILD 4 : the fit of something (as a coat) 5 : an artificial setting for the scene of a play or motion picture 6 : a group of tennis games in which one side wins at least six 7 : a group of persons or things of the same kind or having a common characteristic usu. classed together 8 : a collection of things and esp. of mathematical elements (as numbers or points) 9 : an electronic apparatus ⟨a television ~⟩

³**set** adj 1 : DELIBERATE, INTENT 2 : fixed by authority or custom ⟨a ~ price⟩ 3 : RIGID ⟨a ~ frown⟩ 4 : PERSISTENT

set·back \'set-ˌbak\ n : a temporary defeat : REVERSE

set back vb 1 : HINDER, DELAY; also : REVERSE 2 : COST

set piece n : a composition (as in literature or music) executed in fixed or ideal form often with brilliant effect 2 : a scene, depiction, speech, or event obviously designed to have an imposing effect

set·screw \'set-ˌskrü\ n : a screw screwed through one part tightly upon or into another part to prevent relative movement

set·tee \se-'tē\ n : a bench or sofa with a back and arms

set·ter \'se-tər\ n : a large long-coated hunting dog

set·ting \'se-tiŋ\ n 1 : the frame in which a gem is set 2 : the time, place, and circumstances in which something occurs or develops; also : SCENERY 3 : music written for a text (as of a poem) 4 : the eggs that a fowl sits on for hatching at one time

set·tle \'se-t°l\ vb set·tled; set·tling [ME settlen to seat, bring to rest, come to rest, fr. OE setlan, fr. setl seat] 1 : to place so as to stay 2 : to establish in residence; also : COLONIZE 3 : to make compact 4 : QUIET, CALM 5 : to establish or secure permanently 6 : to direct one's efforts 7 : to fix by agreement 8 : to give legally 9 : ADJUST, ARRANGE 10 : DECIDE, DETERMINE 11 : to make a final disposition of ⟨~ an account⟩ 12 : to come to rest 13 : to reach an agreement on 14 : to sink gradually to a lower level 15 : to become clear by depositing sediment — **set·tler** n

set·tle·ment \'se-t°l-mənt\ n 1 : the act or process of set-

tling **2** : BESTOWAL ⟨a marriage ∼⟩ **3** : payment or adjustment of an account **4** : COLONY **5** : a small village **6** : an institution providing various community services esp. to large city populations **7** : adjustment of doubts and differences
set–to \'set-ˌtü\ *n, pl* **set–tos** : FIGHT
set·up \'set-ˌəp\ *n* **1** : the manner or act of arranging **2** : glass, ice, and nonalcoholic beverage for mixing served to patrons who supply their own liquor **3** : something (as a plot) that has been constructed or contrived; *also* : FRAME-UP
set up *vb* **1** : to place in position; *also* : ASSEMBLE **2** : CAUSE **3** : FOUND, ESTABLISH ⟨*set up* a school⟩ **4** : FRAME **5**
sev·en \'se-vən\ *n* **1** : one more than six **2** : the 7th in a set or series **3** : something having seven units — **seven** *adj or pron* — **sev·enth** \-vənth\ *adj or adv or n*
sev·en·teen \ˌse-vən-'tēn\ *n* : one more than 16 — **seventeen** *adj or pron* — **sev·en·teenth** \-'tēnth\ *adj or n*
seventeen–year locust *n* : a cicada of the U.S. that has in the North a life of 17 years and in the South of 13 years of which most is spent underground as a nymph and only a few weeks as a winged adult
sev·en·ty \'se-vən-tē\ *n, pl* **-ties** : seven times 10 — **sev·en·ti·eth** \-tē-əth\ *adj or n* — **seventy** *adj or pron*
sev·er \'se-vər\ *vb* **sev·ered; sev·er·ing** : DIVIDE; *esp* : to separate by or as if by cutting ⟨∼ed ties with his brother⟩ — **sev·er·ance** \'sev-rəns, 'se-və-\ *n*
sev·er·al \'sev-rəl, 'se-və-\ *adj* [ME, fr. AF, fr. ML *separalis,* fr. L *separ* separate, fr. *separare* to separate] **1** : INDIVIDUAL, DISTINCT ⟨federal union of the ∼ states⟩ **2** : consisting of an indefinite number but yet not very many ⟨ate ∼ cookies⟩ — **sev·er·al·ly** *adv*
severance pay *n* : extra pay given an employee on termination of employment
se·vere \sə-'vir\ *adj* **se·ver·er; -est 1** : marked by strictness or sternness : AUSTERE **2** : strict in discipline **3** : causing distress and esp. physical discomfort or pain ⟨∼ weather⟩ ⟨a ∼ wound⟩ **4** : hard to endure ⟨∼ trials⟩ **5** : SERIOUS ⟨∼ depression⟩ ♦ *Synonyms* STERN, ASCETIC, ASTRINGENT — **se·vere·ly** *adv* — **se·ver·i·ty** \-'ver-ə-tē\ *n*
sew \'sō\ *vb* **sewed; sewn** \'sōn\ *or* **sewed; sew·ing 1** : to unite or fasten by stitches **2** : to engage in sewing
sew·age \'sü-ij\ *n* : waste materials carried off by sewers
¹sew·er \'sō-ər\ *n* : one that sews
²sew·er \'sü-ər\ *n* : an artificial pipe or channel to carry off waste matter
sew·er·age \'sü-ə-rij\ *n* **1** : a system of sewers **2** : SEWAGE
sew·ing *n* **1** : the activity of one who sews **2** : material that has been or is to be sewed
sex \'seks\ *n* **1** : either of the two major forms that occur in many living things and are designated male or female according to their role in reproduction; *also* : the qualities by which these sexes are differentiated and which directly or indirectly function in reproduction involving two parents **2** : sexual activity or behavior; *also* : SEXUAL INTERCOURSE — **sexed** \'sekst\ *adj* — **sex·less** *adj*
sex·a·ge·nar·i·an \ˌsek-sə-jə-'ner-ē-ən\ *n* : a person whose age is in the sixties — **sexagenarian** *adj*
sex appeal *n* : personal appeal or physical attractiveness esp. for members of the opposite sex
sex cell *n* : an egg cell or sperm cell
sex chromosome *n* : one of usu. a pair of chromosomes that are usu. similar in one sex but different in the other sex and are concerned with the inheritance of sex
sex hormone *n* : a steroid hormone (as estrogen or testosterone) that is produced esp. by the gonads or adrenal cortex and chiefly affects the growth or function of the reproductive organs
sex·ism \'sek-ˌsi-zəm\ *n* : prejudice or discrimination based on sex; *esp* : discrimination against women — **sex·ist** \'sek-sist\ *adj or n*
sex·ol·o·gy \sek-'sä-lə-jē\ *n* : the study of sex or of the interactions of the sexes — **sex·ol·o·gist** \-jist\ *n*
sex·pot \'seks-ˌpät\ *n* : a conspicuously sexy woman
sex symbol *n* : a usu. renowned person (as an entertainer) noted and admired for conspicuous attractiveness
sex·tant \'sek-stənt\ *n* [NL *sextant-, sextans* sixth part of a circle, fr. L, sixth part, fr. *sextus* sixth] : a navigational instrument for determining latitude
sex·tet \sek-'stet\ *n* **1** : a musical composition for six voices or instruments; *also* : the performers of such a composition **2** : a group or set of six
sex·ting \'sek-stiŋ\ *n* : the sending of sexually explicit messages or images by cell phone
sex·ton \'sek-stən\ *n* : one who takes care of church property
sex·u·al \'sek-shə-wəl\ *adj* : of, relating to, or involving sex or the sexes ⟨a ∼ spore⟩ ⟨∼ relations⟩ — **sex·u·al·i·ty** \ˌsek-shə-'wa-lə-tē\ *n* — **sex·u·al·ly** \'sek-shə-wə-lē\ *adv*
sexual intercourse *n* **1** : intercourse between a male and a female in which the penis is inserted into the vagina **2** : intercourse between individuals involving genital contact other than insertion of the penis into the vagina
sexually transmitted disease *n* : a disease (as syphilis, gonorrhea, AIDS, or the genital form of herpes simplex) that is caused by a microorganism or virus usu. or often transmitted by direct sexual contact
sexual relations *n pl* : SEXUAL INTERCOURSE
sexy \'sek-sē\ *adj* **sex·i·er; -est** : sexually suggestive or stimulating : EROTIC — **sex·i·ly** \-sə-lē\ *adv* — **sex·i·ness** \-sē-nəs\ *n*
SF *abbr* **1** sacrifice fly **2** science fiction **3** square feet
SFC *abbr* sergeant first class
¹SG *abbr* **1** sergeant **2** solicitor general **3** surgeon general
²SG *symbol* seaborgium
sgd *abbr* signed
Sgt *abbr* sergeant
Sgt Maj *abbr* sergeant major
sh *abbr* share
shab·by \'sha-bē\ *adj* **shab·bi·er; -est 1** : dressed in worn clothes **2** : threadbare and faded from wear **3** : DESPICABLE, MEAN; *also* : UNFAIR ⟨∼ treatment⟩ — **shab·bi·ly** \'sha-bə-lē\ *adv* — **shab·bi·ness** \-bē-nəs\ *n*
shack \'shak\ *n* : HUT, SHANTY
¹shack·le \'sha-kəl\ *n* **1** : something (as a manacle or fetter) that confines the legs or arms **2** : a check on free action made as if by fetters **3** : a device for making something fast or secure
²shackle *vb* **shack·led; shack·ling** : to bind or fasten with shackles
shad \'shad\ *n, pl* **shad** : any of several sea fishes related to the herrings that swim up rivers to spawn and include some important food fishes
¹shade \'shād\ *n* **1** : partial obscurity **2** : space sheltered from the light esp. of the sun **3** : PHANTOM **4** : something that shelters from or intercepts light or heat; *also, pl* : SUNGLASSES **5** : a dark color or a variety of a color **6** : a small difference
²shade *vb* **shad·ed; shad·ing 1** : to shelter from light and heat **2** : DARKEN, OBSCURE **3** : to mark with degrees of light or color **4** : to show slight differences esp. in color or meaning
shad·ing *n* : the color and lines representing darkness or shadow in a drawing or painting
¹shad·ow \'sha-dō\ *n* **1** : partial darkness in a space from which light rays are cut off **2** : SHELTER **3** : shade cast upon a surface by something intercepting rays from a light ⟨the ∼ of a tree⟩ **4** : PHANTOM **5** : a shaded portion of a picture **6** : a small portion or degree : TRACE ⟨a ∼ of doubt⟩ **7** : a source of gloom or unhappiness — **shad·owy** *adj*
²shadow *vb* **1** : to cast a shadow on **2** : to represent faintly or vaguely **3** : to follow and watch closely : TRAIL
shad·ow·box \'sha-dō-ˌbäks\ *vb* : to box with an imaginary opponent esp. for training
shady \'shā-dē\ *adj* **shad·i·er; -est 1** : affording shade **2** : of questionable honesty or reputation ⟨a ∼ politician⟩
¹shaft \'shaft\ *n, pl* **shafts 1** : the long handle of a spear or lance **2** : SPEAR, LANCE **3** *or pl* **shaves** \'shavz\ : POLE; *esp* : one of two poles between which a horse is hitched to pull a vehicle **4** : something (as a column) long and slender **5** : a bar to support a rotating piece or to transmit power by rotation **6** : an inclined opening in the ground (as for finding or mining ore) **7** : a

vertical opening (as for an elevator) through the floors of a building **8** : harsh or unfair treatment — usu. used with *the*

²**shaft** *vb* **1** : to fit with a shaft **2** : to treat unfairly or harshly

shag \'shag\ *n* : a shaggy tangled mass or covering (as of wool) : long coarse or matted fiber, nap, or pile

shag·gy \'sha-gē\ *adj* **shag·gi·er; -est 1** : rough with or as if with long hair or wool **2** : tangled or rough in surface

shah \'shä, 'shò\ *n, often cap* : a sovereign of Iran

Shak *abbr* Shakespeare

¹**shake** \'shāk\ *vb* **shook** \'shùk\; **shak·en** \'shā-kən\; **shak·ing 1** : to move or cause to move jerkily or irregularly **2** : BRANDISH, WAVE ⟨*shaking* his fist⟩ **3** : to disturb emotionally ⟨*shaken* by her death⟩ **4** : WEAKEN ⟨*shook* his faith⟩ **5** : to bring or come into a certain position, condition, or arrangement by or as if by moving jerkily **6** : to clasp (hands) in greeting or as a sign of goodwill or agreement ✦ **Synonyms** TREMBLE, QUAKE, QUAVER, SHIVER, QUIVER — **shak·able** *or* **shake·able** \'shā-kə-bəl\ *adj*

²**shake** *n* **1** : the act or a result of shaking **2** : DEAL, TREATMENT ⟨a fair ∼⟩

shake·down \'shāk-,daùn\ *n* **1** : an improvised bed **2** : EXTORTION ⟨was a victim of a ∼⟩ **3** : a process or period of adjustment **4** : a test (as of a new ship or airplane) under operating conditions

shake down *vb* **1** : to take up temporary quarters **2** : to occupy a makeshift bed **3** : to become accustomed esp. to new surroundings or duties **4** : to settle down **5** : to give a shakedown test to **6** : to obtain money from in a deceitful or illegal manner **7** : to bring about a reduction of

shak·er \'shā-kər\ *n* **1** : one that shakes ⟨pepper ∼⟩ **2** *cap* : a member of a religious sect founded in England in 1747

Shake·spear·ean *or* **Shake·spear·ian** \shāk-'spir-ē-ən\ *adj* : of, relating to, or having the characteristics of Shakespeare or his writings

shake·up \'shāk-,əp\ *n* : an extensive often drastic reorganization

shaky \'shā-kē\ *adj* **shak·i·er; -est** : UNSOUND, WEAK ⟨a ∼ ladder⟩ — **shak·i·ly** \'shā-kə-lē\ *adv* — **shak·i·ness** \-kē-nəs\ *n*

shale \'shāl\ *n* : a finely layered rock formed from clay, mud, or silt

shall \shəl, 'shal\ *vb, past* **should** \shəd, 'shùd\ *pres sing & pl* **shall** — used as an auxiliary to express a command, what seems inevitable or likely in the future, simple futurity, or determination

shal·lop \'sha-ləp\ *n* : a light open boat

shal·lot \shə-'lät, 'sha-lət\ *n* [modif. of F *échalote*] **1** : a small clustered bulb that is used in seasoning and is produced by a perennial herb belonging to a subspecies of the onion; *also* : this herb **2** : GREEN ONION

¹**shal·low** \'sha-lō\ *adj* **1** : not deep **2** : not intellectually profound

²**shallow** *n* : a shallow place in a body of water — usu. used in pl.

¹**sham** \'sham\ *n* **1** : an ornamental covering for a pillow **2** : COUNTERFEIT, IMITATION **3** : a person who shams

²**sham** *vb* **shammed; sham·ming** : FEIGN, PRETEND — **sham·mer** *n*

³**sham** *adj* : not genuine : FALSE, FEIGNED

sha·man \'shä-mən, 'shā-\ *n* [ultim. fr. Evenki (a language of Siberia) *šamán*] : a priest or priestess who uses magic to cure the sick, to divine the hidden, and to control events

sham·ble \'sham-bəl\ *vb* **sham·bled; sham·bling** : to shuffle along — **sham·ble** *n*

sham·bles \'sham-bəlz\ *n* **1** : a scene of great slaughter **2** : a scene or state of great destruction or disorder; *also* : MESS

¹**shame** \'shām\ *n* **1** : a painful sense of having done something wrong, improper, or immodest **2** : DISGRACE, DISHONOR **3** : a cause of feeling shame **4** : something to be regretted ⟨it's a ∼ you'll miss the party⟩ — **shame·ful** \-fəl\ *adj* — **shame·ful·ly** *adv* — **shame·less** *adj* — **shame·less·ly** *adv*

²**shame** *vb* **shamed; sham·ing 1** : DISGRACE **2** : to make ashamed

shame·faced \'shām-,fāst\ *adj* : ASHAMED, ABASHED — **shame·faced·ly** \-,fā-səd-lē, -,fāst-lē\ *adv*

¹**sham·poo** \sham-'pü\ *vb* [Hindi *cāpo*, imper. of *cāpnā* to press, shampoo] : to wash (as the hair) with soap and water or with a special preparation; *also* : to clean (as a rug) similarly

²**shampoo** *n, pl* **shampoos 1** : the act or an instance of shampooing **2** : a preparation for use in shampooing

sham·rock \'sham-,räk\ *n* [Ir *seamróg*, dim. of *seamar* clover] : a plant of folk legend with leaves composed of three leaflets that is associated with St. Patrick and Ireland

shang·hai \shaŋ-'hī\ *vb* **shang·haied; shang·hai·ing** [*Shanghai*, China] : to force aboard a ship for service as a sailor; *also* : to trick or force into an undesirable position

Shan·gri-la \,shaŋ-gri-'lä\ *n* [*Shangri-La*, imaginary land depicted in the novel *Lost Horizon* (1933) by James Hilton] : a remote idyllic hideaway

shank \'shaŋk\ *n* **1** : the part of the leg between the knee and the human ankle or a corresponding part of a quadruped **2** : a cut of meat from the leg **3** : the narrow part of the sole of a shoe beneath the instep **4** : the part of a tool or instrument (as a key or anchor) connecting the functioning part with a part by which it is held or moved

shan·tung \shan-'təŋ\ *n* : a fabric in plain weave having a slightly irregular surface

shan·ty \'shan-tē\ *n, pl* **shanties** [prob. fr. CanF *chantier* lumber camp, hut, fr. F, builder's yard, ways, support for barrels, fr. OF, support, fr. L *cantherius* rafter, trellis] : a small roughly built shelter or dwelling

¹**shape** \'shāp\ *vb* **shaped; shap·ing 1** : to form esp. in a particular shape **2** : DESIGN **3** : ADAPT, ADJUST **4** : REGULATE ✦ **Synonyms** MAKE, FASHION, FABRICATE, MANUFACTURE, FRAME, MOLD

²**shape** *n* **1** : APPEARANCE ⟨the ∼ of an apple⟩ **2** : surface configuration : FORM **3** : bodily contour apart from the head and face : FIGURE **4** : PHANTOM **5** : CONDITION ⟨was in fine ∼⟩ — **shaped** *adj*

shape·less \'shā-pləs\ *adj* **1** : having no definite shape **2** : not shapely — **shape·less·ly** *adv* — **shape·less·ness** *n*

shape·ly \'shā-plē\ *adj* **shape·li·er; -est** : having a pleasing shape ⟨a ∼ model⟩ — **shape·li·ness** *n*

shape-shift·er \'shāp-,shif-tər\ *n* : one that seems able to change form or identity at will

shard \'shärd\ *also* **sherd** \'shərd\ *n* : a broken piece : FRAGMENT

¹**share** \'sher\ *n* : PLOWSHARE

²**share** *n* **1** : a portion belonging to one person or group **2** : any of the equal interests into which the capital stock of a corporation is divided

³**share** *vb* **shared; shar·ing 1** : APPORTION **2** : to use or enjoy with others **3** : PARTICIPATE — **shar·er** *n*

share·crop·per \-,krä-pər\ *n* : a farmer who works another's land in return for a share of the crop — **share·crop** *vb*

share·hold·er \-,hōl-dər\ *n* : STOCKHOLDER

share·ware \'sher-,wer\ *n* : software available for usu. limited trial use at little or no cost but that can be upgraded for a fee

¹**shark** \'shärk\ *n* : any of various active, usu. predatory, and mostly large marine cartilaginous fishes

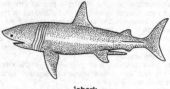

¹**shark**

²**shark** *n* : a greedy crafty person

shark·skin \-,skin\ *n* **1** : the hide of a shark or leather made from it **2** : a fabric woven from strands of many fine threads and having a sleek appearance and silky feel

¹**sharp** \'shärp\ *adj* **1** : having a thin cutting edge or fine point : not dull or blunt **2** : COLD, NIPPING ⟨a ~ wind⟩ **3** : keen in intellect, perception, or attention **4** : BRISK, ENERGETIC **5** : IRRITABLE ⟨a ~ temper⟩ **6** : causing intense distress ⟨a ~ pain⟩ **7** : HARSH, CUTTING ⟨a ~ rebuke⟩ **8** : affecting the senses as if cutting or piercing ⟨a ~ sound⟩ ⟨a ~ smell⟩ **9** : not smooth or rounded ⟨~ features⟩ **10** : involving an abrupt or extreme change ⟨a ~ turn⟩ **11** : CLEAR, DISTINCT ⟨mountains in ~ relief⟩; *also* : easy to perceive ⟨a ~ contrast⟩ **12** : higher than the true pitch; *esp* : raised by a half step **13** : STYLISH ⟨a ~ dresser⟩ ✦ *Synonyms* KEEN, ACUTE, QUICK-WITTED, PENETRATIVE — **sharp·ly** *adv* — **sharp·ness** *n*
²**sharp** *adv* **1** : in a sharp manner **2** : EXACTLY, PRECISELY ⟨left at 8 ~⟩
³**sharp** *n* **1** : a sharp edge or point **2** : a character ♯ which indicates that a specified note is to be raised by a half step; *also* : the resulting note **3** : SHARPER
⁴**sharp** *vb* : to raise in pitch by a half step
shar·pei \ˌshä-'pā, ˌshär-\ *n, pl* **shar·peis** *often cap S&P* [Chin (Guangdong dial.) *sà* sand + *péi* fur] : any of a Chinese breed of dogs that have loose wrinkled skin esp. when young
sharp·en \'shär-pən\ *vb* : to make or become sharp — **sharp·en·er** *n*
sharp·er \'shär-pər\ *n* : SWINDLER; *esp* : a cheating gambler
sharp·ie *or* **sharpy** \'shär-pē\ *n, pl* **sharp·ies** **1** : SHARPER **2** : a person who is exceptionally keen or alert
sharp·shoot·er \'shärp-ˌshü-tər\ *n* : a proficient marksman — **sharp·shoot·ing** *n*
shat·ter \'sha-tər\ *vb* : to dash or burst into fragments — **shat·ter·proof** \'sha-tər-ˌprüf\ *adj*
¹**shave** \'shāv\ *vb* **shaved**; **shaved** *or* **shav·en** \'shā-vən\; **shav·ing 1** : to slice in thin pieces **2** : to make bare or smooth by cutting the hair from **3** : to cut or pare off by the sliding movement of a razor **4** : to skim along or near the surface of
²**shave** *n* **1** : any of various tools for cutting thin slices : an act or process of shaving
shav·er \'shā-vər\ *n* **1** : an electric razor **2** : BOY, YOUNGSTER
shaves *pl of* SHAFT
shaving *n* **1** : the act of one that shaves **2** : something shaved off
shawl \'shȯl\ *n* : a square or oblong piece of fabric used esp. by women as a loose covering for the head or shoulders
Shaw·nee \shȯ-'nē, shä-\ *n, pl* **Shawnee** *or* **Shawnees** : a member of an American Indian people orig. of the central Ohio valley; *also* : their language
shd *abbr* should
she \'shē\ *pron* : that female one ⟨who is ~⟩; *also* : that one regarded as feminine ⟨~'s a fine ship⟩
sheaf \'shēf\ *n, pl* **sheaves** \'shēvz\ **1** : a bundle of stalks and ears of grain **2** : a group of things bound together
¹**shear** \'shir\ *vb* **sheared**; **sheared** *or* **shorn** \'shȯrn\; **shear·ing 1** : to cut the hair or wool from : CLIP, TRIM **2** : to deprive by or as if by cutting ⟨*shorn* of power⟩ **3** : to cut or break sharply
²**shear** *n* **1** : any of various cutting tools that consist of two blades fastened together so that the edges slide one by the other — usu. used in pl. **2** *chiefly Brit* : the act, an instance, or the result of shearing **3** : an action or stress caused by applied forces that causes two parts of a body to slide on each other
shear·wa·ter \'shir-ˌwȯ-tər, -ˌwä-\ *n* : any of several seabirds related to the petrels that often skim along waves in flight
sheath \'shēth\ *n, pl* **sheaths** \'shēthz, 'shēths\ **1** : a case for a blade (as of a knife); *also* : an anatomical covering suggesting such a case **2** : a close-fitting dress usu. worn without a belt
sheathe \'shēth\ *also* **sheath** \'shēth\ *vb* **sheathed**; **sheath·ing 1** : to put into a sheath **2** : to cover with something that guards or protects
sheath·ing \'shē-thiŋ, -thiŋ\ *n* : material used to sheathe something; *esp* : the first covering of boards or of waterproof material on the outside wall of a frame house or on a timber roof

sheave \'shiv, 'shēv\ *n* : a grooved wheel or pulley (as on a pulley block)
she·bang \shi-'baŋ\ *n* : everything involved in what is under consideration ⟨sold the whole ~⟩
¹**shed** \'shed\ *vb* **shed**; **shed·ding 1** : to cause to flow from a cut or wound ⟨~ blood⟩ **2** : to pour down in drops ⟨~ tears⟩ **3** : to give out (as light) : DIFFUSE **4** : to throw off (as a natural covering) : DISCARD ⟨~ skin⟩
²**shed** *n* : a slight structure built for shelter or storage
sheen \'shēn\ *n* : a subdued luster
sheep \'shēp\ *n, pl* **sheep 1** : any of various cud-chewing mammals that are stockier than the related goats and lack a beard in the male; *esp* : one raised for meat or for its wool or skin **2** : a timid or defenseless person **3** : SHEEPSKIN
sheep·dog \'shēp-ˌdȯg\ *n* : a dog used to tend, drive, or guard sheep
sheep·fold \'shēp-ˌfōld\ *n* : a pen or shelter for sheep
sheep·herd·er \-ˌhər-dər\ *n* : a worker in charge of sheep esp. on open range — **sheep·herd·ing** *n*
sheep·ish \'shē-pish\ *adj* : BASHFUL, TIMID; *esp* : embarrassed by consciousness of a fault — **sheep·ish·ly** *adv*
sheep·skin \'shēp-ˌskin\ *n* **1** : the hide of a sheep or leather prepared from it; *also* : PARCHMENT **2** : DIPLOMA
¹**sheer** \'shir\ *vb* : to turn from a course
²**sheer** *adj* **1** : very thin or transparent **2** : UNQUALIFIED ⟨~ folly⟩ **3** : very steep ✦ *Synonyms* PURE, SIMPLE, ABSOLUTE, UNADULTERATED, UNMITIGATED — **sheer** *adv*
¹**sheet** \'shēt\ *n* **1** : a broad piece of cloth (as for a bed); *also* : SAIL **1 2** : a single piece of paper **3** : a broad flat surface ⟨a ~ of ice⟩ **4** : something broad and long and relatively thin
²**sheet** *n* : a rope used to trim a sail
sheet·ing \'shē-tiŋ\ *n* : material in the form of sheets or suitable for forming into sheets
sheikh *or* **sheik** \'shēk, 'shāk\ *n* : an Arab chief — **sheikh·dom** *or* **sheik·dom** \-dəm\ *n*
shek·el *or* **sheq·el** \'she-kəl\ *n* — see MONEY table
shelf \'shelf\ *n, pl* **shelves** \'shelvz\ **1** : a thin flat usu. long and narrow structure fastened horizontally (as on a wall) above the floor to hold things **2** : something (as a sandbar) that suggests a shelf
shelf life *n* : the period of storage time during which a material will remain useful
¹**shell** \'shel\ *n* **1** : a hard or tough often thin outer covering of an animal (as a beetle, turtle, or mollusk) or of an egg or a seed or fruit (as a nut); *also* : something that resembles a shell ⟨a pastry ~⟩ **2** : a light narrow racing boat propelled by oarsmen **3** : a case holding an explosive and designed to be fired from a cannon; *also* : a case holding the charge of powder and shot or bullet for small arms **4** : a plain usu. sleeveless blouse or sweater — **shelled** \'sheld\ *adj* — **shelly** \'she-lē\ *adj*
²**shell** *vb* **1** : to remove from a shell or husk **2** : BOMBARD — **shell·er** *n*
¹**shel·lac** \shə-'lak\ *n* **1** : a purified lac **2** : lac dissolved in alcohol and used as a wood filler or finish
²**shellac** *vb* **shel·lacked**; **shel·lack·ing 1** : to coat or treat with shellac **2** : to defeat decisively ⟨*shellacked* their opponents⟩
shellacking *n* : a sound drubbing
shell bean *n* : a bean grown esp. for its edible seeds; *also* : its edible seed
shell·fish \-ˌfish\ *n* : an invertebrate water animal (as an oyster or lobster) with a shell
shell out *vb* : PAY
shell shock *n* : COMBAT FATIGUE — **shell–shocked** \'shel-ˌshäkt\ *adj*
¹**shel·ter** \'shel-tər\ *n* : something that gives protection : REFUGE
²**shelter** *vb* **shel·tered**; **shel·ter·ing** : to give protection or refuge to
shelve \'shelv\ *vb* **shelved**; **shelv·ing 1** : to slope gradually **2** : to store on shelves **3** : to dismiss from service or use **4** : to put aside : DEFER ⟨~ a proposal⟩
shelv·ing \'shel-viŋ\ *n* : material for shelves; *also* : SHELVES
she·nan·i·gan \shə-'na-ni-gən\ *n* **1** : an underhand trick **2** : questionable conduct — usu. used in pl. **3** : high-spirited or mischievous activity — usu. used in pl.

shepherd • shiver

¹shep·herd \'she-pərd\ n 1 : one who tends sheep 2 : GERMAN SHEPHERD

²shepherd vb : to tend as or in the manner of a shepherd

shep·herd·ess \'she-pər-dəs\ n : a woman who tends sheep

shepherd's pie n : a meat pie with a mashed potato crust

sheqel n, pl sheqalim var of SHEKEL

sher·bet \'shər-bət\ n [Turk şerbet, fr. Pers sharbat, fr. Ar sharba drink] 1 : a drink of sweetened diluted fruit juice 2 also sher·bert \-bərt\ : a frozen dessert of fruit juices, sugar, milk or water, and egg whites or gelatin

sherd var of SHARD

sher·iff \'sher-əf\ n [ME shirreve, fr. OE scīrgerēfa, lit., shire reeve (local official)] : a county officer charged with the execution of the law and the preservation of order

sher·ry \'sher-ē\ n, pl sherries [alter. of earlier sherris (taken as pl.), fr. Xeres (now Jerez), Spain] : a fortified wine with a nutty flavor

Shet·land pony \'shet-lənd-\ n : any of a breed of small stocky hardy ponies

shew \'shō\ Brit var of SHOW

Shia \'shē-(-)ä\ n 1 : one of the two main branches of Islam 2 : a Muslim who is a member of this branch

shi·at·su also shi·at·zu \shē-'ät-sü\ n : a form of acupressure originating in Japan

shib·bo·leth \'shi-bə-ləth\ n [Heb shibbōleth stream; fr. the use of this word as a test to distinguish the men of Gilead from members of the tribe of Ephraim (Judges 12:5, 6)] 1 : CATCHPHRASE 2 : language that is a criterion for distinguishing members of a group

¹shield \'shēld\ n 1 : a broad piece of defensive armor carried on the arm 2 : something that protects or hides 3 : a police officer's badge

²shield vb : to protect or hide with a shield ✦ Synonyms PROTECT, GUARD, SAFEGUARD

shier comparative of SHY

shiest superlative of SHY

¹shift \'shift\ vb 1 : EXCHANGE, REPLACE 2 : to change place, position, or direction : MOVE; also : to change gears 3 : GET BY, MANAGE

²shift n 1 : SCHEME, TRICK 2 : a woman's slip or loose-fitting dress 3 : a change in direction, emphasis, or attitude 4 : a group working together alternating with other groups 5 : TRANSFER 6 : GEARSHIFT

shift·less \'shift-ləs\ adj : LAZY, INEFFICIENT — shift-less·ness n

shifty \'shif-tē\ adj shift·i·er; -est 1 : TRICKY; also : ELUSIVE 2 : indicative of a tricky nature ⟨~ eyes⟩

shih tzu \'shēd-'zü, 'shēt-'sü\ n, pl shih tzus also shih tzu often cap S&T [Chin (Beijing) shīzi (gǒu), fr. shīzi lion + gǒu dog] : any of a breed of small short-legged dogs of Chinese origin that have a short muzzle and a long dense coat

shii·ta·ke \shē-'tä-kē\ n [Jp] : a dark Asian mushroom widely cultivated for its edible cap

Shi·ite \'shē,īt\ n : a Muslim of the Shia branch of Islam

shill \'shil\ n : one who acts as a decoy (as for a pitchman) — shill vb

shil·le·lagh also shil·la·lah \shə-'lā-lē\ n [Shillelagh, town in Ireland] : CUDGEL, CLUB

shil·ling \'shi-liŋ\ n — see MONEY table

shil·ly–shally \'shi-lē-,sha-lē\ vb shilly–shall·ied; shilly–shally·ing 1 : to show hesitation or lack of decisiveness 2 : to waste time

shim \'shim\ n : a thin often tapered piece of wood, metal, or stone used (as in leveling) to fill in space

shim·mer \'shi-mər\ vb : to shine waveringly or tremulously : GLIMMER ⟨~ing light⟩ ✦ Synonyms FLASH, GLEAM, GLINT, SPARKLE, GLITTER — shimmer n — shim·mery adj

shim·my \'shi-mē\ n, pl shimmies : an abnormal vibration esp. in the front wheels of a motor vehicle — shimmy vb

¹shin \'shin\ n : the front part of the leg below the knee

²shin vb shinned; shin·ning : to climb (as a pole) by gripping alternately with arms and hands and legs

shin·bone \'shin-,bōn\ n : TIBIA

¹shine \'shīn\ vb shone \'shōn\ or shined; shin·ing 1 : to give or cause to give light 2 : GLEAM, GLITTER 3 : to be eminent, conspicuous, or distinguished ⟨gave her a chance to ~⟩ 4 : POLISH ⟨~ your shoes⟩

²shine n 1 : BRIGHTNESS, RADIANCE 2 : LUSTER, BRILLIANCE 3 : fair weather : SUNSHINE ⟨rain or ~⟩ 4 : LIKING, FANCY ⟨took a ~ to them⟩ 5 : a polish given to shoes

shin·er \'shī-nər\ n 1 : a silvery fish; esp : any of numerous small freshwater American fishes related to the carp 2 : BLACK EYE

¹shin·gle \'shiŋ-gəl\ n 1 : a small thin piece of building material used in overlapping rows for covering a roof or outside wall 2 : a small sign

²shingle vb shin·gled; shin·gling : to cover with shingles

³shingle n : a beach strewn with gravel; also : coarse gravel (as on a beach)

shin·gles \'shiŋ-gəlz\ n : an acute inflammation of the spinal and cranial nerves caused by reactivation of the chicken pox virus and associated with eruptions and pain along the course of the affected nerves

shin·ny \'shi-nē\ vb shin·nied; shin·ny·ing : SHIN

shin splints n sing or pl : a condition marked by pain and sometimes tenderness and swelling in the shin caused by repeated small injuries to muscles and associated tissue esp. from running

Shin·to \'shin-,tō\ n : the indigenous religion of Japan consisting esp. in reverence of the spirits of natural forces and imperial ancestors — Shin·to·ism n — Shin·to·ist n or adj

shiny \'shī-nē\ adj shin·i·er; -est : BRIGHT, RADIANT; also : POLISHED

¹ship \'ship\ n 1 : a large oceangoing boat 2 : a ship's officers and crew 3 : AIRSHIP, AIRCRAFT, SPACECRAFT

²ship vb shipped; ship·ping 1 : to put or receive on board a ship for transportation 2 : to have transported by a carrier 3 : to take or draw into a boat ⟨~ oars⟩ ⟨~ water⟩ 4 : to engage to serve on a ship — ship·per n

-ship \,ship\ n suffix 1 : state : condition : quality ⟨friendship⟩ 2 : office : dignity : profession ⟨lordship⟩ ⟨clerkship⟩ 3 : art : skill ⟨horsemanship⟩ 4 : something showing, exhibiting, or embodying a quality or state ⟨township⟩ 5 : one entitled to a (specified) rank, title, or appellation ⟨his Lordship⟩ 6 : the body of persons engaged in a specified activity ⟨readership⟩

ship·board \'ship-,bórd\ n

ship·build·er \-,bil-dər\ n : one who designs or builds ships

ship·fit·ter \-,fi-tər\ n 1 : one who constructs ships 2 : a naval enlisted person who works as a plumber

ship·mate \-,māt\ n : a fellow sailor

ship·ment \-mənt\ n : the process of shipping; also : the goods shipped

shipping n 1 : SHIPS; esp : ships in one port or belonging to one country 2 : transportation of goods

ship·shape \'ship-,shāp\ adj : TRIM, TIDY

ship·worm \-,wərm\ n : any of various wormlike marine clams that have a shell used for burrowing in wood and damage wooden ships and wharves

¹ship·wreck \-,rek\ n 1 : a wrecked ship 2 : destruction or loss of a ship 3 : total loss or failure : RUIN

²shipwreck vb : to cause or meet disaster at sea through destruction or foundering

ship·wright \'ship-,rīt\ n : a carpenter skilled in ship construction and repair

ship·yard \-,yärd\ n : a place where ships are built or repaired

shire \'shī-(ə)r, in place-name compounds ,shir, shər\ n : a county in Great Britain

shirk \'shərk\ vb : to avoid performing (duty or work) — shirk·er n

shirr \'shər\ vb 1 : to make shirring in 2 : to bake (eggs removed from the shell) until set

shirr·ing \'shər-iŋ\ n : a decorative gathering in cloth made by drawing up parallel lines of stitches

shirt \'shərt\ n 1 : a loose cloth garment usu. having a collar, sleeves, a front opening, and a tail long enough to be tucked inside pants or a skirt 2 : UNDERSHIRT — shirt·less adj

shirt·ing \'shər-tiŋ\ n : cloth suitable for making shirts

shish ke·bab \'shish-kə-,bäb\ n [Turk şiş kebabı, fr. şiş spit + kebap roast meat] : kebab cooked on skewers

shiv \'shiv\ n, slang : KNIFE

¹shiv·er \'shi-vər\ vb : TREMBLE, QUIVER ✦ Synonyms SHUDDER, QUAVER, SHAKE, QUAKE

²shiver n : an instance of shivering — shiv·ery adj

shlemiel *var of* SCHLEMIEL

shlub *var of* SCHLUB

shmooze *var of* SCHMOOZE

Sho·ah \'shō-ə, -ˌä\ *n* : HOLOCAUST 2

¹**shoal** \'shōl\ *n* **1** : SHALLOW **2** : a sandbank or bar creating a shallow

²**shoal** *n* : a large group (as of fish)

shoat \'shōt\ *n* : a weaned young pig

¹**shock** \'shäk\ *n* : a pile of sheaves of grain or cornstalks set up in a field

²**shock** *n* [MF *choc*, fr. *choquer* to strike against] **1** : a sharp impact or violent shake or jar **2** : a sudden violent mental or emotional disturbance **3** : a state of bodily collapse that is often marked by a drop in blood pressure and volume and that is caused esp. by crushing wounds, blood loss, or burns **4** : the effect of a charge of electricity passing through the body **5** : SHOCK ABSORBER — **shock·proof** \-ˌprüf\ *adj*

³**shock** *vb* **1** : to strike with surprise, horror, or disgust **2** : to subject to the action of an electrical discharge

⁴**shock** *n* : a thick bushy mass (as of hair)

shock absorber *n* : any of several devices for absorbing the energy of sudden shocks in machinery

shock·er \'shä-kər\ *n* : one that shocks; *esp* : a sensational work of fiction or drama

shock·ing \'shä-kiŋ\ *adj* : extremely startling and offensive — **shock·ing·ly** *adv*

shock therapy *n* : the treatment of mental disorder by induction of coma or convulsions by drugs or electricity

shock wave *n* : a wave formed by the sudden violent compression of the medium through which it travels

¹**shod·dy** \'shä-dē\ *n* **1** : wool reclaimed from old rags; *also* : a fabric made from it **2** : inferior or imitation material

²**shoddy** *adj* **shod·di·er; -est 1** : made of shoddy **2** : poorly done or made ⟨~ workmanship⟩ — **shod·di·ly** \'shä-də-lē\ *adv* — **shod·di·ness** \-dē-nəs\ *n*

¹**shoe** \'shü\ *n* **1** : a covering for the human foot **2** : HORSESHOE **3** : the part of a brake that presses on the wheel

²**shoe** *vb* **shod** \'shäd\ *also* **shoed** \'shüd\; **shoe·ing** \'shü-iŋ\ : to put a shoe or shoes on

shoebox \'shü-ˌbäks\ *n* **1** : a box that shoes are sold in **2** : a very small space ⟨a ~ apartment⟩

shoe·horn \-ˌhȯrn\ *n* : a curved implement (as of horn or plastic) used in putting on a shoe

shoe·lace \-ˌlās\ *n* : a lace or string for fastening a shoe

shoe·mak·er \-ˌmā-kər\ *n* : one who makes or repairs shoes

shoe·string \-ˌstriŋ\ *n* **1** : SHOELACE **2** : a small sum of money

sho·gun \'shō-gən\ *n* [Jp *shōgun* general] : any of a line of military governors ruling Japan until the revolution of 1867–68 — **sho·gun·ate** \'shō-gə-nət, -ˌnāt\ *n*

shone *past and past part of* SHINE

shook *past of* SHAKE

shook–up \ˌ(ˌ)shůk-'əp\ *adj* : nervously upset : AGITATED

¹**shoot** \'shüt\ *vb* **shot** \'shät\; **shoot·ing 1** : to drive (as an arrow or bullet) forward quickly or forcibly **2** : to hit, kill, or wound with a missile **3** : to cause a missile to be driven forth or forth from ⟨~ a gun⟩ **4** : to send forth (as a ray of light) **5** : to thrust forward or out **6** : to pass rapidly along ⟨~ the rapids⟩ **7** : PHOTOGRAPH, FILM **8** : to move swiftly : DART **9** : to grow by or as if by sending out shoots; *also* : MATURE, DEVELOP — **shoot·er** *n*

²**shoot** *n* **1** : a plant stem with its leaves and branches esp. when not yet mature **2** : an act of shooting **3** : a shooting match

shooting iron *n* : FIREARM

shooting star *n* : METEOR 2

shoot up *vb* : to inject a narcotic into a vein

¹**shop** \'shäp\ *n* [ME *shoppe*, fr. OE *sceoppa* booth] **1** : a place where things are made or worked on : FACTORY, MILL **2** : a retail store ⟨dress ~⟩

²**shop** *vb* **shopped; shop·ping** : to visit stores for purchasing or examining goods — **shop·per** *n*

shop·keep·er \'shäp-ˌkē-pər\ *n* : a retail merchant

shop·lift \-ˌlift\ *vb* : to steal goods on display from a store — **shop·lift·er** *n*

shopping cart *n* **1** : a cart used for holding merchandise when shopping in a store **2** : a temporary record of items selected for purchase from a website

shop·talk \-ˌtȯk\ *n* : talk about one's business or special interests

shop·worn \-ˌwȯrn\ *adj* : soiled or frayed from much handling in a store

¹**shore** \'shȯr\ *n* : land along the edge of a body of water — **shore·less** *adj*

²**shore** *vb* **shored; shor·ing** : to give support to : BRACE

³**shore** *n* : ¹PROP

shore·bird \-ˌbərd\ *n* : any of a suborder of birds (as the plovers and sandpipers) found mostly along the seashore

shore patrol *n* : a branch of a navy that exercises guard and police functions

shor·ing \'shȯr-iŋ\ *n* : a group of things that shore something up

shorn *past part of* SHEAR

¹**short** \'shȯrt\ *adj* **1** : not long or tall **2** : not great in distance **3** : brief in time **4** : not coming up to standard or to an expected amount **5** : CURT, ABRUPT ⟨was ~ with the busybody⟩ **6** : insufficiently supplied ⟨~ of cash⟩ **7** : made with shortening : FLAKY **8** : consisting of or relating to a sale of securities or commodities that the seller does not possess or has not contracted for at the time of the sale ⟨~ sale⟩ — **short·ness** *n*

²**short** *adv* **1** : ABRUPTLY, CURTLY **2** : at some point before a goal aimed at

³**short** *n* **1** : something shorter than normal or standard **2** *pl* : drawers or pants of less than knee length **3** : SHORT CIRCUIT

⁴**short** *vb* : SHORT-CIRCUIT

short·age \'shȯr-tij\ *n* : LACK, DEFICIT

short·cake \'shȯrt-ˌkāk\ *n* : a dessert consisting of short biscuit spread with sweetened fruit

short·change \-'chānj\ *vb* : to cheat esp. by giving less than the correct amount of change

short circuit *n* : a connection made between points in an electric circuit where current is not intended to flow — **short–circuit** *vb*

short·com·ing \'shȯrt-ˌkə-miŋ\ *n* : FAULT 1, FLAW

short·cut \-ˌkət\ *n* **1** : a route more direct than that usu. taken **2** : a quicker way of doing something

short·en \'shȯr-tᵊn\ *vb* : to make or become short ♦ **Synonyms** CURTAIL, ABBREVIATE, ABRIDGE, RETRENCH

short·en·ing \'shȯr-tᵊn-iŋ\ *n* : a substance (as lard or butter) that makes pastry tender and flaky

short·hand \'shȯrt-ˌhand\ *n* : a method of writing rapidly by using symbols and abbreviations for letters, words, or phrases : STENOGRAPHY

short·hand·ed \ˌshȯrt-'han-dəd\ *adj* : short of the needed number of people

short·horn \'shȯrt-ˌhȯrn\ *n, often cap* : any of a breed of red, roan, or white cattle of English origin

short hundredweight *n* — see WEIGHT table

short–lived \'shȯrt-ˌlivd, -'līvd\ *adj* : of short life or duration

short·ly \'shȯrt-lē\ *adv* **1** : in a few words : in a short time : SOON

short–or·der \'shȯrt-ˌȯr-dər\ *adj* : preparing or serving food that can be quickly cooked ⟨a ~ cook⟩

short shrift *n* **1** : a brief respite from death **2** : little consideration

short·sight·ed \'shȯrt-ˌsī-təd\ *adj* **1** : lacking foresight **2** : NEARSIGHTED — **short·sight·ed·ness** *n*

short·stop \-ˌstäp\ *n* : a baseball player defending the area between second and third base

short story *n* : a short work of fiction usu. dealing with a few characters and a single event

short–tem·pered \ˌshȯrt-'tem-pərd\ *adj* : having a quick temper

short–term \'shȯrt-ˌtərm\ *adj* **1** : occurring over or involving a relatively short period of time **2** : of or relating to a financial transaction based on a term usu. of less than a year

short ton *n* — see WEIGHT table

short·wave \'shȯrt-ˌwāv\ *n* : a radio wave with a wavelength between 10 and 100 meters

Sho·sho·ne *or* **Sho·sho·ni** \shə-'shō-nē\ *n, pl* **Shoshones** *or* **Shoshoni** : a member of an American Indian people orig. ranging through California, Idaho, Nevada, Utah, and Wyoming

¹shot \'shät\ *n* **1** : an act of shooting **2** : a stroke or throw in some games **3** : something that is shot : MISSILE, PROJECTILE; *esp* : small pellets forming a charge for a shotgun **4** : a metal sphere that is thrown for distance in the shot put **5** : RANGE, REACH **6** : MARKSMAN **7** : a single photographic exposure **8** : a single sequence of a motion picture or a television program made by one camera **9** : an injection (as of medicine) into the body **10** : a small serving of undiluted liquor or other beverage

²shot *past and past part of* SHOOT

shot·gun \'shät-ˌgən\ *n* : a gun with a smooth bore used to fire shot at short range

shot put *n* : a field event in which a shot is heaved for distance

should \'shu̇d, shəd\ *past of* SHALL — used as an auxiliary to express condition, obligation or propriety, probability, or futurity from a point of view in the past

¹shoul·der \'shōl-dər\ *n* **1** : the part of the body of a person or animal where the arm or foreleg joins the body **2** : either edge of a roadway **3** : a rounded or sloping part (as of a bottle) where the neck joins the body

²shoulder *vb* **1** : to push or thrust with the shoulder **2** : to bear on the shoulder **3** : to take the responsibility of

shoulder belt *n* : an automobile safety belt worn across the torso and over the shoulder

shoulder blade *n* : a flat triangular bone at the back of each shoulder

shout \'shau̇t\ *vb* : to utter a sudden loud cry — **shout** *n*

shove \'shəv\ *vb* **shoved; shov·ing** : to push along, aside, or away — **shove** *n*

¹shov·el \'shə-vəl\ *n* **1** : a broad long-handled scoop used to lift and throw material **2** : the amount a shovel will hold — **shov·el·ful** \'shə-vəl-ˌful\ *n*

²shovel *vb* **-eled** *or* **-elled; -el·ing** *or* **-el·ling** **1** : to take up and throw with a shovel **2** : to dig or clean out with a shovel

¹show \'shō\ *vb* **showed** \'shōd\; **shown** \'shōn\ *or* **showed; show·ing** **1** : to cause or permit to be seen : EXHIBIT ⟨~ anger⟩ **2** : CONFER, BESTOW ⟨~ mercy⟩ **3** : REVEAL, DISCLOSE ⟨~ed courage in battle⟩ **4** : INSTRUCT ⟨~ me how⟩ **5** : PROVE ⟨~s he was guilty⟩ **6** : APPEAR **7** : to be noticeable **8** : to be third in a horse race

²show *n* **1** : a demonstrative display **2** : outward appearance ⟨a ~ of resistance⟩ **3** : SPECTACLE **4** : a theatrical presentation **5** : a radio or television program **6** : third place in a horse race

¹show·case \'shō-ˌkās\ *n* : a cabinet for displaying items (as in a store)

²showcase *vb* **show·cased; show·cas·ing** : EXHIBIT

show·down \'shō-ˌdau̇n\ *n* : a decisive confrontation or contest; *esp* : the showing of poker hands to determine the winner of a pot

¹show·er \'shau̇(-ə)r\ *n* **1** : a brief fall of rain **2** : a party given by friends who bring gifts **3** : a bath in which water is showered on the person; *also* : a facility (as a stall) for such a bath — **show·ery** *adj*

²shower *vb* **1** : to rain or fall in a shower **2** : to bathe in a shower

show·man \'shō-mən\ *n* : a notably spectacular, dramatic, or effective performer — **show·man·ship** *n*

show-off \'shō-ˌȯf\ *n* : one that seeks to attract attention by conspicuous behavior

show off *vb* **1** : to display proudly **2** : to act as a show-off

show·piece \'shō-ˌpēs\ *n* : an outstanding example used for exhibition

show·place \-ˌplās\ *n* : an estate or building that is a showpiece

show up *vb* : ARRIVE

showy \'shō-ē\ *adj* **show·i·er; -est** : superficially impressive or striking ⟨a ~ orchid⟩ — **show·i·ly** \'shō-ə-lē\ *adv* — **show·i·ness** \-ē-nəs\ *n*

shpt *abbr* shipment

shrap·nel \'shrap-nəl\ *n, pl* **shrapnel** [Henry *Shrapnel* †1842 Eng. artillery officer] : bomb, mine, or shell fragments

¹shred \'shred\ *n* : a narrow strip cut or torn off : a small fragment

²shred *vb* **shred·ded; shred·ding** : to cut or tear into shreds

shrew \'shrü\ *n* **1** : any of a family of very small mammals with short velvety fur that are related to the moles **2** : a scolding woman

shrewd \'shrüd\ *adj* : CLEVER, ASTUTE — **shrewd·ly** *adv* — **shrewd·ness** *n*

shrew·ish \'shrü-ish\ *adj* : having an irritable disposition : ILL-TEMPERED — **shrew·ish·ly** *adv* — **shrew·ish·ness** *n*

shriek \'shrēk\ *n* : a shrill cry : SCREAM, YELL — **shriek** *vb*

shrift \'shrift\ *n, archaic* : the act of shriving : CONFESSION

shrike \'shrīk\ *n* : any of numerous usu. largely grayish or brownish birds that often impale their usu. insect prey upon thorns before devouring it

¹shrill \'shril\ *vb* : to make a high-pitched piercing sound

²shrill *adj* : high-pitched : PIERCING ⟨~ whistle⟩ — **shril·ly** *adv*

shrimp \'shrimp\ *n, pl* **shrimps** *or* **shrimp** **1** : any of various small marine crustaceans related to the lobsters **2** *usu disparaging* : a small or puny person

shrimp 1

shrine \'shrīn\ *n* [ME, receptacle for the relics of a saint, fr. OE *scrīn*, fr. L *scrinium* case, chest] **1** : the tomb of a saint; *also* : a place where devotion is paid to a saint or deity **2** : a place or object hallowed by its associations

¹shrink \'shriŋk\ *vb* **shrank** \'shraŋk\ *or* **shrunk** \'shrəŋk\; **shrunk** *or* **shrunk·en** \'shrəŋ-kən\; **shrink·ing** **1** : to draw back or away **2** : to become smaller or more compact **3** : to lessen in value ♦ *Synonyms* CONTRACT, CONSTRICT, COMPRESS, CONDENSE — **shrink·able** *adj*

²shrink *n* : a clinical psychiatrist or psychologist

shrink·age \'shriŋ-kij\ *n* **1** : the act of shrinking **2** : the amount lost by shrinkage

shrive \'shrīv\ *vb* **shrived** *or* **shrove** \'shrōv\; **shriv·en** \'shri-vən\ *or* **shrived** [ME, fr. OE *scrīfan* to prescribe, allot, shrive, fr. L *scribere* to write] : to administer the sacrament of reconciliation to

shriv·el \'shri-vəl\ *vb* **-eled** *or* **-elled; -el·ing** *or* **-el·ling** : to shrink and draw into wrinkles : DWINDLE

¹shroud \'shrau̇d\ *n* **1** : something that covers or screens **2** : a cloth placed over a dead body **3** : any of the ropes leading from the masthead of a ship to the side to support the mast

²shroud *vb* : to veil or screen from view

shrub \'shrəb\ *n* : a low usu. several-stemmed woody plant — **shrub·by** *adj*

shrub·bery \'shrə-bə-rē\ *n, pl* **-ber·ies** : a planting or growth of shrubs

shrug \'shrəg\ *vb* **shrugged; shrug·ging** : to hunch (the shoulders) up to express aloofness, indifference, or uncertainty — **shrug** *n*

shrug off *vb* **1** : to brush aside : MINIMIZE ⟨she *shrugged* off their concerns⟩ **2** : to shake off **3** : to remove (a garment) by wriggling out

shtick *also* **schtick** *or* **shtik** \'shtik\ *n* [Yiddish *shtik* pranks, lit., piece] **1** : a usu. comic or repetitious performance or routine **2** : one's special trait, interest, or activity

¹shuck \'shək\ *n* : SHELL, HUSK

²shuck *vb* : to strip of shucks

shud·der \'shə-dər\ *vb* : TREMBLE, QUAKE — **shudder** *n*

shuf·fle \'shə-fəl\ *vb* **shuf·fled; shuf·fling** **1** : to mix in a disorderly mass **2** : to rearrange the order of (cards in a pack) by mixing two parts of the pack together **3** : to shift from place to place **4** : to move with a sliding or dragging gait **5** : to dance in a slow lagging manner — **shuffle** *n*

shuf·fle·board \'shə-fəl-ˌbȯrd\ *n* : a game in which players use long-handled cues to shove disks into scoring areas marked on a smooth surface

shun \'shən\ *vb* **shunned; shun·ning** : to avoid deliberately or habitually ♦ *Synonyms* EVADE, ELUDE, ESCAPE, DUCK

¹shunt \'shənt\ *vb* [ME, to turn away] : to turn off to one side; *esp* : to switch (a train) from one track to another

²shunt *n* **1** : a method or device for turning or thrusting aside **2** : a conductor joining two points in an electrical circuit forming an alternate path through which a portion of the current may pass

shut \'shət\ *vb* **shut; shut·ting 1** : CLOSE **2** : to forbid entrance into **3** : to lock up **4** : to fold together ⟨∼ a penknife⟩ **5** : to cease or suspend activity ⟨∼ down an assembly line⟩

shut·down \-ˌdau̇n\ *n* : a temporary cessation of activity (as in a factory)

shut–in \'shət-ˌin\ *n* : a person confined to home, a room, or bed because of illness or incapacity

shut-out \'shət-ˌau̇t\ *n* : a game or contest in which one side fails to score

shut out *vb* **1** : EXCLUDE **2** : to prevent (an opponent) from scoring in a game or contest

shut·ter \'shə-tər\ *n* **1** : a movable cover for a door or window : BLIND **2** : the part of a camera that opens and closes to allow light to enter

shut·ter·bug \'shə-tər-ˌbəg\ *n* : a photography enthusiast

¹shut·tle \'shə-tᵊl\ *n* **1** : an instrument used in weaving for passing the horizontal threads between the vertical threads **2** : a vehicle traveling back and forth over a short route ⟨a ∼ bus⟩ **3** : SPACE SHUTTLE

²shuttle *vb* **shut·tled; shut·tling** : to move back and forth frequently

shut·tle·cock \'shə-tᵊl-ˌkäk\ *n* : a light conical object (as of cork or plastic) used in badminton

shut up *vb* : to cease or cause to cease talking

¹shy \'shī\ *adj* **shi·er** *or* **shy·er** \'shī-ər\; **shi·est** *or* **shy·est** \'shī-əst\ **1** : easily frightened : TIMID **2** : WARY **3** : BASHFUL **4** : DEFICIENT, LACKING ⟨a nickel ∼ of a quarter⟩ — **shy·ly** *adv* — **shy·ness** *n*

²shy *vb* **shied; shy·ing 1** : to show a dislike : RECOIL **2** : to start suddenly aside through fright ⟨the horse *shied*⟩

shy·ster \'shīs-tər\ *n* : an unscrupulous lawyer or politician

Si *symbol* silicon

SI *abbr* [F *Système International d'Unités*] International System of Units

Si·a·mese \ˌsī-ə-ˈmēz, -ˈmēs\ *n, pl* **Sia·mese** : THAI — **Siamese** *adj*

Siamese cat *n* : any of a breed of slender blue-eyed short-haired domestic cats of Asian origin

Siamese twin *n* [fr. Chang †1874 and Eng †1874 twins born in Siam with bodies united] : one of a pair of twins with bodies joined together at birth

Siberian husky *n* : any of a breed of thick-coated compact dogs orig. developed in Siberia to pull sleds

¹sib·i·lant \'si-bə-lənt\ *adj* : having, containing, or producing the sound of or a sound resembling that of the *s* or the *sh* in *sash* — **sib·i·lant·ly** *adv*

²sibilant *n* : a sibilant speech sound (as English \s\, \z\, \sh\, \zh\, \ch (=tsh)\, or \j (=dzh)\)

sib·ling \'si-bliŋ\ *n* : a brother or sister considered irrespective of sex; *also* : one of two or more offspring having one common parent

sib·yl \'si-bəl\ *n, often cap* : PROPHETESS — **sib·yl·line** \-bə-ˌlīn, -ˌlēn\ *adj*

sic \'sik, 'sēk\ *adv* : intentionally so written — used after a printed word or passage to indicate that it exactly reproduces an original ⟨said he seed [∼] it all⟩

sick \'sik\ *adj* **1** : not in good health : ILL; *also* : of, relating to, or intended for use in sickness ⟨∼ pay⟩ **2** : NAUSEATED **3** : DISGUSTED **4** : PINING **5** : mentally or emotionally unsound **6** : MACABRE, SADISTIC ⟨∼ jokes⟩ — **sick·ly** *adj*

sick·bed \'sik-ˌbed\ *n* : a bed on which one lies sick

sick·en \'si-kən\ *vb* : to make or become sick — **sick·en·ing·ly** *adv*

sick·le \'si-kəl\ *n* : a cutting tool consisting of a curved metal blade with a short handle

sickle–cell anemia *n* : an inherited anemia in which red blood cells tend to become crescent-shaped and clog small blood vessels and which occurs esp. in individuals of African, Mediterranean, or southwest Asian ancestry

sick·ness \'sik-nəs\ *n* **1** : ill health; *also* : a specific disease **2** : NAUSEA

side \'sīd\ *n* **1** : the right or left part of the trunk of a body **2** : a place away from a central point or line **3** : a border of an object; *esp* : one of the longer borders as contrasted with an end **4** : an outer surface of an object **5** : a position regarded as opposite to another **6** : a body of contestants — **side** *adj* — **on the side** : in addition to the main portion

side·arm \-ˌärm\ *adj* : made with a sideways sweep of the arm ⟨a ∼ pitch⟩ — **sidearm** *adv*

side arm *n* : a weapon worn at the side or in the belt

side·bar \'sīd-ˌbär\ *n* : a short news story accompanying a major story and presenting related information

side·board \-ˌbȯrd\ *n* : a piece of dining-room furniture for holding articles of table service

side·burns \-ˌbərnz\ *n pl* : whiskers on the side of the face in front of the ears

side by side *adv* **1** : beside one another **2** : in the same place, time, or circumstance — **side–by–side** *adj*

side·car \-ˌkär\ *n* : a one-wheeled passenger car attached to the side of a motorcycle

side effect *n* : a secondary and usu. adverse effect (as of a drug)

side·kick \'sīd-ˌkik\ *n* : PAL, PARTNER

side·line \'sīd-ˌlīn\ *n* **1** : an activity pursued in addition to one's regular occupation **2** : the space immediately outside the lines of an athletic field or court **3** : a sphere of little or no participation — usu. used in pl.

¹side·long \'sīd-ˌlȯŋ\ *adv* : in the direction of or along the side : OBLIQUELY

²sidelong *adj* : directed to one side ⟨∼ look⟩

side·man \'sīd-ˌman\ *n* : a member of a jazz or swing orchestra

side·piece \-ˌpēs\ *n* : a piece forming or contained in the side of something

si·de·re·al \sī-ˈdir-ē-əl, sə-\ *adj* [L *sidereus*, fr. *sider-, sidus* star, constellation] **1** : of or relating to the stars **2** : measured by the apparent motion of the stars

side·sad·dle \'sīd-ˌsa-dᵊl\ *n* : a saddle for women in which the rider sits with both legs on the same side of the horse — **sidesaddle** *adv*

side·show \'sīd-ˌshō\ *n* **1** : a minor show offered in addition to a main exhibition (as of a circus) **2** : an incidental diversion

side·step \-ˌstep\ *vb* **1** : to step aside **2** : AVOID, EVADE ⟨*sidestepped* the question⟩

side·stroke \-ˌstrōk\ *n* : a swimming stroke which is executed on the side and in which the arms are swept backward and downward and the legs do a scissors kick

side·swipe \-ˌswīp\ *vb* : to strike with a glancing blow along the side — **sideswipe** *n*

¹side·track \-ˌtrak\ *n* : SIDING 1

²sidetrack *vb* **1** : to switch from a main railroad line to a siding **2** : to turn aside from a purpose

side·walk \'sīd-ˌwȯk\ *n* : a paved walk at the side of a road or street

side·wall \-ˌwȯl\ *n* **1** : a wall forming the side of something **2** : the side of an automobile tire

side·ways \-ˌwāz\ *adv or adj* **1** : from the side **2** : with one side to the front **3** : to, toward, or at one side

side·wind·er \-ˌwīn-dər\ *n* : a small pale-colored desert rattlesnake of the southwestern U.S.

sid·ing \'sī-diŋ\ *n* **1** : a short railroad track connected with the main track **2** : material (as boards) covering the outside of frame buildings

si·dle \'sī-dᵊl\ *vb* **si·dled; si·dling** : to move sideways or with one side foremost

SIDS *abbr* sudden infant death syndrome

siege \'sēj\ *n* **1** : the placing of an army around or before a fortified place to force its surrender **2** : a persistent attack (as of illness)

sie·mens \'sē-mənz, 'zē-\ *n* : a unit of conductance equivalent to one ampere per volt

si·er·ra \sē-ˈer-ə\ *n* [Sp, lit., saw, fr. L *serra*] : a range of mountains esp. with jagged peaks

si·es·ta \sē-ˈes-tə\ *n* [Sp, fr. L *sexta (hora)* noon, lit., sixth hour] : a midday rest or nap

sieve \'siv\ *n* : a utensil with meshes or holes to separate finer particles from coarser or solids from liquids

sift \'sift\ *vb* **1** : to pass through a sieve **2** : to separate with or as if with a sieve **3** : to examine carefully **4** : to scatter by or as if by passing through a sieve — **sift·er** *n*

sig *abbr* signature

SIG *abbr* special interest group

sigh \'sī\ *vb* **1** : to let out a deep audible breath (as in weariness or sorrow) **2** : GRIEVE, YEARN — **sigh** *n*

¹sight \'sīt\ *n* **1** : something seen or worth seeing **2** : the process or power of seeing; *esp* : the sense of which the eye is the receptor and by which qualities of appearance (as position, shape, and color) are perceived **3** : INSPECTION **4** : a device (as a small bead on a gun barrel) that aids the eye in aiming **5** : VIEW, GLIMPSE **6** : the range of vision — **sight·less** *adj*

²sight *vb* **1** : to get sight of **2** : to aim by means of a sight

sight·ed \'sī-təd\ *adj* : having sight

sight·ly \-lē\ *adj* : pleasing to the sight

sight·see·ing \'sīt-ˌsē-iŋ\ *adj* : engaged in or used for seeing sights of interest — **sight·seer** \-ˌsē-ər\ *n*

sig·ma \'sig-mə\ *n* : the 18th letter of the Greek alphabet — Σ *or* σ *or* ς

¹sign \'sīn\ *n* **1** : a gesture expressing a command, wish, or thought **2** : SYMBOL **3** : a notice publicly displayed for advertising purposes or for giving direction or warning **4** : OMEN, PORTENT **5** : TRACE, VESTIGE ⟨left without a ∼⟩

²sign *vb* **1** : to mark with a sign **2** : to represent by a sign **3** : to make a sign or signal **4** : to write one's name on in token of assent or obligation **5** : to assign legally **6** : to use sign language — **sign·er** *n*

¹sig·nal \'sig-nəl\ *n* **1** : a sign agreed on as the start of some joint action **2** : a sign giving warning or notice of something **3** : the message, sound, or image transmitted in electronic communication (as radio)

²signal *vb* **-naled** *or* **-nalled; -nal·ing** *or* **-nal·ling** **1** : to notify by a signal **2** : to communicate by signals

³signal *adj* : DISTINGUISHED ⟨a ∼ honor⟩ — **sig·nal·ly** *adv*

sig·nal·ize \'sig-nə-ˌlīz\ *vb* **-ized; -iz·ing** : to point out or make conspicuous — **sig·nal·i·za·tion** \ˌsig-nə-lə-'zā-shən\ *n*

sig·nal·man \'sig-nəl-mən, -ˌman\ *n* : a person who signals or works with signals

sig·na·to·ry \'sig-nə-ˌtȯr-ē\ *n, pl* **-ries** : a person or government that signs jointly with others — **signatory** *adj*

sig·na·ture \'sig-nə-ˌchùr\ *n* **1** : the name of a person written by himself or herself **2** : the sign placed after the clef to indicate the key or the meter of a piece of music

sign·board \'sīn-ˌbȯrd\ *n* : a board bearing a sign or notice

sig·net \'sig-nət\ *n* : a small intaglio seal (as in a ring)

sig·nif·i·cance \sig-'ni-fi-kəns\ *n* **1** : something signified : MEANING **2** : SUGGESTIVENESS **3** : CONSEQUENCE, IMPORTANCE ⟨the ∼ of the treaty⟩

sig·nif·i·cant \-kənt\ *adj* **1** : having meaning; *esp* : having a hidden or special meaning **2** : having or likely to have considerable influence or effect : IMPORTANT — **sig·nif·i·cant·ly** *adv*

sig·ni·fy \'sig-nə-ˌfī\ *vb* **-fied; -fy·ing** **1** : to show by a sign **2** : MEAN, IMPORT **3** : to have significance — **sig·ni·fi·ca·tion** \ˌsig-nə-fə-'kā-shən\ *n*

sign in *vb* : to make a record of arrival (as by signing a register)

sign language *n* : a formal system of hand gestures used for communication (as by the deaf)

sign off *vb* : to announce the end (as of a program or broadcast)

sign of the cross : a gesture of the hand forming a cross (as to invoke divine blessing)

sign on *vb* **1** : ENLIST **2** : to announce the start of broadcasting for the day

sign out *vb* : to make a record of departure (as by signing a register)

sign·post \'sīn-ˌpōst\ *n* : a post bearing a sign

sign up *vb* : to sign one's name in order to obtain, do, or join something

Sikh \'sēk\ *n* : an adherent of a religion of India marked by rejection of caste — **Sikh·ism** *n*

si·lage \'sī-lij\ *n* : fodder fermented (as in a silo) to produce a rich moist animal feed

¹si·lence \'sī-ləns\ *n* **1** : the state of being silent **2** : STILLNESS **3** : SECRECY

²silence *vb* **si·lenced; si·lenc·ing** **1** : to reduce to silence : STILL **2** : to cause to cease hostile firing or criticism

si·lenc·er \'sī-lən-sər\ *n* : a device for muffling the noise of a gunshot

si·lent \'sī-lənt\ *adj* **1** : not speaking : MUTE; *also* : TACITURN **2** : STILL, QUIET **3** : performed or borne without utterance ⟨a ∼ prayer⟩ ✦ *Synonyms* RETICENT, RESERVED, CLOSEMOUTHED, CLOSE — **si·lent·ly** *adv*

¹sil·hou·ette \ˌsi-lə-'wet\ *n* [F] **1** : a representation of the outlines of an object filled in with black or some other uniform color **2** : OUTLINE ⟨∼ of a ship⟩

²silhouette *vb* **-ett·ed; -ett·ing** : to represent by a silhouette; *also* : to show against a light background

sil·i·ca \'si-li-kə\ *n* : a mineral that consists of silicon and oxygen

sil·i·cate \'si-lə-ˌkāt, 'si-li-kət\ *n* : a chemical salt that consists of a metal combined with silicon and oxygen

si·li·ceous *also* **si·li·cious** \sə-'li-shəs\ *adj* : of, relating to, or containing silica or a silicate

sil·i·con \'si-li-kən, 'si-lə-ˌkän\ *n* : a nonmetallic chemical element that occurs in combination as the most abundant element next to oxygen in the earth's crust and is used esp. in alloys and semiconductors

sil·i·cone \'si-li-ˌkōn\ *n* : an organic silicon compound used esp. for lubricants and varnishes

sil·i·co·sis \ˌsi-lə-'kō-səs\ *n* : a lung disease caused by prolonged inhaling of silica dusts

silk \'silk\ *n* **1** : a fine strong lustrous protein fiber produced by insect larvae usu. for their cocoons; *esp* : one from moth larvae (**silk·worms** \-ˌwərmz\) used for cloth **2** : thread or cloth made from silk — **silk·en** \'sil-kən\ *adj* — **silky** *adj*

silk screen *n* : a stencil process in which coloring matter is forced through the meshes of a prepared silk or organdy screen; *also* : a print made by this process — **silk–screen** *vb*

sill \'sil\ *n* : a heavy crosspiece (as of wood or stone) that forms the bottom member of a window frame or a doorway; *also* : a horizontal supporting piece at the base of a structure

sil·ly \'si-lē\ *adj* **sil·li·er; -est** [ME *sely, silly* happy, innocent, pitiable, feeble, fr. OE *sǣlig,* fr. *sǣl* happiness] : FOOLISH, ABSURD, STUPID — **sil·li·ness** *n*

si·lo \'sī-lō\ *n, pl* **silos** [Sp] **1** : a trench, pit, or esp. a tall cylinder for making and storing silage **2** : an underground structure for housing a guided missile

¹silt \'silt\ *n* **1** : fine earth; *esp* : particles of such soil floating in rivers, ponds, or lakes **2** : a deposit (as by a river) of silt — **silty** *adj*

²silt *vb* : to obstruct or cover with silt — **silt·ation** \sil-'tā-shən\ *n*

Si·lu·ri·an \sī-'lùr-ē-ən\ *adj* : of, relating to, or being the period of the Paleozoic era between the Ordovician and the Devonian marked by the appearance of the first land plants — **Silurian** *n*

¹sil·ver \'sil-vər\ *n* **1** : a white ductile metallic chemical element that takes a high polish and is a better conductor of heat and electricity than any other substance **2** : coin made of silver **3** : FLATWARE **4** : a grayish white color — **sil·very** *adj*

²silver *adj* **1** : relating to, made of, or coated with silver **2** : SILVERY

³silver *vb* **sil·vered; sil·ver·ing** : to coat with or as if with silver — **sil·ver·er** *n*

silver bromide *n* : a light-sensitive compound used esp. in photography

sil·ver·fish \'sil-vər-ˌfish\ *n* : any of various small wingless insects found in houses and sometimes injurious esp. to sized paper and starched clothes

silver iodide *n* : a light-sensitive compound used in photography, rainmaking, and medicine

silver maple *n* : a No. American maple with deeply cut leaves that are green above and silvery white below

silver nitrate *n* : a soluble compound used in photography and as an antiseptic

sil·ver·ware \'sil-vər-ˌwer\ *n* : FLATWARE

sim *abbr* simulation; simulator

sim·i·an \'si-mē-ən\ *n* : MONKEY, APE — **simian** *adj*

simian immunodeficiency virus *n* : SIV

sim·i·lar \'si-mə-lər\ *adj* : marked by correspondence or resemblance ✦ *Synonyms* ALIKE, AKIN, COMPARABLE,

PARALLEL — sim·i·lar·i·ty \ˌsi-mə-ˈler-ə-tē\ n — sim·i·lar·ly adv

sim·i·le \ˈsi-mə-(ˌ)lē\ n [ME, fr. L, likeness, comparison, fr. neut. of *similis* like, similar] : a figure of speech in which two dissimilar things are compared by the use of *like* or *as* (as in "cheeks like roses")

si·mil·i·tude \sə-ˈmi-lə-ˌtüd, -ˌtyüd\ n : LIKENESS, RESEMBLANCE

sim·mer \ˈsi-mər\ vb sim·mered; sim·mer·ing 1 : to stew at or just below the boiling point 2 : to be on the point of bursting out with violence or emotional disturbance — simmer n

simmer down vb : to become calm or peaceful

si·mo·nize \ˈsī-mə-ˌnīz\ vb -nized; -niz·ing : to polish with or as if with wax

si·mo·ny \ˈsī-mə-nē, ˈsi-\ n [ME *symonie*, fr. AF *simonie*, fr. LL *simonia*, fr. *Simon* Magus sorcerer of Samaria in Acts 8:9–24] : the buying or selling of a church office

sim·pa·ti·co \sim-ˈpä-ti-ˌkō, -ˈpa-\ adj : CONGENIAL, LIKABLE

sim·per \ˈsim-pər\ vb : to smile in a silly manner — sim·per n

sim·ple \ˈsim-pəl\ adj sim·pler \-pə-lər\; sim·plest \-pə-ləst\ [ME, fr. AF, plain, uncomplicated, artless, fr. L *simplus, simplex*, lit., single; L *simplus* fr. *sim-* one + *-plus* multiplied by; L *simplex* fr. *sim-* + *-plex* -fold] 1 : free from dishonesty or vanity : INNOCENT 2 : free from ostentation 3 : of humble origin or modest position 4 : STUPID 5 : not complex : PLAIN ⟨a ~ melody⟩ ⟨~ directions⟩ 6 : lacking education, experience, or intelligence 7 : developing from a single ovary ⟨a ~ fruit⟩ ◆ **Synonyms** EASY, FACILE, LIGHT, EFFORTLESS — sim·ple·ness n — sim·ply adv

simple interest n : interest paid or computed on the original principal only of a loan or on the amount of an account

sim·ple·ton \ˈsim-pəl-tən\ n : FOOL

sim·plic·i·ty \sim-ˈpli-sə-tē\ n, pl -ties 1 : lack of complication : CLEARNESS ⟨the ~ of his reasoning⟩ 2 : CANDOR, ARTLESSNESS 3 : plainness in manners or way of life 4 : SILLINESS, FOLLY

sim·pli·fy \ˈsim-plə-ˌfī\ vb -fied; -fy·ing : to make less complex — sim·pli·fi·ca·tion \ˌsim-plə-fə-ˈkā-shən\ n

sim·plis·tic \sim-ˈplis-tik\ adj : excessively simple : tending to overlook complexities ⟨a ~ solution⟩

sim·u·late \ˈsim-yə-ˌlāt\ vb -lat·ed; -lat·ing : to give or create the effect or appearance of : IMITATE; *also* : to make a simulation of — sim·u·la·tor \ˈsim-yə-ˌlā-tər\ n

sim·u·la·tion \ˌsim-yə-ˈlā-shən\ n 1 : the act or process of simulating 2 : an object that is not genuine 3 : the imitation by one system or process of the way in which another system or process works

si·mul·ta·ne·ous \ˌsī-məl-ˈtā-nē-əs, ˌsi-\ adj : occurring or operating at the same time — si·mul·ta·ne·ous·ly adv — si·mul·ta·ne·ous·ness n

¹sin \ˈsin\ n 1 : an offense esp. against God 2 : FAULT 3 : a weakened state of human nature in which the self is estranged from God — sin·less adj

²sin vb sinned; sin·ning : to commit a sin — sin·ner n

³sin abbr sine

¹since \ˈsins\ adv 1 : from a past time until now 2 : backward in time : AGO 3 : after a time in the past

²since conj 1 : from the time when 2 : seeing that : BECAUSE

³since prep 1 : in the period after ⟨changes made ~ the war⟩ 2 : continuously from ⟨has been here ~ 1980⟩

sin·cere \sin-ˈsir\ adj sin·cer·er; sin·cer·est 1 : free from hypocrisy : HONEST 2 : GENUINE, REAL — sin·cere·ly adv — sin·cer·i·ty \-ˈser-ə-tē\ n

sine \ˈsīn\ n [ML *sinus*, fr. L, curve] : the trigonometric function that is the ratio between the side opposite an acute angle in a right triangle and the hypotenuse

si·ne·cure \ˈsī-ni-ˌkyùr, ˈsi-\ n : a paying job that requires little or no work

si·ne die \ˌsī-ni-ˈdī-ˌē, ˌsi-nā-ˈdē-ˌā\ adv [L, without day] : INDEFINITELY ⟨the meeting adjourned *sine die*⟩

si·ne qua non \ˌsi-ni-ˌkwä-ˈnän, -ˈnōn\ n, pl sine qua nons also sine qui·bus non \-ˌkwi-(ˌ)bùs-\ [LL, without which not] : something indispensable or essential

sin·ew \ˈsin-yü\ n 1 : TENDON 2 : physical strength — sin·ewy adj

sin·ful \ˈsin-fəl\ adj : marked by or full of sin : WICKED — sin·ful·ly adv — sin·ful·ness n

¹sing \ˈsiŋ\ vb sang \ˈsaŋ\ or sung \ˈsəŋ\; sung; sing·ing 1 : to produce musical tones with the voice; *also* : to utter with musical tones 2 : to make a prolonged shrill sound ⟨locusts ~ing⟩ 3 : to produce harmonious sustained sounds ⟨birds ~ing⟩ 4 : CHANT, INTONE 5 : to write poetry; *also* : to celebrate in song or verse 6 : to give information or evidence — sing·er n

²sing abbr singular

singe \ˈsinj\ vb singed; singe·ing : to scorch lightly the outside of; *esp* : to remove the hair or down from usu. by passing over a flame

¹sin·gle \ˈsiŋ-gəl\ adj 1 : UNMARRIED 2 : being alone : being the only one 3 : having only one feature or part 4 : made for one person ◆ **Synonyms** SOLE, UNIQUE, LONE, SOLITARY, SEPARATE, PARTICULAR — sin·gle·ness n — sin·gly adv

²single n 1 : a separate person or thing; *also* : an unmarried person 2 : a hit in baseball that enables the batter to reach first base 3 pl : a tennis match with one player on each side

³single vb sin·gled; sin·gling 1 : to select (one) from a group 2 : to hit a single

single bond n : a chemical bond in which one pair of electrons is shared by two atoms in a molecule

single–lens reflex n : a camera having a single lens that forms an image which is reflected to the viewfinder or recorded on film

sin·gle–mind·ed \ˌsiŋ-gəl-ˈmīn-dəd\ adj : having one driving purpose or resolve ⟨~ determination⟩ — sin·gle·mind·ed·ly adv — sin·gle–mind·ed·ness n

sing·song \ˈsiŋ-ˌsòŋ\ n 1 : verse with marked and regular rhythm and rhyme 2 : a voice delivery marked by monotonous rhythm — sing·songy \-ˌsòŋ-ē\ adj

sin·gu·lar \ˈsiŋ-gyə-lər\ adj 1 : of, relating to, or constituting a word form denoting one person, thing, or instance 2 : OUTSTANDING, EXCEPTIONAL 3 : of unusual quality 4 : ODD, PECULIAR — singular n — sin·gu·lar·i·ty \ˌsiŋ-gyə-ˈler-ə-tē\ n — sin·gu·lar·ly adv

sin·is·ter \ˈsi-nəs-tər\ adj [ME *sinistre*, fr. AF *senestre* on the left, fr. L *sinister* on the left side, inauspicious] 1 : singularly evil or productive of evil 2 : accompanied by or leading to disaster ◆ **Synonyms** BALEFUL, MALIGN, MALEFIC, MALEFICENT — sin·is·ter·ly adv

¹sink \ˈsiŋk\ vb sank \ˈsaŋk\ or sunk \ˈsəŋk\; sunk; sink·ing 1 : SUBMERGE 2 : to descend lower and lower 3 : to grow less in volume or height 4 : to slope downward 5 : to penetrate downward 6 : to fail in health or strength 7 : LAPSE, DEGENERATE 8 : to cause (a ship) to descend to the bottom 9 : to make (a hole or shaft) by digging, boring, or cutting 10 : INVEST — sink·able adj

²sink n 1 : DRAIN, SEWER 2 : a basin connected with a drain 3 : an extensive depression in the land surface

sink·er \ˈsiŋ-kər\ n : a weight for sinking a fishing line or net

sink·hole \ˈsiŋk-ˌhōl\ n : a hollow place in which drainage collects

si·nol·o·gy \sī-ˈnä-lə-jē\ n, often cap : the study of the Chinese and esp. their language, history, and culture — si·no·log·i·cal \ˌsī-nə-ˈlä-ji-kəl\ adj, often cap — si·nol·o·gist \sī-ˈnä-lə-jist\ n, often cap

sin tax n : a tax on substances or activities considered sinful or harmful

sin·u·ous \ˈsin-yə-wəs\ adj : bending in and out : WINDING — sin·u·os·i·ty \ˌsin-yə-ˈwä-sə-tē\ n — sin·u·ous·ly adv

si·nus \ˈsī-nəs\ n [ME, fr. ML, fr. L, curve, hollow] 1 : any of several cavities of the skull usu. connecting with the nostrils 2 : a space forming a channel (as for the passage of blood)

si·nus·itis \ˌsī-nə-ˈsī-təs\ n : inflammation of a sinus of the skull

Sioux \ˈsü\ n, pl Sioux \same or ˈsüz\ [AmerF, short for *Nadouessioux*, fr. Ojibwa *na·towe·ssiw-*, prob. fr. Algonquian *a·towe-* speak another language] : DAKOTA

sip \ˈsip\ vb sipped; sip·ping : to drink in small quantities — sip n

¹si·phon also sy·phon \ˈsī-fən\ n 1 : a bent tube through which a liquid can be transferred by means of air pressure up and over the edge of one container and into an-

siphon • skim 466

other container placed at a lower level **2** *usu* **sy·phon** : a bottle that ejects soda water through a tube when a valve is opened

²**siphon** *also* **syphon** *vb* **si·phoned** *also* **sy·phoned**; **si·phon·ing** *also* **sy·phon·ing** : to draw off by means of a siphon

sip·py cup \'si-pē-\ *n* : a cup having a lid with a perforated spout for a young child

sir \'sər\ *n* [ME *sir, sire,* fr. AF, lord, feudal superior, fr. VL *seior,* alter. of L *senior,* compar. of *senex* old, old man] **1** : a man of rank or position — used as a title before the given name of a knight or baronet **2** — used as a usu. respectful form of address

Si·rach \'sī-rak, sə-'räk\ *n* — see BIBLE table

¹**sire** \'sī(-ə)r\ *n* **1** : FATHER; *also, archaic* : FOREFATHER **2** *archaic* : LORD — used as a form of address and a title **3** : the male parent of an animal (as a horse or dog)

²**sire** *vb* **sired; sir·ing** : BEGET

si·ren \'sī-rən\ *n* **1** : a seductive or alluring woman **2** : an electrically operated device for producing a loud shrill warning signal — **siren** *adj*

sir·loin \'sər-ˌlȯin\ *n* [alter. of earlier *surloin,* modif. of MF *surlonge,* fr. *sur* over (fr. L *super*) + *longe* loin] : a cut of beef taken from the part in front of the round

sirup *var of* SYRUP

si·sal \'sī-səl, -zəl\ *n* : a strong cordage fiber from an agave; *also* : this agave

sis·sy \'si-sē\ *n, pl* **sissies** *disparaging* : an effeminate boy or man; *also* : a timid or cowardly person

sis·ter \'sis-tər\ *n* **1** : a female having one or both parents in common with another individual **2** : a member of a religious order of women : NUN **3** *chiefly Brit* : NURSE **4 a** : a girl or woman regarded as a comrade **b** : a girl or woman who shares with another a common national or racial origin — **sis·ter·ly** *adj*

sis·ter·hood \-ˌhu̇d\ *n* **1** : the state of being a sister **2** : a community or society of sisters **3** : the solidarity of women based on shared conditions

sis·ter–in–law \'sis-tə-rən-ˌlȯ\ *n, pl* **sisters–in–law** : the sister of one's spouse; *also* : the wife of one's sibling or of one's spouse's sibling

sit \'sit\ *vb* **sat** \'sat\; **sit·ting 1** : to rest upon the buttocks or haunches **2** : ROOST, PERCH **3** : to occupy a seat **4** : to hold a session **5** : to cover eggs for hatching : BROOD **6** : to pose for a portrait **7** : to remain quiet or inactive **8** : FIT **9** : to cause (oneself) to be seated **10** : to place in position **11** : to keep one's seat on ⟨∼ a horse⟩ **12** : BABYSIT — **sit·ter** *n*

si·tar \si-'tär\ *n* [Hindi & Urdu *sitār*] : an Indian lute with a long neck and a varying number of strings

sit·com \'sit-ˌkäm\ *n* : SITUATION COMEDY

site \'sīt\ *n* **1** : LOCATION **2** : WEBSITE

sit–in \'sit-ˌin\ *n* : an act of sitting in the seats or on the floor of an establishment as a means of organized protest

sit·u·at·ed \'si-chə-ˌwā-təd\ *adj* : LOCATED, PLACED

sit·u·a·tion \ˌsi-chə-'wā-shən\ *n* **1** : LOCATION, SITE **2** : JOB **3** : CONDITION, CIRCUMSTANCES — **sit·u·a·tion·al** \-shə-nəl\ *adj*

situation comedy *n* : a radio or television comedy series that involves a continuing cast of characters in a succession of episodes

sit–up \'sit-ˌəp\ *n* : an exercise performed from a supine position by raising the torso to a sitting position and returning to the original position without lifting the feet

SIV \ˌes-ˌī-'vē\ *n* [simian immunodeficiency virus] : a retrovirus related to HIV that causes a disease in monkeys similar to AIDS

six \'siks\ *n* **1** : one more than five **2** : the 6th in a set or series **3** : something having six units — **six** *adj or pron* — **sixth** \'siksth\ *adj or adv or n*

six–gun \'siks-ˌgən\ *n* : a 6-chambered revolver

six–pack \-ˌpak\ *n* : six bottles or cans (as of beer) packaged and purchased together; *also* : the contents of a six-pack

six·pence \-pəns, *US also* -ˌpens\ *n* : the sum of six pence; *also* : an English silver coin of this value

six–shoot·er \'siks-ˌshü-tər\ *n* : SIX-GUN

six·teen \ˌsiks-'tēn\ *n* : one more than 15 — **sixteen** *adj or pron* — **six·teenth** \-'tēnth\ *adj or n*

six·ty \'siks-tē\ *n, pl* **sixties** : six times 10 — **six·ti·eth** \'siks-tē-əth\ *adj or n* — **sixty** *adj or pron*

siz·able *or* **size·able** \'sī-zə-bəl\ *adj* : quite large — **siz·ably** \-blē\ *adv*

¹**size** \'sīz\ *n* [ME *sise* assize, judgment, quantity, fr. AF, short for *assise* assize] : physical extent or bulk : DIMENSIONS; *also* : considerable proportions — **sized** \'sīzd\ *adj*

²**size** *vb* **sized; siz·ing 1** : to grade or classify according to size **2** : to form a judgment of ⟨∼ up the situation⟩

³**size** *n* : a gluey material used for filling the pores in paper, plaster, or textiles — **siz·ing** *n*

⁴**size** *vb* **sized; siz·ing** : to cover, stiffen, or glaze with size

siz·zle \'si-zəl\ *vb* **siz·zled; siz·zling** : to fry or shrivel up with a hissing sound — **sizzle** *n*

SJ *abbr* Society of Jesus

SK *abbr* Saskatchewan

ska \'skä\ *n* : popular music of Jamaican origin combining traditional Caribbean rhythms and jazz

¹**skate** \'skāt\ *n, pl* **skates** *also* **skate** : any of a family of rays with thick broad winglike fins

²**skate** *n* **1** : a metal frame and runner attached to a shoe and used for gliding over ice **2** : ROLLER SKATE; *esp* : IN-LINE SKATE — **skate** *vb* — **skat·er** *n*

skate·board \'skāt-ˌbȯrd\ *n* : a short board mounted on small wheels — **skateboard** *vb* — **skate·board·er** *n*

skeet \'skēt\ *n* : trapshooting in which clay targets are thrown in such a way that their angle of flight simulates that of a flushed game bird

skein \'skān\ *n* : a loosely twisted quantity of yarn or thread wound on a reel

skel·e·ton \'ske-lə-tᵊn\ *n* **1** : a usu. bony supporting framework of an animal body **2** : a bare minimum **3** : FRAMEWORK — **skel·e·tal** \-lə-tᵊl\ *adj*

skep·tic \'skep-tik\ *n* **1** : one who believes in skepticism **2** : a person disposed to skepticism esp. regarding religion — **skep·ti·cal** \-ti-kəl\ *adj* — **skep·ti·cal·ly** \-k(ə-)lē\ *adv*

skep·ti·cism \'skep-tə-ˌsi-zəm\ *n* **1** : a doubting state of mind **2** : a doctrine that certainty of knowledge cannot be attained **3** : doubt concerning religion

sketch \'skech\ *n* [D *schets,* fr. It *schizzo,* lit., splash] **1** : a rough drawing or outline **2** : a short or light literary composition (as a story or essay); *also* : a short comedy piece — **sketch** *vb* — **sketchy** *adj*

¹**skew** \'skyü\ *vb* : TWIST, SWERVE

²**skew** *n* : SLANT

skew·er \'skyü-ər\ *n* : a long pin for holding small pieces of meat and vegetables for broiling — **skewer** *vb*

¹**ski** \'skē\ *n, pl* **skis** [Norw, fr. ON *skīth* stick of wood, ski] : one of a pair of long strips (as of wood, metal or plastic) curving upward in front that are used for gliding over snow or water

²**ski** *vb* **skied** \'skēd\; **ski·ing** : to glide on skis — **ski·able** \'skē-ə-bəl\ *adj* — **ski·er** *n*

¹**skid** \'skid\ *n* **1** : a plank for supporting something above the ground **2** : a device placed under a wheel to prevent turning **3** : a timber or rail over or on which something is slid or rolled **4** : the act of skidding **5** : a runner on the landing gear of an aircraft **6** : ²PALLET

²**skid** *vb* **skid·ded; skid·ding 1** : to slide without rotating ⟨a *skidding* wheel⟩ **2** : to slide sideways on the road ⟨the car *skidded* on ice⟩ **3** : SLIDE, SLIP

skid row *n* : a district of cheap saloons frequented by vagrants and alcoholics

skiff \'skif\ *n* : a small boat

ski jump *n* : a jump made by a person wearing skis; *also* : a course or track prepared for such jumping — **ski jump** *vb* — **ski jumper** *n*

skil·ful *chiefly Brit var of* SKILLFUL

ski lift *n* : a mechanical device (as a chairlift) for carrying skiers up a long slope

skill \'skil\ *n* **1** : ability to use one's knowledge effectively in doing something **2** : developed or acquired ability ♦ **Synonyms** ART, CRAFT, CUNNING, DEXTERITY, EXPERTISE, KNOW-HOW — **skilled** \'skild\ *adj*

skil·let \'ski-lət\ *n* : a frying pan

skill·ful \'skil-fəl\ *adj* **1** : having or displaying skill : EXPERT **2** : accomplished with skill — **skill·ful·ly** *adv* — **skill·ful·ness** *n*

¹**skim** \'skim\ *vb* **skimmed; skim·ming 1** : to take off from the top of a liquid; *also* : to remove (scum or cream) from ⟨∼ milk⟩ **2** : to read rapidly and superficially **3** : to pass swiftly over — **skim·mer** *n*

²**skim** *adj* : having the cream removed

skimp \'skimp\ *vb* : to give insufficient attention, effort, or funds; *also* : to save by skimping

skimpy \'skim-pē\ *adj* **skimp·i·er; -est** : deficient in supply or execution — **skimp·i·ly** \-pə-lē\ *adv*

¹**skin** \'skin\ *n* 1 : the outer limiting layer of an animal body; *also* : the usu. thin tough tissue of which this is made 2 : an outer or surface layer (as a rind or peel) — **skin·less** *adj* — **skinned** *adj*

²**skin** *vb* **skinned; skin·ning** : to free from skin : remove the skin of ⟨∼ a rabbit⟩

³**skin** *adj* : devoted to showing nudes ⟨∼ magazines⟩

skin diving *n* : the sport of swimming under water with a face mask and flippers and esp. without a portable breathing device — **skin–dive** *vb* — **skin diver** *n*

skin·flint \'skin-ˌflint\ *n* : a very stingy person

skin graft *n* : a piece of skin surgically removed from one area to replace skin in another area — **skin grafting** *n*

skin·head \'skin-ˌhed\ *n* : a person whose hair is cut very short

¹**skin·ny** \'ski-nē\ *adj* **skin·ni·er; -est** 1 : resembling skin 2 : very thin

²**skinny** *n* : inside information

skin·ny–dip \'ski-nē-ˌdip\ *vb* : to swim in the nude — **skin·ny–dip·per** \-ˌdi-pər\ *n*

skin·tight \'skin-'tīt\ *adj* : closely fitted to the figure ⟨∼ pants⟩

¹**skip** \'skip\ *vb* **skipped; skip·ping** 1 : to move with leaps and bounds 2 : to leap lightly over 3 : to pass from point to point (as in reading) disregarding what is in between 4 : to pass over without notice or mention

²**skip** *n* : a light bouncing step; *also* : a gait of alternate hops and steps

skip·jack \'skip-ˌjak\ *n* : a small sailboat with vertical sides and a bottom similar to a flat V

skip·per \'ski-pər\ *n* [ME, fr. MD *schipper*, fr. *schip* ship] : the master of a ship; *also* : the manager of a baseball team — **skipper** *vb*

skir·mish \'skər-mish\ *n* : a minor engagement in war; *also* : a minor dispute or contest — **skirmish** *vb*

¹**skirt** \'skərt\ *n* : a free-hanging garment or part of a garment extending from the waist down

²**skirt** *vb* 1 : to pass around the outer edge of 2 : BORDER 3 : EVADE ⟨∼ the issue⟩

skit \'skit\ *n* : a brief dramatic sketch

ski tow *n* : SKI LIFT

skit·ter \'ski-tər\ *vb* : to glide or skip lightly or quickly : skim along a surface

skit·tish \'ski-tish\ *adj* 1 : CAPRICIOUS 2 : easily frightened ⟨a ∼ horse⟩; *also* : WARY ⟨∼ investors⟩

ski·wear \'skē-ˌwer\ *n* : clothing suitable for wear while skiing

skosh \'skōsh\ *n* [Jp *sukoshi*] : a small amount : BIT ⟨has a ∼ more room⟩

skul·dug·gery *or* **skull·dug·gery** \ˌskəl-'də-gə-rē\ *n, pl* **-ger·ies** : underhanded or unscrupulous behavior

skulk \'skəlk\ *vb* : to move furtively : SNEAK, LURK — **skulk·er** *n*

skull \'skəl\ *n* : the skeleton of the head of a vertebrate that protects the brain and supports the jaws

skull and crossbones *n, pl* **skulls and crossbones** : a depiction of a human skull over crossbones usu. indicating a danger

skull·cap \'skəl-ˌkap\ *n* : a close-fitting brimless cap

¹**skunk** \'skəŋk\ *n, pl* **skunks** *also* **skunk** 1 : any of various black-and-white New World mammals related to the weasels that can forcibly eject an ill-smelling fluid when startled 2 : a contemptible person

²**skunk** *vb* : to defeat decisively; *esp* : to prevent entirely from scoring in a game

skunk cabbage *n* : either of two No. American perennial herbs related to the arums that occur in shaded wet to swampy areas and have a fetid odor suggestive of a skunk

sky \'skī\ *n, pl* **skies** [ME, sky, cloud, fr. ON *skȳ* cloud] 1 : the upper air 2 : HEAVEN — **sky·ey** \'skī-ē\ *adj*

sky·cap \-ˌkap\ *n* : a person employed to carry luggage at an airport

sky·div·ing \-ˌdī-viŋ\ *n* : the sport of jumping from an airplane and executing various body maneuvers before opening a parachute — **skydiver** *n*

sky·jack \-ˌjak\ *vb* : to commandeer an airplane in flight by threat of violence — **sky·jack·er** *n* — **sky·jack·ing** *n*

¹**sky·lark** \-ˌlärk\ *n* : a European lark noted for singing during flight

²**skylark** *vb* : FROLIC, SPORT

sky·light \'skī-ˌlīt\ *n* : a window in a roof or ceiling — **sky·light·ed** \-ˌlī-təd\ *adj*

sky·line \-ˌlīn\ *n* 1 : HORIZON 2 : an outline (as of buildings) against the sky

¹**sky·rock·et** \-ˌrä-kət\ *n* : ROCKET 1

²**skyrocket** *vb* : ROCKET 2

sky·scrap·er \-ˌskrā-pər\ *n* : a very tall building

sky·surf·ing \-ˌsər-fiŋ\ *n* : skydiving with a short modified surfboard attached to the feet — **sky·surf·er** \-fər\ *n*

sky·walk \-ˌwȯk\ *n* : an aerial walkway connecting two buildings

sky·ward \-wərd\ *adv* : toward the sky

sky·writ·ing \-ˌrī-tiŋ\ *n* : writing in the sky formed by smoke emitted from an airplane — **sky·writ·er** *n*

sl *abbr* 1 slightly 2 slip 3 slow

slab \'slab\ *n* : a thick flat piece or slice

¹**slack** \'slak\ *adj* 1 : CARELESS, NEGLIGENT 2 : SLUGGISH, LISTLESS 3 : not taut : LOOSE 4 : not busy or active ⟨a ∼ season⟩ ✦ *Synonyms* LAX, REMISS, NEGLECTFUL, DELINQUENT, DERELICT — **slack·ly** *adv* — **slack·ness** *n*

²**slack** *vb* 1 : to make or become slack : LOOSEN, RELAX 2 : SLAKE 2

³**slack** *n* 1 : cessation of movement or flow : LETUP 2 : a part that hangs loose without strain ⟨∼ of a rope⟩ 3 : pants esp. for casual wear — usu. used in pl.

slack·en \'sla-kən\ *vb* : to make or become slack

slack·er \'sla-kər\ *n* 1 : one that shirks work or evades military duty 2 : a young person perceived to be disaffected, apathetic, cynical, or lacking ambition

slag \'slag\ *n* : the waste left after the melting of ores and the separation of metal from them

slain *past part of* SLAY

slake \'slāk, *for 2 also* 'slak\ *vb* **slaked; slak·ing** 1 : to relieve or satisfy with or as if with refreshing drink ⟨∼ thirst⟩ 2 : to cause (lime) to crumble by mixture with water

sla·lom \'slä-ləm\ *n* [Norw *slalam*, lit., sloping track] : skiing in a zigzag course between obstacles

¹**slam** \'slam\ *n* : the winning of every trick or of all tricks but one in bridge

²**slam** *n* 1 : a heavy jarring impact : BANG 2 : harsh criticism 3 : a poetry competition

³**slam** *vb* **slammed; slam·ming** 1 : to shut violently and noisily 2 : to throw or strike with a loud impact 3 : to criticize harshly ⟨was *slammed* in the press⟩

slam·mer \'sla-mər\ *n* : JAIL, PRISON

¹**slan·der** \'slan-dər\ *vb* : to utter slander against : DEFAME — **slan·der·er** *n*

²**slander** *n* [ME *sclaundre, slaundre*, fr. AF *esclandre*, alter. of *escandle*, fr. LL *scandalum* stumbling block, offense] : a false report maliciously uttered and tending to injure the reputation of a person — **slan·der·ous** *adj*

slang \'slaŋ\ *n* : an informal nonstandard vocabulary composed typically of invented words, arbitrarily changed words, and extravagant figures of speech — **slangy** *adj*

¹**slant** \'slant\ *n* 1 : a sloping direction, line, or plane 2 : a particular or personal viewpoint ⟨has a liberal ∼⟩ — **slant** *adj* — **slant·wise** \-ˌwīz\ *adv or adj*

²**slant** *vb* 1 : SLOPE 2 : to interpret or present in accordance with a special viewpoint or bias ⟨∼ed the story for their benefit⟩ ✦ *Synonyms* INCLINE, LEAN, LIST, TILT, HEEL — **slant·ing·ly** *adv*

slap \'slap\ *vb* **slapped; slap·ping** 1 : to strike sharply with the open hand 2 : REBUFF, INSULT — **slap** *n*

slap·stick \-ˌstik\ *n* : comedy stressing horseplay

¹**slash** \'slash\ *vb* 1 : to cut with sweeping strokes 2 : to cut slits in (a garment) 3 : to reduce sharply ⟨∼ed prices⟩ — **slash·er** \'sla-shər\ *n*

²**slash** *n* 1 : GASH 2 : an ornamental slit in a garment 3 : a mark / used to denote "or" (as in *and/or*), "and or" (as in *straggler/deserter*), or "per" (as in *feet/second*)

slat \'slat\ *n* : a thin narrow flat strip

¹**slate** \'slāt\ *n* 1 : a dense fine-grained rock that splits into thin layers 2 : a roofing tile or a writing tablet made from this rock 3 : a written or unwritten record

⟨start with a clean ∼⟩ **4** : a list of candidates for election

²**slate** *vb* **slat·ed; slat·ing 1** : to cover with slate **2** : to designate for action or appointment ⟨is *slated* to open soon⟩

slath·er \'sla-thər\ *vb* : to spread with or on thickly or lavishly

slat·tern \'sla-tərn\ *n* : a slovenly woman — **slat·tern·ly** *adj*

¹**slaugh·ter** \'slȯ-tər\ *n* **1** : the butchering of livestock for market **2** : great destruction of lives esp. in battle

²**slaughter** *vb* **1** : to kill (animals) for food : BUTCHER **2** : to kill in large numbers or in a bloody way : MASSACRE

slaugh·ter·house \-ˌhaûs\ *n* : an establishment where animals are butchered

Slav \'släv\ *n* : a person speaking a Slavic language

¹**slave** \'släv\ *n* [ME *sclave*, fr. AF or ML; AF *esclave*, fr. ML *sclavus*, fr. *Sclavus* Slav; fr. the enslavement of Slavs in central Europe in the Middle Ages] **1** : a person held in servitude as property **2** : a device (as the printer of a computer) that is directly responsive to another — **slave** *adj*

²**slave** *vb* **slaved; slav·ing** : to work like a slave : DRUDGE ⟨*slaved* away at his work⟩

¹**sla·ver** \'sla-vər, 'slä-\ *n* : SLOBBER — **slaver** *vb*

²**slav·er** \'slä-vər\ *n* : a ship or a person engaged in transporting slaves

slav·ery \'släv-rē, 'slä-və-\ *n* **1** : wearisome drudgery **2** : the condition of being a slave **3** : the practice of owning slaves ♦ **Synonyms** SERVITUDE, BONDAGE, ENSLAVEMENT

¹**Slav·ic** \'slä-vik, 'slä-\ *n* : a branch of the Indo-European language family including various languages (as Russian or Polish) of eastern Europe

²**Slavic** *adj* : of or relating to the Slavs or their languages

slav·ish \'slä-vish\ *adj* **1** : SERVILE **2** : obeying or imitating with no freedom of judgment or choice — **slav·ish·ly** *adv*

slaw \'slȯ\ *n* : COLESLAW

slay \'slā\ *vb* **slew** \'slü\; **slain** \'slān\; **slay·ing** : KILL — **slay·er** *n*

SLBM *abbr* submarine-launched ballistic missile

sleaze \'slēz\ *n* : a sleazy quality, appearance, or behavior

slea·zy \'slē-zē\ *adj* **slea·zi·er; -est 1** : FLIMSY, SHODDY **2** : marked by low character or quality ⟨a ∼ lawyer⟩

¹**sled** \'sled\ *n* : a vehicle usu. on runners adapted esp. for sliding on snow

²**sled** *vb* **sled·ded, sled·ding** : to ride or carry on a sled

¹**sledge** \'slej\ *n* : SLEDGEHAMMER

²**sledge** *n* : a strong heavy sled

sledge·ham·mer \'slej-ˌha-mər\ *n* : a large heavy hammer wielded with both hands — **sledgehammer** *adj or vb*

¹**sleek** \'slēk\ *vb* **1** : to make smooth or glossy **2** : to gloss over

²**sleek** *adj* **1** : having a smooth well-groomed look **2** : trim and graceful in design ⟨a ∼ car⟩

¹**sleep** \'slēp\ *n* **1** : the natural periodic suspension of consciousness during which bodily powers are restored **2** : a state (as death or coma) suggesting sleep — **sleep·less** *adj* — **sleep·less·ness** *n*

²**sleep** *vb* **slept** \'slept\; **sleep·ing 1** : to rest or be in a state of sleep; *also* : to spend in sleep **2** : to have sexual intercourse — usu. used with *with* **3** : to provide sleeping space for

sleep·er \'slē-pər\ *n* **1** : one that sleeps **2** : a horizontal beam to support something on or near ground level **3** : SLEEPING CAR **4** : someone or something unpromising or unnoticed that suddenly attains prominence or value

sleeping bag *n* : a warmly lined bag for sleeping esp. outdoors

sleeping car *n* : a railroad car with berths for sleeping

sleeping pill *n* : a drug in tablet or capsule form taken to induce sleep

sleeping sickness *n* : a serious disease of tropical Africa that is marked by fever, lethargy, confusion, and sleep disturbances and is caused by protozoans transmitted by the tsetse fly

sleep·over \'slēp-ˌō-vər\ *n* : an overnight stay (as at another's home)

sleep·walk·er \'slēp-ˌwȯ-kər\ *n* : one that walks while or as if while asleep — **sleep·walk** \-ˌwȯk\ *vb*

sleepy \'slē-pē\ *adj* **sleep·i·er; -est 1** : ready for sleep **2** : quietly inactive — **sleep·i·ly** \'slē-pə-lē\ *adv* — **sleep·i·ness** \-pē-nəs\ *n*

sleet \'slēt\ *n* : frozen or partly frozen rain — **sleet** *vb* — **sleety** *adj*

sleeve \'slēv\ *n* **1** : a part of a garment covering an arm **2** : a tubular part designed to fit over another part — **sleeved** *adj* — **sleeve·less** *adj*

¹**sleigh** \'slā\ *n* : an open usu. horse-drawn vehicle on runners for use on snow or ice

²**sleigh** *vb* : to drive or travel in a sleigh

sleight \'slīt\ *n* **1** : TRICK **2** : DEXTERITY

sleight of hand : a trick requiring skillful manual manipulation

slen·der \'slen-dər\ *adj* **1** : SLIM, THIN **2** : WEAK, SLIGHT **3** : MEAGER, INADEQUATE ⟨∼ opportunities⟩

slen·der·ize \-də-ˌrīz\ *vb* **-ized; -iz·ing** : to make slender

sleuth \'slüth\ *n* [short for *sleuthhound* bloodhound, fr. ME (Sc) *sleuth hund*, fr. ME *sleuth, sloith, sloth* track of an animal or person, fr. ON *slōth*] : DETECTIVE

¹**slew** \'slü\ *past of* SLAY

²**slew** *vb* : TURN, VEER, SKID

¹**slice** \'slīs\ *vb* **sliced; slic·ing 1** : to cut a slice from; *also* : to cut into slices **2** : to hit (a ball) so that a slice results

²**slice** *n* **1** : a thin flat piece cut from something **2** : a flight of a ball (as in golf) that curves in the direction of the dominant hand of the player hitting it

¹**slick** \'slik\ *vb* : to make smooth or sleek

²**slick** *adj* **1** : very smooth : SLIPPERY **2** : CLEVER, SMART ⟨a ∼ salesperson⟩

³**slick** *n* **1** : a smooth patch of water covered with a film of oil **2** : a popular magazine printed on coated paper

slick·er \'sli-kər\ *n* **1** : a long loose raincoat **2** : a sly tricky person **3** : a city dweller esp. of natty appearance or sophisticated mannerisms

¹**slide** \'slīd\ *vb* **slid** \'slid\; **slid·ing** \'slī-diŋ\ **1** : to move smoothly along a surface **2** : to fall or dive towards a base in baseball **3** : to fall by a loss of support **4** : to pass unobtrusively **5** : to move or pass smoothly; *also* : to pass unnoticed ⟨let it ∼ by⟩ **6** : to become worse gradually

²**slide** *n* **1** : an act or instance of sliding **2** : something (as a cover or fastener) that operates by sliding **3** : a fall of a mass of earth or snow down a hillside **4** : a surface on which something slides **5** : a glass plate on which a specimen is mounted for examination under a microscope **6** : a small transparent photograph that can be projected on a screen

slid·er \'slī-dər\ *n* **1** : one that slides **2** : a baseball pitch that looks like a fastball but curves slightly **3** : a small hamburger

slide rule *n* : a manual device for calculation consisting of a ruler and a movable middle piece graduated with logarithmic scales

slier *comparative of* SLY

sliest *superlative of* SLY

¹**slight** \'slīt\ *adj* **1** : SLENDER; *also* : FRAIL **2** : UNIMPORTANT ⟨a ∼ movie⟩ **3** : small of its kind or in amount ⟨a ∼ odor⟩ — **slight·ly** *adv*

²**slight** *vb* **1** : to treat as unimportant **2** : to ignore discourteously ⟨∼ed the mayor⟩ **3** : to perform or attend to carelessly

³**slight** *n* : a humiliating discourtesy

¹**slim** \'slim\ *adj* **slim·mer; slim·mest** [D, bad, inferior, fr. MD, *slimp* crooked, bad] **1** : SLENDER, SLIGHT, THIN **2** : SMALL, SLIGHT ⟨a ∼ chance⟩

²**slim** *vb* **slimmed; slim·ming** : to make or become slender

slime \'slīm\ *n* **1** : sticky mud **2** : a slippery substance (as on the skin of a slug or catfish) — **slimy** *adj*

¹**sling** \'sliŋ\ *vb* **slung** \'sləŋ\; **sling·ing 1** : to throw forcibly : FLING **2** : to hurl with or as if with a sling

²**sling** *n* **1** : a short strap with strings attached for hurling stones or shot **2** : something (as a rope or chain) used to hoist, lower, support, or carry; *esp* : a bandage hanging from the neck to support an arm or hand

sling·shot \'sliŋ-ˌshät\ *n* : a forked stick with elastic bands for shooting small stones or shot

slink \'sliŋk\ *vb* **slunk** \'sləŋk\ *also* **slinked** \'sliŋkt\; **slink·ing 1** : to move stealthily or furtively **2** : to move sinuously — **slinky** *adj*

¹**slip** \'slip\ *vb* **slipped; slip·ping 1** : to escape quietly or

secretly **2** : to slide along or cause to slide along smoothly **3** : to make a mistake **4** : to pass unnoticed or undone **5** : to fall off from a standard or level

²**slip** n **1** : a ramp for repairing ships **2** : a ship's berth between two piers **3** : secret or hurried departure, escape, or evasion **4** : BLUNDER **5** : a sudden mishap **6** : a thin one-piece garment worn under a dress or skirt **7** : PILLOWCASE

³**slip** n **1** : a shoot or twig from a plant for planting or grafting **2** : a long narrow strip; esp : one of paper used for a record ⟨deposit ∼⟩

⁴**slip** vb **slipped; slip·ping** : to take slips from (a plant)

slip·knot \'slip-ˌnät\ n : a knot that slips along the rope around which it is made

slipped disk n : a protrusion of one of the disks of cartilage between vertebrae with pressure on spinal nerves resulting esp. in low back pain

slip·per \'sli-pər\ n : a light low shoe that may be easily slipped on and off

slip·pery \'sli-pə-rē\ adj **slip·per·i·er; -est 1** : icy, wet, smooth, or greasy enough to cause one to fall or lose one's hold **2** : not to be trusted : TRICKY ⟨a ∼ salesman⟩ — **slip·per·i·ness** n

slip·shod \'slip-ˈshäd\ adj : SLOVENLY, CARELESS ⟨∼ work⟩

slip·stream \'slip-ˌstrēm\ n : a stream (as of air) driven aft by a propeller

slip-up \'slip-ˌəp\ n **1** : MISTAKE **2** : ACCIDENT

¹**slit** \'slit\ vb **slit; slit·ting 1** : SLASH **2** : to cut off or away

²**slit** n : a long narrow cut or opening

slith·er \'sli-thər\ vb : to slip or glide along like a snake — **slith·ery** adj

sliv·er \'sli-vər\ n : SPLINTER

slob \'släb\ n : a slovenly or boorish person

slob·ber \'slä-bər\ vb **slob·bered; slob·ber·ing** : to dribble saliva — **slobber** n

sloe \'slō\ n : the fruit of the blackthorn

slog \'släg\ vb **slogged; slog·ging 1** : to hit hard : BEAT **2** : to work hard and steadily

slo·gan \'slō-gən\ n [alter. of earlier slogorn, fr. ScGael sluagh-ghairm, fr. sluagh army, host + gairm cry] : a word or phrase expressing the spirit or aim of a party, group, or cause

slo-mo \'slō-ˌmō\ n : SLOW MOTION — **slo-mo** adj

sloop \'slüp\ n [D sloep] : a single-masted sailboat with a jib and a fore-and-aft mainsail

¹**slop** \'släp\ n **1** : thin tasteless drink or liquid food — usu. used in pl. **2** : food waste for animal feed : SWILL **3** : excreted body waste — usu. used in pl.

²**slop** vb **slopped; slop·ping 1** : SPILL **2** : to feed with slop ⟨∼ hogs⟩

¹**slope** \'slōp\ vb **sloped; slop·ing** : SLANT, INCLINE

²**slope** n **1** : upward or downward slant or degree of slant **2** : ground that forms an incline **3** : the part of a landmass draining into a particular ocean

slop·py \'slä-pē\ adj **slop·pi·er; -est 1** : MUDDY, SLUSHY **2** : SLOVENLY, MESSY

sloppy joe \-'jō\ n : ground beef cooked in a thick spicy sauce and usu. served on a bun

slosh \'släsh\ vb **1** : to flounder through or splash about in or with water, mud, or slush **2** : to move with a splashing motion

slot \'slät\ n **1** : a long narrow opening or groove **2** : a position in a sequence

slot car n : an electric toy racing car that runs on a grooved track

sloth \'slóth\ n, pl **sloths** \'slóths, 'slóthz\ **1** : LAZINESS, INDOLENCE **2** : any of several slow-moving plant-eating arboreal mammals of So. and Central America — **sloth·ful** adj

slot machine n **1** : a machine whose operation is begun by dropping a coin into a slot **2** : a coin-operated gambling machine that pays off according to the matching of symbols on wheels spun by a handle

¹**slouch** \'slaúch\ n **1** : a lazy or incompetent person **2** : a loose or drooping gait or posture

²**slouch** vb : to walk, stand, or sit with a slouch : SLUMP

¹**slough** \'slü, 2 usu 'slaù\ n **1** : a wet and marshy or muddy place (as a swamp) **2** : a discouraged state of mind

²**slough** \'sləf\ also **sluff** n : something that has been or may be shed or cast off

³**slough** \'sləf\ also **sluff** vb : to cast off

Slo·vak \'slō-ˌväk, -ˌvak\ n **1** : a member of a Slavic people of Slovakia **2** : the language of the Slovaks — **Slovak** adj — **Slo·va·ki·an** \slō-'vä-kē-ən, -'va-\ adj or n

slov·en \'slə-vən\ n [ME sloveyn slut, rascal, perh. fr. MD slof negligent] : an untidy person

Slo·vene \'slō-ˌvēn\ n **1** : a member of a Slavic people living largely in Slovenia **2** : the language of the Slovenes — **Slovene** adj — **Slo·ve·nian** \slō-'vē-nē-ən\ adj or n

slov·en·ly \'slə-vən-lē\ adj **1** : untidy in dress or person **2** : lazily or carelessly done : SLIPSHOD ⟨∼ thinking⟩

¹**slow** \'slō\ adj **1** : SLUGGISH; also : dull in mind : STUPID **2** : moving, flowing, or proceeding at less than the usual speed **3** : taking more than the usual time **4** : registering behind the correct time **5** : not lively : BORING ♦ **Synonyms** DILATORY, LAGGARD, DELIBERATE, LEISURELY — **slow** adv — **slow·ly** adv — **slow·ness** n

²**slow** vb **1** : to make slow : hold back **2** : to go slower

slow motion n : motion-picture action photographed so as to appear much slower than normal — **slow–motion** adj

SLR abbr single-lens reflex

sludge \'sləj\ n : a slushy mass : OOZE; esp : solid matter produced by sewage treatment processes

slue var of ²SLEW

¹**slug** \'sləg\ n **1** : a small mass of metal; esp : BULLET **2** : a metal disk for use (as in a slot machine) in place of a coin **3** : any of numerous wormlike mollusks related to the snails **4** : a quantity of liquor drunk

²**slug** vb **slugged; slug·ging** : to strike forcibly and heavily — **slug·ger** n

slug·gard \'slə-gərd\ n : a lazy person

slug·gish \'slə-gish\ adj **1** : SLOTHFUL, LAZY **2** : slow in movement, flow, or growth ⟨a ∼ economy⟩ **3** : STAGNANT, DULL — **slug·gish·ly** adv — **slug·gish·ness** n

¹**sluice** \'slüs\ n [ME sluse, scluse, fr. AF escluse, fr. LL exclusa, fem. of exclusus, pp. of excludere to shut out, exclude] **1** : an artificial passage for water with a gate for controlling the flow; also : the gate so used **2** : a channel that carries off surplus water **3** : an inclined trough or flume for washing ore or floating logs

²**sluice** vb **sluiced; sluic·ing 1** : to draw off through a sluice **2** : to wash with running water : FLUSH

¹**slum** \'sləm\ n : a thickly populated area marked by poverty and dirty or deteriorated houses — **slum·my** \'slə-mē\ adj

²**slum** vb **slummed; slum·ming** : to visit slums esp. out of curiosity; also : to go somewhere or do something that might be considered beneath one's station

¹**slum·ber** \'sləm-bər\ vb **slum·bered; slum·ber·ing 1** : DOZE; also : SLEEP **2** : to be in a sluggish or torpid state

²**slumber** n : SLEEP

slum·ber·ous \'sləm-bə-rəs\ or **slum·brous** \-brəs\ adj **1** : SLUMBERING, SLEEPY **2** : PEACEFUL, INACTIVE

slum·lord \'sləm-ˌlórd\ n : a landlord who receives unusually large profits from substandard properties

slump \'sləmp\ vb **1** : to sink down suddenly : COLLAPSE **2** : SLOUCH **3** : to decline sharply — **slump** n

sloth 2

slung *past and past part of* SLING
slunk *past and past part of* SLINK
¹slur \'slər\ *n* : a slighting remark : ASPERSION — **slur** *vb*
²slur *vb* **slurred; slur·ring** 1 : to slide or slip over without due mention or emphasis 2 : to perform two or more successive notes of different pitch in a smooth or connected way
³slur *n* : a curved line connecting notes to be slurred; *also* : a group of slurred notes
slurp \'slərp\ *vb* : to eat or drink noisily — **slurp** *n*
slur·ry \'slər-ē\ *n, pl* **slur·ries** : a watery mixture of insoluble matter
slush \'sləsh\ *n* 1 : partly melted or watery snow 2 : soft mud — **slushy** *adj*
slush fund *n* : an unregulated fund often for illicit purposes
slut \'slət\ *n* 1 *dated* **a** *chiefly Brit, disparaging* : a slovenly woman **b** : MINX 2 *offensive* : a lewd, dissolute, or promiscuous woman — **slut·tish** *adj*
sly \'slī\ *adj* **sly·er** *also* **sli·er** \'slī-ər\; **sly·est** *also* **sli·est** \'slī-əst\ 1 : CRAFTY, CUNNING 2 : SECRETIVE, FURTIVE 3 : ROGUISH ♦ *Synonyms* TRICKY, WILY, ARTFUL, FOXY, GUILEFUL — **sly·ly** *also* **sli·ly** *adv* — **sly·ness** *n*
sm *abbr* small
Sm *symbol* samarium
SM *abbr* 1 master of science 2 sergeant major 3 service mark 4 stage manager
SMA *abbr* sergeant major of the army
¹smack \'smak\ *n* : characteristic flavor; *also* : a slight trace
²smack *vb* 1 : to have a taste 2 : to have a trace or suggestion ⟨~s of treason⟩
³smack *vb* 1 : to move (the lips) so as to make a sharp noise 2 : to kiss or slap with a loud noise
⁴smack *n* 1 : a sharp noise made by the lips 2 : a loud kiss or slap
⁵smack *adv* : squarely and sharply
⁶smack *n* : a sailing ship used in fishing
⁷smack *n, slang* : HEROIN
smack·down \'smak-ˌdau̇n\ *n* 1 : the act of knocking down an opponent 2 : a wrestling match 3 : a decisive defeat 4 : a competition between rivals
SMaj *abbr* sergeant major
¹small \'smȯl\ *adj* 1 : little in size or amount 2 : operating on a limited scale 3 : little or close to zero (as in number or value) 4 : made up of little things 5 : TRIFLING, UNIMPORTANT 6 : MEAN, PETTY ♦ *Synonyms* DIMINUTIVE, PETITE, WEE, TINY, MINUTE — **small·ish** *adj* — **small·ness** *n*
²small *n* : a small part or product ⟨the ~ of the back⟩
small·pox \'smȯl-ˌpäks\ *n* : a contagious virus disease of humans formerly common but now eradicated
small talk *n* : light or casual conversation
small–time \'smȯl-'tīm\ *adj* : insignificant in performance and standing : MINOR — **small–tim·er** *n*
smarmy \'smär-mē\ *adj* **smarm·i·er; -est** : marked by a smug, ingratiating, or false earnestness ⟨~ politeness⟩
¹smart \'smärt\ *adj* 1 : making one smart ⟨a ~ blow⟩ 2 : mentally quick : BRIGHT 3 : WITTY, CLEVER 4 : STYLISH 5 : being a guided missile 6 : containing a microprocessor for limited computing capability ⟨~ terminal⟩ ♦ *Synonyms* KNOWING, QUICK-WITTED, INTELLIGENT, BRAINY, SHARP — **smart·ly** *adv* — **smart·ness** *n*
²smart *vb* 1 : to cause or feel a stinging pain 2 : to feel or endure distress — **smart** *n*
smart al·eck \'smärt-ˌa-lik\ *n* : a person given to obnoxious cleverness
smart card *n* : a small plastic card that has a built-in microprocessor to store and handle data
smart·en \'smär-tᵊn\ *vb* : to make smart or smarter — usu. used with *up*
smart·phone \'smärt-ˌfōn\ *n* : a cell phone that includes additional software functions (as e-mail or an Internet browser)
¹smash \'smash\ *n* 1 : a smashing blow 2 : a hard, overhand stroke in tennis 3 : the act or sound of smashing 4 : collision of vehicles : CRASH 5 : COLLAPSE, RUIN; *esp* : BANKRUPTCY 6 : a striking success : HIT — **smash up**
²smash *vb* 1 : to break or be broken into pieces 2 : to

move forward with force and shattering effect 3 : to destroy utterly : WRECK
smat·ter·ing \'sma-tə-riŋ\ *n* 1 : superficial knowledge 2 : a small scattered number or amount
¹smear \'smir\ *n* 1 : a spot left by an oily or sticky substance 2 : material smeared on a surface (as of a microscope slide)
²smear *vb* 1 : to overspread esp. with something oily or sticky 2 : SMUDGE, SOIL 3 : to injure by slander or insults
¹smell \'smel\ *vb* **smelled** \'smeld\ *or* **smelt** \'smelt\; **smell·ing** 1 : to perceive the odor of by sense organs of the nose; *also* : to detect or seek with or as if with these organs 2 : to have or give off an odor
²smell *n* 1 : ODOR, SCENT 2 : the process or power of perceiving odor; *also* : the sense by which one perceives odor 3 : an act of smelling — **smelly** *adj*
smelling salts *n pl* : an aromatic preparation used as a stimulant and restorative (as to relieve faintness)
¹smelt \'smelt\ *n, pl* **smelts** *or* **smelt** : any of a family of small food fishes of coastal or fresh waters that are related to the trouts and salmons
²smelt *vb* : to melt or fuse (ore) in order to separate the metal; *also* : REFINE
smelt·er \'smel-tər\ *n* 1 : one that smelts 2 : an establishment for smelting
smid·gen *also* **smid·geon** *or* **smid·gin** \'smi-jən\ *n* : a small amount : BIT
smi·lax \'smī-ˌlaks\ *n* 1 : any of various mostly climbing and prickly plants related to the lilies 2 : an ornamental plant related to the asparagus
¹smile \'smī(-ə)l\ *vb* **smiled; smil·ing** 1 : to look with a smile 2 : to be favorable 3 : to express by a smile
²smile *n* : a change of facial expression to express amusement, pleasure, or affection — **smile·less** \'smī(-ə)l-ləs\ *adj*
smil·ey \'smī-lē\ *adj* : exhibiting a smile : frequently smiling
smiley face *n* : a line drawing that symbolizes a smiling face
smirch \'smərch\ *vb* 1 : to make dirty or stained 2 : to bring disgrace on — **smirch** *n*
smirk \'smərk\ *vb* : to smile in an affected or smug manner : SIMPER — **smirk** *n*
smite \'smīt\ *vb* **smote** \'smōt\; **smit·ten** \'smi-tᵊn\ *or* **smote; smit·ing** \'smī-tiŋ\ 1 : to strike heavily; *also* : to kill by striking 2 : to affect as if by a heavy blow
smith \'smith\ *n* : a worker in metals; *esp* : BLACKSMITH
smith·er·eens \ˌsmi-thə-'rēnz\ *n pl* [perh. fr. Ir *smidiríní*] : FRAGMENTS, BITS
smithy \'smi-thē\ *n, pl* **smith·ies** 1 : a smith's workshop 2 : BLACKSMITH
¹smock \'smäk\ *n* : a loose garment worn over other clothes as a protection
²smock *vb* : to gather (cloth) in regularly spaced tucks — **smock·ing** *n*
smog \'smäg, 'smȯg\ *n* [blend of *smoke* and *fog*] : a thick haze caused by the action of sunlight on air polluted by smoke and automobile exhaust fumes — **smog·gy** *adj*
¹smoke \'smōk\ *n* 1 : the gas from burning material (as coal, wood, or tobacco) in which are suspended particles of soot 2 : a mass or column of smoke 3 : something (as a cigarette) to smoke; *also* : the act of smoking — **smoke·less** *adj* — **smoky** *adj*
²smoke *vb* **smoked; smok·ing** 1 : to emit smoke 2 : to inhale and exhale the fumes of burning tobacco; *also* : to use in smoking ⟨~ a pipe⟩ 3 : to stupefy or drive away by smoke 4 : to discolor with smoke 5 : to cure (as meat) with smoke — **smok·er** *n*
smoke detector *n* : an alarm that sounds automatically when it detects smoke
smoke jumper *n* : a forest firefighter who parachutes to locations otherwise difficult to reach
smoke screen *n* 1 : a screen of smoke to hinder enemy observation 2 : something designed to obscure, confuse, or mislead
smoke·stack \'smōk-ˌstak\ *n* : a pipe or funnel through which smoke and gases are discharged
smol·der *or* **smoul·der** \'smōl-dər\ *vb* **smol·dered** *or* **smoul·dered; smol·der·ing** *or* **smoul·der·ing** 1 : to burn and smoke without flame 2 : to burn inwardly — **smolder** *n*

smooch \'smüch\ *vb* : KISS, PET — **smooch** *n*

¹**smooth** \'smü<u>th</u>\ *adj* **1** : not rough or uneven **2** : not jarring or jolting **3** : BLAND, MILD **4** : fluent in speech and agreeable in manner — **smooth·ly** *adv* — **smooth·ness** *n*

²**smooth** *vb* **1** : to make smooth **2** : to free from trouble or difficulty

smooth muscle *n* : muscle with no cross striations that is typical of visceral organs (as the stomach and bladder) and is not under voluntary control

smoothy *or* **smooth·ie** \'smü-thē\ *n, pl* **smooth·ies** **1** : an artfully suave person **2** *smoothie* : a creamy beverage of fruit blended with juice, milk, or yogurt

s'more \'smór\ *n* : a dessert of marshmallow and pieces of chocolate sandwiched between graham crackers

smor·gas·bord \'smór-gəs-ˌbórd\ *n* [Sw *smörgåsbord,* fr. *smörgås* open sandwich + *bord* table] : a luncheon or supper buffet consisting of many foods

smote *past and past part of* SMITE

¹**smoth·er** \'smə-thər\ *n* **1** : thick stifling smoke **2** : a dense cloud (as of fog or dust) **3** : a confused multitude of things

²**smother** *vb* **smoth·ered; smoth·er·ing** **1** : to be overcome by or die from lack of air **2** : to kill by depriving of air **3** : SUPPRESS **4** : to cover thickly

SMSgt *abbr* senior master sergeant

¹**smudge** \'sməj\ *vb* **smudged; smudg·ing** : to soil or blur by rubbing or smearing ⟨his face was *smudged* with grease⟩

²**smudge** *n* : a dirty or blurred spot — **smudgy** *adj*

smug \'sməg\ *adj* **smug·ger; smug·gest** : conscious of one's virtue and importance : SELF-SATISFIED ⟨was ∼ about her victory⟩ — **smug·ly** *adv* — **smug·ness** *n*

smug·gle \'smə-gəl\ *vb* **smug·gled; smug·gling** **1** : to import or export secretly, illegally, or without paying the duties required by law **2** : to convey secretly — **smug·gler** \'smə-glər\ *n*

smut \'smət\ *n* **1** : something (as soot) that smudges; *also* : SMUDGE, SPOT **2** : any of various destructive diseases of plants caused by fungi; *also* : a fungus causing smut **3** : indecent language or matter — **smut·ty** *adj*

Sn *symbol* [LL *stannum*] tin

SN *abbr* seaman

snack \'snak\ *n* : a light meal : BITE — **snack** *vb*

snaf·fle \'sna-fəl\ *n* : a simple jointed bit for a horse's bridle

¹**snag** \'snag\ *n* **1** : a stump or piece of a tree esp. when under water **2** : an unexpected difficulty ♦ *Synonyms* OBSTACLE, OBSTRUCTION, IMPEDIMENT, BAR

²**snag** *vb* **snagged; snag·ging** **1** : to become caught on or as if on a snag **2** : to seize quickly : SNATCH

snail \'snāl\ *n* : any of numerous small gastropod mollusks with a spiral shell into which they can withdraw

snail mail *n* **1** : mail delivered by a postal system **2** : MAIL 2

snake \'snāk\ *n* **1** : any of numerous long-bodied limbless reptiles **2** : a treacherous person **3** : something that resembles a snake — **snake·like** \-ˌlīk\ *adj* — **snaky** *adj*

snake·bite \-ˌbīt\ *n* : the bite of a snake and esp. a venomous snake

¹**snap** \'snap\ *vb* **snapped; snap·ping** **1** : to grasp or slash at something with the teeth **2** : to get or buy quickly **3** : to utter sharp or angry words **4** : to break suddenly with a sharp sound **5** : to give a sharp cracking noise **6** : to throw with a quick motion **7** : FLASH ⟨her eyes *snapped*⟩ **8** : to put a football into play — **snap·per** *n* — **snap·pish** *adj*

²**snap** *n* **1** : the act or sound of snapping **2** : something very easy to do : CINCH **3** : a short period of cold weather **4** : a catch or fastening that closes with a click **5** : a thin brittle cookie **6** : ENERGY, VIM; *also* : smartness of movement **7** : the putting of the ball into play in football

snap bean *n* : a bean grown primarily for its long pods that are cooked as a vegetable when young and tender

snap·drag·on \'snap-ˌdra-gən\ *n* : any of a genus of herbs with long spikes of showy flowers

snapping turtle *n* : either of two large American turtles with powerful jaws and a strong musky odor

snap·py \'sna-pē\ *adj* **1** : quickly made or done **2** : marked by vigor **3** : STYLISH ⟨a ∼ dresser⟩

snap·shot \'snap-ˌshät\ *n* : a photograph taken usu. with an inexpensive hand-held camera

snare \'sner\ *n* : a trap often consisting of a noose for catching birds or mammals — **snare** *vb*

¹**snarl** \'snärl\ *vb* : to cause to become knotted and intertwined

²**snarl** *n* : TANGLE — **snarly** \'snär-lē\ *adj*

³**snarl** *vb* : to growl angrily or threateningly

⁴**snarl** *n* : an angry ill-tempered growl

¹**snatch** \'snach\ *vb* **1** : to try to grasp something suddenly **2** : to seize or take away suddenly ♦ *Synonyms* CLUTCH, SEIZE, GRAB, NAB

²**snatch** *n* **1** : a short period **2** : an act of snatching **3** : something brief or fragmentary ⟨∼*es* of song⟩

¹**sneak** \'snēk\ *vb* **sneaked** \'snēkt\ *or* **snuck** \'snək\; **sneak·ing** : to move, act, or take in a furtive manner ⟨∼*ed* past the guard⟩ — **sneak·ing·ly** *adv*

²**sneak** *n* **1** : one who acts in a furtive or shifty manner **2** : a stealthy or furtive move or escape — **sneak·i·ly** \'snē-kə-lē\ *adv* — **sneaky** *adj*

sneak·er \'snē-kər\ *n* : a sports shoe with a pliable rubber sole

sneer \'snir\ *vb* : to show scorn or contempt by curling the lip or by a jeering tone — **sneer** *n*

sneeze \'snēz\ *vb* **sneezed; sneez·ing** [ME *snesen,* alter. of *fnesen,* fr. OE *fnēosan*] : to force the breath out suddenly and violently as a reflex act — **sneeze** *n*

SNF *abbr* skilled nursing facility

snick·er \'sni-kər\ *n* : a partly suppressed laugh — **snicker** *vb*

snide \'snīd\ *adj* **1** : MEAN, LOW ⟨a ∼ trick⟩ **2** : slyly disparaging ⟨a ∼ remark⟩ — **snide·ly** *adv* — **snide·ness** *n*

sniff \'snif\ *vb* **1** : to draw air audibly up the nose esp. for smelling **2** : to show disdain or scorn **3** : to detect by or as if by smelling — **sniff** *n*

snif·fle \'sni-fəl\ *n* **1** *pl* : a head cold marked by nasal discharge **2** : SNUFFLE — **sniffle** *vb*

¹**snip** \'snip\ *n* **1** : a fragment snipped off **2** : a simple stroke of the scissors or shears

²**snip** *vb* **snipped; snip·ping** : to cut off by bits : CLIP; *also* : to remove by cutting off ⟨∼ a flower⟩

¹**snipe** \'snīp\ *n, pl* **snipes** *or* **snipe** : any of several long-billed game birds esp. of marshy areas that belong to the same family as the sandpipers

²**snipe** *vb* **sniped; snip·ing** : to shoot at an exposed enemy from a concealed position — **snip·er** *n*

snip·py \'sni-pē\ *adj* **snip·pi·er; -est** : CURT, SNAPPISH ⟨∼ comments⟩ — **snip·pi·ly** \'sni-pə-lē\ *adv*

snips \'snips\ *n pl* : hand shears used esp. for cutting sheet metal ⟨tin ∼⟩

snitch \'snich\ *vb* **1** : INFORM, TATTLE **2** : PILFER, SNATCH — **snitch** *n*

sniv·el \'sni-vəl\ *vb* **-eled** *or* **-elled; -el·ing** *or* **-el·ling** **1** : to have a running nose; *also* : SNUFFLE **2** : to whine in a snuffling manner — **snivel** *n*

snob \'snäb\ *n* : one who seeks association with persons of higher social position and looks down on those considered inferior — **snob·bish** *adj* — **snob·bish·ly** *adv* — **snob·bish·ness** *n* — **snob·by** \'snä-bē\ *adj*

snob·bery \'snä-bə-rē\ *n, pl* **-ber·ies** : snobbish conduct

¹**snoop** \'snüp\ *vb* [D *snoepen* to buy or eat on the sly] : to pry in a furtive or meddlesome way

²**snoop** *n* : a prying meddlesome person

snoopy \'snü-pē\ *adj* **snoop·i·er; -est** : given to snooping

snooty \'snü-tē\ *adj* **snoot·i·er; -est** : DISDAINFUL, SNOBBISH ⟨∼ rich people⟩ — **snoot·i·ly** \'snü-tə-lē\ *adv*

snooze \'snüz\ *vb* **snoozed; snooz·ing** : to take a nap : DOZE — **snooze** *n*

snore \'snór\ *vb* **snored; snor·ing** : to breathe with a rough hoarse noise while sleeping — **snore** *n*

snor·kel \'snór-kəl\ *n* [G *Schnorchel*] : a tube projecting above the water used by swimmers for breathing with the face under water — **snorkel** *vb*

snort \'snórt\ *vb* **1** : to force air violently and noisily through the nose ⟨his horse ∼*ed*⟩ **2** : to inhale (a drug) through the nostrils — **snort** *n*

snot \'snät\ *n* **1** *often vulgar* : nasal mucus **2** : a snotty person

snot·ty \'snä-tē\ *adj* **snot·ti·er, -est** **1** : soiled with snot **2** : rude and arrogant ⟨a ∼ remark⟩ ⟨a ∼ person⟩

snout \'snaút\ *n* 1 : a long projecting muzzle (as of a pig) 2 : a usu. large or grotesque nose

¹snow \'snō\ *n* 1 : crystals of ice formed from water vapor in the air 2 : a descent or shower of snow crystals

²snow *vb* 1 : to fall or cause to fall in or as snow 2 : to cover or shut in with or as if with snow

snow·ball \'snō-,ból\ *n* : a round mass of snow pressed into shape in the hand for throwing

²snowball *vb* 1 : to throw snowballs at 2 : to increase or expand at a rapidly accelerating rate

snow·bank \-,baŋk\ *n* : a mound or slope of snow

snow·belt \-,belt\ *n, often cap* : a region that receives an appreciable amount of annual snowfall

snow·blow·er \-,blō-ər\ *n* : a machine in which a rotating spiral blade picks up and propels snow aside

snow·board \-,bórd\ *n* : a board like a wide ski ridden in a surfing position downhill over snow

snow·drift \-,drift\ *n* : a bank of drifted snow

snow·drop \-,dräp\ *n* : a plant with narrow leaves and a nodding white flower that blooms early in the spring

snow·fall \-,fól\ *n* : a fall of snow

snow fence *n* : a fence across the path of prevailing winds to protect something (as a road) from drifting snow

snow·field \'snō-,fēld\ *n* : a mass of perennial snow at the head of a glacier

snow·mo·bile \'snō-mō-,bēl\ *n* : any of various automotive vehicles for travel on snow — **snow·mo·bil·er** \-,bē-lər\ *n* — **snow·mo·bil·ing** \-liŋ\ *n*

snow pea *n* : a cultivated pea with flat edible pods

snow·plow \'snō-,plaú\ *n* 1 : a device for clearing away snow 2 : a skiing maneuver in which the heels of both skis are slid outward for slowing down or stopping

¹snow·shoe \-,shü\ *n* : a lightweight platform for the foot designed to enable a person to walk on soft snow without sinking

²snowshoe *vb* **snow·shoed; snow·shoe·ing** : to travel on snowshoes

snow·storm \-,stórm\ *n* : a storm of falling snow

snow thrower *n* : SNOWBLOWER

snowy \'snō-ē\ *adj* **snow·i·er; -est** 1 : marked by snow 2 : white as snow

snowy egret *n* : a white American egret with a slender black bill

snub \'snəb\ *vb* **snubbed; snub·bing** : to treat with disdain : SLIGHT — **snub** *n*

snub–nosed \'snəb-,nōzd\ *adj* : having a nose slightly turned up at the end

snuck *past and past part of* SNEAK

¹snuff \'snəf\ *vb* 1 : to pinch off the charred end of (a candle) 2 : to put out (a candle) — **snuff·er** *n*

²snuff *vb* 1 : to draw forcibly into or through the nose 2 : SMELL

³snuff *n* : SNIFF

⁴snuff *n* : pulverized tobacco

snuf·fle \'snə-fəl\ *vb* **snuf·fled; snuf·fling** 1 : to snuff or sniff audibly and repeatedly 2 : to breathe with a sniffing sound — **snuf·fle** *n*

snug \'snəg\ *adj* **snug·ger; snug·gest** 1 : fitting closely and comfortably 2 : CONCEALED ⟨a ~ position⟩ — **snug·ly** *adv* — **snug·ness** *n*

snug·gle \'snə-gəl\ *vb* **snug·gled; snug·gling** : to curl up or draw close comfortably : NESTLE

¹so \'sō\ *adv* 1 : in the manner indicated 2 : in the same way ⟨he's hungry and ~ am I⟩ 3 : THUS 4 : FINALLY 5 : to an indicated or great extent ⟨I'm ~ bored⟩ 6 : THEREFORE

²so *conj* : for that reason ⟨he wanted it, ~ he took it⟩

³so *pron* 1 : the same ⟨became chairman and remained ~⟩ 2 : approximately that ⟨a dozen or ~⟩

⁴so *abbr* south; southern

SO *abbr* strikeout

¹soak \'sōk\ *vb* 1 : to remain in a liquid 2 : WET, SATURATE 3 : to draw in by or as if by absorption ⟨~ up the sunshine⟩ ◆ *Synonyms* DRENCH, STEEP, IMPREGNATE

²soak *n* 1 : the act of soaking 2 : the liquid in which something is soaked 3 : DRUNKARD

soap \'sōp\ *n* : a cleansing substance made usu. by action of alkali on fat — **soap** *vb* — **soapy** *adj*

soap·box \'sōp-,bäks\ *n* : an improvised platform used for delivering informal speeches

soap opera *n* [fr. its sponsorship by soap manufacturers] : a radio or television daytime serial drama

soap·stone \'sōp-,stōn\ *n* : a soft talc-containing stone with a soapy feel

soar \'sór\ *vb* : to fly upward or at a height on or as if on wings

sob \'säb\ *vb* **sobbed; sob·bing** : to weep with convulsive heavings of the chest or contractions of the throat — **sob** *n*

so·ba \'sō-bə\ *n* [Jp] : a Japanese noodle made from buckwheat flour

so·ber \'sō-bər\ *adj* **so·ber·er** \-bər-ər\; **so·ber·est** \-bə-rəst\ 1 : temperate in the use of liquor 2 : not drunk 3 : serious or grave in mood or disposition 4 : having a quiet tone or color ◆ *Synonyms* SOLEMN, EARNEST, STAID, SEDATE — **so·ber·ly** *adv* — **so·ber·ness** *n*

so·bri·ety \sō-'brī-ə-tē\ *n* : the quality or state of being sober

so·bri·quet \'sō-bri-,kā, -,ket\ *n* [F] : NICKNAME

soc *abbr* 1 social; society 2 sociology

so·ca \'sō-kə, -kä\ *n* : soul music blended with calypso

so–called \'sō-'kóld\ *adj* : commonly but often inaccurately so termed

soc·cer \'sä-kər\ *n* [by shortening & alter. fr. *association football*] : a game played on a field by two teams with a round inflated ball that is kicked or hit with any body part other than the hands or arms

¹so·cia·ble \'sō-shə-bəl\ *adj* 1 : liking companionship : FRIENDLY 2 : characterized by pleasant social relations ◆ *Synonyms* GRACIOUS, CORDIAL, AFFABLE, GENIAL — **so·cia·bil·i·ty** \,sō-shə-'bi-lə-tē\ *n* — **so·cia·bly** \'sō-shə-blē\ *adv*

²sociable *n* : SOCIAL

¹so·cial \'sō-shəl\ *adj* 1 : marked by pleasant companionship with one's friends 2 : naturally living and breeding in organized communities ⟨~ insects⟩ 3 : of or relating to human society ⟨~ institutions⟩ 4 : of, relating to, or based on rank in a particular society ⟨~ circles⟩; *also* : of or relating to fashionable society — **so·cial·ly** *adv*

²social *n* : a social gathering

so·cial·ise *Brit var of* SOCIALIZE

so·cial·ism \'sō-shə-,li-zəm\ *n* : any of various social systems based on shared or government ownership and administration of the means of production and distribution of goods — **so·cial·ist** \'sō-shə-list\ *n or adj* — **so·cial·is·tic** \,sō-shə-'lis-tik\ *adj*

so·cial·ite \'sō-shə-,līt\ *n* : a person prominent in fashionable society

so·cial·ize \'sō-shə-,līz\ *vb* **-ized; -iz·ing** 1 : to regulate according to the theory and practice of socialism 2 : to adapt to social needs or uses 3 : to participate actively in a social gathering — **so·cial·i·za·tion** \,sō-shə-lə-'zā-shən\ *n*

social media *n pl* : forms of electronic communication (as websites) for sharing content (such as messages, photos, or videos) with other users

social networking *n* : the creation and maintenance of personal and business relationships especially online

social science *n* : a science (as economics or political science) dealing with a particular aspect of human society — **social scientist** *n*

social work *n* : services, activities, or methods providing social services esp. to the economically or socially disadvantaged — **social worker** *n*

so·ci·e·ty \sə-'sī-ə-tē\ *n, pl* **-ties** [MF *societé*, fr. L *societat-, societas*, fr. *socius* companion] 1 : COMPANY ⟨in the ~ of others⟩ 2 : an association of persons for some purpose ⟨a literary ~⟩ 3 : a part of a community bound together by common interests and values; *esp* : the group or set of fashionable people ⟨high ~⟩ 4 : people in general ⟨the benefit of ~⟩ — **so·ci·e·tal** \-t°l\ *adj*

so·cio·eco·nom·ic \,sō-sē-ō-,e-kə-'nä-mik, ,sō-shē-, -,ē-kə-\ *adj* : of, relating to, or involving both social and economic factors

sociol *abbr* sociologist; sociology

so·ci·ol·o·gy \,sō-sē-'ä-lə-jē, ,sō-shē-\ *n* : the science of society, social institutions, and social relationships — **so·ci·o·log·i·cal** \,sō-sē-ə-'lä-ji-kəl, ,sō-shē-\ *adj* — **so·ci·ol·o·gist** \-'ä-lə-jist\ *n*

so·cio·path \'sō-sē-ə-,path, 'sō-sh(ē-)ə-\ *n* : a person exhibiting antisocial behavior : PSYCHOPATH — **so·cio·path·ic** \ˌsō-sē-ə-ˈpa-thik, ˌsō-sh(ē-)ə-\ *adj*

¹**sock** \ˈsäk\ *n, pl* **socks** *or* **sox** \ˈsäks\ : a stocking with a short leg

²**sock** *vb* : to hit, strike, or apply forcefully

³**sock** *n* : a vigorous blow : PUNCH

sock·et \ˈsä-kət\ *n* : an opening or hollow that forms a holder for something

socket wrench *n* : a wrench usu. in the form of a bar and removable socket made to fit a bolt or nut

socket wrench

sock·eye salmon \ˈsäk-ˌī-\ *n* : a commercially important Pacific salmon

¹**sod** \ˈsäd\ *n* : TURF 1

²**sod** *vb* **sod·ded; sod·ding** : to cover with sod

so·da \ˈsō-də\ *n* 1 : SODIUM CARBONATE 2 : SODIUM BICARBONATE 3 : SODIUM 4 : SODA WATER 5 : SODA POP 6 : a sweet drink of soda water, flavoring, and often ice cream

soda pop *n* : a carbonated, sweetened, and flavored soft drink

soda water *n* : a beverage of water charged with carbon dioxide

sod·den \ˈsä-dᵊn\ *adj* 1 : lacking spirit : DULLED 2 : SOAKED, DRENCHED 3 : heavy or doughy from being improperly cooked ⟨~ biscuits⟩

so·di·um \ˈsō-dē-əm\ *n* : a soft waxy silver white metallic chemical element occurring in nature in combined form (as in salt)

sodium bicarbonate *n* : a white weakly alkaline salt used esp. in baking powders, fire extinguishers, and medicine

sodium carbonate *n* : a carbonate of sodium used esp. in washing and bleaching textiles

sodium chloride *n* : SALT 1

sodium fluoride *n* : a salt used chiefly in tiny amounts (as in fluoridation) to prevent tooth decay

sodium hydroxide *n* : a white brittle caustic substance used in making soap and rayon and in bleaching

sodium nitrate *n* : a crystalline salt used as a fertilizer and in curing meat

sodium thiosulfate *n* : a hygroscopic crystalline salt used as a photographic fixing agent

sod·omy \ˈsä-də-mē\ *n* : anal or oral sexual intercourse with a member of the same or opposite sex; *also* : sexual intercourse with an animal — **sod·om·ize** \ˈsä-də-ˌmīz\ *vb*

so·ev·er \sō-ˈe-vər\ *adv* 1 : in any degree or manner ⟨how bad ~⟩ 2 : at all : of any kind ⟨any help ~⟩

so·fa \ˈsō-fə\ *n* [earlier, raised carpeted floor, fr. It *sofà*, fr. Turk *sofa*, fr. Ar *suffa* carpet, divan] : a couch usu. with upholstered back and arms

soft \ˈsȯft\ *adj* 1 : not hard or rough : NONVIOLENT 2 : RESTFUL, GENTLE, SOOTHING 3 : emotionally susceptible 4 : not prepared to endure hardship 5 : not containing certain salts that prevent lathering ⟨~ water⟩ 6 : occurring at such a speed as to avoid destructive impact ⟨~ landing of a spacecraft on the moon⟩ 7 : BIODEGRADABLE ⟨a ~ pesticide⟩ 8 : not alcoholic ⟨~ drinks⟩ 9 : less detrimental than a hard narcotic ⟨~ drugs⟩ — **soft·ly** *adv* — **soft·ness** *n*

soft·ball \ˈsȯft-ˌbȯl\ *n* : a game similar to baseball played with a ball larger and softer than a baseball; *also* : the ball used in this game

soft·bound \-ˌbau̇nd\ *adj* : not bound in hard covers ⟨~ books⟩

soft coal *n* : BITUMINOUS COAL

soft·en \ˈsȯ-fən\ *vb* : to make or become soft — **soft·en·er** *n*

soft palate *n* : the fold at the back of the hard palate that partially separates the mouth from the pharynx

soft·ware \ˈsȯft-ˌwer\ *n* : the entire set of programs, procedures, and related documentation associated with a system; *esp* : computer programs

soft·wood \-ˌwu̇d\ *n* 1 : the wood of a coniferous tree as compared to that of a broad-leaved deciduous tree 2 : a tree yielding softwood — **softwood** *adj*

sog·gy \ˈsä-gē\ *adj* **sog·gi·er; -est** : heavy with water or moisture — **sog·gi·ly** \ˈsä-gə-lē\ *adv* — **sog·gi·ness** \-gē-nəs\ *n*

soi·gné *or* **soi·gnée** \swän-ˈyā\ *adj* : elegantly maintained; *esp* : WELL-GROOMED

¹**soil** \ˈsȯi(-ə)l\ *vb* 1 : CORRUPT, POLLUTE 2 : to make or become dirty 3 : STAIN, DISGRACE ⟨~ed his reputation⟩

²**soil** *n* 1 : STAIN, DEFILEMENT 2 : EXCREMENT, WASTE

³**soil** *n* 1 : firm land : EARTH 2 : the upper layer of earth in which plants grow 3 : COUNTRY, REGION

soi·ree *or* **soi·rée** \swä-ˈrā\ *n* [F *soirée* evening period, evening party, fr. MF, fr. *soir* evening, fr. L *sero* at a late hour] : an evening party

so·journ \ˈsō-jərn, sō-ˈjərn\ *vb* : to dwell in a place temporarily — **so·journ** *n* — **so·journ·er** *n*

¹**sol** \ˈsäl, ˈsȯl\ *n* — see MONEY table

²**sol** *n* : a fluid colloidal system

³**sol** *abbr* 1 solicitor 2 soluble 3 solution

Sol \ˈsäl\ *n* : SUN

¹**sol·ace** \ˈsä-ləs\ *n* : COMFORT

²**solace** *vb* **so·laced; so·lac·ing** : to give solace to : CONSOLE

so·lar \ˈsō-lər\ *adj* 1 : of, derived from, or relating to the sun 2 : measured by the earth's course in relation to the sun ⟨the ~ year⟩ 3 : operated by or using the sun's light or heat ⟨~ energy⟩

solar cell *n* : a photoelectric cell used as a power source

solar collector *n* : a device for the absorption of solar radiation for the heating of water or buildings or the production of electricity

solar flare *n* : a sudden temporary outburst of energy from a small area of the sun's surface

so·lar·i·um \sō-ˈler-ē-əm\ *n, pl* **-ia** \-ē-ə\ *also* **-i·ums** : a room exposed to the sun; *esp* : a room (as in a hospital) for exposure of the body to sunshine

solar mass *n* : a unit of mass equal to the mass of the sun or about 2×10^{30} kilograms

solar plexus *n* : the general area of the stomach below the sternum

solar system *n* : the sun together with the group of celestial bodies that revolve around it

solar wind *n* : plasma continuously ejected from the sun's surface

sold *past and past part of* SELL

sol·der \ˈsä-dər, ˈsȯ-\ *n* : a metallic alloy used when melted to mend or join metallic surfaces — **solder** *vb*

soldering iron *n* : a metal device for applying heat in soldering

¹**sol·dier** \ˈsōl-jər\ *n* [ME *soudeour*, fr. AF, mercenary, fr. *soudee* shilling's worth, wage, fr. *sou, soud* shilling, fr. LL *solidus* a Roman coin, fr. L, solid] : a person in military service; *esp* : an enlisted man or woman — **sol·dier·ly** *adj or adv*

²**soldier** *vb* **sol·diered; sol·dier·ing** 1 : to serve as a soldier 2 : to pretend to work while actually doing nothing

soldier of fortune *n* : ADVENTURER 2

sol·diery \ˈsōl-jə-rē\ *n* : a body of soldiers

¹**sole** \ˈsōl\ *n* : any of various flatfishes including some used for food

²**sole** *n* 1 : the undersurface of the foot 2 : the bottom of a shoe

³**sole** *vb* **soled; sol·ing** : to furnish (a shoe) with a sole

⁴**sole** *adj* : SINGLE, ONLY ⟨the ~ survivor⟩ — **sole·ly** \ˈsōl-lē\ *adv*

so·le·cism \ˈsä-lə-ˌsi-zəm, ˈsō-\ *n* 1 : a mistake in grammar 2 : a breach of etiquette

sol·emn \ˈsä-ləm\ *adj* 1 : marked by or observed with full religious ceremony ⟨a ~ oath⟩ 2 : FORMAL, CEREMONIOUS 3 : highly serious : GRAVE ⟨a ~ gathering⟩ 4 : SOMBER, GLOOMY ⟨a ~ city⟩ — **so·lem·ni·ty** \sə-ˈlem-nə-tē\ *n* — **sol·emn·ly** \ˈsä-ləm-lē\ *adv*

sol·em·nize \ˈsä-ləm-ˌnīz\ *vb* **-nized; -niz·ing** 1 : to observe or honor with solemnity 2 : to celebrate (a marriage) with religious rites — **sol·em·ni·za·tion** \ˌsä-ləm-nə-ˈzā-shən\ *n*

so·le·noid \ˈsō-lə-ˌnȯid, ˈsä-\ *n* : a coil of wire usu. in cylindrical form that when carrying a current acts like a magnet

so·lic·it \sə-'li-sət\ vb 1 : ENTREAT, BEG 2 : to approach with a request or plea 3 : TEMPT, LURE 4 : to try to obtain by request ⟨~ donations⟩ — **so·lic·i·ta·tion** \-,li-sə-'tā-shən\ n

so·lic·i·tor \sə-'li-sə-tər\ n 1 : one that solicits 2 : LAWYER; esp : a legal official of a city or state

so·lic·i·tous \sə-'li-sə-təs\ adj 1 : WORRIED, CONCERNED 2 : EAGER, WILLING ♦ Synonyms AVID, IMPATIENT, KEEN, ANXIOUS — **so·lic·i·tous·ly** adv

so·lic·i·tude \sə-'li-sə-,tüd, -,tyüd\ n : CONCERN, ANXIETY

¹**sol·id** \'sä-ləd\ adj 1 : not hollow; also : written as one word without a hyphen ⟨a ~ compound⟩ 2 : having, involving, or dealing with three dimensions or with solids ⟨~ geometry⟩ 3 : not loose or spongy : COMPACT ⟨a ~ mass of rock⟩; also : neither gaseous nor liquid : HARD, RIGID ⟨~ ice⟩ 4 : of good substantial quality or kind ⟨~ comfort⟩ 5 : thoroughly dependable : RELIABLE ⟨a ~ citizen⟩; also : serious in purpose or character ⟨~ reading⟩ 6 : UNANIMOUS, UNITED ⟨~ for pay increases⟩ 7 : of one substance or character — **solid** adv — **so·lid·i·ty** \sə-'li-də-tē\ n — **sol·id·ly** adv — **sol·id·ness** n

²**solid** n 1 : a geometrical figure (as a cube or sphere) having three dimensions 2 : a solid substance

sol·i·dar·i·ty \,sä-lə-'der-ə-tē\ n : unity based on shared interests, objectives, and standards

so·lid·i·fy \sə-'li-də-,fī\ vb -fied; -fy·ing : to make or become solid — **so·lid·i·fi·ca·tion** \-,li-də-fə-'kā-shən\ n

solid–state adj 1 : relating to the structure and properties of solid material 2 : using semiconductor devices rather than vacuum tubes

so·lil·o·quize \sə-'li-lə-,kwīz\ vb -quized; -quiz·ing : to talk to oneself : utter a soliloquy

so·lil·o·quy \sə-'li-lə-kwē\ n, pl -quies [LL soliloquium, fr. L solus alone + loqui to speak] 1 : the act of talking to oneself 2 : a dramatic monologue that represents unspoken reflections by a character

sol·i·taire \'sä-lə-,ter\ n 1 : a single gem (as a diamond) set alone 2 : a card game for one person

sol·i·tary \'sä-lə-,ter-ē\ adj 1 : being or living apart from others 2 : LONELY, SECLUDED 3 : SOLE, ONLY ⟨a ~ example⟩

sol·i·tude \'sä-lə-,tüd, -,tyüd\ n 1 : the state of being alone : SECLUSION ⟨worked in ~⟩ 2 : a lonely place

soln abbr solution

¹**so·lo** \'sō-lō\ n, pl **solos** [It, fr. solo alone, fr. L solus] 1 : a piece of music for a single voice or instrument with or without accompaniment 2 : an action in which there is only one performer — **solo** adj or vb — **so·lo·ist** n

²**solo** adv : without a companion : ALONE

so·lon \'sō-lən\ n 1 : a wise and skillful lawgiver 2 : a member of a legislative body

sol·stice \'säl-stəs, 'sōl-\ n [ME, fr. L solstitium, fr. sol sun + -stit-, -stes standing] : the time of the year when the sun is farthest north of the equator (**summer solstice**) about June 22 or farthest south (**winter solstice**) about Dec. 22 — **sol·sti·tial** \säl-'sti-shəl, sōl-\ adj

sol·u·ble \'säl-yə-bəl\ adj 1 : capable of being dissolved in or as if in a liquid 2 : capable of being solved or explained — **sol·u·bil·i·ty** \,säl-yə-'bi-lə-tē\ n

sol·ute \'säl-,yüt\ n : a dissolved substance

so·lu·tion \sə-'lü-shən\ n 1 : an action or process of solving a problem; also : an answer to a problem 2 : an act or the process by which one substance is homogeneously mixed with another usu. liquid substance; also : a mixture thus formed

solve \'sälv\ vb **solved; solv·ing** : to find the answer to or a solution for — **solv·able** adj

sol·ven·cy \'säl-vən-sē\ n : the condition of being solvent

¹**sol·vent** \-vənt\ adj 1 : able or sufficient to pay all legal debts 2 : dissolving or able to dissolve

²**solvent** n : a usu. liquid substance capable of dissolving or dispersing one or more other substances

som \'sōm\ n, pl **som** 1 — see MONEY table 2 : the sum of Uzbekistan

so·mat·ic \sō-'ma-tik\ adj : of, relating to, or affecting the body in contrast to the mind or the sex cells and their precursors

som·ber or **som·bre** \'säm-bər\ adj 1 : DARK, GLOOMY 2 : GRAVE, MELANCHOLY ⟨a ~ mood⟩ — **som·ber·ly** adv

som·bre·ro \səm-'brer-ō\ n, pl **-ros** [Sp, fr. sombra shade] : a broad-brimmed felt hat worn esp. in the Southwest and in Mexico

¹**some** \'səm\ adj 1 : one unspecified ⟨~ man called⟩ 2 : an unspecified or indefinite number of ⟨~ berries are ripe⟩ 3 : at least a few or a little ⟨~ years ago⟩

²**some** pron : a certain number or amount ⟨~ of the berries are ripe⟩ ⟨~ of it is missing⟩

¹**-some** \səm\ adj suffix : characterized by a (specified) thing, quality, state, or action ⟨awesome⟩ ⟨burdensome⟩

²**-some** n suffix : a group of (so many) members and esp. persons ⟨foursome⟩

¹**some·body** \'səm-,bä-dē, -bə-\ pron : some person

²**somebody** n : a person of importance

some·day \'səm-,dā\ adv : at some future time

some·how \-,haú\ adv : by some means

some·one \-(,)wən\ pron : some person

som·er·sault also **sum·mer·sault** \'sə-mər-,sólt\ n [MF sombresaut leap, ultim. fr. L super over + saltus leap, fr. salire to jump] : a leap or roll in which a person turns heels over head — **somersault** vb

som·er·set \-,set\ n or vb : SOMERSAULT

some·thing \'səm-thiŋ\ pron : some undetermined or unspecified thing

some·time \-,tīm\ adv 1 : at a future time 2 : at an unknown or unnamed time

some·times \-,tīmz\ adv : OCCASIONALLY

¹**some·what** \-,hwät, -,hwət\ pron : SOMETHING

²**somewhat** adv : in some degree

some·where \-,hwer\ adv : in, at, or to an unknown or unnamed place

som·nam·bu·lism \säm-'nam-byə-,li-zəm\ n : performance of motor acts (as walking) during sleep; also : an abnormal condition of sleep characterized by this — **som·nam·bu·list** \-list\ n

som·no·lent \'säm-nə-lənt\ adj : SLEEPY, DROWSY — **som·no·lence** \-ləns\ n

so·mo·ni \sō-mō-'nē\ n, pl **somoni** — see MONEY table

son \'sən\ n 1 : a male offspring or descendant 2 cap : Jesus Christ 3 : a person deriving from a particular source (as a country, race, or school)

so·nar \'sō-,när\ n [sound navigation ranging] : a method or device for detecting and locating submerged objects (as submarines) by sound waves

so·na·ta \sə-'nä-tə\ n [It] : an instrumental composition with three or four movements differing in rhythm and mood but related in key

son·a·ti·na \,sä-nə-'tē-nə\ n [It, dim. of sonata] : a short usu. simplified sonata

song \'sóŋ\ n 1 : vocal music; also : a short composition of words and music 2 : poetic composition 3 : a distinctive or characteristic sound (as of a bird) 4 : a small amount ⟨sold for a ~⟩

song·bird \'sóŋ-,bərd\ n : a bird that utters a series of musical tones

Song of Sol·o·mon \-'sä-lə-mən\ — see BIBLE table

Song of Songs — see BIBLE table

song·ster \'sóŋ-stər\ n : one that sings

song·stress \-strəs\ n : a girl or woman who is a singer

son·ic \'sä-nik\ adj : of or relating to sound waves or the speed of sound

sonic boom n : an explosive sound produced by an aircraft traveling at supersonic speed

son–in–law \'sən-ən-,lò\ n, pl **sons–in–law** : the husband of one's daughter or son

son·net \'sä-nət\ n : a poem of 14 lines usu. in iambic pentameter with a definite rhyme scheme

son of a gun n, pl **sons of guns** : an offensive or disagreeable person

so·no·rous \sə-'nór-əs, 'sä-nə-rəs\ adj 1 : giving out sound when struck 2 : loud, deep, or rich in sound : RESONANT ⟨a ~ voice⟩ 3 : high-sounding : IMPRESSIVE — **so·nor·i·ty** \sə-'nór-ə-tē\ n

soon \'sün\ adv 1 : before long 2 : PROMPTLY, QUICKLY 3 archaic : EARLY 4 : WILLINGLY, READILY

soot \'sút, 'sət, 'süt\ n : a fine black powder consisting chiefly of carbon that is formed when something burns and that colors smoke — **sooty** adj

sooth \'süth\ n, archaic : TRUTH

soothe \'süth\ vb **soothed; sooth·ing** 1 : to please by flattery or attention 2 : RELIEVE, ALLEVIATE ⟨~ a

burn〉 3 : to calm down : COMFORT 〈~ a child〉 —
sooth·er n — **sooth·ing·ly** adv
sooth·say·er \'süth-,sā-ər\ n : one who foretells events —
sooth·say·ing n
¹sop \'säp\ n : a conciliatory bribe, gift, or concession
²sop vb sopped; sop·ping 1 : to steep or dip in or as if
in a liquid 2 : to wet thoroughly : SOAK; also : to mop
up (a liquid)
SOP abbr standard operating procedure; standing operating procedure
soph abbr sophomore
soph·ism \'sä-,fi-zəm\ n 1 : an argument correct in form
but embodying a subtle fallacy 2 : SOPHISTRY
soph·ist \'sä-fist\ n : PHILOSOPHER; esp : a captious or
fallacious reasoner
so·phis·tic \sä-'fis-tik, sə-\ or **so·phis·ti·cal** \-ti-kəl\ adj : of
or characteristic of sophists or sophistry ♦ **Synonyms**
FALLACIOUS, ILLOGICAL, UNREASONABLE, SPECIOUS
so·phis·ti·cat·ed \sə-'fis-tə-,kā-təd\ adj 1 : COMPLEX 〈~
instruments〉 2 : made worldly-wise by wide experience
3 : intellectually appealing 〈a ~ novel〉 — **so·phis-
ti·ca·tion** \-,fis-tə-'kā-shən\ n
soph·ist·ry \'sä-fə-strē\ n : subtly deceptive reasoning or
argument
soph·o·more \'säf-,mòr, 'sä-fə-\ n : a student in the second year of high school or college
soph·o·mor·ic \,säf-'mòr-ik, ,sä-fə-\ adj 1 : being over-
confident of knowledge but poorly informed and immature 〈~ reasoning〉 2 : of, relating to, or characteristic
of a sophomore 〈~ humor〉
So·pho·ni·as \,sä-fə-'nī-əs, ,sō-\ n : ZEPHANIAH
sop·o·rif·ic \,sä-pə-'ri-fik\ adj 1 : causing sleep or drowsiness 2 : LETHARGIC
so·pra·no \sə-'pra-nō, -'prä-\ n, pl -nos [It, fr. sopra
above, fr. L supra] 1 : the highest singing voice; also
: a singer with this voice 2 : the highest part in a 4-part
chorus — **soprano** adj
sor·bet \sòr-'bā\ n : a usu. fruit-flavored ice served for
dessert or between courses as a palate refresher
sor·cery \'sòr-sə-rē\ n [ME sorcerie, fr. AF, fr. sorcer sorcerer, fr. ML sortiarius, fr. L sort-, sors chance, lot] : the
use of magic : WITCHCRAFT — **sor·cer·er** \-rər\ n —
sor·cer·ess \-rəs\ n
sor·did \'sòr-dəd\ adj 1 : marked by baseness or gross-
ness : VILE 2 : DIRTY, SQUALID 〈~ living conditions〉
— **sor·did·ly** adv — **sor·did·ness** n
¹sore \'sòr\ adj sor·er; sor·est 1 : causing pain or distress 〈a ~ bruise〉 2 : painfully sensitive 〈~ muscles〉
3 : SEVERE, INTENSE 4 : IRRITATED, ANGRY — **sore·ly**
adv — **sore·ness** n
²sore n 1 : a sore spot on the body; esp : one (as an ulcer)
with the tissues broken and usu. infected 2 : a source of
pain or vexation
sore·head \'sòr-,hed\ n : a person easily angered and discontented
sore throat n : painful throat due to inflammation of the
fauces and pharynx
sor·ghum \'sòr-gəm\ n : a tall variable Old World tropical
grass grown widely for its edible seed, for forage, or for
its sweet juice which yields a syrup
so·ror·i·ty \sə-'ròr-ə-tē\ n, pl -ties [ML sororitas sister-
hood, fr. L soror sister] : a club or organization usu. of
female students for social purposes
¹sor·rel \'sòr-əl\ n : a brownish orange to light brown
color; also : a sorrel-colored animal (as a horse)
²sorrel n : any of various herbs having a sour juice
sor·row \'sär-ō\ n 1 : deep distress, sadness, or regret;
also : resultant unhappy or unpleasant state 2 : a cause
of grief or sadness 3 : a display of grief or sadness —
sorrow vb — **sor·row·ful** \-fəl\ adj — **sor·row·ful·ly**
\-f(ə-)lē\ adv
sor·ry \'sär-ē\ adj sor·ri·er; -est 1 : feeling sorrow, regret, or penitence 〈~ for yelling at her〉 2 : MOURN-
FUL, SAD 3 : causing sorrow, pity, or scorn : PITIFUL 〈a
~ lot of ragamuffins〉
¹sort \'sòrt\ n 1 : a group of persons or things that have
similar characteristics : CLASS 2 : QUALITY, NATURE 3
: an instance of sorting — **all sorts of** : many different
— **out of sorts** 1 : somewhat ill 2 : GROUCHY, IRRI-
TABLE
²sort vb 1 : to put in a certain place according to kind,

class, or nature 2 : to be in accord : AGREE 3 : SEARCH
〈~ through this mess〉 — **sort·er** n
sor·tie \'sòr-tē, sòr-'tē\ n 1 : a sudden issuing of troops
from a defensive position against the enemy 2 : one
mission or attack by one airplane
sort of adv : to a moderate degree
SOS \,es-(,)ō-'es\ n : a call or request for help or rescue
so–so \'sō-'sō\ adv or adj : PASSABLY
sot \'sät\ n : a habitual drunkard — **sot·tish** adj — **sot-
tish·ly** adv
souf·flé \sü-'flā\ n [F, fr. soufflé, pp. of souffler to blow,
puff up, fr. OF sufler, fr. L sufflare, fr. sub- up + flare
to blow] : a spongy dish made light in baking by stiffly
beaten egg whites
sough \'saù, 'səf\ vb : to make a moaning or sighing
sound — **sough** n
sought past and past part of SEEK
¹soul \'sōl\ n 1 : the immaterial essence of an individual
life 2 : the spiritual principle embodied in human beings or the universe 3 : an active or essential part 4
: the moral and emotional nature of human beings 5
: spiritual or moral force 6 : PERSON 〈a kindly ~〉 7
: a strong, positive feeling (as of intense sensitivity and
emotional fervor) conveyed esp. by African American
performers 8 : SOUL MUSIC — **souled** \'sōld\ adj —
soul·less \'sōl-ləs\ adj
²soul adj 1 : of, relating to, or characteristic of African
Americans or their culture 〈~ food〉 2 : designed for
or controlled by African Americans 〈~ radio stations〉
soul brother n : an African American male
soul·ful \'sōl-fəl\ adj : full of or expressing deep feeling
〈a ~ ballad〉 — **soul·ful·ly** adv
soul music n : music that is closely related to rhythm
and blues and characterized by intensity of feeling
¹sound \'saùnd\ adj 1 : not diseased or sickly 2 : free
from flaw or defect 〈a ~ structure〉 3 : FIRM, STRONG
4 : free from error or fallacy : RIGHT 〈~ logic〉 5 : LE-
GAL, VALID 6 : THOROUGH 7 : UNDISTURBED 〈~
sleep〉 8 : showing good judgment 〈~ reasoning〉 —
sound·ly adv — **sound·ness** n
²sound n 1 : the sensation of hearing; also : mechanical energy transmitted by longitudinal pressure waves
(sound waves) (as in air) that is the stimulus to hearing
2 : something heard : NOISE, TONE; also : hearing distance : EARSHOT 3 : a musical style 〈the band's ~〉 —
sound·less adj — **sound·less·ly** adv
³sound vb 1 : to make or cause to make a sound 2 : to
order or proclaim by a sound 〈~ the alarm〉 3 : to
convey a certain impression : SEEM 〈that ~s like fun〉
4 : to examine the condition of by causing to give out
sounds — **sound·able** \'saùn-də-bəl\ adj
⁴sound n : a long passage of water wider than a strait often connecting two larger bodies of water
⁵sound vb 1 : to measure the depth of (water) esp. by a
weighted line dropped from the surface : FATHOM 2
: PROBE 3 : to dive down suddenly 〈the hooked fish
~ed〉 — **sound·ing** n
sound bite n : a brief recorded statement broadcast esp.
on a news program — **sound–bite** adj
sound card n : a circuit board in a computer system designed to produce or reproduce sound
sound·er \'saùn-dər\ n : one that sounds; esp : a device
for making soundings
sound·proof \'saùn(d)-,prüf\ vb : to insulate so as to obstruct the passage of sound — **soundproof** adj
sound·stage \'saùnd-,stāj\ n : the part of a motion-picture studio in which a production is filmed
sound·track \'saùn(d)-,trak\ n : music recorded to accompany a film or videotape
soup \'süp\ n 1 : a liquid food with stock as its base and
often containing pieces of solid food 2 : something having the consistency of soup 3 : an unfortunate predicament 〈in the ~〉
soup·çon \süp-'sōⁿ\ n [F, lit., suspicion] : a little bit
〈a ~ of garlic〉
soup up vb : to increase the power of — **souped–up**
\'süpt-'əp\ adj
soupy \'sü-pē\ adj soup·i·er; -est 1 : having the consistency of soup 2 : densely foggy or cloudy
¹sour \'saù(-ə)r\ adj 1 : having an acid or tart taste 〈~
as vinegar〉 2 : SPOILED, PUTRID 〈a ~ odor〉 3 : UN-

PLEASANT, DISAGREEABLE ⟨∼ disposition⟩ — **sour·ish** *adj* — **sour·ly** *adv* — **sour·ness** *n*

²**sour** *vb* : to become or make sour

source \'sȯrs\ *n* 1 : ORIGIN, BEGINNING 2 : a supplier of information 3 : the beginning of a stream of water

source code *n* : a computer program in its original programming language and before translation (as by a compiler)

¹**souse** \'saus\ *vb* **soused; sous·ing** 1 : PICKLE 2 : to plunge into a liquid 3 : DRENCH 4 : to make drunk

²**souse** *n* 1 : something (as pigs' feet) steeped in pickle 2 : a soaking in liquid 3 : DRUNKARD

¹**south** \'sauth\ *adv* : to or toward the south; *also* : into a state of decline

²**south** *adj* 1 : situated toward or at the south 2 : coming from the south

³**south** *n* 1 : the direction to the right of one facing east 2 : the compass point directly opposite to north 3 *cap* : regions or countries south of a specified or implied point; *esp* : the southeastern part of the U.S. — **south·er·ly** \'sə-thər-lē\ *adj or adv* — **south·ern** \'sə-thərn\ *adj* — **South·ern·er** *n* — **south·ern·most** \-ˌmōst\ *adj* — **south·ward** \'sauth-wərd\ *adv or adj* — **south·wards** \-wərdz\ *adv*

south·east \sau-'thēst, *naut* sau-'ēst\ *n* 1 : the general direction between south and east 2 : the compass point midway between south and east 3 *cap* : regions or countries southeast of a specified or implied point — **southeast** *adj or adv* — **south·east·er·ly** *adv or adj* — **south·east·ern** \-'ēs-tərn\ *adj*

south·paw \'sauth-ˌpȯ\ *n* : a left-handed person; *esp* : a left-handed baseball pitcher — **southpaw** *adj*

south pole *n, often cap S&P* : the southernmost point of the earth

south·west \sauth-'west, *naut* sau-'west\ *n* 1 : the general direction between south and west 2 : the compass point midway between south and west 3 *cap* : regions or countries southwest of a specified or implied point — **southwest** *adj or adv* — **south·west·er·ly** *adv or adj* — **south·west·ern** \-'wes-tərn\ *adj*

sou·ve·nir \ˌsü-və-'nir\ *n* [F] : something serving as a reminder

sou'·west·er \sau-'wes-tər\ *n* : a long waterproof coat worn at sea in stormy weather; *also* : a waterproof hat

¹**sov·er·eign** \'sä-vrən, -və-rən\ *n* 1 : one possessing the supreme power and authority in a state 2 : a gold coin of the United Kingdom

²**sovereign** *adj* 1 : EXCELLENT, FINE 2 : supreme in power or authority 3 : CHIEF, HIGHEST 4 : having independent authority ♦ **Synonyms** DOMINANT, PREDOMINANT, PARAMOUNT, PREPONDERANT

sov·er·eign·ty \-tē\ *n, pl* **-ties** 1 : supremacy in rule or power 2 : power to govern without external control 3 : the supreme political power in a state

so·vi·et \'sō-vē-ˌet, 'sä-, -ət\ *n* 1 : an elected governmental council in a Communist country 2 *pl, cap* : the people and esp. the leaders of the U.S.S.R. — **soviet** *adj, often cap* — **so·vi·et·ize** *vb, often cap*

¹**sow** \'sau\ *n* : an adult female swine

²**sow** \'sō\ *vb* **sowed; sown** \'sōn\ *or* **sowed; sow·ing** 1 : to plant seed for growing esp. by scattering 2 : to strew with seed 3 : to scatter abroad — **sow·er** \'sō-ər\ *n*

sow bug \'sau-\ *n* : WOOD LOUSE

sox *pl of* SOCK

soy \'sȯi\ *n* : a sauce made from soybeans fermented in brine

soy·bean \'sȯi-ˌbēn\ *n* : an Asian legume widely grown for forage and for its edible seeds that yield a valuable oil (**soybean oil**); *also* : its seed

sp *abbr* 1 special 2 species 3 specimen 4 spelling 5 spirit

Sp *abbr* Spain

SP *abbr* 1 shore patrol; shore patrolman 2 shore police 3 specialist

spa \'spä\ *n* [*Spa*, watering place in Belgium] 1 : a mineral spring; *also* : a resort with mineral springs 2 : a health and fitness facility 3 : a hot tub with a whirlpool device

¹**space** \'spās\ *n* 1 : a period of time 2 : some small measurable distance, area, or volume 3 : the limitless area in which all things exist and move 4 : an empty place 5

: the region beyond the earth's atmosphere 6 : a definite place (as a seat on a train or ship) 7 : the distance from others that a person needs for comfort

²**space** *vb* **spaced; spac·ing** : to place at intervals — **spac·er** *n*

space–age \'spās-ˌāj\ *adj* : of or relating to the age of space exploration

space·craft \-ˌkraft\ *n* : a vehicle for travel beyond the earth's atmosphere

space·flight \-ˌflīt\ *n* : flight beyond the earth's atmosphere

space heater *n* : a usu. portable device for heating a relatively small area

space·man \'spās-ˌman, -mən\ *n* : one who travels outside the earth's atmosphere

space out *vb* : to become distracted or inattentive

space·ship \-ˌship\ *n* : a vehicle used for space travel

space shuttle *n* : a reusable spacecraft designed to transport people and cargo between earth and space

space station *n* : a large artificial satellite serving as a base (as for scientific observation)

space suit *n* : a suit equipped to make life in space possible for its wearer

space walk *n* : a period of activity outside a spacecraft by an astronaut in space — **space·walk** \'spās-ˌwȯk\ *vb* — **space·walk·er** *n*

spa·cious \'spā-shəs\ *adj* : very large in extent : ROOMY ♦ **Synonyms** COMMODIOUS, CAPACIOUS, AMPLE — **spa·cious·ly** *adv* — **spa·cious·ness** *n*

¹**spade** \'spād\ *n* : a shovel with a blade for digging — **spade·ful** *n*

²**spade** *vb* **spad·ed; spad·ing** : to dig with a spade — **spad·er** *n*

³**spade** *n* : any of a suit of playing cards marked with a black figure resembling an inverted heart with a short stem at the bottom

spa·dix \'spā-diks\ *n, pl* **spa·di·ces** \'spā-də-ˌsēz\ : a floral spike with a fleshy or succulent axis usu. enclosed in a spathe

spa·ghet·ti \spə-'ge-tē\ *n* [It, fr. pl. of *spaghetto*, dim. of *spago* cord, string] : pasta made in thin solid strings

spam \'spam\ *n* : unsolicited usu. commercial e-mail sent to a large number of addresses — **spam** *vb*

¹**span** \'span\ *n* 1 : an English unit of length equal to nine inches (about 23 centimeters) 2 : a limited portion of time 3 : the spread (as of an arch) from one support to another

²**span** *vb* **spanned; span·ning** 1 : MEASURE 2 : to extend across

³**span** *n* : a pair of animals (as mules) driven together

Span *abbr* Spanish

span·dex \'span-ˌdeks\ *n* : any of various elastic synthetic textile fibers

span·gle \'spaŋ-gəl\ *n* : a small disk of shining metal or plastic used esp. on a dress for ornament — **spangle** *vb*

Span·glish \'spaŋ-glish\ *n* : Spanish with many English words included; *also* : a combination of Spanish and English

Span·iard \'span-yərd\ *n* : a native or inhabitant of Spain

span·iel \'span-yəl\ *n* [ME *spaynel, spaniell*, fr. AF *espainnel*, alter. of *espaignol*, Spaniard] : a dog of any of several breeds of mostly small and short-legged dogs usu. with long wavy hair and large drooping ears

Span·ish \'spa-nish\ *n* 1 : the chief language of Spain and of the countries colonized by the Spanish 2 **Spanish** *pl* : the people of Spain — **Spanish** *adj*

Spanish American *n* : a resident of the U.S. whose native language is Spanish; *also* : a native or inhabitant of one of the countries of America in which Spanish is the national language — **Spanish–American** *adj*

Spanish fly *n* : a toxic preparation of dried green European beetles that causes the skin to blister and is thought to be an aphrodisiac

Spanish moss *n* : a plant related to the pineapple that grows in pendent tufts of grayish green filaments on trees from the southern U.S. to Argentina

Spanish onion *n* : a large mild-flavored onion

spank \'spaŋk\ *vb* : to hit on the buttocks with the open hand — **spank** *n*

spank·ing \'spaŋ-kiŋ\ *adj* : BRISK, LIVELY ⟨∼ breeze⟩ — **spanking** *adv*

¹**spar** \'spär\ *n* : a rounded wood or metal piece (as a mast, yard, boom, or gaff) for supporting sail rigging

²**spar** *vb* **sparred; spar·ring** : to box for practice without serious hitting; *also* : SKIRMISH, WRANGLE

¹**spare** \'sper\ *vb* **spared; spar·ing 1** : to refrain from punishing or injuring : show mercy to **2** : to exempt from something **3** : to get along without ⟨can you ∼ ten dollars?⟩ **4** : to use frugally or rarely

²**spare** *adj* **spar·er; spar·est 1** : held in reserve **2** : SUPERFLUOUS **3** : not liberal or profuse **4** : LEAN, THIN **5** : SCANTY ✦ *Synonyms* MEAGER, SPARSE, SKIMPY, EXIGUOUS, SCANT — **spare·ness** *n*

³**spare** *n* **1** : a duplicate kept in reserve; *esp* : a spare tire **2** : the knocking down of all the bowling pins with the first two balls

sparing *adj* : SAVING, FRUGAL ✦ *Synonyms* THRIFTY, ECONOMICAL, PROVIDENT — **spar·ing·ly** *adv*

¹**spark** \'spärk\ *n* **1** : a small particle of a burning substance or a hot glowing particle struck from a mass (as by steel on flint) **2** : a short bright flash of electricity between two points **3** : SPARKLE **4** : a particle capable of being kindled or developed : GERM

²**spark** *vb* **1** : to emit or produce sparks **2** : to stir to activity : INCITE

³**spark** *vb* : WOO, COURT

¹**spar·kle** \'spär-kəl\ *vb* **spar·kled; spar·kling 1** : FLASH, GLEAM **2** : to perform brilliantly **3** : EFFERVESCE ⟨*sparkling* wine⟩ — **spar·kler** *n*

²**sparkle** *n* **1** : GLEAM **2** : ANIMATION

spark plug *n* : a device that produces a spark to ignite the fuel mixture in an engine cylinder

spark plug

spar·row \'spa-rō\ *n* : any of several small dull-colored singing birds

sparse \'spärs\ *adj* **spars·er; spars·est** : thinly scattered : SCANTY ⟨∼ vegetation⟩ ✦ *Synonyms* MEAGER, SPARE, SKIMPY, EXIGUOUS, SCANT — **sparse·ly** *adv* — **sparse·ness** *n*

¹**Spar·tan** \'spär-tᵊn\ *n* **1** : a native or inhabitant of ancient Sparta **2** : a person of great courage and self-discipline

²**Spartan** *adj* **1** : of or relating to Sparta or Spartans **2** *often not cap* : marked by simplicity, frugality, or avoidance of luxury and comfort ⟨a ∼ room⟩

spasm \'spa-zəm\ *n* **1** : an involuntary and abnormal muscular contraction **2** : a sudden, violent, and temporary effort, emotion, or sensation — **spas·mod·ic** \spaz-'mä-dik\ *adj* — **spas·mod·i·cal·ly** \-di-k(ə-)lē\ *adv*

spas·tic \'spas-tik\ *adj* : of, relating to, marked by, or affected with muscular spasm ⟨∼ paralysis⟩ — **spastic** *n*

¹**spat** \'spat\ *past and past part of* SPIT

²**spat** *n*, *pl* **spat** *or* **spats** : a young bivalve mollusk (as an oyster)

³**spat** *n* : a gaiter covering instep and ankle

⁴**spat** *n* : a brief petty quarrel : DISPUTE

⁵**spat** *vb* **spat·ted; spat·ting** : to quarrel briefly

spate \'spāt\ *n* : a sudden outburst

spathe \'spāth\ *n* : a sheathing bract or pair of bracts enclosing an inflorescence (as of the calla lily) and esp. a spadix on the same axis

spa·tial \'spā-shəl\ *adj* : of or relating to space or to the facility to perceive objects in space — **spa·tial·ly** *adv*

spat·ter \'spa-tər\ *vb* **1** : to splash with drops of liquid ⟨clothes ∼ed with paint⟩ **2** : to sprinkle around — **spatter** *n*

spat·u·la \'spa-chə-lə\ *n* : a flexible knifelike implement for scooping, spreading, or mixing soft substances

spav·in \'spa-vən\ *n* : a bony enlargement of the hock of a horse — **spav·ined** \-vənd\ *adj*

¹**spawn** \'spȯn\ *vb* [ME, fr. AF *espandre* to spread out, shed, scatter, spawn, fr. L *expandere*, fr. *ex-* out + *pandere* to spread] **1** : to produce eggs or offspring esp. in large numbers **2** : GENERATE ⟨∼ed much protest⟩ — **spawn·er** *n*

²**spawn** *n* **1** : the eggs of water animals (as fishes or oysters) that lay many small eggs **2** : offspring esp. when produced in great numbers

spay \'spā\ *vb* **spayed; spay·ing** : to remove the ovaries of (a female animal)

SPCA *abbr* Society for the Prevention of Cruelty to Animals

SPCC *abbr* Society for the Prevention of Cruelty to Children

speak \'spēk\ *vb* **spoke** \'spōk\; **spo·ken** \'spō-kən\; **speak·ing 1** : to utter words **2** : to express orally **3** : to mention in speech or writing **4** : to address an audience **5** : to use or be able to use (a language) in talking — **to speak of** : worthy of mention ⟨no progress *to speak of*⟩

speak·easy \'spēk-ˌē-zē\ *n*, *pl* **-eas·ies** : an illicit drinking place

speak·er \'spē-kər\ *n* **1** : one that speaks **2** : the presiding officer of a deliberative assembly **3** : LOUDSPEAKER

¹**spear** \'spir\ *n* **1** : a long-shafted weapon with a sharp point for thrusting or throwing **2** : a sharp-pointed instrument with barbs used in spearing fish — **spear·man** \-mən\ *n*

²**spear** *vb* : to strike or pierce with or as if with a spear — **spear·er** *n*

³**spear** *n* : a usu. young blade, shoot, or sprout (as of asparagus)

spear·head \-ˌhed\ *n* : a leading force, element, or influence — **spearhead** *vb*

spear·mint \-ˌmint\ *n* : a common highly aromatic garden mint

¹**spec** *abbr* **1** special; specialist **2** specifically

²**spec** \'spek\ *n* : SPECIFICATION 2 — usu. used in pl.

spe·cial \'spe-shəl\ *adj* **1** : UNCOMMON, NOTEWORTHY **2** : particularly favored **3** : INDIVIDUAL, UNIQUE **4** : EXTRA, ADDITIONAL **5** : confined to or designed for a definite field of action, purpose, or occasion ⟨a ∼ assignment⟩ — **special** *n*

special delivery *n* : delivery of mail by messenger for an extra fee

special effects *n pl* : visual or sound effects introduced into a motion picture, video recording, or taped television production

Special Forces *n pl* : a branch of the army composed of soldiers specially trained in guerrilla warfare

spe·cial·ise *Brit var of* SPECIALIZE

spe·cial·ist \'spe-shə-list\ *n* **1** : a person who specializes in a particular branch of learning or activity **2** : a rank in the U.S. Army corresponding to that of corporal

spe·cial·ize \'spe-shə-ˌlīz\ *vb* **-ized; -iz·ing** : to concentrate one's efforts in a special activity or field; *also* : to change in an adaptive manner — **spe·cial·i·za·tion** \ˌspe-shə-lə-'zā-shən\ *n*

spe·cial·ly \'spe-shə-lē\ *adv* **1** : in a special manner **2** : for a special purpose : in particular

spe·cial·ty \'spe-shəl-tē\ *n*, *pl* **-ties 1** : a particular quality or detail **2** : a product of a special kind or of special excellence **3** : a skill or discipline in which one specializes ⟨the doctor's ∼ is dermatology⟩

spe·cie \'spē-shē, -sē\ *n* : money in coin

spe·cies \'spē-shēz, -sēz\ *n*, *pl* **spe·cies** [ME, fr. L, appearance, kind, species, fr. *specere* to look] **1** : SORT, KIND **2** : a category of biological classification ranking just below the genus or subgenus and comprising closely related organisms potentially able to breed with one another

specif *abbr* specific; specifically

¹**spe·cif·ic** \spi-'si-fik\ *adj* **1** : having a unique effect or influence or reacting in only one way or with only one thing ⟨∼ antibodies⟩ ⟨∼ enzymes⟩ **2** : DEFINITE, EXACT ⟨a ∼ agreement⟩ **3** : of, relating to, or constituting a species — **spe·cif·i·cal·ly** \-fi-k(ə-)lē\ *adv* — **spec·i·fic·i·ty** \ˌspe-sə-'fi-sə-tē\ *n*

²**specific** *n* : something specific : DETAIL, PARTICULAR — usu. used in pl.

spec·i·fi·ca·tion \ˌspe-sə-fə-'kā-shən\ *n* **1** : the act or process of specifying 2 : a description of work to be done and materials to be used (as in building) — usu. used in pl.

specific gravity *n* : the ratio of the density of a substance to the density of some substance (as water) taken as a standard when both densities are obtained by weighing in air

spec·i·fy \'spe-sə-ˌfī\ *vb* **-fied; -fy·ing** : to mention or name explicitly

spec·i·men \'spe-sə-mən\ *n* : an item or part typical of a group or whole

spe·cious \'spē-shəs\ *adj* : seeming to be genuine, correct, or beautiful but not really so ⟨~ reasoning⟩

speck \'spek\ *n* 1 : a small spot or blemish 2 : a small particle — **speck** *vb*

speck·le \'spe-kəl\ *n* : a little speck — **speckle** *vb*

specs \'speks\ *n pl* : GLASSES

spec·ta·cle \'spek-ti-kəl\ *n* 1 : an unusual or impressive public display 2 *pl* : GLASSES — **spec·ta·cled** \-kəld\ *adj*

spec·tac·u·lar \spek-'ta-kyə-lər\ *adj* : exciting to see : SENSATIONAL

spec·ta·tor \'spek-ˌtā-tər\ *n* : a person who looks on (as at a sports event) ◆ **Synonyms** OBSERVER, WITNESS, BYSTANDER, ONLOOKER, EYEWITNESS

spec·ter *or* **spec·tre** \'spek-tər\ *n* : a visible disembodied spirit : GHOST

spec·tral \'spek-trəl\ *adj* 1 : of, relating to, or resembling a specter 2 : of, relating to, or made by a spectrum

spec·tro·gram \'spek-trə-ˌgram\ *n* : a photograph, image, or diagram of a spectrum

spec·tro·graph \-ˌgraf\ *n* : an instrument for dispersing radiation into a spectrum and recording or mapping the spectrum — **spec·tro·graph·ic** \ˌspek-trə-'gra-fik\ *adj* — **spec·tro·graph·i·cal·ly** \-fi-k(ə-)lē\ *adv*

spec·trom·e·ter \spek-'trä-mə-tər\ *n* : an instrument for measuring spectra — **spec·tro·met·ric** \ˌspek-trə-'me-trik\ *adj* — **spec·trom·e·try** \spek-'trä-mə-trē\ *n*

spec·tro·scope \'spek-trə-ˌskōp\ *n* : an instrument that produces spectra esp. of visible electromagnetic radiation — **spec·tro·scop·ic** \ˌspek-trə-'skä-pik\ *adj* — **spec·tro·scop·i·cal·ly** \-pi-k(ə-)lē\ *adv* — **spec·tros·co·pist** \spek-'träs-kə-pist\ *n* — **spec·tros·co·py** \-pē\ *n*

spec·trum \'spek-trəm\ *n, pl* **spec·tra** \-trə\ *or* **spectrums** [NL, fr. L, appearance, fr. *specere* to look] 1 : a series of colors formed when a beam of white light is dispersed (as by a prism) so that its parts are arranged in the order of their wavelengths 2 : a series of radiations arranged in regular order 3 : a continuous sequence or range ⟨a wide ~ of political opinions⟩

spec·u·late \'spe-kyə-ˌlāt\ *vb* **-lat·ed; -lat·ing** [L *speculari* to spy out, examine, fr. *specula* lookout post, fr. *specere* to look, look at] 1 : to think or wonder about a subject 2 : to take a business risk in hope of gain ◆ **Synonyms** REASON, THINK, DELIBERATE, COGITATE — **spec·u·la·tion** \ˌspe-kyə-'lā-shən\ *n* — **spec·u·la·tive** \'spe-kyə-ˌlā-tiv\ *adj* — **spec·u·la·tive·ly** *adv* — **spec·u·la·tor** \-ˌlā-tər\ *n*

speech \'spēch\ *n* 1 : the act of speaking 2 : TALK, CONVERSATION 3 : a public talk or lecture 4 : LANGUAGE, DIALECT 5 : an individual manner of speaking 6 : the power of speaking — **speech·less** *adj*

¹speed \'spēd\ *n* 1 *archaic* : SUCCESS 2 : SWIFTNESS, RAPIDITY 3 : rate of motion or performance 4 : a transmission gear (as of a bicycle) 5 : METHAMPHETAMINE; *also* : a related drug ◆ **Synonyms** HASTE, HURRY, DISPATCH, CELERITY — **speed·i·ly** \'spē-də-lē\ *adv* — **speedy** *adj*

²speed *vb* **sped** \'sped\ *or* **speed·ed; speed·ing** 1 *archaic* : PROSPER; *also* : GET ALONG, FARE 2 : to go fast; *esp* : to go at an excessive or illegal speed 3 : to cause to go faster — **speed·er** *n*

speed·boat \-ˌbōt\ *n* : a fast motorboat

speed bump *n* : a low raised ridge across a roadway (as in a parking lot) to limit vehicle speed

speed of light *n* : a fundamental physical constant that is the speed of electromagnetic radiation propagation in a vacuum and has the value of 299,792,458 meters per second

speed·om·e·ter \spi-'dä-mə-tər\ *n* : an instrument for indicating speed

speed·up \'spēd-ˌəp\ *n* : ACCELERATION

speed·way \-ˌwā\ *n* : a racecourse for motor vehicles

speed·well \'spēd-ˌwel\ *n* : VERONICA

¹spell \'spel\ *vb* **spelled** \'speld, 'spelt\; **spell·ing** [ME, to signify, read by spelling out, fr. AF *espeleir*, of Gmc origin] 1 : to name, write, or print in order the letters of a word 2 : MEAN ⟨another drought may ~ famine⟩

²spell *n* [ME, talk, tale, fr. OE] 1 : a magic formula : INCANTATION 2 : a compelling influence ⟨under the ~ of a guru⟩

³spell *n* 1 : one's turn at work or duty 2 : a stretch of a specified kind of weather 3 : a period of bodily or mental distress or disorder : ATTACK ⟨a dizzy ~⟩

⁴spell *vb* **spelled** \'speld\; **spell·ing** : to take the place of for a time in work or duty : RELIEVE

spell·bind·er \-ˌbīn-dər\ *n* : a speaker of compelling eloquence; *also* : one that compels attention

spell·bound \-ˌbau̇nd\ *adj* : held by or as if by a spell : FASCINATED

spell·check·er \'spel-ˌche-kər\ *n* : a computer program that identifies possible misspellings in a block of text — **spell-check** \-ˌchek\ *vb*

spell·er \'spe-lər\ *n* 1 : one who spells words 2 : a book with exercises for teaching spelling

spelt \'spelt\ *chiefly Brit past and past part of* ¹SPELL

spe·lunk·er \spi-'ləŋ-kər, 'spē-ˌləŋ-kər\ *n* [L *spelunca* cave, fr. Gk *spēlynx*] : one who makes a hobby of exploring caves — **spe·lunk·ing** *n*

spend \'spend\ *vb* **spent** \'spent\; **spend·ing** 1 : to pay out : EXPEND 2 : WEAR OUT, EXHAUST; *also* : to consume wastefully 3 : to cause or permit to elapse : PASS — **spend·er** *n*

spend·thrift \'spend-ˌthrift\ *n* : one who spends wastefully or recklessly

spent \'spent\ *adj* : drained of energy

sperm \'spərm\ *n, pl* **sperm** *or* **sperms** 1 : SEMEN 2 : a male gamete

sper·ma·to·zo·on \(ˌ)spər-ˌma-tə-'zō-ˌän, -'zō-ən\ *n, pl* **-zoa** \-'zō-ə\ : a motile male gamete of an animal usu. with a rounded or elongated head and a long posterior flagellum

sperm cell *n* : SPERM 2

sper·mi·cide \'spər-mə-ˌsīd\ *n* : a preparation or substance used to kill sperm — **sper·mi·cid·al** \ˌspər-mə-'sī-dəl\ *adj*

sperm whale *n* : a large whale with a massive square-shaped head containing a fluid-filled cavity

sperm whale

spew \'spyü\ *vb* : VOMIT

SPF *abbr* sun protection factor

sp gr *abbr* specific gravity

sphag·num \'sfag-nəm\ *n* : any of a genus of atypical mosses that grow in wet acid areas where their remains become compacted with other plant debris to form peat; *also* : a mass of these mosses

sphere \'sfir\ *n* [ME *spere* globe, celestial sphere, fr. AF *espere*, fr. L *sphaera*, fr. Gk *sphaira*, lit., ball] 1 : a globe-shaped body : BALL 2 : a celestial body 3 : a solid figure so shaped that every point on its surface is an equal distance from the center 4 : range of action or influence — **spher·i·cal** \'sfir-i-kəl, 'sfer-\ *adj* — **spher·i·cal·ly** \-i-k(ə-)lē\ *adv*

spher·oid \'sfir-ˌoid, 'sfer-\ *n* : a figure similar to a sphere but not perfectly round — **sphe·roi·dal** \sfir-'oi-dəl\ *adj*

sphinc·ter \'sfiŋk-tər\ *n* : a muscular ring that closes a bodily opening

sphinx \'sfiŋks\ *n, pl* **sphinx·es** *or* **sphin·ges** \'sfin-ˌjēz\ 1 : a winged monster in Greek mythology having a woman's head and a lion's body and noted for killing anyone unable to answer its riddle 2 : an enigmatic or mysterious person 3 : an ancient Egyptian image having the body of a lion and the head of a man, ram, or hawk

spice \'spīs\ *n* 1 : any of various aromatic plant products (as pepper or nutmeg) used to season or flavor foods **2** : something that adds interest and relish — **spice** *vb* — **spicy** *adj*

spick–and–span *or* **spic–and–span** \,spik-ənd-'span\ *adj* : quite new; *also* : spotlessly clean

spic·ule \'spi-kyül\ *n* : a slender pointed body esp. of calcium or silica ⟨sponge ~s⟩

spi·der \'spī-dər\ *n* **1** : any of an order of arachnids that have a 2-part body, eight legs, and two or more pairs of abdominal organs for spinning threads of silk used esp. in making webs for catching prey **2** : a cast-iron frying pan — **spi·dery** *adj*

spider mite *n* : any of various small web-spinning mites that feed on and are pests of plants

spider plant *n* : a houseplant of the lily family having long green leaves usu. striped with white and producing tufts of small plants on long hanging stems

spi·der·web \'spī-dər-,web\ *n* : the web spun by a spider

spiel \'spēl\ *vb* : to talk in a fast, smooth, and usu. colorful manner — **spiel** *n*

spig·ot \'spi-gət, -kət\ *n* : FAUCET

¹spike \'spīk\ *n* **1** : a very large nail **2** : any of various pointed projections (as on the sole of a shoe to prevent slipping) — **spiky** *adj*

²spike *vb* **spiked**; **spik·ing** **1** : to fasten with spikes **2** : to put an end to : QUASH ⟨~ a rumor⟩ **3** : to pierce with or impale on a spike **4** : to add alcoholic liquor to (a drink)

³spike *n* **1** : an ear of grain **2** : a long cluster of usu. stemless flowers

¹spill \'spil\ *vb* **spilled** \'spild, 'spilt\ *also* **spilt** \'spilt\; **spill·ing** **1** : to cause or allow to fall, flow, or run out esp. unintentionally **2** : to cause (blood) to be lost by wounding **3** : to run out or over with resulting loss or waste **4** : to let out : DIVULGE — **spill·able** *adj*

²spill *n* **1** : an act of spilling; *also* : a fall from a horse or vehicle or an erect position **2** : something spilled

spill·way \-,wā\ *n* : a passage for surplus water to run over or around an obstruction (as a dam)

¹spin \'spin\ *vb* **spun** \'spən\; **spin·ning** **1** : to draw out (fiber) and twist into thread; *also* : to form (thread) by such means **2** : to form thread by extruding a sticky quickly hardening fluid; *also* : to construct from such thread ⟨spiders ~ their webs⟩ **3** : to produce slowly and by degrees ⟨~ a story⟩ **4** : TWIRL **5** : WHIRL, REEL ⟨my head is *spinning*⟩ **6** : to move rapidly along **7** : to present (as information) with a particular spin — **spin·ner** *n*

²spin *n* **1** : a rapid rotating motion **2** : an excursion in a wheeled vehicle **3** : a particular point of view, emphasis, or interpretation

spi·na bi·fi·da \,spī-nə-'bi-fə-də\ *n* : a birth defect in which the spinal column has a fissure

spin·ach \'spi-nich\ *n* : a dark green herb grown for its edible leaves

spi·nal \'spī-nᵊl\ *adj* : of or relating to the backbone or spinal cord — **spi·nal·ly** *adv*

spinal column *n* : BACKBONE 1

spinal cord *n* : the thick cord of nervous tissue that extends from the brain along the back in the cavity of the backbone and carries nerve impulses to and from the brain

spinal nerve *n* : any of the paired nerves which arise from the spinal cord and pass to various parts of the body and of which there are normally 31 pairs in human beings

spin control *n* : the act or practice of attempting to manipulate the way an event is interpreted

spin·dle \'spin-dᵊl\ *n* **1** : a round tapering stick or rod by which fibers are twisted in spinning **2** : a turned part of a piece of furniture ⟨the ~s of a chair⟩ **3** : a slender pin or rod which turns or on which something else turns

spin·dling \'spind-liŋ\ *adj* : SPINDLY

spin·dly \'spind-lē\ *adj* : being long or tall and thin and usu. weak

spin·drift \'spin-,drift\ *n* : spray blown from waves

spine \'spīn\ *n* **1** : BACKBONE **2** : a stiff sharp process esp. on a plant or animal **3** : the part of a book where the pages are attached — **spiny** *adj*

spi·nel \spə-'nel\ *n* : a hard crystalline mineral of variable color used as a gem

spine·less \'spīn-ləs\ *adj* **1** : having no spines, thorns, or prickles **2** : lacking a backbone **3** : lacking courage or determination ⟨a ~ politician⟩

spin·et \'spi-nət\ *n* **1** : an early harpsichord having a single keyboard and only one string for each note **2** : a small upright piano

spin·na·ker \'spi-ni-kər\ *n* : a large triangular sail set on a long light pole

spinning jen·ny \-'je-nē\ *n* : an early multiple-spindle machine for spinning wool or cotton

spinning wheel *n* : a small machine for spinning thread or yarn in which a large wheel drives a single spindle

spin–off \'spin-,öf\ *n* **1** : a usu. useful by-product **2** : something (as a TV show) derived from an earlier work — **spin off** *vb*

spin·ster \'spin-stər\ *n* : an unmarried woman past the common age for marrying — **spin·ster·hood** \-,hüd\ *n*

spiny lobster *n* : any of several edible crustaceans differing from the related lobsters in lacking the large front claws and in having a spiny carapace

¹spi·ral \'spī-rəl\ *adj* : winding or coiling around a center or axis and usu. getting closer to or farther away from it — **spi·ral·ly** *adv*

²spiral *n* **1** : something that has a spiral form; *also* : a single turn in a spiral object **2** : a continuously spreading and accelerating increase or decrease

³spiral *vb* **-raled** *or* **-ralled**; **-ral·ing** *or* **-ral·ling** **1** : to move and esp. to rise or fall in a spiral course **2** : to form into a spiral

spi·rant \'spī-rənt\ *n* : a consonant (as \f\, \s\, \sh\) uttered with decided friction of the breath against some part of the oral passage — **spirant** *adj*

spire \'spī(-ə)r\ *n* **1** : a slender tapering stalk (as of grass) **2** : a pointed tip (as of an antler) **3** : STEEPLE — **spiry** *adj*

spi·rea *or* **spi·raea** \spī-'rē-ə\ *n* : any of a genus of shrubs related to the roses with dense clusters of small usu. white or pink flowers

¹spir·it \'spir-ət\ *n* [ME, fr. AF or L; AF, fr. L *spiritus*, lit., breath, fr. *spirare* to blow, breathe] **1** : a life-giving force; *also* : the animating principle : SOUL **2** *cap* : HOLY SPIRIT **3** : SPECTER, GHOST **4** : PERSON ⟨a bold ~⟩ **5** : DISPOSITION, MOOD ⟨in good ~s⟩ **6** : VIVACITY, ARDOR **7** : essential or real meaning : INTENT **8** : distilled alcoholic liquor **9** : LOYALTY ⟨school ~⟩ — **spir·it·less** *adj*

²spirit *vb* : to carry off secretly or mysteriously

spir·it·ed \'spir-ə-təd\ *adj* : full of energy, animation, or courage

¹spir·i·tu·al \'spir-i-chəl, -chə-wəl\ *adj* **1** : of, relating to, consisting of, or affecting the spirit : INCORPOREAL ⟨~ needs⟩ **2** : of or relating to sacred matters **3** : ecclesiastical rather than lay or temporal — **spir·i·tu·al·i·ty** \,spir-i-chə-'wa-lə-tē\ *n* — **spir·i·tu·al·ize** \'spir-i-chə-,līz, -chə-wə-\ *vb* — **spir·i·tu·al·ly** *adv*

²spiritual *n* : a religious song originating among African Americans of the southern U.S.

spir·i·tu·al·ism \'spir-i-chə-,li-zəm, -chə-wə-\ *n* : a belief that spirits of the dead communicate with the living usu. through a medium — **spir·i·tu·al·ist** \-list\ *n*, *often cap* — **spir·i·tu·al·is·tic** \,spir-i-chə-'lis-tik, -chə-wə-\ *adj*

spir·i·tu·ous \'spir-i-chəs, -chə-wəs; 'spir-ə-təs\ *adj* : containing alcohol

spi·ro·chete *also* **spi·ro·chaete** \'spī-rə-,kēt\ *n* : any of an order of spirally undulating bacteria including those causing syphilis and Lyme disease

spirt *var of* SPURT

¹spit \'spit\ *n* **1** : a thin pointed rod for holding meat over a fire **2** : a point of land that runs out into the water

²spit *vb* **spit·ted**; **spit·ting** : to pierce with or as if with a spit

³spit *vb* **spit** *or* **spat** \'spat\; **spit·ting** **1** : to eject (saliva) from the mouth **2** : to express by or as if by spitting **3** : to rain or snow lightly

⁴spit *n* **1** : SALIVA **2** : perfect likeness ⟨~ and image of his father⟩

spit·ball \'spit-,böl\ *n* **1** : paper chewed and rolled into a ball to be thrown as a missile **2** : a baseball pitch delivered after the ball has been moistened with saliva or sweat

¹spite \'spīt\ *n* : ill will with a wish to annoy, anger, or frustrate : petty malice ♦ *Synonyms* MALIGNITY, SPLEEN, GRUDGE, MALEVOLENCE — **spite·ful** \-fəl\ *adj*

— **spite·ful·ly** adv — **spite·ful·ness** n — **in spite of** : in defiance or contempt of : NOTWITHSTANDING

²**spite** vb **spit·ed; spit·ing** : to treat maliciously : ANNOY, OFFEND

spit·tle \'spi-tᵊl\ n : SALIVA

spit·tle·bug \-,bəg\ n : any of a family of leaping insects with froth-secreting larvae that are related to aphids

spit·toon \spi-'tün\ n : a receptacle for spit

splash \'splash\ vb 1 : to dash a liquid about 2 : to scatter a liquid on : SPATTER 3 : to fall or strike with a splashing noise ◆ Synonyms SPRINKLE, BESPATTER, DOUSE, SPLATTER — **splash** n

splash·down \'splash-,daún\ n : the landing of a manned spacecraft in the ocean — **splash down** vb

splashy \'spla-shē\ adj **splash·i·er; -est** : conspicuously showy : OSTENTATIOUS

¹**splat·ter** \'spla-tər\ vb : SPATTER — **splatter** n

²**splatter** adj : extremely gory or violent ⟨a ~ movie⟩

¹**splay** \'splā\ vb : to spread outward or apart ⟨~ed out her fingers⟩ — **splay** n

²**splay** adj 1 : spread out : turned outward 2 : AWKWARD, CLUMSY

spleen \'splēn\ n 1 : a vascular organ located near the stomach in most vertebrates that is concerned esp. with the filtration and storage of blood, destruction of red blood cells, and production of lymphocytes 2 : SPITE, MALICE ◆ Synonyms MALIGNITY, GRUDGE, MALEVOLENCE, ILL WILL, SPITEFULNESS

splen·did \'splen-dəd\ adj [L splendidus, fr. splendēre to shine] 1 : SHINING, BRILLIANT 2 : SHOWY, GORGEOUS 3 : ILLUSTRIOUS 4 : EXCELLENT ⟨a ~ opportunity⟩ ◆ Synonyms RESPLENDENT, GLORIOUS, SUBLIME, SUPERB — **splen·did·ly** adv

splen·dor \'splen-dər\ n 1 : BRILLIANCE ⟨the ~ of the sun⟩ 2 : POMP, MAGNIFICENCE

splen·dour \'splen-dər\ chiefly Brit var of SPLENDOR

sple·net·ic \spli-'ne-tik\ adj : marked by bad temper or spite

splen·ic \'sple-nik\ adj : of, relating to, or located in the spleen

splice \'splīs\ vb **spliced; splic·ing** 1 : to unite (as two ropes) by weaving the strands together 2 : to unite (as two lengths of film) by connecting the ends together — **splice** n

splint \'splint\ n 1 : a thin strip of wood interwoven with others to make something (as a basket) 2 : material or a device used to protect and keep in place an injured body part (as a broken arm)

¹**splin·ter** \'splin-tər\ n : a thin piece of something split off lengthwise : SLIVER

²**splinter** vb : to split into splinters

split \'split\ vb **split; split·ting** 1 : to divide lengthwise or along a grain or seam 2 : to burst or break in pieces 3 : to divide into parts or sections 4 : LEAVE ⟨~ the party⟩ ◆ Synonyms REND, CLEAVE, RIP, TEAR — **split** n

split-lev·el \'split-'le-vəl\ n : a house divided so that the floor in one part is about halfway between two floors in the other

split personality n : SCHIZOPHRENIA; also : MULTIPLE PERSONALITY DISORDER

split–second \'split-'se-kənd\ adj 1 : occurring in a very brief time 2 : extremely precise ⟨~ timing⟩

split·ting adj : causing a piercing sensation ⟨a ~ headache⟩

splotch \'spläch\ n : BLOTCH

splurge \'splərj\ vb **splurged; splurg·ing** : to spend more than usual esp. on oneself — **splurge** n

splut·ter \'splə-tər\ n : SPUTTER — **splutter** vb

¹**spoil** \'spói(-ə)l\ n : PLUNDER ⟨~s of war⟩

²**spoil** vb **spoiled** \'spói(-ə)ld, 'spói(-ə)lt\ or **spoilt** \'spói(-ə)lt\; **spoil·ing** 1 : ROB, PILLAGE 2 : to damage seriously : RUIN 3 : to impair the quality or effect of 4 : to damage the disposition of by pampering; also : INDULGE, CODDLE 5 : DECAY, ROT 6 : to have an eager desire ⟨~ing for a fight⟩ ◆ Synonyms INJURE, HARM, HURT, MAR — **spoil·age** \'spói-lij\ n

spoil·er \'spói-lər\ n 1 : one that spoils 2 : a device (as on an airplane or automobile) used to disrupt airflow and decrease lift 3 : information about a movie or TV plot that can spoil a viewer's sense of surprise or suspense

spoil·sport \'spói(-ə)l-,spórt\ n : one who spoils the fun of others

¹**spoke** \'spōk\ past & archaic past part of SPEAK

²**spoke** n : any of the rods extending from the hub of a wheel to the rim

spo·ken \'spō-kən\ past part of SPEAK

spokes·man \'spōks-mən\ n : a person who speaks as the representative of another or others

spokes·mod·el \-,mä-dᵊl\ n : a model who is a spokesman or spokeswoman

spokes·per·son \-,pər-sən\ n : SPOKESMAN

spokes·wom·an \-,wù-mən\ n : a woman who speaks as the representative of another or others

spo·li·a·tion \,spō-lē-'ā-shən\ n : the act of plundering : the state of being plundered

¹**sponge** \'spənj\ n 1 : an elastic porous water-absorbing mass of fibers that forms the skeleton of various primitive sea animals; also : any of a phylum of chiefly marine sea animals that are the source of natural sponges 2 : a spongelike or porous mass or material — **spongy** \'spən-jē\ adj

²**sponge** vb **sponged; spong·ing** 1 : to bathe or wipe with a sponge 2 : to live at another's expense 3 : to gather sponges — **spong·er** n

sponge cake n : a light cake made without shortening

sponge rubber n : a cellular rubber resembling natural sponge

spon·sor \'spän-sər\ n [LL, fr. L, guarantor, surety, fr. spondēre to promise] 1 : one who takes the responsibility for some other person or thing : SURETY 2 : GODPARENT 3 : a business firm that pays the cost of a radio or television program usu. in return for advertising time during its course — **sponsor** vb — **spon·sor·ship** n

spon·ta·ne·ous \spän-'tā-nē-əs\ adj [LL spontaneus, fr. L sponte of one's free will, voluntarily] 1 : done or produced freely or naturally 2 : acting or taking place without external force or cause ◆ Synonyms IMPULSIVE, INSTINCTIVE, AUTOMATIC, UNPREMEDITATED — **spon·ta·ne·ity** \,spän-tə-'nē-ə-tē, -'nā-\ n — **spon·ta·ne·ous·ly** adv

spontaneous combustion n : a bursting into flame of material through heat produced within itself by chemical action (as oxidation)

spoof \'spüf\ vb 1 : DECEIVE, HOAX 2 : to make good-naturedly fun of ⟨the movie ~s horror films⟩ — **spoof** n

¹**spook** \'spük\ n 1 : GHOST, APPARITION 2 : SPY 2 — **spooky** adj

²**spook** vb : FRIGHTEN

¹**spool** \'spül\ n : a cylinder on which flexible material (as thread) is wound

²**spool** vb 1 : to wind on a spool 2 : to regulate data flow by means of a spooler

spool·er \'spü-lər\ n : a computer program or routine for regulating data flow

spoon \'spün\ n [ME, fr. OE spōn splinter, chip] 1 : an eating or cooking implement consisting of a small shallow bowl with a handle 2 : a metal piece used on a fishing line as a lure — **spoon** vb — **spoon·ful** n

spoon·bill \'spün-,bil\ n : any of several wading birds related to the ibises that have a bill with a broad flat tip

spoon–feed \-,fēd\ vb **-fed** \-,fed\; **-feed·ing** : to feed by means of a spoon

spoor \'spúr, 'spór\ n, pl **spoor** or **spoors** : a track, a trail, a scent, or droppings esp. of a wild animal

spo·rad·ic \spə-'ra-dik\ adj : occurring now and then ⟨~ outbreaks of disease⟩ ◆ Synonyms OCCASIONAL, RARE, SCARCE, INFREQUENT, UNCOMMON — **spo·rad·i·cal·ly** \-di-k(ə-)lē\ adv

spore \'spór\ n : a primitive usu. one-celled often environmentally resistant dormant or reproductive body produced by plants, fungi, and some microorganisms

¹**sport** \'spórt\ vb [ME, to divert, amuse, short for disporten, fr. AF desporter, to carry away, comfort, entertain, fr. des- (fr. L dis- apart) + porter to carry, fr. L portare] 1 : to amuse oneself : FROLIC 2 : SHOW OFF 1 ⟨~ing new shoes⟩ — **sport·ive** adj

²**sport** n 1 : a source of diversion : PASTIME 2 : physical activity engaged in for pleasure 3 : JEST 4 : MOCKERY ⟨make ~ of his efforts⟩ 5 : BUTT, LAUGHINGSTOCK 6 : one who accepts results cheerfully whether favorable or not 7 : an individual exhibiting marked devia-

tion from its normal type esp. as a result of mutation ◆ **Synonyms** PLAY, FROLIC, FUN, RECREATION — **sporty** *adj*

³sport *or* **sports** *adj* : of, relating to, or suitable for sport or casual wear ⟨∼ coats⟩

sport fish *n* : a fish noted for the sport it affords anglers

sports·cast \'spȯrts-ˌkast\ *n* : a broadcast dealing with sports events — **sports·cast·er** \-ˌkas-tər\ *n*

sports·man \'spȯrts-mən\ *n* **1** : a person who engages in sports (as in hunting or fishing) **2** : one who plays fairly and wins or loses gracefully — **sports·man·like** \-ˌlīk\ *adj* — **sports·man·ship** *n*

sports medicine *n* : a field of medicine dealing with the prevention and treatment of sports-related injuries

sports·wom·an \-ˌwu̇-mən\ *n* : a woman who engages in sports

sports·writ·er \-ˌrī-tər\ *n* : one who writes about sports esp. for a newspaper — **sports·writ·ing** *n*

sport–util·i·ty vehicle \'spȯrt-yü-'ti-lə-tē-\ *n* : SUV

¹spot \'spät\ *n* **1** : STAIN, BLEMISH **2** : a small part different (as in color) from the main part **3** : LOCATION, SITE — **spot·less** *adj* — **spot·less·ly** *adv* — **on the spot 1** : at the place of action **2** : in difficulty or danger

²spot *vb* **spot·ted; spot·ting 1** : to mark or disfigure with spots **2** : to pick out : RECOGNIZE, IDENTIFY

³spot *adj* **1** : being, done, or originating on the spot ⟨a ∼ broadcast⟩ **2** : paid upon delivery **3** : made at random or at a few key points ⟨a ∼ check⟩

spot–check \'spät-ˌchek\ *vb* : to make a spot check of

spot·light \-ˌlīt\ *n* **1** : a circle of brilliant light projected upon a particular area, person, or object (as on a stage); *also* : the device that produces this light **2** : public notice — **spotlight** *vb*

spot–on \'spät-'än\ *adj* : exactly correct ⟨a ∼ forecast⟩

spotted owl *n* : a rare large dark brown dark-eyed owl of humid old growth forests and thickly wooded canyons from British Columbia to southern California and central Mexico

spot·ter \'spä-tər\ *n* **1** : one that keeps watch : OBSERVER **2** : one that removes spots

spot·ty \'spä-tē\ *adj* **spot·ti·er; -est** : uneven in quality; *also* : sparsely distributed ⟨∼ attendance⟩

spou·sal \'spau̇-zəl, -səl\ *n* : MARRIAGE 2, WEDDING — usu. used in pl.

spouse \'spau̇s\ *n* : one's husband or wife — **spou·sal** \'spau̇-zəl, -səl\ *adj*

¹spout \'spau̇t\ *vb* **1** : to eject or issue forth forcibly and freely ⟨wells ∼*ing* oil⟩ **2** : to speak pompously

²spout *n* **1** : a pipe or hole through which liquid spouts **2** : a jet of liquid; *esp* : WATERSPOUT 2

spp *abbr* species (*pl*)

¹sprain \'sprān\ *n* : a sudden or severe twisting of a joint with stretching or tearing of ligaments; *also* : a sprained condition

²sprain *vb* : to subject to sprain

sprat \'sprat\ *n* : a small European fish related to the herring; *also* : SARDINE

sprawl \'sprȯl\ *vb* **1** : to lie or sit with limbs spread out awkwardly **2** : to spread out irregularly — **sprawl** *n*

¹spray \'sprā\ *n* : a usu. flowering branch; *also* : a decorative arrangement of flowers and foliage

²spray *n* **1** : liquid flying in small drops like water blown from a wave **2** : a jet of fine vapor (as from an atomizer) **3** : an instrument (as an atomizer) for scattering fine liquid

³spray *vb* **1** : to discharge spray on or into **2** : to scatter or let fall in a spray — **spray·er** *n*

spray can *n* : a pressurized container from which aerosols are sprayed

spray gun *n* : a device for spraying liquids (as paint or insecticide)

¹spread \'spred\ *vb* **spread; spread·ing 1** : to scatter over a surface **2** : to flatten out : open out **3** : to distribute over a period of time or among many persons **4** : to cover something with ⟨∼ rugs on the floor⟩ **5** : to prepare for a meal ⟨∼ a table⟩ **6** : to pass on from person to person **7** : to stretch, force, or push apart ⟨a bird ∼*ing* its wings⟩ — **spread·er** *n*

²spread *n* **1** : the act or process of spreading **2** : EXPANSE, EXTENT **3** : a prominent display in a periodical **4** : a food to be spread on bread or crackers **5** : a cloth cover for a bed **6** : distance between two points : GAP

spread·sheet \'spred-ˌshēt\ *n* : an accounting program for a computer

spree \'sprē\ *n* **1** : an unrestrained outburst ⟨buying ∼⟩; *also* : a drinking bout

sprig \'sprig\ *n* : a small shoot or twig

spright·ly \'sprīt-lē\ *adj* **spright·li·er; -est** : LIVELY, SPIRITED ⟨a ∼ musical⟩ ◆ **Synonyms** ANIMATED, VIVACIOUS, GAY — **spright·li·ness** *n*

¹spring \'sprin\ *vb* **sprang** \'spran\ *or* **sprung** \'sprən\; **sprung; spring·ing 1** : to move suddenly upward or forward **2** : to grow quickly ⟨weeds *sprang* up overnight⟩ **3** : to come from by birth or descent **4** : to move quickly by elastic force **5** : WARP **6** : to develop (a leak) through the seams **7** : to cause to close suddenly ⟨∼ a trap⟩ **8** : to make known suddenly ⟨∼ a surprise⟩ **9** : to make lame : STRAIN ⟨*sprang* a leg muscle⟩

²spring *n* **1** : a source of supply; *esp* : an issuing of water from the ground **2** : SOURCE, ORIGIN; *also* : MOTIVE **3** : the season between winter and summer **4** : an elastic body or device that recovers its original shape when it is released after being distorted **5** : the act or an instance of leaping up or forward **6** : RESILIENCE — **springy** *adj*

spring·board \'sprin-ˌbȯrd\ *n* : a springy board used in jumping or vaulting or for diving

spring fever *n* : a lazy or restless feeling often associated with the onset of spring

spring tide *n* : a tide of greater-than-average range that occurs at each new moon and full moon

spring·time \'sprin-ˌtīm\ *n* : the season of spring

¹sprin·kle \'sprin-kəl\ *vb* **sprin·kled; sprin·kling** : to scatter in small drops or particles — **sprin·kler** *n*

²sprinkle *n* : a light rainfall

sprin·kling *n* : SMATTERING

¹sprint \'sprint\ *vb* : to run at top speed esp. for a short distance — **sprint·er** *n*

²sprint *n* **1** : a short run at top speed **2** : a short distance race

sprite \'sprīt\ *n* **1** : GHOST, SPIRIT **2** : ELF, FAIRY

spritz \'sprits, 'shprits\ *vb* : SPRAY ⟨∼ the plants⟩ — **spritz** *n*

sprock·et \'sprä-kət\ *n* : a toothed wheel whose teeth engage the links of a chain

sprocket

¹sprout \'sprau̇t\ *vb* : to send out new growth ⟨∼*ing* seeds⟩

²sprout *n* : a usu. young and growing plant shoot (as from a seed)

¹spruce \'sprüs\ *vb* **spruced; spruc·ing** : to make or become spruce

²spruce *adj* **spruc·er; spruc·est** : neat and smart in appearance ◆ **Synonyms** STYLISH, FASHIONABLE, MODISH, DAPPER, NATTY

³spruce *n, pl* **spruc·es** *also* **spruce** : any of a genus of evergreen pyramid-shaped trees related to the pines and having soft light wood; *also* : the wood of a spruce

sprung *past and past part of* SPRING

spry \'sprī\ *adj* **spri·er** *or* **spry·er** \'sprī-ər\; **spri·est** *or* **spry·est** \'sprī-əst\ : NIMBLE, ACTIVE ⟨a ∼ 75-year-old⟩ ◆ **Synonyms** AGILE, BRISK, LIVELY, SPRIGHTLY

spud \'spəd\ *n* **1** : a sharp narrow spade **2** : POTATO

spume \'spyüm\ *n* : frothy matter on liquids : FOAM — **spumy** \'spyü-mē\ *adj*

spu·mo·ni *also* **spu·mo·ne** \spu̇-'mō-nē\ *n* [It *spumone*, fr. *spuma* foam] : ice cream in layers of different colors, flavors, and textures often with candied fruits and nuts

spun *past and past part of* SPIN

spun glass *n* : FIBERGLASS

spunk \'spəŋk\ *n* [fr. *spunk* tinder, fr. ScGael *spong* sponge, tinder, fr. Middle Irish *spongc,* fr. L *spongia* sponge] : PLUCK, COURAGE — **spunky** *adj*

¹**spur** \'spər\ *n* 1 : a pointed device fastened to a rider's boot and used to urge on a horse 2 : something that urges to action 3 : a stiff sharp spine (as on the leg of a cock); *also* : a hollow projecting appendage of a flower (as a columbine) 4 : a ridge extending sideways from a mountain 5 : a branch of railroad track extending from the main line ♦ *Synonyms* GOAD, MOTIVE, IMPULSE, INCENTIVE, INDUCEMENT — **spurred** \'spərd\ *adj* — **on the spur of the moment** : on hasty impulse

²**spur** *vb* **spurred; spur·ring** 1 : to urge a horse on with spurs 2 : INCITE

spurge \'spərj\ *n* : any of a family of herbs and woody plants with a bitter milky juice

spu·ri·ous \'spyur-ē-əs\ *adj* [LL *spurius* false, fr. L, *spurius,* n., son of an unknown father] : not genuine : FALSE

spurn \'spərn\ *vb* 1 : to kick away or trample on 2 : to reject with disdain

¹**spurt** \'spərt\ *vb* : to gush out : SPOUT

²**spurt** *n* : a sudden gushing or spouting

³**spurt** *n* 1 : a sudden brief burst of effort, speed, or development 2 : a sharp increase of activity ⟨~ in sales⟩

⁴**spurt** *vb* : to make a spurt

sput·ter \'spə-tər\ *vb* 1 : to spit small scattered particles : SPLUTTER 2 : to utter words hastily or explosively in excitement or confusion 3 : to make small popping sounds — **sputter** *n*

spu·tum \'spyü-təm\ *n, pl* **spu·ta** \-tə\ [L] : material (as phlegm) that is spit out or coughed up esp. during illness

¹**spy** \'spī\ *vb* **spied; spy·ing** 1 : to watch or search for information secretly : act as a spy 2 : to get a momentary or quick glimpse of : SEE

²**spy** *n, pl* **spies** 1 : one who secretly watches others 2 : a secret agent who tries to get information for one country in the territory of an enemy

spy·glass \'spī-ˌglas\ *n* : a small telescope

sq *abbr* 1 squadron 2 square

squab \'skwäb\ *n, pl* **squabs** *or* **squab** : a young bird and esp. a pigeon

squab·ble \'skwä-bəl\ *n* : a noisy altercation : WRANGLE ♦ *Synonyms* QUARREL, SPAT, ROW, TIFF — **squabble** *vb*

squad \'skwäd\ *n* 1 : a small organized group of military personnel 2 : a small group engaged in a common effort

squad car *n* : a police car connected by two-way radio with headquarters

squad·ron \'skwä-drən\ *n* : any of several units of military organization

squal·id \'skwä-ləd\ *adj* 1 : filthy or degraded through neglect or poverty 2 : SORDID, DEBASED ⟨a ~ political ploy⟩ ♦ *Synonyms* NASTY, FOUL, DIRTY, GRUBBY

squall \'skwól\ *n* : a sudden violent gust of wind often with rain or snow — **squally** *adj*

squa·lor \'skwä-lər\ *n* : the quality or state of being squalid

squa·mous cell \'skwä-məs-\ *n* : a scalelike cell of the outer layers of the skin from which a type of carcinoma arises

squan·der \'skwän-dər\ *vb* : to spend wastefully or foolishly

¹**square** \'skwer\ *n* 1 : an instrument used to lay out or test right angles 2 : a rectangle with all four sides equal 3 : something square 4 : the product of a number multiplied by itself 5 : an area bounded by four streets 6 : an open area in a city where streets meet 7 : a highly conventional person

²**square** *adj* **squar·er; squar·est** 1 : having four equal sides and four right angles 2 : forming a right angle ⟨cut a ~ corner⟩ 3 : multiplied by itself : SQUARED ⟨x² is the symbol for x ~⟩ 4 : being a unit of square measure equal to a square each side of which measures one unit ⟨a ~ foot⟩ 5 : being of a specified length in each of two dimensions ⟨an area 10 feet ~⟩ 6 : exactly adjusted 7 : JUST, FAIR ⟨a ~ deal⟩ 8 : leaving no balance ⟨make accounts ~⟩ 9 : SUBSTANTIAL ⟨a ~ meal⟩ 10 : highly conservative or conventional — **square·ly** *adv*

³**square** *vb* **squared; squar·ing** 1 : to form with four equal sides and right angles or with flat surfaces ⟨~ a timber⟩ 2 : to multiply (a number) by itself 3 : CONFORM, AGREE 4 : BALANCE, SETTLE ⟨~ an account⟩

square dance *n* : a dance for four couples arranged to form a square

square measure *n* : a unit or system of units for measuring area — see METRIC SYSTEM table, WEIGHT table

square–rigged \'skwer-ˈrigd\ *adj* : having the chief sails extended on yards that are fastened to the masts horizontally and at their center

square–rig·ger \-ˌri-gər\ *n* : a square-rigged craft

square root *n* : either of the two numbers whose squares are equal to a given number ⟨the *square root* of 9 is +3 or –3⟩

¹**squash** \'skwäsh, 'skwósh\ *vb* 1 : to beat or press into a pulp or flat mass 2 : QUASH, SUPPRESS ⟨~ a revolt⟩

²**squash** *n* 1 : the impact of something soft and heavy; *also* : the sound of such impact 2 : a crushed mass 3 : a game played on a 4-wall court with a racket and rubber ball

³**squash** *n, pl* **squash·es** *or* **squash** : any of various fruits of plants of the gourd family that are used esp. as vegetables; *also* : a plant and esp. a vine bearing squashes

squash racquets *n* : SQUASH 3

¹**squat** \'skwät\ *vb* **squat·ted; squat·ting** [ME *squatten* to crush, crouch in hiding, fr. MF (dial. of Picardy) *esquatir, escuater,* fr. OF *es-* ex- + *quatir* to hide, fr. VL **coactire* to squeeze, alter. of L *coactare* to compel, fr. *cogere* to compel] 1 : to sit down upon the hams or heels 2 : to settle on land without right or title; *also* : to settle on public land with a view to acquiring title — **squat·ter** *n*

²**squat** *adj* **squat·ter; squat·test** : low to the ground; *also* : short and thick in stature ♦ *Synonyms* THICKSET, STOCKY, HEAVYSET, STUBBY

³**squat** *n* : the act or posture of squatting

squawk \'skwók\ *n* : a harsh loud cry; *also* : a noisy protest — **squawk** *vb*

squeak \'skwēk\ *vb* 1 : to utter or speak in a weak shrill tone 2 : to make a thin high-pitched sound ⟨the door ~s⟩ — **squeak** *n* — **squeaky** *adj*

¹**squeal** \'skwēl\ *vb* 1 : to make a shrill sound or cry 2 : to betray a secret or turn informer 3 : COMPLAIN, PROTEST

²**squeal** *n* : a shrill sharp cry or noise

squea·mish \'skwē-mish\ *adj* 1 : easily nauseated; *also* : NAUSEATED 2 : easily disgusted ♦ *Synonyms* FUSSY, NICE, DAINTY, FASTIDIOUS, PERSNICKETY — **squea·mish·ness** *n*

squee·gee \'skwē-jē\ *n* : a blade set crosswise on a handle and used for spreading or wiping liquid on, across, or off a surface — **squeegee** *vb*

¹**squeeze** \'skwēz\ *vb* **squeezed; squeez·ing** 1 : to exert pressure on the opposite sides or parts of 2 : to obtain by pressure ⟨~ juice from a lemon⟩ 3 : to force or move into a small space ⟨*squeezed* into her jeans⟩ — **squeez·er** *n*

²**squeeze** *n* 1 : an act of squeezing 2 : a quantity squeezed out

squeeze bottle *n* : a flexible plastic bottle that dispenses its contents when it is squeezed

squelch \'skwelch\ *vb* 1 : to suppress completely : CRUSH ⟨~ resistance⟩ 2 : to move in soft mud — **squelch** *n*

squib \'skwib\ *n* : a brief witty writing or speech

squid \'skwid\ *n, pl* **squid** *or* **squids** : any of an order of long-bodied sea mollusks having eight short arms and two longer tentacles and usu. a slender internal shell

squint \'skwint\ *vb* 1 : to look or aim obliquely 2 : to look or peer with the eyes partly closed ⟨~*ing* into the sun⟩ 3 : to be cross-eyed — **squint** *n or adj*

¹**squire** \'skwī(-ə)r\ *n* [ME *squier,* fr. AF *esquier,* fr. LL *scutarius,* fr. L *scutum* shield] 1 : an armor-bearer of a knight 2 : a man gallantly devoted to a lady 3 : a member of the British gentry ranking below a knight and above a gentleman; *also* : a prominent landowner 4 : a local magistrate

²**squire** *vb* **squired; squir·ing** : to attend as a squire or escort

squirm \'skwərm\ *vb* : to twist about like a worm : WRIGGLE

¹**squir·rel** \'skwər-əl\ *n, pl* **squirrels** *also* **squirrel** [ME *squirel,* fr. AF *escurel, esquirel,* fr. VL **scuriolus,* dim. of **scurius,* alter. of L *sciurus,* fr. Gk *skiouros,* prob. fr. *skia*

shadow + *oura* tail] : any of various rodents usu. with a long bushy tail and strong hind legs; *also* : the fur of a squirrel

²**squirrel** *vb* **-reled** *or* **-relled**; **-rel·ing** *or* **-rel·ling** : to store up for future use

¹**squirt** \'skwərt\ *vb* : to eject liquid in a thin spurt

²**squirt** *n* **1** : an instrument (as a syringe) for squirting **2** : a small forcible jet of liquid

¹**Sr** *abbr* **1** senior **2** sister

²**Sr** *symbol* strontium

SR *abbr* seaman recruit

¹**SRO** \ˌes-(ˌ)är-'ō\ *n* [*single-room* *o*ccupancy] : a house or apartment building in which low-income tenants live in single rooms

²**SRO** *abbr* standing room only

SS *abbr* **1** saints **2** Social Security **3** steamship **4** sworn statement

SSA *abbr* Social Security Administration

SSE *abbr* south-southeast

SSG *or* **SSgt** *abbr* staff sergeant

SSI *abbr* supplemental security income

SSM *abbr* staff sergeant major

SSN *abbr* Social Security Number

ssp *abbr* subspecies

SSR *abbr* Soviet Socialist Republic

SSS *abbr* Selective Service System

SST \ˌes-(ˌ)es-'tē\ *n* [*s*upersonic *t*ransport] : a supersonic passenger airplane

SSW *abbr* south-southwest

st *abbr* **1** stanza **2** state **3** stitch **4** stone **5** street

St *abbr* saint

ST *abbr* **1** short ton **2** standard time

-st — see -EST

sta *abbr* station; stationary

¹**stab** \'stab\ *n* **1** : a wound produced by a pointed weapon **2** : a quick thrust **3** : a brief attempt

²**stab** *vb* **stabbed**; **stab·bing** : to pierce or wound with or as if with a pointed weapon; *also* : THRUST, DRIVE

sta·bile \'stā-ˌbēl\ *n* : an abstract sculpture or construction similar to a mobile but made to be stationary

sta·bi·lize \'stā-bə-ˌlīz\ *vb* **-lized**; **-liz·ing 1** : to make stable **2** : to hold steady ⟨~ prices⟩ — **sta·bi·li·za·tion** \ˌstā-bə-lə-'zā-shən\ *n* — **sta·bi·liz·er** \'stā-bə-ˌlī-zər\ *n*

¹**sta·ble** \'stā-bəl\ *n* : a building in which domestic animals are sheltered and fed — **sta·ble·man** \-mən, -ˌman\ *n*

²**stable** *vb* **sta·bled**; **sta·bling** : to put or keep in a stable

³**stable** *adj* **sta·bler**; **sta·blest 1** : firmly established; *also* : mentally and emotionally healthy **2** : steady in purpose : CONSTANT **3** : DURABLE, ENDURING ⟨~ civilizations⟩ **4** : resistant to chemical or physical change ✦ *Synonyms* LASTING, PERMANENT, PERPETUAL, PERDURABLE — **sta·bil·i·ty** \stə-'bi-lə-tē\ *n*

stac·ca·to \stə-'kä-tō\ *adj or adv* [It] : cut short so as not to sound connected ⟨~ notes⟩

¹**stack** \'stak\ *n* **1** : a large pile (as of hay or grain) **2** : an orderly pile (as of poker chips) **3** : a large quantity **4** : a vertical pipe : SMOKESTACK **5** : a rack with shelves for storing books ⟨library ~s⟩

²**stack** *vb* **1** : to pile up **2** : to arrange (cards) secretly for cheating

stack up *vb* : MEASURE UP ⟨how do they *stack up* against the competition?⟩

sta·di·um \'stā-dē-əm\ *n, pl* **-dia** \-dē-ə\ *or* **-di·ums** : a structure with tiers of seats for spectators built around a field for sports events

¹**staff** \'staf\ *n, pl* **staffs** \'stafs, 'stavz\ *or* **staves** \'stavz, 'stävz\ **1** : a pole, stick, rod, or bar used for supporting, for measuring, or as a symbol of authority; *also* : CLUB, CUDGEL **2** : something that sustains ⟨bread is the ~ of life⟩ **3** : the five horizontal lines on which music is written **4** : a body of assistants to an executive **5** : a group of officers holding no command but having duties concerned with planning and managing

²**staff** *vb* : to supply with a staff or with workers ⟨~ a hotel⟩

staff·er \'sta-fər\ *n* : a member of a staff (as of a newspaper)

staff sergeant *n* : a noncommissioned officer ranking in the army next below a sergeant first class, in the air force next below a technical sergeant, and in the marine corps next below a gunnery sergeant

¹**stag** \'stag\ *n, pl* **stags** *or* **stag** : an adult male of various large deer

²**stag** *adj* : restricted to or intended for men ⟨a ~ party⟩ ⟨~ movies⟩

³**stag** *adv* : unaccompanied by a date

¹**stage** \'stāj\ *n* [ME, fr. AF *estage* abode, story of a building, stage, fr. VL **staticum*, fr. L *stare* to stand] **1** : a raised platform on which an orator may speak or a play may be presented **2** : the acting profession : THEATER **3** : the scene of a notable action or event **4** : a station or resting place on a traveled road **5** : STAGECOACH **6** : a degree of advance in an undertaking, process, or development **7** : a propulsion unit in a rocket — **stagy** \'stā-jē\ *adj*

²**stage** *vb* **staged**; **stag·ing** : to produce or perform on or as if on a stage ⟨~ a play⟩ — **stage·able** *adj*

stage·coach \'stāj-ˌkōch\ *n* : a horse-drawn coach that runs regularly between stations

stage manager *n* : one who supervises the physical aspects of a stage production

stag·fla·tion \ˌstag-'flā-shən\ *n* : inflation with stagnant economic activity and high unemployment

¹**stag·ger** \'sta-gər\ *vb* **1** : to reel from side to side : TOTTER **2** : to begin to doubt : WAVER **3** : to cause to reel or waver **4** : to arrange in overlapping or alternating positions or times ⟨~ working hours⟩ **5** : ASTONISH ⟨their indifference ~s me⟩ — **stag·ger·ing·ly** *adv*

²**stagger** *n* **1** *sing or pl* : an abnormal condition of domestic animals associated with damage to the central nervous system and marked by lack of coordination and a reeling unsteady gait **2** : a reeling or unsteady gait or stance

stag·ing \'stā-jiŋ\ *n* **1** : SCAFFOLDING **2** : the assembling of troops and matériel in transit in a particular place

staging post *n* : STOPOVER 2

stag·nant \'stag-nənt\ *adj* **1** : not flowing : MOTIONLESS ⟨~ water in a pond⟩ **2** : DULL, INACTIVE ⟨~ business⟩

stag·nate \'stag-ˌnāt\ *vb* **stag·nat·ed**; **stag·nat·ing** : to be or become stagnant — **stag·na·tion** \stag-'nā-shən\ *n*

staid \'stād\ *adj* : SOBER, SEDATE ✦ *Synonyms* GRAVE, SERIOUS, EARNEST

¹**stain** \'stān\ *vb* **1** : DISCOLOR, SOIL **2** : TAINT, CORRUPT **3** : DISGRACE **4** : to color (as wood, paper, or cloth) by processes affecting the material itself

²**stain** *n* **1** : a small soiled or discolored area **2** : a taint of guilt : STIGMA **3** : a preparation (as a dye or pigment) used in staining — **stain·less** *adj*

stainless steel *n* : steel alloyed with chromium that is highly resistant to stain, rust, and corrosion

stair \'ster\ *n* **1** : a series of steps or flights of steps for passing from one level to another — often used in pl. **2** : one step of a stairway

stair·case \-ˌkās\ *n* : a flight of steps with their supporting framework, casing, and balusters

stair·way \-ˌwā\ *n* : one or more flights of stairs with connecting landings

stair·well \-ˌwel\ *n* : a vertical shaft in which stairs are located

¹**stake** \'stāk\ *n* **1** : a pointed piece of material (as of wood) driven into the ground as a marker or a support **2** : a post to which a person is bound for death by burning; *also* : execution by burning at the stake **3** : something that is staked for gain or loss **4** : the prize in a contest

²**stake** *vb* **staked**; **stak·ing 1** : to mark the limits of by or as if by stakes **2** : to tie to a stake **3** : to support or secure with stakes **4** : BET, WAGER

stake·out \'stāk-ˌaut\ *n* : a surveillance by police (as of a suspected criminal)

¹staff 3

sta·lac·tite \stə-'lak-ˌtīt\ *n* [NL *stalactites,* fr. Gk *stalaktos* dripping, fr. *stalassein* to let drip] : an icicle-shaped deposit hanging from the roof or sides of a cavern

sta·lag·mite \stə-'lag-ˌmīt\ *n* [NL *stalagmites,* fr. Gk *stalagma* drop or *stalagmos* dripping, fr. *stalassein* to let drip] : a deposit resembling an inverted stalactite rising from the floor of a cavern

stale \'stāl\ *adj* **stal·er; stal·est** **1** : having lost good taste and quality from age ⟨~ bread⟩ **2** : used or heard so often as to be dull ⟨~ news⟩ **3** : not as strong or effective as before ⟨~ from lack of practice⟩ — **stale·ness** *n*

stale·mate \'stāl-ˌmāt\ *n* : a drawn contest : DEADLOCK — **stalemate** *vb*

¹stalk \'stȯk\ *n* : a plant stem; *also* : any slender usu. upright supporting or connecting part — **stalked** \'stȯkt\ *adj*

²stalk *vb* **1** : to pursue (game) stealthily **2** : to walk stiffly or haughtily **3** : to follow (a person) obsessively

¹stall \'stȯl\ *n* **1** : a compartment in a stable or barn for one animal **2** : a booth or counter where articles may be displayed for sale **3** : a seat in a church choir; *also* : a church pew **4** *chiefly Brit* : a front orchestra seat in a theater

²stall *vb* : to bring or come to a standstill unintentionally ⟨~ an engine⟩

³stall *n* : the condition of an airfoil or aircraft in which lift is lost and the airfoil or aircraft tends to drop

⁴stall *n* [alter. of *stale* lure] : a ruse to deceive or delay

⁵stall *vb* : to hold off, divert, or delay by evasion or deception

stal·lion \'stal-yən\ *n* : a male horse

stal·wart \'stȯl-wərt\ *adj* : STOUT, STRONG; *also* : BRAVE, VALIANT

sta·men \'stā-mən\ *n* : an organ of a flower that produces pollen

stam·i·na \'sta-mə-nə\ *n* [L, pl. of *stamen* warp, thread of life spun by the Fates] : VIGOR, ENDURANCE ⟨had the ~ to win⟩

sta·mi·nate \'stā-mə-nət, 'sta-mə-, -ˌnāt\ *adj* **1** : having or producing stamens **2** : having stamens but no pistils

stam·mer \'sta-mər\ *vb* : to hesitate or stumble in speaking — **stammer** *n* — **stam·mer·er** *n*

¹stamp \'stamp; *for 2 also* 'stämp *or* 'stȯmp\ *vb* **1** : to pound or crush with a heavy instrument **2** : to strike or beat with the bottom of the foot **3** : IMPRESS, IMPRINT ⟨~ "paid" on the bill⟩ **4** : to cut out or indent with a stamp or die **5** : to attach a postage stamp to

²stamp *n* **1** : a device or instrument for stamping **2** : the mark made by stamping; *also* : a distinctive mark or quality **3** : the act of stamping **4** : a stamped or printed paper affixed to show that a charge has been paid ⟨postage ~⟩

¹stam·pede \stam-'pēd\ *n* : a wild headlong rush or flight esp. of frightened animals

²stampede *vb* **stam·ped·ed; stam·ped·ing** **1** : to flee or cause to flee in panic **2** : to act or cause to act together suddenly and heedlessly

stance \'stans\ *n* : a way of standing

¹stanch \'stȯnch, 'stänch, 'stanch\ *or* **staunch** \'stȯnch, 'stänch\ *vb* : to check the flowing of (as blood); *also* : to cease flowing or bleeding

²stanch *var of* ²STAUNCH

stan·chion \'stan-chən\ *n* : an upright bar, post, or support

¹stand \'stand\ *vb* **stood** \'stu̇d\; **stand·ing** **1** : to take or be at rest in an upright or firm position **2** : to assume a specified position **3** : to remain stationary or unchanged **4** : to be steadfast **5** : to act in resistance ⟨~ against a foe⟩ **6** : to maintain a relative position or rank **7** : to gather slowly and remain ⟨tears *stood* in her eyes⟩ **8** : to set upright **9** : ENDURE, TOLERATE ⟨I won't ~ for that⟩ **10** : to submit to ⟨~ trial⟩ — **stand pat** : to oppose or resist change

²stand *n* **1** : an act of standing, staying, or resisting **2** : a stop made to give a performance **3** : POSITION, VIEWPOINT **4** : a place taken by a witness to testify in court **5** *pl* : tiered seats for spectators **6** : a raised platform (as for speakers) **7** : a structure for a small retail business **8** : a structure for supporting or holding something upright ⟨music ~⟩ **9** : a group of plants growing in a continuous area

stand–alone \'stan-də-ˌlōn\ *adj* : SELF-CONTAINED; *esp* : capable of operation independent of a computer system

¹stan·dard \'stan-dərd\ *n* **1** : a figure adopted as an emblem by a people **2** : the personal flag of a ruler; *also* : FLAG **3** : something set up as a rule for measuring or as a model to be followed **4** : an upright support ⟨lamp ~⟩

²standard *adj* **1** : used as or meeting a standard established by law or custom **2** : regularly and widely used ⟨a ~ practice⟩ **3** : well established by usage in speech or writing

stan·dard–bear·er \-ˌber-ər\ *n* : the leader of a cause

standard deviation *n* : a measure of dispersion in a set of data

stan·dard·ise *Brit var of* STANDARDIZE

stan·dard–is·sue \ˌstan-dərd-'i-shü\ *adj* : STANDARD, TYPICAL ⟨a ~ blue suit⟩

stan·dard·ize \'stan-dər-ˌdīz\ *vb* **-ized; -iz·ing** : to make standard or uniform — **stan·dard·i·za·tion** \ˌstan-dər-də-'zā-shən\ *n*

standard of living : the necessities, comforts, and luxuries that a person or group is accustomed to

standard time *n* : the time established by law or by general usage over a region or country

¹stand·by \'stand-ˌbī\ *n, pl* **stand·bys** \-ˌbīz\ **1** : one that can be relied on **2** : a substitute in reserve — **on standby** : ready or available for immediate action or use

²standby *adj* **1** : ready for use **2** : relating to airline travel in which the passenger must wait for an available unreserved seat — **standby** *adv*

stand–in \'stan-ˌdin\ *n* **1** : someone employed to occupy an actor's place while lights and camera are readied **2** : SUBSTITUTE

¹stand·ing \'stan-diŋ\ *adj* **1** : ERECT ⟨~ timber⟩ **2** : not flowing : STAGNANT **3** : remaining at the same level or amount for an indefinite period ⟨~ offer⟩ **4** : PERMANENT ⟨a ~ army⟩ **5** : done from a standing position ⟨a ~ jump⟩

²standing *n* **1** : length of service; *also* : relative position in society or in a profession : RANK **2** : DURATION ⟨a custom of long ~⟩

stand·off \'stan-ˌdȯf\ *n* : TIE, DRAW

stand·off·ish \stan-'dȯ-fish\ *adj* : somewhat cold and reserved

stand·out \'stan-ˌdau̇t\ *n* : something conspicuously excellent

stand·pipe \'stand-ˌpīp\ *n* : a high vertical pipe or reservoir for water used to produce a uniform pressure

stand·point \-ˌpȯint\ *n* : a position from which objects or principles are judged

stand·still \-ˌstil\ *n* : a state of rest

stand–up \'stan-ˌdəp\ *adj* : done or performing in a standing position ⟨a ~ comic⟩ ⟨~ comedy⟩

stank *past of* STINK

stan·za \'stan-zə\ *n* [It] : a group of lines forming a division of a poem

sta·pes \'stā-ˌpēz\ *n, pl* **stapes** *or* **sta·pe·des** \'stā-pə-ˌdēz\ : the innermost bone of the middle ear of mammals

staph \'staf\ *n* : STAPHYLOCOCCUS

staph·y·lo·coc·cus \ˌsta-fə-lō-'kä-kəs\ *n, pl* **-coc·ci** \-'kä-ˌkī, -'käk-ˌsī\ : any of a genus of spherical bacteria including some pathogens of skin and mucous membranes — **staph·y·lo·coc·cal** \-'kä-kəl\ *adj*

¹sta·ple \'stā-pəl\ *n* : a U-shaped piece of metal or wire with sharp points to be driven into a surface or through thin layers (as paper) for attaching or holding together — **staple** *vb* — **sta·pler** *n*

²staple *n* **1** : a chief commodity or product **2** : a chief part of something ⟨a ~ of their diet⟩ **3** : unmanufactured or raw material **4** : a textile fiber suitable for spinning into yarn

³staple *adj* **1** : regularly produced in large quantities **2** : PRINCIPAL, MAIN ⟨the ~ crop⟩

¹star \'stär\ *n* **1** : a celestial body that appears as a fixed point of light; *esp* : such a body that is gaseous, self-luminous, and of great mass **2** : a planet or configuration of planets that is held in astrology to influence one's fortune — usu. used in pl. **3** *obs* : DESTINY **4** : a conventional figure representing a star; *esp* : ASTERISK **5** : an actor or actress playing the leading role **6** : a brilliant performer — **star·dom** \'stär-dəm\ *n* — **star·less** *adj* — **star·like** *adj* — **star·ry** *adj*

²**star** *vb* **starred; star·ring** **1** : to adorn with stars **2** : to mark with an asterisk **3** : to play the leading role

star anise *n* : the small brown star-shaped fruit of an Asian tree used as a spice esp. in Chinese cooking

star·board \'stär-bərd\ *n* [ME *sterbord*, fr. OE *stēorbord*, fr. *stēor-* steering oar + *bord* ship's side] : the right side of a ship or airplane looking forward — **starboard** *adj*

star·burst \'stär-bərst\ *n* : a pattern that resembles diverging rays of light

¹**starch** \'stärch\ *vb* : to stiffen with or as if with starch

²**starch** *n* : a complex carbohydrate that is stored in plants, is an important foodstuff, and is used in adhesives and sizes, in laundering, and in pharmacy — **starchy** *adj*

stare \'ster\ *vb* **stared; star·ing** : to look fixedly with wide-open eyes ⟨*stared* in disbelief⟩ — **stare** *n* — **star·er** *n*

star·fish \'stär-ˌfish\ *n* : any of a class of echinoderms that have usu. five arms arranged around a central disk and feed largely on mollusks

star fruit *n* : CARAMBOLA 1

¹**stark** \'stärk\ *adj* **1** : rigid as if in death; *also* : STRICT **2** *archaic* : STRONG, ROBUST **3** : SHEER, UTTER ⟨~ nonsense⟩ **4** : BARREN, DESOLATE ⟨~ landscape⟩; *also* : UNADORNED ⟨~ realism⟩ **5** : sharply delineated — **stark·ly** *adv*

²**stark** *adv* : WHOLLY, ABSOLUTELY ⟨~ naked⟩

star·light \'stär-ˌlīt\ *n* : the light given by the stars

star·ling \'stär-liŋ\ *n* : a dark brown or in summer glossy greenish black European bird that is naturalized nearly worldwide and often considered a pest

¹**start** \'stärt\ *vb* **1** : to give an involuntary twitch or jerk (as from surprise) **2** : BEGIN, COMMENCE **3** : to set going ⟨~ an engine⟩ **4** : to enter or cause to enter a game or contest; *also* : to be in the starting lineup — **start·er** *n*

²**start** *n* **1** : a sudden involuntary motion : LEAP **2** : a spasmodic and brief effort or action **3** : BEGINNING; *also* : the place of beginning

start·er \'stär-tər\ *adj* : being an item acquired with the expectation that a more elaborate one will be acquired in the future ⟨a ~ home⟩

star·tle \'stär-tᵊl\ *vb* **star·tled; star·tling** : to frighten or surprise suddenly : cause to start ⟨the noise *startled* the dog⟩

star·tling *adj* : causing sudden fear, surprise, or anxiety — **star·tling·ly** *adv*

starve \'stärv\ *vb* **starved; starv·ing** [ME *sterven* to die, fr. OE *steorfan*] **1** : to die or cause to die from hunger **2** : to suffer extreme hunger or deprivation ⟨*starving* for affection⟩ **3** : to subdue by famine — **star·va·tion** \stär-'vā-shən\ *n*

starve·ling \'stärv-liŋ\ *n* : one that is thin from lack of nourishment

stash \'stash\ *vb* : to store in a secret place for future use — **stash** *n*

sta·sis \'stā-səs, 'sta-\ *n, pl* **sta·ses** \'stā-ˌsēz, 'sta-\ **1** : a stoppage or slowing of the normal flow of a bodily fluid (as blood) **2** : a state of static balance : STAGNATION

¹**stat** \'stat\ *adv* [L *statim*] : without delay : IMMEDIATELY

²**stat** *abbr* statute

¹**state** \'stāt\ *n* [ME *stat*, fr. AF & L; AF *estat*, fr. L *status*, fr. *stare* to stand] **1** : mode or condition of being ⟨the four ~s of matter⟩ **2** : condition of mind **3** : social position **4** : a body of people occupying a territory and organized under one government; *also* : the government of such a body of people **5** : one of the constituent units of a nation having a federal government — **state·hood** \-ˌhùd\ *n*

²**state** *vb* **stat·ed; stat·ing** **1** : to set by regulation or authority **2** : to express in words

state·craft \'stāt-ˌkraft\ *n* : the art of conducting state affairs

state·house \-ˌhaùs\ *n* : the building in which a state legislature meets

state·ly \'stāt-lē\ *adj* **state·li·er; -est** **1** : having lofty dignity : HAUGHTY **2** : IMPRESSIVE, MAJESTIC ⟨~ homes⟩ ♦ *Synonyms* MAGNIFICENT, IMPOSING, AUGUST — **state·li·ness** *n*

state·ment \'stāt-mənt\ *n* **1** : the act or result of presenting in words **2** : a summary of a financial account

state·room \'stāt-ˌrüm, -ˌrùm\ *n* : a private room on a ship or railroad car

state·side \'stāt-ˌsīd\ *adj* : of or relating to the U.S. as regarded from outside its continental limits — **stateside** *adv*

states·man \'stāts-mən\ *n* : a person engaged in fixing the policies and conducting the affairs of a government; *esp* : one wise and skilled in such matters — **states·man·like** *adj* — **states·man·ship** *n*

¹**stat·ic** \'sta-tik\ *adj* **1** : acting by mere weight without motion ⟨~ pressure⟩ **2** : relating to bodies at rest or forces in equilibrium **3** : showing little change **4** : not moving : not active **5** : of or relating to stationary charges of electricity **6** : of, relating to, or caused by radio static

²**static** *n* : noise produced in a radio or television receiver by atmospheric or other electrical disturbances

stat·in \'sta-tᵊn\ *n* : any of a group of drugs that inhibit the synthesis of cholesterol

¹**sta·tion** \'stā-shən\ *n* **1** : the place where a person or thing stands or is assigned to remain **2** : a regular stopping place on a transportation route : DEPOT **3** : a place where a fleet is assigned for duty **4** : a stock farm or ranch esp. in Australia or New Zealand **5** : social standing **6** : a complete assemblage of radio or television equipment for sending or receiving

²**station** *vb* : to assign to a station

sta·tion·ary \'stā-shə-ˌner-ē\ *adj* **1** : fixed in a station, course, or mode **2** : unchanging in condition ⟨a ~ population⟩

stationary front *n* : the boundary between two air masses neither of which is advancing

station break *n* : a pause in a radio or television broadcast to announce the identity of the network or station

sta·tio·ner \'stā-shə-nər\ *n* : one that sells stationery

sta·tio·nery \'stā-shə-ˌner-ē\ *n* : materials (as paper, pens, or ink) for writing; *esp* : letter paper with envelopes

station wagon *n* : an automobile having a long interior, one or more folding or removable rear seats, and usu. a door at the rear

sta·tis·tic \stə-'tis-tik\ *n* **1** : a single term or datum in a collection of statistics **2** : a quantity (as the mean) that is computed from a sample

sta·tis·tics \-tiks\ *n sing or pl* [G *Statistik* study of political facts and figures, fr. NL *statisticus* of politics, fr. L *status* state] : a branch of mathematics dealing with the collection, analysis, and interpretation of masses of numerical data; *also* : a collection of such numerical data — **sta·tis·ti·cal** \-ti-kəl\ *adj* — **sta·tis·ti·cal·ly** \-ti-k(ə-)lē\ *adv* — **stat·is·ti·cian** \ˌsta-tə-'sti-shən\ *n*

stat·u·ary \'sta-chə-ˌwer-ē\ *n, pl* **-ar·ies** **1** : the art of making statues **2** : STATUES

stat·ue \'sta-chü\ *n* : a likeness (as of a person or animal) sculptured, modeled, or cast in a solid substance

stat·u·esque \ˌsta-chə-'wesk\ *adj* : tall and shapely

stat·u·ette \ˌsta-chə-'wet\ *n* : a small statue

stat·ure \'sta-chər\ *n* **1** : natural height (as of a person) **2** : quality or status gained (as by achievement)

sta·tus \'stā-təs, 'sta-\ *n* **1** : the condition of a person in the eyes of others or of the law **2** : state or condition with respect to circumstances

sta·tus quo \-'kwō\ *n* [L, state in which] : the existing state of affairs

stat·ute \'sta-chüt\ *n* : a law enacted by a legislative body

stat·u·to·ry \'sta-chə-ˌtòr-ē\ *adj* : imposed by statute : LAWFUL

statutory rape *n* : sexual intercourse with a person who is below the statutory age of consent

¹**staunch** *var of* ¹STANCH

²**staunch** \'stònch, 'stänch\ *adj* **1** : WATERTIGHT ⟨a ~ ship⟩ **2** : FIRM, STRONG; *also* : STEADFAST, LOYAL ⟨a ~ supporter⟩ ♦ *Synonyms* RESOLUTE, CONSTANT, TRUE, FAITHFUL — **staunch·ly** *adv*

¹**stave** \'stāv\ *n* **1** : CUDGEL, STAFF **2** : any of several narrow strips of wood placed edge to edge to make something (as a barrel) **3** : STANZA

²**stave** *vb* **staved** *or* **stove** \'stōv\; **stav·ing** **1** : to break in the staves of; *also* : to break a hole in **2** : to drive or thrust away ⟨~ off hunger⟩

staves *pl of* STAFF

¹**stay** \'stā\ *n* **1** : a strong rope or wire used to support a mast **2** : ¹GUY

²**stay** *vb* **stayed** \'stād\ *also* **staid** \'stād\; **stay·ing** **1**

: PAUSE, WAIT   **2** : REMAIN   **3** : to stand firm   **4** : LIVE, DWELL   **5** : DELAY, POSTPONE   **6** : to last out (as a race)   **7** : STOP, CHECK   **8** : to satisfy (as hunger) for a time ◆ *Synonyms* REMAIN, ABIDE, LINGER, TARRY
³stay *n*   **1** : STOP, HALT   **2** : a residence or sojourn in a place
⁴stay *n*   **1** : PROP, SUPPORT   **2** : CORSET — usu. used in pl.
⁵stay *vb* : to hold up : PROP
staying power *n* : STAMINA
stbd *abbr* starboard
std *abbr* standard
STD \ˌes-(ˌ)tē-ˈdē\ *n* : SEXUALLY TRANSMITTED DISEASE
Ste *abbr* [F *sainte*] saint (female)
stead \ˈsted\ *n*   **1** : ADVANTAGE ⟨stood him in good ∼⟩   **2** : the place or function ordinarily occupied or carried out by another ⟨acted in her brother's ∼⟩
stead·fast \ˈsted-ˌfast\ *adj*   **1** : firmly fixed in place   **2** : not subject to change   **3** : firm in belief, determination, or adherence : LOYAL ◆ *Synonyms* RESOLUTE, TRUE, FAITHFUL, STAUNCH — **stead·fast·ly** *adv* — **stead·fast·ness** *n*
¹steady \ˈste-dē\ *adj* **steadi·er; -est**   **1** : direct or sure in movement; *also* : CALM   **2** : FIRM, FIXED ⟨held the pole ∼⟩   **3** : STABLE ⟨∼ prices⟩   **4** : not easily disturbed   **5** : RELIABLE ⟨∼ friends⟩   **6** : temperate in character or demeanor ◆ *Synonyms* UNIFORM, EVEN — **steadi·ly** \-də-lē\ *adv* — **steadi·ness** \-dē-nəs\ *n* — **steady** *adv*
²steady *vb* **stead·ied; steady·ing** : to make or become steady
steak \ˈstāk\ *n* : a slice of meat and esp. beef; *also* : a slice of a large fish
¹steal \ˈstēl\ *vb* **stole** \ˈstōl\; **sto·len** \ˈstō-lən\; **steal·ing**   **1** : to take and carry away without right or permission   **2** : to come or go secretly or gradually   **3** : to get for oneself slyly or by skill and daring ⟨∼ a kiss⟩ ⟨∼ the ball in basketball⟩   **4** : to gain or attempt to gain a base in baseball by running without the aid of a hit or an error ◆ *Synonyms* PILFER, FILCH, PURLOIN, SWIPE
²steal *n*   **1** : an act of stealing   **2** : BARGAIN
¹stealth \ˈstelth\ *n*   **1** : secret or unobtrusive procedure   **2** : an aircraft design intended to produce a weak radar return
²stealth *adj* : STEALTHY ⟨a ∼ campaign⟩
stealthy \ˈstel-thē\ *adj* **stealth·i·er; -est** : done by stealth : FURTIVE, SLY ⟨a ∼ burglar⟩ ◆ *Synonyms* SECRET, COVERT, CLANDESTINE, SURREPTITIOUS, UNDERHANDED — **stealth·i·ly** \ˈstel-thə-lē\ *adv*
¹steam \ˈstēm\ *n*   **1** : the vapor into which water is changed when heated to the boiling point   **2** : water vapor when compressed so that it supplies heat and power   **3** : POWER, FORCE, ENERGY — **steamy** *adj*
²steam *vb*   **1** : to pass off as vapor   **2** : to emit vapor   **3** : to move by or as if by the agency of steam — **steam·er** *n*
steam·boat \ˈstēm-ˌbōt\ *n* : a boat driven by steam
steam engine *n* : a reciprocating engine having a piston driven by steam
steam·fit·ter \ˈstēm-ˌfi-tər\ *n* : a worker who puts in or repairs equipment (as steam pipes) for heating, ventilating, or refrigerating systems
steam·punk \ˈstēm-ˌpəŋk\ *n* : science fiction involving historical or imagined steam-powered technology
steam·roll·er \-ˌrō-lər\ *n* : a machine for compacting roads or pavements — **steam·roll·er** *also* **steam·roll** \-ˌrōl\ *vb*
steam·ship \-ˌship\ *n* : a ship driven by steam
steed \ˈstēd\ *n* : HORSE
¹steel \ˈstēl\ *n*   **1** : iron treated with intense heat and mixed with carbon to make it hard and tough   **2** : an article made of steel   **3** : a quality (as hardness of mind) that suggests steel — **steel** *adj* — **steely** *adj*
²steel *vb* : to fill with courage or determination ⟨∼ed himself for her rage⟩
steel wool *n* : long fine steel shavings used esp. for cleaning and polishing
¹steep \ˈstēp\ *adj*   **1** : having a very sharp slope : PRECIPITOUS   **2** : too high ⟨∼ prices⟩ — **steep·ly** *adv* — **steep·ness** *n*
²steep *n* : a steep slope
³steep *vb*   **1** : to soak in a liquid; *esp* : to extract the essence of by soaking ⟨∼ tea⟩   **2** : SATURATE ⟨∼ed in learning⟩

stee·ple \ˈstē-pəl\ *n* : a tall tapering structure built on top of a church tower; *also* : a church tower
stee·ple·chase \-ˌchās\ *n* [fr. the use of church steeples as landmarks to guide the riders] : a horse race across country; *also* : a race over a course obstructed by hurdles
¹steer \ˈstir\ *n* : a male bovine animal castrated before sexual maturity and usu. raised for beef
²steer *vb*   **1** : to direct the course of (as by a rudder or wheel)   **2** : GUIDE, CONTROL   **3** : to pursue a course of action   **4** : to be subject to guidance or direction — **steers·man** \ˈstirz-mən\ *n*
steer·age \ˈstir-ij\ *n*   **1** : DIRECTION, GUIDANCE   **2** : a section in a passenger ship for passengers paying the lowest fares
stego·sau·rus \ˌste-gə-ˈsȯr-əs\ *n* : any of a genus of plant-eating armored dinosaurs with a series of bony plates along the backbone
stein \ˈstīn\ *n* : an earthenware mug
stel·lar \ˈste-lər\ *adj* : of or relating to stars : resembling a star
¹stem \ˈstem\ *n*   **1** : the main stalk of a plant; *also* : a plant part that supports another part (as a leaf or fruit)   **2** : the bow of a ship   **3** : a line of ancestry : STOCK   **4** : that part of an inflected word which remains unchanged throughout a given inflection   **5** : something resembling the stem of a plant — **stem·less** *adj* — **stemmed** \ˈstemd\ *adj*
²stem *vb* **stemmed; stem·ming** : to have a specified source : DERIVE
³stem *vb* **stemmed; stem·ming** : to make headway against ⟨∼ the tide⟩
⁴stem *vb* **stemmed; stem·ming** : to stop or check by or as if by damming
STEM *abbr* science, technology, engineering, and math
stem cell *n* : an undifferentiated cell that may give rise to many different types of cells
stench \ˈstench\ *n* : STINK
sten·cil \ˈsten-səl\ *n* [prob. ultim. fr. ME *stanseld* ornamented, fr. AF *estencelé* spangled, pp. of *estenceler* to sparkle, fr. *estencele* spark, fr. VL *stincilla*, alter. of L *scintilla*] : an impervious material (as metal or paper) perforated with lettering or a design through which a substance (as ink or paint) is applied to a surface to be printed — **stencil** *vb*
ste·nog·ra·phy \stə-ˈnä-grə-fē\ *n* : the art or process of writing in shorthand — **ste·nog·ra·pher** \-fər\ *n* — **steno·graph·ic** \ˌste-nə-ˈgra-fik\ *adj*
ste·no·sis \stə-ˈnō-səs\ *n, pl* **-no·ses** \-ˌsēz\ : a narrowing of a bodily passage or orifice
stent \ˈstent\ *n* : a short narrow tube inserted into an anatomical vessel esp. to keep a passage open
sten·to·ri·an \sten-ˈtȯr-ē-ən\ *adj* : extremely loud ⟨∼ tones⟩
¹step \ˈstep\ *n*   **1** : a rest for the foot in ascending or descending : STAIR   **2** : an advance made by raising one foot and putting it down elsewhere   **3** : manner of walking   **4** : a small space or distance   **5** : a degree, rank, or plane in a series   **6** : a sequential measure leading to a result
²step *vb* **stepped; step·ping**   **1** : to advance or recede by steps   **2** : to go on foot : WALK   **3** : to move along briskly   **4** : to press down with the foot   **5** : to measure by steps   **6** : to construct or arrange in or as if in steps
step aerobics *n sing or pl* : aerobics that involves repeatedly stepping on and off a raised platform
step aside *vb* : STEP DOWN 1
step·broth·er \ˈstep-ˌbrə-thər\ *n* : the son of one's stepparent by a former marriage
step·child \-ˌchī(-ə)ld\ *n* : a child of one's husband or wife by a former marriage
step·daugh·ter \-ˌdȯ-tər\ *n* : a daughter of one's wife or husband by a former marriage
step down *vb*   **1** : to give up a position : RETIRE, RESIGN   **2** : to lower (a voltage) by means of a transformer
step·fa·ther \-ˌfä-thər\ *n* : the husband of one's parent when distinct from one's natural or legal father
step·lad·der \ˈstep-ˌla-dər\ *n* : a light portable set of steps in a hinged frame
step·moth·er \-ˌmə-thər\ *n* : the wife of one's parent when distinct from one's natural or legal mother

step·par·ent \-ˌper-ənt\ *n* : a person who is a stepfather or stepmother

steppe \'step\ *n* [Russ *step'*] : dry level grass-covered treeless land in regions of wide temperature range esp. in southeastern Europe and Asia

step·sis·ter \'step-ˌsis-tər\ *n* : the daughter of one's stepparent by a former marriage

step·son \-ˌsən\ *n* : a son of one's wife or husband by a former marriage

step up *vb* **1** : to increase (a voltage) by means of a transformer **2** : INCREASE, ACCELERATE **3** : to come forward — **step–up** \'step-ˌəp\ *n*

ster *abbr* sterling

ste·reo \'ster-ē-ˌō, 'stir-\ *n, pl* **ste·re·os 1** : stereophonic reproduction **2** : a stereophonic sound system — **stereo** *adj*

ste·reo·phon·ic \ˌster-ē-ə-'fä-nik, ˌstir-\ *adj* : of or relating to sound reproduction designed to create the effect of listening to the original — **ste·reo·phon·i·cal·ly** \-'fä-ni-k(ə-)lē\ *adv*

ster·e·o·scope \'ster-ē-ə-ˌskōp, 'stir-\ *n* [Gk *stereos* solid + *-skopion* means for viewing] : an optical instrument that blends two slightly different pictures of the same subject to give the effect of depth

ste·reo·scop·ic \ˌster-ē-ə-'skä-pik, ˌstir-\ *adj* **1** : of or relating to the stereoscope **2** : characterized by the seeing of objects in three dimensions ⟨∼ vision⟩ — **ste·reo·scop·i·cal·ly** \-'skä-pi-k(ə-)lē\ *adv* — **ste·re·os·co·py** \ster-ē-'äs-kə-pē, ˌstir-\ *n*

ste·reo·type \'ster-ē-ə-ˌtīp, 'stir-\ *n* **1** : a metal printing plate cast from a mold made from set type **2** : something agreeing with a pattern; *esp* : an idea that many people have about a thing or a group and that may often be untrue or only partly true — **stereotype** *vb* — **ste·reo·typ·i·cal** \ˌster-ē-ə-'ti-pi-kəl\ *adj* — **ste·reo·typ·i·cal·ly** \-pi-k(ə-)lē\ *adv*

ste·reo·typed \-ˌtīpt\ *adj* : lacking originality or individuality ♦ **Synonyms** TRITE, CLICHÉD, COMMONPLACE, HACKNEYED, STALE, THREADBARE

ster·ile \'ster-əl\ *adj* **1** : unable to bear fruit, crops, or offspring **2** : free from living things and esp. germs — **ste·ril·i·ty** \stə-'ri-lə-tē\ *n*

ster·il·ize \'ster-ə-ˌlīz\ *vb* **-ized; -iz·ing** : to make sterile; *esp* : to free from germs — **ster·il·i·za·tion** \ˌster-ə-lə-'zā-shən\ *n* — **ster·il·iz·er** \'ster-ə-ˌlī-zər\ *n*

¹ster·ling \'stər-liŋ\ *n* **1** : British money **2** : sterling silver

²sterling *adj* **1** : of, relating to, or calculated in terms of British sterling **2** : having a fixed standard of purity represented by an alloy of 925 parts of silver with 75 parts of copper **3** : made of sterling silver **4** : EXCELLENT ⟨a ∼ record of achievement⟩

¹stern \'stərn\ *adj* **1** : SEVERE, AUSTERE ⟨∼ taskmasters⟩ **2** : STOUT, STURDY ⟨∼ resolve⟩ — **stern·ly** *adv* — **stern·ness** *n*

²stern *n* : the rear end of a boat

ster·num \'stər-nəm\ *n, pl* **sternums** *or* **ster·na** \-nə\ : a long flat bone or cartilage at the center front of the chest connecting the ribs of the two sides

ste·roid \'stir-ˌȯid, 'ster-\ *n* : any of various compounds including numerous hormones (as anabolic steroids) and sugar derivatives — **steroid** *or* **ste·roi·dal** \stə-'rȯi-dᵊl\ *adj*

stetho·scope \'ste-thə-ˌskōp\ *n* : an instrument used to detect and listen to sounds produced in the body

ste·ve·dore \'stē-və-ˌdȯr\ *n* [Sp *estibador*, fr. *estibar* to pack, fr. L *stipare* to press together] : one who works at loading and unloading ships

ste·via \'stē-vē-ə\ *n* [NL, plant from which it is derived, fr. Petrus *Stevus* †1555 Sp. botanist] : a plant-derived powder used as a noncaloric sweetener

¹stew \'stü, 'styü\ *n* **1** : a dish of stewed meat and vegetables served in gravy **2** : a state of agitation, worry, or resentment

²stew *vb* **1** : to boil slowly : SIMMER **2** : to be in a state of agitation, worry, or resentment ⟨∼ed about her predicament⟩

stew·ard \'stü-ərd, 'styü-\ *n* [ME, fr. OE *stīweard*, fr. *stī, stig* hall, sty + *weard* ward] **1** : one employed on a large estate to manage domestic concerns **2** : one who supervises the provision and distribution of food (as on a ship); *also* : an employee on a ship or airplane who serves passengers **3** : one actively concerned with the direction of the affairs of an organization — **stew·ard·ship** *n*

stew·ard·ess \'stü-ər-dəs, 'styü-\ *n* : a woman who is a steward esp. on an airplane

stg *abbr* sterling

¹stick \'stik\ *n* **1** : a cut or broken branch or twig; *also* : a long slender piece of wood **2** : ROD, STAFF **3** : something resembling a stick **4** : a dull uninteresting person **5** *pl* : remote usu. rural areas

²stick *vb* **stuck** \'stək\; **stick·ing 1** : STAB, PRICK **2** : IMPALE **3** : ATTACH, FASTEN **4** : to thrust or project in some direction or manner **5** : to be unable to proceed or move freely **6** : to hold fast by or as if by gluing : ADHERE **7** : to hold to something firmly or closely : CLING **8** : to become jammed or blocked ⟨the door ∼s⟩

stick·er \'sti-kər\ *n* : one that sticks (as a bur) or causes sticking (as glue); *esp* : an adhesive label

sticker shock *n* : astonishment and dismay on being informed of a product's unexpectedly high price

stick insect *n* : any of various usu. wingless insects with a long round body resembling a stick

stick·ler \'sti-klər, -kə-lər\ *n* : one who insists on exactness or completeness

stick shift *n* : a manually operated automobile gearshift usu. mounted on the floor

stick–to–it·ive·ness \stik-'tü-ə-tiv-nəs\ *n* : dogged perseverance : TENACITY

stick up *vb* : to rob at gunpoint — **stick-up** \'stik-ˌəp\ *n*

sticky \'sti-kē\ *adj* **stick·i·er; -est 1** : ADHESIVE **2** : VISCOUS, GLUEY **3** : tending to stick ⟨∼ valve⟩ **4** : DIFFICULT ⟨a ∼ problem⟩

¹stiff \'stif\ *adj* **1** : not pliant : RIGID **2** : not limber ⟨∼ joints⟩; *also* : TENSE, TAUT **3** : not flowing or working easily ⟨∼ paste⟩ **4** : not natural and easy : FORMAL **5** : STRONG, FORCEFUL ⟨∼ breeze⟩ **6** : HARSH, SEVERE ⟨a ∼ penalty⟩ ♦ **Synonyms** INFLEXIBLE, INELASTIC — **stiff·ly** *adv* — **stiff·ness** *n*

²stiff *vb* : to refuse to pay or tip

stiff–arm \'stif-ˌärm\ *vb* : to treat with disdain or neglect ⟨∼ed her advice⟩

stiff·en \'sti-fən\ *vb* : to make or become stiff — **stiff·en·er** *n*

stiff–necked \'stif-'nekt\ *adj* : STUBBORN, HAUGHTY ⟨too ∼ to ask for help⟩

sti·fle \'stī-fəl\ *vb* **sti·fled; sti·fling 1** : to kill by depriving of or die from lack of oxygen or air : SMOTHER **2** : to keep in check by effort : SUPPRESS ⟨∼ a sneeze⟩ — **sti·fling·ly** *adv*

stig·ma \'stig-mə\ *n, pl* **stig·ma·ta** \stig-'mä-tə, 'stig-mə-tə\ *or* **stigmas** [L] **1** : a mark of disgrace or discredit **2** **stigmata** *pl* : bodily marks resembling the wounds of the crucified Jesus **3** : the upper part of the pistil of a flower that receives the pollen in fertilization — **stig·mat·ic** \stig-'ma-tik\ *adj*

stig·ma·tize \'stig-mə-ˌtīz\ *vb* **-tized; -tiz·ing 1** : to mark with a stigma **2** : to characterize as disgraceful ⟨was *stigmatized* by the scandal⟩

stile \'stī(-ə)l\ *n* : steps used for crossing a fence or wall

sti·let·to \stə-'le-tō\ *n, pl* **-tos** *or* **-toes** [It, dim. of *stilo* stylus, dagger] : a slender dagger

¹still \'stil\ *adj* **1** : MOTIONLESS **2** : making no sound : SILENT — **still·ness** *n*

²still *vb* : to make or become still

³still *adv* **1** : without motion ⟨sit ∼⟩ **2** : up to and during this or that time **3** : in spite of that : NEVERTHELESS **4** : EVEN ⟨ran ∼ faster⟩ **5** : YET ⟨has ∼ to be recognized⟩

⁴still *n* **1** : STILLNESS, SILENCE **2** : a static photograph esp. from a motion picture

⁵still *n* **1** : DISTILLERY **2** : apparatus used in distillation

still·birth \'stil-ˌbərth\ *n* : the birth of a dead fetus

still·born \-'bȯrn\ *adj* : born dead

still life *n, pl* **still lifes** : a picture of inanimate objects

stilt \'stilt\ *n* : one of a pair of poles for walking with each having a step or loop for the foot to elevate the wearer above the ground; *also* : a polelike support of a structure above ground or water level

stilt·ed \'stil-təd\ *adj* : not easy and natural ⟨∼ language⟩

Stil·ton \'stil-tᵊn\ *n* : a blue cheese of English origin

stim·u·lant \'sti-myə-lənt\ n 1 : an agent (as a drug) that temporarily increases the activity of an organism or any of its parts 2 : STIMULUS 3 : an alcoholic beverage — **stimulant** adj

stim·u·late \-ˌlāt\ vb **-lat·ed; -lat·ing** : to make active or more active < ANIMATE, AROUSE <~ interest> ◆ **Synonyms** EXCITE, PROVOKE, MOTIVATE, QUICKEN — **stim·u·la·tion** \ˌsti-myə-'lā-shən\ n — **stim·u·la·tive** \'sti-myə-ˌlā-tiv\ adj — **stim·u·la·tor** \-ˌlā-tər\ n — **stim·u·la·to·ry** \-lə-ˌtȯr-ē\ adj

stim·u·lus \'sti-myə-ləs\ n, pl **-li** \-ˌlī\ [L] 1 : something that moves to activity 2 : an agent that directly influences the activity of a living organism or one of its parts

¹sting \'stiŋ\ vb **stung** \'stəŋ\; **sting·ing** 1 : to prick painfully esp. with a sharp or poisonous process 2 : to cause to suffer acutely — **sting·er** n

²sting n 1 : an act of stinging; also : a resultant wound, sore, or pain 2 : a pointed often venom-bearing organ (as of a bee) : STINGER 3 : an elaborate confidence game; esp : one worked by undercover police to trap criminals

sting·ray \'stiŋ-ˌrā\ n : any of numerous rays with sharp stinging spines on a whiplike tail

stin·gy \'stin-jē\ adj **stin·gi·er; -est** : not generous : giving or spending as little as possible — **stin·gi·ness** n

stink \'stiŋk\ vb **stank** \'staŋk\ or **stunk** \'stəŋk\; **stunk; stink·ing** : to give forth a strong and offensive smell; also : to be extremely bad in quality or repute — **stink** n — **stink·er** n

stink·bug \'stiŋk-ˌbəg\ n : any of various true bugs that emit a disagreeable odor

¹stint \'stint\ vb 1 : to be sparing or frugal 2 : to cut short in amount

²stint n 1 : an assigned amount of work 2 : RESTRAINT, LIMITATION 3 : a period of time spent at a particular activity

sti·pend \'stī-ˌpend, -pənd\ n [ME, alter. of stipendy, fr. L stipendium, fr. stips gift + pendere to weigh, pay] : a fixed sum of money paid periodically for services or to defray expenses

stip·ple \'sti-pəl\ vb **stip·pled; stip·pling** 1 : to engrave by means of dots and light strokes 2 : to apply (as paint or ink) with small short touches — **stipple** n

stip·u·late \'sti-pyə-ˌlāt\ vb **-lat·ed; -lat·ing** : to make an agreement; esp : to make a special demand for something as a condition in an agreement — **stip·u·la·tion** \ˌsti-pyə-'lā-shən\ n

¹stir \'stər\ vb **stirred; stir·ring** 1 : to move slightly 2 : AROUSE, EXCITE 3 : to mix, dissolve, or make by continued circular movement <~ eggs into cake batter> 4 : to move to activity (as by pushing, beating, or prodding)

²stir n 1 : a state of agitation or activity 2 : an act of stirring

stir-fry \'stər-ˌfrī\ vb : to fry quickly over high heat while stirring continuously — **stir-fry** n

¹stir·ring \'stər-iŋ\ adj 1 : ACTIVE, BUSTLING 2 : ROUSING, INSPIRING <a ~ speech>

²stirring n : a beginning of activity <the first ~s of revolution>

stir·rup \'stər-əp\ n [ME stirop, fr. OE stigrāp, lit., mounting rope] 1 : a light frame hung from a saddle to support the rider's foot 2 : STAPES

¹stitch \'stich\ n 1 : a sudden sharp pain esp. in the side 2 : one of the series of loops formed by or over a needle in sewing

²stitch vb 1 : to fasten or join with stitches 2 : to make (as a design) with stitches 3 : SEW

stk abbr stock

stoat \'stōt\ n, pl **stoats** also **stoat** : the common Old and New World ermine esp. in its brown summer coat

¹stock \'stäk\ n 1 archaic : a block of wood 2 : a stupid person 3 : a wooden part of a thing serving as its support, frame, or handle 4 pl : a device for publicly punishing offenders consisting of a wooden frame with holes in which the feet and hands can be locked 5 : the original from which others derive; also : a group having a common origin : FAMILY 6 : LIVESTOCK 7 : a supply of goods 8 : the ownership element in a corporation divided to give the owners an interest and usu. voting power 9 : a company of actors playing at a particular theater and presenting a series of plays 10 : liquid in

which meat, fish, or vegetables have been simmered that is used as a basis for soup, gravy, or sauce

²stock vb : to provide with stock

³stock adj : kept regularly for sale or use; also : commonly used : STANDARD

stock·ade \stä-'kād\ n [Sp estacada, fr. estaca stake, pale, of Gmc origin] : an enclosure (as of posts and stakes) for defense or confinement

stock·bro·ker \-ˌbrō-kər\ n : one who executes orders to buy and sell securities

stock car n : a racing car that is similar to a regular car

stock exchange n : a place where the buying and selling of securities is conducted

stock·hold·er \'stäk-ˌhōl-dər\ n : one who owns corporate stock

stock·i·nette or **stock·i·net** \ˌstä-kə-'net\ n : an elastic knitted fabric used esp. for infants' wear and bandages

stock·ing \'stä-kiŋ\ n : a close-fitting knitted covering for the foot and leg

stock market n 1 : STOCK EXCHANGE 2 : a market for stocks

stock·pile \'stäk-ˌpī(-ə)l\ n : a reserve supply esp. of something essential — **stockpile** vb

stocky \'stä-kē\ adj **stock·i·er; -est** : being short and relatively thick : STURDY ◆ **Synonyms** THICKSET, SQUAT, HEAVYSET, STUBBY

stock·yard \'stäk-ˌyärd\ n : a yard for stock; esp : one for livestock about to be slaughtered or shipped

stodgy \'stä-jē\ adj **stodg·i·er; -est** 1 : thick in texture : HEAVY <~ bread> 2 : not interesting : DULL <a ~ accountant> 3 : extremely old-fashioned

¹sto·ic \'stō-ik\ n [ME, fr. L stoicus, fr. Gk stōïkos, lit., of the portico, fr. Stoa (Poikilē) the Painted Portico, portico at Athens where the philosopher Zeno taught] : one who suffers without complaining

²stoic or **sto·i·cal** \-i-kəl\ adj : not affected by passion or feeling; esp : showing indifference to pain ◆ **Synonyms** IMPASSIVE, PHLEGMATIC, APATHETIC, STOLID — **sto·ical·ly** \-i-k(ə-)lē\ adv — **sto·icism** \'stō-ə-ˌsi-zəm\ n

stoke \'stōk\ vb **stoked; stok·ing** 1 : to stir up a fire 2 : to tend and supply fuel to a furnace — **stok·er** n

STOL abbr short takeoff and landing

¹stole past of STEAL

²stole \'stōl\ n 1 : a long narrow band worn round the neck by some members of the clergy 2 : a long wide scarf or similar covering worn by women

stolen past part of STEAL

stol·id \'stä-ləd\ adj : not easily aroused or excited : showing little or no emotion <a ~ face> ◆ **Synonyms** PHLEGMATIC, APATHETIC, IMPASSIVE, STOIC — **sto·lid·i·ty** \stä-'li-də-tē\ n — **stol·id·ly** adv

sto·lon \'stō-lən, -ˌlän\ n : RUNNER 6

¹stom·ach \'stə-mək\ n 1 : a saclike digestive organ of a vertebrate into which food goes from the mouth by way of the throat and which opens below into the intestine 2 : a cavity in an invertebrate animal that is analogous to a stomach 3 : ABDOMEN 4 : desire for food caused by hunger : APPETITE 5 : INCLINATION, DESIRE <had no ~ for an argument>

²stomach vb : to bear without open resentment : put up with

stom·ach·ache \-ˌāk\ n : pain in or in the region of the stomach

stom·ach·er \'stə-mi-kər, -chər\ n : the front of a bodice often appearing between the laces of an outer garment (as in 16th century costume)

stomp \'stämp, 'stȯmp\ vb : STAMP — **stomp** n

¹stone \'stōn\ n 1 : hardened earth or mineral matter : ROCK 2 : a small piece of rock 3 : a precious stone : GEM 4 : CALCULUS 3 5 : a hard stony seed (as of a date) or one (as of a plum) with a stony covering 6 pl usu **stone** : a British unit of weight equal to 14 pounds — **stony** also **ston·ey** \'stō-nē\ adj

²stone vb **stoned; ston·ing** 1 : to pelt or kill with stones 2 : to remove the stones of (a fruit)

Stone Age n : the first known period of prehistoric human culture characterized by the use of stone tools

stoned \'stōnd\ adj 1 : DRUNK 2 : being under the influence of a drug

stone·wall \'stōn-ˌwȯl\ vb : to refuse to comply or cooperate with

stone·washed \'stōn-ˌwȯsht, -ˌwäsht\ *adj* : having been washed with stones during manufacture to create a softer fabric ⟨~ jeans⟩

stood *past and past part of* STAND

stooge \'stüj\ *n* 1 : a person who plays a subordinate or compliant role to a principal 2 : STRAIGHT MAN

stool \'stül\ *n* 1 : a seat usu. without back or arms 2 : FOOTSTOOL 3 : a seat used while urinating or defecating 4 : a discharge of fecal matter

stool pigeon *n* : DECOY, INFORMER

¹**stoop** \'stüp\ *vb* 1 : to bend forward and downward 2 : CONDESCEND 3 : to lower oneself morally ⟨~ to lying⟩

²**stoop** *n* 1 : an act of bending forward 2 : a bent position of head and shoulders

³**stoop** *n* [D *stoep*] : a porch, platform, or entrance stairway at a house door

¹**stop** \'stäp\ *vb* **stopped**; **stop·ping** 1 : to close (an opening) by filling or covering closely 2 : BLOCK, HALT 3 : to cease to go on 4 : to bring activity or operation to an end 5 : STAY, TARRY ✦ *Synonyms* QUIT, DISCONTINUE, DESIST, CEASE

²**stop** *n* 1 : END, CESSATION 2 : a set of organ pipes of one tone quality; *also* : a control knob for such a set 3 : OBSTRUCTION 4 : PLUG, STOPPER 5 : an act of stopping : CHECK 6 : a delay in a journey : STAY 7 : a place for stopping 8 *chiefly Brit* : any of several punctuation marks 9 : a function of an electronic device that stops a recording

stop–ac·tion \'stäp-'ak-shən\ *n* : STOP-MOTION

stop·gap \'stäp-ˌgap\ *n* : something that serves as a temporary expedient

stop·light \-ˌlīt\ *n* : TRAFFIC LIGHT

stop–mo·tion \'stäp-'mō-shən\ *n* : a filming technique in which successive positions of objects are photographed to produce the appearance of movement

stop·over \'stäp-ˌō-vər\ *n* 1 : a stop at an intermediate point in one's journey 2 : a stopping place on a journey

stop·page \'stä-pij\ *n* : the act of stopping : the state of being stopped

stop·per \'stä-pər\ *n* : something (as a cork) for sealing an opening

stop·watch \'stäp-ˌwäch\ *n* : a watch that can be started or stopped at will for exact timing

stor·age \'stȯr-ij\ *n* 1 : space for storing; *also* : cost of storing 2 : MEMORY 6 3 : the act of storing; *esp* : the safekeeping of goods (as in a warehouse)

storage battery *n* : a group of connected rechargeable electrochemical cells used to provide electric current

¹**store** \'stȯr\ *vb* **stored**; **stor·ing** 1 : to place or leave in a safe location for preservation or future use 2 : to provide esp. for a future need ⟨~ information⟩

²**store** *n* 1 : something accumulated and kept for future use 2 : a large or ample quantity 3 : STOREHOUSE 4 : a retail business establishment

store·house \-ˌhaus\ *n* : a building for storing goods or supplies; *also* : an abundant source or supply

store·keep·er \-ˌkē-pər\ *n* : one who operates a retail store

store·room \-ˌrüm, -ˌrum\ *n* : a room for storing goods or supplies

sto·ried \'stȯr-ēd\ *adj* : celebrated in story or history ⟨a ~ career⟩

stork \'stȯrk\ *n* : any of various large stout-billed Old World wading birds related to the herons and ibises

¹**storm** \'stȯrm\ *n* 1 : a heavy fall of rain, snow, or hail with high wind 2 : a violent outbreak or disturbance 3 : a mass attack on a defended position — **storm·i·ly** \'stȯr-mə-lē\ *adv* — **storm·i·ness** \-mē-nəs\ *n* — **stormy** *adj*

²**storm** *vb* 1 : to blow with violence; *also* : to rain, snow, or hail heavily 2 : to make a mass attack against 3 : to be violently angry : RAGE 4 : to rush along furiously ⟨~ed out of the room⟩

¹**sto·ry** \'stȯr-ē\ *n, pl* **stories** 1 : NARRATIVE, ACCOUNT 2 : REPORT, STATEMENT 3 : ANECDOTE 4 : SHORT STORY 5 : LIE, FALSEHOOD 6 : a news article or broadcast ✦ *Synonyms* UNTRUTH, TALE, CANARD

²**story** *also* **sto·rey** \'stȯr-ē\ *n, pl* **stories** *also* **storeys** : a floor of a building or the space between two adjacent floor levels

sto·ry·tell·er \-ˌte-lər\ *n* : a teller of stories

sto·tin \stō-'tēn\ *n, pl* **sto·ti·nov** \stō-'tē-ˌnóv\ : a monetary unit equal to ¹/₁₀₀ tolar formerly used in Slovenia

sto·tin·ka \stō-'tiŋ-kə\ *n, pl* **-tin·ki** \-kē\ — see *lev* at MONEY table

¹**stout** \'staut\ *adj* 1 : BRAVE 2 : FIRM ⟨a ~ refusal⟩ 3 : STURDY 4 : STAUNCH, ENDURING ⟨~ loyalty⟩ 5 : SOLID 6 : FORCEFUL, VIOLENT ⟨a ~ attack⟩ ⟨a ~ wind⟩ 7 : BULKY, THICKSET ✦ *Synonyms* FLESHY, FAT, PORTLY, CORPULENT, OBESE, PLUMP — **stout·ly** *adv* — **stout·ness** *n*

²**stout** *n* : a dark heavy ale

¹**stove** \'stōv\ *n* : an apparatus that burns fuel or uses electricity to provide heat (as for cooking or heating)

²**stove** *past and past part of* STAVE

stow \'stō\ *vb* 1 : HIDE, STORE ⟨~ baggage⟩ 2 : to pack in a compact mass

stow·away \'stō-ə-ˌwā\ *n* : one who hides on a vehicle to ride free

STP *abbr* standard temperature and pressure

strad·dle \'stra-d²l\ *vb* **strad·dled**; **strad·dling** 1 : to stand, sit, or walk with legs spread apart 2 : to favor or seem to favor two apparently opposite sides — **straddle** *n*

strafe \'strāf\ *vb* **strafed**; **straf·ing** [G *Gott strafe England* may God punish England, propaganda slogan during World War I] : to fire upon with machine guns from a low-flying airplane

strag·gle \'stra-gəl\ *vb* **strag·gled**; **strag·gling** 1 : to wander from the direct course : ROVE, STRAY 2 : to become separated from others of the same kind — **strag·gler** *n* — **strag·gly** \'stra-g(ə-)lē\ *adj*

¹**straight** \'strāt\ *adj* 1 : free from curves, bends, angles, or irregularities 2 : not wandering from the main point or proper course ⟨~ thinking⟩ 3 : HONEST ⟨a ~ answer⟩ 4 : having the elements in correct order 5 : UNMIXED, UNDILUTED ⟨~ whiskey⟩ 6 : CONVENTIONAL, SQUARE 7 : HETEROSEXUAL

²**straight** *adv* : in a straight manner

³**straight** *n* 1 : a straight line, course, or arrangement 2 : the part of a racetrack between the last turn and the finish 3 : a sequence of five cards in a poker hand

straight–arm \'strāt-ˌärm\ *n* : an act of warding off a person with the arm fully extended — **straight–arm** *vb*

straight·away \'strā-tə-ˌwā\ *n* : a straight stretch (as at a racetrack)

straight·edge \'strāt-ˌej\ *n* : a piece of material with a straight edge for testing straight lines and surfaces or for cutting along or drawing straight lines

straight·en \'strā-t²n\ *vb* : to make or become straight

straight flush *n* : a poker hand containing five cards of the same suit in sequence

straight·for·ward \strāt-'fȯr-wərd\ *adj* 1 : FRANK, CANDID, HONEST ⟨a ~ account⟩ 2 : proceeding in a straight course or manner

straight man *n* : an entertainer who feeds lines to a comedian who replies with usu. humorous quips

straight shooter *n* : a thoroughly upright straightforward person

straight·way \'strāt-'wā, -ˌwā\ *adv* : IMMEDIATELY ⟨get ~ to work⟩

¹**strain** \'strān\ *n* [ME *streen* progeny, lineage, fr. OE *strēon* gain, acquisition] 1 : LINEAGE, ANCESTRY 2 : a group (as of people or plants) of presumed common ancestry 3 : an inherited or inherent character or quality ⟨a ~ of madness in the family⟩ 4 : STREAK, TRACE ⟨a ~ of fanaticism⟩ 5 : MELODY 6 : the general style or tone

²**strain** *vb* [ME, fr. AF *estreindre*, fr. L *stringere* to bind or draw tight, press together] 1 : to draw taut 2 : to exert to the utmost 3 : to strive violently 4 : to injure by improper or excessive use 5 : to filter or remove by filtering 6 : to stretch beyond a proper limit — **strain·er** *n*

³**strain** *n* 1 : excessive tension or exertion (as of body or mind) 2 : bodily injury from excessive tension, effort, or use; *esp* : one in which muscles or ligaments are unduly stretched usu. from a wrench or twist 3 : deformation of a material body under the action of applied forces

¹**strait** \'strāt\ *adj* [ME, fr. AF *estreit*, fr. L *strictus* strait, strict, fr. pp. of *stringere*] 1 *archaic* : STRICT 2 *archaic* : NARROW 3 *archaic* : CONSTRICTED 4 : DIFFICULT, STRAITENED

²**strait** *n* **1** : a narrow channel connecting two bodies of water **2** *pl* : DISTRESS

strait·en \'strā-tᵊn\ *vb* **1** : to hem in : CONFINE **2** : to subject to distress or difficulty ⟨∼ed by misfortune⟩

strait·jack·et *also* **straight·jack·et** \'strāt-ˌja-kət\ *n* : a cover or garment of strong material (as canvas) used to bind the body and esp. the arms closely in restraining a violent prisoner or patient — **straitjacket** *vb*

strait·laced *or* **straight·laced** \-'lāst\ *adj* : strict in manners, morals, or opinion

¹**strand** \'strand\ *n* : SHORE, BEACH

²**strand** *vb* **1** : to run, drift, or drive upon the shore ⟨a ∼ed ship⟩ **2** : to place or leave in a helpless position

³**strand** *n* **1** : one of the fibers twisted or plaited together into a cord, rope, or cable; *also* : a cord, rope, or cable made up of such fibers **2** : a twisted or plaited ropelike mass ⟨a ∼ of pearls⟩ — **strand·ed** \'stran-dəd\ *adj*

¹**strange** \'strānj\ *adj* **strang·er; strang·est** [ME, fr. AF *estrange,* fr. L *extraneus,* lit., external, fr. *extra* outside] **1** : of external origin, kind, or character **2** : NEW, UNFAMILIAR ⟨moved to a ∼ neighborhood⟩ **3** : DISTANT 6 **4** : UNACCUSTOMED, INEXPERIENCED ⟨she was ∼ to his ways⟩ ♦ **Synonyms** SINGULAR, PECULIAR, ECCENTRIC, ERRATIC, ODD, QUEER, QUAINT, CURIOUS — **strange·ly** *adv* — **strange·ness** *n*

²**strange** *n* : a quark with a charge of −¹/₃ and a measured energy of approximately 150 million electron volts

strang·er \'strān-jər\ *n* **1** : FOREIGNER **2** : INTRUDER **3** : a person with whom one is unacquainted

stran·gle \'straŋ-gəl\ *vb* **stran·gled; stran·gling 1** : to choke to death : THROTTLE **2** : STIFLE, SUPPRESS ⟨repression ∼s free speech⟩ — **stran·gler** *n*

strangler fig *n* : any of several figs that begin life atop a host tree and then send down roots that surround it

stran·gu·late \'straŋ-gyə-ˌlāt\ *vb* **-lat·ed; -lat·ing 1** : STRANGLE, CONSTRICT **2** : to become so constricted as to stop circulation

stran·gu·la·tion \ˌstraŋ-gyə-'lā-shən\ *n* : the act or process of strangling or strangulating; *also* : the state of being strangled or strangulated

¹**strap** \'strap\ *n* : a narrow strip of flexible material used esp. for fastening, holding together, or wrapping

²**strap** *vb* **strapped; strap·ping 1** : to secure with a strap **2** : BIND, CONSTRICT **3** : to flog with a strap **4** : STROP

strap·less \-ləs\ *adj* : having no straps; *esp* : having no shoulder straps

¹**strapping** *adj* : LARGE, STRONG, HUSKY

²**strapping** *n* : material for a strap

strat·a·gem \'stra-tə-jəm, -ˌjem\ *n* **1** : a trick to deceive or outwit the enemy; *also* : a deceptive scheme **2** : skill in deception

strat·e·gy \'stra-tə-jē\ *n, pl* **-gies** [Gk *stratēgia* generalship, fr. *stratēgos* general, fr. *stratos* camp, army + *agein* to lead] **1** : the science and art of military command aimed at meeting the enemy under conditions advantageous to one's own force **2** : a careful plan or method esp. for achieving an end — **stra·te·gic** \strə-'tē-jik\ *adj* — **strat·e·gist** \'stra-tə-jist\ *n*

strat·i·fy \'stra-tə-ˌfī\ *vb* **-fied; -fy·ing** : to form or arrange in layers — **strat·i·fi·ca·tion** \ˌstra-tə-fə-'kā-shən\ *n*

stra·tig·ra·phy \strə-'ti-grə-fē\ *n* : geology that deals with rock strata — **strati·graph·ic** \ˌstra-tə-'gra-fik\ *adj*

strato·sphere \'stra-tə-ˌsfir\ *n* : the part of the earth's atmosphere between about 7 miles (11 kilometers) and 31 miles (50 kilometers) above the earth — **strato·spher·ic** \ˌstra-tə-'sfir-ik, -'sfer-\ *adj*

stra·tum \'strā-təm, 'stra-\ *n, pl* **stra·ta** \'strā-tə, 'stra-\ [NL, fr. L, spread, bed, fr. neut. of *status,* pp. of *sternere* to spread out] **1** : a bed, layer, or sheetlike mass (as of one kind of rock lying between layers of other kinds of rock) **2** : a level of culture; *also* : a group of people representing one stage in cultural development

¹**straw** \'strȯ\ *n* **1** : stalks of grain after threshing; *also* : a single coarse dry stem (as of a grass) **2** : a thing of small worth : TRIFLE **3** : a tube (as of paper or plastic) for sucking up a beverage

²**straw** *adj* **1** : made of straw **2** : having no real force or validity ⟨a ∼ vote⟩

straw·ber·ry \'strȯ-ˌber-ē, -bə-rē\ *n* : an edible juicy usu. red pulpy fruit of any of several low herbs with white flowers and long slender runners; *also* : one of these herbs

straw boss *n* : a foreman of a small group of workers

straw·flow·er \'strȯ-ˌflau̇(-ə)r\ *n* : any of several plants whose flowers can be dried with little loss of form or color

¹**stray** \'strā\ *n* **1** : a domestic animal wandering at large or lost **2** : WAIF

²**stray** *vb* **1** : to wander or roam without purpose **2** : DEVIATE ⟨∼ed from the topic⟩

³**stray** *adj* **1** : having strayed : separated from the group or the main body **2** : occurring at random ⟨∼ remarks⟩

¹**streak** \'strēk\ *n* **1** : a line or mark of a different color or texture from its background **2** : a narrow band of light; *also* : a lightning bolt **3** : a slight admixture : TRACE **4** : a brief run (as of luck); *also* : an unbroken series ⟨a winning ∼⟩

²**streak** *vb* **1** : to form streaks in or on **2** : to move very swiftly

¹**stream** \'strēm\ *n* **1** : a body of water (as a river) flowing on the earth; *also* : any of flowing fluid (as water or gas) **2** : a continuous procession ⟨a ∼ of traffic⟩

²**stream** *vb* **1** : to flow in or as if in a stream **2** : to pour out streams of liquid **3** : to trail out in length **4** : to move forward in a steady stream **5** : to transfer (digital data, such as audio or video material) in a continuous stream esp. for immediate processing or playback

stream·bed \'strēm-ˌbed\ *n* : the channel occupied by a stream

stream·er \'strē-mər\ *n* **1** : a long narrow ribbonlike flag **2** : a long ribbon on a dress or hat **3** : a newspaper headline that runs across the entire sheet **4** *pl* : AURORA

stream·ing \'strē-miŋ\ *adj* : relating to or being the transfer of data (as music or videos) in a continuous stream esp. for immediate processing or playback

stream·let \'strēm-lət\ *n* : a small stream

stream·lined \-ˌlīnd\ *adj* **1** : made with contours to reduce resistance to motion through water or air **2** : SIMPLIFIED **3** : MODERNIZED — **stream·line** *vb*

street \'strēt\ *n* [ME *strete,* fr. OE *strǣt,* fr. LL *strata* paved road, fr. L, fem. of *status,* pp. of *sternere* to spread out] **1** : a thoroughfare esp. in a city, town, or village **2** : the occupants of the houses on a street ⟨the whole ∼ objects to the proposal⟩

street·car \-ˌkär\ *n* : a passenger vehicle running on rails on city streets

streetcar

street fighter *n* : a tough belligerent person

street hockey *n* : a game resembling ice hockey played on a hard surface with hockey sticks and a small ball

street railway *n* : a company operating streetcars or buses

street·walk·er \'strēt-ˌwȯ-kər\ *n* : PROSTITUTE

strength \'streŋth\ *n* **1** : the quality of being strong : ability to do or endure : POWER **2** : TOUGHNESS, SOLIDITY **3** : power to resist attack **4** : INTENSITY **5** : force as measured in numbers ⟨the ∼ of an army⟩

strength·en \'streŋ-thən\ *vb* : to make or become stronger — **strength·en·er** *n*

stren·u·ous \'stren-yə-wəs\ *adj* **1** : VIGOROUS, ENERGETIC **2** : requiring energy or stamina — **stren·u·ous·ly** *adv*

strep \'strep\ *n* : STREPTOCOCCUS

strep throat *n* : an inflammatory sore throat caused by streptococci and marked by fever, prostration, and toxemia

strep·to·coc·cus \,strep-tə-'kä-kəs\ *n, pl* **-coc·ci** \-'kä-,kī, -'käk-,sī, -'kä-,kē, -'käk-,sē\ : any of various spherical bacteria that usu. grow in chains and include some causing serious diseases — **strep·to·coc·cal** \-kəl\ *adj*

strep·to·my·cin \-'mī-s³n\ *n* : an antibiotic produced by soil bacteria and used esp. in treating tuberculosis

¹**stress** \'stres\ *n* 1 : PRESSURE, STRAIN; *esp* : a force that tends to distort a body 2 : a factor that induces bodily or mental tension; *also* : a state induced by such a stress 3 : EMPHASIS 4 : relative prominence of sound 5 : ACCENT; *also* : any syllable carrying the accent — **stress·ful** \'stres-fəl\ *adj*

²**stress** *vb* 1 : to put pressure or strain on 2 : to put emphasis on : ACCENT

¹**stretch** \'strech\ *vb* 1 : to spread or reach out : EXTEND ⟨~ed out her arm⟩ 2 : to draw out in length or breadth : EXPAND 3 : to make tense : STRAIN 4 : EXAGGERATE ⟨~ed the truth⟩ 5 : to become extended without breaking ⟨rubber ~es easily⟩ — **stretchy** \'stre-chē\ *adj*

²**stretch** *n* 1 : an act of extending or drawing out beyond ordinary or normal limits 2 : a continuous extent in length, area, or time 3 : the extent to which something may be stretched 4 : either of the straight sides of a racecourse

³**stretch** *adj* : easily stretched ⟨~ pants⟩

¹**stretch·er** \'stre-chər\ *n* 1 : one that stretches 2 : a device for carrying a sick, injured, or dead person

²**stretcher** *vb* : to carry or transport on a stretcher

stretch marks *n pl* : striae on the skin (as of the abdomen) due to excessive stretching and rupture of elastic fibers (as from pregnancy)

strew \'strü\ *vb* **strewed; strewed** *or* **strewn** \'strün\; **strew·ing** 1 : to spread by scattering 2 : to cover by or as if by scattering something over or on ⟨a floor *strewn* with toys⟩ 3 : DISSEMINATE

stria \'strī-ə\ *n, pl* **stri·ae** \'strī-,ē\ 1 : STRIATION 3 2 : a stripe or line (as in the skin)

stri·at·ed muscle \'strī-,ā-təd-\ *n* : muscle tissue made up of long thin cells with many nuclei and alternate light and dark stripes that includes esp. the muscle of the heart and muscle that moves the vertebrate skeleton and is mostly under voluntary control

stri·a·tion \strī-'ā-shən\ *n* 1 : the state of being marked with stripes or lines 2 : arrangement of striations or striae 3 : a minute groove, scratch, or channel esp. when one of a parallel series

strick·en \'stri-kən\ *adj* 1 : afflicted by or as if by disease, misfortune, or sorrow : WOUNDED ⟨was ~ by an arrow⟩

strict \'strikt\ *adj* 1 : allowing no evasion or escape : RIGOROUS ⟨~ discipline⟩ 2 : ACCURATE, PRECISE ⟨the ~ sense of the word⟩ ♦ **Synonyms** STRINGENT, RIGID — **strict·ly** *adv* — **strict·ness** *n*

stric·ture \'strik-chər\ *n* 1 : an abnormal narrowing of a bodily passage; *also* : the narrowed part 2 : hostile criticism : a critical remark

¹**stride** \'strīd\ *vb* **strode** \'strōd\; **strid·den** \'strī-d³n\; **strid·ing** : to walk or run with long regular steps — **strid·er** *n*

²**stride** *n* 1 : a long step 2 : a stage of progress 3 : manner of striding : GAIT

stri·dent \'strī-d³nt\ *adj* : harsh sounding : GRATING, SHRILL ⟨a ~ voice⟩

strife \'strīf\ *n* : CONFLICT, FIGHT, STRUGGLE ♦ **Synonyms** DISCORD, CONTENTION, DISSENSION

¹**strike** \'strīk\ *vb* **struck** \'strək\; **struck** *also* **strick·en** \'stri-kən\; **strik·ing** 1 : to take a course : GO ⟨*struck* off through the brush⟩ 2 : to touch or hit sharply; *also* : to deliver a blow 3 : to produce by or as if by a blow ⟨*struck* terror in the foe⟩ 4 : to lower (as a flag or sail) 5 : to collide with; *also* : to injure or destroy by collision 6 : DELETE, CANCEL 7 : to produce by impressing ⟨*struck* a medal⟩; *also* : COIN ⟨~ a new cent⟩ 8 : to cause to sound ⟨~ a bell⟩ 9 : to afflict suddenly : lay low ⟨*stricken* with a high fever⟩ 10 : to appear to; *also* : to appear to as remarkable : IMPRESS 11 : to reach by reckoning ⟨~ an average⟩ 12 : to stop work in order to obtain a change in conditions of employment 13 : to cause (a match) to ignite by rubbing 14 : to come upon ⟨~ gold⟩ 15 : TAKE ON, ASSUME ⟨~ a pose⟩ — **strik·er** *n*

²**strike** *n* 1 : an act or instance of striking 2 : a sudden discovery of rich ore or oil deposits 3 : a pitched baseball that is swung at but not hit 4 : the knocking down of all the bowling pins with the 1st ball 5 : a military attack

strike·break·er \-,brā-kər\ *n* : a person hired to replace a striking worker

strike·out \-,aút\ *n* : an out in baseball as a result of a batter's being charged with three strikes

strike out *vb* 1 : to enter upon a course of action 2 : to start out vigorously 3 : to make an out in baseball by a strikeout

strike–slip \'strīk-,slip\ *n* : a fault about which movement is predominantly horizontal

strike up *vb* 1 : to begin or cause to begin to sing or play ⟨*strike up* the band⟩ 2 : BEGIN ⟨~ a conversation⟩

strike zone *n* : the area over home plate through which a pitched baseball must pass to be called a strike

striking *adj* : attracting attention : very noticeable ♦ **Synonyms** ARRESTING, SALIENT, CONSPICUOUS, OUTSTANDING, REMARKABLE, PROMINENT — **strik·ing·ly** *adv*

¹**string** \'striŋ\ *n* 1 : a line usu. composed of twisted threads 2 : a series of things arranged as if strung on a cord 3 : a plant fiber (as a leaf vein) 4 *pl* : the stringed instruments of an orchestra ♦ **Synonyms** SUCCESSION, PROGRESSION, SEQUENCE, CHAIN, TRAIN

²**string** *vb* **strung** \'strəŋ\; **string·ing** 1 : to provide with strings ⟨~ a racket⟩ 2 : to make tense 3 : to thread on or as if on a string ⟨~ pearls⟩ 4 : to hang, tie, or fasten by a string 5 : to take the strings out of ⟨~ beans⟩ 6 : to extend like a string

string bean *n* : a bean of one of the older varieties of kidney bean that have stringy fibers on the lines of separation of the pods; *also* : SNAP BEAN

string bikini *n* : a scanty bikini

string cheese *n* : cheese that can be pulled apart in narrow strips

stringed \'striŋd\ *adj* 1 : having strings ⟨~ instruments⟩ 2 : produced by strings

strin·gen·cy \'strin-jən-sē\ *n* 1 : STRICTNESS, SEVERITY 2 : SCARCITY ⟨~ of money⟩ — **strin·gent** \-jənt\ *adj*

string·er \'striŋ-ər\ *n* 1 : a long horizontal member in a framed structure or a bridge 2 : a news correspondent paid by the amount of copy

stringy \'striŋ-ē\ *adj* **string·i·er; -est** 1 : resembling string esp. in tough, fibrous, or disordered quality ⟨~ meat⟩ ⟨~ hair⟩ 2 : lean and sinewy in build

¹**strip** \'strip\ *vb* **stripped** \'stript\ *also* **stript; strip·ping** 1 : to take the covering or clothing from 2 : to take off one's clothes 3 : to pull or tear off 4 : to make bare or clear (as by cutting or grazing) 5 : PLUNDER, PILLAGE ♦ **Synonyms** DIVEST, DENUDE, DEPRIVE, DISMANTLE — **strip·per** *n*

²**strip** *n* 1 : a long narrow flat piece 2 : AIRSTRIP

¹**stripe** \'strīp\ *vb* **striped** \'strīpt\; **strip·ing** : to make stripes on

²**stripe** *n* 1 : a line or long narrow division having a different color from the background 2 : a strip of braid (as on a sleeve) indicating military rank or length of service 3 : TYPE, CHARACTER — **striped** \'strīpt, 'strī-pəd\ *adj*

striped bass *n* : a large black-striped marine bony fish that occurs along the Atlantic and Pacific coasts of the U.S. and is an excellent food and sport fish

strip·ling \'stri-pliŋ\ *n* : YOUTH, LAD

strip mall *n* : a long building or group of buildings housing several retail stores or service establishments

strip mine *n* : a mine that is worked from the earth's surface by the stripping of the topsoil — **strip–mine** *vb*

strip·tease \'strip-,tēz\ *n* : a burlesque act in which a performer removes clothing piece by piece — **strip·teas·er** *n*

strive \'strīv\ *vb* **strove** \'strōv\ *also* **strived** \'strīvd\; **striv·en** \'stri-vən\ *or* **strived; striv·ing** 1 : to make effort : labor hard 2 : to struggle in opposition : CONTEND ♦ **Synonyms** ENDEAVOR, ATTEMPT, TRY, ASSAY

strobe \'strōb\ *n* 1 : STROBOSCOPE 2 : a device for high-speed intermittent illumination (as in photography)

stro·bo·scope \'strō-bə-,skōp\ *n* : an instrument for studying rapid motion by means of a rapidly flashing light

strode *past of* STRIDE

¹stroke \'strōk\ *vb* **stroked; strok·ing** **1** : to rub gently **2** : to flatter in a manner designed to persuade

²stroke *n* **1** : the act of striking : BLOW, KNOCK **2** : a sudden action or process producing an impact ⟨~ of lightning⟩; *also* : an unexpected result **3** : sudden weakening or loss of consciousness or the power to move or feel caused by rupture or obstruction (as by a clot) of a blood vessel of the brain **4** : one of a series of movements against air or water to get through or over it ⟨the ~ of a bird's wing⟩ **5** : a rower who sets the pace for a crew **6** : a vigorous effort **7** : the sound of striking (as of a clock) **8** : a single movement with or as if with a tool or implement (as a pen)

stroll \'strōl\ *vb* : to walk in a leisurely or idle manner — **stroll** *n* — **stroll·er** *n*

strong \'strȯŋ\ *adj* **stron·ger** \'strȯŋ-gər\; **stron·gest** \'strȯŋ-gəst\ **1** : POWERFUL, VIGOROUS **2** : HEALTHY, ROBUST **3** : of a specified number ⟨an army 10 thousand ~⟩ **4** : not mild or weak **5** : VIOLENT ⟨~ wind⟩ **6** : ZEALOUS ⟨a ~ supporter⟩ **7** : not easily broken **8** : FIRM, SOLID ⟨~ beliefs⟩ ♦ **Synonyms** STOUT, STURDY, STALWART, TOUGH — **strong·ly** *adv*

strong-arm \'strȯŋ-'ärm\ *adj* : having or using undue force ⟨~ operatives⟩

strong force *n* : the physical force responsible for binding together nucleons in the atomic nucleus

strong·hold \-ˌhōld\ *n* : a fortified place : FORTRESS

strong·man \-ˌman\ *n* : one who leads or controls by force of will and character or by military strength

stron·tium \'strän-chē-əm, 'strän-tē-əm\ *n* : a soft malleable metallic chemical element

¹strop \'sträp\ *n* : STRAP; *esp* : one for sharpening a razor

²strop *vb* **stropped; strop·ping** : to sharpen a razor on a strop

stro·phe \'strō-fē\ *n* [Gk *strophē*, lit., act of turning] : a division of a poem — **stroph·ic** \'strä-fik\ *adj*

strove *past of* STRIVE

struck *past and past part of* STRIKE

¹struc·ture \'strək-chər\ *n* [ME, fr. L *structura*, fr. *structus*, pp. of *struere* to heap up, build] **1** : the action of building : CONSTRUCTION **2** : something built (as a house or a dam); *also* : something made up of interdependent parts in a definite pattern of organization **3** : arrangement or relationship of elements (as particles, parts, or organs) in a substance, body, or system — **struc·tur·al** *adj*

²structure *vb* **struc·tured; struc·tur·ing** : to make into a structure

stru·del \'strü-dᵊl, 'shtrü-\ *n* [G, lit., whirlpool] : a pastry made of a thin sheet of dough rolled up with filling and baked ⟨apple ~⟩

¹strug·gle \'strə-gəl\ *vb* **strug·gled; strug·gling** **1** : to make strenuous efforts against opposition : STRIVE **2** : to proceed with difficulty or with great effort ♦ **Synonyms** ENDEAVOR, ATTEMPT, TRY, ASSAY

²struggle *n* **1** : CONTEST, STRIFE **2** : a violent effort or exertion

strum \'strəm\ *vb* **strummed; strum·ming** : to play on a stringed instrument by brushing the strings with the fingers ⟨~ a guitar⟩

strum·pet \'strəm-pət\ *n* : PROSTITUTE

strung \'strəŋ\ *past and past part of* STRING

¹strut \'strət\ *vb* **strut·ted; strut·ting** : to walk with an affectedly proud gait

²strut *n* **1** : a bar or rod for resisting lengthwise pressure **2** : a haughty or pompous gait

strych·nine \'strik-ˌnīn, -nən, -ˌnēn\ *n* : a bitter poisonous plant alkaloid used as a poison (as for rats) and medicinally as a stimulant of the central nervous system

¹stub \'stəb\ *n* **1** : STUMP **2** : a short blunt end **3** : a small part of each leaf (as of a checkbook) kept as a memorandum of the items on the detached part

²stub *vb* **stubbed; stub·bing** : to strike (as one's toe) against something

stub·ble \'stə-bəl\ *n* **1** : the cut stem ends of herbs and esp. grasses left in the soil after harvest **2** : a rough surface or growth resembling stubble ⟨his face covered with ~⟩ — **stub·bly** \-b(ə-)lē\ *adj*

stub·born \'stə-bərn\ *adj* **1** : FIRM, DETERMINED **2** : done or continued in a willful, unreasonable, or persis-

tent manner **3** : not easily controlled or remedied ⟨a ~ cold⟩ — **stub·born·ly** *adv* — **stub·born·ness** *n*

stub·by \'stə-bē\ *adj* : short, blunt, and thick like a stub ⟨~ fingers⟩

stuc·co \'stə-kō\ *n, pl* **stuccos** *or* **stuccoes** [It] : plaster for coating exterior walls — **stuc·coed** \'stə-kōd\ *adj*

stuck *past and past part of* STICK

stuck–up \'stək-'əp\ *adj* : CONCEITED

¹stud \'stəd\ *n* : a male animal and esp. a horse **(stud·horse** \-ˌhȯrs\) kept for breeding

²stud *n* **1** : one of the smaller uprights in a building to which the wall materials are fastened **2** : a removable device like a button used as a fastener or ornament ⟨shirt ~s⟩ **3** : a projecting nail, pin, or rod

³stud *vb* **stud·ded; stud·ding** **1** : to supply with or adorn with studs **2** : DOT ⟨the sky was *studded* with stars⟩

⁴stud *abbr* student

stud·book \'stəd-ˌbu̇k\ *n* : an official record of the pedigree of purebred animals (as horses or dogs)

studding *n* : the studs in a building or wall

stu·dent \'stü-dᵊnt, 'styü-\ *n* : SCHOLAR, PUPIL; *esp* : one who attends a school

stud·ied \'stə-dēd\ *adj* : INTENTIONAL ⟨a ~ insult⟩ ♦ **Synonyms** DELIBERATE, CONSIDERED, PREMEDITATED, DESIGNED

stu·dio \'stü-dē-ˌō, 'styü-\ *n, pl* **-dios** **1** : a place where an artist works; *also* : a place for the study of an art **2** : a place where motion pictures are made **3** : a place equipped for the transmission of radio or television programs

stu·di·ous \'stü-dē-əs, 'styü-\ *adj* : devoted to study — **stu·di·ous·ly** *adv*

¹study \'stə-dē\ *n, pl* **stud·ies** **1** : the use of the mind to gain knowledge **2** : the act or process of learning about something **3** : careful examination **4** : INTENT, PURPOSE **5** : a branch of learning **6** : a room esp. for reading and writing

²study *vb* **stud·ied; study·ing** **1** : to engage in study or the study of **2** : to consider attentively or in detail ♦ **Synonyms** CONSIDER, CONTEMPLATE, WEIGH

¹stuff \'stəf\ *n* [ME, fr. AF *estuffes* goods, fr. *estuffer* to fill in (with rubble), furnish, equip, of Gmc origin] **1** : personal property **2** : raw material **3** : a finished textile fabric; *esp* : a worsted fabric **4** : writing, talk, or ideas of little or transitory worth **5** : an unspecified material substance or aggregate of matter **6** : fundamental material **7** : special knowledge or capability

²stuff *vb* **1** : to fill by packing things in : CRAM **2** : to eat greedily : GORGE **3** : to prepare (as meat) by filling with a stuffing **4** : to fill (as a cushion) with a soft material **5** : to stop up : PLUG

stuffed shirt \'stəft-\ *n* : a smug, conceited, and usu. pompous and inflexibly conservative person

stuff·ing *n* : material used to fill tightly; *esp* : a mixture of bread crumbs and spices used to stuff food

stuffy \'stə-fē\ *adj* **stuff·i·er; -est** **1** : STODGY **2** : lacking fresh air : CLOSE; *also* : blocked up ⟨a ~ nose⟩

stul·ti·fy \'stəl-tə-ˌfī\ *vb* **-fied; -fy·ing** **1** : to cause to appear foolish or stupid **2** : to impair, invalidate, or make ineffective **3** : to have a dulling effect on — **stul·ti·fi·ca·tion** \ˌstəl-tə-fə-'kā-shən\ *n*

stum·ble \'stəm-bəl\ *vb* **stum·bled; stum·bling** **1** : to blunder morally **2** : to trip in walking or running **3** : to walk unsteadily; *also* : to speak or act in a blundering or clumsy manner **4** : to happen by chance — **stumble** *n*

stumbling block *n* : an obstacle to belief, understanding, or progress

¹stump \'stəmp\ *n* **1** : the base of a bodily part (as a leg or tooth) left after the rest is removed **2** : the part of a plant and esp. a tree remaining with the root after the trunk is cut off **3** : a place or occasion for political public speaking — **stumpy** *adj*

²stump *vb* **1** : BAFFLE, PERPLEX **2** : to clear (land) of stumps **3** : to tour (a region) making political speeches **4** : to walk clumsily and heavily

stun \'stən\ *vb* **stunned; stun·ning** **1** : to make senseless or dizzy by or as if by a blow **2** : BEWILDER, STUPEFY ⟨*stunned* by the news⟩

stung *past and past part of* STING

stunk *past and past part of* STINK

stun·ning *adj* **1** : causing astonishment or disbelief **2** : strikingly beautiful — **stun·ning·ly** *adv*

¹**stunt** \'stənt\ *vb* : to hinder the normal growth or progress of

²**stunt** *n* : an unusual or spectacular feat

stu·pe·fy \'stü-pə-ˌfī, 'styü-\ *vb* **-fied; -fy·ing** **1** : to make stupid, groggy, or insensible **2** : ASTONISH — **stu·pe·fac·tion** \ˌstü-pə-'fak-shən, ˌstyü-\ *n*

stu·pen·dous \stü-'pen-dəs, styü-\ *adj* : causing astonishment esp. because of great size or height ◆ **Synonyms** TREMENDOUS, PRODIGIOUS, MONUMENTAL, MONSTROUS — **stu·pen·dous·ly** *adv*

stu·pid \'stü-pəd, 'styü-\ *adj* [MF *stupide,* fr. L *stupidus,* fr. *stupēre* to be numb, be astonished] **1** : very dull in mind **2** : showing or resulting from dullness of mind — **stu·pid·i·ty** \stü-'pi-də-tē, styü-\ *n* — **stu·pid·ly** *adv*

stu·por \'stü-pər, 'styü-\ *n* **1** : a condition of greatly dulled or completely suspended sense or feeling **2** : a state of extreme apathy or torpor often following stress or shock — **stu·por·ous** *adj*

stur·dy \'stər-dē\ *adj* **stur·di·er; -est** [ME, brave, stubborn, fr. AF *esturdi* stunned, fr. pp. of *esturdir* to stun, fr. VL **exturdire,* fr. L *ex-* + VL **turdus* simpleton, fr. L *turdus* thrush] **1** : STRONG, ROBUST **2** : RESOLUTE, UNYIELDING ◆ **Synonyms** STOUT, STALWART, TOUGH, TENACIOUS — **stur·di·ly** \-də-lē\ *adv* — **stur·di·ness** \-dē-nəs\ *n*

stur·geon \'stər-jən\ *n* : any of a family of large bony fishes including some whose roe are made into caviar

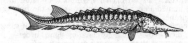

sturgeon

stut·ter \'stə-tər\ *vb* : to speak with involuntary disruption or blocking of sounds — **stutter** *n* — **stut·ter·er** *n*

stutter step *n* : a move made by a runner (as in football) done to fake a defender out of position

¹**sty** \'stī\ *n, pl* **sties** : PIGPEN

²**sty** *or* **stye** *n, pl* **sties** *or* **styes** : an inflamed swelling of a skin gland on the edge of an eyelid

¹**style** \'stī(-ə)l\ *n* **1** : mode of address : TITLE **2** : a way of speaking or writing; *esp* : one characteristic of an individual, period, school, or nation ⟨ornate ~⟩ **3** : manner or method of acting, making, or performing; *also* : a distinctive or characteristic manner **4** : a slender pointed instrument or process; *esp* : STYLUS **5** : a fashionable manner or mode **6** : overall excellence, skill, or grace in performance, manner, or appearance **7** : the custom followed in spelling, capitalization, punctuation, and typography — **sty·lis·tic** \stī-'lis-tik\ *adj*

²**style** *vb* **styled; styl·ing** **1** : NAME, DESIGNATE **2** : to make or design in accord with a prevailing mode ⟨~ hair⟩

styling *n* : the way in which something is styled

styl·ise *Brit var of* STYLIZE

styl·ish \'stī-lish\ *adj* : conforming to current fashion ◆ **Synonyms** MODISH, SMART, CHIC — **styl·ish·ly** *adv* — **styl·ish·ness** *n*

styl·ist \'stī-list\ *n* **1** : one (as a writer) noted for a distinctive style **2** : a developer or designer of styles

styl·ize \'stī-ˌlīz, 'stī-ə-\ *vb* **styl·ized; styl·iz·ing** : to conform to a style; *esp* : to represent or design according to a pattern or style rather than according to nature or tradition ⟨*stylized* flower prints⟩ — **styl·i·za·tion** \ˌstī-lə-'zā-shən\ *n*

sty·lus \'stī-ləs\ *n, pl* **sty·li** \'stī-ˌlī\ *also* **sty·lus·es** \'stī-lə-səz\ [L *stylus, stilus* spike, stylus] **1** : a pointed implement used by the ancients for writing on wax **2** : a phonograph needle **3** : a pen-shaped pointing device for entering data into a computer

sty·mie \'stī-mē\ *vb* **sty·mied; sty·mie·ing** : BLOCK, FRUSTRATE ⟨managed to ~ the opposition⟩

styp·tic \'stip-tik\ *adj* : tending to check bleeding — **styptic** *n*

suave \'swäv\ *adj* [F, fr. MF, pleasant, sweet, fr. L *suavis*] : persuasively pleasing : smoothly agreeable ◆ **Synonyms** URBANE, SMOOTH, BLAND — **suave·ly** *adv* — **sua·vi·ty** \'swä-və-tē\ *n*

¹**sub** \'səb\ *n* : SUBSTITUTE — **sub** *vb*

²**sub** *n* : SUBMARINE

³**sub** *abbr* **1** subtract **2** suburb

sub- \'səb\ *prefix* **1** : under : beneath **2** : subordinate : secondary **3** : subordinate portion of : subdivision of **4** : with repetition of a process described in a simple verb so as to form, stress, or deal with subordinate parts or relations **5** : somewhat **6** : falling nearly in the category of : bordering on

subacute	subliterate
subagency	subminimal
subagent	subminimum
subaqueous	suboptimal
subarctic	suborder
subarea	subparagraph
subatmospheric	subparallel
subaverage	subphylum
subbasement	subplot
subcategory	subpopulation
subcellular	subproblem
subchapter	subprofessional
subclass	subprogram
subclassify	subregion
subcommittee	subroutine
subcontract	subsection
subcontractor	subsense
subculture	subsoil
subcutaneous	substage
subdiscipline	substation
subentry	subsystem
subfamily	subteen
subfield	subthreshold
subfreezing	subtopic
subgenre	subtotal
subgenus	subtreasury
subgroup	subtype
subhead	subunit
subheading	subvariety
subhuman	subvisible
subkingdom	subzero
sublethal	

sub·al·pine \ˌsəb-'al-ˌpīn\ *adj* **1** : of or relating to the region about the foot and lower slopes of the Alps **2** : of, relating to, or inhabiting high upland slopes esp. just below the timberline

sub·al·tern \sə-'bȯl-tərn\ *n* : SUBORDINATE; *esp* : a junior officer (as in the British army)

sub·as·sem·bly \ˌsəb-ə-'sem-blē\ *n* : an assembled unit to be incorporated with other units in a finished product

sub·atom·ic \ˌsəb-ə-'tä-mik\ *adj* : of or relating to the inside of the atom or to particles smaller than atoms

sub·clin·i·cal \ˌsəb-'kli-ni-kəl\ *adj* : not detectable by the usual clinical tests ⟨a ~ infection⟩

sub·com·pact \'səb-'käm-ˌpakt\ *n* : an automobile smaller than a compact

¹**sub·con·scious** \ˌsəb-ə-'kän-chəs, 'səb-\ *adj* : existing in the mind without entering conscious awareness — **sub·con·scious·ly** *adv* — **sub·con·scious·ness** *n*

²**subconscious** *n* : mental activities just below the threshold of consciousness

sub·con·ti·nent \ˌsəb-'kän-tə-nənt\ *n* : a major subdivision of a continent — **sub·con·ti·nen·tal** \ˌsəb-ˌkän-tə-'nen-tᵊl\ *adj*

sub·di·vide \ˌsəb-də-'vīd, 'səb-də-ˌvīd\ *vb* : to divide the parts of into more parts; *esp* : to divide (a tract of land) into building lots — **sub·di·vi·sion** \-'vi-zhən, -ˌvi-\ *n*

sub·duc·tion \səb-'dək-shən\ *n* : the descent of the edge of one crustal plate beneath the edge of an adjacent plate

sub·due \səb-'dü, -'dyü\ *vb* **sub·dued; sub·du·ing** **1** : to bring into subjection : VANQUISH **2** : to bring under control : CURB **3** : to reduce the intensity of

subj *abbr* **1** subject **2** subjunctive

¹**sub·ject** \'səb-jikt\ *n* [ME *suget, subget,* fr. AF, fr. L *subjectus* one under authority *& subjectum* subject of a proposition, fr. *subicere* to subject, lit., to throw under, fr. *sub-* under + *jacere* to throw] **1** : a person under the authority of another **2** : a person subject to a sovereign **3** : an individual that is studied or experimented on **4** : the person or thing discussed or treated : TOPIC, THEME **5** : a word or word group denoting that of which something is predicated

²**subject** *adj* **1** : being under the power or rule of another **2** : LIABLE, EXPOSED ⟨~ to floods⟩ **3** : dependent on some act or condition ⟨appointment ~ to senate approval⟩ ✦ *Synonyms* SUBORDINATE, SECONDARY, TRIBUTARY, COLLATERAL, DEPENDENT

³**sub·ject** \səb-'jekt\ *vb* **1** : to bring under control : CONQUER **2** : to make liable **3** : to cause to undergo or endure — **sub·jec·tion** \-'jek-shən\ *n*

sub·jec·tive \(ˌ)səb-'jek-tiv\ *adj* **1** : of, relating to, or constituting a subject **2** : of, relating to, or arising within one's self or mind in contrast to what is outside : PERSONAL ⟨~ judgments⟩ ⟨a ~ sensation⟩ — **sub·jec·tive·ly** *adv* — **sub·jec·tiv·i·ty** \-ˌjek-'ti-və-tē\ *n*

subject matter *n* : matter presented for consideration, discussion, or study

sub·join \(ˌ)səb-'jóin\ *vb* : APPEND ⟨~ed a statement of expenses to her report⟩

sub ju·di·ce \(ˌ)süb-'yü-di-ˌkā, 'səb-'jü-də-(ˌ)sē\ *adv* [L] : before a judge or court : not yet legally decided

sub·ju·gate \'səb-ji-ˌgāt\ *vb* **-gat·ed; -gat·ing** : CONQUER, SUBDUE; *also* : ENSLAVE ✦ *Synonyms* REDUCE, OVERCOME, OVERTHROW, VANQUISH, DEFEAT, BEAT — **sub·ju·ga·tion** \ˌsəb-ji-'gā-shən\ *n*

sub·junc·tive \səb-'jəŋk-tiv\ *adj* : of, relating to, or constituting a verb form that represents an act or state as contingent or possible or viewed emotionally (as with desire) ⟨the ~ mood⟩ — **subjunctive** *n*

sub·lease \'səb-ˌlēs, -ˌlēs\ *n* : a lease by a lessee of part or all of leased premises to another person with the original lessee retaining some right under the original lease — **sublease** *vb*

¹**sub·let** \'səb-'let\ *vb* **-let; -let·ting** : to let all or a part of (a leased property) to another; *also* : to rent (a property) from a lessee

²**sublet** \-ˌlet\ *n* : property and esp. housing obtained by or available through a sublease

sub·li·mate \'səb-lə-ˌmāt\ *vb* **-mat·ed; -mat·ing** **1** : SUBLIME **2** : to direct the expression of (as a desire or impulse) from a primitive to a more socially and culturally acceptable form — **sub·li·ma·tion** \ˌsəb-blə-'mā-shən\ *n*

¹**sub·lime** \sə-'blīm\ *vb* **sub·limed; sub·lim·ing** : to pass or cause to pass directly from the solid to the vapor state

²**sublime** *adj* **1** : EXALTED, NOBLE **2** : having awe-inspiring beauty or grandeur ✦ *Synonyms* GLORIOUS, SPLENDID, SUPERB, RESPLENDENT, GORGEOUS — **sub·lime·ly** *adv* — **sub·lim·i·ty** \-'bli-mə-tē\ *n*

sub·lim·i·nal \(ˌ)səb-'li-mə-n°l, 'səb-\ *adj* [*sub-* + L *limin-, limen* threshold] **1** : inadequate to produce a sensation or mental awareness ⟨~ stimuli⟩ **2** : existing or functioning below the threshold of consciousness ⟨the ~ mind⟩ ⟨~ advertising⟩

sub·ma·chine gun \ˌsəb-mə-'shēn-ˌgən\ *n* : an automatic firearm fired from the shoulder or hip

¹**sub·ma·rine** \'səb-mə-ˌrēn, ˌsəb-mə-'rēn\ *adj* : UNDERWATER; *esp* : UNDERSEA

²**submarine** *n* **1** : a naval vessel designed to operate underwater **2** : a large sandwich made from a long split roll with any of a variety of fillings

sub·merge \səb-'mərj\ *vb* **sub·merged; sub·merg·ing** **1** : to put or plunge under the surface of water **2** : INUNDATE — **sub·mer·gence** \-'mər-jəns\ *n*

sub·merse \səb-'mərs\ *vb* **sub·mersed; sub·mers·ing** : SUBMERGE — **sub·mer·sion** \-'mər-zhən\ *n*

¹**sub·mers·ible** \səb-'mər-sə-bəl\ *adj* : capable of being submerged

²**submersible** *n* : something that is submersible; *esp* : a small underwater craft used for deep-sea research

sub·mi·cro·sco·pic \ˌsəb-ˌmī-krə-'skä-pik\ *adj* : too small to be seen in an ordinary light microscope

sub·min·ia·ture \ˌsəb-'mi-nē-ə-ˌchùr, 'səb-, -'mi-ni-ˌchùr, -chər\ *adj* : very small

sub·mit \səb-'mit\ *vb* **sub·mit·ted; sub·mit·ting** **1** : to commit to the discretion or decision of another or of others **2** : YIELD, SURRENDER **3** : to put forward as an opinion — **sub·mis·sion** \-'mi-shən\ *n* — **sub·mis·sive** \-'mi-siv\ *adj*

sub·nor·mal \ˌsəb-'nór-məl\ *adj* : falling below what is normal; *also* : having less of something and esp. intelligence than is normal — **sub·nor·mal·i·ty** \ˌsəb-nór-'ma-lə-tē\ *n*

sub·or·bit·al \ˌsəb-'ór-bə-t°l, 'səb-\ *adj* : being or involving less than one orbit

sub·or·di·nate \sə-'bór-də-nət\ *adj* **1** : of lower class or rank ⟨a ~ officer⟩ **2** : INFERIOR **3** : submissive to authority **4** : subordinated to other elements in a sentence : DEPENDENT ⟨~ clause⟩ ✦ *Synonyms* SECONDARY, SUBJECT, TRIBUTARY, COLLATERAL

²**subordinate** *n* : one that is subordinate

³**sub·or·di·nate** \sə-'bór-də-ˌnāt\ *vb* **-nat·ed; -nat·ing** **1** : SUBDUE **2** : to place in a lower rank or class — **sub·or·di·na·tion** \-ˌbór-də-'nā-shən\ *n*

sub·orn \sə-'bórn\ *vb* **1** : to induce secretly to do an unlawful thing **2** : to induce to commit perjury — **sub·or·na·tion** \ˌsə-ˌbór-'nā-shən\ *n*

¹**sub·poe·na** \sə-'pē-nə\ *n* [ME *suppena*, fr. L *sub poena* under penalty] : a writ commanding the person named in it to attend court under penalty for failure to do so

²**subpoena** *vb* **-naed; -na·ing** : to summon with a subpoena

sub–Sa·ha·ran \ˌsəb-sə-'her-ən\ *adj* : of, relating to, or being the part of Africa south of the Sahara

sub·scribe \səb-'skrīb\ *vb* **sub·scribed; sub·scrib·ing** **1** : to sign one's name to a document **2** : to give consent by or as if by signing one's name **3** : to promise to contribute by signing one's name with the amount promised **4** : to place an order by signing **5** : to receive a periodical or service regularly on order **6** : FAVOR, APPROVE ⟨~ to the theory⟩ ✦ *Synonyms* AGREE, ACQUIESCE, ASSENT, ACCEDE — **sub·scrib·er** *n*

sub·script \'səb-ˌskript\ *n* : a symbol (as a letter or number) immediately below or below and to the right or left of another written character — **subscript** *adj*

sub·scrip·tion \səb-'skrip-shən\ *n* **1** : the act of subscribing : SIGNATURE **2** : a purchase by signed order

sub·se·quent \'səb-si-kwənt, -sə-ˌkwent\ *adj* : following after : SUCCEEDING ⟨~ events⟩ — **sub·se·quent·ly** *adv*

sub·ser·vi·ence \səb-'sər-vē-əns\ *n* **1** : a subordinate place or condition **2** : SERVILITY — **sub·ser·vi·en·cy** \-ən-sē\ *n* — **sub·ser·vi·ent** \-ənt\ *adj*

sub·set \'səb-ˌset\ *n* : a set each of whose elements is an element of an inclusive set

sub·side \səb-'sīd\ *vb* **sub·sid·ed; sub·sid·ing** [L *subsidere,* fr. *sub-* under + *sidere* to sit down, sink] **1** : to settle to the bottom of a liquid **2** : to tend downward : DESCEND **3** : SINK, SUBMERGE ⟨*subsided* into a chair⟩ **4** : to become quiet and tranquil ✦ *Synonyms* ABATE, WANE, MODERATE, SLACKEN — **sub·sid·ence** \səb-'sī-d°ns, 'səb-sə-dəns\ *n*

¹**sub·sid·iary** \səb-'si-dē-ˌer-ē\ *adj* **1** : furnishing aid or support **2** : of secondary importance **3** : of or relating to a subsidy ✦ *Synonyms* AUXILIARY, CONTRIBUTORY, SUBSERVIENT, ACCESSORY

²**subsidiary** *n, pl* **-iar·ies** : one that is subsidiary; *esp* : a company controlled by another

sub·si·dise *Brit var of* SUBSIDIZE

sub·si·dize \'səb-sə-ˌdīz\ *vb* **-dized; -diz·ing** : to aid or furnish with a subsidy

sub·si·dy \'səb-sə-dē\ *n, pl* **-dies** [ME, *subsidie,* fr. AF, fr. L *subsidium* reserve troops, support, assistance, fr. *sub-* near + *sedēre* to sit] : a gift of public money to a private person or company or to another government

sub·sist \səb-'sist\ *vb* **1** : EXIST, PERSIST **2** : to have the means (as food and clothing) of maintaining life; *esp* : to nourish oneself

sub·sis·tence \səb-'sis-təns\ *n* **1** : EXISTENCE **2** : means of subsisting : the minimum (as of food and clothing) necessary to support life

sub·son·ic \ˌsəb-'sä-nik, 'səb-\ *adj* : being or relating to a speed less than that of sound; *also* : moving at such a speed

sub·spe·cies \'səb-ˌspē-shēz, -ˌspē-ˌsēz\ *n* : a subdivision of a species; *esp* : a category in biological classification ranking just below a species that designates a geographic population genetically distinct from other such populations and potentially able to breed with them where its range overlaps theirs

sub·stance \'səb-stəns\ *n* **1** : essential nature : ESSENCE ⟨divine ~⟩; *also* : the fundamental or essential part or quality ⟨the ~ of the speech⟩ **2** : physical material from which something is made or which has discrete existence; *also* : matter of particular or definite chemical constitution **3** : something (as drugs or alcohol) deemed harmful and usu. subject to legal restriction ⟨~ abuse⟩ **4** : material possessions : PROPERTY, WEALTH

sub·stan·dard \ˌsəb-ˈstan-dərd\ *adj* : falling short of a standard or norm

sub·stan·tial \səb-ˈstan-chəl\ *adj* **1** : existing as or in substance : MATERIAL; *also* : not illusory : REAL **2** : IMPORTANT, ESSENTIAL ⟨a ~ difference in the stories⟩ **3** : NOURISHING, SATISFYING ⟨~ meal⟩ **4** : having means : WELL-TO-DO **5** : CONSIDERABLE ⟨~ profit⟩ **6** : STRONG, FIRM — **sub·stan·tial·ly** *adv*

sub·stan·ti·ate \səb-ˈstan-chē-ˌāt\ *vb* **-at·ed; -at·ing 1** : to give substance or body to **2** : VERIFY, PROVE ⟨~ a charge⟩ — **sub·stan·ti·a·tion** \-ˌstan-chē-ˈā-shən\ *n*

¹sub·stan·tive \ˈsəb-stən-tiv\ *n* : NOUN; *also* : a word or phrase used as a noun

²substantive *adj* : having substance : REAL ⟨~ changes⟩

¹sub·sti·tute \ˈsəb-stə-ˌtüt, -ˌtyüt\ *n* : a person or thing replacing another — **substitute** *adj*

²substitute *vb* **-tut·ed; -tut·ing 1** : to put or use in the place of another **2** : to serve as a substitute — **sub·sti·tu·tion** \ˌsəb-stə-ˈtü-shən, -ˈtyü-\ *n*

sub·strate \ˈsəb-ˌstrāt\ *n* **1** : the base on which a plant or animal lives **2** : a substance acted upon (as by an enzyme)

sub·stra·tum \ˈsəb-ˌstrā-təm, -ˌstra-\ *n, pl* **-stra·ta** \-tə\ : the layer or structure (as subsoil) lying underneath

sub·struc·ture \ˈsəb-ˌstrək-chər\ *n* : FOUNDATION, GROUNDWORK

sub·sume \səb-ˈsüm\ *vb* **sub·sumed; sub·sum·ing** : to include or place within something larger or more comprehensive

sub·sur·face \ˈsəb-ˌsər-fəs\ *n* : earth material near the surface of the ground — **subsurface** *adj*

sub·ter·fuge \ˈsəb-tər-ˌfyüj\ *n* : a trick or device used in order to conceal, escape, or evade ◆ *Synonyms* FRAUD, DECEPTION, TRICKERY

sub·ter·ra·nean \ˌsəb-tə-ˈrā-nē-ən\ *adj* **1** : lying or being underground **2** : SECRET, HIDDEN ⟨a ~ network of criminals⟩

sub·tile \ˈsə-t⁰l\ *adj* **sub·til·er** \ˈsə-t⁰l-ər\; **sub·til·est** \ˈsə-t⁰l-əst\ : SUBTLE ⟨a ~ aroma⟩

sub·ti·tle \ˈsəb-ˌtī-t⁰l\ *n* **1** : a secondary or explanatory title (as of a book) **2** : printed matter projected on a motion-picture screen during or between the scenes

sub·tle \ˈsə-t⁰l\ *adj* **sub·tler** \ˈsə-t⁰l-ər\; **sub·tlest** \ˈsə-t⁰l-əst\ **1** : hardly noticeable ⟨~ differences⟩ **2** : SHREWD, PERCEPTIVE ⟨a ~ mind⟩ **3** : CLEVER, SLY ⟨a ~ rogue⟩ — **sub·tle·ty** \-tē\ *n* — **sub·tly** \ˈsə-t⁰l-ē\ *adv*

sub·tract \səb-ˈtrakt\ *vb* : to take away (as one part or number) from another; *also* : to perform the operation of deducting one number from another — **sub·trac·tion** \-ˈtrak-shən\ *n*

sub·tra·hend \ˈsəb-trə-ˌhend\ *n* : a number that is to be subtracted from another

sub·trop·i·cal \ˌsəb-ˈträ-pi-kəl, ˈsəb-\ *also* **sub·trop·ic** \-pik\ *adj* : of, relating to, or being regions bordering on the tropical zone ⟨a ~ environment⟩ — **sub·trop·ics** \-piks\ *n pl*

sub·urb \ˈsə-ˌbərb\ *n* **1** : an outlying part of a city; *also* : a small community adjacent to a city **2** *pl* : a residential area adjacent to a city — **sub·ur·ban** \sə-ˈbər-bən\ *adj or n* — **sub·ur·ban·ite** \sə-ˈbər-bə-ˌnīt\ *n*

sub·ur·bia \sə-ˈbər-bē-ə\ *n* **1** : SUBURBS **2** : suburban people or customs

sub·ven·tion \səb-ˈven-chən\ *n* : SUBSIDY, ENDOWMENT

sub·vert \səb-ˈvərt\ *vb* **1** : OVERTHROW, RUIN **2** : CORRUPT ⟨~ the rule of law⟩ — **sub·ver·sion** \-ˈvər-zhən\ *n* — **sub·ver·sive** \-ˈvər-siv\ *adj*

sub·way \ˈsəb-ˌwā\ *n* : an underground way; *esp* : an underground electric railway

sub·woof·er \ˈsəb-ˈwü-fər\ *n* : a loudspeaker responsive only to the lowest acoustic frequencies

suc·ceed \sək-ˈsēd\ *vb* **1** : to follow next in order or next after another; *esp* : to inherit sovereignty, rank, title, or property **2** : to attain a desired object or end : be successful

suc·cess \sək-ˈses\ *n* **1** : favorable or desired outcome **2** : the gaining of wealth and fame **3** : one that succeeds — **suc·cess·ful** \-fəl\ *adj* — **suc·cess·ful·ly** *adv*

suc·ces·sion \sək-ˈse-shən\ *n* **1** : the order, act, or right of succeeding to a property, title, or throne **2** : the act or process of following in order **3** : a series of persons or things that follow one after another ◆ *Synonyms* PROGRESSION, SEQUENCE, CHAIN, TRAIN, STRING

suc·ces·sive \sək-ˈse-siv\ *adj* : following in order : CONSECUTIVE ⟨three ~ days⟩ — **suc·ces·sive·ly** *adv*

suc·ces·sor \sək-ˈse-sər\ *n* : one that succeeds (as to a throne, title, estate, or office)

suc·cinct \(ˌ)sək-ˈsiŋkt, sə-ˈsiŋkt\ *adj* : BRIEF, CONCISE ⟨a ~ description⟩ ◆ *Synonyms* TERSE, LACONIC, SUMMARY, CURT, SHORT — **suc·cinct·ly** *adv* — **suc·cinct·ness** *n*

suc·cor \ˈsə-kər\ *n* [ME *socour, sucurs* (taken as pl.), fr. AF *sucur, sucors,* fr. ML *succursus,* fr. L *succurrere* to run to the rescue, bring aid] : AID, HELP, RELIEF — **succor** *vb*

suc·co·tash \ˈsə-kə-ˌtash\ *n* [Narragansett *msíckquatash* boiled corn kernels] : beans and corn kernels cooked together

suc·cour *chiefly Brit var of* SUCCOR

¹suc·cu·lent \ˈsə-kyə-lənt\ *adj* : full of juice : JUICY; *also* : having fleshy tissues that conserve moisture ⟨~ plants⟩ — **suc·cu·lence** \-ləns\ *n*

²succulent *n* : a succulent plant (as a cactus or an aloe)

suc·cumb \sə-ˈkəm\ *vb* **1** : to yield to superior strength or force or overpowering appeal or desire **2** : DIE ◆ *Synonyms* SUBMIT, CAPITULATE, RELENT, DEFER

¹such \ˈsəch, ˈsich\ *adj* **1** : of this or that kind **2** : having a quality just specified or to be specified

²such *pron* **1** : such a one or ones ⟨he's a star, and acted as ~⟩ **2** : that or those similar or related thereto ⟨boards and nails and ~⟩

³such *adv* : to that degree : so

such·like \ˈsəch-ˌlīk\ *adj* : SIMILAR

¹suck \ˈsək\ *vb* **1** : to draw in liquid and esp. mother's milk with the mouth **2** : to draw liquid from by action of the mouth ⟨~ an orange⟩ **3** : to take in or up or remove by or as if by suction **4** *slang* : to be objectionable

²suck *n* **1** : a sucking movement or force **2** : the act of sucking

suck·er \ˈsə-kər\ *n* **1** : one that sucks **2** : a part of an animal's body used for sucking or for clinging **3** : any of numerous freshwater fishes with thick soft lips for sucking in food **4** : a shoot from the roots or lower part of a plant **5** : a person easily deceived **6** — used as a generalized term of reference ⟨see if you can get that ~ working again⟩

suck·le \ˈsə-kəl\ *vb* **suck·led; suck·ling** : to give or draw milk from the breast or udder; *also* : NURTURE

suck·ling \ˈsə-kliŋ\ *n* : a young unweaned mammal

suck–up \ˈsək-ˌəp\ *n* : a person who seeks to gain favor by flattery ⟨a ~ to the teacher⟩

su·cre \ˈsü-(ˌ)krā\ *n* : the basic monetary unit of Ecuador until 2000

su·crose \ˈsü-ˌkrōs, -ˌkrōz\ *n* : a sweet sugar obtained commercially esp. from sugarcane or sugar beets

suc·tion \ˈsək-shən\ *n* **1** : the act of sucking **2** : the act or process of drawing something (as liquid or dust) into a space (as in a vacuum cleaner or a pump) by partially exhausting the air in the space — **suc·tion·al** \-shə-nəl\ *adj*

suction cup *n* : a cup-shaped device in which a partial vacuum is produced when applied to a surface

sud·den \ˈsə-d⁰n\ *adj* [ME *sodain,* fr. AF *sudain,* fr. L *subitaneus,* fr. *subitus* sudden, fr. pp. of *subire* to come up] **1** : happening or coming unexpectedly ⟨~ shower⟩; *also* : changing angle or character all at once ⟨~ turn⟩ ⟨~ descent⟩ **2** : HASTY, RASH ⟨~ decision⟩ **3** : made or brought about in a short time : PROMPT ⟨~ cure⟩ ◆ *Synonyms* PRECIPITATE, HEADLONG, IMPETUOUS — **sud·den·ly** *adv* — **sud·den·ness** *n*

sudden infant death syndrome *n* : death due to unknown causes of an apparently healthy infant usu. before one year of age and esp. during sleep

su·do·ku \sü-ˈdō-kü\ *n* [Jp *sūdoku,* short for *sūji wa dokushin ni kagiru* "the numerals must remain single"] : a puzzle in which several numbers are to be filled into a 9x9 grid of squares so that every row, every column, and every 3x3 box contains the numbers 1 through 9

suds \ˈsədz\ *n pl* : soapy water esp. when frothy — **sudsy** \ˈsəd-zē\ *adj*

sue \ˈsü\ *vb* **sued; su·ing** [ME *sewen, siuen* to follow, strive for, petition, fr. AF *sivre, siure,* fr. VL **sequere,* fr. L *sequi* to follow] **1** : PETITION, SOLICIT ⟨sued for peace⟩ **2** : to seek justice or right by bringing legal action ⟨sued the company⟩

suede *also* **suède** \'swād\ *n* [F *gants de Suède* Swedish gloves] **1** : leather with a napped surface **2** : a fabric with a suedelike nap

su·et \'sü-ət\ *n* : the hard fat from beef and mutton that yields tallow

suff *abbr* **1** sufficient **2** suffix

suf·fer \'sə-fər\ *vb* **suf·fered; suf·fer·ing** **1** : to feel or endure pain **2** : EXPERIENCE, UNDERGO ⟨~ a defeat⟩ **3** : to bear loss, damage, or injury **4** : ALLOW, PERMIT ✦ **Synonyms** ENDURE, ABIDE, TOLERATE, STAND, BROOK, STOMACH — **suf·fer·able** \'sə-fə-rə-bəl\ *adj* — **suf·fer·er** *n*

suf·fer·ance \'sə-frəns, -fə-rəns\ *n* **1** : consent or approval implied by lack of interference or resistance **2** : ENDURANCE, PATIENCE

suf·fer·ing \'sə-friŋ, -fə-riŋ\ *n* : PAIN, MISERY, HARDSHIP ⟨human ~⟩

suf·fice \sə-'fīs\ *vb* **suf·ficed; suf·fic·ing** **1** : to satisfy a need : be sufficient **2** : to be capable or competent

suf·fi·cien·cy \sə-'fi-shən-sē\ *n* **1** : a sufficient quantity to meet one's needs **2** : ADEQUACY

suf·fi·cient \sə-'fi-shənt\ *adj* : adequate to accomplish a purpose or meet a need — **suf·fi·cient·ly** *adv*

¹suf·fix \'sə-,fiks\ *n* : an affix occurring at the end of a word

²suf·fix \'sə-,fiks, (,)sə-'fiks\ *vb* : to attach as a suffix — **suf·fix·ation** \,sə-,fik-'sā-shən\ *n*

suf·fo·cate \'sə-fə-,kāt\ *vb* **-cat·ed; -cat·ing** : STIFLE, SMOTHER, CHOKE — **suf·fo·cat·ing·ly** *adv* — **suf·fo·ca·tion** \,sə-fə-'kā-shən\ *n*

suf·fra·gan \'sə-fri-gən\ *n* : an assistant bishop; *esp* : one not having the right of succession — **suffragan** *adj*

suf·frage \'sə-frij\ *n* [L *suffragium*] **1** : VOTE **2** : the right to vote : FRANCHISE

suf·frag·ette \,sə-fri-'jet\ *n* : a woman who advocates suffrage for women

suf·frag·ist \'sə-fri-jist\ *n* : one who advocates extension of suffrage esp. to women

suf·fuse \sə-'fyüz\ *vb* **suf·fused; suf·fus·ing** : to spread over or through in the manner of a fluid or light ✦ **Syn·onyms** INFUSE, IMBUE, INGRAIN, STEEP — **suf·fu·sion** \-'fyü-zhən\ *n*

¹sug·ar \'shu̇-gər\ *n* **1** : a sweet substance that is colorless or white when pure and is chiefly sucrose from sugarcane or sugar beets **2** : a water-soluble compound (as glucose) similar to sucrose — **sug·ary** *adj*

²sugar *vb* **sug·ared; sug·ar·ing** **1** : to mix, cover, or sprinkle with sugar **2** : SWEETEN ⟨~ advice with flattery⟩ **3** : to form sugar ⟨a syrup that ~s⟩ **4** : GRANULATE

sugar beet *n* : a large beet with a white root from which sugar is made

sug·ar·cane \'shu̇-gər-,kān\ *n* : a tall grass widely grown in warm regions for the sugar in its stalks

sugar daddy *n* **1** : a well-to-do usu. older man who supports or spends lavishly on a mistress, girlfriend, or boyfriend **2** : a generous benefactor of a cause

sugar maple *n* : a maple with a sweet sap; *esp* : one of eastern No. America with sap that is the chief source of maple syrup and maple sugar

sugar pea *n* : SNOW PEA

sug·ar·plum \'shu̇-gər-,pləm\ *n* : a small ball of candy

sug·gest \səg-'jest, sə-\ *vb* **1** : to put (as a thought, plan, or desire) into a person's mind **2** : to remind or evoke by association of ideas ✦ **Synonyms** IMPLY, HINT, INTIMATE, INSINUATE, CONNOTE

sug·gest·ible \səg-'jes-tə-bəl, sə-\ *adj* : easily influenced by suggestion

sug·ges·tion \-'jes-chən\ *n* **1** : an act or instance of suggesting; *also* : something suggested **2** : a slight indication

sug·ges·tive \-'jes-tiv\ *adj* : tending to suggest something; *esp* : suggesting something improper or indecent — **sug·ges·tive·ly** *adv* — **sug·ges·tive·ness** *n*

¹sui·cide \'sü-ə-,sīd\ *n* **1** : the act of killing oneself purposely **2** : one that commits or attempts suicide — **sui·cid·al** \,sü-ə-'sī-dᵊl\ *adj*

²suicide *adj* : being or performing a deliberate act resulting in the voluntary death of the person who does it ⟨a ~ mission⟩ ⟨a ~ bomber⟩

sui ge·ner·is \,sü-,ī-'je-nə-rəs, ,sü-ē-\ *adj* [L, of its own kind] : being in a class by itself : UNIQUE

¹suit \'süt\ *n* **1** : an action in court to recover a right or claim **2** : an act of suing or entreating; *esp* : COURTSHIP **3** : a number of things used together ⟨~ of clothes⟩ **4** : all the playing cards in a pack bearing the same symbol

²suit *vb* **1** : to be appropriate or fitting **2** : to be becoming to **3** : to meet the needs or desires of : PLEASE

suit·able \'sü-tə-bəl\ *adj* : FITTING, PROPER, APPROPRIATE ⟨~ dress⟩ ✦ **Synonyms** FIT, MEET, APT, HAPPY — **suit·abil·i·ty** \,sü-tə-'bi-lə-tē\ *n* — **suit·able·ness** \'sü-tə-bəl-nəs\ *n* — **suit·ably** \-tə-blē\ *adv*

suit·case \'süt-,kās\ *n* : a portable case designed to hold a traveler's clothing and personal articles

suite \'swēt, *for 4 also* 'süt\ *n* **1** : RETINUE **2** : a group of rooms occupied as a unit **3** : a modern instrumental composition in several movements of different character; *also* : a long orchestral concert arrangement in suite form of material drawn from a longer work **4** : a set of matched furniture for a room

suit·ing \'sü-tiŋ\ *n* : fabric for suits of clothes

suit·or \'sü-tər\ *n* **1** : one who sues or petitions **2** : one who courts a woman or seeks to marry her

su·ki·ya·ki \skē-'yä-kē, su̇-kē-'yä-\ *n* : thin slices of meat, tofu, and vegetables cooked in soy sauce and sugar

sul·fa drug \'səl-fə-\ *n* : any of various synthetic organic bacteria-inhibiting drugs

sul·fate \'səl-,fāt\ *n* : a salt or ester of sulfuric acid

sul·fide \'səl-'fīd\ *n* : a compound of sulfur

sul·fur *also* **sul·phur** \'səl-fər\ *n* : a nonmetallic chemical element used esp. in the chemical and paper industries and in vulcanizing rubber

sulfur di·ox·ide \-dī-'äk-sīd\ *n* : a heavy pungent toxic gas that is used esp. in bleaching, as a preservative, and as a refrigerant, and is a major air pollutant

sul·fu·ric \səl-'fyu̇r-ik\ *adj* : of, relating to, or containing sulfur

sulfuric acid *or* **sul·phu·ric acid** \,səl-'fyu̇r-ik-\ *n* : a heavy corrosive oily strong acid

sul·fu·rous *also* **sul·phu·rous** \'səl-fə-rəs, -fyə-, *also esp for 1* ,səl-'fyu̇r-əs\ *adj* **1** : of, relating to, or containing sulfur **2** : of or relating to brimstone or the fire of hell : INFERNAL **3** : FIERY, INFLAMED ⟨~ sermons⟩

¹sulk \'səlk\ *vb* : to be or become moodily silent or irritable

²sulk *n* : a sulky mood or spell

¹sulky \'səl-kē\ *adj* **sulk·i·er; -est** : inclined to sulk : MOROSE, MOODY ⟨a ~ mood⟩ ✦ **Synonyms** SURLY, GLUM, SULLEN, GLOOMY — **sulk·i·ly** \'səl-kə-lē\ *adv* — **sulk·i·ness** \-kē-nəs\ *n*

²sulky *n, pl* **sulkies** : a light 2-wheeled horse-drawn vehicle with a seat for the driver and usu. no body

sul·len \'sə-lən\ *adj* **1** : gloomily silent : MOROSE **2** : DISMAL, GLOOMY ⟨a ~ sky⟩ ✦ **Synonyms** GLUM, SURLY, DOUR, SATURNINE — **sul·len·ly** *adv* — **sul·len·ness** *n*

sul·ly \'sə-lē\ *vb* **sul·lied; sul·ly·ing** : SOIL, SMIRCH, DEFILE ⟨~ his name⟩

sul·tan \'səl-t³n\ *n* : a sovereign esp. of a Muslim state — **sul·tan·ate** \-,āt\ *n*

sul·ta·na \,səl-'ta-nə\ *n* **1** : a female member of a sultan's family **2** : a pale seedless grape; *also* : a raisin of this grape

sul·try \'səl-trē\ *adj* **sul·tri·er; -est** [obs. E *sulter* to swelter, alter. of E *swelter*] : very hot and moist : SWELTERING; *also* : exciting sexual desire ⟨a ~ look⟩

¹sum \'səm\ *n* [ME *summe*, fr. AF *sume, somme*, fr. L *summa*, fr. fem. of *summus* highest] **1** : a quantity of money **2** : the whole amount **3** : GIST ⟨the ~ of an argument⟩ **4** : the result obtained by adding numbers **5** : a problem in arithmetic

²sum *vb* **summed; sum·ming** : to find the sum of by adding or counting

³sum *n* : — see MONEY table

su·mac *also* **su·mach** \'sü-,mak, 'shü-\ *n* : any of a genus of trees, shrubs, and woody vines having spikes or loose clusters of red or whitish berries

sum·ma·rise *Brit var of* SUMMARIZE

sum·ma·rize \'sə-mə-,rīz\ *vb* **-rized; -riz·ing** : to tell in a summary

¹sum·ma·ry \'sə-mə-rē\ *adj* **1** : covering the main points briefly : CONCISE **2** : done without delay or formality ⟨~ punishment⟩ ✦ **Synonyms** TERSE, SUCCINCT, LACONIC — **sum·mar·i·ly** \(,)sə-'mer-ə-lē, 'sə-mə-rə-lē\ *adv*

²**summary** *n, pl* **-ries** : a concise statement of the main points
sum·ma·tion \(ˌ)sə-'mā-shən\ *n* : a summing up; *esp* : a speech in court summing up the arguments in a case
sum·mer \'sə-mər\ *n* : the season of the year in a region in which the sun shines most directly : the warmest period of the year — **sum·mery** *adj*
sum·mer·house \'sə-mər-ˌhaůs\ *n* : a covered structure in a garden or park to provide a shady retreat
summersault *var of* SOMERSAULT
summer squash *n* : any of various squashes (as zucchini) used as a vegetable while immature
sum·mit \'sə-mət\ *n* **1** : the highest point **2** : a conference of highest-level officials ⟨an economic ∼⟩
sum·mon \'sə-mən\ *vb* [ME *somnen, somonen,* fr. AF *somondre,* fr. VL *summonere,* alter. of L *summonēre* to remind secretly] **1** : to call to a meeting : CONVOKE **2** : to send for; *also* : to order to appear in court **3** : to evoke esp. by an act of the will ⟨∼ up courage⟩ — **sum·mon·er** *n*
sum·mons \'sə-mənz\ *n, pl* **sum·mons·es 1** : an authoritative call to appear at a designated place or to attend to a duty **2** : a warning or citation to appear in court at a specified time to answer charges
sump·tu·ous \'səmp-shə-wəs, -chə-\ *adj* : LAVISH, LUXURIOUS ⟨a ∼ banquet⟩ ⟨a ∼ residence⟩
sum up *vb* : SUMMARIZE
¹**sun** \'sən\ *n* **1** : the shining celestial body around which the earth and other planets revolve and from which they receive light and heat **2** : a celestial body like the sun **3** : SUNSHINE — **sun·less** *adj* — **sun·ny** *adj*
²**sun** *vb* **sunned; sun·ning 1** : to expose to or as if to the rays of the sun **2** : to sun oneself
Sun *abbr* Sunday
sun·bath \'sən-ˌbath, -ˌbäth\ *n* : an exposure to sunlight or a sunlamp — **sun·bathe** \-ˌbāth\ *vb*
sun·beam \-ˌbēm\ *n* : a ray of sunlight
sun·block \'sən-ˌbläk\ *n* : a preparation used on the skin to prevent sunburn (as by blocking ultraviolet radiation)
sun·bon·net \-ˌbä-nət\ *n* : a bonnet with a wide brim to shield the face and neck from the sun
¹**sun·burn** \-ˌbərn\ *vb* **-burned** \-ˌbərnd\ *or* **-burnt** \-ˌbərnt\; **-burn·ing** : to cause or become affected with sunburn
²**sunburn** *n* : a skin inflammation caused by overexposure to ultraviolet radiation esp. from sunshine
sun·dae \'sən-(ˌ)dā, -dē\ *n* : ice cream served with topping
Sun·day \'sən-ˌdā, -dē\ *n* : the 1st day of the week : the Christian Sabbath
sun·der \'sən-dər\ *vb* : to force apart ⟨a family ∼ed by scandal⟩ ♦ **Synonyms** SEVER, PART, DISJOIN, DISUNITE
sun·di·al \'sən-ˌdī(-ə)l\ *n* : a device for showing the time of day from the shadow cast on a plate by an object with a straight edge

sundial

sun·down \-ˌdaůn\ *n* : SUNSET 2
sun·dries \'sən-drēz\ *n pl* : various small articles or items
sun·dry \'sən-drē\ *adj* : SEVERAL, DIVERS, VARIOUS ⟨for ∼ reasons⟩
sun·fish \'sən-ˌfish\ *n* **1** : a large marine fish with a deep flattened body **2** : any of numerous often brightly colored No. American freshwater fishes related to the perches and usu. having the body flattened from side to side
sun·flow·er \-ˌflaů(-ə)r\ *n* : any of a genus of tall New World plants related to the daisies and often grown for the oil-rich seeds of their yellow-petaled dark-centered flower heads

sung *past and past part of* SING
sun·glasses \'sən-ˌgla-səz\ *n pl* : glasses to protect the eyes from the sun
sunk *past and past part of* SINK
sunk·en \'sən-kən\ *adj* **1** : SUBMERGED ⟨∼ ships⟩ **2** : fallen in : HOLLOW ⟨∼ cheeks⟩ **3** : lying in a depression ⟨∼ garden⟩; *also* : constructed below the general floor level ⟨a ∼ living room⟩
sun·lamp \'sən-ˌlamp\ *n* : an electric lamp designed to emit radiation of wavelengths from ultraviolet to infrared
sun·light \-ˌlīt\ *n* : SUNSHINE
sun·lit \-ˌlit\ *adj* : lighted by or as if by the sun
sun protection factor *n* : a number that is the factor by which the time required for unprotected skin to become sunburned is increased when a sunscreen is used
sun·rise \-ˌrīz\ *n* **1** : the apparent rising of the sun above the horizon **2** : the time at which the sun rises
sun·roof \-ˌrüf, -ˌrůf\ *n* : a panel in an automobile roof that can be opened
sun·screen \-ˌskrēn\ *n* : a preparation on the skin to prevent sunburn (as by absorbing ultraviolet radiation]
sun·set \-ˌset\ *n* **1** : the apparent descent of the sun below the horizon **2** : the time at which the sun sets
sun·shade \'sən-ˌshād\ *n* : something (as a parasol or awning) used as a protection from the sun's rays
sun·shine \-ˌshīn\ *n* : the direct light of the sun — **sun·shiny** *adj*
sun·spot \-ˌspät\ *n* : any of the dark spots that appear at times on the sun's surface
sun·stroke \-ˌstrōk\ *n* : heatstroke caused by direct exposure to the sun
sun·tan \-ˌtan\ *n* : a browning of the skin from exposure to the sun's rays
sun·up \-ˌəp\ *n* : SUNRISE 2
¹**sup** \'səp\ *vb* **supped; sup·ping** : to take or drink in swallows or gulps
²**sup** *n* : a mouthful esp. of liquor or broth; *also* : a small quantity of liquid
³**sup** *vb* **supped; sup·ping 1** : to eat the evening meal **2** : to make one's supper ⟨*supped* on roast beef⟩
⁴**sup** *abbr* **1** superior **2** supplement; supplementary **3** supply **4** supra
¹**su·per** \'sü-pər\ *adj* **1** : very fine : EXCELLENT **2** : EXTREME, EXCESSIVE ⟨∼ secrecy⟩
²**super** *n* : SUPERINTENDENT
super- \ˌsü-pər\ *prefix* **1** : over and above : higher in quantity, quality, or degree than : more than **2** : in addition : extra **3** : exceeding a norm **4** : in excessive degree or intensity **5** : surpassing all or most others of its kind **6** : situated above, on, or at the top of **7** : next above or higher **8** : more inclusive than **9** : superior in status or position

superabsorbent	superpatriotism
superachiever	superpremium
superagency	superrich
superblock	supersalesman
superbomb	supersecret
supercity	supersize
superclean	supersized
superexpensive	supersmart
superfast	supersophisticated
superfine	superspy
superheat	superstar
superheavy	superstate
superhero	superstore
superhuman	superstratum
superhumanly	superstrength
superindividual	superstrong
superliner	supersubtle
superman	supersystem
supernormal	supertanker
superpatriot	superthin
superpatriotic	superwoman

su·per·abun·dant \ˌsü-pər-ə-'bən-dənt\ *adj* : more than ample — **su·per·abun·dance** \-dəns\ *n*
su·per·an·nu·ate \ˌsü-pər-'an-yə-ˌwāt\ *vb* **-at·ed; -at·ing 1** : to make out-of-date **2** : to retire and pension because of age or infirmity — **su·per·an·nu·at·ed** *adj*
su·perb \sů-'pərb\ *adj* [L *superbus* excellent, proud,

fr. *super* above] : marked to the highest degree by excellence, brilliance, or competence ✦ *Synonyms* RESPLENDENT, GLORIOUS, GORGEOUS, SUBLIME — **superb·ly** *adv*

su·per·charg·er \'sü-pər-,chär-jər\ *n* : a device for increasing the amount of air supplied to an internal combustion engine

su·per·cil·ious \,sü-pər-'si-lē-əs\ *adj* [L *superciliosus*, fr. *supercilium* eyebrow, haughtiness] : haughtily contemptuous ✦ *Synonyms* DISDAINFUL, OVERBEARING, ARROGANT, LORDLY, SUPERIOR

su·per·com·pu·ter \'sü-pər-kəm-,pyü-tər\ *n* : a large very fast mainframe

su·per·con·duc·tiv·i·ty \,sü-pər-,kän-,dək-'ti-və-tē\ *n* : a complete disappearance of electrical resistance in a substance esp. at very low temperatures — **super·con·duc·tive** \-kən-'dək-tiv\ *adj* — **su·per·con·duc·tor** \-'dək-tər\ *n*

su·per·con·ti·nent \'sü-pər-,kän-tə-nənt\ *n* : a former large continent from which other continents are held to have broken off and drifted away

su·per·ego \,sü-pər-'ē-gō\ *n* : the one of the three divisions of the psyche in psychoanalytic theory that functions to reward and punish through a system of moral attitudes, conscience, and a sense of guilt

su·per·fi·cial \,sü-pər-'fi-shəl\ *adj* 1 : of or relating to the surface or appearance only 2 : not thorough : SHALLOW ⟨a ∼ analysis⟩ — **su·per·fi·ci·al·i·ty** \-,fi-shē-'a-lə-tē\ *n* — **su·per·fi·cial·ly** *adv*

su·per·flu·ous \sü-'pər-flə-wəs\ *adj* : exceeding what is sufficient or necessary : SURPLUS ⟨∼ details⟩ ✦ *Synonyms* EXTRA, SPARE, SUPERNUMERARY — **su·per·flu·i·ty** \,sü-pər-'flü-ə-tē\ *n*

su·per·high·way \,sü-pər-'hī-,wā\ *n* : a broad highway designed for high-speed traffic

su·per·im·pose \-im-'pōz\ *vb* : to lay (one thing) over or above something else

su·per·in·tend \,sü-pə-rin-'tend\ *vb* : to have or exercise the charge and oversight of : DIRECT ⟨∼ed the school system⟩ — **su·per·in·ten·dence** \-'ten-dəns\ *n* — **su·per·in·ten·den·cy** \-dən-sē\ *n* — **su·per·in·ten·dent** \-dənt\ *n*

¹**su·pe·ri·or** \su̇-'pir-ē-ər\ *adj* 1 : situated higher up, over, or near the top; *also* : higher in rank or numbers 2 : of greater value or importance 3 : courageously indifferent (as to pain or misfortune) 4 : better than most others of its kind 5 : ARROGANT, HAUGHTY — **su·pe·ri·or·i·ty** \-,pir-ē-'ȯr-ə-tē\ *n*

²**superior** *n* 1 : one who is above another in rank, office, or station; *esp* : the head of a religious house or order 2 : one higher in quality or merit

¹**su·per·la·tive** \su̇-'pər-lə-tiv\ *adj* 1 : of, relating to, or constituting the degree of grammatical comparison that denotes an extreme or unsurpassed level or extent 2 : surpassing others : SUPREME ✦ *Synonyms* PEERLESS, INCOMPARABLE, SUPERB — **su·per·la·tive·ly** *adv*

²**superlative** *n* 1 : the superlative degree or a superlative form in a language 2 : the utmost degree : ACME

su·per·mar·ket \'sü-pər-,mär-kət\ *n* : a self-service retail market selling foods and household merchandise

su·per·mod·el \'sü-pər-,mä-d°l\ *n* : a famous and successful fashion model

su·per·mom \'sü-pər-,mäm\ *n* : an exemplary mother; *also* : a woman who performs the traditional duties of housekeeping and raising children while also having a full-time job

su·per·nal \su̇-'pər-nəl\ *adj* 1 : being or coming from on high 2 : of heavenly or spiritual character

su·per·nat·u·ral \,sü-pər-'na-chə-rəl\ *adj* : of or relating to phenomena beyond or outside of nature; *esp* : relating to or attributed to a divinity, ghost, or devil — **su·per·nat·u·ral·ly** *adv*

su·per·no·va \,sü-pər-'nō-və\ *n* : the explosion of a very large star

¹**su·per·nu·mer·ary** \-'nü-mə-,rer-ē, -'nyü-\ *adj* : exceeding the usual or required number : EXTRA ✦ *Synonyms* SURPLUS, SUPERFLUOUS, SPARE

²**supernumerary** *n, pl* **-ar·ies** : an extra person or thing; *esp* : an actor hired for a nonspeaking part

su·per·pose \,sü-pər-'pōz\ *vb* **-posed; -pos·ing** : SUPERIMPOSE — **su·per·po·si·tion** \-pə-'zi-shən\ *n*

su·per·pow·er \'sü-pər-,pau̇(-ə)r\ *n* 1 : excessive or superior power 2 : one of a few politically and militarily dominant nations

su·per·sat·u·rat·ed \-'sa-chə-,rā-təd\ *adj* : containing an amount of a substance greater than that required for saturation

su·per·script \'sü-pər-,skript\ *n* : a symbol (as a numeral or letter) written immediately above or above and to one side of another character

su·per·sede \,sü-pər-'sēd\ *vb* **-sed·ed; -sed·ing** [ME (Sc) *superceden* to defer, fr. MF *superceder*, fr. L *supersedēre* to be superior to, refrain from, fr. *super-* above + *sedēre* to sit] : to take the place of : REPLACE ⟨this edition ∼s the previous one⟩

su·per·son·ic \-'sä-nik\ *adj* 1 : ULTRASONIC 2 : being or relating to speeds from one to five times the speed of sound; *also* : capable of moving at such a speed ⟨a ∼ airplane⟩

su·per·sti·tion \,sü-pər-'sti-shən\ *n* 1 : beliefs or practices resulting from ignorance, fear of the unknown, or trust in magic or chance 2 : an unreasoning fear of nature, the unknown, or God resulting from superstition — **su·per·sti·tious** \-shəs\ *adj*

su·per·struc·ture \'sü-pər-,strək-chər\ *n* : something built on a base or as a vertical extension

su·per·ti·tle \'sü-pər-,tī-t°l\ *n* : a translation of foreign-language dialogue displayed above a screen or performance

su·per·vene \,sü-pər-'vēn\ *vb* **-vened; -ven·ing** : to occur as something additional or unexpected

su·per·vise \'sü-pər-,vīz\ *vb* **-vised; -vis·ing** : OVERSEE, SUPERINTEND — **su·per·vi·sion** \,sü-pər-'vi-zhən\ *n* — **su·per·vi·sor** \'sü-pər-,vī-zər\ *n* — **su·per·vi·so·ry** \,sü-pər-'vī-zə-rē\ *adj*

su·pine \su̇-'pīn\ *adj* 1 : lying on the back or with the face upward 2 : LETHARGIC, SLUGGISH; *also* : ABJECT ⟨a ∼ legislature⟩ ✦ *Synonyms* INACTIVE, INERT, PASSIVE, IDLE

supp *or* **suppl** *abbr* supplement; supplementary

sup·per \'sə-pər\ *n* : the evening meal esp. when dinner is taken at midday — **sup·per·time** \-,tīm\ *n*

sup·plant \sə-'plant\ *vb* 1 : to take the place of (another) esp. by force or trickery 2 : REPLACE

sup·ple \'sə-pəl\ *adj* **sup·pler; sup·plest** 1 : COMPLIANT, ADAPTABLE 2 : capable of bending without breaking or creasing : LIMBER ✦ *Synonyms* RESILIENT, ELASTIC, FLEXIBLE

¹**sup·ple·ment** \'sə-plə-mənt\ *n* 1 : something that supplies a want or makes an addition 2 : DIETARY SUPPLEMENT 3 : a continuation (as of a book) containing corrections or additional material — **sup·ple·men·tal** \,sə-plə-'men-t°l\ *adj* — **sup·ple·men·ta·ry** \-'men-tə-rē\ *adj*

²**sup·ple·ment** \'sə-plə-,ment\ *vb* : to fill up the deficiencies of : add to — **sup·ple·men·ta·tion** \,sə-plə-,men-'tā-shən, -mən-\ *n*

sup·pli·ant \'sə-plē-ənt\ *n* : one who supplicates : PETITIONER, PLEADER

sup·pli·cant \'sə-pli-kənt\ *n* : SUPPLIANT

sup·pli·cate \'sə-plə-,kāt\ *vb* **-cat·ed; -cat·ing** 1 : to make a humble entreaty; *esp* : to pray to God 2 : to ask earnestly and humbly : BESEECH ✦ *Synonyms* IMPLORE, BEG, ENTREAT, PLEAD — **sup·pli·ca·tion** \,sə-plə-'kā-shən\ *n*

¹**sup·ply** \sə-'plī\ *vb* **sup·plied; sup·ply·ing** [ME *supplien*, to complete, compensate for, fr. MF *soupplier* fr. L *supplēre* to fill up, supplement, supply, fr. *sub-* under, up to + *plēre* to fill] 1 : to add as a supplement 2 : to satisfy the needs of 3 : FURNISH, PROVIDE — **sup·pli·er** *n*

²**supply** *n, pl* **supplies** 1 : the quantity or amount (as of a commodity) needed or available; *also* : PROVISIONS, STORES — usu. used in pl. 2 : the act or process of filling a want or need : PROVISION 3 : the quantities of goods or services offered for sale at a particular time or at one price

sup·ply-side \sə-'plī-,sīd\ *adj* : of, relating to, or being an economic theory that recommends the reduction of tax rates to expand economic activity

¹**sup·port** \sə-'pȯrt\ *vb* 1 : BEAR, TOLERATE 2 : to take sides with : BACK, ASSIST 3 : to provide with food, clothing, and shelter 4 : to hold up or serve as a founda-

tion for ✦ *Synonyms* UPHOLD, ADVOCATE, CHAMPION — **sup·port·able** *adj* — **sup·port·er** *n* — **sup·port·ive** \-'pȯr-tiv\ *adj*

²**support** *n* 1 : the act of supporting : the state of being supported 2 : one that supports : PROP, BASE 3 : help given in the form of money, information, or services

support group *n* : a group of people with common experiences and concerns who provide emotional and moral support for one another

sup·pose \sə-'pōz\ *vb* **sup·posed; sup·pos·ing** 1 : to assume to be true (as for the sake of argument) 2 : EXPECT ⟨I am *supposed* to go⟩ 3 : to think probable ⟨I ~ so⟩ — **sup·pos·al** *n*

sup·posed \sə-'pōzd, -'pō-zəd\ *adj* : BELIEVED; *also* : mistakenly believed ⟨a ~ cure⟩ — **sup·pos·ed·ly** \-'pō-zəd-lē, -'pōzd-lē\ *adv*

sup·pos·ing *conj* : if by way of hypothesis : on the assumption that ⟨~ I did agree with you⟩

sup·po·si·tion \,sə-pə-'zi-shən\ *n* 1 : something that is supposed : HYPOTHESIS 2 : the act of supposing

sup·pos·i·to·ry \sə-'pä-zə-,tȯr-ē\ *n, pl* **-ries** [ME *suppositorie*, fr. AF, fr. ML *suppositorium*, fr. LL, neut. of *suppositorius* placed beneath] : a small easily melted mass of usu. medicated material for insertion (as into the rectum)

sup·press \sə-'pres\ *vb* 1 : to put down by authority or force : SUBDUE ⟨~ a revolt⟩ 2 : to keep from being known; *also* : to stop the publication or circulation of 3 : to hold back : REPRESS ⟨~ anger⟩ ⟨~ a cough⟩ — **sup·press·ible** \-'pre-sə-bəl\ *adj* — **sup·pres·sion** \-'pre-shən\ *n* — **sup·pres·sor** \-'pre-sər\ *n*

sup·pres·sant \sə-'pre-sᵊnt\ *n* : an agent (as a drug) suppressing rather than eliminating something ⟨a cough ~⟩

sup·pu·rate \'sə-pyə-,rāt\ *vb* **-rat·ed; -rat·ing** : to form or give off pus — **sup·pu·ra·tion** \,sə-pyə-'rā-shən\ *n*

su·pra \'sü-prə, -,prä\ *adv* : earlier in this writing : ABOVE

su·pra·na·tion·al \,sü-prə-'na-shə-nəl, -,prä-\ *adj* : going beyond national boundaries, authority, or interests ⟨~ organizations⟩

su·prem·a·cist \su̇-'pre-mə-sist\ *n* : an advocate of group supremacy

su·prem·a·cy \su̇-'pre-mə-sē\ *n, pl* **-cies** : supreme rank, power, or authority

su·preme \su̇-'prēm\ *adj* [L *supremus*, superl. of *superus* upper, fr. *super* over, above] 1 : highest in rank or authority 2 : highest in degree or quality ⟨~ among poets⟩ 3 : ULTIMATE ⟨the ~ sacrifice⟩ ✦ *Synonyms* SUPERLATIVE, SURPASSING, PEERLESS, INCOMPARABLE — **su·preme·ly** *adv* — **su·preme·ness** *n*

Supreme Being *n* : GOD 1

supt *abbr* superintendent

sur·cease \'sər-,sēs\ *n* : CESSATION, RESPITE ⟨a ~ from pain⟩

¹**sur·charge** \'sər-,chärj\ *vb* 1 : to fill to excess : OVERLOAD 2 : to apply a surcharge to (postage stamps)

²**surcharge** *n* 1 : an extra fee or cost 2 : an excessive load or burden 3 : something officially printed on a postage stamp esp. to change its value

sur·cin·gle \'sər-,siŋ-gəl\ *n* : a band put around a horse's body to make something (as a saddle) fast

¹**sure** \'shu̇r\ *adj* **sur·er; sur·est** [ME, *seur, sure,*fr. AF *seur*, fr. L *securus* secure] 1 : firmly established 2 : TRUSTWORTHY, RELIABLE ⟨a ~ friend⟩ 3 : CONFIDENT ⟨I'm ~ I'm right⟩ 4 : not to be disputed : UNDOUBTED 5 : bound to happen 6 : careful to remember or attend to something ⟨be ~ to lock the door⟩ ✦ *Synonyms* CERTAIN, COCKSURE, POSITIVE — **sure·ness** *n*

²**sure** *adv* : SURELY

sure·fire \'shu̇r-'fī(-ə)r\ *adj* : certain to get results : DEPENDABLE

sure·ly \'shu̇r-lē\ *adv* 1 : in a sure manner 2 : without doubt 3 : INDEED, REALLY ⟨~, you don't believe that⟩

sure·ty \'shu̇r-ə-tē\ *n, pl* **-ties** 1 : SURENESS, CERTAINTY 2 : something that makes sure : GUARANTEE 3 : one who is a guarantor for another person

¹**surf** \'sərf\ *n* : waves that break upon the shore; *also* : the sound or foam of breaking waves

²**surf** *vb* 1 : to ride the surf (as on a surfboard) 2 : to scan the offerings of (as television or the Internet) for something of interest — **surf·er** *n* — **surf·ing** *n*

¹**sur·face** \'sər-fəs\ *n* 1 : the outside of an object or body 2 : outward aspect or appearance — **surface** *adj*

²**surface** *vb* **sur·faced; sur·fac·ing** 1 : to give a surface to : make smooth 2 : to rise to the surface

surf·board \'sərf-,bȯrd\ *n* : a buoyant board used in surfing

¹**sur·feit** \'sər-fət\ *n* 1 : EXCESS, SUPERABUNDANCE 2 : excessive indulgence (as in food or drink) 3 : disgust caused by excess

²**surfeit** *vb* : to feed, supply, or indulge to the point of surfeit : CLOY

surg *abbr* surgeon; surgery; surgical

¹**surge** \'sərj\ *vb* **surged; surg·ing** 1 : to rise and fall actively : TOSS 2 : to move in waves 3 : to rise suddenly to an excessive or abnormal value

²**surge** *n* 1 : a sweeping onward like a wave of the sea ⟨a ~ of emotion⟩ 2 : a large billow 3 : a transient sudden increase of current or voltage in an electrical circuit

sur·geon \'sər-jən\ *n* : a physician who specializes in surgery

sur·gery \'sər-jə-rē\ *n, pl* **-ger·ies** [ME *surgerie*, fr. AF *cirurgerie, surgerie*, fr. L *chirurgia*, fr. Gk *cheirourgia*, fr. *cheirourgos* surgeon, fr. *cheirourgos* doing by hand, fr. *cheir* hand + *ergon* work] 1 : a branch of medicine concerned with the correction of physical defects, the repair of injuries, and the treatment of disease esp. by operations 2 : a room or area where surgery is performed 3 : the work done by a surgeon

sur·gi·cal \'sər-ji-kəl\ *adj* : of, relating to, or associated with surgeons or surgery — **sur·gi·cal·ly** \-k(ə-)lē\ *adv*

sur·ly \'sər-lē\ *adj* **sur·li·er; -est** [alter. of ME *serreli* lordly, imperious, prob. fr. *sire, ser* sire] : having a rude unfriendly disposition ⟨a ~ customer⟩ ✦ *Synonyms* MOROSE, GLUM, SULLEN, SULKY, GLOOMY — **sur·li·ness** \-lē-nəs\ *n*

sur·mise \sər-'mīz\ *vb* **sur·mised; sur·mis·ing** : to form a notion of from scanty evidence ✦ *Synonyms* CONJECTURE, PRESUME, SUPPOSE — **surmise** *n*

sur·mount \sər-'mau̇nt\ *vb* 1 : to prevail over : OVERCOME ⟨~ a problem⟩ 2 : to get to or lie at the top of

sur·name \'sər-,nām\ *n* 1 : NICKNAME 2 : the name borne in common by members of a family

sur·pass \sər-'pas\ *vb* 1 : to be superior to in quality, degree, or performance : EXCEL 2 : to go beyond the reach or powers of ✦ *Synonyms* TRANSCEND, OUTDO, OUTSTRIP, EXCEED — **sur·pass·ing·ly** *adv*

sur·plice \'sər-pləs\ *n* : a loose white outer vestment usu. of knee length

sur·plus \'sər-(,)pləs\ *n* 1 : quantity left over : EXCESS 2 : the excess of assets over liabilities ✦ *Synonyms* SUPERFLUITY, OVERABUNDANCE, SURFEIT

¹**sur·prise** \sər-'prīz\ *n* 1 : an attack made without warning 2 : a taking unawares 3 : something that surprises 4 : AMAZEMENT, ASTONISHMENT

²**surprise** *vb* **sur·prised; sur·pris·ing** 1 : to come upon and attack unexpectedly 2 : to take unawares 3 : AMAZE ⟨his conduct *surprised* me⟩ 4 : to cause astonishment or surprise ⟨her success didn't ~⟩ ✦ *Synonyms* ASTONISH, ASTOUND, DUMBFOUND — **sur·pris·ing** *adj*

sur·pris·ing·ly \-'prī-ziŋ-lē\ *adv* 1 : in a surprising manner or degree 2 : it is surprising that ⟨~, voter turnout was high⟩

sur·re·al \sə-'rē-əl, -'rēl\ *adj* 1 : having the intense irrational reality of a dream 2 : of or relating to surrealism ⟨~ art⟩ — **sur·re·al·ly** *adv*

sur·re·al·ism \sə-'rē-ə-,li-zəm\ *n* : art, literature, or theater characterized by fantastic or incongruous imagery or effects produced by unnatural juxtapositions and combinations — **sur·re·al·ist** \-list\ *n or adj* — **sur·re·al·is·tic** \sə-,rē-ə-'lis-tik\ *adj* — **sur·re·al·is·ti·cal·ly** \-ti-k(ə-)lē\ *adv*

¹**sur·ren·der** \sə-'ren-dər\ *vb* 1 : to yield to the power of another : give up under compulsion 2 : RELINQUISH

²**surrender** *n* : the act of giving up or yielding oneself or the possession of something to another

sur·rep·ti·tious \,sər-əp-'ti-shəs\ *adj* : done, made, or acquired by stealth : CLANDESTINE ⟨a ~ relationship⟩ ✦ *Synonyms* UNDERHAND, COVERT, FURTIVE — **sur·rep·ti·tious·ly** *adv*

sur·rey \'sər-ē\ *n, pl* **surreys** : a 2-seated horse-drawn carriage

surrey

sur·ro·ga·cy \'sər-ə-gə-sē\ *n* : SURROGATE MOTHERHOOD
sur·ro·gate \'sər-ə-ˌgāt, -gət\ *n* 1 : DEPUTY, SUBSTITUTE 2 : a law officer in some states with authority in the probate of wills, the settlement of estates, and the appointment of guardians 3 : SURROGATE MOTHER
surrogate mother *n* : a woman who becomes pregnant (as by surgical implantation of a fertilized egg) in order to carry the fetus for another woman — **surrogate motherhood** *n*
sur·round \sə-'raund\ *vb* 1 : to enclose on all sides : ENCIRCLE 2 : to enclose so as to cut off retreat or escape
sur·round·ings \sə-'raun-diŋz\ *n pl* : conditions by which one is surrounded
surround sound *n* : sound reproduction that uses three or more transmission channels
sur·tax \'sər-ˌtaks\ *n* : an additional tax over and above a normal tax
sur·tout \(ˌ)sər-'tü\ *n* [F, fr. *sur* over + *tout* all] : a man's long close-fitting overcoat
surv *abbr* survey; surveying; surveyor
sur·veil·lance \sər-'vā-ləns\ *n* [F] : close watch; *also* : SUPERVISION
¹**sur·vey** \sər-'vā\ *vb* **sur·veyed; sur·vey·ing** [ME, fr. AF *surveer* to look over, fr. *sur-* over + *veer* to see, fr. L *vidēre*] 1 : to look over and examine closely 2 : to find and represent the contours, measurements, and position of a part of the earth's surface (as a tract of land) 3 : to view or study something as a whole ◆ **Synonyms** SCRUTINIZE, EXAMINE, INSPECT, STUDY — **sur·vey·or** \-ˌər\ *n*
²**sur·vey** \'sər-ˌvā\ *n, pl* **surveys** : the act or an instance of surveying; *also* : something that is surveyed
sur·viv·al·ism \sər-'vī-və-ˌli-zəm\ *n* : an attitude, policy, or practice based on the primacy of survival as a value — **sur·viv·al·ist** \-və-list\ *n or adj*
sur·vive \sər-'vīv\ *vb* **sur·vived; sur·viv·ing** 1 : to remain alive or existent 2 : OUTLIVE, OUTLAST — **sur·viv·al** *n* — **sur·vi·vor** \-'vī-vər\ *n*
sus·cep·ti·ble \sə-'sep-tə-bəl\ *adj* 1 : of such a nature as to permit ⟨words ∼ of being misunderstood⟩ 2 : having little resistance to a stimulus or agency ⟨∼ to colds⟩ 3 : IMPRESSIONABLE, RESPONSIVE ⟨a ∼ mind⟩ ◆ **Synonyms** SENSITIVE, SUBJECT, EXPOSED, PRONE, LIABLE, OPEN — **sus·cep·ti·bil·i·ty** \-ˌsep-tə-'bi-lə-tē\ *n*
su·shi \'sü-shē\ *n* [Jp] : cold rice formed into various shapes and garnished esp. with bits of raw fish or seafood
¹**sus·pect** \'səs-ˌpekt, sə-'spekt\ *adj* : regarded with suspicion; *also* : QUESTIONABLE ⟨his claim is ∼⟩
²**sus·pect** \'səs-ˌpekt\ *n* : one who is suspected (as of a crime)
³**sus·pect** \sə-'spekt\ *vb* 1 : to have doubts of : MISTRUST 2 : to imagine to be guilty without proof 3 : SURMISE
sus·pend \sə-'spend\ *vb* 1 : to bar temporarily from a privilege, office, or function 2 : to stop temporarily : make inactive for a time 3 : to withhold (judgment) for a time 4 : HANG; *esp* : to hang so as to be free except at one point 5 : to put or hold in suspension 6 : to keep from falling or sinking by some invisible support
sus·pend·er \sə-'spen-dər\ *n* : one of two supporting straps which pass over the shoulders and to which the pants are fastened
sus·pense \sə-'spens\ *n* 1 : SUSPENSION 2 : mental uncertainty : ANXIETY 3 : excitement as to an outcome — **sus·pense·ful** *adj*

sus·pen·sion \sə-'spen-chən\ *n* 1 : the act of suspending : the state or period of being suspended 2 : the state of a substance when its particles are mixed with but undissolved in a fluid or solid; *also* : a substance in this state 3 : something suspended 4 : the system of devices supporting the upper part of a vehicle on the axles
sus·pi·cion \sə-'spi-shən\ *n* 1 : the act or an instance of suspecting something wrong without proof 2 : TRACE, SOUPÇON ⟨a ∼ of garlic⟩ ◆ **Synonyms** MISTRUST, UNCERTAINTY, DOUBT, SKEPTICISM
sus·pi·cious \sə-'spi-shəs\ *adj* 1 : open to or arousing suspicion 2 : inclined to suspect 3 : showing suspicion ⟨is ∼ of strangers⟩ — **sus·pi·cious·ly** *adv*
sus·tain \sə-'stān\ *vb* 1 : to provide with nourishment 2 : to keep going : PROLONG ⟨∼ed effort⟩ 3 : to hold up : PROP 4 : to hold up under : ENDURE 5 : SUFFER ⟨∼ a broken arm⟩ 6 : to support as true, legal, or valid ⟨the objection was ∼ed⟩ 7 : PROVE, CORROBORATE — **sus·tain·able** \sə-'stā-nə-bəl\ *adj*
sus·te·nance \'səs-tə-nəns\ *n* 1 : FOOD, NOURISHMENT 2 : a supplying with the necessities of life 3 : something that sustains or supports
su·ture \'sü-chər\ *n* 1 : material or a stitch for sewing a wound together 2 : a seam or line along which two things or parts are joined by or as if by sewing
SUV \ˌes-ˌyü-'vē\ *n* [*sport-utility vehicle*] : a vehicle similar to a station wagon but built on a light-truck chassis
su·zer·ain \'sü-zə-rən, -ˌrān\ *n* [F] 1 : a feudal lord 2 : a nation that has political control over the foreign relations of another nation — **su·zer·ain·ty** \-tē\ *n*
svc *or* **svce** *abbr* service
svelte \'sfelt, 'svelt\ *adj* [F, fr. It *svelto*, fr. pp. of *svellere* to pluck out, modif. of L *evellere*, fr. *e-* out + *vellere* to pluck] : SLENDER, LITHE ⟨a ∼ figure⟩
svgs *abbr* savings
SW *abbr* 1 shortwave 2 southwest
¹**swab** \'swäb\ *n* 1 : MOP 2 : a wad of absorbent material esp. for applying medicine or for cleaning; *also* : a sample taken with a swab 3 : SAILOR
²**swab** *vb* **swabbed; swab·bing** : to use a swab on : MOP
swad·dle \'swä-dᵊl\ *vb* **swad·dled; swad·dling** 1 : to bind (an infant) in bands of cloth 2 : to wrap up : SWATHE
swaddling clothes *n pl* : bands of cloth wrapped around an infant
swag \'swag\ *n* : stolen goods : LOOT
swag·ger \'swa-gər\ *vb* 1 : to walk with a conceited swing or strut 2 : BOAST, BRAG — **swagger** *n*
Swa·hi·li \swä-'hē-lē\ *n* : a language that is a trade and governmental language over much of eastern Africa and the Congo region
swain \'swān\ *n* [ME *swein* boy, servant, fr. ON *sveinn*] 1 : RUSTIC; *esp* : SHEPHERD 2 : ADMIRER, SUITOR
SWAK *abbr* sealed with a kiss
¹**swal·low** \'swä-lō\ *n* : any of numerous small long-winged migratory birds that often have a deeply forked tail
²**swallow** *vb* 1 : to take into the stomach through the throat 2 : to envelop or take in as if by swallowing 3 : to accept or believe without question, protest, or anger
³**swallow** *n* 1 : an act of swallowing 2 : an amount that can be swallowed at one time
swal·low·tail \'swä-lō-ˌtāl\ *n* 1 : a deeply forked and tapering tail like that of a swallow 2 : TAILCOAT 3 : any of various large butterflies with the border of each hind wing usu. drawn out into a process resembling a tail — **swal·low-tailed** \-ˌtāld\ *adj*
swam *past of* SWIM
swa·mi \'swä-mē\ *n* [Hindi *svāmī*, fr. Skt *svāmin* owner, lord] : a Hindu ascetic or religious teacher
¹**swamp** \'swämp\ *n* : a spongy wetland — **swamp** *adj* — **swampy** *adj*
²**swamp** *vb* 1 : to fill or become filled with or as if with water 2 : OVERWHELM 3
swamp·land \-ˌland\ *n* : SWAMP
swan \'swän\ *n, pl* **swans** *also* **swan** : any of various heavy-bodied long-necked mostly pure white swimming birds related to the geese
¹**swank** \'swaŋk\ *or* **swanky** \'swaŋ-kē\ *adj* **swank·er** *or* **swank·i·er; -est** : showily smart and dashing; *also* : fashionably elegant ⟨a ∼ hotel⟩
²**swank** *n* 1 : PRETENTIOUSNESS 2 : ELEGANCE
swans·down \'swänz-ˌdaun\ *n* 1 : the very soft down of

a swan used esp. for trimming   **2** : a soft thick cotton flannel

swan song *n* : a farewell appearance, act, or pronouncement

swap \\'swäp\\ *vb* **swapped; swap·ping** : TRADE, EXCHANGE — **swap** *n*

sward \\'swȯrd\\ *n* : the grassy surface of land

¹swarm \\'swȯrm\\ *n* **1** : a great number of honeybees leaving together from a hive with a queen to start a new colony; *also* : a hive of bees   **2** : a large crowd

²swarm *vb* **1** : to form in a swarm and depart from a hive   **2** : to throng together : gather in great numbers

swart \\'swȯrt\\ *adj* : SWARTHY

swar·thy \\'swȯr-t͟hē, -thē\\ *adj* **swar·thi·er; -est** : dark in color or complexion : dark-skinned

swash \\'swäsh\\ *vb* : to move about with a splashing sound — **swash** *n*

swash·buck·ler \\-,bə-klər\\ *n* : a swaggering or daring soldier or adventurer — **swash·buck·ling** *adj*

swas·ti·ka \\'swäs-ti-kə\\ *n* [Skt *svastika*, fr. *svasti* well-being, fr. *su-* well + *as-* to be] : a symbol or ornament in the form of a cross with the ends of the arms bent at right angles

swat \\'swät\\ *vb* **swat·ted; swat·ting** : to hit sharply ⟨~ a fly⟩ ⟨~ a ball⟩ — **swat** *n* — **swat·ter** *n*

SWAT *abbr* Special Weapons and Tactics

swatch \\'swäch\\ *n* : a sample piece (as of fabric) or a collection of samples

swath \\'swäth, 'swȯth\\ *or* **swathe** \\'swät͟h, 'swȯt͟h, 'swāt͟h\\ *n* [ME, fr. OE *swæth* footstep, trace] **1** : a row of cut grass or grain   **2** : the sweep of a scythe or mowing machine or the path cut in mowing

swathe \\'swät͟h, 'swȯt͟h, 'swāt͟h\\ *vb* **swathed; swath·ing** : to bind or wrap with or as if with a bandage

¹sway \\'swā\\ *n* **1** : a gentle swinging from side to side   **2** : controlling influence or power : DOMINION

²sway *vb* **1** : to swing gently from side to side   **2** : RULE, GOVERN   **3** : to cause to swing from side to side   **4** : BEND, SWERVE; *also* : INFLUENCE ⟨tried to ~ the jury⟩

◆ **Synonyms** OSCILLATE, FLUCTUATE, VIBRATE, WAVER

sway·backed \\'swā-,bakt\\ *also* **sway·back** \\-,bak\\ *adj* : having an abnormally sagging back ⟨a ~ mare⟩ — **swayback** *n*

swear \\'swer\\ *vb* **swore** \\'swȯr\\; **sworn** \\'swȯrn\\; **swear·ing** **1** : to make a solemn statement or promise under oath   **2** : to assert or promise emphatically or earnestly   **3** : to administer an oath   **4** : to bind by or as if by an oath   **5** : to use profane or obscene language — **swear·er** *n*

swear in *vb* : to induct into office by administration of an oath

sweat \\'swet\\ *vb* **sweat** *or* **sweat·ed; sweat·ing** **1** : to excrete salty moisture from glands of the skin : PERSPIRE   **2** : to form drops of moisture on the surface   **3** : to work so that one sweats : TOIL   **4** : to cause to sweat   **5** : to draw out or get rid of by or as if by sweating   **6** : to make a person overwork — **sweat** *n* — **sweaty** *adj*

sweat·er \\'swe-tər\\ *n* **1** : one that sweats   **2** : a knitted or crocheted jacket or pullover

sweat·shirt \\'swet-,shərt\\ *n* : a loose collarless pullover or jacket usu. of heavy cotton jersey

sweat·shop \\'swet-,shäp\\ *n* : a shop or factory in which workers are employed for long hours at low wages and under unhealthy conditions

Swed *abbr* Sweden

swede \\'swēd\\ *n* **1** *cap* : a native or inhabitant of Sweden   **2** *chiefly Brit* : RUTABAGA

Swed·ish \\'swē-dish\\ *n* **1** : the language of Sweden   **2** **Swedish** *pl* : the people of Sweden — **Swedish** *adj*

¹sweep \\'swēp\\ *vb* **swept** \\'swept\\; **sweep·ing** **1** : to remove or clean by or as if by brushing   *also* : to destroy completely; *also* : to remove or take with a single swift movement   **3** : to remove from sight or consideration   **4** : to move over with speed and force ⟨the tide *swept* over the shore⟩   **5** : to win an overwhelming victory in; *also* : to win all the games or contests of   **6** : to move or extend in a wide curve — **sweep·er** *n*

²sweep *n* **1** : something (as a long oar) that operates with a sweeping motion   **2** : a clearing off or away   **3** : a winning of all the contests or prizes in a competition   **4** : a sweeping movement   **5** : CURVE, BEND   **6** : RANGE, SCOPE

sweeping *adj* : EXTENSIVE ⟨~ reforms⟩; *also* : indiscriminately inclusive ⟨~ generalities⟩

sweep·ings \\'swē-piŋz\\ *n pl* : things collected by sweeping

sweep–sec·ond hand \\'swēp-,se-kənd-\\ *n* : a hand marking seconds on a timepiece

sweep·stakes \\'swēp-,stāks\\ *also* **sweep·stake** \\-,stāk\\ *n, pl* **sweepstakes** **1** : a race or contest in which the entire prize may go to the winner   **2** : any of various lotteries

¹sweet \\'swēt\\ *adj* **1** : being or causing the one of the four basic taste sensations that is caused esp. by table sugar and is identified esp. by the taste buds at the front of the tongue; *also* : pleasing to the taste   **2** : AGREEABLE ⟨how ~ it is⟩   **3** : pleasing to a sense other than taste ⟨a ~ smell⟩ ⟨~ music⟩   **4** : not stale or spoiled : WHOLESOME ⟨~ milk⟩   **5** : not salted ⟨~ butter⟩ — **sweet·ish** *adj* — **sweet·ly** *adv* — **sweet·ness** *n*

²sweet *n* **1** : something sweet : CANDY   **2** : DARLING

sweet·bread \\'swēt-,bred\\ *n* : the pancreas or thymus of an animal (as a calf or lamb) used for food

sweet·bri·ar *or* **sweet·bri·er** \\-,brī-ər\\ *n* : a thorny Old World rose with fragrant white to deep pink flowers

sweet clover *n* : any of a genus of erect legumes widely grown for soil improvement or hay

sweet corn *n* : corn of a variety having soft kernels containing a high percentage of sugar

sweet·en \\'swē-t³n\\ *vb* **sweet·ened; sweet·en·ing** : to make sweet — **sweet·en·er** *n* — **sweet·en·ing** *n*

sweet·heart \\'swēt-,härt\\ *n* : one who is loved

sweet·meat \\-,mēt\\ *n* : CANDY 1

sweet pea *n* : a garden plant of the legume family with climbing stems and fragrant flowers of many colors; *also* : its flower

sweet pepper *n* : any of various large mild thick-walled fruits of a pepper; *also* : a plant bearing sweet peppers

sweet potato *n* : a tropical vine related to the morning glory; *also* : its large sweet edible root

sweet–talk \\'swēt-,tȯk\\ *vb* : FLATTER, COAX — **sweet talk** *n*

sweet tooth *n* : a craving or fondness for sweet food

sweet wil·liam \\,swēt-'wil-yəm\\ *n, often cap W* : a widely cultivated Old World pink with small white to deep red or purple flowers often showily spotted, banded, or mottled

¹swell \\'swel\\ *vb* **swelled; swelled** *or* **swol·len** \\'swō-lən\\; **swell·ing** **1** : to grow big or make bigger   **2** : to expand or distend abnormally or excessively ⟨a *swollen* joint⟩; *also* : BULGE   **3** : to fill or be filled with emotion (as pride) ◆ **Synonyms** EXPAND, AMPLIFY, DISTEND, INFLATE, DILATE — **swell·ing** *n*

²swell *n* **1** : a long crestless wave or series of waves in the open sea   **2** : the condition of being protuberant   **3** : a person dressed in the height of fashion; *also* : a person of high social position

³swell *adj* **1** : STYLISH; *also* : socially prominent   **2** : EXCELLENT ⟨a ~ party⟩

swelled head *n* : an exaggerated opinion of oneself : SELF-CONCEIT

swel·ter \\'swel-tər\\ *vb* [ME *sweltren*, fr. *swelten* to die, be overcome by heat, fr. OE *sweltan* to die] **1** : to be faint or oppressed with the heat   **2** : to become exceedingly hot — **swel·ter·ing** \\-tə-riŋ\\ *adj*

swept *past and past part of* SWEEP

swerve \\'swərv\\ *vb* **swerved; swerv·ing** : to move abruptly aside from a straight line or course — **swerve** *n*

¹swift \\'swift\\ *adj* **1** : moving or capable of moving with great speed   **2** : occurring suddenly   **3** : READY, ALERT ⟨~ for vengeance⟩ — **swift·ly** *adv* — **swift·ness** *n*

²swift *n* : any of numerous small insect-eating birds with long narrow wings

swig \\'swig\\ *vb* **swigged; swig·ging** : to drink in long drafts — **swig** *n*

¹swill \\'swil\\ *vb* **1** : to swallow greedily : GUZZLE   **2** : to feed (as hogs) on swill

²swill *n* **1** : food for animals composed of edible refuse mixed with liquid   **2** : GARBAGE

¹swim \\'swim\\ *vb* **swam** \\'swam\\; **swum** \\'swəm\\; **swim·ming** **1** : to propel oneself along in water by natural means (as by hands and legs, by tail, or by fins)   **2** : to glide smoothly along   **3** : FLOAT   **4** : to be covered with or as if with a liquid   **5** : to be dizzy ⟨his head *swam⟩* **6** : to cross or go over by swimming ⟨*swam* the river⟩ — **swim·mer** *n*

²**swim** *n* **1** : an act of swimming **2** : the main current of activity ⟨in the ~⟩

swim·ming *n* : the action, art, or sport of swimming and diving

swimming pool *n* : a tank (as of concrete or plastic) designed for swimming

swim·suit \'swim-ˌsüt\ *n* : a suit for swimming or bathing

swim·wear \'swim-ˌwer\ *n* : clothing for wear while swimming or bathing

swin·dle \'swin-d²l\ *vb* **swin·dled; swin·dling** [fr. *swindler*, fr. G *Schwindler* giddy person, fr. *schwindeln* to be dizzy] : CHEAT, DEFRAUD — **swindle** *n* — **swin·dler** *n*

swine \'swīn\ *n, pl* **swine 1** : any of a family of stout short-legged hoofed mammals with bristly skin and a long flexible snout; *esp* : one widely raised as a meat animal **2** : a contemptible person — **swin·ish** *adj*

¹**swing** \'swiŋ\ *vb* **swung** \'swəŋ\; **swing·ing 1** : to move or cause to move rapidly in an arc **2** : to sway or cause to sway back and forth **3** : to hang so as to move freely back and forth or in a curve **4** : to be executed by hanging **5** : to move or turn on a hinge or pivot **6** : to manage or handle successfully **7** : to march or walk with free swaying movements **8** : to have a steady pulsing rhythm; *also* : to play swing music **9** : to be lively and up-to-date; *also* : to engage freely in sex ♦ *Synonyms* WIELD, MANIPULATE, PLY, MANEUVER — **swing·er** *n* — **swing·ing** *adj*

²**swing** *n* **1** : the act of swinging **2** : a swinging blow, movement, or rhythm **3** : the distance through which something swings : FLUCTUATION **4** : progression of an activity or process ⟨in full ~⟩ **5** : a seat suspended by a rope or chain for swinging back and forth for pleasure **6** : jazz music played esp. by a large band and marked by a steady lively rhythm, simple harmony, and a basic melody often submerged in improvisation

³**swing** *adj* **1** : of or relating to musical swing **2** : that may swing decisively either way (as on an issue) ⟨~ voters⟩

¹**swipe** \'swīp\ *n* : a strong sweeping blow

²**swipe** *vb* **swiped; swip·ing 1** : to strike or wipe with a sweeping motion **2** : PILFER, SNATCH **3** : to slide (a card having a magnetic code) through a reading device

swirl \'swərl\ *vb* : to move or cause to move with a whirling motion — **swirl** *n* — **swirly** \'swər-lē\ *adj*

swish \'swish\ *n* **1** : a prolonged hissing sound **2** : a light sweeping or brushing sound — **swish** *vb*

Swiss \'swis\ *n* **1** *pl* **Swiss 1** : a native or inhabitant of Switzerland **2** : a hard cheese with large holes — **Swiss** *adj*

Swiss chard *n* : a beet having large leaves and succulent stalks often cooked as a vegetable

¹**switch** \'swich\ *n* **1** : a slender flexible whip, rod, or twig **2** : a blow with a switch **3** : a shift from one thing to another; *also* : change from the usual **4** : a device for adjusting the rails of a track so that a locomotive or train may be turned from one track to another; *also* : a railroad siding **5** : a device for making, breaking, or changing the connections in an electrical circuit **6** : a heavy strand of hair often used in addition to a person's own hair for some coiffures

²**switch** *vb* **1** : to punish or urge on with a switch **2** : WHISK ⟨a cow ~*ing* her tail⟩ **3** : to shift or turn by operating a switch **4** : CHANGE, EXCHANGE

switch·back \'swich-ˌbak\ *n* : a zigzag road, trail, or section of railroad tracks for climbing a steep hill

switch·blade \-ˌblād\ *n* : a pocket-knife with a spring-operated blade

switch·board \-ˌbōrd\ *n* : a panel for controlling the operation of a number of electric circuits; *esp* : one used to make and break telephone connections

switch–hit·ter \-'hi-tər\ *n* : a baseball player who bats either right-handed or left-handed — **switch–hit** \-'hit\ *vb*

switch·man \'swich-mən\ *n* : one who attends a railroad switch

Switz *abbr* Switzerland

¹**swiv·el** \'swi-vəl\ *n* : a device joining two parts so that one or both can turn freely

²**swivel** *vb* **-eled** *or* **-elled; -el·ing** *or* **-el·ling** : to swing or turn on or as if on a swivel

swiv·et \'swi-vət\ *n* : an agitated state

swiz·zle stick \'swi-zəl-\ *n* : a stick used to stir mixed drinks

swollen *past part of* SWELL

swoon \'swün\ *vb* : FAINT — **swoon** *n*

swoop \'swüp\ *vb* : to move with a sweep ⟨the eagle ~*ed* down on its prey⟩ — **swoop** *n*

swoopy \'swü-pē\ *adj* : having lines that extend in a wide curve ⟨a ~ silhouette⟩

swop *chiefly Brit var of* SWAP

sword \'sōrd\ *n* **1** : a weapon with a long blade for cutting or thrusting **2** : the use of force

sword·fish \-ˌfish\ *n* : a very large ocean fish used for food that has the upper jaw prolonged into a long sword-like beak

swordfish

sword·play \-ˌplā\ *n* : the art or skill of wielding a sword

swords·man \'sōrdz-mən\ *n* : one skilled in swordplay; *esp* : FENCER

sword·tail \'sōrd-ˌtāl\ *n* : a small brightly marked Central American fish often kept in aquariums

swore *past of* SWEAR

sworn *past part of* SWEAR

swum *past part of* SWIM

swung *past and past part of* SWING

syb·a·rite \'si-bə-ˌrīt\ *n* : a lover of luxury : VOLUPTUARY — **syb·a·rit·ic** \ˌsi-bə-'ri-tik\ *adj*

syc·a·more \'si-kə-ˌmōr\ *n* : a large spreading tree chiefly of the eastern and central U.S. that has light brown flaky bark and small round fruits hanging on long stalks

sy·co·phant \'si-kə-fənt\ *n* : a servile flatterer — **sy·co·phan·cy** \'si-kə-fən-sē\ *n* — **sy·co·phan·tic** \ˌsi-kə-'fan-tik\ *adj*

syl *or* **syll** *abbr* syllable

syl·lab·i·ca·tion \sə-ˌla-bə-'kā-shən\ *n* : the division of words into syllables

syl·lab·i·fy \sə-'la-bə-ˌfī\ *vb* **-fied; -fy·ing** : to form or divide into syllables — **syl·lab·i·fi·ca·tion** \-ˌla-bə-fə-'kā-shən\ *n*

syl·la·ble \'si-lə-bəl\ *n* [ME, fr. AF *sillabe, silable*, fr. L *syllaba*, fr. Gk *syllabē*, fr. *syllambanein* to gather together, fr. *syn-* with + *lambanein* to take] : a unit of spoken language consisting of an uninterrupted utterance and forming either a whole word (as *cat*) or a commonly recognized division of a word (as *syl* in *syl-la-ble*); *also* : one or more letters representing such a unit — **syl·lab·ic** \sə-'la-bik\ *adj*

syl·la·bus \'si-lə-bəs\ *n, pl* **-bi** \-ˌbī\ *or* **-bus·es** : a summary containing the heads or main topics of a speech, book, or course of study

syl·lo·gism \'si-lə-ˌji-zəm\ *n* : a logical scheme of a formal argument consisting of a major and a minor premise and a conclusion which must logically be true if the premises are true — **syl·lo·gis·tic** \ˌsi-lə-'jis-tik\ *adj*

sylph \'silf\ *n* **1** : an imaginary being inhabiting the air **2** : a slender graceful woman or girl

syl·van \'sil-vən\ *adj* **1** : living or located in a wooded area; *also* : of, relating to, or characteristic of forest **2** : abounding in woods or trees

sym *abbr* **1** symbol **2** symmetrical

sym·bi·o·sis \ˌsim-ˌbī-'ō-səs, -bē-\ *n, pl* **-o·ses** \-ˌsēz\ : the living together in close association of two dissimilar organisms esp. when mutually beneficial — **sym·bi·ot·ic** \-'ä-tik\ *adj*

sym·bol \'sim-bəl\ *n* **1** : something that stands for something else; *esp* : something concrete that represents or suggests another thing that cannot in itself be pictured ⟨the lion is a ~ of bravery⟩ **2** : a letter, character, or sign used in writing or printing to represent operations, quantities, elements, sounds, or other ideas — **sym·bol·ic** \sim-'bä-lik\ *also* **sym·bol·i·cal** \-li-kəl\ *adj* — **sym·bol·i·cal·ly** \-k(ə-)lē\ *adv*

sym·bol·ise *Brit var of* SYMBOLIZE

sym·bol·ism \'sim-bə-ˌli-zəm\ *n* : representation of abstract or intangible things by means of symbols

sym·bol·ize \'sim-bə-ˌlīz\ vb **-ized; -iz·ing 1 :** to serve as a symbol of **2 :** to represent by symbols — **sym·bol·i·za·tion** \ˌsim-bə-lə-'zā-shən\ n

sym·me·try \'si-mə-trē\ n, pl **-tries 1 :** an arrangement marked by regularity and balanced proportions **2 :** correspondence in size, shape, and position of parts that are on opposite sides of a dividing line or center — **sym·met·ri·cal** \sə-'me-tri-kəl\ or **sym·met·ric** \sə-'me= trik\ adj — **sym·met·ri·cal·ly** \-k(ə-)lē\ adv

sympathetic nervous system n **:** the part of the autonomic nervous system that is concerned esp. with the body's response to stress and that tends to decrease the tone and contractility of smooth muscle and increase blood pressure and the activity of the heart

sym·pa·thise chiefly Brit var of SYMPATHIZE

sym·pa·thize \'sim-pə-ˌthīz\ vb **-thized; -thiz·ing :** to feel or show sympathy — **sym·pa·thiz·er** n

sym·pa·thy \'sim-pə-thē\ n, pl **-thies 1 :** a relationship between persons or things wherein whatever affects one similarly affects the other **2 :** harmony of interests and aims **3 :** FAVOR, SUPPORT **4 :** the capacity for entering into and sharing the feelings or interests of another; also **:** COMPASSION, PITY **5 :** an expression of sorrow for another's loss, grief, or misfortune — **sym·pa·thet·ic** \ˌsim-pə-'the-tik\ adj — **sym·pa·thet·i·cal·ly** \-ti-k(ə-)lē\ adv

sym·pho·ny \'sim-fə-nē\ n, pl **-nies 1 :** harmony of sounds **2 :** a large and complex composition for a full orchestra **3 :** a large orchestra of a kind that plays symphonies — **sym·phon·ic** \sim-'fä-nik\ adj

sym·po·sium \sim-'pō-zē-əm\ n, pl **-sia** \-zē-ə\ or **-siums :** a conference at which a particular topic is discussed by various speakers; also **:** a collection of opinions about a subject

symp·tom \'simp-təm\ n [LL symptoma, fr. Gk symptōma happening, attribute, symptom, fr. sympiptein to happen, fr. syn- with + piptein to fall] **1 :** something that indicates the presence of disease or abnormality; esp **:** something (as a headache) that can be sensed only by the individual affected **2 :** SIGN, INDICATION ⟨∼s of inner turmoil⟩ — **symp·tom·at·ic** \ˌsimp-tə-'ma-tik\ adj

syn abbr synonym; synonymous; synonymy

syn·a·gogue also **syn·a·gog** \'si-nə-ˌgäg\ n [ME synagoge, fr. AF, fr. LL synagoga, fr. Gk synagōgē assembly, synagogue, fr. synagein to bring together] **1 :** a Jewish congregation **2 :** the house of worship of a Jewish congregation

syn·apse \'si-ˌnaps, sə-'naps\ n **:** the point at which a nervous impulse passes from one neuron to another — **syn·ap·tic** \sə-'nap-tik\ adj

¹**sync** also **synch** \'siŋk\ vb synced also synched \'siŋkt\; **sync·ing** also **synch·ing** \'siŋ-kiŋ\ **:** SYNCHRONIZE

²**sync** also **synch** n **:** SYNCHRONIZATION, SYNCHRONISM — sync adj

syn·chro·ni·sa·tion, syn·chro·nise Brit var of SYNCHRONIZATION, SYNCHRONIZE

syn·chro·nize \'siŋ-krə-ˌnīz, 'sin-\ vb **-nized; -niz·ing 1 :** to occur or cause to occur at the same instant **2 :** to represent, arrange, or tabulate according to dates or time **3 :** to cause to agree in time **4 :** to make synchronous in operation — **syn·chro·nism** \-ˌni-zəm\ n — **syn·chro·ni·za·tion** \ˌsiŋ-krə-nə-'zā-shən, ˌsin-\ n — **syn·chro·niz·er** n

syn·chro·nous \'siŋ-krə-nəs, 'sin-\ adj **1 :** happening at the same time; CONCURRENT **2 :** working, moving, or occurring together at the same rate and at the proper time

syn·co·pa·tion \ˌsiŋ-kə-'pā-shən, ˌsin-\ n **:** a shifting of the regular musical accent **:** occurrence of accented notes on the weak beat — **syn·co·pate** \'siŋ-kə-ˌpāt, 'sin-\ vb

syn·co·pe \'siŋ-kə-(ˌ)pē, 'sin-\ n **:** the loss of one or more sounds or letters in the interior of a word (as in fo'c'sle for forecastle)

¹**syn·di·cate** \'sin-di-kət\ n **1 :** a group of persons who combine to carry out a financial or industrial undertaking **2 :** a loose association of racketeers **3 :** a business concern that sells materials for publication in many newspapers and periodicals at the same time

²**syn·di·cate** \-də-ˌkāt\ vb **-cat·ed; -cat·ing 1 :** to combine into or manage as a syndicate **2 :** to publish through a syndicate — **syn·di·ca·tion** \ˌsin-də-'kā-shən\ n

syn·drome \'sin-ˌdrōm\ n **:** a group of signs and symptoms that occur together and characterize a particular abnormality or condition

syn·er·gism \'sin-ər-ˌji-zəm\ n **:** interaction of discrete agencies (as industrial firms), agents (as drugs), or conditions such that the total effect is greater than the sum of the individual effects — **syn·er·gist** \-jist\ n — **syn·er·gis·tic** \ˌsi-nər-'jis-tik\ adj — **syn·er·gis·ti·cal·ly** \-ti-k(ə-)lē\ adv

syn·er·gy \'si-nər-je\ n, pl **-gies :** SYNERGISM

syn·fuel \'sin-ˌfyül\ n [synthetic] **:** a fuel derived esp. from a fossil fuel

syn·od \'si-nəd\ n **:** COUNCIL, ASSEMBLY; esp **:** a religious governing body — **syn·od·al** \-nə-dᵊl, -ˌnä-dᵊl\ adj — **syn·od·ic** \sə-'nä-dik\ or **syn·od·i·cal** \-di-kəl\ adj

syn·o·nym \'si-nə-ˌnim\ n **:** one of two or more words in the same language which have the same or very nearly the same meaning — **syn·on·y·mous** \sə-'nä-nə-məs\ adj — **syn·on·y·my** \-mē\ n

syn·op·sis \sə-'näp-səs\ n, pl **-op·ses** \-ˌsēz\ **:** a condensed statement or outline (as of a treatise) **:** ABSTRACT

syn·op·tic \sə-'näp-tik\ also **syn·op·ti·cal** \-ti-kəl\ adj **:** characterized by or affording a comprehensive view

syn·tax \'sin-ˌtaks\ n **:** the way in which words are put together to form phrases, clauses, or sentences — **syn·tac·tic** \sin-'tak-tik\ or **syn·tac·ti·cal** \-ti-kəl\ adj

syn·the·sis \'sin-thə-səs\ n, pl **-the·ses** \-ˌsēz\ **:** the combination of parts or elements into a whole; esp **:** the production of a substance by union of chemically simpler substances — **syn·the·size** \-ˌsīz\ vb — **syn·the·siz·er** n

syn·thet·ic \sin-'the-tik\ adj **:** produced artificially esp. by chemical means; also **:** not genuine — **synthetic** n — **syn·thet·i·cal·ly** \-ti-k(ə-)lē\ adv

syph·i·lis \'si-fə-ləs\ n [NL, fr. Syphilus, hero of the poem Syphilis sive Morbus Gallicus (Syphilis or the French disease) (1530) by Girolamo Fracastoro †1553 Ital. physician] **:** an infectious usu. venereal disease caused by a spirochete — **syph·i·lit·ic** \ˌsi-fə-'li-tik\ adj or n

syphon var of SIPHON

Sy·rah \sē-'rä\ n **:** a red wine

¹**sy·ringe** \sə-'rinj\ n **:** a device used esp. for injecting liquids into or withdrawing them from the body

²**syringe** vb **sy·ringed; sy·ring·ing :** to flush or cleanse with or as if with a syringe

syr·up also **sir·up** \'sər-əp, 'sir-əp\ n **1 :** a thick sticky solution of sugar and water often flavored or medicated **2 :** the concentrated juice of a fruit or plant — **syr·upy** adj

syst abbr system

sys·tem \'sis-təm\ n **1 :** a group of units so combined as to form a whole and to operate in unison **2 :** the body as a functioning whole; also **:** a group of bodily organs (as the nervous system) that together carry on some vital function **3 :** a definite scheme or method of procedure or classification **4 :** regular method or order — **sys·tem·at·ic** \ˌsis-tə-'ma-tik\ — **sys·tem·at·i·cal·ly** \-ti-k(ə-)lē\ adv

sys·tem·a·tise Brit var of SYSTEMATIZE

sys·tem·a·tize \'sis-tə-mə-ˌtīz\ vb **-tized; -tiz·ing :** to make into a system **:** arrange methodically

¹**sys·tem·ic** \sis-'te-mik\ adj **1 :** of, relating to, or affecting the whole body ⟨∼ disease⟩ **2 :** of, relating to, or being a pesticide that when absorbed into the sap or bloodstream makes the entire plant or animal toxic to a pest (as an insect or fungus)

²**systemic** n **:** a systemic pesticide

systemic lupus er·y·the·ma·to·sus \ˌer-ə-ˌthē-mə-'tō-səs\ n **:** a systemic disease esp. of women characterized by fever, skin rash, and arthritis, often by anemia, by small hemorrhages of the skin and mucous membranes, and in serious cases by involvement of internal organs

sys·tem·ize \'sis-tə-ˌmīz\ vb **-ized; -iz·ing :** SYSTEMATIZE

systems analyst n **:** a person who studies a procedure or business to determine its goals or purposes and to discover the best ways to accomplish them — **systems analysis** n

sys·to·le \'sis-tə-(ˌ)lē\ n **:** a rhythmically recurrent contraction of the heart — **sys·tol·ic** \sis-'tä-lik\ adj

¹t \'tē\ *n, pl* t's *or* ts \'tēz\ *often cap* : the 20th letter of the English alphabet

²t *abbr, often cap* 1 tablespoon 2 teaspoon 3 temperature 4 ton 5 transitive 6 troy 7 true

T *abbr* 1 toddler 2 T-shirt

Ta *symbol* tantalum

TA *abbr* teaching assistant

¹tab \'tab\ *n* 1 : a short projecting flap, loop, or tag; *also* : a small insert or addition 2 : close surveillance : WATCH ⟨keep ∼s on him⟩ 3 : BILL, CHECK 4 : a key on a keyboard esp. for putting data in columns

²tab *vb* tabbed; tab·bing : DESIGNATE

tab·by \'ta-bē\ *n, pl* tabbies : a usu. striped or mottled domestic cat; *also* : a female domestic cat

tab·er·na·cle \'ta-bər-,na-kəl\ *n* [ME, fr. AF, fr. LL *tabernaculum*, fr. L, tent, fr. *taberna* hut] 1 *often cap* : a tent sanctuary used by the Israelites during the Exodus 2 : a receptacle for the consecrated elements of the Eucharist 3 : a house of worship

¹ta·ble \'tā-bəl\ *n* 1 : TABLET 2 : a piece of furniture consisting of a smooth flat top fixed on legs 3 : a supply of food : BOARD, FARE 4 : a group of people assembled at or as if at a table 5 : an orderly arrangement of data usu. in rows and columns 6 : a short list ⟨∼ of contents⟩ — ta·ble·top \-,täp\ *n*

²table *vb* ta·bled; ta·bling 1 *Brit* : to place on the agenda 2 : to remove (a parliamentary motion) from consideration indefinitely

tab·leau \'ta-,blō\ *n, pl* tab·leaux \-,blōz\ *also* tableaus [F] : a scene or event usu. presented on a stage by silent and motionless costumed participants

ta·ble·cloth \'tā-bəl-,klóth\ *n* : a covering spread over a dining table before the table is set

ta·ble·land \'tā-bəl-,land\ *n* : PLATEAU

ta·ble·spoon \-,spün\ *n* 1 : a large spoon used esp. for serving 2 : a unit of measure equal to ½ fluid ounce (15 milliliters)

ta·ble·spoon·ful \-,fùl\ *n, pl* -spoonfuls \-,fùlz\ *also* -spoons·ful \-,spünz-,fùl\ : TABLESPOON 2

tab·let \'ta-blət\ *n* 1 : a flat slab suited for or bearing an inscription 2 : a collection of sheets of paper glued together at one edge 3 : a compressed or molded block of material; *esp* : a usu. disk-shaped medicated mass 4 : GRAPHICS TABLET 5 *or* tablet computer : a mobile computing device that has a flat rectangular form, is usually controlled by means of a touch screen, and is typically used for accessing the Internet, watching videos, and reading e-books

table tennis *n* : a game resembling tennis played on a tabletop with wooden paddles and a small hollow plastic ball

ta·ble·ware \'tā-bəl-,wer\ *n* : utensils (as of china or silver) for table use

¹tab·loid \'ta-,blòid\ *adj* : condensed into small scope

²tabloid *n* : a newspaper marked by small pages, condensation of the news, and usu. many photographs

¹ta·boo *also* ta·bu \tə-'bü, ta-\ *adj* [Tongan (a Polynesian language) *tabu*] : prohibited by a taboo

²taboo *also* tabu *n, pl* taboos *also* tabus 1 : a prohibition against touching, saying, or doing something for fear of immediate harm from a supernatural force 2 : a prohibition imposed by social custom

ta·bor *also* ta·bour \'tā-bər\ *n* : a small drum used to accompany a pipe or fife played by the same person

tab·u·lar \'ta-byə-lər\ *adj* 1 : having a flat surface 2 : arranged in a table; *esp* : set up in rows and columns 3 : computed by means of a table

tab·u·late \-,lāt\ *vb* -lat·ed; -lat·ing : to put into tabular form — tab·u·la·tion \,ta-byə-'lā-shən\ *n* — tab·u·la·tor \'ta-byə-,lā-tər\ *n*

TAC \'tak\ *abbr* Tactical Air Command

tach \'tak\ *n* : TACHOMETER

ta·chom·e·ter \ta-'kä-mə-tər, tə-\ *n* [ultim. fr. Gk *tachos* speed] : a device to indicate speed of rotation

tachy·car·dia \,ta-ki-'kär-dē-ə\ *n* : relatively rapid heart action

tachy·on \'ta-kē-,än\ *n* : a hypothetical particle held to travel faster than light

tac·it \'ta-sət\ *adj* [F or L; F *tacite*, fr. L *tacitus* silent, fr. *tacēre* to be silent] 1 : expressed without words or speech 2 : implied or indicated but not actually expressed ⟨∼ consent⟩ — tac·it·ly *adv* — tac·it·ness *n*

tac·i·turn \'ta-sə-,tərn\ *adj* : disinclined to talk ✦ Synonyms UNCOMMUNICATIVE, RESERVED, RETICENT, CLOSEMOUTHED — tac·i·tur·ni·ty \,ta-sə-'tər-nə-tē\ *n*

¹tack \'tak\ *vb* 1 : to fasten with tacks; *also* : to add on 2 : to change the direction of (a sailing ship) from one tack to another 3 : to follow a zigzag course

²tack *n* 1 : a small sharp nail with a broad flat head 2 : the direction toward the wind that a ship is sailing ⟨starboard ∼⟩; *also* : the run of a ship on one tack 3 : a change of course from one tack to another 4 : a zigzag course 5 : a course of action

³tack *n* : gear for harnessing a horse

¹tack·le \'ta-kəl, *naut often* 'tā-\ *n* 1 : GEAR, APPARATUS, EQUIPMENT 2 : the rigging of a ship 3 : an arrangement of ropes and pulleys for hoisting or pulling heavy objects 4 : the act or an instance of tackling; *also* : a football lineman playing between guard and end

²tackle *vb* tack·led; tack·ling 1 : to attach and secure with or as if with tackle 2 : to seize, grapple with, or throw down with the intention of subduing or stopping 3 : to set about dealing with ⟨∼ a problem⟩ — tack·ler *n*

¹tacky \'ta-kē\ *adj* tack·i·er; -est : sticky to the touch

²tacky *adj* tack·i·er; -est 1 : SHABBY, SEEDY 2 : marked by lack of style or good taste; *also* : cheaply showy ⟨a ∼ publicity stunt⟩ ⟨a ∼ outfit⟩

ta·co \'tä-kō\ *n, pl* tacos \-kōz\ [MexSp] : a usu. fried tortilla rolled up with or folded over a filling

tact \'takt\ *n* [F, sense of touch, fr. L *tactus*, fr. *tangere* to touch] : a keen sense of what to do or say to keep good relations with others ⟨a diplomat with ∼⟩ — tact·ful \-fəl\ *adj* — tact·ful·ly *adv* — tact·less *adj* — tact·less·ly *adv*

tac·tic \'tak-tik\ *n* : a planned action for accomplishing an end

tac·tics \'tak-tiks\ *n sing or pl* 1 : the science of maneuvering forces in combat 2 : the skill of using available means to accomplish an end — tac·ti·cal \-ti-kəl\ *adj* — tac·ti·cian \tak-'ti-shən\ *n*

tac·tile \'tak-t⁹l, 'tak-,tī(-ə)l\ *adj* : of, relating to, or perceptible through the sense of touch

tad·pole \'tad-,pōl\ *n* [ME *taddepol*, fr. *tode* toad + *polle* head] : an aquatic larva of a frog or toad that has a tail and gills

tadpole: in stages

tae kwon do \'tī-'kwän-'dō\ *n* : a Korean martial art of self-defense

taf·fe·ta \'ta-fə-tə\ *n* : a crisp lustrous fabric (as of silk or rayon)

taff·rail \'taf-,rāl, -rəl\ *n* : the rail around a ship's stern

taf·fy \'ta-fē\ *n, pl* **taffies** : a candy usu. of molasses or brown sugar stretched until porous and light-colored

¹tag \'tag\ *n* **1** : a metal or plastic binding on an end of a shoelace **2** : a piece of hanging or attached material **3** : a hackneyed quotation or saying **4** : a descriptive or identifying epithet

²tag *vb* **tagged; tag·ging 1** : to provide or mark with or as if with a tag; *also* : IDENTIFY **2** : to attach as an addition **3** : to follow closely and persistently ⟨∼s along everywhere we go⟩ **4** : to hold responsible for something

³tag *n* : a game in which one player chases others and tries to touch one of them

⁴tag *vb* **tagged; tag·ging 1** : to touch in or as if in a game of tag **2** : SELECT

TAG *abbr* the adjutant general

tag sale *n* : GARAGE SALE

Ta·hi·tian \tə-'hē-shən\ *n* **1** : a native or inhabitant of Tahiti **2** : the Polynesian language of the Tahitians — **Tahitian** *adj*

tai·ga \'tī-gə\ *n* [Russ *taĭga*] : a moist coniferous subarctic forest extending south from the tundra

¹tail \'tāl\ *n* **1** : the rear end or a process extending from the rear end of an animal **2** : something resembling an animal's tail **3** *pl* : full evening dress for men **4** : the back, last, lower, or inferior part of something; *esp* : the reverse of a coin — usu. used in pl. ⟨∼s, I win⟩ **5** : one who follows or keeps watch on someone — **tailed** \'tāld\ *adj* — **tail·less** \'tāl-ləs\ *adj*

²tail *vb* : FOLLOW; *esp* : to follow for the purpose of surveillance

tail·coat \-'kōt\ *n* : a coat with tails; *esp* : a man's full-dress coat with two long tapering skirts at the back

¹tail·gate \-ˌgāt\ *n* : a board or gate at the back end of a vehicle that can be let down (as for loading)

²tailgate *vb* **tail·gat·ed; tail·gat·ing 1** : to drive dangerously close behind another vehicle **2** : to hold a tailgate picnic

³tailgate *adj* : relating to or being a picnic set up on a tailgate ⟨a ∼ party⟩

tail·light \-ˌlīt\ *n* : a usu. red warning light mounted at the rear of a vehicle

¹tai·lor \'tā-lər\ *n* [ME *taillour*, fr. AF *taillur*, fr. *tailler* to cut, fr. LL *taliare*, fr. L *talea* twig, cutting] : a person whose occupation is making or altering garments

²tailor *vb* **1** : to make or fashion as the work of a tailor **2** : to make or adapt to suit a special purpose

tail·pipe \'tāl-ˌpīp\ *n* : an outlet by which engine exhaust gases are expelled from a vehicle (as an automobile)

tail·spin \'tāl-ˌspin\ *n* : a rapid descent or downward spiral

tail·wind \'tāl-ˌwind\ *n* : a wind blowing in the same general direction as a course of movement (as of an aircraft)

¹taint \'tānt\ *vb* **1** : CORRUPT, CONTAMINATE **2** : to affect or become affected with something bad (as putrefaction)

²taint *n* : a contaminating mark or influence

ta·ka \'tä-kə\ *n* — see MONEY table

¹take \'tāk\ *vb* **took** \'tuk\; **tak·en** \'tā-kən\; **tak·ing** [ME, fr. OE *tacan*, fr. ON *taka*] **1** : to get into one's hands or possession : GRASP, SEIZE **2** : CAPTURE; *also* : DEFEAT **3** : to obtain or secure for use **4** : to catch or attack through the effect of a sudden force or influence ⟨*taken* ill⟩ **5** : CAPTIVATE, DELIGHT **6** : to bring into a relation ⟨∼ a wife⟩ **7** : REMOVE, SUBTRACT ⟨∼ three from eight⟩ **8** : to pick out : CHOOSE **9** : ASSUME, UNDERTAKE **10** : RECEIVE, ACCEPT **11** : to use for transportation ⟨∼ a bus⟩ **12** : to become impregnated with : ABSORB ⟨∼s a dye⟩ **13** : to receive into one's body (as by swallowing) ⟨∼ a pill⟩ **14** : ENDURE, UNDERGO ⟨∼ a cut in pay⟩ **15** : to lead, carry, or cause to go along to another place ⟨∼s a size nine shoe⟩ **16** : NEED, REQUIRE ⟨∼s a size nine shoe⟩ **17** : to obtain as the result of a special procedure ⟨∼ a snapshot⟩ **18** : to undertake and do, make, or perform ⟨∼ a walk⟩ **19** : to take effect : ACT, OPERATE ✦ *Synonyms* GRAB, CLUTCH, SNATCH, SEIZE, NAB, GRAPPLE — **tak·er** *n* — **take advantage of 1** : to profit by **2** : EXPLOIT — **take after** : RESEMBLE — **take care** : to be careful — **take care of** : to attend to — **take effect** : to become operative — **take exception** : OBJECT — **take for** : to suppose to be; *esp* : to mistake for — **take place** : HAPPEN — **take to 1** : to go to **2** : to apply or devote oneself to **3** : to conceive a liking for

²take *n* **1** : the number or quantity taken; *also* : PROCEEDS, RECEIPTS **2** : an act or the action of taking **3** : a television or movie scene filmed or taped at one time; *also* : a sound recording made at one time **4** : a distinct or personal point of view

take·off \'tāk-ˌȯf\ *n* **1** : IMITATION; *esp* : PARODY ⟨did a ∼ of the president⟩ **2** : an act or instance of taking off

take off *vb* **1** : REMOVE **2** : DEDUCT **3** : to set out : go away **4** : to begin flight

take on *vb* **1** : to begin to perform or deal with; *also* : to contend with as an opponent **2** : ENGAGE, HIRE **3** : to assume or acquire as or as if one's own **4** : to make an unusual show of one's feelings esp. of grief or anger

take over *vb* : to assume control or possession of or responsibility for ⟨*took over* the company⟩ — **take·over** \'tāk-ˌō-vər\ *n*

take up *vb* **1** : PICK UP **2** : to begin to occupy (land) **3** : to absorb or incorporate into itself ⟨plants *taking up* nutrients⟩ **4** : to begin to engage in ⟨*took up* jogging⟩ **5** : to make tighter or shorter ⟨*take up* the slack⟩

tak·ings \'tā-kiŋz\ *n pl, chiefly Brit* : receipts esp. of money

ta·la \'tä-lə\ *n, pl* **tala** *or* **talas** — see MONEY table

talc \'talk\ *n* : a soft mineral with a soapy feel used esp. in making a soothing powder (**tal·cum powder** \'tal-kəm-\) for the skin

tale \'tāl\ *n* **1** : a relation of a series of events **2** : a report of a confidential matter **3** : idle talk; *esp* : harmful gossip **4** : a usu. imaginative narrative **5** : FALSEHOOD **6** : COUNT, TALLY

tal·ent \'ta-lənt\ *n* **1** : an ancient unit of weight and value **2** : the natural endowments of a person **3** : a special often creative or artistic aptitude **4** : mental power : ABILITY **5** : a person of talent ✦ *Synonyms* GENIUS, GIFT, FACULTY, APTITUDE, KNACK — **tal·ent·ed** *adj*

ta·ler \'tä-lər\ *n* : any of numerous silver coins issued by German states from the 15th to the 19th centuries

tal·is·man \'ta-ləs-mən, -ləz-\ *n, pl* **-mans** [F *talisman* or Sp *talismán* or It *talismano*, fr. Ar *ṭilsam*, fr. MGk *telesma*, fr. Gk, consecration, fr. *telein* to initiate into the mysteries, complete, fr. *telos* end] : an object thought to act as a charm

¹talk \'tȯk\ *vb* **1** : to express in speech : utter words : SPEAK **2** : DISCUSS ⟨∼ business⟩ **3** : to influence or cause by talking ⟨∼ed him into going⟩ **4** : to use (a language) for communicating **5** : CONVERSE **6** : to reveal confidential information; *also* : GOSSIP **7** : to give a talk : LECTURE — **talk·er** *n* — **talk back** : to answer impertinently

²talk *n* **1** : the act of talking **2** : a way of speaking **3** : a formal discussion **4** : REPORT, RUMOR **5** : the topic of comment or gossip ⟨the ∼ of the town⟩ **6** : an informal address or lecture

talk·ative \'tȯ-kə-tiv\ *adj* : given to talking ✦ *Synonyms* LOQUACIOUS, CHATTY, GABBY, GARRULOUS — **talk·ative·ly** *adv* — **talk·ative·ness** *n*

talk·ing-to \'tȯ-kiŋ-ˌtü\ *n* : REPRIMAND, REPROOF

talk radio *n* : radio programming consisting of call-in shows

tall \'tȯl\ *adj* **1** : high in stature; *also* : of a specified height ⟨six feet ∼⟩ **2** : LARGE, FORMIDABLE ⟨a ∼ order⟩ **3** : UNBELIEVABLE, IMPROBABLE ⟨a ∼ story⟩ — **tall·ness** *n*

tal·low \'ta-lō\ *n* : a hard white fat rendered usu. from cattle or sheep tissues and used esp. in candles

¹tal·ly \'ta-lē\ *n, pl* **tallies 1** : a device for visibly recording or accounting esp. business transactions **2** : a recorded account **3** : a corresponding part; *also* : CORRESPONDENCE

²tally *vb* **tal·lied; tal·ly·ing 1** : to mark on or as if on a tally **2** : to make a count of : RECKON; *also* : SCORE **3** : CORRESPOND, MATCH ✦ *Synonyms* SQUARE, ACCORD, HARMONIZE, CONFORM, JIBE

tal·ly·ho \ˌta-lē-'hō\ *n, pl* **-hos** : a call of a huntsman at sight of the fox

Tal·mud \'täl-ˌmud, 'tal-məd\ *n* [Late Heb *talmūdh*, lit., instruction] : the authoritative body of Jewish tradition — **Tal·mu·dic** \tal-'mü-dik, -'myü-, -'mə-; täl-'mu-\ *adj* — **Tal·mud·ist** \'täl-ˌmu-dist, 'tal-mə-\ *n*

tal·on \'ta-lən\ *n* : the claw of an animal and esp. of a bird of prey

ta·lus \'tā-ləs, 'ta-\ *n* : rock debris at the base of a cliff

tam \'tam\ *n* : TAM-O'-SHANTER

ta·ma·le \tə-'mä-lē\ *n* [MexSp *tamales*, pl. of *tamal* ta-male, fr. Nahuatl *tamalli* steamed cornmeal dough] : ground meat seasoned with chili, rolled in cornmeal dough, wrapped in corn husks, and steamed

tam·a·rack \'ta-mə-ˌrak\ *n* : a larch of northern No. America; *also* : its hard resinous wood

tam·a·rin \'ta-mə-rən\ *n* : any of several small So. American monkeys related to the marmosets

tam·a·rind \'ta-mə-rənd, -ˌrind\ *n* [Sp & Pg *tamarindo*, fr. Ar *tamr hindī*, lit., Indian date] : a tropical tree of the legume family with hard yellowish wood and feathery leaves; *also* : its acid fruit

tam·ba·la \täm-'bä-lə\ *n, pl* **-la** *or* **-las** — see *kwacha* at MONEY table

tam·bou·rine \ˌtam-bə-'rēn\ *n* : a small shallow drum with loose disks at the sides played by shaking or striking with the hand

¹tame \'tām\ *adj* **tam·er; tam·est** **1** : reduced from a state of native wildness esp. so as to be useful to humans : DOMESTICATED **2** : made docile : SUBDUED **3** : lacking spirit or interest : INSIPID ✦ *Synonyms* SUBMISSIVE, DOMESTIC, DOMESTICATED — **tame·ly** *adv* — **tame·ness** *n*

²tame *vb* **tamed; tam·ing** **1** : to make or become tame; *also* : to subject (land) to cultivation **2** : HUMBLE, SUBDUE — **tam·able** *or* **tame·able** \'tā-mə-bəl\ *adj* — **tame·less** *adj* — **tam·er** *n*

tam–o'–shan·ter \'ta-mə-ˌshan-tər\ *n* [fr. poem *Tam o' Shanter* (1790) by Robert Burns †1796 Scot. poet] : a Scottish woolen cap with a wide flat circular crown and usu. a pom-pom in the center

ta·mox·i·fen \tə-'mäk-sə-ˌfen\ *n* : a drug used esp. to treat breast cancer

tamp \'tamp\ *vb* : to drive down or in by a series of light blows

tam·per \'tam-pər\ *vb* **1** : to carry on underhand negotiations (as by bribery) ⟨∼ with a witness⟩ **2** : to interfere so as to weaken or change for the worse ⟨∼ with a document⟩ **3** : to try foolish or dangerous experiments

tam·pon \'tam-ˌpän\ *n* [F, lit., plug] : a plug (as of cotton) introduced into a body cavity usu. to absorb secretions (as from menstruation) or to arrest bleeding

¹tan \'tan\ *vb* **tanned; tan·ning** **1** : to change (hide) into leather esp. by soaking in a liquid containing tannin **2** : to make or become brown (as by exposure to the sun) **3** : WHIP, THRASH

²tan *n* **1** : a brown skin color induced by sun or weather **2** : a light yellowish brown color

³tan *abbr* tangent

tan·a·ger \'ta-ni-jər\ *n* : any of numerous American birds that are often brightly colored

tan·bark \'tan-ˌbärk\ *n* : bark (as of oak or sumac) that is rich in tannin and used in tanning

¹tan·dem \'tan-dəm\ *n* [L, at last, at length (taken to mean "lengthwise"), fr. *tam* so] **1** : a 2-seated carriage with horses hitched tandem; *also* : its team **2** : a bicycle for two persons sitting one behind the other — **in tandem** : in a tandem arrangement

²tandem *adv* : one behind another

³tandem *adj* **1** : consisting of things arranged one behind the other **2** : working in conjunction with each other

tang \'taŋ\ *n* **1** : a part in a tool that connects the blade with the handle **2** : a sharp distinctive flavor; *also* : a pungent odor — **tangy** *adj*

¹tan·gent \'tan-jənt\ *adj* [L *tangent-, tangens*, prp. of *tangere* to touch] : TOUCHING; *esp* : touching a circle or sphere at only one point

²tangent *n* **1** : the trigonometric function that is the ratio between the side opposite and the side adjacent to an acute angle in a right triangle **2** : a tangent line, curve, or surface **3** : an abrupt change of course

tan·gen·tial \tan-'jen-chəl\ *adj* **1** : TANGENT **2** : touching lightly : INCIDENTAL ⟨∼ involvement⟩ — **tan·gen·tial·ly** *adv*

tan·ger·ine \'tan-jə-ˌrēn, ˌtan-jə-'rēn\ *n* : a deep orange loose-skinned citrus fruit; *also* : a tree that bears tangerines

¹tan·gi·ble \'tan-jə-bəl\ *adj* **1** : perceptible esp. by the sense of touch : PALPABLE **2** : substantially real : MATERIAL ⟨∼ rewards⟩ **3** : capable of being appraised ⟨∼ assets⟩ ✦ *Synonyms* APPRECIABLE, PERCEPTIBLE, SENSIBLE, DISCERNIBLE — **tan·gi·bil·i·ty** \ˌtan-jə-'bi-lə-tē\ *n*

²tangible *n* : something tangible; *esp* : a tangible asset

¹tan·gle \'taŋ-gəl\ *vb* **tan·gled; tan·gling** **1** : to involve so as to hamper or embarrass; *also* : ENTRAP **2** : to unite or knit together in intricate confusion : ENTANGLE

²tangle *n* **1** : a tangled twisted mass **2** : a confusedly complicated state : MUDDLE

tan·go \'taŋ-gō\ *n, pl* **tangos** : a dance of Latin-American origin — **tango** *vb*

tank \'taŋk\ *n* **1** : a large artificial receptacle for liquids **2** : a heavily armed and armored combat vehicle that moves on tracks — **tank·ful** *n*

tan·kard \'taŋ-kərd\ *n* : a tall one-handled drinking vessel

tank·er \'taŋ-kər\ *n* : a vehicle equipped for transporting a liquid

tank top *n* : a sleeveless collarless pullover shirt with shoulder straps

tank town *n* : a small town

tan·ner \'ta-nər\ *n* : one that tans hides

tan·nery \'ta-nə-rē\ *n, pl* **-ner·ies** : a place where tanning is carried on

tan·nic acid \'ta-nik-\ *n* : TANNIN

tan·nin \'ta-nən\ *n* : any of various plant substances used esp. in tanning and dyeing, in inks, and as astringents

tan·sy \'tan-zē\ *n, pl* **tansies** : a common weedy herb related to the daisies with an aromatic odor and bitter-tasting finely divided leaves

tan·ta·lise *Brit var of* TANTALIZE

tan·ta·lize \'tan-tə-ˌlīz\ *vb* **-lized; -liz·ing** [fr. *Tantalus*, king of Greek myth punished in Hades by having to stand up to his chin in water that receded as he bent to drink] : to tease or torment by presenting something desirable but keeping it out of reach — **tan·ta·liz·er** *n* — **tan·ta·liz·ing·ly** *adv*

tan·ta·lum \'tan-tə-ləm\ *n* : a gray-white ductile metallic chemical element

tan·ta·mount \'tan-tə-ˌmaunt\ *adj* : equivalent in value or meaning ⟨a relationship ∼ to marriage⟩

tan·trum \'tan-trəm\ *n* : a fit of bad temper

Tao·ism \'tau-ˌi-zəm, 'dau-\ *n* : a Chinese mystical philosophy; *also* : a religion developed from Taoist philosophy and Buddhism — **Tao·ist** \-ist\ *adj or n*

¹tap \'tap\ *n* **1** : FAUCET, COCK **2** : liquor drawn through a tap **3** : the removing of fluid from a container or cavity by tapping **4** : a tool for forming an internal screw thread **5** : a point in an electric circuit where a connection may be made

²tap *vb* **tapped; tap·ping** **1** : to release or cause to flow by piercing or by drawing a plug from a container or cavity **2** : to pierce so as to let out or draw off a fluid **3** : to draw from ⟨∼ resources⟩ **4** : to cut in on (as a telephone signal) to get information **5** : to form an internal screw thread in by means of a tap **6** : to connect (as a gas or water main) with a local supply — **tap·per** *n*

³tap *vb* **tapped; tap·ping** **1** : to rap lightly **2** : to bring about by repeated light blows **3** : SELECT; *esp* : to elect to membership

⁴tap *n* **1** : a light blow or stroke; *also* : its sound **2** : a small metal plate for the sole or heel of a shoe

ta·pa \'tä-pə, 'ta-\ *n* [Sp, lit., cover, lid] : an hors d'oeuvre served with drinks esp. in Spanish bars — usu. used in pl.

¹tape \'tāp\ *n* **1** : a narrow flexible band or strip (as of woven fabric) **2** : MAGNETIC TAPE; *also* : CASSETTE

²tape *vb* **taped; tap·ing** **1** : to fasten or support with tape **2** : to record on magnetic tape

tape deck *n* : a device used to play back cassette tapes that usu. has to be connected to an audio system

tape measure *n* : a tape marked off in units (as inches) for measuring

¹ta·per \'tā-pər\ *n* **1** : a slender wax candle; *also* : a long waxed wick **2** : a gradual lessening of thickness or width in a long object

²taper *vb* **ta·pered; ta·per·ing** **1** : to make or become gradually smaller toward one end **2** : to diminish gradually

tape–re·cord \ˌtāp-ri-'kord\ *vb* : to make a recording of on magnetic tape — **tape recorder** *n* — **tape recording** *n*

tap·es·try \'ta-pə-strē\ *n, pl* **-tries** : a heavy reversible textile that has designs or pictures woven into it and is used esp. as a wall hanging

tape·worm \'tāp-ˌwərm\ *n* : any of a class of long flat segmented worms parasitic esp. in vertebrate intestines

tap·i·o·ca \ˌta-pē-'ō-kə\ *n* : a usu. granular preparation of cassava starch used esp. in puddings; *also* : a dish (as pudding) that contains tapioca

ta·pir \'tā-pər\ *n, pl* **tapirs** *also* **tapir** [Pg *tapir, tapira*, fr. Tupinambà (American Indian language of Brazil) *tapiĩra*] : any of a genus of large herbivorous hoofed mammals of tropical America and southeastern Asia

tap·pet \'ta-pət\ *n* : a lever or projection moved by some other piece (as a cam) or intended to move something else

tap·room \'tap-ˌrüm, -ˌrùm\ *n* : BARROOM

tap·root \-ˌrüt, -ˌrùt\ *n* : a large main root growing straight down and giving off small side roots

taps \'taps\ *n sing or pl* : the last bugle call at night blown as a signal that lights are to be put out; *also* : a similar call blown at military funerals and memorial services

tap·ster \'tap-stər\ *n* : BARTENDER

¹**tar** \'tär\ *n* 1 : a thick dark sticky liquid distilled from organic material (as wood or coal) 2 : SAILOR, SEAMAN

²**tar** *vb* **tarred; tar·ring** : to cover or smear with or as if with tar

tar·an·tel·la \ˌtä-rən-'te-lə\ *n* : a lively folk dance of southern Italy in 6/8 time

ta·ran·tu·la \tə-'ran-chə-lə, -tə-lə\ *n, pl* **tarantulas** *also* **ta·ran·tu·lae** \-'ran-chə-ˌlē, -tə-ˌlē\ : any of a family of large hairy American spiders with a sharp bite that is not very poisonous to human beings

tar·dy \'tär-dē\ *adj* **tar·di·er; -est** 1 : moving slowly : SLUGGISH 2 : LATE ⟨was ~ to work⟩ ♦ *Synonyms* BEHINDHAND, OVERDUE, BELATED — **tar·di·ly** \-də-lē\ *adv* — **tar·di·ness** \-dē-nəs\ *n*

¹**tare** \'ter\ *n* : a weed of grain fields

²**tare** *n* : a deduction from the gross weight of a substance and its container made in allowance for the weight of the container — **tare** *vb*

¹**tar·get** \'tär-gət\ *n* [ME, fr. MF *targette*, dim. of *targe* light shield, of Gmc origin] 1 : a mark to shoot at 2 : an object of ridicule or criticism 3 : a goal to be achieved

²**target** *vb* : to make a target of

tar·iff \'ta-rəf\ *n* [It *tariffa*, fr. Ar *ta'rīf* notification] 1 : a schedule of duties imposed by a government esp. on imported goods; *also* : a duty or rate of duty imposed in such a schedule 2 : a schedule of rates or charges

tar·mac \'tär-ˌmak\ *n* : a surface paved with crushed stone covered with tar

tarn \'tärn\ *n* : a small mountain lake

tar·nish \'tär-nish\ *vb* : to make or become dull or discolored — **tarnish** *n*

ta·ro \'tär-ō, 'ter-\ *n, pl* **taros** : a large-leaved tropical plant related to the arums that is grown for its edible starchy corms; *also* : its corms

tar·ot \'ter-ō, 'ta-rō\ *n* : one of a set of usu. 78 playing cards used esp. for fortune-telling

tar·pau·lin \tär-'pò-lən, 'tär-pə-\ *n* : a piece of material (as durable plastic) used for protecting exposed objects

tar·pon \'tär-pən\ *n, pl* **tarpon** *or* **tarpons** : a large silvery bony fish often caught for sport in the warm coastal waters of the Atlantic esp. off Florida

tar·ra·gon \'ter-ə-gän\ *n* [MF *targon*, ultim. fr. Ar *ṭarkhūn*] : a small widely cultivated perennial wormwood with aromatic leaves used as a seasoning; *also* : its leaves

¹**tar·ry** \'ta-rē\ *vb* **tar·ried; tar·ry·ing** 1 : to be tardy : DELAY; *esp* : to be slow in leaving 2 : to stay in or at a place : SOJOURN ♦ *Synonyms* REMAIN, WAIT, LINGER, ABIDE

²**tar·ry** \'tär-ē\ *adj* : of, resembling, or smeared with tar

tar sand *n* : sand or sandstone that is naturally soaked with the heavy sticky portions of petroleum

tar·sus \'tär-səs\ *n, pl* **tar·si** \-ˌsī\ [NL] : the part of a vertebrate foot between the metatarsus and the leg; *also* : the small bones that support this part — **tar·sal** \-səl\ *adj or n*

¹**tart** \'tärt\ *adj* 1 : agreeably sharp to the taste : PUNGENT 2 : BITING, CAUSTIC ⟨~ comments⟩ — **tart·ly** *adv* — **tart·ness** *n*

²**tart** *n* 1 : a small pie or pastry shell containing jelly, custard, or fruit 2 : PROSTITUTE

tar·tan \'tärt-ᵊn\ *n* : a plaid textile design of Scottish origin usu. distinctively patterned to designate a particular clan

tar·tar \'tär-tər\ *n* 1 : a substance in the juice of grapes deposited (as in wine casks) as a reddish crust or sediment 2 : a crust on the teeth formed from plaque hardened by calcium salts

tar·tar sauce *or* **tar·tare sauce** \'tär-tər-\ *n* : mayonnaise with chopped pickles, olives, or capers

¹**task** \'task\ *n* [ME *taske*, fr. MF dial. *tasque*, fr. ML *tasca* tax or service imposed by a feudal superior, fr. *taxare* to tax] : a piece of assigned work ♦ *Synonyms* JOB, DUTY, CHORE, STINT, ASSIGNMENT

²**task** *vb* : to oppress with great labor

task bar *n* : a strip of icons usually at the bottom of a computer screen showing programs that may be used by selecting their icons

task force *n* : a temporary grouping to accomplish a particular objective

task·mas·ter \'task-ˌmas-tər\ *n* : one that imposes a task or burdens another with labor

¹**tas·sel** \'ta-səl, 'tä-\ *n* 1 : a hanging ornament made of a bunch of cords of even length fastened at one end 2 : something suggesting a tassel; *esp* : a male flower cluster of corn

²**tassel** *vb* **-seled** *or* **-selled; -sel·ing** *or* **-sel·ling** : to adorn with or put forth tassels

¹**taste** \'tāst\ *vb* **tast·ed; tast·ing** 1 : EXPERIENCE, UNDERGO 2 : to try or determine the flavor of by taking a bit into the mouth 3 : to eat or drink esp. in small quantities : SAMPLE 4 : to have a specific flavor ⟨the milk ~s sour⟩

²**taste** *n* 1 : a small amount tasted 2 : BIT; *esp* : a sample of experience 3 : the special sense that perceives and identifies sweet, sour, bitter, or salty qualities and is mediated by taste buds on the tongue 4 : a quality perceptible to the sense of taste; *also* : the sensation obtained from a substance in the mouth : FLAVOR 5 : individual preference 6 : critical judgment, discernment, or appreciation; *also* : aesthetic quality ♦ *Synonyms* TANG, RELISH, FLAVOR, SAVOR — **taste·ful** \-fəl\ *adj* — **taste·ful·ly** *adv* — **taste·less** *adj* — **taste·less·ly** *adv* — **tast·er** *n*

taste bud *n* : a sense organ mediating the sensation of taste

tasty \'tā-stē\ *adj* **tast·i·er; -est** : pleasing to the taste : SAVORY ⟨a very ~ meal⟩ ♦ *Synonyms* PALATABLE, APPETIZING, TOOTHSOME, FLAVORSOME — **tast·i·ness** \'tä-stē-nəs\ *n*

tat \'tat\ *vb* **tat·ted; tat·ting** : to work at or make by tatting

¹**tat·ter** \'ta-tər\ *vb* : to make or become ragged

²**tatter** *n* 1 : a part torn and left hanging 2 *pl* : tattered clothing

tat·ter·sall \'ta-tər-ˌsòl, -səl\ *n* : a pattern of colored lines forming squares on solid background; *also* : a fabric in a tattersall pattern

tat·ting \'ta-tiŋ\ *n* : a delicate handmade lace formed usu. by looping and knotting with a single thread and a small shuttle; *also* : the act or process of making such lace

tat·tle \'ta-tᵊl\ *vb* **tat·tled; tat·tling** 1 : CHATTER, PRATE 2 : to tell secrets; *also* : to inform against another — **tat·tler** *n*

tat·tle·tale \'ta-tᵊl-ˌtāl\ *n* : one that tattles : INFORMER

¹**tat·too** \ta-'tü\ *n, pl* **tattoos** [alter. of earlier *taptoo*, fr. D *taptoe*, fr. the phrase *tap toe!* taps shut!] 1 : a call sounded before taps as notice to go to quarters 2 : a rapid rhythmic rapping

²**tattoo** *vb* : to mark (the skin) with tattoos

³**tattoo** *n, pl* **tattoos** [Tahitian *tatau*] : an indelible figure fixed upon the body esp. by insertion of pigment under the skin

tartan

tau \\'taů, 'tô\\ *n* : the 19th letter of the Greek alphabet — T or τ

taught *past and past part of* TEACH

¹taunt \\'tónt\\ *n* : a sarcastic challenge or insult

²taunt *vb* : to reproach or challenge in a mocking manner : jeer at ⟨the boys ∼ed each other⟩ ✦ *Synonyms* MOCK, DERIDE, RIDICULE, TWIT — **taunt·er** *n*

taupe \\'tōp\\ *n* : a brownish gray

Tau·rus \\'tòr-əs\\ *n* [L, lit., bull] **1** : a zodiacal constellation between Aries and Gemini usu. pictured as a bull **2** : the 2d sign of the zodiac in astrology; *also* : one born under this sign

taut \\'tòt\\ *adj* **1** : tightly drawn : not slack **2** : extremely nervous : TENSE **3** : TRIM, TIDY ⟨a ∼ ship⟩ — **taut·ly** *adv* — **taut·ness** *n*

tau·tol·o·gy \\tò-'tä-lə-jē\\ *n, pl* **-gies** : needless repetition of an idea, statement, or word; *also* : an instance of such repetition — **tau·to·log·i·cal** \\,tòt-ə-'lä-ji-kəl\\ *adj* — **tau·to·log·i·cal·ly** \\-ji-k(ə-)lē\\ *adv* — **tau·tol·o·gous** \\tò-'tä-lə-gəs\\ *adj* — **tau·tol·o·gous·ly** *adv*

tav·ern \\'ta-vərn\\ *n* [ME *taverne*, fr. AF, fr. L *taberna* hut, shop] **1** : an establishment where alcoholic liquors are sold to be drunk on the premises **2** : INN

taw \\'tò\\ *n* **1** : a marble used as a shooter **2** : the line from which players shoot at marbles

taw·dry \\'tò-drē\\ *adj* **taw·dri·er; -est** [*tawdry lace* a tie of lace for the neck, fr. *St. Audrey* (St. Etheldreda) †679 queen of Northumbria] : cheap and gaudy in appearance and quality ⟨∼ decorations⟩ ✦ *Synonyms* GARISH, FLASHY, CHINTZY, MERETRICIOUS — **taw·dri·ly** *adv*

taw·ny \\'tò-nē\\ *adj* **taw·ni·er; -est** : of a brownish orange color

¹tax \\'taks\\ *vb* **1** : to levy a tax on **2** : CHARGE, ACCUSE **3** : to put under pressure — **tax·able** \\'tak-sə-bəl\\ *adj* — **tax·a·tion** \\tak-'sā-shən\\ *n*

²tax *n* **1** : a charge usu. of money imposed by authority on persons or property for public purposes **2** : a heavy charge : STRAIN

¹taxi \\'tak-sē\\ *n, pl* **tax·is** \\-sēz\\ *also* **tax·ies** : TAXICAB; *also* : a similarly operated boat or aircraft

²taxi *vb* **tax·ied; taxi·ing** *or* **taxy·ing; tax·is** *or* **tax·ies 1** : to move along the ground or on the water under an aircraft's own power when starting or after a landing **2** : to go by taxicab

taxi·cab \\'tak-sē-,kab\\ *n* : an automobile that carries passengers for a fare usu. based on the distance traveled

taxi·der·my \\'tak-sə-,dər-mē\\ *n* : the skill or occupation of preparing, stuffing, and mounting skins of animals — **taxi·der·mist** \\-mist\\ *n*

tax·on \\'tak-,sän\\ *n, pl* **taxa** \\-sə\\; *also* **taxons** : a taxonomic group or entity

tax·on·o·my \\tak-'sä-nə-mē\\ *n* : classification esp. of animals or plants according to natural relationships — **tax·o·nom·ic** \\,tak-sə-'nä-mik\\ *adj* — **tax·on·o·mist** \\tak-'sä-nə-mist\\ *n*

tax·pay·er \\'taks-,pā-ər\\ *n* : one who pays or is liable for a tax — **tax·pay·ing** *adj*

Tay–Sachs disease \\'tā-'saks-\\ *n* : a hereditary disorder caused by the absence of an enzyme needed to break down fatty material, marked by buildup of lipids in nervous tissue, and causing death in childhood

tb *abbr* tablespoon; tablespoonful

Tb *symbol* terbium

TB \\,tē-'bē\\ *n* : TUBERCULOSIS

TBA *abbr, often not cap* to be announced

T–bar \\'tē-,bär\\ *n* : a ski lift with a series of T-shaped bars

tbs *or* **tbsp** *abbr* tablespoon; tablespoonful

Tc *symbol* technetium

TC *abbr* teachers college

T cell *n* : any of several lymphocytes (as a helper T cell) specialized esp. for activity in and control of immunity and the immune response

TCP/IP \\,tē-(,)sē-'pē-,ī-'pē\\ *n* [*transmission control protocol/Internet protocol*] : a set of communications protocols used over networks and esp. the Internet

TD **1** touchdown **2** Treasury Department

TDD *abbr* telecommunications device for the deaf

TDY *abbr* temporary duty

Te *symbol* tellurium

tea \\'tē\\ *n* [Chin (dialect of Fujian province) *dé*] **1** : the cured leaves and leaf buds of a shrub grown chiefly in China, Japan, India, and Sri Lanka; *also* : this shrub **2** : a drink made by steeping tea in boiling water **3** : refreshments usu. including tea served in late afternoon; *also* : a reception at which tea is served

teach \\'tēch\\ *vb* **taught** \\'tòt\\; **teach·ing 1** : to cause to know something : act as a teacher **2** : to show how ⟨∼ a child to swim⟩ **3** : to make to know the disagreeable consequences of an action **4** : to guide the studies of **5** : to impart the knowledge of ⟨∼ algebra⟩ — **teach·able** *adj* — **teach·er** *n*

teach·ing *n* **1** : the act, practice, or profession of a teacher **2** : something taught; *esp* : DOCTRINE

tea·cup \\'tē-,kəp\\ *n* : a small cup used with a saucer for hot beverages

teak \\'tēk\\ *n* : the hard durable yellowish brown wood of a tall tropical Asian timber tree related to the vervains; *also* : this tree

tea·ket·tle \\'tē-,ke-t³l\\ *n* : a covered kettle with a handle and spout for boiling water

teal \\'tēl\\ *n, pl* **teal** *or* **teals 1** : any of various small short-necked wild ducks **2** : a dark greenish blue color

¹team \\'tēm\\ *n* [ME *teme*, fr. OE *tēam* offspring, lineage, group of draft animals] **1** : two or more draft animals harnessed to the same vehicle or implement **2** : a number of persons associated in work or activity; *esp* : a group on one side in a match

²team *adj* : of or performed by a team; *also* : marked by devotion to teamwork ⟨a ∼ player⟩

³team *vb* **1** : to haul with or drive a team **2** : to form a team : join forces

team·mate \\-,māt\\ *n* : a fellow member of a team

team·ster \\'tēm-stər\\ *n* : one who drives a team or truck

team·work \\-,wərk\\ *n* : the work or activity of a number of persons acting in close association as members of a unit

tea·pot \\'tē-,pät\\ *n* : a vessel with a spout for brewing and serving tea

¹tear \\'tir\\ *n* **1** : a drop of the salty liquid that moistens the eye and inner side of the eyelids; *also, pl* : an act of weeping or grieving — **tear·ful** \\-fəl\\ *adj* — **tear·ful·ly** *adv* — **teary** \\'tir-ē\\ *adj*

²tear \\'tir\\ *vb* : to fill with or shed tears

³tear \\'ter\\ *vb* **tore** \\'tòr\\; **torn** \\'tòrn\\; **tear·ing 1** : to separate parts of or pull apart by force : REND **1** : LACERATE **3** : to disrupt by the pull of contrary forces **4** : to remove by force : WRENCH ⟨∼ down a house⟩ **5** : to move or act with violence, haste, or force ✦ *Synonyms* RIP, SPLIT, CLEAVE, REND

⁴tear \\'ter\\ *n* **1** : the act of tearing **2** : a hole or flaw made by tearing : RENT

tear gas \\'tir-\\ *n* : a substance that on dispersion in the atmosphere blinds the eyes with tears — **tear gas** *vb*

tear·jerk·er \\'tir-,jər-kər\\ *n* : an extravagantly pathetic story, song, play, movie, or broadcast

¹tease \\'tēz\\ *vb* **teased; teas·ing 1** : to disentangle and lay parallel by combing or carding ⟨∼ wool⟩ **2** : to scratch the surface of (cloth) so as to raise a nap **3** : to annoy persistently esp. in fun by goading, coaxing, or tantalizing ⟨stop *teasing* the dog⟩ **4** : to comb (hair) by taking a strand and pushing the short hairs toward the scalp with the comb ✦ *Synonyms* HARASS, WORRY, PESTER, ANNOY

²tease *n* **1** : the act of teasing or state of being teased **2** : one that teases

tea·sel \\'tē-zəl\\ *n* : a prickly herb or its flower head covered with stiff hooked bracts and used to raise the nap on cloth; *also* : an artificial device used for this purpose

tea·spoon \\'tē-,spün\\ *n* **1** : a small spoon suitable for stirring beverages **2** : a unit of measure equal to ⅙ fluid ounce (5 milliliters)

tea·spoon·ful \\-,fůl\\ *n, pl* **-spoonfuls** *also* **-spoons·ful** \\-,spünz-,fůl\\ : TEASPOON 2

teat \\'tit, 'tēt\\ *n* : the protuberance through which milk is drawn from an udder or breast

tech *abbr* **1** technical; technically; technician **2** technological; technology

tech·ne·tium \\tek-'nē-shē-əm\\ *n* : a radioactive metallic chemical element

tech·nic \\'tek-nik, tek-'nēk\\ *n* : TECHNIQUE 1

tech·ni·cal \\'tek-ni-kəl\\ *adj* [Gk *technikos* of art, skillful, fr. *technē* art, craft, skill] **1** : having special knowledge esp. of a mechanical or scientific subject ⟨∼ experts⟩ **2** : of or relating to a particular and esp. a practical or scientific subject ⟨∼ training⟩ **3** : according to a strict interpretation of the rules **4** : of or relating to technique — **tech·ni·cal·ly** \-k(ə-)lē\ *adv*

tech·ni·cal·i·ty \ˌtek-nə-ˈka-lə-tē\ *n, pl* **-ties 1** : a detail meaningful only to a specialist **2** : the quality or state of being technical

technical sergeant *n* : a noncommissioned officer in the air force ranking next below a master sergeant

tech·ni·cian \tek-ˈni-shən\ *n* : a person who has acquired the technique of a specialized skill or subject

tech·nique \tek-ˈnēk\ *n* [F] **1** : the manner in which technical details are treated or basic physical movements are used **2** : technical methods

tech·no \ˈtek-nō\ *n* : dance music featuring a fast beat and electronically created sounds usu. without vocals

tech·noc·ra·cy \tek-ˈnä-krə-sē\ *n* : management of society by technical experts — **tech·no·crat** \ˈtek-nə-ˌkrat\ *n* — **tech·no·crat·ic** \ˌtek-nə-ˈkra-tik\ *adj*

tech·nol·o·gy \tek-ˈnä-lə-jē\ *n, pl* **-gies** : ENGINEERING; *also* : a manner of accomplishing a task using technical methods or knowledge — **tech·no·log·i·cal** \ˌtek-nə-ˈlä-ji-kəl\ *adj*

tec·ton·ics \tek-ˈtä-niks\ *n sing or pl* **1** : geological structural features **2** : geology dealing esp. with the faulting and folding of a planet or moon — **tec·ton·ic** \-nik\ *adj*

ted·dy bear \ˈte-dē-ˌber\ *n* [*Teddy* Roosevelt; fr. a cartoon depicting the president sparing the life of a bear cub while hunting] : a stuffed toy bear

te·dious \ˈtē-dē-əs\ *adj* : tiresome because of length or dullness ⟨a ∼ speech⟩ ♦ **Synonyms** BORING, TIRING, IRKSOME — **te·dious·ly** *adv* — **te·dious·ness** *n*

te·di·um \ˈtē-dē-əm\ *n* : TEDIOUSNESS; *also* : BOREDOM

¹tee \ˈtē\ *n* : a small mound or peg on which a golf ball is placed to be hit at the beginning of play on a hole; *also* : the area from which the ball is hit to begin play

²tee *vb* **teed; tee·ing** : to place (a ball) on a tee

teem \ˈtēm\ *vb* : to become filled to overflowing : ABOUND ♦ **Synonyms** SWARM, CRAWL, FLOW

teen \ˈtēn\ *n* : a teenage person : TEENAGER — **teen** *adj*

teen·age \ˈtēn-ˌāj\ *or* **teen·aged** \-ˌnājd\ *adj* : of, being, or relating to people in their teens — **teen·ag·er** \-ˌnā-jər\ *n*

teens \ˈtēnz\ *n pl* : the numbers 13 to 19 inclusive; *esp* : the years 13 to 19 in a person's life

tee·ny \ˈtē-nē\ *adj* **tee·ni·er; -est** : TINY

teepee *var of* TEPEE

tee shirt *var of* T-SHIRT

tee·ter \ˈtē-tər\ *vb* **1** : to move unsteadily **2** : SEESAW — **teeter** *n*

teeth *pl of* TOOTH

teethe \ˈtēth\ *vb* **teethed; teeth·ing** : to experience the rising of one's teeth through the gums : to grow teeth

teething *n* : growth of the first set of teeth through the gums with its accompanying phenomena

tee·to·tal·er *or* **tee·to·tal·ler** \ˈtē-ˈtō-tᵊl-ər\ *n* : a person who practices complete abstinence from alcoholic drinks — **tee·to·tal** \ˈtē-ˈtō-tᵊl, -ˌtō-\ *adj* — **tee·to·tal·ism** \-tᵊl-ˌi-zəm\ *n*

TEFL *abbr* teaching English as a foreign language

Te·ja·no \tā-ˈhä-(ˌ)nō\ *n, pl* **-nos** [Mex Sp, fr. *Tejas* Texas] : a Texan of Hispanic descent

tek·tite \ˈtek-ˌtīt\ *n* : a glassy body of probably meteoric origin

tel *abbr* **1** telegram **2** telegraph **3** telephone

tele·cast \ˈte-li-ˌkast\ *vb* **-cast** *also* **-cast·ed; -cast·ing** : to broadcast by television — **telecast** *n* — **tele·cast·er** *n*

tel·e·com \ˈte-li-ˌkäm\ *n* : TELECOMMUNICATION; *also* : the telecommunications industry

tele·com·mu·ni·ca·tion \ˌte-li-kə-ˌmyü-nə-ˈkā-shən\ *n* : communication at a distance (as by telephone or radio)

tele·com·mute \ˈte-li-kə-ˌmyüt\ *vb* : to work at home by the use of an electronic linkup with a central office

tele·con·fer·ence \ˈte-li-ˌkän-fə-rəns\ *n* : a conference among people remote from one another held using telecommunications — **tele·con·fer·enc·ing** *n*

teleg *abbr* telegraphy

tele·ge·nic \ˌte-lə-ˈje-nik, -ˌjē-\ *adj* : markedly attractive to television viewers

tele·gram \ˈte-lə-ˌgram\ *n* : a message sent by telegraph

¹tele·graph \-ˌgraf\ *n* : an electric apparatus or system for sending messages by a code over wires — **tele·graph·ic** \ˌte-lə-ˈgra-fik\ *adj*

²telegraph *vb* : to send or communicate by or as if by telegraph — **te·leg·ra·pher** \tə-ˈle-grə-fər\ *n*

te·leg·ra·phy \tə-ˈle-grə-fē\ *n* : the use or operation of a telegraph apparatus or system

tele·mar·ket·ing \ˌte-lə-ˈmär-kə-tiŋ\ *n* : the marketing of goods or services by telephone — **tele·mar·ket·er** \-tər\ *n*

tele·med·i·cine \ˌte-lə-ˈme-də-sən\ *n* : the practice of medicine using two-way voice and visual communication

te·lem·e·try \tə-ˈle-mə-trē\ *n* : the transmission esp. by radio of measurements made by automatic instruments to a distant station — **tele·me·ter** \ˈte-lə-ˌmē-tər\ *n*

tel·e·no·ve·la \ˌte-lə-nō-ˈve-lə\ *n* : a soap opera televised in or from many Latin-American countries

te·lep·a·thy \tə-ˈle-pə-thē\ *n* : apparent communication from one mind to another by extrasensory means — **tele·path·ic** \ˌte-lə-ˈpa-thik\ *adj* — **tele·path·i·cal·ly** \-thi-k(ə-)lē\ *adv*

¹tele·phone \ˈte-lə-ˌfōn\ *n* : an instrument for sending and receiving sounds over long distances by electricity

²telephone *vb* **-phoned; -phon·ing 1** : to send or communicate by telephone **2** : to speak to (a person) by telephone — **tele·phon·er** *n*

te·le·pho·ny \tə-ˈle-fə-nē, ˈte-lə-ˌfō-\ *n* : use or operation of an apparatus for transmission of sounds as electrical signals between distant points — **tel·e·phon·ic** \ˌte-lə-ˈfä-nik\ *adj*

tele·pho·to \ˌte-lə-ˈfō-tō\ *adj* : being a camera lens giving a large image of a distant object — **tele·pho·tog·ra·phy** \-fə-ˈtä-grə-fē\ *n*

tele·play \ˈte-li-ˌplā\ *n* : a story prepared for television production

tele·print·er \ˈte-lə-ˌprin-tər\ *n* : TELETYPEWRITER

tele·prompt·er \ˈte-lə-ˌprämp-tər\ *n* : a device for displaying prepared text to a speaker or performer

¹tele·scope \ˈte-lə-ˌskōp\ *n* **1** : a cylindrical instrument equipped with lenses or mirrors for viewing distant objects **2** : RADIO TELESCOPE

²telescope *vb* **-scoped; -scop·ing 1** : to slide or pass or cause to slide or pass one within another like the sections of a collapsible hand telescope **2** : COMPRESS, CONDENSE

tele·scop·ic \ˌte-lə-ˈskä-pik\ *adj* **1** : of or relating to a telescope **2** : seen only by a telescope **3** : able to discern objects at a distance **4** : having parts that telescope — **tele·scop·i·cal·ly** \-pi-k(ə-)lē\ *adv*

tele·text \ˈte-lə-ˌtekst\ *n* : a system for broadcasting text over a television signal and displaying it on a decoder-equipped television

tele·thon \ˈte-lə-ˌthän\ *n* : a long television program usu. to solicit funds for a charity

tele·type·writ·er \ˌte-lə-ˈtīp-ˌrī-tər\ *n* : a printing device resembling a typewriter used to send and receive signals over telephone lines

tele·vise \ˈte-lə-ˌvīz\ *vb* **-vised; -vis·ing** : to broadcast by television

tele·vi·sion \ˈte-lə-ˌvi-zhən\ *n* [F *télévision*, fr. Gk *tēle* far, at a distance + F *vision* vision] : a system for transmitting images and sound by converting them into electrical or radio waves which are converted back into images and sound by a receiver; *also* : a television receiving set

tell \ˈtel\ *vb* **told** \ˈtōld\; **tell·ing 1** : COUNT, ENUMERATE **2** : to relate in detail : NARRATE ⟨*told* us what happened⟩ **3** : SAY, UTTER **4** : to make known : REVEAL **5** : to report to : INFORM ⟨*told* me her name⟩ **6** : ORDER, DIRECT **7** : to find out by observing ⟨can ∼ the difference⟩ **8** : to have a marked effect **9** : to serve as evidence ♦ **Synonyms** DISCLOSE, DISCOVER, BETRAY

tell·er \ˈte-lər\ *n* **1** : one that relates : NARRATOR **2** : one that counts **3** : a bank employee handling money received or paid out

tell·ing \ˈte-liŋ\ *adj* : producing a marked effect : EFFECTIVE ⟨∼ evidence⟩ ♦ **Synonyms** COGENT, CONVINCING, SOUND

tell off *vb* : REPRIMAND, SCOLD

tell·tale \ˈtel-ˌtāl\ *n* **1** : INFORMER, TATTLETALE **2** : something that serves to disclose : INDICATION — **telltale** *adj*

tel·lu·ri·um \tə-ˈlu̇r-ē-əm\ *n* : a chemical element used esp. in alloys

tem·blor \ˈtem-blər\ *n* [Sp, lit., trembling] : EARTHQUAKE

te·mer·i·ty \tə-ˈmer-ə-tē\ *n, pl* **-ties** : rash or presumptuous

daring : BOLDNESS ♦ *Synonyms* AUDACITY, EFFRON-
TERY, GALL, NERVE, CHEEK

¹temp \'temp\ *n* **1** : TEMPERATURE **2** : a temporary worker

²temp *abbr* temporary

¹tem·per \'tem-pər\ *vb* **1** : to dilute or soften by the addition of something else ⟨∼ justice with mercy⟩ **2** : to
bring (as steel) to a desired hardness by reheating and
cooling **3** : to toughen (glass) by gradual heating and
cooling **4** : TOUGHEN **5** : TUNE

²temper *n* **1** : characteristic tone : TENDENCY **2** : the
hardness or toughness of a substance ⟨the ∼ of a knife
blade⟩ **3** : a characteristic frame of mind : DISPOSITION
4 : calmness of mind : COMPOSURE **5** : state of feeling
or frame of mind at a particular time **6** : heat of mind
or emotion ♦ *Synonyms* TEMPERAMENT, CHARACTER,
PERSONALITY, MAKEUP — **tem·pered** \'tem-pərd\ *adj*

tem·pera \'tem-pə-rə\ *n* [It] : a painting process using an
albuminous or colloidal medium as a vehicle; *also* : a
painting done in tempera

tem·per·a·ment \'tem-prə-mənt, -pər-mənt\ *n* **1** : characteristic or habitual inclination or mode of emotional
response : DISPOSITION ⟨nervous ∼⟩ **2** : excessive
sensitiveness or irritability ♦ *Synonyms* CHARACTER,
PERSONALITY, NATURE, MAKEUP — **tem·per·a·men·tal**
\ˌtem-prə-'men-tᵊl, -pər-'ment-\ *adj*

tem·per·ance \'tem-prəns, -pə-rəns\ *n* : habitual moderation in the indulgence of the appetites or passions; *esp*
: moderation in or abstinence from the use of alcoholic
beverages

tem·per·ate \'tem-prət, -pə-rət\ *adj* **1** : not extreme or
excessive : MILD **2** : moderate in indulgence of appetite
or desire **3** : moderate in the use of alcoholic beverages
4 : having a moderate climate ♦ *Synonyms* SOBER,
CONTINENT, ABSTEMIOUS

temperate zone *n, often cap T&Z* : the region between
the Tropic of Cancer and the arctic circle or between the
Tropic of Capricorn and the antarctic circle

tem·per·a·ture \'tem-pər-ˌchúr, -prə-ˌchúr, -chər\ *n* **1** : degree of hotness or coldness of something (as air, water, or
the body) as shown by a thermometer **2** : FEVER **1**

tem·pest \'tem-pəst\ *n* [ME *tempeste*, fr. AF, ultim. fr.
L *tempestas* season, weather, storm, fr. *tempus* time] : a
violent storm

tempest in a teapot : a great commotion over an unimportant matter

tem·pes·tu·ous \tem-'pes-chə-wəs\ *adj* : of, involving, or
resembling a tempest : STORMY — **tem·pes·tu·ous·ly**
adv — **tem·pes·tu·ous·ness** *n*

tem·plate \'tem-plət\ *n* : a gauge, mold, or pattern that
functions as a guide to the form or structure of something being made

¹tem·ple \'tem-pəl\ *n* **1** : a building reserved for religious
practice **2** : a place devoted to a special or exalted purpose ⟨a ∼ of cuisine⟩

²temple *n* : the flattened space on each side of the forehead esp. of humans

tem·po \'tem-pō\ *n, pl* **tem·pi** \-(ˌ)pē\ *or* **tempos** [It, lit.,
time] **1** : the rate or speed of a musical piece or passage
2 : rate of motion or activity : PACE

¹tem·po·ral \'tem-pə-rəl\ *adj* **1** : of, relating to, or limited
by time ⟨∼ and spatial bounds⟩ **2** : of or relating to
earthly life or secular concerns ⟨∼ power⟩

²temporal *adj* : of or relating to the temples or the sides
of the skull

¹tem·po·rary \'tem-pə-ˌrer-ē\ *adj* : lasting for a time only
: TRANSITORY ♦ *Synonyms* TRANSIENT, EPHEMERAL,
MOMENTARY, IMPERMANENT — **tem·po·rar·i·ly** \ˌtem-
pə-'rer-ə-lē\ *adv*

²temporary *n, pl* **-rar·ies** : one serving for a limited time

tem·po·rise *Brit var of* TEMPORIZE

tem·po·rize \'tem-pə-ˌrīz\ *vb* **-rized; -riz·ing 1** : to adapt
one's actions to the time or the dominant opinion : COM-
PROMISE **2** : to draw out matters so as to gain time —
tem·po·riz·er *n*

tempt \'tempt\ *vb* **1** : to entice to do wrong by promise
of pleasure or gain **2** : PROVOKE ⟨∼ fate⟩ **3** : to risk
the dangers of **4** : to induce to do something : INCITE
♦ *Synonyms* INVEIGLE, DECOY, SEDUCE, LURE —
tempt·er *n* — **tempt·ing·ly** *adv*

temp·ta·tion \temp-'tā-shən\ *n* **1** : the act of tempting
: the state of being tempted **2** : something that tempts

tempt·ress \'temp-trəs\ *n* : a woman who tempts

ten \'ten\ *n* **1** : one more than nine **2** : the 10th in a
set or series **3** : something having 10 units — **ten** *adj or
pron* — **tenth** \'tenth\ *adj or adv or n*

ten·a·ble \'te-nə-bəl\ *adj* : capable of being held, maintained, or defended

te·na·cious \tə-'nā-shəs\ *adj* **1** : not easily pulled apart
: COHESIVE, TOUGH ⟨a ∼ metal⟩ **2** : holding fast
⟨∼ of his rights⟩ **3** : RETENTIVE ⟨a ∼ memory⟩ —
te·na·cious·ly *adv* — **te·nac·i·ty** \tə-'na-sə-tē\ *n*

ten·an·cy \'te-nən-sē\ *n, pl* **-cies** : the temporary possession or occupancy of something (as a house) that belongs
to another; *also* : the period of a tenant's occupancy

ten·ant \'te-nənt\ *n* **1** : one who rents or leases (as a
house) from a landlord **2** : DWELLER, OCCUPANT —
tenant *vb*

tenant farmer *n* : a farmer who works land owned by another and pays rent either in cash or in shares of produce

Ten Commandments *n pl* : the commandments of God
given to Moses on Mount Sinai

¹tend \'tend\ *vb* **1** : to apply oneself ⟨∼ to your affairs⟩
2 : to take care of ⟨∼ a plant⟩ **3** : to manage the operations of ⟨∼ a machine⟩

²tend *vb* **1** : to move or develop one's course in a particular direction **2** : to show an inclination or tendency

ten·den·cy \'ten-dən-sē\ *n, pl* **-cies 1** : DRIFT, TREND
2 : a proneness to or readiness for a particular kind of
thought or action : PROPENSITY ⟨a ∼ to overreact⟩
♦ *Synonyms* BENT, LEANING, DISPOSITION, INCLINATION

ten·den·tious \ten-'den-chəs\ *adj* : marked by a tendency
in favor of a particular point of view : BIASED ⟨∼ re-
marks⟩ — **ten·den·tious·ly** *adv* — **ten·den·tious·ness** *n*

¹ten·der \'ten-dər\ *adj* [ME, fr. AF *tendre*, fr. L *tener*] **1**
: having a soft texture : easily broken, chewed, or cut **2**
: physically weak : DELICATE; *also* : IMMATURE **3** : expressing or responsive to love or sympathy : LOVING,
COMPASSIONATE ⟨a ∼ smile⟩ **4** : SENSITIVE, TOUCHY
⟨a ∼ ego⟩ ♦ *Synonyms* SYMPATHETIC, WARM, WARM-
HEARTED — **ten·der·ly** *adv* — **ten·der·ness** *n*

²tender *n* [AF *tendre*, fr. *tendre*, v., to stretch, hold out,
offer, fr. L *tendere* to stretch, direct] **1** : an offer or proposal made for acceptance; *esp* : an offer of a bid for a
contract **2** : something (as money) that may be offered
in payment

³tender *vb* : to present for acceptance

⁴tend·er \'ten-dər\ *n* **1** : one that tends or takes care **2**
: a boat carrying passengers and freight to a larger ship
3 : a car attached to a steam locomotive for carrying fuel
and water

⁵tender *n* [prob. short for *tenderloin*] : a strip of meat (as
chicken) often breaded

ten·der·foot \'ten-dər-ˌfút\ *n, pl* **-feet** \-ˌfēt\ *also* **-foots**
\-ˌfúts\ **1** : one not hardened to frontier or rough outdoor life **2** : an inexperienced beginner

ten·der·heart·ed \ˌten-dər-'här-təd\ *adj* : easily moved to
love, pity, or sorrow

ten·der·ize \'ten-də-ˌrīz\ *vb* **-ized; -iz·ing** : to make (meat)
tender — **ten·der·iz·er** \'ten-də-ˌrī-zər\ *n*

ten·der·loin \'ten-dər-ˌlóin\ *n* **1** : a tender strip of beef
or pork from near the backbone **2** : a district of a city
largely devoted to vice

ten·di·ni·tis *or* ten·don·itis \ˌten-də-'nī-təs\ *n* : inflammation of a tendon

ten·don \'ten-dən\ *n* : a tough cord of dense white fibrous
tissue uniting a muscle with another part (as a bone) —
ten·di·nous \-də-nəs\ *adj*

ten·dril \'ten-drəl\ *n* : a slender coiling organ by which
some climbing plants attach themselves to a support

ten·e·brous \'te-nə-brəs\ *adj* : shut off from the light
: GLOOMY, OBSCURE

ten·e·ment \'te-nə-mənt\ *n* **1** : a house used as a dwelling
2 : a building divided into apartments for rent to families; *esp* : one meeting only minimum standards of safety
and comfort **3** : APARTMENT, FLAT

te·net \'te-nət\ *n* [L, he holds, fr. *tenēre* to hold] : one of
the principles or doctrines held in common by members
of a group (as a church or profession) ♦ *Synonyms*
DOCTRINE, DOGMA, BELIEF

ten·fold \'ten-ˌfōld, -'fōld\ *adj* : being 10 times as great or
as many — **ten·fold** \-'fōld\ *adv*

tenge \'teŋ-ˌgä\ *n, pl* **tenge** — see MONEY table

ten–gallon hat *n* : a wide-brimmed hat with a large soft crown

Tenn *abbr* Tennessee

ten·ne \'teŋ-ā\ *n, pl* **ten·e·si** \'teŋ-ə-sē\ *or* **tenne** *or* **ten·ne·si** \'teŋ-ə-sē\ — see *manat* at MONEY table

ten·nes·sine \'te-nə-ˌsēn\ *n* : a short-lived artificially produced radioactive element

ten·nis \'te-nəs\ *n* : a game played with a ball and racket on a court divided by a net

ten·on \'te-nən\ *n* : a projecting part in a piece of material (as wood) for insertion into a mortise to make a joint

ten·or \'te-nər\ *n* **1** : the general drift of something spoken or written ⟨his speech had an angry ∼⟩ **2** : the highest natural adult male voice; *also* : a singer having this voice **3** : a continuing in a course, movement, or activity ⟨the ∼ of my life⟩

tenpenny nail *n* : a nail three inches (about 7.6 centimeters) long

ten·pin \'ten-ˌpin\ *n* : a bottle-shaped bowling pin set in groups of 10 and bowled at in a game (**tenpins**)

¹tense \'tens\ *n* [ME *tens* time, tense, fr. AF, fr. L *tempus*] : distinction of form of a verb to indicate the time of the action or state

²tense *adj* **tens·er; tens·est** [L *tensus*, fr. pp. of *tendere* to stretch] **1** : stretched tight : TAUT **2** : feeling or showing nervous tension ⟨a ∼ smile⟩ ✦ *Synonyms* STIFF, RIGID, INFLEXIBLE — **tense·ly** *adv* — **tense·ness** *n* — **ten·si·ty** \'ten-sə-tē\ *n*

³tense *vb* **tensed; tens·ing** : to make or become tense

ten·sile \'ten-səl, -ˌsī(-ə)l\ *adj* : of or relating to tension ⟨∼ strength⟩

ten·sion \'ten-chən\ *n* **1** : the act of straining or stretching; *also* : the condition of being strained or stretched **2** : a state of mental unrest often with signs of bodily stress **3** : a state of latent hostility or opposition

ten–speed \'ten-ˌspēd\ *n* : a bicycle with a derailleur having 10 possible combinations of gears

¹tent \'tent\ *n* **1** : a collapsible shelter of material stretched and supported by poles **2** : a canopy placed over the head and shoulders to retain vapors or oxygen given for medical reasons

²tent *vb* **1** : to lodge in tents **2** : to cover with or as if with a tent

ten·ta·cle \'ten-ti-kəl\ *n* : any of various long flexible projections about the head or mouth (as of an insect, mollusk, or fish) — **ten·ta·cled** \-kəld\ *adj* — **ten·tac·u·lar** \ten-'ta-kyə-lər\ *adj*

ten·ta·tive \'ten-tə-tiv\ *adj* **1** : not fully worked out or developed ⟨∼ plans⟩ **2** : HESITANT, UNCERTAIN ⟨a ∼ smile⟩ — **ten·ta·tive·ly** *adv* — **ten·ta·tive·ness** *n*

ten·u·ous \'ten-yə-wəs\ *adj* **1** : not dense : RARE ⟨a ∼ fluid⟩ **2** : not thick : SLENDER ⟨a ∼ rope⟩ **3** : having little substance : FLIMSY, WEAK ⟨∼ influences⟩ **4** : lacking stability : SHAKY ⟨∼ reasoning⟩ — **te·nu·i·ty** \te-'nü-ə-tē, tə-, -'nyü-\ *n* — **ten·u·ous·ly** *adv* — **ten·u·ous·ness** *n*

ten·ure \'ten-yər\ *n* : the act, right, manner, or period of holding something (as a landed property, an office, or a position)

ten·ured \'ten-yərd\ *adj* : having tenure ⟨∼ faculty members⟩

te·o·sin·te \ˌtā-ō-'sin-tē\ *n* : a tall annual grass of Mexico that is closely related to and usu. considered ancestral to corn

te·pee *or* **tee·pee** \'tē-(ˌ)pē\ *n* [Dakota *tʰ-ípi*, fr. *tʰ-i-* to dwell] : an American Indian conical tent usu. of skins

tep·id \'te-pəd\ *adj* **1** : moderately warm : LUKEWARM **2** : HALFHEARTED

te·qui·la \tə-'kē-lə, tā-\ *n* : a Mexican liquor distilled from an agave's sap

ter *abbr* **1** terrace **2** territory

tera·byte \'ter-ə-ˌbīt\ *n* [*tera-* trillion (10¹²), fr. Gk *terat-, teras* monster] : 1024 gigabytes; *also* : one trillion bytes

ter·bi·um \'tər-bē-əm\ *n* : a metallic chemical element

ter·cen·te·na·ry \ˌtər-ˌsen-'te-nə-rē, tər-'sen-tə-ˌner-ē\ *n, pl* **-ries** : a 300th anniversary or its celebration — **tercentenary** *adj*

ter·cen·ten·ni·al \ˌtər-ˌsen-'te-nē-əl\ *adj or n* : TERCENTENARY

te·re·do \tə-'rē-dō, -'rā-\ *n, pl* **-dos** [L] : SHIPWORM

ter·i·ya·ki \ˌter-ē-'yä-kē\ *n* [Jp] : a Japanese dish of meat or fish soaked in a soy marinade and cooked

¹term \'tərm\ *n* **1** : END, TERMINATION **2** : DURATION; *esp* : a period of time fixed esp. by law or custom **3** : a mathematical expression connected with another by a plus or minus sign; *also* : an element (as a numerator) of a fraction or proportion **4** : a word or expression that has a precise meaning in some uses or is limited to a particular subject or field **5** *pl* : PROVISIONS, CONDITIONS ⟨∼s of a contract⟩ **6** *pl* : mutual relationship ⟨on good ∼s⟩ **7** : AGREEMENT, CONCORD **8** : a state of acceptance ⟨come to ∼s with his grief⟩

²term *vb* : to apply a term to : CALL

ter·ma·gant \'tər-mə-gənt\ *n* : an overbearing or nagging woman : SHREW

¹ter·mi·nal \'tər-mə-nᵊl\ *adj* **1** : of, relating to, or forming an end, limit, or terminus **2** : FATAL **2** ⟨∼ cancer⟩; *also* : being in or relating to the final stages of a fatal disease ⟨a ∼ patient⟩ ✦ *Synonyms* FINAL, CONCLUDING, LAST, LATEST — **ter·mi·nal·ly** *adv*

²terminal *n* **1** : EXTREMITY, END **2** : a device at the end of a wire or on electrical equipment for making a connection **3** : either end of a transportation line (as a railroad) with its offices and freight and passenger stations; *also* : a freight or passenger station **4** : a device (as in a computer system) for data entry and display

ter·mi·nate \'tər-mə-ˌnāt\ *vb* **-nat·ed; -nat·ing** : to bring or come to an end ✦ *Synonyms* CONCLUDE, FINISH, COMPLETE — **ter·mi·na·ble** \-nə-bəl\ *adj* — **ter·mi·na·tion** \ˌtər-mə-'nā-shən\ *n* — **ter·mi·na·tor** \'tər-mə-ˌnā-tər\ *n*

ter·mi·nol·o·gy \ˌtər-mə-'nä-lə-jē\ *n, pl* **-gies** : the technical or special terms used in a business, art, science, or special subject

ter·mi·nus \'tər-mə-nəs\ *n, pl* **-ni** \-ˌnī\ *or* **-nus·es** [L] **1** : final goal : END **2** : either end of a transportation line or travel route; *also* : the station or city at such a place

ter·mite \'tər-ˌmīt\ *n* : any of numerous pale soft-bodied social insects that feed on wood

tern \'tərn\ *n* : any of various chiefly marine birds with narrow wings and often a forked tail

ter·na·ry \'tər-nə-rē\ *adj* **1** : of, relating to, or proceeding by threes **2** : having three elements or parts

terr *abbr* territory

¹ter·race \'ter-əs\ *n* **1** : a flat roof or open platform **2** : a level area next to a building **3** : an embankment with level top **4** : a bank or ridge on a slope to conserve moisture and soil **5** : a row of houses on raised land; *also* : a street with such a row of houses **6** : a strip of park in the middle of a street

²terrace *vb* **ter·raced; ter·rac·ing** : to form into a terrace or supply with terraces

ter·ra–cot·ta \ˌter-ə-'kä-tə\ *n* [It *terra cotta*, lit., baked earth] : a reddish brown earthenware

terra fir·ma \-'fər-mə\ *n* [NL] : solid ground

ter·rain \tə-'rān\ *n* : the surface features of an area of land ⟨a rough ∼⟩

ter·ra in·cog·ni·ta \ˌter-ə-ˌin-ˌkäg-'nē-tə\ *n, pl* **ter·rae in·cog·ni·tae** \'ter-ˌī-ˌin-ˌkäg-'nē-ˌtī\ [L] : an unexplored area or field of knowledge

ter·ra·pin \'ter-ə-pən\ *n* : any of various turtles of fresh or brackish water

terrapin

ter·rar·i·um \tə-'rer-ē-əm\ *n, pl* **-ia** \-ē-ə\ *or* **-i·ums** : a usu. transparent enclosure for keeping or raising plants or small animals indoors

ter·res·tri·al \tə-'res-trē-əl\ *adj* **1** : of or relating to the earth or its inhabitants **2** : living or growing on land ⟨∼ plants⟩ ✦ *Synonyms* MUNDANE, EARTHLY, WORLDLY

ter·ri·ble \'ter-ə-bəl\ *adj* **1** : exciting terror : FEARFUL, DREADFUL ⟨∼ weapons⟩ **2** : hard to bear : DISTRESSING ⟨a ∼ situation⟩ **3** : extreme in degree : INTENSE ⟨∼ heat⟩ **4** : of very poor quality : AWFUL ⟨a ∼ play⟩

✦ **Synonyms** FRIGHTFUL, HORRIBLE, SHOCKING, APPALLING — **ter·ri·bly** \-blē\ *adv*

ter·ri·er \'ter-ē-ər\ *n* [ME *terryer, terrer,* fr. AF (*chen*) *terrer,* lit., earth dog, fr. *terre* earth, fr. L *terra*] : any of various usu. small energetic dogs orig. used by hunters to drive small game animals from their holes

ter·rif·ic \tə-'ri-fik\ *adj* 1 : exciting terror ⟨a ~ explosion⟩ 2 : EXTRAORDINARY, ASTOUNDING ⟨~ speed⟩ 3 : MAGNIFICENT ⟨makes ~ chili⟩

ter·ri·fy \'ter-ə-ˌfī\ *vb* **-fied; -fy·ing** : to fill with terror : FRIGHTEN ✦ **Synonyms** SCARE, TERRORIZE, STARTLE, ALARM — **ter·ri·fy·ing·ly** *adv*

ter·ri·to·ri·al·i·ty \ˌter-ə-ˌtór-ē-'a-lə-tē\ *n* : persistent attachment to a specific territory ⟨~ in bears⟩

ter·ri·to·ry \'ter-ə-ˌtór-ē\ *n, pl* **-ries** 1 : a geographic area belonging to or under the jurisdiction of a governmental authority 2 : a part of the U.S. not included within any state but organized with a separate legislature 3 : REGION, DISTRICT; *also* : a region in which one feels at home 4 : a field of knowledge or interest 5 : an assigned area 6 : an area occupied and defended by one or a group of animals — **ter·ri·to·ri·al** \ˌter-ə-'tór-ē-əl\ *adj* — **go with the territory** *or* **come with the territory** : to accompany a situation naturally

ter·ror \'ter-ər\ *n* 1 : a state of intense fear : FRIGHT 2 : one that inspires fear 3 : violent or destructive acts committed to intimidate a people or government ✦ **Synonyms** PANIC, CONSTERNATION, DREAD, ALARM, DISMAY, HORROR, TREPIDATION

ter·ror·ism \'ter-ər-ˌi-zəm\ *n* : the systematic use of terror esp. as a means of coercion — **ter·ror·ist** \-ist\ *adj or n*

ter·ror·ize \'ter-ər-ˌīz\ *vb* **-ized; -iz·ing** 1 : to fill with terror : SCARE 2 : to coerce by threat or violence ✦ **Synonyms** TERRIFY, FRIGHTEN, ALARM, STARTLE

ter·ry \'ter-ē\ *n, pl* **terries** : an absorbent fabric with a loose pile of uncut loops

terse \'tərs\ *adj* **ters·er; ters·est** [L *tersus* clean, neat, fr. pp. of *tergēre* to wipe off] : effectively brief : CONCISE — **terse·ly** *adv* — **terse·ness** *n*

ter·tia·ry \'tər-shē-ˌer-ē\ *adj* 1 : of third rank, importance, or value 2 *cap* : of, relating to, or being the earlier period of the Cenozoic era 3 : occurring in or being the third stage ⟨~ medical care⟩

Tertiary *n* : the Tertiary period

TESL *abbr* teaching English as a second language

TESOL *abbr* Teachers of English to Speakers of Other Languages

¹test \'test\ *n* [ME, vessel in which metals were assayed, potsherd, fr. AF, pot, fr. L *testum* earthen vessel] 1 : a critical examination or evaluation : TRIAL 2 : a means or result of testing

²test *vb* 1 : to put to test : TRY, EXAMINE 2 : to undergo or score on tests

³test *adj* : relating to or used in testing ⟨a ~ group⟩

tes·ta·ment \'tes-tə-mənt\ *n* 1 *cap* : either of two main divisions of the Bible 2 : EVIDENCE, WITNESS 3 : CREED 4 : the legal instructions for the disposition of one's property after death : WILL — **tes·ta·men·ta·ry** \ˌtes-tə-'men-tə-rē\ *adj*

tes·tate \'tes-ˌtāt, -tət\ *adj* : having left a valid will

tes·ta·tor \'tes-ˌtā-tər, tes-'tā-\ *n* : a person who dies leaving a valid will

tes·ta·trix \tes-'tā-triks\ *n* : a woman who is a testator

¹tes·ter \'tēs-tər, 'tes-\ *n* : a canopy over a bed, pulpit, or altar

²test·er \'tes-tər\ *n* : one that tests

tes·ti·cle \'tes-ti-kəl\ *n* : TESTIS; *esp* : one of a mammal usu. with its enclosing structures — **tes·tic·u·lar** *adj*

tes·ti·fy \'tes-tə-ˌfī\ *vb* **-fied; -fy·ing** 1 : to make a statement based on personal knowledge or belief : bear witness 2 : to serve as evidence or proof

tes·ti·mo·ni·al \ˌtes-tə-'mō-nē-əl\ *n* 1 : a statement testifying to benefits received; *also* : a character reference 2 : an expression of appreciation : TRIBUTE — **testimonial** *adj*

tes·ti·mo·ny \'tes-tə-ˌmō-nē\ *n, pl* **-nies** 1 : evidence based on observation or knowledge 2 : an outward sign : SYMBOL 3 : a solemn declaration made by a witness under oath esp. in a court ✦ **Synonyms** EVIDENCE, CONFIRMATION, PROOF, TESTAMENT

tes·tis \'tes-təs\ *n, pl* **tes·tes** \'tes-ˌtēz\ [L, witness, testis] : a typically paired male reproductive gland that produces sperm and testosterone and that in most mammals is contained within the scrotum at sexual maturity

tes·tos·ter·one \te-'stäs-tə-ˌrōn\ *n* : a male sex hormone causing development of the male reproductive system and secondary sex characteristics

test–tube *adj* 1 : IN VITRO ⟨~ experiments⟩ 2 : produced by in vitro fertilization ⟨~ babies⟩

test tube *n* : a glass tube closed at one end and used esp. in chemistry and biology

tes·ty \'tes-tē\ *adj* **tes·ti·er; -est** [ME *testif*, fr. AF, headstrong, fr. *teste* head, fr. LL *testa* skull, fr. L, shell] : easily annoyed; *also* : marked by ill humor

tet·a·nus \'te-tə-nəs\ *n* : an infectious disease caused by bacterial poisons and marked by muscle stiffness and spasms esp. of the jaws — **tet·a·nal** \-əl\ *adj*

tetchy \'te-chē\ *adj* **tetchi·er; -est** : irritably or peevishly sensitive

¹tête–à–tête \'tāt-ə-ˌtät\ *n* [F, lit., head to head] : a private conversation between two persons

²tête–à–tête \ˌtāt-ə-'tät\ *adv* : in private

³tête–à–tête \'tāt-ə-ˌtät\ *adj* : being face-to-face : PRIVATE

¹teth·er \'te-thər\ *n* 1 : something (as a rope) by which an animal is fastened 2 : the limit of one's strength or resources

²tether *vb* : to fasten or restrain by or as if by a tether

tet·ra·eth·yl lead \ˌte-trə-'e-thəl-\ *n* : a heavy oily poisonous liquid used esp. formerly as an antiknock agent in gasoline

tet·ra·he·dron \-'hē-drən\ *n, pl* **-drons** *or* **-dra** \-drə\ : a polyhedron that has four faces — **tet·ra·he·dral** \-drəl\ *adj*

tet·ra·hy·dro·can·nab·i·nol \-ˌhī-drə-kə-'na-bə-ˌnól, -ˌnōl\ *n* : THC

te·tram·e·ter \te-'tra-mə-tər\ *n* : a line of verse consisting of four metrical feet

tet·ri \'te-trē\ *n, pl* **tetri** — see *lari* at MONEY table

Teu·ton·ic \tü-'tä-nik, tyü-\ *adj* : GERMANIC

Tex *abbr* Texas

Tex–Mex \'teks-'meks\ *adj* : characteristic of Mexican-American culture and esp. that of southern Texas

¹text \'tekst\ *n* 1 : the actual words of an author's work 2 : the main body of printed or written matter on a page 3 : a scriptural passage chosen as the subject esp. of a sermon 4 : THEME, TOPIC 5 : matter handled with a computer that is chiefly in the form of words 6 : TEXTBOOK 7 : TEXT MESSAGE — **tex·tu·al** \'teks-chə-wəl\ *adj*

²text *vb* : to communicate by text messaging — **texting** *n*

text·book \'tekst-ˌbúk\ *n* : a book used in the study of a subject

tex·tile \'tek-ˌstī(-ə)l, 'teks-t⁰l\ *n* : CLOTH; *esp* : a woven or knit cloth

text message *n* : a short message sent electronically usu. from one cell phone to another

text messaging *n* : the sending of short text messages electronically esp. from one cell phone to another

tex·ture \'teks-chər\ *n* 1 : the visual or tactile surface characteristics and appearance of something ⟨a coarse ~⟩ 2 : essential part 3 : basic scheme or structure : FABRIC 4 : overall structure — **tex·tur·al** \-chə-rəl\ *adj*

TGIF *abbr* thank God it's Friday

¹Th *abbr* Thursday

²Th *symbol* thorium

¹-th — see ¹-ETH

²-th *or* **-eth** *adj suffix* — used in forming ordinal numbers ⟨hundred*th*⟩

³-th *n suffix* 1 : act or process 2 : state or condition ⟨dear*th*⟩

Thai \'tī\ *n, pl* **Thai** *or* **Thais** 1 : a native or inhabitant of Thailand 2 : the official language of Thailand — **Thai** *adj*

thal·a·mus \'tha-lə-məs\ *n, pl* **-mi** \-ˌmī\ [NL] : a subdivision of the brain that serves as a relay station to and from the cerebral cortex and functions in arousal and the integration of sensory information — **tha·lam·ic** \thə-'la-mik\ *adj*

thal·as·se·mia \ˌtha-lə-'sē-mē-ə\ *n* : any of a group of inherited disorders of hemoglobin synthesis

tha·las·so·ther·a·py \thə-ˌla-sō-'ther-ə-pē\ *n* [Gk *thalassa* sea] : the use of seawater or sea products (as seaweed) for the benefit of health or beauty

thal·li·um \'tha-lē-əm\ *n* : a poisonous metallic chemical element

¹than \'than, 'than\ *conj* **1** — used after a comparative adjective or adverb to introduce the second part of a comparison expressing inequality ⟨older ∼ I am⟩ **2** — used after *other* or a word of similar meaning to express a difference of kind, manner, or identity ⟨adults other ∼ parents⟩

²than *prep* : in comparison with ⟨older ∼ me⟩

thane \'thān\ *n* **1** : a free retainer of an Anglo-Saxon lord **2** : a Scottish feudal lord

thank \'thaŋk\ *vb* : to express gratitude to ⟨∼ed them for the present⟩

thank·ful \'thaŋk-fəl\ *adj* **1** : conscious of benefit received **2** : expressive of thanks **3** : GLAD — **thank·ful·ness** *n*

thank·ful·ly \-fə-lē\ *adv* **1** : in a thankful manner **2** : as makes one thankful

thank·less \'thaŋk-ləs\ *adj* **1** : UNAPPRECIATED **2** : UNGRATEFUL

thanks \'thaŋks\ *n pl* : an expression of gratitude

thanks·giv·ing \thaŋks-'gi-viŋ\ *n* **1** : the act of giving thanks **2** : a prayer expressing gratitude **3** *cap* : the 4th Thursday in November observed as a legal holiday for giving thanks for divine goodness

¹that \'that, thət\ *pron, pl* **those** \'thōz\ **1** : the one indicated, mentioned, or understood ⟨∼ is my house⟩ **2** : the one farther away or first mentioned ⟨this is an elm, ∼'s a maple⟩ **3** : what has been indicated or mentioned ⟨after ∼, we left⟩ **4** : the one or ones : IT, THEY ⟨those who wish to leave may do so⟩

²that \that, 'that\ *conj* **1** : the following, namely ⟨he said ∼ he would⟩; *also* : which is, namely ⟨there's a chance ∼ it may fail⟩ **2** : to this end or purpose ⟨shouted ∼ all might hear⟩ **3** : as to result in the following, namely ⟨so heavy ∼ it can't be moved⟩ **4** : for this reason, namely : BECAUSE ⟨we're glad ∼ you came⟩

³that *adj, pl* **those 1** : being the one mentioned, indicated, or understood ⟨∼ boy⟩ ⟨those people⟩ **2** : being the one farther away or less immediately under discussion ⟨this chair or ∼ one⟩

⁴that \that, 'that\ *pron* **1** : WHO, WHOM, WHICH ⟨the woman ∼ saw you⟩ ⟨the woman ∼ you saw⟩ ⟨the money ∼ was spent⟩ **2** : in, on, or at which ⟨the way ∼ he drives⟩ ⟨the day ∼ it rained⟩

⁵that \'that\ *adv* : to such an extent or degree ⟨I like it, but not ∼ much⟩

¹thatch \'thach\ *vb* : to cover with or as if with thatch — **thatch·er** *n*

²thatch *n* **1** : plant material (as straw) for use as roofing **2** : a mat of grass clippings accumulated next to the soil on a lawn **3** : a covering of or as if of thatch ⟨a ∼ of white hair⟩

thaw \'thȯ\ *vb* **1** : to melt or cause to melt **2** : to become so warm as to melt ice or snow **3** : to abandon aloofness or hostility — **thaw** *n*

THC \ˌtē-(ˌ)āch-'sē\ *n* [*tetra*hydrocannabinol] : a physiologically active chemical from hemp plant resin that is the chief intoxicant in marijuana

¹the \thə, *before vowel sounds usu* thē\ *definite article* **1** : that in particular **2** — used before adjectives functioning as nouns ⟨a word to ∼ wise⟩

²the *adv* **1** : to what extent ⟨∼ sooner, the better⟩ **2** : to that extent ⟨the sooner, ∼ better⟩

theat *abbr* theater; theatrical

the·ater *or* **the·atre** \'thē-ə-tər\ *n* [ME *theatre*, fr. MF, fr. L *theatrum*, fr. Gk *theatron*, fr. *theasthai* to view, fr. *thea* act of seeing] **1** : a building or area for dramatic performances; *also* : a building or area for showing motion pictures **2** : a place of enactment of significant events ⟨∼ of war⟩ **3** : a place (as a lecture room) resembling a theater **4** : dramatic literature or performance

theater–in–the–round *n* : a theater with the stage in the center of the auditorium

the·at·ri·cal \thē-'a-tri-kəl\ *also* **the·at·ric** \-trik\ *adj* **1** : of or relating to the theater **2** : marked by artificiality of emotion : HISTRIONIC ⟨a ∼ gesture⟩ **3** : marked by extravagant display : SHOWY

the·at·ri·cals \-kəlz\ *n pl* : the performance of plays

the·at·rics \thē-'a-triks\ *n pl* **1** : THEATRICALS **2** : staged or contrived effects

the·be \'thā-bā\ *n, pl* **thebe** — see *pula* at MONEY table

thee \'thē\ *pron, archaic objective case of* THOU

theft \'theft\ *n* : the act of stealing

thegn \'thān\ *n* : THANE 1

their \thər, 'ther\ *adj* : of or relating to them or themselves

theirs \'therz\ *pron* : their one : their ones

the·ism \'thē-ˌi-zəm\ *n* : belief in the existence of a god or gods — **the·ist** \-ist\ *n or adj* — **the·is·tic** \thē-'is-tik\ *adj*

them \thəm, 'them\ *pron, objective case of* THEY

theme \'thēm\ *n* **1** : a subject or topic of discourse or of artistic representation **2** : a written exercise : COMPOSITION **3** : a melodic subject of a musical composition or movement — **the·mat·ic** \thi-'ma-tik\ *adj*

them·selves \thəm-'selvz, them-\ *pron pl* : THEY, THEM — used reflexively, for emphasis, or in absolute constructions ⟨they govern ∼⟩ ⟨they ∼ came⟩ ⟨∼ busy, they sent me⟩

¹then \'then\ *adv* **1** : at that time **2** : soon after that : NEXT **3** : in addition : BESIDES **4** : in that case **5** : CONSEQUENTLY

²then *n* : that time ⟨since ∼⟩

³then *adj* : existing or acting at that time ⟨the ∼ attorney general⟩

thence \'thens, 'thens\ *adv* **1** : from that place **2** *archaic* : THENCEFORTH **3** : from that fact : THEREFROM

thence·forth \-ˌfȯrth\ *adv* : from that time forward : THEREAFTER

thence·for·ward \thens-'fȯr-wərd, thens-\ *also* **thence·for·wards** \-wərdz\ *adv* : onward from that place or time

the·oc·ra·cy \thē-'ä-krə-sē\ *n, pl* **-cies 1** : government by officials regarded as divinely inspired **2** : a state governed by a theocracy — **the·o·crat·ic** \ˌthē-ə-'kra-tik\ *adj*

theol *abbr* theological; theology

the·ol·o·gy \thē-'ä-lə-jē\ *n, pl* **-gies 1** : the study of religious faith, practice, and experience; *esp* : the study of God and of God's relation to the world **2** : a theory or system of theology — **the·o·lo·gian** \ˌthē-ə-'lō-jən\ *n* — **the·o·log·i·cal** \-'lä-ji-kəl\ *adj*

the·o·rem \'thē-ə-rəm, 'thir-əm\ *n* **1** : a statement esp. in mathematics that has been or is to be proved **2** : an idea accepted or proposed as a demonstrable truth : PROPOSITION

the·o·ret·i·cal \ˌthē-ə-'re-ti-kəl\ *also* **the·o·ret·ic** \-tik\ *adj* **1** : relating to or having the character of theory **2** : existing only in theory : HYPOTHETICAL — **the·o·ret·i·cal·ly** \-ti-k(ə-)lē\ *adv*

the·o·rise *Brit var of* THEORIZE

the·o·rize \'thē-ə-ˌrīz\ *vb* **-rized; -riz·ing** : to form a theory : SPECULATE — **the·o·rist** \-rist\ *n*

the·o·ry \'thē-ə-rē, 'thir-ē\ *n, pl* **-ries 1** : abstract thought **2** : the general principles of a subject **3** : a plausible or scientifically acceptable general principle offered to explain observed facts **4** : HYPOTHESIS, CONJECTURE

theory of games : GAME THEORY

the·os·o·phy \thē-'ä-sə-fē\ *n* : belief about God and the world held to be based on mystical insight — **theo·soph·i·cal** \ˌthē-ə-'sä-fi-kəl\ *adj* — **the·os·o·phist** \thē-'ä-sə-fist\ *n*

ther·a·peu·tic \ˌther-ə-'pyü-tik\ *adj* [Gk *therapeutikos*, fr. *therapeuein* to attend, treat, fr. *theraps* attendant] : of, relating to, or dealing with healing and esp. with remedies for diseases — **ther·a·peu·ti·cal·ly** \-ti-k(ə-)lē\ *adv*

ther·a·peu·tics \ˌther-ə-'pyü-tiks\ *n* : a branch of medical or dental science dealing with the use of remedies

ther·a·py \'ther-ə-pē\ *n, pl* **-pies** : treatment of bodily, mental, or behavioral disorders — **ther·a·pist** \-pist\ *n*

¹there \'ther\ *adv* **1** : in or at that place — often used interjectionally **2** : to or into that place ⟨went ∼ after work⟩ **3** : in that matter or respect

²there \'ther, thər\ *pron* — used as a function word to introduce a sentence or clause ⟨∼'s a pen here⟩

³there \'ther\ *n* **1** : that place ⟨get away from ∼⟩ **2** : that point ⟨you take it from ∼⟩

there·abouts \ˌther-ə-'baȯts, 'ther-ə-ˌbaȯts\ *or* **there·about** \-'baȯt, -ˌbaȯt\ *adv* **1** : near that place or time **2** : near that number, degree, or quantity

there·af·ter \ther-'af-tər\ *adv* : after that : AFTERWARD

there·at \-'at\ *adv* **1** : at that place **2** : at that occurrence : on that account

there·by \ther-'bī, 'ther-ˌbī\ *adv* **1** : by that : by that means **2** : connected with or with reference to that

there·for \ther-'fòr\ *adv* : for or in return for that ⟨wanted a refund ∽⟩
there·fore \'ther-ˌfòr\ *adv* : for that reason : CONSEQUENTLY
there·from \ther-'frəm\ *adv* : from that or it
there·in \ther-'in\ *adv* 1 : in or into that place, time, or thing 2 : in that respect
there·of \-'əv, -'äv\ *adv* 1 : of that or it 2 : from that : THEREFROM
there·on \-'òn, -'än\ *adv* 1 : on that 2 *archaic* : THEREUPON 3
there·to \ther-'tü\ *adv* : to that
there·un·to \ther-'ən-(ˌ)tü, ˌther-ən-'tü\ *adv, archaic* : THERETO
there·upon \'ther-ə-ˌpòn, -ˌpän; ˌther-ə-'pòn, -'pän\ *adv* 1 : on that matter 2 : THEREFORE 3 : immediately after that : at once
there·with \ther-'with -with\ *adv* 1 : with that 2 *archaic* : THEREUPON, FORTHWITH
there·with·al \'ther-wi-ˌthòl, -ˌthòl\ *adv* 1 *archaic* : BESIDES 2 : THEREWITH
therm *abbr* thermometer
ther·mal \'thər-məl\ *adj* 1 : of, relating to, or caused by heat 2 : designed to prevent the loss of body heat ⟨∽ underwear⟩ — **ther·mal·ly** *adv*
thermal pollution *n* : the discharge of heated liquid (as waste water from a factory) into natural waters at a temperature harmful to the environment
therm·is·tor \'thər-ˌmis-tər\ *n* : an electrical resistor whose resistance varies sharply with temperature
ther·mo·cline \'thər-mə-ˌklīn\ *n* : the region in a thermally stratified body of water that separates warmer surface water from cold deep water
ther·mo·cou·ple \'thər-mə-ˌkə-pəl\ *n* : a device for measuring temperature by measuring the temperature-dependent potential difference created at the junction of two dissimilar metals
ther·mo·dy·nam·ics \ˌthər-mə-dī-'na-miks\ *n* : physics that deals with the mechanical action or relations of heat — **ther·mo·dy·nam·ic** \-mik\ *adj* — **ther·mo·dy·nam·i·cal·ly** \-mi-k(ə-)lē\ *adv*
ther·mom·e·ter \thər-'mä-mə-tər\ *n* [F *thermomètre*, fr. Gk *thermē* heat + *metron* measure] : an instrument for measuring temperature typically by the rise or fall of a liquid (as mercury) in a thin glass tube — **ther·mo·met·ric** \ˌthər-mə-'me-trik\ *adj* — **ther·mo·met·ri·cal·ly** \-tri-k(ə-)lē\ *adv*
ther·mo·nu·cle·ar \ˌthər-mō-'nü-klē-ər, -'nyü-\ *adj* 1 : of or relating to changes in the nucleus of atoms of low atomic weight (as hydrogen) that require a very high temperature (as in the hydrogen bomb) 2 : utilizing or relating to a thermonuclear bomb ⟨∽ war⟩
ther·mo·plas·tic \ˌthər-mə-'plas-tik\ *adj* : capable of softening when heated and of hardening again when cooled ⟨∽ resins⟩ — **thermoplastic** *n*
ther·mos \'thər-məs\ *n* : a cylindrical container with a vacuum between an inner and an outer wall used to keep liquids hot or cold
ther·mo·sphere \'thər-mə-ˌsfir\ *n* : the part of the earth's atmosphere that lies above the mesosphere and that is characterized by steadily increasing temperature with height
ther·mo·stat \'thər-mə-ˌstat\ *n* : a device that automatically controls temperature — **ther·mo·stat·ic** \ˌthər-mə-'sta-tik\ *adj* — **ther·mo·stat·i·cal·ly** \-ti-k(ə-)lē\ *adv*
the·sau·rus \thi-'sòr-əs\ *n, pl* **-sau·ri** \-'sòr-ˌī\ *or* **-sau·rus·es** \-'sòr-ə-səz\ [NL, fr. L, treasure, collection, fr. Gk *thēsauros*] : a book of words and their synonyms — **the·sau·ral** \-'sòr-əl\ *adj*
these *pl of* THIS
the·sis \'thē-səs\ *n, pl* **the·ses** \'thē-ˌsēz\ 1 : a proposition that a person advances and offers to maintain by argument 2 : an essay embodying results of original research; *esp* : one written for an academic degree
¹**thes·pi·an** \'thes-pē-ən\ *adj, often cap* [fr. *Thespis*, 6th cent. B.C. Greek poet and reputed originator of tragedy] : relating to the drama : DRAMATIC
²**thespian** *n* : ACTOR
Thess *abbr* Thessalonians
Thes·sa·lo·nians \ˌthe-sə-'lō-nyənz, -nē-ənz\ *n* — see BIBLE table
the·ta \'thā-tə\ *n* : the 8th letter of the Greek alphabet — Θ or θ

thew \'thü, 'thyü\ *n* : MUSCLE, SINEW — usu. used in pl.
they \'thā\ *pron* 1 : those individuals under discussion : the ones previously mentioned or referred to 2 : unspecified persons : PEOPLE
thi·a·mine \'thī-ə-mən, -ˌmēn\ *also* **thi·a·min** \-mən\ *n* : a vitamin of the vitamin B complex essential to normal metabolism and nerve function
¹**thick** \'thik\ *adj* 1 : having relatively great depth or extent from one surface to its opposite ⟨a ∽ plank⟩; *also* : heavily built : THICKSET 2 : densely massed : CROWDED; *also* : FREQUENT, NUMEROUS 3 : dense or viscous in consistency ⟨∽ syrup⟩ 4 : marked by haze, fog, or mist ⟨∽ weather⟩ 5 : measuring in thickness ⟨one meter ∽⟩ 6 : imperfectly articulated : INDISTINCT ⟨∽ speech⟩ 7 : STUPID, OBTUSE 8 : associated on close terms : INTIMATE 9 : EXCESSIVE ♦ *Synonyms* COMPACT, CLOSE, TIGHT — **thick·ly** *adv*
²**thick** *n* 1 : the most crowded or active part 2 : the part of greatest thickness
thick and thin *n* : every difficulty and obstacle ⟨was loyal through *thick and thin*⟩
thick·en \'thi-kən\ *vb* : to make or become thick — **thick·en·er** *n*
thick·et \'thi-kət\ *n* : a dense growth of bushes or small trees
thick·ness \-nəs\ *n* 1 : the smallest of three dimensions ⟨length, width, and ∽⟩ 2 : the quality or state of being thick 3 : LAYER, SHEET ⟨a single ∽ of canvas⟩
thick·set \'thik-'set\ *adj* 1 : closely placed or planted 2 : having a thick body : BURLY
thick–skinned \-'skind\ *adj* 1 : having a thick skin 2 : not easily bothered by criticism or insult ⟨a ∽ politician⟩
thief \'thēf\ *n, pl* **thieves** \'thēvz\ : one that steals esp. secretly
thieve \'thēv\ *vb* **thieved; thiev·ing** : STEAL, ROB ♦ *Synonyms* FILCH, PILFER, PURLOIN, SWIPE
thiev·ery \'thē-və-rē\ *n, pl* **-er·ies** : the act of stealing : THEFT
thigh \'thī\ *n* : the part of the vertebrate hind or lower limb between the knee and the hip
thigh·bone \'thī-ˌbōn\ *n* : FEMUR
thim·ble \'thim-bəl\ *n* : a cap or guard worn on the finger to push the needle in sewing — **thim·ble·ful** *n*
¹**thin** \'thin\ *adj* **thin·ner; thin·nest** 1 : having little extent from one surface through to its opposite : not thick : SLENDER 2 : not closely set or placed : SPARSE ⟨∽ hair⟩ 3 : not dense or not dense enough : more fluid or rarefied than normal ⟨∽ air⟩ ⟨∽ syrup⟩ 4 : lacking substance, fullness, or strength ⟨∽ broth⟩ 5 : FLIMSY ⟨a ∽ excuse⟩ — **thin·ly** *adv* — **thin·ness** *n*
²**thin** *vb* **thinned; thin·ning** : to make or become thin
thine \'thīn\ *pron, archaic* : one or the ones belonging to thee
thing \'thiŋ\ *n* 1 : a matter of concern : AFFAIR ⟨∽s to do⟩ 2 *pl* : state of affairs ⟨∽s are improving⟩ 3 : EVENT, CIRCUMSTANCE ⟨the crime was a terrible ∽⟩ 4 : DEED, ACT ⟨expected great ∽s of him⟩ 5 : a distinct entity : OBJECT 6 : an inanimate object distinguished from a living being 7 *pl* : POSSESSIONS, EFFECTS 8 : an article of clothing 9 : DETAIL, POINT ⟨checks every little ∽⟩ 10 : IDEA, NOTION ⟨says the first ∽ he thinks of⟩ 11 : something one likes to do : SPECIALTY ⟨doing her ∽⟩
think \'thiŋk\ *vb* **thought** \'thòt\; **think·ing** 1 : to form or have in the mind 2 : to have as an opinion : BELIEVE 3 : to reflect on : PONDER 4 : to call to mind : REMEMBER 5 : REASON 6 : to form a mental picture of : IMAGINE 7 : to devise by thinking ⟨thought up a plan to escape⟩ ♦ *Synonyms* CONCEIVE, FANCY, REALIZE, ENVISAGE — **think·er** *n*
think tank *n* : an institute, corporation, or group organized for interdisciplinary research (as in technological or social problems)
thin·ner \'thi-nər\ *n* : a volatile liquid (as turpentine) used to thin paint
thin–skinned \'thin-'skind\ *adj* 1 : having a thin skin or rind 2 : extremely sensitive to criticism or insult
¹**third** \'thərd\ *adj* : next after the second — **third** *or* **third·ly** *adv*
²**third** *n* 1 : one of three equal parts of something 2 : one that is number three in a countable series 3 : the 3d forward gear in an automotive vehicle

third degree *n* : the subjection of a prisoner to mental or physical torture to force a confession

third dimension *n* 1 : thickness, depth, or apparent thickness or depth that confers solidity on an object 2 : a quality that confers reality — **third–dimensional** *adj*

third world *n, often cap T&W, sometimes offensive* : the aggregate of the underdeveloped nations of the world

¹**thirst** \'thərst\ *n* 1 : a feeling of dryness in the mouth and throat associated with a desire to drink; *also* : a bodily condition producing this 2 : an ardent desire : CRAVING ⟨a ∼ for knowledge⟩ — **thirsty** *adj*

²**thirst** *vb* 1 : to need drink : suffer thirst 2 : to have a strong desire : CRAVE

thir·teen \ˌthər-'tēn\ *n* : one more than 12 — **thirteen** *adj or pron* — **thir·teenth** \-'tēnth\ *adj or n*

thir·ty \'thər-tē\ *n, pl* **thirties** : three times 10 — **thir·ti·eth** \-tē-əth\ *adj or n* — **thirty** *adj or pron*

¹**this** \'this\ *pron, pl* **these** \'thēz\ 1 : the one close or closest in time or space ⟨∼ is your book⟩ 2 : what is in the present or under immediate observation or discussion ⟨∼ is a mess⟩; *also* : what is happening or being done now ⟨after ∼ we'll leave⟩

²**this** *adj, pl* **these** 1 : being the one near, present, just mentioned, or more immediately under observation ⟨∼ book⟩ 2 : constituting the immediate past or future ⟨friends all *these* years⟩

³**this** *adv* : to such an extent or degree ⟨didn't expect to wait ∼ long⟩

this·tle \'thi-səl\ *n* : any of various tall prickly composite plants with often showy heads of tightly packed tubular flowers

this·tle·down \-ˌdaůn\ *n* : the down from the ripe flower head of a thistle

¹**thith·er** \'thi-thər\ *adv* : to that place

²**thither** *adj* : being on the farther side

thith·er·ward \-wərd\ *adv* : toward that place : THITHER

thong \'thȯŋ\ *n* 1 : a strip esp. of leather or hide 2 : a sandal held on the foot by a thong between the toes 3 : a narrow strip of swimwear or underwear that passes between the thighs

tho·rax \'thȯr-ˌaks\ *n, pl* **tho·rax·es** *or* **tho·ra·ces** \'thȯr-ə-ˌsēz\ 1 : the part of the body of a mammal between the neck and the abdomen; *also* : its cavity containing the heart and lungs 2 : the middle of the three main divisions of the body of an insect — **tho·rac·ic** \thə-'ra-sik\ *adj*

tho·ri·um \'thȯr-ē-əm\ *n* : a radioactive metallic chemical element

thorn \'thȯrn\ *n* 1 : a woody plant bearing sharp processes 2 : a sharp rigid plant process that is usu. a modified leafless branch 3 : something that causes distress — **thorny** *adj*

thor·ough \'thər-ō\ *adj* 1 : COMPLETE, EXHAUSTIVE ⟨a ∼ search⟩ 2 : very careful : PAINSTAKING ⟨a ∼ scholar⟩ 3 : having full mastery — **thor·ough·ly** *adv* — **thor·ough·ness** *n*

¹**thor·ough·bred** \'thər-ə-ˌbred\ *adj* 1 : bred from the best blood through a long line 2 *cap* : of or relating to the Thoroughbred breed of horses 3 : marked by high-spirited grace

²**thoroughbred** *n* 1 *cap* : any of an English breed of light speedy horses kept chiefly for racing 2 : one (as a pedigreed animal) of excellent quality

thor·ough·fare \-ˌfer\ *n* : a public road or street

thor·ough·go·ing \ˌthər-ə-'gō-iŋ\ *adj* : marked by thoroughness or zeal

those *pl of* THAT

¹**thou** \'thaů\ *pron, archaic* : the person addressed

²**thou** \'thaů\ *n, pl* **thou** : a thousand of something (as dollars)

¹**though** \'thō\ *conj* 1 : despite the fact that ⟨∼ the odds are hopeless, they fight on⟩ 2 : granting that ⟨∼ it may look bad, still, all is not lost⟩

²**though** *adv* : HOWEVER, NEVERTHELESS ⟨not for long, ∼⟩

¹**thought** \'thȯt\ *past and past part of* THINK

²**thought** *n* 1 : the process of thinking 2 : serious consideration : REGARD 3 : reasoning power 4 : the power to imagine : CONCEPTION 5 : IDEA, NOTION 6 : OPINION, BELIEF ⟨spoke his ∼s freely⟩

thought·ful \'thȯt-fəl\ *adj* 1 : absorbed in thought 2 : marked by careful thinking ⟨a ∼ essay⟩ 3 : consid-

erate of others ⟨a ∼ host⟩ — **thought·ful·ly** *adv* — **thought·ful·ness** *n*

thought·less \-ləs\ *adj* 1 : insufficiently alert : CARELESS ⟨a ∼ worker⟩ 2 : RECKLESS ⟨a ∼ act⟩ 3 : lacking concern for others : INCONSIDERATE ⟨∼ remarks⟩ — **thought·less·ly** *adv* — **thought·less·ness** *n*

thou·sand \'thaůz-ᵊnd\ *n, pl* **thousands** *or* **thousand** : 10 times 100 — **thousand** *adj* — **thou·sandth** \-ᵊnth\ *adj or n*

thousands place *n* : the place four to the left of the decimal point in an Arabic number

thrall \'thrȯl\ *n* 1 : SLAVE, BONDMAN 2 : a state of servitude — **thrall·dom** *or* **thral·dom** \'thrȯl-dəm\ *n*

¹**thrash** \'thrash\ *vb* 1 : THRESH 1 2 : BEAT, WHIP; *also* ': DEFEAT 3 : to move about violently 4 : to go over again and again ⟨∼ over the matter⟩; *also* : to hammer out ⟨∼ out a plan⟩

²**thrash** *n* : rock music that is extremely fast and loud

¹**thrash·er** \'thra-shər\ *n* : one that thrashes or threshes

²**thrasher** *n* : any of various long-tailed American songbirds related to the mockingbird

¹**thread** \'thred\ *n* 1 : a thin continuous strand of spun and twisted textile fibers 2 : something resembling a textile thread 3 : the ridge or groove that winds around a screw 4 : a line of reasoning or train of thought 5 : a continuing element 6 : a tenuous or feeble support

²**thread** *vb* 1 : to pass a thread through the eye of (a needle) 2 : to pass (as film) through something 3 : to make one's way through or between 4 : to put together on a thread ⟨∼ beads⟩ 5 : to form a screw thread on or in

thread·bare \-ˌber\ *adj* 1 : having the nap worn off so that the thread shows : SHABBY 2 : TRITE ⟨∼ excuses⟩

thready \'thre-dē\ *adj* 1 : consisting of or bearing fibers of filaments ⟨a ∼ bark⟩ 2 : lacking in fullness, body, or vigor ⟨a ∼ voice⟩

threat \'thret\ *n* 1 : an expression of intent to do harm 2 : one that threatens

threat·en \'thre-tᵊn\ *vb* 1 : to utter threats against 2 : to give signs or warning of : PORTEND 3 : to hang over as a threat : MENACE 4 : to cause to feel insecure or anxious — **threat·en·ing·ly** *adv*

threat·ened \-tᵊnd\ *adj* : having an uncertain chance of continued survival; *esp* : likely to become an endangered species

three \'thrē\ *n* 1 : one more than two 2 : the 3d in a set or series 3 : something having three units — **three** *adj or pron*

3–D \'thrē-'dē\ *n* : a three-dimensional form or picture

three–dimensional *adj* 1 : relating to or having three dimensions 2 : giving the illusion of varying distances ⟨a ∼ picture⟩

three·fold \'thrē-ˌfōld, -'fōld\ *adj* 1 : having three parts : TRIPLE 2 : being three times as great or as many — **three·fold** \-'fōld\ *adv*

three·pence \'thre-pəns, 'thri-, 'thrə-, US also 'thrē-pens\ *n* 1 *pl* **threepence** *or* **three·penc·es** : a coin worth three pennies 2 : the sum of three British pennies

three·score \'thrē-'skȯr\ *adj* : being three times twenty : SIXTY

three·some \'thrē-səm\ *n* : a group of three persons or things

thren·o·dy \'thre-nə-dē\ *n, pl* **-dies** : a song of lamentation : ELEGY

thresh \'thresh, 'thrash\ *vb* 1 : to separate (as grain from straw) mechanically 2 : THRASH — **thresh·er** *n*

thresh·old \'thresh-ˌhōld\ *n* 1 : the sill of a door 2 : a point or place of beginning or entering : OUTSET ⟨on the ∼ of a new era⟩ 3 : a point at which a physiological or psychological effect begins to be produced ⟨pain ∼s⟩

threw *past of* THROW

thrice \'thrīs\ *adv* 1 : three times 2 : in a threefold manner or degree

thrift \'thrift\ *n* [ME, fr. ON, prosperity, fr. *thrīfask* to thrive] : careful management esp. of money : FRUGALITY — **thrift·i·ly** \'thrif-tə-lē\ *adv* — **thrift·less** *adj* — **thrifty** *adj*

thrill \'thril\ *vb* [ME *thirlen, thrillen* to pierce, fr. OE *thyrlian,* fr. *thyrel* hole, fr. *thurh* through] 1 : to have or cause to have a sudden sharp feeling of excitement ⟨was *thrilled* by their decision⟩; *also* : TINGLE, SHIVER 2 : TREMBLE, VIBRATE — **thrill** *n* — **thrill·er** *n* — **thrill·ing·ly** *adv*

thrips \'thrips\ *n, pl* **thrips** : any of an order of minute sucking insects including many plant-feeding pests

thrive \'thrīv\ *vb* **thrived** *or* **throve** \'thrōv\; **thrived** *also* **thriv·en** \'thri-vən\; **thriv·ing** **1** : to grow luxuriantly : FLOURISH **2** : to gain in wealth or possessions : PROSPER ⟨her business ~*s*⟩

throat \'thrōt\ *n* : the part of the neck in front of the spinal column; *also* : the passage through it to the stomach and lungs — **throat·ed** *adj*

throaty \'thrō-tē\ *adj* **throat·i·er; -est** **1** : uttered or produced from low in the throat ⟨a ~ voice⟩ **2** : heavy, thick, or deep as if from the throat ⟨~ notes of a horn⟩ — **throat·i·ly** \-tə-lē\ *adv* — **throat·i·ness** \-tē-nəs\ *n*

¹throb \'thräb\ *vb* **throbbed; throb·bing** : to pulsate or pound esp. with abnormal force or rapidity : BEAT, VIBRATE

²throb *n* : BEAT, PULSE

throe \'thrō\ *n* **1** : PANG, SPASM ⟨death ~*s*⟩ **2** *pl* : a hard or painful struggle

throm·bo·lyt·ic \,thräm-bə-'li-tik\ *adj* : destroying or breaking up a thrombus — **thrombolytic** *n*

throm·bo·sis \thräm-'bō-səs\ *n, pl* **-bo·ses** \-,sēz\ : the formation or presence of a clot in a blood vessel — **throm·bot·ic** \-'bä-tik\ *adj*

throm·bus \'thräm-bəs\ *n, pl* **throm·bi** \-,bī\ [NL, fr. Gk *thrombos* lump, clot] : a clot of blood formed within a blood vessel and remaining attached to its place of origin

throne \'thrōn\ *n* **1** : the chair of state of a sovereign or high dignitary **2** : royal power : SOVEREIGNTY

¹throng \'thrȯŋ\ *n* **1** : MULTITUDE **2** : a crowding together of many persons

²throng *vb* **thronged; throng·ing** : CROWD

¹throt·tle \'thrä-t³l\ *vb* **throt·tled; throt·tling** [ME *throtlen*, fr. *throte* throat] **1** : CHOKE, STRANGLE **2** : SUPPRESS ⟨policies that ~ creativity⟩ **3** : to reduce the speed of (an engine) by closing the throttle — **throt·tler** *n*

²throttle *n* : a valve regulating the flow of steam or fuel to an engine; *also* : the lever controlling this valve

¹through \'thrü\ *prep* **1** : into at one side and out at the other side of ⟨go ~ the door⟩ **2** : by way of ⟨entered ~ a skylight⟩ **3** : in the midst of ⟨a path ~ the trees⟩ **4** : by means of ⟨succeeded ~ hard work⟩ **5** : over the whole of ⟨rumors swept ~ the office⟩ **6** : during the whole of ⟨~ the night⟩ **7** : to and including ⟨Monday ~ Friday⟩

²through *adv* **1** : from one end or side to the other **2** : from beginning to end : to completion ⟨see it ~⟩ **3** : to the core : THOROUGHLY ⟨he was wet ~⟩ **4** : into the open : OUT ⟨break ~⟩

³through *adj* **1** : permitting free passage ⟨a ~ street⟩ **2** : going from point of origin to destination without change or transfer ⟨a ~ train⟩ **3** : coming from or going to points outside a local area ⟨~ traffic⟩ **4** : FINISHED ⟨~ with the job⟩

¹through·out \thrü-'aut\ *adv* **1** : EVERYWHERE **2** : from beginning to end

²throughout *prep* **1** : in or to every part of **2** : during the whole period of

through·put \'thrü-,put\ *n* : OUTPUT, PRODUCTION ⟨the ~ of a computer⟩

throve *past of* THRIVE

¹throw \'thrō\ *vb* **threw** \'thrü\; **thrown** \'thrōn\; **throw·ing** [ME, to cause to twist, throw, fr. OE *thrāwan* to cause to twist] **1** : to propel through the air esp. with a forward motion of the hand and arm ⟨~ a ball⟩ **2** : to cause to fall or fall off **3** : to put suddenly in a certain position or condition ⟨~ into panic⟩ **4** : to put on or take off hastily ⟨~ on a coat⟩ **5** : to lose intentionally ⟨~ a game⟩ **6** : to move (a lever) so as to connect or disconnect parts of something (as a clutch) **7** : to put (an automobile) into a different gear **8** : to act as host for ⟨~ a party⟩ ✦ *Synonyms* TOSS, FLING, PITCH, SLING — **throw·er** *n*

²throw *n* **1** : an act of throwing, hurling, or flinging; *also* : CAST **2** : the distance a missile may be thrown **3** : a light coverlet **4** : a woman's scarf or light wrap

¹throw·away \'thrō-ə-,wā\ *n* : something that is or is designed to be thrown away esp. after one use

²throwaway *adj* : overly wasteful ⟨a ~ society⟩

throw·back \-,bak\ *n* : reversion to an earlier type or phase; *also* : an instance or product of this

throw up *vb* **1** : to build hurriedly **2** : VOMIT

thrum \'thrəm\ *vb* **thrummed; thrum·ming** : to play or pluck a stringed instrument idly : STRUM

thrush \'thrəsh\ *n* : any of numerous small or medium-sized songbirds that are mostly of a plain color often with spotted underparts

¹thrust \'thrəst\ *vb* **thrust; thrust·ing** **1** : to push or drive with force : SHOVE **2** : STAB, PIERCE **3** : INTERJECT **4** : to press the acceptance of upon someone

²thrust *n* **1** : a lunge with a pointed weapon **2** : ATTACK **3** : the pressure of one part of a construction against another (as of an arch against an abutment) **4** : the force produced by a propeller or jet or rocket engine that drives a vehicle (as an aircraft) forward **5** : a violent push : SHOVE **6** : prominent or essential element ⟨the ~ of the argument⟩

thrust·er *also* **thrust·or** \'thrəs-tər\ *n* : one that thrusts; *esp* : a rocket engine

thru·way \'thrü-,wā\ *n* : EXPRESSWAY

¹thud \'thəd\ *n* **1** : ⁴BLOW **2** : a dull sound

²thud *vb* **thud·ded; thud·ding** : to move or strike so as to make a thud

thug \'thəg\ *n* [Hindi & Urdu *thag*, lit., thief] : a brutal ruffian or assassin — **thug·ish** *adj*

thu·li·um \'thü-lē-əm, 'thyü-\ *n* : a rare metallic chemical element

¹thumb \'thəm\ *n* **1** : the short thick first digit of the human hand or a corresponding digit of a lower animal **2** : the part of a glove or mitten that covers the thumb

²thumb *vb* **1** : to leaf through (pages) with the thumb **2** : to wear or soil with the thumb by frequent handling **3** : to request or obtain (a ride) in a passing automobile by signaling with the thumb

thumb drive *n* : FLASH DRIVE

¹thumb·nail \'thəm-,nāl\ *n* : the nail of the thumb

²thumbnail *adj* : BRIEF, CONCISE ⟨a ~ description⟩ ⟨a ~ picture⟩

thumb·print \-,print\ *n* : an impression made by the thumb

thumb·screw \-,skrü\ *n* **1** : a device of torture for squeezing the thumb **2** : a screw with a head that may be turned by the thumb and index finger

thumb·tack \-,tak\ *n* : a tack with a broad flat head for pressing with one's thumb into a board or wall

¹thump \'thəmp\ *vb* **1** : to strike with or as if with something thick or heavy so as to cause a dull sound **2** : POUND

²thump *n* : a blow with or as if with something blunt or heavy; *also* : the sound made by such a blow

¹thun·der \'thən-dər\ *n* **1** : the sound following a flash of lightning; *also* : a noise like such a sound **2** : a loud utterance or threat

²thunder *vb* **1** : to produce thunder **2** : ROAR, SHOUT ⟨jets ~ed overhead⟩

thun·der·bolt \-,bōlt\ *n* : a flash of lightning with its accompanying thunder

thun·der·clap \-,klap\ *n* : a crash of thunder

thun·der·cloud \-,klaud\ *n* : a cloud charged with electricity and producing lightning and thunder

thun·der·head \-,hed\ *n* : a large cumulus or cumulonimbus cloud often appearing before a thunderstorm

thun·der·ous \'thən-də-rəs\ *adj* : producing thunder; *also* : making a noise like thunder — **thun·der·ous·ly** *adv*

thun·der·show·er \'thən-dər-,shau(-ə)r\ *n* : a shower accompanied by thunder and lightning

thun·der·storm \-,stȯrm\ *n* : a storm accompanied by thunder and lightning

thun·der·struck \-,strək\ *adj* : stunned as if struck by a thunderbolt

Thurs *or* **Thu** *abbr* Thursday

Thurs·day \'thərz-,dā, -dē\ *n* [ME, fr. OE *thursdæg*, fr. ON *thōrsdagr*, lit., day of Thor (Norse god)] : the 5th day of the week

thus \'thəs\ *adv* **1** : in this or that manner **2** : to this degree or extent : SO **3** : because of this or that : HENCE

¹thwack \'thwak\ *vb* : to strike with or as if with something flat or heavy

²thwack *n* : a heavy blow : WHACK

¹thwart \'thwȯrt\ *vb* **1** : FOIL, BAFFLE **2** : BLOCK, DEFEAT ⟨~ed the attack⟩ ✦ *Synonyms* BALK, OUTWIT, FRUSTRATE

²thwart \'thwȯrt, *naut often* 'thȯrt\ *adv* : ATHWART

³thwart *adj* : situated or placed across something else

⁴thwart n : a seat extending across a boat

thy \'thī\ adj, archaic : of, relating to, or done by or to thee or thyself

thyme \'tīm, 'thīm\ n [ME, fr. AF time, fr. L thymum, fr. Gk thymon, prob. fr. thyein to make a burnt offering, sacrifice] : a garden mint with small aromatic leaves used esp. in seasoning; also : its leaves so used

thy·mine \'thī-,mēn\ n : a pyrimidine base that is one of the four bases coding genetic information in the molecular chain of DNA

thy·mus \'thī-məs\ n, pl **thy·mus·es** : a glandular organ of the neck region that is composed largely of lymphoid tissue, functions esp. in the development of the immune system, and tends to atrophy in the adult

thy·ris·tor \thī-'ris-tər\ n : a semiconductor device that acts as a switch, rectifier, or voltage regulator

thy·roid \'thī-,ròid\ adj [NL thyroides, fr. Gk thyreoeidēs shield-shaped, thyroid, fr. thyreos shield shaped like a door, fr. thyra door] : a large 2-lobed endocrine gland that lies at the base of the neck and produces several iodine-containing hormones that affect growth, development, and metabolism — **thyroid** also **thy·roi·dal** \thī-'ròi-d²l\ adj

thy·rox·ine or **thy·rox·in** \thī-'räk-,sēn, -sən\ n : an iodine-containing hormone that is produced by the thyroid gland, increases metabolic rate, and is used to treat thyroid disorders

thy·self \thī-'self\ pron, archaic : YOURSELF

Ti symbol titanium

ti·ara \tē-'er-ə, -'är-\ n 1 : a 3-tiered crown worn by the pope 2 : a decorative headband or semicircle for formal wear by women

Ti·bet·an \tə-'be-t²n\ n 1 : the language of the Tibetan people 2 : a native or inhabitant of Tibet — **Tibetan** adj

tib·ia \'ti-bē-ə\ n, pl **-i·ae** \-bē-,ē\ also **-i·as** [L] : the inner of the two bones of the vertebrate hind or lower limb between the knee and the ankle

tic \'tik\ n : a local and habitual twitching of muscles esp. of the face

¹tick \'tik\ n : any of a large group of small bloodsucking arachnids

²tick n : the fabric case of a mattress or pillow; also : a mattress consisting of a tick and its filling

³tick n 1 : a light rhythmic audible tap or beat 2 : a small mark used to draw attention to or check something

⁴tick vb 1 : to make the sound of a tick or series of ticks 2 : to mark, count, or announce by or as if by ticking beats 3 : to mark or check with a tick 4 : to function as an operating mechanism : RUN

⁵tick n, chiefly Brit : CREDIT; also : a credit account

tick·er \'ti-kər\ n 1 : something (as a watch) that ticks 2 : a telegraph instrument that prints information (as stock prices) on paper tape 3 slang : HEART

ticker tape n : the paper ribbon on which a telegraphic ticker prints

¹tick·et \'ti-kət\ n [MF etiquet, estiquette notice attached to something, fr. MF dial. estiquier to attach, fr. MD steken to stick] 1 : CERTIFICATE, LICENSE, PERMIT; esp : a certificate or token showing that a fare or admission fee has been paid 2 : TAG, LABEL 3 : SLATE 4 4 : a summons issued to a traffic offender

²ticket vb 1 : to attach a ticket to 2 : to furnish or serve with a ticket

tick·ing \'ti-kiŋ\ n : a strong fabric used in upholstering and as a mattress covering

tick·le \'ti-kəl\ vb **tick·led; tick·ling** 1 : to excite or stir up agreeably : PLEASE, AMUSE 2 : to have a tingling sensation 3 : to touch (as a body part) lightly so as to cause uneasiness, laughter, or spasmodic movements ⟨tickled her under the chin⟩ — **tickle** n — **tick·ler** n

tick·lish \-kə-lish\ adj 1 : OVERSENSITIVE, TOUCHY 2 : UNSTABLE ⟨a ~ foothold⟩ 3 : requiring delicate handling ⟨~ subject⟩ 4 : sensitive to tickling — **tick·lish·ly** adv — **tick·lish·ness** n

tidal wave n 1 : an unusually high sea wave that sometimes follows an earthquake 2 : an unusual rise of water alongshore due to strong winds

tid·bit \'tid-,bit\ n : a choice morsel

¹tide \'tīd\ n [ME, time, fr. OE tīd] 1 : the alternate rising and falling of the surface of the ocean 2 : something that fluctuates like the tides of the sea ⟨the ~ of public opinion⟩ — **tid·al** \'tī-d²l\ adj

²tide vb **tid·ed; tid·ing** : to carry through or help along as if by the tide ⟨a loan to ~ us over⟩

tide·land \'tīd-,land, -lənd\ n 1 : land overflowed during flood tide 2 : land under the ocean within a nation's territorial waters — often used in pl.

tide·wa·ter \-,wò-tər, -,wä-\ n 1 : water overflowing land at flood tide 2 : low-lying coastal land

tid·ings \'tī-diŋz\ n pl : NEWS, MESSAGE

¹ti·dy \'tī-dē\ adj **ti·di·er; -est** 1 : well ordered and cared for : NEAT 2 : LARGE, SUBSTANTIAL ⟨a ~ sum⟩ — **ti·di·ness** \'tī-dē-nəs\ n

²tidy vb **ti·died; ti·dy·ing** 1 : to put in order 2 : to make things tidy

³tidy n, pl **tidies** : a decorated covering used to protect the back or arms of a chair from wear or soil

¹tie \'tī\ n 1 : a line, ribbon, or cord used for fastening, uniting, or closing 2 : a structural element (as a beam or rod) holding two pieces together 3 : one of the cross supports to which railroad rails are fastened 4 : a connecting link : BOND ⟨family ~s⟩ 5 : an equality in number (as of votes or scores); also : an undecided or deadlocked contest 6 : NECKTIE

²tie vb **tied; ty·ing** or **tie·ing** 1 : to fasten, attach, or close by means of a tie 2 : to bring together firmly : UNITE 3 : to form a knot or bow in ⟨~ a scarf⟩ 4 : to restrain from freedom of action : CONSTRAIN 5 : to make or have an equal score with

tie·back \'tī-,bak\ n : a decorative strip for draping a curtain to the side of a window

tie-dye·ing \'tī-,dī-iŋ\ n : a method of producing patterns in textiles by tying parts of the fabric so that they will not absorb the dye — **tie-dyed** \-,dīd\ adj

tie-in \'tī-,in\ n : CONNECTION

tier \'tir\ n : ROW, LAYER; esp : one of two or more rows arranged one above another — **tiered** \'tird\ adj

tie-rod \'tī-,räd\ n : a rod used as a connecting member or brace

tie-up \-,əp\ n 1 : a slowing or stopping of traffic or business 2 : CONNECTION

¹tiff \'tif\ n : a petty quarrel — **tiff** vb

Tif·fa·ny \'ti-fə-nē\ adj : made of pieces of stained glass ⟨a ~ lamp⟩

ti·ger \'tī-gər\ n : a very large tawny black-striped Asian cat — **ti·ger·ish** adj

tiger

¹tight \'tīt\ adj 1 : so close in structure as to prevent passage of a liquid or gas 2 : strongly fixed or held : SECURE 3 : TAUT 4 : fitting usu. too closely ⟨~ shoes⟩ 5 : set close together : COMPACT ⟨a ~ formation⟩ 6 : DIFFICULT, TRYING ⟨get in a ~ spot⟩ 7 : STINGY, MISERLY 8 : evenly contested : CLOSE 9 : INTOXICATED 10 : low in supply : hard to get ⟨money is ~⟩ — **tight·ly** adv — **tight·ness** n

²tight adv 1 : TIGHTLY, FIRMLY 2 : SOUNDLY ⟨sleep ~⟩

tight·en \'tī-t²n\ vb : to make or become tight

tight-fist·ed \'tīt-'fis-təd\ adj : STINGY

tight·rope \-,rōp\ n : a taut rope or wire for acrobats to perform on

tights \'tīts\ n pl : skintight garments covering the body esp. below the waist; also, Brit : PANTY HOSE

tight·wad \'tīt-,wäd\ n : a stingy person

ti·gress \'tī-grəs\ n : a female tiger

ti·la·pia \tə-'lä-pē-ə, -'lä-\ n, pl tilapia also **ti·la·pi·as** : any of numerous chiefly African freshwater fishes widely raised for food

til·de \'til-də\ n [Sp, fr. ML titulus tittle] : a mark ˜ placed esp. over the letter n (as in Spanish señor sir) to denote the sound \n\ or over vowels (as in Portuguese *irmã* sister) to indicate nasal quality

¹tile \'tī(-ə)l\ *n* **1** : a flat or curved piece of fired clay, stone, or concrete used for roofs, floors, or walls; *also* : a pipe of earthenware or concrete used for a drain **2** : a thin piece (as of linoleum) used for covering walls or floors — **til·ing** \'tī-liŋ\ *n*

²tile *vb* **tiled; til·ing** : to cover with tiles — **til·er** *n*

¹till \'til\ *prep or conj* : UNTIL

²till *vb* : to work by plowing, sowing, and raising crops : CULTIVATE — **till·able** *adj*

³till *n* : DRAWER; *esp* : a money drawer in a store or bank

till·age \'ti-lij\ *n* **1** : the work of tilling land **2** : cultivated land

¹til·ler \'ti-lər\ *n* [OE *telgor, telgra* twig, shoot] : a sprout or stalk esp. from the base or lower part of a plant

²til·ler \'ti-lər\ *n* : one that tills

³til·ler \'ti-lər\ *n* [ME *tiler* stock of a crossbow, tiller, fr. AF *teiler* stock of a crossbow] : a lever used for turning a boat's rudder from side to side

¹tilt \'tilt\ *n* **1** : a contest in which two combatants charging usu. with lances try to unhorse each other : JOUST; *also* : a tournament of tilts **2** : a verbal contest : DISPUTE **3** : a sloping surface : SLANT

²tilt *vb* **1** : to move or shift so as to incline : TIP **2** : to engage in or as if in combat with lances : JOUST, ATTACK

tilth \'tilth\ *n* **1** : TILLAGE 2 **2** : the state of a soil esp. in relation to the suitability of its particle size and structure for growing crops

Tim *abbr* Timothy

tim·ber \'tim-bər\ *n* [ME, fr. OE, building, wood] **1** : growing trees or their wood — often used interjectionally to warn of a falling tree **2** : wood for use in making something **3** : a usu. large squared or dressed piece of wood

tim·bered \'tim-bərd\ *adj* : having walls framed by exposed timbers

tim·ber·land \'tim-bər-ˌland\ *n* : wooded land

tim·ber·line \'tim-bər-ˌlīn\ *n* : the upper limit of tree growth in mountains or high latitudes

timber rattlesnake *n* : a widely distributed rattlesnake of the eastern U.S.

timber wolf *n* : GRAY WOLF

tim·bre *also* **tim·ber** \'tam-bər, 'tim-\ *n* [F, fr. MF, bell struck by a hammer, fr. OF, drum, fr. MGk *tymbanon* kettledrum, fr. Gk *tympanon*] : the distinctive quality given to a sound by its overtones

tim·brel \'tim-brəl\ *n* : a small hand drum or tambourine

¹time \'tīm\ *n* **1** : a period during which an action, process, or condition exists or continues ⟨gone a long ∼⟩ **2** : LEISURE ⟨found ∼ to read⟩ **3** : a point or period when something occurs : OCCASION ⟨the last ∼ we met⟩ **4** : a set or customary moment or hour for something to occur ⟨arrived on ∼⟩ **5** : AGE, ERA **6** : state of affairs : CONDITIONS ⟨hard ∼s⟩ **7** : a rate of speed : TEMPO **8** : a moment, hour, day, or year as indicated by a clock or calendar ⟨what ∼ is it⟩ **9** : a system of reckoning time ⟨solar ∼⟩ **10** : one of a series of recurring instances; *also, pl* : added or accumulated quantities or examples ⟨five ∼s greater⟩ **11** : a person's experience during a particular period ⟨had a good ∼⟩ **12** : the hours or days of one's work; *also* : an hourly pay rate ⟨straight ∼⟩ **13** : TIME-OUT 1

²time *vb* **timed; tim·ing** **1** : to arrange or set the time of : SCHEDULE ⟨∼s his calls conveniently⟩ **2** : to set the tempo or duration of ⟨∼ a performance⟩ **3** : to cause to keep time with **4** : to determine or record the time, duration, or rate of ⟨∼ a sprinter⟩ — **tim·er** *n*

time bomb *n* **1** : a bomb so made as to explode at a predetermined time **2** : something with a potentially dangerous delayed reaction

time clock *n* : a clock that records the time workers arrive and depart

time frame *n* : a period of time esp. with respect to some action or project

time–hon·ored \'tīm-ˌä-nərd\ *adj* : honored because of age or long usage

time·keep·er \-ˌkē-pər\ *n* **1** : a clerk who keeps records of the time worked by employees **2** : one appointed to mark and announce the time in an athletic game or contest

time·less \-ləs\ *adj* **1** : ETERNAL **2** : not limited or affected by time ⟨∼ works of art⟩ — **time·less·ly** *adv* — **time·less·ness** *n*

time·ly \-lē\ *adj* **time·li·er; -est** **1** : coming early or at the right time ⟨a ∼ decision⟩ ⟨∼ payment⟩ **2** : appropriate to the time ⟨a ∼ book⟩ — **time·li·ness** *n*

time–out \'tīm-ˈaut\ *n* **1** : a brief suspension of activity esp. in an athletic game **2** : a quiet period used esp. as a disciplinary measure for a child

time·piece \-ˌpēs\ *n* : a device (as a clock) to show the passage of time

times \'tīmz\ *prep* : multiplied by ⟨2 ∼ 2 is 4⟩

time–shar·ing \'tīm-ˌsher-iŋ\ *n* **1** : simultaneous use of a computer by many users **2** *or* **time–share** \-ˌsher\ : joint ownership or rental of a vacation lodging by several persons with each taking turns using the place

times sign *n* : the symbol × used to indicate multiplication

time·ta·ble \'tīm-ˌtā-bəl\ *n* **1** : a table of the departure and arrival times (as of trains) **2** : a schedule showing a planned order or sequence

time warp *n* : an anomaly, discontinuity, or suspension held to occur in the progress of time

time·worn \-ˌwȯrn\ *adj* **1** : worn by time **2** : HACKNEYED, STALE ⟨a ∼ joke⟩

tim·id \'ti-məd\ *adj* : lacking in courage or self-confidence : FEARFUL — **ti·mid·i·ty** \tə-ˈmi-də-tē\ *n* — **tim·id·ly** *adv*

tim·o·rous \'ti-mə-rəs\ *adj* : of a timid disposition : AFRAID ⟨a ∼ kitten⟩ — **tim·o·rous·ly** *adv* — **tim·o·rous·ness** *n*

tim·o·thy \'ti-mə-thē\ *n* : a perennial grass with long cylindrical spikes widely grown for hay in the U.S.

Tim·o·thy \'ti-mə-thē\ *n* — see BIBLE table

tim·pa·ni \'tim-pə-nē\ *n sing or pl* [It] : a set of kettledrums played by one performer in an orchestra — **tim·pa·nist** \-nist\ *n*

¹tin \'tin\ *n* **1** : a soft white crystalline metallic chemical element malleable at ordinary temperatures that is used esp. in solders and alloys **2** : a container (as a can) made of metal (as tinplate)

²tin *vb* **tinned; tin·ning** **1** : to cover or plate with tin **2** : to pack in tins

TIN *abbr* taxpayer identification number

tinct \'tiŋkt\ *n* : TINCTURE, TINGE

¹tinc·ture \'tiŋk-chər\ *n* **1** *archaic* : a substance that colors **2** : a slight admixture : TRACE **3** : an alcoholic solution of a medicinal substance ♦ *Synonyms* TOUCH, SUGGESTION, SUSPICION, TINGE

²tincture *vb* **tinc·tured; tinc·tur·ing** **1** : COLOR, TINGE **2** : AFFECT

tin·der \'tin-dər\ *n* **1** : a very flammable substance used as kindling **2** : something serving to incite or inflame

tin·der·box \'tin-dər-ˌbäks\ *n* **1** : a metal box for holding tinder and usu. flint and steel for striking a spark **2** : a highly flammable object or place

tine \'tīn\ *n* : a slender pointed part (as of a fork or an antler) : PRONG

tin·foil \'tin-ˌfȯi(-ə)l\ *n* : a thin metal sheeting usu. of aluminum or tin-lead alloy

¹tinge \'tinj\ *vb* **tinged; tinge·ing** *or* **ting·ing** **1** : to color slightly : TINT **2** : to affect or modify esp. with a slight odor or taste

²tinge *n* : a slight coloring, flavor, or quality : TRACE ⟨a ∼ of color⟩ ⟨a ∼ of regret⟩ ♦ *Synonyms* TOUCH, SUGGESTION, SUSPICION, TINCTURE, SOUPÇON

tin·gle \'tiŋ-gəl\ *vb* **tin·gled; tin·gling** **1** : to feel a prickling or thrilling sensation **2** : TINKLE — **tingle** *n*

¹tin·ker \'tiŋ-kər\ *n* **1** : a usu. itinerant mender of household utensils **2** : an unskillful mender : BUNGLER

²tinker *vb* : to repair or adjust something in an unskillful or experimental manner — **tin·ker·er** *n*

¹tin·kle \'tiŋ-kəl\ *vb* **tin·kled; tin·kling** : to make or cause to make a tinkle

²tinkle *n* : a series of short high ringing or clinking sounds

tin·ni·tus \'tī-nə-təs, tə-ˈnī-təs\ *n* : a sensation of noise (as ringing or roaring) in the ears

tin·ny \'ti-nē\ *adj* **tin·ni·er; -est** **1** : abounding in or yielding tin **2** : resembling tin; *also* : LIGHT, CHEAP **3** : thin in tone ⟨a ∼ voice⟩ — **tin·ni·ly** \-nə-lē\ *adv* — **tin·ni·ness** \-nē-nəs\ *n*

tin·plate \'tin-ˈplāt\ *n* : thin sheet iron or steel coated with tin — **tin–plate** *vb*

tin·sel \'tin-səl\ *n* [ME *tyneseyle* cloth interwoven with metallic thread, prob. fr. AF *tencelé*, pp. of *tenceler*, *estenceler* to sparkle] **1** : threads, strips, or sheets of metal, paper, or plastic used to produce a glittering appearance **2** : something superficially attractive but of little worth

tin·smith \'tin-ˌsmith\ *n* : one that works with sheet metal (as tinplate)

¹tint \'tint\ *n* **1** : a slight or pale coloration : HUE **2** : any of various shades of a color

²tint *vb* : to impart a tint to : COLOR

tin·tin·nab·u·la·tion \ˌtin-tə-ˌna-byə-'lā-shən\ *n* **1** : the ringing of bells **2** : a tinkling or jingling sound as if of bells

tin·ware \'tin-ˌwer\ *n* : articles and esp. utensils made of tinplate

ti·ny \'tī-nē\ *adj* **ti·ni·er; -est** : very small : MINUTE ◆ *Synonyms* MINIATURE, DIMINUTIVE, WEE, LILLIPUTIAN

¹tip \'tip\ *vb* **tipped; tip·ping 1** : OVERTURN, UPSET **2** : LEAN, SLANT; *also* : to raise and tilt forward ⟨*tipped* his hat⟩

²tip *n* : the act or an instance of tipping

³tip *vb* **tipped; tip·ping 1** : to furnish with a tip **2** : to cover or adorn the tip of

⁴tip *n* **1** : the usu. pointed end of something **2** : a small piece or part serving as an end, cap, or point

⁵tip *n* : a light touch or blow

⁶tip *vb* **tipped; tip·ping** : to strike lightly : TAP

⁷tip *n* : a piece of advice or expert or confidential information : HINT

⁸tip *vb* **tipped; tip·ping** : to impart a piece of information about or to

⁹tip *vb* **tipped; tip·ping** : to give a gratuity to — **tip·per** *n*

¹⁰tip *n* : a gift or small sum given for a service performed or anticipated

tip–off \'tip-ˌȯf\ *n* : WARNING, TIP

tip·pet \'ti-pət\ *n* : a long scarf or shoulder cape

tipping point *n* : the critical point in a situation or process beyond which a significant effect takes place

tip·ple \'ti-pəl\ *vb* **tip·pled; tip·pling** : to drink intoxicating liquor esp. habitually or excessively — **tipple** *n* — **tip·pler** *n*

tip·ster \'tip-stər\ *n* : a person who gives or sells tips esp. for gambling

tip·sy \'tip-sē\ *adj* **tip·si·er; -est** : unsteady or foolish from the effects of alcohol — **tip·si·ly** \-sə-lē\ *adv* — **tip·si·ness** \-sē-nəs\ *n*

¹tip·toe \'tip-ˌtō\ *n* : the position of being balanced on the balls of the feet and toes with the heels raised; *also* : the ends of the toes

²tiptoe *adv or adj* : on or as if on tiptoe

³tiptoe *vb* **tip·toed; tip·toe·ing** : to walk or proceed on or as if on tiptoe ⟨∼ around the issue⟩

¹tip–top \'tip-'täp\ *n* : the highest point

²tip–top *adj* : EXCELLENT, FIRST-RATE

ti·rade \'tī-ˌrād\ *n* [F, shot, tirade, fr. MF, fr. It *tirata*, fr. *tirare* to draw, shoot] : a prolonged speech of abuse or condemnation

tir·a·mi·su \ˌtir-ə-'mē-sü, -mē-'sü\ *n* [It *tiramisù*] : a dessert made with ladyfingers, mascarpone, and espresso

¹tire \'tī(-ə)r\ *vb* **tired; tir·ing 1** : to make or become weary : FATIGUE **2** : to wear out the patience of : BORE

²tire *n* **1** : a metal hoop that forms the tread of a wheel **2** : a rubber cushion usu. containing compressed air that encircles a wheel (as of a bike)

tired *adj* **1** : WEARY, FATIGUED **2** : HACKNEYED — **tired·ness** *n*

tire·less \'tī(-ə)r-ləs\ *adj* : not tiring : UNTIRING, INDEFATIGABLE ⟨∼ workers⟩ — **tire·less·ly** *adv* — **tire·less·ness** *n*

tire·some \-səm\ *adj* : tending to bore : WEARISOME, TEDIOUS ⟨∼ lectures⟩ — **tire·some·ly** *adv* — **tire·some·ness** *n*

ti·ro *chiefly Brit var of* TYRO

tis·sue \'ti-shü\ *n* [ME *tysshewe, tyssew*, a rich fabric, fr. AF, fr. *tistre* to weave, fr. L *texere*] **1** : a fine lightweight often sheer fabric **2** : NETWORK, WEB ⟨a ∼ of lies⟩ **3** : a soft absorbent paper **4** : a mass or layer of cells forming a basic structural material of an animal or plant

¹tit \'tit\ *n* : TEAT

²tit *n* : any of various small plump Old World songbirds related to the titmice

Tit *abbr* Titus

ti·tan \'tī-t°n\ *n* **1** *cap* : one of a family of giants overthrown by the gods in Greek mythology **2** : one gigantic in size or power ⟨a media ∼⟩

ti·tan·ic \tī-'ta-nik\ *adj* : enormous in size, force, or power ◆ *Synonyms* IMMENSE, GIGANTIC, GIANT, COLOSSAL, MAMMOTH

ti·ta·ni·um \tī-'tā-nē-əm\ *n* : a gray light strong metallic chemical element used esp. in alloys

titbit *var of* TIDBIT

tithe \'tīth\ *n* [ME, fr. OE *teogotha* tenth] : a 10th part paid or given esp. for the support of a church — **tithe** *vb* — **tith·er** *n*

tit·il·late \'ti-t°l-ˌāt\ *vb* **-lat·ed; -lat·ing 1** : to excite pleasurably **2** : TICKLE 3 — **tit·il·la·tion** \ˌti-t°l-'ā-shən\ *n*

ti·tle \'tī-t°l\ *n* **1** : CLAIM, RIGHT; *esp* : a legal right to the ownership of property **2** : the distinguishing name of a written, filmed, or musical production or a work of art **3** : an appellation of honor, rank, or office **4** : CHAMPIONSHIP ◆ *Synonyms* DESIGNATION, DENOMINATION, APPELLATION

ti·tled \'tī-t°ld\ *adj* : having a title esp. of nobility

title page *n* : a page of a book bearing the title and usu. the names of the author and publisher

tit·mouse \'tit-ˌmaùs\ *n, pl* **tit·mice** \-ˌmīs\ : any of several small long-tailed No. American songbirds related to the chickadees

ti·tra·tion \tī-'trā-shən\ *n* : a process of finding the concentration of a solution (as of an acid) by adding small portions of a second solution of known concentration (as of a base) to a fixed amount of the first until an expected change (as in color) occurs

tit·ter \'ti-tər\ *vb* : to laugh in an affected or in a nervous or half-suppressed manner : GIGGLE — **titter** *n*

tit·tle \'ti-t°l\ *n* : a tiny part

tit·tle–tat·tle \'ti-t°l-ˌta-t°l\ *n* : idle talk : GOSSIP — **tittle·tattle** *vb*

tit·u·lar \'ti-chə-lər\ *adj* **1** : existing in title only : NOMINAL ⟨∼ ruler⟩ **2** : of, relating to, or bearing a title ⟨∼ role⟩

Ti·tus \'tī-təs\ *n* — see BIBLE table

ti·yin \'tē-ēn\ *n, pl* **tiyin** *or* **tiyins** — see *sum* at MONEY table

ti·yn \'tē-in\ *n* — see *tenge* at MONEY table

tiz·zy \'ti-zē\ *n, pl* **tizzies** : a highly excited and distracted state of mind

tk *abbr* **1** tank **2** truck

TKO \ˌtē-ˌkā-'ō\ *n* [*technical knockout*] : the termination of a boxing match when a boxer is declared unable to continue the fight

tkt *abbr* ticket

Tl *symbol* thallium

TLC *abbr* tender loving care

T lymphocyte *n* : T CELL

Tm *symbol* thulium

TM *abbr* trademark

T–man \'tē-ˌman\ *n* : a special agent of the U.S. Treasury Department

tn *abbr* **1** ton **2** town

TN *abbr* Tennessee

tng *abbr* training

tnpk *abbr* turnpike

TNT \ˌtē-(ˌ)en-'tē\ *n* : a flammable toxic compound used as a high explosive and in chemical synthesis

¹to \tə, 'tü\ *prep* **1** : in the direction of and reaching ⟨drove ∼ town⟩ **2** : in the direction of : TOWARD **3** : ON, AGAINST ⟨apply salve ∼ a burn⟩ **4** : as far as ⟨can pay up ∼ a dollar⟩ **5** : so as to become or bring about ⟨beaten ∼ death⟩ ⟨broken ∼ pieces⟩ **6** : BEFORE ⟨it's five minutes ∼ six⟩ **7** : UNTIL ⟨from May ∼ December⟩ **8** : fitting or being a part of : FOR ⟨key ∼ the lock⟩ **9** : with the accompaniment of ⟨sing ∼ the music⟩ **10** : in relation or comparison with ⟨similar ∼ that one⟩ ⟨won 10 ∼ 6⟩ **11** : in accordance with ⟨add salt ∼ taste⟩ **12** : within the range of ⟨∼ my knowledge⟩ **13** : contained, occurring, or included in ⟨two pints ∼ a quart⟩ **14** : as regards ⟨agreeable ∼ everyone⟩ **15** : affecting as the receiver or beneficiary ⟨whispered ∼ her⟩ ⟨gave it ∼ me⟩ **16** : for no one except ⟨a room ∼ myself⟩ **17** : into the action of ⟨we got ∼ talking⟩ **18** — used for marking the following verb as an infinitive ⟨wants ∼ go⟩ and often used by itself at the end of a clause in place of an infinitive suggested by the preceding context ⟨goes to town whenever he wants ∼⟩

²**to** \ˈtü\ *adv* **1** : in a direction toward ⟨run ∼ and fro⟩ **2** : into contact esp. with the frame of a door ⟨the door slammed ∼⟩ **3** : to the matter in hand ⟨fell ∼ and ate heartily⟩ **4** : to a state of consciousness or awareness ⟨he came ∼ hours later⟩

TO *abbr* turn over

toad \ˈtōd\ *n* : any of numerous tailless leaping amphibians differing typically from the related frogs in having a shorter stockier build, rough dry warty skin, and less aquatic habits

toad·stool \-ˌstül\ *n* : MUSHROOM; *esp* : one that is poisonous or inedible

toady \ˈtō-dē\ *n, pl* **toad·ies** : a person who flatters in the hope of gaining favors : SYCOPHANT — **toady** *vb*

to–and–fro \ˌtü-ən-ˈfrō\ *adj* : forward and backward — **to–and–fro** *n*

¹**toast** \ˈtōst\ *vb* **1** : to warm thoroughly **2** : to make (as bread) crisp, hot, and brown by heat **3** : to become toasted

²**toast** *n* **1** : sliced toasted bread **2** : someone or something in whose honor persons drink **3** : an act of drinking in honor of a toast

³**toast** *vb* : to propose or drink to as a toast

toast·er \ˈtō-stər\ *n* : an electrical appliance for toasting

toaster oven *n* : a portable electrical appliance that bakes, broils, and toasts

toast·mas·ter \ˈtōst-ˌmas-tər\ *n* : a person who presides at a banquet and introduces the after-dinner speakers

toast·mis·tress \-ˌmis-trəs\ *n* : a woman who acts as toastmaster

toasty \ˈtō-stē\ *adj* **toast·i·er; -est** : pleasantly warm

Tob *abbr* Tobit

to·bac·co \tə-ˈba-kō\ *n, pl* **-cos** [Sp *tabaco*] **1** : a tall broad-leaved herb related to the potato; *also* : its leaves prepared for smoking or chewing or as snuff **2** : manufactured tobacco products; *also* : smoking as a practice

to·bac·co·nist \tə-ˈba-kə-nist\ *n* : a dealer in tobacco

To·bi·as \tō-ˈbī-əs\ *n* : TOBIT

To·bit \ˈtō-bət\ *n* — see BIBLE table

¹**to·bog·gan** \tə-ˈbä-gən\ *n* : a long flat-bottomed light sled made of thin boards curved up at one end

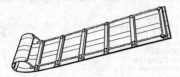

toboggan

²**toboggan** *vb* **1** : to coast on or as if on a toboggan **2** : to decline suddenly (as in value) — **to·bog·gan·er** *n*

toc·sin \ˈtäk-sən\ *n* **1** : an alarm bell **2** : a warning signal

¹**to·day** \tə-ˈdā\ *adv* **1** : on or for this day **2** : at the present time

²**today** *n* : the present day, time, or age

tod·dle \ˈtä-dᵊl\ *vb* **tod·dled; tod·dling** : to walk with short tottering steps in the manner of a young child — **toddle** *n* — **tod·dler** *n*

tod·dy \ˈtä-dē\ *n, pl* **toddies** [Hindi & Urdu *tāṛī* juice of a palm, fr. *tāṛ* a palm, fr. Skt *tāla*] : a drink made of liquor, sugar, spices, and hot water

to–do \tə-ˈdü\ *n, pl* **to–dos** \-ˈdüz\ : BUSTLE, STIR, FUSS

¹**toe** \ˈtō\ *n* **1** : one of the jointed parts of the front end of the vertebrate foot **2** : the front part of a foot or hoof

²**toe** *vb* **toed; toe·ing** : to touch, reach, or drive with the toes

toea \ˈtói-ə\ *n* — see *kina* at MONEY table

toe·hold \ˈtō-ˌhōld\ *n* **1** : a place of support for the toes **2** : a slight footing

toe·nail \ˈtō-ˌnāl\ *n* : a nail of a toe

tof·fee *or* **tof·fy** \ˈtó-fē, ˈtä-\ *n, pl* **toffees** *or* **toffies** : candy of brittle but tender texture made by boiling sugar and butter together

to·fu \ˈtō-(ˌ)fü\ *n* [Jp *tōfu*] : a soft white food product made from soybeans

tog \ˈtäg, ˈtòg\ *vb* **togged; tog·ging** : to put togs on : DRESS

to·ga \ˈtō-gə\ *n* : the loose outer garment worn in public by citizens of ancient Rome — **to·gaed** \-gəd\ *adj*

¹**to·geth·er** \tə-ˈge-thər\ *adv* **1** : in or into one place or group **2** : in or into contact or association ⟨mix ∼⟩ **3** : at one time : SIMULTANEOUSLY ⟨talk and work ∼⟩ **4** : in succession ⟨for days ∼⟩ **5** : in or into harmony or coherence ⟨get ∼ on a plan⟩ **6** : as a group : JOINTLY — **to·geth·er·ness** *n*

²**together** *adj* : composed in mind or manner

together with *prep* : in addition to : in association with

tog·gery \ˈtä-gə-rē, ˈtò-\ *n* : CLOTHING

tog·gle \ˈtä-gəl\ *vb* : to switch between two options esp. of an electronic device

toggle switch *n* : an electric switch operated by pushing a projecting lever through a small arc

togs \ˈtägz, ˈtògz\ *n pl* : CLOTHING; *esp* : clothes for a specified use ⟨riding ∼⟩

¹**toil** \ˈtói(-ə)l\ *n* **1** : laborious effort **2** : long fatiguing labor — DRUDGERY — **toil·ful** \-fəl\ *adj* — **toil·some** *adj*

²**toil** *vb* [ME, to argue, struggle, fr. AF *toiller* to make dirty, fight, wrangle, fr. L *tudiculare* to crush, grind, fr. *tudicula* machine for crushing olives, dim. of *tudes* hammer] **1** : to work hard and long **2** : to proceed with great effort : PLOD — **toil·er** *n*

³**toil** *n* [ME *toile* cloth, net, fr. OF *teile*, fr. L *tela* cloth on a loom] : NET, TRAP — usu. used in pl. ⟨caught in the ∼s of the law⟩

toi·let \ˈtói-lət\ *n* **1** : the act or process of dressing and grooming oneself **2** : BATHROOM **3** : a fixture for use in urinating and defecating; *esp* : one consisting essentially of a water-flushed bowl and seat — **toilet** *vb*

toilet paper *n* : an absorbent paper for drying or cleaning oneself after defecation and urination

toi·let·ry \ˈtói-lə-trē\ *n, pl* **-ries** : an article or preparation used in cleaning or grooming oneself — usu. used in pl.

toi·lette \twä-ˈlet\ *n* **1** : TOILET 1 **2** : formal attire; *also* : a particular costume

toilet training *n* : the process of training a child to control bladder and bowel movements and to use the toilet — **toilet train** *vb*

toil·worn \ˈtói(-ə)l-ˌwōrn\ *adj* : showing the effects of toil

To·kay \tō-ˈkā\ *n* : naturally sweet wine from Hungary

toke \ˈtōk\ *n, slang* : a puff on a marijuana cigarette or pipe

¹**to·ken** \ˈtō-kən\ *n* **1** : an outward sign **2** : SYMBOL, EMBLEM **3** : SOUVENIR, KEEPSAKE **4** : a small part representing the whole **5** : a piece resembling a coin issued as money or for use by a particular group on specified terms

²**token** *adj* **1** : done or given as a token esp. in partial fulfillment of an obligation **2** : representing only a symbolic effort : MINIMAL, PERFUNCTORY

to·ken·ism \ˈtō-kə-ˌni-zəm\ *n* : the policy or practice of making only a symbolic effort (as to desegregate)

tolar \ˈtō-lär\ *n, pl* **to·lar·ja** \ˈtō-lär-ˌyä\ *or* **to·lar·jev** \ˈtō-lär-ˌyev\ *or* **tolars** : the basic monetary unit of Slovenia from 1992 to 2007

told *past and past part of* TELL

tole \ˈtōl\ *n* : sheet metal and esp. tinplate for use in domestic and ornamental wares

tol·er·a·ble \ˈtä-lə-rə-bəl\ *adj* **1** : capable of being borne or endured **2** : moderately good : PASSABLE — **tol·er·a·bly** \-blē\ *adv*

tol·er·ance \ˈtä-lə-rəns\ *n* **1** : the act or practice of tolerating; *esp* : sympathy or indulgence for beliefs or practices differing from one's own **2** : the allowable deviation from a standard (as of size) **3** : the body's capacity to become less responsive over time to something (as a drug used repeatedly) — **tol·er·ant** *adj* — **tol·er·ant·ly** *adv*

tol·er·ate \ˈtä-lə-ˌrāt\ *vb* **-at·ed; -at·ing** **1** : to exhibit physiological tolerance for (as a drug) **2** : to allow to be or to be done without hindrance ♦ *Synonyms* ABIDE, BEAR, SUFFER, STAND, BROOK — **tol·er·a·tion** \ˌtä-lə-ˈrā-shən\ *n*

¹**toll** \ˈtōl\ *n* **1** : a tax paid for a privilege (as for passing over a bridge) **2** : a charge for a service (as for a long-distance telephone call) **3** : the cost in life, health, loss, or suffering

²**toll** *vb* **1** : to cause the slow regular sounding of (a bell)

esp. by pulling a rope **2** : to give signal of : SOUND **3** : to sound with slow measured strokes **4** : to announce by tolling
³**toll** *n* : the sound of a tolling bell
toll·booth \'tōl-,büth\ *n* : a booth where tolls are paid
toll·gate \-,gāt\ *n* : a point where vehicles stop to pay a toll
toll·house \-,haús\ *n* : a house or booth where tolls are paid
tol·u·ene \'täl-yə-,wēn\ *n* : a liquid hydrocarbon used esp. as a solvent
tom \'täm\ *n* : the male of various animals (as a cat or turkey)
¹**tom·a·hawk** \'tä-mə-,hȯk\ *n* : a light ax used as a missile and as a hand weapon esp. by No. American Indians
²**tomahawk** *vb* : to strike or kill with a tomahawk
to·ma·til·lo \,tō-mə-'tē-(,)yō\ *n, pl* **-los** : a small round usu. pale green edible fruit of a Mexican herb related to the tomato; *also* : this herb
to·ma·to \tə-'mā-tō, -'mä-\ *n, pl* **-toes** [alter. of earlier *tomate*, fr. Sp, fr. Nahuatl *tomatl*] : a usu. large, rounded, and red or yellow pulpy edible berry of a widely grown tropical herb related to the potato; *also* : this herb
tomb \'tüm\ *n* **1** : a place of burial : GRAVE **2** : a house, chamber, or vault for the dead — **tomb** *vb*
tom·boy \'täm-,bȯi\ *n* : a girl who behaves in a manner usu. considered boyish — **tom·boy·ish** *adj*
tomb·stone \'tüm-,stōn\ *n* : a stone marking a grave
tom·cat \'täm-,kat\ *n* : a male domestic cat
Tom Col·lins \'täm-'kä-lənz\ *n* : a tall iced drink with a base of gin
tome \'tōm\ *n* : BOOK; *esp* : a large or weighty one
tom·fool·ery \täm-'fü-lə-rē\ *n* : playful or foolish behavior
tom·my gun \'tä-mē-,gən\ *n* : SUBMACHINE GUN — **tommy–gun** *vb*
to·mog·ra·phy \tō-'mä-grə-fē\ *n* : a method of producing a three-dimensional image of the internal structures of a solid object (as the human body or the earth) — **to·mo·graph·ic** \,tō-mə-'gra-fik\ *adj*
to·mor·row \tə-'mär-ō\ *adv* : on or for the day after today — **tomorrow** *n*
tom–tom \'täm-,täm\ *n* : a small-headed drum beaten with the hands
ton \'tən\ *n, pl* **tons** *also* **ton** **1** — see WEIGHT table **2** : a unit equal to the volume of a long ton weight of seawater used in reckoning the displacement of ships and equal to 35 cubic feet
to·nal·i·ty \tō-'na-lə-tē\ *n, pl* **-ties** : tonal quality
¹**tone** \'tōn\ *n* [ME, fr. L *tonus* tension, tone, fr. Gk *tonos*, lit., act of stretching; fr. the dependence of the pitch of a musical string on its tension] **1** : vocal or musical sound; *esp* : sound quality **2** : a sound of definite pitch **3** : WHOLE STEP **4** : accent or inflection expressive of an emotion **5** : the pitch of a word often used to express differences of meaning **6** : style or manner of expression **7** : color quality; *also* : SHADE, TINT **8** : the effect in painting of light and shade together with color **9** : healthy and vigorous condition of a living body or bodily part; *also* : the state of partial contraction characteristic of normal muscle **10** : general character, quality, or trend ◆ **Synonyms** ATMOSPHERE, FEELING, MOOD, VEIN — **ton·al** \'tō-nᵊl\ *adj*
²**tone** *vb* **toned; ton·ing** **1** : to give a particular intonation or inflection to **2** : to impart tone to **3** : SOFTEN, MELLOW ⟨~ down your language⟩ **4** : to harmonize in color : BLEND
tone·arm *n* : the movable part of a record player that carries the pickup and the needle
toney *var of* TONY
tong \'tän, 'tȯn\ *n* : a Chinese secret society in the U.S.
tongs \'tänz, 'tȯnz\ *n pl* : a grasping device consisting of two pieces joined at one end by a pivot or hinged like scissors — **tong** *vb*
¹**tongue** \'təŋ\ *n* **1** : a fleshy movable process of the floor of the mouth used in tasting and in taking and swallowing food and in humans as a speech organ **2** : the flesh of a tongue (as of the ox) used as food **3** : the power of communication **4** : LANGUAGE 1 **5** : manner or quality of utterance; *also* : intended meaning **6** : ecstatic unintelligible utterance accompanying religious excitation — usu. used in pl. **7** : something resembling an ani-

mal's tongue esp. in being elongated and fastened at one end only — **tongued** \'təŋd\ *adj* — **tongue·less** *adj*
²**tongue** *vb* **tongued; tongu·ing** **1** : to touch or lick with the tongue **2** : to articulate notes on a wind instrument
tongue–in–cheek *adj* : characterized by insincerity, irony, or whimsical exaggeration — **tongue in cheek** *adv*
tongue–lash \'təŋ-,lash\ *vb* : CHIDE, REPROVE — **tongue–lash·ing** \-iŋ\ *n*
tongue–tied \-,tīd\ *adj* : unable or disinclined to speak clearly or freely (as from shyness or a tongue impairment)
tongue twister *n* : an utterance that is difficult to articulate because of a succession of similar consonants
¹**ton·ic** \'tä-nik\ *adj* **1** : of, relating to, or producing a healthy physical or mental condition : INVIGORATING **2** : relating to or based on the 1st tone of a scale — **to·nic·i·ty** \tō-'ni-sə-tē\ *n*
²**tonic** *n* **1** : the 1st degree of a musical scale **2** : something that invigorates, restores, or refreshes
tonic water *n* : a carbonated beverage flavored with a bit of quinine, lemon, and lime
¹**to·night** \tə-'nīt\ *adv* : on this present night or the coming night
²**tonight** *n* : the present or the coming night
ton·nage \'tə-nij\ *n* **1** : a duty on ships based on tons carried **2** : ships in terms of the number of tons registered or carried **3** : total weight in tons shipped, carried, or mined
ton·sil \'tän-səl\ *n* : either of a pair of oval masses of lymphoid tissue that lie one on each side of the throat at the back of the mouth
ton·sil·lec·to·my \,tän-sə-'lek-tə-mē\ *n, pl* **-mies** : the surgical removal of the tonsils
ton·sil·li·tis \-'lī-təs\ *n* : inflammation of the tonsils
ton·so·ri·al \tän-'sȯr-ē-əl\ *adj* : of or relating to a barber or a barber's work
ton·sure \'tän-chər\ *n* [ME, fr. AF, ML *tonsura*, fr. L, act of shearing, fr. *tonsus*, pp. of *tondēre* to shear] **1** : the rite of admission to the clerical state by the clipping or shaving of the head **2** : the shaven crown or patch worn by clerics (as monks) — **tonsure** *vb*
tony *also* **ton·ey** \'tō-nē\ *adj* **ton·i·er; -est** : marked by an aristocratic manner or style
too \'tü\ *adv* **1** : in addition : ALSO **2** : EXCESSIVELY ⟨the music is ~ loud⟩ **3** : to such a degree as to be regrettable **4** : VERY ⟨didn't seem ~ interested⟩
took *past of* TAKE
¹**tool** \'tül\ *n* **1** : a hand instrument that aids in accomplishing a task **2** : the cutting or shaping part in a machine; *also* : a machine for shaping metal in any way **3** : something used in doing a job ⟨a scholar's books are his ~s⟩; *also* : a means to an end **4** : a person used by another : DUPE **5** *pl* : natural ability
²**tool** *vb* **1** : to shape, form, or finish with a tool; *esp* : to letter or decorate (as a book cover) by means of hand tools **2** : to equip a plant or industry with machines and tools for production **3** : DRIVE, RIDE ⟨~ing along at 60 miles per hour⟩
tool bar *n* : a strip of icons on a computer display providing quick access to the pictured functions
¹**toot** \'tüt\ *vb* **1** : to sound or cause to sound in short blasts **2** : to blow an instrument (as a horn) — **toot·er** *n*
²**toot** *n* : a short blast (as on a horn)
tooth \'tüth\ *n, pl* **teeth** \'tēth\ **1** : one of the hard bony structures borne esp. on the jaws of vertebrates and used for seizing and chewing food and as weapons; *also* : a hard sharp structure esp. around the mouth of an invertebrate **2** : something resembling an animal's tooth **3** : any of the projections on the edge of a wheel that fits into corresponding projections on another wheel **4** *pl* : effective means of enforcement — **toothed** \'tütht\ *adj* — **tooth·less** *adj*
tooth·ache \'tüth-,āk\ *n* : pain in or about a tooth
tooth·brush \-,brəsh\ *n* : a brush for cleaning the teeth
tooth·paste \-,pāst\ *n* : a paste for cleaning the teeth
tooth·pick \-,pik\ *n* : a pointed instrument for removing food particles caught between the teeth
tooth powder *n* : a powder for cleaning the teeth
tooth·some \'tüth-səm\ *adj* **1** : AGREEABLE, ATTRACTIVE **2** : pleasing to the taste : DELICIOUS ◆ **Synonyms** PALATABLE, APPETIZING, SAVORY, TASTY
toothy \'tü-thē\ *adj* **tooth·i·er; -est** : having or showing prominent teeth

top • torture

¹top \'täp\ *n* **1** : the highest part, point, or level of something **2** : the part of a plant with edible roots lying above the ground ⟨beet ~s⟩ **3** : the upper end, edge, or surface ⟨the ~ of a page⟩ **4** : an upper piece, lid, or covering **5** : the highest degree, pitch, or rank **6** : a quark with a charge of +²/₃ and a measured energy of approximately 175 billion electron volts

²top *vb* **topped; top·ping 1** : to remove or trim the top of : PRUNE ⟨~ a tree⟩ **2** : to cover with a top or on the top : CROWN, CAP **3** : to be superior to : EXCEL, SURPASS **4** : to go over the top of **5** : to strike (a ball) above the center **6** : to make an end or conclusion ⟨~ off a meal with coffee⟩

³top *adj* **1** : of, relating to, or being at the top : HIGHEST ⟨is ~ in her class⟩ **2** : CHIEF

⁴top *n* : a toy that has a tapering point on which it is made to spin

to·paz \'tō-ˌpaz\ *n* : a hard silicate of aluminum; *esp* : a yellow transparent topaz used as a gem

top·coat \'täp-ˌkōt\ *n* **1** : a lightweight overcoat **2** : a protective coating (as of paint)

top dollar *n* : the highest amount being paid for a commodity or service

top–dress \-ˌdres\ *vb* : to apply material to (as land) without working it in; *esp* : to scatter fertilizer over

top–dress·ing \-ˌdre-siŋ\ *n* : a material used to top-dress soil

top–end \'täp-ˈend\ *adj* : TOPFLIGHT

top·flight \'täp-ˈflīt\ *adj* : of, relating to, or being the highest level of excellence or rank ⟨a ~ staff⟩ — **top flight** *n*

top hat *n* : a tall-crowned hat usu. of beaver or silk

top–heavy \'täp-ˌhe-vē\ *adj* : having the top part too heavy for the lower part

to·pi·ary \'tō-pē-ˌer-ē\ *n, pl* **-ar·ies** : the art of training and trimming trees or shrubs with decorative shapes — **topiary** *adj*

top·ic \'tä-pik\ *n* **1** : a heading in an outlined argument **2** : the subject of a discourse or a section of it : THEME

top·i·cal \-pi-kəl\ *adj* **1** : of, relating to, or arranged by topics ⟨a ~ outline⟩ **2** : relating to current or local events **3** : designed to be applied to or to work on a part (as of the body) — **top·i·cal·ly** \-k(ə-)lē\ *adv*

top·knot \'täp-ˌnät\ *n* **1** : an ornament (as a knot of ribbons) forming a headdress **2** : a crest of feathers or tuft of hair on the top of the head

top·less \-ləs\ *adj* **1** : wearing no clothing on the upper body **2** : featuring topless waitresses or entertainers

top·mast \'täp-ˌmast, -məst\ *n* : the 2d mast above a ship's deck

top·most \'täp-ˌmōst\ *adj* : highest of all : UPPERMOST

top–notch \-ˈnäch\ *adj* : of the highest quality : FIRST-RATE

top–of–the–line *adj* : being or belonging to the highest or most expensive class

to·pog·ra·phy \tə-ˈpä-grə-fē\ *n* **1** : the art of showing in detail on a map or chart the physical features of a place or region **2** : the outline of the form of a place showing its relief and the position of features (as rivers, roads, or cities) — **to·pog·ra·pher** \-fər\ *n* — **top·o·graph·ic** \ˌtä-pə-ˈgra-fik\ *or* **top·o·graph·i·cal** \-fi-kəl\ *adj*

topping *n* : a food served on top of another to make it look or taste better

top·ple \'tä-pəl\ *vb* **top·pled; top·pling 1** : to fall from or as if from being top-heavy **2** : to push over : OVERTURN; *also* : OVERTHROW ⟨*toppled* the dictator⟩

¹tops \'täps\ *adj* : topmost in quality or importance ⟨~ in his field⟩

²tops *adv* : at the very most

top·sail \'täp-ˌsāl, -səl\ *also* **top·s'l** \-səl\ *n* : the sail next above the lowest sail on a mast in a square-rigged ship

top secret *adj* : demanding complete secrecy among those concerned

top·side \'täp-ˈsīd\ *adv or adj* **1** : to or on the top or surface **2** : on deck

top·sides \-ˈsīdz\ *n pl* : the top portion of the outer surface of a ship on each side above the waterline

top·soil \'täp-ˌsȯi(-ə)l\ *n* : surface soil usu. including the organic layer in which plants have most of their roots

top·sy–tur·vy \ˌtäp-sē-ˈtər-vē\ *adv* **1** : in utter confusion **2** : UPSIDE DOWN — **topsy–turvy** *adj*

toque \'tōk\ *n* : a woman's small hat without a brim

tor \'tȯr\ *n* : a high craggy hill

To·rah \'tȯr-ə\ *n* **1** : a scroll of the first five books of the Old Testament used in a synagogue; *also* : these five books **2** : the body of divine knowledge and law found in the Jewish scriptures and tradition

¹torch \'tȯrch\ *n* **1** : a flaming light made of something that burns brightly and usu. carried in the hand **2** : something that resembles a torch in giving light, heat, or guidance **3** : a portable burner for producing a hot flame **4** *chiefly Brit* : FLASHLIGHT

²torch *vb* : to set fire to

torch·bear·er \'tȯrch-ˌber-ər\ *n* **1** : a person who carries a torch **2** : one in the forefront (as of a political campaign)

torch·light \-ˌlīt\ *n* : light given by torches

torch song *n* : a popular sentimental song of unrequited love

tore *past of* TEAR

to·re·ador \'tȯr-ē-ə-ˌdȯr\ *n* : BULLFIGHTER

to·re·ro \tə-ˈrer-ō\ *n, pl* **-ros** [Sp] : BULLFIGHTER

¹tor·ment \'tȯr-ˌment\ *n* **1** : extreme pain or anguish of body or mind **2** : a source of vexation or pain

²tor·ment \tȯr-ˈment\ *vb* **1** : to cause severe suffering of body or mind to **2** : DISTORT, TWIST ♦ **Synonyms** RACK, AFFLICT, TRY, TORTURE — **tor·men·tor** \-ˈmen-tər\ *n*

torn *past part of* TEAR

tor·na·do \tȯr-ˈnā-dō\ *n, pl* **-does** *or* **-dos** [modif of Sp *tronada* thunderstorm, fr. *tronar* to thunder, fr. L *tonare*] : a violent destructive whirling wind accompanied by a funnel-shaped cloud that moves over a narrow path

¹tor·pe·do \tȯr-ˈpē-dō\ *n, pl* **-does** : a thin cylindrical self-propelled underwater weapon

²torpedo *vb* **tor·pe·doed; tor·pe·do·ing 1** : to hit or destroy with or as if with a torpedo

torpedo boat *n* : a small very fast boat for firing torpedoes

tor·pid \'tȯr-pəd\ *adj* **1** : having lost motion or the power of exertion : DORMANT **2** : SLUGGISH **3** : lacking vigor — **tor·pid·i·ty** \tȯr-ˈpi-də-tē\ *n*

tor·por \'tȯr-pər\ *n* **1** : DULLNESS, APATHY **2** : extreme sluggishness : STAGNATION ♦ **Synonyms** STUPOR, LETHARGY, LANGUOR, LASSITUDE

¹torque \'tȯrk\ *n* : a force that produces or tends to produce rotation or torsion

²torque *vb* **torqued; torqu·ing** : to impart torque to : cause to twist (as about an axis)

tor·rent \'tȯr-ənt\ *n* [F, fr. L *torrent-, torrens*, fr. *torrent-, torrens* burning, seething, rushing, fr. prp. of *torrēre* to parch, burn] **1** : a tumultuous outburst **2** : a rushing stream (as of water)

tor·ren·tial \tȯ-ˈren-chəl\ *adj* : relating to or resembling a torrent ⟨~ rains⟩

tor·rid \'tȯr-əd\ *adj* **1** : parched with heat esp. of the sun : HOT **2** : ARDENT

torrid zone *n* : the region of the earth between the Tropic of Cancer and the Tropic of Capricorn

tor·sion \'tȯr-shən\ *n* **1** : a wrenching by which one part of a body is under pressure to turn about a longitudinal axis while the other part is held fast or is under pressure to turn in the opposite direction **2** : a twisting of a bodily organ or part on its own axis — **tor·sion·al** \'tȯr-shə-nəl\ *adj* — **tor·sion·al·ly** *adv*

tor·so \'tȯr-sō\ *n, pl* **torsos** *or* **tor·si** \'tȯr-ˌsē\ [It, lit., stalk] : the trunk of the human body

tort \'tȯrt\ *n* : a wrongful act which does not involve a breach of contract and for which the injured party can recover damages in a civil action

tor·til·la \tȯr-ˈtē-ə\ *n* : a round thin cake of unleavened cornmeal or wheat flour bread

tor·toise \'tȯr-təs\ *n* : TURTLE; *esp* : any of a family of land turtles

tor·toise·shell \-ˌshel\ *n* : the mottled horny substance of the shell of some turtles used in inlaying and in making various ornamental articles — **tortoiseshell** *adj*

tor·to·ni \tȯr-ˈtō-nē\ *n* : rich ice cream often made with minced almonds and chopped cherries and flavored with rum

tor·tu·ous \'tȯr-chə-wəs\ *adj* **1** : marked by twists or turns : WINDING ⟨a ~ path⟩ **2** : DEVIOUS, TRICKY

¹tor·ture \'tȯr-chər\ *n* **1** : anguish of body or mind **2**

: the infliction of severe pain esp. to punish or coerce — **tor·tur·ous** \'tȯrch-rəs, 'tȯr-chə-\ *adj*

²**torture** *vb* **tor·tured; tor·tur·ing** **1** : to cause intense suffering to : TORMENT **2** : to punish or coerce by inflicting severe pain **3** : TWIST, DISTORT ♦ **Synonyms** RACK, HARROW, AFFLICT, TRY — **tor·tur·er** *n*

To·ry \'tȯr-ē\ *n, pl* **Tories** **1** : a member of a chiefly 18th century British party upholding the established church and the traditional political structure **2** : an American supporter of the British during the American Revolution **3** *often not cap* : an extreme conservative — **Tory** *adj*

¹**toss** \'tȯs, 'täs\ *vb* **1** : to fling to and fro or up and down **2** : to throw with a quick light motion; *also* : BANDY **3** : to fling or lift with a sudden motion ⟨~ed her head angrily⟩ **4** : to move restlessly or turbulently ⟨~es on the waves⟩ **5** : to twist and turn repeatedly **6** : FLOUNCE **7** : to accomplish readily ⟨~ off an article⟩ **8** : to decide an issue by flipping a coin

²**toss** *n* : an act or instance of tossing; *esp* : TOSS-UP 1

toss–up \-ˌəp\ *n* **1** : a deciding by flipping a coin **2** : an even chance **3** : something that offers no clear basis for choice

¹**tot** \'tät\ *n* **1** : a small child **2** : a small drink of alcoholic liquor : SHOT

²**tot** *vb* **tot·ted; tot·ting** : to add up

³**tot** *abbr* total

¹**to·tal** \'tō-t³l\ *adj* **1** : making up a whole : ENTIRE ⟨~ amount⟩ **2** : COMPLETE, UTTER ⟨a ~ failure⟩ ⟨a ~ stranger⟩ **3** : involving a complete and unified effort esp. to achieve a desired effect — **to·tal·ly** *adv*

²**total** *n* **1** : SUM **4** **2** : the entire amount ♦ **Synonyms** AGGREGATE, WHOLE, GROSS, TOTALITY

³**total** *vb* **to·taled** *or* **to·talled; to·tal·ing** *or* **to·tal·ling** **1** : to add up : COMPUTE **2** : to amount to : NUMBER **3** : to make a total wreck of (a car)

to·tal·i·tar·i·an \tō-ˌta-lə-'ter-ē-ən\ *adj* : of, relating to, or advocating a political regime based on subordination of the individual to the state and strict control of all aspects of life esp. by coercive measures — **totalitarian** *n* — **to·tal·i·tar·i·an·ism** \-ē-ə-ˌni-zəm\ *n*

to·tal·i·ty \tō-'ta-lə-tē\ *n, pl* **-ties** **1** : an aggregate amount : SUM, WHOLE **2** : ENTIRETY, WHOLENESS

to·tal·iza·tor *or* **to·tal·isa·tor** \'tō-t³l-ə-ˌzā-tər\ *n* : a machine for registering and indicating the number of bets and the odds on a horse or dog race

¹**tote** \'tōt\ *vb* **tot·ed; tot·ing** : CARRY

²**tote** *vb* **tot·ed; tot·ing** : ADD, TOTAL — usu. used with *up*

to·tem \'tō-təm\ *n* [Ojibwa *oto·te·man* his totem] : an object (as an animal or plant) serving as the emblem of a family or clan and often as a reminder of its ancestry; *also* : something usu. carved or painted to represent such an object

totem pole *n* : a pole that is carved with a series of totems and is erected before the houses of some northwest American Indians

tot·ter \'tä-tər\ *vb* **1** : to tremble or rock as if about to fall : SWAY **2** : to move unsteadily : STAGGER

tou·can \'tü-ˌkan\ *n* [F, fr. Pg *tucano*, fr. Tupinambá (American Indian language of Brazil) *tukána*] : any of a family of chiefly fruit-eating birds of tropical America with brilliant coloring and a very large bill

¹**touch** \'təch\ *vb* **1** : to bring a bodily part (as the hand) into contact with so as to feel **2** : to be or cause to be in contact **3** : to strike or push lightly esp. with the hand or foot **4** : DISTURB, HARM **5** : to make use of ⟨never ~es alcohol⟩ **6** : to induce to give or lend **7** : to get to : REACH **8** : to refer to in passing : MENTION **9** : to affect the interest of : CONCERN **10** : to leave a mark on; *also* : BLEMISH **11** : to move to sympathetic feeling **12** : to come close : VERGE **13** : to have a bearing : RELATE **14** : to make a usu. brief or incidental stop in port ♦ **Synonyms** AFFECT, INFLUENCE, IMPRESS, STRIKE, SWAY

²**touch** *n* **1** : a light stroke or tap **2** : the act or fact of touching or being touched **3** : the sense by which pressure or traction on the skin or mucous membrane is perceived; *also* : a particular sensation conveyed by this sense **4** : mental or moral sensitiveness : TACT **5** : a small quantity : HINT ⟨a ~ of spring in the air⟩ **6** : a manner of striking or touching esp. the keys of a keyboard instrument **7** : an improving detail ⟨add a few ~es to the painting⟩ **8** : distinctive manner or skill ⟨the ~ of

a master⟩ **9** : the state of being in contact ⟨keep in ~⟩ ♦ **Synonyms** SUGGESTION, SUSPICION, TINCTURE, TINGE

touch·down \'təch-ˌdau̇n\ *n* : the act of scoring six points in American football by being lawfully in possession of the ball on, above, or behind an opponent's goal line

tou·ché \tü-'shā\ *interj* [F] — used to acknowledge a hit in fencing or the success of an argument, an accusation, or a witty point

touch football *n* : football in which touching is substituted for tackling

touch·ing \'tə-chiṅ\ *adj* : capable of stirring emotions ♦ **Synonyms** MOVING, IMPRESSIVE, POIGNANT, AFFECTING

touch off *vb* **1** : to describe with precision **2** : to start by or as if by touching with fire ⟨*touched off* a riot⟩

touch screen *n* : a display screen (as for a computer) on which the user selects options by touching the screen

touch·stone \'təch-ˌstōn\ *n* : a test or criterion of genuineness or quality ♦ **Synonyms** STANDARD, GAUGE, BENCHMARK, YARDSTICK

touch–tone \'təch-'tōn\ *adj* : of, relating to, or being a telephone having push buttons that produce tones corresponding to numbers

touch up *vb* **1** : to improve or perfect by small additional strokes or alterations ⟨*touch up* a photo⟩ — **touch–up** \'təch-ˌəp\ *n*

touchy \'tə-chē\ *adj* **touch·i·er; -est** **1** : easily offended : PEEVISH **2** : calling for tact in treatment ⟨a ~ subject⟩ ♦ **Synonyms** IRASCIBLE, CRANKY, CROSS, TETCHY, TESTY

¹**tough** \'təf\ *adj* **1** : strong or firm in texture but flexible and not brittle **2** : not easily chewed **3** : characterized by severity and determination ⟨a ~ policy⟩ **4** : capable of enduring strain or hardship : ROBUST **5** : hard to influence : STUBBORN **6** : difficult to accomplish, resolve, or cope with ⟨a ~ problem⟩ **7** : ROWDYISH ♦ **Synonyms** TENACIOUS, STOUT, STURDY, STALWART — **tough·ly** *adv* — **tough·ness** *n*

²**tough** *n* : a tough person : ROWDY

tough·en \'tə-fən\ *vb* **tough·ened; tough·en·ing** : to make or become tough ⟨training camp ~ed him up⟩

tou·pee \tü-'pā\ *n* [F *toupet* forelock] : a small wig for a bald spot

¹**tour** \'tu̇r, *1 is also* 'tau̇(-ə)r\ *n* **1** : one's turn : SHIFT **2** : a journey in which one returns to the starting point

²**tour** *vb* : to make a tour

tour de force \ˌtu̇r-də-'fȯrs\ *n, pl* **tours de force** *same*\ [F] : a feat or display of strength, skill, or ingenuity

Tou·rette's syndrome \tü-'rets-\ *n* : a familial neurological disorder marked by recurrent involuntary tics and vocal sounds

tour·ism \'tu̇r-ˌi-zəm\ *n* **1** : the practice of traveling for recreation **2** : promotion of touring **3** : accommodation of tourists — **tour·ist** \-ist\ *n*

tourist class *n* : economy accommodations (as on a ship)

tour·ma·line \'tu̇r-mə-lən, -ˌlēn\ *n* : a mineral that when transparent is valued as a gem

tour·na·ment \'tu̇r-nə-mənt, 'tər-\ *n* **1** : a medieval sport in which mounted armored knights contended with blunted lances or swords **2** : a championship series of games or athletic contests

tour·ney \-nē\ *n, pl* **tourneys** : TOURNAMENT

tour·ni·quet \'tu̇r-ni-kət, 'tər-\ *n* : a device (as a tight bandage) to check bleeding or blood flow

tou·sle \'tau̇-zəl\ *vb* **tou·sled; tou·sling** : to disorder by rough handling : DISHEVEL, MUSS ⟨*tousled* his hair⟩

tout \'tau̇t, *2 is also* 'tüt\ *vb* **1** : to give a tip or solicit bets on a racehorse **2** : to praise or publicize loudly — **tout** *n*

¹**tow** \'tō\ *vb* : to draw or pull along behind

²**tow** *n* **1** : an act of towing or condition of being towed **2** : something (as a barge) that is towed

³**tow** *n* : short or broken fiber (as of flax or hemp) used esp. for yarn, twine, or stuffing

to·ward \'tōrd, 'tō-ərd, tə-'wȯrd\ *or* **to·wards** \'tōrdz, 'tō-ərdz, tə-'wȯrdz\ *prep* **1** : in the direction of ⟨heading ~ the river⟩ **2** : along a course leading to ⟨efforts ~ reconciliation⟩ **3** : in regard to ⟨tolerance ~ minorities⟩ **4** : so as to face ⟨turn the chair ~ the window⟩ **5** : close upon ⟨it was getting along ~ sundown⟩ **6** : for part payment of ⟨here's $100 ~ your tuition⟩

tow·boat \'tō-ˌbōt\ *n* : TUGBOAT

tow·el \'taù(-ə)l\ *n* : an absorbent cloth or paper for wiping or drying

tow·el·ing *or* **tow·el·ling** *n* : a cotton or linen fabric for making towels

¹**tow·er** \'taù(-ə)r\ *n* **1** : a tall structure either isolated or built upon a larger structure ⟨an observation ~⟩ **2** : a towering citadel **3** : a personal computer case that stands in an upright position — **tow·ered** *adj*

²**tower** *vb* : to reach or rise to a great height

tow·er·ing \'taù(-ə)r-iŋ\ *adj* **1** : LOFTY ⟨~ pines⟩ **2** : reaching high intensity ⟨a ~ rage⟩ **3** : EXCESSIVE ⟨~ ambition⟩

tow·head \'tō-ˌhed\ *n* : a person having whitish blond hair — **tow·head·ed** \-ˌhe-dəd\ *adj*

to·whee \'tō-ˌhē, 'tō-(ˌ)ē, tō-'hē\ *n* : a common finch of eastern No. America having the male black, white, and reddish; *also* : any of several closely related finches

to wit *adv* : NAMELY

town \'taùn\ *n* **1** : a compactly settled area usu. larger than a village but smaller than a city **2** : CITY **3** : the inhabitants of a town **4** : a New England territorial and political unit usu. containing both rural and urban areas; *also* : a New England community in which matters of local government are decided by a general assembly **(town meeting)** of qualified voters

town house *n* **1** : the city residence of a person having a country home **2** : a single-family house of two or sometimes three stories connected to another house by a common wall

town·ie *or* **towny** \'taù-nē\ *n, pl* **townies** : a permanent resident of a town as distinguished from a member of another group

towns·folk \'taùnz-ˌfōk\ *n pl* : TOWNSPEOPLE

town·ship \'taùn-ˌship\ *n* **1** : TOWN 4 **2** : a unit of local government in some states **3** : an unorganized subdivision of a county **4** : a division of territory in surveys of U.S. public land containing 36 square miles **5** : an area in the Republic of South Africa segregated for occupation by persons of non-European descent

towns·man \'taùnz-mən\ *n* **1** : a native or resident of a town or city **2** : a fellow citizen of a town

towns·peo·ple \-ˌpē-pəl\ *n pl* **1** : the inhabitants of a town or city **2** : town-bred persons

towns·wom·an \-ˌwù-mən\ *n* **1** : a woman who is a native or resident of a town or city **2** : a woman who is a fellow citizen of a town

tow·path \'tō-ˌpath, -ˌpäth\ *n* : a path (as along a canal) traveled esp. by draft animals towing boats

tow truck *n* : a truck equipped for towing vehicles

tox·emia \täk-'sē-mē-ə\ *n* : a bodily disorder associated with the presence of toxic substances in the blood

tox·ic \'täk-sik\ *adj* [LL *toxicus*, fr. L *toxicum* poison, fr. Gk *toxikon* arrow poison, fr. neut. of *toxikos* of a bow, fr. *toxon* bow, arrow] : of, relating to, or caused by poison or a toxin : POISONOUS — **tox·ic·i·ty** \täk-'si-sə-tē\ *n*

tox·i·col·o·gy \ˌtäk-si-'kä-lə-jē\ *n* : a science that deals with poisons and esp. with problems of their use and control — **tox·i·co·log·i·cal** \-kə-'lä-ji-kəl\ *also* **tox·i·co·log·ic** \-kə-'lä-jik\ *adj* — **tox·i·col·o·gist** \-'kä-lə-jist\ *n*

toxic shock syndrome *n* : an acute disease associated with the presence of a bacterium that is characterized by fever, diarrhea, nausea, diffuse erythema, and shock and occurs esp. in menstruating females using tampons

tox·in \'täk-sən\ *n* : a poisonous substance produced by metabolic activities of a living organism that is usu. unstable, very toxic when introduced into the tissues, and usu. capable of inducing antibodies

¹**toy** \'tói\ *n* **1** : something trifling **2** : a small ornament : BAUBLE **3** : something for a child to play with

²**toy** *vb* **1** : to deal with something lightly : TRIFLE **2** : FLIRT **3** : to amuse oneself as if with a plaything

³**toy** *adj* **1** : DIMINUTIVE ⟨a ~ dog⟩ **2** : designed for use as a toy

tp *abbr* **1** title page **2** township

tpk *or* **tpke** *abbr* turnpike

tr *abbr* **1** translated; translation; translator **2** transpose **3** troop

¹**trace** \'trās\ *n* **1** : a mark (as a footprint or track) left by something that has passed **2** : a minute or barely detectable amount ⟨disappeared without a ~⟩

²**trace** *vb* **traced; trac·ing** **1** : to mark out : SKETCH **2**

: to form (as letters) carefully **3** : to copy (a drawing) by marking lines on transparent paper laid over the drawing to be copied **4** : to follow the trail of : track down **5** : to study out and follow the development of ⟨~ed his family's history⟩ — **trace·able** *adj*

³**trace** *n* : either of two lines of a harness for fastening a draft animal to a vehicle

trac·er \'trā-sər\ *n* **1** : one that traces **2** : ammunition containing a chemical to mark the flight of projectiles by a trail of smoke or light

trac·ery \'trā-sə-rē\ *n, pl* **-er·ies** : ornamental work having a design with branching or interlacing lines

tracery

tra·chea \'trā-kē-ə\ *n, pl* **-che·ae** \-kē-ˌē\ *also* **-che·as** *or* **-chea** : the main tube by which air passes from the larynx to the lungs of vertebrates — **tra·che·al** \-kē-əl\ *adj*

tra·che·ot·o·my \ˌtrā-kē-'ä-tə-mē\ *n, pl* **-mies** : the surgical operation of cutting into the trachea esp. through the skin

tracing *n* **1** : the act of one that traces **2** : something that is traced **3** : a graphic record made by an instrument for measuring vibrations or pulsations

¹**track** \'trak\ *n* **1** : a mark left in passing **2** : PATH, ROUTE, TRAIL **3** : a course laid out for racing; *also* : track-and-field sports **4** : one of a series of paths along which material (as music) is recorded (as on a CD or magnetic tape) **5** : the course along which something moves; *esp* : a way made by two parallel lines of metal rails **6** : awareness of a fact or progression ⟨lost ~ of time⟩ **7** : either of two endless metal belts on which a vehicle (as a bulldozer) travels

²**track** *vb* **1** : to follow the tracks or traces of : TRAIL **2** : to observe the moving path of (as a missile) **3** : to make tracks on **4** : to carry (as mud) on the feet and deposit — **track·er** *n*

track·age \'tra-kij\ *n* : lines of railway track

track–and–field *adj* : of or relating to athletic contests held on a running track or on the adjacent field

¹**tract** \'trakt\ *n* **1** : an area without precise boundaries ⟨huge ~s of land⟩ **2** : a defined area of land **3** : a system of body parts or organs that act together to perform some function ⟨the digestive ~⟩

²**tract** *n* : a pamphlet of political or religious propaganda

trac·ta·ble \'trak-tə-bəl\ *adj* : easily controlled : DOCILE
   ♦ **Synonyms** AMENABLE, OBEDIENT, BIDDABLE

tract house *n* : any of many similar houses built on a tract of land

trac·tion \'trak-shən\ *n* **1** : the act of drawing : the state of being drawn **2** : the drawing of a vehicle by motive power; *also* : the particular form of motive power used **3** : the adhesive friction of a body on a surface on which it moves **4** : a pulling force applied to a skeletal structure (as a broken bone) by means of a special device; *also* : a state of tension created by such a pulling force ⟨a leg in ~⟩ — **trac·tion·al** \-shə-nəl\ *adj* — **trac·tive** \'trak-tiv\ *adj*

trac·tor \'trak-tər\ *n* **1** : an automotive vehicle used esp. for drawing farm equipment **2** : a truck for hauling a trailer

¹**trade** \'trād\ *n* **1** : one's regular business or work : OCCUPATION **2** : an occupation requiring manual or mechanical skill **3** : the persons engaged in a business or industry **4** : the business of buying and selling or bartering commodities **5** : an act of trading : TRANSACTION

²**trade** *vb* **trad·ed; trad·ing** **1** : to give in exchange for

another commodity : BARTER **2** : to engage in the exchange, purchase, or sale of goods **3** : to deal regularly as a customer — **trade on** : EXPLOIT ⟨*trades on* his family name⟩

trade–in \'trād-ˌin\ *n* : an item of merchandise traded in

trade in *vb* : to turn in as part payment for a purchase

¹**trade·mark** \'trād-ˌmärk\ *n* : a device (as a word or mark) that points distinctly to the origin or ownership of merchandise to which it is applied and that is legally reserved for the exclusive use of the owner; *also* : something that identifies a person or thing

²**trademark** *vb* : to secure the trademark rights for ⟨that name is ∼*ed*⟩

trade name *n* : a name that is given by a manufacturer or merchant to a product to distinguish it as made or sold by that manufacturer or merchant and that may be used and protected as a trademark

trad·er \'trā-dər\ *n* **1** : a person whose business is buying or selling **2** : a ship engaged in trade

trades·man \'trādz-mən\ *n* **1** : one who runs a retail store : SHOPKEEPER **2** : CRAFTSMAN

trades·peo·ple \-ˌpē-pəl\ *n pl* : people engaged in trade

trade union *n* : LABOR UNION

trade wind *n* : a wind blowing almost constantly in one direction

trading stamp *n* : a printed stamp given as a premium to a retail customer that when accumulated may be redeemed for merchandise

tra·di·tion \trə-'di-shən\ *n* **1** : an inherited, established, or customary pattern of thought or action **2** : the handing down of beliefs and customs by word of mouth or by example without written instruction; *also* : a belief or custom thus handed down — **tra·di·tion·al** \-ˌdi-shə-nəl\ *adj* — **tra·di·tion·al·ly** *adv*

tra·duce \trə-'düs, -'dyüs\ *vb* **tra·duced; tra·duc·ing** : to lower the reputation of : DEFAME, SLANDER ⟨he was *traduced* in the past⟩ ✦ *Synonyms* MALIGN, LIBEL, CALUMNIATE — **tra·duc·er** *n*

¹**traf·fic** \'tra-fik\ *n* **1** : the business of bartering or buying and selling **2** : communication or dealings between individuals or groups **3** : the movement (as of vehicles) along a route; *also* : the vehicles, people, ships, or planes moving along a route **4** : the passengers or cargo carried by a transportation system

²**traffic** *vb* **traf·ficked; traf·fick·ing 1** : to carry on business dealings **2** : DEAL, TRADE ⟨*trafficked* in illegal drugs⟩ — **traf·fick·er** *n*

traffic circle *n* : ROTARY 2

traffic light *n* : a visual signal (as a system of lights) for controlling traffic

tra·ge·di·an \trə-'jē-dē-ən\ *n* **1** : a writer of tragedies **2** : an actor who plays tragic roles

tra·ge·di·enne \trə-ˌjē-dē-'en\ *n* [F] : an actress who plays tragic roles

trag·e·dy \'tra-jə-dē\ *n, pl* **-dies** [ME *tragedie*, fr. MF, fr. L *tragoedia*, fr. Gk *tragōidia*, fr. *tragos* goat + *aeidein* to sing] **1** : a serious drama with a sorrowful or disastrous conclusion **2** : a disastrous event : CALAMITY; *also* : MISFORTUNE **3** : tragic quality or element ⟨the ∼ of life⟩

trag·ic \'tra-jik\ *also* **trag·i·cal** \-ji-kəl\ *adj* **1** : of, relating to, or expressive of tragedy **2** : appropriate to tragedy **3** : LAMENTABLE, UNFORTUNATE ⟨a ∼ mistake⟩ — **trag·i·cal·ly** \-ji-k(ə-)lē\ *adv*

¹**trail** \'trāl\ *vb* **1** : to hang down so as to drag along or sweep the ground **2** : to draw or drag along behind **3** : to extend over a surface in a straggling manner **4** : to lag behind **5** : to follow the track of : PURSUE **6** : DWINDLE ⟨her voice ∼*ed* off⟩

²**trail** *n* **1** : something that trails or is trailed ⟨a ∼ of smoke⟩ **2** : a trace or mark left by something that has passed or been drawn along : SCENT, TRACK ⟨a ∼ of blood⟩ **3** : a beaten path; *also* : a marked path through woods

trail bike *n* : a small motorcycle for off-road use

trail·blaz·er \-ˌblā-zər\ *n* : PATHFINDER, PIONEER — **trail·blaz·ing** *adj or n*

trail·er \'trā-lər\ *n* **1** : one that trails; *esp* : a creeping plant (as an ivy) **2** : a vehicle that is hauled by another (as a tractor) **3** : a vehicle equipped to serve wherever parked as a dwelling or place of business **4** : PREVIEW 3

trailer park *n* : a site equipped to accommodate mobile homes

trailing arbutus *n* : a creeping spring-flowering plant of the heath family with fragrant pink or white flowers

¹**train** \'trān\ *n* [ME, fr. AF, fr. *trainer* to draw, drag] **1** : a part of a gown that trails behind the wearer **2** : RETINUE **3** : a moving file of persons, vehicles, or animals **4** : a connected series ⟨a ∼ of thought⟩ **5** : AFTERMATH **6** : a connected line of railroad cars usu. hauled by a locomotive ✦ *Synonyms* SUCCESSION, SEQUENCE, PROCESSION, CHAIN

²**train** *vb* [ME, to trail, drag, train, fr. AF *trainer*] **1** : to cause to grow as desired ⟨∼ a vine on a trellis⟩ **2** : to form by instruction, discipline, or drill **3** : to make or become prepared (as by exercise) for a test of skill **4** : to aim or point at an object ⟨∼ guns on a fort⟩ ✦ *Synonyms* DISCIPLINE, SCHOOL, EDUCATE, INSTRUCT — **train·er** *n*

train·ee \trā-'nē\ *n* : one who is being trained esp. for a job

train·ing \'trā-niŋ\ *n* **1** : the act, process, or method of one who trains **2** : the skill, knowledge, or experience gained by one who trains

train·man \-mən\ *n* : a member of a train crew

traipse \'trāps\ *vb* **traipsed; traips·ing** : TRAMP, WALK ⟨∼ the countryside⟩

trait \'trāt\ *n* **1** : a distinguishing quality (as of personality) **2** : an inherited characteristic

trai·tor \'trā-tər\ *n* [ME *traytour*, fr. AF *traitre*, fr. L *traditor*, fr. *tradere* to hand over, deliver, betray, fr. *trans-* across + *dare* to give] **1** : one who betrays another's trust or is false to an obligation **2** : one who commits treason — **trai·tor·ous** *adj*

tra·jec·to·ry \trə-'jek-tə-rē\ *n, pl* **-ries** : the curve that a body (as a planet in its orbit) describes in space

tram \'tram\ *n* **1** : a boxlike car running on rails (as in a mine) **2** *chiefly Brit* : STREETCAR **3** : an overhead cable car

¹**tram·mel** \'tra-məl\ *n* [ME *tramayle*, a kind of net, fr. OF *tramail*, fr. LL *tremaculum*, fr. L *tres* three + *macula* mesh, spot] : something impeding activity, progress, or freedom — usu. used in pl.

²**trammel** *vb* **-meled** *or* **-melled; -mel·ing** *or* **-mel·ling 1** : to catch and hold in or as if in a net **2** : HAMPER ✦ *Synonyms* CLOG, FETTER, SHACKLE, HOBBLE

¹**tramp** \'tramp, *1 & 3 are also* 'trämp, 'trömp\ *vb* **1** : to walk, tread, or step heavily **2** : to walk about or through; *also* : HIKE ⟨∼*ed* through the woods⟩ **3** : to tread on forcibly and repeatedly

²**tramp** \'tramp, *5 is also* 'trämp, 'trömp\ *n* **1** : VAGRANT **2** : a foot traveler **3** : an immoral woman; *esp* : PROSTITUTE **4** : a walking trip : HIKE **5** : the succession of sounds made by the beating of feet on a road **6** : a ship that does not follow a regular course but takes cargo to any port — **trampy** \'tram-pē\ *adj*

tram·ple \'tram-pəl\ *vb* **tram·pled; tram·pling 1** : to tread heavily so as to bruise, crush, or injure **2** : to inflict injury or destruction **3** : to press down or crush by or as if by treading — **trample** *n* — **tram·pler** *n*

tram·po·line \ˌtram-pə-'lēn, 'tram-pə-ˌlēn\ *n* [It *trampolino* springboard] : a resilient sheet or web (as of nylon) supported by springs in a metal frame and used as a springboard in tumbling — **tram·po·lin·ist** \-'lē-nist, -ˌlē-\ *n*

trance \'trans\ *n* [ME, fr. AF *transe*, death, coma, rapture, fr. *transir* to depart, die, fr. L *transire* to cross, pass by, fr. *trans-* across + *ire* to go] **1** : STUPOR, DAZE **2** : a sleeplike state of altered consciousness (as of deep hypnosis) **3** : a state of very deep absorption — **trance·like** \-ˌlīk\ *adj*

tran·quil \'traŋ-kwəl, 'tran-\ *adj* : free from agitation or disturbance : QUIET ✦ *Synonyms* SERENE, PLACID, PEACEFUL — **tran·quil·li·ty** *or* **tran·quil·i·ty** \tran-'kwi-lə-tē, traŋ-\ *n* — **tran·quil·ly** *adv*

tran·quil·ize *also* **tran·quil·lize** \'traŋ-kwə-ˌlīz, 'tran-\ *vb* **-ized** *also* **-lized; -iz·ing** *also* **-liz·ing** : to make or become tranquil; *esp* : to relieve of mental tension and anxiety by means of drugs

tran·quil·iz·er *also* **tran·quil·liz·er** \-ˌlī-zər\ *n* : a drug used to relieve mental disturbance (as tension and anxiety)

¹**trans** \'tranz\ *adj* : TRANSGENDER, TRANSSEXUAL

²**trans** *abbr* **1** transaction **2** transitive **3** translated; translation; translator **4** transmission **5** transportation **6** transverse

trans·act \tran-'zakt, -'sakt\ *vb* : CARRY OUT, PERFORM; *also* : CONDUCT

trans·ac·tion \-'zak-shən, -'sak-\ *n* **1** : something transacted; *esp* : a business deal **2** : an act or process of transacting **3** *pl* : the records of the proceedings of a society or organization — **trans·ac·tion·al** \-shnəl, -shə-nᵊl\ *adj*

trans·at·lan·tic \ˌtrans-ət-'lan-tik, ˌtranz-\ *adj* : crossing or extending across or situated beyond the Atlantic Ocean ⟨a ~ flight⟩

trans·ax·le \trans-'ak-səl\ *n* : a unit combining the transmission and differential gear of a front-wheel-drive automobile

trans·ceiv·er \tran-'sē-vər\ *n* : a radio transmitter-receiver that uses many of the same components for both transmission and reception

tran·scend \tran-'send\ *vb* **1** : to rise above the limits of ⟨music that ~s cultural boundaries⟩ **2** : SURPASS ♦ **Synonyms** EXCEED, OUTDO, OUTSHINE, OUTSTRIP

tran·scen·dent \-'sen-dənt\ *adj* **1** : exceeding usual limits : SURPASSING **2** : transcending material existence ♦ **Synonyms** SUPERLATIVE, SUPREME, PEERLESS, INCOMPARABLE

tran·scen·den·tal \ˌtran-ˌsen-'den-tᵊl, -sən-\ *adj* **1** : TRANSCENDENT **2** : of, relating to, or characteristic of transcendentalism; *also* : ABSTRUSE

tran·scen·den·tal·ism \-tə-ˌli-zəm\ *n* : a philosophy holding that ultimate reality is unknowable and asserting the primacy of the spiritual over the material and empirical — **tran·scen·den·tal·ist** \-tə-list\ *adj or n*

trans·con·ti·nen·tal \ˌtrans-ˌkän-tə-'nen-tᵊl\ *adj* : extending or going across a continent ⟨a ~ railroad⟩

tran·scribe \tran-'skrīb\ *vb* **tran·scribed; tran·scrib·ing 1** : to write a copy of **2** : to make a copy of (dictated or recorded matter) in longhand or on a typewriter **3** : to represent (speech sounds) by means of phonetic symbols; *also* : to make a musical transcription of

tran·script \'tran-ˌskript\ *n* **1** : a written, printed, or typed copy **2** : an official copy esp. of a student's educational record

tran·scrip·tion \tran-'skrip-shən\ *n* **1** : an act or process of transcribing **2** : COPY, TRANSCRIPT **3** : an arrangement of a musical composition for some instrument or voice other than the original **4** : the process of constructing a messenger RNA molecule using a DNA molecule as a template

tran·scrip·tion·ist \-shə-nist\ *n* : one that transcribes; *esp* : a typist who transcribes medical reports

trans·der·mal \trans-'dər-məl, 'tranz-\ *adj* : relating to, being, or supplying a medication in a form for absorption through the skin ⟨~ nicotine patch⟩

trans·duc·er \trans-'dü-sər, tranz-, -'dyü-\ *n* : a device that is actuated by power from one system and supplies power usu. in another form to a second system

tran·sept \'tran-ˌsept\ *n* : the part of a cruciform church that crosses at right angles to the greatest length; *also* : either of the projecting ends

trans fat \'tran(t)s-, 'tranz-\ *n* : a fat containing unsaturated fatty acids (**trans–fatty acids**) that have been linked to an increase in blood cholesterol

¹trans·fer \trans-'fər, 'trans-ˌfər\ *vb* **trans·ferred; trans·fer·ring 1** : to pass or cause to pass from one person, place, or situation to another : MOVE, TRANSMIT **2** : to make over the possession of : CONVEY **3** : to print or copy from one surface to another by contact **4** : to change from one vehicle or transportation line to another — **trans·fer·able** \trans-'fər-ə-bəl\ *adj* — **trans·fer·al** \-əl\ *n*

²trans·fer \'trans-ˌfər\ *n* **1** : conveyance of right, title, or interest in property from one person to another **2** : an act or process of transferring **3** : one that transfers or is transferred **4** : a ticket entitling a passenger to continue a trip on another route

trans·fer·ence \trans-'fər-əns\ *n* : an act, process, or instance of transferring

trans·fig·ure \trans-'fi-gyər\ *vb* **-ured; -ur·ing 1** : to change the form or appearance of **2** : EXALT, GLORIFY — **trans·fig·u·ra·tion** \ˌtrans-ˌfi-gyə-'rā-shən, -gə-\ *n*

trans·fix \trans-'fiks\ *vb* **1** : to pierce through with or as if with a pointed weapon **2** : to hold motionless by or as if by piercing ⟨stood ~ed by her gaze⟩

trans·form \trans-'fòrm\ *vb* : to change in structure, appearance, or character ♦ **Synonyms** TRANSMUTE, TRANSFIGURE, TRANSMOGRIFY — **trans·for·ma·tion** \ˌtrans-fər-'mā-shən\ *n* — **trans·for·ma·tive** \trans-'fòr-mə-tiv\ *adj*

trans·form·er \trans-'fòr-mər\ *n* : one that transforms; *esp* : a device for converting variations of current in one circuit into variations of voltage and current in another circuit

trans·fuse \trans-'fyüz\ *vb* **trans·fused; trans·fus·ing 1** : to cause to pass from one to another **2** : to diffuse into or through **3** : to transfer (as blood) into a vein or an artery of a person or animal — **trans·fu·sion** \-'fyü-zhən\ *n*

trans·gen·der \tranz-'jen-dər\ *also* **trans·gen·dered** \-dərd\ *adj* : of, relating to, or being a person whose gender identity differs from, or the sex the person had or was identified as having at birth

trans·gen·ic \tran(t)s-'je-nik\ *adj* : being or used to produce an organism or cell with genes introduced from another species of organism ⟨~ crops⟩

trans·gress \trans-'gres, tranz-\ *vb* [ME, fr. MF *transgresser*, fr. L *transgressus*, pp. of *transgredi* to step beyond or across, fr. *trans-* across + *gradi* to step] **1** : to go beyond the limits set by ⟨~ the divine law⟩ **2** : to go beyond : EXCEED **3** : SIN — **trans·gres·sion** \-'gre-shən\ *n* — **trans·gres·sor** \-'gre-sər\ *n*

¹tran·sient \'tran-shənt; -sē-ənt, -shē-, -zē-\ *adj* **1** : not lasting long : SHORT-LIVED ⟨~ visitors⟩ **2** : passing through a place with only a brief stay ⟨~ visitors⟩ ♦ **Synonyms** TRANSITORY, PASSING, MOMENTARY, FLEETING — **tran·sient·ly** *adv*

²transient *n* : one that is transient; *esp* : a transient guest

tran·sis·tor \tran-'zis-tər, -'sis-\ *n* [*transfer* + *resistor*; fr. its transferring an electrical signal across a resistor] **1** : a small electronic semiconductor device used in electronic equipment **2** : a radio having transistors

tran·sis·tor·ized \-tə-ˌrīzd\ *adj* : having or using transistors

tran·sit \'tran-sət, -zət\ *n* **1** : a passing through, across, or over : PASSAGE **2** : conveyance of persons or things from one place to another **3** : usu. local transportation esp. of people by public conveyance **4** : a surveyor's instrument for measuring angles

tran·si·tion \tran-'si-shən, -'zi-\ *n* : passage from one state, place, stage, or subject to another : CHANGE — **tran·si·tion·al** \-'si-shə-nəl, 'zi-\ *adj*

tran·si·tive \'tran-sə-tiv, -zə-\ *adj* **1** : having or containing an object required to complete the meaning ⟨a ~ verb⟩ **2** : TRANSITIONAL — **tran·si·tive·ly** *adv* — **tran·si·tive·ness** *n* — **tran·si·tiv·i·ty** \ˌtran-sə-'ti-və-tē, -zə-\ *n*

tran·si·to·ry \'tran-sə-ˌtòr-ē, -zə-\ *adj* : of brief duration : SHORT-LIVED, TEMPORARY ♦ **Synonyms** TRANSIENT, PASSING, MOMENTARY, FLEETING

transl *abbr* translated; translation

trans·late \trans-'lāt, tranz-\ *vb* **trans·lat·ed; trans·lat·ing 1** : to change from one place, state, or form to another **2** : to convey to heaven without death **3** : to turn into one's own or another language — **trans·lat·able** *adj* — **trans·la·tor** \-'lā-tər\ *n*

trans·la·tion \tran(t)s-'lā-shən, tranz-\ *n* **1** : an act, process, or instance of translating **2** : the process of forming a protein molecule from information in messenger RNA — **trans·la·tion·al** \-shnəl, -shə-nᵊl\ *adj*

trans·lit·er·ate \trans-'li-tə-ˌrāt, tranz-\ *vb* **-at·ed; -at·ing** : to represent or spell in the characters of another alphabet — **trans·lit·er·a·tion** \ˌtrans-ˌli-tə-'rā-shən, ˌtranz-\ *n*

trans·lu·cent \trans-'lü-sᵊnt, tranz-\ *adj* : not transparent but clear enough to allow light to pass through — **trans·lu·cence** \-sᵊns\ *n* — **trans·lu·cen·cy** \-sᵊn-sē\ *n* — **trans·lu·cent·ly** *adv*

trans·mi·grate \-'mī-ˌgrāt\ *vb* : to pass at death from one body or being to another — **trans·mi·gra·tion** \ˌtrans-mī-'grā-shən, ˌtranz-\ *n* — **trans·mi·gra·to·ry** \trans-'mī-grə-ˌtòr-ē\ *adj*

trans·mis·sion \-'mi-shən\ *n* **1** : an act or process of transmitting **2** : the passage of radio waves between transmitting stations and receiving stations **3** : the gears by which power is transmitted from the engine of an automobile to the axle that propels the vehicle **4** : something transmitted

trans·mit \-'mit\ *vb* **trans·mit·ted; trans·mit·ting 1** : to transfer from one person or place to another : FORWARD

2 : to pass on by or as if by inheritance **3** : to cause or allow to spread abroad or to another ⟨∼ a disease⟩ **4** : to cause (as light, electricity, or force) to pass through space or a medium **5** : to send out (radio or television signals) ✦ *Synonyms* CONVEY, COMMUNICATE, IMPART — **trans·mis·si·ble** \-'mi-sə-bəl\ *adj* — **trans·mit·ta·ble** \-'mi-tə-bəl\ *adj* — **trans·mit·tal** \-'mit-ᵊl\ *n*

trans·mit·ter \-'mi-tər\ *n* : one that transmits; *esp* : an apparatus for transmitting telegraph, radio, or television signals

trans·mog·ri·fy \trans-'mä-grə-ˌfī, tranz-\ *vb* **-fied; -fy·ing** : to change or alter often with grotesque or humorous effect — **trans·mog·ri·fi·ca·tion** \-ˌmä-grə-fə-'kā-shən\ *n*

trans·mute \-'myüt\ *vb* **trans·muted; trans·mut·ing** : to change or alter in form, appearance, or nature ✦ *Synonyms* TRANSFORM, CONVERT, TRANSFIGURE, METAMORPHOSE — **trans·mu·ta·tion** \ˌtrans-myü-'tā-shən, tranz-\ *n*

trans·na·tion·al \-'na-shə-nəl\ *adj* : extending beyond national boundaries

trans·oce·an·ic \ˌtrans-ˌō-shē-'a-nik, ˌtranz-\ *adj* **1** : lying or dwelling beyond the ocean **2** : crossing or extending across the ocean

tran·som \'tran-səm\ *n* **1** : a piece (as a crossbar in the frame of a window or door) that lies crosswise in a structure **2** : a window above an opening (as a door) built on and often hinged to a horizontal crossbar

tran·son·ic *also* **trans·son·ic** \trans-'sä-nik\ *adj* : being or relating to speeds near that of sound in air or about 741 miles (1185 kilometers) per hour

trans·pa·cif·ic \ˌtrans-pə-'si-fik\ *adj* : crossing, extending across, or situated beyond the Pacific Ocean

trans·par·ent \trans-'per-ənt\ *adj* **1** : clear enough to be seen through **2** : SHEER, DIAPHANOUS ⟨a ∼ fabric⟩ **3** : readily understood : CLEAR; *also* : easily detected ⟨a ∼ lie⟩ ✦ *Synonyms* LUCID, TRANSLUCENT, LUCENT — **trans·par·en·cy** \-ən-sē\ *n* — **trans·par·ent·ly** *adv*

tran·spire \trans-'pī(-ə)r\ *vb* **trans·pired; trans·pir·ing** [MF *transpirer*, fr. ML *transpirare*, fr. L *trans-* across + *spirare* to breathe] **1** : to pass or give off (as water vapor) through pores or a membrane **2** : to become known **3** : to take place : HAPPEN — **tran·spi·ra·tion** \ˌtrans-pə-'rā-shən\ *n*

¹**trans·plant** \trans-'plant\ *vb* **1** : to dig up and plant elsewhere **2** : to remove from one place and settle or introduce elsewhere : TRANSPORT **3** : to transfer (an organ or tissue) from one part or individual to another — **trans·plan·ta·tion** \ˌtrans-ˌplan-'tā-shən\ *n*

²**trans·plant** \'trans-ˌplant\ *n* **1** : a person or thing transplanted **2** : the act or process of transplanting

trans·po·lar \trans-'pō-lər\ *adj* : going or extending across either of the polar regions

tran·spon·der \tran-'spän-dər\ *n* [*transmitter* + re*sponder*] : a radio or radar set that upon receiving a certain signal emits a radio signal and that is used to locate and identify objects and in satellites to relay communications signals

¹**trans·port** \trans-'pȯrt\ *vb* **1** : to convey from one place to another : CARRY **2** : to carry away by strong emotion : ENRAPTURE **3** : to send to a penal colony overseas ✦ *Synonyms* BEAR, CARRY — **trans·por·ta·tion** \ˌtrans-pər-'tā-shən\ *n* — **trans·port·er** *n*

²**trans·port** \'trans-ˌpȯrt\ *n* **1** : an act of transporting **2** : strong or intensely pleasurable emotion ⟨∼s of joy⟩ **3** : a ship used in transporting troops or supplies; *also* : a vehicle (as a truck or plane) used to transport persons or goods

trans·pose \trans-'pōz\ *vb* **trans·posed; trans·pos·ing** **1** : to change the position or sequence of ⟨∼ the letters in a word⟩ **2** : to write or perform (a musical composition) in a different key — **trans·po·si·tion** \ˌtrans-pə-'zi-shən\ *n*

trans·sex·u·al \(ˌ)tran(t)s-'sek-sh(ə-)wəl, -shəl\ *adj* : of, relating to, or being a person whose gender identity is opposite the sex the person had or was identified as having at birth

trans·ship \tran-'ship, trans-\ *vb* : to transfer for further transportation from one ship or conveyance to another — **trans·ship·ment** *n*

tran·sub·stan·ti·a·tion \ˌtran-səb-ˌstan-chē-'ā-shən\ *n* : the change in the eucharistic elements from the substance of

bread and wine to the substance of the body of Christ with only the appearances of bread and wine remaining

trans·verse \trans-'vərs, tranz-\ *adj* : lying across : set crosswise — **transverse** \'trans-ˌvərs, 'tranz-\ *n* — **trans·verse·ly** *adv*

trans·ves·tite \trans-'ves-ˌtīt, tranz-\ *n* : a person and esp. a male who adopts the dress and often the behavior of the opposite sex — **transvestite** *adj* — **trans·ves·tism** \-ˌti-zəm\ *n*

¹**trap** \'trap\ *n* **1** : a device for catching animals **2** : something by which one is caught unawares; *also* : a situation from which escape is difficult or impossible **3** : a machine for throwing clay pigeons into the air; *also* : SAND TRAP **4** : a light one-horse carriage on springs **5** : a device to allow some one thing to pass through while keeping other things out ⟨a ∼ in a drainpipe⟩ **6** *pl* : a group of percussion instruments (as in a dance orchestra)

²**trap** *vb* **trapped; trap·ping** **1** : to catch in or as if in a trap; *also* : CONFINE **2** : to provide or set (a place) with traps **3** : to set traps for animals esp. as a business ✦ *Synonyms* SNARE, ENTRAP, ENSNARE, BAG, LURE, DECOY — **trap·per** *n*

trap·door \'trap-'dȯr\ *n* : a lifting or sliding door covering an opening in a floor or roof

tra·peze \tra-'pēz\ *n* : a gymnastic apparatus consisting of a horizontal bar suspended by two parallel ropes

trap·e·zoid \'tra-pə-ˌzȯid\ *n* [NL *trapezoides*, fr. Gk *trapezoeidēs* trapezoidal, fr. *trapeza* table, fr. *tra-* four + *peza* foot] : a 4-sided polygon with exactly two sides parallel — **trap·e·zoi·dal** \ˌtra-pə-'zȯi-dᵊl\ *adj*

trap·pings \'tra-piŋz\ *n pl* **1** : CAPARISON 1 **2** : outward decoration or dress; *also* : outward sign ⟨∼ of success⟩

traps \'traps\ *n pl* : personal belongings : LUGGAGE

trap·shoot·ing \'trap-ˌshü-tiŋ\ *n* : shooting at clay pigeons sprung from a trap into the air away from the shooter

¹**trash** \'trash\ *n* **1** : something of little worth : RUBBISH **2** : empty or disparaging talk **3** : a worthless person; *also* : such persons as a group : RIFFRAFF — **trashy** *adj*

²**trash** *vb* **1** : to dispose of : DISCARD ⟨∼ed the plans⟩ **2** : VANDALIZE, DESTROY **3** : ATTACK **4** : SPOIL, RUIN **5** : to criticize or disparage harshly

trau·ma \'traú-mə, 'trȯ-\ *n, pl* **traumas** *also* **trau·ma·ta** \-mə-tə\ [Gk, wound] : a bodily or mental injury usu. caused by an external agent; *also* : a cause of trauma — **trau·mat·ic** \trə-'ma-tik, trȯ-, traú-\ *adj*

trau·ma·tize \-ˌtīz\ *vb* **-tized; -tiz·ing** : to inflict trauma upon

¹**tra·vail** \trə-'vāl, 'tra-ˌvāl\ *n* **1** : painful work or exertion : TOIL **2** : AGONY, TORMENT **3** : CHILDBIRTH, LABOR

²**travail** *vb* : to labor hard : TOIL

¹**trav·el** \'tra-vəl\ *vb* **-eled** *or* **-elled; -el·ing** *or* **-el·ling** [ME *travailen* to torment, labor, journey, fr. AF *travailler* strive, fr. VL **trepaliare* to torture, fr. LL *trepalium* instrument of torture] **1** : to go on or as if on a trip or tour : JOURNEY **2** : to move as if by traveling ⟨news ∼s fast⟩ **3** : ASSOCIATE **4** : to go from place to place as a sales representative **5** : to move from point to point ⟨light waves ∼ very fast⟩ **6** : to journey over or through ⟨∼ing the highways⟩ **7** : to take excessive steps while holding a basketball — **trav·el·er** *or* **trav·el·ler** *n*

²**travel** *n* **1** : the act of traveling : PASSAGE **2** : JOURNEY, TRIP — often used in pl. **3** : the number traveling : TRAFFIC **4** : the motion of a piece of machinery and esp. when to and fro

traveler's check *n* : a check paid for in advance that is signed when bought and signed again when cashed

traveling bag *n* : SUITCASE

trav·el·ogue *or* **trav·el·og** \'tra-və-ˌlȯg, -ˌläg\ *n* : a usu. illustrated lecture on travel

¹**tra·verse** \'tra-vərs\ *n* : something that crosses or lies across

²**tra·verse** \trə-'vərs, tra-'vərs *or* 'tra-vərs\ *vb* **tra·versed; tra·vers·ing** **1** : to go or travel across or over **2** : to move or pass along or through **3** : to extend over **4** : SWIVEL

³**tra·verse** \'tra-ˌvərs\ *adj* : TRANSVERSE

trav·er·tine \'tra-vər-ˌtēn, -tən\ *n* : a crystalline mineral formed by deposition from spring waters

¹**trav·es·ty** \'tra-və-stē\ *vb* **-tied; -ty·ing** : to make a travesty of

²**travesty** *n, pl* **-ties** [obs. E *travesty* disguised, parodied, fr. F *travesti*, pp. of *travestir* to disguise, fr. It *travestire*, fr.

tra- across (fr. L *trans-*) + *vestire* to dress] : an imitation that makes crude fun of something; *also* : an inferior imitation

¹**trawl** \'trȯl\ *vb* : to fish or catch with a trawl — **trawl·er** *n*

²**trawl** *n* **1** : a large conical net dragged along the sea bottom in fishing **2** : a long heavy fishing line equipped with many hooks in series

tray \'trā\ *n* : an open receptacle with flat bottom and low rim for holding, carrying, or exhibiting articles

treach·er·ous \'tre-chə-rəs\ *adj* **1** : characterized by treachery **2** : UNTRUSTWORTHY, UNRELIABLE ⟨a ~ co-worker⟩ **3** : providing insecure footing or support ⟨a ~ slope⟩ ♦ *Synonyms* TRAITOROUS, FAITHLESS, FALSE, DISLOYAL — **treach·er·ous·ly** *adv*

treach·ery \'tre-chə-rē\ *n, pl* **-er·ies** : violation of allegiance or trust

trea·cle \'trē-kəl\ *n* [ME *triacle* a medicinal compound, fr. AF, fr. L *theriaca*, fr. Gk *thēriakē* antidote against a poisonous bite, fr. *thērion* wild animal] *chiefly Brit* : MOLASSES — **trea·cly** \-k(ə-)lē\ *adj*

¹**tread** \'tred\ *vb* **trod** \'träd\; **trod·den** \'trä-d°n\ *or* **trod**; **tread·ing 1** : to step or walk on or over **2** : to move on foot : WALK; *also* : DANCE **3** : to beat or press with the feet — **tread water** : to stay afloat and upright in water by sustaining a walking motion

²**tread** *n* **1** : a mark made by or as if by treading **2** : the manner or sound of stepping **3** : the part of a wheel that makes contact with a road **4** : the horizontal part of a step

trea·dle \'tre-d°l\ *n* : a lever device pressed by the foot to drive a machine — **treadle** *vb*

tread·mill \'tred-ˌmil\ *n* **1** : a mill worked by persons who tread on steps around the edge of a wheel or by animals that walk on an endless belt **2** : a device with an endless belt on which a person walks or runs in place **3** : a wearisome routine

treas *abbr* treasurer; treasury

trea·son \'trē-z°n\ *n* : the offense of attempting to overthrow the government of one's country or of assisting its enemies in war — **trea·son·able** \-z°n-ə-bəl\ *adj* — **trea·son·ous** \-z°n-əs\ *adj*

¹**trea·sure** \'tre-zhər, 'trā-\ *n* [ME *tresor*, fr. AF, fr. L *thesaurus*, fr. Gk *thēsauros*] **1** : wealth stored up or held in reserve **2** : something of great value

²**treasure** *vb* **trea·sured; trea·sur·ing 1** : HOARD **2** : to keep as precious : CHERISH ♦ *Synonyms* PRIZE, VALUE, APPRECIATE, ESTEEM

trea·sur·er \'tre-zhə-rər, 'trā-\ *n* : an officer of a club, business, or government who has charge of money taken in and paid out

treasure trove \-ˌtrōv\ *n* **1** : treasure of unknown ownership found buried or hidden **2** : a valuable discovery

trea·sury \'tre-zhə-rē, 'trā-\ *n, pl* **-sur·ies 1** : a place in which stores of wealth are kept **2** : the place where collected funds are stored and paid out **3** *cap* : a governmental department in charge of finances

¹**treat** \'trēt\ *vb* **1** : NEGOTIATE **2** : to deal with esp. in writing; *also* : HANDLE **3** : to pay for the food or entertainment of **4** : to behave or act toward ⟨~ them well⟩ **5** : to regard in a specified manner ⟨~ as inferiors⟩ **6** : to give medical or surgical care to **7** : to subject to some action ⟨~ soil with lime⟩

²**treat** *n* **1** : an entertainment given free to those invited; *also* : food, drink, or entertainment provided at another's expense **2** : a source of joy or amusement

trea·tise \'trē-təs\ *n* : a systematic written exposition or argument

treat·ment \'trēt-mənt\ *n* : the act or manner or an instance of treating someone or something; *also* : a substance or method used in treating

trea·ty \'trē-tē\ *n, pl* **treaties** : an agreement made by negotiation or diplomacy esp. between two or more states or governments

¹**tre·ble** \'tre-bəl\ *n* **1** : the highest of the four voice parts in vocal music : SOPRANO **2** : a high-pitched or shrill voice or sound **3** : the upper half of the musical pitch range

²**treble** *adj* **1** : triple in number or amount **2** : relating to or having the range of a musical treble **3** : high-pitched : SHRILL — **tre·bly** *adv*

³**treble** *vb* **tre·bled; tre·bling** : to make or become three times the size, amount, or number

¹**tree** \'trē\ *n* **1** : a woody perennial plant usu. with a single main stem and a head of branches and leaves at the top **2** : a piece of wood adapted to a particular use ⟨a shoe ~⟩ **3** : something resembling a tree ⟨a genealogical ~⟩ — **tree·less** *adj*

²**tree** *vb* **treed; tree·ing** : to drive to or up a tree ⟨~ a raccoon⟩

tree farm *n* : an area of forest land managed to ensure continuous commercial production

tree frog *n* : any of numerous small usu. tree-dwelling amphibians with adhesive disks on the toes

tree line *n* : TIMBERLINE

tree of heaven *n* : a Chinese ailanthus widely grown as an ornamental tree

tree surgery *n* : operative treatment of diseased trees esp. for control of decay — **tree surgeon** *n*

tre·foil \'trē-ˌfȯi(-ə)l, 'tre-\ *n* **1** : an herb (as a clover) with leaves that have three leaflets **2** : a decorative design with three leaflike parts

¹**trek** \'trek\ *vb* **trekked; trek·king 1** *chiefly southern Africa* : to travel or migrate by ox wagon **2** : to make one's way arduously

²**trek** *n* **1** *chiefly southern Africa* : a migration esp. of settlers by ox wagon **2** : a slow or difficult journey

trel·lis \'tre-ləs\ *n* [ME *trelis*, fr. AF *treleis*, fr. OF *treille* arbor, fr. L *trichila* summerhouse] : a frame of latticework used esp. to support climbing plants

²**trellis** *vb* : to provide with a trellis; *esp* : to train (as a vine) on a trellis

trem·a·tode \'tre-mə-ˌtōd\ *n* : any of a class of parasitic worms

¹**trem·ble** \'trem-bəl\ *vb* **trem·bled; trem·bling 1** : to shake involuntarily (as with fear or cold) : SHIVER **2** : to move, sound, pass, or come to pass as if shaken or tremulous **3** : to be affected with fear or doubt

²**tremble** *n* : a spell of shaking or quivering

tre·men·dous \tri-ˈmen-dəs\ *adj* **1** : causing dread, awe, or terror : TERRIFYING **2** : unusually large, powerful, great, or excellent ⟨~ strength⟩ ♦ *Synonyms* STUPENDOUS, MONUMENTAL, MONSTROUS — **tre·men·dous·ly** *adv*

trem·o·lo \'tre-mə-ˌlō\ *n, pl* **-los** [It] : a rapid fluttering of a tone or alternating tones

trem·or \'tre-mər\ *n* **1** : a trembling or shaking esp. from weakness, emotional stress, or disease **2** : a quivering motion of the earth (as during an earthquake)

trem·u·lous \'trem-yə-ləs\ *adj* **1** : marked by trembling or tremors : QUIVERING ⟨~ hands⟩ **2** : TIMOROUS, TIMID — **trem·u·lous·ly** *adv*

¹**trench** \'trench\ *n* [ME *trenche* track cut through a wood, fr. AF, act of cutting, fr. *trencher* to cut, prob. fr. VL **trinicare* to cut in three, fr. L *trini* three each] **1** : a long narrow cut in the ground : DITCH; *esp* : a ditch protected by banks of earth and used to shelter soldiers **2** *pl* : a place or situation likened to warfare conducted from trenches **3** : a long narrow steep-sided depression in the ocean floor

²**trench** *vb* **1** : to cut or dig trenches in **2** : to protect (troops) with trenches **3** : to come close : VERGE

tren·chant \'tren-chənt\ *adj* **1** : vigorously effective; *also* : CAUSTIC ⟨~ comments⟩ **2** : sharply perceptive : KEEN ⟨a ~ wit⟩ **3** : CLEAR-CUT, DISTINCT

tren·cher \'tren-chər\ *n* : a wooden platter for serving food

tren·cher·man \'tren-chər-mən\ *n* : a hearty eater

trench foot *n* : a painful foot disorder resembling frostbite and resulting from exposure to cold and wet

trench mouth *n* : a progressive painful bacterial infection of the mouth and adjacent parts marked by ulceration, bleeding gums, and foul breath

¹**trend** \'trend\ *vb* **1** : to have or take a general direction : TEND **2** : to show a tendency : INCLINE

²**trend** *n* **1** : a general direction taken (as by a stream or mountain range) **2** : a prevailing tendency : DRIFT **3** : a current style or preference : VOGUE

trendy \'tren-dē\ *adj* **trend·i·er; -est** : very fashionable; *also* : marked by superficial or faddish appeal or taste

trep·i·da·tion \ˌtre-pə-ˈdā-shən\ *n* : nervous agitation : APPREHENSION ♦ *Synonyms* HORROR, TERROR, PANIC, CONSTERNATION, DREAD, FRIGHT, DISMAY

¹**tres·pass** \'tres-pəs, -ˌpas\ *n* **1** : SIN, OFFENSE **2** : unlawful entry on someone else's land ♦ *Synonyms* TRANSGRESSION, VIOLATION, INFRACTION, INFRINGEMENT

²**tres·pass** \vb\ **1** : to commit an offense : ERR, SIN **2** : INTRUDE, ENCROACH; *esp* : to enter unlawfully upon the land of another — **tres·pass·er** *n*

tress \'tres\ *n* : a long lock of hair — usu. used in pl.

tres·tle *also* **tres·sel** \'tre-səl\ *n* **1** : a supporting framework consisting usu. of a horizontal piece with spreading legs at each end **2** : a braced framework of timbers, piles, or steel for carrying a road or railroad over a depression

T. rex \'tē-'reks\ *n* : TYRANNOSAUR

trey \'trā\ *n, pl* **treys** : a card or the side of a die with three spots

tri·ad \'trī-,ad, -əd\ *n* : a union or group of three usu. closely related persons or things

tri·age \trē-'äzh, 'trē-,äzh\ *n* [F, sorting] : the sorting of and allocation of treatment to patients and esp. battle or disaster victims according to a system of priorities designed to maximize the number of survivors

tri·al \'trī-əl\ *n* **1** : the action or process of trying or putting to the proof : TEST **2** : the hearing and judgment of a matter in issue before a competent tribunal **3** : a source of vexation or annoyance **4** : an experiment to test quality, value, or usefulness **5** : EFFORT, ATTEMPT ✦ **Synonyms** CROSS, ORDEAL, TRIBULATION, AFFLICTION — **trial** *adj*

tri·an·gle \'trī-,aŋ-gəl\ *n* **1** : a polygon that has three sides **2** : something shaped like a triangle — **tri·an·gu·lar** \trī-'aŋ-gyə-lər\ *adj* — **tri·an·gu·lar·ly** *adv*

triangle 1: three kinds

tri·an·gu·la·tion \(,)trī-,aŋ-gyə-'lā-shən\ *n* : a method using trigonometry to find the location of a point using bearings from two fixed points a known distance apart — **tri·an·gu·late** \trī-'aŋ-gyə-,lāt\ *vb*

Tri·as·sic \trī-'a-sik\ *adj* : of, relating to, or being the earliest period of the Mesozoic era marked by the first appearance of the dinosaurs — **Triassic** *n*

tri·ath·lon \trī-'ath-lən, -,län\ *n* : an athletic contest consisting of three phases (as swimming, bicycling, and running)

trib *abbr* tributary

tribe \'trīb\ *n* **1** : a social group comprising numerous families, clans, or generations **2** : a group of persons having a common character, occupation, or interest **3** : a group of related plants or animals ⟨the cat ∼⟩ — **trib·al** \'trī-bəl\ *adj*

tribes·man \'trībz-mən\ *n* : a member of a tribe

trib·u·la·tion \,tri-byə-'lā-shən\ *n* [ME *tribulacion*, fr. AF, fr. L *tribulatio*, fr. *tribulare* to press, oppress, fr. *tribulum* drag used in threshing] : distress or suffering resulting from oppression or persecution; *also* : a trying experience ✦ **Synonyms** TRIAL, AFFLICTION, CROSS, ORDEAL

tri·bu·nal \trī-'byü-n³l, tri-\ *n* **1** : the seat of a judge **2** : a court of justice **3** : something that decides or determines ⟨the ∼ of public opinion⟩

tri·bune \'tri-,byün, tri-'byün\ *n* **1** : an official in ancient Rome with the function of protecting the interests of plebeian citizens from the patricians **2** : a defender of the people

¹**trib·u·tary** \'tri-byə-,ter-ē\ *adj* **1** : paying tribute : SUBJECT **2** : flowing into a larger stream or a lake ✦ **Synonyms** SUBORDINATE, SECONDARY, DEPENDENT

²**tributary** *n, pl* **-tar·ies** **1** : a ruler or state that pays tribute **2** : a tributary stream

trib·ute \'tri-(,)byüt, -byət\ *n* **1** : a payment by one ruler or nation to another as an act of submission or price of protection **2** : a usu. excessive tax, rental, or levy exacted by a sovereign or superior **3** : a gift or service showing respect, gratitude, or affection; *also* : PRAISE ✦ **Synonyms** EULOGY, CITATION, ENCOMIUM, PANEGYRIC

trice \'trīs\ *n* : INSTANT, MOMENT

tri·ceps \'trī-,seps\ *n, pl* **triceps** : a large muscle along the back of the upper arm that is attached at its upper end by three main parts and acts to extend the forearm at the elbow joint

tri·cer·a·tops \(,)trī-'ser-ə-,täps\ *n, pl* **-tops** *also* **-tops·es** [NL, fr. Gk *tri-* three + *kerat-, keras* horn + *ōps* face] : any of a genus of large plant-eating Cretaceous dinosaurs with three horns, a bony crest on the neck, and hoofed toes

tri·chi·na \tri-'kī-nə\ *n, pl* **-nae** \-(,)nē\ *also* **-nas** : a small slender nematode worm that in the larval state is parasitic in the striated muscles of flesh-eating mammals (as humans)

trich·i·no·sis \,tri-kə-'nō-səs\ *n* : infestation with or disease caused by trichinae and marked esp. by muscular pain, fever, and swelling

¹**trick** \'trik\ *n* **1** : a crafty procedure meant to deceive **2** : a mischievous action : PRANK **3** : a childish action **4** : a deceptive or ingenious feat designed to puzzle or amuse **5** : PECULIARITY, MANNERISM **6** : a quick or artful way of getting a result : KNACK ⟨∼s of the trade⟩ **7** : the cards played in one round of a card game **8** : a tour of duty : SHIFT ✦ **Synonyms** RUSE, MANEUVER, ARTIFICE, WILE, FEINT

²**trick** *vb* **1** : to deceive by cunning or artifice : CHEAT **2** : to dress ornately

trick·ery \'tri-kə-rē\ *n* : deception by tricks and strategems

trick·le \'tri-kəl\ *vb* **trick·led; trick·ling** **1** : to run or fall in drops **2** : to flow in a thin gentle stream — **trickle** *n*

trick·ster \'trik-stər\ *n* : one who tricks or cheats

tricky \'tri-kē\ *adj* **trick·i·er; -est** **1** : inclined to trickery **2** : requiring skill or caution ⟨a ∼ situation to handle⟩ **3** : UNRELIABLE ⟨a ∼ lock⟩

tri·col·or \'trī-,kə-lər\ *n* : a flag of three colors ⟨the French ∼⟩

tri·cy·cle \'trī-(,)si-kəl\ *n* : a 3-wheeled vehicle usu. propelled by pedals

tri·dent \'trī-d³nt\ *n* [L *trident-, tridens,* fr. *tri-* three + *dent-, dens* tooth] : a 3-pronged spear

tried \'trīd\ *adj* **1** : found trustworthy through testing **2** : subjected to trials

tri·en·ni·al \trī-'e-nē-əl\ *adj* **1** : occurring or being done every three years **2** : lasting for three years — **triennial** *n*

¹**tri·fle** \'trī-fəl\ *n* **1** : something of little value or importance **2** : a dessert of cake soaked with liqueur and served with toppings (as fruit or cream)

²**trifle** *vb* **tri·fled; tri·fling** **1** : to talk in a jesting or mocking manner **2** : to treat someone or something as unimportant **3** : DALLY, FLIRT **4** : to handle idly : TOY — **tri·fler** *n*

tri·fling \'trī-fliŋ\ *adj* **1** : FRIVOLOUS **2** : TRIVIAL, INSIGNIFICANT ⟨∼ details⟩ ✦ **Synonyms** PETTY, PALTRY, MEASLY, INCONSEQUENTIAL

tri·fo·cals \'trī-'fō-kəlz\ *n pl* : eyeglasses with lenses having one part for close focus, one for intermediate focus, and one for distant focus

tri·fo·li·ate \trī-'fō-lē-ət\ *adj* : having three leaves or leaflets

¹**trig** \'trig\ *adj* : stylishly trim : SMART

²**trig** *n* : TRIGONOMETRY

¹**trig·ger** \'tri-gər\ *n* [alter. of earlier *tricker,* fr. D *trekker,* fr. MD *trecker* one that pulls, fr. *trecken* to pull] : a movable lever that activates a device when it is squeezed; *esp* : the part of a firearm lock moved by the finger to fire a gun — **trigger** *adj* — **trig·gered** *adj*

²**trigger** *vb* **1** : to fire by pulling a trigger **2** : to initiate, actuate, or set off as if by a trigger ⟨remarks that ∼ed a fight⟩

tri·glyc·er·ide \trī-'gli-sə-,rīd\ *n* : any of a group of lipids that are formed from glycerol and fatty acids and are widespread in animal tissue

trig·o·nom·e·try \,tri-gə-'nä-mə-trē\ *n* : the branch of mathematics dealing with the properties of triangles and esp. with finding unknown angles or sides given the size or length of some angles or sides — **trig·o·no·met·ric** \-nə-'me-trik\ *also* **trig·o·no·met·ri·cal** \-tri-kəl\ *adj*

trike \'trīk\ *n* : TRICYCLE

¹**trill** \'tril\ *n* **1** : the alternation of two musical tones a scale degree apart **2** : WARBLE **3** : the rapid vibration of one speech organ against another (as of the tip of the tongue against the teeth)

²**trill** *vb* : to utter as or with a trill

tril·lion \'tril-yən\ *n* **1** : a thousand billions **2** *Brit* : a million billions — **trillion** *adj* — **tril·lionth** \-yənth\ *adj or n*

tril·li·um \'tri-lē-əm\ n : any of a genus of spring-blooming herbs that are related to the lilies and have an erect stem bearing a whorl of three leaves and a solitary flower

tril·o·gy \'tri-lə-jē\ n, pl **-gies** : a series of three dramas or literary or musical compositions that are closely related and develop one theme

¹trim \'trim\ vb **trimmed; trim·ming** [OE trymian, trymman to strengthen, arrange, fr. trum strong, firm] **1** : to put ornaments on : ADORN **2** : to defeat esp. resoundingly **3** : to make trim, neat, regular, or less bulky by or as if by cutting ⟨~ a beard⟩ ⟨~ a budget⟩ **4** : to cause (a boat) to assume a desired position in the water by arrangement of the load; also : to adjust (as a submarine or airplane) esp. for horizontal motion **5** : to adjust (a sail) to a desired position **6** : to change one's views for safety or expediency — **trim·ly** adv — **trim·mer** n — **trim·ness** n

²trim adj **trim·mer; trim·mest** : showing neatness, good order, or compactness ⟨a ~ figure⟩ ◆ **Synonyms** TIDY, TRIG, SMART, SPRUCE, SHIPSHAPE

³trim n **1** : good condition : FITNESS **2** : material used for ornament or trimming; esp : the woodwork in the finish of a house esp. around doors and windows **3** : the position of a ship or boat esp. with reference to the horizontal; also : the relation between the plane of a sail and the direction of a ship **4** : the position of an airplane at which it will continue in level flight with no adjustments to the controls **5** : something that is trimmed off

tri·ma·ran \'trī-mə-ˌran, ˌtrī-mə-'ran\ n : a sailboat with three hulls

tri·mes·ter \trī-'mes-tər, 'trī-ˌmes-tər\ n **1** : a period of three or about three months (as in pregnancy) **2** : one of three terms into which an academic year is sometimes divided

trim·e·ter \'tri-mə-tər\ n : a line of verse consisting of three metrical feet

trim·ming \'tri-miŋ\ n **1** : DEFEAT **2** : the action of one that trims **3** : something that trims, ornaments, or completes

tri·month·ly \trī-'mənth-lē\ adj : occurring every three months

trine \'trīn\ adj : THREEFOLD, TRIPLE

Trin·i·da·di·an \ˌtri-nə-'dä-dē-ən, -'da-\ n : a native or inhabitant of the island of Trinidad — **Trinidadian** adj

Trin·i·tar·i·an \ˌtri-nə-'ter-ē-ən\ n : a believer in the doctrine of the Trinity — **Trin·i·tar·i·an·ism** \-ē-ə-ˌni-zəm\ n

Trin·i·ty \'tri-nə-tē\ n **1** : the unity of Father, Son, and Holy Spirit as three persons in one Godhead **2** not cap : TRIAD

trin·ket \'triŋ-kət\ n **1** : a small ornament (as a jewel or ring) **2** : TRIFLE 1

trio \'trē-ō\ n, pl **tri·os** **1** : a musical composition for three voices or three instruments **2** : the performers of a trio **3** : a group or set of three

¹trip \'trip\ vb **tripped; trip·ping** **1** : to move with light quick steps **2** : to catch the foot against something so as to stumble or cause to stumble **3** : to make a mistake : SLIP; also : to detect in a misstep : EXPOSE **4** : to release (as a spring or switch) by moving a catch; also : ACTIVATE ⟨~ an alarm⟩ **5** : to get high on a usu. hallucinatory drug

²trip n **1** : JOURNEY, VOYAGE **2** : a quick light step **3** : a false step : STUMBLE; also : ERROR **4** : the action of tripping mechanically; also : a device for tripping **5** : an intense experience; esp : one triggered by a hallucinatory drug **6** : absorption in an attitude or state of mind ⟨an ego ~⟩

tri·par·tite \trī-'pär-ˌtīt\ adj **1** : divided into three parts **2** : having three corresponding parts or copies **3** : made between three parties ⟨a ~ treaty⟩

tripe \'trīp\ n **1** : stomach tissue esp. of a ruminant (as an ox) used as food **2** : something poor, worthless, or offensive : TRASH

¹tri·ple \'tri-pəl\ vb **tri·pled; tri·pling** **1** : to make or become three times as great or as many **2** : to hit a triple

²triple n **1** : a triple quantity **2** : a group of three **3** : a hit in baseball that lets the batter reach third base

³triple adj **1** : being three times as great or as many **2** : having three units or members **3** : repeated three times

triple bond n : a chemical bond in which three pairs of electrons are shared by two atoms in a molecule

triple point n : the condition of temperature and pressure under which the gaseous, liquid, and solid forms of a substance can exist in equilibrium

trip·let \'tri-plət\ n **1** : a unit of three lines of verse **2** : a group of three of a kind **3** : one of three offspring born at one birth

tri·plex \'tri-ˌpleks, 'trī-\ adj : THREEFOLD, TRIPLE

¹trip·li·cate \'tri-pli-kət\ adj : made in three identical copies

²trip·li·cate \-plə-ˌkāt\ vb **-cat·ed; -cat·ing** **1** : TRIPLE **2** : to provide three copies of ⟨~ a document⟩

³trip·li·cate \-pli-kət\ n : three copies all alike — used with in ⟨typed in ~⟩

tri·ply \'tri-plē, 'tri-pə-lē\ adv : in a triple degree, amount, or manner

tri·pod \'trī-ˌpäd\ n : something (as a caldron, stool, or camera stand) that rests on three legs — **tripod** or **tri·po·dal** \'tri-pə-dᵊl, 'trī-ˌpä-\ adj

trip·tych \'trip-tik\ n : a picture or carving in three panels side by side

tri·reme \'trī-ˌrēm\ n : an ancient galley having three banks of oars

tri·sect \'trī-ˌsekt, trī-'sekt\ vb : to divide into three usu. equal parts — **tri·sec·tion** \'trī-ˌsek-shən\ n

trite \'trīt\ adj **trit·er; trit·est** [L tritus, fr. pp. of terere to rub, wear away] : used so commonly that the novelty is worn off : STALE ◆ **Synonyms** HACKNEYED, STEREOTYPED, COMMONPLACE, CLICHÉD

tri·ti·um \'tri-tē-əm, 'tri-shē-\ n : a radioactive form of hydrogen with one proton and two neutrons in its nucleus and three times the mass of ordinary hydrogen

tri·ton \'trī-tᵊn\ n : any of various large marine gastropod mollusks with a heavy elongated conical shell; also : the shell of a triton

trit·u·rate \'tri-chə-ˌrāt\ vb **-rat·ed; -rat·ing** : to rub or grind to a fine powder

¹tri·umph \'trī-əmf\ n **1** : the joy or exultation of victory or success **2** : VICTORY, CONQUEST — **tri·um·phal** \trī-'əm-fəl\ adj

²triumph vb **1** : to obtain victory : PREVAIL **2** : to celebrate victory or success exultantly — **tri·um·phant** \trī-'əm-fənt\ adj — **tri·um·phant·ly** adv

tri·um·vir \trī-'əm-vər\ n, pl **-virs** also **-vi·ri** \-və-ˌrī\ : a member of a triumvirate

tri·um·vi·rate \-və-rət\ n : a ruling body of three persons

tri·une \'trī-ˌün, -ˌyün\ adj : being three in one ⟨the ~ God⟩

triv·et \'tri-vət\ n **1** : a 3-legged stand : TRIPOD **2** : a usu. metal stand with short feet for use under a hot dish

triv·ia \'tri-vē-ə\ n sing or pl : unimportant matters : obscure facts or details ⟨movie ~⟩

triv·i·al \'tri-vē-əl\ adj [L trivialis found everywhere, commonplace, fr. trivium crossroads, fr. tri- three + via way] : of little importance — **triv·i·al·i·ty** \ˌtri-vē-'a-lə-tē\ n

triv·i·um \'tri-vē-əm\ n, pl **triv·ia** \-vē-ə\ : the three liberal arts of grammar, rhetoric, and logic in a medieval university

tri·week·ly \trī-'wē-klē\ adj **1** : occurring or appearing three times a week **2** : occurring or appearing every three weeks — **triweekly** adv

tro·che \'trō-kē\ n : LOZENGE 2

tro·chee \'trō-(ˌ)kē\ n : a metrical foot of one accented syllable followed by one unaccented syllable — **tro·cha·ic** \trō-'kā-ik\ adj

trod past and past part of TREAD

trodden past part of TREAD

troi·ka \'troi-kə\ n [Russ troĭka, fr. troe three] : a group of three; esp : an administrative or ruling body of three

¹troll \'trōl\ vb **1** : to sing the parts of (a song) in succession **2** : to fish by trailing a lure or baited hook from a moving boat **3** : to sing or play jovially **4** : to deliberately antagonize (others) esp. online

²troll n **1** : a lure used in trolling; also : the line with its lure **2** : a person who trolls others esp. online

³troll n : a dwarf or giant in Scandinavian folklore inhabiting caves or hills

trol·ley also **trol·ly** \'trä-lē\ n, pl **trolleys** also **trollies** **1** : a device (as a grooved wheel on the end of a pole) to carry current from a wire to an electrically driven vehicle **2** : a streetcar powered electrically by overhead wires **3** : a wheeled carriage running on an overhead rail or track

trol·ley·bus \'trä-lē-ˌbəs\ n : a bus powered electrically by overhead wires

trolley car n : TROLLEY 2

trol·lop \'trä-ləp\ *n* : a disreputable woman; *esp* : one who engages in sex promiscuously

trom·bone \träm-'bōn, 'träm-ˌbōn\ *n* [It, fr. *tromba* trumpet] : a brass wind instrument that consists of a long metal tube with two turns and a flaring end and that usu. has a movable slide to vary the pitch — **trom·bon·ist** \-'bō-nist, -ˌbō-\ *n*

tromp \'trämp, 'trómp\ *vb* 1 : TRAMP, MARCH 2 : to stamp with the foot 3 : to defeat decisively

trompe l'oeil \(ˌ)trómp-'lə̄-ē, trōⁿp-'lœi\ *n* [F *trompe-l'oeil*, lit., deceives the eye] : a style of painting in which objects are depicted with photographic detail

¹troop \'trüp\ *n* 1 : a cavalry unit corresponding to an infantry company 2 *pl* : armed forces : SOLDIERS 3 : a collection of people, animals, or things 4 : a unit of Girl Scouts or Boy Scouts under an adult leader

²troop *vb* : to move or gather in crowds

troop·er \'trü-pər\ *n* 1 : an enlisted cavalryman; *also* : a cavalry horse 2 : a mounted or a state police officer

troop·ship \'trüp-ˌship\ *n* : a ship or aircraft for carrying troops

trope \'trōp\ *n* : a word or expression used in a figurative sense

tro·phic \'trō-fik\ *adj* : of or relating to nutrition

tro·phy \'trō-fē\ *n, pl* **trophies** : something gained or given in conquest or victory esp. when preserved or mounted as a memorial

trop·ic \'trä-pik\ *n* [ME *tropik*, fr. L *tropicus* of the solstice, fr. Gk *tropikos*, fr. *tropē* turn] 1 : either of the two parallels of latitude approximately 23½ degrees north (**Tropic of Can·cer**) or south (**Tropic of Cap·ri·corn**) of the equator where the sun is directly overhead when it reaches its most northerly or southerly point in the sky 2 *pl, often cap* : the region lying between the tropics — **trop·i·cal** \-pi-kəl\ *or* **tropic** *adj*

tro·pism \'trō-ˌpi-zəm\ *n* : an automatic movement by an organism in response to a source of stimulation; *also* : a reflex reaction involving this

tro·po·sphere \'trō-pə-ˌsfir, 'trä-\ *n* : the part of the atmosphere between the earth's surface and the stratosphere in which most weather changes occur — **tro·po·spher·ic** \ˌtrō-pə-'sfir-ik, ˌträ-, -'sfer-\ *adj*

¹trot \'trät\ *n* 1 : a moderately fast gait of a 4-footed animal (as a horse) in which the legs move in diagonal pairs 2 : a human jogging gait between a walk and a run

²trot *vb* **trot·ted; trot·ting** 1 : to ride, drive, or go at a trot 2 : to proceed briskly : HURRY — **trot·ter** *n*

troth \'träth, 'tróth, 'trōth\ *n* 1 : pledged faithfulness 2 : one's pledged word; *also* : BETROTHAL

trou·ba·dour \'trü-bə-ˌdór\ *n* [F, fr. Old Occitan *trobador*, fr. *trobar* to compose] : any of a class of poet-musicians flourishing esp. in southern France and northern Italy during the 11th, 12th, and 13th centuries

¹trou·ble \'trə-bəl\ *vb* **trou·bled; trou·bling** 1 : to agitate mentally or spiritually : DISTURB, WORRY 2 : to produce physical disorder in : AFFLICT 3 : to put to inconvenience 4 : RUFFLE ⟨~ the waters⟩ 5 : to make an effort ♦ **Synonyms** DISTRESS, AIL, UPSET — **trou·ble·some** *adj* — **trou·ble·some·ly** *adv* — **trou·blous** \-bə-ləs\ *adj*

²trouble *n* 1 : the quality or state of being troubled esp. mentally 2 : an instance of distress or annoyance 3 : DISEASE, AILMENT ⟨heart ~⟩ 4 : EXERTION, PAINS ⟨took the ~ to phone⟩ 5 : a cause of disturbance or distress

trou·ble·mak·er \-ˌmā-kər\ *n* : a person who causes trouble

trou·ble·shoot·er \-ˌshü-tər\ *n* 1 : a worker employed to locate trouble and make repairs in equipment 2 : an expert in resolving disputes or problems — **trou·ble·shoot** *vb*

trough \'tróf, 'tróth\ *n, pl* **troughs** \'trófs, 'tróvz; 'tróths, 'tróthz\ 1 : a long shallow open boxlike container esp. for water or feed for livestock 2 : a gutter along the eaves of a house 3 : a long channel or depression (as between waves or hills) 4 : an elongated area of low barometric pressure

trounce \'traúns\ *vb* **trounced; trounc·ing** 1 : to thrash or punish severely 2 : to defeat decisively

troupe \'trüp\ *n* : COMPANY; *esp* : a group of performers on the stage — **troup·er** *n*

trou·sers \'traú-zərz\ *n pl* [alter. of earlier *trouse*, fr. ScGael *triubhas*] : PANTS — **trouser** *adj*

trous·seau \'trü-sō, trü-'sō\ *n, pl* **trous·seaux** \-sōz, -'sōz\ *or* **trous·seaus** [F] : the personal outfit of a bride

trout \'traút\ *n, pl* **trout** *also* **trouts** [ME, fr. OE *trūht*, fr. LL *tructa*, a fish with sharp teeth, fr. Gk *trōktēs*, lit., gnawer] : any of various mostly freshwater food and game fishes usu. smaller than the related salmons

trout

trow \'trō\ *vb, archaic* : THINK, SUPPOSE

trow·el \'traú-(ə)l\ *n* 1 : a hand tool used for spreading, shaping, or smoothing loose or plastic material (as mortar or plaster) 2 : a scoop-shaped tool used in gardening — **trowel** *vb*

troy \'trói\ *adj* : expressed in troy weight ⟨~ ounce⟩

troy weight *n* : a system of weights based on a pound of 12 ounces and an ounce of 480 grains (31 grams) — see WEIGHT table

tru·ant \'trü-ənt\ *n* [ME, vagabond, idler, fr. AF, of Celt origin] : a student who stays out of school without permission — **tru·an·cy** \-ən-sē\ *n* — **truant** *adj*

truce \'trüs\ *n* 1 : ARMISTICE 2 : a respite esp. from something unpleasant

¹truck \'trək\ *vb* 1 : EXCHANGE, BARTER 2 : to have dealings : TRAFFIC

²truck *n* 1 : BARTER 2 : DEALINGS 3 : small goods or merchandise; *esp* : vegetables grown for market

³truck *n* 1 : a wheeled vehicle (as a strong heavy automobile) designed for carrying heavy articles or hauling a trailer 2 : a swiveling frame with springs and one or more pairs of wheels used to carry and guide one end of a locomotive or railroad car

⁴truck *vb* 1 : to transport on a truck ⟨~s vegetables⟩ 2 : to be employed in driving a truck — **truck·er** *n*

truck farm *n* : a farm growing vegetables for market — **truck farmer** *n*

truck·le \'trə-kəl\ *vb* **truck·led; truck·ling** : to yield slavishly to the will of another : SUBMIT ♦ **Synonyms** FAWN, TOADY, CRINGE, COWER

truc·u·lent \'trə-kyə-lənt\ *adj* 1 : feeling or showing ferocity : SAVAGE 2 : aggressively self-assertive : BELLIGERENT — **truc·u·lence** \-ləns\ *n* — **truc·u·len·cy** \-lən-sē\ *n* — **truc·u·lent·ly** *adv*

trudge \'trəj\ *vb* **trudged; trudg·ing** : to walk or march steadily and usu. laboriously ⟨*trudged* through the snow⟩

¹true \'trü\ *adj* **tru·er; tru·est** 1 : STEADFAST, LOYAL 2 : agreeing with facts or reality ⟨a ~ description⟩ 3 : CONSISTENT ⟨~ to expectations⟩ 4 : properly so called ⟨~ love⟩ 5 : RIGHTFUL ⟨~ and lawful king⟩ 6 : conformable to a standard or pattern; *also* : placed or formed accurately ♦ **Synonyms** CONSTANT, STAUNCH, RESOLUTE, STEADFAST

²true *adv* 1 : TRUTHFULLY 2 : ACCURATELY ⟨the bullet flew straight and ~⟩; *also* : without variation from type ⟨breed ~⟩

³true *n* 1 : TRUTH, REALITY — usu. used with *the* 2 : the state of being accurate (as in alignment) ⟨out of ~⟩

⁴true *vb* **trued; true·ing** *also* **tru·ing** : to bring or restore to a desired precision

true–blue *adj* : marked by unswerving loyalty ⟨a ~ patriot⟩

true bug *n* : BUG 2

true·heart·ed \'trü-'här-təd\ *adj* : FAITHFUL, LOYAL ⟨a ~ soldier⟩

truf·fle \'trə-fəl, 'trü-\ *n* 1 : the dark or light edible spore-bearing organ of any of several European fungi that grow underground; *also* : one of these fungi 2 : a candy made of chocolate, butter, and sugar shaped into balls and coated with cocoa

tru·ism \'trü-ˌi-zəm\ *n* : an undoubted or self-evident truth
◆ **Synonyms** COMMONPLACE, PLATITUDE, CLICHÉ

tru·ly \'trü-lē\ *adv* 1 : in all sincerity ⟨is ∼ sorry⟩ 2 : in agreement with fact ⟨report it ∼⟩ 3 : ACCURATELY 4 : in a proper or suitable manner

¹**trump** \'trəmp\ *n* : TRUMPET

²**trump** *n* : a card of a designated suit any of whose cards will win over a card that is not of this suit; *also* : the suit itself — often used in pl.

³**trump** *vb* : to take with a trump

trumped–up \'trəmpt-'əp\ *adj* : fraudulently concocted : SPURIOUS ⟨∼ charges⟩

trum·pery \'trəm-pə-rē\ *n* 1 : NONSENSE 2 : trivial articles : JUNK

¹**trum·pet** \'trəm-pət\ *n* 1 : a wind instrument consisting of a long curved metal tube flaring at one end and with a cup-shaped mouthpiece at the other 2 : something that resembles a trumpet or its tonal quality 3 : a funnel-shaped instrument for collecting, directing, or intensifying sound

²**trumpet** *vb* 1 : to blow a trumpet 2 : to proclaim on or as if on a trumpet ⟨∼ the news⟩ — **trum·pet·er** *n*

¹**trun·cate** \'trən-ˌkāt, 'trən-\ *adj* : having the end square or blunt

²**truncate** *vb* **trun·cat·ed; trun·cat·ing** : to shorten by or as if by cutting : LOP — **trun·ca·tion** \ˌtrən-'kā-shən\ *n*

trun·cheon \'trən-chən\ *n* : a police officer's billy club

trun·dle \'trən-dᵊl\ *vb* **trun·dled; trun·dling** : to roll along : WHEEL

trundle bed *n* : a low bed that can be stored under a higher bed

trunk \'trəŋk\ *n* 1 : the main stem of a tree 2 : the body of a person or animal apart from the head and limbs 3 : the main or central part of something 4 : a box or chest used to hold usu. clothes or personal effects (as of a traveler); *also* : the enclosed luggage space in the rear of an automobile 5 : the long muscular nose of an elephant 6 *pl* : men's shorts worn chiefly for sports ⟨swimming ∼s⟩ 7 : a usu. major channel or passage

trunk line *n* : a transportation system handling long-distance through traffic

¹**truss** \'trəs\ *vb* 1 : to secure tightly : BIND 2 : to arrange for cooking by binding close the wings or legs of (a fowl) 3 : to support, strengthen, or stiffen by or as if by a truss

²**truss** *n* 1 : a collection of structural parts (as beams) forming a rigid framework (as in bridge or building construction) 2 : a device worn to reduce a hernia by pressure

¹**trust** \'trəst\ *n* 1 : assured reliance on the character, strength, or truth of someone or something 2 : a basis of reliance, faith, or hope 3 : confident hope 4 : financial credit 5 : a property interest held by one person for the benefit of another 6 : a combination of firms formed by a legal agreement; *esp* : one that reduces competition 7 : something entrusted to one to be cared for in the interest of another 8 : CARE, CUSTODY ◆ **Synonyms** CONFIDENCE, DEPENDENCE, FAITH, RELIANCE

²**trust** *vb* 1 : to place confidence : DEPEND 2 : to be confident : HOPE 3 : ENTRUST 4 : to permit to stay or go or to do something without fear or misgiving 5 : to rely on or on the truth of : BELIEVE 6 : to extend credit to

trust·ee \ˌtrəs-'tē\ *n* 1 : a person to whom property is legally committed in trust 2 : a country charged with the supervision of a trust territory

trust·ee·ship \ˌtrəs-'tē-ˌship\ *n* 1 : the office or function of a trustee 2 : supervisory control by one or more nations over a trust territory

trust·ful \'trəst-fəl\ *adj* : full of trust : CONFIDING — **trust·ful·ly** *adv* — **trust·ful·ness** *n*

trust territory *n* : a non-self-governing territory placed under a supervisory authority by the Trusteeship Council of the United Nations

trust·wor·thy \-ˌwər-thē\ *adj* : worthy of confidence : DEPENDABLE ⟨a ∼ assistant⟩ ◆ **Synonyms** TRUSTY, TRIED, RELIABLE — **trust·wor·thi·ness** *n*

¹**trusty** \'trəs-tē\ *adj* **trust·i·er; -est** : TRUSTWORTHY, DEPENDABLE ⟨a ∼ friend⟩

²**trusty** \'trəs-tē, ˌtrəs-'tē\ *n, pl* **trust·ies** : a trusted person; *esp* : a convict considered trustworthy and allowed special privileges

truth \'trüth\ *n, pl* **truths** \'trüthz, 'trüths\ 1 : TRUTHFULNESS, HONESTY 2 : the real state of things : FACT 3 : the body of real events or facts : ACTUALITY 4 : a true or accepted statement or proposition ⟨the ∼s of science⟩ 5 : agreement with fact or reality : CORRECTNESS ◆ **Synonyms** VERACITY, VERITY

truth·ful \'trüth-fəl\ *adj* : telling or disposed to tell the truth — **truth·ful·ly** *adv* — **truth·ful·ness** *n*

truth serum *n* : a drug held to induce a subject under questioning to talk freely

¹**try** \'trī\ *vb* **tried; try·ing** [ME *trien*, fr. AF *trier* to select, sort, examine, prob. fr. LL *tritare* to grind] 1 : to examine or investigate judicially 2 : to conduct the trial of 3 : to put to test or trial 4 : to subject to strain, affliction, or annoyance 5 : to extract or clarify (as lard) by melting 6 : to make an effort to do something : ATTEMPT, ENDEAVOR ◆ **Synonyms** ESSAY, ASSAY, STRIVE, STRUGGLE

²**try** *n, pl* **tries** : an experimental trial

try·ing *adj* : severely straining the powers of endurance

try on *vb* : to put on (a garment) to test the fit and looks

try out *vb* : to participate in competition esp. for a position on an athletic team or a part in a play — **try·out** \'trī-ˌaut\ *n*

tryp·to·phan \'trip-tə-ˌfan\ *n* : a crystalline essential amino acid that is widely distributed in proteins

tryst \'trist\ *n* 1 : an agreement (as between lovers) to meet 2 : an appointed meeting or meeting place — **tryst** *vb* — **tryst·er** *n*

Ts *symbol* tennessine

TSA *abbr* Transportation Security Administration

tsar, tsarist *var of* CZAR, CZARIST

tsarina *var of* CZARINA

tset·se fly \'tset-sē-, 'tsēt-, 'tet-, 'tēt-, 'set-, 'sēt-\ *n* : any of several sub-Saharan African dipteran flies including the vector of sleeping sickness

TSgt *abbr* technical sergeant

T–shirt \'tē-ˌshərt\ *n* : a collarless short-sleeved or sleeveless cotton undershirt; *also* : an outer shirt of similar design — **T–shirt·ed** \-ˌshər-təd\ *adj*

tsk \a *click; often read as* 'tisk\ *interj* — used to express disapproval

tsp *abbr* teaspoon; teaspoonful

T square *n* : a ruler with a crosspiece at one end for making parallel lines

tsu·na·mi \sü-'nä-mē, tsù-\ *n* [Jp] : a tidal wave caused esp. by an underwater earthquake or volcanic eruption

TT *abbr* Trust Territories

TTY *abbr* teletypewriter

Tu *abbr* Tuesday

tub \'təb\ *n* 1 : a wide low bucketlike vessel 2 : BATHTUB; *also* : BATH 3 : the amount that a tub will hold

tu·ba \'tü-bə, 'tyü-\ *n* : a large low-pitched brass wind instrument

tub·al \'tü-bəl, 'tyü-\ *adj* : of, relating to, or involving a tube and esp. a fallopian tube ⟨∼ infection⟩

tube \'tüb, 'tyüb\ *n* 1 : any of various usu. cylindrical structures or devices; *esp* : one to convey fluids 2 : a slender hollow anatomical part (as a fallopian tube) functioning as a channel in a plant or animal body : DUCT 3 : a soft round container from which a paste is squeezed 4 : a tunnel for vehicular or rail travel 5 *Brit* : SUBWAY 6 : INNER TUBE 7 : ELECTRON TUBE 8 : TELEVISION — **tubed** \'tübd, 'tyübd\ *adj* — **tube·less** *adj* — **tube·like** \'tüb-ˌlīk, 'tyüb-\ *adj*

tu·ber \'tü-bər, 'tyü-\ *n* : a short fleshy usu. underground stem (as of a potato plant) bearing minute scalelike leaves each with a bud at its base

tu·ber·cle \'tü-bər-kəl, 'tyü-\ *n* 1 : a small knobby prominence or outgrowth esp. on an animal or plant 2 : a small abnormal lump in an organ or on the skin; *esp* : one caused by tuberculosis

tubercle bacillus *n* : a bacterium that is the cause of tuberculosis

tu·ber·cu·lar \tù-'bər-kyə-lər, tyù-\ *adj* 1 : TUBERCULOUS 2 : of, resembling, or being a tubercle

tu·ber·cu·lin \tù-'bər-kyə-lən, tyù-\ *n* : a sterile liquid extracted from the tubercle bacillus and used in the diagnosis of tuberculosis esp. in children and cattle

tu·ber·cu·lo·sis \tù-ˌbər-kyə-'lō-səs, tyù-\ *n, pl* **-lo·ses** \-ˌsēz\ : a communicable bacterial disease that affects esp. the lungs and is typically marked by fever, cough, difficulty in breathing, and formation of tubercles — **tu·ber·cu·lous** \-'bər-kyə-ləs\ *adj*

tube·rose \'tüb-ˌrōz, 'tyüb-\ *n* : a bulbous herb related to the agaves and often grown for its spike of fragrant waxy= white flowers

tu·ber·ous \'tü-bə-rəs, 'tyü-\ *adj* : of, resembling, or being a tuber

tub·ing \'tü-biŋ, 'tyü-\ *n* 1 : material in the form of a tube; *also* : a length of tube 2 : a series or system of tubes

tu·bu·lar \'tü-byə-lər, 'tyü-\ *adj* : having the form of or consisting of a tube; *also* : made with tubes

tu·bule \'tü-byül, 'tyü-\ *n* : a small tube

¹**tuck** \'tək\ *vb* 1 : to pull up into a fold ⟨~ed up her skirt⟩ 2 : to make tucks in 3 : to put into a snug often concealing place ⟨~ a book under the arm⟩ 4 : to secure in place by pushing the edges under ⟨~ in a blanket⟩ 5 : to cover by tucking in bedclothes

²**tuck** *n* 1 : a fold stitched into cloth to shorten, decorate, or control fullness 2 : a cosmetic surgical operation for the removal of excess skin or fat ⟨a tummy ~⟩

tuck·er \'tə-kər\ *vb* **tuck·ered**; **tuck·er·ing** : EXHAUST, FATIGUE ⟨was ~ed out after a long day's work⟩

Tues *or* **Tue** *abbr* Tuesday

Tues·day \'tüz-dē, 'tyüz-, -dā\ *n* : the 3d day of the week

tu·fa \'tü-fə, 'tyü-\ *n* : a porous rock (as travertine) formed as a deposit from springs or streams

tuff \'təf\ *n* : a rock composed of volcanic detritus

¹**tuft** \'təft\ *n* 1 : a small cluster of long flexible outgrowths (as hairs); *also* : a bunch of soft fluffy threads cut off short and used as ornament 2 : CLUMP, CLUSTER — **tuft·ed** *adj*

²**tuft** *vb* 1 : to provide or adorn with a tuft 2 : to make (as a mattress) firm by stitching at intervals and sewing on tufts — **tuft·er** *n*

¹**tug** \'təg\ *vb* **tugged**; **tug·ging** 1 : to pull hard 2 : to struggle in opposition : CONTEND 3 : to move by pulling hard : HAUL 4 : to tow with a tugboat

²**tug** *n* 1 : a harness trace 2 : an act of tugging : PULL 3 : a straining effort 4 : a struggle between opposing people or forces 5 : TUGBOAT

tug·boat \-ˌbōt\ *n* : a strongly built boat used for towing or pushing

tug–of–war \ˌtəg-əv-'wȯr\ *n, pl* **tugs–of–war** 1 : a struggle for supremacy 2 : an athletic contest in which two teams pull against each other at opposite ends of a rope

tu·grik *or* **tu·ghrik** \'tü-grik\ *n* — see MONEY table

tu·ition \tü-'i-shən, tyü-\ *n* : money paid for instruction ⟨college ~⟩

tu·la·re·mia \ˌtü-lə-'rē-mē-ə, ˌtyü-\ *n* : an infectious bacterial disease esp. of wild rabbits, rodents, humans, and some domestic animals that in humans is marked by symptoms (as fever) similar to those of influenza

tu·lip \'tü-ləp, 'tyü-\ *n* [NL *tulipa*, fr. Turk *tülbent* turban] : any of a genus of Eurasian bulbous herbs related to the lilies and grown for their large showy erect cup-shaped flowers; *also* : a flower or bulb of a tulip

tulip tree *n* : a tall No. American timber tree that is related to the magnolias and has greenish tulip-shaped flowers and soft white wood

tulle \'tül\ *n* : a sheer often stiffened silk, rayon, or nylon net ⟨a veil of ~⟩

¹**tum·ble** \'təm-bəl\ *vb* **tum·bled**; **tum·bling** [ME, fr. *tumben* to dance, fr. OE *tumbian*] 1 : to fall or cause to fall suddenly and helplessly 2 : to fall into ruin 3 : to perform gymnastic feats of rolling and turning 4 : to roll over and over : TOSS 5 : to issue forth hurriedly and confusedly 6 : to come to understand 7 : to throw together in a confused mass

²**tumble** *n* 1 : a disorderly state 2 : an act or instance of tumbling

tum·ble·down \'təm-bəl-'daún\ *adj* : DILAPIDATED, RAMSHACKLE ⟨a ~ shack⟩

tum·bler \'təm-blər\ *n* 1 : one that tumbles; *esp* : ACROBAT 2 : a drinking glass without foot or stem 3 : a movable obstruction in a lock that must be adjusted to a particular position (as by a key) before the bolt can be thrown

tum·ble·weed \'təm-bəl-ˌwēd\ *n* : a plant that breaks away from its roots in autumn and is driven about by the wind

tum·brel *or* **tum·bril** \'təm-brəl\ *n* 1 : CART 2 : a vehicle carrying condemned persons (as during the French Revolution) to a place of execution

tu·mid \'tü-məd, 'tyü-\ *adj* 1 : SWOLLEN, DISTENDED 2 : BOMBASTIC, TURGID

tum·my \'tə-mē\ *n, pl* **tummies** : BELLY, ABDOMEN, STOMACH

tu·mor \'tü-mər, 'tyü-\ *n* : an abnormal and functionless new growth of tissue that arises from uncontrolled cellular proliferation — **tu·mor·ous** *adj*

tu·mour *chiefly Brit var of* TUMOR

tu·mult \'tü-ˌməlt, 'tyü-\ *n* 1 : UPROAR 2 : violent agitation of mind or feelings

tu·mul·tu·ous \tü-'məl-chə-wəs, tyü-, -chəs\ *adj* 1 : marked by tumult ⟨~ applause⟩ 2 : tending to incite a tumult 3 : marked by violent upheaval ⟨~ war years⟩

tun \'tən\ *n* : a large cask

tu·na \'tü-nə, 'tyü-\ *n, pl* **tuna** *or* **tunas** : any of several mostly large marine fishes related to the mackerels and caught for food and sport; *also* : the flesh of a tuna

tun·able \'tü-nə-bəl, 'tyü-\ *adj* : capable of being tuned — **tun·abil·i·ty** \ˌtü-nə-'bi-lə-tē, ˌtyü-\ *n*

tun·dra \'tən-drə\ *n* [Russ] : a treeless plain of arctic and subarctic regions

¹**tune** \'tün, 'tyün\ *n* 1 : a succession of pleasing musical tones : MELODY 2 : correct musical pitch 3 : harmonious relationship : AGREEMENT ⟨in ~ with the times⟩ 4 : general attitude ⟨changed his ~⟩ 5 : AMOUNT, EXTENT ⟨in debt to the ~ of millions⟩

²**tune** *vb* **tuned**; **tun·ing** 1 : to adjust in musical pitch 2 : to bring or come into harmony : ATTUNE 3 : to put in good working order 4 : to adjust a radio or television receiver so as to receive a broadcast 5 : to adjust the frequency of the output of (a device) to a chosen frequency — **tun·er** *n*

tune·ful \-fəl\ *adj* : MELODIOUS, MUSICAL ⟨a ~ ballad⟩ — **tune·ful·ly** *adv* — **tune·ful·ness** *n*

tune·less \-ləs\ *adj* 1 : UNMELODIOUS 2 : not producing music — **tune·less·ly** *adv*

tune–up \'tün-ˌəp, 'tyün-\ *n* : an adjustment to ensure efficient functioning ⟨an engine ~⟩

tung·sten \'təŋ-stən\ *n* [Sw, fr. *tung* heavy + *sten* stone] : a gray-white hard heavy ductile metallic chemical element used esp. in carbide materials, electrical components, and alloys

tu·nic \'tü-nik, 'tyü-\ *n* 1 : a usu. knee-length belted garment worn by ancient Greeks and Romans 2 : a hip-length or longer blouse or jacket

tuning fork *n* : a 2-pronged metal implement that gives a fixed tone when struck and is useful for tuning musical instruments

¹**tun·nel** \'tə-nᵊl\ *n* : an enclosed passage (as a tube or conduit); *esp* : one underground (as in a mine)

²**tunnel** *vb* **-neled** *or* **-nelled**; **-nel·ing** *or* **-nel·ling** : to make a tunnel through or under — **tun·nel·er** \'tən-lər, 'tə-nᵊl-ər\ *n*

tun·ny \'tə-nē\ *n, pl* **tunnies** *also* **tunny** : TUNA

tuque \'tük, 'tyük\ *n* [CanF] : a warm knitted cone-shaped cap

tur·ban \'tər-bən\ *n* 1 : a headdress worn esp. by Muslims and made of a cap around which is wound a long cloth 2 : a headdress resembling a turban; *esp* : a woman's close-fitting hat without a brim

tur·bid \'tər-bəd\ *adj* [L *turbidus* confused, turbid, fr. *turba* confusion, crowd] 1 : cloudy or discolored by suspended particles ⟨a ~ stream⟩ 2 : CONFUSED, MUDDLED — **tur·bid·i·ty** \ˌtər-'bi-də-tē\ *n*

tur·bine \'tər-bən, -ˌbīn\ *n* [F, fr. L *turbin-, turbo* top, whirlwind, whirl] : an engine whose central driveshaft is fitted with curved vanes spun by the pressure of water, steam, or gas

tur·bo·fan \'tər-bō-ˌfan\ *n* : a jet engine having a fan driven by a turbine for supplying air for combustion

tur·bo·jet \-ˌjet\ *n* : an airplane powered by a jet engine **(turbojet engine)** having a turbine-driven air compressor supplying compressed air to the combustion chamber

tur·bo·prop \-ˌpräp\ *n* : an airplane powered by a jet engine **(turboprop engine)** having a turbine-driven propeller

tur·bot \'tər-bət\ *n, pl* **turbot** *also* **turbots** : a European flatfish that is a popular food fish; *also* : any of several similar flatfishes

tur·bu·lence \'tər-byə-ləns\ *n* : the quality or state of being turbulent

tur·bu·lent \-lənt\ *adj* **1** : causing violence or disturbance **2** : marked by agitation or tumult : TEMPESTUOUS ⟨a ~ marriage⟩ — **tur·bu·lent·ly** *adv*

tu·reen \tə-'rēn, tyū-\ *n* [F *terrine*, fr. MF, fr. fem. of *terrin* of earth] : a deep bowl from which foods (as soup) are served at the table

¹**turf** \'tərf\ *n, pl* **turfs** \'tərfs\ *also* **turves** \'tərvz\ **1** : the upper layer of soil bound by grass and roots into a close mat; *also* : a piece of this **2** : an artificial substitute for turf (as on a playing field) **3** : a piece of peat dried for fuel **4** : a track or course for horse racing; *also* : horse racing as a sport or business

²**turf** *vb* : to cover with turf

tur·gid \'tər-jəd\ *adj* **1** : being in a swollen state **2** : excessively embellished in style or language : BOMBASTIC ⟨~ writing⟩ — **tur·gid·i·ty** \ˌtər-'ji-də-tē\ *n*

tur·key \'tər-kē\ *n, pl* **turkeys** [*Turkey*, country in western Asia and southeastern Europe; fr. confusion with the guinea fowl, supposed to be imported from Turkish territory] : a large No. American bird related to the domestic chicken and widely raised for food

turkey buzzard *n* : TURKEY VULTURE

turkey vulture *n* : an American vulture with a red head and whitish bill

Turk·ish \'tər-kish\ *n* : the language of Turkey — **Turkish** *adj*

tur·mer·ic \'tər-mə-rik\ *n* : a spice or dyestuff obtained from the large aromatic deep-yellow rhizome of an Indian perennial herb related to the ginger; *also* : this herb

tur·moil \'tər-ˌmȯi(-ə)l\ *n* : an extremely confused or agitated condition

¹**turn** \'tərn\ *vb* **1** : to move or cause to move around an axis or center : ROTATE, REVOLVE ⟨~ a wheel⟩ **2** : to effect a desired end by turning something ⟨~ the oven on⟩ **3** : WRENCH ⟨~ an ankle⟩ **4** : to change or cause to change position by moving through an arc of a circle ⟨~ed her chair to the fire⟩ **5** : to cause to move around a center so as to show another side of ⟨~ a page⟩ **6** : to revolve mentally : PONDER **7** : to become dizzy : REEL **8** : to reverse the sides or surfaces of ⟨~ a pancake⟩ **9** : UPSET, DISORDER ⟨things were ~ed topsy-turvy⟩ **10** : to set in another esp. contrary direction **11** : to change one's course or direction **12** : to go around ⟨~ a corner⟩ **13** : BECOME ⟨my hair ~ed gray⟩ ⟨~ed twenty-one⟩ **14** : to direct toward or away from something; *also* : DEVOTE, APPLY **15** : to have recourse **16** : to become or make hostile **17** : to cause to become of a specified nature or appearance ⟨~s the leaves yellow⟩ **18** : to make or become spoiled : SOUR **19** : to pass from one state to another ⟨water ~s to ice⟩ **20** : CONVERT, TRANSFORM **21** : TRANSLATE, PARAPHRASE **22** : to give a rounded form to; *esp* : to shape by means of a lathe **23** : to gain by passing in trade ⟨~ a quick profit⟩ — **turn·able** \'tər-nə-bəl\ *adj* — **turn color 1** : BLUSH **2** : to become pale — **turn loose** : to set free

²**turn** *n* **1** : a turning about a center or axis : REVOLUTION, ROTATION **2** : the action or an act of giving or taking a different direction ⟨make a left ~⟩ **3** : a change of course or tendency ⟨a ~ for the better⟩ **4** : a place at which something turns : BEND, CURVE **5** : a short walk or trip round about ⟨take a ~ around the block⟩ **6** : an act affecting another ⟨did him a good ~⟩ **7** : a place, time, or opportunity accorded in a scheduled order ⟨waited his ~ in line⟩ **8** : a period of duty : SHIFT **9** : a short act esp. in a variety show **10** : a special purpose or requirement ⟨the job serves his ~⟩ **11** : a skillful fashioning ⟨neat ~ of phrase⟩ **12** : a single round (as of rope passed around an object) **13** : natural or special aptitude **14** : a usu. sudden and brief disorder of body or spirits; *esp* : a spell of nervous shock or faintness

turn·about \'tərn-ə-ˌbaût\ *n* **1** : a reversal of direction, trend, or policy **2** : RETALIATION

turn·buck·le \'tərn-ˌbə-kəl\ *n* : a link with a screw thread at one or both ends for tightening a rod or stay

turn·coat \-ˌkōt\ *n* : one who switches to an opposing side or party : TRAITOR

turn down *vb* : to decline to accept : REJECT — **turn·down** \'tərn-ˌdaûn\ *n*

turn·er \'tər-nər\ *n* **1** : one that turns or is used for turning **2** : one that forms articles with a lathe

turn·ery \'tər-nə-rē\ *n, pl* **-er·ies** : the work, products, or shop of a turner

turn in *vb* **1** : to deliver up **2** : to inform on **3** : to acquit oneself of ⟨*turn in* a good job⟩ **4** : to go to bed

turn·ing \'tər-niŋ\ *n* **1** : the act or course of one that turns **2** : a place of a change of direction

tur·nip \'tər-nəp\ *n* **1** : a garden herb related to the cabbage with a thick edible usu. white root **2** : RUTABAGA **3** : the root of a turnip

turn·key \'tərn-ˌkē\ *n, pl* **turnkeys** : one who has charge of a prison's keys

turn·off \'tərn-ˌȯf\ *n* : a place for turning off esp. from an expressway

turn off *vb* **1** : to deviate from a straight course or a main road **2** : to stop the functioning or flow of **3** : to cause to lose interest; *also* : to evoke a negative feeling in ⟨violence on TV *turns* her *off*⟩

turn on *vb* **1** : to cause to flow, function, or operate **2** : to get high or cause to get high as a result of using a drug (as marijuana) **3** : EXCITE, STIMULATE

turn·out \'tərn-ˌaût\ *n* **1** : an act of turning out **2** : the number of people who participate or attend an event **3** : a widened place in a highway for vehicles to pass or park **4** : manner of dress **5** : net yield : OUTPUT

turn out *vb* **1** : EXPEL, EVICT **2** : PRODUCE **3** : to cause to stop functioning by turning a switch **4** : to come forth and assemble **5** : to get out of bed **6** : to prove to be the end

¹**turn·over** \'tərn-ˌō-vər\ *n* **1** : UPSET **2** : SHIFT, REVERSAL **3** : a filled pastry made by turning half of the crust over the other half **4** : the volume of business done **5** : movement (as of goods or people) into, through, and out of a place **6** : the number of persons hired within a period to replace those leaving or dropped **7** : an instance of a team's losing possession of the ball esp. through error

²**turnover** *adj* : capable of being turned over

turn over *vb* : TRANSFER ⟨*turn* the job *over* to her⟩

turn·pike \'tərn-ˌpīk\ *n* [ME *turnepike* revolving frame bearing spikes and serving as a barrier, fr. *turnen* to turn + *pike*] **1** : TOLLGATE; *also* : an expressway on which tolls are charged **2** : a main road

turn·stile \-ˌstī(-ə)l\ *n* : a post with arms pivoted on the top set in a passageway so that persons can pass through only on foot one by one

turn·ta·ble \-ˌtā-bəl\ *n* : a circular platform that revolves (as for turning a locomotive or a phonograph record)

turn to *vb* : to apply oneself to work

turn up *vb* **1** : to come to light or bring to light : DISCOVER, APPEAR **2** : to raise or increase by or as if by turning a control **3** : to arrive at an appointed time or place **4** : to happen unexpectedly

tur·pen·tine \'tər-pən-ˌtīn\ *n* **1** : a mixture of oil and resin obtained from various cone-bearing trees (as pines) **2** : an oil distilled from turpentine or pine wood and used as a solvent and paint thinner

tur·pi·tude \'tər-pə-ˌtüd, -ˌtyüd\ *n* : inherent baseness : DEPRAVITY

tur·quoise *also* **tur·quois** \'tər-ˌkȯiz, -ˌkwȯiz\ *n* [ME *turkeys*, fr. AF *turkeise*, fr. fem. of *turkeis* Turkish, fr. *Turc* Turk] **1** : a blue, bluish green, or greenish gray mineral that is valued as a gem **2** : a light greenish blue color

tur·ret \'tər-ət\ *n* **1** : a little ornamental tower often at a corner of a building **2** : a low usu. revolving structure (as on a tank or warship) in which one or more guns are mounted — **tur·ret·ed** \'tər-ə-təd\ *adj*

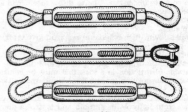

turnbuckles

¹tur·tle \'tər-t³l\ *n, archaic* : TURTLEDOVE

²turtle *n, pl* **turtles** *also* **turtle** : any of an order of horny=
beaked land, freshwater, or sea reptiles with the trunk
enclosed in a bony shell

tur·tle·dove \'tər-t³l-ˌdəv\ *n* : any of several small pigeons
noted for plaintive cooing

tur·tle·neck \-ˌnek\ *n* : a high close-fitting turnover collar
(as on a sweater); *also* : a sweater or shirt with a turtle-
neck — **tur·tle·necked** \-ˌnekt\ *adj*

turves *pl of* TURF

Tus·ca·ro·ra \ˌtəs-kə-'rȯr-ə\ *n, pl* **Tuscarora** *or* **Tusca-**
roras : a member of an American Indian people of No.
Carolina and later of New York and Ontario

tusk \'təsk\ *n* : a long enlarged protruding tooth (as of an
elephant, walrus, or boar) used esp. to dig up food or as
a weapon — **tusked** \'təskt\ *adj*

tusk·er \'təs-kər\ *n* : an animal with tusks; *esp* : a male
elephant with two normally developed tusks

¹tus·sle \'tə-səl\ *n* **1** : a physical struggle : SCUFFLE **2** : an
intense argument, controversy, or struggle

²tussle *vb* **tus·sled; tus·sling** : to struggle roughly ⟨play-
ers *tussled* for the ball⟩

tus·sock \'tə-sək\ *n* : a dense tuft esp. of grass or sedge;
also : a hummock in a marsh or bog bound together by
roots — **tus·socky** *adj*

tu·te·lage \'tü-t³l-ij, 'tyü-\ *n* **1** : an act of guarding or protecting **2** : the state of being under a guardian or tutor
3 : instruction esp. of an individual

tu·te·lary \'tü-tə-ˌler-ē, 'tyü-\ *adj* : acting as a guardian
⟨~ deity⟩

¹tu·tor \'tü-tər, 'tyü-\ *n* **1** : a person charged with the instruction and guidance of another **2** : a private teacher

²tutor *vb* **1** : to have the guardianship of **2** : to teach or
guide individually : COACH ⟨~ed her in Latin⟩ **3** : to receive instruction esp. privately

tu·to·ri·al \tü-'tȯr-ē-əl, tyü-\ *n* : a class conducted by a tutor for one student or a small number of students

tut·ti \'tü-tē, 'tü-, -ˌtē\ *adj or adv* [It, pl. of *tutto* all] : with
all voices and instruments playing together — used as a
direction in music

tut·ti-frut·ti \ˌtü-ti-'frü-tē, ˌtü-\ *n* [It, lit., all fruits] : a confection or ice cream containing chopped usu. candied
fruits

tu·tu \'tü-(ˌ)tü\ *n* [F] : a short projecting skirt worn by a
ballerina

tux·e·do \ˌtək-'sē-dō\ *n, pl* **-dos** *or* **-does** [*Tuxedo* Park,
N.Y.] **1** : a usu. black or blackish blue jacket **2** : a
semiformal evening suit for men

TV \'tē-'vē\ *n* : TELEVISION

TVA *abbr* Tennessee Valley Authority

TV dinner *n* : a frozen packaged dinner that needs only
heating before serving

twad·dle \'twä-d³l\ *n* : silly idle talk : DRIVEL — **twaddle**
vb

twain \'twān\ *n* **1** : TWO **2** : PAIR

¹twang \'twaŋ\ *n* **1** : a harsh quick ringing sound like that
of a plucked bowstring **2** : nasal speech or resonance **3**
: the characteristic speech of a region

²twang *vb* **twanged; twang·ing** **1** : to sound or cause to
sound with a twang **2** : to speak with a nasal twang

tweak \'twēk\ *vb* **1** : to pinch and pull with a sudden jerk
and twitch **2** : to make small adjustments to — **tweak** *n*

tweed \'twēd\ *n* **1** : a rough woolen fabric made usu. in
twill weaves **2** *pl* : tweed clothing; *esp* : a tweed suit

tweedy \'twē-dē\ *adj* **tweed·i·er; -est** **1** : of or resembling
tweed **2** : given to wearing tweeds **3** : suggestive of the
outdoors in taste or habits **4** : ACADEMIC, SCHOLARLY

¹tween \'twēn\ *prep* : BETWEEN

²tween *n* : PRETEEN

¹tweet \'twēt\ *n* **1** : a chirping note **2** : a short message
posted on the Twitter online service

²tweet *vb* **1** : to make a chirping sound **2** : to post a
tweet

tweet·er \'twē-tər\ *n* : a small loudspeaker that reproduces sounds of high pitch

twee·zers \'twē-zərz\ *n pl* [obs. E *tweeze*, n., case for
small implements, short for obs. E *etweese*, fr. pl. of obs.
E *etwee*, fr. F *étui*] : a small pincerlike implement usu.
held between the thumb and index finger and used for
grasping something

twelve \'twelv\ *n* **1** : one more than 11 **2** : the 12th in

a set or series **3** : something having 12 units — **twelfth**
\'twelfth\ *adj or n* — **twelve** *adj or pron*

twelve-month \-ˌmənth\ *n* : YEAR

12–step \'twelv-ˌstep\ *adj* : of, relating to, or being a program designed esp. to help someone overcome a problem
(as an addiction) by following 12 tenets

twen·ty \'twen-tē\ *n, pl* **twenties** : two times 10 —
twen·ti·eth \-tē-əth\ *adj or n* — **twenty** *adj or pron*

twenty–twenty *or* **20/20** \ˌtwen-tē-'twen-tē\ *adj* : characterized by a visual capacity for seeing detail that is normal for the human eye ⟨~ vision⟩

twice \'twīs\ *adv* **1** : on two occasions **2** : two times ⟨~
two is four⟩

¹twid·dle \'twi-d³l\ *vb* **twid·dled; twid·dling** **1** : to be busy
with trifles; *also* : to play idly with something **2** : to rotate lightly or idly

²twiddle *n* : TURN, TWIST

twig \'twig\ *n* : a small branch — **twig·gy** *adj*

twi·light \'twī-ˌlīt\ *n* **1** : the light from the sky between
full night and sunrise or between sunset and full night **2**
: a state of imperfect clarity **3** : a period of decline

twilight zone *n* **1** : an area just beyond ordinary legal or
ethical limits **2** : TWILIGHT 2 **3** : a world of fantasy or
unreality

twill \'twil\ *n* [ME *twyll*, fr. OE *twilic* having a double thread,
part trans. of L *bilic-, bilix*, fr. *bi-* two + *licium* thread] **1**
: a fabric with a twill weave **2** : a textile weave that gives
an appearance of diagonal lines

twilled \'twild\ *adj* : made with a twill weave

¹twin \'twin\ *n* **1** : either of two offspring produced at a
birth **2** : one of two persons or things closely related to
or resembling each other

²twin *vb* **twinned; twin·ning** **1** : to be coupled with another **2** : to bring forth twins

³twin *adj* **1** : born with one other or as a pair at one birth
⟨~ brother⟩ ⟨~ girls⟩ **2** : made up of two similar or related members or parts **3** : being one of a pair ⟨~ city⟩

¹twine \'twīn\ *n* **1** : a strong thread of two or three
strands twisted together **2** : an act of entwining or interlacing — **twiny** *adj*

²twine *vb* **twined; twin·ing** **1** : to twist together; *also* : to
form by twisting **2** : INTERLACE, WEAVE **3** : to coil
about a support **4** : to stretch or move in a sinuous
manner — **twin·er** *n*

¹twinge \'twinj\ *vb* **twinged; twing·ing** *or* **twinge·ing** : to
affect with or feel a sharp sudden pain

²twinge *n* : a sudden sharp stab (as of pain or distress)

¹twin·kle \'twiŋ-kəl\ *vb* **twin·kled; twin·kling** **1** : to shine
or cause to shine with a flickering or sparkling light **2**
: to appear bright with merriment **3** : to flutter or flit
rapidly — **twin·kler** *n*

²twinkle *n* **1** : a wink of the eyelids; *also* : the duration of
a wink **2** : an intermittent radiance **3** : a rapid flashing
motion — **twin·kly** \'twiŋ-klē\ *adj*

twin·kling \'twiŋ-kliŋ\ *n* : the time required for a wink
: INSTANT

¹twirl \'twərl\ *vb* : to turn or cause to turn rapidly ⟨~ a
baton⟩ ✦ **Synonyms** REVOLVE, ROTATE, CIRCLE, SPIN,
SWIRL, PIROUETTE — **twirl·er** *n*

²twirl *n* **1** : an act of twirling **2** : COIL, WHORL — **twirly**
\'twər-lē\ *adj*

¹twist \'twist\ *vb* **1** : to unite by winding one thread or
strand round another **2** : WREATHE, TWINE **3** : to use so
as to hurt : SPRAIN ⟨~ed my ankle⟩ **4** : to twirl into spiral shape **5** : to subject (as a shaft) to torsion **6** : to turn
from the true form or meaning **7** : to pull off or break by
torsion **8** : to follow a winding course **9** : to turn around

²twist *n* **1** : something formed by twisting or winding **2**
: an act of twisting : the state of being twisted **3** : a spiral
turn or curve; *also* : SPIN **4** : a turning aside **5** : ECCEN-
TRICITY **6** : a distortion of meaning **7** : an unexpected
turn or development **8** : DEVICE, TRICK **9** : a variant approach or method

twist·er \'twis-tər\ *n* **1** : one that twists; *esp* : a ball with
a forward and spinning motion **2** : TORNADO; *also* : WA-
TERSPOUT 2

¹twit \'twit\ *n* : a silly or foolish person

²twit *vb* **twit·ted; twit·ting** : to ridicule as a fault; *also*
: TAUNT ✦ **Synonyms** DERIDE, MOCK, RAZZ

¹twitch \'twich\ *vb* **1** : to move or pull with a sudden motion
: JERK **2** : to move jerkily : QUIVER **3** : to have a twitch

²**twitch** *n* **1** : an act or movement of twitching **2** : a brief spasmodic contraction of muscle fibers

¹**twit·ter** \'twi-tər\ *vb* **1** : to make a succession of chirping noises **2** : to talk in a chattering fashion **3** : to tremble with agitation : FLUTTER

²**twitter** *n* **1** : a slight agitation of the nerves **2** : a small tremulous intermittent noise (as made by a swallow) **3** : a light chattering

twixt \'twikst\ *prep* : BETWEEN ⟨∼ the two extremes⟩

two \'tü\ *n, pl* **twos** **1** : one more than one **2** : the second in a set or series **3** : something having two units — **two** *adj or pron*

two cents *n* **1** *or* **two cents' worth** : an opinion offered on a topic under discussion **2** : a sum or object of very small value

two–faced \'tü-'fāst\ *adj* **1** : DOUBLE-DEALING, FALSE **2** : having two faces

two·fold \'tü-,fōld, -'fōld\ *adj* **1** : having two units or members **2** : being twice as much or as many — **two-fold** \-'fōld\ *adv*

2,4–D \,tü-,fór-'dē\ *n* : an irritant compound used esp. as a weed killer

2,4,5–T \-,fīv-'tē\ *n* : an irritant compound used esp. as an herbicide and defoliant

two·pence \'tə-pəns, *US also* 'tü-,pens\ *n* : the sum of two pence

two·pen·ny \'tə-pə-nē, *US also* 'tü-,pe-nē\ *adj* : of the value of or costing twopence

two–ply \'tü-'plī\ *adj* **1** : woven as a double cloth **2** : consisting of two strands or thicknesses ⟨∼ toilet paper⟩

two·some \'tü-səm\ *n* **1** : a group of two persons or things : COUPLE **2** : a golf match between two players

two–step \'tü-,step\ *n* : a ballroom dance performed with a sliding step in march or polka time; *also* : a piece of music for this dance — **two–step** *vb*

two–time \'tü-,tīm\ *vb* : to betray (a spouse or lover) by secret lovemaking with another — **two–tim·er** *n*

two–way *adj* : involving two elements or allowing movement or use in two directions or manners

2WD *abbr* two-wheel drive

twp *abbr* township

TWX *abbr* teletypewriter exchange

TX *abbr* Texas

ty·coon \tī-'kün\ *n* [Jp *taikun* feudal lord] **1** : a masterful leader (as in politics) **2** : a powerful businessman or industrialist

tying *pres part of* TIE

ty·iyn \tē-'en\ *n, pl* **tyiyn** — see *som* at MONEY table

tyke \'tīk\ *n* : a small child

tym·pan·ic membrane \tim-'pa-nik-\ *n* : EARDRUM

tym·pa·num \'tim-pə-nəm\ *n, pl* **-na** \-nə\ *also* **-nums** : EARDRUM; *also* : MIDDLE EAR — **tym·pan·ic** \tim-'pa-nik\ *adj*

¹**type** \'tīp\ *n* [ME, fr. LL *typus*, fr. L & Gk; L *typus* image, fr. Gk *typos* blow, impression, model, fr. *typtein* to strike, beat] **1** : a person, thing, or event that foreshadows another to come : TOKEN, SYMBOL **2** : MODEL, EXAMPLE **3** : a distinctive stamp, mark, or sign : EMBLEM **4** : rectangular blocks usu. of metal each having a face so shaped as to produce a character when printed **5** : the letters or characters printed from or as if from type **6** : general character or form common to a number of individuals and setting them off as a distinguishable class ⟨horses of draft ∼⟩ **7** : a class, kind, or group set apart by common characteristics ⟨a seedless ∼ of orange⟩; *also* : something distinguishable as a variety ⟨reactions of this ∼⟩ ✦ *Synonyms* SORT, NATURE, CHARACTER, DESCRIPTION

²**type** *vb* **typed; typ·ing 1** : to represent beforehand as a type **2** : to produce a copy of; *also* : REPRESENT, TYPIFY **3** : to write with a typewriter or computer keyboard **4** : to identify as belonging to a type **5** : TYPECAST

type A *adj* : relating to, having, or being a personality marked esp. by impatience and aggressiveness

type·cast \-,kast\ *vb* **-cast; -cast·ing 1** : to cast (an actor) in a part calling for characteristics possessed by the actor **2** : to cast repeatedly in the same type of role

type·face \-,fās\ *n* : all type of a single design

type 1 diabetes \'tīp-'wən-\ *n* : a form of diabetes mellitus usu. developing before adulthood and marked by severe insulin deficiency

type·script \'tīp-,skript\ *n* : typewritten matter

type·set \-,set\ *vb* **-set; -set·ting** : to set in type : COMPOSE — **type·set·ter** *n*

type 2 diabetes \-'tü-\ *n* : a form of diabetes mellitus developing esp. in adults and usu. in obese individuals and marked by excess sugar in the blood

type·write \-,rīt\ *vb* **-wrote** \-,rōt\; **-writ·ten** \-,ri-tᵊn\ : TYPE 3

type·writ·er \-,rī-tər\ *n* **1** : a machine for writing in characters similar to those produced by printers' type by means of types striking a ribbon to transfer ink or carbon impressions onto paper **2** : TYPIST

type·writ·ing \-,rī-tiŋ\ *n* : the use of a typewriter ⟨teach ∼⟩; *also* : writing produced with a typewriter

¹**ty·phoid** \'tī-,fòid, tī-'fòid\ *adj* : of, relating to, or being a communicable bacterial disease (**typhoid fever**) marked by fever, diarrhea, prostration, and intestinal inflammation

²**typhoid** *n* : TYPHOID FEVER

ty·phoon \tī-'fün\ *n* : a hurricane occurring esp. in the region of the Philippines or the China sea

ty·phus \'tī-fəs\ *n* : a severe infectious disease transmitted esp. by body lice, caused by a rickettsia, and marked by high fever, stupor and delirium, intense headache, and a dark red rash

typ·i·cal \'ti-pi-kəl\ *adj* **1** : being or having the nature of a type **2** : exhibiting the essential characteristics of a group **3** : conforming to a type — **typ·i·cal·i·ty** \,ti-pə-'ka-lə-tē\ *n* — **typ·i·cal·ness** *n*

typ·i·cal·ly \-pi-k(ə-)lē\ *adv* **1** : in a typical manner **2** : in typical circumstances

typ·i·fy \'ti-pə-,fī\ *vb* **-fied; -fy·ing 1** : to represent by an image, form, model, or resemblance **2** : to embody the essential or common characteristics of

typ·ist \'tī-pist\ *n* : a person who types esp. as a job

ty·po \'tī-pō\ *n, pl* **typos** : an error (as of spelling) in typed or typeset material

ty·pog·ra·pher \tī-'pä-grə-fər\ *n* : one who designs or arranges printing

ty·pog·ra·phy \tī-'pä-grə-fē\ *n* : the art of printing with type; *also* : the style, arrangement, or appearance of printed matter — **ty·po·graph·ic** \,tī-pə-'gra-fik\ *or* **ty·po·graph·i·cal** \-fi-kəl\ *adj* — **ty·po·graph·i·cal·ly** *adv*

ty·ran·ni·cal \tə-'ra-ni-kəl, tī-\ *also* **ty·ran·nic** \-nik\ *adj* : of or relating to a tyrant : DESPOTIC ✦ *Synonyms* ARBITRARY, ABSOLUTE, AUTOCRATIC — **ty·ran·ni·cal·ly** \-ni-k(ə-)lē\ *adv*

tyr·an·nise *Brit var of* TYRANNIZE

tyr·an·nize \'tir-ə-,nīz\ *vb* **-nized; -niz·ing** : to act as a tyrant : rule with unjust severity — **tyr·an·niz·er** *n*

ty·ran·no·saur \tə-'ra-nə-,sòr\ *n* : a massive American flesh-eating dinosaur of the Cretaceous that had small forelegs and walked on its hind legs

tyr·an·no·sau·rus \tə-,ra-nə-'sòr-əs\ *n* : TYRANNOSAUR

tyr·an·nous \'tir-ə-nəs\ *adj* : unjustly severe — **tyr·an·nous·ly** *adv*

tyr·an·ny \'tir-ə-nē\ *n, pl* **-nies** **1** : oppressive power **2** : the rule or authority of a tyrant : government in which absolute power is vested in a single ruler **3** : a tyrannical act

ty·rant \'tī-rənt\ *n* **1** : an absolute ruler : DESPOT **2** : a ruler who governs oppressively or brutally **3** : one who uses authority or power harshly

tyre *chiefly Brit var of* ²TIRE

ty·ro \'tī-rō\ *n, pl* **tyros** [ML, fr. L *tiro* young soldier, tyro] : a beginner in learning : NOVICE

tzar, tzarist *var of* CZAR, CZARIST

¹u \'yü\ *n, pl* **u's** *or* **us** \'yüz\ *often cap* : the 21st letter of the English alphabet

²u *abbr, often cap* unit

¹U \'yü\ *adj* : characteristic of the upper classes

²U *abbr* 1 [abbr. of *Union of Orthodox Hebrew Congregations*] kosher certification — often enclosed in a circle 2 university 3 unsatisfactory

³U *symbol* uranium

UAE *abbr* United Arab Emirates

UAR *abbr* United Arab Republic

UAW *abbr* United Automobile Workers

ubiq·ui·tous \yü-'bi-kwə-təs\ *adj* : existing or being everywhere at the same time : OMNIPRESENT — **ubiq·ui·tous·ly** *adv* — **ubiq·ui·ty** \-kwə-tē\ *n*

U–boat \'yü-ˌbōt\ *n* [trans. of G *U-boot,* short for *Unterseeboot,* lit., undersea boat] : a German submarine

UC *abbr* uppercase

ud·der \'ə-dər\ *n* : an organ (as of a cow) consisting of two or more milk glands enclosed in a large hanging sac and each provided with a nipple

UFO \ˌyü-(ˌ)ef-'ō\ *n, pl* **UFO's** *or* **UFOs** \-'ōz\ : an unidentified flying object; *esp* : FLYING SAUCER

ug·ly \'ə-glē\ *adj* **ug·li·er; -est** [ME, fr. ON *uggligr,* fr. *uggr* fear] 1 : FRIGHTFUL, DIRE 2 : offensive to the sight : HIDEOUS 3 : offensive or unpleasant to any sense 4 : morally objectionable : REPULSIVE 5 : likely to cause inconvenience or discomfort 6 : SURLY, QUARRELSOME ⟨an ~ disposition⟩ — **ug·li·ness** \-glē-nəs\ *n*

UHF *abbr* ultrahigh frequency

UK *abbr* United Kingdom

ukase \yü-'kās, -'kāz\ *n* [F & Russ; F, fr. Russ *ukaz,* fr. *ukazat'* to show, order] : an edict esp. of a Russian emperor or government

Ukrai·ni·an \yü-'krā-nē-ən\ *n* 1 : a native or inhabitant of Ukraine 2 : a Slavic language of the Ukrainian people — **Ukrainian** *adj*

uku·le·le *also* **uke·le·le** \ˌyü-kə-'lā-lē\ *n* [Hawaiian *'ukulele,* fr. *'uku* flea + *lele* jumping] : a small usu. 4-stringed guitar popularized in Hawaii

ul·cer \'əl-sər\ *n* 1 : an open eroded sore of skin or mucous membrane often discharging pus 2 : something that festers and corrupts like an open sore — **ul·cer·ous** *adj*

ul·cer·ate \'əl-sə-ˌrāt\ *vb* **-at·ed; -at·ing** : to become affected with an ulcer — **ul·cer·a·tive** \'əl-sə-ˌrā-tiv\ *adj*

ul·cer·a·tion \ˌəl-sə-'rā-shən\ *n* 1 : the process of forming or state of having an ulcer 2 : ULCER 1

ul·na \'əl-nə\ *n* : the bone on the little-finger side of the human forearm; *also* : a corresponding bone of the forelimb of vertebrates above fishes

ul·ster \'əl-stər\ *n* : a long loose overcoat

ult *abbr* 1 ultimate 2 ultimo

ul·te·ri·or \ˌəl-'tir-ē-ər\ *adj* 1 : lying farther away : more remote 2 : situated beyond or on the farther side 3 : going beyond what is openly said or shown : HIDDEN ⟨~ motives⟩

¹**ul·ti·mate** \'əl-tə-mət\ *adj* 1 : most remote in space or time : FARTHEST 2 : last in a progression : FINAL 3 : the best or most extreme of its kind 4 : arrived at as the last resort 5 : FUNDAMENTAL, ABSOLUTE, SUPREME ⟨~ reality⟩ 6 : incapable of further analysis or division : ELEMENTAL 7 : MAXIMUM ♦ *Synonyms* CONCLUDING, EVENTUAL, LATEST, TERMINAL — **ul·ti·mate·ly** *adv*

²**ultimate** *n* : something ultimate

ul·ti·ma·tum \ˌəl-tə-'mā-təm, -'mä-\ *n, pl* **-tums** *or* **-ta** \-tə\ : a final condition or demand whose rejection will bring about a resort to forceful action

ul·ti·mo \'əl-tə-ˌmō\ *adj* [L *ultimo mense* in the last month] : of or occurring in the month preceding the present

¹**ul·tra** \'əl-trə\ *adj* : going beyond others or beyond due limits : EXTREME

²**ultra** *n* : EXTREMIST

ul·tra·con·ser·va·tive \-kən-'sər-və-tiv\ *adj* : extremely conservative

ul·tra·high frequency \-'hī-\ *n* : a radio frequency between 300 and 3000 megahertz

¹**ul·tra·light** \'əl-trə-ˌlīt\ *adj* : extremely light esp. in weight

²**ultralight** *n* : a very light recreational aircraft typically carrying only one person

ul·tra·ma·rine \ˌəl-trə-mə-'rēn\ *n* 1 : a deep blue pigment 2 : a very bright deep blue color

ul·tra·mi·cro·scop·ic \-ˌmī-krə-'skä-pik\ *adj* : too small to be seen with an ordinary microscope

ul·tra·mod·ern \-'mä-dərn\ *adj* : extremely or excessively modern in idea, style, or tendency

ul·tra·pure \-'pyúr\ *adj* : of the utmost purity

ul·tra·short \-'shórt\ *adj* 1 : having a wavelength below 10 meters 2 : very short in duration

ul·tra·son·ic \ˌəl-trə-'sä-nik\ *adj* : having a frequency too high to be heard by the human ear — **ul·tra·son·i·cal·ly** \-ni-k(ə-)lē\ *adv*

ul·tra·son·ics \-'sä-niks\ *n sing or pl* 1 : ultrasonic vibrations 2 : the science of ultrasonic phenomena

ul·tra·sound \ˌsaúnd\ *n* 1 : ultrasonic vibrations 2 : the diagnostic or therapeutic use of ultrasound and esp. a technique involving the formation of a two-dimensional image of internal body structures 3 : a diagnostic examination using ultrasound

ul·tra·vi·o·let \-'vī-ə-lət\ *adj* : having a wavelength shorter than those of visible light and longer than those of X-rays ⟨~ radiation⟩; *also* : producing or employing ultraviolet radiation — **ultraviolet** *n*

ul·tra vi·res \'əl-trə-'vī-rēz\ *adv or adj* [NL, lit., beyond power] : beyond the scope of legal power or authority

ul·u·late \'əl-yə-ˌlāt\ *vb* **-lat·ed; -lat·ing** : HOWL, WAIL

uma·mi \ú-'mä-mē\ *n* [Jp, flavor] : a meaty or savory taste sensation produced esp. by monosodium glutamate

um·bel \'əm-bəl\ *n* : a flat-topped or rounded flower cluster in which the individual flower stalks all arise near one point on the main stem

um·ber \'əm-bər\ *n* : a brown earthy substance valued as a pigment either in its raw state or burnt — **umber** *adj*

umbilical cord *n* : a cord containing blood vessels that connects the navel of a fetus with the placenta of its mother

um·bi·li·cus \ˌəm-'bi-li-kəs, ˌəm-bə-'lī-\ *n, pl* **um·bi·li·ci** \ˌəm-'bi-lə-ˌkī; ˌəm-bə-'lī-ˌkī, -ˌsī\ *or* **um·bil·i·cus·es** : NAVEL — **um·bil·i·cal** \ˌəm-'bi-li-kəl\ *adj*

um·bra \'əm-brə\ *n, pl* **umbras** *or* **um·brae** \-(ˌ)brē, -ˌbrī\ 1 : SHADE, SHADOW 2 : the conical part of the shadow of a celestial body from which the sun's light is completely blocked

um·brage \'əm-brij\ *n* 1 : SHADE; *also* : FOLIAGE 2 : RESENTMENT, OFFENSE ⟨take ~ at a remark⟩

um·brel·la \ˌəm-'bre-lə\ *n* 1 : a collapsible shade for protection against weather consisting of fabric stretched over hinged ribs radiating from a center pole 2 : something that provides protection 3 : something that covers a range of elements

umi·ak \'ü-mē-ˌak\ *n* : an open Inuit boat made of a wooden frame covered with skins

ump \'əmp\ *n* : UMPIRE

um·pire \'əm-ˌpī(-ə)r\ *n* [ME *oumpere,* alter. of *noumpere* (the phrase *a noumpere* being understood as *an oumpere*), fr. AF *nounpier* single, odd, fr. *non* not + *per* equal, fr. L *par*] 1 : one having authority to decide finally a controversy or question between parties 2 : an official in a sport who rules on plays — **umpire** *vb*

ump·teen \'əmp-ˌtēn\ *adj* : very many : indefinitely numerous — **ump·teenth** \-ˌtēnth\ *adj*

UN *abbr* United Nations

un- \ˌən, ˈən\ *prefix* **1** : not : IN-, NON- **2** : opposite of
: contrary to

unabashed
unabated
unabsorbed
unabsorbent
unacademic
unaccented
unacceptable
unacclimatized
unaccommodating
unaccredited
unacknowledged
unacquainted
unadapted
unadjusted
unadorned
unadventurous
unadvertised
unaesthetic
unaffiliated
unafraid
unaggressive
unaided
unalike
unaltered
unambiguous
unambiguously
unambitious
unanchored
unannounced
unanswerable
unanswered
unanticipated
unapologetic
unapparent
unappealing
unappeased
unappetizing
unappreciated
unappreciative
unapproachable
unappropriated
unapproved
unarguable
unarguably
unarmored
unartistic
unashamed
unasked
unassertive
unassisted
unathletic
unattainable
unattended
unattested
unattractive
unauthentic
unauthorized
unavailable
unavowed
unawakened
unbaked
unbaptized
unbeloved
unbleached
unblemished
unblinking
unbound
unbranched
unbranded
unbreakable
unbridgeable
unbruised
unbrushed
unbudging
unburied
unburned
uncanceled
uncanonical

uncap
uncapitalized
uncared-for
uncataloged
uncaught
uncensored
uncensured
unchallenged
unchangeable
unchanged
unchanging
unchaperoned
uncharacteristic
unchaste
unchastely
unchasteness
unchastity
unchecked
unchivalrous
unchristened
unclad
unclaimed
unclassified
uncleaned
unclear
uncleared
unclouded
uncluttered
uncoated
uncollected
uncolored
uncombed
uncombined
uncomely
uncomic
uncommercial
uncompensated
uncomplaining
uncompleted
uncomplicated
uncomplimentary
uncompounded
uncomprehending
unconcealed
unconfined
unconfirmed
unconformable
uncongenial
unconnected
unconquered
unconsecrated
unconsidered
unconsolidated
unconstrained
unconsumed
unconsummated
uncontaminated
uncontested
uncontrolled
uncontroversial
unconverted
unconvincing
uncooked
uncooperative
uncoordinated
uncorrected
uncorroborated
uncountable
uncreative
uncredited
uncropped
uncrowded
uncrowned
uncrystallized
uncultivated
uncultured
uncured
uncurious

uncurtained
uncustomary
undamaged
undamped
undated
undecided
undecipherable
undeclared
undecorated
undefeated
undefended
undefiled
undefinable
undefined
undemanding
undemocratic
undenominational
undependable
undeserved
undeserving
undesired
undetected
undetermined
undeterred
undeveloped
undifferentiated
undigested
undignified
undiluted
undiminished
undimmed
undiplomatic
undirected
undisciplined
undisclosed
undiscovered
undiscriminating
undisguised
undismayed
undisputed
undissolved
undistinguished
undistributed
undisturbed
undivided
undogmatic
undomesticated
undone
undoubled
undramatic
undraped
undreamed
undressed
undrinkable
undulled
undutiful
undyed
uneager
uneatable
uneaten
uneconomic
uneconomical
unedifying
unedited
uneducated
unembarrassed
unemotional
unemphatic
unenclosed
unencumbered
unendurable
unenforceable
unenforced
unenlightened
unenterprising
unenthusiastic
unenviable
unequipped
unessential
unethical
unexamined

unexcelled
unexceptional
unexcited
unexciting
unexpired
unexplained
unexploded
unexplored
unexposed
unexpressed
unexpurgated
unfading
unfaltering
unfashionable
unfashionably
unfathomable
unfavorable
unfavorably
unfeasible
unfeminine
unfenced
unfermented
unfertilized
unfilled
unfiltered
unfitted
unflagging
unflattering
unflavored
unfocused
unfolded
unforced
unforeseeable
unforeseen
unforgivable
unforgiving
unformulated
unfortified
unframed
unfree
unfulfilled
unfunded
unfunny
unfurnished
unfussy
ungentle
ungentlemanly
ungerminated
unglamorous
unglazed
ungoverned
ungraceful
ungracefully
ungraded
ungrammatical
unground
ungrudging
unguided
unhackneyed
unhampered
unhardened
unharmed
unharvested
unhatched
unhealed
unhealthful
unheated
unheeded
unhelpful
unheralded
unheroic
unhesitating
unhindered
unhistorical
unhonored
unhoused
unhurried
unhurt
unhygienic
unidentifiable
unidentified

unidiomatic	unmusical	unready	unspent
unimaginable	unnameable	unrealistic	unspiritual
unimaginative	unnamed	unrealized	unspoiled
unimpaired	unnecessary	unrecognizable	unspoken
unimpassioned	unneeded	unrecognized	unsportsmanlike
unimpeded	unnewsworthy	unrecorded	unstained
unimportant	unnoticeable	unrecoverable	unstated
unimposing	unnoticed	unredeemable	unsterile
unimpressed	unobjectionable	unrefined	unstructured
unimpressive	unobservant	unreflecting	unstylish
unimproved	unobserved	unreflective	unsubdued
unincorporated	unobstructed	unregistered	unsubstantiated
uninfected	unobtainable	unregulated	unsubtle
uninfluenced	unofficial	unrehearsed	unsuccessful
uninformative	unofficially	unrelated	unsuccessfully
uninformed	unopened	unreliable	unsuitable
uninhabitable	unopposed	unrelieved	unsuited
uninhabited	unoriginal	unremarkable	unsullied
uninitiated	unorthodox	unremembered	unsupervised
uninjured	unorthodoxy	unremovable	unsupportable
uninspired	unostentatious	unrepentant	unsupported
uninstructed	unowned	unreported	unsure
uninstructive	unpaged	unrepresentative	unsurpassed
uninsured	unpaid	unrepresented	unsurprising
unintelligent	unpainted	unrepressed	unsurprisingly
unintelligible	unpaired	unresistant	unsuspected
unintelligibly	unpalatable	unresisting	unsuspecting
unintended	unpardonable	unresolved	unsuspicious
unintentional	unpasteurized	unresponsive	unsweetened
unintentionally	unpatriotic	unresponsiveness	unsymmetrical
uninteresting	unpaved	unrestful	unsympathetic
uninterrupted	unpeeled	unrestricted	unsystematic
uninvited	unperceived	unreturnable	untactful
uninviting	unperceptive	unrewarding	untainted
unjointed	unperformed	unrhymed	untalented
unjustifiable	unpersuaded	unrhythmic	untamed
unjustified	unpersuasive	unripened	untanned
unkept	unperturbed	unromantic	untapped
unknowable	unplanned	unromantically	untarnished
unknowledgeable	unplanted	unsafe	untaxed
unlabeled	unpleasing	unsaid	unteachable
unladylike	unplowed	unsalable	untenable
unlamented	unpoetic	unsalted	untenanted
unleavened	unpolished	unsanctioned	untended
unlicensed	unpolitical	unsanitary	untested
unlighted	unpolluted	unsatisfactory	unthrifty
unlikable	unposed	unsatisfied	untidy
unlimited	unpractical	unscented	untilled
unlined	unpredictability	unscheduled	untitled
unlit	unpredictable	unscholarly	untraceable
unliterary	unprejudiced	unsealed	untraditional
unlivable	unpremeditated	unseasoned	untrained
unlovable	unprepared	unseaworthy	untrammeled
unloved	unpreparedness	unsegmented	untranslatable
unloving	unprepossessing	unself-conscious	untranslated
unmade	unpressed	unself-consciously	untraveled
unmalicious	unpretending	unsensational	untraversed
unmanageable	unpretty	unsentimental	untreated
unmanned	unprivileged	unserious	untrimmed
unmapped	unprocessed	unserviceable	untrod
unmarked	unproductive	unsexual	untrodden
unmarketable	unprofessed	unshaded	untroubled
unmarred	unprofessional	unshakable	untrustworthy
unmarried	unprogrammed	unshaken	untruthful
unmasculine	unprogressive	unshapely	untypical
unmatched	unpromising	unshaven	unusable
unmeant	unprompted	unshorn	unvaried
unmeasurable	unpronounceable	unsifted	unvarying
unmeasured	unpropitious	unsigned	unventilated
unmelodious	unproven	unsinkable	unverifiable
unmentioned	unprovided	unsmiling	unverified
unmerited	unprovoked	unsociable	unversed
unmilitary	unpublished	unsoiled	unvisited
unmilled	unpunished	unsold	unwanted
unmixed	unquenchable	unsoldierly	unwarranted
unmodified	unquestioned	unsolicited	unwary
unmolested	unraised	unsolvable	unwashed
unmotivated	unrated	unsolved	unwavering
unmounted	unratified	unsorted	unweaned
unmovable	unreachable	unspecified	unwearable
unmoved	unreadable	unspectacular	unwearied

unweathered
unwed
unwelcome
unwilling
unwillingly
unwillingness

unwomanly
unworkable
unworn
unworried
unwounded
unwoven

un·able \ˌən-ˈā-bəl\ *adj* **1** : not able **2** : UNQUALIFIED, INCOMPETENT

un·abridged \ˌən-ə-ˈbrijd\ *adj* **1** : not abridged 〈an ~ edition of Shakespeare〉 **2** : complete of its class : not based on one larger 〈an ~ dictionary〉

un·ac·com·pa·nied \ˌən-ə-ˈkəm-pə-nēd\ *adj* : not accompanied; *esp* : being without instrumental accompaniment

un·ac·count·able \ˌən-ə-ˈkaůn-tə-bəl\ *adj* **1** : not to be accounted for : INEXPLICABLE **2** : not responsible — **un·ac·count·ably** \-blē\ *adv*

un·ac·count·ed \-ˈkaůn-təd\ *adj* : not accounted 〈the loss was ~ for〉

un·ac·cus·tomed \ˌən-ə-ˈkəs-təmd\ *adj* **1** : not customary : not usual or common **2** : not accustomed or habituated 〈~ to noise〉

un·adul·ter·at·ed \ˌən-ə-ˈdəl-tə-ˌrā-təd\ *adj* : PURE, UNMIXED 〈~ meat〉 ♦ **Synonyms** ABSOLUTE, SHEER, SIMPLE, UNALLOYED, UNDILUTED, UNMITIGATED

un·af·fect·ed \ˌən-ə-ˈfek-təd\ *adj* **1** : not influenced or changed mentally, physically, or chemically **2** : free from affectation : NATURAL, GENUINE — **un·af·fect·ed·ly** *adv*

un·alien·able \-ˈāl-yə-nə-bəl, -ˈā-lē-ə-\ *adj* : INALIENABLE

un·aligned \ˌən-ə-ˈlīnd\ *adj* : not associated with any one of competing international blocs 〈~ nations〉

un·al·loyed \ˌən-ə-ˈlȯid\ *adj* **1** : UNMIXED, UNQUALIFIED, PURE 〈~ happiness〉

un·al·ter·able \ˌən-ˈȯl-tə-rə-bəl\ *adj* : not capable of being altered or changed 〈an ~ rule〉 — **un·al·ter·ably** \-blē\ *adv*

un–Amer·i·can \ˌən-ə-ˈmer-ə-kən\ *adj* : not characteristic of or consistent with American customs or principles

unan·i·mous \yů-ˈna-nə-məs\ *adj* [L *unanimus,* fr. *unus* one + *animus* mind] **1** : being of one mind : AGREEING **2** : formed with or indicating the agreement of all — **una·nim·i·ty** \yü-nə-ˈni-mə-tē\ *n* — **unan·i·mous·ly** *adv*

un·arm \ˌən-ˈärm\ *vb* : DISARM

un·armed \-ˈärmd\ *adj* : not armed or armored 〈~ civilians〉

un·as·sail·able \ˌən-ə-ˈsā-lə-bəl\ *adj* : not liable to doubt, attack, or question 〈an ~ argument〉

un·as·sum·ing \ˌən-ə-ˈsü-miŋ\ *adj* : MODEST 〈an ~ librarian〉 〈an ~ manner〉 〈an ~ neighborhood〉 ♦ **Synonyms** HUMBLE, LOWLY, MEEK

un·at·tached \ˌən-ə-ˈtacht\ *adj* **1** : not married or engaged **2** : not joined or united

un·avail·ing \ˌən-ə-ˈvā-liŋ\ *adj* : being of no avail — **un·avail·ing·ly** *adv*

un·avoid·able \ˌən-ə-ˈvȯi-də-bəl\ *adj* : not avoidable : INEVITABLE 〈an ~ fact〉 ♦ **Synonyms** CERTAIN, INELUCTABLE, INESCAPABLE, NECESSARY — **un·avoid·ably** \-blē\ *adv*

¹un·aware \ˌən-ə-ˈwer\ *adv* : UNAWARES

²unaware *adj* : not aware : IGNORANT 〈~ of the danger〉 — **un·aware·ness** *n*

un·awares \-ˈwerz\ *adv* **1** : without knowing : UNINTENTIONALLY **2** : without warning : by surprise 〈taken ~〉

un·bal·anced \ˌən-ˈba-lənst\ *adj* **1** : not in a state of balance **2** : mentally disordered **3** : not adjusted so as to make credits equal to debits

un·bar \-ˈbär\ *vb* : UNBOLT, OPEN

un·bear·able \ˌən-ˈber-ə-bəl\ *adj* : greater than can be borne 〈~ pain〉 ♦ **Synonyms** INSUFFERABLE, INSUPPORTABLE, INTOLERABLE, UNENDURABLE, UNSUPPORTABLE — **un·bear·ably** \-blē\ *adv*

un·beat·able \-ˈbē-tə-bəl\ *adj* : not capable of being defeated ♦ **Synonyms** INDOMITABLE, INVINCIBLE, INVULNERABLE, UNCONQUERABLE

un·beat·en \-ˈbē-tᵊn\ *adj* **1** : not pounded, beaten, or whipped **2** : UNTRODDEN **3** : UNDEFEATED

un·be·com·ing \ˌən-bi-ˈkə-miŋ\ *adj* : not becoming : UNSUITABLE, IMPROPER 〈conduct ~ an officer〉 ♦ **Synonyms** INDECOROUS, INDECENT, INDELICATE, UNSEEMLY — **un·be·com·ing·ly** *adv*

un·be·knownst \ˌən-bi-ˈnȯnst\ *also* **un·be·known** \-ˈnȯn\ *adj* : happening or existing without one's knowledge

un·be·lief \ˌən-bə-ˈlēf\ *n* : the withholding or absence of belief : DOUBT — **un·be·liev·ing** \-ˈlē-viŋ\ *adj*

un·be·liev·able \-ˈlē-və-bəl\ *adj* : too improbable for belief; *also* : of such a superlative degree as to be hard to believe 〈an ~ catch for a touchdown〉 ♦ **Synonyms** INCONCEIVABLE, UNIMAGINABLE, UNTHINKABLE — **un·be·liev·ably** \-blē\ *adv*

un·be·liev·er \-ˈlē-vər\ *n* **1** : INFIDEL **2** : DOUBTER

un·bend \-ˈbend\ *vb* **-bent** \-ˈbent\; **-bend·ing** **1** : to free from being bent : make or become straight **2** : UNTIE **3** : to make or become less stiff or more affable : RELAX

un·bend·ing *adj* : formal and distant in manner : INFLEXIBLE

un·bi·ased \ˌən-ˈbī-əst\ *adj* : free from bias; *esp* : UNPREJUDICED 〈an ~ opinion〉 ♦ **Synonyms** DISINTERESTED, DISPASSIONATE, IMPARTIAL, NONDISCRIMINATORY, NONPARTISAN, OBJECTIVE, UNCOLORED

un·bid·den \-ˈbi-dᵊn\ *also* **un·bid** \-ˈbid\ *adj* : not bidden : UNASKED

un·bind \-ˈbīnd\ *vb* **-bound** \-ˈbaůnd\; **-bind·ing** **1** : to remove bindings from : UNTIE **2** : RELEASE

un·blessed *also* **un·blest** \ˌən-ˈblest\ *adj* **1** : not blessed **2** : EVIL

un·block \-ˈbläk\ *vb* : to free from being blocked

un·blush·ing \-ˈblə-shiŋ\ *adj* **1** : not blushing **2** : SHAMELESS 〈~ greed〉 — **un·blush·ing·ly** *adv*

un·bod·ied \-ˈbä-dēd\ *adj* **1** : having no body; *also* : DISEMBODIED **2** : FORMLESS

un·bolt \ˌən-ˈbōlt\ *vb* : to open or unfasten by withdrawing a bolt

un·bolt·ed \-ˈbōl-təd\ *adj* : not fastened by bolts

un·born \-ˈbȯrn\ *adj* : not yet born

un·bos·om \-ˈbů-zəm, -ˈbü-\ *vb* **1** : DISCLOSE, REVEAL **2** : to disclose the thoughts or feelings of oneself

un·bound·ed \-ˈbaůn-dəd\ *adj* : having no bounds or limits 〈~ enthusiasm〉 ♦ **Synonyms** BOUNDLESS, ENDLESS, IMMEASURABLE, LIMITLESS, MEASURELESS, UNLIMITED

un·bowed \ˌən-ˈbaůd\ *adj* **1** : not bowed down **2** : UNSUBDUED 〈~ by failure〉

un·bri·dled \-ˈbrī-dᵊld\ *adj* **1** : UNRESTRAINED 〈~ enthusiasm〉 **2** : not confined by a bridle

un·bro·ken \-ˈbrō-kən\ *adj* **1** : not damaged **2** : not subdued or tamed **3** : not interrupted : CONTINUOUS

un·buck·le \-ˈbə-kəl\ *vb* : to loose the buckle of : UNFASTEN 〈~ a belt〉

un·bur·den \-ˈbər-dᵊn\ *vb* **1** : to free or relieve from a burden **2** : to relieve oneself of (as cares or worries)

un·but·ton \-ˈbə-tᵊn\ *vb* : to unfasten the buttons of 〈~ your coat〉

un·called-for \ˌən-ˈkȯld-ˌfȯr\ *adj* : not called for, needed, or wanted

un·can·ny \-ˈka-nē\ *adj* **1** : GHOSTLY, MYSTERIOUS, EERIE **2** : suggesting superhuman or supernatural powers ♦ **Synonyms** SPOOKY, UNEARTHLY, WEIRD — **un·can·ni·ly** \-ˈka-nə-lē\ *adv*

un·ceas·ing \-ˈsē-siŋ\ *adj* : never ceasing ♦ **Synonyms** CEASELESS, CONTINUOUS, ENDLESS, INTERMINABLE, UNENDING, UNREMITTING — **un·ceas·ing·ly** *adv*

un·cer·e·mo·ni·ous \ˌən-ˌser-ə-ˈmō-nē-əs\ *adj* : acting without or lacking ordinary courtesy : ABRUPT 〈his ~ dismissal〉 — **un·cer·e·mo·ni·ous·ly** *adv*

un·cer·tain \ˌən-ˈsər-tᵊn\ *adj* **1** : not determined or fixed 〈an ~ quantity〉 **2** : subject to chance or change : not dependable 〈~ weather〉 **3** : not definitely known **4** : not sure 〈~ of the truth〉 — **un·cer·tain·ly** *adv*

un·cer·tain·ty \-tᵊn-tē\ *n* **1** : lack of certainty : DOUBT **2** : something that is uncertain ♦ **Synonyms** CONCERN, DOUBT, DUBIETY, INCERTITUDE, SKEPTICISM, SUSPICION

un·chain \ˌən-ˈchān\ *vb* : to free by or as if by removing a chain

un·charged \ˌən-ˈchärjd\ *adj* : having no electrical charge

un·char·i·ta·ble \-ˈcha-rə-tə-bəl\ *adj* : not charitable; *esp* : severe in judging others — **un·char·i·ta·ble·ness** *n* — **un·char·i·ta·bly** \-blē\ *adv*

un·chart·ed \-ˈchär-təd\ *adj* **1** : not recorded on a map, chart, or plan **2** : UNKNOWN 〈discussion moving into ~ territory〉

un·chris·tian \-ˈkris-chən\ *adj* **1** : not of the Christian faith **2** : contrary to the Christian spirit

un·churched \-ˈchərcht\ *adj* : not belonging to or connected with a church

un·cial \'ən-shəl, -chəl; 'ən-sē-əl\ *adj* : relating to or written in a form of script with rounded letters used esp. in early Greek and Latin manuscripts — **uncial** *n*

un·cir·cu·lat·ed \ˌən-'sər-kyə-ˌlā-təd\ *adj* : issued for use as money but kept out of circulation

un·cir·cum·cised \ˌən-'sər-kəm-ˌsīzd\ *adj* 1 : not circumcised 2 : HEATHEN

un·civ·il \ˌən-'si-vəl\ *adj* 1 : not civilized : BARBAROUS 2 : DISCOURTEOUS, ILL-MANNERED, IMPOLITE ⟨∼ remarks⟩

un·civ·i·lized \-'si-və-ˌlīzd\ *adj* 1 : not civilized : BARBAROUS 2 : remote from civilization : WILD

un·clasp \-'klasp\ *vb* : to open by or as if by loosing the clasp

un·cle \'əŋ-kəl\ *n* [ME, fr. AF, fr. L *avunculus* mother's brother] 1 : the brother of one's father or mother 2 : the husband of one's aunt or uncle

un·clean \ˌən-'klēn\ *adj* 1 : morally or spiritually impure 2 : prohibited by ritual law for use or contact 3 : DIRTY, SOILED — **un·clean·li·ness** \-lē-nəs\ *n* — **un·clean·ly** *adj* — **un·clean·ness** *n*

un·clench \-'klench\ *vb* : to open from a clenched position : RELAX

Uncle Tom \-'täm\ *n* [fr. *Uncle Tom,* faithful slave in Harriet Beecher Stowe's novel *Uncle Tom's Cabin* (1851-52)] *disparaging* : a black person who is eager to win the approval of whites

un·cloak \ˌən-'klōk\ *vb* 1 : to remove a cloak or cover from 2 : UNMASK, REVEAL ⟨∼ an impostor⟩

un·clog \-'kläg\ *vb* : to remove an obstruction from

un·close \-'klōz\ *vb* : OPEN — **un·closed** \-'klōzd\ *adj*

un·clothe \-'klōth\ *vb* : to strip of clothes or a covering — **un·clothed** \-'klōthd\ *adj*

un·coil \ˌən-'kȯi(-ə)l\ *vb* : to release or become released from a coiled state

un·com·fort·able \ˌən-'kəmf-tə-bəl, -'kəm-fər-tə-\ *adj* 1 : causing discomfort 2 : feeling discomfort — **un·com·fort·ably** \-blē\ *adv*

un·com·mit·ted \ˌən-kə-'mi-təd\ *adj* : not committed; *esp* : not pledged to a particular belief, allegiance, or program ⟨∼ voters⟩

un·com·mon \ˌən-'kä-mən\ *adj* 1 : not ordinarily encountered : UNUSUAL, RARE 2 : REMARKABLE, EXCEPTIONAL ⟨a soldier of ∼ courage⟩ ✦ *Synonyms* EXTRAORDINARY, PHENOMENAL, SINGULAR, UNIQUE — **un·com·mon·ly** *adv*

un·com·mu·ni·ca·tive \ˌən-kə-'myü-nə-ˌkā-tiv, -ni-kə-\ *adj* : not inclined to talk or impart information : RESERVED ✦ *Synonyms* CLOSEMOUTHED, RETICENT, SILENT, TACITURN

un·com·pro·mis·ing \ˌən-'käm-prə-ˌmī-ziŋ\ *adj* : not making or accepting a compromise : UNYIELDING ✦ *Synonyms* ADAMANT, INFLEXIBLE, OBDURATE, RIGID, UNBENDING

un·con·cern \ˌən-kən-'sərn\ *n* 1 : lack of care or interest : INDIFFERENCE 2 : freedom from excessive concern

un·con·cerned \-'sərnd\ *adj* 1 : not having any part or interest 2 : not anxious or upset : free of worry ✦ *Synonyms* ALOOF, DETACHED, INCURIOUS, REMOTE, UNCURIOUS, UNINTERESTED — **un·con·cern·ed·ly** \-'sər-nəd-lē\ *adv*

un·con·di·tion·al \ˌən-kən-'di-shə-nəl\ *adj* : not limited in any way ⟨∼ surrender⟩ — **un·con·di·tion·al·ly** *adv*

un·con·di·tioned \-'di-shənd\ *adj* 1 : not subject to conditions 2 : not acquired or learned : NATURAL ⟨∼ responses⟩ 3 : producing an unconditioned response ⟨∼ stimuli⟩

un·con·quer·able \ˌən-'käŋ-kə-rə-bəl\ *adj* : incapable of being conquered or overcome : INDOMITABLE

un·con·scio·na·ble \-'kän-shə-nə-bəl\ *adj* 1 : not guided or controlled by conscience 2 : not in accordance with what is right or just ⟨∼ sales practices⟩ ✦ *Synonyms* UNREASONABLE, UNDUE, UNJUSTIFIABLE, UNWARRANTABLE, UNWARRANTED — **un·con·scio·na·bly** \-blē\ *adv*

¹**un·con·scious** \ˌən-'kän-chəs, -shəs\ *adj* 1 : not knowing or perceiving : not aware 2 : not done consciously or on purpose 3 : having lost consciousness 4 : of or relating to the unconscious — **un·con·scious·ly** *adv* — **un·con·scious·ness** *n*

²**unconscious** *n* : the part of one's mental life of which one is not ordinarily aware but which is often a powerful force in influencing behavior

un·con·sti·tu·tion·al \ˌən-ˌkän-stə-'tü-shə-nəl, -'tyü-\ *adj* : not according to or consistent with the constitution of a state or society — **un·con·sti·tu·tion·al·i·ty** \-ˌtü-shə-'na-lə-tē, -ˌtyü-\ *n* — **un·con·sti·tu·tion·al·ly** \-'tü-shə-nə-lē, -'tyü-\ *adv*

un·con·trol·la·ble \ˌən-kən-'trō-lə-bəl\ *adj* : incapable of being controlled : UNGOVERNABLE — **un·con·trol·la·bly** \-blē\ *adv*

un·con·ven·tion·al \-'ven-chə-nəl\ *adj* : not conventional : being out of the ordinary — **un·con·ven·tion·al·i·ty** \-ˌven-chə-'na-lə-tē\ *n* — **un·con·ven·tion·al·ly** \-'ven-chə-nə-lē\ *adv*

un·cork \ˌən-'kȯrk\ *vb* 1 : to draw a cork from 2 : to release from a sealed or pent-up state; *also* : to let go

un·count·ed \-'kaun-təd\ *adj* 1 : not counted 2 : INNUMERABLE

un·cou·ple \-'kə-pəl\ *vb* : DISCONNECT ⟨∼ railroad cars⟩

un·couth \-'küth\ *adj* [ME, unfamiliar, fr. OE *uncūth,* fr. *un-* + *cūth* known] 1 : strange, awkward, and clumsy in shape or appearance 2 : vulgar in conduct or speech : RUDE ✦ *Synonyms* DISCOURTEOUS, ILL-MANNERED, IMPOLITE, UNGRACIOUS, UNMANNERED, UNMANNERLY

un·cov·er \-'kə-vər\ *vb* 1 : to make known : DISCLOSE, REVEAL 2 : to expose to view by removing some covering 3 : to take the cover from 4 : to remove the hat from; *also* : to take off the hat as a token of respect — **un·cov·ered** *adj*

un·crit·i·cal \ˌən-'kri-ti-kəl\ *adj* 1 : not critical : lacking in discrimination 2 : showing lack or improper use of critical standards or procedures — **un·crit·i·cal·ly** \-k(ə-)lē\ *adv*

un·cross \-'krȯs\ *vb* : to change from a crossed position ⟨∼ed his legs⟩

unc·tion \'əŋk-shən\ *n* 1 : the act of anointing as a rite of consecration or healing 2 : exaggerated or insincere earnestness of language or manner

unc·tu·ous \'əŋk-chə-wəs\ *adj* [ME, fr. MF or ML; MF *unctueus,* fr. ML *unctuosus,* fr. L *unctus* act of anointing, fr. *unguere* to anoint] 1 : FATTY, OILY 2 : insincerely smooth in speech and manner ⟨an ∼ politician⟩ — **unc·tu·ous·ly** *adv*

un·curl \ˌən-'kərl\ *vb* : to make or become straightened out from a curled or coiled position

un·cut \ˌən-'kət\ *adj* 1 : not cut down or into 2 : not shaped by cutting ⟨an ∼ diamond⟩ 3 : not having the folds of the leaves slit ⟨an ∼ book⟩ 4 : not abridged or curtailed ⟨the ∼ version of the film⟩ 5 : not diluted ⟨∼ heroin⟩

un·daunt·ed \-'dȯn-təd\ *adj* : not daunted : not discouraged or dismayed ✦ *Synonyms* BOLD, BRAVE, DAUNTLESS, FEARLESS, INTREPID, VALIANT — **un·daunt·ed·ly** *adv*

un·de·ceive \ˌən-di-'sēv\ *vb* : to free from deception, illusion, or error

un·de·mon·stra·tive \ˌən-di-'män-strə-tiv\ *adj* : restrained in expression of feeling : RESERVED

un·de·ni·able \ˌən-di-'nī-ə-bəl\ *adj* 1 : plainly true : INCONTESTABLE 2 : unquestionably excellent or genuine ✦ *Synonyms* INCONTROVERTIBLE, INDISPUTABLE, INDUBITABLE, UNQUESTIONABLE — **un·de·ni·ably** \-blē\ *adv*

¹**un·der** \'ən-dər\ *adv* 1 : in or into a position below or beneath something 2 : below some quantity, level, or limit ⟨$10 or ∼⟩ 3 : in or into a condition of subjection, subordination, or unconsciousness ⟨the ether put him ∼⟩

²**un·der** \ˌən-dər, 'ən-\ *prep* 1 : lower than and overhung, surmounted, or sheltered by ⟨∼ a tree⟩ 2 : subject to the authority or guidance of ⟨served ∼ him⟩ ⟨was ∼ contract⟩ 3 : subject to the action or effect of ⟨∼ the influence of alcohol⟩ 4 : within the division or grouping of ⟨items ∼ this heading⟩ 5 : less or lower than (as in size, amount, or rank) ⟨earns ∼ $5000⟩

³**under** \'ən-dər\ *adj* 1 : lying below, beneath, or on the ventral side 2 : facing or protruding downward 3 : SUBORDINATE 4 : lower than usual, proper, or desired in amount, quality, or degree

un·der·achiev·er \ˌən-dər-ə-'chē-vər\ *n* : one (as a student) who performs below an expected level of proficiency

un·der·act \-'akt\ *vb* : to perform feebly or with restraint

un·der·ac·tive \-'ak-tiv\ *adj* : characterized by abnormally low activity ⟨an ∼ thyroid gland⟩ — **un·der·ac·tiv·i·ty** \-ˌak-'ti-və-tē\ *n*

un·der·age \-'āj\ *adj* : of less than mature or legal age

un·der·arm \-'ärm\ *adj* 1 : UNDERHAND 2 ⟨an ~ throw⟩ 2 : placed under or on the underside of the arms ⟨~ seams⟩ — **underarm** *adv or n*

un·der·bel·ly \'ən-dər-ˌbe-lē\ *n* 1 : a vulnerable area 2 : the underside of a body or mass

un·der·bid \ˌən-dər-'bid\ *vb* -**bid**; -**bid·ding** 1 : to bid less than another 2 : to bid too low

un·der·body \'ən-dər-ˌbä-dē\ *n* : the lower parts of the body of a vehicle

un·der·bred \ˌən-dər-'bred\ *adj* : marked by lack of good breeding

un·der·brush \'ən-dər-ˌbrəsh\ *n* : shrubs, bushes, or small trees growing beneath large trees

un·der·car·riage \-ˌka-rij\ *n* 1 : a supporting framework or underside (as of an automobile) 2 : the landing gear of an airplane

undercarriage 2

un·der·charge \ˌən-dər-'chärj\ *vb* : to charge (as a person) too little — **undercharge** \'ən-dər-ˌchärj\ *n*

un·der·class \'ən-dər-ˌklas\ *n* : LOWER CLASS

un·der·class·man \ˌən-dər-'klas-mən\ *n* : a member of the freshman or sophomore class

un·der·clothes \'ən-dər-ˌklō͟t͟hz\ *n pl* : UNDERWEAR

un·der·cloth·ing \-ˌklō-thiŋ\ *n* : UNDERWEAR

un·der·coat \-ˌkōt\ *n* 1 : a coat worn under another 2 : a growth of short hair or fur partly concealed by the longer and usu. coarser hairs of a mammal 3 : a coat of paint under another

un·der·coat·ing \-ˌkō-tiŋ\ *n* : a special waterproof coating applied to the underside of a vehicle

un·der·cov·er \ˌən-dər-'kə-vər\ *adj* : acting or executed in secret; *esp* : employed or engaged in secret investigation ⟨an ~ agent⟩

un·der·croft \ˌən-dər-ˌkróft\ *n* [ME, fr. *under* + *crofte* crypt, fr. MD, fr. ML *crupta*, fr. L *crypta*] : a vaulted chamber under a church

un·der·cur·rent \-ˌkər-ənt\ *n* 1 : a current below the surface 2 : a hidden tendency of feeling or opinion ⟨an ~ of dread⟩

un·der·cut \ˌən-dər-'kət\ *vb* -**cut**; -**cut·ting** 1 : to cut away the underpart of 2 : to offer to sell or to work at a lower rate than 3 : to strike (the ball) obliquely downward so as to give a backward spin or elevation to the shot — **un·der·cut** \'ən-dər-ˌkət\ *n*

un·der·de·vel·oped \ˌən-dər-di-'ve-ləpt\ *adj* 1 : not normally or adequately developed ⟨~ muscles⟩ 2 : having a relatively low level of economic development ⟨the ~ nations⟩

un·der·dog \'ən-dər-ˌdóg\ *n* : the loser or predicted loser in a struggle

un·der·done \ˌən-dər-'dən\ *adj* : not thoroughly done or cooked : RARE

un·der·draw·ers \'ən-dər-ˌdrórz, -ˌdró-ərz\ *n pl* : UNDERPANTS

un·der·draw·ing \'ən-dər-ˌdró-iŋ\ *n* : a preliminary sketch made prior to painting

un·der·em·pha·size \ˌən-dər-'em-fə-ˌsīz\ *vb* : to emphasize inadequately — **un·der·em·pha·sis** \-səs\ *n*

un·der·em·ployed \-im-'plóid\ *adj* : having less than fulltime or adequate employment

un·der·es·ti·mate \-'es-tə-ˌmāt\ *vb* : to set too low a value on

un·der·ex·pose \-ik-'spōz\ *vb* : to expose (a photographic plate or film) for less time than is needed — **un·der·ex·po·sure** \-'spō-zhər\ *n*

un·der·feed \ˌən-dər-'fēd\ *vb* -**fed** \-'fed\; -**feed·ing** : to feed with too little food

un·der·foot \-'fút\ *adv* 1 : under the feet ⟨flowers trampled ~⟩ 2 : close about one's feet : in the way

un·der·fur \'ən-dər-ˌfər\ *n* : an undercoat of fur esp. when thick and soft

un·der·gar·ment \-ˌgär-mənt\ *n* : a garment to be worn under another

un·der·gird \ˌən-dər-'gərd\ *vb* : to brace up : STRENGTHEN

un·der·go \ˌən-dər-'gō\ *vb* -**went** \-'went\; -**gone** \-'gón, -'gän\; -**go·ing** 1 : to submit to : ENDURE 2 : to go through : EXPERIENCE ⟨~ a change⟩

un·der·grad \'ən-dər-ˌgrad\ *n* : UNDERGRADUATE

un·der·grad·u·ate \ˌən-dər-'gra-jə-wət, -jə-ˌwāt\ *n* : a student at a university or college who has not received a first degree

¹un·der·ground \ˌən-dər-'graúnd\ *adv* 1 : beneath the surface of the earth 2 : in or into hiding or secret operation

²un·der·ground \'ən-dər-ˌgraúnd\ *n* 1 : a space under the surface of the ground; *esp* : SUBWAY 2 : a secret political movement or group; *esp* : an organized body working in secret to overthrow a government or an occupying power 3 : an avant-garde group or movement that operates outside the establishment

³underground \'ən-dər-ˌgraúnd\ *adj* 1 : being, growing, operating, or located below the surface of the ground ⟨~ stems⟩ 2 : conducted by secret means 3 : produced or published by the underground ⟨~ publications⟩; *also* : of or relating to the avant-garde underground

un·der·growth \'ən-dər-ˌgrōth\ *n* : low growth (as of herbs and shrubs) on the floor of a forest

¹un·der·hand \'ən-dər-ˌhand\ *adv* 1 : in an underhanded or secret manner 2 : with an underhand motion

²underhand *adj* 1 : UNDERHANDED 2 : made with the hand kept below the level of the shoulder ⟨an ~ pitch⟩

¹un·der·hand·ed \ˌən-dər-'han-dəd\ *adv* : UNDERHAND

²underhanded *adj* : marked by secrecy and deception ⟨~ tactics⟩ — **un·der·hand·ed·ly** *adv* — **un·der·hand·ed·ness** *n*

un·der·lie \-'lī\ *vb* -**lay** \-'lā\; -**lain** \-'lān\; -**ly·ing** \-'lī-iŋ\ 1 : to lie or be situated under 2 : to be at the basis of : form the foundation of : SUPPORT

un·der·line \'ən-dər-ˌlīn\ *vb* 1 : to draw a line under 2 : EMPHASIZE, STRESS — **underline** *n*

un·der·ling \'ən-dər-liŋ\ *n* : SUBORDINATE, INFERIOR

un·der·lip \ˌən-dər-'lip\ *n* : the lower lip

un·der·ly·ing \ˌən-dər-'lī-iŋ\ *adj* 1 : lying under or below 2 : FUNDAMENTAL, BASIC ⟨~ principles⟩

un·der·mine \-'mīn\ *vb* 1 : to excavate beneath 2 : to weaken or wear away secretly or gradually ⟨~ authority⟩

un·der·most \'ən-dər-ˌmōst\ *adj* : lowest in relative position — **undermost** *adv*

¹un·der·neath \ˌən-dər-'nēth\ *prep* 1 : directly under 2 : under subjection to

²underneath *adv* 1 : below a surface or object : BENEATH 2 : on the lower side

un·der·nour·ished \ˌən-dər-'nər-isht\ *adj* : supplied with insufficient nourishment — **un·der·nour·ish·ment** \-'nər-ish-mənt\ *n*

un·der·pants \'ən-dər-ˌpants\ *n pl* : a usu. short undergarment for the lower trunk : DRAWERS

un·der·part \-ˌpärt\ *n* : a part lying on the lower side (as of a bird or mammal)

un·der·pass \-ˌpas\ *n* : a crossing of a highway and another way (as a road) at different levels; *also* : the lower level

un·der·pay \ˌən-dər-'pā\ *vb* : to pay less than what is normal or required

un·der·pin·ning \'ən-dər-ˌpi-niŋ\ *n* : the material and construction (as a foundation) used for support of a structure — **un·der·pin** \ˌən-dər-'pin\ *vb*

un·der·play \ˌən-dər-'plā\ *vb* : to treat or handle with restraint; *esp* : to play a role with subdued force

un·der·pop·u·lat·ed \ˌən-dər-'pä-pyə-ˌlā-təd\ *adj* : having a lower than normal or desirable density of population

un·der·priv·i·leged \-'priv-lijd, -'pri-və-lijd\ *adj* : having fewer esp. economic and social privileges than others

un·der·pro·duc·tion \ˌən-dər-prə-'dək-shən\ *n* : the production of less than enough to satisfy the demand or of less than the usual supply

un·der·rate \-'rāt\ *vb* : to rate or value too low

un·der·rep·re·sent·ed \ˌ-re-pri-'zen-təd\ *adj* : inadequately represented

un·der·score \'ən-dər-ˌskór\ *vb* 1 : to draw a line under : UNDERLINE 2 : EMPHASIZE — **underscore** *n*

¹**un·der·sea** \ˌən-dər-'sē\ *adj* : being, carried on, or used beneath the surface of the sea

²**undersea** *or* **un·der·seas** \-'sēz\ *adv* : beneath the surface of the sea

un·der·sec·re·tary \ˌən-dər-'se-krə-ˌter-ē\ *n* : a secretary immediately subordinate to a principal secretary ⟨~ of state⟩

un·der·sell \-'sel\ *vb* **-sold** \-'sōld\; **-sell·ing** : to sell articles cheaper than

un·der·sexed \-'sekst\ *adj* : deficient in sexual desire

un·der·shirt \'ən-dər-ˌshərt\ *n* : a collarless undergarment with or without sleeves

un·der·shoot \ˌən-dər-'shüt\ *vb* **-shot** \-'shät\; **-shoot·ing** 1 : to shoot short of or below (a target) 2 : to fall short of (a runway) in landing an airplane

un·der·shorts \'ən-dər-ˌshórts\ *n pl* : underpants for men or boys

un·der·shot \'ən-dər-ˌshät\ *adj* 1 : moved by water passing beneath ⟨an ~ waterwheel⟩ 2 : having the lower front teeth projecting beyond the upper when the mouth is closed

un·der·side \'ən-dər-ˌsīd, ˌən-dər-'sīd\ *n* : the side or surface lying underneath

un·der·signed \'ən-dər-ˌsīnd\ *n, pl* **undersigned** : one whose name is signed at the end of a document

un·der·sized \ˌən-dər-'sīzd\ *also* **un·der·size** \-'sīz\ *adj* : of a size less than is common, proper, or normal

un·der·skirt \'ən-dər-ˌskərt\ *n* : a skirt worn under an outer skirt; *esp* : PETTICOAT

un·der·staffed \ˌən-dər-'staft\ *adj* : inadequately staffed

un·der·stand \ˌən-dər-'stand\ *vb* **-stood** \-'stúd\; **-stand·ing** 1 : to grasp the meaning of : COMPREHEND 2 : to have thorough or technical acquaintance with or expertness in ⟨~ finance⟩ 3 : to have reason to believe ⟨I ~ you are leaving tomorrow⟩ 4 : INTERPRET ⟨we ~ this to be a refusal⟩ 5 : to have a sympathetic attitude 6 : to accept as settled ⟨it is *understood* that he will pay the expenses⟩ — **un·der·stand·able** \-'stan-də-bəl\ *adj*

un·der·stand·ably \-blē\ *adv* : as can be easily understood

¹**un·der·stand·ing** \ˌən-dər-'stan-diŋ\ *n* 1 : knowledge and ability to judge : INTELLIGENCE ⟨a person of ~⟩ 2 : agreement of opinion or feeling 3 : a mutual agreement informally or tacitly entered into

²**understanding** *adj* : endowed with understanding : TOLERANT, SYMPATHETIC

un·der·state \ˌən-dər-'stāt\ *vb* 1 : to represent as less than is the case 2 : to state with restraint esp. for effect — **un·der·state·ment** *n*

un·der·stood \ˌən-dər-'stúd\ *adj* 1 : agreed upon 2 : IMPLICIT

un·der·sto·ry \'ən-dər-ˌstòr-ē\ *n* : the vegetative layer between the top layer of a forest and the ground cover

un·der·study \'ən-dər-ˌstə-dē\ *n* : one who is prepared to act another's part or take over another's duties — **understudy** \'ən-dər-ˌstə-dē, ˌən-dər-'stə-dē\ *vb*

un·der·sur·face \'ən-dər-ˌsər-fəs\ *n* : UNDERSIDE

un·der·take \ˌən-dər-'tāk\ *vb* **-took** \-'túk\; **-tak·en** \-'tā-kən\; **-tak·ing** 1 : to take upon oneself : set about ⟨~ a task⟩ 2 : to put oneself under obligation 3 : GUARANTEE, PROMISE

un·der·tak·er \'ən-dər-ˌtā-kər\ *n* : one whose business is to prepare the dead for burial and to arrange and manage funerals

un·der·tak·ing \'ən-dər-ˌtā-kiŋ, ˌən-dər-'tā-kiŋ; *2 is* 'ən-dər-ˌtā-kiŋ *only*\ *n* 1 : the act of one who undertakes or engages in any project 2 : the business of an undertaker 3 : something undertaken 4 : PROMISE, GUARANTEE

under–the–counter *adj* : UNLAWFUL, ILLICIT ⟨~ sale of drugs⟩

un·der·tone \'ən-dər-ˌtōn\ *n* 1 : a low or subdued tone or utterance 2 : a subdued color (as seen through and modifying another color)

un·der·tow \-ˌtō\ *n* : the current beneath the surface that flows seaward when waves are breaking upon the shore

un·der·val·ue \ˌən-dər-'val-yü\ *vb* 1 : to value or estimate below the real worth 2 : to esteem lightly

un·der·wa·ter \ˌən-dər-'wó-tər, -'wä-\ *adj* : lying, growing, worn, or operating below the surface of the water ⟨an ~ camera⟩ — **un·der·wa·ter** *adv*

under way \-'wā\ *adv* 1 : into motion from a standstill 2 : in progress

un·der·wear \'ən-dər-ˌwer\ *n* : clothing or a garment worn next to the skin and under other clothing

un·der·weight \ˌən-dər-'wāt\ *adj* : weighing below what is normal, average, or necessary — **underweight** *n*

un·der·wire \'ən-dər-ˌwī(-ə)r\ *n* : a wire running through the bottom of a brassiere to aid in support

un·der·world \'ən-dər-ˌwərld\ *n* 1 : the place of departed souls : HADES 2 : the side of the world opposite to one 3 : the world of organized crime

un·der·write \'ən-dər-ˌrīt, ˌən-dər-'rīt\ *vb* **-wrote** \-ˌrōt, -'rōt\; **-writ·ten** \-ˌri-tⁿn, -'ri-tⁿn\; **-writ·ing** 1 : to write under or at the end of something else 2 : to set one's name to an insurance policy and thereby become answerable for a designated loss or damage 3 : to subscribe to : agree to 4 : to guarantee financial support of — **un·der·writ·er** *n*

un·de·sign·ing \ˌən-di-'zī-niŋ\ *adj* : having no artful, ulterior, or fraudulent purpose : SINCERE

un·de·sir·able \-'zī-rə-bəl\ *adj* : not desirable — **undesirable** *n*

un·de·vi·at·ing \ˌən-'dē-vē-ˌā-tiŋ\ *adj* : keeping a true course

un·dies \'ən-dēz\ *n pl* : UNDERWEAR; *esp* : women's underwear

un·do \ˌən-'dü\ *vb* **-did** \-'did\; **-done** \-'dən\; **-do·ing** 1 : to make or become unfastened or loosened : OPEN 2 : to make null or as if not done : REVERSE 3 : to bring to ruin; *also* : UPSET

un·doc·u·ment·ed \ən-'dä-kyə-ˌmen-təd\ *adj* 1 : not supported by documentary evidence 2 : lacking documents required for legal immigration

un·do·ing *n* : a cause of ruin

un·doubt·ed \-'daú-təd\ *adj* : not doubted or called into question : CERTAIN — **un·doubt·ed·ly** *adv*

¹**un·dress** \ˌən-'dres\ *vb* : to remove the clothes or covering of : STRIP, DISROBE

²**undress** *n* 1 : informal dress; *esp* : a loose robe or dressing gown 2 : ordinary dress 3 : NUDITY

un·due \-'dü, -'dyü\ *adj* 1 : not due 2 : exceeding or violating propriety or fitness : EXCESSIVE ⟨~ force⟩

un·du·lant \'ən-jə-lənt, 'ən-də-, -dyə-\ *adj* : rising and falling in waves ⟨~ hills⟩

undulant fever *n* : a human disease caused by bacteria from infected domestic animals or their products and marked by intermittent fever, chills, headache, weakness, and weight loss

un·du·late \-ˌlāt\ *vb* **-lat·ed**; **-lat·ing** [LL *undula* small wave, fr. L *unda* wave] 1 : to have a wavelike motion or appearance 2 : to rise and fall in pitch or volume ⟨*undulating* music⟩

un·du·la·tion \ˌən-jə-'lā-shən, ˌən-də-, -dyə-\ *n* 1 : wavy or wavelike motion 2 : pulsation of sound 3 : a wavy appearance or outline — **un·du·la·to·ry** \'ən-jə-lə-ˌtòr-ē, 'ən-də-, -dyə-\ *adj*

un·du·ly \ˌən-'dü-lē, 'ən-, -'dyü-\ *adv* : in an undue manner : EXCESSIVELY

un·dy·ing \-'dī-iŋ\ *adj* : not dying : IMMORTAL, PERPETUAL

un·earned \-'ərnd\ *adj* : not earned by labor, service, or skill ⟨~ income⟩

un·earth \ˌən-'ərth\ *vb* 1 : to dig out of or as if out of the earth ⟨~ buried treasure⟩ 2 : to bring to light : DISCOVER ⟨~ a secret⟩

un·earth·ly \-lē\ *adj* 1 : not of or belonging to the earth 2 : SUPERNATURAL, WEIRD; *also* : ABSURD

un·easy \ˌən-'ē-zē\ *adj* 1 : AWKWARD, EMBARRASSED ⟨~ among strangers⟩ 2 : disturbed by pain or worry; *also* : RESTLESS 3 : UNSTABLE ⟨an ~ truce⟩ — **un·eas·i·ly** \-'ē-zə-lē\ *adv* — **un·eas·i·ness** \-'ē-zē-nəs\ *n*

un·em·ployed \ˌən-im-'plóid\ *adj* : not being used; *also* : having no job

un·em·ploy·ment \-'plói-mənt\ *n* 1 : lack of employment 2 : money paid at regular intervals (as by a government agency) to an unemployed person

un·end·ing \ˌən-'en-diŋ\ *adj* : having no ending : ENDLESS

un·equal \ˌən-'ē-kwəl\ *adj* 1 : not alike (as in size, amount, number, or value) 2 : not uniform : VARIABLE 3 : badly balanced or matched 4 : INADEQUATE, INSUFFICIENT ⟨~ to the task⟩ — **un·equal·ly** *adv*

un·equaled *or* **un·equalled** \-kwəld\ *adj* : not equaled : UNPARALLELED ⟨an ~ artist of ~ talent⟩

un·equiv·o·cal \ˌən-i-'kwi-və-kəl\ *adj* : leaving no doubt : CLEAR — **un·equiv·o·cal·ly** *adv*

un·err·ing \ˌən-'er-iŋ, ˌən-'ər-\ *adj* : making no errors : CERTAIN, UNFAILING ⟨∼ accuracy⟩ — **un·err·ing·ly** *adv*

UNES·CO \yü-'nes-kō\ *abbr* United Nations Educational, Scientific, and Cultural Organization

un·even \ˌən-'ē-vən\ *adj* 1 : ODD 3 2 : not even : not level or smooth : RUGGED, RAGGED 3 : IRREGULAR; *also* : varying in quality — **un·even·ly** *adv* — **un·even·ness** *n*

un·event·ful \ˌən-i-'vent-fəl\ *adj* : lacking interesting or noteworthy incidents — **un·event·ful·ly** *adv*

un·evolved \ˌən-i-'välvd\ *adj* 1 : not fully developed ⟨an ∼ wine⟩ 2 : lacking cultural refinement

un·ex·am·pled \ˌən-ig-'zam-pəld\ *adj* : UNPRECEDENTED, UNPARALLELED ⟨fought with ∼ passion⟩

un·ex·cep·tion·able \ˌən-ik-'sep-shə-nə-bəl\ *adj* : not open to exception or objection : beyond reproach

un·ex·pect·ed \ˌən-ik-'spek-təd\ *adj* : not expected : UNFORESEEN — **un·ex·pect·ed·ly** *adv*

un·fail·ing \ˌən-'fā-liŋ\ *adj* 1 : not failing, flagging, or waning 2 : INEXHAUSTIBLE ⟨a subject of ∼ interest⟩ 3 : INFALLIBLE, SURE ⟨an ∼ test⟩ — **un·fail·ing·ly** *adv*

un·fair \-'fer\ *adj* 1 : marked by injustice, partiality, or deception : UNJUST 2 : not equitable in business dealings — **un·fair·ly** *adv* — **un·fair·ness** *n*

un·faith·ful \ˌən-'fāth-fəl\ *adj* 1 : not observant of vows, allegiance, or duty : DISLOYAL 2 : INACCURATE, UNTRUSTWORTHY ⟨an ∼ copy of a document⟩ — **un·faith·ful·ly** *adv* — **un·faith·ful·ness** *n*

un·fa·mil·iar \ˌən-fə-'mil-yər\ *adj* 1 : not well-known : STRANGE ⟨an ∼ place⟩ 2 : not well acquainted ⟨∼ with the subject⟩ — **un·fa·mil·iar·i·ty** \-ˌmi-lē-'er-ə-te, -'yer-\ *n*

un·fas·ten \ˌən-'fa-sⁿn\ *vb* : to make or become loose : UNDO, DETACH

un·feel·ing \ˌən-'fē-liŋ\ *adj* 1 : lacking feeling : INSENSATE 2 : HARDHEARTED, CRUEL — **un·feel·ing·ly** *adv*

un·feigned \-'fānd\ *adj* : not feigned : not hypocritical : GENUINE

un·fet·ter \-'fe-tər\ *vb* 1 : to free from fetters 2 : LIBERATE

un·fil·ial \ˌən-'fi-lē-əl, -'fil-yəl\ *adj* : not observing the obligations of a child to a parent : UNDUTIFUL

un·fin·ished \ˌən-'fi-nisht\ *adj* 1 : not brought to an end 2 : being in a rough or unpolished state

¹un·fit \-'fit\ *adj* : not fit or suitable; *esp* : physically or mentally unsound ⟨∼ for army service⟩ — **un·fit·ness** *n*

²unfit *vb* : to make unfit : DISQUALIFY

un·fix \-'fiks\ *vb* 1 : to loosen from a fastening : DETACH 2 : UNSETTLE

un·flap·pa·ble \-'fla-pə-bəl\ *adj* : not easily upset or panicked — **un·flap·pa·bly** *adv*

un·fledged \ˌən-'flejd\ *adj* : not feathered or ready for flight; *also* : IMMATURE, CALLOW

un·flinch·ing \-'flin-chiŋ\ *adj* : not flinching or shrinking : STEADFAST — **un·flinch·ing·ly** *adv*

un·fold \-'fōld\ *vb* 1 : to open the folds of : open up 2 : to lay open to view : DISCLOSE 3 : BLOSSOM, DEVELOP

un·for·get·ta·ble \ˌən-fər-'ge-tə-bəl\ *adj* : incapable of being forgotten ⟨an ∼ event⟩ — **un·for·get·ta·bly** \-blē\ *adv*

un·formed \-'fȯrmd\ *adj* : not regularly formed or ordered : UNDEVELOPED

un·for·tu·nate \-'fȯr-chə-nət\ *adj* 1 : not fortunate : UNLUCKY 2 : attended with misfortune 3 : UNSUITABLE ⟨an ∼ choice of words⟩ — **unfortunate** *n*

un·for·tu·nate·ly \-nət-lē\ *adv* 1 : in an unfortunate manner 2 : it is unfortunate

un·found·ed \ˌən-'faùn-dəd\ *adj* : lacking a sound basis : GROUNDLESS

un·freeze \-'frēz\ *vb* **-froze** \-'frōz\; **-fro·zen** \-'frō-zⁿn\; **-freez·ing** 1 : to cause to thaw 2 : to remove from a freeze ⟨∼ prices⟩

un·fre·quent·ed \ˌən-frē-'kwen-təd; ˌən-'frē-kwən-\ *adj* : seldom visited or traveled over

un·friend·ly \ˌən-'frend-lē\ *adj* 1 : not friendly or kind : HOSTILE 2 : UNFAVORABLE ⟨∼ to new business⟩ — **un·friend·li·ness** \-lē-nəs\ *n*

un·frock \-'fräk\ *vb* : DEFROCK

un·fruit·ful \-'früt-fəl\ *adj* 1 : not producing fruit or offspring : BARREN 2 : yielding no valuable result : UNPROFITABLE — **un·fruit·ful·ness** *n*

un·furl \-'fərl\ *vb* : to loose from a furled state : UNFOLD

un·gain·ly \-'gān-lē\ *adj* [*un-* + obs. *gainly* proper, becoming, fr. *gain* direct, handy, fr. ME *geyn*, fr. OE *gēn*, fr. ON *gegn* against] : CLUMSY, AWKWARD — **un·gain·li·ness** \-lē-nəs\ *n*

un·gen·er·ous \ˌən-'je-nə-rəs\ *adj* : not generous or liberal : STINGY

un·glued \ˌən-'glüd\ *adj* : UPSET, DISORDERED ⟨became ∼ when she was refused⟩

un·god·ly \ˌən-'gäd-lē, -'gȯd-\ *adj* 1 : IMPIOUS, IRRELIGIOUS 2 : SINFUL, WICKED 3 : OUTRAGEOUS ⟨an ∼ hour⟩ — **un·god·li·ness** \-lē-nəs\ *n*

un·gov·ern·able \-'gə-vər-nə-bəl\ *adj* : not capable of being governed, guided, or restrained : UNRULY

un·gra·cious \-'grā-shəs\ *adj* 1 : not courteous : RUDE 2 : not pleasing : DISAGREEABLE ⟨an ∼ task⟩

un·grate·ful \ˌən-'grāt-fəl\ *adj* 1 : not thankful for favors 2 : DISAGREEABLE; *also* : THANKLESS — **un·grate·ful·ly** *adv* — **un·grate·ful·ness** *n*

un·guard·ed \-'gär-dəd\ *adj* 1 : UNPROTECTED 2 : DIRECT, INCAUTIOUS ⟨∼ remarks⟩

un·guent \'əŋ-gwənt, 'ən-\ *n* : a soothing or healing salve : OINTMENT

¹un·gu·late \'əŋ-gyə-lət, 'ən-, -ˌlāt\ *adj* [LL *ungulatus*, fr. L *ungula* hoof, fr. *unguis* nail, hoof] : having hoofs

²ungulate *n* : a hoofed mammal (as a cow, horse, or rhinoceros)

un·hal·lowed \ˌən-'ha-lōd\ *adj* 1 : not consecrated : UNHOLY 2 : IMPIOUS, PROFANE 3 : contrary to accepted standards : IMMORAL

un·hand \ˌən-'hand\ *vb* : to remove the hand from : let go

un·hand·some \-'han-səm\ *adj* 1 : not beautiful or handsome 2 : UNBECOMING 3 : DISCOURTEOUS, RUDE

un·handy \-'han-dē\ *adj* : INCONVENIENT; *also* : AWKWARD

un·hap·py \-'ha-pē\ *adj* 1 : UNLUCKY, UNFORTUNATE ⟨an ∼ coincidence⟩ 2 : SAD, MISERABLE 3 : INAPPROPRIATE ⟨an ∼ choice⟩ — **un·hap·pi·ly** \-'ha-pə-lē\ *adv* — **un·hap·pi·ness** \-pē-nəs\ *n*

un·har·ness \-'här-nəs\ *vb* : to remove the harness from (as a horse)

un·healthy \-'hel-thē\ *adj* 1 : not conducive to health : UNWHOLESOME ⟨∼ foods⟩ 2 : SICKLY, DISEASED

un·heard \-'hərd\ *adj* 1 : not heard 2 : not granted a hearing

unheard–of *adj* : previously unknown; *esp* : UNPRECEDENTED ⟨moving at ∼ speeds⟩

un·hinge \ˌən-'hinj\ *vb* 1 : to make unstable esp. mentally ⟨∼ by grief⟩ 2 : to take from the hinges

un·hitch \-'hich\ *vb* : to UNFASTEN, LOOSE

un·ho·ly \-'hō-lē\ *adj* 1 : not holy : PROFANE, WICKED 2 : very unpleasant ⟨an ∼ mess⟩ — **un·ho·li·ness** \-lē-nəs\ *n*

un·hook \-'hùk\ *vb* : to loose from a hook

un·horse \-'hȯrs\ *vb* : to dislodge from or as if from a horse

uni·cam·er·al \ˌyü-ni-'ka-mə-rəl\ *adj* : having a single legislative house or chamber

UNI·CEF \'yü-nə-ˌsef\ *abbr* [United Nations International Children's Emergency Fund, its former name] United Nations Children's Fund

uni·cel·lu·lar \ˌyü-ni-'sel-yə-lər\ *adj* : having or consisting of a single cell

uni·corn \'yü-nə-ˌkȯrn\ *n* [ME *unicorne*, fr. AF, fr. LL *unicornis*, fr. L, having one horn, fr. *unus* one + *cornu* horn] : a mythical animal with one horn in the middle of the forehead

uni·cy·cle \'yü-ni-ˌsī-kəl\ *n* : a vehicle that has a single wheel and is usu. propelled by pedals

uni·di·rec·tion·al \ˌyü-ni-də-'rek-shə-nəl, -dī-\ *adj* : having, moving in, or responsive in a single direction

uni·fi·ca·tion \ˌyü-nə-fə-'kā-shən\ *n* : the act, process, or result of unifying : the state of being unified

¹uni·form \'yü-nə-ˌfȯrm\ *adj* 1 : not varying ⟨∼ procedures⟩ 2 : of the same form with others — **uni·form·ly** *adv*

²uniform *vb* : to clothe with a uniform

³uniform *n* : distinctive dress worn by members of a particular group (as an army or a police force)

uni·for·mi·ty \ˌyü-nə-'fȯr-mə-tē\ *n, pl* **-ties** : the state of being uniform

uni·fy \'yü-nə-ˌfī\ *vb* **-fied; -fy·ing** : to make into a coherent whole : UNITE

uni·lat·er·al \ˌyü-nə-'la-tə-rəl\ *adj* : of, having, affecting, or done by one side only — **uni·lat·er·al·ly** *adv*

un·im·peach·able \ˌən-im-'pē-chə-bəl\ *adj* : not liable to accusation : IRREPROACHABLE ⟨an ∼ reputation⟩

un·in·hib·it·ed \ˌən-in-'hi-bə-təd\ *adj* : free from inhibition; *also* : boisterously informal — **un·in·hib·it·ed·ly** *adv*

un·in·stall \ˌən-in-'stól\ *vb* : to remove (software) from a computer system

un·in·tel·li·gent \-'te-lə-jənt\ *adj* : lacking intelligence

un·in·tel·li·gi·ble \-jə-bəl\ *adj* : not intelligible : OBSCURE ⟨an ∼ voice mail⟩ — **un·in·tel·li·gi·bly** \-blē\ *adv*

un·in·ter·est·ed \ˌən-'in-trəs-təd, -tə-rəs-, -tə-ˌres-\ *adj* : not interested : not having the mind or feelings engaged or aroused

un·in·ter·rupt·ed \ˌən-ˌin-tə-'rəp-təd\ *adj* : not interrupted : CONTINUOUS

union \'yün-yən\ *n* **1** : an act or instance of uniting two or more things into one : the state of being so united : COMBINATION, JUNCTION **2** : a uniting in marriage **3** : something formed by a combining of parts or members; *esp* : a confederation of independent individuals (as nations or persons) for some common purpose **4** : an organization of workers (as a labor union or a trade union) formed to advance its members' interests esp. in respect to wages and working conditions **5** : a device emblematic of union used on or as a national flag; *also* : the upper inner corner of a flag **6** : a device for connecting parts (as of a machine); *esp* : a coupling for pipes

union·ise *Brit var of* UNIONIZE

union·ism \'yün-yə-ˌni-zəm\ *n* **1** : the principle or policy of forming or adhering to a union; *esp, cap* : adherence to the policy of a firm federal union before or during the U.S. Civil War **2** : the principles or system of trade unions — **union·ist** *n*

union·ize \'yün-yə-ˌnīz\ *vb* **-ized; -iz·ing** : to form into or cause to join a labor union — **union·i·za·tion** \ˌyün-yə-nə-'zā-shən\ *n*

union jack *n* **1** : a flag consisting of the part of a national flag that signifies union **2** *cap U&J* : the national flag of the United Kingdom

unique \yu̇-'nēk\ *adj* **1** : being the only one of its kind : SINGLE, SOLE ⟨each snowflake is ∼⟩ **2** : very unusual : NOTABLE — **unique·ly** *adv* — **unique·ness** *n*

uni·sex \'yü-nə-ˌseks\ *adj* : not distinguishable as male or female; *also* : suitable or designed for both males and females ⟨∼ clothing⟩ — **unisex** *n*

uni·sex·u·al \ˌyü-nə-'sek-shə-wəl\ *adj* **1** : having only male or only female sex organs **2** : UNISEX

uni·son \'yü-nə-sən, -zən\ *n* [ME unisoun, fr. MF unisson, fr. ML unisonus having the same sound, fr. L unus one + sonus sound] **1** : sameness or identity in musical pitch **2** : the condition of being tuned or sounded at the same pitch or in octaves ⟨sing in ∼⟩ **3** : harmonious agreement or union : ACCORD

unit \'yü-nət\ *n* **1** : the smallest whole number greater than zero : ONE **2** : a definite amount or quantity used as a standard of measurement **3** : a single thing, person, or group that is a constituent of a whole; *also* : a part of a military establishment that has a prescribed organization — **unit** *adj*

Uni·tar·i·an \ˌyü-nə-'ter-ē-ən\ *n* : a member of a religious denomination stressing individual freedom of belief — **Uni·tar·i·an·ism** *n*

uni·tary \'yü-nə-ˌter-ē\ *adj* **1** : of or relating to a unit **2** : not divided — **uni·tar·i·ly** \ˌyü-nə-'ter-ə-lē\ *adv*

unite \yu̇-'nīt\ *vb* **unit·ed; unit·ing** **1** : to put or join together so as to make one : COMBINE, COALESCE **2** : to join by a legal or moral bond; *also* : to join in interest or fellowship **3** : AMALGAMATE, CONSOLIDATE **4** : to act in concert

unit·ed \yu̇-'nī-təd\ *adj* **1** : made one : COMBINED **2** : relating to or produced by joint action **3** : being in agreement : HARMONIOUS

unit·ize \'yü-nə-ˌtīz\ *vb* **-ized; -iz·ing** **1** : to form or convert into a unit **2** : to divide into units

uni·ty \'yü-nə-tē\ *n, pl* **-ties** **1** : the quality or state of being or being made one : ONENESS **2** : a definite quantity or combination of quantities taken as one or for which 1 is made to stand in calculation **3** : CONCORD, ACCORD,

HARMONY **4** : continuity without change ⟨∼ of purpose⟩ **5** : reference of all the parts of a literary or artistic composition to a single main idea **6** : totality of related parts **✦ Synonyms** SOLIDARITY, UNION, INTEGRITY

univ *abbr* **1** universal **2** university

uni·valve \'yü-ni-ˌvalv\ *n* : a mollusk having a shell with only one piece; *esp* : GASTROPOD — **univalve** *adj*

uni·ver·sal \ˌyü-nə-'vər-səl\ *adj* **1** : including, covering, or affecting the whole without limit or exception : available or applying to everyone ⟨∼ privileges⟩ ⟨a ∼ rule⟩ **2** : present or occurring everywhere **3** : used or for use among all ⟨a ∼ language⟩ **4** : adaptable for various purposes ⟨a ∼ remote control⟩ — **uni·ver·sal·ly** *adv*

uni·ver·sal·i·ty \-vər-'sa-lə-tē\ *n* : the quality or state of being universal

uni·ver·sal·ize \-'vər-sə-ˌlīz\ *vb* **-ized; -iz·ing** : to make universal : GENERALIZE ⟨would ∼ equal rights⟩ — **uni·ver·sal·i·za·tion** \-ˌvər-sə-lə-'zā-shən\ *n*

universal joint *n* : a shaft coupling for transmitting rotation from one shaft to another not in a straight line with it

universal joint

Universal Product Code *n* : a combination of a barcode and numbers by which a scanner can identify a product and usu. assign a price

uni·verse \'yü-nə-ˌvərs\ *n* [ME, fr. L universum, fr. neut. of universus entire, whole, fr. unus one + versus turned toward, fr. pp. of vertere to turn] : the whole body of things observed or assumed : COSMOS

uni·ver·si·ty \ˌyü-nə-'vər-sə-tē\ *n, pl* **-ties** : an institution of higher learning authorized to confer degrees in various special fields (as theology, law, and medicine) as well as in the arts and sciences generally

un·just \ˌən-'jəst\ *adj* : characterized by injustice — **un·just·ly** *adv*

un·kempt \-'kempt\ *adj* **1** : lacking order or neatness; *also* : ROUGH, UNPOLISHED **2** : not combed : DISHEVELED

un·kind \-'kīnd\ *adj* : not kind or sympathetic ⟨an ∼ remark⟩ — **un·kind·ly** *adv* — **un·kind·ness** *n*

un·kind·ly \-'kīnd-lē\ *adj* : UNKIND — **un·kind·li·ness** *n*

un·know·ing \ˌən-'nō-iŋ\ *adj* : not knowing — **un·know·ing·ly** *adv*

un·known \-'nōn\ *adj* : not known or not well-known — **unknown** *n*

un·lace \-'lās\ *vb* : to loose by undoing a lace

un·lade \-'lād\ *vb* **lad·ed; -laded** *or* **-lad·en** \-'lā-dᵊn\; **-lad·ing** : to take the load or cargo from : UNLOAD

un·latch \-'lach\ *vb* **1** : to open or loose by lifting the latch **2** : to become loosed or opened

un·law·ful \ˌən-'lȯ-fəl\ *adj* **1** : not lawful : ILLEGAL **2** : ILLEGITIMATE — **un·law·ful·ly** *adv*

un·lead·ed \-'le-dəd\ *adj* : not treated or mixed with lead or lead compounds

un·learn \-'lərn\ *vb* : to put out of one's knowledge or memory; *also* : to discard the habit of

un·learned \-'lər-nəd for 1; -'lərnd for 2\ *adj* **1** : UNEDUCATED, ILLITERATE **2** : not gained by study or training

un·leash \-'lēsh\ *vb* : to free from or as if from a leash : let loose

un·less \ən-'les, 'ən-ˌles\ *conj* : except on condition that ⟨won't go ∼ you⟩

un·let·tered \ˌən-'le-tərd\ *adj* : not educated : ILLITERATE

¹un·like \-'līk\ *adj* **1** : not like : DISSIMILAR, DIFFERENT **2** : UNEQUAL — **un·like·ness** *n*

²unlike *prep* **1** : different from ⟨she's quite ∼ her sister⟩ **2** : unusual for ⟨it's ∼ you to be late⟩ **3** : differently from ⟨behaves ∼ his brother⟩

un·like·li·hood \ˌən-'lī-klē-ˌhu̇d\ *n* : IMPROBABILITY

un·like·ly \-'lī-klē\ adj 1 : not likely : IMPROBABLE 2 : likely to fail

un·lim·ber \ˌən-'lim-bər\ vb : to get ready for action

un·list·ed \ˌən-'lis-təd\ adj 1 : not appearing on a list; esp : not appearing in a telephone book 2 : not listed on a stock exchange

un·load \-'lōd\ vb 1 : to take away or off : REMOVE ⟨∼ cargo from a hold⟩; also : to get rid of 2 : to take a load from ⟨∼ the ship⟩; also : to relieve or set free : UNBURDEN ⟨∼ one's mind of worries⟩ 3 : to draw the charge from ⟨∼ed the gun⟩ 4 : to sell in volume

un·lock \-'läk\ vb 1 : to open or unfasten through release of a lock 2 : RELEASE ⟨∼ a flood of emotions⟩ 3 : DISCLOSE, REVEAL ⟨∼ nature's secrets⟩

un·looked–for \-'lukt-fòr\ adj : UNEXPECTED

un·loose \ˌən-'lüs\ vb : to relax the strain of : set free; also : UNTIE

un·loos·en \-'lü-sᵊn\ vb : UNLOOSE

un·love·ly \-'ləv-lē\ adj : having no charm or appeal : not amiable

un·luck·i·ly \-'lə-kə-lē\ adv : UNFORTUNATELY

un·lucky \-'lə-kē\ adj 1 : UNFORTUNATE, ILL-FATED 2 : likely to bring misfortune : INAUSPICIOUS 3 : REGRETTABLE

un·man \ˌən-'man\ vb 1 : to deprive of manly courage 2 : CASTRATE

un·man·ly \-'man-lē\ adj : not manly : COWARDLY; also : EFFEMINATE

un·man·ner·ly \-'ma-nər-lē\ adj : RUDE, IMPOLITE — **unmannerly** adv

un·mask \ˌən-'mask\ vb 1 : to strip of a mask or a disguise : EXPOSE 2 : to remove one's mask

un·mean·ing \-'mē-niŋ\ adj : having no meaning : SENSELESS

un·me·di·at·ed \ˌən-'mē-dē-ˌā-təd\ adj : not mediated : not communicated or transformed by an intervening agency

un·meet \-'mēt\ adj : not meet or fit : UNSUITABLE, IMPROPER

un·men·tion·able \-'men-chə-nə-bəl\ adj : not fit or proper to be talked about ⟨an ∼ topic⟩

un·mer·ci·ful \-'mər-si-fəl\ adj : not merciful : CRUEL, MERCILESS — **un·mer·ci·ful·ly** adv

un·mind·ful \-'mīnd-fəl\ adj : not mindful : CARELESS, UNAWARE

un·mis·tak·able \ˌən-mə-'stā-kə-bəl\ adj : not capable of being mistaken or misunderstood : CLEAR, OBVIOUS — **un·mis·tak·ably** \-blē\ adv

un·mit·i·gat·ed \ˌən-'mi-tə-ˌgā-təd\ adj 1 : not softened or lessened 2 : ABSOLUTE, DOWNRIGHT ⟨an ∼ liar⟩

un·moor \-'mur\ vb : to loose from or as if from moorings

un·mor·al \-'mòr-əl\ adj : having no moral perception or quality : AMORAL — **un·mo·ral·i·ty** \ˌən-mə-'ra-lə-tē\ n

un·muz·zle \-'mə-zəl\ vb : to remove a muzzle from

un·nat·u·ral \ˌən-'na-chə-rəl\ adj : contrary to or acting contrary to nature or natural instincts; also : ABNORMAL — **un·nat·u·ral·ly** adv — **un·nat·u·ral·ness** n

un·nec·es·sar·i·ly \ˌən-ˌne-sə-'ser-ə-lē\ adv 1 : not by necessity 2 : to an unnecessary degree ⟨∼ harsh⟩

un·nerve \ˌən-'nərv\ vb : to deprive of courage, strength, or steadiness ⟨fear *unnerved* them⟩; also : UPSET

un·num·bered \ˌən-'nəm-bərd\ adj : not numbered or counted : INNUMERABLE

un·ob·tru·sive \ˌən-əb-'trü-siv\ adj : not obtrusive or forward : not bold : INCONSPICUOUS — **un·ob·tru·sive·ly** adv

un·oc·cu·pied \ˌən-'ä-kyə-ˌpīd\ adj 1 : not busy : UNEMPLOYED 2 : not occupied : EMPTY, VACANT

un·or·ga·nized \-'òr-gə-ˌnīzd\ adj 1 : not formed or brought into an integrated or ordered whole 2 : not organized into unions ⟨∼ labor⟩

un·pack \ˌən-'pak\ vb 1 : to separate and remove things packed 2 : to open and remove the contents of

un·par·al·leled \ˌən-'pa-rə-ˌleld\ adj : having no parallel; esp : having no equal or match ⟨an ∼ achievement⟩

un·par·lia·men·ta·ry \ˌən-ˌpär-lə-'men-tə-rē\ adj : contrary to parliamentary practice

un·peg \ˌən-'peg\ vb 1 : to remove a peg from 2 : to unfasten by or as if by removing a peg

un·per·son \'ən-'pər-sᵊn, -ˌpər-\ n : a person who usu. for political or ideological reasons is removed from recognition or consideration

un·pile \ˌən-'pī(-ə)l\ vb : to take or disentangle from a pile

un·pin \-'pin\ vb : to remove a pin from : UNFASTEN

un·pleas·ant \-'ple-zᵊnt\ adj : not pleasant : DISAGREEABLE — **un·pleas·ant·ly** adv — **un·pleas·ant·ness** n

un·plug \ˌən-'pləg\ vb 1 : UNCLOG 2 : to remove (a plug) from a receptacle; also : to disconnect from an electric circuit by removing a plug

un·plumbed \-'pləmd\ adj 1 : not tested or measured with a plumb line 2 : not thoroughly explored

un·pop·u·lar \ˌən-'pä-pyə-lər\ adj : not popular : looked upon or received unfavorably — **un·pop·u·lar·i·ty** \ˌən-ˌpä-pyə-'la-rə-tē\ n

un·prec·e·dent·ed \ˌən-'pre-sə-ˌden-təd\ adj : having no precedent : NOVEL

un·pre·ten·tious \ˌən-pri-'ten-chəs\ adj : not pretentious : MODEST

un·prin·ci·pled \ˌən-'prin-sə-pəld\ adj : lacking sound or honorable principles : UNSCRUPULOUS ⟨an ∼ criminal⟩

un·print·able \-'prin-tə-bəl\ adj : unfit or too offensive to be printed ⟨∼ remarks⟩

un·prof·it·able \ˌən-'prä-fə-tə-bəl\ adj : not profitable : USELESS, VAIN

un·pro·tect·ed \ˌən-prə-'tek-təd\ adj 1 : lacking protection 2 : performed without measures to prevent pregnancy or sexually transmitted disease ⟨∼ sex⟩

un·qual·i·fied \ˌən-'kwä-lə-ˌfīd\ adj 1 : not having requisite qualifications 2 : not modified or restricted by reservations : COMPLETE — **un·qual·i·fied·ly** \-ˌfī-əd-lē\ adv

un·ques·tion·able \-'kwes-chə-nə-bəl\ adj : not questionable : INDISPUTABLE — **un·ques·tion·ably** \-blē\ adv

un·ques·tion·ing \-chə-niŋ\ adj : not questioning : accepting without examination or hesitation ⟨∼ obedience⟩ — **un·ques·tion·ing·ly** adv

un·qui·et \-'kwī-ət\ adj 1 : not quiet : AGITATED, DISTURBED 2 : physically, emotionally, or mentally restless : UNEASY

un·quote \'ən-ˌkwōt\ n — used orally to indicate the end of a direct quotation

un·rav·el \ˌən-'ra-vəl\ vb 1 : to separate the threads of 2 : SOLVE ⟨∼ a mystery⟩ 3 : to become unraveled

un·read \-'red\ adj 1 : not read; also : left unexamined 2 : lacking the benefits or the experience of reading

un·re·al \-'rēl\ adj : lacking in reality, substance, or genuineness — **un·re·al·i·ty** \ˌən-rē-'a-lə-tē\ n

un·rea·son·able \-'rē-zᵊn-ə-bəl\ adj 1 : not governed by or acting according to reason; also : not conformable to reason : ABSURD 2 : exceeding the bounds of reason or moderation — **un·rea·son·able·ness** n — **un·rea·son·ably** adv

un·rea·soned \-'rē-zᵊnd\ adj : not based on reason or reasoning ⟨∼ fears⟩

un·rea·son·ing \-'rē-zᵊn-iŋ\ adj : not using or showing the use of reason as a guide or control

un·re·con·struct·ed \ˌən-ˌrē-kən-'strək-təd\ adj : not reconciled to some political, economic, or social change; esp : holding stubbornly to a particular belief, view, place, or style

un·reel \ˌən-'rēl\ vb 1 : to unwind from or as if from a reel 2 : to perform successfully

un·re·gen·er·ate \ˌən-ri-'je-nə-rət\ adj : not regenerated or reformed

un·re·lent·ing \-'len-tiŋ\ adj 1 : not yielding in determination : STERN ⟨∼ leader⟩ 2 : not letting up or weakening in vigor or pace : CONSTANT — **un·re·lent·ing·ly** adv

un·re·mit·ting \-'mi-tiŋ\ adj : CONSTANT, INCESSANT ⟨∼ pain⟩ — **un·re·mit·ting·ly** adv

un·re·quit·ed \ˌən-ri-'kwī-təd\ adj : not requited or not reciprocated or returned in kind ⟨∼ love⟩

un·re·served \-'zərvd\ adj 1 : not limited or partial ⟨∼ enthusiasm⟩ 2 : not cautious or reticent : FRANK, OPEN 3 : not set aside for special use — **un·re·serv·ed·ly** \-'zər-vəd-lē\ adv

un·rest \ˌən-'rest\ n : a disturbed or uneasy state : TURMOIL

un·re·strained \ˌən-ri-'strānd\ adj 1 : IMMODERATE, UNCONTROLLED ⟨∼ anger⟩ 2 : SPONTANEOUS

un·re·straint \-ri-'strānt\ n : lack of restraint

un·righ·teous \ˌən-'rī-chəs\ adj 1 : SINFUL, WICKED 2 : UNJUST — **un·righ·teous·ness** n

un·ripe \-'rīp\ *adj* : not ripe : IMMATURE
un·ri·valed *or* **un·ri·valled** \ˌən-'rī-vəld\ *adj* : having no rival : SUPREME
un·robe \-'rōb\ *vb* : DISROBE, UNDRESS
un·roll \-'rōl\ *vb* **1** : to unwind a roll of : open out **2** : DISPLAY, DISCLOSE **3** : to become unrolled or spread out
un·roof \-'rüf, -'ruf\ *vb* : to strip off the roof or covering of
un·ruf·fled \ˌən-'rə-fəld\ *adj* **1** : not agitated or upset **2** : not ruffled : SMOOTH ⟨∼ water⟩
un·ruly \-'rü-lē\ *adj* [ME *unreuly*, fr. *un-* + *reuly* disciplined, fr. *reule* rule, fr. AF, fr. L *regula* straightedge, rule, fr. *regere* to direct] : not submissive to rule or restraint : TURBULENT ⟨∼ passions⟩ — **un·rul·i·ness** \-'rü-lē-nəs\ *n*
un·sad·dle \ˌən-'sa-dᵊl\ *vb* **1** : to remove the saddle from a horse **2** : UNHORSE
un·sat·u·rat·ed \-'sa-chə-ˌrā-təd\ *adj* **1** : capable of absorbing or dissolving more of something **2** : containing double or triple bonds between carbon atoms ⟨∼ fat⟩ — **un·sat·u·rate** \-rət\ *n*
un·saved \ˌən-'sāvd\ *adj* : not saved; *esp* : not rescued from eternal punishment
un·sa·vory \-'sā-və-rē\ *adj* **1** : TASTELESS **2** : unpleasant to taste or smell **3** : morally offensive ⟨∼ characters⟩
un·say \-'sā\ *vb* **-said** \-'sed\; **-say·ing** : to take back (something said) : RETRACT, WITHDRAW
un·scathed \-'skāᵺd\ *adj* : wholly unharmed : not injured
un·schooled \-'sküld\ *adj* : not schooled : UNTAUGHT, UNTRAINED
un·sci·en·tif·ic \ˌən-ˌsī-ən-'ti-fik\ *adj* : not scientific : not in accord with the principles and methods of science
un·scram·ble \ˌən-'skram-bəl\ *vb* **1** : RESOLVE, CLARIFY **2** : to restore (as a radio message) to intelligible form
un·screw \-'skrü\ *vb* **1** : to draw the screws from **2** : to loosen by turning
un·scru·pu·lous \-'skrü-pyə-ləs\ *adj* : not scrupulous : UNPRINCIPLED — **un·scru·pu·lous·ly** *adv* — **un·scru·pu·lous·ness** *n*
un·seal \-'sēl\ *vb* : to break or remove the seal of : OPEN
un·search·able \-'sər-chə-bəl\ *adj* : not capable of being searched or explored ⟨∼ forests⟩
un·sea·son·able \-'sē-zᵊn-ə-bəl\ *adj* : not seasonable : happening or coming at the wrong time : UNTIMELY — **un·sea·son·ably** \-blē\ *adv*
un·seat \-'sēt\ *vb* **1** : to throw from one's seat esp. on horseback **2** : to remove from political office
un·seem·ly \-'sēm-lē\ *adj* : not according with established standards of good form or taste ⟨∼ behavior⟩; *also* : not suitable — **un·seem·li·ness** *n*
un·seen \ˌən-'sēn\ *adj* : not seen : INVISIBLE ⟨∼ dangers⟩
un·seg·re·gat·ed \-'se-gri-ˌgā-təd\ *adj* : not segregated; *esp* : free from racial segregation
un·self·ish \-'sel-fish\ *adj* : not selfish : GENEROUS — **un·self·ish·ly** *adv* — **un·self·ish·ness** *n*
un·set·tle \ˌən-'se-tᵊl\ *vb* : to move or loosen from a settled position : DISPLACE, DISTURB
un·set·tled \-'se-tᵊld\ *adj* **1** : not settled : not fixed (as in position or character) **2** : not calm : DISTURBED **3** : not decided in mind : UNRESOLVED **4** : not paid ⟨∼ accounts⟩ **5** : not occupied by settlers
un·shack·le \-'sha-kəl\ *vb* : to free from shackles
un·shaped \-'shāpt\ *adj* : not shaped; *esp* : not being in finished, final, or perfect form ⟨∼ ideas⟩ ⟨∼ timber⟩
un·sheathe \ˌən-'shēᵺ\ *vb* : to draw from or as if from a sheath
un·ship \-'ship\ *vb* **1** : to remove from a ship **2** : to remove or become removed from position ⟨∼ an oar⟩
un·shod \ˌən-'shäd\ *adj* : not wearing or provided with shoes
un·sight·ly \ˌən-'sīt-lē\ *adj* : unpleasant to the sight : UGLY ⟨an ∼ mess⟩
un·skilled \-'skild\ *adj* **1** : not skilled; *esp* : not skilled in a specified branch of work **2** : not requiring skill
un·skill·ful \-'skil-fəl\ *adj* : lacking in skill or proficiency — **un·skill·ful·ly** *adv*
un·sling \-'sliŋ\ *vb* **-slung** \-'sləŋ\; **-sling·ing** : to remove from being slung
un·snap \-'snap\ *vb* : to loosen or free by or as if by undoing a snap

un·snarl \-'snärl\ *vb* : to remove snarls from : UNTANGLE
un·so·phis·ti·cat·ed \ˌən-sə-'fis-tə-ˌkā-təd\ *adj* **1** : not worldly-wise : lacking sophistication **2** : SIMPLE ⟨∼ designs⟩
un·sought \ˌən-'sòt\ *adj* : not sought : not searched for or asked for : not obtained by effort ⟨∼ honors⟩
un·sound \-'saund\ *adj* **1** : not healthy or whole; *also* : not mentally normal ⟨of ∼ mind⟩ **2** : not valid **3** : not firmly made or fixed ⟨structurally ∼⟩ — **un·sound·ly** *adv* — **un·sound·ness** *n*
un·spar·ing \-'sper-iŋ\ *adj* **1** : HARD, RUTHLESS ⟨∼ criticism⟩ **2** : not frugal : LIBERAL, PROFUSE ⟨∼ generosity⟩
un·speak·able \-'spē-kə-bəl\ *adj* **1** : impossible to express in words **2** : extremely bad ⟨∼ offenses⟩ — **un·speak·ably** \-blē\ *adv*
un·spool \ˌən-'spül\ *vb* **1** : to unwind from a spool **2** : to present artfully ⟨∼ a new film⟩
un·spot·ted \-'spä-təd\ *adj* : not spotted or stained; *esp* : free from moral stain
un·sprung \-'sprəŋ\ *adj* : not sprung; *esp* : not equipped with springs
un·sta·ble \-'stā-bəl\ *adj* **1** : not stable **2** : FICKLE, VACILLATING; *also* : lacking effective emotional control **3** : readily changing (as by decomposing) in chemical or physical composition or in biological activity ⟨an ∼ atomic nucleus⟩
un·steady \ˌən-'ste-dē\ *adj* : not steady : UNSTABLE — **un·stead·i·ly** \-'ste-də-lē\ *adv* — **un·stead·i·ness** \-'ste-dē-nəs\ *n*
un·stint·ing \-'stin-tiŋ\ *adj* **1** : not restricting or holding back **2** : giving or being given freely or generously ⟨∼ praise⟩
un·stop \-'stäp\ *vb* **1** : UNCLOG **2** : to remove a stopper from
un·stop·pa·ble \ˌən-'stä-pə-bəl\ *adj* : incapable of being stopped
un·strap \-'strap\ *vb* : to remove or loose a strap from
un·stressed \ˌən-'strest\ *adj* : not stressed; *esp* : not bearing a stress or accent ⟨∼ syllables⟩
un·strung \-'strəŋ\ *adj* **1** : having the strings loose or detached **2** : made weak, disordered, or unstable
un·stud·ied \-'stə-dēd\ *adj* **1** : not acquired by study **2** : NATURAL, UNFORCED ⟨moved with ∼ grace⟩
un·sub·stan·tial \ˌən-səb-'stan-chəl\ *adj* : INSUBSTANTIAL
un·sung \ˌən-'səŋ\ *adj* **1** : not sung **2** : not celebrated in song or verse ⟨∼ heroes⟩
un·swerv·ing \ˌən-'swər-viŋ\ *adj* **1** : not swerving or turning aside **2** : STEADY
un·tan·gle \-'taŋ-gəl\ *vb* **1** : DISENTANGLE **2** : to straighten out : RESOLVE ⟨∼ a problem⟩
un·taught \-'tòt\ *adj* **1** : not instructed or taught : IGNORANT **2** : NATURAL, SPONTANEOUS ⟨∼ kindness⟩
un·think·able \-'thiŋ-kə-bəl\ *adj* : not to be thought of or considered as possible ⟨∼ cruelty⟩
un·think·ing \ˌən-'thiŋ-kiŋ\ *adj* : not thinking; *esp* : THOUGHTLESS, HEEDLESS ⟨∼ remarks⟩ — **un·think·ing·ly** *adv*
un·thought \ˌən-'thòt\ *adj* : not anticipated : UNEXPECTED — often used with *of* ⟨unthought-of development⟩
un·tie \-'tī\ *vb* **-tied**; **-ty·ing** *or* **-tie·ing** **1** : to free from something that ties, fastens, or restrains : UNBIND **2** : DISENTANGLE, RESOLVE **3** : to become loosened or unbound
¹un·til \ˌən-'til\ *prep* : up to the time of ⟨worked ∼ 5 o'clock⟩
²until *conj* **1** : up to the time that ⟨wait ∼ he calls⟩ **2** : to the point or degree that ⟨ran ∼ she was breathless⟩
¹un·time·ly \ˌən-'tīm-lē\ *adv* : at an inopportune time : UNSEASONABLY; *also* : PREMATURELY
²untimely *adj* : PREMATURE ⟨∼ death⟩; *also* : INOPPORTUNE, UNSEASONABLE
un·tir·ing \ˌən-'tī-riŋ\ *adj* : not becoming tired : INDEFATIGABLE ⟨an ∼ worker⟩ — **un·tir·ing·ly** *adv*
un·to \ˌən-ˌtü\ *prep* : TO
un·told \ˌən-'tōld\ *adj* **1** : too great or numerous to count **2** : not told : not revealed
¹un·touch·able \ˌən-'tə-chə-bəl\ *adj* : forbidden to the touch
²untouchable *n* : a member of the lowest social class in

India having in traditional Hindu belief the quality of defiling by contact a member of a higher caste

un·touched \ən-'təcht\ *adj* **1** : not subjected to touching **2** : not described or dealt with **3** : not tasted **4** : being in a primeval state or condition **5** : UNAFFECTED ⟨~ by scandals⟩

un·tow·ard \ən-'tórd, -'tō-ərd; ˌən-tə-'wórd\ *adj* **1** : difficult to manage : STUBBORN, WILLFUL ⟨an ~ child⟩ **2** : INCONVENIENT, TROUBLESOME ⟨an ~ encounter⟩

un·tried \ən-'trīd\ *adj* : not tested or proved by experience or trial; *also* : not tried in court

un·true \-'trü\ *adj* **1** : not faithful : DISLOYAL **2** : not according with a standard of correctness **3** : FALSE

un·truth \ən-'trüth, 'ən-ˌtrüth\ *n* **1** : lack of truthfulness **2** : FALSEHOOD

un·tune \-'tün, -'tyün\ *vb* **1** : to put out of tune **2** : DISARRANGE, DISCOMPOSE

un·tu·tored \-'tü-tərd, -'tyü-\ *adj* : UNTAUGHT, UNLEARNED, IGNORANT

un·twine \-'twīn\ *vb* : UNWIND, DISENTANGLE

un·twist \ən-'twist\ *vb* **1** : to separate the twisted parts of : UNTWINE **2** : to become untwined

un·used \-'yüst, -'yüzd *for 1;* -'yüzd *for 2*\ *adj* **1** : UNACCUSTOMED ⟨~ to such treatment⟩ **2** : not used

un·usu·al \-'yü-zhə-wəl\ *adj* : not usual : UNCOMMON, RARE — **un·usu·al·ly** *adv*

un·ut·ter·able \ən-'ə-tə-rə-bəl\ *adj* : being beyond the powers of description : INEXPRESSIBLE ⟨~ shame⟩ — **un·ut·ter·ably** \-blē\ *adv*

un·var·nished \-'vär-nisht\ *adj* **1** : not varnished **2** : not embellished : PLAIN ⟨the ~ truth⟩

un·veil \ən-'vāl\ *vb* **1** : to remove a veil or covering from : DISCLOSE **2** : to remove a veil : reveal oneself

un·voiced \-'vóist\ *adj* **1** : not verbally expressed : UNSPOKEN **2** : VOICELESS 2

un·war·rant·able \-'wór-ən-tə-bəl\ *adj* : not justifiable : INEXCUSABLE — **un·war·rant·ably** \-blē\ *adv*

un·weave \-'wēv\ *vb* **-wove** \-'wōv\; **-wo·ven** \-'wō-vən\; **-weav·ing** : DISENTANGLE, RAVEL

un·well \ən-'wel\ *adj* : SICK, AILING

un·whole·some \-'hōl-səm\ *adj* **1** : harmful to physical, mental, or moral well-being ⟨~ food⟩ **2** : CORRUPT, UNSOUND ⟨~ deals⟩; *also* : offensive to the senses : LOATHSOME ⟨an ~ stench⟩

un·wieldy \-'wēl-dē\ *adj* : not easily managed, handled, or used (as because of bulk, weight, or complexity) : AWKWARD ⟨an ~ tool⟩

un·wind \-'wīnd\ *vb* **-wound** \-'waünd\; **-wind·ing** **1** : to undo something that is wound : loose from coils **2** : to become unwound : be capable of being unwound **3** : RELAX ⟨~ after work⟩

un·wise \ən-'wīz\ *adj* : not wise : FOOLISH — **un·wise·ly** *adv*

un·wit·ting \-'wi-tiŋ\ *adj* **1** : not knowing : UNAWARE **2** : not intended : INADVERTENT ⟨~ mistake⟩ — **un·wit·ting·ly** *adv*

un·wont·ed \-'wón-təd, -'wōn-\ *adj* **1** : RARE, UNUSUAL **2** : not accustomed by experience — **un·wont·ed·ly** *adv*

un·world·ly \-'wərld-lē\ *adj* **1** : not of this world; *esp* : SPIRITUAL **2** : NAIVE **3** : not swayed by worldly considerations — **un·world·li·ness** \-lē-nəs\ *n*

un·wor·thy \ən-'wər-thē\ *adj* **1** : BASE, DISHONORABLE **2** : not meritorious : not worthy : UNDESERVING **3** : not deserved : UNMERITED ⟨~ treatment⟩ — **un·wor·thi·ly** \-thə-lē\ *adv* — **un·wor·thi·ness** \-thē-nəs\ *n*

un·wrap \-'rap\ *vb* : to remove the wrapping from : DISCLOSE

un·writ·ten \-'ri-t⁹n\ *adj* **1** : not in writing : ORAL, TRADITIONAL ⟨an ~ law⟩ **2** : containing no writing : BLANK

un·yield·ing \ən-'yēl-diŋ\ *adj* **1** : characterized by lack of softness or flexibility **2** : characterized by firmness or obduracy ⟨~ opposition⟩

un·yoke \-'yōk\ *vb* : to remove a yoke from; *also* : SEPARATE, DISCONNECT

un·zip \-'zip\ *vb* : to zip open : open by means of a zipper

¹up \'əp\ *adv* **1** : in or to a higher position or level; *esp* : away from the center of the earth **2** : from beneath a surface (as ground or water) **3** : from below the horizon **4** : in or into an upright position; *esp* : out of bed **5** : with greater intensity ⟨speak ~⟩ **6** : to or at a greater rate or amount ⟨prices went ~⟩ **7** : in or into a better

or more advanced state or a state of greater intensity or activity ⟨stir ~ a fire⟩ **8** : into existence, evidence, or knowledge ⟨the missing book turned ~⟩ **9** : into consideration ⟨brought the matter ~⟩ **10** : to or at bat **11** : into possession or custody ⟨gave himself ~⟩ **12** : ENTIRELY, COMPLETELY ⟨eat it ~⟩ **13** — used for emphasis ⟨clean ~ a room⟩ **14** : ASIDE, BY ⟨lay ~ supplies⟩ **15** : so as to arrive or approach ⟨ran ~ the path⟩ **16** : in a direction opposite to down **17** : in or into parts ⟨tear ~ paper⟩ **18** : to a stop ⟨pull ~ at the curb⟩ **19** : for each side ⟨the score was 15 ~⟩

²up *adj* **1** : risen above the horizon ⟨the sun is ~⟩ **2** : being out of bed ⟨~ by 6 o'clock⟩ **3** : relatively high ⟨prices are ~⟩ **4** : RAISED, LIFTED ⟨windows are ~⟩ **5** : BUILT, CONSTRUCTED ⟨the house is ~⟩ **6** : grown above a surface ⟨the corn is ~⟩ **7** : moving, inclining, or directed upward **8** : marked by agitation, excitement, or activity **9** : READY; *esp* : highly prepared **10** : going on : taking place ⟨find out what is ~⟩ **11** : EXPIRED, ENDED ⟨the time is ~⟩ **12** : extensively aware or informed ⟨~ on the news⟩ **13** : being ahead or in advance of an opponent ⟨one hole ~ in a match⟩ **14** : presented for or being under consideration ⟨~ for promotion⟩ **15** : charged before a court ⟨~ for robbery⟩

³up *prep* **1** : to, toward, or at a higher point of ⟨~ a ladder⟩ **2** : to or toward the source of ⟨~ the river⟩ **3** : to or toward the northern part of ⟨~ the coast⟩ **4** : in or toward the interior of ⟨traveling ~ the country⟩ **5** : ALONG ⟨walk ~ the street⟩

⁴up *n* **1** : an upward course or slope **2** : a period or state of prosperity or success ⟨he had his ~s and downs⟩ **3** : a quark with a charge of +²/₃ that is one of the constituents of the proton and neutron

⁵up *vb* **upped** \'əpt\ *or in 2* **up**; **upped**; **up·ping**; **ups** *or in 2* **up** **1** : to rise from a lying or sitting position **2** : to act abruptly or surprisingly ⟨she *upped* and left home⟩ **3** : to move or cause to move upward ⟨*upped* the prices⟩

Upa·ni·shad \ü-'pän-i-ˌshäd\ *n* : one of a set of Vedic philosophical treatises

¹up·beat \'əp-ˌbēt\ *n* : an unaccented beat in a musical measure; *esp* : the last beat of the measure

²upbeat *adj* : OPTIMISTIC, CHEERFUL

up·braid \ˌəp-'brād\ *vb* : to criticize, reproach, or scold severely

up·bring·ing \'əp-ˌbriŋ-iŋ\ *n* : the process of bringing up and training

UPC *abbr* Universal Product Code

up·chuck \'əp-ˌchək\ *vb* : VOMIT

up·com·ing \'əp-ˌkə-miŋ\ *adj* : FORTHCOMING, APPROACHING ⟨the ~ election⟩

up–coun·try \'əp-ˌkən-trē\ *adj* : of or relating to the interior of a country or a region — **up–country** \'əp-'kən-\ *adv*

up·date \ˌəp-'dāt\ *vb* : to bring up to date — **update** \'əp-ˌdāt\ *n*

up·draft \'əp-ˌdraft, -ˌdräft\ *n* : an upward movement of gas (as air)

up·end \ˌəp-'end\ *vb* : to set, stand, or rise on end; *also* : OVERTURN

up–front \'əp-ˌfrənt, ˌəp-'frənt\ *adj* **1** : HONEST, CANDID ⟨an ~ answer⟩ **2** : ADVANCE ⟨~ payment⟩

up front *adv* : in advance ⟨paid *up front*⟩

¹up·grade \'əp-ˌgrād\ *n* **1** : an upward grade or slope **2** : INCREASE, RISE

²up·grade \'əp-ˌgrād, ˌəp-'grād\ *vb* **1** : to raise to a higher grade or position; *esp* : to advance to a job requiring a higher level of skill **2** : to improve or replace (as software or a device) for increased usefulness

up·growth \'əp-ˌgrōth\ *n* : the process of growing upward : DEVELOPMENT; *also* : a product or result of this

up·heav·al \ˌəp-'hē-vəl\ *n* **1** : the action or an instance of uplifting esp. of part of the earth's crust **2** : a violent agitation or change

¹up·hill \'əp-'hil\ *adv* : upward on a hill or incline; *also* : against difficulties

²up·hill \-ˌhil\ *adj* **1** : situated on elevated ground **2** : ASCENDING **3** : DIFFICULT, LABORIOUS ⟨an ~ struggle⟩

up·hold \ˌəp-'hōld\ *vb* **-held** \-'held\; **-hold·ing** **1** : to give support to ⟨~ the law⟩ **2** : to support against an opponent **3** : to keep elevated — **up·hold·er** *n*

up·hol·ster \ˌəp-'hōl-stər\ *vb* : to furnish with or as if with upholstery — **up·hol·ster·er** *n*

up·hol·stery \-stə-rē\ *n, pl* **-ster·ies** [ME *upholdester* upholsterer, fr. *upholden* to uphold, fr. *up* + *holden* to hold] : materials (as fabrics, padding, and springs) used to make a soft covering esp. for a seat

UPI *abbr* United Press International

up·keep \'əp-ˌkēp\ *n* : the act or cost of keeping up or maintaining; *also* : the state of being maintained

up·land \'əp-lənd, -ˌland\ *n* : high land esp. at some distance from the sea — **upland** *adj*

¹**up·lift** \ˌəp-'lift\ *vb* **1** : to lift or raise up : ELEVATE **2** : to improve the condition of esp. morally, socially, or intellectually

²**up·lift** \'əp-ˌlift\ *n* **1** : a lifting up; *esp* : an upheaval of the earth's surface **2** : moral or social improvement ⟨spiritual ∼⟩; *also* : a movement to make such improvement

up·load \(ˌ)əp-'lōd, 'əp-ˌlōd\ *vb* : to transfer (information) from a computer to a remote computer or other device

up·mar·ket \ˌəp-'mär-kət\ *adj* : appealing to wealthy consumers

up·most \'əp-ˌmōst\ *adj* : UPPERMOST

up·on \ə-'pȯn, -'pän\ *prep* : ON

¹**up·per** \'ə-pər\ *adj* **1** : higher in physical position, rank, or order ⟨∼ management⟩ **2** : constituting the smaller and more restricted branch of a bicameral legislature **3** *cap* : being a later part or formation of a specific geological period **4** : being toward the interior ⟨the ∼ Amazon⟩ **5** : NORTHERN ⟨∼ Minnesota⟩

²**upper** *n* : one that is upper; *esp* : the parts of a shoe or boot above the sole

up·per·case \ˌə-pər-'kās\ *adj* : CAPITAL 1 — **uppercase** *n*

upper class *n* : a social class occupying a position above the middle class and having the highest status in a society — **upper–class** *adj*

up·per·class·man \ˌə-pər-'klas-mən\ *n* : a junior or senior in a college or high school

upper crust *n* : the highest social class or group; *esp* : the highest circle of the upper class

up·per·cut \'ə-pər-ˌkət\ *n* : a short swinging punch delivered (as in boxing) in an upward direction usu. with a bent arm

upper hand *n* : MASTERY, ADVANTAGE

up·per·most \'ə-pər-ˌmōst\ *adv* : in or into the highest or most prominent position — **uppermost** *adj*

up·pish \'ə-pish\ *adj* : UPPITY

up·pi·ty \'ə-pə-tē\ *adj* : ARROGANT, PRESUMPTUOUS ⟨an ∼ sales clerk⟩

up·raise \ˌəp-'rāz\ *vb* : to lift up : ELEVATE

¹**up·right** \'əp-ˌrīt\ *adj* **1** : PERPENDICULAR, VERTICAL **2** : erect in carriage or posture **3** : morally correct : JUST ⟨an ∼ citizen⟩ — **upright** *adv* — **up·right·ly** *adv* — **up·right·ness** *n*

²**upright** *n* **1** : the state of being upright : a vertical position **2** : something that stands upright

upright piano *n* : a piano whose strings run vertically

upright piano

up·ris·ing \'əp-ˌrī-ziŋ\ *n* : INSURRECTION, REVOLT, REBELLION

up·riv·er \'əp-'ri-vər\ *adv or adj* : toward or at a point nearer the source of a river

up·roar \'əp-ˌrȯr\ *n* [D *oproer*, fr. MD, fr. *op* up + *roer* motion] : a state of commotion, excitement, or violent disturbance

up·roar·i·ous \ˌəp-'rȯr-ē-əs\ *adj* **1** : marked by uproar **2** : extremely funny — **up·roar·i·ous·ly** *adv*

up·root \ˌəp-'rüt, -'rut\ *vb* **1** : to remove by or as if by pulling up by the roots **2** : DISPLACE 1 ⟨families were ∼ed⟩

¹**up·set** \ˌəp-'set\ *vb* **-set**; **-set·ting** **1** : to force or be forced out of the usual upright, level, or proper position **2** : to disturb emotionally : WORRY; *also* : to make somewhat ill **3** : UNSETTLE, DISARRANGE **4** : to defeat unexpectedly

²**up·set** \'əp-ˌset\ *n* **1** : an upsetting or being upset; *esp* : a minor illness **2** : a derangement of plans or ideas **3** : an unexpected defeat

³**up·set** \(ˌ)əp-'set\ *adj* : emotionally disturbed or agitated ⟨∼ about the divorce⟩

up·shot \'əp-ˌshät\ *n* : the final result

¹**up·side** \'əp-ˌsīd\ *n* **1** : the upper side **2** : a positive aspect **3** : PROMISE ⟨rookies with much ∼⟩

²**up·side** \ˌəp-'sīd\ *prep* : up on or against the side of ⟨knocked him ∼ the head⟩

up·side down \ˌəp-ˌsīd-'daun\ *adv* **1** : with the upper and the lower parts reversed in position **2** : in or into confusion or disorder — **upside–down** *adj*

up·si·lon \'üp-sə-ˌlän, 'yüp-, 'əp-\ *n* : the 20th letter of the Greek alphabet — Y or υ

¹**up·stage** \'əp-ˌstāj\ *adv or adj* : toward or at the rear of a theatrical stage

²**up·stage** \ˌəp-'stāj\ *vb* : to draw attention away from (as an actor)

¹**up·stairs** \ˌəp-'sterz\ *adv* **1** : up the stairs : to or on a higher floor **2** : to or at a higher position

²**up·stairs** \'əp-'sterz\ *adj* : situated above the stairs esp. on an upper floor ⟨∼ bedroom⟩

³**up·stairs** \'əp-ˌsterz, 'əp-'sterz\ *n sing or pl* : the part of a building above the ground floor

up·stand·ing \ˌəp-'stan-diŋ, 'əp-\ *adj* **1** : ERECT **2** : STRAIGHTFORWARD, HONEST ⟨∼ citizens⟩

¹**up·start** \ˌəp-'stärt\ *vb* : to jump up suddenly

²**up·start** \'əp-ˌstärt\ *n* : one that has risen suddenly; *esp* : one that claims more personal importance than is warranted — **up·start** \-'stärt\ *adj*

up·state \'əp-ˌstāt\ *adj* : of, relating to, or characteristic of a part of a state away from a large city and esp. to the north — **upstate** *adv* — **upstate** *n*

up·stream \'əp-'strēm\ *adv* : at or toward the source of a stream — **upstream** *adj*

up·stroke \'əp-ˌstrōk\ *n* : an upward stroke (as of a pen)

up·surge \-ˌsərj\ *n* : a rapid or sudden rise ⟨an ∼ in interest⟩

up·swept \'əp-ˌswept\ *adj* : swept upward ⟨∼ hairdo⟩

up·swing \'əp-ˌswiŋ\ *n* : an upward swing; *esp* : a marked increase or rise (as in activity)

up·take \'əp-ˌtāk\ *n* **1** : UNDERSTANDING, COMPREHENSION ⟨quick on the ∼⟩ **2** : an act or instance of absorbing and incorporating esp. into a living organism, tissue, or cell

up·thrust \'əp-ˌthrəst\ *n* : an upward thrust (as of the earth's crust) — **upthrust** *vb*

up·tight \'əp-'tīt\ *adj* **1** : TENSE, NERVOUS, UNEASY; *also* : ANGRY, INDIGNANT **2** : rigidly conventional

up–to–date *adj* **1** : extending up to the present time **2** : abreast of the times : MODERN — **up–to–date·ness** *n*

up·town \'əp-ˌtaun\ *n* : the upper part of a town or city; *esp* : the residential district — **up·town** \'əp-'taun\ *adj or adv*

¹**up·turn** \'əp-ˌtərn, ˌəp-'tərn\ *vb* **1** : to turn (as earth) up or over **2** : to turn or direct upward

²**up·turn** \'əp-ˌtərn\ *n* : an upward turn esp. toward better conditions or higher prices

¹**up·ward** \'əp-wərd\ *or* **up·wards** \-wərdz\ *adv* **1** : in a direction from lower to higher **2** : toward a higher or better condition **3** : toward a greater amount or higher number, degree, or rate

²**upward** *adj* : directed or moving toward or situated in a higher place or level : ASCENDING — **up·ward·ly** *adv*

upwards of *also* **upward of** *adv* : more than : in excess of ⟨they cost *upwards of* $25 each⟩

up·well \ˌəp-'wel\ *vb* : to move or flow upward

up·well·ing \-'we-liŋ\ *n* : a rising or an appearance of rising to the surface and flowing outward; *esp* : the movement of deep cold usu. nutrient-rich ocean water to the surface

up·wind \'əp-'wind\ *adv or adj* : in the direction from which the wind is blowing

ura·cil \'yür-ə-,sil\ *n* : a pyrimidine base that is one of the four bases coding genetic information in the molecular chain of RNA

ura·ni·um \yü-'rā-nē-əm\ *n* : a silvery heavy radioactive metallic chemical element used as a source of atomic energy

Ura·nus \'yür-ə-nəs, yü-'rā-\ *n* [LL, the sky personified as a god, fr. Gk *Ouranos*, fr. *ouranos* sky, heaven] : the planet 7th in order from the sun

ur·ban \'ər-bən\ *adj* : of, relating to, characteristic of, or constituting a city

ur·bane \,ər-'bān\ *adj* [L *urbanus* urban, urbane, fr. *urbs* city] : very polite and polished in manner : SUAVE

ur·ban·ite \'ər-bə-,nīt\ *n* : a person who lives in a city

ur·ban·i·ty \,ər-'ba-nə-tē\ *n, pl* **-ties** : the quality or state of being urbane

ur·ban·ize \'ər-bə-,nīz\ *vb* **-ized; -iz·ing** : to cause to take on urban characteristics — **ur·ban·i·za·tion** \,ər-bə-nə-'zā-shən\ *n*

ur·chin \'ər-chən\ *n* [ME, hedgehog, fr. AF *heriçun, hirechoun*, ultim. fr. L *ericius*] : a pert or mischievous youngster

Ur·du \'ur-dü, 'ər-\ *n* [Hindi & Urdu *urdū*, fr. Pers *zabān-e-urdū-e-muallā* language of the Exalted Comp (the imperial bazaar in Delhi)] : an Indo-Aryan language that is the official language of Pakistan and that is widely used by Muslims in urban areas of India

urea \yü-'rē-ə\ *n* : a soluble nitrogenous compound that is the chief solid constituent of mammalian urine

ure·mia \yü-'rē-mē-ə\ *n* : accumulation in the blood of materials normally passed off in the urine resulting in a poisoned condition — **ure·mic** \-mik\ *adj*

ure·ter \'yür-ə-tər\ *n* : a duct that carries the urine from a kidney to the bladder

ure·thra \yü-'rē-thrə\ *n, pl* **-thras** *or* **-thrae** \-(,)thrē\ : the canal that in most mammals carries off the urine from the bladder and in the male also serves to carry semen from the body — **ure·thral** \-thrəl\ *adj*

ure·thri·tis \,yür-i-'thrī-təs\ *n* : inflammation of the urethra

¹urge \'ərj\ *vb* **urged; urg·ing** **1** : to present, advocate, or demand earnestly **2** : to try to persuade or sway ⟨∼ a guest to stay⟩ **3** : to serve as a motive or reason for **4** : to impress or impel to some course or activity ⟨the dog *urged* the sheep onward⟩

²urge *n* **1** : the act or process of urging **2** : a force or impulse that urges or drives

ur·gent \'ər-jənt\ *adj* **1** : calling for immediate attention : PRESSING **2** : urging insistently — **ur·gen·cy** \-jən-sē\ *n* — **ur·gent·ly** *adv*

uric \'yür-ik\ *adj* : of, relating to, or found in urine

uric acid *n* : a nearly insoluble acid that is the chief nitrogenous excretory product of birds but is present in only small amounts in mammalian urine

uri·nal \'yür-ə-n⁰l\ *n* **1** : a receptacle for urine **2** : a place for urinating

uri·nal·y·sis \,yür-ə-'na-lə-səs\ *n* : chemical analysis of urine

uri·nary \'yür-ə-,ner-ē\ *adj* **1** : relating to, occurring in, or being organs for the formation and discharge of urine **2** : of, relating to, or for urine

urinary bladder *n* : a membranous sac in many vertebrates that serves for the temporary retention of urine and discharges by the urethra

uri·nate \'yür-ə-,nāt\ *vb* **-nat·ed; -nat·ing** : to release or give off urine — **uri·na·tion** \,yür-ə-'nā-shən\ *n*

urine \'yür-ən\ *n* : a waste material from the kidneys that is usu. a yellowish watery liquid in mammals but is semisolid in birds and reptiles

URL \,yü-(,)är-'el, 'ər(-ə)l\ *n* [*uniform (or universal) resource locator*] : a series of usu. alphanumeric characters that specifies the storage location of a resource on the Internet

urn \'ərn\ *n* **1** : a vessel that typically has the form of a vase on a pedestal and often is used to hold the ashes of the dead **2** : a closed vessel usu. with a spout for serving a hot beverage

uro·gen·i·tal \,yür-ō-'je-nə-t⁰l\ *adj* : of, relating to, or being the excretory and reproductive organs or functions

urol·o·gy \yù-'rä-lə-jē\ *n* : a branch of medical science dealing with the urinary or urogenital tract and its disorders — **uro·log·i·cal** \,yür-ə-'lä-ji-kəl\ *also* **uro·log·ic** \-jik\ *adj* — **urol·o·gist** \yü-'rä-lə-jist\ *n*

Ur·sa Ma·jor \,ər-sə-'mā-jər\ *n* [L, lit., greater bear] : the northern constellation that contains the stars which form the Big Dipper

Ursa Mi·nor \-'mī-nər\ *n* [L, lit., lesser bear] : the constellation including the north pole of the heavens and the stars that form the Little Dipper with the North Star at the tip of the handle

ur·sine \'ər-,sīn\ *adj* : of, relating to, or resembling a bear

ur·ti·car·ia \,ər-tə-'ker-ē-ə\ *n* [NL, fr. L *urtica* nettle] : HIVES

us \'əs\ *pron, objective case of* WE

US *abbr* United States

USA *abbr* **1** United States Army **2** United States of America

us·able *also* **use·able** \'yü-zə-bəl\ *adj* : suitable or fit for use — **us·abil·i·ty** \,yü-zə-'bi-lə-tē\ *n*

USAF *abbr* United States Air Force

us·age \'yü-sij, -zij\ *n* **1** : habitual or customary practice or procedure **2** : the way in which words and phrases are actually used **3** : the action or mode of using **4** : manner of treating

USB \,yü-(,)es-'bē\ *n* [*universal serial bus*] : a standardized computer interface for attaching peripherals

USCG *abbr* United States Coast Guard

USDA *abbr* United States Department of Agriculture

¹use \'yüs\ *n* **1** : the act or practice of using or employing something : EMPLOYMENT, APPLICATION **2** : the fact or state of being used **3** : the way of using **4** : USAGE, CUSTOM **5** : the privilege or benefit of using something **6** : the ability or power to use something (as a limb) **7** : the legal enjoyment of property that consists in its employment, occupation, or exercise; *also* : the benefit or profit esp. from property held in trust **8** : USEFULNESS, UTILITY; *also* : the end served : OBJECT, FUNCTION **9** : something useful or beneficial ⟨it's no ∼ arguing⟩ **10** : the occasion or need to employ ⟨he had no more ∼ for it⟩ **11** : ESTEEM, LIKING ⟨had no ∼ for modern art⟩

²use \'yüz\ *vb* **used** \'yüzd; "*used to*" *usu* 'yüs-tə\; **us·ing 1** : to put into action or service : EMPLOY **2** : to consume or take (as drugs) regularly **3** : UTILIZE ⟨∼ tact⟩; *also* : MANIPULATE ⟨*used* his friends to get ahead⟩ **4** : to expend or consume by putting to use **5** : to behave toward : TREAT ⟨*used* the horse cruelly⟩ **6** : to benefit from ⟨house could ∼ a coat of paint⟩ **7** — used in the past with *to* to indicate a former practice, fact, or state ⟨we *used* to work harder⟩ — **us·er** *n*

used \'yüzd\ *adj* **1** : having been used by another : SECONDHAND ⟨∼ cars⟩ **2** : ACCUSTOMED, HABITUATED ⟨∼ to the heat⟩

use·ful \'yüs-fəl\ *adj* : capable of being put to use : ADVANTAGEOUS; *esp* : serviceable for a beneficial end — **use·ful·ly** *adv* — **use·ful·ness** *n*

use·less \-ləs\ *adj* : having or being of no use : WORTHLESS, INEFFECTUAL — **use·less·ly** *adv* — **use·less·ness** *n*

us·er·name \'yü-zər-,nām\ *n* : a sequence of characters that identifies a user when logging onto a computer or website — called also user ID

USES *abbr* United States Employment Service

use up *vb* : to consume completely

¹ush·er \'ə-shər\ *n* [ME *ussher*, fr. AF *ussier, usscher*, fr. VL **ustiarius* doorkeeper, fr. L *ostium, ustium* door, mouth of a river] **1** : an officer who walks before a person of rank **2** : one who escorts people to their seats (as in a church or theater)

²usher *vb* **1** : to conduct to a place **2** : to precede as an usher, forerunner, or harbinger **3** : INAUGURATE, INTRODUCE ⟨∼ in a new era⟩

ush·er·ette \,ə-shə-'ret\ *n* : a girl or woman who is an usher (as in a theater)

USIA *abbr* United States Information Agency

USMC *abbr* United States Marine Corps

USN *abbr* United States Navy

USO *abbr* United Service Organizations

USP *abbr* United States Pharmacopeia

USPS *abbr* United States Postal Service

USS *abbr* United States ship

USSR *abbr* Union of Soviet Socialist Republics
usu *abbr* usual; usually
usu·al \'yü-zhə-wəl\ *adj* **1** : accordant with usage, custom, or habit : NORMAL **2** : commonly or ordinarily used **3** : ORDINARY ✦ *Synonyms* CUSTOMARY, HABITUAL, ACCUSTOMED, ROUTINE — **usu·al·ly** \'yü-zhə-wə-lē, 'yü-zhə-lē\ *adv*
usu·fruct \'yü-zə-ˌfrəkt\ *n* [L *ususfructus,* fr. *usus et fructus* use and enjoyment] : the legal right to use and enjoy the benefits and profits of something belonging to another
usu·rer \'yü-zhər-ər\ *n* : one that lends money esp. at an exorbitant rate
usu·ri·ous \yü-'zhùr-ē-əs\ *adj* : practicing, involving, or constituting usury ⟨a ∼ rate of interest⟩
usurp \yü-'sərp, -'zərp\ *vb* [ME, fr. AF *usorper,* fr. L *usurpare,* to take possession of without legal claim, fr. *usu* (abl. of *usus* use) + *rapere* to seize] : to seize and hold by force or without right ⟨∼ a throne⟩ — **usur·pa·tion** \ˌyü-sər-'pā-shən, -zər-\ *n* — **usurp·er** \yü-'sər-pər, -'zər-\ *n*
usu·ry \'yü-zhə-rē\ *n, pl* **-ries** **1** : the lending of money with an interest charge for its use **2** : an excessive rate or amount of interest charged; *esp* : interest above an established legal rate
UT *abbr* Utah
Ute \'yüt\ *n, pl* **Ute** *or* **Utes** : a member of an American Indian people orig. ranging through Utah, Colorado, Arizona, and New Mexico
uten·sil \yü-'ten-səl\ *n* [ME, vessels for domestic use, fr. MF *utensile,* fr. L *utensilia,* fr. neut. pl. of *utensilis* useful, fr. *uti* to use] **1** : an instrument or vessel used in a household and esp. a kitchen **2** : a useful tool
uter·us \'yü-tə-rəs\ *n, pl* **uter·us·es** *or* **uteri** \'yü-tə-ˌrī\ : the muscular organ of a female mammal in which the young develop before birth — **uter·ine** \-ˌrīn, -rən\ *adj*
utile \'yüt-ᵊl, 'yü-ˌtī(-ə)l\ *adj* : USEFUL
uti·lise *Brit var of* UTILIZE
¹util·i·tar·i·an \yü-ˌti-lə-'ter-ē-ən\ *n* : a person who believes in utilitarianism
²utilitarian *adj* **1** : of or relating to utilitarianism **2** : of or relating to utility : aiming at usefulness rather than beauty; *also* : serving a useful purpose
util·i·tar·i·an·ism \yü-ˌti-lə-'ter-ē-ə-ˌni-zəm\ *n* : a theory that the greatest good for the greatest number should be the main consideration in making a choice of actions
¹util·i·ty \yü-'ti-lə-tē\ *n, pl* **-ties** **1** : USEFULNESS **2** : something useful or designed for use **3** : a business organization performing a public service and subject to special governmental regulation **4** : a public service or a commodity (as electricity or water) provided by a public utility; *also* : equipment to provide such or a similar service
²utility *adj* **1** : capable of serving esp. as a substitute in various uses or positions ⟨a ∼ outfielder⟩ ⟨a ∼ cord⟩ **2** : being of a usable but poor quality ⟨∼ beef⟩
utility knife *n* : a knife designed for general use; *esp* : one with a retractable blade
uti·lize \'yü-tə-ˌlīz\ *vb* **-lized; -liz·ing** : to make use of : turn to profitable account or use — **uti·li·za·tion** \ˌyü-tə-lə-'zā-shən\ *n*
ut·most \'ət-ˌmōst\ *adj* **1** : situated at the farthest or most distant point : EXTREME **2** : of the greatest or highest degree, quantity, number, or amount — **utmost** *n*
uto·pia \yü-'tō-pē-ə\ *n* [*Utopia,* imaginary island described in Sir Thomas More's *Utopia,* fr. Gk *ou* not, no + *topos* place] **1** *often cap* : a place of ideal perfection esp. in laws, government, and social conditions **2** : an impractical scheme for social improvement
¹uto·pi·an \-pē-ən\ *adj, often cap* **1** : of, relating to, or resembling a utopia **2** : proposing ideal social and political schemes that are impractical **3** : VISIONARY
²utopian *n* **1** : a believer in the perfectibility of human society **2** : one who proposes or advocates utopian schemes
¹ut·ter \'ə-tər\ *adj* [ME, remote, fr. OE *ūtera* outer, compar. adj. fr. *ūt* out, adv.] : ABSOLUTE, TOTAL ⟨∼ ruin⟩ — **ut·ter·ly** *adv*
²utter *vb* [ME *uttren,* fr. *utter* outside, adv., fr. OE *ūtor,* compar. of *ūt* out] **1** : to send forth as a sound : express in usu. spoken words : PRONOUNCE, SPEAK **2** : to put (as currency) into circulation — **ut·ter·er** *n*
ut·ter·ance \'ə-tə-rəns\ *n* **1** : something uttered; *esp* : an oral or written statement **2** : the action of uttering with the voice : SPEECH **3** : power, style, or manner of speaking
ut·ter·most \'ə-tər-ˌmōst\ *adj* : EXTREME, UTMOST ⟨the ∼ parts of the earth⟩ — **uttermost** *n*
U–turn \'yü-ˌtərn\ *n* : a turn resembling the letter U; *esp* : a 180-degree turn made by a vehicle in a road
UV *abbr* ultraviolet
uvu·la \'yü-vyə-lə\ *n, pl* **-las** *or* **-lae** \-ˌlē, -ˌlī\ : the fleshy lobe hanging at the back of the roof of the mouth — **uvu·lar** \-lər\ *adj*
UW *abbr* underwriter
ux·o·ri·ous \ˌək-'sòr-ē-əs, ˌəg-'zòr-\ *adj* : excessively devoted or submissive to a wife

¹v \'vē\ *n, pl* **v's** *or* **vs** \'vēz\ *often cap* : the 22d letter of the English alphabet
²v *abbr, often cap* **1** vector **2** velocity **3** verb **4** verse **5** versus **6** very **7** victory **8** vide **9** voice **10** voltage **11** volume **12** vowel
V *symbol* **1** vanadium **2** volt
Va *abbr* Virginia
VA *abbr* **1** Veterans Administration **2** vice admiral **3** Virginia
va·can·cy \'vā-kən-sē\ *n, pl* **-cies** **1** : a vacating esp. of an office, position, or piece of property **2** : a vacant office, position, or tenancy; *also* : the period during which it stands vacant **3** : empty space : VOID **4** : the state of being vacant
va·cant \'vā-kənt\ *adj* **1** : not occupied ⟨∼ seat⟩ ⟨∼ room⟩ **2** : EMPTY ⟨∼ space⟩ **3** : free from business or care ⟨a few ∼ hours⟩ **4** : devoid of thought, reflection, or expression ⟨a ∼ smile⟩ — **va·cant·ly** *adv*
va·cate \'vā-ˌkāt\ *vb* **va·cat·ed; va·cat·ing** **1** : to make void : ANNUL **2** : to make vacant (as an office or house); *also* : to give up the occupancy of
¹va·ca·tion \vā-'kā-shən, və-\ *n* : a period of rest from work : HOLIDAY
²vacation *vb* : to take or spend a vacation — **va·ca·tion·er** *n*
va·ca·tion·ist \-shə-nist\ *n* : a person taking a vacation
va·ca·tion·land \-shən-ˌland\ *n* : an area with recreational attractions and facilities for vacationists
vac·ci·nate \'vak-sə-ˌnāt\ *vb* **-nat·ed; -nat·ing** : to administer a vaccine to usu. by injection
vac·ci·na·tion \ˌvak-sə-'nā-shən\ *n* **1** : the act of vaccinating **2** : the scar left by vaccinating
vac·cine \vak-'sēn, 'vak-ˌsēn\ *n* [F *vaccin,* fr. *vaccine* cowpox, fr. NL *vaccina* (in *variolae vaccinae* cowpox), fr. L, fem. of *vaccinus* of or from cows, fr. *vacca* cow] : a preparation of material (as of killed or weakened viruses or bacteria) used in vaccinating to produce or increase immunity to a disease
vac·cin·ia \vak-'si-nē-ə\ *n* : COWPOX
vac·il·late \'va-sə-ˌlāt\ *vb* **-lat·ed; -lat·ing** **1** : SWAY, TOTTER; *also* : FLUCTUATE **2** : to incline first to one course or opinion and then to another : WAVER — **vac·il·la·tion** \ˌva-sə-'lā-shən\ *n*
va·cu·ity \va-'kyü-ə-tē\ *n, pl* **-ities** **1** : an empty space **2** : the state, fact, or quality of being vacuous **3** : something that is vacuous
vac·u·ole \'va-kyə-ˌwōl\ *n* : a usu. fluid-filled cavity esp.

in the cytoplasm of an individual cell — **vac·u·o·lar** \ˌva-kyə-ˈwō-lər, -ˌlär\ adj

vac·u·ous \ˈva-kyə-wəs\ adj 1 : EMPTY, VACANT, BLANK 2 : DULL, STUPID, INANE ⟨∼ movies⟩ — **vac·u·ous·ly** adv — **vac·u·ous·ness** n

¹**vac·u·um** \ˈva-(ˌ)kyüm, -kyəm\ n, pl **vacuums** or **vac·ua** \-kyə-wə\ [L, fr. neut. of vacuus empty] 1 : a space entirely empty of matter 2 : a space from which most of the air has been removed (as by a pump) 3 : VOID, GAP 4 : VACUUM CLEANER — **vacuum** adj

²**vacuum** vb : to use a vacuum device (as a vacuum cleaner) on ⟨∼ the den⟩

vacuum bottle n : THERMOS

vacuum cleaner n : a household appliance for cleaning (as floors or rugs) by suction

vacuum–packed adj : having much of the air removed before being hermetically sealed ⟨∼ fish⟩

vacuum tube n : an electron tube from which most of the air has been removed

va·de me·cum \ˌvä-dē-ˈmē-kəm, ˌvä-dē-ˈmä-\ n, pl **vade mecums** [L, go with me] : something (as a handbook or manual) regularly carried about

VADM abbr vice admiral

¹**vag·a·bond** \ˈva-gə-ˌbänd\ adj 1 : WANDERING, HOMELESS 2 : of, characteristic of, or leading the life of a vagrant or tramp 3 : leading an unsettled or irresponsible life

²**vagabond** n : one leading a vagabond life; esp : VAGRANT, TRAMP

va·ga·ry \ˈva-gə-rē, və-ˈger-ē\ n, pl **-ries** : an odd or eccentric idea or action : WHIM, CAPRICE ⟨vagaries of the weather⟩

va·gi·na \və-ˈjī-nə\ n, pl **-nae** \-(ˌ)nē\ or **-nas** [L, lit., sheath] : a canal that leads from the uterus to the external opening of the female sex organs — **vag·i·nal** \ˈva-jə-nᵊl\ adj — **vag·i·nal·ly** \-nᵊl-ē\ adv

vag·i·ni·tis \ˌva-jə-ˈnī-təs\ n : inflammation of the vagina

va·gran·cy \ˈvā-grən-sē\ n, pl **-cies** 1 : the quality or state of being vagrant; also : a vagrant act or notion 2 : the offense of being a vagrant

¹**va·grant** \ˈvā-grənt\ n : a person who has no job and wanders from place to place

²**vagrant** adj 1 : of, relating to, or characteristic of a vagrant 2 : following no fixed course : RANDOM, CAPRICIOUS ⟨∼ thoughts⟩ — **va·grant·ly** adv

vague \ˈvāg\ adj **vagu·er; vagu·est** [MF, fr. L vagus, lit., wandering] 1 : not clear, definite, or distinct ⟨a ∼ plan⟩ ⟨∼ silhouettes⟩ 2 : not clearly felt or analyzed ⟨a ∼ unrest⟩ ✦ **Synonyms** OBSCURE, DARK, ENIGMATIC, AMBIGUOUS, EQUIVOCAL — **vague·ly** adv — **vague·ness** n

vain \ˈvān\ adj [ME, fr. AF, empty, futile, fr. L vanus] 1 : of no real value : IDLE, WORTHLESS 2 : FUTILE, UNSUCCESSFUL 3 : proud of one's looks or abilities ✦ **Synonyms** CONCEITED, NARCISSISTIC, VAINGLORIOUS — **vain·ly** adv — **in vain** 1 : without success ⟨her efforts were in vain⟩ 2 : in a blasphemous manner ⟨took the Lord's name in vain⟩

vain·glo·ri·ous \ˌvān-ˈglȯr-ē-əs\ adj : marked by vainglory : BOASTFUL

vain·glo·ry \ˈvān-ˌglȯr-ē\ n 1 : excessive or ostentatious pride esp. in one's own achievements 2 : vain display : VANITY

val abbr value; valued

va·lance \ˈva-ləns, ˈvā-\ n 1 : drapery hanging from an edge (as of an altar, table, or bed) 2 : a drapery or a decorative frame across the top of a window

vale \ˈvāl\ n : VALLEY, DALE

vale·dic·tion \ˌva-lə-ˈdik-shən\ n [L valedicere to say farewell, fr. vale farewell + dicere to say] : an act or utterance of leave-taking : FAREWELL

vale·dic·to·ri·an \-ˌdik-ˈtȯr-ē-ən\ n : the student usu. of the highest rank in a graduating class who delivers the valedictory address at commencement

vale·dic·to·ry \-ˈdik-tə-rē\ adj : bidding farewell : delivered as a valediction ⟨a ∼ address⟩ — **valedictory** n

va·lence \ˈvā-ləns\ n [LL valentia power, capacity, fr. L valēre to be strong] : the combining power of an atom as shown by the number of its electrons that are lost, gained, or shared in the formation of chemical bonds

Va·len·ci·ennes \və-ˌlen-sē-ˈen, ˌvä-lən-sē-, -ˈenz\ n : a fine handmade lace

val·en·tine \ˈva-lən-ˌtīn\ n : a sweetheart chosen or complimented on Valentine's Day; also : a gift or greeting given on this day

Valentine's Day also **Valentine Day** n : February 14 observed in honor of St. Valentine and as a time for exchanging valentines

¹**va·let** \ˈva-lət, -(ˌ)lā; va-ˈlā\ n 1 : a male servant who takes care of a man's clothes and performs personal services 2 : an attendant in a hotel or restaurant who performs personal services (as parking cars) for customers

²**valet** vb : to serve as a valet

val·e·tu·di·nar·i·an \ˌva-lə-ˌtü-də-ˈner-ē-ən, -ˌtyü-\ n : a person of a weak or sickly constitution; esp : one whose chief concern is his or her ill health — **val·e·tu·di·nar·i·an·ism** \-ē-ə-ˌni-zəm\ n

val·iant \ˈval-yənt\ adj : having or showing valor : BRAVE, HEROIC ✦ **Synonyms** VALOROUS, DOUGHTY, COURAGEOUS, BOLD, AUDACIOUS, DAUNTLESS, UNDAUNTED, INTREPID — **val·iant·ly** adv

val·id \ˈva-ləd\ adj 1 : having legal force ⟨a ∼ contract⟩ 2 : founded on truth or fact : capable of being justified or defended ⟨a ∼ argument⟩ ⟨∼ reasons⟩ — **va·lid·i·ty** \və-ˈli-də-tē\ n — **val·id·ly** adv

val·i·date \ˈva-lə-ˌdāt\ vb **-dat·ed; -dat·ing** 1 : to make legally valid 2 : to confirm the validity of 3 : VERIFY — **val·i·da·tion** \ˌva-lə-ˈdā-shən\ n

va·lise \və-ˈlēs\ n [F] : SUITCASE

val·ley \ˈva-lē\ n, pl **valleys** : a long depression between ranges of hills or mountains

val·or \ˈva-lər\ n [ME valour worth, worthiness, bravery, fr. AF, fr. ML valor, fr. L valēre to be strong] : personal bravery ✦ **Synonyms** HEROISM, PROWESS, GALLANTRY — **val·or·ous** \ˈva-lə-rəs\ adj

val·o·ri·za·tion \ˌva-lə-rə-ˈzā-shən\ n : the support of commodity prices by any of various forms of government subsidy — **val·o·rize** \ˈva-lə-ˌrīz\ vb

val·our chiefly Brit var of VALOR

¹**valu·able** \ˈval-yə-bəl, -yə-wə-bəl\ adj 1 : having money value 2 : having great money value 3 : of great use or service ✦ **Synonyms** INVALUABLE, PRICELESS, COSTLY, EXPENSIVE, DEAR, PRECIOUS

²**valuable** n : a usu. personal possession of considerable value ⟨their ∼s were stolen⟩

val·u·ate \ˈval-yə-ˌwāt\ vb **-at·ed; -at·ing** : to place a value on : APPRAISE — **val·u·a·tor** \-ˌwā-tər\ n

val·u·a·tion \ˌval-yə-ˈwā-shən\ n 1 : the act or process of valuing; esp : appraisal of property 2 : the estimated or determined market value of a thing

¹**val·ue** \ˈval-yü\ n 1 : a fair return or equivalent in money, goods, or services for something exchanged 2 : the monetary worth of a thing; also : relative worth, utility, or importance ⟨nothing of ∼ to say⟩ 3 : an assigned or computed numerical quantity ⟨the ∼ of x in an equation⟩ 4 : relative lightness or darkness of a color : LUMINOSITY 5 : the relative length of a tone or note 6 : something (as a principle or ideal) intrinsically valuable or desirable ⟨human rather than material ∼s⟩ — **val·ue·less** adj

²**value** vb **val·ued; valu·ing** 1 : to estimate the monetary worth of : APPRAISE 2 : to rate in usefulness, importance, or general worth 3 : to consider or rate highly : PRIZE, ESTEEM ⟨valued your opinions⟩ — **val·u·er** n

val·ue–add·ed tax n : an incremental excise tax that is levied on the value added at each stage of the processing of a raw material or the production and distribution of a commodity

valve \ˈvalv\ n 1 : a structure (as in a vein) that temporarily closes a passage or that permits movement in one direction only 2 : a device by which the flow of a fluid material may be regulated by a movable part; also : the movable part of such a device 3 : a device in a brass wind instrument for quickly varying the tube length in order to change the fundamental tone by some definite interval 4 : one of the separate usu. hinged pieces of which the shell of some animals and esp. bivalve mollusks consists 5 : one of the pieces into which a ripe seed capsule or pod separates — **valved** \ˈvalvd\ adj — **valve·less** adj

val·vu·lar \ˈval-vyə-lər\ adj : of, relating to, or affecting a valve esp. of the heart ⟨∼ heart disease⟩

va·moose \va-ˈmüs, və-\ vb **va·moosed; va·moos·ing** [Sp vamos let us go] : to leave or go away quickly

¹**vamp** n 1 : the part of a boot or shoe upper covering

esp. the front part of the foot **2** : a short introductory musical passage often repeated

²vamp \'vamp\ *vb* · **1** : to provide with a new vamp **2** : to patch up with a new part **3** : INVENT, IMPROVISE ⟨∼ up an excuse⟩

³vamp *n* : a woman who uses her charm or wiles to seduce and exploit men

⁴vamp *vb* : to practice seductive wiles on : to act like a vamp

vam·pire \'vam-ˌpī(-ə)r\ *n* [F, fr. G *Vampir*, fr. Serbian *vampir*] **1** : a reanimated corpse of folklore that bites and sucks the blood of the living **2** : a person who preys on other people; *esp* : a woman who exploits and ruins her lover **3** : VAMPIRE BAT

vampire bat *n* : any of various bats of Central and South America that feed on the blood of animals; *also* : any of several other bats that do not feed on blood but are sometimes reputed to do so

¹van \'van\ *n* : VANGUARD

²van *n* : a usu. enclosed wagon or motortruck for moving goods or animals; *also* : a versatile enclosed box-like motor vehicle

va·na·di·um \və-'nā-dē-əm\ *n* : a soft grayish ductile metallic chemical element used esp. to form alloys

Van Al·len belt \van-'a-lən-\ *n* : a belt of intense radiation in the magnetosphere composed of charged particles trapped by earth's magnetic field

van·co·my·cin \ˌvaŋ-kə-'mī-sᵊn\ *n* : an antibiotic used esp. against staphylococci

van·dal \'van-dᵊl\ *n* **1** *cap* : a member of a Germanic people who sacked Rome in A.D. 455 **2** : a person who willfully mars or destroys property

van·dal·ise *Brit var of* VANDALIZE

van·dal·ism \'van-də-ˌli-zəm\ *n* : willful or malicious destruction or defacement of public or private property

van·dal·ize \-ˌlīz\ *vb* **-ized**; **-iz·ing** : to subject to vandalism : DAMAGE

Van·dyke \van-'dīk\ *n* : a trim pointed beard

vane \'vān\ *n* [ME, fr. OE *fana* banner] **1** : a movable device attached to a high object for showing wind direction **2** : a thin flat or curved object that is rotated about an axis by a flow of fluid or that rotates to cause a fluid to flow or that redirects a flow of fluid ⟨the ∼s of a windmill⟩ **3** : a feather fastened near the back end of an arrow for stability in flight

van·guard \'van-ˌgärd\ *n* **1** : the troops moving at the front of an army **2** : the forefront of an action or movement

va·nil·la \və-'ni-lə\ *n* [NL, genus name, fr. Sp *vainilla* vanilla (plant and fruit), dim. of *vaina* sheath, fr. L *vagina*] : a flavoring extract made synthetically or obtained from the long beanlike pods (**vanilla beans**) of a tropical American climbing orchid; *also* : this orchid

van·ish \'va-nish\ *vb* : to pass from sight or existence : disappear completely — **van·ish·er** *n*

van·i·ty \'va-nə-tē\ *n, pl* **-ties** **1** : something that is vain, empty, or useless **2** : the quality or fact of being useless or futile : FUTILITY **3** : undue pride in oneself or one's appearance : CONCEIT **4** : a small case for cosmetics : COMPACT

vanity plate *n* : an automobile license plate bearing distinctive letters or numbers designated by the owner

van·quish \'vaŋ-kwish, 'van-\ *vb* **1** : to overcome in battle or in a contest **2** : to gain mastery over (as an emotion)

van·tage \'van-tij\ *n* **1** : superiority in a contest **2** : a position giving a strategic advantage or a commanding perspective

va·pid \'va-pəd, 'vā-\ *adj* : lacking spirit, liveliness, or zest : FLAT, INSIPID ⟨∼ gossip⟩ — **va·pid·i·ty** \va-'pi-də-tē\ *n* — **va·pid·ly** *adv* — **va·pid·ness** *n*

va·por \'vā-pər\ *n* **1** : fine separated particles (as fog or smoke) floating in the air and clouding it **2** : a substance in the gaseous state; *esp* : one that is liquid under ordinary conditions **3** : something insubstantial or fleeting **4** *pl* : a depressed or hysterical nervous condition

va·por·ing \'vā-pə-riŋ\ *n* : an idle, boastful, or high-flown expression or speech — usu. used in pl. ⟨political ∼s⟩

va·por·ise *Brit var of* VAPORIZE

va·por·ize \'vā-pə-ˌrīz\ *vb* **-ized**; **-iz·ing** **1** : to convert into vapor **2** : to destroy as if by converting to vapor ⟨*vaporized* enemy tanks⟩ — **va·por·i·za·tion** \ˌvā-pə-rə-'zā-shən\ *n*

va·por·iz·er \-ˌrī-zər\ *n* : a device that vaporizes something (as a medicated liquid)

vapor lock *n* : an interruption of flow of a fluid (as fuel in an engine) caused by the formation of vapor in the feeding system

va·por·ous \'vā-pə-rəs\ *adj* **1** : full of vapors : FOGGY, MISTY **2** : UNSUBSTANTIAL, VAGUE ⟨∼ speculations⟩ — **va·por·ous·ly** *adv* — **va·por·ous·ness** *n*

va·pour *chiefly Brit var of* VAPOR

va·que·ro \vä-'ker-ō\ *n, pl* **-ros** [Sp, fr. *vaca* cow, fr. L *vacca*] : a ranch hand : COWBOY

var *abbr* **1** variable **2** variant; variation **3** variety **4** various

¹var·i·able \'ver-ē-ə-bəl\ *adj* **1** : able or apt to vary : CHANGEABLE **2** : FICKLE **3** : not true to type : ABERRANT ⟨a ∼ wheat⟩ — **var·i·abil·i·ty** \ˌver-ē-ə-'bi-lə-tē, ˌvar-\ *n* — **var·i·ably** \-blē\ *adv*

²variable *n* **1** : a quantity that may take on any of a set of values; *also* : a mathematical symbol representing a variable **2** : something that is variable

var·i·ance \'ver-ē-əns\ *n* **1** : variation or a degree of variation : DEVIATION **2** : DISAGREEMENT, DISPUTE **3** : a license to do something contrary to the usual rule ⟨a zoning ∼⟩ **4** : the square of the standard deviation ✦ **Synonyms** DISCORD, CONTENTION, DISSENSION, STRIFE, CONFLICT

¹var·i·ant \'ver-ē-ənt\ *adj* **1** : differing from others of its kind or class **2** : varying usu. slightly from the standard or type

²variant *n* **1** : one that exhibits variation from a type or norm **2** : one of two or more different spellings or pronunciations of a word

var·i·a·tion \ˌver-ē-'ā-shən\ *n* **1** : the act, process, or an instance of varying : a change in form, position, or condition : MODIFICATION, ALTERATION **2** : extent of change or difference **3** : divergence in the characteristics of an organism from those typical or usual for its group; *also* : one exhibiting such variation **4** : repetition of a musical theme with modifications in rhythm, tune, harmony, or key

vari·col·ored \'ver-i-ˌkə-lərd\ *adj* : having various colors : VARIEGATED

var·i·cose \'va-rə-ˌkōs\ *adj* : abnormally swollen and dilated ⟨∼ veins⟩ — **var·i·cos·i·ty** \ˌva-rə-'kä-sə-tē\ *n*

var·ied \'ver-ēd\ *adj* **1** : having many forms or types : DIVERSE ⟨∼ interests⟩ **2** : VARIEGATED — **var·ied·ly** *adv*

var·ie·gat·ed \'ver-ē-ə-ˌgā-təd\ *adj* **1** : having patches, stripes, or marks of different colors ⟨∼ flowers⟩ **2** : VARIED 1 — **var·ie·gate** \-ˌgāt\ *vb* — **var·ie·ga·tion** \ˌver-ē-ə-'gā-shən\ *n*

¹va·ri·etal \və-'rī-ə-tᵊl\ *adj* : of or relating to a variety; *esp* : of, relating to, or producing a varietal

²varietal *n* : a wine bearing the name of the principal grape from which it is made

va·ri·ety \və-'rī-ə-tē\ *n, pl* **-et·ies** **1** : the state of being varied or various : DIVERSITY **2** : a collection of different things : ASSORTMENT **3** : something varying from others of the same general kind **4** : any of various groups of plants or animals within a species distinguished by characteristics insufficient to separate species : SUBSPECIES **5** : entertainment such as is given in a stage presentation comprising a series of performances (as songs, dances, or acrobatic acts)

var·i·o·rum \ˌver-ē-'ȯr-əm\ *n* : an edition or text of a work containing notes by various persons or variant readings of the text

var·i·ous \'ver-ē-əs\ *adj* **1** : VARICOLORED **2** : of differing kinds : MULTIFARIOUS **3** : UNLIKE ⟨animals as ∼ as the jaguar and the sloth⟩ **4** : having a number of different aspects **5** : NUMEROUS, MANY **6** : INDIVIDUAL, SEPARATE ✦ **Synonyms** DIVERGENT, DISPARATE, DIFFERENT, DISSIMILAR, DIVERSE, UNLIKE — **var·i·ous·ly** *adv*

var·let \'vär-lət\ *n* **1** : ATTENDANT **2** : SCOUNDREL, KNAVE

var·mint \'vär-mənt\ *n* [alter. of *vermin*] **1** : an animal considered a pest; *esp* : one classed as vermin and unprotected by game law **2** : a contemptible person : RASCAL

¹var·nish \'vär-nish\ *n* **1** : a liquid preparation that is applied to a surface and dries into a hard glossy coating; *also* : the glaze of this coating **2** : something suggesting varnish by its gloss **3** : outside show : deceptive or superficial appearance

²**varnish** *vb* **1** : to cover with varnish **2** : to cover or conceal with something that gives a fair appearance : GLOSS

var·si·ty \'vär-sə-tē\ *n, pl* **-ties** [by shortening & alter. fr. *university*] **1** *Brit* : UNIVERSITY **2** : the principal team representing a college, school, or club

vary \'ver-ē\ *vb* **var·ied; vary·ing** **1** : ALTER, CHANGE **2** : to make or be of different kinds : introduce or have variety : DIVERSIFY, DIFFER **3** : DEVIATE, SWERVE **4** : to change in bodily structure or function away from what is usual for members of a group

vas·cu·lar \'vas-kyə-lər\ *adj* [NL *vascularis,* fr. L *vasculum* small vessel, dim. of *vas* vase, vessel] : of or relating to a channel or system of channels for the conveyance of a body fluid (as blood or sap); *also* : supplied with or containing such vessels and esp. blood vessels ⟨the ~ system⟩

vascular plant *n* : a plant having a specialized system for carrying fluids that includes xylem and phloem

vas def·er·ens \'vas-'de-fə-rənz\ *n, pl* **va·sa def·er·en·tia** \'vā-zə-,de-fə-'ren-shē-ə\ : a sperm-carrying duct of the testis

vase \'vās, 'vāz\ *n* : a usu. round vessel of greater depth than width used chiefly for ornament or for flowers

va·sec·to·my \və-'sek-tə-mē, vā-'zek-\ *n, pl* **-mies** : surgical excision of all or part of the vas deferens usu. to induce sterility

va·so·con·stric·tion \,vā-zō-kən-'strik-shən\ *n* : narrowing of the interior diameter of blood vessels

va·so·con·stric·tor \-tər\ *n* : an agent (as a nerve fiber or a drug) that initiates or induces vasoconstriction

vas·sal \'va-səl\ *n* **1** : a person under the protection of a feudal lord to whom he owes homage and loyalty : a feudal tenant **2** : one occupying a dependent or subordinate position — **vassal** *adj*

vas·sal·age \-sə-lij\ *n* **1** : the state of being a vassal **2** : the homage and loyalty due from a vassal **3** : SERVITUDE, SUBJECTION

¹**vast** \'vast\ *adj* : very great in size, amount, degree, intensity, or esp. extent ⟨~ plains⟩ ⟨~ knowledge⟩ ✦ *Synonyms* ENORMOUS, HUGE, GIGANTIC, COLOSSAL, MAMMOTH — **vast·ly** *adv* — **vast·ness** *n*

²**vast** *n* : a great expanse : IMMENSITY

vasty \'vas-tē\ *adj* : VAST, IMMENSE

vat \'vat\ *n* : a large vessel (as a tub or barrel) esp. for holding liquids in manufacturing processes

VAT *abbr* value-added tax

vat·ic \'va-tik\ *adj* : PROPHETIC, ORACULAR ⟨~ pronouncements⟩

Vat·i·can \'va-ti-kən\ *n* **1** : the papal headquarters in Rome **2** : the papal government

vau·de·ville \'vod-vəl, 'väd-, 'vōd-, -,vil\ *n* [F, fr. MF, satirical song, alter. of *vaudevire,* fr. *vau-de-Vire* valley of Vire, town in northwest France where such songs were composed] : a stage entertainment consisting of unrelated acts (as of acrobats, comedians, dancers, or singers)

¹**vault** \'vȯlt\ *n* **1** : an arched masonry structure usu. forming a ceiling or roof; *also* : something (as the sky) resembling a vault **2** : a room or space covered by a vault esp. when underground **3** : a room or compartment for the safekeeping of valuables **4** : a burial chamber; *also* : a usu. metal or concrete case in which a casket is enclosed at burial — **vaulty** *adj*

²**vault** *vb* : to form or cover with a vault

³**vault** *vb* : to leap vigorously esp. by aid of the hands or a pole — **vault·er** *n*

⁴**vault** *n* : an act of vaulting : LEAP

vault·ed \'vȯl-təd\ *adj* **1** : built in the form of a vault : ARCHED **2** : covered with a vault

vault·ing \-tiŋ\ *adj* : reaching for the heights ⟨~ ambition⟩

vaunt \'vȯnt\ *vb* [ME, fr. AF *vanter,* fr. LL *vanitare,* ultim. fr. L *vanus* vain] : to boast of ⟨~s his successes⟩ — **vaunt** *n*

vaunt·ed \'vȯn-təd\ *adj* : much praised or boasted of

vb *abbr* verb; verbal

V–chip \'vē-,chip\ *n* : a computer chip in a television set used to block based on content the viewing of certain programs

VCR \,vē-(,)sē-'är\ *n* [*videocassette recorder*] : a device that records and plays back videotapes

VD *abbr* venereal disease

VDT *abbr* video display terminal

veal \'vēl\ *n* : the flesh of a young calf

vec·tor \'vek-tər\ *n* **1** : a quantity that has magnitude and direction **2** : an organism (as a fly or tick) that transmits a pathogen

Ve·da \'vā-də\ *n* [Skt, lit., knowledge] : any of a class of Hindu sacred writings — **Ve·dic** \'vā-dik\ *adj*

Ve·dan·ta \vā-'dän-tə, və-, -'dan-\ *n* : an orthodox Hindu philosophy based on the Upanishads

vee·jay \'vē-,jā\ *n* : an announcer of a program featuring music videos

veep \'vēp\ *n* : VICE PRESIDENT

veer \'vir\ *vb* : to shift from one direction or course to another ✦ *Synonyms* TURN, AVERT, DEFLECT, DIVERT — **veer** *n*

veg·an \'vē-gən, 'vā-; 've-jən, -,jan\ *n* : a strict vegetarian who consumes no animal food or dairy products — **veg·an·ism** \'vē-gə-,ni-zəm, 'vā-, 've-\ *n*

¹**veg·e·ta·ble** \'vej-tə-bəl, 've-jə-\ *adj* [ME, fr. ML *vegetabilis,* vegetative, fr. *vegetare* to grow, fr. L, to animate, fr. *vegetus* lively, fr. *vegēre* to enliven] **1** : of, relating to, or growing like plants ⟨the ~ kingdom⟩ **2** : made from, obtained from, or containing plant or plant products ⟨~ oils⟩ **3** : suggesting that of a plant (as in inertness) ⟨a ~ existence⟩

²**vegetable** *n* **1** : PLANT 1 **2** : a usu. herbaceous plant grown for an edible part that is usu. eaten as part of a meal; *also* : such an edible part

veg·e·tal \'ve-jə-tᵊl\ *adj* **1** : VEGETABLE **2** : VEGETATIVE

veg·e·tar·i·an \,ve-jə-'ter-ē-ən\ *n* : one that believes in or practices living on a diet of vegetables, fruits, grains, nuts, and sometimes animal products (such as milk and cheese) — **vegetarian** *adj* — **veg·e·tar·i·an·ism** \-ē-ə-,ni-zəm\ *n*

veg·e·tate \'ve-jə-,tāt\ *vb* **-tat·ed; -tat·ing** : to live or grow in the manner of a plant; *esp* : to lead a dull inert life

veg·e·ta·tion \,ve-jə-'tā-shən\ *n* **1** : the act or process of vegetating; *also* : inert existence **2** : plant life or cover (as of an area) — **veg·e·ta·tion·al** \-shə-nəl\ *adj*

veg·e·ta·tive \'ve-jə-,tā-tiv\ *adj* **1** : of or relating to nutrition and growth esp. as contrasted with reproduction **2** : of, relating to, or composed of vegetation ⟨~ cover⟩ **3** : VEGETABLE 3

veg out \'vej-\ *vb* **vegged out; vegging out** [short for *vegetate*] : to spend time idly or passively

ve·he·ment \'vē-ə-mənt\ *adj* **1** : marked by great force or energy **2** : marked by strong feeling or expression : PASSIONATE, FERVID ⟨~ opposition⟩ — **ve·he·mence** \-məns\ *n* — **ve·he·ment·ly** *adv*

ve·hi·cle \'vē-ə-kəl, 'vē-,hi-\ *n* **1** : a medium by which a thing is applied or administered ⟨linseed oil is a ~ for pigments⟩ **2** : a medium through or by means of which something is conveyed or expressed **3** : a means of transporting persons or goods ✦ *Synonyms* INSTRUMENT, AGENT, AGENCY, ORGAN, CHANNEL — **ve·hic·u·lar** \vē-'hi-kyə-lər\ *adj*

¹**veil** \'vāl\ *n* **1** : a piece of often sheer or diaphanous material used to screen or curtain something or to cover the head or face **2** : the life of a nun ⟨take the ~⟩ **3** : something that hides or obscures like a veil ⟨a ~ of secrecy⟩

²**veil** *vb* : to cover with or as if with a veil : wear a veil

¹**vein** \'vān\ *n* **1** : a fissure in rock filled with mineral matter; *also* : a bed of useful mineral matter **2** : any of the tubular branching vessels that carry blood from the capillaries toward the heart **3** : any of the bundles of vascular vessels forming the framework of a leaf **4** : any of the thickened ribs that stiffen the wings of an insect **5** : something (as a wavy variegation in marble) suggesting veins **6** : a distinctive style of expression **7** : a distinctive element or quality : STRAIN **8** : MOOD, HUMOR — **veined** \'vānd\ *adj*

²**vein** *vb* : to pattern with or as if with veins — **vein·ing** *n*

vel *abbr* velocity

ve·lar \'vē-lər\ *adj* : of or relating to a velum and esp. that of the soft palate

veld *or* **veldt** \'velt, 'felt\ *n* [Afrikaans *veld,* fr. D, field] : an open grassland esp. in southern Africa usu. with scattered shrubs or trees

vel·lum \'ve-ləm\ *n* [ME *velym,* fr. AF *velim, veeslin,* fr. **veelin,* adj., of a calf, fr. *veel* calf] **1** : a fine-grained lambskin, kidskin, or calfskin prepared for writing on or for binding books **2** : a strong cream-colored paper — **vellum** *adj*

ve·loc·i·pede \və-'lä-sə-ˌpēd\ n : an early bicycle

ve·loc·i·rapt·or \və-'lä-sə-ˌrap-tər\ n : any of a genus of agile flesh-eating bipedal dinosaurs of the Cretaceous having a sickle-shaped claw on each foot

ve·loc·i·ty \və-'lä-sə-tē\ n, pl **-ties** : quickness of motion : SPEED ⟨the ~ of light⟩

ve·lour or **ve·lours** \və-'lu̇r\ n, pl **velours** \-'lu̇rz\ : any of various textile fabrics with pile like that of velvet

ve·lum \'vē-ləm\ n, pl **ve·la** \-lə\ : a membranous body part (as the soft palate) resembling a veil

vel·vet \'vel-vət\ n [ME *veluet, velvet*, fr. AF, fr. *velu* shaggy, ultim. fr. L *villus* shaggy hair] 1 : a fabric having a short soft dense warp pile 2 : something resembling or suggesting velvet (as in softness or luster) 3 : the soft skin covering the growing antlers of deer — **velvet** adj — **velvety** adj

vel·ve·teen \ˌvel-və-'tēn\ n 1 : a fabric woven usu. of cotton in imitation of velvet 2 pl : clothes made of velveteen

Ven abbr venerable

ve·nal \'vē-nᵊl\ adj : capable of being bought or bribed : MERCENARY, CORRUPT ⟨~ legislators⟩ — **ve·nal·i·ty** \vi-'na-lə-tē\ n — **ve·nal·ly** \'vē-nᵊl-ē\ adv

ve·na·tion \ve-'nā-shən, vē-\ n : an arrangement or system of veins ⟨the ~ of the hand⟩ ⟨leaf ~⟩

vend \'vend\ vb : SELL; esp : to sell as a hawker or peddler — **vend·ible** adj

vend·ee \ven-'dē\ n : one to whom a thing is sold : BUYER

ven·det·ta \ven-'de-tə\ n : a feud marked by acts of revenge

vending machine n : a coin-operated machine for selling merchandise

ven·dor \'ven-dər, for 1 also ven-'dȯr\ n 1 : one that vends : SELLER 2 : VENDING MACHINE

¹ve·neer \və-'nir\ n [G *Furnier*, fr. *furnieren* to veneer, fr. F *fournir* to furnish] 1 : a thin usu. superficial layer of material ⟨brick ~⟩; esp : a thin layer of fine wood glued over a cheaper wood 2 : superficial display : GLOSS

²veneer vb : to overlay with a veneer

ven·er·a·ble \'ve-nə-rə-bəl\ adj 1 : deserving to be venerated — often used as a religious title 2 : made sacred by association

ven·er·ate \'ve-nə-ˌrāt\ vb **-at·ed; -at·ing** : to regard with reverential respect ✦ **Synonyms** ADORE, REVERE, REVERENCE, WORSHIP — **ven·er·a·tion** \ˌve-nə-'rā-shən\ n

ve·ne·re·al \və-'nir-ē-əl\ adj : of or relating to sexual intercourse or to diseases transmitted by it ⟨a ~ infection⟩

venereal disease n : a contagious disease (as gonorrhea or syphilis) usu. acquired by having sexual intercourse with someone who already has it

ve·ne·tian blind \və-'nē-shən-\ n : a blind having thin horizontal parallel slats that can be adjusted to admit a desired amount of light

ven·geance \'ven-jəns\ n : punishment inflicted in retaliation for an injury or offense : REVENGE

venge·ful \'venj-fəl\ adj : filled with a desire for revenge : VINDICTIVE ⟨a ~ former employee⟩ — **venge·ful·ly** adv

ve·nial \'vē-nē-əl\ adj : capable of being forgiven : EXCUSABLE ⟨~ sin⟩

ve·ni·re \və-'nī-rē\ n : a panel from which a jury is drawn

ve·ni·re fa·ci·as \-'fā-shē-əs\ n [ME, fr. ML, you should cause to come] : a writ summoning persons to appear in court to serve as jurors

ve·ni·re·man \və-'nī-rē-mən, -'nir-ē-\ n : a member of a venire

ven·i·son \'ven-ə-sən, -zən\ n, pl **venisons** also **venison** [ME, fr. AF *veneisun* game, venison, fr. L *venatio*, fr. *venari* to hunt, pursue] : the edible flesh of a deer

ven·om \'ve-nəm\ n [ME *venim*, fr. AF, ultim. fr. L *venenum* magic charm, drug, poison] 1 : poisonous material secreted by some animals (as snakes, spiders, or bees) and transmitted usu. by biting or stinging 2 : ILL WILL, MALEVOLENCE

ven·om·ous \'ve-nə-məs\ adj 1 : full of venom : POISONOUS 2 : SPITEFUL, MALEVOLENT ⟨~ comments⟩ 3 : secreting and using venom ⟨~ snakes⟩ — **ven·om·ous·ly** adv

ve·nous \'vē-nəs\ adj 1 : of, relating to, or full of veins 2 : being purplish red oxygen-deficient blood rich in carbon dioxide that is present in most veins

¹vent \'vent\ vb 1 : to provide with a vent 2 : to serve as a vent for 3 : EXPEL, DISCHARGE 4 : to relieve oneself by vigorous or emotional expression

²vent n 1 : an opportunity or way of escape or passage : OUTLET 2 : an opening for the escape of a gas or liquid or for the relief of pressure

³vent n : a slit in a garment esp. in the lower part of a seam (as of a jacket or skirt)

ven·ti·late \'ven-tə-ˌlāt\ vb **-lat·ed; -lat·ing** 1 : to discuss freely and openly ⟨~ a question⟩ 2 : to give vent to ⟨~ one's grievances⟩ 3 : to cause fresh air to circulate through (as a room or mine) so as to replace foul air 4 : to provide with a vent or outlet ✦ **Synonyms** EXPRESS, VENT, AIR, UTTER, VOICE, BROACH — **ven·ti·la·tor** \-ˌlā-tər\ n

ven·ti·la·tion \ˌven-tə-'lā-shən\ n 1 : the act or process of ventilating 2 : circulation of air (as in a room) 3 : a system or means of providing fresh air

ven·tral \'ven-trəl\ adj 1 : of or relating to the belly : ABDOMINAL 2 : of, relating to, or located on or near the surface of the body that in humans is the front but in most other animals is the lower surface — **ven·tral·ly** adv

ven·tri·cle \'ven-tri-kəl\ n 1 : a chamber of the heart that receives blood from the atrium of the same side and pumps it into the arteries 2 : any of the communicating cavities of the brain that are continuous with the central canal of the spinal cord — **ven·tric·u·lar** \ven-'tri-kyə-lər\ adj

ven·tril·o·quism \ven-'tri-lə-ˌkwi-zəm\ n [LL *ventriloquus* ventriloquist, fr. L *venter* belly + *loqui* to speak; fr. the belief that the voice is produced from the ventriloquist's stomach] : the production of the voice in such a manner that the sound appears to come from a source other than the speaker — **ven·tril·o·quist** \-kwist\ n

ven·tril·o·quy \-kwē\ n : VENTRILOQUISM

¹ven·ture \'ven-chər\ vb **ven·tured; ven·tur·ing** 1 : to expose to hazard : RISK 2 : to undertake the risks of : BRAVE 3 : to offer at the risk of rebuff, rejection, or censure ⟨~ an opinion⟩ 4 : to proceed despite danger : DARE

²venture n 1 : an undertaking involving chance or risk; esp : a speculative business enterprise 2 : something risked in a speculative venture : STAKE

ven·ture·some \'ven-chər-səm\ adj 1 : involving risk : DANGEROUS, HAZARDOUS 2 : inclined to venture : BOLD, DARING ✦ **Synonyms** ADVENTUROUS, VENTUROUS, RASH, RECKLESS, FOOLHARDY — **ven·ture·some·ly** adv — **ven·ture·some·ness** n

ven·tur·ous \'ven-chə-rəs\ adj : VENTURESOME — **ven·tur·ous·ly** adv — **ven·tur·ous·ness** n

ven·ue \'ven-yü\ n [AF, alter. of *vinné, visné*, lit., neighborhood, neighbors, ultim. fr. L *vicinitas* vicinity] 1 : the place from which the jury is taken and where the trial is held 2 : the place in which the alleged events from which a legal action arises took place 3 : a place where events are held ⟨music ~s⟩

Ve·nus \'vē-nəs\ n : the planet 2d in order from the sun

Venus fly·trap or **Ve·nus's–fly·trap** \'vē-nə-səz-'flī-ˌtrap\ n : an insect-eating plant of the Carolina coast that has the leaf tip modified into an insect trap

Ve·nu·sian \vi-'nü-zhən, -'nyü-\ adj : of or relating to the planet Venus

ve·ra·cious \və-'rā-shəs\ adj 1 : TRUTHFUL, HONEST 2 : TRUE, ACCURATE ⟨~ details⟩ — **ve·ra·cious·ly** adv

ve·rac·i·ty \və-'ra-sə-tē\ n, pl **-ties** 1 : devotion to truth : TRUTHFULNESS 2 : conformity with fact : ACCURACY 3 : something true

ve·ran·da or **ve·ran·dah** \və-'ran-də\ n : a long open usu. roofed porch

veranda

verb \'vərb\ *n* : a word that is the grammatical center of a predicate and expresses an act, occurrence, or mode of being

¹ver·bal \'vər-bəl\ *adj* **1** : of, relating to, or consisting of words; *esp* : having to do with words rather than with the ideas to be conveyed **2** : expressed in usu. spoken words : not written : ORAL ⟨a ~ contract⟩ **3** : of, relating to, or formed from a verb ⟨a ~ adjective⟩ **4** : LITERAL, VERBATIM — **ver·bal·ly** *adv*

²verbal *n* : a word that combines characteristics of a verb with those of a noun or adjective

verbal auxiliary *n* : an auxiliary verb

ver·bal·ize \'vər-bə-ˌlīz\ *vb* **-ized; -iz·ing** **1** : to speak or write in wordy or empty fashion **2** : to express something in words : describe verbally ⟨*verbalized* her feelings⟩ **3** : to convert into a verb — **ver·bal·i·za·tion** \ˌvər-bə-lə-'zā-shən\ *n*

verbal noun *n* : a noun derived directly from a verb or verb stem and in some uses having the sense and constructions of a verb

ver·ba·tim \(ˌ)vər-'bā-təm\ *adv or adj* : in the same words : word for word

ver·be·na \(ˌ)vər-'bē-nə\ *n* : VERVAIN; *esp* : any of several garden vervains of hybrid origin with showy spikes of bright often fragrant flowers

ver·biage \'vər-bē-ij, -bij\ *n* **1** : superfluity of words usu. of little or obscure content **2** : DICTION, WORDING

ver·bose \(ˌ)vər-'bōs\ *adj* : using more words than are needed : WORDY ✦ *Synonyms* PROLIX, DIFFUSE, REDUNDANT, WINDY — **ver·bos·i·ty** \-'bä-sə-tē\ *n*

ver·bo·ten \vər-'bō-tᵊn, fər-\ *adj* [G] : forbidden usu. by dictate

ver·dant \'vər-dᵊnt\ *adj* : green with growing plants — **ver·dant·ly** *adv*

ver·dict \'vər-(ˌ)dikt\ *n* [ME *verdit, verdict,* fr. AF *veirdit,* fr. *veir* true (fr. L *verus*) + *dit* saying, dictum, fr. L *dictum,* fr. *dicere* to say] **1** : the finding or decision of a jury **2** : DECISION, JUDGMENT

ver·di·gris \'vər-də-ˌgrēs, -ˌgris\ *n* : a green or bluish deposit that forms on copper, brass, or bronze surfaces

ver·dure \'vər-jər\ *n* : the greenness of growing vegetation; *also* : such vegetation

¹verge \'vərj\ *n* [ME, rod, measuring rod, margin, fr. AF, rod, area of jurisdiction, fr. L *virga* twig, rod, line] **1** : a staff carried as an emblem of authority or office **2** : something that borders or bounds : EDGE, MARGIN **3** : BRINK, THRESHOLD ⟨on the ~ of collapse⟩

²verge *vb* **verged; verg·ing** **1** : to be contiguous **2** : to be on the verge

³verge *vb* **verged; verg·ing** **1** : to move or extend in some direction or toward some condition : INCLINE **2** : to be in transition or change

verg·er \'vər-jər\ *n* **1** *chiefly Brit* : an attendant who carries a verge (as before a bishop) **2** : SEXTON

ve·rid·i·cal \və-'ri-di-kəl\ *adj* **1** : TRUTHFUL **2** : not illusory : GENUINE

ver·i·fy \'ver-ə-ˌfī\ *vb* **-fied; -fy·ing** **1** : to confirm in law by oath **2** : to establish the truth, accuracy, or reality of ⟨~ the claim⟩ ✦ *Synonyms* AUTHENTICATE, CORROBORATE, SUBSTANTIATE, VALIDATE — **ver·i·fi·able** *adj* — **ver·i·fi·ca·tion** \ˌver-ə-fə-'kā-shən\ *n*

ver·i·ly \'ver-ə-lē\ *adv* **1** : in very truth : CERTAINLY **2** : TRULY, CONFIDENTLY

veri·si·mil·i·tude \ˌver-ə-sə-'mi-lə-ˌtüd, -ˌtyüd\ *n* : the quality or state of appearing to be true or real

ver·i·ta·ble \'ver-ə-tə-bəl\ *adj* : ACTUAL, GENUINE, TRUE — **ver·i·ta·bly** *adv*

ver·i·ty \'ver-ə-tē\ *n, pl* **-ties** **1** : the quality or state of being true or real : TRUTH, REALITY **2** : something (as a statement) that is true **3** : HONESTY, VERACITY

ver·meil *n* [MF] **1** \'vər-məl, -ˌmāl\ : VERMILION **2** \ver-'mā\ : gilded silver

ver·mi·cel·li \ˌvər-mə-'che-lē, -'se-\ *n* [It, fr. pl. of *vermicello,* dim. of *verme* worm] : a pasta made in thinner strings than spaghetti

ver·mic·u·lite \ˌvər-'mi-kyə-ˌlīt\ *n* : any of various lightweight water-absorbent minerals derived from mica

ver·mi·form appendix \'vər-mə-ˌform-\ *n* : APPENDIX 2

ver·mil·ion *also* **ver·mil·lion** \vər-'mil-yən\ *n* : a bright reddish orange color; *also* : any of various red pigments

ver·min \'vər-mən\ *n, pl* **vermin** **1** : small common harmful or objectionable animals (as lice or mice) that are difficult to get rid of **2** : birds and mammals that prey on game — **ver·min·ous** *adj*

ver·mouth \vər-'müth\ *n* [F *vermout,* fr. G *Wermut* wormwood] : a dry or sweet wine flavored with herbs and often used in mixed drinks

¹ver·nac·u·lar \vər-'na-kyə-lər\ *adj* [L *vernaculus* native, fr. *verna* slave born in the master's house, native] **1** : of, relating to, or being a language or dialect native to a region or country rather than a literary, cultured, or foreign language **2** : of, relating to, or being the normal spoken form of a language **3** : applied to a plant or animal in common speech as distinguished from biological nomenclature ⟨~ names⟩

²vernacular *n* **1** : a vernacular language **2** : the mode of expression of a group or class **3** : a vernacular name of a plant or animal

ver·nal \'vər-nᵊl\ *adj* : of, relating to, or occurring in the spring ⟨~ equinox⟩

ver·ni·er \'vər-nē-ər\ *n* : a short scale made to slide along the divisions of a graduated instrument to indicate parts of divisions

ve·ron·i·ca \və-'rä-ni-kə\ *n* : any of a genus of herbs related to the snapdragons that have small usu. bluish flowers

ver·sa·tile \'vər-sə-tᵊl\ *adj* : turning with ease from one thing or position to another; *esp* : having many aptitudes — **ver·sa·til·i·ty** \ˌvər-sə-'ti-lə-tē\ *n*

¹verse \'vərs\ *n* **1** : a line of poetry; *also* : STANZA **2** : metrical writing distinguished from poetry esp. by its lower level of intensity **3** : POETRY **4** : POEM **5** : one of the short divisions of a chapter in the Bible

²verse *vb* **versed; vers·ing** : to familiarize by experience, study, or practice ⟨well *versed* in the theater⟩

ver·si·cle \'vər-si-kəl\ *n* : a verse or sentence said or sung by a leader in public worship and followed by a response from the people

ver·si·fi·ca·tion \ˌvər-sə-fə-'kā-shən\ *n* **1** : the making of verses **2** : metrical structure

ver·si·fy \'vər-sə-ˌfī\ *vb* **-fied; -fy·ing** **1** : to write verse **2** : to turn into verse — **ver·si·fi·er** \-ˌfī-ər\ *n*

ver·sion \'vər-zhən\ *n* **1** : TRANSLATION; *esp* : a translation of the Bible **2** : an account or description from a particular point of view esp. as contrasted with another **3** : a form or variant of a type or original

vers li·bre \ˌver-'lēbrᵊ\ *n, pl* **vers li·bres** *same*\ [F] : FREE VERSE

ver·so \'vər-sō\ *n, pl* **versos** : a left-hand page

ver·sus \'vər-səs\ *prep* **1** : AGAINST 1 ⟨the champion ~ the challenger⟩ **2** : in contrast or as an alternative to ⟨free trade ~ protection⟩

vert *abbr* vertical

ver·te·bra \'vər-tə-brə\ *n, pl* **-brae** \-ˌbrā, -(ˌ)brē\ *or* **-bras** [L] : one of the segments of bone or cartilage making up the backbone

ver·te·bral \(ˌ)vər-'tē-brəl, 'vər-tə-\ *adj* : of, relating to, or made up of vertebrae : SPINAL

vertebral column *n* : BACKBONE 1

¹ver·te·brate \'vər-tə-brət, -ˌbrāt\ *adj* **1** : having a backbone **2** : of or relating to the vertebrates

²vertebrate *n* : any of a large group of animals (as mammals, birds, reptiles, amphibians, or fishes) that have a backbone or in some primitive forms (as a lamprey) a flexible rod of cells and that have a tubular nervous system arranged along the back and divided into a brain and spinal cord

ver·tex \'vər-ˌteks\ *n, pl* **ver·ti·ces** \'vər-tə-ˌsēz\ *also* **ver·tex·es** [ME, top of the head, fr. L *vertex, vortex* whirl, whirlpool, top of the head, summit, fr. *vertere* to turn] **1** : the point opposite to and farthest from the base of a geometrical figure **2** : the point where the sides of an angle or three or more edges of a polyhedron (as a cube) meet **3** : the highest point : TOP, SUMMIT

ver·ti·cal \'vər-ti-kəl\ *adj* **1** : of, relating to, or located at the vertex : directly overhead **2** : rising perpendicularly from a level surface : UPRIGHT — **vertical** *n* — **ver·ti·cal·i·ty** \ˌvər-tə-'ka-lə-tē\ *n* — **ver·ti·cal·ly** \-k(ə-)lē\ *adv*

ver·tig·i·nous \(ˌ)vər-'ti-jə-nəs\ *adj* : marked by, affected with, or tending to cause dizziness

ver·ti·go \'vər-ti-ˌgō\ *n, pl* **-goes** *or* **-gos** : DIZZINESS, GIDDINESS

vertu *var of* VIRTU

ver·vain \'vər-ˌvān\ *n* : any of a genus of chiefly American herbs or low woody plants with often showy heads or spikes of tubular flowers

verve \'vərv\ *n* : liveliness of imagination; *also* : VIVACITY

¹**very** \'ver-ē\ *adj* **veri·er; -est** [ME *verray*, *verry*, fr. AF *verai*, ultim. fr. L *verax* truthful, fr. *verus* true] **1** : EXACT, PRECISE ⟨the ~ heart of the city⟩ **2** : exactly suitable ⟨the ~ tool for the job⟩ **3** : ABSOLUTE, UTTER ⟨the *veriest* nonsense⟩ **4** — used as an intensive esp. to emphasize identity ⟨before my ~ eyes⟩ **5** : MERE, BARE ⟨the ~ idea scared him⟩ **6** : SELFSAME, IDENTICAL ⟨the ~ man I saw⟩

²**very** *adv* **1** : in actual fact : TRULY **2** : to a high degree : EXTREMELY

very high frequency *n* : a radio frequency of between 30 and 300 megahertz

ves·i·cant \'ve-si-kənt\ *n* : an agent that causes blistering — **vesicant** *adj*

ves·i·cle \'ve-si-kəl\ *n* : a membranous and usu. fluid-filled cavity in a plant or animal; *also* : BLISTER — **ve·sic·u·lar** \və-'si-kyə-lər\ *adj*

¹**ves·per** \'ves-pər\ *n* **1** *cap, archaic* : EVENING STAR **2** : a vesper bell **3** *archaic* : EVENING, EVENTIDE

²**vesper** *adj* : of or relating to vespers or the evening ⟨a ~ service⟩

ves·pers \-pərz\ *n pl, often cap* : a late afternoon or evening worship service

ves·sel \'ve-səl\ *n* **1** : a container (as a barrel, bottle, bowl, or cup) for holding something **2** : a person held to be the recipient of a quality (as grace) **3** : a craft bigger than a rowboat **4** : a tube in which a body fluid (as blood or sap) is contained and circulated

¹**vest** \'vest\ *vb* **1** : to place or give into the possession or discretion of some person or authority **2** : to grant or endow with a particular authority, right, or property **3** : to become legally vested **4** : to clothe with or as if with a garment; *esp* : to garb in ecclesiastical vestments

²**vest** *n* **1** : a sleeveless garment for the upper body usu. worn over a shirt **2** *chiefly Brit* : a man's sleeveless undershirt **3** : a front piece of a dress resembling the front of a vest

¹**ves·tal** \'ves-t³l\ *adj* : CHASTE

²**vestal** *n* : VESTAL VIRGIN

vestal virgin *n* **1** : a virgin consecrated to the Roman goddess Vesta and to the service of watching the sacred fire perpetually kept burning on her altar **2** : a chaste woman

vest·ed \'ves-təd\ *adj* : fully and unconditionally guaranteed as a legal right, benefit, or privilege

vested interest *n* : an interest (as in an existing political, economic, or social arrangement) to which the holder has a strong commitment; *also* : one (as a corporation) having a vested interest

ves·ti·bule \'ves-tə-ˌbyül\ *n* **1** : a passage or room between the outer door and the interior of a building **2** : any of various bodily cavities forming or suggesting an entrance to some other cavity or space — **ves·tib·u·lar** \ve-'sti-byə-lər\ *adj*

ves·tige \'ves-tij\ *n* [F, fr. L *vestigium* footprint, track, vestige] : a trace or visible sign left by something lost or vanished; *also* : a minute remaining amount — **ves·ti·gial** \ve-'sti-jē-əl, -jəl\ *adj* — **ves·ti·gial·ly** *adv*

vest·ing \'ves-tiŋ\ *n* : the conveying to an employee of inalienable rights to share in a pension fund; *also* : the right so conveyed

vest·ment \'vest-mənt\ *n* **1** : an outer garment; *esp* : a ceremonial or official robe **2** *pl* : CLOTHING, GARB **3** : a garment or insignia worn by a cleric when officiating or assisting at a religious service

vest–pocket *adj* : very small ⟨a ~ park⟩

ves·try \'ves-trē\ *n, pl* **vestries 1** : a room in a church for vestments, altar linens, and sacred vessels **2** : a room used for church meetings and classes **3** : a body administering the temporal affairs of an Episcopal parish

ves·try·man \-mən\ *n* : a member of a vestry

ves·ture \'ves-chər\ *n* **1** : a covering garment **2** : CLOTHING, APPAREL

¹**vet** \'vet\ *n* : VETERINARIAN

²**vet** *adj or n* : VETERAN

³**vet** *vb* : to evaluate for appraisal or acceptance ⟨~ a manuscript⟩

vetch \'vech\ *n* : any of a genus of twining leguminous herbs including some grown for fodder and green manure

vet·er·an \'ve-trən, -tə-rən\ *n* [L *veteranus*, fr. *veteranus* old, of long experience, fr. *veter-*, *vetus* old] **1** : an old soldier of long service **2** : a former member of the armed forces **3** : a person of long experience usu. in an occupation or skill — **veteran** *adj*

Veterans Day *n* : November 11 observed as a legal holiday in commemoration of the end of hostilities in 1918 and 1945

vet·er·i·nar·i·an \ˌve-trə-'ner-ē-ən, ˌve-tə-rə-\ *n* : one qualified and authorized to practice veterinary medicine

¹**vet·er·i·nary** \'ve-trə-ˌner-ē, 've-tə-rə-\ *adj* : of, relating to, or being the medical care of animals and esp. domestic animals

²**veterinary** *n, pl* **-nar·ies** : VETERINARIAN

¹**ve·to** \'vē-tō\ *n, pl* **vetoes** [L, I forbid] **1** : an authoritative prohibition **2** : a power of one part of a government to forbid the carrying out of projects attempted by another part; *esp* : a power vested in a chief executive to prevent the carrying out of measures adopted by a legislature **3** : the exercise of the power of veto

²**veto** *vb* **1** : FORBID, PROHIBIT **2** : to refuse assent to (a legislative bill) so as to prevent enactment or cause reconsideration — **ve·to·er** *n*

vex \'veks\ *vb* **vexed** *also* **vext; vex·ing 1** : to bring trouble, distress, or agitation to ⟨a ~*ing* problem⟩ **2** : to annoy continually with little irritations

vex·a·tion \vek-'sā-shən\ *n* **1** : the act of vexing **2** : the quality or state of being vexed : IRRITATION **3** : a cause of trouble or annoyance

vex·a·tious \-shəs\ *adj* **1** : causing vexation : ANNOYING **2** : full of distress or annoyance : TROUBLED — **vex·a·tious·ly** *adv* — **vex·a·tious·ness** *n*

vexed \'vekst\ *adj* : fully debated or discussed ⟨a ~ question⟩

VF *abbr* **1** video frequency **2** visual field

VFD *abbr* volunteer fire department

VFW *abbr* Veterans of Foreign Wars

VG *abbr* **1** very good **2** vicar-general

VHF *abbr* very high frequency

VI *abbr* Virgin Islands

via \'vī-ə, 'vē-ə\ *prep* **1** : by way of **2** : by means of

vi·a·ble \'vī-ə-bəl\ *adj* **1** : capable of living; *esp* : sufficiently developed as to be capable of surviving outside the mother's womb ⟨a ~ fetus⟩ **2** : capable of growing and developing ⟨~ seeds⟩ **3** : capable of being put into practice : WORKABLE **4** : having a reasonable chance of succeeding ⟨a ~ candidate⟩ — **vi·a·bil·i·ty** \ˌvī-ə-'bi-lə-tē\ *n* — **vi·a·bly** \'vī-ə-blē\ *adv*

via·duct \'vī-ə-ˌdəkt\ *n* : a long elevated roadway usu. consisting of a series of short spans supported on arches, piers, or columns

vi·al \'vī-əl\ *n* : a small vessel for liquids

vi·and \'vī-ənd\ *n* : an article of food

vi·at·i·cum \vī-'a-ti-kəm, vē-\ *n, pl* **-cums** *or* **-ca** \-kə\ **1** : the Christian Eucharist given to a person in danger of death **2** : an allowance esp. in money for traveling needs and expenses

vibes \'vībz\ *n pl* **1** : VIBRAPHONE **2** : VIBRATIONS

vi·brant \'vī-brənt\ *adj* **1** : VIBRATING, PULSATING **2** : pulsating with vigor or activity ⟨a ~ personality⟩ **3** : readily set in vibration : RESPONSIVE **4** : sounding from vibration **5** : BRIGHT ⟨~ colors⟩ — **vi·bran·cy** \-brən-sē\ *n*

vi·bra·phone \'vī-brə-ˌfōn\ *n* : a percussion instrument like the xylophone but with metal bars and motor-driven resonators

vi·brate \'vī-ˌbrāt\ *vb* **vi·brat·ed; vi·brat·ing 1** : OSCILLATE **2** : to set in vibration **3** : to be in vibration **4** : WAVER, FLUCTUATE **5** : to respond sympathetically : THRILL

vi·bra·tion \vī-'brā-shən\ *n* **1** : a rapid to-and-fro motion of the particles of an elastic body or medium (as a stretched cord) that produces sound **2** : an act of vibrating : a state of being vibrated : OSCILLATION **3** : a trembling motion **4** : VACILLATION **5** : a feeling or impression that someone or something gives off — usu. used in pl. ⟨good ~*s*⟩ — **vi·bra·tion·al** \-shə-nəl\ *adj*

vi·bra·to \vi-'brä-tō\ *n, pl* **-tos** [It] : a slightly tremulous effect imparted to vocal or instrumental music

vi·bra·tor \'vī-ˌbrā-tər\ *n* : one that vibrates or causes vibration; *esp* : a vibrating electrical device used in massage or for sexual stimulation

vi·bra·to·ry \'vī-brə-ˌtȯr-ē\ *adj* : consisting of, capable of, or causing vibration

vi·bur·num \vī-'bər-nəm\ *n* : any of a genus of widely distributed shrubs or small trees related to the honeysuckle and bearing small usu. white flowers in broad clusters

vic *abbr* vicinity

Vic *abbr* Victoria

vic·ar \'vi-kər\ *n* 1 : an administrative deputy 2 : a minister in charge of a church who serves under the authority of another minister — **vi·car·i·ate** \vī-'ker-ē-ət\ *n*

vic·ar·age \'vi-kə-rij\ *n* : a vicar's home

vicar–general *n, pl* **vicars–general** : an administrative deputy (as of a Roman Catholic or Anglican bishop)

vi·car·i·ous \vī-'ker-ē-əs\ *adj* [L *vicarius*, fr. *vicis* change, alternation, stead] 1 : acting for another 2 : done or suffered by one person on behalf of another or others ⟨a ∼ sacrifice⟩ 3 : sharing in someone else's experience through the use of the imagination or sympathetic feelings ⟨∼ thrills⟩ — **vi·car·i·ous·ly** *adv* — **vi·car·i·ous·ness** *n*

¹**vice** \'vīs\ *n* 1 : DEPRAVITY, WICKEDNESS 2 : a moral fault or failing 3 : a habitual usu. trivial fault 4 : an undesirable behavior pattern in a domestic animal

²**vice** *chiefly Brit var of* VISE

³**vi·ce** \'vī-sē\ *prep* : in the place of; *also* : rather than

vice admiral *n* : a commissioned officer in the navy or coast guard ranking above a rear admiral

vice-ge·rent \vīs-'jir-ənt\ *n* : an administrative deputy of a king or magistrate — **vice·ge·ren·cy** \-ən-sē\ *n*

vi·cen·ni·al \vī-'se-nē-əl\ *adj* : occurring once every 20 years

vice presidency *n* : the office of vice president

vice president *n* 1 : an officer ranking next to a president and usu. empowered to act for the president during an absence or disability 2 : any of several of a president's deputies

vice·re·gal \vīs-'rē-gəl\ *adj* : of or relating to a viceroy

vice·roy \'vīs-ˌrȯi\ *n* : the governor of a country or province who rules as representative of the sovereign — **vice·roy·al·ty** \-əl-tē\ *n*

vice ver·sa \ˌvī-si-'vər-sə, 'vīs-'vər-\ *adv* : with the order reversed

vi·chys·soise \ˌvi-shē-'swäz, ˌvē-\ *n* [F] : a soup made esp. from leeks or onions and potatoes, cream, and chicken stock and usu. served cold

vic·i·nage \'vi-sə-nij\ *n* : a neighboring or surrounding district : VICINITY

vi·cin·i·ty \və-'si-nə-tē\ *n, pl* **-ties** [MF *vicinité*, fr. L *vicinitas*, fr. *vicinus* neighboring, fr. *vicus* row of houses, village] 1 : NEARNESS, PROXIMITY 2 : a surrounding area : NEIGHBORHOOD

vi·cious \'vi-shəs\ *adj* 1 : having the quality of vice : WICKED, DEPRAVED 2 : DEFECTIVE, FAULTY; *also* : INVALID 3 : IMPURE, FOUL 4 : having a savage disposition; *also* : marked by violence or ferocity ⟨a ∼ attack⟩ 5 : MALICIOUS, SPITEFUL ⟨∼ gossip⟩ 6 : worsened by internal causes that augment each other ⟨∼ wage-price spiral⟩ — **vi·cious·ly** *adv* — **vi·cious·ness** *n*

vi·cis·si·tude \və-'si-sə-ˌtüd, vī-, -ˌtyüd\ *n* : an irregular, unexpected, or surprising change ⟨the ∼s of business⟩

vic·tim \'vik-təm\ *n* 1 : a living being offered as a sacrifice in a religious rite 2 : an individual injured or killed (as by disease or accident) 3 : a person cheated, fooled, or injured ⟨a ∼ of circumstances⟩

vic·tim·ise *Brit var of* VICTIMIZE

vic·tim·ize \'vik-tə-ˌmīz\ *vb* **-ized; -iz·ing** : to make a victim of — **vic·tim·i·za·tion** \ˌvik-tə-mə-'zā-shən\ *n* — **vic·tim·iz·er** \'vik-tə-ˌmī-zər\ *n*

vic·tim·less \'vik-təm-ləs\ *adj* : having no victim ⟨considered gambling to be a ∼ crime⟩

vic·tor \'vik-tər\ *n* : WINNER, CONQUEROR

vic·to·ria \vik-'tȯr-ē-ə\ *n* : a low 4-wheeled carriage with a folding top and a raised driver's seat in front

¹**Vic·to·ri·an** \vik-'tȯr-ē-ən\ *adj* 1 : of or relating to the reign of Queen Victoria of England or the art, letters, or tastes of her time 2 : typical of the standards, attitudes, or conduct of the age of Victoria esp. when considered prudish or narrow

²**Victorian** *n* 1 : a person and esp. an author of the Victo-

rian period 2 : a typically large ornate house built during Queen Victoria's reign

vic·to·ri·ous \vik-'tȯr-ē-əs\ *adj* 1 : having won a victory 2 : of, relating to, or characteristic of victory ⟨∼ exuberance⟩ — **vic·to·ri·ous·ly** *adv*

vic·to·ry \'vik-tə-rē\ *n, pl* **-ries** 1 : the overcoming of an enemy or an antagonist 2 : achievement of mastery or success in a struggle or endeavor

¹**vict·ual** \'vi-t³l\ *n* [ME *vitaille, victuayle*, fr. AF, fr. LL *victualia*, pl., provisions, food, fr. neut. pl. of *victualis* of nourishment, fr. L *victus* nourishment, way of living, fr. *vivere* to live] 1 : food fit for humans 2 *pl* : food supplies

²**victual** *vb* **-ualed** *or* **-ualled; -ual·ing** *or* **-ual·ling** 1 : to supply with food 2 : to store up provisions

vict·ual·ler *or* **vict·ual·er** \'vi-t³l-ər\ *n* : one that supplies provisions (as to an army or a ship)

vi·cu·ña *or* **vi·cu·na** \vi-'kün-yə, vī-; vī-'kü-nə, -'kyü-\ *n* 1 : a So. American wild mammal related to the llama and alpaca; *also* : its wool 2 : a soft fabric woven from the wool of the vicuña; *also* : a sheep's wool imitation of this

vi·de \'vī-dē, 'vē-ˌdā\ *vb imper* [L] : SEE — used to direct a reader to another item

vi·de·li·cet \və-'de-lə-ˌset, vī-; vi-'dā-li-ˌket\ *adv* [ME, fr. L, fr. *vidēre* to see + *licet* it is permitted] : that is to say : NAMELY

¹**vid·eo** \'vi-dē-ˌō\ *n* 1 : TELEVISION 2 : VIDEOTAPE; *also* : a recording similar to a videotape but stored in digital form 3 : a videotaped performance ⟨music ∼s⟩

²**video** *adj* 1 : relating to or used in transmission or reception of the television image 2 : relating to or being images on a television screen or computer display ⟨a ∼ terminal⟩

video camera *n* : a camera that records visual images and usu. sound; *esp* : CAMCORDER

vid·eo·cas·sette \ˌvi-dē-ō-kə-'set\ *n* 1 : a case containing videotape for use with a VCR 2 : a recording (as of a movie) on a videocassette

videocassette recorder *n* : VCR

vid·eo·con·fer·enc·ing \ˌvi-dē-ō-'kän-f(ə-)rən-siŋ\ *n* : the holding of a conference among people at remote locations by means of transmitted audio and video signals

vid·eo·disc *or* **vid·eo·disk** \'vi-dē-ō-ˌdisk\ *n* 1 : OPTICAL DISK 2 : a recording (as of a movie) on a videodisc

video game *n* : an electronic game played on a video screen

vid·e·o·gen·ic \ˌvi-dē-ō-'je-nik\ *adj* : TELEGENIC

vid·eo·phone \'vid-ē-ə-ˌfōn\ *n* : a telephone for transmitting both audio and video signals

¹**vid·eo·tape** \'vid-ē-ō-ˌtāp\ *n* : a recording of visual images and sound made on magnetic tape; *also* : the magnetic tape used for such a recording

²**videotape** *vb* : to make a videotape

videotape recorder *n* : a device for recording and playing back videotapes

vie \'vī\ *vb* **vied; vy·ing** \'vī-iŋ\ : to compete for superiority : CONTEND — **vi·er** \'vī-ər\ *n*

Viet·cong \vē-'et-'käŋ, ˌvē-ət-, -'kȯŋ\ *n, pl* **Vietcong** : a guerrilla member of the Vietnamese communist movement

¹**view** \'vyü\ *n* 1 : the act of seeing or examining : INSPECTION; *also* : SURVEY 2 : a way of looking at or regarding something 3 : ESTIMATE, JUDGMENT ⟨stated his ∼s⟩ 4 : a sight (as of a landscape) regarded for its pictorial quality 5 : extent or range of vision ⟨within ∼⟩ 6 : OBJECT, PURPOSE ⟨done with a ∼ to promotion⟩ 7 : a picture of a scene

²**view** *vb* 1 : to look at attentively : EXAMINE 2 : SEE, WATCH ⟨∼ a film⟩ 3 : to examine mentally : CONSIDER ⟨∼ a problem⟩ — **view·er** *n*

victoria

view·er·ship \\'vyü-ər-ˌship\\ *n* : a television audience esp. with respect to size or makeup

view·find·er \\'vyü-ˌfīn-dər\\ *n* : a device on a camera for showing the view to be included in the picture

view·point \\-ˌpȯint\\ *n* : POINT OF VIEW, STANDPOINT

vi·ges·i·mal \\vī-'je-sə-məl\\ *adj* : based on the number 20

vig·il \\'vi-jəl\\ *n* **1** : a religious observance formerly held on the night before a religious feast **2** : the day before a religious feast observed as a day of spiritual preparation **3** : evening or nocturnal devotions or prayers — usu. used in pl. **4** : an act or a time of keeping awake when sleep is customary; *esp* : WATCH 1

vigilance committee *n* : a committee of vigilantes

vig·i·lant \\'vi-jə-lənt\\ *adj* : alertly watchful esp. to avoid danger — **vig·i·lance** \\-ləns\\ *n* — **vig·i·lant·ly** *adv*

vig·i·lan·te \\ˌvi-jə-'lan-tē\\ *n* : a member of a volunteer committee organized to suppress and punish crime summarily (as when the processes of law are viewed as inadequate); *also* : a self-appointed doer of justice — **vig·i·lan·tism** \\-'lan-ˌti-zəm\\ *n*

¹vi·gnette \\vin-'yet\\ *n* [F, fr. MF *vignete*, fr. dim. of *vigne* vine] **1** : a small decorative design **2** : a picture (as an engraving or a photograph) that shades off gradually into the surrounding ground **3** : a short descriptive literary sketch

²vignette *vb* **vi·gnett·ed; vi·gnett·ing** **1** : to finish (as a photograph) like a vignette **2** : to describe briefly

vig·or \\'vi-gər\\ *n* **1** : active strength or energy of body or mind **2** : INTENSITY, FORCE ⟨the ~ of their quarrel⟩

vig·or·ous \\'vi-gə-rəs\\ *adj* **1** : having vigor : ROBUST **2** : done with force and energy ⟨a ~ debate⟩ — **vig·or·ous·ly** *adv* — **vig·or·ous·ness** *n*

vig·our *chiefly Brit var of* VIGOR

Vi·king \\'vī-kiŋ\\ *n* [ON *vīkingr*] : any of the pirate Norsemen who raided or invaded the coasts of Europe in the 8th to 10th centuries

vile \\'vī(-ə)l\\ *adj* **vil·er; vil·est** **1** : morally despicable **2** : physically repulsive : FOUL **3** : of little worth **4** : DEGRADING, IGNOMINIOUS **5** : utterly bad or contemptible ⟨~ weather⟩ — **vile·ly** \\'vī(-ə)l-lē\\ *adv* — **vile·ness** *n*

vil·i·fy \\'vi-lə-ˌfī\\ *vb* **-fied; -fy·ing** : to blacken the character of with abusive language : DEFAME ♦ **Synonyms** MALIGN, CALUMNIATE, SLANDER, LIBEL, TRADUCE — **vil·i·fi·ca·tion** \\ˌvi-lə-fə-'kā-shən\\ *n* — **vil·i·fi·er** \\'vi-lə-ˌfī-ər\\ *n*

vil·la \\'vi-lə\\ *n* **1** : a country estate **2** : the rural or suburban residence of a wealthy person

vil·lage \\'vi-lij\\ *n* [ME, fr. AF *vilage*, fr. *vile* manorial estate, farmstead, fr. L *villa*] **1** : a settlement usu. larger than a hamlet and smaller than a town **2** : an incorporated minor municipality **3** : the people of a village

vil·lag·er \\'vi-li-jər\\ *n* : an inhabitant of a village

vil·lain \\'vi-lən\\ *n* **1** : VILLEIN **2** : an evil person : SCOUNDREL

vil·lain·ess \\-lə-nəs\\ *n* : a woman who is a villain

vil·lain·ous \\-lə-nəs\\ *adj* **1** : befitting a villain : WICKED, EVIL **2** : highly objectionable : DETESTABLE ♦ **Synonyms** VICIOUS, INIQUITOUS, NEFARIOUS, INFAMOUS, CORRUPT, DEGENERATE — **vil·lain·ous·ly** *adv* — **vil·lain·ous·ness** *n*

vil·lainy \\-lə-nē\\ *n, pl* **-lain·ies** **1** : villainous conduct; *also* : a villainous act **2** : villainous character or nature

vil·lein \\'vi-lən, -ˌlān\\ *n* **1** : a free villager of Anglo-Saxon times **2** : an unfree peasant having the status of a slave to a feudal lord

vil·lous \\'vi-ləs\\ *adj* : covered with fine hairs or villi

vil·lus \\'vi-ləs\\ *n, pl* **vil·li** \\-ˌlī, -(ˌ)lē\\ : a slender usu. vascular process; *esp* : one of the tiny projections of the mucous membrane of the small intestine that function in the absorption of food

vim \\'vim\\ *n* : robust energy and enthusiasm : VITALITY

VIN *abbr* vehicle identification number

vin·ai·grette \\ˌvi-ni-'gret\\ *n* [F] : a sauce made typically of oil, vinegar, and seasonings

vin·ci·ble \\'vin-sə-bəl\\ *adj* : capable of being overcome or subdued

vin·di·cate \\'vin-də-ˌkāt\\ *vb* **-cat·ed; -cat·ing** **1** : AVENGE **2** : EXONERATE, ABSOLVE **3** : CONFIRM, SUBSTANTIATE **4** : to provide defense for : JUSTIFY **5** : to maintain a right to : ASSERT — **vin·di·ca·tor** \\-ˌkā-tər\\ *n*

vin·di·ca·tion \\ˌvin-də-'kā-shən\\ *n* : the act of vindicating

or the state of being vindicated; *esp* : justification against denial or censure : DEFENSE

vin·dic·tive \\vin-'dik-tiv\\ *adj* **1** : disposed to revenge **2** : intended for or involving revenge ⟨~ punishment⟩ **3** : VICIOUS, SPITEFUL — **vin·dic·tive·ly** *adv* — **vin·dic·tive·ness** *n*

vine \\'vīn\\ *n* [ME, fr. AF *vigne*, fr. L *vinea* vine, vineyard, fr. fem. of *vineus* of wine, fr. *vinum* wine] **1** : GRAPE 2 **2** : a plant whose stem requires support and which climbs (as by tendrils) or trails along the ground; *also* : the stem of such a plant

vin·e·gar \\'vi-ni-gər\\ *n* [ME *vinegre*, fr. AF *vin egre*, lit., sour wine] : a sour liquid obtained by fermentation (as of cider, wine, or malt) and used to flavor or preserve foods

vin·e·gary \\-gə-rē\\ *adj* **1** : resembling vinegar : SOUR **2** : disagreeable in manner or disposition : CRABBED

vine·yard \\'vin-yərd\\ *n* **1** : a field of grapevines esp. to produce grapes for wine production **2** : a sphere of activity : field of endeavor

vi·nous \\'vī-nəs\\ *adj* **1** : of, relating to, or made with wine ⟨~ medications⟩ **2** : showing the effects of the use of wine ⟨~ bloodshot eyes⟩

¹vin·tage \\'vin-tij\\ *n* **1** : a season's yield of grapes or wine **2** : WINE; *esp* : a usu. superior wine which comes from a single year **3** : the act or period of gathering grapes or making wine **4** : a period of origin ⟨clothes of 1890 ~⟩

²vintage *adj* **1** : of, relating to, or produced in a particular vintage **2** : of old, recognized, and enduring interest, importance, or quality : CLASSIC ⟨~ cars⟩ **3** : of the best and most characteristic — used with a proper noun

vint·ner \\'vint-nər\\ *n* : a dealer in wines

vi·nyl \\'vī-nᵊl\\ *n* **1** : a chemical derived from ethylene by the removal of one hydrogen atom **2** : a polymer of a vinyl compound or a product (as a textile fiber) made from one

vinyl chloride *n* : a flammable gaseous carcinogenic compound used esp. to make vinyl resins

vi·ol \\'vī-əl\\ *n* : a bowed stringed instrument chiefly of the 16th and 17th centuries having a fretted neck and usu. six strings

¹vi·o·la \\vī-'ō-lə, 'vī-ə-lə\\ *n* : VIOLET 1; *esp* : any of various hybrid garden plants with white, yellow, purple, or variously colored flowers that resemble but are smaller than those of the related pansies

²vi·o·la \\vē-'ō-lə\\ *n* : an instrument of the violin family slightly larger and tuned lower than a violin — **vi·o·list** \\-list\\ *n*

vi·o·la·ble \\'vī-ə-lə-bəl\\ *adj* : capable of being violated ⟨~ boundaries⟩

vi·o·late \\'vī-ə-ˌlāt\\ *vb* **-lat·ed; -lat·ing** **1** : BREAK, DISREGARD ⟨~ a law⟩ ⟨~ a frontier⟩ **2** : RAPE **3** : PROFANE, DESECRATE **4** : INTERRUPT, DISTURB ⟨*violated* his privacy⟩ — **vi·o·la·tor** \\-ˌlā-tər\\ *n*

vi·o·la·tion \\ˌvī-ə-'lā-shən\\ *n* : an act or instance of violating : the state of being violated ♦ **Synonyms** BREACH, INFRACTION, TRESPASS, INFRINGEMENT, TRANSGRESSION

vi·o·lence \\'vī-ləns, 'vī-ə-\\ *n* **1** : exertion of physical force so as to injure or abuse **2** : injury by or as if by infringement or profanation **3** : intense or furious often destructive action or force **4** : vehement feeling or expression : INTENSITY **5** : jarring quality : DISCORDANCE ♦ **Synonyms** COMPULSION, COERCION, DURESS, CONSTRAINT

vi·o·lent \\-lənt\\ *adj* **1** : marked by extreme force or sudden intense activity **2** : caused by or showing strong feeling ⟨~ words⟩ **3** : EXTREME, INTENSE ⟨~ pain⟩ ⟨~ colors⟩ **4** : emotionally agitated to the point of loss of self-control **5** : caused by force : not natural ⟨~ death⟩ — **vi·o·lent·ly** *adv*

vi·o·let \\'vī-ə-lət\\ *n* **1** : any of a genus of herbs or small shrubs usu. with heart-shaped leaves and both aerial and underground flowers; *esp* : one with small usu. solid-colored flowers **2** : a reddish blue color

vi·o·lin \\ˌvī-ə-'lin\\ *n* : a bowed stringed instrument with four strings that has a shallow body, a fingerboard without frets, and a curved bridge — **vi·o·lin·ist** \\-'li-nist\\ *n*

vi·o·lon·cel·lo \\ˌvī-ə-lən-'che-lō\\ *n* [It] : CELLO — **vi·o·lon·cel·list** \\-list\\ *n*

VIP \\ˌvē-ˌī-'pē\\ *n, pl* **VIPs** \\-'pēz\\ [*very important person*] : a person of great influence or prestige; *esp* : a high official with special privileges

vi·per \'vī-pər\ *n* **1** : a common stout-bodied Eurasian venomous snake having a bite only rarely fatal to humans; *also* : any snake (as a pit viper) of the same family as the viper **2** : any venomous or reputedly venomous snake **3** : a vicious or treacherous person — **vi·per·ine** \-pə-,rīn\ *adj*

vi·ra·go \və-'rä-gō, -'rā-\ *n, pl* **-goes** *or* **-gos** [ME, fr. L, strong or heroic woman, fr. *vir* man] **1** : a loud overbearing woman **2** : a woman of great strength and courage

vi·ral \'vī-rəl\ *adj* **1** : of, relating to, or caused by a virus ⟨a ∼ infection⟩ **2** : quickly and widely spread or popularized esp. by means of social media ⟨a ∼ video⟩ — **vi·ral·ly** *adv*

vir·eo \'vir-ē-,ō\ *n, pl* **-e·os** [L, a small bird, fr. *virēre* to be green] : any of various small insect-eating American songbirds mostly olive green and grayish in color

¹vir·gin \'vər-jən\ *n* **1** : an unmarried woman devoted to religion **2** : an unmarried girl or woman **3** *cap* : the mother of Jesus **4** : a person who has not had sexual intercourse

²virgin *adj* **1** : free from stain : PURE, SPOTLESS **2** : CHASTE **3** : befitting a virgin : MODEST **4** : FRESH, UNSPOILED; *esp* : not altered by human activity ⟨∼ forest⟩ **5** : INITIAL, FIRST

¹vir·gin·al \'vər-jə-n°l\ *adj* : of, relating to, or characteristic of a virgin or virginity ⟨∼ innocence⟩ — **vir·gin·al·ly** *adv*

²virginal *n* : a small rectangular spinet without legs popular in the 16th and 17th centuries

Vir·gin·ia creeper \vər-'jin-yə-\ *n* : a No. American vine related to the grapes that has leaves with five leaflets and bluish-black berries

Virginia reel *n* : an American country-dance

vir·gin·i·ty \vər-'ji-nə-tē\ *n, pl* **-ties** **1** : the quality or state of being virgin; *esp* : MAIDENHOOD **2** : the unmarried life : CELIBACY

Vir·go \'vər-,gō\ *n* [L, lit., virgin] **1** : a zodiacal constellation between Leo and Libra usu. pictured as a young woman **2** : the 6th sign of the zodiac in astrology; *also* : one born under this sign

vir·gule \'vər-gyül\ *n* : ²SLASH 3

vir·i·des·cent \,vir-ə-'de-s°nt\ *adj* : slightly green : GREENISH

vir·ile \'vir-əl\ *adj* **1** : having the nature, properties, or qualities of a man **2** : MASCULINE, MALE **3** : MASTERFUL, FORCEFUL — **vi·ril·i·ty** \və-'ri-lə-tē\ *n*

vi·ri·on \'vī-rē-,än, 'vir-ē-\ *n* : a complete virus particle consisting of an RNA or DNA core with a protein coat

vi·rol·o·gy \vī-'rä-lə-jē\ *n* : a branch of science that deals with viruses and viral diseases — **vi·rol·o·gist** \-jist\ *n*

vir·tu \,vər-'tü, ,vir-\ *or* **ver·tu** \,vər-, ,ver-\ *n* [It *virtù*, lit., virtue] **1** : a love of or taste for objects of art **2** : objects of art (as curios and antiques)

vir·tu·al \'vər-chə-wəl\ *adj* **1** : being in essence or in effect though not formally recognized or admitted ⟨a ∼ dictator⟩ **2** : being on or simulated on a computer or computer network ⟨∼ shopping⟩

vir·tu·al·ly \'vər-chə-wə-lē\ *adv* **1** : almost entirely : NEARLY **2** : for all practical purposes ⟨∼ unknown⟩

virtual reality *n* : an artificial environment that is experienced through sensory stimuli (as sights and sounds) provided by an interactive computer program; *also* : the technology used to create or access a virtual reality

vir·tue \'vər-chü\ *n* [ME *vertu*, fr. AF, fr. L *virtus* strength, manliness, virtue, fr. *vir* man] **1** : conformity to a standard of right : MORALITY **2** : a particular moral excellence **3** : manly strength or courage : VALOR **4** : a commendable quality : MERIT **5** : active power to accomplish a given effect : POTENCY, EFFICACY **6** : chastity esp. in a woman

vir·tu·os·i·ty \,vər-chə-'wä-sə-tē\ *n, pl* **-ties** : great technical skill in the practice of a fine art

vir·tu·o·so \,vər-chə-'wō-sō, -zō\ *n, pl* **-sos** *or* **-si** \-sē, -zē\ [It] **1** : one skilled in or having a taste for the fine arts **2** : one who excels in the technique of an art; *esp* : a highly skilled musical performer ✦ *Synonyms* EXPERT, ADEPT, ARTIST, DOYEN, MASTER — **virtuoso** *adj*

vir·tu·ous \'vər-chə-wəs\ *adj* **1** : having or showing virtue and esp. moral virtue **2** : CHASTE — **vir·tu·ous·ly** *adv*

vir·u·lent \'vir-ə-lənt, 'vir-yə-\ *adj* **1** : highly infectious ⟨a ∼ germ⟩; *also* : marked by a rapid, severe, and often deadly course ⟨a ∼ disease⟩ **2** : extremely poisonous or venomous : NOXIOUS **3** : full of malice : MALIGNANT — **vir·u·lence** \-ləns\ *n* — **vir·u·lent·ly** *adv*

vi·rus \'vī-rəs\ *n, pl* **vi·rus·es** [L, venom, poisonous emanation] **1** : any of a large group of submicroscopic infectious agents that have an outside coat of protein around a core of RNA or DNA, that can grow and multiply only in living cells, and that cause important diseases in human beings, lower animals, and plants; *also* : a disease caused by a virus **2** : something (as a corrupting influence) that poisons the mind or spirit **3** : a computer program that is usu. hidden within another program and that reproduces itself and inserts the copies into other programs and usu. performs a malicious action (as destroying data)

vis *abbr* **1** visibility **2** visual

¹vi·sa \'vē-zə, -sə\ *n* [F] **1** : an endorsement by the proper authorities on a passport to show that it has been examined and the bearer may proceed **2** : a signature by a superior official signifying approval of a document

²visa *vb* **vi·saed** \-zəd, -səd\; **vi·sa·ing** \-zə-iŋ, -sə-\ : to give a visa to (a passport)

vis·age \'vi-zij\ *n* : the face or countenance of a person or sometimes an animal; *also* : LOOK, APPEARANCE

¹vis-à-vis \,vēz-ə-'vē, ,vēs-\ *prep* [F, lit., face-to-face] **1** : face-to-face with : OPPOSITE **2** : in relation to **3** : as compared with

²vis-à-vis *n, pl* **vis-à-vis** *same or* -'vēz\ **1** : one that is face-to-face with another **2** : ESCORT **3** : COUNTERPART **4** : TÊTE-À-TÊTE

³vis-à-vis *adv* : in company : TOGETHER

viscera *pl of* VISCUS

vis·cer·al \'vi-sə-rəl\ *adj* **1** : felt in or as if in the viscera **2** : not intellectual : INSTINCTIVE **3** : of or relating to the viscera — **vis·cer·al·ly** *adv*

vis·cid \'vi-səd\ *adj* : VISCOUS — **vis·cid·i·ty** \vi-'si-də-tē\ *n*

vis·cos·i·ty \vis-'kä-sə-tē\ *n, pl* **-ties** : the quality of being viscous; *esp* : the property of resistance to flow in a fluid

vis·count \'vī-,kaùnt\ *n* : a member of the British peerage ranking below an earl and above a baron

vis·count·ess \-,kaùn-təs\ *n* **1** : the wife or widow of a viscount **2** : a woman who holds the rank of viscount in her own right

vis·cous \'vis-kəs\ *adj* [ME *viscouse*, fr. AF *viscos*, fr. LL *viscosus* full of birdlime, viscous, fr. L *viscum* mistletoe, birdlime] **1** : having the sticky consistency of glue **2** : having or characterized by viscosity

vis·cus \'vis-kəs\ *n, pl* **vis·cera** \'vi-sə-rə\ : an internal organ of the body; *esp* : one (as the heart or liver) located in the cavity of the trunk

vise \'vīs\ *n* [ME *vys, vice* screw, fr. AF *vyz*, fr. L *vitis* vine] : a tool with two jaws for holding work that typically close by a screw or lever

vise

vis·i·bil·i·ty \,vi-zə-'bi-lə-tē\ *n, pl* **-ties** **1** : the quality, condition, or degree of being visible **2** : the degree of clearness of the atmosphere

vis·i·ble \'vi-zə-bəl\ *adj* : capable of being seen ⟨∼ stars⟩; *also* : MANIFEST, APPARENT ⟨has no ∼ means of support⟩ — **vis·i·bly** \-blē\ *adv*

¹vi·sion \'vi-zhən\ *n* **1** : something seen otherwise than by ordinary sight (as in a dream or trance) **2** : a vivid picture created by the imagination ⟨∼s of fame and fortune⟩ **3** : the act or power of imagination **4** : unusual wisdom in foreseeing what is going to happen **5** : the act or power of seeing : SIGHT **6** : something seen; *esp* : a lovely sight

²vision *vb* : IMAGINE, ENVISION

¹**vi·sion·ary** \'vi-zhə-ˌner-ē\ *adj* **1** : of the nature of a vision : ILLUSORY, UNREAL **2** : not practical : UTOPIAN **3** : seeing or likely to see visions : given to dreaming or imagining ♦ *Synonyms* IMAGINARY, FANTASTIC, CHIMERICAL, QUIXOTIC

²**visionary** *n, pl* **-ar·ies** **1** : one whose ideas or projects are impractical : DREAMER **2** : one who sees visions

¹**vis·it** \'vi-zət\ *vb* **1** : to go to see in order to comfort or help **2** : to call on either as an act of courtesy or friendship **3** : to dwell with for a time as a guest **4** : to come to or upon as a reward, affliction, or punishment **5** : INFLICT ⟨~ed his wrath upon them⟩ **6** : to make a visit or regular or frequent visits **7** : CHAT, CONVERSE ⟨enjoys ~ing with the neighbors⟩ — **vis·it·able** *adj*

²**visit** *n* **1** : a short stay : CALL **2** : a brief residence as a guest **3** : a journey to and stay at a place **4** : a formal or professional call (as by a doctor)

vis·i·tant \'vi-zə-tənt\ *n* : VISITOR

vis·i·ta·tion \ˌvi-zə-'tā-shən\ *n* **1** : VISIT; *esp* : an official visit **2** : a special dispensation of divine favor or wrath; *also* : a severe trial

visiting nurse *n* : a nurse employed to visit sick persons or perform public health services in a community

vis·i·tor \'vi-zə-tər\ *n* : one that visits

vi·sor \'vī-zər\ *n* **1** : the front piece of a helmet; *esp* : a movable upper piece **2** : VIZARD **3** : a projecting part (as on a cap) to shade the eyes — **vi·sored** \-zərd\ *adj*

vis·ta \'vis-tə\ *n* **1** : a distant view through or along an avenue or opening **2** : an extensive mental view over a series of years or events

VISTA *abbr* Volunteers in Service to America

¹**vi·su·al** \'vi-zhə-wəl\ *adj* **1** : of, relating to, or used in vision ⟨~ organs⟩ **2** : perceived by vision ⟨a ~ impression⟩ **3** : VISIBLE ⟨~ objects⟩ **4** : done by sight only ⟨~ navigation⟩ **5** : of or relating to instruction by means of sight ⟨~ aids⟩ — **vi·su·al·ly** *adv*

²**visual** *n* : something (as a graphic) that appeals to the sight and is used for illustration, demonstration, or promotion — usu. used in pl.

vi·su·al·ize \'vi-zhə-wə-ˌlīz\ *vb* **-ized; -iz·ing** : to make visible; *esp* : to form a mental image of — **vi·su·al·i·za·tion** \ˌvi-zhə-wə-lə-'zā-shən\ *n* — **vi·su·al·iz·er** *n*

vi·ta \'vē-tə, 'vī-tə\ *n, pl* **vi·tae** \'vē-ˌtī, 'vī-tē\ [L, lit., life] : a brief autobiographical sketch

vi·tal \'vīt-ᵊl\ *adj* **1** : concerned with or necessary to the maintenance of life ⟨~ organs⟩ **2** : full of life and vigor : ANIMATED **3** : of, relating to, or characteristic of life or living beings **4** : FATAL, MORTAL ⟨~ wound⟩ **5** : FUNDAMENTAL, INDISPENSABLE — **vi·tal·ly** *adv*

vi·tal·i·ty \vī-'ta-lə-tē\ *n, pl* **-ties** **1** : the property distinguishing the living from the nonliving **2** : mental and physical vigor **3** : enduring quality **4** : ANIMATION, LIVELINESS ⟨the ~ of youth⟩

vi·tal·ize \'vīt-ə-ˌlīz\ *vb* **-ized; -iz·ing** : to impart life or vigor to : ANIMATE — **vi·tal·i·za·tion** \ˌvīt-ə-lə-'zā-shən\ *n*

vi·tals \'vīt-ᵊlz\ *n pl* **1** : vital organs (as the heart and brain) **2** : essential parts

vital signs *n pl* : the pulse rate, respiratory rate, body temperature, and often blood pressure of a person

vital statistics *n pl* : statistics dealing with births, deaths, marriages, health, and disease

vi·ta·min \'vī-tə-mən\ *n* : any of various organic substances that are essential in tiny amounts to the nutrition of most animals and some plants and are mostly obtained from foods

vitamin A *n* : any of several vitamins (as from egg yolk or fish-liver oils) required esp. for good vision

vitamin B *n* **1** : VITAMIN B COMPLEX **2** *or* **vitamin B₁** : THIAMINE

vitamin B complex *n* : a group of vitamins that are found widely in foods and are essential for normal function of certain enzymes and for growth

vitamin B₆ \-'bē-'siks\ *n* : any of several compounds that are considered essential to vertebrate nutrition

vitamin B₁₂ \-'bē-'twelv\ *n* : a complex cobalt-containing compound that occurs esp. in liver and is essential to normal blood formation, neural function, and growth; *also* : any of several compounds of similar action

vitamin C *n* : a vitamin found esp. in fruits and vegetables that is needed by the body to prevent scurvy

vitamin D *n* : any or all of several vitamins that are needed for normal bone and tooth structure and are found esp. in fish-liver oils, egg yolk, and milk or are produced by the body in response to ultraviolet light

vitamin E *n* : any of various oily fat-soluble liquid vitamins whose absence in the body is associated with such ailments as infertility, the breakdown of muscles, and vascular problems and which are found esp. in leaves and in seed germ oils

vitamin K *n* : any of several vitamins needed for blood to clot properly

vi·ti·ate \'vi-shē-ˌāt\ *vb* **-at·ed; -at·ing** **1** : CONTAMINATE, POLLUTE; *also* : DEBASE, PERVERT **2** : to make legally ineffective : INVALIDATE ⟨~ a contract⟩ — **vi·ti·a·tion** \ˌvi-shē-'ā-shən\ *n* — **vi·ti·a·tor** \'vi-shē-ˌā-tər\ *n*

vi·ti·cul·ture \'vi-tə-ˌkəl-chər\ *n* : the growing of grapes — **vi·ti·cul·tur·al** \ˌvi-tə-'kəl-chə-rəl\ *adj* — **vi·ti·cul·tur·ist** \-rist\ *n*

vit·re·ous \'vi-trē-əs\ *adj* **1** : of, relating to, or resembling glass : GLASSY ⟨~ rocks⟩ **2** : of, relating to, or being the clear colorless transparent jelly (**vitreous humor**) behind the lens in the eyeball

vit·ri·ol \'vi-trē-əl\ *n* : something resembling acid in being caustic, corrosive, or biting — **vit·ri·ol·ic** \ˌvi-trē-'ä-lik\ *adj*

vit·tles \'vi-tᵊlz\ *n pl* : VICTUALS

vi·tu·per·ate \vī-'tü-pə-ˌrāt, və-, -'tyü-\ *vb* **-at·ed; -at·ing** : to abuse in words : SCOLD ♦ *Synonyms* REVILE, BERATE, RATE, UPBRAID, RAIL, LASH — **vi·tu·per·a·tive** \-'tü-pə-rə-tiv, -'tyü-, -ˌrā-\ *adj* — **vi·tu·per·a·tive·ly** *adv*

vi·tu·per·a·tion \(ˌ)vī-ˌtü-pə-'rā-shən, və-, -ˌtyü-\ *n* : lengthy harsh criticism or abuse

vi·va \'vē-və\ *interj* [It & Sp, long live] — used to express goodwill or approval

vi·va·ce \vē-'vä-chā\ *adv or adj* [It] : in a brisk spirited manner — used as a direction in music

vi·va·cious \və-'vā-shəs, vī-\ *adj* : lively in temper, conduct, or spirit : SPRIGHTLY ⟨a ~ personality⟩ — **vi·va·cious·ly** *adv* — **vi·va·cious·ness** *n*

vi·vac·i·ty \-'va-sə-tē\ *n* : the quality or state of being vivacious

viva vo·ce \ˌvī-və-'vō-sē, ˌvē-və-'vō-ˌchā\ *adj* [ML, with the living voice] : expressed or conducted by word of mouth : ORAL — **viva voce** *adv*

viv·id \'vi-vəd\ *adj* **1** : BRILLIANT, INTENSE ⟨a ~ red⟩ **2** : having the appearance of vigorous life **3** : producing a strong impression on the senses; *esp* : producing distinct mental pictures ⟨a ~ description⟩ — **viv·id·ly** *adv* — **viv·id·ness** *n*

viv·i·fy \'vi-və-ˌfī\ *vb* **-fied; -fy·ing** **1** : to put life into : ANIMATE ⟨details that ~ a story⟩ **2** : to make vivid — **viv·i·fi·ca·tion** \ˌvi-və-fə-'kā-shən\ *n* — **viv·i·fi·er** *n*

vi·vip·a·rous \vī-'vi-pə-rəs, və-\ *adj* : producing living young from within the body rather than from eggs — **vi·vi·par·i·ty** \ˌvī-və-'pa-rə-tē, ˌvi-\ *n*

viv·i·sec·tion \ˌvi-və-'sek-shən, 'vi-və-ˌsek-\ *n* : the cutting of or operation on a living animal; *also* : animal experimentation esp. if causing distress to the subject

vix·en \'vik-sən\ *n* **1** : an ill-tempered scolding woman **2** : a female fox

viz *abbr* videlicet

viz·ard \'vi-zərd\ *n* : a mask for disguise or protection

vi·zier \və-'zir\ *n* : a high executive officer of many Muslim countries

VJ *abbr* veejay

vlog \'vlȯg, 'vläg\ *n* [video + b*log*] : a blog that contains video material — **vlog** *vb* — **vlog·ger** *n*

VOA *abbr* Voice of America

voc *abbr* **1** vocational **2** vocative

vocab *abbr* vocabulary

vo·ca·ble \'vō-kə-bəl\ *n* : TERM, NAME; *esp* : a word as such without regard to its meaning

vo·cab·u·lary \vō-'ka-byə-ˌler-ē\ *n, pl* **-lar·ies** **1** : a list or collection of words usu. alphabetically arranged and defined or explained : LEXICON **2** : a stock of words in a language used by a class or individual or in relation to a subject

vocabulary entry *n* : a word (as the noun *book*), hyphened or open compound (as the verb *cross-refer* or the noun *boric acid*), word element (as the affix *-an*), abbreviation (as *agt*), verbalized symbol (as *Na*), or term (as *master of ceremonies*) entered alphabetically in a dictionary for the purpose of definition or identification or expressly included as an inflected form (as the noun *mice* or the verb *saw*) or as a derived form (as the noun *godlessness* or the adverb *globally*) or related phrase (as *in spite of*) run on at its base word and usu. set in a type (as boldface) readily distinguishable from that of the lightface running text which defines, explains, or identifies the entry

¹**vo·cal** \ˈvō-kəl\ *adj* **1** : uttered by the voice : ORAL **2** : relating to, composed or arranged for, or sung by the human voice ⟨~ music⟩ **3** : given to expressing oneself freely or insistently : OUTSPOKEN ⟨a ~ critic⟩ **4** : of or relating to the voice

²**vocal** *n* **1** : a vocal sound **2** : a vocal composition or its performance

vocal cords *n pl* : either of two pairs of elastic folds of mucous membrane that project into the cavity of the larynx and function in the production of vocal sounds

vo·cal·ic \vō-ˈka-lik\ *adj* : of, relating to, or functioning as a vowel

vo·cal·ise *Brit var of* VOCALIZE

vo·cal·ist \ˈvō-kə-list\ *n* : SINGER

vo·cal·ize \-ˌlīz\ *vb* **-ized; -iz·ing 1** : to give vocal expression to : UTTER; *esp* : SING **2** : to make voiced rather than voiceless — **vo·cal·iz·er** *n*

vo·ca·tion \vō-ˈkā-shən\ *n* **1** : a summons or strong inclination to a particular state or course of action ⟨religious ~⟩ **2** : regular employment : OCCUPATION, PROFESSION — **vo·ca·tion·al** \-shə-nəl\ *adj*

vo·ca·tion·al·ism \-shə-nə-ˌli-zəm\ *n* : emphasis on vocational training in education

voc·a·tive \ˈvä-kə-tiv\ *adj* : of, relating to, or constituting a grammatical case marking the one addressed — **vocative** *n*

vo·cif·er·ate \vō-ˈsi-fə-ˌrāt\ *vb* **-at·ed; -at·ing** [L *vociferari,* fr. *voc-, vox* voice + *ferre* to bear] : to cry out loudly : CLAMOR, SHOUT — **vo·cif·er·a·tion** \-ˌsi-fə-ˈrā-shən\ *n*

vo·cif·er·ous \vō-ˈsi-fə-rəs\ *adj* : making or given to loud outcry — **vo·cif·er·ous·ly** *adv* — **vo·cif·er·ous·ness** *n*

vod·ka \ˈväd-kə\ *n* [Russ, fr. *voda* water] : a colorless liquor distilled from a mash (as of rye or wheat)

vogue \ˈvōg\ *n* [MF, action of rowing, course, fashion, fr. *voguer* to sail, fr. OF, fr. OIt *vogare* to row] **1** : popular acceptance or favor : POPULARITY **2** : a period of popularity **3** : one that is in fashion at a particular time ◆ *Synonyms* MODE, FAD, RAGE, CRAZE, TREND, FASHION

vogu·ish \ˈvō-gish\ *adj* **1** : FASHIONABLE, SMART **2** : suddenly or temporarily popular ⟨~ expressions⟩

¹**voice** \ˈvȯis\ *n* **1** : sound produced through the mouth by vertebrates and esp. by human beings (as in speaking or singing) **2** : musical sound produced by the vocal cords : the power to produce such sound; *also* : one of the melodic parts in a vocal or instrumental composition **3** : the vocal organs as a means of tone production ⟨train the ~⟩ **4** : sound produced by vibration of the vocal cords as heard in vowels and some consonants **5** : the power of speaking **6** : a sound suggesting a voice ⟨the ~ of the sea⟩ **7** : an instrument or medium of expression **8** : a choice, opinion, or wish openly expressed; *also* : right of expression **9** : distinction of form of a verb to indicate the relation of the subject to the action expressed by the verb

²**voice** *vb* **voiced; voic·ing** : to give voice or expression to : UTTER ⟨~ a complaint⟩ ◆ *Synonyms* EXPRESS, VENT, AIR, VENTILATE

voice box *n* : LARYNX

voiced \ˈvȯist\ *adj* **1** : having a voice ⟨soft-*voiced*⟩ **2** : uttered with voice ⟨a ~ consonant⟩ — **voiced·ness** \ˈvȯist-nəs, ˈvȯi-səd-nəs\ *n*

voice·less \ˈvȯis-ləs\ *adj* **1** : having no voice **2** : not pronounced with voice — **voice·less·ly** *adv* — **voice·less·ness** *n*

voice mail *n* : an electronic communication system in which spoken messages are recorded for later playback to the intended recipient; *also* : such a message

voice-over *n* : the voice in a film or television program of a person who is heard but not seen or not seen talking

voice·print \ˈvȯis-ˌprint\ *n* : an individually distinctive pattern of voice characteristics that is spectrographically produced

¹**void** \ˈvȯid\ *adj* **1** : UNOCCUPIED, VACANT ⟨a ~ bishopric⟩ **2** : containing nothing : EMPTY **3** : LACKING, DE-

VOID ⟨proposals ~ of sense⟩ **4** : VAIN, USELESS **5** : of no legal force or effect : NULL

²**void** *n* **1** : empty space : EMPTINESS, VACUUM **2** : a feeling of want or hollowness

³**void** *vb* **1** : to make or leave empty; *also* : VACATE, LEAVE **2** : DISCHARGE, EMIT ⟨~ urine⟩ **3** : to render void : ANNUL, NULLIFY ⟨~ a contract⟩ — **void·able** *adj* — **void·er** *n*

voi·là \vwä-ˈlä\ *interj* [F] — used to call attention to or to express satisfaction or approval

voile \ˈvȯi(-ə)l\ *n* : a sheer fabric used esp. for women's clothing and curtains

vol *abbr* **1** volume **2** volunteer

vol·a·tile \ˈvä-lə-tᵊl\ *adj* **1** : readily becoming a vapor at a relatively low temperature ⟨a ~ liquid⟩ **2** : tending to erupt into violence **3** : likely to change suddenly — **vol·a·til·i·ty** \ˌvä-lə-ˈti-lə-tē\ *n* — **vol·a·til·ize** \ˈvä-lə-lə-ˌlīz\ *vb*

vol·ca·nic \väl-ˈka-nik\ *adj* **1** : of, relating to, or produced by a volcano **2** : explosively violent ⟨~ emotions⟩

vol·ca·nism \ˈväl-kə-ˌni-zəm\ *n* : volcanic action or activity

vol·ca·no \väl-ˈkā-nō\ *n, pl* **-noes** *or* **-nos** [It or Sp; It *vulcano,* fr. Sp *vulcán,* ultim. fr. L *Volcanus,* Roman god of fire and metalworking] : an opening in the crust of the earth, a planet, or a moon from which molten rock and steam issue; *also* : a hill or mountain composed of the ejected material

vol·ca·nol·o·gy \ˌväl-kə-ˈnä-lə-jē\ *n* : a branch of geology that deals with volcanic phenomena — **vol·ca·nol·o·gist** \-kə-ˈnä-lə-jist\ *n*

vole \ˈvōl\ *n* : any of various small rodents that are closely related to the lemmings and muskrats

vo·li·tion \vō-ˈli-shən\ *n* **1** : the act or the power of making a choice or decision : WILL **2** : a choice or decision made — **vo·li·tion·al** \-ˈli-shə-nəl\ *adj*

¹**vol·ley** \ˈvä-lē\ *n, pl* **volleys 1** : a flight of missiles (as arrows) **2** : simultaneous discharge of a number of missile weapons **3** : an act of volleying **4** : a burst of many things at once ⟨a ~ of angry letters⟩

²**volley** *vb* **vol·leyed; vol·ley·ing 1** : to discharge or become discharged in or as if in a volley **2** : to hit an object of play (as a ball) in the air before it touches the ground

vol·ley·ball \-ˌbȯl\ *n* : a game played by volleying an inflated ball over a net; *also* : the ball used in this game

volt \ˈvōlt\ *n* : the meter-kilogram-second unit of electrical potential difference and electromotive force equal to the difference in potential between two points in a wire carrying a constant current of one ampere when the power dissipated between the points is equal to one watt

volt·age \ˈvōl-tij\ *n* : potential difference measured in volts

vol·ta·ic \väl-ˈtā-ik, vōl-\ *adj* : of, relating to, or producing direct electric current by chemical action

volte-face \vȯlt-ˈfäs, ˌvȯl-tə-\ *n* : a reversal in policy : ABOUT-FACE

volt·me·ter \ˈvōlt-ˌmē-tər\ *n* : an instrument for measuring in volts the difference in potential between different points of an electrical circuit

vol·u·ble \ˈväl-yə-bəl\ *adj* : fluent and smooth in speech : GLIB ◆ *Synonyms* GARRULOUS, LOQUACIOUS, TALKATIVE — **vol·u·bil·i·ty** \ˌväl-yə-ˈbi-lə-tē\ *n* — **vol·u·bly** \ˈväl-yə-blē\ *adv*

vol·ume \ˈväl-yəm, -(ˌ)yüm\ *n* [ME, fr. AF, fr. L *volumen* roll, scroll, fr. *volvere* to roll] **1** : a series of printed sheets bound typically in book form; *also* : an arbitrary number of issues of a periodical **2** : space occupied as measured by cubic units ⟨the ~ of a cylinder⟩ **3** : sufficient matter to fill a book ⟨her glance spoke ~s⟩ **4** : AMOUNT ⟨increasing ~ of business⟩ **5** : the degree of loudness of a sound ◆ *Synonyms* BODY, BULK, MASS

vo·lu·mi·nous \və-ˈlü-mə-nəs\ *adj* : having or marked by great volume or bulk : LARGE — **vo·lu·mi·nous·ly** *adv* — **vo·lu·mi·nous·ness** *n*

¹**vol·un·tary** \ˈvä-lən-ˌter-ē\ *adj* **1** : done, made, or given freely and without compulsion ⟨a ~ sacrifice⟩ **2** : done on purpose : INTENTIONAL ⟨~ manslaughter⟩ **3** : of, relating to, or regulated by the will ⟨~ behavior⟩ **4** : having power of free choice **5** : provided or

supported by voluntary action ⟨a ~ organization⟩ ✦ **Synonyms** DELIBERATE, WILLFUL, WILLING, WITTING — **vol·un·tar·i·ly** \ˌvä-lən-'ter-ə-lē\ adv

²voluntary n, pl **-tar·ies** : an organ solo played in a religious service

voluntary muscle n : muscle (as most striated muscle) under voluntary control

¹vol·un·teer \ˌvä-lən-'tir\ n 1 : a person who voluntarily undertakes a service or duty 2 : a plant growing spontaneously esp. from seeds lost from a previous crop

²volunteer vb 1 : to offer or give voluntarily 2 : to offer oneself as a volunteer

vo·lup·tu·ary \və-'ləp-chə-ˌwer-ē\ n, pl **-ar·ies** : a person whose chief interest in life is the indulgence of sensual appetites

vo·lup·tu·ous \-chə-wəs\ adj 1 : giving sensual gratification 2 : given to or spent in enjoyment of luxury or pleasure ✦ **Synonyms** LUXURIOUS, EPICUREAN, SENSUOUS — **vo·lup·tu·ous·ly** adv — **vo·lup·tu·ous·ness** n

vo·lute \və-'lüt\ n : a spiral or scroll-shaped decoration

¹vom·it \'vä-mət\ n : an act or instance of throwing up the contents of the stomach through the mouth; also : the matter thrown up

²vomit vb 1 : to throw up the contents of the stomach through the mouth 2 : to belch forth : GUSH

voo·doo \'vü-dü\ n, pl **voodoos** 1 : a religion that is derived from African polytheism and is practiced chiefly in Haiti 2 : a person who deals in spells and necromancy 3 : a charm used in voodoo; also : ²SPELL 1 — **voodoo** adj

voo·doo·ism \-ˌi-zəm\ n 1 : VOODOO 1 2 : the practice of witchcraft

vo·ra·cious \vȯ-'rā-shəs, və-\ adj 1 : having a huge appetite : RAVENOUS 2 : very eager ⟨a ~ reader⟩ ✦ **Synonyms** GLUTTONOUS, RAVENING, RAPACIOUS — **vo·ra·cious·ly** adv — **vo·ra·cious·ness** n — **vo·rac·i·ty** \-'ra-sə-tē\ n

vor·tex \'vȯr-ˌteks\ n, pl **vor·ti·ces** \'vȯr-tə-ˌsēz\ also **vor·tex·es** \'vȯr-ˌtek-səz\ : WHIRLPOOL; also : something resembling a whirlpool

vo·ta·ry \'vō-tə-rē\ n, pl **-ries** 1 : ENTHUSIAST, DEVOTEE; also : a devoted adherent or admirer 2 : a devout or zealous worshiper

¹vote \'vōt\ n [ME (Sc), fr. L votum vow, wish, fr. vovēre to vow] 1 : a choice or opinion of a person or body of persons expressed usu. by a ballot, spoken word, or raised hand; also : the ballot, word, or gesture used to express a choice or opinion 2 : the decision reached by voting 3 : the right of suffrage 4 : a group of voters with some common characteristics ⟨the big city ~⟩ — **vote·less** adj

²vote vb **vot·ed; vot·ing** 1 : to cast a vote 2 : to elect, decide, pass, defeat, grant, or make legal by a vote 3 : to declare by general agreement 4 : to offer as a suggestion : PROPOSE 5 : to cause to vote esp. in a given way — **vot·er** n

vo·tive \'vō-tiv\ adj : consisting of or expressing a vow, wish, or desire

vou abbr voucher

vouch \'vau̇ch\ vb 1 : PROVE, SUBSTANTIATE 2 : to verify by examining documentary evidence 3 : to give a guarantee 4 : to supply supporting evidence or testimony; also : to give personal assurance

vouch·er \'vau̇-chər\ n 1 : an act of vouching 2 : one that vouches for another 3 : a documentary record of a business transaction 4 : a written affidavit or authorization 5 : a form indicating a credit against future purchases or expenditures

vouch·safe \vau̇ch-'sāf\ vb **vouch·safed; vouch·saf·ing** : to grant or give as or as if by a privilege or a special favor

¹vow \'vau̇\ n : a solemn promise or statement; esp : one by which a person is bound to an act, service, or condition ⟨marriage ~s⟩

²vow vb 1 : to make a vow or as a vow 2 : to bind or commit by a vow — **vow·er** n

vow·el \'vau̇(-ə)l\ n 1 : a speech sound produced without obstruction or friction in the mouth 2 : a letter representing such a sound

vox po·pu·li \'väks-'pä-pyə-ˌlī\ n [L, voice of the people] : popular sentiment

¹voy·age \'vȯi-ij\ n [ME, viage, veyage, fr. AF veiage, fr. LL viaticum, fr. L, traveling money, fr. neut. of viaticus of a journey, fr. via way] : a journey esp. by water from one place or country to another

²voyage vb **voy·aged; voy·ag·ing** : to take or make a voyage — **voy·ag·er** n

voya·geur \ˌvȯi-ə-'zhər, ˌvwä-yä-\ n [CanF] : a person employed by a fur company to transport goods to and from remote stations esp. in the Canadian Northwest

voy·eur \vwä-'yər, vȯi-'ər\ n 1 : one who obtains sexual pleasure from viewing esp. covertly the nudity or sexual activity of others 2 : an observer of the sordid — **voy·eur·ism** \-ˌi-zəm\ n — **voy·eur·is·tic** \ˌvwä-(ˌ)yər-'is-tik, ˌvȯi-ər-\ adj

VP abbr 1 verb phrase 2 vice president

vs abbr 1 verse 2 versus

vss abbr 1 verses 2 versions

V/STOL abbr vertical or short takeoff and landing

Vt or **VT** abbr Vermont

VTOL abbr vertical takeoff and landing

VTR abbr videotape recorder

vul·ca·nize \'vəl-kə-ˌnīz\ vb **-nized; -niz·ing** : to treat rubber or rubberlike material chemically to give useful properties (as elasticity and strength)

Vulg abbr Vulgate

vul·gar \'vəl-gər\ adj [ME, fr. L vulgaris of the mob, vulgar, fr. vulgus mob, common people] 1 : VERNACULAR ⟨the ~ tongue⟩ 2 : of or relating to the common people : GENERAL, COMMON 3 : lacking cultivation or refinement : BOORISH; also : offensive to good taste or refined feelings ⟨~ language⟩ ✦ **Synonyms** GROSS, OBSCENE, RIBALD, DIRTY, INDECENT, PROFANE — **vul·gar·ly** adv

vul·gar·i·an \ˌvəl-'ger-ē-ən\ n : a vulgar person

vul·gar·ism \'vəl-gə-ˌri-zəm\ n 1 : VULGARITY 2 : a word or expression originated or used chiefly by illiterate persons 3 : a coarse expression : OBSCENITY

vul·gar·i·ty \ˌvəl-'ga-rə-tē\ n, pl **-ties** 1 : something vulgar 2 : the quality or state of being vulgar

vul·gar·ize \'vəl-gə-ˌrīz\ vb **-ized; -iz·ing** : to make vulgar — **vul·gar·i·za·tion** \ˌvəl-gə-rə-'zā-shən\ n — **vul·gar·iz·er** \'vəl-gə-ˌrī-zər\ n

Vul·gate \'vəl-ˌgāt\ n [ML vulgata, fr. LL vulgata editio edition in general circulation] : a Latin version of the Bible used by the Roman Catholic Church

vul·ner·a·ble \'vəl-nə-rə-bəl\ adj 1 : capable of being wounded : susceptible to wounds 2 : open to attack 3 : liable to increased penalties in contract bridge — **vul·ner·a·bil·i·ty** \ˌvəl-nə-rə-'bi-lə-tē\ n — **vul·ner·a·bly** \'vəl-nə-rə-blē\ adv

vul·pine \'vəl-ˌpīn\ adj : of, relating to, or resembling a fox esp. in cunning ⟨~ charms⟩

vul·ture \'vəl-chər\ n 1 : any of various large birds (as a turkey vulture) related to the hawks, eagles, and falcons but having weaker claws and the head usu. naked and living chiefly on carrion 2 : a rapacious person

vul·va \'vəl-və\ n, pl **vul·vae** \-ˌvē\ [ME, fr. ML, fr. L volva, vulva womb, female genitals] : the external parts of the female genital organs — **vul·val** \'vəl-vəl\ or **vul·var** \-vər, -ˌvär\ adj

vv abbr 1 verses 2 vice versa

VX \ˌvē-'eks\ n : an extremely toxic chemical weapon

vying pres part of VIE

¹w \'də-bəl-(ˌ)yü\ *n, pl* w's *or* ws *often cap* : the 23d letter of the English alphabet

²w *abbr, often cap* 1 water 2 watt 3 week 4 weight 5 west; western 6 wide; width 7 wife 8 with

W *symbol* [G *Wolfram*] tungsten

WA *abbr* 1 Washington 2 Western Australia

wacky \'wa-kē\ *adj* wack·i·er; -est : ECCENTRIC, CRAZY

¹wad \'wäd\ *n* 1 : a little mass, bundle, or tuft ⟨~s of clay⟩ 2 : a soft mass of usu. light·fibrous material 3 : a pliable plug (as of felt) used to retain a powder charge (as in a cartridge) 4 : a considerable amount (as of money) 5 : a roll of paper money

²wad *vb* wad·ded; wad·ding 1 : to push a wad into ⟨~ a gun⟩ 2 : to form into a wad 3 : to hold in by a wad ⟨~ a bullet in a gun⟩ 4 : to stuff or line with a wad : PAD

wad·ding \'wä-diŋ\ *n* 1 : WADS; *also* : material for making wads 2 : a soft mass or sheet of short loose fibers used for stuffing or padding

wad·dle \'wä-dᵊl\ *vb* wad·dled; wad·dling : to walk with short steps swaying from side to side like a duck — wad·dle *n*

wade \'wād\ *vb* wad·ed; wad·ing 1 : to step in or through a medium (as water) more resistant than air 2 : to move or go with difficulty or labor and often with determination ⟨~ through a dull book⟩ — wad·able *or* wade·able \'wä-də-bəl\ *adj* — wade *n*

wad·er \'wä-dər\ *n* 1 : one that wades 2 : SHOREBIRD; *also* : WADING BIRD 3 *pl* : a waterproof garment consisting of pants with attached boots for wading

wa·di \'wä-dē\ *n* [Ar *wādī*] : a streambed of southwest Asia and northern Africa that is dry except in the rainy season

wading bird *n* : any of an order of long-legged birds (as sandpipers, cranes, or herons) that wade in water in search of food

wa·fer \'wā-fər\ *n* 1 : a thin crisp cake or cracker 2 : a thin round piece of unleavened bread used in the Eucharist 3 : something (as a piece of candy) that resembles a wafer

¹waf·fle \'wä-fəl\ *n* : a soft but crisped cake of batter cooked in a special hinged metal utensil (waffle iron)

²waffle *vb* waf·fled; waf·fling \-f(ə)liŋ\ : to speak or write in a vague or evasive manner ⟨*waffled* on important issues⟩

¹waft \'wäft, 'waft\ *vb* : to cause to move or go lightly by or as if by the impulse of wind or waves

²waft *n* 1 : a slight breeze : PUFF 2 : the act of waving

¹wag \'wag\ *vb* wagged; wag·ging 1 : to sway or swing shortly from side to side or to-and-fro ⟨the dog *wagged* his tail⟩ 2 : to move in chatter or gossip ⟨scandal caused tongues to ~⟩

²wag *n* : an act of wagging : a wagging movement

³wag *n* : WIT, JOKER

¹wage \'wāj\ *n* 1 : payment for labor or services usu. according to contract 2 *pl* : RECOMPENSE, REWARD

²wage *vb* waged; wag·ing 1 : to engage in : CARRY ON ⟨~ a war⟩ 2 : to be in process of being waged

¹wa·ger \'wā-jər\ *n* 1 : BET, STAKE 2 : something on which bets are laid : GAMBLE

²wager *vb* : BET — wa·ger·er *n*

wag·gish \'wa-gish\ *adj* 1 : resembling or characteristic of a wag : MISCHIEVOUS 2 : SPORTIVE, HUMOROUS

wag·gle \'wa-gəl\ *vb* wag·gled; wag·gling : to move backward and forward or from side to side : WAG — waggle *n*

wag·on \'wa-gən\ *chiefly Brit var of* WAGON

wag·on \'wa-gən\ *n* 1 : a 4-wheeled vehicle; *esp* : one drawn by animals and used for freight or merchandise 2 : PADDY WAGON 3 : a child's 4-wheeled cart 4 : STATION WAGON

wag·on·er \'wa-gə-nər\ *n* : the driver of a wagon

wag·on·ette \ˌwa-gə-'net\ *n* : a light wagon with two facing seats along the sides behind a cross seat in front

wa·gon–lit \vä-gōⁿ-'lē\ *n, pl* wagons–lits *or* wagon–lits *same or* -'lēz\ [F, fr. *wagon* railroad car + *lit* bed] : a railroad sleeping car

wagon train *n* : a column of wagons traveling overland

wag·tail \'wag-ˌtāl\ *n* : any of various slender-bodied mostly Old World birds with a long tail that jerks up and down

wa·hi·ne \wä-'hē-nē, -ˌnā\ *n* 1 : a Polynesian woman 2 : a female surfer

wa·hoo \'wä-ˌhü\ *n, pl* wahoos : a large vigorous food and sport fish related to the mackerel and found in warm seas

waif \'wāf\ *n* 1 : something found without an owner and esp. by chance 2 : a stray person or animal; *esp* : a homeless child

wail \'wāl\ *vb* 1 : LAMENT, WEEP 2 : to make a sound suggestive of a mournful cry 3 : COMPLAIN — wail *n*

wail·ful \-fəl\ *adj* : SORROWFUL, MOURNFUL ♦ Synonyms MELANCHOLY, DOLEFUL, LUGUBRIOUS, LAMENTABLE, PLAINTIVE, WOEFUL — wail·ful·ly *adv*

wain \'wān\ *n* : a usu. large heavy farm wagon

wain·scot \'wän-skət, -ˌskōt, -ˌskät\ *n* 1 : a usu. paneled wooden lining of an interior wall of a room 2 : the lower part of an interior wall when finished differently from the rest — wainscot *vb*

wain·scot·ing *or* wain·scot·ting \-ˌskō-tiŋ, -ˌskä-, -skə-\ *n* : material for a wainscot; *also* : WAINSCOT

waist \'wāst\ *n* 1 : the narrowed part of the body between the chest and hips 2 : a part resembling the human waist esp. in narrowness or central position ⟨the ~ of a ship⟩ 3 : a garment or part of a garment (as a blouse or bodice) for the upper part of the body

waist·band \-ˌband\ *n* : a band (as on pants or a skirt) that fits around the waist

waist·coat \'wes-kət, 'wāst-ˌkōt\ *n, chiefly Brit* : VEST 1

waist·line \'wāst-ˌlīn\ *n* 1 : a line around the waist at its narrowest part; *also* : the length of this 2 : the line at which the bodice and skirt of a dress meet

¹wait \'wāt\ *vb* 1 : to remain inactive in readiness or expectation : AWAIT ⟨~ for orders⟩ 2 : to delay serving (a meal) 3 : to act as attendant or servant ⟨~ on customers⟩ 4 : to attend as a waiter : SERVE ⟨~ tables⟩ ⟨~ at a banquet⟩ 5 : to be ready ⟨a letter ~*ing* for you⟩

²wait *n* 1 : a position of concealment usu. with intent to attack or surprise ⟨lie in ~⟩ 2 : an act or period of waiting

wait·er \'wā-tər\ *n* 1 : one that waits on another; *esp* : a person who waits tables 2 : TRAY

waiting game *n* : a strategy in which one or more participants withhold action in the hope of an opportunity for more effective action later

waiting room *n* : a room (as at a doctor's office) for the use of persons who are waiting

wait·per·son \'wāt-ˌpər-sən\ *n* : a waiter or waitress

wait·ress \'wā-trəs\ *n* : a woman who waits tables

waive \'wāv\ *vb* waived; waiv·ing [ME *weiven* to decline, reject, give up, fr. AF *waiver, gaiver*, fr. *waif* lost, stray] 1 : to give up claim to ⟨*waived* his right to a trial⟩ 2 : POSTPONE

waiv·er \'wā-vər\ *n* : the act of waiving right, claim, or privilege; *also* : a document containing a declaration of such an act

¹wake \'wāk\ *vb* woke \'wōk\ *also* waked \'wākt\; wo·ken \'wō-kən\ *also* waked *or* woke; wak·ing 1 : to be or remain awake; *esp* : to keep watch (as over a corpse) 2 : AWAKE, AWAKEN ⟨the baby *woke* up early⟩

²wake *n* 1 : the state of being awake 2 : a watch held over the body of a dead person prior to burial

³wake *n* : the track left by a ship in the water; *also* : a track left behind

wake·board \'wāk-ˌbȯrd\ *n* : a short board with foot bindings on which a rider is towed by a motorboat across its wake — wake·board·er *n* — wake·board·ing *n*

wake·ful \'wāk-fəl\ adj : not sleeping or able to sleep : SLEEPLESS, ALERT — **wake·ful·ness** n
wak·en \'wā-kən\ vb : WAKE
wake–rob·in \'wāk-ˌrä-bən\ n : TRILLIUM
wak·ing \'wā-kiŋ\ adj : passed in a conscious or alert state ⟨every ~ hour⟩
wale \'wāl\ n : a ridge esp. on cloth; also : the texture esp. of a fabric
¹**walk** \'wȯk\ vb [partly fr. ME walken, fr. OE wealcan to roll, toss and partly fr. ME walkien, fr. OE wealcian to roll up, muffle up] 1 : to move or cause to move on foot usu. at a natural unhurried gait ⟨~ to town⟩ ⟨~ a horse⟩ 2 : to pass over, through, or along by walking ⟨~ the streets⟩ 3 : to perform or accomplish by walking ⟨~ guard⟩ 4 : to follow a course of action or way of life ⟨~ humbly in the sight of God⟩ 5 : WALK OUT 6 : to receive a base on balls; also : to give a base on balls to — **walk·er** n
²**walk** n 1 : a going on foot ⟨go for a ~⟩ 2 : a place, path, or course for walking 3 : distance to be walked ⟨a quarter-mile ~ from here⟩ 4 : manner of living : CONDUCT, BEHAVIOR 5 : social or economic status ⟨various ~s of life⟩ 6 : manner of walking : GAIT; esp : a slow 4-beat gait of a horse 7 : BASE ON BALLS
walk·away \'wȯ-kə-ˌwā\ n : an easily won contest
walk·ie–talk·ie \ˌwȯ-kē-'tȯ-kē\ n : a small portable radio transmitting and receiving set
¹**walk–in** \'wȯk-ˌin\ adj : large enough to be walked into ⟨a ~ refrigerator⟩
²**walk–in** n 1 : an easy election victory 2 : one that walks in
walking papers n pl : DISMISSAL, DISCHARGE
walking stick n 1 : a stick used in walking 2 : STICK INSECT; esp : one of the U.S. and Canada

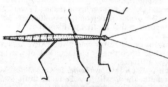

walking stick 2

walk–on \'wȯk-ˌȯn, -ˌän\ n : a small part in a dramatic production
walk·out \-ˌaùt\ n 1 : a labor strike 2 : the action of leaving a meeting or organization as an expression of disapproval
walk out vb 1 : to leave suddenly often as an expression of disapproval 2 : to go on strike
walk·over \-ˌō-vər\ n : a one-sided contest : an easy victory
walk–up \'wȯk-ˌəp\ n : a building or apartment house without an elevator — **walk–up** adj
walk·way \-ˌwā\ n : a passage for walking
¹**wall** \'wȯl\ n [ME, fr. OE weall, fr. L vallum rampart, fr. vallus stake, palisade] 1 : a structure (as of stone or brick) intended for defense or security or for enclosing something 2 : one of the upright enclosing parts of a building or room 3 : the inside surface of a cavity or container ⟨the ~ of a boiler⟩ 4 : something like a wall in appearance, function, or effect ⟨a tariff ~⟩ — **walled** \'wȯld\ adj
²**wall** vb 1 : to provide, separate, or surround with or as if with a wall ⟨~ in a garden⟩ 2 : to close (an opening) with or as if with a wall ⟨~ up a door⟩
wal·la·by \'wä-lə-bē\ n, pl **wallabies** also **wallaby** : any of various small or medium-sized kangaroos
wall·board \'wȯl-ˌbȯrd\ n : a structural material (as of wood pulp or plaster) made in large sheets and used for sheathing interior walls and ceilings
wal·let \'wä-lət\ n 1 : a bag or sack for carrying things on a journey 2 : a pocketbook with compartments (as for personal papers and usu. unfolded money) : BILLFOLD
wall·eye \'wȯl-ˌī\ n 1 : an eye with a whitish iris or an opaque white cornea 2 : a large vigorous No. American

food and sport fish related to the perches — **wall·eyed** \-ˌīd\ adj
wall·flow·er \'wȯl-ˌflaù(-ə)r\ n 1 : any of several Old World herbs related to the mustards; esp : one with showy fragrant flowers 2 : a person who usu. from shyness or unpopularity remains alone (as at a dance)
Wal·loon \wä-'lün\ n : a member of a people of southern and southeastern Belgium and adjacent parts of France — **Walloon** adj
¹**wal·lop** \'wä-ləp\ vb 1 : to beat soundly : TROUNCE 2 : to hit hard : SOCK ♦ **Synonyms** BATTER, BEAT, LAMBASTE, POUND, PUMMEL, THRASH
²**wallop** n 1 : a powerful blow or impact 2 : the ability to hit hard 3 : emotional, sensory, or psychological force : IMPACT ⟨a story with a ~⟩
wal·lop·ing \'wä-lə-piŋ\ adj 1 : LARGE, WHOPPING ⟨a ~ storm⟩ 2 : exceptionally fine or impressive ⟨a ~ fun party⟩
¹**wal·low** \'wä-lō\ vb 1 : to roll oneself about sluggishly in or as if in deep mud ⟨hogs ~ing in the mire⟩ 2 : to indulge oneself excessively ⟨~ in luxury⟩ 3 : to become or remain helpless ⟨~ in ignorance⟩ ♦ **Synonyms** BASK, INDULGE, LUXURIATE, REVEL, WELTER
²**wallow** n : a muddy or dust-filled area where animals wallow
wall·pa·per \'wȯl-ˌpā-pər\ n 1 : decorative paper for the walls of a room 2 : the background image or set of images displayed on a computer screen — **wallpaper** vb
wall–to–wall adj 1 : covering the entire floor ⟨wall-to-wall carpeting⟩ 2 : covering or filling one entire space or time ⟨crowds of wall-to-wall people⟩
wal·nut \'wȯl-(ˌ)nət\ n [ME walnut, fr. OE wealhhnutu, lit., foreign nut, fr. Wealh Welshman, foreigner + hnutu nut] 1 : a nut with a furrowed usu. rough shell and an adherent husk from any of a genus of trees related to the hickories; esp : the large edible nut of a Eurasian tree 2 : a tree that bears walnuts 3 : the usu. reddish to dark brown wood of a walnut used esp. in cabinetwork and veneers
wal·rus \'wȯl-rəs, 'wäl-\ n, pl **walrus** or **wal·rus·es** : a large mammal of arctic waters that is related to the seals and has long ivory tusks
¹**waltz** \'wȯlts\ n [G Walzer, fr. walzen to roll, dance] 1 : a gliding dance done to music having three beats to the measure 2 : music for or suitable for waltzing
²**waltz** vb 1 : to dance a waltz 2 : to move or advance easily, successfully, or conspicuously ⟨he ~ed off with the championship⟩ — **waltz·er** n
wam·ble \'wäm-bəl\ vb **wam·bled**; **wam·bling** : to progress unsteadily or with a lurching shambling gait
Wam·pa·no·ag \ˌwäm-pə-'nō-(ˌ)ag; ˌwȯm-\ n, pl **Wampanoag** or **Wampanoags** [Narragansett, lit., easterners] : a member of an American Indian people of parts of Rhode Island and Massachusetts
wam·pum \'wäm-pəm\ n [short for wampumpeag, fr. Massachuset (an Algonquian Indian language) wampompeag, fr. wampan white + api string + -ag, pl. suffix] 1 : beads made of shells strung in strands, belts, or sashes and used by No. American Indians as money and ornaments 2 slang : MONEY
wan \'wän\ adj **wan·ner**; **wan·nest** 1 : SICKLY, PALLID; also : FEEBLE 2 : DIM, FAINT 3 : LANGUID ⟨a ~ smile⟩ ♦ **Synonyms** ASHEN, BLANCHED, DOUGHY, LIVID, PALE, WAXEN — **wan·ly** adv — **wan·ness** n
wand \'wänd\ n 1 : a slender staff carried in a procession 2 : the staff of a fairy, diviner, or magician
wan·der \'wän-dər\ vb 1 : to move about aimlessly or without a fixed course or goal : RAMBLE 2 : to go astray in conduct or thought; esp : to become delirious ♦ **Synonyms** GAD, GALLIVANT, MEANDER, RANGE, ROAM, ROVE — **wan·der·er** n
wandering Jew n : either of two trailing or creeping plants cultivated for their showy and often white-striped foliage
wan·der·lust \'wän-dər-ˌlȯst\ n : strong longing for or impulse toward wandering
¹**wane** \'wän\ vb **waned**; **wan·ing** 1 : to grow gradually smaller or less ⟨the full moon ~s to new⟩ ⟨his strength waned⟩ 2 : to lose power, prosperity, or influence 3 : to draw near an end ⟨summer is waning⟩ ♦ **Synonyms** ABATE, EBB, MODERATE, RELENT, SLACKEN, SUBSIDE

²**wane** *n* : a waning (as in size or power); *also* : a period in which something is waning

wan·gle \'waŋ-gəl\ *vb* **wan·gled**; **wan·gling** **1** : to obtain by sly or devious means; *also* : to use trickery or questionable means to achieve an end **2** : MANIPULATE; *also* : FINAGLE

wan·na·be *also* **wan·na·bee** \'wä-nə-ˌbē\ *n* : a person who wants or aspires to be someone or something else or who tries to look or act like someone else

¹**want** \'wȯnt, 'wänt\ *vb* **1** : to fail to possess : LACK ⟨they ~ the necessities of life⟩ **2** : to feel or suffer the need of **3** : NEED, REQUIRE ⟨the house ~s painting⟩ **4** : to desire earnestly : WISH

²**want** *n* **1** : a lack of a required or usual amount : SHORTAGE **2** : dire need : DESTITUTION **3** : something wanted : DESIRE **4** : personal defect : FAULT

¹**want·ing** \'wȯnt-, 'wän-\ *adj* **1** : not present or in evidence : ABSENT **2** : falling below standards or expectations **3** : lacking in ability or capacity : DEFICIENT ⟨~ in common sense⟩

²**wanting** *prep* **1** : LESS, MINUS ⟨a month ~ two days⟩ **2** : WITHOUT ⟨a book ~ a cover⟩

¹**wan·ton** \'wȯn-t°n, 'wän-\ *adj* [ME, undisciplined, fr. *wan-* deficient, wrong + *towen*, pp. of *teen* to draw, train, discipline] **1** : UNCHASTE, LEWD, LUSTFUL; *also* : SENSUAL **2** : having no regard for justice or for other persons' feelings, rights, or safety : MERCILESS, INHUMANE ⟨~ cruelty⟩ **3** : having no just cause ⟨a ~ attack⟩ — **wan·ton·ly** *adv* — **wan·ton·ness** *n*

²**wanton** *n* : a wanton individual; *esp* : a lewd or immoral person

³**wanton** *vb* **1** : to be wanton : act wantonly **2** : to pass or waste wantonly

wa·pi·ti \'wä-pə-tē\ *n, pl* **wapiti** *or* **wapitis** : ELK 2

¹**war** \'wȯr\ *n* **1** : a state or period of usu. open and declared armed fighting between states or nations **2** : the art or science of warfare **3** : a state of hostility, conflict, or antagonism **4** : a struggle between opposing forces or for a particular end ⟨~ against disease⟩ — **war·less** \-ləs\ *adj*

²**war** *vb* **warred**; **war·ring** : to engage in warfare : be in conflict

³**war** *abbr* warrant

¹**war·ble** \'wȯr-bəl\ *n* **1** : a melodious succession of low pleasing sounds **2** : a musical trill

²**warble** *vb* **war·bled**; **war·bling** **1** : to sing or utter in a trilling manner or with variations **2** : to express by or as if by warbling

³**warble** *n* : a swelling under the skin esp. of the back of cattle, horses, and wild mammals caused by the maggot of a fly (**warble fly**); *also* : its maggot

war·bler \'wȯr-blər\ *n* **1** : SONGSTER **2** : any of various small slender-billed chiefly Old World songbirds related to the thrushes and noted for their singing **3** : any of numerous small bright-colored insect-eating American birds with a usu. weak and unmusical song

war·bon·net \'wȯr-ˌbä-nət\ *n* : a feathered American Indian ceremonial headdress

war crime *n* : a crime (as genocide) committed during or in connection with war

war cry **1** : a cry used by fighters in war **2** : a slogan used esp. to rally people to a cause

¹**ward** \'wȯrd\ *n* **1** : a guarding or being under guard or guardianship; *esp* : CUSTODY **2** : a body of guards **3** : a division of a prison **4** : a division in a hospital **5** : a division of a city for electoral or administrative purposes **6** : a person (as a child) under the protection of a guardian or a law court **7** : a person or body of persons under the protection or tutelage of a government **8** : a means of defense : PROTECTION

²**ward** *vb* : to turn aside : DEFLECT — usu. used with *off* ⟨~ off a blow⟩

¹**-ward** *also* **-wards** *adj suffix* **1** : that moves, tends, faces, or is directed toward ⟨wind*ward*⟩ **2** : that occurs or is situated in the direction of ⟨sea*ward*⟩

²**-ward** *or* **-wards** *adv suffix* **1** : in a (specified) direction ⟨up*wards*⟩ ⟨after*ward*⟩ **2** : toward a (specified) point, position, or area ⟨sky*ward*⟩

war dance *n* : a dance performed (as by American Indians) before going to war or in celebration of victory

war·den \'wȯr-d°n\ *n* **1** : GUARDIAN, KEEPER **2** : the governor of a town, district, or fortress **3** : an official charged with special supervisory or enforcement duties ⟨game ~⟩ ⟨air raid ~⟩ **4** : an official in charge of the operation of a prison **5** : one of two ranking lay officers of an Episcopal parish **6** : any of various British college officials

ward·er \'wȯr-dər\ *n* : WATCHMAN, WARDEN

ward heel·er \-ˌhē-lər\ *n* : a local worker for a political boss

ward·robe \'wȯr-ˌdrōb\ *n* [ME *warderobe*, fr. AF **warderobe, garderobe*, fr. *warder, garder* to guard + *robe* robe] **1** : a room or closet where clothes are kept; *also* : CLOTHESPRESS **2** : a collection of wearing apparel ⟨his summer ~⟩

ward·room \-ˌdrüm, -ˌdrum\ *n* : the dining area for officers aboard a warship

ward·ship \'wȯrd-ˌship\ *n* **1** : GUARDIANSHIP **2** : the state of being under care of a guardian

ware \'wer\ *n* **1** : manufactured articles or products of art or craft : GOODS ⟨glass*ware*⟩ **2** : an article of merchandise ⟨a peddler hawking his ~s⟩ **3** : items (as dishes) of fired clay : POTTERY

ware·house \-ˌhaüs\ *n* : a place for the storage of merchandise or commodities : STOREHOUSE — **warehouse** *vb* — **ware·house·man** \-mən\ *n* — **ware·hous·er** \-ˌhaü-zər, -sər\ *n*

ware·room \'wer-ˌrüm, -ˌrum\ *n* : a room in which goods are exhibited for sale

war·fare \'wȯr-ˌfer\ *n* **1** : military operations between enemies : WAR; *also* : an activity undertaken by one country to weaken or destroy another ⟨economic ~⟩ **2** : STRUGGLE, CONFLICT

war·fa·rin \'wȯr-fə-rən\ *n* : an anticoagulant compound used as a rodent poison and in medicine

war·head \'wȯr-ˌhed\ *n* : the section of a missile containing the charge

war·horse \-ˌhȯrs\ *n* **1** : a horse for use in war **2** : a veteran soldier or public person (as a politician) **3** : a musical composition that is often performed

war·like \-ˌlīk\ *adj* **1** : fond of war ⟨~ peoples⟩ **2** : of, relating to, or useful in war : MILITARY, MARTIAL ⟨~ supplies⟩ **3** : befitting or characteristic of war or of soldiers ⟨~ attitudes⟩

war·lock \-ˌläk\ *n* [ME *warloghe*, fr. OE *wǣrloga* one that breaks faith, the Devil, fr. *wǣr* faith, troth + *-loga* (fr. *lēogan* to lie)] : SORCERER, WIZARD

war·lord \-ˌlȯrd\ *n* **1** : a high military leader **2** : a military commander exercising local civil power by force ⟨former Chinese ~s⟩

¹**warm** \'wȯrm\ *adj* **1** : having or giving out heat to a moderate or adequate degree ⟨~ milk⟩ ⟨a ~ stove⟩ **2** : serving to retain heat ⟨~ clothes⟩ **3** : feeling or inducing sensations of heat ⟨~ from exercise⟩ ⟨a ~ climb⟩ **4** : showing or marked by strong feeling : ARDENT ⟨~ support⟩ **5** : marked by tense excitement or hot anger ⟨a ~ campaign⟩ **6** : giving a pleasant impression of warmth, cheerfulness, or friendliness ⟨~ colors⟩ ⟨a ~ tone of voice⟩ **7** : marked by or tending toward injury, distress, or pain ⟨made things ~ for the enemy⟩ **8** : newly made : FRESH ⟨a ~ scent⟩ **9** : near to a goal ⟨getting ~ in a search⟩ — **warm·ly** *adv*

²**warm** *vb* **1** : to make or become warm **2** : to give a feeling of warmth or vitality to **3** : to experience feelings of affection or pleasure ⟨she ~ed to her guest⟩ **4** : to reheat for eating ⟨~ed over the roast⟩ **5** : to make ready for operation or performance by preliminary exercise or operation ⟨~ up the motor⟩ **6** : to become increasingly ardent, interested, or competent ⟨the speaker ~ed to his topic⟩ — **warm·er** *n*

warm–blood·ed \-'blə-dəd\ *adj* : able to maintain a relatively high and constant body temperature relatively independent of that of the surroundings

warmed–over \'wȯrmd-'ō-vər\ *adj* **1** : REHEATED ⟨~ cabbage⟩ **2** : not fresh or new ⟨~ ideas⟩

warm front *n* : an advancing edge of a warm air mass

warm·heart·ed \'wȯrm-'här-təd\ *adj* : marked by warmth of feeling : CORDIAL — **warm·heart·ed·ness** *n*

warming pan *n* : a long-handled covered pan filled with live coals and formerly used to warm a bed

war·mon·ger \'wȯr-ˌməŋ-gər, -ˌmäŋ-\ *n* : one who urges or attempts to stir up war — **war·mon·ger·ing** \-g(ə-)riŋ\ *n*

warmth \'wȯrmth\ *n* **1** : the quality or state of being warm **2** : ZEAL, ARDOR, FERVOR

warm up *vb* : to engage in exercise or practice esp. before entering a game or contest — **warm–up** \'wȯrm-ˌəp\ *n*

warn \'wȯrn\ *vb* **1** : to put on guard : CAUTION; *also* : ADMONISH, COUNSEL **2** : to notify esp. in advance : INFORM **3** : to order to go or keep away

¹**warn·ing** \'wȯr-niŋ\ *n* **1** : the act of warning : the state of being warned **2** : something that warns or serves to warn ⟨a tornado ~⟩

²**warning** *adj* : serving as an alarm, signal, summons, or admonition ⟨a ~ bell⟩ — **warn·ing·ly** *adv*

¹**warp** \'wȯrp\ *n* **1** : the lengthwise threads on a loom or in a woven fabric **2** : a twist out of a true plane or straight line ⟨a ~ in a board⟩

²**warp** *vb* [ME, fr. OE *weorpan* to throw] **1** : to turn or twist out of shape; *also* : to become so twisted **2** : to lead astray : PERVERT; *also* : FALSIFY, DISTORT

war paint *n* : paint put on the face and body by American Indians as a sign of going to war

war·path \'wȯr-ˌpath, -ˌpäth\ *n* : the course taken by a party of American Indians going on a hostile expedition — **on the warpath** : ready to fight or argue

war·plane \-ˌplān\ *n* : a military airplane; *esp* : one armed for combat

warp speed *n* : the highest possible speed

¹**war·rant** \'wȯr-ənt, 'wär-\ *n* **1** : AUTHORIZATION; *also* : JUSTIFICATION, GROUND **2** : evidence (as a document) of authorization; *esp* : a legal writ authorizing an officer to take action (as in making an arrest, seizure, or search) **3** : a certificate of appointment issued to an officer of lower rank than a commissioned officer

²**warrant** *vb* **1** : to guarantee security or immunity to : SECURE **2** : to declare or maintain positively ⟨I ~ this is so⟩ **3** : to assure (a person) of the truth of what is said **4** : to guarantee to be as it appears or as it is represented ⟨~ goods as of the first quality⟩ **5** : SANCTION, AUTHORIZE **6** : to give proof of : ATTEST; *also* : GUARANTEE **7** : JUSTIFY ⟨his need ~s the expenditure⟩

warrant officer *n* **1** : an officer in the armed forces ranking next below a commissioned officer **2** : a commissioned officer ranking below an ensign in the navy or coast guard and below a second lieutenant in the marine corps

war·ran·ty \'wȯr-ən-tē, 'wär-\ *n, pl* **-ties** : an expressed or implied statement that some situation or thing is as it appears to be or is represented to be; *esp* : a usu. written guarantee of the integrity of a product and of the maker's responsibility for the repair or replacement of defective parts

war·ren \'wȯr-ən, 'wär-\ *n* **1** : an area where rabbits breed; *also* : a structure where rabbits are bred or kept **2** : a crowded tenement or district

war·rior \'wȯr-yər, 'wȯr-ē-ər, 'wär-\ *n* : a person engaged or experienced in warfare

war·ship \'wȯr-ˌship\ *n* : a naval vessel

wart \'wȯrt\ *n* **1** : a small usu. horny projecting growth on the skin; *esp* : one caused by a virus **2** : a protuberance resembling a wart (as on a plant) — **warty** *adj*

wart·hog \'wȯrt-ˌhȯg, -ˌhäg\ *n* : a wild African hog that has large tusks and in the male two pairs of rough warty protuberances below the eyes

warthog

war·time \'wȯr-ˌtīm\ *n* : a period during which a war is in progress

wary \'wer-ē\ *adj* **war·i·er; -est** : very cautious; *esp* : care-

ful in guarding against danger or deception — **war·i·ly** \'wer-ə-lē\ *adv* — **war·i·ness** \'wer-ē-nəs\ *n*

was *past 1st & 3d sing of* BE

wa·sa·bi \'wä-sə-bē; wä-'sä-\ *n* [Jp] : a condiment prepared from the ground greenish root of an Asian herb and similar in flavor and use to horseradish; *also* : the herb or its root

¹**wash** \'wȯsh, 'wäsh\ *vb* **1** : to clean with water and usu. soap or detergent ⟨~ clothes⟩ ⟨~ your hands⟩ **2** : to wet thoroughly : DRENCH **3** : to flow along the border of ⟨waves ~ the shore⟩ **4** : to pour or flow in a stream or current **5** : to move or remove by or as if by the action of water **6** : to cover or daub lightly with a liquid (as whitewash) **7** : to run water over (as gravel or ore) in order to separate valuable matter from refuse ⟨~ sand for gold⟩ **8** : to undergo laundering ⟨a dress that doesn't ~ well⟩ **9** : to stand a test ⟨that story will not ~⟩ **10** : to be worn away by water

²**wash** *n* **1** : the act or process or an instance of washing or being washed **2** : articles to be washed or being washed **3** : a thin coat of paint (as watercolor) **4** : the flow or action of a mass of water (as a wave) **5** : worthless esp. liquid waste : REFUSE, SWILL **6** : erosion by waves (as of the sea) **7** : a disturbance in a fluid (as water or the air) caused by the passage of a wing or propeller **8** *West* : the dry bed of a stream

³**wash** *adj* : WASHABLE

Wash *abbr* Washington

wash·able \'wȯ-shə-bəl, 'wä-\ *adj* : capable of being washed without damage — **wash·abil·i·ty** \ˌwȯ-shə-'bi-lə-tē, ˌwä-\ *n*

wash–and–wear *adj* : of, relating to, or being a fabric or garment that needs little or no ironing after washing

wash·ba·sin \'wȯsh-ˌbā-sᵊn, 'wäsh-\ *n* : WASHBOWL

wash·board \-ˌbȯrd\ *n* : a grooved board to scrub clothes on

wash·bowl \-ˌbōl\ *n* : a large bowl for water for washing hands and face

wash·cloth \-ˌklȯth\ *n* : a cloth used for washing one's face and body

washed–out \'wȯsht-'aút, 'wäsht-\ *adj* **1** : faded in color **2** : EXHAUSTED ⟨felt ~ after working all night⟩

washed–up \-'əp\ *adj* : no longer successful, popular, skillful, or needed

wash·er \'wȯ-shər, 'wä-\ *n* **1** : a ring or perforated plate used around a bolt or screw to ensure tightness or relieve friction **2** : one that washes; *esp* : a machine for washing

wash·er·wom·an \-ˌwu-mən\ *n* : a woman whose occupation is washing clothes

wash·ing \'wȯ-shiŋ, 'wä-\ *n* **1** : material obtained by washing **2** : articles washed or to be washed

washing soda *n* : SODIUM CARBONATE

Wash·ing·ton's Birthday \'wȯ-shiŋ-tənz-, 'wä-\ *n* : the 3d Monday in February observed as a legal holiday

wash·out \'wȯsh-ˌaút, 'wäsh-\ *n* **1** : the washing away of earth (as from a road); *also* : a place where earth is washed away **2** : a complete failure

wash·room \-ˌrüm, -ˌrúm\ *n* : BATHROOM

wash·stand \-ˌstand\ *n* **1** : a stand holding articles needed for washing face and hands **2** : LAVATORY 1

wash·tub \-ˌtəb\ *n* : a tub for washing or soaking clothes

wash·wom·an \'wȯsh-ˌwu-mən, 'wäsh-\ *n* : WASHERWOMAN

washy \'wȯ-shē, 'wä-\ *adj* **wash·i·er; -est** **1** : WEAK, WATERY **2** : PALLID ⟨a ~ yellow⟩ **3** : lacking in vigor, individuality, or definiteness

wasp \'wäsp, 'wȯsp\ *n* : any of numerous social or solitary winged insects related to the bees and ants with biting mouthparts and in females and workers an often formidable sting

WASP *or* **Wasp** *n* [*white Anglo-Saxon Protestant*] *sometimes disparaging* : an American of northern European and esp. British ancestry and of Protestant background

wasp·ish \'wäs-pish, 'wȯs-\ *adj* **1** : SNAPPISH, IRRITABLE ⟨a ~ temper⟩ **2** : resembling a wasp in form; *esp* : slightly built ◆ **Synonyms** FRACTIOUS, FRETFUL, HUFFY, PEEVISH, PETULANT, QUERULOUS

wasp waist *n* : a very slender waist

¹**was·sail** \'wä-səl, wä-'sāl\ *n* [ME *wæs hæil, washayl,* fr. ON *ves heill* be well] **1** : an early English toast to some-

one's health **2** : a hot drink made with wine, beer, or cider, spices, sugar, and usu. baked apples and traditionally served at Christmas **3** : riotous drinking : REVELRY
²**wassail** *vb* **1** : CAROUSE **2** : to drink to the health of — **was·sail·er** *n*
Was·ser·mann test \'wä-sər-mən-, 'vä-\ *n* : a blood test for the detection of syphilis
wast·age \'wā-stij\ *n* : WASTE 3
¹**waste** \'wāst\ *n* **1** : a sparsely settled or barren region : DESERT; *also* : uncultivated land **2** : the act or an instance of wasting : the state of being wasted **3** : gradual loss or decrease by use, wear, or decay **4** : material left over, rejected, or thrown away; *also* : an unwanted by-product of a manufacturing or chemical process **5** : refuse (as garbage) that accumulates about habitations **6** : material (as feces) produced but not used by a living organism — **waste·ful** \-fəl\ *adj* — **waste·ful·ly** *adv* — **waste·ful·ness** *n*
²**waste** *vb* **wast·ed; wast·ing 1** : DEVASTATE **2** : to wear away or diminish gradually : CONSUME **3** : to spend or use carelessly or uselessly : SQUANDER **4** : to lose or cause to lose weight, strength, or energy ⟨*wasting* away from fever⟩ **5** : to become diminished in bulk or substance : DWINDLE ♦ **Synonyms** DEPREDATE, DESOLATE, DESPOIL, RAVAGE, SPOIL, STRIP — **wast·er** *n*
³**waste** *adj* **1** : being wild and uninhabited : BARREN, DESOLATE; *also* : UNCULTIVATED **2** : being in a ruined condition **3** : discarded as worthless after being used ⟨~ water⟩ **4** : excreted from or stored in inert form in a living organism as a by-product of vital activity ⟨~ matter from birds⟩
waste·bas·ket \'wāst-bas-kət\ *n* : a receptacle for refuse
waste·land \-land, -lənd\ *n* : land that is barren or unfit for cultivation
waste·pa·per \-'pā-pər\ *n* : paper thrown away as used, not needed, or not fit for use
wast·rel \'wā-strəl\ *n* : a person who wastes resources : SPENDTHRIFT
¹**watch** \'wäch, 'wȯch\ *vb* **1** : to be or stay awake intentionally : keep vigil ⟨~ed by the patient's bedside⟩ : to wake and pray⟩ **2** : to be on the lookout for danger : be on one's guard **3** : to keep guard ⟨~ outside the door⟩ **4** : OBSERVE ⟨~ a game⟩ **5** : to keep in view so as to prevent harm or warn of danger ⟨~ a brush fire carefully⟩ **6** : to keep oneself informed about ⟨~ his progress⟩ **7** : to lie in wait for esp. so as to take advantage of ⟨~ed her opportunity⟩ — **watch·er** *n*
²**watch** *n* **1** : the act of keeping awake to guard, protect, or attend; *also* : a state of alert and continuous attention **2** : a public weather alert ⟨a winter storm ~⟩ **3** : close observation **4** : LOOKOUT, WATCHMAN, GUARD **5** : a period during which a part of a ship's crew is on duty; *also* : the part of a crew on duty during a watch **6** : a portable timepiece carried on the person
watch·band \'wäch-band, 'wȯch-\ *n* : the bracelet or strap of a wristwatch
watch·dog \-dȯg\ *n* **1** : a dog kept to guard property **2** : one that guards or protects
watch·ful \-fəl\ *adj* : steadily attentive and alert esp. to danger : VIGILANT — **watch·ful·ly** *adv* — **watch·ful·ness** *n*
watch·mak·er \-mā-kər\ *n* : a person who makes or repairs watches — **watch·mak·ing** \-mā-kiŋ\ *n*
watch·man \-mən\ *n* : a person assigned to watch : GUARD
watch night *n* : a devotional service lasting until after midnight esp. on New Year's Eve
watch·tow·er \'wäch-taù(-ə)r, 'wȯch-\ *n* : a tower for a lookout
watch·word \-wərd\ *n* **1** : a secret word used as a signal or sign of recognition **2** : a word or motto used as a slogan or rallying cry
¹**wa·ter** \'wȯ-tər, 'wä-\ *n* **1** : the liquid that descends as rain and forms rivers, lakes, and seas **2** : a natural mineral water — usu. used in pl. **3** *pl* : the water occupying or flowing in a particular bed; *also* : a band of seawater bordering on and under the control of a country **4** : any of various liquids containing or resembling water; *esp* : a watery fluid (as tears, urine, or sap) formed or circulating in a living organism **5** : a specified degree of thoroughness or completeness ⟨a scoundrel of the first ~⟩

²**water** *vb* **1** : to supply with or get or take water ⟨~ horses⟩ ⟨the ship ~ed at each port⟩ **2** : to treat (as cloth) so as to give a lustrous appearance in wavy lines **3** : to dilute by or as if by adding water to **4** : to form or secrete water or watery matter ⟨her eyes ~ed⟩ ⟨my mouth ~ed⟩
wa·ter·bed \'wȯ-tər-bed, 'wä-\ *n* : a bed whose mattress is a watertight bag filled with water
wa·ter·borne \-bȯrn\ *adj* : supported, carried, or transmitted by water
water buffalo *n* : a common oxlike often domesticated Asian bovine
water chestnut *n* : a whitish crunchy vegetable used esp. in Chinese cooking that is the peeled tuber of a widely cultivated Asian sedge; *also* : the tuber or the sedge itself
water closet *n* : a compartment or room with a toilet bowl : BATHROOM; *also* : a toilet bowl along with its accessories
wa·ter·col·or \'wȯ-tər-kə-lər, 'wä-\ *n* **1** : a paint whose liquid part is water **2** : the art of painting with watercolors **3** : a picture made with watercolors
wa·ter·course \-kȯrs\ *n* : a stream of water; *also* : the bed of a stream
wa·ter·craft \-kraft\ *n* : a craft for water transport : SHIP, BOAT
wa·ter·cress \-kres\ *n* : an aquatic perennial Eurasian cress that is naturalized in the U.S. and has edible leaves used esp. in salads
wa·ter·fall \-fȯl\ *n* : a very steep descent of the water of a stream
wa·ter·fowl \'wȯ-tər-faù(-ə)l, 'wä-\ *n, pl* **-fowl** *also* **-fowls** : a bird that frequents water; *esp* : a swimming bird (as a duck) hunted as game
wa·ter·front \-frənt\ *n* : land or a section of a town fronting or abutting on a body of water
water gap *n* : a pass in a mountain ridge through which a stream runs
water glass *n* : a drinking glass
water hyacinth *n* : a showy floating aquatic plant of tropical America that often clogs waterways (as in the southern U.S.)
watering hole *n* : a place (as a bar) where people gather socially
watering place *n* : a resort that features mineral springs or bathing
water lily *n* : any of various aquatic plants with floating roundish leaves and showy solitary flowers
wa·ter·line \'wȯ-tər-līn, 'wä-\ *n* : a line that marks the level of the surface of water on something (as a ship or the shore)
wa·ter·logged \-lȯgd, -lägd\ *adj* : so filled or soaked with water as to be heavy or unmanageable ⟨a ~ boat⟩
wa·ter·loo \wȯ-tər-'lü, wä-\ *n, pl* **-loos** [*Waterloo,* Belgium, scene of Napoleon's defeat in 1815] : a decisive or final defeat or setback
¹**wa·ter·mark** \'wȯ-tər-märk, 'wä-\ *n* **1** : a mark indicating height to which water has risen **2** : a marking in paper visible when the paper is held up to the light
²**watermark** *vb* : to mark (paper) with a watermark
wa·ter·mel·on \-me-lən\ *n* : a large roundish or oblong fruit with sweet juicy usu. red pulp; *also* : a widely grown African vine related to the squashes that produces watermelons
water moccasin *n* : a venomous pit viper chiefly of the southeastern U.S. that is related to the copperhead
water ou·zel \-'ü-zəl\ *n* : DIPPER 1
water park *n* : an amusement park with a pool and wetted slides
water pill *n* : DIURETIC
water pipe *n* : a pipe for smoking that has a long flexible tube whereby the smoke is cooled by passing through water
water pistol *n* : a toy pistol for squirting a jet of liquid
water polo *n* : a team game played in a swimming pool with a ball resembling a soccer ball
wa·ter·pow·er \'wȯ-tər-paù(-ə)r, 'wä-\ *n* : the power of moving water used to run machinery
¹**wa·ter·proof** \'wȯ-tər-prüf, 'wä-\ *adj* : not letting water through; *esp* : covered or treated with a material to prevent permeation by water — **wa·ter·proof·ing** *n*
²**waterproof** *n* **1** : a waterproof fabric **2** *chiefly Brit* : RAINCOAT

³**waterproof** *vb* : to make waterproof
wa·ter·re·pel·lent \ˌwȯ-tər-ri-'pe-lənt, ˌwä-\ *adj* : treated with a finish that is resistant to water penetration
wa·ter·re·sis·tant \-ri-'zis-tənt\ *adj* : WATER-REPELLENT
wa·ter·shed \'wȯ-tər-ˌshed, 'wä-\ *n* 1 : a dividing ridge between two drainage areas 2 : the region or area drained by a particular body of water
wa·ter·side \-ˌsīd\ *n* : the land bordering a body of water
water ski *n* : a ski used on water when the wearer is towed — **wa·ter·ski** *vb* — **wa·ter·ski·er** \-ˌskē-ər\ *n*
water snake *n* : any of various snakes found in or near freshwater and feeding largely on aquatic animals
wa·ter·spout \'wȯ-tər-ˌspau̇t, 'wä-\ *n* 1 : a pipe for carrying water from a roof 2 : a funnel-shaped cloud extending from a cloud down to a spray torn up by whirling winds from an ocean or lake
water strider *n* : any of various long-legged bugs that move about swiftly on the surface of water
water table *n* : the upper limit of the portion of the ground wholly saturated with water
wa·ter·tight \ˌwȯ-tər-'tīt, ˌwä-\ *adj* 1 : constructed so as to keep water out 2 : allowing no possibility for doubt or uncertainty ⟨a ~ case against the accused⟩
wa·ter·way \'wȯ-tər-ˌwā, 'wä-\ *n* : a navigable body of water
wa·ter·wheel \-ˌhwēl, -ˌwēl\ *n* : a wheel made to turn by water flowing against it
water wings *n pl* : an air-filled device to give support to a person's body esp. when learning to swim
wa·ter·works \'wȯ-tər-ˌwərks, 'wä-\ *n pl* : a system for supplying water (as to a city)
wa·tery \'wȯ-tə-rē, 'wä-\ *adj* 1 : containing, full of, or giving out water ⟨~ clouds⟩ 2 : being like water : THIN, WEAK ⟨~ lemonade⟩; *also* : being soft and soggy ⟨~ turnips⟩
WATS \'wäts\ *abbr* Wide-Area Telecommunications Service
watt \'wät\ *n* [James *Watt* †1819 Scottish engineer and inventor] : the metric unit of power equal to the work done at the rate of one joule per second or to the power produced by a current of one ampere across a potential difference of one volt
watt·age \'wä-tij\ *n* : amount of power expressed in watts
wat·tle \'wä-t³l\ *n* 1 : a framework of rods with flexible branches or reeds interlaced used esp. formerly in building; *also* : material for this framework 2 : a naked fleshy process hanging usu. from the head or neck (as of a bird) — **wat·tled** \-t³ld\ *adj*
W Aust *abbr* Western Australia
¹**wave** \'wāv\ *vb* **waved; wav·ing** 1 : FLUTTER ⟨flags *waving* in the breeze⟩ 2 : to motion with the hands or with something held in them in signal or salute 3 : to become moved or brandished to-and-fro; *also* : BRANDISH, FLOURISH ⟨~ a sword⟩ 4 : to move before the wind with a wavelike motion ⟨fields of *waving* grain⟩ 5 : to curve up and down like a wave : UNDULATE
²**wave** *n* 1 : a moving ridge or swell on the surface of water 2 : a wavelike formation or shape ⟨a ~ in the hair⟩ 3 : the action or process of making wavy or curly 4 : a waving motion; *esp* : a signal made by waving something 5 : FLOW, GUSH ⟨a ~ of anger swept over her⟩ 6 : a peak of activity ⟨a ~ of selling⟩ 7 : a disturbance that transfers energy progressively from point to point in a medium ⟨light travels in ~s⟩ ⟨a sound ~⟩ 8 : a period of hot or cold weather — **wave·like** *adj*
wave·length \'wāv-ˌleŋth\ *n* 1 : the distance in the line of advance of a wave from any one point (as a crest) to the next corresponding point 2 : a line of thought that reveals a common understanding
wave·let \-lət\ *n* : a little wave : RIPPLE
wa·ver \'wā-vər\ *vb* 1 : to fluctuate in opinion, allegiance, or direction 2 : REEL, TOTTER; *also* : QUIVER, FLICKER ⟨~ing flames⟩ 3 : FALTER 4 : to give an unsteady sound : QUAVER ♦ **Synonyms** FALTER, HESITATE, SHILLY-SHALLY, VACILLATE — **waver** *n* — **wa·ver·er** *n* — **wa·ver·ing·ly** *adv*
wavy \'wā-vē\ *adj* **wav·i·er; -est** : having waves : moving in waves
¹**wax** \'waks\ *n* 1 : a yellowish plastic substance secreted by bees for constructing the honeycomb 2 : any of various substances like beeswax

²**wax** *vb* : to treat or rub with wax — **wax·er** *n*
³**wax** *vb* 1 : to increase in size, numbers, strength, volume, or duration 2 : to increase in apparent size ⟨the moon ~es toward the full⟩ 3 : to take on a quality or state : BECOME ⟨~ed indignant⟩ ⟨the party ~ed merry⟩
wax bean *n* : a kidney bean with pods that turn creamy yellow to bright yellow when mature enough to use as snap beans
wax·en \'wak-sən\ *adj* 1 : made of or covered with wax 2 : resembling wax (as in color or consistency)
wax museum *n* : a place where wax effigies are exhibited
wax myrtle *n* : any of a genus of shrubs or trees with aromatic leaves; *esp* : an evergreen shrub or small tree of the eastern U.S. that produces small hard berries with a thick coating of bluish-white wax used for candles
wax·wing \'waks-ˌwiŋ\ *n* : any of a genus of chiefly brown to gray singing birds with a showy crest and red waxy material on the tips of some wing feathers
wax·work \-ˌwərk\ *n* 1 : an effigy usu. of a person in wax 2 *pl* : an exhibition of wax figures
waxy \'wak-sē\ *adj* **wax·i·er; -est** 1 : made of or full of wax 2 : WAXEN 2
way \'wā\ *n* 1 : a thoroughfare for travel or passage : ROAD, PATH, STREET 2 : ROUTE ⟨knew the ~ home⟩ 3 : a course of action ⟨chose the easy ~⟩; *also* : opportunity, capability, or fact of doing as one pleases ⟨always had your own ~⟩ 4 : a possible course : POSSIBILITY ⟨no two ~s about it⟩ 5 : METHOD, MODE ⟨this ~ of thinking⟩ ⟨a new ~ of painting⟩ 6 : FEATURE, RESPECT ⟨a good worker in many ~s⟩ 7 : the usual or characteristic state of affairs ⟨as is the ~ with old people⟩; *also* : individual characteristic or peculiarity ⟨used to her ~s⟩ 8 : DISTANCE ⟨a short ~ from here⟩ ⟨a long ~ from success⟩ 9 : progress along a course ⟨working my ~ through college⟩ 10 : something having direction : LOCALITY ⟨out our ~⟩ 11 : STATE, CONDITION ⟨the ~ things are⟩ 12 *pl* : an inclined structure upon which a ship is built or is supported in launching 13 : CATEGORY, KIND ⟨get what you need in the ~ of supplies⟩ 14 : motion or speed of a boat through the water — **by the way** : by way of interjection or digression — **by way of** 1 : for the purpose of ⟨*by way of* illustration⟩ 2 : by the route through : VIA — **out of the way** 1 : WRONG, IMPROPER 2 : SECLUDED, REMOTE
way·bill \'wā-ˌbil\ *n* : a paper that accompanies a freight shipment and gives details of goods, route, and charges
way·far·er \'wā-ˌfer-ər\ *n* : a traveler esp. on foot — **way·far·ing** \-ˌfer-iŋ\ *adj*
way·lay \'wā-ˌlā\ *vb* **-laid** \-ˌlād\; **-lay·ing** : to lie in wait for or attack from ambush
way-out \'wā-'au̇t\ *adj* : FAR-OUT
-ways *adv suffix* : in (such) a way, course, direction, or manner ⟨sideways⟩
ways and means *n pl* : methods and resources esp. for raising revenues needed by a state; *also* : a legislative committee concerned with this function
way·side \'wā-ˌsīd\ *n* : the side of or land adjacent to a road or path
way station *n* : an intermediate station on a line of travel (as a railroad)
way·ward \'wā-wərd\ *adj* [ME, short for *awayward* turned away, fr. *away*, adv. + *-ward* directed toward] 1 : following one's own capricious or wanton inclinations ⟨~ children⟩ 2 : UNPREDICTABLE, IRREGULAR ⟨a ~ act⟩
WBC *abbr* white blood cells
WC *abbr* 1 water closet 2 without charge
WCTU *abbr* Women's Christian Temperance Union
we \'wē\ *pron* 1 — used of a group that includes the speaker or writer 2 — used for the singular *I* by a monarch, editor, or writer
weak \'wēk\ *adj* 1 : lacking strength or vigor : FEEBLE 2 : not able to sustain or resist much weight, pressure, or strain 3 : deficient in vigor of mind or character; *also* : resulting from or indicative of such deficiency ⟨a ~ policy⟩ ⟨a ~ will⟩ 4 : not supported by truth or logic ⟨a ~ argument⟩ 5 : lacking skill or proficiency; *also* : indicative of a lack of skill or aptitude 6 : lacking vigor of expression or effect 7 : of less than usual strength ⟨~ tea⟩ 8 : not having or exerting authority ⟨~ government⟩; *also* : INEFFECTIVE, IMPOTENT ⟨~ measures to control crime⟩ 9 : of, relating to, or con-

stituting a verb or verb conjugation that forms the past tense and past participle by adding *-ed* or *-d* or *-t* — **weak·ly** *adv*

weak·en \'wē-kən\ *vb* : to make or become weak ⟨bodies ∼*ed* by hunger⟩ ✦ *Synonyms* ENFEEBLE, DEBILITATE, UNDERMINE, SAP, CRIPPLE, DISABLE

weak·fish \'wēk-ˌfish\ *n* [obs. D *weekvis*, fr. D *week* soft + *vis* fish] : a common marine fish of the Atlantic coast of the U.S. caught for food and sport; *also* : any of several related food fishes

weak force *n* : the physical force responsible for particle decay processes in radioactivity

weak–kneed \'wēk-'nēd\ *adj* : lacking willpower or resolution ⟨∼ appeasers⟩

weak·ling \'wē-klin\ *n* : a person who is physically, mentally, or morally weak

weak·ly \'wē-klē\ *adj* : FEEBLE, WEAK

weak·ness \'wēk-nəs\ *n* **1** : the quality or state of being weak; *also* : an instance or period of being weak ⟨in a moment of ∼ he agreed to go⟩ **2** : FAULT, DEFECT **3** : an object of special desire or fondness ⟨chocolate is her ∼⟩

¹weal \'wēl\ *n* : WELL-BEING, PROSPERITY

²weal *n* : WELT

weald \'wēld\ *n* [The *Weald*, wooded district in England, fr. ME *Weeld*, fr. OE *weald* forest] **1** : FOREST **2** : WOLD

wealth \'welth\ *n* [ME *welthe* welfare, prosperity, fr. *wele* weal] **1** : abundance of possessions or resources : AFFLUENCE, RICHES **2** : abundant supply : PROFUSION ⟨a ∼ of detail⟩ **3** : all property that has a money or an exchange value; *also* : all objects or resources that have economic value ✦ *Synonyms* FORTUNE, PROPERTY, SUBSTANCE, WORTH

wealthy \'wel-thē\ *adj* **wealth·i·er; -est** : having wealth : RICH

wean \'wēn\ *vb* **1** : to accustom (a young mammal) to take food by means other than nursing **2** : to free from a source of dependence; *also* : to free from a usu. unwholesome habit or interest

weap·on \'we-pən\ *n* **1** : something (as a gun, knife, or club) used to injure, defeat, or destroy **2** : a means of contending against another ⟨a ∼ against cancer⟩ — **weap·on·less** \-ləs\ *adj*

weap·on·ry \-rē\ *n* : WEAPONS

¹wear \'wear\ *vb* **wore** \'wòr\; **worn** \'wòrn\; **wear·ing** **1** : to use as an article of clothing or adornment ⟨∼ a coat⟩ ⟨∼*s* earrings⟩; *also* : to carry on the person ⟨∼ a gun⟩ **2** : EXHIBIT, PRESENT ⟨∼ a smile⟩ **3** : to impair, diminish, or decay by use or by scraping or rubbing ⟨clothes *worn* to shreds⟩; *also* : to produce gradually by friction, rubbing, or wasting away ⟨∼ a hole in the rug⟩ **4** : to exhaust or lessen the strength of : WEARY, FATIGUE ⟨*worn* by care and toil⟩ **5** : to endure use : last under use or the passage of time ⟨this cloth ∼*s* well⟩ **6** : to diminish or fail with the passage of time ⟨the day ∼*s* on⟩ ⟨the effect of the drug *wore* off⟩ **7** : to grow or become by attrition, use, or age ⟨the coin was *worn* thin⟩ — **wear·able** \'wer-ə-bəl\ *adj* — **wear·er** *n*

²wear *n* **1** : the act of wearing : the state of being worn ⟨clothes for everyday ∼⟩ **2** : clothing usu. of a particular kind or for a special occasion or use ⟨children's ∼⟩ **3** : wearing or lasting quality ⟨the coat still has lots of ∼ in it⟩ **4** : the result of wearing or use : impairment due to use ⟨the suit shows ∼⟩

wear and tear *n* : the loss, injury, or stress to which something is subjected in the course of use; *esp* : normal depreciation

wear down *vb* : to weary and overcome by persistent resistance or pressure

wea·ri·some \'wir-ē-səm\ *adj* : causing weariness : TIRESOME — **wea·ri·some·ly** *adv* — **wea·ri·some·ness** *n*

wear out *vb* **1** : TIRE **2** : to make or become useless by wear

¹wea·ry \'wir-ē\ *adj* **wea·ri·er; -est** **1** : worn out in strength, energy, or freshness **2** : expressing or characteristic of weariness ⟨a ∼ sigh⟩ **3** : having one's patience, tolerance, or pleasure exhausted ⟨∼ of war⟩ — **wea·ri·ly** \'wir-ə-lē\ *adv* — **wea·ri·ness** \-ē-nəs\ *n*

²weary *vb* **wea·ried; wea·ry·ing** : to become or make weary : TIRE

¹wea·sel \'wē-zəl\ *n, pl* **weasels** : any of various small slender flesh-eating mammals related to the minks — **wea·sel·ly** *also* **wea·sely** \'wēz-lē, 'wē-zə-lē\ *adj*

²weasel *vb* **wea·seled; wea·sel·ing** **1** : to use weasel words : EQUIVOCATE **2** : to escape from or evade a situation or obligation — often used with *out*

weasel word *n* [fr. the weasel's reputed habit of sucking the contents out of an egg while leaving the shell intact] : a word used to avoid a direct or forthright statement or position

¹weath·er \'we-thər\ *n* **1** : the state of the atmosphere with respect to heat or cold, wetness or dryness, calm or storm, clearness or cloudiness **2** : a particular and esp. a disagreeable atmospheric state : RAIN, STORM

²weather *vb* **1** : to expose to or endure the action of weather; *also* : to alter (as in color or texture) by such exposure **2** : to bear up against successfully ⟨∼ a storm⟩ ⟨∼ troubles⟩

³weather *adj* : WINDWARD

weath·er–beat·en \'we-thər-ˌbē-t°n\ *adj* : worn or damaged by exposure to the weather; *also* : toughened or tanned by the weather ⟨∼ face⟩

weath·er·cock \-ˌkäk\ *n* : a weather vane shaped like a rooster

weath·er·ing \'we-thə-rin\ *n* : the action of the weather in altering the color, texture, composition, or form of exposed objects; *also* : alteration thus effected

weath·er·ize \'we-thə-ˌrīz\ *vb* **-ized; -iz·ing** : to make (as a house) better protected against winter weather (as by adding insulation)

weath·er·man \-ˌman\ *n* : one who reports and forecasts the weather : METEOROLOGIST

weath·er·per·son \-ˌpər-sən\ *n* : a person who reports and forecasts the weather : METEOROLOGIST

weath·er·proof \'we-thər-ˌprüf\ *adj* : able to withstand exposure to weather — **weatherproof** *vb*

weath·er·strip·ping \'we-thər-ˌstri-pin\ *n* : material used to seal a door or window at the edges — **weath·er–strip** *vb* — **weather strip** *n*

weather vane *n* : VANE 1

weath·er·worn \'we-thər-ˌwórn\ *adj* : worn by exposure to the weather

¹weave \'wēv\ *vb* **wove** \'wōv\ *or* **weaved; wo·ven** \'wō-vən\ *or* **weaved; weav·ing** **1** : to form by interlacing strands of material; *esp* : to make on a loom by interlacing warp and filling threads ⟨∼ cloth⟩ **2** : to interlace (as threads) into a fabric and esp. cloth **3** : SPIN 2 **4** : to make as if by weaving together parts **5** : to insert as a part : work in **6** : to move in a winding or zigzag course esp. to avoid obstacles ⟨we *wove* our way through the crowd⟩ — **weav·er** *n*

²weave *n* : something woven; *also* : a pattern or method of weaving ⟨a loose ∼⟩

¹web \'web\ *n* **1** : a fabric on a loom or coming from a loom **2** : COBWEB; *also* : SNARE, ENTANGLEMENT ⟨caught in a ∼ of deceit⟩ **3** : an animal or plant membrane; *esp* : one uniting the toes (as in many birds) **4** : NETWORK ⟨a ∼ of highways⟩ **5** : the series of barbs on each side of the shaft of a feather **6** : WORLD WIDE WEB — **webbed** \'webd\ *adj*

²web *vb* **webbed; web·bing** **1** : to make a web **2** : to cover or provide with webs or a network **3** : ENTANGLE, ENSNARE

web·bing \'we-bin\ *n* : a strong closely woven tape designed for bearing weight and used esp. for straps, harness, or upholstery

web·cam \'web-ˌkam\ *n* : a camera used in transmitting live images over the World Wide Web

web·cast \'web-ˌkast\ *n* : a transmission of sound and images via the World Wide Web — **webcast** *vb*

web–foot·ed \'web-'fú-təd\ *adj* : having webbed feet

web·log \'web-ˌlòg, -ˌläg\ *n* : BLOG

web·mas·ter \'web-ˌmas-tər\ *n, often cap* : a person responsible for the creation or maintenance of a website

web page *n* : ³PAGE 2

web·site *or* **Web site** \'web-ˌsīt\ *n* : a group of World Wide Web pages made available online (as by an individual or business)

wed \'wed\ *vb* **wed·ded** *also* **wed; wed·ding** **1** : to take, give, enter into, or join in marriage : MARRY **2** : to unite firmly

Wed *abbr* Wednesday

wed·ding \'we-diŋ\ n 1 : a marriage ceremony usu. with accompanying festivities : NUPTIALS 2 : a joining in close association 3 : a wedding anniversary or its celebration

¹**wedge** \'wej\ n 1 : a piece of wood or metal that tapers to a thin edge and is used to split logs or rocks or to raise heavy weights 2 : something (as an action or policy) that serves to open up a way for a breach, change, or intrusion 3 : a wedge-shaped object or part ⟨a ~ of pie⟩

²**wedge** vb **wedged; wedg·ing** 1 : to hold firm by or as if by driving in a wedge 2 : to force (something) into a narrow space

wed·lock \'wed-,läk\ n [ME wedlok, fr. OE wedlāc marriage bond, fr. wedd pledge + -lāc, suffix denoting activity] : the state of being married : MARRIAGE, MATRIMONY

Wednes·day \'wenz-(,)dā, -dē\ n [ME, fr. OE wōdensdæg, lit., day of Woden (supreme god of the pagan Anglo-Saxons)] : the 4th day of the week

wee \'wē\ adj [ME (Sc) we, fr. we, n., little bit, fr. OE wǣge weight] 1 : very small : TINY 2 : very early ⟨~ hours of the morning⟩

¹**weed** \'wēd\ n 1 : a plant that tends to grow thickly where it is not wanted and to choke out more desirable plants 2 : MARIJUANA

²**weed** vb 1 : to clear of or remove weeds or something harmful, inferior, or superfluous ⟨~ a garden⟩ 2 : to get rid of ⟨~ out the troublemakers⟩ — **weed·er** n

³**weed** n : mourning clothes — usu. used in pl. ⟨widow's ~s⟩

weedy \'wē-dē\ adj 1 : full of weeds 2 : resembling a weed esp. in vigor of growth or spread 3 : noticeably lean and scrawny : LANKY

week \'wēk\ n 1 : seven successive days; esp : a calendar period of seven days beginning with Sunday and ending with Saturday 2 : the working or school days of the calendar week

week·day \'wēk-,dā\ n : a day of the week except Sunday or sometimes except Saturday and Sunday

¹**week·end** \-,end\ n : the period between the close of one working or business or school week and the beginning of the next

²**weekend** vb : to spend the weekend

¹**week·ly** \'wē-klē\ adj 1 : occurring, appearing, or done every week 2 : computed in terms of one week ⟨~ rental rates⟩ — **weekly** adv

²**weekly** n, pl **weeklies** : a weekly publication

ween \'wēn\ vb, archaic : SUPPOSE 3

wee·ny \'wē-nē\ also **ween·sy** \'wēn-sē\ adj : exceptionally small

weep \'wēp\ vb **wept** \'wept\; **weep·ing** 1 : to express emotion and esp. sorrow by shedding tears : BEWAIL, CRY 2 : to give off fluid slowly : OOZE — **weep·er** n

weeping adj 1 : TEARFUL ⟨~ gratitude⟩ 2 : having slender drooping branches

weeping willow n : a willow with slender drooping branches

weepy \'wē-pē\ adj : inclined to weep

wee·vil \'wē-vəl\ n : any of a large group of beetles having a long head usu. curved into a snout and including many whose larvae are destructive plant-feeding pests — **wee·vily** or **wee·vil·ly** \'wē-və-lē\ adj

weft \'weft\ n 1 : a filling thread or yarn in weaving 2 : WEB, FABRIC; also : something woven

¹**weigh** \'wā\ vb [ME weyen, fr. OE wegan to move, carry, weigh] 1 : to find the heaviness of 2 : to have weight or a specified weight 3 : to consider carefully : PONDER 4 : to merit consideration as important : COUNT ⟨evidence ~ing against him⟩ 5 : to raise before sailing ⟨~ anchor⟩ 6 : to press down with or as if with a heavy weight

²**weigh** n [alter. of way] : WAY — used in the phrase under weigh

¹**weight** \'wāt\ n 1 : the amount that something weighs; also : the standard amount that something should weigh 2 : a quantity or object weighing a usu. specified amount 3 : a unit (as a pound or kilogram) of weight or mass; also : a system of such units 4 : a heavy object for holding or pressing something down; also : a heavy object for throwing or lifting in an athletic contest 5 : a mental or emotional burden 6 : IMPORTANCE; also : INFLUENCE

⟨threw his ~ around⟩ 7 : overpowering force 8 : relative thickness (as of a textile) ⟨summer-weight clothes⟩
♦ **Synonyms** SIGNIFICANCE, MOMENT, CONSEQUENCE, IMPORT, AUTHORITY, PRESTIGE, CREDIT

☞ the U.S. WEIGHTS AND MEASURES table is on page 572

²**weight** vb 1 : to oppress with a burden ⟨~ed down with cares⟩ 2 : to load with or as if with a weight

weight·less \'wāt-ləs\ adj : having little weight : lacking apparent gravitational pull ⟨a ~ environment⟩ — **weight·less·ly** adv — **weight·less·ness** n

weighty \'wā-tē\ adj **weight·i·er; -est** 1 : of much importance or consequence : MOMENTOUS, SERIOUS ⟨~ problems⟩ 2 : SOLEMN ⟨a ~ manner⟩ 3 : HEAVY 4 : POWERFUL, TELLING ⟨~ arguments⟩

weiner var of WIENER

weir \'wer, 'wir\ n 1 : a fence set in a waterway for catching fish 2 : a dam in a stream to raise the water level or divert its flow

weird \'wird\ adj [ME wird, werd fate, destiny, fr. OE wyrd] 1 : MAGICAL 2 : ODD, UNUSUAL ⟨~ noises⟩ ♦ **Synonyms** EERIE, UNCANNY, SPOOKY — **weird·ly** adv — **weird·ness** n

weirdo \'wir-(,)dō\ n, pl **weird·os** : a person who is extraordinarily strange or eccentric

Welch var of WELSH

¹**wel·come** \'wel-kəm\ vb **wel·comed; wel·com·ing** 1 : to greet cordially or courteously 2 : to accept, meet, or face with pleasure ⟨he ~s criticism⟩

²**welcome** adj 1 : received gladly into one's presence ⟨a ~ visitor⟩ 2 : giving pleasure : PLEASING ⟨~ news⟩ 3 : willingly permitted or admitted ⟨all are ~ to use the books⟩ 4 — used in the phrase "You're welcome" as a reply to an expression of thanks

³**welcome** n 1 : a cordial greeting or reception 2 : the state of being welcome ⟨overstayed their ~⟩

weld \'weld\ vb 1 : to unite (metal or plastic parts) either by heating and allowing the parts to flow together or by hammering or pressing together 2 : to unite closely or intimately ⟨~ed together in friendship⟩ — **weld·er** n

²**weld** n 1 : a welded joint 2 : union by welding

wel·fare \'wel-,fer\ n 1 : the state of doing well esp. in respect to happiness, well-being, or prosperity 2 : aid in the form of money or necessities for those in need; also : the agency through which the aid is given

welfare state n : a nation or state that assumes primary responsibility for the individual and social welfare of its citizens

wel·kin \'wel-kən\ n : SKY; also : AIR

¹**well** \'wel\ n 1 : a spring with its pool : FOUNTAIN; also : a source of supply ⟨a ~ of information⟩ 2 : a hole sunk in the earth to obtain a natural deposit (as of water, oil, or gas) 3 : an open space (as for a staircase) extending vertically through floors of a structure 4 : something suggesting a well

²**well** vb : to rise up and flow out

³**well** adv **bet·ter** \'be-tər\; **best** \'best\ 1 : in a good or proper manner : RIGHTLY; also : EXCELLENTLY, SKILLFULLY 2 : SATISFACTORILY, FORTUNATELY ⟨the party turned out ~⟩ 3 : ABUNDANTLY ⟨eat ~⟩ 4 : with reason or courtesy : PROPERLY ⟨I cannot ~ refuse⟩ 5 : COMPLETELY, FULLY, QUITE ⟨~ worth the price⟩ ⟨well-hidden⟩ 6 : INTIMATELY, CLOSELY ⟨I know him ~⟩ 7 : CONSIDERABLY, FAR ⟨~ over a million⟩ ⟨~ ahead⟩ 8 : without trouble or difficulty ⟨we could ~ have gone⟩ 9 : EXACTLY, DEFINITELY ⟨remember it ~⟩

⁴**well** adj 1 : PROSPEROUS; also : being in satisfactory condition or circumstances 2 : SATISFACTORY, PLEASING ⟨all is ~⟩ 3 : ADVISABLE, DESIRABLE ⟨it is not ~ to anger him⟩ 4 : free or recovered from ill health : HEALTHY 5 : FORTUNATE ⟨it is ~ that this has happened⟩

well-ad·just·ed \,wel-ə-'jəs-təd\ adj : WELL-BALANCED 2

well-ad·vised \-əd-'vīzd\ adj 1 : PRUDENT ⟨~ restraint⟩ 2 : resulting from, based on, or showing careful deliberation or wise counsel ⟨~ plans⟩

well-ap·point·ed \-ə-'pȯin-təd\ adj : properly fitted out ⟨a ~ house⟩

well-bal·anced \'wel-'ba-lənst\ adj 1 : nicely or evenly balanced or arranged ⟨a ~ meal⟩ 2 : emotionally or psychologically untroubled

well-be·ing \-'bē-iŋ\ n : the state of being happy, healthy, or prosperous

U.S. WEIGHTS AND MEASURES

LENGTH

UNIT (SYMBOL)	U.S. EQUIVALENT	METRIC EQUIVALENT
mile (mi)	5280 feet, 1760 yards	1.609 kilometers
rod (rd)	5.50 yards, 16.5 feet	5.029 meters
yard (yd)	3 feet, 36 inches	0.9144 meter
foot (ft *or* ')	12 inches	30.48 centimeters
inch (in *or* ")	0.083 foot, 0.028 yard	2.54 centimeters

AREA

UNIT (SYMBOL)	U.S. EQUIVALENT	METRIC EQUIVALENT
square mile (sq mi *or* mi²)	640 acres	2.590 square kilometers
acre (ac)	4840 square yards, 43,560 square feet	4047 square meters,
square rod (sq rd *or* rd²)	30.25 square yards	25.293 square meters
square yard (sq yd *or* yd²)	9 square feet	0.836 square meter
square foot (sq ft *or* ft²)	144 square inches	0.093 square meter
square inch (sq in *or* in²)	0.0069 square foot	6.452 square centimeter

VOLUME

UNIT (SYMBOL)	U.S. EQUIVALENT	METRIC EQUIVALENT
cubic yard (cu yd *or* yd³)	27 cubic feet	0.765 cubic meter
cubic foot (cu ft *or* ft³)	1728 cubic inches	0.028 cubic meter
cubic inch (cu in *or* in³)	0.00058 cubic foot	16.387 cubic centimeter

WEIGHT—AVOIRDUPOIS

UNIT (SYMBOL)	U.S. EQUIVALENT	METRIC EQUIVALENT
ton		
short ton	2000 pounds	0.907 metric ton
long ton	2240 pounds	1.016 metric tons
hundredweight (cwt)		
short hundredweight	100 pounds	45.359 kilograms
long hundredweight	112 pounds	50.802 kilograms
pound (lb *also* #)	16 ounces	0.454 kilogram
ounce (oz)	16 drams, 437.5 grains	28.350 grams
dram (dr)	27.344 grains	1.772 grams
grain (gr)	0.037 dram	0.0648 gram

CAPACITY

UNIT (SYMBOL)	U.S. EQUIVALENT	METRIC EQUIVALENT
	LIQUID MEASURE	
gallon (gal)	4 quarts	3.785 liters
quart (qt)	2 pints	0.946 liter
pint (pt)	4 gills	473.176 milliliters
gill (gi)	4 fluid ounces	118.294 milliliters
fluid ounce (fl oz *or* f℥)	8 fluid drams	29.573 milliliters
fluid dram (fl dr *or* f℈)	60 minims	3.697 milliliters
minim (min *or* ♍)	1/60 fluid dram	0.061610 milliliter
	DRY MEASURE	
bushel (bu)	4 pecks	35.239 liters
peck (pk)	8 quarts	8.810 liters
quart (qt)	2 pints	1.101 liters
pint (pt)	½ quart	0.551 liter

well·born \-'bȯrn\ adj : born of noble or wealthy lineage

well–bred \-'bred\ adj : having or indicating good breeding : REFINED

well–de·fined \-di-'fīnd\ adj : having clearly distinguishable limits or boundaries

well–dis·posed \-di-'spōzd\ adj : disposed to be friendly, favorable, or sympathetic ⟨∼ to the idea⟩

well–done \'wel-'dən\ adj 1 : rightly or properly performed 2 : cooked thoroughly

well–en·dowed \'wel-in-'daud\ adj 1 : having plenty of money or property 2 : having large breasts 3 : having a large penis

well–fa·vored \-'fā-vərd\ adj : GOOD-LOOKING, HANDSOME ⟨a ∼ face⟩

well–fixed \-'fikst\ adj : WELL-HEELED

well–found·ed \-'faun-dəd\ adj : based on good reasons

well–groomed \-'grümd, -'grumd\ adj : neatly dressed or cared for

well–ground·ed \-'graun-dəd\ adj 1 : having a firm foundation 2 : WELL-FOUNDED

well·head \-,hed\ n 1 : the source of a spring or a stream 2 : principal source 3 : the top of or a structure built over a well

well–heeled \-'hēld\ adj : financially well-off

well–known \-'nōn\ adj : fully or widely known

well–mean·ing \-'mē-niŋ\ adj : having or based on good intentions

well·ness \-nəs\ n : good health esp. as an actively sought goal ⟨∼ clinics⟩ ⟨lifestyles that promote ∼⟩

well–nigh \-'nī\ adv : ALMOST, NEARLY ⟨∼ impossible⟩

well–off \-'ȯf\ adj : being in good condition or circumstances; esp : WELL-TO-DO

well–or·dered \-'ȯr-dərd\ adj : having an orderly procedure or arrangement

well–placed \-'plāst\ adj : appropriately or advantageously directed or positioned

well–read \-'red\ adj : well informed through reading

well–round·ed \-'raun-dəd\ adj 1 : broadly trained, educated, and experienced 2 : COMPREHENSIVE ⟨a ∼ program of activities⟩

well–spo·ken \'wel-'spō-kən\ adj 1 : speaking well and esp. courteously 2 : spoken with propriety ⟨∼ words⟩

well·spring \-,spriŋ\ n : a source of continuous supply ⟨a ∼ of information⟩

well–timed \-'tīmd\ adj : TIMELY ⟨a ∼ announcement⟩

well–to–do \,wel-tə-'dü\ adj : having more than adequate financial resources : PROSPEROUS

well–turned \'wel-'tərnd\ adj 1 : pleasingly shaped ⟨a ∼ ankle⟩ 2 : pleasingly expressed ⟨a ∼ phrase⟩

well–wish·er \'wel-,wi-shər\ n : an admiring supporter or fan — **well–wish·ing** adj or n

welsh \'welsh, 'welch\ vb 1 now sometimes offensive : to avoid payment 2 now sometimes offensive : to break one's word ⟨∼ed on his promises⟩

Welsh \'welsh\ also **Welch** \'welch\ n [ME walisch, welisch, adj., Welsh, fr. OE wælisc foreign, British, Welsh, fr. Wealh foreigner, Briton, Welshman] 1 **Welsh** pl : the people of Wales 2 : the Celtic language of Wales — **Welsh** adj — **Welsh·man** \-mən\ n

Welsh cor·gi \-'kȯr-gē\ n [W corgi, fr. cor dwarf + ci dog] : a short-legged long-backed dog with foxy head of either of two breeds of Welsh origin

Welsh rabbit n : melted often seasoned cheese served over toast or crackers

Welsh rare·bit \-'rer-bət\ n : WELSH RABBIT

¹welt \'welt\ n 1 : the narrow strip of leather between a shoe upper and sole to which other parts are stitched 2 : a doubled edge, strip, insert, or seam for ornament or reinforcement 3 : a ridge or lump raised on the skin usu. by a blow; also : a heavy blow

²welt vb 1 : to furnish (as a shoe) with a welt 2 : to hit hard

¹wel·ter \'wel-tər\ vb 1 : WRITHE, TOSS; also : WALLOW 2 : to rise and fall or toss about in or with waves 3 : to become deeply sunk, soaked, or involved 4 : to be in turmoil

²welter n 1 : TURMOIL 2 : a chaotic mass or jumble ⟨a ∼ of data⟩

wel·ter·weight \'wel-tər-,wāt\ n : a boxer weighing more than 135 but not over 147 pounds

wen \'wen\ n : an abnormal growth or a cyst protruding from a surface esp. of the skin

wench \'wench\ n [ME wenche, short for wenchel child, fr. OE wencel] 1 : a young woman 2 : a female servant

wend \'wend\ vb : to direct one's course : proceed on (one's way)

went past of GO

wept past and past part of WEEP

were past 2d sing, past pl, or past subjunctive of BE

were·wolf \'wer-,wulf, 'wir-, 'wər-\ n, pl **were·wolves** \-,wulvz\ [ME, fr. OE werwulf, fr. wer man + wulf wolf] : a person who in stories is transformed into a wolf or is capable of assuming a wolf's form

wes·kit \'wes-kət\ n : VEST 1

¹west \'west\ adv : to or toward the west

²west adj 1 : situated toward or at the west 2 : coming from the west

³west n 1 : the general direction of sunset 2 : the compass point directly opposite to east 3 cap : regions or countries west of a specified or implied point 4 cap : Europe and the Americas — **west·er·ly** \'wes-tər-lē\ adv or adj — **west·ward** adv or adj — **west·wards** adv

¹west·ern \'wes-tərn\ adj 1 : lying toward or coming from the west 2 cap : of, relating to, or characteristic of a region conventionally designated West 3 cap : of or relating to the Roman Catholic or Protestant segment of Christianity — **West·ern·er** n

²western n, often cap : a novel, story, film, or radio or television show about life in the western U.S. during the latter half of the 19th century

west·ern·ize \'wes-tər-,nīz\ vb -ized; -iz·ing : to give western characteristics to ⟨wanted to ∼ the country⟩ — **west·ern·i·za·tion** \,wes-tər-nə-'zā-shən\ n

West Nile virus \-'nī(-ə)l-\ n [West Nile province of Uganda] : a virus that is transmitted to humans by mosquitoes and causes an illness marked by fever, headache, muscle ache, and sometimes encephalitis or meningitis; also : this illness

¹wet \'wet\ adj **wet·ter; wet·test** 1 : consisting of or covered or soaked with liquid (as water) 2 : RAINY ⟨∼ days⟩ 3 : not dry ⟨∼ paint⟩ 4 : permitting or advocating the manufacture and sale of alcoholic beverages ⟨a ∼ town⟩ ⟨a ∼ candidate⟩ ✦ **Synonyms** DAMP, DANK, MOIST, HUMID — **wet·ly** adv — **wet·ness** n

²wet n 1 : WATER; also : WETNESS, MOISTURE 2 : rainy weather : RAIN 3 : an advocate of a wet liquor policy

³wet vb **wet** or **wet·ted; wet·ting** : to make or become wet — **wet·ter** n

wet blanket n : one that quenches or dampens enthusiasm or pleasure

weth·er \'we-thər\ n : a castrated male sheep or goat

wet·land \'wet-,land, -lənd\ n : land or areas (as swamps) containing much soil moisture — usu. used in pl.

wet nurse n : a woman who cares for and suckles children not her own

wet suit n : a rubber suit for swimmers that acts to retain body heat by keeping a layer of water against the body as insulation

wh abbr 1 which 2 white

¹whack \'hwak\ vb 1 : to strike with a smart or resounding blow 2 : to cut with or as if with a whack

²whack n 1 : a smart or resounding blow; also : the sound of such a blow 2 : PORTION, SHARE ⟨must each pay our ∼⟩ 3 : CONDITION, STATE ⟨the machine is out of ∼⟩ 4 : an opportunity or attempt to do something : CHANCE 5 : a single action or occasion ⟨made three pies at a ∼⟩

¹whale \'hwāl\ n, pl **whales** 1 or pl **whale** : CETACEAN; esp : one (as a sperm whale or killer whale) of large size 2 : a person or thing impressive in size or quality ⟨a ∼ of a story⟩

²whale vb **whaled; whal·ing** : to fish or hunt for whales

³whale vb **whaled; whal·ing** 1 : THRASH 2 : to strike or hit vigorously

whale·boat \-,bōt\ n : a long narrow rowboat originally used by whalers

whale·bone \-,bōn\ n : BALEEN

whal·er \'hwā-lər\ n 1 : a person or ship that hunts whales 2 : WHALEBOAT

whale shark n : a shark of warm waters that is the largest known fish

wham·my \'hwa-mē\ n, pl **wham·mies** : JINX, HEX ⟨put the ∼ on him⟩

wharf \'hwȯrf\ *n, pl* **wharves** \'hwȯrvz\ *also* **wharfs** : a structure alongside which ships lie to load and unload

¹what \'hwät, 'hwət\ *pron* **1** — used to inquire about the identity or nature of a being, an object, or some matter or situation ⟨~ is he, a salesman⟩ ⟨~'s that⟩ ⟨~ happened⟩ **2** : that which ⟨I know ~ you want⟩ **3** : WHATEVER 1 ⟨take ~ you want⟩

²what *adv* **1** : in what respect : HOW ⟨~ does he care⟩ **2** — used with *with* to introduce a prepositional phrase that expresses cause ⟨kept busy ~ with school and work⟩

³what *adj* **1** — used to inquire about the identity or nature of a person, object, or matter ⟨~ books do you read⟩ **2** : how remarkable or surprising ⟨~ an idea⟩ **3** : WHATEVER

¹what·ev·er \hwät-'e-vər, hwət-\ *pron* **1** : anything or everything that ⟨does ~ he wants to⟩ **2** : no matter what ⟨~ you do, don't cheat⟩ **3** : WHAT 1 — used as an intensive ⟨~ do you mean⟩

²whatever *adj* : of any kind at all ⟨no food ~⟩

³whatever *adv* : in any case : whatever the case may be — often used to suggest the unimportance of an issue or choice ⟨see a movie, watch TV, — ~⟩

¹what·not \'hwät-,nät, 'hwət-\ *pron* : any of various other things that might also be mentioned ⟨needles, pins, and ~⟩

²whatnot *n* : a light open set of shelves for small ornaments

what·so·ev·er \,hwät-sō-'e-vər, ,hwət-\ *pron or adj* : WHATEVER

wheal \'hwēl\ *n* : a rapidly formed flat slightly raised itching or burning patch on the skin; *also* : WELT

wheat \'hwēt\ *n* : a cereal grain that yields a fine white flour used chiefly in breads, baked goods, and pastas; *also* : any of several widely grown grasses yielding wheat — **wheat·en** *adj*

wheat germ *n* : the vitamin-rich wheat embryo separated in milling

whee·dle \'hwē-d²l\ *vb* **whee·dled; whee·dling** **1** : to entice by flattery **2** : to gain or get by wheedling

¹wheel \'hwēl\ *n* **1** : a disk or circular frame that turns on a central axis **2** : a device whose main part is a wheel **3** : something resembling a wheel in shape or motion **4** : a curving or circular movement **5** : machinery that imparts motion : moving power ⟨the ~s of government⟩ **6** : a person of importance **7** *pl, slang* : AUTOMOBILE — **wheeled** \'hwēld\ *adj* — **wheel·less** *adj*

²wheel *vb* **1** : ROTATE, REVOLVE **2** : to change direction as if turning on a pivot **3** : to convey or move on wheels or in a vehicle

wheel·bar·row \-,ber-ō\ *n* : a vehicle with handles and usu. one wheel for carrying small loads

wheel·base \-,bās\ *n* : the distance in inches between the front and rear axles of an automotive vehicle

wheel·chair \-,cher\ *n* : a chair mounted on wheels esp. for the use of disabled persons

wheel·er \'hwē-lər\ *n* **1** : one that wheels **2** : WHEELHORSE **3** : something that has wheels — used in combination ⟨a side-*wheeler*⟩

wheel·er-deal·er \,hwē-lər-'dē-lər\ *n* : a shrewd operator esp. in business or politics

wheel·horse \'hwēl-,hȯrs\ *n* **1** : a horse in a position nearest the front wheels of a wagon **2** : a steady and effective worker esp. in a political body

wheel·house \-,haus\ *n* : PILOTHOUSE

wheel–thrown \'hwēl-,thrōn\ *adj* : made on a potter's wheel

wheel·wright \-,rīt\ *n* : a maker and repairer of wheels and wheeled vehicles

¹wheeze \'hwēz\ *vb* **wheezed; wheez·ing** : to breathe with difficulty usu. with a whistling sound

²wheeze *n* **1** : a sound of wheezing ⟨the ~ of an engine⟩ **2** : an often repeated and well-known joke **3** : a trite saying

wheezy \'hwē-zē\ *adj* **wheez·i·er; -est** **1** : inclined to wheeze **2** : having a wheezing sound — **wheez·i·ly** \-zə-lē\ *adv* — **wheez·i·ness** \-zē-nəs\ *n*

whelk \'hwelk\ *n* : a large sea snail; *esp* : one much used as food in Europe

whelm \'hwelm\ *vb* : to overcome or engulf completely : OVERWHELM

¹whelp \'hwelp\ *n* : any of the young of various carnivorous mammals (as a dog)

²whelp *vb* : to give birth to (whelps); *also* : bring forth young

¹when \'hwen\ *adv* **1** : at what time ⟨~ will you return⟩ **2** : at or during which time ⟨a time ~ things were better⟩

²when *conj* **1** : at or during the time that ⟨leave ~ I do⟩ **2** : every time that ⟨they all clapped ~ he sang⟩ **3** : in the event that : IF ⟨disqualified ~ you cheat⟩ **4** : ALTHOUGH ⟨quit politics ~ he might have had a great career in it⟩

³when *pron* : what or which time ⟨since ~ have you been the boss⟩

⁴when *n* : the time of a happening

whence \'hwens\ *adv or conj* : from what place, source, or cause

when·ev·er \hwe-'ne-vər, hwə-\ *conj or adv* : at whatever time

when·so·ev·er \'hwen-sō-,e-vər\ *conj* : at any or every time that

¹where \'hwer\ *adv* **1** : at, in, or to what place ⟨~ is it⟩ ⟨~ will we go⟩ **2** : at, in, or to what situation, position, direction, circumstances, or respect ⟨~ does this road lead⟩

²where *conj* **1** : at, in, or to what place ⟨knows ~ the house is⟩ **2** : at, in, or to what situation, position, direction, circumstances, or respect ⟨shows ~ the road leads⟩ **3** : WHEREVER ⟨goes ~ she likes⟩ **4** : at, in, or to which place ⟨the town ~ we live⟩ **5** : at, in, or to the place at, in, or to which ⟨stay ~ you are⟩ **6** : in a case, situation, or respect in which ⟨outstanding ~ endurance is called for⟩

³where *n* : PLACE, LOCATION ⟨the ~ and how of the accident⟩

¹where·abouts \-ə-,bauts\ *also* **where·about** \-,baut\ *adv* : about where : near what place ⟨~ does he live⟩

²whereabouts *n sing or pl* : the place where a person or thing is ⟨his present ~ are unknown⟩

where·as \hwer-'az\ *conj* **1** : while on the contrary; *also* : ALTHOUGH **2** : in view of the fact that : SINCE

where·at \-'at\ *conj* **1** : at or toward which **2** : in consequence of which : WHEREUPON

where·by \-'bī\ *conj* : by, through, or in accordance with which ⟨the means ~ we achieved our goals⟩

¹where·fore \'hwer-,fȯr\ *adv* **1** : for what reason or purpose : WHY **2** : THEREFORE

²wherefore *n* : an answer or statement giving an explanation : REASON

¹where·in \hwer-'in\ *adv* : in what : in what respect ⟨~ was I wrong⟩

²wherein *conj* **1** : in which : WHERE ⟨the city ~ we live⟩ **2** : during which **3** : in what way : HOW ⟨showed me ~ I was wrong⟩

where·of \-'əv, -'äv\ *conj* **1** : of what ⟨knows ~ he speaks⟩ **2** : of which or whom ⟨books ~ the best are lost⟩

where·on \-'ȯn, -'än\ *conj* : on which ⟨the base ~ it rests⟩

where·so·ev·er \'hwer-sō-,e-vər\ *conj* : WHEREVER

where·to \'hwer-,tü\ *conj* : to which

where·up·on \'hwer-ə-,pȯn, -,pän\ *conj* **1** : on which **2** : closely following and in consequence of which

¹wher·ev·er \hwer-'e-vər\ *adv* : where in the world ⟨~ did he get that tie⟩

²wherever *conj* **1** : at, in, or to whatever place ⟨thrives ~ he goes⟩ **2** : in any circumstance in which

where·with \'hwer-,with, -,with\ *conj* : with or by means of which ⟨lack the tools ~ to repair the damage⟩

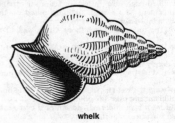

whelk

where·with·al \'hwer-wi-ˌthȯl, -ˌthȯl\ *n* : MEANS, RESOURCES; *esp* : MONEY

wher·ry \'hwer-ē\ *n, pl* **wherries** : a long light rowboat sharp at both ends

whet \'hwet\ *vb* **whet·ted; whet·ting** **1** : to sharpen by rubbing on or with something abrasive (as a whetstone) **2** : to make keen : STIMULATE ⟨~ the appetite⟩

wheth·er \'hwe-thər\ *conj* **1** : if it is or was true that ⟨ask ~ he is going⟩ **2** : if it is or was better ⟨uncertain ~ to go or stay⟩ **3** : whichever is or was the case, namely that ⟨~ we succeed or fail, we must try⟩ **4** : EITHER ⟨turned out well ~ by accident or design⟩

whet·stone \'hwet-ˌstōn\ *n* : a stone for sharpening blades

whey \'hwā\ *n* : the watery part of milk that separates after the milk sours and thickens

¹which \'hwich\ *adj* **1** : being what one or ones out of a group ⟨~ shirt should I wear⟩ **2** : WHICHEVER

²which *pron* **1** : which one or ones ⟨~ is yours⟩ ⟨~ are his⟩ ⟨it's in May or June, I'm not sure ~⟩ **2** : WHICHEVER ⟨we have all kinds; take ~ you like⟩ **3** — used to introduce a relative clause and to serve as a substitute therein for the noun modified by the clause ⟨the money ~ is coming to me⟩

¹which·ev·er \hwich-'e-vər\ *adj* : no matter which ⟨~ way you go⟩

²whichever *pron* : whatever one or ones

which·so·ev·er \ˌhwich-sō-'e-vər\ *pron or adj, archaic* : WHICHEVER

whick·er \'hwi-kər\ *vb* : NEIGH, WHINNY — **whicker** *n*

¹whiff \'hwif\ *n* **1** : a quick puff or slight gust (as of air) **2** : an inhalation of odor, gas, or smoke **3** : a slight trace ⟨a ~ of scandal⟩ **4** : STRIKEOUT

²whiff *vb* **1** : to expel, puff out, or blow away in or as if in whiffs **2** : to inhale an odor **3** : STRIKE OUT 3

Whig \'hwig\ *n* [short for *Whiggamore*, member of a Scottish group that marched to Edinburgh in 1648 to oppose the court party] **1** : a member or supporter of a British political group of the late 17th through early 19th centuries seeking to limit royal authority and increase parliamentary power **2** : an American favoring independence from Great Britain during the American Revolution **3** : a member or supporter of an American political party formed about 1834 to oppose the Democrats

¹while \'hwī(-ə)l\ *n* **1** : a period of time ⟨stay a ~⟩ **2** : the time and effort used : TROUBLE ⟨worth your ~⟩

²while *conj* **1** : during the time that ⟨she called ~ you were out⟩ **2** : AS LONG AS ⟨~ there's life there's hope⟩ **3** : ALTHOUGH ⟨~ he's respected, he's not liked⟩

³while *vb* **whiled; whil·ing** : to cause to pass esp. pleasantly ⟨~ away an hour⟩

¹whi·lom \'hwī-ləm\ *adv* [ME, lit., at times, fr. OE *hwīlum*, dat. pl. of *hwīl* time, while] *archaic* : FORMERLY

²whilom *adj* : FORMER ⟨his ~ friends⟩

whilst \'hwīlst\ *conj, chiefly Brit* : WHILE

whim \'hwim\ *n* : a sudden wish, desire, or change of mind

whim·per \'hwim-pər\ *vb* : to make a low whining plaintive or broken sound — **whimper** *n*

whim·si·cal \'hwim-zi-kəl\ *adj* **1** : full of whims : CAPRICIOUS **2** : resulting from or characterized by whim or caprice : ERRATIC ⟨~ notions⟩ — **whim·si·cal·i·ty** \ˌhwim-zə-'ka-lə-tē\ *n* — **whim·si·cal·ly** \'hwim-zi-k(ə-)lē\ *adv*

whim·sy *also* **whim·sey** \'hwim-zē\ *n, pl* **whimsies** *also* **whimseys** **1** : WHIM, CAPRICE **2** : a fanciful or fantastic device, object, or creation esp. in writing or art ⟨decorative ~⟩

whine \'hwīn\ *vb* **whined; whin·ing** [ME, fr. OE *hwīnan* to whiz] **1** : to utter a usu. high-pitched plaintive or distressed cry; *also* : to make a sound similar to such a cry **2** : to complain with or as if with a whine — **whine** *n* — **whin·er** *n* — **whiny** *also* **whin·ey** \'hwī-nē\ *adj*

¹whin·ny \'hwi-nē\ *vb* **whin·nied; whin·ny·ing** : to neigh usu. in a low or gentle manner

²whinny *n, pl* **whinnies** : NEIGH

¹whip \'hwip\ *vb* **whipped; whip·ping** **1** : to move, snatch, or jerk quickly or forcefully ⟨~ out a gun⟩ **2** : to strike with a slender lithe implement (as a lash) esp. as a punishment; *also* : SPANK **3** : to drive or urge on by or as if by using a whip **4** : to bind or wrap (as a rope or rod) with cord in order to protect and strengthen; *also*

: to wind or wrap around something **5** : DEFEAT **6** : to stir up : INCITE ⟨~ up enthusiasm⟩ **7** : to produce in a hurry ⟨~ up a meal⟩ **8** : to beat (as eggs or cream) into a froth **9** : to proceed nimbly or briskly; *also* : to flap about forcefully ⟨flags *whipping* in the wind⟩ — **whip·per** *n* — **whip into shape** : to bring forcefully to a desired state or condition

²whip *n* **1** : a flexible instrument used for whipping **2** : a stroke or cut with or as if with a whip **3** : a dessert made by whipping a portion of the ingredients ⟨prune ~⟩ **4** : a person who handles a whip **5** : a member of a legislative body appointed by a party to enforce party discipline **6** : a whipping or thrashing motion

whip·cord \-ˌkȯrd\ *n* **1** : a thin tough braided cord **2** : a strong cloth with fine diagonal cords or ribs

whip hand *n* : positive control : ADVANTAGE

whip·lash \'hwip-ˌlash\ *n* **1** : the lash of a whip **2** : injury resulting from a sudden sharp movement of the neck and head (as of a person in a vehicle that is struck from the rear)

whip·per·snap·per \'hwi-pər-ˌsna-pər\ *n* : a small, insignificant, or presumptuous person

whip·pet \'hwi-pət\ *n* : any of a breed of small swift slender dogs that are used for racing

whipping boy *n* : SCAPEGOAT

whip–poor–will \'hwi-pər-ˌwil\ *n* : an American insect-eating bird with dull variegated plumage whose call at nightfall and just before dawn is suggestive of its name

whip·saw \'hwip-ˌsȯ\ *vb* : to beset with two or more adverse conditions or situations at once

¹whir *also* **whirr** \'hwər\ *vb* **whirred; whir·ring** : to move, fly, or revolve with a whir

²whir *also* **whirr** *n* : a continuous fluttering or vibratory sound made by something in rapid motion

¹whirl \'hwərl\ *vb* **1** : to move or drive in a circle or curve esp. with force or speed **2** : to turn or cause to turn rapidly in circles **3** : to turn abruptly : WHEEL **4** : to move or go quickly **5** : to become dizzy or giddy : REEL

²whirl *n* **1** : a rapid rotating or circling movement; *also* : something whirling **2** : COMMOTION, BUSTLE ⟨the social ~⟩ **3** : a state of mental confusion : TRY ⟨gave it a ~⟩

whirl·i·gig \'hwər-li-ˌgig\ *n* [ME *whirlegigg*, fr. *whirlen* to whirl + *gigg* top] **1** : a child's toy having a whirling motion **2** : something that continuously whirls or changes

whirl·pool \'hwərl-ˌpül\ *n* : water moving rapidly in a circle so as to produce a depression in the center into which floating objects may be drawn

whirl·wind \-ˌwind\ *n* **1** : a small whirling windstorm **2** : a confused rush **3** : a violent or destructive force

whirly·bird \'hwər-lē-ˌbərd\ *n* : HELICOPTER

¹whish \'hwish\ *vb* : to move with a whish or swishing sound

²whish *n* : a rushing sound : SWISH

¹whisk \'hwisk\ *n* **1** : a quick light sweeping or brushing motion **2** : a usu. wire kitchen implement for beating food by hand **3** : WHISK BROOM

²whisk *vb* **1** : to move nimbly and quickly **2** : to move or convey briskly ⟨~ed the children off to bed⟩ **3** : to beat or whip lightly ⟨~ eggs⟩ **4** : to brush or wipe off lightly ⟨~ a coat⟩

whisk broom *n* : a small broom with a short handle used esp. as a clothes brush

whis·ker \'hwis-kər\ *n* **1** : one hair of the beard **2** *pl* : the part of the beard that grows on the sides of the face or on the chin **3** : one of the long bristles or hairs growing near the mouth of an animal (as a cat or mouse) — **whis·kered** \-kərd\ *adj*

whis·key *or* **whis·ky** \'hwis-kē\ *n, pl* **whiskeys** *or* **whiskies** [Ir *uisce beatha* & ScGael *uisge beatha*, lit., water of life] : a liquor distilled from fermented wort (as that obtained from rye, corn, or barley mash)

¹whis·per \'hwis-pər\ *vb* **1** : to speak very low or under the breath; *also* : to tell or utter by whispering ⟨~ a secret⟩ **2** : to make a low rustling sound — **whis·per·er** \-pər-ər\ *n*

²whisper *n* **1** : something communicated by or as if by whispering : HINT, RUMOR **2** : an act or instance of whispering

whist \'hwist\ *n* : a card game played by four players in two partnerships with a deck of 52 cards

¹whis·tle \'hwi-səl\ *n* **1** : a device by which a shrill sound is produced ⟨steam ∼⟩ ⟨tin ∼⟩ **2** : a shrill clear sound made by forcing breath out or air in through the puckered lips **3** : the sound or signal produced by a whistle or as if by whistling **4** : the shrill clear note of an animal (as a bird)

²**whistle** *vb* **whis·tled; whis·tling 1** : to utter a shrill clear sound by blowing or drawing air through the puckered lips **2** : to utter a shrill clear note or call resembling a whistle **3** : to make a shrill clear sound esp. by rapid movements ⟨the wind *whistled*⟩ **4** : to blow or sound a whistle **5** : to signal or call by a whistle **6** : to produce, utter, or express by whistling ⟨∼ a tune⟩ — **whis·tler** *n*

whis·tle–blow·er \ˈhwi-səl-ˌblō-ər\ *n* : INFORMER

whis·tle–stop \-ˌstäp\ *n* : a brief personal appearance by a political candidate orig. on the rear platform of a touring train

whit \ˈhwit\ *n* [prob. alter. of ME *wiht, wight* creature, thing, fr. OE *wiht*] : the smallest part or particle : BIT

¹**white** \ˈhwīt\ *adj* **whit·er; whit·est 1** : free from color **2** : of the color of new snow or milk; *esp* : of the color white **3** : light or pallid in color ⟨lips ∼ with fear⟩ **4** : SILVERY; *also* : made of silver **5** : of, relating to, or being a member of a group or race characterized by light-colored skin **6** : free from spot or blemish : PURE, INNOCENT **7** : BLANK 2 ⟨∼ space in printed matter⟩ **8** : not intended to cause harm ⟨a ∼ lie⟩ **9** : wearing white ⟨∼ friars⟩ **10** : marked by snow ⟨∼ Christmas⟩ **11** : consisting of a wide range of frequencies ⟨∼ light⟩ — **white·ness** \-nəs\ *n* — **white·ish** \ˈhwī-tish\ *adj*

²**white** *n* **1** : the color of maximal lightness that characterizes objects which both reflect and transmit light : the opposite of black **2** : a white or light-colored part or thing ⟨the ∼ of an egg⟩; *also, pl* : white garments **3** : the light-colored pieces in a 2-player board game; *also* : the person by whom these are played **4** : one that is or approaches the color white **5** : a person of a light-skinned race

white ant *n* : TERMITE

white blood cell *n* : any of the colorless blood cells (as lymphocytes) that do not contain hemoglobin but do have a nucleus

white–bread \ˈhwīt-ˈbred\ *adj* : being, typical of, or having qualities (as blandness) associated with the white middle class ⟨∼ values⟩

white–cap \ˈhwīt-ˌkap\ *n* : a wave crest breaking into white foam

white chocolate *n* : a whitish confection chiefly of cocoa butter, milk, and sugar

white–col·lar \ˈhwīt-ˈkä-lər\ *adj* : of, relating to, or constituting the class of salaried workers whose duties do not require the wearing of work clothes or protective clothing ⟨∼ jobs⟩

white dwarf *n* : a small very dense whitish star of low luminosity

white elephant *n* **1** : an Indian elephant of a pale color that is sometimes venerated in India, Sri Lanka, Thailand, and Myanmar **2** : something requiring much care and expense and giving little profit or enjoyment

white feather *n* [fr. the superstition that a white feather in the plumage of a gamecock is a mark of a poor fighter] : a mark or symbol of cowardice

white·fish \ˈhwīt-ˌfish\ *n* : any of various freshwater food fishes related to the salmons and trouts

white flag *n* : a flag of pure white used to signify truce or surrender

white gold *n* : a pale alloy of gold resembling platinum in appearance

white goods *n pl* : white fabrics or articles (as sheets or towels) typically made of cotton or linen

White·hall \ˈhwīt-ˌhȯl\ *n* : the British government

white hat *n* **1** : an admirable and honorable person **2** : a mark or symbol of goodness

white·head \-ˌhed\ *n* : a small whitish lump in the skin due to retention of secretion in an oil gland duct

white heat *n* : a temperature higher than red heat at which a body becomes brightly incandescent

white–hot *adj* **1** : being at or radiating white heat **2** : FERVID ⟨∼ enthusiasm⟩

White House \-ˌhaůs\ *n* **1** : a residence of the president of the U.S. **2** : the executive department of the U.S. government

white lead *n* : a heavy white poisonous carbonate of lead used esp. formerly as a pigment in exterior paints

white matter *n* : whitish nerve tissue esp. of the brain and spinal cord that consists largely of neuron processes enclosed in a fatty material and that typically lies under the cortical gray matter

whit·en \ˈhwī-tᵊn\ *vb* : to make or become white ♦ **Synonyms** BLANCH, BLEACH — **whit·en·er** *n*

white oak *n* : any of various oaks with acorns that take one year to mature; *also* : its hard durable wood

white pepper *n* : a spice that consists of the berry of a pepper plant ground after removal of its black husk

white pine *n* : a tall-growing pine of eastern No. America with needles in clusters of five; *also* : its wood

white sale *n* : a sale on white goods

white shark *n* : GREAT WHITE SHARK

white slave *n* : a woman or girl held unwillingly for purposes of prostitution — **white slavery** *n*

white·tail \ˈhwīt-ˌtāl\ *n* : WHITE-TAILED DEER

white–tailed deer *n* : a No. American deer with a rather long tail white on the underside and the males of which have forward-arching antlers

white–tie \-ˈtī\ *adj* : characterized by or requiring formal evening clothes consisting of esp. white tie and tailcoat for men and a formal gown for women

white·wall \ˈhwīt-ˌwȯl\ *n* : an automobile tire having a white band on the sidewall

¹**white·wash** \-ˌwȯsh, -ˌwäsh\ *vb* **1** : to whiten with whitewash **2** : to clear of a charge of wrongdoing by offering excuses, hiding facts, or conducting a perfunctory investigation **3** : SHUT OUT 2

²**whitewash** *n* **1** : a liquid mixture (as of lime and water) for whitening a surface **2** : a clearing of wrongdoing by whitewashing

white water *n* : frothy water (as in breakers, rapids, or falls)

white·wood \-ˌwůd\ *n* : any of various trees and esp. a tulip tree having light-colored wood; *also* : such wood

¹**whith·er** \ˈhwi-thər\ *adv* **1** : to what place **2** : to what situation, position, degree, or end ⟨∼ will this drive him⟩

²**whither** *conj* **1** : to the place at, in, or to which; *also* : to which place **2** : to whatever place

whith·er·so·ev·er \ˌhwi-thər-sō-ˈe-vər\ *conj* : to whatever place

¹**whit·ing** \ˈhwī-tiŋ\ *n, pl* **whiting** *also* **whit·ings** : any of several usu. light or silvery food fishes (as a hake) found mostly near seacoasts

²**whiting** *n* : calcium carbonate in powdered form used esp. as a pigment and in putty

whit·low \ˈhwit-ˌlō\ *n* : a deep inflammation of a finger or toe with pus formation

Whit·sun·day \ˈhwit-ˈsən-dē, -sən-ˌdā\ *n* [ME *Whitsonday*, fr. OE *hwīta sunnandæg*, lit., white Sunday; prob. fr. the custom of wearing white robes by those newly baptized at this season] : PENTECOST

whit·tle \ˈhwi-tᵊl\ *vb* **whit·tled; whit·tling 1** : to pare or cut off chips from the surface of (wood) with a knife; *also* : to cut or shape by such paring **2** : to reduce as if by paring down ⟨∼ down expenses⟩

¹**whiz** *or* **whizz** \ˈhwiz\ *vb* **whizzed; whiz·zing** : to hum, whir, or hiss like a speeding object (as an arrow or ball) passing through air

²**whiz** *or* **whizz** *n, pl* **whiz·zes** : a hissing, buzzing, or whizzing sound

³**whiz** *n, pl* **whiz·zes** : WIZARD 2

who \ˈhü\ *pron* **1** : what or which person or persons ⟨∼ did it⟩ ⟨∼ is he⟩ ⟨∼ are they⟩ **2** : the person or persons that ⟨knows ∼ did it⟩ **3** — used to introduce a relative clause and to serve as a substitute therein for the substantive modified by the clause ⟨the person ∼ lives there is rich⟩

WHO *abbr* World Health Organization

whoa \ˈwō, ˈhwō, ˈhō\ *vb imper* **1** — a command to an animal to stand still **2** : cease or slow a course of action or a line of thought

who·dun·it *also* **who·dun·nit** \hü-ˈdə-nət\ *n* : a detective or mystery story

who·ev·er \hü-ˈe-vər\ *pron* : whatever person : no matter who

¹**whole** \ˈhōl\ *adj* [ME *hool* healthy, unhurt, entire, fr. OE *hāl*] **1** : being in healthy or sound condition : free from

defect or damage **2** : having all its proper parts or elements ⟨~ milk⟩ **3** : constituting the total sum of : ENTIRE ⟨owns the ~ island⟩ **4** : each or all of the ⟨the ~ family⟩ **5** : not scattered or divided : CONCENTRATED ⟨gave me his ~ attention⟩ **6** : seemingly complete or total ⟨the ~ idea is to help, not hinder⟩ **♦ Synonyms** PERFECT, INTACT, SOUND — **whole·ness** *n*

²whole *n* **1** : a complete amount or sum **2** : something whole or entire — **on the whole 1** : in view of all the circumstances or conditions **2** : in general

³whole *adv* : COMPLETELY, WHOLLY, ENTIRELY ⟨a ~ new term⟩

whole food *n* : a food eaten in its natural state with little or no artificial additives

whole·heart·ed \'hōl-'här-təd\ *adj* : undivided in purpose, enthusiasm, will, or commitment

whole hog *adv* : to the fullest extent : COMPLETELY ⟨accepted the proposals *whole hog*⟩

whole note *n* : a musical note equal to one measure of four beats

whole number *n* : any of the set of nonnegative integers; *also* : INTEGER

¹whole·sale \'hōl-,sāl\ *n* : the sale of goods in quantity usu. for resale by a retail merchant

²wholesale *adj* **1** : performed on a large scale without discrimination ⟨~ slaughter⟩ **2** : of, relating to, or engaged in wholesaling — **wholesale** *adv*

³wholesale *vb* **whole·saled; whole·sal·ing** : to sell at wholesale — **whole·sal·er** *n*

whole·some \'hōl-səm\ *adj* **1** : promoting mental, spiritual, or bodily health or well-being ⟨a ~ environment⟩ **2** : sound in body, mind, or morals : HEALTHY **3** : PRUDENT ⟨~ respect for the law⟩ — **whole·some·ness** *n*

whole step *n* : a musical interval comprising two half steps (as C–D or F♯–G♯)

whole wheat *adj* : made of ground entire wheat kernels

whol·ly \'hōl-lē\ *adv* **1** : COMPLETELY, TOTALLY **2** : SOLELY, EXCLUSIVELY

whom \'hüm\ *pron, objective case of* WHO

whom·ev·er \hü-'me-vər\ *pron, objective case of* WHOEVER

whom·so·ev·er \,hüm-sō-'e-vər\ *pron, objective case of* WHOSOEVER

¹whoop \'hwüp, 'hwùp, 'hüp, 'hùp\ *vb* **1** : to shout or call loudly and vigorously **2** : to make the characteristic whoop of whooping cough **3** : to go or pass with a loud noise **4** : to utter or express with a whoop; *also* : to urge, drive, or cheer with a whoop

²whoop *n* **1** : a whooping sound or utterance : SHOUT, HOOT **2** : a crowing intake of breath after a fit of coughing in whooping cough

¹whoop·ee \'hwù-(,)pē, 'hwü-\ *interj* — used to express exuberance

²whoopee *n* **1** : boisterous fun **2** : sexual play — usu. used with *make*

whooping cough *n* : an infectious bacterial disease esp. of children marked by convulsive coughing fits often followed by a shrill gasping intake of breath

whooping crane *n* : a large white nearly extinct No. American crane noted for its loud whooping call

whoop·la \'hwüp-,lä, 'hwùp-\ *n* **1** : HOOPLA **2** : boisterous merrymaking

whop·per \'hwä-pər\ *n* : something unusually large or extreme of its kind; *esp* : a monstrous lie

whop·ping \'hwä-pin\ *adj* : extremely large ⟨a ~ increase⟩

whore \'hòr\ *n* : PROSTITUTE

whorl \'hwòrl, 'hwərl\ *n* **1** : a group of parts (as leaves or petals) encircling an axis and esp. a plant stem **2** : something that whirls or coils around a center : COIL, SPIRAL **3** : one of the turns of a snail shell

whorled \'hwòrld, 'hwərld\ *adj* : having or arranged in whorls

¹whose \'hüz\ *adj* : of or relating to whom or which esp. as possessor or possessors, agent or agents, or object or objects of an action ⟨asked ~ bag it was⟩

²whose *pron* : whose one or ones ⟨~ is this car⟩ ⟨~ are those books⟩

who·so \'hü-,sō\ *pron* : WHOEVER

who·so·ev·er \,hü-sō-'e-vər\ *pron* : WHOEVER

whs *or* **whse** *abbr* warehouse

whsle *abbr* wholesale

¹why \'hwī\ *adv* : for what reason, cause, or purpose ⟨~ did you do it?⟩

²why *conj* **1** : the cause, reason, or purpose for which ⟨that is ~ you did it⟩ **2** : for which : on account of which ⟨knows the reason ~ you did it⟩

³why *n, pl* **whys** : REASON, CAUSE ⟨the ~s of racial prejudice⟩

⁴why \'wī, 'hwī\ *interj* — used to express surprise, hesitation, approval, disapproval, or impatience ⟨~, here's what I was looking for⟩

WI *abbr* **1** West Indies **2** Wisconsin

WIA *abbr* wounded in action

Wic·ca \'wi-kə\ *n* [prob. fr. OE *wicca* wizard] : a religion that affirms the existence of supernatural power (as magic) and of deities who inhere in nature and that ritually observes seasonal and life cycles

wick \'wik\ *n* : a loosely bound bundle of soft fibers that draws up oil, tallow, or wax to be burned in a candle, oil lamp, or stove

wick·ed \'wi-kəd\ *adj* **1** : morally bad : EVIL, SINFUL **2** : FIERCE, VICIOUS **3** : ROGUISH ⟨a ~ glance⟩ **4** : REPUGNANT, VILE ⟨a ~ odor⟩ **5** : HARMFUL, DANGEROUS ⟨a ~ attack⟩ **6** : impressively excellent ⟨throws a ~ fastball⟩ — **wick·ed·ly** *adv* — **wick·ed·ness** *n*

wick·er \'wi-kər\ *n* **1** : a small pliant branch (as an osier or a withe) **2** : WICKERWORK — **wicker** *adj*

wick·er·work \-,wərk\ *n* : work made of osiers, twigs, or rods : BASKETRY

wick·et \'wi-kət\ *n* **1** : a small gate or door; *esp* : one forming a part of or placed near a larger one **2** : a window-like opening usu. with a grille or grate (as at a ticket office) **3** : a set of three upright rods topped by two crosspieces bowled at in cricket **4** : an arch or hoop in croquet

wick·i·up \'wi-kē-,əp\ *n* : a hut used by nomadic Indians of the western and southwestern U.S. with a usu. oval base and a rough frame covered with reed mats, grass, or brushwood

wid *abbr* widow, widower

¹wide \'wīd\ *adj* **wider; wid·est 1** : covering a vast area **2** : measured across or at right angles to the length **3** : not narrow : BROAD; *also* : ROOMY **4** : opened to full width ⟨eyes ~ with wonder⟩ **5** : not limited : EXTENSIVE ⟨~ experience⟩ **6** : far from the goal, mark, or truth ⟨was ~ of the truth⟩ — **wide·ly** *adv*

²wide *adv* **wid·er; wid·est 1** : over a great distance or extent : WIDELY ⟨searched far and ~⟩ **2** : over a specified distance, area, or extent **3** : so as to leave a wide space between ⟨~ apart⟩ **4** : so as to clear by a considerable distance ⟨ran ~ around left end⟩ **5** : COMPLETELY, FULLY ⟨opened her eyes ~⟩

wide area network *n* : a computer network (as the Internet) over a large area (as a country or the globe) for sharing resources or exchanging data

wide–awake \,wīd-ə-'wāk\ *adj* : fully awake; *also* : KNOWING, ALERT

wide–body \'wīd-,bä-dē\ *n* : a large jet aircraft having a wide cabin

wide–eyed \'wīd-'īd\ *adj* **1** : having the eyes wide open esp. with wonder or astonishment **2** : NAIVE ⟨~ innocence⟩

wide–mouthed \-'maùthd, -'maùtht\ *adj* **1** : having one's mouth opened wide (as in awe) **2** : having a wide mouth ⟨~ jars⟩

wid·en \'wī-d°n\ *vb* : to increase in width, scope, or extent

wide·spread \'wīd-'spred\ *adj* **1** : widely scattered or prevalent **2** : widely extended or spread out ⟨~ wings⟩

widgeon *var of* WIGEON

¹wid·ow \'wi-dō\ *n* : a woman who has lost her spouse or partner by death and has not married again — **wid·ow·hood** *n*

²widow *vb* : to cause to become a widow or widower

wid·ow·er \'wi-də-wər\ *n* : a man who has lost his spouse or partner by death and has not married again

width \'width\ *n* **1** : a distance from side to side : the measurement taken at right angles to the length : BREADTH **2** : largeness of extent or scope; *also* : FULLNESS **3** : a measured and cut piece of material ⟨a ~ of calico⟩

wield \'wēld\ *vb* **1** : to use or handle esp. effectively ⟨~ a broom⟩ **2** : to exert authority by means of : EMPLOY ⟨~ influence⟩ — **wield·er** *n*

wie·ner *also* **wei·ner** \'wē-nər\ *n* [short for *wienerwurst*, fr. G, lit., Vienna sausage] : FRANKFURTER

wife \'wīf\ *n, pl* **wives** \'wīvz\ **1** *dial* : WOMAN **2** : a woman acting in a specified capacity — used in combination ⟨fish*wife*⟩ **3** : a female partner in a marriage — **wife·hood** *n* — **wife·less** *adj* — **wife·ly** *adj*

wig \'wig\ *n* [short for *periwig*, modif. of MF *perruque*, fr. It *parrucca, perrucca* hair, wig] : a manufactured covering of natural or synthetic hair for the head; *also* : TOUPEE

wi·geon *or* **wid·geon** \'wi-jən\ *n, pl* **wigeon** *or* **wigeons** *or* **widgeon** *or* **widgeons** : any of several medium-sized freshwater ducks

wig·gle \'wi-gəl\ *vb* **wig·gled; wig·gling 1** : to move to and fro with quick jerky or shaking movements : JIGGLE ⟨*wiggled* his toes⟩ **2** : WRIGGLE — **wiggle** *n*

wig·gler \'wi-glər, -gə-lər\ *n* **1** : a larva or pupa of a mosquito **2** : one that wiggles

wig·gly \'wi-glē, -gə-lē\ *adj* **1** : tending to wiggle ⟨a ∼ worm⟩ **2** : WAVY ⟨∼ lines⟩

wight \'wīt\ *n* : a living being : CREATURE

wig·let \'wi-glət\ *n* : a small wig used esp. to enhance a hairstyle

¹wig·wag \'wig-ˌwag\ *vb* **1** : to signal by or as if by a flag or light waved according to a code **2** : to make or cause to make a signal (as with the hand or arm)

²wigwag *n* : the art or practice of wigwagging

wig·wam \'wig-ˌwäm\ *n* : a hut of the Indians of the eastern U.S. having typically an arched framework of poles overlaid with bark, rush mats, or hides

wigwam

¹wild \'wī(-ə)ld\ *adj* **1** : living in a state of nature and not ordinarily tamed ⟨∼ ducks⟩ **2** : growing or produced without human aid or care ⟨∼ honey⟩ ⟨∼ plants⟩ **3** : WASTE, DESOLATE ⟨∼ country⟩ **4** : UNCONTROLLED, UNRESTRAINED, UNRULY ⟨∼ passions⟩ ⟨a ∼ young stallion⟩ **5** : TURBULENT, STORMY ⟨a ∼ night⟩ **6** : EXTRAVAGANT, FANTASTIC, CRAZY ⟨∼ ideas⟩ **7** : indicative of strong passion, desire, or emotion ⟨a ∼ stare⟩ **8** : UNCIVILIZED, SAVAGE **9** : deviating from the natural or expected course : ERRATIC ⟨a ∼ throw⟩ **10** : able to represent any playing card designated by the holder ⟨deuces ∼⟩ — **wild·ly** *adv* — **wild·ness** *n*

²wild *adv* **1** : WILDLY **2** : without regulation or control ⟨running ∼⟩

³wild *n* **1** : WILDERNESS **2** : a natural or undomesticated state or existence

wild boar *n* : an Old World wild hog from which most domestic swine have been derived

wild card *n* **1** : an unknown or unpredictable factor **2** : one picked to fill a leftover play-off or tournament position **3** *usu* **wild·card** : a symbol (as ? or *) used in a keyword search to represent the presence of unspecified characters

wild carrot *n* : QUEEN ANNE'S LACE

¹wild·cat \'wī(-ə)ld-ˌkat\ *n, pl* **wildcats 1** : any of various small or medium-sized cats (as a lynx or ocelot) **2** : a quick-tempered hard-fighting person

²wildcat *adj* **1** : not sound or safe ⟨∼ schemes⟩ **2** : initiated by a group of workers without formal union approval ⟨∼ strike⟩

³wildcat *vb* **wild·cat·ted; wild·cat·ting** : to drill an oil or gas well in a region not known to be productive

wil·de·beest \'wil-də-ˌbēst\ *n, pl* **wildebeests** *also* **wildebeest** [Afrikaans *wildebees*, fr. *wilde* wild + *bees* ox] : either of two large African antelopes with an oxlike head and horns and a horselike mane and tail

wil·der·ness \'wil-dər-nəs\ *n* [ME, fr. *wildern* wild, fr. OE *wilddēoren* of wild beasts] : an uncultivated and uninhabited region

wild·fire \'wī(-ə)ld-ˌfī(-ə)r\ *n* : an uncontrollable fire — **like wildfire** : very rapidly

wild·flow·er \-ˌflaů(-ə)r\ *n* : the flower of a wild or uncultivated plant or the plant bearing it

wild·fowl \-ˌfaů(-ə)l\ *n* : a bird and esp. a waterfowl hunted as game

wild–goose chase *n* : the pursuit of something unattainable

wild·life \'wī(-ə)ld-ˌlīf\ *n* : nonhuman living things and esp. wild animals living in their natural environment

wild oat *n* **1** : any of several Old World wild grasses **2** *pl* : offenses and indiscretions attributed to youthful exuberance — usu. used in the phrase *sow one's wild oats*

wild rice *n* : a No. American aquatic grass; *also* : its edible seed

wild type *n* : a gene or trait that is typical of a natural population of organisms in contrast to that of mutant forms; *also* : an organism with such a gene or trait

wild·wood \'wī(-ə)ld-ˌwůd\ *n* : a wood unaltered or unfrequented by humans

¹wile \'wī(-ə)l\ *n* **1** : a trick or stratagem intended to ensnare or deceive; *also* : a playful trick **2** : TRICKERY, GUILE

²wile *vb* **wiled; wil·ing** : LURE, ENTICE

¹will \'wil\ *vb, past* **would** \'wůd\ *pres sing & pl* **will 1** : WISH, DESIRE ⟨call it what you ∼⟩ **2** — used as an auxiliary verb to express (1) desire, willingness, or in negative constructions refusal ⟨∼ you have another⟩ ⟨he *won't* do it⟩, (2) customary or habitual action ⟨∼ get angry over nothing⟩, (3) simple futurity ⟨tomorrow we ∼ go shopping⟩, (4) capability or sufficiency ⟨the back seat ∼ hold three⟩, (5) determination or willfulness ⟨I ∼ go despite them⟩, (6) probability ⟨that ∼ be the mailman⟩, (7) inevitability ⟨accidents ∼ happen⟩, or (8) a command ⟨you ∼ do as I say⟩

²will *n* **1** : wish or desire often combined with determination ⟨the ∼ to win⟩ **2** : something desired; *esp* : a choice or determination of one having authority or power **3** : the act, process, or experience of willing : VOLITION **4** : the mental powers manifested as wishing, choosing, desiring, or intending **5** : a disposition to act according to principles or ends **6** : power of controlling one's own actions or emotions ⟨a leader of iron ∼⟩ **7** : a legal document in which a person declares to whom his or her possessions are to go after death

³will *vb* **1** : to dispose of by or as if by a will : BEQUEATH **2** : to determine by an act of choice; *also* : DECREE, ORDAIN **3** : INTEND, PURPOSE; *also* : CHOOSE

will·ful *or* **wil·ful** \'wil-fəl\ *adj* **1** : governed by will without regard to reason : OBSTINATE **2** : INTENTIONAL ⟨∼ murder⟩ — **will·ful·ly** *adv*

wil·lies \'wi-lēz\ *n pl* : a fit of nervousness : JITTERS — used with *the*

will·ing \'wi-liŋ\ *adj* **1** : inclined or favorably disposed in mind : READY ⟨∼ to go⟩ **2** : prompt to act or respond ⟨∼ workers⟩ **3** : done, borne, or accepted voluntarily or without reluctance **4** : of or relating to the will : VOLITIONAL — **will·ing·ly** *adv* — **will·ing·ness** *n*

wil·li·waw \'wi-lē-ˌwȯ\ *n* : a sudden violent gust of cold land air common along mountainous coasts of high latitudes

will–o'–the–wisp \ˌwil-ə-thə-'wisp\ *n* **1** : a light that appears at night over marshy grounds **2** : a misleading or elusive goal or hope

wil·low \'wi-lō\ *n* **1** : any of a genus of quick-growing shrubs and trees with tough pliable shoots **2** : an object made of willow wood

wil·low·ware \-ˌwer\ *n* : dinnerware that is usu. blue and white and that is decorated with a story-telling design featuring a large willow tree by a little bridge

wil·lowy \'wi-lə-wē\ *adj* : PLIANT; *also* : gracefully tall and slender

will·pow·er \'wil-ˌpaů(-ə)r\ *n* : energetic determination : RESOLUTENESS

wil·ly–nil·ly \ˌwi-lē-'ni-lē\ *adv or adj* [alter. of *will I nill I* or *will ye nill ye* or *will he nill he*; *nill* fr. archaic *nill* to be unwilling, fr. ME *nilen*, fr. OE *nyllan*, fr. *ne* not + *wyllan* to wish] : without regard for one's choice : by compulsion ⟨they rushed us along ∼⟩

¹wilt \'wilt\ *vb* **1** : to lose or cause to lose freshness and become limp esp. from lack of water : DROOP ⟨the roses were ∼*ing*⟩ **2** : to grow weak or faint : LANGUISH

²wilt *n* : any of various plant disorders marked by wilting and often shriveling

wily \'wī-lē\ *adj* **wil·i·er; -est** : full of guile : TRICKY — **wil·i·ness** \-lē-nəs\ *n*

wimp \'wimp\ *n* : a weak, cowardly, or ineffectual person — **wimpy** \'wim-pē\ *adj*

¹wim·ple \'wim-pəl\ *n* : a cloth covering worn over the head and around the neck and chin by women esp. in the late medieval period and by some nuns

²wimple *vb* **wim·pled; wim·pling** **1** : to cover with or as if with a wimple **2** : to ripple or cause to ripple

¹win \'win\ *vb* **won** \'wən\; **win·ning** [ME *winnen,* fr. OE *winnan* to struggle] **1** : to get possession of esp. by effort : GAIN; *also* : to obtain by work : EARN **2** : to gain in or as if in battle or contest; *also* : to be the victor in ⟨*won* the war⟩ **3** : to solicit and gain the favor of; *esp* : to induce to accept oneself in marriage

²win *n* : VICTORY; *esp* : 1st place at the finish (as of a horse race)

wince \'wins\ *vb* **winced; winc·ing** : to shrink back involuntarily (as from pain) : FLINCH — **wince** *n*

winch \'winch\ *n* : a machine that has a drum on which is wound a rope or cable for hauling or hoisting — **winch** *vb*

¹wind \'wind\ *n* **1** : a movement of the air **2** : a prevailing force or influence : TENDENCY, TREND **3** : BREATH ⟨he had the ~ knocked out of him⟩ **4** : gas produced in the stomach or intestines **5** : something insubstantial; *esp* : idle words **6** : air carrying a scent (as of game) **7** : INTIMATION ⟨they got ~ of our plans⟩ **8** : WIND INSTRUMENTS; *also, pl* : players of wind instruments

²wind *vb* **1** : to get a scent of ⟨the dogs ~*ed* the game⟩ **2** : to cause to be out of breath ⟨he was ~*ed* from the climb⟩ **3** : to allow (as a horse) to rest so as to recover breath

³wind \'wīnd, 'wind\ *vb* **wind·ed** \'wīn-dəd, 'win-\ *or* **wound** \'waund\; **wind·ing** : to sound by blowing ⟨~ a horn⟩

⁴wind \'wīnd\ *vb* **wound** \'waund\ *also* **wind·ed; wind·ing** **1** : ENTANGLE, INVOLVE **2** : to introduce stealthily : INSINUATE **3** : to encircle or cover with something pliable : WRAP, COIL, TWINE ⟨~ a bobbin⟩ **4** : to hoist or haul by a rope or chain and a winch **5** : to tighten the spring of; *also* : CRANK **6** : to raise to a high level (as of excitement) **7** : to cause to move in a curving line or path **8** : to have a curving course or shape ⟨a river ~*ing* through the valley⟩ **9** : to move or lie so as to encircle

⁵wind \'wīnd\ *n* : COIL, TURN

wind·age \'win-dij\ *n* : the influence of the wind in deflecting the course of a projectile through the air; *also* : the amount of such deflection

wind·bag \'wind-,bag\ *n* : an overly talkative person

wind·blown \-,blōn\ *adj* : blown by the wind; *also* : having the appearance of being blown by the wind ⟨~ hair⟩

wind·break \-,brāk\ *n* : a growth of trees or shrubs serving to break the force of the wind; *also* : a shelter from the wind

wind·burned \-,bərnd\ *adj* : irritated and inflamed by exposure to the wind — **wind·burn** \-,bərn\ *n*

wind·chill \-,chil\ *n* : a still-air temperature that would have the same cooling effect on exposed human skin as a given combination of temperature and wind speed

windchill factor *n* : WINDCHILL

wind down *vb* **1** : to draw toward an end **2** : RELAX, UNWIND

wind·er \'wīn-dər\ *n* : one that winds

wind·fall \'wind-,fol\ *n* **1** : something (as a tree or fruit) blown down by the wind **2** : an unexpected or sudden gift, gain, or advantage ⟨won a ~ from the lottery⟩

wind·flow·er \-,flaü-(ə)r\ *n* : ANEMONE

¹wind·ing \'wīn-diŋ\ *n* : material (as wire) wound or coiled about an object

²winding *adj* **1** : having a pronounced curve or spiral ⟨~ stairs⟩ **2** : having a course that winds ⟨a ~ road⟩

wind·ing–sheet \-,shēt\ *n* : SHROUD

wind instrument *n* : a musical instrument (as a flute or horn) sounded by wind and esp. by the breath

wind·jam·mer \'wind-,ja-mər\ *n* : a sailing ship; *also* : one of its crew

wind·lass \'wind-ləs\ *n* [ME *wyndlas,* alter. of *wyndase,* fr. OF *guindas, windas,* fr. ON *vindáss,* fr. *vinda* to wind

+ *áss* pole] : a winch used esp. on ships for hoisting or hauling

wind·mill \'wind-,mil\ *n* : a mill or machine worked by the wind turning sails or vanes that radiate from a central shaft

win·dow \'win-dō\ *n* [ME *windowe,* fr. ON *vindauga,* fr. *vindr* wind + *auga* eye] **1** : an opening in the wall of a building to let in light and air; *also* : the framework with fittings that closes such an opening **2** : WINDOWPANE **3** : an opening resembling or suggesting that of a window in a building **4** : an interval of time during which certain conditions or an opportunity exists **5** : a rectangular box appearing on a computer screen on which information (as files or program output) is displayed — **win·dow·less** *adj*

window box *n* : a box for growing plants in or by a window

window dressing *n* **1** : display of merchandise in a store window **2** : a showing made to create a deceptively favorable impression

win·dow·pane \'win-dō-,pān\ *n* : a pane in a window

win·dow–shop \-,shäp\ *vb* : to look at the displays in store windows without going inside the stores to make purchases — **win·dow–shop·per** *n*

win·dow·sill \-,sil\ *n* : the horizontal member at the bottom of a window

wind·pipe \'wind-,pīp\ *n* : TRACHEA

wind·proof \-'prüf\ *adj* : impervious to wind ⟨a ~ jacket⟩

wind·row \'wind-,rō\ *n* **1** : hay raked up into a row to dry **2** : a row of something (as dry leaves) swept up by or as if by the wind

wind shear *n* : a radical shift in wind speed and direction that occurs over a very short distance

wind·shield \'wind-,shēld\ *n* : a transparent screen (as of glass) in front of the occupants of a vehicle

wind sock *n* : an open-ended truncated cloth cone mounted in an elevated position to indicate wind direction

wind·storm \-,storm\ *n* : a storm with high wind and little or no rain

wind·surf·ing \-,sər-fiŋ\ *n* : the sport or activity of riding a sailboard — **wind·surf** \-,sərf\ *vb* — **wind·surf·er** *n*

wind·swept \'wind-,swept\ *adj* : swept by or as if by wind ⟨~ plains⟩

wind tunnel *n* : an enclosed passage through which air is blown to investigate air flow around an object

wind–up \'wīn-,dəp\ *n* **1** : CONCLUSION, FINISH **2** : a series of regular and distinctive motions made by a pitcher preliminary to delivering a pitch

wind up *vb* **1** : to bring or come to a conclusion : END ⟨*wind up* the meeting⟩ **2** : to put in order for the purpose of bringing to an end **3** : to arrive in a place, situation, or condition at the end or as a result of a course of action ⟨*wound up* as paupers⟩ **4** : to make a pitching windup

¹wind·ward \'win-dwərd\ *n* : the side or direction from which the wind is blowing

²windward *adj* : being in or facing the direction from which the wind is blowing

windy \'win-dē\ *adj* **wind·i·er; -est** **1** : having wind : exposed to winds ⟨a ~ day⟩ ⟨a ~ prairie⟩ **2** : STORMY **3** : FLATULENT **4** : indulging in or characterized by useless talk : VERBOSE

¹wine \'wīn\ *n* [ME *win,* fr. OE *wīn,* ultim. fr. L *vinum*] **1** : fermented grape juice used as a beverage **2** : the usu. fermented juice of a plant product (as fruit) used as a beverage ⟨rice ~⟩

²wine *vb* **wined; win·ing** : to treat to or drink wine

wine cellar *n* : a room for storing wines; *also* : a stock of wines

wine·grow·er \-,grō-ər\ *n* : one that cultivates a vineyard and makes wine

wine·press \-,pres\ *n* : a vat in which juice is pressed from grapes

win·ery \'wī-nə-rē, 'wīn-rē\ *n, pl* **-eries** : a wine-making establishment

¹wing \'wiŋ\ *n* **1** : one of the movable feathered or membranous paired appendages by means of which a bird, bat, or insect flies **2** : something suggesting a wing; *esp* : an airfoil that develops the lift which supports an aircraft in flight **3** : a plant or animal appendage or part likened to a wing **4** : a turned-back or extended edge on an article of clothing **5** : a means of flight or rapid progress **6** : the act or manner of flying : FLIGHT **7** *pl* : the area at the side of the stage out of sight **8** : one of the positions or players on either side of a center position or line **9** : either of two opposing groups within an organization : FACTION **10** : a unit in military aviation consisting of two or more squadrons — **wing·less** *adj* — **wing·like** \-ˌlīk\ *adj* — **on the wing** : in flight : FLYING — **under one's wing** : in one's charge or care

²**wing** *vb* **1** : to fit with wings; *also* : to enable to fly easily **2** : to pass through in flight : FLY ⟨~ the air⟩ ⟨swallows ~ing southward⟩ **3** : to let fly : DISPATCH **4** : to wound in the wing ⟨~ a bird⟩; *also* : to wound without killing **5** : to perform without preparation : IMPROVISE ⟨~ing it⟩

wing·ding \ˈwiŋ-ˌdiŋ\ *n* : a wild, lively, or lavish party

winged \ˈwiŋd, ˈwiŋ-əd, *in compounds* ˈwiŋd\ *adj* **1** : having wings esp. of a specified character **2** : soaring with or as if with wings : ELEVATED **3** : SWIFT, RAPID

wing nut *n* : a nut with winglike extensions that can be gripped with the thumb and finger

wing·span \ˈwiŋ-ˌspan\ *n* : the distance between the tips of a pair of wings

wing·spread \-ˌspred\ *n* : the spread of the wings; *esp* : the distance between the tips of the fully extended wings of a winged animal

¹**wink** \ˈwiŋk\ *vb* **1** : to close and open one eye quickly as a signal or hint **2** : to close and open the eyes quickly : BLINK **3** : to avoid seeing or noticing something ⟨~ at a traffic violation⟩ **4** : TWINKLE, FLICKER — **wink·er** \ˈwiŋ-kər\ *n*

²**wink** *n* **1** : a brief period of sleep : NAP **2** : an act of winking; *esp* : a hint or sign given by winking : INSTANT ⟨dries in a ~⟩

win·ner \ˈwi-nər\ *n* : one that wins

¹**win·ning** \ˈwi-niŋ\ *n* **1** : VICTORY **2** : something won; *esp* : money won at gambling ⟨large ~s⟩

²**winning** *adj* **1** : successful esp. in competition **2** : ATTRACTIVE, CHARMING

win·now \ˈwi-nō\ *vb* **1** : to remove (as chaff) by a current of air; *also* : to free (as grain) from waste in this manner **2** : to sort or separate as if by winnowing

wino \ˈwī-nō\ *n, pl* **win·os** : one who is addicted to drinking wine

win·some \ˈwin-səm\ *adj* [ME *winsum*, fr. OE *wynsum*, fr. *wynn* joy] **1** : generally pleasing and engaging ⟨a ~ smile⟩ **2** : CHEERFUL, GAY — **win·some·ly** *adv* — **win·some·ness** *n*

¹**win·ter** \ˈwin-tər\ *n* : the season of the year in any region in which the noonday sun shines most obliquely : the coldest period of the year

²**winter** *vb* **1** : to pass the winter ⟨~ed in Florida⟩ **2** : to feed or find food during the winter ⟨~ed on hay⟩

³**winter** *adj* : sown in autumn for harvesting in the following spring or summer ⟨~ wheat⟩

win·ter·green \ˈwin-tər-ˌgrēn\ *n* **1** : a low evergreen plant of the heath family with white bell-shaped flowers and spicy red berries **2** : an aromatic oil or its flavor from the wintergreen

win·ter·ize \ˈwin-tə-ˌrīz\ *vb* **-ized; -iz·ing** : to make ready for winter

win·ter–kill \ˈwin-tər-ˌkil\ *vb* : to kill or die by exposure to winter weather

winter squash *n* : any of various hard-shelled squashes that keep well in storage

win·ter·tide \-ˌtīd\ *n* : WINTER

win·ter·time \-ˌtīm\ *n* : WINTER

win·try \ˈwin-trē\ *also* **win·tery** \ˈwin-tə-rē\ *adj* **win·tri·er; -est** **1** : of, relating to, or characteristic of winter ⟨~ weather⟩ **2** : CHILLING, CHEERLESS ⟨a ~ welcome⟩

¹**wipe** \ˈwīp\ *vb* **wiped; wip·ing** **1** : to clean or dry by rubbing ⟨~ dishes⟩ **2** : to remove by or as if by rubbing ⟨~ away tears⟩ **3** : to erase completely : OBLITERATE **4** : to pass or draw over a surface ⟨*wiped* his hand across his face⟩ — **wip·er** *n*

²**wipe** *n* **1** : an act or instance of wiping; *also* : BLOW, STRIKE, SWIPE **2** : something used for wiping ⟨disposable ~s⟩

wipe out *vb* : to destroy completely

¹**wire** \ˈwī(-ə)r\ *n* **1** : metal in the form of a thread or slender rod; *also* : a thread or rod of metal **2** : hidden or secret influences controlling the action of a person or organization — usu. used in pl. ⟨pull ~s⟩ **3** : a line of wire for conducting electric current **4** : a telegraph or telephone wire or system **5** : TELEGRAM, CABLEGRAM **6** : the finish line of a race

²**wire** *vb* **wired; wir·ing** **1** : to provide or equip with wire ⟨~ a house⟩ **2** : to bind, string, or mount with wire **3** : to send or send word to by telegraph

wired *adj* **1** : furnished with wires **2** : connected to the Internet **3** : feverishly excited ⟨~ fans⟩

wire·hair \ˈwī(-ə)r-ˌher\ *n* : a wirehaired dog or cat

wire·haired \-ˈherd\ *adj* : having a stiff wiry outer coat of hair

¹**wire·less** \-ləs\ *adj* **1** : having no wire or wires **2** : RADIO **3** : of or relating to data communications using radio waves

²**wireless** *n* **1** : telecommunication involving signals transmitted by radio waves; *also* : the technology used in radio telecommunication **2** *chiefly Brit* : RADIO

wire service *n* : a news agency that sends out syndicated news copy to subscribers by wire or satellite

wire·tap \-ˌtap\ *n* : the act or an instance of tapping a telephone or telegraph wire to get information; *also* : an electrical connection used for such tapping — **wiretap** *vb* — **wire·tap·per** \-ˌta-pər\ *n*

wire·worm \-ˌwərm\ *n* : any of various slender hard-coated beetle larvae esp. destructive to plant roots

wir·ing \ˈwī(-ə)r-iŋ\ *n* : a system of wires

wiry \ˈwī(-ə)r-ē\ *adj* **wir·i·er** \ˈwī-rē-ər\; **-est** **1** : made of or resembling wire **2** : slender yet strong and sinewy ⟨~ arms⟩ — **wir·i·ness** \ˈwī-rē-nəs\ *n*

Wis *or* **Wisc** *abbr* Wisconsin

Wisd *abbr* Wisdom

wis·dom \ˈwiz-dəm\ *n* [ME, fr. OE *wīsdom*, fr. *wīs* wise] **1** : accumulated philosophic or scientific learning : KNOWLEDGE; *also* : INSIGHT **2** : good sense : JUDGMENT **3** : a wise attitude or course of action

Wisdom *n* — see BIBLE table

Wisdom of Sol·o·mon \-ˈsä-lə-mən\ — see BIBLE table

wisdom tooth *n* : the last tooth of the full set on each side of the upper and lower jaws of humans

¹**wise** \ˈwīz\ *n* : WAY, MANNER, FASHION ⟨in no ~⟩ ⟨in this ~⟩

²**wise** *adj* **wis·er; wis·est** **1** : having wisdom : SAGE **2** : having or showing good sense or good judgment **3** : aware of what is going on : KNOWING ⟨got ~ to his secrets⟩; *also* : CRAFTY, SHREWD **4** : possessing inside information ⟨~ to the deal⟩ **5** : INSOLENT, FRESH ⟨a ~ retort⟩ — **wise·ly** *adv*

-wise \-ˌwīz\ *adv comb form* : in the manner or direction of ⟨slantwise⟩

wise·acre \ˈwīz-ˌā-kər\ *n* [MD *wijssegger* soothsayer] : SMART ALECK

¹**wise·crack** \ˈwīz-ˌkrak\ *n* : a clever, smart, or flippant remark

²**wisecrack** *vb* : to make a wisecrack

wise guy *n* : SMART ALECK

¹**wish** \ˈwish\ *vb* **1** : to have a desire : long for ⟨~ you were here⟩ ⟨~ for a puppy⟩ **2** : to form or express a wish concerning ⟨~ed him a happy birthday⟩ **3** : BID ⟨he ~ed me good morning⟩ **4** : to request by expressing a desire ⟨I ~ you to go now⟩

²**wish** *n* **1** : an act or instance of wishing or desire : WANT; *also* : GOAL **2** : an expressed will or desire

wish·bone \-ˌbōn\ *n* : a forked bone in front of the breastbone in most birds

wish·ful \ˈwish-fəl\ *adj* **1** : expressive of a wish; *also* : having a wish **2** : according with wishes rather than fact ⟨~ thinking⟩

wishy–washy \ˈwi-shē-ˌwȯ-shē, -ˌwä-\ *adj* : WEAK, INSIPID; *also* : morally feeble

wisp \ˈwisp\ *n* **1** : a small handful (as of hay or straw) **2** : a thin strand, strip, or fragment ⟨a ~ of hair⟩; *also* : a thready streak ⟨a ~ of smoke⟩ **3** : something frail, slight, or fleeting ⟨a ~ of a smile⟩ — **wispy** *adj*

wis·te·ria \wis-ˈtir-ē-ə\ *also* **wis·tar·ia** \-ˈtir-ē-ə *also* -ˈter-\ *n* : any of a genus of chiefly Asian mostly woody vines related to the peas and widely grown for their long showy clusters of blue, white, purple, or rose flowers

wist·ful \'wist-fəl\ *adj* : feeling or showing a timid desire ⟨∼ memories⟩ — **wist·ful·ly** *adv* — **wist·ful·ness** *n*

wit \'wit\ *n* **1** : reasoning power : INTELLIGENCE **2** : mental soundness : SANITY — usu. used in pl. **3** : RESOURCEFULNESS, INGENUITY; *esp* : quickness and cleverness in handling words and ideas **4** : a talent for making clever remarks; *also* : a person noted for making witty remarks — **wit·ted** \'wi-təd\ *adj* — **at one's wit's end** : at a loss for a means of solving a problem

¹witch \'wich\ *n* **1** : a person believed to have magic power; *esp* : SORCERESS **2** : an ugly old woman : HAG **3** : a charming or alluring girl or woman **4** : an adherent of Wicca

²witch *vb* : BEWITCH

witch·craft \'wich-ˌkraft\ *n* **1** : the power or practices of a witch : SORCERY **2** : WICCA

witch doctor *n* : a person in a primitive society who uses magic to treat sickness and to fight off evil spirits

witch·ery \'wi-chə-rē\ *n, pl* **-er·ies** **1** : SORCERY **2** : FASCINATION, CHARM

witch·grass \'wich-ˌgras\ *n* : any of several grasses that are weeds in cultivated areas

witch ha·zel \'wich-ˌhā-zəl\ *n* **1** : a shrub of eastern No. America bearing small yellow flowers in the fall **2** : a soothing alcoholic lotion made from witch hazel bark

witch·hunt \'wich-ˌhənt\ *n* **1** : a searching out and persecution of persons accused of witchcraft **2** : the searching out and deliberate harassment esp. of political opponents

witch·ing \'wi-chin\ *adj* : of, relating to, or suitable for sorcery or supernatural occurrences

with \'with, 'with\ *prep* **1** : AGAINST ⟨a fight ∼ his brother⟩ **2** : FROM ⟨parting ∼ friends⟩ **3** : in mutual relation to ⟨talk ∼ a friend⟩ **4** : in the company of ⟨went there ∼ her⟩ **5** : AS REGARDS, TOWARD ⟨is patient ∼ children⟩ **6** : compared to ⟨on equal terms ∼ another⟩ **7** : in support of ⟨I'm ∼ you all the way⟩ **8** : in the presence of : CONTAINING ⟨tea ∼ sugar⟩ **9** : in the opinion of : as judged by ⟨their arguments had weight ∼ her⟩ **10** : BECAUSE OF, THROUGH ⟨pale ∼ anger⟩; *also* : by means of ⟨hit him ∼ a club⟩ **11** : in a manner indicating ⟨work ∼ a will⟩ **12** : GIVEN, GRANTED ⟨∼ your permission I'll leave⟩ **13** : HAVING ⟨came ∼ good news⟩ ⟨stood there ∼ his mouth open⟩ **14** : characterized by ⟨boys ∼ good morals⟩ **15** : at the time of : right after ⟨∼ that we left⟩ **16** : DESPITE ⟨∼ all her cleverness, she failed⟩ **17** : in the direction of ⟨swim ∼ the tide⟩

with·al \wi-'thól, -'thól\ *adv* **1** : together with this : BESIDES **2** : on the other hand : NEVERTHELESS

with·draw \with-'dró, with-\ *vb* **-drew** \-'drü\; **-drawn** \-'drón\; **-draw·ing** \-'dró-in\ **1** : to take back or away : REMOVE **2** : to call back (as from consideration); *also* : RETRACT **3** : to go away : RETREAT, LEAVE **4** : to terminate one's participation in or use of something

with·draw·al \-'dró-əl\ *n* **1** : an act or instance of withdrawing **2** : the discontinuance of the use or administration of a drug and esp. an addicting drug; *also* : the period following such discontinuance marked by often painful physiological and psychological symptoms **3** : a pathological retreat from the real world (as in some schizophrenic states)

with·drawn \with-'drón\ *adj* **1** : ISOLATED, SECLUDED **2** : socially detached and unresponsive ⟨became depressed and ∼⟩

withe \'with\ *n* : a slender flexible twig or branch

with·er \'wi-thər\ *vb* **1** : to shrivel from or as if from loss of bodily moisture and esp. sap **2** : to lose or cause to lose vitality, force, or freshness ⟨their enthusiasm ∼ed⟩ **3** : to cause to feel shriveled ⟨∼ed him with a glance⟩

with·ers \'wi-thərz\ *n pl* : the ridge between the shoulder bones of a horse; *also* : the corresponding part in other 4-footed animals

with·hold \with-'hōld, with-\ *vb* **-held** \-'held\; **-hold·ing** **1** : to hold back : RESTRAIN; *also* : RETAIN **2** : to refrain from granting, giving, or allowing ⟨∼ permission⟩ ⟨∼ names⟩

withholding tax *n* : a tax on income withheld at the source

¹with·in \wi-'thin, -'thin-\ *adv* **1** : in or into the interior : INSIDE **2** : inside oneself : INWARDLY

²within *prep* **1** : inside the limits or influence of ⟨∼ call⟩ **2** : in the limits or compass of ⟨∼ a mile⟩ **3** : in or to the inner part of ⟨∼ the room⟩

with–it \'wi-thət, -thət\ *adj* : socially or culturally up-to-date

¹with·out \wi-'thaut, -'thaut\ *prep* **1** : OUTSIDE **2** : LACKING ⟨∼ hope⟩; *also* : not accompanied by or showing ⟨spoke ∼ thinking⟩

²without *adv* **1** : on the outside : EXTERNALLY **2** : with something lacking or absent ⟨has learned to do ∼⟩

with·stand \with-'stand, with-\ *vb* **-stood** \-'stud\; **-stand·ing** : to stand against : RESIST; *esp* : to oppose (as an attack) successfully

wit·less \'wit-ləs\ *adj* : lacking wit or understanding : FOOLISH — **wit·less·ly** *adv* — **wit·less·ness** *n*

¹wit·ness \'wit-nəs\ *n* [ME *witnesse*, fr. OE *witnes* knowledge, testimony, witness, fr. *wit* mind, intelligence] **1** : TESTIMONY ⟨bear ∼ to the fact⟩ **2** : one that gives evidence; *esp* : one who testifies in a cause or before a court **3** : one present at a transaction so as to be able to testify that it has taken place **4** : one who has personal knowledge or experience of something **5** : something serving as evidence or proof : SIGN

²witness *vb* **1** : to bear witness : TESTIFY **2** : to act as legal witness of **3** : to furnish proof of : BETOKEN **4** : to be a witness of **5** : to be the scene of ⟨this region has ∼ed many wars⟩

wit·ti·cism \'wi-tə-ˌsi-zəm\ *n* : a witty saying or phrase

wit·ting \'wi-tin\ *adj* : done knowingly : INTENTIONAL — **wit·ting·ly** *adv*

wit·ty \'wi-tē\ *adj* **wit·ti·er; -est** : marked by or full of wit : AMUSING ⟨a ∼ writer⟩ ⟨a ∼ remark⟩ ✦ *Synonyms* HUMOROUS, FACETIOUS, JOCULAR, JOCOSE — **wit·ti·ly** \-tə-lē\ *adv* — **wit·ti·ness** \-tē-nəs\ *n*

wive \'wīv\ *vb* **wived; wiv·ing** : to take a wife

wives *pl of* WIFE

wiz·ard \'wi-zərd\ *n* [ME *wysard* wise man, fr. *wys* wise] **1** : MAGICIAN, SORCERER **2** : a very clever or skillful person ⟨a ∼ at chess⟩

wiz·ard·ry \'wi-zər-drē\ *n, pl* **-ries** **1** : magic skill : SORCERY **2** : great skill or cleverness in an activity

wiz·en \'wi-zᵊn, 'wē-\ *vb* : to become or cause to become dry, shrunken, or wrinkled ⟨a face ∼ed by age⟩

wk *abbr* **1** week **2** work

WL *abbr* wavelength

wmk *abbr* watermark

WNW *abbr* west-northwest

WO *abbr* warrant officer

w/o *abbr* without

woad \'wōd\ *n* : a European herb related to the mustards; *also* : a blue dyestuff made from its leaves

wob·ble \'wä-bəl\ *vb* **wob·bled; wob·bling** **1** : to move or cause to move with an irregular rocking or side-to-side motion **2** : TREMBLE, QUAVER **3** : WAVER, VACILLATE — **wobble** *n* — **wob·bly** \-bə-lē\ *adj*

woe \'wō\ *n* **1** : deep suffering from misfortune, affliction, or grief **2** : TROUBLE, MISFORTUNE ⟨economic ∼s⟩

woe·be·gone \'wō-bi-ˌgón\ *adj* : exhibiting woe, sorrow, or misery ⟨∼ faces⟩; *also* : being in a sorry condition

woe·ful *also* **wo·ful** \'wō-fəl\ *adj* **1** : full of woe : AFFLICTED **2** : involving, bringing, or relating to woe ⟨∼ stories⟩ **3** : DEPLORABLE ⟨∼ test scores⟩ — **woe·ful·ly** *adv*

wok \'wäk\ *n* [Chin (Guangzhou & Hong Kong dial.) *wohk*] : a bowl-shaped cooking utensil used esp. in stir=frying

¹woke *past and past part of* WAKE

²woke \'wōk\ *adj* **wok·er; wok·est** *slang* : aware of and actively attentive to important facts and issues (especially issues of racial and social justice)

woken *past part of* WAKE

wold \'wōld\ *n* : an upland plain or stretch of rolling land without woods

¹wolf \'wulf\ *n, pl* **wolves** \'wulvz\ **1** : any of several large erect-eared bushy-tailed doglike predatory mammals that live and hunt in packs; *esp* : GRAY WOLF **2** : a fierce or destructive person — **wolf·ish** *adj* — **wolf in sheep's clothing** : one who hides a hostile intention with a friendly manner

²wolf *vb* : to eat greedily : DEVOUR

wolf·hound \-ˌhaund\ *n* : any of several large dogs orig. used in hunting wolves

wol·fram \'wul-frəm\ *n* : TUNGSTEN
wol·ver·ine \ˌwul-və-'rēn\ *n, pl* **wolverines** *also* **wol·verine** : a dark shaggy-coated flesh-eating mammal of northern forests and associated tundra that is related to the weasels
wom·an \'wu̇-mən\ *n, pl* **wom·en** \'wi-mən\ [ME, fr. OE *wīfman,* fr. *wīf* woman, wife + *man* human being, man] **1** : an adult female person **2** : WOMANKIND **3** : feminine nature : WOMANLINESS **4** : a female servant or attendant
wom·an·hood \'wu̇-mən-ˌhu̇d\ *n* **1** : the state of being a woman : the distinguishing qualities of a woman or of womankind **2** : WOMEN, WOMANKIND
wom·an·ish \'wu̇-mə-nish\ *adj* **1** : associated with or characteristic of women rather than men **2** : suggestive of a weak character : EFFEMINATE ⟨a ∼ voice⟩
wom·an·ize \'wu̇-mə-ˌnīz\ *vb* **1** : to pursue casual sexual relationships with numerous women — **wom·an·iz·er** *n*
wom·an·kind \'wu̇-mən-ˌkīnd\ *n* : female human beings : women esp. as distinguished from men
wom·an·like \-ˌlīk\ *adj* : WOMANLY
wom·an·ly \-lē\ *adj* : having qualities characteristic of a woman — **wom·an·li·ness** \-lē-nəs\ *n*
woman suffrage *n* : possession and exercise of suffrage by women
womb \'wüm\ *n* **1** : UTERUS **2** : a place where something is generated
wom·bat \'wäm-ˌbat\ *n* : any of several stocky burrowing Australian marsupials that resemble small bears
wom·en·folk \'wi-mən-ˌfōk\ *also* **wom·en·folks** \-ˌfōks\ *n pl* : WOMEN
¹won \'wən\ *past and past part of* WIN
²won \'wän\ *n, pl* **won** — see MONEY table
¹won·der \'wən-dər\ *n* **1** : a cause of astonishment or surprise : MARVEL; *also* : MIRACLE **2** : the quality of exciting wonder ⟨the charm and ∼ of the scene⟩ **3** : a feeling (as of awed astonishment or uncertainty) aroused by something extraordinary or affecting
²wonder *vb* **1** : to feel surprise or amazement **2** : to feel curiosity or doubt ⟨∼ about the future⟩
wonder drug *n* : MIRACLE DRUG
won·der·ful \'wən-dər-fəl\ *adj* **1** : exciting wonder : MARVELOUS, ASTONISHING **2** : unusually good : ADMIRABLE ⟨did a ∼ job⟩ — **won·der·ful·ly** \-f(ə-)lē\ *adv* — **won·der·ful·ness** *n*
won·der·land \-ˌland, -lənd\ *n* **1** : an imaginary place of delicate beauty or magical charm **2** : a place that excites admiration or wonder ⟨a scenic ∼⟩
won·der·ment \-mənt\ *n* **1** : ASTONISHMENT, SURPRISE **2** : a cause of or occasion for wonder **3** : curiosity about something
won·drous \'wən-drəs\ *adj* : WONDERFUL, MARVELOUS ⟨a ∼ feat⟩ — **won·drous·ly** *adv* — **won·drous·ness** *n*
wonk \'wäŋk, 'wȯŋk\ *n* : one who works in a specialized usu. intellectual field ⟨computer ∼s⟩
¹wont \'wȯnt, 'wōnt\ *adj* [ME *woned, wont,* fr. pp. of *wonen* to dwell, be used to, fr. OE *wunian*] **1** : ACCUSTOMED, USED ⟨as we are ∼ to do⟩ **2** : INCLINED, APT
²wont *n* : CUSTOM, USAGE, HABIT ⟨according to her ∼⟩
won't \'wōnt\ : will not
wont·ed \'wȯn-təd, 'wōn-\ *adj* : ACCUSTOMED, CUSTOMARY ⟨his ∼ courtesy⟩
woo \'wü\ *vb* **1** : to try to gain the love of : COURT **2** : SOLICIT, ENTREAT **3** : to try to gain or bring about ⟨∼ public favor⟩ — **woo·er** *n*
¹wood \'wu̇d\ *n* **1** : a dense growth of trees usu. larger than a grove and smaller than a forest — often used in pl. **2** : a hard fibrous substance that is basically xylem and forms the bulk of trees and shrubs beneath the bark; *also* : this material fit or prepared for some use (as burning or building) **3** : something made of wood
²wood *adj* **1** : WOODEN **2** : suitable for holding, cutting, or working with wood **3** *or* **woods** \'wu̇dz\ : living or growing in woods
³wood *vb* **1** : to supply or load with wood esp. for fuel **2** : to cover with a growth of trees
wood alcohol *n* : METHANOL
wood·bine \'wu̇d-ˌbīn\ *n* : any of several honeysuckles; *also* : VIRGINIA CREEPER
wood·block \-ˌbläk\ *n* : WOODCUT
wood·chop·per \-ˌchä-pər\ *n* : one engaged esp. in chopping down trees

wood·chuck \-ˌchək\ *n* : a thickset grizzled marmot of Alaska, Canada, and the northeastern U.S.

woodchuck

wood·cock \'wu̇d-ˌkäk\ *n, pl* **woodcocks** : a brown eastern No. American game bird with a short neck and long bill that is related to the snipe; *also* : a related and similar Old World bird
wood·craft \-ˌkraft\ *n* **1** : skill and practice in matters relating to the woods and esp. in how to take care of oneself in them **2** : skill in shaping or constructing articles from wood
wood·cut \-ˌkət\ *n* **1** : a relief printing surface engraved on a block of wood **2** : a print from a woodcut
wood·cut·ter \-ˌkə-tər\ *n* : a person who cuts wood
wood duck *n* : a showy crested American duck of which the male has iridescent multicolored plumage
wood·ed \'wu̇-dəd\ *adj* : covered with woods or trees ⟨∼ slopes⟩
wood·en \'wu̇-d⁼n\ *adj* **1** : made of wood **2** : lacking flexibility : awkwardly stiff ⟨∼ acting⟩ — **wood·en·ly** *adv* — **wood·en·ness** *n*
wood·en·ware \'wu̇-d⁼n-ˌwer\ *n* : articles made of wood for domestic use
wood·land \'wu̇d-lənd, -ˌland\ *n* : land covered with trees : FOREST — **woodland** *adj*
wood·lot \'wu̇d-ˌlät\ *n* : a restricted area of woodland usu. privately kept to meet fuel and timber needs
wood louse *n* : any of various small flat crustaceans that live esp. in ground litter and under stones and bark
wood·man \'wu̇d-mən\ *n* : WOODSMAN
wood·note \-ˌnōt\ *n* : verbal expression that is natural and artless
wood nymph *n* : a nymph living in the woods
wood·peck·er \'wu̇d-ˌpe-kər\ *n* : any of numerous usu. brightly marked climbing birds with stiff spiny tail feathers and a chiselike bill used to drill into trees for insects
wood·pile \-ˌpī(-ə)l\ *n* : a pile of wood and esp. firewood
wood rat *n* : PACK RAT
wood·shed \-ˌshed\ *n* : a shed for storing wood and esp. firewood
woods·man \'wu̇dz-mən\ *n* : a person who frequents or works in the woods; *esp* : one skilled in woodcraft
woodsy \'wu̇d-zē\ *adj* **woods·i·er; -est** : relating to or suggestive of woods ⟨a ∼ odor⟩
wood·wind \'wu̇d-ˌwind\ *n* : one of a group of wind instruments including flutes, clarinets, oboes, bassoons, and sometimes saxophones
wood·work \-ˌwərk\ *n* : work made of wood; *esp* : interior fittings (as moldings or stairways) of wood
woody \'wu̇-dē\ *adj* **wood·i·er; -est** **1** : abounding with or overgrown with woods ⟨a ∼ trail⟩ **2** : of or containing wood or wood fibers ⟨∼ plants⟩ **3** : characteristic of or suggestive of wood ⟨a ∼ flavor⟩ — **wood·i·ness** \'wu̇-dē-nəs\ *n*
woof \'wu̇f\ *n* [alter. of ME *oof,* fr. OE *ōwef,* fr. ō- (fr. *on* on) + *wefan* to weave] **1** : WEFT **1** **2** : a woven fabric; *also* : its texture
woof·er \'wu̇-fər\ *n* : a loudspeaker that reproduces sounds of low pitch
wool \'wu̇l\ *n* **1** : the soft wavy or curly hair of some mammals and esp. the domestic sheep; *also* : something (as a textile or garment) made of wool **2** : material that resembles a mass of wool — **wooled** \'wu̇ld\ *adj*
¹wool·en *or* **wool·len** \'wu̇-lən\ *adj* **1** : made of wool **2** : of or relating to the manufacture or sale of woolen products ⟨∼ mills⟩
²woolen *or* **woollen** *n* **1** : a fabric made of wool **2** : garments of woolen fabric — usu. used in pl.
wool·gath·er·ing \-ˌga-thə-riŋ\ *n* : idle daydreaming
¹wool·ly *also* **wooly** \'wu̇-lē\ *adj* **wool·li·er; -est** **1** : of,

relating to, or bearing wool **2** : consisting of or resembling wool **3** : mentally confused ⟨~ thinking⟩ **4** : marked by a lack of order or restraint ⟨the wild and ~ West⟩

²**wool·ly** *also* **wool·ie** *or* **wooly** \'wu̇-lē\ *n, pl* **wool·lies** : a garment made from wool; *esp* : underclothing of knitted wool — usu. used in pl.

woolly adel·gid \-ə-'del-jəd\ *n* : either of two aphids accidentally introduced into No. America where they are serious pests of firs and hemlocks

woolly bear *n* : any of numerous very hairy moth caterpillars

woolly mammoth *n* : a heavy-coated mammoth formerly inhabiting colder parts of the northern hemisphere

woo·zy \'wü-zē\ *adj* **woo·zi·er; -est 1** : BEFUDDLED **2** : somewhat dizzy, nauseated, or weak ⟨~ from fatigue⟩ **3** : somewhat indistinct or unfocused : FUZZY — **woo·zi·ness** \'wü-zē-nəs\ *n*

¹**word** \'wərd\ *n* **1** : something that is said; *esp* : a brief remark **2** : a speech sound or series of speech sounds that communicates a meaning; *also* : a graphic representation of such a sound or series of sounds **3** : ORDER, COMMAND **4** *often cap* : the 2d person of the Trinity; *also* : GOSPEL **5** : NEWS, INFORMATION **6** : PROMISE **7** *pl* : QUARREL, DISPUTE **8** : a verbal signal : PASSWORD — **word·less** *adj*

²**word** *vb* : to express in words : PHRASE

word·age \'wər-dij\ *n* **1** : WORDS **2** : number of words **3** : WORDING

word·book \'wərd-ˌbu̇k\ *n* : VOCABULARY, DICTIONARY

word·ing \'wər-diŋ\ *n* : verbal expression : PHRASEOLOGY

word of mouth : oral communication

word·play \'wərd-ˌplā\ *n* : playful use of words

word processing *n* : the production of typewritten documents with automated and usu. computerized text-editing equipment — **word process** *vb*

word processor *n* : a keyboard-operated terminal for use in word processing; *also* : software to perform word processing

wordy \'wər-dē\ *adj* **word·i·er; -est** : using or having too many words ⟨~ sentences⟩ ♦ *Synonyms* PROLIX, DIFFUSE, REDUNDANT — **word·i·ness** \-dē-nəs\ *n*

wore *past of* WEAR

¹**work** \'wərk\ *n* **1** : TOIL, LABOR; *also* : EMPLOYMENT ⟨out of ~⟩ **2** : TASK, JOB ⟨have ~ to do⟩ **3** : the energy used when a force is applied over a given distance **4** : DEED, ACHIEVEMENT **5** : a fortified structure **6** *pl* : engineering structures **7** *pl* : a place where industrial labor is done : PLANT, FACTORY **8** *pl* : the moving parts of a mechanism **9** : something produced by mental effort or physical labor; *esp* : an artistic production (as a book or needlework) **10** : WORKMANSHIP ⟨careless ~⟩ **11** : material in the process of manufacture **12** *pl* : everything possessed, available, or belonging ⟨the whole ~s went overboard⟩; *also* : drastic treatment ⟨gave him the ~s⟩ ♦ *Synonyms* OCCUPATION, EMPLOYMENT, BUSINESS, PURSUIT, CALLING — **in the works** : in process of preparation

²**work** *adj* **1** : used for work ⟨~ elephants⟩ **2** : suitable or styled for wear while working ⟨~ clothes⟩

³**work** *vb* **worked** \'wərkt\ *or* **wrought** \'rȯt\; **work·ing 1** : to bring to pass : EFFECT **2** : to fashion or create a useful or desired product through labor or exertion **3** : to prepare for use (as by kneading) **4** : to bring into a desired form by a manufacturing process ⟨~ cold steel⟩ **5** : to set or keep in operation : OPERATE ⟨a pump ~ed by hand⟩ **6** : to solve by reasoning or calculation ⟨~ out a problem⟩ **7** : to cause to toil or labor ⟨~ed the team hard⟩; *also* : to make use of ⟨~ a mine⟩ **8** : to pay for with labor or service ⟨~ off a debt⟩ **9** : to bring or get into some position or condition by stages ⟨the stream ~ed itself clear⟩ ⟨the knot ~ed loose⟩ **10** : CONTRIVE, ARRANGE ⟨~ it so you can leave early⟩ **11** : to practice trickery or cajolery on ⟨~ed the management for a free ticket⟩ **12** : EXCITE, PROVOKE ⟨~ed himself into a rage⟩ **13** : to exert oneself physically or mentally; *esp* : to perform work regularly for wages **14** : to function according to plan or design **15** : to produce a desired effect : SUCCEED ⟨the plan ~ed⟩ **16** : to make way slowly and with difficulty ⟨he ~ed forward through the crowd⟩ **17** : to permit of being worked

⟨this wood ~s easily⟩ **18** : to be in restless motion; *also* : FERMENT 1 — **work on 1** : AFFECT **2** : to try to influence or persuade — **work upon** : to have effect upon : operate on : INFLUENCE

work·able \'wər-kə-bəl\ *adj* **1** : capable of being worked ⟨~ clay⟩ **2** : PRACTICABLE, FEASIBLE — **work·able·ness** *n*

work·a·day \'wər-kə-ˌdā\ *adj* **1** : relating to or suited for working days **2** : PROSAIC, ORDINARY ⟨~ chores⟩

work·a·hol·ic \ˌwər-kə-'hȯ-lik, -'hä-\ *n* : a compulsive worker

work·bench \-ˌbench\ *n* : a bench on which work esp. of mechanics, machinists, and carpenters is performed

work·book \-ˌbu̇k\ *n* **1** : a worker's manual **2** : a student's book of problems to be answered directly on the pages

work·day \'wərk-ˌdā\ *n* **1** : a day on which work is done as distinguished from a day off **2** : the period of time in a day when work is performed

work·er \'wər-kər\ *n* **1** : one that works; *esp* : a person who works for wages **2** : any of the sexually undeveloped individuals of a colony of social insects (as bees, ants, or termites) that perform the work of the community

workers' compensation *n* : a system of insurance that reimburses an employer for damages paid to an employee who was injured while working

work ethic *n* : belief in work as a moral good

work farm *n* : a farm on which persons guilty of minor law violations are confined

work·horse \'wərk-ˌhȯrs\ *n* **1** : a horse used for hard work **2** : a person who does most of the work of a group task **3** : something that is useful, durable, or dependable

work·house \-ˌhau̇s\ *n* **1** *Brit* : POORHOUSE **2** : a house of correction for persons guilty of minor law violations

¹**work·ing** \'wər-kiŋ\ *n* **1** : manner of functioning — usu. used in pl. **2** *pl* : an excavation made in mining or tunneling

²**working** *adj* **1** : engaged in work ⟨a ~ journalist⟩ **2** : adequate to allow work to be done ⟨a ~ majority⟩ ⟨a ~ knowledge of French⟩ **3** : adopted or assumed to help further work or activity ⟨a ~ draft⟩ **4** : spent at work ⟨~ life⟩

work·ing·man \'wər-kiŋ-ˌman\ *n* : WORKER 1

work·man \'wərk-mən\ *n* **1** : WORKER 1 **2** : ARTISAN, CRAFTSMAN

work·man·like \-ˌlīk\ *adj* : worthy of a good workman : SKILLFUL

work·man·ship \-ˌship\ *n* : the art or skill of a workman : CRAFTSMANSHIP; *also* : the quality of a piece of work ⟨a vase of exquisite ~⟩

work·out \'wərk-ˌau̇t\ *n* **1** : a practice or exercise to test or improve one's fitness, ability, or performance **2** : a test or trial to determine ability or capacity or suitability

work out *vb* **1** : to bring about esp. by resolving difficulties **2** : DEVELOP, ELABORATE **3** : to prove effective, practicable, or suitable ⟨our plan didn't *work out*⟩ **4** : to amount to a total or calculated figure — used with *at* **5** : to engage in a workout

work·place \'wərk-ˌplās\ *n* : a place (as an office) where work is done

work·room \'wərk-ˌrüm, -ˌru̇m\ *n* : a room used for work

work·shop \-ˌshäp\ *n* **1** : a shop where manufacturing or handicrafts are carried on **2** : a seminar emphasizing exchange of ideas and practical methods

work·sta·tion \-ˌstā-shən\ *n* : an area with equipment for the performance of a specialized task; *also* : a personal computer usu. connected to a computer network

world \'wərld\ *n* [ME, fr. OE *woruld* human existence, this world, age, fr. a prehistoric compound whose first constituent is represented by OE *wer* man and whose second constituent is akin to OE *eald* old] **1** : the earth with its inhabitants and all things upon it **2** : people in general : HUMANKIND **3** : human affairs ⟨withdraw from the ~⟩ **4** : CREATION **3 5** : a state of existence : scene of life and action ⟨the ~ of the future⟩ **6** : a distinctive class of persons or their sphere of interest ⟨the musical ~⟩ **7** : a part or section of the earth or its inhabitants by itself **8** : a great number or quantity ⟨a ~ of troubles⟩ **9** : a celestial body

world–beat·er \-ˌbē-tər\ *n* : one that excels all others of its kind : CHAMPION

world–class *adj* : of the highest caliber in the world ⟨a ~ athlete⟩

world·ling \-liŋ\ *n* : a person absorbed in the concerns of the present world

world·ly \-lē\ *adj* **1** : of, relating to, or devoted to this world and its pursuits rather than to religion or spiritual affairs ⟨~ pleasures⟩ **2** : WORLDLY-WISE, SOPHISTICATED — **world·li·ness** \-lē-nəs\ *n*

world·ly–wise \-,wīz\ *adj* : possessing a practical and often shrewd understanding of human affairs

world·wide \'wərld-'wīd\ *adj* : extended throughout the entire world ⟨attracted ~ attention⟩ — **worldwide** *adv*

World Wide Web *n* : a part of the Internet usu. accessed through a browser and containing files connected by hyperlinks

¹worm \'wərm\ *n* **1** : any of various small long usu. naked and soft-bodied round or flat invertebrate animals (as an earthworm, nematode, tapeworm, or maggot) **2** : a human being who is an object of contempt, loathing, or pity : WRETCH **3** : something that inwardly torments or devours **4** *pl* : infestation with or disease caused by parasitic worms **5** : a spiral or wormlike thing (as the thread of a screw) — **worm·like** \-,līk\ *adj* — **wormy** *adj*

²worm *vb* **1** : to move or cause to move or proceed slowly and deviously **2** : to insinuate or introduce (oneself) by devious or subtle means **3** : to obtain or extract by artful or insidious pleading, asking, or persuading ⟨~ed the truth out of him⟩ **4** : to treat (an animal) with a drug to destroy or expel parasitic worms

worm–eat·en \'wərm-,ē-t³n\ *adj* : eaten or burrowed by worms

worm gear *n* : a mechanical linkage consisting of a short rotating screw whose threads mesh with the teeth of a gear wheel

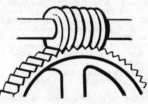

worm gear

worm·hole \'wərm-,hōl\ *n* : a hole or passage burrowed by a worm

worm·wood \-,wu̇d\ *n* **1** : any of a genus of aromatic woody plants (as a sagebrush); *esp* : one of Europe used in absinthe **2** : something bitter or grievous : BITTERNESS

worn *past part of* WEAR

worn–out \'wōrn-'au̇t\ *adj* : exhausted or used up by or as if by wear

wor·ri·some \'wər-ē-səm\ *adj* **1** : causing distress or worry ⟨~ news⟩ **2** : inclined to worry or fret ⟨a ~ mother⟩

¹wor·ry \'wər-ē\ *vb* **wor·ried; wor·ry·ing** **1** : to shake and mangle with the teeth ⟨a terrier ~ing a rat⟩ **2** : to make anxious or upset ⟨her poor health *worries* me⟩ **3** : to feel or express great care or anxiety : FRET ⟨~ing about his health⟩ — **wor·ri·er** *n*

²worry *n, pl* **worries** **1** : ANXIETY **2** : a cause of anxiety : TROUBLE

wor·ry·wart \'wər-ē-,wȯrt\ *n* : one who is inclined to worry unduly

¹worse \'wərs\ *adj, comparative of* BAD *or of* ILL **1** : bad or evil in a greater degree : less good **2** : more unfavorable, unpleasant, or painful; *also* : SICKER

²worse *n* **1** : one that is worse **2** : a greater degree of ill or badness ⟨a turn for the ~⟩

³worse *adv, comparative of* BAD *or of* ILL : in a worse manner : to a worse extent or degree ⟨you drive ~ than he does⟩

wors·en \'wər-s³n\ *vb* : to make or become worse ⟨the rash ~ed⟩

¹wor·ship \'wər-shəp\ *n* [ME *worshipe* worthiness, respect, reverence paid to a divine being, fr. OE *weorthscipe* worthiness, respect, fr. *weorth* worthy, worth + *-scipe* -ship, suffix denoting quality or condition] **1** *chiefly Brit* : a person of importance — used as a title for officials **2**

: reverence toward a divine being or supernatural power; *also* : the expression of such reverence **3** : extravagant respect or admiration or devotion ⟨~ of the dollar⟩

²worship *vb* **-shipped** *also* **-shiped; -ship·ping** *also* **-ship·ing** **1** : to honor or reverence as a divine being or supernatural power **2** : IDOLIZE ⟨~s his brother⟩ **3** : to perform or take part in worship — **wor·ship·er** *or* **wor·ship·per** *n*

wor·ship·ful \'wər-shəp-fəl\ *adj* **1** *archaic* : NOTABLE, DISTINGUISHED **2** *chiefly Brit* — used as a title for various persons or groups of rank or distinction **3** : VENERATING, WORSHIPING ⟨~ fans⟩

¹worst \'wərst\ *adj, superlative of* BAD *or of* ILL **1** : most bad, evil, ill, or corrupt ⟨the ~ criminals⟩ **2** : most unfavorable, unpleasant, or painful ⟨the ~ scenario⟩; *also* : most unsuitable, faulty, or unattractive **3** : least skillful or efficient ⟨her ~ students⟩

²worst *adv, superlative of* ILL *or of* BAD *or* BADLY **1** : to the extreme degree of badness or inferiority ⟨the ~ dressed person⟩ : in the worst manner **2** : MOST ⟨those who need help ~⟩

³worst *n* : one that is worst

⁴worst *vb* : DEFEAT

wor·sted \'wu̇s-təd, 'wər-stəd\ *n* [ME, fr. *Worsted* (now *Worstead*), England] : a smooth compact yarn from long wool fibers; *also* : a fabric made from such yarn

wort \'wərt, 'wȯrt\ *n* : a sweet liquid drained from mash and fermented to form beer and whiskey

¹worth \'wərth\ *n* **1** : monetary value; *also* : the equivalent of a specified amount or figure ⟨$5 ~ of gas⟩ **2** : the value of something measured by its qualities **3** : MERIT, EXCELLENCE

²worth *prep* **1** : equal in value to; *also* : having possessions or income equal to **2** : deserving of ⟨well ~ the effort⟩

worth·less \'wərth-ləs\ *adj* **1** : lacking worth : VALUELESS; *also* : USELESS **2** : LOW, DESPICABLE ⟨a ~ coward⟩ — **worth·less·ness** *n*

worth·while \'wərth-'hwī(-ə)l\ *adj* : being worth the time or effort spent

¹wor·thy \'wər-thē\ *adj* **wor·thi·er; -est** **1** : having worth or value : ESTIMABLE ⟨a ~ cause⟩ **2** : HONORABLE, MERITORIOUS ⟨my ~ opponent⟩ **3** : having sufficient worth ⟨~ of the honor⟩ — **wor·thi·ly** \'wər-thə-lē\ *adv* — **wor·thi·ness** \-thē-nəs\ *n*

²worthy *n, pl* **worthies** : a worthy person

would \'wu̇d\ *past of* WILL **1** *archaic* : wish for : WANT **2** : strongly desire : WISH ⟨I ~ I were young again⟩ **3** — used as an auxiliary to express (1) preference ⟨~ rather run than fight⟩, (2) wish, desire, or intent ⟨those who ~ forbid gambling⟩, (3) habitual action ⟨we ~ meet often for lunch⟩, (4) a contingency or possibility ⟨if he were coming, he ~ be here by now⟩, (5) probability ⟨~ have won if he hadn't tripped⟩, or (6) a request ⟨~ you help us⟩ **4** : COULD **5** : SHOULD

would–be \'wu̇d-'bē\ *adj, disparaging* : desiring or pretending to be ⟨a ~ artist⟩

¹wound \'wu̇nd\ *n* **1** : an injury involving cutting or breaking of bodily tissue (as by violence, accident, or surgery) **2** : an injury or hurt to feelings or reputation

²wound *vb* : to inflict a wound to or in

³wound \'wau̇nd\ *past and past part of* WIND

wove *past of* WEAVE

woven *past part of* WEAVE

¹wow \'wau̇\ *n* : a striking success : HIT

²wow *vb* : to arouse enthusiastic approval ⟨~ed the critics⟩

WP *abbr* word processing; word processor

WPM *abbr* words per minute

wpn *abbr* weapon

wrack \'rak\ *n* [ME, fr. OE *wræc* misery, punishment, something driven by the sea] : violent or total destruction

wraith \'rāth\ *n, pl* **wraiths** \'rāths, 'rā͟ths\ **1** : GHOST, SPECTER **2** : an insubstantial appearance : SHADOW

¹wran·gle \'raŋ-gəl\ *vb* **wran·gled; wran·gling** **1** : to quarrel angrily or peevishly : BICKER **2** : ARGUE ⟨they *wrangled* about money⟩ **3** : to obtain by persistent arguing **4** : to herd and care for (livestock) on the range — **wran·gler** *n*

²wrangle *n* : an angry, noisy, or prolonged dispute; *also* : CONTROVERSY

¹wrap \'rap\ *vb* **wrapped; wrap·ping** **1** : to cover esp. by winding or folding   **2** : to envelop and secure for transportation or storage   **3** : to enclose wholly : ENFOLD   **4** : to coil, fold, draw, or twine about something   **5** : SURROUND, ENVELOP ⟨*wrapped* in mystery⟩   **6** : INVOLVE, ENGROSS ⟨*wrapped* up in a hobby⟩   **7** : to complete filming or recording

²**wrap** *n*   **1** : WRAPPER, WRAPPING   **2** : an article of clothing that may be wrapped around a person   **3** *pl* : SECRECY ⟨kept under ∼*s*⟩   **4** : completion of filming or recording   **5** : a thin piece of bread that is rolled around a filling

wrap·around \'ra-pǝ-ˌraůnd\ *n* : a garment (as a dress) adjusted to the figure by wrapping around

wrap·per \'ra-pǝr\ *n*   **1** : that in which something is wrapped   **2** : one that wraps   **3** : an article of clothing worn wrapped around the body

wrap·ping \'ra-piŋ\ *n* : something used to wrap an object : WRAPPER

wrap—up \'rap-ˌǝp\ *n* : SUMMARY

wrap up *vb*   **1** : SUMMARIZE, SUM UP   **2** : to bring to a usu. successful conclusion

wrasse \'ras\ *n* : any of a large family of usu. brightly colored marine fishes including many food fishes

wrath \'rath\ *n*   **1** : violent anger : RAGE   **2** : divine punishment ✦ **Synonyms** INDIGNATION, IRE, FURY, ANGER

wrath·ful \-fǝl\ *adj*   **1** : filled with wrath : very angry   **2** : showing, marked by, or arising from anger ⟨a ∼ assault⟩ — **wrath·ful·ly** *adv* — **wrath·ful·ness** *n*

wreak \'rēk\ *vb* [ME *wreken*, fr. OE *wrecan* to drive, punish, avenge]   **1** : to exact as a punishment : INFLICT ⟨∼ vengeance on an enemy⟩   **2** : to give free scope or rein to ⟨∼*ed* his wrath⟩   **3** : BRING ABOUT, CAUSE ⟨∼ havoc⟩

wreath \'rēth\ *n, pl* **wreaths** \'rēthz, 'rēths\ : a circular band of flowers or leaves usu. for decoration; *also* : something having a circular or coiling form ⟨a ∼ of smoke⟩

wreathe \'rēth\ *vb* **wreathed; wreath·ing**   **1** : to shape or take on the shape of a wreath   **2** : to crown, decorate, or cover with or as if with a wreath ⟨a face *wreathed* in smiles⟩

¹**wreck** \'rek\ *n*   **1** : something (as goods) cast up on the land by the sea after a shipwreck   **2** : SHIPWRECK   **3** : a destructive crash ⟨a car ∼⟩   **4** : the action of breaking up or destroying something   **5** : broken remains (as of a vehicle after a crash)   **6** : something disabled or in a state of ruin; *also* : an individual broken in health, strength, or spirits ⟨he's a nervous ∼⟩

²**wreck** *vb*   **1** : SHIPWRECK   **2** : to ruin or damage by breaking up ⟨∼*ed* his marriage⟩ : involve in disaster or ruin

wreck·age \'re-kij\ *n*   **1** : the act of wrecking : the state of being wrecked : RUIN   **2** : the remains of a wreck

wreck·er \'re-kǝr\ *n*   **1** : one that searches for or works upon the wrecks of ships   **2** : TOW TRUCK   **3** : one that wrecks; *esp* : one whose work is the demolition of buildings

wren \'ren\ *n* : any of a family of small mostly brown singing birds with short wings and often a tail that points upward

¹**wrench** \'rench\ *vb*   **1** : to move with a violent twist   **2** : to pull, strain, or tighten with violent twisting or force   **3** : to injure or disable by a violent twisting or straining ⟨∼*ed* her back⟩   **4** : to snatch forcibly : WREST

²**wrench** *n*   **1** : a forcible twisting; *also* : an injury (as to one's ankle) by twisting   **2** : a tool for holding, twisting, or turning (as nuts or bolts)

¹**wrest** \'rest\ *vb*   **1** : to pull or move by a forcible twisting movement   **2** : to gain with difficulty by or as if by force or violence ⟨∼ control of the government from the dictator⟩

²**wrest** *n* : a forcible twist : WRENCH

¹**wres·tle** \'re-sǝl, 'ra-\ *vb* **wres·tled; wres·tling**   **1** : to grapple with and try to throw down an opponent   **2** : to compete against one in wrestling   **3** : to struggle for control (as of something difficult) ⟨∼ with a problem⟩ — **wres·tler** \'res-lǝr, 'ras-\ *n*

²**wrestle** *n* : the action or an instance of wrestling : STRUGGLE

wres·tling \'res-liŋ\ *n* : the sport in which two opponents wrestle each other

wretch \'rech\ *n* [ME *wrecche*, fr. OE *wrecca* outcast, exile]   **1** : a miserable unhappy person   **2** : a base, despicable, or vile person

wretch·ed \'re-chǝd\ *adj*   **1** : deeply afflicted, dejected, or distressed : MISERABLE   **2** : WOEFUL, GRIEVOUS ⟨a ∼ accident⟩   **3** : DESPICABLE ⟨a ∼ trick⟩   **4** : poor in quality or ability : INFERIOR ⟨∼ workmanship⟩ — **wretch·ed·ly** *adv* — **wretch·ed·ness** *n*

wrig·gle \'ri-gǝl\ *vb* **wrig·gled; wrig·gling**   **1** : to twist and move to and fro like a worm : SQUIRM ⟨*wriggled* in his chair⟩ ⟨∼ your toes⟩; *also* : to move along by twisting and turning ⟨a snake *wriggled* along the path⟩   **2** : to extricate oneself as if by wriggling ⟨∼ out of difficulty⟩ — **wriggle** *n*

wrig·gler *n*   **1** : one that wriggles   **2** : WIGGLER 1

wring \'riŋ\ *vb* **wrung** \'rǝŋ\; **wring·ing** \'riŋ-iŋ\   **1** : to squeeze or twist esp. so as to make dry or to extract moisture or liquid ⟨∼ wet clothes⟩   **2** : to get by or as if by twisting or pressing ⟨∼ the truth out of him⟩   **3** : to twist so as to strain or sprain : CONTORT ⟨∼ his neck⟩   **4** : to twist together as a sign of anguish ⟨*wrung* her hands⟩   **5** : to affect painfully as if by wringing : TORMENT ⟨her plight *wrung* my heart⟩

wring·er \'riŋ-ǝr\ *n* : one that wrings; *esp* : a device for squeezing out liquid or moisture ⟨clothes ∼⟩

¹**wrin·kle** \'riŋ-kǝl\ *n*   **1** : a crease or small fold on a smooth surface (as in the skin or in cloth)   **2** : a clever or new method, trick, or idea — **wrin·kly** \-k(ǝ-)lē\ *adj*

²**wrinkle** *vb* **wrin·kled; wrin·kling** : to develop or cause to develop wrinkles

wrist \'rist\ *n* : the joint or region between the hand and the arm; *also* : a corresponding part in a lower animal

wrist·band \-ˌband\ *n* : a band or the part of a sleeve encircling the wrist

wrist·let \-lǝt\ *n* : WRISTBAND; *esp* : a close-fitting knitted band attached to the top of a glove or the end of a sleeve

wrist·watch \-ˌwäch\ *n* : a small watch attached to a bracelet or strap to fasten about the wrist

writ \'rit\ *n*   **1** : something written   **2** : a written legal order signed by a court officer

writ·able \'rī-tǝ-bǝl\ *adj* : being an electronic storage medium on which it is possible to introduce new data ⟨a ∼ DVD⟩

write \'rīt\ *vb* **wrote** \'rōt\; **writ·ten** \'ri-tᵊn\ *also* **writ** \'rit\; **writ·ing** \'rī-tiŋ\ [ME, fr. OE *wrītan* to scratch, draw, inscribe]   **1** : to form characters, letters, or words on a surface ⟨learn to read and ∼⟩   **2** : to form the letters or the words of ⟨∼ your name⟩ ⟨∼ a check⟩   **3** : to put down on paper : express in writing   **4** : to make up and set down for others to read ⟨∼ a book⟩ ⟨∼ music⟩   **5** : to write a letter to   **6** : to communicate by letter : CORRESPOND

write-in \'rīt-ˌin\ *n* : a vote cast by writing in the name of a candidate; *also* : a candidate whose name is written in

write in *vb* : to insert (a name not listed on a ballot) in an appropriate space; *also* : to cast (a vote) in this manner

write off *vb* : to eliminate (an asset) from a bookkeeping record : enter as a loss or expense

writ·er \'rī-tǝr\ *n* : one that writes esp. as a business or occupation : AUTHOR

writer's cramp *n* : a painful spasmodic contraction of muscles of the hand or fingers brought on by excessive writing

write-up \'rīt-ˌǝp\ *n* : a written account (as in a newspaper); *esp* : a flattering article

writhe \'rīth\ *vb* **writhed; writh·ing**   **1** : to twist and turn this way and that ⟨∼ in pain⟩   **2** : to suffer with shame or confusion

writing *n*   **1** : the act of one that writes; *also* : HANDWRITING   **2** : something that is written or printed   **3** : a style or form of composition   **4** : the occupation of a writer

Writings \'rī-tiŋz\ *n pl* : the third part of the Jewish scriptures

wrnt *abbr* warrant

¹**wrong** \'rȯŋ\ *n*   **1** : an injurious, unfair, or unjust act   **2** : a violation of the legal rights of another person   **3** : something that is wrong : wrong principles, practices, or conduct ⟨know right from ∼⟩   **4** : the state, position, or fact of being wrong ⟨was in the ∼⟩

²**wrong** *adj* **wrong·er** \'rȯŋ-ǝr\; **wrong·est** \'rȯŋ-ǝst\   **1** : SINFUL, IMMORAL   **2** : not right according to a standard or code : IMPROPER   **3** : INCORRECT ⟨a ∼ solution⟩   **4**

: UNSATISFACTORY **5** : UNSUITABLE, INAPPROPRIATE **6** : constituting a surface that is considered the back, bottom, inside, or reverse of something ⟨iron only on the ∼ side of the fabric⟩ ◆ *Synonyms* FALSE, ERRONEOUS, INCORRECT, INACCURATE, UNTRUE — **wrong·ly** *adv*
³wrong *adv* **1** : INCORRECTLY **2** : in a wrong direction, manner, or relation
⁴wrong *vb* **wronged; wrong·ing** \'rȯŋ-iŋ\ **1** : to do wrong to : INJURE, HARM **2** : to treat unjustly : DISHONOR, MALIGN ◆ *Synonyms* OPPRESS, PERSECUTE, AGGRIEVE
wrong-do·er \'rȯŋ-ˌdü-ər\ *n* : a person who does wrong and esp. moral wrong — **wrong·do·ing** \-ˌdü-iŋ\ *n*
wrong·ful \'rȯŋ-fəl\ *adj* **1** : WRONG, UNJUST **2** : UNLAWFUL ⟨∼ conduct⟩ — **wrong·ful·ly** *adv* — **wrong·ful·ness** *n*
wrong·head·ed \-'he-dəd\ *adj* : stubborn in clinging to wrong opinion or principles — **wrong·head·ed·ly** *adv* — **wrong·head·ed·ness** *n*
wrote *past of* WRITE
wroth \'rȯth, 'rōth\ *adj* : filled with wrath : ANGRY
wrought \'rȯt\ *adj* [ME, fr. pp. of *worken* to work] **1** : FASHIONED, FORMED ⟨carefully ∼ essays⟩ **2** : ORNAMENTED **3** : beaten into shape by tools : HAMMERED ⟨∼ metals⟩ **4** : deeply stirred : EXCITED ⟨gets easily ∼ up⟩

wrung *past and past part of* WRING
wry \'rī\ *adj* **wry·er** \'rī-ər\; **wry·est** \'rī-əst\ **1** : having a bent or twisted shape ⟨a ∼ smile⟩; *also* : turned abnormally to one side : CONTORTED ⟨a ∼ neck⟩ **2** : cleverly and often ironically humorous — **wry·ly** *adv* — **wry·ness** *n*
wry·neck \'rī-ˌnek\ *n* **1** : either of two Old World woodpeckers that differ from typical woodpeckers in having a peculiar manner of twisting the head and neck **2** : an abnormal twisting of the neck and head to one side caused by muscle spasms
WSW *abbr* west-southwest
wt *abbr* weight
wurst \'wərst, 'wu̇rst\ *n* : SAUSAGE
wu·shu \'wü-'shü\ *n* [Chin (Beijing) *wǔshù*, fr. *wǔ* martial + *shù* art] : Chinese martial arts
wuss \'wu̇s\ *n* : WIMP — **wussy** \'wu̇-sē\ *adj*
WV *or* **W Va** *abbr* West Virginia
WW *abbr* World War
w/w *abbr* wall-to-wall
WY *or* **Wyo** *abbr* Wyoming
WYS·I·WYG \'wi-zē-ˌwig\ *adj* [what you see is what you get] : of, relating to, or being a computer display that shows a document exactly as it will appear when printed out

¹x \'eks\ *n, pl* **x's** *or* **xs** \'ek-səz\ *often cap* **1** : the 24th letter of the English alphabet **2** : an unknown quantity
²x *vb* **x-ed** *also* **x'd** *or* **xed** \'ekst\; **x-ing** *or* **x'ing** \'ek-siŋ\ : to cancel or obliterate with a series of x's — usu. used with *out*
³x *abbr* **1** ex **2** experimental **3** extra
⁴x *symbol* **1** times ⟨3 x 2 is 6⟩ **2** by ⟨a 3 x 5 index card⟩ **3** *often cap* power of magnification
Xan·a·du \'za-nə-ˌdü, -ˌdyü\ *n* [fr. *Xanadu*, locality in *Kubla Khan* (1798), poem by Eng. poet Samuel Taylor Coleridge †1834] : an idyllic, exotic, or luxurious place
Xan·thip·pe \zan-'thi-pē, -'ti-\ *or* **Xan·tip·pe** \-'ti-pē\ *n* [Gk *Xanthippē*, shrewish wife of Socrates] : an ill-tempered woman
x–ax·is \'eks-ˌak-səs\ *n* : the axis of a graph or of a system of coordinates in a plane parallel to which abscissas are measured
X–C *abbr* cross-country
X chromosome *n* : a sex chromosome that usu. occurs paired in each female cell and single in each male cell in organisms (as humans) in which the male normally has two unlike sex chromosomes
Xe *symbol* xenon
xe·non \'zē-ˌnän, 'ze-\ *n* [Gk, neut. of *xenos* strange] : a heavy gaseous chemical element occurring in minute quantities in air
xe·no·pho·bia \ˌze-nə-'fō-bē-ə, ˌzē-\ *n* : fear and hatred of strangers or foreigners or of what is strange or foreign — **xe·no·phobe** \'ze-nə-ˌfōb, 'zē-\ *n* — **xe·no·pho·bic** \ˌze-nə-'fō-bik, ˌzē-\ *adj*
xe·ric \'zir-ik, 'zer-\ *adj* : characterized by or requiring only a small amount of moisture ⟨a ∼ habitat⟩
xeri·scape \'zir-ə-ˌskāp, 'zer-\ *n, often cap* : a landscaping method utilizing water-conserving techniques
xe·rog·ra·phy \zə-'rä-grə-fē\ *n* : a process for copying printed matter by the action of light on an electrically charged surface in which the latent image is developed with a powder — **xe·ro·graph·ic** \ˌzir-ə-'gra-fik\ *adj*
xe·ro·phyte \'zir-ə-ˌfīt\ *n* : a plant adapted for growth with a limited water supply — **xe·ro·phyt·ic** \ˌzir-ə-'fi-tik\ *adj*
xi \'zī, 'ksī\ *n* : the 14th letter of the Greek alphabet — Ξ or ξ
XL *abbr* **1** extra large **2** extra long

Xmas \'kris-məs *also* 'eks-məs\ *n* [*X* (symbol for *Christ*, fr. the Gk letter chi (Χ), initial of *Christos* Christ) + *-mas* (in *Christmas*)] : CHRISTMAS
XML \ˌeks-(ˌ)em-'el\ *n* : a markup language that indicates the structural type of data
XO *abbr* executive officer
x–ra·di·a·tion \ˌeks-ˌrā-dē-'ā-shən\ *n, often cap* **1** : exposure to X-rays **2** : radiation consisting of X-rays
x–ray \'eks-ˌrā\ *vb, often cap* : to examine, treat, or photograph with X-rays
X–ray \'eks-ˌrā\ *n* **1** : a radiation with an extremely short wavelength of less than 100 angstroms that is able to penetrate through various thicknesses of solids and to act on photographic film **2** : a photograph taken with X-rays — **X–ray** *adj*
XS *abbr* extra small
xu \'sü\ *n, pl* **xu** — see *dong* at MONEY table
xy·lem \'zī-ləm, -ˌlem\ *n* : a woody tissue of vascular plants that transports water and dissolved materials upward, functions in support and storage, and lies central to the phloem
xy·lo·phone \'zī-lə-ˌfōn\ *n* [Gk *xylon* wood + *phōnē* voice, sound] : a musical instrument consisting of a series of wooden bars graduated in length to produce the musical scale, supported on belts of straw or felt, and sounded by striking with two small wooden hammers — **xy·lo·phon·ist** \-ˌfō-nist\ *n*

xylophone

¹y \'wī\ *n, pl* y's *or* ys \'wīz\ *often cap* : the 25th letter of the English alphabet

²y *abbr* 1 yard 2 year

¹Y \'wī\ *n* : YMCA, YWCA

²Y *symbol* yttrium

¹-y *also* -ey \ē\ *adj suffix* 1 : characterized by : full of ⟨dirt*y*⟩ ⟨clay*ey*⟩ 2 : having the character of : composed of ⟨ic*y*⟩ 3 : like : like that of ⟨home*y*⟩ ⟨wintr*y*⟩ ⟨stag*y*⟩ 4 : tending or inclined to ⟨sleep*y*⟩ ⟨chatt*y*⟩ 5 : giving occasion for (specified) action ⟨tear*y*⟩ 6 : performing (specified) action ⟨curl*y*⟩

²-y \ē\ *n suffix, pl* -ies 1 : state : condition : quality ⟨beggar*y*⟩ 2 : activity, place of business, or goods dealt with ⟨laundr*y*⟩ 3 : whole body or group ⟨soldier*y*⟩

³-y *n suffix, pl* -ies : instance of a (specified) action ⟨entreat*y*⟩ ⟨inquir*y*⟩

YA *abbr* young adult

¹yacht \'yät\ *n* [obs. D *jaght*, fr. Middle Low German *jacht*, short for *jachtschip*, lit., hunting ship] : a usu. large recreational watercraft

²yacht *vb* : to race or cruise in a yacht

yacht·ing \'yä-tiŋ\ *n* : the sport of racing or cruising in a yacht

yachts·man \'yäts-mən\ *n* : a person who owns or sails a yacht

ya·hoo \'yä-hü, 'yä-\ *n, pl* yahoos [fr. *Yahoo*, one of a race of brutes having the form of humans in Jonathan Swift's *Gulliver's Travels*] : a boorish, crass, or stupid person

Yah·weh \'yä-ˌwä\ *also* Yah·veh \-ˌvä\ *n* : GOD 1 — used esp. by the Hebrews

¹yak \'yak\ *n, pl* yaks *also* yak : a large long-haired wild or domesticated ox of Tibet and adjacent Asian uplands

²yak *also* yack \'yak\ *n* : persistent or voluble talk — yak *also* yack *vb*

yam \'yam\ *n* 1 : the edible starchy root of various twining plants used as a staple food in tropical areas; *also* : a plant that produces yams 2 : a usu. deep orange sweet potato

yam·mer \'ya-mər\ *vb* [ME *yameren*, alter. of *yomeren* to murmur, be sad, fr. OE *gēomrian*] 1 : WHIMPER 2 : CHATTER — yammer *n*

¹yank \'yaŋk\ *vb* : to pull with a quick vigorous movement

²yank *n* : a strong sudden pull : JERK

Yank \'yaŋk\ *n* : YANKEE

Yan·kee \'yaŋ-kē\ *n* 1 : a native or inhabitant of New England; *also* : a native or inhabitant of the northern U.S. 2 : AMERICAN 2

yan·qui \'yäŋ-kē\ *n, often cap* [Sp] : a citizen of the U.S. as distinguished from a Latin American

¹yap \'yap\ *vb* yapped; yap·ping 1 : BARK, YELP 2 : GAB

²yap *n* 1 : a quick sharp bark 2 : CHATTER

¹yard \'yärd\ *n* [ME, fr. OE *geard* enclosure, yard] 1 : a small enclosed area open to the sky and adjacent to a building 2 : the grounds of a building 3 : the grounds surrounding a house usu. covered with grass 4 : an enclosure for livestock 5 : an area set aside for a particular business or activity 6 : a system of railroad tracks for storing cars and making up trains

²yard *n* [ME *yarde*, fr. OE *gierd* twig, measure, yard] 1 — see WEIGHT table 2 : a long spar tapered toward the ends that supports and spreads the head of a sail — the whole nine yards : all of a set of circumstances, conditions, or details

yard·age \'yär-dij\ *n* : an aggregate number of yards; *also* : the length, extent, or volume of something as measured in yards

yard·arm \'yärd-ˌärm\ *n* : either end of the yard of a square-rigged ship

yard·man \-mən, -ˌman\ *n* : a person employed in or about a yard

yard·mas·ter \-ˌmas-tər\ *n* : the person in charge of a railroad yard

yard·stick \-ˌstik\ *n* 1 : a graduated measuring stick three feet long 2 : a standard for making a critical judgment : CRITERION ♦ *Synonyms* GAUGE, TOUCHSTONE, BENCHMARK, MEASURE

yar·mul·ke \'yä-mə-kə, 'yär-, -məl-\ *n* [Yiddish *yarmlke*] : a skullcap worn esp. by Jewish males in the synagogue and the home

yarn \'yärn\ *n* 1 : a continuous often plied strand composed of fibers or filaments and used in weaving and knitting to form cloth 2 : STORY; *esp* : a tall tale

yar·row \'ya-rō\ *n* : a strong-scented herb related to the daisies that has white or pink flowers in flat clusters

yaw \'yó\ *vb* : to deviate erratically from a course ⟨the ship ∼*ed* in the heavy seas⟩ — yaw *n*

yawl \'yól\ *n* : a 2-masted sailboat with the shorter mast aft of the rudder

¹yawn \'yón\ *vb* : to open wide; *esp* : to open the mouth wide and take a deep breath usu. as an involuntary reaction to fatigue or boredom — yawn·er *n*

²yawn *n* : the act of yawning

yawp *or* yaup \'yóp\ *vb* 1 : to make a raucous noise : SQUAWK 2 : CLAMOR, COMPLAIN — yawp·er *n*

yaws \'yóz\ *n pl* : a contagious tropical disease caused by a spirochete closely resembling the causative agent of syphilis and marked by skin lesions

y–ax·is \'wī-ˌak-səs\ *n* : the axis of a graph or of a system of coordinates in a plane parallel to which the ordinates are measured

Yb *symbol* ytterbium

YB *abbr* yearbook

Y chromosome *n* : a sex chromosome that is characteristic of male cells in organisms (as humans) in which the male typically has two unlike sex chromosomes

yd *abbr* yard

¹ye \'yē\ *pron* : YOU 1

²ye \yē, yə, *originally same as* THE\ *definite article, archaic* : THE — used by early printers to represent the manuscript word *þe* (*the*)

¹yea \'yā\ *adv* 1 : YES — used in oral voting 2 : INDEED, TRULY

²yea *n* : an affirmative vote; *also* : a person casting such a vote

yeah \'yeə, 'yaə\ *adv* : YES

year \'yir\ *n* 1 : the period of about 365¼ solar days required for one revolution of the earth around the sun; *also* : the time in which a planet completes a revolution about the sun 2 : a cycle of 365 or 366 days beginning with January 1; *also* : a calendar year specified usu. by a number 3 *pl* : a time of special significance ⟨their glory ∼*s*⟩ 4 *pl* : AGE ⟨advanced in ∼*s*⟩ 5 : a period of time other than a calendar year ⟨the school ∼⟩

year·book \-ˌbúk\ *n* 1 : a book published annually esp. as a report 2 : a school publication recording the history and activities of a graduating class

year·ling \'yir-liŋ, 'yər-lən\ *n* 1 : one that is a year old 2 : a racehorse between January of the year after the year in which it was born and the next January

year·long \'yir-ˈlóŋ\ *adj* : lasting through a year

¹year·ly \'yir-lē\ *adj* : ANNUAL

²yearly *adv* : every year

yearn \'yərn\ *vb* 1 : to feel a longing or craving ⟨∼*ing* for freedom⟩ 2 : to feel tenderness or compassion ♦ *Synonyms* LONG, PINE, HANKER, HUNGER, THIRST

yearn·ing *n* : a tender or urgent longing

year–round \'yir-ˈraúnd\ *adj* : effective, employed, or operating for the full year : not seasonal ⟨a ∼ resort⟩

yeast \'yēst\ *n* 1 : a surface froth or a sediment in sugary liquids (as fruit juices) that consists largely of cells of a tiny fungus and is used in making alcoholic liquors and as a leaven in baking 2 : a commercial product containing yeast fungi in a moist or dry medium **3** : a minute one-celled fungus present and functionally active in yeast that reproduces by budding; *also* : any of several similar fungi **4** *archaic* : the foam of waves : SPUME **5** : something that causes ferment or activity

yeast infection *n* : infection of the vagina with an excess growth of a normally present fungus that resembles a yeast

yeasty \'yē-stē\ *adj* **yeast·i·er; -est** **1** : of, relating to, or resembling yeast **2** : UNSETTLED **3** : full of vitality ⟨∼ youths⟩; *also* : FRIVOLOUS

¹yell \'yel\ *vb* : to utter a loud cry or scream — SHOUT — **yell·er** *n*

²yell *n* **1** : SHOUT **2** : a cheer used esp. to encourage an athletic team (as at a college)

¹yel·low \'ye-lō\ *adj* **1** : of the color yellow **2** *sometimes offensive* : having a yellow complexion or skin **3** : SENSATIONAL ⟨∼ journalism⟩ **4** : COWARDLY ⟨was too ∼ to fight⟩ — **yel·low·ish** \'ye-lə-wish\ *adj*

²yellow *n* **1** : a color between green and orange in the spectrum : the color of ripe lemons or sunflowers **2** : something yellow; *esp* : the yolk of an egg **3** *pl* : any of several plant diseases marked by stunted growth and yellowing of foliage

³yellow *vb* : to make or turn yellow

yellow birch *n* : a No. American birch with thin lustrous gray or yellow bark; *also* : its strong hard wood

yellow fever *n* : an acute infectious viral disease marked by prostration, jaundice, fever, and often hemorrhage and transmitted by a mosquito

yellow jack *n* : YELLOW FEVER

yellow jacket *n* : any of various small social wasps having the body barred with bright yellow

yel·low·tail \'ye-lō-ˌtāl\ *n* : any of various fishes with a yellow or yellowish tail including several valuable food fishes

yelp \'yelp\ *vb* [ME, to boast, cry out, fr. OE *gielpan* to boast, exult] : to utter a sharp quick shrill cry — **yelp** *n*

Ye·me·ni \'ye-mə-nē\ *n* : YEMENITE — **Yemeni** *adj*

Ye·men·ite \'ye-mə-ˌnīt\ *n* : a native or inhabitant of Yemen — **Yemenite** *adj*

¹yen \'yen\ *n, pl* **yen** — see MONEY table

²yen *n* [obs. E argot *yen-yen* craving for opium, fr. Chin (Guangdong dial.) *yīn-yáhn*, fr. *yīn* opium + *yáhn* craving] : a strong desire : LONGING ⟨a ∼ to travel⟩

yeo·man \'yō-mən\ *n* **1** : an attendant or officer in a royal or noble household **2** : a naval petty officer who performs clerical duties **3** : a person who owns and cultivates a small farm; *esp* : one of a class of English freeholders below the gentry — **yeo·man·ly** \-lē\ *adj*

yeo·man·ry \-rē\ *n* : the body of yeomen and esp. of small landed proprietors

-yer — see -ER

¹yes \'yes\ *adv* — used as a function word esp. to express assent or agreement or to introduce a more emphatic or explicit phrase

²yes *n* : an affirmative reply

ye·shi·va *also* **ye·shi·vah** \yə-'shē-və\ *n, pl* **yeshivas** *or* **ye·shi·voth** \-ˌshē-'vōt, -'vōth\ : a Jewish school esp. for religious instruction

yes-man \'yes-ˌman\ *n* : a person who endorses uncritically every opinion or proposal of a superior

¹yes·ter·day \'yes-tər-dē, -ˌdā\ *adv* **1** : on the day preceding today **2** : only a short time ago

²yesterday *n* **1** : the day last past **2** : time not long past

yes·ter·year \'yes-tər-ˌyir\ *n* **1** : last year **2** : the recent past

¹yet \'yet\ *adv* **1** : in addition : BESIDES; *also* : EVEN **6 2** : up to now; *also* : STILL **3** : so soon as now ⟨not time to go ∼⟩ **4** : EVENTUALLY **5** : NEVERTHELESS, HOWEVER

²yet *conj* : but nevertheless : BUT

ye·ti \'ye-tē, 'yā-\ *n* : ABOMINABLE SNOWMAN

yew \'yü\ *n* **1** : any of a genus of evergreen trees and shrubs with dark stiff poisonous needles and fleshy fruits **2** : the wood of a yew; *esp* : that of an Old World yew

Yid·dish \'yi-dish\ *n* [Yiddish *yidish*, short for *yidish daytsh*, lit., Jewish German] : a language derived from medieval German and spoken by Jews esp. of eastern European origin — **Yiddish** *adj*

¹yield \'yēld\ *vb* **1** : to give as fitting, owed, or required **2** : GIVE UP; *esp* : to give up possession of on claim or

demand **3** : to bear as a natural product **4** : PRODUCE, SUPPLY **5** : to bring in : RETURN **6** : to give way (as to force or influence) **7** : to give place ✦ **Synonyms** RELINQUISH, CEDE, WAIVE, SURRENDER

²yield *n* : something yielded; *esp* : the amount or quantity produced or returned

yield·ing \'yēl-diŋ\ *adj* **1** : not rigid or stiff : FLEXIBLE **2** : SUBMISSIVE, COMPLIANT

yikes \'yīks\ *interj* — used to express fear or astonishment

yip \'yip\ *vb* **yipped; yip·ping** : YAP

YK *abbr* Yukon; Yukon Territory

YMCA \ˌwī-ˌem-(ˌ)sē-'ā\ *n* : Young Men's Christian Association

YMHA \ˌwī-ˌem-ˌāch-'ā\ *n* : Young Men's Hebrew Association

yo \'yō\ *interj* — used to call attention, indicate attentiveness, or express affirmation

YOB *abbr* year of birth

yo·del \'yō-dᵊl\ *vb* **yo·deled** *or* **yo·delled; yo·del·ing** *or* **yo·del·ling** : to sing by suddenly changing from chest voice to falsetto and back; *also* : to shout or call in this manner — **yodel** *n* — **yo·del·er** *n*

yo·ga \'yō-gə\ *n* [Skt, lit., yoking, fr. *yunakti* he yokes] **1** *cap* : a Hindu theistic philosophy teaching the suppression of all activity of body, mind, and will in order that the self may realize its distinction from them and attain liberation **2** : a system of exercises for attaining bodily or mental control and well-being — **yo·gic** \-gik\ *adj, often cap*

yo·gi \'yō-gē\ *also* **yo·gin** \-gən, -ˌgin\ *n* **1** : a person who practices yoga **2** *cap* : an adherent of Yoga philosophy

yo·gurt *also* **yo·ghurt** \'yō-gərt\ *n* [Turk *yoğurt*] : a soured slightly acid often flavored semisolid food made of milk and milk solids to which cultures of bacteria have been added

¹yoke \'yōk\ *n, pl* **yokes** **1** : a wooden bar or frame by which two draft animals (as oxen) are coupled at the heads or necks for working together; *also* : a frame fitted to a person's shoulders to carry a load in two equal portions **2** : a clamp that embraces two parts to hold or unite them in position **3** *pl usu* **yoke** : two animals yoked together **4** : SERVITUDE, BONDAGE **5** : TIE, LINK ⟨the ∼ of matrimony⟩ **6** : a fitted or shaped piece esp. at the shoulder of a garment ✦ **Synonyms** COUPLE, PAIR, BRACE

²yoke *vb* **yoked; yok·ing** **1** : to put a yoke on : couple with a yoke **2** : to attach a draft animal to ⟨∼ a plow⟩ **3** : JOIN; *esp* : MARRY

yo·kel \'yō-kəl\ *n* : a naive or gullible country person

yolk \'yōk\ *n* **1** : the yellow rounded inner mass of the egg of a bird or reptile **2** : the stored food material of an egg that supplies nutrients (as proteins and cholesterol) to the developing embryo — **yolked** \'yōkt\ *adj*

Yom Kip·pur \ˌyōm-ki-'pùr, ˌyäm-, -'ki-pər\ *n* [Heb *yōm kippūr*, lit., day of atonement] : a Jewish holiday observed in September or October with fasting and prayer as a day of atonement

¹yon \'yän\ *adj* : YONDER

²yon *adv* **1** : YONDER **2** : THITHER ⟨ran hither and ∼⟩

¹yon·der \'yän-dər\ *adv* : at or to that place

²yonder *adj* **1** : more distant ⟨the ∼ side of the river⟩ **2** : being at a distance within view ⟨∼ hills⟩

yore \'yōr\ *n* [ME, fr. *yore*, adv., long ago, fr. OE *geāra*, fr. *gēar* year] : time long past ⟨in days of ∼⟩

York·ie \'yòr-kē\ *n* : YORKSHIRE TERRIER

York·shire terrier \'yòrk-ˌshir-, -shər-\ *n* : any of a breed of compact toy terriers with long straight silky hair

you \'yü\ *pron* **1** : the person or persons addressed ⟨∼ are a nice person⟩ ⟨∼ are nice people⟩ **2** : ONE 2 ⟨∼ turn this knob to open it⟩

¹young \'yəŋ\ *adj* **youn·ger** \'yəŋ-gər\; **youn·gest** \'yəŋ-gəst\ **1** : being in the first or an early stage of life, growth, or development **2** : having little experience **3** : recently come into being **4** : YOUTHFUL **5** *cap* : belonging to or representing a new or revived usu. political group or movement — **young·ish** \'yəŋ-ish\ *adj*

²young *n, pl* **young** : young persons; *also* : young animals

young·ling \'yəŋ-liŋ\ *n* : one that is young — **youngling** *adj*

young·ster \-stər\ *n* **1** : a young person **2** : CHILD

your \'yùr, 'yòr, yər\ *adj* : of or relating to you or yourself

yours \'yùrz, 'yòrz\ *pron* : one or the ones belonging to you

your·self \yər-'self\ *pron, pl* **yourselves** \-'selvz\ : YOU —

used reflexively, for emphasis, or in absolute constructions ⟨you'll hurt ~⟩ ⟨do it ~⟩

youth \'yüth\ *n, pl* **youths** \'yüthz, 'yüths\ **1** : the period of life between childhood and maturity **2** : a young man; *also* : young persons **3** : YOUTHFULNESS

youth·ful \'yüth-fəl\ *adj* **1** : of, relating to, or appropriate to youth **2** : being young and not yet mature **3** : FRESH, VIGOROUS ⟨~ fervor⟩ — **youth·ful·ly** *adv* — **youth·ful·ness** *n*

youth hostel *n* : HOSTEL 2

yowl \'yaù(-ə)l\ *vb* : to utter a loud long mournful cry : WAIL — **yowl** *n*

yo–yo \'yō-(ˌ)yō\ *n, pl* **yo–yos** [prob. fr. Ilocano (a Philippine language) *yóyo*] : a thick grooved double disk with a string attached to its center that is made to fall and rise to the hand by unwinding and rewinding on the string — **yo–yo** *vb*

yr *abbr* **1** year **2** your

yrbk *abbr* yearbook

YT *abbr* Yukon Territory

yt·ter·bi·um \i-'tər-bē-əm\ *n* : a rare metallic chemical element

yt·tri·um \'i-trē-əm\ *n* : a rare metallic chemical element

yu·an \'yü-ən, yü-'än\ *n, pl* **yuan** — see MONEY table

yuc·ca \'yə-kə\ *n* : any of a genus of plants related to the agaves that grow esp. in warm dry regions and bear large clusters of white cup-shaped flowers atop a long stiff stalk

yuck *also* **yuk** \'yək\ *interj* — used to express rejection or disgust

yule \'yül\ *n, often cap* : CHRISTMAS

Yule log *n* : a large log formerly put on the hearth on Christmas Eve as the foundation of the fire

yule·tide \'yül-ˌtīd\ *n, often cap* : CHRISTMASTIDE

yum·my \'yə-mē\ *adj* **yum·mi·er; -est** : highly attractive or pleasing

yup·pie \'yə-pē\ *n* [prob. fr. *y*oung *u*rban *p*rofessional + *-ie* (as in hipp*ie*)] : a young college-educated adult employed in a well-paying profession and living and working in or near a large city — **yup·pie·dom** \-dəm\ *n*

yurt \'yùrt\ *n* : a light round tent of skins or felt stretched over a lattice framework used by pastoral peoples of inner Asia

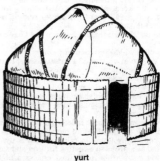

yurt

YWCA \ˌwī-də-bəl-yü-(ˌ)sē-'ā\ *n* : Young Women's Christian Association

YWHA \-ˌāch-'ā\ *n* : Young Women's Hebrew Association

Z

¹z \'zē\ *n, pl* **z's** *or* **zs** \'zēz\ *often cap* : the 26th letter of the English alphabet

²z *abbr* **1** zero **2** zone

Z *symbol* atomic number

Zach *abbr* Zacharias

Zach·a·ri·as \ˌza-kə-'rī-əs\ *n* : ZECHARIAH

¹za·ny \'zā-nē\ *n, pl* **zanies** [It *zanni*, a traditional masked clown, fr. It dial. *Zanni*, nickname for It *Giovanni* John] **1** : CLOWN, BUFFOON **2** : a silly or foolish person

²zany *adj* **za·ni·er; -est 1** : characteristic of a zany **2** : CRAZY, FOOLISH ⟨a ~ movie⟩ — **za·ni·ly** \'zā-nə-lē\ *adv* — **za·ni·ness** \'zā-nē-nəs\ *n*

zap \'zap\ *vb* **zapped; zap·ping 1** : DESTROY, KILL **2** : to heat or cook in a microwave oven ⟨*zapped* the soup⟩

zeal \'zēl\ *n* : eager and ardent interest in the pursuit of something : FERVOR ✦ **Synonyms** ENTHUSIASM, PASSION, ARDOR

zeal·ot \'ze-lət\ *n* : a zealous person; *esp* : a fanatical partisan ⟨a religious ~⟩ ✦ **Synonyms** ENTHUSIAST, BIGOT

zeal·ous \'ze-ləs\ *adj* : filled with, characterized by, or due to zeal — **zeal·ous·ly** *adv* — **zeal·ous·ness** *n*

ze·bra \'zē-brə\ *n, pl* **zebras** *also* **zebra** : any of several African mammals related to the horse but conspicuously striped with black or dark brown and white or buff

zebra mussel *n* : a freshwater Eurasian mollusk introduced into U.S. waterways where it colonizes and clogs water intake pipes

ze·bu \'zē-bü, -byü\ *n* : any of various breeds of domestic oxen developed in India that have a large fleshy hump over the shoulders, a dewlap, drooping ears, and marked resistance to heat and to insect attack

Zech *abbr* Zechariah

Zech·a·ri·ah \ˌze-kə-'rī-ə\ *n* — see BIBLE table

zed \'zed\ *n, chiefly Brit* : the letter z

zeit·geist \'tsīt-ˌgīst, 'zīt-\ *n* [G, fr. *Zeit* time + *Geist* spirit] : the general intellectual, moral, and cultural state of an era

Zen \'zen\ *n* : a Japanese Buddhist sect that teaches self-discipline, meditation, and attainment of enlightenment through direct intuitive insight

ze·na·na \zə-'nä-nə\ *n* : HAREM

ze·nith \'zē-nəth\ *n* **1** : the point in the heavens directly overhead **2** : the highest point : ACME ⟨the ~ of her career⟩ ✦ **Synonyms** CULMINATION, PINNACLE, APEX

ze·o·lite \'zē-ə-ˌlīt\ *n* : any of various feldsparlike silicates used esp. as water softeners

Zeph *abbr* Zephaniah

Zeph·a·ni·ah \ˌze-fə-'nī-ə\ *n* — see BIBLE table

zeph·yr \'ze-fər\ *n* : a breeze from the west; *also* : a gentle breeze

zep·pe·lin \'ze-plən, -pə-lən\ *n* [Count Ferdinand von *Zeppelin* †1917 Ger. airship manufacturer] : a cylindrical rigid blimplike airship

¹ze·ro \'zē-rō, 'zir-ō\ *n, pl* **zeros** *also* **zeroes** [ultim. fr. Ar *ṣifr*] **1** : the numerical symbol 0 **2** : the number rep-

zebra

resented by the symbol 0 **3** : the point at which the graduated degrees or measurements on a scale (as of a thermometer) begin **4** : the lowest point

²**zero** *adj* **1** : of, relating to, or being a zero **2** : having no magnitude or quantity **3** : ABSENT, LACKING; *esp* : having no modified inflectional form

³**zero** *vb* : to adjust the sights of a firearm to hit the point aimed at — usu. used with *in*

zero hour *n* : the time at which an event (as a military operation) is scheduled to begin

zest \'zest\ *n* **1** : a quality of enhancing enjoyment : PIQUANCY **2** : keen enjoyment : GUSTO ⟨a ∼ for life⟩ — **zest·ful** \-fəl\ *adj* — **zest·ful·ly** *adv* — **zest·ful·ness** *n* — **zesty** \'zes-tē\ *adj*

ze·ta \'zā-tə, 'zē-\ *n* : the 6th letter of the Greek alphabet — Z or ζ

zi·do·vu·dine \zi-'dō-vyü-ˌdēn\ *n* : AZT

¹**zig·zag** \'zig-ˌzag\ *n* : one of a series of short sharp turns, angles, or alterations in a course; *also* : something marked by such a series

²**zigzag** *adv* : in or by a zigzag path

³**zigzag** *adj* : having short sharp turns or angles

⁴**zigzag** *vb* **zig·zagged; zig·zag·ging** : to form into or proceed along a zigzag

zil·lion \'zil-yən\ *n* : a large indeterminate number

zinc \'ziŋk\ *n* : a bluish-white metallic chemical element that is commonly found in minerals and is used esp. in alloys and as a protective coating for iron and steel

zinc oxide *n* : a white solid used esp. as a pigment, in compounding rubber, and in ointments and sunblocks

zine \'zēn\ *n* : a noncommercial publication usu. devoted to specialized subject matter

zin·fan·del \'zin-fən-ˌdel\ *n, often cap* : a dry red table wine made chiefly in California

zing \'ziŋ\ *n* **1** : a shrill humming noise **2** : VITALITY 4 — **zing** *vb*

zing·er \'ziŋ-ər\ *n* : a pointed witty remark or retort

zin·nia \'zi-nē-ə, 'zēn-yə\ *n* : any of a genus of tropical American herbs or low shrubs related to the daisies and widely grown for their showy long-lasting flowers

Zi·on \'zī-ən\ *n* **1** : the Jewish people **2** : the Jewish homeland as a symbol of Judaism or of Jewish national aspiration **3** : HEAVEN **4** : UTOPIA

Zi·on·ism \'zī-ə-ˌni-zəm\ *n* : an international movement orig. for the establishment of a Jewish national or religious community in Palestine and later for the support of modern Israel — **Zi·on·ist** \-nist\ *adj or n*

¹**zip** \'zip\ *vb* **zipped; zip·ping** : to move, act, or function with speed or vigor

²**zip** *n* **1** : a sudden sharp hissing sound **2** : ENERGY, VIM ⟨the performance lacked ∼⟩

³**zip** *n* : NOTHING, ZERO ⟨the score was 27 to ∼⟩

⁴**zip** *vb* **zipped; zip·ping** : to close or open with a zipper

zip code *n, often cap Z&I&P* [*zone improvement plan*] : a number that identifies each postal delivery area in the U.S.

zip line *n* : a cable suspended usu. over an incline to which a rider is harnessed

zip·per \'zi-pər\ *n* : a fastener consisting of two rows of metal or plastic teeth on strips of tape and a sliding piece that closes an opening by drawing the teeth together

zip·py \'zi-pē\ *adj* **zip·pi·er; -est 1** : very speedy ⟨a ∼ car⟩ **2** : strikingly appealing ⟨∼ clothes⟩

zir·con \'zər-ˌkän\ *n* : a zirconium-containing mineral transparent varieties of which are used as gems

zir·co·ni·um \ˌzər-'kō-nē-əm\ *n* : a gray corrosion-resistant metallic chemical element used esp. in alloys and ceramics

zit \'zit\ *n* : PIMPLE

zith·er \'zi-thər, -thər\ *n* : a musical instrument having 30 to 40 strings played with plectrum and fingers

zi·ti \'zē-tē\ *n, pl ziti* [It] : medium-size tubular pasta

zlo·ty \'zlȯ-tē\ *n, pl zlo·tys* \-tēz\ *or* **zloty** — see MONEY table

Zn *symbol* zinc

zo·di·ac \'zō-dē-ˌak\ *n* [ME, fr. AF, fr. L *zodiacus*, fr. Gk *zōidiakos*, fr. *zōidion* carved figure, sign of the zodiac, fr. dim. of *zōion* living being, figure] **1** : an imaginary belt in the heavens that encompasses the paths of most of the planets and that is divided into 12 constellations or signs **2** : a figure representing the signs of the zodiac and their symbols — **zo·di·a·cal** \zō-'dī-ə-kəl\ *adj*

zom·bie *also* **zom·bi** \'zäm-bē\ *n* : a person who is be-

lieved to have died and been brought back to life without speech or free will

zon·al \'zō-nᵊl\ *adj* : of, relating to, or having the form of a zone — **zon·al·ly** *adv*

¹**zone** \'zōn\ *n* [ME, fr. AF, fr. L *zona* belt, zone, fr. Gk *zōnē*] **1** : any of five great divisions of the earth's surface made according to latitude and temperature including the torrid zone, two temperate zones, and two frigid zones **2** : something that forms an encircling band ⟨a ∼ of tissue⟩ **3** : a region or area set off as distinct from surrounding parts ⟨business ∼⟩ ⟨postal ∼⟩

²**zone** *vb* **zoned; zon·ing 1** : ENCIRCLE **2** : to arrange in or mark off into zones; *esp* : to divide (as a city) into sections reserved for different purposes

zonked \'zäŋkt\ *adj* : being or acting as if under the influence of alcohol or a drug : HIGH

zoo \'zü\ *n, pl* **zoos** : a park where wild animals are kept for exhibition

zoo·ge·og·ra·phy \ˌzō-ə-jē-'ä-grə-fē\ *n* : a branch of biogeography concerned with the geographical distribution of animals — **zoo·ge·og·ra·pher** \-fər\ *n* — **zoo·geo·graph·ic** \-ˌjē-ə-'gra-fik\ *also* **zoo·geo·graph·i·cal** \-fi-kəl\ *adj*

zoo·keep·er \'zü-ˌkē-pər\ *n* : a person who cares for animals in a zoo

zool *abbr* zoological; zoology

zoological garden *n* : ZOO

zo·ol·o·gy \zō-'ä-lə-jē\ *n* : a branch of biology that deals with the classification and the properties and vital phenomena of animals — **zo·o·log·i·cal** \ˌzō-ə-'lä-ji-kəl\ *adj* — **zo·ol·o·gist** \zō-'ä-lə-jist\ *n*

zoom \'züm\ *vb* **1** : to move with a loud hum or buzz **2** : to gain altitude quickly **3** : to focus a camera or microscope using a special lens that permits the apparent distance of the object to be varied — **zoom** *n*

zoom lens *n* : a camera lens in which the image size can be varied continuously while the image remains in focus

zoo·mor·phic \ˌzō-ə-'mȯr-fik\ *adj* **1** : having the form of an animal **2** : of, relating to, or being the representation of a deity in the form or with the attributes of an animal

zoo·plank·ton \ˌzō-ə-'plaŋk-tən, -ˌtän\ *n* : plankton composed of animals

zoo·spore \'zō-ə-ˌspȯr\ *n* : a motile spore

zoot suit \'züt-\ *n* : a flashy suit of extreme cut typically consisting of a thigh-length jacket with wide padded shoulders and pants that are wide at the top and narrow at the bottom — **zoot-suit·er** \-ˌsü-tər\ *n*

Zo·ro·as·tri·an·ism \ˌzȯr-ə-'was-trē-ə-ˌni-zəm\ *n* : a religion founded by the Persian prophet Zoroaster — **Zo·ro·as·tri·an** \-trē-ən\ *adj or n*

zounds \'zaúndz\ *interj* [euphemism for *God's wounds*] — used as a mild oath

zoy·sia \'zȯi-shə, -zhə, -sē-ə, -zē-ə\ *n* : any of a genus of creeping perennial grasses having fine wiry leaves and including some used as lawn grasses

ZPG *abbr* zero population growth

Zr *symbol* zirconium

zuc·chet·to \zü-'ke-tō, tsü-\ *n, pl* **-tos** [It] : a small round skullcap worn by Roman Catholic ecclesiastics

zuc·chi·ni \zù-'kē-nē\ *n, pl* **-ni** *or* **-nis** [It] : a smooth cylindrical usu. dark green summer squash; *also* : a plant that bears zucchini

Zu·lu \'zü-ˌlü\ *n, pl* **Zulu** *or* **Zulus** : a member of a Bantuspeaking people of South Africa; *also* : the Bantu language of the Zulus

Zu·ni \'zü-nē\ *or* **Zu·ñi** \-nyē\ *n, pl* **Zuni** *or* **Zunis** *or* **Zuñi** *or* **Zuñis** : a member of an American Indian people of western New Mexico; *also* : the language of the Zuni people

zwie·back \'swē-ˌbak, 'swī-, 'zwē-, 'zwī-, -ˌbäk\ *n* [G, lit., twice baked, fr. *zwie-* twice + *backen* to bake] : a usu. sweetened bread that is baked and then sliced and toasted until dry and crisp

Zwing·li·an \'zwiŋ-glē-ən, 'swiŋ-, -lē-; 'tsfiŋ-lē-\ *adj* : of or relating to the Swiss religious reformer Ulrich Zwingli or his teachings — **Zwinglian** *n*

zy·de·co \'zī-də-ˌkō\ *n* : popular music of southern Louisiana that combines tunes of French origin with elements of Caribbean music and the blues

zy·gote \'zī-ˌgōt\ *n* : a cell formed by the union of two sexual cells; *also* : the developing individual produced from such a cell — **zy·got·ic** \zī-'gä-tik\ *adj*

FOREIGN WORDS & PHRASES

These words and phrases occur frequently enough in English context to be included in a general English dictionary, but they merit a special section because they have not become a part of the English vocabulary.

---

ab·eunt stu·dia in mo·res \'ä-be-,ṵnt-'stü-dē-,ä-,in-'mō-,räs\ [L] : practices zealously pursued pass into habits

à bien·tôt \ä-byaⁿ-tò\ [F] : so long

ab in·cu·na·bu·lis \,äb-,in-kú-'nä-bú-,lēs\ [L] : from the cradle : from infancy

à bon chat, bon rat \ä-bōⁿ-'shä bōⁿ-'rä\ [F] : to a good cat, a good rat : retaliation in kind

à bouche ou·verte \ä-bü-shü-vert\ [F] : with open mouth : eagerly : uncritically

ab ovo us·que ad ma·la \äb-'ō-vō-,ús-kwe-,äd-'mä-lä\ [L] : from egg to apples : from soup to nuts : from beginning to end

à bras ou·verts \ä-brä-zü-ver\ [F] : with open arms : cordially

ab·sit in·vi·dia \'äb-,sit-in-'wi-dē-,ä\ [L] : let there be no envy or ill will

ab uno dis·ce om·nes \äb-'ú-nō-,dis-ke-'óm-,näs\ [L] : from one learn to know all

ab ur·be con·di·ta \äb-'úr-be-'kòn-di-,tä\ [L] : from the founding of the city (Rome, founded 753 B.C.) — used by the Romans in reckoning dates

ab·usus non tol·lit usum \'ä-,bü-sùs-,nōn-,tò-lit-'ü-sùm\ [L] : abuse does not take away use, i.e., is not an argument against proper use

à compte \ä-'kōⁿt\ [F] : on account

à coup sûr \ä-kü-sṵr\ [F] : with sure stroke : surely

acte gra·tuit \äk-tə-grä-tw^yē\ [F] : gratuitous impulsive act

ad ar·bi·tri·um \,ad-är-'bi-trē-ùm\ [L] : at will : arbitrarily

ad as·tra per as·pe·ra \ad-'as-trə-,pər-'as-pə-rə\ [L] : to the stars by hard ways — motto of Kansas

ad ex·tre·mum \,äd-ek-'strä-,mùm, ,ad-ik-'strē-məm\ [L] : to the extreme : at last

ad ma·jo·rem Dei glo·ri·am \äd-mä-'yòr-,em-'de-,ē-'glòr-ē-,äm\ [L] : to the greater glory of God — motto of the Society of Jesus

ad pa·tres \äd-'pä-,träs\ [L] : (gathered) to his fathers : deceased

ad re·fe·ren·dum \,äd-,re-fe-'ren-dùm\ [L] : for reference : for further consideration by one having the authority to make a final decision

à droite \ä-drwät\ [F] : to or on the right hand

ad utrum·que pa·ra·tus \äd-ú-'trùm-kwe-pä-'rä-tús\ [L] : prepared for either (event)

ad vi·vum \äd-'wē-,wùm\ [L] : to the life

ae·gri som·nia \,ī-grē-'sóm-nē-,ä\ [L] : a sick man's dreams

ae·quam ser·va·re men·tem \'ī-,kwäm-ser-,wä-rä-'men-,tem\ [L] : to preserve a calm mind

ae·quo ani·mo \,ī-,kwō-'ä-ni-,mō\ [L] : with even mind : calmly

à gauche \ä-gōsh\ [F] : to or on the left hand

age quod agis \'ä-ge-,kwòd-'ä-,gis\ [L] : do what you are doing : to the business at hand

à grands frais \ä-gräⁿ-fre\ [F] : at great expense

à huis clos \ä-w^yē-klō\ [F] : with closed doors : behind closed doors

aide–toi, le ciel t'ai·dera \ed-twä lə-'syel-te-drä\ [F] : help yourself (and) heaven will help you

aî·né \e-nä\ [F] : elder : senior (masc.)

aî·née \e-nä\ [F] : elder : senior (fem.)

à l'aban·don \ä-lä-bäⁿ-dōⁿ\ [F] : carelessly : in disorder

à la belle étoile \ä-lä-bel-ä-twäl\ [F] : under the beautiful star : in the open air at night

à la bonne heure \ä-lä-bó-nœr\ [F] : at a good time : well and good : all right

à la fran·çaise \ä-lä-fräⁿ-sez\ [F] : in the French manner

à l'amé·ri·caine \ä-lä-mä-rē-ken\ [F] : in the American manner : of the American kind

à l'an·glaise \ä-läⁿ-glez\ [F] : in the English manner

à la page \ä-lä-päzh\ [F] : at the page : up-to-the-minute

à la russe \ä-lä-rṵes\ [F] : in the Russian manner

alea jac·ta est \'ä-lē-,ä-,yäk-tä-'est\ [L] : the die is cast

à l'im·pro·viste \ä-laⁿ-prò-vēst\ [F] : unexpectedly

alis vo·lat pro·pri·is \'ä-,lēs-'wò-,lät-'prō-prē-,ēs\ [L] : she flies with her own wings — motto of Oregon

al·ki \'al-,kī, -kē\ [Chinook Jargon] : by and by — motto of Washington

alo·ha oe \ä-,lō-hä-'òi, -'ō-ē\ [Hawaiian] : love to you : greetings : farewell

al·ter idem \,òl-tər-'ī-,dem, ,äl-ter-'ē-\ [L] : second self

à mer·veille \ä-mer-vä\ [F] : marvelously : wonderfully

ami·cus hu·ma·ni ge·ne·ris \ä-'mē-kús-hü-,mä-nē-'ge-ne-ris\ [L] : friend of the human race

ami·cus us·que ad aras \-,ús-kwe-,äd-'är-,äs\ [L] : a friend as far as to the altars, i.e., except in what is contrary to one's religion; *also* : a friend to the last extremity

ami de cour \ä-,mē-də-'kùr\ [F] : court friend : insincere friend

amor pa·tri·ae \'ä-,mòr-'pä-trē-,ī\ [L] : love of one's country

amor vin·cit om·nia \'ä-,mòr-,win-kit-'òm-nē-ä\ [L] : love conquers all things

an·guis in her·ba \, äŋ-gwis-in-'her-,bä\ [L] : snake in the grass

ani·mal bi·pes im·plu·me \'ä-ni-,mäl-,bi-,pās-im-'plü-me\ [L] : two-legged animal without feathers (i.e., the human race)

ani·mis opi·bus·que pa·ra·ti \'ä-ni-,mēs-,ó-pi-'bús-kwe-pä-'rä-tē\ [L] : prepared in mind and resources — one of the mottoes of South Carolina

an·no ae·ta·tis su·ae \'ä-nō-ī-,tä-tis-'sü-,ī\ [L] : in the (specified) year of his (or her) age

an·no mun·di \,ä-nō-'mùn-dē\ [L] : in the year of the world — used in reckoning dates from the supposed period of the creation of the world, esp. as fixed by James Ussher at 4004 B.C. or by the Jews at 3761 B.C.

an·no ur·bis con·di·tae \,ä-nō-,úr-bis-'kòn-di-,tī\ [L] : in the year of the founded city : in the year that the city was founded (Rome, founded 753 B.C.)

an·nu·it coep·tis \,ä-nü-,it-'kóip-,tēs\ [L] : He (God) has approved our beginnings — motto on the reverse of the Great Seal of the United States

à peu près \ä-pœ-pre\ [F] : nearly : approximately

à pied \ä-pyä\ [F] : on foot

à point \ä-pwaⁿ\ [F] : at the right time

après moi le dé·luge \ä-pre-mwä-lə-dā-lṵezh\ *or* **après nous le déluge** \ä-pre-nü-\ [F] : after me the deluge — attributed to Louis XV

à pro·pos de rien \ä-prə-pō-də-ryaⁿ\ [F] : apropos of nothing

aqua et ig·ni in·ter·dic·tus \,ä-kwä-et-'ig-nē-,in-ter-'dik-tús\ [L] : forbidden to be furnished with water and fire : outlawed

Ar·ca·des am·bo \'är-kä-,des-'äm-bō\ [L] : both Arcadians : two persons of like occupations or tastes; *also* : two rascals

ar·rec·tis au·ri·bus \ä-'rek-,tēs-'aù-ri-,bús\ [L] : with ears pricked up : attentively

ar·ri·ve·der·ci \,är-ē-vä-'der-chē\ [It] : till we meet again : farewell

ars lon·ga, vi·ta bre·vis \ärs-'lòŋ-,gä ,wē-,tä-'bre-wis\ [L] : art is long, life is short : human life span limits all that might be accomplished

as–sa·laam alai·kum \əs-sə-'läm-ə-'lī-kùm\ [Ar *as-salāmu 'alaykum*] : peace to you — used as a traditional greeting among Muslims

a ter·go \ä-'ter-(,)gō\ [L] : from behind

à tort et à tra·vers \ä-tȯr-ä-ä-trä-ver\ [F] : wrong and crosswise : at random : without rhyme or reason

au bout de son la·tin \ō-büd-sōⁿ-lä-taⁿ, -bü-də-\ [F] : at the end of one's Latin : at the end of one's mental resources

au con·traire \ō-kōⁿ-trer\ [F] : on the contrary

au·de·mus ju·ra nos·tra de·fen·de·re \au̇-'dä-mús-‚yūr-ä-'nó-strä-dä-'fen-de-rä\ [L] : we dare defend our rights — motto of Alabama

au·den·tes for·tu·na ju·vat \au̇-'den-‚tās-fȯr-‚tü-nä-'yù-‚wät\ [L] : fortune favors the bold

au·di al·te·ram par·tem \'au̇-‚dē-‚äl-te-‚räm-'pär-‚tem\ [L] : hear the other side

au fait \ō-fet, -fe\ [F] : to the point : fully competent : fully informed : socially correct

au fond \ō-fōⁿ\ [F] : at bottom : fundamentally

au grand sé·rieux \ō-grä̈ⁿ-sä-ryœ\ [F] : in all seriousness

au mieux \ō-myœ\ [F] : on the best terms : on intimate terms

au pays des aveugles les borgnes sont rois \ō-pä-ē-dä-zä-vœglᵊ-lä-bȯrnᵞ-ə-sōⁿ-rwä\ [F] : in the country of the blind the one-eyed men are kings

au·rea me·di·o·cri·tas \'au̇-rē-ä-‚me-dē-'ó-kri-‚tás\ [L] : the golden mean

au reste \ō-rest\ [F] : for the rest : besides

au sé·rieux \ō-sä-ryœ\ [F] : seriously

aus·si·tôt dit, aus·si·tôt fait \ō-sē-tō-dē ō-sē-tō-fe\ [F] : no sooner said than done

aut Cae·sar aut ni·hil \au̇t-'kī-sär-‚au̇t-'ni-‚hil\ [L] : either a Caesar or nothing

au·tres temps, au·tres mœurs \ō-trə-täⁿ ō-trə-mœrs\ [F] : other times, other customs

aut vin·ce·re aut mo·ri \au̇t-'wiŋ-ke-rä-‚au̇t-'mó-‚rē\ [L] : either to conquer or to die

aux armes \ō-zärm\ [F] : to arms

avant la lettre \ä-väⁿ-lä-letrᵃ\ [F] : before the letter : before a (specified) name or entity existed

ave at·que va·le \'ä-‚wä-‚ät-kwe-'wä-‚lä\ [L] : hail and farewell

à vo·tre san·té \ä-vȯt-säⁿ-tä, -vó-trə-\ [F] : to your health — used as a toast

ax·is mun·di \'ak-səs-'mún-dē\ [L] : turning point of the world : line through the earth's center around which the universe revolves

bel·la fi·gu·ra \'bel-lə-fē-'gü-rä\ [It] : fine appearance or impression

bel·lum om·ni·um con·tra om·nes \'be-lùm-'òm-nē-ùm-‚kòn-trä-'óm-‚näs\ [L] : war of all against all

bien en·ten·du \byaⁿ-näⁿ-täⁿ-dœ\ [F] : well understood : of course

bien—pen·sant \byaⁿ-päⁿ-säⁿ\ [F] : right-minded : one who holds orthodox views

bis dat qui ci·to dat \'bis-‚dät-kwē-'ki-tō-‚dät\ [L] : he gives twice who gives promptly

bon ap·pé·tit \bȯ-nä-pä-tē\ [F] : good appetite : enjoy your meal

bon gré, mal gré \'bōⁿ-‚grä 'mäl-‚grä\ [F] : whether with good grace or bad : willy-nilly

bon·jour \bōⁿ-zhür\ [F] : good day : good morning

bonne foi \bón-fwä\ [F] : good faith

bon·soir \bōⁿ-swär\ [F] : good evening

bru·tum ful·men \‚brü-tùm-'fúl-men\ [L] : insensible thunderbolt : a futile threat or display of force

ca·dit quae·stio \‚kä-dit-'kwī-stē-‚ō\ [L] : the question drops : the argument collapses

carte d'iden·ti·té \kärt-dē-däⁿ-tē-tä\ [F] : identity card

cau·sa si·ne qua non \'kau̇-‚sä-‚si-nä-kwä-'nōn\ [L] : an indispensable cause or condition

ça va sans dire \sä-vä-säⁿ-dir\ [F] : it goes without saying

ca·ve ca·nem \‚kä-wä-'kä-‚nem\ [L] : beware the dog

ce·dant ar·ma to·gae \'kä-‚dänt-‚är-mə-'tō-‚gi\ [L] : let arms yield to the toga : let military power give way to civil power — motto of Wyoming

ce n'est que le pre·mier pas qui coûte \snek-lə-prə-myä-pä-kē-küt\ [F] : it is only the first step that costs

c'est-à-dire \se-tä-dir\ [F] : that is to say : namely

c'est au·tre chose \se-tōt-shōz, -tō-trə-\ [F] : that's a different thing

c'est la guerre \se-lä-ger\ [F] : that's war : it cannot be helped

c'est la vie \se-lä-vē\ [F] : that's life : that's how things happen

c'est plus qu'un crime, c'est une faute \se-plœ-kœⁿ-krēm se-tœn-fōt\ [F] : it is worse than a crime, it is a blunder

ce·te·ra de·sunt \‚kā-te-‚rä-'dä-‚sùnt\ [L] : the rest is missing

cha·cun à son goût \shä-kœⁿ-nä-sōⁿ-gü\ [F] : everyone to his taste

châ·teau en Es·pagne \shä-tō-äⁿ-nes-pänᵞ\ [F] : castle in Spain : a visionary project

cher·chez la femme \sher-shä-lä-fäm\ [F] : look for the woman

che sa·rà, sa·rà \‚kä-sä-‚rä sä-'rä\ [It] : what will be, will be

che·val de ba·taille \shə-väl-də-bä-täᵞ\ [F] : warhorse : argument constantly relied on : favorite subject

co·gi·to, er·go sum \'kō-gi-‚tō ‚er-gō-'sùm\ [L] : I think, therefore I exist

co·mé·die hu·maine \kȯ-mä-dē-œ-men\ [F] : human comedy : the whole variety of human life

comme ci, comme ça \kòm-sē kòm-sä\ [F] : so-so

com·pa·gnon de voy·age \kōⁿ-pä-nᵞōⁿ-də-vwä-yäzh\ [F] : traveling companion

compte ren·du \kōⁿt-räⁿ-dœ\ [F] : report (as of proceedings in an investigation)

con·cor·dia dis·cors \kòn-'kȯr-dē-ä-'dis-‚kȯrs\ [L] : discordant harmony

con·fes·sio fi·dei \kòn-'fe-sē-ō-'fi-dē-‚ē\ [L] : confession of faith

cor·rup·tio op·ti·mi pes·si·ma \kȯ-'rùp-tē-‚ō-'äp-ti-‚mē-'pe-si-‚mä\ [L] : the corruption of the best is the worst of all

coup de maî·tre \küd-metrᵃ, kü-də-\ [F] : masterstroke

coup d'es·sai \kü-dä-se\ [F] : experiment : trial

coûte que coûte \küt-kə-küt\ [F] : cost what it may

cre·do quia ab·sur·dum est \‚krä-dō-'kwē-ä-äp-‚sùr-dùm-'est\ [L] : I believe it because it is absurd

cres·cit eun·do \‚kres-kit-'eùn-dō\ [L] : it grows as it goes — motto of New Mexico

crise de nerfs or **crise des nerfs** \krēz-də-ner\ [F] : crisis of nerves : nervous collapse : hysterical fit

cu·jus re·gio, ej·us re·li·gio \‚kü-yùs-'re-gē-‚ō ‚e-yùs-re-'li-gē-‚ō\ [L] : whose region, his or her religion : subjects are to accept the religion of their ruler

cum gra·no sa·lis \kùm-‚grä-nō-'sä-lis\ [L] : with a grain of salt

cus·tos mo·rum \‚kùs-tōs-'mȯr-ùm\ [L] : guardian of manners or morals : censor

d'ac·cord \dä-kȯr\ [F] : in accord : agreed

dame d'hon·neur \däm-dò-nœr\ [F] : lady-in-waiting

dam·nant quod non in·tel·li·gunt \'däm-‚nänt-‚kwòd-‚nōn-in-'te-li-‚gùnt\ [L] : they condemn what they do not understand

de bonne grâce \də-bòn-gräs\ [F] : with good grace : willingly

de gus·ti·bus non est dis·pu·tan·dum \dä-'gùs-tə-‚bùs-‚nōn-‚est-‚dis-pù-'tän-‚dùm\ [L] : there is no disputing about tastes

Dei gra·tia \‚de-‚ē-'grä-tē-‚ä\ [L] : by the grace of God

de in·te·gro \dä-'in-te-‚grō\ [L] : anew : afresh

de·len·da est Car·tha·go \dä-'len-dä-‚est-kär-'tä-gō\ [L] : Carthage must be destroyed

de mal en pis \də-mä-läⁿ-pē\ [F] : from bad to worse

de mi·ni·mis non cu·rat lex \dä-'mi-ni-‚mēs-‚nōn-‚kü-‚rät-'leks\ [L] : the law takes no account of trifles

de mor·tu·is nil ni·si bo·num \dä-'mȯr-tü-‚ēs-‚nēl-ni-sē-'bò-‚nùm\ [L] : of the dead (say) nothing but good

de nos jours \də-nō-zhür\ [F] : of our time : contemporary — used postpositively esp. after a proper name

Deo fa·ven·te \‚dä-ō-fä-'ven-tä\ [L] : with God's favor

Deo gra·ti·as \‚dä-ō-'grä-tē-‚äs\ [L] : thanks (be) to God

de pro·fun·dis \‚dä-prō-'fùn-dēs\ [L] : out of the depths

de·si·pe·re in lo·co \dä-'si-pe-rä-in-'lò-kō\ [L] : to indulge in trifling at the proper time

de te fa·bu·la nar·ra·tur \‚dä-‚tä-'fä-bù-lä-nä-'rä-‚tùr\ [L] : the story applies to you

De·us ab·scon·di·tus \‚dä-ùs-‚äp-'skòn-di-‚tùs\ [L] : hidden God : God unknowable by the human mind

De·us vult \‚dä-ùs-'wùlt\ [L] : God wills it — rallying cry of the First Crusade

di·es fau·stus \‚dē-‚äs-'fau̇-stùs\ [L] : lucky day

dies in·fau·stus \-in-‚fau̇-stùs\ [L] : unlucky day

dies irae \-ē-‚rī, -‚rä\ [L] : day of wrath — used of the Judgment Day

Dieu et mon droit \dyœ-ä-móⁿ-drwä\ [F] : God and my right — motto on the British royal arms

Dieu vous garde \dyœ-vü-gärd\ [F] : God keep you

di·ri·go \'dē-ri-ˌgō\ [L] : I direct — motto of Maine

dis ali·ter vi·sum \ˌdēs-ˌä-li-ˌter-'wē-ˌsùm\ [L] : the Gods decreed otherwise

di·tat De·us \ˌdē-ˌtät-'dā-ˌùs\ [L] : God enriches — motto of Arizona

di·vi·de et im·pe·ra \'dē-wi-ˌde-ˌet-'im-pe-ˌrä\ [L] : divide and rule

do·cen·do dis·ci·mus \dò-ˌken-dō-'dis-ki-ˌmùs\ [L] : we learn by teaching

Do·mi·ne, di·ri·ge nos \'dò-mi-ˌne 'dē-ri-ˌge-'nōs\ [L] : Lord, direct us — motto of the City of London

Do·mi·nus vo·bis·cum \ˌdò-mi-ˌnùs-wō-'bēs-ˌkúm\ [L] : the Lord be with you

dul·ce et de·co·rum est pro pa·tria mo·ri \ˌdùl-ˌke-et-de-'kór-ùm-ˌest-prō-ˌpä-trē-ˌä-'mò-ˌrē\ [L] : it is sweet and seemly to die for one's country

dum spi·ro, spe·ro \dùm-'spē-rō 'spä-rō\ [L] : while I breathe, I hope — one of the mottoes of South Carolina

dum vi·vi·mus vi·va·mus \dùm-'wē-wē-ˌmùs-wē-'vä-mùs\ [L] : while we live, let us live

d'un cer·tain âge \dœⁿ-ser-te-näzh\ [F] : of a certain age : no longer young

dux fe·mi·na fac·ti \ˌdùks-ˌfä-mi-nä-'fäk-ˌtē\ [L] : a woman was leader of the exploit

ec·ce sig·num \ˌe-ke-'sig-ˌnùm\ [L] : behold the sign : look at the proof

e con·tra·rio \ˌä-kòn-'trär-ē-ˌō\ [L] : on the contrary

écra·sez l'in·fâme \ā-krä-zä-laⁿ-fäm\ [F] : crush the infamous thing

eheu fu·ga·ces la·bun·tur an·ni \ˌā-ˌheú-fù-'gä-ˌkäs-lä-'bùn-ˌtùr-'ä-ˌnē\ [L] : alas! the fleeting years glide on

ein' fes·te Burg ist un·ser Gott \in-ˌfes-tə-'bùrk-ist-ˌùn-zər-'gót\ [G] : a mighty fortress is our God

em·bar·ras de choix \äⁿ-bä-rä-də-shwä\ or **embarras du choix** \-dœ-shwä\ [F] : embarrassing variety of choice

em·bar·ras de ri·chesses or **embarras de ri·chesse** \äⁿ-bä-räd-rē-shes, -rä-dò-\ [F] : embarrassing surplus of riches : confusing abundance

en ami \äⁿ-nä-mē\ [F] : as a friend

en ef·fet \äⁿ-nä-fe\ [F] : in fact : indeed

en fa·mille \äⁿ-fä-mē\ [F] : in or with one's family : at home : informally

en·fant ché·ri \äⁿ-fäⁿ-shä-rē\ [F] : loved or pampered child : one that is highly favored

en·fant gâ·té \äⁿ-fäⁿ-gä-tä\ [F] : spoiled child

en·fants per·dus \äⁿ-fäⁿ-per-dœ\ [F] : lost children : soldiers sent to a dangerous post

en·fin \äⁿ-faⁿ\ [F] : in conclusion : in a word

en gar·çon \äⁿ-gär-sōⁿ\ [F] : as or like a bachelor

en garde \äⁿ-gärd\ [F] : on guard

en plein air \äⁿ-ple-ner\ [F] : in the open air

en plein jour \äⁿ-plaⁿ-zhür\ [F] : in broad day

en règle \äⁿ-regl^ə\ [F] : in order : in due form

en re·tard \äⁿr-(ə-)tär\ [F] : behind time : late

en re·traite \äⁿr-(ə-)tret\ [F] : in retreat : in retirement

en re·vanche \äⁿr-(ə-)väⁿsh\ [F] : in return : in compensation

en·se pe·tit pla·ci·dam sub li·ber·ta·te qui·e·tem \ˌen-se-ˌpe-tit-'plä-ki-ˌdäm-sùb-ˌlē-ber-ˌtä-te-kwē-'ä-ˌtem\ [L] : with the sword she seeks calm repose under liberty : by the sword we seek peace, but peace only under liberty — motto of Massachusetts

eo ip·so \ā-ō-'ip-(ˌ)sō\ [L] : by that itself : by that fact alone

épa·ter le bour·geois \ā-pä-tä-lə-bür-zhwä\ or **épater les bour·geois** \-lā-bür-\ [F] : to shock the middle classes

e plu·ri·bus unum \ˌā-ˌplür-ə-bəs-'(y)ü-nəm, ˌä-ˌplür-i-bús-'ü-nùm\ [L] : one out of many — used on the Great Seal of the U.S. and on several U.S. coins

ep·pur si muo·ve \äp-ˌpür-sē-'mwó-vä\ [It] : and yet it does move — attributed to Galileo after recanting his assertion of the earth's motion

Erin go bragh \ˌer-ən-gə-'brò, -gō-'brä\ [Ir go brách or go bráth, lit., till doomsday] : Ireland forever

er·ra·re hu·ma·num est \e-ˌrär-ä-hü-ˌmä-nùm-'est\ [L] : to err is human

es·prit de l'es·ca·lier \es-prēd-les-kä-lyä\ or **es·prit d'es·ca·lier** \-prē-des-\ [F] : wit of the staircase : repartee thought of only too late

es·se quam vi·de·ri \'e-sä-ˌkwäm-wi-'dā-rē\ [L] : to be rather than to seem — motto of North Carolina

est mo·dus in re·bus \est-'mò-ˌdús-in-'rä-ˌbús\ [L] : there is a proper measure in things, i.e., the golden mean should always be observed

es·to per·pe·tua \'es-ˌtō-per-'pe-tù-ˌä\ [L] : may she endure forever — motto of Idaho

et hoc ge·nus om·ne \et-ˌhōk-ˌge-nùs-'òm-ne\ or **et id genus omne** \et-ˌid-\ [L] : and everything of this kind

et sic de si·mi·li·bus \et-ˌsēk-dä-si-'mi-li-ˌbús\ [L] : and so of like things

et tu Bru·te \et-'tü-'brü-te\ [L] : thou too, Brutus — exclamation attributed to Julius Caesar on seeing his friend Brutus among his assassins

eu·re·ka \yù-'rē-kä\ [Gk] : I have found it — motto of California

Ewig–Weib·li·che \ˌā-vik-'vīp-li-kə\ [G] : eternal feminine

ex·al·té \eg-zäl-tä\ [F] : emotionally excited or elated : fanatic

ex ani·mo \eks-'ä-ni-ˌmō\ [L] : from the heart : sincerely

ex·cel·si·or \ik-'sel-sē-ər, eks-'kel-sē-ˌór\ [L] : still higher — motto of New York

ex·cep·tio pro·bat re·gu·lam de re·bus non ex·cep·tis \eks-'kep-tē-ˌō-ˌprō-bät-'rä-gù-ˌläm-dä-'rä-ˌbús-ˌnōn-eks-'kep-ˌtēs\ [L] : an exception establishes the rule as to things not excepted

ex·cep·tis ex·ci·pi·en·dis \eks-'kep-ˌtēs-eks-ˌki-pē-'en-ˌdēs\ [L] : with the proper or necessary exceptions

ex·i·tus ac·ta pro·bat \'ek-si-ˌtùs-ˌäk-tä-'prò-ˌbät\ [L] : the outcome justifies the deed

ex li·bris \eks-'lē-bris\ [L] : from the books of — used on bookplates

ex me·ro mo·tu \ˌeks-ˌmer-ō-'mō-tü\ [L] : out of mere impulse : of one's own accord

ex ne·ces·si·ta·te rei \ˌeks-ne-ˌke-si-'tä-te-'rä(-ˌē)\ [L] : from the necessity of the case

ex ni·hi·lo ni·hil fit \eks-'ni-hi-ˌlō-ˌni-ˌhil-'fit\ [L] : from nothing nothing is produced

ex pe·de Her·cu·lem \eks-ˌpe-de-'her-kù-ˌlem\ [L] : from the foot (we may judge of the size of) Hercules : from a part we may judge of the whole

ex·per·to cre·de \eks-ˌper-tō-'krä-de\ or **experto cre·di·te** \'-krä-di-ˌte\ [L] : believe one who has had experience

ex un·gue le·o·nem \eks-'ùn-gwe-le-'ō-ˌnem\ [L] : from the claw (we may judge of) the lion : from a part we may judge of the whole

ex vi ter·mi·ni \eks-ˌwē-'ter-mə-ˌnē\ [L] : from the force of the term

fa·ci·le prin·ceps \ˌfä-ki-le-'prin-ˌkeps\ [L] : easily first

fa·ci·lis de·scen·sus Aver·no \'fä-ki-ˌlis-dä-ˌskän-ˌsùs-ä-'wer-nō\ or **facilis descensus Aver·ni** \-(ˌ)nē\ [L] : the descent to Avernus is easy : the road to evil is easy

fa·çon de par·ler \fä-sōⁿ-də-pär-lä\ [F] : manner of speaking : figurative or conventional expression

fas est et ab ho·ste do·ce·ri \fäs-'est-et-äb-'hò-ste-dò-'kä-(ˌ)rē\ [L] : it is right to learn even from an enemy

Fa·ta vi·am in·ve·ni·ent \ˌfä-tä-'wē-ˌäm-in-'we-nē-ˌent\ [L] : the Fates will find a way

fat·ti mas·chii, pa·ro·le fe·mi·ne \ˌfät-tē-'mäs-ˌkē pä-ˌrò-lä-'fä-mē-ˌnä\ [It] : deeds are males, words are females : deeds are more effective than words — motto of Maryland, where it is generally interpreted as meaning "manly deeds, womanly words"

faux bon·homme \fō-bò-nòm\ [F] : pretended good fellow

faux–naïf \fœ-nä-ēf\ [F] : spuriously or affectedly childlike : artfully simple

fe·lix cul·pa \'fä-liks-'kùl-pä\ [L] : fortunate fault — used esp. of original sin in relation to the consequent coming of Christ

femme de cham·bre \fäm-də-shäⁿbr^ə\ [F] : chambermaid : lady's maid

fe·sti·na len·te \fe-ˌstē-nä-'len-ˌtä\ [L] : make haste slowly

feux d'ar·ti·fice \fœ-där-tē-fēs\ [F] : fireworks : display of wit

fi·at ju·sti·tia, ru·at cae·lum \ˌfē-ˌät-yùs-'ti-tē-ä ˌrú-ˌät-'kī-ˌlùm\ [L] : let justice be done though the heavens fall

fi·at lux \ˌfē-ˌät-'lùks\ [L] : let there be light

Fi·dei De·fen·sor \ˌfi-de-ē-dā-'fän-ˌsòr\ [L] : Defender of the Faith — a title of the sovereigns of England

fille de cham·bre \fē-də-shäⁿbr^ə\ [F] : lady's maid

fille d'hon·neur \fē-dȯ-nœr\ [F] : maid of honor

fi·nem re·spi·ce \ˌfē-ˌnem-'rā-spi-ˌke\ [L] : consider the end

fi·nis co·ro·nat opus \ˌfē-nis-kȯ-ˌrō-ˌnät-'ō-ˌpu̇s\ [L] : the end crowns the work

flo·re·at \'flō-rē-ˌät\ [L] : may (he, she, or it) flourish — usu. followed by a name

fluc·tu·at nec mer·gi·tur \'flu̇k-tü-ˌät-ˌnek-'mer-gi-ˌtu̇r\ [L] : it is tossed by the waves but does not sink — motto of Paris

fo·lie de gran·deur or **fo·lie des gran·deurs** \fȯ-lē-də-grä°-dœr\ [F] : delusion of greatness : megalomania

force de frappe \fȯrs-də-fräp\ [F] : a force equipped to deal a retaliatory blow

fors·an et haec olim me·mi·nis·se ju·va·bit \ˌfȯr-ˌsän-ˌet-'hīk-ˌō-lim-ˌme-mi-'ni-se-yü-'wä-bit\ [L] : perhaps this too will be a pleasure to look back on one day

for·tes for·tu·na ju·vat \'fȯr-ˌtās-fȯr-ˌtü-nä-'yü-ˌwät\ [L] : fortune favors the brave

fron·ti nul·la fi·des \'frȯn-ˌtē-ˌnu̇-lä-'fi-ˌdās\ [L] : no reliance can be placed on appearance

fu·it Ili·um \'fu̇-it-'i-lē-u̇m\ [L] : Troy has been (i.e., is no more)

fu·ror lo·quen·di \ˌfu̇r-ˌȯr-lȯ-'kwen-(ˌ)dē\ [L] : rage for speaking

furor po·e·ti·cus \-pȯ-'ā-ti-ku̇s\ [L] : poetic frenzy

furor scri·ben·di \-skrē-'ben-(ˌ)dē\ [L] : rage for writing

Gal·li·ce \'gä-li-ˌke\ [L] : in French : after the French manner

gar·çon d'hon·neur \gär-sō°-dȯ-nœr\ [F] : bridegroom's attendant

garde du corps \gärd-du̇-kȯr\ [F] : bodyguard

gar·dez la foi \gär-dā-lä-fwä\ [F] : keep faith

gau·de·a·mus igi·tur \ˌgau̇-dē-'ä-mu̇s-'i-gi-ˌtu̇r\ [L] : let us then be merry

gens d'é·glise \zhä°-dā-glēz\ [F] : church people : clergy

gens de guerre \zhä°-də-ger\ [F] : military people : soldiery

gens du monde \zhä°-du̇-mō°d\ [F] : people of the world : fashionable people

gno·thi se·au·ton \'gnō-thē-ˌse-au̇-'tȯn\ [Gk] : know thyself

goût de ter·roir \gü-də-te-rwär\ [F] : taste of the earth

grand monde \grä°-mō°d\ [F] : great world : high society

gros·so mo·do \'grȯs-(ˌ)sō-'mȯ-(ˌ)dō\ [It] : roughly

guerre à ou·trance \ger-ä-ü-trä°s\ [F] : war to the uttermost

gu·ten Tag \ˌgü-tən-'täk\ [G] : good day

has·ta la vis·ta \ˌäs-tə-lä-'vēs-tə\ [Sp] : good-bye

haute vul·ga·ri·sa·tion \ōt-vu̇el-gä-rē-zä-syō°\ [F] : high popularization : effective presentation of a difficult subject to a general audience

hic et nunc \'hēk-et-'nu̇ŋk\ [L] : here and now

hic et ubi·que \ˌhēk-et-ú-'bē-kwe\ [L] : here and everywhere

hic ja·cet \hik-'jä-sət, hēk-'yä-ket\ [L] : here lies — used preceding a name on a tombstone

hinc il·lae la·cri·mae \ˌhiŋk-ˌi-ˌlī-'lä-kri-ˌmī\ [L] : hence those tears

hoc age \hōk-'ä-ge\ [L] : do this : apply yourself to what you are about

homme d'af·faires \ȯm-dä-fer\ [F] : man of business : business agent

homme d'es·prit \ȯm-des-prē\ [F] : man of wit

homme moyen sen·suel \ȯm-mwä-ya°-sä°-swᵉel\ [F] : the average nonintellectual man

ho·mo sum: hu·ma·ni nil a me ali·e·num pu·to \'hȯ-mō-ˌsu̇m hü-ˌmä-nē-'nēl-ä-ˌmä-ä-lē-'ä-nu̇m-'pu̇-tō\ [L] : I am a human being: I regard nothing of human concern as foreign to my interests

ho·ni soit qui mal y pense \ȯ-nē-swä-kē-mäl-ē-pä°s\ [F] : shamed be he who thinks evil of it — motto of the Order of the Garter

hu·ma·num est er·ra·re \hü-ˌmä-nu̇m-ˌest-e-'rär-ā\ [L] : to err is human

ich dien \ik-'dēn\ [G] : I serve — motto of the Prince of Wales

ici on parle fran·çais \ē-sē-ō°-pärl-frä°-se\ [F] : French is spoken here

idées re·çues \ē-dār-(ə-)sᵫe\ [F] : received ideas : conventional opinions

id est \id-'est\ [L] : that is

ig·no·ran·tia ju·ris ne·mi·nem ex·cu·sat \ˌig-nȯ-ˌrän-tē-ä-ˌyu̇r-is-'nä-mi-ˌnem-eks-'kü-ˌsät\ [L] : ignorance of the law excuses no one

ig·no·tum per ig·no·ti·us \ig-'nō-tu̇m-ˌper-ig-'nō-tē-ˌu̇s\ [L] : (explaining) the unknown by means of the more unknown

il faut cul·ti·ver no·tre jar·din \ēl-fō-ku̇el-tē-vä-nȯt-zhär-da°, -nȯ-trə-zhär-\ [F] : we must cultivate our garden : we must tend to our own affairs

in ae·ter·num \ˌin-ī-'ter-ˌnu̇m\ [L] : forever

in du·bio \in-'du̇-bē-ˌō\ [L] : in doubt : undetermined

in fu·tu·ro \ˌin-fu̇-'tu̇r-ō\ [L] : in the future

in hoc sig·no vin·ces \in-hōk-'sig-nō-'wiŋ-ˌkās\ [L] : by this sign (the Cross) you will conquer

in li·mi·ne \in-'lē-mi-ˌne\ [L] : on the threshold : at the beginning

in om·nia pa·ra·tus \in-'ȯm-nē-ä-pä-'rä-ˌtu̇s\ [L] : ready for all things

in par·ti·bus in·fi·de·li·um \in-'pär-ti-ˌbu̇s-ˌin-fi-'dä-lē-ˌu̇m\ [L] : in the regions of the infidels — used of a titular bishop having no diocesan jurisdiction, usu. in non-Christian countries

in prae·sen·ti \ˌin-prī-'sen-ˌtē\ [L] : at the present time

in sae·cu·la sae·cu·lo·rum \in-'sī-kü-ˌlä-ˌsī-kü-'lȯr-u̇m, -'sä-kü-ˌlä-ˌsä-\ [L] : for ages of ages : forever and ever

in·shal·lah \ˌin-shä-'lä\ [Ar *in shāʼ Allāh*] : if Allah wills : God willing

in·te·ger vi·tae sce·le·ris·que pu·rus \ˌin-te-ˌger-'wē-ˌtī-ˌske-le-'ris-kwe-'pü-ru̇s\ [L] : upright of life and free from wickedness

in·ter nos \in-ter-'nōs\ [L] : between ourselves

in·tra mu·ros \in-trä-'mü-ˌrōs\ [L] : within the walls

in utrum·que pa·ra·tus \in-ü-'tru̇m-kwe-pä-'rä-ˌtu̇s\ [L] : prepared for either (event)

in·ve·nit \in-'wā-nit\ [L] : he or she devised it

in vi·no ve·ri·tas \in-wē-nō-'wā-ri-ˌtäs\ [L] : there is truth in wine

ip·sis·si·ma ver·ba \ip-'si-si-ˌmä-'wer-ˌbä\ [L] : the very words

ira fu·ror bre·vis est \ˌē-rä-'fu̇r-ˌȯr-'bre-wis-ˌest\ [L] : anger is a brief madness

j'ac·cuse \zhä-kᵫez\ [F] : I accuse : bitter denunciation

jac·ta alea est \'yäk-ˌtä-ˌä-lē-ˌä-'est\ [L] : the die is cast

j'adoube \zhä-dübᵊ\ [F] : I adjust — used in chess when touching a piece without intending to move it

ja·nu·is clau·sis \ˌyä-nu̇-ˌēs-'klau̇-ˌsēs\ [L] : behind closed doors

je main·tien·drai \zhə-ma°-tyä°-drā\ [F] : I will maintain — motto of the Netherlands

jeu de mots \zhœd-mō, zhœ-də-\ [F] : play on words : pun

Jo·an·nes est no·men eius \yō-'ä-näs-est-ˌnō-men-'ä-yu̇s\ [L] : John is his name — motto of Puerto Rico

jour·nal in·time \zhür-näl-a°-tēm\ [F] : intimate journal : private diary

jus di·vi·num \ˌyu̇s-di-'wē-ˌnu̇m\ [L] : divine law

jus·ti·tia om·ni·bus \yu̇s-ˌti-tē-ˌä-'ȯm-ni-ˌbu̇s\ [L] : justice for all — motto of the District of Columbia

j'y suis, j'y reste \zhē-swᵉē zhē-rest\ [F] : here I am, here I remain

Kin·der, Kir·che, Küche \'kin-dər 'kir-kə 'kᵫe-kə\ [G] : children, church, kitchen

la belle dame sans mer·ci \lä-bel-däm-sä°-mer-sē\ [F] : the beautiful lady without mercy

la·bo·ra·re est ora·re \'lä-bȯ-ˌrär-ä-ˌest-'ō-ˌrär-ä\ [L] : to work is to pray

la·bor om·nia vin·cit \'lä-ˌbȯr-ˌȯm-nē-ä-'wiŋ-kit\ [L] : labor conquers all things — motto of Oklahoma

la·cri·mae re·rum \ˌlä-kri-ˌmī-'rä-ˌru̇m\ [L] : tears for things : pity for misfortune; *also* : tears in things : tragedy of life

lais·sez-al·ler or **lais·ser-al·ler** \le-sä-ä-lä\ [F] : letting go : lack of restraint

lap·sus ca·la·mi \ˌläp-su̇s-'kä-lä-ˌmē\ [L] : slip of the pen

lap·sus lin·guae \-'liŋ-ˌgwī\ [L] : slip of the tongue

la reine le veut \lä-ren-lo-vœ\ [F] : the queen wills it

la·scia·te ogni spe·ran·za, voi ch'en·tra·te \läsh-'shä-tā-ˌō-nʸē-spä-'rän-tsä ˌvō-ē-kän-'trä-tā\ [It] : abandon all hope, ye who enter

lau·da·tor tem·po·ris ac·ti \lau̇-'dä-ˌtȯr-ˌtem-pȯ-ris-'äk-ˌtē\ [L] : one who praises past times

laus Deo \laùs-'dā-ō\ [L] : praise (be) to God

Le·bens·welt \'lā-bəns-ˌvelt\ [G] : life world : world of lived experience

le cœur a ses rai·sons que la rai·son ne con·naît point \lə-kœr-ä-sā-re-zōⁿk-lä-re-zōⁿn-kȯ-ne-pwäⁿ\ [F] : the heart has its reasons that reason knows nothing of

le roi est mort, vive le roi \lə-rwä-e-mȯr vēv-lə-rwä\ [F] : the king is dead, long live the king

le roi le veut \lə-rwä-lə-vœ\ [F] : the king wills it

le style, c'est l'homme \lə-stēl se-lȯm\ [F] : the style is the man

l'état, c'est moi \lā-tä se-mwä\ [F] : the state, it is I

l'étoile du nord \lā-twäl-dœ-nȯr\ [F] : the star of the north — motto of Minnesota

Lie·der·kranz \'lē-dər-ˌkränts\ [G] : wreath of songs : German singing society

lit·tera scrip·ta ma·net \ˌli-te-ˌrä-ˌskrip-tä-'mä-net\ [L] : the written letter abides

lo·cus in quo \ˌlō-kùs-in-'kwō\ [L] : place in which

l'union fait la force \lœ-nyōⁿ-fe-lä-fȯrs\ [F] : union makes strength — motto of Belgium

lu·sus na·tu·rae \ˌlü-sùs-nä-'tùr-ē, -'tùr-ˌī\ [L] : freak of nature

ma foi \mä-fwä\ [F] : my faith! : indeed

mag·na est ve·ri·tas et prae·va·le·bit \ˌmäg-nä-ˌest-'wä-ri-ˌtäs-et-ˌprī-wä-'lā-bit\ [L] : truth is mighty and will prevail

ma·ha·lo \'mä-hä-lō\ [Hawaiian] : thank you

ma·lade ima·gi·naire \mä-läd-ē-mä-zhē-ner\ [F] : imaginary invalid : hypochondriac

mal de siècle \mäl-də-syeklᵃ\ [F] : illness from worldly concerns : world-weariness

ma·lis avi·bus \ˌmä-ˌlēs-'ä-wi-ˌbùs\ [L] : under evil auspices

man spricht Deutsch \män-shprikt-'dȯich\ [G] : German spoken

ma·riage de con·ve·nance \mä-ryäzh-də-kōⁿv-näⁿs\ [F] : marriage of convenience

ma·ri com·plai·sant \mä-rē-kōⁿ-ple-zäⁿ\ [F] : complaisant husband : cuckold who accepts his wife's infidelity

mau·vaise honte \mȯ-vez-ōⁿt\ [F] : bad shame : bashfulness

mau·vais quart d'heure \mȯ-ve-kär-dœr\ [F] : bad quarter hour : an uncomfortable though brief experience

me·dio tu·tis·si·mus ibis \'me-dē-ˌō-tü-ˌti-si-mùs-'ē-bis\ [L] : you will go most safely by the middle course

me ju·di·ce \mā-'yü-di-ke\ [L] : I being judge : in my judgment

mens sa·na in cor·po·re sa·no \mäns-'sä-nä-in-ˌkȯr-pȯ-re-'sä-nō\ [L] : a sound mind in a sound body

me·um et tu·um \ˌmē-əm-ˌet-'tü-əm, ˌme-ùm-ˌet-'tü-ùm\ [L] : mine and thine : distinction of private property

mi·ra·bi·le vi·su \mi-ˌrä-bi-lä-'wē-sü\ [L] : wonderful to behold

mi·ra·bi·lia \ˌmir-ə-'bi-lē-ˌä\ [L] : wonders : miracles

mœurs \mœr(s)\ [F] : mores : attitudes, customs, and manners of a society

mo·le ru·it sua \'mō-le-'rù-it-ˌsù-ä\ [L] : it collapses from its own bigness

monde \mōⁿd\ [F] : world : fashionable world : society

mon·ta·ni sem·per li·be·ri \mȯn-'tä-nē-ˌsem-per-'lē-be-ˌrē\ [L] : mountaineers are always free — motto of West Virginia

mo·nu·men·tum ae·re per·en·ni·us \ˌmȯ-nù-'men-tùm-ˌī-re-pe-'re-nē-ùs\ [L] : a monument more lasting than bronze — used of an immortal work of art or literature

mo·re suo \ˌmȯr-ā-'sù-ō\ [L] : in his (or her) own manner

mo·ri·tu·ri te sa·lu·ta·mus \ˌmȯr-i-'tùr-ē-ˌtä-sä-lù-'tä-mùs\ *or* **morituri te sa·lu·tant** \-'sä-lù-ˌtänt\ [L] : we (or those) who are about to die salute thee

mul·tum in par·vo \ˌmùl-tùm-in-'pär-vō, -'pär-wō\ [L] : much in little

mu·ta·to no·mi·ne de te fa·bu·la nar·ra·tur \mü-ˌtä-tō-'nō-mi-ne-ˌdā-ˌtä-'fä-bù-lä-nä-'rä-ˌtùr\ [L] : with the name changed the story applies to you

my·ster·i·um tre·men·dum \mi-'ster-ē-ˌùm-tre-'men-dùm\ [L] : overwhelming mystery

na·tu·ram ex·pel·las fur·ca, ta·men us·que re·cur·ret \nä-'tü-ˌräm-ek-ˌspe-läs-'fùr-ˌkä ˌtä-men-'ùs-kwe-re-'kùr-et\ [L] : you may drive nature out with a pitchfork, but she will keep coming back

na·tu·ra non fa·cit sal·tum \nä-'tü-rä-ˌnōn-ˌfä-kit-'säl-ˌtùm\ [L] : nature makes no leap

ne ce·de ma·lis \nā-ˌkä-de-'mä-ˌlēs\ [L] : yield not to misfortunes

ne·mo me im·pu·ne la·ces·sit \'nā-mō-ˌmä-im-ˌpü-nä-lä-'ke-sit\ [L] : no one attacks me with impunity — motto of Scotland and of the Order of the Thistle

ne quid ni·mis \ˌnā-ˌkwid-'ni-mis\ [L] : not anything in excess

n'est–ce pas? \nes-pä\ [F] : isn't it so?

nicht wahr? \nikt-'vär\ [G] : not true? : isn't it so?

nil ad·mi·ra·ri \'nēl-ˌäd-mi-'rär-ē\ [L] : to be excited by nothing : equanimity

nil de·spe·ran·dum \'nēl-ˌdā-spä-'rän-dùm\ [L] : never despair

nil si·ne nu·mi·ne \'nēl-ˌsi-nä-'nü-mi-ne\ [L] : nothing without the divine will — motto of Colorado

n'im·por·te \naⁿ-pȯrt\ [F] : it's no matter

no·lens vo·lens \ˌnō-ˌlenz-'vō-ˌlenz\ [L] : unwilling (or) willing : willy-nilly

non om·nia pos·su·mus om·nes \nōn-'ȯm-nē-ä-ˌpȯ-sù-mùs-'ȯm-ˌnäs\ [L] : we can't all (do) all things

non sans droict \nōⁿ-säⁿ-drwä\ [OF] : not without right — motto on Shakespeare's coat of arms

non sum qua·lis eram \ˌnōn-ˌsùm-ˌkwä-lis-'er-ˌäm\ [L] : I am not what I used to be

nos·ce te ip·sum \ˌnȯs-ke-ˌtä-'ip-ˌsùm\ [L] : know thyself

nos·tal·gie de la boue \nȯs-täl-zhēd-lä-bü, -zhē-də-\ [F] : yearning for the mud : attraction to what is unworthy, crude, or degrading

nous avons chan·gé tout ce·la \nü-zä-vōⁿ-shäⁿ-zhä-tü-sə-lä\ [F] : we have changed all that

nous ver·rons ce que nous ver·rons \nü-ve-rōⁿs-kə-nü-ve-rōⁿ, -rōⁿ-sə-kə-\ [F] : we shall see what we shall see

no·vus ho·mo \ˌnȯ-wùs-'hȯ-mō\ [L] : new man : man newly ennobled : upstart

novus or·do se·clo·rum \-'ȯr-ˌdō-sä-'klȯr-ùm\ [L] : a new cycle of the ages — motto on the reverse of the Great Seal of the United States

nu·gae \'nü-ˌgī\ [L] : trifles

nuit blanche \nwē-bläⁿsh\ [F] : white night : a sleepless night

nyet \'nyet\ [Russ] : no

ob·iit \'ȯ-bē-ˌit\ [L] : he or she died

ob·scu·rum per ob·scu·ri·us \ȯb-'skyùr-ùm-ˌper-ȯb-'skyùr-ē-ùs\ [L] : (explaining) the obscure by means of the more obscure

ode·rint dum me·tu·ant \'ȯ-de-ˌrint-ˌdùm-me-tù-ˌänt\ [L] : let them hate, so long as they fear

odi et amo \'ȯ-ˌdē-et-'ä-(ˌ)mō\ [L] : I hate and I love

omer·tà \ȯ-'mer-tä\ [It] : conspiracy of silence

om·ne ig·no·tum pro mag·ni·fi·co \ˌȯm-ne-ig-'nō-ˌtùm-prō-mäg-'ni-fi-ˌkō\ [L] : everything unknown (is taken) as grand : the unknown tends to be exaggerated in importance or difficulty

om·nia mu·tan·tur, nos et mu·ta·mur in il·lis \ˌȯm-nē-ä-mü-'tän-ˌtùr ˌnȯs-et-mü-ˌtä-mùr-in-'i-ˌlēs\ [L] : all things are changing, and we are changing with them

om·nia vin·cit amor \'ȯm-nē-ä-'wiⁿ-kit-'ä-ˌmȯr\ [L] : love conquers all

onus pro·ban·di \ˌȯ-nùs-prō-'ban-ˌdī, -dē\ [L] : burden of proof

ora pro no·bis \ˌȯ-rä-prō-'nō-ˌbēs\ [L] : pray for us

ore ro·tun·do \ˌȯr-ē-rō-'tən-dō\ [L] : with round mouth : eloquently

oro y pla·ta \ˌȯr-ō-ē-'plä-tə\ [Sp] : gold and silver — motto of Montana

o tem·po·ra! o mo·res! \ō-'tem-pȯ-rä ō-'mō-ˌräs\ [L] : oh the times! oh the manners!

oti·um cum dig·ni·ta·te \'ō-tē-ˌùm-kùm-ˌdig-ni-'tä-te\ [L] : leisure with dignity

où sont les neiges d'an·tan? \ü-sōⁿ-lā-nezh-däⁿ-täⁿ\ [F] : where are the snows of yesteryear?

outre–mer \ütrᵃ-mer\ [F] : overseas : distant lands

pal·li·da Mors \ˌpa-li-dä-'mȯrz\ [L] : pale Death

pa·nem et cir·cen·ses \'pä-ˌnem-et-kir-'kän-ˌsäs\ [L] : bread and circuses : provision of the means of life and recreation by government to appease discontent

pan·ta rhei \ˌpän-ˌtä-'rä\ [Gk] : all things are in flux

par avance \pär-ä-väⁿs\ [F] : in advance : by anticipation

par avion \pär-ä-vyōⁿ\ [F] : by airplane — used on airmail

par ex·em·ple \pär-äg-zäⁿplᵃ\ [F] : for example

pars pro to·to \'pärs-(ˌ)prō-'tō-(ˌ)tō\ [L] : part (taken) for the whole

par·tu·ri·unt mon·tes, nas·ce·tur ri·di·cu·lus mus \pär-'tůr-ē-,ůnt-'món-,tās näs-'kā-,tůr-ri-,di-ků-lůs-'müs\ [L] : the mountains are in labor, and a ridiculous mouse will be brought forth

pa·ter pa·tri·ae \'pä-,ter-'pä-trē-,i\ [L] : father of his country

pau·cis ver·bis \,paů-,kēs-'wer-,bēs\ [L] : in a few words

pax vo·bis·cum \,päks-vō-'bēs,kům\ [L] : peace (be) with you

peine forte et dure \pen-fôr-tā-dʉer\ [F] : strong and hard punishment : torture

per an·gus·ta ad au·gus·ta \per-'än-,gůs-tä-äd-'aů-,gůs-tä\ [L] : through difficulties to honors

per·fide Al·bion \per-fēd-äl-byōⁿ\ [F] : perfidious Albion (England)

peu à peu \pœ-à-pœ\ [F] : little by little

peu de chose \pœd-shōz, pœ-də-\ [F] : a trifle

pinx·it \'piŋk-sit\ [L] : he or she painted it

place aux dames \pläs-ō-däm\ [F] : (make) room for the ladies

ple·no ju·re \,plä-nō-'yůr-e\ [L] : with full right

plus ça change, plus c'est la même chose \plʉe-sä-shäⁿ plʉe-se-lä-mem-shōz\ [F] : the more that changes, the more it's the same thing — often shortened to *plus ça change*

plus roy·a·liste que le roi \plʉe-rwä-yä-lēst-kəl-rwä\ [F] : more royalist than the king

po·cas pa·la·bras \pō-käs-pä-'lä-vräs\ [Sp] : few words

po·eta nas·ci·tur, non fit \pō-,ā-tä-'näs-ki-,tůr nōn-'fit\ [L] : a poet is born, not made

po·ète mau·dit \pó-et-mō-dē\ [F] : accursed poet : a writer dogged by misfortune and lack of recognition

pol·li·ce ver·so \pó-li-ke-'wer-sō\ [L] : with thumb turned : with a gesture or expression of condemnation

post hoc, er·go prop·ter hoc \'pòst-,hōk ,er-gō-'pròp-ter-,hōk\ [L] : after this, therefore on account of it (a fallacy of argument)

post ob·itum \pòst-'ō-bi-,tům\ [L] : after death

pour en·cou·ra·ger les autres \půr-äⁿ-kü-rä-zhä-lä-zōtrⁿ\ [F] : in order to encourage the others — said ironically of an action (as an execution) carried out in order to compel others to obey

pri·mum non no·ce·re \,prē-mům-,nōn-nó-'kä-rä\ [L] : the first thing (is) to do no harm

pro bo·no pu·bli·co \prō-,bó-nō-'pü-bli-,kō\ [L] : for the public good

pro hac vi·ce \prō-,häk-'wi-ke\ [L] : for this occasion

pro pa·tria \prō-'pä-trē-,ä\ [L] : for one's country

pro re·ge, le·ge, et gre·ge \prō-'rä-,ge 'lä-,ge et-'gre-,ge\ [L] : for the king, the law, and the people

pro re na·ta \,prō-,rä-'nä-tä\ [L] : for an occasion that has arisen : as needed — used in medical prescriptions

quand même \käⁿ-mem\ [F] : even so : all the same

quan·tum mu·ta·tus ab il·lo \,kwän-tům-mü-'tä-tůs-äb-'i-lō\ [L] : how changed from what he once was

quan·tum suf·fi·cit \,kwän-təm-'sə-fə-,kit\ [L] : as much as suffices : a sufficient quantity — used chiefly in medical prescriptions

¿quién sa·be? \kyän-'sä-vä\ [Sp] : who knows?

qui fa·cit per ali·um fa·cit per se \kwē-,fä-kit-,per-'ä-lē-,ům-,fä-kit-,per-'sä\ [L] : he who does (something) through another does it through himself

quis cus·to·di·et ip·sos cus·to·des? \,kwis-kůs-'tō-dē-,et-,ip-,sōs-kůs-'tō-,däs\ [L] : who will keep the keepers themselves?

qui s'ex·cuse s'ac·cuse \kē-'sek-,skʉez-'sä-,kʉez\ [F] : he who excuses himself accuses himself

quis se·pa·ra·bit? \,kwis-,sä-pə-'rä-bit\ [L] : who shall separate (us)? — motto of the Order of St. Patrick

qui trans·tu·lit sus·ti·net \kwē-'träns-tů-,lit-'sůs-ti-,net\ [L] : He who transplanted sustains (us) — motto of Connecticut

qui va là? \kē-vä-lä\ [F] : who goes there?

quo·ad hoc \,kwó-,äd-'hōk\ [L] : as far as this : to this extent

quod erat de·mon·stran·dum \,kwòd-'er-,ät-,de-mən-'stran-dəm, -,dä-,mòn-'strän-,dům\ [L] : which was to be proved

quod erat fa·ci·en·dum \-,fä-kē-'en-,dům\ [L] : which was to be done

quod sem·per, quod ubi·que, quod ab om·ni·bus \kwòd-'sem-,per kwòd-'ù-bi-,kwä ,kwòd-äb-'òm-ni-,bůs, -,kwòd-ù-'bē-(,)kwä-\ [L] : what (has been held) always, everywhere, by everybody

quod vi·de \kwòd-'wi-,de\ [L] : which see

quo·rum pars mag·na fui \'kwòr-ùm-,pärs-,mäg-nä-'fú-ē\ [L] : in which I played a great part

quos de·us vult per·de·re pri·us de·men·tat \kwōs-'dä-ùs-,wůlt-'per-de-,rä-,pri-ùs-dä-'men-,tät\ [L] : those whom a god wishes to destroy he first drives mad

quot ho·mi·nes, tot sen·ten·ti·ae \kwòt-'hò-mi-,näs ,tòt-sen-'ten-tē-,i\ [L] : there are as many opinions as there are men

quo va·dis? \kwō-'wä-dis, -'vä-dəs\ [L] : whither are you going?

rai·son d'état \re-zōⁿ-dä-tä\ [F] : reason of state

reg·nat po·pu·lus \,reg-,nät-'pó-pů-,lús\ [L] : the people rule — motto of Arkansas

re in·fec·ta \,rä-in-'fek-,tä\ [L] : the business being unfinished : without accomplishing one's purpose

re·li·gio lo·ci \re-'li-gē-,ō-'lō-,kē\ [L] : religious sanctity of a place

rem acu te·ti·gis·ti \rem-'ä-,kü-,te-ti-'gis-tē\ [L] : you have touched the point with a needle : you have hit the nail on the head

ré·pon·dez s'il vous plaît \rä-pōⁿ-dä-sēl-vü-ple\ [F] : reply, if you please

re·qui·es·cat in pa·ce \,re-kwē-'es-,kät-in-'pä-,ke, ,rä-kwē-'es-,kät-in-'pä,chä\ [L] : may he or she rest in peace — used on tombstones

re·spi·ce fi·nem \,rä-spi-,ke-'fē-,nem\ [L] : look to the end : consider the outcome

re·sur·gam \re-'sůr-,gäm\ [L] : I shall rise again

re·te·nue \rət-nʉe\ [F] : self-restraint : reserve

re·ve·nons à nos mou·tons \rəv-nōⁿ-ä-nō-mü-tōⁿ\ [F] : let us return to our sheep : let us get back to the subject

ruse de guerre \rʉez-də-ger\ [F] : war stratagem

rus in ur·be \,rüs-in-'ůr-,be\ [L] : country in the city

sae·va in·dig·na·tio \,sī-wä-,in-dig-'nä-tē-ō\ [L] : fierce indignation

salle à man·ger \säl-ä-mäⁿ-zhä\ [F] : dining room

sa·lus po·pu·li su·pre·ma lex es·to \,sä-,lüs-'pó-pů-,lē-sù-,prä-mä-,leks-'es-tō\ [L] : let the welfare of the people be the supreme law — motto of Missouri

sanc·ta sim·pli·ci·tas \,säŋk-tä-sim-'pli-ki-,täs\ [L] : holy simplicity — often used ironically in reference to another's naïveté

sans doute \säⁿ-düt\ [F] : without doubt

sans gêne \säⁿ-zhen\ [F] : without embarrassment or constraint

sans peur et sans re·proche \säⁿ-pœr-ä-säⁿ-rə-'prōsh\ [F] : without fear and without reproach

sans sou·ci \säⁿ-sü-sē\ [F] : without worry

sa·yo·na·ra \,sī-ə-'när-ə, ,sä-yə-\ [Jp] : good-bye

sculp·sit \'skŭlp-sət, 'skŭlp-sit\ [L] : he or she carved it

scu·to bo·nae vo·lun·ta·tis tu·ae co·ro·nas·ti nos \'skü-,tō-'bò-,nī-,vó-lùn-,tä-tis-'tù-,ī-'kòr-ò-,näs-tē'nōs\ [L] : Thou hast crowned us with the shield of Thy good will — a motto on the Great Seal of Maryland

se·cun·dum ar·tem \se-,kún-dùm-'är-,tem\ [L] : according to the art : according to the accepted practice of a profession or trade

secundum na·tu·ram \-nä-'tü-,räm\ [L] : according to nature : naturally

se de·fen·den·do \'sä-,dä-,fen-'den-dō\ [L] : in self-defense

se ha·bla es·pa·ñol \sä-,äv-lä-,äs-pä-'nʸòl\ [Sp] : Spanish spoken

sem·per ea·dem \,sem-,per-'e-ä-,dem\ [L] : always the same (fem.) — motto of Queen Elizabeth I

sem·per fi·de·lis \,sem-pər-fə-'dä-ləs\ [L] : always faithful — motto of the U.S. Marine Corps

sem·per idem \,sem-,per-'ē-,dem\ [L] : always the same (masc.)

sem·per pa·ra·tus \,sem-pər-pə-'rä-təs\ [L] : always prepared — motto of the U.S. Coast Guard

se non è ve·ro, è ben tro·va·to \sä-,nōn-e-'vä-rō e-,ben-trō-'vä-tō\ [It] : even if it is not true, it is well conceived

sha·lom alei·chem \shò-lòm-ə-'lä-kəm, ,shō-, -,kəm\ [Heb *shālōm 'alēkhem*] : peace to you — used as a traditional Jewish greeting

sic itur ad as·tra \sēk-'i-,tůr-,äd-'äs-trə\ [L] : thus one goes to the stars : such is the way to immortality

sic sem·per ty·ran·nis \sik-,sem-pər-tə-'ra-nəs\ [L] : thus ever to tyrants — motto of Virginia

sic trans·it glo·ria mun·di \sēk-'trän-sit-,glòr-ē-ä-'mún-dē\ [L] : so passes away the glory of the world

si jeu·nesse sa·vait, si vieil·lesse pou·vait! \sē-'zhœ-nes-'sä-ve sē-'vye-yes-'pü-ve\ [F] : if youth only knew, if age only could!

si·lent le·ges in·ter ar·ma \,si-,lent-'lā-,gās-,in-ter-'är-mä\ [L] : the laws are silent in the midst of arms (i.e., in time of war)

s'il vous plaît \sēl-vü-ple\ [F] : if you please

si·mi·lia si·mi·li·bus cu·ran·tur \si-'mi-lē-ä-si-'mi-li-bùs-kü-'rän-,tùr\ [L] : like is cured by like

si·mi·lis si·mi·li gau·det \'si-mi-lis-'si-mi-lē-'gaù-,det\ [L] : like takes pleasure in like

si mo·nu·men·tum re·qui·ris, cir·cum·spi·ce \,sē-,mó-nù-,men-tùm-re-'kwē-ris kir-'kùm-spi-ke\ [L] : if you seek his monument, look around — epitaph of Sir Christopher Wren in St. Paul's, London, of which he was architect

sim·pliste \saⁿ-plēst\ [F] : simplistic : overly simple or naïve

si quae·ris pen·in·su·lam amoe·nam, cir·cum·spi·ce \sē-'kwī-ris-pā-'nin-sə-,läm-ä-'mòi-,näm kir-'kùm-spi-ke\ [L] : if you seek a beautiful peninsula, look around — motto of Michigan

sis·te vi·a·tor \,sis-te-wē-'ä-,tòr\ [L] : stop, traveler — used on Roman roadside tombs

si vis pa·cem, pa·ra bel·lum \sē-'wēs-'pä-,kem 'pä-rä-'be-,lùm\ [L] : if you wish peace, prepare for war

sol·vi·tur am·bu·lan·do \'sól-wi-,tùr-,äm-bù-'län-dō\ [L] : it is solved by walking : the problem is solved by a practical experiment

spo·lia opi·ma \,spò-lē-ä-ō-'pē-mä\ [L] : rich spoils : the arms taken by the victorious from the vanquished general

sta·tus quo an·te bel·lum \'stä-tùs-kwō-,än-te-'be-lùm\ [L] : the state existing before the war

sua·vi·ter in mo·do, for·ti·ter in re \'swä-wi-,ter-in-'mó-dō 'fór-ti-,ter-in-'rä\ [L] : gently in manner, strongly in deed

sub ver·bo \sùb-'wer-bō, ,səb-'vər-bō\ or sub vo·ce \sùb-'wō-ke, ,səb-'vō-sē\ [L] : under the word — introducing a cross-reference in a dictionary or index

sunt la·cri·mae re·rum \sùnt-,lä-kri-,mī-'rä-rùm\ [L] : there are tears for things : tears attend trials

suo ju·re \,sù-ō-'yùr-e\ [L] : in his or her own right

suo lo·co \-'lō-kō\ [L] : in its proper place

suo Mar·te \-'mär-te\ [L] : by one's own exertions

su·um cui·que \,sù-ùm-'kwi-kwe\ [L] : to each his own

tant mieux \täⁿ-myœ\ [F] : so much the better

tant pis \-pē\ [F] : so much the worse : too bad

tem·po·ra mu·tan·tur, nos et mu·ta·mur in il·lis \,tem-pó-rä-mü-'tän-,tùr ,nōs-,et-mü-,tä-mùr-in-'i-,lēs\ [L] : the times are changing, and we are changing with them

tem·pus edax re·rum \'tem-pùs-,e-,däks-'rä-rùm\ [L] : time, that devours all things

tem·pus fu·git \,tem-pəs-'fyü-jət, ,tem-pùs-'fü-git\ [L] : time flies

ti·meo Da·na·os et do·na fe·ren·tes \,ti-mē-,ō-'dä-nä-,ōs-,et-,dō-nä-fe-'ren,tās\ [L] : I fear the Greeks even when they bring gifts

to·ti·dem ver·bis \,tò-ti-,dem-'wer-,bēs\ [L] : in so many words

to·tis vi·ri·bus \,tō-,tēs-'wē-ri-,bùs\ [L] : with all one's might

to·to cae·lo \,tō-tō-'kī-lō\ or toto coe·lo \-'kòi-lō\ [L] : by the whole extent of the heavens : diametrically

tou·jours per·drix \tü-zhür-per-drē\ [F] : always partridge : too much of a good thing

tour d'ho·ri·zon \tür-dò-rē-zōⁿ\ [F] : circuit of the horizon : general survey

tous frais faits \tü-fre-fe\ [F] : all expenses defrayed

tout à fait \tü-tä-fe\ [F] : altogether : quite

tout au con·traire \tü-tō-kōⁿ-trer\ [F] : quite the contrary

tout à vous \tü-tä-vü\ [F] : wholly yours : at your service

tout bien ou rien \tü-'byaⁿ-nü-'ryaⁿ\ [F] : everything well (done) or nothing (attempted)

tout com·pren·dre c'est tout par·don·ner \'tü-kōⁿ-präⁿ-drə-se-'tü-pär-dó-nä\ [F] : to understand all is to forgive all

tout court \tü-kür\ [F] : quite short : and nothing else : simply : just; also : brusquely

tout de même \tüt-mem\ [F] : all the same : nevertheless

tout de suite \tüt-swᵉēt\ [F] : immediately; also : all at once : consecutively

tout en·sem·ble \tü-täⁿ-säⁿblᵊ\ [F] : all together : general effect

tout est per·du fors l'hon·neur \tü-te-per-dœ-fór-ló-nœr\ or tout est perdu hors l'honneur \-dœ-òr-\ [F] : all is lost save honor

tout le monde \tü-lə-mōⁿd\ [F] : all the world : everybody

tra·hi·son des clercs \trä-ē-zōⁿ-dä-klerk\ [F] : treason of the intellectuals

tranche de vie \träⁿsh-də-'vē\ [F] : slice of life

trist·esse \trē-stes\ [F] : melancholy

tu·e·bor \tù-'ā-,bòr\ [L] : I will defend — a motto on the Great Seal of Michigan

ua mau ke ea o ka ai·na i ka po·no \,ù-ä-'mä-ù-kā-'ā-ä-ō-kä-'ä-ē-nä,-ē-kä-'pō-nō\ [Hawaiian] : the life of the land is perpetuated in righteousness — motto of Hawaii

über al·les \,ᴇ-ber-'ä-les\ [G] : above everything else

Über·mensch \'ᴇ-bər-,mench\ [G] : superman

ul·ti·ma ra·tio re·gum \'ùl-ti-mä-,rä-tē-ō-'rä-gùm\ [L] : the final argument of kings, i.e., war

und so wei·ter \ùnt-zō-'vī-tər\ [G] : and so on

uno ani·mo \,ù-nō-'ä-ni,-mō\ [L] : with one mind : unanimously

ur·bi et or·bi \,ùr-bē-,et-'òr-bē\ [L] : to the city (Rome) and the world : to everyone

uti·le dul·ci \,ü-ti-le-'dùl,-kē\ [L] : the useful with the agreeable

ut in·fra \ùt-'in-frä\ [L] : as below

ut su·pra \ùt-'sü-prä\ [L] : as above

va·de re·tro me, Sa·ta·na \,wä-de-'rä-trō-,mä 'sä-tä-,nä\ [L] : get thee behind me, Satan

vae vic·tis \wī-'wik-,tēs\ [L] : woe to the vanquished

va·ri·um et mu·ta·bi·le sem·per fe·mi·na \,wär-ē-ùm-,et-,mü-'tä-bi-le-,sem-,per-'fä-mi-nä\ [L] : woman is ever a fickle and changeable thing

ve·di Na·po·li e poi mo·ri \,vä-dē-'nä-pò-lē-ä-,pò-ē-'mò-rē\ [It] : see Naples and then die

ve·ni, vi·di, vi·ci \,wä-nē ,wē-dē 'wē-kē, ,vä-nē ,vē-dē 'vē-chē\ [L] : I came, I saw, I conquered

ven·tre à terre \,väⁿ-trä-ter\ [F] : belly to the ground : at very great speed

ver·ba·tim ac lit·te·ra·tim \wer-'bä-tim-,äk-,li-te-'rä-tim\ [L] : word for word and letter for letter

ver·bum sat sa·pi·en·ti est \,wer-bùm-'sät-,sä-pē-'en-tē-,est\ [L] : a word to the wise is sufficient

via cru·cis \wē-ä-'krü-sis\ [L] : Way of the Cross : path of suffering

vieux jeu \vyœ-zhœ\ [F] : old game : old hat

vin·cit om·nia ve·ri·tas \,wiⁿ-kit-'óm-nē-ä-'wä-ri-,täs\ [L] : truth conquers all things

vin·cu·lum ma·tri·mo·nii \,wiⁿ-kù-lùm-,mä-tri-'mō-nē-,ē\ [L] : bond of marriage

vin du pays \vaⁿ-dœ-pä-ē\ or vin de pays \vaⁿ-də-\ [F] : wine of the locality

vir·gi·ni·bus pu·e·ris·que \wir-'gi-ni-bùs-,pù-e-'rēs-kwe\ [L] : for girls and boys

vir·go in·tac·ta \'wir-gō-in-'täk-tä\ [L] : untouched virgin

vir·tu·te et ar·mis \wir-'tü-te-,et-'är-mēs\ [L] : by valor and arms — motto of Mississippi

vis me·di·ca·trix na·tu·rae \'wēs-,me-di-'kä-triks-nä-'tü-,rī\ [L] : the healing power of nature

vive la dif·fé·rence \vēv-lä-dē-fä-räⁿs\ [F] : long live the difference (between the sexes)

vive la reine \vēv-lä-ren\ [F] : long live the queen

vive le roi \vēv-lə-rwä\ [F] : long live the king

vogue la ga·lère \vóg-lä-gä-ler\ [F] : let the galley be kept rowing : keep on, whatever may happen

voi·là tout \vwä-lä-tü\ [F] : that's all

vox et prae·te·rea ni·hil \'wōks-et-prī-'ter-e-ä-'ni,-hil\ [L] : voice and nothing more

vox po·pu·li vox Dei \wōks-'pò-pù-,lē-,wōks-'dā-ē\ [L] : the voice of the people is the voice of God

Wan·der·jahr \'vän-dər-,yär\ [G] : year of wandering

wie geht's? \vē-'gäts\ [G] : how goes it? : how is it going? — used as a greeting

wun·der·bar \'vùn-dər-,bär\ [G] : wonderful

BIOGRAPHICAL NAMES

This section gives basic information on many notable figures from contemporary culture, history, legend, mythology, and biblical tradition. Figures from the Bible, myth, and legend are clearly identified as such.

In cases where individuals have alternate names, they are entered under the name by which they are best known. Names are generally alphabetized by the main element of the surname, without regard for connectives such as *da, de, van,* or *von* (as **Gama** . . . Vasco da). Names appearing in the entry in italics are original names, maiden names, or nicknames.

The first dates given in the entry are birth/death dates; other dates refer to terms in office, reigns, achievements, or honors. Abbreviations used here are listed in the front section Abbreviations in This Work.

Aar·on \'er-ən\ brother of Moses and 1st high priest of the Hebrews in the Bible
Aaron Hank 1934– *Henry Louis Aaron* Amer. baseball player
Abel \'ā-bəl\ son of Adam and Eve and brother of Cain in the Bible
Abra·ham \'ā-brə-,ham\ patriarch and founder of the Hebrew people in the Bible; also revered by Muslims
Achil·les \ə-'ki-lēz\ hero of the Trojan War in Greek mythology
Ad·am \'a-dəm\ the 1st man in biblical tradition
Ad·ams \'a-dəmz\ Abigail 1744–1818 née *Smith* Amer. writer; wife of John Adams
Adams Ansel Easton 1902–1984 Amer. photographer
Adams John 1735–1826 2d pres. of the U.S. (1797–1801)
Adams John Quin·cy \'kwin-zē, -sē\ 1767–1848 6th pres. of the U.S. (1825–29); son of John and Abigail Adams
Adams Samuel 1722–1803 patriot in the Amer. Revolution
Ad·dams \'a-dəmz\ Jane 1860–1935 Amer. social worker; Nobel Prize winner (1931)
Ado·nis \ə-'dä-nəs, -'dō-\ youth in Greek mythology loved by Aphrodite
Ae·ne·as \i-'nē-əs\ Trojan hero in Greek and Roman mythology
Ae·o·lus \'ē-ə-ləs\ god of the winds in Greek mythology
Aes·chy·lus \'es-kə-ləs, 'ēs-\ 525–456 B.C. Greek dramatist
Aes·cu·la·pi·us \,es-k(y)ə-'lā-pē-əs\ god of medicine in Roman mythology — compare ASCLEPIUS
Ae·sop \'ē-,säp, -səp\ legendary Greek writer of fables
Ag·a·mem·non \,a-gə-'mem-,nän, -nən\ leader of the Greeks during the Trojan War in Greek mythology
Ag·nes \'ag-nəs\ Saint *died* 304 A.D. Christian martyr
Ahab \'ā-,hab\ king of Israel in the 9th cent. B.C. and husband of Jezebel
Ajax \'ā-,jaks\ hero in Greek mythology who kills himself because the armor of Achilles is awarded to Odysseus during the Trojan War
Alad·din \ə-'la-dᵊn\ youth in the *Arabian Nights' Entertainments* who acquires a magic lamp
Al·bee \'ól-(,)bē, 'al-\ Edward Franklin 1928–2016 Amer. dramatist
Al·bright \'ól-,brīt\ Madeleine 1937– née *Korbel* Amer. (Czech-born) diplomat; U.S. secretary of state (1997–2001)
Al·cott \'ól-kət, 'al-, -,kät\ Louisa May 1832–1888 Amer. author
Al·ex·an·der \,a-lig-'zan-dər, ,e-\ name of eight popes: esp. VI 1431–1503 (pope 1492–1503)
Alexander the Great 356–323 B.C. *Alexander III* king of Macedonia (336–323)
Al·fred \'al-frəd, -fərd\ 849–899 *Alfred the Great* king of the West Saxons (871–899)
Ali \ä-'lē\ Muhammad 1942–2016 orig. *Cassius Clay* Amer. boxer
Ali Ba·ba \,a-lē-'bä-bə, ,ä-lē-\ woodcutter in the *Arabian Nights' Entertainments* who enters the cave of the Forty Thieves by using the password *Sesame*
Al·len \'a-lən\ Ethan 1738–1789 Amer. Revolutionary soldier
Al·va·rez \'al-və-,rez\ Luis 1911–1988 Amer. physicist

Amerigo Vespucci — see VESPUCCI
Am·herst \'a-(,)mərst\ Jeffery 1717–1797 Baron *Amherst* Brit. general in America
Amund·sen \'ä-mən-sən\ Roald 1872–1928 Norwegian explorer
An·a·ni·as \,a-nə-'nī-əs\ early Christian in the Bible struck dead for lying
An·der·sen \'an-dər-sən\ Hans Christian 1805–1875 Danish writer of fairy tales
An·der·son \'an-dər-sən\ Marian 1897–1993 Amer. contralto
An·ge·lou \'an-jə-(,)lō, *commonly* -,lü\ Maya 1928–2014 orig. *Marguerite Johnson* Amer. author
Anne \'an\ 1665–1714 queen of Great Britain (1702–14)
An·tho·ny \'an(t)-thə-nē\ Susan Brownell 1820–1906 Amer. suffragist
An·tig·o·ne \an-'ti-gə-(,)nē\ daughter of Oedipus and Jocasta in Greek mythology
An·to·ny \'an-tə-nē\ Mark *ca* 82–30 B.C. *Marc Anthony*; *Marcus An·to·ni·us* \an-'tō-nē-əs\ Roman general and triumvir (43–30)
Aph·ro·di·te \,a-frə-'dī-tē\ goddess of love and beauty in Greek mythology — compare VENUS
Apol·lo \ə-'pä-(,)lō\ god of sunlight, prophecy, music, and poetry in Greek and Roman mythology
Ap·ple·seed \'ap-əl-,sēd\ Johnny 1774–1845 orig. *John Chapman* Amer. pioneer
Aqui·nas \ə-'kwī-nəs\ Saint Thomas 1224/25–1274 Ital. theologian
Ar·chi·me·des \,är-kə-'mē-dēz\ *ca* 287–212 B.C. Greek mathematician and inventor
Ares \'a-(,)rēz, 'er-(,)ēz\ god of war in Greek mythology — compare MARS
Ar·is·toph·a·nes \,a-rə-'stä-fə-,nēz\ *ca* 450–*ca* 388 B.C. Greek playwright
Ar·is·tot·le \'a-rə-,stä-tᵊl\ 384–322 B.C. Greek philosopher
Arm·strong \'ärm-,stróŋ\ Lance 1971– Amer. cyclist
Armstrong Louis 1901–1971 *Satch·mo* \'sach-,mō\ Amer. jazz musician
Armstrong Neil Alden 1930–2012 Amer. astronaut; 1st person on the moon (1969)
Ar·nold \'är-nᵊld\ Benedict 1741–1801 Amer. Revolutionary general and traitor
Ar·te·mis \'är-tə-məs\ goddess of the moon, wild animals, and hunting in Greek mythology — compare DIANA
Ar·thur \'är-thər\ legendary king of the Britons whose story is based on traditions of a 6th-century military leader — **Ar·thu·ri·an** \är-'thùr-ē-ən, -'thyùr-\ *adj*
Arthur Chester Alan 1829–1886 21st pres. of the U.S. (1881–85)
As·cle·pi·us \ə-'sklē-pē-əs\ god of medicine in Greek mythology — compare AESCULAPIUS
Astaire \ə-'ster\ Fred 1899–1987 orig. *Frederick Austerlitz* Amer. dancer and actor
As·tor \'as-tər\ John Jacob 1763–1848 Amer. (Ger.-born) fur trader and capitalist
Athe·na \ə-'thē-nə\ *or* **Athe·ne** \-nē\ goddess of wisdom in Greek mythology — compare MINERVA
At·las \'at-ləs\ Titan in Greek mythology forced to bear the heavens on his shoulders
At·ti·la \'a-tə-lə, ə-'ti-lə\ 406?–453 A.D. king of the Huns

At·tucks \\'a-təks\ Crispus 1723?–1770 Amer. patriot
At·wood \\'at-ˌwúd\ Margaret 1939–   Canad. author
Au·den \\'ȯ-dᵊn\ Wystan Hugh 1907–1973 Amer. (Eng.-born) poet
Au·du·bon \\'ȯ-də-bən, -ˌbän\ John James 1785–1851 Amer. (Haitian-born) artist and naturalist
Au·gus·tine \\'ȯ-gə-ˌstēn; ȯ-'gəs-tən, ə-\ Saint 354–430 A.D. church father; bishop of Hippo (396–430)
Au·gus·tus \ȯ-'gəs-təs, ə-\ or Caesar Augustus or Oc·ta·vi·an \äk-'tā-vē-ən\ 63 B.C.–14 A.D. 1st Roman emperor (27 B.C.–14 A.D.)
Aus·ten \\'ȯs-tən, 'äs-\ Jane 1775–1817 Eng. author
Bab·bage \\'ba-bij\ Charles 1791–1871 Eng. mathematician and inventor
Bac·chus \\'ba-kəs, 'bä-\ — see DIONYSUS
Bach \\'bäk, 'bäk\ Johann Sebastian 1685–1750 Ger. composer
Ba·con \\'bā-kən\ Francis 1561–1626 Eng. philosopher and author
Ba·den–Pow·ell \\'bā-dᵊn-'pō-əl\ Robert Stephenson Smyth 1857–1941 Baron Baden-Powell Brit. general and founder of Boy Scout movement
Baf·fin \\'ba-fən\ William ca 1584–1622 Eng. navigator
Bal·an·chine \ˌba-lən-'shēn\ George 1904–1983 orig. Georgy Melitonovich Balanchivadze Amer. (Russ.-born) choreographer
Bal·boa \bal-'bō-ə\ Vasco Núñez de 1475–1519 Span. explorer
Bal·zac \\'bȯl-ˌzak, 'bal-\ Honoré de 1799–1850 French author
Ba·rab·bas \bə-'ra-bəs\ prisoner in the Bible released in preference to Jesus at the demand of the multitude
Bar·num \\'bär-nəm\ P. T. 1810–1891 Phineas Taylor Barnum Amer. showman
Bar·rie \\'ba-rē\ Sir James Matthew 1860–1937 Scot. author
Bar·thol·di \bär-'täl-dē, -'tȯl-, -'thäl-, -'thȯl-\ Frédéric-Auguste 1834–1904 French sculptor of the Statue of Liberty
Bar·tók \\'bär-ˌtäk\ Béla 1881–1945 Hung. composer
Bar·ton \\'bär-tᵊn\ Clara 1821–1912 founder of American Red Cross
Beau·re·gard \\'bȯr-ə-ˌgärd\ Pierre Gustave Toutant 1818–1893 Amer. Confederate general
Beck·et \\'be-kət\ Saint Thomas ca 1118–1170 Thomas à Becket archbishop of Canterbury (1162–70)
Beck·ett \\'be-kət\ Samuel 1906–1989 Irish playwright in France; Nobel Prize winner (1969)
Bee·tho·ven \\'bā-ˌtō-vən\ Ludwig van 1770–1827 Ger. composer
Bell \\'bel\ Alexander Graham 1847–1922 Amer. (Scot.-born) inventor of the telephone
Bel·low \\'be-(ˌ)lō\ Saul 1915–2005 Amer. (Canad.-born) author
Ben·e·dict \\'be-nə-ˌdikt\ name of 16 popes: esp. XIV 1675–1758 (pope 1740–58); XV 1854–1922 (pope 1914–22); XVI 1927–   (pope 2005–13)
Be·nét \bə-'nā\ Stephen Vincent 1898–1943 Amer. author
Ben·ja·min \\'ben-jə-mən\ youngest son of Jacob and ancestor of one of the 12 tribes of Israel in the Bible
Ben·ton \\'ben-tᵊn\ Thomas Hart 1889–1975 Amer. painter
Be·o·wulf \\'bā-ə-ˌwúlf\ legendary warrior and hero of the Old Eng. poem Beowulf
Berg·man \\'bərg-mən\ Ingmar 1918–2007 Swed. film director
Be·ring \\'ber-iŋ, 'bir-\ Vitus 1681–1741 Danish navigator and explorer for Russia
Ber·lin \(ˌ)bər-'lin\ Irving 1888–1989 Amer. (Russ.-born) composer
Ber·ners-Lee \\'bər-nərz-'lē\ Sir Timothy John 1955–   Brit. inventor
Ber·ni·ni \ber-'nē-nē\ Gian Lorenzo 1598–1680 Ital. sculptor, architect, and painter
Bern·stein \\'bərn-ˌstīn, -ˌstēn\ Leonard 1918–1990 Amer. conductor and composer
Bes·se·mer \\'be-sə-mər\ Sir Henry 1813–1898 Eng. engineer and inventor
Bi·den \\'bī-dᵊn\ Joseph Robinette, Jr. 1942–   vice pres. of the U.S. (2009–17)
Bish·op \\'bi-shəp\ Elizabeth 1911–1979 Amer. poet
Bi·zet \bē-'zā\ Georges 1838–1875 French composer

Black Hawk \\'blak-ˌhȯk\ 1767–1838 Sauk Indian chief
Black·well \\'blak-ˌwel, -wəl\ Elizabeth 1821–1910 Amer. (Eng.-born) physician
Blair \\'bler\ Tony 1953–   Anthony Charles Lynton Blair Brit. prime minister (1997–2007)
Blake \\'blāk\ William 1757–1827 Eng. poet and artist
Bloom·er \\'blü-mər\ Amelia 1818–1894 née Jenks Amer. social reformer
Boc·cac·cio \bō-'kä-ch(ē-ˌ)ō\ Giovanni 1313–1375 Ital. author
Bohr \\'bȯr\ Niels 1885–1962 Danish physicist; Nobel Prize winner (1922)
Bo·leyn \bú-'lin, -'lēn\ Anne 1507?–1536 2d wife of Henry VIII and mother of Elizabeth I of England
Bo·lí·var \bə-'lē-ˌvär; 'bä-lə-ˌvär, -vər\ Si·món \sē-ˌmōn, ˌsī-mən\ 1783–1830 South Amer. liberator
Bon·i·face \\'bä-nə-fəs, -ˌfäs\ name of 9 popes: esp. VIII ca 1235 (or 1240)–1303 (pope 1294–1303)
Boone \\'bün\ Daniel 1734–1820 Amer. pioneer
Booth \\'büth\ John Wilkes 1838–1865 Amer. actor; assassin of Abraham Lincoln
Bo·re·as \\'bȯr-ē-əs\ god of the north wind in Greek mythology
Bosch \\'bäsh, 'bȯsh\ Hieronymus ca 1450–ca 1516 Dutch painter
Bot·ti·cel·li \ˌbä-tə-'che-lē\ Sandro 1445–1510 Ital. painter
Bow·ie \\'bü-ē, 'bō-\ Jim 1796–1836 James Bowie hero of the Texas revolution
Boyle \\'bȯi(-ə)l\ Robert 1627–1691 Eng. physicist and chemist
Brad·bury \\'brad-ˌber-ē, -b(ə-)rē\ Ray Douglas 1920–2012 Amer. author
Brad·dock \\'bra-dək\ Edward 1695–1755 Brit. general in America
Brad·ford \\'brad-fərd\ William 1590–1657 Pilgrim leader
Brad·street \\'brad-ˌstrēt\ Anne ca 1612–1672 Amer. poet
Bra·dy \\'brā-dē\ Mathew B. 1823?–1896 Amer. photographer
Brahe \\'brä; 'brä-hē, -hə\ Tycho 1546–1601 Danish astronomer
Brah·ma \\'brä-mə\ creator god of the Hindu sacred triad — compare SHIVA, VISHNU
Brahms \\'brämz\ Johannes 1833–1897 Ger. composer
Braille \\'brāl, 'brī\ Louis 1809–1852 French blind teacher of the blind
Bran·deis \\'bran-ˌdīs, -ˌdīz\ Louis Dembitz 1856–1941 Amer. jurist
Brant \\'brant\ Joseph 1742–1807 Thayendanegea Mohawk Indian chief
Brant Mary 1736?–1796 Molly Brant Mohawk Indian leader; sister of Joseph Brant
Braun \\'braún\ Wernher von 1912–1977 Amer. (Ger.-born) rocket engineer
Brezh·nev \\'brezh-ˌnef\ Leonid Ilich 1906–1982 Soviet leader of the Communist Party (1964–82); pres. of the U.S.S.R. (1960–64; 1977–82)
Brit·ten \\'bri-tᵊn\ Edward Benjamin 1913–1976 Baron Britten of Aldeburgh Eng. composer
Bron·të \\'brän-tē, -(ˌ)tā\ family of Eng. writers: Charlotte 1816–1855 and her sisters Emily 1818–1848 and Anne 1820–1849
Brooks \\'brúks\ Gwendolyn Elizabeth 1917–2000 Amer. poet
Brown \\'braún\ John 1800–1859 Amer. abolitionist
Brown James Gordon 1951–   Brit. prime minister (2007–10)
Brow·ning \\'braú-niŋ\ Elizabeth Barrett 1806–1861 Eng. poet
Browning Robert 1812–1889 Eng. poet; husband of the preceding
Brue·ghel \\'brü-gəl, 'brȯi-\ Pieter ca 1525–1569 known as Pieter Brughel the Elder Flemish painter
Bru·tus \\'brü-təs\ Marcus Junius 85–42 B.C. Roman politician; one of Julius Caesar's assassins
Bry·an \\'brī-ən\ William Jennings 1860–1925 Amer. lawyer and politician
Bu·chan·an \byü-'ka-nən, bə-\ James 1791–1868 15th pres. of the U.S. (1857–61)
Buck \\'bək\ Pearl S. 1892–1973 née Sydenstricker Amer. author; Nobel Prize winner (1938)
Bud·dha \\'bü-də, 'bú-\ ca 563–ca 483 B.C. orig. Siddhartha Gautama Indian founder of Buddhism

Buffalo Bill — see W. F. CODY
Bun·yan \\'bən-yən\\ John 1628–1688 Eng. preacher and author
Bunyan Paul — see PAUL BUNYAN
Bur·bank \\'bər-ˌbaŋk\\ Luther 1849–1926 Amer. horticulturist
Bur·goyne \\(ˌ)bər-'gȯin, 'bər-ˌ\\ John 1722–1792 Brit. general in America
Burns \\'bərnz\\ Robert 1759–1796 Scot. poet
Burn·side \\'bərn-ˌsīd\\ Ambrose Everett 1824–1881 Amer. general
Burr \\'bər\\ Aaron 1756–1836 vice pres. of the U.S. (1801–5)
Bush \\'bu̇sh\\ George (Herbert Walker) 1924–2018 41st pres. of the U.S. (1989–93)
Bush George W. 1946– *George Walker Bush* 43rd pres. of the U.S. (2001–09); son of the preceding
By·ron \\'bī-rən\\ Lord 1788–1824 *George Gordon Byron*, 6th Baron *Byron* Eng. poet
Cab·ot \\'ka-bət\\ John *ca* 1450–*ca* 1499 orig. *Giovanni Ca·bo·to* \\kä-'bō-tō\\ Ital. navigator; explorer for England
Cabot Sebastian 1476?–1557 Eng. navigator; son of J. Cabot
Ca·bri·ni \\kə-'brē-nē\\ Saint Frances Xavier 1850–1917 *Mother Cabrini* 1st Amer. (Ital.-born) saint (1946)
Cae·sar \\'sē-zər\\ (Gaius) Julius 100?–44 B.C. Roman general, political leader, and writer
Cain \\'kān\\ son of Adam and Eve and brother of Abel in the Bible
Calamity Jane \\kə-'la-mə-tē-\\ 1852?–1903 *Martha Jane Burk* \\'bərk\\ née *Can·nary* \\'ka-nə-rē\\ Amer. frontier figure
Cal·houn \\kal-'hün\\ John Caldwell 1782–1850 vice pres. of the U.S. (1825–32)
Ca·lig·u·la \\kə-'li-gyə-lə\\ 12–41 A.D. Roman emperor (37–41)
Cal·li·ope \\kə-'lī-ə-(ˌ)pē\\ muse of heroic poetry in Greek mythology
Cal·vert \\'kal-vərt\\ George 1580?–1632 Baron *Baltimore* Eng. colonist in America
Cal·vin \\'kal-vən\\ John 1509–1564 *Jean Calvin* or *Cau·vin* \\kō-'van\\ French theologian and reformer
Ca·mus \\kä-'mᵫ\\ Albert 1913–1960 French author; Nobel Prize winner (1957)
Ca·nute \\kə-'nüt, -'nyüt\\ *died* 1035 *Canute the Great* Danish king of England (1016–35); of Denmark (1018–35); of Norway (1028–35)
Ca·ra·vag·gio \\ˌka-rə-'vä-j(ē-)ˌō\\ Michelangelo da 1571–1610 orig. *Michelangelo Merisi* Ital. painter
Car·ne·gie \\'kär-'ne-gē, 'kär-nə-gē\\ Andrew 1835–1919 Amer. (Scot.-born) industrialist and philanthropist
Car·roll \\'ka-rəl\\ Lewis 1832–1898 pseud. of *Charles Lutwidge Dodgson* Eng. author and mathematician
Car·son \\'kär-sⁿn\\ Kit 1809–1868 *Christopher Carson* Amer. frontiersman and guide
Carson Rachel Louise 1907–1964 Amer. scientist and writer
Car·ter \\'kär-tər\\ Jimmy 1924– orig. *James Earl Carter, Jr.* 39th pres. of the U.S. (1977–81); Nobel Prize winner (2002)
Car·tier \\kär-'tyā, 'kär-tē-ˌā\\ Jacques 1491–1557 French explorer
Ca·ru·so \\kə-'rü-(ˌ)sō, -(ˌ)zō\\ En·ri·co \\en-'rē-kō\\ 1873–1921 Ital. tenor
Car·ver \\'kär-vər\\ George Washington 1861?–1943 Amer. agricultural chemist and agronomist
Ca·sa·no·va \\ˌka-zə-'nō-və, ˌka-sə-\\ Giovanni Giacomo 1725–1798 Ital. adventurer
Cas·san·dra \\kə-'san-drə, -'sän-\\ daughter of Priam in Greek mythology who is endowed with the gift of prophecy but fated never to be believed
Cas·satt \\kə-'sat\\ Mary 1845–1926 Amer. painter
Cas·tro \\'käs-(ˌ)trō\\ (**Ruz**) Fidel 1926–2016 Cuban leader (1959–2008)
Cath·er \\'ka-thər\\ Willa 1873–1947 Amer. author
Cath·er·ine \\'ka-th(ə-)rən\\ name of 1st, 5th, and 6th wives of Henry VIII of England: Catherine of Aragon 1485–1536; Catherine Howard 1520?–1542; Catherine Parr 1512–1548
Catherine I 1684–1727 wife of Peter the Great; empress of Russia (1725–27)
Catherine II 1729–1796 *Catherine the Great* empress of Russia (1762–96)

Catherine de Mé·di·cis \\-də-ˌmā-dē-'sēs, -'me-də-(ˌ)chē\\ 1519–1589 Ital. *Ca·te·ri·na de' Me·di·ci* \\ˌkä-tā-'rē-nä-dä-'me-dē-(ˌ)chē\\ queen consort of Henry II of France (1547–59) and regent of France (1560–74)
Cav·en·dish \\'ka-vən-(ˌ)dish\\ Henry 1731–1810 Eng. scientist
Ce·ci·lia \\sə-'sēl-yə, -'sil-\\ Saint *fl.* 3d cent. A.D. Christian martyr; patron saint of music
Ce·res \\'sir-(ˌ)ēz\\ goddess of agriculture in Roman mythology — compare DEMETER
Cer·van·tes \\sər-'van-ˌtēz, -'vän-ˌtās\\ Miguel de 1547–1616 Span. author
Cé·zanne \\sā-'zan\\ Paul 1839–1906 French painter
Cha·gall \\shə-'gäl, -'gal\\ Marc 1887–1985 Russ. painter in France
Cham·plain \\ˌsham-'plān, shän-'plaⁿ\\ Samuel de 1567–1635 French explorer in America
Chap·lin \\'cha-plən\\ Charlie 1889–1977 Sir *Charles Spencer Chaplin* Brit. actor and producer
Chapman \\'chap-mən\\ John — see Johnny APPLESEED
Char·le·magne \\'shär-lə-ˌmān\\ 742–814 A.D. *Charles the Great* or *Charles I* Frankish king (768–814); Holy Roman emperor (800–814)
Charles \\'chär(-ə)lz\\ name of 10 kings of France: esp. **II** 823–877 A.D. *Charles the Bald* (r. 840–77); Holy Roman emperor (875–77); **IV** 1294–1328 *Charles the Fair* (r. 1322–28); **V** 1337–1380 *Charles the Wise* (r. 1364–80); **VI** 1368–1422 *Charles the Mad* (or *the Beloved*) (r. 1380–1422); **VII** 1403–1461 *Charles the Well-Served* or *the Victorious* (r. 1422–61); **IX** 1550–1574 (r. 1560–74); **X** 1757–1836 (r. 1824–30)
Charles name of 2 kings of Great Britain: **I** 1600–1649 (r. 1625–49); **II** 1630–1685 (r. 1660–85); son of Charles I
Charles V 1500–1558 Holy Roman emperor (1519–56); king of Spain as *Charles I* (1516–56)
Charles Edward Stuart — see Charles Edward STUART
Charles Mar·tel \\-mär-'tel\\ *ca* 688–741 A.D. Frankish ruler (719–41); grandfather of Charlemagne
Cha·ryb·dis \\kə-'rib-dəs\\ whirlpool off the coast of Sicily personified in Greek mythology as a female monster
Chau·cer \\'chȯ-sər\\ Geoffrey *ca* 1342–1400 Eng. poet
Cha·vez \\'chä-vəs, -ˌvez\\ Cesar Estrada 1927–1993 Amer. labor leader
Che·khov \\'che-ˌkȯf, -ˌkȯv\\ Anton Pavlovich 1860–1904 Russ. author
Che·ney \\'chē-nē, *commonly* 'chā-\\ Richard Bruce 1941– vice pres. of the U.S. (2001–2009)
Cheops — see KHUFU
Ches·ter·ton \\'ches-tər-tən\\ G. K. 1874–1936 *Gilbert Keith Chesterton* Eng. author
Chiang Kai-shek \\jē-'äŋ-'kī-'shek, 'chaŋ-\\ 1887–1975 Chinese general and politician; president of China (1948–1949; Taiwan, 1950–1975)
Cho·pin \\'shō-ˌpan, -ˌpaⁿ\\ Frédéric François 1810–1849 Polish composer
Chou En–lai or **Zhou Enlai** \\'jō-'en-'lī\\ 1898–1976 Chinese Communist politician; premier (1949–76)
Chré·tien \\krä-'tyaⁿ\\ Jean 1934– Canad. prime minister (1993–2003)
Christ Jesus — see JESUS
Chris·tie \\'kris-tē\\ Dame Agatha 1890–1976 née *Miller* Eng. author
Chur·chill \\'chər-ˌchil, 'chȯrch-ˌhil\\ Sir Winston Leonard Spencer 1874–1965 Brit. prime minister (1940–45; 1951–55) Nobel Prize winner (1953)
Cic·ero \\'si-sə-ˌrō\\ Marcus Tullius 106–43 B.C. Roman statesman, orator, and author
Clark \\'klärk\\ George Rogers 1752–1818 Amer. soldier and frontiersman
Clark William 1770–1838 Amer. explorer (with Meriwether Lewis)
Clay \\'klā\\ Henry 1777–1852 Amer. politician and orator
Clem·ens \\'kle-mənz\\ Samuel Langhorne — see Mark TWAIN
Cle·o·pa·tra \\ˌklē-ə-'pa-trə, -'pä-\\ 69–30 B.C. queen of Egypt (51–30)
Cleve·land \\'klēv-lənd\\ (Stephen) Grover 1837–1908 22nd and 24th pres. of the U.S. (1885–89; 1893–97)
Clin·ton \\'klin-tⁿn\\ Hillary Rodham née *Rodham* 1947– Amer. politician; U.S. secretary of state (2009–13); wife of W.J. Clinton

Clinton William Jefferson 1946– *Bill Clinton* 42nd pres. of the U.S. (1993–2001)

Cly·tem·nes·tra \ˌklī-təm-ˈnes-trə\ wife of Agamemnon in Greek mythology

Cobb \ˈkäb\ Ty 1886–1961 *Tyrus Raymond Cobb* Amer. baseball player

Co·chise \kō-ˈchēs\ 1812?–1874 Apache Indian chief

Co·dy \ˈkō-dē\ William Frederick 1846–1917 *Buffalo Bill* Amer. hunter, guide, and showman

Co·han \ˈkō-ˌhan\ George Michael 1878–1942 Amer. composer

Cole·ridge \ˈkōl-rij, ˈkō-lə-rij\ Samuel Taylor 1772–1834 Eng. poet

Co·lette \kō-ˈlet\ 1873–1954 orig. *Sidonie-Gabrielle Colette* French author

Co·lum·bus \kə-ˈləm-bəs\ Christopher 1451–1506 Ital. navigator and explorer for Spain

Con·fu·cius \kən-ˈfyü-shəs\ 551–479 B.C. Chinese philosopher

Con·rad \ˈkän-ˌrad\ Joseph 1857–1924 Brit. (Polish-born) author

Con·sta·ble \ˈkən(t)-stə-bəl, ˈkän(t)-\ John 1776–1837 Eng. painter

Con·stan·tine I \ˈkän(t)-stən-ˌtēn, -ˌtīn\ *after* 280–337 A.D. *Constantine the Great* Roman emperor (306–37)

Cook \ˈku̇k\ Captain James 1728–1779 Eng. navigator

Coo·lidge \ˈkü-lij\ (John) Calvin 1872–1933 30th pres. of the U.S. (1923–29)

Coo·per \ˈkü-pər, ˈku̇-\ James Fenimore 1789–1851 Amer. author

Co·per·ni·cus \kō-ˈpər-ni-kəs\ Nicolaus 1473–1543 Polish astronomer

Cop·land \ˈkō-plənd\ Aaron 1900–1990 Amer. composer

Cop·ley \ˈkä-plē\ John Singleton 1738–1815 Amer. painter

Corn·wal·lis \kȯrn-ˈwä-ləs\ Charles 1738–1805 1st Marquess *Cornwallis* Brit. general in America

Co·ro·na·do \ˌkȯr-ə-ˈnä-(ˌ)dō, ˌkär-\ Francisco Vásquez de *ca* 1510–1554 Span. explorer of southwestern U.S.

Cor·tés \kȯr-ˈtez, ˈkȯr-,\ Hernán *or* Hernando 1485–1547 Span. conqueror of Mexico

Cous·teau \kü-ˈstō\ Jacques-Yves 1910–1997 French marine explorer

Crane \ˈkrān\ Stephen 1871–1900 Amer. author

Crazy Horse \ˈkrā-zē-ˌhȯrs\ 1842?–1877 *Ta-sunko-witko* Sioux Indian chief

Crock·ett \ˈkrä-kət\ Davy 1786–1836 *David Crockett* Amer. frontiersman

Crom·well \ˈkräm-ˌwel, ˈkrəm-, -wəl\ Oliver 1599–1658 Eng. general; lord protector of England (1653–58)

Cro·nus \ˈkrō-nəs, ˈkrä-\ Titan in Greek mythology overthrown by his son Zeus

Cum·mings \ˈkə-miŋz\ Edward Estlin 1894–1962 known as *e. e. cummings* Amer. poet

Cu·pid \ˈkyü-pəd\ god of love in Roman mythology — compare EROS

Cu·rie \kyu̇-ˈrē, ˈkyu̇r-(ˌ)ē\ Marie 1867–1934 née *Sklo·dow·ska* \sklə-ˈdȯf-skə\ French (Polish-born) chemist; Nobel Prize winner (1903, 1911)

Curie Pierre 1859–1906 French chemist; husband of M. Curie; Nobel Prize winner (1903)

Cus·ter \ˈkəs-tər\ George Armstrong 1839–1876 Amer. general

Cy·ra·no de Ber·ge·rac \ˈsir-ə-ˌnō-də-ˈber-zhə-ˌrak\ Savinien 1619–1655 French playwright

Cy·rus II \ˈsī-rəs\ *ca* 585–*ca* 529 B.C. *Cyrus the Great* king of Persia (*ca* 550–529)

Dae·da·lus \ˈde-də-ləs, ˈdē-\ builder in Greek mythology of the Cretan labyrinth and inventor of wings by which he and his son Icarus escape imprisonment

Da·lí \ˈdä-lē, *by himself* dä-ˈlē\ Salvador 1904–1989 Span. painter

Dal·ton \ˈdȯl-tᵊn\ John 1766–1844 Eng. chemist and physicist

Dan·iel \ˈdan-yəl\ prophet in the Bible who is held captive in Babylon and delivered from a den of lions

Dan·te \ˈdän-(ˌ)tā, ˈdan-, -(ˌ)tē\ 1265–1321 *Dante Ali·ghie·ri* \ˌa-lə-ˈgyer-ē\ Ital. poet

Da·ri·us I \də-ˈrī-əs\ 550–486 B.C. *Darius the Great* king of Persia (522–486)

Dar·row \ˈda-(ˌ)rō\ Clarence Seward 1857–1938 Amer. lawyer

Dar·win \ˈdär-wən\ Charles Robert 1809–1882 Eng. naturalist

Da·vid \ˈdā-vəd\ a youth in the Bible who slays Goliath and succeeds Saul as king of Israel

Da·vis \ˈdā-vəs\ Jefferson 1808–1889 pres. of the Confederate States of America (1861–65)

Davis Miles 1926–1991 Amer. jazz musician

Debs \ˈdebz\ Eugene Victor 1855–1926 Amer. socialist and labor organizer

De·bus·sy \ˌde-byü-ˈsē, ˌdā-\ Claude 1862–1918 French composer

De·ca·tur \di-ˈkā-tər\ Stephen 1779–1820 Amer. naval officer

De·foe \di-ˈfō\ Daniel 1660–1731 Eng. author

De·gas \də-ˈgä\ Edgar 1834–1917 French painter

de Gaulle \di-ˈgōl, -ˈgȯl\ Charles 1890–1970 French general; pres. of Fifth Republic (1958–69)

De·li·lah \di-ˈlī-lə\ mistress and betrayer of Samson in the Bible

De·me·ter \di-ˈmē-tər\ goddess of agriculture in Greek mythology — compare CERES

de Mille \də-ˈmil\ Agnes 1905–1993 Amer. dancer and choreographer

De·mos·the·nes \di-ˈmäs-thə-ˌnēz\ 384–322 B.C. Athenian orator and statesman

Demp·sey \ˈdem(p)-sē\ Jack 1895–1983 orig. *William Harrison Dempsey* Amer. boxer

Des·cartes \dā-ˈkärt\ René 1596–1650 French mathematician and philosopher

de So·to \thä-ˈsō-(ˌ)tō, di-\ Hernando *ca* 1496–1542 Span. explorer

Dew·ey \ˈdü-ē, ˈdyü-\ George 1837–1917 Amer. admiral

Dewey John 1859–1952 Amer. philosopher and educator

Di·ana \dī-ˈa-nə\ ancient Ital. goddess of the forest and of childbirth who was identified with Artemis by the Romans

Dick·ens \ˈdi-kənz\ Charles 1812–1870 pseud. *Boz* \ˈbäz, ˈbōz\ Eng. author

Dick·in·son \ˈdi-kən-sən\ Emily Elizabeth 1830–1886 Amer. poet

Di·do \ˈdī-(ˌ)dō\ legendary queen of Carthage who falls in love with Aeneas and kills herself when he leaves her

Di·Mag·gio \də-ˈmä-zhē-(ˌ)ō, -ˈma-jē-(ˌ)ō\ Joe 1914–1999 *Joseph Paul DiMaggio* Amer. baseball player

Di·o·ny·sus \ˌdī-ə-ˈnī-səs, -ˈnē-\ god of wine and ecstasy in classical mythology

Dis·ney \ˈdiz-nē\ Walt 1901–1966 *Walter Elias Disney* Amer. film producer and cartoonist

Dis·rae·li \diz-ˈrā-lē\ Benjamin 1804–1881 Earl of *Beaconsfield* Brit. prime minister (1868; 1874–80)

Dix \ˈdiks\ Dorothea Lynde 1802–1887 Amer. social reformer

Dodg·son \ˈdäd-sən, ˈdäj-\ Charles Lutwidge — see Lewis CARROLL

Donne \ˈdən\ John 1572–1631 Eng. poet and clergyman

Don Qui·xote \ˌdän-kē-ˈ(h)ō-tē, ˌdän-\ hero of Cervantes' *Don Quixote*

Dos·to·yev·sky \ˌdäs-tə-ˈyef-skē, -ˈyev-\ Fyodor Mikhaylovich 1821–1881 Russ. novelist

Doug·las \ˈdə-gləs\ Stephen Arnold 1813–1861 Amer. politician

Doug·lass \ˈdə-gləs\ Frederick 1817–1895 Amer. abolitionist

Doyle \ˈdȯi(-ə)l\ Sir Arthur Conan 1859–1930 Brit. physician and author

Drake \ˈdrāk\ Sir Francis *ca* 1540–1596 Eng. navigator, explorer, and admiral

Drei·ser \ˈdrī-sər, -zər\ Theodore 1871–1945 Amer. author

DuBois \dü-ˈbȯis, dyü-\ William Edward Burghardt 1868–1963 Amer. educator and writer

Du·mas \dü-ˈmä, dyü-\ Alexandre 1802–1870 *Dumas père* \ˈper\ French author

Dun·can \ˈdəŋ-kən\ Isadora 1877–1927 Amer. dancer

Dü·rer \ˈdu̇r-ər, ˈdyu̇r-, ˈduer-\ Albrecht 1471–1528 Ger. painter and engraver

Dy·lan \ˈdi-lən\ Bob 1941– orig. *Robert Allen Zimmerman* Amer. singer and songwriter

Ea·kins \ˈā-kənz\ Thomas 1844–1916 Amer. artist

Ear·hart \ˈer-ˌhärt, ˈir-\ Amelia 1897–1937 Amer. aviator

Earp \ˈərp\ Wyatt 1848–1929 Amer. frontiersman and lawman

Ed·dy \'e-dē\ Mary Baker 1821–1910 Amer. founder of Christian Science

Ed·i·son \'e-də-sən\ Thomas Alva 1847–1931 Amer. inventor

Ed·ward \'ed-wərd\ name of 8 post-Norman kings of England: **I** 1239–1307 *Edward Longshanks* (r. 1272–1307); **II** 1284–1327 (r. 1307–27); **III** 1312–1377 (r. 1327–77); **IV** 1442–1483 (r. 1461–70; 1471–83); **V** 1470–1483 (r. 1483); **VI** 1537–1553 (r. 1547–53); son of Henry VIII and Jane Seymour; **VII** 1841–1910 (r. 1901–10); son of Queen Victoria; **VIII** 1894–1972 (r. 1936; abdicated) *Duke of Windsor*; son of George V

Ein·stein \'īn-ˌstīn\ Albert 1879–1955 Amer. (Ger.-born) physicist; Nobel Prize winner (1921)

Ei·sen·how·er \'ī-z°n-ˌhaù(-ə)r\ Dwight David 1890–1969 Amer. general; 34th pres. of the U.S. (1953–61)

Elec·tra \i-'lek-trə\ sister of Orestes in Greek mythology who aids him in avenging their father's murder

Eli·jah \i-'lī-jə\ Hebrew prophet of the 9th cent. B.C.

El·i·on \'e-lē-ən\ Gertrude Belle 1918–1999 Amer. pharmacologist; Nobel Prize winner (1988)

El·iot \'e-lē-ət, 'el-yət\ George 1819–1880 pseud. of *Mary Ann Evans* Eng. author

Eliot T. S. 1888–1965 *Thomas Stearns Eliot* Brit. (Amer.-born) poet; Nobel Prize winner (1948)

Eliz·a·beth I \i-'li-zə-bəth\ 1533–1603 queen of England (1558–1603); daughter of Henry VIII and Anne Boleyn

Elizabeth II 1926– queen of the United Kingdom (1952–); daughter of George VI

El·ling·ton \'e-liŋ-tən\ Duke 1899–1974 *Edward Kennedy Ellington* Amer. bandleader and composer

Em·er·son \'e-mər-sən\ Ralph Waldo 1803–1882 Amer. essayist and poet

En·dym·i·on \en-'di-mē-ən\ beautiful youth in Greek mythology loved by the goddess of the moon

Ep·i·cu·rus \ˌe-pi-'kyùr-əs\ 341–270 B.C. Greek philosopher

Er·ik the Red \'er-ik\ *fl.* 10th cent. orig. *Erik Thorvaldson* Norwegian explorer; father of Leif Eriksson

Eriksson Leif — see LEIF ERIKSSON

Eros \'er-ˌäs, 'ir-\ god of love in Greek mythology — compare CUPID

Esau \'ē-(ˌ)sò\ son of Isaac and Rebekah and elder twin brother of Jacob in the Bible

Es·ther \'es-tər\ Hebrew woman in the Bible who as the queen of Persia delivers her people from destruction

Eu·clid \'yü-kləd\ *fl. ca.* 300 B.C. Greek mathematician

Eu·rip·i·des \yù-'ri-pə-ˌdēz\ *ca* 484–406 B.C. Greek playwright

Eu·ro·pa \yù-'rō-pə\ princess in Greek mythology who was carried off by Zeus disguised as a white bull

Eu·ryd·i·ce \yù-'ri-də-(ˌ)sē\ wife of Orpheus in Greek mythology

Eve \'ēv\ the 1st woman in biblical tradition; wife of Adam

Eze·kiel \i-'zē-kyəl, -kē-əl\ Hebrew prophet of the 6th cent. B.C.

Fahr·en·heit \'fa-rən-ˌhīt, 'fär-ən-\ Daniel Gabriel 1686–1736 Ger. physicist

Far·a·day \'fa-rə-ˌdā, -dē\ Michael 1791–1867 Eng. chemist and physicist

Far·ra·gut \'fa-rə-gət\ David Glasgow 1801–1870 Amer. admiral

Faulk·ner \'fók-nər\ William 1897–1962 Amer. author; Nobel Prize winner (1949)

Faust \'faùst\ *or* **Fau·stus** \'faù-stəs, 'fò-\ magician in Ger. legend who sells his soul to the devil for knowledge and power

Fawkes \'fóks\ Guy 1570–1606 Eng. conspirator

Fel·li·ni \fə-'lē-nē\ Federico 1920–1993 Ital. film director

Fer·di·nand \'fər-də-ˌnand\ **V** of Castile *or* **II** of Aragon 1452–1516 *Ferdinand the Catholic* king of Castile (1474–1504), of Aragon (1479–1516), of Naples (1504–16); husband of Isabella I

Fer·mi \'fer-(ˌ)mē\ Enrico 1901–1954 Amer. (Ital.-born) physicist; Nobel Prize winner (1938)

Fiel·ding \'fēl-diŋ\ Henry 1707–1754 Eng. author

Fill·more \'fil-ˌmór\ Millard 1800–1874 13th pres. of the U.S. (1850–53)

Fitz·ger·ald \fits-'jer-əld\ Ella 1917–1996 Amer. singer

Fitzgerald F. Scott 1896–1940 *Francis Scott Key Fitzgerald* Amer. author

Flem·ing \'fle-miŋ\ Sir Alexander 1881–1955 Brit. bacteriologist; Nobel Prize winner (1945)

Flying Dutchman legendary Dutch mariner condemned to sail the seas until Judgment Day

Ford \'fórd\ Gerald Rudolph 1913–2007 38th pres. of the U.S. (1974–77)

Ford Henry 1863–1947 Amer. automobile manufacturer

Fos·sey \'fò-sē, 'fä-\ Dian 1932–1985 Amer. zoologist

Fos·ter \'fòs-tər, 'fäs-\ Stephen Collins 1826–1864 Amer. songwriter

Fran·cis \'fran(t)-səs\ 1936– pope (2013–)

Francis of As·si·si \-ˌsv-ə-'si-sē, -'sē-\ Saint 1181/1182–1226 Ital. friar; founder of Franciscan order

Fran·co \'frän-(ˌ)kō, 'fraŋ-\ Francisco 1892–1975 Span. general, dictator, and head of Span. state (1936–75)

Frank \'fraŋk, 'fräŋk\ Anne 1929–1945 Ger.-born diarist during the Holocaust

Frank·lin \'fraŋ-klən\ Benjamin 1706–1790 Amer. patriot, author, and inventor

Fred·er·ick I \'fre-d(ə-)rik\ *ca* 1123–1190 *Frederick Barbarossa* Holy Roman emperor (1152–90)

Frederick II 1712–1786 *Frederick the Great* king of Prussia (1740–86)

Fré·mont \'frē-ˌmänt\ John Charles 1813–1890 Amer. general and explorer

French \'french\ Daniel Chester 1850–1931 Amer. sculptor

Freud \'fròid\ Sigmund 1856–1939 Austrian neurologist; founder of psychoanalysis

Fried·man \'frēd-mən\ Milton 1912–2006 Amer. economist

Frig·ga \'fri-gə\ wife of Odin and goddess of married love and the hearth in Norse mythology

Frost \'fròst\ Robert Lee 1874–1963 Amer. poet

Full·er \'fù-lər\ (Richard) Buckminster 1895–1983 Amer. engineer and architect

Fuller (Sarah) Margaret 1810–1850 Amer. author and reformer

Ful·ton \'fùl-t°n\ Robert 1765–1815 Amer. inventor

Ga·bri·el \'gā-brē-əl\ archangel named in Hebrew tradition — compare MICHAEL, RAPHAEL, URIEL

Ga·ga·rin \gə-'gär-ən\ Yury Alekseyevich 1934–1968 Russ. astronaut; 1st person in space (1961)

Gage \'gāj\ Thomas 1721–1787 Brit. general in America

Gal·a·had \'ga-lə-ˌhad\ knight of the Round Table in medieval legend who finds the Holy Grail

Gal·a·tea \ˌga-lə-'tē-ə\ female figure sculpted by Pygmalion in Greek mythology and given life by Aphrodite in answer to the sculptor's prayer

Ga·len \'gā-lən\ 129–*ca* 216 A.D. Greek physician and writer

Ga·li·leo \ˌga-lə-'lē-(ˌ)ō, -'lā-\ 1564–1642 *Galileo Galilei* Ital. astronomer and physicist

Gall \'gól\ 1840?–1894 Sioux Indian leader

Ga·ma \'ga-mə, 'gä-\ Vasco da *ca* 1460–1524 Portuguese navigator and explorer

Gan·dhi \'gän-dē, 'gan-\ Indira 1917–1984 Indian prime minister (1966–77; 1980–84); daughter of Jawaharlal Nehru

Gandhi Mohandas Karamchand 1869–1948 *Ma·hat·ma* \mə-'hät-mə, -'hat-\ *Gandi* Indian leader

Gar·cía Már·quez \gär-'sē-ə-'mär-ˌkäs\ Gabriel 1928–2014 Colombian author; Nobel Prize winner (1982)

Gar·field \'gär-ˌfēld\ James Abram 1831–1881 20th pres. of the U.S. (1881)

Gar·i·bal·di \ˌga-rə-'bòl-dē\ Giuseppe 1807–1882 Ital. patriot

Gar·ri·son \'ga-rə-sən\ William Lloyd 1805–1879 Amer. abolitionist

Gates \'gāts\ Bill 1955– *William Henry Gates III* Amer. computer software manufacturer

Gau·guin \gō-'gaⁿ\ Paul 1848–1903 French painter

Geh·rig \'ger-ig\ Lou 1903–1941 *Henry Louis Gehrig* Amer. baseball player

Gehry \'ger-ē\ Frank Owen 1929– orig. *Ephraim Owen Goldberg* Amer. (Canad.-born) architect

Gei·sel \'gī-zəl\ Theodor Seuss 1904–1991 pseud. *Dr. Seuss* \'süs\ Amer. author and illustrator

Gen·ghis Khan \ˌjeŋ-gəs-'kän, ˌgeŋ-\ *ca* 1162–1227 Mongol conqueror

George \'jòrj\ name of 6 kings of Great Britain: **I** 1660–1727 (r. 1714–27); **II** 1683–1760 (r. 1727–60); **III** 1738–1820

(r. 1760–1820); **IV** 1762–1830 (r. 1820–30); **V** 1865–1936 (r. 1910–36); **VI** 1895–1952 (r. 1936–52); father of Elizabeth II

Ge·ron·i·mo \jə-'rä-nə-ˌmō\ 1829–1909 Apache Indian leader

Gersh·win \'gər-shwən\ George 1898–1937 Amer. composer

Gil·bert \'gil-bərt\ Sir William Schwenck 1836–1911 Eng. librettist and poet; collaborator with Sir Arthur Sullivan

Gins·burg \'ginz-ˌbərg\ Ruth Bader 1933–   Amer. jurist

Glad·stone \'glad-ˌstōn, *chiefly Brit* -stən\ William Ewart 1809–1898 Brit. prime minister (1868–74; 1880–85; 1886; 1892–94)

Glenn \'glen\ John Herschel 1921–2016 Amer. astronaut and politician; 1st Amer. to orbit the earth (1962)

Go·di·va \gə-'dī-və\ an Eng. gentlewoman who in legend rode naked through Coventry to save its citizens from a tax

Goe·thals \'gō-thəlz\ George Washington 1858–1928 Amer. engineer who directed the building of the Panama Canal

Goe·the \'gə(r)-tə, 'gœ-tə\ Johann Wolfgang von 1749–1832 Ger. author

Gogh, van \van-'gō, -'gäk̲\ Vincent Willem 1853–1890 Dutch painter

Gol·ding \'gōl-diŋ\ William Gerald 1911–1993 Eng. author; Nobel Prize winner (1983)

Go·li·ath \gə-'lī-əth\ Philistine giant who is killed by David in the Bible

Gom·pers \'gäm-pərz\ Samuel 1850–1924 Amer. (Brit.-born) labor leader

Goo·dall \'gu̇-(ˌ)dȯl, -(ˌ)däl\ Jane 1934–   Brit. zoologist

Good·year \'gu̇d-ˌyir\ Charles 1800–1860 Amer. inventor

Gor·ba·chev \ˌgȯr-bə-'chȯf, -'chef\ Mikhail Sergeyevich 1931–   Soviet leader of Communist party (1985–91); pres. of U.S.S.R. (1990–91); Nobel Prize winner (1990)

Gore \'gȯr\ Albert, Jr. 1948–   vice pres. of the U.S. (1993–2001); Nobel Prize winner (2007)

Gor·gas \'gȯr-gəs\ William Crawford 1854–1920 Amer. army surgeon

Go·ya (y Lu·cien·tes) \'gȯi-ə-ˌē-ˌlü-sē-'en-ˌtäs\ Francisco José de 1746–1828 Span. painter

Gra·ham \'grä-əm, 'gra(-ə)m\ Martha 1893–1991 Amer. dancer and choreographer

Grant \'grant\ Ulysses S. 1822–1885 orig. *Hiram Ulysses Grant* Amer. general; 18th pres. of the U.S. (1869–77)

Gre·co, El \el-'gre-(ˌ)kō\ 1541–1614 *Doménikos Theotokópoulos* Span. (Cretan-born) painter

Gree·ley \'grē-lē\ Horace 1811–1872 Amer. journalist and politician

Greene \'grēn\ (Henry) Graham 1904–1991 Brit. author

Greene Nathanael 1742–1786 Amer. Revolutionary general

Greg·o·ry \'gre-g(ə-)rē\ name of 16 popes: esp. **I** Saint *ca* 540–604 A.D. *Gregory the Great* (pope 590–604); **VII** Saint *ca* 1020–1085 (pope 1073–85); **XIII** 1502–1585 (pope 1572–85)

Grey \'grā\ Lady Jane 1537–1554 queen of England for 9 days (1553)

Grey Zane 1872–1939 Amer. author

Grieg \'grēg\ Edward Hagerup 1843–1907 Norwegian composer

Grimm \'grim\ Jacob 1785–1863 and his brother Wilhelm 1786–1859 Ger. philologists and folklorists

Gro·pi·us \'grō-pē-əs\ Walter 1883–1969 Amer. (Ger.-born) architect

Gue·va·ra \ge-'vär-ə, gä-\ Che 1928–1967 orig. *Ernesto* Cuban (Arg.-born) revolutionary

Guin·e·vere \'gwi-nə-ˌvir\ legendary wife of King Arthur and lover of Lancelot

Gu·ten·berg \'gü-tᵊn-ˌbərg\ Johannes *ca* 1400–1468 Ger. inventor of printing method from movable type

Ha·des \'hā-(ˌ)dēz\ — see PLUTO

Ha·dri·an \'hā-drē-ən\ 76–138 A.D. Roman emperor (117–138)

Hai·le Se·las·sie \'hī-lē-sə-'la-sē, -'lä-\ 1892–1975 emperor of Ethiopia (1930–36; 1941–74)

Hale \'hāl\ Edward Everett 1822–1909 Amer. minister and author

Hale Nathan 1755–1776 Amer. Revolutionary hero

Hal·ley \'ha-lē\ Edmond *or* Edmund 1656–1742 Eng. astronomer and mathematician

Hal·sey \'hȯl-sē, -zē\ William Frederick 1882–1959 Amer. admiral

Ham·il·ton \'ha-məl-tən\ Alexander 1755–1804 Amer. political leader

Ham·mu·ra·bi \ˌha-mə-'rä-bē\ *died ca* 1750 B.C. king of Babylon (*ca* 1792–50)

Han·cock \'han-ˌkäk\ John 1737–1793 Amer. Revolutionary patriot

Han·del \'han-dᵊl\ George Frideric 1685–1759 Brit. (Ger.-born) composer

Han·dy \'han-dē\ W. C. 1873–1958 *William Christopher Handy* Amer. blues musician and composer

Han·ni·bal \'ha-nə-bəl\ 247–183? B.C. Carthaginian general

Har·ding \'här-diŋ\ Warren Gamaliel 1865–1923 29th pres. of the U.S. (1921–23)

Har·dy \'här-dē\ Thomas 1840–1928 Eng. author

Har·per \'här-pər\ Stephen 1959–   Canad. prime minister (2006–15)

Har·ri·son \'ha-rə-sən\ Benjamin 1833–1901 23rd pres. of the U.S. (1889–93); grandson of W. H. Harrison

Harrison William Henry 1773–1841 Amer. general; 9th pres. of the U.S. (1841)

Harte \'härt\ Bret 1836–1902 orig. *Francis Brett Harte* Amer. author

Har·vey \'här-vē\ William 1578–1657 Eng. physician and anatomist

Haw·king \'hȯ-kiŋ\ Stephen William 1942–2018 Brit. physicist

Haw·thorne \'hȯ-ˌthȯrn\ Nathaniel 1804–1864 Amer. author

Haydn \'hī-dᵊn\ Franz Joseph 1732–1809 Austrian composer

Hayes \'hāz\ Rutherford Birchard 1822–1893 19th pres. of the U.S. (1877–81)

Hearst \'hərst\ William Randolph 1863–1951 Amer. newspaper publisher

Hec·tor \'hek-tər\ son of Priam and Hecuba; Trojan hero slain by Achilles in Greek mythology

Hec·u·ba \'he-kyə-bə\ wife of Priam in Greek mythology

He·gel \'hā-gəl\ Georg Wilhelm Friedrich 1770–1831 Ger. philosopher

Hei·sen·berg \'hī-zᵊn-bərg, -ˌberk\ Werner Karl 1901–1976 Ger. physicist

Hel·en of Troy \ˌhe-lən-əv-'trȯi\ wife of Menelaus whose abduction by Paris in Greek mythology causes the Trojan War

He·li·os \'hē-lē-əs, -(ˌ)ōs\ god of the sun in Greek mythology — compare SOL

Hem·ing·way \'he-miŋ-ˌwā\ Ernest Miller 1899–1961 Amer. author; Nobel Prize winner (1954)

Hen·ry \'hen-rē\ name of 8 kings of England: **I** 1068–1135 (r. 1100–35); **II** 1133–1189 (r. 1154–89); **III** 1207–1272 (r. 1216–72); **IV** 1366–1413 (r. 1399–1413); **V** 1387–1422 (r. 1413–22); **VI** 1421–1471 (r. 1422–61; 1470–71); **VII** 1457–1509 (r. 1485–1509); **VIII** 1491–1547 (r. 1509–47)

Henry name of 4 kings of France: **I** *ca* 1008–1060 (r. 1031–60); **II** 1519–1559 (r. 1547–59); **III** 1551–1589 (r. 1574–89); **IV** 1553–1610 *Henry of Navarre* (r. 1589–1610)

Henry O. 1862–1910 pseud. of *William Sydney Porter* Amer. author

Henry Patrick 1736–1799 Amer. patriot and orator

Hen·son \'hen(t)-sən\ Matthew Alexander 1866–1955 Amer. arctic explorer

He·phaes·tus \hi-'fes-təs, -'fēs-\ god of fire and of metalworking in Greek mythology — compare VULCAN

He·ra \'hir-ə, 'he-rə, 'her-ə\ sister and wife of Zeus and goddess of women and marriage in Greek mythology — compare JUNO

Her·cu·les \'hər-kyə-ˌlēz\ *or* **Her·a·cles** \'her-ə-ˌklēz-, 'he-rə-\ hero in Greek mythology noted for his strength

Her·mes \'hər-(ˌ)mēz\ god of commerce, eloquence, invention, travel, and theft who serves as herald and messenger of the other gods in Greek mythology — compare MERCURY

Her·od \'her-əd\ 73–4 B.C. *Herod the Great* Roman king of Judea (37–4)

Herod An·ti·pas \'an-tə-pəs, -ˌpas\ 21 B.C.–39 A.D. Roman governor of Galilee (4 B.C.–39 A.D.); son of Herod the Great

Her·schel \'hər-shəl\ Sir William 1738–1822 Eng. astronomer

Hes·se \\'he-sə\\ Hermann 1877–1962 Ger. author; Nobel Prize winner (1946)

Hey·er·dahl \\'hā-ər-ˌdäl\\ Thor 1914–2002 Norwegian explorer and author

Hi·a·wa·tha \\ˌhī-ə-'wò-thə, ˌhē-ə-, -'wä-\\ legendary Iroquois Indian chief

Hick·ok \\'hi-ˌkäk\\ Wild Bill 1837–1876 orig. *James Butler Hickok* Amer. frontiersman and U.S. marshal

Hi·dal·go (y Cos·ti·lla) \\ē-'thäl-gō-ē-kò-'stē-yä\\ Miguel 1753–1811 Mex. priest and revolutionary leader

Hil·ton \\'hil-tᵊn\\ James 1900–1954 Eng. novelist

Hip·poc·ra·tes \\hi-'pä-krə-ˌtēz\\ *ca* 460–*ca* 377 B.C. Greek physician

Hi·ro·hi·to \\ˌhir-ō-'hē-(ˌ)tō\\ 1901–1989 emperor of Japan (1926–89)

Hitch·cock \\'hich-ˌkäk\\ Sir Alfred Joseph 1899–1980 Eng. film director

Hit·ler \\'hit-lər\\ Adolf 1889–1945 Ger. (Austrian-born) chancellor and dictator (1933–45)

Hodg·kin \\'häj-kin\\ Dorothy Mary 1910–1994 née *Crowfoot* Brit. physicist; Nobel Prize winner (1964)

Hol·i·day \\'hä-lə-ˌdā\\ Billie 1915–1959 orig. *Eleanora Fagan* Amer. jazz singer

Holmes \\'hōmz, 'hōlmz\\ Oliver Wendell 1809–1894 Amer. physician and author

Holmes Oliver Wendell, Jr. 1841–1935 Amer. jurist; son of the preceding

Ho·mer \\'hō-mər\\ *fl.* 9th *or* 8th cent. B.C. Greek epic poet

Homer Winslow 1836–1910 Amer. painter

Hooke \\'hùk\\ Robert 1635–1703 Eng. scientist

Hook·er \\'hù-kər\\ Thomas 1586?–1647 Eng. colonist; a founder of Connecticut

Hoo·ver \\'hü-vər\\ Herbert Clark 1874–1964 31st pres. of the U.S. (1929–33)

Hoover John Edgar 1895–1972 Amer. director of the Federal Bureau of Investigation (1924–72)

Hop·per \\'hä-pər\\ Edward 1882–1967 Amer. painter

Hopper Grace 1906–1992 née *Murray* Amer. admiral, mathematician, and computer scientist

Hou·di·ni \\hü-'dē-nē\\ Harry 1874–1926 orig. *Erik Weisz* Amer. magician

Hous·ton \\'hyü-stən, 'yü-\\ Sam 1793–1863 *Samuel Houston* Amer. politician; pres. of the Republic of Texas (1836–38; 1841–44)

Howe \\'haù\\ Elias 1819–1867 Amer. inventor

Howe Julia 1819–1910 née *Ward* Amer. suffragist and reformer

Hub·ble \\'hə-bəl\\ Edwin Powell 1889–1953 Amer. astronomer

Hud·son \\'həd-sən\\ Henry *ca* 1565–1611 Eng. explorer

Hughes \\'hyüz\\ Charles Evans 1862–1948 Amer. jurist; chief justice U.S. Supreme Court (1930–1941)

Hughes (James) Langston 1902–1967 Amer. author

Hugo \\'hyü-(ˌ)gō, 'yü-\\ Victor 1802–1885 French author

Hus·sein I \\hü-'sān\\ 1935–1999 king of Jordan (1952–99)

Hussein Saddam 1937–2006 pres. of Iraq (1979–2003)

Hutch·in·son \\'hə-chə(n)-sən\\ Anne 1591–1643 née *Marbury* Eng. colonist and religious leader in America

Hutchinson Thomas 1711–1780 Amer. colonial administrator

Hux·ley \\'həks-lē\\ Aldous Leonard 1894–1963 Eng. author

Hy·men \\'hī-mən\\ god of marriage in Greek mythology

Ib·sen \\'ib-sən, 'ip-\\ Henrik 1828–1906 Norwegian playwright

Ic·a·rus \\'i-kə-rəs\\ son of Daedalus who in Greek mythology falls into the sea when the wax of his artificial wings melts as he flies too near the sun

Ig·na·tius \\ig-'nä-sh(ē-)əs\\ Saint 1491–1556 *Ignatius of Loyola* Span. priest; founder of Society of Jesus (Jesuits)

In·no·cent \\'i-nə-sənt\\ name of 13 popes: esp. **III** 1160/61–1216 (pope 1198–1216); **IV** *died* 1254 (pope 1243–54)

Ir·ving \\'ər-viŋ\\ Washington 1783–1859 Amer. author

Isaac \\'ī-zik, -zək\\ son of Abraham and father of Jacob in the Bible

Is·a·bel·la I \\ˌi-zə-'be-lə\\ 1451–1504 queen of Castile (1474–1504) and of Aragon (1479–1504); wife of Ferdinand V

Isa·iah \\ī-'zā-ə, *chiefly Brit* -'zī-\\ Hebrew prophet of the 8th cent. B.C.

Ish·ma·el \\'ish-(ˌ)mā-əl, -mē-\\ outcast son of Abraham and Hagar in the Bible

Ives \\'īvz\\ Charles Edward 1874–1954 Amer. composer

Jack·son \\'jak-sən\\ Andrew 1767–1845 Amer. general; 7th pres. of the U.S. (1829–37)

Jackson Thomas Jonathan 1824–1863 *Stonewall Jackson* Amer. Confederate general

Ja·cob \\'jā-kəb\\ son of Isaac and Rebekah and younger twin brother of Esau in the Bible

James \\'jāmz\\ one of the 12 apostles in the Bible

James *the Less* one of the 12 apostles in the Bible

James name of 2 kings of Great Britain: **I** 1566–1625 (r. 1603–25); king of Scotland as *James VI* (r. 1567–1625); **II** 1633–1701 (r. 1685–88)

James Henry 1843–1916 Brit. (Amer.-born) author

Ja·nus \\'jā-nəs\\ god of gates and doors and of all beginnings in Roman mythology and that is pictured with two opposite faces

Ja·son \\'jā-sᵊn\\ hero in Greek mythology noted for his successful quest of the Golden Fleece

Jay \\'jā\\ John 1745–1829 Amer. jurist and statesman; 1st chief justice of the U.S. Supreme Court (1789–95)

Jef·fer·son \\'je-fər-sən\\ Thomas 1743–1826 3d pres. of the U.S. (1801–09)

Jer·e·mi·ah \\ˌjer-ə-'mī-ə\\ Hebrew prophet of the 7th–6th cent. B.C.

Je·sus \\'jē-zəs, -zəz\\ *or* **Jesus Christ** *ca* 6 B.C.–*ca* 30 A.D. source of the Christian religion and Savior in the Christian faith

Jez·e·bel \\'je-zə-ˌbel\\ queen of Israel and wife of Ahab who is noted for her wickedness in the Bible

Joan of Arc \\ˌjōn-əv-'ärk\\ Saint *ca* 1412–1431 *the Maid of Orléans* French national heroine

Job \\'jōb\\ man in the Bible who has many sufferings but keeps his faith

Jobs \\'jäbz\\ Steven Paul 1955–2011 Amer. computer entrepreneur

Jo·cas·ta \\jō-'kas-tə\\ queen of Thebes in Greek mythology who unknowingly marries her son Oedipus

John \\'jän\\ one of the 12 apostles believed to be the author of the 4th Gospel, three Epistles, and the Book of Revelation

John name of 21 popes: esp. **XXIII** 1881–1963 (pope 1958–63)

John 1167–1216 *John Lackland* king of England (1199–1216)

John Paul \\'pòl\\ name of 2 popes; esp. **II** 1920–2005 (pope 1978–2005)

John·son \\'jän(t)-sən\\ Andrew 1808–1875 17th pres. of the U.S. (1865–69)

Johnson Lyndon Baines 1908–1973 36th pres. of the U.S. (1963–69)

Johnson Samuel 1709–1784 *Dr. Johnson* Eng. lexicographer and author

John the Baptist Saint, 1st cent. A.D. prophet and baptizer of Jesus in the Bible

Jol·liet *or* **Jo·liet** \\zhòl-'yä\\ Louis 1645–1700 French-Canad. explorer

Jo·nah \\'jō-nə\\ Hebrew prophet who in the Bible spends three days in the belly of a great fish

Jones \\'jōnz\\ John Paul 1747–1792 Amer. (Scot.-born) naval officer

Jop·lin \\'jä-plən\\ Scott 1868–1917 Amer. pianist and composer

Jor·dan \\'jòr-dᵊn\\ Michael 1963– Amer. basketball player

Jo·seph \\'jō-zəf\\ son of Jacob in the Bible who rises to high office in Egypt after being sold into slavery by his brothers

Joseph Chief *ca* 1840–1904 Nez Percé Indian chief

Joseph Saint, husband of Mary, the mother of Jesus, in the Bible

Josh·ua \\'jä-sh(ə-)wə\\ Hebrew leader in the Bible who succeeds Moses during the settlement of the Israelites in Canaan

Joyce \\'jòis\\ James Augustine 1882–1941 Irish author

Juan Car·los \\'(h)wän-'kär-ˌlōs\\ 1938– king of Spain (1975–2014)

Juá·rez \\'(h)wär-əs\\ Benito Pablo 1806–1872 president of Mexico (1861–65; 1867–72)

Ju·dah \\'jü-də\\ son of Jacob and ancestor of one of the 12 tribes of Israel in the Bible

Ju·das \'jü-dəs\ *or* Judas Is·car·i·ot \-is-'ka-rē-ət\ one of the 12 apostles and the betrayer of Jesus in the Bible

Jung \'yùn\ Carl Gustav 1875–1961 Swiss psychologist

Ju·no \'jü-(,)nō\ queen of heaven, wife of Jupiter, and goddess of light, birth, women, and marriage in Roman mythology — compare HERA

Ju·pi·ter \'jü-pə-tər\ chief god and god of light, of the sky and weather, and of the state in Roman mythology — compare ZEUS

Kaf·ka \'käf-kə, 'kaf-\ Franz 1883–1924 Czech author

Kalb \'kälp, 'kalb\ Johann 1721–1780 Baron *de Kalb* \di-'kalb\ Ger. general in Amer. Revolutionary army

Ka·me·ha·me·ha I \kə-,mä-ə-'mä-(,)hä\ 1758?–1819 orig. *Paiea* Hawaiian king (1795–1819)

Kant \'kant, 'känt\ Immanuel 1724–1804 Ger. philosopher

Keats \'kēts\ John 1795–1821 Eng. poet

Kel·ler \'ke-lər\ Helen Adams 1880–1968 Amer. deaf and blind lecturer and author

Kel·vin \'kel-vən\ 1st Baron 1824–1907 *William Thomson* Brit. mathematician and physicist

Ken·ne·dy \'ke-nə-dē\ John Fitzgerald 1917–1963 35th pres. of the U.S. (1961–63)

Kennedy Robert Francis 1925–1968 attorney general of the U.S. (1961–64); brother of the preceding

Ke·o·kuk \'kē-ə-,kək\ 1780?–1848 Sauk and Fox tribal leader

Kep·ler \'ke-plər\ Johannes 1571–1630 Ger. astronomer

Key \'kē\ Francis Scott 1779–1843 Amer. lawyer; author of "The Star-Spangled Banner"

Keynes \'kānz\ John Maynard 1883–1946 Eng. economist

Khayyám Omar — see OMAR KHAYYÁM

Khru·shchev \krüsh-'chof, -'chòv\ Nikita Sergeyevich 1894–1971 premier of U.S.S.R. (1958–64)

Khu·fu \'kü-(,)fü\ *or Greek* Che·ops \'kē-,äps\ *fl.* 25th cent. B.C. king of Egypt and pyramid builder

Kidd \'kid\ William *ca* 1645–1701 *Captain Kidd* Scot. pirate

Kier·ka·gaard \'kir-kə-,gär(d), -,gòr\ Søren 1813–1855 Danish philosopher

King \'kin\ Billie Jean 1943– Amer. tennis player

King Martin Luther, Jr. 1929–1968 Amer. minister and civil rights leader; Nobel Prize winner (1964)

Kip·ling \'kip-lin\ Rudyard 1865–1936 Eng. author; Nobel Prize winner (1907)

Kis·sin·ger \'ki-sᵊn-jər\ Henry Alfred 1923– Amer. (Ger.-born) government official; U.S. secretary of state (1973–77); Nobel Prize winner (1973)

Knox \'näks\ John *ca* 1514–1572 Scot. religious reformer

Koch \'kòk, 'kòk, 'kōk, 'kōk\ Robert 1843–1910 Ger. bacteriologist; Nobel Prize winner (1905)

Koś·ciusz·ko \kòsh-'chùsh-(,)kō, ,kä-sē-'əs-,kō\ Tadeusz 1746–1817 Polish patriot and general in Amer. Revolutionary army

Krish·na \'krish-nə, 'krēsh-\ god worshipped in later Hinduism

Ku·blai Khan \'kü-,blə-'kän, -,blī-\ 1215–1294 Mongol leader; grandson of Genghis Khan

La·fa·yette \,lä-fē-'et, ,la-\ Marquis de 1757–1834 French general in Amer. Revolutionary army

La·ius \'lā-əs, 'lī-əs\ king of Thebes who in Greek mythology is killed by his son Oedipus

Lan·ce·lot \'lan(t)-sə-,lät, 'län(t)-, -s(ə-)lət\ legendary knight of the Round Table and lover of Queen Guinevere

Lange \'lan\ Dorothea 1895–1965 Amer. photographer

Lao-tzu \'laùd-'zə\ *fl.* 6th cent. B.C. Chinese philosopher

La Salle \lə-'sal\ Sieur de 1643–1687 *René-Robert Cavelier* French explorer

La·voi·sier \ləv-'wä-zē-,ā\ Antoine-Laurent 1743–1794 French chemist

Law·rence \'lòr-ən(t)s, 'lär-\ D. H. 1885–1930 *David Herbert Lawrence* Eng. author

Lawrence Thomas Edward 1888–1935 *Lawrence of Arabia* Brit. soldier and author

Laz·a·rus \'laz-rəs, 'la-zə-\ brother of Mary and Martha who in the Bible is raised by Jesus from the dead

Lazarus beggar in the biblical parable of the rich man and the beggar

Le·da \'lē-də\ Spartan princess in Greek mythology who is courted by Zeus in the form of a swan

Lee \'lē\ Ann 1736–1784 Eng. mystic; founder of Shaker society in the U.S.

Lee Robert Edward 1807–1870 Amer. Confederate general

Leeu·wen·hoek \'lā-vən-,hùk\ Antonie van 1632–1723 Dutch naturalist

Leib·niz \'līb-nəts\ Gottfried Wilhelm 1646–1716 Ger. philosopher and mathematician

Leif Er·iks·son *or* Er·ics·son \,lāv-'er-ik-sən, ,lēf-\ *fl.* 1000 Norwegian explorer; son of Erik the Red

Le·nin \'le-nən\ 1870–1924 orig. *Vladimir Ilyich Ul·ya·nov* \ùl-'yän-əf, -,of, -,òv\ Russ. Communist leader

Leo \'lē-(,)ō\ name of 13 popes: esp. I Saint *died* 461 A.D. *Leo the Great* (pope 440–61); III Saint *died* 816 (pope 795–816); XIII 1810–1903 (pope 1878–1903)

Le·o·nar·do da Vin·ci \,lē-ə-'när-(,)dō-də-'vin-chē, ,lā-, -'vēn-\ 1452–1519 Ital. painter, sculptor, architect, and engineer

Lew·is \'lü-əs\ C. S. 1898–1963 *Clive Staples Lewis* Brit. author

Lewis John Llewellyn 1880–1969 Amer. labor leader

Lewis Meriwether 1774–1809 Amer. explorer (with William Clark)

Lewis Sinclair 1885–1951 Amer. author; Nobel Prize winner (1930)

Lin·coln \'lin-kən\ Abraham 1809–1865 16th pres. of the U.S. (1861–65)

Lind·bergh \'lin(d)-,bərg\ Charles Augustus 1902–1974 Amer. aviator

Lin·nae·us \lə-'nē-əs, -'nā-\ Carolus 1707–1778 *Carl von Linné* Swedish botanist

Lis·ter \'lis-tər\ Joseph 1827–1912 Eng. surgeon and medical scientist

Liszt \'list\ Franz 1811–1886 Hungarian pianist and composer

Liv·ing·stone \'li-vin-stən\ David 1813–1873 Scot. missionary in Africa

Locke \'läk\ John 1632–1704 Eng. philosopher

Lon·don \'lən-dən\ Jack 1876–1916 *John Griffith London* Amer. author

Long·fel·low \'lòn-,fe-(,)lō\ Henry Wadsworth 1807–1882 Amer. poet

Lou·is \'lü-ē, lü-'ē\ name of 18 kings of France: esp. IX Saint 1214–1270 (r. 1226–70); XI 1423–1483 (r. 1461–83); XII 1462–1515 (r. 1498–1515); XIII 1601–1643 (r. 1610–43); XIV 1638–1715 (r. 1643–1715); XV 1710–1774 (r. 1715–74); XVI 1754–1793 (r. 1774–92; guillotined); XVII 1785–1795 (r. in name 1793–95); XVIII 1755–1824 (r. 1814–15; 1815–24)

Lou·is \'lü-əs\ Joe 1914–1981 orig. *Joseph Louis Barrow* Amer. boxer

Low \'lō\ Juliette 1860–1927 née *Gordon* Amer. founder of the Girl Scouts

Low·ell \'lō-əl\ Amy 1874–1925 Amer. poet

Lowell James Russell 1819–1891 Amer. author

Luke \'lük\ physician and companion of the apostle Paul believed to be the author of the 3d Gospel and the Book of Acts

Lu·ther \'lü-thər\ Martin 1483–1546 Ger. Reformation leader

Ly·on \'lī-ən\ Mary 1797–1849 Amer. educator

Mac·Ar·thur \mə-'kär-thər\ Douglas 1880–1964 Amer. general

Mac·don·ald \mək-'dä-nᵊld\ Sir John Alexander 1815–1891 first prime minister of Canada (1867–1873; 1878–1891)

Ma·chi·a·vel·li \,ma-kē-ə-'ve-lē\ Niccolò 1469–1527 Ital. political philosopher

Mad·i·son \'ma-də-sən\ James 1751–1836 4th pres. of the U.S. (1809–17)

Ma·gel·lan \mə-'je-lən, *chiefly Brit* -'ge-\ Ferdinand *ca* 1480–1521 Portuguese navigator and explorer

Mah·ler \'mä-lər\ Gustav 1860–1911 Austrian composer

Mal·colm X \'mal-kəm-'eks\ *Malcolm Little* 1925–1965 Amer. civil rights leader

Man·dela \man-'de-lə\ Nelson Rolihlahla 1918–2013 pres. of South Africa (1994–99); Nobel Prize winner (1993)

Ma·net \ma-'nā, mä-\ Édouard 1832–1883 French painter

Mann \'man\ Horace 1796–1859 Amer. educator

Mao Tse–tung *or* Mao Zedong \'maù-(')dzə-'dùn, -(')tsə-\ 1893–1976 leader of People's Republic of China (1949–76)

Mar·co·ni \mär-'kō-nē\ Guglielmo 1874–1937 Ital. physicist and inventor; Nobel Prize winner (1909)

Marco Polo — see POLO

Ma·rie An·toi·nette \,an-twə-'net, -tə-\ 1755–1793 wife of Louis XVI of France

Mar·i·on \'mer-ē-ən\ Francis 1732?–1795 *the Swamp Fox* Amer. commander in Revolution

Mark \'märk\ evangelist believed to be the author of the 2d Gospel

Mark Antony — see ANTONY

Mar·quette \mär-'ket\ Jacques 1637–1675 *Père Marquette* French-born Jesuit missionary and explorer in America

Mars \'märz\ god of war in Roman mythology — compare ARES

Mar·shall \'mär-shəl\ George Catlett 1880–1959 Amer. general and diplomat; Nobel Prize winner (1953)

Marshall John 1755–1835 Amer. jurist; chief justice of the U.S. Supreme Court (1801–35)

Marshall Thurgood 1908–1993 Amer. jurist

Mar·tha \'mär-thə\ sister of Lazarus and Mary and friend of Jesus in the Bible

Mar·tin \'mär-tⁿn, mär-'taⁿ\ Saint 316–397 *Martin of Tours* \-'tùr\ patron saint of France

Mar·tin \'mär-tⁿn\ Paul (Edgar Phillipe) 1938–   Canad. prime minister (2003–06)

Marx \'märks\ Karl 1818–1883 Ger. political philosopher and socialist

Mary \'mer-ē, 'ma-rē, 'mā-rē\ *Saint Mary*; *Virgin Mary* mother of Jesus

Mary sister of Lazarus and Martha in the Bible

Mary I 1516–1558 *Mary Tudor*; *Bloody Mary* queen of England (1553–58)

Mary II 1662–1694 joint Brit. sovereign with William III (1689–94)

Mary Mag·da·lene \'mag-də-lən, -,lēn\ woman in the Bible who sees the risen Christ

Mary, Queen of Scots 1542–1587 *Mary Stuart* queen of Scotland (1542–67)

Mas·sa·soit \,ma-sə-'sòit\ *died* 1661 Wampanoag Indian chief

Math·er \'ma-thər, -thər\ Cotton 1663–1728 Amer. religious leader and author

Mather Increase 1639–1723 Amer. minister and author; father of Cotton Mather

Ma·tisse \ma-'tēs, mə-\ Henri 1869–1954 French painter

Mat·thew \'ma-(,)thyü\ apostle believed to be the author of the 1st Gospel

Mau·pas·sant \,mō-pə-'säⁿ\ Guy de 1850–1893 French author

Max·well \'maks-,wel, -,wəl\ James Clerk 1831–1879 Scot. physicist

Mays \'māz\ Willie Howard 1931–   Amer. baseball player

Mc·Au·liffe \mə-'kòl-əf\ Christa 1948–1986 Amer. teacher; chosen to be 1st private citizen in space (1986)

Mc·Car·thy \mə-'kär-thē\ Joseph Raymond 1908–1957 Amer. politician

Mc·Clel·lan \mə-'kle-lən\ George Brinton 1826–1885 Amer. general

Mc·Clin·tock \mə-'klin-tək\ Barbara 1902–1992 Amer. botanist; Nobel Prize winner (1983)

Mc·Cor·mick \mə-'kór-mik\ Cyrus Hall 1809–1884 Amer. inventor

Mc·Kin·ley \mə-'kin-lē\ William 1843–1901 25th pres. of the U.S. (1897–1901)

Mead \'mēd\ Margaret 1901–1978 Amer. anthropologist

Meade \'mēd\ George Gordon 1815–1872 Amer. Civil War general

Mea·ny \'mē-nē\ George 1894–1980 Amer. labor leader

Me·dea \mə-'dē-ə\ woman with magic powers in Greek mythology who helps Jason to win the Golden Fleece and who kills her children when he leaves her

Medici Catherine de' — see CATHERINE DE MÉDICIS

Me·di·ci \'me-də-chē\ Lorenzo de' 1449–1492 *Lorenzo the Magnificent* Florentine statesman, ruler, and patron of the arts

Me·du·sa \mi-'dü-sə, -'dyü-, -zə\ Gorgon in Greek mythology slain by Perseus

Me·ir \mā-'ir\ Golda 1898–1978 prime minister of Israel (1969–74)

Mel·ville \'mel-,vil\ Herman 1819–1891 Amer. author

Men·del \'men-dᵊl\ Gregor Johann 1822–1884 Austrian botanist

Men·dels·sohn (–Bar·thol·dy) \'men-dᵊl-sən(-bär-'tòl-dē, -'thòl-)\ Felix 1809–1847 Ger. composer

Men·e·la·us \,me-nə-'lā-əs\ king of Sparta, brother of Agamemnon, and husband of Helen of Troy in Greek mythology

Meph·is·toph·e·les \,me-fə-'stä-fə-,lēz\ chief devil in the Faust legend

Mer·ca·tor \(,)mər-'kā-tər\ Gerardus 1512–1594 orig. *Gerhard Kremer* Flemish cartographer

Mer·cu·ry \'mər-kyə-rē, -k(ə-)rē\ god of commerce, eloquence, travel, and theft who serves as messenger of the other gods in Roman mythology — compare HERMES

Mer·lin \'mər-lən\ prophet and magician in the legend of King Arthur

Met·a·com \'me-tə-,käm\ *or* **King Philip** *ca* 1638–1676 *Met·a·com·et* \,me-tə-'käm-ət\ Wampanoag Indian chief; son of Massasoit

Mi·chael \'mī-kəl\ archangel named in Hebrew tradition — compare GABRIEL, RAPHAEL, URIEL

Mi·chel·an·ge·lo \,mī-kə-'lan-jə-,lō, ,mi-, ,mē-kə-'län-\ 1475–1564 Ital. sculptor, painter, architect, and poet

Mi·das \'mī-dəs\ legendary king having the power to turn everything he touched into gold

Mil·lay \mi-'lā\ Edna St. Vincent 1892–1950 Amer. poet

Mil·ler \'mi-lər\ Arthur 1915–2005 Amer. playwright

Milne \'mil(n)\ A. A. 1882–1956 *Alan Alexander Milne* Eng. author

Mil·ton \'mil-tᵊn\ John 1608–1674 Eng. poet

Mi·ner·va \mə-'nər-və\ goddess of wisdom in Roman mythology — compare ATHENA

Mi·no·taur \'mi-nə-,tòr, 'mī-\ monster in Greek mythology shaped half like a man and half like a bull

Min·u·it \'min-yə-wət\ Peter *ca* 1580–1638 Dutch colonial administrator in America

Mitch·ell \'mi-chəl\ Maria 1818–1889 Amer. astronomer

Mo·lière \mōl-'yer, 'mōl-,\ 1622–1673 orig. *Jean-Baptiste Poquelin* French actor and playwright

Mo·net \mō-'nā\ Claude 1840–1926 French painter

Mon·roe \mən-'rō\ James 1758–1831 5th pres. of the U.S. (1817–25)

Mont·calm \mänt-'kälm-, -'käm-\ Marquis de 1712–1759 *Louis-Joseph de Montcalm-Grozon* French field marshal in Canada

Mon·tes·so·ri \,män-tə-'sòr-ē\ Maria 1870–1952 Ital. educator

Mon·te·ver·di \,män-tə-'ver-dē, -'vər-\ Claudio 1567–1643 Ital. composer

Mon·te·zu·ma II \,män-tə-'zü-mə\ 1466–1520 last Aztec emperor of Mexico (1502–20)

Moore \'mòr, 'mùr\ Marianne 1887–1972 Amer. poet

More \'mòr\ Sir Thomas 1478–1535 *Saint Thomas More* Eng. public official and author

Mor·gan \'mòr-gən\ J. P. 1837–1913 *John Pierpont Morgan* Amer. financier

Mor·ri·son \'mòr-ə-sən, 'mär-\ Toni 1931–   orig. *Chloe Anthony Wofford* Amer. author; Nobel Prize winner (1993)

Morse \'mòrs\ Samuel Finley Breese 1791–1872 Amer. artist and inventor

Mo·ses \'mō-zəz\ Hebrew prophet and lawgiver in the Bible

Moses Grandma 1860–1961 *Anna Mary Moses* née *Robertson* Amer. painter

Mott \'mät\ Lucretia 1793–1880 Amer. reformer

Mo·zart \'mōt-,särt\ Wolfgang Amadeus 1756–1791 Austrian composer

Mu·ham·mad \mō-'ha-məd, -'hä-\ *ca* 570–632 A.D. Arab prophet and founder of Islam

Mun·ro \(,)mən-'rō\ Alice 1931–   née *Laidlaw* Canadian writer; Nobel Prize Winner (2013)

Mur·row \'mər-(,)ō, 'mə-(,)rō\ Edward Roscoe 1908–1965 Amer. journalist

Mus·so·li·ni \,mü-sə-'lē-nē, ,mú-\ Be·ni·to \bə-'nēt-ō\ 1883–1945 *Il Du·ce* \ēl-'dü-chā\ Ital. fascist premier (1922–43)

Na·bo·kov \nə-'bò-kəf\ Vladimir 1899–1977 Amer. (Russ.-born) author

Na·po·le·on I \nə-'pōl-yən, -'pō-lē-ən\ *or* **Napoleon Bo·na·parte** \'bō-nə-,pärt\ 1769–1821 French general and emperor of the French (1804–15)

Nar·cis·sus \när-'si-səs\ beautiful youth in Greek mythology who pines away for love of his own reflection and is then turned into the narcissus flower

Nash \'nash\ Ogden 1902–1971 Amer. poet
Na·tion \'nā-shən\ Car·ry \'kar-ē\ Amelia 1846–1911 née *Moore* Amer. temperance agitator
Nav·ra·ti·lo·va \ˌnav-rə-tə-'lō-və\ Martina 1956–   Amer. (Czech-born) tennis player
Neb·u·cha·drez·zar II \ˌne-byə-kə-'dre-zər, -bə-\ *or* Neb·u·chad·nez·zar \-kəd-'ne-\ *ca* 630–*ca* 561 B.C. Chaldean king of Babylon (605–562)
Neh·ru \'ner-(ˌ)ü, 'nā-(ˌ)rü\ Ja·wa·har·lal \jə-'wä-hər-ˌläl\ 1889–1964 1st prime minister of Republic of India (1947–64)
Nel·son \'nel-sən\ Horatio 1758–1805 Viscount *Nelson* Brit. admiral
Nem·e·sis \'ne-mə-səs\ goddess of reward and punishment in Greek mythology
Nep·tune \'nep-ˌtün, -ˌtyün\ god of the sea in Roman mythology — compare POSEIDON
Ne·ro \'nē-(ˌ)rō, 'nir-(ˌ)ō\ 37–68 A.D. Roman emperor (54–68)
Ne·ru·da \nä-'rü-də, -(ˌ)thä\ Pablo 1904–1973 orig. *Neftalí Ricardo Reyes Basoalto* Chilean poet
Nev·el·son \'ne-vəl-sən\ Louise 1900?–1988 Amer. sculptor
New·ton \'nü-tᵊn, 'nyü-\ Sir Isaac 1642–1727 Eng. mathematician and physicist
Nich·o·las \'ni-k(ə-)ləs\ Saint *fl.* 4th cent. A.D. Christian bishop
Nicholas I 1796–1855 czar of Russia (1825–55)
Nicholas II 1868–1918 last czar of Russia (1894–1917)
Nietz·sche \'nē-chə, -chē\ Friedrich Wilhelm 1844–1900 Ger. philosopher
Night·in·gale \'nī-tᵊn-ˌgāl, -tiŋ-\ Florence 1820–1910 *Lady of the Lamp* Eng. nurse and philanthropist
Ni·ke \'nī-kē\ goddess of victory in Greek mythology
Ni·o·be \'nī-ə-bē\ bereaved mother in Greek mythology who while weeping for her slain children is turned into a stone from which her tears continue to flow
Nix·on \'nik-sən\ Richard Milhous 1913–1994 37th pres. of the U.S. (1969–74)
No·ah \'nō-ə\ biblical builder of the ark in which he, his family, and living creatures of every kind survive the biblical Flood
No·bel \nō-'bel\ Alfred Bernhard 1833–1896 Swedish manufacturer, inventor, and philanthropist
Oak·ley \'ōk-lē\ Annie 1860–1926 orig. *Phoebe Anne Oakley Moses* Amer. sharpshooter
Oba·ma \ō-'bä-mə\ Ba·rack \bə-'räk\ Hussein, Jr. 1961–   44th pres. of the U.S. (2009–17); Nobel Prize winner (2009)
Oce·anus \ō-'sē-ə-nəs\ Titan who rules over a great river encircling the earth in Greek mythology
O'·Con·nor \ō-'kä-nər\ (Mary) Flannery 1925–1964 Amer. author
O'Connor Sandra Day 1930–   Amer. jurist
Odin \'ō-dᵊn\ *or* Wo·den \'wō-dᵊn\ chief god, god of war, and patron of heroes in Norse mythology
Odys·seus \ō-'di-sē-əs, -'dis-yəs, -'di-shəs, -'di-ˌshüs\ *or* Ulys·ses \yù-'li-(ˌ)sēz\ king of Ithaca and hero in Greek mythology
Oe·di·pus \'e-də-pəs, 'ē-\ son of Laius and Jocasta who in Greek mythology kills his father and marries his mother not knowing their identity
Ogle·thorpe \'ō-gəl-ˌthȯrp\ James Edward 1696–1785 Eng. general and founder of Georgia
O'·Keeffe \ō-'kēf\ Georgia 1887–1986 Amer. painter
Olaf V \'ō-ləf, -läf, -laf; 'ü-läf\ 1903–1991 king of Norway (1957–91)
Omar Khay·yám \ˌō-ˌmär-ˌkī-'yäm, ˌō-mər-, -'yam\ 1048–1131 Persian poet and astronomer
O'·Neill \ō-'nēl\ Eugene Gladstone 1888–1953 Amer. playwright; Nobel Prize winner (1936)
Or·pheus \'ȯr-ˌfyüs, -fē-əs\ poet and musician in Greek mythology
Or·well \'ȯr-ˌwel, -wəl\ George 1903–1950 pseud. of *Eric Arthur Blair* Eng. author
Osce·o·la \ˌä-sē-'ō-lə, ˌō-\ *ca* 1804–1838 Seminole Indian chief
Otis \'ō-təs\ James 1725–1783 Amer. Revolutionary patriot
Ov·id \'ä-vəd\ 43 B.C.–17 A.D.? Roman poet
Ow·en \'ō-ən\ Robert 1771–1858 Welsh social reformer

Ow·ens \'ō-ənz\ Jesse 1913–1980 orig. *James Cleveland Owens* Amer. track-and-field athlete
Paine \'pān\ Thomas 1737–1809 Amer. (Eng.-born) political philosopher and author
Pan \'pan\ god of pastures, flocks, and shepherds in Greek mythology who is usu. represented as being part goat
Pan·do·ra \pan-'dȯr-ə\ woman in Greek mythology who out of curiosity opens a box and lets loose all of the evils that trouble humans
Pank·hurst \'paŋk-ˌhərst\ Emmeline 1858–1928 née *Goulden* Eng. suffragist
Par·is \'pa-rəs\ son of Priam whose abduction of Helen of Troy in Greek mythology leads to the Trojan War
Park·man \'pärk-mən\ Francis 1823–1893 Amer. historian
Parks \'pärks\ Rosa 1913–2005 née *McCauley* Amer. civil rights activist
Pas·cal \pa-'skal, päs-'käl\ Blaise 1623–1662 French mathematician and philosopher
Pas·ter·nak \'pas-tər-ˌnak\ Boris Leonidovich 1890–1960 Russ. author; Nobel Prize winner (1958)
Pas·teur \pas-'tər\ Louis 1822–1895 French chemist and microbiologist
Pat·rick \'pa-trik\ Saint *fl.* 5th cent. A.D. apostle and patron saint of Ireland
Pat·ton \'pa-tᵊn\ George Smith 1885–1945 Amer. general
Paul \'pȯl\ Saint *died ca.* 67 A.D. Christian missionary and author of several New Testament epistles
Paul name of 6 popes: esp. III 1468–1549 (pope 1534–49); V 1552–1621 (pope 1605–21); VI 1897–1978 (pope 1963–78)
Paul Bun·yan \'bən-yən\ giant lumberjack in Amer. folklore
Pau·ling \'pȯ-liŋ\ Linus Carl 1901–1994 Amer. chemist; Nobel Prize winner (1954, 1962)
Pav·lov \'päv-ˌlȯf, 'pav-, -ˌlȯv\ Ivan Petrovich 1849–1936 Russ. physiologist; Nobel Prize winner (1904)
Pav·lo·va \'pav-lə-və, pav-'lō-\ Anna 1881–1931 Russ. ballerina
Pea·ry \'pir-ē\ Robert Edwin 1856–1920 Amer. arctic explorer
Peg·a·sus \'pe-gə-səs\ winged horse in Greek mythology
Pei \'pā\ Ieoh Ming 1917–   Amer. (Chinese-born) architect
Pence \'pens\ Mike 1959–   *Michael Richard Pence* vice pres. of the U.S. (2017–   )
Penn \'pen\ William 1644–1718 Eng. Quaker leader and founder of Pennsylvania
Per·i·cles \'per-ə-ˌklēz\ *ca* 495–429 B.C. Athenian political leader
Per·ry \'per-ē\ Matthew Calbraith 1794–1858 Amer. commodore
Per·seph·o·ne \pər-'se-fə-nē\ daughter of Zeus and Demeter who in Greek mythology is abducted by Pluto to rule with him over the underworld
Per·shing \'pər-shiŋ, -zhiŋ\ John Joseph 1860–1948 Amer. general
Pe·ter \'pē-tər\ Saint *died ca.* 64 A.D. orig. *Si·mon* \'sī-mən\ one of the 12 apostles in the Bible
Peter I 1672–1725 *Peter the Great* czar of Russia (1682–1725)
Phil·ip \'fi-ləp\ Saint, one of the 12 apostles in the Bible
Philip King — see METACOM
Philip name of 6 kings of France: esp. II *or* Philip Augus·tus 1165–1223 (r. 1179–1223); IV 1268–1314 *Philip the Fair* (r. 1285–1314); VI 1293–1350 (r. 1328–50)
Philip name of 5 kings of Spain: esp. II 1527–1598 (r. 1556–98); V 1683–1746 (r. 1700–46)
Philip II 382–336 B.C. king of Macedon (359–336); father of Alexander the Great
Pi·cas·so \pi-'kä-(ˌ)sō, -'ka-\ Pablo 1881–1973 Span. painter and sculptor in France
Pic·card \pi-'kär, -'kärd\ Auguste 1884–1962 and his son Jacques 1922–2008 Swiss scientists and developers of the bathyscaphe
Pick·ett \'pi-kət\ George Edward 1825–1875 Amer. Confederate general
Pierce \'pirs\ Franklin 1804–1869 14th pres. of the U.S. (1853–57)
Pi·late \'pī-lət\ Pon·tius \'pän-chəs, 'pən-chəs\ *died after* 36 A.D. Roman governor of Judea (26–36)

Biographical Names

608

Pinkerton \'piŋ-kər-t°n\ Allan 1819–1884 Amer. (Scot.‐born) detective

Pis·sar·ro \pə-'sär-(ˌ)ō\ Camille 1830–1903 French (West Indian-born) painter

Pitt \'pit\ William 1759–1806 *the Younger Pitt* Eng. prime minister (1783–1801; 1804–6)

Pi·us \'pī-əs\ name of 12 popes: esp. **VII** 1742–1823 (pope 1800–23); **IX** 1792–1878 (pope 1846–78); **X** Saint 1835–1914 (pope 1903–14); **XI** 1857–1939 (pope 1922–39); **XII** 1876–1958 (pope 1939–58)

Pi·zar·ro \pə-'zär-(ˌ)ō\ Francisco *ca* 1475–1541 Span. conqueror of Peru

Planck \'pläŋk\ Max Karl Ernst Ludwig 1858–1947 Ger. physicist

Pla·to \'plā-(ˌ)tō\ *ca* 428–348 (*or* 347) B.C. Greek philosopher

Plu·to \'plü-(ˌ)tō\ god of the underworld in Greek mythology

Po·ca·hon·tas \ˌpō-kə-'hän-təs\ *ca* 1595–1617 Amer. Indian friend of the colonists at Jamestown; daughter of Powhatan

Poe \'pō\ Edgar Allan 1809–1849 Amer. author

Polk \'pōk\ James Knox 1795–1849 11th pres. of the U.S. (1845–49)

Pol·lock \'pä-lək\ (Paul) Jackson 1912–1956 Amer. painter

Po·lo \'pō-(ˌ)lō\ Marco *ca* 1254–1324 Venetian merchant and traveler

Poly·phe·mus \ˌpä-lə-'fē-məs\ a one-eyed creature in Greek mythology that is blinded by Odysseus

Ponce de Le·ón \ˌpän(t)-sə-ˌdā-lē-'ōn, ˌpänts-də-, -'lē-ən\ Juan 1460–1521 Span. explorer

Pon·ti·ac \'pän-tē-ˌak\ *ca* 1720–1769 Ottawa Indian chief

Por·ter \'pȯr-tər\ Cole Albert 1891–1964 Amer. composer

Porter Katherine Anne 1890–1980 Amer. author

Porter William Sydney — see O. HENRY

Po·sei·don \pə-'sī-d°n\ god of the sea in Greek mythology — compare NEPTUNE

Pot·ter \'pä-tər\ (Helen) Beatrix 1866–1943 Brit. author and illustrator

Pound \'paùnd\ Ezra Loomis 1885–1972 Amer. poet

Pound·mak·er \'paùnd-ˌmā-kər\ 1826–1886 Cree Indian chief

Pow·ell \'paù(-ə)l\ Colin Luther 1937– Amer. general; U.S. secretary of state (2001–05)

Pow·ha·tan \ˌpaù-ə-'tan, paù-'ha-t°n\ 1550?–1618 Amer. Indian chief of a confederacy of Algonquian-speaking tribes; father of Pocahontas

Pres·ley \'pres-lē, 'prez-\ Elvis Aaron 1935–1977 Amer. popular singer

Pri·am \'prī-əm, -ˌam\ king of Troy during the Trojan War in Greek mythology

Price \'prīs\ (Mary) Leontyne 1927– Amer. soprano

Pro·me·theus \prə-'mē-thē-əs, -ˌthyüs\ Titan in Greek mythology who is punished by Zeus for stealing fire from heaven and giving it to humans

Pro·teus \'prō-tyüs, -tē-əs\ sea god in Greek mythology who is capable of assuming different forms

Proust \'prüst\ Marcel 1871–1922 French novelist

Ptol·e·my \'tä-lə-mē\ *fl.* 2d cent. A.D. Greco-Egyptian astronomer, geographer, and mathematician in Alexandria

Puc·ci·ni \pü-'chē-nē\ Giacomo 1858–1924 Ital. composer

Pu·las·ki \pə-'las-kē, pyü-\ Kazimierz 1747–1779 Polish soldier in Amer. Revolutionary army

Pu·lit·zer \'pù-lət-sər *(family's pron)*, 'pyü-\ Joseph 1847–1911 Amer. (Hungarian-born) journalist

Pu·tin \'pü-tin\ Vladimir Vladimirovich 1952– pres. of Russia (2000–08; 2012–)

Pyg·ma·lion \pig-'māl-yən, -'mā-lē-ən\ sculptor in Greek mythology who creates Galatea

Py·thag·o·ras \pə-'tha-gə-rəs, pī-\ *ca* 580–*ca* 500 B.C. Greek philosopher and mathematician

Ra \'rä\ god of the sun and chief deity of ancient Egypt

Ra·leigh *or* **Ra·legh** \'rȯ-lē, 'rä- *also* 'ra-\ Sir Walter 1554?–1618 Eng. navigator and courtier

Ram·ses \'ram-ˌsēz\ *or* **Ram·e·ses** \'ra-mə-ˌsēz\ name of 12 kings of Egypt: esp. **II** (r. 1279–1213 B.C.); **III** (r. 1187–1156 B.C.)

Ran·dolph \'ran-ˌdälf\ Asa Philip 1889–1979 Amer. labor and civil rights leader

Ra·pha·el \'ra-fē-əl, 'rä-, -ˌel\ archangel named in Hebrew tradition — compare GABRIEL, MICHAEL, URIEL

Ra·pha·el \'ra-fē-əl, 'rä-, 'rä-\ 1483–1520 orig. *Raffaello Sanzio* or *Santi* Ital. painter

Ras·pu·tin \ra-'spyü-t°n, -'spü-, -'spù-\ Grigory Yefimovich 1872–1916 Russ. mystic

Ra·vel \rä-'vel, ra-\ Joseph Maurice 1875–1937 French composer

Rea·gan \'rā-gən\ Ronald Wilson 1911–2004 40th pres. of the U.S. (1981–89)

Re·bek·ah \ri-'be-kə\ wife of Isaac and mother of Jacob in the Bible

Red Cloud \'red-ˌklaùd\ 1822–1909 Sioux Indian chief

Red Jack·et \'red-ˌja-kət\ 1758?–1830 *Sa·go·ye·wa·tha* \sä-ˌgȯi-(y)ə-'wä-thə\ Seneca Indian chief

Reed \'rēd\ Walter 1851–1902 Amer. army surgeon

Rehn·quist \'ren-ˌkwist, 'reṇ-kwəst\ William Hubbs 1924–2005 Amer. jurist; chief justice of the U.S. Supreme Court (1986–2005)

Rem·brandt \'rem-ˌbrant *also* -ˌbränt\ 1606–1669 *Rembrandt (Harmenszoon) van Rijn* Dutch painter

Rem·ing·ton \'re-miṇ-tən\ Frederic 1861–1909 Amer. painter and sculptor

Re·mus \'rē-məs\ son of Mars who in Roman mythology is killed by his twin brother Romulus

Re·noir \'ren-ˌwär, rən-'\ (Pierre-) Auguste 1841–1919 French painter

Re·vere \ri-'vir\ Paul 1735–1818 Amer. patriot and silversmith

Rich·ard \'ri-chərd\ name of 3 kings of England: **I** 1157–1199 *Richard the Lion-Hearted* (r. 1189–99); **II** 1367–1400 (r. 1377–99); **III** 1452–1485 (r. 1483–85)

Ride \'rīd\ Sally Kristen 1951–2012 Amer. astronaut; 1st Amer. woman in space (1983)

Rob·erts \'rä-bərts\ John Glover Jr. 1995– Amer. jurist; chief justice of the U.S. Supreme Court (2005–)

Rob·in Good·fel·low \'rä-bən-'gùd-ˌfe-(ˌ)lō\ mischievous elf in Eng. folklore

Robin Hood \ˌhùd\ legendary Eng. outlaw who gave to the poor what he stole from the rich

Rob·in·son \'rä-bən-sən\ Edwin Arlington 1869–1935 Amer. poet

Robinson Jackie 1919–1972 *Jack Roosevelt Robinson* Amer. baseball player

Rob·in·son Cru·soe \'rä-bə(n)-sən-'krü-(ˌ)sō\ shipwrecked sailor in Daniel Defoe's *Robinson Crusoe* who lives for many years on a desert island

Ro·cham·beau \ˌrō-ˌsham-'bō\ Comte de 1725–1807 French general in Amer. Revolution

Rocke·fel·ler \'rä-ki-ˌfe-lər\ John Davison 1839–1937 and his son John Davison, Jr. 1874–1960 Amer. oil magnates and philanthropists

Ro·din \'rō-ˌda°(n)\ François-Auguste-René 1840–1917 French sculptor

Ro·ma·nov \rō-'mä-nəf, 'rō-mə-ˌnäf\ Michael 1596–1645 1st czar (1613–45) of Russ. Romanov dynasty (1613–1917)

Rom·u·lus \'räm-yə-ləs\ son of Mars in Roman mythology who is the twin brother of Remus and the founder of Rome

Rönt·gen *or* **Roent·gen** \'rent-gən, 'rənt-, -jən\ Wilhelm Conrad 1845–1923 Ger. physicist; Nobel Prize winner (1901)

Roo·se·velt \'rō-zə-vəlt, -ˌvelt\ (Anna) Eleanor 1884–1962 Amer. lecturer and writer; wife of F. D. Roosevelt

Roosevelt Franklin Delano 1882–1945 32nd pres. of the U.S. (1933–45)

Roosevelt Theodore 1858–1919 26th pres. of the U.S. (1901–09); Nobel Prize winner (1906)

Ross \'rȯs\ Betsy 1752–1836 née *Griscom* reputed maker of 1st Amer. flag

Ros·si·ni \rȯ-'sē-nē, rə-\ Gioacchino Antonio 1792–1868 Ital. composer

Roth \'rȯth\ Philip Milton 1933–2018 Amer. author

Rous·seau \rù-'sō, 'rü-\ Jean-Jacques 1712–1778 French (Swiss-born) philosopher and writer

Rowl·ing \'rō-liŋ\ J. K. 1965– *Joanne Kathleen Rowling* Brit. author

Ru·bens \'rü-bənz\ Peter Paul 1577–1640 Flemish painter

Ru·dolph \'rü-ˌdȯlf, -ˌdälf\ Wilma Glodean 1940–1994 Amer. athlete

Rus·sell \'rə-səl\ Bertrand Arthur William 1872–1970 3d Earl *Russell* Eng. mathematician and philosopher; Nobel Prize winner (1950)

Ruth \\'rüth\ woman in the Bible who was one of the ancestors of King David

Ruth Babe 1895–1948 *George Herman Ruth* Amer. baseball player

Ruth·er·ford \\'rə-t͟hə(r)-fərd, -t͟hə(r)-\ Ernest 1871–1937 Baron *Rutherford* Brit. physicist; Nobel Prize winner (1908)

Sa·bin \\'sā-bin\ Albert Bruce 1906–1993 Amer. (Polish-born) physician and microbiologist

Sac·a·ga·wea \ˌsa-kə-jə-'wē-ə\ 1786?–1812 Shoshone Indian guide to Lewis and Clark

Sa·dat \sə-'dat, -'dät\ Anwar el- 1918–1981 pres. of Egypt (1970–81); Nobel Prize winner (1978)

Sa·gan \\'sā-gən\ Carl Edward 1934–1996 Amer. astronomer and science writer

Saint Nicholas — see Saint NICHOLAS, SANTA CLAUS

Sal·a·din \\'sa-lə-ˌdēn, -dən\ 1137 (or 1138)–1193 Kurdish general; sultan of Egypt and Syria

Sal·in·ger \\'sa-lən-jər\ J. D. 1919–2010 *Jerome David Salinger* Amer. author

Salk \\'sö(l)k\ Jonas Edward 1914–1995 Amer. physician and medical researcher

Sa·lo·me \sə-'lō-mē, 'sa-lə-(ˌ)mā\ niece of Herod Antipas who in the Bible is given the head of John the Baptist as a reward for her dancing

Sa·mo·set \\'sa-mə-ˌset, sə-'mä-sət\ *died ca.* 1653 Abenaki leader

Sam·son \\'sam(p)-sən\ powerful Hebrew hero in the Bible who fights against the Philistines but is betrayed by Delilah

Sam·u·el \\'sam-yə-wəl, -yəl\ Hebrew judge in the Bible who appoints Saul and then David king

Sand·burg \\'san(d)-ˌbərg\ Carl 1878–1967 Amer. author

Sang·er \\'saŋ-ər\ Margaret 1883–1966 née *Higgins* Amer. birth-control activist

San·ta Claus \\'san-tə-ˌklöz\ plump white-bearded and red-suited old man in modern folklore who delivers presents to good children at Christmastime

Sap·pho \\'sa-(ˌ)fō\ *fl. ca* 610–*ca* 580 B.C. Greek poet

Sa·rah \\'ser-ə, 'sā-rə\ wife of Abraham and mother of Isaac in the Bible

Sar·gent \\'sär-jənt\ John Singer 1856–1925 Amer. painter

Sar·tre \\'särtrᵊ\ Jean-Paul 1905–1980 French philosopher and author

Sat·urn \\'sa-tərn\ god of agriculture in Roman mythology

Saul \\'söl, 'säl\ 1st king of Israel in the Bible

Saul *or* **Saul of Tarsus** the apostle Paul in the Bible

Sche·her·a·zade \shə-ˌher-ə-'zäd\ fictional wife of a sultan and narrator of the tales in the *Arabian Nights' Entertainments*

Schin·dler \\'shind-lər\ Oskar 1908–1974 Ger. humanitarian during the Holocaust

Schoen·berg \\'shə(r)n-ˌbərg, 'shœn-ˌberk\ Arnold Franz Walter 1874–1951 Amer. (Austrian-born) composer

Schu·bert \\'shü-bərt, -ˌbert\ Franz Peter 1797–1828 Austrian composer

Schu·mann \\'shü-ˌmän, -mən\ Clara 1819–1896 née *Wieck* \\'vēk\ Ger. pianist; wife of R. Schumann

Schumann Robert Alexander 1810–1856 Ger. composer

Schweit·zer \\'shwīt-sər, 'shvīt-, 'swīt-\ Albert 1875–1965 French theologian, philosopher, physician, and music scholar; Nobel Prize winner (1952)

Scott \\'skät\ Dred \\'dred\ 1795?–1858 Amer. slave

Scott Robert Falcon 1868–1912 Brit. polar explorer

Scott Sir Walter 1771–1832 Scot. author

Scott Winfield 1786–1866 Amer. general

Scyl·la \\'si-lə\ nymph in Greek mythology who is changed into a monster and inhabits a cave opposite the whirlpool Charybdis off the coast of Sicily

Se·at·tle \sē-'a-tᵊl\ 1786?–1866 Amer. Indian chief

Se·le·ne \sə-'lē-nē\ goddess of the moon in classical mythology

Se·quoy·ah *or* **Se·quoia** \si-'kwòi-ə\ *ca* 1760–1843 *George Guess* Cherokee Indian scholar

Ser·ra \\'ser-ə\ Junípero 1713–1784 Span. missionary in Mexico and California

Se·ton \\'sē-tᵊn\ Saint Elizabeth Ann 1774–1821 *Mother Seton* née *Bayley* Amer. religious leader

Seu·rat \sə-'rä\ Georges 1859–1891 French painter

Seuss Dr. — see GEISEL, THEODOR SEUSS

Sew·ard \\'sü-ərd, 'sùrd\ William Henry 1801–1872 Amer. politician; U.S. secretary of state (1861–69)

Shack·le·ton \\'sha-kəl-tən\ Sir Ernest Henry 1874–1922 Brit. polar explorer

Shake·speare \\'shāk-ˌspir\ William 1564–1616 Eng. playwright and poet

Shaw \\'shò\ George Bernard 1856–1950 Brit. playwright; Nobel Prize winner (1925)

Shaw Robert Gould 1837–1863 Amer. soldier

Shel·ley \\'she-lē\ Mary Wollstonecraft 1797–1851 née *Godwin* Eng. author; wife of P. B. Shelley

Shelley Percy Bysshe \\'bish\ 1792–1822 Eng. poet

Shep·ard \\'she-pərd\ Alan Bartlett, Jr. 1923–1998 Amer. astronaut; 1st Amer. in space (1961)

Sher·i·dan \\'sher-ə-dən\ Philip Henry 1831–1888 Amer. general

Sher·lock Holmes \\'shər-ˌläk-'hōmz, -'hōlmz\ detective in stories by Sir Arthur Conan Doyle

Sher·man \\'shər-mən\ John 1823–1900 Amer. statesman; brother of W. T. Sherman

Sherman William Tecumseh 1820–1891 Amer. general

Shi·va \\'shi-və, 'shē-\ *or* **Si·va** \\'si-və, 'shi-, 'sē-, 'shē-\ god of destruction and regeneration in the Hindu sacred triad — compare BRAHMA, VISHNU

Sieg·fried \\'sig-ˌfrēd, 'sēg-\ hero in Germanic legend who kills a dragon guarding a gold hoard

Si·mon \\'sī-mən\ *or* **Simon the Zealot** one of the 12 apostles in the Bible

Si·na·tra \sə-'nä-trə\ Frank 1915–1998 *Francis Albert Sinatra* Amer. singer and actor

Sind·bad the Sailor \\'sin-ˌbad\ citizen of Baghdad whose adventures are narrated in the *Arabian Nights' Entertainments*

Sis·y·phus \\'si-sə-fəs\ king of Corinth who in Greek mythology is condemned to roll a heavy stone up a hill in Hades only to have it roll down again as it nears the top

Sit·ting Bull \ˌsi-tiŋ-'bùl\ *ca* 1831–1890 Sioux Indian chief

Siva — see SHIVA

Smith \\'smith\ Adam 1723–1790 Scot. economist

Smith Bessie 1894?–1937 Amer. blues singer

Smith John *ca* 1580–1631 Eng. colonist in America

Smith Joseph 1805–1844 Amer. founder of the Mormon Church

Soc·ra·tes \\'sä-krə-ˌtēz\ *ca* 470–399 B.C. Greek philosopher

Sol \\'säl\ god of the sun in Roman mythology — see HELIOS

Sol·o·mon \\'sä-lə-mən\ 10th-century B.C. king of Israel noted for his wisdom

Sond·heim \\'sänd-(ˌ)hīm\ Stephen Joshua 1930– Amer. composer and songwriter

Soph·o·cles \\'sä-fə-ˌklēz\ *ca* 496–406 B.C. Greek playwright

Sou·sa \\'sü-zə, 'sü-sə\ John Philip 1854–1932 Amer. bandmaster and composer

Spar·ta·cus \\'spär-tə-kəs\ *died* 71 B.C. Roman slave and gladiator

Sphinx \\'sfiŋ(k)s\ monster in Greek mythology having a lion's body, wings, and the head and bust of a woman

Spiel·berg \\'spēl-ˌbərg\ Steven 1947– Amer. filmmaker

Spi·no·za \spi-'nō-zə\ Benedict de 1632–1677 Hebrew *Baruch Spinoza* Dutch philosopher

Squan·to \\'skwän-tō\ *died* 1622 Amer. Indian friend of the Pilgrims

Sta·lin \\'stä-lən, 'sta-, -ˌlēn\ Joseph 1879–1953 Soviet Communist party leader (1922–53), premier (1941–53), and dictator

Stan·dish \\'stan-dish\ Myles *or* Miles 1584?–1656 Amer. colonist

Stan·ley \\'stan-lē\ Sir Henry Morton 1841–1904 Brit. explorer in Africa

Stan·ton \\'stan-tᵊn\ Elizabeth Cady 1815–1902 Amer. suffragist

Stein \\'stīn\ Gertrude 1874–1946 Amer. author

Stein·beck \\'stīn-ˌbek\ John Ernst 1902–1968 Amer. author; Nobel Prize winner (1962)

Steu·ben \\'stü-bən, 'styü-, 'shtöi-\ Friedrich Wilhelm von 1730–1794 Prussian-born general in Amer. Revolution

Ste·vens \\'stē-vənz\ Wallace 1879–1955 Amer. poet

Ste·ven·son \\'stē-vən-sən\ Adlai Ewing 1900–1965 Amer. politician

Stevenson Robert Louis 1850–1894 Scot. author

Sto·ker \'stō-kər\ Bram 1847–1912 *Abraham Stoker* Irish author

Stowe \'stō\ Harriet Beecher 1811–1896 Amer. author

Stra·di·va·ri \ˌstra-də-'vär-ē, -'ver-\ Antonio 1644?–1737 Ital. violin maker

Strauss \'shtraùs, 'straùs\ Johann 1804–1849 and his sons Johann, Jr. 1825–1899 and Josef 1827–1870 Austrian composers

Strauss Richard 1864–1949 Ger. composer

Stra·vin·sky \strə-'vin(t)-skē\ Igor 1882–1971 Amer. (Russ.-born) composer

Stu·art \'stü-ərt, 'styü-; 'st(y)ùrt\ Charles Edward 1720–1788 *the Young Pretender; Bonnie Prince Charlie* claimant to the Brit. throne

Stuart Gilbert Charles 1755–1828 Amer. painter

Stuart Jeb 1833–1864 *James Ewell Brown Stuart* Amer. Confederate general

Stuy·ve·sant \'stī-və-sənt\ Peter *ca* 1610–1672 Dutch colonial administrator in America

Sul·li·van \'sə-lə-vən\ Sir Arthur Seymour 1842–1900 Eng. composer; collaborator with Sir William Gilbert

Sullivan Louis Henri 1856–1924 Amer. architect

Sum·ner \'səm-nər\ Charles 1811–1874 Amer. politician

Sun Yat–sen \'sùn-'yät-'sen\ 1866–1925 Chinese statesman

Sut·ter \'sə-tər, 'sü-\ John Augustus 1803–1880 Amer. (Ger.-born) pioneer in California

Swift \'swift\ Jonathan 1667–1745 Eng. (Irish-born) author

Synge \'siŋ\ John Millington 1871–1909 Irish playwright

Taft \'taft\ William Howard 1857–1930 27th pres. of the U.S. (1909–13); chief justice of the U.S. Supreme Court (1921–30)

Ta·gore \tə-'gór\ Ra·bin·dra·nath \rə-'bin-drə-ˌnät\ 1861–1941 Indian poet; Nobel Prize winner (1913)

Tall·chief \'tól-ˌchēf\ Maria 1925–2013 Amer. dancer

Tan \'tan\ Amy 1952– Amer. author

Ta·ney \'tò-nē\ Roger Brooke 1777–1864 Amer. jurist; chief justice of the U.S. Supreme Court (1836–64)

Tan·ta·lus \'tan-tə-ləs\ king in Greek mythology who is condemned to stand up to his chin in a pool of water in Hades and beneath fruit-laden boughs only to have the water or fruit go out of reach at each attempt to drink or eat

Tay·lor \'tā-lər\ Zachary 1784–1850 Amer. general; 12th pres. of the U.S. (1849–50)

Tchai·kov·sky \chī-'kóf-skē, chə-, -'kóv-\ Pyotr Ilich 1840–1893 Russ. composer

Te·cum·seh \tə-'kəm(p)-sə, -sē\ 1768–1813 Shawnee Indian chief

Tek·a·kwitha \ˌte-kə-'kwi-thə\ Kateri 1656–1680 *Lily of the Mohawks* canonized Mohawk Indian religious

Ten·ny·son \'te-nə-sən\ Alfred 1809–1892 Baron *Tennyson* known as *Alfred, Lord Tennyson* Eng. poet

Te·re·sa \tə-'rā-zə, -'rē-sə\ Mother 1910–1997 beatified Albanian religious in India; Nobel Prize winner (1979)

Teresa of Ávi·la \'ä-vi-lə\ Saint 1515–1582 Span. nun and mystic

Tes·la \'tes-lə\ Nikola 1856–1943 Amer. (Croatian-born) electrical engineer and inventor

Thatch·er \'tha-chər\ Margaret Hilda 1925–2013 Baroness *Thatcher of Kesteven* née *Roberts* Brit. prime minister (1979–90)

The·seus \'thē-ˌsüs, -sē-əs\ hero in Greek mythology who kills the Minotaur and conquers the Amazons

Thom·as \'tä-məs\ apostle in the Bible who demanded proof of Jesus' resurrection

Thomas à Becket — see Saint Thomas BECKET

Thomas Aquinas Saint — see AQUINAS

Thor \'thór\ god of thunder, weather, and crops in Norse mythology

Tho·reau \thə-'rō, thò-\ Henry David 1817–1862 Amer. author

Thorpe \'thórp\ Jim 1888–1953 *James Francis Thorpe* Amer. athlete

Thur·ber \'thər-bər\ James Grover 1894–1961 Amer. author

Ti·be·ri·us \tī-'bir-ē-əs\ 42 B.C.–37 A.D. Roman emperor (14–37)

Ti·tian \'ti-shən\ *ca* 1488–1576 orig. *Tiziano Vecellio* Ital. painter

Tocque·ville \'tōk-ˌvil, 'tòk-, 'täk-, -ˌvēl, -vəl\ Alexis de 1805–1859 French politician and author

Tol·kien \'tòl-ˌkēn\ J. R. R. 1892–1973 *John Ronald Reuel Tolkien* Brit. author

Tol·stoy \tòl-'stòi, tōl-', täl-', 'tòl-ˌ, 'tōl-ˌ, 'täl-ˌ\ Leo 1828–1910 Count *Lev Nikolayevich Tolstoy* Russ. author

Tou·louse–Lau·trec \tü-ˌlüz-lō-'trek\ Henri de 1864–1901 French painter

Tri·ton \'trī-tᵊn\ sea god in Greek mythology who is half man and half fish

Trots·ky \'trät-skē\ Leon 1879–1940 orig. *Lev Davidovich Bronstein* Russ. Communist leader

Tru·deau \'trü-(ˌ)dō, trü-'\ Justin (Pierre James) 1971– Canad. prime minister (2015–)

Trudeau Pierre Elliott 1919–2000 Canad. prime minister (1968–79, 1980–84)

Tru·man \'trü-mən\ Harry S. 1884–1972 33rd pres. of the U.S. (1945–53)

Trump \'trəmp\ Donald J. 1946– *Donald John Trump* 45th pres. of the U.S. (2017–)

Truth \'trüth\ Sojourner 1797?–1883 Amer. abolitionist

Tub·man \'təb-mən\ Harriet *ca* 1820–1913 Amer. abolitionist

Tu·ring \'tùr-iŋ\ Alan Mathison 1912–1954 Eng. mathematician and logician

Tur·ner \'tər-nər\ Joseph Mallord William 1775–1851 Eng. painter

Tut·ankh·a·men \ˌtü-ˌtaŋ-'kä-mən, -ˌtäŋ-\ originally *Tutankh·a·ten* \-'kä-tᵊn\ *ca* 1370–1352 B.C. king of Egypt (1361–1352 B.C.)

Twain \'twān\ Mark 1835–1910 pseud. of *Samuel Langhorne Clem·ens* \'klem-ənz\ Amer. author

Tweed \'twēd\ William Marcy 1823–1878 *Boss Tweed* Amer. politician

Ty·ler \'tī-lər\ John 1790–1862 10th pres. of the U.S. (1841–45)

Ulysses — see ODYSSEUS

Up·dike \'əp-ˌdīk\ John 1932–2009 Amer. author

Ura·nus \'yùr-ə-nəs, yù-'rā-\ the sky personified as a god and father of the Titans in Greek mythology

Ur·ban \'ər-bən\ name of eight popes: esp. II *ca* 1035–1099 (pope 1088–99)

Uri·el \'yùr-ē-əl\ archangel named in Hebrew tradition — compare GABRIEL, MICHAEL, RAPHAEL

Val·en·tine \'va-lən-ˌtīn\ Saint, 3d cent. Christian martyr

Van Bu·ren \van-'byùr-ən, vən-\ Martin 1782–1862 8th pres. of the U.S. (1837–41)

Van Dyck *or* **Van·dyke** \van-'dīk, vən-\ Sir Anthony 1599–1641 Flemish painter

van Gogh Vincent — see GOGH, VAN

Ve·láz·quez \və-'las-kəs, -'läs-, -kwiz, -(ˌ)käs\ Diego 1599–1660 Span. painter

Ve·nus \'vē-nəs\ goddess of love and beauty in Roman mythology — compare APHRODITE

Ver·di \'ver-dē\ Giuseppe 1813–1901 Ital. composer

Ver·meer \vər-'mer, -'mir\ Jan *or* Johannes 1632–1675 Dutch painter

Verne \'vərn, 'vern\ Jules \'jülz\ 1828–1905 French author

Ves·puc·ci \ve-'spü-chē, -'spyü-\ Ame·ri·go \ə-'mer-i-ˌgō\ 1454–1512 Latin *Amer·i·cus Ves·pu·cius* \ə-'mer-ə-kəs,-ves-'pyü-sh(ē-)əs\ Ital. navigator for Spain and namesake of America

Vic·to·ria \vik-'tòr-ē-ə\ 1819–1901 *Alexandrina Victoria* queen of the United Kingdom (1837–1901)

Vinci, da Leonardo — see LEONARDO DA VINCI

Vir·gil *also* **Ver·gil** \'vər-jəl\ 70–19 B.C. Roman poet

Vish·nu \'vish-(ˌ)nü\ god of preservation in the Hindu sacred triad — compare BRAHMA, SHIVA

Vi·val·di \vi-'väl-dē, -'vòl-\ Antonio Lucio 1678–1741 Ital. composer

Vol·ta \vōl-'tə, väl-, vòl-\ Alessandro 1745–1827 Ital. physicist

Vol·taire \vōl-'tar, väl-, vòl-, -'ter\ 1694–1778 orig. *François* Marie Arouet French author

Vul·can \'vəl-kən\ god of fire and metalworking in Roman mythology — compare HEPHAESTUS

Wag·ner \'väg-nər\ Ri·chard \'ri-ˌkärt, -ˌkärt\ 1813–1883 Ger. composer

Walk·er \'wò-kər\ Alice Malsenior 1944– Amer. writer

Wal·lace \'wä-ləs\ Alfred Russel 1823–1913 Eng. naturalist

Wal·len·berg \\'wä-lən-ˌbərg\ Raoul 1912–1947? Swedish diplomat and hero of the Holocaust

War·hol \\'wär-ˌhȯl, -ˌhōl\ Andy 1928–1987 orig. *Andrew Warhola* Amer. artist

War·ren \\'wȯr-ən, 'wär-\ Earl 1891–1974 Amer. jurist; chief justice of the U.S. Supreme Court (1953–69)

Wash·ing·ton \\'wȯ-shiŋ-tən, 'wä-\ Booker Tal·ia·ferro \\'tä-lə-vər\ 1856–1915 Amer. educator

Washington George 1732–1799 Amer. general; 1st pres. of the U.S. (1789–97)

Watt \\'wät\ James 1736–1819 Scot. inventor

Wayne \\'wān\ Anthony 1745–1796 *Mad Anthony* Amer. general

Web·ster \\'web-stər\ Daniel 1782–1852 Amer. politician

Webster Noah 1758–1843 Amer. lexicographer

Wel·ling·ton \\'we-liŋ-tən\ Duke of 1769–1852 *Arthur Wellesley; the Iron Duke* Brit. general and statesman

Wells \\'welz\ H. G. 1866–1946 *Herbert George Wells* Eng. author and historian

Wel·ty \\'wel-tē\ Eudora 1909–2001 Amer. author

Wes·ley \\'wes-lē, 'wez-\ John 1703–1791 Eng. founder of Methodism

Wes·ting·house \\'wes-tiŋ-ˌhau̇s\ George 1846–1914 Amer. inventor and industrialist

Whar·ton \\'hwȯr-tᵊn, 'wȯr-\ Edith 1862–1937 née *Jones* Amer. author

Whis·tler \\'hwis-lər, 'wis-\ James (Abbott) McNeill 1834–1903 Amer. artist

Whit·man \\'hwit-mən, 'wit-\ Walt 1819–1892 Amer. poet

Whit·ney \\'hwit-nē, 'wit-\ Eli 1765–1825 Amer. inventor

Whit·ti·er \\'hwi-tē-ər, 'wit-\ John Greenleaf 1807–1892 Amer. poet

Wie·sel \vē-'zel, wē-\ Elie 1928–2016 Amer. (Romanian⸗ born) author; Nobel Prize winner (1986)

Wilde \\'wī(-ə)ld\ Oscar 1854–1900 Irish author

Wil·der \\'wī(-ə)l-dər\ Thornton Niven 1897–1975 Amer. author

Wil·liam \\'wil-yəm\ name of 4 kings of England: **I** *ca* 1028–1087 *William the Conqueror* (r. 1066–87); **II** *ca* 1056–1100 *William Rufus* \\'rü-fəs\ (r. 1087–1100); **III** 1650–1702 (r. 1689–1702); **IV** 1765–1837 (r. 1830–37)

Wil·liam Tell \ˌwil-yəm-'tel\ legendary Swiss patriot commanded to shoot an apple off his son's head

Wil·liams \\'wil-yəmz\ Roger 1603?–1683 Eng. colonist

Williams Ted 1918–2002 *Theodore Samuel Williams* Amer. baseball player

Williams Tennessee 1911–1983 orig. *Thomas Lanier Williams* Amer. playwright

Williams Venus 1980– and her sister Serena 1981– Amer. tennis players

Wil·son \\'wil-sən\ August 1945–2005 orig. *Frederick August Kittel* Amer. playwright

Wilson Edward Osborne 1929– Amer. biologist

Wilson (Thomas) Woodrow 1856–1924 28th pres. of the U.S. (1913–21); Nobel Prize winner (1919)

Win·throp \\'win(t)-thrəp\ John 1588–1649 1st governor of Massachusetts Bay Colony

Witt·gen·stein \\'vit-gən-ˌshtīn, -ˌstīn\ Ludwig Josef Johan 1889–1951 Eng. (Austrian-born) philosopher

Woden — see ODIN

Woll·stone·craft \\'wu̇l-stən-ˌkraft\ Mary 1759–1797 Eng. feminist and writer

Woods \\'wu̇dz\ Tiger 1975– *Eldrick Woods* Amer. golfer

Woolf \\'wu̇lf\ Virginia 1882–1941 Eng. author

Words·worth \\'wərdz-(ˌ)wərth\ William 1770–1850 Eng. poet

Wo·vo·ka \wō-'vō-kə\ 1858?–1932 *Jack Wilson* Paiute Indian mystic

Wren \\'ren\ Sir Christopher 1632–1723 Eng. architect

Wright \\'rīt\ Frank Lloyd 1867–1959 Amer. architect

Wright Orville 1871–1948 and his brother Wilbur 1867–1912 Amer. pioneers in aviation

Wright Richard 1908–1960 Amer. author

Wy·eth \\'wī-əth\ Andrew Newell 1917–2009 Amer. painter

Xi Jin·ping \\'shē-'jin-'piŋ\ 1953– general secretary of Chinese Communist Party (2012–); president of China (2013–)

Yeats \\'yāts\ William Butler 1865–1939 Irish author

Yel·tsin \\'yelt-sən, 'yel-sin\ Boris Nikolayevich 1931–2007 pres. of Russia (1990–99)

York \\'yȯrk\ Alvin Cullum 1887–1964 Amer. hero in World War I

Young \\'yəŋ\ Brig·ham \\'brig-əm\ 1801–1877 Amer. Mormon leader

Za·har·i·as \zə-'ha-rē-əs\ Babe Didrikson 1914–1956 *Mildred Ella Zaharias* née *Didrikson* Amer. athlete

Za·pa·ta \sä-'pä-tä\ Emiliano 1879–1919 Mex. revolutionary

Zech·a·ri·ah \ˌze-kə-'rī-ə\ Hebrew prophet of the 6th cent. B.C.

Zeng·er \\'zeŋ-gər, -ər\ John Peter 1697–1746 Amer. (Ger.⸗ born) journalist and printer

Zeph·y·rus \\'ze-fə-rəs\ god of the west wind in Greek mythology

Zeus \\'züs\ chief god and ruler of the sky and weather in Greek mythology — compare JUPITER

GEOGRAPHICAL NAMES

This section gives basic information about the worldHs countries, regions, cities, and major physical features. The latest population figures are given for nations, cities, and some regions. For many of these entries, derived nouns and adjectives are also listed (as **Iceland . . . Icelander . . . n**). Other derived words not shown here have been separately entered in the main A-Z section, because of the presence of additional senses (as **Chinese**).

Abbreviations used here are listed in the front section Abbreviations in This Work. The capital letters N, E, S, and W, used singly or in combination and without a period, indicate direction. For example, "N India" means "northern India." Where direction is a part of the name, the word is spelled out.

The symbol * denotes a capital. Sizes are given in conventional U.S. units, with metric equivalents following.

Ab·er·deen \,a-bər-'dēn\ city NE Scotland; *pop* 223,000 — **Ab·er·do·ni·an** \,a-bər-'dō-nē-ən\ *adj or n*

Ab·i·djan \,ä-bē-'jän, ,a-bi-\ city, seat of government of Cote d'Ivoire; *pop* 1,934,342

Ab·i·lene \'a-bə-,lēn\ city NW *cen* Texas; *pop* 117,063

Abu Dha·bi \ä-bü-'dä-bē, -'thä-\ city, * of United Arab Emirates; *pop* 2,394,000

Abu·ja \ä-'bü-jä\ city *cen* Nigeria; its *; *pop* 1,144,000

Ab·ys·sin·ia \,a-bə-'si-nē-ə, -nyə\ — see ETHIOPIA — **Ab·ys·sin·i·an** \-nē-ən, -nyən\ *adj or n*

Aca·dia \ə-'kā-dē-ə\ *or French* **Aca·die** \ä-kä-'dē\ NOVA SCOTIA — an early name — **Aca·di·an** \-ē-ən\ *adj or n*

Aca·pul·co \,ä-kä-'pül-(,)kō, ,a-\ city & port S Mexico on the Pacific; *pop* 789,971

Ac·cra \'ä-krə, 'a-; ə-'krä\ city & port, * of Ghana; *pop* 1,849,000

Acon·ca·gua \,ä-kōn-'kä-gwä\ mountain 22,834 ft. (6960 m.) W Argentina; highest in the Andes & in Western Hemisphere

Ad·dis Aba·ba \'ä-dis-'ä-bä-,bä, ,a-dəs-'a-bə-bə\ city, * of Ethiopia; *pop* 2,740,000

Ad·e·laide \'a-də-,lād\ city S Australia, * of South Australia; *pop* 1,103,979

Aden \'ä-dᵊn, 'ā-\ city & port S Yemen; *pop* 240,370

Aden, Gulf of arm of Indian Ocean between Yemen (Arabia) & Somalia (Africa)

Ad·i·ron·dack \,a-də-'rän-,dak\ mountains NE New York; highest Mount Marcy 5344 ft. (1629 m.)

Admiralty \'ad-m(ə-)rəl-tē\ 1 island SE Alaska 2 islands W Pacific N of New Guinea; part of Papua New Guinea

Adri·at·ic Sea \,ā-drē-'a-tik, ,a-\ arm of Mediterranean between Italy & Balkan Peninsula

Ae·ge·an Sea \i-'jē-ən\ arm of Mediterranean between Asia Minor & Greece

Af·ghan·i·stan \af-'ga-nə-,stan, -'gä-nə-,stän\ country W Asia E of Iran; *, Kabul; *pop* 22,576,000

Af·ri·ca \'a-fri-kə\ continent S of the Mediterranean

Agana — see HAGÄTÑA

Agra \'ä-grə, 'ə-\ city N India SSE of Delhi; *pop* 1,585,704

Aguas·ca·lien·tes \,ä-gwäs-,käl-'yen-,tās\ city *cen* Mexico NE of Guadalajara; *pop* 797,010

Agul·has, Cape \ə-'gə-ləs\ cape Republic of South Africa; most southerly point of Africa, at 34° 52′ S latitude

Ahag·gar \ə-'hä-gər, ,ä-hə-'gär\ mountains S Algeria in W *cen* Sahara

Ah·mad·abad \'ä-mə-də-,bäd, -,bad\ city W India N of Bombay; *pop* 5,577,940

Ak·ron \'a-krən\ city NE Ohio; *pop* 199,110

Al·a·bama \,a-lə-'ba-mə\ state SE U.S.; *, Montgomery; *pop* 4,779,736 — **Al·a·bam·i·an** \-'ba-mē-ən\ *or* **Al·a·bam·an** \-'ba-mən\ *adj or n*

Alas·ka \ə-'las-kə\ 1 peninsula SW Alaska SW of Cook Inlet 2 state of U.S. in NW North America; *, Juneau; *pop* 710,231 3 mountain range S Alaska extending from Alaska Peninsula to Yukon boundary — **Alas·kan** \-kən\ *adj or n*

Alaska, Gulf of inlet of Pacific off S Alaska between Alaska Peninsula on W & Alexander Archipelago on E

Al·ba·nia \al-'bā-nē-ə, -nyə\ country S Europe in Balkan Peninsula on Adriatic; *, Tirane; *pop* 3,823,000

Al·ba·ny \'òl-bə-nē\ city, * of New York; *pop* 97,856

Albemarle Sound \'al-bə-,märl\ inlet of the Atlantic in NE North Carolina

Albert, Lake \'al-bərt\ lake E Africa between Uganda & Democratic Republic of the Congo in course of the Nile

Al·ber·ta \al-'bər-tə\ province W Canada; *, Edmonton; *pop* 3,290,350 — **Al·ber·tan** \-'bər-tᵊn\ *adj or n*

Al·bu·quer·que \'al-bə-,kər-kē\ city *cen* New Mexico; *pop* 545,852

Al·ca·traz \'al-kə-,traz\ island California in San Francisco Bay

Al·da·bra \äl-'dä-brə\ island NW Indian Ocean N of Madagascar; belongs to Seychelles

Al·der·ney \'òl-dər-nē\ — see CHANNEL

Alep·po \ə-'le-(,)pō\ city N Syria; *pop* 1,445,000

Aleu·tian \ə-'lü-shən\ islands SW Alaska extending 1700 mi. (2735 km.) W from Alaska Peninsula

Al·ex·an·der \,al-ig-'zan-dər, ,el-\ archipelago SE Alaska

Al·ex·an·dria \,a-lig-'zan-drē-ə, ,e-\ 1 city N Virginia S of District of Columbia; *pop* 139,966 2 city N Egypt on the Mediterranean; *pop* 4,123,869 — **Al·ex·an·dri·an** \-drē-ən\ *adj or n*

Al·ge·ria \al-'jir-ē-ə\ country NW Africa on Mediterranean; *, Algiers; *pop* 34,200,000 — **Al·ge·ri·an** \-ē-ən\ *adj or n*

Al·giers \al-'jirz\ city, * of Algeria; *pop* 2,364,230 — **Al·ge·rine** \,al-jə-'rēn\ *adj or n*

Al·lah·a·bad \'ä-lä-hä-,bäd, 'a-lə-hə-,bad\ city N India on the Ganges; *pop* 1,212,395

Al·le·ghe·ny \,a-lə-'gā-nē\ 1 river 325 mi. (523 km.) long W Pennsylvania & SW New York 2 mountains of Appalachian system E U.S. in Pennsylvania, Maryland, Virginia, & West Virginia

Al·len·town \'a-lən-,taùn\ city E Pennsylvania; *pop* 118,032

Al·ma·ty \əl-'mä-tē\ *or* **Al·ma–Ata** \əl-'mä-ə-'tä; ,al-mə-'ä-tə, -ə-'tä\ city, former * of Kazakhstan; *pop* 1,365,632

Alps \'alps\ mountain system *cen* Europe — see MONT BLANC

Al·tai *or* **Al·tay** \,al-'tī\ mountain system *cen* Asia between Mongolia & W China & between Kazakhstan & Russia

Ama·ga·sa·ki \,ä-mä-gä-'sä-kē\ city Japan in W *cen* Honshu; *pop* 453,748

Am·a·ril·lo \,a-mə-'ri-(,)lō, -lə\ city NW Texas; *pop* 190,695

Am·a·zon \'a-mə-,zän, -zən\ river 3900 mi. (6436 km.) long N South America flowing from Peruvian Andes into Atlantic in N Brazil

Amer·i·ca \ə-'mer-ə-kə, -'me-rə-\ 1 either continent (**North America** *or* **South America**) of Western Hemisphere 2 *or* **the Amer·i·cas** \-kəz\ lands of Western Hemisphere including North, Central, & South America & West Indies 3 UNITED STATES OF AMERICA — **American** *adj or n*

American Falls — see NIAGARA FALLS

American Samoa *or* **Eastern Samoa** islands SW *cen* Pacific; U.S. territory; *, Pago Pago (on Tutuila Island); *pop* 55,519

Am·man \ä-'män, a-, -'man\ city, * of Jordan; *pop* 627,505

Am·ster·dam \'am(p)-stər-,dam, ,äm(p)-stər-,däm\ city, official * of the Netherlands; *pop* 810,767

Amur \ä-'mùr\ river 1780 mi. (2784 km.) long E Asia flowing into the Pacific & forming part of boundary between China & Russia

An·a·heim \'a-nə-ˌhīm\ city SW California E of Long Beach; *pop* 336,265

An·a·to·lia \ˌa-nə-'tō-lē-ə, -'tōl-yə\ — see ASIA MINOR — **An·a·to·li·an** \-'tō-lē-ən, -'tōl-yən\ *adj or n*

An·chor·age \'aŋ-k(ə-)rij\ city S *cen* Alaska; *pop* 291,826

An·da·man \'an-də-mən, -ˌman\ 1 islands India in Bay of Bengal S of Myanmar & N of Nicobar Islands 2 sea, arm of Bay of Bengal S of Myanmar — **An·da·man·ese** \ˌan-də-mə-'nēz, -'nēs\ *adj or n*

An·des \'an-(ˌ)dēz\ mountain system W South America extending from Panama to Tierra del Fuego — see ACONCAGUA — **An·de·an** \'an-(ˌ)dē-ən, an-'\ *adj* — **An·dine** \'an-ˌdēn, -ˌdīn\ *adj*

An·dor·ra \an-'dor-ə, -'där-ə\ country SW Europe in E Pyrenees between France & Spain; ✳, Andorra la Vella; *pop* 76,100 — **An·dor·ran** \-ən\ *adj or n*

Andorra la Vel·la \lä-'vel-yä\ town, ✳ of Andorra; *pop* 21,513

An·dros \'an-drəs\ island, largest of Bahamas

An·gel Falls \'än-jəl\ waterfall 3212 ft. (979 m.) SE Venezuela; world's highest waterfall

Ang·kor \'aŋ-ˌkor\ ruins of ancient city NW Cambodia

An·gle·sey \'aŋ-gəl-sē\ island NW Wales

An·go·la \aŋ-'gō-lə, an-\ country SW Africa S of mouth of Congo River; ✳, Luanda; *pop* 24,383,000 — **An·go·lan** \-lən\ *adj or n*

An·i·ak·chak Crater \ˌa-nē-'ak-ˌchak\ volcanic crater SW Alaska on Alaska Peninsula; 6 mi. (10 km.) in diameter

An·ka·ra \'aŋ-kə-rə, 'äŋ-\ city, ✳ of Turkey in N *cen* Anatolia; *pop* 4,609,000

An·nap·o·lis \ə-'na-pə-lis\ city, ✳ of Maryland; *pop* 38,394

Ann Ar·bor \(ˌ)an-'är-bər\ city SE Michigan; *pop* 113,934

An·shan \'än-'shän\ city NE China; *pop* 1,203,986

An·ta·nan·a·ri·vo \ˌän-tä-ˌnä-nä-'rē-(ˌ)vō\ city, ✳ of Madagascar; *pop* 958,929

Ant·arc·ti·ca \ˌant-'ärk-ti-kə, -'är-ti-\ body of land around the South Pole; plateau covered by great ice cap

An·ti·gua \an-'tē-gə, -gwə\ island West Indies in the Leewards; with Barbuda forms independent **Antigua and Barbuda**; ✳, Saint John's; *pop* 83,700

An·til·les \an-'ti-lēz\ the West Indies except for the Bahamas — see GREATER ANTILLES, LESSER ANTILLES — **An·til·le·an** \-lē-ən\ *adj*

An·trim \'an-trəm\ district E Northern Ireland; *pop* 54,000

Ant·werp \'ant-ˌwərp, 'an-ˌtwərp\ city N Belgium; *pop* 493,517

Aomen — see MACAO

Aoraki — see COOK, MOUNT

Ap·en·nines \'a-pə-ˌnīnz\ mountain chain Italy extending length of the peninsula; highest peak Monte Corno (NE of Rome) 9560 ft. (2897 m.) — **Ap·en·nine** \'a-pə-ˌnīn\ *adj*

Apia \ä-'pē-ä\ town, ✳ of Samoa; *pop* 36,735

Apo, Mount \'ä-(ˌ)pō\ volcano Philippines in SE Mindanao 9692 ft. (2954 m.); highest peak in the Philippines

Ap·pa·la·chia \ˌa-pə-'lā-chə, -'la-chə, -'lā-shə\ region E U.S. including Appalachian Mountains from S *cen* New York to *cen* Alabama

Ap·pa·la·chian Mountains \ˌa-pə-'lā-ch(ē-)ən, -sh(ē-)ən\ mountain system E North America extending from S Quebec to *cen* Alabama — see MITCHELL, MOUNT

Aqa·ba, Gulf of \'ä-kä-bə\ arm of Red Sea E of Sinai Peninsula

Aquid·neck \ə-'kwid-ˌnek\ *or* **Rhode** island SE Rhode Island in Narragansett Bay

Ara·bia \ə-'rā-bē-ə\ peninsula of SW Asia including Saudi Arabia, Yemen, Oman, & Persian Gulf States

Ara·bi·an Sea \ə-'rā-bē-ən\ NW section of Indian Ocean between Arabia & India

Ara·fu·ra \ˌä-rä-'fū-rä\ sea between N Australia & W New Guinea

Ar·al Sea \'a-rəl\ *formerly* **Lake Aral** formerly large lake W Asia which has shrunk into sections some of which are now entirely in Kazakhstan and others between Kazakhstan & Uzbekistan

Ar·a·rat \'a-rə-ˌrat\ mountain 16,946 ft. (5165 m.) E Turkey near border of Iran

Arc·tic \'ärk-tik, 'är-tik\ 1 ocean N of Arctic Circle 2 Arctic regions 3 archipelago N Canada in Nunavut & Northwest Territories

Ar·da·bil *or* **Ar·de·bil** \ˌär-də-'bēl\ city NW Iran; *pop* 418,000

Ards \'ärdz\ district E Northern Ireland; *pop* 78,000

Are·ci·bo \ˌä-rä-'sē-(ˌ)bō\ city & port N Puerto Rico; *pop* 96,440

Ar·gen·ti·na \ˌär-jən-'tē-nə\ country S South America between the Andes & the Atlantic; ✳, Buenos Aires; *pop* 40,117,000 — **Ar·gen·tine** \'är-jən-ˌtīn, -ˌtēn\ *adj or n* — **Ar·gen·tin·ean** *or* **Ar·gen·tin·i·an** \ˌär-jən-'ti-nē-ən\ *adj or n*

Ar·gos \'är-ˌgös, -gəs\ ancient Greek city-state S Greece

Ar·i·zo·na \ˌa-rə-'zō-nə\ state SW U.S.; ✳, Phoenix; *pop* 6,392,017 — **Ar·i·zo·nan** \-nən\ *or* **Ar·i·zo·nian** \-nē-ən, -nyən\ *adj or n*

Ar·kan·sas \'är-kən-ˌso\ 1 river 1450 mi. (2334 km.) long SW *cen* U.S. flowing SE into the Mississippi 2 state S *cen* U.S.; ✳, Little Rock; *pop* 2,915,918 — **Ar·kan·san** \är-'kan-zən\ *adj or n*

Ar·ling·ton \'är-liŋ-tən\ city N Texas; *pop* 365,438

Ar·magh \är-'mä, 'är-ˌ\ 1 district S Northern Ireland; *pop* 59,000 2 town *cen* Armagh district; *pop* 14,265

Ar·me·nia \är-'mē-nē-ə, -nyə\ 1 region W Asia in mountainous area SE of Black Sea & SW of Caspian Sea divided among Iran, Turkey, & Armenia (country) 2 country W Asia; ✳, Yerevan; *pop* 3,018,854

Arn·hem Land \'är-nəm\ region N Australia on N coast of Northern Territory

Ar·no \'är-(ˌ)nō\ river 150 mi. (241 km.) long *cen* Italy flowing through Florence

Aru·ba \ə-'rü-bə\ Dutch island in Caribbean Sea off coast of NW Venezuela; *pop* 101,484

Ar·va·da \är-'va-də\ city N *cen* Colorado N of Denver; *pop* 106,433

Ash·ga·bat \'äsh-gə-ˌbät\ *or* **Ashkh·a·bad** \'ash-kə-ˌbad, -ˌbäd\ city, ✳ of Turkmenistan; *pop* 412,200

Asia \'ā-zhə, -shə\ continent of Eastern Hemisphere N of the Equator — see EURASIA

Asia Mi·nor \-'mī-nər\ *or* **An·a·to·lia** \ˌa-nə-'tō-lē-ə, -'tōl-yə\ peninsula in modern Turkey between Black Sea on N & the Mediterranean on S

As·ma·ra \az-'mä-rə, -'ma-rə\ city, ✳ of Eritrea; *pop* 342,706

As·syr·ia \ə-'sir-ē-ə\ ancient empire W Asia extending along the middle Tigris & over foothills to the E — **As·syr·i·an** \-ē-ən\ *adj or n*

As·ta·na \ä-stä-'nä\ city, ✳ of Kazakhstan; *pop* 814,400

Asun·ción \ä-sün-'syön\ city, ✳ of Paraguay; *pop* 502,426

As·wân \a-'swän, ä-\ city S Egypt on the Nile near site of **Aswân High Dam**; *pop* 265,500

Ata·ca·ma \ˌä-tä-'kä-mä\ desert N Chile

Atchaf·a·laya \(ə-)ˌcha-fə-'lī-ə\ river 225 mi. (362 km.) long S Louisiana flowing S into Gulf of Mexico

Ath·a·bas·ca \ˌa-thə-'bas-kə, -a-\ river 765 mi. (1231 km.) long NE Alberta flowing into **Lake Athabasca** on Alberta–Saskatchewan border

Ath·ens \'a-thənz\ 1 city NE Georgia; *pop* 115,452 2 city, ✳ of Greece; *pop* 664,046 — **Athe·nian** \ə-'thē-nē-ən, -nyən\ *adj or n*

At·lan·ta \ət-'lan-tə, at-\ city, ✳ of Georgia; *pop* 420,003

At·lan·tic \ət-'lan-tik, at-\ ocean separating North America & South America from Europe & Africa; often divided into **North Atlantic** and **South Atlantic** — **Atlantic** *adj*

At·las \'at-ləs\ mountains NW Africa from SW Morocco to N Tunisia

At·ti·ca \'a-ti-kə\ ancient state E Greece; chief city Athens — **At·tic** \'at-ik\ *adj*

Auck·land \'o-klənd\ city N New Zealand on NW North Island; *pop* 404,658

Au·gus·ta \o-'gəs-tə, ə-\ 1 city E Georgia; *pop* 195,844 2 city, ✳ of Maine; *pop* 19,136

Au·ro·ra \ə-'ror-ə, o-\ 1 city NE *cen* Colorado; *pop* 325,078 2 city NE Illinois; *pop* 197,899

Auschwitz — see OSWIECIM

Aus·tin \'os-tən\ city, ✳ of Texas; *pop* 790,390

Aus·tral·asia \ˌos-trə-'lā-zhə, äs-, -'lā-shə\ Australia, Tasmania, New Zealand, & Melanesia — **Aus·tral·asian** \-zhən, -shən\ *adj or n*

Aus·tra·lia \o-'strāl-yə, ä-, ə-\ 1 continent of Eastern Hemisphere SE of Asia 2 country including continent of Australia & island of Tasmania; ✳, Canberra; *pop* 21,508,000 — **Aus·tra·lian** \-yən\ *adj or n*

Australian Alps mountain range SE Australia in E Victoria & SE New South Wales; part of Great Dividing Range

Australian Capital Territory district SE Australia including two areas, one containing Canberra (✳ of Australia) & the other on Jervis Bay (inlet of the South Pacific); surrounded by New South Wales

Aus·tria \\'òs-trē-ə, 'äs-\\ country *cen* Europe; ✳, Vienna; *pop* 8,402,000 — **Aus·tri·an** \\-ən\\ *adj or n*

Aus·tria–Hun·ga·ry \\-'həŋ-gə-rē\\ country 1867–1918 *cen* Europe including Bohemia, Moravia, Transylvania, Galicia, and what are now Austria, Hungary, Slovenia, Croatia, & part of NE Italy — **Aus·tro–Hun·gar·i·an** \\'òs-(,)trō-,həŋ-'ger-ē-ən, 'äs-\\ *adj or n*

Aus·tro·ne·sia \\,òs-trə-'nē-zhə, ,äs-, -'nē-shə\\ **1** islands of the South Pacific **2** area extending from Madagascar through Malay Peninsula & Malay Archipelago to Hawaii & Easter Island — **Aus·tro·ne·sian** \\-zhən, -shən\\ *adj or n*

Avon \\'ā-vən, 'a-\\ river 96 mi. (154 km.) long *cen* England flowing WSW into the Severn

Ayers Rock — see ULURU

Ayles·bury \\'ālz-b(ə-)rē\\ town SE *cen* England; *pop* 41,288

Ayr \\'er\\ *or* **Ayr·shire** \\-,shir, -shər\\ former county SW Scotland

Azer·bai·jan \\,a-zər-,bī-'jän, ,ä-\\ country W Asia & SE Europe bordering on Caspian Sea; ✳, Baku; *pop* 9,477,000 — **Azer·bai·ja·ni** \\,a-zər-,bī-'jä-nē, ,ä-\\ *adj or n*

Azores \\'ā-,zòrz, ə-'\\ islands Portugal in North Atlantic lying 800 mi. (1287 km.) W of Portuguese coast; *pop* 246,800 — **Azor·e·an** \\ā-'zòr-ē-ən, ə-\\ *adj or n*

Bab·y·lon \\'ba-bə-lən, -,län\\ ancient city, ✳ of Babylonia; site 55 mi. (89 km.) S of Baghdad near the Euphrates — **Bab·y·lo·nian** \\,ba-bə-'lō-nyən, -nē-ən\\ *adj or n*

Bab·y·lo·nia \\,ba-bə-'lō-nyə, -nē-ə\\ ancient country W Asia in valley of lower Euphrates and Tigris rivers

Bac·tria \\'bak-trē-ə\\ ancient country W Asia in present NE Afghanistan — **Bac·tri·an** \\'bak-trē-ən\\ *adj or n*

Bad·lands barren region SW South Dakota & NW Nebraska

Baf·fin \\'ba-fən\\ **1** bay of the Atlantic between W Greenland & E Baffin Island **2** island NE Canada in Arctic Archipelago N of Hudson Strait

Bagh·dad \\'bag-,dad, ,bäg-'däd\\ city, ✳ of Iraq on the Tigris; *pop* 3,841,000

Ba·guio \\,bä-gē-'ō\\ city, former summer ✳ of the Philippines in NW *cen* Luzon; *pop* 318,676

Ba·ha·mas \\bə-'hä-məz\\ islands in N Atlantic SE of Florida; ✳, Nassau; *pop* 367,000 — **Ba·ha·mi·an** \\bə-'hä-mē-ən, -'hä-\\ *or* **Ba·ha·man** \\-'hä-mən, -'häm-ən\\ *adj or n*

Bahia — see SALVADOR

Bah·rain \\bä-'rān\\ islands in Persian Gulf off coast of Arabia; country; ✳, Manama; *pop* 651,000 — **Bah·raini** \\-'rā-nē\\ *adj or n*

Bai·kal, Lake *or* **Lake Bay·kal** \\bī-'käl, -'kal\\ lake Russia, in mountains N of Mongolia

Ba·ja California \\'bä-(,)hä\\ peninsula NW Mexico W of Gulf of California

Ba·kers·field \\'bā-kərz-,fēld\\ city S California; *pop* 347,483

Ba·ku \\bä-'kü\\ city, ✳ of Azerbaijan on W coast of Caspian Sea; area *pop* 2,046,000

Bal·a·ton \\'ba-lə-,tän, 'bò-lò-,tōn\\ lake W Hungary

Bal·boa Heights \\(,)bal-'bō-ə\\ town Panama; formerly the center of administration for Canal Zone

Bal·e·ar·ic Islands \\,ba-lē-'a-rik\\ islands E Spain in the W Mediterranean

Ba·li \\'bä-lē, 'ba-\\ island Indonesia off E end of Java; *pop* 3,891,000 — **Ba·li·nese** \\,bä-li-'nēz, ,bal-, -'nēs\\ *adj or n*

Bal·kans \\'bòl-kənz\\ **1** *or* **Balkan Mountains** mountains N Bulgaria extending from Serbia border to Black Sea; highest (est.) 7,793 ft. (2375 m.) **2** *or* **Balkan Peninsula** peninsula SE Europe between Adriatic & Ionian seas on the W & Aegean & Black seas on the E **3** *or* **Balkan States** countries occupying the Balkan Peninsula: Slovenia, Croatia, Bosnia and Herzegovina, Macedonia, Kosovo, Serbia, Montenegro, Romania, Bulgaria, Albania, Greece, Turkey (in Europe)

Bal·ly·me·na \\,ba-lē-'mē-nə\\ district NE *cen* Northern Ireland; *pop* 64,000

Bal·ly·mon·ey \\,ba-lē-'mə-nē\\ district N Northern Ireland; *pop* 31,000

Bal·tic Sea \\'bòl-tik\\ arm of the Atlantic N Europe E of Scandinavian Peninsula

Bal·ti·more \\'bòl-tə-,mòr, -mər\\ city N Maryland; *pop* 620,961

Ba·ma·ko \\'bä-mä-,kō\\ city, ✳ of Mali on the Niger; *pop* 1,016,000

Ban·bridge \\ban-'brij\\ district SE *cen* Northern Ireland; *pop* 48,000

Ban·dar Se·ri Be·ga·wan \\,bən-dər-,ser-ē-bə-'gä-wän\\ town, ✳ of Brunei; *pop* 27,285

Ban·dung \\'bän-,dùn\\ city Indonesia in W Java SE of Jakarta; *pop* 2,394,873

Ban·ga·lore \\'baŋ-gə-,lòr\\ city S India W of Madras; *pop* 8,482,000

Bang·kok \\'baŋ-,käk, baŋ-'\\ city, ✳ of Thailand; *pop* 6,160,000

Ban·gla·desh \\,bäŋ-glə-'desh, ,baŋ-, ,bəŋ-, -'däsh\\ country S Asia E of India; ✳, Dhaka; *pop* 149,772,000 — see EAST PAKISTAN — **Ban·gla·deshi** \\-'de-shē, -'dä-\\ *adj or n*

Ban·gor \\'baŋ-,gòr, 'ban-,gòr\\ town E Northern Ireland; *pop* 46,585

Ban·gui \\bäŋ-'gē\\ city, ✳ of Central African Republic; *pop* 532,000

Ban·jul \\'bän-jül\\ *formerly* **Bath·urst** \\'bath-(,)ərst\\ city & port, ✳ of Gambia; *pop* 44,188

Bao·tou *or* **Pao–t'ou** \\'baù-'tō\\ city N China; *pop* 1,999,000

Bar·ba·dos \\bär-'bā-(,)dōs, -dəs, -(,)dōz\\ island West Indies in Lesser Antilles E of Windward Islands; country, ✳, Bridgetown; *pop* 277,821 — **Bar·ba·di·an** \\-'bā-dē-ən\\ *adj or n*

Bar·bu·da \\bär-'bü-də\\ island West Indies; part of independent Antigua and Barbuda; *pop* 1600

Bar·ce·lo·na \\,bär-sə-'lō-nə\\ city NE Spain on the Mediterranean; chief city of Catalonia; *pop* 1,611,013

Bar·king and Dag·en·ham \\'bär-kiŋ-ən(d)-'da-gə-nəm\\ borough of E Greater London, England; *pop* 186,000

Bar·na·ul \\,bär-nə-'ül\\ city S Russia; *pop* 612,000

Bar·net \\'bär-nət\\ borough of N Greater London, England; *pop* 356,000

Bar·ran·qui·lla \\,bär-än-'kē-yä\\ city N Colombia; *pop* 1,142,000

Barren Grounds treeless plains N Canada W of Hudson Bay

Bar·row, Point \\'ba-(,)rō\\ most northerly point of Alaska & of U.S. at about 71°25′ N latitude

Ba·si·lan \\bä-'sē-,län\\ island S Philippines SW of Mindanao

Bas·il·don \\'ba-zəl-dən\\ town SE England; *pop* 157,500

Bass \\'bas\\ strait separating Tasmania & continent of Australia

Basse·terre \\bas-'ter, bäs-\\ seaport Saint Kitts, ✳ of Saint Kitts and Nevis; *pop* 14,725

Basutoland — see LESOTHO

Bathurst — see BANJUL

Bat·on Rouge \\,ba-t°n-'rüzh\\ city, ✳ of Louisiana; *pop* 229,493

Ba·var·ia \\bə-'ver-ē-ə\\ *or German* **Bay·ern** \\'bī-ərn\\ state SE Germany bordering on Czech Republic & Austria; *pop* 12,397,614 — **Ba·var·i·an** \\bə-'ver-ē-ən, -'var-\\ *adj or n*

Ba·ya·mon \\,bī-ä-'mōn\\ city NE *cen* Puerto Rico; *pop* 208,116

Beau·fort \\'bō-fərt\\ sea consisting of part of Arctic Ocean NE of Alaska & NW of Canada

Beau·mont \\'bō-,mänt, bō-'\\ city SE Texas; *pop* 118,296

Bech·u·a·na·land \\,bech-'wä-nə-,land, ,be-chə-\\ **1** region S Africa N of Orange River **2** — see BOTSWANA

Bed·ford·shire \\'bed-fərd-,shir, -shər\\ *or* **Bedford** county SE England

Bedloe's — see LIBERTY

Bei·jing \\'bā-'jiŋ\\ *or* **Pe·king** \\'pē-'kiŋ, 'pā-\\ city, ✳ of China; *pop* 10,819,407

Bei·rut \\bā-'rüt\\ city, ✳ of Lebanon; urban area *pop* 1,100,000

Be·la·rus \\,be-lə-'rüs, ,bye-lə-\\ country *cen* Europe; ✳, Minsk; *pop* 9,468,100 — **Be·la·ru·si·an** \\-'rü-sē-ən, -'rə-shən\\ *or* **Be·la·rus·sian** \\-'rə-shən\\ *adj or n*

Belau — see PALAU

Be·lém \\be-'lem\\ city N Brazil; *pop* 1,393,399

Bel·fast \\'bel-,fast, bel-'\\ city, ✳ of Northern Ireland; *pop* 281,000

Bel·gium \\'bel-jəm\\ *or French* **Bel·gique** \\bel-'zhēk\\ *or Flemish* **Bel·gië** \\'bel-kē-ə\\ country W Europe; ✳, Brussels; *pop* 11,125,500 — **Bel·gian** \\'bel-jən\\ *adj or n*

Bel·grade \'bel-ˌgrad, -ˌgräd, -ˌgrad, bel-'\ *or* **Beo·grad** \bā-'oˌ-ˌgräd\ city, ✳ of Serbia on the Danube; *pop* 1,120,000
Be·lize \bə-'lēz\ *formerly* **British Honduras** country Central America on the Caribbean; ✳, Belmopan; *pop* 324,500 — **Be·liz·ean** \bə-'liz-ē-ən\ *adj or n*
Belize City seaport E Belize; *pop* 55,400
Belle·vue \'bel-ˌvyü\ city W Washington E of Seattle; *pop* 122,363
Bel·mo·pan \ˌbel-mō-'pän\ city, ✳ of Belize; *pop* 13,931
Be·lo Ho·ri·zon·te \'bā-lō-ˌōr-ē-'zōn-tē\ city E Brazil N of Rio de Janeiro; *pop* 2,375,151
Be·lo·rus·sia \ˌbe-lō-'rə-shə, ˌbye-lō-\ *or* **Bye·lo·rus·sia** \bē-ˌe-lō-, ˌbye-lō-\ former republic of U.S.S.R.; became independent Belarus in 1991 — **Belo·rus·sian** \ˌbe-lō-'rə-shən, ˌbye-\ *adj or n*
Ben·gal \ben-'gȯl, beŋ-, -'gäl\ region S Asia including delta of Ganges & Brahmaputra rivers; divided between Bangladesh & India — **Ben·gal·ese** \ˌben-gə-'lēz, ˌben-, -'lēs\ *adj or n*
Bengal, Bay of arm of Indian Ocean between India & Myanmar
Be·nin \bə-'nēn, -'nin; 'be-nin\ *formerly* **Da·ho·mey** \də-'hō-mē\ country W Africa on Gulf of Guinea; ✳, Porto-Novo; *pop* 9,984,000 — **Ben·i·nese** \bə-ˌni-'nēz, -ˌnē-, -'nēs; ˌbe-ni-'nēz, -'nēs\ *adj or n*
Ben Nev·is \ben-'ne-vəs\ mountain 4406 ft. (1343 m.) W Scotland in the Grampians; highest in Great Britain
Beograd — *see* BELGRADE
Ber·gen \'bər-gən, 'ber-\ city & port SW Norway; *pop* 271,949
Be·ring \'bir-iŋ, 'ber-\ **1** sea, arm of the North Pacific between Alaska & NE Siberia **2** strait at narrowest point 53 mi. (85 km.) wide between North America (Alaska) and Asia (Russia)
Berke·ley \'bər-klē\ city W California on San Francisco Bay N of Oakland; *pop* 112,580
Berk·shire \'bərk-ˌshir, -shər\ hills W Massachusetts; highest point Mount Greylock 3491 ft. (1064 m.)
Ber·lin \(ˌ)bər-'lin, *G* ber-'lēn\ city, ✳ of Germany; divided 1945–90 into **East Berlin** (✳ of East Germany) & **West Berlin** (city of West Germany lying within East Germany; *pop* 3,292,365 — **Ber·lin·er** \(ˌ)bər-'li-nər\ *n*
Ber·mu·da \(ˌ)bər-'myü-də\ islands W Atlantic ESE of Cape Hatteras; a British colony; ✳, Hamilton; *pop* 71,000 — **Ber·mu·dan** \-d°n\ *or* **Ber·mu·di·an** \-dē-ən\ *adj or n*
Bern \'bərn, 'bern\ city, ✳ of Switzerland; *pop* 128,848 — **Ber·nese** \(ˌ)bər-'nēz, -'nēs\ *adj or n*
Bes·sa·ra·bia \ˌbe-sə-'rā-bē-ə\ region SE Europe now chiefly in Moldova — **Bes·sa·ra·bi·an** \-bē-ən\ *adj or n*
Beth·le·hem \'beth-li-ˌhem, -lē-həm, -lē-əm\ town of ancient Palestine in Judaea; the present-day town is SW of Jerusalem in the West Bank; *pop* 30,200
Bev·er·ly Hills \'be-vər-lē\ city SW California within Los Angeles; *pop* 34,109
Bex·ley \'bek-slē\ borough of E Greater London, England; *pop* 211,200
Bho·pal \bō-'päl\ city N *cen* India; *pop* 1,886,100
Bhu·tan \bü-'tän, -'tan\ country S Asia in the Himalayas on NE border of India; ✳, Thimphu; *pop* 753,000 — **Bhu·ta·nese** \ˌbü-tə-'nēz, -'nēs\ *adj or n*
Bi·ki·ni \bi-'kē-nē\ atoll W Pacific in Marshall Islands
Bil·lings \'bi-liŋz\ city S *cen* Montana; largest in state; *pop* 104,170
Bi·loxi \bə-'lək-sē, -'läk-\ city & port SE Mississippi on Gulf of Mexico; *pop* 44,054
Bi·o·ko \bē-'ō-(ˌ)kō\ *formerly* **Fer·nan·do Póo** \fer-'nän-(ˌ)dō-'pō\ island portion of Equatorial Guinea in Gulf of Guinea
Bir·ken·head \'bər-kən-ˌhed, ˌbər-kən-'\ borough NW England on the Mersey opposite Liverpool; *pop* 123,907
Bir·ming·ham \'bər-miŋ-ˌham\ **1** city N *cen* Alabama; *pop* 212,237 **2** city W *cen* England; *pop* 1,086,000
Bis·cay, Bay of \'bis-ˌkā, -kē\ inlet of the Atlantic between W coast of France & N coast of Spain
Bish·kek \bish-'kek\ *formerly* **1926–91** **Frun·ze** \'frün-zi\ city, ✳ of Kyrgyzstan; *pop* 794,000
Bis·marck \'biz-ˌmärk\ **1** city, ✳ of North Dakota; *pop* 61,272 **2** archipelago W Pacific N of E end of New Guinea
Bis·sau \bi-'saù\ city, ✳ of Guinea-Bissau; *pop* 386,500

Bi·thyn·ia \bə-'thi-nē-ə\ ancient country NW Asia Minor bordering on Sea of Marmara and Black Sea — **Bi·thyn·i·an** \-nē-ən\ *adj or n*
Bit·ter·root \'bi-tə(r)-ˌrüt, -ˌrút\ range of the Rockies along Idaho–Montana boundary
Black·burn \'blak-(ˌ)bərn\ town NW England; *pop* 132,800
Black Forest forested mountain region Germany along E bank of the upper Rhine
Black Hills mountains W South Dakota & NE Wyoming
Black·pool \'blak-ˌpül\ town NW England on Irish Sea; *pop* 144,500
Black Sea sea between Europe & Asia connected with Aegean Sea through the Bosporus, Sea of Marmara, & Dardanelles
Blanc, Mont — *see* MONT BLANC
Blan·tyre \'blan-ˌtī(-ə)r\ city S Malawi; *pop* 661,000
Bloem·fon·tein \'blüm-fən-ˌtān, -ˌfän-\ city Republic of South Africa, judicial ✳ of the country; *pop* 149,836
Blue Ridge E range of the Applachians E U.S. extending from S Pennsylvania to N Georgia
Bodh Gaya \'bȯd-'gī-ä\ village NE India; one of the holiest sites of Buddhism
Boe·o·tia \bē-'ō-sh(ē-)ə\ ancient state E *cen* Greece NW of Attica; chief ancient city, Thebes — **Boe·o·tian** \bē-'ō-shən\ *adj or n*
Bo·go·tá \ˌbō-gō-'tä, -'tȯ, 'bō-gə-ˌ\ city, ✳ of Colombia; *pop* 6,850,500
Bo Hai *or* **Po Hai** \'bō-'hī\ *or* **Gulf of Chih·li** \'chē-'lē, 'jir-\ arm of Yellow Sea NE China
Bo·he·mia \bō-'hē-mē-ə\ region W Czech Republic; chief city, Prague
Bo·hol \bō-'hȯl\ island S *cen* Philippines
Boi·se \'bȯi-sē, -zē\ city, ✳ of Idaho; *pop* 205,761
Bo·liv·ia \bə-'li-vē-ə\ country W *cen* South America; administrative ✳, La Paz; constitutional ✳, Sucre; *pop* 8,274,325 — **Bo·liv·i·an** \-vē-ən\ *adj or n*
Bo·lo·gna \bō-'lō-nyä\ city N Italy; *pop* 371,000
Bol·ton \'bōl-t°n\ town NW England; *pop* 253,300
Bom·bay \bäm-'bā\ *or* **Mum·bai** \'məm-ˌbī\ city & port W India; area *pop* 12,442,373
Bonn \'bän, 'bȯn\ city Germany on the Rhine SSE of Cologne, formerly (1949–99) ✳ of West Germany; *pop* 305,765
Boo·thia \'bü-thē-ə\ peninsula N Canada W of Baffin Island; its N tip is most northerly point in mainland North America
Bor·ders \'bȯr-dərz\ former administrative region SE Scotland
Bor·neo \'bȯr-nē-ˌō\ island Malay Archipelago SW of the Philippines; divided between Brunei, Indonesia, and Malaysia
Bos·nia \'bäz-nē-ə, 'bȯz-\ region S Europe; with Herzegovina forms independent **Bosnia** and **Her·ze·go·vi·na** \ˌhert-sə-gō-'vē-nə, ˌhərt-, -'gō-və-nə\; ✳, Sarajevo; *pop* 3,832,000 — **Bos·ni·an** \-nē-ən\ *adj or n*
Bos·po·rus \'bäs-p(ə-)rəs\ strait 18 mi. (29 km.) long between Turkey in Europe & Turkey in Asia connecting Sea of Marmara & Black Sea
Bos·ton \'bȯs-tən\ city, ✳ of Massachusetts; *pop* 617,594 — **Bos·to·nian** \bȯ-'stō-nē-ən, -nyən\ *adj or n*
Bot·a·ny Bay \'bä-tə-nē\ inlet of South Pacific SE Australia in New South Wales S of Sydney
Both·nia, Gulf of \'bäth-nē-ə\ arm of Baltic Sea between Sweden & Finland
Bo·tswa·na \bät-'swä-nə\ *formerly* **Bech·u·a·na·land** \ˌbech-'wä-nə-ˌland\ country S Africa; ✳, Gaborone; *pop* 1,680,863
Boul·der \'bōl-dər\ city N *cen* Colorado; *pop* 97,385
Boulder Dam — *see* HOOVER DAM
Bourne·mouth \'bȯrn-məth, 'bùrn-\ town S England on English Channel; *pop* 154,400
Brad·ford \'brad-fərd\ city N England; *pop* 350,000
Brah·ma·pu·tra \ˌbrä-mə-'pü-trə\ river about 1800 mi. (2900 km.) long S Asia flowing from the Himalayas in Tibet to Ganges Delta
Bra·síl·ia \brə-'zil-yə\ city, ✳ of Brazil; *pop* 2,570,160
Bra·ti·sla·va \ˌbra-tə-'slä-və, ˌbrä-\ city on the Danube; ✳ of Slovakia; *pop* 411,000
Bra·zil \brə-'zil\ country E & *cen* South America; ✳, Brasília; *pop* 190,733,000 — **Bra·zil·ian** \brə-'zil-yən\ *adj or n*

Braz·za·ville \\'bra-zə-ˌvil, 'brä-zə-ˌvēl\ city, * of Republic of the Congo on W bank of lower Congo River; *pop* 1,373,000

Bre·men \\'bre-mən, 'brā-\ city & port NW Germany; *pop* 542,707

Bren·ner \\'bre-nər\ pass 4495 ft. (1370 m.) high in the Alps between Austria & Italy

Brent \\'brent\ borough of W Greater London, England; *pop* 311,200

Bret·on, Cape \kāp-'bre-tᵊn, kə-'bre-, -'bri-\ cape Canada; most easterly point of Cape Breton Island & of Nova Scotia

Bridge·port \\'brij-ˌpȯrt\ city SW Connecticut on Long Island Sound; *pop* 144,229

Bridge·town \\'brij-ˌtau̇n\ city, * of Barbados; *pop* 5996

Brigh·ton \\'brī-tᵊn\ town S England on English Channel; *pop* 133,400

Bris·bane \\'briz-bən, -ˌbān\ city & port E Australia, * of Queensland; *pop* 1,874,427

Bris·tol \\'bris-tᵊl\ **1** city & port SW England; *pop* 536,000 **2** channel between S Wales & SW England

Brit·ain \\'bri-tᵊn\ **1** the island of Great Britain **2** UNITED KINGDOM

British Columbia province W Canada on Pacific coast; *, Victoria; *pop* 4,113,487

British Commonwealth — see COMMONWEALTH, THE

British Empire former empire consisting of Great Britain & the British dominions & dependencies

British Guiana — see GUYANA

British Honduras — see BELIZE

British India the part of India formerly under direct British administration

British Indian Ocean Territory British colony in Indian Ocean consisting of Chagos Archipelago

British Isles island group W Europe consisting of Great Britain, Ireland, & nearby islands

British Virgin Islands E islands of Virgin Islands; a British possession; *pop* 14,786

British West Indies islands of the West Indies including Jamaica, Trinidad and Tobago, & the Bahama & Cayman islands, Windward Islands, Leeward Islands, & British Virgin Islands

Brit·ta·ny \\'bri-tə-nē\ region NW France SW of Normandy

Brom·ley \\'bräm-lē\ borough of SE Greater London, England; *pop* 309,000

Bronx \\'brä̇ŋks\ *or* **The Bronx** borough of New York City NE of Manhattan; *pop* 1,385,108

Brook·lyn \\'bru̇k-lən\ borough of New York City at SW end of Long Island; *pop* 2,504,700

Brooks Range \\'bru̇ks\ mountains N Alaska

Browns·ville \\'brau̇nz-ˌvil, -vəl\ city S Texas on the Rio Grande; *pop* 175,023

Bru·nei \brü-'nī, 'brü-ˌnī\ country NE Borneo; *, Bandar Seri Begawan; *pop* 406,200 — **Bru·nei·an** \brü-'nī-ən\ *adj or n*

Brus·sels \\'brə-səlz\ city, * of Belgium; *pop* 163,000

Bu·cha·rest \\'bü-kə-ˌrest, 'byü-\ city, * of Romania; *pop* 1,926,000

Buck·ing·ham·shire \\'bə-kiŋ-əm-ˌshir\ *or* **Buckingham** county SE *cen* England

Bu·da·pest \\'bü-də-ˌpest\ city, * of Hungary; *pop* 1,729,040

Bue·nos Ai·res \ˌbwā-nəs-'a-rēz, Sp ˌbwā-nōs-'ī-räs\ city, * of Argentina; *pop* 2,960,976

Buf·fa·lo \\'bə-fə-ˌlō\ city W New York on Lake Erie; *pop* 261,310

Bu·jum·bu·ra \ˌbü-jəm-'bu̇r-ə\ city, * of Burundi; *pop* 497,166

Bu·ko·vi·na \ˌbü-kō-'vē-nə\ region E *cen* Europe in foothills of E Carpathians

Bul·gar·ia \ˌbəl-'ger-ē-ə, bu̇l-\ country SE Europe on Black Sea; *, Sofia; *pop* 7,246,000 — **Bul·gar·i·an** \ˌbəl-'ger-ē-ən, bu̇l-\ *adj or n*

Bull Run \\'bəl-'rən\ stream NE Virginia

Bun·ker Hill \\'bəŋ-kər\ height in Boston, Massachusetts

Bur·bank \\'bər-ˌbaŋk\ city SW California; *pop* 103,340

Bur·gun·dy \\'bər-gən-dē\ region E France — **Bur·gun·di·an** \(ˌ)bər-'gən-dē-ən\ *adj or n*

Bur·ki·na Fa·so \bu̇r-'kē-nə-'fä-sō, bər-\ *formerly* **Upper Vol·ta** \\'vōl-tə, 'vȯl-\ country W Africa N of Cote d'Ivoire, Ghana, & Togo; *, Ouagadougou; *pop* 14,017,000

Bur·ling·ton \\'bər-liŋ-tən\ city NW Vermont; largest in state; *pop* 42,417

Bur·ma \\'bər-mə\ — see MYANMAR — **Bur·mese** \ˌbər-'mēz, -'mēs\ *adj or n*

Bu·run·di \bu̇-'rün-dē, -'rün-\ country E *cen* Africa; *, Bujumbura; *pop* 8,300,000 — **Bu·run·di·an** \-dē-ən\ *adj or n*

Bu·san \\'bü-ˌsän\ *or* **Pu·san** \'pü-ˌsän, 'bü-\ city SE South Korea; *pop* 3,655,437

Bute \\'byüt\ island SW Scotland in Firth of Clyde

Butte \\'byüt\ city SW Montana; county *pop* 32,996

Byelorussia — see BELORUSSIA

By·zan·tine Empire \\'bi-zᵊn-ˌtēn, 'bī-, -ˌtīn; bə-'zan-ˌtēn, -tīn, bī-\ empire of SE & S Europe and W Asia from 4th to 15th century

By·zan·ti·um \bə-'zan-sh(ē-)əm, -'zant-ē-əm\ ancient city on site of modern Istanbul

Cabo Verde — see CAPE VERDE

Caer·nar·von \kär-'när-vən, kə(r)-\ town & seaport NW Wales; *pop* 9506

Ca·guas \\'kä-ˌgwäs\ town E *cen* Puerto Rico; *pop* 142,893

Cai·ro \\'kī-(ˌ)rō\ city, * of Egypt; *pop* 7,787,000 — **Cai·rene** \kī-'rēn\ *adj or n*

Ca·la·bria \kə-'lä-brē-ə, -'lä-\ district of ancient Italy consisting of area forming heel of Italian Peninsula — **Ca·la·bri·an** \kə-'lä-brē-ən, -'lä-\ *adj or n*

Cal·cut·ta \kal-'kə-tə\ *or* **Kol·ka·ta** \kōl-'kä-tä\ city E India on Hugli River; *pop* 4,496,694 — **Cal·cut·tan** \-'kə-tᵊn\ *adj or n*

Cal·e·do·nia \ˌka-lə-'dō-nyə, -nē-ə\ — see SCOTLAND — **Cal·e·do·nian** \-nyən, -nē-ən\ *adj or n*

Cal·ga·ry \\'kal-gə-rē\ city SW Alberta, Canada; *pop* 1,096,833

Ca·li \\'kä-lē\ city W Colombia; *pop* 2,326,500

Cal·i·for·nia \ˌka-lə-'fȯr-nyə\ state SW U.S.; *, Sacramento; *pop* 37,253,956 — **Cal·i·for·nian** \-nyən\ *adj or n*

California, Gulf of arm of the Pacific NW Mexico

Cal·va·ry \\'kal-v(ə-)rē\ place outside ancient Jerusalem where Jesus was crucified

Cambay, Gulf of — see KHAMBHAT (Gulf of)

Cam·bo·dia \kam-'bō-dē-ə\ *or* **Kam·pu·chea** \ˌkam-pu̇-'chē-ə\ country SE Asia in S Indochina; *, Phnom Penh; *pop* 13,396,000 — **Cam·bo·di·an** \kam-'bō-dē-ən\ *adj or n*

Cam·bria \\'kam-brē-ə\ WALES — an old name

Cam·bridge \\'kām-brij\ **1** city E Massachusetts W of Boston; *pop* 105,162 **2** city E England; *pop* 92,772

Cam·bridge·shire \\'kām-brij-ˌshir, -shər\ *or* **Cambridge** county E England

Cam·den \\'kam-dən\ borough of N Greater London, England; *pop* 220,000

Cam·er·oon *or French* **Cam·er·oun** \ˌka-mə-'rün\ country W Africa; *, Yaoundé; *pop* 17,464,000 — **Cam·er·oo·nian** \-'rü-nē-ən, -rü-nyən\ *adj or n*

Ca·mi·guin \ˌkä-mē-'gēn\ island Philippines, off N coast of Mindanao

Ca·naan \\'kā-nən\ the part of ancient Palestine between Jordan River & Mediterranean Sea; sometimes used to refer to all of ancient Palestine — **Ca·naan·ite** \'kā-nə-ˌnīt\ *adj or n*

Can·a·da \\'ka-nə-də\ country N North America; *, Ottawa; *pop* 33,476,688 — **Ca·na·di·an** \kə-'nā-dē-ən\ *adj or n*

Canadian Falls — see NIAGARA FALLS

Canadian Shield *or* **Lau·ren·tian Plateau** \lȯ-'ren(t)-shən\ plateau region E Canada & NE U.S. extending from Mackenzie River basin E to Davis Strait & S to S Quebec, S *cen* Ontario, NE Minnesota, N Wisconsin, NW Michigan, and NE New York including the Adirondacks

Canal Zone *or* **Panama Canal Zone** strip of territory Panama leased to U.S. (until 1979) for Panama Canal

Ca·nary \kə-'ner-ē\ islands Spain in the Atlantic off NW coast of Africa; *pop* 2,118,679

Ca·nav·er·al, Cape \kə-'nav-rəl, -'na-və-\ *or* *1963–73* **Cape Ken·ne·dy** \-'ken-ə-dē\ cape E Florida in the Atlantic on Canaveral Peninsula E of Indian River

Can·ber·ra \\'kan-b(ə-)rə, -ˌber-ə\ city, * of Australia in Australian Capital Territory; *pop* 355,596

Cannes \\'kan, 'kän\ port SE France; *pop* 73,671

Can·ter·bury \\'kan-tə(r)-ˌber-ē, -b(ə-)rē\ city SE England; *pop* 34,404

Canton — see GUANGZHOU

Cape Bret·on Island \käp-'bret-tᵊn, kə-'bre-, -'bri-\ island NE Nova Scotia

Cape Coral city SW Florida; *pop* 154,305

Cape Horn — see HORN, CAPE

Cape of Good Hope — see GOOD HOPE, CAPE OF

Cape Province *or* **Cape of Good Hope** *or before 1910* **Cape Colony** former province S Republic of South Africa

Cape Town \'kāp-,taun\ city, legislative * of Republic of South Africa and formerly * of Cape Province; *pop* 3,740,026

Cape Verde \'vərd\ *or* **Ca·bo Ver·de** \,kä-bü-'ver-də\ islands in the North Atlantic off W Africa; country; *, Praia; *pop* 303,673 — **Cape Verd·ean** \'vər-dē-ən\ *adj or n*

Cape York Peninsula \'york\ peninsula NE Australia in N Queensland

Ca·pri \kä-'prē, kə-; 'kä-(,)prē, 'kä-\ island Italy S of Bay of Naples; *pop* 7270

Ca·ra·cas \kä-'rä-käs\ city, * of Venezuela; *pop* 1,836,000

Car·diff \'kär-dif\ city, * of Wales; *pop* 335,000

Ca·rib·be·an Sea \,ka-rə-'bē-ən, kə-'ri-bē-\ arm of the Atlantic; on N & E are the West Indies, on S is South America, & on W is Central America — **Caribbean** *adj*

Car·lisle \kär-'lī(-ə)l, kər-, 'kär-,\ city NW England; *pop* 99,800

Carls·bad Caverns \'kär(-ə)lz-,bad\ series of caves SE New Mexico

Car·mar·then \kär-'mär-thən, kə(r)-\ port S Wales; *pop* 54,800

Car·o·li·na \,ka-rə-'lī-nə\ English colony on E coast of North America founded 1663 & divided 1729 into North Carolina & South Carolina (the **Carolinas**) — **Car·o·lin·i·an** \,ka-rə-'li-nē-ən, -nyən\ *adj or n*

Ca·ro·li·na \,kä-rō-'lē-nä\ city NE Puerto Rico; *pop* 176,762

Car·o·line \'ka-rə-,līn, -lən\ islands W Pacific E of S Philippines; comprising Palau & the Federated States of Micronesia

Car·pa·thi·an \kär-'pā-thē-ən\ mountains E *cen* Europe along boundary between Slovakia & Poland & in N & *cen* Romania; highest Gerlachovsky 8711 ft. (2655 m.)

Car·pen·tar·ia, Gulf of \,kär-pən-'ter-ē-ə\ inlet of Arafura Sea N of Australia

Car·rick·fer·gus \,ka-rik-'fər-gəs\ district E Northern Ireland; *pop* 39,000

Car·roll·ton \'ka-rəl-tən\ city N Texas; *pop* 119,097

Car·son City \'kär-sᵊn\ city, * of Nevada; *pop* 55,274

Car·thage \'kär-thij\ ancient city N Africa NE of modern Tunis; * of an empire that once included much of NW Africa, E Spain, & Sicily — **Car·tha·gin·ian** \,kär-thə-'ji-nyən, -nē-ən\ *adj or n*

Ca·sa·blan·ca \,ka-sə-'blaŋ-kə, ,kä-sə-'bläŋ-, -zə-\ city W Morocco on the Atlantic; *pop* 3,102,000

Cas·cade Range \(,)kas-'kād\ mountains NW U.S. in Washington, Oregon, & N California — see RAINIER, MOUNT

Cas·per \'kas-pər\ city *cen* Wyoming; *pop* 55,316

Cas·pi·an Sea \'kas-pē-ən\ salt lake between Europe and Asia about 90 ft. (27 m.) below sea level

Cas·tile \ka-'stēl\ *or in full* **Cas·ti·lla** \kä-'stēl-yä, -'stē-yä\ region & ancient kingdom *cen* & N Spain

Cast·le·reagh \'ka-səl-(,)rā\ district E Northern Ireland; *pop* 67,000

Cas·tries \'kas-,trēz, -,trēs\ seaport, * of Saint Lucia; *pop* 11,900

Cat·a·lo·nia \,ka-tə-'lō-nyə, -nē-ə\ region NE Spain bordering on France & the Mediterranean; chief city, Barcelona; *pop* 7,519,843 — **Cat·a·lo·nian** \-'ō-nyən, -nē-ən\ *adj or n*

Ca·thay \ka-'thā\ an old name for China

Cats·kill \'kat-,skil\ mountains in Appalachian system SE New York W of the Hudson

Cau·ca·sus \'kó-kə-səs\ mountain system SE Europe between Black & Caspian seas in Russia, Georgia, Azerbaijan, & Armenia

Cay·enne \kī-'en, kā-\ city, * of French Guiana; *pop* 37,097

Cay·man \(,)kā-'man, *attributively* 'kā-mən\ islands West Indies NW of Jamaica; a British colony; *pop* 56,700

Ce·bu \sā-'bü\ island E *cen* Philippines

Ce·dar Rapids \'sē-dər\ city E Iowa; *pop* 126,326

Cel·tic Sea \'kel-tik, 'sel-\ inlet of the Atlantic in British Isles SE of Ireland, SW of Wales, & W of SW England

Central African Republic country N *cen* Africa; *, Bangui; *pop* 2,998,000

Central America narrow portion of North America from S border of Mexico to South America — **Central American** *adj or n*

Central Valley valley of Sacramento & San Joaquin rivers in California between Sierra Nevada & Coast Ranges

Cey·lon \si-'län, sā-\ 1 island in Indian Ocean off S India 2 — see SRI LANKA — **Cey·lon·ese** \,sā-lə-'nēz, ,sē-, ,se-, -'nēs\ *adj or n*

Chad \'chad\ country N *cen* Africa; *, N'Djamena; *pop* 9,253,000 — **Chad·ian** \'cha-dē-ən\ *adj or n*

Chad, Lake shallow lake N *cen* Africa at junction of boundaries of Chad, Niger, & Nigeria

Cha·gos Archipelago \'chä-gəs\ island group *cen* Indian Ocean; forms British Indian Ocean Territory — see DIEGO GARCIA

Chal·dea \kal-'dē-ə\ ancient region SW Asia on Euphrates River & Persian Gulf — **Chal·de·an** \-'dē-ən\ *adj or n* — **Chal·dee** \'kal-,dē\ *n*

Cham·pagne \sham-'pān\ region NE France

Cham·plain, Lake \sham-'plān\ lake between New York & Vermont extending N into Quebec

Chan·di·garh \'chən-dē-gər\ city N India N of Delhi; *pop* 809,000

Chan·dler \'chan(d)-lər\ city SW *cen* Arizona; *pop* 236,123

Chang \'chäŋ\ *or traditionally* **Yang·tze** \'yaŋ-'sē, 'yaŋ(k)t-'sē; 'yäŋ-'tsə\ river 3434 mi. (5525 km.) long *cen* China flowing into East China Sea

Chang·chun \'chäŋ-'chùn\ city NE China; *pop* 3,802,000

Chang·sha \'chäŋ-'shä\ city SE *cen* China; *pop* 3,094,000

Channel islands in English Channel including Jersey, Guernsey, & Alderney & belonging to United Kingdom; *pop* 135,694

Charles \'chär(-ə)lz\ river 47 mi. (76 km.) long E Massachusetts flowing into Boston harbor

Charles, Cape cape E Virginia N of entrance to Chesapeake Bay

Charles·ton \'chär(-ə)l-stən\ 1 seaport SE South Carolina; *pop* 120,083 2 city, * of West Virginia; *pop* 51,400

Char·lotte \'shär-lət\ city S North Carolina; *pop* 731,424

Charlotte Ama·lie \ə-'mäl-yə, 'a-mə-lē\ city, * of Virgin Islands of the U.S.; on island of Saint Thomas; *pop* 11,004

Char·lottes·ville \'shär-ləts-,vil, -vəl\ city *cen* Virginia; *pop* 43,475

Char·lotte·town \'shär-lət-,taun\ city, * of Prince Edward Island, Canada; *pop* 32,174

Chat·ta·noo·ga \,cha-tə-'nü-gə\ city SE Tennessee; *pop* 167,674

Chech·nya \chech-'nyä, 'chech-nyə\ republic of SE Russia in Europe; *, Grozny

Chelms·ford \'chemz-fərd\ town SE England; *pop* 150,000

Che·lya·binsk \chel-'yä-bən(t)sk\ city W Russia; *pop* 1,130,000

Cheng·chou — see ZHENGZHOU

Cheng·du *or* **Ch'eng·tu** \'chən-'dü\ city SW *cen* China; *pop* 7,416,000

Chennai — see MADRAS

Cher·no·byl \chər-'nō-bəl, (,)cher-\ site N Ukraine of town abandoned after 1986 nuclear accident

Ches·a·peake \'che-sə-,pēk, 'ches-,pēk\ city SE Virginia; *pop* 222,209

Chesapeake Bay inlet of the Atlantic in Virginia & Maryland

Chesh·ire \'che-shər, -,shir\ *or* **Ches·ter** \'ches-tər\ former county W England bordering on Wales

Chester \'ches-tər\ city NW England; *pop* 58,436

Chev·i·ot \'che-vē-ət, 'che-\ hills along English–Scottish border

Chey·enne \shī-'an, -'en\ city, * of Wyoming; *pop* 59,466

Chi·ba \'chē-bä\ city E Japan on Honshu on Tokyo Bay E of Tokyo; *pop* 961,749

Chi·ca·go \shə-'kä-(,)gō, -'kó-, -gə\ city & port NE Illinois on Lake Michigan; *pop* 2,695,598 — **Chi·ca·go·an** \-'kä-gō-ən, -'kó-\ *n*

Chi·chén It·zá \chē-,chen-ēt-'sä, -'ēt-sə\ ruined Mayan city SE Mexico in Yucatán Peninsula

Chich·es·ter \'chi-chəs-tər\ city S England; *pop* 24,189

Ch'i–ch'i–ha–erh — see QIQIHAR

Chihli, Gulf of — see BO HAI

Chi·le \'chi-lē, 'chē-()lā\ country SW South America; *,

Santiago; *pop* 16,341,929 — **Chil·ean** \'chi-lē-ən, chə-'lā-ən\ *adj or n*

Chim·bo·ra·zo \ˌchēm-bō-'rä-(ˌ)zō\ mountain 20,561 ft. (6267 m.) W *cen* Ecuador

Chi·na \'chī-nə\ 1 country E Asia; ✳, Beijing; *pop* 1,335,000,000 — *see* TAIWAN 2 sea section of the W Pacific; divided into East China & South China seas

Chin–chou *or* **Chinchow** — see JINZHOU

Chi·și·năus \ˌkē-shē-'naú\ *or* **Ki·shi·nev** \ˌki-shi-'nyôf; 'ki-shə-ˌnef, -ˌnev\ city *cen* Moldova; its ✳; *pop* 664,700

Chit·ta·gong \'chi-tə-ˌgäŋ, -ˌgôŋ\ city SE Bangladesh on Bay of Bengal; *pop* 3,920,222

Chong·qing *or* **Ch'ung–ch'ing** \'chùŋ-'chiŋ\ *or* **Chung·king** \'chùŋ-'kiŋ\ city SW *cen* China; *pop* 6,861,000

Christ·church \'krīs(t)-ˌchərch\ city New Zealand on E coast of South Island; urban area *pop* 341,469

Christ·mas \'kris-məs\ island E Indian Ocean SW of Java; governed by Australia; *pop* 1000

Chu·la Vis·ta \ˌchü-lə-'vis-tə\ city SW California S of San Diego; *pop* 243,916

Chuuk \'chük\ *or* **Truk** \'trək, 'trük\ islands *cen* Carolines, part of Federated States of Micronesia; *pop* 53,300

Cin·cin·na·ti \ˌsin(t)-sə-'na-tē, -'na-tə\ city SW Ohio; *pop* 296,943

Ci·u·dad Juá·rez \syü-'thäth-'hwär-es, 'wär-; ˌsē-ü-'dad-\ city Mexico on Texas border; *pop* 1,332,131

Ciudad Trujillo — see SANTO DOMINGO

Clarks·ville \'klärks-ˌvil, -vəl\ city N Tennessee NW of Nashville; *pop* 132,929

Clear·wa·ter \'klir-ˌwò-tər, -ˌwä-\ city W Florida NW of St. Petersburg; *pop* 107,685

Cleve·land \'klēv-lənd\ city & port NE Ohio on Lake Erie; *pop* 396,815

Clyde \'klīd\ river 106 mi. (171 km.) long SW Scotland flowing into **Firth of Clyde** (estuary)

Coast Mountains mountain range W British Columbia, Canada; the N continuation of Cascade Range

Coast Ranges chain of mountain ranges W North America extending along Pacific coast W of Sierra Nevada & Cascade Range & through Vancouver Island into S Alaska to Kenai Peninsula & Kodiak Island

Cod, Cape \-'käd\ peninsula SE Massachusetts

Coim·ba·tore \ˌkòim-bə-'tòr\ city S India; *pop* 1,050,721

Cole·raine \kōl-'rān, 'kōl-ˌ\ 1 district N Northern Ireland; *pop* 59,000 2 port in Coleraine district

Co·logne \kə-'lōn\ city W Germany on the Rhine; *pop* 1,005,775

Co·lom·bia \kə-'ləm-bē-ə\ country NW South America; ✳, Bogotá; *pop* 41,468,000 — **Co·lom·bi·an** \-bē-ən\ *adj or n*

Co·lom·bo \kə-'ləm-bō\ city ✳ of Sri Lanka; *pop* 647,100

Col·o·ra·do \ˌkä-lə-'ra-(ˌ)dō\ 1 river 1450 mi. (2334 km.) long SW U.S. & NW Mexico flowing from N Colorado into Gulf of California 2 desert SE California 3 plateau region SW U.S. W of Rocky Mountains 4 state W U.S.; ✳, Denver; *pop* 5,029,196 — **Col·o·rad·an** \-'ra-dᵊn, -'rä-\ *or* **Co·lo·ra·do·an** \-'ra-dō-ən, -'rä-\ *adj or n*

Colorado Springs city *cen* Colorado E of Pikes Peak; *pop* 416,427

Co·lum·bia \kə-'ləm-bē-ə\ 1 river 1214 mi. (1953 km.) long SW Canada & NW U.S. flowing S & W from SE British Columbia into the Pacific 2 plateau in Columbia River basin in E Washington, E Oregon, & SW Idaho 3 city, ✳ of South Carolina; *pop* 129,272

Co·lum·bus \kə-'ləm-bəs\ 1 city W Georgia; *pop* 189,885 2 city, ✳ of Ohio; *pop* 787,033

Com·mon·wealth, the \'käm-ən-ˌwel(t)th\ *or* **Commonwealth of Nations** *formerly* **British Commonwealth** the United Kingdom & most of the countries formerly dependent on it

Com·o·ros \'kä-mə-ˌrōz\ islands off SE Africa NW of Madagascar; country (except for Mayotte Island); ✳, Moroni; *pop* 752,000

Con·a·kry \'kä-nə-krē\ city, ✳ of Guinea; *pop* 1,668,000

Con·cord \'kä-ˌkòrd, 'käŋ-\ 1 city W California; *pop* 122,067 2 town E Massachusetts NW of Boston; *pop* 17,668 3 city, ✳ of New Hampshire; *pop* 42,695

Con·go \'käŋ-(ˌ)gō\ 1 *or* **Zaire** \zä-'ir\ river over 2700 mi. (4344 km.) long W Africa flowing into the Atlantic 2 *officially* **Democratic Republic of the Congo** *formerly* *1971–97* **Zaire** country *cen* Africa consisting of most of Congo River basin E of lower Congo River; ✳, Kinshasa;

pop 67,800,000 3 *or officially* **Republic of the Congo** country W *cen* Africa W of lower Congo River; ✳, Brazzaville; *pop* 3,697,000 — **Con·go·lese** \ˌkäŋ-gə-'lēz, -'lēs\ *adj or n*

Con·nacht \'kä-ˌnòt\ province W Ireland; *pop* 464,296

Con·nect·i·cut \kə-'ne-ti-kət\ 1 river 407 mi. (655 km.) long NE U.S. flowing S from N New Hampshire into Long Island Sound 2 state NE U.S.; ✳, Hartford; *pop* 3,574,097

Constantinople — see ISTANBUL

Continental Divide line of highest points of land separating the waters flowing W from those flowing N or E and extending SSE from NW Canada across W U.S. through Mexico & Central America to South America where it joins the Andes Mountains

Cook \'kúk\ 1 inlet of the Pacific S Alaska W of Kenai Peninsula 2 islands South Pacific SW of Society Islands belonging to New Zealand; *pop* 19,600 3 strait New Zealand between North Island & South Island

Cook, Mount *or* **Ao·ra·ki** \aú-'rä-kē\ mountain 12,349 ft. (3764 m.) New Zealand in W *cen* South Island in Southern Alps; highest in New Zealand

Cooks·town \'kúks-ˌtaún\ district *cen* Northern Ireland; *pop* 37,000

Co·pen·ha·gen \ˌkō-pən-'hä-gən, -'hā-\ city, ✳ of Denmark; *pop* 579,513

Cor·al Sea \'kòr-əl, 'kär-\ arm of the W Pacific NE of Australia

Coral Springs city SE Florida; *pop* 121,096

Cór·do·ba \'kòr-də-bə, 'kòr-thō-ˌvä\ city N *cen* Argentina; *pop* 1,293,000

Cor·inth \'kòr-ən(t)th, 'kär-\ 1 region of ancient Greece 2 ancient city; site SW of present city of Corinth — **Co·rin·thi·an** \kə-'rin(t)-thē-ən\ *adj or n*

Corinth, Gulf of inlet of Ionian Sea *cen* Greece N of the Peloponnese

Cork \'kòrk\ city S Ireland; *pop* 198,582

Corn·wall \'kòrn-ˌwòl, -wəl\ *or* *1974-2009* **Cornwall and Isles of Scilly** \'si-lē\ former county SW England

Co·ro·na \kə-'rō-nə\ city SW California E of Los Angeles; *pop* 152,374

Cor·pus Chris·ti \ˌkòr-pəs-'kris-tē\ city & port S Texas; *pop* 305,215

Cor·reg·i·dor \kə-'re-gə-ˌdòr\ island Philippines at entrance to Manila Bay

Cor·si·ca \'kòr-si-kə\ island France in the Mediterranean N of Sardinia; *pop* 309,693 — **Cor·si·can** \'kòr-si-kən\ *adj or n*

Cos·ta Me·sa \'kòs-tə-'mā-sə\ city SW California; *pop* 109,960

Costa Ri·ca \'rē-kə\ country Central America between Nicaragua & Panama; ✳, San José; *pop* 4,301,712 — **Cos·ta Ri·can** \-kən\ *adj or n*

Côte d'Ivoire \ˌkōt-dē-'vwär\ *or* *English* **Ivory Coast** country W Africa on Gulf of Guinea; official ✳, Yamoussoukro; seat of government, Abidjan; *pop* 22,650,000

Cots·wold \'kät-ˌswōld, -swəld\ hills SW *cen* England

Cov·en·try \'kə-vən-trē\ city *cen* England; *pop* 326,000

Craig·av·on \krā-'ga-vən\ district *cen* Northern Ireland; *pop* 93,000

Cra·ter \'krā-tər\ lake 1932 ft. (589 m.) deep SW Oregon in Cascade Range

Crete \'krēt\ island Greece in E Mediterranean; *pop* 623,065 — **Cre·tan** \'krē-tᵊn\ *adj or n*

Cri·mea \krī-'mē-ə, krə-\ peninsula SE Europe extending into Black Sea — **Cri·me·an** \krī-'mē-ən, krə-\ *adj*

Cro·atia \krō-'ā-sh(ē-)ə\ country SE Europe; ✳, Zagreb; *pop* 4,288,000 — **Croat** \'krō-ˌat\ *n*

Croy·don \'kròi-dᵊn\ borough of S Greater London, England; *pop* 363,000

Cu·ba \'kyü-bə, 'kü-vä\ island in the West Indies; country; ✳, Havana; *pop* 11,167,000 — **Cu·ban** \'kyü-bən\ *adj or n*

Cum·ber·land \'kəm-bər-lənd\ river 687 mi. (1106 km.) long S Kentucky & N Tennessee

Cumberland Gap pass through Cumberland Plateau NE Tennessee

Cumberland Plateau mountain region E U.S.; part of S Appalachian Mountains extending from S West Virginia to NE Alabama

Cum·bria \'kəm-brē-ə\ county NW England; *pop* 499,858

Cum·bri·an \\'kəm-brē-ən\\ mountains NW England chiefly in Cumbria county

Cu·par \\'kü-pər\\ town E Scotland; *pop* 6642

Cu·ri·ti·ba \\ˌkür-ə-'tē-bə\\ city S Brazil SW of São Paulo; *pop* 1,751,907

Cush \\'kəsh, 'kùsh\\ ancient country NE Africa in upper Nile valley S of Egypt — **Cush·ite** \\'kə-ˌshīt, 'kù-\\ *n* — **Cush·it·ic** \\ˌkə-'shi-tik, kù-\\ *adj*

Cuz·co \\'küs-(ˌ)kō\\ city S *cen* Peru; *pop* 348,935

Cymru — see WALES

Cy·prus \\'sī-prəs\\ island E Mediterranean S of Turkey; country; ✻, Nicosia; *pop* 1,100,000 — **Cyp·ri·ot** \\'si-prē-ət, -ˌät\\ *or* **Cyp·ri·ote** \\-ˌōt, -ət\\ *adj or n*

Cy·re·na·ica \\ˌsir-ə-'nā-ə-kə, ˌsī-rə-\\ ancient region N Africa on coast W of Egypt — **Cy·re·na·i·can** \\-'nā-ə-kən\\ *adj or n*

Czecho·slo·va·kia \\ˌche-kə-slō-'vä-kē-ə, -slə-, -'va-\\ former country *cen* Europe divided into the independent states of the Czech Republic & Slovakia — **Czecho·slo·vak** \\-'slō-ˌväk, -ˌvak\\ *adj or n* — **Czecho·slo·va·ki·an** \\-slō-'vä-kē-ən, -slə-, -'va-\\ *adj or n*

Czech Republic country *cen* Europe; ✻, Prague; *pop* 10,522,000

Dae·gu \\'dä-gü\\ *or* **Tae·gu** \\'tä-gü, 'dä-\\ city SE South Korea; *pop* 2,444,000

Daejeon — see TAEJON

Dahomey — see BENIN

Dairen — see DALIAN

Da·kar \\'da-ˌkär, də-'kär\\ city, ✻ of Senegal; *pop* 2,200,000

Da·ko·ta **1** *or* **James** river 710 mi. (1143 km.) long North Dakota & South Dakota flowing S into the Missouri **2** territory 1861–89 NW U.S. divided 1889 into states of North Dakota & South Dakota (the **Dakotas** \\-təz\\ )

Da·lian *or* **Ta·lien** \\'dä-'lyen\\ *or* **Lü·da** *or* **Lü–ta** \\'lü-'dä\\ *or* **Dai·ren** \\'dī-'ren\\ city NE China; *pop* 3,995,000

Dal·las \\'da-ləs, -lis\\ city NE Texas; *pop* 1,197,816

Dal·ma·tia \\dal-'mā-sh(ē-)ə\\ region W Balkan Peninsula on the Adriatic — **Dal·ma·tian** \\-shən\\ *adj or n*

Da·ly City \\'dā-lē\\ city W California S of San Francisco; *pop* 101,123

Da·mas·cus \\də-'mas-kəs\\ city, ✻ of Syria; *pop* 1,451,000

Dan·ube \\'dan-(ˌ)yüb\\ river 1771 mi. (2850 km.) long S Europe flowing from SW Germany into Black Sea — **Da·nu·bi·an** \\də-'nü-bē-ən, da-, -'nyü-\\ *adj*

Dar·da·nelles \\ˌdär-də-'nelz\\ *or* **Hel·les·pont** \\'he-lə-ˌspänt\\ strait NW Turkey connecting Sea of Marmara & the Aegean

Dar es Sa·laam \\ˌdär-ˌe(s)-sə-'läm\\ city, historic ✻ of Tanzania; *pop* 4,365,000

Dar·ling \\'där-liŋ\\ river about 1700 mi. (2735 km.) long SE Australia in Queensland & New South Wales flowing SW into the Murray

Dar·win \\'där-wən\\ city Australia, ✻ of Northern Territory; *pop* 103,016

Da·vao \\'dä-ˌvaù, dä-'vaù\\ city S Philippines in E Mindanao on Davao Gulf; *pop* 1,449,000

Dav·en·port \\'da-vən-ˌpōrt\\ city E Iowa; *pop* 99,685

Da·vis \\'dä-vəs\\ strait between SW Greenland & E Baffin Island connecting Baffin Bay & the Atlantic

Day·ton \\'dā-tᵊn\\ city SW Ohio; *pop* 141,527

Dead Sea salt lake between Israel & Jordan; 1312 ft. (400 m.) below sea level

Death Valley dry valley E California & S Nevada containing lowest point in U.S. (282 ft. *or* 86 m. below sea level)

Dec·can \\'de-kən, -ˌkan\\ plateau region S India

Del·a·ware \\'de-lə-ˌwer, -wər\\ **1** river 296 mi. (476 km.) long E U.S. flowing S from S New York into Delaware Bay **2** state E U.S.; ✻, Dover; *pop* 897,934 — **Del·a·war·ean** *or* **Del·a·war·ian** \\ˌde-lə-'wer-ē-ən\\ *adj or n*

Delaware Bay inlet of the Atlantic between SW New Jersey & E Delaware

Del·hi \\'de-lē\\ city N India; *pop* 11,034,555 — see NEW DELHI

De·los \\'dē-ˌläs\\ island Greece — **De·lian** \\'dē-lē-ən, 'dēl-yən\\ *adj or n*

Del·phi \\'del-ˌfī\\ ancient town *cen* Greece on S slope of Mt. Parnassus

Democratic Republic of the Congo — see CONGO 2

De·na·li \\də-'nä-lē\\ *or unofficially* **Mount Mc·Kin·ley** \\mə-'kin-lē\\ mountain 20,320 *ft* (6149 *m*) *cen* Alaska Range; highest in U.S. and N. America; in **Denali National Park**

Den·mark \\'den-ˌmärk\\ country N Europe occupying most of Jutland & neighboring islands; ✻, Copenhagen; *pop* 5,604,000

Den·ver \\'den-vər\\ city, ✻ of Colorado; *pop* 600,158

Der·by \\'där-bē\\ city N *cen* England; *pop* 252,000

Der·by·shire \\'där-bē-ˌshir, -shər\\ *or* **Derby** county N *cen* England

Der·ry \\'der-ē\\ *or* **Lon·don·der·ry** \\ˌlən-dən-'der-ē\\ city & port NW Northern Ireland; *pop* 62,697

Des Moines \\di-'mòin\\ city, ✻ of Iowa; *pop* 203,433

De·troit \\di-'tròit\\ **1** river 31 mi. (50 km.) long between SE Michigan & Ontario connecting Lake Saint Clair & Lake Erie **2** city SE Michigan; *pop* 713,777

Dev·on \\'de-vən\\ *or* **De·von·shire** \\'de-vən-ˌshir, -shər\\ county SW England

Dha·ka \\'dä-kə\\ city, ✻ of Bangladesh; *pop* 7,033,000

Die·go Gar·cia \\dē-ˌā-gō-ˌgär-'sē-ə\\ island in Indian Ocean; chief island of Chagos Archipelago

Di·li \\'di-lē\\ city & port N Timor, ✻ of East Timor; *pop* 192,652

Di·nar·ic Alps \\də-'na-rik\\ range of the E Alps in W Slovenia, W Croatia, Bosnia and Herzegovina, & Montenegro

District of Co·lum·bia \\kə-'ləm-bē-ə\\ federal district E U.S. coextensive with city of Washington; *pop* 601,723

Djakarta — see JAKARTA

Dji·bou·ti \\jə-'bü-tē\\ **1** country E Africa on Gulf of Aden; *pop* 818,000 **2** city, its ✻; *pop* 339,500

Dni·pro·pe·trovs'k *or* **Dne·pro·pe·trovsk** \\də-ˌnye-prə-pə-'tròfsk\\ city E *cen* Ukraine; *pop* 996,500

Dodge City \\'däj\\ city S Kansas on Arkansas River; *pop* 27,340

Do·do·ma \\dō-'dō-(ˌ)mä\\ city, legislative ✻ of Tanzania; *pop* 312,500

Do·ha \\'dō-(ˌ)hä\\ city & port, ✻ of Qatar on Persian Gulf; *pop* 521,000

Dom·i·ni·ca \\ˌdä-mə-'nē-kə\\ island West Indies in the Leeward Islands; country; ✻, Roseau; *pop* 71,300

Do·min·i·can Republic \\də-'mi-ni-kən\\ country West Indies in E Hispaniola; ✻, Santo Domingo; *pop* 9,445,000 — **Dominican** *adj or n*

Don \\'dän\\ river 1224 mi. (1969 km.) long SW Russia

Do·nets'k \\də-'nyetsk\\ city E Ukraine; *pop* 980,000

Dor·ches·ter \\'dòr-chəs-tər, -ˌches-\\ town S England; *pop* 14,049

Dor·set \\'dòr-sət\\ *or* **Dor·set·shire** \\-ˌshir, -shər\\ county S England on English Channel

Dort·mund \\'dòrt-ˌmùnt, -mənd\\ city W Germany in the Ruhr; *pop* 571,143

Dou·a·la \\dü-'ä-lä\\ seaport W Cameroon; *pop* 1,900,000

Dou·ro \\'dòr-(ˌ)ü\\ *or Spanish* **Due·ro** \\'dwe(ə)r-ō\\ river 556 mi. (895 km.) long N Spain & N Portugal flowing into the Atlantic

Do·ver \\'dō-vər\\ city, ✻ of Delaware; *pop* 36,047

Dover, Strait of channel between SE England & N France; the most easterly section of English Channel

Down \\'daùn\\ district SE Northern Ireland; *pop* 69,750

Dow·ney \\'daù-nē\\ city SW California SE of Los Angeles; *pop* 111,772

Down·pat·rick \\daùn-'pa-trik\\ town E Northern Ireland; *pop* 8245

Dra·kens·berg \\'drä-kənz-ˌbərg\\ mountain range E Republic of South Africa & Lesotho; highest peak Thabana Ntlenyana 11,425 ft. (3482 m.)

Dres·den \\'drez-dən\\ city E Germany; *pop* 512,354

Du·bayy *or* **Du·bai** \\(ˌ)dü-'bī\\ **1** sheikhdom, member of United Arab Emirates; *pop* 1,790,000 **2** city, its ✻ *pop* 265,702

Dub·lin \\'də-blən\\ city, ✻ of Ireland; *pop* 527,612

Dud·ley \\'dəd-lē\\ town W *cen* England; *pop* 312,550

Duis·burg \\'dü-əs-ˌbərg, 'düz-ˌ, 'dyüz-ˌ\\ city W Germany at junction of Rhine & Ruhr rivers; *pop* 488,468

Du·luth \\də-'lüth\\ city & port NE Minnesota at W end of Lake Superior; *pop* 86,265

Dum·fries \\ˌdəm-'frēs, -'frēz\\ burgh S Scotland; *pop* 32,084

Dumfries and Gal·lo·way \\'ga-lə-ˌwā\\ administrative subdivision of S Scotland

Dun·dee \\ˌdən-'dē\\ city E Scotland; *pop* 147,000

Dun·gan·non \\ˌdən-'ga-nən\\ district W Northern Ireland; *pop* 53,000

Dur·ban \\'dər-bən\\ city and seaport E Republic of South Africa; *pop* 736,852

Dur·ham \'dər-əm, 'də-rəm, 'dùr-əm\ city N *cen* North Carolina; *pop* 228,330

Du·shan·be \dü-'sham-bə, dyü-, -'shäm-, 'dyü-,; ‚dyü-shäm-'bä\ city, ✻ of Tajikistan; *pop* 749,500

Düs·sel·dorf \'dü-səl-‚dörf, 'dyü-, 'due-\ city W Germany on the Rhine; *pop* 586,291

Ea·ling \'ē-liŋ\ borough of W Greater London, England; *pop* 338,000

East An·glia \'aŋ-glē-ə\ region E England; *pop* 1,586,051

East China Sea — see CHINA

Eas·ter \'ē-stər\ island Chile SE Pacific about 2000 mi. (3200 km.) W of Chilean coast

Eastern Cape province SE Republic of South Africa; *pop* 6,562,053

Eastern Desert desert E Egypt between the Nile & the Red Sea

Eastern Ghats \'gäts, 'góts, 'gəts\ chain of low mountains SE India along coast

Eastern Hemisphere the half of the earth E of the Atlantic Ocean including Europe, Asia, Australia, and Africa

Eastern Roman Empire the Byzantine Empire from 395 to 474

Eastern Samoa — see AMERICAN SAMOA

East Germany — see GERMANY

East Indies the Malay Archipelago — **East Indian** *adj or n*

East London city S Republic of South Africa; *pop* 296,000

East Pakistan the former E division of Pakistan consisting of E portion of Bengal; now Bangladesh

East River strait SE New York connecting upper New York Bay & Long Island Sound and separating Manhattan & Long Island

East Sea — see JAPAN, SEA OF

East Sus·sex \'sə-siks\ county SE England; *pop* 526,671

East Timor or **Ti·mor—Les·te** \'tē-mōr-'lesh-‚tā\ country SE Asia on E Timor; ✻, Dili; *pop* 1,066,000

Ebro \'ā-(‚)brō\ river 565 mi. (909 km.) long NE Spain flowing into the Mediterranean

Ec·ua·dor \'e-kwə-‚dòr, ‚e-kwä-'thòr\ country W South America; ✻, Quito; *pop* 14,483,000 — **Ec·ua·dor·an** \‚e-kwə-'dòr-ən\ or **Ec·ua·dor·ean** or **Ec·ua·dor·ian** \-ē-ən\ *adj or n*

Ed·in·burgh \'e-dᵊn-‚bər-ə\ city, ✻ of Scotland; *pop* 459,000

Ed·mon·ton \'ed-mən-tən\ city, ✻ of Alberta, Canada; *pop* 812,201

Edom \'ē-dəm\ ancient country SW Asia S of Judaea & Dead Sea — **Edom·ite** \'ēd-ə-‚mīt\ *n*

Egypt \'ē-jipt\ country NE Africa & Sinai Peninsula of SW Asia bordering on Mediterranean & Red seas; ✻, Cairo; *pop* 72,798,000

Eire — see IRELAND

Elam \'ē-ləm\ ancient country SW Asia at head of Persian Gulf E of Babylonia — **Elam·ite** \'ē-lə-‚mīt\ *n*

Elbe \'el-bə, 'elb\ river 720 mi. (1159 km.) long N Czech Republic & NE Germany flowing NW into North Sea

El·bert, Mount \'el-bərt\ mountain 14,433 ft. (4399 m.) W *cen* Colorado; highest in Colorado & the Rocky Mountains

El·brus, Mount \el-'brüz, -'brüs\ mountain 18,510 ft. (5642 m.) Russia; highest in the Caucasus & in Europe

El·burz \el-'bùrz\ mountains N Iran

Eliz·a·beth \i-'li-zə-bəth\ city NE New Jersey; *pop* 124,969

Elles·mere \'elz-‚mir\ island N Canada in Nunavut

Ellice — see TUVALU

El·lis Island \'e-ləs\ island SE New York S of Manhattan; served as immigration station 1892–1954

El Mon·te \el-'män-tē\ city SW California E of Los Angeles; *pop* 113,475

El Paso \el-'pa-(‚)sō\ city W Texas on Rio Grande; *pop* 649,121

El Sal·va·dor \el-'sal-və-‚dòr, -‚sal-və-'; ‚el-‚säl-vä-'thòr\ country Central America bordering on the Pacific; ✻, San Salvador; *pop* 5,744,113

Ely, Isle of \'ē-lē\ area of high ground amid marshes in East Anglia, England

En·field \'en-‚fēld\ borough of N Greater London, England; *pop* 316,500

En·gland \'iŋ-glənd, 'iŋ-lənd\ country S Great Britain; a division of United Kingdom; ✻, London; *pop* 53,012,456

English Channel arm of the Atlantic between S England & N France

En·nis·kil·len \‚e-nə-'ski-lən\ town SW Northern Ireland in Fermanagh district

Ephra·im \'ē-frē-əm\ 1 hilly region N Jordan E of Jordan River 2 — see ISRAEL — **Ephra·im·ite** \'ē-frē-ə-‚mīt\ *n*

Equatorial Guinea *formerly* **Spanish Guinea** country W Africa including Mbini & Bioko; ✻, Malabo; *pop* 722,000

Erie \'ir-ē\ 1 city & port NW Pennsylvania; *pop* 101,786 2 canal New York between Hudson River at Albany & Lake Erie at Buffalo; now superseded by New York State Barge Canal

Erie, Lake lake E *cen* North America in U.S. & Canada; one of the Great Lakes

Er·in \'er-ən\ poetic name of Ireland

Er·i·trea \‚er-ə-'trē-ə, -'trā-\ country NE Africa; ✻, Asmara; *pop* 4,252,000 — **Er·i·tre·an** \-ən\ *adj or n*

Es·con·di·do \‚es-kən-'dē-(‚)dō\ city SW California N of San Diego; *pop* 143,911

Es·fa·han \‚es-fə-'hän, -'han\ or **Is·fa·han** \‚is-\ city W *cen* Iran; *pop* 1,756,126

Española — see HISPANIOLA

Es·sen \'e-sᵊn\ city W Germany in the Ruhr; *pop* 566,201

Es·sex \'e-siks\ county SE England on North Sea; *pop* 1,393,587

Es·to·nia \e-'stō-nē-ə, -nyə\ country E Europe on Baltic Sea; ✻, Tallinn; *pop* 1,298,000 — **Es·to·nian** \e-'stō-nē-ən, -nyən\ *adj or n*

Eswa·ti·ni \‚e-swä-'tē-nē\ or **Swa·zi·land** \'swä-zē-‚land\ country SE Africa between South Africa & Mozambique; ✻, Mbabane; *pop* 1,018,000 — **Swa·zi** \'swä-zē\ *adj or n*

Ethi·o·pia \‚ē-thē-'ō-pē-ə\ *historically* **Ab·ys·sin·ia** \‚a-bə-'si-nē-ə, -nyə\ country E Africa; ✻, Addis Ababa; *pop* 73,835,000 — **Ethi·o·pi·an** \-pē-ən\ *adj or n*

Et·na, Mount \'et-nə\ volcano 10,902 ft. (3323 m.) Italy in NE Sicily

Eto·bi·coke \e-'tō-bi-‚kō\ former city Canada in SE Ontario; now part of Toronto

Etru·ria \i-'trùr-ē-ə\ ancient country *cen* peninsula of Italy

Eu·gene \yü-'jēn\ city W Oregon; *pop* 156,185

Eu·phra·tes \yù-'frā-(‚)tēz\ river 1700 mi. (2736 km.) long SW Asia flowing from E Turkey & uniting with the Tigris to form the Shatt al Arab

Eur·asia \yù-'rā-zhə, -shə\ landmass consisting of Europe & Asia — **Eur·asian** \-zhən, -shən\ *adj or n*

Eu·rope \'yùr-əp\ continent of the Eastern Hemisphere between Asia & the Atlantic

European Union economic, scientific, & political organization consisting of Belgium, France, Italy, Luxembourg, Netherlands, Germany, Denmark, Greece, Ireland, United Kingdom, Spain, Portugal, Austria, Finland, Sweden, Cyprus, Czech Republic, Estonia, Hungary, Latvia, Lithuania, Malta, Poland, Slovakia, Slovenia, Bulgaria, Romania, & Croatia

Ev·ans·ville \'e-vənz-‚vil\ city SW Indiana; *pop* 117,429

Ev·er·est, Mount \'ev-rəst, 'ev-ə-rəst\ mountain 29,035 ft. (8850 m.) S Asia in the Himalayas on border between Nepal & Tibet; highest in the world

Ev·er·glades \'e-vər-‚glādz\ swamp region S Florida now partly drained

Ex·e·ter \'ek-sə-tər\ city SW England; *pop* 101,100

Faer·oe or **Far·oe** \'fer-(‚)ō\ islands NE Atlantic NW of the Shetlands belonging to Denmark; *pop* 48,250 — **Faero·ese** \‚far-ə-'wēz, ‚fer-, -'wēs\ *adj or n*

Fair·banks \'fer-‚baŋks\ city E *cen* Alaska; *pop* 31,535

Fai·sa·la·bad \‚fī-sä-lə-'bäd, -‚sa-lə-'bad\ *formerly* **Ly·all·pur** \‚lī-‚äl-'pùr\ city NE Pakistan W of Lahore

Falk·land Islands \'fó-klənd, 'fól-\ or *Spanish* **Is·las Mal·vi·nas** \‚ēs-läs-mäl-'vē-näs\ island group SW Atlantic E of S end of Argentina; a British colony; ✻, Stanley

Far East the countries of E Asia & the Malay Archipelago — usually thought to consist of the Asian countries bordering on the Pacific but sometimes including also India, Sri Lanka, Bangladesh, Tibet, & Myanmar — **Far Eastern** *adj*

Far·go \'fär-(‚)gō\ city E North Dakota; largest in state; *pop* 105,549

Faroe — see FAEROE

Fay·ette·ville \'fā-ət-‚vil, -vəl\ city SE *cen* North Carolina; *pop* 200,564

Fear, Cape \'fir\ cape SE North Carolina

Fer·man·agh \fər-'ma-nə\ district SW Northern Ireland

Fernando Póo — see BIOKO

Fes \'fes\ city N *cen* Morocco; *pop* 947,000

Fife \'fīf\ administrative subdivision of E Scotland

Fi·ji \'fē-(,)jē\ islands SW Pacific; country; ✳, Suva; *pop* 837,000 — **Fi·ji·an** \'fē-(,)jē-ən, fi-'\ *adj or n*

Fin·land \'fin-lənd\ country NE Europe; ✳, Helsinki; *pop* 5,453,000 — **Fin·land·er** *n*

Flan·ders \'flan-dərz\ 1 region W Belgium & N France on North Sea 2 semiautonomous region W Belgium; *pop* 6,396,000

Flat·tery, Cape \'fla-tə-rē\ cape NW Washington at entrance to Strait of Juan de Fuca

Flint \'flint\ city SE Michigan; *pop* 102,434

Flor·ence \'flör-ən(t)s, 'flär-\ *or Italian* **Fi·ren·ze** \fē-'rent-sä\ city *cen* Italy; *pop* 358,079 — **Flor·en·tine** \'flör-ən-,tēn, 'flär-, -,tīn\ *adj or n*

Flor·i·da \'flör-ə-də, 'flär-\ state SE U.S.; ✳, Tallahassee; *pop* 18,801,310 — **Flo·rid·i·an** \flə-'ri-dē-ən\ *or* **Flor·i·dan** \'flör-ə-dən, 'flär-\ *adj or n*

Florida, Straits of channel between Florida Keys on NW & Cuba & Bahamas on S & E connecting Gulf of Mexico & the Atlantic

Florida Keys chain of islands off S tip of Florida

Foochow — see FUZHOU

For·a·ker, Mount \'fôr-i-kər, 'fär-\ mountain 17,400 ft. (5304 m.) S *cen* Alaska in Alaska Range

For·mo·sa \fôr-'mō-sə, fər-, -zə\ — see TAIWAN — **For·mo·san** \fôr-'mō-sᵊn, fər-, -zᵊn\ *adj or n*

For·ta·le·za \,fôr-tə-'lā-zə\ city & port NE Brazil on the Atlantic; *pop* 2,452,185

Fort Col·lins \'kä-lənz\ city N Colorado; *pop* 143,986

Fort–de–France \fôr-də-'fräⁿs\ city West Indies, ✳ of Martinique on W coast; *pop* 87,216

Forth \'fôrth\ river 116 mi. (187 km.) long S *cen* Scotland flowing E into North Sea through **Firth of Forth**

Fort Knox \'näks\ military reservation N *cen* Kentucky SSW of Louisville; location of U.S. Gold Bullion Depository

Fort Lau·der·dale \'lö-dər-,däl\ city SE Florida; *pop* 165,521

Fort Wayne \'wān\ city NE Indiana; *pop* 253,691

Fort Worth \'wərth\ city NE Texas; *pop* 741,206

Fox \'fäks\ islands SW Alaska in the E Aleutians

Foxe Basin \'fäks\ inlet of the Atlantic N Canada in E Nunavut W of Baffin Island

France \'fran(t)s, 'fräⁿs\ country W Europe between the English Channel & the Mediterranean; ✳, Paris; *pop* 64,613,000

Frank·fort \'fraŋk-fərt\ city, ✳ of Kentucky; *pop* 25,527

Frank·furt \'fraŋk-fərt, 'fräŋk-,fûrt\ *or in full* **Frankfurt am Main** \-(,)äm-'mīn\ city W Germany on Main River; *pop* 667,925

Frank·lin \'fraŋ-klən\ former district N Canada in Northwest Territories including Arctic Archipelago & Boothia & Melville peninsulas

Fra·ser \'frā-zər, -zhər\ river 850 mi. (1368 km.) long Canada in S *cen* British Columbia flowing into the Pacific

Fred·er·ic·ton \'fre-drik-tən, 'fre-də-rik-\ city, ✳ of New Brunswick, Canada; *pop* 50,535

Free State *formerly* **Or·ange Free State** \'ör-inj, 'är-, -ənj\ province E *cen* Republic of South Africa; *pop* 2,745,590

Free·town \'frē-,taun\ city, ✳ of Sierra Leone; *pop* 178,600

Fre·mont \'frē-,mänt\ city W California; *pop* 214,089

French Guiana country N South America on the Atlantic; an overseas division of France; ✳, Cayenne; *pop* 239,849

French Indochina — see INDOCHINA

Fres·no \'frez-(,)nō\ city S *cen* California SE of San Francisco; *pop* 494,665

Frunze — see BISHKEK

Fu·ji, Mount \'fü-jē\ *or* **Fu·ji·ya·ma** \,fü-jē-'yä-mä\ mountain 12,388 ft. (3776 m.) Japan in S *cen* Honshu; highest in Japan

Fu·ku·o·ka \,fü-kü-'ō-kä\ city Japan in N Kyushu; *pop* 1,463,743

Ful·ler·ton \'fù-lər-tən\ city SW California; *pop* 135,161

Fu·na·fu·ti \,fü-nä-'fü-tē\ city, ✳ of Tuvalu; *pop* 1328

Fun·dy, Bay of \'fən-dē\ inlet of the Atlantic SE Canada between New Brunswick & Nova Scotia

Fu·shun \'fü-'shun\ city NE China E of Shenyang; *pop* 1,319,000

Fu·zhou \'fü-'jō\ *or* **Foo·chow** \'fü-'jō, -'chau\ city & port SE China; *pop* 2,873,000

Ga·bon \gä-'bōⁿ\ country W Africa on the Equator; ✳, Libreville; *pop* 1,600,000 — **Gab·o·nese** \,ga-bə-'nēz, -'nēs\ *adj or n*

Ga·bo·rone \,gä-bō-'rō-(,)nā, ,kä-\ city, ✳ of Botswana; *pop* 229,500

Gads·den Purchase \'gadz-dən\ area of land S of Gila River in present Arizona & New Mexico purchased 1853 by the U.S. from Mexico

Ga·la·pa·gos Islands \gə-'lä-pə-gəs, -'la-, -,gōs\ island group Ecuador in the Pacific 600 mi. (965 km.) W of South America; *pop* 25,000

Ga·la·tia \gə-'lä-sh(ē-)ə\ ancient country *cen* Asia Minor in region around modern Ankara, Turkey — **Ga·la·tian** \-shən\ *adj or n*

Ga·li·cia \gə-'li-sh(ē-)ə\ 1 region E *cen* Europe now divided between Poland & Ukraine 2 region NW Spain on the Atlantic — **Ga·li·cian** \-'li-shən\ *adj or n*

Gal·i·lee \'ga-lə-,lē\ hilly region N Israel — **Gal·i·le·an** \,ga-lə-'lē-ən\ *adj or n*

Galilee, Sea of *or modern* **Lake Ti·be·ri·as** \tī-'bir-ē-əs\ lake N Israel on Syrian border; crossed by Jordan River

Gal·lo·way \'ga-lə-,wā\ former administrative district of SW Scotland — see DUMFRIES AND GALLOWAY

Gam·bia \'gam-bē-ə, 'gäm-\ *or* **the Gambia** *or* **Republic of the Gambia** country W Africa; ✳, Banjul; *pop* 1,882,000 — **Gam·bi·an** \-bē-ən\ *adj or n*

Gan·ges \'gan-,jēz\ river 1550 mi. (2494 km.) long N India flowing from the Himalayas SE & E to unite with the Brahmaputra and empty into Bay of Bengal through a vast delta — **Gan·get·ic** \gan-'je-tik\ *adj*

Gao·xiong \'gau-'shyun\ *or* **Kao–hsiung** \'kau-'shyun, 'gau\-\ city & port SW Taiwan; *pop* 2,780,000

Garden Grove city SW California; *pop* 170,883

Gar·land \'gär-lənd\ city NE Texas NNE of Dallas; *pop* 226,876

Ga·ronne \gə-'rän, gä-'rön\ river 355 mi. (571 km.) long SE France flowing NW

Gary \'ger-ē\ city NW Indiana on Lake Michigan; *pop* 80,294

Gas·co·ny \'gas-kə-nē\ region SW France — **Gas·con** \'gas-kən\ *adj or n*

Gas·pé \ga-'spā, 'ga-,\ peninsula SE Quebec E of mouth of the Saint Lawrence — **Gas·pe·sian** \ga-'spē-zhən\ *adj or n*

Gaul \'göl\ *or Latin* **Gal·lia** \'ga-lē-ə\ ancient country W Europe chiefly consisting of region occupied by modern France & Belgium

Gau·teng \'gau-,teŋ\ province *cen* NE Republic of South Africa; *pop* 12,272,000

Ga·za Strip \'gä-zə, 'ga-\ district NE Sinai Peninsula on the Mediterranean

Ge·ne·va \jə-'nē-və\ city SW Switzerland on Lake Geneva; *pop* 187,000 — **Ge·ne·van** \-vən\ *adj or n* — **Gen·e·vese** \,je-nə-'vēz, -'vēs\ *adj or n*

Geneva, Lake lake on border between SW Switzerland & E France

Gen·oa \'je-nō-ə\ *or Italian* **Ge·no·va** \'je-nō-(,)vä\ city & port NW Italy; *pop* 586,180 — **Gen·o·ese** \,je-nō-'ēz, -'ēs\ *or* **Gen·o·vese** \-nə-'vēz, -'vēs\ *adj or n*

George·town \'jörj-,taun\ 1 a W section of Washington, District of Columbia 2 city & port, ✳ of Guyana; *pop* 162,000

Geor·gia \'jör-jə\ 1 state SE U.S.; ✳, Atlanta; *pop* 9,687,653 2 *or* **Republic of Georgia** country SW Asia on Black Sea S of Caucasus Mountains; ✳, Tbilisi; *pop* 4,630,000 — **Geor·gian** \'jör-jən\ *adj or n*

Georgia, Strait of channel Canada & U.S. between Vancouver Island & main part of British Columbia NW of Puget Sound

Georgian Bay inlet of Lake Huron in S Ontario

Ger·man·town \'jər-mən-,taun\ a NW section of Philadelphia, Pennsylvania

Ger·ma·ny \'jər-mə-nē\ country *cen* Europe bordering on North & Baltic seas; ✳, Berlin; divided 1946–90 into two independent states: the **Federal Republic of Germany** (West Germany; ✳, Bonn) & the **German Democratic Republic** (East Germany; ✳, East Berlin); *pop* 80,219,695

Get·tys·burg \'ge-tēz-,bərg\ town S Pennsylvania; *pop* 7620

Gha·na \'gä-nə, 'ga-\ *formerly* **Gold Coast** country W Africa on Gulf of Guinea; ✳, Accra; *pop* 24,659,000 — **Gha·na·ian**

\gä-'nä-ən, ga-, -'nī-ən\ *or* **Gha·ni·an** \'gä-nē-ən, 'ga-, -nyən\ *adj or n*

Ghats \'gòts\ two mountain chains S India consisting of **Eastern Ghats** & **Western Ghats**

Ghent \'gent\ city NW *cen* Belgium; *pop* 250,000

Gi·bral·tar \jə-'bról-tər\ British colony on S coast of Spain including Rock of Gibraltar; *pop* 31,000

Gibraltar, Rock of cape on S coast of Spain in Gibraltar at E end of Strait of Gibraltar; highest point 1396 ft. (426 m.)

Gibraltar, Strait of passage between Europe & Africa connecting the Atlantic & the Mediterranean

Gi·la \'hē-lə\ river 630 mi. (1014 km.) long SW New Mexico and S Arizona flowing W into the Colorado

Gil·bert \'gil-bərt\ town SW *cen* Arizona; *pop* 208,453

Gilbert and El·lice Islands \'e-lis\ island group W Pacific; divided into Kiribati and Tuvalu

Gil·e·ad \'gi-lē-əd\ mountain region of NE ancient Palestine E of Jordan River; now in NW Jordan — **Gil·e·ad·ite** \-lē-ə-₂dīt\ *n*

Gi·za \'gē-zə\ city N Egypt on the Nile SW of Cairo; *pop* 2,865,000

Gla·cier Bay \'glā-shər\ inlet SE Alaska at S end of Saint Elias Range

Glas·gow \'glas-(₂)kō, 'glas-(₂)gō, 'glaz-(₂)gō\ city S *cen* Scotland on the Clyde; *pop* 586,000 — **Glas·we·gian** \gla-'swē-jən, glaz-\ *adj or n*

Glen·dale \'glen-₂dāl\ **1** city *cen* Arizona NW of Phoenix; *pop* 226,721 **2** city S California NE of Los Angeles; *pop* 191,719

Glouces·ter \'gläs-tər, 'glòs-\ town SW *cen* England; *pop* 91,800

Glouces·ter·shire \'gläs-tər-₂shir, -shər, 'glòs-\ *or* **Gloucester** county SW *cen* England; *pop* 596,984

Goa \'gō-ə\ state W India on Malabar coast; *pop* 1,458,545

Goat Island island W New York in Niagara River — see NIAGARA FALLS

Go·bi \'gō-(₂)bē\ desert E *cen* Asia in Mongolia & N China

Godthab — see NUUK

Godwin Austen — see K2

Go·lan Heights \'gō-₂län, -lən\ hilly region NE of Sea of Galilee

Gol·con·da \gäl-'kän-də\ ruined city *cen* India W of Hyderabad

Gold Coast 1 — see GHANA **2** coast region W Africa on N shore of Gulf of Guinea E of Côte d'Ivoire

Golden Gate strait W California connecting San Francisco Bay with Pacific Ocean

Good Hope, Cape of \₂gùd-'hōp\ cape S Republic of South Africa on SW coast of Western Cape province

Gorki — see NIZHNIY NOVGOROD

Gö·te·borg \₂yœ-tə-'bór-ē\ city & port SW Sweden; *pop* 538,000

Gram·pi·an \'gram-pē-ən\ hills N *cen* Scotland

Grand Banks shallow area in the W North Atlantic SE of Newfoundland

Grand Canyon gorge of Colorado River NW Arizona

Grand Canyon of the Snake — see HELLS CANYON

Grande, Rio — see RIO GRANDE

Grand Prairie city NE *cen* Texas W of Dallas; *pop* 175,396

Grand Rapids city SW Michigan; *pop* 188,040

Graz \'gräts\ city S Austria; *pop* 253,000

Great Australian Bight wide bay on S coast of Australia

Great Barrier Reef coral reef Australia off NE coast of Queensland

Great Basin region W U.S. between Sierra Nevada & Wasatch Range including most of Nevada & parts of California, Idaho, Utah, Wyoming, & Oregon; has no drainage to ocean

Great Bear lake Canada in Northwest Territories draining through Great Bear River into Mackenzie River

Great Brit·ain \'bri-tᵊn\ **1** island W Europe NW of France consisting of England, Scotland, & Wales; *pop* 61,371,000 **2** UNITED KINGDOM

Great Dividing Range mountain system E Australia extending S from Cape York Peninsula into Tasmania — see KOSCIUSKO, MOUNT

Greater Antilles group of islands of the West Indies including Cuba, Hispaniola, Jamaica, & Puerto Rico — see LESSER ANTILLES

Greater London metropolitan county SE England consisting of City of London & 32 surrounding boroughs

Greater Manchester metropolitan county NW England including city of Manchester

Greater Sudbury — see SUDBURY, GREATER

Great Lakes chain of five lakes (Superior, Michigan, Huron, Erie, & Ontario) *cen* North America in U.S. & Canada

Great Plains elevated plains region W *cen* U.S. & W Canada E of the Rockies; extending from W Texas to NE British Columbia & NW Alberta

Great Rift Valley basin SW Asia & E Africa extending with several breaks from valley of the Jordan S to *cen* Mozambique

Great Salt Lake lake N Utah having salty waters & no outlet

Great Slave Lake lake NW Canada in S Northwest Territories drained by Mackenzie River

Great Smoky mountains between W North Carolina & E Tennessee

Greece \'grēs\ country S Europe at S end of Balkan Peninsula; *, Athens; *pop* 10,816,286

Green \'grēn\ **1** mountains E North America in the Appalachians extending from S Quebec S through Vermont into W Massachusetts **2** river 730 mi. (1175 km.) long W U.S. flowing from W Wyoming S into the Colorado in SE Utah

Green Bay 1 inlet of NW Lake Michigan 120 mi. (193 km.) long in NW Michigan & NE Wisconsin **2** city NE Wisconsin on Green Bay; *pop* 104,057

Green·land \'grēn-lənd, -₂land\ island in the North Atlantic off NE North America belonging to Denmark; *, Nuuk; *pop* 56,300

Greens·boro \'grēnz-₂bər-ō\ city N *cen* North Carolina; *pop* 296,666

Green·wich \'gre-nich, 'grēn-₂wich, 'grin-₂wich\ borough of SE Greater London, England; *pop* 254,557

Green·wich Village \'gre-nich\ section of New York City in W Manhattan

Gre·na·da \grə-'nä-də\ island West Indies in S Windward Islands; independent country; *, Saint George's; *pop* 103,300

Gren·a·dines, the \₂gre-nə-'dēnz, 'gre-nə-₂\ islands West Indies in *cen* Windward Islands; N islands part of Saint Vincent and the Grenadines; S islands dependency of Grenada

Groz·ny \'gróz-nē, 'gräz-\ city S Russia in Europe; * of Chechnya; *pop* 271,600

Gua·da·la·ja·ra \₂gwä-də-lə-'här-ə, ₂gwä-thä-lä-'hä-rä\ city W *cen* Mexico; *pop* 1,495,189

Gua·dal·ca·nal \₂gwä-dᵊl-kə-'nal, ₂gwä-də-kə-\ island W Pacific in the SE Solomons; *pop* 93,600

Gua·dal·qui·vir \₂gwä-dᵊl-ki-'vir, -'kwi-vər\ river 408 mi. (656 km.) long S Spain flowing into the Atlantic

Gua·de·loupe \'gwä-də-₂lüp\ two islands separated by a narrow channel in West Indies in *cen* Leeward Islands; an overseas division of France; *pop* 403,400

Gua·lla·ti·ri \₂gwä-yə-'tir-ē, ₂gwī-ə-\ volcano 19,882 ft. (6060 m.) high N Chile

Guam \'gwäm\ island W Pacific in S Marianas belonging to U.S.; *, Hagåtña; *pop* 159,400 — **Gua·ma·ni·an** \gwä-'mä-nē-ən\ *adj or n*

Gua·na·ba·ra Bay \₂gwä-nä-'bär-ə\ inlet of the Atlantic SE Brazil on which city of Rio de Janeiro is located

Guang·dong \'gwän-'dùn\ *or* **Kwang·tung** \'gwän-'dún, 'kwän-, -'tùn\ province SE China bordering on South China Sea & Gulf of Tonkin; *, Guangzhou; *pop* 104,320,459

Guang·zhou \'gwän-'jō\ *or* **Can·ton** \'kan-₂tän, kan-'\ city & port SE China; *pop* 11,000,000

Guan·tá·na·mo Bay \gwän-'tä-nä-₂mō\ inlet of the Caribbean in SE Cuba; site of U.S. naval station

Gua·te·ma·la \₂gwä-tə-'mä-lə, -tä-'mä-lä\ **1** country Central America; *pop* 15,073,000 **2** *or* **Guatemala City**, its *; *pop* 942,000 — **Gua·te·ma·lan** \-'mä-lən\ *adj or n*

Gua·ya·quil \₂gwī-ə-'kēl, -'kil\ city & port W Ecuador; *pop* 2,285,000

Guay·na·bo \gwī-'nä-(₂)bō, -(₂)vō\ city NE *cen* Puerto Rico; *pop* 97,924

Guern·sey \'gərn-zē\ — see CHANNEL

Gui·a·na \gē-'a-nə, -'ä-nə; gī-'a-nə\ region N South America on the Atlantic; includes Guyana, French Guiana, Suriname, & nearby parts of Brazil & Venezuela — **Gui·a·nan** \-nən\ *adj or n*

Guin·ea \'gi-nē\ **1** region W Africa on the Atlantic extending along coast from Gambia to Angola **2** country W Africa N of Sierra Leone & Liberia; ✳, Conakry; *pop* 10,629,000 — **Guin·ean** \'gi-nē-ən\ *adj or n*

Guinea, Gulf of arm of the Atlantic W *cen* Africa

Guin·ea–Bis·sau \,gi-nē-bi-'saù\ country W Africa; ✳, Bissau; *pop* 1,521,000

Gui·yang \'gwä-'yäŋ\ *or* **Kuei–yang** \'gwä-'yäŋ\ city S China; *pop* 2,750,000

Gulf States states of U.S. bordering on Gulf of Mexico: Florida, Alabama, Mississippi, Louisiana, and Texas

Gulf Stream warm current of the Atlantic Ocean flowing from Gulf of Mexico NE along coast of U.S. to Nantucket Island and from there eastward

Guy·ana \gī-'an-ə\ *formerly* **British Guiana** country N South America on the Atlantic; ✳, Georgetown; *pop* 748,000 — **Guy·a·nese** \,gī-ə-'nēz, -'nēs\ *adj or n*

Gwangju — *see* KWANGJU

Gwent \'gwent\ former county SE Wales

Gwyn·edd \'gwi-ne<u>th</u>\ administrative area NW Wales; *pop* 121,874

Hack·ney \'hak-nē\ borough of N Greater London, England; *pop* 246,000

Ha·gât·ña \hə-'gät-nyə\ *formerly* **Aga·na** \ä-'gä-nyä\ town, ✳ of Guam; *pop* 1051

Hague, The \<u>th</u>ə-'häg\ city, seat of government of Netherlands; *pop* 825,018

Hai·kou \'hī-'kō\ city & port SE China; *pop* 1,517,000

Hai·phong \'hī-'fóŋ, -'fäŋ\ city & port N Vietnam; *pop* 808,000

Hai·ti \'hā-tē\ country West Indies in W Hispaniola; ✳, Port-au-Prince; *pop* 9,923,000 — **Hai·tian** \'hā-shən\ *adj or n*

Ha·le·a·ka·la Crater \,hä-lä-,ä-kä-'lä\ crater over 2500 ft. (762 m.) deep Hawaii in E Maui

Hal·i·fax \'ha-lə-,faks\ municipality & port, ✳ of Nova Scotia, Canada; *pop* 390,096

Ham·burg \'ham-,bərg; 'häm-,bùrg, -,bùrk\ city N Germany on the Elbe; *pop* 1,706,696 — **Ham·burg·er** \-,bər-gər, -,bùr-\ *n*

Ham·hung *or* **Ham·heung** \'häm-,hùŋ\ city E *cen* North Korea; *pop* 704,000

Ham·il·ton \'ha-məl-tən\ **1** town, ✳ of Bermuda; *pop* 1010 **2** city & port, S Ontario, Canada on Lake Ontario; *pop* 519,949

Ham·mer·smith and Ful·ham \'ha-mər-,smith-ənd-'fù-ləm\ borough of SW Greater London, England; *pop* 182,000

Hamp·shire \'hamp-,shir, -shər\ county S England on English Channel

Hamp·ton \'hamp-tən\ city SE Virginia; *pop* 137,436

Hampton Roads channel SE Virginia through which James River flows into Chesapeake Bay

Hang·zhou \'häŋ-'jō\ *or* **Hang·chow** \'haŋ-'chaù, 'häŋ-'jō\ *or* **Hang–chou** \-'jō\ city E China; *pop* 5,700,000

Han·ni·bal \'ha-nə-bəl\ city NE Missouri on the Mississippi River; *pop* 17,916

Han·no·ver *or* **Han·o·ver** \'ha-,nō-vər, -nə-vər, *G* hä-'nō-fər\ city N *cen* Germany; *pop* 506,416

Ha·noi \ha-'nói, hə-, hä-\ city ✳ of Vietnam; *pop* 2,481,000

Hao·ra \'haù-rə\ city E India on Hugli River opposite Calcutta; *pop* 1,077,000

Ha·ra·re \hə-'rä-(,)rā\ *formerly* **Salis·bury** \'sòlz-,ber-ē, -b(ə-)rē\ city, ✳ of Zimbabwe; *pop* 1,485,000

Har·bin \'här-bən, här-'bin\ *or* **Ha–erh–pin** \'hä-'ər-'bin\ city NE China; *pop* 5,237,000

Har·in·gey \'ha-riŋ-,gā\ borough of N Greater London, England; *pop* 259,000

Har·lem \'här-ləm\ section of New York City in N Manhattan

Har·ris·burg \'ha-rəs-,bərg\ city, ✳ of Pennsylvania; *pop* 49,528

Har·row \'ha-(,)rō\ borough of NW Greater London, England; *pop* 241,000

Hart·ford \'härt-fərd\ city, ✳ of Connecticut; *pop* 124,775

Hat·ter·as, Cape \'ha-tə-rəs\ cape North Carolina on **Hatteras Island**

Ha·vana \hə-'va-nə\ city, ✳ of Cuba; *pop* 2,106,000

Hav·ant \'ha-vənt\ town S England; *pop* 47,125

Ha·ver·ing \'hāv-riŋ, 'hā-və-riŋ\ borough of NE Greater London, England; *pop* 237,000

Ha·waii \hə-'wä-yē, -'wä-,ē\ **1** *or* **Ha·wai·ian Islands** *formerly* **Sand·wich Islands** \,san-(d)wich-\ group of islands *cen* Pacific belonging to U.S. **2** island, largest of the group **3** state of U.S., ✳, Honolulu; *pop* 1,360,301

Hay·ward \'hā-wərd\ city W California SE of Oakland; *pop* 144,186

Heb·ri·des \'he-brə-,dēz\ islands W Scotland in the North Atlantic consisting of **Outer Hebrides** (to W) and **Inner Hebrides** (to E); *pop* 30,660 — **Heb·ri·de·an** \,he-brə-'dē-ən\ *adj or n*

Hel·e·na \'he-lə-nə\ city, ✳ of Montana; *pop* 28,190

Hellespont — *see* DARDANELLES

Hells Canyon \'helz\ canyon of Snake River on Idaho–Oregon boundary

Hel·sin·ki \'hel-,siŋ-kē, hel-'\ city, ✳ of Finland; *pop* 612,664

Hen·der·son \'hen-dər-sən\ city S Nevada; *pop* 257,729

Hen·ry, Cape \'hen-rē\ cape E Virginia S of entrance to Chesapeake Bay

Her·e·ford and Wor·ces·ter \'her-ə-fərd-ən-'wùs-tər\ former county W England

Hert·ford·shire \'här-fərd-,shir, 'härt-, -shər\ *or* **Hertford** county SE England

Her·ze·go·vi·na \,hert-sə-gō-'vē-nə, ,hərt-, -'gō-və-nə\ *or Serb* **Her·ce·go·vi·na** \'kert-sə-gō-vē-nə\ region S Europe; with Bosnia to the N forms Bosnia and Herzegovina — **Her·ze·go·vi·nian** \,hert-sə-gō-'vē-nē-ən, ,hərt-, -nyən\ *n*

Hi·a·le·ah \,hī-ə-'lē-ə\ city SE Florida; *pop* 224,669

Hi·ber·nia \hī-'bər-nē-ə\ — *see* IRELAND — **Hi·ber·ni·an** \-ən\ *adj or n*

Hi·ga·shi·ōsa·ka \hē-,gä-shē-'ō-sä-kä\ city Japan in S Honshu E of Osaka; *pop* 509,533

High·land \'hī-lənd\ administrative subdivision of NW Scotland; *pop* 232,132

High·lands \'hī-ləndz\ the mountainous N part of Scotland lying N & W of the Lowlands

High Plains the Great Plains esp. from Nebraska southward

Hil·ling·don \'hi-liŋ-dən\ borough of W Greater London, England; *pop* 274,000

Hi·ma·la·yas, the \,hi-mə-'lā-əz\ *or* **the Himalaya** mountain system S Asia on border between India & Tibet and in Kashmir, Nepal, & Bhutan — *see* EVEREST, MOUNT — **Hi·ma·la·yan** \,him-ə-'lā-ən, hə-'mäl-(ə-)yən\ *adj*

Hin·du Kush \'hin-(,)dü-'kùsh, -'kəsh\ mountain range *cen* Asia SW of the Pamirs on border of Kashmir and in Afghanistan

Hin·du·stan \,hin-(,)dü-'stan, -də-, -'stän\ **1** a name for N India **2** the subcontinent of India **3** the country of India

Hi·ro·shi·ma \,hir-ə-'shē-mə, hə-'rō-shə-mə\ city Japan in SW Honshu on Inland Sea; *pop* 1,173,843

His·pan·io·la \,his-pə-'nyō-lə\ *or Spanish* **Es·pa·ño·la** \,es-,pä-'nyō-lä\ island West Indies in Greater Antilles; divided between Haiti on W & Dominican Republic on E

Ho·bart \'hō-bərt\ city Australia, ✳ of Tasmania; *pop* 170,975

Ho Chi Minh City \'hō-,chē-'min\ *formerly* **Sai·gon** \sī-'gän, 'sī-,\ city S Vietnam; *pop* 5,950,000

Hoh·hot \'hō-'hōt\ *or* **Hu·he·hot** \'hü-(,)hä-'hōt\ city N China, ✳ of Inner Mongolia; *pop* 1,497,000

Hok·kai·do \hō-'kī-(,)dō\ island N Japan N of Honshu; *pop* 5,506,419

Hol·land \'hä-lənd\ **1** county of Holy Roman Empire bordering on North Sea & consisting of area now forming part of W Netherlands **2** — *see* NETHERLANDS — **Hol·land·er** \-lən-dər\ *n*

Hol·ly·wood \'hä-lē-,wùd\ **1** section of Los Angeles, California, NW of downtown district **2** city SE Florida; *pop* 140,768

Holy Roman Empire empire consisting mainly of German & Italian territories & existing from 9th or 10th century to 1806

Hon·du·ras \hän-'dùr-əs, -'dyùr-; òn-'dü-räs\ country Central America; ✳, Tegucigalpa; *pop* 8,100,000 — **Hon·du·ran** \-ən\ *adj or n*

Hong Kong \'häŋ-,käŋ, -,käŋ\ *or Chinese* **Xiang·gang** \'shyäŋ-,gäŋ\ special administrative region China on SE coast including Hong Kong Island & Jiulong Peninsula; chief city Victoria; *pop* 7,072,000

Ho·ni·a·ra \,hō-nē-'är-ə\ town, ✳ of Solomon Islands; *pop* 49,107

Ho·no·lu·lu \,hä-nə-'lü-(,)lü, ,hō-nə-\ city, ✳ of Hawaii on Oahu; *pop* 390,738

Hon·shu \'hän-(,)shü, 'hon-\ island Japan; largest of the four chief islands; *pop* 100,254,208

Hood, Mount \'hùd\ mountain 11,235 ft. (3424 m.) NW Oregon in Cascade Range

Hoo·ver Dam \'hü-vər\ *or* Boul·der Dam \'bōl-dər\ dam 726 ft. (221 m.) high in Colorado River between Arizona & Nevada — see MEAD, LAKE

Hor·muz, Strait of \'(h)òr-,məz, (h)òr-'müz\ strait connecting Persian Gulf & Gulf of Oman

Horn, Cape \'hòrn\ cape S Chile on an island in Tierra del Fuego; the most southerly point of South America at 56° S latitude

Horn of Africa the easternmost projection of Africa; variously used to refer to Somalia, SE or all of Ethiopia, often Djibouti, & sometimes Eritrea, Sudan, & Kenya

Horseshoe Falls — see NIAGARA FALLS

Houns·low \'haùnz-(,)lō\ borough of SW Greater London, England; *pop* 254,000

Hous·ton \'hyüs-tən, 'yüs-\ city SE Texas; *pop* 2,096,798

Hsi–an — see XI'AN

Huang *or* Hwang \'hwäŋ\ *or* Yellow river about 3396 mi. (5464 km.) long N China flowing into Bo Hai

Hud·ders·field \'hə-dərz-,fēld\ town N England NE of Manchester; *pop* 123,888

Hud·son \'həd-sən\ 1 river 306 mi. (492 km.) long E New York flowing S 2 bay, inlet of the Atlantic in N Canada 3 strait NE Canada connecting Hudson Bay & the Atlantic

Hu·gli *or* Hoo·ghly \'hü-glē\ river 120 mi. (193 km.) long E India flowing S into Bay of Bengal

Huhehot — see HOHHOT

Hull \'həl\ *or* Kings·ton upon Hull \'kiŋ-stən\ city & port N England; *pop* 284,000

Hun·ga·ry \'həŋ-gə-rē\ country *cen* Europe; ✳, Budapest; *pop* 9,937,628

Hunt·ing·ton Beach \'hən-tiŋ-tən\ city SW California; *pop* 189,992

Hunts·ville \'hənts-,vil, -vəl\ city N Alabama; *pop* 180,105

Hu·ron, Lake \'hyùr-,än, 'yùr-\ lake E *cen* North America in U.S. & Canada; one of the Great Lakes

Hy·der·abad \'hī-d(ə-)rə-,bad, -,bäd\ 1 city S *cen* India; *pop* 7,204,000 2 city SE Pakistan on the Indus; *pop* 1,166,894

Iba·dan \i-'bä-dᵊn, 'ba-\ city SW Nigeria; *pop* 2,600,000

Ibe·ri·an \ī-'bir-ē-ən\ peninsula SW Europe occupied by Spain & Portugal

Ice·land \'īs-lənd, 'īs-,land\ island SE of Greenland between Arctic & Atlantic oceans; country; ✳, Reykjavik; *pop* 315,600 — Ice·land·er \'īs-,lan-dər, 'īs-lən-\ *n*

Ida·ho \'ī-də-,hō\ state NW U.S.; ✳, Boise; *pop* 1,567,582 — Ida·ho·an \,ī-də-'hō-ən\ *adj or n*

Igua·çú *or* Igua·zú \,ē-gwə-'sü\ river 745 mi. (1199 km.) long S Brazil flowing W

IJs·sel *or* Ijs·sel \'ī-səl, 'ā-\ river 70 mi. (113 km.) long E Netherlands flowing out of Rhine N into IJsselmeer

IJs·sel·meer \'ī-səl-,mer, 'ā-\ *or* Lake Ijs·sel freshwater lake N Netherlands separated from North Sea by a dike; part of former Zuider Zee (inlet of North Sea)

Ilium — see TROY

Il·li·nois \,i-lə-'nói\ state N *cen* U.S.; ✳, Springfield; *pop* 12,830,632 — Il·li·nois·an \,i-lə-'nói-ən\ *adj or n*

Il·lyr·ia \i-'lir-ē-ə\ ancient country S Europe and Balkan Peninsula on the Adriatic — Il·lyr·i·an \-ē-ən\ *adj or n*

Im·pe·ri·al Valley \im-'pir-ē-əl\ valley SE corner of California & partly in NE Baja California, Mexico

In·chon *or* In·cheon \'in-,chən\ city South Korea on Yellow Sea; *pop* 2,650,000

In·de·pen·dence \,in-də-'pen-dən(t)s\ city W Missouri E of Kansas City; *pop* 116,830

In·dia \'in-dē-ə\ 1 subcontinent S Asia S of the Himalayas between Bay of Bengal & Arabian Sea 2 country consisting of major portion of the subcontinent; ✳, New Delhi; *pop* 1,210,855,000 3 *or* Indian Empire before 1947 those parts of the subcontinent of India under British rule or protection

In·di·an \'in-dē-ən\ ocean E of Africa, S of Asia, W of Australia, & N of Antarctica

In·di·ana \,in-dē-'a-nə\ state E *cen* U.S.; ✳, Indianapolis; *pop* 6,483,802 — In·di·an·an \-'a-nən\ *or* In·di·an·i·an \-'a-nē-ən\ *adj or n*

In·di·a·nap·o·lis \,in-dē-ə-'na-pə-lis\ city, ✳ of Indiana; *pop* 820,445

Indian River lagoon 165 mi. (266 km.) long E Florida between main part of the state & coastal islands

Indian Territory former territory S U.S. in present state of Oklahoma

In·dies \'in-(,)dēz\ 1 EAST INDIES 2 WEST INDIES

In·do·chi·na \,in-(,)dō-'chī-nə\ 1 peninsula SE Asia including Myanmar, Malay Peninsula, Thailand, Cambodia, Laos, & Vietnam 2 *or* French Indochina former country SE Asia consisting of area now forming Cambodia, Laos, & Vietnam — In·do–Chi·nese \-chī-'nēz, -'nēs\ *adj or n*

In·do·ne·sia \,in-də-'nē-zhə, -shə\ country SE Asia in Malay Archipelago consisting of Sumatra, Java, S & E Borneo, Sulawesi, W New Guinea, & many smaller islands; ✳, Jakarta; *pop* 237,641,000 — In·do·ne·sian \-zhən, -shən\ *adj or n*

In·dore \in-'dòr\ city W *cen* India; *pop* 2,067,000

In·dus \'in-dəs\ river 1800 mi. (2897 km.) long S Asia flowing from Tibet NW & SSW through Pakistan into Arabian Sea

In·gle·wood \'iŋ-gəl-,wùd\ city SW California; *pop* 109,673

In·land Sea \'in-,land, -lənd\ inlet of the Pacific in SW Japan between Honshu on N and Shikoku and Kyushu on S

Inner Hebrides — see HEBRIDES

Inner Mon·go·lia \män-'gōl-yə, mäŋ-, -'gō-lē-ə\ *or* Nei Mong·gol \'nā-'män-,gōl, -'mäŋ-\ region N China; *pop* 24,706,291

Inside Passage protected shipping route between Puget Sound, Washington, & the lower part of Alaska

In·ver·ness \,in-vər-'nes\ town NW Scotland; *pop* 48,000

Io·ni·an \ī-'ō-nē-ən\ sea, arm of the Mediterranean between SE Italy & W Greece

Io To — see IWO JIMA

Io·wa \'ī-ə-wə\ state N *cen* U.S.; ✳, Des Moines; *pop* 3,046,355 — Io·wan \-wən\ *adj or n*

Ips·wich \'ip-(,)swich\ town SE England; *pop* 139,000

Iqa·lu·it \ē-'ka-lü-ət\ town Canada, ✳ of Nunavut on Baffin Island; *pop* 6184

Iran \i-'rän, -'ran\ *formerly by outsiders* Per·sia \'pər-zhə\ country SW Asia; ✳, Tehran; *pop* 75,150,000 — Irani \-'rä-nē, -'ra-\ *adj or n* — Ira·nian \i-'rā-nē-ən, -'ran-ē-, -'rän-ē-\ *adj or n*

Iraq \i-'räk, -'rak\ country SW Asia in Mesopotamia; ✳, Baghdad; *pop* (est.) 34,500,000 — Iraqi \-'räk-ē, -'rak-\ *adj or n*

Ire·land \'ī(-ə)r-lənd\ 1 *or Latin* Hi·ber·nia \hī-'bər-nē-ə\ island W Europe in the North Atlantic; one of the British Isles 2 *or* Eire \'er-ə\ country occupying major portion of Ireland (island); ✳, Dublin; *pop* 4,588,000

Irish Sea arm of the North Atlantic between Great Britain & Ireland

Ir·kutsk \ir-'kütsk, ,ər-\ city S Russia near Lake Baikal; *pop* 587,500

Ir·ra·wad·dy \,ir-ə-'wä-dē\ river 1300 mi. (2092 km.) long Myanmar flowing S into Bay of Bengal

Ir·tysh \ir-'tish, ,ər-\ river over 2600 mi. (4180 km.) long *cen* Asia flowing NW & N from Altay Mountains in China, through Kazakhstan, & into W *cen* Russia

Ir·vine \'ər-,vīn\ city SW California; *pop* 212,375

Ir·ving \'ər-viŋ\ city NE Texas NW of Dallas; *pop* 216,290

Isfahan — see ESFAHAN

Is·lam·abad \is-'lä-mə-,bäd, iz-, -'la-mə-,bad\ city, ✳ of Pakistan; *pop* 529,180

Islas Malvinas — see FALKLAND ISLANDS

Isle of Man — see MAN, ISLE OF

Isle of Wight \'wīt\ island England in English Channel

Isle Roy·ale \ī(-ə)l-'ròi(-ə)l\ island Michigan in Lake Superior

Isles of Scilly 1 — see CORNWALL AND ISLES OF SCILLY 2 — see SCILLY

Is·ling·ton \'iz-liŋ-tən\ borough of N Greater London, England; *pop* 206,000

Ispahan — see ESFAHAN

Is·ra·el \'iz-rē(-ə)l, -(,)rā(-ə)l\ 1 kingdom in ancient Palestine consisting of lands occupied by the Hebrew people 2 *or* Ephra·im \'ē-frē-əm\ the N part of the Hebrew kingdom after about 933 B.C. 3 country SW Asia; ✳, Jerusalem; *pop* 7,412,000 — Is·rae·li \iz-'rā-lē\ *adj or n*

Is·tan·bul \,is-tən-'bül, -,tan-, -,tän-, -'bùl, 'is-tən-,, *or with* m *for* n\ *formerly* Con·stan·ti·no·ple \,kän-,stan-tə-'nō-pəl\ city NW Turkey on the Bosporus & Sea of Marmara; *pop* 12,500,000

Is·tria \'is-trē-ə\ peninsula in Croatia & Slovenia extending into the N Adriatic — **Is·tri·an** \-trē-ən\ *adj or n*

It·a·ly \'i-tə-lē\ country S Europe including a boot-shaped peninsula & the islands of Sicily & Sardinia; ✳, Rome; *pop* 59,434,000

Itas·ca, Lake \ī-'tas-kə\ lake NW *cen* Minnesota; source of the Mississippi

Ivory Coast — see COTE D'IVOIRE — **Ivor·i·an** \(,)ī-'vòr-ē-ən\ *adj or n* — **Ivory Coast·er** \'kō-stər\ *n*

Iwo Ji·ma \ē-(,)wō-'jē-mə\ *or* **Io To** \ē-(,)ō-'tō\ island Japan in W Pacific SSE of Tokyo

Izhevsk \'ē-,zhefsk\ *or 1985–87* **Usti·nov** \'üs-ti-,nòf, -,nòv\ city W Russia; *pop* 628,000

Iz·mir \iz-'mir\ *formerly* **Smyr·na** \'smər-nə\ city W Turkey; *pop* 3,100,000

Jack·son \'jak-sən\ city, ✳ of Mississippi; *pop* 173,514

Jack·son·ville \'jak-sən-,vil\ city NE Florida; *pop* 821,784

Jai·pur \'jī-,pùr\ city NW India; *pop* 3,046,000

Ja·kar·ta *also* **Dja·kar·ta** \jə-'kär-tə\ city, ✳ of Indonesia in NW Java; *pop* 9,608,000

Ja·mai·ca \jə-'mā-kə\ island West Indies in Greater Antilles; country; ✳, Kingston; *pop* 2,698,000 — **Ja·mai·can** \-kən\ *adj or n*

James \'jāmz\ 1 — see DAKOTA 2 river 340 mi. (547 km.) long Virginia flowing E into Chesapeake Bay

James Bay the S extension of Hudson Bay between NE Ontario & W Quebec

James·town \'jāmz-,taùn\ ruined village E Virginia on James River; first permanent English settlement in America (1607)

Jam·shed·pur \'jäm-,shed-,pùr\ city E India; *pop* 570,349

Ja·pan \jə-'pan, ja-\ country E Asia consisting of Honshu, Hokkaido, Kyushu, Shikoku, & other islands in the W Pacific; ✳, Tokyo; *pop* 128,057,000

Japan, Sea of *also* **East Sea** arm of the Pacific between Japan & Korea

Ja·va \'jä-və, 'ja-\ island Indonesia SW of Borneo; chief city, Jakarta; *pop* 107,581,306 — **Ja·va·nese** \ja-və-'nēz, jä-, -'nēs\ *n*

Jef·fer·son City \'je-fər-sən\ city, ✳ of Missouri; *pop* 43,079

Jer·sey \'jər-zē\ — see CHANNEL

Jersey City city NE New Jersey on Hudson River; *pop* 247,597

Je·ru·sa·lem \jə-'rü-s(ə-)ləm, -'rü-z(ə-)ləm\ city NW of Dead Sea, ✳ of Israel; *pop* 765,000

Jid·da *or* **Jid·dah** \'ji-də\ *or* **Jed·da** *or* **Jed·dah** \'je-də\ city W Saudi Arabia on Red Sea; *pop* 561,104

Ji·lin \'jē-'lin\ *or* **Ki·rin** \'kē-'rin\ city NE China; *pop* 1,470,000

Ji·nan *or* **Tsi·nan** \'jē-'nän\ city E China; *pop* 3,932,000

Jin·zhou *or* **Chin–chou** *or* **Chin-chow** \'jin-'jō\ city NE China; *pop* 946,000

Jiu·long *or* **Kow·loon** \'jü-'lòŋ\ *or* \'kaù-'lün\ 1 peninsula SE China in Hong Kong opposite Hong Kong Island 2 city on Jiulong Peninsula; *pop* 1,975,265

Jo·han·nes·burg \jō-'hä-nəs-,bərg, -'ha-\ city NE Republic of South Africa; *pop* 4,434,827

Jo·li·et \jō-lē-'et\ city NE Illinois; *pop* 147,433

Jor·dan \'jòr-dᵊn\ 1 river 200 mi. (322 km.) long Israel & Jordan flowing S from Syria into Dead Sea 2 country SW Asia in NW Arabia; ✳, Amman; *pop* 6,350,000 — **Jor·da·ni·an** \jòr-'dā-nē-ən\ *adj or n*

Juan de Fu·ca, Strait of \,wän-də-'fyü-kə, ,hwän-\ strait 100 mi. (161 km.) long between Vancouver Island, British Columbia, & Olympic Peninsula, Washington

Ju·ba \'jü-bə, -,bä\ town, ✳ of South Sudan

Ju·daea *or* **Ju·dea** \jü-'dē-ə, -'dā-\ region of ancient Palestine forming its S division under Persian, Greek, & Roman rule — **Ju·dae·an** *or* **Ju·dean** \-ən\ *adj or n*

Ju·neau \'jü-(,)nō, jù-'\ city, ✳ of Alaska; *pop* 31,275

Ju·ra \'jùr-ə\ mountain range extending along boundary between France & Switzerland N of Lake of Geneva

Jut·land \'jət-lənd\ 1 peninsula N Europe extending into North Sea and consisting of main part of Denmark & N portion of Germany 2 the main part of Denmark

Ka·bul \'kä-bəl, -,bül; kə-'bül\ city, ✳ of Afghanistan; *pop* 1,424,000

Ka Lae \kä-'lä-ā\ *or* **South Cape** *or* **South Point** most southerly point of Hawaii & of U.S.

Kal·a·ha·ri \,ka-lə-'här-ē, ,kä-\ desert region S Africa N of Orange River in S Botswana & NW Republic of South Africa

Kalgan — see ZHANGJIAKOU

Ka·li·man·tan \,ka-lə-'man-,tan, ,kä-lē-'män-,tän\ 1 BORNEO — its Indonesian name 2 the S & E portion of Borneo belonging to Indonesia

Ka·li·nin·grad \kə-'lē-nən-,grad, -nyən-, -,grät\ *formerly* **Kö·nigs·berg** \'kä-nigz-,bərg\ city & port W Russia; *pop* 431,500

Kam·chat·ka \kam-'chat-kə, -'chät-\ peninsula 750 mi. (1207 km.) long E Russia

Kam·pa·la \käm-'pä-lä, kam-\ city, ✳ of Uganda; *pop* 1,516,000

Kampuchea — see CAMBODIA

Kan·da·har \'kən-də-,här\ city SE Afghanistan; *pop* 130,200

Ka·no \'kä-(,)nō\ city N *cen* Nigeria; *pop* 3,000,000

Kan·pur \'kän-,pùr\ city N India on the Ganges; *pop* 2,900,000

Kan·sas \'kan-zəs\ state W *cen* U.S.; ✳, Topeka; *pop* 2,853,118 — **Kan·san** \'kan-zən\ *adj or n*

Kansas City 1 city NE Kansas bordering on Kansas City, Missouri; *pop* 145,786 2 city W Missouri; *pop* 459,787

Kao–hsiung — see GAOXIONG

Ka·ra·chi \kə-'rä-chē\ city S Pakistan on Arabian Sea; *pop* 12,100,000

Ka·ra·gan·da \,kär-ə-'gän-də\ *or* **Qa·ra·ghan·dy** \-dē\ city *cen* Kazakhstan *pop* 460,000

Kar·a·ko·ram Pass \,kär-ə-'kòr-əm\ mountain pass NE Kashmir in **Karakoram Range** (system connecting the Himalayas with the Pamirs)

Ka·re·lia \kə-'rē-lē-ə, -'rēl-yə\ region NE Europe in Finland & Russia; *pop* 643,548 — **Ka·re·lian** \kə-'rē-lē-ən, -'rēl-yən\ *adj or n*

Ka·roo *or* **Kar·roo** \kə-'rü\ plateau region W Republic of South Africa W of Drakensberg Mountains

Kash·mir \'kash-,mir, 'kazh-, kash-', kazh-'\ disputed territory N subcontinent of India; claimed by India & Pakistan — **Kash·miri** \kash-'mi(ə)r-ē, kazh-\ *adj or n*

Ka·thi·a·war \,kä-tē-ə-'wär\ peninsula W India N of Gulf of Khambhat

Kath·man·du *or* **Kat·man·du** \,kat-,man-'dü, ,kät-,män-\ city, ✳ of Nepal; *pop* 1,003,000

Kat·mai, Mount \'kat-,mī\ volcano 6715 ft. (2047 m.) Alaska on Alaska Peninsula

Kat·te·gat \'ka-ti-,gat\ arm of North Sea between Sweden & E coast of Jutland Peninsula of Denmark

Kau·ai \kä-'wä-ē\ island Hawaii NW of Oahu; *pop* 67,091

Kau·nas \'kaù-nəs, -näs\ city C Lithuania; *pop* 315,993

Ka·wa·sa·ki \,kä-wä-'sä-kē\ city Japan in E Honshu S of Tokyo; *pop* 1,425,512

Ka·zakh·stan *also* **Ka·zak·stan** \,ka-(,)zak-'stan\ country NW *cen* Asia; ✳, Astana; *pop* 16,010,000 — **Ka·zakh** *also* **Ka·zak** \kə-'zak, -'zäk\ *n*

Ka·zan \kə-'zan\ city W Russia; *pop* 1,144,000

Kee·wa·tin \kē-'wä-tᵊn, -'wä-\ former district N Canada in E Northwest Territories NW of Hudson Bay; area now part of Nunavut

Ke·me·ro·vo \'kye-mə-rə-və\ city S *cen* Russia; *pop* 533,000

Ke·nai \'kē-,nī\ peninsula S Alaska E of Cook Inlet

Kennedy, Cape — see CANAVERAL, CAPE

Ken·sing·ton and Chel·sea \'ken-ziŋ-tən-ənd-'chel-sē, 'ken(t)-siŋ-\ borough of W Greater London, England; *pop* 158,500

Kent \'kent\ county SE England; *pop* 1,463,740 — **Kent·ish** \'ken-tish\ *adj*

Ken·tucky \kən-'tə-kē\ state E *cen* U.S.; ✳, Frankfort; *pop* 4,339,367 — **Ken·tuck·i·an** \-kē-ən\ *adj or n*

Ken·ya \'ke-nyə, 'kē-\ 1 mountain 17,058 ft. (5199 m.) *cen* Kenya 2 country E Africa S of Ethiopia; ✳, Nairobi; *pop* 38,610,000 — **Ken·yan** \-nyən\ *adj or n*

Key West \'west\ city SW Florida on Key West (island); *pop* 24,649

Kha·ba·rovsk \kə-'bär-əfsk, kə-\ city SE Russia; *pop* 577,500

Kham·bhat, Gulf of \'kəm-bət\ *or* **Gulf of Cam·bay** \kam-'bā\ inlet of Arabian Sea in India N of Bombay

Khar·kiv \'kär-kəf, 'kär-\ *or* **Khar·kov** \'kär-,kòf, 'kär-, -,kòv, -kəf\ city NE Ukraine; *pop* 1,446,000

Khar·toum \kär-'tüm\ city, ✳ of Sudan; *pop* 1,950,000

Khy·ber \'kī-bər\ pass 33 mi. (53 km.) long on border between Afghanistan & Pakistan

Ki·bo \'kē-(ˌ)bō\ mountain peak 19,340 ft. (5895 m.) NE Tanzania; highest peak of Kilimanjaro & highest point in Africa

Kiel \'kēl\ — see NORD-OSTSEE

Ki·ev \'kē-ˌef, -ˌev, -if\ *or Ukrainian* **Kyiv** \'kyē-ü\ city, ✳ of Ukraine; *pop* 2,800,000

Ki·ga·li \kē-'gä-lē\ city, ✳ of Rwanda; *pop* 859,000

Ki·lau·ea \ˌkē-ˌlä-'wä-ä\ volcanic crater Hawaii on Hawaii Island on E slope of Mauna Loa

Kil·i·man·ja·ro \ˌki-lə-mən-'jär-(ˌ)ō, -'ja-(ˌ)rō\ mountain NE Tanzania; highest in Africa — see KIBO

Kil·lar·ney, Lakes of \ki-'lär-nē\ three lakes SW Ireland

Kings·ton \'kiŋ-stən\ city & port, ✳ of Jamaica; *pop* 103,771

Kingston upon Hull — see HULL

Kingston upon Thames borough of SW Greater London, England; *pop* 160,000

Kings·town \'kiŋz-ˌtaùn\ seaport, ✳ of Saint Vincent and the Grenadines; *pop* 12,900

Kin·sha·sa \kin-'shä-sə\ city, ✳ of Democratic Republic of the Congo; *pop* 3,804,000

Ki·ri·bati \'kir-ə-ˌbas\ island group W Pacific; country; ✳, Tarawa; *pop* 103,000

Kirin — see JILIN

Kirk·wall \'kər-ˌkwól\ town and port N Scotland, ✳ of Orkney Islands; *pop* 7000

Kishinev — see CHIȘINĂU

Ki·ta·kyu·shu \kē-ˌtä-'kyü-(ˌ)shü\ city Japan in N Kyushu; *pop* 976,846

Kitch·e·ner \'kich-nər, 'ki-chə-\ city SE Ontario, Canada; *pop* 219,153

Kit·ty Hawk \'kit-ē-ˌhók\ town E North Carolina; *pop* 3272

Klon·dike \'klän-ˌdīk\ region NW Canada in *cen* Yukon in valley of Klondike River

Knox·ville \'näks-ˌvil, -vəl\ city E Tennessee; *pop* 178,874

Ko·be \'kō-bē, -ˌbā\ city Japan in S Honshu; *pop* 1,544,200

Ko·di·ak \'kō-dē-ˌak\ island S Alaska E of Alaska Peninsula

Ko·la \'kō-lə\ peninsula NW Russia bordering on Finland

Ko·rea \kə-'rē-ə\ peninsula E Asia between Yellow Sea & East Sea (Sea of Japan); divided 1948 into independent countries of North Korea & South Korea — **Ko·re·an** \kə-'rē-ən\ *adj or n*

Ko·ror \'kòr-ˌòr\ town, former ✳ of Palau; *pop* 13,303

Kos·ci·us·ko, Mount \ˌkä-zē-'əs-(ˌ)kō, ˌkä-sē-\ mountain 7310 ft. (2228 m.) SE Australia in SE New South Wales; highest in Great Dividing Range & in Australia

Ko·so·vo \'kò-sò-ˌvō, 'kä-\ country S Europe in the Balkans; *pop* 1,757,000

Kowloon — see JIULONG

Krak·a·tau \ˌkra-kə-'taù\ *or* **Krak·a·toa** \-'tō-ə\ island & volcano Indonesia between Sumatra & Java

Kra·kow \'krä-ˌkaù, 'kra-, 'krä-, -(ˌ)kò, *Pol* 'krä-ˌküf\ city S Poland; *pop* 758,000

Kras·no·dar \ˌkräs-nə-'där\ city SW Russia; *pop* 745,000

Kras·no·yarsk \ˌkräs-nə-'yärsk\ city S *cen* Russia; *pop* 973,850

Kry·vyy Rih \kri-'vē-'rik\ *or* **Kri·voy Rog** \ˌkri-ˌvòi-'ròg, -'rók\ city SE *cen* Ukraine; *pop* 675,000

K2 \ˌkä-'tü\ *or* **God·win Aus·ten** \ˌgä-dwən-'òs-tən, ˌgò-, -'äs-\ mountain 28,250 ft. (8611 m.) N Kashmir in Karakoram Range; second highest in the world

Kua·la Lum·pur \ˌkwä-lə-'lùm-ˌpùr, -'ləm-, -ˌlùm-'\ city, ✳ of Malaysia; *pop* 1,145,075

Kuei·yang — see GUIYANG

Kun·lun \'kün-'lün\ mountain system W China extending E from the Pamirs; highest peak Muztag 25,340 ft. (7724 m.)

Kun·ming \'kùn-'miŋ\ city S China; *pop* 3,567,000

Kur·di·stan \ˌkùr-də-'stan, ˌkər-, -'stän; 'kər-də-ˌ\ region SW Asia chiefly in E Turkey, NW Iran, & N Iraq — **Kurd** \'kùrd, 'kərd\ *n* — **Kurd·ish** \'kùr-dish, 'kər-\ *adj*

Ku·ril *or* **Ku·rile** \kyùr-ˌēl, 'kùr-; kyù-'rēl, kù-\ islands Russia in W Pacific between Kamchatka Peninsula & Hokkaido Island

Ku·wait \kù-'wät\ 1 country SW Asia in Arabia at head of Persian Gulf; *pop* 3,986,000 2 city, its ✳; *pop* 28,859 — **Ku·waiti** \-'wä-tē\ *adj or n*

Kuybyshev — see SAMARA

Kuz·netsk Basin \kùz-'netsk\ *or* **Kuz·bas** *or* **Kuz·bass** \'kùz-ˌbas\ basin S *cen* Russia

Kwa·ja·lein \'kwä-jə-lən, -ˌlän\ island W Pacific in Marshall Islands

Kwang·ju *or* **Gwang·ju** \'gwäŋ-(ˌ)jü\ city SW South Korea; *pop* 1,472,000

Kwa·Zu·lu–Na·tal \kwä-'zü-(ˌ)lü-nə-'täl\ province E Republic of South Africa; *pop* 10,267,300

Kyo·to \kē-'ōt-ō\ city Japan in W *cen* Honshu; *pop* 1,474,015

Kyr·gyz·stan \ˌkir-gi-'stan, -'stän\ country W *cen* Asia; ✳, Bishkek; *pop* 5,234,000

Kyu·shu \'kyü-(ˌ)shü\ island Japan S of W end of Honshu; *pop* 13,445,561

Lab·ra·dor \'la-brə-ˌdòr\ 1 peninsula E Canada between Hudson Bay & the Atlantic divided between the provinces of Quebec & Newfoundland and Labrador 2 the part of the peninsula belonging to the province of Newfoundland and Labrador — **Lab·ra·dor·ean** *or* **Lab·ra·dor·ian** \ˌla-brə-'dòr-ē-ən\ *adj or n*

Lac·ca·dive \'la-kə-ˌdēv, -ˌdīv, -div\ islands India in Arabian Sea N of Maldive Islands

La·co·nia \lə-'kō-nē-ə, -nyə\ ancient country S Greece in SE Peloponnese; ✳, Sparta — **La·co·nian** \-nē-ən, -nyən\ *adj or n*

La·fay·ette \ˌla-fē-'et, ˌlä-\ city S Louisiana; *pop* 120,623

La·gos \'lä-ˌgäs, -ˌgòs\ city, former ✳ (1960–91) of Nigeria; *area pop* 9,114,000

La·hore \lə-'hòr\ city E Pakistan; *pop* 5,143,495

Lake District region NW England containing many lakes & mountains

Lake·hurst \'lāk-(ˌ)hərst\ borough E New Jersey; *pop* 2654

Lake·wood \'lāk-ˌwúd\ city *cen* Colorado; *pop* 142,980

Lam·beth \'lam-bəth, -ˌbeth\ borough of S Greater London, England; *pop* 303,000

La·nai \lə-'nī, lä-\ island Hawaii W of Maui

Lan·ca·shire \'laŋ-kə-ˌshir, -shər\ *or* **Lan·cas·ter** \'laŋ-kəs-tər\ county NW England — **Lan·cas·tri·an** \laŋ-'kas-trē-ən, lan-\ *adj or n*

Lan·cas·ter \'laŋ-kəs-tər, 'lan-ˌkas-tər\ city NW England; *pop* 48,000

Land's End \'landz-'end\ cape SW England; most westerly point of England

Lan·sing \'lan-siŋ\ city, ✳ of Michigan; *pop* 114,297

Lan·zhou *or* **Lan·chou** \'län-'jō\ city W China; *pop* 2,533,000

Laos \'laùs, 'lä-(ˌ)ōs, 'lä-ˌäs\ country SE Asia in Indochina NE of Thailand; ✳, Vientiane; *pop* 6,514,000 — **Lao·tian** \lä-'ō-shən, 'laù-shən\ *adj or n*

La Paz \lä-'päz, -'päs\ city, administrative ✳ of Bolivia; *pop* 762,000

Lap·land \'lap-ˌland, -lənd\ region N Europe above the Arctic Circle in N Norway, N Sweden, N Finland, & Kola Peninsula of Russia — **Lap·land·er** \-ˌlan-dər, -lən-\ *n*

La·re·do \lə-'rā-(ˌ)dō\ city S Texas on the Rio Grande; *pop* 236,091

Larne \'lärn\ district NE Northern Ireland; *pop* 32,000

Las·sen Peak \'la-s³n\ volcano 10,457 ft. (3187 m.) N California at S end of Cascade Range

Las Ve·gas \läs-'vā-gəs\ city SE Nevada; *pop* 583,756

Latin America 1 Spanish America and Brazil 2 all of the Americas S of the U.S. — **Latin–American** *adj* — **Latin American** *n*

Latin Quarter section of Paris, France S of the Seine

Lat·via \'lat-vē-ə\ country E Europe on Baltic Sea; ✳, Riga; *pop* 2,070,000

Lau·ren·tian Mountains \lò-'ren(t)-shən\ hills E Canada in S Quebec N of the Saint Lawrence on S edge of Canadian Shield

Laurentian Plateau — see CANADIAN SHIELD

La·val \lə-'val\ city S Quebec NW of Montreal; *pop* 401,553

Law·rence \'lòr-ən(t)s, 'lär-\ 1 city NE Kansas *pop* 87,643 2 city NE corner of Massachusetts; *pop* 76,377

League of Nations political organization established at the end of World War I; replaced by United Nations 1946

Leb·a·non \'le-bə-nən\ 1 mountains Lebanon (country) running parallel to coast 2 country SW Asia on the Mediterranean; ✳, Beirut; *pop* 4,100,000 — **Leb·a·nese** \ˌle-bə-'nēz, -'nēs\ *adj or n*

Leeds \\'lēdz\\ city N England; *pop* 475,000

Lee·ward Islands \\'lē-wərd, 'lü-ərd\\ **1** islands Hawaii extending WNW from main islands of the group **2** islands South Pacific in W Society Islands **3** islands West Indies in N Lesser Antilles extending from Virgin Islands (on N) to Dominica (on S)

Le Ha·vre \\lə-'hävrᵊ, -'häv\\ city N France on English Channel; *pop* 175,497

Leh·man Caves \\'lē-mən\\ limestone caverns E Nevada

Leices·ter \\'les-tər\\ city *cen* England ENE of Birmingham; *pop* 444,000

Leices·ter·shire \\'les-tər-ˌshir, -shər\\ *or* **Leicester** county *cen* England

Lein·ster \\'len(t)-stər\\ province E Ireland; *pop* 2,504,814

Leip·zig \\'līp-sig, -sik\\ city E Germany; *pop* 502,979

Le·na \\'lē-nə, 'lā-\\ river about 2700 mi. (4345 km.) long E Russia, flowing NE & N from mountains W of Lake Baikal into Arctic Ocean

Leningrad — see SAINT PETERSBURG

Le·ón \\lā-'ōn\\ city *cen* Mexico; *pop* 1,436,000

Ler·wick \\'lər-ˌwik, 'ler-\\ town and port N Scotland in the Shetlands; *pop* 7223

Le·so·tho \\lə-'sō-ˌtō, -'sü-ˌtü\\ *formerly* **Ba·su·to·land** \\bə-'sütō-ˌland\\ country S Africa surrounded by Republic of South Africa; ✳, Maseru; *pop* 1,877,000

Lesser Antilles islands in the West Indies including Virgin Islands, Leeward Islands, & Windward Islands, Barbados, Trinidad, Tobago, & islands in the S Caribbean N of Venezuela — see GREATER ANTILLES

Le·vant \\lə-'vant\\ the countries bordering on the E Mediterranean — **Lev·an·tine** \\'lev-ən-ˌtīn, -ˌtēn, lə-'van-\\ *adj or n*

Lew·es \\'lü-əs\\ town S England

Lew·i·sham \\'lü-ə-shəm\\ borough of SE Greater London, England; *pop* 276,000

Lew·is with Har·ris \\'lü-əs-with-'ha-rəs, -with-\\ island NW Scotland in Outer Hebrides

Lex·ing·ton \\'lek-siŋ-tən\\ **1** city NE *cen* Kentucky; area *pop* 295,803 **2** town NE Massachusetts; *pop* 31,394

Ley·te \\'lā-tē\\ island Philippines S of Samar

Lha·sa \\'lä-sə, 'la-\\ city SW China, ✳ of Tibet; *pop* 199,000

Li·be·ria \\lī-'bir-ē-ə\\ country W Africa on the North Atlantic; ✳, Monrovia; *pop* 3,477,000 — **Li·be·ri·an** \\-ē-ən\\ *adj or n*

Lib·er·ty \\'li-bər-tē\\ *formerly* **Bed·loe's** \\'bed-ˌlōz\\ island SE New York; site of the Statue of Liberty

Li·bre·ville \\'lē-brə-ˌvil, -ˌvēl\\ city, ✳ of Gabon; *pop* 419,596

Lib·ya \\'li-bē-ə\\ country N Africa on the Mediterranean W of Egypt; ✳, Tripoli; *pop* 5,491,000 — **Lib·y·an** \\'li-bē-ən\\ *adj or n*

Libyan desert N Africa W of the Nile in Libya, Egypt, & Sudan

Liech·ten·stein \\'lik-tən-ˌstīn, 'lik-tən-ˌshtīn\\ country W Europe between Austria & Switzerland; ✳, Vaduz; *pop* 36,000 — **Liech·ten·stein·er** \\-ˌstī-nər, -ˌshtī-\\ *n*

Lif·fey \\'li-fē\\ river 50 mi. (80 km.) long E Ireland

Li·gu·ria \\lə-'gyùr-ē-ə\\ region NW Italy on Ligurian Sea — **Li·gu·ri·an** \\-ē-ən\\ *adj or n*

Ligurian Sea arm of the Mediterranean N of Corsica

Li·lon·gwe \\li-'lóŋ-ˌ(ˌ)gwā\\ city, ✳ of Malawi; *pop* 674,448

Li·ma \\'lē-mə\\ city, ✳ of Peru; *pop* 8,039,000

Lim·a·vady \\ˌli-mə-'va-dē\\ district NW Northern Ireland; *pop* 34,000

Lim·po·po \\lim-'pō-(ˌ)pō\\ river 1000 mi. (1609 km.) long Africa flowing from Republic of South Africa into Indian Ocean in Mozambique

Lin·coln \\'liŋ-kən\\ **1** city, ✳ of Nebraska; *pop* 258,379 **2** city E England; *pop* 100,000

Lin·coln·shire \\'liŋ-kən-ˌshir, -shər\\ *or* **Lincoln** county E England

Line \\'līn\\ islands Kiribati S of Hawaii; *pop* 4782

Lis·bon \\'liz-bən\\ *or Portuguese* **Lis·boa** \\lēzh-'vō-ə\\ city, ✳ of Portugal; *pop* 547,733

Lis·burn \\'liz-(ˌ)bərn\\ district E Northern Ireland; *pop* 120,000

Lith·u·a·nia \\ˌli-thə-'wā-nē-ə, ˌli-thyə-, -nyə\\ country E Europe; ✳, Vilnius; *pop* 3,043,000

Lit·tle Rock \\'li-tᵊl-ˌräk\\ city, ✳ of Arkansas; *pop* 193,524

Liv·er·pool \\'li-vər-ˌpül\\ city NW England; *pop* 509,000

Li·vo·nia \\lə-'vō-nē-ə, -nyə\\ city SE Michigan; *pop* 96,942

Lju·blja·na \\lē-ˌü-blē-'ä-nə\\ city, ✳ of Slovenia; *pop* 272,000

Lla·no Es·ta·ca·do \\'la-(ˌ)nō-ˌes-tə-'kä-(ˌ)dō, 'lä-, 'yä-\\ *or* **Staked Plain** \\'stāk(t)-\\ plateau region SE New Mexico & NW Texas

Lo·bam·ba \\lō-'bäm-bə\\ town, legislative ✳ of Eswatini; *pop* (est.) 10,000

Lodz \\'lüj, 'lädz\\ city *cen* Poland WSW of Warsaw; *pop* 729,000

Lo·fo·ten \\'lō-ˌfō-tᵊn\\ islands NW Norway

Lo·gan, Mount \\'lō-gən\\ mountain 19,551 ft. (5959 m.) NW Canada in Saint Elias Range; highest in Canada & second highest in North America

Loire \\lə-'wär, 'lwär\\ river 634 mi. (1020 km.) long *cen* France flowing NW & W into Bay of Biscay

Lo·mé \\lō-'mā\\ city, ✳ of Togo; *pop* 838,500

Lo·mond, Loch \\'lō-mənd\\ lake S *cen* Scotland

Lon·don \\'lən-dən\\ **1** city SE Ontario, Canada; *pop* 366,151 **2** city, ✳ of England & of United Kingdom on the Thames; consists of **City of London** & Greater London metropolitan county; *pop* 8,174,000 — **Lon·don·er** \\-də-nər\\ *n*

Londonderry — see DERRY

Long Beach city SW California S of Los Angeles; *pop* 462,257

Long Island island 118 mi. (190 km.) long SE New York S of Connecticut

Long Island Sound inlet of the Atlantic between Connecticut & Long Island, New York

Lon·gueuil \\lòŋ-'gäl\\ city Canada in S Quebec E of Montreal; *pop* 231,409

Lor·raine \\lə-'rān, lò-\\ region NE France

Los An·ge·les \\lòs-'an-jə-ləs\\ city SW California; *pop* 3,792,621

Lou·ise, Lake \\lü-'ēz\\ lake SW Alberta, Canada

Lou·i·si·ana \\lü-ˌē-zē-'a-nə, ˌlü-ə-zē-, ˌlü-zē-\\ state S U.S.; ✳, Baton Rouge; *pop* 4,533,372 — **Lou·i·si·an·ian** \\-'a-nē-ən, -'a-nyən\\ *or* **Lou·i·si·an·an** \\-'a-nən\\ *adj or n*

Louisiana Purchase area W *cen* U.S. between Rocky Mountains & the Mississippi purchased 1803 from France

Lou·is·ville \\'lü-i-ˌvil, -vəl\\ city N Kentucky on the Ohio River; *pop* 597,337

Low Countries region W Europe consisting of modern Belgium, Luxembourg, & the Netherlands

Low·ell \\'lō-əl\\ city NE Massachusetts NW of Boston; *pop* 106,519

Lower 48 the continental states of the U.S. excluding Alaska

Low·lands \\'lō-ləndz, -ˌlandz\\ the *cen* & E part of Scotland

Lu·an·da \\lü-'än-də\\ city, ✳ of Angola; *pop* 2,600,000

Lub·bock \\'lə-bək\\ city NW Texas; *pop* 229,573

Lu·bum·ba·shi \\lü-büm-'bä-shē\\ city SE Democratic Republic of the Congo; *pop* 739,000

Luck·now \\'lək-ˌnaú\\ city N India ESE of Delhi; *pop* 2,817,105

Lüda *or* **Lü·ta** — see DALIAN

Lu·ray Caverns \\'lü-ˌrā, lü-'\\ series of caves N Virginia

Lu·sa·ka \\lü-'sä-kä\\ city, ✳ of Zambia; *pop* 1,747,000

Lü·shun \\'lü-'shún, 'lᴜᵊ-\\ *or* **Port Ar·thur** \\-'är-thər\\ seaport NE China; part of greater Dalian

Lu·ton \\'lü-tᵊn\\ town SE *cen* England; *pop* 211,000

Lux·em·bourg *or* **Lux·em·burg** \\'lək-səm-ˌbərg, 'lük-səm-ˌbùrk\\ **1** country W Europe bordered by Belgium, France, & Germany; *pop* 512,000 **2** city, its ✳; *pop* 95,000 — **Lux·em·bourg·er** \\-ˌbər-gər, -ˌbùr-\\ *n* — **Lux·em·bourg·ian** \\ˌlək-səm-'bər-gē-ən, ˌlùk-səm-'bùr-\\ *adj*

Lu·zon \\lü-'zän\\ island N Philippines; *pop* 42,784,360

L'viv \\lə-'vē-ü, -'vēf\\ *or* **L'vov** \\lə-'vóf, -'vòv\\ *or Polish* **Lwów** \\lə-'vüf, -'vüv\\ city W Ukraine; *pop* 729,400

Lyallpur — see FAISALABAD

Lyd·ia \\'li-dē-ə\\ ancient country W Asia Minor on the Aegean — **Lyd·i·an** \\-ē-ən\\ *adj or n*

Lyon \\'lyōⁿ\\ *or* **Lyons** \\lē-'ōⁿ, 'li-ənz\\ city SE *cen* France; *pop* 505,094

Ma·cao *or Portuguese* **Ma·cau** \\mə-'kaú\\ *or Chinese* **Ao·men** \\'aú-'mən\\ **1** special administrative region on coast of SE China W of Hong Kong; *pop* 553,000 **2** city, its ✳; *pop* 460,000 — **Ma·ca·nese** \\ˌmä-kə-'nēz, -'nēs\\ *n*

Mac·e·do·nia \\ˌma-sə-'dō-nē-ə, -nyə\\ **1** region S Europe in Balkan Peninsula in NE Greece, the former Yugoslav section & now independent country of Macedonia, & SW Bulgaria including territory of ancient kingdom of Macedonia (**Mac·e·don** \\'mas-ə-dən, -ə-ˌdän\\ ) **2** country

S *cen* Balkan Peninsula; ✳, Skopje; a former republic of Yugoslavia; *pop* 2,063,000 — **Mac·e·do·nian** \‚mas-ə-'dō-nyən, -nē-ən\ *adj or n*

Mac·gil·li·cud·dy's Reeks \mə-'gi-lə-‚kə-dēz-'rēks\ mountains SW Ireland; highest Carrantuohill 3414 ft. (1041 m.)

Ma·chu Pic·chu \‚mä-(‚)chü-'pē-(‚)chü, -'pēk-\ site SE Peru of ancient Inca city

Mac·ken·zie \mə-'ken-zē\ river 1120 mi. (1802 km.) long NW Canada flowing from Great Slave Lake NW into Beaufort Sea

Mack·i·nac, Straits of \'ma-kə-‚nò, -‚nak\ channel N Michigan connecting Lake Huron & Lake Michigan

Ma·con \'mā-kən\ city *cen* Georgia; *pop* 91,351

Mad·a·gas·car \‚ma-də-'gas-kər, -kär\ *formerly* **Mal·a·gasy Re·public** \‚ma-lə-'ga-sē\ island country W Indian Ocean off SE Africa; ✳, Antananarivo; *pop* 21,842,000 — **Mad·a·gas·can** \‚ma-də-'gas-kən\ *adj or n*

Ma·dei·ra \mə-'dir-ə, -'der-ə\ 1 river 2013 mi. (3239 km.) long W Brazil flowing NE into the Amazon 2 islands Portugal in the North Atlantic N of the Canary Islands; *pop* 261,313 3 island; chief of the Madeira group — **Ma·dei·ran** \-'dir-ən, -'der-\ *adj or n*

Ma·di·nat ash Sha'b \mə-'dē-‚nə-tash-'shab\ city S Yemen

Mad·i·son \'ma-də-sən\ city, ✳ of Wisconsin; *pop* 233,209

Ma·dras \mə-'dras, -'dräs\ *or* **Chen·nai** \'che-‚nī\ city SE India; *pop* 4,646,732

Ma·drid \mə-'drid\ city, ✳ of Spain; *pop* 3,198,645

Ma·du·rai \‚mä-də-'rī\ city S India; *pop* 1,241,000

Mag·da·len Islands \'mag-də-lən\ *or F* **Îles de la Ma·de·leine** \‚ēl-də-lä-mäd-'len, -mä-də-'len\ islands Canada in Gulf of Saint Lawrence between Newfoundland & Prince Edward Island

Ma·gel·lan, Strait of \mə-'je-lən, *chiefly Brit* -'ge-\ strait at S end of South America between mainland & Tierra del Fuego

Magh·er·a·felt \'mär-ə-‚felt, 'ma-kə-rə-‚felt\ district *cen* Northern Ireland; *pop* 45,000

Maid·stone \'mād-stən, -‚stōn\ town SE England; *pop* 108,000

Main \'mīn, 'mān\ river 325 mi. (523 km.) long S *cen* Germany flowing W into the Rhine

Maine \'mān\ state NE U.S.; ✳, Augusta; *pop* 1,328,361 — **Main·er** \'mā-nər\ *n*

Ma·jor·ca \mä-'jòr-kə, mə-, -'yòr-\ *or Spanish* **Ma·llor·ca** \mä-'yòr-kä\ island Spain in W Mediterranean — **Ma·jor·can** \-'jòr-kən, -'yòr\ *adj or n*

Ma·ju·ro \mä-'jür-(‚)ō\ atoll that contains ✳ of Marshall Islands; *pop* 27,797

Mal·a·bar Coast \'ma-lə-‚bär\ region SW India on Arabian Sea

Ma·la·bo \mä-'lä-(‚)bō\ city, ✳ of Equatorial Guinea; *pop* 134,400

Ma·lac·ca, Strait of \mə-'la-kə, -'lä-\ channel between S Malay Peninsula & island of Sumatra

Ma·la·wi \mə-'lä-wē\ *formerly* **Ny·asa·land** \nī-'a-sə-‚land, nē-\ country SE Africa on Lake Nyasa; ✳, Lilongwe; *pop* 13,077,000 — **Ma·la·wi·an** \-ən\ *adj or n*

Ma·lay \mə-'lā, 'mā-(‚)lā\ 1 archipelago SE Asia including Sumatra, Java, Borneo, Sulawesi, Moluccas, & Timor; usu. thought to include the Philippines & sometimes New Guinea 2 peninsula SE Asia divided between Thailand & Malaysia (country)

Ma·laya \mə-'lā-ə, mä-\ 1 the Malay Peninsula 2 former country SE Asia on Malay Peninsula; now part of Malaysia

Ma·lay·sia \mə-'lā-zh(ē-)ə, -sh(ē-)ə\ 1 the Malay Archipelago 2 the Malay Peninsula & Malay Archipelago 3 country SE Asia; ✳, Kuala Lumpur; *pop* 27,566,000 — **Ma·lay·sian** \mə-'lā-zhən, -shən\ *adj or n*

Mal·dives \'mòl-‚dēvz, -‚dīvz\ islands in Indian Ocean SW of Sri Lanka; country; ✳, Male Atoll; *pop* 299,000 — **Mal·div·i·an** \mòl-'di-vē-ən, mal-\ *adj or n*

Ma·le \'mä-lē\ atoll containing national ✳ of Maldives; *pop* 103,693

Ma·li \'mä-lē, 'ma-\ country W Africa; ✳, Bamako; *pop* 14,500,000 — **Ma·li·an** \-lē-ən\ *adj or n*

Mal·ta \'mòl-tə\ islands in the Mediterranean S of Sicily; country since 1964; ✳, Valletta; *pop* 417,000 — **Mal·tese** \mòl-'tēz, -'tēs\ *adj or n*

Malvinas, Islas — see FALKLAND ISLANDS

Mam·moth Cave \'ma-məth\ limestone caverns SW *cen* Kentucky

Man, Isle of \'man\ island British Isles in Irish Sea; has own legislature & laws; *pop* 60,496

Ma·na·gua \mä-'nä-gwä\ city, ✳ of Nicaragua; *pop* 1,007,000

Ma·na·ma \mə-'na-mə\ city, ✳ of Bahrain; *pop* 143,045

Man·ches·ter \'man-‚ches-tər, -chəs-tər\ 1 city S *cen* New Hampshire; *pop* 109,565 2 city NW England; *pop* 503,000

Man·chu·ria \man-'chùr-ē-ə\ region NE China S of the Amur — **Man·chu·ri·an** \-ē-ən\ *adj or n*

Man·hat·tan \man-'ha-t°n, mən-\ 1 island SE New York in New York City 2 borough of New York City consisting chiefly of Manhattan Island; *pop* 1,585,873

Ma·nila \mə-'ni-lə\ city, ✳ of Philippines in W Luzon; *pop* 1,661,000

Man·i·to·ba \‚ma-nə-'tō-bə\ province *cen* Canada; ✳, Winnipeg; *pop* 1,208,268 — **Man·i·to·ban** \-bən\ *adj or n*

Man·i·tou·lin \‚ma-nə-'tü-lən\ island 80 mi. (129 km.) long S Ontario in Lake Huron

Ma·pu·to \mä-'pü-(‚)tō, -(‚)tü\ city, ✳ of Mozambique; *pop* 1,094,628

Mar·a·cai·bo \‚ma-rə-'kī-(‚)bō, ‚mär-ä-\ city NW Venezuela; *pop* 1,207,513

Maracaibo, Lake extension of a gulf of the Caribbean NW Venezuela

Mar·a·thon \'ma-rə-‚thän\ plain E Greece NE of Athens

Mar·i·ana \‚mer-ē-'a-nə\ islands W Pacific N of Caroline Islands; comprise Commonwealth of Northern Mariana Islands & Guam

Mariana Trench ocean trench W Pacific extending from SE of Guam to NW of Mariana Islands; deepest in world

Ma·rin·du·que \‚ma-rən-'dü-(‚)kā, ‚mär-ēn-\ island *cen* Philippines; *pop* 173,715

Maritime Provinces the Canadian provinces of New Brunswick, Nova Scotia, & Prince Edward Island & formerly thought by some to include Newfoundland and Labrador

Ma·ri·u·pol \‚ma-rē-'ü-‚pól, -pəl\ *or 1949–89* **Zhda·nov** \zhə-'dä-nəf\ city E Ukraine; *pop* 461,000

Mar·ma·ra, Sea of \'mär-mə-rə\ sea NW Turkey connected with Black Sea by the Bosporus & with Aegean Sea by the Dardanelles

Marne \'märn\ river 325 mi. (523 km.) long NE France flowing W into the Seine

Mar·que·sas \mär-'kā-zəz, -zəs, -səz, -səs\ islands South Pacific; belonging to France; *pop* 7358 — **Mar·que·san** \-zən, -sən\ *adj or n*

Mar·ra·kech \‚ma-rə-'kesh, 'ma-rə-‚, mə-'rä-kish\ city *cen* Morocco; *pop* 823,154

Mar·seille \mär-'sā\ *or* **Mar·seilles** \mär-'sā, -'sālz\ city SE France; *pop* 850,726

Mar·shall Islands \'mär-shəl\ islands W Pacific E of the Carolines; republic, in association with U.S.; ✳, Majuro; *pop* 53,200

Martha's Vineyard \'mär-thəz\ island SE Massachusetts off SW coast of Cape Cod WNW of Nantucket

Mar·ti·nique \‚mär-tə-'nēk\ island West Indies in the Windward Islands; an overseas division of France; ✳, Fort-de-France; *pop* 394,173

Mary·land \'mer-ə-lənd\ state E U.S.; ✳, Annapolis; *pop* 5,773,552 — **Mary·land·er** \-lən-dər, -‚lan-\ *n*

Mas·ba·te \mäz-'bä-tē, mäs-\ island *cen* Philippines

Mas·e·ru \'ma-sə-‚rü, -zə-\ city, ✳ of Lesotho; *pop* 204,000

Mash·had \mə-'shad\ city NE Iran; *pop* 2,749,374

Ma·son–Dix·on Line \'mā-s°n-'dik-sən\ boundary between Maryland & Pennsylvania; often considered the boundary between N & S states

Masqat — see MUSCAT

Mas·sa·chu·setts \‚ma-sə-'chü-səts, -zəts\ state NE U.S.; ✳, Boston; *pop* 6,547,629

Mat·a·be·le·land \‚ma-tə-'bē-lē-‚land, ‚mä-tä-'bā-lä-\ region SW Zimbabwe

Mat·lock \'mat-‚läk\ town N England; *pop* 20,610

Mat·ter·horn \'ma-tər-‚hòrn, 'mä-\ mountain 14,691 ft. (4478 m.) on border between Switzerland & Italy

Maui \'maù-ē\ island Hawaii NW of Hawaii Island; *pop* 154,834

Mau·na Kea \‚maù-nä-'kā-ä, ‚mó-\ extinct volcano 13,796 ft. (4205 m.) Hawaii in N *cen* Hawaii Island

Mau·na Loa \-'lō-ə\ volcano 13,680 ft. (4170 m.) Hawaii in S *cen* Hawaii Island

Mau·re·ta·nia *or* **Mau·ri·ta·nia** \,mȯr-ə-'tā-nē-ə, ,mär-, -nyə\ ancient country NW Africa in modern Morocco & W Algeria — **Mau·re·ta·ni·an** *or* **Mau·ri·ta·ni·an** \-nē-ən, -nyən\ *adj or n*

Mauritania country NW Africa on the Atlantic N of Senegal River; ✳, Nouakchott; *pop* 3,537,000 — **Mauritanian** *adj or n*

Mau·ri·tius \mȯ-'ri-sh(ē-)əs\ island in Indian Ocean E of Madagascar; country; ✳, Port Louis; *pop* 1,237,091 — **Mau·ri·tian** \-'ri-shən\ *adj or n*

May, Cape \'mā\ cape S New Jersey at entrance to Delaware Bay

Ma·yon, Mount \mä-'yōn\ volcano 8077 ft. (2462 m.) Philippines in SE Luzon

Ma·yotte \mä-'yät, -'yȯt\ island Comoros group; French dependency; *pop* 213,000 — see COMOROS

Ma·za·ma, Mount \mə-'zäm-ə\ prehistoric mountain SW Oregon the collapse of whose top formed Crater Lake

Mba·bane \əm-bä-'bä-nā\ city, ✳ of Eswatini; *pop* 57,992

Mbi·ni \em-'bē-nē\ *formerly* **Río Mu·ni** \,rē-ō-'mü-nē\ mainland portion of Equatorial Guinea; *pop* 750,000

Mc·Al·len \mə-'ka-lən\ city S Texas; *pop* 129,877

McKinley, Mount — see DENALI

Mead, Lake \'mēd\ reservoir NW Arizona & SE Nevada formed by Hoover Dam in Colorado River

Mec·ca \'me-kə\ city W Saudi Arabia; contains Islam's Great Mosque; *pop* 1,294,106

Me·dan \mā-'dän\ city Indonesia, in N Sumatra; *pop* 2,097,610

Me·de·llín \,me-də-'lēn, ,mä-thā-'yēn\ city NW Colombia; *pop* 2,400,000

Me·di·na \mə-'dī-nə\ city W Saudi Arabia; *pop* 1,100,000

Med·i·ter·ra·nean \,me-də-tə-'rā-nē-ən, -nyən\ sea 2300 mi. (3700 km.) long between Europe & Africa connecting with the Atlantic through Strait of Gibraltar

Me·kong \'mā-'kȯŋ, -'käŋ; 'mā-,\ river 2600 mi. (4184 km.) long SE Asia flowing from E Tibet S & SE into South China Sea in S Vietnam

Mel·a·ne·sia \,me-lə-'nē-zhə, -shə\ islands of the Pacific NE of Australia & S of Micronesia including Bismarck, the Solomons, Vanuatu, New Caledonia, & the Fijis

Mel·bourne \'mel-bərn\ city SE Australia; ✳ of Victoria; metropolitan area *pop* 3,708,000

Mel·e·ke·ok \'mel-ə-,kä-,ȯk\ town, ✳ of Palau

Melos — see MÍLOS

Mel·ville \'mel-,vil\ **1** island N Canada, split between Northwest Territories & Nunavut **2** peninsula Canada in Nunavut

Mem·phis \'mem(p)-fəs\ **1** city SW Tennessee; *pop* 646,889 **2** ancient city N Egypt S of modern Cairo

Mem·phre·ma·gog, Lake \,mem(p)-fri-'mä-,gäg\ lake on border between Canada (Quebec) & United States (Vermont)

Men·do·ci·no, Cape \,men-də-'sē-(,)nō\ cape NW California

Mer·cia \'mər-sh(ē-)ə\ ancient Anglo-Saxon kingdom *cen* England — **Mer·cian** \'mər-shən\ *adj or n*

Mer·sey \'mər-zē\ river 70 mi. (113 km.) long NW England flowing NW & W into Irish Sea

Mer·sey·side \'mər-zē-,sīd\ metropolitan county NW England; includes Liverpool

Mer·ton \'mər-tᵊn\ borough of SW Greater London, England; *pop* 200,000

Me·sa \'mā-sə\ city S *cen* Arizona; *pop* 439,041

Me·sa·bi Range \mə-'sä-bē\ region NE Minnesota that contains iron ore

Mes·o·po·ta·mia \,me-s(ə)-pə-'tä-mē-ə, -myə\ **1** region SW Asia between Euphrates & Tigris rivers **2** the entire Tigris–Euphrates valley — **Mes·o·po·ta·mian** \-mē-ən, -myən\ *adj or n*

Mes·quite \mə-'skēt, me-\ city NE Texas E of Dallas; *pop* 139,824

Meuse \'myüz, 'mə(r)z, 'mœz\ river 580 mi. (933 km.) long W Europe flowing from NE France into North Sea in the Netherlands

Mex·i·co \'mek-si-,kō\ **1** country S North America; *pop* 112,337,000 **2** *or* **Mexico City** city, its ✳; *pop* 8,851,000 — **Mex·i·can** \'mek-si-kən\ *adj or n*

Mexico, Gulf of inlet of the Atlantic SE North America

Mi·ami \mī-'a-mē\ city & port SE Florida; *pop* 399,457

Miami Beach city SE Florida; *pop* 87,779

Mich·i·gan \'mi-shi-gən\ state N *cen* U.S.; ✳, Lansing; *pop* 9,883,640 — **Mich·i·gan·der** \,mi-shi-'gan-dər\ *n* — **Mich·i·ga·ni·an** \,mi-shə-'gā-nē-ən, -'ga-\ *n* — **Mich·i·gan·ite** \'mi-shi-gə-,nīt\ *n*

Michigan, Lake lake N *cen* U.S.; one of the Great Lakes

Mi·cro·ne·sia \,mī-krə-'nē-zhə, -shə\ islands of the W Pacific E of the Philippines & N of Melanesia including Caroline, Kiribati, Mariana, & Marshall groups — **Mi·cro·ne·sian** \-zhən, -shən\ *adj or n*

Micronesia, Federated States of islands W Pacific in the Carolines; country in association with U.S.; ✳, Palikir; *pop* 103,000

Middle East the countries of SW Asia & N Africa — usually thought to include the countries extending from Libya on the W to Afghanistan on the E — **Middle Eastern** *adj*

Mid·dles·brough \'mi-dᵊlz-brə\ town N England; *pop* 175,000

Middle West — see MIDWEST

Mid Gla·mor·gan \'mid-glə-'mȯr-gən\ former county SE Wales

Mid·i·an \'mi-dē-ən\ ancient region NW Arabia E of Gulf of Aqaba — **Mid·i·an·ite** \-ē-ə-,nīt\ *n*

Mid·lands \'mid-ləndz\ the *cen* counties of England

Mid·way \'mid-,wā\ islands *cen* Pacific 1300 mi. (2092 km.) WNW of Honolulu belonging to U.S.

Mid·west \,mid-'west\ *or* **Middle West** region N *cen* U.S. including area around Great Lakes & in upper Mississippi valley from Ohio on the E to North Dakota, South Dakota, Nebraska, & Kansas on the W — **Mid·west·ern** \,mid-'wes-tərn\ *or* **Middle Western** *adj* — **Mid·west·ern·er** \,mid-'wes-tə(r)-nər\ *or* **Middle Westerner** *n*

Mi·lan \mə-'lan, -'län\ *or Italian* **Mi·la·no** \mē-'lä-(,)nō\ city NW Italy; *pop* 1,242,123 — **Mil·a·nese** \,mi-lə-'nēz, -'nēs\ *adj or n*

Mí·los *or* **Me·los** \'mē-,lȯs\ island Greece

Mil·wau·kee \mil-'wȯ-kē\ city SE Wisconsin on Lake Michigan; *pop* 594,833

Mi·nas Basin \'mī-nəs\ bay *cen* Nova Scotia; NE extension of Bay of Fundy

Min·da·nao \,min-də-'nä-,ō, -'naů\ island S Philippines; *pop* 13,966,000

Min·do·ro \min-'dȯr-(,)ō\ island *cen* Philippines; *pop* 473,940

Min·ne·ap·o·lis \,mi-nē-'a-pə-lis\ city SE Minnesota; *pop* 383,578

Min·ne·so·ta \,mi-nə-'sō-tə\ state N *cen* U.S.; ✳, Saint Paul; *pop* 5,303,925 — **Min·ne·so·tan** \-'sō-tᵊn\ *adj or n*

Mi·nor·ca \mə-'nȯr-kə\ island Spain in W Mediterranean — **Mi·nor·can** \mə-'nȯr-kən\ *adj or n*

Minsk \'min(t)sk\ city, ✳ of Belarus; *pop* 1,836,808

Mis·sis·sau·ga \,mi-sə-'sȯ-gə\ city Canada in S Ontario; *pop* 713,443

Mis·sis·sip·pi \,mi-sə-'si-pē\ **1** river 2340 mi. (3765 km.) long *cen* U.S. flowing into Gulf of Mexico — see ITASCA, LAKE **2** state S U.S.; ✳, Jackson; *pop* 2,967,297

Mis·sou·ri \mə-'zůr-ē\ **1** river 2466 mi. (3968 km.) long W U.S. flowing from SW Montana to the Mississippi in E Missouri (state) **2** state *cen* U.S.; ✳, Jefferson City; *pop* 5,988,927 — **Mis·sou·ri·an** \-'zůr-ē-ən\ *adj or n*

Mitch·ell, Mount \'mi-chəl\ mountain 6684 ft. (2037 m.) W North Carolina in the Appalachians; highest in U.S. E of the Mississippi

Mo·bile \mō-'bēl, 'mō-,bēl\ city SW Alabama on Mobile Bay (inlet of Gulf of Mexico); *pop* 195,111

Mo·des·to \mō-'des-(,)tō\ city *cen* California; *pop* 201,165

Mog·a·di·shu \,mä-gə-'di-(,)shü, ,mō-, -'dē-\ *or* **Mog·a·di·scio** \-(,)shō\ city, ✳ of Somalia; *pop* 349,245

Mo·hawk \'mō-,hȯk\ river E *cen* New York flowing into the Hudson

Mo·hen·jo Da·ro \mō-,hen-(,)jō-'där-(,)ō\ prehistoric city in valley of the Indus NE of modern Karachi, Pakistan

Mo·ja·ve *or* **Mo·ha·ve** \mə-'hä-vē, mō-\ desert S California SE of S end of Sierra Nevada

Mol·da·via \mäl-'dā-vē-ə, -vyə\ region E Europe in NE Romania & Moldova — **Mol·da·vian** \-vē-ən, -vyən\ *adj or n*

Mol·do·va \mäl-'dō-və, mȯl-\ country E Europe in E Moldavia region; ✳, Chişinău; *pop* 3,785,000 — **Mol·do·van** \-vən\ *adj or n*

Mol·o·kai \,mä-lə-'kī, ,mō-lō-'kä-ē\ island Hawaii ESE of Oahu

Geographical Names

Mo·luc·cas \mə-'lə-kəz\ islands Indonesia E of Sulawesi; *pop* 2,300,000 — **Mo·luc·ca** \mə-'lə-kə\ *adj* — **Mo·luc·can** \-kən\ *adj or n*

Mom·ba·sa city & port S Kenya; *pop* 926,000

Mo·na·co \'mä-nə-ˌkō\ country W Europe on Mediterranean coast of France; ✳, Monaco; *pop* 31,100 — **Mo·na·can** \'mä-nə-kən, mə-'nä-kən\ *adj or n* — **Mon·e·gasque** \ˌmä-ni-'gask\ *n*

Mon·go·lia \män-'gōl-yə, mäŋ-, -'gō-lē-ə\ **1** region E Asia E of Altay Mountains; includes Gobi Desert **2** country E Asia consisting of major northern portion of Mongolia region; ✳, Ulaanbaatar; *pop* 2,701,000

Mo·non·ga·he·la \mə-ˌnäŋ-gə-'hē-lə, -ˌnäŋ-gə-, -'hä-lə\ river N West Virginia & SW Pennsylvania

Mon·ro·via \(ˌ)mən-'rō-vē-ə\ city, ✳ of Liberia; *pop* 1,016,500

Mon·tana \män-'ta-nə\ state NW U.S.; ✳, Helena; *pop* 989,415 — **Mon·tan·an** \-nən\ *adj or n*

Mont Blanc \ˌmōⁿ-'bläⁿ\ mountain 15,771 ft. (4807 m.) SE France on Italian border; highest in the Alps

Mon·te·go Bay \män-'tē-(ˌ)gō\ city & port NW Jamaica on **Montego Bay** (inlet of the Caribbean); *pop* 110,115

Mon·te·ne·gro \ˌmän-tə-'nē-(ˌ)grō, -'nä-, -'ne-\ country S Europe on the Adriatic Sea; ✳, Podgorica; *pop* 620,029

Mon·ter·rey \ˌmän-tə-'rā\ city NE Mexico; *pop* 1,135,550

Mon·te·vi·deo \ˌmän-tə-və-'dā-(ˌ)ō, -'vi-dē-ˌō; ˌmón-tä-vē-'thä-ō\ city, ✳ of Uruguay; *pop* 1,312,000

Mont·gom·ery \(ˌ)mən(t)-'gə-mə-rē, män(t)-, -'gä-; -'gəm-rē, -'gäm-\ city, ✳ of Alabama; *pop* 205,764

Mont·pe·lier \mänt-'pēl-yər, -'pil-\ city, ✳ of Vermont; *pop* 7855

Mon·tre·al \ˌmän-trē-'ól, ˌmən-\ city S Quebec, Canada on **Montreal Island** in the Saint Lawrence; *pop* 1,649,519

Mont·ser·rat \ˌmän(t)-sə-'rat\ island British West Indies in the Leeward Islands; *pop* 4922

Mo·ra·via \mə-'rä-vē-ə\ region E Czech Republic — **Mo·ra·vi·an** \mə-'rä-vē-ən\ *adj or n*

Mo·re·no Valley \mə-'rē-(ˌ)nō\ city S California; *pop* 193,365

Mo·roc·co \mə-'rä-(ˌ)kō\ country NW Africa; ✳, Rabat; *pop* 31,900,000 — **Mo·roc·can** \-kən\ *adj or n*

Mo·ro·ni \mó-'rō-nē\ city, ✳ of Comoros; *pop* 41,500

Mos·cow \'mäs-(ˌ)kō, -ˌkaü\ *or Russian* **Mos·kva** \mäsk-'vä\ city, ✳ of Russia; *pop* 11,563,000

Mo·selle \mō-'zel\ river about 340 mi. (545 km.) long E France & W Germany

Moyle \'mói(-ə)l\ district N Northern Ireland; *pop* 17,000

Mo·zam·bique \ˌmō-zəm-'bēk\ **1** channel SE Africa between Mozambique (country) & Madagascar **2** country SE Africa; ✳, Maputo; *pop* 20,252,000 — **Mo·zam·bi·can** \ˌmō-zəm-'bē-kən\ *adj or n*

Mpu·ma·lan·ga \əm-ˌpü-mä-'läŋ-gä\ province NE Republic of South Africa; *pop* 4,040,000

Mukden — *see* SHENYANG

Mul·tan \múl-'tän\ city NE Pakistan SW of Lahore; *pop* 1,197,384

Mumbai — *see* BOMBAY

Mu·nich \'myü-nik\ *or German* **Mün·chen** \'mᵫn-kən\ city S Germany in Bavaria; *pop* 1,348,335

Mun·ster \'mən-sh(ē-)stər\ province S Ireland; *pop* 1,246,000

Mur·cia \'mər-sh(ē-)ə\ region & ancient kingdom SE Spain

Mur·ray \'mər-ē, 'mə-rē\ river over 1560 mi. (2510 km.) long SE Australia flowing W from E Victoria into Indian Ocean in South Australia

Mur·rum·bidg·ee \ˌmər-əm-'bi-jē, ˌmə-rəm-\ river almost 1000 mi. (1609 km.) long SE Australia in New South Wales flowing W into the Murray

Mus·cat \'məs-ˌkät, -kat, -kət\ *or* **Mas·qat** \'məs-ˌkät\ town E Arabia; ✳ of Oman Oct 24, 893

Muz·tag \müs-'täg, məz-\ mountain 25,340 ft. (7724 m.) W China; highest in Kunlun Mountains

Myan·mar \'myän-ˌmär\ *or unofficially* **Bur·ma** \'bər-mə\ country SE Asia; ✳, Nay Pyi Taw; *pop* 51,419,000

My·ce·nae \mī-'sē-(ˌ)nē\ ancient city S Greece in NE Peloponnese

Myr·tle Beach \'mər-tᵊl\ city E South Carolina on the Atlantic; *pop* 27,109

My·sore \mī-'sór\ city S India; *pop* 991,000

Nab·a·taea *or* **Nab·a·tea** \ˌna-bə-'tē-ə\ ancient Arab kingdom SE of Palestine — **Nab·a·tae·an** *or* **Nab·a·te·an** \-'tē-ən\ *adj or n*

Na·goya \nə-'gói-ə, 'nä-gó-(ˌ)yä\ city Japan in S *cen* Honshu; *pop* 2,263,894

Nag·pur \'näg-ˌpúr\ city E *cen* India; *pop* 2,452,000

Nai·ro·bi \nī-'rō-bē\ city, ✳ of Kenya; *pop* 3,133,518

Na·mib·ia \nə-'mi-bē-ə\ *formerly* **South–West Africa** country SW Africa on the Atlantic; ✳, Windhoek; *pop* 2,113,000 — **Na·mib·ian** \-bē-ən, -byən\ *adj or n*

Nan·chang \'nän-'chäŋ\ city SE China; *pop* 2,291,000

Nan·jing \'nän-'jiŋ\ *or* **Nan·king** \'nan-'kiŋ, 'nän-\ city E China; *pop* 6,496,000

Nan·tuck·et \nan-'tə-kət\ island SE Massachusetts S of Cape Cod; *pop* 7446

Na·per·ville \'nä-pər-ˌvil\ city NE Illinois W of Chicago; *pop* 141,853

Na·ples \'nā-pəlz\ *or Italian* **Na·po·li** \'nä-pō-lē\ *ancient* **Ne·ap·o·lis** \nē-'a-pə-ləs\ city S Italy on Bay of Naples; *pop* 962,003 — **Ne·a·pol·i·tan** \ˌnē-ə-'päl-ə-tən\ *adj or n*

Nar·ra·gan·sett Bay \ˌna-rə-'gan(t)-sət\ inlet of the Atlantic SE Rhode Island

Nash·ville \'nash-ˌvil, -vəl\ city, ✳ of Tennessee; *pop* 601,222

Nas·sau \'na-ˌsó\ city, ✳ of Bahamas on New Providence Island; *pop* 246,329

Na·tal \nə-'tal, -'täl\ former province E Republic of South Africa

Na·u·ru \nä-'ü-(ˌ)rü\ island W South Pacific; country; ✳, Yaren; *pop* 10,065 — **Na·u·ru·an** \-'ü-rə-wən\ *adj or n*

Nay Pyi Taw *or* **Nay·pyi·daw** \'nē-pyē-ˌdó\ site of ✳ of Myanmar

Naz·a·reth \'na-zə-rəth\ town of ancient Palestine in *cen* Galilee; now a city of N Israel; *pop* 72,000

N'Dja·me·na \ən-jä-'mä-nä, -'mē-\ city, ✳ of Chad; *pop* 951,000

Neagh, Lough \ˌläk-'nä\ lake Northern Ireland; largest in British Isles

Near East the countries of NE Africa & SW Asia — **Near Eastern** *adj*

Ne·bras·ka \nə-'bras-kə\ state *cen* U.S.; ✳, Lincoln; *pop* 1,826,341 — **Ne·bras·kan** \-kən\ *adj or n*

Neg·ev \'ne-ˌgev\ desert region S Israel

Ne·gro \'nä-(ˌ)grō, 'ne-\ river 1400 mi. (2253 km.) long in E Colombia & N Brazil flowing into the Amazon

Ne·gros \'nä-(ˌ)grōs, 'ne-\ island *cen* Philippines

Nei Monggol — *see* INNER MONGOLIA

Ne·pal \nə-'pól, nä-\ country Asia on NE border of India in the Himalayas; ✳, Kathmandu; *pop* 26,495,000 — **Nep·a·lese** \ˌne-pə-'lēz, -'lēs\ *adj or n* — **Ne·pali** \nə-'pól-ē, -'päl-, -'pal-\ *adj or n*

Ness, Loch \'nes\ lake NW Scotland

Neth·er·lands \'ne-thər-ləndz\ **1** *or Dutch* **Ne·der·land** \'nād-ər-ˌlänt\ *also* **Holland** country NW Europe on North Sea; ✳, Amsterdam; seat of the government, The Hague; *pop* 16,829,000 **2** LOW COUNTRIES — an historical usage — **Neth·er·land** \'ne-thər-lənd\ *adj* — **Neth·er·land·er** \-ˌlan-dər, -lən-\ *n* — **Neth·er·land·ish** \-ˌlan-dish, -lən-\ *adj*

Netherlands Antilles islands of the West Indies, formerly an overseas territory of the Netherlands; ✳, Willemstad

Ne·va \'nē-və, 'nä-, nye-'vä\ river 40 mi. (64 km.) long W Russia; flows through Saint Petersburg

Ne·vada \nə-'va-də\ state W U.S.; ✳, Carson City; *pop* 2,700,551 — **Ne·vad·an** \-'va-dᵊn, -'vä-\ *or* **Ne·vad·i·an** \-'va-dē-ən, -'vä-\ *adj or n*

Ne·vis \'nē-vəs\ island West Indies in the Leeward Islands — *see* SAINT KITTS

New Amsterdam town founded 1625 on island of Manhattan by the Dutch; renamed New York 1664 by the British

New·ark \'nü-ərk, 'nyü-\ city NE New Jersey; *pop* 277,140

New Britain island W Pacific in Bismarck group; *pop* 263,500

New Bruns·wick \-'brənz-(ˌ)wik\ province SE Canada; ✳, Fredericton; *pop* 751,171

New Caledonia island SW Pacific SW of Vanuatu; an overseas department of France; ✳, Nouméa; *pop* 245,600

New·cas·tle \'nü-ˌka-səl, 'nyü-\ city SE Australia in E New South Wales; metropolitan area *pop* 308,308

Newcastle *or* **Newcastle upon Tyne** \'tīn\ city N England; *pop* 268,000

New Delhi city, ✳ of India S of Delhi; *pop* 258,000

New England section of NE U.S. consisting of states of

Maine, New Hampshire, Vermont, Massachusetts, Rhode Island, & Connecticut — **New En·gland·er** \'iŋ-glən-dər\ n

New·found·land \'nü-fən(d)-lənd, 'nyü-, -ˌland; ˌnü-fən(d)-'land, ˌnyü-\ island Canada in the Atlantic — **New·found·land·er** \-lən-dər, -ˌlan-\ n

Newfoundland and Labrador province E Canada consisting of Newfoundland Island and Labrador; ✳, Saint John's; *pop* 514,536

New France the possessions of France in North America before 1763

New Guinea 1 island W Pacific N of E Australia; divided between West Papua, Indonesia & independent Papua New Guinea **2** the NE portion of the island of New Guinea together with some nearby islands; now part of Papua New Guinea — **New Guinean** *adj or n*

New·ham \'nü-əm, 'nyü-\ borough of E Greater London, England; *pop* 308,000

New Hamp·shire \'hamp-shər, -ˌshir\ state NE U.S.; ✳, Concord; *pop* 1,316,470 — **New Hamp·shire·man** \-mən\ n — **New Hamp·shir·ite** \-ˌīt\ n

New Ha·ven \'hā-vən\ city S Connecticut; *pop* 129,779

New Hebrides — see VANUATU

New Jersey state E U.S.; ✳, Trenton; *pop* 8,791,894 — **New Jer·sey·an** \-ən\ n — **New Jer·sey·ite** \-ˌīt\ n

New Mex·i·co \'mek-si-ˌkō\ state SW U.S.; ✳, Santa Fe; *pop* 2,059,179 — **New Mex·i·can** \-si-kən\ *adj or n*

New Neth·er·land \'ne-thər-lənd\ former Dutch colony (1613–64) North America along Hudson & lower Delaware rivers

New Or·leans \'òr-lē-ənz, 'òr-lənz, 'òrl-yənz, ˌ(ˌ)òr-'lēnz\ city SE Louisiana; *pop* 343,829

New·port \'nü-ˌpòrt, 'nyü-, -ˌpórt\ **1** town S England in Isle of Wight; *pop* 25,000 **2** city SE Wales; *pop* 128,000

Newport News \'nü-ˌpòrt-'nüz, 'nyü-ˌpòrt-'nyüz, -pərt-\ city SE Virginia; *pop* 180,719

New Providence island NW *cen* Bahamas; chief town, Nassau; *pop* 247,500

New·ry and Mourne \'n(y)ü-rē-ən(d)-'mórn\ district S Northern Ireland; *pop* 99,000

New South Wales state SE Australia; ✳, Sydney; *pop* 6,917,658

New Spain former Spanish possessions in North America, Central America, West Indies, & the Philippines

New Sweden former Swedish colony (1638–55) North America on W bank of Delaware River

New·town·ab·bey \ˌnü-t⁹n-'a-bē, ˌnyü-\ district E Northern Ireland; *pop* 85,000

Newtown Saint Bos·wells \'nü-ˌtaùn-sənt-'bäz-wəlz, 'nyü-, -ˌsänt-\ village S Scotland

New World the Western Hemisphere including North America and South America

New York 1 state NE U.S.; ✳, Albany; *pop* 19,378,102 **2** *or* **New York City** city SE New York (state); *pop* 8,175,133 — **New York·er** \'yòr-kər\ n

New York State Barge Canal — see ERIE

New Zea·land \'zē-lənd\ country SW Pacific ESE of Australia; ✳, Wellington; *pop* 4,242,000 — **New Zea·land·er** \-lən-dər\ n

Ni·ag·a·ra Falls \(ˌ)nī-'a-g(ə-)rə\ falls New York & Ontario in **Niagara River** (flowing N from Lake Erie into Lake Ontario); divided by Goat Island into Horseshoe Falls, or Canadian Falls (158 ft. or 48 m. high) & American Falls (167 ft. or 51 m. high)

Nia·mey \nē-'ä-(ˌ)mā, nyä-'mā\ city, ✳ of Niger; *pop* 1,026,848

Ni·caea \nī-'sē-ə\ *or* **Nice** \'nīs\ ancient city W Bithynia; site at modern village in NW Turkey — **Ni·cae·an** \nī-'sē-ən\ *adj or n* — **Ni·cene** \'nī-ˌsēn, nī-'sēn\ *adj*

Ni·ca·ra·gua \ˌni-kə-'rä-gwə, ˌnē-kä-'rä-gwä\ **1** lake about 100 mi. (160 km.) long S Nicaragua **2** country Central America; ✳, Managua; *pop* 6,100,000 — **Ni·ca·ra·guan** \-'rä-gwən\ *adj or n*

Nice \'nēs\ city & port SE France on the Mediterranean; *pop* 343,304

Nic·o·bar \'ni-kə-ˌbär\ islands India in Bay of Bengal S of the Andamans; *pop* 14,563

Nic·o·sia \ˌni-kə-'sē-ə\ city, ✳ of Cyprus; *pop* 55,014

Ni·ger \'nī-jər, nē-'zher\ **1** river 2600 mi. (4184 km.) long W Africa flowing into Gulf of Guinea **2** country W Africa N of Nigeria; ✳, Niamey; *pop* 17,139,000 —

Ni·ger·ien \ˌnī-'jir-ē-'en, nē-'zher-ē-ən\ *adj or n* — **Ni·ger·ois** \ˌnē-zhər-'wä, -zher-\ n

Ni·ge·ria \nī-'jir-ē-ə\ country W Africa on Gulf of Guinea; ✳, Abuja; *pop* 164,500,000 — **Ni·ge·ri·an** \-ē-ən\ *adj or n*

Nii·hau \'nē-ˌhaù\ island Hawaii WSW of Kauai

Nile \'nī(-ə)l\ river 4160 mi. (6693 km.) long E Africa flowing from Lake Victoria in Uganda N into the Mediterranean in Egypt

Nil·gi·ri \'nil-gə-rē\ hills S India

Nin·e·veh \'ni-nə-və\ ancient city, ✳ of Assyria; ruins in Iraq on the Tigris

Nip·i·gon, Lake \'ni-pə-ˌgän\ lake Canada in W Ontario N of Lake Superior

Nizh·niy Nov·go·rod \'nizh-nē-'näv-gə-ˌräd, -'nóv-gə-rət\ *formerly 1932–89* **Gor·ki** \'gòr-kē\ city W Russia; *pop* 1,250,600

Nord–Ost·see \'nòrt-'òst-'zā\ *or* **Kiel** \'kēl\ canal 61 mi. (98 km.) long N Germany across base of Jutland Peninsula connecting Baltic Sea & North Sea

Nor·folk \'nòr-fək\ city & port SE Virginia; *pop* 242,803

Nor·man·dy \'nòr-mən-dē\ region NW France NE of Brittany

North 1 river estuary of the Hudson between NE New Jersey & SE New York **2** sea, arm of the Atlantic E of Great Britain **3** island N New Zealand; *pop* 3,237,048

North·al·ler·ton \nòr-'tha-lər-tən\ town N England; *pop* 17,000

North America continent of Western Hemisphere NW of South America & N of the Equator — **North American** *adj or n*

North·amp·ton \nòr-'tham(p)-tən, nòrth-'ham(p)-\ town *cen* England; *pop* 215,000

North·amp·ton·shire \-ˌshir, -shər\ *or* **Northampton** county *cen* England

North Cape cape New Zealand at N end of North Island

North Car·o·li·na \ˌker-(-ə)-'lī-nə, ˌka-rə-\ state E U.S.; ✳, Raleigh; *pop* 9,535,483 — **North Car·o·lin·ian** \-'li-nē-ən, -'li-nyən\ *adj or n*

North Da·ko·ta \də-'kō-tə\ state N U.S.; ✳, Bismarck; *pop* 672,591 — **North Da·ko·tan** \-'kō-t⁹n\ *adj or n*

North Down district E Northern Ireland; *pop* 79,000

Northern Cape province W Republic of South Africa; *pop* 1,145,861

Northern Cook islands S *cen* Pacific N of Cook Islands

Northern Hemisphere the half of the earth that lies N of the Equator

Northern Ireland region N Ireland comprising 26 districts of Ulster; a division of United Kingdom; ✳, Belfast; *pop* 1,810,900

Northern Mar·i·ana Islands \ˌmer-ē-'a-nə\ islands W Pacific; commonwealth in association with U.S.; seat of the government on Saipan; *pop* 53,900

Northern Rhodesia — see ZAMBIA

Northern Territory territory N & *cen* Australia; ✳, Darwin; *pop* 211,945

North Korea *or* **Democratic People's Republic of Korea** country N half of Korean Peninsula in E Asia; ✳, Pyongyang; *pop* 24,700,000

North Las Vegas city SE Nevada; *pop* 216,061

North Slope region N Alaska between Brooks Range & Arctic Ocean

North·um·ber·land \nòr-'thəm-bər-lənd\ county N England

North·um·bria \nòr-'thəm-brē-ə\ ancient country Great Britain in what is now N England and S Scotland — **North·um·bri·an** \-brē-ən\ *adj or n*

North Vietnam — see VIETNAM

North West province N Republic of South Africa; *pop* 3,509,953

Northwest Passage sea passage between the Atlantic and the Pacific along the N coast of North America

Northwest Territories territory NW Canada consisting of the area of the mainland north of 60° between Yukon (territory) & Nunavut; ✳, Yellowknife; *pop* 41,462

North York former city Canada in SE Ontario; now part of Toronto

North Yorkshire county N England

Nor·walk \'nòr-ˌwòk\ city SW California SE of Los Angeles; *pop* 105,549

Nor·way \'nòr-ˌwā\ country N Europe in Scandinavia; ✳, Oslo; *pop* 5,156,000

Geographical Names 632

Nor·wich \'nor-(,)wich\ city E England; *pop* 187,000
Not·ting·ham \'nä-tiŋ-əm\ city N *cen* England; *pop* 289,000
Not·ting·ham·shire \'nä-tiŋ-əm-,shir, -shər\ *or* Notting-ham county N *cen* England; *pop* 692,000
Nouak·chott \nù-'äk-,shät\ city, ✻ of Mauritania; *pop* 958,399
Nou·méa \nü-'mā-ə\ city, ✻ of New Caledonia; *pop* 99,000
No·va Sco·tia \,nō-və-'skō-shə\ province SE Canada; ✻, Halifax; *pop* 921,727 — No·va Sco·tian \-shən\ *adj or n*
No·vo·kuz·netsk \,nō-(,)vō-kùz-'netsk, ,nò-və-küz-'nyetsk\ city S Russia in Asia; *pop* 548,000
No·vo·si·birsk \,nō-(,)vō-sə-'birsk, ,nō-və-\ city S Russia in Asia; *pop* 1,474,000
Nu·bia \'nü-bē-ə, 'nyü-\ region NE Africa in Nile valley in S Egypt & N Sudan — Nu·bi·an \'nü-bē-ən, 'nyü-\ *adj or n*
Nu·ku·a·lo·fa \,nü-kü-ä-'lō-fä\ seaport, ✻ of Tonga; *pop* 24,000
Nu·mid·ia \nù-'mi-dē-ə, nyü-\ ancient country N Africa E of Mauretania in modern Algeria — Nu·mid·i·an \-dē-ən\ *adj or n*
Nu·na·vut \'nù-nə-,vùt\ semiautonomous territory NE Canada; ✻, Iqaluit; *pop* 31,906
Nu·rem·berg \'nùr-əm-,bərg, 'nyùr-\ *or German* Nürn·berg \'nuern-,berk\ city S Germany; *pop* 486,314
Nuuk \'nük\ *or Danish* Godt·håb \'got-,hóp\ town, ✻ of Greenland on SW coast; *pop* 16,900
Ny·asa, Lake \nī-'as-ə, nē-\ lake SE Africa in Malawi, Mozambique, & Tanzania
Nyasaland — see MALAWI
Oa·hu \ō-'ä-(,)hü\ island Hawaii; site of Honolulu
Oak·land \'ō-klənd\ city W California on San Francisco Bay E of San Francisco; *pop* 390,724
Ob' \'äb, 'ób\ river over 2250 mi. (3620 km.) long W Russia in Asia flowing NW & N into Arctic Ocean
Oce·a·nia \,ō-shē-'a-nē-ə, -'ä-\ lands of the *cen* & S Pacific: Micronesia, Melanesia, Polynesia including New Zealand, & by some thought to include Australia & Malay Archipelago
Ocean·side \'ō-shən-,sīd\ city SW California NNW of San Diego; *pop* 167,086
Oder \'ō-dər\ *or* Odra \'ò-drə\ river about 565 mi. (909 km.) long *cen* Europe flowing from Silesia NW into Baltic Sea; forms part of boundary between Poland & Germany
Odes·sa \ō-'de-sə\ city & port S Ukraine on Black Sea; *pop* 1,012,500
Ohio \ō-'hī-(,)ō, ə-, -ə\ 1 river about 981 mi. (1578 km.) long E U.S. flowing from W Pennsylvania into the Mississippi 2 state E *cen* U.S.; ✻, Columbus; *pop* 11,536,504 — Ohio·an \-'hī-ō-ən\ *adj or n*
Oka·ya·ma \,ō-kä-'yä-mä\ city Japan in W Honshu on Inland Sea; *pop* 709,584
Okee·cho·bee, Lake \,ō-kə-'chō-bē\ lake S *cen* Florida
Oke·fe·no·kee \,ō-kə-fə-'nō-kē, ,ō-kē-\ swamp SE Georgia & NE Florida
Okhotsk, Sea of \ō-'kätsk, ə-'kótsk\ inlet of the North Pacific E Russia in Asia
Oki·na·wa \,ō-kə-'nä-wə, -'naù-ə\ 1 islands Japan in *cen* Ryukyus 2 island, chief of group — Oki·na·wan \-'nä-wən, -'naù-ən\ *adj or n*
Okla·ho·ma \,ō-klə-'hō-mə\ state S *cen* U.S.; ✻, Oklahoma City; *pop* 3,751,351 — Okla·ho·man \-mən\ *adj or n*
Oklahoma City city, ✻ of Oklahoma; *pop* 579,999
Old·ham \'ōl-dəm\ city NW England; *pop* 225,000
Old Point Comfort cape SE Virginia N of entrance to Hampton Roads
Ol·du·vai Gorge \'ōl-də-,vī\ canyon N Tanzania SE of Serengeti Plain; site of fossil beds
Old World the half of the earth to the E of the Atlantic Ocean including Europe, Asia, and Africa & esp. the continent of Europe
Olym·pia \ə-'lim-pē-ə, ō-\ 1 city, ✻ of Washington; *pop* 46,478 2 plain S Greece in NW Peloponnese
Olym·pic \-pik\ mountains NW Washington on Olympic Peninsula; highest Mt. Olympus 7965 ft. (2428 m.)
Olym·pus \ə-'lim-pəs, ō-\ mountains NE Greece
Omagh \'ō-mə, -(,)mä\ 1 district N Northern Ireland; *pop* 51,000 2 town in Omagh district; *pop* 19,000
Oma·ha \'ō-mə-,hó, -,hä\ 1 beach NW France in Normandy 2 city E Nebraska on Missouri River; *pop* 408,958
Oman \ō-'män, -'man\ country SW Asia in SE Arabia; ✻,

Muscat; *pop* 2,773,479 — Omani \ō-'mä-nē, -'ma-\ *adj or n*
Oman, Gulf of arm of Arabian Sea between Oman & SE Iran
Omsk \'óm(p)sk, 'äm(p)sk\ city SW Russia in Asia; *pop* 1,154,000
On·tar·io \än-'ter-ē-,ō\ 1 city SW California; *pop* 163,924 2 province E Canada; ✻, Toronto; *pop* 12,851,821 — On·tar·i·an \-ē-ən\ *adj or n*
Ontario, Lake lake E *cen* North America in U.S. & Canada; one of the Great Lakes
Oran \ō-'rän\ city & port NW Algeria; *pop* 803,329
Or·ange \'är-inj, 'är(-ə)nj, 'ór-inj, 'ór(-ə)nj\ 1 city SW California; *pop* 136,416 2 river 1300 mi. (2092 km.) long S Africa flowing W from Drakensberg Mountains into the Atlantic
Orange Free State — see FREE STATE
Or·e·gon \'ór-i-gən, 'är-\ state NW U.S.; ✻, Salem; *pop* 3,831,074 — Or·e·go·nian \,ór-i-'gō-nē-ən, ,är-, -nyən\ *adj or n*
Oregon Trail pioneer route to the NW U.S. about 2000 mi. (3220 km.) long from Missouri to Washington
Ori·no·co \,ór-ē-'nō-(,)kō\ river 1336 mi. (2150 km.) long Venezuela flowing into the Atlantic
Ork·ney \'órk-nē\ islands N Scotland; *pop* 19,570
Or·lan·do \ór-'lan-(,)dō\ city *cen* Florida; *pop* 238,300
Osa·ka \ō-'sä-kä, 'ō-sä-,kä\ city Japan in S Honshu; *pop* 2,665,314
Osh·a·wa \'ä-shə-wə, -,wä, -wə\ city SE Ontario, Canada on Lake Ontario ENE of Toronto; *pop* 149,607
Os·lo \'äz-(,)lō, 'äs-\ city, ✻ of Norway; *pop* 636,000
Oś·wię·cim \,ósh-'fyen-chēm\ *or German* Ausch·witz \'aùsh-,vits\ town S Poland W of Krakow; *pop* 40,000
Ot·ta·wa \'ä-tə-wə, -,wä, -,wó\ 1 river 696 mi. (1120 km.) E Canada in SE Ontario & S Quebec flowing E into the Saint Lawrence 2 city, ✻ of Canada in SE Ontario on Ottawa River; *pop* 812,129
Ot·to·man Empire \'ä-tə-mən\ former Turkish sultanate in SE Europe, W Asia, & N Africa
Oua·ga·dou·gou \,wä-gä-'dü-(,)gü\ city, ✻ of Burkina Faso; *pop* 1,475,223
Outer Hebrides — see HEBRIDES
Over·land Park \'ō-vər-lənd\ city NE Kansas; *pop* 173,372
Ox·ford \'äks-fərd\ city *cen* England; *pop* 160,000
Ox·ford·shire \'äks-fərd-,shir, -shər\ *or* Oxford county *cen* England
Ox·nard \'äks-,närd\ city SW California; *pop* 197,899
Ozark Plateau \'ō-,zärk\ *or* Ozark Mountains eroded plateau N Arkansas, S Missouri, & NE Oklahoma with E extension into S Kansas
Pa·cif·ic \pə-'si-fik\ ocean extending from Arctic Circle to the Equator (North Pacific) and from the Equator to the Antarctic regions (South Pacific) & from W North America & W South America to E Asia & Australia — Pacific *adj*
Pacific Islands, Trust Territory of the grouping of islands in W Pacific formerly under U.S. administration: the Carolines & the Marshalls
Pacific Rim the countries bordering on or located in the Pacific Ocean — used esp. of Asian countries on the Pacific
Pa·dang \'pä-,däŋ\ city Indonesia in W Sumatra; *pop* 834,000
Pa·dre \'pä-drē, -drä\ island 113 mi. (182 km.) long S Texas in Gulf of Mexico
Pa·go Pa·go \,pä-(,)gō-'pä-(,)gō, ,päŋ-(,)ō-'päŋ-(,)ō\ town, ✻ of American Samoa on Tutuila Island; *pop* 3656
Painted Desert region N *cen* Arizona
Pak·i·stan \'pa-ki-,stan, ,pä-ki-'stän\ country S Asia NW of India; ✻, Islamabad; *pop* 193,240,000 — see EAST PAKISTAN — Pak·i·stani \,pa-ki-'sta-nē, ,pä-ki-'stä-nē\ *adj or n*
Pa·lau \pə-'laù\ *or* Be·lau \bə-\ island group W Pacific in the W Carolines; country in association with U.S.; ✻, Melekeok; *pop* 17,501 — Pa·lau·an \pə-'laù-ən\ *n*
Pa·la·wan \pə-'lä-wən, -,wän\ island W Philippines between South China & Sulu seas; *pop* 528,287
Pa·lem·bang \,pä-ləm-'bäŋ\ city Indonesia in SE Sumatra; *pop* 1,455,000
Pa·ler·mo \pə-'lər-(,)mō, pä-'ler-\ city Italy, ✻ of Sicily; *pop* 657,561
Pal·es·tine \'pa-lə-,stīn\ region SW Asia dating back to

ancient times with unofficial, disputed, & fluctuating boundaries, but extending from E coast of Mediterranean Sea up to or beyond Jordan River — **Pal·es·tin·ian** \‚pa-lə-'sti-nē-ən, -nyən\ *adj or n*

Pa·li·kir \‚pä-lē-'kir\ town, * of Federated States of Micronesia on Pohnpei Island; *pop* 6227

Pal·i·sades \‚pa-lə-'sädz\ line of high cliffs 15 mi. (24 km.) long on W bank of the Hudson in SE New York & NE New Jersey

Palm·dale \'päm-‚dāl, 'pälm-\ city SW California NE of Los Angeles; *pop* 152,750

Pa·mirs \pə-'mirz\ elevated mountainous region *cen* Asia in E Tajikistan & on borders of China, India, Pakistan, & Afghanistan; many peaks over 20,000 ft. (6096 m.)

Pam·li·co Sound \'pam-li-‚kō\ inlet of the North Atlantic E North Carolina between main part of the state & offshore islands

Pam·pa \'pam-pə\ city NW Texas; *pop* 17,994

Pan·a·ma \'pan-ə-‚mä, -‚mȯ; ‚pan-ə-'mä, -'mȯ\ 1 country S Central America; *pop* 3,406,000 2 *or* **Panama City** city, its * on the Pacific; *pop* 430,000 3 canal 40 mi. (64 km.) long Panama connecting Atlantic & Pacific oceans — **Pan·a·ma·ni·an** \‚pan-ə-'mä-nē-ən\ *adj or n*

Panama, Isthmus of *formerly* **Isthmus of Dar·i·en** \‚der-ē-'en\ strip of land *cen* Panama connecting North America & South America

Panama Canal Zone — see CANAL ZONE

Pa·nay \pə-'nī\ island *cen* Philippines in the Visayans

Pan·gaea \pan-'jē-ə\ land area believed to have once connected the landmasses of the Southern Hemisphere with those of the Northern Hemisphere

Pan·mun·jom *or* **Pan·mun·jeom** \‚pän-‚mùn-'jəm\ village on North Korea–South Korea border

Pao–t'ou — see BAOTOU

Pap·ua, Territory of \'pa-pyü-wə, 'pä-pù-wə\ former British territory consisting of SE New Guinea & offshore islands; now part of Papua New Guinea

Papua New Guinea country SW Pacific; *, Port Moresby; *pop* 7,275,000

Par·a·guay \'pa-rə-‚gwī, -‚gwä\ 1 river 1584 mi. (2549 km.) long *cen* South America flowing from Brazil S into the Paraná in Paraguay 2 country *cen* South America; *, Asunción; *pop* 6,600,000 — **Par·a·guay·an** \‚pa-rə-'gwī-ən, -'gwä-\ *adj or n*

Par·a·mar·i·bo \‚pa-rə-'ma-rə-‚bō\ city, * of Suriname; *pop* 240,924

Pa·ra·ná \‚pär-ə-'nä\ river about 2500 mi. (4022 km.) long *cen* South America flowing S from Brazil into Argentina

Pa·ri·cu·tin \pä-‚rē-kü-'tēn\ volcano Mexico on site of a former village

Par·is \'pa-rəs\ city, * of France; *pop* 2,243,833 — **Pa·ri·sian** \pə-'ri-zhən, -'rē-\ *adj or n*

Par·nas·sus \pär-'na-səs\ mountain *cen* Greece

Par·os \'pär-‚ȯs\ island Greece — **Par·i·an** \'par-ē-ən, 'per-\ *adj*

Par·ra·mat·ta \‚pa-rə-'ma-tə\ city SE Australia in New South Wales; *pop* 166,858

Par·thia \'pär-thē-ə\ ancient country SW Asia in NE modern Iran — **Par·thi·an** \-thē-ən\ *adj or n*

Pas·a·de·na \‚pa-sə-'dē-nə\ 1 city SW California E of Glendale; *pop* 137,122 2 city SE Texas; *pop* 149,043

Pat·a·go·nia \‚pa-tə-'gō-nyə, -nē-ə\ region South America S of about 40° S latitude in S Argentina & S tip of Chile; sometimes thought to include Tierra del Fuego — **Pat·a·go·nian** \-nyən, -nē-ən\ *adj*

Pat·er·son \'pa-tər-sən\ city NE New Jersey; *pop* 146,199

Pat·mos \'pat-məs\ island Greece SSW of Samos

Pat·na \'pət-nə\ city NE India on the Ganges; *pop* 2,049,156

Pearl Harbor inlet Hawaii on S coast of Oahu W of Honolulu

Peking — see BEIJING

Pe·li·on \'pē-lē-ən\ mountain 5089 ft. (1551 m.) NE Greece

Pel·o·pon·nese \'pe-lə-pə-‚nēz, -‚nēs\ *or* **Pel·o·pon·ni·sos** \‚pe-lə-pə-'nē-səs\ peninsula forming S part of mainland of Greece

Pem·broke Pines \'pem-‚brȯk\ city SE Florida; *pop* 154,750

Pen·nine Chain \'pe-‚nīn\ mountains N England; highest Cross Fell 2930 ft. (893 m.)

Penn·syl·va·nia \‚pen(t)-səl-'vā-nyə, -nē-ə\ state E U.S.; *, Harrisburg; *pop* 12,702,379

Pe·o·ria \pē-'ȯr-ē-ə\ 1 town SW *cen* Arizona; *pop* 154,065 2 city N *cen* Illinois; *pop* 115,007

Per·ga·mum \'pər-gə-məm\ *or* **Per·ga·mus** \-məs\ ancient Greek kingdom including most of Asia Minor

Perm \'pərm, 'perm\ city E Russia in Europe; *pop* 991,300

Pernambuco — see RECIFE

Persia — see IRAN

Per·sian Gulf \'pər-zhən\ arm of Arabian Sea between Iran & Arabia

Perth \'pərth\ city, * of Western Australia; area *pop* 1,728,867

Pe·ru \pə-'rü, pā-\ country W South America; *, Lima; *pop* 27,412,000 — **Pe·ru·vi·an** \-'rü-vē-ən\ *adj or n*

Pe·tra \'pē-trə, 'pe-\ ancient city NW Arabia; site in SW Jordan

Petrograd — see SAINT PETERSBURG

Phil·a·del·phia \‚fi-lə-'del-fyə, -fē-ə\ city SE Pennsylvania; *pop* 1,526,006 — **Phil·a·del·phian** \-fyən, -fē-ən\ *adj or n*

Phil·ip·pines \‚fi-lə-'pēnz, 'fi-lə-‚pēnz\ island group approximately 500 mi. (805 km.) off SE coast of Asia; country; *, Manila; *pop* 92,338,000 — **Phil·ip·pine** \‚fi-lə-'pēn, 'fi-lə-‚\ *adj*

Phnom Penh \(pə-)'näm-'pen, (pə-)'nȯm-\ city, * of Cambodia; *pop* 1,200,000

Phoe·ni·cia \fi-'ni-sh(ē-)ə, -'nē-\ ancient country SW Asia on the Mediterranean in modern Syria & Lebanon

Phoe·nix \'fē-niks\ city, * of Arizona; *pop* 1,445,632

Phry·gia \'fri-j(ē-)ə\ ancient country W *cen* Asia Minor

Pic·ar·dy \'pi-kər-dē\ *or F* **Pi·car·die** \pē-kär-'dē\ region & former province N France bordering on English Channel N of Normandy — **Pi·card** \'pi-‚kärd, -kərd\ *adj or n*

Pied·mont \'pēd-‚mänt\ plateau region E U.S. E of the Appalachians between SE New York & NE Alabama

Pierre \'pir\ city, * of South Dakota; *pop* 13,646

Pie·ter·mar·itz·burg \‚pē-tər-'ma-rəts-‚bərg\ city E Republic of South Africa; *pop* 475,000

Pigs, Bay of \'pigz\ *or* **Ba·hía de Co·chi·nos** \bä-'ē-ä-thä-kō-'chē-nōs\ bay W Cuba on S coast

Pikes Peak \'pīks\ mountain 14,110 ft. (4301 m.) E *cen* Colorado in a range of the Rockies

Pin·dus \'pin-dəs\ mountains W Greece; highest point 8136 ft. (2480 m.)

Pi·sa \'pē-zə, *It* -sä\ city W *cen* Italy W of Florence; *pop* 85,900

Pit·cairn \'pit-‚kern\ island South Pacific; a British colony; *pop* 62

Pitts·burgh \'pits-‚bərg\ city SW Pennsylvania; *pop* 305,704

Plac·id, Lake \'pla-səd\ lake NE New York

Pla·no \'plā-(‚)nō\ city NE Texas N of Dallas; *pop* 259,841

Plov·div \'plȯv-‚dif, -‚div\ city S Bulgaria; *pop* 335,000

Plym·outh \'pli-məth\ 1 town SE Massachusetts; *pop* 56,468 2 city & port SW England; *pop* 235,000

Po \'pō\ river 405 mi. (652 km.) N Italy flowing into the Adriatic

Pod·go·ri·ca \'pȯd-‚gȯr-ēt-sä\ city * of Montenegro; *pop* 150,977

Po Hai — see BO HAI

Pohn·pei \'pȯn-‚pä\ island W Pacific in the E Carolines; part of Federated States of Micronesia

Po·land \'pō-lənd\ country *cen* Europe on Baltic Sea; *, Warsaw; *pop* 38,512,000 — **Pole** *n*

Pol·y·ne·sia \‚pä-lə-'nē-zhə, -shə\ islands of the *cen* & S Pacific including Hawaii, the Line, Tonga, Cook, & Samoa islands, & often New Zealand among others

Pom·er·a·nia \‚pä-mə-'rā-nē-ə, -nyə\ region N Europe on Baltic Sea; formerly in Germany, now mostly in Poland

Po·mo·na \pə-'mō-nə\ city SW California E of Los Angeles; *pop* 149,058

Pom·peii \päm-'pā, -'pā-‚ē\ ancient city S Italy SE of Naples destroyed 79 A.D. by eruption of Vesuvius — **Pom·pe·ian** \-'pā-ən\ *adj or n*

Pon·ce \'pȯn(t)-(‚)sä\ city S Puerto Rico; *pop* 166,327

Pon·do·land \'pän-(‚)dō-‚land\ region S Republic of South Africa

Pon·ta Del·ga·da \‚pȯn-tə-del-'gä-də\ city & port Portugal, largest in the Azores; *pop* 41,000

Pont·char·train, Lake \'pänt-shər-‚trān, ‚pänt-shər-'\ lake SE Louisiana E of the Mississippi & N of New Orleans

Pon·tus \'pän-təs\ ancient country NE Asia Minor — **Pon·tic** \'pänt-ik\ *adj or n*

Poole \\'pül\\ town S England on English Channel; *pop* 155,000

Po·po·ca·te·petl \\,pō-pə-'ka-tə-,pe-t^əl, -,ka-tə-'\\ volcano 17,887 ft. (5452 m.) SE *cen* Mexico

Port Arthur — see LÜSHUN

Port–au–Prince \\,pȯrt-ō-'prin(t)s, ,pȯr-(t)ō-'praⁿs\\ city, ✳ of Haiti; *pop* 875,978

Port Jack·son \\'jak-sən\\ inlet of South Pacific SE Australia in New South Wales; harbor of Sydney

Port·land \\'pȯrt-lənd\\ 1 city SW Maine; largest in state; *pop* 66,194 2 city NW Oregon; *pop* 583,776

Port Lou·is \\'lü-əs, 'lü-ē\\ city, ✳ of Mauritius; *pop* 146,876

Port Mores·by \\'mȯrz-bē\\ city, ✳ of Papua New Guinea; *pop* 341,000

Por·to \\'pȯr-(,)tü\\ city & port NW Portugal; *pop* 327,368

Por·to Ale·gre \\'pȯr-(,)tü-ä-'lä-grē\\ city & port S Brazil; *pop* 1,409,351

Port of Spain city NW Trinidad, ✳ of Trinidad and Tobago; *pop* 37,074

Por·to–No·vo \\,pȯr-tō-'nō-(,)vō\\ city, ✳ of Benin; *pop* 263,600

Port Phil·lip Bay \\'fi-ləp\\ inlet of South Pacific SE Australia in Victoria; harbor of Melbourne

Port Said \\sä-'ēd, 'sīd\\ city & port NE Egypt on the Mediterranean at N end of the Suez Canal; *pop* 571,000

Ports·mouth \\'pȯrts-məth\\ 1 city SE Virginia; *pop* 95,535 2 city S England; *pop* 238,000

Por·tu·gal \\'pȯr-chi-gəl, ,pür-tü-'gäl\\ country SW Europe; ✳, Lisbon; *pop* 10,562,178

Portuguese India former Portuguese possession on W coast of India; became part of India 1962

Port–Vi·la \\pȯrt-'vē-lə\\ *or* Vila city, ✳ of Vanuatu; *pop* 44,040

Po·to·mac \\pə-'tō-mək, -mik\\ river 287 mi. (462 km.) long flowing from West Virginia into Chesapeake Bay and forming boundary between Maryland & Virginia

Pough·keep·sie \\pə-'kip-sē, pō-\\ city & river port SE New York on the Hudson; *pop* 32,736

Po·wys \\'pō-əs\\ administrative subdivision E *cen* Wales; *pop* 132,976

Prague \\'präg\\ *or Czech* **Pra·ha** \\'prä-(,)hä\\ city, ✳ of Czech Republic; *pop* 1,169,106

Praia \\'prī-ə\\ town, ✳ of Cape Verde; *pop* 132,000

Prairie Provinces the Canadian provinces of Alberta, Manitoba, & Saskatchewan

Pres·ton \\'pres-tən\\ town NW England; *pop* 98,000

Pre·to·ria \\pri-'tȯr-ē-ə\\ city Republic of South Africa in the municipality of Tshwane, administrative ✳ of the country; *pop* 742,000

Prib·i·lof \\'pri-bə-,lȯf\\ islands Alaska in Bering Sea

Prince Ed·ward Island \\'ed-wərd\\ island SE Canada in Gulf of Saint Lawrence; a province; ✳, Charlottetown; *pop* 140,204

Prince Ru·pert's Land \\'rü-pərts\\ historical region N & W Canada consisting of drainage basin of Hudson Bay

Prince·ton \\'prin(t)-stən\\ borough W *cen* New Jersey; *pop* 12,307

Prín·ci·pe \\'prin(t)-si-pē\\ island W Africa in Gulf of Guinea; *pop* 7450 — see SÃO TOMÉ AND PRÍNCIPE

Pro·vence \\prə-'vän(t)s, prō-'väⁿs\\ region SE France on the Mediterranean

Prov·i·dence \\'prä-və-dən(t)s, -,den(t)s\\ city, ✳ of Rhode Island; *pop* 178,042

Pro·vo \\'prō-(,)vō\\ city N *cen* Utah; *pop* 112,488

Prud·hoe Bay \\'prü-(,)dō, 'prə-\\ inlet of Beaufort Sea N Alaska

Prus·sia \\'prə-shə\\ former kingdom, & later, state Germany — **Prus·sian** \\'prə-shən\\ *adj or n*

Pueb·lo \\'pwe-,blō\\ city SE *cen* Colorado SSE of Colorado Springs; *pop* 106,595

Puer·to Ri·co \\,pwer-tə-'rē-(,)kō, ,pwer-tō-\\ island West Indies E of Hispaniola; a self-governing commonwealth associated with U.S.; ✳, San Juan; *pop* 3,725,789 — **Puer·to Ri·can** \\'rē-kən\\ *adj or n*

Pu·get Sound \\'pyü-jət\\ arm of the North Pacific W Washington

Pu·ne \\'pü-nə\\ city W India, ESE of Bombay; *pop* 5,057,709

Pun·jab \\,pən-'jäb, -'jab, 'pən-,\\ region in Pakistan & NW India in valley of the Indus

Pusan — see BUSAN

Pyong·yang *or* **Pyeong·yang** \\'pyȯŋ-'yaŋ, 'pyəŋ-, -'yäŋ\\ city, ✳ of North Korea; *pop* 2,581,076

Pyr·e·nees \\'pir-ə-,nēz\\ mountains on French–Spanish border extending from Bay of Biscay to the Mediterranean

Qaraghandy — see KARAGANDA

Qa·tar \\'kä-tər, 'gä-, 'gə-; kə-'tär\\ country E Arabia on peninsula extending into Persian Gulf; ✳, Doha; *pop* 1,699,000 — **Qa·tari** \\kə-'tär-ē, gə-\\ *adj or n*

Qing·dao \\'chiŋ-'daù\\ *or* **Tsing·tao** \\'chiŋ-'daù, '(t)siŋ-'daù\\ city & port E China; *pop* 3,855,000

Qi·qi·har \\'chē-'chē-'här\\ *or* **Ch'i-ch'i-ha-erh** \\'chē-'chē-'hä-'ər\\ city NE China; *pop* 1,315,000

Que·bec \\kwi-'bek, ki-\\ *or French* **Qué·bec** \\kā-'bek\\ 1 province E Canada; *pop* 7,903,001 2 city, its ✳, on the Saint Lawrence; *pop* 516,622

Queens \\'kwēnz\\ borough of New York City on Long Island E of Brooklyn; *pop* 2,230,722

Queens·land \\'kwēnz-,land, -lənd\\ state NE Australia; ✳, Brisbane; *pop* 4,332,739 — **Queens·land·er** \\-,lan-dər, -,lən-\\ *n*

Que·zon City \\'kā-,sȯn\\ city Philippines in Luzon; formerly ✳ of the country; *pop* 2,761,720

Qui·to \\'kē-(,)tō\\ city, ✳ of Ecuador; *pop* 1,607,734

Ra·bat \\rə-'bät\\ city, ✳ of Morocco; *pop* 621,480

Rai·nier, Mount \\rə-'nir, rā-\\ mountain 14,410 ft. (4392 m.) W *cen* Washington; highest in Cascade Range

Raj·pu·ta·na \\,räj-pə-'tä-nə\\ *or* **Ra·ja·sthan** \\'räj-ə-,stän\\ region NW India S of Punjab

Ra·leigh \\'rȯ-lē, 'rä-lē\\ city, ✳ of North Carolina; *pop* 403,892

Ran·cho Cu·ca·mon·ga \\'ran-(,)chō-,kü-kə-'mən-gə, 'rän-, -'mäŋ-\\ city SW California; *pop* 165,269

Rand·wick \\'ran-(,)dwik\\ municipality SE Australia in E New South Wales; *pop* 128,989

Rangoon — see YANGON

Ra·wal·pin·di \\,rä-wəl-'pin-dē, raùl-', rȯl-'\\ city NE Pakistan NNW of Lahore; *pop* 1,409,768

Read·ing \\'re-diŋ\\ town S England; *pop* 219,000

Re·ci·fe \\rī-'sē-fē\\ *formerly* **Per·nam·bu·co** \\,pər-nəm-'bü-(,)kō, -'byü-\\ city NE Brazil; *pop* 1,537,704

Red \\'red\\ 1 river 1018 mi. (1638 km.) long flowing E on Oklahoma–Texas boundary and into the Atchafalaya & the Mississippi in Louisiana 2 sea between Arabia & NE Africa

Red·bridge \\'red-(,)brij\\ borough of NE Greater London, England; *pop* 279,000

Re·gi·na \\ri-'jī-nə\\ city, ✳ of Saskatchewan, Canada; *pop* 193,100

Re·no \\'rē-(,)nō\\ city NW Nevada; *pop* 225,221

Republic of the Congo — see CONGO 3

Ré·union \\rē-'yü-nyən, ,rā-ᵫ-'nyōⁿ\\ island W Indian Ocean; an overseas division of France; ✳, Saint-Denis; *pop* 834,000

Reyk·ja·vik \\'rā-kyə-,vik, -,vēk\\ city, ✳ of Iceland; *pop* 117,976

Rhine \\'rīn\\ river 820 mi. (1320 km.) long W Europe flowing from SE Switzerland to North Sea in the Netherlands — **Rhen·ish** \\'re-nish, 'rē-\\ *adj*

Rhine·land \\'rīn-,land, -lənd\\ *or German* **Rhein·land** \\'rīn-,länt\\ the part of Germany W of the Rhine — **Rhine·land·er** \\'rīn-,lan-dər, -lən-\\ *n*

Rhode Is·land \\'rōd-'ī-lənd\\ 1 *or officially* **Rhode Island and Providence Plantations** state NE U.S.; ✳, Providence; *pop* 1,052,567 2 — see AQUIDNECK — **Rhode Is·land·er** \\-lən-dər\\ *n*

Rhodes \\'rōdz\\ island Greece in the SE Aegean

Rho·de·sia \\rō-'dē-zh(ē-)ə\\ — see ZIMBABWE — **Rho·de·sian** \\-zh(ē-)ən\\ *adj or n*

Rhone *or French* **Rhône** \\'rōn\\ river 505 mi. (813 km.) long Switzerland & SE France

Rich·mond \\'rich-mənd\\ 1 — see STATEN ISLAND 2 city, ✳ of Virginia; *pop* 204,214

Richmond upon Thames borough of SW Greater London, England; *pop* 187,000

Ri·ga \\'rē-gə\\ city, ✳ of Latvia; *pop* 658,640

Rio de Ja·nei·ro \\'rē-(,)ō-dā-zhə-'ner-(,)ō, -,dē-\\ city SE Brazil on Guanabara Bay; *pop* 6,320,446

Rio Grande \\,rē-(,)ō-'grand, -'gran-dē\\ *or Mexican* **Rio Bra·vo** \\,rē-(,)ō-'brä-(,)vō\\ river 1885 mi. (3034 km.) long SW U.S., forming part of U.S.–Mexico boundary, and flowing into Gulf of Mexico

Río Muni — see MBINI

Riv·er·side \'ri-vər-ˌsīd\ city S California; *pop* 303,871

Riv·i·era \ˌri-vē-'er-ə\ coast region SE France & NW Italy

Ri·yadh \rē-'yäd\ city, * of Saudi Arabia; *pop* 4,700,000

Ro·a·noke \'rō-(ə-)ˌnōk\ city W Virginia; *pop* 97,032

Roanoke Island island North Carolina S of entrance to Albemarle Sound

Rob·son, Mount \'räb-sən\ mountain 12,972 ft. (3954 m.) W Canada in E British Columbia; highest in the Canadian Rockies

Roch·es·ter \'rä-chəs-tər, -ˌches-tər\ city W New York; *pop* 210,565

Rock·ford \'räk-fərd\ city N Illinois; *pop* 152,871

Rocky Mountains *or* Rock·ies \'rä-kēz\ mountains W North America extending SE from N Alaska to *cen* New Mexico

Roman Empire the empire of ancient Rome

Ro·ma·nia \rù-'mā-nē-ə, rō-, -nyə\ *or* Ru·ma·nia \rù-\ country SE Europe on Black Sea; *, Bucharest; *pop* 20,122,000

Rom·blon \räm-'blōn\ island group *cen* Philippines

Rome \'rōm\ *or Italian* Ro·ma \'rō-mä\ city, * of Italy; *pop* 2,617,175

Ro·sa·rio \rō-'zär-ē-ˌō, -'sär-\ city E *cen* Argentina on the Paraná; *pop* 927,000

Ro·seau \rō-'zō\ seaport, * of Dominica; *pop* 14,725

Ros·tov–on–Don \ˌrä-'stóf-ˌän-'dän, -'stóv, -ˌón-\ city S Russia in Europe; *pop* 1,090,000

Ros·well \'räz-ˌwel, -wəl\ city SE New Mexico; *pop* 48,366

Ro·ta \'rō-tə\ island W Pacific in the Marianas

Rot·ter·dam \'rä-tər-ˌdam, -ˌdäm\ city & port SW Netherlands; *pop* 618,357

Ru·an·da–Urun·di \rü-'än-dä-ü-'rün-dē\ former trust territory E *cen* Africa bordering on Lake Tanganyika; now divided into Burundi & Rwanda

Rudolf, Lake — see TURKANA, LAKE

Ruhr \'rúr\ 1 river 146 mi. (235 km.) long W Germany flowing NW & W to the Rhine 2 industrial district W Germany E of the Rhine in valley of Ruhr River

Rumania — see ROMANIA

Rupert's Land PRINCE RUPERT'S LAND

Rush·more, Mount \'rəsh-ˌmór\ mountain 5600 ft. (1707 m.) W South Dakota in Black Hills

Rus·sia \'rə-shə\ 1 former empire largely having the same boundaries as U.S.S.R. 2 UNION OF SOVIET SOCIALIST REPUBLICS 3 country E Europe & N Asia; *, Moscow; *pop* 143,300,000

Ru·the·nia \rü-'thē-nyə, -nē-ə\ region W Ukraine W of the N Carpathians — Ru·the·nian \-'thē-nyən, -nē-ən\ *adj or n*

Ru·wen·zo·ri \ˌrü-ən-'zór-ē\ mountain group E *cen* Africa between Uganda & Democratic Republic of the Congo; highest Mount Margherita 16,763 ft. (5109 m.)

Rwan·da *formerly* Ru·an·da \rü-'än-dä\ country E *cen* Africa; *, Kigali; *pop* 10,516,000 — Rwan·dan \-dən\ *adj or n*

Ryu·kyu \rē-'yü-(ˌ)kyü, -(ˌ)kü\ islands Japan extending in an arc from S Japan, to N tip of Taiwan; *pop* 1,222,458 — Ryu·kyu·an \-'kyü-ən, -ˌkü-\ *adj or n*

Saar \'sär, 'zär\ 1 river about 150 mi. (241 km.) long Europe flowing from E France to W Germany 2 *or* Saar·land \'sär-ˌland, 'zär-\ region W Europe in valley of Saar River between France & Germany

Sac·ra·men·to \ˌsa-krə-'men-(ˌ)tō\ 1 river 382 mi. (615 km.) long N California flowing S into Suisun Bay 2 city, * of California; *pop* 466,488

Sag·ue·nay \'sa-gə-ˌnā, ˌsa-gə-'\ 1 river 105 mi. (169 km.) long Canada in S Quebec flowing E into the Saint Lawrence 2 city Canada in S Quebec; *pop* 144,746

Sa·ha·ra \sə-'her-ə, -'här-\ desert region N Africa extending from Atlantic coast to Red Sea — Sa·ha·ran \-ən\ *adj*

Sa·hel \'sa-hil, sə-'hil\ the S fringe of the Sahara

Saigon — see HO CHI MINH CITY

Saint Al·bans \'ól-bənz\ city SE England; *pop* 82,000

Saint Cath·a·rines \'ka-th(ə-)rənz\ city Canada in SE Ontario; *pop* 131,400

Saint Christopher — see SAINT KITTS

Saint Clair, Lake \'kler\ lake SE Michigan & SE Ontario connected by Saint Clair River (40 mi. or 64 km. long) with Lake Huron & draining by Detroit River into Lake Erie

Saint Croix \sänt-'krói, sənt-\ 1 river 129 mi. (208 km.)

long Canada & U.S. on border between New Brunswick & Maine 2 island West Indies; largest of Virgin Islands of the U.S.; *pop* 50,601

Saint Eli·as, Mount \i-'lī-əs\ mountain 18,008 ft. (5489 m.) on Alaska–Canada boundary in Saint Elias Range

Saint George's \'jór-jəz\ town, * of Grenada; *pop* 4000

Saint George's Channel channel British Isles between SW Wales & Ireland

Saint Gott·hard \sänt-'gä-tərd, sənt-, 'gät-hərd\ pass S *cen* Switzerland in Saint Gotthard Range of the Alps

Saint He·le·na \ˌsänt-ə-'lē-nə, ˌsänt-hə-'lē-\ island South Atlantic; a British colony; *pop* 4100

Saint Hel·ens, Mount \sänt-'he-lənz, sənt-\ volcano S Washington

Saint John \sänt-'jän, sənt-\ city & port Canada in New Brunswick; *pop* 70,063

Saint John's \sänt-'jänz, sənt-\ 1 city, * of Antigua and Barbuda; *pop* 23,000 2 city, * of Newfoundland and Labrador, Canada; *pop* 106,172

Saint Kitts \'kits\ *or* Saint Chris·to·pher \'kris-tə-fər\ island West Indies in the Leeward Islands; with Nevis forms independent Saint Kitts and Nevis; *, Basseterre (on Saint Kitts); *pop* 51,000

Saint Law·rence \sänt-'lór-ən(t)s, sənt-, -'lär-\ 1 river 760 mi. (1223 km.) long E Canada in Ontario & Quebec bordering on U.S. in New York & flowing from Lake Ontario NE into the Gulf of Saint Lawrence (inlet of the Atlantic) 2 seaway Canada & U.S. in and along the Saint Lawrence between Lake Ontario & Montreal

Saint Lou·is \sänt-'lü-əs, sənt-\ city E Missouri on the Mississippi; *pop* 319,294

Saint Lu·cia \sänt-'lü-shə, sənt-\ island West Indies in the Windwards S of Martinique; country; *, Castries; *pop* 166,500

Saint Mo·ritz \ˌsänt-mə-'rits, ˌsaⁿ-mə-\ *or G* Sankt Mo·ritz \ˌzäŋkt-mə-'rits\ town E Switzerland; *pop* 5000

Saint Paul \'pól\ city, * of Minnesota; *pop* 285,068

Saint Pe·ters·burg \'pē-tərz-ˌbərg\ 1 city W Florida; *pop* 244,769 2 *or 1914–24* Pet·ro·grad \'pe-trə-ˌgrad, -ˌgrät\ *or 1924–91* Le·nin·grad \'le-nən-ˌgrad, -ˌgrät\ city W Russia in Europe; *pop* 4,864,500

Saint Thom·as \'tä-məs\ island West Indies, one of Virgin Islands of the U.S.; chief town, Charlotte Amalie

Saint Vin·cent \sänt-'vin(t)-sənt, sənt-\ island West Indies in the *cen* Windward Islands; with N Grenadines forms independent Saint Vincent and the Grenadines; *, Kingstown (on Saint Vincent); *pop* 110,000

Sai·pan \sī-'pan, -'pän, 'sī-ˌ\ island W Pacific in S *cen* Marianas; *pop* 48,220

Sa·kai \(ˌ)sä-'kī\ city Japan in S Honshu; *pop* 841,966

Sa·kha·lin \ˌsa-kə-ˌlēn, -lən; ˌsä-kä-'lēn\ island SE Russia in W Pacific N of Hokkaido, Japan

Sal·a·mis \'sa-lə-məs\ ancient city Cyprus on E coast

Sa·lem \'sā-ləm\ city, * of Oregon; *pop* 154,637

Sa·li·nas \sə-'lē-nəs\ city W California; *pop* 150,441

Salisbury — see HARARE

Salisbury Plain plateau S England; site of Stonehenge

Salop — see SHROPSHIRE

Salt Lake City city, * of Utah; *pop* 186,440

Sal·ton Sea \'sól-tᵊn\ saline lake about 235 ft. (72 m.) below sea level SE California; formed by diversion of water from Colorado River

Sal·va·dor \'sal-və-ˌdór, ˌsal-və-'\ *or* Ba·hia \bä-'ē-ə\ city NE Brazil on the Atlantic; *pop* 2,675,656 — Sal·va·dor·an \ˌsal-və-'dór-ən\ *or* Sal·va·dor·ean *or* Sal·va·dor·ian \-ē-ən\ *adj or n*

Sal·ween \'sal-ˌwēn\ river about 1500 mi. (2415 km.) long SE Asia flowing from Tibet S into Bay of Bengal in Myanmar

Sa·mar \'sä-ˌmär\ island *cen* Philippines

Sa·ma·ra \sə-'mär-ə\ *or 1935–91* Kuy·by·shev \'kwē-bə-ˌshef, 'kü-ē-bə-, -ˌshev\ city W Russia, on the Volga; *pop* 1,165,000

Sa·mar·ia \sə-'mer-ē-ə\ district of ancient Palestine W of the Jordan between Galilee & Judaea

Sam·ar·qand *or* Sam·ar·kand \'sa-mər-ˌkand\ city E Uzbekistan; *pop* 370,500

Sam·ni·um \'sam-nē-əm\ ancient country S *cen* Italy — Sam·nite \'sam-ˌnīt\ *adj or n*

Sa·moa \sə-'mō-ə\ 1 islands SW *cen* Pacific N of Tonga; divided at longitude 171° W into American Samoa (or

Eastern Samoa) & independent Samoa **2** *formerly* **Western Samoa** islands Samoa W of 171° W; country; ✳ Apia; *pop* 187,800 — **Sa·mo·an** \sə-'mō-ən\ *adj or n*

Sa·mos \'sā-ˌmäs, 'sä-ˌmòs\ island Greece in the Aegean off coast of Turkey

San·aa *or* **Sana** \sä-'nä, 'sa-ˌnä\ city SW Arabia, ✳ of Yemen; *pop* 1,700,000

San An·dre·as Fault \ˌsan-an-'drā-əs\ zone of faults in California extending from N coast toward head of Gulf of California

San An·to·nio \ˌsan-ən-'tō-nē-ˌō\ city S Texas; *pop* 1,327,407

San Ber·nar·di·no \ˌsan-ˌbər-nə(r)-'dē-(ˌ)nō\ city S California; *pop* 209,924

San Di·ego \ˌsan-dē-'ā-(ˌ)gō\ coastal city SW California; *pop* 1,307,402

San·i·bel Island \'sa-nə-bəl, -ˌbel\ island SW Florida

Sand·wich \'san(d)-(ˌ)wich\ town SE England; *pop* 4600

Sandwich Islands — see HAWAII

San Fran·cis·co \ˌsan-frən-'sis-(ˌ)kō\ city W California on San Francisco Bay & Pacific Ocean; *pop* 805,235

San Joa·quin \ˌsan-wä-'kēn, -wò-\ river 350 mi. (563 km.) long *cen* California flowing NW into the Sacramento

San Jo·se \ˌsan-(h)ō-'zā\ city W California SE of San Francisco; *pop* 945,942

San Jo·sé \ˌsän-hō-'sā, ˌsan-(h)ō-'zā\ city, ✳ of Costa Rica; *pop* 288,000

San Juan \san-'wän, ˌsän-'hwän\ city, ✳ of Puerto Rico; *pop* 395,326

San Ma·ri·no \ˌsan-mə-'rē-(ˌ)nō\ **1** small country S Europe surrounded by Italy ENE of Florence near Adriatic Sea; *pop* 32,500 **2** town, its ✳; *pop* 4100 — **Sam·mar·i·nese** \ˌsa(m)-ˌma-rə-'nēz, -'nēs\ *n* — **San Mar·i·nese** \ˌsan-ˌma-\ *adj or n*

San Pe·dro Su·la \sän-'pā-(ˌ)thrō-'sü-lä\ city NW Honduras; *pop* 646,000

San Sal·va·dor \san-'sal-və-ˌdòr, ˌsän-'säl-vä-ˌthòr\ **1** island *cen* Bahamas **2** city, ✳ of El Salvador; *pop* 316,090

San·ta Ana \ˌsan-tə-'a-nə, ˌsän-tä-'ä-nä\ city SW California ESE of Long Beach; *pop* 324,528

San·ta Bar·ba·ra \'bär-b(ə-)rə\ *or* **Channel** islands California off SW coast in the North Pacific

Santa Clara \'kler-ə\ city W California NW of San Jose; *pop* 116,468

Santa Cla·ri·ta \klə-'rē-tə\ city S California N of Los Angeles; *pop* 176,320

San·ta Fe \ˌsan-tə-'fā\ city, ✳ of New Mexico; *pop* 67,947

Santa Fe Trail pioneer route to the SW U.S. about 1200 mi. (1930 km.) long used esp. 1821–80 from vicinity of Kansas City, Missouri, to Santa Fe, New Mexico

San·ta Ro·sa \ˌsan-tə-'rō-zə\ city W California N of San Francisco; *pop* 167,815

San·ti·a·go \ˌsan-tē-'ä-(ˌ)gō, ˌsän-\ city, ✳ of Chile; metropolitan area *pop* 4,668,500

San·to Do·min·go \ˌsan-tə-də-'miŋ-(ˌ)gō\ *formerly* **Tru·ji·llo** \trü-'hē-(ˌ)yō\ city, ✳ of Dominican Republic; *pop* 2,582,000

São Pau·lo \saùⁿ-'paù-(ˌ)lü, -(ˌ)lō\ city SE Brazil; *pop* 11,253,503

São To·mé \saùⁿ-tə-'mā\ town, ✳ of São Tomé and Príncipe; *pop* 43,420

São Tomé and Príncipe country W Africa; ✳ São Tomé; *pop* 192,000

Sap·po·ro \'sä-pō-ˌrō; sä-'pór-(ˌ)ō\ city Japan on W Hokkaido; *pop* 1,913,545

Sa·ra·je·vo \ˌsa-rə-'yä-(ˌ)vō, ˌsär-ə-\ city SE *cen* Bosnia and Herzegovina, its ✳; *pop* 330,500

Sa·ra·tov \sə-'rä-təf\ city W Russia, on the Volga; *pop* 838,000

Sar·din·ia \sär-'di-nē-ə, -'di-nyə\ island Italy in the Mediterranean S of Corsica; *pop* 1,639,362 — **Sar·din·ian** \sär-'di-nē-ən, -'din-yən\ *adj or n*

Sar·gas·so Sea \sär-'ga-(ˌ)sō\ area of nearly still water in the North Atlantic lying chiefly between 20° & 35° N latitude & 30° & 70° W longitude

Sas·katch·e·wan \sa-'ska-chə-wən, sa-, -ˌwän\ province W Canada; ✳, Regina; *pop* 1,033,381

Sas·ka·toon \ˌsas-kə-'tün\ city *cen* Saskatchewan, Canada; *pop* 222,189

Sau·di Ara·bia \ˌsaú-dē, 'sò-dē, ˌsä-'ü-dē\ country SW Asia occupying largest part of Arabian Peninsula; ✳, Riyadh; *pop* 27,000,000 — **Saudi** *adj or n* — **Saudi Arabian** *adj or n*

Sault Sainte Ma·rie Canals \'sü-(ˌ)sänt-mə-'rē\ *or* **Soo Canals** \ˌsü\ three ship canals, two in U.S. (Michigan) & one in Canada (Ontario), at rapids in river connecting Lake Superior & Lake Huron

Sa·vaii \sə-'vī-ˌē\ island, largest in independent Samoa

Sa·van·nah \sə-'va-nə\ city & port E Georgia; *pop* 136,286

Sa·voy \sə-'vòi\ *or French* **Sa·voie** \sä-'vwä\ region SE France SW of Switzerland bordering on Italy — **Sa·voy·ard** \sə-'vòi-ˌärd, ˌsa-ˌvòi-'ärd, ˌsa-ˌvwä-'yär(d)\ *adj or n*

Sca·fell Pike \ˌskò-'fel\ mountain 3210 ft. (978 m.) NW England; highest in Cumbrian Mountains & in England

Scan·di·na·via \ˌskan-də-'nä-vē-ə, -vyə\ **1** peninsula N Europe occupied by Norway & Sweden **2** Denmark, Norway, Sweden, & as used by some also Iceland & Finland — **Scan·di·na·vian** \ˌskan-də-'nä-vē-ən, -vyən\ *adj or n*

Scar·bor·ough \'skär-ˌbər-ō\ former city Canada in SE Ontario; now part of Toronto

Schel·de \'skel-də\ *or* **Scheldt** \'skelt\ river 270 mi. (434 km.) long W Europe flowing from N France through Belgium into North Sea in Netherlands

Schuyl·kill \'skü-kᵊl, 'skül-ˌkil\ river 131 mi. (211 km.) long SE Pennsylvania flowing SE into the Delaware River at Philadelphia

Scil·ly, Isles of \'si-lē\ island group SW England off Land's End; *pop* 2900

Sco·tia \'skō-shə\ SCOTLAND — the Medieval Latin name

Scot·land \'skät-lənd\ *or Latin* **Cal·e·do·nia** \ˌka-lə-'dō-nyə, -nē-ə\ country N Great Britain; a division of United Kingdom; ✳, Edinburgh; *pop* 5,295,000

Scotts·dale \'skäts-ˌdāl\ city SW *cen* Arizona E of Phoenix; *pop* 217,385

Scyth·ia \'si-thē-ə, -thē\ ancient area of Europe & Asia N & NE of Black Sea & E of Aral Sea — **Scyth·i·an** \'si-thē-ən, -thē\ *adj or n*

Se·at·tle \sē-'a-tᵊl\ city & port W Washington; *pop* 608,660

Seine \'sān, 'sen\ river 480 mi. (772 km.) long N France flowing NW into English Channel

Sel·kirk \'sel-ˌkərk\ range of the Rocky Mountains SE British Columbia, Canada; highest peak, 11,555 ft. (3522 m.)

Se·ma·rang \sə-'mär-ˌäŋ\ city Indonesia in *cen* Java; *pop* 1,556,000

Sen·dai \(ˌ)sen-'dī\ city Japan in NE Honshu; *pop* 1,045,986

Sen·e·ca Falls \'se-ni-kə\ village W *cen* New York; *pop* 6681

Sen·e·gal \ˌse-ni-'gól, -'gäl, 'se-ni-ˌ\ **1** river 1015 mi. (1633 km.) long W Africa flowing W into the North Atlantic **2** country W Africa; ✳, Dakar; *pop* 13,509,000 — **Sen·e·ga·lese** \ˌse-ni-gə-'lēz, -'lēs\ *adj or n*

Seoul \'sōl\ city, ✳ of South Korea; *pop* 9,750,000

Ser·bia \'sər-bē-ə\ country S Europe in the Balkans; ✳ Belgrade; *pop* 7,150,000

Serbia and Montenegro *or 1992-2003* **Yugoslavia** former country S Europe on Balkan Peninsula

Ser·en·ge·ti Plain \ˌser-ən-'ge-tē\ area N Tanzania

Seven Hills the seven hills upon and about which was built the city of Rome, Italy

Sev·ern \'se-vərn\ river 210 mi. (338 km.) long Wales & England flowing from E *cen* Wales into Bristol Channel

Se·ville \sə-'vil\ *or Spanish* **Se·vi·lla** \sā-'vē-(ˌ)yä\ city SW Spain; *pop* 700,169

Sew·ard Peninsula \'sü-ərd\ peninsula 180 mi. (290 km.) long W Alaska projecting into Bering Sea

Sey·chelles \sā-'shel(z)\ islands W Indian Ocean NE of Madagascar; country; ✳, Victoria; *pop* 90,900 — **Sey·chel·lois** \ˌsā-shəl-'wä, -ˌshel-\ *n*

Shang·hai \shaŋ-'hī\ city & port E China; *pop* 21,126,600

Shan·non \'sha-nən\ river 230 mi. (370 km.) long W Ireland flowing S & W into the North Atlantic

Shar·on, Plain of \'sher-ən\ region Israel on the coast

Shas·ta, Mount \'shas-tə\ mountain 14,162 ft. (4316 m.) N California in Cascade Range

Shatt al Ar·ab \ˌshat-al-'a-rəb\ river 120 mi. (193 km.) long SE Iraq formed by flowing together of Euphrates & Tigris rivers and flowing SE into Persian Gulf

Shef·field \'she-ˌfēld\ city N England; *pop* 518,000

Shen·an·do·ah \ˌshe-nən-'dō-ə\ valley Virginia between the Alleghany & Blue Ridge mountains

Shen·yang \'shən-'yäŋ\ *or traditionally* **Muk·den** \'mùk-dən, 'mək-; mùk-'den\ city NE China; chief city of Manchuria; *pop* 5,987,000

Sher·brooke \\'shər-ˌbrúk\\ city Quebec, Canada E of Montreal; *pop* 154,601

Sher·wood Forest \\'shər-ˌwúd\\ ancient royal forest *cen* England

Shet·land \\'shet-lənd\\ islands N Scotland NE of the Orkneys; *pop* 23,000

Shi·jia·zhuang *or* **Shih–chia–chuang** \\'shir-'jyä-'jwäŋ, 'shē-\\ city NE China; *pop* 2,802,500

Shi·ko·ku \\shē-'kō-(ˌ)kü\\ island S Japan E of Kyushu; *pop* 4,154,039

Shi·raz \\shi-'räz, -'raz\\ city SW *cen* Iran; *pop* 1,460,665

Shreve·port \\'shrēv-ˌpórt\\ city NW Louisiana on Red River; *pop* 199,311

Shrews·bury \\'sh(r)üz-ˌber-ē, -b(ə-)rē\\ town W England; *pop* 72,000

Shrop·shire \\'shräp-shər, -ˌshir\\ *or* *1974–80* **Sal·op** \\'sal-əp\\ county W England bordering on Wales; *pop* 306,000

Shu·ma·gin \\'shü-mə-gən\\ islands SW Alaska S of Alaska Peninsula

Siam — see THAILAND

Siam, Gulf of — see THAILAND, GULF OF

Si·be·ria \\sī-'bir-ē-ə\\ region N Asia in Russia between the Urals & the North Pacific — **Si·be·ri·an** \\-ən\\ *adj or n*

Sic·i·ly \\'si-s(ə-)lē\\ *or Italian* **Si·ci·lia** \\sē-'chēl-yä\\ island S Italy SW of toe of peninsula of Italy; *, Palermo; *pop* 5,002,904 — **Si·cil·ian** \\sə-'sil-yən\\ *adj or n*

Si·er·ra Le·one \\sē-ˌer-ə-lē-'ōn, ˌsir-ə-, -lē-'ō-nē\\ country W Africa on the North Atlantic; *, Freetown; *pop* 4,491,000 — **Si·er·ra Le·on·ean** \\-'ō-nē-ən\\ *adj or n*

Si·er·ra Ma·dre \\sē-ˌer-ə-'mä-drā, 'syer-ä-'mä-ˌthrä\\ mountain system Mexico including **Sierra Madre Oc·ci·den·tal** \\ˌäk-sə-ˌden-'täl, ˌōk-sē-ˌthen-'täl\\ range W of the *cen* plateau, **Sierra Madre Ori·en·tal** \\ˌór-ē-ˌen-'täl\\ range E of the plateau, & **Sierra Madre del Sur** \\'sür, 'sür\\ range to the S

Sierra Ne·va·da \\nə-'va-də, -'vä-\\ 1 mountain range E California & W Nevada — see WHITNEY, MOUNT 2 mountain range S Spain

Sik·kim \\'si-kəm, -ˌkim\\ former country SE Asia on S slope of the Himalayas between Nepal & Bhutan; state of India since 1975; *pop* 610,577

Si·le·sia \\sī-'lē-zh(ē-)ə, sə-, -sh(ē-)ə\\ region E *cen* Europe in valley of the upper Oder; formerly chiefly in Germany now chiefly in E Czech Republic & SW Poland — **Si·le·sian** \\-zh(ē-)ən, -sh(ē-)ən\\ *adj or n*

Silk Road *or* **Silk Route** ancient trade route that extended from China to the Mediterranean

Sim·coe, Lake \\'sim-(ˌ)kō\\ lake Canada in SE Ontario

Si·mi Valley \\sē-'mē\\ city SW California W of Los Angeles; *pop* 124,237

Sim·plon Pass \\'sim-ˌplän\\ mountain pass 6590 ft. (2009 m.) between Switzerland & Italy

Si·nai \\'sī-ˌnī\\ 1 mountain on Sinai Peninsula where according to the Bible the Law was given to Moses 2 peninsula extension of continent of Asia NE Egypt between Red Sea & the Mediterranean

Sin·ga·pore \\'siŋ-ə-ˌpór\\ 1 island off S end of Malay Peninsula; country; *pop* 5,077,000 2 city, its *; *pop* 206,500 — **Sin·ga·por·ean** \\ˌsiŋ-ə-'pór-ē-ən\\ *adj or n*

Sinkiang Uighur — see XINJIANG UYGUR

Sioux Falls \\'sü\\ city SE South Dakota; largest in state; *pop* 153,888

Skag·ge·rak \\'ska-gə-ˌrak\\ arm of North Sea between S Norway & N Denmark

Skop·je \\'skó-pye, -pyə\\ city, * of independent Macedonia; *pop* 487,000

Sla·vo·nia \\slə-'vō-nē-ə, -nyə\\ region E Croatia; *pop* 78,000 — **Sla·vo·ni·an** \\-nē-ən, -nyən\\ *adj or n*

Slo·va·kia \\slō-'vä-kē-ə, -'va-\\ country *cen* Europe; *, Bratislava; *pop* 5,397,036

Slo·ve·nia \\slō-'vē-nē-ə, -nyə\\ country S Europe; *, Ljubljana; *pop* 2,050,000

Smyrna — see IZMIR

Snake \\'snäk\\ river NW U.S. flowing from NW Wyoming into the Columbia in SE Washington

Snow·don \\'snō-dᵊn\\ massif 3560 ft. (1085 m.) in **Snow·do·nia** \\snō-'dō-nē-ə, -nyə\\ (mountainous district) NW Wales; highest point in Wales

So·ci·e·ty \\sə-'sī-ə-tē\\ islands South Pacific; belonging to France; chief island, Tahiti; *pop* 162,573

So·fia \\'sō-fē-ə, 'só-, sō-'\\ city, * of Bulgaria; *pop* 1,291,600

So·ho \\'sō-ˌhō\\ district of *cen* London, England

So·li·hull \\ˌsō-li-'həl\\ city *cen* England; *pop* 123,000

Sol·o·mon \\'sä-lə-mən\\ 1 islands W Pacific E of New Guinea divided between Papua New Guinea & independent Solomon Islands 2 sea, arm of Coral Sea W of the Solomons

Solomon Islands country, SW Pacific E of New Guinea; *, Honiara (on Guadalcanal); *pop* 516,000

Sc·ma·lia \\sō-'mä-lē-ə, sə-, -'mäl-yə\\ country E Africa on Gulf of Aden & Indian Ocean; *, Mogadishu; *pop* 10,250,000 — **So·ma·li·an** \\-'mä-lē-ən, -'mäl-yən\\ *adj or n*

So·ma·li·land \\sō-'mä-lē-ˌland, sə-\\ historical region E Africa consisting of Somalia, Djibouti, & part of E Ethiopia — **So·ma·li** \\sō-'mä-lē, sə-\\ *n*

Som·er·set \\'sə-mər-ˌset, -sət\\ *or* **Som·er·set·shire** \\-ˌshir, -shər\\ county SW England

So·nor·an \\sə-'nór-ən\\ *or* **So·no·ra** \\sə-'nór-ə\\ desert SW U.S. & NW Mexico

Soo Canals — see SAULT SAINTE MARIE CANALS

South Africa, Republic of *formerly* **Union of South Africa** country S Africa; administrative *, Pretoria; legislative *, Cape Town; judicial *, Bloemfontein; *pop* 51,771,000 — **South African** *adj or n*

South America continent of Western Hemisphere SE of North America and chiefly S of the Equator — **South American** *adj or n*

South·amp·ton \\saù-'tham(p)-tən, saùth-'ham(p)-\\ city S England; *pop* 254,000

South Australia state S Australia; *, Adelaide; *pop* 1,596,572 — **South Australian** *adj or n*

South Bend \\'bend\\ city N Indiana; *pop* 101,168

South Cape *or* **South Point** — see KA LAE

South Car·o·li·na \\ˌker(-ə)-'lī-nə, ˌka-rə-\\ state SE U.S.; *, Columbia; *pop* 4,625,364 — **South Car·o·lin·i·an** \\-'li-nē-ən, -'li-nyən\\ *adj or n*

South China Sea — see CHINA

South Da·ko·ta \\də-'kō-tə\\ state NW *cen* U.S.; *, Pierre; *pop* 814,180 — **South Da·ko·tan** \\-'kō-tᵊn\\ *adj or n*

South·end–on–Sea \\ˌsaù-ˌthend-ˌón-'sē, -ˌän-\\ seaside resort SE England E of London; *pop* 176,000

Southern Alps mountain range New Zealand in W South Island extending almost the length of the island

Southern Hemisphere the half of the earth that lies S of the Equator

South Georgia island S Atlantic E of Tierra del Fuego; administered by United Kingdom

South Island island S New Zealand; *pop* 1,004,397

South Korea *or* **Republic of Korea** country S half of Korean Peninsula in E Asia; *, Seoul; *pop* 48,400,000

South Seas the areas of the Atlantic, Indian, & Pacific oceans in the Southern Hemisphere

South Shields \\'shēldz\\ seaport N England; *pop* 75,000

South Sudan country E Africa formed 2011 from the S part of Sudan; *, Juba; *pop* 8,260,500

South Vietnam — see VIETNAM

South·wark \\'sə-thərk, 'saùth-wərk\\ borough of S Greater London, England; *pop* 288,000

South–West Africa — see NAMIBIA

South Yorkshire metropolitan county N England; *pop* 1,343,600

Soviet Central Asia portion of *cen* & SW Asia formerly belonging to U.S.S.R. and including the former soviet socialist republics of present-day Kyrgyzstan, Tajikistan, Turkmenistan, Uzbekistan & by some thought also to include Kazakhstan

Soviet Union — see UNION OF SOVIET SOCIALIST REPUBLICS

So·we·to \\sō-'wä-tō, -'we-, -tü\\ residential area NE Republic of South Africa adjoining SW Johannesburg

Spain \\'spān\\ country SW Europe on Iberian Peninsula; *, Madrid; *pop* 48,815,916

Spanish America 1 the Spanish-speaking countries of America 2 the parts of America settled and formerly governed by the Spanish

Spanish Guinea — see EQUATORIAL GUINEA

Spanish Sahara — see WESTERN SAHARA

Spar·ta \\'spär-tə\\ ancient city S Greece in Peloponnese; * of Laconia

Spo·kane \\spō-'kan\\ city E Washington; *pop* 208,916

Spring·field \\'spriŋ-ˌfēld\\ 1 city, * of Illinois; *pop* 116,250 2 city SW Massachusetts; *pop* 153,060 3 city SW Missouri; *pop* 159,498

Sri Lan·ka \(,)srē-'läŋ-kə, (,)shrē-, -'laŋ-\ *formerly* Cey·lon \si-'län, sā-\ country having the same boundaries as island of Ceylon; ✳, Colombo; *pop* 20,300,000 — Sri Lan·kan \-'läŋ-kən, -'laŋ-\ *adj or n*

Sri·na·gar \srē-'nə-gər\ city N India; *pop* 1,260,500

Staf·ford \'sta-fərd\ town W *cen* England; *pop* 68,000

Staf·ford·shire \'sta-fərd-,shir, -shər\ *or* Stafford county W *cen* England

Staked Plain — see LLANO ESTACADO

Stam·ford \'stam-fərd\ city SW Connecticut; *pop* 122,643

Stan·ley \'stan-lē\ town, ✳ of Falkland Islands; *pop* 2100

Stat·en Island \'sta-tᵊn\ 1 island SE New York SW of mouth of the Hudson 2 *formerly* Rich·mond \'rich-mənd\ borough of New York City including Staten Island; *pop* 468,730

Ster·ling Heights \'stər-liŋ\ city SE Michigan; *pop* 129,699

Stir·ling \'stər-liŋ\ town *cen* Scotland; *pop* 36,000

Stock·holm \'stäk-,hō(l)m\ city, ✳ of Sweden; *pop* 896,500

Stock·port \'stäk-,pȯrt\ town NW England; *pop* 285,000

Stock·ton \'stäk-tən\ city *cen* California; *pop* 291,707

Stoke–on–Trent \'stōk-,än-'trent, -,ȯn-\ city *cen* England; *pop* 271,000

Stone·henge \'stōn-,henj, (,)stōn-'\ prehistoric assemblage of megaliths S England in Wiltshire on Salisbury Plain

Stone Mountain mountain 1686 ft. (514 m.) NW Georgia E of Atlanta

Stor·no·way \'stȯr-nə-,wä\ seaport NW Scotland; chief town of Lewis with Harris Island; *pop* 5700

Stra·bane \strə-'ban\ district W Northern Ireland; *pop* 39,843

Strath·clyde \strath-'klīd\ former region SW Scotland; included Glasgow

Strom·bo·li \'sträm-bō-(,)lē\ volcano 2500 ft. (758 m.) Italy on Stromboli Island in Tyrrhenian Sea

Stutt·gart \'shtut-,gärt, 'stut-, 'stȧt-\ city SW Germany; *pop* 585,890

Styx \'stiks\ chief river of the underworld in Greek mythology

Süchow — see XUZHOU

Su·cre \'sü-(,)krā\ city, constitutional ✳ of Bolivia; *pop* 244,000

Su·dan \sü-'dan, -'dän\ 1 region N Africa S of the Sahara between the Atlantic & the upper Nile 2 country NE Africa S of Egypt; ✳, Khartoum; *pop* 30,900,000 — Su·da·nese \,sü-də-'nēz, -'nēs\ *adj or n*

Sud·bury, Greater \'səd-,ber-ē, -b(ə-)rē\ city SE Ontario, Canada; *pop* 160,274

Su·ez, Gulf of \sü-'ez, 'sü-,ez\ arm of Red Sea

Suez, Isthmus of isthmus NE Egypt between Mediterranean & Red seas connecting Africa & Asia

Suez Canal canal 100 mi. (161 km.) long NE Egypt across the Isthmus of Suez

Suf·folk \'sə-fək\ county E England on North Sea; *pop* 728,163

Sui·sun Bay \sə-'sün\ inlet of San Francisco Bay, W *cen* California

Su·la·we·si \,sü-lä-'wä-sē\ island Indonesia E of Borneo; *pop* 12,520,711

Su·lu \'sü-(,)lü\ 1 archipelago SW Philippines SW of Mindanao 2 sea W Philippines

Su·ma·tra \su̇-'mä-trə\ island W Indonesia S of Malay Peninsula — Su·ma·tran \-trən\ *adj or n*

Su·mer \'sü-mər\ the S division of ancient Babylonia — Su·me·ri·an \sü-'mer-ē-ən, -'mir-\ *adj or n*

Sun·belt \'sən-,belt\ region S & SW U.S.

Sun·da \'sün-də, 'sən-\ strait between Java & Sumatra

Sun·der·land \'sən-dər-lənd\ seaport N England; *pop* 174,000

Sun·ny·vale \'sə-nē-,vāl\ city W California; *pop* 140,081

Sun Valley resort center *cen* Idaho

Su·pe·ri·or, Lake \su̇-'pir-ē-ər\ lake E *cen* North America in U.S. & Canada; largest of the Great Lakes

Su·ra·ba·ya \,su̇r-ə-'bī-ə\ city Indonesia in NE Java; *pop* 2,765,000

Su·ri·na·me \,su̇r-ə-'nä-mə\ country N South America between Guyana & French Guiana; ✳, Paramaribo; *pop* 542,000 — Su·ri·nam·er \'su̇r-ə-,nä-mər, ,su̇r-ə-'nä-\ *n* — Su·ri·nam·ese \,su̇r-ə-nə-'mēz, -'mēs\ *adj or n*

Sur·rey \'sər-ē, 'sə-rē\ city Canada in SW British Columbia; *pop* 468,251

Sut·ton \'sə-tᵊn\ borough of S Greater London, England; *pop* 190,000

Su·va \'sü-və\ city & port, ✳ of Fiji on Viti Levu Island; *pop* 74,850

Su·wan·nee \sə-'wä-nē, 'swä-\ river 250 mi. (400 km.) long SE U.S. flowing SW into Gulf of Mexico

Sverdlovsk — see YEKATERINBURG

Swan·sea \'swän-zē\ city & port SE Wales; *pop* 179,000

Swa·zi·land \'swä-zē-,land\ — see ESWATINI— Swa·zi \'swä-zē\ *adj or n*

Swe·den \'swē-dᵊn\ country N Europe on Scandinavia (peninsula) bordering on Baltic Sea; ✳, Stockholm; *pop* 8,016,000

Swit·zer·land \'swit-sər-lənd\ country W Europe in the Alps; ✳, Bern; *pop* 7,800,000

Syd·ney \'sid-nē\ city SE Australia, ✳ of New South Wales; *pop* 3,908,642

Syr·a·cuse \'sir-ə-,kyüs, -,kyüz\ city *cen* New York; *pop* 145,170

Syr·ia \'sir-ē-ə\ 1 ancient region SW Asia bordering on the Mediterranean 2 country S of Turkey; ✳, Damascus; *pop* 17,952,000 — Syr·i·an \'sir-ē-ən\ *adj or n*

Syrian Desert desert region between Mediterranean coast & the Euphrates in N Saudi Arabia, SE Syria, W Iraq, & NE Jordan

Table Bay harbor of Cape Town, Republic of South Africa

Ta·briz \tə-'brēz\ city NW Iran; *pop* 1,494,998

Ta·co·ma \tə-'kō-mə\ city & port W Washington S of Seattle; *pop* 198,397

Taegu — see DAEGU

Tae·jon \'tā-,jon, 'dä-\ *or* Dae·jeon \'dä-\ city *cen* South Korea NW of Taegu; *pop* 1,495,000

Ta·gus \'tä-gəs\ *or Spanish* Ta·jo \'tä-(,)hō\ *or Portuguese* Te·jo \'tä-(,)zhü\ river 626 mi. (1007 km.) long Spain & Portugal flowing W into the North Atlantic

Ta·hi·ti \tä-'hē-tē\ island South Pacific in Society Islands; *pop* 131,309

Tai·bei \'tī-'bā\ *or* Tai·pei \'tī-'pā, -'bā\ city, ✳ of (Nationalist) China in N Taiwan; *pop* 2,700,000

T'ai–nan \'tī-'nän\ city SW Taiwan; *pop* 1,883,000

Tai·wan \'tī-'wän\ *formerly* For·mo·sa \fȯr-'mō-sə, fər-, -zə\ 1 island China off SE coast of mainland; seat of government of (Nationalist) Republic of China; ✳, Taibei; *pop* 23,340,000 2 strait between Taiwan & mainland of China connecting East China & South China seas — Tai·wan·ese \,tī-wə-'nēz, -'nēs\ *adj or n*

Tai·yuan \'tī-'ywen, -'ywän\ city N China; *pop* 3,290,500

Tai·zhong \'tī-'jüŋ\ *or* Tai·chung \'tī-'chu̇ŋ\ city W Taiwan; *pop* 2,702,500

Ta·jik·i·stan \tä-,ji-ki-'stan, tə-, -,jē-, -'stän\ country W *cen* Asia bordering on China & Afghanistan; ✳, Dushanbe; *pop* 7,564,500

Ta·kli·ma·kan *or* Ta·kla Ma·kan \,tä-klə-mə-'kän\ desert W China

Ta·lien — see DALIAN

Tal·la·has·see \,ta-lə-'ha-sē\ city, ✳ of Florida; *pop* 181,376

Tal·linn \'ta-lən, 'tä-\ city, ✳ of Estonia; *pop* 405,000

Tam·pa \'tam-pə\ city W Florida on Tampa Bay (inlet of Gulf of Mexico); *pop* 335,709

Tan·gan·yi·ka \,tan-gə-'nyē-kə, ,taŋ-gə-, -'nē-\ former country E Africa S of Kenya; now part of Tanzania

Tanganyika, Lake lake E Africa between Tanzania & Democratic Republic of the Congo

Tang·shan \'däŋ-'shän, 'täŋ-\ city NE China; *pop* 2,750,000

Tan·za·nia \,tan-zə-'nē-ə, ,tän-\ country E Africa on Indian Ocean, including Zanzibar; legislative ✳, Dodoma; historic ✳, Dar es Salaam; *pop* 44,929,000 — Tan·za·ni·an \-'nē-ən\ *adj or n*

Ta·ra·wa \tə-'rä-wə, 'ta-rə-,wä\ island *cen* Pacific, contains ✳ of Kiribati; *pop* 56,284

Tar·ry·town \'ta-rē-,tau̇n\ village SE New York; *pop* 11,277

Tar·sus \'tär-səs\ ancient city of S Asia Minor; now a city in S Turkey

Tash·kent \tash-'kent, täsh-\ city, ✳ of Uzbekistan; *pop* 2,200,000

Tas·ma·nia \taz-'mā-nē-ə, -nyə\ *or earlier* Van Die·men's Land \van-'dē-mənz\ island SE Australia S of Victoria; a state; ✱, Hobart; *pop* 495,354 — **Tas·ma·nian** \taz-'mā-nē-ən, -nyən\ *adj or n*

Tas·man Sea \'taz-mən\ the part of the South Pacific between SE Australia & New Zealand

Ta·try \'tä-trē\ *or* **Ta·tra** \'tä-trə\ mountains N Slovakia & S Poland in *cen* Carpathian Mountains

Taun·ton \'tȯn-tⁿn, 'tän-\ town SW England; *pop* 60,000

Tbi·li·si \tə-'bē-lə-sē, tə-bə-'lē-sē\ *or* **Tif·lis** \'ti-fləs, tə-'flēs\ city, ✱ of Republic of Georgia; *pop* 1,106,500

Te·gu·ci·gal·pa \tə-ˌgü-sə-'gal-pə, tä-ˌgü-sē-'gäl-pä\ city, ✱ of Honduras; *pop* 879,000

Teh·ran \ˌtā-(ə-)'ran, te-'ran, -'rän\ city, ✱ of Iran; at foot of S slope of Elburz Mountains; *pop* 8,154,051

Tel Aviv \ˌtel-ə-'vēv\ *or officially* **Tel Aviv–Ya·fo** \-'yä-fō\ city W Israel on the Mediterranean; *pop* 410,000

Tem·pe \tem-'pē\ city S *cen* Arizona; *pop* 158,000

Ten·nes·see \ˌte-nə-'sē, 'te-nə-ˌ\ 1 river 652 mi. (1049 km.) long in Tennessee, N Alabama, & W Kentucky 2 state E *cen* U.S.; ✱, Nashville; *pop* 6,346,105 — **Ten·nes·se·an** *or* **Ten·nes·see·an** \ˌte-nə-'sē-ən\ *adj or n*

Te·noch·ti·tlan \tä-ˌnȯch-tēt-'län\ ancient name of Mexico City

Tex·as \'tek-səs, -siz\ state S U.S.; ✱, Austin; *pop* 25,145,561 — **Tex·an** \-sən\ *adj or n*

Texas Panhandle the NW projection of land in Texas

Thai·land \'tī-ˌland, -lənd\ *formerly* **Si·am** \sī-'am\ country SE Asia on Gulf of Thailand; ✱, Bangkok; *pop* 65,982,000 — **Thai·land·er** \-ˌlan-dər, -lən-\ *n*

Thailand, Gulf of *formerly* **Gulf of Siam** arm of South China Sea between Indochina & Malay Peninsula

Thames \'temz\ river over 200 mi. (322 km.) long S England flowing E from the Cotswolds into the North Sea

Thar \'tär\ desert E Pakistan & NW India (country) E of Indus River

Thebes \'thēbz\ 1 *or* **The·bae** \'thē-(ˌ)bē\ ancient city S Egypt on the Nile 2 ancient city E Greece NNW of Athens — **The·ban** \'thē-bən\ *adj or n*

Thes·sa·lo·ní·ki \ˌthe-sä-lō-'nē-kē\ city N Greece; *pop* 325,000

Thim·phu \tim-'pü\ city, ✱ of Bhutan; *pop* 79,185

Thi·ru·van·an·tha·pur·am \ˌtir-ü-və-ˌnən-tə-'pùr-əm\ city S India; *pop* 1,679,754

Thousand Islands island group Canada & U.S. in the Saint Lawrence River in Ontario & New York

Thousand Oaks city SW California W of Los Angeles; *pop* 126,683

Thrace \'thrās\ *or ancient* **Thra·cia** \'thrā-sh(ē-)ə\ region SE Europe in Balkan Peninsula N of the Aegean now divided between Greece & Turkey; in ancient times extended N to the Danube — **Thra·cian** \'thrā-shən\ *adj or n*

Thunder Bay city SW Ontario, Canada on Lake Superior; *pop* 108,359

Tian·jin \'tyän-'jin\ *or* **Tien·tsin** \'tyen-'tsin, 'tin-\ city NE China SE of Beijing; *pop* 10,190,000

Tian Shan *or* **Tien Shan** \'tyen-'shän, -'shan\ mountain system *cen* Asia extending NE from Pamirs

Ti·ber \'tī-bər\ *or Italian* **Te·ve·re** \'tä-vä-rā\ river 252 mi. (405 km.) long *cen* Italy flowing through Rome into Tyrrhenian Sea

Tiberias, Lake — see GALILEE, SEA OF

Ti·bes·ti \tə-'bes-tē\ mountains N *cen* Africa in *cen* Sahara in NW Chad; highest 11,204 ft. (3415 m.)

Ti·bet \tə-'bet\ *or* **Xi·zang** \'shēd-'zäŋ\ region SW China on high plateau at average altitude 16,000 ft. (4877 m.) N of the Himalayas; ✱, Lhasa; *pop* 3,002,165

Tier·ra del Fue·go \tē-'er-ə-(ˌ)del-fü-'ā-(ˌ)gō, 'tyer-ä-(ˌ)thel-'fwā-gō\ 1 island group off S South America 2 chief island of the group; divided between Argentina & Chile

Tiflis — see TBILISI

Ti·gris \'tī-grəs\ river 1180 mi. (1899 km.) long Turkey & Iraq flowing SSE and uniting with the Euphrates to form the Shatt al Arab

Ti·jua·na \ˌtē-ə-'wä-nə, tē-'hwä-nä\ city NW Mexico on the U.S. border; *pop* 1,559,683

Timbuktu — see TOMBOUCTOU

Ti·mor \'tē-ˌmȯr, tē-\ island S Malay Archipelago SE of Sulawesi; W half part of Indonesia, E half independent East Timor

Timor–Leste — see EAST TIMOR

Ti·ra·ne *or* **Ti·ra·na** \ti-'rä-nə, tē-\ city, ✱ of Albania; *pop* 418,495

Ti·rol *or* **Ty·rol** \tə-'rōl\ *or Italian* **Ti·ro·lo** \tē-'rò-(ˌ)lō\ region in E Alps in W Austria & NE Italy — **Ti·ro·le·an** \tə-'rō-lē-ən, tī-\ *or* **Tir·o·lese** \ˌtir-ə-'lēz, ˌtī-rə-, -'lēs\ *adj or n*

Ti·ti·ca·ca, Lake \ˌti-ti-'kä-kä, ˌte-tē-\ lake on Bolivia–Peru boundary at altitude of 12,500 ft. (3810 m.)

To·ba·go \tə-'bā-(ˌ)gō\ island West Indies NE of Trinidad; part of independent Trinidad and Tobago; *pop* 60,874 — **To·ba·go·ni·an** \ˌtō-bə-'gō-nē-ən, -nyən\ *n*

To·go \'tō-(ˌ)gō\ country W Africa on Gulf of Guinea; ✱, Lomé; *pop* 6,191,000 — **To·go·lese** \ˌtō-gə-'lēz, -'lēs\ *adj or n*

To·kyo \'tō-kē-ˌō, -ˌkyō\ city, ✱ of Japan in SE Honshu on Tokyo Bay; *pop* 8,945,695 — **To·kyo·ite** \'tō-kē-(ˌ)ō-ˌīt\ *n*

To·le·do \tə-'lē-(ˌ)dō, -'lē-də\ city NW Ohio; *pop* 287,208

Tol'·yat·ti \tȯl-'yä-tē\ city W Russia; NW of Samara; *pop* 720,000

Tom·bouc·tou \tōⁿ-bük-'tü\ *or* **Tim·buk·tu** \ˌtim-ˌbək-'tü, tim-'bək-(ˌ)tü\ town W Africa in Mali near Niger River; *pop* 55,000

Ton·ga \'täŋ-gə, 'täŋ-ə, 'tòŋ-ä\ islands SW Pacific E of Fiji Islands; country; ✱, Nukualofa; *pop* 103,300 — **Ton·gan** \-(g)ən\ *adj or n*

Ton·kin, Gulf of \'täŋ-kən\ arm of South China Sea E of N Vietnam

To·pe·ka \tə-'pē-kə\ city, ✱ of Kansas; *pop* 127,473

Tor·bay \(ˌ)tȯr-'bā\ district SW England; *pop* 131,000

To·ron·to \tə-'rän-(ˌ)tō, -'rän-tə\ city, ✱ of Ontario, Canada; *pop* 2,615,060

Tor·rance \'tȯr-ən(t)s, 'tär-\ city SW California; *pop* 145,438

Tor·res \'tȯr-əs\ strait between New Guinea & Cape York Peninsula, Australia

Tou·louse \tü-'lüz\ city SW France; *pop* 441,802

Tower Hamlets borough of E Greater London, England; *pop* 254,000

Trans·vaal \tran(t)s-'väl, tranz-\ former province NE Republic of South Africa

Tran·syl·va·nia \ˌtran(t)-səl-'vā-nyə, -nē-ə\ region W Romania — **Tran·syl·va·nian** \-nyən, -nē-ən\ *adj or n*

Transylvanian Alps a S extension of Carpathian Mountains in *cen* Romania

Tren·ton \'tren-tⁿn\ city, ✱ of New Jersey; *pop* 84,913

Trin·i·dad \'tri-nə-ˌdad\ island West Indies off NE coast of Venezuela; with Tobago forms the independent country of Trinidad and Tobago; ✱, Port of Spain; *pop* 1,328,000 — **Trin·i·da·di·an** \ˌtri-nə-'dä-dē-ən, -'da-\ *adj or n*

Trip·o·li \'tri-pə-lē\ 1 city & port NW Lebanon; *pop* 127,611 2 city & port, ✱ of Libya; *pop* 591,062

Tris·tan da Cu·nha \ˌtris-tən-də-'kü-nə, -nyə\ island South Atlantic, chief of the Tristan da Cunha Islands (part of British colony of Saint Helena); *pop* 274

Tro·bri·and \'trō-brē-ˌänd, -ˌand\ islands SW Pacific in Solomon Sea belonging to Papua New Guinea

Trond·heim \'trän-ˌhām\ city & port *cen* Norway; *pop* 182,035

Trow·bridge \'trō-(ˌ)brij\ town S England; *pop* 39,000

Troy \'trȯi\ *or* **Il·i·um** \'i-lē-əm\ *or* **Tro·ja** \'trō-jə, -yə\ ancient city NW Asia Minor SW of the Dardanelles

Truk — see CHUUK

Tru·ro \'trür-(ˌ)ō\ city SW England; *pop* 20,000

Tshwa·ne \'chwä-nā\ municipality Republic of South Africa which includes city of Pretoria; *pop* 2,921,488

Tsinan — see JINAN

Tsingtao — see QINGDAO

Tuc·son \'tü-ˌsän\ city SE Arizona; *pop* 520,116

Tu·la \'tü-lä\ city W Russia S of Moscow; *pop* 501,000

Tul·sa \'tǝl-sə\ city NE Oklahoma; *pop* 391,906

Tu·nis \'tü-nəs, 'tyü-\ city, ✱ of Tunisia; *pop* 699,000

Tu·ni·sia \tü-'nē-zh(ē-)ə, tyü-, -'ni-\ country N Africa on the Mediterranean E of Algeria; ✱, Tunis; *pop* 10,983,000 — **Tu·ni·sian** \-zh(ē-)ən\ *adj or n*

Tu·rin \'tùr-ən, 'tyùr-\ city NW Italy on the Po; *pop* 872,367

Tur·ka·na, Lake \tər-'ka-nə\ *or* **Lake Ru·dolf** \'rü-ˌdȯlf, -ˌdälf\ lake N Kenya in Great Rift Valley

Tur·key \'tər-kē\ country W Asia & SE Europe between Mediterranean & Black seas; ✱, Ankara; *pop* 73,085,000 — **Turk** \'tərk\ *n*

Turk·men·i·stan \(ˌ)tərk-ˌme-nə-'stan, -'stän\ country *cen* Asia; ✱, Ashkhabad; *pop* 5,479,000 — **Turk·me·ni·an** \ˌtərk-'mē-nē-ən\ *adj*

Turks and Cai·cos \'tərks-ənd-'kā-kəs, -ˌkŏs\ two groups of islands West Indies at SE end of the Bahamas; a British colony; *pop* 31,458

Tu·tu·i·la \ˌtü-tü-'wē-lä\ island South Pacific, chief of American Samoa group

Tu·va·lu \tü-'vä-(ˌ)lü, -'vär-(ˌ)ü\ *formerly* **El·lice** \'e-lis\ islands W Pacific N of Fiji; country; ✳, Funafuti; *pop* 11,000 — see GILBERT AND ELLICE ISLANDS

Tyne and Wear \'tīn-ənd-'wir\ metropolitan county N England; *pop* 1,105,000

Tyre \'tī(-ə)r\ ancient city, ✳ of Phoenicia; now a town of S Lebanon — **Tyr·i·an** \'tir-ē-ən\ *adj or n*

Tyrol — see TIROL — **Ty·ro·le·an** \tə-'rō-lē-ən, tī-\ *adj or n* — **Ty·ro·lese** \ˌtir-ə-'lēz, ˌtī-rə-, -'lēs\ *adj or n*

Tyr·rhe·ni·an Sea \tə-'rē-nē-ən\ the part of the Mediterranean SW of Italy, N of Sicily, & E of Sardinia & Corsica

Ufa \ü-'fä\ city W Russia NE of Samara; *pop* 1,062,000

Ugan·da \ü-'gän-də, yü-, -'gan-\ country E Africa N of Lake Victoria; ✳, Kampala; *pop* 34,857,000 — **Ugan·dan** \-dən\ *adj or n*

Ukraine \yü-'krān, 'yü-ˌ\ country E Europe on N coast of Black Sea; ✳, Kiev; *pop* 45,500,000 — **Ukrai·ni·an** \yü-'krā-nē-ən\ *adj or n*

Ulaan·baa·tar *or* **Ulan Ba·tor** \ˌü-ˌlän-'bä-ˌtȯr\ city, ✳ of Mongolia; *pop* 1,088,000

Ul·san \'ül-'sän\ city SE South Korea; *pop* 1,082,000

Ul·ster \'əl-stər\ 1 region N Ireland (island) consisting of Northern Ireland & N Ireland (country) 2 province N Ireland (country); *pop* 295,000 3 NORTHERN IRELAND

Ulu·ru \ü-'lü-rü\ *or* **Ayers Rock** \'erz\ outcrop *cen* Australia in SW Northern Territory

Um·bria \'əm-brē-ə\ region *cen* Italy in the Apennines; *pop* 884,268

Un·ga·va \ˌən-'ga-və\ 1 bay, inlet of Hudson Strait NE Canada 2 peninsula region NE Canada in N Quebec

Union of South Africa — see SOUTH AFRICA, REPUBLIC OF

Union of Soviet Socialist Republics *or* **U.S.S.R.** *or* **Soviet Union** country 1922–91 E Europe & N Asia; former union of 15 republics comprising present-day countries of Armenia, Azerbaijan, Belarus, Estonia, Georgia, Kazakhstan, Krygyzstan, Latvia, Lithuania, Moldova, Russia, Tajikistan, Turkmenistan, Ukraine, & Uzbekistan

United Arab Emir·ates \'e-mə-rəts, -ˌrāts\ country E Arabia on Persian Gulf; composed of seven emirates; ✳, Abu Dhabi; *pop* 7,000,000

United Kingdom *or in full* **United Kingdom of Great Britain and Northern Ireland** country W Europe in British Isles consisting of England, Scotland, Wales, Northern Ireland, Channel Islands, & Isle of Man; ✳, London; *pop* 63,182,000

United Nations political organization established in 1945 with headquarters in international territory in New York City

United States of America *or* **United States** country North America bordering on Atlantic, Pacific, & Arctic oceans & including Hawaii; ✳, Washington; *pop* 308,745,538

Upper Volta — see BURKINA FASO — **Upper Vol·tan** \'väl-tᵊn, 'vȯl-, 'vȯl-\ *adj or n*

Ural \'yur-əl\ 1 mountains Russia & Kazakhstan extending about 1640 mi. (2640 km.); usually thought of as dividing line between Europe & Asia; highest about 6214 ft. (1894 m.) 2 river over 1500 mi. (2414 km.) long Russia & Kazakhstan flowing from S end of Ural Mountains into Caspian Sea

Uru·guay \'ur-ə-ˌgwī, 'yur-\ 1 river about 1000 mi. (1609 km.) long SE South America 2 country SE South America; ✳, Montevideo; *pop* 3,286,314 — **Uru·guay·an** \ˌur-ə-'gwī-ən, ˌyur-\ *adj or n*

Ürüm·qi \ü-'rüm-'chē\ *or* **Urum·chi** \ü-'rüm-chē, ˌür-əm-'\ city NW China; *pop* 2,941,000

Us·pa·lla·ta \ˌüs-pä-'yä-tä, -'zhä-\ mountain pass S South America in the Andes between Argentina & Chile

Ustinov — see IZHEVSK

Utah \'yü-ˌtȯ, -ˌtä\ state W U.S.; ✳, Salt Lake City; *pop* 2,763,885 — **Utah·an** \-ˌtȯ(-ə)n, -ˌtä(-ə)n\ *adj or n* — **Utahn** \-ˌtȯ(-ə)n, -ˌtä(-ə)n\ *n*

Uz·bek·i·stan \(ˌ)üz-ˌbe-ki-'stan, ˌəz-, -'stän\ country W *cen* Asia between Aral Sea & Afghanistan; ✳, Tashkent; *pop* 30,000,000

Va·duz \vä-'düts\ town, ✳ of Liechtenstein; *pop* 5200

Val·dez \val-'dēz\ city & port S Alaska; *pop* 4949

Va·len·cia \və-'len(t)-sh(ē-)ə, -sē-ə\ 1 region & ancient kingdom E Spain 2 city, its ✳, on the Mediterranean; *pop* 792,000

Val·le·jo \və-'lā-(ˌ)ō\ city W California; *pop* 115,942

Valley Forge locality SE Pennsylvania

Val·let·ta \və-'le-tə\ city, ✳ of Malta; *pop* 5760

Van·cou·ver \van-'kü-vər\ 1 city SW Washington on Columbia River opposite Portland, Oregon; *pop* 161,791 2 island W Canada in SW British Columbia 3 city & port SW British Columbia, Canada; *pop* 603,502

Van Diemen's Land — see TASMANIA

Van·u·atu \ˌvan-ə-'wä-ˌtü, ˌvän-\ *formerly* **New Heb·ri·des** \'he-brə-ˌdēz\ islands SW Pacific W of Fiji; country; ✳, Port-Vila; *pop* 234,000

Va·ra·na·si \və-'rä-nə-sē\ city N India; *pop* 1,432,280

Vat·i·can City \'va-ti-kən\ independent state within Rome, Italy; *pop* 800

Ven·e·zu·e·la \ˌve-nə-'zwā-lə, -zə-'wä-; ˌbä-nä-'swä-lä\ country N South America; ✳, Caracas; *pop* 27,228,000 — **Ven·e·zu·e·lan** \-lən\ *adj or n*

Ven·ice \'ve-nəs\ *or Italian* **Ve·ne·zia** \ve-'net-sē-ä\ city N Italy on islands in Lagoon of Venice; *pop* 261,362 — **Ve·ne·tian** \və-'nē-shən\ *adj or n*

Ven·tu·ra \ven-'tùr-ə, -'tyùr-\ city & port SW California; *pop* 106,433

Ve·ra·cruz \ver-ə-'krüz, -'krüs\ city E Mexico; *pop* 552,156

Ver·mont \vər-'mänt\ state NE U.S.; ✳, Montpelier; *pop* 625,741 — **Ver·mont·er** \-'mänt-ər\ *n*

Ve·ro·na \və-'rō-nä\ city N Italy W of Venice; *pop* 252,520

Ver·sailles \(ˌ)vər-'sī, ver-\ city N France, WSW suburb of Paris; *pop* 86,110

Ve·su·vi·us \və-'sü-vē-əs\ volcano about 4190 ft. (1277 m.) S Italy near Bay of Naples

Vicks·burg \'viks-ˌbərg\ city W Mississippi; *pop* 23,856

Vic·to·ria \vik-'tȯr-ē-ə\ 1 city, ✳ of British Columbia, Canada on Vancouver Island; *pop* 80,017 2 island N Canada in Arctic Archipelago 3 state SE Australia; ✳, Melbourne; *pop* 5,354,042 4 city & port, Hong Kong; *pop* 992,000 5 seaport, ✳ of Seychelles; *pop* 26,000 — **Vic·to·ri·an** \vik-'tȯr-ē-ən\ *adj or n*

Victoria, Lake lake E Africa in Tanzania, Kenya, & Uganda

Victoria Falls waterfall 355 ft. (108 m.) S Africa in the Zambezi on border between Zambia & Zimbabwe

Vi·en·na \vē-'e-nə\ *or German* **Wien** \'vēn\ city, ✳ of Austria on the Danube; *pop* 1,700,000 — **Vi·en·nese** \ˌvē-ə-'nēz, -'nēs\ *adj or n*

Vien·tiane \(ˌ)vyen-'tyän\ city, ✳ of Laos; *pop* 200,000

Vie·ques \vē-'ā-kās\ island Puerto Rico off E end of main island; *pop* 9301

Viet·nam \vē-'et-'näm, vyet-, ˌvē-ət-, vēt-, -'nam\ country SE Asia in Indochina; ✳, Hanoi; *pop* 85,847,000; divided 1954–75 into the independent states of **North Vietnam** (✳, Hanoi) & **South Vietnam** (✳, Saigon) — **Viet·nam·ese** \vē-ˌet-nə-'mēz, ˌvyet-, ˌvē-ət-, ˌvēt-, -nə-, -nä-, -'mēs\ *adj or n*

Vila — see PORT-VILA

Vi·la No·va de Ga·ia \'vē-lə-'nȯ-və-də-'gī-ə\ city NW Portugal; *pop* 302,295

Vil·ni·us \'vil-nē-əs\ city, ✳ of Lithuania; *pop* 524,000

Vin·land \'vīn-lənd\ a portion of the coast of North America visited & so called by Norse voyagers about 1000 A.D.; thought to be located along the North Atlantic in what is now E or NE Canada

Vir·gin·ia \vər-'ji-nyə, -'ji-nē-ə\ state E U.S.; ✳, Richmond; *pop* 8,001,024 — **Vir·gin·ian** \-nyən, -nē-ən\ *adj or n*

Virginia Beach city SE Virginia; *pop* 437,994

Virginia City locality W Nevada; *pop* 855

Virgin Islands island group West Indies E of Puerto Rico — see BRITISH VIRGIN ISLANDS, VIRGIN ISLANDS OF THE UNITED STATES

Virgin Islands of the United States the W islands of the Virgin Islands; U.S. territory; ✳, Charlotte Amalie (on Saint Thomas); *pop* 106,405

Vi·sa·yan \və-'sī-ən\ islands *cen* Philippines

Vish·a·kha·pat·nam \vi-ˌshä-kə-'pət-nəm\ *or* **Vis·a·kha·pat·nam** \vi-ˌsä-\ city E India; *pop* 1,728,128

Vis·tu·la \'vis-chə-lə, 'vish-chə-, 'vis-tə-\ river over 660 mi. (1062 km.) long Poland flowing N from the Carpathians

Vi·ti Le·vu \ˌvē-tē-'le-(ˌ)vü\ island SW Pacific; largest of the Fiji group

Vlad·i·vos·tok \ˌvla-də-və-ˈstäk, -ˈväs-ˌtäk\ city & port SE Russia on an inlet of Sea of Japan; *pop* 592,000
Vol·ga \ˈväl-gə, ˈvȯl-, ˈvōl-\ river about 2300 mi. (3700 km.) long W Russia; longest river in Europe
Vol·go·grad \ˈväl-gə-ˌgrad, ˈvȯl-, ˈvōl-, -ˌgrät\ city S Russia in Europe, on the Volga; *pop* 1,021,000
Vol·ta \ˈväl-tə, ˈvȯl-, ˈvȯl-\ river about 300 mi. (485 km.) long Ghana flowing from **Lake Volta** (reservoir) into Gulf of Guinea
Vo·ro·nezh \və-ˈrȯ-nish\ city S *cen* Russia in Europe; *pop* 932,500
Vosges \ˈvōzh\ mountains NE France on W side of Rhine valley
Wa·co \ˈwā-(ˌ)kō\ city *cen* Texas; *pop* 124,805
Wad·den·zee \ˌvä-d°n-ˈzä\ inlet of the North Sea N Netherlands
Wake \ˈwāk\ island North Pacific N of Marshall Islands; U.S. territory
Wake·field \ˈwāk-ˌfēld\ city N England; *pop* 99,000
Wa·la·chia *or* **Wal·la·chia** \wä-ˈlā-kē-ə\ region S Romania between Transylvanian Alps & the Danube
Wales \ˈwālz\ *or Welsh* **Cym·ru** \ˈkəm-ˌrē\ principality SW Great Britain; a division of United Kingdom; ✻, Cardiff; *pop* 3,063,456
Wal·lo·nia \wä-ˈlō-nē-ə\ semiautonomous region S Belgium; *pop* 3,600,000
Wal·sall \ˈwȯl-sȯl, -səl\ town W *cen* England; *pop* 68,000
Wal·tham Forest \ˈwȯl-thəm\ borough of NE Greater London, England; *pop* 258,000
Wal·vis Bay \ˈwȯl-vəs\ town & port W Namibia on Walvis Bay (inlet of the Atlantic); formerly administered by Republic of South Africa; *pop* 61,700
Wands·worth \ˈwän(d)z-(ˌ)wərth\ borough of SW Greater London, England; *pop* 307,000
War·ren \ˈwȯr-ən, ˈwär-\ city SE Michigan; *pop* 134,056
War·saw \ˈwȯr-ˌsȯ\ *or Polish* **War·sza·wa** \vär-ˈshä-vä\ city, ✻ of Poland; *pop* 1,700,000
War·wick \ˈwär-ik\ town *cen* England; *pop* 31,000
War·wick·shire \ˈwär-ik-ˌshir, -shər\ *or* **Warwick** county *cen* England
Wa·satch \ˈwȯ-ˌsach\ range of the Rockies SE Idaho & N *cen* Utah; highest Mount Timpanogos 12,008 ft. (3660 m.), in Utah
Wash·ing·ton \ˈwȯ-shiŋ-tən, ˈwä-\ **1** state NW U.S.; ✻, Olympia; *pop* 6,724,540 **2** city, ✻ of U.S.; having the same boundaries as District of Columbia; *pop* 601,723 — **Wash·ing·to·nian** \ˌwȯ-shiŋ-ˈtō-nē-ən, ˌwä-, -nyən\ *adj or n*
Washington, Mount mountain 6288 ft. (1916 m.) N New Hampshire; highest in White Mountains
Wa·ter·bury \ˈwȯ-tə(r)-ˌber-ē, ˈwä-\ city W *cen* Connecticut; *pop* 110,366
Wei·mar Republic \ˈvī-ˌmär, ˈwī-\ the German republic 1919–33
Wel·land \ˈwe-lənd\ canal 27 mi. (44 km.) long SE Ontario connecting Lake Erie & Lake Ontario
Wel·ling·ton \ˈwe-liŋ-tən\ city, ✻ of New Zealand; *pop* 187,500
Wes·sex \ˈwe-siks\ ancient kingdom S England
West Bank area Middle East W of Jordan River; occupied by Israel since 1967 with parts having been transferred to Palestinian administration since 1993
West Brom·wich \ˈbrä-mich\ town W *cen* England; *pop* 73,000
West Co·vi·na \kō-ˈvē-nə\ city SW California; *pop* 106,098
Western Australia state W Australia; ✻, Perth; *pop* 2,239,170 — **Western Australian** *adj or n*
Western Cape province SW Republic of South Africa; *pop* 5,822,734
Western Ghats — see GHATS
Western Hemisphere the half of the earth lying W of the Atlantic Ocean & comprising North America, South America, & surrounding waters
Western Isles former administrative area of W Scotland consisting of the Outer Hebrides
Western Sahara *formerly* **Spanish Sahara** territory NW Africa; occupied by Morocco; *pop* 522,000
Western Samoa — see SAMOA
West Germany — see GERMANY
West Indies islands lying between SE North America & N South America & consisting of the Greater Antilles, Lesser Antilles, & Bahamas — **West Indian** *adj or n*

West Midlands metropolitan county W *cen* England; includes Birmingham
West·min·ster \ˈwes(t)-ˌmin(t)-stər\ city N *cen* Colorado NW of Denver; *pop* 106,114
West Pakistan the former W division of Pakistan now having the same boundaries as Pakistan
West·pha·lia \west-ˈfāl-yə, -ˈfā-lē-ə\ region W Germany E of the Rhine — **West·pha·lian** \west-ˈfāl-yən, -ˈfā-lē-ən\ *adj or n*
West Point site SE New York of United States Military Academy on W bank of Hudson River N of New York City
West Quod·dy Head \ˈkwä-dē\ cape; most easterly point of Maine & of the Lower 48
West Sus·sex \ˈsə-siks\ county SE England; *pop* 806,892
West Valley City city N Utah S of Salt Lake City; *pop* 129,480
West Virginia state E U.S.; ✻, Charleston; *pop* 1,852,994 — **West Virginian** *adj or n*
West York·shire metropolitan county NW England; includes Wakefield
White sea NW Russia in Europe
White·horse \ˈhwīt-ˌhȯrs, ˈwīt-\ city, ✻ of Yukon, Canada; *pop* 23,276
White Mountains mountains N New Hampshire in the Appalachians — see WASHINGTON, MOUNT
Whit·ney, Mount \ˈhwit-nē, ˈwit-\ mountain 14,495 ft. (4418 m.) SE *cen* California in Sierra Nevada; highest in U.S. outside of Alaska
Wich·i·ta \ˈwi-chə-ˌtȯ\ city S Kansas; *pop* 382,368
Wichita Falls city N Texas; *pop* 104,553
Wien — see VIENNA
Wight, Isle of — see ISLE OF WIGHT
Wil·lem·stad \ˈvi-ləm-ˌstät\ city, formerly ✻ of Netherlands Antilles; *pop* 93,600
Wil·liams·burg \ˈwil-yəmz-ˌbərg\ city SE Virginia; *pop* 14,068
Wil·ming·ton \ˈwil-miŋ-tən\ city N Delaware; largest in state; *pop* 70,851
Wilt·shire \ˈwilt-ˌshir, -shər\ county S England; *pop* 470,981
Win·ches·ter \ˈwin-ˌches-tər, -chəs-tər\ city S England; *pop* 45,000
Win·der·mere \ˈwin-də(r)-ˌmir\ lake NW England in Lake District
Wind·hoek \ˈvint-ˌhùk\ city, ✻ of Namibia; *pop* 324,500
Wind·sor \ˈwin-zər\ city S Ontario, Canada on Detroit River; *pop* 210,891
Wind·ward \ˈwind-wərd\ islands West Indies in the S Lesser Antilles extending S from Martinique but not including Barbados, Tobago, or Trinidad
Win·ni·peg \ˈwi-nə-ˌpeg\ city, ✻ of Manitoba, Canada; *pop* 663,617
Winnipeg, Lake lake S *cen* Manitoba, Canada
Win·ni·pe·sau·kee, Lake \ˌwi-nə-pə-ˈsȯ-kē\ lake *cen* New Hampshire
Win·ston–Sa·lem \ˌwin(t)-stən-ˈsä-ləm\ city N *cen* North Carolina; *pop* 229,617
Wis·con·sin \wi-ˈskän(t)-sən\ state N *cen* U.S.; ✻, Madison; *pop* 5,686,986 — **Wis·con·sin·ite** \-sə-ˌnīt\ *n*
Wit·wa·ters·rand \ˈwit-ˌwȯ-tərz-ˌrand, -ˌwä-, -ˌränd, -ˌränt\ ridge of gold-bearing rock NE Republic of South Africa; *pop* 245,942
Wol·lon·gong \ˈwù-lən-ˌgäŋ, -ˌgȯŋ\ city SE Australia in E New South Wales S of Sydney; *pop* 245,942
Wol·ver·hamp·ton \ˌwùl-vər-ˈham(p)-tən\ town W *cen* England NW of Birmingham; *pop* 210,000
Worces·ter \ˈwùs-tər\ city E *cen* Massachusetts; *pop* 181,045
Wran·gell, Mount \ˈraŋ-gəl\ volcano 14,163 ft. (4317 m.) S Alaska in Wrangell Mountains
Wro·claw \ˈvrȯt-ˌswäf, -ˌsläv\ city SW Poland in Silesia; *pop* 630,500
Wu·han \ˈwü-ˈhän\ city E *cen* China; *pop* 8,663,500
Wu·xi *or* **Wu–hsi** \ˈwü-ˈshē\ city E China; *pop* 3,151,000
Wy·o·ming \wī-ˈō-miŋ\ state NW U.S.; ✻, Cheyenne; *pop* 563,626 — **Wy·o·ming·ite** \-miŋ-ˌīt\ *n*
Xi'·an *or* **Hsi–an** \ˈshē-ˈän\ city E *cen* China; *pop* 5,853,500
Xianggang — see HONG KONG
Xin·jiang Uy·gur *or* **Sin·kiang Ui·ghur** \ˈshin-ˈjyäŋ-ˈwē-gər\ region W China between the Kunlun & Altai mountains; *pop* 21,815,815
Xizang — see TIBET

Xu·zhou \'shü-'jō\ *or* **Sü·chow** \'shü-'jō, 'sü-\ city E China; *pop* 2,634,500

Yak·i·ma \'ya-kə-ˌmó\ city S *cen* Washington; *pop* 91,067

Ya·lu \'yä-(ˌ)lü\ river 500 mi. (804 km.) long SE Manchuria & North Korea

Ya·mous·sou·kro \ˌyä-mə-'sü-krō\ town, official ✻ of Cote d'Ivoire; *pop* 207,412

Yan·gon \ˌyän-'gōn\ *formerly* **Ran·goon** \ran-'gün, raŋ-\ city, former ✻ of Myanmar; *pop* 4,477,600

Yangtze — see CHANG

Yaoun·dé \yaún-'dā\ city, ✻ of Cameroon; *pop* 1,817,524

Yap \'yap, 'yäp\ island W Pacific in the W Carolines; *pop* 11,377

Ya·ren \'yä-ˌrən\ district containing ✻ of Nauru; *pop* 747

Ya·ro·slavl \ˌyär-ə-'slä-vᵊl\ city *cen* Russia in Europe, NE of Moscow; *pop* 591,486

Yaz·oo \ya-'zü, 'ya-(ˌ)zü\ river W *cen* Mississippi

Ye·ka·te·rin·burg \yi-'ka-tə-rən-ˌbərg, yi-ˌkä-ti-rēm-'bùrk\ *formerly* **Sverd·lovsk** \sverd-'lófsk\ city W Russia, in *cen* Ural Mountains; *pop* 1,350,000

Yellow 1 — see HUANG **2** sea, section of East China Sea between N China, North Korea, & South Korea

Yel·low·knife \'ye-lō-ˌnīf\ town, ✻ of Northwest Territories, Canada; *pop* 18,700

Ye·men \'ye-mən\ country S Arabia bordering on Red Sea & Gulf of Aden; ✻, Sanaa; *pop* 24,500,000 — **Ye·me·ni** \'ye-mə-nē\ *adj or n* — **Ye·men·ite** \-mə-ˌnīt\ *adj or n*

Ye·ni·sey *or* **Ye·ni·sei** \ˌyi-ni-'sā\ river over 2500 mi. (4022 km.) long *cen* Russia, flowing N into Arctic Ocean

Ye·re·van \ˌyer-ə-'vän\ city, ✻ of Armenia; *pop* 1,100,000

Yo·ko·ha·ma \ˌyō-kō-'hä-mä\ city Japan in SE Honshu on Tokyo Bay S of Tokyo; *pop* 3,688,773

Yon·kers \'yäŋ-kərz\ city SE New York N of New York City; *pop* 195,976

York \'yórk\ city N England; *pop* 153,000

York, Cape cape NE Australia in Queensland at N tip of Cape York Peninsula

York·shire \-ˌshir, -shər\ former county N England

Yo·sem·i·te Falls \yō-'se-mə-tē\ waterfall E California in Yosemite Valley; includes two falls, the upper 1430 ft. (436 m.) & the lower 320 ft. (98 m.)

Youngs·town \'yəŋz-ˌtaún\ city NE Ohio; *pop* 66,982

Yu·ca·tán \ˌyü-kə-'tan, -kä-'tän\ peninsula SE Mexico & N Central America including Belize & N Guatemala

Yu·go·sla·via \ˌyü-gō-'slä-vē-ə, ˌyü-gə-\ **1** former country S Europe including Serbia, Montenegro, Slovenia, Croatia, Bosnia and Herzegovina, & Macedonia; ✻, Belgrade **2** — see SERBIA AND MONTENEGRO — **Yu·go·slav** \ˌyü-gō-'släv, -'slav; 'yü-gō-ˌ\ *or* **Yu·go·sla·vi·an** \ˌyü-gō-'slä-vē-ən, -gə-\ *adj or n*

Yu·kon \'yü-ˌkän\ **1** river 1979 mi. (3185 km.) long NW Canada & Alaska flowing into Bering Sea **2** *or formerly* **Yukon Territory** territory NW Canada; ✻, Whitehorse; *pop* 33,897

Yu·ma \'yü-mə\ city SW corner of Arizona on the Colorado; *pop* 93,064

Za·greb \'zä-ˌgreb\ city, ✻ of Croatia; *pop* 687,000

Zaire \zä-'ir\ **1** river in Africa — see CONGO 1 **2** country in Africa — see CONGO 2 — **Zair·ean** *or* **Zair·ian** \zä-'ir-ē-ən\ *adj or n*

Zam·be·zi *or* **Zam·be·si** \zam-'bē-zē, zäm-'bä-zē\ river about 1700 mi. (2735 km.) long SE Africa flowing from NW Zambia into Mozambique Channel

Zam·bia \'zam-bē-ə\ *formerly* **Northern Rhodesia** country S Africa N of the Zambezi; ✻, Lusaka; *pop* 13,070,000 — **Zam·bi·an** \'zam-bē-ən\ *adj or n*

Zan·zi·bar \'zan-zə-ˌbär\ island Tanzania off NE Tanganyika coast; united 1964 with Tanganyika forming Tanzania

Za·po·rizh·zhya *or* **Za·po·ro·zh'ye** \ˌzä-pə-'rēzh-zhyə\ city SE Ukraine; *pop* 769,500

Zhang·jia·kou \'jäŋ-'jyä-'kō\ *or* **Kal·gan** \'kal-'gan\ city NE China NW of Beijing; *pop* 925,000

Zhdanov — see MARIUPOL

Zheng·zhou *or* **Cheng–chou** \'jəŋ-'jō\ city NE *cen* China; *pop* 3,965,500

Zim·ba·bwe \zim-'bä-bwē, -(ˌ)bwä\ *formerly* **Rhodesia** country S Africa S of Zambezi River; ✻, Harare; *pop* 13,061,000 — **Zim·ba·bwe·an** \-ən\ *adj or n*

Zui·der Zee \ˌzī-dər-'zä, -'zē\ — see IJSSELMEER

Zu·lu·land \'zü-(ˌ)lü-ˌland\ territory E Republic of South Africa on Indian Ocean

Zu·rich \'zùr-ik\ city N Switzerland; *pop* 373,000

A BRIEF HISTORY OF ENGLISH

With the abundance of words derived from Latin and from Greek by way of Latin, the casual observer might guess that English would be, like French, Spanish, and Italian, a Romance language derivative of the Latin spoken by the ancient Romans. But although the Romans made a few visits to Britain in the first century A.D., long before the English were there—before there was even an England—English is not a Romance language. In terms of its genetic stock, English is a member of the Germanic group, and thus a sister of such extinct tongues as Old Norse and Gothic and such modern ones as Swedish, Dutch, and German.

The history of English is intimately tied to the history of the British Isles over the last 1500 years or so. We may speak of English as having its beginnings with the conquest and settlement of a large part of the island of Britain by Germanic tribes from the European continent in the fifth century, although the earliest written documents of the language belong to the seventh century. Of course these Germanic peoples did not, upon their arrival in England, suddenly begin to speak a new language. They spoke the closely related Germanic tongues of their continental homelands. From these developed the English language. In fact, the words *English* and *England* are derived from the name of one of these early Germanic peoples, the Angles.

The oldest form of English, known as Anglo-Saxon or Old English and dating from the beginning of the language to about A.D. 1100, retained the basic grammatical properties of the Germanic branch of the Indo-European family. For example, some verbs formed their past tense and past participle by adding an ending with *-d* or *-t* while others did this by changing a vowel. Nouns belonged to one of three genders (masculine, feminine, or neuter) and appeared in one of two numbers (singular or plural) and different cases according to their function within the clause (nominative, accusative, genitive, dative). Adjectives not only took inflectional endings for gender, case, and number but also had different sets of endings depending on whether a word like *that* or *your* preceded them or whether they stood alone.

From its beginnings English has been gradually changing and evolving, as language tends to do, until the earliest written records have become all but incomprehensible to the speaker of Modern English without specialized training. To get a sense of how far evolution has taken us from the early tongue, we need only glance at a sample of Old English. Here is the beginning of the Lord's Prayer:

Fæder ūre, þu þe eart on heofonum: si þin nama gehālgod. Tōbecume þin rīce. Geweorþe þin willa on eorþan swāswā on heofonum.

The difference between this language and today's is more radical than just a difference in spelling, since several of the letters signify sounds different from what the same letters signify today. Much of this came about during the Great Vowel Shift in the fifteenth, sixteenth, and seventeenth centuries. That is the name given to a set of changes most readily recognizable in the changing values of long vowels. From the older values that resembled those of vowels in the modern continental languages ($\bar{a}$ \ä\, $\bar{e}$ \ā\, $\bar{\imath}$ \ē\, $\bar{o}$ \ō\, $\bar{u}$ \ü\) came our Modern English pronunciations (a \ā\, e \ē\, i \ī\, oo \ü\ or \u̇\ or \ə\, ou \au̇\). Thus, for example, the Old English ancestor of *five* would have been pronounced \'fēf\, the ancestor of *clean* would have been pronounced something like \'klän-ə\, and the ancestor of *root* would have been pronounced \'rōt\. In looking back at the Old English Lord's Prayer, we see the ninth word þin 'thine' characterized by two distinctive differences from modern *thine:* the first is the unusual letter þ, called thorn (which had a \th\ sound); the second is the long *i* which had a sound closer to the vowel sound of the modern word *mean*. The next word, *nama* 'name', was pronounced something like \'näm-ä\.

Between the vocabularies of Old English and Modern English, there is a certain continuity at the core, since something over half of the thousand most common words of the Old English poetic vocabulary have survived into Modern English more or less intact, apart from normal sound change. And of the thousand most common Modern English words, four-fifths are of Old English origin. But away from this ancestral core of words like *be, water,* and *strong,* the picture is one of radical change. Perhaps five-sixths of the Old English words of which we have a record left no descendants in Modern English. And a majority of the words used in English today are of foreign origin. Of the foreign languages affecting the Old English vocabulary, the most influential was Latin. Ecclesiastical terms especially, like *priest, vicar,* and *mass,* were borrowed from Latin, the language of the Church. But words belonging to aspects of life other than the strictly religious, like *cap, inch, kiln, school,* and *noon,* also entered Old English from Latin.

The Scandinavians, too, influenced the language of England during the Old English period. From the eighth century on, Scandinavians raided and eventually settled in England, especially in the north and the east. This prolonged, if frequently unfriendly, contact had a considerable and varied influence on the English vocabulary. In a few instances the influence of a Scandinavian cognate gave an English word a new meaning. Thus our *dream,* which meant 'joy' in Old English, probably took on the now familiar sense 'a series of thoughts, images, or emotions occurring during sleep' because its Scandinavian cognate *draumr* had that meaning. A considerable number of common words, like *cross, fellow, ball,* and *raise,* also became naturalized as a result of the Viking incursions over the years. The initial consonants *sk-* often reveal the Scandinavian ancestry of words like *sky, skin,* and *skirt,* the last of which has persisted side by side with its native English cognate *shirt.*

The Middle English period, from about 1100 to 1500, was marked by a great extension of foreign influence on English, principally as a result of the Norman Conquest of 1066, which brought England under the rule of French speakers. The English language, though it did not die, was for a long time of only secondary importance in political, social, and cultural matters. French became the language of the upper classes in England. The variety of French spoken then is now called Anglo-French. The lower classes continued to speak English, but many French words were borrowed into English. To this circumstance we owe, for example, a number of distinctions between the words used for animals in the pasture and the words for those animals prepared to be eaten. Living animals were under the care of English-speaking peasants; cooked, the animals were served to the French-speaking nobility. *Swine* in the sty became *pork* on the table, *cow* and *calf* became *beef* and *veal.* Anglo-French also had an influence on the words used in the courts, such as *indict, jury,* and *verdict.* English eventually reestablished itself as the major language of England, but the language did not lose its habit of borrowing, and many foreign words became naturalized in Middle English, especially loanwords taken from Old French and Middle French (such as *date, escape, infant,* and *money*) or directly from Latin (such as *alibi, library,* and *pacify*).

Modern English, from about 1500 to the present, has been a period of even wider borrowing. English still derives much of its learned vocabulary from Latin and Greek. And we have also borrowed words from nearly all of the languages in Europe, though only a few examples can be given here. From Modern French we have words like *bikini, cliché,* and *discotheque,* from Dutch, *easel, gin,* and *yacht,* from German, *delicatessen, pretzel,* and *swindler,* and from Swedish, *ombudsman* and *smorgasbord.* From Italian we have taken *carnival, fiasco,* and *pizza,* as well as many terms from music (including *piano*). Portuguese has given us *cobra* and *molasses,* and the Spanish of Spain has yielded *sherry* and *mosquito,* while the Spanish of the New World has given us *ranch* and *machismo.* From Russian, Czech, and Yiddish we have taken *czar, robot* and *kibitz.*

And in the modern period the linguistic acquisitiveness of English has found opportunities even farther afield. From the period of the Renaissance voyages of discovery through the days when the sun never set upon the British Empire and up to the present, a steady stream of new words has flowed into the language to match the new objects and experiences English speakers have encountered all over the globe. English has drawn words from India (*bandanna*), China (*gung ho*), and Japan (*tycoon*), as well as a number of smaller areas in the Pacific (*amok* and *orangutan* from the Malay language and *ukulele* from Hawaiian). Arabic has been a prolific source of words over the centuries, giving us *hazard, lute, magazine,* and a host of words beginning with the letter *a,* from *algebra* to *azimuth.*

English has also added words to the vocabulary in a variety of ways apart from borrowing. Many new words are compounds of existing words (like *melting pot*) or coinages without reference to any word element in English or other languages (like *quark*). Many words derive from literary characters (like *ignoramus* and *quixotic*), figures from mythology (like *hypnosis* and *panic*), the names of places (like *donnybrook* and *tuxedo*), or the names of people (like *boycott* and *silhouette*). The Roman emperor Julius Caesar has lent his name to a number of English words, including *cesarean, czar, July,* and *kaiser.*

Whether borrowed or created, a word generally begins its life in English with one meaning. Yet no living language is static, and in time words develop new meanings and lose old ones. There are several directions in which semantic development frequently moves. Two common tendencies of language are generalization and specialization. A word used in a specific sense may be extended, or generalized, to cover a host of similar senses. Our *virtue* is derived from the Latin *virtus,* which originally meant 'manliness'. But we apply the term to any excellent quality possessed by man, woman, or beast; even inanimate objects have their virtues. In Latin, *decimare* meant 'to select and kill a tenth part of' and described the Roman way of dealing with mutinous troops. Its English descendant, *decimate,* now simply means 'to destroy a large part of'.

Perhaps more frequent in its operation than generalization is the phenomenon of specialization, or narrowing, in which a word of general application becomes limited to a small part of its former wide range. *Tailleur,* the Old French ancestor of our *tailor,* first meant simply 'one who cuts', whether the cutting was of stone, wood, or cloth. Gradually the meaning was restricted to cloth, and the word came into English with that sense. *Deer* once meant 'animal'. Now only the members of a single family of mammals are called *deer.*

In addition to what could be thought of as a horizontal dimension of change—the extension or contraction of meaning—words also may rise and fall along a vertical scale of value. Perfectly unobjectionable words are sometimes used disparagingly or sarcastically. If we say, "You're a fine one to talk," we are using *fine* in a sense quite different from its usual meaning. If a word is used often enough in negative contexts, the negative coloring may eventually become an integral part of the meaning of the word. A *villain* was once a peasant. His social standing was not high, perhaps, but he was certainly not necessarily a scoundrel. *Scavenger* originally designated the collector of a particular kind of tax in late medieval England. *Puny* first meant no more than 'younger' when it passed from French into English and its spelling was transformed. Only later did it acquire the derogatory meaning more familiar to us now.

Euphemism too, though very well-intentioned, has caused many a word to take on a pejorative meaning. People are often reluctant, from a sense of decency or prudery or even simple kindness, to use a word whose denotation is unpleasant. Eventually, however, the good new word may become as unloved as the bad old one, and a new euphemism must be found. *Cretin* originally meant 'Christian' and was used charitably for a kind of mentally deficient person. The Modern English word retains no trace of its etymological meaning.

The opposite process seems to take place somewhat less frequently, but amelioration of meaning does occasionally occur. In the fourteenth century *nice,* for example, meant 'foolish'. Its present meaning, of course, is quite different, and the attitude it conveys seems to have undergone a complete reversal from contempt to approval. *Pioneer* now has overwhelmingly favorable connotations. A pioneer leads ordinary people along the way to new territory or new realms of knowledge. When the word first appeared in English, however, a pioneer was only a common foot soldier who performed such menial tasks as digging trenches. Another word that has followed the course of amelioration is *urbane*. In its earliest recorded occurrences in English, its meaning was the same as that of its etymological twin *urban*. Yet within a hundred years *urbane* had taken on the honorific sense of 'smoothly courteous or polite' in which we know it today.

There is no question that the spread of English around the world was the result of colonization of areas by the British. And while English trails behind Chinese in the number of native speakers, English is nevertheless widely used as a way for people of diverse cultures and languages to communcate with one another.

The spread of the language has been helped by printing, for in its earliest days, there was an enormous variety in the way people used English words. The first English "dictionaries" were actually bilingual glossaries, the earliest a French-English glossary printed by William Caxton in England in 1480. The first significant dictionary to explain English words in English was that of Robert Cawdrey, published in 1604. It was Samuel Johnson, in 1755, who put out the first truly classic dictionary, with more than 40,000 words and more than 100,000 quotations from established authors as examples of use. This dictionary, and its updates, served as a standard for generations. In the United States, Noah Webster, schoolmaster and spelling reformer, undertook to produce a dictionary that would cover the range of English of his day, including Americanisms. In 1828, after working on it nearly 20 years, Webster published his *An American Dictionary of the English Language*. It was an immediate success, selling out the first printing in less than a year.

The language continues to grow with the addition of new words and new senses, at a rate of hundreds every year. In just the past 50 years we have seen an explosion of new words from new experiences, from the "Space Race" of the 1960s, to the Information Age and beyond. And as the language grows, so it is necessary for dictionaries to keep up. And how do words make it into the dictionary? Editors keep a watch on what words are used, gathering examples from a wide variety of print and online sources. A word, along with the source information and enough context to show how it is used—this information is called a "citation"—is stored in a database, and when enough examples have been collected from a variety of sources and over a period of time, an individual word may be considered for dictionary entry. There is no one formula for determining when a word may be entered; the size and type of dictionary often affects the decision, as does whether the dictionary in question is being updated or completely re-edited.

Whatever the history of their meanings, words are finally as individual—even sometimes eccentric—in their development as the people using them.

ENGLISH WORD ROOTS

The capitalized word elements here are the ancient roots of the derived modern English words that appear in italics in the discussion and following in boldface.

AB/ABS comes to us from Latin, and means "from," "away," or "off." *Abuse* is the use of something in the wrong way. To *abduct* is to "lead away from" or kidnap. *Aberrant* behavior is behavior that "wanders away from" what is usually acceptable. But there are so many words that include these roots, it would be *absurd* to try to list them all here. **abscond, abstemious, abstraction, abstruse**

AM/IM comes from the Latin word *amor*, "love." *Amiable* means "friendly or good-natured," and *amigo* is Spanish for "friend." **amicable, enamored, inimical, paramour**

AMBI/AMPHI means "on both sides" or "around"; *ambi-* comes from Latin and *amphi-* from Greek. An *ambidextrous* person can use the right and the left hand equally well. An *amphibian*, such as a frog or salamander, is able to live both on land and in the water. **ambient, ambiguous, ambivalent, amphitheater**

ANIM comes from Latin *anima*, meaning "breath" or "soul," and it generally describes something that is alive or lively. An *animal* is a living, breathing thing. *Animism* is the belief that all things have a spirit and an awareness. **animated, animosity, inanimate, magnanimous**

ANN/ENN comes from Latin *annus* and means "year." An *annual* event occurs yearly. A wedding or birthday *anniversary* is an example, although the older you get the more frequent they seem to be. **annuity, millennium, perennial, superannuated**

ANT/ANTI is opposite to or opposes something else. An *antiseptic* or an *antibiotic* fights germs; an *anticlimax* is the opposite of a climax; an *antidote* is given against a poison; and an *antacid* fights acid in the stomach. Be careful not to confuse *anti-* with *ante-*, meaning "before": *antebellum* means "before a war," not "opposed to war." **antagonist, antigen, antipathy, antithesis**

ANTE is Latin for "before" or "in front of." *Antediluvian*, a word describing something very old or outdated, literally means "before the flood"— that is, the flood described in the Bible. *Antebellum* literally means "before the war," usually the American Civil War. **antechamber, antedate, ante meridiem, anterior**

ANTHROP comes from the Greek word for "human being." An *anthropomorphic* god, such as Zeus or Athena, basically looks and acts like a human. **anthropoid, anthropology, misanthropic, philanthropy**

ART comes from the Latin word for "skill." Until a few centuries ago, almost no one made a strong distinction between skilled craftsmanship and what we would call "art." *Art* could also mean simply "cleverness." The result is that this root appears in some words where we might not expect it. **artful, artifact, artifice, artisan**

AUD, from the Latin verb *audire*, is the root that has to do with hearing. What is *audible* is "hearable", and an *audience* is a group of people that listen, sometimes in an *auditorium*. **audition, auditor, auditory, inaudible**

BELL comes from a Latin word meaning "war." Bellona was the little-known Roman goddess of war; her husband, Mars, was the god of war. **antebellum, bellicose, belligerence, rebellion**

BI means "two" or "double." A *bicycle* has two wheels; *binoculars* consist of two little telescopes; *bigamy* is marriage to two people at once. A road through the middle of a neighborhood *bisects* it into two pieces. **biennial, binary, bipartisan, bipolar**

BIO comes from the Greek word for "life." It forms the base for many English words: a *biosphere* is a body of life forms in an environment; *biology* is the study of all living forms and life processes; and *biotechnology* uses the knowledge acquired through biology. **biodegradable, bionic, biopsy, symbiosis**

CAD/CID/CAS all come from the same Latin verb, *cadere*, meaning "to fall, fall down, drop," or from the related noun *casus*, "fall or chance." An *accident* happens to you out of the blue. By *coincidence*, things fall together in a pattern. *Casual* dress is what you put on almost by chance. **cadaver, casualty, decadent, recidivism**

CANT, from the Latin verbs *canere* and *cantare*, meaning "sing," produces several words that come directly from Latin, and others that come by way of French and add an *h* to the root: for example, *chant* and *chantey*. **cantata, cantor, descant, incantation**

CAP/CEP comes from *capere*, the Latin verb meaning "take, seize." *Capture*, which is what a *captor* does to a *captive*, has the same meaning. *Captivate* once meant literally "capture," but now means only to capture mentally through charm or appeal. In some other English words this root produces, its meaning is harder to find. **incipient, perceptible, reception, susceptible**

CAPIT, from the Latin word for "head," *caput*, turns up in some pretty important places. The *captain* of a ship is the head of the whole operation; the *capital* of a state or country is the seat of government, where the head of state is located. A *capital* letter stands head and shoulders above a lowercase letter, as well as at the head of a sentence. **capitalism, capitulate, decapitate, recapitulate**

CARN comes from *caro*, the Latin word for "flesh," and words including this root usually refer to flesh in some form. The word *carnivore*, for example, means "an eater of meat." **carnage, carnal, carnival, incarnation**

CATA comes from Greek *kata*, one of whose meanings was "down." A *catalogue* is a list of items put down on paper. A *catapult* is an ancient military weapon for hurling missiles down on one's enemies. **cataclysm, catalyst, cataract, catatonic**

CED/CESS, from the Latin verb *cedere*, meaning "to go" or "to proceed," produces many English words, from *procession*, meaning something that goes forward, to *recession*, which is a moving back or away. **accede, antecedent, concession, precedent**

CENT means "one hundred," from Latin *centum*. The dollar is made up of a hundred *cents;* other monetary systems use *centavos* or *centimes* as the smallest coin. A *centipede* has what appears to be a hundred pairs of legs, though the actual number varies greatly. But there really are a hundred years in a *century*. **centenary, centigrade, centimeter, centurion**

CENTR/CENTER comes from Greek *kentron* and Latin *centrum*, meaning "sharp point" or "exact middle of a circle." A *centrifuge* is a spinning machine that throws things outward from the *center*; the apparent force that pushes them outward is called *centrifugal* force. **concentrate, eccentric, egocentric, epicenter**

CHRON comes from the Greek word for "time." A *chronicle* records the events of a particular time. A *chronometer* is a device for measuring time, usually one that's more accurate (and more expensive) than an ordinary watch or clock. **anachronism, chronic, chronology, synchronous**

CIRCU/CIRCUM means "around" in Latin. So *circumnavigate* is "to navigate around," often describing a trip around the world, and *circumambulate* means "to walk around." A *circuit* can be a tour around an area or territory, or the complete path of an electric current. **circuitous, circumference, circumspect, circumvent**

CIS comes from the Latin verb meaning "to cut, cut down, or slay." An *incisor* is one of the big front biting teeth; beavers and woodchucks have especially large ones. A *decision* "cuts off" previous discussion and uncertainty. **concise, excise, incisive, precision**

CLAM/CLAIM comes from the Latin verb *cla-*

mare, meaning "to shout or cry out." An *exclamation* is a cry of shock, joy, or surprise. A *proclamation* is read loudly enough so that all can hear its important message. **acclamation, clamor, declaim, reclamation**

CLUD/CLUS, from Latin *claudere*, "to close," appears in *include*, which originally meant "to shut up or enclose" and now means "to contain." *Exclude*, its opposite, means "to expel or keep out"—that is, to close the door to something. **occlusion, preclude, recluse, seclusion**

COD/CODI comes from Latin *codex*, meaning "trunk of a tree" or "document written on wooden tablets." A *code* can be either a set of laws or a system of symbols used to write messages. To *encode* a message is to write it in code. A genetic code, transmitted by genes, is a set of instructions for everything from blood type to eye color. **codex, codicil, codify, decode**

COGN comes from the Latin verb *cognoscere*, "to get to know." We may *recognize* ("know again") the root in some words, but in *quaint* and *acquaint* French has altered it beyond *recognition*. **cognitive, cognizance, cognoscente, incognito**

CONTRA is the Latin equivalent of *anti-* and it too means essentially "against" or "contrary to" or "in contrast to." *Contrary* itself comes directly from this prefix and means simply "opposite" or "opposed." A *contrast* "stands against" something else to which it is compared. *Contrapuntal* music sets one melody against another and produces harmony, which no one is opposed to. **contraband, contradict, contraindication, contravene**

CORD, from the Latin word for "heart," turns up in many common English words. For example, the word *concord* (which includes the prefix *con-*, "with") means literally that one heart is *with* another heart, and thus that they are in agreement. So *discord* (with its prefix *dis-*, "apart") means "disagreement" or "conflict." **accord, concordance, cordial, discordant**

CORP comes from *corpus*, the Latin word for "body." A *corporation* is one kind of body, a *corpse* is another, and a *corps*, such as the Marine Corps, is yet another. **corporal, corporeal, corpulent, incorporate**

COSM, from the Greek word meaning both "ornament" and "order," gives us two different groups of words. *Cosmetics* are the stuff we use to ornament our faces. The "order" meaning combines with the Greek belief that the universe was an orderly place, so words in this group relate to the universe and the worlds within it. *Cosmonaut*, for instance, is the word for a space traveler from the former Soviet Union. **cosmogony, cosmology, cosmopolitan, cosmos**

CRAC/CRAT comes from a Greek word meaning "power." Attached to another root, it indicates which group holds the power. With *demos,* the Greek word for "people," it forms *democracy,* a form of government in which the people rule. In a *meritocracy,* people earn power by their own merit. A *theocracy,* from Greek *theos,* "god," is government based on divine guidance. **aristocrat, autocratic, bureaucrat, plutocracy**

CRE/CRET comes from the Latin verb *crescere,* which means both "to come into being" and "to grow." A *crescendo* in music occurs when the music is growing louder, a *decrescendo* when it is growing softer. **accretion, crescent, excrescence, increment**

CRED comes from *credere,* the Latin verb meaning "to believe." If something is *credible* it is believable, and if it is *incredible* it is almost unbelievable. We have a good *credit* rating when institutions believe in our ability to repay a loan, and we carry *credentials* so that others will believe we are who we say we are. **credence, creditable, credulity, creed**

CRIT comes from a Greek verb that means "to judge" or "to decide." A film *critic* judges a movie and tells us what is good or bad about it. Her *critical* opinion may convince us not to go, or we may overlook any negative *criticism* and see it anyway. **criterion, critique, diacritic, hypercritical**

CRYPT comes from a Greek verb meaning "to hide." *Cryptography* is the practice of putting a message into code—that is, hiding its meaning in a secret language. A medical term beginning with *crypto-* means there is something hidden about the condition. **apocryphal, crypt, cryptic, cryptogram**

CUMB/CUB can be traced to the Latin verbs *cubare,* "to lie," and *-cumbere,* "to lie down." A *cubicle* was originally a small room for sleeping that was separated from a larger room, though now it can be any small area set off by partitions, as in an office. An *incubus* is an evil spirit that was once believed to seek out women in order to "lie on" them in their sleep. **incubate, incumbent, recumbent, succumb**

CUR, from the Latin verb *curare,* means basically "care for." Our verb *cure* comes from this root, as do *manicure* ("care of the hands") and *pedicure* ("care of the feet"). **curative, curator, procure, sinecure**

CURR/CURS comes from *currere,* the Latin verb meaning "to run." Although the sense of speed may be lacking from words based on this root, the sense of movement remains. *Current,* for instance, refers to running water in a stream or river. And an *excursion* is a trip from one place to another. **concurrent, cursory, discursive, precursor**

DE/DIV comes from two related Roman words, *deus,* "god," and *divus,* "divine." *Deism,* a philosophy that teaches natural religion, emphasizes morality, and denies that the creator god interferes with the laws of the universe, was the basic faith of many of America's Founding Fathers. **deity, divination, divine, divinity**

DEC comes from both Greek and Latin and means "ten." A *decade* lasts for ten years, and the *decimal* system is based on 10. **decalogue, decibel, decimate**

DEMI/HEMI/SEMI all mean "half." *Hemi-* comes from Greek, *semi-* from Latin, and *demi-* from French. A *hemisphere* is half a sphere. A *demitasse* (the word comes directly from French) is a dainty after-dinner coffee cup, half the size of a regular cup. And a *semicircle* is half a circle. **demigod, demimonde, semiconductor, semisweet**

DEMO comes from the Greek word meaning "people." A *demagogue* leads the people, usually into trouble, by lying and appealing to their prejudices. **demographic, demotic, endemic, pandemic**

DI/DU, the Greek and Latin prefixes meaning "two," show up in both technical and nontechnical terms. A *duel* is a battle between two people. A *duet* is music for a *duo,* or a pair of musicians. If you have *dual* citizenship, you belong to two countries at once. Most birds are *dimorphic,* with feathers of one color for males and another color for females. **dichotomy, diploma, duplex, duplicity**

DIC, from *dicere,* the Latin word meaning "to speak," says a lot. A *contradiction* (with the prefix *contra-,* "against") speaks against or denies something. A *dictionary* is a treasury of words. And *diction* is another word for speech. **edict, interdiction, jurisdiction, malediction**

DIS comes from Latin, where it means "apart." In English, its meanings have increased to include "do the opposite of" (as in *disestablish*), "deprive of" (as in *disfranchise*), "exclude or expel from" (*disbar*), "the opposite or absence of" (*disaffection*), and "not" (*disagreeable*). The original meaning can still be seen in a word like *dissipate,* which means "to break up and scatter." **diffraction, disseminate, dissension, dissipate**

DOC/DOCT comes from the Latin *docere,* which means "to teach." A *doctor* is a highly educated person capable of instructing others in the *doctrines,* or basic principles, of his or her field—which is not necessarily medicine. **docile, doctrinaire, doctrine, indoctrinate**

DOM comes from Latin *domus,* "house," or *dominus,* "master," or the verb *domare,* "to tame or subdue." A *domain* is the area where a person has authority or is *dominant.* Unfortunately, dominant people can also be *domineering,* seeing themselves as the masters of those they live and work with. **domicile, domination, dominion, predominant**

DUC, from the Latin verb *ducere,* "to lead," shows up constantly in English. *Duke* means basically "leader." The Italian dictator Mussolini was known simply as "Il Duce." But such words as *produce* and *reduce* also contain the root, even though their meanings show it less clearly. **conducive, deduction, induce, seduction**

DYNA/DYNAM comes from a Greek verb that means "to be able" or "to have power." *Dynamite* has enough power to blow up the hardest granite bedrock. An instrument that measures force is called a *dynamometer.* **dynamic, dynamo, dynasty, hydrodynamic**

EP/EPI comes from Greek and means variously "upon," "besides," "attached to," "over," "outer," or "after." An *epicenter* is the portion of the earth's surface directly over the focus of an earthquake. The *epidermis* is the outer layer of the skin, overlying the inner layer or "dermis." **ephemeral, epitaph, epithet, epoch**

ERR, from the Latin verb *errare,* means "to wander" or "to stray." This root is easily seen in the word *error,* which means a wandering or straying from what is correct or true. We also use the word *erratum* to mean "a mistake" in a book or other printed material; its plural is *errata,* and the *errata* page is the book page that lists mistakes found too late to correct before publication. **aberrant, errant, erratic, erroneous**

EU comes from the Greek word for "well"; in English words it can also mean "good" or "true." A person delivering a *eulogy* is full of good words, or praise, for the honoree. *Euthanasia* is regarded as a way of providing a hopelessly sick or injured person a "good" or easy death. **eugenic, euphemism, euphoria, evangelism**

EV comes from Latin *aevum,* "age" or "lifetime." This root occurs in only a few English words, but it is related to Greek *aion,* "age," from which we get the English word *eon,* meaning a very long period of time. **coeval, longevity, medieval, primeval**

EXTRA places words outside or beyond their usual or routine territory. *Extraterrestrial* affairs take place beyond the earth. Something *extravagant,* such as an *extravaganza,* goes beyond the limits of reason or necessity. And of course *extra* itself is a word, a shortening of *extraordinary,* "beyond the ordinary." **extracurricular, extramarital, extraneous, extrapolate**

FAC/FEC/FIC comes from the Latin verb *facere,* meaning "to make or do." Thus, a *benefactor* is someone who does good. To *manufacture* is to make, usually in a *factory.* **confection, facile, olfactory, proficient**

FER, from the Latin verb *ferre,* means "to carry." If you *refer* to an incident in your past, you "carry back" to that time. And *transfer* means "to carry across." **confer, deferential, fertile, proliferate**

FID comes from *fides,* the Latin word for "faith." *Fidelity* is another word for "faithfulness." *Confidence* is having faith in someone or something.

And an *infidel* is someone who lacks a particular kind of religious faith. **affidavit, diffident, fiduciary, perfidy**

FIG comes from the Latin verb *fingere,* which means "to shape or mold," and the related noun *figura,* meaning "a form or shape." A *transfiguration* changes the shape or appearance or nature of something. A *disfiguring* injury changes the shape of part of the body. **configuration, effigy, figment, figurative**

FIN comes from the Latin word for "end" or "boundary." *Final* describes last things, and a *finale* or a *finish* is an ending. But its meaning is harder to trace in some of the other English words derived from it. **affinity, definitive, finite, infinitesimal**

FLECT/FLEX comes from *flectere,* the Latin verb meaning "to bend." Things that are *flexible* can be bent. When light is *reflected,* it is bent and bounces back to us. **circumflex, deflect, genuflect, inflection**

FLU comes from the Latin verb *fluere,* "to flow." A *flume* is a narrow gorge with a stream flowing through it. A *fluent* speaker is one from whom words *flow* easily. Originally, *influence* referred to an invisible *fluid* that was believed to flow from the stars and to affect the actions of humans. **affluence, effluent, fluctuation, mellifluous**

FORM is a Latin root meaning "shape" or "form." Marching in *formation* is marching in ordered patterns. A *formula* is a standard form for expressing information, such as a recipe or a rule written in mathematical symbols. **conform, formality, format, formative**

FRAG/FRACT comes from the Latin verb *frangere,* "to break or shatter." A *fraction* is one of the pieces into which a whole can be broken; recipes typically call for *fractional* parts of a stick of butter or a cup of flour. The dinnerware on which food is served is often *fragile* or easily broken. **fractious, fragmentary, infraction, refraction**

FUG comes from the Latin verb *fugere,* meaning "to flee or escape." A *refugee* flees from some threat or danger to a *refuge,* which is a place that provides shelter and safety. **centrifugal, fugitive, fugue, subterfuge**

FUND/FUS, from the Latin verb *fundere,* "to pour out" or "to melt," pours forth English words. A *fuse* depends on melting metal to break an overloaded circuit. A *refund* pours money back into your pocket. *Confusion* results when so many things are poured together that they can't be sorted out. **diffuse, effusive, profusion, suffuse**

FUNG/FUNCT comes from the Latin verb *fungi,* "to perform, carry out, or undergo." A car that is *functional* is able to perform its *function* of providing transportation. A functional illiterate is a person who lacks the skills necessary to carry out the ordinary tasks of reading and writing required by day-to-day life. **defunct, functionary, malfunction, perfunctory**

GEN *generates* many English words. Their basic meaning is "come into being" or "be born." The root occurs in *gene*, the most fundamental of biological architects, and in *genealogy*, the study of family roots. **carcinogenic, congenial, generic, indigenous**

GRAD comes from Latin *gradus*, "step" or "degree." A *grade* is a step up or down on a scale of some kind. A *gradual* change takes place in small steps. The *gradient* of a steep slope might be 45 *degrees*. **degrade, gradation, graduate, retrograde**

GRAT comes from *gratus*, the Latin word meaning "pleasing, welcome, or agreeable," or from *gratia*, meaning "grace, agreeableness, or pleasantness." A meal that is served *graciously* will be received with *gratitude* by *grateful* diners, unless they want to risk being called *ingrates*. **congratulate, gratuitous, gratuity, ingratiate**

GRAV comes from the Latin word meaning "heavy, weighty, serious." Thus, a *grave* matter is serious and important. **aggravate, gravid, gravitate, gravity**

GREG comes from Latin *grex*, "herd" or "flock." Bees, wolves, people—any creatures that like to live together in flocks or herds—are *gregarious* animals. People who greatly enjoy companionship, who are happiest when part of a rowdy herd, are highly gregarious. **aggregate, congregation, egregious, segregate**

HABIT/HIBIT comes from Latin *habere*, "to have" or "to hold." A *habit*, bad or good, has a hold on you. To *prohibit* is to "hold back" or prevent. **exhibitionist, habitual, inhibit, prohibition**

HER/HES, from the Latin verb *haerere*, means "to stick." This has produced words with two kinds of meaning. A word such as *adhesive* means basically "sticking," whereas a word such as *hesitate* means more or less "stuck in one place." **adherent, cohesion, incoherent, inherent**

HOM/HOMO comes from *homos*, the Greek word for "same." In an English word it can mean "one and the same" or "similar" or "alike." A *homograph* is one of two or more words spelled alike but different in meaning or derivation or pronunciation. A *homosexual* is a person who exhibits sexual desire toward others of the same sex. **homogeneous, homologous, homonym, homophone**

HOSP/HOST comes from a Latin word meaning "host." *Hospitality* is what a good *host* or *hostess* offers to a guest. A *hospital* was once a house for religious pilgrims and other travelers or a home for the aged. **hospice, hostage, hostel, inhospitable**

HYDR flows from the Greek word for "water." In the Northwest, rushing rivers provide an abundance of *hydrodynamic* power to convert to electricity. "Water" can also be found in the lovely

flower called *hydrangea*: its seed capsules resemble ancient Greek water vessels. **dehydrate, hydraulic, hydroelectric, hydroponics**

HYPER is a Greek prefix that means "above or beyond it all." To be *hypercritical* or *hypersensitive* is to be critical or sensitive above and beyond what is normal. **hyperactive, hyperbole, hypertension, hyperventilate**

HYPO/HYP as a prefix can mean variously "under," "beneath," "down," or "below normal." Many *hypo-* words are medical. A *hypodermic* needle injects medication under the skin. *Hypoglycemia*, low blood sugar, is an unhealthy condition. **hypochondriac, hypocrisy, hypothetical, hypothyroidism**

JAC/JEC comes from *jacere*, the Latin verb meaning "throw" or "hurl." To *reject* something is to throw (or push) it back. To *eject* something is to throw (or drive) it out. To *object* is to throw something in the way of something else. **adjacent, conjecture, dejected, trajectory**

JUR comes from the Latin verb *jurare*, "to swear or take an oath," and the noun *jur-*, "right or law." A *jury*, made up of *jurors*, makes judgments based on the law. A personal *injury* caused by another person is "not right." **abjure, jurisprudence, objurgate, perjury**

LAT comes from a Latin verb that means "to carry or bear." From this root come *relation* and *relative*, a person you are *related* to, whether you like it or not. You might be *elated*, or "carried away by joy," to get free tickets to a rock concert, but your elderly relative might not share your *elation*. **collate, correlate, prelate, relativity**

LEV comes from the Latin adjective *levis*, meaning "light," and the verb *levare*, meaning "to raise or lighten." *Levitation* is the magician's trick in which a body seems to rise into the air by itself. And a *lever* is a bar used to lift something by means of *leverage*. **alleviate, elevate, leavening, levity**

LOCU/LOQU comes from the Latin verb *loqui*, "to talk." An *eloquent* preacher speaks fluently, forcefully, and expressively. A dummy's words come out of a *ventriloquist's* mouth. **circumlocution, colloquial, elocution, loquacious**

LOG, from the Greek word *logos*, meaning "word, speech, reason," is found particularly in English words that end in *-logy* and *-logue*. The ending *-logy* often means "the study of": *biology* is the study of life, and *anthropology* is the study of humans. The ending *-logue* usually indicates a type of discussion: *dialogue* is conversation between two people or groups, and an *epilogue* is an author's last words on a subject. **eulogy, genealogy, monologue, neologism**

LUC comes from the Latin noun *lux*, "light," and the verb *lucere*, "to shine or glitter." *Lucid* prose is clear in meaning, as if light were shining through it. *Lucifer*, a name for the devil, means

"Light-bearer," the name he had before he fell from heaven. **elucidate, lucent, lucubration, translucent**

LUD/LUS comes from Latin *ludere,* "to play," and *ludum,* "play" or "game." An *interlude* thus is something "between games" (*inter-* meaning "between"). A *delusion* or an *illusion* plays tricks on a person. **allude, collusion, ludicrous, prelude**

MAL as a combining form means "bad." *Malpractice* is bad medical practice. A *malady* is a bad condition—a disease or illness—of the body or mind. *Malodorous* things smell bad. And a *malefactor* is someone guilty of bad deeds. **malevolent, malicious, malign, malnourished**

MAND/MEND comes from *mandare,* Latin for "entrust" or "order." A *command* and a *commandment* are both orders. A *commando* unit carries out orders for special military actions. A *recommendation* may entrust, praise, or advise. **commendation, mandate, mandatory, remand**

MAR, from the Latin word *mare,* meaning "sea," brings its salty tang to English in words like *marine,* "having to do with the sea," and *submarine,* "under the sea." **aquamarine, marina, mariner, maritime**

MATR/METR comes from the Greek and Latin words for "mother." A *matron* is a mature woman with children; *matrimony* is marriage itself, traditionally a first step toward motherhood; and a *matrix* is something in which something else is embedded or takes form, the way a baby takes form inside the mother. **maternity, matriarch, matriculate, metropolitan**

MENS comes from the Latin noun *mensura,* "measure," and the verb *metiri,* "to measure." **commensurate, dimension, immensity, mensurable**

METR comes to us from Greek by way of Latin; in both languages it refers to "measure." A *thermometer* measures heat; a *perimeter* is the measure around something; and things that are *isometric* are equal in measure. **metric, odometer, symmetrical, tachometer**

MIT/MIS, from the Latin verb *mittere,* "to send," appears in such English words as *missionary, missile,* and *emit.* A missionary is sent out to convert others to a new faith; a missile is sent to explode on some far spot; and to emit is to send something out. **emissary, manumission, missive, remittance**

MONI comes from the Latin verb *monere,* "to warn" or "to remind." Warning and reminding often are rather similar, since some reminders warn against the consequences of forgetting. **admonish, monitor, monitory, premonition**

MONO is Greek for "one" or "only." So a *monorail* is a railroad that has only one rail, a *monotonous* voice seems to have only one tone, and a *monopoly* puts all ownership in the hands of a single

company, eliminating any competition. **monogamous, monograph, monolithic, monotheism**

MOR/MORT comes from the Latin noun *mors* (stem *mort-*), meaning "death," and verb *mori,* meaning "to die." A *mortuary* is a place where dead bodies are kept until burial. A *postmortem* examination is one conducted on a recently dead body. And a *memento mori* (a Latin phrase meaning literally "Remember that you must die") is a reminder of death; the death's head carved onto an old gravestone is an example. **immortality, moribund, mortician, mortify**

MORPH comes from the Greek word for "shape." *Morph* is itself an English word with a brand-new meaning; by morphing, filmmakers can now alter photographic images or shapes digitally, making them move or transform themselves in astonishing ways. **amorphous, anthropomorphic, metamorphosis, morphology**

MUT comes from the Latin *mutare,* "to change." Plenty of science-fiction movies have been made on the subject of weird *mutations,* changes in normal people or animals that end up causing no end of death and destruction. More often than not, it is some mysterious or alien force that causes the unfortunate victim to *mutate.* **commutation, immutable, permutation, transmute**

NASC/NAT/NAI comes from the Latin verb *nasci,* meaning "to be born." Words that have come directly from Latin carry the root *nasc-* or *nat-,* but those that took a detour through French bear a telltale *nai-* —words like *renaissance,* "rebirth," or *naive,* "unsophisticated." **cognate, innate, nascent, native**

NEC/NIC/NOX, from the Latin nouns *nex* (stem *nec-*) and *noxa,* have to do with violent death. These roots are related to Greek *nekros,* "corpse," found in such words as *necrology,* "a list of the recently dead," and *necromancy,* "the art of conjuring up spirits of the dead." **internecine, necrosis, noxious, pernicious**

NEG and its variants *nec-* and *ne-* are the prefixes of denial or refusal in Latin. The Latin verb *negare,* "to say no," is the source of our English verb *negate.* A *negative* is something that denies, contradicts, refuses, or reverses. **abnegation, negligible, renegade, renege**

NOM comes from the Latin word for "name." A *nominee* is "named"—or *nominated*—to run for or serve in office. A *binomial* ("two names") is the scientific name for a species; the domestic cat, for example, has the binomial *Felis catus.* A *polynomial,* with "many names," is an algebraic equation involving several terms. **ignominious, misnomer, nomenclature, nominal**

PAN comes from Greek with its spelling and meaning intact. It simply means "all" in Greek; as an English prefix it can also mean "completely," "whole," or "general." A *panoramic* view is a complete view in every direction. *Panchromatic* film is sensitive to the reflected light of all colors in the spectrum. *Pantheism* is the worship of all gods. A *pantheon* is a temple dedicated to all the gods of a particular religion. **panacea, pandemonium, panegyric, panoply**

PARA can mean "beside": *parallel* lines run beside each other. It can mean "beyond or outside": *paranoid*, in which *para-* combines with the Greek word *nous*, "mind," means a little outside of one's mind. Finally, *para-* can mean "associated with, especially as an assistant": *paramedics* and *paralegals* assist doctors and lawyers, and a *paramilitary* force assists regular military forces. **paradigm, paradox, paragon, parameter**

PART, from the Latin word *pars*, meaning "part," comes into English most obviously in our word *part* but also in words like *apartment, compartment*, and *particle*, all of which are parts of a larger whole. **impart, impartial, participle, partisan**

PATER/PATR, from both the Greek and the Latin word for "father," is the source of many English words. A *patriarchy* is a society or institution in which ultimate authority rests with the father or with the men of the family. A *patron* is one who assumes a fatherly role toward an institution or project, typically giving moral and financial support. **expatriate, paternal, patrician, patrimony**

PED comes from the Greek word for "child." It is like the PED that means "foot." The two usually aren't hard to tell apart—but don't mistake a *pediatrician* for a *podiatrist*. **encyclopedic, orthopedics, pedagogy, pediatrics**

PED comes from the Latin word *pes*, closely related to the Greek roots *pod* and *pous*, meaning "foot." From *ped-* we get *pedicure*, "care of the feet, toes, and toenails." From *pod-* we get *podiatrist*, "a foot doctor." **expedient, expedite, impediment, pedestrian**

PEL/PULS comes from the Latin verb *pellere*, meaning "to move or drive." A *propeller* moves an airplane forward. When soldiers *repel* an enemy charge, they drive it back. And to *dispel* something is to drive it away. **compel, expel, impel, repulsion**

PEN/PUN comes from the Latin words *poena*, "penalty," and *poenire* or *punire*, "to punish." From them come such English words as *penalty* and *repentance*; when a penalty is given to someone, it is expected that he or she will be moved to repentance. **impunity, penal, penance, punitive**

PEND/PENS, meaning "to hang, weigh, or cause to hang down," comes from the Latin verb *pendere*. We find it in English in words like *pensive*, meaning "thoughtful," and *appendix*, that useless and sometimes troublesome piece that hangs from the intestine. **appendage, expend, propensity, suspend**

PER, a Latin prefix that generally means "through," "throughout," or "thoroughly," has been a thoroughly useful root throughout its history and through all its many meanings. The "through" and "throughout" meanings are seen in *perforate*, "to bore through," *perennial*, "throughout the years," and *permanent*, "remaining throughout." And the "thoroughly" sense shows up in *persuade*, for "thoroughly advise," and *perverted*, "thoroughly turned around." **percolate, peremptory, permeate, persevere**

PERI usually means "going around something." With a *periscope*, you can see around corners. *Peristalsis* is the bodily function that moves food around the intestines; without it, digestion would grind to a halt. The moon's *perigee* is the point in its orbit where it is closest to the earth. The point in the earth's orbit around the sun that brings it closest to the sun is its *perihelion*. **perimeter, periodontal, peripatetic, peripheral**

PHAN/PHEN, from the Greek verbs that mean "to appear or seem" or "to present to the mind," has to do with the way things seem or appear rather than the way they really are. From these roots come words such as *fanciful* and *fantasy*, in which the imagination plays an important part. **diaphanous, phantasm, phantasmagoria, phenomenon**

PHIL comes from the Greek word meaning "love." In *philosophy*, it is joined with *sophia*, "wisdom," so philosophy means literally "love of wisdom." When joined with *biblio-*, "book," the result is *bibliophile*, or "lover of books." *Philadelphia*, containing the Greek word *adelphos*, "brother," is the city of "brotherly love." **philanthropy, philatelist, philology, philter**

PHON is a Greek root meaning "sound," "voice," or "speech." It is similar to the Latin *voc* in meaning but typically means only "sound" when used in such words as *telephone* ("far sound"), *microphone* ("small sound"), or *xylophone* ("wood sound"). **cacophony, phonetic, polyphonic, symphony**

PHOS/PHOT comes from the Greek word for "light." *Phos* can be seen in the word *phosphorus*, which refers generally to anything that glows in the dark and also to a particular glowing chemical element. *Phot*, the more familiar root, appears in words like *photography*, which is the use of light to create an image on film or paper. **phosphorescent, photogenic, photon, photosynthesis**

PLE comes from a Latin word meaning "to fill." It can be seen in the word *complete*, meaning "possessing all necessary parts." A *supplement* is an addition that makes something fuller. **complement, deplete, implement, replete**

PLIC comes from the Latin verb *plicare*, "to fold," A *complicated* subject has many folds or wrinkles. A person who is *implicated* in a crime is "wrapped up" in it somehow. The person's involvement may become *explicit*—"unwrapped" or revealed—

when the details of the crime unfold. **complicity, explicate, implicit, replicate**

POLIS/POLIT comes from the Greek word for "city." "City-states" operated much like separate nations in ancient Greece, so all their *politics* was local, like all their public *policy*. **acropolis, cosmopolitan, megalopolis, politic**

POLY comes from *polys*, the Greek word for "many." *Polysyllabic* words are words of many syllables. *Polygamy* is marriage in which one has many spouses, or at least more than the legal limit of one. A *polygraph* is an instrument for recording variations in many different bodily pulsations simultaneously to reveal whether someone is lying. **polyglot, polyhedron, polymer, polyphony**

PON/POS, from the Latin verb *ponere*, means "put" or "place." You *expose* film by "placing it out" in the light. You *oppose* an *opponent* by "putting yourself against" him or her. You *postpone* a trip by "placing it after" its original date. **component, disposition, repository, superimpose**

POPUL comes from the Latin word meaning "people," and in fact forms the basis of the word *people* itself. *Popular* means not only "liked by many people" but also "relating to the general public." The *population* is the people of an area. **populace, populist, populous, vox populi**

POST comes from a Latin word meaning "after" or "behind." A *postscript* is a note that comes after an otherwise completed letter, usually as an afterthought. *Postpartum* refers to the period following childbirth and all of its related events and complications. To *postdate* a check is to give it a date after the day when it was written. **posterior, posterity, posthumous, postmortem**

PRE, one of the most common of all English *prefixes*, comes from *prae*, the Latin word meaning "before" or "in front of." A television program *precedes* another by coming on the air earlier. You make a *prediction* by saying something will happen before it occurs. A person who *presumes* to know makes an assumption before he or she has all the facts. Someone with a *prejudice* against a class of people has formed an opinion of individuals before having met them. **precept, precocious, predispose, prerequisite**

PRIM comes from *primus*, the Latin word for "first." Something that is *primary* is first in time, development, rank, or importance. A *primer* is a book of first instructions on a subject. A *primate* is a bishop or archbishop of the first rank. Something *primitive* is in its first stage of development. **primal, primeval, primogeniture, primordial**

PRO comes from Latin, where it means "before," "forward," or "for." As a prefix, it can also mean "earlier than," "front," or "in front of." A lifetime of anger or bitterness can *proceed*, or "come forth," from an unhappy childhood. An ambi-

tious army officer expects to be *promoted*, or "moved forward," rapidly. Those who *provide* for the future by laying away money are "looking ahead." **procrastinate, prodigious, progress, propitious**

PROB/PROV comes from Latin words meaning "good, honest" and "show to be good, prove." *Probate* court is where the genuineness of the wills of deceased people must be *proved*. **approbation, disprove, probity, reprobate**

PROPER/PROPR come from the Latin word *proprius*, meaning "own." A *proprietor* is an owner. *Property* is what he or she owns. **appropriate, expropriate, proprietary, propriety**

PROT/PROTO comes from Greek and has the basic meaning "first in time" or "first formed." *Protozoans* are one-celled animals, such as amoebas and paramecia, that are among the most basic members of the biological kingdom. A *proton* is an elementary particle that, along with neutrons, can be found in all atomic nuclei. **protagonist, protocol, protoplasm, prototype**

PUNG/PUNCT comes from the Latin verb *pungere*, meaning "to prick or stab," and the noun *punctum*, meaning "point." A period is a form of *punctuation* that is literally a point. A *punctured* tire, pricked by a sharp point, can make it hard to be *punctual*—that is, to arrive "on the dot" or at a precise point in time. **compunction, expunge, punctilious, pungent**

PURG comes from the Latin verb *purgare*, "to clean or cleanse." An *unexpurgated* version of Ovid's *Metamorphoses* has not been cleansed of its vulgar or "dirty" sections. *Purging* literature of passages that might harm youthful readers has kept many an editor occupied; even in ancient times, some of Ovid's poetry was carefully *purged*. **expurgate, purgation, purgative, purgatory**

PUT, from the Latin verb *putare*, meaning "to think, consider, or reckon," has come into English in a variety of forms. A *reputation*, for example, is what others think of you; a *deputy* is someone "considered as" the person who appointed him or her. **disputatious, impute, putative, reputed**

QUADR/QUART means "four" and comes from Latin *quadr-*, "four," *quartus*, "fourth." In English, a *quart* is one-fourth of a gallon, just as a *quarter* is one-fourth of a dollar. A *quadrangle* has four sides but is not necessarily square; a *quadrant* is one of four equal parts. **quadrennial, quadrille, quadruple, quartet**

QUINT comes from the Latin word meaning "fifth." A *quintessence* is literally the "fifth essence," the fifth and highest element of ancient and medieval philosophy, which was supposed to be in the celestial bodies. **quintessential, quintet, quintuplet**

QUIS is derived from the Latin verb *quaerere,* meaning "to seek or obtain." You can see it in our word *acquisitive,* which means "having a strong wish to possess things." The roots *quir* and *ques* are also derived from this word and give us words such as *inquiry,* "a search or request for information," and *question,* "something asked." **acquisitive, inquisition, perquisite, requisition**

RECT comes from the Latin word *rectus,* which means "straight" or "right." A *rectangle* is a four-sided figure whose parallel, straight sides meet at right angles. *Rectus,* short for Latin *rectus musculus,* may refer to any of several straight muscles, such as those of the abdomen. To *correct* something is to make it right. **rectify, rectilinear, rectitude, rector**

RETRO means "back," "behind," or "backward" in Latin. A *retrospective* is a "looking back" at events from the past. **retroactive, retrofit, retrograde, retrogress**

ROG comes from *rogare,* the Latin verb meaning "to ask." The ancient Romans also used this word to mean "to propose," thinking perhaps that when we propose an idea, we are actually asking someone to consider it. So *interrogate* means "to question systematically," and a *surrogate* (for example, a surrogate mother) is a substitute, someone who is proposed to stand in for another. **abrogate, arrogate, derogatory, prerogative**

SACR/SANCT, meaning "holy," comes from the Latin words *sacer,* "holy," and *sancire,* "to make holy." A *sacrament* such as the bread and wine of Christian communion is a way of receiving holy grace. The person who receives it is *sanctified* or "made holy" by it; this holiness or *sanctity* is believed to result from God's grace. **sacrilege, sacrosanct, sanction, sanctuary**

SCAND/SCEND comes from the Latin verb *scandere,* "to climb." *Ascend,* "go up," and *descend,* "go down," are the most familiar of the English words it has produced. **ascendancy, condescend, descendant, transcend**

SCI comes from the Latin verb *scire,* "to know" or "to understand." This root appears in the word *science,* which refers to factual knowledge, and in *conscience,* which refers to moral knowledge. And to be *conscious* is to be in a state where you are able to know or understand. **conscientious, omniscience, prescient, unconscionable**

SCRIB/SCRIP comes from the Latin verb *scribere,* "to write." *Scribble* is a word meaning to write or draw carelessly. A written work that hasn't been published is a *manuscript.* To *describe* is to picture something in words. **circumscribe, conscription, inscription, proscribe**

SECU/SEQU comes from the Latin verb *sequi,* meaning "to follow." A *sequel* follows the original novel, film, or television show. The *second* follows the first. But a *non sequitur* is a conclusion

that does "not follow" from what was said before. **consequential, execute, obsequious, sequential**

SERV means "to be subject to." A *servant* is the person who *serves* you with meals and provides other necessary *services.* A tennis or volleyball *serve* puts the ball in play much as a servant puts food on the table. **serviceable, servile, servitude, subservient**

SIGN comes from the Latin noun *signum,* "sign or mark." An architect's *design* marks out the pattern for a building; if the owner *designates* that design as the one he wants, he so indicates by putting a *signature,* his own special mark, on an agreement. **assignation, resign, signatory, signet**

SOLV/SOLU comes from the Latin verb *solvere,* "to loosen, free, release." The number of English words that have been spawned by this root is seemingly without end. For example, to *solve* a problem—that is, to find its *solution*—is to free up a situation, and a *solvent dissolves* and releases oil or paint. **absolve, dissolution, resolve, soluble**

SON is the Latin root meaning "sound," as in our word *sonata,* meaning a kind of music usually played by one or two instruments, and *sonorous,* usually meaning "full, loud, or rich in sound." **assonance, dissonant, resonance, sonic**

SOPH is a Greek root from the word meaning "wise" or "wisdom." In our language, the root often appears in words where the "wise" is of the "wiseguy" variety. But in words such as *philosophy* we see a more respectful attitude toward wisdom. **sophisticated, sophistry, sophomoric, theosophy**

SPHER comes from the Greek word for "ball," and it appears in words for things that have something round about them. A ball is itself a *sphere.* The *stratosphere* and the *ionosphere* are parts of the *atmosphere* that encircles the earth. **biosphere, hemisphere, spherical, troposphere**

SPIC/SPEC comes from the Latin verb *specere* or *spicere,* meaning "to look at or behold." Closely related is the root *specta-,* which produces such words as *spectator, spectacles,* and *spectacular.* **auspicious, conspicuous, introspection, perspicacious**

STRU/STRUCT comes from the Latin verb *struere,* meaning "to put together," "to put in order," and "to build or devise." A *structure* is something *constructed,* "built" or "put together"; *instructions* tell how the pieces should be arranged. Something that *obstructs* is "built up in the way." **construe, destructive, infrastructure, instrumental**

SUB means "under," as in *subway, submarine,* and *substandard.* A *subject* is a person who is under the authority of another. The word *subscribe* once meant "to write one's name underneath," and *subscription* was the act of signing at the end of a document or agreement. **subconscious, subjugate, subliminal, subversion**

TANG/TACT comes from the Latin verb *tangere*, "to touch." A person who shows *tact* has a delicate touch when it comes to dealing with other people. To make *contact* is to touch or "get in touch." **intact, tactile, tangential, tangible**

TELE has as its basic meanings "distant" or "at a distance." A *telescope* looks at faraway objects, a *telephoto* lens on a camera magnifies distant objects for a photograph, and a *television*, for better or worse, allows us to watch things taking place far away. **telecommunication, telegenic, telemetry, telepathic**

TEMPER comes from the Latin verb *temperare*, "to moderate or keep within limits" or "to mix." It comes into English in words like *temperature*. *Tempered* (as in tempered steel) means "hardened by reheating and cooling in oil or water." *Tempered* enthusiasm, similarly, is enthusiasm that has cooled a bit. **intemperate, temper, tempera, temperance**

TEMPOR comes from Latin *tempus*, meaning "time." The Latin phrase *tempus fugit* means "time flies," an observation that somehow seems more true during summer vacation than in the dead of winter. A *temporary* repair is meant to last only a short time. The *tempo*, or speed, of a country-and-western ballad is usually different from that of a heavy metal song. **contemporary, extemporaneous, temporal, temporize**

TEN/TIN, from the Latin verb *tenere* and the related word *tenax*, basically means "hold" or "hold on to." A *tenant* is the "holder" of an apartment, house, or land, but not necessarily the owner. A *lieutenant* governor may "hold the position" or "serve in lieu" of the governor when necessary. **abstinence, sustenance, tenable, tenacious**

TEND/TENT, from Latin *tendere*, meaning "to stretch, extend, or spread," can be seen most simply in the English word *tent*, meaning "a piece of material stretched or extended over a frame." It can also be seen in the word *extend*, which means "to stretch forth or stretch out," and in *tendon*, the word for a tough band of tissue that stretches from a muscle to a bone. **contentious, distend, portend, tendentious**

TERM/TERMIN comes from the Latin verb *terminare*, "to limit, bound, or set limits to," or the related noun *terminus*, a "limit or boundary." In English, those boundaries or limits tend to be final: to *terminate* a sentence or a meeting or a ballgame means to end it, and a *term* goes on for a given amount of time and then ends. **coterminous, indeterminate, interminable, terminal**

TERR comes from Latin *terra*, "earth." *Terra firma* is a Latin phrase that means "firm ground" as opposed to the swaying seas; a *terrace* is a leveled area along a sloping hill; the French call potatoes

pommes de terre, literally "apples of the earth"; *territory* is a specific piece of land. **parterre, subterranean, terrarium, terrestrial**

THE comes from the Greek word meaning "god." *Theology* is the study of gods or religion. *Monotheism* is the worship of a single god; someone who is *polytheistic*, however, worships many gods. **apotheosis, atheistic, pantheistic, theocracy**

THERM/THERMO comes from the Greek word meaning "heat." A *thermometer* measures the amount of warmth in a body, the air, or an oven; a *thermostat* makes sure the temperature stays at the same level. In a *thermodynamic* process, heat affects the behavior of atoms, particles, or molecules. **thermal, thermocline, thermocouple, thermonuclear**

TOP comes from *topos*, the Greek word for "place." A *topic* is the subject of a paper or discussion. Its root originally meant "commonplace"—that is, a common subject. **isotope, topical, topography, utopia**

TORS/TORT comes from two forms of the Latin verb *torquere*, meaning "to twist" or "to wind" or "to wrench." A sideshow *contortionist* twists his or her body into bizarre shapes. This may appear to be a form of *torture*, which itself often involves a merciless wrenching and twisting of the body. **extort, torsion, tort, tortuous**

TRACT comes from *trahere*, the Latin verb meaning "drag or draw." Something *attractive* draws us toward it. A *tractor* drags other vehicles behind it, with the help of the *traction* of its wheels. **detract, intractable, protracted, retraction**

TRANS comes from Latin to indicate movement "through, across, or beyond" something. *Translation* carries the meaning from one language to another. A television signal is sent or *transmitted* through the air (or a cable) to your set. When making your way through a city on public *transportation*, you may have to *transfer* from one bus or subway across to another. **transcendent, transfiguration, transfuse, transient**

TRI means "three," whether derived from Greek or Latin. A *tricycle* has three wheels. A *triangle* has three sides and three angles. And a *triumvirate* is a board or government of three people. **triceratops, trident, trilogy, trinity**

TURB comes from the Latin verb *turbare*, "to throw into disorder," and the noun *turba*, "crowd" or "confusion." A *disturbance*, for example, confuses and upsets normal order or routine. **perturb, turbid, turbine, turbulent**

TUT/TUI, from the Latin verb *tueri*, originally meant "to look at," but the English meaning of the root gradually came to be "to guide, guard, or teach." A *tutor* guides a student through a subject, saving the most careful tutoring for the most difficult areas. **intuition, tuition, tutelage, tutorial**

UMBR, from Latin *umbra,* "shadow," is a shady customer. The familiar *umbrella,* with its ending meaning "little," casts a "little shadow" to keep off the sun or the rain. **adumbrate, penumbra, umber, umbrage**

UND comes into English from the Latin words *unda,* "wave," and *undare,* "to rise in waves," "to surge or flood." *Undulations* are waves or wavelike things or motions. To *undulate* is to rise and fall in a wavelike way. **abundant, inundate, redundancy, undulant**

UNI comes from the Latin word for "one." A *uniform* is a single design worn by everyone. A *united* group has one single opinion or forms a single *unit.* A *unicorn* is a mythical animal with one horn; a *unicycle* has only one wheel. **unicameral, unilateral, unison, unitarian**

UT/US comes from the Latin verb *uti,* "to use, make use of, employ," and the related adjective *utilis,* "useful, fit." It is *used* in such words as *abuse,* "improper use," and *reuse,* "to use again." **usufruct, usury, utilitarian, utility**

VEN/VENT comes from *venire,* the Latin verb meaning "come." To *intervene* in a case or an argument is to "come between" the two opponents. An *avenue* is a street, or originally an access road by which to "come toward" something. Groups "come together" at a *convention.* **advent, provenance, venturesome, venue**

VER comes from the Latin word for "truth." A *verdict* in a trial is "the truth spoken." But a just verdict may depend on the *veracity,* or "truthfulness," of the witnesses. **aver, verify, verisimilitude, verity**

VERB comes from Latin *verbum,* meaning "word." A *verb*—or action word—appears in some form in every complete sentence. To express something *verbally*—or to *verbalize* something—is to say it or write it. **proverb, verbatim, verbiage, verbose**

VERT/VERS, from the Latin verb *vertere,* means "to turn" or "to turn around." An *advertisement* turns your attention to a product or service. *Vertigo* is the dizziness that results from turning too rapidly or that makes you feel as if everything else is turning. **avert, divert, perverse, versatile**

VEST comes from the Latin verb *vestire,* "to clothe" or "to dress," and the related noun *vestis,* "clothing" or "garment." *Vest* is the shortest English word we have from this root, and is the name of a rather small piece of clothing. **divest, investiture, transvestite, travesty**

VID/VIS comes from the Latin verb *videre,* and appears in words having to do with seeing and sight. A *videotape* is a collection of *visual* images—that is, images *visible* to our eyes. But this root does not always involve eyes. To *envision* something, for instance, is to see it with your imagination. **revise, visage, visionary, visitation**

VINC/VICT comes from the Latin verb *vincere,* which means "to conquer" or "to overcome." The *victor* defeats an enemy, whether on a battlefield or a football field. To *convince* someone that you're right is a *victory* of another kind. **conviction, evince, invincible, victorious**

VIR is Latin for "man." A *virtue* is a good quality—originally, the kind of quality an ideal man possessed. And *virtuous* behavior is morally excellent. All in all, the Romans seemed to believe that being a man was a good thing. **triumvirate, virago, virility, virtuosity**

VIV comes from *vivere,* the Latin verb meaning "to live or be alive." A *survivor* has lived through something terrible. A *revival* brings something back to life, whether an old film, interest in a long-dead novelist, or the religious faith of a group. **convivial, revivify, vivacious, vivisection**

VOC/VOK, from the Latin noun *vox* and the verb *vocare,* has to do with speaking and calling and the use of the voice. So a *vocation* is a calling to a type of work; an *evocative* sight or smell calls forth memories and feelings; and a *vocal* ensemble is a singing group. **equivocate, irrevocable, provoke, vociferous**

VOLU/VOLV comes from the Latin verb *volvere,* meaning "to roll, wind, turn around, or twist around." From this source come words like *volume,* which was originally the name of a scroll or roll of papyrus, and *revolve,* which simply means "turn in circles." **convoluted, devolution, evolution, voluble**

VOR, from the Latin verb *vorare,* means "to eat." The ending *-ivorous* shows up in words that refer to eaters of certain kinds of food. Some *-ivorous* words such as *insectivorous* are easy to understand at a glance. **carnivorous, herbivorous, omnivorous, voracious**

657

CONFUSED & MISUSED WORDS

This section contains words that are similar or identical in sound and therefore easily confused, but that are quite different in meaning, as well as words that are often misused in other ways. The guidance provided below may help you avoid embarrassing mistakes.

a/an *A* is used before a word beginning with a consonant or consonant sound ("a door," "a one-time deal"). *An* is usually used before a word beginning with a vowel or vowel sound ("an operation"). *A* is used before *h* when the h is pronounced ("a headache"); *an* is used if the *h* is not pronounced ("an honor").

accept/except The verb *accept* means "to agree to, receive" ("accept a gift"). *Except* most often means "not including" ("will visit all national parks except the Grand Canyon").

adapt/adopt The verb *adapt* means "to change or modify" ("adapt to the warmer climate"); the verb *adopt* means "to take as one's own" ("adopt a child").

adverse/averse *Adverse* usually means "unfavorable" ("adverse conditions"); *averse* means "having an active feeling of dislike or reluctance" ("was averse to change").

affect/effect The verb *affect* means to "cause a change in something" ("rain affects plant growth"); the noun *effect* means "the result" ("the effect of rain on plant growth").

ain't *Ain't* is used by some people in informal speech to mean "are not," "is not," or "am not," among other things. Because *ain't* is considered very informal, it is not generally used in schoolwork, or in formal speech and writing.

aisle/isle *Aisle* means "a walkway between seats"; *isle* is a poetic word meaning "island."

allude/elude To *allude* is "to refer indirectly" ("alluded to her earlier comment"); to *elude* is "to evade or escape" ("eluded the police," "eluded capture," "her name eludes me").

allusion/illusion An *allusion* is an indirect reference ("the poem makes allusions to classical literature"); an *illusion* is a mistaken idea ("was under no illusions about their chances of winning") or a misleading image ("used mirrors to give the illusion of a larger space").

a lot/allot *A lot*, meaning "a great number," is spelled as two words; it is sometimes written incorrectly as *alot*. *Allot* is a verb meaning "to give out in portions" ("alloted one hour for homework").

an See *a/an*.

apt See *liable/likely/apt*.

as . . . as Is it more correct to say "she is as smart as I" or "she is as smart as me"? Actually, both ways are correct. In comparisons with "as . . . as," it's acceptable to use either subject pronouns (like "I," "you," "he," "she," "it," "we," and "they") or object pronouns (like "me," "you," "him," "her," "it," "us," and "them") after the second *as*. However, subject pronouns are more formal, so you may want to use subject pronouns in your comparisons when you are speaking formally or in writing.

as/like Sometimes *as* is used with the same meaning as *like* ("do as I do"), ("do like I do"). At other times, *as* means "in the role of" ("acted as a substitute teacher").

assent/ascent To *assent* is "to agree" ("assented to the proposal"); someone's *assent* is their agreement ("gave his assent"); an *ascent* is a climb or slope ("completed their ascent of the mountain"; "went up a steep ascent").

assure/ensure/insure To *assure* is "to make certain" ("assured their success") or "to state confidently to" ("assured him it was OK"); to *ensure* means "to make certain" ("will ensure their safety"); to *insure* means "to make certain" ("will insure their safety") or "to provide or obtain insurance on or for" ("insured their home").

as well as When *as well as* is used in a comparison, the pronoun following the second *as* is usually in the subject form ("she can spell as well as I [can]," not "she can spell as well as me"). (For a list of subject pronouns, see *as...as*.)

aural/oral *Aural* and *oral* are sometimes pronounced the same, but they have different meanings. *Aural* means "of or relating to the ear or sense of hearing." It comes from the Latin word for "ear." *Oral* means "of, relating to, given by, or near the mouth," and comes from a Latin word for "mouth." (See also *verbal/oral*.)

averse See *adverse/averse*.

bare/bear *Bare* means "without clothes or a covering" ("bare feet"); *bear* means "to carry."

bazaar/bizarre *Bazaar* is a fair or an exhibition of things for sale; *bizarre* means *weird*.

beside/besides *Beside* generally means "next to or at the side of" something; *besides* means "in addition to."

born/borne *Born* is having come into life; *borne* means "carried."

bring/take *Bring* usually means "to carry to a closer place"; *take*, "to carry to a farther place."

can/may *Can* usually means "to be able to or know how to" ("they can read and write"); *may* means "to have permission to" ("may I go?"). In casual conversation, *can* also means "to have permission to" ("can I go?"), but *may* is used instead in more formal speech or in writing.

canvas/canvass *Canvas* is a cloth; *canvass* means to ask people's opinions.

capital/capitol *Capital* is the place or city of government; *capitol* is the building of government.

cereal/serial *Cereal* is a breakfast food; *serial* is a story presented in parts.

cite/sight/site The verb *cite* often means "to quote" ("be sure to cite your sources"); the verb *sight* usually means "to get sight of" ("sighted a rare bird"); the noun *site* means "location" ("a construction site") or "website" ("updated the company's site").

colonel/kernel *Colonel* is a military rank; *kernel* is a part of a seed.

compliment/complement A *compliment* is a nice thing to say; a *complement* is something that completes.

confidant/confident A *confidant* is someone to whom secrets are confided; *confident* means "certain" ("confident of success") or "self-assured" ("a confident person/manner").

conscience/conscious A *conscience* is one's awareness of right and wrong ("had a guilty conscience"); *conscious* usually refers to being awake or aware ("the patient is conscious"), or to doing something with awareness ("was conscious of the risks involved").

council/counsel A *council* is a group of people meeting; *counsel* is advice.

country/county *Country* is a nation; *county* is a small, local government area.

data This was originally a plural form, but today it is used as both a singular and a plural noun.

desert/dessert *Desert* (with one *s*) is a dry, barren place; *dessert* is a sweet eaten after a meal.

die/dye To *die* is to cease to live; to *dye* is to change the color of.

diluted See *deluded/diluted*.

dived/dove Both spellings are common as a past tense of the verb *dive* ("she dived into the pool," "she dove into the pool").

effect See *affect/effect*.

e.g./i.e. *E.g.* stands for *exempli gratia* in Latin, which means "for example" ("many countries, e.g., France, Germany, and Japan"). *I.e.* stands for *id est*, which means "that is" in Latin. It introduces a rewording or a clarification ("a short period of time, i.e., three to five days").

elude See *allude/elude*.

ensure See *assure/ensure/insure*.

every day/everyday *Every day* means "each day" ("goes running every day"); *everyday* means "ordinary" ("her everyday clothes," "everyday life").

except See *accept/except*.

farther/further *Farther* usually refers to distance ("he ran farther than I did"). *Further* refers to degree or extent ("she further explained the situation").

flammable/inflammable Both words mean "capable of catching fire," but *inflammable* is also sometimes used to mean "excitable."

flaunt/flout *Flaunt* most commonly means "to show or display ostentatiously" ("flaunted their wealth"). Both *flout* and *flaunt* can mean "treat contemptuously" ("flouted/flaunted the law"), although *flaunt* used in this way is often considered a mistake.

flounder/founder The verb *flounder* usually means "to struggle" ("floundered in the mud," "floundering for words"); the verb *founder* usually means "to sink" ("the ship foundered") or "to fail" ("their marriage foundered").

flout See *flaunt/flout*.

forth/fourth *Forth* means "forward"; *fourth* means "number four in a sequence."

founder See *flounder/founder*.

further See *farther/further*.

good/well To *feel good* generally means "to be in good health and good spirits." *To feel well* usually means "to be healthy."

half/half a/half a The *l* in *half* is silent — it is used in writing, but it is not pronounced. *Half* is often used with the word *a*, which can either come before *half* or after it ("ate a half sandwich," "ate half a sandwich"). In casual speech, *a half a* is sometimes used ("ate a half a sandwich"), but it is avoided in more formal speech and in writing.

hanged/hung Both *hanged* and *hung* are used as the past tense of the verb *to hang*. *Hanged* is used when referring to execution by hanging; *hung* is used in all other senses.

hardy/hearty *Hardy* (suggestive of *hard*) means "strong"; *hearty* (suggestive of *heart*) means "friendly, enthusiastic."

i.e. See *e.g./i.e.*

illusion See *allusion/illusion*.

incite/insight *Incite* means "to arouse to action" ("incited the crowd to riot"); *insight* refers to understanding or to the ability to understand ("a person of great insight," "had a sudden insight," "gained some insight into the situation").

insure See *assure/ensure/insure*.

isle See *aisle/isle*.

its/it's *Its* means "of or relating to it or itself" ("the dog wagged its tail"). *It's* is a contraction of *it is* ("it's polite to say *thank you*").

kernel See *colonel/kernel*.

later/latter *Later* is the comparative form of *late*; it means "after a given time" ("they started later than they had intended"). *Latter* is an adjective that refers to the second of two things mentioned, or the last one of a sequence ("of the two choices, the latter is preferred").

lay/lie *Lay* means "to put (something) down"; *lie* means "to put one's body in a flat position."

lead/led These two words are pronounced the same, but have different meanings. *Lead* is a metal; *led* is the past tense of the verb *to lead*.

less/fewer *Less* is usually used with things that cannot be counted ("there is less sunshine today") and *fewer* with things that can be counted ("there are fewer people today").

liable/likely/apt All three words mean the same thing, but *likely* and *apt* are more often used in situations that could have a positive or neutral outcome ("she's apt to burst out laughing," "they'll likely visit today"). *Liable* is usually used where there is a possibility of a negative outcome ("you're liable to get hurt").

lie See *lay/lie*.

like See *as/like*.

liter/litter A *liter* is a unit of measurement; *litter* is a messy collection of things.

loose/lose *Loose* means "not tight"; *lose* means "to misplace or fail to win."

marital/martial *Marital* has to do with marriage; *martial* has to do with the military.

may See *can/may*.

moral/morale *Moral* has to do with high ideals ("a person of good moral character"); *morale* is the state of feelings of a person or group ("after the victory, morale was high").

naval/navel *Naval* has to do with the Navy; a *navel* is a belly button.

no way *No way* is an expression meaning "no" or "not at all." It is used in everyday speech, but is usually considered too casual for formal speech and writing.

oral See *verbal/oral and aural/oral*.

peace See *piece/peace*.

pedal/peddle *Pedal* means "to use or work the pedals of something" ("pedal a bicycle"). *Peddle* means "to sell from house to house."

piece/peace A *piece* is a portion of something ("a piece of cake"); *peace* is the freedom from war or fighting.

pore/pour To *pore* is usually "to read studiously" ("pored over the report"); to *pour* is "to flow or cause to flow" ("water poured from the broken pipe," "can I pour you some tea?").

precede/proceed *Precede* means "to go ahead of or come before"; *proceed* means "to start or move forward."

principle/principal A *principle* is a rule or guiding truth; *principal* is "the main one" — as an adjective or a noun: "the principal meal of the day," "the head of a school is a principal." It may help you to remember that *principle* and *rule* end with the same two letters.

respectfully/respectively *Respectfully* means "in a manner that shows respect" ("greeted them respectfully"; "she respectfully disagreed"); *respectively* usually means "each in the order given" ("she and I are 30 and 31 years old, respectively").

serial See *cereal/serial*.

set/sit The verb *set* means "to rest on eggs to hatch them"; *sit* means "to rest on the part of the body where the hips and legs join."

sight See *cite/sight/site*.

sit See *set/sit*.

site See *cite/sight/site*.

stationary/stationery Something that is *stationary* stands still; *stationery* is paper that is used for writing letters. It's easy to tell these two words apart if you remember that *stationery* and *letter* are both spelled with *er*.

tack/tact A *tack* is usually a small nail ("attached it with a tack") or a course of direction or action ("a tack from port to starboard," "it didn't work, so she tried a different tack"). *Tact* is social sensitivity ("his lack of tact got him in trouble").

take See *bring/take*.

than/then *Than* is a conjunction used to indicate a comparison ("better than that"); *then* means "at that time" ("then we went home").

there/their/they're *There* points to a place ("there it is"); *their* refers to "what belongs to them" ("this is their house"); *they're* is a contraction of *they* and *are* ("they're running late").

to/too/two *To* implies a direction ("went to the store"). *Too* means "also," "very," or "excessively" ("brought a pen and pencil too," "not too difficult," "too much"). *Two* is the number 2.

used to/use to The phrases *used to* and *use to* are often confused since they have the same pronunciation. *Used to* is correct in most instances ("we used to go to the lake every summer," "I used to know that"). But when it follows *did* or *didn't*, the correct spelling is *use to* ("that didn't use to be a problem").

verbal/oral Both *verbal* and *oral* are sometimes used to mean "spoken rather than written" ("a verbal agreement," "an oral agreement"). *Verbal* can also mean "of, relating to, or formed by a verb," or "of, relating to, or consisting of words." (For more about *oral*, see *aural/oral*.)

want See *won't/want*.

were/we're *Were* is a past tense verb form of *be* ("they were very young"); *we're* is a contraction of *we are* ("we're glad to see you").

who/whom *Who* is used as the subject of a clause (where one would use *he, she,* or *they*). *Whom* is used as the object of a clause (where one would use *him, her,* or *them*), and often follows prepositions like *to, for, from,* or *with*. Subject: "Who is coming to the party?" "He is coming to the party." Object: "John is coming with whom?" "John is coming with them."

who's/whose The word *who's* is a contraction of *who is* ("Who's there?"); *whose* is an adjective indicating ownership or quality ("Whose book is this?")

won't/want *Won't* is a contraction of *will not* ("I won't go"); *want* is a verb meaning "to need or desire" ("do you want some milk?").

Xmas *Xmas* is a shortened form of the word *Christmas*; the *X* comes from a Greek letter, which is the first letter of the Greek word for *Christ*. *Xmas* is used in very casual writing, but it is inappropriate for formal writing or school work.

your/you're *Your* is an adjective meaning "that which belongs to you" ("is that your sister?"). *You're* is a contraction of *you are* ("you're going, aren't you?").

A GUIDE TO COMMON VERB COLLOCATIONS

Collocation, as used here, describes verbs and the prepositional, infinitive, and gerund phrases and clauses that frequently accompany them. Also included here are combinations that include particles (adverbs) that frequently are used to intensify or modify the force or meaning of the verb. While this guide is not exhaustive, it covers the most common verb patterns about which the user is likely to have questions.

absolve *Absolve* uses the preposition *from* or *of* ⟨absolved from their obligations⟩ ⟨cannot be absolved of blame⟩.

abstain The preposition normally used with *abstain* is *from* ⟨abstain from meat⟩. In reference to voting, *abstain* frequently stands alone ⟨20 delegates abstained⟩.

abstract When *abstract* takes a preposition, it is generally *from* or *by* ⟨abstracted the essential data from the report⟩ ⟨abstracted by a researcher⟩.

abut *On* is the preposition most frequently used with *abut* ⟨land abuts on the road⟩.

accede *Accede* is normally followed by *to* ⟨acceding to their demands⟩.

accommodate The preposition following intransitive *accommodate* is usually *to* ⟨she accommodated to the change⟩. *To* is also used after a reflexive pronoun object ⟨he accommodated himself to these demands⟩.

account *Account* is normally followed by the preposition *for* ⟨fails to account for the results⟩.

accrue *Accrue* as an intransitive verb usually takes *to, on,* or *with* ⟨interest accrues to her account⟩ ⟨interest accrues on a daily basis⟩ ⟨the wisdom that accrues with age⟩.

acquaint *Acquaint* is most often followed by the preposition *with* ⟨is acquainted with them⟩.

acquiesce *Acquiesce* is frequently followed by *in* ⟨acquiesced in the decision⟩, less frequently by *to* ⟨would acquiesce to those demands⟩.

act up *Act* is often used with *up* to indicate an unusual or unwanted action ⟨children acted up when there were visitors⟩ ⟨the computer is acting up again⟩.

affiliate The verb *affiliate* in participial form commonly takes the preposition *with* ⟨he is affiliated with the university⟩.

amount *Amount* is regularly followed by *to* ⟨amounted to more than $200⟩.

amuse The verb *amuse* and its past participle *amused* are commonly followed by *at, by,* and *with* ⟨amused at this observation⟩ ⟨he was amused by the play⟩ ⟨amusing themselves with video games⟩ or by an infinitive ⟨I was amused to find an article about it⟩.

append *Append* usually takes *to* ⟨should append it to the file⟩.

apportion *Apportion* may take the prepositions *among, between,* and *to* ⟨to be apportioned among the states⟩ ⟨apportioned responsibility between the higher and lower courts⟩ ⟨will apportion duties to her subordinates⟩.

approve *Approve,* used as an intransitive verb meaning "to have a favorable opinion," takes *of* ⟨approves of the effort⟩. Used as a transitive verb, usually in the sense "to ratify," it can take *by* to indicate the agent ⟨the plan was approved by the board⟩.

arise *Arise* is often followed by a prepositional phrase indicating the state something is coming from ⟨arising from sleep⟩ ⟨problems that arose out of the clash of two cultures⟩.

array When used in the sense of "dress," *array* usually takes *in* ⟨arrayed in finery⟩. When meaning "to get or place in order," many prepositions are possible, usually indicating position ⟨marchers arrayed on the parade grounds⟩ ⟨Secret Service members arrayed before the podium⟩.

arrive When the place of arrival is the object, *in* and *at* are used ⟨arrived in New York⟩ ⟨arrive at the courtroom⟩; *on* may also be used ⟨arrived on the scene⟩. When things arrive, we find *in, at,* or *on* ⟨word arrived in the classroom⟩ ⟨the letter arrived at her desk⟩ ⟨the dinghy arrived on the beach⟩. If the object is the point of departure, *from* is the most common ⟨arrived from Seattle⟩. When the object is the means of arrival, we find *by, on,* and occasionally *in*

⟨arriving by limousine⟩ ⟨arrive on horseback⟩ ⟨arrived in a skiff⟩.

ask *Ask* may use an infinitive ⟨was asked to return⟩ or a clause ⟨I ask that you not use it⟩ ⟨she asked how you were⟩. When prepositions are used, one convention is this: "Ask *of* a person, *for* what is wanted, *after* one's health."

aspire *To* is the preposition most often used with *aspire* ⟨aspires to a singing career⟩. An infinitive is also common ⟨aspired to be champion⟩.

assent When *assent* takes a preposition, it is *to* ⟨assented to their demands⟩.

assimilate When the verb *assimilate* takes a preposition, it is most often *to* or sometimes *into* ⟨assimilate to the conditions⟩ ⟨was assimilated into the platoon⟩. *By* indicates the agent ⟨assimilated by her new country⟩.

assist *Assist,* meaning "help," usually takes *in* or *with* ⟨assist in finding the owner⟩ ⟨assisted with clearing the table⟩.

astonish In the passive, *astonish* can be used with *at* or *by* ⟨we were astonished at [by] the force of the hurricane⟩. In the active voice, *astonish* frequently takes *by* and a gerund ⟨he astonished the judges by withdrawing the piece⟩.

attain When used intransitively, *attain* is normally followed by *to* ⟨he could only attain to a low-level job⟩.

attempt *Attempt* is normally followed by the infinitive ⟨we attempted to grow carrots⟩.

back *Back* is sometimes used with particles indicating retreat or withdrawal from a position or commitment ⟨back away from their previous assertions⟩ ⟨the bully backed down from the fight⟩ ⟨they backed out at the last minute⟩.

base *Base* is usually followed by *on, upon,* and *in* ⟨based on the facts⟩ ⟨based upon the sources⟩ ⟨based in a thorough modernism⟩.

blend *Blend* is followed by *with* or *into* ⟨blending these ideas with similar ones of his partner⟩ ⟨the structure blends into its surroundings⟩.

border When *border* is used to mean "to verge on the nature of a specific thing," it is usually followed by *on* ⟨a statement bordering on the ridiculous⟩. When the literal sense of *border* is used in the passive, the preposition is most often *by* ⟨grounds bordered by potted flowers⟩.

call *Call,* when the complement indicates purpose, often takes an infinitive ⟨was called to testify in court⟩ or a prepositional phrase with *for* or *to* ⟨call for help⟩ ⟨called for an investigation⟩ ⟨called to active duty in the reserves⟩. When indicating the object, the prepositions may be *at* or *on* ⟨called at the home of a friend⟩ ⟨a salesman calling on customers⟩. Sometimes *call* is followed by particles as intensives ⟨call up the electric company with a question about the bill⟩ ⟨call off the numbers⟩.

capitalize When used intransitively, *capitalize* is followed by *on* ⟨hoped to capitalize on his new-found fame by running for public office⟩.

care *Care* is often followed by *for* and *about* ⟨the animal was being cared for by shelter volunteers⟩ ⟨I don't care about that⟩. An infinitive may also follow *care* ⟨do you care to comment?⟩.

catch Used in the passive voice, *catch* is usually followed by *in* or *by* ⟨caught in a web of lies⟩ ⟨caught in a sudden storm⟩ ⟨the fugitive was caught by a persistent detective⟩.

center Prepositions used with *center* are usually *in, around,* or *on* ⟨the action is centered in a small Midwest town⟩ ⟨community activities centered around the church⟩ ⟨their thoughts were centered on history⟩.

check *Check* is used with a number of common particles.

Check into means "investigate" ⟨check into these rumors⟩. *Check out* has several meanings ⟨check out the competition⟩ ⟨check out his story⟩ ⟨check it out with Barbara⟩. *Check on* is also common ⟨check on the baby⟩ ⟨check on his progress⟩ as is *check over* ⟨I checked over my test before submitting it⟩.

choke When followed by a preposition, *choke* usually takes *on* or *with* ⟨he choked on a fish bone⟩ ⟨stores were choked with shoppers⟩. Transitive *choke* may be followed by a particle as an intensive ⟨the rule was designed to choke off debate⟩.

claim Aside from a direct object, *claim* can be followed by a clause ⟨claimed [that] he saw a ghost⟩ or an infinitive ⟨some people claim to see beauty in that painting⟩.

clean The transitive use of *clean* often takes various particles before the object ⟨clean up the attic⟩ ⟨clean out a drain⟩ ⟨clean off a blackboard⟩. Intransitive *clean* sometimes uses the particle *up* ⟨clean up after working in the yard⟩.

clear Transitive *clear* is often followed by *for* showing intention ⟨clear two downtown blocks for the new civic center⟩, *from* showing place ⟨clear snow from the walk⟩, or *of* showing burden or obstruction ⟨cleared land of brush⟩ ⟨clear your mind of foolish fancies⟩. Intransitive *clear*, referring to the sky, often takes the particle *up* ⟨it cleared up quickly after the rain⟩.

cling *Cling* is usually followed by the preposition *to* ⟨my soaked garments clung to my body⟩ ⟨clinging to the hope that her son had survived⟩.

close Transitive *close* sometimes is followed by prepositional phrases indicating place, reason, duration, or object ⟨close the gate of the plant⟩ ⟨close a street for snow removal⟩ ⟨schools were closed for the holiday⟩ ⟨close a land to new settlers⟩. Intransitive *close* is also followed by prepositional phrases usually indicating where or how ⟨clouds soon closed over the sun⟩ ⟨his comrades closed around him protectively⟩ ⟨the clamshell bucket closed on a load of dirt⟩ ⟨I close with this warning⟩. *Close* is also often used with particles ⟨military intelligence agents closed in on him⟩ ⟨the shop closed up after 20 years in business⟩.

coalesce When *coalesce* occurs with a preposition, *into* is the one used most often ⟨the clouds coalesced into a threateningly dark mass⟩.

coax *Coax* is sometimes followed by an infinitive ⟨coaxing a cold engine to start⟩ but more often by prepositional phrases ⟨coaxed her into changing the date of the ceremony⟩ ⟨coaxing extra servings from the cook⟩.

commiserate *Commiserate* used intransitively is most often followed by *with* ⟨sought to commiserate with her⟩ and sometimes *over* ⟨the actors commiserated over the play's failure⟩.

commune *Commune* is followed by *with* ⟨commune with nature⟩.

communicate *Communicate* is usually followed by *with* ⟨she communicated with him⟩ but by *to* before an indirect object ⟨communicated to him the wishes of her government⟩.

compare The general rule is: when you mean "to liken," use *compare to* ⟨shall I compare thee to a summer's day?⟩; when you mean "to examine so as to discover the likenesses and differences," use *compare with* ⟨these results compare favorably with those of 10 years ago⟩.

concur *Concur* is used primarily with *with*, *in*, and *on* ⟨we concur with his opinion⟩ ⟨they concurred in finding him responsible⟩ ⟨the two of them concur on this point⟩.

confess The intransitive *confess* is often followed by the preposition *to* and either a gerund ⟨confesses to having cheated me⟩ or a noun ⟨confessed to the crime⟩. The transitive *confess* uses *to* before an indirect object ⟨confessed his sins to the priest⟩.

confide *Confide* in its intransitive sense is often used with *in* ⟨they haven't confided in me⟩.

conform When *conform* takes a preposition, it is mostly *to* or *with* ⟨does not conform to the pattern⟩ ⟨this conforms with our understanding⟩.

connect *Connect* is used with the prepositions *with* and *to* ⟨he had been connected with a secret organization⟩ ⟨the white wire connects to switch A⟩. Two or more things may also be connected by still another thing ⟨these items are connected by their relation to a third⟩.

contend The word *contend* is commonly followed by a clause ⟨she contends that she was out at the time⟩. *Contend* is also used with the prepositions *with* and *against* ⟨had difficulty contending with the traffic⟩ ⟨forces against which they could not contend⟩. When the object of the preposition is the focus of the contention, *for* is the choice ⟨contended for the prize⟩.

contrast *Contrast* takes *with* or *to* ⟨contrasted her clean apartment with his messy place⟩ ⟨contrasting their production methods to their rival's⟩.

convict When *convict* is followed by a preposition, the preposition is usually *of* or *on* ⟨convict of perjury⟩ ⟨convicted on two counts of fraud⟩.

convince *Convince* is often followed by a clause ⟨convinced [that] they can win⟩ or by a phrase beginning with *of* ⟨convinced of the need⟩.

cope *Cope* in the sense "to struggle with difficulties" is used with the preposition *with* ⟨she had trouble coping with her mother⟩. *Cope* is also used absolutely, with no preposition or object ⟨so exhausted he could not cope⟩.

correspond *Correspond*, meaning "to be in agreement," may be followed by *to* or *with* ⟨that reference does not correspond to [with] any published source⟩. When meaning "to communicate," *correspond* takes *with* exclusively ⟨we correspond with them frequently⟩.

culminate *Culminate* is usually used with the preposition *in* ⟨culminated in a constitutional amendment⟩ but can also be followed by *with* ⟨the celebration culminates with the sounding of the gong⟩.

cure When the passive form *cured* is followed by a preposition, it is usually *of* ⟨he was cured of the habit⟩.

dabble People usually dabble *in* something ⟨dabbling in politics⟩.

dally *With* is often used with *dally* ⟨dallying with a new idea⟩.

dare As an auxiliary verb, *dare* is followed by an infinitive phrase without *to* ⟨no one dared say a word⟩. As a regular verb, it can be followed by an infinitive phrase with *to* ⟨she dares to criticize me⟩. When preceded by other auxiliaries (such as *might*, *would*, and *do*), *dare* is followed by an infinitive without *to* ⟨I wouldn't dare ask them⟩.

dawn Things usually dawn *on* people ⟨it dawned on me that he was an utter fool⟩.

dazzle People are usually *dazzled with* or *dazzled by* something ⟨he dazzled millions with his speeches⟩ ⟨I was dazzled by the light⟩.

deal Things are often *dealt in* or *dealt with* ⟨they were dealing in matters of no concern to me⟩ ⟨dealt harshly with the rebels⟩. When *deal* is used to mean "distribute," it is frequently accompanied by *out* ⟨dealt out severe punishment⟩ ⟨deal the cards out⟩.

decide Decide is frequently followed by an infinitive ⟨she decided to buy a new hat⟩ or a clause ⟨the president decided that the meeting should be postponed⟩. Often *decide* is followed by the preposition *on* ⟨they could not decide on the right course of action⟩.

decline When decline is used to mean "withhold consent," it is often followed by an infinitive ⟨declined to accept the offer⟩. When used in the sense "descend," it is sometimes used with the preposition *to* ⟨the path declines to the river⟩.

defend *Defend* may be followed by *against* or *from* ⟨playing deep to defend against a pass⟩ ⟨defended herself from criticism⟩.

defer When *defer* means "yield," it is followed by the preposition *to* ⟨everyone deferred to the king⟩.

defile Used with a phrase expressing means or agent, *defile* is followed by *by* or *with* ⟨a view defiled by billboards⟩ ⟨boots defiled with blood⟩.

deliberate People usually deliberate *on* or *about* something ⟨deliberated on the matter⟩ ⟨deliberating about the next step⟩.

delve Things are usually delved *into* ⟨delved into his family history⟩.

depart People *depart from* a starting point or *depart for* a destination ⟨the train departed from the station⟩ ⟨here the river departs from its original course⟩ ⟨it's time to depart for home⟩.

depend In most senses *depend* is followed by *on* or *upon* ⟨life depends on [upon] food⟩ ⟨you can depend on me⟩.

desist When *desist* takes a preposition, it is usually *from*

despair *Despair* often takes *of* with a noun or gerund ⟨we despair of people who do not like poetry⟩ ⟨he despaired of mastering idioms⟩.

destine The participle *destined* commonly takes an infinitive ⟨a relationship destined to last⟩. *Destined* is used with *for* before a noun ⟨a child destined for greatness⟩.

detract When a preposition follows *detract*, it is *from* ⟨exaggerations that detract from the real issues⟩.

deviate People or things *deviate from* one idea or path and *deviate to* [or *toward*] another.

devolve *Devolve* usually appears with *on* or *upon* ⟨his estate devolved on a distant cousin⟩ ⟨when the general fell, command devolved upon the colonel⟩.

die *Die* in the sense of "succumb" or "stop" or "subside" often takes a particle ⟨the noise died away⟩ ⟨flowers die back [or down] after blooming⟩ ⟨her few relatives died off one by one⟩.

differ When *differ* means "to be unlike," the usual preposition is *from* ⟨the laws of this state differ from those of neighboring states⟩. When *differ* means "to disagree," it usually takes *with* ⟨differs with the Pentagon on the use of preemptive strikes⟩.

differentiate It is idiomatic to differentiate *between* two things or differentiate one thing *from* another ⟨difficult to differentiate between the twins⟩ ⟨climate differentiates one coast from the other⟩.

disagree It is possible to disagree *with* someone *about* or *over* or *on* some issue.

disappoint The participle *disappointed* may take *about, at, by, over,* or *with* ⟨disappointed about [at, by, over, with] the decision⟩. *Disappointed in* is also encountered ⟨was disappointed in himself⟩.

disapprove *Of* is the preposition that follows *disapprove* ⟨I disapprove of your attitude⟩.

discourage When a preposition follows *discourage,* it is usually *from,* which often takes a gerund phrase ⟨was discouraged from pursuing a literary career⟩ or a noun phrase ⟨discouraged from the use of medications⟩.

discriminate *Between* is the usual preposition after *discriminate* ⟨could not discriminate between the colors red and green⟩.

dislike The verb *dislike* can take a noun object ⟨dislikes the ocean⟩, a gerund phrase ⟨dislikes having to take the subway⟩ or, less frequently, an infinitive phrase ⟨I dislike to disturb you at home⟩.

dismay *By* is the usual preposition after the passive *dismayed* ⟨dismayed by his girlfriend's refusal⟩. *Dismayed* can also be followed by the infinitive ⟨was dismayed to discover that she had lost⟩.

displease In the passive, *displease* usually takes *with* or *by* ⟨we were displeased with the meal⟩ ⟨I was displeased by their constant arguing⟩.

dispose In the sense "to discard or clear away," *dispose of* is the idiom ⟨dispose of the excess⟩. When *disposed* means "inclined" or "tending to," what follows is an infinitive ⟨we were disposed to accept the offer⟩ or a phrase introduced by *to* or *toward* ⟨favorably disposed toward them⟩.

dissent When *dissent* is followed by a preposition, the preposition is usually *from* ⟨dissenting from the majority opinion⟩.

dissociate, disassociate *Dissociate* and *disassociate* share the sense "to separate from association," and both words often take the preposition *from* ⟨dissociated [disassociated] himself from the business⟩.

distinguish A thing may be set apart *by* a quality ⟨the church was distinguished by the absence of a tower⟩ or one may note distinctions *between* things ⟨could not distinguish between reality and imagination⟩ or one thing may be viewed apart *from* others ⟨nothing distinguished him from his employees⟩.

dive The prepositions that follow *dive* are *to* or *into* ⟨the mercury dived to eight below zero⟩ ⟨dived into her pocketbook for a comb⟩.

diverge The usual preposition after *diverge* is *from* ⟨his talk diverged from the prepared notes⟩.

divest *Divest* normally appears with *of* when occurring with a reflexive pronoun ⟨the firm plans to divest itself of its foreign holdings⟩.

divorce The verb *divorce* is almost always used with *from* when a prepositional phrase follows ⟨a solution divorced from mundane considerations⟩.

do The intransitive *do,* when followed by a prepositional phrase, often has *as, like, with,* or *for* ⟨do as I say⟩ ⟨never knew them to do like this before⟩ ⟨what shall we do for money?⟩ ⟨have done with talking⟩. When the meaning is "treat," the preposition is *by* ⟨you always do well by your friends⟩. Intransitive *do* is also followed by an infinitive ⟨it will not do to neglect your duties⟩. As an auxiliary verb, *do* is sometimes used with the infinitive without *to* ⟨fervently do we pray⟩ ⟨you did forget my birthday⟩ ⟨do be careful!⟩ ⟨don't you see?⟩.

dominate Intransitive *dominate* takes the preposition *over* ⟨he dominated over the proceedings⟩. When *dominate* is used in the passive voice, the agent is named in a phrase using *by* ⟨the debate was dominated by the Republicans⟩.

dote *Dote* usually takes *on* ⟨grandparents who dote on their grandchildren⟩.

dream *Dream* may take either *of* or *about* before a gerund or a noun object ⟨dreamt of [about] you last night⟩ ⟨dreamed of owning a house⟩.

emerge When *emerge* is followed by a preposition, the choice is usually *from* ⟨they emerged from behind the curtain⟩.

enamor The participle form *enamored* usually takes *of* and sometimes *with* ⟨became enamored of the dog⟩ ⟨enamored with foreign films⟩.

engage *Engage* when used with a preposition most often takes *in,* usually followed by a gerund or a noun ⟨engaged in trade for many years⟩.

enthrall When *enthralled* is used with a preposition, it is usually *by* or *with* ⟨enthralled by the spectacle⟩ ⟨enthralled with the campaign⟩.

expect *Expect* is very often followed by the infinitive ⟨researchers expect to find clues to mystery⟩. Less often, *expect* is used with *from* or *of* ⟨what would you expect from the likes of him?⟩ ⟨little was expected of us⟩.

face In its transitive use, *face,* meaning "confront," is usually used with the particles *down* or *out* in active constructions ⟨she faced down all opposition⟩ ⟨determined to face out the situation⟩ and *with* in passive constructions ⟨faced with evidence of treachery⟩. Intransitive *face* can be followed by *up,* which again conveys the meaning "confront" and is often followed by a *to* phrase ⟨finally faces up to his past⟩.

fall away The combination *fall away* can mean "diminish," but more often conveys the notion of "withdrawing" or "moving away" ⟨her troubles beginning to fall away as she gained more confidence⟩ ⟨the path fell away in a steep slope⟩ ⟨our sponsors gradually fell away⟩.

fascinate The preposition used with *fascinate* is *by* with either a human or nonhuman object ⟨is fascinated by her⟩ ⟨was fascinated by carnivals⟩. *Fascinated with* takes only nonhuman objects ⟨fascinated with power⟩.

fend The transitive *fend,* meaning "repel" or "defend against," is often used with *off* ⟨eating well and taking vitamins to fend off the flu⟩. The intransitive *fend,* meaning "manage" or "take care" usually takes a *for* phrase ⟨leaving young children to fend for themselves⟩.

fiddle *Fiddle,* in the sense "to handle something idly, casually, or aimlessly," usually takes *with* ⟨nervously fiddled with his tie⟩ ⟨fiddled with the engine for hours⟩.

filter When removing something with a filter, the idiom is usually *filter out.*

flush In the sense of "excite," *flush* in the passive construction is often followed by a *with* phrase ⟨was flushed with pride at his son's success⟩.

forbid *Forbid* is commonly followed by the infinitive after the direct object ⟨her mother forbids her to go⟩. *Forbid* is also used with *from* followed by a gerund ⟨the law forbids them from selling to minors⟩ and sometimes with a gerund as object ⟨the rules of the game forbid talking⟩.

foreclose In its intransitive use, *foreclose* is normally followed by *on* ⟨the bank foreclosed on the house⟩.

forget *Forget* is typically followed by a direct object ⟨I forgot my keys⟩. Sometimes the usage is *forget to do* something (with an infinitive) or *forget about* something (with a noun or gerund phrase) ⟨I forgot to close the door⟩ ⟨he forgot about the assignment⟩ ⟨forgot about turning down the oven and burned the pie⟩.

freshen up *Freshen* is often followed by *up* in both transitive and intransitive uses ⟨painters are freshening up several rooms⟩ ⟨wanted to freshen up before going to dinner⟩.

frighten *Frighten* in the passive voice often takes *by* ⟨children frightened by thunder⟩ or *of* ⟨frightened of snakes⟩.

fritter *Fritter away* is the usual idiom ⟨frittered away his allowance at the arcade⟩.

front In the sense of "have or take a position with respect to something" or "face," *front* usually takes *on* or *toward* ⟨the house fronts on the street⟩ ⟨the church fronted toward the east⟩.

frown When used in the sense of "express disapproval," *frown* is usually followed by *on* ⟨society frowns on such actions⟩.

furnish When *furnish* is followed by a preposition, the preposition is usually *with* ⟨furnished the police with evidence⟩ ⟨the house is furnished with antiques⟩.

gear The verb *gear* is sometimes used with *up* to mean "increase" or "move faster" ⟨gearing up production to meet military needs⟩.

gird *Gird*, in the sense of "prepare," is usually used reflexively ⟨the worker girded himself for another meeting with his boss⟩.

gloat *Gloat* is frequently used with the preposition *over* ⟨gloating over his successful presentation⟩.

go along The combination *go along* is frequently used to mean "express cooperation or agreement" ⟨declined to take the gamble and go along⟩. Often *go along* takes *with* ⟨were glad enough to go along with his suggestions⟩.

grapple *Grapple* often implies a struggle to deal or cope with something and is usually used with *with* ⟨wanted to grapple with international problems after the election⟩.

gripe *Gripe*, meaning "complain," is usually used with *about* ⟨students griping about food in the dining hall⟩.

haggle *Haggle* is commonly used with *over* ⟨haggling over the price⟩.

happen *Happen* usually occurs with a *to* phrase ⟨all sorts of pleasant things happened to him⟩ or with an infinitive ⟨he happens to be a very rich man⟩.

hasten *Hasten* often takes an infinitive ⟨I hasten to add that I agree⟩.

have As a verbal auxiliary *have* is often used with a past participle to form the perfect tenses ⟨has gone home⟩ ⟨I had read the book before seeing the play⟩. As a regular verb with the meaning "obligation," *have* is usually followed by an infinitive ⟨I have to see a doctor⟩ ⟨we had to be home by six⟩ and sometimes simply as "have to" with the second verb understood ⟨I don't want to go, but I have to⟩.

hesitate *Hesitate* is sometimes used with an infinitive ⟨no qualified student should hesitate to apply to college⟩.

hide *Hide* often occurs with a *from* phrase to indicate the thing being avoided ⟨children playfully hiding from their friends⟩. *Hide* is often used with a *behind* phrase to indicate evading or seeking refuge from something ⟨hiding behind dark glasses to avoid being recognized⟩ ⟨company executives hiding behind union rules when it comes to promotions⟩.

hinge When "contingency" is the concept, *hinge* is used with *on* or *upon* ⟨the success of the company hinges on this decision⟩.

hint *Hint* is usually used with *at* ⟨caught on to what he was hinting at⟩.

hire *Hire* as an intransitive is usually followed by *on* or *out* ⟨hire on as a stuntman in movies⟩ ⟨young women who hire out as nannies⟩.

honor The verb *honor* may take *by* or *with* to indicate "how" ⟨honored by a special dinner⟩ ⟨honored with a commemorative plaque⟩. It occurs less frequently with *for, at,* or *in* to indicate reason, place, or manner ⟨honored for his contribution⟩ ⟨honored at town hall⟩ ⟨honored in grand style⟩.

hope *Hope* is often followed by a *for* phrase ⟨hope for great things from the children⟩ or by a clause ⟨hopes [that] he will win the prize⟩.

hover *Hover* often takes *over* with a noun ⟨clouds of smoke hovered over the building⟩ or *around* with or without an object ⟨the thermometer hovered around 90⟩ ⟨photographers hovering around waiting for the arrival of the star⟩.

huddle The intransitive *huddle* is often used with a number of adverbs, such as *together, close,* or *near,* suggesting closeness or intimacy ⟨they huddled together [close] in the cold shelter⟩.

hunch *Hunch* is often used with an adverb indicating direction ⟨hunches down behind a barrier⟩ ⟨hunched over in pain⟩ ⟨he hunched forward to listen⟩ ⟨hunched up his shoulders⟩ ⟨I hunched my chair closer⟩.

hunger One usually *hungers for* or *after* something ⟨hungering for [after] knowledge⟩.

hunt *Hunt* may be used intransitively with a *for* phrase ⟨hunt for a lost wallet⟩ or transitively with *down* when referring to prey ⟨the escapees were hunted down and arrested⟩ or with *up* or *out* when searching through resources ⟨hunting out obscure meanings in poems⟩ ⟨hunted up a lot of new evidence⟩.

impeach Used with a preposition, *impeach* usually takes *for* ⟨impeached for malfeasance⟩. Occasionally it takes *on* ⟨impeached on several counts⟩.

impose When used with a preposition, *impose* most often takes *on* (or *upon*) ⟨imposed his views on the others⟩ ⟨may I impose upon you for a favor?⟩.

improve *Improve* is most often a transitive verb ⟨the editor improved the wording⟩, but sometimes one can *improve on* something ⟨can't improve on the design⟩.

incline In involving a course of conduct or opinion, one often *inclines* to or *toward* something ⟨we incline to [toward] traditional ways⟩.

indulge We usually *indulge* an action, or *indulge* a person *in* their actions or beliefs, or we may *indulge in* a behavior of our own ⟨indulged the convalescing child with whatever she wished to eat⟩ ⟨he did not indulge in alcohol⟩.

infatuate The participle *infatuated* takes *with* as a prepositional phrase ⟨became infatuated with Italy⟩.

infer *Infer* is commonly followed by *from* ⟨I infer from your letter that everything was satisfactory⟩.

infringe *Infringe* as an intransitive verb is often followed by *on* or *upon* ⟨infringing on [upon] our rights⟩.

inquire When an object follows *inquire,* it is usually the object of *about* or *into* ⟨inquired about their health⟩ ⟨inquired into the girls' activities⟩.

insinuate A common idiomatic usage is *insinuate* (something) *into* (something) ⟨insinuating himself into the conversation⟩.

insist *Insist,* used with a preposition, usually takes *on* or *upon,* sometimes with a gerund phrase as the object ⟨insisted on this point⟩ ⟨insisted on going with them⟩. As a transitive verb, *insist* has a clause as its object ⟨Mr. Bergin insists [that] he has nothing to cover up⟩ ⟨they insisted that we come in⟩.

instruct *Instruct* frequently occurs with an infinitive ⟨was instructed to contact them⟩. *Instruct* is also used with the preposition *in* ⟨were instructed in the art of designing with gold⟩.

intend *Intend* may be followed by an infinitive ⟨never intended to upset them⟩ or by a direct object and an infinitive phrase ⟨apparently intended the money to go to charity⟩ or by a gerund phrase ⟨the parents intended leaving the children with a relative⟩. *Intend* may take a prepositional phrase introduced by *for* ⟨not intended for consumer use⟩.

interfere The usual idiom is *interfere with* (something) ⟨that will interfere with our plans⟩.

intrude Where the action is unwelcome, one is usually *intruding on* or *upon* something or someone ⟨I do not wish to intrude on your good nature⟩.

join *Join* is used with any of several prepositions, most often *in, to,* or *with. In* is followed by a noun or gerund ⟨joined in marriage⟩ ⟨joined in singing⟩. Noun phrases usually follow *to* and *with* ⟨her grieving spirit, joined to her pain, caused her to do it⟩ ⟨images joined with narrative captions⟩.

justify When *justify* takes a preposition, it frequently occurs with *in* and a gerund phrase or *by,* usually followed by a noun or gerund phrase ⟨justified in pressing charges⟩ ⟨action justified by customer responses⟩ ⟨justified himself by claiming ignorance⟩.

know The usual prepositions with *know* are *of* and *about* ⟨knew of her but had not yet met her⟩ ⟨I know about that; you don't need to tell me⟩.

A Guide to Common Verb Collocations

lead *Lead* often takes a prepositional phrase indicating direction, place, or manner ⟨led the officers to his hiding place⟩ ⟨were led through the fog by the distant lights⟩ ⟨leads the world in the steel production⟩ ⟨that door leads to the kitchen⟩.

leaf One typically *leafs through* a book or information resource ⟨leafing through the old newspaper files, I found the right article⟩.

learn *Learn* is often followed by an infinitive ⟨she learned to read very early⟩ or by a clause ⟨we learned that he will arrive shortly⟩. *Learn* is often also followed by prepositions *about* or *of* ⟨what have you learned about this matter?⟩ ⟨I just learned of your recent illness⟩.

lie *Lie* is often followed by adverbs or prepositional phrases indicating direction, position, or manner ⟨the route lay to the west⟩ ⟨books lying on the table⟩ ⟨lying in wait for deer⟩ ⟨they lay motionless for a long time⟩. *Lie down* means "to assume a horizontal position" ⟨he lay down for a nap⟩.

liken One thing is usually *likened to* another ⟨I would liken it to a play by Oscar Wilde⟩ ⟨he likened it to putting a fox in charge of the henhouse⟩.

line When *line* is used to mean "put into or assume an orderly linear arrangement," it is usually used with *up* ⟨line the silverware up on the table⟩ ⟨line up the silverware on the table⟩ ⟨cadets lined up for inspection⟩.

listen This verb is often followed by the prepositions *to* or *for* ⟨listening nervously to the gunfire⟩ ⟨listen to this!⟩ ⟨I listened for his footsteps in the hall⟩.

lobby *Lobby* is frequently followed by a *for* phrase ⟨lobbying for their proposals⟩ ⟨lobbied their congressman for more funding⟩.

long The "strong desire" sense of *long* usually takes an infinitive or a *for* phrase ⟨I long to see my old home again⟩ ⟨longing for summer to come⟩.

lurk *Lurk* is often followed by a prepositional phrase indicating position or direction ⟨guerrillas lurking in the mountains⟩ ⟨smugglers lurking along the shore⟩ ⟨the melancholy that lurks in the eyes of beggars⟩.

lust The usual prepositions used with *lust* are *for* and *after* ⟨my tired body lusted for sleep⟩ ⟨lusting after success⟩.

luxuriate *Luxuriate*, meaning "revel," frequently is followed by the preposition *in* ⟨luxuriating in a warm bath⟩.

mar The participle *marred* usually takes the preposition *by* ⟨marred by a few gaffes⟩.

mediate *Mediate* is most often used with *between* ⟨mediating between the two parties⟩ and occasionally *for* ⟨mediated for the combatants⟩.

meditate The usual idiom is *meditate on* ⟨the teacher asked us to meditate on the meaning of the poem⟩.

meet *Meet* is most often followed by a direct object, often with a following phrase indicating place or time ⟨the delegation went to meet them at the station⟩; sometimes *meet* is followed directly by the preposition *with* ⟨the project met with disaster⟩.

merge Intransitive *merge* is often followed by an infinitive ⟨the two banks merged to form one huge institution⟩ or by a prepositional phrase ⟨mountain slopes spread out and merge into the plain⟩ ⟨my company merged with a competitor⟩.

mess Both transitive and intransitive uses of *mess* are frequently followed by the particle *up* ⟨something happens to mess up the girl's life⟩ ⟨magnetic storms mess up radio communications⟩ ⟨I messed up and forgot to give you credit in the report⟩. Intransitive *mess* can also be followed by prepositions *in* or *with* ⟨messing in other people's affairs⟩ ⟨a nervous child messing with her hair⟩.

mix When *mix* is used with a preposition, it is most often *with* ⟨mixes business with pleasure⟩. Less often, *in* or *into* is used ⟨decided not to mix in politics⟩ ⟨mixing some rather silly notions into this ideological brew⟩.

move *Move*, both transitive and intransitive, is frequently followed by a particle or prepositional phrase indicating direction or manner ⟨moved his chair back when she approached⟩ ⟨moved the flag slowly up and down as a signal⟩ ⟨the weary travelers moved slowly along the road⟩ ⟨prices moved steadily upward⟩. In transitive use, the object is also sometimes followed by an infinitive ⟨the logic of the argument moved them to reconsider⟩.

mull The usual idiom is *mull over* ⟨sat with a cup of coffee to mull over the problem⟩.

must As a verbal auxiliary, *must* is followed by an infinitive without *to* ⟨you must hear my side of the story⟩ ⟨told him what he must do⟩ ⟨it must be dinner time⟩.

need *Need* as an auxiliary verb is followed by an infinitive without *to* ⟨no one need know⟩ ⟨all you need do is apply⟩. As a regular verb the following infinitive requires *to* ⟨he needed to contact them⟩. *Need* can also be followed by a gerund ⟨it doesn't need repeating⟩ ⟨this needs saying⟩.

nod *Nod* often is used with the particle *off* when indicating falling asleep ⟨I nodded off several times in class⟩.

object When the verb *object* takes a preposition, it is usually *to*. What follows *to* may be a noun ⟨didn't object to the proposal⟩, pronoun ⟨has never objected to it⟩, or gerund ⟨objected to going⟩. *Object* may also be followed by a clause ⟨objected that the statement was misleading⟩.

open up *Open* is often used with *up* to add a sense of expansion to the meanings ⟨her account of the accident opened up a new line of investigation⟩ ⟨the road opens up ahead⟩.

opt The verb *opt* is usually followed by a *for* phrase or an infinitive ⟨I would opt for a good jazz band⟩ ⟨we opted to go to Europe⟩.

overwhelm When used in the passive voice, *overwhelmed* is most often followed with *by* ⟨the picnic area was overwhelmed by black flies⟩ ⟨a small building overwhelmed by its towering neighbors⟩ and less frequently by *with* ⟨suddenly overwhelmed with requests for interviews⟩.

own up *Own* is used with *up* to mean "to admit or confess fully" ⟨own up to your mistakes⟩.

partake As an intransitive verb, *partake* may be followed by *in* or *of*. *Partake in* implies active participation ⟨partaking in the revelry⟩. *Partake of* usually means "share" or "possess" ⟨the religion partakes of a certain mysticism⟩.

permeate *Permeate* is used with *by* or *with*. When used with *by*, the verb is almost always in the passive ⟨was permeated by the stench⟩; when followed by *with*, the verb may be active ⟨has permeated her work with her sense of guilt⟩ or passive ⟨a room permeated with tobacco smoke⟩.

pervert The verb *pervert* is often used with *into*, *to*, or *by* ⟨perverted the trial into a media show⟩ ⟨perverted it to their own ends⟩ ⟨perverting the play by introducing new scenes⟩.

pique The preposition used with the passive *piqued* is either *at* or *by* ⟨was piqued at them for discounting her claim⟩ ⟨was piqued by this reversal⟩.

plan *Plan* is usually used with the preposition *on* ⟨plan on fewer guests than the number invited⟩. *Plan* is also frequently followed by an infinitive ⟨had planned to complete the project by May⟩.

please The form *pleased* is often followed by an infinitive ⟨was pleased to arrange the meeting⟩ or by a prepositional phrase beginning with *with*, *about*, or *by* ⟨is pleased with the results⟩ ⟨was pleased about the news⟩ ⟨were pleased by these signs of progress⟩.

possess When *possessed* is used as a participle or adjective meaning "controlled," it takes *by* ⟨possessed by personal demons⟩ or less frequently *with* ⟨possessed with the idea⟩. The phrase *to be possessed of* means "to own" or "to have as an attribute" ⟨is possessed of a certain talent⟩.

preside When it takes a preposition, *preside* most commonly uses *over* ⟨presiding over the festivities⟩. Less frequently, it is used with *at* ⟨presiding at the ceremony⟩.

prohibit *Prohibit* is often followed by *from* and a gerund ⟨were prohibited from selling the property⟩. *Prohibit from* can also be followed by a noun ⟨it was not prohibited from use⟩.

provide When *provide* is used intransitively, it most often takes *for* ⟨provide for the common defense⟩. When used transitively to mean "to supply what is needed," a prepositional phrase beginning with *for* or *to* often introduces an indirect object ⟨provided new uniforms for the band⟩ ⟨provides job opportunities to young people⟩.

reckon When used with a preposition, *reckon* is most often followed by *with* and means "to consider" ⟨a force to be reckoned with⟩.

relate The intransitive sense of *relate* that means "to have a relationship" or "respond favorably" is usually used with a *to* phrase ⟨can't relate to that kind of music⟩.

rob When *rob* takes a preposition, it is usually *of* ⟨robbed them of their dignity⟩, though occasionally it can take *from* ⟨robs intensity from the performance⟩.

sate, satiate Both *sate* and *satiate*, when used as participles, are followed by *with* ⟨readers were sated with sensationalism⟩ ⟨satiated with others' opinions⟩.

saturate When *saturate* is followed by a preposition, the usual choice is *with* ⟨contents saturated with moisture⟩; *by* and *in* are also sometimes used ⟨kids saturated by television advertising⟩ ⟨a room saturated in sunlight⟩. When the object of *saturate* is a reflexive pronoun, the preposition is *in* ⟨saturated himself in the literature of the era⟩.

scare When used with a preposition, *scared* is most often followed by *of*, *about*, *at*, and *by* ⟨scared of snakes⟩ ⟨scared about the change⟩ ⟨scared at the prospect⟩ ⟨scared by the news⟩. It may also take an infinitive ⟨scared to go out⟩.

seek The verb *seek* is frequently used with *after* or *for*. *After* occurs most often with the participle *sought* in the passive voice ⟨the film star was much sought after⟩, but active use also occurs ⟨we should not seek after the cause⟩. *For* is common with all tenses and voices ⟨seeking for clues⟩ ⟨these results were not sought for⟩. *Seek* is also commonly followed by an infinitive ⟨seeking to place him at the scene⟩.

smell *Smell* is frequently followed by a prepositional phrase introduced by *of* ⟨the place smells of money and power⟩.

strive *Strive* is most often followed by an infinitive ⟨striving to keep a balance⟩. It is also used with the preposition *for* ⟨strove for reform⟩.

suffer When followed by a preposition, *suffer* almost always takes *from* ⟨suffers from rheumatism⟩.

surprised The prepositions following the passive form of *surprise* are *at* and *by*. *By* is the choice when *surprise* means "to take unawares" ⟨I was surprised by the force of the wind⟩. Both *at* and *by* occur when *surprise* means "to amaze" ⟨we were surprised at [by] the announcement⟩.

tamper *Tamper* with is the usual idiom ⟨accused of tampering with the witness⟩ ⟨don't tamper with that switch!⟩.

tangle Prepositions following the passive *tangle* typically are *in* and *by* ⟨hopelessly tangled in controversy⟩ ⟨hair tangled by the breeze⟩.

taper off *Taper*, meaning "diminish," is frequently followed by the particle *off* ⟨the magazine's circulation began to taper off⟩ ⟨I will taper off activity and work less⟩.

tend The intransitive *tend*, meaning "take care of," is followed by the preposition *to* ⟨tend to matters at hand⟩.

testify *Testify* typically takes a prepositional phrase introduced by *for*, *against*, or *to* ⟨testify for the defendant⟩ ⟨had been testifying against abuses of power⟩ ⟨I can testify to the importance of this program⟩.

think *Think* is usually followed by a clause ⟨we thought [that] it was a good idea⟩ or by the prepositions *about* or *of* ⟨want to think about it before deciding⟩ ⟨could not think of a reason to leave⟩ ⟨thought of himself as an artist⟩ ⟨We thought well of him⟩. Sometimes *think* is used with particles such as *over* or *through* ⟨think over [through] the situation⟩ ⟨think the situation over [through]⟩.

thirst *Thirst* usually takes *for* or *after* to head a phrase ⟨thirst for water⟩ ⟨thirsting for adventure⟩ ⟨thirsting after every new video game⟩.

threaten *Threaten* is typically followed by an infinitive ⟨he threatened to sell the car⟩ or, with a direct object, by a prepositional phrase using *with* ⟨threatened them with punishment⟩.

thrive When *thrive* is followed by a prepositional phrase, the preposition is usually *on* ⟨he thrives on competition⟩.

tide over *Tide*, in the sense of "carry through," is usually followed by the particle *over* ⟨enough food to tide us over until spring⟩.

tinker *Tinker* is typically followed by a *with* phrase ⟨spend my spare time tinkering with old machines⟩.

tire When *tire* is followed by a preposition, it is usually *of* ⟨never tires of reading the Bible⟩. Sometimes, *tire* is followed by the particle *out* ⟨I was tired out after that climb⟩ ⟨The climb tired me out⟩.

toy *Toy* is frequently used with a *with* phrase ⟨toying with great philosophical issues⟩ ⟨don't toy with my emotions⟩.

trust The prepositions *in* and *to* both occur after the verb *trust* ⟨trust in your intuition⟩ ⟨trust to luck⟩.

urge When *urge* is followed by a complement, it is usually an infinitive ⟨I urge you to vote⟩ or a clause ⟨urged that they reconsider their position⟩.

verge *On* is the preposition used with *verge* ⟨an achievement that verged on greatness⟩ ⟨your courage verges on foolhardiness⟩.

vie *Vie* is typically used with the prepositions *with* and *for* in this kind of context: competitors vie *with* each other *for* a prize.

visit When *visit* is followed by a preposition, it is usually *with*, whether indicating the object of the visit ⟨visited with a sick friend⟩ or the source ⟨visited with plagues⟩. Sometimes a *by* phrase will be used in the passive ⟨visited by the neighbors⟩.

volunteer When *volunteer* is intransitive, it takes an infinitive ⟨volunteered to serve on the committee⟩ or a *for* phrase ⟨volunteered for service in the army⟩.

vote *Vote* most often takes an infinitive ⟨voted to remove them from office⟩ or a *for* phrase ⟨voted for the incumbent⟩; sometimes it takes a clause ⟨I vote [that] we table the motion⟩.

vouch *Vouch for* something is the usual idiom ⟨I can vouch for the truth of it⟩.

wade When followed by a prepositional phrase, *wade* usually takes *through* or *into* ⟨waded through the snow⟩ ⟨wading through piles of documents⟩ ⟨waded into the brawl⟩. When referring to water, *wade* is often followed by the particle *in* ⟨the children waded in up to their waists⟩.

wait *Wait* is often used with particles *up* and *around* ⟨children waiting up for Santa Claus⟩ ⟨we waited around until it was too late for the movie⟩. Referring to remaining in readiness, *wait* is often followed by a prepositional phrase indicating the object of the waiting or the duration ⟨we were waiting for hours⟩ ⟨are you waiting for Mr. Smith?⟩ ⟨we waited until 7 o'clock⟩ ⟨we waited into the night for word from the hospital⟩. When it refers to serving, *wait* is frequently followed by *on* ⟨waiting on tables⟩ ⟨waiting on customers⟩.

wake When arousing from sleep, *wake* is frequently followed by the particle *up* ⟨I woke up refreshed after the nap⟩ ⟨it was difficult to wake you up⟩.

wander Intransitive *wander* is frequently followed by particles *around*, *about*, or *off* ⟨would like to wander about the world⟩ ⟨wandering around in a daze⟩ ⟨my dog wandered off⟩. Prepositional phrases that follow often indicate place or direction ⟨a crowd wandering on a village green⟩ ⟨they wandering to the south⟩ or point of departure ⟨I wandered from a trail⟩.

want *Want* in the sense of "feeling the need of" often takes an infinitive ⟨wanting to rise in the world⟩ ⟨want to be home for the holidays⟩. Sometimes the object of desire is expressed in a prepositional phrase ⟨wants for their happiness⟩.

wash *Wash*, in transitive and intransitive senses, is often followed by a prepositional phrase indicating focus or manner of the washing ⟨wash (the mud) off the car⟩ or the method ⟨wash (the wound) with soap and water⟩. Intransitive *wash* is often followed by the particle *up* ⟨wash up before dinner⟩.

watch *Watch* is frequently followed by a prepositional phrase indicating the object of the watching ⟨watched for the signal⟩ or the one watching ⟨being watched by the police⟩. In the sense of being alert for danger, *watch* often takes the particle *out* ⟨Watch out!⟩; when conveying the notion of care for another, the particle is often *over* ⟨watches over the children⟩.

while The verb *while* is usually used with the particle *away* ⟨whiled away an hour waiting for the rain to stop⟩.

wish *Wish* is frequently followed by a clause ⟨I wish [that] someone would bring back the 5-cent cup of coffee⟩, but typically the object of desire is expressed in a prepositional phrase ⟨wishing for the courage to stand up to a bully⟩. Often *wish* is followed by an infinitive ⟨the point I wish to make⟩; and sometimes *wish* is used humorously or sarcastically without an object ⟨Get an A in math? You wish!⟩.

wonder *Wonder* is frequently followed by clauses ⟨I wonder if he is all right⟩ ⟨I wonder whether it will rain today⟩. Typical prepositions used with *wonder* are *at* and *about* ⟨couldn't help wondering at the size of the servings⟩ ⟨I wonder about the meaning of that word⟩.

worry The most common preposition used with *worry* is *about*, followed by a noun or gerund phrase ⟨I'll let you worry about the details⟩ ⟨began to worry about venturing so far from home⟩.

wrestle *With* is used most often to introduce a prepositional phrase after *wrestle* ⟨wrestled all his life with a feeling of insecurity⟩ ⟨the movers wrestled with our heavy boxes⟩ ⟨I will wrestle with the problem⟩.

yank The verb *yank* is frequently followed by prepositional phrases introduced by *at* or *on* ⟨yanked at the door to open it⟩ ⟨the fish yanked on the line⟩.

yearn People who yearn usually yearn *for* something ⟨yearning for love⟩. Less often, the preposition following *yearn* is *after* ⟨yearns after her lost childhood⟩.

yell Typical prepositional phrases following *yell* are introduced by *with*, *for*, or *to* ⟨the boys yelled with delight⟩ ⟨heard him yell for help⟩ ⟨yelled to them to stop⟩.

yield *Yield*, in the sense of "give way," is often used with *to* ⟨he yielded to pressure and changed his vote⟩.

zero The verb *zero* is often followed by the particle *in* to convey the sense "to focus one's aim" ⟨zeroed in on the target⟩ ⟨investigators zeroing in on the problem⟩.

zoom In the sense "to focus with a variable-focus lens," *zoom* is often used with the particles *in* or *out* ⟨zoomed in on her hands⟩ ⟨I'll zoom out for a wider view⟩.

IRREGULAR ENGLISH VERBS

Regular English verbs, like *call* or *trust*, have a predictable pattern in the past tense and past participle forms (referred to as the principal parts). They form the past and past participle by the addition of *-ed* to the infinitive form. Sometimes the ending results in an added syllable (*trusted* \'trəst-əd\) and sometimes not (*called* \'kȯld\).

Verbs are also considered regular if the final consonant is doubled by the addition of the *-ed* (*abet, abetted, abetted*) or if the final *-e* is dropped in adding the *-ed* ending (*die, died, died*).

Verbs are irregular if the past or past participle have a different pattern from the simple addition of *-ed* (*swim, swam, swum*) or if either or both forms have a variant form in addition to the *-ed*, (*saw, sawed, sawed* or *sawn*). Often this variant form is one in which the *-ed* has been changed to *-t*—which represents a typical pronunciation—(*burn, burned* or *burnt*).

Below is a list of irregular English verbs, showing the past tense and past participle forms, along with any variant forms.

INFINITIVE FORM	PAST TENSE	PAST PARTICIPLE
arise	arose	arisen
awake	awoke *also* awaked	awoken *or* awaked *also* awoke
be	was, were	been
bear	bore	borne *also* born
beat	beat	beaten *or* beat
become	became	become
befall	befell	befallen
begin	began	begun
behold	beheld	beheld
bend	bent	bent
beseech	besought *or* beseeched	besought *or* beseeched
beset	beset	beset
bet	bet *also* betted	bet *also* betted
bid	bade *or* bid	bidden *or* bid *also* bade
bind	bound	bound
bite	bit	bitten *also* bit
bleed	bled	bled
blow	blew	blown
break	broke	broken
breed	bred	bred
bring	brought	brought
build	built	built
burn	burned *or* burnt	burned *or* burnt
burst	burst *also* bursted	burst *also* bursted
buy	bought	bought
can (auxiliary verb)	could	—
cast	cast	cast
catch	caught	caught
choose	chose	chosen
cling	clung	clung
come	came	come
cost	cost	cost

INFINITIVE FORM	PAST TENSE	PAST PARTICIPLE
creep	crept	crept
cut	cut	cut
deal	dealt	dealt
dig	dug	dug
do	did	done
draw	drew	drawn
dream	dreamed *or* dreamt	dreamed *or* dreamt
drink	drank	drunk *or* drank
drive	drove	driven
dwell	dwelt *or* dwelled	dwelt *or* dwelled
eat	ate	eaten
fall	fell	fallen
feed	fed	fed
feel	felt	felt
fight	fought	fought
find	found	found
flee	fled	fled
fling	flung	flung
fly	flew	flown
forbid	forbade *also* forbad	forbidden
forecast	forecast *also* forecasted	forecast *also* forecasted
forego	forewent	foregone
foresee	foresaw	foreseen
foretell	foretold	foretold
forget	forgot	forgotten *or* forgot
forgive	forgave	forgiven
forsake	forsook	forsaken
freeze	froze	frozen
get	got	got *or* gotten
give	gave	given
go	went	gone
grind	ground	ground
grow	grew	grown
hang	hung *also* hanged	hung *also* hanged
have	had	had
hear	heard	heard
hide	hid	hidden *or* hid
hit	hit	hit
hold	held	held
hurt	hurt	hurt
keep	kept	kept
kneel	knelt *or* kneeled	knelt *or* kneeled
know	knew	known
lay	laid	laid
lead	led	led
lean	leaned *also* leant	leaned
leap	leapt *or* leaped	leapt *or* leaped
leave	left	left

INFINITIVE FORM	PAST TENSE	PAST PARTICIPLE
lend	lent	lent
let	let	let
lie (to recline)	lay	lain
light	lit	lit
	or lighted	*or* lighted
lose	lost	lost
make	made	made
may	might	—
mean	meant	meant
meet	met	met
mow	mowed	mowed
		or mown
pay	paid	paid
put	put	put
quit	quit	quit
	also quitted	*also* quitted
read	read	read
rend	rent	rent
rid	rid	rid
	also ridded	*also* ridded
ride	rode	ridden
ring (to sound)	rang	rung
rise	rose	risen
run	ran	run
saw	sawed	sawed
		or sawn
say	said	said
see	saw	seen
seek	sought	sought
sell	sold	sold
send	sent	sent
set	set	set
shake	shook	shaken
shall (auxiliary verb)	should	—
shear	sheared	sheared
		or shorn
shed	shed	shed
shine	shone	shone
	or shined	*or* shined
shoot	shot	shot
show	showed	shown
		or showed
shrink	shrank	shrunk
	or shrunk	*or* shrunken
shut	shut	shut
sing	sang	sung
	or sung	
sink	sank	sunk
	or sunk	
sit	sat	sat
slay	slew	slain
sleep	slept	slept
slide	slid	slid
sling	slung	slung
smell	smelled	smelled
	or smelt	*or* smelt
sow	sowed	sown
		or sowed
speak	spoke	spoken

INFINITIVE FORM	PAST TENSE	PAST PARTICIPLE
speed	sped *or* speeded	sped *or* speeded
spell	spelled	spelled
spend	spent	spent
spill	spilled *also* spilt	spilled *also* spilt
spin	spun	spun
spit (to eject saliva)	spit *or* spat	spit *or* spat
split	split	split
spoil	spoiled *or* spoilt	spoiled *or* spoilt
spread	spread	spread
spring	sprang *or* sprung	sprung
stand	stood	stood
steal	stole	stolen
stick	stuck	stuck
sting	stung	stung
stink	stank *or* stunk	stunk
stride	strode	stridden
strike	struck	struck *also* stricken
swear	swore	sworn
sweep	swept	swept
swell	swelled	swelled *or* swollen
swim	swam	swum
swing	swung	swung
take	took	taken
teach	taught	taught
tear (to rip)	tore	torn
tell	told	told
think	thought	thought
throw	threw	thrown
thrust	thrust	thrust
tread	trod	trodden *or* trod
wake	woke *also* waked	woken *also* waked *or* woke
waylay	waylaid	waylaid
wear	wore	worn
weave	wove *or* weaved	woven *or* weaved
wed	wedded *also* wed	wedded *also* wed
weep	wept	wept
will (auxiliary verb)	would	—
win	won	won
wind (to encircle)	wound *also* winded	wound *also* winded
withdraw	withdrew	withdrawn
withhold	withheld	withheld
withstand	withstood	withstood
wring	wrung	wrung
write	wrote	written *also* writ

BASIC ENGLISH GRAMMAR

The essence of the English language is the sentence. A sentence is a grammatically self-contained group of words that expresses a statement, a question, a command, a wish, or an exclamation. It is composed of a *subject*, about which something is said, and a *predicate*, which expresses what is said about the subject. The subject can be a single noun, a noun phrase, such as *"the strong wind,"* or a noun clause, such as *"what he decides* is important to all of us." The predicate can be a single verb, a verb phrase, such as *"will be going,"* a verb and all its modifiers, such as *"will be going as soon as the bus arrives,"* or a verb and its complements, such as *"gave his client the bad news."*

In English, word order is important. The subject usually comes first, but not necessarily:

An amusement park is across the river.
Across the river is *an amusement park*.
Is *an amusement park* across the river?

The grammar of English is concerned with the structure of these elements that make up a sentence. Every word in a sentence can be classified as a particular part of speech (*noun, verb, adjective,* etc.), according to its function in the sentence. The major parts of speech are briefly discussed in the following guide to basic English grammar.

THE ADJECTIVE

The adjective gives information about a noun or pronoun, such as what kind

the *black* cat
a *joyful* occasion

or which one

a *first* draft
that suggestion

or how many

ten players
few new ideas.

The adjective usually precedes the noun it modifies, but some adjectives can also follow certain verbs:

the house is *white* (→ *white* house)
the speeches seemed *long* (→ *long* speeches)
the chair felt *comfortable* (→ *comfortable* chair)
the tree grew *tall* (→ *tall* tree)

A few adjectives will follow their nouns, but usually only in set phrases:

court-martial
secretary-general

POSITIVE, COMPARATIVE, AND SUPERLATIVE DEGREES OF ADJECTIVES

The positive degree is the basic form of the adjective. It gives basic information about the noun without reference to anything else (a *white* house). The comparative degree relates a noun to another—as having more or less of some quality (this house is *whiter* than that); the superlative degree relates the noun to all others of its class (this is the *whitest* house in the neighborhood).

When the adjective consists of a single syllable, the suffix *-er* is added to form the comparative degree, and the suffix *-est* is added to form the superlative degree. When the adjective consists of two syllables, the suffixes are often used to form the comparative (as *gentler*) and superlative (as *gentlest*), but the adverbs *more/less* can also be used to form the comparative (as *more skillful* and *less skillful*), and likewise, the adverbs *most/least* can be used to form the superlative (as *most skillful* and *least skillful*). For adjectives of more than two syllables, the adverbs are usually used to form the comparative and superlative forms (as *more fortunate, most fortunate*).

There are a few adjectives that have unique comparative and superlative forms:

Positive	Comparative	Superlative
good	better	best
bad	worse	worst
some	more	most
little (amount)	less	least
but		
little (size)	littler	littlest

There are a few adjectives that have no comparative or superlative forms:

an *utter* failure
the *principal* objections

DEMONSTRATIVE ADJECTIVES

The demonstrative adjectives *this* and *that* are used to point out the one person or thing referred to (as "not *this* coat but *that* one"). The plural forms are *these* and *those*, respectively.

These books are mine and *those* books are yours.

DESCRIPTIVE ADJECTIVES

A descriptive adjective describes or indicates a quality, type, or condition:

a *fascinating* conversation
a *positive* attitude
a *fast* computer

INDEFINITE ADJECTIVES

An indefinite adjective is used to designate unspecified person(s) or thing(s):

some children
other projects
any book

INTERROGATIVE ADJECTIVES

An interrogative adjective is used to form a question:

Whose office is this?
Which book do you want?

THE NOUN USED AS ADJECTIVE

A noun sometimes serves to modify another noun and thus functions as an adjective:

the *Vietnam* War
word processing

POSSESSIVE ADJECTIVES

The possessive form of a personal pronoun is called a *possessive adjective*. Following is a list of possessive adjectives and a few examples of how they are used:

Singular	Plural
my	our
your	your
his/her/its	their

Where's *my* magazine?
Your cab is here.
They can read *his* story.
It was *her* idea.
The box and *its* contents were inspected.
She's *our* mother.
Your photos are ready.
We paid for *their* tickets.

PREDICATE ADJECTIVES

A predicate adjective modifies the subject of a linking verb, such as *be*, *become*, *feel*, *taste*, *smell*, or *seem*:

He is *lucky*.
She became *angry*.
They are *happy* with the outcome.
The milk smells *bad*.
The student seems *lonely*.

PROPER ADJECTIVES

A proper adjective is derived from a proper noun and is capitalized:

Victorian furniture
a *Chinese* custom
a *Shakespearean* scholar

THE ADVERB

Adverbs, whether single words or phrases, usually give information about the verbs, such as *when*

We arrived *yesterday*
He woke up *late*

or *where*

I found them *at the restaurant*
He spent time *in [the] hospital*

or *how*

They arose *quickly*
She worked *hard*

Most single-word adverbs end in *-ly* and are formed by adding the suffix *-ly* to an adjective:

mad → madly
wonderful → wonderfully

When the adjective ends in *-y*, the adverb is formed by changing *-y* to *-i* and adding the suffix *-ly*:

happy → happily
dainty → daintily

When the adjective ends in *-ic*, the adverb is formed by adding the suffix *-ally*:

basic → basically
numeric → numerically

When an adjective ends in *-ly*, the adverb retains the same spelling:

a *daily* routine (adjective)
she calls her mother *daily* (adverb)
an *early* meeting (adjective)
the show started *early* (adverb)

Also, there are adverbs that do not end in *-ly*, for example:

again	*now*	*soon*
too	*there*	*how*

POSITIVE, COMPARATIVE, AND SUPERLATIVE DEGREES OF ADVERBS

Adverbs, like adjectives, can have three degrees of comparison: the *positive* form exists without reference to anything else; the *comparative* degree relates to another—as being more or less of the adverb quality; and *superlative* relates to all members of a class. As a general rule, a single-syllable adverb ends in *-er* when it is comparative (as *faster*) and in *-est* when it is superlative (as *fastest*). For adverbs of three or more syllables, the comparative and superlative degrees are formed by using the adverbs *more/less* and *most/least*. The comparative and superlative degrees of an adverb of two syllables are formed by following either one of these methods:

Positive	Comparative	Superlative
early	earlier	earliest
easy	easier	easiest
nearly	more nearly	most nearly
quickly	more quickly	most quickly
satisfactorily	less satisfactorily	least satisfactorily

Some adverbs, such as *only*, *quite*, and *very*, have no comparative or superlative forms.

INTENSIVE ADVERBS

Intensive adverbs, such as *just* and *only*, are usually used only to emphasize other words. The emphasis varies according to the placement of the adverb within the sentence:

He *just* nodded to me as he passed.
He nodded to me *just* as he passed.
I *only* wanted to speak with you.
I wanted to speak *only* with you.

INTERROGATIVE ADVERBS

Interrogative adverbs, such as *when*, *where*, and *why*, are used chiefly to introduce questions:

When will he return?
Where is the remote control?
Why did you hide it?

THE ARTICLE

Articles, sometimes called "determiners," are elements of a noun phrase that indicate whether the noun is "definite," that is, a specific individual, or "indefinite," that is, very general in nature.

THE DEFINITE ARTICLE

There is only one form of the definite article: *the*.

The boys were expelled.
It was *the* best movie I have seen.

THE INDEFINITE ARTICLE

The indefinite article *a* is used with every noun or abbreviation beginning with either a consonant or the sound of a consonant:

a door	*a* union	*a* one-way street
a B.A. degree	*a* hat	*a* U.S. Senator

The indefinite article *an* is used with every noun or abbreviation that begins with a vowel sound, whether or not the first letter of the noun or abbreviation is a vowel or consonant:

an icicle	*an* MP
an honor	*an* FAQ

When the first syllable of a noun is not stressed or has only a slight stress, the article *a* is frequently used:

   a historian   *a* heroic attempt   *a* hilarious performance

However, the article *an* is sometimes used in these cases:

   an historian   *an* heroic attempt   *an* hilarious performance

Both forms are acceptable.

THE CONJUNCTION

There are three main types of conjunctions: *coordinating conjunctions*, *correlative conjunctions*, and *subordinating conjunctions*.

COORDINATING CONJUNCTIONS

Coordinating conjunctions, such as *and*, *but*, *for*, *or*, *nor*, *so*, and *yet*, are used to connect grammatical elements of the same type. These elements may be words, phrases, clauses, or complete sentences. Coordinating conjunctions are used to connect similar elements, to make exclusions or contrasts, to indicate an alternative, to indicate a cause, or to specify a result:

connecting similar elements:	She ordered pencils, pens, *and* erasers.
exclusion or contrast:	He is a brilliant *but* arrogant man.
	They offered a promising plan, *but* it had not yet been tested.
alternative:	She can wait here *or* go on ahead.
cause:	The report is useless, *for* its information is no longer current.
result:	His diction is excellent, *so* every word is clear.

CORRELATIVE CONJUNCTIONS

Correlative conjunctions are used in groups of two to connect choices or elements of the same grammatical type:

   Both Rita *and* Jane attended the conference.
   Either you go *or* you stay.
   He had *neither* looks *nor* wit.

SUBORDINATING CONJUNCTIONS

Subordinating conjunctions are used to connect a subordinate clause to an independent clause. These conjunctions express cause, condition or concession, manner, intention or result, time, place, or circumstance, as well as a possibility.

cause:	*Because* she learns quickly, she is doing well in her new job.
condition or concession:	Don't call *unless* you are coming.
manner:	We'll do it *however* you tell us.
intention or result:	They burned all the bridges *so* that the enemy could not use them.
time:	She kept the meeting to a minimum *when* she could.
place:	*Wherever* he goes, he is welcomed with open arms.

THE NOUN

BASIC USES

The noun may be a single word or a phrase (noun phrase). The noun phrase may consist of an article and/or adjectives and/or prepositional phrases. The noun can function as subject of a sentence, object of a verb, object of a preposition, predicate nominative, complement of an object, in apposition, and in direct discourse:

subject:	*The office* was quiet.
	The house with the green shutters was for sale.
direct object of a verb:	He locked *the office*.
indirect object of a verb:	He gave *his client* the papers.
object of a preposition:	The business was in *bankruptcy*.
	The file is in *the office*.
predicate nominative:	Ms. Adams is *the managing partner*.
complement of an object:	They made Ms. Adams *managing partner*.
in apposition:	Ms. Adams, *the managing partner*, wrote that memo.
in direct discourse:	*Ms. Adams*, may I present Mr. Wilson.

Nouns are often classified as to whether they are proper nouns—capitalized—(*Eiffel Tower*, *White House*) or common nouns (*tower*, *house*), abstract nouns (*honor*, *love*) or concrete nouns (*desk*, *flower*) or collective nouns (*team*, *government*). American English typically uses a singular verb with a collective noun (the team *is*), while British English typically uses a plural verb (the government *are*).

Most nouns are neuter, showing no distinction as to whether having a masculine or feminine reference. However, a few nouns ending in -*ess* (as *empress*, *hostess*) are feminine in gender, and some others have a specific gender. For example: *husband*, *wife*, *father*, *mother*, *brother*, *sister*. The names of certain animals also have a specific gender, for example, *bull/cow*, *stag/doe*. When it is necessary to specify the gender of a neuter noun, the noun is usually modified with words like *male*, *female*, *man*, *woman* (a *male* parrot, *women* painters).

THE NOUN AS ADJECTIVE

The noun has the function of an adjective when it precedes another noun:

olive oil	*business* management
emergency room	*dog* house

THE FORMATION OF THE PLURAL

The plural of most nouns is formed by adding the suffix -*s* to the singular noun:

book → *books*   *cat* → *cats*

When the singular noun ends in -*s*, -*x*, -*z*, -*ch*, or -*sh*, the suffix -*es* is added to the singular:

cross → *crosses*   *fox* → *foxes*
witch → *witches*   *wish* → *wishes*

For a singular noun ending in -*z*, the last letter is doubled before adding the suffix -*es*:

whiz → *whizzes*   *quiz* → *quizzes*

For a singular noun ending in -*y* preceded by a consonant, the -*y* changes to -*i* and the suffix -*es* is added:

fairy → *fairies*   *pony* → *ponies*   *guppy* → *guppies*

For a singular noun ending in -*y* preceded by a vowel, the -*y* usually does not change when the suffix -*s* is added:

boy → *boys*   *attorney* → *attorneys*

Some words that end in -*uy* sometimes change the -*y* to -*i*:

guy → *guys*   *soliloquy* → *soliloquies*

There are a few nouns that do not always change in the plural:

fish → *fish* (or *fishes* when referring to more than one species)
caribou → *caribou* (sometimes *caribous*)
moose → *moose*

There are also some nouns that have a unique plural:

foot → *feet*   *mouse* → *mice*   *knife* → *knives*

THE POSSESSIVE CASE

The possessive case of most singular nouns is formed by adding an apostrophe followed by an *-s*:

Jackie's passport   This hat is *Billy's*

For plural nouns ending in *-s*, only the apostrophe is added:

the *neighbors'* dog   both *boys'* behavior

Proper nouns that end in *-s* often present a special case:

Mr. Douglas's car   *Socrates'* teachings

THE PREPOSITION

The preposition is used with an object (a noun, pronoun, or the equivalent of a noun) to form a phrase that functions generally as an adjective or an adverb.

The man *in the car* is his father. (adjective)
The river winds *through the valley*. (adverb)
I like *to watch sports*. (infinitive phrase used as a noun)

There are two types of prepositions: the simple preposition, which consists of a single word (for example, *against, from, near, of, on, out, in*) and the compound preposition, which consists of more than one element (for example, *according to, on account of, because of, in spite of*).

THE CONJUNCTION VS.
THE PREPOSITION

The words *after*, *before*, *but*, *for*, and *since* can be used as prepositions or conjunctions. Their part of speech is determined by their function in the sentence. Conjunctions are usually used to connect two elements of the same grammatical type, while prepositions are followed by an object to form a phrase.

conjunction:	The playful *but* thoughtful youngsters did well in school.
	(*but* connects two adjectives)
preposition:	I was left with nothing *but* hope.
	(*but* followed by an object)
conjunction:	The device conserves fuel, *for* it is battery-powered.
	(*for* connects two clauses)
preposition:	The device conserves fuel *for* better mileage.
	(*for* followed by an object)

PLACE IN THE SENTENCE

A preposition comes in front of a noun or a pronoun (*under* the desk, *beside* them), after an adjective (antagonistic *to*, insufficient *for*, symbolic *of*), or after a verb as a particle (take *over*, put *on*, come *across*). The preposition may end a sentence, especially if it is a verb particle.

What does this all *add up to*?
After Amy left, Sandra *took over*.

THE PRONOUN

Pronouns are often said to stand in place of the noun or noun phrase in a sentence. Usually, the pronoun stands for something previously specified or generally understood.

Pronouns have the following characteristics: *case* (nominative, possessive, or objective); *number* (singular or plural); *person* (first, second, or third); and *gender* (masculine, feminine, or neuter). Pronouns can be classed in seven main categories, each having a specific function.

DEMONSTRATIVE PRONOUNS

The words *this, that, these*, and *those* are considered as pronouns when they function as nouns. (They are classed as demonstrative adjectives when they modify a noun.) The demonstrative pronoun designates a person or thing in order to distinguish it from another person or thing:

This is the one I want.
I was happy about ***that***.
These are the best designs.
I picked ***those*** as the prettiest flowers.

The demonstrative pronoun also serves to distinguish a person or thing nearby from one that is farther away (*this* is my desk; *that* is yours).

INDEFINITE PRONOUNS

Indefinite pronouns are used to designate a person or thing of which the identity is unknown or is not immediately evident. The indefinite pronouns include the following:

all	either	none	another	everybody	no one
any	everyone	one	anybody	everything	other(s)
anyone	few	several	anything	many	some
both	much	somebody	each	neither	someone
each one	nobody	something			

The indefinite pronoun and the verb that follows it should agree in number. The following pronouns are used with a singular verb: *another, anything, each one, everything, much, nobody, no one, other, someone, something*:

> ***Much*** is being done.   ***No one*** wants to go.

The indefinite pronouns *both, few, many,* and *several* are used with plural verbs:

> ***Many*** are called; ***few*** are chosen.

Certain pronouns, such as *all, any, none,* and *some,* sometimes present difficulties, since they can be used with a singular or a plural verb. As a general rule, a pronoun that is used with a noun that cannot be counted requires a singular verb, while a pronoun that is used with a noun that can be counted requires a plural verb.

with an uncountable noun: All of the property is affected.
None of the soup was spilled.
Some of the money was spent.
with a countable noun: All of my shoes are black.
None of the clerks were available.
Some of your friends were here.

INTERROGATIVE PRONOUNS

The interrogative pronouns *what, which, who, whom,* and *whose,* as well as those bound with the word *-ever* (*whatever, whichever,* etc.) are used to introduce a direct or an indirect question:

Who is she?   He asked me ***who*** she was.
Whoever can that be?   We wondered ***whoever*** that could be.

PERSONAL PRONOUNS

The personal pronoun reflects the person, number, and gender of the being or the thing it represents. Each category is made up of distinct personal pronouns:

Person		Nominative	Possessive	Objective
First	(sing.)	I	my, mine	me
	(pl.)	we	our, ours	us
Second	(sing.)	you	your, yours	you
	(pl.)	you	your, yours	you
Third	(sing.)	he	his	him
		she	her, hers	her
		it	its	it
	(pl.)	they	their, theirs	them

RECIPROCAL PRONOUNS

The reciprocal pronouns *each other* and *one another* indicate a mutual action or relationship:

> Jim and Andy saw *each other* at the party.
> They do not quarrel with *one another*.

The reciprocal pronoun is also used as a possessive:

> The two companies depend on *each other's* success.
> The members enjoyed *one another's* company.

REFLEXIVE PRONOUNS

Reflexive pronouns are formed from the personal pronouns *him, her, it, my, our, them*, and *your*, to which the combining form *-self* or *-selves* is added. The reflexive pronoun is usually used to express a reflexive action or to emphasize the subject of a sentence, clause, or phrase:

> She dressed *herself*.
> He asked *himself* if it was worth it.
> I *myself* am not involved.
> They wanted to do it *themselves*.

RELATIVE PRONOUNS

The relative pronouns are *who, whom, whose, which*, and *that*, as well as the compounds formed by adding the ending *-ever*. These pronouns are used to introduce subordinate clauses that function as a noun or an adjective.

> a man *who* sought success
> a woman *whom* we can trust
> an author *whose* first novel was a success
> a move *which* was unforeseen
> a boy *that* behaves well
> give it to *whomever* you wish
> *whoever* thought of it
> pick *whichever* you want

In certain cases the relative pronoun may be omitted:

> The man [*whom*] I was talking to is the senator.

THE VERB

Verbs have essentially three classes: ordinary verbs of action, such as *go*, auxiliary verbs, like *can* and *shall*, and fundamental verbs like *be, have*, and *do*, which can function as both ordinary verbs and as auxiliaries.

The verb has the following characteristics: *inflection* (for example, helps, helping, helped), *person* (first, second, third), *number* (singular, plural), *tense* (present, past, future), *aspect* (categories of time other than the simple tenses of present, past, future), *voice* (active, passive), and *mood* (indicative, subjunctive, and imperative).

INFLECTION

Regular verbs have three inflections that are formed by adding the suffixes *-s* or *-es*, *-ed*, and *-ing* (for example, *asks, asked, asking*) Most of the irregular verbs have four inflections (for example, *sees, saw, seen, seeing*). The verb *be* has seven inflections: *is, am, are, was, were, being, been*).

Verbs ending in silent *-e* in general keep the *-e* when a consonantal suffix (such as *-s*) is added to the word, but the *-e* is dropped when the suffix begins with a vowel (such as *-ed, -ing*):

> *arrange; arranges; arranged; arranging*
> *hope; hopes; hoped; hoping*

However, certain verbs keep the *-e* in order to avoid confusion with another verb:

> *dye* (color); *dyes*; *dyed*; *dyeing*
> *but*
> *die* (cease to live); *dies*; *died*; *dying*
> *singe* (burn); *singes*; *singed*; *singeing*
> *but*
> *sing* (produce music); *sings*; *sang*; *singing*

If a single-syllable verb ends in a single consonant preceded by a single vowel, the final consonant is often doubled before the addition of *-ed* or *-ing*:

> *brag; brags; bragged; bragging*
> *grip; grips; gripped; gripping*

When a multi-syllable verb ends in the same way, and the last syllable is stressed, the final consonant is also doubled:

> *commit; commits; committed; committing*
> *occur; occurs; occurred; occurring*

It frequently happens that a verb ending in *-y* preceded by a consonant changes *-y* to *-i*, except when the suffix is *-ing*:

> *carry; carries; carried; carrying*
> *study; studies; studied; studying*

When a verb ends in *-c*, a *-k* is added to inflections if the suffix begins with *-e* or *-i*:

> *mimic; mimics; mimicked; mimicking*
> *traffic; traffics; trafficked; trafficking*

TENSE AND ASPECT

The present and past tenses are generally formed as a single word:

> I *do*, I *did*
> we *write*, we *wrote*

The future tense is conjugated with the auxiliary verbs *shall* or *will* and the present or progressive forms:

> I *shall do* it.
> We *will come* tomorrow.
> I *shall be leaving* tomorrow.

Aspect concerns the tense of the verb other than the present, the past, or the future. Aspect has four forms: the *progressive*, the *present perfect*, the *past perfect*, and the *future perfect*.

The *progressive* is used to express an ongoing action that takes place in the present, past, or future:

> He *is reading* the paper at the moment.
> I *was studying* for the test.
> I *will be going* to India.

The *present perfect* tense is used to express an action done in the past but which may be continuing in the present, or to express an action that occurred at an indefinite moment in the past. It is conjugated with the auxiliary verbs *has* or *have* and the past participle:

> She *has written* many books.
> They *have regretted* their mistake.

The *past perfect* expresses a completed action that occurred before another action in the past. It is conjugated with the auxiliary verb *had* and the past participle:

> She *had written* several books previously.
> We *had left* the house before they arrived.

The *future perfect* tense indicates that a future action will take place before another action or occurrence still to come. It is conjugated with the auxiliary verbs *will* or *shall* and *have* and the past participle:

> We *will have finished* the project by then.
> They *will have gone* before we will arrive.

VOICE

The *active* voice indicates that the subject of the sentence is the doer of the action of the verb; the *passive* voice, consisting of a form of the verb *be* and a past participle, indicates that the subject of the sentence is the object of the action:

Active voice: His colleagues *respect* him.
Passive voice: He *was respected* by his colleagues.

MOOD

There are three moods: the *indicative*, the *subjunctive*, and the *imperative*. The *indicative* is used to indicate a fact or to ask a question:

He *is* here.
Is he here?

The *subjunctive* is used to express a condition contrary to fact, especially in clauses introduced by *if*, and after the verb *wish*:

If she *were* there, she could answer that.
I wish he *were* here.

The *subjunctive* is also used in clauses beginning with the word *that* following verbs that request, demand, or recommend:

They asked that the books *be* returned.
She insisted that the door *remain* open.
The law required that he *report* his earnings.

The imperative is used to express a command or a demand:

Come here!
Pay attention!

TRANSITIVE AND INTRANSITIVE VERBS

A transitive verb takes a direct object:

She *sold* her car.

An intransitive verb has no direct object:

He *talked* all day.

A HANDBOOK OF STYLE

PUNCTUATION

Punctuation marks are used in written English to separate groups of words for meaning and emphasis; to convey an idea of the variations of pitch, volume, pauses, and intonation of the spoken language; and to help avoid ambiguity. The uses of the standard punctuation marks are discussed and illustrated in the following pages. For an explanation of the punctuation marks used in the entries in this dictionary, see the Explanatory Notes in the front of the book.

APOSTROPHE '

1. Indicates the possessive of nouns and indefinite pronouns. The possessive of singular nouns and some plural nouns is formed by adding -'s. The possessive of plural nouns ending in an *s* or *z* sound is usually formed by adding only an apostrophe; the possessive of irregular plurals is formed by adding -'s.

the boy's mother   birds' migrations

Douglas's crimes   the Stevenses' house

anyone's guess   people's opinions

Degas's drawings   children's laughter

2. Marks the omission of letters in contracted words.

didn't   they're   she'd

3. Marks the omission of digits in numerals.

class of '03   in the '90s

4. Often forms plurals of letters, figures, abbreviations, symbols, and words referred to as words.

dot your *i*'s and cross your *t*'s

three 8's   *or*   three 8s

these Ph.D.'s   *or*   these Ph.D.s

used &'s instead of *and*'s

BRACKETS [ ]

1. Enclose editorial comments or clarifications inserted into quoted material.

His embarrassment had peaked [sic] her curiosity.

2. Enclose insertions that supply missing letters or that alter the form of the original word.

His letter continues, "If D[eutsch] won't take the manuscript, perhaps someone at Faber will."

He dryly observed that they bought the stock because "they want[ed] to see themselves getting richer."

3. Function as parentheses within parentheses.

Posner's recent essays (like his earlier *Law and Literature* [1988]) bear this out.

COLON :

1. Introduces an amplifying word, phrase, or clause that acts as an appositive.

That year Handley's old obsession was replaced with a new one: jazz.

The issue comes down to this: Will we offer a reduced curriculum, or will we simply cancel the program?

2. Introduces a list or series.

Three abstained: Britain, France, and Belgium.

3. Introduces a clause or phrase that explains, illustrates, amplifies, or restates what has gone before.

Dawn was breaking: the distant peaks were already glowing with the sun's first rays.

4. Introduces lengthy quoted material set off from the rest of the text by indentation but not by quotation marks. It may also be used before a quotation enclosed by quotation marks in running text.

The *Rumpole* series has been well described as follows:

Rumpled, disreputable, curmudgeonly barrister Horace Rumpole often wins cases despite the disdain of his more aristocratic colleagues. Fond of cheap wine ("Château Thames Embankment") and. . . .

The inscription reads: "Here lies one whose name was writ in water."

5. Separates elements in bibliographic publication data and page references, in biblical citations, and in formulas used to express time and ratios.

Boston: Houghton Mifflin, 1997

Scientific American 240 (Jan.):122-33

John 4:10   8:30 a.m.   a ratio of 3:5

6. Separates titles and subtitles.

Southwest Stories: Tales from the Desert

7. Follows the salutation in formal correspondence.

Dear Judge Wright: Ladies and Gentlemen:

8. Follows headings in memorandums and business letters.

TO: Reference:

9. Is placed outside quotation marks and parentheses when it punctuates the larger sentence.

The problem becomes most acute in "Black Rose and Destroying Angel": plot simply ceases to exist.

COMMA   ,

1. Separates main clauses joined by a coordinating conjunction (such as *and, but, or, nor, so*), and occasionally short parallel clauses not joined by conjunctions.

She knew very little about the new system, and he volunteered nothing.

The trial lasted for nine months, but the jury took only four hours to reach its verdict.

She came, she saw, she conquered.

2. Sets off adverbial clauses and phrases that begin or interrupt a sentence. If the sentence can be easily read without a comma, the comma may be omitted.

Having agreed to disagree, they turned to other matters.

The report, after being read aloud, was put up for consideration.

In January the roof fell in.

As cars age they depreciate.

3. Sets off transitional words and phrases (such as *indeed, however*) and words that introduce examples (such as *namely, for example*).

Indeed, no one seemed to have heard of him.

They concluded, however, that it was meaningless.

Three have complied, namely, Togo, Benin, and Ghana.

4. Sets off contrasting expressions within a sentence.

This project will take six months, not six weeks.

5. Separates words, phrases, or clauses in a series. Many writers omit the comma before the last item in a series whenever this would not result in ambiguity.

Men, women[,] and children crowded aboard the train.

Her job required her to pack quickly, to travel often[,] and to have no personal life.

He came down the steps as reporters shouted questions, flashbulbs popped[,] and the crowd pushed closer.

6. Separates two or more adjectives that modify a noun. It is not used between two adjectives when the first modifies the combination of the second plus the noun it modifies.

in a calm, reflective manner

the harsh, damp, piercing wind

the lone bald eagle   a good used car

7. Sets off a nonrestrictive (nonessential) word, phrase, or clause that is in apposition to a preceding or following noun.

We visited Verdun, site of the famous battle.

A cherished landmark, the Hotel Sandburg was spared.

Its author, Maria Olevsky, was an expert diver.

8. Separates a direct quotation from a phrase identifying its source or speaker. The comma is omitted when the quotation ends with a question mark or exclamation point, and usually omitted when the quoted phrase itself is the subject or object of the larger sentence.

She answered, "I'm leaving."

"I suspect," Bob observed, "we'll be hearing more."

"How about another round?" Elaine piped up.

"The network is down" was the reply she feared.

9. Sets off words in direct address and mild interjections.

The facts, my fellow Americans, are very different.

This is our final notice, Mr. Sutton.

Ah, the mosaics in Ravenna are matchless.

10. Precedes a tag question.

That's obvious, isn't it?

11. Indicates the omission of a word or phrase used in a parallel construction earlier in the sentence. In short sentences, the comma may be omitted.

Eight councillors cast their votes for O'Reilly; six, for Mendez.

Seven voted in favor, three against.

12. Is used to avoid ambiguity that might arise from adjacent words.

Under Mr. James, Madison High School flourished.

13. Groups numerals into units of three to separate thousands, millions, and so on. It is not used in street addresses, page numbers, and four-digit years.

2,000 case histories	12537 Wilshire Blvd.
a fee of $12,500	page 1415
numbering 3,450,000	in 3000 B.C.

14. Separates a surname from a following title or degree, and often from the abbreviations *Jr.* and *Sr.*

Sandra H. Cobb, Vice President

Lee Herman Melville, M.D.

Douglas Fairbanks, Jr.
or Douglas Fairbanks Jr.

15. Sets off elements of an address (except for zip codes) and full dates. When only the month and year are given, the comma is usually omitted.

Write to Bureau of the Census, Washington, DC 20233.

In Reno, Nevada, their luck ran out.

On July 26, 2000, the court issued its opinion.

October 1929 brought an end to all that.

16. Follows the salutation in informal correspondence and follows the complimentary close in a letter.

Dear Aunt Sarah,   Sincerely yours,

DASH —

1. Marks an abrupt change or break in the structure of a sentence.

The students seemed happy enough with the new plan, but the alumni—there was the problem

2. Is used in place of commas or parentheses to emphasize parenthetical or amplifying material. In general, no punctuation immediately precedes an opening dash or immediately follows a closing dash.

It will prevent corporations—large and small—from buying influence with campaign contributions.

3. Introduces defining phrases and lists.

The motion was then tabled—that is, removed indefinitely from consideration.

Davis was a leading innovator in at least three styles—bebop, cool jazz, and jazz-rock fusion.

4. Often precedes the attribution of a quotation, either immediately after the quotation or on the next line.

Only the sign is for sale. —Søren Kierkegaard

or

Only the sign is for sale.
                                    —Søren Kierkegaard

5. Sets off an interrupting clause or phrase. An exclamation point or question mark may immediately precede a dash.

If we don't succeed—and the critics say we won't—then the whole project is in jeopardy.

His hobby was getting on people's nerves—especially mine!—and he was very good at it.

ELLIPSIS ...

1. Indicates the omission of one or more words within a quoted sentence. Omission of a word or phrase is indicated by three ellipsis points. If an entire sentence or more is omitted, the end punctua-

tion of the preceding sentence (including a period) is followed by three ellipsis points. Punctuation used in the original that falls on either side of the ellipsis is often omitted; however, it may be retained, especially if this helps clarify the sentence structure. (The second and third examples below are shortened versions of the first.)

> Is it so bad, then, to be misunderstood? Pythagoras was misunderstood, and Socrates, and Jesus, and Luther, and Copernicus, and Galileo, and Newton, and every pure and wise spirit that ever took flesh. To be great is to be misunderstood.—Emerson

> Is it so bad, then, to be misunderstood? Pythagoras was misunderstood, and Socrates, and Jesus, . . . and every pure and wise spirit that ever took flesh.

> Is it so bad, then, to be misunderstood? . . . To be great is to be misunderstood.

2. Indicates that one or more lines have been omitted from a poem. The row of ellipsis points usually matches the length of the line above.

> When I heard the learned astronomer,
> . . . .
> How soon unaccountable I became tired and sick,
> Til rising and gliding out I wandered off by myself,

3. Indicates faltering speech or an unfinished sentence in dialogue.

> "I mean . . . " he stammered, "like . . . How?"

EXCLAMATION POINT !

1. Ends an emphatic phrase, sentence, or interjection.

> Without a trace!

> There is no alternative!

> Encore!

2. Is placed within brackets, dashes, parentheses, and quotation marks when it punctuates only the enclosed material. It is placed outside them when it punctuates the entire sentence. If it falls where a comma could also go, the comma is dropped.

> All of this proves—at long last!—that we were right from the start.

> Somehow the dog got the gate open (for the third time!) and ran into the street.

> He sprang to his feet and shouted "Point of order!"

> At this rate, the national anthem will soon be replaced by "You Are My Sunshine"!

> "Absolutely not!" he snapped.

> They wouldn't dare! she told herself over and over.

HYPHEN -

1. Is often used to link elements in compound words. Consult the dictionary in doubtful cases.

secretary-treasurer	spin-off
cost-effective	light-year
middle-of-the-road	president-elect

2. Is used to separate a prefix, suffix, or combining form from an existing word if the base word is capitalized, and often when the base word is more than two syllables long, or when identical letters would otherwise be adjacent to each other. Consult the dictionary in doubtful cases.

pre-Victorian	wall-like
industry-wide	co-opted
recession-proof	anti-inflationary

3. Is used in compound nouns containing a particle (usually a preposition or adverb).

on-ramp	falling-out
runner-up	right-of-way

4. Is used in most compound modifiers when placed before the noun.

> the fresh-cut grass   a made-up excuse

> her gray-green eyes   the well-worded statement

5. Is used with the first of two prefixes or modifiers forming a compound with the same base word.

> pre- and postoperative care

> anti- or pro-Revolutionary sympathies

> early- and mid-20th-century painters

6. Is used with written-out numbers, both cardinal and ordinal, between 21 and 99.

> forty-one years old   his forty-first birthday

> one hundred forty-one

7. Is used in a written-out fraction employed as a modifier. A fraction used as a noun is often left open.

> a one-half share

> three fifths of the vote   *or*   three-fifths of the vote

> one one-hundredth of an inch

8. Is used between numbers and dates with the meaning "(up) to and including." In typeset material the hyphen is replaced by the longer en dash.

pages 128–34

the years 1995–99

9. Is used as the equivalent of *to, and,* or *versus* to indicate linkage or opposition. In typeset material the longer en dash is used.

the New York–Paris flight

the Lincoln–Douglas debates

a final score of 7–2.

10. Marks an end-of-line division of a word.

Stanley's search came to an end at Lake Tanganyika, in the Arab settlement of Ujiji.

PARENTHESES ( )

1. Enclose phrases and clauses that provide examples, explanations, or supplementary facts.

Nominations for principal officers (president, vice president, treasurer, and secretary) were approved.

Four computers (all outdated models) were replaced.

Although we liked Mille Fiori (their risotto was the best), we hadn't been there in several months.

2. Enclose numerals that confirm a spelled-out number in a business or legal context.

Delivery will be made in thirty (30) days.

The fee is four thousand dollars ($4,000.00).

3. Enclose numbers or letters indicating individual items in a series within a sentence.

Sentences can be classified as (1) simple, (2) multiple or compound, and (3) complex.

4. Enclose abbreviations that follow their spelled-out forms, or spelled-out forms that follow their abbreviations.

the Food and Drug Administration (FDA)

the ABA (American Booksellers Association)

5. Indicate alternative terms.

Please sign and return the enclosed form(s).

6. Often enclose cross-references and bibliographic references, as well as publishing data in bibliographic citations.

Specialized services are also available (see list below).

The diagram (Fig. 3) illustrates the action of the pump.

Subsequent studies (Braxton 1998; Roh and Weinglass 2002) have confirmed these findings.

3. See Stendhal, *Love* (New York: Penguin, 1975), 342.

7. Are used with other punctuation marks as follows: If an independent sentence is enclosed in parentheses, its first word is capitalized and a period is placed inside the parentheses. If the parenthetical expression occurs within a sentence, it is uncapitalized unless it is a quotation, and does not end with a period but may end with an exclamation point, a question mark, or quotation marks. No punctuation immediately precedes an opening parenthesis within a sentence; if punctuation is required, it follows the closing parenthesis.

The discussion was held in the boardroom. (The results are still confidential.)

This short section (musicians would call it the *bridge*) has the song's most distinctive harmonies.

The background music is always Bach (does the chairman have such good taste?).

He was distraught ("It's my whole career!") and refused to see anyone.

I'll get back to you tomorrow (Friday), when I have more details.

PERIOD .

1. Ends a sentence or a sentence fragment that is neither a question nor an exclamation. Only one period ends a sentence.

She asked if we were swing dancers.

Give it your best.

Unlikely. In fact, inconceivable.

She liked best the sentence that read "Leda Rubin has made the impossible possible."

2. Follows most abbreviations and some contractions.

Calif.	e.g.	Dr.
Sept.	p.m.	Jr.
etc.	dept.	Assn.
Ph.D. *or* PhD		C.E.O. *or* CEO

3. Is used with a person's initials.

F. Scott Fitzgerald   J. B. S. Haldane

4. Follows numerals and letters when used without parentheses in outlines and vertical lists.

I. Objectives
A. Economy
   1. Low initial cost
   2. Low maintenance cost
B. Ease of operation

QUESTION MARK ?

1. Ends a direct question.

"When do they arrive?" she asked.

Was anyone seen in the area after 10 p.m.?

2. Ends a question that forms part of a sentence, but does not follow an indirect question.

What was her motive? you may be asking.

I naturally wondered, Will it really work?

He asked when the club normally closed.

3. Indicates uncertainty about a fact.

Geoffrey Chaucer, English poet (1342?–1400)

4. Is used with other punctuation marks exactly like the exclamation point.

QUOTATION MARKS, DOUBLE " "

1. Enclose direct quotations but not indirect quotations.

"I'm leaving," she whispered. "This could last forever."

She whispered that she was leaving.

He asked, "What went wrong?"

The question is, What went wrong?

2. Enclose words or phrases borrowed from others, and words of obvious informality.

They required a "biodata summary"—that is, a résumé.

He called himself "emperor," but he was really just a dictator.

They were afraid the patient had "stroked out"—had had a cerebrovascular accident.

3. Enclose titles of poems, short stories, essays, articles in periodicals, chapters of books, and episodes of radio and television programs.

the article "After the Genocide" in the *New Yorker*

"The Death of the Hired Man" by Robert Frost

Poe's "The Murders in the Rue Morgue"

John Barth's essay "The Literature of Exhaustion"

The Jungle Book's ninth chapter, "Rikki-tikki-tavi"

*M*A*S*H*'s finale, "Goodbye, Farewell and Amen"

4. Enclose lines of poetry run in with the text.

When Gilbert advised, "Stick close to your desks and never go to sea, / And you all may be rulers of the Queen's Navee!" this latest appointee was obviously paying attention.

5. Are used with other punctuation marks as follows: A period or comma is placed within the quotation marks. A colon or semicolon is placed outside them. A dash, question mark, or exclamation point is placed inside the quotation marks when it punctuates the quoted matter only, but outside when it punctuates the whole sentence.

He smiled and said, "I'm happy for you."

"Too easy," she shot back.

There was only one real "issue": noise.

She spoke of her "little cottage in the country"; she might better have called it a mansion.

"I can't see how—" he started to say.

Saturdays there were dances—"sock hops"—in the gym.

He asked, "When did she leave?"

What is the meaning of "the open door"?

She collapsed in her seat with a stunned "Good grief!"

Save us from his "mercy"!

QUOTATION MARKS, SINGLE ' '

1. Enclose quoted material within quoted material.

"I distinctly heard him say, 'Don't be late,' and then I heard the door close."

This analysis is indebted to Del Banco's "Elizabeth Bishop's 'Insomnia': An Inverted View."

2. In British usage, may enclose quoted material, in which case a quotation within a quotation is set off by double quotation marks.

'I distinctly heard him say, "Don't be late," and then I heard the door close.'

SEMICOLON ;

1. Separates related independent clauses joined without a coordinating conjunction.

> Cream the butter and sugar; add the eggs and beat well.

> The river overflowed its banks; roads vanished; freshly plowed fields turned into lakes.

2. Joins two clauses when the second includes a conjunctive adverb (such as *however, indeed, thus*) or a phrase that acts like one (such as *in that case, as a result, on the other hand*).

> It won't be easy to sort out the facts; a decision must be made, however.

> The case could take years; as a result, many plaintiffs will accept settlements.

3. Is often used before introductory expressions such as *for example, that is,* and *namely*.

> We were fairly successful; that is, we made our deadlines and met our budget.

4. Separates phrases or items in a series when they contain commas.

> The assets include $22 million in land, buildings, and equipment; $34 million in cash and investments; and $8 million in inventory.

> The Pissarro exhibition will travel to Washington, D.C.; Manchester, N.H.; Portland, Ore.; and Oakland, Cal.

> The votes against were: Precinct 1, 418; Precinct 2, 332; Precinct 3, 256.

5. Is placed outside quotation marks and parentheses.

> They again demanded "complete autonomy"; the demand was again rejected.

> She found him urbane and entertaining (if somewhat overbearing); he found her charmingly ingenuous.

SLASH /

1. Separates alternatives, usually representing the words *or* or *and/or*.

> alumni/ae   his/her

2. Replaces the word *to* or *and* in some compound terms and ranges.

> 1998/99   *or*   1998–99

> the May/June issue   *or*   the May–June issue

3. Separates lines of poetry that are run in with the text. A space usually precedes and follows the slash.

> In Pope's words: "'Tis with our judgments as our watches, none / Go just alike, yet each believes his own."

4. Separates the elements in a numerical date, and numerators and denominators in fractions.

> on 9/11/01   a 7/8-mile course

5. Represents the word *per* or *to* when used between units of measure or the terms of a ratio.

> 400,000 tons/year   price/earnings ratio

> 29 mi/gal   20/20 vision

6. Punctuates some abbreviations.

> w/o [*for* without]   I/O [*for* input/output]

> c/o [*for* care of]   P/E [*for* price/earnings]

7. Punctuates Internet addresses.

> http://unabridged.Merriam-Webster.com/

FOREIGN MARKS

1. Guillemets « » often enclose quotations in French and other European languages.

> Marie Antoinette est censée dire «qu'ils mangent de la brioche».

2. Spanish exclamation points ¡ ! are used in pairs to enclose an exclamatory sentence in Spanish writing.

> ¡Qué buen día!

3. Spanish question marks ¿ ? are used in pairs to enclose an interrogatory sentence in Spanish writing.

> ¿Qué es esto?

CAPITALS AND ITALICS

Words and phrases are capitalized or italicized to indicate that they have a special significance in particular contexts. The following rules and examples describe the most common uses of capitals and italics.

BEGINNINGS

1. The first word of a sentence or sentence fragment is capitalized.

The play lasted nearly three hours.

So many people, so many opinions.

Bravo!

2. The first word of a sentence contained within parentheses is capitalized. However, a parenthetical sentence within another sentence is not capitalized unless it is a complete quoted sentence.

No one answered the telephone. (They were probably on vacation.)

Having waited in line for an hour (why do we do these things?), we finally left.

After some initial defensiveness ("Was it my fault?"), he gradually got over it.

3. The first word of a direct quotation is capitalized. However, if the quotation is interrupted in mid-sentence, the second part does not begin with a capital. When a quotation is syntactically dependent on the sentence in which it occurs, it usually does not begin with a capital.

Hart repeated, "We have no budget for new computers."

"We have no budget for new computers," repeated Hart, "but we may next year."

Hart made it clear that "we have no budget for new computers."

4. The first word of a sentence within a sentence that is not a direct quotation is usually capitalized. Examples include mottoes and rules, unspoken or imaginary dialogue, and direct questions.

You know the saying "Fools rush in where angels fear to tread."

The first rule is, When in doubt, spell it out.

My first thought was, How can I avoid this assignment?

The question is, When can we go?

5. The first word following a colon is usually lowercased, even when it begins a complete sentence. However, when the sentence introduced is lengthy and distinctly separate from the preceding clause, it is often capitalized.

The advantage of this system is clear: it's inexpensive.

The situation is critical: This company cannot hope to recoup the fourth-quarter losses that were sustained in five operating divisions.

6. The first word of a line of poetry is traditionally capitalized. However, in modern poetry the line beginnings are often lowercased. The poem's original capitalization should always be retained.

The best lack all conviction, while the worst
Are full of passionate intensity.
                                        —W. B. Yeats

     If tributes cannot
be implicit
give me diatribes and the fragrance of iodine,
the corn oak acorn grown in Spain. . .
                                        —Marianne Moore

7. The first words of items in vertical lists are usually capitalized. However, numbered phrases within a sentence are lowercased.

The English peerage consists of five ranks:
  1. Duke (Duchess)
  2. Marquess (Marchioness)
  3. Earl (Countess)
  4. Viscount (Viscountess)
  5. Baron (Baroness)

Among the fastest animals are (1) the cheetah, clocked at 70 mph; (2) the pronghorn, at 61 mph; (3) the lion, at 50 mph; (4) the quarter horse, at 47 mph; and (5) the elk, at 45 mph.

8. The first word in an outline heading is capitalized.

  I. Prose texts
    A. Typeface
      1. Alphabets
      2. Characteristics
    B. Type page and trim size

9. The first word and courtesy titles of the salutation of a letter and the first word of a complimentary close are capitalized.

Dear Sir or Madam: Sincerely yours,

To whom it may concern: Love,

PROPER NOUNS AND ADJECTIVES

Awards and Prizes

1. Names of awards and prizes are capitalized. Words and phrases that are not actually part of the award's name are lowercased.

Academy Award	Rhodes Scholarship
Nobel Prize in medicine	Rhodes scholar

Derivatives of Proper Nouns

2. Derivatives of proper nouns are capitalized when used in their primary sense. If the derived term has taken on a specialized meaning, it is often lowercased. Consult the dictionary when in doubt.

Roman sculpture	chinaware
Edwardian era	Hodgkin's disease
french fries	quixotic

Geographical References

3. Terms that identify divisions of the earth's surface and distinct regions, places, or districts are capitalized, as are derivative nouns and adjectives.

Tropic of Cancer	the Highlands
Asia Minor	Highland attitudes
the Great Lakes	Burgundy
Arnhem Land	Burgundians

4. Popular names of localities are capitalized.

the Left Bank	the Sunbelt
Little Italy	the Loop

5. Words designating global, national, regional, or local political divisions are capitalized when they are essential elements of specific names. They are usually lowercased when they precede a proper noun or are not part of a specific name.

the Roman Empire	New York City
the fall of the empire	the city of New York

6. Generic geographical terms (such as *lake, mountain*) are capitalized if they are part of a proper noun.

Lake Tanganyika	Atlas Mountains
Yosemite Valley	Mount Everest

7. Generic geographical terms preceding two or more names are usually capitalized.

Lakes Huron and Erie

Mounts McKinley, Whitney, and Shasta

8. Generic terms that are not used as part of a single proper noun are not capitalized. These include plural terms that follow two or more proper nouns, and terms that are used descriptively or alone.

Maine and Oak streets

the Oder and Nysa rivers

the Pacific coast of Mexico

the river delta

9. Compass points are capitalized when they refer to a geographical region or form part of a place-name or street name. They are lowercased when they refer to a simple direction.

the Southwest	East Coast
North Pole	north of the Rio Grande
West 12th Street	went west on 12th Street

10. Nouns and adjectives that are derived from compass points and that designate or refer to a specific geographical region are usually capitalized.

Easterners	Southern hospitality
Northern Europeans	Southwestern recipes

11. Names of streets, monuments, parks, landmarks, and other public places are capitalized. Generic terms (such as *street, park, bridge*) are lowercased when used alone.

State Street	the Plaza Hotel
Golden Gate Bridge	back to the hotel

Governmental and Judicial Bodies

12. Full names of legislative, executive, and administrative bodies are capitalized, as are easily recognizable short forms of these names. However, nonspecific noun and adjective references to them are usually lowercased.

United States Congress

Congress

congressional hearings

Federal Trade Commission

a federal agency

13. Full names of high courts are capitalized. Short forms of such names are usually lowercased, as are names of city and county courts. However, both the full and short names of the U.S. Supreme Court are capitalized.

International Court of Justice

the state supreme court

Springfield municipal court

small-claims court

the Supreme Court of the United States

the Court

Historical Periods and Events

14. Names of some historical and cultural periods and movements are capitalized. When in doubt, consult a dictionary or encyclopedia.

Bronze Age	Third Reich
the Renaissance	Victorian era
Fifth Republic	Age of Pericles
Prohibition	the atomic age

15. Names of conferences, councils, and specific historical, cultural, and sporting events are capitalized.

Yalta Conference	San Francisco Earthquake
Council of Trent	Cannes Film Festival
Boston Tea Party	World Cup

16. Full names of specific treaties, laws, and acts are capitalized.

Treaty of Versailles	First Amendment rights
the Bill of Rights	Clean Air Act of 1990

Legal Cases

17. Names of the plaintiff and defendant in legal case titles are italicized, as are short forms of case titles. The *v.* (for *versus*) may be roman or italic. When the party involved rather than the case itself is being discussed, the reference is not italicized.

Smith et al. v. [or v.] *Jones*

a quick decision in the *Jones* case

She covered the Lemuel Jones trial for the newspaper.

Military Units

18. Full titles of branches and units of the U.S. armed forces are capitalized, as are standard short forms. However, the plurals of *army, navy, air force,* and *coast guard* are lowercased.

U.S. Marine Corps	the Third Army
the Marines	allied armies

Organizations

19. Names of organizations, corporations, and institutions are capitalized, as are derivative terms to designate their members. However, common nouns occurring after the names of two or more organizations are lowercased.

the Rotary Club	AT&T Corporation
all Rotarians	League of Women Voters
University of Wisconsin	
Yale and Harvard universities	

20. Words such as *agency, department, division, group,* or *office* that designate corporate and organizational units are capitalized only as part of a specific proper noun.

manager of the Sales Division of K2 Outfitters

a memo to the sales divisions of both companies

People

21. Names and initials of persons are capitalized. If a name is hyphenated, both elements are capitalized. Particles forming the initial elements of surnames (such as *de, della, du, la, ten, ter, van,* and *von*) may or may not be capitalized, depending on the practice of the individual. The prefixes *Mac, Mc,* and *O'* are always capitalized.

Cecil Day-Lewis	Martin Van Buren
Cecil B. DeMille	Wernher von Braun
Agnes de Mille	Archibald MacLeish
W. E. B. DuBois	Sean O'Casey

22. Titles preceding the name of a person and epithets or nicknames used instead of a name are capitalized. However, titles used alone or as part of a phrase following a name are usually lowercased.

President Lincoln

Honest Abe

King Henry VIII

Henry VIII, king of England

Logex Corp.'s president

23. Words of family relationship preceding or used in place of a person's name are capitalized; otherwise they are lowercased.

Uncle Fred	Mother's birthday
Cousin Julia	my mother's birthday

24. Words designating languages, nationalities, peoples, races, religious groups, and tribes are capitalized. Designations based on skin color are usually lowercased.

Spanish	Iroquois
Spaniards	Asians
Muslims	blacks and whites

Personifications

25. Abstract concepts or qualities are capitalized when they are personified.

as Autumn paints each leaf in fiery colors

the statue of Justice with her scales

Religious Terms

26. Words designating the supreme being are capitalized. Plural references to deities are lowercased.

Allah	the Almighty
Brahma	in the eyes of God
Jehovah	the angry gods

27. Personal pronouns referring to the supreme being are often capitalized in religious writing.

God made His presence known

28. Traditional designations of apostles, prophets, and saints are capitalized.

the Madonna	the Twelve
the Prophet	St. John of the Cross
Moses the Lawgiver	John the Baptist

29. Names of religions, denominations, creeds and confessions, and religious orders are capitalized, as are derivatives of these names.

Judaism	Apostles' Creed
Islam	a Buddhist
Eastern Orthodox	Society of Jesus
Church of England	Jesuit teachers

30. Full names of specific places of worship are capitalized, but terms such as *church, synagogue,* and *mosque* are lowercased when used alone.

| Hunt Memorial Church | the Blue Mosque |
| Beth Israel Synagogue | the mosque's minaret |

31. Names of the Bible and other sacred works, their books and parts, and versions or editions of them are capitalized but not italicized. Adjectives derived from such names are capitalized except for the words *biblical* and *scriptural.*

Bible	Talmud
the Scriptures	Bhagavad Gita
Old Testament	Revised Standard Version
Koran *also* Quran *or* Qur'an	
Koranic *also* Quranic *or* Qur'anic	

Scientific Terms

32. Names of planets and their satellites, stars, constellations, and other specific celestial objects are capitalized. However, the words *sun, earth,* and *moon* are usually lowercased unless they occur with other astronomical names.

Jupiter	Halley's comet
Ganymede	Mars, Venus, and Earth
the North Star	life on earth
Ursa Major	the new moon

33. New Latin genus names in zoology and botany are capitalized and italicized. The second term in binomial scientific names, identifying the species, is lowercased and italicized, as are the names of races, varieties, or subspecies.

the California condor (*Gymnogyps californianus*)

a common buttercup (*Ranunculus acris*)

the Florida panther (*Felis concolor coryi*)

34. In zoology and botany, New Latin names of all groups above genus (such as class or family) are capitalized but not italicized. Their derivative nouns and adjectives are lowercased.

the class Gastropoda	the order Diptera
gastropod	dipteran flies
the family Ascaridae	Bryophyta
ascarid	bryophytic

35. Names of geological time divisions are capitalized. The generic terms that follow them are lowercased.

| Mesozoic era | Paleocene epoch |
| Quaternary period | the Upper Cretaceous |

Time Periods and Dates

36. Names of days of the week, months, and holidays and holy days are capitalized. Names of the seasons are lowercased.

| Tuesday | Veterans Day | Easter |
| January | Yom Kippur | winter |

Titles of Works

37. Words in titles of books, magazines, newspapers, plays, movies, long poems, and works of art such as paintings and sculpture are capitalized except for internal articles, coordinating conjunctions, prepositions, and the *to* of infinitives. Prepositions of four or more letters are often capitalized. The entire title is italicized. (Titles of articles in periodicals, short poems, short stories, essays, lectures, chapters of books, and episodes of radio and television programs are similarly capitalized but enclosed in quotation marks rather than italicized; see examples at "Quotation Marks, Double" above.)

Of Mice and Men	*Lawrence of Arabia*
Publishers Weekly	Eliot's *The Waste Land*
USA Today	Monet's *Water-Lily Pool*
Miller's *The Crucible*	Rodin's *Thinker*

38. Titles of long musical compositions are usually capitalized and italicized; the titles of songs and short compositions are capitalized and enclosed in quotation marks, as are the popular names of longer works. The titles of compositions identified by their musical forms (such as *quartet, sonata, concerto*) are capitalized only, as are movements.

Mozart's *The Magic Flute*

Loesser's *Guys and Dolls*

"My Funny Valentine"

Beethoven's "Für Elise"

the "Moonlight" Sonata

his Violin Concerto in D

Quartet in D, Op. 64, No. 5

the Adagietto movement

39. Common titles of book sections (such as *chapter, preface, index*) are usually capitalized only when they refer to a section of the same book in which the reference appears.

See the Appendix for further information.

In a long introduction, the author explained her goals.

40. Nouns used with numbers or letters to designate major reference headings in books or periodicals are usually capitalized. Nouns designating minor elements are usually lowercased.

in Volume 5   see page 101

of Chapter 2   at paragraph 6.1

in Table 3   in line 8

Trademarks

41. Registered trademarks, service marks, and brand names are capitalized.

Coke	Kleenex	Xerox
Walkman	Band-Aid	Prozac
Levi's	Jacuzzi	Express Mail

Transportation

42. Names of ships, airplanes, and space vehicles are capitalized and italicized. The designations *USS, SS,* and *HMS* are not italicized.

HMS *Bounty*   *Challenger*

Spirit of St. Louis   *Apollo 13*

43. Names of train lines, types of aircraft, and space programs are capitalized but not italicized.

Metroliner   Concorde

Boeing 727   Pathfinder Program

OTHER STYLING CONVENTIONS

44. Italics are used to emphasize or draw attention to words in a sentence.

Students must notify the dean's office *in writing* of any added or dropped courses.

She was not *the* star, merely *a* star.

45. Italics are often used for letters referred to as letters, words referred to as words, and numerals referred to as numerals.

The *g* in *align* is silent.

Purists still insist that *data* is a plural noun.

The first *2* and the last *0* are barely legible.

46. Unfamiliar words or words having a specialized meaning are italicized when first introduced and defined in a text, but not subsequently.

In the *direct-to-consumer* transaction, the publisher markets directly to the individual by mail.

Vitiligo is a condition in which skin pigment cells stop making pigment. Treatment for vitiligo includes . . .

47. Foreign words and phrases that have not been fully adopted into English are italicized. In general, any word that appears in the main A-Z vocabulary of this dictionary does not need to be italicized.

At the club such behavior was distinctly *mal vu.*

The prix fixe lunch was $25.

DOCUMENTATION OF SOURCES

Writers are often required to specify the source of a quotation or piece of information borrowed from another work. Though formal documentation is omitted from popular writing, where quotations or information sources are acknowledged only casually (e.g., "As Stephen Hawking observed in his *Brief History of Time,* . . ."), the systematic use of notes, references, and bibliographies is required in most serious nonfiction and all scholarly writing, in which such documentation is an important indicator of the quality of the writer's research.

Footnotes, which are placed at the bottom of a page, and *endnotes,* which are placed at the end of an article, chapter, or book, have been the preferred form of documentation in serious works intended for a wide general readership and traditionally also in scholarly works in the humanities. Numbers within the text refer the reader to the footnotes or endnotes, which contain full bibliographical information on the works cited.

In scholarly works in the social and natural sciences, and increasingly in the humanities as well, *parenthetical references*—very brief references enclosed in parentheses within the actual text—refer the reader to a list of sources at the end. In works that employ parenthetical references, footnotes or endnotes may be used to provide ancillary information.

Regardless of which system is used, most carefully documented works include a *bibliography* or *list of sources* at the end.

The following paragraphs discuss and illustrate standard styles for references, notes, and bibliographic entries in scholarly fields. Fuller treatment can be found in *Merriam-Webster's Manual for Writers and Editors, The Chicago Manual of Style,* Kate Turabian's *Manual for Writers of Term Papers, Theses, and Dissertations,* the *MLA Handbook for Writers of Research Papers* (for the humanities), the *Publication Manual of the American Psychological Association* (for the social sciences), and *Scientific Style and Format* (for the natural sciences). However, the most efficient way to master the standard documentation style employed in any given discipline may be simply to study the citations in one of its leading journals.

FOOTNOTES AND ENDNOTES

Footnotes and endnotes are indicated by superscript numerals, usually placed immediately after the borrowed text. In an article, the numbering is consecutive throughout; in a book, it starts over with each new chapter. The notes themselves begin with numbers (either superscript, or now more commonly, full size with a period) that correspond to the superscript reference numbers in the text. Word-processing programs have greatly simplified the placement and numbering of footnotes and endnotes.

The first thirteen examples below (each of which is keyed to an item in the "Bibliographies" section at the end) illustrate the style to be used for the first reference to a book (nos. 1–9) or article (nos. 10–13). For journals, the abbreviations *vol.* and *no.* are now usually omitted. The reference normally ends with a page reference, though the abbreviations *p.* and *pp.* are usually omitted. In typescript, underlining may be used in place of italics. Any element of the reference that appears in the text itself (e.g., the author's name) can be omitted from the note. Note that citations of online sources (nos. 14–15) replace any physical place of publication with an Internet address, and end with the date on which the user consulted the source. An example of a substantive note (a note providing information other than straight bibliographical data) is also included (no. 16). Subsequent references to a book or article (nos. 17–18) generally consist of only the author's name and the new page reference; a shortened version of the work's title may be added to distinguish two or more cited works by the same author.

One author	1. Ta-Nehisi Coates, *Between the World and Me* (New York: Random House Publishing Group, 2015), 5.
Two or more authors	2. Albert C. Baugh and Thomas Cable, *A History of the English Language,* 6th ed. (Upper Saddle River, N.J.: Pearson, 2013), 14.
	3. Randolph Quirk et al., *A Comprehensive Grammar of the English Language* (London: Longman, 1985), 135.
Edition and/or translation	4. Tom Lansford, ed., *Political Handbook of the World: 2016–2017* (Thousand Oaks, California: CQ Press, 2017), 719–22.
	5. Vladimir Vladimirovich Nabokov and Vera Nabokova, *Letters to Véra,* trans. and ed. Olga Voronina and Brian Boyd (New York: Alfred A. Knopf, 2014), 4.
Second or later edition	6. Albert Hourani and Malise Ruthven, *A History of the Arab Peoples,* 2d ed. (Belknap–Harvard Univ. Press, 2002), 66.

Article in a collection	7. Chester Himes, "Headwaiter," in *Calling the Wind*, ed. Clarence Major (New York: HarperCollins, 1993), 83.
Work in two or more volumes	8. Frederic G. Cassidy and Joan Houston Hall, eds., *Dictionary of American Regional English* (Belknap–Harvard Univ. Press, 1985–2013), 3:447.
Corporate author	9. *Who's Who in America: 2016* (New Providence, N.J.: Marquis Who's Who, 2016), 1:995.
Monthly magazine	10. Vannevar Bush, "As We May Think," *Atlantic Monthly*, July 1945, 101–8.
Weekly magazine	11. Christopher Hitchens, review of *C. L. R. James* by Farrukh Dhondy, *Times Literary Supplement*, 18 Jan. 2002, 34.
Journal paginated consecutively throughout annual volume	12. Lawrence M. Davis, Charles L. Houck, and Clive Upton, "'Sett Out Verry Eairly Wensdy': The Spelling and Grammar in the Lewis and Clark Journals," *American Speech* 75 (Summer 2000): 138.
Newspaper	13. Carol Kaesuk Yoon, "Scientists Say Orangutans Can Exhibit 'Culture,'" *New York Times*, 3 Jan. 2003, A14.
Electronic source	14. Corey Sparks, "18.11.12, Wallace, Geoffrey Chaucer," January 18, 2018, *The Medieval Review* ⟨https://scholarworks.iu.edu/journals/index.php/tmr/article/view/26104⟩ (18 Dec. 2018).
	15. John Rothgeb, "The Tristan Chord: Identity and Origin," *Music Theory Online*, 1.1 (Jan. 1995), ⟨http://www.societymusictheory.org/mto/issues/mto.95.1.1/mto.95.1.1.rothgeb.art⟩ (12 June 1999).
Substantive note	16. Both "globalization" and "global village" date at least from the 1960s, with Zbigniew Brzezinski and Marshall McLuhan emphasizing respectively the universal status of the North American model of modernity and the technological convergence of the world. See Mattelart, 115.
Subsequent reference	17. Quirk et al., 106.
	18. Nabokov, *Letters to Véra*, 4.

PARENTHETICAL REFERENCES

Parenthetical references, though not used in works intended for a wide audience, are standard in scholarly works in the social sciences and natural sciences, and are increasingly being used in the humanities as well. These highly abbreviated references are embedded within the text itself and direct the reader to the more complete source information given in a bibliography at the end.

In the natural sciences, parenthetical references include only the author's last name and the year of publication ("author-date style," or "name-year style"). In the social sciences, writers use either the author-date style or an alternative style that also includes a page reference ("author-date-page style"). In the humanities, a page reference normally takes the place of the year of publication ("author-page style"). To distinguish two works published in the same year, the date may be followed by a lowercase letter—"(Chavis 1999a)," "(Chavis 1999b)." To distinguish among cited works by the same author, a shortened form of the work's title may be added—"(Faulkner, *Absalom* 220)," "(Faulkner, *Intruder* 151)."

The examples below illustrate the use of parenthetical references in, respectively, the natural sciences, the social sciences, and the humanities.

A historical assessment of many small, isolated populations found that every group with fewer than 50 individuals became extinct within 50 years (Berger 1990).

The land in West Africa was quite difficult to settle, and the mortality rate during the passage was "shockingly high" (Schick 1980, 27).

García Lorca critics have pointed out that, although Pepe sets the action of *La casa de Bernarda Alba* in motion, he never appears onstage (Gabriele 388; Urrea 51).

As with footnotes and endnotes, any information evident from the textual context—name, date, or title—is omitted from the reference. As a result, many references in the social sciences and humanities consist simply of page numbers.

References to electronic sources, which usually lack page references, may instead use paragraph numbers, if provided—"(Mather ¶ 16)"—or the number of the paragraph under a given heading within the article—"(Ortiz & Lane, Conclusions, para. 4)."

OTHER SYSTEMS

A newer style of citation, now often used in the natural sciences, is the *citation-sequence system.* Every source is given a number corresponding to the order of its first appearance in the article, and every later citation of that source employs the same number. The numbers themselves are either set in the main text as superscripts or are shown full-size in parentheses or brackets. There is usually no bibliography. The excerpt below (in which the source with the lower number had first appeared earlier in the article) is followed by the corresponding entries in the article's list of sources, in a style employing minimal punctuation and italicization.

> The relation between bone mass and breast cancer may also involve endogenous androgens, which are determinants of bone mass[100] and which have also been associated with the risk of breast cancer.[21]

> **21**. Zhang Y, Kiel DP, Kreger BE, et al. Bone mass and the risk of breast cancer among postmenopausal women. N Engl J Med 1997;336:611–7.

> **100**. Buchanan JR, Myers C, Lloyd T, Leuenberger P, Demers LM. Determinants of peak trabecular bone density in women: the role of androgens, estrogen, and exercise. J Bone Miner Res 1988;3:673–80.

Another newer system, sometimes used when the intended audience includes both general readers and scholars, is the *white-copy system,* which provides endnotes but omits any reference to them at all on the text pages. The general reader can thus completely ignore the documentation, while the scholar can check sources at will. The excerpt is followed by its corresponding endnotes.

> Aiken was on his way out of the flat when Ezra asked him if there was nobody genuinely *modern* he could recommend? Maybe someone at Harvard, 'something DIFFERENT'? Aiken thought for a moment, and answered: 'Oh well, there is Eliot.' Ezra asked who Eliot was, and was told: 'A guy at Harvard doing funny stuff.' Actually, added Aiken, Eliot was in England at the moment, so Ezra could meet him if he wanted to. Ezra told Aiken to arrange it.

> 257 'something DIFFERENT', PH 21 Dec '56. 'Oh well', Doob 128. 'A guy', Lyndall Gordon, *Eliot's Early Years,* Oxford University Press, 1977, 66.

The style of white-copy endnotes continues to vary widely from publication to publication. Here the abbreviations "PH" (indicating an unpublished collection of letters) and "Doob" (indicating a book) are explained in the book's bibliographic appendix; the third item, not being one of the book's important sources, is omitted from the appendix and instead given its full citation here.

BIBLIOGRAPHIES

A bibliography is usually provided at the end of any properly documented work (except those using the citation-sequence style). In works that rely on parenthetical references, a bibliography is essential, since the full citations are given nowhere else. In works that rely on footnotes or endnotes, the bibliography generally simply provides a convenient listing, alphabetized by the author's last name, of the bibliographic information that first appeared in the notes. Bibliography entries differ from notes chiefly in their punctuation. They include all the information in a full footnote or endnote except specific page references; however, when a journal article or a piece in a collection is being cited, the entry provides the range of pages for the entire article or piece.

The following bibliographies illustrate standard styles employed in, respectively, the humanities and the social and natural sciences. These differ principally in four respects: in the sciences, (1) the author's first and middle names are abbreviated, often without periods, (2) the date directly follows the author's name, (3) all words in book and article titles are lowercased except the first word, the first word of any subtitle, and proper nouns and adjectives, and (4) article titles are not enclosed in quotation marks. Also, in many scientific publications today, book and journal titles are not italicized. In journal citations, the abbreviations *vol.* and *no.* are generally omitted; the issue number either appears in parentheses or is omitted altogether, since pagination alone is sufficient to identify the issue when pagination is continuous throughout the volume. The titles of scientific journals are usually given in standard abbreviated forms.

Humanities

Baugh, Albert C., and Thomas Cable. *A History of the English Language,* 6th ed. Upper Saddle River, N.J.: Pearson, 2013.

Bush, Vannevar. "As We May Think." *Atlantic Monthly.* July 1945: 101–8.

Cassidy, Frederic G., and Joan Houston Hall, eds. *Dictionary of American Regional English.* 5 vols. Cambridge, Mass.: Belknap–Harvard Univ. Press, 1985–2013.

Coates, Ta-Nehisi. *Between the World and Me.* New York: Random House Publishing Group, 2015.

Davis, Lawrence M., Charles L. Houck, and Clive Upton. "'Sett Out Verry Eairly Wensdy': The Spelling and Grammar in the Lewis and Clark Journals." *American Speech* 75 (Summer 2000): 137–148.

Himes, Chester. "Headwaiter." In Clarence Major, ed., *Calling the Wind.* New York: HarperCollins, 1993: 79–93.

Hitchens, Christopher. Review of *C. L. R. James,* by Farrukh Dhondy. *Times Literary Supplement.* 18 Jan. 2002: 34.

Hourani, Albert, and Malise Ruthven. *A History of the Arab Peoples.* 2d ed. Cambridge, Mass.: Belknap—Harvard Univ. Press, 2002.

Lansford, Tom, ed. *Political Handbook of the World: 2016–2017.* Thousand Oaks, California: CQ Press, 2017.

Nabokov, Vladimir Vladimirovich, and Vera Nabokova. *Letters to Véra.* Trans. and ed. Olga Voronina and Brian Boyd. New York: Alfred A. Knopf, 2014.

Quirk, Randolph, et al. *A Comprehensive Grammar of the English Language.* London: Longman, 1985.

Rothgeb, John. "The Tristan Chord: Identity and Origin." *Music Theory Online* 1.1 (Jan. 1995). ⟨http://societymusictheory.org/mto/issues/mto.95.1.1/mto.95.1.1.rothgeb.art⟩ (12 June 1999).

Sparks, Corey. "18.11.12, Wallace, Geoffrey Chaucer." *The Medieval Review.* 18 Jan. 2018. ⟨https://scholarworks.iu.edu/journals/index.php/tmr/article/view/26104⟩ (18 Dec. 2018).

Who's Who in America: 2003. 3 vols. New Providence, N.J.: Marquis Who's Who, 2002.

Yoon, Carol Kaesuk. "Scientists Say Orangutans Can Exhibit 'Culture.'" *New York Times.* 3 Jan. 2003: A14.

Sciences

American Ornithologists' Union. 1998. *The A.O.U. checklist of North American birds.* 7th ed. Washington, D.C.: American Ornithologists' Union.

Borio, L., et al. 2001. Death Due to bioterrorism-related inhalational anthrax. *JAMA* 286:2554–59.

Charney, R., and A. Lytchak. 2001. Metric characterizations of spherical and Euclidean buildings. *Geom. and Topol.* 5, paper 17: 521–550. ⟨http://www.maths.warwick.ac.uk/gt/GTVol5/paper17.abs.html⟩ (8 Aug. 2002).

Gould, S.J., and N. Eldredge. 1977. Punctuated equilibria: The tempo and mode of evolution reconsidered. *Paleobiology* 3: 115–151.

Hölldobler, B., and E.O. Wilson. 1990. *The ants.* Cambridge, Mass.: Belknap–Harvard Univ. Press.

Mayr, E. 1982. Processes of speciation in animals. In: C. Barigozzi, ed. *Mechanisms of speciation.* New York: Alan R. Liss. 1–19.

McGraw-Hill yearbook of science and technology: 2003. 2003. New York: McGraw-Hill.

Nowak, R.M. 1999. *Walker's mammals of the world.* 6th ed. 2 vols. Baltimore: Johns Hopkins Univ. Press.

SIGNS AND SYMBOLS

Astronomy

⊙ the sun; Sunday
◑, ☾, *or* ☽ the moon; Monday
● new moon
☽, ◑, ☽ first quarter
○, ☽ full moon
☾, ◑, ☽ last quarter
☿ Mercury; Wednesday
♀ Venus; Friday
♁ the earth

♂ Mars; Tuesday
♃ Jupiter; Thursday
♄ Saturn; Saturday
♅ Uranus
♆ Neptune
♇ Pluto
☄ comet
∗ fixed star

Business

@ at; each; ⟨4 apples @ 25¢ = $1.00⟩
c/o care of
number if it precedes a numeral ⟨track #3⟩; pounds if it follows ⟨a 5# sack of sugar⟩
lb pound; pounds

% percent
‰ per thousand
$ dollars
¢ cents
£ pounds
© copyrighted
® registered trademark

Mathematics

+ plus; positive ⟨$a + b = c$⟩
− minus; negative
± plus or minus ⟨the square root of $4a^2$ is $\pm 2a$⟩
× multiplied by; times ⟨$6 \times 4 = 24$⟩— also indicated by placing a dot between the numbers ⟨$6 \cdot 4 = 24$⟩
÷ *or* : divided by ⟨$24 \div 6 = 4$⟩—also indicated by writing the divisor under the dividend with a line between ⟨$\frac{24}{6} = 4$⟩ or by writing the divisor after the dividend with a diagonal between ⟨$^3/_8$⟩
= equals ⟨$6 + 2 = 8$⟩
≠ or ≠ is not equal to
> is greater than ⟨$6 > 5$⟩
< is less than ⟨$3 < 4$⟩
≧ *or* ≥ is greater than or equal to
≦ *or* ≤ is less than or equal to
≯ is not greater than
≮ is not less than
≈ is approximately equal to
: is to; the ratio of
∴ therefore
∞ infinity
∠ angle; the angle ⟨∠ABC⟩
∟ right angle ⟨∟ABC⟩
⊥ the perpendicular; is perpendicular to ⟨AB⊥CD⟩

∥ parallel; is parallel to ⟨AB∥CD⟩
⊙ *or* ○ circle
⌒ arc of a circle
△ triangle
□ square
▭ rectangle
√ square root ⟨as in $\sqrt{4} = 2$⟩
( ) parentheses ⎫ indicate that quantities
[ ] brackets ⎬ enclosed by them
{ } braces ⎭ are to be taken together
π pi; the number 3.14159265+; the ratio of the circumference of a circle to its diameter
° degree ⟨60°⟩
′ minute(s); foot (feet) ⟨30′⟩
″ second(s); inch(es) ⟨30″⟩
2,3, etc. —used as exponents placed above and at the right of an expression to indicate that it is raised to a power indicated by the figure ⟨a^2 is the square of a⟩
∪ union of two sets
∩ intersection of two sets
⊂ is included in, is a subset of
⊃ contains as a subset
∈ is an element of
∉ is not an element of
Λ *or* 0 *or* Ø *or* { } empty set

Miscellaneous

&	and	$f/$ or f:	relative aperture of a photographic lens
&c	et cetera; and so forth	☠	poison
/	diagonal *or* slant; used to mean "or" (as in *and/or*); "per" (as in *meters/second*); indicates end of a line of verse; separates the figures of a date (9/29/99)	℞	take—used on prescriptions
		♀	female
		♂	male
		☮	peace
†	died—used esp. in genealogies	×	by ⟨3 × 5 cards⟩

Reference Marks

These marks are placed in written or printed text to direct attention to a footnote:

*	asterisk *or* star	§	section *or* numbered clause
†	dagger	‖	parallels
‡	double dagger	¶	paragraph

AN OVERVIEW OF THE INTERNET

The Internet is a massive electronic communications network that links smaller networks around the world, and that allows the transmission of information from any one connected computing device to another.

The modern Internet had its beginnings in a U.S. Department of Defense program called ARPANET (Advanced Research Projects Agency Network), which was developed in the late 1960's for the purpose of providing a secure, decentralized communications network that could survive a nuclear attack.

The Internet is now accessed by billions of people worldwide, and encompasses numerous electronic systems and services. Some of these are discussed in more detail below.

WORLD WIDE WEB

Established in the 1990's, the World Wide Web (or simply "the web") is the part of the Internet that makes use of *hypertext transfer protocol* (or *HTTP*). It is accessible through web browser software, and through applications that include such software.

Web pages are typically written in a special programming language called *HTML*, for *hypertext markup language*. This language was developed to ensure that basic instructions for displaying text could be interpreted by any computer or operating system.

The web now consists of trillions of pages of information. A collection of these pages in one location is known as a *website*. Websites vary widely in size and scope, are offered by an enormous variety of individuals and organizations, and provide access to a broad range of information (such as news and reference content) and services (such as shopping, games, blogging platforms, file storage, and more).

Although the web has become an indispensable part of modern life, it also has its dangers and disadvantages. The security of one's personal data can be compromised, and one's online activities may be logged, analyzed, and shared for commercial purposes. Some dangers can be posed by fellow users, as in cases of cyberbullying or cyberstalking. And it is not always clear which information on the Internet is trustworthy and which is not.

E-MAIL

Electronic mail, or e-mail, is a means or system for transmitting messages electronically over a computer network (especially the Internet). Invented in 1971, e-mail revolutionized personal communications.

E-mail is typically sent and received either through a stand-alone e-mail application installed on a device such as a computer or phone, or through a web browser interface.

An e-mail address typically consists of the addressee's name, nickname, or alias, followed by the commercial "at sign" (@) and then a domain name (such as "merriam-webster.com"). One can send a message to several recipients at once by including their addresses in the "TO:" line of the message. There may also be lines for sending a copy of the e-mail to other recipients as a "cc" (originally meaning "carbon copy"), or hiding the names of recipients receiving a copy in a "bcc" (blind cc). The recipient of an e-mail can reply by clicking or tapping a "Reply" button or link, or forward the message to others by clicking or tapping a "Forward" button or link.

Most e-mail applications allow the user to save commonly used addresses; to save a group of addresses together under an alias that can be used to e-mail all addresses in the group at once; to include documents or files along with the e-mail; to customize their personal interface; to automate certain frequent tasks; to mark or flag specific messages; to organize messages into folders; and to receive notifications when new mail arrives.

Most users receive at least some unsolicited e-mail. Some such messages are electronic junk mail, or "spam." Others are scam (or "phishing") e-mails, or have attached malware. Some e-mail systems filter some spam and quarantine or flag potentially dangerous messages.

SOCIALIZING ONLINE

Since the early days of personal computing, people have created systems for using networked computers for group discussions.

Mailing Lists, *Bulletin Boards*, Newsgroups, and Forums

Among the earliest such systems to be developed was the e-mail *mailing list*, in which list subscribers send their comments by e-mail to a communal address from which the e-mails are forwarded to each subscriber.

Other early developments included electronic *bulletin boards* and *newsgroups*. Bulletin board users could connect directly with a host's computer by dialing that computer's modem to leave messages; download text or computer programs; or upload their own content for others to access. Newsgroups are electronic message boards devoted to specific topics. They are most often associated with Usenet, a large network of newsgroups. Bulletin boards and newsgroups have declined significantly in popularity, but are still in use.

A user *forum* allows users to post messages publicly through a website, or to respond publicly to such posts made by other users. There are websites dedicated to hosting user forums, but other kinds of sites may offer user forum areas for discussions relating to the site's main focus (such as a company's product line), or they may provide a comments section similar to a forum beneath each of their content posts.

Chat and Messaging

While the systems mentioned above generally provide one-at-a-time communication, other systems allow a number of people to communicate at the same time. One such form of synchronous communication is Internet-based *chat*, or real-time online interactive discussion. Although chat tends to be associated primarily with text-based communication, some systems also support audio or audiovisual chat. Chat is still available as a stand-alone service, and many Internet-based systems, such as some video games and videoconferencing services, include a real-time chat feature as part of their user interface.

Text-based chat differs from *instant messaging* in that people who post chat messages cannot designate a specific recipient; all active participants can read the message. With instant messaging, written messages are sent privately in real-time be-tween two or more parties designated by the initial sender. However, some chat systems also include a private messaging feature.

Some forms of *text messaging* (the sending of short text messages electronically especially from one cell phone to another) are Internet-based, and can therefore be considered a type of instant messaging.

Social Media

Many of the forms of online group discussion mentioned above have declined significantly with the rise of *social media*, which encompass many of the same features.

Social media are forms of electronic communication, such as social networking or blogging sites and applications, through which users create online communities to share information, ideas, personal messages, and other content (such as photos and videos).

When a social media user posts content, the post is generally visible to all of the other users who "follow" (subscribe to the feed of) that user, though the creator of a post typically has some control over which other users can see it. Typically, other users may respond to a post by adding a comment, by clicking or tapping on a reaction icon (as to indicate approval), or by sharing the post with their own followers. Many social media services offer additional features such as instant messaging, voice and video calling, and more.